MOST
POPULAR
WEB
SITES,
2ND EDITION

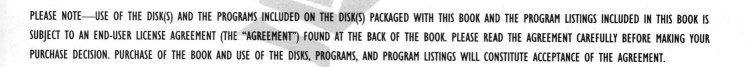

MOST POPULAR WEB SITES

THE BEST OF THE NET FROM

2ND EDITION

PRESS
AN IMPRINT OF QUE®

LYCOS PRESS
AN IMPRINT OF MACMILLAN COMPUTER PUBLISHING USA
INDIANAPOLIS, INDIANA

Title Manager	Lorna Gentry
Cover Design	Dan Armstrong
Illustration	Mina Reimer
Production	Debra Kincaid, Julie Searls, Jenny Earhart

Lycos Press books are developed as a joint effort of Lycos and Que. They are published by Macmillan Computer Publishing USA, a Simon & Schuster Company.

Lycos™ is a trademark of Carnegie Mellon University

Lycos Press books are produced on a Macintosh computer system with the following applications: FrameMaker®, Microsoft® Word, QuarkXPress®, Adobe Illustrator®, Adobe Photoshop®, Adobe Streamline™, MacLink®Plus, Aldus® FreeHand™, Collage Plus™.

Lycos Press, an imprint of
Macmillan Computer Publishing USA
201 West 103rd Street
Indianapolis, IN 46290-1097

Library of Congress No.: 97-69185
ISBN 0-78970-1348-9
Manufactured in the United States of America
10 9 8 7 6 5 4 3 2 1

TABLE OF CONTENTS

xx TABLE OF CONTENTS

PREFACE

The Web is both a wondrous and an accursed place: wondrous, because of the vast amount of information it makes available to millions of people around the world, yet accursed by its very nature—global, without borders, and often confusing. With no signposts to guide the virtual traveler, the Web can be a bit like a library without a card catalog.

I became involved in creating the a2z directory with the idea in mind that people needed more than mere directional signals—go here, turn there; they needed labels, in much the same way we expect our food to provide labeling for nutritional content. What the heck is in this worldwide can, and how good will it be when you open it?

Telling you what's in the can is the easy part—well, sort of. I hadn't bargained on the diversity and complexity of information available, or that it would depart so dramatically from the way we house and store information in a conventional library. It made sorting and cataloging the Web a challenging task, and underscored the most fascinating peculiarity of this new medium: Suddenly, we are all publishers. As such, almost anything goes, from the unique perspectives of some 30 million authors around the globe.

So how can anyone say for sure how good any one can will be once you open it? One person's nirvana could be another's mismatched sock drawer. So at a2z, we decided to let the users do the talking; our editors tell you what's in the can, then you decide how much you like it. That strategy is at the heart of the "most popular" approach. We think you know as well as anyone how you like your Web. And we know what you like because you've told us—you've linked out to these sites hundreds of times from your own home pages, providing your own signposts and endorsements along the virtual highway. We know, because we counted—we counted all the links to all the pages in the Lycos catalog and found the ones you liked the best (and linked the most).

Now we're bringing them to you in this book, which we hope will be a handy reference while you get your ethereal feet wet in this wave of new technology. We figure that if enough of your friends and colleagues were willing to give these sites a double thumbs-up, you will, too. Oh yeah, and because we're editors, we couldn't help telling you about a few of our own favorites, so we've included those here as well.

So go get it. Enjoy a bit of the wonder, without the curse.

ABOUT LYCOS, INC.

In the brief time since the world has had point-and-click access to the multigraphic, multimedia World Wide Web, the number of people going online has exploded to 30 million at last count, all roaming about the tens of millions of places to visit in Cyberspace.

As the Web makes its way into our everyday lives, the kinds of people logging on are changing. Today, there are as many webmasters as novices, or newbies, and all are struggling to get the most from the vast wells of information scattered about the Web. Even well-prepared surfers stumble aimlessly through cyberspace using hit-or-miss methods in search of useful information, with few results, little substance, and a lot of frustration.

In 1994, the Lycos technology was created by a scientist at Carnegie Mellon University to help those on the Web regain control of the Web. The company's powerful technology is the bedrock underlying a family of guides that untangle the Web, offering a simple and intuitive interface for all types of Web surfers, from GenXers to seniors, from net vets to newbies.

Lycos (http://www.lycos.com) is a premium navigation tool for cyberspace, providing not just searches but unique editorial content and Web reviews that all draw on the company's extensive catalog of over 60 million Web sites (and growing).

DESTINATION, LYCOS

Lycos designed its home base on the premise that people want to experience the Web in three fundamentally different ways: they want to search for specific subjects or destinations, they want to browse interesting categories, or they want recommendations on sites that have been reviewed for quality of their content and graphics. Traditionally, Internet companies have provided part of this solution, but none has offered a finding tool that accommodates all degrees and types of curiosity. Lycos has.

Lycos utilizes its CentiSpeed spider technology as the foundation for finding and cataloging the vast variety of content on the World Wide Web. CentiSpeed processes a search faster than earlier technologies, featuring Virtual Memory Control, User-Level Handling and Algorithmic Word Compaction. This advanced technology allows the engine to execute more than 4,000 queries per second. CentiSpeed provides faster search results and unparalleled power to search the most comprehensive catalog of the World Wide Web. Lycos uses statistical word calculations and avoids full-word indexing, which helps provide the most relevant search results available on the Web.

In mid 1995, Lycos acquired Point Communications, widely recognized by Web veterans for its collection of critical reviews of the Web. Now an integrated part on the Lycos service, Point continues to provide thousands of in-depth site reviews and a thorough rating of the top Web sites throughout the world. The reviews are conducted by professional reviewers and editors who rate sites according to content, presentation and overall experience on a scale of 1 to 50. Reviews are presented as comprehensive abstracts that truly provide the user with subjective critiques widely heralded for their accuracy and perceptiveness. In addition, Point's top five percent ratings for Web sites receive a special "Top 5% Badge" icon, the Web's equivalent to the famed consumer "Good Housekeeping Seal."

And for Web browsers who don't need a touring list of well-reviewed sites but who may not be destination-specific, Lycos offers its Sites by Subject. Organizing thousands of Web sites into subject categories, Lycos Sites by Subject gives the cybersurfer at-a-glance Web browsing, including sports, entertainment, social issues, and children's sites. A compilation of the most popular sites on the Internet by the Lycos standard-- those with the greatest number of links from other sites--the directory provides Web travelers with a more organized approach to finding worthwhile places to visit on the Web.

SPIDERS ON STEROIDS

Lycos was originally developed at Carnegie Mellon University by Dr. Michael "Fuzzy" Mauldin, who holds a Ph.D. in conceptual information retrieval. Now chief scientist at the company, Dr. Mauldin continues to expand the unique exploration and indexing technology. Utilizing this technology, Lycos strives to deliver a family of guides to the Internet that are unparalleled for their accuracy, relevance and comprehensiveness. Lycos is one of the most frequently visited sites on the Web and is one of the leading sites for advertisers.

The Lycos database is constantly being refined by dozens of software robots, or agents, called "spiders." These spiders roam the Web endlessly, finding and downloading Web pages. Once a page is found, the spiders create abstracts which consist of the title, headings and subheading, 100 most weighty words, first 20 lines, size in bytes and number of words. Heuristic (self-teaching) software looks at where the words appear in the document, their proximity to other words, frequency and site popularity to determine relevance.

Lycos eliminates extraneous words like "the," "a," "and," "or," and "it" that add no value and slow down finding capabilities. The resulting abstracts are merged, older versions discarded, and a new, up-to-date database is distributed to all Lycos servers and licensees. This process is repeated continuously, resulting in a depth and comprehensiveness that makes Lycos a top information guide company.

Online providers or software makers can license Lycos-- the spider, search engine, catalog, directory and Point reviews--to make them available to users.

Lycos, Inc., an Internet exploration company, was founded specifically to find, index and filter information on the Internet and World Wide Web. CMG Information Services, Inc. (NASDAQ: CMGI) is a majority shareholder in Lycos, Inc. through its strategic investment and development business unit, CMG@Ventures. CMGI is a leading provider of direct marketing services investing in and integrating advanced Internet, interactive media and database management technologies.

ARTS AND HUMANITIES

THE 25 MOST POPULAR ARTS AND HUMANITIES SITES

Avalon: Arthurian Heaven
http://reality.sgi.com/employees/chris_
manchester/arthur.html

Columbia University Digital Design Lab
http://www.arch.columbia.edu/

Ever The Twain Shall Meet
http://www.lm.com/~joseph/mtwain.html

Galaxy: Religion (Community)
http://www.einet.net/galaxy/Community/
Religion.html

Genealogy in Australia
http://www.pcug.org.au/~mpahlow/
welcome.html

Karl Marx/Friedrich Engels Archives
http://csf.colorado.edu/psn/marx/

The Museum of Antiquities
http://www.ncl.ac.uk/~nantiq/

Natural History Museum
http://www.nhm.ac.uk/

Palace of Diocletian at Split
http://sunsite.unc.edu/expo/palace.exhibit/
intro.html

Palmer Museum of Art
http://cac.psu.edu/~mtd120/palmer/

Religious Resources on the Net
http://convex.cc.uky.edu/~jatuck00/Religion/
Religion.html

Research Institute for the Humanities
http://www.arts.cuhk.hk/

Smithsonian Institution
http://www.si.edu/

Studio 2000
http://este.darmstadt.gmd.de:5000/cgi-bin/
capture.pl

Su Tzu's Chinese Philosophy Page
http://mars.superlink.net/user/fsu/philo.html

University of Pennsylvania Classical Studies Department
http://ccat.sas.upenn.edu/clst/clst.html

University of Pennsylvania School of Arts and Sciences
http://www.sas.upenn.edu/

W. H. Calvin's The Ascent of Mind
http://weber.u.washington.edu/wcalvin/
bk5.html

Worlds of Late Antiquity
http://ccat.sas.upenn.edu/jod/wola.html

World Wide Stage
http://ireland.iol.ie/~westrock/

WWW Virtual Library: Architecture
http://www.clr.toronto.edu:1080/VIRTUALLIB/
arch.html

WWW Virtual Library: Religion
http://marvin.biologie.uni-freiburg.de/
~amueller/religion/

ARCHITECTURE

ANCIENT

Architecture & Architectural Sculpture of the Mediterranean Basin
http://www.ncsa.uiuc.edu/SDG/Experimental/anu-art-history/architecture.html

Classical and Hellenistic architecture of the Mediterranean basin is featured in this collection of research images. Visitors will find architecture and architectural sculpture from the pre-classical period to the 19th century.

Images of Architecture & Architectural Sculpture
http://www.ncsa.uiuc.edu/SDG/Experimental/anu-art-history/architecture.images.html

Presented by the Australian National University's art history department, this page features digitized images of European (mainly Roman) architecture and architectural sculpture. Visitors can follow links to the departmental home page.

Palace of Diocletian at Split
http://sunsite.unc.edu/expo/palace.exhibit/intro.html

Travel back to the Later Roman Empire for a look at the structure, style and history of Spalato's Palace of Diocletian. Find a discussion of the architectural site in text and pictures here.

WebAcropol
http://www.mechan.gsd.ntua.gr/webacropol/

WebAcropol features a historical guided tour of the Acropolis of Athens, the imposing rock on which the Parthenon was built. The tour includes images, history and explanations.

ARCHITECTURAL HISTORY

Architecture & Architectural Sculpture of the Mediterranean Basin
http://www.ncsa.uiuc.edu/SDG/Experimental/anu-art-history/architecture.html

Classical and Hellenistic architecture of the Mediterranean basin is featured in this collection of research images. Visitors will find architecture and architectural sculpture from the pre-classical period to the 19th century.

Gargoyle Home Page
http://ils.unc.edu/garg/garghp4.html

This site features information about gargoyles, a natural and unnatural history, cathedral tours and images of gargoyles at Duke University. Includes links to other pages as well.

Renaissance and Baroque Architecture
http://www.lib.virginia.edu/dic/colls/arh102/index.html

Renaissance and Baroque Architecture is a University of Virginia resource for students of its Architectural History 102 class. Images from 15th-17th century Italy and France and England are provided.

Society of Architectural Historians
http://www.ccsf.caltech.edu/~mac/sah/index.htm

The Southern California Chapter of the Society of Architectural Historians maintains this site with general information and resource access. Visit here to learn about the society's aims and objectives, view its calendar of events, find related publications, and more.

ARCHIVES AND INDICES

Architecture of Islam
http://rubens.anu.edu.au/islam2/index_1.html

Interested in the architecture of Islam? Australian National University maintains this archive, organized by countries, which offers .jpg files of architecture from Egypt to Syria. This archive is part of ArtServe, which features art and architecture from the Mediterranean Basin.

ArtServe
http://rubens.anu.edu.au/index.html

From Australian National University, ArtServe features nearly 16,000 images devoted to the history of art and architecture, mainly from the Mediterranean Basin. Resources also include art history tutorials, access to reference works and source images.

Images of Architecture & Architectural Sculpture
http://www.ncsa.uiuc.edu/SDG/Experimental/anu-art-history/architecture.images.html

From the Australian National University's art history department, this page features digitized images of European (mainly Roman) architecture and architectural sculpture. Visitors can follow links to the departmental home page.

Planning and Architecture Internet Resource Center
http://www.arch.buffalo.edu/pairc/

The Planning and Architecture Internet Resource Center, a service of the University of Buffalo, N.Y., maintains this informational site. Visit here for resources in building and landscape design, city and regional planning, land use and related educational resources. An index of professional firms, conferences and image galleries is also available.

Rice University Architecture Gopher
gopher://riceinfo.rice.edu/11/Subject/Architecture

Rice University maintains this gopher with links to architectural information on the Internet. Links include "Architronic: The Electronic Journal of Architecture," the Chicago Architecture Foundation and information about online discussion groups.

University of California, Berkeley, Architecture Slide Library
http://www.arch.buffalo.edu/pairc/

The Architecture Slide Library at the University of California, Berkeley, provides this query form to access 35mm slides of thousands of images. Find directions on how to use it and link to additional online collections.

WWW Virtual Library: Architecture
http://www.clr.toronto.edu:1080/VIRTUALLIB/arch.html

The Virtual Library's architecture stacks are primarily filled with links to educational institutions, professional organizations, design firms and publications. Includes pointers to conferences, competitions and related engineering research. Search tool provided.

ASSOCIATIONS AND ORGANIZATIONS

American Institute of Architects
http://www.aia.org/

The American Institute of Architects (AIA) is a professional association that serves to foster communication between architects and the general public. This site offers information on the AIA's mission, history and membership benefits. Also, find tips on selecting an architect, careers in architecture and K-12 classroom resources.

American Institute of Architects, Baltimore

http://www.goucher.edu/aia

The Baltimore Chapter of The American Institute of Architects provides an overview of its work here. Visitors will find a list of the group's board of directors and pointers to two other groups created by the chapter. The page also includes an index to architecture-related sites on the Web.

California Division of the State Architect

http://www.dsa.ca.gov/

California's Division of the State Architect includes general information about its services and projects at its Web site. It also has links to the Office of Construction Services and the Office of Regulation Services.

Canadian Centre for Architecture

http://cca.qc.ca/

The Canadian Centre for Architecture was established on the conviction that architecture "is a public concern." Visitors to its home page can learn more about the center, its exhibitions, library resources and special projects. Available in English and French.

Megacities 2000 Digital Village

http://valley.interact.nl/MEGACITIES

The Megacities 2000 Foundation "originates from the awareness of the future role of cities as the dominant type of settlement for humanity." Via Digital Village, the foundation offers information about its main project, Codex, a report covering all aspects of sustainable urban management and development. See Editor's Choice, page 3.

Rice Design Alliance

http://riceinfo.rice.edu/ES/Architecture/RDA.html

The Rice Design Alliance (RDA) is a non-profit organization dedicated to the advancement of architecture and urban design in Houston, Texas. Here, the group provides information about its lecture series and a link to its publication "Cite."

Society of Architectural Historians

http://www.ccsf.caltech.edu/~mac/sah/index.htm

The Southern California Chapter of the Society of Architectural Historians maintains this site with general information and resources. Visit here to learn about the society's aims and objectives, view its calendar of events, find related publications and more.

BUILDINGS AND STRUCTURES

Arcosanti

http://www.arcosanti.org/

Arcosanti, 60 miles north of Phoenix, Ariz., is a social and architectural experiment combining compact urban structures with large-scale, solar greenhouses on 20 acres of a 4,000 acre preserve. This Web site provides information on the community and its founder, Paolo Soleri.

Bill's Lighthouse Getaway

http://zuma.lib.utk.edu/lights/

Bill's Lighthouse Getaway, a travel guide to U.S. lighthouses, takes you on a photo and story tour of the nation's historic beacons in regions such as New England, the Great Lakes and the Outer Banks. Features include the top 10 lighthouses, a list of endangered lights and links to lighthouse societies.

Castles on the Web

http://fox.nstn.ca/~tmonk/castle/castle.html

Castles on the Web escorts visitors on a global castle tour, complete with historical profiles and an extensive image gallery. Includes a "Castle of the Week" and a glossary of all-important castle terminology.

Contemporary Architecture in Hong Kong

http://www.ncsa.uiuc.edu/SDG/Experimental/anu-art-history/hongkong.html

Take a look at contemporary architecture at work in Hong Kong at this site which features images of buildings. Photos provided by Michael Greenhalgh of the Australian National University.

A Guide to Old Covered Bridges of Southeastern Pennsylvania

http://william-king.www.drexel.edu/top/bridge/cb1.html

Anyone interested in the architecture of old covered bridges, particularly in southeastern Pennsylvania, should take a look at this guide. Compiled by Dr. Roger McCain, the page documents the 19th-century structures, a symbol of "small-town America."

Isfahan Islamic Architecture

http://www.anglia.ac.uk/~trochford/isfahan.html

Photographs and discussions of the Islamic and Iranian architectural styles of Isfahan, Iran, are featured at this site. Find examples of the city's architecture along with an annotated glossary of architectural concepts and ideas.

Maine Solar House

http://solstice.crest.org/renewables/wlord/index.html

Keep up with the construction of a solar house at this instructional site with plans, documentation and news about the construction from the ground up. Technical details and a Frequently Asked Question (FAQ) file are provided for curious visitors.

Palace of Diocletian at Split

http://sunsite.unc.edu/expo/palace.exhibit/intro.html

Travel back to the Later Roman Empire for a look at the structure, style and history of Spalato's Palace of Diocletian. Find a discussion of the architectural site in text and pictures here.

COMPANIES

Aaron Cohen Associates

http://www.acohen.com/

Architectural and library design consultants Aaron Cohen & Associates details its services at this informational site. Includes links to images of some of the firm's projects, as well as its philosophy on library construction.

Architects Abroad

http://www.rahul.net/arctour/

Architects Abroad, a San Francisco, Calif.-based provider of architecture-oriented travel packages, maintains this site with information about its tours, schedules, programs, accommodations, trip costs and other aspects of the company's service.

Arete' Designs: Builds

http://www.nwlink.com/~luckeyjo/arete.html

This Seattle, Wash., architectural design firm helps individuals and businesses create floorplans and construction drawings without first having to retain an architect. Find information at this promotional site about the company's CAD design development services.

Boreskie

http://www.mbnet.mb.ca/boreskie/

This unique Canadian architectural firm is committed to "Integral Architecture," and "the human art of placemaking"—in short, transforming a site owner's mission and vision into a structure that reflects and embodies that vision. Visitors can learn more about the company, its projects, and rate structures here.

Building Research Establishment

http://www.bre.co.uk/

The Building Research Establishment offers advice and information to building engineers and the construction industry. Visitors can review the British government agency's consulting services and online resources.

Hermann Zillgens Associates

http://www.infopost.com/sandiego/architects/index.html

The San Diego, Calif., architectural firm Hermann Zillgens Associates maintains this site with information about its planning, engineering and GIS services for public and private institutions.

Jonathan Cohen and Associates

http://www.dnai.com/~kvetcher/index.html

Jonathan Cohen and Associates are architects and planners in San Francisco. This site provides information about the firm and its services, as well as a portfolio of its projects.

Kajima Corporation

http://www.kajima.co.jp/

Kajima Corporation, a construction company located in Japan, offers hardcore company news along with a look at the lighter side of cultural- and sports-related activities sponsored by Kajima. A book collection on interior and exterior design is also available.

Kisho Kurokawa

http://www.kisho.co.jp/

Kisho Kurokawa, an architect, details his books, theses, works and projects on his personal home page. A curriculum vitae and profile of his company are also included.

Moriyama & Teshima

http://www.magic.ca/mtarch/

The online presence of architectural firm Moriyama and Teshima includes information about the company's team of architects and designers, along with a look at its corporate philosophy. Visitors also can check out the firm's project gallery or link to sites of interest to architects, including the InterPRO Resources service listing for those in the construction trades.

Murokami Associates

http://www.murokami.com/

The Murokami Associates home page contains information on the architectural design firm, including past and current projects, staff profiles and links to other design, engineering and architectural Web pages.

Netcad Corporation

http://www.netcad.com/base.html

Netcad Corporation, a CAD consulting and Web publishing firm in Springfield, Va., maintains this site with online CAD examples, Minicad software sales and training information, and links to HVAC resources and Sigma Phi Epsilon. Its Web development services are also detailed here.

O'Donnell, Wicklund, Pigozzi and Peterson Architects, Inc.

http://www.automatrix.com/owp/

An Illinois architecture firm posts information about itself and its work here. Visitors can download photos of the firm's work and link to architecture resources elsewhere on the Internet.

Robert P. Davis Architects

ftp://ftp.sccsi.com/pub/local/rpd611/rpd.html

Robert P. Davis Architects, Houston, Texas, specializes in general residential, commercial and industrial architecture in the gulf coast and great plains regions. Guests here can tour the firm's current projects and samples of recent work and learn a bit about architectural design.

 EDITOR'S CHOICE

Megacities 2000 Digital Village

http://valley.interact.nl/MEGACITIES

We all know that the world's population is exploding, but the growth of "megacities," cities with over 10 million inhabitants, pose special ecological, economical, structural, and human rights challenges. According to the Megacities Foundation, formed by the International Academy of Architecture, Mexico City and Calcutta already have 20 million inhabitants, and by the year 2000 it's predicted there will be 21 megacities. To be better prepared to deal with these massive settlements of the very near future, the Megacities Foundation is hosting a series of international congresses and assembling a Codex that will cover solutions in urban management and development while taking into account geographic, cultural and economic diversity. Scholars and activists in architecture, the environmental and human rights movements, urban planning, public administration, and many other related disciplines, may find the beginnings to solutions—and many more questions—at the Megacities 2000 page. A project overview and details about its founders' academic and personal backgrounds is presented, as well as conference reports and meeting information. However, the site's central feature is the evolving Megacities Codex itself, which covers such topics as interculturality, city sizes, reaction to urban development, liveability and needed space. Visit this interesting and thought-provoking site to see why the Megacities Foundation is based on "the awareness of the future role of cities as the dominant type of settlement for humanity."—*Reviewed by Amy Hembree*

Megacities 2000 Digital Village

Background of Megacities 2000

Megacities 2000 Foundation

Megacities Codex

Megacities Link Library

May conference report

About the Digital Village and mailing list

Stefan Jauslin

http://a77.ethz.ch/~stefan/

On his personal page, Stefan Jauslin, an architectural scholar at the Swiss Federal Institute of Technology, Zurich, includes a research paper, "Transitory Spaces," and examples of his work.

DESIGNS AND PLANS

Architectural Visualisation

http://archpropplan.auckland.ac.nz/Archivis/archivis.html

The Department of Architecture at the University of Auckland, New Zealand, provides information on computer-assisted design and visualization, a student gallery and a collection of images and ideas in the world of architecture. Includes descriptions of reconstruction projects, ecological design paradigms and links to other architectural sites.

Maine Solar House

http://solstice.crest.org/renewables/wlord/index.html

Keep up with the construction of a solar house at this instructional site with plans, documentation and news about the construction from the ground up. Technical details and a Frequently Asked Question (FAQ) file are provided for curious visitors.

FAMOUS AND NOTEWORTHY ARCHITECTS

Chesley Bonestell Gallery

http://www.secapl.com/bonestell/top.html

At this site devoted to architect, astronomical artist and filmmaker, Chesley Bonestell, visitors can take a virtual tour of Bonestall's life, work and interests.

Frank Lloyd Wright in Wisconsin

http://flw.badgernet.com:2080/

The Frank Lloyd Wright Wisconsin Heritage Association was organized to promote, preserve and protect the renowned architect's structures in the state of Wisconsin. Visit here to view the organization's tour brochure and multimedia gallery. Membership information is also available.

Frank Lloyd Wright Page

http://www.mcs.com/~tgiesler/flw_home.htm

Frank Lloyd Wright reigns as one of the greatest American architects of the 20th century. This Web page has information about the man and his work, and visitors can follow links to images and other Wright-related and architectural sites.

INSTITUTES AND SCHOOLS

California Institute of the Arts

http://www.calarts.edu/

The California Institute of the Arts, located in Valencia, Calif., details information on the school and its fine art programs. Visitors can also browse a collection of artistic home pages from CalArts students and faculty.

Careers in Architecture

http://www.aia.org/career.htm

The American Institute of Architects and the American Architectural Foundation provide this resource for those considering a career in architecture. Data on scholarships and internship opportunities and a listing of accredited architecture schools are accompanied by informative articles.

Carnegie Mellon Department of Architecture

http://www.arc.cmu.edu/

Carnegie Mellon University's architecture department provides visitors with information on graduate and undergraduate programs, facilities and faculty at its home page. Includes a departmental calendar and a forum enabling department members to discuss issues online.

The Chinese University of Hong Kong Department of Architecture

http://www.arch.cuhk.hk/

The Chinese University of Hong Kong Department of Architecture provides an overview for prospective students here. The site includes information about the department's research projects, faculty and students.

Columbia University Digital Design Lab

http://www.arch.columbia.edu/

The Digital Design Lab (DDL) at Columbia University invites visitors to its home page to examine online reports and essays and review its students' work in the gallery. Links to other sites of interest on and off campus are also provided.

Columbia University Graduate School of Architecture, Planning and Preservation

http://www.columbia.edu/~archpub/

Columbia University's Graduate School of Architecture, Planning and Preservation page features sections on computer-aided and urban design, a link to City on the Bias from the Istanbul Workshop project, and information about building technologies.

Digital Communities : Urban Design & Planning in Cyberspace

http://alberti.mit.edu/arch/4.207/homepage.html

This Massachusetts Institute of Technology site describes a graduate seminar in urban planning and design in cyberspace. Includes a course description, prerequisites for registration and profiles of course instructors.

Energy Research Group

http://erg.ucd.ie/

The Energy Research Group, based in the School of Architecture, University College, Dublin, specializes in research and education in climate-sensitive architectural design and building energy utilization. Learn more about the group's activities, staff and publications here.

Fraunhofer Institut Solare Energiesysteme

http://www.ise.fhg.de/

Fraunhofer Institut Solare Energiesysteme, Germany, provides information about its projects, including self-sufficient solar houses and the Radiance Synthetic Image System. Links to press releases and information about Freiburg, Germany, is also available.

Group for the Application of Scientific Methods to Architecture and Urban Planning

http://www-gams.cnrs-mrs.fr/

The Group for the Application of Scientific Methods to Architecture and Urban Planning maintains this searchable overview of its current scientific program. Information on research activities, education programs and the people involved are featured, along with images from its various projects. In French and English.

Mississippi State University School of Architecture

http://wright.sarc.msstate.edu/

The School of Architecture at Mississippi State University, State College, Miss., maintains this page with information about its research, faculty and students. Prospective graduate students will also find details about the school's program and curriculum.

MIT School of Architecture and Planning

http://alberti.mit.edu/ap/

The Massachusetts Institute of Technology School of Architecture and Planning takes visitors through its gallery space by way of a video. The study of animation, information about women in architecture and a design studio of the future are also housed here.

Prairie View A&M University College of Engineering and Architecture
http://www.pvamu.edu/

Information, services and departments at Prairie View A&M University's College of Engineering and Architecture are featured here. An index includes pointers to the High Energy Physics Department, the Texas Space Grant Consortium home page and the Student Organizations Home Page.

Rensselaer Polytechnic Institute Lighting Research Center
http://www.lrc.rpi.edu/

Flash on the home page of the Lighting Research Center located at Rensselaer Polytechnic Institute's School of Architecture in Troy, N.Y. Visitors can learn about the center's academic program, research projects, publications and affiliations.

South Bank University Department of Architecture & Civil Engineering
http://www.sbu.ac.uk/Architecture/home.html

South Bank University's Department of Architecture & Civil Engineering targets potential engineering students with access to architecture-related Internet sites. The site also includes a department catalog, admissions info, course and project descriptions.

State University of New York, Buffalo, School of Architecture and Planning
http://www.arch.buffalo.edu/

From the School of Architecture and Planning at the State University of New York, Buffalo, this page contains curriculum overviews, faculty research projects, and admissions guidelines. Includes information about student services, campus organizations, and links to other campus servers.

University of California, Berkeley, College of Environmental Design
http://www.ced.berkeley.edu/

The College of Environmental Design at UC-Berkeley invites visitors to explore its departments and review its academic programs. Departments include architecture, city and regional planning, and landscape architecture.

University of Dundee School of Architecture
http://bagpuss.architecture.dundee.ac.uk/

The University of Dundee, Scotland, gives prospective students an overview of its architectural courses and faculty here. The site includes pictures of the campus and sights around Dundee.

University of Hannover Landscape Architecture & Environmental Development
http://www.laum.uni-hannover.de/

The faculty of Landscape Architecture and Environmental Development at the University of Hannover, Germany, offers a glimpse at the school's history and current research at this site. In German and English.

University of Oregon School of Architecture and Allied Arts
http://laz.uoregon.edu/

Information on departments, programs, research activities and student organizations is available at the School of Architecture and Allied Arts site at the University of Oregon. Schoolwide information is also provided.

University of Sydney College of Architecture
http://www.arch.su.edu.au/

The College of Architecture at the University of Sydney maintains this home page containing information about its academic programs, departments, faculty and research projects. There's also a link to general university information.

University of Southern California School of Architecture
http://www.usc.edu/dept/architecture/

The University of Southern California's School of Architecture details its program and introduces its faculty here. Stop by for samples of student work, course descriptions and virtual tours of campus.

Victoria University School of Architecture
http://www.arch.vuw.ac.nz/

The School of Architecture at Victoria University of Wellington in New Zealand features rotating exhibits which welcome visitors to its home page. The site also introduces the school, its programs, and course offerings.

Vienna University of Technology
http://info.archlab.tuwien.ac.at/

The Vienna University of Technology's Architecture and Urban Planning Department posts a program overview at this VRML supported site. In German.

INTERIOR DESIGN

Combo Directory
http://www.combo.com/

Calgary's Allscan Distributors, Inc., maintains the Combo directory containing links to office furniture manufacturers worldwide. Information about office-wide ergonomics is also available, as well as details about ergonomically designed furnishings.

i3
http://www.i3.se/

i3 is a forum for those interested in furniture and interior design. At i3's designers' forum, visitors can search for information by design pictures, designers or manufacturers. Publications and essays are available under Skrift and commercial pages are ergonomically located but a click away.

Indesign
http://www.intergate.bc.ca/business/indesign/

Indesign creates drapery hardware and accessories, including finials, rods, rings and supports, all available in a variety of materials and finishes. Online ordering is available.

LANDSCAPE ARCHITECTURE

Arcosanti
http://www.arcosanti.org/

Arcosanti, 60 miles north of Phoenix, Ariz., is a social and architectural experiment combining compact urban structures with large-scale, solar greenhouses on 20 acres of a 4,000 acre preserve. This Web site provides information on the community and its founder, Paolo Soleri.

Centre for Landscape Research Network
http://www.clr.toronto.edu:1080/clr.html/

This site informs visitors of designs, planning and policies relating to the environment. Includes links to related sites on landscape architecture, research, projects and schools.

University of Guelph Landscape Architecture
http://tdg.uoguelph.ca/nav/LA_startingpoints.html

The University of Guelph provides this index to landscape architecture resources on the Internet. The page also includes links to forestry school sites and the EnviroGopher.

WWW Virtual Library: Landscape Architecture
http://www.clr.toronto.edu:1080/VIRTUALLIB/larch.html

Visitors to this searchable, information-heavy site can harvest huge amounts of information regarding landscape architecture. Includes links to historical, educational and professional Web sites related to landscaping, plus listings of events, conferences and competitions.

MODELS AND MODELING

SiteX
http://architecture.mcgill.ca/siteX/homepage.html

McGill University's School of Architecture showcases a variety of architectural modeling projects at this site, including entries that use both traditional and computer modeling methods.

Sonata Building Modeling System
http://www.biw.co.uk/sonata/

Not a CAD system, the Sonata Building Modeling System creates an actual model from which drawings can be generated. The Sonata documentation here includes software information, downloadable libraries, images, VRML files, parametric files and more.

PROFESSIONAL RESOURCES

AEC Infocenter
http://www.aecinfo.com/

The Canadian AEC InfoCenter features resources relevant to the daily workings of the architectural, engineering, construction and home building industries. The center provides classifieds, a product library and the SpecCenter, which provides manufacturers' specs for a variety of materials and products.

ArchiWeb Consulting Services
http://www.archiweb.com/

ArchiWeb is a gateway to more than 750 architectural information services online. Includes links to design firms, major building projects, computer-aided design software, related exhibits and other resources. Information is in Japanese and English.

Building Information Warehouse
http://www.biw.co.uk/

Established to encourage the U.K. construction industry to publish information in a highly accessible form, Building Information Warehouse contains links to the sites of contractors, product and service suppliers, institutes, research and publications.

Building Research Establishment
http://www.bre.co.uk/

Building Research Establishment offers advice and information to building engineers and the construction industry. Visitors can review the British government agency's consulting services and online resources here.

Computer Architecture Home Page
http://www.cs.wisc.edu/~arch/www/

Maintained by researchers at the University of Wisconsin, this index of computer architecture resources, provides a wealth of Internet links. Visit here to connect with professional organizations, technical materials, employment opportunities and more.

Planning and Architecture Internet Resource Center
http://www.arch.buffalo.edu/pairc/

The Planning and Architecture Internet Resource Center, a service of the University of Buffalo, N.Y., maintains this informational site. Visit here for resources in building and landscape design, city and regional planning, land use and related educational resources. An index of professional firms, conferences and image galleries is also available.

PUBLICATIONS AND INDUSTRY NEWS

Architronic: The Electronic Journal of Architecture
http://arcrs4.saed.kent.edu/Architronic/homepage.html

"Architronic," an online critical architectural journal, "aims to gather and disseminate articles not only of occasional but also of permanent interest" to architects and students of architecture. At its home page, visitors can browse articles or perform key word searches for specific topics.

City of Bits
http://www-mitpress.mit.edu/City_of_Bits/index.html

"City of Bits," written by MIT School of Architecture Dean William J. Mitchell, explores the implications of "a largely invisible but increasingly important system of virtual spaces." Visitors can read a synopsis of the book here.

SOFTWARE

Softdesk, Inc.
http://www.softdesk.com/

Architecture, engineering and construction application software comprise the product line of Softdesk, Inc. Get a product list, company profile and technical support at this promotional site.

Sonata Building Modeling System
http://www.biw.co.uk/sonata/

Not a CAD system, the Sonata Building Modeling System creates an actual model from which drawings can be generated. The Sonata documentation here includes software information, downloadable libraries, images, VRML files, parametric files and more.

URBAN PLANNING

Arcosanti
http://www.arcosanti.org/

Arcosanti, 60 miles north of Phoenix, Ariz., is a social and architectural experiment combining compact urban structures with large-scale, solar greenhouses on 20 acres of a 4,000 acre preserve. This Web site provides information on the community and its founder, Paolo Soleri.

Digital Communities : Urban Design & Planning in Cyberspace
http://alberti.mit.edu/arch/4.207/homepage.html

This Massachusetts Institute of Technology site describes a graduate seminar in urban planning and design in cyberspace. Includes a course description, prerequisites for registration and profiles of course instructors.

Group for the Application of Scientific Methods to Architecture and Urban Planning
http://www-gams.cnrs-mrs.fr/

The Group for the Application of Scientific Methods to Architecture and Urban Planning maintains this searchable overview of its current scientific program. Information on research activities, education programs and the people involved are featured, along with images from their various projects. In French and English.

ART

ARCHIVES AND INDICES

Art E-boulevard
http://www.ccc.nl/

Art E-boulevard is a Dutch site focusing on art guides, an art 'zine, galleries and artists. A world art tour, a different featured artist and gallery each month, and the most-frequented pages are easily found here.

Art Gallery
http://heiwww.unige.ch/art/
Visitors to this page will find a couple of online art exhibits. More predominant, however, is the list of links to other art sites on the Web.

Art Links
http://sunsite.unc.edu/otis/art-links.html
Offering no more—yet no less—than its title promises, this index is organized by categories: Collections of Links, Multidisciplinary, One-Person Shows, Uncategorized, Mostly Textual Experiments and Comic.

Art Search
http://www.pacific.net:80/~joy/art/
Joy Calonico, Founder of this Web site, describes Art Search as "a directory of fine artists, sculptors and craftsmen [sic]." Visitors can search portfolios of individual artists, search by gallery, or browse an alpha list. Instructions for artists wishing to join the index are also included.

Arts Site of the Day
http://wwar.com/index.html
The Arts Site of the Day was designed to take visitors to a new and interesting art-related Web creation every day. What's more, the site hosts a searchable index of arts resources, covering everything from antiques to education to performance art and beyond.

ArtsNet
http://artsnet.heinz.cmu.edu/
Carnegie Mellon University's Master of Arts Management program offers this index of arts management and cultural resources on the Internet. Visitors can link directly to dozens of sites.

ArtSource
http://www.uky.edu/Artsource/artsourcehome.html
This mega-resource houses pointers to a wide array of selective art sites on the Net, from architecture libraries and gopher sites, to virtual image collections and professional organizations. Entries are chosen by the Webmasters from Net-wide resources, in addition to original materials submitted by librarians, artists, and art historians.

Civilized Explorer—Art on the Internet
http://www.cieux.com/~philip/Arthome.html
This site provides links to "artistic" Web locations, from hipster electronic magazines and virtual galleries of traditional artwork to interactive pages which allow visitors to create in cyberspace. Links are categorized according to content, with helpful descriptions to Web wanderers.

Fantasy Directory
ftp://ftp.sunet.se/pub/pictures/fantasy/
The Fantasy Art FTP index is Valhalla for the elf and unicorn set. This cornucopia of muscle-bound illustration runneth over with eye-popping images of Nordic maidens, mythical beasts, sylvan glades, and sword-wielding uber-men. Indexed by artist and the fantasy authors who inspired them.

Find Arts
http://www.find-arts.com/First.html
As the name implies, visitors can search for artists, galleries, artwork, associations and other art sites here. The site also details Find Arts' Web site design service.

Indian Classical Arts
http://www.cis.ohio-state.edu/~sundar/
This guide to Indian classical arts, part of a personal home page, provides in-depth information and graphic images. Visit here to learn about Carnatic and Hindustani music styles, classical dance forms, contemporary performers, and more.

Internet ArtResources
http://www.ftgi.com/
Not exactly one page but a collection of six pages, the Internet ArtResources site features links to its GalleryWalk, StudioVisit, MuseumStroll, ArtNewsstand and ArtShows pages. At each location find pointers to topical sites from around the world.

Internet for the Fine Arts
http://www.fine-art.com/
Visitors to the Internet for the Fine Arts page will find "a network of on-line artists, galleries, museums, and resources for the fine arts." Besides links to all the above, IFA also features publications, an events calendar and its own gallery.

Jon's Image Archive
http://lynx.uio.no/jon/gif/
Visitors here can browse the images at Jon's Image Archive on topics from art to comics to boys and girls, or download the pictures for their own use. Some pictures do contain nudity. Guests can also sign Jon's petition to save the Eurasian Lynx from extinction by the Norwegian government.

M.C. Escher's Virtually Gone Gallery
http://server.berkeley.edu/Escher/
The Virtual Escher Gallery which once lived here has now been removed—at least when last we checked. However, visitors can peruse a list of links to other Escher-related sites.

Millennium Productions' Arts-Online
http://www.arts-online.com/
This page contains the gateway to Millennium Production's Arts-Online, offering selected links to information about various artistic disciplines. Dance, music, writing, painting and theater arts are featured.

Not Waiting for the Information Highway: The Art Site on the World Wide Web
http://cwis.usc.edu/dept/annenberg/artfinal.html
This site contains a paper by Margaret L. McLaughlin of the Annenberg School for Communication at the University of Southern California. The paper analyzes art sites on the Web and includes numerous links to art galleries.

Online Art References
http://www.art.net/Links/artref.html
This reference server provides a wealth of links to art-related sites. Visitors can link to galleries, journals, museums and auctions. Also find links to various artists' studios, shows and projects.

OTIS On-Line Artchives
http://sunsite.unc.edu/otis/gallery.html
This arts index sorts a large collection of links and resources according to medium and content, then cross-references search results to particular artists working in the user's selected discipline. Submissions are welcome; forms and guidelines provided.

Prints Database
http://rubens.anu.edu.au/prints_form.html
A form allows users to search the Australian National University database of art prints. Multiple criteria options allow for both broad and narrow searches.

Project Runeberg
http://www.lysator.liu.se/runeberg/
Project Runeberg creates and collects electronic editions of classic Nordic literature and art. Its site provides information on the volunteer project as well as the online works, which are indexed by artist and author. The page is available in a variety of languages.

Reverse Solidus
http://www.teleport.com/~bbrace/bbrace.html
The Arte Art Kunst Foto is an online gallery of selected art and photography drawn from a wide range of sources. The site also includes links to newsgroups and FTP archives. Text available in English, Italian, French and German.

The Dragon Hawthorne
http://www.best.com/~wooldri/fantasy/
A fan of the fantastical presents this guide to "fantasy" art and writing. This extensive index of primarily image-related Web sites will lead you to ASCII dragon art, role playing games, book reviews and more.

Univ. of Victoria, Canada-Faculty of Fine Arts Gopher System

gopher://kafka.uvic.ca:70/1

The Faculty of Fine Arts Computer Facilities at the University of Victoria, Canada, provides access to its image library, the university library and a directory of test GIFs on this gopher menu. Includes recipes from the university and job postings.

Virtual Image Archive

http://imagiware.com/via.cgi

This extensive index to digital arts images is organized by topic and ranges from fractals to animals to movie stars.

World Art Treasures

http://sgwww.epfl.ch/BERGER/

This page from the Jacques-Edouard Berger Foundation houses the organization's 100,000 fine art slides, representing work from all over the world, in all periods and genres. Categories include the Renaissance, ancient Rome and most of the major artistic movements.

World-Wide Web Virtual Library: Art

http://www.w3.org/pub/DataSources/
bySubject/Literature/Overview.html

Part of the larger World Wide Web Virtual Library, this index of arts resources includes pointers to museums, galleries, art by genre, artists, publications, and a host of other art- and literature-related resources.

ART HISTORY

Architecture & Architectural Sculpture of the Mediterranean Basin

http://www.ncsa.uiuc.edu/SDG/Experimental/
anu-art-history/architecture.html

Classical and Hellenistic architecture of the Mediterranean basin is featured in this collection of research images. Visitors will find architecture and architectural sculpture from the preclassical period to the 19th century.

Art History Visual Guide

http://www.dsu.edu/departments/liberal/
artwork/ArtH.html

A fine arts graduate of Dakota State University takes browsers on a nuts-and-bolts tour of the important developments in Classical European art history here. Each of the major art-historical periods is addressed, along with pictures of representative works and explanatory text.

Art of China

http://pasture.ecn.purdue.edu/~agenhtml/
agenmc/china/china.html

This well-rounded cultural page serves up a variety of Chinese visual art images, musical selections and language resources. Take a virtual tour of China, ponder your Chinese Zodiac sign or link to other Chinese-related sites.

ArtServe

http://rubens.anu.edu.au/index.html

This Australian National University site features nearly 16,000 images concerned with the history of art and architecture mainly from the Mediterranean Basin. Resources also include art history tutorials, access to reference works and source images. See Editor's Choice, page 9.

The Getty Institute for the History of Arts and Humanities

http://www.getty.edu/gri/

This page acts as a gateway to the Getty Art History Information Program, a project of the J. Pau Getty Trust. Beyond the gateway, find information on the program, its initiatives, projects, publications and news. A searchable database and links to other resources are also featured.

---

a2z   EDITOR'S CHOICE

ArtServe

http://rubens.anu.edu.au/

From an Australian National University art history professor comes ArtServe, where visitors will find around 16,000 images concerned with the history of art and architecture, mostly from the Mediterranean basin. Not for the timid and packed with images and information, the main menu offers a variety of choices from classical art to prehistoric ritual monuments of the British isles, to Islamic architecture and contemporary architecture in Hong Kong. Not satisfied with this mere explosion of tutorials, guides, photographs and graphics, Artserve also documents exactly how the recording of all this was done, including information about currently employed technologies, help on graphics techniques and a link to "Computers & the History of Art: Teaching, Images, Internet." Not exactly a simple stop on the Web, scholars, students, and amateurs alike will want to camp out for several days, exploring each of the hundreds of links and pages in detail. ArtServe is not only a valuable resource for art history information and research, it's also indispensable for those who wish to set up similar pages, implement graphics imaging and iconic systems, learn more about the teaching of art history or simply find links to include on their own pages.—*Reviewed by Amy Hembree*

ArtServe

Art & Architecture mainly from the Mediterranean Basin

Welcome to the
Australian National University!

Images for Art History at ANU
http://www.ahip.getty.edu/ahip/home.html
Maintained by an art history professor at the Australian National University, this page offers a gateway to trial pages featuring image projects under construction. Find a tutorial on the history of prints and a point-and-click system accessing the National Gallery of Australia.

Images of Orality and Literacy in Greek Iconography of the Fifth, Fourth and Third Centuries BCE
http://ccat.sas.upenn.edu/awiesner/oralit.html
Experience the origin and invention of western writing technologies at the Images of Orality and Literacy in Greek Iconography of the Fifth, Fourth and Third Centuries BCE site. Historical images and explanatory texts are archived here.

The Institute of Egyptian Art and Archaeology
http://www.memphis.edu/egypt/main.html
The Institute of Egyptian Art and Archaeology at the University of Memphis offers this page with a collection of exhibition images and information about the institute. Visitors can also take a short tour of Egyptian sites along the Nile.

ARTISTS A2Z

Christo & Jeanne-Claude Home Page
http://www.nbn.com/youcan/christo/
Fans of contemporary conceptual and environmental artists Christo and Jeanne-Claude can peruse text and pictures from recent installations here, including the Reichstag installation and updates on works in progress.

Fuertes Collection
http://oitnext.cit.cornell.edu/library-images/fuertes-birds.html
The Louis Agassiz Fuertes page contains a collection of the artist's letters, notebooks, sketchbooks, diaries and other personal papers. This page includes a gallery of over 1,000 of his bird sketches in ink, pencil and watercolor.

Ilan Hasson Museum & Art
http://shani.net/~akatz/hass/hass1.html
At Ilan Hasson's Museum and Art page, visitors can take a virtual tour of the Israeli artist's online exhibition and learn more about worldwide exhibitions and the dedication of Hasson's painting at a special meeting with Madam Jehan Sadat concerning the Egyptian/Israeli peace process.

Frida Kahlo Tribute
http://www.cascade.net/kahlo.html
This Web site is devoted to Mexican surrealist painter Frida Kahlo. Contains biographical information about Kahlo, examples of her work, a sampling of self-portraits, and a link to the Frida Kahlo Commercial Art Gallery.

Paintings of Vermeer
http://www.ccsf.caltech.edu/~roy/vermeer/
This online gallery presents selected works of the 17th Century Dutch painter, Jan Vermeer. Visitors can learn more about the artist and his home, view thumbnails of his paintings and link to other topic-related sites.

Rossetti Archive
http://jefferson.village.virginia.edu/rossetti/rossetti.html
Find the writings and paintings of the Pre-Raphaelite poet and painter, Dante Gabriel Rossetti, archived at this site. Scholarly annotations and notes provide commentary and insight into the work.

World of Escher
http://www.texas.net/escher/
The World of Escher is an online company specialising in products based on the work of Dutch artist M.C. Escher. Visitors can read discussions of Escher's work or articles relating to Professor Roger Penrose, the author of a collection of mathematically based puzzles.

ASSOCIATIONS AND ORGANIZATIONS

American Arts Alliance
http://www.tmn.com/0h/Artswire/www/aaa/aaahome.html
The American Arts Alliance is an advocate of America's professional non-profit arts organizations. Visitors to its home page will find art news and legislation updates, and reports on the economic impact of funding cutbacks on the arts.

Australia's Federal Department of Communications and the Arts
http://www.dca.gov.au/
The Federal Department of Communications and the Arts from the land downunder features information on state supported culture. Visitors can access links to Australian arts organizations and keep up with country-wide events using the information resources supplied.

Leonardo Online
http://www-mitpress.mit.edu/Leonardo/home.html
Leonardo is a society serving professionals active in the use of science and technology in contemporary art. The organization's support site includes general information, forums, almanacs and other resources, as well as links to related sites.

McLuhan Probes
http://www.mcluhan.ca/mcluhan/
The Canadian-based Herbert Marshall McLuhan Foundation offers downloadable art works and copies of its online publication, "The McLuhan Probes," here. Links to art, as well as a description of the foundation's mission is also featured.

Public Domain
http://noel.pd.org/
This site is the Web home of Public Domain, Inc., a non-profit organization dedicated to exploring "the interface between art, technology, and theory." Visitors to this home page can find information on the group, its Working Papers series and its journal, "Perforations."

BODY ART

Body art
http://www.cis.ohio-state.edu/text/faq/usenet/bodyart/top.html
Tattooing, piercing and other forms of body manipulation are explored and explained at this site, which includes a frequently asked questions (FAQ) file regarding bodyart.

Tatoos
http://ziris.syr.edu/dj/dj.tatoos/tatoos.html
Visitors to this interactive, show-and-tell page can ponder tattoos. Options to wax poetic and exhibit personal art are featured.

CALLIGRAPHY

Vellum Gallery
http://www.catalog.com/gallery/welcome.html
Promoting "an appreciation and understanding of the art of lettering" is the goal of this virtual calligraphy gallery. Webmasters offer an illustration of calligraphic and illumination techniques, an electronic exhibition of lettering and book arts, and an opportunity to purchase works online. Resources for calligraphers are also included.

CENTERS AND PROGRAMS

The Centre for Contemporary Art

http://www.catalog.com/gallery/welcome.html

Poland's Centre for Contemporary Art, located in Warsaw's Ujazdowski Castle, operates as a multi-disciplinary exhibition hall and documentary archive for the arts. At the heart of the Centre's goals is an initiative to collect and display contemporary Central and Eastern European art. Read more about the Centre's activities here, browse an index of upcoming events, or stroll through a virtual collection of the Centre's holdings.

Dia Center for the Arts, New York, NY

http://www.diacenter.org/

New York-based Dia Center for the Arts is a multi-disciplinary contemporary arts organization, aiming to serve as a "conduit for realizing extraordinary projects." Browsers can link to a variety of pages here, including the center's permanent collection, exhibitions, poetry, dance and publications.

French National Center for Art and Culture Home Page

http://www.cnac-gp.fr/

The French National Center for Art and Culture in Paris, France, maintains this site for news, activities updates and exhibits information. Visit here to learn about the center and its related programs. Available in French and English

Jubilee Community Arts

http://funnelweb.utcc.utk.edu/~tkoosman/jca/

The Jubilee Community Arts site is an online cultural center dedicated to the traditional arts in the Knoxville, Tenn., area. Upcoming concerts and events for the Southern Appalachian area are listed.

Media and Visual Arts

http://www-nmr.banffcentre.ab.ca/

The Banff Centre for the Arts in Canada offers information about its current exhibits and profiles its staff on this home page. The page also includes links to the works of artists in residence at the center.

Mito Arts Foundation

http://www.soum.co.jp/mito/

Japan's Mito Arts Foundation maintains this site as part of its effort to promote art, music and culture. Visitors will find information on the Art Tower Mito concept, as well as links to information on local art, music and theatre presentations. Pages are offered in both Japanese and English.

Powersource Native American Art & Education Center

http://www.powersource.com/powersource/gallery/default.html

Native American art graces the virtual walls of the Powersource Gallery. In addition to the art collection, access Native American cultural, historical and political guides here.

CHILDREN'S ART

The Fridge Gallery

http://www.ibm.com/Stretch/EOS/fridge.html

IBM's Fridge Gallery brings kids' refrigerator art into cyberspace. Webmasters encourage kids of all ages to submit, but warns those over age 12 that their digital hipness may be of questionable authenticity (translation: "Grownups, go play in your own cyberyards!"). The company also, and not surprisingly, showcases its new image search technology here, which offers gallery queries by image color and pattern.

Peace in Pictures

http://www.macom.co.il/peace/index.html

This international project encourages children around the world to draw their visions of peace and submit the artwork for display here. Visitors to the site can learn more about the project and view the artwork already received.

CLIP ART

Deep Visions Clip Art

http://www.kiva.net/~deepvis/dv/

When divers look at scuba art, what they see is outdated equipment, regulators on the wrong side, masks on foreheads—all wrong, and dangerous images for this sport. Deep Vision Scuba Clip Art sets out to correct that with downloadable samples and ordering information online.

COMPUTER ART

ComputerArt

http://ourworld.compuserve.com/homepages/Maushart/

This ComputerArt page features Florian Maushart's Raytrace picture gallery along with a link to the e-zine, "The Stick." Visitors can take a guided tour through the gallery or get a "quickview" of pre-selected pieces.

Computer Graphics

http://mambo.ucsc.edu/psl/cg.html

This page puts visitors in touch with a variety of online resources related to computer graphics. Included are links to Frequently Asked Questions (FAQ) lists and a variety of commercial and educational Web sites.

Contours of the Mind

http://online.anu.edu.au/ITA/ACAT/contours/contours.html

This "celebration of fractals, feedback and chaos" was a 1994 exhibition of sonic and visual art at Australian National University. The exhibition's long-standing informational site includes a catalog of submissions and a "digital gallery."

Cyber Art Gallery Eindhoven

http://asterix.urc.tue.nl/~rcrolf/cage/cage.shtml

This virtual art gallery was created by Dutch artist Rolf van Gelder in order to display his works to a wider audience. Van Gelder exhibits paintings and digital work, and offers a guide to his real-time exhibitions.

Fractal Design Digital Art Gallery

http://www.fractal.com/gallery/

The Fractal Design Corporation showcases digital art made with its graphics software. The site displays work from Fractal's Digital Art Contest finalists, a rotating artist of the month, and curates a "Poser Gallery," a collection of ... well, digitally created poses (honest).

Implicate Beauty—Art by Brian Evans

http://www.vanderbilt.edu/VUCC/Misc/Art1/Beauty.html

"Implicate Beauty" is the name given to artist/composer Brian Evans' computer art. At his personal page, you can view some of his artwork, watch animation excerpts or try out some interactive algorithmic art generators for yourself.

Interactive Genetic Art

http://robocop.modmath.cs.cmu.edu:8001/

The Interactive Genetic Art site from Carnegie Mellon's School of Computer Science offers three interactive art projects which can be explored and rated on a scale of one to ten

Optical Illusions: A Collection

http://www.lainet.com/~ausbourn/

This personal home page provides links to a variety of optical illusions. Visit here to view images that challenge the mind and stir the imagination.

Space-Time Travel Machine

http://blanche.polytechnique.fr/lactamme/
Mosaic/descripteurs/demo_14.html

In the Space-Time Travel Machine, computers, mathematics and art collide. View the results at this online exhibit. The artist also offers his philosophical perspective on the work and its implications for the future.

Three-Dimensional and SIRDS Images

http://www.comlab.ox.ac.uk/archive/3d.html

This graphics archive stocks SIRDS (single image random dot stereo) images which are 3-D graphics comprised only of dots or text. Consider the advantages of wall-eyed viewing, cross-eyed viewing and "focus to infinity," or for a taste of superheroism, download a Batman stereogram.

Vern's SIRDS Gallery

http://www.sirds.com/

Vern's SIRDS Gallery contains a collection of Single Image (Random Dot) Stereograms that can be viewed online, along with an informative article and Frequently Asked Questions (FAQ) file on the subject. The site's creator invites stereogram authors to add their works to the exhibition.

CONSERVATION AND RESTORATION

IsabelDeco Gallery

http://www.isabel.com/

If you're an Old Master enthusiast with a small pocketbook, this reproduction service could be the answer to your collecting prayers. Curators specialize in the creation of handcrafted replicas, right down to "technique, type of brushes and mixing of colour." Ordering info and a virtual gallery are available here.

Vintage Ink and Paint

http://home.earthlink.net/~sworth/

Restoration and sale of vintage animation art is Vintage Ink and Paint's line. The company explains its services and posts artwork available for purchase. The page also contains information for the novice collector and a glossary of animation terminology.

CRAFTS

CraftWeb Home Page

http://www.craftweb.com/

This unusual project hopes to create an online community where "professional craftspeople and artisans meet, share information and promote fine crafts worldwide." Resources here include real-time chat, an FTP site, links to individual artisans, an online gallery, and access to newsletters and related books.

FolkArt & Craft Exchange™

http://www.folkart.com/

The FolkArt & Craft Exchange, a service of Sunnyvale, Calif.-based promoter Latitude International, provides a forum for buying and selling handmade crafts by American indigenous peoples. Visit here for an index of resources in English, Japanese and Spanish.

Not Just Mud

http://www.njmgallery.com/index.htm

Glassblowers are featured at this site based in rural Portsmouth, N.H., where exhibits of glass artistry, jewelry and kaleidoscopes are displayed and offered for sale.

The Origami Page

http://www.cs.ubc.ca/spider/jwu/origami.html

Origami enthusiast Joseph Wu maintains this home page containing a wealth of information and graphics. Visit this site to find out how to make origami, see interesting examples and link to other origami sites.

White House Collection of American Crafts Home Page

http://www.nmaa.si.edu/whc/
whcmainpage.html

This White House exhibition features the work of 77 individual artisans. Visitors can take a virtual video and audio tour, or search for artists by name and medium.

FUNDING, ENDOWMENTS, AND GRANTS

Grantseeker's Resource Center

http://oeonline.com/~ricknot2/grant_
seekers.html

The Grantseeker's Resource Center specializes in helping organizations, businesses and individuals get their hands on grant funding. Visitors to this Web site can learn about the center's research, grant-writing and educational services.

GrantsWeb

http://web.fie.com/cws/sra/resource.html

GrantsWeb organizes links to grant and funding-related information and resources on the Internet. This page includes info on the service and a topic index including general funding opportunities, grants databases, policy developments and professional activities.

New York Foundation for the Arts

http://www.tmn.com/Artswire/www/nyfa.html

The New York Foundation for the Arts helps contemporary artists and art organizations complete and exhibit their work. Readers are invited to explore financial and networking resources offered by the nonprofit organization, and check out the latest art world news.

GALLERIES AND WORKS FOR SALE

ARTISTS' COLLECTIVES

Apparitions

http://www-apparitions.ucsd.edu/

Apparitions is an online art installation focusing on virtual environments. Visitors can view its online catalog and portfolio of text and images, read about its creators or link to other interesting art sites on the World Wide Web.

@art gallery

http://gertrude.art.uiuc.edu/@art/gallery.html

This electronic art gallery is an offering of the University of Illinois at Urbana-Champaign. The goal is to provide a "viewing space for talented and mature artists of outstanding merit." Visitors can choose from the current exhibition, or browse an archive of past presentations here.

Art Gallery

http://heiwww.unige.ch/art/

Visitors to this page will find a couple of online art exhibits. More predominant, however, is the list of links to other art sites on the Web

Art on the Net

http://www.art.net/

This vast virtual exhibition hall features an array of artists' studios, from visual and performance art to video and animation, musicians, hackers and electronic poet laureates. For .au fans with time on their hands, an index of artists' downloadable sound bites should please.

Art to Lift Your Spirit

http://www.mindspring.com/~tentmakr/
spirart.html

Visitors can wander through an exhibition of scripture-laced fractals at this online art gallery. Includes links to churches, Christian publications and schools, and the Cyberspace Catacombs, a meeting place for the saved.

Arthole

http://www.mcs.com/~wallach/arthole.html

View a panic movie, tour an online nightmare ("in a more or less organized way"), relax in meditative contemplation, or browse through an exhibition of photo images from Guatemala at this eclectic and engaging art site. Among the innovative entries: "Bald Dali Panic," "An Internet Trans-Global Exquisite Corpse Project," and "New York Postcards."

Artnetweb

http://artnetweb.com

The third phase of an attempt to build an art colony in cyberspace, the artnetweb provides a "curated area for projects, writings and resources." Visitors will also find info on arts organizations and an arts commerce section.

Atelier Nord

http://www.sn.no/home/atelier/

Artists in residence at Atelier Nord in Norway create electronic art that includes video, performance and animation. Visitors here can browse through a virtual gallery of the artists' work. The page also contains a message bulletin board. In English.

Bas van Reek

http://www.xs4all.nl/~basvreek/

The Bas van Reek Art Building features five virtual floors of Dutch art and culture. Areas include the Webmaster's own gallery, guest rooms featuring the work of other artists, a giftshop and a feature no art gallery should be without, a toilet.

Black Hole of the Web

http://www.ravenna.com/blackhole.html

Is it art? Is it social commentary? Once you enter the Black Hole of the Web, it's impossible to say. With each flicker of the screen, visitors fall deeper into the darkness, and await the terse comments that began the journey. What they find is utter, empty space—a black hole.

Cirque de la Mama

http://lancet.mit.edu/cirque/cirque.html

In more colloquial terms, "Mom's Circus" is a virtual exhibition hall "born to bring works of art to people and to bring people to works of art." The site's author claims the space is experimental, and as a result, online exhibits change and rearrange frequently.

Cloud Gallery

http://www.commerce.digital.com/palo-alto/CloudGallery/home.html

This online gallery offers visitors some ethereal renderings of cloud photography; float through the exhibition or download selected images for your own home page. Includes a photographer's essay on tapping into "angel power," plus contact information.

Fluxus Online

http://www.panix.com/~fluxus/

Fluxus, the postmodern art movement born in the 1960s which declared that all realities are constantly changing, is celebrated and explored at this bright site. Poetry, photography, large-scale installations, performance and video are among the art forms presented.

Gallery of Artists

http://branch.com/artists/artists.html

This artists' collective, based in New York City, hopes to present work from artists around the world in this unique virtual setting: 12 different images from a single artist will be shown for 12 consecutive weeks, with a different image on display each week. Contact info for submissions is included.

HypArt Project Home Page

http://rzsun01.rrz.uni-hamburg.de/cgi-bin/HypArt.sh

Visitors can join in a worldwide art initiative at the HypArt Project page. Artists are invited to submit a drawing based on the current theme and to integrate that contribution online into the single image displayed at the site.

interARTisrael

http://www.interart.co.il/

From Jerusalem, the interARTisrael page features works by Israeli artists along with design concepts from the area and works by international artists. Visitors can also contact art sales houses or browse catalogs of art books and publications.

Linda's Gallery

http://www.tricon.net/Comm/linda/index.html

Painter Linda Coven curates this online exhibition of four artists' works, which includes landscape and portrait painting, wildlife and still life, and "romantic" oils on canvas. All works are for sale, and all artists are available for commissioned work.

95Global

http://www.mech.gla.ac.uk/~gsapd/sig.htm

Students and faculty at Scotland's Glasgow School of Art invite visitors to view a collection of "vanity cases for sanity cases," "digital happy families," "ambient video dentistry," and "mustardy mopeds." If that doesn't satisfy your curiosity, link to the institution's departments and academic programs, or take a virtual tour of "the crew" home pages.

Old Schoolhouse Virtual Art Gallery

http://www.cuug.ab.ca:8001/~dicka/gallery.html

The Old Schoolhouse is a virtual art gallery showcasing the work of various artists. Visitors will find art exhibits and artists' biographies.

The Place

http://gertrude.art.uiuc.edu/ludgate/the/place/place2.html

An evolving gallery of artwork created with Web distribution in mind, this site includes images and text, plus information about The Place's curator and reviews of the online exhibition house.

Santa Fe Fine Art

http://www.sffa.com/

The Santa Fe Fine Art site has monthly featured artists, and exhibitions by photographers, painters, sculptors and printmakers. A link to the Southwestern Artists home page is also featured.

Starving Artists

http://www.starving.com/

"Starving Artists" offers a place for visitors to satiate their hunger for art and poetry online. Artists' biographies and links to related sites are provided, and comments are invited.

SWD Home Page

http://www.ism.net/~swd/index.html

Stone Worship Design is the brainchild of a group of friends in Missoula, Mont. The group acts as a research consortium to explore different ways that computer technology manifests itself as media. The resulting home page is full of artful images, fiction and poetry, and links to other colorful places on the Net.

Temple Gallery of the Arts

http://betty.music.temple.edu:80/Gallery/

Temple University's Gallery of Arts features student art, music and film. Sample the works online and link to listings of campus cultural happenings.

Virtual Gallery

http://www.daum.co.kr/gallery/

The Virtual Gallery features online exhibitions of the world's great painters, sculptors and artists. Visitors to its home page can review a schedule of events, view online portfolios, or wander through the galleries.

Virtual Gallery on the Pixerver

http://papin.HRZ.uni-marburg.de/~meyerh/

Dubbed an "experimental forum," this server hosts discussions and exhibitions of digital art and painting. Visitors are invited to explore digital collages and material surface paintings, post comments and questions, and submit their own works for display. In English and German.

COMMERCIAL GALLERIES

Art Cellar Exchange

http://www.artcellarex.com/ace/

The Art Cellar Exchange is a fine art consultancy offering international art brokering services for collectors, corporations and institutions. Includes descriptions of company services, brokerage fees, a catalog of artwork for sale and information on buying and selling art on the secondary market.

The ARTA Gallery, Jerusalem.

http://www.macom.co.il/arta/index.html

The Arta Gallery of Israel presents an exhibit of the works of Marc Chagall. Included are images of lithographs, the Kidush Cup, candlesticks and windows.

ArtCom Art Collectors Corner

http://www.artcom.com/

This art dealers' gallery offers a variety of orginal works for sale. The site also includes links to museum tours and upcoming international art expos.

The Electric Art Gallery

http://www.egallery.com/index.html

This virtual collectors' space, self-described as "the Premier Art Source on the Web since April 1994," offers online purchasing of original paintings from galleries and dealers around the world. Select from contemporary, folk, Byzantine and regional styles.

The Electric Art Gallery: Jazz and Blues Wing

http://www.egallery.com/jazz.html

Stroll down this wing of the Electric Gallery to look at contemporary art that celebrates American jazz and blues. Browsers can purchase the paintings, read about the artists and download a snippet from blues giant B.B. King.

Gondwana Fine African Art

http://www.gondwana.com/

Visitors can browse through online fine African art galleries here. The extensive site also includes links to travel information and environmental groups working on African issues. Webmasters also promise tribal pages, social & policial issues, and current African affairs.

Isaacs/Innuit Gallery

http://www.novator.com/UC-Catalog/Isaacs-Catalog/Isaacs-Internet.html

The Isaacs/Innuit Gallary of Toronto, Canada exhibits sculptures, drawings, wall hangings and other works created by Innuit artists. Visit this site to view its collection, search for artists and works by region, and learn about the gallery. Ordering information is also available

IsabelDeco Gallery

http://www.isabel.com/

If you're an Old Master enthusiast with a small pocketbook, this reproduction service could be the answer to your collecting prayers. Curators specialize in the creation of handcrafted replicas, right down to "technique, type of brushes and mixing of colour." Ordering info and a virtual gallery are available here.

Kaleidospace

http://kspace.com/

Kaleidospace claims to have been the first company to commercially distribute works by independent artists and musicians via the Web. This colorful site offers all indies (from CD-ROM authors to filmmakers) the opportunity to display (or advertise) their work for sale.

MauiWeb Gallery

http://maui.net/stuart/MWG.html

Visitors to this page will find a virtual art gallery "showcasing the work of artists from the Valley Isle and around the Pacific Rim." Most of the featured works are for sale—some as prints, others only as originals.

Miramar

http://useattle.uspan.com/miramar/

Miramar Images, Inc. sells music and art from a variety of new age artists. Visit here to browse their catalog and stroll through a virtual gallery.

911 Gallery Home Page

http://www.iquest.net/911/iq_911.html

Here, the 911 Gallery in Boston, Mass., presents a selection of its works online, including information about current exhibits and directions to the gallery itself.

Print Emporium

http://web2.airmail.net/tself/

A commercial gateway leads to the online gallery of the Fine Art Print Emporium, a dealer based in Aubrey, Texas. Visitors can view prints bycategory or place orders online.

Robischon Gallery Home Page

http://artresources.com/guide/clients/2.html

The Robischon Gallery in Denver, Colo., focuses on contemporary works from artists living in the Southwestern and Mountain states, but also includes pieces by notable artists residing outside the region. The institution's home page provides a list of featured artists and directions to the gallery.

The Vienna Kunstlerhaus

http://www.kunstart.co.at/kunstart/

The Vienna Kunstlerhaus claims to be "virtually the last and only privately owned Artist-Society's Exhibition Hall." On its home page are assembled examples of paintings and drawings from current and upcoming exhibits.

Wentworth Gallery Home Page

http://www.kunstart.co.at/kunstart/

Wentworth Gallery owns 36 fine art galleries across the United States. It offers a selection of its works in this virtual gallery and also posts information about its artists, exhibitions and gift certificates.

INDIVIDUAL ARTISTS' GALLERIES

Abulafia Gallery

http://www.cgrg.ohio-state.edu/~mlewis/Gallery/gallery.html

Painter Matthew Lewis hosts this virtual gallery space to exhibit his series entitled "Dennett's Dream..." The series was created as a "storyboard for an animation of a skeptic nightmare." This electronic version includes both VRML and animated presentations.

Ancestry: Religion, Death and Culture

http://gort.ucsd.edu/mw/bdl.html

Artist Belinda Di Leo curates this site as a virtual exhibition hall for her MFA project, a series of paintings documenting her experiences as a native of Central Appalachia in North America. The work explores Appalachian culture using landscape, still life and portrait techniques.

Art of Maria Kazanskaya

http://www.kulichki.com/centralit/manin/gal.html

View the oil paintings of Maria Kazanskaya in this three-room virtual gallery, from still life to landscape. Webmaster Dmitrii Manin curates the show complete with an artist's biography and purchasing information.

The ARTA Gallery, Jerusalem.

http://www.macom.co.il/arta/index.html

The Arta Gallery of Israel presents an exhibit of the works of Marc Chagall. Included are images of lithographs, the Kidush Cup, candlesticks and windows.

Burtz Virtual Atelier

http://www.burtz.ch/

This is the manual link to an artist's "atelier" or workshop in Switzerland. An artist in the virtual realm, Marcy Burtz offers her work, solicits opinions (which she then posts) on a 13-month year, provides hotlinks free of "smut" and "dangerous" material, and signs her work digitally.

Chavi Feldman Judaica Art Gallery

http://www.io.org/~yfeldman/chavi.htm

Patterned after art galleries along the streets of Jerusalem, this online gallery features the work of artist Chavi Feldman. Visitors are invited to browse and review her work and its Judaic themes, as well as talk to the artist.

Chesley Bonestell Gallery

http://www.secapl.com/bonestell/Top.html

Paintings of space and planetary scenes are featured at the Chesley Bonestell Interactive Art Gallery. Each work by Bonestell is accompanied by a brief narrative; familiar subjects include Earth, Jupiter, Mars and Saturn.

Danner Studios

http://www.infi.net/~ddanner/index.html

This online exhibition of wildlife sculptures from Danner Studios of Roanoke, Va. showcases the work of artist Dennis Danner. Danner's handiwork includes owls, rabbits, chipmunks and other woodland creatures. Ordering info included.

Jef Morlan

http://www.sos.net/home/jef/

Jef Morlan brings his art works to the Web here at his personal page. Visitors are invited to view landscapes, nudes, portraits and other works.

The Mark Vinsel Gallery

http://www.lanminds.com/local/vinnie/gallery.html

Artist Mark Vinsel's paintings reflect one of his other keen interests—fishing. Paintings of landscapes are here, and each is accompanied by a caption describing the work's inspiration.

Nathan Wagoner's Gallery of Allegory

http://heiwww.unige.ch/art/wagoner/

The artwork of Nathan Wagoner is featured on this page. He presents images of his allegorical paintings — including Fat Betty and Dream House — which he allows to be used or reproduced for any non-commercial purpose.

Sarabel's Studio

http://www.art.net/Studios/Visual/Sarabel/sarabel.html

Sarabel's Studio is a virtual tour of the artist's Santa Fe studio and a description of how she works. Includes a gallery of paintings and sketches.

Shremagraphs Home Page

http://www.webscope.com/shremagraphs/info.html

This home page exhibits "Shremagraphs," three-dimensional, kinetic artwork created by Stephan Shrem. Includes background on the artist, plus pricing and ordering information.

Strange Interactions

gopher://amanda.physics.wisc.edu/11/show

Strange Interactions is an experimental one-person art exhibit of drawings, paintings and prints. John Jacobsen created this online exhibit from a show of his work in Madison, Wis., in 1993. He includes an artist statement and related essays

GENRES

!Surréalisme!

http://pharmdec.wustl.edu/juju/surr/

Surrealism and its associated oddities come to life on the Web through this creative page. It contains odd bits of text and pictures that examine Surrealism, along with Surrealist games and writings. See Editor's Choice, page 15.

GRAFFITI

Art Crimes

http://www.gatech.edu/desoto/graf/

Art or vandalism? Visitors decide at this online gallery featuring graffiti from city walls and train cars around the world. Related links include articles and interviews, featured artists, an events calendar and pointers to other Web sites dedicated to graffiti. See Editor's Choice.

---

a2z   EDITOR'S CHOICE

!Surréalisme!

http://pharmdec.wustl.edu/juju/surr/

In Surrealistic art, "images swim congruently," and it is for the paintings and graphic works of such artists as Salvador Dali that the movement became famous (or possibly) infamous. With this in mind, put your expectations aside, and more than once visit !Surréalisme!, where you'll find much to amaze, astound and most likely confound. What is the "Vice of Surrealism?" Find out here…maybe. Who qualifies as a famous Surrealist? Mmmmmaybe that's here, too. There's also plenty…or not…of critical paranoia, Surrealist Games (is that redundant?), and writings and leftings. Visit the Department of Objects and Delusions, the Cadaveric Enigma Engine Generator and the ever-popular Surrealist Compliment Generator for wisdoms like, "Your unexpected explosion entangles us in a web of premature umbrellas and precocious timepieces." And if it becomes too much, you could always run home to your Dada.—*Reviewed by Amy Hembree*

GRAPHIC DESIGN

DESIGNERS AND COMPANIES

Atom Co., Ltd.

http://www.atom.co.jp/

This Japanese graphic design and multimedia company's home page contains an online publication, graphics image gallery, music archives and user comment links. English and Japanese.

CMC Interactive

http://www.atom.co.jp/

CMC is a visual design and marketing company, specializing in print and electronic media and presentation graphics. Visit this home page for service overviews, client listings, employment opportunities and contact information.

PROFESSIONAL RESOURCES

Communication Arts

http://www.commarts.com/

Communication Arts, a trade journal for graphic artists and print media professionals, offers an online version here that aims to highlight artists' work and careers, and link pros to resources. Visit for online exhibits, job postings, and indices of printer info, service bureaus and paper companies.

Design Online

http://www.dol.com/

designOnline offers a broad range of interactive services and resources for design professionals, educators, students and amateurs. Includes a Bulletin Board System (BBS) allowing visitors to download software anddocuments.

Designlink

http://206.14.15.5/designlink/

Designlink is a San Francisco-based bulletin board system for artists and photographers. Visitors to its Web site can download shareware, browse through portfolios from graphic artists and photographers, and look for jobs. The site also posts information on Designlink's user group meetings.

The European Association for Computer Graphics

http://www.cwi.nl/Eurographics/

Here's a nonprofit association for researchers, developers, educators and others who provide or use computer graphics. Member services include conferences, publications, working groups and workshops. Read about the organization's activities and find contact info here.

Fractal Design Corp. FTP Archive

ftp://ftp.fractal.com/

The anonymous FTP server maintained by graphics software developer, Fractal Design, provides a place for visitors to pick up images, files and tips useful for computer design work.

The Graphix Exchange

http://www.rust.net/TGX_WWW_pgs/TGX.html

The Graphix Exchange maintains this site for its directory of illustrators, graphic designers, photographers, animators and other graphic-related professionals. Visit here to search its art resource database of more than 600 members from around the world.

VIRTUAL DISPLAYS

Design Research Centre's Virtual Gallery

http://dougal.derby.ac.uk/gallery/

Images of photography, electronic art and virtual reality art are featured at the Virtual Gallery of the Design Research Centre. Visitors can also check out a selected show of "unusual and innovative work" and public art such as billboards and graffiti.

---

a2z EDITOR'S CHOICE

Art Crimes

http://www.gatech.edu/desoto/graf/

Think of the Web as a huge, online wall for graffiti artists. Started in 1994, the volunteer Art Crimes project provides cultural information and resources related to the art form, and emphasizes that much of the world's graffiti is created by artists, not gangs. Art Crimes also provides information about shows, events, stickers, and styles, but the main attraction here is the work that's found mostly on city walls and trains—graffiti artists' favorite canvases. The works are categorized by country and region, and in the train gallery, some works are pinned down to a regional freight line. Many of the artists are represented by more than their graffiti art, as Art Crimes proprietors regularly feature interviews and articles, inviting all interested artists to submit work from a variety of media. And what do the artists like to see besides graffiti art? How about the Phatlist, a collection of links to "Hip Hop Places," music, zines, and personal home pages. If the art is spray-painted and phat, then it's probably here.—*Reviewed by Amy Hembree*

Art Crimes: The Writing on the Wall

Such & KA - Mesa, Arizona

> What's New
> Graffiti Shows and Events
> City Walls
> Trains
> Featured Artists

HOLOGRAMS AND 3-D ART

Holocom!

http://www.holo.com/

Holy holograms! Holocom! is a hall of holography holdings. The hullabaloo includes a hologram image gallery, information about the Art in Holography symposium, a holographic image generator, industry news and a holographic site search.

Royal Holographic Art Gallery

http://www.islandnet.com/~royal/index.htm

"Enter the World of 3-D," beckons this page from the Royal Holographic Art Gallery in Victoria, B.C., Canada. The site offers a preview of gallery holdings, and provides ordering info for most items, including a do-it-yourself photogram kit for would-be holographers.

StereoArt

http://www.crl.com/~dow/stereoart.html

At the StereoArt Gallery, those little red-and-blue glasses are required to experience the full effect of the 3-D JPEG images. Never fear, however; the glasses can be ordered here.

ILLUSTRATION AND CARTOON ART

Fractal Movie Archive

http://www.cnam.fr/fractals/anim.html

This movie archive boasts the "biggest collection of fractal animations online." Visitors can choose from more than 100 titles, from "Cruise through an alien landscape" to "Chaotic smoke." Available in a variety of still and animation formats.

INSTITUTES AND SCHOOLS

Advanced Computing Center for the Arts

http://www.cgrg.ohio-state.edu/

Ohio State University's Advanced Computing Center for the Arts andDesign teaches computer graphics, animation, software development and more. It details its program, faculty and students here. Visitors candownload course information and take a look at examples of the center's work dating back to 1970.

Appalachian State University Department of Art

http://www.acs.appstate.edu/art/

The Department of Art at Appalachian State University in North Carolina offers a tour of the Rosen Outdoor Sculpture Exhibitions and a collection of links to art resources. This demo page also features a pointer to departmental academic info, and a newly under-construction home page.

AusArts

http://ausarts.anu.edu.au/ITA/AusArts/index.html

Sponsored by the Australian National University's Institute of the Arts Library, this server acts as a gateway to the Canberra Schools of Art and Music, as well as the Australian Centre for the Arts and Technology. Find info here on academic course work, gallery and concert schedules, and links to ANU's electronic art and music resources.

Centennial's Bell Centre for Creative Communications

http://www.bccc.com/

Centennial College presents this site, which details the new Bell Centre for Creative Communications, Canada's largest interactive multimedia training centre, offering full time studies in advertising, book and magazine publishing, journalism and more.

Center for Research in Computing & the Arts

http://crca-www.ucsd.edu/index.html

The Center for Research in Computing and the Arts, part of the University of California in San Diego, gives an overview of its programs and research projects here. The page also provides a link to the center's FTP archive.

The Cooper Union Home Page

http://www.cooper.edu/

Prospective students of the Cooper Union for the Advancement of Science and Art in New York will find an overview of the school here. The private college grants full-tuition scholarships to all of its students.

Department of Photography and Instructional Graphics

http://www.dopig.uab.edu/

This departmental page from the University of Alabama at Birmingham contains information on courses of study, course offerings, admissions, and faculty profiles. Includes links to other campus servers and related resources

Illinois State University College of Fine Arts

http://orathost.cfa.ilstu.edu/

The Illinois State University College of Fine Arts home page contains information on academic departments, courses of study and faculty pro-

files. Includes a gallery of fine art, links to the computer laboratory, software and pointers to other art resources.

The Institute of Egyptian Art and Archaeology

http://www.memst.edu/egypt/main.html

The Institute of Egyptian Art and Archaeology at The University of Memphis, Tenn., maintains this informational site. Visit here to learn about the institute and take a virtual tour of its artifact exhibits.

Kyushu Institute of Design

http://www.kyushu-id.ac.jp/

The Kyushu Institute of Design is a Japanese graduate school for professional training in the design disciplines. Campus information and an electronic access guide are posted at this site.

MICANet

http://www.mica.edu/

Expand your creative side by touring the facilities at the Maryland Institute College of Art. Information about the campus, programs of study, and student portfolios is available.

Minneapolis College of Art & Design

http://www.mcad.edu/

The Minneapolis College of Art and Design in Minneapolis, Minn. provides information here on its people and programs. Visit here to learn about the college, check into its online classrooms and visit its gallery of student works.

National Conservatory for Arts and Crafts

http://www.cnam.fr/

The home page for the National Conservatory for Arts and Crafts in Paris provides general information about CNAM, pictures, a library catalog, and technical information. In French and English.

Satakunta Polytechnic

http://www.spt.fi/

The Satakunta Polytechnic in Finland provides more than academic information at its web site. It also provides the Jazz.Bit 96 contest, an international competition for computer animation. In English and Finnish.

Scholes Library at NYS College of Ceramics

http://scholes.alfred.edu/

This server provides access to resources offered by the New York State College of Ceramics, and acts as a gateway to global resources in the areas of Art and Design (particularly in ceramics), Engineering and Science.

School of Visual Arts (SVA)

http://www.sva.edu/

Prospective students of New York City's School of Visual Arts can get an overview of the school and admissions information here. Visitors can also take a virtual tour through graduate student exhibitions.

Surrey Institute of Art & Design

http://www.surrart.ac.uk/

England's Surrey Institute of Art and Design has set up this page of Web links to art, design and media resources and sites. Information on academic programs; keyword search also available.

Syracuse University—Art Media Studies and Computer Graphics

http://ziris.syr.edu/

Syracuse University's College of Visual and Performing Arts, Art Media Studies and Computer Graphics presents this collaborative online art exhibition. Visitors will find digital images and selections of student work on display.

Tasmanian School of Art Home Page

http://ziris.syr.edu/

The Tasmanian School of Art provides facilities for research and training in design and the visual arts. Visit this site to learn about the school, its course offerings and its teaching staff

University of Art and Design Helsinki UIAH

http://www.uiah.fi/default.html

Finland's University of Art and Design Helsinki invites visitors to its home page to learn more about the university and its academic programs, publications, conferences and exhibitions. Also provided is access to the school's online Internet guide.

University of Waterloo Faculty of Arts

http://watarts.uwaterloo.ca/

The Faculty of Arts at Canada's University of Waterloo provides information on its academic departments, administration and support services, and student organizations. Links to related sites of interest on campus are also featured.

METALSMITHING

The ArtMetal Project

http://wuarchive.wustl.edu/edu/arts/metal/ArtMetal.html

A group of metalsmiths launched this project "to disseminate information about ... artistic metalworking and to provide a forum for artists and art lovers." An array of metalworking resources can be accessed here, along with an ArtMetal Gallery, and metalworking news "from around the globe."

Enrique Vega Metalsmith

http://wuarchive.wustl.edu/edu/arts/metal/Gallery/vega_e.html

This Web site exhibits the creations of metalwork artist Enrique Vega Visitors can read descriptions and browse accompanying images of the artist's architectural and public artwork.

MUSEUMS

AUSTRALIA/OCEANIA

La Trobe University Art Museum

http://www.latrobe.edu.au/Glenn/Museum/ArtMuseumHome.html

Browsers can wander through online exhibits from the art museum at La Trobe University in Australia here. The site also contains links to other art sites on the Net.

EUROPE

Ashmolean Museum of Art & Archaeology

http://www.ashmol.ox.ac.uk/

The home page of the Ashmolean Museum of Art & Archeology provides information about this venerable University of Oxford institution. Listings of current and upcoming temporary exhibitions, plus historical information and descriptions of the museum's permanent collection.

Louvre

http://mistral.culture.fr/louvre/

The Web site of the Louvre Museum in Paris, France provides information about the museum's exhibits and publications. Available in French, soon available in English and Spanish

Musee Arts Metiers

http://web.cnam.fr/museum/

Visitors can take a virtual tour of Paris's Musee des Arts et Metiers here. The site also includes general information about the museum, its exhibits, and programs. In French.

The Vienna Kunstlerhaus

http://www.kunstart.co.at/kunstart/

The Vienna Kunstlerhaus claims to be "virtually the last and only privately owned Artist-Society's Exhibition Hall." On its home page are assembled examples of paintings and drawings from current and upcoming exhibits.

NORTH AMERICA

African Art: Aesthetics and Meaning

http://www.kunstart.co.at/kunstart/

The Bayly Art Museum at the University of Virginia hosted an exhibit in 1993 called African Art: Aesthetics and Meaning Browsers can tour an electronic version of the exhibit here that includes accompanying essays.

The Andy Warhol Museum

http://www.warhol.org/warhol/

Located in Pittsburgh, Pa., this museum features the work of influential American pop artist Andy Warhol, who received far more than his share of 15 minutes of fame. Visitors will find a preview of the museum's permanent collections and archives, as well as temporary exhibits from other artists.

Dallas Museum of Art Online

http://www.unt.edu/dfw/dma/www/dma.htm

At the Dallas Museum of Art Online, visitors can view museum galleries and sculpture gardens or stop by the education resource center.

Exhibits from The University of Texas at Austin

http://www.lib.utexas.edu/Exhibits/Exhibits.html

The University of Texas at Austin offers this page detailing art exhibits on campus. Visitors will find calendars, background information and artwork from the shows. A select list of art exhibits on the Internet is also provided.

The Fine Arts Museums of San Francisco

http://www.famsf.org/

Take a virtual tour of San Francisco's Fine Arts Museums, the deYoung and The Legion. The online exhibits include samplings from the deYoung's American art collection and a look at the newly renovated Legion.

Kelsey Museum Online

http://www.umich.edu/~kelseydb/

Greek, Roman and Near Eastern artifacts and art objects call the Kelsey Museum home. Find online versions of the museum's exhibits of classical art and archaeology at this site. Includes text, pictures and maps.

Krannert Art Museum

http://www.art.uiuc.edu/kam/

The Krannert Art Museum and Kinkead Pavilion at the University of Illinois, Urbana-Champaign, features 8,000 works of art, including some from the fourth millennium B.C.E. Visitors can take a hypermedia tour, browse the permanent collection, plan a visit or sip virtual coffee in the coffeeshop.

Metropolitan Museum of Art

http://www.metmuseum.org/

Tour the Metropolitan Museum of Art in New York. Visitors are asked to sign a registry to receive updates about museum news, and inside they will find glimpses of museum collections, as well as access to the museum store.

The Minneapolis Institute of Arts

http://artsMIA.org/

This North American museum, "the most comprehensive fine arts museum in the upper midwest,"
houses a permanent collection of some 85,000 objects which span a period of 4,000 years. Its Web site offers virtual access to some of its many exhibitions, educational programs (both real-time and online), the museum shop, and an index of volunteer opportunities.

National Museum of American Art

http://www.nmaa.si.edu/

The National Museum of American Art maintains this multimedia site offering visitors a variety of online exhibits containing almost 1,000 pieces of art. General museum information, a calendar of
events, and links to the museum's departments and publications are also featured

Palmer Museum of Art

http://cac.psu.edu/~mtd120/palmer/

This electronic museum, sponsored by Pennsylvania State University, features a guided tour of its galleries, a directory of represented artists and works, online "art supplies," and more. Links to other art-related sites are also available

University Art Museum Pacific Film Archive

http://www.uampfa.berkeley.edu/

Visitors can take a virtual tour of the University of California, Berkeley's, University Art Museum/Pacific Film Archive here. The site includes full online exhibits from the art museum and an events calendar for the film theater.

Weisman Art Museum

http://hudson.acad.umn.edu/

The Frederick R. Weisman Art Museum, at the University of Minnesota, Minneapolis, presents images from the museum's 13,000-object permanent collection. Exhibitions and current events are listed here as well.

Whitney Museum of American Art

http://www.echonyc.com/~whitney/

New York's famous—if often controversial—Whitney Museum of American Art offers this electronic preview of its temporary exhibits and permanent collections. Digital artists will find an invitation to contribute to the site's continuously evolving interface.

VIRTUAL

Expo

http://sunsite.unc.edu/expo/ticket_office.html

Expo makes "interesting exhibitions" from throughout the Web available to the general public. Visit its "ticket office" to find detailed exhibit information and take a "shuttle bus" to one of the attractions. Don't worry; tickets are free. See Editor's Choice, page 20.

Internet Arts Museum

http://www.artnet.org/iamfree/

The Internet Arts Museum features music, text, photographs, digital manipulations, and animation. The material here is free and visitors are welcome to download what they like.

---

a2z   EDITOR'S CHOICE

EXPO

http://sunsite.unc.edu/expo/ticket_office.html

Presented quite literally as an exhibition, EXPO offers its visitors virtual "tickets" to a series of "pavilions" it has created from space, text and images donated by the U.S. Library of Congress. A variety of displays are featured, among them Rome Reborn: The Vatican Library and Renaissance Culture, which presents about 200 of the Vatican Library's most precious manuscripts and maps, many of which were instrumental in the re-discovery of the classical heritage of Greece and Rome. The Soviet Archive Exhibit is the "first public display of the hitherto highly secret internal record of Soviet Communist rule." 1492: An Ongoing Voyage is an examination of the interactions between native Americans and Europeans in the years between 1492 and 1600. And the Dead Sea Scrolls exhibit examines the mysteries surrounding ancient documents from the settlement of Qumran and the effects the scrolls have had on modern religious, biblical and historical study. Other pavilions include a paleontology exhibit from the University of California, Berkeley, and the Palace of Diocletian at Split, a fascinating structure from the late Roman empire. Tourists at the EXPO will also find a restaurant, post office and exhibit catalogs for sale. Complete, yet diverse in its subject matter, EXPO is one of the most comprehensive Web museums on the Internet.—*Reviewed by Amy Hembree*

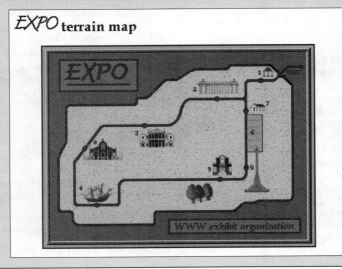

EXPO terrain map

Leonardo da Vinci Museum

http://cellini.leonardo.net/museum/main.html

This virtual display brings you the inventive and artful work of Leonardo da Vinci. Filled with the master's magnificent genius, this site also features links to related Leonardo resources.

Net in Arcadia

http://www.parnasse.com/net.in.arcadia.html

This electronic museum is "dedicated to contemporary classicism," and houses works by Alfred Russell, Andree Descharnes and Elsie Russell. The works are chronicled according to date, media and size; biographies and statements from the artists are also available

University of North Carolina Virtual Museum

http://sunsite.unc.edu/exhibits/vmuseum/vmuseumhome.html

The Workstation Development Group at the University of North Carolina maintains this online museum. Visitors can peruse a number of exhibits, including the Soviet Archive and the Mathematical Art Gallery.

Vatican Exhibit—Rome Reborn

http://www.ncsa.uiuc.edu/SDG/Experimental/vatican.exhibit/Vatican.exhibit.html

The Library of Congress takes browsers on a virtual tour of its Vatican Exhibit here. The exhibit includes a close look at the history of the papal city and the arts that flourished within it.

Vomitus Maximus Museum

http://www.vomitus.com

The Vomitus Maximus Museum is a collection of strange, sometimes graphically violent, paintings and drawings by artist R.S. Connett. This welcome page explains the nature of the site and the artist, providing ample warning for the weak of stomach

WebMuseum Technical Tips

http://sunsite.unc.edu/louvre/about/tech.html

This page from the WebMuseum site in Paris details how Web cruisers can tune up their software to make the most of the inline images at the site. The technical page includes links to download Web browsers

Yoruba and Akan Art in Wood and Metal: The Doorway

http://www.fa.indiana.edu/~conner/africart/home.html

This online catalog for an African art exhibit first displayed in Peoria, Ill., displays photographs of the pieces plus informational texts describing the processes used in their creation. Visitors also can link to a page providing information about people who assembled the exhibit.

NEWSGROUPS

FineArt Forum

http://www.msstate.edu/Fineart_Online/home.html

The FineArt Forum was created as a network for the exchange of information and ideas about art and technology. Visitors here can download the forum's newsletters, browse through its online gallery or use the gopher service. Links to museums, publications, exhibitions, schools, and selected resources.

PAINTING

The Electric Art Gallery

http://www.egallery.com/

Have an art critic's eye but a shallow pocket? At The Electric Art Gallery, "the first commercial art gallery on the Web," choose from a variety of genres, complete with prices, to order a critic's original or a more affordable print.

The HoLing Gallery

http://www.webconn.com/holing/

The HoLing Gallery of St. Paul, Minn., displays some of artist HoLing Hui's works online. HoLing paints in the traditional Chinese style called Ling Nan where natural plant colors are applied to rice paper and mounted on a scroll. The paintings are offered for sale here.

PERFORMANCE ART

Digger Archives

http://www.webcom.com/~enoble/diggers/diggers.html

The San Francisco Diggers became legend during the years 1966-68. A roving guerrilla performance and social action group, their random "happenings" are chronicled in this archive: "Free Food," the "Free Store," and a history of the group's formation and eventual disbanding are explored.

The Kitchen

http://www.panix.com/kitchen/

The Kitchen, a New York home for the arts, makes its Web home on this page to encourage visitors to learn more about the center, its history, and future plans. Current performance schedules, video catalogs and merchandise offerings are also available.

Knitting Factory

http://www.knittingfactory.com/

A performance space located in New York City, the Knitting Factory has been bringing cutting-edge creative expression to the public since 1987. Director Michael Dorf describes it as "an artistic laboratory for experimental rock, jazz, funk, poetry, dance, film, video, performance art, and everything in between." Get more of the lowdown at this Web site, along with schedules and an overview of the Factory's record label ventures.

Laurie Anderson: HOMEpage of the Brave

http://www.c3.lanl.gov:8080/cgi/jimmyd/quoter?home

Followers of singer, musician, technical wizard and performance artist Laurie Anderson can find art of, for, and about their multimedia heroine at the Home Page of the Brave. Explore her discography and performance schedule, or link to the artist's official Web sites.

Seemen

http://robotics.eecs.berkeley.edu/SEEMEN/

The Seemen Web site bursts to life with descriptions and video clips of this unique performance art troupe, whose hallmark is staging shows which explore viewers' tastes for violence and danger. Among themes explored by the group are propaganda, exploitation, machines and history.

PHOTOGRAPHY

The Athenaeum of Photography

http://www.shore.net/~axenios/

Visitors will find photographer Andrew Xenios' virtual studio here. His work includes a photo essay of aloneness, photogravures from the Yucatan, and street and cafe drawings. All art is for sale, but browsers can enjoy the artistry for no charge.

Designlink

http://206.14.15.5/designlink/

Designlink is a San Francisco-based bulletin board system for artists and photographers. Visitors to its Web site can download shareware, browse through portfolios from graphic artists and photographers, and look for jobs. The site also posts information on Designlink's user group meetings.

Fox Studio Limited

http://www.webcom.com/~foxstu/

Fox Studio Limited of Minneapolis, Minn., presents selected images from its photographers' portfolios and works-in-progress. The page also has an index of businesses geared toward clients and colleagues.

Reverse Solidus

http://www.teleport.com/~bbrace/bbrace.html

The Arte Art Kunst Foto is an online gallery of selected art and photography drawn from a wide range of sources. The site also includes links to newsgroups and FTP archives. Text available in English, Italian, French and German.

PRINTMAKING

Bill Curr

http://www.printspace.com/billcurr/index.html

Visitors to this page can access the imagery of Bill Curr, a "printmaker gone digital." The work is arranged in a thumbnail index with a special link to Curr's newest work.

PROFESSIONAL RESOURCES AND SUPPLIES

Artnetweb

http://artnetweb.com/

The third phase of an attempt to build an art colony in cyberspace, the artnetweb provides a "curated area for projects, writings and resources." Visitors will also find info on arts organizations and an arts commerce section.

Arts Wire Home Page

http://www.tmn.com/Oh/Artswire/www/aaa/aaahome.html

ArtsWire is a subscriber-based network of arts resources and information, sponsored by the New York Foundation for the Arts. ArtsWire also publishes a free weekly digest of current news in the art world

ArtsEdge

http://artsedge.kennedy-center.org/

Arts Edge is a budding network of information for artists and art educators based at Washington D.C.'s Kennedy Center. A full palate of services and links are provided, from Internet beginner's resources to a calendar of art conferences and calls for entries.

ArtSource

http://www.uky.edu/Artsource/artsourcehome.html

This mega-resource houses pointers to a wide array of selective art sites on the Net, from architecture libraries and gopher sites, to virtual image collections and professional organizations. Entries are chosen by the Webmasters from Net-wide resources, in addition to "original materials submitted by librarians, artists and art historians."

ArtsWire Current News

http://artswire.org/Artswire/www/current.html

This page from ArtsWire, a network serving the arts community, offers a mixed palette of news. Visit to read about the latest art and politics collision, to find job openings or find recommended artworld events. Includes funding updates for artists seeking to board the gravy train.

New York Foundation for the Arts

http://www.tmn.com/Artswire/www/nyfa.html

The New York Foundation for the Arts helps contemporary artists and art organizations complete and exhibit their work. Readers are invited to explore financial and networking resources offered by the nonprofit organization, and check out the latest art world news.

Starving Artists

http://www.starving.com/

"Starving Artists" offers a place for visitors to satiate their hunger for art and poetry online. Artists' biographies and links to related sites are provided, and comments are invited.

PUBLICATIONS AND INDUSTRY NEWS

Art Bin

http://www.nisus.se/artbin

"The Art Bin," a Sweden-based online culture magazine, provides articles and columns about art, literature, information technology and politics. Visit here for access to the publication in Swedish and English.

ArtScene

http://artscenecal.com/

An electronic exhibition listing for Southern California's art cognoscenti, ArtScene's directory service hits all the major galleries and museums, in addition to providing detailed area maps, a calendar of openings and special events, and a users' forum. Reviews and commentary also provided.

ArtsUSA

http://www.artsusa.org/

ArtsUSA, a service of the American Council for the Arts, lists a broad selection of articles, news and primary documents on American arts and culture. Includes a menu of choices listed by subject.

ArtsWire Current News

http://artswire.org/Artswire/www/current.html

This page from ArtsWire, a network serving the arts community, offers a mixed palette of news. Visit to read about the latest art and politics collision, to find job openings or find recommended artworld events. Includes funding updates for artists seeking to board the gravy train

Asian Arts

http://www.webart.com/asianart/index.html

This online "journal" explores the breadth and history of Asian art, and includes articles and commentary, a vast image gallery, and a calendar of Asian art-related events and exhibitions.

Communication Arts

http://www.commarts.com/

Communication Arts, a trade journal for graphic artists and print media professionals, offers an online version here that aims to highlight artists' work and careers, and link pros to resources. Visit for online exhibits, job postings, and indices of printer info, service bureaus, and paper companies.

Departure from Normal

http://www.xwinds.com/dfn/dfn.html

This electronic arts journal hosts a diverse selection of digitized expressions, from poetry and short fiction to paintings and graphics. Submission guidelines assert, "If we like it, we publish it."

FineArt Forum Online—Mississippi State University

gopher://gopher.msstate.edu/11/Online_services/fineart_online

This gopher hole houses current and back issues of "FineArt Forum," a monthly newsletter published on the Internet and distributed exclusively via e-mail. The focus of the publication is the interelationship between art, science and technology. Electronic subscription info included.

McLuhan Probes

http://www.mcluhan.ca/mcluhan/

The Canadian-based Herbert Marshall McLuhan Foundation offers downloadable art works and copies of its online publication, "The McLuhan Probes," here. Links to art, as well as a description of the foundation's mission is also featured.

Not Waiting for the Information Highway: The Art Site on the World Wide Web

http://cwis.usc.edu/dept/annenberg/artfinal.html

This site contains a paper by Margaret L. McLaughlin of the Annenberg School for Communication at the University of Southern California. The paper analyzes art sites on the Web and includes numerous links to art galleries.

NWHQ

http://www.knosso.com/NWHQ/

A novel (if less-than-straightforward) Web journal of literature and art, nwhq is described by its editor as "a labyrinth" where art and text may be links that spin the reader to other areas of the document. This gateway page features an image map offering numerous entry points into the work.

Parallel Gallery

http://www.camtech.com.au/parallel/x2/index.html

This art publication examines cross-disciplinary work from artists and writers, and explores topics ranging from architecture and art to film and fiction. Visitors will find samples of work from a variety of authors and artists.

Who's Got the Body?

http://www.sva.edu/WGTB/flypaper.html

In response to efforts to censor the Internet, graduate students from New York's School of Visual Arts Computer Art Department recommend a series of sites about censorship, and provide their own artistic responses to the censorship initiative.

ONLINE COLLABORATIONS

Breaking Out (of the Virtual Closet)

http://math240.lehman.cuny.edu/art/

This exhibit sponsored by the Lehman College Art Gallery aims to bridge the gap between computer terminal and artist. Included here are images, videos, "sound bursts" and anopportunity to add to the "world's first collaborative sentence."

DigitalJourneys

http://ziris.syr.edu/digjourney.html

From Syracuse University's College of Visual and Performing Arts comes Digital Journeys, a "collaborative Internet art projectt" that presents a multitude of variations on myriad themes. Visitors are encouraged to respond to the work here and submit their own images and writings.

SCULPTURE

Danner Studios

http://www.infi.net/~ddanner/index.html

This online exhibition of wildlife sculptures from Danner Studios of Roanoke, Va. showcases the work of artist Dennis Danner. Danner's handiwork includes owls, rabbits, chipmunks and other woodland creatures. Ordering info included.

Images of Architecture & Architectural Sculpture

http://www.ncsa.uiuc.edu/SDG/Experimental/anu-art-history/architecture.images.html

This page, presented by the Australian National University's art history department, features digitized images of European (mainly Roman)

architecture and architectural sculpture. Visitors can follow links to the departmental home page.

Telematic Sculpture 4

http://iis.joanneum.ac.at/kriesche/biennale95.html

Like a wrecking ball driven by a mathematical equation, Richard Kriesche's bizarre, kinetic sculpture was designed to crash through the wall of the gallery where it was displayed if postings to computer newsgroups outpaced art newsgroup traffic. Learn more about the interactive artwork, which was part of the 1995 Venice Biennale..

Zimbabwean Stone Sculpture

http://www.twi.tudelft.nl/Local/ShonaSculpture/ShonaSculpture.html

Visitors here will learn about Shona sculpture, stone carvings crafted by Zimbabwean artisans. Wander through an image gallery or link to biographical information about the artists.

SOFTWARE

Fractal Design Digital Art Gallery

http://www.fractal.com/gallery/

The Fractal Design Corporation showcases digital art made with its graphics software. The site displays work from Fractal's Digital Art Contest finalists, a rotating artist of the month, and curates a "Poser Gallery," a collection of ... well, digitally created poses (honest).

GENERAL HUMANITIES RESOURCES

The American Humanist Association

http://freethought.tamu.edu/org/aha/

The American Humanist Association is an organization dedicated to the study of mankind and to promoting human well-being. Visitors to its home page can read articles on humanism that range from a basic primer to humanism as it relates to religion.

ARIADNE Network WWW Server

http://ithaki.servicenet.ariadne-t.gr/default.html

Greece's National Academic and Research Network of Computer Communication serves as the main access to the Hellenic Civilization database.

The visual and performing arts, literature and museums are featured as are links to the Hellenistic News database, an online art gallery and other Internet links.

Basilik Journal Home Page

http://www.webart.com/asianart/index.html

Basilik, a "quarterly journal of film, architecture, philosophy, literature, music and perception," maintains this site as an archive for its articles and graphics. Visitors will find thought-provoking materials on the "operative realms of the virtual."

Carnegie Mellon University English Server

http://english-server.hss.cmu.edu/

Carnegie Mellon University provides files for a variety of disciplines in English studies here. The gopher includes listings on literature, cultural theory, related journals, linguistics and semantics, and other areas of interest. See Editor's Choice.

Chorus: Reviews & Resources for "Real World" Computing

http://www-writing.berkeley.edu

The Chorus describes itself as a collection of reviews and resources for "Real World" computing, combining the voices of the humanities disciplines with technology. This page presents a network of resources aimed at assisting scholars, and includes educational software, bibliographic programs and electronic education reviews.

Grantseeker's Resource Center

http://oeonline.com/~ricknot2/grant_seekers.html

The Grantseeker's Resource Center specializes in helping organizations, businesses and individuals get their hands on grant funding. Visitors to this Web site can learn about the center's research, grant-writing and educational services.

GrantsWeb

http://infoserv.rttonet.psu.edu/gweb.htm

GrantsWeb organizes links to grant and funding-related information and resources on the Internet. This page includes info on the service and a topic index including general funding opportunities, grants databases, policy developments and professional activities.

Humanités Canada / Humanities Canada

http://www.hssfc.ca/

Sponsored by the Canadian Federation for the Humanities, this site is an electronic resource and networking tool for "humanists in Canada (and elsewhere)." Canadian member associations post info here on their research in the humanities, publications, teaching and their roles within local communities. In French and English.

Postmodern Culture

http://jefferson.village.virginia.edu/pmc/contents.all.html

The "Postmodern Culture" home page contains tables of contents for current and back issues of the electronic journal of interdisciplinary criticism. The journal's archives can be searched by subject or keyword.

Research Institute for the Humanities

http://www.arts.cuhk.hk/

This Chinese University of Hong Kong site presents an index of humanities resources. The site includes an extensive list of directories and libraries containing information on art, music, languages, literature, philosophy and more.

Social Sciences & Humanities INFOMINE

http://lib-www.ucr.edu/rivera/

Social sciences and humanities Web resources can be accessed along with the latest related news through the INFOMINE Web site. The pages are maintained by the University of California.

Stanford Electronic Humanities Review

http://shr.stanford.edu/shreview/

The Stanford Electronic Humanities Review opens up an intellectual landscape by providing a forum for scholarly dialogue. This page includes articles that deal with cognitive science, artificial intelligence and similar topics. Includes a link to the Stanford University home page.

Voice of the Shuttle

http://humanitas.ucsb.edu/

This comprehensive Web directory indexes humanities resources on the Internet. Subjects range from anthropology and history to linguistics, philosophy, and women's studies. Includes links to related journals, libraries, publishers, and reference and teaching resources.

WWW Virtual Library: Humanities

http://www.hum.gu.se/w3vl/w3vl.html

These electronic stacks of the WWW Virtual Library contain a comprehensive index of Web resources and informational sites relating to the humanities. Pointers to archives, databases, organizations and institutions are among the materials presented.

HISTORY

THE AMERICAS

Alcatraz

http://www.nps.gov/alcatraz/

Once called "The Rock" and "Hellcatraz," the maximum-security federal penitentiary Alcatraz served a 29-year sentence housing some of America's worst criminals. Here visitors can learn more about the prison island's various histories, including its military, Native American and natural pasts.

American and British History Resources on the Internet

http://libraries.rutgers.edu/rulib/socsci/hsit/amhist.html

If you've got the time, this page has the information, much from original documents. Pick your period and find stats, laws, people, maps and more. From Rutgers University Libraries.

The American Civil War, 1861-1865

http://www.access.digex.net/~bdboyle/cw.html

Visitors can take a long, detailed look at the Civil War here with resources that include a link to the Library of Congress Civil War archive and various historical preservation groups.

American Civil War Home Page

http://funnelweb.utcc.utk.edu/~hoemann/cwarhp.html

The American Civil War page, maintained by a University of Tennessee historian, offers links to a wide range of Internet resources about the "war between the states." Visit here for texts, soldiers' rosters, battle descriptions, links to museums and more.

American Historical Documents Gopher

gopher://ucsbuxa.ucsb.edu:3001/11/.stacks/.historical

The University of California at Santa Barbara maintains this primer of historic American political documents, including the Bill of Rights, the Constitutional amendments, the Declaration of Independence and more.

American Memory from the Library of Congress

http://rs6.loc.gov/amhome.html

American Memory is a collection of primary source material on American culture and history held by the Library of Congress. Here, visitors can download electronic reproductions in the collection, including photographs, sound, manuscripts and early movies of such things as Pres. William McKinley at the 1901 Pan-American Exposition.

American South

http://sunsite.unc.edu/doug_m/pages/south/south.html

Electronic resources for southern regional studies are consolidated at the American South Home Page. Access two major academic centers, the University of North Carolina's Center for the Study of the American South, and the University of Mississippi's Center for the Study of Southern Culture, at this site.

Anti-Imperialism in the United States

http://www.rochester.ican.net/~fjzwick/ail98-35.html

Syracuse University provides this document about anti-imperialism in the United States from 1898-1935. Visitors will find a historical background, literature and primary texts on this movement.

British Columbia History

http://www.freenet.victoria.bc.ca/bchistory.html

If there was ever any question about the history of Canada's British Columbia, the answers are probably here. The page links to academic history departments, museums and societies, all with a focus on days long past.

Canadian Heritage Information Network

http://www.chin.gc.ca/

Find out more about the Great White North at the Canadian Heritage Information Network with features that include a guide to Canadian museums and galleries, online Canadian cultural and historical exhibits, and information about Canadian publications and courses. In French and English.

Canadian Museum of Civilization: Mystery of the Maya

http://www.civilization.ca/membrs/civiliz/maya/mminteng.html

The Mystery of the Maya features a look at the history of the ancient civilization of Mexico and Guatemala. The page is a joint effort of the Canadian Museum of Civilization and the makers of a new IMAX film.

Canadian War Museum

http://www.cmcc.muse.digital.ca/cwm/cwmeng/cwmeng.html

The Canadian War Museum, dedicated to Canadians lost in war, examines the effect of war upon the nation and documents Canada's international peacekeeping efforts. This site offers exhibitions, educational programs, collections, and other links.

California Indian Library Collections
http://www.mip.berkeley.edu/cilc/brochure/brochure.html

Thousands of texts concerning California's Native American population, both historical and modern, are archived in California's Indian library collections and deposited in California libraries. Here, the collection is introduced, including information about sound recordings, photos, and texts of historical value from the collections and contact info for collections administrators.

Declaration of Independence
http://www.cs.indiana.edu/statecraft/decl.html

Read the background and full text of the Declaration of Independence of the 13 American colonies at this site. Adopted by the Continental Congress on July 4, 1776, the document is an explanation of why the colonies, now states, declared their independence.

Declaration of Independence
http://www.law.emory.edu/FEDERAL/independ/declar.html

The Declaration of Independence page provides the full text of the 1776 document that announced America's independence from British rule. (Elaborate penmanship not included.)

A Deeper Shade of Black
http://www.ai.mit.edu/~isbell/HFh/black/bhcal-toc.html

Charles Isbell's offers this look at black films, literature and history. The artificial intelligence researcher at the Massachusetts Institute of Technology provides film reviews and quite a bit of information on events and people in black history.

Flag of the United States of America
http://www.icss.com/usflag/

Everything you ever wanted to know about the American flag flies proud at this page. Visit here to learn about the flag's history, evolution and the attempts to amend the U.S. Constitution with a flag protection rider.

French and Indian War Home Page
http://web.syr.edu/~laroux/

A writer chronicling the 18th century French and Indian War offers research materials on the soldiers, battles and strategies of the war. Find a special emphasis on French soldiers who went to Canada to fight.

From Revolution to Reconstruction
http://grid.let.rug.nl/~welling/usa/revolution.html

Historians will find kindred spirits at the site for hypertext collective writing to discuss the American Revolution and struggle for independence. Texts include papers on the colonial period, westward expansion and section conflict, with links to original sources and an opportunity to comment on every subject.

Gettysburg Address
http://lcweb.loc.gov/exhibits/G.Address/ga.html

The U.S. Library of Congress maintains this site with the text of Abraham Lincoln's 1863 Gettysburg Address. Visitors will find full text of the speech and related documents.

The Great Arabian Discovery
http://www.chevron.com/explore/history/arab50/index.html

"The discovery required seven wells, five years, millions of dollars spent during the Great Depression, and a band of dedicated explorers fighting heat and sand in a remote desert. But the payoff was enormous." Read more about the history of Chevron's oil discovery in the Saudi Arabian desert here.

The Heritage Post Interactive
http://heritage.excite.sfu.ca/hpost.html

Dubbed "the Web's first interactive Canadian history magazine," Heritage Post celebrates Canadian heritage with a historical synopsis and links to subjects such as art and key players. Available in English and French.

Historic Mount Vernon
http://www.mountvernon.org/

Preview the grounds at George Washington's Mount Vernon Estate and gardens at this page, which includes a virtual tour, archaeological details and pointers to related educational resources.

In the Beginning Was the Word: The Russian Church and Native Alaskan Cultures
http://lcweb.loc.gov/exhibits/russian/s1a.html

At this Library of Congress online exhibit, visitors will find items from the Alaskan Russian Church Archives documenting the interaction between Alaskan natives and priests of the Russian Orthodox Church from 1794 to 1915.

Letters Home From a Soldier in the U. S. Civil War
http://www.ucsc.edu/civil-war-letters/home.html

The letters found here were written during the Civil War by a private in the 36th Infantry, Iowa Volunteers, to his faithful companion (and future wife) at home. They detail his life as he traveled in Mississippi, Missouri, Iowa, and Arkansas. The site was compiled by the private's great-grandson.

Maryland State Archives
http://www.mdarchives.state.md.us/

The Maryland State Archives houses records dating back to its founding in 1634. The archives contain governmental, church and business records, maps, photographs and newspapers. Dig through indices, exhibits and preservation news here.

New York State Archive gopher
gopher://unix6.nysed.gov:70/1

The New York State Archive is a storehouse of records and information about New York's colonial-era and modern state government agencies, legislatures, and judiciary.

Selected Civil War Photographs
http://rs6.loc.gov/cwphome.html

The U.S. Library of Congress exhibits over 1,000 electronic images in its Selected Civil War Photographs Collection. Portraits of military personnel and battle scene landscapes make up this historic online archive.

The State Historical Archives of Wisconsin
http://www.wisc.edu/shs-archives/

Was that progressive Wisconsin senator Robert LaFollette or Lafollette? The State Historical Archives of Wisconsin could tell you. There's also information about major U.S. sociopolitical movements, including labor and working class history, the New Left, the battle over reproductive rights and others.

U.S. Civil War Center
http://www.cwc.lsu.edu/civlink.htm

The U.S. Civil War Center provides an exhaustive array of information on the bloody conflict between North and South. Visitors can check out a wealth of historical information—including maps, diaries, university archives and much more—or link to hundreds of related sites.

University of Saskatchewan Department of History
http://www.usask.ca/history/

The Department of History at the University of Saskatchewan provides information on graduate and undergraduate programs of study, admissions, course offerings, class schedules, faculty and research projects.

Utah State Archives
http://utstdpww.state.ut.us/~archives/

The Utah State Archives serve as a repository for historical records derived from official government business. County, court and statewide resources are available and searchable, and there are sections on Utah state history and on using the Web for genealogical research.

Works Progress Administration Life Histories
http://rs6.loc.gov/wpaintro/wpahome.html

The Manuscript Division of the Library of Congress presents these life history documents from the Folklore Project. The collection consists of nearly 3,000 documents from 300 writers across America. Visitors can view the archive lists by state, title or topic, or search the entire collection.

The World of Mayan Culture

http://www.yucatan.com.mx/mayas/
mapamay.htm

Mayan culture, cuisine, history, travel and more are addressed in The World of Mayan Culture, available in English and Spanish versions. A link-sensitive map lets visitors explore Mayan regions in Mexico, Belice, Honduras, and Guatemala and El Salvador to learn more on this ancient culture.

ANCIENT

The Akkadian Language

http://www.sron.ruu.nl/~jheise/akkadian/
index.html

This tutorial on Akkadian, a dialect spoken in Mesopotamia in 3000 B.C., is provided here by the Netherland's Space Research Organization. Visitors will find instructional materials, sample texts and a downloadable user's dictionary.

The American Society of Papyrologists

http://scholar.cc.emory.edu/scripts/ASP/ASP-MENU.html

At the American Society of Papyrologists page visitors can explore the papyrus archives at Duke University. Also included is a checklist of editions of Greek and Latin Papyri, Ostraca and tablets.

Ancient City of Athens

http://www.indiana.edu/~kglowack/Athens/
Athens.html

The Ancient City of Athens site presents a photographic archive of archaeological and architectural remains of the ancient Greek city. Intended primarily as a resource for students of classical languages, civilization, art, archaeology and history at Indiana University.

Ancient History Bulletin

http://www.ucalgary.ca/~ahb/

This quarterly publication contains scholarly articles covering ancient history and related topics, such as the study of age-old manuscripts, currency and inscriptions. This site offers access to indexed volumes, previews of pieces to be published and information about submitting articles for consideration.

Ancient World Web

http://atlantic.evsc.virginia.edu/julia/
AncientWorld.html

The Ancient World Web presents a compendium of Internet resources containing searchable geographic, subject and alphabetical indices. A link to the recent news in the field is also available.

Assyria Online

http://www.cs.toronto.edu/~jatou/

Scratch the surface of thousands of years of history, culture and literature at Assyria Online. Ancient and modern civilizations are both represented here, from the history of Mesopotamian times to details about the modern Assyrians of Sweden and Germany.

Bryn Mawr Classical Review

gopher://gopher.lib.virginia.edu/11/alpha/bmcr

The Bryn Mawr Classical Review contains several hundred classical studies-related articles dating back to 1990. Visit here to read more about the review or to search the entire database.

Cassiodorus

http://ccat.sas.upenn.edu/jod/cassiodorus.html

Roman senator, monk and writer Flavius Magnus Aurelius Cassiodorus is the topic of this site. The full text of a historical treatise on Cassiodorus is available here, as well as works by him and links to related sites.

Celebrating 17 Centuries of the City of Split

http://www.st.carnet.hr/split/

Hey, there's a party at Diocletian's! Visitors here can virtually celebrate the 1,700th anniversary of the Roman emperor Diocletian's palace at Split in Dalmatia. Learn more about the ancient structure and the city that has taken on its unique character.

Classical Association of Canada

http://www.trentu.cal/rac

Classical literature takes center stage at this page from the Classical Association of Canada. Visitors can read the association's publications and the "Canadian Classical Bulletin." In French and English.

Classics Subject Guide

http://www.ualberta.ca/~slis/guides/classics/
home.htm

The Classics Subject Guide is a starting point for finding classics Internet resources and exists specifically for classicists at the University of Alberta, Canada. However, visitors are invited to peruse the variety of resources in the three categories of classical art, archaeology, and history.

 EDITOR'S CHOICE

Carnegie Mellon University English Server

http://english-www.hss.cmu.edu/

Managed by student, staff and faculty at Carnegie Mellon, the English Server has been publishing Internet humanities texts—primarily research, criticism, novels and hypertext works—since 1990. Quite a collection has accumulated since then, and the site provides one of the widest, original varieties of humanities texts available online (or anywhere else, for that matter). Not merely a directory of links to other sites, the work here includes "Bad Subjects," a journal of progressive issues, "Cultronix," another journal dealing with contemporary art and cultural theory, and a section devoted exclusively to Marx and Engels. Topics here encompass a variety of humanities concerns, both traditional (18th century studies, feminism) and the new-fangled (cyber and multimedia collections). Rich in resources, yet simply designed and easily navigated by either the text or graphical views, the English Server is a primary Web resource for both scholars and casual visitors.—*Reviewed by Amy Hembree*

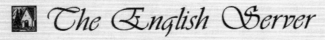

The English Server

The English Server at CMU is managed by students, faculty and staff in the English Department at Carnegie Mellon University. It has been publishing humanities texts to the Internet since 1990. Feel free to read about this site, send comments or contributions to our editors, browse our text collections, talk on our telnet conference line, and join our public mailing lists.

[ABOUT THIS SITE | COMMENTS | SEARCH | OTHER SITES]
[GOPHER | TELNET | LISTSERV | RECENT | EMAIL | FTP]
[Graphical View]

Diotima

http://www.uky.edu/ArtsSciences/Classics/gender.html

Diotima provides information on patterns of gender in the ancient Mediterranean world, as well as a forum for instructors teaching courses about women and gender in the ancient world. Diotima offers course materials, book reviews, online articles, images, and a bibliography of recent work in the field.

Duke University Papyrus Archive

http://odyssey.lib.duke.edu/papyrus/

The Duke University Papyrus Archive features information about and images of 1,373 papyri from ancient Egypt. Instructions for using the archive, general information about Egypt and papyri, and an online catalog search are featured.

Egyptology Resources

http://www.newton.cam.ac.uk/egypt/

This page, maintained by the Newton Institute at the University of Cambridge in England, provides an abundance of Egypt-related resources. Visitors will find news, history and gossip, announcements of conferences and exhibitions, and an Egyptology bulletin board.

Electronic Antiquity: Communicating the Classics

gopher://info.utas.edu.au:70/11/Publications/Electronic%20Antiquity%20%3a%20Communicating%20The%20Classics

The University of Tasmania gopher provides this index of "Electronic Antiquity: Communicating the Classics," an online academic journal about the classics and ancient history. This index contains articles, guidelines, reviews, back issue archive and table of contents.

Exploring Ancient World Cultures

http://cedar.evansville.edu/~wcweb/wc101/

Explore the mysteries of eight far-flung cultures of the ancient world in an online classroom which traces the history of cultures that shaped the development of mankind. Follow cultural avenues into essay collections, museums and other Internet resources at this award-winning site.

Greek Astronomy

http://sunsite.unc.edu/expo/vatican.exhibit/exhibit/d-mathematics/Greek_astro.html

Greek astronomy, created by Hipparchus in the second century B.C.E. and perfected by Ptolemy in the second century C.E., is explored here at the Library of Congress Vatican Exhibit. Links to the ancient works "Almagest," "Tadhkira" and "Geography" are featured.

Greek Mythology

http://www.intergate.net/uhtml/.jhunt/greek_myth/greek_myth.html

Greek gods, those mythological beings who got their jollies swilling ambrosia on Mount Olympus and confusing humans, are the focus here with plenty of information on the gods and Greek myths.

Images of Orality and Literacy in Greek Iconography of the Fifth, Fourth and Third Centuries BCE

http://ccat.sas.upenn.edu/awiesner/oralit.html

Experience the origin and invention of western writing technologies at the Images of Orality and Literacy in Greek Iconography of the Fifth, Fourth and Third Centuries BCE site. Historical images and explanatory texts are archived here.

KMT: A Modern Journal of Ancient Egypt

http://www.egyptology.com/kmt

"KMT: A Modern Journal of Ancient Egypt" online features selected articles from the current issue of this scholarly journal of research and discovery. Complete back issues are also available.

Learning to Read Rome's Ruins

http://sunsite.unc.edu/expo/vatican.exhibit/exhibit/b-archeology/Archaeology.html

Learn about what the ruins of Rome tell us about the people and the times at this archaeological page. Visitors can read a short report and follow links to images of the ruins. The page is part of the U.S. Library of Congress Vatican Exhibit.

Material Culture of the Ancient Canaanites, Israelites and Related Peoples

http://staff.feldberg.brandeis.edu/~jacka/ANEP/ANEP.html

This electronic resource for the University of Pennsylvania course, Introduction to Biblical Archaeology, details materials from "excavations at Beth Shan, Gibeon, Sarepta and Tell es-Sa'idiyeh as well as Haverford College's excavation at Beth Shemesh." Review articles from the Iron Age through the Persian Period.

Mount Athos Greek Manuscripts Catalog

http://abacus.bates.edu/~rallison/

This server is the primary repository of information related to the Philotheou Monastery Catalog Project, located at Bates College, Lewiston, Maine. Visitors will find information on the project here, in addition to such features as Greek monastery manuscripts and methodological papers.

Palace of Diocletian at Split

http://sunsite.unc.edu/expo/palace.exhibit/intro.html

Travel back to the Later Roman Empire for a look at the structure, style and history of Spalato's Palace of Diocletian. Find a discussion of the architectural site in text and pictures here.

Papyrus of Ani: Egyptian Book of the Dead

http://www.sas.upenn.edu/African_Studies/Books/Papyrus_Ani.html

The Department of African Studies at the University of Pennsylvania maintains this site for text of the "Papyrus of Ani: Egyptian Book of the Dead." Visitors can read the English translation of the text, written in 240 B.C.

Perseus Project

http://www.perseus.tufts.edu/

The Perseus Project is an "evolving digital library on Ancient Greece." Visitors will find extensive resources on archaeology, art and literature. This page also contains information on using Perseus in the classroom.

Pompeii

http://www.tulane.edu/pompeii/text/pompeii.html

Pompeii, part of a Tulane University hypercard stack devoted to the ancient city, is intended for students taking "Pompeii: Roman Society and Culture in Microcosm." However, Web guests will also be rewarded by a dig through information revealing the House of Faun and a mosaic of the Battle of Issus.

Reeder's Egypt Page

http://www.egyptology.com/reeder

Reeder's Egypt Page, "...dedicated to examining the art, archaeology, religion and history of Egypt," features links to "KMT: A Modern Journal of Ancient Egypt," the study of a fascinating tomb at Saqqara and an image gallery. Also, learn more about the mysterious Tekenu, who's found in certain ancient funeral ceremonies. See Editor's Choice.

Roman Law

http://www.jura.uni-sb.de/Rechtsgeschichte/Ius.Romanum/origo.html

The original version of this Latin server may have its visitors scrambling for their high school primers. But for speakers of English, Italian or German, an alternative exists. In the language of your choice, access a collection of detailed information on ancient Roman law, or peruse biographical data on Roman and medieval lawyers.

A Simple List of Roman Emperors

http://rome.classics.lsa.umich.edu/emperors.html

How many Roman emperors were named Constantine? This simple list of Roman emperors may answer some of your questions. The emperors are listed in chronological order from Augustus to the fall of Constantinople.

TOCS-IN

ftp://ftp.epas.utoronto.ca/pub/tocs-in/Search.html

TOCS-IN is a searchable archive of the contents of more than 150 journals of interest to classicists. The data is divided into classics, archaeology, religion and near eastern studies, and miscellaneous.

University of Pennsylvania Classical Studies Department

http://ccat.sas.upenn.edu/clst/clst.html

The home page of the Classical Studies Department at the University of Pennsylvania provides a variety of department and classical studies information here. Read about academics, faculty, lectures, workshops and events, and link to personal home pages and related Web sites.

WebAcropol

http://www.mechan.ntua.gr/webacropol

WebAcropol features a historical guided tour of the Acropolis of Athens, the imposing rock on which the Parthenon was built. The tour includes images, history and explanations.

Worlds of Late Antiquity

http://ccat.sas.upenn.edu/jod/wola.html

This site sweeps the dust off of Mediterranean history and culture dating from 200-700 C.E. Prepared by a University of Pennsylvania faculty member, this site offers history buffs recommended reading lists, searchable databases, scholarly commentary and online ancient texts, in addition to a class syllabus.

---

a2z EDITOR'S CHOICE

Reeder's Egypt Page

http://www.sirius.com/~reeder/egypt.html

Want to learn more about ancient Egypt, but afraid of curses and those nasty asp bites? Then try Reeder's Egypt Page for the beginning of deeper study or an overview of some fascinating Egyptological subjects. Start your tour with current issues of "KMT," the quarterly journal devoted to the study of "Kemet" or "The Black Land," which is what the ancient Egyptians called their home. After learning more about the subject, and maybe picking up some vocabulary there, continue to the page's main features. The Saqqara tomb of Niankhkhnum and Khnumhotep, two male manicurists to fifth dynasty king Niusere, is fascinating to many Egyptologists because of how it details the lives of its two occupants, who shared an identical title in the palace and whose names are joined forever above the tomb's entrance. And who are the Muu? Why are they dancing? This page delves into one of the "most obscure and occult" subjects of Egyptology, and includes an article from "KMT." Far from being a stodgy, academic site, Reeder's Egypt Page is gorgeously presented and features all the photographs and images expected of such a fascinating—and timeless—subject.—*Reviewed by Amy Hembree*

WELCOME TO REEDER'S EGYPT PAGE

ANTIQUES AND ARTIFACTS

American Antiquarian Society Gopher

gopher://mark.mwa.org/

The American Antiquarian Society promotes the study of American history through the preservation and collection of rare books. Visitors to its gopher will learn more about the group and find a calendar of upcoming events for book lovers and history buffs.

Chronology of Events in the History of Microcomputers

http://www.islandnet.com/~kpolsson/comphist.htm

Trace the history of the microcomputers all the way from 1926 until the present at the Chronology of Events in the History of Microcomputers. Many historical events on the timeline are linked to further information on the Web.

The Hill Monastic Manuscript Library

http://www.csbsju.edu/hmml/

"Fire, flood, theft, war. It only takes a minute to destroy history's greatest ideas." Working since 1965, the Hill Monastic Manuscript Library is one of the world's most comprehensive archives of medieval and Renaissance sources. Learn more about the library's microfilm collection, manuscript catalogs and study centers here.

Images of Orality and Literacy in Greek Iconography of the Fifth, Fourth and Third Centuries BCE

http://ccat.sas.upenn.edu/awiesner/oralit.html

Experience the origin and invention of western writing technologies at the Images of Orality and Literacy in Greek Iconography of the Fifth, Fourth and Third Centuries BCE site. Historical images and explanatory texts are archived here.

Interpreting Ancient Manuscripts

http://www.stg.brown.edu/projects/mss/overview.html

Interpreting Ancient Manuscripts, a navigable hypertext study of ancient manuscripts that are the bases for the New Testament, is presented by Brown University. Critical discussions of the texts, glossaries and tables aid in the reader's study.

The Lindisfarne Gospels

http://portico.bl.uk/access/treasures/lindisfarne.html

A seventh-century manuscript, "written and illuminated in honour of God and St. Cuthbert," and the British Library's gift book and videotape celebrating the artistic treasure are described at this site. Visitors can read the life story of the historic text here.

Mount Athos Greek Manuscripts Catalog

http://abacus.bates.edu/~rallison/

This server is the primary repository of information related to the Philotheou Monastery Catalog Project, located at Bates College, Lewiston, Maine. Visitors will find information on the project here, in addition to such features as Greek monastery manuscripts and methodological papers.

Runer

http://gonzo.hd.uib.no/NCCH-docs/runes.html

Developments in the computer-based study of runes, as well as ancient and medieval inscriptions, are published and linked at this Norwegian site. Mac users can download rune fonts here. In Norwegian and English.

Scientific and Medical Antiques

http://www.duke.edu/~tj/sci.ant.html

The Scientific and Medical Antiques site provides information for enthusiasts and collectors of old telescopes, scales and surgical equipment. Visitors can find out about online auctions and learn about rare and antiquarian books, among other services.

Therion's Armor and Weapons Page

http://www.io.com/~therion1

Not nearly as menacing as the title would imply, this enthusiast's informational page contains a clanking collection of photographs and descriptions of European and Asian arms and armor.

ARCHIVES AND INDICES

Ari's Today in History Page

http://www.uta.fi/~blarku/tanaan.html

This Web site answers the question, "what happened on today's date throughout history?" Site features also include a 30-day preview of upcoming holidays on the current Christian, Jewish and Islamic calendars. In Finnish and English.

Bodleian Library Electronic Texts Gopher

gopher://rsl.ox.ac.uk/11/lib-corn/hunter/Browse%20Alex/Browse%20by%20Date/Browse%20by%20Date%3a%201600s

The works of writers such as Blaise Pascal, Thomas Hobbes and John Milton are featured on this gopher server from the United Kingdom. It also includes works from John Locke and the first Thanksgiving proclamation from Charlestown, Mass.

Carnegie Mellon University History and Historiography Index

http://english-server.hss.cmu.edu/History.html

The English Department of Carnegie Mellon University maintains this index of history texts. Visit here to find texts covering a wide variety of international historical events.

Chronology of Events in the History of Microcomputers

http://www.islandnet.com/~kpolsson/comphist.htm

Trace the history of the microcomputers all the way from 1926 until the present at the Chronology of Events in the History of Microcomputers. Many historical events on the timeline are linked to further information on the Web.

Economic History Services

http://cs.muohio.edu/

Operated by the Cliometric Society under a grant from the U.S. National Science Foundation, the Economic History Services site aims to be a central source of information for academicians. Visitors will find book reviews, data files, and links to home pages and course materials from economics institutes around the world.

Eighteenth Century Resources

http://www.english.upenn.edu/~jlynch/18th/

Journey back in time via this Web site, which offers visitors information on the literature, history, philosophy, art, architecture and music of the 1700s. Includes scholarly papers, sound files and scads of links to 18th-century resources.

Eighteenth Century Studies Archive Page

http://english-www.hss.cmu.edu/18th/

Part of the English server archive maintained by Carnegie Mellon University, this page provides visitors with an alphabetical list of writings from the 18th century. Visitors can peruse poems, treatises, novels, plays, historical texts and more.

Galaxy: Social Sciences and History

http://galaxy.einet.net/galaxy/Social-Sciences/History.html

Galaxy, an Internet directory, provides this index to historical pages that relate to the social sciences.

Historical Documents Gopher

gopher://gopher.vt.edu:10010/10/33

Historical documents, philosophical teachings and literary works by famous authors are on file and ready to download at this gopher. Selections range from "The Gettysburg Address" to works from Confucius.

Historical Text Archives

gopher://dewey.lib.ncsu.edu:70/11/library/disciplines/history/archives

Maintained by Mississippi State University, the Historical Text Archives provides FTP access for the download of historical texts from around the world, although the current collection is predominantly American.

History Computerization Project

http://www.directnet.com/history/

The University of Southern California and the Los Angeles City Historical Society are building a database for historians, librarians and researchers. Visitors here can read about the project and request a tutorial for the database.

The History of Computing

http://ei.cs.vt.edu/~history/index.html

The History of Computing, collected and written by J. A. N. Lee, former editor-in-chief of the "IEEE Annals of the History of Computing," is a subject-indexed archive that includes details about people and pioneers, archives and museums.

Index of Resources for Historians

http://kuhttp.cc.ukans.edu/history/index.html

Visitors to this index maintained by the University of Kansas can view a comprehensive list of links to historical resources on the Internet. Use this list of pointers to find out about the languages of ancient Greece, view historical art archives and more.

Joan's Witch Directory

http://www.ucmb.ulb.ac.be:80/~joan/witches/index.html

If you have an interest in the history of witch hunts, you'll find dozens of links and resources here, spanning from Salem, Mass., to Finland. Includes a topical glossary and book excerpts describing torture methods that often resulted in "confessions."

Mississippi State University Historical Text Archive

http://www.msstate.edu/Archives/History/index.html

Mississippi State University's Historical Text Archive contains geographically and topically indexed collections of historically important documents. Also includes links to similar archives, databases and history departments, plus photos, maps, bibliographies and scholarship information.

Research Institute for the Humanities: History

http://www.arts.cuhk.hk/His.html

The history page from the Research Institute for the Humanities Web site contains links to history servers around the world covering five historical periods: ancient, medieval, renaissance, modern and World War II. The links are grouped by regions.

Resources for History

http://www.arts.gla.ac.uk/www/ctich/histlinks.html

History students in the throes of term paper despair, panic no more. If you've waited too long to get the information through traditional channels, try the University of Glasgow's Resources for History. Search for information by topic or read samples of other student projects for ideas.

WWW Services for Historians

http://grid.let.rug.nl/ahc/hist.html

This site provides historians with a wealth of important resources. Here they will find updates on grants, archives, various organizations and links to history-related sites around the world. There's also a section on historical articles and exhibitions.

WWW Virtual Library: History

http://history.cc.ukans.edu/history/WWW_history_main.html

This segment of the WWW Virtual Library points to a wealth of history resources organized alphabetically, by era, or by region. Visitors can also access historical news groups and discussion lists, or get details on topical conferences here.

ASIA

A-Bomb WWW Museum

http://www.csi.ad.jp/ABOMB/index.html

Students and faculty of Hiroshima City University constructed this project to provide "accurate information concerning the impact the first atomic bomb had on Hiroshima" and to provide the context for thorough discussion of the topic.

The Great Arabian Discovery

http://www.chevron.com/explore/history/arab50/index.html

"The discovery required seven wells, five years, millions of dollars spent during the Great Depression, and a band of dedicated explorers fighting heat and sand in a remote desert. But the payoff was enormous." Read more about the history of Chevron's oil discovery in the Saudi Arabian desert here.

History of Mathematics: China

http://aleph0.clarku.edu/~djoyce/mathhist/china.html

The Department of Mathematics and Computer Science at Clark University in Worcester, Mass., maintains this site to outline the history of mathematics in China. Visit here to view a chronology of Chinese math studies, read profiles of noted mathematicians, and link to other Chinese historic and cultural resources.

Netherlands Institute for the Near East

http://www.leidenuniv.nl/nino/nino.html

The Netherlands Institute for the Near East in Leiden has long been a center of Oriental studies. Founded in 1939, it produces research and journals on Near East issues. Its home page has information about the institute, its publications and links to related sites.

Philippine History 101

http://pubweb.acns.nwu.edu/~flip/history.html

Culled from various sources, these colorful recountings of social customs and historical timelines provide an introduction to the history and culture of the Philippine people. Includes photos and details on the islands' occupation by the Spanish and the United States.

Mark Twain on the Philippines

http://www.rochester.ican.net/~fjzwick/twain/

Mark Twain, who served as a vice president of the Anti-Imperialist League, thought the United States never should have become involved in the internal affairs of the Philippines. Check out this page and find out why; it's filled with Twain's ideas on the subject, as well as a profile of the writer.

Virtual Memorial Hall of the Victims in Nanjing Massacre

http://www.arts.cuhk.hk/NanjingMassacre/NM.html

Approximately 300,000 people were killed and over 20,000 were reported raped in the December 1937 fall of Nanjing, China to the Japanese Imperial Army. This Virtual Memorial Hall commemorates the victims. It includes photos, videos and book suggestions.

ASSOCIATIONS AND ORGANIZATIONS

The American Antiquarian Society

gopher://mark.mwa.org:70/1

The American Antiquarian Society in Worcester, Mass., maintains a research library of American history and culture that has 3 million books, newspapers and pamphlets collected since 1812. Visitors can search an online catalog here and learn about the society's programs and fellowships.

The American Society of Papyrologists

http://scholar.cc.emory.edu/scripts/ASP/ASP-MENU.html

American Society of Papyrologists (experts on the paper and writings of the ancient world) calls for papers for the 1996 ASP Annual Meeting. Check out the papyrus archives at Duke University. Included in this site is a checklist of Editions of Greek and Latin Papyri, Ostraca and Tablets. Links also to the Papyrology Home Page.

Leonard Peltier Defense Committee International Office

http://www.unicom.net/peltier/index.html

Here, the Leonard Peltier Defense Committee International Office gives visitors the whole story behind this Native American's involvement at Wounded Knee and his subsequent arrest, providing Frequently Asked Questions (FAQs) and articles. This site also includes artwork by Leonard Peltier.

National Civil War Association

http://ncwa.org/

You'd never expect to find the National Civil War Association in Northern ... California. But this group offers re-enactment camps, historic resources to research Confederate and Union forces, and links to other U.S. Civil War sites.

Palo Alto Historical Association

http://www.commerce.digital.com/palo-alto/historical-assoc/home.html

The home page for the Palo Alto Historical Association describes how the city of Palo Alto, Calif., got its name and provides a list of its publications.

Skeptics Society Web

http://www.skeptic.com/

The Skeptics Society promotes science and critical thinking, and disseminates information on pseudoscience, pseudohistory, the paranormal, etc. This site highlights skeptical resources, including an electronic version of "Skeptic" magazine.

Society for the History of Authorship, Reading & Publishing
http://www.indiana.edu/~sharp/

The Society for the History of Authorship, Reading and Publishing is a network aimed at scholars, librarians, publishing professionals and authors interested in the history of print. Visit here to learn how to join the society, track down publishers' archives and link to historical sites.

BIOGRAPHY

Britannica's Lives
http://www.eb.com/calendar/calendar.html

Britannica's Lives is a collection of all the biographies listed in the Encyclopedia Britannica. Visitors can enter a birthdate and age range, and Britannica will then provide all the biographies that fit that description.

Cassiodorus
http://ccat.sas.upenn.edu/jod/cassiodorus.html

Roman senator, monk and writer Flavius Magnus Aurelius Cassiodorus is the topic of this site. The full text of a historical treatise on Cassiodorus is available here, as well as works by him and links to related sites.

Discovery of X-Rays—Wilhelm Conrad Roentgen
http://www.fh-wuerzburg.de/roentgen/index_e.html

Science historians can relive the late 19th-century discovery of X-rays at the Wilhelm Conrad Roentgen page. Visitors can access background information on both the discoverer and his important find here. In German and English.

The Martin Luther King, Jr., Directory
http://www-leland.stanford.edu/group/King/

The Martin Luther King, Jr., Directory, from the project at Stanford University, contains documents written by and about the civil rights leader. Links to a biography, articles and reference sources and the King Center are included.

EUROPE

The Alexander Palace Time Machine
http://www.travelogix.com/emp/batchison/

The Alexander Palace, located in Tsarskoe Selo outside St. Petersburg, was the home of the last Russian Tsar and his family. The Alexander Palace Time Machine lets visitors tour its various rooms and treasures, provides floor plans and introduces its former residents with images and biographies.

American and British History Resources on the Internet
http://info.rutgers.edu/rulib/artshum/amhist.html

If you've got the time, this page has the information, much from original documents. Pick your period and find stats, laws, people, maps and more. From Rutgers University Libraries.

Arthuriana
http://dc.smu.edu/Arthuriana/

"Arthuriana" is a scholarly journal about the legend of King Arthur published quarterly by the North American branch of the International Arthurian Society. Visitors will find sample articles, subscription information and related products such as King Arthur t-shirts.

Classics Ireland
http://www.ucd.ie/~classics/ClassicsIreland.html

Classics Ireland, from the University College Dublin, is the online version of a journal published by the Classical Association of Ireland (CAI). On this page find recent volumes with articles relating to the ancient world, its literature and ideas.

Electronics Sources for West European History and Culture
gopher://dewey.lib.ncsu.edu:70/0ftp%3adewey.lib.ncsu.edu%40/pub/stacks/guides/european-guide

Electronics Sources for West European History and Culture offers information about European history resources on the Internet. Sources are categorized in several fashions including by chronological period, country, academic sub- discipline and alphabetically by subject.

EuroDocs: Primary Historical Documents From Western Europe
http://library.byu.edu/~rdh/eurodocs/

Scholars looking for primary sources can stop here to graze on the offerings of transcribed and translated materials. Find historical information on medieval and Renaissance Europe or more modern material on individual countries.

Library of Congress Soviet Archives Exhibit
http://www.ncsa.uiuc.edu/SDG/Experimental/soviet.exhibit/soviet.archive.html

The U.S. Library of Congress presents its Soviet archives exhibit online. Visit here to explore its collection of documents from the "previously top secret archives of the Central Committee of the Communist Party."

Macedonia: History and Politics
http://vislab-www.nps.navy.mil/~fapapoul/macedonia/macedon.html

Macedonia: History and Politics, part of a virtual tour of the Peloponnese, presents a comprehensive look at the country from antiquity to modern times. A table of contents and annotated list of links to photographs are provided.

Muslims in the 19th Century Russian Empire
http://www.uoknor.edu/cybermuslim/russia/rus_home.html

This page, maintained by the CyberMuslim Information Collective, features an exhibit of photography and historical information regarding the Turks and Tatars. Part of an interactive history project, this site's growth depends on the contributions of visitors' ideas and memories.

Northwestern University Library Special Collections: The Siege and Commune of Paris, 1870-1871
http://www.library.nwu.edu/spec/siege/

Northwestern University maintains this searchable collection of links to over 1,200 photographs and images recorded during the Siege and Commune of Paris. The collection is indexed by subject.

Norwegian Historical Data Center
http://www.isu.uit.no/seksjon/rhd/

The Norwegian Historical Data Center maintains electronic records of "censuses from the years 1865, 1875, 1891 and 1900 together with the parish registers for the 18th and 19th centuries." General information about the NHDC is featured, as are price lists for its data products. In Norwegian and English.

Richard III Society
http://www.r3.org/

The American branch of the Richard III Society offers Web resources for those interested in the interpretations of Richard III, the controversial 15th-century English king and Shakespearean drama. Here the curious will find publications, and topics that include the Battle of Bosworth Field.

Tito
http://www.fri.uni-lj.si/~tito/tito-eng.html

Presented with a first person perspective, this multimedia "home page" of the deceased Yugoslavian dictator, Tito, offers a collection of recorded speeches, galleries of photos and other memorabilia from his years in power.

Ulster Historical Publications
http://www.gpl.net/users/bradley/

Publications about the history, culture and heritage of Northern Ireland can be researched at the

Ulster Historical Publications home page. The site offers lists of publications that are available by mail order.

Vatican Exhibit—Rome Reborn

http://www.ncsa.uiuc.edu/SDG/Experimental/vatican.exhibit/Vatican.exhibit.html

The Library of Congress takes its visitors on a virtual tour of its Vatican Exhibit here. The exhibit includes a close look at the history of the papal city and the arts that flourished within it.

Victorian Web

http://www.stg.brown.edu/projects/hypertext/landow/victorian/victov.html

At Brown University's Victorian Web, visitors will find a wealth of information about the unique era named after the famed British queen. Aspects here include economics, religion, philosophy, literature, and visual arts. Gender matters, science, and technology are also covered.

The Viking Home Page

http://control.chalmers.se/vikings/viking.html

The Control Engineering Laboratory at Chalmers University of Technology in Goteborg, Sweden, maintains this site for The Viking Home Page. Visit here to learn about Viking culture and history through an extensive index of internal and related Web links.

Viking Network Web

http://odin.nls.no/viking/vnethome.htm

Targeting its presentations to primary and secondary schools, the Viking Network Web separates myth from fact to present the lifestyle, travels and heritage of the Viking people. The network is a joint project of the Local History Resource Centre in Fetsund, Norway, and the Summerhill Education Centre in Aberdeen, Scotland.

World of the Vikings

http://www.pastforward.co.uk/vikings/index.html

The World of the Vikings links to Viking history resources available on the Internet. A project of the National Museum of Denmark, this page traces electronically available museum exhibitions, excavations and research projects in this brief but informative index.

GENEALOGY

Acadian Genealogy

http://tdg.uoguelph.ca/~ycyr/genealogy/

Samples from the CD-ROM ``In Search of Our Acadian Roots'' and background on the author are available here. Support for "the first French Canadian/Acadian genealogy CD-ROM of its kind" also is provided.

Ancestors Home Page

http://kbyuwww.byu.edu/ancestor.htm

KBYU-TV, in association with the Public Broadcasting Service, presents this home page promoting "Ancestors," a new "family history and genealogy series set to air in 1996." Visit the set, meet the host, review an in-depth series overview or follow pointers to various genealogy sites.

Australian Family History Compendium

http://www.ozemail.com.au/~coherent/

This online resource aids those rooting out the details of their family trees. Visitors will find a wide variety of genealogical resources, although the site does lean toward Australian information. Includes geographical, historical and software information, plus links to genealogical databases.

A Barrel of Links

http://cpcug.org/user/jlacombe/mark.html

Detectives searching the sea of humanity for ancient relatives and long-forgotten surnames can sift through A Barrel of Links for tools useful on the genealogical voyage. Links include map resources, indices, national and regional resources and heraldry.

Churchyard/Orr Family Museum

http://uts.cc.utexas.edu/~churchh/genealgy.html

The Churchyard/Orr Family Museum traces the genealogy of these two families. Visitors will find an ancestral line that branches out to over 360 different family names, with a summary of main ancestral lines, a list of principal family names and indexes of lineal ancestors.

Directory of Royal Genealogical Data

http://www.dcs.hull.ac.uk/public/genealogy/royal/catalog.html

The Directory of Royal Genealogical Data page traces the British royal family and other royal family lineages. The database includes over 12,000 individuals and can be searched by lineage, surname, forename, date or title. The directory also lists links by culture and country.

Everton's Genealogical Helper

http://www.everton.com/

The online edition of Everton's Genealogical Helper is a multimedia offering from the world's largest genealogy magazine. Not an electronic reprint of the paper version, this site focuses specifically on genealogy resources online.

The Genealogy Bulletin Board Systems

http://www.genealogy.org/PAF/www/gbbs/

The Genealogy Bulletin Board Systems (GBBS) is published monthly and includes more than 1,000 computer bulletin board systems around the world. The GBBS is presented in two formats: table-based pages and pages that do not use tables.

Genealogy Calendar

http://www.genealogy.org/PAF/www/events/

The Genealogy Calendar site contains a schedule of upcoming genealogical events and conferences between 1995 and 2000. Includes guidelines for submissions, indexes by month and location.

Genealogy Home Page

http://www.genhomepage.com/full.html

With a variety of genealogy-related resources ranging from standard Web indices and helpful software to maps and details for contacting genealogists, this page includes a link to a U.S. Geological Survey document explaining how maps can help trace family history.

Genealogy in Australia

http://www.pcug.org.au/~mpahlow/welcome.html

Genealogists will find a host of Australian resources at this site, sponsored by the Canberra Dead Persons Society. The page lists dozens of related links and gives visitors tips on how and where to start their research.

Genealogy Information Center

http://www.astarte.ch/cgr/cgre.html

The Genealogy Information Center has published dozens of resources for people who want to find their ancestors with the help of computers and databases. There is also link to a book on genealogy, "The Descendants of Richard Austin of Charlestown, MA, 1638."

Genealogy in Newfoundland & Labrador

http://www.iosphere.net/~;holwell/nlgrif/nlgrif-l.html

Find detailed information on Newfoundland and Labrador families at this home page. Visitors can access land records, family histories, archives, libraries and associations.

Genealogy Listservers, Newsgroups and Special Home Pages

http://www.eskimo.com/~chance/

Genealogists or hobbyists searching for their ancestral roots may find value in this alphabetical index of genealogy listservers, newsgroups and Web pages. Find links to resources around the world.

Genealogy Online

http://genealogy.emcee.com/

Genealogy Online's archive houses the Emcee Internet Directory which provides links to genealogical collections and related software products. Visitors here also can find U.S. Federal Census results, a link to the National Genealogical Society's home page and related resources.

GenWeb
http://demo.genweb.org/gene/genedemo.html

Genealogists hope to create a coordinated world-wide genealogy database using the Web. For a discussion of the GenWeb concept and proposals to make it a reality, consult this introductory page.

Georgia Genealogical Information
http://www.mindspring.com/~bevr/index.html

This page shares genealogical resources gathered by a woman whose family tree took root in the state of Georgia. Includes links to libraries, public records sources, Georgia genealogical societies and Church of Jesus Christ of Latter-day Saints family history resources.

Helm's Genealogy Toolbox Frequently Asked Questions
http://www.staff.uiuc.edu/~al-helm/genealogy.html

The Genealogy Toolbox is designed to provide access to genealogy research tools on the Internet. Find guides and indexes, surname data, geographic and ethnic resources, commercial resources, software and much more.

The Irish Family History Foundation
http://www.mayo-ireland.ie/Roots.htm

The Irish Family History Foundation, which coordinates government-approved genealogical research in the Republic of Ireland and Northern Ireland, has computerized millions of Irish ancestral records. Visitors here can learn more about the foundation's services and how to interpret such information as surname variations and birthdates.

Italian Genealogy
http://www.italgen.com/

Highlights of this genealogy resource include links to the Italian Surname Database, Civil Records Repositories in Italy and the POINT network. Also find links to family home pages, the history of Italian regions, a list of common Italian surname prefixes and more.

Kansas Interactive Genealogy
http://raven.cc.ukans.edu/heritage/research/inter-gen/

Genealogists tracing their roots to Kansas will find a wealth of information here detailing the lives of Kansas pioneers and modern family histories. The site also posts links to genealogy sites on the Web.

National Archives and Records Administration Gopher
gopher://gopher.nara.gov:70/1

America's file cabinet, the National Archives and Records Administration (NARA), makes information available electronically through the CLIO system. Visitors here can download the Federal Register, genealogy files, government documents and much more.

National Genealogical Society
http://genealogy.org/NGS/

The National Genealogical Society (NGS) is a Virginia-based, non-profit organization devoted to the study and research of genealogy. A wealth of NGS info is provided here, including a calendar of events, special publications and program details.

Odessa: A German-Russian Genealogical Library
http://pixel.cs.vt.edu/library/odessa.html

The Odessa library of German-Russian genealogy at Virginia Tech University is an ongoing experiment in using the Web to reconstruct family histories. The site includes articles, cemetery records, census records, family histories and obituaries from Eastern Europe.

Rand Genealogy Club
http://www.rand.org/personal/Genea/

Employees of Rand, a west coast public policy think tank, have created this page "to share information about genealogical resources ... on the information highway." Genealogy buffs can access a variety of databases and Web sites, including surname lists, online elephone books, the Federal Census Bureau and Queen Victoria's family tree.

Roots Location List Name Finder
http://www.rand.org/personal/Genea/

This interactive site provides a search tool that generates a list of all registered persons doing genealogical research in specified locations. The page includes search suggestions and information about the project.

Spencer Genealogical and Historical Society
http://iquest.com/~lcrowe/shgs.shtml

The document on this page describes the efforts of the Spencer Historical and Genealogical Society and the purpose of its database detailing the family tree. An invitation to join the society, reunion information and links to other genealogical sites are featured.

Tim Doyle Home Page
http://www.doit.com/tdoyle/

Tim Doyle's home page features a vast database of genealogy resources along with pointers to some of the best genealogy sites on the Web.

WWW Genealogy Databases
http://www.genhomepage.com/genwww.html

A vast database of genealogy information, this index includes pointers to royal ancestral resources, a genealogy demo for newbies, links to family trees around the world, and a number of discussion groups. Although the site is no longer being regularly updated, Webmaster Stephen Wood still maintains the page, and points visitors to an active "What's New" repository for genealogy resources.

INSTITUTES AND SCHOOLS

Institute of Historical Research
http://ihr.sas.ac.uk/

The Institute of Historical Research at the University of London maintains this server with access to electronic publications, the Centre for Metropolitan History and various online resources for historians in London and worldwide.

Rochester University History Department
http://www.history.rochester.edu/

The University of Rochester presents the home page for its History Department at this site. Visitors will find information on academics, faculty, courses and departmental events. Extensive links to history sites on the Internet are also featured.

University of Glasgow CTI Centre for History, Archaeology and Art History
http://www.arts.gla.ac.uk/www/ctich/homepage.html

The University of Glasgow CTI Centre for History, Archaeology and Art History specializes in history, economic and social history, archaeology, and the history of art. Resources here are categorized by subject.

University of Kansas History Department Index
http://history.cc.ukans.edu/history/index.html

The History Department at the University of Kansas maintains this searchable index offering hundreds of links to history resources on the Web. The index is arranged alphabetically, by subject and individual site.

University of Melbourne Classics and Archaeology Department
http://www.arts.unimelb.edu.au/Dept/ClassArch/

The Department of Classics and Archaeology at the University of Melbourne, Australia, provides information here on its undergraduate studies and projects, which include ancient Greek, Latin, and medieval studies.

University of Michigan Department of Classics and Mediterranean Archaeology

http://rome.classics.lsa.umich.edu/welcome.html

The Department of Classics and Mediterranean Archaeology at the University of Michigan maintains this site for related literature and academic resources. Visitors can link to texts, journals, bibliographies, image files, and World Wide Web sites.

University of Pennsylvania Classical Studies Department

http://ccat.sas.upenn.edu/clst/clst.html

The home page of the Classical Studies Department at the University of Pennsylvania provides a variety of department and classical studies info. Read about academics, faculty, lectures, workshops and events, and link to personal home pages and related Web sites.

University of Saskatchewan Department of Classics

http://www.usask.ca/classics/

Learn what you can do with a background in classics or delve into the ancient world of theater at the Department of Classics, University of Saskatchewan. Prospective students can also find out more about the program and degree requirements here.

MAPS AND CARTOGRAPHY

Heritage Map Museum

http://www.carto.com/

The Heritage Map Museum home page details its educational services here, as well as pointers to its collection of 15th- to 19th-century maps, many of which are for sale. Appraisal and collection development services are also outlined.

History of Cartography

http://elvis.neep.wisc.edu/~cdean/index.html

The University of Wisconsin's History of Cartography project works to understand the cultural context and historical functions of maps, as well as how they were made. Geographers can get an extensive overview of the project here.

Paris Maps, 1716-1887 Gopher

gopher://gutentag.cc.columbia.edu/11/fun/pictures/art-history

How much liberty did those 18th- and 19th-century French novelists take when they described the streets of Paris? Fact-check their routes with this collection of historic Parisian maps.

University of California, San Diego, Maps and Spatial Data Home Page

http://gort.ucsd.edu/mw/maps.html

The University of San Diego's Map and Spatial Data site features a description of the school's map room, San Diego census data, land and ocean info systems, atmosphere and planetary data, and much more.

MARITIME HISTORY

A Guide to Maritime History Information on the Internet

http://ils.unc.edu/maritime/home.html

Visitors seeking information about maritime and shipping history will find resources for their searches at A Guide to Maritime History Information on the Internet. Dig up recent findings in nautical archaeology and read about maritime themes in music and art here.

Maritime History Virtual Archives

http://pc-78-120.udac.se:8001/WWW/Nautica/Nautica.html

The Maritime History Virtual Archives includes a wealth of information of interest to nautical enthusiasts. Visitors will find links to information on conferences, naval museums, antiquarian bookshops and much more.

MEDIEVAL

Arthuriana

http://dc.smu.edu/Arthuriana/

"Arthuriana" is a scholarly journal about King Arthur published quarterly by the North American branch of the International Arthurian Society. Visitors will find sample articles, subscription information, and related products such as King Arthur t-shirts.

Avalon: Arthurian Heaven

http://reality.sgi.com/employees/chris_manchester/arthur.html

Travel to the isle of Avalon to learn more about the legend of King Arthur. Links are provided to books, articles, related resources—like the script to the Monty Python version of the story—and an Arthurian study course.

Bryn Mawr Medieval Review

gopher://gopher.lib.virginia.edu:70/11/alpha/bmmr

The "Bryn Mawr Medieval Review" provides access to a broad range of documents and electron-

ic texts focusing on medieval studies. Includes a searchable index, an archive of previous issues and subscription information.

Castles on the Web

http://fox.nstn.ca/~tmonk/castle/castle.html

Castles on the Web escorts browsers on a global castle tour, complete with historical profiles and an extensive image gallery. Includes a "Castle of the Week" and a glossary of all-important castle terminology.

Exemplaria: A Journal of Theory in Medieval and Renaissance Studies

http://www.clas.ufl.edu/english/exemplaria/

Exemplaria: A Journal of Theory in Medieval and Renaissance Studies is an academic publication offering a refereed look at critical issues within the discipline. Read back issues, retrieve submissions guidelines or request a subscription to the publication of, by and for medievalists and Renaissance scholars.

The Hill Monastic Manuscript Library

http://www.csbsju.edu/hmml/

"Fire, flood, theft, war. It only takes a minute to destroy history's greatest ideas." Working since 1965, the Hill Monastic Manuscript Library is one of the world's most comprehensive archives of medieval and Renaissance sources. Learn more about the library's microfilm collection, manuscript catalogs and study centers here.

Khazaria Info Center

http://www.khazaria.com

The medieval Jewish kingdom of Khazaria is the topic of the history, timeline and quotes featured on this page. A map, an illustration of Turkic runes and links to many topic-related sites are also included.

Labyrinth

http://www.georgetown.edu/labyrinth/labyrinth-home.html

Sponsored by Georgetown University, this page offers access to a vast collection of medieval studies resources, from electronic texts to databases worldwide. Virtual library holdings are available in French, Italian, English and Latin, as well as Middle and Old English. Search by subject on topics ranging from Arthurian Studies to Viking culture.

Medieval Resources

http://ebbs.english.vt.edu/medieval/medieval.ebbs.html

For those who take nostalgia to extremes, Medieval Resources offers links to materials devoted to art, literature and daily life. It also offers links to archives of texts in Old and Middle English and other European languages.

Society for Creative Anachronism

http://www.sca.org/

Visit the Current Middle Ages page for an introduction to the Society for Creative Anachronism (SCA), which researches and recreates Middle Age history and culture. Stressing active participation, the SCA stages historical reenactments and role-playing events.

The Texas Medieval Association

http://www.towson.edu/~duncan/ tmahome.html

The Texas Medieval Association (TEMA) sponsors conferences, projects, and workshops for aficionados of the Middle Ages. Find out more about joining TEMA and about attending or submitting papers for the next conference. Links are provided to other Web sites related to medieval studies.

WWW Virtual Library: Medieval Studies

http://www.georgetown.edu/labyrinth/Virtual_ Library/Medieval_Studies.html

The Labyrinth, part of the Virtual Library and provided by the Department of Medieval Studies at Georgetown University, offers links to a variety of online resources. Visitors will find links to an extensive library collection and other professional organizations and scholarly publications.

MILITARY HISTORY

A-Bomb WWW Museum

http://www.csi.ad.jp/ABOMB/index.html

Students and faculty of Hiroshima City University constructed this project to provide "accurate information concerning the impact the first atomic bomb had on Hiroshima" and to provide the context for thorough discussion of the topic.

American Civil War Home Page

http://funnelweb.utcc.utk.edu/~hoemann/ cwarhp.html

The American Civil War page, maintained by a University of Tennessee historian, offers links to a wide range of Internet resources about the "war between the states." Visit here for texts, soldiers' rosters, battle descriptions, links to museums and more.

Canadian Museum of Civilization Corporation

http://www.cmcc.muse.digital.ca/

The Canadian Museum of Civilization Corporation (CMCC) presents entryways to each of its two museums, the Canadian Museum of Civilization and the Canadian War Museum, and directions to each facility.

Concentration Camps: A Factual Report on Crimes Committed Against Humanity

http://zero.tolerance.org/zt/kz.html

Visitors to this page will find a report detailing the medical experiments and other horrors which occurred in Nazi concentration camps during World War II. Attached to the document is a list of witnesses.

Enola Gay Perspectives

http://www.glue.umd.edu/~enola/ welcome.html

Enola Gay Perspectives focuses on the Smithsonian Museum's exhibit of the first airplane to drop an atomic bomb. The site exhaustively examines the history and the controversy that took place over the exhibit.

First Division Museum at Cantigny

http://www.xnet.com/~fdmuseum/

The Big Red One, the 1st Infantry Division of the U.S. Army, is the focus of the First Division Museum at Cantigny in Wheaton, Ill. This site contains information on Col. Robert R. McCormick, on whose estate the museum sits, as well as information on the museum, the division, exhibits and more.

French and Indian War Home Page

http://web.syr.edu/~laroux/

A writer chronicling the 18th-century French and Indian War offers research materials on the soldiers, battles and strategies of the war. Find a special emphasis on French soldiers who went to Canada to fight.

From Revolution to Reconstruction

http://grid.let.rug.nl/~welling/usa/ revolution.html

Historians will find kindred spirits at the site for hypertext collective writing to discuss the American Revolution and struggle for independence. Texts include papers on the colonial period, westward expansion and section conflict, with links to original sources and an opportunity to comment on every subject.

The High Energy Weapons Archive

http://www.pal.xgw.fi/hew/

The High Energy Weapons Archive offers a sobering look at the Nuclear Age and the proliferation of nuclear weapons across the Earth. The Web site features essays, articles and news reports, plus eyewitness accounts provided by survivors of the Hiroshima and Nagasaki bombings.

Holocaust Index

http://www.cs.washington.edu/homes/ tdnguyen/Holocaust.html

Historians and students of the Holocaust will find links to a wealth of information at this index. Links to Usenet newsgroups, libraries and the Holocaust Museum are featured here.

The Holocaust Memorial

http://wahoo.netrunner.net/~holomem/

Tour the Holocaust Memorial, located in Miami Beach, Fla., at this site. The sculptures by Kenneth Treister personify the anguish of individuals caught up in Holocaust horror.

L'Chaim: A Holocaust Web Project

http://www.charm.net/~rbennett/l'chaim.html

L'Chaim, developed by a University of Baltimore grad student, provides a historical perspective on the Holocaust. Survivors' stories, a virtual tour of Dachau, and a link to the United States Holocaust Museum can be found here.

Liberation Force/Occupation Power

http://www.image.co.at/image/salzburg/

The Forschungsgemeinschaft Boltzmann Institute in Salzburg, Austria, presents its online project, "Liberation Force/Occupation Power" with a request for reactions and responses. Here, visitors can read about Austrian-American diplomacy following the end of World War II and find links to a variety of related information.

Nizkor Project

http://nizkor.almanac.bc.ca/

The Nizkor Project dedicates itself to the preservation and dissemination of electronic resources documenting and commemorating the Holocaust. Find a special emphasis on exposing and refuting revisionist movements that seek to deny the historical existence of the Holocaust.

Operation Desert Storm Debriefing Book

http://www.nd.edu/~aleyden/contents.html

The Operation Desert Storm Debriefing Book, a personal collection of research materials and related links, offers a comprehensive look at the war. Visit here for an extensive index of articles covering the politics, logistics, weaponry and media coverage of the conflict.

Remembering Nagasaki

http://www.exploratorium.edu/nagasaki/

This site, presented by the Exploratorium, observes the 50th anniversary of the bombing of Nagasaki, presenting Yosuke Yamahata's photographs of the Japanese Army and a public forum on issues related to the Atomic Age.

Trinity Atomic Web Site

http://www.envirolink.org/issues/nuketesting/

Visitors here will find information about the Trinity test site, where the United States exploded the first atomic bomb, on this page. The page includes photos of high-energy weapons tested since World War II and a description of the upcoming commemorative events at the Trinity site.

United States Holocaust Memorial Museum

http://www.ushmm.org/

The home page of the United States Holocaust Memorial Museum in Washington, D.C., offers information on the center, its research and programs, plus help in planning a visit. Also find online access to the data archive and pointers to sites of related interest.

U-Web

http://rvik.ismennt.is/~gummihe/Uboats/u-boats.htm

Learn about the U-boat battles of World War II at this site, which includes information on the unique submersible boats and the men who sailed them. Also available is a bibliography, a glossary, and information on the Sharkhunters, an organization dedicated to submarine history.

Virtual Memorial Hall of the Victims in Nanjing Massacre

http://www.arts.cuhk.hk/NanjingMassacre/NM.html

Approximately 300,000 people were killed and over 20,000 were reported raped in the December 1937 fall of Nanjing, China to the Japanese Imperial Army. This Virtual Memorial Hall commemorates the victims with photos, videos and book suggestions.

Warsaw Uprising

http://www.princeton.edu/~mkporwit/uprising/top.html

Lasting two months during World War II and leaving 200,000 people dead, Poland's Warsaw Uprising against the Nazi occupation is commemorated on this page. Features include maps, photos and background information.

World War II Archive

http://192.253.114.31/D-Day/GVPT_stuff/new.html

This World War II archive was created by students at Patch American High School in Stuttgart, Germany. It contains a huge collection of war-related historical documents, photos, movies, and sounds, including speeches by Harry Truman and Douglas MacArthur.

World War II: The World Remembers

http://192.253.114.31/D-Day/Table_of_contents.html

The students and faculty of Patch American High School in Vaihingen, a small section of Stuttgart, Germany, have compiled a wealth of info on World War II at this site, including documents from government and military archives, famous speeches, maps and battle plans and much more.

MODERN

The Computer Museum

http://www.tcm.org/

If you can't make it to Boston to visit the real thing, drop by The Computer Museum page to examine the history and workings of the computer. Visitors to the page can link to information on the museum and its projects and exhibits.

The Farnsworth Chronicles

http://www.edge.net/noma/philo/index.html

The Farnsworth Chronicles details the story of the prescient fellow who invented video. Philo Farnsworth died in 1971, with few knowing his story. The Webmaster interviewed surviving relatives and posts a lively biography here.

History of Space Exploration Archive

http://www.ksc.nasa.gov/history/history.html

Presented by NASA, this historical archive details the history of U.S. space exploration. Includes rocket history, manned missions and mission patches.

Kennedy Assassination Home Page

http://mcadams.posc.mu.edu/home.htm

Whether or not you accept either the "grassy knoll" or the "lone nut" theory, you can learn more about Lee Harvey Oswald and the assassination of President John F. Kennedy at this information-packed page which attempts to deflate rumors of conspiracy surrounding the incident.

Smithsonian

http://www.smithsonianmag.si.edu

The online version of Smithsonian magazine features columns and articles about the arts, environment, culture and entertainment, history and science—just what you'd expect from the museum known as "America's attic." Online subscription ordering is also available, as well as a gift shop.

MUSEUMS

Glenbow

http://www.glenbow.org/

Glenbow, "western Canada's foremost centre of history and art," is a museum featuring international cultural collections, an art gallery, and a library and archives of western Canadian history. Here, visitors can learn more about Glenbow's holdings, peruse This Week in Western Canadian History and delve into "story robes."

Michigan Digital Historical Initiative in the Health Sciences

http://www.med.umich.edu/HCHS/

The Michigan Digital Historical Initiative in the Health Sciences (MDHI) serves as a guide to Web-based repositories of museum materials, photographs, artifacts and online galleries, all containing objects of interest to medical historians. Visitors here can view historical information about African-Americans' experiences with health care.

Smithsonian Institution

http://www.si.sgi.com/sgistart.htm

"America's Treasure House of Learning," The Smithsonian Institution sponsors this page as a central jump station to its individual museums and resources. Explore the institution's vast array of galleries, research centers and exhibitions, from historic Americana to aerospace technology and engineering.

PUBLISHERS AND PUBLICATIONS

Essays in History

http://www.lib.virginia.edu/journals/EH/EH.html

Essays in History, a journal from University of Virginia Department of History, is featured here. Issues from 1991 to 1995 are available, as well as submission instructions and journal information.

KMT: A Modern Journal of Ancient Egypt

http://library.uwaterloo.ca/ejournals/history_ej.html

"KMT: A Modern Journal of Ancient Egypt" online features selected articles from the current issue of this scholarly journal of research and discovery. Complete back issues are also available.

Smithsonian

http://www.smithsonianmag.si.edu

The online version of Smithsonian magazine features columns and articles about the arts, environment, culture and entertainment, history and science—just what you'd expect from the museum known as "America's attic." Online subscription ordering is also available, as well as a gift shop.

Society for the History of Authorship, Reading & Publishing

http://www.indiana.edu/~sharp/

The Society for the History of Authorship, Reading and Publishing is a network aimed at scholars, librarians, publishing professionals and authors interested in the history of print. Visit here to learn how to join the society, track down publishers' archives and link to historical sites.

RENAISSANCE

The Art of Renaissance Science: Galileo and Perspective

http://bang.lanl.gov/video/stv/arshtml/arstoc.html

The Art of Renaissance Science: Galileo and Perspective analyzes Galileo's contribution to the technology revolution of the 17th century.

Electric Renaissance

http://www.idbsu.edu/courses/hy309/

Electric Renaissance was a course conducted entirely over the Internet in 1995. Visitors here can download the syllabus, outlines of course topics, and maps, pictures and sounds used as course materials.

Exemplaria: A Journal of Theory in Medieval and Renaissance Studies

http://www.clas.ufl.edu/english/exemplaria/

Exemplaria: A Journal of Theory in Medieval and Renaissance Studies is an academic publication offering a refereed look at critical issues within the discipline. Read back issues, retrieve submissions guidelines or request a subscription to the publication of, by and for medievalists and Renaissance scholars.

The Hill Monastic Manuscript Library

http://www.csbsju.edu/hmml/

"Fire, flood, theft, war. It only takes a minute to destroy history's greatest ideas." Working since 1965, the Hill Monastic Manuscript Library is one of the world's most comprehensive archives of medieval and Renaissance sources. Learn more about the library's microfilm collection, manuscript catalogs and study centers here.

Renaissance Faire Homepage

http://www.resort.com/~banshee/Faire/index.html

Intended primarily as a reference for Renaissance Faire workers, visitors to this page will find pointers to period information, as well as general resources for faires and reenactments. Featured topics include authentic costuming, language usage and working with the public.

WORLD HISTORY AND EVENTS

Significant Events from 1890 to 1940

http://weber.u.washington.edu/~eckman/timeline.html

Significant Events from 1890 to 1940 covers "any event (publication, invention, election, exhibition, exposition, etc.) ...important in terms of modernism as a Literary Period." A hyperlink timeline is featured, and submissions of "significant events" are invited.

Today in History

http://lcweb2.loc.gov/ammem/today/today.html

You'll want to visit this Web page every day to find out what happened "Today in History" throughout the world. You'll also get a famous quote, and, if you'd prefer, you can arrange to receive "Today in History" via e-mail.

LITERATURE

ARCHIVES AND INDICES

A.Word.A.Day

http://www.wordsmith.org/words/today.html

A.Word.A.Day is a literary service that provides a new word and its definition each day. Visitors can have this daily word offering automatically delivered via e-mail. A philosophical quotation comes with each serving.

ArtServe TextSearch

http://rubens.anu.edu.au/searchmenu.html

Perform keyword searches of classical literature at this site. Works available for text searching include Pascal's *Pensees,* Shakespeare's *Sonnets* and Homer's *Iliad* and *Odyssey.*

La Bibliotheque d'ABU

http://www.cnam.fr/ABU/principal/bibABU.html

Visitors to this site will find a selection of classic literature online for reading and reference purposes. Included are works from Moliere, Balzac and Rousseau. In French.

Bodleian Library Electronic Texts Gopher

gopher://rsl.ox.ac.uk/11/lib-corn/hunter/Browse%20Alex/Browse%20by%20Date/Browse%20by%20Date%3a%201600s

The works of writers such as Blaise Pascal, Thomas Hobbes and John Milton are featured at this U.K. gopher, which also includes works from John Locke and the first Thanksgiving proclamation from Charlestown, Mass.

Carnegie Mellon University English Department

http://english-www.hss.cmu.edu/

The English Department at Carnegie Mellon University maintains this site with a comprehensive list of links to English literature and language resources. Topics here include drama, feminism, fiction and literacy, just to name a few.

Eighteenth Century Studies Archive Page

http://english-www.hss.cmu.edu/18th/

Part of the English server archive maintained by Carnegie Mellon University, this page provides visitors with an alphabetical list of writings from the 18th century. Visitors can peruse poems, treatises, novels, plays, historical texts and more.

Etext Archives

http://www.etext.org/

The Etext Archives provides access to electronic texts of all descriptions. Personal and professional 'zines, electronic books, mailing lists, religious tracts and texts, legal documents and political materials are here, as are the contents of other selected archives.

European Literature Electronic Texts

http://www.lib.virginia.edu/wess/etexts.html

This collection of western European literature is provided by the Western European Specialists Section of the Association of College and Research Libraries. Visit here for fiction and non-fiction titles in a variety of non-English languages.

Guide to Christian Literature on the Internet

http://www.iclnet.org/pub/resources/christian-books.html

The Institute for Christian Leadership hosts this guide to Christian literature on the Internet Visitors will find links to several versions of the Bible, plus church-related news, books, newsletters, essays, articles and sermons.

Historical Documents Gopher

gopher://gopher.vt.edu:10010/10/33

Historical documents, philosophical teachings and literary works by famous authors are on file and ready to download at this gopher. Selections range from "The Gettysburg Address" to works from Confucius.

Humanities Text Initiative

http://www.hti.umich.edu/

The Humanities Text Initiative (HTI) at the University of Michigan, Ann Arbor, creates and maintains online texts, including examples of Middle English prose and American poetry. This site has links to reference documents, the main "stacks," journals and other resources.

A Hundred Highlights from the Koninklijke Bibliotheek

http://www.konbib.nl/100hoogte/hh-en.html

The Netherlands Department of Special Collections published this book in 1994 to provide a "selection of manuscripts, printed works, book bindings, and specimens from the paper history collection in the Department." Visit here to read excerpts from the book and to take guided tours of literary, religious and historical subjects.

Internet Arts Museum for Free

http://www.rahul.net/iamfree/

The Internet Arts Museum is a diverse collection of online arts, music and literature. Visitors are invited to take a tour of the galleries and download the exhibit materials.

The Internet Book Information Center

http://sunsite.unc.edu/ibic/IBIC-homepage.html

Literature and the Internet Book Information Center are the focus on this Virtual Library page. The wide-ranging site includes links to current literature, retail and online booksellers, libraries, books on tape, rare editions and other literary Web sites.

Internet Wiretap Gopher

gopher://wiretap.spies.com/11/Books

Literature buffs can download hundreds of classic and contemporary literary works from Aesop to Jane Austen via this gopher.

Labyrinth

http://www.georgetown.edu/labyrinth/labyrinth-home.html

Sponsored by Georgetown University, this page offers access to a vast collection of medieval studies resources, from electronic texts to databases worldwide. Virtual library holdings are available in French, Italian, English and Latin, as well as Middle and Old English. Search by subject on topics ranging from Arthurian Studies to Viking culture.

Literary Resources on the Net

http://www.english.upenn.edu/~jlynch/Lit/

A University of Pennsylvania doctoral candidate maintains this index of links to Web sites "dealing especially with English and American literature." Search by genre, including Classical, Victorian, Renaissance and 20th century selections. Information about related mailing lists and scholarly publications is included.

The Modern English Collection

http://etext.lib.virginia.edu/modeng.browse.html

The Electronic Text Center at the University of Virginia provides access to this collection of hundreds of complete literary works available for download. Arranged in alphabetical order, selections range from Horatio Alger to Bram Stoker.

The On-line Books Page

http://www.cs.cmu.edu/Web/books.html

Hundreds of hypertext books are available on the Internet, and this index, which includes a search function, will help readers find them.

Pulitzer Prizes

http://www.pulitzer.org/

The Pulitzer Prizes are among the highest awards bestowed upon newspaper reporters, authors, playwrights and composers in America. Features here include a current list of winners, audio excerpts, full texts of selected news articles and synopses of honored books.

Significant Events from 1890 to 1940

http://weber.u.washington.edu/~eckman/timeline.html

Significant Events from 1890 to 1940 covers "any event (publication, invention, election, exhibition, exposition, etc.) ...important in terms of modernism as a Literary Period." A hyperlink timeline is featured, and submissions of "significant events" are invited.

Text Archives

http://ccat.sas.upenn.edu/txtarch.html

Visitors here will find indices of text archives available on the Internet, including the CCAT text archives, the English Server at Carnegie Mellon University, the Gutenberg Project and more.

UNCAT

http://www.sapphire.com/UNCAT/

The UNCAT site is an electronic catalog of textual materials generally not available in libraries and bookstores. UNCAT, a special system of cataloging designed exclusively for the Web, is used by people working in the television, radio and print industries.

The Voice of the Shuttle: English Literature

http://humanitas.ucsb.edu/shuttle/english.html

A professor at the Department of English at the University of California, Santa Barbara, provides this index to a variety of English literature and humanities sites.

ASSOCIATIONS AND ORGANIZATIONS

The Association des Bibliophiles Universels

http://www.cnam.fr/ABU/

Offering "as many French public domain texts as possible," the Association des Bibliophiles Universels also hosts a local copy of the Project Gutenberg e-texts. Enjoy access to the electronic stacks, plus find answers to Frequently Asked Questions (FAQs). In French, with some English.

Association for the Study of Literature & Environment

http://faraday.clas.virginia.edu/~djp2n/asle.html

The Association for the Study of Literature & Environment (ASLE) posts its publications, conference schedules and archives at this site. Find essays on the intersection of the two disciplines and links to related Internet resources.

Society for the History of Authorship, Reading & Publishing

http://www.indiana.edu/~sharp/

The Society for the History of Authorship, Reading and Publishing is a network aimed at scholars, librarians, publishing professionals and authors interested in the history of print. Visit here to learn how to join the society, track down publishers' archives, and link to historical sites.

Voltaire Foundation

http://www.voltaire.ox.ac.uk/

"Welcome to the Enlightenment!" proclaims this page from the Voltaire Foundation at England's Oxford University. Find publications, images, societies and more, all related to the great French poet, dramatist, satirist, and historian. In French and English.

AUTHORS AND POETS

Emily Dickinson Page

http://lal.cs.byu.edu/people/black/dickinson.html

Begun in 1995 after a fruitless Web search for material related to Emily Dickinson, this site has flowered into a repository of points and pointers. Biographical data, online poetry, annotations, summaries, reviews and references are featured, along with information about the Emily Dickinson International Society.

Ever The Twain Shall Meet

http://www.lm.com/~joseph/mtwain.html

Ever The Twain Shall Meet is a literary reference and resource devoted to Mark Twain. This page has links to some of his works in their entirety, including *The Adventures of Huckleberry Finn* and *The Adventures of Tom Sawyer*.

Lewis Carroll Home Page

http://www.students.uiuc.edu/~jbirenba/carroll.html

Devoted to author Lewis Carroll, this page provides information about the author and links to illustrated, electronic texts of his works, including "Alice's Adventures in Wonderland." Visitors will also find a featured discussion topic and a list of organizations devoted to the writer. See Editor's Choice, page 42.

Literary Kicks

http://www.charm.net/~brooklyn/LitKicks.html

"Beat" fans will enjoy this home page, featuring links to the works of Jack Kerouac, Allen Ginsberg, William S. Burroughs and more. Maintained by an avid reader of the genre, this site provides an in-depth look at the authors who set the literary stage for the American cultural revolution of the 1960s.

Mark Twain Resources on the World Wide Web

http://web.syr.edu/~fjzwick/twainwww.html

Mark Twain fans will enjoy this site, with information about the author and his work. Maintained by Jim Zwick of Syracuse University, the site offers full text as well as interpretations and adaptations of his stories.

Phil Carson's Raymond Carver Page

http://world.std.com/~ptc/

A fan of late American poet and short story author Raymond Carver presents a pertinent overview of this Guggenheim Fellow's works and related literary criticism here. "Vaguely interesting" photographs are included as is the Web author's graduate thesis.

Rossetti Archive

http://jefferson.village.virginia.edu/rossetti/rossetti.html

Find the writings and paintings of the Pre-Raphaelite poet and painter, Dante Gabriel Rossetti, archived at this site. Scholarly annotations and notes provide commentary and insight into the work.

Tolkien Language List

http://www.dcs.ed.ac.uk/staff/jcb/TolkLang/

The world and language of author J.R.R. Tolkien are featured on the home page for the Tolkien Language List Usenet newsgroup. Visitors to the site can view texts and resources about the fictional language created by the fantasy writer or read archival newsgroup postings.

Walker Percy

http://sunsite.unc.edu/wpercy/

Southern favorite son Walker Percy is characterized as a "philosophical novelist" by the University of North Carolina archive that collects and presents his work online. Visitors can peruse Percy's papers, fiction and philosophical treatises here.

William Faulkner on the Web

http://www.mcsr.olemiss.edu/~egjbp/faulkner/faulkner.html

Literary fans of William Faulkner can explore the author's mythical and actual stomping grounds at this site. The site also includes a trivia page, notes and synopses of the author's works and resource listings for students.

CHILDREN'S LITERATURE

Alice's Adventures in Wonderland

http://www.cs.indiana.edu/metastuff/wonder/wonderdir.html

Project Gutenberg serves up this hypertext version of Lewis Carroll's fantastic classic, *Alice's Adventures in Wonderland*.

 EDITOR'S CHOICE

Lewis Carroll Home Page

http://www.students.uiuc.edu/~jbirenba/carroll.html

Who was the Rev. Charles Lutwidge Dodgson? He was a man who, according to this page, "didn't want his true identity linked to his best work," which is why he wrote his best work under the name Lewis Carroll. Not only a writer, Dodgson lectured in mathematics at Christ Church Oxford and was a clergyman. As a photographer, his favorite subject was Alice Liddell, who became the Alice of his most famous works. Exhaustive and packed with biographical info, photographs and links, the Lewis Carroll page is a lot like a crowded attic: There's stuff that's both familiar and strange, new and well-worn, surprising, and commonplace. Available goodies include electronic texts, graphics from the original "Alice" books, biographies, a lesson plan for teaching "Jabberwocky," articles, mathematical puzzles and riddles, the reason why *Alice's Adventures in Wonderland* was banned in China, and trunks full of Carroll trinkets and doodads. And lots of photographs. So prepare to get lost and "just follow the grin."—*Reviewed by Amy Hembree*

LEWIS CARROLL Home Page

 Welcome to the Lewis Carroll home page. We hope to provide useful information for the Carroll enthusiast as well as the novice and all those in between. Cyberspace seems a suitable home for information regarding a man who didn't want his true identity linked to his best work.

What follows is a guide to Lewis Carroll resources and documents on-line and in print.

Life what is it but a dream?

Table of Contents

Some of the links in this table of contents point to sections of this page, and some point to separate pages. This means that if you just scroll down this page, you'll miss some good stuff. Click here to go to:

Children's Literature Web Guide

http://www.ucalgary.ca/~dkbrown/index.html

The Children's Literature Web Guide contains a huge searchable archive of Internet resources related to books for children. Visitors will find lists of recommended books, discussion groups, online stories and much more.

The Page at Pooh Corner

http://www.public.iastate.edu/~jmilne/pooh.html

Dedicated to the stories of *Winnie the Pooh* and *House at Pooh Corner,* this unofficial site highlights the misadventures of Pooh, Piglet, Tigger and all their fictional friends. Includes biographical information on the stories' creators, A. A. Milne and E.H. Shepard.

Story Resources

http://www.swarthmore.edu/~sjohnson/stories/

An index to storytelling information and resources found on the Web is featured on this page. Organizations, tales by culture, children's stories and stories by children, familiar folk tales and hyperfiction highlight the list of links.

CLASSICAL STUDIES

Interpreting Ancient Manuscripts

http://www.stg.brown.edu/projects/mss/overview.html

Interpreting Ancient Manuscripts, a navigable hypertext study of ancient manuscripts that are the bases for the New Testament, is presented by Brown University. Critical discussions of the texts, glossaries and tables aid in the reader's study.

Italian Literature in HTML

http://www.crs4.it/HTML/Literature.html

The Centre for Advanced Studies, Research and Development in Sardinia hosts this page of Italian literature. It includes electronic-text versions of classic poems, plays, religious and philosophical works. In Italian only.

James J. O'Donnell

http://ccat.sas.upenn.edu/jod/jod.html

A University of Pennsylvania professor provides links to a variety of classical text translations here. Visit to read the texts and access the resources of the university's Center for Computer Analysis of Texts.

Perseus Project

http://www.perseus.tufts.edu/

The Perseus Project is an "evolving digital library on Ancient Greece." Visitors will find extensive resources on archaeology, art and literature. This page also contains information on using Perseus in the classroom.

Tech Classics Archive

http://the-tech.mit.edu/Classics/index.html

Maintained at the Massachusetts Institute of Technology, this searchable e-text archive contains 376 Greek and Roman literary classics. Find the well-known works of Homer, Virgil and Plato, plus Aristophanes, Sophocles and others. English texts, commentaries and author information are also featured.

INSTITUTES AND SCHOOLS

University of Kentucky Classics Department

http://www.uky.edu/ArtsSciences/Classics/

The University of Kentucky at Lexington provides information about its Classics Department here. Visitors will find descriptions of its faculty, graduate and undergraduate degree programs, courses, publications, study abroad options and more.

University of Minnesota English Department

http://www-engl.cla.umn.edu/

The University of Minnesota sponsors this Web site for its Department of English. Information on faculty, classes and departmental events is featured.

JOURNALS AND PERIODICALS

Beatrice

http://www.beatrice.com/contents/

"Beatrice," an online monthly magazine, offers a spread of original fiction, essays, book reviews and interviews.

Crossconnect

http://tech1.dccs.upenn.edu/~xconnect

"Crossconnect" is an online journal of contemporary art and writing, presented by Ivy League smarties at the University of Pennsylvania in Philadelphia. Visitors can access current and back is-

sues here, including a poetry section praised by the *Philadelphia Weekly.*

De Proverbio

http://info.utas.edu.au/docs/flonta/

"De Proverbio" is an e-journal on international proverb studies. Included at this site are journal issues, a catalog of multilingual Internet resources, and links to schools, libraries, literature, linguistic departments and online publications.

Deep South

http://elwing.otago.ac.nz:889/dsouth/home-page.html

Deep South is a quarterly journal published by the graduate students of the English Department at the University of Otago in Dunedin, New Zealand. The current and back issues can be accessed at this site, which also contains information about staff, submissions, and subscriptions.

Didaskalia

http://www.warwick.ac.uk/didaskalia/didaskalia.html

"Didaskalia," an online journal devoted to Greek and Roman drama performed today, is found here. The page links to current and former issues of the journal, based at University of Warwick, England. It also announces upcoming productions.

Dogwood Blossom

http://glwarner.samford.edu/haiku.htm

"Dogwood Blossom," an electronic haiku journal maintained by a researcher at Samford University in Birmingham, Ala., offers poetry, book reviews and articles about the Japanese writing form. Includes submission forms and links to other haiku-related sites.

JAC Online

http://nosferatu.cas.usf.edu/JAC/index.html

Sponsored by the Association of Teachers of Advanced Composition and the University of South Florida, JAC Online is a scholarly journal concerned with such aspects of composition theory as postmodern signification and multicultural literacy. Visitors can browse the archive of past issues, but a password is required for access to the current issue.

Keats-Shelley Journal

http://www.luc.edu/publications/keats-shelley/ksjweb.htm

The *Keats-Shelley Journal,* published in print form each year at Loyola University in Chicago, goes online with conference announcements, reviews, academic studies and links to author pages.

RhetNet: A CyberJournal

http://www.missouri.edu/~rhetnet/

RhetNet is a repository for resources on the Internet of interest to the rhetoric and writing community. It provides articles and essays, Internet conversations and a "general call for participation."

LITERARY CLASSICS

Alice's Adventures in Wonderland

http://www.cs.indiana.edu/metastuff/wonder/wonderdir.html

Project Gutenberg serves up this hypertext version of Lewis Carroll's fantastic classic, *Alice's Adventures in Wonderland.*

Chinese Classics

http://www.cnd.org/Classics/index.html

Electronic editions of China's literary classics are collected here, including poetry, prose and philosophy as well as a brief chronology of Chinese history presented by the "China News Digest."

Collected Works of Shakespeare

http://www.gh.cs.usyd.edu.au/~matty/Shakespeare/index.html

So final exams are coming up, your roommate's skipped town with your English lit paperbacks, and you haven't taken the semester seriously until now. Well, at the Collected Works of Shakespeare, you can search for words, lines or characters and get those citations.

MYTHOLOGY AND LEGEND

Arthuriana

http://dc.smu.edu/Arthuriana/

Arthuriana is a scholarly journal about King Arthur published quarterly by the North American branch of the International Arthurian Society. Visitors will find sample articles, subscription information and related products such as King Arthur t-shirts.

Avalon: Arthurian Heaven

http://reality.sgi.com/employees/chris_manchester/arthur.html

Travel to the isle of Avalon to learn more about the legend of King Arthur. Links are provided to books, articles, related resources—like the script to the Monty Python version of the story—and an Arthurian study course.

POETRY

The Alsop Review

http://www.hooked.net/users/jalsop/

Northern California poet Jaimes Alsop shares his own work and work that inspires him here. Find contemporary poetic offerings, plus a list of links, including pointers to Internet tools, humor and job search resources.

B.A.W.P.: Best-quality Audio Web Poems

http://www.cs.brown.edu/fun/bawp/

Best-quality Audio Web Poems provides visitors recordings of spoken word performances in both Sun .au and mono .mpg formats. Visitors can select from the current list of poets and performers, or link to other related sites.

Best Fiction and Poetry from CSUN: 1962-1988

http://www.csun.edu/~hceng029/thebest/bestcontents.html

The Best Fiction and Poetry from California State University, Northridge: 1962-1988, offers an extensive sampling of works during this 25-year span.

British Poetry 1780-1910

http://www.lib.virginia.edu/etext/britpo/britpo.html

With annotated and illustrated texts of notable British poetry, this archive contains guidelines for submissions, and links to the Alderman Library at the University of Virginia and other campus servers.

Cowboy Poetry

http://agricomm.com/agricomm/cp

The spirit of the Old West lives on in Cowboy Poetry, poems and prose that celebrate the uniquely American cowboy mystique. Poems by and about men and women who ride the range bring home the life of the cowboy, and other text spells out current gatherings and projects of interest to modern cowboys.

Czeslaw Milosz's Poetry

http://sunsite.unc.edu/dykki/poetry/milosz/milcov.html

Poet Czeslaw Milosz comes to life online with readings of "Conversation with Jeanne" and "A Poem for the End of the Century." Both are read in Polish and English. A biography of Milosz, a select bibliography and link to the Internet Poetry Archive cover page also included.

Emily Dickinson Page

http://lal.cs.byu.edu/people/black/dickinson.html

Begun in 1995 after a fruitless Web search for material related to Emily Dickinson, this site has flowered into a repository of points and pointers.

Biographical data, online poetry, annotations, summaries, reviews and references are featured, along with information about the Emily Dickinson International Society.

Internet Poetry Archive

http://sunsite.unc.edu/dykki/poetry/home.html

Works of the poets Seamus Heaney, Czeslaw Milosz and others are electronically reproduced at the Internet Poetry Archive. Find a description of the archive project or access the poetical texts collected here.

Labyrinth Electronic Publishing Project

http://www.honors.indiana.edu/lepp/index.html

Honor students from Indiana University host the Labyrinth Electronic Publishing Project, a collection of online poetry, art and fiction. In addition to viewing the works and images on display, visitors can read about the project's history here.

Mark's Poem of the Day

http://www.dataimages.com/poetry/

Maintained by a University of Arizona engineering student, this page offers a daily poem selection. Visit here to read the latest prose and contribute to the collection.

Poems Pace

http://www.teleport.com/~rawdirt/poemspace.html

An online poetry chapbook, this Web space houses poems and some related images. Visitors also can link to literary Web sites and Web-design resources.

Turkish Poetry Home Page

http://www.cs.rpi.edu/~sibel/poetry/

"Here we speak with a Turkish accent," the Webmasters write. They appear to do so in a variety of tongues. This page offers Turkish poetry in Turkish, English, Spanish, French and Italian.

The White Man's Burden and Its Critics

http://www.rochester.ican.net/fjzwick/kipling/

This poetry site, maintained by a doctoral candidate at Syracuse University, offers criticism on Rudyard Kipling's "The White Man's Burden." Visit here to read the poem and read a range of critical viewpoints from the turn of the 20th century.

World Wide Stage

http://ireland.iol.ie/~westrock/

The World Wide Stage, a forum for international fiction, poetry, and stage writers, offers access to "some of the best writing available on the Internet today." Visit here for author biographies and the latest additions to this writing collection.

HAIKU

Haiku for People
http://www.oslonett.no/home/keitoy/
haiku.html

Visitors can dabble in the art of haiku, a form of
Japanese poetry, at this site. The page contains a
history of haiku and some famous examples.

The Shiki Internet Haiku Salon
http://mikan.cc.matsuyama-u.ac.jp/~shiki/

This site dedicated to Haiku, a type of Japanese poetry, introduces visitors to the form and sheds light
on its history. This site offers mailing list information, a contest, an Internet Haiku salon and more.
See Editor's Choice.

QUOTATIONS

Commonplace Book
http://sunsite.unc.edu/ibic/Commonplace-
Book.html

A service of the Internet Book Information Center,
this page provides a forum for people to share
any striking passages they have encountered in
literature. The entire collection of submissions is
available here and readers are encouraged to add
their own.

Shakespearean Insult Generator
http://www.nova.edu/Inter-Links/cgi-bin/
bard.pl

For help coming up with more than the everyday
four-letter insult, consult this site for an old English style jab. Visitors are greeted with a new insult upon loading the page, such as "thou puny
beetle-headed clotpole."

STORIES AND STORY COLLECTIONS

Best Fiction and Poetry from CSUN: 1962-1988
http://www.csun.edu/~hceng029/thebest/
bestcontents.html

The Best Fiction and Poetry from California State
University, Northridge: 1962-1988, offers an extensive sampling of works during this 25-year span.

Creating A Celebration of Women Writers
http://www.cs.cmu.edu/Web/People/mmbt/
women/celebration.html

Creating a Celebration of Women Writers is an effort to post public-domain or copyright-authorized
works of female authors. The evolving site lists
women writers and instructions for submitting
work.

The Gift of the Magi
http://www.auburn.edu/~vestmon/Gift_of_the_
Magi.html

This file contains the O. Henry short story "Gift of
the Magi" from Project Gutenberg. Information
on the project is included, as are hypertext links to
the definitions of words such as "imputation" and
"parsimony."

Labyrinth Electronic Publishing Project
http://www.honors.indiana.edu/lepp/
index.html

Honor students from Indiana University host the
Labyrinth Electronic Publishing Project, a collection of online poetry, art and fiction. In addition to
viewing the works and images on display, visitors
can read about the project's history here.

19th-Century German Stories
http://128.172.170.24/menu.html

This Web site archives 19th-century German stories by the Brothers Grimm, Wilhem Busch and
Heinrich Hoffman. Includes original manuscript illustrations and a link to Virginia Commonwealth
University's Foreign Languages Department
home page.

---

a2z EDITOR'S CHOICE

The Shiki Internet Haiku Salon
http://mikan.cc.matsuyama-u.ac.jp/~shiki/

Named for famous Japanese Haiku poet Shiki Masaoka, the Shiki Internet
Haiku Salon seeks to introduce the beauty of Haiku with details about its
form, history and artful aspects, as well as by encouraging others to practice its writing. Nature and the seasons are of special significance in
Haiku—the word "shiki" can also mean "the four seasons" in Japanese—
and the format is very strict: each poem must consist of only three lines
of five, seven, and five syllables respectively. Fans of Haiku, as well as
those new to the form, will enjoy this delicately-designed page which
takes visitors step-by-step from the cultural and historical background of
Haiku to an explanation of its international popularity and appreciation.
Detailed instructions for writing Haiku are featured, including ancient and
modern examples, a lesson plan, and, most important, the rules. Writers
and readers are never alone in their enjoyment of Haiku: information
about mailing lists, Haiku archives, contests and links to related sites are
also featured, emphasizing the importance of Haiku as an interest that is
best shared.—*Reviewed by Amy Hembree*

THE SHIKI INTERNET HAIKU SALON

surprising cool breeze

Story Resources

http://www.swarthmore.edu/~sjohnson/stories/

An index to storytelling information and resources found on the Web is featured on this page. Organizations, tales by culture, children's stories and stories by children, familiar folk tales and hyperfiction highlight the list of links.

World Wide Stage

http://ireland.iol.ie/~westrock/

The World Wide Stage, a forum for international fiction, poetry and stage writers, offers access to "some of the best writing available on the Internet today." Visit here for author biographies and the latest additions to this writing collection.

TEACHING RESOURCES

Eighteenth Century Studies Archive Page

http://english-www.hss.cmu.edu/18th/

Part of the English server archive maintained by Carnegie Mellon University, this page provides visitors with an alphabetical list of writings from the 18th century. Visitors can peruse poems, treatises, novels, plays, historical texts and more.

Electronic Archives for Teaching the American Literatures

http://www.georgetown.edu/tamlit/tamlit-home.html

The Electronic Archives for Teaching the American Literatures site contains essays, syllabi and bibliographies for teaching.

WOMEN IN LITERATURE

Creating A Celebration of Women Writers

http://www.cs.cmu.edu/Web/People/mmbt/women/celebration.html

Creating a Celebration of Women Writers is an effort to post public-domain or copyright-authorized works of female authors. The evolving site lists women writers and instructions for submitting work.

Emily Dickinson Page

http://lal.cs.byu.edu/people/black/dickinson.html

Begun in 1995 after a fruitless Web search for material related to Emily Dickinson, this site has flowered into a repository of points and pointers. Biographical data, online poetry, annotations, summaries, reviews and references are featured, along with information about the Emily Dickinson International Society.

Kassandra Project

http://www.reed.edu/~ccampbel/tkp

The Kassandra Project offers a series of pages that feature German women writers, artists and thinkers from the second half of the 1800s to the first decades of the 1900s. The project seeks to "clear the cultural shadows" cast by Goethe, Schiller and Kant.

MUSEUMS

Academy of Natural Sciences

http://www.acnatsci.org/

The Academy of Natural Sciences, an educational institution andnatural history museum located in Philadelphia, Pa, maintains this informational site. Visit here to learn about the academy, it's education and research programs, membership benefits, and more.

Adler Planetarium and Museum

http://astro.uchicago.edu/adler/

The first planetarium in the Western Hemisphere, Chicago's Adler Planetarium and Museum maintains this information server as part of its tradition for bringing the universe and its exploration to the widest possible audience. Visitors can preview exhibits and shows, learn about special events and courses, and link to the online resources.

Ashmolean Museum of Art & Archaeology

http://www.ashmol.ox.ac.uk/

The home page of the Ashmolean Museum of Art & Archeology provides information about this venerable University of Oxford institution. Listings of current and upcoming temporary exhibitions, plus historical information and descriptions of the museum's permanent collection.

Bishop Museum

http://www.bishop.hawaii.org/

This Web site is maintained by the Hawaiian state museum of cultural and natural history. Includes an ongoing inventory of native and non-native species of flora and fauna found in the archipelago, information about a traveling AIDS exhibition, a hands-on science display and links to museum departments.

California Museum of Photography

http://www.cmp.ucr.edu/frames/

The California Museum of Photography at the University of California, Riverside, maintains this page with exhibits of contemporary and historical photography and information about upcoming shows. Includes interactive essays and a museum store.

Canadian Museum of Civilization

http://www.cmcc.muse.digital.ca/cmc/cmceng/welcmeng.html

Visitors to the Canadian Museum of Civilization's Web site will find information about the museum, calendars and tours. There are also image galleries of the museum's collections, including the children's museum and the National Postal Museum.

Canadian War Museum

http://www.cmcc.muse.digital.ca/cwm/cwmeng/cwmeng.html

The Canadian War Museum, dedicated to Canadians lost in war, examines the effect of war upon the nation and documents Canada's international peacekeeping efforts. This site offers exhibitions, educational programs, collections and other links.

Computer Museum

http://www.net.org/

Boston's Computer Museum sponsors this page featuring information about the museum and its exhibits. On our last visit, the site was in the process of becoming an online interactive museum.

Czars Lobby

http://www.times.st-pete.fl.us/Treasures/TC.Lobby.html

Visitors here can take a virtual tour of Treasures of the Czars, an exhibit on loan from the Moscow Kremlin Museums to the Florida International Museum. The exhibit includes great artworks that give visitors a feel for czarist Russia.

ExploraNet

http://www.exploratorium.edu/

San Francisco's Exploratorium houses a collection of interactive exhibits for teachers, students and science enthusiasts. ExploraNet, its online museum, offers electronic tours and demonstations.

Field Museum of Natural History

http://www.bvis.uic.edu/museum/

The Field Museum of Natural History in Chicago offers information on worldwide nature and cultures. Visitors will enjoy imaginative exhibits, essays and related references to topics as diverse as ethnography, archaeology and nature conservation.

Florida Museum of Natural History

http://www.flmnh.ufl.edu/

The Florida Museum of Natural History at the University of Florida, Gainesville, features more than 10 million animal and fossil specimens. Visit this site for information about museum exhibits and staff, and learn more about its public education programs.

The German Historical Museum, Berlin

http://www.dhm.de/index.html

The German Historical Museum, Berlin, maintains this site with information about its collections and exhibitions. A list of publications and information about the museum's historic building, the Zeughaus, which houses its photo gallery, library and cinema, is featured. In German, French and English.

Heritage Map Museum

http://www.carto.com/

The Heritage Map Museum home page details its educational services here, as well as pointers to its collection of 15th to 19th century maps, many of which are for sale. Appraisal and collection development services are also outlined.

Honolulu Community College Dinsosaur Exhibit

http://www.hcc.hawaii.edu/dinos/dinos.1.html

Dinosaurs in Hawaii? You betcha. Honolulu Community College presents its permanent collection of "fossils"—actually replicas from the American Museum of Natural History, New York City. Visitors can browse fossil pictures and explanations or take the narrated tour.

Illinois State Museum

http://www.museum.state.il.us/

The Illinois State Museum in Springfield maintains this site containing information about the museum, its collections, research and programs. By touring online exhibits, visitors can learn more about the ice age, fossils and the ancient midwestern United States.

The Institute of Egyptian Art and Archaeology

http://www.memphis.edu/egypt/main.html

The Institute of Egyptian Art and Archaeology at the University of Memphis offers this page with a collection of exhibition images and information about the institute. Visitors can also take a short tour of Egyptian sites along the Nile.

Kelsey Museum Online

http://www.umich.edu/~kelseydb/

Greek, Roman and Near Eastern artifacts and art objects call the Kelsey Museum home. Find online versions of the museum's exhibits of classical art and archaeology at this site. Includes text, pictures and maps.

Mary Rose Virtual Maritime Museum

http://www.maryrose.org

Nautical archaeology buffs can tour wreckage of the "Mary Rose," a warship built in 1510 and sunk in 1545. Visit this virtual maritime museum to discover how the ship was originally operated and recently excavated.

Museo de las Momias

http://www.sirius.com/~dbh/mummies/

Mummies are the featured attraction at the Museo de las Momias of Guanajuato, Mexico. Here visitors can learn more about the town's unique practice of preserving some of its deceased citizens for public display (why?—'cause the families couldn't afford to pay the graveyard upkeep). Also included are images of the local cemetery and historical details about the museum.

The Museum of Antiquities

http://www.ncl.ac.uk/~nantiq/

The Museum of Antiquities, an archaeological museum in northeast England, specializes in the region's history, especially Hadrian's Wall. Features here include an exhibition centered around Stone Age European hunter-gatherers, object of the month and general museum information.

Museum of the City of New York

http://www.netresource.com/mcny/

Visitors can take a virtual tour of the Museum of the City of New York here. The site includes images from current exhibitions, biographical sketches of artists, exhibition information and an online membership form.

Enter Evolution: Theory and History

http://www.ucmp.berkeley.edu/history/evolution.html

The University of California Museum of Paleontology presents this online exhibit devoted to the theory of evolution and its importance as "the binding force of all biological research." Neatly arranged, the exhibit opens with a quote from Charles Darwin and links to four important topics in the theory's study: systematics, taxonomy, dinosaur discoveries and vertebrate flight, "a case study in convergent evolution." In introducing important scientists, the exhibit reaches back to the likes of Leonardo da Vinci and Carolus Linnaeus, among others, with descriptions of their work and how it relates to the formulation and eventual study of evolutionary theory. The final link in the exhibit's evolution is to the full text of Darwin's *On The Origin Of Species By Means of Natural Selection, Or The Preservation of Favoured Races In The Struggle For Life.* Clear and interesting, Enter Evolution offers a sound presentation of a sometimes confusing, still controversial topic.—*Reviewed by Amy Hembree*

ENTER EVOLUTION:
Theory and History

DARWIN COLLECTION

Museum Online Resource Review

http://www.okc.com/morr/

The Museum Online Resource Review is a directory of resources for museum professionals. Resources are arranged by category and alphabetically, and a search is available. Links include Usenet groups and FTP sites.

Museums of Paris

http://www.paris.org/Musees/

An offering of the Paris Pages, this site links to detailed information about the many museums of Paris. An interactive map is included, as are links to related sites. In French and English.

National Air and Space Museum

http://ceps.nasm.edu:2020/NASMpage.html

Located at the Smithsonian Institution in Washington, D.C., the National Air and Space Museum specializes in aeronautics and planetary studies. This site enables visitors to explore the museum via an interactive map and learn about its events.

Natural History Museum

http://www.nhm.ac.uk/

The U.K.'s Natural History Museum brings its "unrivalled collections" and "world-class exhibitions and education" to the Web. Visitors will find pages for each of the museum's scientific departments (botany, zoology, mineralogy, etc.), as well as access to a number of its databases. [Find Related Sites]

Natural History Museum, Berne, Switzerland

http://www-nmbe.unibe.ch/index.html

The Natural History Museum of Berne, Switzerland, offers general information about the museum, its departments, events, exhibits and staff contacts. Includes links to various scientific museum sites, the University of Berne and other resources.

New Mexico Museum of Natural History and Science

http://www.aps.edu/HTMLPages/NMMNH.html

The vibrant home page for New Mexico's Museum of Natural History and Science includes info about the museum, including details on its projects, teacher support services and individual exhibits. Visitors also will find links to the Sandia Mountain Natural History Center and related sites.

North Carolina Museum of Life and Science

http://ils.unc.edu/NCMLS/ncmls.html

The home page for North Carolina's Museum of Life and Science, Durham, N.C., features an array of online exhibits. Visitors will also find information about the museum, its programs and services, and links to related sites.

On-line Exhibitions and Images

http://155.187.10.12/fun/exhibits.html

Find links to dozens of biology- and natural history-related online museum exhibitions and image archives here. Includes links to home pages of the Smithsonian Institution and the Grand Canyon National Park.

Oriental Institute

http://www-oi.uchicago.edu/OI/default.html

The Oriental Institute at the University of Chicago is a museum and research body "devoted to the study of the ancient Near East." This site offers visitors a look at the institute's museum, its archives, archaeology, and philology projects, plus related publications and databases.

Smithsonian Institution Home Page

http://www.si.edu/

"America's Treasure House of Learning," The Smithsonian Institution sponsors this page as a central jump station to its individual museums and resources. Explore the Insitution's vast array of galleries, research centers and exhibitions, from historic Americana to aerospace technology and engineering

Smithsonian Natural History Home Page

http://nmnhwww.si.edu/nmnhweb.html

The Smithsonian Museum of Natural History home page contains information on anthropology, botany, entomology, zoology, mineral sciences and more. Visitors will also find a museum guide and information on programs and activities here.

Stark's Museum of Vacuum Cleaners

http://www.reed.edu/~karl/vacuum/vacuum.html

A part-time janitor and vacuum maintainer at the Stark's Museum of Vacuum Cleaners in Portland, Oregon "smuggled a camera inside" the museum. He posts the resulting virtual museum here, which details one hundred years of vacuums with pictures and text.

Tech Museum of Innovation

http://www.thetech.org/

The Tech Museum of Innovation of San Jose, Calif., provides this interactive page intended to make technology accessible to anyone. Find out what's in store for the future, or link to various educational programs and publications.

Tridentino Museum of Natural Science

http://www.itc.it/mtsn/museo.html

Italy's Tridentino Museum of Natural Science maintains this informative page. Researchers can download its publications, abstracts and preprints, while browsers can read general facts about the museum and its exhibits. In Italian and English.

United States Holocaust Memorial Museum

http://www.ushmm.org/

The home page of the United States Holocaust Memorial Museum in Washington, D.C., offers information on the center, its research and programs, plus help in planning a visit. Also find online access to the data archive and pointers to sites of related interest.

University of North Carolina Virtual Museum

http://sunsite.unc.edu/exhibits/vmuseum/vmuseumhome.html

The Workstation Development Group at the University of North Carolina maintains this online museum. Visitors can peruse a number of exhibits, including the Soviet Archive and the Mathematical Art Gallery.

Vatican Exhibit Main Hall

http://www.ncsa.uiuc.edu/SDG/Experimental/vatican.exhibit/exhibit/Main_Hall.html

The U.S. Library of Congress presents this online Vatican Exhibit, which provides pointers to historical information about Rome. Visitors can dig through archaeological, mathematical and medical information, search for a specific artifact using the online object index, or read an overview of the exhibition.

Virtual Museum of Computing

http://www.comlab.ox.ac.uk/archive/other/museums/computing.html

The Virtual Museum of Computing is a compilation of Internet links to places offering exhibits and displays on the history of computers and technology.

WebAcropol

http://www.mechan.gsd.ntua.gr/webacropol/

WebAcropol features a historical guided tour of the Acropolis of Athens, the imposing rock on which the Parthenon was built. The tour includes images, history and explanations.

WWW Virtual Library: Museums

http://www.comlab.ox.ac.uk/archive/other/museums/search.html

An extensive directory of museums categorized by continent, subject, language and nationality is featured here. A search function is included, as well as links to museums with online exhibits, plus a host of recommendations.

PHILOSOPHY

Analytical Philosophy
http://college.antioch.edu/~smauldin/

Antioch College graduate student Shannon Mauldin features a collection of analytical philosophy links at her personal Web site. Includes links to many university philosophy department home pages and to collections of individual philosophers' works.

Applied Ethics Resources
http://www.ethics.ubc.ca/papers/AppliedEthics.html

Visitors to this page will find an index of links dealing with applied ethics. Categories include business ethics, environmental ethics, media ethics and others.

Australasian Philosophy Network
http://www.arts.su.edu.au/Arts/departs/philos/APS/APS.home.html

The Australasian Philosophy home page provides information "for and about the philosophical community in Australia and New Zealand." Includes links to philosophy department home pages, the Australasian Association of Philosophy Web site and a directory of Australasian philosophers.

Bertrand Russell Archives at McMaster University
http://www.mcmaster.ca/russdocs/russell.htm

McMaster University in Ontario, Canada marks the epicenter for scholarly study of Bertrand Russell, the renowned British philosopher, logician, essayist, and socio/political activist. The University sponsors the online Bertrand Russell Archive, featuring Russell's writings, the Russell Editorial Project, favorite quotations from Russell's works, and much more.

Bjorn's Guide to Philosophy
http://www-und.ida.liu.se/~y92bjoch/

Maintained by a student of political science at the University of Linköping, Sweden, Björn's Guide to Philosophy features information about philosophers, as well as links to journals, university departments and electronic texts. In Swedish and English.

Brown Electronic Article Review Service
http://www.brown.edu/Departments/Philosophy/bears/homepage.html

The Brown Electronic Article Review Service attempts to get around the time delays of traditional publishing by placing academic criticism online. Visitors to this page will find a list of reviews in the area of moral and political philosophy.

Contemporary Philosophy of Mind: An Annotated Bibliography
http://ling.ucse.edu/~chalmers/biblio.html

An annotated bibliography of "Contemporary Philosophy of the Mind" is provided here by David Chalmers at Washington University in St Louis. The work consists of 1,800 entries with brief summaries, divided into five sections of Consciousness and Qualia, Mental Context, Pychophysical and Psychological Explanation, the Philosophy of Artificial Intelliegence and other topics.

Deoxyribonucleic Hyperdimension
http://www.intac.com/~dimitri/dh/deoxy.html

The contemporary philosophers represented on this page "peer into bits and zones of Chaos," exploring alternate realities and expanded levels of consciousness. Contemplate the writings of Alan Watts, Timothy Leary, Terrence McKenna and Robert Anton Wilson.

Electronic Journal of Analytic Philosophy
http://www.phil.indiana.edu/ejap/

The "Electronic Journal of Analytic Philosophy" explores various topics of philosophical research. Current and back issues are offered here along with mailing list information and submission guidlelines.

Engaged Buddhist Dharma
http://www.maui.com/~lesslie/

Engaged Buddhist Dharma features information about human rights concerns, world news, and environmental concerns. Link to Buddhist art and writings as well.

Ereignis: The Heidegger Home Page
http://www.webcom.com/~paf/ereignis.html

Martin Heidegger no longer leaves a paper trail, but an abundance of thought about his writings is posted on the Internet. This page devoted to the German philosopher contains links to Heidegger resources around the Internet including the archive of the Heidegger mailing list.

Friedrich Wilhelm Nietzsche
http://www.usc.edu/dept/annenberg/thomas/nietzsche.html

The Annenberg School of Communications at the University of Southern California maintains this page dedicated to the German philosopher Friedrich Wilhelm Nietzsche. Features include a biography and works bibliography in German and English, links to Nietzsche societies and organizations, and access to selected writings.

Gateless Gate
http://sunsite.unc.edu/zenbin/koan-index.pl

This site hosts a collection of more than 30 philosophical vingettes pertaining to Taoism and Buddhism. Check out classic moral ponderings here,

such as "Two Monks Roll Up the Screen" and "This Mind is Buddha."

Hartlib Papers Project
http://www2.shef.ac.uk/hartlib/hartlib.html

The Hartlib Papers Project, devoted to the papers of the 17th-century polymath Samuel Hartlib, is archived at the Sheffield University Library, England. These papers are considered one of the great collections relating to the development of modern Western thought. This page includes information about project personnel and the project itself.

Indiana University Philosophy Department
http://www.phil.indiana.edu/

Indiana University offers information on its philosopy department and links to other philosophy organizations here. Visitors will find a list of classes and schedules of seminars.

Indiana University-Bloomington Program in Pure and Applied Logic
http://www.phil.indiana.edu/~iulg/iulg.html

The Program in Pure and Applied Logic at Indiana University-Bloomington maintains this page profiling its multidisciplinary course of study. Find information on the faculty, seminar schedules, abstracts of publications and class offerings.

International Philosophical Preprint Exchange
http://phil-preprints.l.chiba-u.ac.jp/IPPE.html

Philosophers worldwide share their ideas on this electronic swap meet of published and unpublished scholarly investigations. The service is coordinated by the Department of Philosophy, Chiba University, Japan. See Editor's Choice.

Internet Services for Philosophers
http://www.phil.ruu.nl/philosophy_services.html

The Internet Services for Philosophers provides a compilation of selected Web sites relevant to the study of philosophy. Visitors will find links to archives, mailing lists and other resources.

Kansas Religion & Philosophy Center
http://falcon.cc.ukans.edu/~mahyarp/

The Kansas Religion & Philosophy Center, part of a personal home page, guides visitors through "the deeper meanings of life." Visit here for an index of world religions, cultures and philosophies.

Karl Marx/Friedrich Engels Archives
http://csf.colorado.edu/psn/marx/

"There's no way to monetarily profit from this project," of putting the Karl Marx/Friedrich Engels archives online, the archivist of this site says, but he hopes the material will be pleasurable and enlightening. The works are accompanied by photos of the two thinkers.

Krishnamurti
http://www.well.com/user/jct/
Works by and about Indian philosopher and author U.G. Krishnamurti are provided here. His book *Mind is a Myth* is available for downloading, as are video clips, transcriptions of conversations with Krishnamurti and related articles.

Metaphysical Review
http://www.meta.unh.edu/
"Metaphysical Review," an electronic journal of the University of New Hampshire, provides essays, comments, letters and book reviews for subscribers in more than 20 countries worldwide. Visit here for current and back issues, a keyword search of its article database and subscription information.

New Paradigms Project
http://www.access.digex.net/~kknisely/
philosophy.tv.html
A virtual library of conspiracy theories, the New Paradigms Project catalogs bibliographic information and links regarding assassination conspiracies, secret societies and more.

No Dogs or Philosophers Allowed
http://www.access.digex.net/~kknisely/
philosophy.tv.html
No Dogs or Philosphers Allowed is an interactive multimedia forum for discussion of the human condition. Includes information on NDOPA and how to access the philosophy-centered live TV show.

Philosophy at Large
http://www.liv.ac.uk/~srlclark/philos.html
From the staff and students at Liverpool University's Philosophy Department comes this index of pointers to all things philosophical on the Web (and in the United Kingdom in particular). Pointers to Usenet newsgroups, Listservs, electronic texts and journals are just a small sampling of the vast resources compiled here.

Philosophy on the Web
http://www.phil.ruu.nl/philosophy-sites.html
The search for meaning on the Internet is made easier by a visit to Philosophy on the Web. This extensive collection of links to journals, texts, academic departments and other philosophical fodder caters to both the serious academician and the armchair existentialist.

Postmodern Culture
http://jefferson.village.virginia.edu/pmc/
contents.all.html
The "Postmodern Culture" home page contains tables of contents for current and back issues of the electronic journal of interdisciplinary criticism. The journal's archives can be searched by subject or keyword.

Principia Cybernetica Web
http://pespmc1.vub.ac.be/
The Principia Cybernetica Project "tries to tackle age-old philosophical questions with the help of the most recent cybernetic theories and technologies." Subjects discussed here include metasystem transition theory, cybernetics and systems theory. See Editor's Choice.

RhetNet: A CyberJournal
http://www.missouri.edu/~rhetnet/
RhetNet is a repository for resources on the Internet of interest to the rhetoric and writing community. It provides articles and essays, Internet conversations and a "general call for participation."

The Robot Wisdom Pages
http://www.mcs.net/~jorn/home.html
"Home of the new, conservative-left Responsible Party," Robot Wisdom proposes creating a computer model of the human predicament. This will help clear the path for a new political paradigm, where "cynical predators" can no longer feed. Visitors here will find political, philosophical, and social looks at the plan.

Sean's One-Stop Philosophy Shop
http://www.rpi.edu/~cearls/phil.html
Attempting to "create the ultimate philosophy link list," the Webmaster presents visitors to his page with a good start to that end. Categories of links include university departments, gophers, real-life philosophers, famous works and discussions, various "isms" and more.

Spoon Collective
http://jefferson.village.virginia.edu/~spoons/
Spoon Collective devotes this page to philosophical discussion and archived information. Learn about and discuss such heady topics as the theory of artistic avant-garde, Marxist discourse and a number of other philosophical ideas from an extensive listing.

Stanford Unversity Department of Philosophy
http://csli-www.stanford.edu/philosophy/
philosophy.html
The Department of Philosophy at Stanford University in California presents this site with a wide range of departmental resources. Visitors can

---

a2z EDITOR'S CHOICE
International Philosophical Preprint Exchange
http://phil-preprints.l.chiba-u.ac.jp/IPPE.html
From Chiba University, Japan, the International Philosophical Preprint Exchange (IPPE) provides access to prepublication philosophical papers categorized by subject areas including aesthetics, epistemology, ethics, logic, metaphysics, political philosophy, and more. Abstracts of the most recent preprints and instructions for submission are also available, as is information about journals, books, and conferences. The organization of the IPPE page is very straightforward, navigable by either graphical or text maps, with alternatives for both quick and full access. IPPE has also published many of its preprints on CD-ROM, which can be ordered from this site.—*Reviewed by Amy Hembree*

International · Philosophical · Preprin
Internet mail: <Phil-Preprints-Admin@Phil-Preprints.

QUICK ACCESS

[Preprint subject areas][Journals, Books, and Conferences][Recent Abstracts][Call for Submissions] browse phone indices, mailing lists and information on faculty members, or review the Philosopher's Index.

Su Tzu's Chinese Philosophy Page

http://mars.superlink.net/user/fsu/philo.html

Visitors to this page will find a generous collection of links to Chinese philosophy resources on the Web. Find electronic texts, as well as centers and institutions, offering a variety of general information and instructional teaching. In Chinese and English.

Theosophical Society

http://ezinfo.ucs.indiana.edu/~mcooke/mcooke/theosophy.html

Founded in 1875, the Theosophical Society is a worldwide association "dedicated to the uplifting of humanity" through the teaching of universal brotherhood, and study of ancient and modern religion, science and philosophy. This home page sheds light on the organization and its history.

University of Chicago Philosophy Project

http://csmaclab-www.uchicago.edu/philosophyProject/philos.html

The University of Chicago Philosophy Project is an electronically-mediated forum for scholarly discussion. The site offers visitors a seat in the audience, or the option to suggest or join a discussion group. Includes links to current discussions, the sponsoring university and a variety of related resources.

University of Massachusetts Philosophy Department

http://www.umassd.edu/1Academic/CArtsandSciences/Philosophy/Philosophyhomepage.html

The Philosophy Department of the University of Massachusetts at Dartmouth maintains this departmental overview. Meet the faculty, review the course requirements and link to related sites on and off campus.

University of Sydney School of Philosophy

http://www.arts.su.edu.au/Arts/departs/philos/philosophy.home.html

The School of Philosophy at the University of Sydney, Australia, maintains this site with administrative information and academic resources. Visit here to learn about the school and find links to philosophy-related information, including research reports, conferences updates and employment opportunities.

University of Texas Philosophy Department

http://www.dla.utexas.edu/depts/philosophy/main.html

The University of Texas Philosophy Department provides information on its programs, course offerings and faculty here. The site includes links to scholarly and whimsical philosophy Internet resources, and other pages from the university.

University of Waterloo Department of Philosophy

http://watarts.uwaterloo.ca/PHIL/cpshelle/philosophy.html

The Philosophy Department at the University of Waterloo in Ontario, Canada, profiles its faculty and programs at this home page. Visitors can check out the course calendars, visit the gallery of philosophers or read the "Eidos" journal.

Utrecht University Philosophy Department

http://www.phil.ruu.nl/

The Philosophy Department at Utrecht University in the Netherlands provides an overview of its programs and faculty here. The page also contains a look at the university's environs.

Walker Percy

http://sunsite.unc.edu/wpercy/

Southern favorite son Walker Percy is characterized as a "philosophical novelist" by the University of North Carolina archive that collects and presents his work online. Visitors can peruse Percy's papers, fiction and philosophical treatises here.

---

a2z EDITOR'S CHOICE

Principia Cybernetica Web

http://pespmc1.vub.ac.be/

Who am I? Where do I come from? Where am I going? Need help with these questions and a lot more? Queries like these are the basis of philosophy, and the Principia Cybernetica Project, an international organization, attempts to deal with them in a interesting and up-to-date fashion, that is, "with the help of the most recent cybernetic theories and technologies." The folks at Principia Cybernetica believe that the best way to form contemporary philosophy is through the use of information science, that all systems are constructed by a "continuing process of self-organization." The Principia Cybernetica Web, based at the Free University of Brussels, introduces, annotates and explains the project's theories and methods and offers links to sites that deal with complexity, human-machine interaction, cognition and related topics. The main theory, MetaSystem Transition Theory, is detailed in a short, hyperlinked essay, and an extensive background for Cybernetics and Systems Theory is also provided, including a dictionary of important terms. The site is easily navigable via the text links or an image map that not only takes readers to each major topic, but also serves as a visual aid for understanding Principia Cybernetica issues. Have something to say about the ideas here? Feel free to submit suggestions or general comments to the User Annotations.—*Reviewed by Amy Hembree*

PRINCIPIA CYBERNETICA WEB - ©

Author : Editors ,
Date : May 24, 1996 (modified); Jul 8, 1993 (created)

Welcome to the Principia Cybernetica Web

This is the WWW server of the **Principia Cybernetica Project** (PCP), an international organization. The Project's aim is the *computer-supported collaborative development of an evolutionary-systemic philosophy*. Put more simply, PCP tries to tackle age-old philosophical questions with the help of the most recent cybernetic theories and technologies.

W. H. Calvin's The Ascent of Mind

http://weber.u.washington.edu/wcalvin/bk5.html

A complete chapter-by-chapter summary of William H. Calvin's *Ascent of the Mind: Ice Age Climates and the Evolution of Intelligence* is provided here, in Dutch and English. Visitors who like what they read can download chapters individually.

RELIGION

ARCHIVES AND INDICES

Cosmic Web

http://www.sirius.com/~cosmic/welcome.html

Cosmic Web intends to open minds and "awaken souls" with inspirational answers to the question of evolution. Find books, publications and a child's education section.

Facets of Religion

http://www.servtech.com/public/mcroghan/religion.html

Facets of Religion is a listing of the major faiths worldwide. It contains general and interreligious information along with related topics and skeptical studies.

Finding God in Cyberspace

http://users.ox.ac.uk/~mikef/durham/gresham.html

An online guide to Internet-based religious information, this site offers links to theological and religious studies libraries, publishers and more. Visit here for pointers to a variety of references on world religions and philosophies. See Editor's Choice, page 54.

Galaxy: Religion

http://www.einet.net/galaxy/Humanities/Religion.html

Galaxy's Religion page provides links to readings and discussions of religion in the cultural and philosophical context. With more deconstructionists than devotees, the resources provided are largely academic and include theology and mythology.

Galaxy: Religion (Community)

http://www.einet.net/galaxy/Community/Religion.html

Resources on religious communities worldwide are provided at this Galaxy page. From Bahai to

Islam, Judaism to Voodoo, most bases are covered. In addition to pointers, the site offers a variety of articles, books and guides on related topics.

The Green Pages

http://www.oakgrove.org/GreenPages

These pages contain links to resources for pagans, including listings of gatherings, covens and groups. Visitors also will find general information submitted by participating organizations, along with links to pagan publications and Web sites.

Kansas Religion & Philosophy Center

http://falcon.cc.ukans.edu/~mahyarp/

The Kansas Religion & Philosophy Center, part of a personal home page, guides visitors through "the deeper meanings of life." Visit here for an index of world religions, cultures and philosophies.

The Library of Congress Religion and Philosophy Gopher

gopher://marvel.loc.gov:70/11/global/phil

Philosophers and theologians will find plenty to delve into here. The Library of Congress's philosophy and religion gopher provides access to journals, Kierkegaard discussion archives, academic sites and much more.

North Carolina State University Library Religion Gopher State University

gopher://dewey.lib.ncsu.edu/11/library/disciplines/religion

Religion and philosophy scholars can use this gopher to search religious texts and find religion bibliographic resources on the Internet. Users can also access the American Philosophical Association gopher and the King James Bible.

 EDITOR'S CHOICE

Big Dummies Guide to Theology, Philosophy, and Ethics

http://www.industrial.com/~simon/bdintro.html

This "Big Dummies" guide bills itself as "a starter kit for technoids," those, ah...computer geeks perhaps unfamiliar with the less virtual (but no less conceptual) aspects of humanity: spirituality, religion, metaphysics, ethics and philosophy. The author also comes forward with the confession that "this book will probably offend nearly everyone." The guide is divided into three sections covering religion, philosophy and ethics, but doesn't let its users jump into any topic too early. From the home page, readers can step gingerly to the Vocabulary of Deep Thought or, if they already know all the words, proceed with confidence to the Seven Deadly Arguments which include original sin, creationism, evil done in the name of religion and the ever-popular Does God Exist? Ever under construction, this guide provides a solid and simple start to those just beginning to grapple with the mysteries of existence and the existence of mysteries.—*Reviewed by Amy Hembree*

Big Dummies Guide to Theology, Philosophy, and Ethics

A Starter Kit for Technoids

By Orrin R. Onken, aka "Simon"

Copyright 1995 - Orrin R. Onken

Religion and Philosophy Resources on the Internet
http://web.bu.edu/LIBRARY/Religion/contents.html

From Boston University, this gateway site contains a comprehensive listing of worldwide religion and philosophy resources. Includes links to selected library catalogs, research guides and other resources.

The Religious Freedom Home Page
http://northshore.shore.net/rf/

Learn about religious freedom from a national, international and non-denominational perspective at this Web site. The Religious Freedom Home Page provides pointers to related legal and constitutional documents on the Web.

Religious Resources on the Net
http://convex.cc.uky.edu/~jatuck00/Religion/Religion.html

Religious Resources on the Net features links to Catholic resources across the Internet, as well as other religion pages, including the Jewish Home Page, the Islamic Texts and Resources MetaPage, the Zen Page and Finding God in Cyberspace.

Rice University Philosophy-Religion Gopher
gopher://riceinfo.rice.edu/11/Subject/RelPhil

Rice University offers this gopher of "information by subject area." This sub-directory hosts pointers to Internet-wide resources relating to philosophy and religion.

WWW Virtual Library: Religion
http://sunfly.ub.uni-freiburg.de/religion/

The World Wide Web Virtual Library offers links to religious sites and texts here. The index includes entries for the world's major religions as well as ancient religions and pagan sites. It also includes pointers to newsgroups and mailing lists.

ASSOCIATIONS AND ORGANIZATIONS

Computers for Christ
http://www.cforc.com/

Computers for Christ is an organization dedicated to the use of computer technology for spreading the "good news" of the Gospel of Christ. Visitors will find a database of online Christian resources, including church home pages, and links to a variety of religious hypertexts.

Creation Research Society
http://www.iclnet.org/pub/resources/text/crs/crs-home.html

Here, the Creation Research Society welcomes members of the Internet community who share its interest in creationism.

The FARMS Home Page
http://farmsresearch.com

The Foundation for Ancient Research and Mormon studies (FARMS) supports research about the Book of Mormon. It gives visitors an overview of its publications here and posts membership information.

Peregrine Foundation
http://www.matisse.net/~peregrin/index.html

A non-profit group dedicated to the dissemination of information about "high-demand" religious groups, totalitarian sects, and communes, the Peregrine Foundation offers access to its newsletters and archives via this Web site.

Theosophical Society
http://ezinfo.ucs.indiana.edu/~mcooke/mcooke/theosophy.html

Founded in 1875, the Theosophical Society is a worldwide association "dedicated to the uplifting of humanity" through the teaching of universal brotherhood, and study of ancient and modern religion, science and philosophy. This home page sheds light on the organization and its history.

A Unitarian Universalist Hotlist
http://www.wolfe.net/~uujim/uusrc.html

Find out what a Unitarian Universalist (UU) is and discover answers to other Frequently Asked Questions (FAQ) at this informative site. Links to UU church and organization home pages, plus UU newsgroups and mailing lists are also featured.

World Council of Churches
http://www.wcc-coe.org/oikumene.html

The World Council of Churches (WCC) maintains this site with links to a member church list, meetings calendar, press releases, aid and relief information, and ecumenical resources. In French and English.

ATHEISTS AND AGNOSTICS

The Atheism Web
http://freethought.tamu.edu/news/atheism/

The basic, but comprehensive, Atheism Web contains an introduction to atheism, its arguments, links to its online organizations and short synopses of atheist books, movies and other media. Links to the Usenet newsgroups alt.atheism and soc.atheism are also provided.

The Left Hemisphere Web
http://www.xnet.com/~blatura/left_hem.shtml

The Left Hemisphere Web features links to skeptic, religious and secular resources on the Web. Visitors can follow links to magazines and organizations covering the three topic areas.

The Secular Web
http://freethought.tamu.edu/

Maintained by the Internet Infidels, this "free-thinking" Web site offers—surprise!—many links to atheist, agnostic, and humanist Internet resources. Visitors will find links to topical magazines, organizations and newsgroups here, along with criticism and debate.

DAILY SCRIPTURE AND GUIDANCE

Daily Wisdom
http://www.gospelcom.net/gf/dw/

"Daily Wisdom," provided by the Gospel Communications Network, offers a Christian grain of wisdom each day on the Internet. Visitors can see the daily offering or search a categorized archive of past wisdom.

Our Daily Bread
http://www.gospelcom.net/rbc/odb/odb.shtml

Our Daily Bread presents a Christian homily-of-the-day from RBC Ministries on the Gospel Communications Network. Visitors can access an archive of previous articles and arrange for delivery of Our Daily Bread.

Promises—A Daily Guide to Supernatural Living
http://www.mdalink.com/cgi-bin/promises.cgi

The Campus Crusade for Christ provides this daily installment from the book, "Promises—A Daily Guide to Supernatural Living." Each entry features a biblical quotation and an inspiring vignette for Christians.

Words of Hope
http://www.gospelcom.net/devo/woh/

The Gospel Communications Network and Online Christian Resources sponsor "Words of Hope," offering meditations and inspirational thoughts for every day of the year.

INSPIRATIONAL ART

Art to Lift Your Spirit

http://www.mindspring.com/~tentmakr/spirart.html

Visitors can wander through an exhibition of scripture-laced fractals at this online art gallery. Includes links to churches, Christian publications and schools, and the Cyberspace Catacombs, a meeting place for the saved.

New Orleans Cemetery Images

http://www.webcorp.com/images/nocems.htm

New Orleans Cemetery Images is a collection of photographs documenting the religious, sometimes superstitious, affinity for religious imagery this community has traditionally embraced. Sound clips and brief explanations accompany each image.

INSTITUTES AND SCHOOLS

Abilene Christian University College of Biblical and Family Studies

gopher://bible.acu.edu/

Abilene Christian University, Texas, maintains this gopher with information about its College of Biblical and Family Studies, information about technology and Christianity, and Bible and theological links.

Acton Institute Online

http://www.acton.org/

The Acton Institute for the Study of Religion and Liberty is a non-profit educational center in Grand Rapids, Mich., that promotes religious pluralism, individual liberty and governmental conservatism. This Web site states the institution's history and purpose, and presents news, publications and opinions.

Bethel College and Theological Seminary

http://www.bethel.edu/

Bethel College and Theological Seminary in St. Paul, Minn., maintains this searchable site containing general information, including news about its campus, libraries, Center for Continuing Studies and more.

Catholic University of America

http://www.cua.edu/

The Catholic University of America is a private educational facility located in Washington, D.C. Visitors to its Web server will find access to schools and admissions, libraries, alumni resources, news and events.

Friends Just Peace Institute

http://www.ipt.com/htmlpub/jpi/jpi.htm

Friends Just Peace Institute is an organization from the Friends Congregational Church that encourages social justice and tolerance. Visitors to this page will find an overview of the organization, a forum for discussion and other resources that provide justice-related information.

Goshen College

http://www.goshen.edu/

A ministry of the Mennonite Church, Goshen College, Goshen, Ind., maintains this site with information about the school and academic departments and links to news and campus services.

ICLnet Home Page

http://www.iclnet.org/

The Institute for Christian Leadership (ICL) provides resources to Christian institutions of higher education. ICLnet, its online branch, invites visitors to join ICL hosted discussion groups and to access numerous Christian resources on the Web. Also found here is a "Guide to Christian Literature on the Internet."

University of Durham Department of Theology Gopher

gopher://delphi.dur.ac.uk/11/Academic/P-T/Theology/Computing

The Department of Theology at the University of Durham, England, provides this gopher menu that features theological resources. It includes links to discussion groups, software and texts.

INTERFAITH RESOURCES

Celebrating the Spirit

http://www.crc.ricoh.com/~rowanf/CTS/cts.html

A spiritual revival is envisioned by authors of the Berkeley Area Interfaith Council's Web site. The

---

a2z EDITOR'S CHOICE

Finding God in Cyberspace

http://users.ox.ac.uk/~mikef/durham/gresham.html

According to this page, God is everywhere, even in this void we call cyberspace. A guide to religious studies resources on the Internet, the material here is categorized by resource type with a special section of links to important and popular topics such as Buddhism, Christianity, Islam, and mythology. The print resources directory has information for finding dissertations, publishers, booksellers and libraries. A directory of people links to a variety of electronic conferences and scholarly societies. At digital resources, visitors will find the usual set of Internet links, including electronic texts and journals, software and multimedia items. Easy to browse or search, this page, which was designed by a scholar in library science and religious studies, provides an excellent starting point for finding God in cyberspace...or anywhere else you choose to look.—*Reviewed by Amy Hembree*

FINDING GOD IN CYBERSPACE

A GUIDE TO RELIGIOUS STUDIES RESOURCES ON THE INTERNET

New 1995 Edition

by John L. Gresham, MLS, PhD

- About this Author
- Table of Contents

council's Global Ethic project beckons visitors to explore the page; the council promises updates on its interfaith project.

Centre for Religious Tolerance

http://www.kosone.com/people/ocrt/ocrt_hp.htm

The Ontario Centre for Religious Tolerance strives to expose and remedy religious hatred. At its home page, visitors can access a variety of documents which seek to promote an understanding of all religions. Explore topics from atheism to Zoroastrianism.

International Lutheran Marriage Encounter

http://www.pic.net/~speed/lme.html

The International Lutheran Marriage Encounter weekend program is designed to give married couples of all faiths a chance to get to know one another all over again through God. Couples can visit this site to learn more about the program.

Renewal Outreach

http://users.deltanet.com/users/nco/public_html/

Part of the Swedenborg Centre, Renewal Outreach offers to help you improve your spiritual health, your marriage, your family, and even society by recognizing and accepting the love of God.

Saddleback Valley Community Church

http://www.saddleback.com

Saddleback Valley Community Church in Lake Forest, Calif., features a message from pastor Dr. Rick Warren and information about its services here. Visitors can also stop by for daily devotionals and the Fax of Life.

JOURNALS AND PERIODICALS

Index of Newspaper Articles

http://www.ucalgary.ca/~elsegal/Shokel/Art_Index.html

Here, a writer in Calgary posts over 100 articles he has published in the *Jewish Free Press* and *Jewish Star*. The articles cover religious holidays, scholarship, trivia, exotica, and community affairs.

IOUDAIOS Review

http://www.lehigh.edu/lists/ioudaios-review/

Religious scholars can read reviews of books on early Judaic history and related fields here. "IOUDAIOS Review" is an online journal dedicated to making these reviews accessible to all professional scholars. Guidelines are also available.

Jewish Post of New York

http://www.jewishpost.com/

For the latest news relating to Judaism, turn to the Jewish Post of New York. This electronic bimonthly covers such issues as bigotry and anti-Semitism. The site also includes information on subscribing to the hard-copy version.

The Journal of Biblical Ethics in Medicine

http://www.usit.net/public/CAPO/jbem.html

The Center for the Advancement of Paleo Orthodoxy (CAPO), a biblical and historic consortium, provides articles on a variety of topics, including ethical and religious conflicts in medical practice and teen sexuality. Visitors can link to CAPO's home page, the Augustine Institute (Ethics) or the Calvin Institute (Theology).

Mount Athos Greek Manuscripts Catalog

http://abacus.bates.edu/~rallison/

This server is the primary repository of information related to the Philotheou Monastery Catalog Project, located at Bates College, Lewiston, Maine. Visitors will find information on the project here, in addition to such features as Greek monastery manuscripts and methodological papers.

Scripture Studies

http://www.kaiwan.com/~ssper/sstdys.html

Scripture Studies, a journal dedicated to Bible commentary, is published 10 times a year with studies of New and Old Testament books. The current issue is available here and can also be downloaded in plain text or as .zip or .hqx files.

Sojourners

http://www.sojourners.com/sojourners/home.html

Check here for the online version of *Sojourners,* a magazine that explores faith, politics and culture. "Rooted in the solid ground of the prophetic biblical tradition," this publication offers articles intended for readers with diverse religions and ethnic backgrounds.

Wire

http://www.roehampton.ac.uk/link/wire/

In its printed form, *Wire* is mailed free to thousands of churches and schools in southern England. Visitors here can download the newsletter, which includes features for and about the Catholic church and how it communicates. Available in Adobe Acrobat.

LIBRARIES

The Christia Library

http://www.ihi.aber.ac.uk/~spk/christia.html

Essays devoted to "practical Christian life" hit the Web at the Christia Library site. Readers can browse the collection sorted by author or subject, or opt to subscribe to the Christia mailing list.

MISSIONS AND SOCIAL WORK

Bethany Christian Services

http://www.bethany.org/

The protection of the lives of children and families is the goal of this Christian organization. The site describes the group's mission and provides links to related Internet sites.

International Union of Gospel Missions

http://www.iugm.org

The International Union of Gospel Missions serves more than 27 million meals each year and offers warm shelter to the needy. It offers information on homelessness and its efforts to battle it on this page. The union invites others to join its ranks.

Mennonite Central Committee

http://www.mennonitecc.ca/mcc/

The Webmaster of the Mennonite Central Committee describes this organization as the "relief and development arm of the North American Mennonite and Brethren in Christ churches." Visitors will find background and volunteer information on programs for disaster relief and third world development.

Youth With a Mission International

http://www.ywam.org/

Youth With a Mission International (YWAM) is an organization of Christians active in support of the needy. Visitors here will find information about training programs, ministries and frontier missions around the world.

MONASTERIES

Russell's Monastic Den

http://www.efn.org/~russelln/

Russell's Monastic Den contains links to all things monkish on the Internet. Monastery links include the Benedictine home page and the 1,000-year-old Hungarian Archabbey of Pannonhalma. Other items of interest include ancient texts, Coptic sites and St. Benedict's Beer Label.

Tsurphu Foundation Homepage
http://www.maui.net/~tsurphu/karmapa/

The Tsurphu Foundation is a U.S.-based group devoted to raising awareness and funds for monasteries of His Holiness the Gyalwa Karmapa, particularly those monasteries in Tibet. This home page is an introduction to the spiritual dogma and provides a look at Karmapa lineage, prophecies and prayers.

NEWSGROUPS

The Church of Scientology
http://www.maui.net/~tsurphu/karmapa/

The founder of the Usenet newsgroup alt.religion.scientology hosts this site with information about the newsgroup, its history and notes on the Webmaster's scraps with Scientology officials. There are also links to related sites.

PUBLISHERS

Ignatius Press
http://www.ignatius.com/

This virtual catalog details information about Catholic books, periodicals and other resources offered by Ignatius Press. Also includes news of interest to Catholics and information about the publishing company.

Religio
http://www.thur.de/religio/start.html

Religio is a German publisher of Christian and cult-awareness materials. The Religio site offers sections on popular alternative sects and their recruiting tactics, beliefs and logos, as well as advice for families or individuals who may be under the spell of a cult. In German and English.

Saint Mary's Press
http://wwwsmp.smumn.edu/

Saint Mary's Press, a Christian publishing house based in Winona, Minn., provides title and ordering information on this site. Visitors here can search for books by title and author, and use the electronic order form.

RELIGIONS A2Z

BUDDHISM

Asynchronous School of Buddhist Dialectics Buddhist Dialectics
http://faraday.clas.Virginia.EDU/~wam7c/

This Buddhist site offers translations of selected Tibetan Buddhist texts, including current and historic documents.

Dark Zen: The Teachings of Mystical Zen
http://www.teleport.com/~zennist/zennist.html

There's plain Zen, and then there's Dark Zen, that which is "directed towards achieving mystical union with Buddha Mind." Searchers upon this Web path can learn about the study of Dark Zen and find answers to their more mundane questions about the Buddha Mind Institute.

Dharma Rain Zen Center
http://www.teleport.com/~ryanjb/STILLPOINT/SP.shtml

The Dharma Rain Zen Center (DRZC), a Soto Zen lay practice temple in Portland, Ore., maintains its home page with information about its meditation schedule and links to current and previous issues of the newsletter, "StillPoint."

DharmaNet
http://www.dharmanet.org/

Presented as a public service by DharmaNet International, this site contains the DharmaNet Electronic Files Archive. The links featured include Buddhist InfoWeb, Buddhist Meditation Retreats and Events, Dharma Newsstand, and the Buddhis.

Dzogchen Foundation
http://www.dzogchen.org/

This page presents Dzogchen, the "ultimate teaching of the Non-Sectarian Practice Lineage of Tibetan Buddhism." Includes article reprints and historical information illuminating the Dzogchen Foundation and "the innate great perfection."

Electronic Buddhist FTP Archive
ftp://coombs.anu.edu.au/coombspapers/otherarchives/electronic-buddhist-archives/

From the Australian National University, this FTP archive contains files for teachers and students of Buddhism and other Asian religions. Visitors here can download everything from lists of Buddhist centers to ancient texts and sermons. Part of the Coombspapers Social Sciences Research Data Bank.

Gateless Gate
http://sunsite.unc.edu/zenbin/koan-index.pl

This site hosts a collection of more than 30 philosophical vignettes pertaining to Taoism and Buddhism. Check out classic moral ponderings here, such as "Two Monks Roll Up the Screen" and "This Mind is Buddha."

IRIZ Home Page
http://www.iijnet.or.jp/iriz/irizhtml/irizhome.htm

The International Research Institute for Zen Buddhism shares its extensive collection of Buddhist primary texts at this site. Visitors will find Zen literature, art, and links to Zen masters and centers around the globe.

Lama Surya Das
http://www.dzogchen.org/surya/

Western Buddhists will find many photos and links to teachings at American-born Lama Surya Das' home page. Das, founder of the Dzogchen Foundation, posts his writings and those of other Zen masters here, along with a photo gallery.

Osel Shen Phen Ling Tibetan Buddhist Dharma Community
http://www.ism.net/~ose/index.html

The Tibetan Buddhist Center site provides devotees with prayers, meditations and other practices of the faith. Includes an introduction to Tibetan Buddhism, videos of learned priests and links to related Web pages.

Shambhala
http://www.shambhala.org/

No mere abstract and esoteric vision, Shambhala seeks to use mediation and spirituality in forming an enlightened society. Interested guests can hook up with mediation centers nationwide or learn more about this program founded by a master of Tibetan Buddhist traditions.

The White Path Temple
http://www.mew.com/shin/

The White Path Temple is described by the Webmaster as "a virtual Shin Buddhist Temple in Cyberspace." Visitors are encouraged to examine Shin texts, sutras, mandalas and documents, meditate upon Shin Buddhist art, visit a Shinran exhibit, reflect upon poetry, and learn the ways, philosophy and teachings of Buddha.

WWW Virtual Library: Buddhist Studies
http://coombs.anu.edu.au/WWWVL-Buddhism.html

Maintained by the Virtual Library, this index of Buddhist studies resources is a comprehensive, classified collection of information with links to news, texts, publications, and other sources covering the study of Buddhism in its many forms.

The Zen Garden

http://www.nomius.com/~zenyard/
zenyard.htm

The subCultureNet from Nomius Eye on the Web provides this Zen page. Stories, images, sounds and enigmatic "koans" tat illustrate the Zen worldview (or lack thereof) are featured.

Zen@SunSITE

http://sunsite.unc.edu/zen/

Visitors will find information about the teachings and practice of Zen Buddhism here. Download Frequently Asked Questions (FAQ) files from alt.zen, link to Zen Buddhist texts and learn about monasteries and retreats.

CHRISTIANITY

AlaPadre's Catholic Corner

http://www.wsnet.com:80/~alapadre/

AlaPadre's Catholic Corner plumbs the depths of Catholic theology and ethics. hundreds of links on this index point to sites on the rituals of mass, theology and Catholic schools, among others. It is maintained by a priest and also spotlights a site called "Ask Father."

All Topics for Contradictions

http://www.ugcs.caltech.edu/cgi-bin/
webnews/read/contradictions/0

This page contains a reply to a list of 143 purported contradictions found in the text of the Bible that was originally posted to the newsgroup soc.religion.christian. An index to the contradictions is provided for quick reference.

Anglicans Online

http://www.anglican.org/online/

This gateway leads to information on Anglican churches throughout the U.S., Canada and worldwide. Visitors can stop by the news room for church news, join discussion groups or link to resources for biblical study.

Archdiocese of Mobile

http://www.wsnet.com/~alapadre/
deanimax.html

The Roman Catholic archdiocese of Mobile, Ala., goes online here with information about its bishop and organization, history and parishes. "Sister Lister" lets visitors identify nuns in the diocese by their first names. Links are provided to Spring Hill College in Mobile and to the Catholic Corner.

Association of Christians in Higher Education

http://www.bham.ac.uk/uccf/ache/

The Association of Christians in Higher Education is a fellowship of Christians who work as academics and administrative staff at colleges and universities in the United Kingdom. Visitors to its home page can learn more about the association and its organizing principles.

Calculation of the Ecclesiastical Calendar

http://cssa.stanford.edu/~marcos/ec-cal.html

Pinpoint the dates of Easter and Lenten rites with this tool that calculates ecclesiastical dates. Simply enter the year, and a calendar listing Catholic and Eastern Orthodox dates will pop up. Histories, algorithms and a list of feasts related to Easter are also available.

Campus Crusade for Christ

http://www.mdalink.com/CCC/index.html

This evangelical group claims to spread the gospel world-wide, and describes its ministry on this home page. Visitors can follow the organization's missions, download Christian writings and link to other Christian resources on the Internet.

Catholic Answers

http://www.catholic.com/cgi-shl/index.p/

This lay organization promotes the Catholic faith through publications, seminars, tapes, and television and radio appearances. site includes access to *This Rock* magazine and other organizational information.

Catholic Files

http://listserv.american.edu/catholic/

This site lists a variety of resources on Catholicism and items of interest to Catholics. Includes links to Church servers, documents, organizations and other religious resources on the Internet.

Catholic Goldmine

http://web.sau.edu/~cmiller/religion.html

The Catholic Goldmine features pointers to a host of Web pages and newsgroups related to the Catholic church. Stop by for the latest scoop on apparitions that are reported from around the globe, as well as details about prayers and devotions.

Catholic Information Center

http://www.catholic.net/

A free service of the Path to Peace Foundation, this site features the news and philosophy of the Roman Catholic Church. Also find links to periodicals, past issues of the CIC page and related services.

Catholic Resources on the Net

http://www.cs.cmu.edu/Web/People/spok/
catholic.html

Lay Catholic John Mark Ockerbloom has compiled an extensive look at the Catholic church at this home page. Visitors will find explanations of and pointers to Catholic teachings, mass, writings, saints and organizations. The site also includes links to official Catholic pages on the Web.

Catholic Youth Ministry

http://www.microserve.net/~fabian/ym.html

A director at St. Luke's Church in Stroudsburg, Penn., provides the Catholic Youth Ministry page, a networking resource. Catholic directories, discussion groups and youth programs are available here.

Celtic Christianity

http://www.shsu.edu/~lib_maa/celt_christ.html

With an extensive collection of Celtic Christianity Web resources, this page also links to just about everything else relating to Celtic culture on the Internet. Visitors here can find music, newsgroups, merchandise, books and more.

Center for the Advancement of Paleo Orthodoxy

http://capo.org/

The Center for the Advancement of Paleo Orthodoxy attempts to bring ancient biblical light to modern issues by exploring ethics, politics and current trends. On this page, link to the center's various research institutions and related publications.

Christian Answers Network

http://www.christiananswers.net/
canhome.html

The Christian Answers Network, provided by a cooperative ministry of Christian organizations, answers questions relating to contemporary problems. This page also offers a selection of links that lead to children's resources, video recommendations and sponsoring organizations.

ChristianAnswers.Net

http://www.christiananswers.net/

Eden Communications provides this extensive site for Christians seeking "biblical answers to important contemporary questions." With over 800 files, this in-depth resource includes kids' coloring competitions, theological pondering, news and more.

Christian Broadcasting Network, Inc.

http://the700club.org/

The Christian Broadcasting Network, Inc., maintains this page with information on the network, a viewer guide, 700 Club information and various press releases. Includes a list of stations carrying Christian programming and access to ministry information.

Christian Coalition

http://cc.org/

The Christian Coalition home page provides detailed information on its political agenda, philosophy and campaigns, including Congressional and Virginia General Assembly scorecards. Visitors can also link to other Christian-related sites on the Web.

Christian Connections

http://tcm.nbs.net/~cc/cchome.html

Christian Connections' purpose is to inspire Christians to use, "online technology for the care and support of God's people in their various ministries wherever that ministry takes place." Resources and contacts for organizations, a job bank and publications are available here.

The Christian Coptic Orthodox Church of Egypt

http://cs-www.bu.edu/faculty/best/pub/cn/Home.html

This is a collection of links to sites devoted to the study and history of the Coptic Orthodox Church of Egypt. Visitors here will find extensive articles, prayers, hymnals, letters and music relating to this faith.

Christian Cyberspace

http://www.net-connect.net/~tonyscot/chrsites.htm

Christian Cyberspace, an index to Christian Internet resources, features links to the home pages of Christian individuals and churches, online devotionals, Usenet newsgroups, online Bibles, publications and more. Visitors can also join a mailing list for regular updates.

Christian Cyberspace Companion

http://www.bakerbooks.com/ccc/

This page features a promotion for Jason A. Baker's book, *Christian Cyberspace Companion: A Guide to the Internet and Christian Online Resources.* Also featured is the Christian Internet Directory, an index and online search tool for finding Christian-related Web sites.

Christian Home Exchange Worldwide Net

http://www.gate.net/~sthans/sthans.htm

This group promotes Christian home exchanges as a means of broadening the quality of family, church, and community life. site offers an overview of the exchange system, and provides a directory of home exchange listings.

Christian Internet Directory

http://www.bakerbooks.com/ccc/appcmain.htm

Part of the Christian Cyberspace Companion, the Christian Internet Directory features links to a host of Internet resources, including campus ministries, denominations, politics and theology.

Christian Reformed Church in North America

http://www.crcna.org

Find out more about the Christian Reformed Church (CRC) in North America, as well as its beliefs, mission, and activities. site has CRC news, plus information on publications, personnel, and congregations.

Christian Research Institute

http://www.iclnet.org/pub/resources/text/cri/cri-home.html

The Christian Research Institute features online editions of its journals and newsletters here. Readers can browse writings from the California-based institute or click to guides to other Christian sites.

Christian Resources

http://www.calvin.edu/Christian/

Links to Christian resources from Christian literature to daily Bible verses are available at the Christian Resources page. Visitors will also find links to daily devotionals and the "Internet for Christians Newsletter."

Christus Rex et Redemptor Mundi

http://www.christusrex.org/

The Sistine Chapel, the Vatican, the Pope's letter to women, the Evangelium Vitae and more from the Roman Catholic Church can be found here, including a link to Radio Vatican. Visitors can also see some of the art collected by the church over the centuries.

Church of Jesus Christ Latter-day Saints Resource Page

http://www.primenet.com/~kitsonk/mormon.html

Here, visitors will find pointers to online resources for members of the Church of Jesus Christ Latter-day Saints. Resources available here include pages on the Church, electronic Mormon texts and links to a variety of related Web sites.

Claretian Missionaries Communications Worldwide

http://http1.brunel.ac.uk:8080/depts/chaplncy/cmfs.htm

Claretian Communications Worldwide unveils information about the Claretian Missionaries at this home page. Visitors can find out more about the Claretian Ideal, a description of what the missionaries do and a collection of Claretian prayers.

Creation Science

http://emporium.turnpike.net/C/cs/

A group of Christian engineers at AT&T Bell Laboratories "who believe strongly that people need to become better informed on this most important question of our origins," attack the theory of human evolution and offer their support for the idea of Creationism.

CrossSearch

http://www.crosssearch.com/

This listing provides a variety of links to Christian resources. These range from the very general ("What is Christianity all about?") to information about specific churches, ministries, and denominations. There's also a reference section for Internet resources.

Cyberspace Catacombs

http://www.mindspring.com/~tentmakr/pphp/landlord.html

These virtual catacombs host underground electronic meetings for Christians from around the world. Visitors who aspire to join this community of faith may contact current members here.

Demon Possession Handbook

http://www.opendoor.com/higher.ground/hs.html

Here, Disk Books presents the full text of the *Demon Possession Handbook* by J. F. Cogan. Written for "human service workers," the handbook covers deliverance from possession, the origin of Satan, rock music, and spiritual warfare. A link to Cogan's other book, *Bible Sex Facts,* is also available.

Discipleship Journal

http://www.gospelcom.net/navs/djhome.html

The *Discipleship Journal* unveils its monthly news for Christian disciples here with tips for a one-on-one approach to bringing more people into the church in their local neighborhoods and around the world.

Divine Mercy

http://www.cais.com/npacheco/mercy/faustina.html

In 1931, Sister Faustina Kowalska of Poland received the message of mercy from Christ. At this page learn about the revelation and how to pray for and perform the Devotion of Divine Mercy. Visitors will find history of and resources for the devotion.

Ecole Initiative

http://www.evansville.edu/~ecoleweb/

The Ecole Initiative seeks to create a hypertext encyclopedia of early Christian church history. Chronological listings, a bibliography, documents and a glossary all can be found here, along with information about the project.

Encyclicals and Other Papal Documents

http://listserv.american.edu/catholic/church/papal/papal.html

Encyclicals, letters and documents from recent popes are available here from the Catholic Files at American University.

Episcopal Church

http://www.ai.mit.edu/people/mib/anglican/

Here visitors can find out more about the Episcopal Church, including worship practices, beliefs, texts and religious orders. site also features documents from church officials, as well as resources such as libraries, pictures, mailing lists and church-oriented links.

Episcopal Daily Office Rite Two

http://alumni.caltech.edu/~shrum/

Updated weekly, the Episcopal Daily Office Rite Two provides the full text of appropriate daily Episcopal evening and morning prayers, taken from *Book of Common Prayers*.

Evangelical Free Church of America

http://www.halcyon.com/churches/efca/efca.html

Evangelical Free Church of America home page provides an overview of the association's commitment to ministerial and fellowship cooperation between 1,100 autonomous churches. Link to those individual organizations and to EFCA missionary pages.

Evangelical Lutheran Church in America

http://elca.org/

The official online site for the Evangelical Lutheran Church in America features details about how the group was formed and the latest news from fellow churches. It also includes a link to the library and the Lutheran Center in Chicago.

Fasting & Prayer '95

http://www.mdalink.com/fasting-prayer/

Fasting & Prayer '95 is a report on a gathering of Christian leaders in the United States for a day of concentrated spiritual devotion. This site also offers a seven-step program for those who wish to pursue fasting as a means of spiritual regeneration and a call for an even larger gathering in 1996.

Focus on the Family

http://www.cs.albany.edu/~ault/fof/fof.html

Focus on the Family is a non-profit, evangelical Christian organization that works to strengthen families. Turn here for information about the group and its radio programs, an online newsletter and a profile of the group's leader.

Gospel Communications Network

http://www.gospelcom.net/

Gospel Communications Network (GCN) is a gathering of Christian ministries. This site provides daily Bible verses, member organization links and information about activities and partner organizations.

Grace Notes

http://www.realtime.net/~wdoud/

A Christian publication ministry, Grace Notes offers Biblical passages and topical insights into "the basics of the Christian way of life." Visitors to this page can review the Grace Notes library of materials, link to the Grace Notes Prayer Net or follow pointers to topical sites.

Guide to Christian Literature on the Internet

http://www.iclnet.org/pub/resources/christian-books.html

The Institute for Christian Leadership hosts this guide to Christian literature on the Internet. Visitors will find links to several versions of the Bible, plus church-related news, books, newsletters, essays, articles and sermons.

Institute for Christian Leadership ICLnet Primer

http://www.iclnet.org/pub/resources/iclnet-primer.html

Institute for Christian Leadership, providing resources to Christian higher education institutions, maintains this informational site. Visit here for the ICLnet primer, featuring links to its reading room and software collection.

International Bible Society

http://www.gospelcom.net/ibs/

Dedicated to outreach in Evangelical Christianity, the International Bible Society page links visitors to Biblical literature, scripture and information, lets them listen to audio files of Christian music, offers prayers for visitors who e-mail requests, and provides links to other Christian sites.

International Churches of Christ

HTTP://www.INTLCC.com/

The International Churches of Christ presents its official home page with information about the church, its doctrines and mission. Church members, or disciples, can peruse Kingdom News Net, which presents highlights and features about its news-making disciples.

Internet for Christians

http://www.gospelcom.net/ifc/

The Internet for Christians page invites visitors to subscribe to a Christian newsletter and preview the upcoming publication of "Internet for Christians." Additional selections here include links to Christian e-mail groups and media enterprises.

Jesus Army

http://www.jesus.org.uk/

The Jesus Army is marching your way bearing this page intent upon briefing you about the Jesus Fellowship Church and its "charismatic emphasis." Spiritual c-rations here include e-mail prayer request, the "Streetpaper," interviews with Christian leaders and more.

Jesus Christ's Eternal Abundant Life, Inc.

http://jceal.org/top.html

Jesus Christ's Eternal Abundant Life, Inc., is a non-profit corporation established "for the sole

purpose of spreading the good news of the gospel of Jesus Christ to every creature." Learn more about the corporation and its quest for "universal linguistics" and request a sermon tape or literature here.

Jews for Jesus

http://www.jews-for-jesus.org/

Jews for Jesus, a movement within the Jewish community which is centered around the belief that that Jesus was the Messiah, hosts this home page. Includes an essay on reconciling Judaism with belief in Jesus, access to publications, testifying opportunities and event schedules.

LDS Info on the Internet

http://www.ldsworld.com/links/

This unofficial page about the Church of Jesus Christ of Latter-Day Saints contains basic LDS information, including Mormon beliefs and pointers to Church resources. Included are scriptures, books, articles, organizations, colleges, projects and more.

LDS Mission Alumni Pages

http://www.et.byu.edu/~harmanr/all_missions_links.html

If you served a mission with Church of Jesus Christ of Latter-day Saints, visit this site to connect with others who served in the same area. Each mission area has its own site that may include updates about events in each mission area as well as mailing lists and reunion news.

LDS Resource on the Internet

http://www.npl.com/ldsirc.html

The Latter Day Saints Resource on the Internet, a personal collection of Mormon religion-related information, offers extensive links to mailing lists, chat rooms, home pages, literature and more. Includes index of Internet-based genealogy resources.

LDS Resources

http://fas-www.harvard.edu/~brown5/lds.html

This annotated index provides pointers to sites related to or about the Mormon Church. It includes an audio file from a church elder, images and dozens of links.

Letter to Women

http://listserv.american.edu/catholic/church/papal/jp.ii/jp2wom95.html

Here, visitors can read the papal letter written to women on the eve of the Fourth World Conference on Women in Beijing, China. letter was issued by the Vatican in July, 1995.

Living Stones
http://www.stainedglass.com/~stainglass/ls/ls.htm

The monthly issues of *Living Stones,* a journal of testimonials and essays about Christianity, are available here. Readers can follow advice about such things as spiritual Web wandering or submit articles to be included in future issues.

Maranatha
http://www.infi.net/~stegner/

Sponsored by the Gospel Baptist Church of Richmond, Va., this page cites Biblical prophesies and relates them to current events. Personal testimonies and links to other Christian resources on the Web also are featured.

Matthew Fox
http://boris.qub.ac.uk/tony/Fox/

Here, visitors can learn more about modern religious writer Matthew Fox. Included here area bibliography of Fox's work, listings of articles about Fox and links to related religious works. There's also information about the Matthew Fox mailing list; visitors can search the list's archives here.

New Advent
http://www.sni.net/advent/

New Advent presents resources about and from the Roman Catholic Church. Included are an introduction to Catholicism, church documents, listings of saints and popes, and Catholic humor.

New Heaven, New Earth
http://nen.sedona.net//nhne/

New Heaven, New Earth is a grassroots network that believes the planet is spiraling toward Armageddon; it aims to "safely pass through whatever changes may come our way and help give birth to a new way of life on our planet." Visitors here can get an overview of the network, read prophesies and join the network's mailing list.

New Jersey Online Faith Page
http://www.nj.com/popepage/

It's not every day that the pope drops by, so if you missed the last tour, Pope John Paul II's October 1995 visit to the United States is commemorated at this site from New Jersey Online. Included are photos, the text of his United Nations address, and an index of the pontiff's world travels.

Newman Centers and Catholic Student Associations
http://www.cco.caltech.edu/~newman/OtherNC.html

Here, links to Newman Centers and Catholic Student Associations are listed by geographical region in both the U.S. and worldwide.

Northlake Unitarian Universalist Church
http://www.wolfenet.com/~uujim/

Northlake Unitarian Universalist Church, of Kirland, Wash., provides general information on Unitarian Universalism and a "tour" of Seattle here. Other site features include "How Do I Make a Home Page?" and a "UU Hotlist."

Order of St. Benedict
http://www.osb.org/osb/

Maintained by a monk at Saint John's Abbey in Collegeville, Minn., the Order of Saint Benedict page contains history and beliefs of the order, as well as listings of its abbeys, priories, monasteries, convents and academic institutions.

Orthodox Christian Page
http://www.ocf.org/OrthodoxPage/

The Orthodox Christian Page in America provides information on this traditional branch of the faith. Here, visitors can learn more about Orthodox practice and beliefs, read scriptures and prayers, and get updates on related news.

Our Lady of Fatima
http://www.cais.com/npacheco/fatima/fatima.html

Check the accuracy of the prophecies of Our Lady of Fatima at her home page. Frequently Asked Questions (FAQ) will tells you about the small town in Portugal and the child visionaries who saw the Virgin Mary. Links to Shroud of Turin and other Catholic resources are provided.

Papal Visit to the U.S–Catholic University of America
http://www.cua.edu/www/pbaf/pope.htm

The Catholic University of America hosts this page highlighting Pope John Paul II's 1995 visit to the United States. Includes images and excerpts from papal speeches.

Presbyterian Church (U.S.A.)
http://www.pcusa.org/

The Presbyterian Church in America maintains this site containing religious news and resources. Visit here for an overview of the church, related software archives, online services, and "good, clean religious humor."

Project 21st. Century
http://www.webhelp.com/future.htm

Forward-looking Web travelers may want to visit this site to sample visions of the future—both gloomy and cheery—or offer their own ideas about what will take place in the 21st century. Links here include related newsgroups, Biblical sources of prophecy, Presidential press releases and more.

Promise Keepers Information Network
http://www.primenet.com/~jsavin/pkhome.htm

An unofficial site providing information on the Promise Keepers, a ministry of men dedicated to honoring Jesus Christ, this page contains information on the group and its events, plus a link to its official magazine, *New Man.* Includes a chat room and newsgroup.

Radio Vaticana Kurznachrichten
http://www.uni-passau.de/ktf/vatican.archiv.html

An archive of transcripts from Radio Vatican broadcasts dating to May 1995 is provided at this site. All information is in German.

Rapture Index
http://www.novia.net/~todd/

The Christian prophecy of the Rapture, found in the Bible's last book of Revelation, states that sometime in the future, after a series of signs, believers will be taken bodily into heaven. At the Rapture Index, learn more about this prophecy and read news items and world indicators purported to be signs of its imminence.

Reasons To Believe
http://www.gospelcom.net/rbc/10rsn.home/

For those whose faith needs fortifying, this site offers reasons to believe in the Christian cosmology. It lays out, via Biblical verses, why we should believe in the existence of God, the divine foundations of Christianity and that a humble Jewish carpenter rose from the dead to save us from eternal damnation.

Religious Society of Friends
http://www.quaker.org/

The Religious Society of Friends, otherwise known as Quakers, offers this list of dozens of links to information about the religion, recommended books, discussion groups, and Quaker personal pages.

The Roman Catholic Archdiocese of St. John's
http://delweb.com/rcec/

This archdiocese in Newfoundland, Canada, features a parish directory, as well as links to its adult ministry leadership program and Basilica of St. John the Baptist. Religious visitors might also enjoy Newfoundland's Catholic journal *Monitor.*

Saint Francis Episcopal Church
http://eliza.netaxis.com/ahynes/stf/stf.html

The Saint Francis Episcopal Church in Stamford, Conn., hosts this Web page containing information about church activities, services and publications. Read the church's weekly bulletin for regular updates and a schedule of services.

Scripture Union Online

http://www.scripture.org.uk/

Find Jesus online. Scripture Union, headquartered in Bletchley, Great Britain, is a group of volunteer evangelists who are working to share the Bible with people around the world. Find out about their work and how to join them at their home site.

SEBC: Resources for Christian Growth

http://sebc.com/~resource/000sebc.html

The Southeast Bible Community (SEBC) is a Christian study group based in southeast Portland, Ore. This home page includes the community's basic philosophies, ministry notes, and charts and maps.

Selected Works of Martin Luther 1483–1546

http://www.iclnet.org/pub/resources/text/wittenberg/wittenberg-luther.html

The Selected Works of Martin Luther, 1483—1546, presents his "Definitions of Faith," "Devotional Thoughts," and other writings, as well as hymns and a great deal of related Lutheran content.

Theology on the Web

http://www.dma.org/~thawes

Theology on the Web features an index of links to such sites as the newsletter "Classical Christianity," philosophical documents, and various creeds of orthodoxy and confessions of faith.

Triumphing Over London Cults

http://www.ftech.net/~hamrag/

Triumphing Over London Cults (TOLC) is dedicated to those who have "experienced the loss of their personal freedom...." Here, TOLC features news about the London Church of Christ, including interviews with church leaders and former members and a link to the Usenet newsgroup alt.religion.christian.boston-church.

United Church of Christ

http://www.apk.net/ucc/

Guests who find their way to the United Church of Christ Home Page can link to information and news from this Christian denomination. Visitors can find out about the church mission and ministries, newsletters, and more.

United Methodist Church

http://www.netins.net/showcase/umsource/

The United Methodist Church provides information on church issues, news, and online conferences here. Also, find links to other churches on the Internet and a Methodist e-mail directory. Links to colleges, seminaries, and specific ministry types also provided.

Unity Church of Victoria

http://www.vic.uimc.ca/

The Unity Church of Victoria, British Columbia, is based on the principles of "the teachings of Jesus Christ, stating that humanity is inseparable from the Spirit of God." In addition to book and video titles, there's an overview of the church's fundamental tenets and information about special events.

Unravelling Wittgenstein's Net: A Christian ThinkTank

http://www.webcom.com/~ctt/

The Christian ThinkTank Web page features a tongue-in-cheek examination of religious matters with pointers to suggested readings such as a detailed syllabi of the author's Sunday adult education courses, as well as links to related pages.

The Westminster Confession of Faith

gopher://cs1.presby.edu/00/religion/west.conf.faith

Presbyterian College posts the full text of the Westminster Confession of Faith, a religious doctrine of the church, here.

World Wide Christian Web

http://www.superb.com/www/pages/wwcw/index.html

The World Wide Christian Web beckons believers and non-believers with Biblical questions-and-answers, links to Christian-related sites, prayer requests, book reviews and news from a religious perspective.

Yahweh's New Covenant Assembly

http://www.pair.com/gallery/

Yahweh's New Covenant Assembly, located in Kingdom City, Mo., maintains this worship page with information about its Sunday services, links to its literature, and information about audio and video tapes. Pictures from the church's India and Philippines assemblies are also available.

HARE KRISHNA

Dvaita

http://www.rit.edu/~mrreee/dvaita.html

Dvaita, the doctrine propounded by Ananda Tiirtha, asserts that the difference between the individual soul and the Creator is eternal and real. Learn about the five "differences" here, as well as the doctrine's scholars and Ananda Tiirtha himself. Translated hymns can also be downloaded.

Hare Krishna Home Page

http://www.webcom.com/~ara/

The Hare Krishna page explains the eastern religion and offers visitors access to graphics, books and magazines for more detailed information. The site also includes locations of Hare Krishna centers and information on ordering a free catalog.

Official Hare Krishna Home Page

http://www.algonet.se/~krishna/

The official Hare Krishna page features "a treasure of knowledge and insight" about the movement. Information about Hare Krishna origins, structure, philosophy, temples and programs is available here. Recent news and links to related organizations and its worldwide address list are also provided.

HINDUISM

Avatar Meher Baba Ki Jai

http://www.oslonett.no/home/erics/index.html

Avatar Meher Baba Ki Jai is a Hindu spiritual leader with a large following in Norway. Visitors to his home page will find related news articles and descriptions of his teachings.

Chinmaya Mission

http://www.tezcat.com/~bnaik/chinmiss.html

Visitors will find a religious roadmap leading to vedantic truths at the Chinmaya Mission home page. Centers across the world are listed here, along with links to study groups, religious texts and a biography of founder Swami Chinmayananda.

Global Hindu Electronic Networks: The Hindu Universe

http://rbhatnagar.csm.uc.edu:8080/hindu_universe.html

The Global Hindu Electronic Network is a collection of links to a variety of Hindu-related newsgroups and Web sites. Visitors can jump to scriptural archives, temple photos and Hindu festival and organization listings.

Guidance Through Gita

http://www.tezcat.com/~bnaik/gita/guide.html

Visitors to the Guidance through Bhagavad Gita page can follow the links while they consider their place in the world. It features information about a series of fundamental topics as told by Swami Chinmayananda.

JUDAISM

Boston University Hillel

http://web.bu.edu/HILLEL/

Boston University Hillel allows it is known throughout the Boston community as the heart of Jewish student life—its house includes chapels, a library and meeting rooms. The group details Jewish living on campus on this page and includes information on Kosher dining, student groups, counseling and a calendar of events.

Center for Jewish Life
http://www.princeton.edu/~hillel/

Located at Princeton University, the Center for Jewish Life maintains this online resource. Find a holiday calendar, information about Jewish campus organizations worldwide, and links to Internet sites relevant to Israel and Judaism.

Chabad Jewish Student Organization
http://www.utexas.edu/students/cjso/

More than just basic information about this Jewish student group, the Chabad Jewish Student Organization Home Page also links users to information on the religion itself, such as holiday dates, a mikve for married couples and more.

Cornell Jewish Infoline
http://www.ithaca.ny.us/Orgs/YoungIsrael/cji/

Visit the Cornell Jewish Infoline for the who, what, when and where of Jewish-related activities around campus. The site is updated each week and includes an extensive index to Jewish campus groups around the world.

A Guide to Chabad Literature
http://www.utexas.edu/students/cjso/Chabad/chabad.html

A Guide to Chabad Literature includes archives, essays, classic Jewish songs, an art and picture gallery, and special effects gallery with 3-D graphics and animations. There's also the hypertext book "A New Day Breaks" and electronic journals.

Harvard-Radcliffe Hillel Home Page
http://hcs.harvard.edu/~hrhillel/

Jewish Harvard and Radcliffe students can consult this site for a listing activities at Hillel, the center for Jewish life on campus. The site also links to dozens of other Jewish-related student groups and Internet-wide resources.

Hillel at the University of Pennsylvania
http://dolphin.upenn.edu/~hillel/

Here, students and members of the University of Pennsylvania community will find information on Jewish-related activities there. A link to the upenn.hillel newsgroup and the national Hillel gopher is included.

Israel Action Committee
http://www.ocf.berkeley.edu/~iac/

This student group is dedicated to "promoting Israel awareness" on the campus of the University of California, Berkeley. To this end, the group sponsors films, discussions, classes and other pro-Israel activities. Read all about their efforts here and browse the collection of Israeli and Middle Eastern links.

Jewish Communication Network
http://www.jcn18.com/

The Jewish Communication Network takes its effort to create an on-line center for Jewish families, teachers and professionals to the Web with this site. It offers a collection of the top 12 humor lists as well as information about Israel and a Jewish newsstand.

Jewish Feminist Resources
http://world.std.com/~alevin/jewishfeminist.html

Jewish Feminist Resources contains a rich collection of links related to the arts, Jewish texts and liturgy, lesbian issues, Israel-related organizations, and periodicals of Judaism and feminism.

Jewish Student Union
http://www.brown.edu/Students/Jewish_Student_Union/

The Jewish Student Union is a student coordinating body whose activities include sharing resources for programs and debates to form a response from the Jewish community. Includes a calendar of events, minutes from meetings and links to other Jewish resources on the Internet.

Jewish Student Union at Columbia
http://www.columbia.edu/cu/jsu/

This Web site indexes Jewish academic and living resources at Columbia University in New York. Includes links to the Jewish Electronic Calendar, the Jewish Student Union, the Center for Israel and Jewish Studies and more.

Jewishnet
http://jewishnet.net/

This global Jewish information network offers links to Israeli and Jewish mailing lists, home pages of Jewish interest and electronic Jewish libraries. Links to gopher and FTP sites are also included.

The Judaica Web World
http://www.nauticom.net/users/rafie/judaica-world.html

The Jewish Web World is a diverse collection of links to Judaica around the globe. Visitors will find pointers to Jewish calendars, software, museums and galleries, activities for children and a host of other resources too numerous to mention.

Keddem Congregation
http://www.next.com/~amarcum/Keddem.html

News, announcements, events and services of the Keddem Congregation, a Palo Alto, Calif., Jewish congregation, are provided here. Find a pointer to the San Francisco Bay Area Volunteer Information Center and links to other Keddem resources.

A Network for Jewish Youth
http://www.ort.org/anjy/anjy.htm

ANJY (A Network for Jewish Youth) offers an A to Z Jewish resource list for young people, a penpal service, a diary of events, and access to "Jewish Youth Work" magazine.

Project Genesis
http://www.ucalgary.ca/~elsegal/Shokel/Art_Index.html

Project Genesis is an Internet center for Jewish philosophy, Kabbalah, ethics and law. Includes links to online classes in Torah and other Jewish educational materials.

Shamash: The Jewish Internet Consortium
http://shamash.nysernet.org/

The Shamash Judaica server provides pointers to Jewish-related information and resources, including a bookstore, Torah readings, links to organizations, access to a cultural network, and Jewish studies.

Union of Jewish Studies
http://www.dircon.co.uk/ujs/

The World Wide Web's Union of Jewish Students provides a multitude of services, including an opportunity to subscribe to their newsletter, national conference information, resources, links to Jewish societies, and more.

Virtual Jerusalem
http://www.jerl.co.il/

An Israel-based information service, Jerusalem One's home page catalogs a variety of resources for the worldwide Jewish community. Included are a calendar of events and holidays, software, clipart, and business and government information.

Yale Hillel
http://www.cis.yale.edu/hillel/

The Hillel organization at Yale University supplies information here on its activities and services for Jewish students and organizations on campus. Links to other Hillel organizations and Jewish resources are provided, as is subscription information for the Yale Hillel mailing list.

MUSLIM/ISLAM

Ahmadiyya Muslim Student's Organization
http://www.utexas.edu/ftp/student/amso/

The Ahmadiyya Muslim Student's Organization is based at the University of Texas, Austin. The Islam home page provides information on the creed of Islam as well as articles. Visitors can also link to other sites about the religion on the Web.

CyberMuslim Information Collective
http://www.uoknor.edu/cybermuslim/

Dunya is a comprehensive resource page for Muslims provided by the CyberMuslim Information Collective. Visitors will find Islamic books, magazines, newspapers, cultural resources, an interactive Qur'aan and much more here.

Dunya: CyberMuslim Information Collective

http://www.uoknor.edu:80/cybermuslim/

Assalamu-alaikum and welcome to Dunya, where CyberMuslim Selim guides visitors to Muslim activist information, online Islamic newspapers and a primer on Islamic beliefs. Feel like chatting? Hook up with Muslim newsgroups to discuss Muslim religious practices or culture.

The HyperQur'aan Project

http://www.uoknor.edu/cybermuslim/cy_quraan.html

A "CyberMuslim experiment," this page offers a hypermedia presentation of Islamic text in six translations. Audio recitations accompany the project.

Islamic Association for Palestine Home Page Palestine

http://www.iap.org

The Islamic Association for Palestine (IAP) presents an Islamic perspective on Palestine here in an effort to support the people living under occupation. Besides an overview of IPA and its mission, the links here point to various organizations and news carriers that focus on Islamic issues.

Islamic Resources

http://sparc.latif.com/welcome.html

Islamic Resources provides information about Islamic beliefs, resources, events, businesses and organizations at this site. Visitors also are invited to post and read answers to the question, "what does Islam mean to you?"

Islamic Texts and Resources Texts and Resources

http://wings.buffalo.edu/student-life/sa/muslim/isl/isl.html

The Muslim Students Association at New York's University of Buffalo offers a variety of informational resources at this site. Visitors will find answers to questions about Islam, plus links to related texts, Muslim news and issue forums.

KampungNet

http://irdu.nus.sg/kampungnet/

KampungNet is an online community for Muslims living in Singapore. Visitors will find community news, arts and entertainment, publications and a list of Muslim buildings in the area. Available in English and Malay.

Muslim Resources Gopher

gopher://latif.com/

Information of interest to the Muslim community is available here at this gopher, including the "Middle East Studies Association Bulletin," events listings and an English-language version of the *Quran*.

Muslim Students Association at Caltech

http://www.cco.caltech.edu/~calmsa/calmsa.html

The Muslim Students Association at the California Institute of Technology offers visitors information about Islam and access to the Quran database. Links to related resources are also available, including a list of local Halal restaurants.

The Nation of Gods and Earths

http://sunsite.unc.edu/nge/

This Islamic home page provides lessons on Islam, links to music files, information about black gods of the inner city, and audio and photo files.

Nation of Islam

http://www.afrinet.net/~islam/

The Nation of Islam page provides a link to an Islam index and a look at current and upcoming events.

New York State University Muslim Student Association

gopher://wings.buffalo.edu/hh/student-life/sa/muslim/

The Muslim Student Association of New York State University, Buffalo, maintains this page with information and resources of interest to Muslims and "those in touch with Islam and Muslims." Information about local mosques and communities, Islam and the association's location are featured.

The Online Islamic Bookstore

http://www.sharaaz.com/

The Online Islamic Bookstore Web site serves as a one-stop market for the Muslim community's book needs. Visitors can browse the book, video or audio tape catalogs and place online orders.

Sufi Center Bookstore

http://home.worldweb.net/sufi/

This virtual bookshop sells books, videos, audio tapes and music of interest to members of this Muslim mystic sect. There's also information about Sufi centers around the world, plus links to Sufi-related Internet sites.

University of Essex Islamic Society

http://cswww2.essex.ac.uk/users/rafiam/

The Islamic Society from the University of Essex offers primers on the background of the religion at this site. Also included are articles such as Abdur-Raheem Green's work about the "authenticity and proof of the Quran as a revelation from Allaah."

University of Southern California Muslim Students Association Islamic Server

http://www.usc.edu/dept/MSA/

The University of Southern California presents the home page for its Muslim Students Organization. Visitors will find an introduction to the fundamentals of Islam and its place in modern society. Islamic stories and schedules of campus events are included.

OCCULTISM

Hell: The Online Guide to Satanism

http://webpages.marshall.edu/~allen12/index.html

This page is devoted to providing information about Satanic organizations and belief systems. Links to organizations, the Church of Satan, the Temple of Set and related groups are provided, along with pointers to devilish news and publications.

PAGANISM AND MYSTICISM

CoGweb

http://www.cog.org/cog/

The Covenant of the Goddess Web site explains the activities of the international organization of cooperating, autonomous Wiccan congregations and practitioners. This site offers information on witchcraft and answers to commonly asked questions. It also posts events and offers links to various covens.

Covenant of the Goddess, Northern California Local

http://www.crc.ricoh.com/~rowanf/COG/cog.html

The home page for the Northern California affiliate of the Covenant of the Goddess contains general information on the council, which practices a religion known as Wicca. The page also includes information on other Wiccan and pagan resources.

SCIENTOLOGY

Church of Scientology International vs. Fishman and Geertz

http://www.cs.cmu.edu/~dst/Fishman/

A Web site devoted to criticism of the Church of Scientology, this page contains a vast number of documents, including articles and correspondence, as well as links to related newsgroups.

Church of Scientology vs. the Internet

http://www.cybercom.net/~rnewman/
scientology/home.html

This personal home page rounds up the Church of Scientology's alleged attempts to quash free speech on the Internet. Includes summaries of the most current news stories on this topic, plus a comprehensive listing of newspaper and magazine articles available online.

Road to Xenu

http://www.demon.co.uk/castle/xenu/
xenu.html

Readers can download the entire text of the book *Road to Xenu* from this page. The work, by Margery Wakefield, details the influences of cults and Scientology. Each chapter is posted as a text file.

Scamizdat Memorial—Yet Another Scientology Home Page

http://www.well.com/user/jerod23/clam.html

The Scamizdat Memorial tells you right up front that when compared to other Scientology home pages, this one is "not as good." In a bizarre and humorous introduction, learn that this site depicts the "Church" in an unfavorable light, pulling from material that is lurid and sensational.

Scientology Acronym/Terminology FAQ

http://www.amazing.com/scientology/dict.html

Taken from the Usenet newsgroup alt.religion.scientology, this dictionary is as advertised by its title. Presented on a single page, the document's entries are cross-indexed with one another via hyperlink.

Scientology Critics' Info Page

http://www.xs4all.nl/~kspaink/mpoulter/
scum.html

This page pulls no punches as it takes on Scientology with news, article reprints and numerous links.

Scientology Gopher

ftp://rtfm.mit.edu/pub/usenet-by-group/
news.answers/scientology/new-reader-faq

Postings from the alt.religion.scientology newsgroup have been archived here. This site includes a Frequently Asked Questions (FAQ) file and an overview of the Scientology catechism.

Scientology's Private Investigators

http://www.primenet.com/~lippard/pis.html

Church of Scientology critics have posted a cyber wanted poster here for the Church's lead private investigator, Eugene Martin Ingram, who is wanted for arrest in Florida. This page also describes some of the church's investigations of church skeptics and includes photos.

Sloth's Suppressive Person's Page

http://www.sky.net/~sloth/sci/sci_index.html

An anti-Church of Scientology page provides newcomers with a narrative of the author's response to Scientologists' statements and actions. The page links to newsgroups, other Web documents and the Webmaster's own topic-based document.

Temporary Restraining Order

http://www.eff.org/pub/Censorship/CoS_v_
the_Net/erlich_tro_021095.order

Visitors to this site will find a copy of the temporary restraining order filed in the United States District Court in the Web-shaking case of the Religious Technology Center and Bridge Publications, Inc. vs. Dennis Erlich, et al. The plaintiff is the Church of Scientology; the defendant is one of its most persistent, Internet-based critics.

XS4ALL Internet Scientology Press Release

http://www.xs4all.nl/~felipe/cos/pers.eng.html

This Web site offers a press release regarding a copyright-infringement lawsuit filed by the Church of Scientology against an Amsterdam-based Internet service provider, XS4ALL. Includes information on a police visit to the XS4ALL offices and links to censorship and Scientology-related Web sites. In Dutch and English.

SIKHISM

The Sikhism Home Page

http://www.sikhs.org/

At the Sikhism home page, visitors can learn more about the religion's philosophies and browse translations of religious texts. Various gurus are featured and Sikh codes of conduct are explained. Other religions are also examined.

TAOISM

Thigpen's Taoism Page

http://www.ccs.neu.edu/home/thigpen/html/
tao.html

A brief description of Taoism, the Chinese philosophy and religious system based on the sixth-century B.C. writings of Lao-tse, is accompanied by translations of Taoist poems and writings from Sun Tzu's *Art of War*.

UNIFICATION CHURCH

Unification Home Page

http://www.cais.net/unification/

A member of the Unification Church of the Rev. Sun Myung Moon maintains this page featuring links to Unification resources on the Internet. The church's international works and artistic activities are featured, as are the religion's articles of faith.

ZOROASTRIANISM

Stanford University Zoroastrian Group

http://www-leland.stanford.edu/group/
zoroastrians/

The home page of Stanford University's Zoroastrian Group hopes to provide common ground for those interested in the religion. Visitors here will find listings of upcoming events, support groups, historical information and prayer samples.

RELIGIOUS PHILOSOPHY

Bruderhof Communities

http://www.bruderhof.org/

This Christian religious community puts its philosophy on the web. Established in 1920 in Sannerz, Germany, exiled to England in 1937 and later to Paraguay, the group now is based in the northeastern U.S. and England.

Firewatch

http://140.190.128.190/merton/merton.html

The Firewatch home page is devoted to the works of Thomas Merton and religious contemplation. The group is affiliated with the Merton Research Consortium, an association of groups, centers, institutes and organizations interested in the contemplative life.

General Theory of Religion Page

http://world.std.com/~awolpert

This personal philosophy page, maintained by an independent religion scholar, offers "an introduction to a general theory of religion." Visit here to learn about one person's study of religion, based on "the cybernetic technique of Forrester-style system dynamics."

Provenzano & Sons Philosophy and Theology

http://www.smartlink.net/~joepro/

Provenzano & Sons offer their take on philosophy and theology here. Links to philosophical definitions, an essay list, a book synopsis, and information about Pierre Teilhard de Chardin, an evolutionary paleontologist, Catholic priest and thinker, are offered here.

SHOPS, SALES, AND SERVICES

GOSHEN: Global Online Service Helping Evangelize Nations
http://www.goshen.net/

Goshen designs and provides access to Christian Web sites. Visitors here will find an extensive directory to Christian sites and information on Goshen's Web site design services.

Iron Rod, Inc.
http://www.xmission.com/~ironrod

Iron Rod presents a menu of religious products: books, scriptures software, music, videos, pictures, statuary, toys, and more. An order form is included.

Logos Research Systems, Inc.
http://www.logos.com

Jump on over to the home page for Logos Research Systems, Inc., a worldwide leader in Christian software and multilingual electronic publishing. Get the facts on Logos and its software, with additional links to product news and user tips.

The Online Islamic Bookstore
http://www.sharaaz.com

The Online Islamic Bookstore Web site serves as a one-stop market for the Muslim community's book needs. Visitors can browse the book, video, or audio tape catalogs and place online orders.

STUDENT AND YOUTH RESOURCES

Boston University Hillel
http://web.bu.edu/HILLEL/

Boston University Hillel allows it is known throughout the Boston community as the heart of Jewish student life—its house includes chapels, a library and meeting rooms. The group details Jewish living on campus on this page and includes information on Kosher dining, student groups, counseling and a calendar of events.

Chabad Jewish Student Organization
http://www.utexas.edu/students/cjso/

More than just basic information about this Jewish student group, the Chabad Jewish Student Organization Home Page also links users to information on the religion itself, such as holiday dates, a mikve for married couples and more.

Cornell Jewish Infoline
http://www.ithaca.ny.us/Orgs/YoungIsrael/cji/

Visit the Cornell Jewish Infoline for the who, what, when and where of Jewish-related activities around campus. The site is updated each week and includes an extensive index to Jewish campus groups around the world.

First Orthodox Youth
http://www.orthodoxyouth.com/

The Orthodox Youth Page from the Antiochian Orthodox Christian Archdiocese contains information about its summer camps and ministry platform. Read about the church program's youth directors and upcoming training events.

Harvard-Radcliffe Hillel Home Page
http://hcs.harvard.edu/~hrhillel/

Jewish Harvard and Radcliffe students can consult this site for a listing activities at Hillel, the center for Jewish life on campus. The site also links to dozens of other Jewish-related student groups and Internet-wide resources.

Hillel at the University of Pennsylvania
http://dolphin.upenn.edu/~hillel/

Here, students and members of the University of Pennsylvania community will find information on Jewish-related activities there. A link to the upenn.hillel newsgroup and the national Hillel gopher is included.

InterVarsity Christian Fellowship
http://www.gospelcom.net/iv/

College students interested in Jesus Christ and the Bible can visit the Web home of the InterVarsity Christian Fellowship, "...a trans-denominational campus ministry." Lists of campus chapters, graduate members and other Christian Internet resources are available here.

Jewish Student Union
http://www.brown.edu/Students/Jewish_Student_Union/

The Jewish Student Union is a student coordinating body whose activities include sharing resources for programs and debates to form a response from the Jewish community. Includes a calendar of events, minutes from meetings and links to other Jewish resources on the Internet.

Jewish Student Union at Columbia
http://www.columbia.edu/cu/jsu/

This Web site indexes Jewish academic and living resources at Columbia University in New York. Includes links to the Jewish Electronic Calendar, the Jewish Student Union, the Center for Israel and Jewish Studies and more.

Network for Jewish Youth
http://www.ort.org/anjy/anjy.htm

ANJY (A Network for Jewish Youth) offers an A to Z Jewish resource list for young people, a penpal service, a diary of events and access to "Jewish Youth Work" magazine.

New York State University Muslim Student Association
gopher://wings.buffalo.edu/hh/student-life/sa/muslim/

The Muslim Student Association of New York State University, Buffalo, maintains this page with information and resources of interest to Muslims and "those in touch with Islam and Muslims." Information about local mosques and communities, Islam and the association's location are featured.

Union of Jewish Students
http://www.dircon.co.uk/ujs/

The World Wide Web's Union of Jewish Students provides a multitude of services, including an opportunity to subscribe to their newsletter, national conference information, resources, links to Jewish societies and more.

Yale Hillel
http://www.cis.yale.edu/hillel/

The Hillel organization at Yale University supplies information here on its activities and services for Jewish students and organizations on campus. Links to other Hillel organizations and Jewish resources are provided, as is subscription information for the Yale Hillel mailing list.

TELEVISION AND RADIO BROADCASTS

CCM Online
http://www.ccmcom.com/

CCM Online provides news, reviews, features and columns on Christian music. Included here is information on CCM radio and television programming, and concert listings.

Radio Vaticana Kurznachrichten
http://www.uni-passau.de/ktf/vatican.html

Radio Vaticana Kurznachrichten is a German-language digest of news from the official Vatican radio broadcasts.

This Week in Bible Prophecy
http://www.twibp.com/

"This Week in Bible Prophecy," a television show that discusses Christian prophecy, maintains this page with an air schedule, selected articles from its magazine and newspaper, and transcripts of recent shows. A product catalog and a link to the newsgroup alt.bible.prophecy are also provided.

Trans World Radio Canada

http://www.twr.org/

Trans World Radio is a Christian evangelical organization that utilizes short-wave and AM radio to spread its message of faith. The Canadian group's home page lists the program schedule, broadcast frequencies, core beliefs and highlights from its 41-year history.

Trinity Broadcasting Network

http://www.tbn.org/

The gateway of the Trinity Broadcasting Network (TBN), an independent Christian television network, invites visitors on a tour of TBN's products and services. A newsletter, broadcasting schedules and station information are available at the main page.

World Changers

http://www.mdalink.com/worldchangers/index.html

The radio program "World Changers" is designed to help people grow in their faith. This home page links with materials from Campus Crusade for Christ as well as with audio samples of the program. Find programming schedules from stations throughout the country.

The World, the Word and You

http://www.wwy.org

Downloadable transcripts from the Christian radio show "The World, the Word and You!" are featured here. This site also has information on the show's philosophy and the Independent Fundamental Churches of America.

TEXTS AND TRACTS

ARTFL Project: Bibles

http://humanities.uchicago.edu/homes/BIBLES.html

As part of an experiment on multi-lingual processing, ARTFL has built this Web site with four versions of the bible in French, German, Latin and English, searchable by chapter.

Augustine

http://ccat.sas.upenn.edu/jod/augustine.html

This page devoted to St. Augustine—arguably the father of early Christian thought—includes full text of the *Confessions* (in Latin and English),

On Christian Doctrine and a selection of lesser works, critical commentaries, research materials and essays.

Bible Text Gopher Menu

gopher://ftp.std.com/11/obi/book/Religion/Vulgate

Visitors to this gopher menu can access text files of the individual books of the Bible.

The Book of Mormon

http://www.sci.dixie.edu/mormon/contents.html

Visitors to this page will find an e-text edition of *The Book of Mormon.*

Christian Classics Ethereal Library

http://ccel.wheaton.edu/

Christian Classics Ethereal Library presents an online collection that visitors can browse by author and type or search. Selections include non-fiction from St. Thomas Aquinas, fiction from Fydor Dostoevsky and references such as the World Wide Study Bible and various Bible dictionaries.

Guide to Early Church Documents

http://www.iclnet.org/pub/resources/christian-history.html

This guide, provided by the Institute of Christian Leadership, covers early canons and creeds, the writings of the Apostolic Fathers, and other historical works. Visit here for full text of many historically significant biblical passages.

The Hill Monastic Manuscript Library

http://www.csbsju.edu/hmml/

"Fire, flood, theft, war. It only takes a minute to destroy history's greatest ideas." Working since 1965, the Hill Monastic Manuscript Library is one of the world's most comprehensive archives of medieval and Renaissance sources. Learn more about the library's microfilm collection, manuscript catalogs and study centers here.

Interpreting Ancient Manuscripts

http://www.stg.brown.edu/projects/mss/overview.html

Interpreting Ancient Manuscripts, a navigable hypertext study of ancient manuscripts which are the bases for the New Testament, is presented by Brown University. Critical discussions of the texts, glossaries and tables aid in the reader's study.

King James Bible Gopher

gopher://ccat.sas.upenn.edu:3333/11/Religious/Biblical/KJVBible

The University of Pennsylvania posts the King James version of the Bible on this gopher menu. Includes a search tool.

La Bibbia

http://www.crs4.it/~riccardo/Letteratura/Bibbia/Bibbia.html

The Italian Episcopalian Conference sponsors this online version of the Bible. Available in Italian only.

Luther Bibel

http://nobi.ethz.ch/bibel/buecher.html

Luther Bibel is an online version of the Bible in German. Visitors will find both New and Old Testaments here.

Project Wittenberg

http://www.iclnet.org/pub/resources/text/wittenberg/wittenberg-home.html

This project represents the combined efforts of "an ad hoc group of individuals dedicated to posting on the internet ... a cross-section of classic and historic texts written by Lutherans." Historic treatises, hymnals and catechisms are among the works offered.

Quran in Arabic

http://www.wam.umd.edu/~lilsistr/Quran/quran.html

Visitors here can read the Quran, broken down by sura number, in Arabic. It's an offshoot of the Islam Page.

Scrolls from the Dead Sea: The Ancient Library of Qumran and Modern Scholarship

http://sunsite.unc.edu/expo/deadsea.scrolls.exhibit/intro.html

Examine the Dead Sea Scrolls at an exhibit curated by the U.S. Library of Congress. Delve into the scholarly controversy surrounding the ancient religious texts or view scroll fragments and other objects comprising the exhibit.

Summa Theologica

http://www.knight.org/advent/summa/summa.htm

Translated by the Fathers of the English Dominican Province, New Advent offers a hypertext version of St. Thomas Aquinas' *Summa Theologica* at this site. Visit the home page for a plethora of related literature and religious information.

That They May Be One

http://listserv.american.edu/catholic/church/papal/jp.ii/jp2utunu.html

This page contains Pope John Paul II's encyclical entitled, "That They May Be One." The entire text of the May 1995 papal letter is available in hypertext.

Torah Fax in Cyberspace

http://www.netaxis.qc.ca/torahfax/

"Torah on the spot for people on the go!," is the motto of this service based in Montreal, Canada. TorahFax began as a way for busy people to learn the Torah via a regular fax delivery—it now offers its services by e-mail, fax or this daily Web posting.

Virtual Christianity

http://www.mit.edu:8001/people/aaronc/bibles.html

Virtual Christianity features links to online Bibles, literature and Bible study resources. The Web author provides short synopses of each link and has indicated his favorites with bold type.

World Scripture

http://rain.org/~origin/ws.html

The International Religious Foundation in New York, N.Y., maintains this site to provide a comparative anthology of sacred texts. Visit World Scripture to view its collection of more than 4,000 scriptural passages organized by theme. Background information about the foundation and its founders is available.

World Wide Study Bible

http://ccel.wheaton.edu/wwsb/

Begin with Genesis, skip to the harrowing Revelations at the end or peruse any book of the Bible via this e-text edition. Find the Old and New Testaments, plus the Apocrypha, presented with search options and resources by the Christian Classics Ethereal Library at Wheaton College.

SCHOOLS AND INSTITUTES

CLA Home Page

http://cla-net.cla.umn.edu/clahome.htm

The home page of the College of Liberal Arts (CLA) at the University of Minnesota is maintained at this site. Visitors can obtain information about the College's academics, administration, departments and programs, read CLA and University of Minnesota publications or link to the Colleges FTP site.

Faculty of Arts, Goteberg University

http://www.hum.gu.se/humeng.html

The Faculty of Arts at Sweden's Goteburg University introduces the itself and describes the departments of archaeology, classical studies, history of art and linguistics. Other information sources are described. In Swedish and English.

Harvard University Faculty of Arts and Sciences

http://fas-www.harvard.edu/

The Faculty of Arts and Sciences at Harvard University maintains this informational site. Visit here to learn about its facilities, programs, resources and student life. Links to local weather and community information are also available.

Michigan Technological University Humanities Department

http://www.hu.mtu.edu/

Michigan Technological University rounds out its scientific education offerings with a healthy dose of the liberal arts. Review the academic programs of the school's Humanities Department at this site.

Rose-Hulman Institute of Technology

http://www.sla.purdue.edu/

The School of Liberal Arts at Purdue University provides information here on its departments, student services and academic programs. Visit here to learn about the school and its information technology resources.

University of Florida College of Liberal Arts and Sciences

http://www.clas.ufl.edu/

In addition to a course catalog and program overviews, the University of Florida's College of Liberal Arts and Sciences home page offers details on its computing and networking facilities. Pointers to related campus departments and Web search tools are also provided.

University of Pennsylvania Classical Studies Department

http://ccat.sas.upenn.edu/clst/clst.html

The home page of the Classical Studies Department at the University of Pennsylvania provides a variety of department and classical studies info. Read about academics, faculty, lectures, workshops and events, and link to personal home pages and related Web sites.

University of Pennsylvania School of Arts and Sciences

http://www.sas.upenn.edu/

The School of Arts and Sciences at the University of Pennsylvania provides descriptions of its graduate and undergraduate programs, academic departments and admissions guidelines. Includes info on computing facilities, alumni services, publications and links to other campus servers.

BUSINESS AND INVESTING

THE 25 MOST POPULAR BUSINESS AND INVESTING SITES

Advertising Age
http://www.adage.com

Bestagents.com
http://www.bestagents.com

Better Business Bureau
http://www.igc.apc.org/cbbb/

Chiat/Day Idea Factory
http://www.chiatday.com/factory

CNN Financial Network
http://www.cnnfn.com

Currency Converter
http://www.olsen.ch/cgi-bin/exmenu

Dow Jones
http://www.dowjones.com/

European Patent Office
http://www.epo.co.at/epo/

FedEx
http://www.fedex.com

First Virtual
http://www.fv.com

Gannett Co., Inc.
http://www.gannett.com/

Harvard Business School
http://www.hbs.harvard.edu/

Internal Revenue Service
http://www.irs.ustreas.gov/prod/cover.html

JobSource
http://www.jobsource.com

JOBTRAK
http://www.jobtrak.com

Melanet
http://www.melanet.com/melanet/

Money Abroad—Europe
http://www.inria.fr/robotvis/personnel/laveau/
money-faq/europe.html

NYNEX Interactive Yellow Pages
http://www.niyp.com

PR Newswire
http://www.prnewswire.com

**Print Publications Related to Business
Use of the Internet**
http://arganet.tenagra.com/Tenagra/
books.html

**Securities and Exchange Commission
EDGAR Archive**
http://www.sec.gov/edgarhp.htm

Sharper Image
http://www.sharperimage.com

Strategis
http://strategis.ic.gc.ca

Tax Wizard
http://taxwizard.com

Telecommuting Advisory Council
http://www.telecommute.org

ADVERTISING, MARKETING, AND PUBLIC RELATIONS

ADVERTISING

Advertising Age
http://www.adage.com

Consult the bible of the advertising industry. See Editor's Choice.

Advertising Media Internet Center
http://www.amic.com

Telmar Advertising's Media Internet Center is an online stomping ground for browsers interested in the interaction of the ad biz and the Web. Check in with the Telmar Media Gurus for answers to common questions about advertising or sign up for a free account to receive industry news briefs.

American Association of Advertising Agencies
http://www.commercepark.com/AAAA

With more than 600 member agencies, the New York-based American Association of Advertising Agencies acts as the industry's spokesperson with government, media and the public. Visit its home page to connect to member services, regulatory updates, agency search tools and trade publications.

Dahlin Smith White
http://www.dsw.com

Dahlin Smith White, an advertising agency with such high-profile computer-biz clients as Intel, Corel WordPerfect, Iomega and Sybase, presents a doodle-filled legal pad tour of its services. Visitors can flip through its portfolio, case studies, and staff pages, or contact its offices in Salt Lake City or San Francisco.

Fallon McElligott
http://www.fallon.com

The Fallon McElligott home page offers detailed information about the firm, which was recently named "Agency of the Year" by Advertising Age magazine. Visitors can take examine work the firm has done for such prestigious clients as BMW and The Prudential.

The Gallery of Advertising Parody
http://www.dnai.com/~sharrow/parody.html

Pokes fun at the advertisers who try to sell us things. See Editor's Choice.

gekko GbR
http://www.gekko.technopark.gmd.de

A German advertising agency with the irresistible name of gekko GbR introduces its wide range of services here. Visitors also will find examples of the company's previous work. In German.

Idea Factory
http://www.chiatday.com/factory

The Chiat/Day ad agency touts its Idea Factory through this creative home page. The site explains Chiat/Day's unique vision, its current projects and its concept of a virtual office focusing on emerging media. Visitors can even influence the future direction of the media by engaging in an online focus group.

Laran Communications Online Advertising
http://www.web-ads.com

Laran Communications is a full-service advertising firm located in Winfield, Ill. Visitors to this promotional site, which contains the company's "online classifieds," will learn about options for advertising both the traditional way and the Web way.

Risdall Linnihan Advertising
http://www.rladvert.com

New Brighton, Minn.-based Risdall Linnihan Advertising is a full-service agency providing creative services and marketing in traditional and emerging media. Visitors to its intriguing home page will find a unique graphics-based introduction to the firm and its work.

Rubin Postaer and Associates
http://www.rpa.com

RPA is a brassy, L.A.-based advertising company that believes in thoroughly understanding both the consumer and the product so that a brand personality can be developed. Its motto? "Ideas are the whole idea."

MARKETING

GENERAL

Advanced Multimedia System Design

http://www.amsd.ru

Moscow-based Advanced Multimedia System Design offers details about its software development expertise and unique abilities to aid companies in Russia and around the world. Check out the AMSD Ariadna Web browser that is available in beta release.

Black Box

http://www.ot.com/blackbox

Black Box, a marketing and design agency, promotes its services here. The company designs brochures, annual reports, multimedia presentations and Web pages.

BMG Ariola Studios

http://www.bmgstudios.de

BMG Ariola Studios, a "complete production network," helps its clients find audio, video and graphic solutions to multimedia and commercial needs, including casting and production consulting. Find out more about the German company here.

Business Product Review

http://www.sofcom.com.au/BPR

The Australian magazine Business Product Review is a bimonthly, direct-marketing publication. Visitors to the online version of the publication can read the latest issue or browse the archive of past issues.

Capital Relations, Inc.

http://www.caprel.com

Capital Relations is a public-relations and marketing firm specializing in technological clientele. Capital offers market research, product positioning, Internet communications (including home-page development and maintenance), print and broadcast exposure, and more.

Computer-Aided Research & Media Analysis International

http://www.carma.com/carma/index.html

Washington, D.C.-based Computer-Aided Research & Media Analysis, or CARMA, examines trends in print and electronic media for a variety of clients. Visitors to its home page will find staff profiles and current-events analysis.

A Day at the Consumer Electronics Show

http://www.halcyon.com/ces/welcome.html

A smorgasboard of all the latest in computer technology. See Editor's Choice.

Direct Marketing Group

http://www.teleport.com/~web/dmginc.html

This home page illuminates a company specializing in direct-mail campaigns. Visitors can receive a free marketing analysis for their Web businesses and read the Digital Marketing Group's monthly electronic newsletter.

Equifax National Decision Systems

http://www.ends.com

Equifax National Decision Systems, a San Diego-based marketing research firm, maintains this promotional site. Visit here to learn about the company and its consumer information resources.

Forrester Research Inc.

http://www.forrester.com

Forrester Research Inc., a technology market research consulting firm, maintains this promotional page. Visitors are encouraged to learn more about the company and the services it provides.

Frost Yellow Pages Inc.

http://www.frostyp.com/fyp

Frost Yellow Pages Inc. uses this page to promote its particular twist on effective "yellow pages" advertising. Businesses can check out the consulting firm's services and preview the "90 Minute Guide to Yellow Pages Advertising (It'll Save You Money)."

---

a2z **EDITOR'S CHOICE**

The Gallery of Advertising Parody

http://www.dnai.com/~sharrow/parody.html

Juxtaposing bad ads with clever send-ups, the insiders at the Sharrow Advertising agency take some well deserved potshots at the worst of the profession. The targets range from Absolut Vodka ("So tasteful. So au courant. It makes a DUI almost worth it.") to IBM ("It's embarrassing to see old farts pretend they're hip and cool. Especially when they're all warped and twisted.") to the Gap. Graphic designers with an Xacto wit are welcome to submit their own parodies for inclusion here. The challenge: to be even worse than the original.—*Reviewed by Joe Williams*

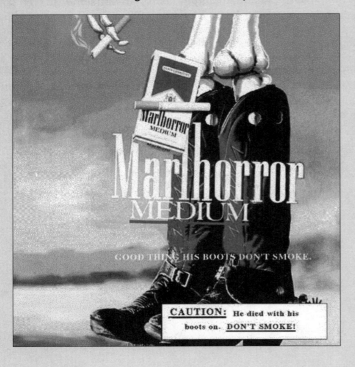

Internet VALS Survey

http://future.sri.com

At this site, SRI International presents a survey that translates Web users' likes and dislikes into valuable currency for marketers. Compare yourself to the "average" Web denizen or examine the trends revealed by these virtual demographic researchers.

Liggett-Stashower

http://www.liggett.com

Liggett-Stashower is an integrated marketing communications company performing a wide range of traditional and electronic marketing services. Its Web site includes descriptions of it services, consulting programs, creative departments, public relations and customer support.

Market Research Center

http://www.asiresearch.com

ASI Market Research of Glendale, Calif., provides information on its research in advertising, entertainment and new media. This corporate site includes access to industry news and publications as well as details about the Internet Market Research & Advertising Industry E-mail Directory published by ASI.

Master-McNeil, Inc.

http://www.naming.com/naming.html

Provides that all-important memorable company name. See Editor's Choice.

New Marketing Imperatives

http://www.siva.com/nmi/nmhome.html

Eavesdrop on this group of corporate executives and market strategists while they deliberate on challenging marketing problems. The Roundtable Web server and its video series (for sale here) provide candid glimpses into these high rollers' insights as they grapple with critical corporate issues.

Nomura Research Institute

http://www.nri.co.jp

Japan's Nomura Research Institute is a marketing research and systems consultation company. In addition to providing information about the company, its services and publications, the company's home page offers links to a variety of information on Japanese corporations. In Japanese and English.

O'Keefe Marketing

http://www.okeefe.com

O'Keefe Marketing provides details on its conventional business services, such as advertising, direct mail, corporate communications and consumer merchandising; also included here are details on O'Keefe Interactive, which works in CD-ROM development, interactive kiosk design and online marketing. A directory of online clients is included.

RW Lynch Company

http://www.rwlynch.com

RW Lynch spells out its marketing and advertising services for the legal profession through this page. It includes links to radio and TV ad campaigns, along with print ad strategies and marketing plans for cementing a law firm's "name awareness."

Southwest Multimedia

http://www.swmm.com

Southwest Multimedia's Web site explains the company's products and services. Those in the market for catalogs on disk, multimedia presentations or media-buying assistance can peruse the company's newsletters or sample its work here.

Wahlstrom & Co.

http://www.wahlstrom.com

This promotional site is the Web home of Wahlstrom & Co., a direct-marketing consulting firm that specializes in Yellow Pages advertising. Visitors to its page can learn more about the company, read its current newsletter and review its online client portfolio.

X Communications' World

http://www.xworld.com/

X-Communications, a New York City-based multimedia design firm, shows off its efforts on this sleek page. It promotes its services, but also provides a site called Music View, which "provides a cornucopia of cool crap from an eclectic selection of artists that have appeared on the Music View Radio Show."

WEB CONSULTING AND MARKETING

AAA Internet Promotions

http://www.west.net/~solution

AAA Internet Promotions, located in lovely Santa Barbara, Calif., promises to help you achieve "your maximum potential of traffic, clients and sales" with its Web-promotion service. The site includes an international client directory, so you can check whether what they say is true.

ABACUSnet

http://www.abacus.net

Abacus provides information and pricing on its Web services, which include virtual storefronts, training and secured credit-card transactions. The

---

a2z EDITOR'S CHOICE

A Day at the Consumer Electronics Show

http://www.halcyon.com/ces/welcome.html

The Consumer Electronic Show, held annually in the timelessly elegant confines of the Las Vegas convention center, is "the one show where you can go to see the latest in computers, software, home electronics, games, peripherals, household convenience products [and] entertainers." This virtual recap of the 1995 soiree only hints at the overkill weirdness of the event, where the likes of Bill Gates rub elbows with moonlighting Vegas showgirls, Penn & Teller, and tipsy, tapped-out programmers from Anytown, USA. Includes a preview of upcoming conventions with a similar gee-whiz factor.—*Reviewed by Joe Williams*

Welcome to *A Day At CES* - a virtual tour of the 1995 Winter Consumer Electronics Show that took place in Las Vegas, Nevada. The CES is the one show where you can go to see the latest in computers, software, home electronics, games, peripherals, household convenience products, entertainers and...BOB.

Abacus Mall features businesses such as Shawn's Internet Resume Center; CD Now; Sunglasses, Shavers and More; and Jan's Custom Knits.

Activ Media's Online Marketer Help Desk

http://www.activmedia.com

This data and resource locator points visitors toward online marketing information. A diverse collection of resources and information is available here, from marketing reports and surveys to an index of Net directories providing site-registration services.

Acxes.com

http://www.acxes.com/hm

Evergreen, Colo.-based acxes.com offers "affordable and effective" home page creation services. Visit here to learn about its capabilities, rates and client base, which mainly comprises real-estate firms.

The Aframian Webnet

http://www.he.net/~awe

The Aframian WebNet describes itself as a "centralized repository of afrocentric links," providing visitors with a collection of Web sites of interest to African Americans. The company also designs Web sites for like-minded clientele.

Agency.Com Ltd.

http://www.agency.com

Agency.Com helps corporations develop interesting, creative and easily navigable Web sites. Visit this corporate home page to see a copy of Urban Desires, a very cool Web-based arts-and-lifestyles publication, or peruse samples of current and past projects.

Amaranth Communications

http://www.amaranth.com

Amaranth Communications of Pensacola, Fla., provides information on its Internet-access, Web-advertising and Web-design services. It presents a marketplace of its businesses, a guide to Pensacola and more.

America.Net

http://www.america.net

Georgia-based America.Net supplies the lowdown on its Net access and site-design capabilities. Featured here is a far-flung index of Internet resources, including reference tools and search engines, plus members' business sites and home pages.

American Information Systems Inc.

http://www.ais.net

An Internet access provider and consulting firm in Chicago gives an overview of its services on this promotional page. The company also describes its knack for Java programming.

Anderson Internet Development Group

http://www.aidg.com

Based in Research Triangle Park, N.C., the Anderson Internet Development Group promotes its business services at this Web site. Visit here to learn about its dial-up account service and its Web-site development, design and hosting capabilities.

Argus Associates Inc.

http://argus-inc.com/

Argus Associates Inc. specializes in design of large-scale information systems. Visitors to the company's home page will find information on its Web-site design services, content-driven advertising and Internet training sessions.

ARRAY Development

http://www.arraydev.com

Located in Ottawa, Canada, ARRAY Development offers companies and organizations services such as Web-site design and technology analysis.

AspenMedia

http://www.aspenmedia.com

AspenMedia touts its publishing services on the Web through this home page. Visitors can click into details about the California company's consulting and graphics services or follow links to Saturday fun in the Weekend Warriors section.

Atlantic Computing Technology Corp. Home Page

http://www.atlantic.com

Atlantic Computing Technology Corp. boasts, "Our whole business is placing other businesses on the Internet." For a recitation of products, services and a general sales pitch, visit the company's home page.

Audit Bureau of Circulations

http://www.accessabc.com

Want to know who's watching and reading what on the Internet? Check the Audit Bureau of Circulations for details about its efforts at Web auditing, or check out some of the more than 4,000 publishers, advertisers and agencies that use its services.

Automatrix Main Page

http://www.automatrix.com

Automatrix, Inc. is an Internet marketing firm based in Rexford, New York. Visitors to its site will find a list of advertisers, rates and a description of services that allows companies to get their message and products on the Net.

---

a2z **EDITOR'S CHOICE**

Master-McNeil, Inc.

http://www.naming.com/naming.html

What's in a name, you ask? Well, there's a reason that Burroughs Inc. is now called Unisys and Western Electric is now called Lucent Technologies. The average Joe might not know the reason, but Master-McNeil does. This Berkeley-based firm has a knack for names. When corporations need new monikers to spruce up their images, this is one place where they turn. This home page offers an explanation of Master-McNeil's naming philosophy for the digital age, a surprisingly extensive glossary of naming terms, and a list of clients (before and after). Be on the lookout for the names MemBrain, Symbios and dpiX, all of which were hatched by the company and embraced by their high-tech clientele.—*Reviewed by Joe Williams*

MemBrain

Master-McNeil created this name for Marmot Mountain Ltd.'s new high-performance Smart Fabric Technology(TM). The name plays on the "smart," adaptable nature of the fiber technology, which is used in rugged outdoor clothing.

MemBrain(TM) is a shape-change polymer that responds precisely to climatic conditions, adjusting its form to keep the wearer comfortable.

Logo design: Kevin McPhee and Associates, San Carlos, California

BBN Planet

http://www.bbnplanet.com

BBN Planet offers Internet service packages to business organizations worldwide. At the BBN Planet home page, visitors can read the company's history, related publications, profiles, and news.

Bedrock Information Solutions Inc.

http://end2.bedrock.com

Bedrock Information Solutions Inc. offers technical support, training and systems-integration services to companies conducting business on the Internet. Visitors can review the company's products and services at this promotional site.

Benemann Translation Center

http://www.translate.com

Parlez-vous Internet? Benemann Translation Center in California offers its Web-page translation services on this promotional page, which can be read in English, French, German, Spanish, Japanese and Mandarin Chinese. (What, no Esperanto?)

Berbee Information Networks Corp.

http://www.binc.net

This site serves as an electronic welcome mat for clients of the Berbee Information Networks Corp., a Wisconsin-based provider of Internet services for businesses. Visitors can find out more about the company, link to its clients' home pages or follow the other general-interest pointers that are provided.

Berkeley Internet Connections

http://www.berkeleyic.com

Berkeley Internet Connections supplies information on its Web-design services at this commercial site. Included are links to some of its works, such as the Grand Old Page and the Phil Gramm for President site.

Berkeley NetCentral

http://www.berkeleynetcentral.com

At this commercial Web site, Berkeley NetCentral supplies information on its online services such as custom Web-page design and database creation. Visitors also will find company addresses, phone numbers, a client listing and rate information.

Bien Logic Bold Design

http://www.bienlogic.com

This promotional site is the home of Bien Logic, a Web design firm located in San Diego, Calif. Learn more about the company and visit its online gallery at this highly graphical site.

BizNet Technologies

http://www.bnt.com

If you didn't know already, any business of any kind is capable of commerce on the Internet. BizNet Technologies has been formed to help the global business community expand and explore its fullest potential on the Web with a wide range of services.

BizPro Inc.

http://www.bizpro.com/bizpro

An Internet marketing firm posts a promotional page here outlining its Web-page creation and hosting services. Visitors will get an overview of the company, its work and rates for custom work.

Black Box

http://www.ot.com/blackbox

Black Box, a marketing and design agency, promotes its services here. The company designs brochures, annual reports, multimedia presentations and Web pages.

Black Star Photo and Web Resources

http://www.blackstar.com

Headquartered in New York City, Black Star represents a network of 350 photographers from around the world. Visitors to this commercial site can browse the organization's photojournalism gallery, check out an online stock photo library, or learn about the company's World Wide Web publishing services.

BMG Ariola Studios

http://www.bmgstudios.de

BMG Ariola Studios, a "complete production network," helps its clients find audio, video and graphic solutions to multimedia and commercial needs, including casting and production consulting. Find out more about the German company here.

BonAire Communications

http://www.mbeacon.com

Self-described as "Maine's premiere online publishing company" (a heady boast, indeed), BonAire Communications hosts this site offering links to its electronic newspaper, the Coastal Beacon, as well as its Maine Index.

Bonsai Software Inc.

http://www.bonsai.com

Visitors to this commercial Web site can peruse the portfolio of a company specializing in Web applications. Bonsai Software Inc.'s programmers and designers build Web tools, create Web pages and perform server administration tasks. Its Web also site includes corporate information about the California-based company.

Brad's Apple Internet Server 6150

http://brad.net

This is the home page of Brad Schrick, who creates Web sites for commercial clients and public-service organizations. Information is available here about Brad's special-interest projects and Web authoring, along with links to miscellaneous sites.

Brainstorm Networks

http://www.brainstorm.net

Brainstorm Networks' promotional site provides details on Internet connection, consulting and tools offered by the San Francisco Bay Area company. Includes price listings for high-speed Internet connections for business and personal use.

Buck Information Systems Inc.

http://bisinc.com

Ontario-based Buck Information Systems publishes electronic catalogs and corporate home pages at this commercial site. A business-to-business area and classified ads also are available.

Burma Shave Today

http://www.charm.net/~windsor/daily.html

See the future of advertising today. See Editor's Choice.

Business Resource Center

http://www.kciLink.com:80/brc

Khera Communications Inc., an Internet publishing and consulting firm based in Rockville, Md., offers small business owners and other entrepreneurs marketing, management and financing tips at this site. Includes links to the Government Contractor Resource Center and other business-related pages.

By-the-Web

http://www.nettuno.it/btw

By-the-Web provides online marketing and design services to Italian companies looking to get on the Internet. Potential customers are invited to review examples of the company's work by visiting the Web sites of current clients. Includes a schedule of rates and services. In Italian with limited English translations.

The CallAmerica Nexus

http://www.callamer.com

The CallAmerica Nexus is a Web marketing site featuring information about the California firm's clients and services. Includes background info on the company, its services and prices.

CaribNet

http://www.caribnet.net

A Caribbean Web-development company and Internet site host outlines opportunities for commercial or individual Web presences on this corporate home page. Find out what kind of services CaribNet has to offer, and visit some of its Barbados clients from here.

Centripedus

http://www.centripedus.com

Centripedus is a design firm that concocts eye-catching artwork and photo enhancements for corporate and online clients. Its home site says little but shows much.

China Internet Corporation

http://www.china.com

The goal of Hong Kong-based China Internet Corporation is "to promote trade between China and the world using the technology and resources of the Internet" and provide all provinces in the country with Web hosting services. Visitors can connect to the growing client list here. In Mandarin and English.

Convergence Systems Inc.

http://www.convergence.com

Networking consultant firm Convergence Systems assists cable providers in connecting to the "Fast Internet." Visit its home page for service descriptions, client lists and a variety of cable industry-related information resources.

Coolware Inc.

http://none.coolware.com

Coolware Inc., a San Francisco-based Internet marketing company, maintains this promotional site. Visit here to learn about its Web-site creation and promotion services and to link to its many online resources, including classified advertisements, health and fitness guides, community information and more.

Coral Technologies, Inc.

http://www.coral.net/

Florida-based Coral technologies is a Web-service provider and site designer with an emphasis on sun and fun. Its home page has information about vacation destinations, real estate and scuba diving, along with the company's client list, descriptions of products and services, and related Web sites.

Cove Software Systems

http://www.covesoft.com

Maryland's Cove Software Systems Inc. assists advertisers on its Web server (and elsewhere) to market their products and services. Visitors to its home page can learn more about the company and its services, or access the networks and home pages it hosts.

Creative Internet Solutions

http://www.creativeis.com

This promotional site is the Web home of Creative Internet Solutions, an Internet marketing company based in Minneapolis. Visitors are invited to find out more about the company and the services it provides.

CultNet Finland

http://www.cultnet.fi

CultNet Finland calls itself a "virtual company" providing design and marketing services to commercial entities developing presences on the Web. Visitors can get a taste of the company's methods for developing online advertising campaigns.

Cyberagentes

http://www.eunet.es/InterStand/cyberagentes

Cyberagentes boasts a collection of online marketing and research services for businesses in Spain. Visit sites of current clients for examples of the company's promotional work. In Spanish and English.

The CyberMarketing Group

http://www.cybermarket.com

Businesses seeking counsel about putting their identity online can consult the CyberMarketing Group. A summary of the company's Internet-related products and services is offered.

Cybernet Marketing Services

http://www.cyberms.com

Wooster, Ohio-based Cybernet provides Web-based advertising and marketing services. Visitors to its home page will find service overviews, client lists and Internet-related information resources.

Cyber Publishing Japan

http://www.toppan.co.jp

Cyber Publishing Japan provides an online home to Japanese commercial entities. Follow the links provided to a diverse collection of promotional sites. In Japanese and English.

Cyber Resources

http://www.netins.net/showcase/cyber

Iowa-based Cyber Resources highlights its Web design and maintenance business at its promotional home page with 20 reasons that your company should be on the Web.

CyberSmart Marketing

http://www.martinagency.com

Businesses hoping to launch a Web marketing campaign need look no further than this, the Martin Agency's home page. It's filled with helpful pointers and examples of successful (and not so successful) Web pages.

Cyber Technologies International

http://www.cyber.ad.jp

This promotional page is the Web home of Cyber Technologies International, a full-service Web consulting, marketing and programming company located in Tokyo. Visitors are invited to learn more about the company, its products and its services. In English and Japanese.

---

a2z EDITOR'S CHOICE

Burma Shave Today

http://www.charm.net/~windsor/daily.html

In the golden age of Route 66 Americana, the Burma Shave Company made a name for itself with a series of clever, sequential billboards. The premise of the Burma Shave Today site is that Web pages represent a new kind of corporate billboard, and this site shines its virtual headlights on the best of the bunch. By its own admission, this weekly review focuses on a lot more corporate heavyweights than unknown entrepreneurs (after all, the giants can afford the best designers and programmers), but such fun home pages as the Molson, Crayola and Joe Boxer sites are invariably worthy of the praise they receive here. The Webmaster also promises critical discussions of the advertising biz in the near future.—*Reviewed by Joe Williams*

Burma Shave

The Best Advertising on the Net

D&D Consulting Ltd.
http://www.disaster.com

At this commercial site, New York's D&D Consulting Ltd. presents information on its Web-authoring, computer-networking and Internet-connection services for businesses. A company history and client list also are featured.

Darkmass Media
http://www.eden.com/~darkmass

DARKMASS Productions displays its slightly dark and quirkily animated Web-design finesse on this promotional page. Browsers can learn about the firm's services and admire its clients' sites.

DDB Needham Interactive Communications
http://www.ddbniac.com

The new-media and technologies subsidiary of advertising concern DDB Needham Worldwide displays general information about its operations and resources at this corporate site. Visitors can sample its services, visit a virtual gallery and browse an index of employment opportunities.

DigiMark Center
http://www.digimark.net

DigiMark specializes in putting companies online. Visitors will find information on the company's services, along with developer resources and travel and arts information.

Digital Creations
http://www.digicool.com

This commercial site introduces Virginia-based Digital Creations, a company that helps businesses establish their own Web sites. Visitors here can find descriptions of the company's products and services, along with local information.

digitalNATION
http://www.dn.net

This promotional site is maintained by digitalNATION, an Internet design and marketing company located in Alexandria, Va. Visitors to its home page are invited to learn more about the company, its products and services.

Digital Planet
http://www.digiplanet.com

Located in Culver City, Calif., Digital Planet describes itself as "a full service development and production studio" that provides "a comprehensive approach to publishing, advertising, and marketing for an interactive medium." Learn more about the company and review its online portfolio at this promotional home page.

Dimension X Inc.
http://www.dimensionx.com

This site is the Web home of Dimension X Inc., a red-hot San Francisco-based Web designer that develops its own Java-based 3D design tools. Visitors will learn about the company and its tools, clients and talents.

Direct Marketing Group
http://www.teleport.com/~web/dmginc.html

This home page makes a pitch for a company specializing in direct-mail campaigns. Visitors can receive a free marketing analysis for their Web businesses and read the Digital Marketing Group's monthly electronic newsletter.

DISCscribe Ltd.
http://www.discribe.ca

DISCscribe Ltd. of Fredericton, New Brunswick, maintains this site to promote its Internet host services. Visit here to learn about the company and link to an A-Z list of its customer sites. Available in French and English.

The Door: 3 Loop 9 Design
http://www.3loop9.com

Behind this door, 3 Loop 9 Design invites us into a vast space filled with the myriad marvels and mysteries of the Internet. Visitors can enjoy 3 Loop 9's print work, logos and Web designs before launching into the ether.

Ecosys, Ltd.
http://www.eccosys.com/JPN

The Japanese Internet consulting firm Ecosys, Ltd. provides product and service information in English and Japanese on this corporate home page. Included is a list of current clients and a map indicating where its headquarters are in Tomigaya. (Turn left at the ramen noodle shack.)

e.doc
http://www.edoc.com

The Baltimore, Md.-based electronic publishing group has designed sites for such organizations as Science magazine and the American Physical Therapy Association. Visit e.doc's corporate home page to access client, service and contact info.

Education Showcase
http://www.infomall.org/Showcase

This promotional page is the Internet home of Education Showcase, an Internet publishing company that helps other companies market to schools through the Internet. Includes descriptions of products, services and customer support.

Electronic Dimensions
http://www.edime.com.au

Electronic Dimensions provides Internet consulting services for Australian government and commercial organizations. Visit here to learn about its World Wide Web design, publishing and marketing services.

The Electronic Pen Inc.
http://www.epen.com

Located in the San Francisco Bay Area, the Electronic Pen Inc. is an Internet marketing and graphics communications company. Visitors to its home page are invited to learn more about the company and its services and to review its portfolio of work.

Entercom
http://www.entercom.net

Wisconsin-based Internet access provider and Web-site developer Entercom introduces itself to the Web community and describes its service plans and options through its home page. The company specializes in Web document design, consulting and Internet training.

Entrepreneur On-Line
http://www.netaccess.on.ca/entrepr

Entrepreneur On-Line offers itself as a Internet marketing tool. Visitors can subscribe to the service to have their information circulated among subscribers or find out what Entrepreneur On-Line can do to expose their products to the public.

Evergreen Internet
http://cybermart.com

Evergreen Internet specializes in creating commercial Web sites for service-intensive businesses. Visitors can find out about Evergreen's services and fees, plus link to shopping, entertainment and tourism sites created by the company.

The Executive Guide to Marketing on the New Internet
http://www.industry.net/guide.html

The Industry.Net Marketing and Research Group offers an executive guide to marketing on the Internet through this corporate page. The report covers the Internet's growth, explains how it can pay off for marketers and theorizes about the future.

FGCNet's Presence Index
http://www.fcg.com

A page from the Flying Color Graphics site, this index lists businesses and other info servers in Illinois. Find examples of the online design services offered by FCG, a Web publishing firm.

Fine.com
http://fine.com

An Internet marketing firm in idyllic Seattle details its services and provides an online portfolio here.

Finite Systems Consulting

http://www.finite-systems.com/fsc

At its support site, Finite Systems Consulting, a Toronto, Ontario-based Internet consulting firm, provides information on its technology, services, products and resources. Live demonstrations are available here as well.

First Virtual InfoHaus

http://www.infohaus.com

This mall allows clients to post their commercial information services. Includes listings of info shops, along with instructions for establishing a site and uploading information.

Fleet House Information Management Solutions

http://www.fleethouse.com

Fleet House, based in Vancouver, British Columbia, is an electronic publications company that designs newsletters, brochures, catalogs and other Internet-ready business documents. This corporate site contains several of the firm's publications, many related to Canadian travel and tourism.

ForumNet Inc.

http://www.forum.net

This promotional page is the Web home of ForumNet Inc., a Web-site design and marketing firm based in Madison, Wis. Visitors can learn more about the company and its services.

Free Range Media

http://www.freerange.com

Seattle, Wash.-based Free Range Media, a full-service Web production and Internet services company, maintains this site to exhibit its creative services. Visitors can follow links to find additional examples of the company's work.

The Futuris Internet Business Center

http://www.futuris.net

Futuris is an Internet design, consulting and hosting service located in Hartford, Conn. Businesses can learn about becoming a member here, while visitors can shop for a variety of services and products at the virtual mall of clients' sites.

FX Media

http://fxmedia.com

FX Media, Inc., a Web-development and multimedia company in sunny Sarasota, Fla., walks its talk by offering a collection of sample site designs (including Jagermeister liquor and Troma Film Studios) for your inspection.

Ganymede Corporation

http://www.ganymede.net

Ganymede Corporation unveils its work as an Internet designer and Web-site host at its home page. These self-styled "Internet architects" post information about their design services, complete with pricing options.

GemiNet

http://www.chataqua.com

Gemini Internet Marketing Services promotes its Web-development services here. Details on pricing, design strategy and GemiNet "virtual marketplaces" accompany pointers to existing clients.

Global-X-Change Communications Inc.

http://www.globalx.net

This promotional page is the Web home of Global-X-Change Communications Inc., a Canadian firm offering Web design and marketing services. Visitors will find company info, links to client pages and pointers to selected "hot" Web sites.

Graham Technology Solutions

http://www.graham.com

Visitors to Graham Technology Solutions' home page will find information about the Internet consulting firm. Includes an overview of the company's services and a link to Rolling Stones pages created by GTS.

Graphical Business Interfaces

http://www.gbi.com

Various Web sites designed and supported by Graphical Business Interfaces are a click away via this page. Among them are GBI Software Solutions and Musicwaves, an online music source. The firm also designs plug-ins for Web browsers.

Graphic Communication

http://www.graph.com

Graphic Communication, a Hawaiian Internet publishing and advertising firm, describes its Web marketing services and corporate background here. Visitors can review the company's online portfolio or amuse themselves with the collection of optical illusions.

Great Circle Associates

http://www.greatcircle.com

Great Circle Associates is a California-based company that specializes in Internet training and consulting. Visitors are encouraged to find out more about the company's Internet Security Firewalls Tutorial, as well as its other products and services.

Heilmann Graphics

http://www.hgraphics.com

The Heilmann Graphics page promotes the Web consulting services of this company. It can get your own marketing page started and keep it going, offering expertise in graphics, programming, image maps and forms.

The Idea Factory & Gallery

http://www.dnai.com/~sharrow/ideas.html

For people who are full of ideas but have no one to listen to them, this site is the perfect sounding board. Sharrow Davies Townsend, a San Francisco-based marketing, planning and communications consulting firm, provides a series of forms here to submit ideas about marketing, new products and other promotions.

Ikonic Interactive

http://www.ikonic.com

Ikonic Interactive provides creative cybersolutions for some of the biggest names around (you've heard of Sprint and GTE, haven't you?), including online services and networks, interactive television and personal digital assistants.

Imagex

http://sandpiper.rtd.com/~imagex/index.html

Imagex 2.0 is the Web-design portfolio of IP Squared, a company providing creative Internet services. Visitors here can check out the company's gallery, news and features.

The Information Server Co.

http://www.tisco.com/

The Information Server Co. is a full-service advertising and design firm located near Boston. Visitors to this corporate home page can learn more about the company and the Internet marketing services it provides.

Insanely Interactive Systems Inc.

http://www.iisys.com/iishome.htm

Insanely Interactive Systems Inc. specializes in Internet services for Web-site development, Internet consulting, and personalized corporate training. Visitors will find details on its services and clients at the company's home page.

Interactive Factory

http://www.ifactory.com

A Boston-based design firm promotes its services here. The firm designs CD-ROMs and Web pages, and it consults on marketing strategies. Visitors can get an overview of the firm and download its portfolio from this page.

Interactive Media Communications

http://www.route-one.co.uk/route-one

Interactive Media Communications maintains this site to introduce its Web authoring services, offering full-motion video, sound, graphics, text and interactivity. Includes a downloadable demonstration and descriptions of products and services.

International Internet Group, Inc.
http://iigi.com

A mix of business, legal and outdoor-sports resources share space on the home page of the International Internet Group, a Web hosting service.

InternationalNet
http://international.com

InternationalNet is an online access provider and open-systems consulting firm that promises low rates. The California-based firm also designs Web pages and provides audio, video and animation demos here.

Internet Access Group Inc.
http://www.iagi.net

Located in Bethesda, Md., this Web site publisher and Internet access provider maintains a home page to provide information about its services and prices. Includes the Hub, a collection of home pages constructed for the company's clients.

Internet Advertising Solutions
http://iaswww.com

Internet Advertising Solutions aims to convince businesses of the efficacy of advertising on the Web. Visitors can examine demographics profiles of potential competitors already making their mark on this modern medium, plus cost and design specifics.

Internet Commerce Corp. Surf Shop
http://www.wisdom.com/pcs/surf.htm

The Internet Commerce Corp. Surf Shop delivers links to a smorgasbord of topics, including the latest news and weather in the Louisiana area. The Internet access and Web consulting firm also offers info on its products and services.

The Internet Convention Center
http://www.apk.net

The Internet Convention Center is an advertising resource for entrepreneurs and a gateway to products and services for consumers. This site categorizes businesses in Yellow Pages fashion, offering links to a variety of destinations, from high-tech companies to dating services.

Internet Direct Inc.
http://www.indirect.com

Internet Direct Inc., based in Phoenix, Ariz., provides Internet services and solutions for businesses, including the GoSite "virtual Internet server." Product and services info, demonstrations, support and a company overview flesh out this commercial site.

Internet Directory Australia
http://www.ida.com.au

This is the home page of Internet Directory Australia, an Internet access provider and Web publishing company. Check out info on Australian travel, tourism and commercial businesses, or find out about company services and pricing here.

Internet Distribution Services Inc.
http://www.service.com

Located in Palo Alto, Calif., Internet Distribution Services Inc. provides electronic marketing, publishing and distribution services on the World Wide Web. Visit this site for more information about the company and its clients, including Hitachi Data Systems, and the University of California, Berkeley.

The Internet Factory
http://www.netfactory.com

The Internet Factory, bravely hammering out Internets beneath the smokestacks of Birmingham, Mich., provides a variety of commercial Web presence services. Visit its home page to find how it can set up your organization's home page for maximum exposure and effectiveness.

The Internet Group
http://www.tig.com/IBC/index.html

This promotional site is sponsored by The Internet Group, a supplier of turnkey solutions for marketing on the Internet. Visitors can learn more about the company, its products and services, and contact the company with comments or questions.

Internet Information Services Inc.
http://www.iis.com

Internet Information Services of Rockville, Md., provides Internet integration, consulting and security services. This site includes information on the company and its services.

Internet Information Systems
http://www.internet-is.com

Internet Information Systems of Fremont, Calif., is a designer of custom Web sites for businesses. Visitors will find service information and links to customer sites here at the company's home page.

Internet International
http://interinc.com/

This site, maintained by Internet access provider and Web-page designer, SSP International Inc., features information for businesses interested in leasing space for commercial Web sites. Visitors also will find a list of current Internet International customers.

Internet Literacy Consultants
http://www.matisse.net

Invoking the motto, "Knowledge will forever govern ignorance" (whatever that means), Internet Literacy Consultants of San Francisco, Calif., showcases its Web design and advertising talents on this home page. Prices, clients, projects and a political page are available for perusal.

Internet Marketing Services
http://www.inmarket.com

"Full-service Internet presence provider" Internet Marketing Services tells all about its Web site design, hosting and publicity services on this commercial home page. Visitors can learn about the company and link to its client's pages here.

Internet Marketing Services Ltd.
http://www.digimark.net/dundas/ims

Internet Marketing Services Ltd. is an Internet consultant for businesses that designs, publishes and places Web sites. It provides a list of clients' pages and its pricing structure here.

Internet Rockhouse
http://www.rockhouse.com/

Aspiring musicians of all kinds can hype their talent here. See Editor's Choice.

Internet Services Corp.
http://www.netservices.com

Internet Services Corporation assists organizations in creating an online presence and expanding into global markets. Visit this site for information about its projects and services.

Internet Training & Consulting Services
http://www.itcs.com

Internet Training & Consulting Services hawks its Web design and tutelage at this promotional site. Potential customers can link to client Web pages, training presentations and a company overview.

Internet Yellow Web Pages
http://warlight.com/warlight

The Internet Yellow Web Pages provide listings of online businesses and services that are alphabetized and sorted by topic. Featured at this site are the Real Estate Section and Outdoor Adventures Magazine.

Interse' Corp.
http://www.interse.com

Interse' Corp. is a marketer specializing in online communications. The company also produces software to analyze user interaction within Web sites. The company's home page has information about Web trends, details on its analysis software, and links to its own Web sites.

Intervid
http://www.intervid.co.uk/

Intervid, a London Web-design firm, creates pages that will catch the eyes of most visitors: a flashing Santa selling books, an art show and more. Find out more about the company's services here.

INTERWEB Computer Solutions

http://www.relay.net/~gcw/consult.html

INTERWEB Computer Solutions of Chicago offers HTML page-design services and discount memory, peripherals and accessories. Visitors can check out the company's services and products here, along with a list of prices.

Intuitive Systems

http://www.intuitive.com/

Intuitive Systems, a computer systems and Website design agency based in Redwood City, Calif., maintains this site for general information. Visit here for company and service information, programming resources and client lists.

IntuMediaWorks

http://www.intumedia.com/intumedia

IntuMediaWorks, an Internet-based sales, marketing and consulting company located in Cary, N.C., maintains this promotional site. Visit here to learn about the company and its education and training programs.

The Isotropic Media Group

http://isotropic.com

Atlanta's Isotropic Media Group puts companies and organizations on the Internet. This home site outlines the firm's services and supplies a list of clients and work samples.

Knossopolis

http://www.knosso.com

This promotional site is the Web home of Knossopolis, a Web design, marketing and consulting firm located in British Columbia. Visitors are invited to learn more about the company, its philosophy and the services it provides.

Knowledge Computing

http://www.knowledge.co.uk/xxx

U.K.-based Knowledge Computing supplies details on its Web publishing services and Multilingual PC Directory for foreign-language software at this commercial site.

Lavondyss Productions

http://www.lavondyss.com

Lavondyss Productions, a Web-design company based in Savannah, Ga., maintains this promotional page with information about its clients and links to a variety of art, entertainment and leisure sites designed by the company.

Left Bank Operation

http://www.ksr.com

A Massachusetts-based network consulting firm gives an overview of its services and profiles its hard-working, talented, slightly bohemian employees here.

Liberty Hill Cyberwerks

http://cyberwerks.com

Along with its Web consulting business, Liberty Hill Cyberwerks is dedicated to promoting "Internet literacy." Visitors to this home page can learn more about Liberty Hill's services and can link to hip Bay Area organizations the company has put online, including New Albion Records and the Modern Times Bookstore.

Lightside Inc.

http://www.lightside.com

Lightside, a Los Angeles-based Internet access provider and Web marketing firm, gives an overview of its services here. The site also contains links to its clients' pages.

LinkStar Internet Directory

http://www.powerlink.com

Florida-based LinkStar Communications Corp.'s stated aim is to make doing business on the Web easy (and cheap). The company's maiden product, offered here, allows anybody with an e-mail address to add an electronic business card to a searchable database.

LiveSite

http://netbrochure.com

LiveSite is an online, instant Web site creator for businesses and individuals. This site has information about LiveSite's pricing, newsgroup and experiments, plus details on creating and editing a site.

Lycos Advertising

http://www.lycos.com/lycosinc/advertising.html

Banner advertisements on Web services such as Lycos reach millions of users daily. Businesses looking for a new marketing angle can visit this site and find out how to place an advertisement with the Web's largest (and most lovable) catalog and search-engine service.

---

a2z EDITOR'S CHOICE

Internet Rockhouse

http://www.rockhouse.com/

Let's say you're the manager of a neo-psychedelic folk-pop combo called Righteous Broccoli and the bigwigs at the major labels won't give you the time of day. You can jumpstart the careers of your young protegees with the help of the Internet Rockhouse, a Web marketing service for musicians. The Rockhouse can help you develop a home page or place your band in its directory of hopefuls, which is sorted by musical category (original rock, classical, folk, blues, punk, even—touchingly—new wave). There are also chat rooms, classifieds, gigging and equipment info and more, all of which can make that long and winding road to the Rock and Roll Hall of Fame that much smoother.—*Reviewed by Joe Williams*

A New January
Chicago, USA
Price per gig: price negotiable
Contact: january@rockhouse.com
Description digital electro-dance music

Soup
Youngstown, OH, USA
Price per gig: price negotiable
Contact: Room43@rockhouse.com
Description Death-Disco

Alarming Trends
USA, USA
Price per gig: price negotiable
Contact: rcramer@ix.netcom.com
Description A modern female-vocals-hard-edged-guitar type outfit

Foothill Farms Jr. High Bands

weaving/winding sounds of the piano.

EscapeEase
Dayton, Ohio, USA
Price per gig: price negotiable
Contact: frontier@dnaco.net
Description Escape with the weaving/winding sounds of the piano.

Lisa Morse
Jacksonville, NC, USA
Price per gig: Price Negotiable
Contact: lisamorse@rockhouse.com
Description Pianist, composer, sounds similar to John Tesch's music.

Behaviorial scIences
New York City, USA

MaineStreet Communications

http://www.maine.com

MaineStreet Communications offers Internet access, publishing and electronic commerce services to Maine residents. Includes information on the company's products and pricing, plus links to client advertising sites.

Making the Most of the World Wide Web for Your Organization

http://www.gsfc.nasa.gov/documents/making most www.html

Written under contract to NASA, this all-text document explores the Web as a business application. Suggestions for additional reading are attached to the end of the presentation.

MarCom Center

http://wweb.netcomart/marcom

MarCom Center, a marketing communications firm based in Lake Forest, Calif., maintains this site, which offers a corporate overview. Visit here to view Web sites of the company's high-technology clients, learn about its marketing capabilities and link to related sites around the world.

Matterform Media

http://www.matterform.com/welcome.html

Matterform Media is dedicated to "exploring the interplay between figure and ground as it manifests itself in new electronic media." In other words, the company designs Web sites. Visitors to this home page will find details on design services and interface proposals, in addition to sample creations.

Maxcor Consulting

http://www.interlog.com/~pjm/maxcor.html

Maxcor Consulting in Ontario, Canada, offers a variety of service information here, along with company contact info. Browsers can read pages on Maxcor's services for Unix system integration, Internet training, Web-page design and multimedia authoring.

media@web

http://www.tbo.nl

A service of the Box Office, a film and television production company, media@web distributes media press kits and information over the Internet. Visitors are welcome to browse currently posted packages. In English and Dutch.

Mediabridge Infosystems Inc.

http://www.mediabridge.com

The city that never sleeps is renowned for its diverse culture, landmark architecture and rich history. New York City-based Mediabridge Infosystems aims to promote commerce in the Big Apple. Here the electronic publishing company offers a virtual tour of the city, along with an online art gallery.

Media Connection of New York Inc.

http://www.mcny.com

The interactive advertising agency that maintains this site provides information on its Web-design and marketing services here. Visitors also will find a client list and topically indexed links to sites dealing with subjects such as the arts, business, graphics and Internet law.

Mediapolis Inc.

http://www.digitopia.com/mediapolis.html

A New York City-based online marketing and Web-design firm posts its promotional page here. Visitors will get an overview of the company and its services at this site.

Medium for Global Access Inc.

http://www.mgainc.com

Medium for Global Access Inc. is a St. Petersburg, Fla., company that seeks to help businesses make the shift to electronic commerce. Visitors will find information on the company's services, which include networking solutions and designing and maintaining Web sites.

Mesh

http://www.meshnet.or.jp

This home page describes the services of C&C Internet, a Japanese access provider and Web designer for commercial accounts. Includes background on the company, listings of services and links to client sites. In Japanese and English.

Meta Info Labs

http://sunsite.unc.edu/dbarbericommunications.html

David Barberi's Meta Info Labs is an Internet design and consulting firm based in West Chester, Pa. Visitors to this site can link to some of Meta Info's award-winning Web sites.

The Microstate Network

http://www.microstate.com/pub/micros

Microstate Ltd. is a commercial Internet-based marketing service specializing in "very small states, autonomous territories, colonies, islands and similar domains." Interested visitors can read about the company's divisions and its services in communications, marketing, training and publishing.

Middle Volga Communications

http://www.stc.simbirsk.su

Middle Volga Communications outlines its Internet services and highlights the wonders of the World Wide Web at its home page. The site also includes information about the 1995 Russian elections. In Russian and English.

Mr. Digital and Associates

http://mrdigital.com

Mr. Digital and Associates, a Pittsburgh-based digital-publishing and data-conversion company, maintains this promotional site. Visit here to find out how it can convert your existing inventories of publications and other information into digital format.

MJA Technologies Inc.

http://www.mja.net

MJA Technologies is in the business of Internet advertising. Visitors can review the company's marketing services or shop in a "cybermall" populated by MJA's clients' commercial Web shops.

Mmedia.com

http://www.mmedia.com

Mmedia, a Manhattan, Kansas-based Internet presence provider, maintains this site for promotional material and local resources. Visitors can learn about its commercial Web-site creation services or link to a host of state business, community and media organizations.

Mountain Wide Web Design

http://www.csn.net/~scotto

Mountain Wide Web Design of Colorado provides businesses with a Web presence. Information on its services is included here, as are links to the pages of its clients.

Mouse Tracks Home Page

http://nsns.com/MouseTracks

Mouse Tracks, provided by Tallahassee, Fla.-based New South Network Services, offers news and commentary from the world of Internet-based marketing. Visit here for online shopping centers, marketing lists, academic resources and other related World Wide Web links.

Multimedia Marketing Group—Home of WebStep

http://www.mmgco.com/

The Multimedia Marketing Group (MMG) offers digital-marketing consultation services. Visit this page to access the home sites of clients, peruse indices of interesting sites, read white papers and find out how MMG can help your company.

Myhouse Communications

http://204.156.22.13

Based in Washington, D.C., Myhouse Communications leases server space to businesses wanting to store Web publications. This home site offers service information and rates, plus a mixed bag of links to the company's clients' pages.

NetCreations Inc.

http://www.netcreations.com

You can review projects, inspect the client portfolio and check out software at this site maintained by NetCreations, a New York City-based company that performs Web-site construction and Internet marketing.

Net Daemons Associates Inc.

http://www.nda.com

Net Daemons Associates provides expertise in computer-network administration and Internet connectivity for small and medium-sized businesses. This corporate home page includes a description of services and pricing information.

NetFront Information Services

http://www.netfront.com

Based in San Jose, Calif., NetFront Information Services is a business consultancy focused on re-engineering business communications via the Internet and related technologies. This promotional site gives details on the organization's consulting and technical services.

Nethead Limited

http://www.nethead.co.uk

Nethead Limited spotlights its Internet service plans for the United Kingdom on this page. Visitors also can check out the company's clients and their Web pages.

Net Impact Electronic Marketplace

http://www.netimpact.com/biz/netimpact

Net Impact, a company specializing in creating "large-scale" World Wide Web sites for recreation and travel companies, maintains this site for its Electronic Marketplace information service. Visit here for an overview of its authoring capabilities and training services. Includes links to client Web sites.

Net-Mark Enterprises

http://www.net-mark.mb.ca/netmark

Net-Mark Enterprises is a Canadian company specializing in Internet marketing and advertising. At its home page, visitors can read detailed service information, view the Net-Mark gallery of creative work or search the entire Net-Mark directory.

Netmar World Wide Web Marketing

http://netmar.com

Netmar is a full-service Internet provider that features corporate and personal server leasing and award-winning Web-page design. Includes links to account information, Web guide service, and a pointer to the Triangle Realty Network.

Netopia

http://netopia.com

Netopia provides advertising, publishing and consulting services for businesses wishing to develop a presence on the World Wide Web. Visitors will find service descriptions and examples of Web pages designed by the company.

net.presence

http://arganet.tenagra.com/Tenagra/net-presence.html

At this comprehensive tip site, business-minded Webmasters can learn how to create and capitalize on an Internet presence. The site's sponsor, the Tenagra Corp., offers publications, instructions and examples for profitable Web-based marketing.

Netsurfer Marketplace

http://www.netsurf.com/nsm/latest.mktplace.html

Netsurfer Marketplace is the commercial supplement to Netsurfer Digest, which is available on the Web and by e-mail. The Marketplace provides information on companies, services and products, with links to those home pages and, when appropriate, ordering information.

NETView Communications

http://www.netview.com

NETView Communications is a San Jose, Calif. company directing businesses to advertising opportunities on the Internet. Visitors can sample a grab bag of predominantly San Francisco Bay Areas products and services.

NetWorX, Inc., HomePage

http://www.clark.net/pub/networx/networx.html

NetWorX, Inc., an Internet marketing firm, provides an organizational overview, lays out its services, and shows examples of its Webwork at this promotional site. Includes links to current projects.

New South Network Services

http://nsns.com

This online marketing company, based in Tallahassee, Fla., hawks its Web-based business services here. Find out how it can put your company online.

new3 Inc.

http://www.new3.com

new3 Inc., an Internet access provider based in Huntsville, Ala., maintains this promotional site to introduce its Web site design and development services. Visit here to learn about its multimedia capabilities and link to client Web sites.

Next Online

http://www.next.com.au

Produced by Next Media, this Web site describes the Australian publishing company's rapidly growing battery of Internet-based services. Includes information on Next's design, marketing, public relations and systems integration offerings, plus access to online music and gaming resources.

Nielsen Interactive Services

http://www.nielsenmedia.com

At this site, curious visitors can find out about the interactive services of Nielsen Media Research, the same folks who monitor our TV-viewing habits. Visitors can browse the results of Nielsen's Internet demographics survey, read press releases and a Frequently Asked Question file, peruse employment opportunities (you have to be good at asking questions) or delve deeper into company details.

1995 Tenagra Award for Internet Marketing Excellence

http://arganet.tenagra.com/awards95.html

See who demonstrates the best Internet marketing concepts according to the Tenagra Corporation and a panel of marketing experts. In 1995, Federal Express and Ragu Spaghetti Sauce were among the winners. Visit this site to see why they won.

Northern Lights Internet Solutions

http://www.lights.com

Northern Lights Internet Solutions, based in scenic Saskatoon, Saskatchewan, offers Internet marketing strategies for companies diving into cyberspace. Its clients include a safety audit firm, a wheat pool, a local Mexican restaurant and a greeting card printer, with samples online.

Northwest Voyager

http://caboose.com

Based in Battle Ground, Wash., Little Red Caboose Electronic Publishing Group bills itself as a mom-and-pop Internet storefront. Window shop among the commercial businesses and nonprofits residing here or rent space for your own company.

Novia Internetworking

http://www.novia.net

Novia is an Internet service provider and consulting firm based in Nebraska. The company's home page contains information about its connectivity products, publications and consulting services. Includes pricing info and links to customers' sites.

NPiX Interactive

http://npixi.webmaster.net

NPiX Interactive designs electronic marketing and communication materials, including Web sites. Visitors to the NPiX home page can browse the NPiX Interactive Media Gallery.

OneEarth

http://www.1earth.com/1e

OneEarth profiles its Internet services through this site, which also outlines the company's goal of promoting socially and environmentally conscious agendas through the Net. The site includes pricing information and service profiles.

Online Ad Agency

http://advert.com

This online ad agency details its projects and services here, including the latest edition of its "Web Digest for Marketers," a marketing handbook for online initiatives.

On Ramp Inc.

http://metaverse.com/vibe/onramp/onramp.html

With "presences" in major U.S. cities, On Ramp Inc. specializes in building Internet domains for its customers. Visit this page to learn more about the company, its products and its services.

onShore Inc.

http://www.onshore.com

Chicago-based software-development and multimedia-consulting company onShore Inc. maintains this promotional site. Visit here to learn about the company and its offerings, including tasteful Internet presentations, delicious Linux kernel patches, shiny Perl source code and more.

Orbit Interactive Communications

http://www.orbitint.com

This promotional site is the Web home of Orbit Interactive Communications, Inc., a Web design and marketing firm. Find company info, links to sites created and maintained by the company, and an index to other selected Web sites.

Pacific Internet

http://www.pacific.net

An Internet access provider and Web-page designer based in Mendocino, Calif., details its services and rates here. The company also posts links to its customers' home pages and other Internet resources.

PageAlert

http://www.nfic.com/pagealert.html

PageAlert, from Cambridge, Mass.-based New Frontiers Information Corporation, monitors your Web pages and tells you if anyone is having problems accessing them. Find out more here, and take advantage of an introductory offer.

PagOne Internet Advertising Services

http://www.pagone.com

PagOne provides online advertising, Web-page design, site development and placement. Its home page includes a description of services and background information on the company.

PeachWeb Corporation

http://www.peachweb.com

PeachWeb is an Atlanta-based World Wide Web development company that offers Internet consulting and Web-site creation services to the business community.

Phrantic's Flea Market

http://www.quadrunner.com/~phrantic

Phrantic's Flea Market offers affordable Web advertising to small businesses. This home site includes client listings, descriptions of services and price information.

Pixelsight

http://www.pixelsight.com

Pixelsight is a Web-based design service that specializes in user interfaces, page design and icons. The Pixelsight page presents a portfolio of work, as well as downloadable clip art, ASCII designs and user-interface tools.

PlanetCom

http://www.planetcom.com/homepage.html

Maryland-based PlanetCom offers its customers "complete and custom solutions to their Internet needs." This access provider and Web consulting company provides information here about its services, including prices and a client list.

Poppe Tyson Advertising & Public Relations

http://www.poppe.com

Anyone in the marketing, communications or software industries will want to pay a visit to the Sales and Marketing Exchange directory. This site offers free access and inclusion in its extensive, classified directory of professional services.

Portia Communication and Internet Services

http://www.portia.com

Portia Communication and Internet Services offers a comprehensive approach to taking a business online. From system development to content engineering to Internet access, the Ohio company provides soup-to-nuts solutions for internetworking needs.

Potomac Interactive Corporation

http://www.picnet.com

Potomac Interactive Corporation invites businesses who want to set up shop online to engage its Web-site design and management services. The company hosts business pages both on its own server and at the corporate site of the client's choosing.

Presence Information Design

http://www.presence.com

Presence Information Design is a Web-page design firm in Pasadena, California. Visitors here will find a profile of the company, examples of its sleek design work and a client list.

Primenet Web Services

http://com.primenet.com

Primenet is a Web-page design and marketing firm. Visitors to its site will learn about its design services and its commerce server, which uses encryption to ensure safe transactions. The site includes a client list and a demo of the secure server.

Print Publications Related to Business Use of the Internet

http://arganet.tenagra.com/Tenagra/books.html

Maintained by the Tenagra Corp., this publications index concentrates on print-media references to business use of the Internet. Includes indices of books, periodicals and subscription services that help businesses utilize Internet resources for marketing products and services.

Promote-It!

http://www.cam.org/~psarena/promote-it.html

Web Promote offers online marketing services for businesses. Register your site for free here, link to other registration sites or peruse specialty catalogs and "site of the day" picks.

Pronet Global Interactive Business Centre

http://www.pronett.com

British Columbia-based Pronet Enterprises Ltd. provides Internet access and Web-page development for businesses around the world. This commercial page contains pricing and contact information for the company.

PSINet Ltd.

http://www.psinet.co.uk

U.K.-based PSINet (not affiliated with the U.S.-based company of the same name) offers a wide variety of organizational and personal Internet services. Visit here to learn about its Web-based marketing strategies, help resources and software archives.

RayneWaters Studio Arts Online

http://rwsa.com

RayneWaters Studio Arts offers information about its Internet advertising and graphics-design services through this page. It offers links to sites built and maintained by the Seattle-based company along with a sampler of its graphics and online marketing packages.

Renaissance Internet Services

http://www.ro.com

Renaissance Internet Services' (RIS) home page lists businesses (mostly in the Huntsville, Ala., area) that advertise on the Internet using RIS's services. Also here: information about RIS, listings of Internet shopping sites, Web directories and information about Internet tools and privacy issues.

Rescue Island

http://www.comcomsystems.com

The jaunty Rescue Island site calls itself a "safe haven" amidst the Internet's "stormy seas." The site, which includes fun links, a photo gallery a directory search engine of businesses on the Net, is a promotional service from ComCom Systems, purveyor of networked forms-processing and image-archiving services.

Réseau Interordinateurs Scientifique Québécois

http://www.risq.net

RISQ provides Web marketing, design and training services in the Canadian province of Quebec. Link here to read descriptions of services. French only.

Results Direct

http://www.resultsdirect.com

Results Direct specializes in creating Web presentations for businesses. This support page features information on the company's products, services and clients. Web-page tips, marketing advice and entertainment links also are offered here.

Rissa & Järvinen Oy

http://www.mroy.fi

Maintained by a management consulting firm based in Helsinki, this Web site trumpets the company's expertise in information technology and Internet development. Available in Finnish.

RubySlippers

http://www.rubyslippers.com

The wizards at the RubySlippers advertising firm can help a business conjure up a corporate presence on the Web. Visitors also can peek behind the electronic curtain for a look at some clients' home pages.

Sally's Place

http://www.bpe.com

Sally Bernstein is a food enthusiast, Internet provider and media personality in San Francisco. She dubs her page "A Worldwide Perspective on the Finer Things in Life." Visitors here can link to Bernstein's client pages, which celebrate good food and drink, fine restaurants and hot travel spots.

Schober O'Neal Inc.

http://www.schoneal.com

This promotional site, maintained by Schober O'Neal Inc., provides information on the Web marketing agency. Visitors will find a Frequently Asked Questions file illuminating the Austin, Texas, company and its services.

Sea Horse Designs

http://www.seahorse.com

Billed as an "Internet ad connection," the home page of Sea Horse Designs attempts to attract cli-ents to its services. Includes information about the company's consultation, estimating and software offerings, plus tips for Internet advertisers.

Select HyperMedia

http://www.selectsite.com

Select Hypermedia is a California firm specializing in Web publishing and consultation. Visitors to its Web site will find examples of clients' pages, detailed information about its Web-design services and pricing information.

Shade's Landing Inc.

http://www.shadeslanding.com

Minnesota-based Shade's Landing Inc. lets visitors know what's cool in the world of Web design and marketing. The company lists its services and shines the light on award-winning sample pages.

Sharrow Advertising and Marketing Resource Center

http://www.dnai.com/~sharrow

Sharrow shows off its stuff in this inventive and amusing example of a corporate home page. Comprehensive yet easy-to-read information on the company's promotion service is provided, as well as hilarious parodies of advertisements, an arch history of sex in advertising, advice on creating usable Web pages and other fun links.

Silicon Forest Media Inc.

http://www.sfm.com/about-sfm.html

Silicon Forest Media Inc., a San Francisco-based Web-design company, provides corporate information at this page. Visitors also will find personnel and contact information and an index of clients' pages.

SilverPlatter World

http://www.silverplatter.com

SilverPlatter Information, a company that assists others in adding sites to the Web, provides this resource page. Visitors can learn more about the company and its Web technology, products and services.

Slik Designs

http://www.ssp-ii.com/ssp/Slik

The home page of Slik Designs, a multimedia company specializing in Web development for business and marketing, offers details about the Los Angeles-based business. Browsers can view samples of Slik's creative work, obtain pricing information, and use a secure ordering form for Web-design services.

Smart Store Virtual

http://smartstore.ac.com/smartstore

Andersen Consulting sponsors research and dialogue related to virtual retailing and other electronic-commerce issues at this corporate site. Includes links to top-notch cyber shops and Andersen's home page.

Sojourn Systems Ltd.

http://www.sojourn.com

Internet management for businesses and individual users, including full Web services, are available from Sojourn Systems Ltd. Visitors can learn about the company at this site, which also features a listing of classified ads.

Solutions Online

http://www.solon.com

Solutions Online is a consulting company for businesses interested in establishing a presence on the Internet. Includes descriptions of services, account information, links to client sites and listings of Internet resources.

Southwest Multimedia

http://www.swmm.com

Southwest Multimedia's Web site explains the company's products and services. Those in the market for catalogs on disk, multimedia presentations or media-buying assistance can peruse the company's newsletters or sample its work here.

Southwind Technologies Inc.

http://www.southwind.com

Internet access provider Southwind Technologies Inc. also offers computer networking and programming services. Visitors to Southwind's corporate home page can learn about the company's rates and sample its clients' Web sites.

SpectraCom

http://www.spectracom.com

SpectraCom is a Wisconsin-based marketing and Web-page design firm. Visitors to its promotional page will get an overview of the company and its services.

Spinners Inc.

http://www.spinners.com/welcome.html

The home page for Spinners Inc. trumpets the company's ability to build interactive Web sites. This page features links to its clients' Web sites and information about its products and services.

Steve Rapport's Web World

http://hammers.wwa.com/hammers

The home page of Steve Rapport promotes his Web-design company, Ironworks Designs, and his activities as a celebrity photographer. Examples of his works in both areas are featured here.

Streams Online Media Development

http://streams.com

This is the home page of Streams Online Media Development, a Chicago, Ill.-based company specializing in online media planning. Visitors can read about Streams' Internet media planning and assessment tool "Lily Pad" or find out about current employment opportunities with Stream Online.

Strickland & Associates

http://www.strickland.com

Strickland & Associates describes itself as "a full-service information technology consulting firm and Internet presence provider." Visit the company's home page to find out more about the firm's background, services and clients.

Studio Archetype

http://www.cmdesigns.com

Formerly known as Clement Mok Designs, Studio Archetype has produced some of the world's most outstanding Web pages. Visit here to learn about the company and its client base, including Nintendo and 24 Hours in Cyberspace.

Studio X

http://www.nets.com

Located in Santa Fe, N.M., Studio X is an experimental media company and Internet access provider. It gives an overview of its services, including Web site design and storage, and posts a gallery of its work here.

SuperBusiness NET Inc.

http://www.sbusiness.com

This promotional page is maintained by Super-Business NET Inc., a consulting firm and network space provider offering Web site design services. Visitors are invited to learn more about the company and its services here.

Supernet Club

http://www.itl.net/barclaysquare

The Supernet Club tracks movements of the Information Highway to inform developers of future applications about Internet usage habits. Visitors may enter the site as members or as guests, and once inside can roam the club's selected offerings, including interactive sites as well as discount shopping and travel opportunities.

SWA Web Advertising and Development

http://www.metropolis.nl/~swa

SWA Web Advertising and Development provides a Web-page design and maintenance service. Visitors to this site will find descriptions of services, pricing information, marketing and advertising expertise. Dutch and English.

Tab Net Internet Services

http://www.tab.com

Tab Net Internet Services hosts the "Austin Minority Business Journal" and the "Home Business Review" on its Web server. Find out about the business-oriented connectivity products offered by the Texas-based access provider and Web site designer.

Tachyon Communications Corp.

http://www.tach.net

Tachyon Communications Corp. is an Internet service and presence provider based in Melbourne, Fla. Visit here to learn about its wide range of services, from standard dial-up connections to worldwide Internet-based advertising campaigns. In English, French, Spanish, Italian, German, Nihongo and Hangukmal.

Target Marketing

http://www.targeting.com

Target Marketing, a firm in Santa Barbara, Calif., wants to help you learn how to make money off of the Web. Consult this promotional site to review the firm's strategy and design services.

Telebase Systems Inc.

http://www.telebase.com

This corporate Web site describes Telebase System Inc.'s five Internet services: World Wide Library, Music Boulevard, Stones World, David Bowie Outside and EasyNet 2.0. Includes details about the company and links to its online offerings.

TeleCommons Development Group Research Home Page

http://tdg.uoguelph.ca

Canadian-based TeleCommons Development Group offers information about its research activities on this page. It also includes details about the company, which attempts to provide creative Internet and networking solutions for communities, businesses and organizations.

Tenagra

http://arganet.tenagra.com/Tenagra/tenagra.html

The far-flung Tenagra Corp. provides clients with expertise in Internet marketing, advertising, public relations and Web site design. Its corporate Web site provides details on Tenagra's services, along with company background, client listings and news items.

Tenagra Award 94

http://arganet.tenagra.com/Tenagra/awards94.html

Internet marketing and consulting business Tenagra Corp. announces its awards for the top five business sites on the Internet in this online press release. Browsers can read about and link to the sites, and learn why Tenagra selected them.

Texas Internet Consulting

http://www.tic.com/index.html

Based in Austin, Texas, this firm does network and open-systems consulting. Visitors to its corporate home page will find information about the organization, along with reprints of articles written by the firm's founders.

Thomas Consulting

http://nwlink.com/joker

Thomas Consulting provides Web pages and Internet consulting for businesses. Information on Web-site design and consulting, and access to the Seattle-based company's portfolio, are offered at this home page.

ThoughtPort Authority Inc.

http://www.thoughtport.com

The ThoughtPort Authority Inc. is a growing national Internet-access provider (offering connections in such hipster locales as New York and Springfield, Mo.) that also offers network solutions and Web site design.

TIESoft Home Page

http://www.tiesoft.com/tiesoft

TIESoft, a Quebec, Canada-based Internet marketing services company, maintains this site to introduce its World Wide Web publishing projects. Visit here to see client Web sites and find instructional information on setting up your own Web page.

Trade Point Tampere Finland

http://www.tradepoint.fi

Finnish businesses that have joined the online gold rush are indexed at the Trade Point Tampere Finland site. The page, part of a United Nations group working to promote trade online, invites visitors to learn about the program's philosophy. In English.

Tradewatch International

http://www.tradewatch.com

Tradewatch International is an online business directory. The company provides free listings for businesses and offers to design larger web sites for a fee.

TradeWave Galaxy

http://galaxy.einet.net

TradeWave, a premier provider of Web services for business, maintains the Galaxy site, a guide to worldwide info services and business news coupled with a handy Internet subject index. Visitors who like what they see of this newfangled Internet can then talk with TradeWave about creating a "corporate Virtual Private Internet."

TriNet Services Inc.

http://trinet.com

TriNet Services Inc. is a Web consulting, marketing and training service based in North Carolina. Its corporate home page offers descriptions of company services, staff and employment listings and links to clients' portfolios.

Trytel Internet Inc.

http://www.trytel.com

Ottawa-based Trytel Internet Inc. provides Internet access, Web-page design, sales, repairs and other services. This site includes information about the company's services and prices, along with links to customer home pages.

UltraPLEX Information Systems

http://www.uplex.net

UltraPLEX Information Systems provides Web-page development services for individuals and businesses. The company's Web site includes descriptions of UltraPLEX's services and fees.

Unirom Internet Services

http://www.unirom.com

Unirom offers information at this site on its Web consulting, Web design and related services. Storefronts such as the CD-ROM Store and Comprehensive Connections, which markets monitors and accessories, also are available here.

Up All Night

http://www.allnight.com

San Francisco-based Up All Night produces custom Web sites for a variety of businesses and organizations. Visitors to its home page will find service descriptions, staff profiles and links to client creations.

UUNET Primer and Business Guide

http://www.uu.net/primer.htm

Internet newbies looking for direction can find basic as well as advanced techniques at this site, focusing on the business of the Internet. Nationwide Internet access provider, UUNET, serves up tips for business people looking to get the most out of the online market.

ValleyNet

http://www.valleynet.com

ValleyNet Communications of Fresno, Calif., is an Internet access provider that doubles as a commercial Web-page designer. This promotional site provides links to client home pages, a tutorial on creating Web pages and a directory of businesses.

Veronica Internet

http://www.veronica.nl

The Veronica Interactive Plaza offers international companies a way to "reach the thousands of Internet users in Holland who are young, hip, and searching for that special cyber-something." Companies and browsers can check out retail and service opportunities and offerings. In Dutch and English.

Vidya Media Ventures

http://www.vidya.com

Vidya Media Ventures takes potential customers on a tour of client Web sites to demonstrate the company's Web-design, multimedia and online marketing services. Visitors can review the multimedia publisher's products and services at this promotional site.

Virtual Advertising

http://www.halcyon.com/zz/top.html

The Virtual Advertising home page provides details about the company's Internet advertising and product-placement services. Includes pricing information and an index of the firm's clients.

Virtual Artists

http://www.va.com.au/va

Visitors will find specialists in the fields of Web authoring, video and radio production and Macintosh software consulting at the Virtual Artists page. This Australian design enterprise demonstrates its expertise here with a sampling of pages it has developed for its clients.

Virtual Creations

http://www.creation.com

Web-development company Virtual Creations provides information on its services here. Includes a puzzle page.

VirtualLynx

http://www.virtualynx.com

An Internet marketing firm details its services on this promotional page. Visitors here can browse through its commerce market and classifieds or link to the company's pick for cool sites.

Visual Radio, Inc.

http://www.visualradio.com

Visual Radio, Inc., is a new-media and Internet service company based in New York City. Visitors to its promotional site will find details on the company, its clients, and its services, which include Web design and Net marketing.

Vivid Studios

http://www.vivid.com

San Francisco-based Vivid Studios is a multimedia production company specializing in the development of interactive Web sites. Visitors can read about its products and browse job listings here, or embark on a virtual tour of Multimedia Gulch, "home of green burritos and the hippest nerds on earth."

Voice Creative Engineering

http://fleet.britain.eu.net/cims/herald html/home.html

Based in Glasgow, Scotland, the multimedia division of Caledonian Information and Media Services describes its "turnkey" Internet packages for businesses wanting to venture into the wired world here. Visitors can virtually tour the company's design studios or sample sites created for clients.

Volant TurnPike

http://turnpike.net/index.html

This commercial site is sponsored by the Volant Corporation, a hosting server and Web marketing company. Visitors will find an interactive map with links to shopping, user forums, libraries and other commercial and non-commercial pages.

Washington Web

http://www.washweb.net

An Internet access provider called Internet Interstate presents Washington Web, with resources on and from the Washington, D.C., area. Includes the arts, business, education, news, travel and more. A demonstration page shows features that clients can include on their own Web pages.

WebCorp

http://www.webcorp.com

WebCorp's home page features audio of historical speeches, a "randomizer" of bits of speeches from politicians that sound "frighteningly realistic," images from New Orleans cemeteries and much more.

The Web Foundry

http://www.medical-web.com

The Web Foundry is an Internet service provider and Web-design company boasting commercial clients and reduced rates for nonprofits. The company has designed and hosts such sites as The Medical Web and a bed and breakfast guide. The company offers info on its "particular expertise in applying database technology to Web design."

WebLink Inc.

http://www.weblink.com

Based in Berkeley, Calif., WebLink Inc. offers Internet marketing services. The company introduces itself here, providing details on its custom Web-site designs, online catalogs, interactive forms, e-mail and more. Includes links to client sites and other business-related resources.

Webmedia

http://www.webmedia.com

Webmedia designs and maintains—what else?—Web sites. Visitors can learn about the company's services and clients on this promotional page.

WebNet Technologies

http://www.wn.com

WebNet Technologies is a Web-page design firm in Dallas, Texas. Visit here for a look at its client pages, services and prices.

Web Professionals Inc.
http://www.professionals.com

Web Professionals Inc. primarily traffics in design and publishing services for businesses on the Web. The company also provides dial-up access to Cupertino, Calif.-area residents. Find a run-down of services and rates at this promotional site.

WebSavvy Internet Consulting Sources
http://www.websavvy.com

A Dubuque, Iowa, company that specializes in on-line marketing and Web-site development outlines its expertise and services here. Examples of its work are posted: Its clients include the Windows INTERNetworking headquarters and the city of Dubuque.

WebTrack
http://www.webtrack.com

This is the home page of WebTrack, an online service providing information and resources for on-line marketing and advertisement. Access WebTrack's services here, including directories, newsletters, tracking software and databases of major U.S. advertisers.

Webworks Internet Consulting Co.
http://www.ari.net/webworks

A Web-page design and consulting company markets its services on this page. The site features a general collection of links to commercial sites, development resources and search engines.

Westward Connections
http://www.westward.com

Albuquerque, N.M.-based Westward Communications provides a variety of electronic communications and marketing services. Visit here to learn about its Web site creation and online promotional capabilities. Clients include local public broadcasters and outdoor events.

Whitey's Web Works
http://www.rmii.com/~whitey

Whitey's Web Works is a Boulder, Colo.-based Web consulting company specializing in site development, online marketing and research, and Internet tutoring. Links to customer pages and HTML tutorials are available.

What's New on Wimsey
http://www.wimsey.com

Burnaby, Canada-based Wimsey Internet Consulting maintains this site for company news. Visitors can learn about recent activities and link to local commercial resources and publications.

Wilmington Internet Service Enterprises Inc.
http://www.wilmington.net

Wilmington Internet Service Enterprises Inc. is a North Carolina company offering promotional Internet services to area businesses. WISE's home page serves up contact and service information, plus Wilmington Online, an interactive magazine about the greater Wilmington, N.C., area.

WinNET Communications Inc.
http://www.win.net

Lousiville, Ky.-based WinNET presents its menu of Internet access and site-design services through this home page. The site explains who WinNET is, describes its services, and includes links to its customers' Web sites, which include pages for local radio stations and a fan site for the guy who starred in "The Equalizer."

Wognum Art
http://www.pi.se/wognum-art

Wognumart is a full-service design studio located in Stockholm. It posts an online portfolio here, along with details about its services, including Web design, typography and CD programming.

Wombat on the Web
http://www.wombat.com.au/wombat

A South Australia Web marketing firm posts links to commercial, nonprofit, governmental and entertainment sites here. The site also contains tourist and travel information.

World IntuAction Press
http://www.crocker.com/intuaction

World IntuAction Press specializes in helping businesses maintain a presence on the Web. Visit this promotional home page to learn more about the company and its services, plus find links to its clients' pages.

World Publishing Systems Home Page
http://www.wps.com.au

Australia's InterNet World Publishing Systems publishes business, real-estate and travel information on the Web. This page also includes travel and tourism notes, employment and general Web information.

World Wide Business Center
http://wwbc.com

The World Wide Business Center profiles companies, offers training information, helps search for employees, markets business services and hosts Web sites. Based in Georgia, site of the 1996 Summer Olympics, the center also lists homes that are available for rent in the area!

World Wide Web Consulting, Inc.
http://www.goodies.com

World Wide Web Consulting, Inc. maintains this site to promote the businesses, real-estate listings and entertainment resources of Riverhead, New York. Links are also provided to the city's Web-based local government resources.

X Communications' World
http://www.webcom.com/~xcomm

X-Communications, a New York City-based multimedia design firm, shows off its efforts on this sleek page. It promotes its services, but also provides a site called Music View, which "provides a cornucopia of cool crap from an eclectic selection of artists that have appeared on the Music View Radio Show."

X'it Group
http://www.xgroup.com

X'it Group, a SoCal Web site developer, promotes it services in Web design, multimedia engineering and traditional graphic work here. Visitors will get an overview of the firm and its philosophy and can link to examples of its online work.

Xynergy Interactive Web Services
http://www.nets.com/xynergy.html

Xynergy Interactive Web Services tempts businesses with the come-on, "Your virtual wish is our command!" Find out what the Santa Fe, N.M.-based company can do to hook your business up to the Internet by checking out this promotional site. Get a look at some sample Web-page designs, check out Xynergy's client portfolio, and read about Xynergy's business philosophy.

Zyzzyva Enterprises
http://www.zyzzyva.com

Zyzzyva Enterprises pitches its Web-design and consulting services at its corporate home page. Find out how Zyzzyva built sites for clients such as Lincoln Online and the Nebraska Who's Who, plus what they can do for you.

PUBLIC RELATIONS

Business Wire Home Page
http://www.hnt.com/bizwire

Business Wire dubs itself "The International Media Relations Wire Service." Visitors can learn how Business Wire might help their business get its message to media outlets around the world.

Morse-McFadden Communications Home Page

http://www.morsepr.com

Morse-McFadden Communications is a public-relations firm in Washington State with an advanced-technology clientele that stretches "from Budapest to Silicon Valley."

Niehaus Ryan Haller Public Relations, Inc.

http://www.nrh.com:8400

San Francisco-based hi-tech public relations firm Niehaus Ryan Haller maintains this promotional site. Visit here to find industry news, client lists, and a variety of reports for companies trying to learn the art of communicating on the Internet.

Oak Ridge Public Relations Inc.

http://www.oakridge.com

Oak Ridge Public Relations Inc. of Cupertino, Calif., specializes in technology and business promotion. The company's promotional page provides information about the company and its services, along with a client list, a newsletter and ordering instructions for those interested in snagging a copy of "The High Tech Joke Book."

Ogilvy & Mather Home Page

http://www.ogilvy.com

Public relations giant Ogilvy & Mather is online here. Browsers can download samples of the firm's print, radio and film work, or join in the Ask Ogilvy forum for small businesses. The firm also gives an overview of its online services here.

PR Newswire

http://www.prnewswire.com/

PR Newswire has been a distributor of corporate news since 1954. This online version of the wire service offers news from public and private companies, government agencies, associations and organizations. Includes a number of links to related sites.

Wiley Brooks Co.

http://www.wileyco.com/

Seattle's Wiley Brooks Co. is a public-relations firm "specializing in damage control, crisis management, media relations and advocacy." Visit the company's Wiley Web to learn more about the firm and its services.

wolfBayne Communications

http://www.bayne.com/wolfBayne

Colorado-based wolfBayne Communications introduces its public-relations and Internet-marketing plans on this home page. The site contains a calendar of upcoming seminars and workshops along with a selection of articles about marketing communications on the Internet.

BANKS, BANKING, AND FINANCIAL INSTITUTIONS

ASSOCIATIONS AND ORGANIZATIONS

Federal Deposit Insurance Corporation

http://www.fdic.gov

Founded in 1933 by the U.S. Congress, the Federal Deposit Insurance Corporation "promotes the safety and soundness" of the nation's banking system. Visit its home page for current assets sales and information on financial institutions across the United States.

Financial Services Technology Consortium

http://www.fstc.org/

This consortium of financial-services providers, national laboratories, universities, industrial powers and government agencies aims to enhance the competitiveness of the U.S. financial-services industry. Topics featured at this site include fraud prevention and electronic commerce and checking.

BANKS AND ONLINE BANKING

CREDIT UNIONS

Credit Union Home Page

http://www.cu.org

Maintained by the Florida Credit Union League Inc., a nonprofit association of Florida-based credit unions, this home page shares statistical and consumer information and explains the credit-union philosophy. Include pointers to individual credit unions' home pages.

Credit Union National Association and Affiliates

http://www.cuna.org

The Credit Union National Association and Affiliates maintains this site to promote its industry's unique delivery of financial services. Discover what a credit union is and how to join one, plus find news and consumer financial information.

Stanford Federal Credit Union

http://www.sfcu.org

Owned and operated by members of the Stanford University community, Palo Alto, Calif.-based Stanford Federal Credit Union maintains this promotional site. Visitors will find information on its financial services, including car loans and home mortgages.

CYBER-CASH AND MONEY SUBSTITUTES

CyberCash

http://www.cybercash.com

The future of doing business and commerce—without money. See Editor's Choice.

First Virtual Account Application

http://www.fv.com/merchant.html

Working toward becoming the Internet's answer to secure financial transactions, First Virtual offers registration at this site for its "virtual accounts." With this service, users can buy or sell without passing credit card numbers through cyberspace.

LETSystems

http://www.gmlets.u-net.com/

Claiming that "money is only information," LETSystems aims to re-invent the world's exchange systems. Visit its home page to learn about the group's theories, practices and information resources.

Money - Past, Present and Future

http://www.ex.ac.uk/~RDavies/arian/money.html

Maintained by a science librarian from Exeter University, this site offers a discussion of the evolution of currency, up to the dawning of the age of "cyber-cash." Visit here for a variety of related Web links and articles from the book, "History of Money from Ancient Times to the Present Day."

NetBank

http://www.teleport.com/~netcash

Software Agents, Inc. maintains this site to introduce its NetBank NetCash system, offering "easy, natural and secure" cash transactions over the Internet. Visitors will find service descriptions and cash standards and security updates.

NetCash

http://www.netbank.com/~netcash

NetCash, a service of NetBank, allows online vendors and its customers to conduct "virtual" cash transactions over the Internet. At this home page, visitors can get more information about accessing the system and how it works.

Net1

http://www.netchex.com

Net1 is the online home of NetChex, a virtual checking account that facilitates online transactions. The page presents information about NetChex and its technology, including a virtual marketplace.

Versatile Virtual Vending

http://rainer.bnt.com/vvv.html

The home page of Versatile Virtual Vending, a cross-platform software system that provides a secure front end for online retail ordering, allows visitors to view a demonstration copy of the software and obtain additional system info.

INTERNATIONAL

Asian Development Bank

http://www.asiandevbank.org

Promoting the economic and social progress of its member countries, the Asian Development Bank maintains this site to introduce its financial services and programs. Visit here for news releases, environmental impact assessments, project profiles and related resources.

Bank of Montreal

http://www.bmo.com

Visitors to the Bank of Montreal's home page will find an overview of the bank's services, including current rates, home mortgage information, bank news and Canadian economic forecasts. Small-business help and mutual funds info is also available.

Banque Nationale de Paris

http://www.calvacom.fr/BNP

BNP, an international banking concern, provides financial news and information about its investments and global projects. Also offered here is a review of the bank's more personal services, including checkingsavings accounts to investment services. In French and English.

Canada Trust Mortgage Co.

http://www.canadatrust.com

Canada Trust, one of the country's largest non-bank financial institutions, maintains this site to introduce its personal and corporate services. In addition to an extensive index of financial information, visitors will find links to local and national consumer organizations.

CCF

http://www.calvacom.fr/ccf/accueil.html

Paris-based financial institution CCF provides information here on its corporate structure and its latest service additions. Includes an extensive index of finance-related World Wide Web links and publications. In French and English.

Rabobank

http://rabobank.info.nl

The Dutch bank Rabobank supplies a biweekly survey of the Dutch economy, an economic survey of The Netherlands, agribusiness reports and socioeconomic reports on Dutch regions. The bank also provides information on its structure and services. Available in Dutch, with some information in English.

Royal Bank of Canada

http://www.royalbank.com

The Royal Bank of Canada offers details about its personal financial services, business banking, international services and royal mutual funds here. Visitors also will find corporate news and employment opportunities listings. Available in English and French.

Royal Bank of Scotland

http://www.royalbankscot.co.uk

The United Kingdom's sixth-largest financial institution, The Royal Bank of Scotland, maintains this promotional site. Visitors will find industry news, financial service descriptions and updated account interest rate listings.

Toronto-Dominion Bank

http://www.tdbank.ca/tdbank

The Toronto-Dominion Bank provides information about its financial services and resources here. The site also includes answers to questions about homes and personal finances.

---

a2z EDITOR'S CHOICE

CyberCash

http://www.cybercash.com

If we can believe what we read, it's time to roll up that penny collection, because cash money as we know it will soon be history. Online financial transactions are fast becoming a reality, and several competing technologies are already trying to divvy up the digital pie. The cyber-cash faction, which has several heavy-hitting allies, describes the principles and advantages of cashless commerce at this site. Find something you want to buy online? CyberCash offers "secure purchases" for consumers and merchants on the Web. You can even use it for "pay as you play" video games. O, brave new world ...—*Reviewed by Joe Williams*

World Bank Gopher Menu

gopher:ftp.worldbank.org/1

Visitors to the World Bank gopher server can access general information about this international-development bank as well as World Bank publications and information about African Development Studies.

PUBLIC INFORMATION RESOURCES

Bayshore Trust Company

http://www.bayshoretrust.com/

Boasting its place as the "world's first financial institution to offer on-line loan approval on the Internet," Bayshore Trust Company requires visitors to use an SSL (Secure Sockets Layer) compliant Web browser. Find out more about the browser and Bayshore Trust via this gateway.

College Money Matters

http://www.txbanc.com/

Signet Bank's resource for money-hungry college students includes information on federal student aid, loan options and alternatives. Visitors here can browse the titles in Signet's virtual bookstore or read informational texts relating to college budget planning.

Currencies and Currency-Exchange

http://www.wiso.gwdg.de/ifbg/currency.html

Before leaving on that trip abroad, visit this currency-exchange site hosted by the Institute of Finance and Banking at Germany's University of Gottingen. Visitors can access several exchange rate sites, as well as explanatory information about different currencies.

Czech National BankEUnet Gopher Menu

gopher://gopher.eunet.cz/11/Documents/Economy/kursy

The Czech National Bank and EUnet Czechia collaborate to bring this currency guide to the Web. Visitors to this gopher server will find an index of past and present world currency exchange rates.

First Access Network Library

http://www.powersource.com/ccs/

First Union Corporation opens the door to its First Access Network online library through this page. It contains information about credit services and credit-related products as well as the banking industry. Check out a consumer's guide to credit and what every consumer needs to know about plastic.

Informal Credit Homepage

http://titsoc.soc.titech.ac.jp/titsoc/higuchi-lab/icm/index.html

Japan's Tokyo Institute of Technology maintains this site for information on "alternative non-con-

ventional financial systems." Visit this site to learn about informal credit markets, offering consumers the advantages of unregulated and easily accessible money supplies.

Money Abroad—Europe

http://www.inria.fr/robotvis/personnel/laveau/money-faq/europe.html

If you can't wait for a uniform European currency, visit this site to learn the basics of currency exchange and banking in Europe. Includes coin and bill denominations, travelers'-check exchange charges and information on the presence of automated teller machines for most European countries.

Swiss Banks Directory

http://www.swconsult.ch/chbanks/index.html

Swiss bank accounts have long been favored by discrete customers worldwide because of the tight lips of Swiss bank officials. Netizens hankering for their own Swiss account can get contact information here for hundreds of Swiss banks as well as link to other pages in peace-loving Switzerland.

UNITED STATES

Bank of America

http://www.bofa.com

Bank of America, the financial institution begun by an Italian immigrant and established during the great 1906 earthquake crisis in San Francisco, offers a "money tip of the day," credit cards, special offers on computer checks, home loans, business and corporate banking services, and an interactive way to figure how much you should be saving for retirement.

Bank of the Commonwealth

http://www.infi.net/boc

Norfolk, Va.-based Bank of the Commonwealth provides a wide range of commercial banking and financial services to individuals and organizations in the Hampton Roads area. Visitors to its home page will find financial product descriptions, certificate rates and customer service resources.

Barnett Banks Inc.

http://www.barnett.com

Jacksonville, Fla.-based Barnett Banks maintains this site to introduce its financial products and services. Includes tourism and commercial resources for cities in Florida and South Georgia.

Citibank

http://www.citicorp.com

Citibank, a U.S.-headquartered banking corporation with branches in more than 40 countries, provides information here on its latest services. Includes a branch-locator feature to find the Citibank nearest you.

Compass Bank: CompassWeb

http://www.compassweb.com

Compass Bank is a financial institution with offices in Alabama, Texas and Florida. It offers this home page to provide information about its services and products as well as mortgage rates and branch locations.

Federal Reserve Bank Philadelphia

http://www.phil.frb.org/

They won't be offering you a Visa card, but if you need more information on the Federal Reserve Bank of Philadelphia, visit this home page. Visitors can get more information on this bank or reserve banks and the U.S. monetary system in general.

First Hawaiian Bank

http://www.fhb.com/fhb

Actor Pat Morita greets visitors to the First Hawaiian Bank page. Besides reading the obligatory account information, prospective college students can check out the availability of student loans and job seekers can find out what it's like to work at FHB.

First Union Corp.—The Internet Cyberbank

http://www.firstunion.com

Charlotte, N.C.-based First Union National Bank, touting itself as "the original Cyberbank," maintains this site to introduce its Internet-based banking services. Visit here for investment reports, economic forecasts, employment opportunities and online credit applications.

J.P. Morgan & Co. Inc.

http://www.jpmorgan.com

Global financial services firm J.P. Morgan serves governments, corporations, individuals and privately held firms through a variety of financial planning capabilities. Visitors to its home page will find company news, product and service descriptions and employment opportunities.

Kingfield Bank

http://www.maine.com/kingfield

Kingfield Bank in Kingfield, Maine, maintains this site to provide current rates for loans, CDs, IRAs, savings accounts and money markets. Visit here for the latest on all its financial packages and a look at other local business sectors.

Merchants Bank

http://www.bnt.com/~mnb

Aurora, Ill.-based Merchants Bank maintains this site to introduce its consumer and business financial services. Includes credit and loan information, corporate profile and branch locations.

NationsBank

http://www.nationsbank.com

NationsBank, a retail banking institution serving the American Southeast, Southwest and Mid-Atlantic states, maintains this promotional site. Visitors will find financial services descriptions, press releases, investor's resources and more.

On Finances

http://www.crestar.com

Sure money talks. But when it does, can you understand it? Click on the lucky penny at the On Finance page for financial tips and banking needs from Crestar Bank. Includes rates and mortgage information.

The People's Bank

http://www.peoples.com

The People's Bank, "the largest independent bank in Connecticut," links visitors with information about its financial services for both consumers and businesses.

Wells Fargo & Co.

http://www.wellsfargo.com

West Coast banking institution Wells Fargo introduces its financial products and services at this corporate home page. Includes information on personal finance, small business loans, online banking and commercial services.

BDO Dunwoody

http://www.bdo.ca

Accounting and consulting firm BDO Dunwoody, based in Toronto and with more than 70 offices across Canada, specializes in accounting for independent and community-based organizations. Visitors to its home page will find service descriptions, online document libraries and a branch office directory.

KMPG Canada

http://www.kpmg.ca

The Canadian arm of the accounting and management-consulting megafirm KMPG maintains this promotional site. Visitors can look up locations of offices, descriptions of services, online tax information and career opportunities without having to suit up.

Rutgers Accounting Web

http://www.rutgers.edu/Accounting/raw.htm

This accounting information resource provides number crunchers with educational materials and professional tools, including a software shopping guide. Includes links to Rutgers University's various accounting departments.

ADVICE AND OPPORTUNITIES

BidCast

http://www.bidcast.com

BidCast is a service that brings together government purchasers and suppliers. After bid notices are found, BidCast notifies the appropriate supplier to initiate the bidding process. Federal, state and municipal bids are included in this service as well as grant opportunities. Find a registration form here to participate.

Business Incorporating Guide

http://www.corporate.com

Wilmington, Del.-based consultancy Corporate Agents maintains this site for a guide to incorporating businesses. Visitors to this promotional site will find legal resources, government publications and helpful tips for seeking corporate protection in the American business market.

BUSINESS AND CORPORATE NEWS AND SERVICES

ACCOUNTING

Accountants Home Page

http://www.servtech.com/re/acct.html

All the latest in the world of accounting. See Editor's Choice.

ANet

http://anet.scu.edu.au/ANetHomePage.html

Part of the International Accounting Network, the Australia-based ANet provides an electronic forum for the discussion of accounting and auditing issues. Visit its home page for course offerings, conference updates and service descriptions.

---

a2z EDITOR'S CHOICE

Accountants Home Page

http://www.servtech.com/re/acct.html

The rough-and-tumble world of accounting isn't for everyone, but if you have the mettle to crunch the numbers, come hoist a flagon of mead with your mates at the Accountant's Home Page. This site, maintained by Rochester, N.Y.-based Cohen Computer Consulting, offers a jackpot of links to public and private accounting organizations, business and financial news, tax law, workplace humor (Dilbert, anyone?) and trade publications such as True Accounting, Lusty Ledgers and Two-Fisted Tales of Embezzlement (just kidding).—*Reviewed by Joe Williams*

WWW Sites for Accounting

The Accounting Professional's Choice

Top financial sites
- What's your government doing? THOMAS: Legislative Information on the Internet
- Tax forms and official tax advice from the IRS. The Internal Revenue Service
- What plans are they making for your money in Albany? The New York State Assembly
- Business advice for small businesses. The Small Business Administration
- Links, lists and home to the AICPA Microcomputer Conference home page. K2 Enterprises WWW Server

Click on the link below to go to the area of interest:
- Governmental Resources
- Other Tax related resources
- Accounting and Educational Organizations
- Business on the Web
- Cash and Stocks on the Web
- Business resources on the Web
- CPAs on the Web
- These don't really belong here, but ...

CyberSpace Japan

http://www.csj.co.jp

CyberSpace Japan is a resource for those interested in doing business in Japan. Visitors will find classified ads, financial advice, management consulting and critical tips on opening an office in Japan. In English and Japanese.

Grantseeker's Resource Center

http:oeonline.com/~ricknot2/grant seekers.html

The Grantseeker's Resource Center specializes in helping organizations, businesses and individuals get their hands on grant funding. Visitors to this Web site can learn about the center's research, grant-writing and educational services.

Internet Business Opportunity Showcase

http://www.ibos.com/pub/ibos

The Internet Business Opportunity Showcase, a service of Maryland-based NetWorks Marketing, provides a variety of business-related resources through this site. Visit here for links to franchise offerings, network marketing opportunities, online business services and more.

NASA Office of Procurement

http://www.hq.nasa.gov/office/procurement

The U.S. National Aeronautics and Space Administration maintains this site to offer information to businesses competing for upcoming contracts. Visitors will find an acquisition forecast, procurement initiatives, the "Procurement Countdown" newsletter, and links to various facilities' procurement home pages.

ARCHIVES AND INDICES

Finance.Wat.ch

http://finance.wat.ch

Finance.Wat.ch provides informational services to people interested in financial and investing news. Available databases cover topics such as futures, options, world indices and more. Also available is news of the stock exchange and the financial yellow pages.

International Business Resources on the World Wide Web

http://ciber.bus.msu.edu/busres.htm

This Web site is packed with links to news, journals, directories and other indices of interest to the global commerce community. Maintained by Michigan State University Center for International Business Education and Research, it includes governmental and corporate Internet directories.

Lookup USA

http://www.abii.com

Omaha, Neb.-based American Business Information, Inc. maintains this site for free access to its database of more than 11 million business listings. Visit here to locate organizations across the United States organized by name and type of business.

National Trade Data Bank

http://www.stat-usa.gov/BEN/Services/ntdbhome.html

The National Trade Data Bank is the U.S. government's "most comprehensive" source of international trade data. Registration is available at this site, and subscribers have access to thousands of files, including export information, statistics, market research reports, overseas contacts and trade opportunities.

U.S. International Trade Statistics

http://www.census.gov/ftp/pub/foreign-trade/www

The U.S. International Trade Statistics site provides data on American exports. Includes a guide to using the database, a "who's who" listing and press reports.

University of Michigan Economic Data Gopher

gopher://una.hh.lib.umich.edu:70/11/ebb

Maintained by the University of Michigan Library, this gopher server offers a variety of in-depth reports from the U.S. Department of Commerce. Visitors will find an extensive index of economic materials and a keyword search of its contents.

ASSOCIATIONS AND ORGANIZATIONS

Electronic Commerce Association

http://www.globalx.net/eca

Ottawa, Ontario-based Electronic Commerce Association provides networking and educational opportunities for members of high-technology industries. Visitors to its home page will find events calendars, membership information and professional resources.

Registered International Correspondents for Exporting

http://www.calvacom.fr/ccio/index.html

This French organization dedicated to developing international business opportunities, offers general information on its services here. Visitors can read about ongoing projects and browse international company profiles.

Texas Association of Mexican American Chambers of Commerce

http://www.tamacc.org

This Texas organization, which serves as an advocate for the Mexican-American business community, presents information on its convention, leadership and corporate partners here. The site also features the Texas Business Center, with information on business opportunities, legislative summaries and more.

U.S. Chamber of Commerce

http://www.chamber-of-commerce.com

The Chamber of Commerce is a venerable American institution, bringing together a locality's commercial resources into a central body for ease of contact and information dispersal. The American Chamber of Commerce offers an online directory of its member organizations, sorted by state and searchable by keyword.

CYBER-BUSINESS RESOURCES

Electronic Commerce World Institute

http://www.ecworld.org

This nonprofit organization works to promote electronic data interchange and commerce. Visitors will get an overview of the organization's members and can wander through a virtual exhibit hall.

Fairfax Electronic Commerce Resource Center

http://www.ecrc.gmu.edu/index.html

The Fairfax Electronic Commerce Resource Center (ECRC) provides information and assistance to government and industrial bodies seeking to establish or expand their presence on the Internet. The ECRC provides a mission statement, program descriptions, contact information and a calendar of events.

Octagon Technology Group Inc.

http://www.otginc.com

For the growing number of businesses trying to make an honest buck on the Internet, the Octagon Technology Group showcases its multifaceted computing and financial services. Octagon offers tools to help businesses make the most of the Internet marketplace, from sales-lead generation and order capturing to secure credit-card transactions and international wire transfers.

Online Market Research

http://www.ora.com/survey

The demographic lowdown on who actually uses the Internet. See Editor's Choice.

DIRECTORIES AND GUIDES

Access Business Online

http://www.clickit.com/touch/welcome.html

Promising links to more than 40,000 business services "within three mouse clicks," Access Business Online aims to be *the* businessperson's comprehensive guide to the Internet. This site offers an extensive index of news, corporate information resources, press releases, newswires and much, much more.

Asia Business Connection

http://asiabiz.com

Updated daily, the Asia Business Connection provides an extensive index of companies and business services in Asia and Oceania. Visit here for resources organized by country and industry.

Austrian Worldport

http://www.channel1.com/websites/directory/

Vienna-based Austrian Worldport promises links to 3,000 business home pages from around the world at this site. Also includes job listings, telephone directories and IRC (Internet relay chat) service.

Avon Internet Business Park

http://www.avonibp.co.uk

Sponsored by Hewlett-Packard of Bristol, England, this "experiment in electronic commerce" offers links to a variety of British technology and service companies. Includes an index of affiliated nonprofit organizations.

Berner Technopark

http://www.marktplatz.ch/berner-technopark

Housing more than 40 high-tech companies, the Berner Technopark in Berne, Switzerland, maintains this promotional site. Visit here for a list of its corporate tenants and descriptions of the Technopark's meeting and entertainment facilities.

BizWeb

http://www.bizweb.com

Atlanta-based BizWeb offers links to more than 3,000 national products and services at this index site. Visitors will find everything from computer software to flower delivery here, organized by industry and area.

Business and Income Solutions

http://www.bizsol.com

Offering a variety of classified advertising listings, BIZSOL claims to attract more than 20,000 visitors to this site each month. Visit here to learn about learn about its rates and "membership awards."

Canadian Business Pages

http://www.cban.com

The Canadian Business Pages provide a comprehensive, searchable index of Canada-based companies doing business on the Web. Other features include business-card services, opportunities for job seekers, and an online business magazine called (perhaps ironically) Error 404.

CyberCity InfoLink

http://www.ridgeco.com/

CyberCity InfoLink puts visitors in touch with Canada's business community, including a list of entrepreneurs and service companies. General info on Canada and links to Canadian newsgroups are also here for the linking.

Da Vinci Design Co.

http://www.sccsi.com/DaVinci/davinci.html

Owned and operated by an independent inventor, Texas-based Da Vinci Design Company specializes in patent, engineering and business consulting. Visit its home page for service descriptions and contact information.

DePaul University Institute for Business and Professional Ethics

http://www.depaul.edu/ethics

The Institute for Business and Professional Ethics at Chicago's DePaul University provides this overview of the school. It offers links to the "Ethics Calendar," professional resources, ethics resources and related news items.

---

a2z EDITOR'S CHOICE

Online Market Research

http://www.ora.com/survey

You might have guessed that more men than women use the Internet. But did you know that the largest percentage of users make between $50,000 and $75,000 a year? That the largest employment sector among users is Sales? That the average Web surfer spends 22.5 hours per day online? All right, we made up that last one, but you can separate Internet fact from fiction by checking the numbers in the Online Market Research survey from California-based publisher O'Reilly & Associates. Armed with these numbers, marketers can target their Web resources to the people who are really online—which, at least for now, seems to be 35-year-old white male college graduates with an obsessive interest in "Star Trek" and spokesmodels.—*Reviewed by Joe Williams*

Results

All survey results reflect the Internet population between May-August 1995

Table of Contents: Final Report

- Phase II: Internet Users
- Phase III: Commercial Online Service Subscribers

Size of Online User Population

- Size of U.S. Adult Online User Population
- 1996 Projected U.S. Online User Population

U.S. Internet Users

These charts show the percentage of U.S. Internet users, grouped by gender, age, income, and number of employees per company.

- Internet Users, by Gender
- Internet Users, by Age
- Internet Users, by Income
- Internet Users, by Job Function
- Internet Users, by Number of Employees per Company

European Patent Office

http://www.epo.co.at/epo

The European Patent Office, headquartered in Munich, Germany, provides a centralized patent-grant system for all European Union member countries. Visit its home page for news, public information archives and patent application resources.

GreenMoney On-Line Guide

http://www.greenmoney.com

GreenMoney promotes awareness of socially and environmentally responsible businesses and investments. It gives an overview of its work here and showcases the products and services of participating companies. Visitors can also download the Socially Responsible Business Guide and articles from The GreenMoney Journal.

Industry.Net

http://www.industry.net

Industry.Net is a collection of business Web sites from companies all over the United States. Businesses will find information on becoming a member, and visitors can link directly to the business Web sites.

Infopark Online Service

http://www.infopark.de

Infopark presents a laundry list of links to German commercial and informational sites. Visitors will find commercial and banking services, financial news, cultural resources and more. Entirely in German.

Information Center

http://www.greatinfo.com

This "opportunity and informational magazine for today's entrepreneur" provides a guide to on-line resources to assist users in building a successful business or career. Visitors will find business-opportunity reports, a shareware/software center, and a career-search center, among many other resources.

Italia.Com

http://www.italia.com

Billing itself as "the Italian Internet business center," Italia.Com makes its Web home at this site. Features include a directory of 250 Web servers from "important Italian companies," among them, Internet access providers and international concerns. In Italian and English.

iWorld's Guide to Electronic Commerce

http://e-comm.iworld.com

Mecklermedia's iWorld maintains this guide to commercial and financial Web resources. Visitors will find a variety of useful tools, from small-business promotions to corporate banking and marketing Web sites.

Lookup USA

http://www.abii.com

Omaha, Neb.-based American Business Information, Inc. maintains this site for free access to its database of more than 11 million business listings. Visit here to locate organizations across the United States, sorted by name and type of business.

MELANET

http://www.melanet.com/melanet

MELANET, a service for African American business people, provides an index of online goods and services. Visit here to search for companies, browse informational links and download graphics and Quicktime movies.

Michigan BizServe

http://bizserve.com

Michigan BizServe lists Michigan businesses and organizations along with the services and products each has to offer. An online advertising forum, this site includes a membership directory, business news and a discussion group.

NYNEX Interactive Yellow Pages

http://www.niyp.com/home lycos.html

Now you can let your mouse do the walking. The NYNEX Interactive Yellow Pages is a searchable directory of 16.5 million business across the United States.

Pittsburgh Internet Business Pages

http://www.ibp.com/pit/index.html

Pittsburgh's edition of "The Internet Business Pages" features a "What's New" section for the greater Pittsburgh area, an alphabetical listing of local advertisers, and a complete business directory. Includes links to similar resources for other cities.

Texas Marketplace

http://www.texas-one.org

At the Texas Marketplace, registered users trade business directories, procurement leads and international business opportunities. Produced by the Texas Department of Commerce, this service connects Texas small businesses with state, national and global information resources.

U.K. Business Directory

http://www.milfac.co.uk/milfac

England-based Millenium Facilities Ltd. maintains this site for its extensive index of British businesses. Visit here to search by name or category for information on more than 50,000 companies in the United Kingdom.

U.K. Business on the Web

http://www.u-net.com/ukcom

U-Net Ltd., provides this comprehensive index of British business pages on the Web. Visitors here can view the listings by subject category or alpha-

betical listing. The business pages here include retail, food and drink and travel.

ECONOMICS

ASSOCIATIONS AND ORGANIZATIONS

Centre de Recherche Public Henri Tudor

http://www.crpht.lu

Hosted by the Luxembourg Institute of Technology, this research center aims to improve the innovation capabilities of industries located in the European country. This site presents information about special events, services, annual reports and more.

European Community Information Society Project Office

http://www.ispo.cec.be

Say a German supplier of banking software is looking for European customers, or an Italian hospital wants to take part in worldwide telemedicine field trials. The quasi-governmental EC Information Society Project Office aims to promote growth, competitiveness and employment through European development of emerging computer technologies.

Organisation for Economic Co-operation and Development Online

http://www.oecd.org

The Organisation for Economic Co-operation and Development monitors economic trends in 26 free-market democracies in North America, Europe and the Pacific. At this site, it offers information about environmental health and safety, science and technology, and finance. In English and French.

ECONOMIC RESEARCH

Al Roth's Game Theory and Experimental Economics Page

http://www.pitt.edu/~alroth/alroth.html

Economics professor Al Roth of the University of Pittsburgh reveals his thoughts on game theory and experimental economics at his home page, which also serves as an extensive index for other resources on these subjects.

Corporate Information Bank

http://www.dir.co.jp/cib

Tokyo-based Daiwa Institute of Research provides a variety of financial-, economic- and industrial-research services. Visitors to its Corporate Information Bank will find finance-related news, publications and research reports.

Daiwa Institute of Research Ltd.

http://www.dir.co.jp/welcome.html

A think tank involved in microeconomic and macroeconomic research and systems consulting, Japan's Daiwa Institute of Research posts this page offering an overview of the organization, its services and products. Also find publications, research reports and data resources. In Japanese and English.

Dun & Bradstreet Corp.

http://www.dnb.com

Dun & Bradstreet Corp. provides marketing info, software and services for organizations around the world and owns subsidiaries like Moody's Investors Service and Nielsen Media Research. Visit this site to link to its general information and specific company Web sites.

Economic Consequences of the World Wide Web

http://www.homefair.com/homefair/webeconc.html

Presented at the Second International WWW Conference in 1994, this white paper attempts to project the economic benefits of marketing on the World Wide Web. Visit here for one perspective on how the Web will change the world economy in "some unusual ways."

Economic History Services

http://cs.muohio.edu

Operated by the Cliometric Society under a grant from the U.S. National Science Foundation, the Economic History Services site aims to be a central source of information for academicians. Visitors will find book reviews, data files, and links to home pages and course materials from economics institutes around the world.

Economics Working Paper Archive

http://econwpa.wustl.edu/Welcome.html

Provided by the Economics Department of Washington University in St. Louis, this site offers free access to working papers covering 22 subject areas of economics. Includes paper-submission and subscription forms, test posting areas, and a boatload of texts in a variety of downloadable formats.

Institute for Fiscal Studies

http://www1.ifs.org.uk

The Institute for Fiscal Studies provides information here on its research, publications and membership services. Visitors can access historical information about this European policy research institution here.

Law and Economics

http://www-leland.stanford.edu/~tstanley/lawecon.html

Maintained by a Ph.D. candidate in the Engineering-Economic Systems program of Stanford University's engineering school, this page assembles a variety of economics- and law-related links and references. Visitors will find pointers to university departments, bibliographies, working papers and journals.

Michael Trick's Operations Research Page

http://mat.gsia.cmu.edu

A professor at Carnegie Mellon University's Graduate School of Industrial Administration maintains this site devoted to all aspects of operations research. Includes answers to Frequently Asked Questions (and we've got plenty) along with links to related organizations and resources.

NetEc

http://netec.mcc.ac.uk/NetEc.html

NetEc is an English volunteer effort aiming to use electronic media to improve communication about economics research. Visitors to this Web site can access four databases: printed working papers, electronic working papers, econometrics, and Web resources on economics. A search engine also is provided.

Ohio State University Department of Economics

http://ecolan.sbs.ohio-state.edu

The Department of Economics at Ohio State University in Columbus, Ohio, maintains this site to introduce its people and programs. Visit here for faculty profiles, departmental listings, and other academic and administrative resources.

Olsen & Associates

http://www.olsen.ch

Olsen & Associates, a Zurich-based economic-research firm, specializes in forecasting and historical analysis of currency-exchange rates, interest rates and world market indices. Visitors to its home page will find company information and a variety of financial-information resources.

Resources for Economists on the Internet

http://econwpa.wustl.edu/EconFAQ/EconFAQ.html

The University of Southern Mississippi offers this index to the many online resources of interest to academic and practicing economists.

PUBLICATIONS AND INDUSTRY NEWS

Journal of Applied Econometrics Database Archive

http://qed.econ.queensu.ca/jae

Database access to the Journal of Applied Econometrics is provided here by Canada's Queen's University. Visitors will find free access to issues dating back to January 1994.

The RAND Journal of Economics

http://www.rand.org/misc/rje

This journal supports research of regulated industries, the economic analysis of organizations and applied microeconomics. Visit this site to read articles and article abstracts, subscribe to the publication or find submission guidelines.

EMPLOYMENT AND LABOR ISSUES

Cornell University Industrial and Labor Relations School

http://www.ilr.cornell.edu

The School of Industrial and Labor Relations at New York's Cornell University provides information on employer-employee relations and workplace issues at this site. Also included are an overview of academic programs offered, an electronic library and links to related institutions.

Integrity Center Inc.

http://www.integctr.com

The Integrity Center provides nationwide employment screening services for client companies. Browsers here can read a newsletter, learn about background checks or take an online tutorial on pre-employment screening.

U.S. Bureau of Labor Statistics

http://stats.bls.gov

The Bureau of Labor Statistics publishes economic surveys and data related to U.S. employment trends at this Web site. Visitors can access data, publications, regional information and the "economy at a glance" from this site.

MANAGEMENT ISSUES

Alfred P. Sloan Foundation

http://www.sloan.org

At its home page, the Alfred P. Sloan Foundation relates its founder's scientific approach to managerial techniques. Site features also include information on the foundation's interests and programs.

Andersen Consulting

http://www.ac.com

This global management and technology leader maintains this site to introduce its corporate services. Visitors will find company news, trade publications, industry-specific resources and employment opportunities.

Booz-Allen & Hamilton

http://www.bah.com

Booz-Allen & Hamilton, based in McLean, Va., is an international management and technology consulting firm. This home page provides information on the firm, its clients and services, as well as contact information.

Business Policy and Strategy

http://comsp.com.latrobe.edu.au/bps.html

The Business Policy and Strategy Division of the U.S. Academy of Management deals with the roles and problems of general managers employed in diversified firms or multifunction business units. This home page includes information on strategy formulation, decision processes and resource allocation.

Business Strategies

http://www.bizstrat.com

Rochester, N.Y.-based Business Strategies newspaper maintains this site to supplement its regular print edition. Visit here for current and back issues as well as links to Rochester's Yellow Page Business Directory.

Economic Conversion Information Exchange Gopher

gopher://ecix.doc.gov

The Economic Conversion Information Exchange gopher is a site for companies planning to downsize. Workers who may be laid off could also use this economic and legal data.

Global Business Network

http://www.gbn.org

Global Business Network, a group "specializing in scenario thinking and collaborative learning about the future," offers corporate planning resources to its members. Visitors to this home page can learn about GBN's services and the theories behind its foundation.

How to Save Time and Money in Legal Auditing

http://www.primenet.com/~awong/legaudit.html

California-based Hummingbird Software explains the legal auditing process and profiles its Fee $aver software application and related company services on this promotional page. The software is designed to streamline in-house auditing of legal bills.

Institute of Management and Administration

http://ioma.com/ioma

The Institute of Management and Administration is a publisher of management and business-information resources. Visitors to its home page will find organizational newsletters and a directory of business-related sites and news publications on the Internet.

International Association of Business Communicators

http://www.iabc.com

The International Association of Business Communicators strives to "achieve excellence in organizational communication." Visitors to IABC's home page can learn about its mission, services and memberships, or peruse the magazine CW Online.

Occupational Safety Consultants Inc.

http://www.mindspring.com/~stephens/oschome.html

Occupational Safety Consultants Inc. is an Atlanta-based safety management company that specializes in helping small- to medium-sized businesses reduce the cost of complying with U.S. Occupational Safety and Health Administration regulations. Its page describes its services and offers links to related federal-government sites.

Quality Resources Online

http://www.casti.com/qc/

Quality Resources Online, a collection of quality assurance-related resources, offers links to government, private and nonprofit organizations. Visit here for pointers to federal agencies, national publications, discussion groups and more.

OFFICE TECHNOLOGY

All Makes Office Machine Co.

http://mmink.cts.com/mmink/dossiers/allmakes.html

California-based All Makes Office Machine Company recounts its history dating back to 1945 and spells out its current mission to serve its customers with office-automation products and dictation systems from Novell, Epson, Sanyo and other manufacturers. The page includes contact information.

Elan GMK

http://elan-gmk.com/elan.htm

Elan GMK, an electronic scanning, drafting and data-storage company based in Moorpark, Calif., outlines its services at this promotional site. Visit here to learn about its capabilities, including engineering document scanning, vector conversion and re-drafting, CD-ROM recording, and Internet marketing.

The Electronic Conferencing Co.

http://www.tecc.co.uk

This corporate site provides information about the Electronic Conferencing Co. and its services and products, including software designed to assist the exchange of information via the Internet. TECC also is the Web home for businesses such as Top Gear Magazine and Illuminations.

FedEx U.S. Domestic Service Availability Form

http://www.fedex.com/cgi-bin/svcform

Federal Express provides this handy page on U.S. domestic availability of its delivery services. Visitors can enter the date, time and location to find the best method for getting packages delivered.

The Olivetti Active Badge System

http://www.cam-orl.co.uk/ab.html

Locates your employees' whereabouts via electronic badges. See Editor's Choice.

Printing House Ltd.

http://www.tph.ca

This promotional site is the Internet home of the Printing House Ltd., a Canadian print and copy company. Visitors are invited to learn about the company as well as its printing services, store locations and prices.

TDC Consulting

http://www.shore.net/~pgraham

TDC (That Damn Computer) Consulting offers technophobes non-threatening computing solutions. Find out how the company proposes to ease computers into your business life at this promotional site.

United Parcel Service Package Tracking

http://www.ups.com/tracking/tracking.html

Electronically locate packages shipped by the United Parcel Service via the UPS Package Tracking site. (The package's 11-digit tracking number is a requirement for search performance, so don't lose that number.)

Visual Manufacturing

http://mfginfo.com/cadcam/visual/visual.htm

Visual Manufacturing is a Windows-based manufacturing software product that lets users sort multiple operations and materials for a job in one window, calculates accurate delivery dates, and enables different workstations to access the same data.

PUBLICATIONS AND INDUSTRY NEWS

Asia, Inc. Online

http://www.asia-inc.com

Touted as "Asia's first interactive business magazine," this online publication includes features from current and past issues of the paper version, in addition to exclusive articles and daily financial news. Includes daily technical financial-market commentary.

Australian Financial Review

http://www.afr.com.au

The Financial Review is an Australian publication that covers business, market and industry news. In this electronic version, browsers will find daily "editor's choice" articles, a guide to interactive Web sites and information about upcoming conferences.

Bisk Publishing Co. Accounting Site

http://www.bisk.com

Tampa, Fla.-based Bisk Publishing Company markets professional educational products for accountants, including software, audio-visual materials and books. Visit its home page provides product descriptions, technical support, a mailing list and a toll-free number for phone orders.

CNNfn

http://www.cnnfn.com/index.html

The network that revolutionized television news may be doing the same for the Internet. Visit its Financial News site for an impressive array of headlines, features, and updated stock and mutual fund quotes.

Infomart Dialog Ltd.

http://www.infomart.ca

Infomart Dialog Ltd. is a Canadian company specializing in online search tools and automated news-clipping services for business people. Visitors to the site can read a company overview, browse the Infomart database or link to related pages and services on the Web.

Information Access Co.

http://www.iacnet.com

This home page outlines Information Access Co.'s products and services. The company offers full-text magazines and newspapers via a database for corporate and individual users.

Information Providers Limited

http://www.ipl.co.uk

Break into business in the United Kingdom with the Business Information Service, offering specialized Internet searches, periodicals and more. The service is sponsored by Information Providers Limited, a commercial purveyor of online news and research to the British business community.

Knight-Ridder Financial Publishing Services

http://www.route-one.co.uk/route-one/ridder

Visitors to this site will learn about the financial and commodity news and statistics available from Knight-Ridder Inc.'s financial publishing division. Includes access to a historical database and an end-of-day stock quote service, plus downloadable demo software.

Miller Freeman Inc.

http://www.mfi.com

Miller Freeman is a fast-growing publishing company that markets business and special-interest magazines, books and directories, newsletters and CD-ROMs. Visitors can learn about the publisher and its products here.

NewsPage

http://www.newspage.com

NewsPage boasts a comprehensive listing of more than 500 online business-news resources and 25,000 pages of related information. Browsers can register to access articles, organized by industry. Topics covered range from multimedia and banking to insurance and environmental services.

Online Journal of Ethics

http://condor.depaul.edu/ethics/ethg1.html

Seeking to prove that "business ethics" is not just another oxymoron, the On-Line Journal of Ethics researches and analyzes business and professional behavior. Review related papers, event calendars and professional resources at this site.

PennWell Publishing Co.

http://www.pennwell.com

This promotional site is maintained by the PennWell Publishing Co., a publisher of business magazines and newsletters based in Tulsa, Okla. Visitors to its home page are invited to learn more about the company and its diverse publications.

PR Newswire

http://www.prnewswire.com

PR Newswire has been a distributor of corporate news since 1954. This online version of the wire service offers news from public and private companies, government agencies, associations and organizations. Includes a number of links to related sites.

Providence Business News

http://www.pbn.com

The online version of Providence Business News offers a weekly examination of the sometimes chilly but always colorful business climate in southern New England. Visitors can read current and back issues here.

Singapore Business Times

http://www.asia1.com.sg/biztimes

The Singapore Business Times Web page is a complete, online version of this financial newspaper. Visitors will find feature articles, news, analysis and an Asian business database. Also includes entertainment coverage.

Stanford Journal of Law, Business & Finance

http://www-leland.stanford.edu/group/sjlbf

Stanford University provides the home page for the Stanford Journal of Law, Business & Finance. Visitors will find writers' guidelines, subscription info and an archive of past issues and articles. This journal specializes in emerging legal issues affecting the business and finance communities.

---

a2z EDITOR'S CHOICE

The Olivetti Active Badge System

http://www.cam-orl.co.uk/ab.html

Olivetti is the Italian computer (and typewriter) company. Visitors to this page will find information on its Active Badge System, which allows companies to track employees electronically by location, thanks to a little badge they wear. (They're actually quite proud of this.) Thus if you think that Smithers is spending a little too much time in the john, you can get your proof without actually hiring a stoolie. Of course, there are also less-invasive uses of the technology, as demonstrated here on the employees of the Olivetti lab in Cambridge, England. This site is available in English and Italian.—*Reviewed by Joe Williams*

olivetti Research Laboratory   People at ORL

News from ORL _____ La versione in Italiano

TitleNet
http://www.infor.com
Supported by a network of international publishers that includes Microsoft Press and McGraw-Hill, TitleNet offers free access to a large online catalog of books, journals, software and publications. Visitors can read excerpts and tables of contents, and can choose to place an online order.

World Wide Trade Service
http://www.nas.com/~westg/index.html
World Wide Trade Service provides information about its trade books, manuals, directories and dealership services here. Visitors to this site can browse pages about foreign and domestic wholesale products and import-export trade sources, read detailed company info or obtain a price list and order form.

SMALL BUSINESS DIGEST

Big Dreams Newsletter
http://www.wimsey.com/~duncans
A selection of articles on personal development and topics related to starting a small business await readers of the Big Dreams Newsletter, a publication from Coquitlam, British Columbia-based Alpine Training and Development. Includes monthly installments of features, book reviews and Web links.

Business Resource Center
http://www.kcilink.com/brc
Khera Communications Inc., an Internet publishing and consulting firm based in Rockville, Md., provides information for small-business owners here. Visitors will find marketing and financing guides, management resources, and links to a variety of Web sites related to business development.

The Company Corporation
http://www.service.com/tcc/home.html
Wilmington, Del.-based Company Corporation advises businesses on proper incorporating procedures. Visitors to its home page will find basic incorporation costs, sample forms and a variety of helpful tips.

International Small Business Consortium
http://www.isbc.com
The International Small Business Consortium is an online "showplace for emerging businesses" from around the globe. Find out how to be listed in the database and access company indices, or peruse a small sampling of ISBC's clients.

Mail Order Mall
http://www.nas.com/~westg/BizOp/Bizop.html
This site includes work-at-home and money-saving opportunities, "adults only" listings, health and nutrition sales information and other too-good-to-be-true situations for would-be entrepreneurs.

NetMarquee
http://nmq.com
Visitors to this page will find a business center dedicated to the needs of small, emerging companies as well as those run by families. Market trends, news, technology information and products of strategic value are featured.

San Antonio Electronic Commerce Resource Center
http://www.saecrc.org
Funded by the U.S. Department of Defense, the San Antonio Electronic Commerce Resource Center offers education and consulting services to small businesses selling goods and services to the federal body. Visitors to its home page will find a variety of contractor resources, including registration software, procurement updates, industry publications and much more.

Small Business Advancement National Center
http://wwwsbanet.uca.edu
This site provides small business owners and other entrepreneurs with business and economic resources and information. Visitors will find information about the organization's staff and consulting services, with tips, newsletters and links to related sites, including U.S. Congress member e-mail lists.

Small Business Resource Center
http://www.webcom.com/~seaquest
Would-be small business owners can download free guides on starting and maintaining a business here. The site also includes an online catalog of products for business owners.

Ultra B-O-N-D Contractor Opportunities
http://www.ibos.com/pub/ibos/ultrabon/ultra.html
An online infomercial, the Ultra B-O-N-D Inc. home page reveals how entrepreneurs can employ the corporation's patented method for repairing cracked windshields to earn a six-figure income. Complete with "before" and "after" pictures (of the windows, not the clients) and ordering information.

U.S. Small Business Administration
http://www.sbaonline.sba.gov
The U.S. Small Business Administration aids, counsels, assists and protects the interests of small businesses in America. Visit this site for information about running your own company and access links to related organizations. Also features government contracting statistics, legal regulations for small businesses and contact information for when you have to talk to a real live person.

BUSINESS SCHOOLS AND INSTITUTES

ARCHIVES AND INDICES

Amos Tuck Business School Index
http://www.dartmouth.edu/pages/tuck/bschools.html
The Amos Tuck School of Business Administration at Dartmouth presents a thorough index of business schools throughout the world here.

Education, Training and Development Resource Center for Business and Industry
http://www.tasl.com/tasl/home.html
This page, maintained by Training and Seminar Locators Inc., provides help in finding business education resources. It includes an index of qualified training providers and information about products and services.

The MBA Page
http://www.cob.ohio-state.edu/dept/fin/mba.htm
Ohio State University's Fisher College of Business offers a survival guide to the dog-eat-dog world of the MBA student. Find a collection of resources ranging from games MBAs play to MBA program rankings at this educational site.

INDEPENDENT BUSINESS SCHOOLS

Bryant College
http://www.bryant.edu
Bryant College, located in Rhode Island, offers undergraduate and graduate programs in business. Visitors to its home page will find an overview of the school, including information on its academic departments, programs of study, faculty and student services.

Helsinki School of Economics and Business

http://www.hkkk.fi

This home page contains details about the academic programs and services offered by the Helsinki School of Economics and Business. Includes faculty and contact info. In English and Finnish.

Rotterdam School of Management

http://www.rsm.eur.nl

Netherlands-based Rotterdam School of Management maintains this site to introduce its programs and facilities. Visit here to learn about its degree programs, publications and projects relating to management techniques.

Stockholm School of Economics

http://www.hhs.se

Training the next generation of Swedish stockbrokers, the Stockholm School of Economics provides general information here, as well as details on its academic departments, institutes, services, news and personnel.

Turku School of Economics and Business Administration

http://www.tukkk.fi

Prospective students can learn about the Turku School of Economics and Business Administration in Finland at this academic home page. Visitors will get an overview of the school and its research here. In Finnish and English.

University of Economics and Business Administration

http://rektorat.wu-wien.ac.at

Wirtschaftsuniversitat Wien, the University of Economics and Business Administration in Vienna, Austria, maintains this site to introduce its programs and services. Visitors will find faculty contacts, school publications, research funding updates, and other academic and administrative resources.

INSTITUTES

Institute for Fiscal Studies

http://www1.ifs.org.uk

The Institute for Fiscal Studies provides information here on its research, publications and membership services. Visitors can access historical information about this European policy research institution here.

Institute of Management and Administration

http://ioma.com/ioma

The Institute of Management and Administration is a publisher of management and business-information resources. Visitors to its home page will

find organizational newsletters and a directory of business-related sites and news publications on the Internet.

U.S.-Japan Technology Management Center

http://fuji.stanford.edu

Stanford University introduces its U.S.-Japan Technology Management Center here. Visitors to the site will find information and course details regarding Japan's unique business and technology culture. A guide to Japanese information resources also is included.

UNIVERSITY DEPARTMENTS

INTERNATIONAL

Cranfield Centre for Logistics and Transportation

http://www.cranfield.ac.uk/som/cclt/cclt.html

The Centre for Logistics and Transportation of England's Cranfield School of Management presents information about programs, staff and research projects. Visitors will find an extensive list of job information sources, as well as links to related sites.

Dalhousie University Faculty of Management

http://quasar.sba.dal.ca:2000

The home page of the Faculty of Management at Dalhousie University in Halifax, Canada, provides information on the department's programs and on the local community. Visit here for an overview of academic courses offered and an introduction to the city of Halifax.

Flinders University School of Commerce

http://www.law.flinders.edu.au

The School of Commerce at the Flinders University of South Australia maintains this site to introduce its people and programs. Visit here for staff listings, research and training overviews, business information, annual reports, school publications and other academic and administrative resources.

Humboldt University of Berlin Economics Department

http://www.wiwi.hu-berlin.de

The Economics Department of Germany's Humboldt University of Berlin provides this informational site. Visit here to learn about its programs and people, access academic materials, and link with a variety of German Internet resources.

Imperial College Management School

http://graph.ms.ic.ac.uk

London, England's Imperial College of Science, Technology and Medicine maintains this site to introduce its school of business administration studies. Visitors will find an introduction to the school's faculty, departmental resources and course offerings.

Lund University Economics and Management School

http://www.ec.lu.se

The School of Economics and Management at Sweden's Lund University maintains this site for academic and electronic resources. Visitors will find departmental listings, research and reference materials, and a variety of Internet search tools.

Macquarie Graduate School of Management

http://www.gsm.mq.edu.au

The Macquarie Graduate School of Management in Sydney, Australia, provides information on its postgraduate programs here. Includes information on the institution's research centers and profiles of faculty members.

Nijenrode University Business School

http://www.nijenrode.nl

The Netherlands Business School at Nijenrode University hosts this Web site containing a variety of information about the institution's programs and activities. Visitors can read an overview of information sessions and master's degree fairs or obtain details on conferences.

Simon Fraser University Faculty of Business Administration

http://www.bus.sfu.ca

Vancouver, British Columbia-based Simon Fraser University's business school maintains this site to introduce its people and programs. Visitors will find faculty profiles, course offerings and other academic and administrative resources.

Strathclyde University Information Science Department

http://www.dis.strath.ac.uk

This home page, maintained by the information-science department of the business school at Scotland's Strathclyde University, contains details about the department, its course offerings and its faculty. Includes pointers to departmental research groups and facilities.

University of Bristol Department of Economics

http://www.ecn.bris.ac.uk

The Department of Economics at England's University of Bristol maintains this informational site. Visit here for course descriptions, university publications, and other academic and administrative resources.

University of Tokyo Faculty of Economics

http://www.e.u-tokyo.ac.jp

This page, from the University of Tokyo, provides information about the Faculty of Economics, and guides browsers to academics, staff and coursework. Access info on the Ecomomic Society 7th World Congress here.

University of Victoria Economics Department

http://sol.uvic.ca/econ

The Department of Economics at Canada's University of Victoria profiles its programs, faculty and publications here. Prospective students can survey the school's graduate and undergraduate courses of study. Includes a listing of scheduled seminars.

University of Victoria Economics Institutes Index

http://castle.uvic.ca/econ/depts.html

The University of Victoria Department of Economics conveniently compiles listings of worldwide university economics departments' Web sites. Organized by nation.

University of Western Ontario, Western Business School

http://www.business.uwo.ca/

The Western School of Business at the University of Ontario provides a wealth of information about its programs, academics, publications, services, students and admissions. Includes descriptions of its unique teaching methods and business research projects.

UNITED STATES

Abilene Christian University MBA Program

http://150.252.25.26/aboutMBA.html

The master's of business administration program at Abilene Christian University in Texas is the subject of this departmental page. Peruse course offerings, faculty listings and alumni resources, or telnet directly to the Margaret and Herman Brown Library.

Cornell University Graduate School of Management

http://www.gsm.cornell.edu

The Johnson Graduate School of Management at Cornell University maintains this page featuring information about its academic offerings, international programs and career-development services. Links to the school's publications, faculty directory and alumni network are provided.

Cornell University Industrial and Labor Relations School

http://www.ilr.cornell.edu

The School of Industrial and Labor Relations at New York's Cornell University provides information on employer-employee relations and workplace issues at this site. Also included are an overview of academic programs offered, an electronic library and links to related institutions.

Dartmouth University School of Business Administration

http://www.dartmouth.edu/pages/tuck/tuckhome.html

Dartmouth's Amos Tuck School of Business maintains this site to introduce its people and programs. Visit here for course offerings, alumni listings and career services links.

Freeman Unplugged

http://freeman.sob.tulane.edu

The unofficial home page of Tulane University's A.B. Freeman School of Business, this site serves as an informal gathering place for student recipes, hobbies and photos. It links to the official page, but there's no mistaking one for the other.

Harvard Business School

http://www.hbs.harvard.edu

Harvard University's Graduate School of Business Administration maintains this overview of its academic programs, faculty and division research. Links to related sites also are featured.

Iowa Electronic Markets

http://www.biz.uiowa.edu/iem/index.html

Allows you to play the big investor—with no risk! See Editor's Choice.

Kent State University College of Business

http://business.kent.edu

The College of Business and Graduate School of Management at Ohio's Kent State University maintains this site to introduce its programs and facilities. Visitors will find departmental overviews, activities listings, and other academic and administrative resources.

---

a2z EDITOR'S CHOICE

Iowa Electronic Markets

http://www.biz.uiowa.edu/iem/index.html

Like the weather, everybody talks about politics but few people do anything about it. Now savvy investors can put their money where their mouths are with this civic-minded twist on fantasy investing. Sponsored by University of Iowa's College of Business Administration, the Iowa Electronic Markets site allows investors to bet real money (yes, real money) on the outcome of the U.S. presidential elections and other global events (such as the Russian elections and the status of Hong Kong). Specialized indices enable players to predict winners as well as specific margins of victory. It's supposed to be educational, but we say it's a new dimension in vote peddling.—*Reviewed by Joe Williams*

Iowa Electronic Markets

The Iowa Electronic Markets are real-money futures markets where contract payoffs depend on economic and political events such as elections. These markets are operated by faculty at the University of Iowa College of Business as part of our research and teaching mission.
We invite you to join us in this mission.

US Political Markets including Presidential Election (WTA) Presidential Election (Vote-Share) Republican Convention	Non-US Political Markets including Austria British Columbia Russia	Earnings and Returns including Computer Returns Microsoft Price Level Minnesota Returns
IEM in the News	FAQ	Documents and Forms
Write to Us		

Michigan State University Eli Broad College of Business and Graduate School of Management

http://www.bus.msu.edu

This home page provides information about the departments within Michigan State University's Eli Broad College of Business and Graduate School of Management. Find also links to an index of library holdings and an online course catalog.

Oregon State University College of Business

http://www.bus.orst.edu

Departments, programs and services at the College of Business at Oregon State University are the focus here. There also are directories of research, student organizations, local Web pages, personnel, software tools and other resources.

Southern Methodist University School of Business

http://www.cox.smu.edu

The Southern Methodist University's Edwin L. Cox School of Business maintains this site to introduce its people and programs. Visit here to learn about its degree programs, academic departments and campus events.

Stanford University Department of Economics

http://www-econ.stanford.edu

The Stanford University Department of Economics home page features a current list of its Ph.D. candidates who are available for employment (hint, hint), as well as a working papers archive. Information about its research and graduate and undergraduate programs is also available.

Stanford University Graduate School of Business

http://gsb-www.stanford.edu/home.html

The Graduate School of Business at Stanford University offers this Web site containing information on its faculty, a mission statement and admissions policy details. Visitors also can view a number of multimedia presentations produced by department members.

University of California, Berkeley, School of Business

http:haas.berkeley.edu

The University of California, Berkeley's Haas School of Business maintains this site for general information. Visit here to learn about its facilities, academic programs, faculty and students. Includes an events calendars and links to the publications HaasWeek and California Management Review.

University of Iowa's College of Business Administration

http://www.biz.uiowa.edu

The College of Business Administration at the University of Iowa in Iowa City has set up this home page with information about the department, faculty and programs. Course catalog information and links to related sites are offered.

University of Michigan Business School

http://www.bus.umich.edu

Look into the course requirements for getting a master's degree at the University of Michigan Business School home page. Visitors can engage in a question-and-answer session with the dean or order application materials here.

Weatherhead School of Management

http://nexxus.som.cwru.edu

Case Western Reserve University in Cleveland, Ohio, presents this home page for its Weatherhead School of Management. Visitors here will find information about academics, faculty, career resources and departmental events.

CAREERS AND JOBS

CAREER DEVELOPMENT AND ADVANCEMENT RESOURCES

California School-to-Career Information System

http://wwwstc.cahwnet.gov

The California School-to-Career Information System is a joint project of the state's public school system and local business partners. This home page tells about the system's career guidance activities, aimed at helping students move easily from school into employment.

Career Resumes

http://branch.com/cr/cr.html

This promotional site is the Web home of Career Resumes, an employment counseling service based in Goldens Bridge, N.Y. Find out why "if your resume isn't a winner, it's a killer," and what the company can do to help.

Getting Past Go - A Survival Guide for College Graduates

http:lattanze.loyola.edu/MonGen/home.html

Maintained by a management information-systems major at Loyola University, this career resource page offers a step-by-step guide to finding a job. Includes tips for recent and soon-to-be college graduates.

Recruiters OnLine Network

http://www.ipa.com

The Internet Professional Association is an online arm of the employment industry. Company recruiters and job seekers alike can use this forum for filling their respective work-related needs. Prospective members can review IPA's products and services at this site.

Society for Human Resource Management

http://www.shrm.org

The Society for Human Resource Management home page offers information about the group along with industry news and access to articles in the society's HR Magazine. Includes a frequently asked questions file that provides legal information for human-resources professionals.

CLASSIFIED ADVERTISING

CareerNet's Career Resource Center

http://www.careers.org

This site provides a job resource center with links to more than 15,000 jobs and pointers to other career-related Web sites. Visitors will find links to associations, franchising opportunities and library resources.

CareerSite

http://www.careersite.com

Job seekers can pound the digital pavement by searching this database by employer name or occupation. Employers can find out how to sign on with this virtual placement agency.

C.E. Weekly Online

http://www.ceweekly.wa.com

Contract Employment Weekly Online posts job listings and links to contract firms. Employment seekers can visit libraries for reference materials and resume writing guidelines.

Computer Register

http://www.computerregister.com

Browsers in the market for computer consultants or services can check out relevant advertisements here. Employment classifieds are provided for job-seekers and employers.

Employment Opportunities and Resume Postings

http://galaxy.einet.net/GJ/employment.html

TradeWave's Galaxy Internet guide maintains this site for a variety of career resources. Visit here for an index of academic, high-tech and governmental job listings.

Get a Job!

http://sensemedia.net/getajob

This site, a service of SenseMedia, offers an exhaustive collection of employment opportunities for "hypermedia professionals." Visit here to link to job listings, employment agencies, and many other online resources for Internet and computing-savvy career seekers.

Institute of Electrical and Electronics Engineers Employment Services

http://www.ieee.org/jobs.html

The Institute of Electrical and Electronics Engineers Inc. maintains this online employment service for its members. Job listings by geographic area, a resume bank and links to employment resources are featured among other items of interest.

Jobs in Mathematics

http://www.cs.dartmouth.edu/~gdavis/policy/jobmarket.html

The market for PhDs in Mathematics is not exactly brimming with opportunities; just take a look at the market statistics on this career page. But all is not lost. Find information on marketable skills in the field, listings of job openings, solutions to the problems in job hunting and documentation of labor policies. Mathemeticians unite—you have only your unemployment to lose!

MacTemps

http://www.mactemps.com

If you know Macintosh (or even PCWindows) software and are in search of employment, MacTemps is a good place to start. As this home page explains, the organization specializes in providing businesses with computer experts, filling temporary and permanent positions around the world. In English and French.

The Monster Board

http://www.monster.com

The Monster Board promotes itself as the "#1 Career Site on the WWW." Visitors can find out what's new on the server, conduct a career search of the nearly 50,000 job listings, or post a resume online.

National Center for Supercomputing Applications Job Announcements

http://www.ncsa.uiuc.edu/General/Jobs/00Jobs.html

The National Center for Supercomputing Applications, on the campus of the University of Illinois at Urbana-Champaign, maintains this site for updated job announcements. Visitors will find descriptions and contact information for currently available technical positions.

DIRECTORIES AND GUIDES

America's Job Bank

http://www.ajb.dni.us

Funded by employers' federal unemployment taxes, America's Job Bank presents job-search and employer services. Includes information about career resources, search engines for job seekers and a customer comments form.

CareerMosaic

http://www.careermosaic.com

Bernard Hodes Advertising maintains this site for its award-winning CareerMosaic job resource service. Visitors will find an extensive collection of resources for job seekers and employers.

CareerWEB

http://www.cweb.com

Recruiters, employers and individuals hunting for jobs are all welcome at CareerWEB. Find general career resources along with lists of position openings, company profiles and a resume database.

Designlink

http://www.designlink.com

Designlink is a San Francisco-based bulletin-board system for artists and photographers. Visitors to its Web site can download shareware, browse through portfolios from graphic artists and photographers, and look for jobs. The site also posts information on Designlink's user group meetings.

Finding A Job

http://www.dbisna.com/dbis/jobs/vjobhunt.htm

Dun & Bradstreet Inc. offers this resources page to help those seeking employment find "the perfect job." Visitors can read job-search tips, check out employment trends, sample the company's employment solutions or become a charter member free of charge.

helpwanted.com

http:helpwanted.com

A service of Massachusetts-based recruiting services and software company Your Software Solutions Inc., this site provides a variety of job-search tools. Visitors will find company listings, a jobs database and related information services.

IntelliMatch

http://www.intellimatch.com/intellimatch

IntelliMatch is an electronic job-placement agency. It promotes its services for employers here and invites job seekers to utilize its free resume posting page.

Jobs, Labor, and Management

http://www.fedworld.gov/jobs.htm

Visitors will find an annotated index of links to job-, labor- and management-related U.S. government servers here. Employment opportunities listings, labor statistics and pointers to other government information servers also are offered.

National Technical Employment Services

http://iquest.com/~ntes

This organization recruits contract professionals for employment with technical firms. Visit this page to review the company's products and services, including its resume database, job postings magazine and links to the home pages of selected companies.

Online Career Center

http://www.occ.com

The Online Career Center boasts that it is the Internet's "first and most frequently accessed career center." Visitors will find a searchable database of job search resources for a wide range of industries.

Professionals Online

http://www.prosonline.com

Professionals Online presents a directory of Web resources categorized by profession. Among the areas covered are business, finance, accounting, law, computers and technology, and government. Also included is a job-finder service.

Rensselaer Career Development Center

http://www.rpi.edu/dept/cdc

Although primarily intended for students or grads of Rensselaer Polytechnic Institute, job seekers and employers from around the country can find links to employment-related Internet sites at the Career Resource home page. Visitors will find links to job listings, professional organizations and career services.

The Riley Guide

http://www.jobtrak.com/jobguide

Massachusetts-based career and recruitment consultant Margaret Riley maintains this extensive and handy index of employment resources. Job seekers will find job postings, industry listings and a variety of self-help guides.

JOB SEARCH AND PLACEMENT AGENCIES

INTERNATIONAL

Asia-Net
http://www.asia-net.com
Asia-Net is a clearinghouse of job listings for bilingual (Japanese/Korean/Chinese and English) professionals. Visitors can browse the listings, forward their resumes and subscribe to an e-mail list. In English, with limited Japanese translations.

TeleJob
http://ezinfo.ethz.ch/ETH/TELEJOB/tjb home e.html
TeleJob is the job exchange board for assistants and doctoral students at the technological institutes of Zurich and Lausanne, Switzerland. The site includes listings of available positions, resume postings and other job-related services. In German, French and English.

UNITED STATES

California Career & Employment Center
http://www.webcom.com/~career/welcome.html
The California Career & Employment Center is an online job service that caters to employers and job seekers. Access links to post both career opportunities and personal resumes. Other links lead to various career-related and educational resources.

California Employment Development Department
http://wwwedd.cahwnet.gov
California's Employment Development Department page provides a description of the agency and links to information about its services. Among other items, visitors will find links to the State Job Training Council and the Governor's Committee for Employment of Disabled Persons.

Catapult
http://www.wm.edu/catapult/catapult.html
The College of William and Mary in Williamsburg, Va., maintains this site to provide access to the Catapult, its career services guide. Visit here to use the university's employment resources, including job-search tools, career libraries, links to graduate schools and more.

JobCenter
http://www.jobcenter.com
he JobCenter matches employers and applicants online. For a fee, job-seekers and recent grads can post their resumes to this central database for the perusal of potential bosses. For the same fee, a resume-critiquing service is also provided. Potential job leads are delivered straight to their e-mail in-boxes.

Job Search
http://www.adnetsol.com/jsearch/jshome1.html
Job Search provides an employment service for professionals, managers and executives seeking work in Southern California. The site provides information on 40,000 area firms, along with press releases and a description of services.

J. Robert Scott
http://j-robert-scott.com
J. Robert Scott, a Boston-based senior level executive search firm, maintains this promotional site. Visit here for a company overview, employment opportunities and contact information

North Carolina Employment Security Commission
http://www.esc.state.nc.us
This site contains general information on North Carolina employment services, labor markets and unemployment insurance. Includes news releases and links to other state-government sites.

PursuitNet Jobs
http://www.tiac.net/users/jobs/index.html
Billed as a discreet job search engine, PursuitNet matches skills and desires with compatible open positions submitted by companies. Resumes may be e-mailed for inclusion, and a Hot Job page lists positions of particular interest.

SkillSearch
http://www.internet-is.com/skillsearch/index.html
SkillSearch is a professional membership organization linking individuals with two-to-30 years of experience in the workplace to organizations that need their talents. Services enable members to network with active employers online.

Snelling Personnel Services
http://www.snelling.com
Snelling Personnel Services, one of the nation's largest employment agencies, maintains this link to its employment-opportunity database and other job-search services. Visitors will find info on contract, temporary and full-time positions, including jobs in California's Silicon Valley.

Twin Cities Jobs Page
http://www.fentonnet.com/jobs.html
At the Twin Cities Jobs Pages, supply and demand bring potential bosses and workers together, and resumes and cover letters can be traded without the waste of paper. Hunt for a job in Minneapolis-St. Paul online or look for a Web-savvy employee here.

RESUMES ONLINE

American Resource Co.
http://www.arcfile.com
This Milwaukee-based electronic advertising firm offers a Worldwide Resume Talent Bank and other career-advancement resources. Includes online shopping opportunities as well.

Drexel University Employer-Directed Resume Search
http://cmc.www.drexel.edu
The Employer Directed Resume Search site from Drexel University offers the resumes of nearly all of its graduating seniors and some alumni in a searchable database targeted at employers. Users have to receive a validated request form before viewing resumes.

Shawn's Internet Resume Center
http://www.inpursuit.com/sirc
InPursuit Web Services maintains this site for Shawn's Internet Resume Center, an extensive collection of employment resources for companies and individuals. Visitors will find resume and job postings, company directories, a keyword search engine, and an online "personal home-page creation center."

CORPORATE HOME PAGES

INTERNATIONAL

Fujitsu Ltd.
http://www.fujitsu.co.jp/index-e.html
Japanese manufacturing powerhouse Fujitsu Ltd. serves up background and product information on its corporate home page. Includes information on the electronic devices, computers and information-processing and communications systems sold by the company. Available in English and Japanese.

Hitachi Ltd.

http://www.hitachi.co.jp

Japan's Hitachi Ltd., manufacturer of consumer and industrial electronic products, power systems and materials, maintains this promotional site. Visitors will find company news, product descriptions, and research and development overviews. In Japanese and English.

Korean Telecom

http://nac.kotel.co.kr

At the Korean Telecom CO-LAN site, review the company's products and services and link to related sites. In Korean only.

Matsushita Electrical Industrial Co., Ltd.

http://www.mei.co.jp/index.html

Tokyo-based Matsushita, known in many countries by the Panasonic brand, produces a wide variety of electronics, including home appliances, industrial components and computer networking equipment. Visitors to its home page will find news, press releases and links to its worldwide network of subsidiary companies.

Merck & Co., Inc.

http://www.merck.com

Merck & Co., an international marketer of animal and human health products and services, maintains this promotional site. Visitors will find in-depth research overviews, health services publications and product information.

Mitsubishi Electric Corporation

http://www.melco.co.jp

Tokyo-based international electronics manufacturer Mitsubishi maintains this promotional site. Visitors will find a brief introduction to the company, including financial performance data and worldwide subsidiary listings.

NEC Corporation

http://www.nec.com

The NEC Corporation, a Japanese manufacturer of communications products, computer and semiconductor components, maintains this site for general information. Visit here for corporate and product information, sales and support services, details on upcoming trade events, and more.

Nikko

http://www.nikko.co.jp

At this corporate home page, visitors can access information about any of Nikko's subsidiary organizations: Nikko Securities Co. Ltd., Nikko Research Center Ltd., Nikko System Center Ltd. or Nikko Investor Relations Co. Ltd. Available in Japanese and English.

Nintendo

http://www.nintendo.com

Nintendo, creators of video-game mainstays Super Mario and Donkey Kong, presents this promotional home page. Designed for businesspeople and game addicts alike, the site offers corporate information, as well as fun and interesting resources from Nintendo's broad line of games.

Philips Electronics

http://www.philips.com

Dutch-based Philips Electronics is a multinational consumer-electronics manufacturer. (They invented the CD). Visitors to the corporation's home page will find product information, research details and an overview of the organization, which also includes the PolyGram record labels.

Seiko Epson Corp.

http://www.epson.co.jp

Nagano, Japan-based Seiko Epson Corporation manufactures computers and peripherals, semiconductors and really nice wrist watches. Visit its home page for corporate information, product descriptions and customer service resources. In Japanese and English.

Shell Oil Co.

http://www.shellus.com

Shell Oil Company does a lot more than sell gasoline. Visitors to its home page will find links to its many community, sports and alternative energy exploration programs.

Sony Online

http://www.sony.com

Sony Corp.'s Web server provides pointers to the entertainment and electronics giant's many subsidiaries. Visitors can access information about Sony musical artists, movies, television shows, electronic products and more. Includes a link to Sony's Tokyo Web site.

Sumitomo Electric Industries Ltd.

http://www.sumiden.co.jp

Sumitomo Electric Industries Ltd. manufactures optical fibers, synthetic diamonds, compound semiconductors, cabling and high-tech ceramics. Its corporate home page offers a company overview, press releases and product descriptions. In Japanese, Mandarin and English.

UNITED STATES

Ameritech

http://www.ameritech.com

Ameritech provides local phone service for several states in the American Midwest, in addition to offering celular, paging, interactive video and wireless data communications for much of the

country and many parts of Europe. Visitors will find company news and details on products and services here.

Apple Computer Inc.

http://www.apple.com/

Apple Computer, Inc., creators of the Macintosh line of personal computers, offers this home page, featuring a variety of company and product updates. Includes links to resources for consumers, educators and third-party developers.

AT&T

http://www.att.com/

American telecommunications mainstay AT&T provides product, service and corporate information at its home site. The Ma Bell page includes a variety of resources for Web surfers, including a topic-oriented Internet directory and info about At&T's new WorldNet service.

Bell Atlantic Corp.

http://www.bell-atl.com/

At the home page of the East Coast "baby Bell," visitors can find out what's new at the ever-growing company; review its finances, products and services; or learn about Bell Atlantic's forays into new technology.

Chevron Corp.

http://www.chevron.com

This promotional page is the Web home of the San Francisco-based Chevron Corp. Browsers are invited to "drill" the site's geological map interface for info on the company, its operations, products and services, and financial data.

Chrysler Technology Center

http://www.chryslercorp.com/

Once you enter your name and e-mail address (it needn't be real), you're cleared to enter this site, which offers a wealth of historical and technical information for armchair gearheads. get a sneak peek at Chrysler concept cars and alternate-energy plans, or stroll through a vitual showroom containing Chrysler, Plymouth, Dodge, Jeep and Eagle cars and trucks.

Citibank

http://www.citicorp.com

Citibank, a U.S.-headquartered banking corporation with branches in more than 40 countries, provides information here on its latest services. Includes a branch-locator feature to find the Citibank nearest you.

Coca-Cola Co.

http://www.cocacola.com/

Thirsty for information on Coca-Cola? The Atlanta-based soft drink company's corporate site offers slick advertisements, product information and Coca-Cola lore galore.

Disney.com

http://www.disney.com

International entertainment kingpin Disney packs its home page with cartoons, games, catalogs and just plain fun stuff. Includes links to all Disney subsidiaries, including the Disney Channel, Walt Disney Records and its worldwide network of family theme parks ("the happiest places on earth").

Federal Express

http://www.fedex.com

Leading international express-delivery company FedEx maintains this promotional site for package tracking services and software. Includes delivery-option descriptions and customer-service information.

Gannett Co. Inc.

http://www.gannett.com/index.html

Media conglomerate Gannett blankets the U.S. market with its newspapers, radio and television stations, and billboards. Review Gannett's corporate profile or link to online presences of its news outlets at this company home page.

General Electric Co.

http://www.ge.com

General Electric, the diversified technology, manufacturing and services company that brings us both light bulbs and "Seinfeld," maintains this promotional site. Visitors will find news, products and services descriptions, worldwide operations overviews, and divisional information resources.

Goodyear Tire & Rubber Co.

http://www.goodyear.com

Get the good news about Goodyear at this corporate site for the tire and rubber giant. Company news, dealer locations and an events calendar are featured here, along with consumer info about tire care, tire wear and tire replacement.

IBM

http://www.ibm.com/

IBM provides information here on its broad range of business products and services, from workstations to microelectronics. Visitors will find company news, product descriptions and links to its worldwide network of manufacturers and distributors.

Intel

http://www.intel.com

Santa Clara, Calif.-based Intel Corporation produces high-powered microprocessors, networking products, videoconferencing systems and probably a few really cool things that the general public hasn't heard about yet. Visitors to its home page will find product updates, customer support resources and employment opportunities.

JCPenney

http://www.jcpenney.com

Department store chain JCPenney provides consumer and investor information at this promotional site. Includes a variety of online-shopping and ordering services, as well as detailed corporate and financial information resources.

Lockheed Martin Corp.

http://www.lockheed.com

Lockheed Martin, the result of a merger of the Lockheed and Martin Marietta corporations, is a world leader in the manufacture of space systems, missiles, aeronautics and electronics. Its Web site offers a video tour of the giant corporation, as well as fast facts, financial reports and a list of its operating units and subsidiaries.

MCAUniversal

http://www.mca.com

Entertainment mega-corporation MCAUniversal, parent company of Universal Pictures, Putnam Berkeley Publishing, Winterland Productions and many others, maintains this promotional site. Visitors will find links to subsidiary companies and an online tour of the Universal Studios theme parks.

MCI

http://www.mci.com

Telecommunications giant MCI, providing long distance, wireless, local access, paging and Internet services, offers this corporate home page. Visitors can learn about its latest connectivity promotions and find detailed information about its products for business and home.

Mobil Corp.

http://www.mobil.com

Mobil Corporation, with oil, gas and petrochemical operations in more than 100 countries, offers company information and consumer services at this home page. Visit here for a variety of resources, from shareholder information to online gasoline credit card applications.

Motorola Inc.

http://www.mot.com

Motorola, a major manufacturer of semiconductors, electronics and wireless communications products, provides detailed company information and comprehensive product listings here. Includes links to the Motorola University Press and Internet archive sites containing data related to the communications company.

---

a2z EDITOR'S CHOICE

T-Net

http://www.usscreen.com

In case you thought that "I'm With Stupid" or the yellow smiley-face phenomenon just happened by accident, T-Net is here to set you straight about the genius and hard work that underlies this free-thinking arm of the apparel industry. The U.S. Screen Printing Institute's home page provides news from the screen-graphics, airbrush and t-shirt printing industries, along with an industry buyer's guide, trade-show listings and supplier links. A highlight is the T-Shirt Mall, where shrewd retailers can pick up everything "from funny slogans to slightly off color" togs and tees. Just do it!—*Reviewed by Joe Williams*

Check out a T-Shirt Mall Sponsor by clicking on the image below.

W.A.S.P. A Polo Classically Styled in 100% Pure Combed Cotton.

Visit our Featured Site of the Month. Enter their T-Shirt contest.

Net Sweats & Tees
cybershop extraordinaire - since October 1994

T-Shirt Mall Directory of Stores

PacifiCorp Energy Planet

http://www.upl.com

PacifiCorp Electric is an energy utility and tele-communications company with headquarters in Oregon. It provides a corporate overview, information about its products and services and stock-holder information here. Much of the site requires a password.

Pacific Telesis Group

http://www.pactel.com

U.S. telecommunications product and service provider Pacific Telesis Group maintains this site for corporate and financial information. Visit here to perform a keyword search of press releases from Pacific Telesis and its subsidiary, Pacific Bell.

Raytheon

http://www.raytheon.com

Raytheon is an international technology company that offers products in the realms of commercial electronics, engineering and construction, aviation, major appliances and bombs. Find a company history, press releases, shareholder information and employment opportunities at its corporate home page.

Reebok International

http://www.planetreebok.com

The Planet Reebok home page provides a gateway to information on sports and fitness, outdoor adventure, company-sponsored special events and Reebok brand athletic footwear. Visitors also will find Reebok corporate information, press releases, and a round-up of celebrity endorsers.

Rockwell International Corp.

http://www.rockwell.com

Global high-tech player Rockwell International packs its corporate home page with information on its many areas of expertise, which include avionics, defense electronics and semiconductor systems. Visitors will find departmental information and more.

Southwestern Bell

http://www.sbc.com

Southwestern Bell provides a "digital drive-in" for visitors to its home page. Cruise into the market for this Midwestern phone company's products and services, steer around the new technology reports, and park a while at its "cartoons and concessions" entertainment stand.

Sprint's World of Communications

http://www.sprint.com

Sprint provides long distance calling, video conferencing, network security and a host of other telecommunications services. Visitors to its home page will find product and service descriptions, special offers and Internet-based productivity solutions for business.

Sun Microsystems Inc.

http://www.sun.com/index.html

The home of Sun Microsystems—Silicon Valley's workstation powerhouse—offers more than mere product promotion. It's a graphics-driven company magazine that dishes the goods on everything from bandwidth to Sun's high-tech offerings. Visitors can link to Sun developers or browse corporate info.

Tele-Communications Inc.

http://www.tcinc.com

Denver-based cable television giant Tele-Communications Inc., or TCI, maintains this corporate home page. Visit here for information on its many holdings and its commitment to quality, uplifting television.

Texas Instruments Inc.

http://www.ti.com

This commercial site for Texas Instruments Inc. provides a comprehensive company profile with descriptions of new products, articles such as "The Digital Future," and employment opportunities.

T-Net

http://www.usscreen.com

The U.S. Screen Printing Institute's home page. See Editor's Choice.

---

a2z EDITOR'S CHOICE

Union Pacific Railroad

http://www.uprr.com

America has had a love affair with the railroads for as long as there's been an American dream, and the Union Pacific Corp. is an ongoing embodiment of that love affair. Sure, its home page has all the usual corporate information—financial and organizational notes, press releases, a system map—but it is in the ancillary materials that this site really shines. It is packed with the stuff of popular lore: the rich history of the frontier expansion, images of the great trains, scenic vistas along the railbed, and a gallery of yesteryear celebrities embarking on train trips. Visitors can also buy their own railroading gear at the company store, and those who fancy a life on the rails can check out the job opportunities.—*Reviewed by Joe Williams*

Henry Fonda departing on the City of Los Angeles for a vacation April 27, 1939

TRW Inc.

http://www.trw.com

Cleveland-based TRW, a provider of high-tech products and services to the automotive, space and defense industries, maintains this promotional site. Visit here for a company profile, plus information on the company's financial services (which include collecting and disseminating your credit report).

Union Pacific Railroad

http://www.uprr.com

The history and lore surrounding a great railroad. See Editor's Choice.

Unisys

http://www.unisys.com

This commercial Web site details corporate information and career opportunities at information management company Unisys. Visitors can stroll through the digital aisles of the company's online software store or thumb through recent press releases here.

United Parcel Service

http://www.ups.com

This home page for the United Parcel Service offers a wealth of information about its U.S. and international delivery services. Visitors can check out interactive assistance pages, U.S. service guides, detailed packaging information and more here.

U.S. West Inc.

http://www.uswest.com

U.S. West is a communications conglomerate producing and marketing directory services, cellular communications systems and communications software. At this corporate Web site, visitors will learn about the company and the products and services it offers.

Warner-Lambert Home Page

http://www.warner-lambert.com

The Warner-Lambert home page contains an encyclopedia of its brand-name items categorized by product type, such as cough and cold remedies, shaving products, gums and mints, skin care and antacids. Includes quizzes, games and answers to questions about ingredients, flavors and product usage.

Xerox Corp.

http://www.xerox.com

At the home page for "the document company," visitors will find extensive product documentation, research information, technical reports, financial data—and nary a smeared piece of mimeograph paper.

INSURANCE AND INSURANCE COMPANIES

CNA Insurance Companies

http://www.cna.com

Chicago.-based CNA Insurance Companies provides a variety of property and health services for businesses and individuals. Visit its home page for investor information, product descriptions and employment opportunities.

DPIC Companies Inc.

http://www.dpic.com

Marketing professional liability insurance programs in the U.S. and Canada, Design Professionals Insurance Company's group of companies maintains this promotional site. Visitors are encouraged to learn more about the group, its products and services.

Great-West Life

http://www.gwl.ca

Great-West Life, a Canadian insurance company, provides a corporate profile, press releases and quarterly results here. In French and English.

Hartford Steam Boiler Inspection & Insurance Company

http://www.hsb.com

This Connecticut company performs safety inspections and offers insurance on boilers, machinery, computers and other types of business property. Visit its home page for service descriptions and corporate profiles.

Hodge & Hodge

http://insurehodge.com/insurehodge

Hodge & Hodge is an auto-insurance brokerage firm located in Irvine, Calif. Visitors to the firm's home page will find a general corporate overview and information about its services.

Insurance News Network

http://www.insure.com

The Insurance News Network site features information about the insurance industry, surveys of insurance costs and auto safety, and Standard & Poor's ratings and reports. Links are included to specific insurance-information servers and providers.

Northwestern Mutual Life

http://www.northwesternmutual.com

Learn more about the life insurance corporation that calls itself the "quiet" company at the Northwestern Mutual Life home page. Visitors can find life-insurance policy information and state-by-state listings of local agents.

INVESTING AND INVESTMENTS

ARCHIVES AND INDICES

Canada Net Financial Pages

http://www.visions.com/netpages/finance/finance.html

This online financial resource features Canadian stock quotes, a searchable database of all Canadian mutual funds and links to financial articles. The page is part of the Canada Net Pages site, offering a comprehensive list of Canadian businesses.

Canadian Financial Network Inc.

http://www.canadianfinance.com

The Canadian Financial Network Inc. introduces its free Internet-based investment guide at this corporate site. Visit here for resource summaries and catalogs, and learn how to contribute information to its growing database.

Interactive Nest Egg

http://nestegg.iddis.com

If you feel guilty when you see articles on financial planning, this financial resource may make your entrance into the wonderful world of investment less stressful. Visitors will find links to the stock market news, mutual funds info and books for the beginning investor.

InvestSIG

http://cpcug.org/user/invest

InvestSIG, a special interest group of the Capital Personal Computer User Group, provides a variety of financial information here. Visitors will find links to books and publications covering economics, investing, stock markets and related topics.

Misc.invest FAQ on General Investment Topics

http://www.cis.ohio-state.edu/hypertext/faq/usenet/investment-faq/general/top.html

Usenet postings on a variety of financial topics are available at this general-use site. Visitors will find helpful information on investment instruments, including stocks, bonds, options, life insurance and others.

Wall Street Directory
http://www.cts.com/~wallst

This home page presents more than 2,500 pages of information and links for traders and investors. Includes pointers to the Sponsor's Mall, featuring thousands of products and services, and online information request forms.

ASSOCIATIONS AND ORGANIZATIONS

Financial Services Technology Consortium
http://www.llnl.gov/fstc

This consortium of financial-services providers, national laboratories, universities, industry powers and government agencies aims to enhance the competitiveness of the U.S. financial-services industry. Topics featured at this site include fraud prevention and electronic commerce and checking.

Securities & Exchange Commission
http://www.sec.gov

The U.S. Securities and Exchange Commission maintains this server featuring SEC news and general information, public statements, policies and answers to frequently asked questions.

BROKERAGE FIRMS

INTERNATIONAL

Altamira Investment Services Inc.
http://www.altamira.com

Toronto-based Altamira Investment Services, Inc. offers a variety of financial services, including "no load" mutual funds. Visitors to its investment library will find market commentary, financial-planning tips and related publications.

RINACO Plus
http://www.fe.msk.ru/infomarket/rinacoplus

This Moscow-based brokerage house offers various investment services related to the Russian securities market. Visitors will find market information including samples of industry reports, daily bids, quotes on liquid Russian securities and the "Institutional Investors' Guide to Russia."

UNITED STATES

PAWWS Financial Network
http:pawws.secapl.com

The PAWWS Financial Network provides a wide variety of Web-based investment tools, including integrated portfolio accounting, securities and market research tools, real-time quotations and online trading. Visit here to learn more about its subscription services.

Prudential Securities
http://www.prusec.com

Information about the financial services offered by Prudential Securities is featured at this site, along with resources for the beginning investor. Included are daily market commentaries, a document on planning for retirement and an investment personality quiz.

FRANCHISING

FranNet
http://www.frannet.com

Run your own business through franchising. See Editor's Choice.

INVESTMENT RESEARCH RESOURCES

inSight inFormation
http://avidinfo.com

The inSight inFormation home page is an online source of technical market opinions and investment strategies in U.S. equities, currencies, precious metals and world markets. Includes an overview of the company, editorials, client responses and a three-day trial subscription offer.

InvestorsEdge
http://www.irnet.com

InvestorsEdge, an online financial information service of Ethos Corp., offers news and corporate reports about publicly traded companies. Visit here for the latest investment-related news and links to stock quotes, worldwide financial markets and mutual funds.

MoneyLine
http://www.moneyline.com

MoneyLine, a provider of real-time financial information, offers visitors information about U.S. Treasury notes, municipal bonds, money markets and many other securities. The corporate site also includes details of the MoneyLine Corp.'s investor services.

NETworth
http://networth.galt.com/www/home/networth.html

The Quicken Financial Network site is home to NETworth, a service that dubs itself the "Internet Investor Network." Receive the latest stock market quotes, mutual fund news and other financial info of vital importance to investors and the state of U.S. and world markets.

NumaWeb
http://www.numa.com

Numa Financial Systems Ltd. of Bradford on Avon, England, offers this extensive guide to derivatives and other financial instruments. Includes company information, employment opportunites and investment resources.

Quote.Com
http://www.quote.com

This page provides an introduction to Quote.Com, an Internet-based financial-information provider. Registered guests get free access to services ranging from stock quotes and market-performance graphs to complete portfolio profiles. Registration information is provided on this page.

Silicon Investor
http://www.techstocks.com

Silicon Investor maintains this site for its technology-stock buyer's guide and news service. Visitors will find updated stock quotes, charts, discussion forums, and links to other high-tech stock Web resources. Includes a headline service and expert columns.

Technical Charts
http://www.homecom.com/timely/timely.html

Atlanta.-based HomeCom communications maintains this page for access to Standard & Poor's financial graphics. Visit here to view S&P 500 Index Daily Bar charts, updated five times a week.

STOCKS, BONDS, AND MUTUAL FUNDS

MUTUAL FUNDS

Dynamic Mutual Funds
http://www.dynamic.ca

Financial movers and shakers interested in Canadian mutual funds can check out the latest offerings from Dynamic Mutual Funds through its home page. Visitors can read about recent fund prices or check the market index.

Fast EDGAR Mutual Funds Reporting

http://edgar.stern.nyu.edu/mutual.html

New York University's Stern School of Business maintains this site to provide access to mutual funds reports. Visit here for date- and category-focused searches of a variety of mutual funds databases.

The Fund Library Inc.

http://www.fundlib.com

Closed-end funds, relatives of mutual funds, often are available at steep discounts, according to the information posted here. The site's maintainer aims to educate investors about these financial instruments and their peculiarities here.

Internet Closed-End Fund Investor

http://www.icefi.com

This site provides an introduction to closed-end funds, a quasi mutual-fund investment that is often available at a discount. It also serves as the front end of a subscription tip service and performance report.

Investors FastTrack Mutual Fund Tracking Service

http://www.fasttrack.net

Confused by the thousands of mutual funds and the outdated recommendations from magazines, newsletters, brokers and friends? Investors Fast Track offers updated information on more than 1,200 mutual funds for strategic investment planning.

Mutual Funds Magazine Online

http://www.mfmag.com

Mutual Funds Magazine, published by the Institute for Econometric Research, maintains this site to supplement its print version. Visit here for features and columns about mutual funds, retirement planning, mortgage management and many other financial matters. Includes online and print subscription information.

OPTIONS, COMMODITIES, AND FUTURES

Chicago Board of Trade

http://www.cbot.com

The Chicago Board of Trade offers a wealth of information for cybertourists and professional traders alike. Traders can download 10-minute-delayed quotes, global commodity prices and analysts' forecasts. Includes a virtual tour of the Board of Trade.

Chicago Board Options Exchange

http://www.cboe.com

The Chicago Board Options Exchange maintains this informational site to explain its investment

services. Visit here to learn about options investing, check the latest news listings, browse product literature and link to its educational extension, the Options Institute.

Chicago Mercantile Exchange

http://www.cme.com

The Chicago Mercantile Exchange's home page provides business news and information about the organization and its financial services and products. Includes a listing of member firms, a rundown of trading floor rules and a catalog of educational courses offered by the exchange.

PUBLICATIONS AND INDUSTRY NEWS

Closing Bell

http://www.merc.com/cbell2.html

Denver-based Mercury Mail Inc. provides a variety of online subscription services, including stocks, sports and weather reports. Visitors to its Closing Bell page will find out how to subscribe to its stock quote service, offering daily delivery of user-selected listings.

Financial Times Group

http://www.ft.com

The online adjunct of the respected Financial Times newspaper offers the highlights of each day's print version and a guide to other services from the Financial Times Group. Other sections include news briefs and world stock-market indices.

Investing News Online

http://www.ino.com

Investing News Online provides up-to-date information on all areas of financial investments. Visitors will find financial newsletters, magazines, libraries, charts and data here.

Knight-Ridder Financial Publishing Services

http://www.route-one.co.uk/route-one/ridder

Visitors to this site will learn about the financial and commodity news and statistics available from Knight-Ridder Inc.'s financial publishing division. Includes access to a historical database and an end-of-day stock quote service, plus downloadable demo software.

---

a2z EDITOR'S CHOICE

FranNet

http://www.frannet.com

Are you sick of kowtowing to the man? Do you want to be your own boss? Do you dream of wearing a paper hat and handing sacks of food through drive-up windows? Then you might have what it takes to be a franchise owner. But as FranNet points out, there are far more franchise money-making opportunities than just the traditional fast-food route. This page can connect you to franchisers ranging from tax-preparation firms to weight-loss centers. General-interest tips and topics covered here include selecting and financing a franchise, and a quick test to help visitors determine whether they're good candidates for owning a franchise operation in the first place.—*Reviewed by Joe Williams*

FranNet *Franchise Listings*

Accounting & Tax

Audio/Video

Automotive Products

Auto/Truck Rentals

Business Products & Services

Childrens' Services & Products

Network Information Services

http://www.nis.za

Investors can catch up on the latest South African financial news here. Visit here to monitor the Johannesburg Stock Exchange and purchase stocks through Sharenet, an online investing resource. Includes links to other stock exchanges and Inter-Shop, "South Africa's first online CyberShop."

U.S. Stock Market News

http://www.nando.net/newsroom/nt/stocks.html

The Nando Times provides this roundup of news stories focusing on the U.S. stock market. The page includes a summary of the day's stock activities, as well as headlines and stories about other markets.

STOCKS

African Stock Exchange Guide

http://africa.com/pages/jse/page1.htm

Part of McGregor Information Services' Virtual Africa site, this financial guide provides an overview of companies listed on the stock exchanges in Africa. Visitors can search the alphabetized and sector-based listings or link to sites offering other exchange-rate rundowns.

American Stock Exchange

http://www.amex.com

The world's largest stock market provides financial market services to more than 800 companies. Visitors to the American Stock Exchange home page will find financial updates, market summaries, an index of listed companies and pointers to related resources.

American Stock Exchange Market Summary

http://www.amex.com/summary/summary.htm

Investors and followers of happenings at the American Stock Exchange can take a look back at each day's market activities through this Web page. It is updated daily at approximately 6 p.m. Eastern Standard Time.

Asian Stock Market Closings

http://www.asia-inc.com/lippo/index.html

The regional trade publication Asia, Inc. maintains this update of Asian stock market closings. Visitors will find composite and weighted indexes for major Asian stock markets, including Hong Kong, Japan, Taiwan and others.

Digital Ink Financial Information— Vancouver Stock Exchange

http://giant.mindlink.net/financial/main_idx.html

This page from the larger Digital Ink Financial Information series focuses on the Vancouver Stock

Exchange. Insider trading reports, a list of public issuers in default, and exchange notices are featured along with an index to the companies listed on the exchange.

Electronic Share Information Ltd.

http://www.esi.co.uk

Electronic Share Information Ltd. is a British company offering free, up-to-the-minute prices and basic information on issues listed on the London Stock Exchange. Visitors can access online trading opportunities and other financial services.

LineWise

http://www.public.se

Sweden's LineWise Web site offers 30-minute delayed stock quotes from the Stockholm Stock Exchange. Visitors can find updated financial indices and submit their company's name to the database.

Nasdaq Financial Executive Journal

http://www.law.cornell.edu/nasdaq/nasdtoc.html

This Nasdaq publication offers stock market and investment news and analysis geared to industry professionals. Visitors will find an emphasis on information bearing on "corporate finance and investor relations."

NETworth Quote Server

http://quotes.galt.com

Galt Technologies Inc. provides a personalized stock-quote server that allows visitors to query information about designated stocks and to chart the stocks' progress.

R.R. Donnelley Library of SEC Materials

http://edgar.stern.nyu.edu/sponsors/sponsors.html

International printing services company R.R. Donnelly Financial maintains this site for a guide to U.S. Securities and Exchange Commission materials. Visit here for filer's manuals, trade law publications and links to New York University Business School resources.

Zacks Analyst Watch on the Internet

http://aw.zacks.com

Zacks Investment Research Inc., a Chicago-based investment-analysis firm, maintains this promotional site. Visit here for company information, links to related Internet resources and a demonstration of its database of more than 5,000 equities.

VENTURE CAPITAL COMPANIES

Hummer Winblad Venture Partners

http://www.humwin.com

Hummer Winblad Venture Partners is a California-based company that invests in new and growing software companies. The firm gives an overview of its services on this promotional page. It posts a "cool jobs @ hot companies" listing here, too.

PERSONAL FINANCES AND TAXES

DIRECTORIES AND GUIDES

LawTalk - Business Law and Personal Finance

http://www.law.indiana.edu/law/bizlaw.html

This "talking" index of business law and personal finance information links to audio files on a variety of related topics; from bounced checks to investment opportunities. It's an offering of the Indiana University, Bloomington, School of Law.

PERSONAL FINANCIAL SERVICES

CONSUMER CREDIT COMPANIES

Barclaycard Netlink

http://www.barclaycard.co.uk

Barclaycard, an English credit-card company, provides information here on its financial services. Visit here to learn about the company and its membership benefits.

MasterCard

http://www.mastercard.com

MasterCard maintains this site to highlight its credit-card services, accepted by more than 12 million businesses worldwide. Visitors will find customer support resources, financial-security tips and an automated teller-machine locator for world travelers.

Visa Expo

http://www.visa.com

Credit card monolith Visa offers its financial products to the masses at this promotional site. Consumers can review the company's financial tips, explore its Internet commerce standards or apply for credit online.

TAX RETURN PREPARATION AND ADVICE

Ernst & Young International

http://www.ey.com

The accounting firm of Ernst & Young International maintains this map-based, interactive corporate page offering links to its member firms around the world. Visitors also will find information about the organization's accounting, auditing, tax preparation and consulting services.

1-800-TAX-LAWS

http://www.5010geary.com

U.S. taxpayers can file online via this home page from a national network of tax professionals. Find a step-by-step set of forms, tax humor, and information about the company, including contact numbers.

Tax Wizard

http://taxwizard.com

Hargrave & Hargrave, a Los Angeles-based accounting firm, provides the Tax Wizard for a user-friendly tour of available taxpayer resources. Visitors can download tax information search tools, find legislation updates and ask the Wizard questions about current tax laws.

U.S. Tax Code On-Line

http://www.fourmilab.ch/ustax/ustax.html

Though not a site sponsored by the U.S. government, this page allows access to the complete text of the U.S. Internal Revenue Title 26 of the Code (26 U.S.C). For ease of cross-referencing, hyperlinks have been embedded in the text.

REAL ESTATE

AGENTS AND BROKERS ONLINE

COMMERCIAL

Concord Pacific Place

http://www.concordpacific.com

Fancy some beachfront property in the Pacific Northwest? This promotional page is maintained by the Concord Pacific Developments Corp., a property developer in Vancouver, British Columbia. Visitors are encouraged to learn more about the $3 billion community development.

Marcus & Millichap

http://www.mmreibc.com

This promotional site is the Web home of Marcus & Millichap, a national real-estate investment brokerage specializing in "the acquisition and disposition of income producing property including offices, apartments, retail and industrial properties, mobile-home parks, single-tenant, net-leased properties, senior housing facilities and land." Visitors can find out more about the company and its office locations or review its listings of properties for sale.

RESIDENTIAL

bestagents.com

http://www.bestagents.com/

bestagents.com offers an extensive directory of qualified real-estate agents and helpful property purchasing tips. Visit here to learn the basics of real estate and find professionals in the field.

Homefinders' Real Estate

http://www.homefinders.com

Homefinders' Real Estate Services is a real-estate agency serving Maryland and Virginia. Home shoppers can access information about the company, along with pointers on determining spending limits, finding financing options and choosing an area to live in.

Pam Golding Properties

http://www.os2.iaccess.za/pgp

This Internet property portfolio lists homes for sale in South Africa. A company profile is available, as is information on property trends, tips on buying and selling homes, and a currency converter.

Rubloff Residential Real Estate Home Page

http://rubloff.com

Rubloff Residential Real Estate specializes in the downtown and near north areas of Chicago. This site features images and links to related sites.

WaterFront

http://www.islands.com

The WaterFrontSunshine Dreams Real Estate home page from Coral Technologies Inc. (CTI) provides pointers to a number of realtors specializing in real estate available in Florida and the Caribbean. Also available at this site are links to the home pages of CTI's clients and sites related to tropical diving and resort locations.

Windermere Real Estate

http:windermere.com

The Windermere Real Estate page offers visitors access to the real-estate brokerage services of this regional firm located in the Northwest. Property listings are featured along with advice for buying and selling real estate.

ARCHIVES AND INDICES

Ask Sherlock

http://accnet.com/cgi-bin/listings.pl

This search engine, provided by ACCNET real-estate services, allows visitors to scan the Internet for property listings. Includes helpful instructions on running simple keyword searches.

Home NetCenter Net

http://www.netprop.com

Net Properties is a Web publisher whose goal is to provide the most comprehensive real-estate information to the industry and general public. Visitors to this site can browse (or list with) residential and commercial real-estate "information superstores."

Homes & LandRental Guide

http://www.homes.com/Welcome.html

Homes & Land Publishing Corp. runs an electronic open house here. A real-estate information center, this site offers a national database of available properties, rentals and real-estate agents. Includes information on Smart Moves personal relocation software.

REonline

http://www.reonline.com/re

This online selling block offers listings of business, commercial and recreational properties. Visitors can search for real estate at international locations. Includes pointers to other real-estate resources.

ASSOCIATIONS AND ORGANIZATIONS

National Association of Realtors Home Page

http://www.realtor.com

Realtors can check here for information on their profession through the Realtors Information Network and other resources. Net users looking to buy a home can also stop by for advice on mortgages, property rights and taxation or to view thousands of homes-for-sale listings.

National Association of Residential Property Managers

http://www.marketnet.com/mktnet/narpm

The National Association of Residential Property Managers is a national organization representing landlords. Visitors will find an overview of the group here, along with membership information and an application form.

LISTINGS

COMMERCIAL

Flick Resource Center

http://www.tpoint.net/flickrpt/flickhome.html

If you're buying, selling or negotiating for commercial property in central Texas, the Flick Resource Center offers market research and geographic market sector reviews. There's an office building directory for greater Austin, tax and commercial sales services, and a bushel of other information for real-estate professionals.

Market ICI World Real Estate Network

http://www.iciworld.com

The Market Industrial, Commercial and Investment Real Estate Network, based in Toronto, Ontario, offers advertising and directory services to professional property buyers and sellers. Visit here for company news, subscription offers and an extensive index of real-estate resources.

RESIDENTIAL

Apartment Relocation Service

http://www.homefair.com/apt/search.html

This page, from the Homebuyer's Fair site, offers apartment relocation services. Find online help apartment hunting in Massachusetts, Rhode Island, New Hampshire and Connecticut, plus various Northern metro areas and other regions of the U.S.

BayNet Real Estate

http://www.baynet.com/re.html

If you're looking to buy housing in the San Francisco Bay area, BayNet provides maps, photos and a search function to save driving from town to town. Demographic breakdowns of towns are also available here, and estimated total housing costs.

Estate Net

http://www.estate.de

House hunters can access a worldwide real-estate database through the Estate Net site. Prospective buyers can view listings by selecting from a world map or check the special offers section for hot properties. The site is based in Germany but is available in English.

FosTech Homes Online

http://www.cyberstore.ca/FosTech

Canada's FosTech Homes Online features real-estate listings for scenic Vancouver, British Columbia. Users can check residential and commercial listings describing properties for sale and homes for rent. Visitors also can read profiles of area realtors.

Homes & LandRental Guide

http://www.homes.com/Welcome.html

Homes & Land Publishing Corp. runs an electronic open house here. A real-estate information center, this site offers a national database of available properties, rentals and real estate agents. Includes information on Smart Moves personal relocation software.

Homes4Sale

http://www.homes4sale.com

The Homes4Sale Web site provides information about property for sale in California. The page includes listings of residential, condominium and commercial real estate.

Houston Real Estate Web

http://www.sccsi.com/hrew/houston.html

The Houston Real Estate Web provides consumers with online home and property listings for the Houston metroplex. A clickable map of the area connects visitors with information on homes in various suburbs. Includes a mortgage calculator that figures estimated monthly payments.

Real Estate Connection

http://www.austinre.com

The Austin Real Estate Connection provides public access to real-estate listings and services in that area of Texas. Visitors can search through residential and commercial listings—including apartments—and access mortgage lenders, title-insurance companies and more.

Real Estate Maine

http://www.biddeford.com/real_estate

Real Estate Maine maintains this site for online guided tours and detailed property information. Visit here to learn about the company and link to property pricing and availability listings.

Real Estate Online's New York City Guide

http://www.nyrealty.com

This real-estate page contains information on rentals, residential properties, vacation homes and commercial properties in New York City and its surrounding areas. It includes market analyses and posts lists of real estate agencies, architects and designers.

Rent.Net

http://www.rent.net

Looking for a new apartment? It couldn't be easier with Rent.Net, an interactive database of more than 300,000 furnished and unfurnished apartments across the United States and Canada. Each entry comes complete with photographs, floor plans and location maps.

Scott Sells Seattle

http:oneworld.wa.com/realestate/scott1.html

This promotional page is the Internet home of Scott Aiken, Seattle real estate broker. Buyers, sellers and renters alike are welcome to stop by and browse the information on housing in the city that's becoming the new San Francisco.

Toronto Real Estate for Sale

http://www.onramp.ca/realestate

This site features real estate for sale in the city of Toronto, Canada, and surrounding areas. Also included is a listing of real estate agencies and a listing of Toronto and Ontario properties.

Westate: Real Estate Server in Belgium

http://www.westate.be

Via this site, well-heeled visitors can shop for a house in Belgium. The service includes real-estate listings with photos. In English, French and Dutch.

LOANS AND LENDERS

Canada Trust Mortgage Co.

http://www.canadatrust.com

Canada Trust, one of the country's largest non-bank financial institutions, maintains this site to introduce its personal and corporate services. In addition to an extensive index of financial information, visitors will find links to local and national consumer organizations.

Consumer Mortgage Information Network

http://www.human.com/proactive/index.html

The Consumer Mortgage Information Network helps home buyers connect with favorable residential financing plans by arming them with pointers to software, articles and reference materials related to home finance.

Fannie Mae

http://www.fanniemae.com

This Fannie Mae is a diversified financial company (not a chocolatier) and a provider of mortgage funds. At the Fannie Mae Web site, browsers can link to pages on personal finance, home buying and real estate.

HomeOwners Finance

http://www.homeowners.com

California-based HomeOwners Finance provides complete mortgage brokerage services, including fixed- and adjustable-rate mortgages. Visitors are invited to take the Refi TestDrive to see how much they might save by refinancing with HomeOwners Finance.

HomeOwners Finance Center Loan Calculation Page

http://www.internet-is.com/homeowners/calculator.html

The HomeOwners Finance Center Loan Calculation Page is a simple yet very useful page that asks home owners to fill in information about their home loan in a calculator screen and then calculates monthly payments and divides the payments into principal and interest.

Mortgage Finance Resources

http://www.homefair.com/homefair/mortgage.html

Mortgage Finance Resources, part of the Homebuyer's Fair web site, helps potential U.S. homebuyers figure out the best financing options. How to shop for a mortgage, figuring out what is affordable, loan cost comparisons, insurance, and 15-year versus 30-year loans are all discussed.

Mortgage Guaranty Insurance Corp.

http://www.mgic.com

The Mortgage Guaranty Insurance Corp. home page offers a checklist and files to teach people how secure a home loan. The commercial site also includes detailed corporate information about the Milwaukee-based corporation.

P.A. Mortgage Service Inc.

http://www.cftnet.com/mall/munzo

A loan officer at Florida-based P.A. Mortgage Service introduces potential customers to the company's financial and loan products at this promotional site. Find out about arranging home loans in the Sunshine State.

LOCATORS

Florida Internet Real Estate Guide

http://www.lynqs.com/floridaguide

This real estate information service provides a variety of resources for those looking for a home in Florida. Visit here to link with home-finding services, government and business information and more. Includes a clickable map for honing the home search.

PUBLICATIONS AND INDUSTRY NEWS

House Buying and Financing

http://www.gsa.gov/staff/pa/cic/housing.htm

This Web site, maintained by the General Services Administration's Consumer Information Center, indexes consumer information for homeowners and homebuyers. Visitors can sample low-cost pamphlets on buying and financing a house, homeowners' insurance, home improvement and more.

HSH Associates

http://www.hsh.com

Financial publishers HSH Associates offer a variety of services online, including mortgage and consumer loan information. Aimed at lenders, real estate agents and consumers, services include national average mortgage rates, products and market trends.

TRADE AND LABOR RESOURCES

CONSTRUCTION AND REPAIR

American Society of Home Inspectors

http://www1.mhv.net/~dfriedman/ashihome.htm

This unofficial guide to the American Society of Home Inspectors, certifying inspectors in the United States and Canada, is maintained by a local Internet service provider. Visitors will find an extensive index of trade resources, including online technical libraries, industry publications and home buyer services.

InterPRO Resources Inc.

http://www.ipr.com

This Orlando, Fla.-based company offers a wide variety of information and services for architects, engineers and contractors. Visitors will find publications and lists of construction industry firms and professional organizations.

ENTERTAINMENT

The Virtual Headbook

http://www.xmission.com/~wintrnx/virtual.html

The Virtual Headbook provides a talent pool for casting agents on the Internet. Visitors will find actors' headshots, resumes, membership information for actors and models, and casting call services for directors, agents and talent scouts.

COMPUTER SCIENCE

THE 25 MOST POPULAR COMPUTER SCIENCE SITES

The Atomic Diner
http://atomic.com/

Bellcore Home Page
http://www.bellcore.com/

Chip Directory
http://www.xs4all.nl/~ganswijk/chipdir/

CMP Publications
http://techweb.cmp.com/techweb/docs/list-o-pubs.html

The Commodore 8-bit WWW server
http://www.hut.fi/~msmakela/cbm/

Computing Dictionary
http://wombat.doc.ic.ac.uk/

Dell.com
http://www.dell.com/

Die DFN-CERT Home Page
http://www.cert.dfn.de/

Digital Equipment Corporation
http://www.dec.com/

Directory of /SimTel
ftp://oak.oakland.edu/SimTel

Fellowbug's Laboratory
http://www.dtd.com/bug/

Iomega Home Page
http://www.iomega.com/

JAVA™— Programming for the Internet
http://java.sun.com

Kai's Power Tips and Tricks for Photoshop
http://the-tech.mit.edu/KPT/

Macworld Online
http://www.macworld.com/

Microsoft Support Online Knowledge Base
http://www.microsoft.com/KB/

NCSA Software Tools
http://www.ncsa.uiuc.edu/SDG/Software/SDGSoftDir.html

NIIP Homepage
http://www.niiip.org/

Novell NetWare
http://www.netware.com/

SCRI Home Page
http://www.scri.fsu.edu/

SGI DOOM FAQ
http://www.cmpharm.ucsf.edu/~troyer/sgidoomfaq.html

Shareware! Shareware! Shareware! - Jumbo! - Shareware!
http://www.jumbo.com/

Welcome to Computer Life Online
http://www.complife.ziff.com/~complife/

Why Macintosh?
http://www2.apple.com/whymac/

WWW Home Page at the CTR
http://www.ctr.columbia.edu/

ASSOCIATIONS AND ORGANIZATIONS

Advanced Radiodata Research Centre (ARRC)

http://www.arrc.ca/

The Advanced Radiodata Research Centre in Richmond, British Columbia, is an initiative of Motorola and the Canadian federal government to provide funding and support to Canadian software developers and universities for research in wireless data technology.

American Committee for Interoperable Systems

http://www.sun.com/ACIS/

Issues regarding software interoperability and copyrights are the focus of the American Committee for Interoperable Systems page. Includes a Frequently Asked Questions sheet, a list of members and links to related papers and discussions.

American National Standards Institute

http://www.ansi.org/home.html

The American National Standards Institute hosts a wealth of info about its mission, developments, people, resources and membership. Browse ANSI's latest news, calendar of events and reference library or link to other pages with standards info.

ARPA Knowledge Sharing Effort Public Library

http://www-ksl.stanford.edu/ knowledge-sharing/README.html

The ARPA Knowledge Sharing Effort is a consortium that seeks to develop standards for sharing knowledge bases and knowledge-based systems. Find here a public directory for information and software related to ARPA projects.

ATM Forum

http://www.atmforum.com/

More than 700 companies belong to the ATM (Asynchronous Transfer Mode) Forum, which promotes and develops this method of communication that can be used on networks to carry voice, data, and video. Visitors will get an overview of the forum and ATM here.

The Cell Relay Retreat

http://cell-relay.indiana.edu/

An association of vendors, carriers, consultants and users, the Frame Relay Forum maintains this site in support of its efforts to implement cell relay technology. Find technical and group info, newsletters, the newsgroup archive, and related links.

CI Labs

http://www.cilabs.org/

Computer industry scions Apple, IBM, and Novell have established this nonprofit organization (CI Labs) to develop applications incorporating the cross-platform OpenDoc software architecture.

The Coalition for Networked Information

http://www.cni.org/CNI.homepage.html

The Coalition for Networked Information, a Washington, D.C.-based organization working to advance the role of computer networks in society, maintains this site for general information. Visit here to learn about its programs, initiatives, leadership, and computing resources.

The Coalition for Networked Information Gopher

gopher://gopher.cni.org/

The Coalition for Networked Information works to hone information management skills. At this gopher server visitors will find a brief overview of the group, as well as access to its FTP archives.

The Corporation for National Research Initiatives

http://www.cnri.reston.va.us/

The Corporation for National Research Initiatives is a nonprofit organization that researches initiatives on the use of information technology. It gives an overview of its programs and a biography of its president here.

CPSR

http://www.cpsr.org/dox/home.html

Computer Professionals for Social Responsibility is an alliance of scientists and professionals devoted to advising policymakers and the public on the potential of computer technologies. Visitors to its site will find an organizational overview, articles on electronic ethics, and more.

IHETS

http://www.ind.net/

The Indiana Higher Education Telecommunication System is a statewide consortium for all higher education shared voice, video, and data networks. Documentation on the networks, a directory of Internet starter pages, and a link to INDnet, the state's Internet backbone, are available here.

IMA: The Best Minds in Multimedia

http://www.ima.org/

The Interactive Multimedia Association offers a wealth of information about its multimedia products, services, and events. Check out IMA's digital media products, books, documents, digital video systems, and video games or peruse upcoming expo information.

Independant Group of Unix-Alikes and Network Activists

http://www.innet.net/iguana/

A nonprofit organization, IGUANA supports and provides information to its members, primarily "users of 'Free Operating Systems' and users wishing to connect several computer platforms through networks." Visit this page for membership and event info, links to members and staff, plus Linux resources.

International Federation for Information Processing

http://www.acs.org.au/ifip96.html

The International Federation for Information Processing site is sponsored by the Australian Computer Society. Visitors will find schedules and information on computer conferences and seminars taking place in Australia.

IIT Software Engineering

http://wwwsel.iit.nrc.ca/

The Institute for Information Technology's Software Engineering Group develops software tools and techniques that assist Canadian software companies. Visitors here will learn about the group's research and can download technical papers. The group also provides pointers to its favorite software sites. In English or French.

Lone Star SIGCHI

http://www.utdallas.edu/orgs/sigchi/ LSCHI.html

Texas-based Lone Star SIGCHI is an official chapter of the Special Interest Group for Computer-Human Interaction of the Association for Computing Machinery. Visitors to this organizational site will find an online newsletter, as well as e-mail contacts and a list of "favorite CHI resources."

National Multimedia Association of America

http://nmaa.org/

The National Multimedia Association of America's mission is "to improve its members' knowledge and abilities while promoting and developing new markets and uses for multimedia applications." Visit here for information about the association and how to become a member.

The NetBSD Project

http://www.netbsd.org/

The NetBSD Project is a volunteer effort to produce a free Unix-like operating system. Visit this site for updates on its progress and access to the latest software release.

NIIIP

http://www.niiip.org/

Avoiding the digital debacle of competing software protocol standards is the task of the National Industrial Information Infrastructure Protocols Consortium. Visitors to the group's home page can learn about the consortium's efforts to aid U.S. companies by setting up a common standard.

Object Database Management Group

http://www.odmg.org/

The Object Database Management Group, a consortium of vendors and third party organizations developing cross-platform computer standards, maintains this site for news, member information, and technical specifications. Includes links to related Web sites.

ShowNet 365

http://www.shownet.com/

The online conference calendar, ShowNet 365, features information about computer industry trade shows and expositions on its home page. Includes links to such events as PC Expo in New York and DB/Expo in San Francisco.

SIGGRAPH Online

http://siggraph.org/

SIGGRAPH is the ACM special interest group on computer graphics. Includes information on SIGGRAPH workshops and conferences, resources, publications, searchable archives, and calendar.

Softbank Exposition

http://www.sbexpos.com/

Softbank Exposition organizes conferences, exhibitions and seminars for technology vendors and buyers. Visitors to its promotional site will find schedules and information on Softbank's upcoming events.

The Software Publishers Association

http://www.spa.org/

The Software Publishers Association is a trade organization for the PC software industry. Visitors can find information on member companies, addresses and contacts, SPA publications and membership guidelines.

SPARC International

http://www.sparc.com/

SPARC International is a nonprofit organization that promotes SPARC microprocessor architecture, establishes hardware and software specifications and ensures compatability of SPARC products. This support page includes links to standards organizations, technical information and more.

UniForum

http://www.uniforum.org/

UniForum is an international vendor association offering products and services to information systems professionals. At the UniForum home page browsers can read about UniForum '96 conferences, trade shows, products, and publications.

Usenix Association

http://www.usenix.org/

This home page for Usenix, the advanced computing systems professional and technical association, also provides information on SAGE, the System Administrators Guild. Designed for members, options include links to the calendar of events, the membership directory, and publications.

Versit

http://www.versit.com/

The focus here is news and information about Versit, an alliance founded by Apple Computer Inc., AT&T, IBM, and Siemens to create interoperability specifications. The site includes a FAQ sheet, technical specifications, and a discussion group.

XIWT

http://www.cnri.reston.va.us:3000/XIWT/public.html

XIWT is a multi-industry coalition dedicated to "providing and maintaining the architecture for a powerful, sustainable national information infrastructure." Read their "White Papers" and reports or simply learn about their short-term goals.

FREEWARE AND SHAREWARE REPOSITORIES

AMIGA (TOASTER)

ALynx

http://www.fhi-berlin.mpg.de/amiga/alynx.html

Information about the ALynx ASCII Web browser for Amiga computers is the topic of this page. Visitors can download the latest version of the program, read the documentation or find out facts about the people who ported the popular, lo-fi Lynx browser to the Amiga platform.

APPLE MACINTOSH AND CLONES

mirror.apple.com

http://mirror.apple.com/

At the mirror.apple.com server, Apple Computer Inc. offers Macintosh users access to a selection of Macintosh software archives. Visitors can download public domain applications and software documentation.

MULTI-PLATFORM

AMINET FTP mirror

ftp://wuarchive.wustl.edu/

The Washington University FTP archive offers the usual collection of public domain software and documentation files available for anonymous download. Search for Web connectivity packages, operating system info or multimedia utilities. The site also includes the Digital Equipment User Society's archives.

CSIRO Australia Telescope National Facility FTP Archive

ftp://ftp.atnf.csiro.au/pub/software/karma/

Karma is the anonymous FTP software archive operated by the CSIRO Australia Telescope National Facility in Sydney. Look here for data and utilities useful to radiophysics researchers.

Everyday Computing: Systems, Languages and Software

http://www.cs.cmu.edu/Web/computing.html

Find pointers "to various resources for hacking, programming and otherwise getting along in your computing environment" on the Everyday Computing: Systems, Languages and Software page. Platforms covered range from Amiga to Unix and from archives to Web servers with little left out in between.

FTP Interface for Motorola Archives

http://nyquist.ee.ualberta.ca/html/motorola.html

This online archive provides working tools for engineers working on Motorola microprocessor development. Included here are links to the site's host, the University of Alberta's electrical engineering department and to Motorola's home page and freeware services.

Games on the Internet

http://happypuppy.com/games/lordsoth/
index.html

Pointing to freeware, shareware, and demos, this site covers over 1,200 games on the Internet and the number continues to grow. In addition to the games, find cheats, hints, walkthroughs, FAQs, offset lists, and other useful resources.

Garbo Anonymous FTP Archive

http://garbo.uwasa.fi/

Garbo is an Finnish archive of shareware available for anonymous download. Visitors will find software offerings in all categories for MS-DOS, Windows, Unix, and Macintosh platforms.

Jumbo! Official Web Shareware Site

http://www.jumbo.com/

You'll find all the shareware you could ever want. See Editor's choice, page 126.

Motorola Microcontroller's Freeware Data Services

http://freeware.aus.sps.mot.com/freeweb/
index.html

Motorola's Advanced Microcontroller Group Freeware Data Services provides digital data services via modem and the Internet. Visit this page to find links to FTP files, bulletin board services and other sites of interest to users of Motorola microcontrollers.

NCSA Software Tools

http://www.ncsa.uiuc.edu/SDG/Software/
SDGSoftDir.html

The National Center for Supercomputing Applications provides free public access to its software tools at this site. With a concentration on the development of scientific tools, the NCSA creates applications for Macintosh, IBM-compatible and Unix-based systems.

pub directory

ftp://ftp2.cc.ukans.edu/pub/

The University of Kansas archives software and documentation for various computer platforms here. The files are available for anonymous download.

Shareware by Category from many of STAR's 100+ Software Authors

http://www.shareware.org/

Visitors can download a wide array of shareware from this Shareware Trade Association and Resources (STAR) site. The group also includes a profile of its work.

SunSITE Hong Kong (SunSITE.ust.hk)

http://sunsite.ust.hk/

This multimedia information service is maintained by the Hong Kong University of Science and Technology. Visitors to this SunSITE—Sun Software, Information and Technology Exchange site—will find archives and documents relating to Sun Microsystems computers and tips for producing cross-platform multimedia applications.

University of Michigan Software Gopher Server

gopher://gopher.archive.merit.edu:70/11/
.software-archives

The University of Michigan provides this gopher server, containing a large archive of shareware and freeware. Visitors can access public domain titles and even licensed software, browsable by software type.

---

a2z EDITOR'S CHOICE

Jumbo! Official Web Shareware Site

http://www.jumbo.com/

Shareware is Bingo for the 1990s. Every once in a while you win. Oftentimes, it's just fun to play the game. After all, the company's good and the stakes are just right. In that case, think of Jumbo! as the world's largest church basement, with over 59,208 titles available for anonymous download at almost any time of the day. The catch? Advertisements, about five small ones per page. The latch? Turn "Auto Load Images" off. But even if you make it past the tantalizing, animated billboards at the top of the page, you're not guaranteed to find the game, utility or system tool you're looking for—when you're looking for it. The site allows for a maximum of 60 connections from 11 p.m. 'til 4 a.m., Monday through Friday, and only 10 users are allowed to download files during weekday "business hours." But then, would anything Bingo-esque be immediate delivery? If you're fully in touch with the Bingo vibe, you can get a winning ticket, faster, by eschewing the hi-fi "http" connection and opting for a no-frills "ftp" route. Jumbo provides several mirror sites for players who don't mind the uncertain loss of graphics—and advertisements—for the certain gain of a quicker queue. There might be other archives this big, but none are this Jumbo!—*Reviewed by José Marquez*

THE COOLEST SHAREWARE SITE ON THE WEB!

Shareware! Games! Freeware!

FREE! FREE! FREE!

The Most Mind-Boggling, Most Eye-Popping, Most Death-Defying Conglomeration of Freeware and Shareware Programs on the Known-Web!

59,208 PROGRAMS! Count 'em! *59,208*

PC

LINUX

Linux FTP Archive

ftp://tsx-11.mit.edu/pub/linux/

The Linux FTP archive offers an assortment of resources for Linux users, including DOS utilities and software documentation. It also posts an archive of the Linux-Activists mailing lists.

Linux FTP Archive

ftp://sunsite.unc.edu/pub/Linux/

This University of North Carolina SUNSITE FTP archive includes various Linux files and utilities which are available for anonymous download.

OS/2

Hobbes Virtual Mirror

http://www.columbia.edu/~chs11/hvm.html

This virtual mirror page is designed to ease the retrieval of files from the Hobbes OS/2 archive and its mirrors. Includes links to supporting servers.

OS/2 Warp Shareware and Freeware

http://www.mit.edu:8001/activities/os2/faq/os2faq0302.html

This site provides information on obtaining OS/2 Warp shareware and freeware, with information about BBSs, Usenet newsgroups and FTP sites. Links to related sites are also offered.

Software Library - OS/2 Software

http://www.state.ky.us/software/os2.html

Kentucky's Web Services maintains this site to provide utilities for IBM's OS/2 operating system. Visit here for a variety of resources for use in Internet connectivity, multimedia programming, graphics applications and more.

WINDOWS

The Best Windows 95 Software!

http://biology.queensu.ca/~jonesp/win95/software/software.html

A selective archive of Windows 95 shareware available on the Web is offered here. Windows 95 users can access a wide variety of software including Internet applications, games, graphics, and utilities.

Galt Shareware and Software

http://www.galttech.com/

Galt Technology produces shareware for Windows-based platforms. Their site includes screen savers, utilities, games, downloading information, and a company newsletter.

InfoWest Windows 95 Software Archive

http://www.netex.net/w95/

The InfoWest Windows 95 software archive features applications, discussion forums, a page devoted to tips and tricks and links to related sites.

Inter-Links

http://www.nova.edu/Inter-Links/

The CICA computer software archive offers an index of pointers to its Microsoft Windows-related subdirectories at this site. Link to file collections organized around a variety of subjects including printer drivers, programming information, utilities and more.

Microsoft Software FTP Site

ftp://ftp.microsoft.com/

Here's the FTP directory for Microsoft Corporation. Visitors will find files packed with information on Microsoft, its support, services and products.

Process Software Windows 95 FTP Site!

http://www.process.com/win95/win95ftp.htm

Process Software Corporation provides this archive of shareware and freeware for Windows 95. The site contains Internet utilities, multimedia software, Windows 95 enhancements, and graphics utilities.

Sophos Software's NetSpace

http://www.mindspring.com/~sophos/sophos.html

The home page for Sophos Software includes news, registration information and downloadable programs. Featured shareware includes Collegio Football '95, Collegio Basketball '96, utilities and multimedia products for Windows.

UNIX-LIKE WORKSTATIONS

ftp.digital.com World-Wide Web Server

http://gatekeeper.dec.com/hypertext/gatekeeper.home.html

This FTP archive is maintained by the Digital Equipment Corp. An unsupported service of Digital's corporate research division, it is searchable and provides access to DEC software, usage guidelines, and other information.

The HENSA Unix Archive - JISC funded - SGI powered

http://unix.hensa.ac.uk/hensa.unix.html

The Higher Education National Software Archives, or HENSA, at the University of Kent at Canterbury, England, maintains this site for its Unix programming archive. Visit here for news, automated searches, browsable archives, online documentation, and other services.

PICO Web Server

http://picossc.et.tudelft.nl/

The PICO Web Server page offers links to downloadable HPUX, COMPASS, VANTAGE, XILINX, OCEAN/NELSIS, and PUBLICAD software plus computer hardware and chip processing information. In Dutch.

HARDWARE

APPLE MACINTOSH AND CLONES

DIRECT

Apple Solutions Server

http://www.solutions.apple.com/

The Apple Solutions Server offers information on the computer maker's Web-related hardware product line. Find a special focus on educational market strategies and resources for disabled users.

DayStar

http://www.daystar.com/

Flowery Branch, Ga.-based DayStar Digital Inc. develops, manufactures and markets high performance MacOS-based workstations for media-publishing professionals. Visitors to its home page will find company news, downloadable software and technical support resources.

CAPTURE

Radius Inc.

http://www.radius.com/

Radius Inc., a computer hardware and software supplier specializing in graphics and video solutions for the Macintosh, maintains this promotional page. Visitors are invited to learn more about the company, its line of products and customer services and to browse the online software library.

CHIPS, ETC.

Clock Chipping
http://violet.berkeley.edu/~schrier/mhz.html

The Clock Chipping home page, maintained by a University of California, Berkeley researcher, provides updated information about crystal oscillator swapping technology. Visit here for related software and resources for Apple Macintosh computer systems.

INTERNET AND RELATED WIDE AREA NETWORKS

What's New on Apple Servers?
http://www.apple.com/documents/whatsnew.html

Apple Computer Inc., makers of the Macintosh, updates visitors on the content of the company's many Web servers at this site. The page announces new areas and topics of discussion, as well as news and announcements categorized by date.

NETWORKING AND NETWORKING CONSULTANTS

Sonic Systems Inc.
http://www.sonicsys.com/

Sonic Systems Inc. soups up Macintosh systems with its high performance networking products. Review the company's offerings which include hardware bridges, remote booting software, ethernet cards, and transceivers and software bridges at this promotional site.

VARS

Sun Remarketing Inc.
http://www.sunrem.com/

Sun Remarketing Inc., a Logan, Utah-based Apple computer reseller, maintains this promotional site. Visit here for new and used product price lists and company contact information.

ELECTRONICS

Advanced Micro Devices Inc.
http://www.amd.com/

Advanced Micro Devices Inc. is an integrated circuit manufacturing company. Its home page includes information on AMD's microprocessors and programmable logic devices.

Advanced Microelectronics
http://www.aue.com/

Advanced Microelectronics, an integrated circuit design center in Jackson, Mississippi, provides examples of its custom designs, a list of clients and a list of technology associates here. The detailed site also includes a close look at the company's technical abilities and hardware.

Altera Corp.
http://www.altera.com/

The Altera Corp., an international supplier of high density, programmable logic devices, maintains this promotional page. Visitors are invited to learn more about the company, its products and its programs here. Includes employment opportunities listings.

Applied Microsystems Corporation— The Embedded Systems Experts
http://www.amc.com/

Applied Microsystems Corporation is a manufacturer of integrated development systems for embedded design. Visitors to its support site will find sales information, technical documentation, press releases, customer support and job listings.

Avnet Inc.
http://www.avnet.com/

New York-based Avnet Inc.'s home page features information about the electronic components and computer products the company makes and distributes. Visitors will find a corporate profile and news about the company and its products.

IBM Microelectronics
http://www.chips.ibm.com/

The Microelectronics Division of IBM sponsors this page. Check out the latest developments in the industry, browse product information, access employment opportunities or link to the main IBM server.

National Electronics Test Center
http://www.netc.ie/

The Forbairt Corporation of Dublin, Ireland, presents the home page for its National Electronics Test Center. This division offers testing and consulting services for electronic and electrical systems.

Silicon Systems Inc.
http://www.ssi1.com/

Those looking for an integrated circuit, particularly one that's application-specific and mixed-signal, may want to visit the Silicon Systems Web site. A wholly owned subsidiary of the TDK USA Corp., the company specializes in combining analog and digital circuitry.

MULTI-PLATFORM

CAPTURE

The Connectix QuickCam
http://www.indstate.edu/msattler/sci-tech/comp/hardware/quickcam.html

Information about the Connectix QuickCam computer-mounted video camera is provided here by a product beta tester. Visit here for unofficial software and platform compatibility information, product overviews, user instructions, and direct links to Connectix Corporation.

Geac Computer Corporation
http://www.geac.com/

Geac Computer Corporation Ltd. will outfit businesses and institutions with top to bottom computing systems, including hardware, software, service, and support. With offices across the globe, the company pitches its products and services to an international market at this promotional site.

Play Incorporated
http://www.play.com/

Play Incorporated, a computer-based video editing software company, maintains this site for general information and product samples. Visit here to learn about its video graphics tools and download demonstration software.

Videomedia
http://www.videomedia.com/

Videomedia helps professional video and multimedia developers connect VCRs to hard drives. Visitors to Videomedia's home page can check out the company's controllers and desktop editing software.

Vigra
http://www.vigra.com/

Vigra, a supplier of high performance audio and video capture hardware, maintains this promotional page. Visitors can learn more about the company's products, access its product manuals and visit its anonymous FTP site for software downloads.

Visioneer
http://www.visioneer.com/

Visioneer provides products that integrate paper and electronic information, including the PaperPort desktop scanner. The site includes company and product info, links to the sales department and a software library.

CHIPS, ETC.

Chip Directory

http://www.xs4all.nl/~ganswijk/chipdir/

The Chip Directory Web page offers a search engine for locating information about computer chips online. This page points users to six mirror sites around the world for quick and easy access of the site.

Cirrus Logic

http://www.cirrus.com/

This promotional page for Cirrus Logic, a computer chip manufacturer, outlines the company's products, financial data, support services, and job opportunities. Includes a company store where browsers can check out Cirrus Logic apparel and gifts.

Enhanced Peripherals & PostScript Systems (EPPS)

http://www.epps.ch/

Switzerland's Enhanced Peripherals & PostScript Systems specializes in the distribution and installation of memory chips, disk drives, and other peripherals for workstations and personal computers. The company's home page has information about its memory expansion kits for Apple, Hewlett-Packard, IBM and Sun products, among others.

Harris Semiconductor Corp.

http://www.semi.harris.com/

The home page of the Harris Semiconductor Corp. details its product line, including wireless communications, analog and digital signal products and transient voltage suppressors. General corporate news and info also can be found at this commercial site.

Intel

http://www.intel.com/

Santa Clara, Calif.-based Intel Corporation produces high-powered microprocessors, networking products and videoconferencing systems. Visitors to its home page will find product updates, customer support resources, and employment opportunities.

Microchip Technology Inc.

http://www.microchip.com//

Microchip Technology Inc. is a RISC microcontroller and serial EEPROM manufacturer located in Chandler, Ariz. Visitors to the company's site will find corporate and product information, data sheets, specs, and applications notes.

MIPS Technologies Inc.

http://www.mips.com/

MIPS Technologies Inc. is a RISC microprocessor supplier. The company's home page hosts a glossy presentation combining product pitches, development tools, and company press releases.

Mitel Corp.'s Semiconductor Division

http://www.semicon.mitel.com/

This promotional page is the Web home of the Mitel Corp.'s Semiconductor Division. Visitors will find information on the division, its products and career opportunities. Press clippings and current stock information also are featured.

Motorola Microcontroller Technologies Group.

http://freeware.aus.sps.mot.com/index.html

Visitors can learn about Motorola's microprocessors and microcontrollers at this promotional site. The site also provides a link to the Motorola Freeware Data Services Bulletin Board system.

Motorola Semiconductor Products Sector

http://motserv.indirect.com/

Enter the Motorola Semiconductor Products Sector for promotional news and information about the company's wireless communication systems. Shop for products or seek technical support here. In English and Japanese.

National Semiconductor

http://www.nsc.com/

This promotional site is the Web home of the National Semiconductor Corporation. Browsers are invited to visit the design library, learn the latest in product and corporate news and review the company's product support services.

Philips Semiconductors

http://www.semiconductors.philips.com/

The Web page of Philips Semiconductors offers product information for the company's multimedia, communications and audio and video technologies. Visitors also can access company news and employment opportunities.

Rockwell Semiconductor Systems

http://www.nb.rockwell.com/

Rockwell Semiconductor Systems, a Newport Beach, Calif.-based industrial supplier, maintains this promotional site for an overview of its operating divisions. Visitors will also find press releases, product briefs, help files, employment opportunities and more.

Ultra Technology

http://www.dnai.com/~jfox

The owner of Ultra Technology introduces his company along with tidbits concerning his personal life at this site. Find microchip info, links to free files and a pointer to the Aikido Federation.

Xicor Inc.

http://www.xicor.com/

Xicor Inc. designs, manufactures and markets "advanced nonvolatile memory products." The company's home page provides a corporate overview, information on products and services, investor info, pricing structures, and job listings.

ZyXel

http://www.zyxel.com/

ZyXel is a company specializing in providing modems for the networking communications industry. Visitors can check out the company's online trade shows, brochures, technical support, company background, and related articles.

DIRECT

Advanced Logic Research Inc.

http://www.alr.com/

The Advanced Logic Research site provides product specifications, press releases and technical and sales information. ALR makes and markets everything from servers and workstations to personal computers and peripherals.

Apricot Computers Limited

http://www.apricot.co.uk/

Apricot Computers Limited, an England-based computer manufacturer, maintains this promotional site. Visit here to learn about its consumer and business computers, read press releases and contact its sales and technical support departments.

Digital Equipment Corp.

http://www.dec.com/

Digital Equipment Corporation, supplier of networked computer systems, software and service to more than 100 countries worldwide, maintains this promotional site. Visit here for extensive product descriptions, financial news and investor information, employment opportunities, and more.

NEC Corporation

http://www.nec.co.jp/

Computer and semiconductor producer, NEC, hawks its hardware here. A company overview, product list and research and development news comprise the promotional fodder at this corporate site. In Japanese and English.

Vector Technology Corporation

http://www.vector.com/

Vector Technology Corporation is a Houston, Texas-based company that deals in servers, workstations and networking products. It gives an overview of its products here.

DISPLAY

NEC Corporation

http://www.nec.com/

The NEC Corporation, a Japan-based manufacturer of communications products, computers and semiconductor components, maintains this site for general information. Visit here for corporate and product information, sales and support services, details on upcoming trade events and more.

Tektronix Inc.

http://www.tek.com/

Computer color printing, video and networking comprise the range of high technology products and services offered by Tektronix Inc. At the company's home page, explore corporate profiles, product listings, and career opportunities.

I/O PERIPHERALS

Cybernet Systems Corp.

http://www.cybernet.com/

Cybernet Systems of Ann Arbor, Mich., maintains this Web site to provide information on its computer hardware products. Products include a "force feedback joystick" and a "driver for mice and touchscreens for DOS and Unix."

INTERNET AND RELATED WIDE AREA NETWORKS

Ascend Communications Inc.

http://www.ascend.com/

Ascend Communications Inc. produces network access products for enhancing and extending corporate applications such as Internet and remote local area network access, videoconferencing and telecommunications applications. Visit here for product overviews, a corporate site index and contact information.

Bellcore

http://www.bellcore.com/

This site features an AT&T-related company specializing in global connectivity, information systems and networking solutions. Includes info on the company, consulting, engineering and software services, technology integration and training.

Boca Research Inc.

http://www.bocaresearch.com/

Boca Research Inc. manufactures communication products. Its home page offers product information and technical support and also highlights Internet-only special prices on products.

Cellware Information Service

http://www.cellware.de/

Cellware manufactures and sells ATM computer products. On this home page get information about the German company, its products and its research and technologies. Also find out about exhibitions and Cellware distributors.

Cisco Information Online

http://www.cisco.com/

Cisco Systems Inc. develops and markets Internet networking components and software. Visitors to Cisco Information Online will find product information, software updates and technical support from the self-described "Leading Global Supplier of Internetworking Solutions."

Comtrol Corporation

http://www.comtrol.com/

Comtrol, a supplier of high performance asynchronous and synchronous connectivity products, offers information on products, sales, marketing and technical support. Its page also includes news updates and employment opportunities.

Data Research Associates

http://www.dra.com/

Data Research Associates produces client/server automation systems and networking services for libraries and information providers. This site delivers background information on the company, its products, and clients.

Datametrix

http://www.datametrix.no/

This promotional site is the Web home of Datametrix A/S, a Norwegian supplier of system solutions for local and wide area computer networks and telecommunication systems. Visitors are invited to learn more about the company and its products. In Norwegian with limited English translations.

Data TeleMark

http://www.datatelemark.com/index.html

This promotional site is the Web home of Germany's Data TeleMark, a producer of wireless ISDN transmission technology. Visitors can learn more about the company, its products, and its customer services.

Digital Sound Corp.

http://www.dsc.com/

The Digital Sound Corp. site provides information on its network-based message processing systems, including VoiceServer and InfoMail. Also featured is information on the Carpinteria, Calif.-based company's services, news releases and a clickable map of customers and partners.

Elvis+

http://www.elvis.ru/

In collaboration with Sun Microsystems, the WWW server from Russia is here. See Editor's Choice.

FastComm Communications Corp.

http://www.fastcomm.com/

The home page for FastComm Communications Corp. is a no-nonsense site covering technical issues, sales figures, and biographies of top-level officials in the company. An overview of frame relay products, the mainstay of FastComm's business, is also provided.

Finisar Corporation

http://www.finisar.com/

The California-based Finisar Corporation designs and manufactures high-speed fiber optic data links, network products and gigabit link analyzers. Find more info about the company, its products and services on this corporate home page.

Gandalf Technologies Inc.

http://www.gandalf.ca/

Gandalf Technologies Inc. offers networking products and services designed to help remote businesses connect with central resources. Browsers will find company news, product information and developing technology press releases.

Garbee and Garbee

http://www.gag.com/

Garbee and Garbee, a Colorado-based computer and communications consulting firm, maintains this site to introduce its embedded systems, modem support, system design and data integration services. Visit here to learn about the company and link to related local area resources and commercial Web sites.

GNP Computers

http://www.gnp.com/

GNP Computers is a workstation systems integrator designing LAN's and WAN's for large institutions with Sun Microsystems and Silicon Graphics machines. Their site features information about the company, job opportunities and a virtual art gallery for your leisure.

Guardian Insurance

http://www.gre.co.uk/

A UK operating company that insures personal computers. See Editor's Choice.

Hayes Microcomputer Products Inc.

http://www.hayes.com/

Hayes, the makers of the modem that became the standard for accessing the Internet, hosts this corporate home page to keep browsers attuned to their ever-changing product line and customer service options.

Internet One Corporation

http://www.internetone.com/

Internet One Inc. is an Internet and network consulting, training and products business. This site tells visitors about the various services, products and training offered by the corporation.

IPC Technologies Inc.

http://www.ipctech.com/

IPC Technologies Inc. is a client/server consulting firm located in Richmond, Va. Visitors to the computer company's home page will find product and service descriptions, a corporate overview, and job listings.

James River Group Inc.

http://www.jriver.com/

This promotional site is maintained by the James River Group Inc., a software development and marketing company specializing in connecting PCs to Unix systems. Visitors to its home page are invited to learn more about the company, its products, and customer support services.

Level One Communications

http://www.level1.com/

Level One Communications is a California-based company that develops and distributes a complex line of switchers, transceivers and multiplexers for Web-based WANs, as well as ethernet products for regular LANs. Visitors to the Level One site can read quarter results, link to places of interest to visit on the Web, review the company's fine line of products, and check out Level One employment opportunities.

Livingston Enterprises

http://www.livingston.com/

This gateway page introduces visitors to Livingston Enterprises, a company that develops and manufactures tools enabling remote access of computer networks. Visitors can access Livingston's customer support services, plus detailed corporate and product information.

Molex Incorporated

http://www.molex.com/

This promotional site is the home of Molex Incorporated, an Illinois-based manufacturer of electronic, electrical and fiber optic interconnection systems. The company's history, latest developments, and information about its products are featured for review.

Motorola Inc. Product Information

http://www.mot.com/MIMS/ISG/Products/

This home page provides details about Motorola's home and business communication products, cataloged both alphabetically and by topic. Visitors will find technical info about the company's modems and network management systems.

Multi-Tech Systems Inc.

http://www.multitech.com/

Multi-Tech Systems Inc. manufactures computer communications and networking products, particularly modems and multiplexers. This site provides an overview of the company, information on upgrades, product news, tech notes, and a query form.

 EDITOR'S CHOICE

Elvis+

http://www.elvis.ru/

Americans would like to think that they won the Cold War just like they won the so-called Space Race. Maybe. Maybe not. Maybe we "won" because the other side got tired of playing with us and moved on to work on wireless LAN/WAN hardware. One result of the victory: We can now consider the "other side" from their perspective and the help of Russia's ELVIS+ corporation. Founded in 1991, ELVIS+ borrowed most of its initial staff from the Electronic Apparatus' Systems of the former Ministry of the Electronics Industry of the USSR. Remember the peace dividend? Remember the financial assistance that was promised to fledgling "democratizing" markets in Russia? Well, none of that applied to ELVIS+. Nope. Instead of receiving a helping hand from Uncle Sam, ELVIS+ got a leg up in 1993 from Sun Microsystems Inc., as the expanding Silicon Valley corporation took a 10 percent equity position in the company. So what's the ruckus? While American political culture is wallowing in the quagmire of its dubious New World Order, ELVIS+ and Sun Microsystems—to name but a few—are helping to make erstwhile wide area networks into quite local area networks; transforming, both physically and metaphorically, the—wireless—ties that bind together international communities of workers, managers and consumers. Romeo and Juliet knew the story of ELVIS+ very well, indeed.—*Reviewed by José Marquez*

Welcome to ELVIS+ WWW server from RUSSIA!!!

Our server works in Russian and English language modes. Choose the one you want and able to understand.

ò○□□□□□Ñ○□□□□Ñ □□□□Ø □Å□x°Å□□ (KOI8)

English part of our server

Press here, if you don't see Cyrillic above but wish to

Нажмите здесь, если вы не видите русских символов ни в одной из предыдущих строк

N.E.T.
http://www.net.com/

Network Equipment Technologies supplies multi-service backbone networks for information-intensive enterprises and network service providers. Learn about N.E.T.'s products and services by accessing its case studies and white papers.

Net Daemons Associates Inc.
http://www.nda.com/

Net Daemons Associates provides expertise in computer network administration and Internet connectivity for small and medium-sized businesses. This corporate home page includes a description of services and pricing information.

Netrix Corporation
http://www.netrix.com/

The Netrix Corporation manufactures and markets data, voice and image networks for international communications. Visitors to this home page are invited to learn more about the company, its products and services.

Network General
http://www.ngc.com/

Network General develops and markets computer networking hardware and software. Review the company's products and services or check out its corporate health in the eyes of the stock market at this promotional site.

Phrack Magazine
http://www.fc.net/phrack.html

The magazine for those who want an inside connection to the Web. See Editor's Choice.

Sequent Online
http://www.sequent.com/

Visitors to this corporate home page can read about Sequent Computer Systems Inc., an Oregon-based client/server systems manufacturer. Includes corporate news and financial information, product, and service listings and customer testimonials.

South to the Future
http://www.slip.net/~getaway/sttf/index.html

Get on the information superhighway and head South! See Editor's Choice.

Supra Communications Info Bahn
http://www.supra.com/

Supra Communications produces telecommunications technology for Macintosh and PC users. The company's site features information on its products and services, plus links to related resources.

Tribe Computer Works
http://www.tribe.com/

Tribe makes remote access and Internet connectivity products. With WebManage, Tribe "pioneered the use of the World Wide Web as an interface for remote device management." Get the real deal on TCW at their corporate Web site.

U.S. Robotics
http://www.usr.com/

U.S. Robotics is a major manufacturer of communications hardware and software, most notably modems. The company's home page provides product lists, press releases and a corporate profile.

 **EDITOR'S CHOICE**

Guardian Insurance
http://www.gre.co.uk/

For the most part, commerce conducted on the Internet puts the proverbial cart before the horse. But not at the "Internet site of Guardian Insurance, the UK operating company of the Guardian Royal Exchange Group." You see, the Guardian Insurance site allows UK-based visitors to actually buy an insurance policy for their personal computers directly from the Guardian site. Imagine the following scenario: You jack into cyberspace and are cruising along the blue-light district when suddenly a deadly bot crashes into your souped-up cruiser and demolishes your shell. Sounds fantastic, doesn't it? Consider the same scenario recast in different terms: You log on to the Web and are browsing through various spreadsheet archives when suddenly the Java applet you're downloading crashes your PC and erases your hard drive. Wouldn't you be a bit more at ease if you'd bought Guardian's Networker policy before you started surfing those unpredictably exciting Web waves? Read the fine print of this particularly progressive insurance policy and decide for yourself if the Guardian Royal Exchange Group has the right idea. The site's literature covers the following rhetorically asked questions: "What makes 'Networker' so Simple?", "What protection does 'Networker provide?" and "What are the prices and how do I apply online?"—*Reviewed by José Marquez*

ZyXel

http://www.zyxel.com/

ZyXel is a company specializing in providing modems for the networking communications industry. Visitors can check out the company's online trade shows, brochures, technical support, company background, and related articles.

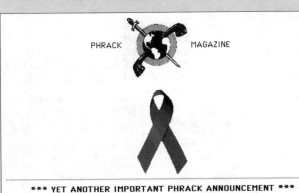

MEMORY HARDWARE

Enhanced Peripherals & PostScript Systems (EPPS)

http://www.epps.ch/

Switzerland's Enhanced Peripherals & PostScript Systems specializes in the distribution and installation of memory chips, disk drives and other peripherals for workstations and personal computers. The company's home page has information about its memory expansion kits for Apple, Hewlett-Packard, IBM and Sun products, among others.

NETWORKING AND NETWORKING CONSULTANTS

3Com

http://www.3com.com/

3Com, a Santa Clara, Calif.-based data networking systems developer, maintains this site to introduce its people, products and services. Visitors will find company news, technology solutions reports, customer support and product and service guides.

Adaptec Inc.

http://www.adaptec.com/

Adaptec Inc. designs, manufactures and markets IOware, computer hardware designed to eliminate performance bottlenecks between microcomputers, networks and peripherals. Visit this site to learn about its products and link to technical support, employment opportunities and more.

ADC Telecommunication

http://www.adc.com/

At ADC Telecommunication's home page, networking-minded browsers can learn more about the company's products and services; including fiber optics, connector modules, a variety of software, and more.

Advanced Computer Communications: RiverWatch

http://www.acc.com/

The Advanced Computer Communication's RiverWatch site provides an interactive guide to office routing. ACC's guide also offers a company profile and product information.

Agile Networks

http://www.agile.com/

Agile Networks creates "intelligent [Ethernet] switches" for local area networks. Explore how the company can ease and simplify network operation by reading the promotional materials posted here.

AMP Incorporated

http://www.amp.com/

AMP Incorporated is a manufacturer of electronic interconnectivity devices. Includes an overview of the company, plus information on products, services, employment opportunities, and related news items.

Arena Logistics

http://www.arena.com.au/

Arena Logistics of Australia is a computer consulting firm that focuses on networking IBM-compatible mainframes to other operating systems. Visitors will get an overview of the company here and can link to software, hardware, and IBM-related sites.

The Burton Group

http://www.tbg.com/

The Burton Group is a consulting firm for businesses that use local area networks. Visitors here will get a look at TBG's services, including biographical sketches of its network analysts.

Cayman Systems Inc.

http://www.cayman.com/

Cayman Systems Inc. is a producer of workgroup connectivity hardware and software located in Woburn, Mass. Visitors will find product descriptions, price lists, technical specifications, and ordering information.

Chipcom Corporation

http://www.chipcom.com/

Chipcom develops and markets computer networking products including terminal servers and network management software. Product descriptions and corporate information is available here.

Compatible Systems Routers

http://www.compatible.com/

Compatible Systems manufactures and markets "internetworking" products, such as routers and client software, to businesses and educational institutions. Visitors here can review the company's product and service offerings.

Computone Corporation

http://www.computone.com/

Computone Corporation, a designer and manufacturer of multi-user hardware and software, gives an overview of its wares at this promotional site. The company specializes in remote access communications servers.

Com Tech Communications

http://www.comtech.com.au/

Com Tech Communications is a networking design firm located in Australia. Visitors to its home page can learn about the company, its network products, technical services, and educational programs.

Datacom Caribe

http://www.coqui.com/

Datacom Caribe, which provides networking products and services in Puerto Rico and the Caribbean, presents general information on the company, its products and services. Includes links to a business center and an index of Puerto Rican links. In Spanish and English.

Destek Group Inc.

http://www.destek.net/

Networking products and services are offered by Destek Group Inc. at this promotional site. Visitors can review the company's commercial offerings and a profile of its corporate holdings and history.

---

a2z **EDITOR'S CHOICE**

South to the Future

http://www.slip.net/~getaway/sttf/index.html

The dukes of the information dirt road and the digital holler let loose their rebel war whoop in the form of this rousing call to arms for the next American—online—revolution. The South to the Future site invokes a world of technology that's no longer brother against brother, machine against man. This TechnoFree future belongs neither to the east nor the west, neither north nor south, neither to the citizens nor the illegal aliens, but, rather, promises "¡Derechos tecnologicos para todos!" On the electronic battlefield of the Web, the future southerners are staking their claims on the brains and backs of the GenX generation. Unleashing an awesome production run of t-shirts, designer eyewear and even their own series of self-help books for the computer depraved, South to the Future will write the fables of the next reconstruction. You can download South to the Future desktop patterns, ergonomic liberation FAQs, and mechanical schematics for personal computing machines not yet imagined. Do yourself, your family and your country a favor: go South (to the Future) and ¡Git Online!—*Reviewed by José Marquez*

Digi International

http://www.digibd.com/

Digi International is a producer of computer network and server products. Visitors to its site will find press releases, product and ordering information, and customer support.

Electronic Systems of Richmond Inc.

http://www.esr.com/

Electronic Systems Richmond boasts services for the design, installation and support of local area networks. Examine what the company has to say about its products and services at its corporate Web site.

Extended Systems Inc.

http://www.extendsys.com/

Extended Systems, a Boise, Idaho-based computer networking products company, maintains this promotional site for product information. Visit here to learn about its connectivity solutions, including network print servers, infrared connections, client/server software, and more.

Farallon Computing Inc.

http://www.farallon.com/

Farallon Computing Inc., an Alameda, Calif.-based supplier of plug-and-play networking products, maintains this promotional site. Visitors will find company news, press releases, product descriptions, technical support, career opportunity listings and more.

Fibronics Mosaic

http://www.fibronics.co.il/

At the home page of Fibronics, a network management and "solutions" provider, browsers can read about the company's products and services, visit the home pages of Fibronics users or link to other sites of interest on the Web.

Infovav

http://www.infovav.se/

Infovav is a Swedish network consulting firm. Visitors here will get an overview of the company's work with local and wide area networks. In English and Swedish.

Lantronix

http://www.lantronix.com/

Lantronix, an Irvine, Calif., company that develops ethernet connectivity products for workgroup applications, presents information on products, sales, marketing and support. Included is an ethernet tutorial and glossary and an FTP site.

Microplex Systems Ltd.

http://www.microplex.com/

Microplex Systems, a Vancouver, Canada-based network communications products company, maintains this promotional site. Visit here to learn

about the company's history, products, and career opportunities.

Morning Star Technologies

http://www.morningstar.com/

Morning Star Technologies, a Columbus, Ohio-based Internet service provider and networking applications developer, maintains this site for product information and technology overviews. Includes career opportunity listings.

Net Guru Technologies Inc.

http://www.internet-is.com/netguru/

Net Guru Technologies Inc. deals in research, training and consulting in the field of computer networking. This corporate page highlights courses the company offers, including registration information and instructor bios.

Network Appliance

http://www.netapp.com/

Network appliances like computer file servers should work as dependably as toasters, the California-based Network Appliance firms tells visitors to its home page. This spiffy, toaster-motif site gives an overview of the company's products, including its data-access servers.

ON Technology Inc.

http://www.on.com/

ON Technology is a supplier of NetWare optimized workgroup applications and Local Area Network utilities based in Cambridge, Mass. Visitors will find product information, technical support, free demos of software and company press releases.

Patton Electronic Co.

http://www.patton.com/

Patton Electronic Co., a manufacturer of data communications equipment based in Gaithersurg, Md., displays a varied array of information about its products here. This commercial site includes corporate information and a searchable online catalog.

Proteon

http://www.proteon.com/

Proteon is a networking systems and connectivity hardware developer. Its home page provides an index to Proteon products—like the Proteon ISDN Router, customer services, and company press releases.

Qualcomm Inc.

http://www.qualcomm.com/

Qualcomm Inc., a San Diego-based developer and manufacturer of advanced communications systems, maintains this corporate home page. Visitors can learn about the company, its products and current employment opportunities.

Racal-Datacom

http://www.racal.com/

At Racal-Datacom's online corporate headquarters, browsers can attend telecommunications product demos and pitches for their professional network services. Find company news and a corporate profile at this commercial site.

Rockwell Network Systems

http://www.rns.com/

This site profiles Rockwell Telecommunications Network Systems products. Includes links to sales and technical support staffs, press releases, the Nikos Web Index, and other Rockwell servers.

Strategic Networks Consulting Inc.

http://www.snci.com/

Strategic Networks Consulting Inc. offers network consulting, research, advisory and testing services. To review the company's communications network services, visitors can visit this promotional site.

Telebit Corporation

http://www.telebit.com/

Telebit Corporation designs, manufactures and markets advanced high speed products for dial-up networking and wide-area communications. This page profiles the corporation and its products and services. Visitors will also find press releases, documentation, and support links.

Thomas-Conrad

http://www.tci.com/

Thomas-Conrad Corporation is a supplier of high-speed computer network products. Technical support and product information are available here, as is background and current information about the corporation, which is based in Austin, Texas.

Wingra Technologies Inc.

http://www.wingra.com/

Wingra Technologies Inc. is a network and messaging system developer. At its corporate home page, visitors will find product descriptions and company information. Includes job opportunities listings.

Xircom Online

http://www.xircom.com/

This corporate home page focuses on the world of mobile connectivity. Includes links to product information, FAQs, technical support and new developments in the realm of data and voice.

Xyplex

http://www.xyplex.com/

Xyplex manufactures networking systems and components. Training is part of the package, too, as the company will show clients how to use and maintain its networks. Potential customers can explore hardware and software products and services at this promotional site.

PCMCIA AND RELATED CARDS

Adaptive Solutions Incorporated

http://www.asi.com/

Adaptive Solutions Incorporated unveils new products such as its PowerShop accelerator board for use with Adobe PhotoShop at this promotional site. The company primarily designs and manufactures parallel computing systems.

ASUSTeK Computer Inc.

http://asustek.asus.com.tw/

ASUSTeK Computer Inc., a Taipei, Taiwan-based computer hardware company, maintains this site for corporate and product information. Visit here to find technical information about its mainboards and add-on cards and to access its public software directory.

ATI Technologies Online

http://www.atitech.ca/

ATI Technologies develops graphics and multimedia accelerator cards. Visit this site for links to company and product information, as well as question and answer guides.

Creative Labs Inc.

http://www.creaf.com/

This home page is devoted to Creative Labs Inc.'s multimedia products. Includes descriptions of Creative Labs' products—like the popular SoundBlaster and 3D Blaster cards—and customer services, as well as links to other sound, video, and game sites.

Diamond Multimedia Systems Inc.

http://www.diamondmm.com/

Diamond Multimedia Systems Inc., a San Jose, Calif.-based computer graphics and communications product company, maintains this promotional site. Visit here to learn about its products for PC and Macintosh computers, including video and animation accelerators, fax/modems and more.

Ensoniq Corporation

http://www.ensoniq.com/

Ensoniq Corporation, a manufacturer of musical instruments, multimedia sound cards and integrated circuits, maintains this promotional page. Visitors are invited to learn more about the company and its musical products.

Number Nine Visual Technology

http://www.nine.com/

The home page of Number Nine Visual Technology tells about the Massachusetts-based company and its graphics acceleration products. Visitors can find technical specifications and a listing of distributors of the company's merchandise.

POWER

Exide Electronics Inc.

http://www.exide.com/exide/

The Exide Electronics site posts information on the company's uninterrupted power system products. Visit here for product reviews, ordering information, a tutorial, news releases and investor information. Demonstration software is also available.

PRINTERS AND OTHER PERIPHERALS

Fargo Electronics

http://www.fargo.com/

This corporate home page describes Fargo Electronics' color printing products. Includes corporate background information and press releases, plus product price listings and profiles of some of Fargo's customers.

Hewlett-Packard Co.

http://www.hp.com/

Hewlett-Packard, an electronics and computer peripheral manufacturer based in Palo Alto, Calif., maintains this site for its Access HP information service. Visit here for news, product descriptions, international branch office links and technical support.

Hewlett-Packard Peripherals Directory

http://www.hp.com/

Hewlett-Packard, a California-based supplier of electronics and computer products, maintains this site for its peripherals directory. Visit here for customer support and information about printers, copiers, plotters, scanners, and other products.

HP Access Guide Directory

http://www.hp.com/Misc/QuickRef.html Browsers who want to navigate through Hewlett Packard's Web site can start here, where HP lists a table of contents, title index, and search function.

Lexmark International Inc.

http://www.lexmark.com/

Look up laser and ink-jet printing industry news, a company profile or product line descriptions at Lexmark International Inc.'s home page. Also find company press releases and technical support information.

STORAGE

APS Technologies

http://www.apstech.com/

APS Technologies, a Kansas City, Mo.-based data storage products company, maintains this promotional site. Visit here to learn about its disk drives and other peripherals, read press releases and news updates and contact its sales and customer service departments.

CD Archive Inc.

http://www.cdarchive.com/

CD Archive Inc. markets CD-ROM recording and archiving peripherals. This site includes specification sheets on recorders, an extensive collection of CD-R information and ordering instructions.

Conner Peripherals

http://www.conner.com/

Conner Peripherals deals in hard drives, tape drives and storage systems. Visitors to its promotional page will get an overview of the company and its products.

Data General Corp.

http://www.dg.com/

Specializing in servers and storage products, Data General provides high-end computing solutions to corporate clients. Find a list of products and services and a corporate profile at this promotional site.

Iomega Corporation

http://www.iomega.com/

Iomega Corporation, the Roy, Utah-based computer information storage services company that created the portable ZIP and Jaz Drives, maintains this promotional site. Visit here for news, press releases, product descriptions, staff directories, and technical support.

Maximum Strategy Inc.

http://www.maxstrat.com/

Maximum Strategy Inc. is a manufacturer of data, storage and file servers located in Milipitas, Calif. Visitors will find product descriptions, customer support and worldwide distribution information at the company's Web site. Links to high performance computing resources on the Internet also are provided.

Maxtor Corporation

http://www.maxtor.com/

Maxtor Corporation, a San Jose, Calif.-based data storage products company, maintains this site for a corporate overview, news, technical support and product descriptions. Includes a bulletin board service and employment listings.

Micropolis Corporation

http://www.micropolis.com/

Micropolis, a California-based computer disk drive manufacturer, maintains this site for general information. Visit here to learn about its products, contact its technical support department, browse its index of job listings, and more.

StorageTek

http://www.stortek.com/

StorageTek, an information storage company, explains its services, corporate profile and company background here. The company develops drives for such companies as IBM and is best-known for its Iceberg, Kodiak, and Arctic Fox models.

Symbios Logic

http://www.symbios.com/

Symbios Logic develops hardware for moving and storing computer data. For a rundown of the company's products and services consult this promotional site. Symbios, an independently operated subsidiary of Hyundai Electronics America, has operations in Wichita, Kansas, Fort Collins and Colorado Springs, Colorado.

Western Digital Corp.

http://www.wdc.com/

Western Digital Corp. designs and manufactures hard disk drives, graphics cards and integrated circuits for the microcomputer industry. Visit this site for product overviews, customer service, technical support, employment opportunities listings and more.

SYSTEM REPAIR AND RECOVERY

Laser Pros International

http://www.inmarket.com/laserpro/

Laser Pros International, of Madison, Wis., provides ordering information here for its printer parts service. The company provides "spare parts" for Hewlett-Packard, Apple, and IBM, among others.

VARs AND CONSULTANTS

BTG Incorporated

http://www.btg.com/

BTG Incorporated, a technology integration company, maintains this site to introduce its value-added services. Visitors will find company news, investor information, product and service descriptions, online ordering systems, employment opportunities and more.

CompAdept Corporation

http://www.compadept.com/

CompAdept Corporation, a Palo Alto, Calif.-based computer consulting firm, maintains this

promotional site. Visit here for company information, technical resources and employment opportunities.

Control Data Systems

http://www.cdc.com/

Control Data Systems builds information management systems which integrate hardware and software. Its Web site provides company announcements, customer and investor services, technical support info, a showcase of its customers, and job openings.

CyberMeridian

http://www.cybermeridian.com/

CyberMeridian promotes its "distribution of computer hardware and software" business on this corporate home page. The company includes information about its Internet-related hardware and software solutions as well as details about its Windows database design expertise.

Geac Computer Corporation

http://www.geac.com/

Geac Computer Corporation Ltd. will outfit businesses and institutions with top to bottom computing systems, including hardware, software, service and support. With offices across the globe, the company pitches its products and services to an international market at this promotional site.

Harris Computer Systems Corporation

http://www.csd.harris.com/

Florida-based Harris Computer Systems Corporation supplies commercial and governmental markets with high performance real-time and multi-level secure computer systems. Visitors to its home page can learn more about the company, its consulting services and system packages.

Intergraph Corporation

http://www.ingr.com/

This promotional site is presented by the Huntsville, Alabama-based Intergraph Corporation, a developer, manufacturer and marketer of interactive computer graphic systems. Visitors can learn about the company as well as its vast array of hardware and software systems, plus link to user groups and related businesses.

PERYT Corp.

http://www.peryt.waw.pl/

PERYT Corp., a Polish computer systems distribution company, makes its Internet home here. Visitors are invited to learn more about the company, its products, and services. In Polish.

Sonic Computers

http://www.human.com/sonicc/index.html

Sonic Computers presents its products and services here at its company home page. Visitors can

check the prices on hard drives, modems and complete systems from the Santa Clara, Calif., company.

Total Systems Inc.

http://www.gotss.com/

Total Systems Inc. is a Kansas-based computer consulting firm that also sells computer and networking systems. It promotes its products and services here and offers online computer configuring tips.

PERSONAL DIGITAL ASSISTANTS

Zoomer Personal Digital Assistant

http://www.grot.com/zoomer/ The home page for the Zoomer personal digital assistant contains mailing list archives, technical information, descriptions of software and hardware products, vendor contacts, and more.

PCs

CHIPS, ETC.

CHIPLIST 8.1 by Aad Offerman, I 8-10-95

http://einstein.et.tudelft.nl/~offerman/chiplist.html

Chiplist 8.1 by Aad Offerman is a compilation of chips for the benefit of the Web community to help answer questions about the differences between various chips used in IBM PC, IBM PC/XT, IBM PC/AT, IBM PS/2 and compatibles.

DIRECT

The Acer Group

http://www.acer.com/

This promotional site is maintained by Acer Incorporated, an international electronics company headquartered in Taiwan. Visitors are invited to find out more about the company, its computer hardware products and customer support services.

Dell.com

http://www.dell.com/

The Dell Computer Corp. produces portable, desktop and mainframe computers and is best known for its competitively priced personal computers. Visit this corporate home page for information about its products, customer support services, international network, and corporate structure.

Sonic Computers

http://www.human.com/sonicc/index.html

Sonic Computers presents its products and services here at its company home page. Visitors can check the prices on hard drives, modems, and complete systems from the Santa Clara, Calif., company.

Stratus Computer Inc.

http://www.stratus.com/

This Web site provides information on Stratus Computer Inc. and its subsidiaries, Isis Distributed Systems and S2. Visitors will find general information about the company's hardware and applications products.

Tadpole Technology Inc.

http://www.tadpole.com/

This promotional site is maintained by Tadpole Technology Inc., a designer, developer and manufacturer of portable computers based in Cambridge, England. Visitors are invited to learn more about the company, its products and customer support services.

Tangent Computer Inc.

http://www.tangent.com/

The Tangent Computers home page contains information on its personal computers, servers and media-specific workstations. Includes links to several PC and Windows-related servers.

INTERNET AND RELATED WIDE AREA NETWORKS

Novell Applications Group

http://wp.novell.com/

From the Novell software company's corporate site, this page focuses on the Applications Group. Find links to info on the company's business applications and GroupWare and a link to the corporate home page.

PCMCIA AND RELATED CARDS

BusLogic Inc.

http://www.buslogic.com/

This promotional page is the Web home of BusLogic Inc., a California-based developer of SCSI cards for the PC. Visitors can learn more about the company, its products, services, and technical support options. A link to information on its reseller programs is also available.

NVIDIA

http://www.nvidia.com/

NVIDIA designs and markets multimedia accelerators for PCs. The company promotes its products here.

VARs

Z-Connect Cyber-Journal

http://www.zds.com/

Zenith Data Systems provides information about its computer products through this "Cyber-Journal". The company has recently entered into an agreeement with Microsoft to practically put a computer in evey college student's lap.

UNIX-BASED AND RELATED SYSTEMS

CHIPS, ETC.

Heurikon Corporation

http://www.heurikon.com/

Heurikon Corporation, a Madison, Wis.-based manufacturer of high performance computer processor boards, maintains this promotional site. Visitors will find news, product descriptions, white papers, publications, and information retrieval services.

DIRECT

IBM AS/400

http://as400.rochester.ibm.com/

IBM's AS/400 advanced application architecture is described and discussed at this site. Visitors will find documentation and product support here.

IBM RISC System/6000

http://www.austin.ibm.com/software/

This IBM RISC System/6000 site contains information on the platform's operating system and educational, business, multimedia and scientific software. Includes descriptions of standards, user services, customer support, news items, and a link to the IBM home page.

HAL Computer Systems

http://www.hal.com/

HAL Computer Systems' home page introduces visitors to the company's 64-bit SPARC/Solaris compatible workstations. Includes information

about the company and its products, as well as current employment opportunities.

Hewlett-Packard Workstations

http://www.hp.com/go/workstations/

Review computer industry giant Hewlett-Packard's line of workstations and technical servers here. Information on hardware, software solutions and technical support is available at this promotional site.

NeXT Computer

http://www.next.com/

Steve Jobs, co-founder of Apple Computers Inc., left Apple to found the next best thing: NeXT Computers. Visit their corporate home page to pick up the latest in news or browse through general information about the dynamic company, its products and services.

Silicon Graphics: Chemistry and Biological Sciences

http://www.sgi.com/ChemBio/

This promotional site presents Silicon Graphics Inc.'s supercomputing offerings to the scientific community. Review the company's computer systems especially equipped for scientific research, as well as a company overview, product information and event announcements.

Sun Microsystems Inc.

http://www.sun.com/index.html

The home of Sun Microsystems—Silicon Valley's computer workstation giant—offers more than mere product promotion. It's a graphics-driven company magazine that dishes the goods on everything from bandwidth to Sun's high-tech offerings. Visitors can link to Sun developers or browse corporate info.

VARs AND CONSULTANTS

Impediment Incorporated

http://www.impediment.com/

This promotional page is the Web home of Impediment Incorporated, a workstations distributor and dealer located in Marshfield, Mass. Find information about the company as well as its products and services.

Unixpac Index

http://www.unixpac.com.au/

Unixpac presents this Web site with online access to Unix hardware and software, VAR services and company information. Also includes customer support services and the company's "cool links."

INFORMATION RESOURCES AND USER GROUPS

GENERAL HELP RESOURCES

Access HP—Comments
http://www.hp.com/Misc/Comments.html
Hardware peripheral developers Hewlett-Packard hosts this feedback site, where visitors can post their comments or questions about HP products and services. Also link to FTP sites for drivers and patches.

BugNet Online
http://www.bugnet.com/~bugnet/
BugNet Online brags that it hosts "the global resource for PC bugs, glitches, incompatibilities...and their fixes." Find the latest news on that nagging computer-related problem and possibly a cure for the pain.

Common Internet File Formats
http://www.matisse.net/files/formats.html
Intended for Macintosh users (and PC users who operate with Windows), this site charts various file formats (.au, .aiff, etc.), providing a description and type for each one.

Compression Frequently Asked Questions (FAQ)
http://www.cis.ohio-state.edu/hypertext/faq/usenet/compression-faq/top.html
Browsers can download an extensive FAQ sheet on compression programs for managing and compressing data, text, images and sound files at this Ohio State University site. The FAQ is in three parts and includes pointers to other compression programs and related resources on the Internet.

Computer Graphics
http://mambo.ucsc.edu/psl/cg.html
This page puts visitors in touch with a variety of online resources related to computer graphics. Included are links to FAQ sheets and a variety of commercial and educational Web sites.

Cornell Information Technologies HelpDesk
http://sckb.ucssc.indiana.edu/kb/
The Cornell Information Technologies HelpDesk provides links to resources offering answers to computer-related problems. Some resources featured are for Cornell students only; others are for general purposes.

CSUWEB: RTFM, Web Style
http://csugrad.cs.vt.edu/manuals/
This Vermont University computer science department site archives online manuals for GNU software packages like elm, emacs, flex and gawk, to name a few. Visitors can search the collection by keyword.

CWI Audio File Formats Guide
http://cuiwww.unige.ch/OSG/AudioFormats
This Web site houses a highly technical guide to audio file formats and players. Information covered includes device characteristics, popular sampling rates, file conversions, and compression schemes.

Damar Group
http://www.dgl.com/
The Damar Group, a computer learning facility in Columbia, Md., maintains this site to assist people in achieving greater productive literacy and computer knowledge. Contains learning publications and an index of computer classes.

Database Archive
http://www.lpac.ac.uk/SEL-HPC/Articles/DBArchive.html
This database archive from the London & South-East Centre for High Performance Computing contains resources for relational databases, object oriented databases and databases with parallel processing. Articles are indexed by author, institution, conference and journal. Keyword search.

Desktop Video Conferencing
http://fiddle.ee.vt.edu/succeed/videoconf.html
An exhaustive discussion of desktop video conferencing is available at this site, including information about products to enhance connectivity, an explanation of bandwith and discussions about the virtues and drawbacks of ISDN and ethernet.

Ethernet Page
http://wwwhost.ots.utexas.edu/ethernet/
Gasping without ether? Take a gander at the ethernet Page which provides background and technical information about ethernet and IEEE 802.3 local area network technology. Includes info about ethernet software, troubleshooting codes, links to FAQ sheets, vendor contact info and related Usenet listings.

Fast Ethernet
http://alumni.caltech.edu/~dank/fe
This personal repository of fast ethernet resources at the California Institute of Technology, offers a wide range of valuable product and technical information. Visit here to link out to ethernet equipment manufacturers and other sites related to the widely-used computer networking device.

The Graphic Utilities' Site & Version FAQ
http://www.public.iastate.edu/~stark/gutil_sv.html
Find out about graphics utilities from this page, which details what the latest versions are, where they can be found and what types of files they can handle. It covers utilities for DOS, Macintosh, OS/2, Windows, Windows 95, and X Windows.

Hewlett-Packard SupportLine Services
http://support.mayfield.hp.com/
This is Hewlett-Packard's customer support online service. Visitors to the site will find trouble shooting tips, documentation and resources, including product news, help databases with engineering notes and patch browsing and downloading instructions.

High Speed Packet Radio
http://hydra.carleton.ca/articles/hispeed.html
This technical document summarizes the hardware options for medium- to high-speed packet radio links. Information on modems, data interfaces, and radios is featured.

Intellectual Property Law Primer for Multimedia Developers
http://www.eff.org/pub/CAF/law/ip-primer
As the title indicates, posted at this site is an intellectual property law primer for multimedia developers written by J. Dianne Brinson and Mark F. Radcliffe. Visitors can read the full text of this legal outline online.

Internaut
http://www.zilker.net/users/internaut/update.html
PC users of TCP/IP Internet software can access documentation and help files for connectivity applications at this site. Visitors will find answers to Frequently Asked Questions, newsgroups, and software updates.

Introduction to PC Hardware
http://pclt.cis.yale.edu/pclt/pchw/platypus.htm
"Introduction to PC Hardware," is a clearly written, simple introduction to the mysteries of buying a personal computer. The page is posted by "PC Lube and Tune," which uses the vehicle metaphor to make sense of CPUs, RAM chips, and megahertz.

JPEG Compression

http://www.cis.ohio-state.edu/hypertext/faq/
usenet/jpeg-faq/faq.html

This simple document page contains a thorough FAQ sheet about JPEG image compression, the advantages and disadvantages of JPEGs versus GIFs and related issues.

Kai's Power Tips and Tricks for Photoshop

http://the-tech.mit.edu/KPT/

Adobe Photoshop users could learn some of tricks of their trade here. Kai's Power Tips and Tricks was originally published on America Online and contains 23 tips to using Photoshop. The page also includes pointers to other tutorials for Web page designers.

Lotus Notes Frequently Asked Questions

http://www.turnpike.net/metro/kyee/
NotesFAQ.html

This FAQ sheet for Lotus Notes, taken from the Usenet newsgroup comp.groupware.lotus-notes.misc and the LNOTES-L mailing list, includes answers in areas such as programming, mail gateways, FTP archives, and books and magazines.

Modems

http://www.cis.ohio-state.edu/hypertext/faq/
usenet/modems/top.html

Untangle the lines of information about modems with the answers provided in Usenet FAQs dedicated to the computer networking hardware. Digicom, NetComm and ZyXEL modem basics are explained in the general info files archived at this Ohio State University site.

MPEG Moving Picture Expert Group FAQ

http://www.crs4.it/HTML/LUIGI/MPEG/
mpegfaq.html

This site is devoted to information on creating and editing MPEGs on Unix and Macintosh platforms. Visitors will find detailed documents and discussions of MPEG techniques.

MPEG Technical Information

http://www.eit.com/techinfo/mpeg/mpeg.html

This site is devoted to information on creating and editing MPEGs on Unix and Macintosh platforms. Visitors will find detailed documents and discussions of MPEG techniques.

Multimedia Authoring Web

http://www.mcli.dist.maricopa.edu/authoring/

Learn everything you ever wanted to know about multimedia but were afraid to ask a consultant at this Web site sponsored by Maricopa Community Colleges of Phoenix, Ariz. Describing the authoring process as "programming by non-programmers," this site offers visitors access to related software, discussions, organizations, and commercial multimedia producers.

Network Buyer's Guide - Strategic Research Corp.

http://www.sresearch.com/

A central buying guide for communications and connectivity, visitors will find pointers to everything from hardware and peripherals to industry publications here. Search storage, networking and general communications products using an online "expert guide," or, for the savvier buyer, a keyword search.

Notes Network Information Center

http://www.notes.net/

The Notes Network Information Center contains a directory of Lotus Notes pages on the Internet which extend the Notes domain across the Web. Includes pointers to Lotus Education Services and related Notes servers.

---

a2z EDITOR'S CHOICE

Introduction to PC Hardware

http://pclt.cis.yale.edu/pclt/pchw/platypus.htm

When the Web works, it works like Howard Gilbert's Introduction to PC Hardware. This casual primer covers the basics and all the bases of the modern Personal Computer. Find out how the CPU is connected to the RAM and how the RAM is connected to the PCI bus and how the PCI bus is connected to the thigh bone. This step-by-step and comprehensive guide explains the minutiae of personal computers with charm and a casual, user-friendly tone. If you would like to build your own PC or simply buy the best PC for your money, Gilbert's suggestions are straightforward and concise. Case in point: "It seems unlikely that anyone would ever try and put an eight-cylinder engine in a Saturn, but most computer vendors overload their systems with CPU power." Some of the topics covered in this primer include the CPU and Memory, the I/O Bus, Video Adapters and IDE or SCSI Disks. Each section relates the particular to the general, the preceding component to the following device. If the sound of computer jocks kvetching over Java makes your blood curdle, sauntering at your own pace through the halls of this veritable PC summer school will help you get the answers you need when you need them.—*Reviewed by José Marquez*

Introduction to PC Hardware

Platypus Computer Systems

PowerPuss P90
90Mh Pentium
256K Cache
8M 70 nsec memory
ISA bus
810M EIDE HD
SVGA
14" NI Display

The Platypus - a creature of spare parts
assembled by a God with a sense of humor

The newspaper ads scream out prices, MHz, upgradable, and SVGA. Do you know what these buzzwords really mean? Does anyone? The PC may be the single most important tool for researchers and executives, but because it is purchased in a camera store or discount food warehouse it is often treated as a commodity item. It should come as no surprise that most people who use the techno-jargon have no real understanding of any of the terms or issues.

Operating Systems Project Information

http://www.cs.arizona.edu/people/bridges/oses.html

This collection of links provides information on operating system projects and research. Sites are listed alphabetically and by operating system type.

Relcom Corp.'s Network Operational Center

http://www.relcom.eu.net/

Relcom Corp.'s Network Operational Center Web page features publicly accessible information and databases, along with links to network registration centers such as InterNIC and the Russian Institute for Public Networks. Visitors also can link to the Russian corporation's home page.

Software Engineering Institute

http://www.sei.cmu.edu/FrontDoor.html

The Software Engineering Institute offers classes and consultations to industry, government and educational clients. Visitors to the company's Web site will find information about its services and classes.

The Soundblaster AWE32

http://www.edu.isy.liu.se/~d93jesno/awe32.html

This unofficial fan site for Creative Lab's sound card features product info, support and links to the manufacturer's home page.

Storm Before the COM

http://pclt.cis.yale.edu/pclt/comisdn/default.htm

Get beyond the modem manual by reading "The Storm Before the Com," an essay all about modems. Written in plain English, this work covers the history of modems and explains how the telecommunications devices work. Includes information on ISDN modems.

Top This Computer Jargon Index

http://www.cis.ohio-state.edu/htbin/info/dir/

Top This is a directory of frequently used computer terms and their definitions. Along with basic and helpful information, find a few not-so-serious selections, such as a satirical dictionary of "crackpot religions."

UCS Knowledge Base

http://sckb.ucssc.indiana.edu/kb/search.html

The UCS Knowledge Base at Indiana University is a search engine containing the answers to over 4,000 general computing questions. This page includes pointers to suggestions, corrections and additions.

The Year 2000 Information Center

http://arganet.tenagra.com/cgi-bin/clock.cgi

Head into the next millenium with the correct time. See Editor's Choice, page 142.

GENERAL PUBLICATIONS AND INFORMATION RESOURCES

Australian Personal Computer

http://www.com.au/apc/

The online digs of paper-and-ink magazine "Australian Personal Computer," this Web site offers up information about the current issue along with many extras, like downloadable software and on-line-only articles.

---

a2z EDITOR'S CHOICE

The Year 2000 Information Center

http://arganet.tenagra.com/cgi-bin/clock.cgi

Dorky, techie, irresistibly redundant: The Year 2000 Project is more than a "patch" vendor list for computer systems that will begin to malfunction when their internal clocks fail to compute the new millennium—it's an adventure in multimediated mixed genres. The pitch: "To save storage space—and perahaps [sic] reduce the amount of keystrokes necessary to enter a year—most IS groups have allocated two digits to the year…These two-digit dates exist on millions of data files used as input to millions of applications…But what happens in the year 2000?" The swing: "We must correct the data residing in all data files or write code to handle the problem." The connection: t-shirts, newsletters, conferences, video tapes, reference information, and more. But hurry, supplies are limited and the clock is ticking…fast. There's even a Year 2000 Users Group so that "YOU DON'T HAVE TO FACE IT ALONE!!" Nor should you face "IT" without a secret decoder ring. Stan Price, of the Year 2000 site/project/clubhouse, recommends that concerned members of the public approach the news media "very carefully" so as to not scare off concerned companies or, worse yet, "out" companies that are secretly well-aware of this Digital Doomsday. If you're a fan of conspiracies, the endtime or the Two Digit Code of the Apocalypse, the Year 2000 organization has your number.—*Reviewed by José Marquez*

The current time is: 21:04:13 UTC Wednesday, June 26, 1996

Time remaining until Jan. 1, 2000 (UTC):
3 years, 187 days, 2 hours, 55 minutes, 47 seconds.

Vendors | User Groups | Conferences/Seminars | Products | Archives | Current Column | Links

The Year 2000 Information Center

The date change to the year 2000 is less than 1400 days away! For many computer and software systems, the year 2000 will bring a host of problems related to software programs that record the year using only the last two digits.

Peter de Jager, in his September 6, 1993 ComputerWorld article DOOMSDAY 2000, describes how this problem can trigger fatal errors in mission-critical systems (a French Version of this article is also available). This web site has been created to provide a forum for making information available about the year 2000 problem and for the discussion of possible solutions.

You are also encouraged to subscribe to the Year2000 mailing list.

CD-ROM Magazine Online

http://www.widearea.co.uk/cdrom "CD-ROM Magazine Online" is packed with information on games, movies, references, publishers' sites, game cheats and software fixes. Visitors can access back issues, examine the index of the current issue, do a database search for major CD-ROM releases, and offer feedback.

Center for Intelligent Information Retrieval

http://ciir.cs.umass.edu/

The Center for Intelligent Information Retrieval is operated by the Computer Science Department at the University of Massachusetts, Amherst. Visitors to the site will find forums and discussions devoted to databases and information storage systems for various disciplines.

Central Processing Unit Info Center

http://infopad.eecs.berkeley.edu/CIC/

The Central Processing Unit Info Center, maintained by a University of California-Berkeley researcher, offers computer industry updates. Visit here to find information about the latest advances in microprocessor manufacturing, system performance reviews, technological timelines, and more.

CERA Research

http://www.cera2.com/

CERA Research maintains this repository of links to vendors and developers in the embedded systems, digital signal processing, real-time computing, and industrial computing industries. Visitors can also check for recent Internet and company news.

Chorus: Reviews & Resources for "Real World" Computing

http://www.peinet.pe.ca:2080/Chorus/home.html

This Canadian e-zine focuses on academic and educational computing in the humanities. Find reviews of educational software, humanities links, an index of bibliographic programs, a Windows utility report, and other items of interest.

Communications Week Interactive

http://techweb.cmp.com/techweb/cw/current/default.html

Networking and telecommunications professionals can track industry trends with "CommunicationsWeek Interactive." Visitors will find industry news, product reviews, and links to related Internet resources.

comp.archives Archives

http://www.mid.net/ARCHIVE

Visitors to this site will find software announcements taken from the Usenet newsgroup comp.archives. Announcements may be accessed by date, title, keyword, and author. Announce-ments for today and this month have their own pages.

Computer and Communications Links

http://www-atp.llnl.gov/atp/link.html

An enormous, searchable index of computer and communications resources and information available on the Web is maintained at this site. Links to hundreds of sites span the spectrum of media, companies, conference listings, organizations, projects, and Usenet newsgroups. A mirror site is also available in Korea.

Computer Currents Interactive

http://www.currents.net/

Technical journalism junkies can catch up on the latest news, reviews and research developments by reading the online edition of "Computer Currents" magazine. In addition to the publication, visitors will find electronic shopping services, "technobabble," and a host of links to computer-related Internet resources.

Computer Information Centre (CompInfo)—Index Page

http://www.compinfo.co.uk/index.htm The Computer Information Center serves the information needs of computer users and buyers with a list of suppliers, technical support pages, an index of publications, and industry employment listings. There are also links to non-computer "fun" sites.

---

a2z   EDITOR'S CHOICE

Computer News Middle East

http://gpg.com/cnme/

In the new world of the Global Village (modem), a quality hometown paper can turn up on the other side of the Web. Computer News Middle East (CNME) is a classic hometown paper for folk who live around these here parts we locals like to call the Net. It's got gossip about new products, new industry alliances, new technology trends and, of course, services that have recently come to the Middle East. All of the articles are written in English and the local culture evident in the journalism is flavored more by San Jose, California silicon than by Riyadh, Saudi Arabia sand. In fact, there's little to the CNME that is specific to the Middle East. Instead of alienating esoterica, the CNME is chock-full of easy-to-digest blurbs, written in a casual, detailed and no-nonsense voice. Sure, you won't find advertisements or links to the mentioned manufacturer's site and there are no illustrative images to fill up your phone line, but hey…what did you expect from the local newsletter? Now, if you're interested in the inside track, the "Analysis of computing in the region" section has tidbits of interest to potential consultants and distributors. If you're looking for a morning paper that rises earlier than you, bookmark the CNME for a brighter tomorrow.—*Reviewed by José Marquez*

Welcome to Computer News Middle East WEB page. CNME was launched in 1991 to meet the demand for a sophisticated computer industry publication that covered all major buying influences. CNME features Arab/English editorial covering local and international developments with in-depth features written by professionals. We will shortly bring you back issues, please visit us often. Below you will find our latest edition.

"Computer-Mediated Communication Magazine"

http://www.december.com/cmc/mag/current/toc.html

"Computer-Mediated Communication Magazine" is an Internet publication devoted to the various aspects of computer-mediated communication. This site includes the current issue, archives, submission guidelines, and policies.

a2z   EDITOR'S CHOICE

Dictionary of Computing

http://wombat.doc.ic.ac.uk/

The Free Online Dictionary of Computing is so hot that if it were included in its very own directory it would be cross-listed under CooL (the Combined object oriented Language), COLD (Computer Output to Laser Disc) and, yes…ICE (Intrusion Countermeasure Electronics). Simply put, the Free On-line Dictionary of Computing (FOLDOC) is one of the most elegant sites on the Web. In fact, FOLDOC might really be the definition of a Web site, par excellence: It's infinitely useful, efficient, attitude free, advertising free and, needless to say, free of charge. Of course, if you already know everything you ever wanted to know about computers and are afraid to ask an anonymous, electronic dictionary displayed on your own PC, then maybe you don't need the FOLDOC. But if you do find yourself wondering what SLIP means or how to get your hands on "brochureware", look no further—ask no more. Plus, for your added convenience, you can visit FOLDOC mirror sites in New Jersey, California, France and Turkey. Doubtful of FOLDOC's versatility? Want to sink your teeth into its encyclopedic bowels? Try browsing through the contents, section by section—there are 500K of entry names, alone. Traveling through the Sahara with your laptop in hopes of writing the new techno-American novel? Download the FOLDOC and run it locally. Looking to get lucky with learning? Try the random definition option. It's all true. We told you so. Right here.—*Reviewed by José Marquez*

[Home] [Contents] [Feedback] [Random] [   ] [Search]

FOLDOC
Free On-Line Dictionary Of Computing

---

600 Contributors!

06 Jun 1996 Thank you **Keith Briggs**, FOLDOC's 600th contributor, and to all the other Guest Editors, contributors, and well-wishers. Let's make it 1000 before 2000!

Searching the dictionary

A search either returns the single entry whose complete heading matches your search string exactly or, failing that, all entries whose headings start with your search string, ignoring case.

FOLDOC mirrors

Princeton (NJ USA), InfoStreet (CA USA), NightFlight (CA USA), Institut Gaspard Monge (France), Bilkent University (Turkey).

Please use the site nearest to you and please contact me if you are thinking of setting up any kind of mirror of the dictionary.

Computer News Middle East

http://gpg.com/cnme/

The current and back issues (dating to April 1995) of Computer News Middle East are contained at this site. The magazine includes news, analysis, commentary and features on the worldwide computer industry, with a focus on the Middle East.

The Computer Paper

http://www.tcp.ca/

Canada-based "The Computer Paper" maintains this site to complement its monthly print edition. Visit here for articles on computer products and trends, small and home office management tips, hardware and software reviews, and more.

Computer Register

http://www.computerregister.com/

Browsers in the market for computer consultants or services can check out relevant advertisements here. Employment classifieds are provided for job-seekers and employers.

DESY GNU Project Overview

http://info.desy.de/gnu/www/GNU.html

"GNU's Not Unix!" and Richard Stallman tells why in an essay on the software system. This German site also contains other GNU information, the GNU bulletin, and links to related sites. In English and German.

Dictionary of Computing

http://wombat.doc.ic.ac.uk/

Thousands of entries of definitions and use information. See Editor's Choice, page 145.

Digital Systems Research Center Research Reports

http://www.research.digital.com/SRC/publications/src-rr.html

The Systems Research Center at Digital provides this index to its research reports with links to abstracts. Visitors can use an online form to order hard copies of reports and videotapes.

Director Web

http://www.mcli.dist.maricopa.edu/director/

An unofficial resource for users of Macromedia Director, this Web site provides tips, demos and links to add-on applications for users of the multimedia authoring program. Visitors can search this site and link to other Director resources on the Internet.

Dr. Dobb's Journal

http://www.ddj.com/

This site for "Dr. Dobb's Journal," a 20-year-old publication for computer programmers, includes selected articles and the organization's monthly newsletter. Visitors will also find a CD-ROM demo library and information on associated publications.

Electronic Data Interchange (EDI) Help Desk

http://www.wwa.com/unidex/edi/

This online help desk links visitors with information about electronic data interchange products, services and organizations. It is maintained by Unidex, a New Jersey-based corporation that provides EDI consulting services.

Engines for Education

http://www.ils.nwu.edu/~e_for_e/nodes/I-M-INTRO-ZOOMER-pg.html

Engines for Education furnishes educators in all fields pointers to research developments and software innovations. Link also to related technology advances in business instruction.

IDG Magazines Sweden

http://www.idg.se/

Computer publications giant International Data Group offers links to some of its popular magazine titles here, in both English and Swedish. Connect to MacWorld, Computer Sweden, PC World, and OS/2 World, among others. Additional pointers to IDG's Swedish resources.

"Infosys"

http://www.fit.qut.edu.au/~mcarthur/infosys

Information Systems Newsletter "Infosys" is an electronic newsletter for information systems faculty, students and professionals. "Infosys" publishes articles, job postings, a calendar of upcoming events, and reviews of recent publications.

InTransNet Services, Ltd. Japanese Information Page

http://www.intransnet.bc.ca/engmen.html

This Web site provides information about InTransNet Services, a Canada-based Japanese PC software developer and distributor. Also listed are informative primers on recent PC technology. In Japanese and English.

KnowledgeWeb Inc.

http://www.kweb.com/

KnowledgeWeb Inc. provides this searchable database of computer industry events. Visitors will find complete listings for all computer-related technical conferences, exhibits, seminars, and trade shows.

LAN Web

http://www.lanmag.com/

LAN Web offers a range of information and resources for local area networks. Visit this site to find about registration or connect to some of LAN Web's online resources, such as the "Java Diary", feature articles, test drives, "LAN Insider", games, and news links.

The Macintosh Advantage

http://www2.apple.com/whymac/

Apple Computer Inc. presents this hypertext document on "why Macintosh computers are better than PCs running Windows 95." Visitors can read a wealth of Macintosh-related info and propaganda here, including a list of key Macintosh advantages and performance comparisons.

Macmillan Bookstore

http://www.mcp.com/cgi-bin/do-bookstore.cgi

Visitors to the Macmillan Information SuperLibrary bookstore can read descriptions of more than 1,100 computer-related books. Many of the titles listed also include sample chapters, tables of contents, and graphics.

MagNet

http://www.cris.com/~milewski/magnet.html

MagNet is a listing of computer and Internet magazines. Part of the Milewski Index, it includes links to Computer Currents, HotWired, the Cybernautics Digest, and many other publications.

Manufacturers Information Net

http://mfginfo.com/home.htm

Manufacturers Information Net offers a wealth of information about producers of computers and computer-related products. Visitors can read the latest news, join discussion groups, browse the classifieds, or read and submit manufacturing articles.

Martin Ramsch - iso8859-1 Table

http://www.uni-passau.de/~ramsch/iso8859-1.html

This site contains an ISO8859-1 table. Includes descriptions of characters, corresponding codes, and entity names.

Matrix Information and Directory Services Inc. (MIDS)

http://www.mids.org/mids/index.html

Matrix Information and Directory Services Inc., sells publications about computer networks and global-societal computing issues. Visitors to its promotional site will find a newsletter, a color map, surveys, and a weather report.

Matrix Maps Quarterly (MMQ)

http://www.jsbus.com/

Find visual blueprints for computer networks in "Matrix Maps Quarterly." Tables, graphs, figures, and text describing various networks are presented in this online publication.

Message Passing Interface

http://www.mcs.anl.gov/mpi/index.html

This Web site describes the Message Passing Interface (MPI) standard. Available here are links to MPI libraries, home pages, and Frequently Asked Questions.

MMWIRE Online

http://www.mmwire.com/

MMWIRE Online circulates insider information for multimedia and interactive entertainment professionals. Includes news, classifieds, related association and conference information, original articles, and a directory of related sites.

National Media Lab

http://www.nml.org/

The National Media Lab, an organization providing advanced computer storage tools for the U.S. government, maintains this site for general information and resource access. Visit here to perform a keyword search of its database, view its publications, contact its operations service, and support departments and more.

Network Computing Online

http://techweb.cmp.com/techweb/nc/current/default.html

The online version of Network Computing tackles all the products and tough issues that confront networked computer users. Bring your LAN and WAN to this e-zine's site and kick back with all the latest in industry news and product reviews.

New Review of Applied Expert Systems

http://www.abdn.ac.uk/~acc025/ijaes.html

The "New Review of Applied Expert Systems" is a journal focusing on the development of expert systems for "organisations and in all branches of industry, commerce, the professions, education, and government." The journal provides information that can help system managers apply proven approaches and techniques to solve their own system problems.

O'Reilly & Associates

http://www.ora.com/

O'Reilly & Associates publishes an extremely popular series of books on everyting from Unix to TCP/IP. If you're looking into a new programming language, chances are O&A have a guide for you. Browse the company's online bookstore and order books or software titles directly.

Pentium Study

http://www.ibm.com/Features/pentium.html

This IBM-sponsored page details a special study of the occurrence of floating point errors in Pentium chips. Visitors will find summaries and statistics from a slew of probability and frequency tests.

PlugIn DATAMATION

http://www.datamation.com/

Information systems managers will find monthy news and reviews in the online trade journal, Datamation. The site claims it delivers " all the important Web pages, FTP sites, USENET and News groups, search engines, and other resources on the Internet that are important to IS managers." See for yourself.

Software Technology Parks of India

http://www.stph.net/

The Software Technology Parks site contains information about software development in India, export arrangements, server usage, and development centers. Includes links to Indian tourism info.

3DSite

http://www.lightside.com/~dani/

3DSite is dedicated to the who, how and what of 3-D computer graphics. Find events and resources related to the field, as well as links to production houses, publications and software developers. A comprehensive listing for the industry and its members.

Trailblazer

http://www.zdnet.com/~zdi/tblazer

Trailblazer, the Ziff-Davis guide to computing resources on the Web, presents an annotated collection of links aimed at Internet resources, software companies, games, search tools, and more.

The University of Edinburgh FTI index /pub/mmaccess

ftp://ftp.ed.ac.uk/pub/mmaccess/

Scotland's University of Edinburgh offers a report entitled "Network Access to Multimedia Information" at this site. The report and its summary are compressed in a number of formats available for download here.

Ventana Communications

http://www.vmedia.com/

Ventana Communications publishes computer-related educational materials in both print and software formats. Visitors are invited to learn about the company, its products and services at this promotional site.

Wide-Area Collaboration and Cooperative Computing

http://www.ai.mit.edu/projects/iiip/colab/workshop.html

This page contains the summary of a workshop on wide-area collaboration and cooperative computing. The workshop was given at The Second International WWW Conference '94: Mosaic and the Web.

World Wide Web Virtual Library: Computing

http://src.doc.ic.ac.uk/bySubject/Computing/Overview.html

The World Wide Web Virtual Library index page for "computing" resources offers information categorized by subject. Topics range from "conferences and exhibitions" to "vendors." The list is extensive.

HELP RESOURCES BY CATEGORY

APPLE AND MACOS

Apple Computer Inc.'s Support and Information Web

http://www.info.apple.com/

Apple provides a company overview, product descriptions, developer services, and software updates here. The site also includes a technical support page, the Tech Info Library, and the Apple Interactive Training System.

Apple Computer World Wide Technical Support

http://www.support.apple.com/

Apple Computer Inc. in Cupertino, Calif., maintains this site for its World Wide Product Technical Support Engineering department. Visitors will find software updates, technical bulletins, Usenet news archives, and access to its technical information library.

Apple Smorgasbord

http://www.info.apple.com/web.pages.html

The Smorgasbord is an extension of Apple Computer's support and educational resources directory. It includes employment opportunity listings, links to personal home pages maintained by Apple employees, and even a QuickTime movie archive.

Apple Tech Support and Library Gopher

gopher://info.hed.apple.com:70/11

Apple Computer posts its technical information library and support services here. Visitors can download press releases, software updates, and a wealth of information on Macintosh products.

Macintosh AV Frequently Asked Questions (FAQ)

http://www.sims.berkeley.edu/~jwang/cgi/au-faq/

This Frequently Asked Questions sheet provides information for users of Macintosh AV computers. Hardware and software information is available here, along with technical details on audio and visual input and output.

Macintosh Frequently Asked Questions (FAQ)

http://www.astro.nwu.edu/lentz/mac/faqs/home-faqs.html

This index of Macintosh FAQs contains reams of information on hardware, applications, and programming.

Macintosh Usenet Frequently Asked Questions (FAQ)

http://www.cis.ohio-state.edu/hypertext/faq/usenet/macintosh/top.html

From Ohio State University, this site concentrates on Usenet FAQ sheets regarding Macintosh computers. Includes answers to questions about purchasing, installing, and using Macintosh hardware and software.

NCSA Mosaic for Macintosh User's Guide

http://www.ncsa.uiuc.edu/SDG/Software/MacMosaic/

NCSA's Macintosh User's Guide for its Mosaic Web browser contains information on setting up and navigating the Web. The site includes a general introduction, directions for customization, navigation hints, and online help and technical support.

OzEmail's Macintosh CyberCentre

http://www.ozemail.com.au/~pkortge/mac/mum.html

Australian Macintosh users can use this extensive index to link with area retailers and resellers of Apple products. Also find Mac-related FTP sites, newsgroups, magazines, mailing lists, and other items of related interest.

Repository of Macintosh Information

http://www.cs.wisc.edu/~tuc/mac A graduate student at the University of Wisconsin's Computer Sciences Department provides a host of Macintosh resources. Includes information on CHRP and the Copland operating system, technical documents, periodicals, and assorted Mac links.

DEC

Digital's Commercial Services

http://www.service.digital.com/

The customer services provided by Digital Equipment Corporation at this Web site include software patches, documentation and publications, access to the COMET search engine, product and service information, and help and chat lines.

IBM

IBM Information Gopher Server

gopher://gopher.ibmlink.ibm.com/

Keep up with news at mega PC power, International Business Machines, at this gopher site. It provides access to internal IBM documents, training plans, and descriptions of products and services. Visitors also can access information by mailing list.

Personal Software Services - Browse and Search

http://ps.boulder.ibm.com/pbin-usa-ps/getobj.pl?/pdocs-usa/support_line_electronic.html

IBM users can browse through or search a technical tips database on this official IBM page, which vows to "help in problem determination and resolution" while letting browsers access technical documents from support centers around the world.

LINUX

ARM Linux

http://whirligig.ecs.soton.ac.uk/~rmk92/armlinux.html

Visitors will learn about the latest developments in ARM Linux, a port of the Unix-based operating system, here. The page contains details about hardware requirements and information on software.

Astronomical Software on Linux

http://bima.astro.umd.edu/nemo/linuxastro/

A collection of pointers to astronomical software resources for Linux platforms, this server links to the linuxastro mailing list, as well as FTP archives containing software updates and releases.

Linux/68k

http://echo-linux.alienor.fr/articles/m68k/cure.html

This site offers an index of pages with information about Linux/68K. Find links to a FAQ sheet, news, installation hints, mailing lists, newsgroups, and more.

Linux at CESDIS

http://cesdis.gsfc.nasa.gov/pub/linux/linux.html

This site provides links to Linux information available through the NASA Goddard Space Flight Center. Visitors can also link to remote sites, such as the "Linux Journal" and the Linux Documentation Project.

Linux for Acorn Machines

http://www.ph.kcl.ac.uk/~amb/linux.html

Visitors to this page will find answers to Frequently Asked Questions about running Linux on the Acorn 486 machine. Multitasking, ARM hard disk, and floppy driver updates are also featured.

Linux Installation and Getting Started

http://sunsite.unc.edu/mdw/LDP/gs/gs.html

This Linux programming resource site, authored by a researcher at the Cornell University Robotics and Vision Laboratory, offers installation and new user informational materials. Visit here to view or download a Linux instructional text.

The Linux Installation HOWTO

http://sunsite.unc.edu/mdw/HOWTO/Installation-HOWTO.html

This informational page provides details on how to obtain and install the Linux operating system, with a focus on the Slackware distribution version. It is intended to be "the first document which a new Linux user should read to get started."

The Linux NIS(YP)/NIS+/NYS HOWTO

http://sunsite.unc.edu/mdw/HOWTO/NIS-HOWTO.html

A how-to guide is posted here for Linux NIS and NYS server software. Visitors can learn to set up a NYS or NIS server and download the necessary software and documentation here.

Linux PCMCIA Information

http://hyper.stanford.edu/HyperNews/get/pcmcia/home.html

Card Services for Linux is a complete PCMCIA support package. This site includes current PCMCIA information and links to topical FTP sites. Includes links to the Linux Laptop Home Page.

The Linux Serial How To

http://sunsite.unc.edu/mdw/HOWTO/Serial-HOWTO.html

A real "how to" for Linux users, this page describes the ins and outs of establishing serial communications devices using a Linux box. Topics include multiport serial boards, hardware requirements, and using "getty."

The Linux Sound HOWTO

http://sunsite.unc.edu/mdw/HOWTO/Sound-HOWTO.html

The Linux Sound HOWTO page lists supported sound hardware and software, as well as installation and configuration procedures. Includes a list of Frequently Asked Questions.

Take the Power of Linux

http://www.fi.muni.cz/~kas/linux/

This Czech-language page addresses the Linux operating system. Includes information for newbies as well as tech heads and pointers to the nearest mirror site.

MISCELLANEOUS

Berkeley Software Design Inc.: Manuals

http://www.bsdi.com/bsdi-man

Berkeley Software Design Inc. provides a searchable index for its software manuals. Visitors can also scroll through indexes and explanations of manual sections.

FreeBSD Operating System

http://www.freebsd.org/

Information on FreeBSD, a "state of the art" personal computer operating system, is provided here. Visitors are invited to learn about the OS which is compatible with Intel's 386, 486, and Pentium architecture.

OS/2

Contribution Guidelines

http://sunsite.nus.sg/pub/os2/pharmacy/Submission.html

The Warp Pharmacy is a cybercenter offering prescriptions to alleviate problems installing or using IBM's OS/2 operating system. Visitors to this page will find guidelines for contributing information to the database of solutions.

Installing Internet Support in OS/2 Warp

http://pclt.cis.yale.edu/pclt/winworld/os2.htm

IBM hosts this Web page, providing information about operating system OS/2's Internet access support features for networks. Visitors can access a variety of OS/2 Warp networking info here, including pages on configuration, login scripts, troubleshooting, and local area network (LAN) Internet access.

OS/2 Warp and TIA Frequently Asked Questions (FAQ) v1.1

http://venus.ee.ndsu.nodak.edu/os2/rupa/tiafaq_idx.html

This Frequently Asked Questions site focuses on IBM's OS/2 Internet Access Kit as well as general Internet access information.

SGI

SGI

http://www.cis.ohio-state.edu/hypertext/faq/usenet/sgi/top.html

Silicon Graphics users and curious onlookers can browse an index of SGI FAQ sheets at this Ohio State University-sponsored site. The newsgroup FAQ sheets cover SGI-related topics in the areas of audio, hardware, security, and more. Includes access to SGI's anonymous FTP archives.

SUN

SunSolve Online

http://sunsolve1.sun.com/

Sun Microsystems Inc. offers solutions for its customers through the SunSolve Online site. Customers can download the latest system patches and pose questions to the help staff through this page.

UNIX

How to make MPEG movies (UNIX)

http://www.arc.umn.edu/GVL/Software/mpeg.html

MPEG is a popular format for storing video files. Unix users can get step-by-step instructions for creating MPEG movies at this site sponsored by the Minnesota Supercomputer Center.

UNIX System Administration Handbook Order Site

http://www.admin.com/

Unix wizards can check out the contents of Prentice Hall's "UNIX System Administration Handbook," 2nd Edition at this site. Readers can view what's new in the book and place online orders for the same.

Unix Workstation Support Group

http://uwsg.ucs.indiana.edu/

The Unix Workstation Support Group of Indiana University maintains this site for system administration support, educational resources, equipment purchasing support, and more. All owners and administrators of Unix workstations are invited to use this helpful resource.

VAX

MPJZ's VMS Resources on the Web

http://axp616.gsi.de:8080/www/vms/sw.html

This page contains links to resources for VMS, the VAX computer system from Digital. Links to software archives, help files, and product info are featured.

WEB-DISTRIBUTED GENERAL APPLICATIONS

Emacs Reference Materials

http://www.eecs.nwu.edu/emacs/emacs.html

Emac editors will find this site filled with questions, answers, and electronic manuals related to Emacs programming—including references for Emacs Lisp resources.

GNU Emacs Manual - Table of Contents

http://csugrad.cs.vt.edu/manuals/emacs/emacs_toc.html

This site contains the full text of the GNU Emacs Manual. If you're having difficulties getting your text work done with Emacs, this is your ticket to a proper control XC.

Gnuplot Information

http://www.cs.dartmouth.edu/gnuplot_info.html

This page provides information about gnuplot, a command-line driven interactive function plotting utility for Unix, MSDOS, and VMS platforms. The page is hosted by the Dartmouth University Computer Science department.

GNU's Not Unix

http://www.cs.pdx.edu/~trent/gnu/

An unofficial archive of GNU information, this site explains the basics of the nicely named computer operating system. Technical information, including manuals for GNU software, can be located here, along with many other related resources.

Introduction to (UNIX) Pine (Internet Version)

http://www.snre.umich.edu/pinedocs/pine.internet.intro.html

Information about the Pine mailing program for Unix can be found at this site, courtesy of the University of Michigan. The document introduces Pine and answers a number of general questions about the program's interface.

KQML - Knowledge Query and Manipulation Language

http://www.cs.umbc.edu/kqml/

This directory page contains information and software related to the design, development, and use of the Knowledge, Query, and Manipulation Language. There's listings of applications, publications, seminars, and conferences related to KQML at this site.

WIN95

Dylan Greene's Windows 95 Starting Page

http://www.dylan95.com/

Dylan Greene's Windows 95 Starting Page compiles the wisdom of hardware, software, applications, networking, and support professionals to assist others in using Windows 95. The site is loaded with Frequently Asked Questions, tips, and other resources.

1,001 Windows 95 Shortcuts

http://www.zdnet.com/~pccomp/1001tips/index.html

Ziff-Davis Publishing Inc. stocks this site with a wealth of handy info for Windows 95 users. Browsers can check out tips for mastering the Microsoft operating system, along with a variety of software, networking, and publisher info here.

Stroud's CWSApps List - Main Menu

http://www8.zdnet.com/pcmag/features/comm/_open.htm

Three Shields Hawaii offers this mirror site for The Consummate Winsock Apps List, maintained by Forrest H. Stroud. Features include popular Internet applications for Windows users. The colorful Web site also provides downloadable software and descriptions.

Stroud's CWSApps List - Windows 95/NT Apps

http://www.netppl.fi/consummate/win95.html

This site explores the seemingly bottomless pit of connectivity options available for Windows NT and Windows 95 users, including a critical look at Winsock, Archie, and Finger.

Windows Frequently Asked Questions (FAQ)

http://scwww.ucs.indiana.edu/FAQ/Windows/

This Microsoft Windows Frequently Asked Questions sheet is maintained by Indiana University. Visitors will find an extensive collection of answers to common queries about the personal computer operating platform.

Windows 95 Dial-Up Networking Tutorial

http://www.castle.net/~ace/cwin95.html

This personal Web site is home to a tutorial designed to help Microsoft Windows 95 users set up the operating system's built-in, dial-up networking system. Visitors will find step-by-step instructions.

The Windows 95 QAID

http://www.kingsoft.com/qaid/win4000.htm

This resource page answers questions about Microsoft's Windows 95 operating system. Visitors can pick up tips and tricks or download the Windows 95 freeware file, the Question-Answer-Information-Database (QAID).

Winsock- und Win95-Software

http://staff-www.uni-marburg.de/~sander/win95.htm

This Germany-based Winsock and Windows 95 resource page provides links to information on the Microsoft operating system and software applications. Includes pointers to related Web pages, Usenet newsgroups, and FAQ sheets.

Winsock Applications – American Mirror

http://cws.wilmington.net/

Windows users can fetch Internet applications at the Consummate Winsock Apps List. A clearinghouse for software resources, the CWS Apps List provides a comprehensive collection of links to Winsock application archives.

The Winsock Frequently Asked Questions (FAQ)

http://www.twinmast.com/

Answers are offered for questions about Winsock Internet access utilities at this site. Interested parties can learn about Winsock applications and related issues such as SLIP/PPP by reading this FAQ file.

WINNT

Rick's Windows NT Info Center

http://rick.wzl.rwth-aachen.de/rick/

This page offers links to Web sites containing information about Microsoft's Windows NT operating system. Newsgroups, mailing lists, white papers, FAQ sheets, and shareware or freeware to download are featured among other items of related interest.

Windows NT Information - Main Menu - Stuttgart, Germany

http://www.informatik.uni-stuttgart.de/misc/nt/nt.html

The German University of Stuttgart offers an online guide to the building blocks and performance capabilities of Microsoft's operating system, Windows NT. Find FAQ sheets, software, and the latest product related news here.

X WINDOWS

X Consortium Server

http://www.x.org/

This welcome page introduces the purpose and scope of the X Consortium and the X Window system. Includes links to current projects, staff, and info on obtaining and using X Window.

X Information

http://www.x.org/consortium/x_info.html

This page, part of the X Consortium site, indexes Web resources related to X Window operating system. Includes a lengthy FAQ sheet.

PUBLICATIONS AND INFORMATION RESOURCES BY CATEGORY

AMIGA

Amiga Report Magazine

http://www.omnipresence.com/Amiga/News/AR/

Past issues of "Amiga Report Magazine," dating to 1993, are collected at this site. Included in each issue are news, columns, reviews, and features on Amiga computer products and Amiga-related services.

APPLE MACINTOSH AND CLONES

Apple Computer Inc. Online Document Index

http://www.apple.com/documents/contents.html

This index page contains Apple-related information ranging from employment opportunities to details on the computer company's board of directors and executive officers. In between, visitors will find heaping helpings of "HotNews," hardware and software information, and customer support.

Apple Internet Sites

http://www.apple.com/documents/otherappleservers.html

Dedicated Mac heads will want to dive into this Apple-hosted site with pointers to its independent public Web pages. Jump to Apple's home page, support sites, Apple Pacific, and a hefty index of connections abroad.

Apple Worldwide Developers Conference

http://wwdc.carlson.com/

Find out what went on at the 1995 Apple Worldwide Developers Conference here. Review the programs and proceedings of the spring conference at this site or check out vendors' product information.

Bottom Line Online

http://www.dgr.com/

Bottom Line Distribution offers an extensive collection of pointers to Macintosh hardware and software resources on the Web. Includes links to third party vendor product catalogs and Mac-related online publications.

Brad's Apple Internet Resources

http://www.ape.com/

Visit this site for a variety of information about Macintosh-based Internet applications. Maintained by a computer programmer, the page provides links to software and Web sites created on Macintosh and Mac OS computers.

ClarisWeb

http://www.claris.com/

Visit ClarisWeb, the online home of software developer Claris Incorporated, for technical support, customer assistance and product demonstrations. Check out the company's publicity materials or link to parent corporation, Apple Computer Inc.

Hayden Books

http://www.mcp.com/hayden/

Hayden Books, publishers of titles for Macintosh users, offers its catalog on this page. Information on Hayden authors, how to order its books and even how to write a book for the publisher can be found. Includes links to the Macmillan Bookstore.

Info-Mac HyperDigests

http://dutera.et.tudelft.nl/people/vdham/info-mac/

This site contains an archive of the hypertext-formatted editions of "Info-Mac Digest," a journal for home Macintosh users. Visitors can search the entire collection by keyword or browse specific issues.

Internet Interstate's Macintosh Web Page

http://www.intr.net/ts/

Everything you wanted to know about the Macintosh but were afraid to ask is provided at Internet Interstate's Macintosh Web. The Internet provider from Washington, D.C., presents such information as recommended software, publications, newsgroups and links to companies.

Macintosh

http://www.astro.nwu.edu/lentz/mac/home-mac.html

The Welcome to Macintosh site is a fanzine for users of Apple's popular platforms. Find hardware reviews and reports on emerging technologies, alongside files filled with Macintosh humor. Links to Mac related Internet sites abound.

The Macintosh Vendor Directory
http://www.macfaq.com/vendor.html
The Macintosh Vendor Directory offers a comprehensive list, with addresses, of U.S. Apple Macintosh vendors. All categories are included from software to user groups.

Macintosh Web browsers
http://www.tokai-ic.or.jp/WWW/Macintosh/browsers.html
This Japanese Web site points visitors to Internet software resources such as Web browsers for Macintosh computers. Visitors can follow links to downloadable versions of Netscape Navigator, NCSA Mosaic and MacWeb. In Japanese with limited English translations.

Macintosh WWW Pointers
http://www.nmia.com/~jjm/home.html
Macintosh WWW Pointers is a personal collection of Web resources for users of Apple Macintosh personal computers. Visit here for an extensive index of links to sites from user groups, third-party developers, and even Apple, itself.

MacInTouch
http://www.macintouch.com/
The MacInTouch home page provides information and services for Macintosh devotees. Includes tips, a resources catalog, and a news archive, all related to the user-friendly computers.

MacMania
http://www.europa.com/~bubba/mac/appleindex.html
MacMania serves as a launching pad to Macintosh-related resources on the Internet. Visitors can join discussion groups, follow links to freeware and shareware or jump to periodicals on the Web.

MacTech Magazine
http://www.mactech.com/
"MacTech Magazine" is dedicated to providing online resources that support Macintosh programmers and developers. Includes an archive of articles, information on how to get the latest Macintosh development tools, and more.

The Mactivity Inc. Info Site
http://www.mactivity.com/
Mactivity organizes conferences and workshops for Macintosh Internet content developers. Visitors to their informative home page can find out about upcoming conferences, visit the resource center and company store, or just ask for help.

Macworld Magazine Online
http://www.macworld.com/
Taking the global perspective, the online version of Macworld magazine provides the latest Mac news for the Internet community. Mac fans can visit here to read articles, browse the software library, post a note on the message boards or loiter in the Technocultural Cafe.

Repository of Macintosh Information
http://www.cs.wisc.edu/~tuc/mac
A graduate student at the University of Wisconsin's Computer Sciences Department provides a host of Macintosh resources. Includes information on CHRP and the Copland operating system, technical documents, periodicals, and assorted Mac links.

TidBITS
http://king.tidbits.com/
"TidBITS" is a weekly electronic publication reporting news in the personal computer industry with an emphasis on the Macintosh. Includes an archive of back issues, subscription information, and Frequently Asked Questions about the company's books and projects.

---

a2z EDITOR'S CHOICE

Macworld Magazine Online
http://www.macworld.com/
Welcome to the party. If you own an Apple product—or just wish you did—this is the place to be. How we do love this site—let me count the ways. Reason numero uno: The Macworld Online site serves up every issue of Macworld ever published, free of charge and in a searchable directory. If you're looking for extensive and comprehensive third-party product reviews, the technically-savvy (and user-friendly) technicians at Macworld's testing facilities are folks you can count on to give you the real deal—sans such corporate-speak gems as "software solutions" and "revolutionary design." Reason numero dos: Not all computer magazines represent computer users, but Macworld Online not only promises helpful tips and tricks, they actually deliver state-of-the-art tools and utilities straight to your own computer via their North Pole-esque Software Directory. Anyone who visits Macworld Online can flip through these well-documented and Macworld-evaluated product listings and download enough freeware and/or shareware to start a Third World software vending empire. The bottom line: Macworld Online's no-nonsense approach to Apple computing is your ticket to a better tomorrow—today.—*Reviewed by José Marquez*

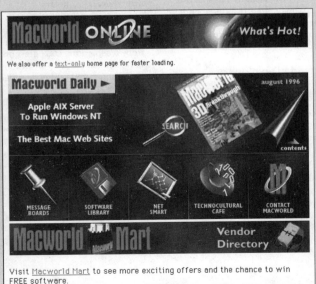

The Ultimate Macintosh

http://www.freepress.com/myee/ultimate_mac.html

This personal home page devoted to Macintosh computers includes many links to Mac-related sites and software archives. Publications, games, newsgroups, and information on new Macintosh products can be accessed here.

Washington University Macintosh Information Gopher Server

http://wuarchive.wustl.edu/systems/mac/info-mac/

Read up on anti-virus software or figure out exactly how to get those graphics to load on your trusty Mac with tips from this subdirectory of the Macintosh archives at Washington University in St. Louis. Includes tutorials and downloadable software.

The Well Connected Mac

http://www.macfaq.com/

The Well Connected Mac, an online guide to Macintosh personal computer resources, offers a variety of user information. Visit here to find software catalogs, trade show calendars, online magazines, newsgroups, and much more.

What's New on Apple Servers?

http://www.apple.com/documents/whatsnew.html

Apple Computer Inc., makers of the Macintosh, updates visitors on the content of the company's many Web servers at this site. The page announces new areas and topics of discussion, as well as news and announcements categorized by date.

DOS

PC Software Announcements

http://www.mid.net/MSDOS_A/

An extensive collection of PC software announcements drawn from the "comp.archives.ms-dos.announce" Usenet newsgroup are available at this site. Visitors can customize their search of the index by specifying title, keyword or other parameters.

IBM

IBM Personal Systems Magazine

http://pscc.dfw.ibm.com/psmag/

IBM, the mother of all PC makers, publishes an online magazine for technical coordinators. "Personal Systems" takes on software, hardware, and industry news issues affecting IBM computer and operating system markets.

IBM's System User International

http://204.254.77.2/ibmsu/

IBM's "System User International" is a bi-weekly online newsletter aimed at the IBM-user community. Back issues, text retrieval, and links to related sites are among the services offered.

LINUX

Linux Counter Reports

http://domen.uninett.no:29659/request-form_eng.html

Visit this site for reports detailing who uses Linux and where. Statistics on machines running Linux are also featured.

Linux Documentation Project

http://sunsite.unc.edu/mdw/

The Linux programming resources at this site includes programming updates, how-to manuals, downloading instructions, and a related products list. Links to user groups and other Linux and Unix sites are also available here.

Linux International

http://www.iinet.com.au/~pdcruze/

At Linux International's home page, find a complete introduction to available Linux hardware and software products, news and announcements, user group info, and more.

Linux Journal

http://www.ssc.com/lj/index.html

This online journal dedicated to the Linux operating system provides references and pointers for Linux users and programmers. Visitors can search through "Linux Journal" issues or browse tables of contents. Ordering and subscription information also available.

Plasma Linux Web

http://plasma-gate.weizmann.ac.il/Linux/

The Plasma Linux Web features links to the latest downloadable software, along with a library of Linux resources and links to other Linux Web sites. Includes a link to the Weizman Institute of Science home page.

Two Linux Books

http://www.cs.cornell.edu/Info/People/mdw/rl.txt

This site details two books on Linux software recently published by O'Reilly & Associates. Includes summaries and ordering information.

OS/2

Best of OS/2

http://www.bestofos2.com

The Best of OS/2 provides news and resources on the IBM operating system. Included are listings of software, organizations, news groups, electronic magazines, and publications. FTP sites are available, including one for the latest version of the IBM WebExplorer.

Don't just get Warped...Get Connected!

http://www.austin.ibm.com/pspinfo/warpflyer.html

This commercial site sings the praises of IBM's 32-bit operating system, OS/2 Warp. Amidst all the hype, visitors will find detailed information about the various versions of the system and a link to IBM's home page.

IBM OS/2 Warp

http://www.austin.ibm.com/pspinfo/os2.html

PC behemoth IBM's operating system is the headliner at the official OS/2 Warp home page. Explore the operating system's capabilities and link to a software archive of associated applications at this site.

IBM Personal Software

http://www.austin.ibm.com/pspinfo/

This guide to IBM personal software, part of the RISC System/6000 home page, offers links to information on its OS/2 operating system, local area network server software, DOS, and special applications. Visit here for news, version updates, compatibility listings, and more.

Indelible Blue Inc.

http://www.indelible-blue.com/ib

Indelible Blue provides information about OS/2 Warp and its available applications. The site contains an online catalog with detailed product information. Visitors can check out the featured product of the week.

Just Add OS/2 Warp

http://www.austin.ibm.com/pspinfo/drkly4.htm

PC users can download or order by mail the Just Add OS/2 Warp kit, which contains an electronic guide to OS/2 and an interactive demo.

OS/2

http://www.mit.edu:8001/activities/os2/os2world.html

The OS/2 Web home page offers users of the IBM operating system the usual array of software and hardware tips, newsgroup listings, and home pages. This page, created by students at the Massachusetts Institute of Technology, links to the official Team OS/2 page.

OS/2 Sites

http://www.auburn.edu/~lestewm/os2.html

An extensive collection of OS/2 Internet resources is offered at this Auburn University site. Visitors can link to Web OS/2 home pages, gopher services, organizations, FAQ sheets, and more.

Newton Medical

http://med-amsa.bu.edu/newton.medical/newton.medical.html

You scoffed, you chuckled and you guffawed—now, prepare to be awed. Apple Computer's Newton, the premiere Personal Digital Assistant, is becoming a lifesaver in the hands of health care professionals who find that they now need more than a pen and paper to make their rounds. The Newton Medical site, hosted by Nader Yaghoubi of the Boston University School of Medicine, brings together many of the software resources and product updates which are making Newton PDAs indispensable to doctors and technicians previously infamous for their indecipherable prescriptions. Webmaster Yaghoubi assures prospective Newtonians that Apple now regards the medical community as a "vertical market" for the now well-tested Newton—a guarantee that translates immediately into free software and upgrades, as well as the eventual delivery of more and better applications geared explicitly for health care professionals. It was this unique brand of personable treatment that made Apple's Macintosh computers as commonplace as notebooks in America's schools over the course of the last decade. The Newton Medical site may be the harbinger of a similar revolution on the PDA front—and in America's hospitals. The site contains links to other health care-oriented Newton sites, Newton software archives (featuring utilities for patient management, reference information and quantitative analysis) and Newton news sites.—*Reviewed by José Marquez*

Newton Medical Web Site and Archive

Welcome to a web site dedicated to medical applications of the Newton PDA. Since the launch of the original Newton MessagePad, we've watched the intended market for the Newton shift away from Apple's original goal of an electronic assistant for the masses towards a more specialized niche in vertical markets. Medicine is one field that can benefit from convenient and online access to large amounts of reference information, as well as handheld access to communications and analysis capabilities. The required application programs that will enable clinical use of the Newton PDA are now beginning to emerge. The survival of the Newton platform seems pretty well established. Recent forecasts are predicting exponential expansion of the PDA market through 1999 with the Newton operating system retaining the largest share of the market (MacWeek 9/26/94). Competing PDA platforms haven't made it off the ground yet, while Newton ftp archives have been accumulating software from the very outset. Important support now comes from Apple Computer, which has targeted health care as a major vertical market for Newton technology.

This web resource is meant to provide information about medical uses of the Newton and to serve as an archive of software presently available at various ftp sites. Download information can be accessed here. These documents are presently being run off a web server at the Boston University School of Medicine. As they'll be under constant development, any information, submissions, or comments will be welcomed.

Applications currently available have been broken down into several general categories. Descriptions of the software, contact information, and links to download available applications can be accessed from the following selections:

- Patient Management
- Reference Information
- Quantitative Analysis
- Wireless Communications

An OS/2 Warp Online Exploration Guide

http://www.cyberblue.com/

This Web site acts as a sort of Internet tour guide for those interested in locating online OS/2 resources. Visitors can access the home page of IBM, the operating system's manufacturer, as well as many other informational Internet sites.

OS/2 Warp vs. Windows95: A Decisionmaker's Guide

http://www.austin.ibm.com/pspinfo/os2vschg.html

This site provides a comparison between Windows95 and OS/2 Warp. Includes discussions on architecture, multitasking, application support, vendor commitments, and other issues. Links to IBM pages.

Stéphane's OS/2 Web Site - Index

http://cyniska.ubishops.ca/os2/os2.html

Users of OS/2 Warp can use this site to find information and resources. Areas covered include games, programming, bitmaps and graphics, fun stuff, and links. Pointers to FTP sites are included.

PERSONAL DIGITAL ASSISTANTS

NewtNews

http://www.ridgecrest.ca.us/NewtNews/NN_top.html

The NewtNews site, a support and information site for Apple's hand held computer product, Newton and related technologies, has product news, a FAQ sheet, reviews and discussion, as well as instructions for joining a mailing list.

Newton Medical

http://med-amsa.bu.edu/newton.medical/newton.medical.html

A web site from the Boston University School of Medicine for medical news and information. See Editor's Choice.

Mobilis

http://www.volksware.com/mobilis/

Mobilis, the mobile computing lifestyle e-zine, offers interviews, product reviews, reader feedback, and tips for PDAs. Back issues are online here as well as the current edition.

UNIX

FlashBack

http://www.flashback.com/

This electronic newsletter is aimed at the open systems computing market. Browsers can access most articles via FTP orthey can jump to "SunWorld Online" for the Flashback-sponsored "New Products" column.

Hot Topic: Unix 25th Anniversary

http://www.amdahl.com/internet/events/unix25.html

The Amdahl corporation posts a "hotlinks" page at this site to spotlight special events or instructive source code. When we visited a special page was posted celebrating the 25th anniversary of the Unix operating system.

NeXT Stuff

http://digifix.digifix.com/

Stepwise bills its site as a single stop on the Internet for NEXTSTEP and Open Step info. Visitors can read up on NeXT Computers or follow links to NEXTSTEP newsgroups.

Unix Resources

http://wwwhost.cc.utexas.edu/cc/services/unix/index.html

This Unix resource page, maintained by the University of Texas at Austin Computation Center, provides an exhaustive index of links to related information. Visit here to search by keyword and browse Unix servers from around the world.

WINDOWS (PC'S)

The Cobb Group

http://www.cobb.com/index.htm

The Cobb Group is a division of the Ziff-Davis publishing empire, specializing in products for Windows aficionados. Visitors to this site will find information on Cobb's Microsoft software books and periodicals, including the "Inside.." line of magazines.

Commercial Winsock Stacks Page

http://www.northernc.on.ca/wasted/stacks/

The Commercial Winsock Stacks Page contains reviews of commercial stacks for Windows users. Visitors can read the Webmaster's evaluations and obtain software vendor contact info.

EMWAC

http://emwac.ed.ac.uk/

The aim of EMWAC at the University of Edinburgh is to support the use of Windows NT in the academic community by sponsoring technical workshops, training courses, and information on Microsoft products and services on the Internet.

Knowledge Computing

http://www.knowledge.co.uk/xxx/

United Kingdom-based Knowledge Computing supplies details on its Web publishing services and Multilingual PC Directory for foreign-language software at this commercial site. Contact information is provided.

The One-Stop Windows 95 Site

http://www.win95.com/

Visit this page to find Windows 95 resources on the Internet. Networks, files, product links, articles, and other goodies are featured.

O'Reilly Windows Center

http://www.ora.com/windows/

O'Reilly & Associates' Windows Center Web site contains a list of online resources and publications about Microsoft Windows and Windows 95. Includes Windows applications descriptions.

PC/Computing

http://www.zdnet.com/~pccomp/

PC/Computing, Ziff-Davis' monthly magazine for the non-Apple set, is available in online form at this site. Visit here for industry dirt, product reviews, sneak previews of new PC software, and humor (i.e., "Woody Allen's Hotlist").

PC SoftDIR - The Automated DOS/Windows Software Reference Guide

http://www.netusa.com/pcsoft/softdir.htm

PC SoftDIR provides a comprehensive online resource for selecting software for DOS, Windows, and OS/2 computers. Visit here for reviews of popular and recently released software titles for the PC.

PC World Online

http://www.pcworld.com/

Consumers and industry denizens alike will find informative news and reviews in the current edition of "PC World" Online. The electronic version of the major computer monthly offers the latest info on hardware, software and PC-related enterprises.

Win95 Magazine - The Online Magazine for Users of Windows 95

http://www.win95mag.com/

The home page for "Win95 Magazine" features the current issue as well as an archive of previous editions. Visitors can also submit articles and letters to the editor orfind out how to advertise in the publication.

Windows Sources

http://www.zdnet.com/~wsources/

"Windows Sources" is an online magazine devoted to Windows software and related topics and products. Features here include weird Web sites, work from cartoonist Michael Fry, reports, reviews, columns and downloadable software. Back issues are also archived here.

Windows95.com

http://www.windows95.com/

Windows95.com, an unofficial guide to Microsoft's personal computer operating system, provides free software and information for all user skill levels. Visit this site for a keyword search and links to a variety of instructional materials.

Windows 95 Information

http://www.mbnet.mb.ca/win/Window95.html

Sponsored by the Canadian user group, the Windows Information Network, this page contains an index to Windows 95 information and resources. Items covered include books, commercial vendors, CD-ROM titles and related sites.

Windows 95 Visual Tour

http://techweb.cmp.com/techweb/techweb/win95/1.htm

The Windows 95 Visual Tour site presents a very thorough overview and thumbnail evaluation of Microsoft's new operating system, Windows 95. The review is casual but thorough. A must-read for anyone considering making the upgrade.

WinMagWeb

http://www.winmag.com/

For a comprehensive source of Windows information, visit the Internet home of Windows magazine. This site complements the print version with articles on systems, software and other Windows-related topics.

USER GROUPS

GENERAL COMPUTING

ACM Living Publications & Services Catalogue

http://info.acm.org/catalog/

ACM is an international scientific and educational computer society that boasts over 80,000 members. It promotes its books, journals, videos and conference proceedings here.

Capital PC User Group (CPCUG)

http://cpcug.org/

The Capital PC User Group Inc. has more than 5,600 members and is located in Rockville, Md. The group includes 27 special interest groups, including Windows, desktop publishing, shareware, investment, OS/2 and APL. There's information here about the group's monthly magazine and BBS, as well as links to Internet, computer and entertainment-related sites.

Harvard Computer Society

http://hcs.harvard.edu/

The Harvard University Computer Society's home page lists computer news and tidbits, along with a host of instructional and informational links.

Melbourne PC User Group

http://www.melbpc.org.au/

The Melbourne Personal Computer User Group maintains this site for general information on the group, its activities and resources. Visit here for links to industry updates, online computer magazines, related databases and software archives.

PC User Group WWW

http://www.ibmpcug.co.uk/

PC fanatics in the U.K. looking for a sense of belonging can consult the PC User Group site. With links to PC shareware, tips and tricks and group event announcements, users can connect with information or with each other.

Texas ISDN Users Group (TIUG)

http://www.crimson.com/isdn/

Internet users who connect through ISDN modems have a resource in the Texas ISDN Users Group home page. Visitors can check out the schedule for upcoming meetings or click through an educational series of links that explains what ISDN is and how it works.

USER GROUPS BY CATEGORY

APPLE MACINTOSH AND CLONES

AMUG's Newton Page

http://www.amug.org/amug_newton.html

Addicts of Apple's Newton, a personal digital assistant, can find related facts, files and fun at the Atlanta Macintosh User Group's Newton page. Link to Newton software applications, utilities and user association sites from here.

Arizona Macintosh Users Group

http://www.amug.org/

The Arizona Macintosh Users Group is a nonprofit organization providing educational resources and assistance to users of Apple Macintosh computers. Visit this site for group activities, services and background information.

BMUG Boston

http://www.xensei.com/users/bmugbos/

The Boston branch of BMUG, a user group for Macintosh, presents general information and membership details at this site. Find also links to the BMUG Berkeley, Calif., page, as well as access to Mac-related gopher and FTP sites.

Johns Hopkins Macintosh Users Group

http://mug.welch.jhu.edu/

The Johns Hopkins Macintosh Users Group site contains an index of user guides, operating hints and links to related resources.

New Jersey Macintosh Users Group

http://www.njmug.org

The New Jersey Macintosh Users Group home page has information about Mac-related BBSs, Internet configurations and tools, as well as Usenet newsgroups. The site also features a collection of pointers to Macintosh software archives on the Web.

San Diego Macintosh User Group

http://www.sdmug.org

The San Diego Macintosh User Group supplies information on it meetings, membership privileges and more at its site. Also included are details on the group's MacINTOUCH magazine, Tele-Mac BBS, local group-sponsored activities and related special interest groups.

Stanford/Palo Alto Macintosh User Group (SMUG)

http://www.mediacity.com/smug/smug.html

The Stanford/Palo Alto Macintosh Users Group invites Macintosh users and Apple devotees to join its ranks for social, technical and informational interactions. Find out how to get the most out of your Mac from fellow enthusiasts.

TopSoft

http://www.topsoft.org/

Macintosh programmers can network online at TopSoft, a nonprofit, Internet-based users' group. Visitors may read up on the group's philosophy or its current projects here. Find also contact and biographical information about TopSoft members.

HEWLETT-PACKARD

Hewlett-Packard DutchWorks

http://hpux.ced.tudelft.nl/

DutchWorks a Hewlett-Packard's technical workstation user group for the Netherlands. Through this home page, the group provides support to technical users, systems and network administrators, programmers and consultants using HP equipment. In English and Dutch.

Interex, The International Association of Hewlett-Packard

http://www.interex.org/

The latest news and information about Interex—the International Association of Hewlett-Packard Computing Professionals—comes to the Web through this home page. The page features an introduction to Interex and its publications.

InterWorks - Technical Users Forum of Interex

http://www.interworks.org/

The InterWorks forum serves Hewlett-Packard users interested in the effective use of their workstations. Answers to Frequently Asked Questions and links to related information services are provided.

LINUX

The Atlanta Linux Enthusiasts

http://www.gatech.edu/ale/

The Atlanta Linux Enthusiasts is a group devoted to the Linux operating system. Visitors will find an organizational overview, member lists and a schedule of meetings and events.

Chippewa Linux Users and Enthusiasts

http://cvfn.org/clubs/clue/

The Chippewa Linux Users and Enthusiasts Web server provides a forum for the exchange of information about Linux, a free Unix clone which runs on IBM PC computers and clones. Visitors can link to Linux-related Web sites or join the CLUE mailing list.

Italian Linux Society

http://svpop.com.dist.unige.it/ILS.html

This is the home page for the Italian Linux Society. In Italian.

Linux User Registration

http://domen.uninett.no:29659/

Linux users stand up to be counted at the Linux User Registration page. A Norwegian user is conducting this worldwide survey. Visit this site to register or check statistics currently available.

MUUG Linux/System-Administration SIG

http://www.muug.mb.ca/linuxsig/

This page from the larger Manitoba Unix User Group's site is maintained by the Linux/System subgroup to post meeting information. Visit here for minutes of past meetings, announcements of upcoming events and links to related resources.

Salt Lake Linux Users Group

http://www.sllug.org/

Utah enthusiasts of the Unix operating system, Linux, unite as SLLUG, the Salt Lake Linux Users Group. Find out about the group's next meeting or access Linux related information, documentation and software files.

Vinny's Linux PC

http://vinny.csd.mu.edu/

This personal page by a Marquette University student mixes an introduction to Linux with a smattering of facts and links of relevancy to his personal life.

MISCELLANEOUS

Digital Equipment Computer Users Society

http://www.decus.org/

Digital Equipment Computer Users Society, an association of information technology profes-

sionals interested in the products, services and technologies of Digital Equipment Corporation, maintains this informational site. Visitors can link to news, local user groups, member services, group publications and more.

Emagic Users Page

http://www.mcc.ac.uk/~emagic/emagic_page.html

Two "enthusiastic users" of Emagic software, a maker of multimedia sound applications, maintain this site for fellow enthusiasts. Full descriptions and uses of applications like SoundSurfer and SoundDiver are provided, along with a mailing list and online tutorial.

University of Waterloo AIX Support Group

http://auk.uwaterloo.ca/

This AIX support group site contains information on services, staff and users of the AIX campus system at the University of Waterloo, Canada. Includes information on IBM RISC system/6000 hardware, the AIX operating system and available software.

UNIX

Calgary Unix Users Group

http://www.cuug.ab.ca:8001/

The Calgary Unix Users Group, the "largest" of its kind in North America, maintains this informational site. Visit here for organizational news and activities updates, educational presentations, member home pages and related newsgroups.

HEPiX

http://wwwcn.cern.ch/hepix/www/Overview.html

HEPix is a group of Unix users in the high energy physics community. This site offers access to the group's archived materials and documentation files stored at different HEPix sites.

The Michigan State University Unix Computing Group

http://rs560.cl.msu.edu/

The Michigan State University Unix Computing Group maintains this page of pointers to available UCG resources, documentation and applications. Links to other school pages are also available.

UK UNIX User Group

http://web.dcs.bbk.ac.uk/

This site is home to the UK UNIX User Group. It offers access to the organization's newsletter, Usenet newsgroup and software archive, as well as providing information about upcoming seminars and workshops related to the Unix operating system.

PROGRAMMING LANGUAGES, ENVIRONMENTS AND GUIDES

COMMERCIAL AND NON-COMMERCIAL KITS AND DEVELOPMENT TOOLS

Applied Testing and Technology

http://www.aptest.com/

Applied Testing and Technology outlines its software testing products and customer services at this promotional site. Check out the company's new test suites or link to other testing resources on the Web.

Asset Source for Software Engineering Technology

http://source.asset.com/

This commercial Web site, maintained by a division of San Diego-based Science Applications International Corp., offers software engineering and information technology resources for developers and scientists. Visitors can access information about the service, visit the electronic marketplace or check out training information and events listings.

Atria Software Inc.

http://www.atria.com/

Atria Software Inc. is a developer of professional progamming and software engineering tools based in Lexington, Mass. Visitors to the company's Web site will find news releases and information on products, services, customer support and training programs.

Borland Online

http://www.borland.com/

Borland Online provides information on its programming products, services and technical data. This page also includes press releases, company background and a user feedback link.

Bristol Technology Inc.

http://bristol.com/

Bristol Technology Inc. develops and markets the Wind/U family of products, which allow programmers to build Windows, Unix and other applications from a single source code base. Find detailed info about the company and its products and services at this promotional site.

Business Basic FTP Server

ftp://ftp.gmcclel.bossnt.com/

The Business Basic FTP Server contains BASIS product information, as well as files of interest to Business Basic programmers.

CASE Tools

http://osiris.sunderland.ac.uk/sst/casehome.html

An extensive site indexing CASE programming tools on the Web, this home page includes links to software and mailing lists across the Internet.

Century Computing Inc.

http://www.cen.com/

Century Computing makes software developmenty tools for image processing, client/server computing and space and defense applications. Visitors will find technical summaries, descriptions of new products, pricing information and interactive demonstrations.

City Zoo Inc.

http://www.mindspring.com/~cityzoo/cityzoo.html

City Zoo Inc., based in Atlanta, Ga., is a software and Web consulting firm, with an emphasis on teaching and training software. Its site features tips and tricks for Borland's Delphi and a link to its FTP site.

Data I/O Corporation

http://www.data-io.com/

The Data I/O Corporation produces Windows EDA software and programmer products. The Redmond, Wash.-based company gives an overview of its wares and provides technical support on this promotional page.

Franz Inc.

http://www.franz.com/

This promotional home page for Berkeley, Calif.-based Franz Inc., gives an overview of the computing company and its products. Franz creates dynamic object oriented programming tools for Unix workstations and PCs.

Freedom Software's Hyperspace Center

http://freedom.lm.com/motif.html

At Freedom Software's Hyperspace Center, visitors can find Motif tools and a tutorial on Motif X Windows. Includes information on other Freedom software products.

Home of Petri Nets at DAIMI

http://www.daimi.aau.dk/~petrinet/

This site features links to a wealth of information on Petri Nets, a graphical language for modelling complex systems. Visitors will find a FAQ section, topical e-mail lists and information about a Petri Nets newsletter.

ICONIX

http://www.iconixsw.com/

ICONIX produces CASE software engineering tools and provides training. Visitors to the ICONIX "PowerPage" can register for free white papers on object-oriented analysis and design.

ILOG Inc.

http://www.ilog.com/

The home page for ILOG, a supplier of C++ software components, offers customer success stories and information about the its products and services. Visitors can complete inquiry form to receive product literature and a CD-ROM containing software demos.

InfoMagic

http://www.infomagic.com/

This commercial site offers information on Info-Magic's computer language and development tools. InfoMagic kits come on CD-ROMS and their titles range from Linux development tools to the Hobbes OS/2. The site also provides information on InfoMagic's Internet service and the Communications Decency Act.

Integrated Computer Solutions

http://www.ics.com/

Headquartered in Cambridge, Mass., Integrated Computer Solutions Inc. promotes its visual development tools, training seminars, consulting services and technical support on this home page. Visitors can also read the ICS newsletter and find out about job opportunities.

Interactive Software Engineering Inc.

http://www.eiffel.com/

Interactive Software Engineering Inc. maintains this promotional site devoted to the company's object-oriented software development tools. Read about ISE's products and services, as well as the company itself.

INTERSOLV

http://www.intersolv.com/

INTERSOLV is a software firm which primarily produces client/server software development tools. Its corporate home page provides links to company information and financial records, product announcements, service plan overviews and career opportunities.

KL Group

http://www.klg.com/

The KL Group supplies Graphical User Interface (GUI) software objects to the X software community. The company's home page includes a company profile and information about products and marketing sites worldwide.

Kuck & Associates Inc.

http://www.kai.com/

Kuck & Associates Inc. is a computer applications producer in Champaign, Ill. Visitors will find product information on the company's numerical applications programs and optimizer applications for C/C++ and 77/90. Complete corporate information, job opportunities and contacts are listed.

Locus Computing Corporation

http://www.locus.com/

This promotional site is maintained by Locus Computing Corporation, a development and implementation company specializing in Unix-based open systems. Visitors to its home page are invited to learn more about the company, its products and its customer support services.

Mabry Software

http://www.mabry.com/

Mabry Software offers technical programming information and ordering instructions for its products at this promotional site. Find also a collection of links to other Visual Basic-related Web sites.

Mainsoft Corporation

http://www.mainsoft.com/

The home page of the Mainsoft Corp., a company that offers tools for multi-platform software developers, serves up general information about the Sunnyvale, Calif., business. Read about Mainsoft's Microsoft-based cross-development environment for porting Windows applications to Unix, company news releases and job opportunities.

Micro Focus Ltd.

http://www.mfltd.co.uk/

Micro Focus Ltd., a computer programming software company, maintains this site for general information. Visit here to learn about its wide range of programming tools, industry events, employment opportunities and more.

The Mops Page

http://www.netaxs.com/~jayfar/mops.html

Mops 2.6 is a powerful freeware public-domain development system for the Macintosh. With Forth and Smalltalk parentage, Mops has extensive OOP capabilities. Downloads are available.

Orion Instruments Inc.

http://www.oritools.com/

Orion Instruments is a developer and manufacturer of highly integrated, cost-effective tools for em-bedded systems designers. This home page provides a corporate overview, product information and information on distribution channels.

Portland Group Inc.

http://www.pgroup.com/

The Portland Group Inc. is a software developer concentrating on the production and sale of scalar and parallel compilers. Look up the company's track record in the industry or get product and sales information at this promotional site.

Powersoft

http://www.powersoft.com/

The Powersoft home page contains an overview of the company and descriptions of its local/server databases and high performance compiler/language tools. Includes information on customer support, training and consulting services, product details and employment opportunities.

SanSoft

http://www.pdantic.com/SanSoft.htm

SanSoft is a software and systems consulting firm offering services to the Macintosh and Newton computing community. Visit this promotional site for a look at the company's products and software programming services.

Silverware

http://rampages.onramp.net/~silver/

Silverware, a Dallas-based corporation, specializes in the development of third party asynchronous communications software libraries for DOS and Windows software developers.

Software Research Associates

http://www.sra.co.jp/

Japan's Software Research Associates presents information on its programming tools—namely, its component-based development environment—at the company's home page. Includes a company overview, technical support sites and ordering info. In Japanese and English.

Soum Corporation

http://www.soum.co.jp/

The Soum Corporation of Japan, a Unix application development company, maintains this promotional site. Visit here to learn about its products and services, including consulting, software development, technical document translation and more.

Taligent Inc.

http://www.taligent.com/

Taligent Inc. develops object-oriented programming tools for a wide variety of programming levels. Visit this site to learn about the company, its products and career opportunities.

Thomson Software Products

http://www.thomsoft.com/

Thompson Software's site offers a company overview, along with its products and services for "mission-critical application development, enterprise-wide data access and reporting." Packages include ActivAda for Windows and TeleUSE/Enterprise.

Tower Concepts Inc.

http://www.tower.com/

Tower Concepts Inc. promotes Razor, an integrated software package that is a configurable problem-tracking and file version control and release management system, at the company's home page. Find an introduction to the company and its complement of products and services at this promotional site.

Wind River

http://www.wrs.com/

Wind River, a software designer specializing in real-time operating systems and development tools, maintains this promotional page. Visitors are invited to learn more about the company, its products, services, user groups, customer support and training opportunities.

WINTERP 2.0

http://www.eit.com/software/winterp/winterp.html

Programmers can get the scoop about the OSF/Motif Widget INTERPreter at this home page. WINTERP is a rapid prototyping environment for creating and delivering GUI-based applications. This site features links to WINTERP downloadable software and documentation.

VBxtras Inc.

http://www.vbxtras.com/

Visual Basics supplies product and ordering information. Its home page features 140 products, including the firm's featured program, the Visual Basic 4.0 programming system for the creation of Windows '95 applications.

X/Open Company Ltd.

http://www.xopen.org/

X/Open Company Ltd., offers this Web site with a wealth of information about its open system design products and services. Visitors to this site can peruse the company's online resources or take a "five minute" virtual tour of the site.

Xilinx

http://www.xilinx.com/

This commercial home page provides information about Xilinx, a company which supplies CMOS programmable logic and related development system software. Visitors can access product information, customer support and job listing data.

PROGRAMMING GUIDES

Association of Logic Programming

http://www.cs.mu.oz.au/~ad/alp/archive.html

The Association of Logic Programming posts an archive of articles from the Logic Programming Newsletter here. The site also contains links to ALP's home page.

Bugtraq Archives for July 1995 - present by thread

http://www.eecs.nwu.edu/~jmyers/bugtraq/index.html

Bugtraq Archives, a personal collection of programming resources, exposes various Unix security holes, what they are and how to fix them. Find a mailing list designed to encourage discussion and create workable solutions.

Catalog of Free Compilers and Interpreters

http://cuiwww.unige.ch/freecomp

The searchable version of the Free Compilers List catalogs free software for language tools, including compilers, compiler generators, interpreters and assemblers. Natural language processing tools are also included.

CERN STING Information Service

http://dxsting.cern.ch/sting/sting.html

The Software Technology Interest Group provides visitors to its page pointers to programming resources and computer science archives on the Web. Site features also include STING organizational data and contact information.

Digitool Inc.

http://www.digitool.com/

The Digitool Web page provides information on the three aspects of the Macintosh Common Lisp phenomenon: the MCL product, the MCL community and the MCL FTP site. The company's expertise is Macintosh and Common Lisp development.

Document Style Semantics and Specification Language

http://www.jclark.com/dsssl/

This site devoted to Document Style Semantics and Specification Language offers information and examples of the DSSSL transformation language. Find resources of interest to the computer science and programming communities.

A First Guide to PostScript

http://www.cs.indiana.edu/docproject/programming/postscript/postscript.html

The Department of Computer Science at Indiana University maintains this site for a simple introduction to the Postscript page description language from Adobe. Comprehensive information on programming, links to the Adobe home page, reference books and other related resources are available here.

Formal Technical Review Archive Web

http://www.ics.hawaii.edu/~johnson/FTR/

The Formal Technical Review Archive Web page is a resource for software review methods such as code inspection, active design reviews, phased inspections and FTArm. The page includes overviews of the methods and links to related Internet resources.

Fortran Market

http://www.fortran.com/fortran/market.html

This site is devoted to products and services related to Fortran, a programming language. Browsers here will find commercial pages selling related books, software and consulting services. The site also posts answers to Frequently Asked Questions about Fortran products and links to Fortran organizations.

Functional Programming Archive

http://www.lpac.ac.uk/SEL-HPC/Articles/FuncArchive.html

The Functional Programming Archive offers links to articles and electronic resources covering a range of related languages, theories and applications. Find descriptions of functional programming events, research and upcoming conferences using the extensive set of pointers to highly technical sites.

IBM Solution Developer Operations

http://www.austin.ibm.com/developer/

IBM maintains this site for its Solution Developer Operations resource index. Visitors will find news, events schedules, developer assistance and an archive of recent articles of interest to developers using IBM's products and services.

Index to Object-Oriented Information Sources

http://cuiwww.unige.ch/OSG/OOinfo/

This page features a searchable index of object-oriented languages and systems information resources on the Web. The links here cover books, programming languages, Frequently Asked Questions (FAQs), newsgroups, search engines, bibliographies and more.

Introduction to the Software Engineering Glossary

http://dxsting.cern.ch/sting/glossary-intro.html

STING, the Software Technology Interest Group, presents a "software engineering glossary and information guide." Features pointers to general development news, upcoming conferences and a searchable index of terms and info by keyword.

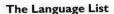

The Language List

http://cuiwww.unige.ch/langlist/

The Language List, a project of the Centre Universitaire d'Informatique of Geneva, Switzerland. The Language List is an attempt to enumerate all known programming languages. It is maintained by Bill Kinnersley and is periodically published on comp.lang.misc.

Linear Programming FAQ

http://www.densis.fee.unicamp.br/pesquisa/faq/lp_faq.html

The Linear Programming Frequently Asked Questions sheet provides a variety of info on linear programming, codes, software tools, test models and more. Visitors can also link to the Non-Linear Programming FAQ from here.

Modula-3

http://www.research.digital.com/SRC/modula-3/html/home.html

Modula-3 is a Pascal-related computer programming language. Find resources, documentation and news related to Modula-3 at this informational site.

Motif Frequently Asked Questions (FAQ)

http://www.cis.ohio-state.edu/hypertext/faq/usenet/motif-faq/top.html

This Usenet site contains a FAQ sheet about Motif, a widely-accepted set of user interface guidelines which specify how an X Window System application should look and feel.

OO Bibliography

http://cuiwww.unige.ch/cgi-bin/bibrefs/

A hypertext database of bibliography references related to object-oriented systems is maintained at this server. Visitors can also browse prepackaged queries or find out how to obtain a copy of the bibliography. This page is a mirror of the OO Bibliography Catalog at IAM.

Patterns

http://st-www.cs.uiuc.edu/users/patterns/patterns.html

The Patterns home page is a source for information about all aspects of patterns and pattern languages. Visitors will find information on pattern books, papers, conferences, mailing lists and archives here.

Rexx Language, IBM Hursley

http://rexx.hursley.ibm.com/rexx/

Computer programmers and software developers will find an index of Internet resources related to the Rexx programming language at this site.

Robert Lentz's Macintosh Programming Resources

http://www.astro.nwu.edu/lentz/mac/programming/home-prog.html

Macintosh Programming Resources provides basic information and tools for professional and aspiring software developers. Find the Apple's Developer's Guide here, as well as the latest news on the revolutionary new OpenDoc technology.

Software Composition Group

http://iamwww.unibe.ch/~scg/

The Software Composition Group, based in Berne, Switzerland, offers information about its current research projects in the use of object-oriented technology in software development. This page includes links to object-oriented information sources, an object-oriented FAQ, an object-oriented bibliography, the CHOOSE Homepage and general C++ resources.

Turbo Pascal Programmers Page

http://www.cs.vu.nl/~jprins/tp.html

This "turbo" page contains a wealth of informative links of value to Pascal programmers. Visitors will find enough book descriptions, lists of FTP sites and Frequently Asked Questions to peruse for days.

Visual Programming

http://www.cogs.susx.ac.uk/users/ianr/vpl.html

Visit this site for a variety of information about visual computer programming systems. Maintained by a programmer, this home page features links to instructional materials on various systems, related professional associations and Internet newsgroups.

What is Object-Oriented Software?

http://www.soft-design.com/softinfo/objects.html

An Introduction Anyone who is in the dark about object-oriented software can learn something by reading this page from Terry Montlick of Software Design Consultants. The introductory document uses real-life metaphors to explain the programming approach.

World Wide Web Virtual Library: Computing, Programming Languages

http://src.doc.ic.ac.uk/bySubject/Computing/Languages.html

Programmers visiting this site will find numerous pointers to online reference materials about computer languages and software development tools.

The Z Notation

http://www.comlab.ox.ac.uk/archive/z.html

According to this home page, "the formal specification notation Z (pronounced 'zed') is based on set theory and first order predicate logic." This page links to information about Z archives,

publications, meetings, courses and various other resources.

PROGRAMMING GUIDES BY LANGUAGE

ADA

The Ada-Belgium Organization

http://www.cs.kuleuven.ac.be/~dirk/ada-belgium/

The Ada-Belgium Organization is a forum for programmers interested in the Ada language and applications. Includes Ada resources as well as membership application forms.

Public Ada Library (PAL)

http://wuarchive.wustl.edu/languages/ada/pal.html

The Public Ada Library is an open archive of software, information and documentation related to the international standard computer programming language. Programmers and other interested visitors can find out how to access PAL's reference materials, courseware, compilers and more.

C / C++

C++ Archive

http://www.quadralay.com/www/CCForum/CCForum.html

The commonly used programming language C++ is the basis for Quadralay Corporation software. On this page, Quadralay points to Internet resources providing explanations of and instruction in C++.

FORTRAN

The High Performance Fortran Forum

http://www.erc.msstate.edu/hpff/home.html

The High Performance Fortran Forum represents a coalition of industry, academic and laboratory professionals working to push the envelope on Fortran 90 research. Featured here are research projects, technical publications and reports on products and services related to Fortran 90 developments.

Netlib Repository High-Performance Fortran Index

http://www.netlib.org/hpf/index.html

The Netlib Repository, a collection of mathematical software, papers and databases provided by the University of Tennessee at Knoxville, maintains this site for high-performance Fortran index. Visitors will find programming materials and links to related resources.

LISP

The Association of Lisp Users

http://www.cs.rochester.edu/u/miller/ALU/home.html

Computer scientists working with the Lisp language can download information from this Association of Lisp Users page maintained by the University of Rochester's computer science department.

Common Lisp Hypermedia Server (CL-HTTP)

http://www.ai.mit.edu/projects/iiip/doc/cl-http/home-page.html

Visitors to this site will find an index to sites relevant to Common Lisp. General information, sources, distribution and bug reports are included.

MISCELLANEOUS

CLIPS: A Tool for Building Expert Systems

http://www.jsc.nasa.gov/~clips/CLIPS.html

CLIPS, an interactive development tool for expert systems, is available here from the U.S. National Aeronautics and Space Administration. Visit this site to learn about and download the software, used by thousands of engineers in the public and private sector.

GLU Parallel Programming System

http://www.csl.sri.com/GLU.html

GLU (Granular Lucid) is "a very high-level programming system for constructing parallel and distributed applications to run on high-performance computing systems." Links to an overview and software, with demo and applications are featured.

Purdue University Compiler Construction Tool Set

http://dynamo.ecn.purdue.edu/~hankd/PCCTS/Index.html

Purdue University maintains this site for its Compiler Construction Tool Set, an archive of public-domain software tools designed for the construction of compilers and other translations systems. Includes tutorials and recent release versions.

SCG Script Archive

http://iamwww.unibe.ch/~scg/Src/

The University of Bern's Institute of Computer Science and Applied Mathematics maintains this site to provide information about its Software Composition Group archive. The page features links to Perl scripts and packages plus an Htgrep FAQ sheet.

PERL

Index of Perl Info

http://www.metronet.com/1h/perlinfo/perl5

Programmers will find the index of a personal FTP site containing dozens of downloadable files relating to the Perl computer language here.

libwww-perl: Distribution Information

http://www.ics.uci.edu/pub/websoft/libwww-perl/

Perl programmers will find a library of Perl4 packages at this informative site maintained by the University of California, Irvine. Visitors here can download a host of information and tools related to the CGI scripting language.

Perl

http://www.metronet.com/perlinfo/perl5/manual/perl.html

The Practical Extraction and Report Language (PERL) is a language for scanning text files, extracting information and then printing reports. This manual site for perl users provides complete technical information, including a list of bugs.

Perl5 Information, Announcements and Discussion - pl5.000

http://www.metronet.com/perlinfo/perl5.html

Perl 5 features informative postings and source sites designed for perl newsgroup users. Route to an online perl manual for expanded technical material.

PERL FAQ

http://pubweb.nexor.co.uk/public/perl/faq/intro.html

Frequently Asked Questions files are the workhorses of the Internet, but this FAQ file on the Perl scripting language has a beautiful stride. Comprehensive and exact, yet written with a sense of humor, the Web page may evoke a smile while visitors looks up the answer to their questions.

Perl Meta-FAQ

http://www.khoros.unm.edu/staff/neilb/perl/metaFAQ/metaFAQ.html

Information is provided here on obtaining another FAQ sheet for the computer programming language Perl 1.4. Visitors can link to HTML, postcript and ASCII versions of the FAQ.

Perl Reference Materials

http://www.eecs.nwu.edu/perl/perl.html

This site is an information resource for programmers using the Perl language. Includes a newsgroup, FAQ sheets, how-to guides and links to other resources.

Tom Christiansens' Mox.Perl.COM

http://mox.perl.com/

Are you going PERL-a-go-go? Programmers using Perl will find links to the Comprehensive Perl Archive Network and dozens of other Perl resources at this PERL-specific corporate Web site.

TCL/TK

A Brief Introduction to Tcl/Tk

http://http2.brunel.ac.uk:8080/~csstddm/TCL2/TCL2.html

An online document serving as a brief introduction to Tcl/Tk, "a programming system ... which has very useful graphical interface facilities," is offered here by a computer programmer. In addition to a system overview, find programming examples, including a simple file browser and a text editor.

Tcl

http://www.pi.infn.it/tcl/Tcl.html

This page serves as a comprehensive resource for information about Tcl/tk, the Tool command language, as well as Tcl/Tk resources on the Web. The site also features links to a FAQ sheet and manual pages.

Tcl Frequently Asked Questions (FAQ)

http://www.cis.ohio-state.edu/hypertext/faq/usenet/tcl-faq/top.html

Visit this page to access the Tcl FAQ sheet from the Usenet newsgroup, comp.lang.tcl. Also find a relevant bibliography and other related files.

Tcl/Tk Project At Sun Microsystems Laboratories

http://www.sunlabs.com/research/tcl/

Sun Microsystems Laboratories, the Mountain View, Calif.-based computing concern, maintains this site for Tcl programming information. Visitors are presented with info about Tcl/Tk, a universal scripting platform for the Internet.

Tcl/Tk Resources

http://web.cs.ualberta.ca/~wade/Auto/Tcl.html

The Tcl/Tk Resources site offers highly technical information and resources regarding the computer languages, Tcl and Tk. Includes usage instructions, troubleshooting tips and lists of Frequently Asked Questions.

Virtual Library: Tcl/Tk

http://cuiwww.unige.ch/eao/www/TclTk.html

An index of software and documentation resources for the programming languages Tcl/Tk resides here. Browsers will find links to Tcl/Tk-based development tools and programs for a variety of programming environments.

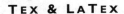
TEX & LATEX

TeX & LaTeX Archives from comp.text.tex

http://www.ucc.ie/info/TeX/TeXmenu.html

The TeX and LaTeX computer languages are detailed at this site. Computer programmers can find related resources, documentation and access to Usenet discussion groups here.

TeX-related Documentation

http://www.cl.cam.ac.uk/TeXdoc/TeXdocs.html

"This page is primarily intended for users of TeX in the Teaching and Research part of the University of Cambridge Computer Laboratory." Disclaimer aside, visitors are invited to peruse and use the documentation provided at this informational site.

VISUAL BASIC

Visual Basic

http://www.apexsc.com/vb/

Devoted to Visual Basic programmers worldwide, this page features links to electronic magazines and articles, files available to download, FAQ sheets and sites of interest to beginners. A jobs page, a marketplace and miscellaneous links are also included.

SECURITY AND ENCRYPTION

CheckPoint Software Technologies Ltd.: Home of FireWall-1

http://www.checkpoint.com/

Checkpoint Software Technologies is a developer of Internet computer network security applications. This page includes background information on the company, product descriptions and instructions for ordering.

Data Fellows World Wide Web Server

http://www.datafellows.fi/

The Finnish Data Fellows Corporation develops and distribute "security" software. Visitors will find information about DF's security and virus-protection products and services. An online database of computer viruses is also provided.

International PGP

http://www.ifi.uio.no/~staalesc/PGP/

For PGP users outside the United States, this site contains updated information, FAQs and relevant links. It includes info on support resources for non-English-speaking users.

NCSA HTTPd/Mosaic: Using PGP/PEM auth

http://hoohoo.ncsa.uiuc.edu/docs/PEMPGP.html

The HTTPd Development Team at the NCSA maintains this FAQ sheet and general information page to disseminate the facts about the PGP/PEM encryption schemes. Sections listed include answers to the following questions: "How bullet-proof is it?" "What does the protocol look like?" and "What do I need to use it?"

PGP 2.6.2 FAQ, Buglist, Fixes and Improvements

http://www.mit.edu:8001/people/warlord/pgp-faq.html

Pretty Good Privacy version 2.6.2, a communications encryption application, can be downloaded from this site, which also posts PGP FAQ sheets and tips for working out the software's bugs.

Portland Software

http://www.portsoft.com/

Portland Software makes ZipLock, an application for digital encryption for Internet transfers. Find information about this software and the company's other products and services at this site, along with press clippings and a link to a biography of Harpo Marx.

RSA Data Security Inc.

http://www.rsa.com/

This California-based computer company produces cryptology and security software. Visitors to its home page will find detailed product information, company news and a FAQ sheet.

SOFTWARE DEVELOPERS AND VENDORS

APPLE MACINTOSH AND CLONES

DAILY PLANNERS, PERSONAL ASSISTANTS, AND VIRTUAL OFFICE GEAR

CE Software

http://www.cesoft.com/

CE Software Inc., a West Des Moines, Iowa-based company, develops and publishes office productivity software for Macintosh personal computers. Visit this site for company and product information, technical support, customer services and other company resources.

ENTERTAINMENT— ADULT, ARCADE, MYSTERY

MacPlay

http://www.macplay.com/

MacPlay is the Macintosh-only division of Interplay Productions. The company provides entertainment and educational software "for the discriminating Macintosh consumer." Visitors to its promotional site can check out product demos and coming attractions or locate tech support.

INTERNET

The Electric Magic Company

http://www.emagic.com/

NetPhone is an application for the Macintosh that allows the user to place audio calls throughout the Internet for no cost. Includes downloading and purchasing instructions.

ROFM CGI

http://rowen.astro.washington.edu/

ROFM CGI, formerly Filemaker Pro CGI for the Macintosh, allows users to search and add records to databases via the Web. Browsers can download the latest version of the application and documentation.

StarNine Technologies

http://www.starnine.com/

This promotional site is the Web home of Star-Nine Technologies, a provider of Internet server software and e-mail software for the Macintosh. Visitors are invited to learn about the company, its products and customer support services.

MULTIMEDIA—CD-ROM AND ELECTRONIC PUBLISHING

Apple Multimedia Program

http://www.amp.apple.com/

Apple Computer's Multimedia Program is featured at this corporate site, which offers members access to the top minds in multimedia development. The site offers membership details, technical resources for multimedia professionals and more.

QuickMedia

http://www.quickmedia.com/

Software developer QuickMedia provides information here on its Living Album for Macintosh, including features, reviews, screen shots and ordering information. The Living Album allows users to store and publish multimedia albums on floppies, CDs and the Internet. A Living Album Lite is available for downloading.

SCIENTIFIC

Chris Smolinski's

http://www.access.digex.net/~cps/

Chris Smolinski produces science and radio-related software for the Macintosh. Visitors to his home page can download demos. This site also provides shortwave radio pages and lots of links.

SYSTEM SOFTWARE, UTILITIES, FONTS

Aladdin Systems, Inc

http://www.aladdinsys.com/

Aladdin Systems of Watsonville, Calif., a Macintosh software developer, supplies information here on products such as StuffIt, SITcomm and Aladdin Desktop Tools. Also included are news, job opportunities, shareware, freeware and an FTP link.

Casady & Greene

http://www.casadyg.com/

Casady & Greene, a Mac shareware software developer, promotes its games to utilities on this not-so-corporate home page. The site features product announcements, updates and demonstrations. Visitors can also find out where on the Web their software—ConflictCatcher, GliderPro—can be downloaded.

Gatekeeper

http://gargravarr.cc.utexas.edu/gatekeeper/gatekeeper.html

The home page for Gatekeeper, a sleek anti-virus program for today's Macintosh computers, contains information about the latest version of the program along with details about how it works. Includes instructions on downloading the program and its documentation.

MacTCP Monitor

http://gargravarr.cc.utexas.edu/mactcp-mon/main.html

MacTCP Monitor is a utility that graphs the interaction between Macs and their network systems. Visitors will find information on the creator, as well as his department at the University of Texas.

Semicolon Software

http://www.opendoor.com/Rick/Semicolon.html

Semicolon Software is the Macintosh shareware software developer responsible for such classics as Solitaire Till Dawn. Visitors can find company news, product descriptions and reviews, as well as shareware to download.

ZipIt

http://www.awa.com/softlock/zipit/zipit.html

Visitors to this site will find a promotion for ZipIt 1.3.4, a Mac shareware program that "zips and unzips archives in a format fully compatible with PKZip for the IBM." Answers to Frequently Asked Questions, info on obtaining and registering the software and author contact info are also available.

3-D OBJECTS—CAD, RENDERING, VR, CGI

Specular Online

http://www.specular.com/

Specular's Web page promotes the company's 3-D rendering tools for the Macintosh. Customers will find technical support and visitors can download ready-made models. Includes a gallery of artwork created with Specular software.

WORD PROCESSING

Alpha

http://www.cs.umd.edu/~keleher/alpha.html

Download a shareware Macintosh text editor at this site. Included is Alpha software, documentation and registration info.

Nisus Software Inc.

http://www.nisus-soft.com/

Nisus Software supplies news and information about its Macintosh software products, including the Nisus Writer word processor, Easy Alarms and Laser TechFonts at this site. Also available

are demos, ordering information, technical support and an FTP site.

MULTI-PLATFORM

BUSINESS—FINANCIAL PLANNING, ACCOUNTING, AND SPREADSHEETS

Dun & Bradstreet Software

http://www.dbss.com/

Financial giant Dun & Bradstreet produces business and financial software. Visitors can take a close look at the company's products and services at this promotional site.

Expertsoft Corporation

http://www.expersoft.com/

Expersoft Corporation, a "distributed object management" software developer, hosts this promotional site. Visit here for its executive summary, marketing forecasts, product information and more.

Grant Tracker

http://www.rahul.net/kendric/

Grant Tracker is a spreadsheet program tailor-made for sorting and accounting grant funding data and expenses over the life of a project. Order the software package online at this commercial site or download a demo.

Intuit

http://www.careermosaic.com/cm/intuit/intuit1.html

Menlo Park, Calif.-based Intuit Inc. markets personal finance, small business accounting and tax preparation software. Visitors to its home page can find out more about the company, its products and customer services.

Peachtree Software

http://www.peachtree.com/

Peachtree Software provides information on its accounting products and services. Also included are demos and information on support for Peachtree products.

Portal Information Network

http://www.portal.com/

The Portal Information Network sells business management software to Internet access providers. The company's support site has information on products and services, staff and customer support.

SBT Accounting Systems

http://www.sbtcorp.com/

This commercial Web site explains the founding principles of (and shows off the product lines offered by) SBT Accounting Systems, a California-based company that sells accounting and business-management software. Includes technical support and seminar information.

The Software Management Resource Center (SM) by Express Systems Inc.

http://www.express-systems.com/

Express Systems Inc. markets software management products, that is electronic solutions to monitoring and maintaining software license compliance and efficient asset distribution. Learn about the company's products and services at this promotional site.

Sterling Software

http://www.sterling.com/

The Sterling Software site provides information on the company, its clients and its electronic banking and management systems software. Includes access to archives containing documents on electronic data interchange, electronic commerce and other topics.

Thinking Machines Corporation

http://www.think.com/

The Thinking Machine corporate page describes the company's software and systems solutions, as well as its products and services. The company develops "analytical software" that take the guesswork out of financial speculation. Information on employment opportunities is also provided here.

Timeslips

http://www.timeslips.com/

Timeslips Corporation produces two types of software: Time Sheet Professional and Timeslips, both billing and accounting programs. This home page provides company info, product listings, ordering details and downloadable demos.

DAILY PLANNERS, PERSONAL ASSISTANTS, AND VIRTUAL OFFICE GEAR

Adaptiv Software

http://www.adaptiv.com/

Adaptiv Software promotes its daily planner-type software program, The People Scheduler, here and offers discounted sales and technical support. Check out the full line of Adaptiv Software at this coporate home page.

Answer Systems, Incorporated

http://www.answer.com/

Answer Systems Lab, a wholly-owned subsidiary of Platinum Technology Inc., is the developer of the Apriori family of software, designed to assist technical support teams. The Answer Systems site offers help for its Desk Help program, a corporate profile, information on Apriori and links to Platinum Technology's other labs.

Blueridge Technologies

http://www.blueridge.com/

Blueridge Technologies is a corporate producer of cross-platform management software for Mac and Windows environments. Visitors will find information on products, update releases, technical support and customer services.

Ex Machina Inc.

http://exmachina.com/

Ex Machina, which develops wireless communications software, provides company information and a product catalog at its site. Includes information on company services, alliance programs and technical support.

InfoImaging Technologies, Inc

http://www.infoimaging.com/

InfoImaging Technologies Inc. welcomes visitors to its home page with an offer to download its digital facsimile software for free. Visitors can access product, tutorial and troubleshooting information, along with facts about the corporation.

NEXOR

http://web.nexor.co.uk/

NEXOR is a British company that develops electronic messaging and directory software. This site offers information on marketing, technical support and research, plus public Web services and personal pages from the staff.

ProNotes Inc.

http://www.speechsolutions.com/

ProNotes Inc. develops and markets voice recognition and free-dictation software. This page serves up an overview of the company, its products and its services.

DATABASES

Amdahl Corp.

http://www.amdahl.com/

Amdahl Corp. develops and integrates large-scale computing systems and enterprise-wide solutions to address the business and information needs of large organizations. Visitors will find information on Amdahl's products, services and support at this corporate home page.

Belmont Research

http://www.belmont.com/

Belmont Research of Cambridge, Mass., supplies information on its products and services for graphical data reporting and related data activities. Also provided here are company information and job openings.

Compusult Limited

http://www.compusult.nf.ca/

Canada's Compusult Limited promotes its computer consulting services, custom software and systems design offerings at this corporate home page. Find access to the company's environmental sites and a link to the Newfoundland and Labrador home page.

Control Data Systems

http://www.cdc.com/

Control Data Systems builds information management systems which integrate hardware and software. Its Web site provides company announcements, customer and investor services, technical support info, a showcase of its customers and job openings.

Empress Software Inc.

http://www.empress.com/

Empress Software Inc. a Canadian distributor of data management software, provides extensive info about its company, products and services on this page. Visitors can find out what's new at Empress and check out career opportunities with the company.

Folio Corporation

http://www.folio.com/

Folio Corporation, a Provo, Utah-based cross-platforjm "infobase" software company, maintains this promotional site. Visit here to learn about the company and its database, electronic publishing and communications products. In Dutch, English, French, Italian and Spanish.

Information Projects Group

http://www.ipgroup.com/

The Information Projects Group is a Reston, Virginia-based database services consultant. Their promotional site includes company background information on the company and an indexed list of its products and services.

InformixLink

http://www.informix.com/

Informix Software Inc. is a supplier of high performance, parallel processor database technology for open systems. The company details on its product line, including development tools and database servers, at this promotional site.

Knowledge Engineering Pty, Ltd.

http://www.ke.com.au/

Knowledge Engineering Pty of Melbourne, Australia, provides information on its database software and other products and services. Includes demonstrations of its Texpress database system, plus a client list, support services, course information and distributors index.

LCS Support Web

http://www.support.lotus.com/

Get Lotus software product support at this commercial site, with information about new applications, an FTP library and a search engine.

Notes Network Information Center

http://www.notes.net/

The Notes Network Information Center contains a directory of Lotus Notes pages on the Internet which extend the Notes domain across the Web. Includes pointers to Lotus Education Services and related Notes servers.

Object Design Inc.

http://www.odi.com/

Object Design Inc. works in the object database market, developing database management systems, tools, connectivity solutions, services and support. Its Web page offers a primer on object technology as well as a pitch for OD Inc. products.

Persimmon IT Inc.

http://www.persimmon.com/

Persimmon IT, an "information technology company," maintains this site to introduce its services, including software development, specialty applications, strategic applications and infrastructure projects. Visit here for a corporate and service overview, staff profiles and employment opportunities.

Schema Research Corp.

http://www.schemaresearch.com/

Schema Research Corp. provides database products and services. Visitors to this corporate site can read a company overview and product descriptions or link to other sites for engineering software.

Teledyne Brown Engineering

http://www.tbe.com/

Teledyne Brown Engineering is a systems engineering and software development company located in Huntsville, Ala. Visitors to its corporate Web site will find a general overview of the corporation, descriptions of its products and services and a listing of career opportunities.

Toyo Engineering Corp.

http://www.toyo-eng.co.jp/

The Toyo Engineering Corp. page contains information on the company and its information systems products. Includes technical documentation and user response forms. In Japanese and English.

Versant Object Technology Corp.

http://www.versant.com/

Versant Object Technology Corp. is a software engineering firm specializing in object database management systems for multi-user, distributed computer environments. This site provides general information about the company, product descriptions and customer support resources.

VNP Software

http://www.vnp.com/

VNP Software offers development tools and consulting expertise to the NEXTSTEP/OpenStep community. The company offers an overview of its products and services, as well as its current efforts toward the development of the Financial Objects Framework.

VTLS Inc.

http://www.vtls.com/

This promotional site is the Web home of VTLS Inc., a developer of library management systems headquartered in Blacksburg, Va. Visitors can read about the company, its products and services.

EDUCATIONAL—GAMES, REFERENCES, ALMANACS

ECSDG Hem-Sida

http://ecsdg.lu.se/

EkonomiCentrum Software Development Group (ECSDG), Lund University, develops software to enable information retrieval in research and education. A data retrieval program, a Swedish version of NCSA Mosaic and other software and documents are available here. In Swedish and English.

iec ProGAMMA

http://www.gamma.rug.nl/

ProGAMMA develops and distributes software for the social and behavioral sciences. Includes links to other social science information technology sites and related Web servers.

KME Corporate Engineering Division

http://www.kme-lab.co.jp/

The Corporate Engineering Division of Kyushu Matsushita Electric Corporation Ltd. introduces Web users to its English-to-Japanese translation software and research and development laboratory. Visitors can also view a Japanese photo gallery. In Japanese and English.

Logos Research Systems Inc.

http://www.logos.com

The Logos Research Systems site features reviews of its Logos Bible Software 2.0, technical support,
news releases and other product information. Links to other Christian resources are included.

NTT Learning Systems Corp.

http://www.nttls.co.jp/

NTT Learning Systems Corp., a Japanese developer of multimedia production products and corporate training software, maintains this Web site to explain its services to visitors. Information is available in English and Japanese.

Rocky Mountain Digital Peeks

http://www.csn.net/malls/rmdp/

Rocky Mountain Digital Peeks is a developer and publisher of nature, science, entertainment and educational CD-ROM titles. Its home page includes information about the company and its products and opportunities to download software updates and images.

SIByL

http://www.gamma.rug.nl/sibyl.html

The Software Information Bank of the inter-university expertise center, ProGAMMA, contains information about software for the social sciences. This site includes details on the project as well as access to the SIByL database.

Waterloo Maple Inc.

http://www.maplesoft.com/

Waterloo Maple Inc., a Waterloo, Canada-based technical and educational mathematics software developer, maintains this promotional site. Visit here for news, product descriptions, demonstration software and ordering information.

ENTERTAINMENT— ADULT, ARCADE, MYSTERY

The Atomic Diner

http://atomic.com/

Texas-based Atomic Games Inc. employs this corporate home page to promote its menu of action computer games, including V for Victory, World at War and Close Combat. Access the company's listserver to join mailing lists and check out the FTP archive for game patches and shareware utilities.

Interplay

http://www.interplay.com/

Interplay Productions is a commercial developer of interactive entertainment software. At its corporate Web site, visitors can learn about the company and demo its popular computer gaming products.

Rocket Science
http://www.rocketsci.com/

This promotional site is sponsored by Rocket Science, a company that designs and manufactures CD-ROM games for all platforms. Visitors can learn about the company, review its products and purchase games or other merchandise.

GRAPHICS—DESIGN AND ILLUSTRATION

Adobe Systems Inc.
http://www.adobe.com/

A leading manufacturer in the computer graphics and desktop publishing market, Adobe Systems provides information about the company's products and services at this corporate home page. Includes training info, user tips and access to Adobe freeware.

Corel Corporation
http://www.corel.ca/

Corel Corporation, a design and graphics software company, hawks its wares here. Visitors are invited to learn about the company, its products (including the latest generation of Corel Draw) and customer support services. In English and German.

Fractal Design Corporation
http://www.fractal.com/

The Fractal Design Corporation home page features a profile of the software company, product descriptions, an art gallery, program downloading instructions and customer support. FD is best known for its electronic painting program, Fractal Painter. The site includes job listings.

Inside EDA: Mentor Graphics on the Web
http://www.mentorg.com/

Mentor Graphics, a professional design software developer, gives an overview of its services and products here. The site also contains trade show information, an online customer training page and a Silicon Valley contest.

Island Graphics
http://www.island.com/

Island Graphics, a Larkspur, Calif.-based developer of image processing, electronic assembly and other graphics software, maintains this promotional site. Visitors are invited to learn more about the company, its history, products and services.

Serif Incorporated
http://www.serif.com/

Serif Incorporated is a desktop publishing and graphics software company in Nashua, N.H. At its support site, the company offers desktop publishing software including downloadable utilities, fonts and clip art, as well as tips and tips and a link to the Serif PDF gallery.

INTERNET

Acrobat and the Web
http://www.adobe.com/Acrobat/AcrobatWWW.html

The Adobe Corporation features its cross-software Acrobat software on this page. The site features downloadable versions of the Acrobat reader as well as information about how Acrobat and PDF files can be integrated into Internet sites.

Agent Newsreader
http://www.forteinc.com/forte/agent/agent.htm

Agent Newsreader is a feature-enhanced newsreader package that includes full e-mail capabilities. This site includes downloading instructions, description of features and press information.

Allaire
http://www.allaire.com/

Allaire is a software company specializing in high-powered Web site development tools, such as its flagship application Cold Fusion. Visit the company's home page to read about Allaire products and services.

Compulink Information eXchange
http://www.compulink.co.uk/

Based in Britain since 1984, Compulink Information eXchange offers a comprehensive range of products and services to meet a wide range of communications needs. Visitors to this organizational site will find information on computer conferencing and Internet connections and a multimedia workshop.

CyberPhone
http://magenta.com/cyberphone/

This commercial site promotes CyberPhone, a real time phone system utilizing the Internet. Visitors can learn about the product, its history, equipment requirements, cost and ordering info.

Cybersource
http://www.cyber.com.au/

Cybersource, which develops software and provides network management, supplies information on its services, products and projects. Also at this site is Brighton Beach Software, which provides details on products such as the JokeBag screen saver.

Firefox Communications Inc.
http://www.firefox.com/

Firefox Communications Inc., a San Jose, Calif.-based software publisher, provides Internet software for Novell's NetWare network operating system. Visit here for a company profile, product information and technical support contacts.

Getstats Documentation
http://www.eit.com/software/getstats/getstats.html

Getstats (formerly called Getsites) is a versatile Web server log analyzer which takes log files from individual servers and prints out detailed and customizable reports on Web traffic to and fro a given Web server. The application is not in the public domain but can still be distributed freely if done according to certain criteria.

Glimpse
http://glimpse.cs.arizona.edu:1994/glimpse.html

Glimpse is a computer indexing and search system that helps users find misplaced files fast. This online user's manual provides both general and detailed information regarding the program which can only be used on Web servers to perform local area searches.

The Global Village
http://www.globalcenter.net/

Global Village Communications produces telecommunications software, including widely popular fax software. Visitors to its promotional site can browse through its online catalog or seek online customer services.

The Harvest Information Discovery and Access System
http://harvest.cs.colorado.edu/

The Harvest Information Discovery and Access System is an "integrated set of tools to gather, extract, organize, search, cache and replicate relevant information across the Internet." This informational site instructs visitors on how to the configure and use the system in order to increase network efficiency.

Internet Control Center
http://www.usefulware.com/icc.html

Usefulware promotes its Internet Control Center at this Web site. The software automates connecting and disconnecting with your Internet provider. Visitors can buy the software and download it on this page.

Lloyd Internetworking
http://www.lloyd.com/

The California-based Internet and offline software design company, Lloyd Internetworking, stocks its corporate Web site with company and product information.

L-Soft international Inc.

http://www.lsoft.com/

L-Soft International in Landover, Md., offers information on its many Listserv products and services. Check out product announcements, press releases and L-Soft job listings or download Windows 95 Listserv shareware here.

McGill Systems Inc.

http://musicm.mcgill.ca/

McGill Systems Inc. offers details about its software products related to networking and the Internet, along with general company facts, at this corporate site. Additionally, texts of recent presentations regarding the Internet are included.

Microsystems Software on the Web

http://www.microsys.com/

Need to police your employees and your children? Check out the Microsystems Software Inc. Web site for the Framington, Mass.-based software developer. Visit here to learn about its home and business computer programs, including CyberPatrol, an Internet filter utility.

NetEdge Systems the Home of the ATM Connect

http://www.netedge.com/

This promotional site for NetEdge's ATM Connect Software previews the versatility of this specialized internetworking package. Delivered as a slow-moving slide presentation, this site and the products listed therein are for serious Webmaters only.

NetOffice Inc.

http://www.netoffice.com/

NetOffice Inc. is an Atlanta, Ga.-based firm specializing in software that allows users to send and receive faxes on the Web. Visitors will find a corporate profile, technical documentation and a demo version of FaxWeb.

Netvideo: QuickTime & MPEG Video Storage & Distribution

http://www.netvideo.com/

The Netvideo site explores the gambut of issues associate with video on on the Internet. The site includes a catalog of client "Web videos," as well as a comparitive discussion of MPEG and Quicktime.

Omni Development Inc.

http://www.omnigroup.com/

Omni Development Inc. is a consulting company specializing in client/server systems and applications for the Web. Visitors can learn about the company's products, order free software and read about employment opportunities at this promotional site.

Open Market Inc.

http://www.openmarket.com/

This site is the home page for Open Market Inc., located in Boston, Mass. The company is a software developer focusing on enterprise-wide applications for electronic commerce; i.e., Web servers that allow for secure and consistent packet exchanges over the Net.

PCNet HOME Page

http://www.pcnet.com/index.html

The home page for this Connecticut Internet service provider includes details about the company's service options as well as links to Internet software for PCs and Macintoshes. Visitors can also look at users' home pages.

Quarterdeck

http://www.qdeck.com/

The Quarterdeck home page provides information on the Internet software company, its Web construction and mangement products and consulting services. Includes a corporate overview, descriptions of products, news releases and leisure activities.

Raptor Systems Inc.

http://www.raptor.com/

Raptor Systems Inc., a computer-security product manufacturer based in Waltham, Mass., maintains this site for general information. Visit here to learn about its integrated and modular firewall security management software and services.

SATAN Release Information

http://www.cs.ruu.nl/cert-uu/satan.html

Release information is available here for Satan 1.1, a tool to help system administrators recognize network-related security problems. A comprehensive index of FTP mirror sites where Satan can be downloaded is also available.

Software.com Inc.

http://www.software.com/

This promotional site, maintained by Software.com Inc., provides visitors with information about its recent Internet "infrastructure" products for Windows NT and Unix servers. Features include a free demo, ordering information, answers to Frequently Asked Questions and company information.

Software Ventures Corporation

http://www.svcdudes.com/

The Software Ventures Corporation, creators of the Internet Valet, provides technical support, software information and a look at the company's history on this corporate home page.

Spyglass Inc.

http://www.spyglass.com/

Spyglass Inc. licenses open, adaptable Web technologies to software developers and integrators, who add the technologies to their products and services. Visitors will find information here on Spyglass products, partnerships and the company itself.

SurfWatch

http://www.surfwatch.com/

SurfWatch is a software that helps parents, educators and employers reduce the risk of children and others uncovering sexually explicit material on the Internet. Visitors here will find an overview of the software and can download a demonstration.

Templar

http://www.templar.net/templar/

Premenos promotes its networking software and service package, Templar, here. The software which utilizes TCP/IP networks is detailed on this promotional page.

Tetherless Access Ltd

http://www.tetherless.com/

Tetherless Access Ltd. sells software to telecommunications service providers. The California-based company describes its products and corporate vision here.

Traffic Software

http://www.trafficsoftware.com/traffic/index.html/

The promotional page from Iceland's Traffic Software Ltd. advertises the company's Object Fax software which permits "high-volume fax broadcasting in a secure environment." Links to marketing information, technical support services and the company's home page are also featured.

Tribe Computer Works

http://www.tribe.com/

Tribe makes remote access and Internet connectivity products. With WebManage, Tribe pioneered the use of the Web as an interface for remote device management.

Virtual Home Space Builder&153; 1.0

http://www.us.paragraph.com/whatsnew/homespce.htm

ParaGraph International provides details on its Virtual Home Space Builder software at this promotional site. The software allows users to build virtual multimedia galleries on the Internet.

White Pine Software

http://www.wpine.com/

White Pine Software, a Nashua, N.H.-based computer internetworking product company, maintains this promotional site. Visit here for updated product information, technical support, employment opportunities and more.

MULTIMEDIA—CD-ROM AND ELECTRONIC PUBLISHING

Advanced Cultural Technologies

http://www.actinc.bc.ca/

Advanced Cultural Technologies Incorporated unveils its Cinemage software series and services focused on integrating multimedia data with high speed computer networks. Its products include interactive multimedia textbooks and museum archiving software.

ANSA and APM

http://www.ansa.co.uk/

This U.K.-based computer networking and multimedia company's home page explains its consulting and training programs. Visitors also can read about Architecture Projects Management Ltd.'s various projects and its ANSAware software.

The Black Box Inc.—Multimedia for the Mind

http://www.theblackbox.com/~whatsup

The Black Box Inc., a Hong Kong-based multimedia publisher, offers product info here. Visit its The Color is Black site to learn about its CD-ROM-based documentaries or perform keyword searches of its database and contact staff members.

BMC Software Inc.

http://www.bmc.com/

BMC Software Inc., is a developer of software products and services. Browsers can read corporate information and product descriptions, search for specific products or browse BMC's current employment opportunities.

Creative Labs Inc.

http://www.creaf.com/

This home page is devoted to Creative Labs's multimedia products. Includes descriptions of products and services as well as links to other sound, video and game sites.

Gryphon Software

http://www.gryphonsw.com/

Gryphon Software develops and publishes graphics software for video professionals as well as childrens' programs with a highly visual orientation. Includes product descriptions, demos, job listings and ordering information.

Macromedia Inc.

http://www.macromedia.com/

Macromedia Inc.'s home page provides information about the corporation's multimedia software offerings. Includes descriptions of plug-ins available for Macromedia Director, technical support info, multimedia industry news and a gallery of projects created using Macromedia products.

Multi-Media Design Inc.

http://www.evansville.net/~mmd/mmdhome.html

Multi-Media Design of Newburgh, Ind., supplies details on its services such as video production, CD-ROM development, interactive training and Web design. There is also information and images on its entertainment software.

Personal Library Software

http://www.pls.com/

Personal Library Software supplies graphical information retrieval software used in CD-ROM and Internet publishing, online services and other applications. Visit this site to learn about its products and people, download software, find employment opportunities and more.

SoftKey International Inc.

http://www.softkey.com/

SoftKey International Inc., a Cambridge, Mass.-based electronic content developer, maintains this promotional site for company and product information. Visit here to learn about its CD-ROM business and consumer software packages, read press releases, enter contests and more.

NETWORKING

Artisoft Inc.

http://www.artisoft.com/

Based in Tucson, Ariz., Artisoft Inc. manufactures Windows and DOS networking software and network management tools. They also develop back-up and multi-platform connectivity systems. Visit this site for company and product information.

Born Information Services Group

http://www.born.com/

Born Information Services Group of Wayzata, Minn., provides consulting and other computer-related services. The company's site includes information on its services, such as AS/400 application development, along with case studies, job openings and client sites.

Computer Associates

http://www.cai.com/

The home page for Computer Associates Inc. describes the multinational company's system software for networking, project management and database security. It also details the Long Island, New York-based company's recent forays into electronic commerce.

Cykic Software

http://cykic.com/

This Web site provides access to information about Cykic Software, a computer connectivity technology company. Visitors can take part in a tutorial-like tour of the company's software products or learn about a variety of businesses using Cykic Software in the Hype-It Online Mall.

Datametrix

http://www.datametrix.no/

This promotional site is the Web home of Datametrix A/S, a Norwegian supplier of system software for local and wide area computer networks and telecommunication systems. Visitors are invited to learn more about the company and its products. In Norwegian with limited English translations.

deltaComm Development

http://delta.com/

The home page for deltaComm Development provides background on the company and descriptions of its connectivity software. Includes instructions for downloading Telix for DOS and Windows, information on staff and news releases.

DXI Corporation

http://isotropic.com/dxicorp/dxihome.html

The DXI Corporation offers information processing and support services to the technology industry. This home page outlines DXI's services and contains the DXI Exchange, a bi-monthly newsletter for information processing professionals.

GLOBEtrotter Software Inc.

http://www.globetrotter.com/

GLOBEtrotter Software Inc. offers detailed information about its many software products for software assessment management, system and network administration, HTML work, licensing and developing software and more. Visitors can link to related training classes, user groups and company info.

JSB

http://www.jsbus.com/

JSB, a Cheshire, England-based client/server environment software developer, maintains this promotional site, featuring company information, product descriptions and technical support listings. Includes FTP link for downloading software.

Novell FTP Index

ftp://ftp.novell.com/

Users of Novell software will find this FTP index, maintained by the company's technical support team, useful for checking out product updates, finding demonstration software or visiting the patches files.

Novell NetWare

http://www.netware.com/

Novell's NetWare site is the source for the latest information and technical support for the networking software system. It also includes facts about upcoming system upgrades.

Premenos' Electronic Commerce Resource Guide

http://www.premenos.com/

Premenos, provider of electronic data interchange software, develops methods for corporations to conduct business using electronic communications systems. Visit this site for information about many of its products.

Stac Electronics

http://www.stac.com/

The Stac Electronics home page contains an overview of the company, its multi-platform networking products and services. Includes information on obtaining Stac products, customer support and career opportunities with the company.

System Integrators Inc.

http://www.sii.com/

California-based System Integrators Inc. designs, integrates and services publishing systems for print news organizations around the world. At this corporate home page, find information about the company and its products and services.

Tivoli Systems Inc.

http://www.tivoli.com/

Tivoli Systems Inc., supplies systems management software for client/server computing. This commercial site showcases the corporation's products, services and technical support. Includes contact info and company news.

TriTeal Corporation

http://www.triteal.com/

California-based TriTeal Corporation develops and sells client/server software. Visitors to its home page can review the company's corporate profile along with a list of its products and services.

SCIENTIFIC

Adept Scientific plc

http://www.adeptscience.co.uk/

Adept Scientific, a Letchworth Garden City, England-based computer consulting firm, supplies and supports software and hardware products for technical applications. Visit here to learn about the company and link to its "Technical Computing" magazine.

CambridgeSoft

http://www.camsci.com/

CambridgeSoft creates computer software applications for chemists and engineers. Visitors will find product information and specs for ChemDraw, Chem3D and ChemFinder.

CASTech virtual castings

http://www.castech.fi/

Castech develops and sells solidification simulation software—indeed, it claims that theirs is the leading simulation software in foundries in northern Europe. Its Web site lets potential customers test this heady boast, study case histories, download a demonstration, and gather price and support information.

DSP Development Corporation

http://www.dadisp.com/

This promotional site is the Web home of the DSP Development Corporation, a developer and marketer of scientific and engineering software. Visitors are invited to learn more about the company, its visual data analysis products and its customer services. A downloadable demo of its DADiSP 4.0 graphical analysis software is featured.

Fluent Incorporated

http://www.fluent.com/

Fluent Inc., a Lebanon, N.H.-based computational fluid dynamics software company, maintains this promotional site. Visit here for company and product information, customer services, press releases and other publications, user tips and more.

GAMS : Guide to Available Mathematical Software

http://gams.nist.gov/

This Guide to Available Mathematical Software is a service of the National Institute of Standards and Technology, a U.S. government agency. As a gateway to mathematical software, GAMS can be searched according to the following criteria: what problem it solves, the software package name, the software module name. A neat service from a no-nonsense organization.

Geomatics International Inc.

http://www.geomatics.com/

This promotional site is the Web home of Geomatics International Inc., a provider of spatial information technology solutions headquartered in Canada. Visitors can learn more about the company, its products and services.

Lateiner Dataspace

http://www.dataspace.com/

The Lateiner Dataspace Corporation offers cutting-edge solutions in "high-speed volume visualization, discrete physical simulation techniques and Dataspace distributed datastructures." Link to their home page to read up on the Company's latest research projects or link to their technical reports archive and FTP server.

The MathWorks Inc.

http://www.mathworks.com/

This promotional site is the Web home of The MathWorks Inc., a Massachusetts-based company that develops and markets interactive engineering and scientific software. Visitors can take the product tour, review the company's tech support and customer services info, browse online publications or check out the software library.

MDL Information Systems Inc.

http://www.mdli.com/

MDL's home page features information about its chemical information management software, databases and related services. ISIS, a client-server system; Project Library, a drug design tool; and MACCS-II and REACCS are also profiled.

National Instruments

http://www.natinst.com/

The National Instruments Home Page provides an overview of its science and engineering-related PC products and workstations. Laboratory applications, instrument control interfaces and numerical analysis software are among the company's major product lines.

NCSA Software Development Group

http://www.ncsa.uiuc.edu/SDG/SDGIntro.html

The Software Development Group at the National Center for Supercomputing Applications develops computer programs to assist scientific discovery. This support site features program information, staff directory and software tools.

PEST

http://gil.ipswichcity.qld.gov.au/comm/pest/index.html

PEST is a software suite that performs nonlinear parameter estimations for any scientific model on both DOS and Unix computers. Ordering information, a downloadable demo and a free version of PESTLITE for DOS is provided.

POSC

http://posc.org/

The Petrotechnical Open Software Corporation supplies interface standards for technical exploration and production software to the Oil industry. Includes descriptions of products and services, training information, press releases, answers to Frequently Asked Questions and listings of employment opportunities.

REDUCE

http://www.rrz.uni-koeln.de/REDUCE/

The REDUCE Computer Algebra System site details a new version of an interactive program for use by scientists, engineers and mathematicians in general algebraic computations. The page also includes information on similar packages offered by other sources, along with a REDUCE network library.

Softaid

http://www.softaid.net/emulators.html

Softaid, Columbia, M.D.-based company, sells in-circuit emulators and source debuggers for 8

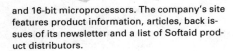
and 16-bit microprocessors. The company's site features product information, articles, back issues of its newsletter and a list of Softaid product distributors.

Synopsys

http://www.synopsys.com/

Synopsys is a corporate producer of logic and behavioral synthesis software. Visitors to its site will find product information and a corporate history.

T&T Research

http://www.io.org/~tmaler/

This company site exposes visitors to T&T Research's family of high-tech products, including DNA Parrot, a talking DNA sequence reader and CourseBuilder a cross-platform multimedia authoring and testing tool.

Teradyne Inc.

http://www.teradyne.com/

Teradyne Inc., a Boston, Mass.-based technology testing systems company, maintains this promotional site. The company develops both hardware and software that can be used to test the reliability of electronic and telecommunications components. Visit here for company information, branch office locations, products and services descriptions and financial performance data.

Viewlogic Systems Inc.

http://www.viewlogic.com/

VIEWlogic Systems Inc., is a computer software company located in Marlborough, Mass. Visitors will find information on the company's design tools for electrical engineers at this promotional site.

Visioneering Research Laboratory Inc.

http://www.vrl.com/

The Visioneering Research Laboratory home page contains information on the company's hardware and software products for designing microchips. Includes a corporate profile and links to new product development info.

Visual Numerics

http://www.vni.com/

Visual Numerics, a data analysis software company, maintains this promotional site. Visit here for product information, distributor and reseller contacts, employment opportunities and more.

Wolfram Research

http://mathsource.wri.com/

Wolfram Research, the makers of the software program Mathematica, promotes its products and services at this site. Review math related books, newsletters and software here. Technical support for Wolfram Research products is also available.

SOUND—COMPOSITION, EDITING, AND MANIPULATION

The Auricle

http://www.webcom.com/~auricle/welcome.html

The Auricle page promotes the Auricle interactive application used to develop musical scores for motion pictures and videos. This site provides information on system requirements, ordering information and screen examples.

DiAcoustics Inc.

http://www.iquest.com/~diac/

DiAcoustics, a Huntsville, Ala.-based multimedia software company, maintains this promotional site. Visit here to learn about its MIDI-based products, view its "Wavelet" newsletter and link to other music software-related Web sites.

DSP Group Inc.

http://www.dspg.com/

DSP Group Inc., located in Silicon Valley, Ca., makes chips and software for personal computers, multimedia and communications products. This site offers information on the company, its financial status and its products—especially TrueSpeech—a compression and decompression application for use with sound.

SoundSite Audio and Video

http://www.soundsite.com/

The SoundSite Web page provides detailed info on the company's audio and video software. A collection of related info is also available here, including industry news and features and pointers to other audio-visual Web sites.

SYSTEM SOFTWARE, UTILITIES, FONTS

BGS Systems

http://www.bgs.com/

BGS Systems is a company offering BEST/1 Performance Assurance software products for performance management and capacity planning for MVS, VM, Unix, OpenVMS, AS/400, OS/2 and other network systems. Visitors to this site can scan a range of company and product information.

PC Center "TECHNO"

http://www.pczz.msk.su/

The PC Center Techno home page explains how to get Russian cyrillic (koi8) fonts.

QNX Software Systems

http://www.qnx.com/

QNX Software Systems provides information on its operating system alternative for personal computers. Includes product information and descrip-

tion of support services, along with links to its distribution network, employment opportunities and related news articles.

Second Nature Software

http://www.secondnature.com/

Second Nature Software produces over 80 screen saver and wallpaper programs for Windows and Macintosh. It donates all its profits to the Nature Conservancy, a land conservation organization. Visitors here can download free samples or browse through an online catalog.

Symantec

http://www.symantec.com/

The giant software maker, Symantec, outlines product information, online services, company news and tech support offerings at its corporate home page. Also find a link to its AntiVirus Research Center.

Ziff-Davis Benchmark Operation

http://www.zdnet.com/~zdbop

Ziff-Davis Benchmark Operation offers information on its development and support of the core benchmark programs that its publications use to evaluate computer software and hardware products.

3-D OBJECTS—CAD, RENDERING, VR, CGI

Ashlar

http://www.ashlar.com/

CAD software developer, Ashlar Inc. pitches its newest version of Ashlar-Vellum 3D at this promotional site. Visitors can review new product offerings and access technical support.

Black Sun Interactive

http://www.blacksun.de/

Black Sun Interactive offers innovative virtual reality software— including CyberGate, CyberHub and CyberKit—which can be downloaded in beta version directly from this home page.

Byte by Byte

http://bytebybyte.com/

Byte by Byte, an Austin, Texas-based supplier of 3-D animation and rendering software, maintains this site for downloadable software and instructional materials. Visit here for demonstration versions of its powerful graphics applications and links to related Web sites.

Evans & Sutherland

http://www.es.com/

Visitors to this commercial Web site can access information about Evans & Sutherland's products and career opportunities. The real-time simulation software developer features an image gallery and links to related Web sites.

Information Solutions Inc.

http://www.spectracom.com/imsc-cad/

Information Solutions Inc. provides Computer Aided Design software and services to the manufacturing, architectural and geographic information system mapping industries. The company's support site has information on products, consulting, events and technical support.

Lightscape Technologies

http://www.lightscape.com/

Lightscape provides information here on its unique visualization application which "combines proprietary radiosity algorithms with a physically based lighting interface." Visitors will find an image library along with loads of information on the company and its software offerings.

Mesa 3-D Graphics Library

http://www.ssec.wisc.edu/~brianp/Mesa.html

Mesa is a 3-D Graphics Library "very similar to that of OpenGL." Find application documentation and downloading instructions at this site.

The MR Toolkit

http://www.cs.ualberta.ca/~graphics/MRToolkit.html

The home page of MR Toolkit features a collection of virtual reality and 3-D user interface software tools. Visitors to this site can read extensive software documentation and link to related sites of interest, including other MR projects.

OrCAD

http://www.orcad.com/

OrCAD of Beaverton, Ore., supplies details on its desktop electronic design automation software. Find also company information, including technical support, customer service and training. Documentation, drivers, macros and the like are available for downloading.

QuickTime.Apple.Com

http://quicktime.apple.com/

QuickTime.Apple.Com offers downloadable versions of QuickTime video and audio software for the Mac and Windows. But it's not just software anymore; visitors can also order clothware (clothes with the Quicktime logo), a virtual reality player and VR movies and music.

Radiance

http://radsite.lbl.gov/radiance/HOME.html

Radiance is a shareware application that supports ray-tracing used for the "analysis and visualization of lighting in design." Visitors will find user documentation and instructions for downloading the latest version.

Sinnott and Associates Inc.

http://sinnott-cgi.com/

Sinnott and Associates Inc. pitches its services to clients in the market for a commercial production company specializing in computer imaging and animation. View Sinnott and Associates' digital commercials in its animation lounge.

Softdesk Inc.

http://www.softdesk.com/

Architecture, engineering and construction application software make up the product line of the Softdesk Corporation. Get a product list, company profile and technical support at this promotional site.

Stereograms

http://eleves.ens.fr:8080/home/massimin/sis/sis.ang.html

This site offers all the information a visitor might need to understand hollusions, SIRDS and SIS and various other terms that refer to stereograms or 3-D images. Images, FAQ sheets and links to other resources are also provided here. In French and English.

Syndesis Corporation

http://www.webmaster.com/syndesis

The Syndesis Corporation describes its Windows graphics utility, InterChange, at this promotional site. Learn the specifics about sharing files between 3-D programs.

Template Graphics Software

http://www.sd.tgs.com/~template/WebSpace/

Template Graphics Software, based in San Diego, Calif., provides cross-platform graphics tools for application developers, independent software vendors and academic and research organizations. Visit this site for an introduction to its WebSpace VRML Navigator browser application.

Virtek International Corporation

http://www.virtek.com/

Virtek International Corporation is a producer of 3-D graphic rendering software. Visitors to this promotional page will find information on the 3D-Ware product line, a download option and online demos.

Virtus Corporation

http://www.virtus.com/

Escape the two-dimensional computing environment with the help of Virtus Corporation's virtual reality and 3-D modeling software products. Review the company's product offerings and services at this promotional site.

Warp California Inc. - Virtual TV Technology

http://www.warp.com/

Warp Limited develops software for dynamically viewing 3-D videos and computer graphics. Their site includes a comparison between their patent pending VTV software and Apple's Quicktime Virtual Reality software, as well as downloadable demos of their product and an online demo.

Xanim Rev 2.68.5

http://www.univ-rennes1.fr/ASTRO/fra/xanim.html

XAnim is a software package that can run animations of varying formats on X11 operating systems. This page includes a listing of supported animation formats, descriptions of features, downloading instructions and documentation.

VIDEO

ATI Technologies Online

http://www.atitech.ca/

Canadia ATI Technologies develops graphics, communications and multimedia video software. Visit this site for links to company and product information, as well as question and answer guides.

Cross-platform QuickTime

http://www.astro.nwu.edu/lentz/mac/qt/home-qt.html

Visitors can download the QuickTime video player for Mac and Windows here. The site also contains other video and audio applications.

Optibase

http://www.optibase.com/

This promotional page is the Internet home of Optibase, an international supplier of MPEG products. Visitors to this site are invited to learn more about the company, its products and services.

WORD PROCESSING

SemWare Corporation

http://www.semware.com/

SemWare, the creators of the shareware application SemWare Editor, offers information here on the latest version release. Check out the newest features of this shareware text editor for DOS and OS/2 and then download a copy.

Working Software Inc.

http://www.webcom.com/~working/

Santa Cruz, Calif.-based Working Software Inc. produces software for Macs and PCs alike. Visitors to its promotional site can read about its utilities and text editors, download demo software versions and order products online.

PCs

BUSINESS—FINANCIAL PLANNING, ACCOUNTING, AND SPREADSHEETS

Telescan Inc.
http://www.telescan.com/
Telescan Inc. touts its investment software and online financial database at this corporate site. The firm outlines its investment industry services and products here, including the Telescan Investor's Platform for Windows software package.

DAILY PLANNERS, PERSONAL ASSISTANTS, AND VIRTUAL OFFICE GEAR

GammaLink
http://www.gammalink.com/
GammaLink, introducer of the first PC-to-fax hardware and software products in 1985, talks about its products here. Includes corporate news and background, plus information on technology, sales, distribution and applications.

DATABASES

NJK
http://www.njk.co.jp/
NJK Corp. of Tokyo presents information on the company's history, operation, business groups, branch locations and products. Among its products are a visual database system and a newspaper shop management system for Windows. In Japanese and English.

Watcom International Corporation
http://www.sybase.com/
Located in Canada, the Watcom International Corporation, a developer of PC-based SQL database servers, sponsors this promotional page offering information about its products and its parent company, the Powersoft Corporation. Visitors are welcome to a free evaluation copy of Watcom SQL.

DESKTOP PUBLISHING

Hamrick Software: VuePrint
http://www.primenet.com/~hamrick/
VuePrint, touted as "the premier program for viewing and printing images on Microsoft Windows," serves as this site's subject. Find links to obtaining and registering the latest version, accessing technical support and getting related information.

EDUCATIONAL—GAMES, REFERENCES, ALMANACS

Open Windows - Educational Software And Utilities
http://delta.com/openwin.com/openwin.htm
Open Windows specializes in utility and educational software for Windows-based platforms. Includes a catalog of shareware and freeware, downloading instructions and links to related resources.

ENTERTAINMENT— ADULT, ARCADE, MYSTERY

FS5 Scenery Design - The South African Way
http://www.nezcom.fltsim
So you can fly with the Microsoft Flight Simulator, now what? Why not simulate a flight over South Africa? Visit the FS5 Scenery Design home page to pick up your flight plan. Browse scenery and flight simulator files and get a look at upcoming Microsoft software at this promotional site.

Winsock Game Clients for Windows
http://homepages.together.net/~shae//client.html
Windows users will find a virtual arcade filled with game enthusiast links. Visitors can connect to game servers MUD, MUSH, MOO and MUX game servers for use with Windows 3.1, Windows For Workgroups or Windows 95.

GRAPHICS—DESIGN AND ILLUSTRATION

LView Pro from MMedia Research
http://world.std.com/~mmedia/lviewp.html
Windows users can visit this page to download the latest version of the shareware graphics viewer and editor, LView Pro. Find software, documentation and customer support at this promotional site.

INTERNET

About URL Grabber
http://brooknorth.com/grabber.html
URL Grabber is a tool bar that resides in the corner of the Windows desktop and allows for direct manipulation of Web addresses. This site includes a downloadable demo and ordering information for the full version.

About WinZip
http://www.winzip.com/
This page features an overview of WinZip and WinZip Self-Extractor software and its features. Visitors can download an evaluation version of WinZip from this site.

Anzio Lite
http://www.anzio.com/anziolite.html
This site provides information about Anzio Lite, a shareware Windows telnet client. Descriptions of the software are available here and visitors can download the latest version and take it for a test drive.

Asymetrix Corporation
http://www.asymetrix.com/
Asymetrix Corporation develops and markets Windows-based software and tools. On this home page, visitors will find outlines on multimedia and client/server tools, technical services and sales information. Details, as well as a demo of their 3-D Web program can be found here.

CUHK's QuickTime Mplayer Extensions
http://www.ncsa.uiuc.edu/SDG/Software/WinMosaic/Viewers/qt.htm
Download freeware QuickTime extensions for Windows Media Player at this site. Information is also available regarding Mosaic configuration set up.

Distinct Corporation
http://www.distinct.com/
Distinct Corporation, a California software company, displays its networking wares on this page. Viewers can order TCP/IP for Windows here or find technical support.

FTP Index of Winsock-I Talk/Voice Software
ftp://papa.indstate.edu/winsock-1/talk_voice
The Papa FTP server maintains this index of Winsock-I talk software compressed in a variety of formats, including .zip. There's also a demo.

Gibbon Computer Products
http://www.gibbon.com/
Gibbon Computer Products develops Internet software for IBM's OS/2 operating system. Visitors to this commercial site are invited to review the company's catalog and order products online.

ICL ProSystems AB
http://www.pro.icl.se/
ICL ProSystems, a Scandinavian computer company, maintains this not-so-corporate home page to promote its Internet software. Featured this months is EMBLA, "a Windows application for Internet e-mail." Visitors can also obtain free evaluation copies of software at this site.

NetDial

http://www.enterprise.net/netdial

The NetDial Home Page provides information and specifications about the Internet dialer for the Microsoft Windows operating system. Visitors can download the software here and learn how it can be customized to fit a variety of systems.

NetManage Inc.

http://www.netmanage.com/

NetManage develops TCP/IP applications for Windows platforms. Visitors can obtain info on Chameleon, terminal and printer emulation, groupware and other NetManage desktop management products here.

NT Mail - Index

http://www.net-shopper.co.uk/software/ntmail/index.htm

NTMail provides Windows NT servers and its workstation versions with SMTP and POP3 services for dial-up and LAN Internet connections. NTMail's home page provides information on its features, documentation and downloading guidelines.

Radient Software

http://www.radient.com/

Radient Software of Sunnyvale, Calif., has set up this site to provide information about and promote its communications and multimedia software products. Currently, this site features the product CommNet for Windows.

Tidewater Systems

http://www.biddeford.com/~jobrien/tidewater.html

Tidewater Systems' home page provides access to its Winsock software. Includes downloading instructions and descriptions of Winsock Finger version 1.5 and Winsock Finger Daemon version 1.3.

Trumpet Software International

http://www.trumpet.com.au/

Trumpet Software International develops and markets WinSock software, an Internet connectivity product for PCs. Visit the company's home page for product updates and downloadable software.

Trumpet Winsock Overview

http://www.trumpet.com.au/wsk/winsock.htm

Visitors to this page will find promotional information about Trumpet Winsock 2.1, a TCP/IP stack for use with the Microsoft Windows operating platform. Includes information on Winsock error messages and applications, as well as a list of Frequently Asked Questions.

Wall Data Incorporated

http://www.walldata.com/

Based in Kirkland, Wa., Wall Data Incorporated promotes its RUMBA and SALSA Web servers for PCs at this commercial site. Visitors can find out about the company, its business products and ONESTEP support services, as well as access free demos.

WINGate Technologies

http://www.wingate.com/

WINGate Technologies manufactures and sells Windows/DOS communications software. The company's support site provides information about programmer tools and user applications, as well as product info and price lists. Also find links to the company's FTP site.

WinZip

http://www.winzip.com/winzip/

WinZip is a shareware utility for Windows users which provides support for popular Internet file formats such as TAR, gzip and Unix compress. Browsers can read further information about WinZip, download an evaluation version or link to other shareware resources.

NETWORKING

Arena Logistics

http://www.arena.com.au/

Arena Logistics of Australia is a computer consulting firm that focuses on networking IBM-compatible mainframes to other operating systems. Visitors will get an overview of the company here and can link to software, hardware and IBM-related sites.

Attachmate

http://www.atm.com/

The Attachmate Corporation develops internetworking software for the PC market. At the company's home page find pitches for products and services, the latest development news and a corporate profile. Customer support is also available.

CSM - Computer Software Manufaktur Ges.m.b.H

http://www.csm.co.at/csm/

This site offers information about the Austrian Computer Software Manufaktur, its Windows-compative Internet server software and related customer services. Includes an overview of the company, details on software offerings, pricing and availability.

FutureSoft

http://www.fse.com/

FutureSoft's DynaComm family of networking software for PCs and Windows-based platforms is presented here. Browsers will get an overview of the company, its products and distributors on this promotional page.

Microsoft BackOffice

http://www.ecssin.com.sg/ms/backoffice.htm

Computer software publisher Microsoft Corporation maintains this site to provide information on its BackOffice networking system, an integrated family of server software built on the Windows NT® Server operating system. Visit here for product descriptions, training information, third party resources and more.

Network Computing Devices

http://www.ncd.com/

Network Computing Devices announces its Win-Center Pro software at this promotional site. Win-Center Pro, Z-MAIL and the company's other offerings for fast retrieval of information on a Windows95 and WindowsNT network are touted by the company as "products that truly make the network the computer."

SCIENTIFIC

O-Matrix for Windows—Visual Data Analysis

http://world.std.com/~harmonic/

O-Matrix for Windows is an interactive analysis and visualization package. This promotional page includes media reports, system requirements, pricing and ordering information.

SYSTEM SOFTWARE, UTILITIES, FONTS

Black Diamond Software

http://blackdiamond.com/

Black Diamond Software is an Oregon-based company specializing in device drivers and system-level firmware for Windows and DOS PC's. Visit this site to read detailed product info, testimonials or link to other interesting Web sites.

Debian Project

http://www.debian.org/

Featured here is the most recent release of the Debian GNU version of Linux, a Unix-compatible operating system for PCs. Also includes a FAQ section and mailing list information.

IBM Software Indexes

http://www.software.ibm.com/software/indexlist.html

IBM provides this comprehensive index of software that will be of interest to developers, systems managers, resellers and personal computer users. Visitors will find descriptions, tech sheets, specifications, FAQ sheets and more.

Linux

http://www.linux.org/

Linux is a freely-distributable implementation of Unix for 386, 486 and Pentium PCs, supporting a wide range of software. This Web site offers an index of links to Linux resources, including FTP addresses, newsgroups and a FAQ sheet.

Microsoft Knowledge Base

http://www.microsoft.com/KB/

Knowledge Base, a service of computer software developer Microsoft Corporation, provides a keyword search of product resources. Visit here to find information on Windows 95, Visual Basic and a host of other operating systems and software applications.

Microsoft Windows 95

http://www.microsoft.com/Windows/

Microsoft Corporation maintains this site for information about its Windows 95 operating system. Visit here for technical information, user support, news, events, free software and more.

Photo Icons

http://www.cin.net/cinusers/photoicn/photoicn.html

Iconation presents this collection of dazzling and vivid photo icons for dressing up Windows desktops. Visitors can download free samples of these miniature works of art or check info on buying collections.

PKWare

http://www.pkware.com/

This promotional page is the Internet home of Wisconsin's PKWare, a company specializing in data compression, including its popular PKZIP standard. Visitors to this site are invited to learn more about the company's products and available employment opportunities.

QNX Software Systems

http://www.qnx.com/

QNX Software Systems provides information on its operating system alternative for personal computers. Includes product information and description of support services, along with links to its distribution network, employment opportunities and related news articles.

Super, Natural British Columbia Screen Saver

http://www.tbc.gov.bc.ca/screensaver.html

Tired of flying toasters or psychedelic swirls? This downloadable Windows 3.1 screensaver will bring the mountains, forests and seashore of British Columbia to your PC. A detailed map of the province is also here.

3-D OBJECTS—CAD, RENDERING, VR, CGI

Cadkey

http://www.cadkey.com/

Cadkey develops, manufactures and markets Computer-Aided Design software for personal computers. Visitors can find information about its products, download demos and visit a gallery of Cadkey designs at this site.

Micrografx

http://www.micrografx.com/

Micrografx deals in graphics software with a "a full range of 3D tools and extensive 3D data for Microsoft Windows, Windows 95 and Windows NT." The company offers downloadable software and technical support at this promotional site.

WORD PROCESSING

COMCOM Systems Inc.

http://www.comcomsystems.com/image.html

This promotional page is the Web home of ComCom Systems Inc., a developer of Windows-based forms processing and image archiving software based in Clearwater, Fla. Visitors can learn about the company and its ELA product line or follow the pointers provided to company-recommended sites.

Gamma Productions Inc.

http://www.gammapro.com/

Gamma Productions Inc. develops foreign language software tools, fonts and related technology for Microsoft Windows. Visitors can learn about its products at this promotional page. Ordering information is also provided.

Intersoft International

http://starbase.neosoft.com/~zkrr01/

Intersoft International Inc. makes tools for Microsoft Windows users. Here it promotes Net-Term, a program that optimizes the use of databases and THEdit, a text editor program. It also provides telnet links to online databases and Windows software archives.

Next Generation Software Inc.—Spell Check

http://www.nextgensoft.com/

Next Generation Software Inc. maintains this site to promote its Spell Check 3.2b program for Windows computers. Download the shareware, register it and find supporting documentation.

Spell Checker for Windows

http://clever.net/quinion/spell/

This spell checker application, provided by a software engineering student, works with a wide range of text editors for the Windows computing environment. Visit this site to read documentation and download the software.

UNIX-BASED AND RELATED SYSTEMS

DAILY PLANNERS, PERSONAL ASSISTANTS, AND VIRTUAL OFFICE GEAR

Faximum Software Inc.

http://www.faximum.com/

Faximum develops fax software for the Unix platform. The company's home page includes links to product information and reviews.

DATABASES

FirstBase RDBMS Application Builder

http://www.firstbase.com/fb_prod.htm

FirstBase Software, a Tucson, Ariz.-based software company, maintains this site to introduce its relational database management application. Visit here for a complete explanation of the software package and download a demonstration copy.

Glimpse

http://glimpse.cs.arizona.edu:1994/

The Glimpse Working Group at the University of Arizona provide this Web site with information on Glimpse, an indexing and query system that allows users to search though files quickly. Visitors can link to demonstration sites, read further documentation or download Glimpse source codes and manual pages.

Schema Research Corp.

http://www.schemaresearch.com/

The Schema Research Corp. provides database products and services and their flagship application is a NEXTSTEP database application. Visitors to this corporate site can read a company overview and product descriptions or link to other sites for reverse engineered solutions comparable to Oracle and Sybase databases.

ENTERTAINMENT— ADULT, ARCADE, MYSTERY

SGI DOOM FAQ

http://www.cmpharm.ucsf.edu/~troyer/sgidoomfaq.html

This FAQ sheet teaches visitors the ins and outs of the popular 3-D arcade game DOOM and its port to the Silicon Graphics Irix platform. Site features include information about how to load the game on an SGI machine and how to register.

INTERNET

Analog

http://www.statslab.cam.ac.uk/~sret1/analog/

Analog is a program that analyzes log files from Web servers on any Unix-based system. This informational page provides a description, source code, links to other programs and statistical reports.

Chimera

http://www.unlv.edu/chimera/

Chimera is a Web browser for Unix-based computers running an X Window system. From this page, visitors can link to a mirror site where for downloading the current version of the Internet navigational software.

The Forum News Gateway

http://forum.swarthmore.edu/forum.news.gateway.html

Forum News Gateway is a utility for reading Usenet news, but it adds the twist of allowing reading and posting of hypertext articles in HTML. Visitors can test demo versions of the product here or link to Forum's home page.

Futplex System

http://gewis.win.tue.nl/applications/futplex/

The Futplex Unix software package creates documents with read/write access on the Web. Visitors can read about the software's features and check out a demo at this site, which also has a user's guide and FTP sites.

GSQL—A Mosaic-SQL Gateway

http://www.ncsa.uiuc.edu/SDG/People/jason/pub/gsql/starthere.html

GSQL is a software program that allows Mosaic forms to interface with SQL databases. Visitors to this site can download the software, plus tips and documentation.

The Harvest Cache and Httpd-Accelerator

http://excalibur.usc.edu/

Soup up speedy Web servers with the Harvest Cache and Httpd-Accelerator offered at this site. Mosaic, Netscape and Lynx Web clients can increase server performance (up to a factor of 10) by downloading and installing this free software.

Hypermail Documentation

http://www.eit.com/software/hypermail/hypermail.html

Hypermail Documentation is an application that takes a file of mail messages in Unix mailbox format and creates a set of cross-referenced HTML documents.

Mortice Kern Systems Inc.

http://www.mks.com/

Mortice Kern Systems Inc., a developer and international supplier of software, open systems and communications applications, makes its Internet home at this site. Visitors are invited to learn more about the company, its products and its support services.

NCSA HTTPd

http://hoohoo.ncsa.uiuc.edu/docs/Overview.html

Browsers can download NCSA's premier server software, HTTPd, here, along with instructions on getting the server running. The site also includes an extensive library of information on writing your own server, if you think you can hack it.

Status of the W3C httpd

http://www.w3.org/hypertext/WWW/Daemon/Overview.html

Get the CERN httpd server at this site. Link to discussion forums for Unix web servers and current version's source code are also listed at this World Wide Web Consortium site.

WebCopy Documentation

http://www.inf.utfsm.cl/~vparada/webcopy.html

The beta 2.0 version of WebCopy and its documentation are available at this site. This perl program retrieves URLs, specific HTML files and file trees.

WebForce Software Environment

http://www.sgi.com/Products/WebFORCE/WebForceSoft.html

Silicon Graphics hawks its Indigo Magic and WebFORCE software environments for easy Web page authoring within the IRIX operating system. This informational page offers info and specs on the Web editors for Silicon Graphics workstations, along with an invitation to download a demo version of WebMagic 2.0.

WWWWAIS Documentation

http://www.eit.com/software/wwwwais/wwwwais.html

This Web page is about wwwwais.c, an ANSI C program that acts as a gateway between programs that create indexed catalogs of files and form-capable Web browsers. The software is downloadable from this site, along with complete directions and information.

MULTIMEDIA—CD-ROM AND ELECTRONIC PUBLISHING

HDS Network Systems

http://www.hds.com/

HDS Network Systems develops multimedia applications for open systems environments with emphasis on a universal desktop application. HSD is also the first company to license Java technology. Peruse software descriptions and special offers or get up-to-date on the company's history.

MetaCard

http://www.metacard.com/

MetaCard is a multimedia authoring tool for Unix/X 11 workstations. Browsers will get a full explanation of MetaCard on this promotional page and can download a demo copy.

NETWORKING

SEA Change Corporation

http://www.seawest.seachange.com/

Canada's SEA Change Corporation produces products and services for Unix and TCP/IP systems. Find corporate news and information as well as a guide to products and services.

Unison Software Inc.

http://www.unison.com/

Unison is a software firm specializing in systems management applications for Hewlett-Packard products. This promotional page includes a company history, product descriptions, customer education and technical help information.

SCIENTIFIC

Confluent Inc.

http://www.confluent.com/

Visitors here will find information on Visual Thought, a Unix diagramming and flowcharting tool. Product and technical information, along with customer support services and an online ordering form round out this site.

GRTensor

http://astro.queensu.ca/~grtensor/GRHome.html

Maintained at Queen's University in Ontario, Canada, this Web site offers information about GRTensor, a computer algebra package for "doing calculations primarily of interest to relativists." Visitors can read documentation including reports, updates and benchmark calculation times.

PVM: Parallel Virtual Machine

http://www.epm.ornl.gov/pvm/

PVM (Parallel Virtual Machine) is a software package that permits a heterogeneous collection of Unix computers hooked together by a network to be used as a single large parallel computer. Download the software and jump on the parallel computing expressway today!

SYSTEM SOFTWARE, UTILITIES, FONTS

Apple-Macintosh Application Environment

http://www.mae.apple.com/

This site provides details on the Macintosh Application Environment, which allows Unix work station users to run Macintosh software. Visitors will find a press release and an MAE 2.0 white paper.

Freedom Software

http://freedom.lm.com/freedom.html

Freedom Software specializes in "open systems" operating system software. This Web site provides information on the Pittsburgh-based company's products and services, contact points and a link to its anonymous FTP server.

Ical

http://clef.lcs.mit.edu/~sanjay/ical.html

Ical is an X-based calendar program. The site provides details on program features, a user guide and links to source code via anonymous FTP.

OpenVMS

http://www.openvms.digital.com/

Digital, which develops hardware and software products primarily for large corporations, promotes the OpenVMS multi-user operating system at this Web site.

Stardock Systems!

http://206.65.85.49/

Stardock Systems develops and publishes OS/2 platform system and desktop environment software for corporate and consumer users. Visit this page to find out more about the company and its software products.

System V

http://www.systemv.com/

The System V home page contains information about the company's Intel-based Unix operating systems. Customers include businesses, technicians, scientists and creative users.

3-D OBJECTS—CAD, RENDERING, VR, CGI

Blue Moon Rendering Tools

http://www.seas.gwu.edu/student/gritz/bmrt.html

Animators can download Blue Moon Rendering Tools (BMRT), programs that adhere to Pixar's RenderMan standard at this site. The page includes downloading directions, an image gallery and links to other RenderMan sites on the Web.

VIDEO

MPEG Player

http://www.geom.umn.edu/docs/mpeg_play/mpeg_play.html

This offering of the Geometry Center allows visitors to obtain information about and download a copy of MPEG Player/MI (motif interface) for Unix. Pointers are also provided to MPEG players for Macintosh and PC.

WORD PROCESSING

AUC TeX

http://www.iesd.auc.dk/~amanda/auctex/

AUC TeX is a software application for writing and formatting TeX files for variants of GNU Emacs. Here the user can download the latest version of the software as well as the 60-page manual. A mailing list is also available for subscription.

Emacs Lisp Introduction

http://www.cs.indiana.edu/elisp/elisp-intro.html

Elisp (Emacs Lisp) is a language used to extend emacs, a customizable text editor. This site includes an online manual on using Elisp and a searchable index of Emacs Lisp packages such as Ange FTP, a package that lets users edit remote files transparently.

SPECIAL COMPUTING

ARTIFICIAL INTELLIGENCE (AI)

Advanced Telecommunications Research Institute International

http://www.atr.co.jp/

The Advanced Telecommunications Research Institute International in Japan works on artificial intelligence and human-machine interactions to help people deal with the deluge of information that comes their way. Cross-language communications and space networks are just part of the work.

Informatics Group

http://avalon.epm.ornl.gov/

The Informatics Group constructs high-performance computing and artificial intelligence-based analysis systems, as well as database access tools. Visitors to this site can learn more about the group and the tools it has developed.

Institute for Information Technology

http://www.iit.nrc.ca/

The National Research Council of Canada's Institute for Information Technology home page contains information on the seven departments participating in its artificial intelligence projects. Includes info on publications, software and a comprehensive index of artificial intelligence-related links.

INNOVATIVE RESEARCH

Advanced Computer Tutoring Project

http://sands.psy.cmu.edu/

The Advanced Computer Tutoring Project develops cognitive architecture systems for teaching and learning. ACT's research, which uses computers to simulate human acquisition of knowledge and intelligent behavior, can be reviewed at this site.

Advanced Laboratory Workstation System
http://www.alw.nih.gov/
The U.S. National Institutes of Health organization maintains this site to provide information about its Advanced Laboratory Workstation System. Visit here to learn about the Unix-based computer system, its design and its applications.

Apple's Advanced Technology Group
http://www.atg.apple.com/
Apple's Advanced Technology Group offers this site, with a wealth of info about its research and work. Check out the group's publications, job opportunities and personal home pages here orlink to resources for online children's education and entertainment.

Arjuna Project Information.
http://www.vocaltec.com/
This site provides information about the Arjuna Project to create an object-oriented programming system for constructing fault-tolerant distributed applications. Includes a project summary, papers and technical manuals for the Arjuna program, plus links to online resources at the project's sponsoring institution.

ART+COM
http://www.artcom.de/
ART+COM, a Berlin, Germany-based research center, integrates the work of scientists and artists to develop new interfaces and software applications for the future. Visit to experience A+C's slick design and to learn more about their cutting edge projects.

ASTER Demonstration
http://www.cs.cornell.edu/Info/People/raman/aster/demo.html
Technophiles can witness a demonstration of the Audio System for Technical Readings, "a computing system for rendering technical documents in audio," at this site. Includes information about the system and its developer.

AT&T Bell Laboratories Research
http://www.research.att.com/
The Bell Labs Research home page features information about the lab, personnel and a text-to-speech demo. There's also a searchable index and fun geeky stuff to do.

BEATMAN
http://www.cs.colorado.edu/homes/batman/public_html/Home.html
The Boulder, Colo., ATM Area Network is an experimental network comprised of local schools, laboratories, companies and research centers. Visitors will find a general overview of the project along with standards documents for ATM networking.

Center for Excellence for Document Analysis and Recognition (CEDAR)
http://www.cedar.buffalo.edu/
The Center for Excellence for Document Analysis and Recognition pursues successful acronyms, digital document analysis and interpretation technologies. Visitors can review CEDAR's publications, projects and resources here.

a2z EDITOR'S CHOICE

Advanced Telecommunications Research Institute International
http://www.atr.co.jp/
Yes, there is a cutting-edge, it is very sharp and you can get a hold of it at the Advanced Telecommunications Research Institute (ATR) Web site. No doubt there are similarly brilliant research projects underway outside of the ATR's maze-like complex in Kyoto, Japan—but then, who knows if there is an Intergalactic Resource Locator (or IRL) for such a home page. The Institute's diverse and stunning array of goals include "realizing communications that facilitate mutual understanding beyond differences in place, time, language and culture," creating technologies that facilitate "mental image expression" and "the Synthesis and Simulation of Living Systems." But you won't find a litany of techno-futuristic jargon at the ATR site. On the contrary, this advanced technology Oz is buzzing with images, diagrams, research abstracts and conference memos. Particularly compelling are the diagrams that accompany the ATR Media Integration & Communications page. These simple, almost intuitive illustrations allow visitors to identify and understand the differences between "Face-to-face communications" and ATR's proposed "Hyper-realistic communications"—the latter consisting of "3D vision, tactile sensation" and "3D audio." Exactly what the future of telecommunications and human-machine interactions will look like is still unclear, but you can bet that image is coming into focus at this very moment somewhere on the ATR Web site.—*Reviewed by José Marquez*

Advanced Telecommunications Research Institute International

Outline of ATR
- ATR International(http://www.ctr.atr.co.jp/)
  Promotion of Integrated R&D Activities
- ATR Media Integration & Communications Research Laboratories(http://www.mic.atr.co.jp/)
  Creating new multi-media communications
- ATR Interpreting Telecommunications Research Laboratories (http://www.itl.atr.co.jp/)

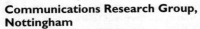
Communications Research Group, Nottingham

http://www.crg.cs.nott.ac.uk/

The Communications Research Group at the University of Nottingham, England, conducts research on the use of technology to support human communications and the work of physically distributed groups. Visit this site to learn about the group and access links to related organizations.

Communications Research Laboratory

http://www.crl.go.jp/

The Communications Research Laboratory of the Japanese Ministry of Posts and Telecommunications is responsible for the study of telecommunications technologies, radio science and radio applications. Visit this site to learn about its mission and activities, link to its public services and access its Internet search resources.

Computer Supported Cooperative Work Research Group

http://orgwis.gmd.de/

The Research Group on Computer Supported Cooperative Work in Germany studies the problems of working groups distributed in time and space and develops support systems. The site presents information on research, projects and publications.

Computer Vision & Image Processing Group

http://poseidon.csd.auth.gr/

The digital image processing team at the University of Thessaloniki in Greece provides information on its research projects, facilities and publications at this site.

DeweyWeb

http://ics.soe.umich.edu/

DeweyWeb is the University of Michigan's School of Education home page. Visitors will find articles and research related to the department as well as a chronicle of an on-going electronic communications project.

Distributed Object Computing

http://info.gte.com/ftp/doc/doc.html

The Distributed Object Computing group, a project of GTE Laboratories, maintains this site concerned with the Distributed Object Management project. The site explains this highly technical research project.

FringeWare Inc.

http://www.fringeware.com/

The FringeWare home page outlines its unique business activities: buying and selling "strange gizmos, non-mainstream software and subversive media," providing online services and publishing zines and comics on the Web. Maintained by "a small bunch of Net-savvy freaks," the site offers other pointers to the strange and unusual.

The Grasshopper Operating System

http://www.gh.cs.su.oz.au/Grasshopper/index.html

The Persistent Systems Research Group maintains this page describing progress on the development of the Grasshopper Operating System. Visitors to this site can learn more about this project in "persistent" computing and the people involved in it, as well as reading the group's papers and technical reports.

HealthNet

http://debra.dgbt.doc.ca/~mike/home.html

The HealthNet project focuses on applying communications technologies toward the development of a health-care information infrastructure for Canada. One feature here is HealthNet to GO!, a software package that helps users access health sites on the Internet. There is also information on a Web Demonstration Project and a HealthNet listserv.

The Hughes-STX Software Engineering Lab

http://info.stx.com/

This site serves as the home page for the Hughes-STX Software Excellence Initiative's software engineering lab. Visitors can learn about the organization's efforts to foster the development of data systems by going through the background information here.

The Institute of Computer Graphics, Vienna University of Technology

http://www.cg.tuwien.ac.at/

The Vienna University of Technology's Institute of Computer Graphics presents information about its research and faculty at this home page. Visitors can check out the Department of Algorithms and Programming Methodology page or jump to the Department of Visualization and Animation.

InterVisions Systems

http://www.intervisionsystems.com/wearable

InterVision specializes in hardware and software engineering and services for field operations, equipment maintenance and training. At the company's home page, find hardware specifications for the company's line of "wearable computers" and other field computing devices.

Mitek Systems Inc.

http://www.cts.com/browse/mitek

Visitors to this Web site will find information about Mitek Systems Inc. and the corporation's intelligent character recognition and optical character recognition products. Find also links to OCR resources and research available via the Internet.

Software Engineering Research Centre

http://www.serc.nl/

The Software Engineering Research Centre's home page provides information about this Neth-erlands-based group concerned with applied software engineering. Topics covered include smart people, neat projects, interesting reports and Centre news.

Tenet Group

http://tenet.berkeley.edu/

The Tenet Group conducts research on real-time and high performance computer networks. Take a look at tomorrow's media applications such as video conferencing at this research and development-oriented site.

Virtual Environments Special Interest Group

http://vered.rose.toronto.edu/HFESVE.html

The Virtual Environments Special Interest Group Web page from the Human Factors and Ergonomics Society explains the group's mission of enhancing human interfaces with virtual environment systems.

XSoft, A Division of the Xerox Corporation

http://www.xerox.com/XSoft/XSoftHome.html

XSoft, a division of Xerox, sells software designed to improve the way documents are created and captured, aiming to manage and communicate ideas and information. Its Web site offers an animated demonstration, tech support and product news.

MONDO COMPUTING

Army High Performance Computing Research Center

http://www.arc.umn.edu/

The Army High Performance Computing Research Center is a collaborative program that unites the U.S. government, academia and industry in the promotion of research and education in the Army's computing environment. Find an in-depth overview of the center and a look at the educational courses it provides.

Atari on the Web!

http://www.mcc.ac.uk/~dlms/atari.html

Computer maker Atari has some devoted fans in cyberspace, including the author of this Web site. Includes links to newsletters, FAQs, newsgroups, game tips and solutions.

Commodore 8-bit World Wide Web Server

http://www.hut.fi/~msmakela/cbm/

Find out what's new at the page that specializes in what's old. This personal resource page is actually about the Commodore 64, the computer with almost as much memory as a present-day digital watch. Visit this site for a stroll down memory lane through user groups, publications and links to related Web sites.

Cyberterm

http://cyberterm.com.au

Cyberterm describes itself as "...a 3-D BBS, a multi-user flight simulator/games programming platform, a VR environment, an operating system, a cyberspace engine..." Still in the alpha testing stage when we visited, the future shareware title is expected to be available for download in early 1996.

The German Research Network Computer Emergency Response Team

http://www.cert.dfn.de/

The German Research Network's Computer Emergency Response Team presents contact information, an overview of the project and searchable documents. The Team is a "member of the international Forum of Incident Response and Security Teams." The site posts information on GRN-CERT services, events, support and more. In German with some information in English.

I Hate Windoze

http://www.tach.net/public/personal/scpayne/ihatewin/ihatewin.html

"I Hate WINdoze," says this Webmaster. Visit this site for an index of of anti-Microsoft humor articles and "hate pages." Hey, why not?

The International MPEG Bizarre 1st Film Festival

http://www.best.com/~johnp/film.html

The I'M B1FF! repository of MPEG movies contains both lighthearted and serious independent films turned digital via the MPEG compression standard. Get a copy of an MPEG viewer and sit back for such renowned neo-classics as David Blair's "David Blair: WAX, or The Discovery of Television Among the Bees."

Laserium—Music For Your Eyes

http://www.laserium.com/

Laserium is a company specializing in the manufacture of laser special effects equipment and laser light show productions for the entertainment industry. Visit this site for information on the company, its products, services and show schedules.

Microsoft Library

http://library.microsoft.com/

The electronic shelves of Microsoft Corp.'s online library contain many resources for computer users. Links to computer company information, technical magazines, Internet search tools and various reference resources can be found along with a listing of "fun & interesting" Internet sites.

NASA/WVU Software Research Laboratory

http://atlantis.ivv.nasa.gov/

The Software Research Laboratory, a joint program of the U.S. National Aeronautics and Space Administration and West Virginia University, maintains this informational site. Visitors here for news, project and technical documentation, lecture and events information, staff profiles and more.

The Online Bonsai Icon Collection

http://www.neosoft.com/~hav/tobic.html

A large collection of bonsai tree icons and images is offered at this Web site. Images are available in BMP, GIF and JPEG format and browsers can download each of several collections individually. Visitors can also link to the official Bonsai Web site from here.

Pictures from The Linux Congress at Heidelberg

http://aorta.tat.physik.uni-tuebingen.de/~flebbe/heidelberg/heidel.html

The Pictures from the Linux Congress at Heidelberg page is a Web gallery of head shots of scientists attending the congress.

Silicon Studio Information

http://www.studio.sgi.com/

Silicon Studio Inc., a subsidiary of Silicon Graphics, develops technology for the entertainment industry. Visit this site to browse its index of projects and resources from the print, broadcast and interactive entertainment fields orlink to the company's international training courses and technical materials.

Teknowledge

http://www.teknowledge.com/

Teknowledge provides consulting services and software products for commercial and defense applications. Includes a company overview and descriptions of products and services.

Trademarks of International Business Machines

http://www.ibm.com/trademarks.html

Find at this site a non-comprehensive alphabetical list of trademarks owned by IBM, the computer industry giant.

V-ONE Corporation

http://www.v-one.com/

Get the lowdown on smartcard technologies at this site from software and hardware developer, the Virtual Open Network Environment Corporation. Technologies featured include V-ONE's Cyber Wallet and SmartCAT, the company's smartcard-based user authentication client.

Yggdrasil Computing, Incorporated

http://www.yggdrasil.com/

Named for the world tree of old Norse mythology, Yggdrasil Computing Inc.'s stated mission is "to provide infrastructure to support the free software world." Find information on the company's products and technical support services, as well as links to freeware archives.

ONLINE MULTIMEDIA GALLERIES AND RESEARCH FACILITIES

The Advanced Communication Technologies Laboratory

http://actlab.rtf.utexas.edu/

The Advanced Communication Technologies Laboratory of the University of Texas, Austin, maintains this site for listing general information and Internet resources. Visit here to learn about ACTLab's programs, faculty and students. Links to its Gopher server and Internet gateways also are available.

Advisory Group on Computer Graphics

http://www.agocg.ac.uk:8080/agocg/

The U.K.'s Advisory Group on Computer Graphics features pointers for higher education groups creating multimedia presentations. Visitors can take a look at the group's publications and current projects at this site.

Alex Lam's Virtual Studio

http://www.alexlam.com/users/lampas

Browsers will wander through a virtual art gallery and multimedia extravaganza here, featuring photography of the Webmaster as well as several other artists. Lam's page also includes links to live radio and television news from Hong Kong and Japan.

Animation Master Hobbyist

http://www.xmission.com/~gastown/animation/index.html

Users of Animation Master and Playmation software exchange information, ideas and creations at this site. Download software reviews and tips files or visit the gallery to see the animation being produced with these software tools.

CAD Lab

http://cad.ucla.edu/

The Computer Aided Design Lab at UCLA maintains this colorful page offering links to UCLA's main info servers as well as the CAD Lab online resources.

CERL Sound Group

http://datura.cerl.uiuc.edu/

Digital audio signal processing is the focus of the CERL Sound Group's home page, a service of the University of Illinois. Includes computer music and sound computation info, sound-related position papers and pointers to other sound computation sites.

CSC Graphics Group

http://www.csc.fi/visualization/graphics_group.html

The Visualization Group at the Center for Scientific Computing (CSC) in Finland focuses on visualization and animation problems. Its graphics guide and course material are presented in Finnish. Visitors also can check out such CSC projects as the Chemistry Art Gallery.

Fractal Explorer

http://www.vis.colostate.edu/~user1209/fractals/index.html

The Fractal Explorer provides background information about these computer-generated images, plus two fractal sets for visitors to enjoy: the Mandelbrot and Julia sets. Includes a link to the home page of the site's author.

GIFs Directory

http://www.acm.uiuc.edu/rml/Gifs/

The GIFs Directory is devoted to digital pictures. An extensive image guide indexed by subject and date, this site contains thousands of GIFs—sit back and enjoy the view ordownload for use with your own Web creations.

Institute for New Media

http://www.inm.de/

Institute for New Media, a site devoted to research in art, science and technology, explores both the staff and projects at INM related to video, audio and interactive media. Visitors can also link to a virtual library of abstracts, available services and software and upcoming events. Pages vary from English to German depending on the link.

Kiernan's Wavefront

http://www.unm.edu/~kholland

Animations are the focus of this home page from Kiernan Holland, a Web server administrator and Wavefront expert at the University of New Mexico. His animations include titles such as "Rise of the Thorax," "The Hand" (don't tell Oliver Stone), and "Box Fungus."

Leviathan Web

http://leviathan.tamu.edu:70/

The Texas Agricultural Extension Service from the Texas A&M University System presents a free keyword search site with access to more than 2,300 clip art images and slides through the Leviathan Web page. Includes Web programming resources and links to related publications.

The MIDI Farm Internet

http://www.midifarm.com/

MIDI sound files sprout at The MIDI Farm, which features a well-fertilized archive, a live chat, a bulletin board and news of the day. There also is a newsletter, a marketplace, and a directory of manufacturers' e-mail addresses.

 EDITOR'S CHOICE

NCSA Education & Outreach

http://www.ncsa.uiuc.edu/Edu/EduHome.html

The expansive, ever-changing Web and open-eyed, curious children were made for each other—the problem is, how should the two connect? The Education Group at the National Center for Supercomputing Applications (NCSA) might just have the answer. Remember, the NCSA was the first to develop and distribute a graphical Web browser, as well as a host of free Web server software. These visionary folk are serious about the Web and, at this site, they're also serious about learning. School administrators, teachers and parents can all benefit from a studious trip through such thought-provoking and inspiring links as: Selected Educational WWW Resources, SuperQuest for Teachers and the Networking Infrastructure for Education. Some of these sections contain classroom-ready materials while others relate some of the NCSA Education Group's long-term and wide-range goals regarding Web-based teaching and learning tools. The Group's own stated goals are to "help enable citizens to prepare for their future by...transferring to all sectors of society...scientific knowledge related to High Performance Computing." In layman's terms, the Education Group is making sure that the kind of well-educated democracy which Thomas Jefferson once described won't be erased by a growing disparity between those with technical "know-how" and those without.—*Reviewed by José Marquez*

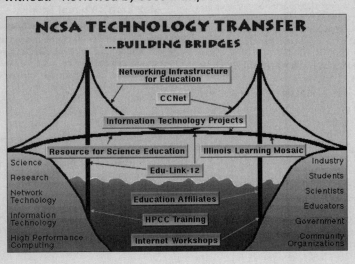

Multimedia Info

http://viswiz.gmd.de/MultimediaInfo/

Find computer audio and visual resources across the Web using this alphabetical index of Internet sites related to multimedia. Categories of information include guides, FAQ sheets, software, archives, research, newsgroups and bibliographies.

NCSA Education & Outreach

http://www.ncsa.uiuc.edu/Edu/EduHome.html

Bridges the gap between high-tech information and the average citizen. See Editor's Choice.

NCSA Exhibits

http://www.ncsa.uiuc.edu/General/NCSAExhibits.html

Among the multimedia exhibits from the National Center for Supercomputing Applications are a fractals demonstration and excerpts from the NCSA Digital Gallery CD-ROM. Visitors can check out the Grand Challenge Cosmology Consortium and the National Metacenter MetaScience Project.

Rob's Multimedia Lab

http://www.andatech.com/videocraft/banners.html

Witness audio and video computer feats at Rob's Multimedia Lab. Access collections of images, sounds and QuickTime movies here. Find also links to wacky multimedia-oriented sites.

Silicon Graphics Image Gallery

http://www.sgi.com/Fun/free/gallery.html

Silicon Graphics' Image Gallery contains dozens of graphics and 3-D "stereogram" images, including the winners of SGI's Third International Contest Awards. The site also lists links to other online image galleries.

SYNERGY:PANIC

http://sunsite.unc.edu/otis/synergy/panic.html

This virtual graphic forum is an "ongoing live image exchange and manipulation gathering" operation. Initiated at a Minneapolis nightclub, participants download GIFs and JPEGs from a central FTP site, manipulate them "in odd and stimulating ways," then upload them for general viewing and discussion.

Thant's Animation Index

http://mambo.ucsc.edu/psl/thant/thant.html

If it moves on the Web, it's probably here. Visit this personal link collection to find hundreds of animations created for entertainment, science and business purposes.

The University of Manchester Computer Graphics Unit

http://info.mcc.ac.uk/CGU/CGU-intro.html

The Computer Graphics Unit (CGU) at the University of Manchester provides interactive computer graphics, multimedia and image-processing facilities at the United Kingdom-based school. Information is available here about CGU's software, research, movies, staff and students.

VIRTUAL REALITY (VR)

Computer Graphics Lab, Swiss Federal Institute of Technology

http://ligwww.epfl.ch/

The Computer Graphics Lab at the Swiss Federal Institute of Technology specializes in computer animation and VR applications. Peruse research projects, computer-generated films, student theses and other related resources.

KAIST Virtual Reality Group

http://dangun.kaist.ac.kr/

The Korea Advance Institute of Science and Technology's Virtual Reality Group invites visitors to learn more about the group, its members, areas of research, publications, and other projects. In English and Korean.

NAVE: Navigating and Acting in Virtual Environments

http://www.cs.colorado.edu/homes/cboyd/public_html/Home.html

Colorado University computer wizards working on SGI workstations have developed a new world of virtual spaces at the Navigating and Acting in Virtual Environments Research Group. Try out experimental navigational models for walking and flying or test out acoustics in a virtual hall at this site.

VETT Project

http://mimsy.mit.edu/

The VETT team at MIT conducts research into the use of virtual environments for training purposes. Browsers can read about the laboratory's staff, projects and publications, as well as link to other sites of interest on the Web.

Virtual Reality

http://www.cs.uidaho.edu/lal/cyberspace/VR/VR.html

The Virtual Reality page provides a description and definition of this emerging technology. Includes links to several VR primers, a look at some practical applications, pointers to "home brew" development guides and listings of related newsgroups.

SUPERCOMPUTING AND PARALLEL COMPUTING

HISTORICAL AND TOPICAL SUPERCOMPUTING INFORMATION

David A. Bader's Parallel Sites

http://www.umiacs.umd.edu/~dbader/sites.html

This page offers a personally compiled listing of parallel computing sites. Topics covered here include "Supercomputing Vendors," "Computer Science Research Groups," "Federal Agencies" and a "List of the World's Most Powerful Computing Sites." See Editor's Choice.

Fourth IEEE International Symposium on High Performance Distributed Computing

http://uvacs.cs.virginia.edu/~hpdc95/

The Fourth IEEE International Symposium on High Performance Distributed Computing, held in Virginia in August 1995, provides its program and demonstrations at this Web site along with other conference-related information.

Internet Parallel Computing Archive

http://www.hensa.ac.uk/parallel/

The Internet Parallel Computing Archive is administered by the University of Kent at Canterbury, England. Visitors to the site will find information and documentation about computer networks and a variety of software designs and applications.

Load Balancing and Optimization

http://www.infomall.org/npac/pcw/node247.html

Parallel computing aficionados can access the text of a technical book called "Parallel Computing Works" through this page, which features the contents of the book's 11th chapter.

NCSA Education & Outreach

http://www.ncsa.uiuc.edu/Edu/EduHome.html

This "outreach" site is designed to educate people about high performance computing and communications. Included here are a number of projects, special exhibits, training and resource information.

Supercomputing '94

http://sc94.ameslab.gov/

Supercomputing '94 details the 1994 conference on high performance computing and communications. Includes info on the conference program, seminars and related educational resources.

Supercomputing and Parallel Computing Research Groups

http://www.cs.cmu.edu/afs/cs.cmu.edu/
project/scandal/public/www/
research-groups.html/

This annotated list of research groups in the fields of supercomputing and parallel computing is part of an index to Supercomputing and Parallel Computing Resources. Pointers to the index's other resources and to similar lists are provided.

---

a2z EDITOR'S CHOICE

David A. Bader's Parallel Sites

http://www.umiacs.umd.edu/~dbader/sites.html

"Would you like to play a game?" An invitation, a warning, a cliché—these legendary lines will forever be associated with America's first supercomputing sweetheart: the fictional W.O.P.R. supercomputer featured in the late Cold War classic, Wargames. While such a pickup line is not likely to be overheard in any of the sites listed at this index of parallel computing sites, the same spirit of voyeuristic fascination that endeared the 1980s generation of would-be cyberpunks to these room-sized supercomputers lives on—the Web, that is. Today, thanks to David Bader's nearly encyclopedic collection of links to supercomputing sites, anyone from an accountant to a zoologist can occupy the same virtual space as the computers the arms race conceived and academia nourished into a peaceful—if busy—adulthood. From the Arctic Region Supercomputing Center to the ZIAM GmbH (Center for Industrial Applications of Massively Parallel Systems), Bader's list accounts for an estimated 600 supercomputing sites. The site is maintained at the University of Maryland Institute for Advanced Computer Studies, where Bader himself is a member of the "administrata." So, if you feel like coming terminal-to-terminal with the steroidal counterpart to your own puny PC, this is the place to be.—*Reviewed by José Marquez*

David A. Bader's List of Parallel Computing Sites

UMIACS

Topics:

- New and Updated Links
- Supercomputing and Parallel Computing
- Supercomputer Vendors
- Federal Agencies

PRIVATE INSTITUTES AND R&D DIVISIONS

Alta Technology

http://www.xmission.com/~altatech/

Utah's Alta Technology, a supplier of modular products for scalable supercomputing systems, sponsors this promotional home page. Visitors can learn more about the company, its hardware and software products, and its customer services.

Center for Display Technology and Manufacturing

http://dtm.eecs.umich.edu/

The Center for Display Technology and Manufacturing at the University of Michigan focuses on research and development in flat-panel display technologies. This site contains information on the center, as well as resources such as a newsletter, research publications, and an FTP site.

Hewlett-Packard Convex Technology Center

http://www.convex.com/

Hewlett-Packard's Convex Technology Center supplies information on its high performance computer systems, including pointers to support services and software. The site features info on user group conferences and exhibitions of computational capabilities.

High Performance Computing from Digital Equipment Corp.

http://www.digital.com/info/hpc/hpc.html

The Digital Equipment Corporation's HPC Info-Center site contains information on hardware, software and applications for high performance computing. Includes breakdown of market segments and announcements of upcoming conferences and events. Includes links to the Digital home page and other sites of related interest.

IBM Research

http://www.research.ibm.com/

Visitors to the IBM Research home page are invited to take the self-guided "Tour de Research." Peek at IBM's latest technology, review research reports in the cyberjournal and find out the latest company news. Links to other IBM sites are also featured.

IBM T.J. Watson Research Center

http://www.watson.ibm.com/

This New York state institution headquarters IBM's research division, working in computer and physical sciences, systems technology, mathematics, and information services. This page provides information about the center, local hotels and a link to the IBM home page.

UNIVERSITIES

Alabama Research and Education Network

http://sgisrvr.asc.edu/index.html

The Alabama Research and Education Network presents the Alabama Supercomputer Network through its home page. The site includes facts about the program and the latest news and research.

ANU Supercomputer Facility

http://anusf.anu.edu.au/

The Australian National University Supercomputer Facility's site contains information on high performance computing. This site includes links to Australian HPC centers and resources, current announcements, documentation, other ANU sites and "fun and interesting stuff."

Calcul parallele au LMFA

http://cephee.mecaflu.ec-lyon.fr/

The Fluid Mechanic Laboratory in Lyon, France, features its experiments in parallel computing at this scientific Web site. The site is available in French, with an English translation under construction.

The Center for Research on Parallel Computation

http://www.crpc.rice.edu/CPRC/

The Center for Research on Parallel Computation is where computer scientists, mathematicians and engineers research ways to make computing faster, stronger and bigger in ways that industry, government and academia need. Its site contains research, reports, outreach notes and other links. The site is searchable.

CESUP - Centro de Supercomputacao da UFRGS

http://www.cesup.ufrgs.br/

This site hosts the National Supercomputer Center at the Federal University at Rio Grande do Sul in Porto Alegre - RS - Brazil. Visitors are invited to learn more about the center, its resources and mission to "serve the Brazillian science and engineering communities." In Portuguese and English.

CINECA

http://www.cineca.it/

CINECA, the Interuniversity Consortium of Northeastern Italy for Automatic Computing, is a large Scientific Computing Center. Visitors to its Web site can explore the Consortium's varied academic uses of supercomputing technology.

Concurrent Supercomputing Consortium

http://www.ccsf.caltech.edu/cscc.html

The Concurrent Supercomputing Consortium is an alliance of universities, research facilities, government and industry agencies combining resources to share computational capabilities and exchange technical information. Includes access to an annual report, online documentation and links to other high performance and parallel computing sites.

Cornell Theory Center

http://www.tc.cornell.edu/

A National Science Foundation supercomputing center, the Cornell Theory Center offers parallel processing resources and information to the scientific community. This Web site describes CTC's research activities and educational offerings.

Edinburgh Parallel Computing Centre

http://www.epcc.ed.ac.uk/

Edinburgh Parallel Computing Center promotes the development and utilization of high performance computing systems in the academic and commercial realms. Explore the Center's programs, publications and educational opportunities at this site.

Flexible Architecture for Shared Memory (FLASH)

http://www-flash.stanford.edu/

Information about the design of the FLASH (Flexible Architecture for Shared Memory) multiprocessor and related work at Stanford University can be found here.

ITI Main Web Page

http://www.iit.nrc.ca/

The Canadian Information Technology Institute site describes its research and devlopment projects, general information about the Institute and pointers to its various services. Includes job listings, staff directory and links to related resources.

London Parallel Applications Centre

http://www.lpac.ac.uk/

Visitors to this Web server will find links to the London Parallel Applications Centre, the London & South-East Centre for High Performance Computing and the Europa Working Group. A link to the World Stock & Commodity Exchanges Handbook is also included.

National Center for Supercomputing Applications

http://www.ncsa.uiuc.edu/General/NCSAHome.html

The National Center for Supercomputing Applications is operated by the University of Illinois at Urbana-Champaign. Visitors will find NCSA general info, news, publications, software tools and job opportunities.

National Consortium for High Performance Computing

http://www.nchpc.lcs.mit.edu/

This MIT server provides information about the activities of the National Consortium for High Performance Computing such as meeting minutes, conference notes, workshops and a list of relevant courses offered by member institutions.

Ohio Supercomputer Center

http://www.osc.edu/welcome.html

The Supercomputer Center in Columbus, Ohio, maintains this site for user services and information. Visitors can learn about its facilities, workshops and events, and more.

Politechnika Wroclaw

http://sun1000.ci.pwr.wroc.pl/

The Wroclaw Centre of Networking and Supercomputing site at the Technical University of Wroclaw in Poland posts information on its academics, services and facilities. Also find links to other Polish sites. In Polish and some English.

San Diego Supercomputer Center

http://www.sdsc.edu/

The San Diego Supercomputer Center researches computational science and engineering. Its site provides information on the center's research, services and publications. Includes detailed images and a link to the National Science Foundation's site.

Scalable Concurrent Programming Laboratory

http://www.scp.caltech.edu/

The Scalable Concurrent Programming Laboratory, part of the Computer Science Department at the California Institute of Technology, focuses on coupling large-scale applications with high performance computing and modern computer science.

Supercomputer Computations Research Institute

http://www.scri.fsu.edu/

The Supercomputer Computations Research Institute at Florida State University provides information here on its research, software, conferences, networks, and people. Links are provided to home pages of associated institutions.

University of Westminster's Centre for Parallel Computing

http://www.cpc.wmin.ac.uk/welcome.html

The home page of the Centre for Parallel Computing at the University of Westminster supplies information on the institution's projects, with a focus on the Copernicus Projects' software engineering and high-performance computing tools. Also here are news, info on staff members and an FTP site.

The Utah Supercomputing Institute

http://ute.usi.utah.edu/

The Utah Supercomputing Institute, a facility of the University of Utah at Salt Lake City, maintains this informational site. Visitors will find news, facilities overviews, user documentation, workshops and events schedules, as well as other research and computing resources.

TELE-COMMUNICATIONS AND INFRASTRUCTURE

Ameritech

http://www.ameritech.com/

Ameritech provides local phone service for several states in the American Midwest, in addition to offering celular, paging, interactive video and wireless data communications for much of the country and many parts of Europe. Visitors will find company news and details on products and services here.

Arasmith Engineering

http://www.arasmith.com/

Arasmith Engineering, a Sunnyvale, Calif.-based computer consulting company, maintains this promotional site to introduce its Internet connectivity services and amateur radio enthusiast resources. Includes link to the Bay Area Communications Society.

Bay Area Gigabit Testbed

http://george.lbl.gov/BAGNet.html

Fourteen San Francisco organizations are working on the Bay Area Gigabit Testbed (BAGNet), an infrastructure that will support the emerging technology age. Visitors here will get detailed technical information on the program and links to the fourteen participants' sites.

Bell Atlantic Public Archive Gopher Menu

gopher://ba.com/

The Bell Atlantic Public Archive gopher contains current documents on Bell Atlantic telecommunications policy. Includes links to related congressional hearings, educational programs ,and other relevant resources.

Coherent Communications Systems Corp.

http://www.coherent.com/

This voice-enhancement and telecommunications technology corporation's home page includes a corporate overview, a products list, articles, press releases, and investor information. Includes a response form for requesting additional info.

Columbia University Center for Telecommunications Research

http://www.ctr.columbia.edu/

The Columbia University Center for Telecommunications Research maintains this site to provide access to its research groups, information resources, and systems managers. Also available are links to FTP and gopher sites as well as a variety of other Internet search tools.

Common Knowledge:Pittsburgh

http://info.ckp.edu/

This site provides information about Common Knowledge: Pittsburgh, a collaborative project started by the Pittsburgh Public Schools, the Pittsburgh Supercomputing Center and the University of Pittsburgh. CK:P is aimed at developing a computer networking infrastructure for educational uses. Visitors here can find out about the project's design and progress.

Corning Optical Fiber Information Center

http://www.usa.net/corning-fiber

The Corning Optical Fiber Information Center, provided by Endicott, N.Y.-based Corning Incorporated, offers company news, product updates and technology case histories. Visit here to learn about the company and the fiber optics products that are "transforming the way the world sends and receives information."

CNET

http://www.cnet.fr/

France Telecom's research and development department reports on its current projects and scientific collaborations here. In French.

Digital Technics Incorporated

http://www.access.digex.net/~dti/index.html

Digital Technics Incorporated, a telecommunications research and development firm, discusses its mission and promotes its primary products on this commercial home page. Products featured include Esopus 2000, a generic switching platform that can be used in a variety of environments.

ElektroPost

http://www.ep.se/

ElektroPost is a company focusing on computer communications via electronic mail and associated telecommunications systems. Includes links to general information on services, e-mail addresses, and entertainment sites. Swedish and English.

Ericsson

http://www.ericsson.com/

Ericsson, a telecommunications firm that specializes in switching, radio and networking, presents info about its company here. Browsers can read press releases, financial reports, or learn about products at this site.

Eureka, from Digital Technics Inc.

http://www.access.digex.net/~dti/eureka/eureka.html

This site, maintained by Digital Technics Inc., is a "telecom neighborhood for telecom professionals and consumers." Visitors can link to corporate and organization home pages or access product and service information from a variety of vendors.

INESC (Portugal) Web Server

http://www.inesc.pt/

INESC, a Portuguese nonprofit organization, provides telecommunications research material and links to other Portuguese Web servers. Text is available in Portuguese and English.

Institute of Technology

http://www.tele.pw.edu.pl/

The Institute of Telecommunications at the Warsaw University of Technology gives an overview of its departments, programs and research here. The site includes information for post doctoral candidates. In Polish and English.

International Telecommunications Satellite Organization—INTELSAT

http://www.intelsat.int:8080/

Nonprofit cooperative of 130 nations provides information on satellite technology that links the global village. See Editor's Choice, page 191.

International Telecommunication Union

gopher://info.itu.ch/

This gopher site archives documents describing the functions, recommendations and members of the International Telecommunication Union (ITU), a United Nations agency that regulates, standardizes, and coordinates development of international telecommunications.

ITU Plenipotentiary Conference 94 in Kyoto

http://www.mpt.go.jp/ITU/ITU-PP94-home.html

This site, maintained by the Japanese Ministry of Posts and Telecommunications, contains program notes from the Plenipotentiary Conference held in Kyoto in 1994. Opening statements by various ministry and conference officials are featured.

MCNC

http://www.mcnc.org/

MCNC is a nonprofit organization that develops information technology strategies for business, education and governmental bodies in North Carolina. Visitors to its home page can find descriptions of its telecommunications and supercomputing facilities.

National Institute of Telecommunications

http://arctique.int-evry.fr/

The National Institute of Telecommunications in Evry, France, discusses its programs and research at this Web site. Visitors can take a look at the campus or read about the institute's mission. In French and English.

Nippon Telegraph and Telephone Corp. Software Laboratories Palo Alto

http://www.nttam.com/

Nippon Telegraph and Telephone Corp. posts links to home pages for its California research lab and corporate headquarters in Japan at this site. Visitors also can read about the company's computer network research here.

Nortel Corp.

http://www.nortel.com/

Canadian-based Nortel (formerly Northern Telecom) is a telecommunications company focusing on network design and implementation. Company news and information along with product descriptions are available here in English, French, German, and Spanish.

Promptus Communications

http://www.promptus.com/promptus

Promptus Communications' home page supplies information on the company's digital telecommunications products. Featured is the Open Access to Switched Integrated Services (OASIS) product family. Company information and a password-protected file library are included.

PTCWeb

http://www.ptc.org/

PTC Web is the online presence of the Pacific Telecommunications Council, an international, nonprofit, non-governmental organization for providers and users of communications services. The site contains information on members, conferences, publications, and technologies.

The Russian Institute for Public Networks

http://www.ripn.net/

The Russian Institute for Public Networks works to develop computer communications and networking in Russia. Visitors here will learn more about the project, its affiliations and its research.

Rutgers Telecommunications Division Server

http://www-ns.rutgers.edu/

The Telecommunications Division supplies documents and services pertaining to the Rutgers University Network, as well as information about the division.

---

a2z EDITOR'S CHOICE

International Telecommunications Satellite Organization—INTELSAT

http://www.intelsat.int:8080/

Ever wonder who keeps the world afloat? Wonder no more. INTELSAT, an international nonprofit cooperative of more than 130 member nations, builds, maintains and leases the satellites that keep our mass-mediated Global Village intact. INTELSAT boasts a fleet of over 24 "spacecraft in geostationary orbit" with 13 more satellites "in order for launch over the next two years." Together, this fleet of "flying toasters" carries more than "half of all international telephone calls, virtually all transoceanic television broadcasts," and a score of domestic transmissions. Impressed yet? The INTELSAT site also features pictures of powerful people and multi-million dollar equipment none of us lowly simulcast television viewers and long-distance telephone callers could ever hope to understand, let alone control. Yet at the INTELSAT site, almost anyone can learn how to operate a multi-billion dollar operation by reading through the Annual Reports section—and, while you're at it, why not add a few of the names under the contacts link to your own rolodex? You never know when this orbital telecommunications leviathan will line up with your destiny. Remember, the Web is like a giant slingshot on a grassy plain...forever under the intangible weight of a giant's shadow.—*Reviewed by José Marquez*

How does INTELSAT work?

Irving Goldstein, Director General and CEO

INTELSAT is an international not for profit cooperative of more than 130 member nations, operated pursuant to sound commercial principles. The owners contribute capital in proportion to their relative use of the system and receive a return on their investment. Users pay a charge for all INTELSAT services. The charges vary depending on the type, amount, and duration of the service. Any nation may use the Intelsat system , whether or not it is a member. INTELSAT basically operates as a wholesaler, providing services to end-users through the INTELSAT member in each country. Some INTELSAT member nations have chosen to authorize several organizations to provide INTELSAT services within their countries. Currently, INTELSAT has more than 300 authorized customers. Most of the decisions which INTELSAT's member nations must make regarding the INTELSAT system is accomplished by consensus, a noteworthy achievement for an international organization with such a large and diverse membership.

Southwestern Bell Technology Resources

http://www.tri.sbc.com/

Southwestern Bell Technology Resources is a research unit of the Southwestern Bell Communications Corporation. Visitors will find information on innovative new technology for the information highway.

SpaceNet Informationen

http://www.space.net/

Space Net is a German firm specializing in Internet and satellite communications networks. Visitors will find corporate news and information on services. Available in English and German.

Stentor: The Alliance of Canada's Telephone Companies

http://www.stentor.ca/

All 11 telephone companies which serve Canada belong to Stentor, "the alliance of Canada's telephone companies." This site offers links to the home pages of each of those companies, plus copious information about Stentor and the Canadian telecommunications industry.

Swiss Post Office and Telecom (PTT)

http://www.telecom.ch/

Switzerland's Post Office and Telecom offers general information about its historical and present communications services. Link directly to departments, sister companies or press releases.

Technical University of Berlin Broadband Communications Project

http://www.tk.tu-berlin.de/

The Technical University of Berlin, Germany, maintains this site for information on its Broadband Communications Project. Visitors will find news and announcements, staff listings, project overviews and related Internet links.

The Telstra Corporation

http://www.telstra.com.au/

The Telstra Corporation is an Australian telecommunications company. Visitors to its site will find a company overview, product and service information and job listings.

Tetherless Access Ltd.

http://www.tetherless.com/

Tetherless Access Ltd. sells software to telecommunications service providers. The California-based company describes its products and corporate vision here.

U.S. West Inc.

http://www.uswest.com/

U.S. West is a communications conglomerate producing and marketing directory services, cellular communications systems and communications software. At this corporate Web site, visitors will learn about the company and the products and services it offers.

University of Limerick Telecommunications Research Laboratory

http://oak.ece.ul.ie/

The Telecommunications Research Laboratory at Ireland's University of Limerick posts information about its research here. The page also contains information on the lab's personnel and upcoming seminars.

Verlag Heinz Heise

http://www.ix.de/

Verlag Heinz Heise is a telecommunications firm located in Wandel, Germany. Visitors to the site will find product and services documentation. Available in German only.

WorldLinx Telecommunications Inc.

http://www.worldlinx.com/

WorldLinx Telecommunications Inc. is a subdivision of Bell Canada. Visitors to the corporation's home page will find press releases, a corporate overview and information on services and customers. Available in English and French.

The World-Wide Web Virtual Library: Communications & Telecommunications

http://www.analysys.co.uk/commslib.htm

This Communications and Telecommunications section of the massive Word-Wide Web Virtual Library covers dozens of areas in its subject index. Subjects include broadcasting, education, mobile communications and multimedia. Includes a search engine and links to other related resources.

EDUCATION

THE 25 MOST POPULAR EDUCATION SITES

Aberdeen High School
http://www.ahs.aberdeen.k12.ms.us/

California State Polytechnic University, Pomona
http://www.csupomona.edu/

Canadian Universities
http://watserv1.uwaterloo.ca/~credmond/univ.html

Catapult
http://www.jobweb.org/catapult/catapult.htm

Central Michigan University
http://www.cmich.edu/

City University of New York
http://www.cuny.edu/

College of the Holy Cross
http://www.holycross.edu/

Data Research Associates
http://www.dra.com/

Georgetown University
http://www.georgetown.edu/guhome.html

Illinois State University
http://www.ilstu.edu/

Massachusetts Institute of Technology
http://web.mit.edu/

Online Educator
http://www.ole.net/ole/

Pica
http://www.pica.nl/

Pojoaque Valley Schools
http://pvs.k12.nm.us/

Purdue University
http://www.purdue.edu/

Sam Houston State University
http://www.shsu.edu/

State University of New York
http://www.sunycentral.edu/

United States Public Libraries
http://galaxy.einet.net/hytelnet/US000PUB.html

U.S. Universities and Community Colleges
http://wwwhost.cc.utexas.edu/world/univ.html

University of California
http://www.reg.uci.edu/SANET/uc.html

University of Central Florida
http://www.ucf.edu/

University of Colorado, Boulder
http://www.colorado.edu/

University of Illinois, Springfield
http://www.uis.edu/

University of Washington
http://www.cac.washington.edu:1180/

University of Wisconsin, Eau Claire
http://www.uwec.edu/

COLLEGE HOME PAGES

AFRICA

Rhodes University
http://www.ru.ac.za
Rhodes University in Grahamstown, South Africa, provides information here on its course offerings, computing services, student groups, employment opportunities, staff directories, and more. Includes links to affiliated institutions.

University of Cape Town
http://www.uct.ac.za
The University of Cape Town, South Africa, maintains this site to introduce its people and programs. Visitors will find staff and student directories, upcoming event and conference listings, and a variety of computer services.

University of Port Elizabeth
http://www.upe.ac.za
The University of Port Elizabeth in South Africa provides information here on its academic programs and current events. Visitors will learn about the institution and its efforts to "establish itself as a democratic, multicultural university accessible to all South Africans."

ASIA

CHINA

Fudan University
http://www.cs.wisc.edu/~mshen/fudan.html
Fudan University is a higher educational facility located in southern China. Visitors to this site will find information about classes, departments, Chinese culture, and the overseas alumni mailing list.

Peking University
http://www.pku.edu.cn
China's Peking University offers this page as a guide to campus academics and information. Visitors can find specific programs and courses offered at this institution, as well as info about research facilities and organizations. Additional Peking resources are also available.

Tsinghua University
http://www.cernet.edu.cn/tsinghua/index.html
Visit the Tsinghua University home page for more details on this Chinese university and its course offerings, library, student life, publications, and more. In Chinese or English.

Xian Jiaotong University
http://www.cs.bham.ac.uk/~yxh/xjtu.html
The Xian Jiaotong University home page, mirrored here in England, provides insight into the school located in Xian, an ancient Chinese city where palace ruins from the Tang Dynasty can be found. Campus photos, tourist information, and other Chinese links are also provided.

HONG KONG

Hong Kong Baptist University
http://www.hkbu.edu.hk
The Hong Kong Baptist University home page provides historical information about the school, along with details on academic programs, campus facilities, publications, and student life. Visitors can also link to the HKBU gopher server to browse additional university resources.

Hong Kong Polytechnic University
http://cwis.polyu.edu.hk
Hong Kong Polytechnic University provides an index to information about the school and its services at this site. Areas covered include academics, students, library, research, personnel, computing, and campus activities.

INDIA

Indian Colleges/Institutes/Universities
http://www.cs.wisc.edu/~shubu/iitk/colleges.html
This is a comprehensive database of the more than 400 universities and colleges in the nation of India. Visitors can search and link to the home pages of many of these educational institutions.

JAPAN

Chiba University
http://www.hike.te.chiba-u.ac.jp/chiba-u
Take a trip to Japan at the Chiba University home page. Guests to the page can listen to the university anthem, learn more about university academics, policies, faculty, students, and the Chiba region, and connect to campus servers. Available in Japanese and English.

Ehime University
http://ccs42.dpc.ehime-u.ac.jp:8000
The Ehime University site indexes information about the Japanese school's academic departments and faculty. An overview of the university can be found here, along with general facts about Japan and a cybertour of the Matsuyama Beer Garden.

Fukuoka Junior College of Technology
http://www.fjct.fit.ac.jp
Fukuoka Junior College of Technology welcomes browsers to this page with an introduction to its campus location, various laboratories, and staff. The information here is available in English, Japanese, and limited Chinese.

Fukushima University
http://www.fukushima-u.ac.jp
Fukushima University gives visitors a look at the university and its surrounding community here. The site includes departmental information, as well as dozens of links to sites about Fukushima, Japan, and other Japanese universities. Available in Japanese and English, the site is enhanced by photos, audio clips, and even a QuickTime movie.

Gunma University
http://www.la.gunma-u.ac.jp
Gunma University, Japan, provides information here on academic departments, courses of study, and faculty listings. Includes links to student services, admissions information, and pointers to other Japanese resources. In English and Japanese.

Hirosaki University
http://www.hirosaki-u.ac.jp/index-j.html
Information on and resources from Hirosaki University in Japan are available at this site. Included are links to servers at the university's schools and faculties, and to other servers in the Tohoku area. Available in Japanese and English.

Hiroshima City University
http://www.hiroshima-cu.ac.jp
Hiroshima City University's fundamental principle is to become "an international university which contributes to world peace and to the prosperity of the community through education and research in science and art." Find out more at the HCU home page. In English and Japanese.

Hiroshima Shudo University
http://www.shudo-u.ac.jp
Hiroshima Shudo University's home page includes both general and detailed information about the university and features a link to a page about the bomb monuments at the Peace Park. In English and Japanese.

Hiroshima University
http://www.hiroshima-u.ac.jp
Japan's Hiroshima University invites browsers to see a bird's eye view of the campus, explore campus maps, and learn about its dozens of departments. Includes a university-wide "Who's Who" directory. In English and Japanese.

Kagoshima University

http://www.kagoshima-u.ac.jp

Information from Japan's Kagoshima University comes to the Web through the college's home page. It features program details, as well as information about current research projects and links to the college's library. In Japanese, with a link to a complete English version.

Kanazawa University

http://kipcwww.ipc.kanazawa-u.ac.jp:8080

Japan's Kanazawa University maintains this site for its international student guide and index to Internet resources. Visit here to learn about the university and its programs and find links to electronic information services in Japan. In Japanese and English.

Keio University

http://www.keio.ac.jp

The Keio University home page is full of info on the areas of study at its five campuses, including economics, law, and medicine. Keio offers undergraduate and graduate programs and is affiliated with numerous junior and senior high schools. In English and Japanese.

Keio University, Shonan Fujisawa Campus

http://www.sfc.keio.ac.jp

The Web server for Keio University's Shonan Fujisawa Campus provides info on SFC's media center, academic and research activities, student organizations, and more. Also find links to personal home pages and Web manuals. In Japanese and English.

Kobe City University of Foreign Studies

http://www.kobe-cufs.ac.jp

The Kobe City University of Foreign Studies in Kobe, Japan, maintains this site for general information. Visit here to learn about its campus, programs, faculty, and students. Information about the 1995 Kobe earthquake is also available here.

Kobe University

http://www.kobe-u.ac.jp

Japan's Kobe University invites visitors to its home page to learn more about the university—its programs, projects, and personnel—as well as the town in which it is located, Kobe City. Information on Japan is also provided.

Kochi National College of Technology

http://www.kochi-ct.ac.jp

The Kochi National College of Technology server offers students and prospective students campus information, university news, and links to specific departments and programs. Links to other Japanese servers for tourism, education, and youth activities are provided. In Japanese and English.

Kumamoto National College of Technology

http://www.cs.knct.ac.jp

Kumamoto National College of Technology presents general information, its college guide, and details on its departments at this Web site. There are links to pages within the college and elsewhere. In Japanese and English.

Kumamoto University

http://www.eecs.kumamoto-u.ac.jp/index.html

Kumamoto University's home page provides visitors with information on Kumamoto prefecture, sightseeing information, and details about the university itself, including links to departmental sites. In Japanese and English.

Kyoto Institute of Technology

http://www.kit.ac.jp

Japan's Kyoto Institute of Technology maintains this home page offering a look at life on campus. Visitors can learn more about the institute, explore its departments and class offerings, and link to related sites. In Japanese and English.

Kyoto University

http://www.kyoto-u.ac.jp/English

Kyoto University, located in Kyoto, Japan, presents information on the university's academic departments and includes a map of the main campus. Links to Japanese Web sites and the Virtual Tourist are provided.

Kyushu Home Page List

http://www.karrn.ad.jp/const/click-e.html

The Kyushu click map links visitors to the servers of the island's colleges and institutes, including Kyushu Institute of Technology, Kyushu University, and Saga University. A searchable list also is provided, as is a Japanese version.

Kyushu Institute of Technology

http://www.kyutech.ac.jp

Kyutech provides information about its academic programs here. The page also includes an entrance exam guide and access to the institute's FTP archive. In English or Japanese.

Kyushu University

http://www.kyushu-u.ac.jp/kyushu-u/INDEX-j.html

Kyushu University's home page includes a link to a campus map in Japanese, information about public transportation to the university, and other campus info. In Japanese with some English.

Meiji University

http://www.meiji.ac.jp

Meiji University in Surugadai, Japan, maintains this informational site. Visit here to learn about its campus, programs, faculty, museums, and library services. Available in Japanese and English.

Meisei University, Ome Campus

http://www.meisei-u.ac.jp/index-e.html

Meisei University's Ome Campus provides information on academic departments, courses of study, and faculty at this test site. Includes info on campus facilities, student organizations, extracurricular events, and links to area servers. Visitors can even listen to the campus song.

Miyazaki University

http://www.miyazaki-u.ac.jp

Miyazaki University's site contains information on academic departments, courses of study, and faculty profiles. Includes info on Internet services, campus FTP servers, and links to university servers. English and Japanese.

Muroran Institute of Technology

http://www.muroran-it.ac.jp

The home page of the Muroran Institute of Technology, Japan, provides general information and links to departmental home pages and related sites. In Japanese and English.

Musashi Institute of Technology

http://www.musashi-tech.ac.jp

The Musashi Institute of Technology home page contains information on the various schools of engineering, programs of study, and research centers. Includes info on admissions, faculty, and links to other Japanese servers. Japanese and English.

Nagasaki University

http://www.cc.nagasaki-u.ac.jp

The 50th anniversary of the atomic bombing of Nagasaki is one of the interesting links at NUNet, the Web site of Nagasaki University's information infrastructure. University, regional and Web information is also here—some in English, most in Japanese.

Nagoya University

http://www.nagoya-u.ac.jp/index-e.html

The home page of Japan's Nagoya University is available in both Japanese and English. Link to campus maps, software development pages, conferencing information, and individual academic departments from Education to Medicine.

Nanzan University

gopher://gopher.nanzan-u.ac.jp:70/1

Nanzan University in Nagoya, Japan, maintains this gopher server to provide information on its Japanese studies programs. Get general campus and academic details here as well as events and research activities. Available in English and Japanese.

Niigata University

http://www.cc.niigata-u.ac.jp

Japan's Niigata University spells out information about academics and programs here, along with a section on research and attached schools. In Japanese and English.

Oita University

http://www.oita-u.ac.jp

Japan's Oita University offers department and research information at this site, pinpointing its location through maps and directions. Anyone interested in knowing more about Oita City, the home of the university, will find those details here. In English and Japanese.

Okayama Prefectural University

http://www.oka-pu.ac.jp

Okayama Prefectural University offers this gateway to its many Web servers. Resources available here include the departmental, computing, and laboratory facility home pages, as well as library services and general university-related info. In Japanese and English.

Osaka Kyoiku University

http://okumedia.cc.osaka-kyoiku.ac.jp

The home page for Osaka Kyoiku University in Osaka, Japan, has only a few pages available in English at this time, including a general introduction and K-12 information.

Osaka University

http://www.osaka-u.ac.jp/Osaka-u.html

Osaka University's Web server goes beyond providing academic information; it offered news of a recent local earthquake when we last visited, with mirror sites available. Three Japanese versions of the page are available, as well as an English language page.

Reitaku University

http://www.reitaku-u.ac.jp

Reitaku University offers home pages in English, Japanese, and German. This gateway page connects visitors with information (in their choice of language) about the Japanese school, along with a university photo album showing various campus buildings.

Ritsumeikan University

http://www.ritsumei.ac.jp

Ritsumeikan University in Japan unveils its programs and campus news through this Web site, which can be read in English with a link to a Japanese page. The page also features information about related high schools and junior high schools.

Saga University

http://www.cc.saga-u.ac.jp

Saga University's home page provides information about this Japanese school. In addition to academic information, tourist and event guides can be accessed from this Web site. Text available in English or Japanese.

Sophia University Home Page

http://www.sophia.ac.jp

Japan's Sophia University presents its home page with info on admissions, alumni events, and a "What's New" link. In English and Japanese.

SUNTechno College

http://www.suntech.ac.jp

The SUN in SUNTechno College stands for Scholarship, Universe, and Network. STC's site contains information on academic departments, courses of study, and faculty profiles. Also includes a listing of personal home pages, general campus services, and links to other servers. In Japanese and English.

Teikyo University

http://www.teikyo-u.ac.jp

Teikyo University's home page offers a message from the school's president and information on the system's various campuses. Visitors also will find entrance requirements for numerous scholastic programs. In Japanese and English.

Tohoku University

http://www.tohoku.ac.jp/index-e.html

Tohoku University in Sendai, Japan, provides institutional information and links to its campus networks here. Includes a guide to the city of Sendai. English and Japanese versions are available.

Tokyo Denki University

http://www.dendai.ac.jp

The Tokyo Denki University home page features general information about the school and links to other university Web servers. Special reports and announcements of job openings also appear. In English with links to Japanese.

Tokyo Institute of Technology

http://www.titech.ac.jp

The Tokyo Institute of Technology is a higher educational facility located in Japan. Visitors to the site will find transportation guides, campus maps, and a general overview of Titech's academic programs. This page is provided in both English and Japanese.

Tokyo Woman's Christian University

http://www.twcu.ac.jp

The Tokyo Woman's Christian University links to its anonymous FTP server and offers an art gallery of student works, a database of access technology for the visually impaired, and Internet links, all in Japanese.

Toyama University

http://www.toyama-u.ac.jp

Toyama University in Toyama, Japan, maintains this site for general information and resource access. Visit here to learn about its programs and

people, contact staff members, and link to a variety of Internet search tools. Available in Japanese and English.

University of Aizu, Faculty Pofiles Brochure

http://www.u-aizu.ac.jp/brochure/Contents.html

Japan's University of Aizu provides this faculty site containing detailed information on researchers and professors at the university, whose motto is "People Advancing Knowledge for Humanity." Includes links to university servers, departmental pages, and illustrations.

University of Tokushima

http://www.tokushima-u.ac.jp

Located in Tokushima, Shikoku, Japan, the University of Tokushima invites visitors to its home page to learn more about the university, its history, and its organization. Links to sites of interest on and off campus are provided. In English and Japanese.

University of Tokyo

http://www.u-tokyo.ac.jp

The University of Tokyo maintains this experimental site of general information about its undergraduate and graduate schools, institutes, and facilities. Links to Internet resources are also featured. Available in Japanese and English.

University of Tokyo, Komaba Campus

http://www.c.u-tokyo.ac.jp/index.html

The Komaba Campus of the University of Tokyo maintains this site for general information. Visit here to learn about its campus, programs, faculty, and students. Links to a variety of other informational sites, including Internet country codes, local weather conditions, and more.

University of Tsukuba

http://www.tsukuba.ac.jp

The home page of Japan's University of Tsukuba provides info on its academic programs—with emphasis on mathematics and science—and offers access to the campus library catalog. Available in both English and Japanese, the site also points to a variety of Web servers in Japan.

Utsunomiya University

http://www.utsunomiya-u.ac.jp

Kegon, the integrated information network of Japan's Utsunomiya University, maintains a Web site in English and Japanese with information about the school. An image map of the campus gives details of selected spots.

Wakayama University

http://www.wakayama-u.ac.jp

Japan's Wakayama University invites prospective students to review its educational programs and

176 EDUCATION

campus facilities at this home page. Visitors can explore academic life in Japan as well as the tourism and industry of the Wakayama Prefecture. In English and Japanese.

Waseda University
http://www.waseda.ac.jp/index-j.html

Japan's Waseda University leaves little out when it comes to general information about the campus and academic programs. This comprehensive package digs deep into degree and research details, reaching both potential students and alumni. In Japanese and English.

KOREA

Inha University
http://nms.inha.ac.kr

The Inha Multimedia Information System provides a searchable collection of pages about Korea's Inha University and serves as a gateway to information about the district of Inchon. Visitors can read the latest campus news here.

Korea University
http://www.korea.ac.kr

Check out the academic programs and campus of Korea University through the school's home page. Visitors can also read a history of the college and find out about faculty and staff in different departments. In Korean with some English.

Pusan Women's University
http://lotus.pwu.ac.kr

Find out about Pusan Women's University in Korea through this home page, which reveals the college's history and programs. Also gives a glimpse of the city and a preview of the 14th Asian Games scheduled to be held in Pusan in 2002.

Seoul National University
http://www.snu.ac.kr

Seoul National University is a higher educational facility located in Korea. Visitors to this site will find departmental overviews, plus information on faculty, research, programs of study, and student organizations.

Sogang University
http://www.sogang.ac.kr

Students of Sogang University, a Catholic college in Korea, can visit this home page to learn about the school's history or to check rules and regulations. Information about courses and faculty is also included here. In English and Korean.

MACAU

University of Macau
http://www.umac.mo

The University of Macau in East Asia supplies information at this home page about the campus, admissions, academics, services, and the like. The site includes pages on centers and faculties, including the Faculties of Education, Law, and Business Administration.

MALAYSIA

Universiti Sains Malaysia
http://www.cs.usm.my

USM in Penang gives an overview of its programs and departments here, plus a calendar of events. The site also contains information on Penang Island.

Universiti Teknologi Malaysia
http://www.utm.my

Learn about the Universiti Teknologi Malaysia's two campuses, administrative and student services, and research activities here. Faculty and facility information is available as well, along with events listings and information on books and journals published by the school.

PHILIPPINES

De La Salle University
http://www.dlsu.edu.ph

Located in the Philippines, De La Salle University invites visitors to its Web page to learn more about the university, its history, academic programs, faculty, and student services. Links to other LaSallian Schools are also available.

Mindanao State University, Iligan Institute of Technology
http://www.msuiit.edu.ph

The Iligan Institute of Technology, one of the seven campuses of Mindanao State University in the Philippines, maintains this site for general information and Internet resources. Visitors will learn about the MSU-ITT campus, programs, faculty, and students. Links to a variety of Internet search tools are also available.

University of San Carlos
http://www.usc.edu.ph

Located in Cebu City, the Philippines, the University of San Carlos invites visitors and prospective students to its home page to tour its campus, explore its academic opportunities, and meet the faculty and students. Links to sites of interest both on and off campus are provided.

SINGAPORE

Nanyang Technological University
http://www.ntu.ac.sg

Nanyang Technological University is a public educational facility located in Singapore. Visitors to this informational site can take a virtual tour of the university's different schools, research and development opportunities, academic services, alumni, and more.

National University of Singapore
http://www.nus.sg/NUShome.html

The National University of Singapore offers a wealth of information at its home page, including the usual campus info, plus teaching vacancies, a calendar of events, and academic linkages with overseas universities. Netscape-capable visitors can also take a cybertour of the NUS campus.

Ngee Ann Polytechnic
http://www.np.ac.sg

Singapore's Ngee Ann Polytechnic, "preparing you for tomorrow's challenges," provides this detailed look at life on campus. Find a campus map and tour the facilities, review the academic departments and support centers, find out about student services and organizations, and read the campus publications.

Singapore Polytechnic
http://www.sp.ac.sg/home.html

Singapore Polytechnic presents visitors with a clickable map to access information about the engineering technology institute. A campus map is provided as are selected press clippings about the school and its graduates.

Temasek Polytechnic
http://www.tp.ac.sg

Temasek Polytechnic, Singapore, features its educational resources at this site with links to detailed course information, the TP Graduates Association, and much more.

TAIWAN

Academia Sinica
http://www.sinica.edu.tw

Browsing in both Chinese and English is accommodated at the Academia Sinica's World Wide Web information server. Individual institutes and programs are listed here, along with access to the library, gopher, and news services.

Academia Sinica

gopher://gopher.sinica.edu.tw

The gopher server at the Computing Center of Academia Sinica in Taipei, Taiwan, provides Chinese-language instruction and assistance in using various Internet search tools. It also provides information about the general course offerings at Academia Sinica.

Chung Cheng University

http://www.ccu.edu.tw/

Chung Cheng University's home page provides information on academic departments, courses of study, and faculty listings. Includes links to other Taiwan sites, news items, and a collection of Web sites. In English and Chinese.

National Chiao Tung University

http://www.nctu.edu.tw

The home page for the National Chiao Tung University offers admissions, registration, historical, course selection, and other information about this Chinese school. Mostly in Chinese.

National Taiwan Normal University

http://www.ntnu.edu.tw

The home page for the National Taiwan Normal University includes general information on the school, its academic departments, courses of study, and student life. Mostly in Chinese.

THAILAND

Bangkok University

http://www.bu.ac.th

Thailand's Bangkok University provides an overview of academic and campus life here. The site includes interactive maps, campus news and links to its gopher server.

Khon Kaen University

http://www.kku.ac.th

In addition to the usual college info, the home page for Khon Kaen University in Thailand features links to general information about Thailand as well as details of the total solar eclipse that could be seen in the country in 1995.

AUSTRALIA/ OCEANIA

AUSTRALIA

The Australian Defence Force Academy

http://www.adfa.oz.au

The Australian Defence Force Academy home page contains information on academic departments, programs of study and military training courses. Includes background on the Academy, info on student life, faculty profiles and details on the officer leadership programs.

Australian Defence Force Academy

gopher://gopher.adfa.oz.au:70/1

The Australian Defence Force Academy, a joint undertaking between the University of New South Wales and the Australian Defence Force, provides this gopher site. Among the resources here are calendars, database searches and information on departments, research, library services and sports.

Australian International Hotel School

http://hotelschool.cornell.edu/aihs

The Australian International Hotel School in Canberra specializes in the education of hospitality industry professionals. Visit this home page to read about the school's academic programs, student activities and affiliations.

Australian National University

http://cis.anu.edu.au/anu/contents.html

The home page for the Australian National University in Canberra contains information about academic departments, programs of study and admissions guidelines, with pointers to research groups, student services and campus facilities.

Bond University

http://bond.edu.au

Australia's first private independent university, Bond University in Queensland maintains this home page to provide information on academic departments, programs of study and admissions criteria. Includes a staff index, descriptions of student services and special educational and research programs.

Claremont College

http://www.clare.tased.edu.au

Located in Hobart, Tasmania, Australia, Claremont College invites visitors to its home page to review the campus photo album and academic programs. Links to sites of interest on and off campus are provided.

Curtin University of Technology

http://www.curtin.edu.au

Australia's Curtin University of Technology introduces its students, faculty and facilities via Curtin Link. Explore Curtin's academic departments and libraries or check out its hot list of Internet sites.

Edith Cowan University

http://www.cowan.edu.au

The Edith Cowan University in Perth, Western Australia, maintains this site for its campus-wide information service. Visitors will find faculty and student directories, departmental course offerings, computer services, library collections, employment opportunities and other academic resources.

Flinders University

http://www.flinders.edu.au

The Flinders University of South Australia in Adelaide maintains this site of general information and Internet resources. Visit here to learn about its campus, programs, faculty and students.

Griffith University

http://www.gu.edu.au

The home page of Australia's Griffith University serves as an online brochure of general information about the school. Academic programs, publications and a student directory are featured.

James Cook University

http://www.jcu.edu.au

The James Cook University home page contains information on this North Queensland university's academic departments, general and administrative services, faculty listings and campus info sites. Includes links to remote services.

La Trobe University

http://www.latrobe.edu.au

The La Trobe University home page supplies general information and statistics regarding its students, faculty, curriculum and campus life in Bundoora. Also featured are links to associated Internet sites.

Macquarie University

http://www.mq.edu.au

Australia's Macquarie University offers access to its general information services at this site. University-only information exists side-by-side with descriptions of academic programs and student life.

Monash University

http://www.monash.edu.au

The home page for Monash University, "Australia's international university," contains departmental and admissions information. In addition, visitors will find such resources as university services and directories, faculty handbooks, newsletters and reports.

Northern Territory University

http://www.ntu.edu.au

Northern Territory University in Australia features links to its library along with profiles of the faculty and administration on a colorful home page. Visitors can view student resources, read about academic departments and programs or search for individuals through the phone and e-mail directory.

Queensland University of Technology

http://www.qut.edu.au

Queensland University of Technology in Brisbane, Australia, provides campus maps and a bus timetable here, along with general information on its students and staff. Includes links to university library and counseling services.

Royal Melbourne Institute of Technology

http://www.rmit.edu.au

Australia's Royal Melbourne Institute of Technology provides information about its campus, programs, faculty and students. Visit here to learn about RMIT and link to affiliated organizations.

University of Adelaide

http://www.adelaide.edu.au

The University of Adelaide home page provides information on programs of study, academic departments, faculty listings and admissions at this South Australia university. Includes info on student services, campus publications, facilities and computer support.

University of Ballarat

http://www.ballarat.edu.au

University of Ballarat students and others wishing to know more about this Australian university can visit and learn about programs offered to the over 4,000 students as well as administrative policies.

University of Canberra

http://www.canberra.edu.au

The University of Canberra (Australia) presents a vast storehouse of info at its campus-wide information service site, including the university handbook, course info, an events calendar, a campus map and Internet resources, to name just a few.

University of Melbourne

http://www.unimelb.edu.au

At the campus information system for the University of Melbourne, Australia, visitors will find university news and events updates, phone and e-mail directory services, links to faculties and departments, and information on research projects.

University of New England

http://www.une.edu.au

Prospective students can retrieve academic, administrative and community information from the home page Australia's University of New England in New South Wales.

University of New South Wales

http://www.unsw.edu.au

Australia's University of New South Wales offers links to its academic departments as well as to other Australian universities, institutions and laboratories. This site also allows visitors to access the university's library catalog.

University of Queensland

http://www.uq.edu.au

The University of Queensland's Web Server introduces visitors to the school's digitalized resources, from its gopher server to news of its external affairs and community services. Student home pages and a listing of staff vacancies are also provided.

University of Southern Queensland

http://www.usq.edu.au

Poke around the campus of the University of Southern Queensland by way of its Funnel Web site. Access people and academic departments for a general view of the school's educational resources and opportunities.

University of Sydney

http://www.usyd.edu.au

The University of Sydney provides information about the campus here. Browsers will find data about libraries, administraion and links to the outside world.

University of Tasmania

gopher://info.utas.edu.au:70/1

This gopher server highlights the University of Tasmania, linking visitors to its various departments and libraries, administrative, computing and networking services, and other information archives.

University of Technology, Sydney

http://www.uts.edu.au

The University of Technology in Sydney, Australia, maintains this site for general information and Internet resources. Visit here to learn about its campus, academic programs and people. Information about its Internet-related courses, such as Website authoring, is also available.

University of Western Sydney, Macarthur

http://www.macarthur.uws.edu.au

The Macarthur campus of Australia's University of Western Sydney offers campus news and educational informational services at this site. Use Macarthur Web to browse the library catalog or contact the school's research offices.

University of Western Sydney, Nepean

http://www.nepean.uws.edu.au

InfoNepean, the campus information system of the University of Western Sydney at Nepean, provides information about its staff, academic and research opportunities, policies and library. Visitors can also connect with other UWS campuses and a variety of Internet resources.

University of Wollongong

http://www.uow.edu.au

The University of Wollongong is a public education facility located in Australia. Its site contains information on the school's academic programs, faculty, departments, clubs and social activities.

NEW ZEALAND

Massey University

http://www.massey.ac.nz

The home page of Massey University in Palmerston North, New Zealand, contains a variety of information about the university's departments, students, faculty, library and resources.

University of Otago

http://www.otago.ac.nz

The University of Otago in Dunedin, New Zealand, profiles its academic programs along with the campus and faculty through its home page. The site includes links to campus maps and maps of the region.

CARIBBEAN ISLANDS

University of the Virgin Islands

http://www.uvi.edu/

At the central Web server for the University of the Virgin Islands, visitors will find information on academic departments, campus news, and Virgin Island cultural connections on the Internet.

University of the West Indies

http://www.uwimona.edu.jm/

The home page for the University of West Indies in Mona, Jamaica, provides information regarding academic departments, campus events, and student life, as well as an Internet directory service.

EUROPE

AUSTRIA

University of Graz

http://www.kfunigraz.ac.at/

Austria's University of Graz maintains this Web server, hosting a range of info about the school's academic programs, administrative departments and campus activities. In German.

University of Innsbruck

http://info.uibk.ac.at/

The University of Innsbruck in Austria provides an overview here of its academic departments, research resources and campus life. The page also includes online directories and other administrative information. In English or German.

University of Klagenfurt

http://info.uni-klu.ac.at/

This page acts as a gateway to the campus wide information system of Austria's University of Klagenfurt. Inside, find facts and figures about the university, information on degree programs and student services, links to faculty pages and a calendar of events.

University of Salzburg

http://www.edvz.sbg.ac.at/

The University of Salzburg, Austria, maintains this Web page with information about its faculty, academics, special institutes and details about postgraduate studies. In English and German.

University of Technology

http://iuinfo.tuwien.ac.at/

The University of Technology in Vienna, Austria, offers a sound file of the Blue Danube, stamp-icons to lead visitors through the site and a gracious reminder to watch your manners. It links to academic and national sites as well.

Vienna University of Economics

http://www.wu-wien.ac.at/

The Vienna University of Economics provides information about its departments, academic programs and links to student home pages. In English and German.

BELGIUM

Brussels Free University

http://www.vub.ac.be/

This site is the home page of the Brussels Free University (VUB), featuring the VUBnet network server. Visitors are welcome to tour the university or link to a variety of Web, gopher and other data servers located on the network.

Faculte Polytechnique de Mons

http://www.fpms.ac.be/

Access the Belgian Faculte Polytechnique de Mons server here. Link to university, faculty and academic departmental information at this site. In French.

Free University of Brussels

http://pespmc1.vub.ac.be/VUBULB.html

A professor at the Free University of Brussels takes visitors on a tour of the free university (free means it allows freedom of inquiry and freedom from religious domination). The tour includes a look at the university's Dutch-speaking counterpart. The author is a member of Principia Cybernetica, which hosts this page.

Royal Military Academy of Belgium

http://www.rma.ac.be/

The Royal Military Academy of Belgium (located in Brussels) presents information on its departments and research at this site. There are links to RMA departments and laboratories and to other military schools worldwide. Information is in English, French and Dutch.

Universite Catholique de Louvain

http://www.ucl.ac.be/

The Universite Catholique de Louvain in Belgium is a higher educational facility affiliated with the Catholic Church. Visitors will find information on studies, research, academic departments and faculty. Available in English and French.

University of Antwerp

http://www.ua.ac.be/

The University of Antwerp comprises three Belgian universities. This home page offers directory services, study guides, library services, local information and a link to the Belgian Academic Network. Some pages in Dutch, some in English.

University of Antwerp, Universitaire Instelling Antwerpen

http://www.uia.ac.be/

The Universitaire Instelling Antwerpen campus of Belgium's University of Antwerp maintains this gateway to information about the university and its information server. Also features a campus directory and student info.

University of Ghent

http://www.rug.ac.be/

The bilingual English/Dutch home page for Belgium's University of Ghent provides info on the various faculties, departments and laboratories, as well as student activities and an online campus telephone directory.

Vesalius College

http://www.vub.ac.be/VECO/VECO-intro.html

Visitors to this site will find admissions and degree program information about Vesalius College in Brussels, Belgium. Academic opportunities and school facilities are outlined.

BULGARIA

American University in Bulgaria

http://www.aubg.bg/

Academic programs and services offered by the American University in Bulgaria are outlined at the school's Web site. Faculty listings and information about student government and other student-run organizations can also be found here.

CROATIA

University of Zagreb

http://www.zvne.etf.hr/uniinfo.html

The University of Zagreb, Croatia, provides an overview of its 25 faculties and colleges here. The page also includes a historical perspective and an online university directory.

CZECH REPUBLIC

Charles University

gopher://gopher.cuni.cz:70/1

The gopher at the Computer Centre for Charles University in Prague, Czech Republic, features links to other gophers in the country and public information services. Highlights include links to the Czech Educational and Scientific Network and the Prague Academic and Scientific Network.

Czech Technical University

http://www.cvut.cz/default.htm

Czech Technical University in Prague provides information about its people and programs. Visit here to learn about the university and link to various engineering and science faculty information servers.

Technical University of Liberec

http://www.vslib.cz/

The home page for the Czech Republic's Technical University of Liberec contains information on academic departments, programs of study and faculty profiles. Also includes admissions guidelines, campus services and links to university servers.

DENMARK

Aalborg University

http://www.auc.dk/

At the home page for Aalborg University in Denmark, visitors will find details on the university's departments, facilities and student organizations.

Roskilde University

http://www.ruc.dk/

This Web site provides information about Roskilde University, a non-traditional Danish school. Visitors will find maps of the university and its surroundings, plus administrative and departmental information in both English and Danish.

University of Copenhagen

http://www.ku.dk/welcome-e.html

The University of Copenhagen, Denmark, maintains this site for general information and resource access. Visitors learn about its campus, programs, faculty and students. In Danish and English.

ENGLAND

Anglia Polytechnic University

http://www.anglia.ac.uk/

Anglia Polytechnic University offers information about the school, its news (including a database of the staff's areas of expertise), master's degree in education classes on the Internet, and home pages put up by others at this UK school.

Aston University

http://www.aston.ac.uk/home.html

Aston University in Birmingham, England, presents campus and course information here. Visitors can also browse the faculty biographies, and look at engineering energy rearch group findings, health studies and more.

Birbeck College

http://www.bbk.ac.uk/

The home page of Birbeck College at the University of London provides an overview of the college, its academic departments and programs of study. Includes pointers to campus services, descriptions of facilities and resources and links to other servers in the London area.

The Cambridge Panorama

http://www.cam-orl.co.uk/cgi-bin/pangen

This site offers a view of Cambridge University as seen from the rooftop of the Olivetti Research Laboratory. Visitors to this page can link to Cambridge's online resources, such as the school's statistical laboratory, library and press. Available in English or Italian.

City University

http://web.city.ac.uk/

City University in London, England, maintains this home page offering visitors a look at university life. Features include information on academic programs and research projects as well as facilities, faculty, and policies.

Cranfield University

http://www.cranfield.ac.uk/

Cranfield University, UK, is a leading international center for the generation and application of knowledge in engineering, science, manufacturing and management. The school offers predominantly post-graduate courses, and its Web page has more information about the school, academics, location and research.

Goldsmiths College

http://www.gold.ac.uk/

Goldsmiths College is a liberal arts institution, part of London University. Visitors to this home page will find information on the school's academic offerings, along with student information and links to the college's Web servers and research pages.

King's College Cambridge

http://www.kings.cam.ac.uk/

A constituent college of the renowned University of Cambridge, King's College offers inside information on all aspects of its student and faculty life. A user-friendly interface lets you navigate through the college's user pages, directories and facilities, read about the chapel, or access a wealth of school-related resources.

King's College London

http://www.kcl.ac.uk/

The Kings College London site contains descriptions of its academic departments, library and student unions as well as numerous links to sites that pertain to London. Includes an enquiries and comments section.

Kingston University

http://www.kingston.ac.uk/

The UK's Kingston University provides information on its faculties, schools and departments, as well as directories of staff and students. This site also has information about Kingston-upon-Thames, a listing of servers at the university and links to Web resources.

Lancaster University

http://www.lancs.ac.uk/

The Lancaster University (UK) site provides general information on academic departments, research projects, faculty and staff. There are also descriptions of services, recreation, admissions requirements and news items.

Liverpool John Moores University

http://www.livjm.ac.uk/

Liverpool John Moores University provides general details about this UK institution along with academic and course particulars, at this site. This page also links browsers to various Liverpool resources and sports organizations and offers online career services.

London School of Economics and Political Science

http://www.blpes.lse.ac.uk/

The London School of Economics and Political Science gives an overview of its programs, courses, staff and club here. The site also includes access to the British Library of Political and Economic Science.

Manchester Metropolitan University

http://www.doc.mmu.ac.uk/mapp.html

The UK's Manchester Metropolitan University hosts this site providing information on its academics, admissions, administration, students, research and faculty. Browsers can link to a score of departmental pages here.

Nottingham Trent University

http://www.ntu.ac.uk/

The home page for Nottingham Trent University offers information on curriculum and programs at this British university. There are also links to specific departments and resources about the outside world.

The Open University of the United Kingdom

http://www.open.ac.uk/

The Open University of the United Kingdom, founded in 1969, has no entry requirements for most of its courses. Included here is information about its degrees offered and academic departments. Studying at the Open University via the Internet is explained here.

Oxford University

http://www.ox.ac.uk/

England's Oxford University Networked Information Service provides links to the main university home page as well as to individual academic departments. There is also access to the library and campus computing services.

Queen Mary and Westfield College

http://www.qmw.ac.uk/

Queen Mary and Westfield College is a higher educational facility located in London, England. Visitors to the QMW site will find academic department servers, campus news and information on students and faculty.

Royal Holloway

http://www.rhbnc.ac.uk/

The home page for the Royal Holloway country campus of the University of London offers information about the Royal Holloway Art Collection, a campus map and virtual campus tour, a Department of Music calendar and much more.

Southampton University

http://www.soton.ac.uk/UofS.html

The UK's University of Southampton provides an electronic presentation of general information about its academic programs and educational opportunities. Link to department resources, campus event calendars and more.

South Bank University

http://www.sbu.ac.uk/

London's South Bank University offers a general overview of its academic programs and educational facilities. Visitors can review research opportunities, university publications and student organizations.

UK Academic Sites

http://src.doc.ic.ac.uk/uk-academic.html

If you're shopping for higher education resources in the United Kingdom, consult the directory of

servers provided at the UK Academic Sites page. Find an extensive list of links to universities and their internal departments at this site.

UK Sensitive Map - Academic
http://scitsc.wlv.ac.uk/ukinfo/uk.map.html

England's University of Wolverhampton sponsors this interactive map that links to all UK colleges and universities on the Web. Jump to Newcastle University, Leeds Metro, Andover and Bournemouth, and more listings in London than you can shake a mouse at, including the famous London School of Economics.

University College London
http://www.ucl.ac.uk/

University College London provides college-wide information plus phone and e-mail directories with links to external directories at this site. Also featured are the standard guidelines on departments, policies and so on.

University of Bath
http://www.bath.ac.uk/

This home page provides general information about England's University of Bath and its surrounding area. Available courses of study, research programs and student services are featured.

University of Birmingham
http://www.bham.ac.uk/

Details on this British university's courses, schools and departments are provided here. Other site features include a campus map and information on the city of Birmingham.

University of Bradford
http://www.brad.ac.uk/

The Peace Studies Department at England's University of Bradford is the world's largest university center for peace studies. The Bradford home page provides a general overview of life on campus. Information on student services, faculty, facilities and academic programs is presented.

University of Brighton
http://www.bton.ac.uk/

The University of Brighton, UK, maintains this site with information about its facilities and academics. Visitors can also read the university prospectus, and link to departmental and faculty pages and other campus information centers here.

University of Bristol
http://www.bris.ac.uk/

The University of Bristol is a higher educational facility located in England. Visitors to the site will find campus directories, maps and an overview of academic departments and faculty.

University of Cambridge
http://www.cam.ac.uk/

The World Wide Web Server for the UK's University of Cambridge contains information about the college and departments, e-mail addresses of students and faculty, the library catalogue and links to Internet search engines.

University of Derby
http://www.derby.ac.uk/

The UK's University of Derby home page supplies an interactive tour as well as information on research, entry requirements, services, learning resources, library and more. Also included here are a phone directory, maps and addresses.

University of East Anglia
http://cpca3.uea.ac.uk/welcome.html

Located in Norwich, England, the University of East Anglia maintains this look at life on its campus. Find a QuickTime movie and links to academic departments, research programs and personnel.

University of East London
http://www.uel.ac.uk/

The University of East London introduces itself, its academic programs and its student population via this Web server. Visitors are invited to take a tour of campus and explore studies at the English school.

University of Essex
http://www.essex.ac.uk/

The University of Essex (UK) home page serves as a gateway to the school's Campus Wide Information Service, including admissions, curriculum and directory information. Arts, libraries, charities and sports on campus are among the resources available.

University of Exeter
http://www.ex.ac.uk/

The University of Exeter introduces guests to its "research of international standing," and scholarly pursuits. Prospective students can access links to virtually every aspect of campus life, including a campus press that boasts titles ranging from garden history to linguistics, poetry and maritime studies.

University of Greenwich
http://www.gre.ac.uk/

The University of Greenwich is a higher educational facility located in London, England. Visitors to its central server will find information on courses, research, faculty and academic departments.

University of Hertfordshire
http://www.herts.ac.uk/

The University of Hertfordshire provides information about its academic departments, programs of study and admissions guidelines at this site. Includes links to student services and organizations, campus facilities and administration.

University of Huddersfield
http://www.hud.ac.uk/

The University of Huddersfield in West Yorkshire, England, has set up this home page with information about the school, its faculty and its academic programs. Prospective students can also look over a campus map and get more information about local towns Huddersfield and Kirklees.

The University of Leeds
http://www.leeds.ac.uk/

The University of Leeds, England, provides information here on its academic departments, general services, centers and institutes, and faculty members. Visit here to learn about the university and its graduate and undergraduate courses of study.

University of Leicester
http://www.le.ac.uk/

England's University of Leicester Campus Wide Information System features news and events, job and course vacancies, and general academic information, including details about the city of Leicester.

University of Liverpool
http://www.liv.ac.uk/

Great Britain's University of Liverpool invites visitors to explore the campus, its academic departments and programs, and its facilities. A tour of the Merseyside region is also featured.

University of Manchester
http://www.man.ac.uk/

The home page for the University of Manchester in the United Kingdom provides a wealth of information about the university and the City of Manchester. Read pages on the school's academic programs, departments, administration, publications, faculty and student organizations.

University of North London
http://www.unl.ac.uk/welcome.html

The University of North London features information about its programs and campus facilities at its home page. The site also includes links to local information throughout London.

University of Northumbria, Newcastle
http://www.unn.ac.uk/

The Web server for the UK's University of Northumbria at Newcastle provides links to a variety of information sources within the university community and all over the Internet as well.

The University of Nottingham
http://www.nott.ac.uk/

The home page for the University of Nottingham, UK, provides complete details on the university, its academic departments and services, and research groups. Visitors will also find such features as weather and recreational information here.

University of Plymouth
http://www.plym.ac.uk/

General information about England's University of Plymouth is available here, as well as information about courses, research, facilities and departments. This site also has contact information and photographs.

University of Portsmouth
http://www.port.ac.uk/

This page contains information about the University of Portsmouth, located on Portsea Island on the south coast of England. The page includes a guide to city of Portsmouth, course and faculty information and links to general university publications.

The University of Reading
http://www.reading.ac.uk/

The home page for the University of Reading, UK, provides information on administration, academic departments and services. Visitors can link to such resources as the library and careers advisory here.

University of Sheffield
http://www.shef.ac.uk/

The UK's University of Sheffield Information Service provides a window on academic activities and student life. Access the university's electronic resources, or tour the city of Sheffield and surrounding regions from this site.

University of Sunderland
http://orac.sund.ac.uk/

The University of Sunderland, England, provides information about its program and departments here and posts announcements for its staff and students. The site also contains detailed information on Northeast England.

University of Teesside
http://www.tees.ac.uk/

The UK's University of Teesside promotes its academic programs and research facilities at this site. Link to the campus information server or explore other regional information services from here.

University of the West of England
http://gate.uwe.ac.uk:8000/uwe/uwe.html

The University of the West of England home page contains information on this Bristol-based institution's academic departments, programs of study and faculty profiles. Also includes admissions info, student activities, campus organizations and job listings.

University of Warwick
http://www.warwick.ac.uk/

Located in Coventry, England, the University of Warwick maintains this home page offering a look at life on campus. Visitors are invited to learn more about the university's academic programs, faculty, facilities and student services. Links to sites of interest off campus are provided as well.

University of Wolverhampton
http://www.wlv.ac.uk/

The University of Wolverhampton, England, maintains this site to introduce its people and programs. Visit here for news, staff and student home pages, course offerings, computer services and other academic and administrative resources.

University of York
http://www.york.ac.uk/

Visit this site to learn general information about England's University of York, its academic departments and staff, services and facilities and university events. This page also links to information about the city of York, as well as other Internet resources and sites.

ESTONIA

Tallinn Technical University
http://zaphod.cc.ttu.ee/

Estonia's Tallinn Technical University provides info on its academic programs, faculty and research opportunities. A brief history of the school and links to other Estonian servers are also included.

FINLAND

Espoo-Vantaa Institute of Technology
http://www.evitech.fi/

Located outside Helsinki, Finland, EVITECH maintains this overview of its academic programs. Also find faculty, staff and student home pages, links to services and Web servers, plus information about the Internet, the Web and HTML.

Helsinki University of Technology
http://www.hut.fi/

The Helsinki University of Technology's home page offers general information on the Finnish school's research and academic activities, as well

as news of the academic community in Otaniemi. Provided in English and Finnish.

Jyvaskyla Polytechnic
http://www.jypoly.fi/

The home page for Jyvaskyla Polytechnic, a Finnish higher educational vocational institute, contains info about degree programs and entrance requirements. In Finnish and English.

Lappeenranta University of Technology
http://www.lut.fi/

The home page for Finland's Lappeenranta University of Technology offers links to information services, university departments, and miscellaneous information for students. Primarily of interest to forestry students and instructors, the site includes study guides, documents and links to users' homepages. In English and Finnish.

Oulu Institute of Technology
http://www.otol.fi/

Finland's Oulo Institute of Technology includes info about its academic programs and departments on its home page. Facts about the city of Oulo and a link to the OuloNet regional server are also featured. In Finnish and English.

Tampere University of Technology
http://www.cc.tut.fi/

Finland's Tampere University of Technology posts this overview of its educational and research programs. Also find links to student activities, a campus directory and selected sites of related interest locally and around the world. In Finnish with some English.

University of Helsinki
http://www.helsinki.fi/eindex.html

The University of Helsinki supplies browsers with information about its academic programs, research and organizations on this page. Links to publications and directories are also located here. In English and Finnish.

University of Joensuu
http://cc.joensuu.fi/

The University of Joensuu is a higher educational facility located in Finland. Visitors will find information on academic departments, faculty and study abroad programs.

University of Jyvaskyla
http://www.jyu.fi/

Finland's University of Jyvaskyla home page boasts a bilingual look at its faculty, curriculum and campus services. The site contains information particularly geared toward prospective students.

University of Kuopio

http://www.uku.fi/

The University of Kuopio is an institute in Finland for the study of natural, health and social sciences. Visitors to this site will find information on degree programs, research projects and faculty. In English and Finnish.

University of Tampere

http://www.uta.fi/

The University of Tampere, Finland, maintains this site to introduce its people and programs. Visit here to learn about its departmental course offerings, library collections, upcoming events, academic course offerings and more. Includes staff and student directories. In Finnish and English.

University of Tampere, Institute for Extension Studies Home Page

http://www.sjoki.uta.fi/

The University of Tampere in Seinajoki, Finland, maintains this home page describing its Institute for Extension Studies. Visitors here will find information about the institute's courses, faculty and students. In Finnish only.

University of Turku

http://www.utu.fi/

Finland's University of Turku site contains information about the school, including faculties and a map of the university area. Although mostly in Finnish, some info is available in English.

Vocational Teacher Education College of Jyvaskyla

http://www.vte.fi/

The Vocational Teacher Education College of Jyvaskyla in Finland offers information about its academic programs on the home page. It includes a link to information about the city, as well as pointers to the college's personnel. In Finnish with English links.

FRANCE

American University of Paris

http://www.aup.fr/

The American University of Paris page describes the academic programs available at this institution. Visitors can tour the campus virtually, find out about study-abroad offerings or get admissions info. The page also provides summer school and continuing education links.

Ecole Normale Superieure

http://www.ens.fr/

This informational site sponsored by the Ecole Normale Superieure of Paris offers visitors a tour of the school's academic departments. In French and English.

National Institute of Telecommunications

http://www.int-evry.fr/

France's National Institute of Telecommunications maintains this overview of its campus, academic programs, research projects and services. In French, with English pages under construction when we last visited.

Telecom Bretagne

http://www.enst-bretagne.fr/

Telecom Bretagne, a graduate school of telecommunication engineering in France, presents an overview of its programs and research projects through this home page. The site can be read in French, with English links.

Universite Bordeaux I

http://graffiti.cribx1.u-bordeaux.fr/aqui.html

The Universite Bordeaux, France, maintains this site with information about the school, its research laboratories, links to other university sites and pages and more. In French.

Universite d'Angers

http://www.univ-angers.fr/

Resources about the University of Angers in France are contained at this site. In addition to information about departments, faculties and institutes, there are pointers to the university's networks and other Web resources. The welcome page is available in French, German and English, but most other information is in French.

Universite de Limoges

http://www.unilim.fr/

France's University of Limoges maintains this Web server offering access to an overview of life on campus. Also find a list of French Web servers and FTP sites, plus links to selected sites across Europe and around the world. In French, with English pages under construction when last we checked.

Université des Sciences et Technologies de Lille I

http://www.univ-lille1.fr/

The Universite des Sciences et Technologies de Lille presents an introduction to its research projects and educational programs at this French-language site.

Universite de Tours

http://www.univ-tours.fr/

The 25-year-old University of Tours in France is a multi-disciplinary school with 27,500 students in the wine-producing region of Touraine. The university's Web page provides links to professors, colloquia and Internet services. In French.

Universite d'Orleans

http://web.univ-orleans.fr/index.html

The University of Orleans in France presents information on the campus, programs, services, research projects and library here. In French.

GERMANY

Clausthal Technical University

http://www.tu-clausthal.de/

The University of Clausthal is a technical school located in Germany. Visitors to their site will find information about faculty, courses of study and library access. This service is offered in English and German.

Fachhochschule Augsburg

http://www.fh-augsburg.de/

This Web server is maintained by the Fachhochschule Augsburg. Visitors are invited to learn about the academic programs and student life on campus. In German only.

Free University of Berlin

http://www.fu-berlin.de/

The Free University of Berlin's Web site offers addresses, research, news, academic course listings and departmental information about this German school. In German and English.

Freiburg University

http://www.uni-freiburg.de/

The Freiburg University home page provides a general introduction to the university. It includes information on academic programs, faculty, central services and an overview of the Freiburg state. Mostly in German, with some English.

Gottingen University

http://www.uni-goettingen.de/

The hypermedia information system at Gottingen University in Germany describes the university faculty, student topics, and events, and gives tourist information and maps of the city of Gottingen. Mostly in German with some English.

Hessian State University of Science and Technology

http://www.th-darmstadt.de/

The Hessian State University of Science and Technology in Darmstadt, Germany, maintains this site to introduce its programs and facilities. Visit here for news, course offerings, departmental listings, local area information, and other academic and administrative resources. In German and English.

Humboldt University of Berlin

http://www.rz.hu-berlin.de/

This site provides an overview of Humboldt University of Berlin, its courses of study and faculty.

Includes information on research projects, admissions and links to other servers. In German and English.

Ludwig-Maximilians University

http://www.uni-muenchen.de/index-e.html

The Ludwig-Maximilians University in Munich, Germany, maintains this home page with information about its departments, university resources and links to other institutions and sites in Munich. Most information here is in German, with some pages in English.

Martin-Luther University

http://www.uni-halle.de/

Martin Luther University in Halle-Wittenberg, Germany, provides an overview of its academic departments, faculty, research and campus events. Available in German only.

Technical University of Berlin

http://www.tu-berlin.de/

The Technical University of Berlin home page provides browsers with information about the school's academic programs, a directory of scientific projects, interdisciplinary programs and library resources, among other info. Available only in German.

Technical University of Chemnitz-Zwickau

http://www.tu-chemnitz.de/index-e.html

The Technical University of Chemnitz-Zwickau, Germany, maintains this site offering a look at the university, its academic programs, facilities and student services. Links to related sites on and off campus are also provided. In English and German.

Technical University of Hamburg-Harburg

http://www.tu-harburg.de/

The Technical University of Hamburg-Harburg home page offers visitors information in German about the school, its libraries, academic departments, study programs, stadium and faculty. There are also links to other German servers.

Technical University of Munich

http://www.tu-muenchen.de/

Germany's Technical University of Munich offers a site that provides access to its various departments, research programs and student organizations. A link to the library, helpful maps of the school and town, and updates on current events are also included. In English and German.

University of Bayreuth

http://www.uni-bayreuth.de/

From the home page of Germany's University of Bayreuth, visitors can learn everything they ever wanted to know about the faculty, students, de-

gree programs, and computing facilities of the university. There is also information about the Bayreuth community at large and pointers to myriad off-campus Web sites. In German.

University of Bielefeld

http://www.techfak.uni-bielefeld.de/

The University of Bielefeld, Germany, offers information here on its faculty, research centers, computer services and important events. Includes links to local and national Internet resources. Available in German and English.

University of Dortmund

http://ls6-www.informatik.uni-dortmund.de/WhoIsWhoAtLS6.html

Meet some of the faculty and students from the University of Dortmund (Germany) at this site, where guests can view images of students and staff, get their e-mail addresses or link to their home pages.

University of Erlangen-Nuremberg

http://www.uni-erlangen.de/

The hypertext information system for the University of Erlangen-Nuremberg in Germany links the university, the city of Erlangen and the Bavarian university network together. This handy service is available in English and German.

University of Essen

http://www.uni-essen.de/

The University of Essen in Germany provides information about its programs and faculty through this college home page. The site includes welcoming information. In German with minimal English.

University of Greifswald

http://www.uni-greifswald.de/

The University of Greifswald, Germany, maintains this site to introduce its people and programs. Visitors will find faculty listings, course offerings, computer services and other academic and administrative resources. In German and English.

University of Hamburg

http://www.uni-hamburg.de/

The University of Hamburg maintains this server offering information about the school and the city in which it is located, as well as links to other German Web sites. Among options available, visitors can browse the university's catalog or tour Hamburg and its surrounding countryside. In German and English.

University of Hannover

http://www.uni-hannover.de/

This site provides an overview of the University of Hannover, including information on academic departments, faculty and student institutions. In-

cludes links to servers at the German university and in the Hannover region. Mostly in German

University of Heidelberg

http://www.urz.uni-heidelberg.de/

The University of Heidelberg presents general institutional and program info here. All in German.

University of Hildesheim

http://www.uni-hildesheim.de/

Germany's University of Hildesheim sponsors this home page and invites visitors to learn more about the university, its academic programs, research projects and student services. Available in German.

University of Hohenheim

http://www.uni-hohenheim.de/

The University of Hohenheim's Web server provides information, in both English and German, about this German university. General information about the institution and its coursework and student groups can be found here, along with links to Internet resources.

University of Jena

http://www.uni-jena.de/

This is the Web server for Germany's University of Jena. Visitors will find university news, links to student services, and details on organizations, clubs and unions. Mostly in German.

University of Kaiserslautern

http://www.uni-kl.de/

The University of Kaiserslautern in Germany offers a Web page mostly in German, with departmental and academic as well as administrative links.

Univeristy of Kiel

http://www.uni-kiel.de/

The University of Kiel serves up information about the school's programs at this educational site. In German.

University of Koblenz

http://www.uni-koblenz.de/

The University of Koblenz, Germany, maintains this home page with information about the school, its departments and a link to the Department of Computer Science. This site also features information about the city; in German, with some English.

University of Konstanz

http://www.uni-konstanz.de/

This site is the home page of the Web server at Germany's University of Konstanz. Visitors are invited to explore the university and its academic programs, or follow the links provided to other sites in Konstanz and Germany. In German only.

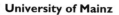

University of Mainz

http://www.uni-mainz.de/Welcome.html

The University of Mainz provides academic and administrative information to visitors of this German site. You can look in on the library and local links and use the FTP archive, gopher server and news lists, but the Webmaster warns visitors that every data transfer costs someone somewhere and requests wise use of the resource. In German and English.

University of Potsdam

http://www.uni-potsdam.de/

The University of Potsdam, Germany, maintains this site of general information about its campus, programs, faculty and students. Available in German and English.

University of Regensburg

http://www.uni-regensburg.de/

The University of Regensburg, Germany, maintains this informational site. Visit here to learn about its campus, programs, faculty and students. Available in German only.

University of Rostock

http://www.uni-rostock.de/

The University of Rostock in Germany offers information about its programs and faculty through this home page. Read about current research and the school's computer resources as well. In German and English.

University of Stuttgart

http://www.uni-stuttgart.de/

The home page for the University of Stuttgart is a German-language site that provides general information about the University of Stuttgart, Germany, and links to Web resources.

University of Trier

http://www.uni-trier.de/

The University of Trier in Germany gives an overview of its programs here. The site also includes access to the university library and posts news of upcoming conferences. In German and English.

University of Ulm

http://www.uni-ulm.de/

The University of Ulm provides an overview of its departments and faculty here. Prospective students can learn about the university's programs of study, student life, organizations and admissions requirements. In German or English.

University of Wurzburg

http://www.uni-wuerzburg.de/

The University of Wurzburg provides a map of its campus and links to academic departments including its computer center. Student listings are also available here. In German and English.

GREECE

Democritus University of Thrace

http://www.cc.duth.gr/

The home page for Democritus University of Thrace provides information on academic departments, programs of study and admissions. Includes faculty listings, links to research groups, descriptions of campus facilities and student life. In English and Greek.

HUNGARY

Hungary University

http://www.fsz.bme.hu/hu-infoservers.html

The Hungary University home page provides a comprehensive overview of department and academic information. Links point to specific disciplines offered at this institution as well as to programs within other educational facilities throughout the country. Available in Hungarian and English.

Jozsef Attila University

http://www.jate.u-szeged.hu/

Josef Attila University in Szeged, Hungary provides information here on its programs, departments, faculty and students. Visit here to learn about the university and its surrounding area. In Hungarian and English.

Lajos Kossuth University of Arts and Sciences

http://www.lib.klte.hu/index.english.html

The Lajos Kossuth University of Arts and Sciences in Hungary offers this campus-wide information server. A wealth of info can be found here on the school's faculty, resources and student activities. Visitors can also link to Web sites with info on the city of Debrecen and local weather forecasts.

ICELAND

University of Iceland

http://www.rhi.hi.is/

The University of Iceland maintains this site with information about its departments, institutes, research and Iceland itself. A searchable campus e-mail directory is also available.

IRELAND

Dublin City University

http://www.dcu.ie/

May the luck of the Irish be with you as you explore Dublin City University's Web site. Review course offerings and student clubs and organizations. When all that mouse clicking has worn you out, visit the Mega Bytes menu to see what you could have for lunch—if you were in Dublin.

Dublin Institute of Technology

http://147.252.133.152/

Ireland's Dublin Institute of Technology invites visitors to its home page to learn more about the school and its academic programs, research and development activities, faculty and student services. Also provided are links to the DIT library and Dublin tourist information.

St. Patrick's College Maynooth

http://www.may.ie/

St. Patrick's College Maynooth provides information here on its people and programs. Visit here to learn about its academic programs in the arts, Celtic studies, philosophy and science. Links to other university sites and international resources are also available here.

University College Dublin

http://www.ucd.ie/

This site contains the home page of University College Dublin in Ireland and offers information about the college, its curriculum and its services. Visitors can explore the campus using a map-based interface, see aerial views of the campus, or link to other sites on campus and off.

University of Dublin, Trinity College

http://www.tcd.ie/

The home page for the Trinity College, the sole constituent college of University of Dublin (Ireland) provides information about the university, courses and departments. Also available at this site is an index of Irish World Wide Web servers and documentation on using the Internet.

University of Limerick

http://www.ul.ie/

Ireland's University of Limerick maintains this overview of its departments, academic programs and student services. A campus directory and related links are also featured, as well as maps and other info for prospective students.

ITALY

International School for Advanced Studies

http://www.sissa.it/

The International School for Advanced Studies is a post-graduate center for teaching and research located in Trieste, Italy. Visitors to this bilingual Web site will find general information on disciplines and activities at the school.

Politecnico di Torino

http://www.polito.it/

Politecnico di Torino, a public university in Turin, Italy, provides information here on its programs and people. Visit here to learn about the university, contact faculty members, access departmental resources and link research activities. In English and Italian.

Scuola Normale Superiore

http://www.sns.it/

Prospective students can visit this Web site to get an overview of programs and degrees offered by the Scuola Normale Superiore in Pisa, Italy. Students can search the library catalog or contact staff members from here. In Italian.

University of Modena

http://www.casa.unimo.it/

Italy's University of Modena offers visitors a glance at its academic programs and educational resources. In Italian.

University of Parma

http://www.unipr.it/

This home page for Italy's University of Parma provides an online catalog of the university's academic programs, course offerings and services. Visitors can learn more about the university as well tour the town of Parma. In Italian and English.

University of Pisa

http://www.unipi.it/welcome.html

The University of Pisa home page presents general information about the Italian university, listings of academic departments and faculty. There's also access to the campus newsletter, info on research programs and student activities. In Italian and English.

University of Trieste

http://www.univ.trieste.it/

The University of Trieste, Italy, provides general information and details on research, teaching activities, computing and library resources at its home page. There are also links to Web and Trieste resources. In Italian and English.

LATVIA

Riga Technical University

http://www.eef.rtu.lv/

The Riga Technical University site contains information about the institution's academic departments, course offerings and faculty members. Also includes details about the Latvian school's research groups, admissions policies and campus services.

NETHERLANDS

Delft University of Technology

http://www.tudelft.nl/

Delft University of Technology is a higher educational facility located in the Netherlands. Visitors can read the weekly campus newspaper and find information on academic departments, research and library resources.

Erasmus University Rotterdam

http://www.eur.nl/

Erasmus Channel, the Web server of Erasmus University Rotterdam, offers information on faculties, organiations, services and facilities at this higher education institution in the Netherlands. There's also a link to Erasmus's foreign exchange program. In English and Dutch.

Hogeschool van Utrecht

http://www.hvu.nl/

The Hogeschool van Utrecht home page offers information about the Dutch school's faculty and coursework. There's also historical information about the school and links to other Web sites. Information is available in English or Dutch.

Katholieke Universiteit Brabant

http://www.kub.nl:2080/

The Netherland's Katholieke Universiteit Brabant maintains this informational site for access to its network of departmental World Wide Web servers. Includes links to student associations and university directories. In Dutch.

University of Amsterdam

http://www.uva.nl/home.html

The University of Amsterdam provides an overview of the the school, its academic departments and course offerings. Includes descriptions of student services, campus facilities, library and faculty. In Dutch.

University of Antwerp, Universitaire Instelling Antwerpen

http://www.uia.ac.be/

The Universitaire Instelling Antwerpen campus of Belgium's University of Antwerp maintains this gateway to information about the university and its information server. Also features a campus directory and student info.

University of Antwerp

http://www.ua.ac.be/index.html

The University of Antwerp's information server gives visitors access to a directory of services, a study guide in Dutch, an academic bibliography of the university, library services and business links. Other regional and world links are also available. In English and Dutch.

University of Groningen

http://www.rug.nl/

The University of Groningen's home page provides information on the Netherlands' second-oldest university, along with links to information services both in and out of the country. In Dutch with limited English translations.

University of Limburg

http://www.rulimburg.nl/

The University of Limburg at Maastricht offers information on its academic departments, faculty and courses of study. Site features also include links to student services, library servers and pointers to outside area resources. In English and Dutch.

University of Nijmegen

http://www.kun.nl/

The University of Nijmegen, located in the Netherlands, maintains this page to offer a look at life on campus. Visitors can view photos of the campus buildings or use the OZIS system to search university research activities and publications. In English and Dutch

University of Twente

http://www.utwente.nl/

The home page for the University of Twente in the Netherlands contains program descriptions, university news updates and online access to the university's library catalog. Text available in Dutch and English.

Utrecht University

http://www.ruu.nl/Home.html

Here, Utrecht University, the Netherlands, details its academic departments and courses of study, with an overview of the institution. Includes information on campus services, organizations, events, symposia and research projects.

Vrije University

http://www.vu.nl/

Visitors to this site will find a general introduction to Vrije University in Amsterdam. Learn about the school's facilities and programs of study, pore over campus maps, or search the university's telecommunication guide here. In Dutch and English.

NORTHERN IRELAND

Queen's University of Belfast

http://www.qub.ac.uk/

The Queen's University of Belfast World Wide Web Information Service serves as a gateway to campus information and electronic resources. Visitors can explore academic, administrative and social institutions at this Northern Ireland university.

University of Ulster

http://www.ulst.ac.uk/

UUWeb is a World Wide Web service operated by the University of Ulster in Northern Ireland. Browsers can read about the university's academic departments and educational facilities or link to a virtual guide to Northern Ireland.

NORWAY

Alesund College
http://www.hials.no/

Alesund College in Norway profiles its programs and employees through this educational home page. The site includes an introduction to the college and maps of Norway. In Norwegian and English.

Bergen College
http://www.hib.no/

This Norwegian university site contains general information about Norway and brief descriptions of Bergen College's courses of study and student population. In Norwegian and English.

Molde College
http://www.himolde.no/

Molde College in Molde, Norway, gives an overview of its programs and research in business administration, economics, informatics, social sciences, and nursing. The site also contains a map of Norway and information on Molde. In English or Norwegian.

Nesna College
http://oter.hinesna.no/

Nesna College in Norway provides information about the college, its academic programs, campus facilities and library. Includes links to student and staff personal home pages and info about the town of Nesna. In English and Norwegian.

Telemark College
http://www.hit.no/

Telemark College in Norway introduces its campus and student body at this introductory page. The college outlines its courses and student services, along with a link to the Norwegian Institute of Technology. In Norwegian and English.

University of Oslo
http://www.uio.no/Struktur/engelsk.html

The University of Oslo's World Wide Web server provides browsers with access to general information about the school's student organizations and academic departments—from theology to dentistry to media and communications. In English and Norwegian.

University of Tromso
http://www.service.uit.no/
homepage-english.uit.no.html

The University of Tromso's home page provides information about the Norwegian school's many programs in social sciences, literature, math, medicine, law, and so on. In English and Norwegina.

POLAND

Adam Mickiewicz University
http://www.amu.edu.pl/welcome.html

Prospective students can check out the Adam Mickiewicz University in Poznan, Poland, here. The site gives an overview of the school, the city and specific information about its University of Medical Sciences. Partially in English; mostly Polish.

Stanislaw Staszic University of Mining and Metallurgy in Cracow
http://www.uci.agh.edu.pl/

The Stanislaw Staszic University of Mining and Metallurgy in Cracow, Poland maintains this home page with information about its research and organizations. Links to related home pages, archives, documents and other resources are available. In English and Polish.

Warsaw University of Technology
http://www.pw.edu.pl/

The Warsaw University of Technology provides a Web site with academic and administrative information, as well as personal links, a history of the school, and research. In Polish and English.

PORTUGAL

Universidade de Coimbra
http://www.uc.pt/

Portugal's University of Coimbra stocks this home page with information about the school's history, facilities and research activities. The page also offers an overview of the Portugese educational system and information about the Machado de Castro National museum. In Portugese, French and English.

University of Minho
http://www.uminho.pt/

The University of Minho's home page contains information about the Portuguese school and its programs. Visitors can check out its engineering and science schools or connect to its library. Information is available in both English and Portuguese.

RUSSIA

Moscow State University
http://www.rector.msu.su/

Moscow State University, Russia, maintains this page with general information about the school, the scientific program and projects and an e-zine called "Alma Mater." Links take visitors to other MSU departmental Web servers.

Novgorod State University
http://www.novsu.ac.ru/

Novgorod State University in Russia presents general information about the school, as well as background on the area around the university and historical information about Lord Novgorod the Great. In Russian and English.

Novosibirsk State University
http://www.nsu.nsk.su/

Information on the history and departments of Novosibirsk State University in Siberia are featured here. Other resources include an FTP site, information on the region, and personal home pages. The home page is available in English.

SCOTLAND

Dundee University
http://alpha.mic.dundee.ac.uk/dusa/dusa.html

This virtual handbook is a guide to the Students' Association at Dundee University, Scotland. In addition to association info, visitors will find links to the central university server, history of the city of Dundee, and that all-important pub guide.

Heriot-Watt University
http://www.hw.ac.uk/

Located in Edinburgh, Scotland, Heriot-Watt University provides a general introduction to the institution with info on its academic departments, courses of study, faculty and staff. Links to student activities, job listings and access to other campus servers are also included.

Napier University
http://www.napier.ac.uk/

Edinburgh, Scotland's Napier University has set up this Local Online Guide with information about the school, divided into general, academic, and community. Also contains Internet hints, tips and courses for newbies.

Queen Margaret College
http://www.qmced.ac.uk/

Latch onto this home page for Edinburgh's Queen Margaret College to get in the know on the college, available courses, and other info students need.

University of Glasgow
http://www.gla.ac.uk/

The GLANCE Information Service of Scotland's University of Glasgow provides extensive information about the school as well as its academic departments, administration and services.

University of Paisley

http://www.online.edu/

The University of Paisley, Scotland, outlines its courses of study in marketing, management, engineering and health via this Online Education WWW Werver. Visitors will also find links to such resources as Health Net and Business Net here and student/staff home pages.

University of St. Andrews

http://www.st-and.ac.uk/

The University of St. Andrews was founded in 1411 and is the oldest university in Scotland. The St. Andrews home page provides information on its people and programs and links to its academic schools and institutes, computing and library services, and staff and student directories.

University of Stirling

http://www.stir.ac.uk/

The home page for the University of Stirling in Scotland offers an overview of the university, including admissions, student life and degree programs. The site also offers links to a number of Internet directories, news and software sites. Available in English and Gaelic.

SLOVAKIA

University of Matej Bel

http://nic.uakom.sk/

The University of Matej Bel in Slovakia maintains this Web site to provide information about the school and the country and town, Banska Bystrica, in which it is located. Includes cultural, legal and weather news, plus a link to SANET, the Slovak Academic Network. In English and Slovak.

SLOVENIA

University of Ljubljana

http://www.uni-lj.si/

The University of Ljubljana, Slovenia, maintains this site to introduce its people and programs. Visit here for staff profiles, course offerings, and other academic and administrative resources.

University of Maribor

http://www.uni-mb.si/

Read up on the state of Slovenian higher education at the University of Maribor home page. In English, with local news offered in Slovene.

SPAIN

Instituto de Física de Cantabria

http://www.gae.unican.es/

The Instituto de Física de Cantabria is a higher educational facility located in Santander, Spain. Vis-

itors to their site will get a general overview of academic departments and resources. Provided in Spanish only.

Universitat Autonoma de Barcelona

http://www.uab.es/

The Universitat Autonoma de Barcelona page contains general information about the university as well as its programs of study, libraries and faculty. Includes links to campus servers, info about computer facilities and software. In Spanish.

University of Granada

http://www.ugr.es/

The University of Granada provides details of its academic departments, programs of study and faculty listings. Includes info on admissions, student services, links to research groups and Spanish servers. In Spanish and English.

University of Oviedo

http://www.uniovi.es/

Spain's University of Oviedo provides an overview of its programs here. The page also includes links to students' and faculty members' home pages (and instructions on how to create one) and a calendar of upcoming events. In Spanish.

SWEDEN

Chalmers University of Technology

http://www.chalmers.se/

Chalmers University of Technology in Goteborg, Sweden, provides information here on academic programs and resources. Visit here to learn about the university, access its reference library and link to related World Wide Web servers. Available in Swedish and English.

Forsmark Technical College

http://www.forsmark.uu.se/

Forsmark Technical College in Sweden profiles its academic programs and highlights the campus with pictures at this home page. The site includes links to student information and the Power Struggle Multi-User Dungeon game.

Halmstad University

http://www.hh.se/

Halmstad University in Sweden features recent school news and an introduction to the college through its home page. The site includes a 3D map of the campus as well as links to departmental home pages and research projects. In Swedish and English.

Mid Sweden University

http://www.forv.mh.se/

The Mid Sweden University home page provides information on the university's divisions, departments and organizations, details of an interactive

course in business writing and a searchable e-mail, address and telephone directory. In Swedish and English.

Royal Institute of Technology

http://www.kth.se/index-eng.html

Sweden's Royal Institute of Technology provides general information about the school as well as news, details on students, research, computer networks and events at this Web site.

Stockholm University

http://www.su.se/

The Stockholm University home page provides an overview of the university's academic departments, programs of study and faculty. Includes listings of university Web servers, library references, folklife and student information. In Swedish and English.

Swedish National Agency for Higher Education

http://www.vhs.se/

The Swedish National Agency for Higher Education offers online reports about activities at universities in Sweden. In Swedish.

Umea University

http://www.umu.se/

Sweden's Umea Univesity maintains this site to provide links to university resources. Information about facilities, faculty and students is available. In English and Swedish.

University of Skovde

http://www.his.se/

Prospective students can visit this Web site to read up on departments, students and faculty at the University of Skovde in Sweden. In English.

Uppsala University

http://www.uu.se/

Sweden's Uppsala University sponsors this home page offering a look at life on campus. Visitors can learn about the university's history and traditions, its academic and research programs, its student services and organizations, or link to related sites off campus. In Swedish and English.

SWITZERLAND

Swiss Federal Institute of Technology, Zurich

http://www.ethz.ch/

The Swiss Federal Institute of Technology in Zurich offers visitors an overview of the school's research and degree programs at its home page. Features include a calendar of events, links to student organizations and other related sites. In German and English.

Graduate Institute of International Studies

http://heiwww.unige.ch/

The Graduate Institute of International Studies in Geneva, Switzerland, maintains this site with information about international relations, its library, programs and students. In English.

Swiss Federal Institute of Technology, Lausanne

http://www.epfl.ch/

The Lausanne campus of the Swiss Federal Institute of Technology maintains this page featuring info about its academic departments, research and development projects, programs for continuing education and the administration. Links to related sites, including the school's campus in Zurich, are also provided. In English, French and German.

University of Geneva, University Center of Information

http://cuiwww.unige.ch/

The home page of University Center of Information (CUI) at the University of Geneva, Switzerland, features links to CUI research groups, Center services and the Computer Science Department. An online search engine assists in keyword queries. In English and French.

University of Lausanne

http://www.unil.ch/

The University of Lausanne's home page offers standard information about the Swiss school's coursework, faculty, campus and the like. Not available in English.

University of Neuchatel

http://www.unine.ch/

The University of Neuchatel in Switzerland welcomes visitors to its academic departments and information services at this introductory site. Find a general overview of educational programs and facilities in French and English.

University of St. Gallen

http://www.unisg.ch/

Switzerland's University of St. Gallen hosts this site offering visitors a look at life on campus. Pictures of the university, research publications and curriculum information are only a few of the items online for review from this university of business administration, economics, law, and social sciences.

TURKEY

Bogazici University

http://www.boun.edu.tr/

The home page for Bogazici University in Istanbul, Turkey, informs visitors about this university's background and how to get more info on its academic and research offerings.

WALES

University of Wales, Aberystwyth

http://www.aber.ac.uk/

Prospective students to the University of Wales at Aberystwyth will learn about the university, its departments and student life here. Includes links to information about Aberystwyth. In English or Welsh.

University of Wales, Bangor

http://www.bangor.ac.uk/

The University of Wales at Bangor maintains this site with information about university academic departments, staff, student union activities, interesting Web links and e-mail directories. This page also includes regional information. Available in English and Welsh.

University of Wales, Cardiff

http://www.cf.ac.uk/

The home page for the University of Wales at Cardiff provides information on its campus, programs, student services and library resources. Visit here to learn about the university and links to a variety of Internet information services.

MIDDLE EAST

ISRAEL

Ben-Gurion University of the Negev

http://www.bgu.ac.il/

The Ben-Gurion Univesity of the Negev is an institution located in Beer-Sheva, the capital of the Negev Desert in Israel. Review research programs and academic course offerings at the school's home page, all in English.

Hebrew University of Jerusalem

http://www1.huji.ac.il/

This Web site directs visitors to the Hebrew University of Jerusalem's information servers. Visitors can access various academic department's Web resources and the school's FTP sites from this gateway page. Information is in English and Hebrew.

Technion: Israel Institute of Technology

http://www.technion.ac.il/

Technion, the Israel Institute of Technology, maintains this page with information about its graduate and undergraduate studies, course lists, research information and an index to departments. Links to Israeli artist exhibitions and the school's projects and journals are also available.

NORTH AMERICA

GENERAL

American Universities

http://www.clas.ufl.edu/CLAS/american-universities.html

This alphabetical index connects Web surfers with the home pages of American universities. Includes links to similar resources listing community colleges and international universities.

Canadian Universities

http://watserv1.uwaterloo.ca/~credmond/univ.html

This site alphabetically indexes members of the Association of Universities and Colleges of Canada and links visitors to their online resources, if any. Also available here are Canadian university phone books, online news and links to other universities around the globe.

Internet College Exchange

http://www.usmall.com/college/

The Internet College Exchange offers detailed information on more than 5,000 U.S. colleges and universities. Visitors can link directly to the central Web servers of those institutions.

U.S. Universities and Community Colleges

http://wwwhost.cc.utexas.edu/world/univ.html

The University of Texas at Austin maintains this list of primary Web servers found at universities and colleges across the U.S. Browsers can view the index in alphabetical order or sort listings by state. Related links are also featured.

University Pages

http://isl-garnet.uah.edu/Universities/

The University Pages site is an online tour of universities and colleges across the U.S. Navigate this Netscape-enhanced collection of home pages by choosing states on the map.

CANADA

Alberta

University of Alberta

http://web.cs.ualberta.ca/UAlberta.html

Meet the faculty, students and staff of the University of Alberta at this site. Canada's major research university offers access to its libraries, academic departments, research centers and electronic publications at this site.

University of Calgary

http://www.ucalgary.ca/Welcome.html

The University of Calgary home page serves up details on the school, its departments and faculty, and student services. Visitors can access an on-line telephone directory and guide to electronic publications.

University of Lethbridge

http://www.uleth.ca/

The University of Lethbridge, Canada, maintains this site with information about the school, research, faculty and campus. Links to information about the surrounding areas are included here, too.

British Columbia

Lambton College of Applied Arts and Technology

http://www.lambton.on.ca/

The server at Lambton College of Applied Arts and Technology in Canada includes information about its Center for Advanced Process Technology, Computer Training Center and Health Sciences and Applied Arts division here.

Simon Fraser University

http://www.sfu.ca/

At the home page for Canada's Simon Fraser University. Visitors will find loads of administrative, academic and student information here. Features include a campus map and an academic calendar.

Simon Fraser University, Harbour Centre

http://www.harbour.sfu.ca/

Find out all about academics and activities at Simon Fraser University's Harbour Centre—a satellite campus of the main university in Burnaby—in Vancouver, B.C. Info provided here includes a list of courses, computing facilites, upcoming events and staff phone list.

Trinity Western University

http://www.twu.ca/

Canada's Trinity Western University is a public Christian school. The site contains a history of the university, admissions guidelines, news, academic information, a map and a campus directory.

University of British Columbia

http://www.ubc.ca/

The University of British Columbia's online information desk dishes out up-to-date academic, administrative, campus and regional weather information. Visitors also can connect to the Canadian school's computer resources and library here.

University of Victoria

http://www.uvic.ca/

UVicINFO, the information service of the University of Victoria in British Columbia, includes university and departmental information, school and world phone books, and Canadian travel and weather information. Visitors can access the university's library and gopher services from this location.

Manitoba

Brandon University

http://www.brandonu.ca/

Prospective students will get an overview of Canada's Brandon University here. The page also posts links to individual departments and student pages.

University of Manitoba

http://www.umanitoba.ca/

The University of Manitoba, located in Winnipeg, Manitoba, Canada, provides visitors access to information on the school's departments, faculty and campus e-mail directory. There is also access to the library, student groups and the computer services department. Weather, news and events in Winnipeg are provided.

University of Winnipeg

http://www.uwinnipeg.ca/

Link to the University of Winnipeg home page for some basic information on this Canadian university, its departments and academic programs, and related colleges and institutions.

New Brunswick

Mount Allison University

http://www.mta.ca/

This home page provides information about Mount Allison University. Visitors can tour the Canadian school's campus, access events and academic department listings, shop the university bookstore or link to a computing services help desk.

Universite de Moncton, Edmundston

http://www.cuslm.ca/

The home page for the University of Moncton's Edmundston, New Brunswick (Canada), campus presents services and information for this francophone school. In French only.

University of New Brunswick

http://www.unb.ca/

The University of New Brunswick offers access to its Fredericton and Saint John campuses here.

For general information take the campus tours offered. To get more specific, consult its academic calendars, course descriptions or simply explore the contents of the campus gophers.

Newfoundland

Cabot College of Applied Arts, Technology and Continuing Education

http://www.cabot.nf.ca/

Cabot College holds an online open house at its official home page. Read a general overview of the college's educational mission, information on academic departments, course offerings, admissions guidelines and explore personal home pages of faculty and students for a personal view of campus life.

Nova Scotia/P.E.I

Acadia University

http://www.acadiau.ca/

Acadia University in Wolfville, Nova Scotia, invites visitors who stop by its home page to learn more about the university—its traditions and history, academic programs and projects, and its cultural and social offerings. Among the site's features, a photographic tour of Acadia stands out.

Mount Saint Vincent University

http://www.msvu.ca/

Visitors will find information on Mount Saint Vincent University academic programs, courses and campus events at the school's home page.

Nova Scotia Teachers College

http://fox.nstn.ca/~ptiwana/nstc.html

Find out what teachers are being taught at the Nova Scotia Teachers College home page. Access the school's administrative offices, educational resources and online library systems here.

Technical University of Nova Scotia

http://www.tuns.ca/

Located in Halifax, the Technical University of Nova Scotia maintains this page offering a look at life on its campus. Visitors are encouraged to learn more about the university, its academic programs, faculty, research projects and facilities. Links to associated universities are also available.

University of Prince Edward Island

http://www.upei.ca/

Canada's University of Prince Edward Island outlines its academic programs and campus facilities at this site. Use this gateway to campus information services to tour the library, departments and student organizations.

Ontario

Brock University
http://www.brocku.ca/

Located in St. Catharines, Ontario, Brock University invites visitors to its home page to explore academic departments and programs. Links to sites of interest on and off campus are provided.

Canadore College
http://www.canadorec.on.ca/index.htm

Make like the smart Canadians and learn more on Canadore College, the Ontario school with a large population of students over the traditional age. Get all the info you need on the school including university policies, courses, degrees offered and more.

Carleton University
http://www.carleton.ca/

Canada's Carleton University leads visitors on a virtual tour of the school's departments and administrative offices. Find access to research activities, educational resources and descriptions of academic programs.

Carleton University
gopher://gopher.carleton.ca:70/1

Carleton University's main gopher server connects visitors to other Internet resources, both on campus and off. It includes admissions and academic information, an events calendar, campus phone and e-mail directories and much more.

Erindale College
http://www.erin.utoronto.ca/

Information about and resources from Erindale College in Mississauga, Ontario, Canada, are presented at this home page. Featured are information about programs, services, organizations and research. Links are provided to the University of Toronto, the city of Mississauga and Internet resources.

Lakehead University
http://www.lakeheadu.ca/menu.html

Lakehead University in Thunder Bay, Ontario, Canada, welcomes visitors to its home page and invites a closer look at the university, its academic programs and administration. Tourist information about Thunder Bay is also available.

McMaster University
http://www.mcmaster.ca/

McMaster University of Ontario, Canada posts general information about its history and programs at this site. Take a virtual tour of the campus or explore the school's electronic resources here.

Northern College
http://www.northernc.on.ca/

Ontario's Northern College home page provides information on the college, its programs, services and faculty, as well as local information for Ontario. Internet service providers and local bulletin board systems are also listed.

Ryerson Polytechnic University
http://www.acs.ryerson.ca/

Ryerson Polytechnic Institute in Toronto provides information here on its academic departments, course offerings and faculty members. Includes links to student services, admissions and library resources.

Sir Sandford Fleming College
http://www.flemingc.on.ca/

Sir Sandford Fleming College, located in south-central Ontario, Canada, details its four campuses here. Visitors will find information on academic programs, alumni, faculty and students.

University of Toronto
http://www.utoronto.ca/

The home page of the University of Toronto provides information about the dozens of degree programs offered by the university as well as information on student life and activities, the faculty, the library and the school's computing facilities.

University of Toronto, Scarborough
http://www.scar.toronto.edu/

Welcome to the Scarborough Campus of the University of Toronto. Visitors here can get information about the academic calendar, the divisons and departments, the campus and the student body.

University of Waterloo
http://www.uwaterloo.ca/home.html

The University of Waterloo, Ontario, Canada, maintains this UWinfo site with information about the school, campus, courses, exams and departments.

University of York
http://www.yorku.ca/

The University of York is located in Toronto, Canada. Visitors to its site can learn about academic life, policies, alumni resources and the campus library system.

Wilfrid Laurier University
http://www.wlu.ca/

Get to know Wilfrid Laurier University in Waterloo, Ontario, Canada, through its home page. It features sports news and admissions information along with details about academic programs.

Quebec

Bishop's University
http://venus.ubishops.ca/

This site informs visitors about Bishop's University in Lenoxville, Quebec. Admissions, calendar and other school-related information can be found here.

Concordia University
http://www.concordia.ca/

Located in Montreal, Concordia University maintains this Web site to provide useful information for its current and prospective students, news about campus activities and academic information. It also offers links to the faculty, departmental and other Concordia Web sites, and links to related pages and resources.

Ecole Polytechnique de Montreal
http://www.polymtl.ca/

The Polytechnical School of Montreal, Canada, maintains this informational site. Visit here to learn about its campus, programs, faculty and students. Available in French, with limited English.

Universite de Sherbrooke
http://www.usherb.ca/

The Universite de Sherbrooke in Quebec, Canada, outlines its academic offerings and campus through this college home page. Visitors can get a glimpse of campus life or read about recent research conducted at the school. In French

Universite Laval
http://www.ulaval.ca/

Quebec City's Universite Laval is Canada's first French-language university. Check out Alerion, the university's online information service, to review its facilities, academic offerings, research projects and faculty. In French with limited English.

Saskatchewan

University of Saskatchewan
http://www.usask.ca/

Located in Saskatoon, Canada's University of Saskatchewan maintains this overview offering searchable information on the school's academic departments, organizations, people and upcoming events. Pointers to a collection of Canadian and worldwide Internet links are also featured.

MEXICO

Instituto Tecnologico y de Estudios Superiores de Monterrey
http://www.mty.itesm.mx/

The Instituto Tecnologico y de Estudios Superiores de Monterrey is in Mexico. Visitors to this site will information on academics, faculty and regional facilities in Mexico. Available in Spanish only.

Universidad Autonoma de Zacatecas

http://bufa.reduaz.mx/

The computing center at Mexico's Universidad Autonoma de Zacatecas features its programs and profiles the campus at this college home page. The site also includes pointers to World Wide Web sites in Mexico. In Spanish, with an English page under construction when we last visited.

Universidad Autonoma Metropolitana

http://tonatiuh.uam.mx/

Mexico City's Universidad Autonoma Metropolitana, a 20-year-old university, takes visitors on a virtual tour of its history, goals, achievements and ideals. In English and Spanish.

University of Colima

http://www.ucol.mx/

The University of Colima in Mexico includes legislative and tourist information at its site, which also features a university directory. Most information is in Spanish, with limited English.

University of Guadalajara

http://www.udg.mx/

News and information in English and Spanish can be found here on the University of Guadalajara, Mexico, and the Guadalajara area.

UNITED STATES

Alabama

Auburn University

http://www.auburn.edu/

Auburn University in Auburn, Ala., maintains this home page with information about academics, research, its library and athletics. Prospective and former students can also find admissions and alumni information.

Birmingham-Southern College

http://www.bsc.edu/

Birmingham-Southern College maintains this Web site offering a look at life on its Alabama campus. Visitors are invited to learn more about the college, its academic programs, student services and administration.

University of Alabama, Huntsville

http://www.uah.edu/

Information on admissions, colleges, student life and research is the focus of the home page of the University of Alabama at Huntsville. News, job listings and links are provided.

University of South Alabama

http://www.usouthal.edu/

The University of South Alabama proudly welcomes guests to the facts on this university in the greater Mobile area, ushering guests in to learn about the school, academic policies, courses offered, student life and more.

Alaska

University of Alaska, Anchorage

http://www.uaa.alaska.edu/

The University of Alaska at Anchorage invites visitors to take an electronic tour of campus resources, student life and academic opportunities at this introductory site. Includes information about extended campuses as well.

Arizona

Arizona State University

http://www.asu.edu/

Arizona State University maintains this home page with information about its campuses, colleges, catalog, research and a link to general information about the state of Arizona.

Embry Riddle Aeronautics University, Prescott

http://www.pr.erau.edu/

Embry Riddle Aeronautics University is an aviation mechanics and flying school in Prescott, Ariz. Its home page features a full catalog of courses, admissions information, administrative facts and links to academic departments.

Glendale Community College

http://www.gc.maricopa.edu/

Glendale Community College in Glendale, Ariz., introduces itself to the Web world through its home page, including links to campus maps and directories as well as a pointer to the student newspaper, "The Voice." Visitors can find out about the school's programs and faculty.

Mesa Community College

http://www.mc.maricopa.edu/

Mesa Community College in Arizona provides information here on its campus, programs, faculty and students. Visit here to learn about the university, access its library services, and link to a variety of Internet-based resources.

Northern Arizona University

http://www.nau.edu/

Northern Arizona University offers general academic and campus information at this site. Find links to an interactive campus map, a calendar of events, the academic colleges, support services

and sites of related interest locally, across the state and around the world.

Scottsdale Community College

http://www.sc.maricopa.edu/

Scottsdale Community College of Scottsdale, Ariz., familiarizes the visitor with its handbook, departments and class schedules. Visitors can embark upon a virtual tour of the campus as well.

University of Arizona

http://www.arizona.edu/

The University of Arizona home page acquaints Web surfers with the Tucson, Ariz., school. Visitors to this site will find information on the university's academic departments, campus, administration and student services.

University of Arizona Graduate College

http://grad.admin.arizona.edu/

The Graduate College of the University of Arizona, Tucson, maintains this site of general college information. Visit here to learn about admissions, financial assistance, study programs and more.

Arkansas

Harding University

http://www.harding.edu/

The Harding University home page provides campus information about this Christian college, located in Searcy, Ark. Also featured are links to Arkansas-related Web sites.

University of Arkanas, Little Rock

http://www.ualr.edu/

The University of Arkanas at Little Rock home page contains a wealth of information about the university, its academic departments and programs of study. Includes info on student services, job openings, a virtual tour of the campus, UALR publications and links to other Arkansas resources.

University of Arkansas, Monticello

http://cotton.uamont.edu/

The University of Arkansas at Monticello provides information on degree programs and a schedule of classes here. The site also includes access to the university's library.

University of Central Arkansas

http://www.uca.edu/

The University of Central Arkansas maintains this index to university information and resources. Links to the school's departments, the Small Business Advancement National Center, a directory of faculty and staff, plus sites in Arkansas are featured.

California

Azusa Pacific University
http://www.apu.edu/
The home page of Azusa Pacific University features programs and academic information about the Christian liberal arts institution in California. Find out about campus services, link to personal home pages or learn about the school's

Barstow College
http://www.barstow.cc.ca.us/
The home page of Barstow College in California provides a wide range of information academic departments, programs of study and faculty. Resources available here include a catalog, academic calendar, reference materials, and the school's online poetry magazine

Biola University
http://www.biola.edu/
Take a virtual campus tour of southern California's Biola University at this site. Biola is a Christian university offering biblically focused educational opportunities. The Biola home page also provides info on campus life and resources.

Butte College
http://www.cin.butte.cc.ca.us/
Butte College in Oroville, Calif., maintains this site with information about the college and campus, including links to class schedules, program descriptions and local educational sites and resources.

California Institute of Technology
http://www.caltech.edu/
The California Institute of Technology home page provides information on academic programs, admissions, research projects and faculty. Includes descriptions of campus facilities, student organizations and extracurricula activities.

California Lutheran University
http://callutheran.edu/
California Lutheran University, a private school in Thousand Oaks, Calif., maintains this home page with information about its mission, academics, admissions and links to its departmental home pages. Visitors and prospective students can request admission material online and take a virtual tour of the campus.

California State Polytechnic University, Pomona
http://www.csupomona.edu/
A campus map, a master calendar of university events, links to the library and classes, the bookstore and admissions office—what more could a student need? Cal Poly Ponoma offers a rich index of its resources at this page.

California State University
http://www.calstate.edu/
The systemwide information server for the California State University system provides info on the 22 constituent campuses, in cluding admissions, job opportunities, and a news and events calendar.

California State University
gopher://gopher.calstate.edu:70/1
The California State university system gopher server provides administrative information for the state's higher education network. Includes access to publications, telephone numbers, admissions requirements, network resources and policy reports.

California State University, Bakersfield
http://www.csubak.edu/
The home page for Cal State at Bakersfield contains information on academic departments, courses of study and faculty profiles. Includes a campus tour, news releases and general info about the institution.

California State University, Chico
http://www.csuchico.edu/
The California State University at Chico serves up info about the school's admissions policies, academic programs and campus facilities at this home page.

California State University, Fresno
http://www.csufresno.edu/
The Fresno campus of California State University provides this site for students and visitors. The page includes campus and local information and links to other sites of interest.

California State University, Los Angeles
http://www.calstatela.edu/
California State University at Los Angeles provides information here on its people and programs. Visit here for news, campus maps, admissions listings and links to university service divisions. Includes links to faculty biographies and government resources.

California State University, Sacramento
http://www.csus.edu/
Look into academic opportunities at California State University at Sacramento, "the capital university." Find course offerings, computer services and student resources outlined here.

California State University, San Bernardino
http://www.csusb.edu/
The home page of California State University at San Bernardino consists of an index that includes information on admissions, academic programs and administrative divisions. Find also campus and city maps.

California State University, Stanislaus
http://lead.csustan.edu/
The California State University at Stanislaus offers links to pages on its academic programs, administrative resources and admissions requirements. Also find links to the campus bulletin board, faculty and staff members' pages and other sites of topical interest.

Chapman University
http://www.chapman.edu/
Chapman University in Orange, Calif., invites visitors to its home page to tour its campus, explore its academic opportunities and meet the faculty and students. Links to sites of interest both on and off campus are provided.

City College of San Francisco
http://hills.ccsf.cc.ca.us:9878/
City College of San Francisco serves up a plethora of useful info for potential students and curious visitors. With a wide range of departmental pages and the complete class schedule online, guests can examine academic offerings in-depth. What's more, City College now offers a variety of Telecourses for couch potatoes, viewable on San Francisco's Cable Channel 52—no, really!

Claremont Colleges
http://www.claremont.edu/
The Claremont Colleges are a consortium of six higher-education facilities located in Northern California. Visitors can link directly to each of the members' home pages and find information on shared resources and educational activities.

Claremont McKenna College
http://www.mckenna.edu/
Claremont McKenna College in Claremont, Calif., provides general information as well as details on students, faculty, administration, research and more here. Information for both prospective students and alumni can be accessed from this home page.

De Anza College
http://wwwdeanza.fhda.edu/
The home page for California's De Anza College provides academic and class information, as well as details on administrative and support services. Visitors will also find information on the De Anza community here.

Diablo Valley College
http://www.dvc.edu/
Diablo Valley College boasts an online catalog and a link to library services at its home page. Review the academic course offerings and information resources here.

Foothill College

http://www.fhda.edu/foothill/

Foothill College, located between San Francisco and Silicon Valley, Calif., offers academic and administrative information, a campus map, photos, on-line courses and international programs at its Web site.

Fullerton College

http://www.fullcoll.edu/

The Fullerton College home page contains information about academic departments, course offerings and faculty profiles. Includes links to campus information servers, local interest items and other educational resources.

Grossmont-Cuyamaca Community College District

http://www.gcccd.cc.ca.us/

The Grossmont-Cuyamaca Community College District home page offers links to Grossmont College and Cuyamaca College—both located in San Diego, Calif. This developing site promises pointers to district newsgroups, FTP archives and gopher services.

Occidental College

http://www.oxy.edu/

Los Angeles's Occidental College provides an on-line college catalog to prospective students, including information about student life and facilities as well as departments.

Pomona College

http://www.pomona.edu/

Pomona College in Claremont, Calif., provides information here about its academic programs and resources. Visit here to learn about its liberal arts and sciences curriculum, special study opportunities, faculty members, and more.

San Diego State University

http://www.sdsu.edu/

Get a glimpse inside the halls of San Diego State University through this Web page. The page introduces the university and includes links to information about the school's departments, research and available majors.

San Francisco State University

http://www.sfsu.edu/

San Francisco State University offers information on its campus, faculty and students at this introductory site. Visitors can access frequently asked questions (FAQ) files, Internet search tools and more.

San Jose State University

http://www.sjsu.edu/

San Jose State University, "Silicon Valley's metropolitan university," maintains this site to provide general information about the school and the San Jose area, as well as links to university resources.

Santa Barbara City College

http://www.sbcc.cc.ca.us/

The Computer Science Department at Santa Barbara City College maintains this unofficial site, which gives an overview of the college. Visit for general information, a schedule of classes and a look at the college's departments.

Santa Monica College

http://www.smc.edu/

The Santa Monica College home page contains information about the school, academic departments, faculty and library services. Includes admissions info, descriptions of campus facilities and student organizations.

Sonoma State University

http://www.sonoma.edu/

This site offers a look at life on campus at Sonoma State University in Rohnert Park, Calif. Among other topics of interest, visitors can learn about the academic departments and programs, student services and school policies.

Southwestern College

http://swc.cc.ca.us/

The home page for Southwestern College in San Diego, Calif., was still under construction when we last visited. At that time it contained a campus map, directions to the campus, and links to the Web servers at UC San Diego and San Diego State University.

Stanford University

http://www.stanford.edu/

This is the central server for Stanford University, located in Palo Alto, Calif. Links include general campus-wide information and admissions, student groups and activities, as well as individual academic departments, research centers and the university libraries. See Editor's Choice, page 218.

Stanford University, The Portfolio Collection

http://www.stanford.edu/home/administration/portfolio.html

Portolio, Stanford University's Campus-Wide Information Service, provides a comprehensive guide to Stanford courses, campus, students and faculty. The site includes schedules, maps and directories as well as press releases and promotional materials from the school.

Stanford University Users' Server

http://www-leland.stanford.edu/

The Stanford Users' Web Server provides a directory of home pages in the Stanford community.

Includes instructions for placing pages in the directory.

Student-Run Cal Berkeley Home Page

http://server.berkeley.edu/

The student-run Cal Berkeley Home Page links us up to an imagemap of the campus, the Bay Area Transit Information, and the Martial Arts Network. Read the campus newspaper, the "Daily Californian," online, consider joining a student group or hang around other cool bay area pages.

University of California

http://www.reg.uci.edu/SANET/uc.html

The Registrar's Office of the University of California maintains this site for general information on admission, transfers and tuition. Visit here to link with the university's many campuses, programs and resources.

University of California, Berkeley

http://www.berkeley.edu/

The University of California at Berkeley maintains this look at life on its campus. Visitors will find information on the academic programs, research units, students and faculty, libraries and museums.

University of California, Berkeley

gopher://infocal.berkeley.edu:70/1

The University of California at Berkeley posts a wealth of campus information at this gopherspace, including a course listing, phonebooks and news from the Health Services department. Visitors will get a look at campus research here, too.

University of California, Campuses and Labs

gopher://gopher-registry.berkeley.edu:4322/1

Information and links to selected resources at University of California campuses and laboratories are contained at this gopher site. Among the resources are the systemwide administration, the Lawrence Berkeley Laboratory and the Lick Observatory.

University of California, Davis

http://www.ucdavis.edu/

The University of California at Davis home page tells visitors about what's happening on and near the campus. Also includes information on the school's computing resources and academic and research programs.

University of California, Irvine

http://www.cwis.uci.edu/

The University of California at Irvine is a member of the University of California public educational system. Its site includes access to the library, academic calandars, computing services, and information on programs and research.

University of California, Irvine

gopher://gopher-server.cwis.uci.edu:70/1

The University of California at Irvine gopher server provides visitors with easy access to text-based resources on the school, its location and attractions, plus academic, administrative and library links.

University of California, Irvine, Schedules

gopher://ka.reg.uci.edu/11/ro/soc

Course info, schedules and addenda for current and past terms are available on this gopher. From anthropology to writing, find out who's teaching and when at UC Irvine.

University of California, Los Angeles

http://www.ucla.edu/

The University of California at Los Angeles's home page provides a tour of the campus, details on academic departments, faculty and courses of study. Includes information on student services, events, jobs and links to other UCLA resources.

University of California, Riverside

http://www.ucr.edu/

At the University of California at Riverside home page, visitors are greeted by the chancellor's welcome and campus news reports. Prospective students are invited to tour the facilities or link to college, library and museum pages.

University of California, San Diego

http://www.ucsd.edu/

InfoPath is a virtual directory service of the University of California at San Diego. Visitors can take a virtual tour of the campus or access a wide variety of info about the library, academic offerings and San Diego area.

University of California, Santa Barbara

http://www.ucsb.edu/

The home page for the University of California at Santa Barbara contains a wealth of information on the school's departments, research, administration, libraries and computing organizations. Also find links to student groups and activities.

University of California, Santa Cruz

http://www.ucsc.edu/public/index.htm

InfoSlug is the name of home page of the University of California at Santa Cruz. Visitors can learn about campus news, events and announcements. UCSC periodicals and information on academic and research projects are included.

University of California Servers

http://www.ucop.edu/ucophome/ucservers.html

The University of California system posts links to all its campuses' Web and gopher servers here. The page also contains links to the organizations affiliated with the university system.

University of San Francisco

http://www.usfca.edu/

The University of San Francisco maintains this site with information about the campus, programs, faculty and students. A variety of Internet search tools are also available here.

University of Southern California

http://www.usc.edu/Univ

This page from the sunstruck University of Southern California campus provides serious information on admissions, the academic curriculum, students services, athletics, library facilities, special events and more. Tanning butter not included.

University of Southern California, Research

http://www.usc.edu/Research

Researchers will find an index of resources available at the University of Southern California on this page. It contains library information as well as links to the university's gopher and FTP archives and campus institutes ranging from the Center for Feminist Research to the Center for Craniofacial Molecular Biology. The page also posts an index to researchers' resources elsewhere on the Net.

University of the Pacific

http://www.uop.edu/

The University of the Pacific in Stockton, Calif., "California's first chartered university," provides information here on its campus, programs, faculty and students. Visit here to link with the liberal arts university and its collection of valuable Internet resources.

---

a2z EDITOR'S CHOICE

Stanford University

http://www.stanford.edu/

Northern California's Stanford University has created an inviting, helpful home page that offers resources for both prospective and current students, as well as alumni and faculty. In addition to the usual departmental info, Stanford provides detailed descriptions of student activities and organizations, plus a complete course catalog and undergraduate and graduate admissions requirements. A plan is even in the works to allow for online purchase of tickets to arts events. Visitors will find maps of the Stanford area and can take a virtual tour of the campus through more than 2,000 photos. The latest addition to the already-brimming Stanford home page is the electronic incarnation of the magazine "Stanford Today," which contains the full text of the print version. Beyond that, students can access the independent newspaper "The Stanford Daily" or log off and tune in to Channel 51, the Stanford Channel, on TV. (Remember TV? that *other* noisy, colorful machine in your room?)—*Reviewed by Karen Wise*

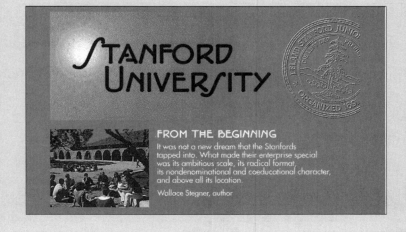

Colorado

Colorado Christian University

http://www.ccu.edu/

Colorado Christian University, Denver, maintains this site with information about admissions, academics and campus events.

Colorado State University

http://www.colostate.edu/

Tour Colorado State University online. Find admissions information, descriptions of academic programming and perspectives on student life. Libraries, news and other electronic resources can also be accessed here.

Metropolitan State College of Denver

http://www.mscd.edu/

The Metropolitan State College of Denver, Colo., maintains this page with information about the campus, events and resources. The site, which includes a listing of indexes to other college Web servers, is searchable.

National Technological University

http://www.ntu.edu/

The National Technological University of Fort Collins, Colo., sponsors this informational catalog. Visitors can learn more about NTU, its programs and its services, or search the university's server.

United States Air Force Academy

http://www.usafa.af.mil/

The United States Air Force Academy in Colorado Springs, Colo., maintains this site for general information and Internet resources. Browsers can learn about the school's campus, programs, faculty and students. Links to related sites and a keyword search of Internet tools are also available.

University of Colorado, Boulder

http://www.colorado.edu/

The University of Colorado at Boulder maintains this site to introduce its people and programs. Visit here for staff and student listings, course offerings, current events, local information, and other academic and administrative resources.

University of Colorado, Colorado Springs

http://www.uccs.edu/

Visitors to the home page of the University of Colorado at Colorado Springs are invited to tour the campus, explore its facilities and review the academic programs. Links to many sites of interest both on and off campus are provided.

The University of Colorado, Denver

http://www.cudenver.edu/

The University of Colorado at Denver offers undergraduate and graduate degree programs in an urban, nonresidential educational community. Tour the campus and academic departments at the school's home page.

University of Denver

http://www.du.edu/

The University of Denver home page provides information on academic departments, courses of study and admissions. Includes info on DU faculty, student organizations, activities, athletics and campus facilities.

University of Northern Colorado

http://www.univnorthco.edu/

The University of Northern Colorado, located in Greeley (just a short distance from major skiing areas), guides visitors through its academic and department information as well as extracurriculars, financial aid and admissions.

Connecticut

Saint Joseph College

http://www.sjc.edu/

This site shows visitors around Saint Joseph College in West Hartford, Conn. Find an online campus tour along with academic, administration, admissions and activities information.

Southern Connecticut State University

http://scwww.ctstateu.edu/

Southern Connecticut State University's home page provides school news and campus information as well as links to SCSU's Web and Gopher servers and other Internet locations.

University of Connecticut

http://www.uconn.edu/

Browsers of the Husky Web Menu will find a number of useful pointers to life on campus in Hartford. From academics to Web servers, anything of interest concerning the University of Connecticut can be found here.

---

a2z EDITOR'S CHOICE

Yale University

http://www.cis.yale.edu/

A fitting home page for an Ivy League institution, Yale University presents five clickable leather-covered tomes, each containing resources relating to a particular aspect of campus life. For instance, in Academics, visitors will find the usual stuff: departmental info, course syllabi, graduate programs and research opportunities. Prospective students will want to check out the campus photos and maps and take a cybertour of the New Haven area. There's also a QuickTime video serving as an introduction to Yale. A special feature, the Yale Sampler, offers a collection of multimedia projects to provide a glimpse of the life of the mind and the community at Yale. Highlights include a gallery of personal home pages from Yale students and faculty and "Wilderness in the North American Imagination," a student project from the American Studies Department. —*Reviewed by Karen Wise*

Yale University
Click on the book title of your choice.

University of Hartford
http://www.hartford.edu/

The University of Hartford's home page contains a wealth of resources about this Connecticut institution. In addition to the usual info about academic programs and campus facilities, there's also a daily-updated bulletin and links to student home pages and resumes.

Wesleyan University
http://www.wesleyan.edu/home/home.html

Wesleyan University in Middletown, Conn., maintains this home page with information about its academics, students and alumni, campus events and an alphabetical index.

YaleInfo
gopher://yaleinfo.yale.edu/

Get graphics-free administrative and academic news at YaleInfo, the Ivy League university's gopher server. Includes New Haven, Conn. weather conditions, course syllabi and public lecture schedules.

Yale University
http://www.cis.yale.edu/

The Yale University home page contains a detailed overview of life on this New Haven, Conn., campus. Site features include general information, departmental listings, admissions guidelines, and links to cultural and scholarly resources. See Editor's Choice.

Yale University Seal and Mottos
http://www.cs.yale.edu/HTML/YALE/Seal.html

This page features an image of the Yale University seal and explanations of its Latin and Hebrew mottos.

Delaware

University of Delaware
http://www.udel.edu/

The University of Delaware's home page offers a tour of the campus, a look at who's who, and a full menu of information related to campus life, services and departments.

District of Columbia

American University
http://www.american.edu/

The American University's EagleInfo site contains information on academic departments, course offerings, campus services and administration. Includes info on student life, news, special events, campus media and links to Washington, D.C. servers.

Georgetown University
http://www.georgetown.edu/guhome.html

The Georgetown University home page mixes traditional campus and administrative information with academic features and graphics. Features include a Latin American political database and the Georgetown academic calendar.

Georgetown University
gopher://gopher.georgetown.edu:70/1

Georgetown University in Washington, D.C., provides this gopher server as an introduction to campus facilities and academic information. Visitors can also link to events, research and publications.

George Washington University
http://www.gwu.edu/

The George Washington University in Washington, D.C., maintains this informational site. Visit here to learn about the university and its academic programs, departments, events and resources.

National Defense University
http://www.ndu.edu/

The National Defense University in Washington, D.C., presents a site filled with information on its institutes and colleges, including the National War College and the Institute for National Strategic Studies. A searchable index of research and publications is provided.

Florida

Barry University
http://www.barry.edu/

Tour the campus of Barry University in Florida through its home page. It offers a complete academic calendar and admissions info along with details about course offerings and degrees.

Broward Community College
http://www.broward.cc.fl.us/

The home page for Broward Community College in Fort Lauderdale, Fla., features general course information and schedules, along with campus news and a collection of Internet starting points.

Embry-Riddle Aeronautical University
http://www.db.erau.edu/

This home page for the Embry-Riddle Aeronautical University in Daytona Beach, Fla., offers a variety of options for students (career services, online publications) and visitors (admissions information, a virtual tour of campus). Other site features include links to an Aerospace Virtual Library and Alumni Services.

Florida Agricultural and Mechanical University
http://www.famu.edu/

Florida Agricultural and Mechanical University, known for its phenomenal marching band The Rattlers, checks into the Web here with all the vital statistics on this primarily African-American university and its constituent schools and colleges.

Florida Atlantic University
http://www.fau.edu/

Florida Atlantic University gives an overview of its facilities and educational programs at this site. Visit its multiple campuses, and consult the course catalog here.

Florida Institute of Technology
http://www.fit.edu/

Florida Tech's home page serves up info on campus life, academics and research, online resources and a link to the school's alumni Association. Programs in aeronautics, business, engineering and liberal arts are explored.

Florida International University
http://www.fiu.edu/

Florida International University in Miami is the largest doctoral-granting public university in South Florida. The FIU home page contains photos, maps and all of the standard info on academics, organizations and special events.

Florida State University
http://www.fsu.edu/

Florida State University, Tallahassee, offers visitors to this home page an online catalog of information detailing all aspects of university life there. Options allow a self-guided tour by topic or use of a keyword search engine.

Hillsborough Community College
http://204.96.208.1/

Located in Tampa, Fla., Hillsborough Community College invites visitors to its home page to learn more about its academic programs and personnel. Links to faculty, administration and student home pages are provided.

Jacksonville University
http://junix.ju.edu/

Jacksonville University introduces prospective students to its academic programs and admissions requirements. Visitors can evaluate the strength of the athletic department or dive into descriptions of student life on campus.

Jones College
http://www.jones.edu/

Located in Jacksonville, Fla., Jones College opens its home page by offering the college's core philosophy and history. Also find links to the collegiate programs, administration, faculty and staff, facilities, special programs and college calendar.

Nova Southeastern University

http://alpha.acast.nova.edu/

Nova Southeastern University in Ft. Lauderdale, Florida provides information on academic programs, descriptions of courses and faculty profiles. Includes pointers to computer and library facilities, student services and campus organizations.

Stetson University

http://www.stetson.edu/

The home page for Stetson University, in DeLand, Fla., provides links to a calendar of special events and activities, a course catalog, and information about the library and various departments, including the Stetson College of Law.

University of Central Florida

http://www.ucf.edu/

The University of Central Florida in Orlando welcomes visitors to its virtual campus at this introductory site. Prospective students can review academic programs, campus facilities and educational opportunities.

University of Florida

http://www.ufl.edu/

The home page for the University of Florida provides potential students and interested visitors with a collection of information about the University, its faculty, departments, course offerings and publications. Includes links to campus organizations, student services and other information resources.

University of Miami

http://www.ir.miami.edu/

Florida's University of Miami maintains this gateway to information about its graduate and undergraduate programs. Links to the Coral Gables campus, the School of Medicine and the Rosenstiel School of Marine and Atmospheric Science are provided.

University of South Florida

http://www.usf.edu/

An electronic visit to the University of South Florida yields academic, student and facility information for the school's five campuses. An illustrated brochure, this site contains general information about the institution's educational programs.

University of West Florida

http://www.uwf.edu/

The University of West Florida is located in Pensacola, Fla. The Argo Information System will supply visitors with info on academic departments, admissions, faculty and student life.

Georgia

Emory University

http://www.emory.edu/

Emory University in Atlanta, Ga., provides information here on its academic departments, courses of study and admissions requirements. Visitors will also find links to professional schools, research centers, job openings and student services.

Georgia Institute of Technology

http://www.gatech.edu/TechHome.html

Georgia Tech maintains this home page offering visitors a look at the academic and social life on campus. Features include links to admissions, athletics, campus news, colleges and schools, research and student organizations.

Georgia State University

http://www.gsu.edu/

Georgia State University in Atlanta, Ga., maintains this site for general information and Internet resources. Visit here to learn about its academic and alumni/ae programs, career services, campus activities and more.

Mercer University

http://www.mercer.peachnet.edu/

Mercer University, the world's second-largest Baptist-affiliated institution, is located in Macon, Ga. Its home page includes links to general and departmental information, tools for researchers and Web projects at Mercer.

Southern College of Technology

http://www.sct.edu/

Southern Tech in Marietta, Ga., takes future students on a campus tour and provides them with the necessary information for enrollment. There's also information about Internet access, news and weather here.

South Georgia College

http://www.sgc.peachnet.edu/

South Georgia College serves up its home page at this site. Find out more about the school and the University of Georgia through online brochures and catalogs.

State University of West Georgia

http://www.westga.edu/

The State University of West Georgia in Carrollton offers this server, with information on the school's history, academics, jobs and resources. Visitors can view a clickable map of the campus, read online course materials or visit the Cool Sites to Surf page.

University of Georgia, Athens

http://www.uga.edu/

The University of Georgia at Athens offers more than the standard school brochure at this site. Investigate student life via a visit to campus organizations online or by reading the extensive news and sports reports available.

Hawaii

Hawaii Pacific University

http://www.hpu.edu/

The central server for Hawaii Pacific University in Honolulu maintains this site to provide general information about its campus, programs, faculty and students. Links to tourist information are also available.

Honolulu Community College

http://www.hcc.hawaii.edu/

Surf the academic options at Honolulu Community College. Campus information and course descriptions are offered, as well as a link to the school's museums and exhibits. Also find general promotional information about the state of Hawaii.

Kapi'olani Community Colege

http://naio.kcc.hawaii.edu/

Maintained by the faculty, staff and students of Kapi'olani Community Colege in Hawaii, this server displays a snapshot of what's going on there. Links to current media center project and the University of Hawaii, computer support resources and interesting finds.

University of Hawaii

gopher://gopher.hawaii.edu:70/1

The UHINFO gopher gives an overview of the University of Hawaii's departments and campus life here. The site also posts phone directories, news and job openings.

University of Hawai'i, West O'ahu

http://www.uhwo.hawaii.edu/

The University of Hawai'i at West O'ahu invites visitors to learn about the university, its academic programs, divisions, faculty and administration. Links to related sites on and off campus are also provided.

Idaho

Albertson College of Idaho

http://www.acofi.edu/

Visitors to the home page for Albertson College of Idaho will find the usual college info on academic programs and student life, plus a campus tour of this Caldwell, Idaho, institution.

Idaho State University
http://www.isu.edu/
Visitors to Idaho State University's official Web site will find academic information (catalogs, course listings), campus resources (directories, maps), and an online help system from the university computer center. Links to several newspaper and weather services are also provided.

Northwest Nazarene College
http://www.nnc.edu/
Northwest Nazarene College unveils info about its campus and programs through this page. Read about the Christian liberal arts school's approach to education as well as its student services and computer resources.

Illinois

Augustana College
http://www.augustana.edu/
Augustana College, a private college in Rock Island, Ill., provides information about the school, its academic programs, library and admissions. Includes alumni news, a calendar of events and a directory of phone numbers.

Blackburn College
http://www.mcs.net/~kwplace/bc.htm
In order to keep tuition costs low for all students, Blackburn College in Carlinville, Ill., has instituted a unique work program. Visit the college's site to find out more about the program and the degree options offered.

Bradley University
http://www.bradley.edu/
Find out why Bradley University will play in Peoria, Ill. This home page provides general information on academics and student life. Includes admissions information, a telephone directory, links to student services and departmental servers.

Concordia University, River Forest
http://www.curf.edu
Concordia University in River Forest, Ill., features its more than 60 undergraduate and graduate programs at this college home page. Visitors can check out admissions requirements and policies for the Christian liberal arts school as well.

Danville Area Community College
http://www.dacc.cc.il.us/
Illinois' Danville Area Community College offers two-year degree programs for youth and adults. Visitors can peruse the school's course catalog or investigate the city of Danville's community resources.

DePaul University
http://www.depaul.edu/
The DePaul University site contains information about academic departments, programs of study, and faculty profiles. Includes info on admissions, students services, campus facilties and links to information servers.

Illinois Institute of Technology
http://www.iit.edu/
At the Illinois Institute of Technology's central Web server, visitors will find information about student life, academics, research and library access.

Illinois State University
http://www.ilstu.edu/
Illinois State University in Normal, Ill., was the first public institution of higher learning in the state. Its founding documents were drafted by Abraham Lincoln in 1857. Illinois State offers academic programs in Arts and Sciences.

John A. Logan College
http://www.jal.cc.il.us/
John A. Logan College is a community college in Illinois, whose district covers Williamson, Jackson and parts of surrounding counties. Students who are thinking about going to the school can visit this site in order to learn more about their options.

Joliet Junior College
http://ac4.jjc.cc.il.us/
Joliet Junior College presents information on admissions, courses of study, class schedules and an academic calendar at this Web site. Includes links to library services, info on lecture series and a brief history of the Illinois institution.

Northern Illinois University
http://www.niu.edu/
At the Northern Illinois University information server, browsers can read a wealth of information about the school's staff, students, academics, libraries, organizations and Internet services.

North Park College
http://www.npcts.edu/
North Park is a Christian liberal arts college located in Chicago. Visitors to its home page will find information on academic departments, campus information systems, and theological seminary.

Northwestern University, Campus Maps
http://nuinfo.nwu.edu/evchi-map/twomaps.html
Maps of Northwestern University's Evanston and Chicago campuses are available at this site. Major buildings are listed and are clickable for a closer look and more information. There is also an index to other information sites at the university.

Olivet Nazarene University
http://www.olivet.edu/
Olivet Nazarene University in Bourbonnais, Ill., provides its history and information about academics programs on its home page. Visitors can learn about the people and learning opportunities at the Christian college.

Saint Xavier University
http://www.sxu.edu/
Saint Xavier University in Chicago briefly profiles its mission as a Catholic school and provides details about the library and computer resources on campus. The college offers graduate and undergraduate degrees.

Southern Illinois University
http://www.siu.edu/
Southern Illinois University is a multicampus university with facilities in the United States and Japan. Visit this site for links to general school information, news, board of directors profiles and more.

Southern Illinois University, Edwardsville
http://www.siue.edu/
The Southern Illinois University at Edwardsville maintains this informational site. Visit here to learn about its campus, programs, faculty and students. An interactive campus map is also available.

University of Chicago
http://www.uchicago.edu/
The University of Chicago introduces visitors, alumni and prospective students to news about the institution. Check of the school's educational offerings, tour the campus, visit the admissions office and evaluate university research facilities here.

University of Illinois, Chicago
http://www.uic.edu/
The University of Illinois at Chicago provides information here on its academic departments, campus units and student organizations. Visit this site to learn about its people, programs and academic resources.

University of Illinois, Springfield
http://www.uis.edu/
Prospective students to the University of Illinois at Springfield can learn about the school's departments, programs and admission policies here. The page also posts some student pages, an online telephone directory and departmental pages.

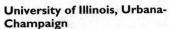

University of Illinois, Urbana-Champaign

http://www.uiuc.edu/

Get to know the University of Illinois at Urbana-Champaign at this introductory site. Maintained by the University's Office of Public Affairs, this page offers admissions, course and campus information. Link to other University of Illinois campuses from here.

University of Illinois, Urbana-Champaign

gopher://gopher.uiuc.edu/

The University of Illinois at Urbana-Champaign gopher server provides a bulletin board as a service to the campus for posting department and student/faculty-related news. Browsers here can find continually updated announcements and directories for a variety of campus resources.

University of Illinois, Urbana-Champaign, Graduate College

http://www.grad.uiuc.edu/

The University of Illinois Urbana-Champaign maintains this Web site, containing detailed information about its graduate college. Visitors can browse a multitude of college publications, course catalogs and handbooks, read financial aid info or link to other campus facilities' home pages from here.

Wheaton College

http://www.wheaton.edu/

Wheaton College, a Christian liberal arts school in Wheaton, Ill., maintains this site for general information and Internet resources. Visit here to learn about its campus, programs, faculty and students. Links to university gopher servers and departmental Web sites also are available.

William Rainey Harper College

http://www.harper.cc.il.us/

Everything Harper College students need for the new quarter— except for books and a nice pair of sensible shoes—can be found at the suburban Chicago school's Web site. Academics and extracurriculars are covered, with events listings, job openings and maps available for inspection.

Indiana

Ball State University

http://bsu.edu/

Ball State University's extensive Web site gives visitors an overview of the Muncie, Ind., campus and offers online courses. Browsers can also catch the latest sports scores and order university merchandise from the online market.

Earlham College

http://http.earlham.edu/

Earlham College of Richmond, Ind., presents an index with pointers to departments with Web pages, along with information on admissions, personnel and campus life. Listings of the library's resources are searchable.

Hanover College

http://www.hanover.edu/

Hanover College is a four-year Presbyterian liberal arts college in Hanover, Ind. The Hanover home page contains campus photos, links to student and alumni pages, and a message from the college president.

Indiana Institute of Technology

http://www.indtech.edu/

Indiana Tech's Web site contains information about academic departments, courses of study and faculty profiles. Includes links to research groups, student services, admissions info and other campus servers.

Indiana State University

http://www.indstate.edu/

Although sponsored by the Department of Life Science, this site is really an Indiana State University catalog and brochure. Visitors can link to information on all courses of study, access faculty, alumni and student facts, and tour the school's reference and Internet centers.

Indiana University

http://www-iub.ucs.indiana.edu/

Indiana University maintains this site to introduce its statewide campuses and programs. Visitors will find links to its system units and services, university mission statements, computer resources and nine campus locations.

Indiana University, Bloomington

http://www.indiana.edu/iub/

This is the central server for the University of Indiana at Bloomington. Visitors will find information on admissions, academic programs and research, recreation, entertainment and campus services.

Indiana University-Purdue University, Fort Wayne

http://www.ipfw.indiana.edu/

Indiana University-Purdue University, Fort Wayne, is a public university that offers associate, bachelor's and master's degrees. This page points out various schools of study and offers campus information.

Indiana University-Purdue University, Indianapolis

http://indyunix.iupui.edu/

The home page of Indiana University-Purdue University, Indianapolis, provides academic, library and service information, along with campus news and information about the institution's medical center.

Indiana University Southeast

http://www.ius.indiana.edu/

Indiana University Southeast at New Albany maintains this directory and overview of life on campus. Find links to the academic departments, student and faculty home pages, the school paper, and related sites on and off campus.

Purdue University

http://www.purdue.edu/

The home page for Purdue University in West Lafayette, Ind., provides details on academics, activities and admissions. Visitors will also find campus news, sports information, and an alumni section here.

Purdue University, Administrative Information Services

http://www.adpc.purdue.edu/

Purdue University's online Administrative Information Services provides access to the official information servers on campus. Selected high traffic links and an alphabetical index assist users for quick reference.

Purdue University, Personnel Lookup

http://www.cc.purdue.edu/PUCC-PDN/ph-query.html

Purdue University offers this search form for locating university staff and students. Visitors can search the database by name and department.

Rose-Hulman Institute of Technology

http://www.rose-hulman.edu/

The Rose-Hulman Institute of Technology, just outside of Terre Haute, Ind., provides university information here on admissions, academic departments and publications.

Taylor University

http://www.tayloru.edu/

Information about Taylor University, a Christian liberal arts college in Upland, Ind., is contained on this home page. Featured here are details on programs, departments, admissions, student life and more. Also included is Taylor World Wide, an online publication with news, events, articles and a Parent Connection.

UCS Support Center

http://www.indiana.edu/~ucssc

The UCS Support Center services Indiana University's campus information system. Review system bugs and news, or contact one of the center's consultants to troubleshoot account problems online.

University of Indianapolis

http://www.uindy.edu/

IndyWeb provides a range of information about the University of Indianapolis's admissions, resources, academics and student activites. Visitors are invited to take a virtual tour of the campus.

University of Notre Dame

http://www.nd.edu/

The home page of the University of Notre Dame provides useful information for prospective students about the university's departments, students, faculty, alumni, sports and religious activities.

Valparaiso University

http://www.valpo.edu/

Valparaiso University, located just outside Chicago but across the state line in Indiana, outlines its academic programs and educational facilities. Find course descriptions, admissions info and campus activity updates.

Wabash College

http://www.wabash.edu/

Wabash College, in Crawfordsville, Ind., offers information about its academic departments, courses of study and faculty listings. This Web site also contains links to the library, admissions and student services.

Iowa

Clarke College

http://www.clarke.edu/

The home page of Clarke College in Dubuque, Iowa, provides information on the school's academic departments, activities and events. In addition, browsers can link to other sites of interest on the Web, including Surf the Net—an Internet summer camp for high school students.

Coe College

http://www.coe.edu/

The Coe College Web site has eight buttons to click for information. The library has resources for exploring the Web and the welcome page contains a viewbook for prospective students.

Cornell College

http://www.cornell-iowa.edu/

Cornell College is a private liberal arts college located in eastern Iowa. Visitors to its home page will find details of its academic programs, facilities and policies.

Drake University

http://www.drake.edu/default.html

Iowa's Drake University offers a wealth of information on its academics, students, faculty and admissions at this site. Browers can also read a hypertext-version of Iowa's presidential caucus, or access the university directories.

Grinnell College

http://www.grin.edu/

Iowa's Grinnell College serves up general information on its academic departments, administrative office and campus-wide resources. Also find sesquicentennial info.

Iowa State University

http://www.iastate.edu/

The Iowa State University home page offers an overview of its educational opportunities and an introduction to student life. Includes listings of academic departments and programs, admissions guidelines and sports news.

North Iowa Area Community College

http://info.niacc.cc.ia.us/

The North Iowa Area Community College home page contains information about academic departments, programs of study, course offerings and faculty. Includes links to student services, campus information centers and admissions guidelines.

Simpson College

http://www.simpson.edu/

Simpson College in Indianola, Iowa, offers this viewbook of general information. Visitors can learn about the school's campus, programs, faculty and students.

Upper Iowa University

http://www.uiu.edu/

Upper Iowa University, located in Fayette, welcomes visitors with information about this liberal arts school. Extended education takes the spotlight here, a program designed for many different types of students, but residential studies also make the page.

William Penn College

http://www.wmpenn.edu/

William Penn College is a private liberal arts college located in Oskaloosa, Iowa. Visitors will find

an overview of academic programs, campus facilities, admissions and student services.

Kansas

Baker University

http://www.bakeru.edu/

The home page of Baker University in Baldwin, Kansas, offers an online catalog from the College of Arts and Sciences, a calendar of campus events, selections from the school newspaper, and pointers to student, departmental and faculty home pages.

Emporia State University

http://www.emporia.edu/

Emporia State University in Kansas unveils information about its academic programs and admissions requirements through this site. Prospective students can check out campus accommodations and safety.

MidAmerica Nazarene College

http://www.manc.edu/

Kansas's MidAmerica Nazarene College describes its academic offerings, departmental resources and library holdings at this educational information site.

University of Kansas

http://kufacts.cc.ukans.edu/cwis/kufacts_start.html

KUfacts is the University of Kansas's online information system. It offers a general overview of the Lawrence main campus, Kansas City Medical Center, and Overland Park Regents Center. Resources include a timetable of classes, course catalog, descriptions and calendar of events and activities, and lists of academic departments and campus organizations.

University of Kansas

http://www.sped.ukans.edu/campus/ku.html

Photos and brief movies bring to life the University of Kansas's online brochure. General overviews are provided of the university's campuses, academic divisions, library collections and cultural activities.

Kentucky

Bowling Green State University

http://www.bgsu.edu/

Kentucky's Bowling Green State University provides this online introduction to its academic departments, athletic programs and student activities. Access admissions information and gain entry to campus electronic resources from this site.

Centre College

http://www.centre.edu/

Centre College in Danville, Ky., maintains this site for information on its campus, programs, faculty and students. Visit here to learn about the college and link to a variety of student and alumni services.

University of Kentucky, Lexington

http://www.uky.edu/

Here's the gateway to the Lexington campus of the University of Kentucky. Access online campus resources or investigate academic programs, student services and the university's medical center.

University of Louisville

http://www.louisville.edu/

The University of Louisville, located in Kentucky, specializes in the fields of medicine, dentistry, law and engineering. Visitors will find general campus and admissions information, news, a searchable databases and Internet resources here.

Louisiana

Nicholls State University

http://server.nich.edu/

The Nicholls State University home page presents a portrait of the university, located in Thibodaux, La. Information is included on departments and faculty. Links go to Internet workshops, the Small Business Development Center and other Louisiana Web servers.

Northeast Louisiana University

http://www.nlu.edu/

Located in Monroe, Northeast Louisiana University offers this campus overview. Find information about its various colleges and degree programs, the facilities and faculty.

Southeastern Louisiana University

http://www.selu.edu/

Southeastern Louisiana University, Hammond, puts its best foot forward at this introductory site. Here, visitors and prospective students can review the school's academic programs, educational opportunities and check out information about the local area.

University of New Orleans

http://www.uno.edu/

Louisiana's University of New Orleans maintains this site for information access. Find descriptions of the school, its academic divisions and course offerings, plus pointers to items about New Orleans.

University of Southwestern Louisiana

http://www.usl.edu/

The University of Southwestern Louisiana home page contains information about the Lafayette university's faculty, research, academic departments, alumni and Ragin' Cajun athletics. Includes items of interest about the area, Cajun culture and publications.

Maine

Bates College

http://www.bates.edu/

Lewiston, Maine's Bates College's campus wide information system contains a complete description of the school, its academic departments, course offerings and faculty. Includes a virtual tour, admissions guidelines, sports, weather and student organizations.

Colby College

http://www.colby.edu/

Colby College in Waterville, Maine, maintains this home page offering a look at life on campus. Visitors can learn about the college and its history, tour the campus, check into the various departments and their course offerings, browse campus publications, and link to the home pages of student organizations.

University of Maine

http://www.ume.maine.edu/

Take a virtual visit to the University of Maine here and find out about the university's faculty, library, campus life, academics and more.

University of Maine, Farmington

http://www.umf.maine.edu/

Visitors to the home page for the Farmington campus of the University of Maine can learn about this small school in west-central Maine. Links are provided to student and alumni home pages, plus info on all the standard academic departments, administrative guidelines, and extracurricular activities.

University of Maine, Fort Kent

http://www.umfk.maine.edu/

The University of Maine at Fort Kent home page features not only information about the college and its programs but the greater community surrounding the campus. The site also hosts The French Connection—a collection of links to French language literature and Web sites.

Maryland

Hood College

http://www.hood.edu/

Resources from and about Hood College in Frederick, Md., are contained on this home page. In addition to information about the college, its programs, departments and services, there are pointers to its career center and library information center.

Johns Hopkins University

http://www.jhu.edu/

Johns Hopkins University—which maintains campuses in Baltimore, Washington, D.C., China and Italy—provides general information about its campuses, programs, faculty and students here. Includes research and alumni news.

Johns Hopkins University

gopher://gopher.jhu.edu/

JHUniverse, the Johns Hopkins University gopher, has information about the school's faculty and academic programs, as well as calendars, library links and alumni news.

Loyola College in Maryland

http://www.loyola.edu/menu.html

The Loyola College in Maryland site offers information on programs of study, academic departments, student services and faculty. Includes telephone numbers and e-mail addresses.

St. John's College

http://www.sjca.edu/

St. John's College unveils information about its twin campuses in Annapolis, Md., and Santa Fe, N.M., through this home page. Visitors can click to either campus for details about course offerings and admissions.

Towson State University

http://www.towson.edu/

The official homepage of Towson State University in Towson, Md., includes links to official information and student homepages, as well as a message from the president and alumni resources.

U.S. Naval Academy

http://www.nadn.navy.mil/

Located in Annapolis, Md., the United States Naval Academy maintains this site offering general information about the undergraduate college for officer training. Links to the school's information resources and an index of U.S. Navy Web pages are featured.

University of Baltimore

http://www.ubalt.edu/

This site presents an overview of the University of Baltimore, including information on its academic departments and faculty. Visitors also will find links to university services and user's groups.

University of Maryland, Baltimore County

http://www.umbc.edu/

This is the main Web site for the University of Maryland, Baltimore County. Visitors will find information on academic departments, student and faculty resources, and campus news and events.

University of Maryland, College Park

http://inform.umd.edu/

The University of Maryland at College Park home page provides information about the school's academic programs and the Baltimore-Washington, D.C., corridor.

University of Maryland System

http://www.umd.edu/

This gateway page is the main Web site for the University of Maryland System. Visitors can access home pages of various UMS learning institutions, or link to state governmental and K-12 educational resources.

Massachusetts

Amherst College

http://www.amherst.edu/

Amherst College's ACCESS Information System presents an overview of the college, its academic programs and faculty listings. Includes a campus tour, campus and area maps, and a gateway to external resources.

Babson College

http://www.babson.edu/

Babson College in Wellesley, Mass., presents an in-depth look for potential students. An overview of both graduate and undergraduate programs is provided, along with a variety of departmental and program pages. Also, check out special events on campus.

Boston College

http://www.bc.edu/

Boston College in Chestnut Hill, Mass., provides information here on its programs and people. Visit here to learn about its academic departments, courses of study and faculty members. Links to campus communications centers and financial aid resources are also available.

Boston University

http://web.bu.edu/

Items of interest found on this page include links to Boston University's colleges, schools and departments, access to its online reference and research tools, and information on how to contact the university, located along the banks of the Charles River.

Brandeis University

http://www.brandeis.edu/

Brandeis University, the only nonsectarian Jewish-sponsored university or college in the Unites States, offers a home page packed with helpful information. You can learn about this Massachusetts-based school's admissions policies, student organizations, faculty, academic departments and up-to-date news about the school itself.

Clark University

http://www.clarku.edu/

Worcester, Mass.'s Clark University opens its doors to the world at this home page. The site highlights the school's programs, along with profiles of the people on campus and a brief history of the institution.

College of the Holy Cross

http://www.holycross.edu/

The College of the Holy Cross in Worcester, Mass., provides information here on its programs and people. Visit here for an overview of academics, computer and research resources, campus and community events, and more.

Hampshire College

http://www.hampshire.edu/

Hampshire College in Amherst, Mass., provides information here on its programs and people. Visit here to learn about its upcoming events, academic courses, reference resources, admissions requirements and more.

Harvard University

http://www.harvard.edu/

Harvard University offers this virtual tour of its storied campus and academic facilities. Visitors can learn about the school's history, its many special programs, its overstuffed library and its thriving student organizations. An online help program ensures easy navigation for those without an Ivy League sheepskin.

Massachusetts Institute of Technology

http://web.mit.edu/

Massachusetts Institute of Technology in Cambridge, Mass., provides information here on its people and programs. Visit here for campus news and activities, staff and student directories, research facilities, computing services and other academic resources.

Massachusetts Institute of Technology, Information Servers

http://www.mit.edu:8001/server-pages.html

This site lists information servers around the Massachusetts Institute of Technology. Includes links to MIT services, academic departments, laboratories, student groups and other Web-related resources.

Mount Holyoke College

http://www.mtholyoke.edu/

Explore educational opportunities and academic resources at Mt. Holyoke, a historic liberal arts college for women, located in South Hadley, Mass.

Northeastern University

http://www.northeastern.edu/

Northeastern University in Boston provides this Web server with information about the school's departments, academics, computing and online publications. Browsers can also read more about the Boston area, or link to other places of interest on the Internet.

Rittners School of Floral Design

http://www.tiac.net/users/stevrt/index.html

Located in Boston, Mass., Rittners School of Floral Design offers courses for the professional and amateur alike. Visit the school's home page to learn more about available courses and careers in floral design, to find answers to Frequently Asked Questions (FAQ), or to link to topic-related sites.

Simon's Rock College

http://www.simons-rock.edu/

Simon's Rock College in Great Barrington, Mass., maintains this site with information about the school, its programs, location and admissions details.

Smith College

http://www.smith.edu/

Smith College in Northampton, Mass., a private liberal arts college for women, maintains this site for providing general information and links to online resources. Visit here to learn about the school's people, programs, admissions policies, campus news and schedules, or to link to the college's library services.

University of Massachusetts, Amherst

http://www.cs.umass.edu/rcfdocs/newhome/index.html

This experimental multimedia Web server from the University of Massachusetts, Amherst, uses text, photos, and audio clips to convey information about the school, campus, departments, research groups and the local area. Visitors can even take a campus HyperTour.

University of Massachusetts, Boston

http://www.umb.edu/

The University of Massachusetts at Boston supplies general information and contact information at this site. Other resources include exam schedules and pointers to Healey Library, Continuing Education, Environmental Sciences and other divisions and programs.

University of Massachusetts, Lowell

http://www.uml.edu/

An online brochure for the University of Massachusetts Lowell, this site provides general statistics about students, faculty and campus life. Explore admissions information or sort through the contents of the school's multimedia labs.

Wellesley College

http://www.wellesley.edu/

Campus information, research resources and Internet tools are presented here by Wellesley College in Wellesley, Mass. This site features schedules, information on programs, college policies, online exhibits, a library catalog and links to other resources.

Wheaton College
http://www.wheatonma.edu/

The Wheaton College site contains information on academic departments, courses of study and admissions. Includes links to the library, a virtual tour of the Norton, Mass., campus and listings of electronic resources.

Michigan

Central Michigan University
http://www.cmich.edu/

Located in Mount Pleasant, Central Michigan University presents this home page offering information about its academic programs and facilities. Take an online tour of the campus, get a feel for student life, and review available services and resources.

Eastern Michigan University
http://www.emich.edu/

Eastern Michigan University maintains this overview of life on its campus. Find information about the academic programs, faculty and staff, resources and activities.

Ferris State University
http://about.ferris.edu/

Ferris State University, of Big Rapids, Mich., provides information here on its academic departments, courses of study and athletic programs. Includes admissions information, student services descriptions and links to various campus servers.

Hillsdale College
http://www.hillsdale.edu/

Hillsdale College presents an introduction to academics, admissions and Internet resources at its home page. Visitors can find a general overview of the Michigan school's educational opportunities here.

Hope College
http://www.hope.edu/

Hope College, a Christian liberal arts college in Holland, Mich., maintains this site with information about admissions, academics, student services and alumni.

Lake Superior State University
http://www.lssu.edu/

Lake Superior State University in Sault Ste. Marie, Mich., opens its doors to the Web world with information about academic offerings and campus activities on this page. After examining the site, test your knowledge by taking the LSSU trivia contest.

Michigan State University
http://burrow.cl.msu.edu/

Michigan State University's well-designed home page includes information on the school's curriculum, faculty, outreach programs, and related areas of interest. Includes campus maps and alumni information.

Michigan Technological University
http://www.mtu.edu/

Michigan Technological University presents information about its academic programs, admissions policies, research facilities and alumni resources.

Michigan Web Servers
http://www.w3.org/hypertext/DataSources/WWW/Michigan.html

Take a look at college Web sites from Michigan through this page. It offers links to better-known state colleges such as the University of Michigan and Michigan State University as well as smaller colleges such as Wayne State University.

University of Michigan
http://www.umich.edu/

The University of Michigan contains information on academic departments, programs of study and faculty profiles. Includes info on admissions, alumni resources, libraries, campus facilities and student services.

Washtenaw Community College
http://northernspy.washtenaw.cc.mi.us/

Washtenaw Community College in Ann Arbor, Mich., provides information here on its courses, departments and faculty members. Visitors will also find student services, special programs, and local directories and maps.

MINNESOTA

Anoka-Ramsey Community College
http://www.an.cc.mn.us/

The Anoka-Ramsey Community College home page contains information on academic departments, courses of study and a virtual tour of the campus. Includes an events calendar, college services and listings of student organizations.

Augsburg College
http://www.augsburg.edu/

The Augsburg College home page contains information on the school's academic departments, library and computer resources, plus an online brochure and campus map. Includes a link to the Minneapolis institution's gopher server.

Bemidji State University
http://bsuweb.bemidji.msus.edu/

Bemidji State University, located in Bemidji, Minn., has set up this Web site with information

about the school, its faculty and a link to the campus library. This site also links to HTML help resources and Roadmap Internet training archives.

College of Saint Benedict and Saint John's University
http://www.csbsju.edu/

This is the combined home page for two sibling Catholic colleges in Minnesota, Saint John's University and the College of Saint Benedict. Includes general information about the schools, plus links to alumni and library resources.

College of St. Scholastica
http://www.css.edu/

The College of St. Scholastica's home page includes information about the Duluth, Minn., institution. Visitors can access facts about the school's academics, activities and admissions policies, along with administrative and alumni information.

Gustavus Adolphus College
http://www.gac.edu/

Gustavus Adolphus College in St. Peter, Minn., provides information here on its campus and programs. Visit here to find news, awards, and admissions and academic information. A keyword search of its database is also available.

Mankato State University
http://www.mankato.msus.edu/

Prospective students are invited to take a virtual tour of campus at the Mankato State University home page. Read about academic offerings and educational opportunities here.

St. Mary's University of Minnesota
http://140.190.128.190/SMC/HomePage.html

The Saint Mary's University of Minnesota home page provides information on the university's academic programs, campus, degree offerings and publications. Includes access to Netphone and video conferencing services with university officers.

St. Olaf College
http://www.stolaf.edu/

St. Olaf College in Northfield, Minn., offers this site with a variety of information about the school's academics, faculty, students and Internet resources.

University of Minnesota
http://www.umn.edu/

The University of Minnesota provides this home page for information on the academic departments, programs of study, faculty and admissions at its four campuses. Includes descriptions of campus facilities, student organizations and athletics.

University of Minnesota, Duluth

http://www.d.umn.edu/

The University of Minnesota at Duluth home page contains a vast assortment of resources, from a student handbook to faculty information to admissions guidelines.

University of St. Thomas

http://www.stthomas.edu/

The University of St. Thomas is a Catholic liberal arts college located in St. Paul/Minneapolis, Minn. Visitors will find information on academics, administrative affairs, campus events and sports programs.

Winona State University

http://www.winona.msus.edu/

Winona State University in Minnesota provides an overview of its academic programs and admissions information here. The site also highlights student interests and offers a glimpse of the town of Winona.

Mississippi

Millsaps College

http://www.millsaps.edu/

Millsaps College, located in Jackson, Miss., offers a Web site that includes a profile of the school and info on its academic departments. Visitors can check out a campus map, drop in to the Career Center or library or check out the dining services.

Mississippi State University

http://www.msstate.edu/

Study an online brochure and catalog for Mississipi State University at this site. Descriptions of its academic, campus and community resources are provided by the Starkville, Miss., institution of higher education.

University of Mississippi

http://www.olemiss.edu/

Ole Miss maintains this site to introduce its people and programs. Visit here to learn about its admissions procedures, access its library collections, link to its medical center and find other academic resources available.

University of Southern Mississippi

http://www.usm.edu/

The University of Southern Mississippi maintains this site to provide general information and Internet resources. Visit here to learn about its campus, programs, faculty and students.

Missouri

Central Missouri State University

http://cmsuvmb.cmsu.edu/

Central Missouri State University in Warrensburg introduces its faculty, students and mascot at this site. Look up campus services and general Missouri information here.

Northeast Missouri State University

http://www.nemostate.edu/

The home page for Northeast Missouri State University, soon to be Truman State University, contains information on academic departments, course offerings and faculty profiles. Also included are info on student services, campus organizations and publications.

Saint Louis University

http://www.slu.edu/

The home page of Saint Louis University, a Jesuit school in Missouri, allows browsers to read pages containing detailed info about SLU's four campuses.

Southeast Missouri State University

http://www.semo.edu/

Southeast Missouri State University in Cape Girardeau offers a general overview of its academic programs and educational facilities. Visit here to learn about its programs and people or to contact faculty and staff.

Stephens College

http://www.stephens.edu/

The second oldest women's college in the nation, Stephens College is a private, four-year institution located on 190 acres in Columbia, Mo. Find an academic overview along with a history of the school, details of campus life and admissions particulars posted to this home page.

University of Missouri, Columbia

http://www.missouri.edu/

The University of Missouri at Columbia offers information here about its courses, department activities and research materials. Visitors to this site will also find beginners' Internet tips, a help desk service and Internet connection account information.

University of Missouri, Kansas City

http://www.umkc.edu/

The home page for the University of Missouri, Kansas City, greets visitors with general overviews of the school's faculty, student body, computing facilities, academic departments and campus resources.

University of Missouri, Rolla

http://www.umr.edu/

The University of Missouri, Rolla, site provides information on academic departments, programs of study and faculty. Visitors will find admissions info, alumni news, a list of student organizations, campus events and maps.

Washington University

http://www.wustl.edu/

Get a bearing on the campus of Washington University in St. Louis, Missouri with links to facts, student services, admission policies, schools, the library and athletics. Tour the campus, the city of St. Louis and examine FTP archives.

William Woods University

http://www.wmwoods.edu/

Billing itself as "the only private women's-centered university in the United States," William Woods University in Fulton, Mo., is proud of its mission to educate, enlighten and empower its 750 students. Learn more about the institution here.

Montana

Montana State University, Bozeman

http://www.montana.edu/

Montana State University offers information for prospective students and a general overview of its programs here. The thorough site also includes financial aid information, a class schedule and a look at the Bozeman area.

Montana State University, Northern

http://cis.nmclites.edu/

Montana State University, Northern opens the gates to its information services and Web and gopher servers at this site. Access coursework and computer information or the student consulting office from this home page.

University of Montana

http://www.umt.edu/

The University of Montana offers visitors a site full of information about "the Berkeley of the Rockies." Take a photo tour of the summer campus, visit the wildlife spatial analysis lab, examine the renowned creative writing program or consider enrolling in anything from environmental studies to economics.

Nebraska

Dana College

http://www.dana.edu/

Dana College is a private liberal arts college located in Blair, Neb. Visitors will find information on academics, special programs and campus events at the Dana home page.

University of Nebraska, Kearney

http://betty-boop.unk.edu/

The University of Nebraska at Kearney maintains this site with information on academic departments, courses of study, research and admissions. This site also includes info on student services, faculty and campus facilities.

University of Nebraska, Lincoln

http://www.unl.edu/

The University of Nebraska, Lincoln Information System provides academic and staffing facts about the school. Visitors also can sample various departments' home pages, scan campus maps or link to NebraskaNet's gopher service.

Nevada

University of Nevada, Las Vegas

http://www.unlv.edu/

The University of Nevada at Las Vegas maintains this online information kiosk offering visitors and prospective students details covering all aspects of university life. Features include course and events listings, a campus map, a telephone directory and links to specific colleges and departments.

University of Nevada, Reno

http://www.unr.edu

The University of Nevada at Reno presents an index with links to colleges, schools and departments. The site also includes phone listings, class schedules, the student newspaper and a photo tour. There's also a special link to UNR's Academic Master Plan.

New Hampshire

Dartmouth College

http://www.dartmouth.edu/

At the official home page of Dartmouth College, visitors will find general information about the college, in addition to details on its individual departments. Other links include academic support centers, student services, and alumni information.

Plymouth State College

http://www.plymouth.edu/

Plymouth State College in New Hampshire gives an overview of its departments and posts its latest news here. Visitors can also take a virtual tour of the college on this site.

University of New Hampshire

http://unhinfo.unh.edu/

This campus-wide information system is a user online gateway to the University of New Hampshire. Find an overview of the school's educational programs, admissions info, course offerings, facilities and campus news at this introductory site.

New Jersey

Drew University

http://www.drew.edu/

Located in Madison, N.J., Drew University is composed of its College of Liberal Arts, Graduate School and Theological School. Visitors to its page will find information on its academic departments, admissions, alumni resources and campus events.

Mercer County Community College

http://www.mccc.edu/

Mercer County Community College, located in Trenton, N.J., uses this Web ite to guide visitors through its courses and programs, providing financial aid information and admission details.

Monmouth University

http://www.monmouth.edu/

Monmouth University in West Long Branch, N.J., provides information here on its people and programs. Visit here to learn about the university and its research facilities, course offerings, academic departments, student activities and current events.

Montclair State University

http://www.montclair.edu/

Montclair State University introduces its campus facilities and academic programs at this official home page. Follow pointers to student organizations as well as news and publications.

New Jersey Institute of Technology

http://www.njit.edu/

At the home page of the New Jersey Institute of Technology, visitors can get a historical overview of the institution, descriptions of its various schools and departments, and application information. Includes photos of the campus and links to related sites on campus and off.

Princeton University

http://www.princeton.edu/index.html

New Jersey's Princeton University maintains this Ivy League Web site with links to the library, leisure activities, news, travel and weather. Includes a special link for students, faculty and staff.

Rider University

http://www.rider.edu/

Lawrenceville, N.J.'s Rider University invites visitors to tour its campus and sample its academic offerings at this site. Find access to online information resources, and faculty and student directories here.

Rowan College of New Jersey

http://www.rowan.edu/

Rowan College of New Jersey offers this overview of its departments and academic programs.

Also find directions to the campus and instructions for applying for admission.

Rutgers, the State University of New Jersey

http://info.rutgers.edu/

This central Web server for Rutgers State University, of New Jersey, provides information on its academic departments, facilities, student life and campus happenings.

Seton Hall University

http://www.shu.edu/

Guests at the Seton Hall University home page can find out more about the curriculum, activities, programs, policies and staff of this private Catholic New Jersey university.

Stevens Institute of Technology

http://www.stevens-tech.edu/

Located in Hoboken, N.J., Stevens Institute of Technology provides this look at its mission, campus and programs. Find information on its academic departments, facilities, faculty and staff, campus events, and organizations. A clickable campus map and links to topical sites are also featured.

Trenton State College

http://www.trenton.edu/

Trenton State College, Ewing, N.J., maintains this site of general information and Internet resources. Visit here to learn about its campus, programs, faculty and students.

New Mexico

New Mexico State University

http://www.nmsu.edu/

New Mexico State University in Las Cruces, N.M., maintains this site with information about its campus, programs, faculty and students. Career placement services resources are also available here.

St. John's College

http://www.sjca.edu/

St. John's College unveils information about its twin campuses in Annapolis, Md., and Santa Fe, N.M., through this home page. Visitors can click to either campus for details about course offerings and admissions.

Santa Fe Community College

http://www.santafe.cc.fl.us/

At the home page of Santa Fe Community College, you can find complete information on the college and its programs, as well as information on the area.

University of New Mexico

http://www.unm.edu/

Here at Albuquerque's University of New Mexico home page, visitors can access student information and the school's various colleges. Links to libraries, campus services and research information are provided as well.

Western New Mexico University

http://www.wnmu.edu/

Western New Mexico University's home page features an undergraduate bulletin, a faculty and staff directory, and a photo exhibit. Also find information on Silver City and its attractions, plus links to other sites in New Mexico and beyond.

New York

Barnard College

http://www.barnard.columbia.edu/

New York-based Barnard College features general admissions and program information along with a school history and details about information technology on campus through this home page.

City University of New York

http://www.cuny.edu/

The City University of New York (CUNY) offers comprehensive information about its academics, departments, history, students and faculty at this site. Visitors can peruse campus maps, read publications or link to helpful resources for exploring the World Wide Web.

City University of New York, Graduate School and University Center

http://www.gc.cuny.edu/

The CUNY Graduate School and University Center presents this overview. Find pointers to information about academics and research, the Mina Rees Library, online documents, computer services, and a gallery of art.

Clarkson University

http://www.clarkson.edu/

Clarkson University in Potsdam, N.Y., invites visitors to peruse its academic information page, with details about graduate/undergraduate programs, scholarships and research. Those interested in the campus setting will find locale info as well.

Columbia University

http://www.columbia.edu/

New York's Columbia University provides individually tailored electronic resources for students, faculty, alumni and prospective students. Launch into the one of these information tours from the Columbia home page.

Cooper Union

http://www.cooper.edu/

Prospective students of the Cooper Union for the Advancement of Science and Art in New York will find an overview of the school here. The private college grants full-tuition scholarships to all of its students.

Cornell University

http://www.cornell.edu/

The home page for Cornell University, of Ithaca, N.Y., provides an extensive and colorful overview of its academic and student life. Visitors will also find information on Ithaca and the surrounding community here.

Daemen College

http://www.daemen.edu/

Tour the campus of Daemen College in western New York or get a sample of campus life through this home page. Prospective students can also check out the surrounding areas of Buffalo, Niagara Falls and Toronto.

Erie Community College

http://davey.sunyerie.edu/

Erie Community College introduces visitors to its educational programs and campus facilities at this site. Includes descriptions of course offerings, links to student services, faculty home pages and campus information servers.

Hamilton College

http://www.hamilton.edu/

Located outside Clinton, N.Y., Hamilton College maintains this page offering a look at life on campus. Visitors are invited to examine the school's academic programs and student services, and to tour the facilities.

Hobart and William Smith Colleges

http://hws3.hws.edu:9000/

Hobart College for men and William Smith College for women are associated institutions in Geneva, N.Y. Visitors will find a quick overview of the colleges along with detailed info on their academic departments and educational resources at this site.

Hudson Valley Community College

http://www.hvcc.edu/

Somewhere in the back of your mind, a strange desire to know more about Hudson Valley Community College has haunted you. Satisfy that craving by checking out the HVCC site with links to the Biology Department, the HVCC gopher and the Center for Effective Teaching.

Long Island University

http://www.liunet.edu/

Long Island University is a private university in the New York City area. Its welcome page contains

pointers to campus-wide information, its six campuses, information resources and Internet starting points. Overviews, details on programs and other resources are available for each campus.

Marist College

http://www.marist.edu/

Marist College in Poughkeepsie, N.Y., provides a wealth of information on its academics, history, resources, administration, campus life and alumni here. Visitors to this site can also read the latest news and events at the college, obtain contact info or browse college online resources, including the library, Web services and academic computing.

Plattsburgh Information Delivery

http://bio444.beaumont.plattsburgh.edu/SUNYInformation.html

Maintained by the State University of New York at Plattsburgh, this page features an index of the info servers on campus. Links to Web resources are also featured.

Polytechnic University

http://www.poly.edu/

Polytechnic University's home page provides information about events scheduled to take place on this venerable New York institution's three campuses. Also here: descriptions of the science and engineering institution's academic and research programs, computer facilities, and student services, projects and publications.

Rensselaer Polytechnic Institute

http://www.rpi.edu/

This university home page describes the Rensselaer Polytechnic Institute and its undergraduate and graduate courses of study. Includes information about this Troy, N.Y., institution's admissions criteria, student life, faculty and staff, administrative services, pointers to regional info and events.

Rockefeller University

http://www.rockefeller.edu/ru.home.html

New York's Rockefeller University, home to the Rockefeller University Hospital, gives an overview of its programs and research efforts here. Visitors can also access its administrative services, including the library.

Sage Colleges

http://www.sage.edu/

Russell Sage College provides this Web site with information on the academics, activities and resources of its four colleges. Prospective students can obtain information here about the schools and their programs.

St. Lawrence University

http://www.stlawu.edu/

St. Lawrence University, Canton, N.Y., serves up information here on its academic programs and student life. Guests can peruse a medley of departmental home pages and student groups, or flip through the academic calendar and publications.

State University of New York
http://www.suny.edu/

The SUNY multicollege public education system that educates 400,000 students a year, comes to the Web with information for the curious guest or prospective student.

State University of New York, Albany
http://www.albany.edu/

Check out the "Feature of the Week" at SUNY Albany's home page. You'll also find info on admissions, majors and graduate study programs, an undergraduate bulletin and a searchable class schedule.

State University of New York, Brockport
http://www.brockport.edu/

The State University of New York at Brockport's home page provides campus and academic department information. Visitors can receive local weather information, link to other SUNY Web pages or access "USA Today" online departments from this site.

State University of New York, Buffalo
http://wings.buffalo.edu/

The State University of New York, Buffalo home page offers up a host of material, including information about the faculty and staff, libraries, academic departments, computing facilities, and events of general interest to the Buffalo community.

State University of New York, Cortland
http://www.cortland.edu/

SUNY Cortland puts its academic and administrative departments online at this site. Review educational opportunities, student life experiences and campus information services here.

State University of New York, Geneseo
http://mosaic.cc.geneseo.edu/

The State University of New York at Geneseo introduces its educational opportunities and campus resources at this site. Included are local news and server offerings.

State University of New York, Plattsburgh
http://bio444.beaumont.plattsburgh.edu/Default.html

The State University of New York at Plattsburgh provides a tour of its campus, course descriptions, program overviews and current campus news. Visitors to this "Digital Rest Area" will also find links to sites of interest in Plattsburgh and around the world.

State University of New York, Potsdam
http://www.potsdam.edu/

The oldest of the 64 units that make up the State University of New York system, SUNY Potsdam offers a 4-year, liberal arts-based education. Take a virtual tour of the college, review its academics, sports and student activities, plus find campus directories, news and events information.

State University of New York, Stony Brook
http://www.sunysb.edu/

The Stony Brook campus of the State University of New York presents Web servers run by different university departments, a campus news and information server, directories of faculty, staff and students, and access to the library.

Syracuse University
http://cwis.syr.edu/

New York's Syracuse University reveals its vital statistics at the introductory page of its Campus-Wide Information System. Explore the campus, the Syracuse region and entry points to the World Wide Web here.

Union College
http://www.union.edu/

Union College provides of an online catalog to assist newcomers in their search for academic information about this Schenectady, N.Y., institution. Also, find a directory of campus services.

United States Military Academy
http://www.usma.edu/

The United States Military Academy at West Point, N.Y., apprises visitors of admissions information, agencies and departments, with links to mailing lists, e-mail addresses, online utilities, references and journals.

University of Rochester
http://www.rochester.edu/

The University of Rochester's online information system contains links to the expected areas: admissions, academic and administrative departments, alumni information, school libraries, and more. A rather useful help link goes somewhat beyond the expected, even offering instruction in setting up a Web server.

Vassar College
http://vasweb.vassar.edu/vc.guide.html

Links to everything you need to know about this New York school are found at Vassar College WebCentral, with links to curriculum information, faculty, admissions policies and more.

North Carolina

Davidson College
http://www.davidson.edu/

Davidson College, just north of Charlotte, N.C., describes its liberal arts and sciences academic program at this home page. Also provided are info on financial aid, athletics, the library and more.

Duke University
http://www.duke.edu/

This is the home page for North Carolina's Duke University. Visitors will find administrative, academic and student information here, as well as links to the university library and medical center.

East Carolina University
http://www.ecu.edu/

East Carolina University serves up a wealth of information about its academics, administration, computing services, student life, athletics and campus organizations. Browsers can also access the schools telephone and e-mail directories.

Guilford College
http://www.guilford.edu/

North Carolina's Guilford College invites visitors to explore its educational history and current programs at the school's home page. Overviews of academic and administrative departments are offered here.

North Carolina State University
http://www.ncsu.edu/

North Carolina State University, located in Raleigh, N.C., maintains this site to introduce its people and programs. Visit here for admissions information, staff and student directories, computer and library services, course offerings and other administrative and academic resources.

University of North Carolina
http://www.ga.unc.edu/

The University of North Carolina General Administration introduces itself here, along with information about campus resources, academics and constituent institutions. It includes scheduling for the North Carolina Research and Education Network as well a directory of the board of governors.

University of North Carolina, Chapel Hill
http://www.unc.edu/

The University of North Carolina, Chapel Hill, maintains this site with information about the school and links to departmental home pages, news and publications. There's also faculty, alumni and student information.

University of North Carolina, Greensboro

http://www2.uncg.edu/

Prospective students to the University of North Carolina, Greensboro will get an overview of the school, its departments and its student life here.

Wake Forest University

http://www.wfu.edu/www-data/start.html

Wake Forest University in Winston-Salem, N.C., maintains this site for general information. Visit here to learn about its programs, faculty and students. Includes maps and aerial photos of the campus and a comprehensive listing of the university's online resources.

Warren Wilson College

http://www.warren-wilson.edu/

The home page of Warren Wilson College in the Blue Ridge Mountains of Asheville, N.C., offers viewers a peek into its educational philosophy, based on academics, work for the school, and service to the community.

Western Carolina University

http://www.wcu.edu/

The Western Carolina University home page contains information on academic departments, programs of study and admissions guidelines for undergraduate and graduate students. Includes pointers to research projects, student services and descriptions of campus facilities.

North Dakota

North Dakota State University

http://www.ndsu.nodak.edu/

North Dakota State University, located in Fargo, welcomes visitors with details about programs and research, plus financial aid and housing information. Find out what's happening on campus and in athletics.

North Dakota University System

http://www.nodak.edu/

The North Dakota University System posts links to its eleven campuses here. The site also contains a link to the system's gopher server and to other servers in the state.

Ohio

Antioch College

http://college.antioch.edu/

The home page for Antioch College provides a range of college news and information. Visitors can read about Antioch's technology resources, academics, library and alumni or link to the psychology and peace studies home pages.

Bluffton College

http://www.bluffton.edu/

Bluffton College in Bluffton, Ohio, utilizes this Web space to introduce potential students to its studies, scholars and faculty. The Office of Academic Affairs dishes up a melange of handy info—such as the current academic calendar and an overview of the school's study center—while the student e-mail directory lets you browse for connected students.

Case Western Reserve University

http://litwww.cwru.edu/

The home page of Case Western Reserve University in Cleveland provides information on the school's academics, activities, services and computing resources. Includes pointers to CWRU publications and community information.

Cleveland State University

http://www.csuohio.edu/

Ohio's Cleveland State University maintains this site to introduce its people and programs. Visitors will find links to student services, departmental course offerings, library resources, administrative offices and associated organizations.

Denison University

http://louie.cc.denison.edu/

Prospective students of Denison University in Granville, Ohio, will learn about its programs and admission policy here. Visitors can also check out the campus and surrounding area.

Heidelberg College

http://www.heidelberg.edu/

Heidelberg College in Tiffin, Ohio, welcomes visitors to the HeiWay, a page of information about the campus and community. Special topics include links to the Fallen Timbers Battlefield Archaeological Project and Heidelberg's Water Quality Laboratory.

Hiram College

http://www.hiram.edu/

Hiram College in Ohio provides information about its faculty and programs here. The page also provides directions on how to reach the college from Cleveland and a weather forecast.

Kenyon College

http://www.kenyon.edu/

Ohio-based liberal arts institution Kenyon College offers an introduction to its admissions policies, academic programs and campus facilities here. Link to student publications and campus news for an insider's view of life at Kenyon.

Miami University

http://www.muohio.edu/

Miami University in Oxford, Ohio, maintains this site to provide information about its campus, faculty, students and educational resources.

Muskingum College

http://www.muskingum.edu/

Muskingum College in New Concord, Ohio, features at its virtual campus a message from its famous graduate, United States Senator and former astronaut John Glenn, along with tuition information and an introduction to its academic programs.

Oberlin College

http://www.oberlin.edu/

Ohio's Oberlin College, a four-year liberal arts school, maintains this overview of life on campus. Visitors will find information on the academic programs, facilities, student services and online resources, plus links to related sites.

Ohio Northern University

http://www.onu.edu/

The home page for Ohio Northern University contains information about the school's academic programs of study, listings of faculty and student services. Includes links to the athletic department, university statistics and area profiles.

Ohio State University

http://www.ohio-state.edu/

When was Ohio State University established? How many students does the university have? What's the record of the women's basketball team? Ohio State's home page can answer all these questions, and it will take you on a tour of campus and show you a movie of graduation to boot!

University of Cincinnati

http://www.uc.edu/

This site presents information on the University of Cincinnati's academic departments and programs, faculty members, student services and admissions policies. Includes links to student newspaper "The News Record," personal home pages maintained by UC community members, and the school's library services.

University of Dayton

http://www.udayton.edu/

The University of Dayton, Ohio, provides this Web site with a variety of information on the school's academics, administration, alumni, sports, and organizations. Browsers can read the University of Dayton Quarterly for weekly updates of the schools news.

Wilmington College
http://www.wilmington.edu/

Wilmington College introduces visitors to its educational opportunities and campus facilities at its home page. Prospective students can review the Ohio school's academic programs, student organizations and calendar of events.

Wright State University
http://www.wright.edu/

Wright State University in Dayton, Ohio, details for the visitor all the ins and outs of campus life, including academics, athletics, employment and student services.

Oklahoma

East Central University
http://student.ecok.edu/

East Central University in Oklahoma unveils information about its departments and provides links to GIF images of the campus. Includes pointers to the various departmental pages, admissions info, academic programs, student activities and organizations.

Langston University
http://www.lunet.edu/

Langston University's home page provides information about its departments, library and faculty, and also features a link to Blues Online, a Blues music information resource. Other links include general Web resources and information about high energy physics and African-American culture.

Oklahoma City University
http://frodo.okcu.edu/

Oklahoma City University provides information here about its academics, facilities, faculty, admissions and student events. Visit here for a virtual tour of its campus or link to a number of useful starter pages for exploring the World Wide Web.

University of Oklahoma
http://www.uoknor.edu/

The home page for the University of Oklahoma holds a variety of information for the campus community and visitors. Features include student and administrative affairs, details on individual colleges and research projects, sports information and a calendar of events.

University of Tulsa
http://www.utulsa.edu/

Oklahoma's University of Tulsa offers undergraduate and graduate degrees focusing on the theme of international and intercultural unity. The site provides general descriptions of programs, resources and student life.

Oregon

Central Oregon Community College
http://www.cocc.edu/

Central Oregon Community College in Bend, Ore., provides information here on its campus, programs, faculty and students. Links to community resources and a variety of Internet search tools are also available.

Lewis & Clark College
http://www.lclark.edu/

Visit Lewis & Clark College without making the long trek to Portland, Ore., at the school's introductory Web page. Find information about academic offerings and upcoming campus events here. Includes photo-studded campus information, along with links to the college's law and professional studies schools.

Linfield College
http://www.linfield.edu/

The home page for Linfield College, in McMinnville, Ore., describes the many services on its information web, including career planning, financial aid, alumni resources, campus schedules, intercollegiate sports, academic departments, and more.

Oregon State University
http://www.orst.edu/

Oregon State University's home page provides information about the school's campuses, students and educational offerings. Visitors also can begin a search of the OSU Web from here.

Portland State University
http://www.pdx.edu/

Portland State University maintains this general overview of the school. Find departmental listings, various resources, student services, an events calendar and news about PSU.

Reed College
http://www.reed.edu/

Reed College in Portland, Ore. maintains this site for general information. Visit here to learn about its campus, academic programs, faculty and students. Information about its annual Educom conference is also available here.

University of Oregon
http://www.uoregon.edu/

The University of Oregon, Eugene maintains this site for general information. Visit here to learn about its campus, programs, faculty and students; also link to the main university server and a variety of other Internet resources.

Western College
http://www.wbc.edu/

Western College, a Christian liberal arts college tucked into the woods of Salem, Ore., maintains this informational page about its academic programs and campus news. Interested students can apply online.

Willamette University
http://www.willamette.edu/

Oregon's Willamette University presents information on its academic departments, students and faculty at this introductory site. Featured are an online course catalog and history of the university.

Pennsylvania

Allegheny College
http://www.alleg.edu/

Northern Pennsylvania's Allegheny College invites visitors to its home page to review its academic programs, student services and campus facilities. A campus map, calendar of events and links to academic departments are featured.

Allentown College
http://www.allencol.edu/

Pennsylvania's Allentown College presents a look at its academic departments and computing facilities here. Visitors can search course offerings and obtain admissions information.

Bloomsburg University
http://www.bloomu.edu/

Pennsylvania's Bloomsburg University sponsors this home page offering a look at life on campus. Visitors are invited to learn about the university, its academic programs, student life and community services.

Bucknell University
http://www.bucknell.edu/

Pennsylvania's Bucknell University maintains this site to provide general information and links to campus resources. Visit this site to learn more about the university. Directions to the campus from nearby cities is also provided.

Carnegie Mellon University
http://www.cmu.edu/

Carnegie Mellon University's home page serves up admissions, research, alumni and student life info, along with historical information about the Pittsburgh institution. Visitors can access the school's various academic departments to get the lowdown on specific courses of study.

Drexel University

http://www.drexel.edu/

Drexel University's home page presents information about the school's academic and administrative setup. Also: admissions and internship details, and links to the Philadelphia learning institution's research and library facilities.

Duquesne University

http://www.duq.edu/

Located in Pittsburgh, Pa., Duquesne University maintains this look at life on its campus. Find information about the university's schools, departments, students, alumni, libraries and Web resources.

Edinboro University

http://www.edinboro.edu/

Pennsylvania's Edinboro University introduces its facilities and educational programs at this site. Visit the library and academic departments from here. A map is provided for navigating ease.

Gettysburg College

http://www.gettysburg.edu/

Gettysburg College provides information on academic departments, programs of study and admissions. Includes links to college publications, descriptions of student life and campus information servers.

Haverford College

http://www.haverford.edu/

Haverford College, the Pennsylvania liberal arts institution, offers an introduction to its academic programs and campus facilities here. Includes links to career development resources, a guide to the Philadelphia area and alumni info.

Indiana University of Pennsylvania

http://www.iup.edu/

The Indiana University of Pennsylvania has three campuses in the Allegheny Mountains. It offers a brief overview here, along with links to its honors college, its information system and an online phone book.

Lebanon Valley College

http://www.lvc.edu/

Lebanon Valley College of Pennsylvania features information about its programs and campus through this home page. Visitors can read about admissions requirements and check on the availability of financial aid.

Lock Haven University

http://www.lhup.edu/

Lock Haven University of Pennsylvania features admissions information and resources for current and former students at its home page. Visitors can access a career services section or view the school's library resources.

Lycoming College

http://www.lycoming.edu/

Founded in 1812 at Williamsport, Pa., Lycoming College is one of the 50 oldest colleges in the United States. Visit the Lycoming home page to learn more about the libraries, student services and academic offerings.

Messiah College

http://www.messiah.edu/

Messiah College is an arts and sciences college located in Grantham, Pa. Visitors to the school's Web page will find information on academic departments, administration, admissions policies and campus publications.

Millersville University

http://marauder.millersv.edu/

Millersville University's home page introduces visitors to the Pennsylvania school. Learn about its campus, academics, administration and student services here, or access its gopher server.

Penn State University

http://www.psu.edu/

Penn State University maintains this overview of life among the Nittany Lions. Site features include information on academic and research programs, student services, the faculty and facilities.

Shippensburg University

http://www.ship.edu/

Pennsylvania's Shippensburg University, a liberal arts and professional programs institution, maintains this site. Visitors can read about the school's academics, admissions and student activities, or link to the home pages of faculty and students.

University of Pennsylvania

http://www.upenn.edu/

The University of Pennsylvania maintains this site to introduce its people and programs. Visit here for staff and student directories, worldwide faculty and colleagues listings, events calendars, and other academic and administrative resources.

University of Pittsburgh

http://www.pitt.edu/

Prospective students to the University of Pittsburgh can learn about admission and faculty information via PittInfo, as well as the latest news about the school and the year's calendar of events.

University of Scranton

http://www.uofs.edu/

The University of Scranton, a private coeducational Catholic institution located in Pennsylvania, invites visitors to take a look at its academic and campus information. Links to admissions information is included.

Ursinus College

http://www.ursinus.edu/

Ursinus College in Collegeville, Pa., presents its catalog of courses and admissions on its home page. Prospective students can take a look at student communications, check out the library's resources or search the college directory of e-mail addresses.

Villanova University

http://www.vill.edu/

An online brochure for Villanova University offers an illustrated look at the school's academic programs, student activities and campus facilities. Visitors can access the university's information services and school news here.

Virtual Media Lab

http://philae.sas.upenn.edu/

Online teaching materials and subject matter resources for several academic disciplines are available at the Virtual Media Lab site. Includes coursework in art history, English, religious studies, languages and other areas. Sponsored by the University of Pennsylvania.

Wilkes University

http://www.wilkes.edu/

Prospective students to Wilkes University in Pennsylvania can take a virtual tour of the university here. This online catalogue includes telephone and e-mail directories among its services.

York College

http://www.yorkcol.edu/

York College's home page provides information about courses, academic resources and events at this York, Penn., school. Includes information about the central Pennsylvania area, plus links connecting visitors to alumni information and the resources available at the school's Schmidt Library.

Rhode Island

Brown University

http://www.brown.edu/

This site contains offers visitors a detailed look at university life. Features include a walking tour of the campus, links to the university's administration, academic departments, athletics program and library. Visitors also can access a Brown University phone book and alumni information.

Johnson & Wales University

http://www.jwu.edu/

Johnson & Wales University is a liberal arts college located in Providence, R.I., with associated campuses in Virginia, South Carolina and Florida. When we last checked this site was still under construction but promises to offer more extensive news on its academics and student activities.

In the meantime, guests can access a variety of departmental pages, flick through the library and bookstore catalogs or find out about admission requirements.

University of Rhode Island

http://www.uri.edu/

The home page for the University of Rhode Island contains information for the campus community and its visitors. Features include admissions information and links to campus clubs and services. Visitors will also find photos and a map of the campus.

South Carolina

Clemson University

http://www.clemson.edu/

South Carolina's Clemson University provides information about the school's admissions, financial aid and housing policies, as well as news and details about its academic and administrative organization. Includes information about the university's Web server. Campus maps available.

College of Charleston

http://www.cofc.edu/

The College of Charleston home page provides general information concerning the South Carolina school's academic programs, departments and student body. Find facility descriptions and electronic resource listings as well.

Furman University

http://www.furman.edu/

Furman University's home page offers a multimedia overview of the Greenville, S.C., campus, its academic curriculum and happenings outside the classroom. Pointers to the Cultural Life Program and various student organizations are included.

University of South Carolina

http://www.sc.edu/

The University of South Carolina's home page offers information from calendars, maps and text files for potential students, staff members and alumni. Its Web site links to academic, administrative and research information, as well as news and favored pages.

University of South Carolina, Aiken

http://www.usca.scarolina.edu/

The University of South Carolina, Aiken maintains this site for general information and Internet resources. Visit here to learn about its programs and people, access its library collection, and link to a variety of Internet search tools.

South Dakota

Dakota State University

http://www.dsu.edu/

Dakota State University's Web page offers a map of the campus and a calendar of upcoming events. Also found here are faculty profiles, course offerings and links to student, faculty, and staff members' personal home pages.

South Dakota State University

http://www.sdstate.edu/

South Dakota State University's home page provides visitors with descriptions of its major courses of study, its museums and organizations of students, faculty and alumni. Links to regional sites center South Dakota State with a sense of place.

University of South Dakota

http://www.usd.edu/

The University of South Dakota at Vermillion provides information here on its campus, programs and resources. Visit here to learn about the university and link to news, events, libraries, research facilities and more.

Tennessee

Belmont University

http://acklen.belmont.edu/

Belmont University is a Christian liberal arts college located in Nashville, Tenn. Visitors to the school's Web site will find information about academics, athletics, faculty and students, plus links to faculty, student and alumni home pages and campus stores like the Computer Connection.

Middle Tennessee State University

http://www.mtsu.edu/

Middle Tennessee State University in Murfreesboro, Tenn., maintains this site for general information and Internet resources. Visit here to learn about its campus, programs, faculty and students. Links to university gopher sites and other Internet servers are available.

Rhodes College

http://www.rhodes.edu/

Rhodes College, Memphis, Tenn., maintains its home page with information about admissions, academics, alumni and links to related sites, including information about Memphis.

Southern College of Seventh-Day Adventists

http://www.southern.edu/

Among the resources presented here by Southern College of Seventh-Day Adventists in Collegedale, Tenn., are departmental information, news releases, a schedule of classes and individuals' home pages. Links to other Seventh-Day Adventists resources are available.

Tennessee Technological University

http://www.tntech.edu/

The home page of the Tennessee Technological University contains information on academic departments and colleges, programs of study and faculty profiles. Includes info on admissions, campus services, computer and scientific facilities.

University of Memphis

http://www.memphis.edu/

The University of Memphis, Tenn., maintains this site for general information. Visit here to learn about its programs, people and the Memphis area. University library access also is available.

University of Tennessee

http://loki.ur.utk.edu/default.html

The University of Tennessee offers this online gateway to its statewide campus system and educational resources. Prospective students can explore academic opportunities and research facilities at this introductory site.

University of Tennessee Office of Academic and Research Services

http://voyager.rtd.utk.edu/

The University of Tennessee Office of Academic and Research Services designs networked information systems to support the university's research mission. This office supplies information on its services here and posts links to the Federal Register, Commerce Business Daily and other campus sites.

University of Tennessee, Knoxville

http://www.utk.edu/

The University of Tennessee, Knoxville, maintains this site to provide links to general information. Visit here to learn more about its facilities, programs, faculty and students.

University of Tennessee, Martin

http://www.utm.edu/

The University of Tennessee at Martin offers undergraduate degree programs in more than 80 specialized fields and graduate programs including business administration, education, and human environmental sciences. This site outlines its academic areas and provides links to other university and Internet resources.

University of Tennessee, Memphis

http://utmgopher.utmem.edu/utm.html

The University of Tennessee at Memphis maintains this site to introduce its programs and people. Visitors will find campus visitor and policy information, job listings, staff and student home page, departmental course offerings, and other academic and administrative resources.

University of the South (Sewanee)

http://www.sewanee.edu/

The University of the South, commonly known as Sewanee, is a small liberal arts school in Tennessee. Prospective students can tour campus, review degree programs and explore educational opportunities at this home page.

Vanderbilt University

http://www.vanderbilt.edu/

A research university located in Nashville, Tenn., Vanderbilt offers visitors to its home page campus news, admissions guidelines, and information on its academic and research programs. Links to the library and other resources both on and off campus are also featured.

Texas

Abilene Christian University

http://www.acu.edu/

The Abilene Christian University, Texas, site contains information about academic departments, courses of study and faculty profiles. The "ACUinfo" site also includes info on admissions, financial aid, an events calendar and campus organizations.

Angelo State University

http://www.angelo.edu/

The home page for Angelo State University in San Angelo, Texas, features the university's entire course catalog with student information, along with a campus map, plenty of pages dedicated to Angelo sports, and even some free self-teaching basic computer programming courses.

Austin Community College

http://www.austin.cc.tx.us/

Austin Community College, a two-year school in Austin, Texas, provides information about its facilities, services, academics, admissions and more at this home page. Publications, computer tools and links also are available.

Baylor University

http://www.baylor.edu/

The Baylor University home page provides an overview of the institution, its academic programs, departments and courses of study. Includes descriptions of campus facilities, services, student organizations and admissions guidelines.

East Texas State University

http://www.etsu.edu/

East Texas State University presents overviews of its administrative, academic and student departments here. Prospective students can review class schedules and library resources.

Houston Community College System

http://www.hccs.cc.tx.us/

The Houston Community College System provides a clickable map here to takes visitors to its six colleges. The page includes a map of Houston Internet sites and a listing of frequently requested sites such as the library, traffic report and software.

Incarnate Word College

http://www.iwctx.edu/

Incarnate Word College in San Antonio, Texas, home of the Crusaders, unveils its mission and academic offerings through this home page. The college includes information about its international programs, career services and sports here.

Rice University

http://www.owlnet.rice.edu/

Students at Rice University and other visitors will find the school's Owlnet Web server packed with links to information about the university, as well as general Internet information resources and cool photos of owls. Includes links to Rice library holdings, student home pages and administrative info.

Richland College

http://www.rlc.dcccd.edu/

Dallas County Community College District's Richland College serves campus, admissions and course information, as well as details about the school's academic departments at this home page. Visitors can also sample views campus or link to other schools within the district.

St. Edward's University

http://www.stedwards.edu/home.htm

A four-year, coeducational liberal arts, Catholic university located on a hilltop overlooking Austin, Texas, St. Edward's University offers programs in the behavioral, social and natural sciences, business, education and the humanities. Learn more about the school, its history and academic programs at this home page.

Sam Houston State University

http://www.shsu.edu/

Sam Houston State University, a member of the Texas State University system, presents this home page for information on its students, faculty and campus. Visitors will also find links to graduate programs and community resources.

Southwest Texas State University

http://www.swt.edu/

Southwest Texas State University in San Marcos, Texas, maintains this site with a description of academic programs, student life and campus facilities. Look for electronic library access and links to online publications here.

Texas A&M University

http://www.tamu.edu/

Texas A&M University's home page provides a searchable guide to Web pages from the university's departments, agencies and organizations. In addition to campus and academic information, visitors will find links here to resources for politics, sports and the arts.

Texas A&M University, Corpus Christi

http://www.tamucc.edu/

The Texas A&M-Corpus Christi page contains information on academic departments, courses of study and administration policies. Includes links to research, computer info and pointers to area servers.

Texas Tech University

http://www.ttu.edu/

Texas Tech University maintains this multimedia home page featuring the sights and sounds of life on campus. Review the academic departments and programs, meet the faculty, check into the student organizations, or link to related sites of interest.

Texas Woman's University

http://www.twu.edu/

The home page of Texas Woman's University serves up a profile of the insitution, an events calendar, and links to student services, departmental pages and academic computing.

Trinity University

http://www.trinity.edu/

Trinity University in San Antonio, Texas, maintains this site with information about the campus and its people. Visit here for links to faculty, student, academic and research resources.

University of Dallas

http://acad.udallas.edu/

This college home page provides information on academic departments, courses of study and research projects at the University of Dallas . Includes faculty profiles and links to student services, the campus gopher server and UD's chemistry, philosophy and physics departments.

University of Houston

http://www.uh.edu/

The University of Houston home page includes general information about the school, its academic programs, course offerings, alumni associations and admissions policies. Includes descriptions of campus facilities, student services and athletic programs.

University of North Texas

http://www.unt.edu/

The University of North Texas loads its site with information for current and prospective students. The site includes an online catalog and admissions information, events announcements, campus computing information and links to the surrounding community of Denton.

University of Texas, Austin

http://www.utexas.edu/

The University of Texas at Austin provides a look at its departments, research, library and student organizations here. The site also includes maps, the Daily Texan and admissions information.

University of Texas Electronic Directory

http://x500.utexas.edu/

This electronic directory allows visitors to search the online records of the University of Texas (UT) at Austin. Visitors can find information on students, faculty and departmental studies, or link to other UT Web sites.

University of Texas, Pan American

http://www.panam.edu/

The home page for the Pan American campus of the University of Texas (in the tropical Rio Grande Valley) contains information on academic departments, programs of study and faculty profiles. Includes a map, plus admissions info, background on the institution, and links to research groups and student services.

Utah

University of Utah

http://www.utah.edu/

Find an introduction to the University of Utah at this site. Explore academic departments, student life and campus facilities here. Access to university computer services is provided.

Utah State University

http://www.usu.edu/

Learn about student life and educational opportunities at the Utah State University home page. Academic departments, research activities and alumni resources are highlighted at this site.

Utah Valley State College

http://www.uvsc.edu/

Utah Valley State College in Orem, Utah, provides information here on its people and programs. Visit here for news, academic course listings, department resources, contact information and more.

Vermont

Champlain College

http://www.champlain.edu/

Champlain College of Vermont seeks to remain "responsive to changing workplace environments," offering career-oriented education to students of all ages. Learn about the school's flexible approach to teaching here. Includes distance learning info.

Saint Michael's College

http://waldo.smcvt.edu/

The World Wide Web server for Saint Michael's College (located in Colchester, Vt.) allows you to take an interactive campus tour, read students' personal home pages, and access various Internet resources.

University of Vermont

http://www.uvm.edu/

Visitors to the University of Vermont home page will find details on admissions, departments, programs and research projects. Other site features include student, faculty and staff directories, and an arts and entertainment section.

Vermont Technical College

http://www.vtc.vsc.edu/

Vermont Technical College includes an overview of its degree programs and a course catalog at this home page. Visitors can read about the faculty, check into student services and much more.

Virginia

College of William and Mary

http://www.wm.edu/

The College of William and Mary home page presents general information about the Virginia school's students, faculty and academic programs. Campus tours and maps.

Eastern Mennonite University

http://www.emu.edu/

The home page for Eastern Mennonite University in Harrisonburg, Va., offers information on admissions, tuition, faculty, services and the Mennonite seminary. Find also links to information on Harrisonburg and the Shenandoah Valley.

George Mason University

http://www.gmu.edu/

At MasonLink, the Web server for George Mason University, visitors will find information on students, faculty and staff, and academic departments. Links to resources from the surrounding community and the state of Virginia are also included.

James Madison University

http://www.jmu.edu/

Virginia's James Madison University provides an index to information at its home page, including a school history, programs, departments, services, events and personnel.

Liberty University

http://www.liberty.edu/

Jerry Falwell's Liberty University gives an overview of its programs and Baptist seminary here. It also posts information on its sports program and publications.

Mary Washington College

http://www.mwc.edu/

Mary Washington College, Fredericksburg, Va., maintains its home page with information about the college, admissions, departments, labs and campus resources, including course Web pages.

Norfolk State University

http://cyclops.nsu.edu/

The home page of Virginia's Norfolk State University provides a wealth of information about the school's academics, student activities, resources and staff. Visitors can view a map of the campus here, or read a hypertext version of the university calender.

Old Dominion University

http://www.odu.edu/

Old Dominion University in Norfolk, Va., maintains this searchable site with information about the school, campus, library, athletics and more.

Radford University

http://www.runet.edu/

Radford University, located in Virginia, presents information about its academic and athletic programs and admissions. Visitors can take a virtual stroll around the campus map and explore a number of Web site links.

Randolph-Macon Woman's College

http://www.rmwc.edu/

Randolph-Macon Woman's College in Lynchburg, Va., supplies information on admissions, academics, student life and international opportunities. Also featured are the college's English as a Second Language program and Maier Museum of Art.

University of Richmond

http://www.urich.edu/

The home page of the University of Richmond provides a variety of information about the school's academic programs, facilities and resources. Visitors can tour the campus, read a university history or look up admissions procedures.

University of Virginia

http://www.virginia.edu/

Take a virtual tour of the University of Virginia at this Web site. The introduction offered here includes information on academic offerings, university news, the school's hospital and library, and facts about Charlottesville, Va.

Virginia Commonwealth University

http://www.vcu.edu/

Richmond's Virginia Commonwealth University home page provides an overview of this urban research institution. This page features information about the academic campus, the student body, faculty and staff, the libraries, graduate studies and the computing department.

Virginia Polytechnic Institute and State University

http://www.vt.edu/

The Virginia Tech home page offers a variety of information about its admissions, academics, resources, students services and activities. Visitors can also browse the University directories and read about Web publishing at the school.

Virginia Polytechnic Institute and State University

gopher://gopher.vt.edu:70/1

This gopher server from Virginia Tech, Blacksburg, Va., acts as the gateway for access to all gopher servers on the campus. Among other things, visitors will find general information here about Virginia Tech, as well as details from its colleges and departments.

Virginia Wesleyan College

http://www.vwc.edu/

Virginia Wesleyan College presents this comprehensive guide to its campus, offering information about academics, departments and programs. Visitors can also find admission details and a calendar of events as well as general info on southeastern Virginia.

Washington and Lee University

http://liberty.uc.wlu.edu/

Washington and Lee University in Lexington, Va., tells about its campus, programs, faculty and students here. A help index for Internet- and computer-related questions is also available at this university home page.

Washington

City University

http://www.cityu.edu/

City University, Bellevue, Wash., was designed to allow working adults to get a higher education. The online courses at this site include those leading to a Master of Business Administration degree, with undergraduate Computer Systems classes coming soon.

Eastern Washington University

http://www.ewu.edu/

Eastern Washington University invites visitors to its home page to learn more about the school, its academic offerings, research resources, faculty and student services. In addition, links to information about the surrounding community, region and state are provided.

Edmonds Community College

http://www.edmonds.ctc.edu/

Edmonds Community College in the state of Washington features its academic programs and admissions information through this Web site. Prospective students can also check out online class opportunities and international programs.

Evergreen State College

http://www.evergreen.edu/

Evergreen State College in Washington State unveils information for prospective students about its academic offerings and campus through this home page. Visitors can also read about current research at the college.

Gonzaga University

http://www.gonzaga.edu/

Gonzaga University, a Spokane, Wash.-based Jesuit school, provides information here about its campus, programs, faculty and students. Visitors will also find course catalogs and admissions materials.

Seattle Pacific University

http://www.spu.edu/

Washington's Seattle Pacific University provides general information about its academic programs, departments and students at this site. Electronic resources at SPU are also available.

University of Puget Sound

http://www.ups.edu/

The University of Puget Sound home page contains information about academic departments, programs of study and faculty profiles. Includes links to student services, other campus servers, organizations and other resources.

University of Washington

http://www.cac.washington.edu:1180/

The home page of the University of Washington provides an array of school and local information and resources. Visitors can read recent university announcements and information about campus events, or link directly to online university services.

Washington State University

http://www.wsu.edu/

Washington State University is a public educational facility located in Pullman, Wash.; visitors to their main Web server will find information on WSU services, academics and student activities.

Whitman College

http://www.whitman.edu/

Whitman College in Walla Walla, Wash., has set up this home page to provide information about the school, faculty and academic programs. Prospective students can learn more about the campus and surrounding area as well as link to other Web sites.

West Virginia

Bethany College

http://info.bethany.wvnet.edu/

The Bethany College, Bethany, W.Va., home page contains information about departments, admissions, courses and athletics. This page also includes an academic calendar, faculty profiles and links to library and Internet resources.

Wisconsin

Carroll College

http://www.cc.edu/

The home page for Carroll College (Wisconsin's first college) contains information about academic departments, course offerings and faculty. Includes admissions guidelines, links to student services and info on regulations for moderation of all campus servers.

Lawrence University

http://www.lawrence.edu/

Lawrence University has been drawing students to its small Wisconsin campus for over 150 years with its nationally recognized Conservatory of Music, proudly exhibited here along with all the facts on this private liberal arts university. See Editor's Choice.

Ripon College

http://www.ripon.edu/

Ripon College in Wisconsin offers links to its students' personal home pages as well as to faculty and departments within the school at this site. The Webmaster also features a collection of Internet starting points and links to alumni information.

University of Wisconsin, Eau Claire

http://www.uwec.edu/

The University of Wisconsin, Eau Claire, introduces visitors to its academic programs and educational facilities. Includes overviews of campus happenings, student organizations and departmental studies.

University of Wisconsin, Extension

http://www.uwex.edu/

The University of Wisconsin, Extension, home page provides visitors with news and issues that are pertinent to the school's community outreach and education programs, which emphasize skill-building for farm families.

University of Wisconsin, Madison

http://www.wisc.edu/

WiscINFO, the University of Wisconsin, Madison, campus-wide information system provides links to information categorized by subject, title or information source. Visitors will find campus directories, events calendars, academic and employment information, and links to campus Web and gopher resources.

University of Wisconsin, Madison, Graduate School

http://www.wisc.edu/grad

The University of Wisconsin, Madison, Graduate School's home page provides news and information about its academic degree programs, publications, calendar and research centers. Links to related sites on and off campus are also featured.

University of Wisconsin, Marathon Center

http://mthwww.uwc.edu/wwwmahes/homepage.htm

The Web server for the University of Wisconsin, Marathon Center, in Wausau, Wis,. offers a college teacher's page, library searches, course descriptions, sports, Big Ten athletic conference links, and a myriad of other materials.

University of Wisconsin, Platteville

http://www.uwplatt.edu/

The University of Wisconsin at Platteville maintains this home page offering a look at life on campus. Visitors are invited to learn more about the university, its academic programs, faculty and administration, and student resources.

University of Wisconsin, River Falls

http://www.uwrf.edu/

The home page for the University of Wisconsin at River Falls contains information about the school, academic departments, courses of study, faculty, student and administrative services, class schedules, events and attractions.

University of Wisconsin, Whitewater

http://www.uww.edu/

The home page for the University of Wisconsin at Whitewater features general campus information, admissions guidelines and academic program facts, as well as links to student organizations. The page also details the university's Internet use policies and guidelines.

REMOTE LEARNING

California Coast University

http://www.calcoastuniv.edu/ccu

California Coast University provides mid-career professionals with off-campus study opportunities. This site includes descriptions of degree completion programs, links to other distance education resources and newsgroups, and background information on the university.

Distance Learning Resources

http://www.crl.com/~gorgon/distance.html

Distance Learning Resources come to your computer desktop through this list of World Wide Web links. The site includes pointers to information from across the Internet, including from the AEDNET mailing list archives.

Educational Courses on the Web

http://lenti.med.umn.edu/~mwd/courses.html

A list of virtual courses offered on the Internet is available at this Web site. Visitors can search for courses by category and academic discipline; most are science-related courses.

New School for Social Research: Distance Learning

http://dialnsa.edu/home.html

The New School for Social Research offers adults a wide variety of courses in its Distance Learning Program. Students log in via modem and download lectures, reading materials and messages from instructors.

---

a2z EDITOR'S CHOICE

Lawrence University

http://www.lawrence.edu/

Who said bigger is better? Top-ranked Lawrence University in Appleton, Wis., has just 1,200 students, but its Conservatory of Music is the only nationally recognized conservatory dedicated exclusively to the education of undergraduates. At LU's handsome home page, audiophiles can listen to some soundbites, and learn more about the university's five-year double-degree program, in which students can obtain both a bachelor of music and a bachelor of arts degree in another discipline. LU's impressive mission statement clearly states the school's goal to help students develop their intellect and talent, acquire knowledge and understanding, and cultivate judgment and values. Visitors to LU's handsome home page can also take a peek at Format, the Lawrence e-zine, learn about the various departments' academic offerings and check out student and faculty home pages.—*Reviewed by Karen Wise*

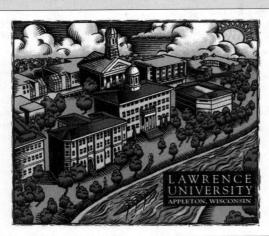

LAWRENCE UNIVERSITY
APPLETON, WISCONSIN

Open University of the United Kingdom

http://www.open.ac.uk/

The Open University of the United Kingdom, founded in 1969, has no entry requirements for most of its courses. Included here is information about its degrees offered and academic departments. Studying at the Open University via the Internet is explained here.

Technology and Distance Education

http://www.etc.bc.ca/home.html

The Technology and Distance Education Branch of the British Columbia Ministry of Education, Skills and Training offers links to info on the Community Learning Network, District Technology Planning, Schoolnet and much more.

TeleEducation NB

http://ollc.mta.ca/tenb.html

TeleEducation NB assists in the delivery of long-distance education courses in New Brunswick, Canada. This home page provides information about TeleEducation, its staff and plans for the future. Links to general interest sites about New Brunswick are also provided. In English and French.

Utah Education Network

http://www.uen.org

The Utah Education Network offers long-distance classes over three television stations and one online network in Utah. It details its course offerings here.

Virtual Online University

http://www.athena.edu

Get your degree in your bathrobe and slippers! The Virtual Online University offers classes and academic programs over the Internet. Visitors to this site will find information on course offerings, faculty, degrees, news and admissions.

World Lecture Hall

http://www.utexas.edu/world/lecture

The World Lecture Hall provides links to faculty pages presenting online class materials and lectures. Visitors can find course materials for all academic disciplines.

SOUTH AMERICA

ARGENTINA

Universidad Nacional de la Plata

http://www.unlp.edu.ar/

The home page for the Universidad Nacional de la Plata in Argentina provides general information on the area and the school. There are links to the faculties within the university and to other sites in Argentina. In Spanish.

BRAZIL

Universidade Estadual de Campinas

http://www.unicamp.br/

At the main Web server for the Universidade Estadual de Campinas, Brazil, visitors will find administrative information and links to the campus libraries and computer servers. In Portuguese.

CHILE

Universidad de Concepcion

gopher://halcon.dpi.udec.cl:70/1

Chile's Universidad de Concepcion maintains this gopher server for university resources, academic materials and links to Internet information services. Visit here to learn about its people and programs. Available in Spanish.

University of Bio-Bio

http://www.dci.ubiobio.cl/

Chile's University of Bio-Bio provides an overview of its programs here. The page also includes links to students' and faculty members' home pages (and instructions on how to create one) and a calendar of upcoming events. In Spanish.

University of Chile

http://www.uchile.cl/

The University of Chile introduces its academic programs and campus to the world through this college home page. It contains facts about day-to-day university life along with links to visitor information about Chile. Mostly in Spanish, with some English.

University of Tarapaca

http://www.quipu.uta.cl/

The University of Tarapaca maintains this page with general info on the school, its outreach programs and its Center for Information Technology. The page also includes a link to other Web resources. In Spanish only.

COLOMBIA

University of the Andes

http://www.uniandes.edu.co/

The University of the Andes in Bogota, Colombia, provides information on the university and its programs of study, faculty and staff. Descriptions of computer and student services, help links and pointers to other Web servers are included. In Spanish with limited English.

PUERTO RICO

University of Puerto Rico

http://www.upr.clu.edu/home.html

The University of Puerto Rico, established in 1903, provides information here on its campuses, programs, research centers and faculty. Visit here to learn about the university and link to other sites in Puerto Rico, Latin America and the Caribbean. In Spanish and English.

VENEZUELA

Universidad Central de Venezuela

http://www.sagi.ucv.edu.ve/

This page, written in Spanish, connects users to information about the Universidad Central de Venezuela, including university FTP sites, a schedule of events, the school's library system and more.

EARLY CHILDHOOD RESOURCES

Flix Productions Animated Shareware

http://www.eden.com/~flixprod

At this site, find shareware from Flix Productions, a company that specializes in animated educational software. Descriptions, screenshots and download options are featured for such titles as Animated Old Testament, Animated Mother Goose and Animated Alphabet.

ParentsPlace.com

http://www.parentsplace.com/

ParentsPlace.com, provides an online index of parenting resources on the Internet. Visitors can read articles and books, chat with other parents, or perform a keyword search of its databases. Links to a variety of parenting centers and related businesses are also available.

FINANCIAL AID

American Indian College Fund, Annual Reports
http://hanksville.phast.umass.edu/defs/independent/AICF.html

Visitors to this page will find links to the 1993 and the 1994 Annual Report of the American Indian College Fund. Contact info for the fund is also featured.

CollegeNET
http://www.collegenet.com/

CollegeNET, an online guide to universities in the United States and Canada, offers links to featured institutions and official home pages. Visitors will also find financial aid and scholarship information and a variety of academic resources.

DO-IT at the University of Washington
http://weber.u.washington.edu/~doit/

The DO-IT program at the University of Washington seeks to provide opportunities for study in the sciences to individuals with disabilities. Computer loans, scholarships and mentorships are among the strategies employed to further this goal. An outline of the program is provided at the DO-IT site.

FinAid: The Financial Aid Information Page
http://www.cs.cmu.edu/afs/cs/user/mkant/Public/FinAid/finaid.html

The Financial Aid Information page, maintained by the author of a scholarship and fellowship guide book, is full of pointers to sites that help students navigate the world of financial aid. Visit here for the author's recommended financial aid sources, scam alerts, downloadable software and links to dozens of university and government information sites.

Student Guide
http://www.ed.gov/prog_info/SFA/StudentGuide/

This Student Guide details financial aid programs available from the U.S. Department of Education. Includes a general overview of programs, descriptions of specific grants, work-study opportunities and loans.

University of California, Irvine, Financial Aid Office
http://www.fao.uci.edu/

The Financial Aid Office of the University of California, Irvine, maintains this online guide for current and prospective students. Visit here to read its Financial Aid Handbook and link to other university information resources.

HIGHER EDUCATION RESOURCES

Addison Wesley Longman
http://www.aw.com/

This promotional site is the Web server of Addison Wesley Longman, parent corporation of the Addison-Wesley Publishing Group. Includes information about the parent organization as well as its subsidiaries and divisions.

Alabama Industrial Development Training
http://www.aidt.edu/

An institute of the state's Department of Postsecondary Education, Alabama Industrial Development Training presents this overview of its services. Links to its centers in Huntsville, Mobile and Montgomery, and its annual report and quarterly newsletter also are featured.

Alpha Phi Omega, Delta Chapter, Auburn University
http://www.auburn.edu/apo/deltawww.html

Get the latest news from the Delta Chapter of the Alpha Phi Omega fraternity at Alabama's Auburn University. Visitors can find out what's up with the tiger or link to current and alumni brothers using the e-mail directory provided.

American Academy of Arts and Sciences
http://www.amacad.org/

The American Academy of Arts and Sciences bestows honors on outstanding scholars in a wide array of academic fields. Read about the award program and its other projects aimed at highlighting and solving societal problems.

Annual Reviews
http://www.annurev.org/

Annual Reviews is a nonprofit organization providing critical summaries of recent research advances in a variety of scientific fields. Users can search reviews online or order volumes of past publications at this site.

Apple Education Worldwide
http://www.education.apple.com

Apple Computer's online educational home invites visitors to tour educational sites on the Web. Browsers can jump to news of Apple products designed for classroom use at all levels, seminars, promotions and more. In English, French and German.

Association for Experiential Education
http://www.princeton.edu/~rcurtis/aee.html

This site's Boulder, Colo.-based creators advise that "experiential education is a process through which a learner constructs knowledge, skill and value from direct experiences." Find out more about the practical applications, link to other groups and browse related publications.

Association of Midwest College Biology Teachers
http://papa.indstate.edu/amcbt

The Association of Midwest College Biology Teachers site contains a database of biology education resources, as well as details on seminars and conferences. Includes membership information and an online application.

Brunel Directory Service
http://echo.brunel.ac.uk:4040/

Brunel University, UK, uses this directory service to locate people and organizations associated with the university.

Brunel University Information Service
http://http1.brunel.ac.uk:8080/

Academic, faculty and research services, plus links to other college libraries and a directory of students, can be found at the home page for the UK's Brunel University.

Caltech Alumni
http://www.alumni.caltech.edu/

Remember your housemates from Caltech? Find out what they are up to now on the Caltech Alumni Web Server. Add your home page to the Caltech alumni computers or link up with classmates via newsgroups and e-mail lists.

Carnegie Mellon University Contributed Home Page
http://www.contrib.andrew.cmu.edu/

Carnegie Mellon University's contributed Web features user-posted and maintained info relating to college life. Topics tackled include Usenet censorship, local bus schedules, library resources and more.

Catapult
http://www.jobweb.org/catapult/catapult.htm

JobWeb maintains this site to provide access to the Catapult, its career services guide. Visit here to use the university's employment resources, including job-search tools, career libraries, links to graduate schools and more.

CAUSE
http://cause-www.colorado.edu/

CAUSE is a professional association whose members facilitate the "transformational changes occuring in higher education through the effective management and use of information resources."

Visitors to the CAUSE home page can learn more about the organization, its current issues, professional development programs and publications.

Center for Teaching and Learning at Duke

http://www.ctl.duke.edu/

The Center for Teaching and Learning, which supports faculty teaching at Duke University, provides an index to resources, services, publications, workshops and a staff directory at this site.

CHANCE Database

http://www.geom.umn.edu/docs/snell/chance/welcome.html

CHANCE is a quantitative literacy course drawing on statistics reported in daily newspapers and journals to improve the statistics knowledge and critical analysis capabilities of students. The CHANCE database contains course syllabi, reference materials and teaching aids.

CollegeNET

http://www.collegenet.com/

CollegeNET, an online guide to universities in the United States and Canada, offers links to featured institutions and official home pages. Visitors will also find financial aid and scholarship information and a variety of academic resources. See Editor's Choice.

College of Education at Virginia Polytechnic Institute and State University

http://infoserver.etl.vt.edu/

The College of Education at Virginia Tech and State University features a profile of its programs and faculty on its home page. Check out the undergraduate and graduate degree requirements, visit the facilities and review the other resources available.

Commonwealth of Learning

http://www.col.org/

The Commonwealth of Learning, an international organization composed of 53 member countries, works to widen access to education and improve its quality through the use of communication technologies and distance learning. This site provides information about the COL, its publications, archives and education programs.

Communications Technology Center

http://www.ctc.edu/

The Communications Technology Center provides information services to Washington state's community and technical colleges. Link to member colleges or access educational technology resources at this site.

Community Research and Development Information Service

http://www.cordis.lu/

Member states of the European Union share research and technology resources via CORDIS, the Community Research and Development Information Service. Access CORDIS databases, publications and policies here. In English, French and German.

Compass in Cyberspace

http://www.clark.net/pub/journalism/brochure.html

John Makulowich, the creator of what's widely acknowledged to be among the best journalism lists on the Internet, offers a course to teach professionals how to explore the Internet at the University of Maryland. You can sign up online but must attend in person. It costs $195.

Council for the Renewal of Undergraduate Education

http://www.hgur.se/

The home page of Sweden's Council for the Renewal of Undergraduate education has information about the council's mission and links to projects and related information. The council promotes efforts to develop the quality and renewal of undergraduate education, awards grants and collects information.

---

a2z EDITOR'S CHOICE

CollegeNET

http://www.collegenet.com/

College-bound high school juniors and seniors will want to beam aboard the CollegeNET spaceship for help in narrowing down a list of colleges. This online guide is packed with info and resources about four-year colleges and universities as well as community, technical and junior colleges throughout the U.S., Canada and New Zealand. Each school is categorized by location, enrollment and tuition, and contains a link to the school's home page whenever available. There are also special categories such as Catholic schools, Ivy League schools, women's schools and historically black schools. Once that all-important shortlist is created, students can even use CollegeNET's ApplyWeb service to apply to certain colleges online! The CollegeNET page also features tons of info on financial aid and scholarships (plus help in figuring out how much it would cost to live in another city as a student), academic resources, and Allsport, a service for matching student-athletes and schools. And, after a long day of college-hunting online, weary students can visit the CollegeNET planetarium and sit back to view the planets of our solar system.—*Reviewed by Karen Wise*

CTI Centre for Economics

http://www.sosig.ac.uk/cticce/

The CTI Centre for Economics, based at the University of Bristol in the United Kingdom, encourages the employment of learning technologies in British higher education. The institution's home page lists its services and related news and provides links to similar resources.

Curry School of Education

http://curry.edschool.virginia.edu/

The home page for the Curry School of Education provides a wealth of information about the school's departments, academics, administration, technology and organizations. Visitors can also link to the University of Virginia's main home page from here.

DANTE

http://www.dante.net/

A European nonprofit company, DANTE was created to "provide advanced international computer network services for the European research community." Visitors to this page can find out more about DANTE, its EuropaNET network, and other projects. DANTE's publications are also featured.

Dewey School of Education

http://ics.soe.umich.edu/

DeweyWeb is the University of Michigan's School of Education home page. Visitors will find articles and research related to the department as well as a chronicle of an on-going electronics communications project.

Digital Campus

http://www.linkmag.com/

Digital Campus is a comprehensive set of links that provides news and information on American colleges and universities. Visitors can link directly to higher educational facility Web servers.

Division of Educational Programs

http://www.dep.anl.gov/

The Division of Educational Programs of the Argonne National Laboratory in Chicago maintains this site for general information and resource access. Visit here to learn about its higher education programs, technology training, catalog of research projects and more.

Educom

http://educom.edu/

Educom, an alliance of institutions formed to address critical issues surrounding information technology in higher education, sponsors this comprehensive guide to the organization, its projects and its programs.

Elderhostel

http://www.elderhostel.org/

The Elderhostel home page describes its innovative, varied educational study programs for older adults. Educational institutions around the world offer courses in everything from Cicero to computers.

Electronic Archives for Teaching the American Literatures

http://www.georgetown.edu/tamlit/tamlit-home.html

The Electronic Archives for Teaching the American Literatures site contains essays, syllabi and bibliographies for teaching.

Experimental Study Group Biology Hypertextbook

http://esg-www.mit.edu:8001/esgbio/7001main.html

Learn biology over the Web with this hypertextbook developed by the Massachusetts Institute of Technology. Find instructional text, practice problems and self-administered quizzes here. Virtual students can contact tutors online from this site.

Federal Information Exchange

http://web.fie.com/

The Federal Information Exchange indexes a broad array of employment, equipment exchange and grant opportunities for educators and researchers looking for a piece of the federal pie. Find listings from minority colleges and universities, a used equipment network, and general research and employment initiatives.

Fuzz's APhiO Pages

http://work1.utsi.edu:8000/fuzz/aphio/

Fuzz's site serves as the unofficial home page of the Alpha Phi Omega fraternity. Stop by the welcome center and pick up a map of the different chapters, or use the online chapter finder. General information about the fraternity, its administration and calendar of conferences is also available.

Global Campus

http://www.csulb.edu/gc/

The Global Campus Web server is an extensive multimedia database offering resources for students and teachers around the globe. Visit this site to check out a wealth of educational materials, including documents, sounds, images and video.

Globewide Network Academy

http://uu-gna.mit.edu:8001/uu-gna/index.html

The Globewide Network Academy is a nonprofit group of educational and research organizations that offer online courses as well as administrative and technical services. Educational institutions are welcome to join the consortium and individuals are asked to submit course applications.

Groupe Ecole Superieure de Commerce Marseille-Provence

http://serveia.u-3mrs.fr/

Find out more about Le Groupe Ecole Superieure de Commerce Marseille-Provence, which represents 2,500 international exchange students. The Groupe ESCMP home page describes the group's history, departments, and research services. In French.

Harvard Graduate School of Education

http://gseweb.harvard.edu/

The home page of the Harvard Grad School of Education is an electronic campus department catalog for potential students. It links browsers to academic and research programs, provides enrollment information and links to library and technical resources. Includes information on upcoming events and online campus publications.

Hiroshima University, Information Processing Center

http://www.ipc.hiroshima-u.ac.jp/

This Hiroshima University site contains information on the school's information-processing center, its services and center staff. Includes links to users' personal pages and telephone and e-mail service. Information is in English and Japanese.

Houghton Mifflin Company

http://www.hmco.com/

Houghton Mifflin, a Boston-based instructional text publisher, maintains this promotional site for company and product information. Visit here to learn about its wide range of educational materials, textbooks, and fiction and nonfiction titles for adults and children.

IBM Kiosk for Education

http://ike.engr.washington.edu/ike.html

IBM's Kiosk for Education offers technology solutions for the higher education community. Find special hardware and software product promotions for students and educators.

Indiana University, Honors Division

http://www.honors.indiana.edu/

Indiana University's Honors Division posts an overview of the program and a list of recommended courses on this page. Here, students can also browse through an electronic journal of art, fiction and poetry written by Honors students.

Indiana University, School of Education

http://education.indiana.edu/

Teaching teachers is the mission of the Indiana University School of Education. Brush up on the latest tricks of the trade or look into graduate study opportunities in the field here. Includes course descriptions and faculty listings.

Information Network of the Society for Information Technology and Teacher Education

http://curry.edschool.virginia.edu/insite/

InSITE explores ways in which the Internet can benefit teacher education programs around the world. Read about the society's mission and its research findings here.

Institute for Learning Technologies

http://www.ilt.columbia.edu/

Developed by Columbia University as part of its Virtual Information Initiative, this site is the gateway to the Institute for Learning Technologies online offerings. The ILTweb contains academic, Internet and computer resource information.

Institute of Computer Based Learning

http://reddwarf.qub.ac.uk/

Located at Queens's University in Belfast, Northern Ireland, the Institute for Computer Based Learning is charged with assisting departments in the development of computer-based teaching and diagnostic materials. Visitors to its home page can find out more about the institute, as well as its teaching and research activities.

International Student Organisations

http://www.informatik.rwth-aachen.de/AEGEE/orgas/imiso.html

The International Student Organisations provides a long index of student group sites here. It is sorted by discipline and includes human sciences, law and economics and general student groups. The information is provided by the German-based Association des Etats Generaux des Etudiants de l'Europe (AEGEE).

Internet Headquarters for Student Governments

http://www.umr.edu/~stuco/national.html

The University of Missouri, Rolla, has compiled this catalog of university-level student governments across the globe. Link to over 100 official student government organizations.

JANET

http://www.ja.net/

JANET is the academic and research network of the United Kingdom. Visit JANET's Web home for a complete list of U.K. academic research servers and sites connected the network, as well as links to JANET documents and user groups.

John Simon Guggenheim Memorial Foundation

http://www.gf.org/

The John Simon Guggenheim Memorial Foundation provides fellowships for advanced professionals in all fields except the performing arts. General information about the foundation and fellowship eligibility, deadlines and application forms can be found here.

Kaplan Online

http://www.kaplan.com/

Kaplan claims to be the world's leader in standardized test preparation classes. At this promotional site visitors can learn about the company by downloading free games, visiting an online classroom or checking out the library. See Editor's Choice.

Knowledge Media Institute

http://hcrl.open.ac.uk/

The Open University, an experimental higher educational campus in London, presents the home page for its Knowledge Media Institute. Visitors will find information on the program and related research.

Learning Resource Server

http://www.ed.uiuc.edu/

This knowledge space from the University of Illinois's College of Education offers links to various distributors of electronic learning resources for students and instructors. Visitors will find information on the college, in addition to such items as networking projects and online publications.

Maricopa Center for Learning and Instruction

http://www.mcli.dist.maricopa.edu/

The Maricopa Center for Learning and Instruction, an Arizona-based educational support organization, works to promote innovation and change in the community college environment. Visit here for general information, teaching resources, employment opportunities and more.

Massachusetts Institute of Technology, Student Information Processing Board

http://www.mit.edu/

The Student Information Processing Board of the Massachusetts Institute of Technology maintains this informational site. Visit here for Internet resources, campus Web servers, staff and student home pages, and other academic and administrative resources.

---

a2z EDITOR'S CHOICE

Kaplan Online

http://www.kaplan.com/

If the letters SAT, ACT, GRE, GMAT, and MCAT give you a sick headache, fear not. Just surf over to Kaplan Online for a huge assortment of resources to help you prepare for standardized tests, college admissions, and even job hunting. Whether you're just thinking about applying to college or considering a graduate program, Kaplan offers a wealth of test preparation hints and registration info here. You can even order Kaplan books and software online or take a practice exam to get yourself into the mood. And, after you've spent the day immersed in exercises and reviews, be sure to head over to the Rathskeller for some R&R. There you can take a quiz to find out if you're a party animal or a scholar, tune in to the Idiot Box, or visit the Junk Food & Dive Bars page. And don't forget to take a peek at Kaplan's Hypnotic Relaxer before you leave. You're getting v-e-r-y sleepy. . . . —*Reviewed by Karen Wise*

Mensa

http://www.mensa.org/

Mensa is an international society whose members score in the top two percent of the population on standardized IQ tests. Visitors can read about the group here, join its special interest groups (SIGs) or scan the Mensa personal ads.

National Center for Science Information Systems

http://www.nacsis.ac.jp/nacsis.index.html

A Japanese Inter-University Research Institute, the National Center for Science Information Systems links libraries, research units and computer centers to provide researchers access to natural sciences, social sciences and humanities scholarship. Find out more about the center at this site. In Japanese and English.

Northwestern University, Institute for the Learning Sciences

http://www.ils.nwu.edu/

The Institute for the Learning Sciences at Northwestern University provides information on its graduate programs in learning, computer and cognitive science. The site includes information on its research, staff and students.

Ohio Board of Regents

http://www.bor.ohio.gov/

Ohio's State Board of Regents describes its mission and offers what's new in higher education through its Web site. It includes links to Ohio state government along with profiles of the schools and programs.

Ontario Institute for Studies in Education

http://www.oise.on.ca/

The Ontario Institute for Studies in Education, affiliated with the University of Toronto, Canada, maintains this site to introduce its people and programs. Visit here for news, publications, staff and student directories, course offerings and other academic resources.

Open Net

http://www.opennet.net.au/

Australia's Open Net Educational Internet Services provides educational news, establishes educational partners, and lists courses of study, conferences and exhibitions. Includes employment listings and educational resources for teachers.

Oxford University Press USA

http://www.oup-usa.org/

Visitors to this home page can learn about the venerable Oxford University Press USA. Information about the company's history and a catalog of its publications wait here alongside its customer service department and links to the publishing house's international branches

Peterson's Education Center

http://www.petersons.com/

Provided by publisher Peterson's Guides, this Education Center is a collection of Web resources for all levels and disciplines. Link areas include K-12, studying abroad, executive education and language study.

Project Muse

http://muse.jhu.edu/

Project Muse digitizes and makes available all journals produced by the Johns Hopkins University Press. This site provides access to these electronic publications and the related database. Includes Frequently Asked Questions (FAQ).

Queensland Open Learning Network

http://www.uq.oz.au/~zzpwhitl

The Queensland Open Learning Network operates 40 Open Learning Centers throughout Queensland, Australia. These centers provide resources for continuing and higher education and other training programs. This support site has the center's background and information about its resources and facilities.

Scholarly Communications Project of Virginia Polytechnic Institute and State University

http://scholar.lib.vt.edu/

Visitors can search academic journals online, courtesy of the Scholarly Communications Project at Virginia Tech and State University. Includes general project info as well as a list of electronically accessible journals, publications and theses and dissertations.

Scholars Press: The Electronically Linked Academy

http://scholar.cc.emory.edu/

The Scholars Press brings you the Electronically Linked Academy, which boasts links to scholarly presses, publications and societies. Find virtual exhibits, catalogs and networking opportunities aimed at an academic audience.

SkillsBank Corporation

http://www.skillsbank.com/

The SkillsBank Corporation is an educational technology firm located in Baltimore, Md. Visitors will find descriptions of the company's products and services at this promotional site.

Special Education, University of Kansas

http://www.sped.ukans.edu/spedadmin/welcome.html

The Department of Special Education at the University of Kansas in Lawrence maintains this overview of its academic programs and research projects. Browsers can also meet the faculty, get an overview of its special technology lab and link to related Internet resources.

State Council of Higher Education for Virginia

http://www.schev.edu/

The State Council of Higher Education for Virginia provides a searchable site with resources for colleges and universities from that state and from around the world. It also links to general Internet sites and weather reports for the local region.

STEM~Net

http://calvin.stemnet.nf.ca/

STEM~Net provides electronic resources for K-12, rural public colleges and Memorial Universities of Newfoundland and Labrador, Canada. Visitors to its home page can access its numerous information and reference options as well as link to Canada's SchoolNet, SchoolNet Rings, and related Web sites and servers.

STILE Project

http://indigo.stile.le.ac.uk/

The STILE Project (Students and Teachers Integrated Learning Environment) is a resource for students of the World Wide Web. Based at the University of Leicester at Loughborough in the UK, the links include esoteric subjects ranging from Contemporary Crafts to Latin American Politics to images from various Archeological Studies.

Sunergy

http://www.sun.com/sunergy/

Sun Microsystems unveils Sunergy, its interactive technology educational program, through this page. It features schedules of satellite TV broadcasts for its programs along with transcripts and audio clips.

Sveriges Forenade Studentkarer

http://www.sfs.se/

The Swedish National Union of Students page links to information and background about the Swedish chapter of this international organization that promotes higher education and student welfare. It provides contact between the various unions and covers major issues of concern. Available in Swedish and English.

Swedish National Union of Students

http://www.sfs.se/

The Swedish National Union of Students page links to information and background about the Swedish chapter of this international organization that promotes higher education and student welfare. It provides contact between the various unions and covers major issues of concern. Available in Swedish and English.

Teachers College

http://www.tc.columbia.edu/

Columbia University's Teachers College introduces itself, its academic departments and admissions requirements via TCWeb. Find support services and information resources for the education profession at this site.

Teacher Talk

http://www.mightymedia.com/talk/working.htm

Teachers can share ideas with each other at the Mighty Media Teachers Lounge. Access to the online forum is free, but visitors must register first.

Teaching and Learning Technology Programme

http://www.icbl.hw.ac.uk/tltp/

The UK's Teaching and Learning Technology Programme, whose mission "is to make teaching and learning more productive and efficient by harnessing modern technology," provides this site with lists of projects, Web workshop details and newsletters.

TELL Consortium

http://www.hull.ac.uk/cti/tell.htm

The home page of the TELL Consortium—a project designed to develop computer-based materials for higher education teaching and learning in the UK—is located here. Browsers can read extensive information about the project's aims and products or link to affiliated home pages.

TERENA Document Store

http://www.rare.nl/

The Trans-European and Education Networking Association (TERENA) works to encourage the development of a high-quality computer networking infrastructure for the European research community. Visitors here will get an overview of the association and its projects and can download its publications.

The Times Higher Education Supplement Internet Service

http://www.timeshigher.newsint.co.uk/

The Times Higher Education Supplement Internet Service (THESIS) provides news and employment opportunities from the post-compulsory education system worldwide. Visit here for news summaries, job listings, book reviews and databases.

21stC

http://www.21stc.org/

Columbia University offers an attractive online magazine, 21stC, at this site. It details for a general audience what Columbia's researchers are doing and why it matters. Topics run the research gamut, from viruses to English literature.

U: The National College Magazine

http://www.umagazine.com/

This page serves as an entryway into the world of the cyber-rag U. Magazine. Departments include u.news, u.views, u.pix and u.sports. See Editor's Choice, page 248.

University and College Education

http://www.cs.fsu.edu/projects/group11/combined.hotlist.html

Students and researchers will find an index to American and international universities on the Web here. The page also contains information on financial aid, libraries and teaching resources.

University of California, Berkeley, California Alumni Association

http://www.alumni.berkeley.edu/

The California Alumni Association of the University of California at Berkeley supplies updates, membership information, club listings and details on programs. Also featured are articles and an alumni calendar from "California Monthly" magazine.

University of California, Santa Cruz

http://www.slugs.com/slugweb/

The banana slug, the unofficial mascot of the University of California, Santa Cruz, lends its name to this student service site. Visitors are apprised of upcoming student activities and hit with a pitch for the school's memorabilia and merchandise.

University of Minnesota, College of Education and Human Development

http://www.coled.umn.edu/

The University of Minnesota's College of Education and Human Development home page is designed to disseminate information about the school and provide educational resources to teachers. This site also links to Web66, a project to ease the Internet into precollege classrooms.

University of Oregon, International Bulletin Board

http://darkwing.uoregon.edu/~oieehome

The University of Oregon serves up an online bulletin board providing browsers with access to international education info on its own campus and abroad. Check out international events and reference material here, or link to starter pages for exploring the World Wide Web.

University of Oulu, Faculty of Education

http://wwwedu.oulu.fi/

Finland's University of Oulu outlines what it teaches its future teachers at its Faculty of Education home page. In Finnish and English.

---

a2z   EDITOR'S CHOICE

U: The National College Magazine

http://www.umagazine.com/

No two ways about it: U. Magazine is the hippest college publication on the Web. If you've got a pulse, you won't be able to get enough of U.Mag's particular brand of relevance and irreverence. It's no wonder U is the most widely read lifestyle and entertainment magazine among college students. On any given rainy afternoon, you can check out the winners of the U.Pix photo contest (yes, some guy did run naked through a fire), visit U.Views to learn the results of the latest U.Polls (for instance, "Knowing what you know now, would you choose the same college?") or read the U.News (everything from race issues on campus to campaign '96). And, just so that you don't think it's *all* fun and games here, U offers an annual scholarship competition and a resume helper for those serious moments.—*Reviewed by Karen Wise*

no, this isn't an astronomy home page. this is **way cooler.**

University of Pennsylvania, Educational Technology Services

http://ccat.sas.upenn.edu/

The University of Pennsylvania presents the home page for its Educational Technology Services Department here. Visitors will find information on faculty, research and facilities, as well as links to related sites.

Victoria Jubilee Technical Institute

http://www.ece.iit.edu/~hchhaya/vjti/vjti.html

A directory of alumni from the Victoria Jubilee Technical Institute in Bombay, India, is featured here, along with a job listings page. There are also indexes of VJTI news and links, plus information on the VJTI Alumni Association.

Web Pages and Gophers of Scholarly Societies

http://www.lib.uwaterloo.ca/society/webpages.html

The Scholarly Societies Project of Canada's University of Waterloo maintains this site for its index of links to other scholarly societies. Visitors can browse for institutions by name and subject and link directly from this page.

World-Wide Web Virtual Library: Education

http://www.csu.edu.au/education/library.html

The World Wide Web Virtual Library provides this searchable, comprehensive list of links to education resources and sites. Links are categorized alphabetically, by education level, resource provided, site type and country.

World-Wide Web Virtual Library: Educational Technology

http://tecfa.unige.ch/info-edu-comp.html

The Educational Technology section of the World Wide Web Virtual Library provides a massive list of links to sites relating to educational software and other electronic educational projects. Heavy on software archives, the list includes brief descriptions of the links provided.

ISSUES

Commonwealth of Learning

http://www.col.org/

The Commonwealth of Learning, an international organization composed of 53 member countries, works to widen access to education and improve its quality through the use of communication technologies and distance learning. This site provides information about the COL, its publications, archives and education programs.

Educom

http://educom.edu/

Educom, an alliance of institutions formed to address critical issues surrounding information technology in higher education, sponsors this comprehensive guide to the organization, its projects and its programs.

Edu.fi

http://www.edu.fi/

Edu.fi, an educational network in Finland, outlines its services and goals through this Web gateway. The network includes links to universities and schools in Finland, as well as the National Board of Education and Ministry of Education. This page is available in Finnish and English.

Engines for Education

http://www.ils.nwu.edu/~e_for_e/

Engines for Education, a hyper-book written by Roger Schank and Chip Cleary, is about the education system's problems and methods for reform. The book is also available in paper and CD-ROM.

From Now On

http://www.fromnowon.org/

From Now On is an electronic educational journal focusing on classroom management techniques, learning strategies and other educational topics related to technology.

National Library of Canada Electronic Collection

http://www.nlc-bnc.ca/eppp/e-coll-e.htm

A mission statement for the National Library of Canada's Electronic Publishing Pilot Project can be found at this Web site. The project aims to "identify and understand issues that libraries will encounter handling electronic publications and online collections."

Northwest Regional Educational Laboratory

http://www.nwrel.org/

The Northwest Regional Educational Laboratory is a nonprofit educational research and development institution in Portland, Ore., dedicated to improving education for children, youth and adults. At the NWERL Web site visitors can read about the institution's programs, publications and events.

Serendip

http://serendip.brynmawr.edu/

Life's instructions are always ambiguous and incomplete, habitues of Serendip assure us. This is an online forum and resource for those interested in intellectual and social change in education. Brain behavior, free will, competition and cooperation, the bell curve and genetics are some of the topics members and guests are invited to explore.

Technology Based Learning Network Canada

http://www.humanities.mcmaster.ca/~misc2/tblca1.htm

The Technology Based Learning Network Canada wants to ensure information technology enfranchisement for the country's students and educators. Read about the nonprofit institution's grand scheme for introducing state-of-the-art teaching technologies into the schools, or sift through its collection of educational Internet index sites.

Texas Education Network

http://www.tenet.edu/

The Texas Education Network is an organization devoted to advancing and enhancing education in Texas. Visitors here can learn about the organization, get updates on its projects and download freeware. The site also posts link to other educational organizations in Texas.

U.S. Department of Education

http://www.ed.gov/index.html

At its online home, the U.S. Department of Education offers the latest education news, guides for teacher and researchers, grant information and more. The tone is refreshingly informal.

U.S. Department of Education, Office of Inspector General

http://www.ed.gov/offices/OIG/edoig.html

The home page of the Department of Education, Office of Inspector General presents the department's goal to assure the continued improvement in the effectiveness and integrity of the national education program. Find links to regional offices and related education sites.

K-12 RESOURCES

Aberdeen High School

http://www.ahs.aberdeen.k12.ms.us/

The Aberdeen High School home page provides information on the Mississippi school's facilities, programs and activities. Includes Internet guidebooks, lessons on Netiquette, community information, local home pages and links to various Web sites.

Academy One

http://www.nptn.org/cyber.serv/AOneP/

An international online education resource for students, teachers and parents, Academy One features projects and special events for the K-12 crowd. Find information about this "global classroom without walls" and links to related sites.

Access Excellence
http://www.gene.com/ae/
High school biology teachers are connected with scientists, scientific information and each other through the online network, Access Excellence. The national education program is sponsored by Genentech, Inc.

Activities Integrating Mathematics and Science Educational Foundation
http://204.161.33.100/AIMS.html
The AIMS Education Foundation—Activities Integrating Mathematics and Science—maintains this site as a resource for its K-9 educational program. Primarily for educators, browsers can access an AIMS discussion forum, a puzzle corner, and an extensive activity archive containing classroom exercises.

Ann Arbor Community High School
http://chs-web.umdl.umich.edu/
Michigan's Ann Arbor Community High School articulates its mission to "prepare our students to be productive citizens, lifelong learners, and responsible, autonomous individuals" at its home page. Visitors can explore student home pages and keep up with current school events.

Answers to Commonly Asked "Primary and Secondary School Internet User" Questions
http://chs.cusd.claremont.edu/www/people/rmuir/rfc1578.html
This long, practical guide provides detailed answers to numerous questions about Internet use for educating the K-12 set. Graphics free but content rich, the document includes a glossary.

Anthology
http://pen.k12.va.us/
A project of the Virginia Public Education Network, Anthology is a first step in developing a client-server system accessible by the state's K-12 teachers and students. Visitors to the Anthology home page can learn more about the project and its aims.

Appalachia Educational Laboratory
http://www.ael.org/
A nonprofit corporation in Charleston, W.Va., the Appalachia Educational Laboratory performs research and development services for education agencies. This searchable site provides info on AEL success stories, plus links to regional and other educational resources.

Appetizers and Lessons for Math and Reason
http://www.cam.org/~aselby/lesson.html
The Appetizers and Lessons for Math and Reason site is an online math and logic classroom. Grade school students learn how to use rules and patterns or click math lessons covering everything from basic arithmetic to calculus.

Apple Education Worldwide
http://www.education.apple.com
Apple Computer's online educational home invites visitors to tour educational sites on the Web. Browsers can jump to news of Apple products designed for classroom use at all levels, seminars, promotions and more. In English, French and German.

AskERIC
http://ericir.syr.edu/
The Educational Resources Information Center offers access to its lesson plans, collections and searchable database. Links to related ERIC sites and other educational resources are also featured.

Bellevue Public Schools
http://belnet.bellevue.k12.wa.us/
Bellevue Public Schools in Bellevue, Wash. maintains this site with links to its area schools and community resources. Visit here to browse its index of elementary, middle and high schools, and learn about its educational and local outreach programs.

Bellingham Public Schools
http://www.bham.wednet.edu/
Visitors are invited to enter the electronic classrooms of Bellingham, Wash.'s elementary, middle and high school system at this site. Find city's schools, administrative offices and even a student art gallery online.

Blake School
http://www.blake.pvt.k12.mn.us/
The home page of the Blake School in Minnesota features a high school literary arts magazine, "FLASH," along with general information about the school, its faculty and academic programs. Visitors are invited to peruse the online art gallery of student works.

Boulder Valley School District
http://bvsd.k12.co.us/
At Colorado's Boulder Valley School District home page, students can access electronic research sources and teachers can find curriculum ideas online. Links to individual schools in the district are also featured.

Branson School
http://www.nbn.com/~branson
The Branson School is an experimental independent secondary school in Ross, Calif., focusing on utilizing new educational technologies to enhance the learning environment. Includes descriptions of new programs, school restructuring strategies and Quicktime videos.

Bronx High School of Science
http://www.bxscience.edu/
The Bronx High School of Science is a public New York school that specializes in the sciences. This home page provides general information about departments, science computing and policies. Interested students can learn more about the people involved by linking to a selection of faculty, student and organization home pages.

Canada's SchoolNet
http://schoolnet2.carleton.ca/
Canada's SchoolNet brings teachers and students a wealth of online educational resources and activites. Explore the Web from an educator's prospective. In French and English.

CEARCH Virtual Schoolhouse
http://sunsite.unc.edu/cisco/schoolhouse.html
The Cisco Educational Archive is a library of links to K-12 resources. Visitors can search this virtual schoolhouse for links in all academic subjects. Search engines for other educational levels and specialized subjects are included.

Cedar Lane Center
http://www.usgs.gov/cedar/
The Cedar Lane Center is a public high school in Vienna, Va. Its site contains a message from the principal, a calendar of events, and a cedar chest brimming with educational resources.

Center for Excellence in Education
http://rsi.cee.org/
Founded by Admiral H. G. Rickover (father of the Nuclear Navy) in McLean, Va., the Center for Excellence in Education sponsors the Research Science Institute, a six-week summer research internship for America's brightest students in science and math. This site provides information about the program, past participants and other CEE projects and events.

Center for the New Engineer
http://cne.gmu.edu/
The Center for the New Engineer (CNE), a project funded by U.S. Department of Defense, aims to create new approaches in engineering- and science-based education. Visit this site to learn about the CNE's activities and staff, publications, tutorial modules and K-12 educational resources.

ChemCAI: Instructional Software for Chemistry
http://www.sfu.ca/chemed/
Simon Fraser University in British Columbia, Canada, features resources for chemistry educators through its Web site. Digital textbook chapters and other materials can serve as alternatives to traditional teaching methods. The pages also include downloadable software.

Cisco Educational Archives

http://sunsite.unc.edu/cisco/cisco-home.html

Cisco Systems, a supplier of interactive network solutions for schools and businesses, maintains this online educational archive and resources catalog (CEARCH) featuring a keyword search engine. Other features at this site include a meta-library called the Virtual Schoolhouse and information about the sponsoring company.

Classroom Connect

http://www.classroom.net

Educators can look to Classroom Connect for pointers and guides to educational resources on the Web. Link to software and info of interest and benefit to the K-12 set.

Common Knowledge: Pittsburgh

http://info.ckp.edu/

This site provides information about Common Knowledge: Pittsburgh, a collaborative project started by the Pittsburgh Public Schools, the Pittsburgh Supercomputing Center and the University of Pittsburgh. CK:P is aimed at developing a computer networking infrastructure for educational uses. Visitors here can find out about the project's design and progress.

Computer as Learning Partner

http://www.clp.berkeley.edu/CLP.html

The mission of the Computer as Learning Partner project at the University of California at Berkeley is to faciliate science education for middle school students nationwide. Find out about CLP's conceptual framework and instructional approach at this Web site, as well as info about their curriculum and software.

Cyber High School

http://www.webcom.com/~cyberhi

Cyber High School is a college preparatory school offering classes via the Internet. Visitors can learn about the philosophy behind this alternative school, how it operates and what kind of curriculum if follows. Admissions information is also available.

Cyberspace Middle School

http://www.scri.fsu.edu/~dennisl/CMS.html

Designed for students in the sixth through ninth grades, the Cyberspace Middle School provides links to educational activities on the Web. Features also include links to the home pages of middle schools across the country, a teacher's resource center and a special announcements board.

Desert View High School

http://wacky.ccit.arizona.edu/~susd/dvhome.html

Arizona's Desert View High School site features information of interest to students, including an electronic magazine, Internet tools and a link to a page for Native American students.

Drexel Hill School of the Holy Child

http://forum.swarthmore.edu/~joanna

Pennsylvania's Drexel Hill School of the Holy Child is a Catholic co-ed institution more than 65 years old. This page gives visitors a brief rundown of its math, computer, science, social studies and foreign language classes.

Educational Online Sources

http://netspace.students.brown.edu/eos/main_image.html

The Educational Online Sources is meant to be a first stop for educators exploring the Internet's potential as a teaching tool. This introductory page explains the EOS project and offers a link into the source list.

Educational Space Simulations Project

http://chico.rice.edu/armadillo/Simulations/simserver.html

The Educational Space Simulations Project is sponsored by the Houston Independent School District and Rice University. Visitors to this page will find information on projects that combine technological simulations with educational programs for children.

Education Showcase

http://www.infomall.org/Showcase

This promotional page is the Internet home of Education Showcase, an Internet publishing company that helps other companies market to schools through the Internet. Includes descriptions of products, services and customer support.

EdWeb

http://k12.cnidr.org:90/

EdWeb is a site dealing with educational reform. Voted by "NetGuide Magazine" as one of the 50 best places to go online, EdWeb offers insightful ideas about improving education in schools around the world with the help of online services such as the Web. Site includes some links to a number of worthy home pages.

EE-Link

http://nceet.snre.umich.edu/

The mission of EE-Link, Environmental Education on the Internet, is to help educators and students explore the environment and investigate current issues. EE-Link comes complete with classroom resources, organizations, an educational directory, regional information and more.

Enlaces Project Information Service

http://www.enlaces.ufro.cl/

The Chilean Ministry of Education's Enlaces Project is designed to study the cost and effectiveness of placing computers in elementary and secondary schools. This site outlines the project, in English and Spanish, and provides links to Chilean education servers.

Environmental Education Network

http://envirolink.org/enviroed

The Environmental Education Network is a collaborative effort of educators, private industry and the environmental community to bring environmental education online. Includes links to libraries, databases, marketplaces and user participation sites.

ERIC/Clearinghouse on Reading, English and Communication

http://www.indiana.edu/~eric_rec/index.html

The Educational Resources Information Center (ERIC) Clearinghouse on Reading, English and Communication provides educational materials, services and coursework to parents, educators and students interested in the language arts. Includes an online bookstore, up-to-date bibliographies and research digests. See Editor's Choice.

Explorer

http://unite.ukans.edu/

At the Explorer Web site browsers can view a database of resources for K-12 mathematics and science education. The database is a joint project of the Great Lakes Collaborative and the University of Kansas, and is funded by the U.S. department of Education.

Explores!

http://thunder.met.fsu.edu/explores/explores.html

At Florida Explores, visitors can read about the state's efforts to implement the NAOO Direct Readout Satellite Ground Station Program in K-12 education. Check out a wealth of Florida-related resources here, including weather, satellite imagery, data sets and more.

Far West Laboratory

http://www.fwl.org/

One of 10 regional educational laboratories created by Congress in 1966, the Far West Laboratory (FWL) provides services and expertise to the education communities in Arizona, California, Nevada and Utah. This organizational site explains FWL's range of services, and provides topical updates and information.

Fermilab Education Office

http://www-ed.fnal.gov/

Information on education programs of the Fermi National Accelerator Laboratory are the focus of this site. Also included are course materials and teachers' resources, including a quarterly journal. Fermilab is home to the world's most powerful particle accelerator, the Tevatron.

German-American School

http://www.rahul.net/dehnbase/das

The German-American School in San Francisco features information about its recognized German foreign school program through this page.

The school includes educational opportunities for K-12 students. In English and German.

Gifted Resources

http://www.eskimo.com/~user/kids.html

The Gifted Resources home page provides "a convenient starting point for gifted students, their parents and educators." Visit here for links to talent searches, summer programs, distance learning opportunities, scholarship information and more.

Global Network Navigator Select: Education

http://gnn.com/gnn/wic/wics/ed.new.html

This page, from the larger Global Network Navigator site, offers an overview of and links into the Education Center, "a resource dedicated to providing educators with dynamic curricula, projects, and connections." Find reading and language, math, social studies and American History covered.

Global Student News

http://www.jou.ufl.edu/forums/gsn/

Global Student News seeks to provide a forum for sharing ideas useful to students and educators involved in news media. Using Internet distribution as a springboard, the site offers learning tools to get student online publications up and running.

GLOBE Program

http://www.globe.gov/

The GLOBE Program unites students, teachers and scientists for the study of the environment. At its home page, GLOBE explains its organizational philosophy, describes current projects and programs.

Hillside Elementary School

http://hillside.coled.umn.edu/

Web 66, a project to introduce K-12 educators and students to Web publishing, hosts this home page for Hillside Elementary School, of Cottage Grove, Minn. Visitors will find school information here, as well as home pages from various classrooms.

Hinsdale Township High School District 86

http://www.district86.k12.il.us/district86_home_page.html

The Hinsdale Township High School District Number 86 makes its home on this page. Visitors can read about the Illinois school district, including its history, staff and students.

Hoffer School

http://cmp1.ucr.edu/exhibitions/hoffer/hoffer.homepage.html

Hoffer Elementary School offers information here on its photography and media-related student projects. Check out group pictures, past exhibits from the California Museum of Photography and highlights of the children's other Internet adventures. See Editor's Choice, page 253.

Houghton Mifflin Company

http://www.hmco.com/

Houghton Mifflin, a Boston, Mass.-based instructional text publisher, maintains this promotional site for company and product information. Visit here to learn about its wide range of educational materials, textbooks, and fiction and nonfiction titles for adults and children.

Houston Independent School District

http://chico.rice.edu/armadillo/hisdabout.html

The Houston Independent School District maintains this site, called Armadillo, detailing its student demographics, instructor salaries and personnel profiles. Link to the School Board's Declaration of Beliefs and Visions for info on the district's restructuring initiatives.

I*EARN

http://www.igc.apc.org/iearn/

The I*EARN page introduces browsers to a network resource involved with international education. Focusing on children 6 to 19, the resource offers global telecommunication opportunities for projects that promote "a meaningful difference" to people and to planet Earth.

Institute for the Academic Advancement of Youth

http://www.jhu.edu/~gifted/

This Web site provides details on programs sponsored by the Center for Talented Youth and Center for Academic Advancement at Johns Hopkins University's Institute for the Academic Advancement of Youth. Includes talent-search information.

Interactive Frog Dissection

http://curry.edschool.virginia.edu/~insttech/frog/home.html

This interactive, online tutorial leads visitors through the dissection of a frog. Designed for high school biology labs, this electronic frog has an advantage over the formaldehyde-packed kind: it can be used over and over.

---

a2z   EDITOR'S CHOICE

ERIC/Clearinghouse on Reading, English and Communication

http://www.indiana.edu/~eric_rec/index.html

ERIC, the Educational Resources Information Center, is the world's largest educational database. The ERIC Clearinghouse on Reading, English and Communication is a vast collection of language arts, educational materials and services geared to parents and teachers alike. Among the many resources available are long distance education courses for credit, professional development workshops for educators, and summaries of current research in education. Parents will find read-along stories to share with their kids, and seniors will want to check out the Senior Partners pen pal program, a unique service that matches adult letter writers with kids throughout the United States. For teachers, the Clearinghouse Bookstore contains a full range of publications and videos on language arts education, plus free lesson plans and info on using the Internet in the classroom. The ERIC/REC home page also contains info on joining the READPRO e-mail list, a forum for educators to discuss language arts education.—*Reviewed by Karen Wise*

Welcome to the ERIC Clearinghouse on Reading, English, and Communication (ERIC/REC). Our site is dedicated to providing educational materials, services, and coursework to everyone interested in the language arts.

Intercultural E-Mail Classroom Connections

http://www.stolaf.edu/network/iecc/

Intercultural E-Mail Classroom Connections is a free service linking teachers and students with e-mail partners in other countries and cultures. At this site you can read about projects and programs, subscribe to IECC or search the archives.

International Olympiad in Informatics

http://www.win.tue.nl/win/ioi/

The International Olympiad in Informatics is an annual computer science competition for seniors at secondary schools around the world. Visitors will find rules and regulations, previous competition task lists and information on the upcoming competition.

Internet Access for Polish High Schools

http://idsserv.waw.ids.edu.pl/ids/
Welcome.html

The Internet home of the Internet dla Szkol project in Poland details plans to provide full Net access to all Polish high schools and train students and teachers about basic Internet services. Visitors can read about the project in Polish or English.

Internet for Learning

http://www.rmplc.co.uk/

RM is a company supplying Internet technology to grade schools in the United Kingdom. The Internet for Learning home page describes RM's subscription service which features direct Internet connections, technical support, a filtered news service, POP mail and a home page creation option.

Internet for Minnesota Schools

http://informns.k12.mn.us/

Internet for Minnesota Schools is a joint public project that helps Minnesota K-12 educators use the Internet as a teaching tool. It also provides Internet access and software. This site contains links to instructional resources and to many Minnesota schools.

Jason Project

http://jasonproject.org/

The Jason Foundation for Education offers this Web site devoted to providing information about the Jason Project, a national program designed to bring eductional technologies to high schools across the U.S. Visitors can read pages on Jason Project news bulletins, discussion groups, student and teacher resources or learn how to participate.

Jason VI: Island Earth

http://seawifs.gsfc.nasa.gov/JASON/HTML/
JASON_6_HOME.html

The Jason Project sponsors an annual scientific expedition that is covered electronically for students in grades 4 - 8. The sixth expedition, which explored Hawaii and the inside of a volcano, took place in 1995 and is detailed here.

Jon's Home-School Resource Page

http://www.midnightbeach.com/hs/

Parents interested in homeschooling will find a wealth of resources at this Web site, including newsgroups and mailing lists, a list of frequently asked questions (FAQ) and links to homeschooling sites all over the Internet.

K-12+ Servers

http://www.tenet.edu/education/main.html

Visitors will find an index to K-12+ educational servers here. The index includes state, international and government categories.

Kaplan Educational Centers

http://www.kaplan.com/

Kaplan claims to be the world's leader in standardized test preparation classes. At this promotional site visitors can learn about the company by downloading free games, visiting an online classroom or checking out the library.

Kids Web: A World Wide Web Digital Library for Schoolkids

http://www.npac.syr.edu/textbook/kidsweb/

Kids Web, part of the Syracuse University Living Schoolbook Project presents a wide-ranging digital library for school kids. Included are links to the arts, sciences, social studies and other items of educational value—and interest—to children. Links to other digital libraries are also available.

Lawrence Berkeley National Laboratory ELSI Project

http://www.lbl.gov/Education/ELSI/ELSI.html

Explore Ethical, Legal and Social Issues in science at the Lawrence Berkeley National Laboratory's ELSI Project. The information here is geared toward teachers and students at a middle school level, with discussions of the politics of cancer, genetics, pollution and privacy.

Learning in Motion

http://www.learn.motion.com/

Learning in Motion is a corporate producer of K-12 educational software. Visitors will find information and demos of the company's math, science and multimedia note-taking programs. Includes a list of top educational sites on the Web.

 EDITOR'S CHOICE

Hoffer School

http://cmp1.ucr.edu/exhibitions/hoffer/hoffer.homepage.html

The third-graders in room eight at the Hoffer Elementary School in Banning, Calif., are doing some way cool things with photography and related media. The Hoffer home page is full of photos, audio clips, videos and text, all created by students. Click on any student's picture for an audio introduction, then go directly to the student's own home page to check out original photos, poems, illustrations, scanned images, and stories. Other Hoffer student adventures include a magazine collage, PhotoShop gallery and various animation projects. All of these exciting learning experiences are conducted in collaboration with the University of California at Riverside and the California Museum of Photography. Before you leave the Hoffer home page, we bet you won't be able to resist clicking on the DO NOT ENTER sign!—*Reviewed by Karen Wise*

UCR/California Museum of Photography presents...

HOFFER ELEMENTARY SCHOOL
in
LOW TECH HIGH TECH

Hello and welcome to Hoffer Elementary School! For the past five years we have collaborated with the UCR/California Museum of Photography on photography and related media projects. Hoffer is now one of four schools participating in the museum's VidKids Media Literacy program. What follows is part of this year's discoveries...have fun!

During your visit you will *see* pictures, *hear* voices, and read works of young artists from room eight. You can meet them and check out what they do by clicking on words and pictures throughout your tour. Start below and enjoy your visit! Click on any words in color & any picture with a color border. To receive sounds you will need sound software such as SoundMachine.

Learning Web at the U.S. Geological Survey

http://info.er.usgs.gov/education/index.html

The U.S. Geological Survey (USGS) maintains The Learning Web, a page dedicated to K-12 education, exploration and learning. This page contains curricula resources and information about a variety of Earth-related topics.

Lexington Bicycle Safety Program

http://larch-www.lcs.mit.edu:8001/~guttag/lbsp/lbsp.html

Bicycle safety comes to the World Wide Web through this site from the Lexington Bicycle Safety Program. The nonprofit organization features a curriculum kit for elementary school teachers and a video public service announcement featuring U.S. sports celebrities.

Los Alamos Middle School

http://lams.losalamos.k12.nm.us/

The Los Alamos Middle School home page offers a calendar of events and links to the student newspaper through its New Mexico-based site. It also has links to educational hot spots and home pages created by students.

Low Bentham County Primary School

http://cres1.lancs.ac.uk/~esarie/school.htm

Low Bentham County Primary School in North Yorkshire, England, offers an introduction to its teachers, students and local community at this site. Visit here for student home pages, children's stories, village scenery and more.

Madison Middle School 2000

http://198.150.8.9/

At the central Web site for Madison Middle School 2000, of Madison, Wis., visitors will find school news, updates on student projects, and information about life in Madison.

Mankato Area Schools

http://www.isd77.k12.mn.us/

Residents of Blue Earth County in Minnesota can check in with their school system here. Parents can take virtual tours of the schools, download educational software and check the latest school news. A search function and staff directory are also posted here.

MathMagic

http://forum.swarthmore.edu/mathmagic/

MathMagic is a project for K-12 students to solve math problems while using the Internet. The challenges are split into grade groupings, with current and past puzzles available. Teachers can use this site to prompt discussions and carry on what kids learn. Registration costs, but unregistered visitors can work the problems, too.

MathMol

http://www.nyu.edu/pages/mathmol/

MathMol (Mathematics and Molecules) from New York University serves as an introduction to the field of molecular modeling. Features here include a software archive, library of structures, a special section on water and MathMol for the K-12 set.

MECC

http://www.mecc.com/

MECC, a leading producer of children's software, posts a company overview and product list on this promotional page. It includes a software primer for parents and links to dozens of child advocacy groups on the Web.

MidLink Magazine

http://longwood.cs.ucf.edu/~MidLink/

MidLink Magazine is an interactive publication for children ages 10 to 15. Includes an index to articles and activities, links to other publications for school-age children and teens, a book fair, and other educational resources. See Editor's Choice, page 255.

Minnesota New Country School

http://mncs.k12.mn.us/

At the Minnesota New Country School's site visitors will get an overview of the Le Sueur, Minn., school and staff and a look at the students' artwork and home pages.

Mississippi School for Mathematics and Science

http://www.msms.doe.k12.ms.us/

Located in Columbus, the Mississippi School for Mathematics and Science is a high school for academically talented students. Visitors to this home page will find information about the campus and the school's disciplinary approaches, news, and publications.

Monroe Middle School

http://monhome.sw2.k12.wy.us/

Monroe Middle School in Green River, Wyo., maintains this site for student projects, school resources, faculty profiles and more. Visit here to learn about the school and link to its Internet directory.

---

a2z   EDITOR'S CHOICE

MidLink Magazine

http://longwood.cs.ucf.edu/~MidLink/

The award-winning e-zine MidLink is geared, appropriately enough, to middle-school students. It's filled with original art and writing created by kids aged 10 to 15 from all over the world. With the help of teacher editors and advisors from the U.S. to Israel to Belarus to Tokyo (and just about everywhere in between!), the student editors create a thematic issue each quarter—the June-September 1996 issue, for example, celebrates the 1996 Summer Olympics. Back issues of MidLink remain accessible on the Web for a year after their first appearance. Schools worldwide are invited to contribute, and MidLink will feature a link to any school's own home page. The MidLink home page also includes info on online student projects, including Book Link (students share their favorite books and authors), the Global Rivers Project and Creative Cuisine.—*Reviewed by Karen Wise*

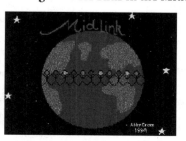

MidLink Magazine:
The Electronic Magazine for Kids in the Middle Grades

Monta Vista High School

http://www.mvhs.edu/

Monta Vista High School, located in Cupertino, Calif., maintains this informational site. Visit here for a school profile, links with community information, and other Internet-based educational resources.

Montgomery County Intermediate Unit

http://www.mciu.k12.pa.us/

Find out how public education is governed in the state of Pennsylvania at the Montgomery County Intermediate Unit home page. A calendar and links to the MCIU Educational Technology Newsletter are also provided.

Mountain Lake Software

http://www.woodwind.com/mtlake/index.html

This promotional site is the Web home of Mountain Lake Software, a California-based publisher of educational software. Visitors can learn more about the company, its products and services, plus find product demos and other free offers.

NASA Lewis Research Center HPCC/IITA K-12 Program

http://www.lerc.nasa.gov/Other_Groups/K-12/K-12_homepage.html

The NASA Lewis Research Center provides this site with information about the High Performance Computing and Communications/Information Infrastructure Technology Applications K-12 Program, an educational program designed to increase the computer literacy of K-12 students.

NASA Online Educational Resources

http://www.gsfc.nasa.gov/nasa_online_education.html

This is NASA's online outreach program to the educational community. Visitors will find articles, videos and animation on astronomy and space exploration. Links are provided for educational resources throughout NASA.

National Energy Foundation

http://www.xmission.com/~nef/

The National Energy Foundation is a nonprofit organization devoted to the development of energy-related instructional materials, teacher training and student programs. This site has more information about the foundation and features a materials catalog and details for ordering.

National Regional Educational Laboratories

http://www.nwrel.org/national/regional-labs.html

Supported in part by the U.S. Dept. of Education, these educational research and development labs are networked regionally, and linked via this Web page. Each lab supports different services and resources: video conferencing, discipline-specific consortiums, virtual libraries, and a variety of resources and tools for educators.

Net-Happenings

http://www.mid.net/NET/

Net-happenings is a service that allows educational network staffers and K-12 educators to inform other Internet users of online educational events and resources. Visitors here can search through archived listings or submit their own Net-based learning tools for publicity.

New Horizons Regional Education Center

http://www.nhgs.tec.va.us/

New Horizons Regional Education Center operates high school programs for autistic and emotionally disturbed children from the Hampton, Va., area. The school focuses on three developed programs: Career-Technical Education, Governor's School for Science and Technology and Special Education. Visitors here can learn more about the programs, get campus information or link to related resources.

New Tools for Teaching

http://ccat.sas.upenn.edu/teachdemo

This report from James J. O'Donnell at the University of Pennsylvania on Internet-based teaching tools, provides an overview of the communications, archiving and information search resources of the growing electronic network. Includes help for beginners.

NonEuclid: Geometry Software

http://riceinfo.rice.edu/projects/NonEuclid/NonEuclid.html

Visit this page to learn about a Rice University software package that offers "an interactive simulation of the Poincare Model of Hyperbolic Geometry for use in high school and undergraduate education." Find an introduction to the software and a discussion of the model it presents.

North Carolina Department of Public Instruction

http://www.dpi.state.nc.us/

Public Schools of North Carolina provides DPI InfoWeb, an education-related information service for both the educators and citizens of the state. Among the features available are an educators' resource center, an Internet library, a personnel directory and a facts and figures file.

Northwest Tri-County Intermediate Unit

http://www.trinet.k12.pa.us/

The Northwest Tri-County Intermediate Unit provides programs and services supporting quality education in Pennsylvania. Its home page offers news, Internet beginners' tutorials and contact information.

Online Educator

http://www.ole.net/ole/

The Online Educator is an online and print subscription-based magazine that provides Internet educational tools. This site has an index of hot links for teachers, sample articles from the print edition and other information.

Patch American High School

http://192.253.114.31/

Located at Patch Barracks, headquarters for the United States European Command (US EUCOM) in Stuttgart, Germany, Patch American High School welcomes visitors to the site of the first high school Web server in Europe. The school's academics, extracurricular and multi-curricular activities are highlighted.

Pathways to School Improvement

http://www.ncrel.org/ncrel/sdrs/pathways.htm

Visitors to this page will find a gateway to Pathways to School Improvement, a service filled with resources for teaching professionals.

Peddie School

http://www.peddie.k12.nj.us/

The Peddie School site contains information on the college-prep boarding school's admissions policies, academic programs and mission statement. Includes descriptions of the Hightstown, N.J., school's nonacademic programs and summer classes and info on high-tech projects.

Peterson's Education Center

http://www.petersons.com/

Provided by publisher Peterson's Guides Inc., this Education Center is a collection of Web resources for all levels and disciplines. Link areas include K-12, studying abroad, executive education and language study.

Pine View High School

http://www.pvhs.wash.k12.ut.us/

Pine View High School in Saint George, Utah, presents general information about the school and its educational programs via PantherNET. Visit here to learn aboutthe school's students and teachers, access student Web sites, download Internet search tools, and more.

Pojoaque Valley Schools

http://pvs.k12.nm.us/

The home page of northern New Mexico's Pojoaque Valley Schools contains links to high and middle school pages by students and faculty, a gallery of student art, poems and a guest book. This page also includes links to other Web sites and the district's other servers.

Princeton Regional Schools

http://www.prs.k12.nj.us/

This site provides general information about the schools and students of Princeton, N.J.'s Regional School District. Here browsers will find school board items, links to specific schools and more.

Project GeoSim

http://geosim.cs.vt.edu/index.html

Project GeoSim is a research program at Virginia Tech to develop educational software modules for introductory geography courses. Site features include listings of completed modules, links to the project library and links to other information servers at the university.

Quest: NASA K-12 Internet Initiative

http://quest.arc.nasa.gov/

Quest is a NASA sponsored K-12 Internet initiative to provide support and services for teachers and students to fully utilize the Internet as a basic tool for learning. Includes links to NASA researchers, research sites and online interactive activities.

Reece High School

http://web.reece.tased.edu.au/

Reece High School in Devonport, Tasmania, Australia, provides a place for the school's students to publish their work and learn about Internet communication technologies. A collection of student work is available, including Haiku poetry and Reece's electronic magazine, Troncartee.

Riley High School

http://sjcpl.lib.in.us/rhshomepage/riley2.html

Teachers and students at Indiana's Riley High School showcase their downloadable software creations at the school's home page. Includes a school profile, photos and access to an alumni page.

Rockingham School

http://www.cfn.cs.dal.ca/Education/RockinghamSch/Rockingham.html

The home page for Rockingham School of Halifax, Nova Scotia, contains an interactive image map and links to student home pages, educational resources, and staff information.

SchoolsNET

http://www.schnet.edu.au/

Australia's Melbourne-based SchoolsNET is dedicated to providing Internet access and online educational resources to schools. Its home page provides teachers and students alike with links to online course materials, electronic conferences and virtual field trips.

Science Bytes

http://loki.ur.utk.edu/ut2kids/science.html

Visit here to find the University of Tennessee's electronic magazine for the K-12 crowd, Science Bytes. Each issue seeks to educate and inspire young minds by describing current research at the university.

Sidwell Friends School

http://www.sidwell.edu/

The home page of the Sidwell Friends School, located in Washington, D. C., features an Internet guide for faculty and students. Visitors to the site can read about the computing resources at the school and get information about academic programs, faculty and alumni activities.

Sites for Educators

http://www.mtjeff.com/~bodenst/page5.html

This site provides a comprehensive list of links to sites for educators, including various search engines, resources from the state of Oregon, and resources in the humanities, sciences and mathematics.

SkillsBank Corporation

http://www.skillsbank.com/

The SkillsBank Corporation is a educational technology firm located in Baltimore, Maryland. Visitors will find descriptions of the company's products and services at this promotional site.

StarChild

http://starchild.gsfc.nasa.gov/

The StarChild Project is a NASA educational initiative aimed at providing learning experiences to K-12 students. Find astronomy-related topics discussed and demonstrated in fun and easy terms at this site.

STEM~Net

http://calvin.stemnet.nf.ca/

STEM~Net provides electronic resources for K-12, rural public colleges and Memorial Universities of Newfoundland and Labrador, Canada. Visitors to its home page can access its numerous information and reference options as well as link to Canada's SchoolNet, SchoolNet Rings, and related Web sites and servers.

Tasmanian Department of Education, Community and Cultural Development

http://www.tased.edu.au/

The Tasmanian Department of Education, Community and Cultural Development presents an index to schools, colleges, the state library and educational programs here. There's also a pointer to the Australian government home page.

Teacher Talk

http://education.indiana.edu/cas/tt/tthmpg.html

The Teacher Talk home page, provided by the Center for Adolescent Studies at Indiana University, is an online publication for preservice, secondary education teachers. Visit here for current and back issues, a topic list, and related resources.

Thomas Jefferson High School for Science and Technology

http://www.tjhsst.edu/

Thomas Jefferson High School for Science and Technology in Alexandria, Va., maintains this site for student home pages, clubs news, and campus athletics and activities updates. Includes index of Internet resources.

Urban Education Web

http://eric-web.tc.columbia.edu/

UEweb is dedicated to assisting urban students and those who teach, guide and mentor them. Among other features, this clearinghouse on urban education includes urban and minority family resources, topical publications, education materials, and links to ERIC (library) databases.

Viking Network Web

http://odin.nls.no/viking/vnethome.htm

Targeting its presentations to primary and secondary schools, the Viking Network Web separates myth from fact to present the lifestyle, travels and heritage of the Viking people. The network is a joint project of the Local History Resource Centre in Fetsund, Norway, and the Summerhill Education Centre in Aberdeen, Scotland.

Virtual FlyLab

http://vflylab.calstatela.edu/edesktop/VirtApps/VflyLab/IntroVflyLab.html

Scientists at California State University have devised the Virtual FlyLab to enable viewers to play the role of a research geneticist. Custom design fruit fly matings to create personalized mutations, learning the correct rules of genetic inheritance as you go.

Vocal Point

http://bvsd.k12.co.us/cent/Newspaper/Newspaper.html

Vocal Point, an online monthly newspaper assembled by students at Centennial Middle School in Boulder, Colo., tackles a new topic each issue. Visitors can check out the current and back issues or link to the Boulder Valley School District's home page.

Vose School Education Resources

http://www.teleport.com/~vincer/starter.html

Look at educational resources on the Internet through the eyes of an Oregon teacher. A special introduction to the Internet for students and education professionals, this site walks beginners through electronically available school and academic subject sites.

Wangaratta Primary School

http://www.ozemail.com.au/~wprimary/wps.htm

Australia's rural Wangaratta Primary School posts fun Aussie activities for children on this page. Introductions to its students and a list of nontraditional gender occupations are also featured.

Weather Unit

http://faldo.atmos.uiuc.edu/WEATHER/weather.html

The Weather Unit provides links to K-12 lessons in a variety of disciplines, including math, science, reading, drama, social sciences and other areas of study. This page also links to the Collaborative Lesson Archive.

WebEd Curriculum Links

http://badger.state.wi.us/agencies/dpi/www/WebEd.html

Started in 1993 as one man's project to find Web resources to support his school district's curriculum, WebEd Curriculum Links is now a thorough listing of K-12 sites hosted by the Wisconsin Department of Public Instruction's server. Categories here include links to sites for children and teachers, humanities subjects, reference, news, and college and career information.

Web 66

http://web66.coled.umn.edu/

The Web 66 Project seeks to facilitate integration of Internet technology into K-12 curricula. Includes information on Web resources for educators, links to a pilot program, and instructional guides for setting up and operating a server.

Whole Frog Project

http://george.lbl.gov/ITG.hm.pg.docs/Whole.Frog/Whole.Frog.html

The Lawrence Berkeley Laboratory ITG Whole Frog Project is designed to introduce concepts of computer-based 3D visualization and demonstrate 3D imaging of a frog's anatomy as a high school biology teaching aid. This site provides step-by-step information on using computers to create 3D images.

WWW Servers Hosted at CNIDR

http://k12.cnidr.org/

Hosted by the Center for Networked Information Discovery and Retrieval, this page provides several pointers to K-12 education-oriented servers on the Web. Links range from Janice's K12 Cyberspace Outpost to Presidential Awardees Internet Pilot.

World-Wide Web Virtual Library: Education

http://www.csu.edu.au/education/library.html

The World Wide Web Virtual Library provides this searchable, comprehensive list of links to education resources and sites. Links are categorized alphabetically, by education level, resource provided, site type and country.

World-Wide Web Virtual Library: Educational Technology

http://tecfa.unige.ch/info-edu-comp.html

The Educational Technology section of the World Wide Web Virtual Library provides a massive list of links to sites relating to educational software and other electronic educational projects. Heavy on software archives, the list includes brief descriptions of the links provided.

LIBRARIES

Alexicon

http://www.konbib.nl/

Alexican, the information service of the National Library of the Netherlands, maintains this site for library and Internet resources. Visit here to access its collection of published works, perform a keyword search of its database and find link to guest organizations. In Dutch and English.

Ameritech Library Services

http://www.notis.com/

Ameritech Library Services provides products and services for libraries. This site supplies academic news and information on Ameritech's products and customer-support services. Includes an electronic newsletter.

Association of Research Libraries

http://arl.cni.org/

The Association of Research Libraries articulates the concerns of research libraries, influences policy development and supports innovation in research library operations. ARL programs, statistics and publications are available here.

Bibliographical Society of America

http://aultnis.rutgers.edu/bsastuff/bsahome.html

The Bibliographical Society of America, a New York-based scholarly society for the textual and bibliographical study of books, maintains this informational site. Visit here for recent publications, officer profiles, fellowship information and links to related Web sites.

BIBSYS

http://www.bibsys.no/english.html

BIBSYS is an online collective library system of all Norwegian University libraries, the National Library and a number of research libraries. A free service for Internet users, it provides access to 1.8 million bibliographic records. In Norwegian and English.

Birmingham Public Library

http://www.bham.lib.al.us/

The Birmingham Public Library home page contains a description of the library system and its collections. Includes details on the Alabama library's departments, access to its catalog and links to Web navigation tools.

Bladen Library

http://library-gopher.scar.utoronto.ca/

The University of Toronto's Scarborough Campus library is online here. Visitors can search its catalogue or link to other pages in the University system from this site.

Bodleian Library at the University of Oxford

http://www.rsl.ox.ac.uk/

The Bodleian Library at the University of Oxford supplies readers' guides to many of its offerings, including its Japanese Library, Law Library and Indian Institute Library. It also provides Bodleian Access to Remote Databases (BARD), Web links and a listing of items from the Bodleian Shop.

Brigham Young University Libraries Information Network

http://library.byu.edu/

Brigham Young University hosts this Web site with a wealth of information on its library services. Check out library news, projects, exhibits, records and projects, or access catalogs, reference tools and databases here. Visitors can also link to the text-based library system via telnet, or read BYLINE: The Next Generation, a hyper-text interface to the library's online catalog.

BUBL Information Service

http://bubl.ac.uk

Although it originated in the UK as a bulletin board for libraries, BUBL has expanded to serve the country's academic and research communities as well. Visitors can search for Internet information and resources by using the the BUBL subject tree, keyword search or other services and tools.

California State Library

http://library.ca.gov/california/State_Library/

You won't need a library card at the California State Library page, but if you want to know more about this state's library system, this is the place to check out. A greeting from the state librarian, details including locations, hours and staffing, and an overview of library service are all available here.

CARL Corporation

http://carl.org/carl.html

The CARL Corporation markets the CARL System, a turnkey library management system, as well as other products and services to libraries and information providers. Browsers can learn about the company, its products and services, and access online references.

Carrie

http://history.cc.ukans.edu/carrie/carrie_main.html

The University of Kansas posts Carrie, a full-text electronic library. Visitors can browse through the stacks or download information from the Kansas Collection. The library also contains periodicals and daily news.

Centre de Ressources Informatiques de l'Université de Rennes 1

http://www.univ-rennes1.fr/

At the home page for the Center for Information Resources at the University of Rennes in France, visitors can look up staff, check the library catalogues and research, or link to on and off-campus sites. French only.

Chicago Public Library

http://cpl.lib.uic.edu/CPL.html

The Chicago Public Library unveils its experimental Web server, providing the masses with access to Internet resources and services. Visitors will find the library's catalog, events listings, and links to sites offering information on Chicago and Illinois.

Columbia University Libraries

http://www.cc.columbia.edu/cu/libraries/index.html

LibraryWeb is the main information site of the Columbia University Libraries. Resources provided here are library search tools; electronic texts, journals and images; and Internet subject guides.

CoOL

http://palimpsest.stanford.edu/

Conservation OnLine (CoOL) posts full text files here for people who preserve library and museum materials. The site, maintained by the Preservation Department of Stanford University Libraries, includes links to related sites.

Cyclops' Internet Toolbox

http://cyclops.idbsu.edu/

This personal home page can link visitors with library resource tools as well as its creator's favorite Web sites. Featured here are pages of library resources compiled by a reference librarian at Albertsons Library at Boise State University.

Data Research Associates

http://www.dra.com/

Data Research Associates produces client/server automation systems and networking services for libraries and information providers. This site delivers background information on the company, its products and clients.

Digital Libraries Project

http://www-diglib.stanford.edu/diglib/

Stanford University's Digital Libraries Project highlights the efforts to establish a single, integrated, universal library. This page offers links to

the people building the library, as well as a Frequently Asked Question (FAQ) file and a glimpse into the library itself.

Dundee University Library and Information Service

http://gotwo.dundee.ac.uk/uldhome.html

The University Library Dundee site contains an overview of the library, its facilities and access to the library catalog. Includes a tour of the library and links to other library-based sites in the United Kingdom.

East Carolina University Academic Library Services

http://fringe.lib.ecu.edu/

The East Carolina University Academic Library Services site contains links to the various departments in the system, an online catalog, periodical indexes and newspapers. Includes job listings, electronic texts and pointers to U.S. government servers.

Edinburgh University Data Library

http://datalib.ed.ac.uk/

Edinburgh University's Data Library site allows browsers to search the university's data library. Links to related projects and other information services are also included.

ELISA

http://info.anu.edu.au/elisa.html

The Electronic Library and Information Service at the Australian National University features general library services information, a campus events calendar and a database directory. Also find links to Internet indexes, electronic journals and texts, and reference materials.

Flinders University Library

http://www.lib.flinders.edu.au/

The Flinders University of South Australia puts its library information system online for all the Web to see. Visitors can search the library's catalog or access electronic document delivery services here.

Galen II

http://www.library.ucsf.edu/

Galen II is the home page for the Digital Library of the University of California, San Francisco. Includes access to numerous databases and archives, a library catalog, the UCSF Interactive Learning Centers and educational/consulting sources for faculty, staff and students. Links to other government and educational resources.

Gerber/Hart Library & Archives

http://www.gerberhart.org/

Chicago's Gerber/Hart Library & Archives is the Midwest's gay, lesbian and bisexual circulation library. Visitors to the institution's home page can access information aimed at the Midwest's gay and bisexual community. Includes

links to pages like Digital Queers Chicago and similar sites.

Helmke Library

http://www-lib.ipfw.indiana.edu/

Located at Indiana University-Purdue University Fort Wayne, the Helmke Library maintains this site offering an overview of the facility and its services. Links to the library's catalogs, databases, indexes and government collections are featured.

HyperPals

http://bingen.cs.csbsju.edu/pals/hyperpals.html

HyperPals is a hypertext Web interface to the PALS (Project for Automated Library Systems) OPAC (Online Public Access Catalog). This informative site answers questions about HyperPals, explains basic operation, and provides hints for users.

Indexes and Abstracts

http://www.lib.utexas.edu/Indexes/Online.html

The library system at the University of Texas at Austin maintains this list of searchable indexes and abstracts. Only limited access is provided to browsers without proper UT ID.

Indiana State Library

http://www.statelib.lib.in.us/

The Indiana State Library maintains this site for public access. Visitors may search the library's wide range of texts and periodicals, connect with local and federal government resources, and find links to a variety of Internet search tools.

Indiana University - Purdue University Indianapolis Library

http://www-lib.iupui.edu/

The IUPUI Library goes online at this site, which features electronic references and online catalogs, as well as application tools, information center and user help links, including a building map, user suggestion page and a checkout service.

Indiana University, School of Library and Information Science

http://www-slis.lib.indiana.edu/

The University of Indiana provides this informational page on its PhD and Masters programs at the School of Library and Information Sciences. Visitors will find info on faculty and the various academic paths and courses.

Information and Library Studies Student Association

http://http2.sils.umich.edu/ILSSA/HomePage.html

The Information and Library Studies Student Association of the University of Michigan serves up a variety of organization information here. Visitors can read the ILSSA Frequently Asked Questions (FAQ), annual reports or link to other student organizations and activities.

Informedia

http://fuzine.mt.cs.cmu.edu/im/informedia.html

The Informedia Digital Library, a project of Carnegie Mellon University, is working to establish an extensive online digital video library for users of desktop computers and metropolitan area networks. Visit this site to learn about the library, its sponsors and its latest advances.

International Federation of Library Associations and Institutions

http://www.nlc-bnc.ca/ifla/home.htm

The International Federation of Library Associations and Institutions, headquartered in the Hague, Netherlands, maintains this site for publications, conference updates, information services and staff contact listings. Includes user feedback survey form.

Internet Cataloging Project: Call for Participation

http://www.oclc.org/oclc/man/catproj/catcall.htm

The Online Computer Library Center strives to further access to the world's information with this Internet cataloging project, a growing database of specially formatted bibliographic records. The project seeks participants and—in addition to the existing database—this site provides a project overview and guidelines.

Internet Public Library

http://ipl.sils.umich.edu/

The Internet Public Library provides links to various reference resources. Visitors can choose from divisions such as Reference and Youth, and browse in such areas as the Reading Room and the Exhibit Hall. A directory and tour are also available here.

Iowa State University Library

http://www.lib.iastate.edu/

The Iowa State University Library home page provides information about the institution and SCHOLAR, its online information system. Includes an online card catalog, a topically indexed listing of databases, and links to other academic libraries' holdings catalogs.

Jump to Library in Japan

http://ss.cc.affrc.go.jp/ric/opac/opac.html

This on-line public access catalog in Japan includes links to national technology laboratory and university sites. Includes link to the Agriculture, Forestry and Fisheries Research Information Center. In Japanese and English.

Jyvaskyla University Library

http://www.jyu.fi/~library/

Jyvaskyla University Library is one of the largest research libraries in Finland housing collections of Finnish prints, databases and publications. It is also a National Resource Library for Education, Sport Sciences and Psychology. In English and Finnish.

Kansas State University Libraries

http://www.lib.ksu.edu/

The Kansas State University Libraries provide information about their services and holdings at this site. Library news, staff telephone numbers and Internet resources are also listed.

Larry's InfoPOWER Page

http://www.clark.net/pub/lschank/home.html

This librarian's personal home page contains pointers to numerous selected sites and Web guides. Includes Internet learner's pages, links to government document servers, shopping sites and resources for professional librarians.

Lehigh University Libraries

http://www.lib.lehigh.edu/

The libraries at Pennsylvania's Lehigh University maintain this informative page providing access to online reference materials and special collections. Visitors are encouraged to learn more about the libraries and the resources they provide.

LibInfo

http://www.lib.uchicago.edu/

LibInfo is a reference service from the University of Chicago Library Information System. Besides providing information on library holdings and pointers to topical Internet resources, the site gives details on services and access to the staff. General information on the university is also included.

LibLink

http://www.lib.utk.edu/

The home page of the University of Tennessee's Knoxville Libraries details the services this facility has to offer, including links to electronic reference material and to general campus information.

Libraries and Internet Electronic Text Collection

http://www.ub2.lu.se/UB2proj/LIS_collection/collection_top.html

The Libraries and Internet Electronic Text Collection maintains this collection of electronic texts on the subject of how libraries are dealing with networked information. Contributions are in English, German and Nordic languages. This page also includes a link to the Lund University electronic library home page.

Libraries of the Claremont Colleges

http://voxlibris.claremont.edu/

The Libraries of the Claremont Colleges open their collections, resources and library system services to interested Web denizens. Includes links to online information centers for the Claremont Colleges.

Library and Information Science

http://www.ub2.lu.se/lisres.html

Sweden's Lund University provides this clearinghouse for online resources in library and information science. Includes a broad collection of Internet resources, directories, conferences and publications. Browse journals, books online or search databases and download software.

Library Catalogs

http://ds.internic.net/cgi-bin/tochtml/library/0intro.library

A large number of libraries that allow access to their catalogs through the Internet are linked at this site presented by the InterNIC Directory of Directories.

Library of Congress

http://www.loc.gov/

This site contains a guide to the U.S. Library of Congress materials available online. Featured categories include exhibits and events, services and publications, digital collections, online systems, and congress and government.

Library of Congress Online Services

http://lcweb.loc.gov/homepage/online.html

This page offers Web searching tools for the Library of Congress. Included are links to LC MARVEL, the gopher-based information system; LOCIS telnet; and anonymous FTP. Search guides, library hours and a link to the Vietnam Prisoner of War/Missing in Action Database are included.

Library of the University of Electro-Communications

http://baloo.cc.uec.ac.jp/

The University of Electro-Communications puts its library online, offering access to services in Japanese and English. Search library holdings by following the links provided.

Library of the University of Illinois at Urbana-Champaign

http://www.grainger.uiuc.edu/

At the home page of the Library of the University of Illinois at Urbana-Champaign, visitors will find general library information, access to its online catalog, and links to other networked library and information resources.

Library-Oriented Lists and Electronic Serials

http://info.lib.uh.edu/liblists/liblists.htm

This Web site is a compilation of electronic discussion lists, distribution lists and electronic serials of interest to library staff and professionals.

Library Resources on the Internet

http://www.library.nwu.edu/resources/library/

Northwestern University in Evanston, Ill., maintains this site for library resources. Visit here to browse indexes of Internet-based library links from around the world.

Louisiana State University Virtual Library

http://www.lib.lsu.edu/

The Virtual Library of Louisiana State University provides access to academic library collections, electronic publications and Internet information resources. Visit here to find user information, perform keyword searches and browse by subject, title and author.

Lund University Electronic Library

http://munin.ub2.lu.se/ub2.html

Sweden's Lund University maintains this library site offering access to a variety of electronic information resources. Online help, search and information options are available to assist new users. In Swedish and English.

Mann Library

http://www.mannlib.cornell.edu/

Cornell University's Mann Library online contains a list of the library's print holdings and access to hundreds of databases for references, full text and statistics. Information is also available here on university course materials, workshops, tutorials, user guides and helper applications.

Massachusetts Institute of Technology Libraries

http://nimrod.mit.edu/

The six libraries and their branches at the Massachusetts Institute of Technology are online and usable by non-students. Visitors will find pointers to the extensive newpaper collection, subject catalog and a spec guide for thesis preparation. The site also offers links to outside collections.

MELVYL System

http://www.dla.ucop.edu/

The MELVYL library system from the University of California allows users to search a variety of bibliographic databases. Includes links to various university servers, MELVYL system contributors, projects and publications.

Michigan State University Vincent Voice Library

http://web.msu.edu/vincent/index.html

The Vincent Voice Library at Michigan State University compiles utterances and holds a collection from over 50,000 people. The site allows browsing of U.S. Presidents' sound samples, as well as a collection of general sound samples.

Morris Library of Southern Illinois University, Carbondale

http://www.lib.siu.edu/

Students at Southern Illinois University can access and search the university's library from this site. Visitors can also browse the university's collections and find out about interlibrary loans.

National Library of Canada

http://www.nlc-bnc.ca/

The National Library of Canada collects and offers access to the country's published heritage. Visitors are invited on a virtual tour of the facility and introduced to the library's archives, exhibitions and publications. In French and English.

New York Public Library

http://gopher.nypl.org/

The New York Public Library opens its collections to the Web masses at this site. Peruse catalogs of the institution's holdings and stay abreast of exhibitions, programs and performances here.

North Carolina State University Libraries

http://www.lib.ncsu.edu/

This Web site provides information about the extensive library system at North Carolina State University in Raleigh, N.C. General library information can be found here, as well as links to library catalogs and journal indexes.

North Carolina State University Libraries: Catalogs, Indexes and Internet Resources

http://dewey.lib.ncsu.edu/disciplines/index.html

This Internet resource index, a service of the North Carolina State University, provides access to its World Wide Web links, library catalogs and an online keyword search. Visitors can search for information by resource or subject classification.

Nordic Libraries: Information Servers

http://www.ub2.lu.se/resbyloc/Nordic_lib.html

The Nordic Libraries: Information Servers page is an extensive directory to Web sites arranged by Nordic country. Subcategories by country classify sites by Web or gopher links. The page has a link to the Lund University Electronic Library home page.

Northwestern University Library

http://www.library.nwu.edu/

The central library at Illinois' Northwestern University hosts this site providing general info on its holdings and services, as well as pointers to main campus servers and a variety of university networked resources.

Nova Scotia Provincial Library

http://rs6000.nshpl.library.ns.ca/

A division of the Policy Branch of the Nova Scotia Department of Education and Culture, the Nova Scotia Provincial Library mantains this site with info about the library and the regional public library system. Links to topic-related sites are also provided.

Online Catalogs with "Webbed" Interfaces

http://www.lib.ncsu.edu/staff/morgan/alcuin/wwwed-catalogs.html

The handy site offers researchers a collection of links to online information resources. Information seekers can find instructions for passing through library Web, gopher and Internet gateways at this index of indexes.

Online Computer Library Center Access Selection

http://www.oclc.org/

The Online Computer Library Center is a nonprofit computer service and research organization that provides online service and CD-ROM products to libraries for assistance in bibliographic verification, cataloging, collection development, loan and reference. Visitors will find full information here on OCLC and its products and services.

Oxford University Libraries Automation Service

http://www.lib.ox.ac.uk/

The Oxford University Libraries Automation Service Web server includes general information about the library along with links to the facility's Early Printed Books Project. It also includes profile pages for library staffers.

Pica

http://www.pica.nl/

The Pica home page describes the library automation systems and online information services provided for Dutch and German academic and public libraries by the nonprofit organization. Includes background information, descriptions of online services, pointers to Dutch libraries and restricted access to technical documentation.

Planet Earth

http://www.nosc.mil/planet_earth/info_modern.html

Planet Earth is a virtual library that includes links to a virtual librarian room, reference shelf and search engines index.

PORTALS

http://portals.lib.pdx.edu/

The Portland Area Library System (PORTALS) is an organization of public and private institutions working to expand and enrich information services in the Portland area. Visitors to the PORTALS home page can find out more about the group and access its collective resources.

Portico

http://portico.bl.uk/

Portico is the British Library's information server. Browse the stacks electronically or access library news and event announcements.

Presidential Libraries IDEA Network

http://sunsite.unc.edu/lia/president

The Presidential Libraries IDEA Network facilitates access to the materials stored in presidential libraries. Find a list of libraries sorted by president, links to related exhibits and a pointer to the First Ladies IDEA Network.

Princeton University Libraries

http://infoshare1.princeton.edu:2003/

The Princeton University Libraries in Princeton, NJ maintain this site to provide general access and Internet resources. Visit here for links to its searching and browsing tools, catalogs, databases, other university Web servers and more.

Provo City Library

http://www.provo.lib.ut.us/

The Provo City Library Web site features quick information through a reference section as well as information about the library's collection and children's programs. Includes links to community servers and the state of Utah. The site is searchable by keywords.

Purdue University Libraries

http://thorplus.lib.purdue.edu/

Thor, the University of Purdue's online library system, allows visitors to access various libraries on campus, a virtual reference desk and Purdue University databases.

Queensland Department of Education Virtual Library

http://cooroomba.client.uq.edu.au/

The Queensland Department of Education provides this virtual library service for access to its book and periodical collection. Includes Internet tutorials and information search resources.

Reseau Documentaire de Grenoble

http://melpomene.upmf-grenoble.fr.POLE/REDOC/

The research libraries of Grenoble, France, offer their work to the world at large, particularly anyone who needs to access research about the Alpine region. Information is in French.

Rice University, Fondren Library

http://riceinfo.rice.edu/Fondren/

The Fondren Library at Rice University offers access to its online publications and services here. Visitors can browse the online catalog, view special collections and exhibits, read about the library or link to campus info.

Royal Holloway Library Information Service

http://fs1.lb.rhbnc.ac.uk/

The Royal Holloway Library Information Service at the University of London, England, maintains this home page with general library and contact information. Links to the library catalog, special collections, guides and related Web sites are available.

Royal Melbourne Institute of Technology Libraries

http://ghmac.lib.rmit.edu.au/

The libraries at the Royal Melbourne Institute of Technology, Australia, maintain this home page with links to their catalog and those of other library systems. Other links include a gopher site, various databases and search functions.

Rudjer Boskovic Institute Library

http://nippur.irb.hr/

The Rudjer Boskovic Institute Library in Zagreb, Croatia, maintains this site for a variety of local and worldwide reference tools. Visit here to access its database of book and periodical collections, national and international libraries, and a host of Internet search and information tools.

St. Joseph County Public Library

http://192.217.111.2/

The St. Joseph County Public Library in South Bend, Ind., maintains this site to provide access to a variety of resources. Visit here to link to databases and Web servers from local media outlets, legislative bodies, government agencies, Internet service providers and the SJCPL itself.

St. Joseph County Public Library's List of Public Libraries with Internet Services

http://sjcpl.lib.in.us/homepage/PublicLibraries/PublicLibraryServers.html

This site routes the user to Web servers hosting the St. Joseph County Public Library index to worldwide libraries offering Internet services. Includes listings of specialized resources and a pointer to search forms.

Saint Mary's College Gaelnet

http://www.stmarys-ca.edu/

Gaelnet is the library server for the Saint Mary's University in Moraga, California. Visitors will discover library collections, research resources, archives and special collections.

Serials in Cyberspace

http://www.uvm.edu/~bmaclenn

Researchers will find a comprehensive index to sites with electronic journal collections and services within and outside of the U.S. here, as well as links to selected electronic journals. The site is maintained by a librarian at the University of Vermont.

Southeastern Library Network

http://www.solinet.net/

The Southeastern Library Network is a nonprofit organization coordinating resource sharing among the library and information community in the southeastern U.S. Read about the institution's mission and services here.

Southern Cross University Library

http://wwwlib.scu.edu.au/

Southern Cross University in Sydney, Australia, unleashes a variety of info here about its academics, computing resources, publications and students. Visitors can search the school's library catalogs and databases or perform a keyword search on pointers to Internet information here.

Stanford University Libraries & Academic Information Resources

http://www-sul.stanford.edu/

The home page of Stanford Universities Libraries and Academic Information Resources consists of campus wide academic information, data resources and computing services. Visitors can read detailed information about library services.

State Library of North Carolina

http://hal.dcr.state.nc.us/ncslhome.htm

The State Library of North Carolina circulates news and information about its services at this site. Browsers can learn of upcoming events as well as recent acquisitions, or link to other North Carolina government resources. Includes a staff directory. See Editor's Choice.

Swets & Zeitlinger

http://www.swets.nl/

Swets & Zeitlinger, a Netherlands-based international supplier of library materials, maintains this promotional site. Visit here to learn about its subscription services, read recent press releases and find contacts at its offices around the world.

Swiss National Library

http://www.snl.ch/

At the home page for the Swiss National Library, visitors are invited to learn about the library and its projects and to access the library's catalog of holdings. In French.

United States Public Libraries

http://galaxy.einet.net/hytelnet/US000PUB.html

This U.S. Public Library server contains links to all the public library systems with Internet sites in the United States. Visitors can link directly through a lengthy list of city and county servers.

University of Adelaide Library Information Service

http://library.adelaide.edu.au/

The Library Information Service at the University of Adelaide, Australia, offers an overview of its collection and an online directory. Visit here to read news and staff profiles and browse its index of books and periodicals.

University of California, Berkeley, Libraries

http://infolib.berkeley.edu/

At the University of California, Berkeley's Libraries site, visitors can browse and search the library catalog, get information on collections and resources and look over a map of the libraries.

University of California, Davis, General Library

http://www.lib.ucdavis.edu/

The University of California, Davis, posts general information about its library system here. Visitors can review library resources by subject, plus access the library's catalog of holdings, CD-ROM network databases and electronic resources.

University of California, Irvine, Libraries Department

http://www.lib.uci.edu/

The Libraries Department of the University of California, Irvine, maintains this site providing access to its reference and literature resources. Visit here to browse its collections, and access a variety of Internet links and instructional materials.

University of Connecticut's Libraries Information

http://spirit.lib.uconn.edu/

The University of Connecticut's main library server allows access to the campus library system. Users can visit the libraries and find general information about the university.

University of Houston Libraries

http://info.lib.uh.edu/

The University of Houston Libraries home page aims to provide easy access to informational and research-oriented Web resources. Visitors will find indexes and subject lists, the university library catalog, and access to library publications here.

University of Idaho Library

http://drseuss.lib.uidaho.edu/

The University of Idaho Library Web server provides access to a wealth of university library information and resources; including online periodicals and university publications.

University of Iowa Libraries

http://www.arcade.uiowa.edu/

The University of Iowa posts an online library catalog and general information about the university's libraries here. The site also includes an index to similar resources on the Internet.

University Libraries and Scholarly Communication

http://www.lib.virginia.edu/mellon/mellon.html

This study prepared for the Andrew W. Mellon Foundation, is provided online here by the University of Virginia. Visit this site for full text of the study and a keyword search of related information.

University of Michigan, School of Information and Library Studies

http://www.sils.umich.edu/

The home page for the School of Information and Library Studies at the University of Michigan provides information on the department, educational initiatives, research projects, associated publications and related resources. Browsers can search the department resources or view an alphabetical list by title.

University of Michigan University Library

http://www.lib.umich.edu/

The University of Michigan's library system offers this site for title catalogs, personnel directories, special programs, and other services. Includes index of Internet resources and answers to frequently asked questions.

---

a2z EDITOR'S CHOICE

State Library of North Carolina

http://hal.dcr.state.nc.us/ncslhome.htm

It was only a matter of time before libraries all over the world started making their presence felt on the Internet. And with the Web's hyperlinking capabilities, the opportunities for finding and accessing information are virtually unlimited. Take the State Library of North Carolina, for example, with its graphics-rich image map. The library aims to serve as a tour guide on the Web, helping anyone in search of information—or the merely curious—to find it. From encyclopedias to periodicals, from software to statistics, you'll find it here. There are even special services and audiovisual materials for the blind and physically challenged. All this (and more) makes it easy to see how the State Library of North Carolina is fulfilling its mission of "increasing knowledge, education, commerce, and business in the state."—Reviewed by Karen Wise

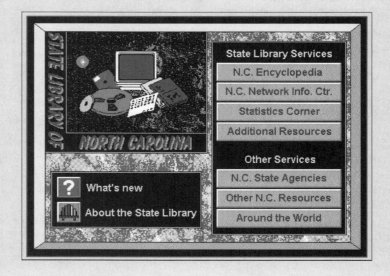

University of Pennsylvania Library

http://www.library.upenn.edu/

The University of Pennsylvania Library offers an online catalog, searchable commercial database services and electronic forms for library transactions. Connect to all 15 University of Pennsylvania libraries from this site.

University of Saskatchewan Libraries

http://library.usask.ca/

Among the resources provided here by the University of Saskatchewan libraries is an online catalog and basic information on locations, hours, policies and interlibrary loans. A search mechanism is included.

University of Texas, Austin, Graduate School of Library and Information Science

http://fiat.gslis.utexas.edu/

The graduate program for Library and Information Science at the University of Texas at Austin provides information here on its courses, faculty and students. The site also features a message board.

University of Texas Library Online Comments

http://www.lib.utexas.edu/Info/comments.html

The University of Texas at Austin offers library users the opportunity to provide online feedback. Browsers can link to the general university library server and main home page.

University of Virginia Library

http://www.lib.virginia.edu/

At the University of Virginia Library site search the library's electronic centers, online publications and selected Internet resources. Heavy on electronic publishing, the library provides access to materials licensed to the University of Virginia as well as links to free Internet sites.

University of Washington Libraries

http://www.lib.washington.edu/

Visitors to this Web site can access the University of Washington Libraries' card catalog, journals and databases. Includes interactive request forms, information about the institution's branches and operating hours, and a link to the UW home page.

University of Waterloo Electronic Library

http://www.lib.uwaterloo.ca/index.html

The University of Waterloo, Canada, provides this electronic library with a wealth of news, information and resources. Visitors can peruse bulletins, documents, Canadian press releases, databases and library catalogs, or search the entire site for something specific.

University of York Library and Information Services

http://www.york.ac.uk/services/library/

The J. B. Morrell Library at the University of York, England, maintains this reference site for resources and directories. Visit here for news, internal staff and facilities listings, text and periodical catalogs, and links to library-related Web sites from around the world.

Virtual Library of Virginia

http://www.viva.lib.va.us/

VIVA, the Virtual Library of Virginia, is a consortium of academic libraries that provides a network of shared electronic resources for students and faculty of local institutions. Visit this site to access academic texts, professional journals, government publications and more.

VTLS

http://www.vtls.com/

This promotional site is the Web home of VTLS, a developer of library management systems headquartered in Blacksburg, Va. Visitors can read about the company, its products and services. In English and Spanish.

Washington University Libraries

http://library.wustl.edu/

The Washington University Libraries has set up WorldWindow, a Web site that helps users access its electronic information resources. From this page, you can access the library's catalog or use the telnet connection provided.

World-Wide Web Virtual Library: Libraries

http://www.w3.org/hypertext/DataSources/bySubject/Libraries.html

Easy access to the world's greatest libraries is one of the foundational strengths of the Internet and this page will direct visitors to some of those institutions: the city library of Helsinki, the national library of Australia, BUBL's United Kingdom-based bulletin board for libraries and the U.S. Library of Congress. Visitors can also search by subject.

World-Wide Web Virtual Library: Library of Congress Classification

http://www.w3.org/hypertext/DataSources/bySubject/LibraryOfCongress.html

This Virtual Library site provides a distributed subject catalog organized by Library of Congress standards. Includes links to other subject catalogs.

Yale University Library

http://www.library.yale.edu/

Information about the Yale University Library is presented here with information about the research workstation, a computer interface that al-

lows access to databases on the campus network. The main catalog and specific collections are also available.

ZWeb Search Engine

http://zweb.cl.msu.edu/

The Zweb Search Engine, a service of Michigan State University, offers a keyword search of university libraries and other information resources around the United States. Users can request that a new site be added to the server.

ENTERTAINMENT AND LEISURE

THE 25 MOST POPULAR ENTERTAINMENT AND LEISURE SITES

American Wine on the Web
http://www.2way.com:80/food/wine/

The Barbie Page
http://silver.ucs.indiana.edu/~jwarf/barbie.html

Beavis and Butt-Head Fan Site
http://calvin.hsc.colorado.edu/

BookWeb
http://www.ambook.org/

Cyrano Server
http://www.nando.net/toys/cyrano.html

The Death of Rock 'n' Roll
http://weber.u.washington.edu/~jlks/pike/DeathRR.html

Disney.com
http://www.disney.com/

The Elvis Shrine
http://www.mit.edu:8001/activities/41West/Elvis.html

E-Motion's Supermodels
http://www.wi.leidenuniv.nl/~pverheij/models.html

Film Festivals Server
http://www.filmfestivals.com/

The Gigaplex!
http://www.gigaplex.com/

Horse Country
http://www.pathology.washington.edu/Horse/index.html

Marilyn Monroe Home Page
http://www.ionet.net/~jellenc/marilyn.html

Mr. Showbiz
http://showbiz.starwave.com/showbiz/

The Monty Python Page
http://www.iia.org/~rosenr1/python/

MTV Online
http://www.mtv.com/

Playbill On-Line
http://wheat.symgrp.com/playbill/home.cgi

R.E.M. Home Page
http://www.halcyon.com/rem/index.htm

Reprise Records Home Page
http://www.repriserec.com/

The Science of Star Trek
http://www.gsfc.nasa.gov/education/just_for_fun/startrek.html

Shangri La Home Page
http://aleph0.clarku.edu/rajs/Shangri_La.html

The Simpsons Archive
http://www.snpp.com/index.html

SonicNet
http://www.sonicnet.com/

Star Wars
http://www.tcfhe.com:80/starwars/

A Visit to Yesterland
http://www.mcs.net/~werner/yester.html

BOOKS

ARCHIVES AND INDEXES

BookWire

http://www.bookwire.com/

BookWire is an extensive guide to books and book-related resources on the Internet. Visit this site for book reviews, bestseller lists and an on-line reading room. Listings of book events and educational resources are among the wealth of data provided.

Book Wire Booksellers

http://www.bookwire.com/links/online_booksellers/online_booksellers.html

BookWire, an extensive site devoted to books, provides this extensive index to booksellers on the Net. The index catalogs the booksellers by the genre of books they offer. The page also includes a link to Book Wire's home page.

Information SuperLibrary

http://www.mcp.com/index.html

The Information SuperLibrary hosts online homes for publishing heavy hitters such as Macmillan, Simon and Schuster and SSI Distribution Services. Visitors are invited to browse reference works, resource directories, software libraries, the Internet Starter Kit, and more.

Online Books

http://www.cs.indiana.edu/metastuff/bookfaq.html

Visitors to this site will find a Frequently Asked Questions (FAQ) file "addressing the availability of public domain sources of e-texts." The site also includes links to public domain archive sites and non public domain texts.

Romance Novel Database

http://www.sils.umich.edu/~sooty/romance/romance.html

Readers weigh in on hundreds of romance novels here. Search by title, author or subgenre to find a brief review, a rating (a scale of hearts, not stars), and publisher information. See Editor's Choice.

ASSOCIATIONS AND ORGANIZATIONS

Association of American University Presses

http://aaup.pupress.princeton.edu/

The Association of American University Presses (AAUP) is compiling a database of book titles from 100 academic presses and soon expects to offer over 100,000 titles. Visitors can search the database and order books here or link to various university press pages.

BookWeb

http://www.ambook.org/

Readers can flip through BookWeb's pages to find schedules of author tours, discussion groups, a searchable bookstore directory and other book-related news. The extensive site is maintained by the American Booksellers Association.

BOOK PROMOTIONS

City of Bits

http://www-mitpress.mit.edu/City_of_Bits/index.html

"City of Bits," written by MIT School of Architecture Dean William J. Mitchell, explores the implications of "a largely invisible but increasingly important system of virtual spaces." Visitors can read a synopsis of the book at this promotional site.

Cleo Odzer, MOO Phreak

http://mosaic.echonyc.com/~cleo/

The steamier side of Asia can be seen at this site, maintained by nonfiction author Dr. Cleo Odzer. Visitors can read excerpts from her books "Patpong Sisters: An American Woman's View of the Bangkok Sex World" and "Goa Freaks: My Hippie Years in India."

The Computer Privacy Handbook

http://www.well.com/user/abacard

Maintained by Andre Bacard, author of the "Computer Privacy Handbook," this site answers Frequently Asked Questions (FAQ) concerning e-mail privacy, anonymous remailers and PGP. Links to topic-related sites are also featured along with details for ordering the author's book.

Contemporary Fiction

http://www.het.brown.edu/people/mende/books/

"See" a new featured novel and "attend" a reading of it at this site, which also provides such information as a dust-jacket biography and reviews. Pointers to other books—mostly by dead people—are provided.

Engines for Education

http://www.ils.nwu.edu/~e_for_e/

"Engines for Education," a "hyper-book" written by Roger Schank and Chip Cleary, is about the education system's problems and methods for reform. The book is also available in paper and CD-ROM. Purchasing info is provided.

50 Greatest Conspiracies of All Time

http://www.webcom.com:80/~conspire/

Conspiracy theorists, the curious and the cynical will delight in the offerings here. The authors of the book "The 50 Greatest Conspiracies of All Time" provide sample chapters, plus dozens of files at this promo site, which covers topics ranging from the assassination of John F. Kennedy to cover-ups of confirmed UFO sightings.

Good Will Toward Men

http://www.butterfly.net/gwtm

"Good Will Toward Men" is a record of conversations between 22 women about men, sexual politics and relationships. This page includes excerpts from the book, ordering information and instructions for booking the author for speaking engagements.

How Birds Fly

http://www.us.net/birds/welcome.html

Periwinkle Books promotes its new title, "How Birds Fly," by David Goodnow on this page. Visitors can look at some of the pictures of flight found in the photo essay and order online.

J.K. Lasser's Your Income Tax 1996

http://www.mcp.com/mgr/lasser/

Macmillan Publishing promotes J.K. Lasser's Your Income Tax 1996 here. This searchable site provides some free tax information, but a paid subscription is needed to access most of the tax tips. Links to other tax sites are also available.

One Horse Rhino

http://www.onehorse.com/index.shtml

One-Horse Rhino, a "one-horse publishing company" in San Francisco, markets its novel "The Voice of the Free Earth" here. Visit for reviews, excerpts, the entire copy or ordering instructions for the print version.

Two Linux Books

http://www.cs.cornell.edu/Info/People/mdw/rl.txt

This site details two books on Linux software recently published by O'Reilly & Associates. Includes summaries and ordering information.

Unity: A Celebration of Gay Games IV and Stonewall

http://www.prowillen.com/Unity.html

Net users who attended Gay Games IV or have memories of the Stonewall riot in New York may want to check out the home page for the book "Unity: A Celebration of Gay Games IV and Stonewall." Visitors can take a look at a book review and order the book, leave their memories and thoughts on the Gay Games, or read what others have written.

The WorldWideWeb Handbook

http://www.ucc.ie/~pflynn/books/wwwbook.html

Peter Flynn promotes his book "The World-WideWeb Handbook" here. Visitors can download a selection from the book and an HTML reference card. The page also provides a link to the publisher's page.

BOOKSTORES, SALES, AND CATALOGS

ACM Living Publications & Services Catalogue

http://info.acm.org/catalog/

ACM is an international scientific and educational computer society with over 80,000 members. Here, it promotes its books, journals, videos and conference proceedings.

Addison-Wesley

http://aw.com/

Addison-Wesley publishes educational and non-fiction titles, and visitors can search its catalog and order books here. The house also posts job openings, newsletters and pointers to its various presses.

The Adventurous Traveler Bookstore

http://www.gorp.com/atbook.htm

Browsers heading for Mount McKinley, the wilds of Kenya, the jungles of the Amazon, or other adventurous locales will find titles to guide them here. This bookstore provides an online catalog specializing in outdoor adventure books and maps for locations worldwide.

Amazon.com Books

http://www.amazon.com/

Claiming to be "Earth's biggest bookstore," Amazon.com Books holds one million titles in its catalog. Customers can browse the full catalog, read about recommended titles and order online. The site contains a search tool, too.

American Journal of Nursing Company Online Services

http://www.ajn.org/

The "American Journal of Nursing" maintains this site with descriptions and ordering details for trade and research publications, books and multimedia products. Practicing nurses may want to check into AJN Online, an interactive forum for discussions of practice, research and ideas.

AP Professional Catalog

http://bookweb.cwis.uci.edu:8042/Books/Academic/index.html

The University of California at Irvine's (UCI) bookstore hosts this page, providing information about Academic Press professional titles. Browse the catalog by author and subject, or find out about UCI's other books and services. Includes ordering instructions.

Arachnoid Writer's Alliance

http://www.vena.com/arachnoid

The Arachnoid Writer's Alliance provides excerpts from unpublished and self-published works here. Visitors can search for books by topic, browse author bios, and order books by mail.

Archway Press

http://branch.com/archway/archway.html

Part of the Branch Mall, Archway Press promotes a 10-book collection of over 500 "dream home" floor plans here. Online and toll-free ordering are featured.

Association of American University Presses

http://aaup.pupress.princeton.edu/

The Association of American University Presses is compiling a database of book titles from 100 academic presses and soon expects to offer over 100,000 titles. Visitors can search the database and order books here or link to various university press pages.

EDITOR'S CHOICE

Romance Novel Database

http://www.sils.umich.edu/~sooty/romance/romance.html

Bodice rippers and swooning maidens, burly chested heroes and myriad barriers to true love are the realm of the romance novel. Here, find readers' comments on hundreds of these steamy tomes, as well as ratings for "sexual explicitness" (ranging from "just kissing" to "very explicit") and a scale of hearts instead of stars (with five hearts being the utmost pinnacle of reader satisfaction). A searchable database makes the titles available by title, author or subgenre, and includes a bit of information about each writer, but more importantly, those reader comments, which range from the gushing ("I love this book more than life itself") to the sedate ("I would check it out of the library but I wouldn't buy it").—*Reviewed by Julene Snyder*

Welcome to the Romance Novel Database. For more information, choose the About this Database button.

List of books by title

List of books by author

Baltzer Science Publishers

http://www.nl.net/~baltzer/

Baltzer Science Publishers maintains this site with its ordering information and submission guidelines. Visit here to browse its index of scientific titles, view its upcoming publication schedule and find manuscript submission details.

Bioenergetics Press

http://www.msn.fullfeed.com/rschenk/bioecat.html

Bioenergetics Press markets books and videos on men's and gender issues. Product and ordering information is available here, as is a men's opinion page and details on a speakers' bureau.

Blue Heron Publishing

http://www.teleport.com/~bhp

Blue Heron Publishing provides a catalog of its titles, a list of its authors and guidelines for queries and submissions here. The site also includes book ordering information and links to related resources.

Booksonline

http://booksonline.com/

A service of Newbridge Communications, Inc., Booksonline is an electronic book store offering a variety of book clubs and continuity programs. Find answers to questions, ordering info, news, and program details at this commercial site.

Book Stacks—Home Page

http://www.books.com/

Book Stacks Unlimited, Inc. bills itself as "your local bookstore - no matter where you live." The Book Stacks page stocks over 330,000 titles, along with audio interviews, book reviews and press releases for upcoming titles. Visitors can buy online here, too.

Brian's Books

http://www.davison.net/books

Brian's Books, the Internet and computer book retailing source of New Brunswick, N.J.-based Davison Computer Services, maintains this promotional site. Visit here for its online ordering catalog, special pricing updates and contact information.

Catalogue of Books Available From CSHL Press

http://www.cshl.org/books/

Cold Spring Harbor Laboratory Press (CSHL), a publisher of biology-related materials, displays its online catalog here. Visitors can browse its index of titles pertaining to plant and molecular biology, laboratory manuals, neurobiology, and more.

Centennial Publications

http://www.gorp.com/cl_angle/bookcat.htm

Fly tiers, rod builders and fishermen who yearn for classic tackle will find books to buy here. Centennial, which specializes in fishing books, promotes its current titles, and posts book reviews. Online ordering available.

Charlesbank

http://med-amsa.bu.edu/medbooks/medbooks.html

The Charlesbank Health Sciences Bookshop, soon to be known as the Boston University Medical Center Bookstore, maintains this site to promote its store, which is one of the largest medical bookstores in the Northeast. The page also publicizes the work of author-physicians who are affiliated with Boston University.

City Lights Publishers and Booksellers

http://town.hall.org/places/city_lights/

City Lights Publishers and Booksellers, the press known for fostering and celebrating the beat poets, provides its online catalog on this site. Visit here to browse and order from its current collection of fiction, nonfiction, and poetry titles.

Claitor's Law Books & Publishing

http://www.premier.net/~CLAITORS

Claitor's Law Books and Publishing in Baton Rouge, La., says it has the "largest inventory of U.S. Government Books outside of the Government Printing Office." Browsers can order those titles, plus volumes on cooking and travel, here.

CompuBooks

http://www.compubooks.com/books.html

This site acts as the virtual lobby of the CompuBooks Online Bookstore, boasting over 6,000 computer-related titles from over 300 publishers. Visitors can access more information about the company, enter the shopping area, find out about worldwide shipping and ordering information, or link to topic-related sites.

Computer Literacy Bookshops

http://www.clbooks.com/

Computer Literacy Bookshops has four stores that specialize in books about computers. Visitors to its online store can browse through its full catalog or check bulletins for new and upcoming titles.

Concertina: Books on the Internet

http://www.digimark.net/iatech/books/intro.htm

Concertina is a Canadian children's print and online book publisher that emphasizes Jewish and Biblical themes. Visitors will find book and ordering information at this promotional site.

Course Technology

http://www.course.com/course.html

Course Technology has two divisions, CTI and Boyd & Fraser, which sell software and books on computing respectively. Visit here for an online catalog from the Cambridge-based company.

Del Rey Books

http://www.randomhouse.com/delrey/

The publishing house provides an online catalog of its titles, sample chapters and news of pending publications here. Links to the current featured title, newsletter, gallery of covers and guidelines for submitting unsolicited works are featured.

Eastgate Systems

http://www.eastgate.com/

Eastgate on the Web claims to feature some of the best in Hypertext writing on the Internet, including Diane Greco's "Cyborg: Engineering The Body Electric." Visitors can request a free copy of Eastgate's hypertext catalog.

East View Publications, Inc. Home Page

http://www.eastview.com/

East View Publications, a clearinghouse for publications from Russia, the Commonwealth of Independent States and Central Europe, maintains this site to introduce its products and services. Visit here for periodicals, "gray" literature, translation services, links to related resources on the World Wide Web and more.

The Exclusive Electronic Computer Book Club

http://www.libhitech.com/libhitech/

The Exclusive Electronic Computer Book Club offers a wide range of titles relating to computers and technology. Visitors can browse the online catalogs of books and software, find answers to Frequently Asked Questions (FAQ), and access topic-related links.

Feral House

http://www.csn.net/central/feralhouse/index.html

Readers can take a walk on the wild side here. Feral House Press publishes exotic, controversial and unorthodox titles that range in topic from the occult to the grunge music scene. The site includes an online catalog, sample pages from some titles and online ordering.

Future Fantasy Bookstore

http://futfan.com/

Venture to another world through the pages of books offered for sale from the Future Fantasy Bookstore. Browse an online catalog by genre or author, then find out how to place online orders.

Goose Lane Editions

http://www.cygnus.nb.ca/glane/glogo.html

Goose Lane Editions, a Canadian book store, posts its electronic catalog of titles on this page, which also incudes an option to request more information.

HarperCollins Publishers

http://www.harpercollins.com/

Information on books in a variety of categories and from several countries is provided here by mega-publisher HarperCollins. Among the other resources are news releases, job opportunities and a history of HarperCollins, which published Mark Twain. Online order forms are available.

Haslam's Book Store

http://www.haslams.com/haslams

Haslam's Book Store stocks thousands of out-of-print and used books. Drop an e-mail to order something special or take a quick peek at new, old and odd books listed in the online catalog.

Hayden Books

http://www.mcp.com/hayden/

Hayden Books, publishers of titles for Macintosh users, offers its catalog on this page. Information on Hayden authors, how to order its books and even how to write a book for the publisher can be found. Includes links to the Macmillan Bookstore.

Hodder & Stoughton Publishers

http://www.u-net.com/hodder

London's Hodder & Stoughton Publishers maintains this page offering an overview of the company and its publishing history. An introduction to its latest title is featured, as is ordering and contact information.

Houghton Mifflin

http://www.hmco.com/trade

At Houghton Mifflin's site, visitors can wander through a virtual bookstore, read excerpts of recently published books, link to discussion groups and learn about authors.

IBM Redbooks

http://www.redbooks.ibm.com/redbooks

This commercial site promotes IBM Redbooks, technical publications providing "how-to" instruction and advice for working with IBM computers and software packages. Visitors can browse the catalog of available titles, place orders or link to other IBM pages.

Ignatius Press

http://www.ignatius.com/

Ignatius Press' virtual catalog details information about Catholic books, periodicals and other resources offered by the company. Also includes news of interest to Catholics and a company overview.

Internaut Books

http://www.zilker.net/users/internaut/index.html

Internaut Books provides an e-zine that serves as a reference guide to books published by the company. Visitors can read sample chapters and order online here.

The Internet Book Shop

http://www.bookshop.co.uk/

The Internet Book Shop, based in the UK, bills itself as "the largest online bookshop in the world." Visitors can browse the offerings and place orders for all literary genres.

Intertain.com

http://intertain.com/store/welcome.html

Intertain.com features books of the week, a children's book section and thousands of adult titles. Visitors can search for a specific title or just browse.

JF Lehmanns Internet Shop

http://www.germany.eu.net/shop/JFL/

Visitors can shop for books and journals online here. The site includes online catalogs and ordering information. In German and English.

Kaiser Books and Computers

http://kbc.com/

Kaiser Books and Computers, a bookstore located in Woodbridge, Va., provides pointers to used book stores around the United States, magazine archives, Internet search tools and more here. Visitors here can also shop for used books from the turn of the century and old "National Geographic" magazines.

Kennys Bookshop and Art Galleries, Galway, Ireland.

http://www.iol.ie/resource/kennys/

The Kennys Bookshop and Art Galleries in Galway, Ireland promotes new and antiquarian Irish books here. Visitors can search its online catalog of Irish titles, read copies of the Kenny Review newsletter or sign up to be a member of the book club.

Login Brothers Book Company

http://www.lb.com/

Login Brother Book Company publishes titles in the health sciences, law and electronic media. Visitors here can search the publisher's database, read about the books or place an order. Links to related industry sites are also provided.

Macmillan HTML Workshop

http://www.mcp.com/general/workshop/

Macmillan Publishing provides resources and information on Hypertext Markup Language (HTML) and on Macmillan's HTML-related books and products, here. Included are listings for beginning, intermediate and advanced users.

Mals og Menningar

http://www.centrum.is/mm

Order books from the largest bookstore in Iceland from this site. Visitors can search a catalog of books or make suggestions about books they think should be added to the catalog. In English.

Midnight Special Bookstore

http://msbooks.com/msbooks/

You can search the books available from the Midnight Special Bookstore in Santa Monica, Calif., by title or author. The site also provides information on the store and a calendar of its events.

The MIT Press Home Page

http://mitpress.mit.edu/

The Massachusetts Institute of Technology (MIT) Press provides online catalogs of its books, journals and other publications here. The site also includes general information about the academic house and ordering information.

Moe's Bookstore

http://moesbooks.com

Moe's Bookstore in Berkeley, California offers this Web site with information about its many books and reference materials. Browse catalogs for dozens of different book categories and link to ordering instructions.

New World Books

http://branch.com/books/books.html

New World Books, a Suffern, N.Y.-based discount book store, promises up to 30 percent savings on books listed at this promotional site. Visit here for a catalog of more than one million books, audio, CD-ROM and video titles.

The New York Law Publishing Company

http://public.ljextra.com/catstart.html

The New York Law Publishing Company provides its catalog of books, newsletters, CD-ROMs and audio tapes for the legal community here. The company also conducts online legal seminars and provides links to law-related resources on the Internet.

NHBS Virtual Environmental Bookstore

http://www.nhbs.co.uk/

The Natural History Book Service Ltd is a mail order bookstore and library supplier based in England that specializes in environmental titles. Visitors here can check out new releases, sale items, software recommendations and highlighted titles, or search the entire catalog of scientific and general-interest publications.

OmniMedia

http://www.awa.com/library/omnimedia/

OmniMedia promotes its electronic publishing efforts, offering a catalog of available titles. The on-line bookstore features works such as "Aesop's Fables" formatted in hypertext for reading on computers.

The On-line Books Page

http://www.dnai.com/~ochobbit/

Hundreds of hypertext books are available on the Internet. This index, which includes a search function, will help browsers find them.

Oryx Press

http://www.oryxpress.com/

Oryx Press publishes books and CD-ROMs for the library and education markets. Visitors to its site can browse catalogs, read a company overview and order products online.

The Other Change of Hobbit

http://www.dnai.com/~ochobbit/

Set up by a bookstore in Berkeley, Calif., that specializes in science fiction and fantasy publications, this commercial site allows browsers to buy recent releases and out-of-print books. Shoppers can use the online ordering form or check store hours here.

Peachpit Press

http://www.peachpit.com/

Peachpit Press, a division of Addison-Wesley, publishes books about computers, digital publishing, and online communications. This site provides excerpts, tutorials, and interviews, as well as a list of titles and ordering information.

Polonia Bookstore, Chicago

http://www.wtinet.com/wti/polonia.htm

Polonia, a publisher and seller of books "dealing with Poland or Polish themes," hosts this online catalog. Browse its selections—offered in both English and Polish—place an order, or subscribe to Polish magazines and newspapers.

Putnam Berkley Online

http://www.mca.com/putnam

Book publisher Putnam Berkley tells about its upcoming releases here. Visitors can access many online books as well.

Reed Interactive

http://www.readbooks.com.au/index.html

Reed Interactive's home page offers information on books available from the Australian company. Visitors can browse an online book shop or read informative pages delving into topics like English, mathematics and technology.

Resolution Business Press, Inc.

http://www.respress.com/

This commercial site promotes the latest book releases of Resolution Business Press, Inc., a Washington state publisher of Internet-related titles. Visitors can browse presentations on the current books and previously published titles, link to selected resources geared for families or learn more about the company.

Saint Mary's Press

http://wwwsmp.smumn.edu/

Saint Mary's Press, a Christian publishing house based in Winona, Minn., provides title and ordering information here. Visitors can search for books by title and author and use the electronic order form.

Shen's Books and Supplies

http://www.shens.com/

The vibrant design of Shen's Books and Supplies' home site reflects the company's philosophy to "share culturally diverse books with all children and parents." Includes prize winning books translated into other languages and teaching tools.

Softpro Books

http://www.softproeast.com

Softpro specializes in computer books and has retail stores in the Boston and Denver areas. It promotes its stores and titles—from Macintosh to Java titles—here.

The Space Between Book Catalog

http://www.tagsys.com/Ads/SpaceBetween/

The Space Between, a New Haven, Conn.-based retailer of "diverse and non-conventional" books, maintains this online catalog. Visit here to browse its collection of new and used titles and use its online ordering utility.

Specialist Science Books Home Page

http://www.demon.co.uk/ssb

Information on more than 3,000 books ranging from botany to zoology is provided here by Specialist Science Books. Included are listings of featured books, details about planned publications, and ordering information.

Stacey's Professional Bookstore

http://www.staceys.com/

San Francisco-based Stacey's Professional Bookstore maintains this site, which lists customers' favorite books, featured publishers, and visiting authors. An index of in-stock titles and a contest flesh out Stacey's online offering.

Stone Bridge Press

http://www.stonebridge.com/~sbp

Stone Bridge Press of Berkeley, Calif., produces books about Japan. This site has complete lists of available books, videos and software, as well as author profiles, a list of distributors, and ordering information.

Storyteller Audio Bookstore

http://www.audio-books.com/

Don't have the time to sit down and read a book? Check the shelves of the Storyteller Audio Bookstore to see if you can listen to that novel instead. Stop by for news about recent releases or sample sections of audio books using RealAudio software.

Sufi Center Bookstore

http://guess.worldweb.net/sufi

This virtual bookshop sells books, videos, audio tapes and music of interest to members of this Muslim mystic sect. There's also information about Sufi centers around the world, plus links to Sufi-related Internet sites.

Taugher Books

http://www.batnet.com/taugher/

Taugher Books is a virtual bookstore specializing in collectible modern first editions, detective fiction/mysteries, black literature and "interesting non-fiction." Visit to browse the catalog and order online.

Tech Bookstore Home Page

http://www.bnt.com/~techbook/

Virginia's Tech Bookstore offers an online shopping place for textbooks as well as hard cover and paperback volumes and selected software. Its home page includes ordering information.

Telos

http://www.telospub.com/

Telos is a scientific books imprint located in New York City. Visitors to this corporate Web site can read reviews of Telos publications, wade through an online file archive, or browse the company's catalog of titles.

Titles Bookstore Home Page

http://bookstore.services.mcmaster.ca/

McMaster University's bookstore provides online access to product info on its range of educational and recreational books, sportswear and gifts. Browsers also can link to the school's computing center and read campus newsletters here.

TRC Publishing

http://www.trc.co.jp/index.htm

TRC, a Japanese publisher, furnishes information on new books of the past week and a retrieval service for books published in the past 10 months. The site also provides directories of publishers and authors. In Japanese and English.

UCI Bookstore Home Page (CWIS)

http://bookweb.cwis.uci.edu:8042/

Shop for books, compact discs and school souvenirs at the University of California, Irvine Bookstore home page. Visitors can order products online at this nonprofit enterprise.

University Book Store

http://www.univbkstr.com/

The University of Wisconsin-Madison Book Store sells general, medical and technical books, computers and typical college bookstore merchandise. Visitors can order online here or link to Project Gutenberg, Shakespeare Online, and other related resources.

University Press Books, Berkeley

http://www.fractals.com/upb/html/upb_intro.html

University Press Books, Berkeley is a bookstore that specializes in books published by university presses. The store promises that soon, its entire catalog will be available online. In the meantime, it asks that browsers request titles via fax or e-mail.

VCH Publishing Group

http://www.vchgroup.de/

VCH Publishing Group is an international firm that deals in scientific books and texts. Visitors to its promotional page will learn about its print and electronic offerings.

Virtual Book Shop

http://www.virtual.bookshop.com/

Books of every type and genre are available in the Virtual Book Shop where visitors can shop for modern fiction, history, science, children's books, and more here.

Virtual WordsWorth

http://www.wordsworth.com/

The Virtual WordsWorth is an online book ordering service. Visitors will find short synopses and ordering information for over 125,000 books of all genres.

West Publishing

http://www.westpub.com/

West Publishing provides information about its legal, educational, news, business and financial publications at this promotional home page. Online ordering and access to the searchable lawyer database are also featured.

W. W. Norton & Company

http://www.wwnorton.com/

W.W. Norton, a publisher based in New York and London, maintains this site with its catalogs, online ordering and author touring schedules. Links to author home pages are also available.

CHILDREN'S BOOKS

Children's Literature Web Guide

http://www.ucalgary.ca/~dkbrown/index.html

The Children's Literature Web Guide contains a huge searchable archive of Internet resources related to books for children. Visitors will find lists of recommended books, discussion groups, online stories and much more.

Cyber-Seuss Welcome Page

http://www.afn.org/~afn15301/drseuss.html

Pile your plate high with green eggs and ham and link to the Cyber-Seuss Welcome Page for more on this famous children's author. The page provides links to Seuss work online, reviews of his books, biographical information and more on the whimsical writer.

Nancy Drew Home Page

http://sunsite.unc.edu/cheryb/nancy.drew/ktitle.html

The Nancy Drew home page contains information on the writers, central themes and characteristics of the juvenile mystery series. Includes character sketches, plot summaries and discussions of the evolution of the books since 1929. See Editor's Choice.

---

a2z EDITOR'S CHOICE

Nancy Drew Home Page

http://sunsite.unc.edu/cheryb/nancy.drew/ktitle.html

Perky girl detective Nancy Drew is the subject of adulation and examination here, where fans can find a plethora of minutia about the fictional teenage gumshoe. Perhaps the most popular children's series ever created, the Nancy Drew books have sold more than 40 million copies in North America, and while formulaic and somewhat dated, they clearly continue to strike a chord with scores of readers. Tidbits include a look at Miss Drew's fascination with the color blue ("Not only were the books blue, but so were Nancy's eyes, along with her sporty roadster"), plot synopses, a look at the character's meaning to feminists, and much, much more. Deft analysis reveals much about the psychology of both the writers of these books and the readers who devour them ("Solving a mystery, in the Nancy books, is actually the fictional equivalent of baking a cake, piecing together a quilt, sewing a fine seam, or spring cleaning"), making this site a must-see spot for fans of the über-sleuth.—*Reviewed by Julene Snyder*

Nancy Drew: Girl Sleuth, Girl Wonder

This Mosaic project describes the authorship, central themes, and characteristics of the Nancy Drew mystery series, first written in 1929 and continuing through the present day. To return to the cover page from any place in the project, click on this icon at the bottom of each screen:

- **The Eternal Prom Queen**: An Introduction to Nancy Drew

  - Find Out about Her **Advantages,**
  - **Brilliance,**
  - And What the Color **Blue** Means for Her!

EVENTS AND FESTIVALS

The Swiftsure Project
http://www.swifty.com/
Swiftsure was a May 1996 arts gala in Victoria, B.C. Visitors here can check out the artists, galleries, writers, and publishers who participated in the event.

INTERACTIVE AND ONLINE BOOKS

ARCHIVES AND INDICES

Bibliobytes Books on Computer
http://www.bb.com/
Bibliobytes Books on Computer sells electronic versions of books in an Acrobat format. The site includes a catalog arranged by category and brief description of each book. Visitors can order online with a First Virtual account. The site also includes up-to-date information on the legal dispute surrounding the Communications Decency Act.

Books On-line: Authors
http://www.cs.cmu.edu/Web/bookauthors.html
This Internet resource lists online books by their authors' names. Visitors can browse alphabetical author listings or jump to listings arranged by title.

Books Online, Listed by Call Number
http://www.cs.cmu.edu/Web/booksubjects.html
Books On-line is an enormous index of books available online. It is categorized by Library of Congress call numbers and includes a subject-area search function.

Books On-line, New Listings
http://www.cs.cmu.edu/Web/booknew.html
Carnegie Mellon University posts titles recently added to Books Online on this page. Books Online is an archive of electronic works—see the entry below for further description and a link to its main page.

Creating a Celebration of Women Writers
http://www.cs.cmu.edu/Web/People/mmbt/women/celebration.html
Creating a Celebration of Women Writers is an effort to post public-domain or copyright-authorized works of female authors. The evolving site lists women writers and instructions for submitting work.

The Modern English Collection
http://etext.lib.virginia.edu/modeng.browse.html
The Electronic Text Center at the University of Virginia provides access to this collection of hundreds of complete literary works available for download. Arranged in alphabetical order, selections range from Horatio Alger to Bram Stoker.

Tech Classics Archive
http://the-tech.mit.edu/Classics/index.html
Maintained at the Massachusetts Institute of Technology, this searchable e-text archive contains 376 Greek and Roman literary classics. Find the well-known works of Homer, Virgil and Plato, plus Aristophanes, Sophocles, and others. English texts, commentaries and author info featured.

Text Archives
http://ccat.sas.upenn.edu/txtarch.html
This gopher server offers indexes of text archives available on the Internet. Visit here to link to the CCAT text archives, the English Server at Carnegie Mellon University, the Gutenberg Project, and more.

The Word
http://www.speakeasy.org/~dbrick/Hot/word.html
The Speakeasy Cafe in Seattle, Wash., provides an extensive index here to online books, poetry and journals. It also provides links to Biblical sites and dozens of literature pages.

FICTION

ArtServe TextSearch
http://rubens.anu.edu.au/searchmenu.html
Perform keyword searches of classical literature at this site. Works available for text searching include Pascal's "Pensees," Shakespeare's "Sonnets" and Homer's "Iliad" and "Odyssey."

Ever The Twain Shall Meet
http://www.lm.com/~joseph/mtwain.html
Ever The Twain Shall Meet is a literary reference and resource devoted to Mark Twain. This page has links to some of his works in their entirety, including "The Adventures of Huckleberry Finn" and "The Adventures of Tom Sawyer."

Hyperizons
http://www.duke.edu/~mshumate/hyperfic.html
Visit here for an extensive repository of original hypertext fiction and previously published fiction converted into hypertext. The site includes discussion on new developments in hypertext fiction and notes on theory and techniques.

The Jayhawk Series by Mary K. Kuhner
http://www.klab.caltech.edu/~flowers/jayhawk/
Serialized into 144 postings, the complete text of "Jayhawk" by Mary K. Kuhner is available here. Included is a story background, also written by the author.

Mark Twain Resources on the World Wide Web
http://web.syr.edu/~fjzwick/twainwww.html
Mark Twain fans will enjoy this site, with information about the author and his work. Maintained by Jim Zwick of Syracuse University, the site offers full text as well as interpretations and adaptations of his stories.

Sherlock Holmes
http://www.cs.cmu.edu/afs/andrew.cmu.edu/usr18/mset/www/holmes.html
Elementary, my dear Watson, this site is not. Rather, it is brimming with a large collection of online Sherlock Holmes books, pictures and sound files. The site also contains links to a multitude of other Holmes-related Web sites.

Steven Shaviro's DOOM PATROLS
http://dhalgren.english.washington.edu/~steve/doom.html
Visitors to this site will find the electronic text of "Doom Patrols," Steven Shaviro's book of "theoretical fiction about postmodernism and popular culture." Read the book online or download its chapters.

Tech Classics Archive
http://the-tech.mit.edu/Classics/index.html
Maintained at the Massachusetts Institute of Technology, this searchable e-text archive contains 376 Greek and Roman literary classics. Find the well-know works of Homer, Virgil and Plato, plus Aristophanes, Sophocles and others. English texts, commentaries and author info featured.

The Waygate
http://www.cc.gatech.edu/ftp/people/viren/www/jordan/jordan.html
An arcane page composed strictly for those "in the know," this site—based upon the "Wheel of Time" series by fantasy author Robert Jordan—revels in its insider nature. Includes links to science fiction and speculative fiction sites.

NONFICTION

Christian Classics Ethereal Library
http://ccel.wheaton.edu/
Christian Classics Ethereal Library presents an online collection that visitors can browse by author and type or search. Selections include nonfiction from St. Thomas Aquinas, fiction from Fydor Dostoevsky and references such as the World Wide Study Bible and various Bible dictionaries.

E for Ecstasy by Nicholas Saunders
http://hyperreal.com/drugs/e4x/

Visitors can download an online version of the book "E is for Ecstasy" by Nicholas Saunders from this site. The book includes a personal account, notes on side effects and warnings about the drug's dangers. It also provides information on laws concerning the drug, which has become popular in recent years within the rave and dance club scenes.

F.E. Potts' Guide to Bush Flying
http://www.fepco.com/Bush_Flying.html

Written by a seasoned Alaskan pilot, this no-nonsense guide to flying in remote Alaska is meant for pilots who have a "commercial level of skill." It covers seasonal conditions, the terrain, flying techniques and navigation tips, among other detailed topics.

54 Ways You Can Help The Homeless
http://ecosys.drdr.virginia.edu/ways/54.html

A hypertext version of Rabbi Charles A. Kroloff's book, "54 Ways You Can Help the Homeless" is available here. Visitors can sift through the author's suggestions and read tips on volunteering.

From Webspace to Cyberspace
http://www.eit.com/~kevinh/cspace

"From Webspace to Cyberspace" is an online book that provides a brief history of the Web and analyzes the future of cyberspace. Visitors can download the 254 page document here.

Promises—A Daily Guide to Supernatural Living
http://www.mdalink.com/cgi-bin/promises.cgi

The Campus Crusade for Christ provides this daily installment from the book, "Promises—A Daily Guide to Supernatural Living." Each entry features a biblical quotation and an inspiring vignette for Christians.

POETRY

British Poetry 1780-1910
http://etext.lib.virginia.edu/britpo.html

This hypertext archive contains texts of notable British poetry, some annotated and illustrated. Includes guidelines for submissions, links to the Alderman Library at the University of Virginia and other campus servers.

Cowboy Poetry
http://agricomm.com/agricomm/cp

The spirit of the Old West lives on in Cowboy Poetry, poems and prose which celebrate the uniquely American cowboy mystique. Poems by and about men and women who ride the range bring home the life of the cowboy, and other text spells out current gatherings and projects of interest to modern cowboys.

Czeslaw Milosz's Poetry
http://sunsite.unc.edu/dykki/poetry/milosz/milcov.html

Poet Czeslaw Milosz comes to life online with readings of "Conversation with Jeanne" and "A Poem for the End of the Century." Both are read in Polish and English. A biography of Milosz, a select bibliography and link to the Internet Poetry Archive cover page also included.

Emily Dickinson Page
http://lal.cs.byu.edu/people/black/dickinson.html

Begun in 1995 after a fruitless Web search for material related to Emily Dickinson, this site has flowered into a respository of points and pointers. Biographical data, online poetry, annotations, summaries, reviews and references are featured, along with information about the Emily Dickinson International Society.

Internet Poetry Archive
http://sunsite.unc.edu/dykki/poetry/home.html

Works of the poets Seamus Heaney, Czeslaw Milosz, and others are electronically reproduced at the Internet Poetry Archive. Find a description of the archive project or access the poetical texts collected here.

What the Welsh and Chinese Have in Common
http://sunsite.unc.edu/pjones/poetry/

Poetry from the pages of "What the Welsh and Chinese Have in Common" by Paul Jones is available via this home page. Visitors can click through this gateway to read the poems or link to the poet's home page.

LIBRARIES

Biblioteca Nacional
http://www.bne.es/

Biblioteca Nacional is the Web home for this Spanish library. The site includes access to cultural information, bibliographic data and catalog links to the institution. In Spanish.

Digital Libraries '95
http://bush.cs.tamu.edu/dl95/README.html

Review the proceedings from the 1995 Second Annual Conference on the Theory and Practice of Digital Libraries. The site includes archived papers presented at the conference, available in full-text format.

EPPP Home Page
http://www.nlc-bnc.ca/eppp/e-coll-e.htm

A mission statement for the National Library of Canada's Electronic Publishing Pilot Project can be found at this home page. The project aims to "identify and understand issues that libraries will encounter handing electronic publications and online collections."

Hi Jolly Library Service
http://www.cascade.net/~hijolly

The Hi Jolly Library Service features links to its catalog of bird books, children's books and library services. The California-based business provides services for educational organizations and schools.

POPULAR AUTHORS

Note: In this section sites are alphabetized by author's last name where applicable.

Isaac Asimov
http://www.clark.net/pub/edseiler/WWW/asimov_FAQ.html

Just how do you pronounce Isaac Asimov? Readers will find out from this Frequently Asked Questions (FAQ) file, posted by the newsgroup alt.books.isaac-asimov. The file also looks at the prolific writer's life—he wrote day and night-- and provides pointers to Asimov texts online.

Hakim Bey
http://www.uio.no/~mwatz/bey/

This site contains selected poetry and writings of Hakim Bey, an avant-garde poet-philosopher, as well as biographical information. Featured texts include "Temporary Autonomous Zone," "The Radio Sermonettes" and "Mailorder Mysticism."

William Burroughs
http://www.peg.apc.org/~firehorse/wsb/wsb.html

Pictures and prose await those who visit this unofficial William Burroughs page, maintained by Firehorse Publications. The beat writer's timeworn visage accompanies interviews, journals, excerpts from his work, and a fact file about the man who pushed the literary envelope.

Lewis Carroll Home Page
http://www.students.uiuc.edu/~jbirenba/carroll.html

The Lewis Carroll home page provides information about the author and links to illustrated, electronic texts of his works, including "Alice's Adventures in Wonderland." Visitors will also find a featured discussion topic and a list of organizations devoted to the writer.

Hitchhiker's Guide to the Galaxy Home Page

http://asylum.cid.com/hhgttg/hhgttg.html

This page invites browsers into the wacky universe of Douglas Adams' popular book "Hitchhiker's Guide to the Galaxy" by providing links to related sites. Visitors can access everything from newsgroup postings to a promotional page from the publisher.

The Intergalactic Home Page

http://asylum.cid.com/hhgttg/hhgttg.html

Do you still hold to the illusion that humans run the planet? Well, we don't. Mice do. Step off the edge of reality and into The Intergalactic Home Page to see why there are so many crazed Douglas Adams fans. Perhaps you'll find the meaning of life.

Petteri Jarvinen Oy

http://www.pjoy.fi/

Petteri Jarvinen is a Finnish author of computer-related books. He promotes his company, Petteri Jarvinen Co., here and posts his columns from Tietokone magazine. In Finnish with an English summary.

Who Is Guy Kawasaki?

http://www.evangelist.macaddict.com

A writer. Browsers can read excerpts from his business book, "How to Drive Your Competition Crazy," or read his columns from "Macworld" and "MacUser" magazines on this page.

Stephen King

http://wwwcsif.cs.ucdavis.edu/~pace/king.html

Horror writer Stephen King is the subject of this bio- and bibliographical tribute presented by a fan. Learn about the man (and the mind) responsible for such dark tales as "Carrie," "The Stand" and "Misery."

A Visit with Elmore Leonard

http://www.bdd.com/athwk/bddathwk.cgi/07-28-95/menu

Bantam Doubleday profiles Elmore Leonard, called the greatest crime writer alive by The New York Times, on this page. Visit for a promotion of his newest title, a biographical sketch and a chance to e-mail a fan letter.

Richard Manning's Author Page

http://www.montana.com/manning

Journalist and author Richard Manning focuses on the environment and the West. Download an excerpt from his latest book "Grassland," or link to prairie restoration groups here. Manning's essays, which range in topic from divorce to fire ecology, are also on file.

Lucy Maud Montgomery

http://www.gov.pe.ca/info/lucy/index.html

Lucy Maud Montgomery was the author of the beloved novel "Anne of Green Gables." This tribute page from the government of Prince Edward Island, Canada, provides a thorough introduction to Montgomery's life and work as well as to the windswept North Atlantic province that inspired her.

Owl Springs Partnership

http://www.ibmpcug.co.uk/~owls/index.html

Husband-and-wife team Peter Morwood and Diane Duane write science fiction books, like to cook and have an avid interest in Ireland. Visitors will find a bit about each of these topics and more on this personal home page.

Walker Percy

http://sunsite.unc.edu/wpercy/

Southern favorite son Walker Percy is characterized as a "philosophical novelist" by the University of North Carolina archive which collects and presents his work online. Visitors can peruse Percy's papers, fiction, and philosophical treatises.

Some Information on Terry Pratchett

http://vangogh.cs.tcd.ie/cbuckley/books/terry.html

This page catalogs the variety of Internet offerings devoted to science fiction author Terry Pratchett. Find links to the Usenet newsgroup alt.fan.pratchett, the Clarecraft Catalogue, the Terry Pratchett Archives, and much more.

Anne Rice: Commotion Strange

http://ecosys.drdr.virginia.edu/~jsm8f/commotion.html

Anne Rice, Queen of the ghoulish and erotic, offers a newsletter to her fans here. This site contains archives of the newsletter, Commotion Strange, and links to other Rice resources. See Editor's Choice.

Bruce Sterling

http://riceinfo.rice.edu/projects/RDA/VirtualCity/Sterling/index.html

This site contains pointers to Web sites relevant to the career of Bruce Sterling, author, journalist, editor and critic. The themes Mr. Sterling explores are often related to the electronic frontier.

 EDITOR'S CHOICE

Anne Rice: Commotion Strange

http://ecosys.drdr.virginia.edu/~jsm8f/commotion.html

Writer Anne Rice—perhaps best known for her novels "Interview With the Vampire" and "The Vampire Lestat"—keeps in contact with her fans via a chatty newsletter, which is reproduced here for fans on the Web. Browsers will get a peek at her house in New Orleans (complete with a street map), an explanation of how the author negotiates film deals for her work, and a fervent paean to the writing process. ("I've never done anything in my life that has given me as much joy as writing a book," Rice confesses.) Interviews, essays and transcripts of phone messages make this the place to go for anyone craving more information on the wildly popular gothic/horror/erotic novelist.—*Reviewed by Julene Snyder*

PUBLISHING

PUBLISHERS

Addison-Wesley
http://aw.com/
Addison-Wesley publishes educational and nonfiction titles. Visitors can search its catalog and order books here. The house also posts job openings, newsletters, and pointers to its various presses.

Addison Wesley Longman FTP Archive
ftp://aw.com/
Educational publishing company Addison Wesley Longman's anonymous FTP archive contains information for its divisions Addison-Wesley, Benjamin/Cummings, Longman Publishing, and Technology Exchange Company.

Association of American University Presses
http://aaup.pupress.princeton.edu/
The Association of American University Presses (AAUP) is compiling a database of book titles from 100 academic presses and soon expects to offer over 100,000 titles. Visitors can search the database and order books here or link to various university press pages.

Baen Books
http://www.baen.com/
Baen Books, a small publisher well-known to science fiction and fantasy fans, shows off its stuff here. Those who check out the page can find out more about Baen books, preview chapters from upcoming titles, read through author biographies or browse the online catalog.

Baltzer Science Publishers
http://www.nl.net/~baltzer/
Baltzer Science Publishers maintains this site for its ordering information and submission guidelines. Visit here to browse its index of scientific titles, view its upcoming publication schedule, and find manuscript submission details.

Bantam-Doubleday-Dell
http://www.bdd.com/
BDD Online features news and press releases from mega-publisher Bantam-Doubleday-Dell. New titles, reviews, and author interviews dot the electronic literary landscape.

Blue Heron Publishing
http://www.teleport.com/~bhp
Blue Heron Publishing provides a catalog of its titles, a list of its authors and guidelines for queries and submissions here. The site also includes book ordering information and links to related resources.

Bookport
http://www.bookport.com/welcome/bookport/point/
Sponsored by the publishing consultants at Fortuity Consulting, this site features selected books, reviews and literary treasures. Readers can stop by to view a clearinghouse of book-related information such as Internet recommended reading lists and online book marketing sites.

Cambridge University Press North American Branch
http://www.cup.org/
The North American branch of Cambridge University Press calls this site its online home. Find a complete online catalog, along with a general overview of the press' history and publications.

Centennial Publications
http://www.gorp.com/cl_angle/bookcat.htm
Fly tiers, rod builders and fishermen who yearn for classic tackle will find books to buy here. Centennial specializes in fishing books. It promotes its current titles and posts book reviews on this site, which also accommodates online ordering.

Cherwell Scientific Publishing
http://www.cherwell.com/index.html
Cherwell Scientific Publishing develops software for science and research in areas including genetics, chemistry and engineering. Here scientific professionals can link to specific software home pages, download demo versions, check the software list, and learn more about the company.

Cold Spring Harbor Laboratory Press
http://www.cshl.org/about_cshl_press.html
This site features the home page of the Cold Spring Harbor Laboratory (CSHL) Press, a publisher of scientific books and other media. Visitors can access the online catalog of book and journal titles as well as the home pages of staff members.

Concertina: Books on the Internet
http://www.digimark.net/iatech/books/intro.htm
Concertina is a Canadian children's print and online book publisher that emphasizes Jewish and Biblical themes. Visitors will find book and ordering information at this promotional site.

Course Technology
http://www.course.com/course/default.html
Course Technology has two divisions, CTI and boyd & fraser, which sell software and books on computing respectively. Visit here for an online catalog from the Cambridge-based company.

Del Rey Books Home Page
http://www.randomhouse.com/delrey/
The publishing house provides an online catalog of its titles, sample chapters and news of pending publications here. The site includes links to the current featured title, a newsletter, a gallery of covers and guidelines for submitting unsolicited works.

Duke Communications International
http://www.duke.com/
Duke Communications publishes "Controller Magazine," "News/400" and "Windows NT Magazine." Visitors can read online versions here. The site also promotes books from Duke Press, which publishes guidebooks and tools for programmers and developers.

Feral House
http://www.csn.net/central/feralhouse/index.html
Browsers can take a walk on the wild side here. Feral House Press publishes exotic, controversial, and unorthodox titles that range in topic from the occult to the grunge music scene. The site includes an online catalog, sample pages from some titles, and online ordering.

Gareth Stevens Home Page
http://market.net/literary/gsinc/index.html
Gareth Stevens Publishing, based in Milwaukee, Wis., is a children's book publisher. The company's support site features an online catalog, ordering instructions, a list of national distributors, and a table of contents by general subject area.

HarperCollins Publishers
http://www.harpercollins.com/
Information on books in a variety categories and from several countries is provided here by mega-publisher HarperCollins. Among the other resources are news releases, job opportunities, and a history of HarperCollins, which published Mark Twain. Online order forms are available.

Hayden Books
http://www.mcp.com/hayden/
Hayden Books, publishers of titles for Macintosh users, offers its catalog on this page. Information on Hayden authors, how to order its books, and even how to write a book for the publisher can be found. Includes links to the Macmillan Bookstore.

Hodder & Stoughton Publishers
http://www.u-net.com/hodder
London, England's Hodder & Stoughton Publishers maintains this page offering an overview of the company and its publishing history. An introduction to its latest title is featured, as is ordering and contact information.

Houghton Mifflin
http://www.hmco.com/trade
Houghton Mifflin promotes its titles here. Visitors to this extensive site can wander through a virtual bookstore, read excerpts of recently published books, link to discussion groups, and learn about authors.

Ignatius Press

http://www.ignatius.com/

This virtual catalog details information about Catholic books, periodicals and other resources offered by Ignatius Press. Also includes news of interest to Catholics and information about the publishing company.

International Thomson Publishing

http://www.thomson.com/

Thomson Publishing is a large international publisher whose offerings range from elementary-school texts to post-graduate science, technology, business, medicine, the humanities, social sciences, and defense. The company promotes its catalog and electronic resources at this site.

Internaut Books

http://www.zilker.net/users/internaut/index.html

Internaut Books provides an e-zine here that serves as a reference guide to books published by the company. Visitors can read sample chapters and order online here.

Knopf Publishing Group

http://www.randomhouse.com/knopf/index.html

The Knopf Publishing Group, a division of Random House Publishing, features news of its "many outstanding books and authors" here. Visitors can peruse comprehensive details of its five imprints which span the literary spectrum of intellectual European literature to contemporary Western fiction.

Kodansha

http://www.toppan.co.jp/kodansha/

A Japanese publisher, Kodansha produces books, as well as 56 weekly and monthly magazines. Visit this promotional page to learn more about the company and to browse its reading materials. In Japanese and English.

Learned InfoNet

http://info.learned.co.uk/

Learned Information Ltd., part of England's VNU Publishing Group, publishes books, conference proceedings, newspapers, newsletters and journals for both providers and users of information in many industrial sectors. Visitors to the company's home page will find the latest conference and publication news.

Login Brothers Book Company

http://www.lb.com/

Login Brother Book Company publishes titles in the health sciences, law and electronic media. Visitors here can search the publisher's database, read about the books or place an order. Links to related industry sites are also provided.

Miller Freeman Inc.

http://www.mfi.com/

Miller Freeman is a fast-growing publishing company that markets business and special-interest magazines, books and directories, newsletters and CD-ROMs. Visitors can learn about the publisher and its products here.

The MIT Press Home Page

http://mitpress.mit.edu/

The Massachusetts Institute of Technology (MIT) Press provides online catalogs of its books, journals, and other publications here. The site also includes general information about the academic house and ordering information.

The New York Law Publishing Company

http://public.ljextra.com/catstart.html

The New York Law Publishing Company provides its catalog of books, newsletters, CD-ROMs and audio-tapes for the legal community here. The company also conducts also online legal seminars and provides links to law-related resources on the Internet.

Oryx Press Home Page

http://www.oryxpress.com/

Oryx Press publishes books and CD-ROMs for the library and education markets. Visitors to its site can browse catalogs, read a company overview,, and order products online.

Oxford University Press

http://www.comlab.ox.ac.uk/archive/publishers/oup.html

Oxford University Press promotes its publications here, such as the venerable, authoritative Oxford English Dictionary and the journal PostModern Culture. Visit for general information about the press, including an e-mail address for editorial queries.

Oxford University Press USA

http://www.oup-usa.org/

Visitors to this home page can learn about the highly respected Oxford University Press USA. Information about the company's history and a catalog of its publications wait here alongside its customer service department and links to the publishing house's international branches.

Peachpit Press

http://www.peachpit.com/

Peachpit Press, a division of Addison-Wesley, publishes books about computers, digital publishing and online communications. This site provides excerpts, tutorials, and interviews, as well as a list of titles and ordering information.

Penguin USA

http://www.penguin.com/usa/

Penguin Books USA provides online book catalogs here. The publisher also posts new release information, publicity material, and a corporate profile.

Publishers on the Internet

http://www.faxon.com/Internet/publishers/pubs.html

Those after trades, journals or books can use this comprehensive index to find publishers on the Internet.

Resolution Business Press, Inc.

http://www.respress.com

This commercial site promotes the latest book releases of Resolution Business Press, Inc., a Washington state publisher of Internet-related titles. Visitors can browse presentations on the current books and previously published titles, link to selected resources geared for families, or learn more about the company.

Routledge OnLine

http://www.routledge.com/routledge.html

Internet users who link to the Routledge OnLine page can learn about this social science and humanities publisher and the books it publishes. Visitors can also order books online, check out Routledge's philosophy resources or link to related publishers.

Saint Mary's Press Home Page

http://wwwsmp.smumn.edu/

Saint Mary's Press, a Christian publishing house based in Winona, Minn., provides title and ordering information on this site. Visitors here can search for books by title and author, and use the electronic order form.

Springer-Verlag Berlin/Heidelberg

http://tick.ntp.springer.de/

The home page of Springer-Verlag Berlin/Heidelberg describes the services and products of the German-based publishing company. Geared toward the scientific and medical communities, the publishing house provides a catalog of its books, journals, and electronic media.

Stone Bridge Press

http://www.stonebridge.com/~sbp

Stone Bridge Press of Berkeley, Calif., produces books about Japan. This site has complete lists of available books, videos, and software, as well as author profiles, a list of distributors and ordering information.

Telos Home Page
http://www.telospub.com/
Telos is a scientific books imprint located in New York City. Visitors to this corporate Web site can read reviews of Telos publications, wade through an online file archive or browse the company's catalog of titles.

TRC Publishing Home Page
http://www.trc.co.jp/index.htm
TRC, a Japanese publisher, furnishes information on new books of the past week and a retrieval service for books published in the past 10 months. The site also provides directories of publishers and authors. In Japanese and English.

VCH Publishing Group
http://www.vchgroup.de/
VCH Publishing Group is an international firm that deals in scientific books and texts. Visitors to its promotional page will learn about its print and electronic offerings.

West Publishing
http://www.westpub.com/
West Publishing provides information about its legal, educational, news, business, and financial publications at this promotional home page. Online ordering and access to the searchable lawyer database are also featured.

W.W. Norton Online
http://www.wwnorton.com/
W.W. Norton is a New York and London based publisher. Visitors here can click through its catalogues, order online, and follow author touring schedules. The page also posts links to its authors' home pages.

RARE BOOKS

Antiquarian Booksellers' Association of America
http://www.clark.net/pub/rmharris/abaa.html
The Antiquarian Booksellers' Association of America (ABAA) specializes in rare and antiquarian books, maps, and prints. Visitors here will find lists of ABAA bookstores and bookfairs and online catalogs.

Howard Karno Books
http://www.cts.com/~karnobks
Howard Karno Books sells rare and out of print books from and about Latin America. Visitors to its online shop can peruse the inventory of titles. Online ordering is available.

Taugher Books on the World Wide Web
http://www.batnet.com/taugher/
Taugher books is a virtual bookstore specializing in collectible first edition books of modern first editions, detective fiction/mysteries, black literature and "interesting non-fiction." Visit to browse the catalog and order online.

EDITOR'S CHOICE

Fiction Addiction
http://www.iol.ie/~westrock/fiction/
Bookworms, rejoice. The word-fix you so desperately crave is right around the virtual corner at Fiction Addiction, where you'll find a vast number of book reviews, sorted by title, genre and writer. Snuggle down with author interviews and reader chat sessions, or simply search for the skinny on the latest best-seller. Editors recommend books for those looking for a new volume to devour, warning readers to "miss these books at your own peril!" Mailing lists keep readers current on new titles, while plenty of behind-the-scenes data feeds the never-sated hunger of fiction aficionados.—*Reviewed by Julene Snyder*

We've received a perfect ten from LynxOfTheWeekList(tm) and have been adjudged to be in the Top 5% of the World Wide Web

Publishers, Publicists and Authors, submit books for review by Fiction Addiction.

REVIEWS

Boston Book Review
http://www.bookwire.com/bbr/bbr-home.html
BookWire provides an online version of "The Boston Book Review" here. Visitors can subscribe to the print version of the review, search its archives online or read reviews from past issues.

Fiction Addiction
http://www.iol.ie/~westrock/fiction/
Readers craving a fix of new titles might turn to the Fiction Addiction page for reviews sorted by title, genre or writer. Mailing lists keep readers current on all featured new material; author interviews feed the hunger for behind-the-scenes information. See Editor's Choice.

The Internet Top 100 SF/Fantasy List
http://www.clark.net/pub/iz/Books/Top100/top100.html
Compiled via a public e-mail voting system, the selected "top" 100 science fiction and fantasy books are listed here. Review the list, or review the list of books that didn't make the top 100.

WRITING RESOURCES

Britannica Online
http://www.eb.com/

People don't necessarily need the shelf space to hold volumes of Encyclopedia Britannica anymore. Britannica Online is a commercial service that allows subscribers to search an electronic edition of the reference work. Visitors can register for a free trial at this site.

University of Texas, Austin, Computer Writing and Research Labs
http://www.en.utexas.edu/

Educational technologies are studied and implemented at the University of Texas, Austin through the work of Computer Writing and Research Labs. Writing and literature classes are taught by the center and other classes are supported by it. Explore online course curricula here.

WritersNet: The Internet Directory of Published Writers
http://www.bocklabs.wisc.edu/ims/writers.html

WritersNet bills itself as "the Internet directory of published writers." Search alphabetically or by category, and auto-print the results of your query. The site also features a download option for offline browsing and an extensive directory of literary agents. See Editor's Choice

Writery
http://www.missouri.edu/~wleric/writery.html

The Online Writery is a comprehensive resource for writers of all stripes. Includes communication sites to contact other writers, marketing information, teachers' resources, links to newsgroups, and writers' home pages.

COMICS AND CARTOONS

ANIMATION

Anime & Stuff
http://server.berkeley.edu/Anime/

From the Student Run Cal Berkeley home page comes Anime & Stuff, a comprehensive list of links to Japanese animation on the Internet. Fans will also find links to the Anime Web Turnpike and cultural information about Japan.

Anime Picture Archive
http://www.lysator.liu.se/~neotron/anime/

The Anime Picture Archive features downloadable cartoon images from Japanese animators. Visitors can search the archive, view a random image, or check out the most recent graphic additions.

Anime Web Turnpike
http://soyokaze.biosci.ohio-state.edu/~jei/anipike/

Here you'll find an exhaustive guide to anime. See Editor's Choice.

Fractal Movie Archive
http://www.cnam.fr/fractals/anim.html

This movie archive boasts the "biggest collection of fractal animations" online. Visitors can choose from more than 100 titles, from "Cruise through an alien landscape" to "Chaotic smoke." Available in a variety of still and animation formats.

Japanese Animation on the WWW
http://www.imsa.edu/~leda/anime/

Fans of those cartoon characters that all look like "Speed Racer" and are capable of everything from unbelievable cuteness and heroism to rape and murder will enjoy this site. Part of a personal home page, this Japanese anime resource offers an overview of the art form and links to related clubs and newsgroups.

Mark Hairston's Anime Page
http://utd500.utdallas.edu/~hairston/animehp.html

Learn more about the art of Japanese animation at this fan-produced site featuring images and background information. Details on television series such as "Sailor Moon" are included, as well as information about Japanese animator Hayao Miyazaki.

---

a2z EDITOR'S CHOICE

WritersNet: The Internet Directory of Published Writers
http://www.bocklabs.wisc.edu/ims/writers.html

The writers' life is a lonely one with few immediate rewards, but at least isolated scribes can connect with other shut-in scribners via the WritersNet, which bills itself "the Internet directory of published writers." A bulletin board steers writers toward freelance opportunities, and an extensive directory of literary agents is a bonus for those looking to write the next Great American Novel and start raking in the Big Bucks. Fiction, nonfiction, poetry, scripts and children's literature are among the searchable options in this extensive database, with dozens of subgenres to further narrow the focus of a budding writer's search.—*Reviewed by Julene Snyder*

Svjetski Festival of Animated Films

http://animafest.hr/

The 11th World Festival of Animated Films in Zagreb, Croatia, is the focus of this site featuring award winners, daily programs, and exhibitions. An announcement for the 1996 festival and links to information about Zagreb and Croatia are also included. In Croatian and English.

Thant's Animation Index

http://mambo.ucsc.edu/psl/thant/thant.html

If it moves on the Web, it's probably here. Visit this personal link collection to find hundreds of animations created for entertainment, science, and business purposes.

ANIMATORS

GAINAX

http://www.stellar.co.jp/GAINAX/index-e.html

GAINAX Network Systems outlines its products and services on this promotional page. Visitors can read in English or Japanese about GAINAX's recent anime cartoon productions and CD-ROM video products.

J. Dyer Animation Studio

http://www.com/bubba/

Located in Atlanta, Georgia, the J. Dyer Animation Studio presents information on its visual products and services at this promotional site. Find an intro to the founder, an online gallery and a link to the cartoon adventures of Dyer's "Bubba Bullmash."

ARCHIVES AND INDICES

AAA Ardvark—WraithSpace Comics Index

http://www.redweb.com/wraithspace/

Funnies, comics, cartoons, whatever you call them, most everything related to their creation and distribution is indexed by subject category in this searchable directory. Find close to 1,500 resources (and counting!)—from animations and characters to strips and Web-comix—with dozens of listings in between. See Editor's Choice.

Al Gore's Cartoon Gallery

http://www.whitehouse.gov/WH/EOP/OVP/html/Cartoon.html

A Democratic White House wins yet another battle against political stuffiness with this official col-lection of political cartoons poking fun at the vice president. Includes downloadable graphics and brief analysis of each of the one-panel comic jabs at the environmental crusader.

CartooNet Home Page

http://www.pavilion.co.uk/cartoonet/

Visitors to the CartooNet page will find an archive of cartoon images and a chance to register for access to select European cartoon art sites. More than 200 graphics are available for viewing, and networking opportunities are provided for fellow cartoonists.

Cartoon World

http://www.cet.com/~rascal

Images, video clips, theme songs, other sound clips, coloring-book pages, and links are available at this cartoon fan page. Among the stars featured here are Scooby Doo, Daffy Duck, Foghorn Leghorn, and the Road Runner. But that's *not* all, folks.

The Comics Hotlist

http://www.uta.fi/yhteydet/sarjikset.html

The Comics Hotlist is a collection of regularly updated comics found on the Web, with links to daily, weekly, and monthly comics. The most current comics are included in a hotlist and visitors can also create personal hotlists.

Comics 'n Stuff!

http://www.missouri.edu/~c617145/comix.html

This repository offers an index to animated character-related sites on the Web and answers to frequently asked questions from the cartoon world. An online search tool and visitors' chatroom round out the offerings on this page.

Doug and Lisa's Disney Home Page

http://www.lido.com/disney/

At this unofficial Walt Disney page, visitors will find loads of trivia and information about Disney theme parks, movie art, and animated films. A host of other Disney resources from fans around the world are provided at this colorful site.

European Comics on the Web

http://grid.let.rug.nl/~erikt/.Comics/welcome.html

Readers of European comic artists will enjoy this online guide and search engine. Visit here for an extensive index of Europe-based creators of humor, fantasy, and adventure comics.

Hitoshi Doi

http://www.tcp.com/doi/doi.html

Hitoshi Doi has had a series of pretty good years, to look at the highlights on his home page. This Japanese native is a major fan of anime and manga, and his page is full of links concerning this Japanese art form.

---

a2z EDITOR'S CHOICE

Anime Web Turnpike

http://soyokaze.biosci.ohio-state.edu/~jei/anipike/

"Speed Racer" and his wrench-wielding monkey Chim-Chim were just the beginning. Take a ride on any Japanese subway nowadays, and you'll see people of all ages, from schoolkids to salarymen, burying their noses in colorful "manga" comic books. Tune into prime-time Japanese television, and you'll find a host of "anime" cartoon series, big-budget productions ranging from well-crafted children's educational programs to soft porn. For an exhaustive guide to Japan's most popular cultural export, visit the Anime Web Turnpike, produced by a North America-based anime and manga expert. Image archives, newsgroups, and fan pages only top the list of resources at this site, and more is on the way as the site's reported 350,000 visitors contribute their own anime-related links.—*Reviewed by Paul Bacon*

ASSOCIATIONS AND ORGANIZATIONS

Association of American Editorial Cartoonists
http://www.detnews.com/AAEC/AAEC.html
The Association of American Editorial Cartoonists unveils information about its benefits for members and provides a computer bulletin board through this home page. Cartoonists also can catch up on the latest industry news or view the membership roster.

Comic Book Legal Defense Fund
http://www.insv.com/cbldf/
Visitors to this site can contribute to the Comic Book Legal Defense Fund and join the fight against humor-impaired bureaucrats. It offers a history of comics censorship along with recent news from the front lines.

KUPLA ("Balloon")
http://www.kaapeli.fi/~sarjaks/
Comics from the risque to the profound are featured here by members of KUPLA, the Finnish Comics Society. Visitors can also find out about the artists and the Helsinki Comics Festival. In English and Finnish.

CARTOON AND COMIX CHARACTERS

The Cult of Tintin
http://www.daimi.aau.dk/~jjuhne/COT/cot_home.html
Fans of "The Adventures of Tintin" comic strip will delight in this in-depth and colorful, fan-created site sponsored by the Internet Bookstore. Visitors can peruse "Tintin" lore in a variety of languages and test their trivia knowledge with the "Tintin" quiz.

The Looney Tunes SoundSource
http://www.nonstick.com/sounds/
Offered "for the fan of good old-fashioned sex and violence in cartoons," this very unofficial site provides an index of downloadable WAV sound files from Warner Brothers animated features. Visit here to hear the familiar voice of Mel Blanc as he brings to life Bugs Bunny, Daffy Duck, Porky Pig, and many others.

The Page at Pooh Corner
http://www.public.iastate.edu/~jmilne/pooh.html
Dedicated to the stories of "Winnie the Pooh" and "House at Pooh Corner," this unofficial site highlights the misadventures of Pooh, Piglet, Tigger, and all their fictional friends. Includes biographical information on the story's creators: A A. Milne and E.H. Shepard.

Simpsons Characters
http://ftoomsh.progsoc.uts.edu.au/~jrwatkin/simpsons
Telemarketers and stalkers alike will enjoy the juicy information presented here for "The Simpsons" family members. Includes biographical information and pictures of Homer, Marge, Bart, and other characters of the long-running animated comedy series.

The World of Lilly Wong
http://www.asiaonline.net/lilywong/
American cartoonist Larry Feign lives and works in Hong Kong and presents a daily dose of his favorite cartoon secretary at this multimedia site. Enjoy the "romance, culture clash and politics" that is "The World of Lilly Wong." In multiple languages.

CARTOONISTS

Business Cartoons by Goff
http://www.fileshop.com/personal/tgoff/
Here, cartoonist Ted Goff posts samples of his work, which often expose little truths about life in the business world. Visitors can browse through the collection and learn how to commission Goff's talents here.

Herge
http://www.netpoint.be/abc/herge/
Fans of the comic "Tintin" can find out about the strip's creator, Herge, and join in ongoing discussions of the strip at this fan page. Read old cartoons and join in the debate about whether Herge was a Fascist.

Tool User Comics Project
http://www.tooluser.com/
Some of today's most inventive and talented cartoon artists are assembled at this art broker's site. Visitors will find links to famous and soon-to-be famous creators of comic strips and science fiction and fantasy cartoons.

a2z   EDITOR'S CHOICE

AAA Aardvark—WraithSpace Comics Index
http://www.redweb.com/wraithspace/
Aptly alphabetized as an animated annex allowing aficionados access to almost all archives, this site by WraithSpace Comics is...well...awesome! A well-organized index of international animation and comics resources greet visitors to this reference page, offering a seemingly endless array of links and information pages. Comic book readers and followers of animated features are just a few clicks away from screens full of links to official and fan-produced Web tributes. Cartoonists and animators will find extensive lists of professional contacts, events, and publications from the world comics community. Easily navigable and frequently updated, AAA Aardvark provides an excellent starting point for fans and creators alike. —*Reviewed by Paul Bacon*

AAA Aardvark - WraithSpace Comics Index

Items so far: 1683   Visits so far: 023844

Virtually Reality

http://www.onramp.net/~scroger/vreality.html

Computer graphics artist Eric Scroger maintains this site to introduce his self-styled approach to comic creation. Visitors to Virtually Reality will find an archive of his latest comic offerings, all rendered with 3-D imaging technology.

Warp Cartoons

http://www.accessone.com/~rufev

Admire the latest offerings from aptly-named cartoonist Kim Warp at the Warp Cartoons home page. See this week's off-kilter scribble, or check out a collection of Warp's greatest hits.

CARTOONS

Akazuki Chacha

http://www.tcp.com/doi/chacha/chacha.html

The antics of magician girl Ayahana Min from the manga comic Akazukin Chacha are featured in this page. Read an introduction to the comic or review a TV episode guide. Beware though! Plot outlines could spoil the mystery of episodes you haven't already seen.

The Complete Mobile Police Patlabor Guide

http://www.cs.purdue.edu/homes/pappasnw/anime/patlabor.html

A fan of "Mobile Police Patlabor," maintains this site for trivia and graphics from the action-comedy animation television series. Visit here for episode guides and character information.

Duckman Fan Site

http://bluejay.creighton.edu/~jduche/duckman.html

"Duckman," a Klasky Csupo/Paramount Television production, is based upon the underground comic of the same name. Visitors to this unofficial site will find series trivia, graphics, memorable quotes, and production and writing credits. Link to official fan page is available here.

Elfquest.Com

http://www.elfquest.com/

Warp Graphics, Inc. maintains this site for information and fan resources for the "Elfquest" animation series. Visit here for character sketches, downloadable graphics, merchandise information, and news about the feature-length animation movie.

Heeere's Ren and Stimpy

http://www.cris.com/~lkarper/rands.html

Nice and steeeenky! "Ren and Stimpy" fans have found their home on the Web at this unofficial site. Features graphics, soundbites, song lyrics, and links to more "Ren and Stimpy"-related than we're willing to admit.

Legend of the Galactic Heroes WWW Info Center

http://wwwhost.cc.utexas.edu/ftp/student/anime/utanime/amos/.LGH/logh.html

Japanese anime featuring the Legend of the Galactic Heroes storylines are based on a series of Japanese sci-fi novels—an unusual twist for usually cartoon-inspired anime. Even an anime newbie can get up to speed with these episode and character guides, scripts, sights, and sounds.

Maison Ikkoku Home Page

http://server.berkeley.edu/Anime/MI/

Fans of the softer side of Japanese anime will enjoy this unofficial tribute to the romantic comedy series "Maison Ikkoku." Described as a "touching love story," the series began as a children's comic book and eventually made it onto Japanese television in the late 1980s.

Maverick's Simpsons Page

http://www.eden.com/~maverick/simpsons.htm

D'oh! Fans of "The Simpsons" need look no further than this unofficial fan page for a huge collection of downloadable sounds, trivia and news. Includes a question-and-answer service with a "Simpsons" panel of experts.

Nadia: The Secret of Blue Water

http://utd500.utdallas.edu/~hairston/nadiahpbck.html

"Nadia: The Secret of Blue Water," a popular Japanese animation series based on Jules Verne's "20,000 Leagues Under the Sea," is showcased at this fan-produced site. Visit here for character and episode guides, song translations, picture galleries, production credits, and much more.

The Original Space Ghost Web Page

http://iquest.com/~cshuffle/sghost/

The unofficial fan page for "Space Ghost" celebrates a black-hooded interplanetary crusader who has been on television in various incarnations since 1966. The site includes episode guides, sound files, and an interview with Space Ghost himself.

Ranma 1/2 Universe

http://iczer1.usacomputers.net/~ranma/ranma.html

Meet the characters and creators of Japanese animation series "Ranma 1/2." Visitors to this unofficial site will find video release information, episode plot descriptions, and Japanese and English character soundbites.

ReBoot

http://uts.cc.utexas.edu/~ifex534/main.html

"ReBoot," an imaginative, computer-generated fantasy television series, is the subject of this unofficial site. Visit here for character and episode guides, production credits, and a call to fans to petition its cancellation.

Sailor Moon Web Page

http://www.engsoc.carleton.ca/~rsavoie/smoon/smoon.shtml

Information about the Japanese animated TV series "Sailor Moon" is featured on this page. Interested visitors can access information on characters, an episode list, storylines, and the animation video vault.

The Simpsons Archive

http://www.digimark.net/TheSimpsons/index.html

"Don't have a cow, man," "Blame the boy," and scores of other memorable "Simpsons" quotes are available at this fan-produced site. Includes extensive collection of series-related trivia, production credits, air dates, and episode guides.

Tenchi Muyo

http://www.cage.curtin.edu.au/~phillips/tenchi

The anime cartoon series "Tenchi Muyo," based on the story of a high school student who meets up with a demon, is profiled on this fan-produced page. Visit here for animations and reference material about characters in the series of related television shows, movies, and comics.

Unoffical ReBoot Home Page

http://www.inwap.com/reboot/

"ReBoot" is a Saturday morning cartoon that airs on ABC. Visit this unofficial page for an episode guide of the computer animated television series, a look at its creators and news of its pending cancellation.

Urusei Yatsura

http://haas.berkeley.edu/~chennav/uy/

"Urusei Yatsura" (translation: obnoxious guys) is a sexy and humorous Japanese cartoon series about an alien invasion of earth. Visit this unofficial site, offering background information on the series' characters and creators. Includes extensive index of downloadable graphics (mostly of scantily clad, cow-eyed young women).

COMIC BOOKS

The Doom Patrol

http://www.rpi.edu/~bulloj/Doom_Patrol/DoomPatrol.html

Visit this repository for information about the third version of DC Comics' "Doom Patrol." The site includes summaries and annotations for most of the books in the long-running, multi-artist series, as well as other information and comics-related links.

New Comic Book Releases
http://www.mnsinc.com/hyworth/comics/new.html

Part of a personal home page, Comic Book Central maintains this site for an updated index of recently released comic books. Visit here for a weekly report of new titles, organized by publisher name.

Tank Girl Fan Site
http://www.cs.ucl.ac.uk/staff/b.rosenberg/tg/index.html

Fans of the "punkster girl that takes no s**t" will enjoy this unofficial "Tank Girl" fan site, offering graphics, merchandise, and comic trivia. Includes links to newsgroups devoted to the comic heroine and answers to frequently asked questions. See Editor's Choice.

COMPANIES

The Comic Strip
http://www.unitedmedia.com/comics/

United Features Syndicate, representing "Peanuts," "Dilbert," and many other popular comic strips, maintains this promotional site. Visitors can view comic strip archives and send e-mail directly to featured artists.

Sirius Entertainment
http://www.insv.com/sirius

Sirius Entertainment publishes comics and places itself "in the nebulous space on the edges of the comic industry where genre classifications are meaningless." Visit here to tour its online gallery and catalog, featuring titles like "Angry Christ Comics" and "Akiko."

EDITORIAL CARTOONS

The Inkwell
http://www.unitedmedia.com/inkwell/

Comic distributor United Features Syndicate provides this collection of some of America's most prolific editorial cartoonists. Visitors will find background information and viewable comics from Ed Stein, Jim Berry, Rob Rogers, and many others.

PUBLICATIONS AND INDUSTRY NEWS

Borderline Netazine
http://www.the-borderline.com/

Created by a teenage cartoonist, "The Borderline Netazine" features a variety of humor, satire and comic offerings. Visit here for daily cartoons, a "sorta" monthly collection of articles and a list of mirror sites around the world.

The Comics Journal
http://www.halcyon.com/fgraphic/home.html

Comic books, known to many as "graphic novels," are not just for kids anymore, and The Comics Journal is here to prove it. Comics fans can preview articles from past or present issues of this periodical covering the comics industry, subscribe to the magazine, visit the parent comics site, or link to more comics on the Net.

fps: The Magazine of Animation on Film and Video
http://www.cam.org/~pawn/fps.html

"fps," a quarterly print publication dedicated to the world of animation, is available in online form at this official site. Visitors will find articles and features covering all aspects and types of animation—from Japanese anime to Hollywood productions. See Editor's Choice.

Friday Daily Cartoon
http://www.fridaymagazine.com/

Get your daily chuckle at the Friday Humor Magazine home page, where a new cartoon is posted every day. You can also look at sample pages from the magazine—similar to Britain's "Punch."

Giggle
http://www.glasswings.com.au/GlassWings/jolly/giggle.html

This comedy zine includes spirited features and comic strips with titles like "The Joke Assortment with Furballs" and "The Bunny People of Planet Pynk!" Check out the latest issue or browse the archive of giggles past.

---

a2z EDITOR'S CHOICE

Tank Girl Fan Site
http://www.dcs.qmw.ac.uk/~bob/stuff/tg/index.html

Blasting traditional cartoon conventions of women as damsels in distress, Tank Girl arrived on the British comic scene in 1988 as a heat-packing punkster with a shaved head and an attitude. Almost a decade later, she's a superheroine of the Apocalypse, starring in countless comic books, popular magazines, and even a feature-length Hollywood film. Visitors to this unofficial homage to the gun-toting comandette are treated to a well-meaning, but frightening, introduction to the sassy skinhead—including her life story and favorite obscenities ("beef curtain," "flippin' heck," and "quim"—to name a few). A gallery of portraits shows Tank Girl in a variety of violent battles and a "clone" page offers snapshots of real women who are dead ringers for the comic strip character. —*Reviewed by Paul Bacon*

The Hype! Comic Cafe

http://www.hype.com/comics/cafe/comicafe.htm

Described as "the launching pad for comic book related gossip and late breaking news," this page leads browsers to news about comic collecting, nostalgia and reviews. Information about new releases and links to comic banter and gossip also are located here.

SHOPS, SALES AND SERVICES

The Cartoon Factory Animation Art Gallery

http://www.cartoon-factory.com/

If you've ever wanted to own an original animation cell from your favorite cartoon, stop by the Cartoon Factory. The site offers an extensive online gallery of official items from top cartoons such as "The Simpsons," and from top studios such as Disney and MCA/Universal.

STRIPS

Alley Oop Official Archive

http://www.unitedmedia.com/comics/alleyoop/

Fans of the enduring prehistoric comic strip "Alley Oop" will enjoy this official site from United Media. Features a daily comic offering and an archive of recent strips.

Arlo & Janis Official Fan Site

http://www.unitedmedia.com/comics/arlonjanis/

United Media's "Arlo & Janis" comic strip is available online, with two weeks of strips archived as well as full-color versions of the most recent Sunday strip. An opportunity to e-mail the artist directly is also available.

Asterix Fan Site

http://www.ifi.uio.no/~janl/ts/asterix.html

Dedicated to long-running comic "Asterix," this Web site offers images and background information describing the strip's characters and plot lines. Includes links to other "Asterix"-related resources—including an annotated listing of stories and the French-language Toon Land Asterix page.

Calvin and Hobbes on the WWW

http://eos.kub.nl:2080/calvin_hobbes/

An extensive personal collection of trivia and resources for fans of the "Calvin and Hobbes" comic strip is available at this unofficial site. Visitors will find information on published anthologies, characters, and the strip's creator, Bill Watterson.

The Dilbert Zone

http://www.unitedmedia.com/comics/dilbert/

United Media maintains this site, offering background on "Dilbert" creator, Scott Adams, and archives of the sidesplitting comic strip that regularly lampoons corporate culture. Visitors can laugh for free or send money for "Dilbert" paraphernalia.

Doctor Fun Archive

http://sunsite.unc.edu/Dave/archive.html

Doctor Fun, a weekly one-panel, "Far Side"-style cartoon, is available online at this artist-maintained site. Visit here for an archive of the strip, formerly carried by the United Media national syndicate. Selected links to SunSite are also available.

Drabble

http://www.unitedmedia.com/comics/drabble/

Kevin Fagan's daily syndicated comic strip, "Drabble," can be viewed through this link to the United Media Web site. Visitors can view the daily update or opt to view a two-week archive of recent strips.

Firehose Tavern Home Page

http://the-tech.mit.edu/Images/Firehose/firehose-home.html

"Firehose Tavern," a regular comic strip from the Massachusetts Institute of Technology student newspaper "The Tech," takes a humorous look at technology and college life. Visit here to view an unofficial index of collected strips.

Fried Society Comic Archive

http://www.fried.com/comix/fried/

Artist Chris Kelly fries modern life to a crisp with this online comic archive. Visitors will find links to current and previous offerings of this multi-paneled comic strip.

Har Broks Kuifje Index

http://www.cs.rulimburg.nl/~wiesman/kuifjeindex/

"Tintin," the most popular comic book series in Europe, is on the Web here in Dutch. Browsers can look up an English translation of the names, but unless they speak Dutch, enjoying the pictures will have to suffice.

---

a2z **EDITOR'S CHOICE**

United Media

http://www.unitedmedia.com/UM_home.html

From the prehistoric antics of "Alley Oop," running since 1933, to today's goofiest corporate spoof "Dilbert," United Media distributes America's most enduring and popular comic strips. Other long-running titles include "Nancy," "Marmaduke," "Rose is Rose," and everybody's favorite philosophical schoolyard gang, Charles Schultz's "Peanuts." The company's home page provides hours of family-approved comic fun, offering two-week archives and a bonus color Sunday strip for all its well-known characters. A pointer to parent company United Features Syndicate's "Inkwell" offers a birdseye view of recent panels from its team of political cartoonists, including Ed Stein and Steve Benson. Special online merchandise areas include "The Dilbert Zone" and Snoopy's "Dog House." —*Reviewed by Paul Bacon*

Kev's World

http://www.S2F.com/kevsworld/index.html

Freelance newspaper cartoonist Kevin Nichols maintains this site to present his one-panel comic offerings in "Kev's World." Visitors will can view recent works and download a copy of his "digital sketchbook."

Marmaduke Official Fan Site

http://www.unitedmedia.com/comics/marmaduke/

Fans of "Marmaduke," a nationally syndicated comic strip about a clumsy, but loveable great dane, will enjoy this official site. Visit here for daily comic offerings, a two-week archive and information about the strip's creator, Brad Anderson.

NetBoy

http://netboy.com

Follow the antics of one of the Internet's very first born! "NetBoy" reaches back, way back, into the annals of the Web, well, almost a couple years ago and serves up great cyberhumor on a regular basis.

Onca Ray

http://www.solarlink.com/~oncaray

The adventures of Egyptian princess Onca Ray, entombed in a time capsule to bring a message of compassion to the future, can be followed online here. Visit this artist-created Web site for an ongoing storyline and related sound and graphics offerings.

One Brick Shy

http://www.citynet.net/diller/diller.html

"One Brick Shy" is a weekly, one-panel comic strip that scratches at the underbelly of America for its sardonic observations and ironic humor. The latest cartoon and a cartoon archive are available.

Over the Hedge

http://www.unitedmedia.com/comics/hedge/

At United Media's "Over the Hedge" site, visitors can download today's strip and check out the archives of recent strips. Those so inclined can also e-mail Michael Fry, the strip's writer.

Pete's Best of The Far Side

http://members.aol.com/HPElzer/index.html

Do you miss the days of the "Boneless Chicken Ranch" and smoking dinosaurs? Fans of Gary Larson's comic, "The Far Side," can get their fill of chuckles on this page, thanks to a collection of 70 favorite cartoons maintained by Hans Peter Elzer.

Robotman Official Fan Site

http://www.unitedmedia.com/comics/robotman/

United Feature Syndicate maintains this site for an archive of "Robotman" comic strips. Visit here to catch the wit of the pint-sized robot stuck in a human society and send your feedback directly to its creator, Jim Meddick.

Snoopy's Dog House

http://www.unitedmedia.com/comics/peanuts/

Snoopy, Charlie Brown, and the rest of the "Peanuts" gang are officially online here, where browsers can download a two-week archive of the latest newspaper strips. The site includes excerpts from Charles M. Schultz's biography, "Peanuts" milestones, and the art world's look at the long-running comic strip.

Star Trek—The Cartoon Generation

http://manor.york.ac.uk/htdocs/tng.html

Blaming a lack of productive ways to spend free time, the creator of this site has assembled a comic strip-style lampoon of "Star Trek: The Next Generation." Visit here to view the strip, assembled with graphic elements lifted from random Web sites.

Stocious

http://fishwrap.mit.edu/Comics/Stocious

A regular feature in Massachusetts Institute of Technology's "Fishwrap" online magazine, "Stocious" offers a bizarre, one-panel comic look at modern life. Visitors can find current and past comic creations.

Where the Buffalo Roam

http://plaza.xor.com/wtbr/

Hans Bjordahl's "Where the Buffalo Roam" comic strip is available online on this Internet Plaza page. Visitors can view current and past strips from the subdued, yet silly Colorado-based cartoonist.

---

a2z **EDITOR'S CHOICE**

fps: The Magazine of Animation on Film and Video

http://www.cam.org/~pawn/fps.html

"fps" is the industry bible for animation artists and producers. The Montreal, Quebec-based quarterly print publication offers in-depth articles about the latest breakthroughs in animation and showcases famous and upcoming creators. Its home on the Web takes the mission one step further by offering a regularly updated index of industry resources, including artist directories, upcoming conventions and production company contacts. Online versions of its well-read articles are also included, as well as mail-order animation video catalogs and a collection of reader "hip lists." One look at the dozens of other sites which link to "fps" shows this is the place for animation. —*Reviewed by Paul Bacon*

DANCE

ARCHIVES AND INDICES

Body and Grace
http://www.i3tele.com/photo_perspectives_museum/faces/abt.html

Here you'll find images of ABT dancers. See Ediotr's Choice.

The Dance Directory
http://www.cyberspace.com/vandehey/dance.html

From ballet to tango, the Dance Directory surveys the Web wide variety of dance resources. Identify clubs, companies, or instructional sites with this collection of links and listings.

Dance Links
http://www.physics.purdue.edu/

Professional dancers, dance students and dance fans alike will find hundreds of pages to spin through in this index. Dance companies, educational institutions, and grant sources are but a few of the types of resources available.

Dance Pages
http://www.ens-lyon.fr/~esouche/danse/dance.html

This personal home page was created to give dancers and dance enthusiasts access to a world-wide network of resources. Visitors can link to various archives and international dance companies, including the Paris Opera Ballet.

Finnish Dance Server
http://www.utu.fi/harrastus/tanssi/english/index.html

Material ranges from listings of folk and competition troupes to information on cool bands and hot discotheques. It's accompanied by a database of facts on Finnish record labels, booking agents, and studios. In Finnish, Swedish, and English.

Henry's Dance Hotlist
http://zeus.ncsa.uiuc.edu:8080/~hneeman/dance_hotlist.html

Henry's Dance Hotlist is an extensive listing of links for all forms of dance. Visitors can locate organizations and clubs offering lessons, classes, and regular dance events.

Southern California Dance and Directory
http://www.usc.edu/dept/dance/

The Southern California Dance and Directory page features links to Los Angeles-based chore-

---

Body and Grace
http://www.i3tele.com/photo_perspectives_museum/faces/abt.html

Those who like to watch will get a kick out of these graceful black-and-white images of bodies in motion. Celebrated photographer Nancy Ellison's portraits of principals, soloists, and corps de ballet from the American Ballet Theatre provide the main attraction. Stylishly commemorating the theatre's 55th anniversary, Ellison's photos pick up on every contortion, rib-bone contour, and flex of muscle. A pictorial history of the ABT is also available on-site, as are a handful of Ellison's celebrity shots of personalities like Mick Jagger and Grace Jones.—*Reviewed by James Fitch*

Dancing on a Line
http://www.danceonline.com/

New York-based e-zine Dancing on a Line is created for "people who know nothing about dance, and people who know everything about dance." (And, perhaps more importantly, people who use Netscape 2.0.) The site is alive with photography, movement and thoughtful commentary. Critics put the eye on current New York performances while feature stories range from "Familiar Movements" to "The Struggle with the Body." For visitors who like things a little soapy, the site's ongoing fiction feature, "The Chronicles of DancerX," is just the ticket. Dance enthusiasts should definitely get on *this* line.—*Reviewed by James Fitch*

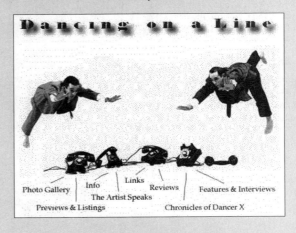

ographers and dancers as well as pointers to dance resources at the University of Southern California.

World Wide Web Virtual Library: Dance

http://www.artswire.org/Artswire/www/dance/dance.html

The World Wide Web Virtual Library's dance section provides a comprehensive listing of links to dance-related information on the Web. Browse by topic, or submit information to the stacks.

COMPANIES

Los Angeles Choreographers & Dancers—The Company

http://www.usc.edu/dept/dance/p2_lacd.html

Los Angeles Choreographers & Dancers is a professional dance company composed of Louise Reichlin & Dancers (modern) and Zapped Taps/Alfred Desio (tap). Visitors to this home page will find out all about the company and its projects.

New York City Ballet

http://www.nycballet.com/

Fans of the New York City Ballet will enjoy this official site, featuring information about the company's performances and cast members. Visitors can also order tickets or ballet merchandise online.

Paris Opera Ballet

http://www.ens-lyon.fr/~esouche/danse/POB.html

The Paris Opera Ballet maintains this site to provide information on its dancers, choreographers and seasonal ballets. Fans will also find an assortment of links to related sites of interest.

INSTITUTES AND SCHOOLS

Ohio State University Department of Dance

http://www.dance.ohio-state.edu/

The Department of Dance at Ohio State University at Columbus, maintains this page with information about the department, personnel, performances, courses, and research. Many links to other dance sites.

PUBLICATIONS AND INDUSTRY NEWS

Dance Ink

http://www.webcom.com/~ink/

If you don't know the difference between a pirouette and a Twyla Tharp, the quarterly issues of Dance Ink will help you tell the dancer from the

dance. The online version offers the latest news and reviews from the world of ballet and modern interpretive dance, along with artist profiles and an archive of back issues.

Dancing on a Line

http://www.danceonline.com/

This site has graphics, reviews, and more. See Editor's Choice.

---

a2z **EDITOR'S CHOICE**

Cajun/Zydeco Music & Dance

http://www.bme.jhu.edu/~jrice/cz.html

Seasoned with squeezebox-playing crawfish, dancing gators, and splashes of Panola and Tabasco, the Cajun/Zydeco Music & Dance page makes the heat of Louisiana a little more accessible to the rest of the world. Link to Cajun/Zydeco connections from Lexington to London. And don't miss the site's no-nonsense online dance lessons, which set out to teach visitors "how to dance, and do it more or less correctly."—*Reviewed by James Fitch*

Cajun/Zydeco Music & Dance

Now more than just Baltimore & Washington Areas

This page has been viewed 24624 times.

Mid-Atlantic Crawfish Net T-shirt Offer

Resource information

Farewell Tornado Alley Page NEW

Places to find Cajun/Zydeco in Washington, D.C.

Places to find Cajun/Zydeco in Baltimore

Places to find Cajun/Zydeco in San Francisco Bay Area

Places to find Cajun/Zydeco across the USA (and UK)

CapAccess Online Service covering local Cajun/Zydeco *Maintained by Gary Hayman*

How to Dance to Cajun and Zydeco Music

Picture Gallery

RECREATIONAL DANCE

FOLK

Cajun/Zydeco Music & Dance
http://www.bme.jhu.edu/~jrice/cz.html

This lively site gets you in touch with the Cajun/Zydeco scene. See Editor's Choice.

Morris & Sword Pages on the Web
http://www.mit.edu:8001/people/jcb/morris-teams.html

Learn the ins and outs of Morris and Sword Sides dance. The site features a link to the World Wide Web Virtual Library's dance section as well as an alphabetical listing of related sites from around the world.

Roda Capoeira
http://www.bnbcomp.net/capoeira/cap1.htm

Learn about this Brazilian art form here. See Editor's Choice.

Steve Allen's Dance Index Page
http://ucowww.ucsc.edu/~sla/dance/dance.html

This folk-dancing home page includes links to regionally indexed dance resources around the world. Includes information—including history, photos, and songs—on English Morris dancing.

SQUARE DANCE

Bob Lafleur's Square Dancing Resource List
http://pages.map.com/~bobl/sdance.htm

Bob Lafleur offers fellow square-dance enthusiasts an extensive index of what's available on the Net. Among the offerings, find an alphabetical list of callers and a state-by-state listing of clubs.

Western Square Dancing
http://suif.stanford.edu/~rfrench/wsd/

The world of square dancing is at your fingertips here. See Editor's Choice.

SWING

The U.S. Swing Dance Server
http://www.cs.cornell.edu/Info/People/aswin/SwingDancing/swing_dancing.html

Swingers can practice their virtual footwork here. The expansive site includes a library of swing steps, a file defining dance terms, and a national events calendar.

TAP

Tap Dance Homepage
http://www.mcphu.edu/~corrp/tap/

The Tap Dance home page features a Who's Who in Tap and links to information about tap dancing events and festivals. Visitors can read a history of tap dancing or view pictures of some of the dance form's biggest names.

SHOPS, SALES, AND SERVICES

Dance Supplies, Etc.
http://www.dancesupply.com/dances/index.htm

Dancers can shop for and purchase such essentials as pointe and tap shoes, ballet slippers, leotards, tights, and more at Dance Supplies, Etc. The site also contains an index of dance-related Web resources.

FAMOUS AND INFAMOUS PEOPLE

ARCHIVES AND INDEXES

Autograph Online
http://www.io.org/~akennedy/

Autograph buffs can peruse a robust collection of online signatures and publications here. Find out more about Autograph Online and how you can

EDITOR'S CHOICE

Roda Capoeira
http://www.bnbcomp.net/capoeira/cap1.htm

Interchangeably described at this information site as a dance, a mischievous art form, a martial art form, a religion, and a cultural identity, it's anyone's guess as to whether or not we've properly categorized the Brazilian practice of Roda Capoeira. In a nutshell, a circle—or roda—is formed, music is played, clapping and singing ensue, and two players "interact" in the circle's center. The site's glossary piques our interest with Portuguese translations for such phrases as "head butt" and "crab's mouth movement," while a "Pictures of Capoeira" section brings things a little more into focus. The terminally curious are free to take in the site's (not so brief) history of the intriguing activity.—*Reviewed by James Fitch*

participate, or link to a number of other auto-
graph-related sites on the Web.

The Babe Test

http://babes.sci.kun.nl/

Test your "babe" (the female kind, not the talking
pig kind) knowledge here. Each day, this quiz
posts photos of 15 famously beautiful women;
you take a multiple choice test to match images
with names.

Directory of Royal Genealogical Data

http://www.dcs.hull.ac.uk/public/genealogy/
royal/catalog.html

The Directory of Royal Genealogical Data page
traces the British royal family and other royal
family lineages. The database includes over
12,000 individuals and can be searched by lineage, surname, forename, date, or title. The directory also lists links by culture and country.

Famous Women JPEGs

ftp://src.doc.ic.ac.uk/media/visual/collections/
funet-pics/jpeg/people/female/

SunSite's Northern European archive is located at
Imperial College in London. This FTP directory
contains pictures of famous women—including
Michelle Pfeiffer and Sherilyn Fenn.

Gangsters!

http://www.well.com/user/mod79/

Devoted to the "gentleman bandit," this amusing
Web resource investigates "the "romantic mystique" of the All-American Mobster. In addition to
info on such renowned gangsters as Al Capone,
an intriguing overview of organized crime internationally is available.

Mr. Showbiz

http://www.mrshowbiz.com/

Mr. Showbiz follows the entertainment world.
The extensive site contains movie and music reviews, articles, star profiles and more. Browsers
can don reviewer caps and submit their thoughts
here, too. See Edior's Choice.

Model's Lynk Home Page

http://www.modelslynk.com/

Models, models, models. Female models. Male
models. Models with swimsuits. Models without.
If you're into looking at bodies, then this is the
page for you. Links to information (and pictures,
of course) about actors and actresseses, casting
for roles and swapmeets. There's also a Webchat
facility to talk about...you guessed it, models.

Past Notable Women of Computing

http://www.cs.yale.edu/HTML/YALE/CS/
HyPlans/tap/past-women.html

The Ada Project (TAP) presents an index of notable women in computing and seeks submissions
to add to the listing. The women featured here begin with women in mathematics, dating to Hypa-

tia (370–415 A.D.), and work their way forward in
time. Included is a photo gallery and links on the
history of computing.

Quotations Home Page

http://www.lexmark.com/data/quote.html

A large index of memorable quotations is maintained at this server, along with detailed reference
information. Quote collections range from advice,
proverbial wisdom and annoying proverbs to serious sarcasm and poetry.

The Quotations Page

http://www.starlingtech.com/quotes/

This personal home page offers a daily selection
of randomly selected quotations. Visit here for the
words of George Bernard Shaw, former U.S. Vice
President Dan Quayle and other quotable legends.

Secret E-Mail Addresses and Fan Pages

http://www2.islandnet.com/~luree/
fanmail.html

The Unknown Psychic hosts this directory.
"Some of the pages are actually maintained by
the celebrity listed, some are 'excellent' examples
of well maintained fan pages." Which are which is
up to visitors to ferret out.

Supermodel.com

http://www.supermodel.com/

Pictures and products dominate the Supermodel
Home Page. The site's "model of the month" and
Supermodel Shop provide one-stop glamor
shopping.

 EDITOR'S CHOICE

Western Square Dancing

http://suif.stanford.edu/~rfrench/wsd/

It ain't much to look at, but we can't imagine a place on Earth that contains
more information on the pastime of Western Square Dance than this server.
From squares who meet at church to squares who meet in Sweden; from
caller associations to caller colleges, world-wide boot-scooters are sure to
locate that vital link here. They can even do a little online shopping while
they're at it—for such essentials as a square dance simulator for DOS and
the latest glossary of calls and concepts.—*Reviewed by James Fitch*

FAMOUS FACES

Note: In this section sites are alphabetized by author's last name where applicable.

Refuse & Resist: Stop the Legal Lynching of Mumia Abu-Jamal

http://www.calyx.com/~refuse/mumia/index.html

Mumia Abu-Jamal is an African-American journalist currently on death row in Pennsylvania, convicted of murdering a policeman. This page is dedicated to an international effort to free him from what many consider a wrongful conviction based on his political beliefs.

Woody Allen

http://www.idt.unit.no/~torp/woody/

Admirers of scandal-ridden legendary comedic actor and film creator Woody Allen can peruse funny lines and some great sound bytes in this site from a dedicated fan. Explore details of Allen's past career, or check out a complete filmography with photos.

Isaac Asimov FAQ

http://www.clark.net/pub/edseiler/WWW/asimov_FAQ.html

Just how do you *pronounce* Isaac Asimov? Readers will find out from this Frequently Asked Questions (FAQs) file, posted by the newsgroup alt.books.isaac-asimov. The file also looks at the prolific writer's life—he wrote day and night—and provides pointers to Asimov texts online.

The Helena Bonham Carter Pages

http://www.student.nada.kth.se/~nv91-gta/www/HBC/welcome.html

A fan of British actress Helena Bonham Carter praises and details her career here. Carter is best known for her various roles in Merchant Ivory Films, but has also appeared on stage and television.

Pat Buchanan for President Home Page

http://www.buchanan.org/

The Pat Buchanan for President home page contains scads of information about the conservative political pundit and his Republican presidential campaign. Includes an overview of his platform, a sampling of his unique political opinions and a bio that proves he's a red-blooded American.

The I Love Sandra Bullock Pages

http://www.webcom.com/~alsplace/sandra_bullock/sandra_main.html

An amorous fan has compiled this significant archive of images and video clips of actress Sandra Bullock. The extensive site includes synopses of her films, trivia, and a list of her magazine appearances, with photos.

William S. Burroughs

http://www.charm.net/~brooklyn/People/WilliamSBurroughs.html

Dress for the afternoon meal and sit down to an online bio of Beat writer William S. Burroughs. Hyperlinks lead to further information about Burroughs' friends, family, writings and places he has visited and lived. A bibliography is included.

Johnny Cash

http://american.recordings.com/American_Artists/Johnny_Cash/cash_home.html

Johnny Cash (who still walks the line) has his followers in both rock and in country music. They congregate at this official American Recordings site, where visitors can hear, see and learn about the man in black and his music. Links to a related newsgroup.

Arthur C. Clarke Unauthorized Home Page

http://www.lsi.usp.br/~rbianchi/clarke/

Dedicated to science fiction writer Arthur C. Clarke, this unofficial site offers information about the author's biography, awards and filmography. Hypertext versions of interviews are online as well.

Rodney Dangerfield

http://www.rodney.com/

This site features a multimedia "laugh break" starring the man who gets no respect, Rodney Dangerfield. Video clips, sound bites, photos and philosophical musings—yes, musings—are featured, along with the Joke of the Day, current news and old annoyances.

---

a2z EDITOR'S CHOICE

Mr. Showbiz

http://www.mrshowbiz.com/

Whattya want? Innuendo? Gossip? Rumor? Quote unquote entertainment news? Well, it's your lucky day, li'l punkin, cuz when you visit Mr. Showbiz, you'll find out the inside skinny on everybody from Demi to Alanis, Joan Crawford to Bogie. With a design to die for—all cool 1950s boomerang shapes and stylish caricatures—this is the spot to get down in the muck and wallow in the latest dirt, vis à vis lifestyles of the rich and infamous. Thrill to the daily water cooler polls! Shiver at the latest antics of fill-in-the-name-of-current-hot-property-here and their wacky propensity for tormenting gerbils! Hurry, hurry, hurry! Content changes daily with a dizziness that mirrors the very culture it follows: News and reviews, features, star bios, chat, and much, much, more await you at the Web's preeminent purveyor of all things popcultish. But don't worry, misanthropes, there's enough smarmy attitude and snot-nose commentary sprinkled in to make this the spot to check out even if you don't care what Heather Locklear's done to her hair this week.—*Reviewed by Julene Snyder*

This is Cal D. and the Place to Be!

http://www.calvertdeforest.com/

Calvert DeForest—the artist formerly known as Larry "Bud" Melman—breaks away from David Letterman with this commercial site of his own. In addition to audio clips, movie clips, photos and biographical information on the rotund celebrity, the page provides games and advice.

Family Life at the White House

http://www.whitehouse.gov/WH/Family/html/Life.html

Have you ever wondered what family life is really like at the White House? If you have, then visit this page and take a tour of First Family life. This page comes with photos and an audio link to Socks, the Clinton family cat.

Allen Ginsberg

http://www.charm.net/~brooklyn/People/AllenGinsberg.html

Levi Asher, a writer from New York City, provides a tribute to poet and performer Allen Ginsberg. Visitors can link to bibliographies of Ginsberg's work, as well as writings about him. An astute bio from Asher leaves readers with insight.

NewtWatch Home Page

http://www.cais.com/newtwatch/

This site offers a one-stop resource for information about the U.S. Speaker of the House, Newt Gingrich. Frequently less than flattering information is here, as well as links to his voting record, campaign finances, staff salaries, image galleries and an abundance of related resources.

Helen Hunt Fan Page

http://www.pitt.edu/~pssst3/helen/end.html

Mad about Helen Hunt? Check out this unofficial fan site for a few pics and poems about the "Mad About You" star.

Janet Jackson: Planet Janet

http://www.mit.edu:8001/people/agoyo1/janet.html

The pop diva Janet Jackson is celebrated here by one of her biggest fans. Includes Janet news, worldwide tour information, a picture gallery, a cache of audio clips, lyrics and a chance for the viewer to submit feedback.

The Michael Jackson Internet Fan Club

http://www.fred.net/mjj/

The Michael Jackson Internet Fan Club will provide fans of "The King of Pop" with lyrics to his songs, current Billboard charts, a list of related books and fan magazines, a complete discography, information on joining, and much more.

The Unofficial Moira Kelly Homepage

http://www.sirius.com/~eaquino/moira/welcome.html

A devoted Moira Kelly fan idolizes her here. Read a few articles, exchange notes with other fans, but

mostly look at the pictures of this actress, who has starred in such films as "Chaplin" and "Billy Bathgate."

Senator Edward M. Kennedy

http://www.senate.gov/member/ma/kennedy/general/

Senator Edward Kennedy's home page contains background on the politician, his voting record and contact information. Includes links to U.S. Government servers, Massachusetts on the Web and pointers to political activist pages.

Being Stephen King

http://www.isisw3.com/sking/

King families around the world occasionally name a son *Stephen*. The Stephen Kings' home page offers an online support group for the regular joes whose given monikers get them mistaken for the famous American horror fiction author.

The Helena Kobrin Love Page

http://www.demon.co.uk/castle/helena/

A lawyer representing the Religious Technology Center, "a branch of the Scientology empire," Helena Kobrin's life and times as a "cult figure" are chronicled by this "tribute to the many welcome [cough] contributions that Helena has made to open communication on the 'net and to the upholding of ethics [cough] in the legal profession."

The Timothy Leary and Robert Anton Wilson Show

http://www.intac.com/~dimitri/dh/learywilson.html

The Timothy Leary and Robert Anton Wilson Show contains information, writings, and interviews with these two outlaw intellectuals. The vast site includes links to publications, research and philosophy.

---

a2z   EDITOR'S CHOICE

The Anti-Rush Limbaugh Page

http://www.cjnetworks.com/~cubsfan/rush/antirush.html

From the opening salvo—a doctored photo of Limbaugh with a rather fetching set of pig-ears (click on the image to hear the man profess his true vision of himself in RealAudio)—this page pulls no punches in skewering the conservative pundit. Equal time is given to the "dittoheads" on a message wall, complete with well-thought-out responses like this: "Rush Limbaugh Rules. It is the mixed up liberal wacos [sic] and feminatsi type [sic] that will destroy this country, along with your partners the gays (fagots) [sic]." Touché! On your way to brain-surgery school, are you? The brain-child of Mike Silverman—who also runs "Turn Left," which he bills as the "Web's leading liberal site"—here's a page that uses wit, actual data and humor to refute Rush Limbaugh's tendency to play fast and loose with the facts. For further fun, check out the "jokes" section for offerings like this: "Q: What is the difference between Rush Limbaugh and the Hindenburg? A: One is a flaming fascist gasbag full of hot air, and the other is a dirigible."—*Reviewed by Julene Snyder*

Anti-Rush Limbaugh Page

OINK IF YOU LOVE RUSH!

"We gather here today not to praise Rush, but to bury him!"

Click on the picture to the left to hear Rush describe himself best!

This page is the work of Mike Silverman who also is the webmaster of **Turn Left**, the Web's leading liberal site.

Rush Limbaugh Articles and Resources on the 'Net

http://www.well.com/user/srhodes/rush.html

This page links to various articles and resources dealing with controversial talk-radio star Rush Limbaugh. The Webmaster compiled information for the site while working on a PBS documentary, "Rush Limbaugh's America."

The Anti-Rush Limbaugh Page

http://www.cjnetworks.com/~cubsfan/rush/antirush.html

The Anti-Rush Limbaugh Page is a scathing look at the conservative pundit. Includes meticulous and humorous critiques of his writings and on-air commentaries, links to related reviews, jokes and reproductions of anti-Rush bumper stickers. See Editor's Choice.

Rush to the Right Side

http://www.clark.net/pub/jeffd/rushpage.html

Rush to the Right Side is another Web valentine to R. Limbaugh, offering a selection of his thoughts on current affairs. Includes info on his radio broadcasts, audio snippets of some conservative musical parodies, the infamous list of "35 Undeniable Truths," a form for ordering the styl-ish Limbaugh necktie collection, and links to related sites on the Internet (of which there are many).

H. P. Lovecraft Page

http://www.primenet.com/~dloucks/hplpage.html

H.P. Lovecraft is a notorious writer of bizarre fantasy fiction. Visitors to this site will find a biography, chronological information, a Frequently Asked Questions (FAQs) file and a list of links to other Lovecraft sites.

The Madonna Home Page

http://www.mit.edu:8001/people/jwb/Madonna.html

This fan-hosted site serves up dish on the all-around American pop star: her hits, her bombs, her contributions to "George" magazine...even the "Top 10 Signs that David Letterman is Obsessed with Madonna."

Steve Martin—A Wild and Crazy Guy

http://qlink.queensu.ca/~4kgd/steve/

The man who hit Hollywood with baloon animals and a brash "Exxxxcuse meee!" is now a comedy institution. Find film and TV clips, soundbites and trivia about Steve at this fan-produced site.

Paul McCartney

http://cip2.e-technik.uni-erlangen.de:8080/hyplan/gernhard/macca.html

This German Web page devoted to ex-Beatle Paul McCartney features recent news and historical references to the singer from his Fab Four and Wings days. The page includes a complete discography of his solo career, along with links to bootleg recordings and videos. In English.

John Muir Exhibit

http://ice.ucdavis.edu/John_Muir/

The John Muir Exhibit home page features the life and writings of the conservationist and naturalist, including a fact sheet on Muir from the Sierra Club. Visitors can read quotations from Muir and view biographical information.

Paulina Porizkova

http://darwin.clas.virginia.edu/~mgk4e/paulina/paulina.html

This unofficial page is devoted to supermodel Paulina Porizkova. Visitors will find a variety of photos of the Polish beauty.

Anne Rice: Commotion Strange

http://ecosys.drdr.virginia.edu/~jsm8f/commotion.html

Anne Rice—Queen of the ghoulish and erotic—offers a newsletter to her fans here. This site contains archives of the newsletter, Commotion Strange, and links to other Rice resources.

The Official Roy Rogers and Dale Evans Web Site

http://www.royrogers.com/

Happy trails are in store for anyone visiting the official Roy Rogers page, offering a trip down memory lane into the world of sagebrush, six-shooters and the sunny western skies of the Mojave. From here, buckaroos can visit the Roy Rogers Museum, the RogersDale USA theme park (opening in Victorville, California in 1997), and a gift shop where they can relive the golden days of the "King of the Cowboys."

RuPaul's House of Love

http://www.teleport.com/~rupaul/

Sit yourself down girl and pull on some lacy togs for an evening of entertainment and shameless self promotion. RuPaul has self-titled—himself/herself?—Queen of Cyberspace. Visit the RuPaul House of Love for a new kind of Internet adventure. See Editor's Choice.

The Meg Ryan Page

http://web.cs.ualberta.ca:80/~davidw/MegRyan/meg.cgi

A devoted fan pays homage to American film star, Meg Ryan of "When Harry Met Sally" at this jam-packed unofficial site. Check out the icons filmography and best quotes, or find out when Meg was last "sighted."

RuPaul's House of Love

http://www.teleport.com/~rupaul/

Here find the world's most snuggly drag queen in full effect, glammed out and ready to play—when RuPaul enters the room, you just know that fun and frolic with a capital "F" is just around the corner. From the "latest dish" to the "media darling" section, RuPaul gets it right. Links to Ru's biography, "Letting It All Hang Out," audio files ("No, I don't do windows, honey"), and more images than you can shake a high-heeled pump at are all offered without apology at the House of Love. Get down, get funky, and go girl, directly to the House of Love. While you're there, give Miss Thing a playful smack on the booty for me, for strutting her stuff in virtual high style.—*Reviewed by Julene Snyder*

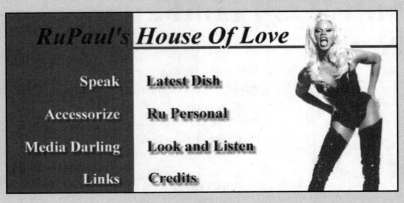

Winona Ryder!

http://www.access.digex.net/~bdecker/afwr.html

This Winona Ryder fan site serves up online homages to the "gen-X gorgeous elfin brainy goddess actress." Visitors can access pictures, newsgroups and links to related sites here.

Santa Claus is Coming...From Norway!

http://www.telepost.no/Santa/Claus.html

Is Santa Claus really Norwegian? Well, the creators of this site sure aim to prove so. Admirers of the world's most benevolent giver (aka Santa Claus, Kris Kringle, Julenisse) can peruse the jolly old elf's history and enjoy a collection of photographs showing Claus in Norway.

Paul Teale/Karla Homolka Information Site

http://www.cs.indiana.edu/canada/karla.html

This home page is devoted to disseminating information about convicted thrill killer Paul Bernardo (aka Paul Teale), whose trial was kept secret by Canadian authorities. Includes news clips from trial coverage and information pulled from the Usenet newsgroups alt.pub-ban.homolka and alt.fan.karla-homolka.

GONE BUT NOT FORGOTTEN

Note: In this section sites are alphabetized by author's last name where applicable.

The J.S. Bach Archive and Bibliography

http://www.let.rug.nl/Linguistics/diversen/bach/intro.html

This personal home page offers a look at classical composer Johann Sebastian Bach. Visit the archive and bibliography to learn about his life and work.

Tribute to Humphrey Bogart

http://www.macconsult.com/mikerose/bogart/bogart.html

Fans of the movie legend can test their Bogie trivia knowledge by playing "Name That Film!" and "Name That Quote!" A film-, bio- and bibliography are also featured, along with a gallery of non-film images.

Phil Carson's Raymond Carver Page

http://world.std.com/~ptc/

A fan of late American poet and short story author Raymond Carver presents a pertinent overview of this Guggenheim Fellow's works and related literary criticism here. "Vaguely interesting" photographs are included as is the Web author's graduate thesis.

Albert Einstein Online

http://www.sas.upenn.edu/~smfriedm/einstein.html

Relativity master Albert Einstein is celebrated and detailed here. Visit for various biographies, Einstein's own writings and pictures. The site also includes quintessential Einstein quotes, including "If I had my life to live over again, I'd be a plumber."

William Faulkner on the Web

http://www.mcsr.olemiss.edu/~egjbp/faulkner/faulkner.html

Literary fans of William Faulkner can explore the author's mythical and actual stomping grounds at this site. The site also includes a trivia page, notes, and synopses of the author's works and resource listings for students.

Jack Kerouac

http://www.charm.net/~brooklyn/People/JackKerouac.html

At this page from Literary Kicks, visitors will find a biography of author Jack Kerouac, as well as a bibliography of his work and publications about him. Links include sites featuring Kerouac's voice and a guide to character names.

The Martin Luther King, Jr., Directory King Martin Luther Jr.

http://www-leland.stanford.edu/group/King/

The Martin Luther King, Jr., Directory, from the project at Stanford University, contains documents written by and about the civil rights leader. Links to a biography, articles and reference sources and the King Center are included.

The Marilyn Pages

http://www.ionet.net:80/~jellenc/marilyn.html

Norma Jean Mortenson, better known as Marilyn Monroe, gets a tribute here from a fan who offers a weighty photo collection of the fallen star, along with biographical information and quotes. Includes a filmography of sights and sounds. See Editor's Choice.

---

a2z **EDITOR'S CHOICE**

The Marilyn Pages

http://www.ionet.net/~jellenc/marilyn.html

A stylish multimedia shrine to the former Norma Jean Mortenson can be found at this compulsively well-organized site, sprinkled with scores of photos showing the many faces of Marilyn. A fairly comprehensive biography, dozens of images, memorabilia and an overview of the actress's film career are all within reach of your mouse, as are plenty of details for the Monroe-obsessed visitor. From the years covering "A Ticket to Tomahawk" to her final completed film, "The Misfits," it's all here in easily digestible bites. And what you don't find out in the Marilyn Pages is sure to be a click away at one of the dozens of other sites devoted to the breathy film star, all helpfully compiled by your Webmaster.—*Reviewed by Julene Snyder*

Marilyn

Marilyn Monroe Home Page

http://www.ionet.net/~jellenc/marilyn.html

This multimedia Marilyn page features a biography of the iconic actress, along with information about the films she starred in and scores of photos. Links to memorabilia information, and other fan pages are available.

Wolfgang Amadeus Mozart

http://classicalmus.com/composers/mozart.html

Is Wolfgang Amadeus Mozart the most popular classical composer? If so, this online bio goes a long way to explain why. Part of the Classics World site, this page recommends recordings that present Mozart's music to best effect.

Brittanica Sampler on Edvard Munch

http://www.eb.com/~jdimm/munch.html

For some more information on the artist that created the famous painting "The Cry," head over to the Brittanica Sampler on Edvard Munch for a list of his works and biographical information.

Friedrich Wilhelm Nietzsche

http://www.usc.edu/dept/annenberg/thomas/nietzsche.html

The Annenberg School of Communications at the University of Southern California maintains this page dedicated to the German philosopher Friedrich Wilhelm Nietzsche. Features include a biography and works bibliography in German and English, links to Nietzsche societies and organizations, and access to selected writings.

Will Rogers

http://www.ionet.net/~jellenc/rogers.html

Find out about Will Rogers, the "Indian Cowboy" from the Cherokee Nation. Visitors can read about the man as performer, journalist, philosopher and ambassador, or link to a couple of related sites.

The Alan Turing Home Page

http://www.wadham.ox.ac.uk/~ahodges/Turing.html

Alan Turing, one of the first to propose the idea of a computer, led an interesting life. Arrested for homosexuality in the 1950s, he was barred from entering the U.S. during the Cold War, and eventually committed suicide—leaving behind a revolutionary body of work. Want more? Visit here for additional tons on Turing.

Mark Twain Resources on the World Wide Web

http://web.syr.edu/~fjzwick/twainwww.html

Mark Twain fans will enjoy this site, with information about the author and his work. Maintained by Jim Zwick of Syracuse University, the site offers full text as well as interpretations and adaptations of his stories.

Daniel Webster: Dartmouth's Favorite Son

http://grafton.dartmouth.edu:8005/~dw/

Daniel Webster, American politician and orator, graduated from Dartmouth College in 1801. As one of the school's more illustrious students, Webster gets his tribute from Dartmouth here, including biographical information and a selection of images and speeches.

THE KING

Elvis in Latin: Frequently Asked Questions

http://www.cs.uoregon.edu/~bhelm/misc/elvis.html

For those who thought Elvis Presley and Latin were both dead, think again. Here browsers will find details of Presley recordings rendered in Latin, as well as ordering information.

The Elvis Shrine

http://www.mit.edu:8001/activities/41West/Elvis.html

"The King Lives!" announces the youthful proprietor of The Elvis Shrine, who has adorned his personal space with an enormous image of Elvis memorabilia. Worshippers who enter the shrine can find a list of similarities between Elvis and J. Christ (Jesus is the Lord's shepherd; Elvis dated Cybill Shepherd) and the results of a monosyllabic seance chat with the King.

---

a2z **EDITOR'S CHOICE**

Elvis: Virtual Voyager

http://www1.chron.com/voyager/elvis/

Visitors here are greeted with a familiar voice drawling, "I can't believe they done this all for me. I'm just a poor old boy from Mississippi." And that's just the beginning of this merry romp through all things Elvisian. Gaze at the velvet gallery, a cyber-vision to behold, stuffed as it is with frightening images of the King, ranging from his lean-jawed younger days to the more paunchy latter ones. The tale of the Webmaster's search for Elvis finds the former staying in hellish dorm rooms, wandering around humid backstreets and admiring a legion of Elvis impersonators, in segments designed for the short-attention-span viewer. From Tupelo to Memphis to Graceland itself, this intrepid voyager looks for Elvis in all the right places—in the end, it's a journey worth taking, if only for the moment where a preacher's vision of Elvis is detailed: "He asked Elvis the question: 'Elvis, can you stay with me a while?' The King spoke. 'Howard,' he said, 'I'm on a tight schedule.'!"—*Reviewed by Julene Snyder*

This impressionistic Elvis, upper left, was purchased at an auction in June benefitting DiverseWorks in Houston. The paunchy, singing Elvis, lower right, came out of the shops of Ciudad Juarez, Mexico.

Elvis: Virtual Voyager

http://www1.chron.com/voyager/elvis/

Browsers can join a virtual search for The King here. While in the neighborhood, why not take an Elvis trivia quiz, download Elvis sounds and software or wander through a gallery of velvet? See Editor's Choice.

Unofficial Elvis Pages

http://sunsite.unc.edu/elvis/elvishom.html

You ain't nothin' but a hound dog if you're an Elvis fan and don't check out this Web site, dedicated to the American rock 'n' roll icon. Photos, historical information, and other wacky stuff related to the King can be found here, including a Graceland tour, souvenir information, a comic strip and a copy of Presley's last will and testament.

FOOD AND COOKING

ARCHIVES AND INDICES

The Dinner Co-op

http://dinnercoop.cs.cmu.edu/dinnercoop/home-page.html

This a group of Pittsburgh food lovers meets regularly to cook for each other. Visit the group's home page to access general information and a Frequently Asked Questions (FAQ) file, plus an archive of resources for fellow gourmands.

The Internet Epicurean

http://www.epicurean.com

The Internet Epicurean covers the culinary universe from soup to nuts. The site offers menus, recipes, magazines, links to restaurant sites, and an epicurean exchange for articles and cooking tips.

Medieval/Renaissance Food Home Page

http://www.pbm.com/~lindahl/food.html

This time-worn page provides information on recipes, techniques and food bibliographies from the Middle Ages and Renaissance periods. Includes articles, descriptions of cooking techniques and Frequently Asked Questions (FAQ).

Mimi's Cyber Kitchen

http://www.cyber-kitchen.com/

"Lauded as the best and largest food site of its kind on the World Wide Web," Mimi's Cyber Kitchen attempts to point out all the food fun there is to be had in cyberspace. Find recipes, cooking tips, humor, newsgroups, dining guides, even mail order sites.

The Solar Cooking Archive

http://www.accessone.com/~sbcn/index.htm

The Solar Cooking Archive features links to a host of information about harnessing the sun's energy to cook everything from bread to steak. Site highlights include construction plans for cookers, a gallery of cooker images and breaking news from the solar cooking grapevine.

ASSOCIATIONS AND ORGANIZATIONS

The National Pork Producers Council

http://www.nppc.org/

Pig out on information about the pork industry through this official page of the National Pork Producers Council. Visitors can stop by for cooking ideas or details about the status of the pork industry.

BEVERAGES

ALCOHOLIC

American Wine on the Web

http://www.2way.com:80/food/wine/

Find vintner profiles, tasting tips, wine country reports and results of wine competitions in "American Wine," an electronic magazine exploring wine making in the Americas—from Canada to Chile. The current issue and archive of past issues are featured.

Association of Brewers

http://www.aob.org/aob

The Association of Brewers' page overflows with comprehensive beer info. Visitors will find home brewing reports, details on events around the world, publications, and a glossary of beer and brewery terms.

The Atlanta Beer Guide

http://www.beerinfo.com/beerinfo/atlbeer/index.html

There's no need to drive the streets of Atlanta, Ga., in search of the best beer when users can check the Atlanta Beer Guide home page. It describes recently opened microbreweries, pubs and hangouts that serious beer connoisseurs won't want to miss.

Avalanche Brewing Company

http://www.dnai.com/~tmurphy/BREW/Welcome.html

Avalanche Brewing Company features information about its beers and ales, as well as pointers to its CU-SeeMe Keg Tapper Net Brewcasts. The San Francisco-based, two-man brewing team also offers visitors a listen to its theme song.

Bath University Student Union Wine Society

http://www.bath.ac.uk/~su3ws/home.html

Students at the United Kingdom's Bath University maintain this page with information about their society's wine tasting events, the Vintage Club and their tastings archive. Also find a handful of links to other topical sites.

Beer & Wine Hobby

http://www.beer-wine.com

Those of you interested in spirits—the drinkable kind—may want to check out the Beer & Wine Hobby page. These folks are professional consultants and suppliers, and can help with your brewing process.

Beer in Cyberspace

http://s-kanslia-3.hut.fi/

The Finnish League of Independent Beer Societies maintains this site for beer lovers and brewers. Visitors will find links to trivia files, home brewing tips, brewing companies, and virtual and real pubs around the world. In Finnish and English.

The Beer Info Source

http://www.beerinfo.com/~jlock/

Beer aficionados and home brew hobbyists can get a taste of beer information on the Net through the Beer Info Source. Find a collection of pointers to top resources and documents, as well as a searchable index.

Beer Master's Tasting Society

http://beermasters.com/BeerMasters/

The Beer Master's Tasting Society is an organization devoted to the art of brewing beer. Visitors to this home page will find membership information, special merchandise and a bimonthly newsletter.

Beer Periodicals List

http://www.beerinfo.com/beerinfo/beermags/index.html

If you're looking for information about home brewing or reviews of more mainstream brews, check the Beer Periodicals List. It features pointers to zines and club newsletters.

BeNeLux Beerguide

http://www.dma.be/p/bier/beer.htm

The BeNeLux Beerguide features hundreds of links to information about beer and breweries in

Belgium, the Netherlands and Luxembourg. Visitors can stop by to view a calendar of beer festivals, read recent reports about Benelux beers or follow links to other beer pages on the Net.

The Brewery

http://alpha.rollanet.org/

The Brewery is an extensive site that will delight home beer brewers. Includes online resources, beer recipes, links to other brewers and home brewer resources.

Brew on Premise Speak Easy

http://www.neosoft.com/internet/paml/ groups.B/brew_on_premise.html

Join the current discussion exploring the various aspects of "brew on premises" commercial breweries (U-Brews or BOP-Shops) where the customers are allowed to brew the beer. Subscribe to the mailing list, or link to related pages.

The Campaign for Real Ale

http://www.camra.org.uk/

A United Kingdom-based consumer group dedicated to true brew explains its mission and its tactics here. This champion of small brewers and public houses offers festival listings and a beer-drinker's glossary, along with membership information and branch contacts.

Cats Meow 3: The Internet Beer Recipe Database

http://alpha.rollanet.org/cm3/CatsMeow3.html

Home brewers will find an extensive database of beer recipes on tap here, offering beverages ranging from ale and cider to mead, porter and stout. The site also includes tasting notes, advice for beginners and a search tool.

Celebrator Beer News

http://celebrator.com/celebrator/

Contained at this site are the archives of the "Celebrator Beer News," a bimonthly magazine covering "brew news, views, rumors, and innuendo." A keyword search for articles and hard copy subscription information are provided.

Dan's Beer Page

http://www.eff.org/~brown/beer.html

A San Francisco Bay Area beer enthusiast and a member of BURP (Brewers United for Real Potables), Dan seems a reliable guide to beer pages in cyberspace. Find pointers to pub home pages, tours, archives, FAQs and related mailing lists.

Eric's Beer and Homebrewing Page

http://pekkel.uthscsa.edu/beer.html

Find news on brews and brewing at this site dedicated to amateur beer brewers. Beer recipes and reviews, a label archive, a list of tastings and competitions and links to beer-related sites are featured.

Fuji Publishing Group Wine Page

http://www.netins.net/showcase/fujiwine

Chicago's Fuji Publishing Group offers this collection of Web links to wine resources. Visitors will find pointers to wine shops, newsletters, tasting events, auctions, software, and more.

Golden Prairie Brewing Company

http://www.mcs.com/~nr706/gp.html

This Chicago brewery describes itself as "one company that really puts the micro in microbrewery." On its home page, visitors can drink it all in, from the brewery's humble beginnings to its current beer-friendly distribution locations. A mini-tour of the brewery is also featured.

Guide to Guinness

http://wombatix.physics.ucg.ie/misc/ guinness.html

Visit this page for answers to Frequently Asked Questions about the Irish brew, Guinness. Also find pub guides for different cities, an archive of ads and postcards, a giftware catalog and an image of the "perfect pint."

Guinness Brewing

http://www.guinness.ie/

The official Guinness Web site contains information about the brewing company, its products and some analysis of the competition. Includes links to a company store, product descriptions and ordering information.

Heineken Home Page

http://www.heineken.nl/

While this site may not taste as good as a frosty brew, Heineken's home page can still tell you how the Dutch beer company originated, why its libations are so popular and where to find good places for good times. Includes an interactive game and info on Heineken-sponsored events.

Houston: Locations Serving Fine Beer

http://arganet.tenagra.com/Beer/Beer.html

Access this geographical list of links to find bars and restaurants in Houston, Texas, that "will serve you a good beer." Reviews and info about microbreweries and brewpubs are on tap, with new sites and reviews being added all the time.

The Interactive Gourmet: Wine

http://www.cuisine.com

Wine lovers can visit the Interactive Gourmet for resources on wine, as well as food services. Do some online shopping or check out restaurants, menus, recipes, reviews and links to wines online.

Jane Brook Estate Wines

http://www.highway1.com.au/business/ janebrook/

Maintained by the Australian winemaker, this commercial site provides background on the es-

tate and descriptions of Jane Brook's wines. You won't need a corkscrew to take part in the virtual wine tasting; it's composed of comments on various vintages.

Kirin Art Tank and Tankard

http://www.toppan.com/kirin

This "art tank" from Kirin is devoted to informing visitors about the Japanese beer manufacturer and its award-winning brew. In Japanese.

London Pubs

http://www.cs.ucl.ac.uk/misc/uk/london/pubs/ index.html

Visitors to this site can almost smell the ale. London pubs are listed by area with information such as addresses, featured beers and special attractions. Most pubs are graded on a 1-4 scale.

The Mead Maker's Page

http://www.atd.ucar.edu/homes/cook/mead/ mead.html

"If it's good for ancient Druids ... it's good enough for me," say the folks behind the Mead Maker's Page. Visit to download recipes for making the ancient drink made with honey, fruit and yeast.

Molson Online

http://www.molson.com/

Molson Breweries, a Canadian beer company, maintains this site for its Brewmaster's Circle. Visit here to learn about the beer-making process, connect with local breweries, view tips for responsible alcohol consumption and more.

Napa Valley Virtual Visit

http://www.freerun.com/cgi-bin/home.o

FreeRun Technologies Inc. sponsors this home page devoted to California's Napa Valley. Visitors can take a virtual tour of vineyards, learn about wine, shop and more.

Napa Valley Wineries

http://www.freerun.com/napavalley/ mwinerie.html

From the Napa Valley Virtual Visit site, this page offers browsers a look at the wineries in Napa Valley. Access info via a clickable map or select wineries by name, location, or a variety of other criteria.

OIR Wine-Tasting Bash World Wine Web

http://cfa160.harvard.edu/winepage/wp.html

This is the home page of the Optical and Infrared (OIR) Astronomy Wine Tasting Bash, a "somewhat-weekly, informal gathering of students, faculty and staff for the tasting of several wines." Visitors will find a wine database in addition to details on the next tasting.

The Real Beer Page

http://realbeer.com/

Beer fans and brewmasters will find fun on tap at this site. Visitors can take virtual tours of micro-breweries, link to topical zines, check out a calendar of beer-related events and more.

rec.food.drink.beer FAQ

http://www.beerinfo.com/beerinfo/rfdb/index.html

Beer drinkers and brewers will find a Frequently Asked Questions (FAQ) file for the newsgroup rec.food.drink.beer here. The page also provides a link to the newsgroup.

Redhook Ale Brewery Home Page

http://www.redhook.com/

Take a virtual tour of the Redhook Ale Brewery in Seattle, Wash. While there, "Meet the Beers," read "The Redhook Story" and find other cold and frothy features.

The Schläger Zone

http://www.schlager.com/

Goldschläger, a cinnamon schnapps imported from Switzerland, is a "21 only" page, daring adults: "Be afraid. Be very afraid." But for all its hype, the information here offers a peek at the "Schläger Zine," a worldwide party guide and accessories catalog. Ordering information is included.

Scotch.com

http://scotch.com/

Of-age Net users who appreciate the smoky taste and subtle nuances of a well-blended knock of scotch should take Scotch.com straight up. Visit here for the straight dope on scotch whiskies, how they're made and enjoyed.

Shiner Bock RamPage

http://www.shiner.com/

Spoetzl Brewery promotes its Shiner Bock brand offering a history of the Texas-based brewery, access to the Spoetzl museum and gift shop, and an introduction to the brewery's beers. Visitors can also use an interactive map to check the availability of Shiner Bock in their state.

Some Delightful Drinks to Rinse Your Throat

http://www.fsz.bme.hu/hungary/cuisine/beverages.html

A Webmaster at the Technical University of Budapest, Hungary, maintains this site for information about Hungarian wines and spirits. Visit here to learn about Unicum, a potent liqueur, and other drinks. Links to a variety of other national and cultural information are also available here.

Spencer's Beer Page

http://realbeer.com/spencer/

Spencer's Beer Page is designed for the beer lover, particularly the home brewer. Includes tips from master brewers, recipe files, an abundant supply of reference material, and links to other beer-related pages.

Stoli Central

http://www.stoli.com/

Stoli Central is the home page for the venerable Russian vodka, Stolichnaya. The site is described as "a place where the individual freedoms of adventure, expression and vodka always hold true." Visitors will find results from a vodka taste test.

The Tequila Home Page

http://www.io.com/~elvis/

Do you know the difference between tequila and mezcal? If you don't (or if you want to check your answer), sidle on over to the Tequila Home Page for the briny liquor's history and production methods. While you're there, sample the recipes and the links to other tequila sites.

UK Homebrew Home Page

http://sun1.bham.ac.uk/GraftonG/homebrew.htm

The UK Homebrew Home Page is an online discussion group for lovers of British beer. Discussion resources include technical documents on beer brewing, cider pages, recipes and links to beer sites around the globe.

Winecountry Virtual Visit

http://www.freerun.com/

Love that vino? Then take a virtual tour of California's wine country. Saunter through Livermore Valley, Sonoma County, Napa Valley, Monterey and Temecula vineyards. There are also jokes, recipes and hangover cures.

Wine Lovers' OnLine Searchable Database

http://www.wines.com/magical/search.html

Wine aficionados can prep for wine tastings on this full-bodied, searchable site. Find complete articles on topics like "taste scoring systems and hundreds of other wine terms from abboccato to zymotechnology!"

Wine Net News

http://http.cs.berkeley.edu/~sethg/Wine/wine.html

Visit this site to access the "Wine Net News" newsletter archive. Wine reviews, notices of wine events and links to topical sites are also featured.

The Wine Page

http://www.speakeasy.org/~winepage/wine.html

The Wine Page will have oenologists running for their corkscrews. Check out the list of Frequently Asked Questions (FAQ), the tasting archive, a Washington wine tour, and light-hearted features like "Rate Robert Parker" and "Guess the Wine."

Wines On-Line

http://www.wine.com/wine/index.html

"Connecting the World Wine Web together," Wines On-Line points to what's new, rare, "hot" and up for auction. Also find forums, online search resources and shopping opportunities.

Wines on the Internet

http://www.wines.com/

Lovers of the grape will find a "cyberspace guide to wine and wineries" at Wines on the Internet. Explore "virtual wine country" or check out the "tasting room." Those seeking "unique or exceptional values" can even order selections online.

The World-Wide Web Virtual Library: Beer & Brewing

http://www.beerinfo.com/~jlock/wwwbeer.html

Beer aficionados and brewing fanatics can find a slew of tips and tricks via this robust index. From online pubs and beer stores to homebrew competitions, there's sure to be something here to tickle the fancy of most every beer fancier.

Zima Beverage Company

http://www.zima.com/

Those who find themselves asking "Whatizit?" will find the answers they seek on this page devoted to the clear, alcoholic beverage, Zima. Visitors can also check out "z spots" on the Web and join "tribe z."

NON-ALCOHOLIC

Caffeinated Home Page

http://net-abuse.org/~lizardo/caffeine.html

This page sporting the "Mr. Coffee" logo (but no indication that it's official) concerns itself with all things caffeinated. Picture collections, textual musings on the drug, and pointers to "caffeinated stuff" complement a caffeine chemical data sheet.

Coca-Cola Co.

http://www.cocacola.com/

Thirsty for information on Coca-Cola? The Atlanta-based soft drink company's corporate site offers slick advertisements, product information and Coca-Cola lore.

The Cooler Site
http://205.217.2.106/

Offering "cool, refreshing stuff for your consumption," this official Gatorade site details the company's current sales promotions, offers online shopping of branded merchandise and features information about the "Thirst Quencher." Also find a section hosted by Gatorade spokesperson, Michael Jordan.

Harvard Espresso Company's Home Page
http://www.coffees.com/

Even though Harvard students may need a good shot of caffeine now and then, this coffee company has nothing to do with the Boston university. What this Seattle-based company offers is a specialty line of coffee for sale over the Net, as well as information on brewing and drinking the perfect cup.

MotherCity Virtual Magazine
http://www.halcyon.com/zipgun/mothercity/mothercity.html

Seattle java junkies who like their coffee "black as hell, strong as death, sweet as love" can locate the finest coffeehouses and bean roasters in the area via this Web site. Includes short reviews of coffee pushers, plus a dictionary of coffee terminology.

The Organic Coffee Company
http://www.bid.com/bid/cybercafe/occ.html

The Organic Coffee Company home page provides information on the naturally grown products offered by the company. Includes descriptions of the various coffees and blends, as well as other merchandise for sale.

Over The Coffee
http://www.cappuccino.com/

The Over the Coffee site is dedicated to coffee enthusiasts and contains general information about the stimulating bean. Includes a reference desk, business section and related resource links.

Perrier: The Art of Refreshment
http://www.perrier.com/

Perrier, the French mineral water bottler, supports this site offering an art gallery, restaurant guides for the United States and a catalog of specialty items sporting the company logo. A corporate overview and product descriptions are also provided.

The SnappleSphere
http://www.snapple.com/

Explore the world of Snapple and learn about the beverage which prides itself on being number three in the industry. In addition to enjoying a drink history, guests who enter the SnappleSphere are also invited to share Snapple anecdotes, play Snapple games and win prizes.

A World of Tea
http://www.teleport.com/~tea/

What would the world do without tea? The creators of the World of Tea page can't imagine. If you can't either, stop by for tea news, history and recipes. Visitors can also place orders with the Stash Tea Company.

CHEFS ONLINE

Star Chefs & Cookbook Authors
http://www.starchefs.com/

Dishing up some of the recipes favored by the chefs it profiles, this cooking resource offers insight into preparing delicious meals like the greats. Also find info on culinary careers and an archive of previously featured chefs.

COMPANIES

Ben & Jerry's Ice Cream
http://www.benjerry.com/

From the Ben & Jerry's Homemade Inc. Web site, this page features a seasonal or topical promotion sponsored by the Vermont-based ice cream company. A site directory affords access to other Ben & Jerry's pages.

Dole 5 A Day Home Page
http://www.dole5aday.com/

The Dole 5 A Day home page reminds visitors to get five servings a day of fruits and vegetables. The "Fun with Fruits and Vegetables Kids Cook-

---

book" attempts to make the concept a little more appealing.

Hershey Foods Corporation

http://www.hersheys.com/~hershey/

Chocoholic alert! Where else could you find recipes to satisfy that craving but at Hershey Foods Corporation. Here, tour the factory and find out how nutritious chocolate is (we always knew it was). Don't forget to check out the new products.

Honeysuckle White

http://www.magibox.net/~hsw/

Cargill's North American Poultry Operation talks turkey here. The site not only offers instructions on how to cook Cargill's gobblers properly, but also provides new recipes and a roaster full of turkey trivia.

Ketchum Kitchen

http://www.recipe.com/

Ketchum Kitchen develops recipes, tests ingredients and tracks food trends for Ketchum Public Relations Worldwide. Visitors to its site can download recipes and cooking tips or post questions to its online food expert, Sandy.

Mama's Cucina

http://www.eat.com/

This saucy commercial Web site dishes out recipes, contests, stories, a tour of Little Italy, even Italian lessons, all the while plugging Van den Bergh Foods, Inc., makers of Ragu.

Michigan Marketing Association Earthy Delights Home Page

http://earthy.com/index.htm

The Michigan Marketing Association (MMA) Earthy Delights distributes specialty produce to restaurants, clubs, hotels and the "adventurous gourmet." Sample MMA's top-shelf products including hot chiles and Southwest cuisine, baby vegetables, edible flowers and purple sticky rice.

MooTown Snackers: The UdderNet

http://www.mootown.com/

Promoting its MooTown Snackers line, Sargento Foods, Inc. targets kids with this fun page featuring the Cow Chip Toss game and MooTown Hide and Seek. An online survey solicits marketing feedback.

Whole Foods Market

http://www.wholefoods.com/wf.html

This promotional site is the Web home of Whole Foods Market, Inc., a Texas-based national chain of 40 natural food supermarkets. Visitors can read about the company's quality standards, pick up some recipe tips, review the company's potential as an investment and find out how to contact its Distribution Centers.

COOKBOOKS

The USENET Cookbook

http://www.lysator.liu.se:7500/etexts/recept/main.html

The "pre-main menu" for this online cookbook offers the option to select either metric units or "the US-system" of measuring units. From there, culinary enthusiasts can go straight to the recipe archives and cook up a mean breeze.

FOOD a2z

Algy's Herb Page

http://www.algy.com/herb/herb.html

Cultivation, harvesting techniques and more are the subjects of this site. See Editor's Choice.

The Burrito Page

http://www.infobahn.com/pages/rito.html

The Burrito page is a comprehensive and humorous examination of everyone's favorite Mexican food. Visitors will find historical and cultural notes, burrito lore and an interactive personality profile that judges users according to the types of burritos they like to eat.

CheeseNet

http://www.wgx.com/cheesenet

See a cheese photospread, review cheese facts, and read cheese fiction (poetry, too!) all at the site dedicated to the proposition that the cheese does indeed stand alone. And if having visited this, "the Internet's cheese resource," browsers find their appetites whetted for more, links lead the way to other sites offering wild and cheesy delights!

The Chile-Heads Home Page

http://neptune.netimages.com/~chile/

The Chile-Heads page contains dozens of links and indexes to chile-related info (that's chile peppers, now—you know, the HOT! ones). Explore the Chile Gallery, rummage the archive, and for a really hot time, check out the eats!

Durian OnLine

http://www.ecst.csuchico.edu/~durian/

Care for a serving of a big thorny fruit that smells bad? Here's a platter full of delicious fun from one fan of durians, "the king of fruit" in Malaysia. Tongue-in-cheek info makes these tidbits easy to swallow.

---

a2z **EDITOR'S CHOICE**

Wild Mushrooms

http://www.ijs.si/slo/country/food/gobe/

Tramp the wild woods of Slovenia and learn about a pastime so popular with the locals "one could call it a national sport." But be warned: some mushrooms are deadly; pickers need to be very picky about what they ingest. And don't pull them up; cut them at the stem so the mycelium is preserved for future growth. That said, hosts Vladimir Alkalaj and Joh Dokler are ready to lead the party, pointing out "a few good mushrooms" and some of "the bad and the ugly" from among more than 400 types which grow in their country. Oggle color photographs and peruse descriptive text about all kinds of 'shrooms. For reference, the Dictionary of the Mushroom offers a diagram of the fleshy fungi, naming and defining its various parts. And of course, what mushroom outing would be complete without a nod toward eating. Featured recipes include sauteed mushrooms with sour cream and mushroom stuffed trout. Mmm-mushrooms!—*Reviewed by Sean McFadden*

Wild mushrooms

How to Find, Cook and Eat Them -- and Survive!

The Electric Cheese Page

http://www.emf.net/~mal/cheese.html

Blue, Swiss, cheddar ... find all the cheese anyone could ever want; this page is filled with places to go on the Web to find blocks of compressed milk curds. Just be thankful when you visit the Limburger page that the Internet isn't capable of reproducing smells.

The Real Cranberry Home Page

http://www.scs.carleton.ca/~palepu/cranberry.html

Maintained by agriculture and information technology consultants Cran Breton Enterprises, this site offers a variety of tips for growing and preparing cranberries. Visitors will find information on cranberry diseases, farming associations, recipes and related links.

Talking About Turkey

http://www.hoptechno.com/book15.htm

This fact-filled tipsheet will negate the need for dialing a turkey hotline (or the in-laws) come holiday time. Read about how to buy, store, thaw, stuff and cook a bird. Compiled from a United States Department of Agriculture bulletin.

Wild Mushrooms

http://www.ijs.si/gobe/

Visitors to this site can learn how to find, cook and eat wild mushrooms without experiencing any painful side effects. Created by mushroom enthusiasts in Slovenia, the site takes pickers on a hand-in-hand 'shrooming tutorial with safety tips. See Editor's Choice.

INSTITUTES AND SCHOOLS

The Expo Restaurant Le Cordon Bleu

http://sunsite.unc.edu/expo/restaurant/restaurant.html

Restaurant Le Cordon Bleu is an online exhibition of L'Art Culinaire—the art of cooking as taught by the world-famous Parisian cooking school, Le Cordon Bleu. Visitors to this site will find a brief history of the establishment and menus for each day of the week.

University of Minnesota Department of Food Science & Nutrition

http://fscn1.fsci.umn.edu/

The University of Minnesota's Department of Food Science & Nutrition maintains this site to provide general information and an online photographic tour of its facilities. Visit here to find class materials, newsletters and more.

PUBLICATIONS AND INDUSTRY NEWS

Epicurious

http://www.epicurious.com/

Self-described as "the taste of the Web," Epicurious hosts this gateway to its two main divisions: Epicurious Food, "for people who eat," and Epicurious Travel. Enjoy!

Epicurious Food

http://www.epicurious.com/epicurious/home.html

Your Pavlovian responses may kick in when you look at Epicurious Food. Among other offerings, each day the online service features a menu composed of recipes from "Gourmet" and "Bon Appetit" magazines. A recent menu featured marinated vegetables and rigatoni with shrimp.

RECIPES

COLLECTIONS

CMU Students' Recipes Folder

http://english-server.hss.cmu.edu/Recipes.html

Favoring the vegetarian flavors, recipes at this Carnegie Mellon University English Server site feature garden variety dishes—beans, eggplant, berries and the like. For meat eaters, a sampling of recipes for "dead cow," "dead bunny," and "dead chicken" are sure to whet the appetite.

Fry Cooks on Venus Recipe Index

http://www.cs.ubc.ca/spider/edmonds/recipes/index.html

Part of a personal home page, this index of popular recipes offers complete instructions for making a variety of breakfast dishes, breads, desserts, sauces and more. Includes recipes for international dishes.

FTP Directory of Recipes

ftp://ftp.cs.ubc.ca/pub/local/RECIPES/

Find recipes for appetizers, entrees, side dishes and desserts at this culinary FTP site. Ethnic cooking, meats, breads, soups and vegetarian dishes are also featured.

Ridiculously Easy Recipes for Students and Other Incompetents

http://www.sar.usf.edu/~zazuetaa/recipe.html

The name of the site says it all. See Editor's Choice.

---

a2z **EDITOR'S CHOICE**

Ridiculously Easy Recipes for Students and Other Incompetents

http://www.sar.usf.edu/~zazuetaa/recipe.html

It's a small collection, admits Auntie Boo, but she guarantees all the recipes indexed at this site are "nearly impossible to mess up." Featured fare ranges from the convenient—for Melissa's Truckstop Frito Pie "you can pick up most, if not all, ingredients at the Texaco Superstore near you"—to more eccentric taste treats like Eggs and Shredded Wheat. (Believe it or not, "so far, no one who has tried it hates it.") Sociable snackers may want to try the Roasted Garlic Sandwiches, or if you're planning a more intimate meal, try Tony's Pork Picatta, which "looks almost as good as it sounds and goes well with a light salad and your favorite cheap wine." Web wanderers, spread the word. Kitchen cretins need no longer starve, nor die from ill-advised consumption. Yoo-hoo! It's Auntie Boo!—*Reviewed by Sean McFadden*

RIDICULOUSLY EASY RECIPES FOR STUDENTS AND OTHER INCOMPETENTS

DESSERTS AND CONFECTIONS

The Pie Page

http://www.teleport.com/~psyched/pie/pie.html

Pastry lovers will just eat up this site devoted to the art of pie baking. Take a step-by-step pie crust making tutorial or dig into yummy recipes for treats like good old-fashioned American apple pie and taffy apple cheesecake pie.

MEATS

Pit Cooking

http://www.cco.caltech.edu/~salmon/pit.html

Team Mumu teaches visitors "how to tell dinner from a hole in the ground." Find anecdotes and complete instructions for cooking a variety of meats in pits dug into the ground.

WORLD FOOD

Eleanor's Kitchen

http://www.columbia.edu/~js322/eleanor/eleanor.html

Eleanor teaches about Czech food. See Editor's Choice.

Manuela's Recipes

http://he1.uns.tju.edu/recipes/

Manuela, an Italian-American student at Ithaca College, presents a collection of mouth-watering Italian recipes from antipasti to dolci. Learn how to make risotto, spaghetti alla carbonara, tiramisu and more.

The Mole Page

http://www.slip.net/~bobnemo/mole.html

Get out the chiles, chocolate and pumpkin seeds for a mole-fest. If you don't know what mole is (pronounced MO-lay), read the description and history here. Then get your pots and pans out to try your hand at over 20 recipes for the Mexican national dish.

Rolling Your Own Sushi

http://www.rain.org/~hutch/sushi.html

Rolling Your Own Sushi, part of a personal home page, is a virtual cookbook for the Japanese seafood delicacy. Visit here for everything you need to know to make sushi like a professional chef. Includes special recipes and links to Japan- and sushi-related Web sites.

The Tamilian Cuisine

http://www.cba.uh.edu/~bala/tamilnadu/food.html

Learn about the delectable food creations that are part of Tamil cuisine. This page includes an introduction to Tamil foods, as well as complete recipes and cooking instructions.

Texas Foods Recipe Page

http://www.microserve.com/~duane/TexasFoods.html

Fans of Texas cooking can sample recipes for appetizers, main dishes, breads and desserts here. Includes links to the Chili! Page and a site containing Tex-Mex recipes.

RESTAURANTS

CITY DINING GUIDES

Atlanta Area Restaurant Guide

http://www.w3.com/atlanta/

Heading to the home of the 1996 Summer Olympic Games? Stop by this guide for pointers to the must-see and must-eat places in the city. Browse the reviews or build your own restaurant itinerary, and check out restaurant guides to several other cities.

---

a2z EDITOR'S CHOICE

Eleanor's Kitchen

http://www.columbia.edu/~js322/eleanor/eleanor.html

"Czech food isn't light but it is good," confides Eleanor Schrabel, a New York City native whose father was Czech and mother Slovak, and whose Web site is as comfortable (and spread with food) as her own kitchen table. Eleanor begins by talking casually about her life, telling of meeting her husband, the "canceled Czech" (an emigrant to the U.S. who escaped the rise of communism in central Europe), then moves into a discussion of Czecho-Slovak food. "Their original Slavik taste for souring foods with sour cream, lemon, vinegar or green grapes is greatly influenced by the schnitzel from Vienna, the goulash from Hungary and the sauerkraut from Germany." Then come the recipes, over a dozen, dishes so authentic their names require translation. Bohemian dumplings; plum dumplings; roasted pork, more dumplings and cabbage. "They love the dumplings, all sorts," says Eleanor, "and the pork is their favorite meat." You might need a pulley to get you up from the table after one of Eleanor's meals, but one of life's little pleasures is an occasional indulgence, no?—*Reviewed by Sean McFadden*

Kuchařské metamorfózy

Welcome to Eleanor's kitchen

* To introduce myself, irrelevantly to the present stateship, I am truly a Czechoslovak, or if you want, a Czecho-Slovak. I was born in 1931 on the east side of Manhattan, near the Gracie Mansion. My father was a Czech origin from Kolin, my mother a Slovak, origin from Mijava. My maiden name was Podhajsky, a name which nobody could pronounce, so I was called "Poboravsky" and all sorts of names. Marrying my husband with name such as Schrabal did not help since many people believed that we are Germans, because his name "Sch" was misspelled from correct czech "Sh" which is difficult to pronounce. I met him in 1952 at the Carnegie Hall after a concert celebrating October 28th, the Czech State holiday. He was with other canceled Czechs (pronounce as "check") who escaped after February 1948 when the communists took over the country.

* The Czech land is located in the center of Europe and under the influence of their neighbors. Their original Slavic taste for souring foods with sour cream, lemon, vinegar or green grapes is greatly influenced by the schnitzel from Vienna, the goulash from Hungary and sauerkraut from Germany.

* Czech food isn't light but it is a good food. They love the dumplings, all sorts, and the pork is their favored meat. From picturesque farms comes geese (much favored over a duck), chickens and trout from mountain streams. They harvest carp from ponds for Christmas eve meal. Many kinds of variety of delicious edible mushrooms come from virgin woods and meadows. They know and like cereal products such as noodles. Their superbly delicious rye breads are served with cold meats and cheeses.

* Their Sunday dinner starts with a soup with liver dumplings, main

The Boston Restaurant Guide

http://www.hubnet.com/

The Boston Restaurant Guide provides an informative look at the city's dining and drinking establishments. Visit here to search for information on a particular restaurant or bar, and read regularly updated articles and columns.

DC's Dining Web

http://dc.myhouse.com/

DC's Dining Web offers an online search tool for finding food and entertainment in the greater Washington, D.C., area. Visit here to find restaurants, bars, and other establishments by neighborhood, cuisine type and special services.

DineSite U.S.A.

http://www.dinesite.com/

DineSite provides links to thousands of U.S. restaurant descriptions and reviews organized by state or city. Users can also check out celebrity restaurants and MenuNet's picks for the best restaurants.

Houston Restaurant Interactive Database

http://pgsa.rice.edu/restdb.html

Fed by the public which has been fed at the restaurants featured, this searchable database offers reviewed listings of Houston, Texas, eateries. A variety of search options allow users to pinpoint suitable restaurant choices quickly and easily.

New Jersey Smokefree Dining

http://www.boutell.com/infact/gasp/gasp.html

New Jersey's Group Against Smoking Pollution (GASP) maintains this directory of smoke-free restaurants in the state. A geographic index provides quick reference. General information about GASP is also featured.

RESTAURANTS a2z

The Gumbo Shop

http://www.accesscom.net/gumbo

If piquant Creole cuisine is your passion, stop by this home page for New Orleans' Gumbo Shop restaurant. Browse the menu and wine list, or enjoy recipes and an outline of the colorful history of New Orleans food. In English, Japanese, Spanish and French.

SWEETS

The Chocolate Lovers' Page

http://bc.emanon.net/chocolate/

The Chocolate Lovers' Page presents a comprehensive list of shops and companies that sell chocolate on the Internet, as well as links to recipes and other chocolate goodies.

I Need My Chocolate!

http://www.qrc.com/~sholubek/choco/start.htm

Devoted to chocolate lovers around the globe, this site includes pointers to recipes, chocolate manufacturers, online catalogs and even chocolate clubs.

The Unofficial Marshmallow Peeps Page

http://www.wam.umd.edu/~ejack/peep.html

The Easter chick marshmallow treat inspired this site. See Editor's Choice.

VEGETARIAN RESOURCES

Toronto Vegetarian Association

http://www.interlog.com/~tva/home.html

The Toronto Vegetarian Association's site includes a definition of vegetarianism, the group's newsletter and membership info. Links to other vegetarian sites are also featured.

---

a2z EDITOR'S CHOICE

The Unofficial Marshmallow Peeps Page

http://www.wam.umd.edu/~ejack/peep.html

Webmaster Jack John Boutros Boutros Ulaf Ute Edward Elvis Telemachus Thomas Eidsness worships the "painfully sweet" chick-shaped Easter confection known as Peeps and insists that everyone, everywhere should be equally devoted to the sugar-coated marshmallow poultry. To that end, he posts a Peeporama and preaches the virtues of "Peepness." Enjoy Peep history quoted from "The Book of Peep," fascinating Peep facts, unforgettable Peep pictures and an especially poignant Peep tale, "An Easter Memory" by Truman Capote. Bizarre sounds add a multimedia aspect to the site, while suggestions of fun things to do with the spongy chicks inspire creativity. Perhaps visitors won't come away converted to the pleasures of popping Peeps into their mouths, but they will see that the possibilities for Peep play are virtually limitless.—*Reviewed by Sean McFadden*

The MARSHMALLOW **Peeps** page

TOP 5% OF ALL WEB SITES POINT

Cool sound bites

What's New

Fun Peep Facts

Peep!

Peep graphics collection

Cool things to do with Peeps

Peep History

Vegetarianism: A Means to a Higher End

http://www.webcom.com/~ara/col/books/VEG/hkvc1.html

For sale from the Bhaktivedanta Book Trust, this "practical cookbook" assists seekers in preparing authentic Indian meals. Learn both the techniques of Vedic and classical Indian vegetarian cooking, and "the Vedic art of eating, which nourishes both the soul and the body and mind."

The Vegetarian Pages

http://www.veg.org./veg

This meatless site dishes up a worldwide guide to vegetarian resources on the Net. Check out everything veggie-related here, from restaurants and stores to organizations and services.

Vegetarian Resource Group

http://envirolink.org/arrs/VRG/home.html

Vegetarianism and animal rights are the focus of the Vegetarian Resource Group home page. Resources include journals, nutrition information, recipes, travel guides and links.

World Guide to Vegetarianism

http://catless.ncl.ac.uk/veg/Guide/

A special link found on the Vegetarian Pages, "this is a hypertext list of restaurants, organizations and other interesting information around the world, separated into regions and sub-regions."

GAMES

ARCADE GAMES

The Foosball Source

http://www.foosball.com/

Everything about foosball is explored on this home page. Visitors can score links to Frequently Asked Questions (FAQ) files, foosball images and cartoons, and a complete schedule of tournaments. Information on the world's top players can be found in the player gallery.

The Pinball Pasture

http://www.lysator.liu.se/pinball/

The Pinball Pasture is devoted to information about pinball machines. Visitors can find game reviews, articles about classic machines, and information on buying and selling pinball machines.

ARCHIVES AND INDICES

Games Kids Play

http://www.corpcomm.net/~gnieboer/gamehome.htm

A great site to refresh your memory about yard games. See Editor's Choice.

Games on the Internet

http://happypuppy.com/games/lordsoth/index.html

Pointing to freeware, shareware, and demos, this site covers over 1,200 games on the Internet and the number continues to grow. In addition to the games, find cheats, hints, walkthroughs, FAQs, offset lists, and other useful resources.

idGames FTP

ftp://ftp.cdrom.com/pub/idgames/

Are you looking for a place to download the latest version of Doom, Doom2, Heretic or Hexen? Look no further. This FTP archive from Walnut Creek CD-ROM offers the latest software and documentation for your downloading pleasure.

Interactive Web Games List

http://einstein.et.tudelft.nl/~mvdlaan/texts/www_games.html

Link to the classics like Hangman, Battleship, Tic Tac Toe, and Blackjack, or try something new like Find-the-Spam. Featured games also include a variety of sliding puzzles and a relatively new offering called WebMind.

SpinnWebe

http://www.thoughtport.com/spinnwebe/

SpinnWebe offers realtime interactive games on the Web. Visitors can play several games, enter contests, and read humorous stories.

---

a2z EDITOR'S CHOICE

Games Kids Play

http://www.corpcomm.net/~gnieboer/gamehome.htm

Red rover, red rover, send Web surfers over! Mother may I? Yes, you may. You may also enjoy this growing, reader-contributed collection of rules for yard games played by children. Find Tag, Kick the Can, Duck Duck Goose, Dodgeball, Steal the Bacon, Red Light/Green Light, Marbles—even Jump Rope Rhymes. Because most games are passed verbally from older children to younger ones, Webmaster Geof Nieboer sees this archive as an attempt "to catalog a fascinating piece of oral tradition, and make sure none of these games are ever lost." To that end, all are invited to submit knowledge, game rules, and variations for the collective enjoyment of yesterday's, today's, and tomorrow's children. Simon says, "Go play."—*Reviewed by Sean McFadden*

Games Kids Play

Remember all those games you played as kid out in the backyard? Where did the those rules come from?

Obviously there was no "official" rule book, just knowledge passed down from older kids to younger kids.

The purpose of this page is two-fold;

- One, to let you remember some of those odd games we used to play and bring a smile to your face.

- Two, to try to catalog a fascinating piece of oral tradition, and make sure none of these games are ever lost forever.

I am, however, going to need your help. There are hundreds of these games, and no one person has played them all. Plus there are undoubtedly hundreds more variations depending on where you

ThreadTreader's World Wide Web Contests Guide

http://www.4cyte.com/ThreadTreader/

Players who like to win real prizes will find opportunities galore posted to this listing of contests, drawings, raffles, sweepstakes, and other promotions on the Web. Listings are arranged alphabetically, by contest theme, and prize type. Also find Contest Chat, with tips, advice, and more.

The 3D Gaming Scene

http://www.3dgaming.se/index.html

Visitors to this site will find a comprehensive list of 3-D games on the Web. Game descriptions and useful pointers are provided for each entry.

World Charts

http://www.xs4all.nl/~jojo/

This site contains information on popular games for personal computers. Includes charts on commercial and Internet games, new games listings, previous editions of the chart, and links to other topical pages.

WorldVillage

http://www.worldvillage.com/

WorldVillage is an Internet stop for software reviews, articles, downloads, contests, chat, and computer games. Check out the Bald Guy's Multimedia Site of the Week.

BOARD GAMES

Chess Pages

http://www.ub.uit.no/chess/

Chess players visiting this site can download games in text and pgn formats. An index of chess-related sites on the Net is also featured.

Chess Space

http://www.redweb.com/chess/

Chess Space features many excellent Internet resources for chess players. Visitors will find an extensive list to choose from including famous games, strategy guides, and newsgroups.

Chinook

http://web.cs.ualberta.ca/~chinook/

Web denizens can challenge a computer to a game of checkers at this site. Includes links to the International Checker Hall of Fame, the American Checker Federation, and Chinook's endgame database.

Go: An Addictive Game

http://www.cwi.nl/~jansteen/go/go.html

Detailed on this page are the goals and strategy behind the ancient Chinese game called Go. Also find the complete rules, a history of the game, topical resources on the Web, and information about computer versions of the game.

Internet Chess Library

http://caissa.onenet.net/chess/

The Internet Chess Library contains a diverse collection of memorabilia for chess players. Site features include a large archive, game databases, rating information, and an art gallery.

Kasparov vs. Deep Blue

http://chess.ibm.park.org/

It's world chess champ Garry Kasparov versus IBM's Deep Blue—the most powerful chess-playing computer on the planet. Kasparov usually wins...but not always. Get all the details here, and replay past games from each match.

Monopoly

http://www.monopoly.com/

"A nice, ruthless, money-hungry Web site," Monopoly offers online excitement in the world of play money finance and plastic property management. Visit often to compete "ruthlessly and globally...against worthy adversaries" and to access insider information.

Steve's Chess Page

http://www.chemeng.ed.ac.uk/people/steve/chess.html

This Web site serves as a compendium of chess-related information. Links to player rankings, reprints of articles, and other online chess resources await those who visit this space.

Sprig's Collectible Card Game Warehouse

http://www.itis.com/other-games/

Created to "provide information about as many Collectible Card Games as possible," the Sprig's Warehouse archives details on over 50 released card games and close to 20 announced games in more than a dozen gaming categories—from anime, children and fantasy to horror, martial combat, and science fiction. In addition, the page points to newsgroups, FTP, and Web sites, over a half dozen magazines online, gaming company home pages, and software resources. Of special interest is Sprig's online Player Registry. Players are grouped by their interest in specific game titles, and entries include names as well as e-mail addresses. A free resource for anyone who wishes to stop by, Sprig's helps to "keep things fresh and exciting" when it comes to the collectible card game craze.—*Reviewed by Sean McFadden*

Sprig's Collectible Card Games Warehouse

This page is dedicated to the collectible trading card game hobby/industry. If you have any information about any such games you'd like to see here, please send email to *whitkenbits.com*

Disclaimer: Sprig's CCG Warehouse is not a game store - we do not have cards for sale, so please don't write asking for our prices.

The **CCG Warehouse** has a lot of new features planned - if you have any ideas you'd like to see, let us know!

Main Menu

Welcome/Mission	Games (alphabetical)	News Bytes
What's New	Games (by category)	News Bytes (by game)
Icon Index	Dice Games	CCG Software
Help Needed	Game Companies	Online Resources
Reader Survey	Artist Lists	Magazines
Free Speech Online		

CARD GAMES

The Blackjack Server of Universal Access Inc.

http:///blackjack.ua.com

Hey, high-roller! Care to play cards for play money? The house will stake all comers to an initial bankroll, but only the skilled will be able to hang on to what they've got and build their pile.

Illuminati: New World Order

http://www.io.com/sjgames/inwo/

Visit this page for information on INWO, the trading card version of the game Illuminati. Features include rules, card lists, announcements, tactics, and dealer information, plus links to newsgroups, mailing lists, and an FTP site. Also find the Illuminati News Flash and archive.

Magic: The Gathering

http://www.itis.com/deckmaster/magic/

Devoted to Wizards of the Coast's Magic: The Gathering collectible trading card games, this site offers general information for rookie players, plus in-depth information for gaming veterans. Includes a glossary, information about specific cards, and Frequently Asked Questions (FAQ) files containing game rules and clarifications.

Sprig's Collectible Card Game Warehouse

http://www.itis.com/other-games/

This site provides info about Collectible Card Games. See Editor's Choice.

CLUBS AND ORGANIZATIONS

The Internet Modem Players Listing

http://www.xmission.com/~morrison/IMPL/home.html

The Internet Modem Players Listing lets game players who play over a modem find other local players. The page lists game players by area code, so players within local calling rates can find each other to play without long distance charges.

COMPANIES

The Atomic Diner

http://atomic.com/

Texas-based Atomic Games, Inc. employs this corporate home page to promote its menu of action computer games, including V for Victory, World at War, and Close Combat. Access the

company's listserver to join mailing lists and check out the FTP archive for game patches and shareware utilities.

Chaosium, Inc.

http://www.sirius.com/~chaosium/chaosium.html

Chaosium, Inc. provides a line of fantasy role-playing games, books, and accessories. This promotional site offers detailed information on products, services, and ordering.

Electronic Arts Online

http://www.ea.com/

Electronic Arts, a major developer of home entertainment software, provides a glimpse at its titles for Sony, 3DO, Sega, and Nintendo game systems. Features include product demos and movies, as well as company information.

GT Interactive Software

http://www.gtinteractive.com/

Be the first on the block to own new computer game titles from GT Interactive Software by using the electronic ordering services offered here. Get press releases on upcoming products or purchase and directly download hot new games via the company's online delivery service.

id Software Inc.

http://www.idsoftware.com/

This promotional site is the Web home of id Software Inc., a producer of action/fantasy software games such as DOOM, DOOM2, and Ultimate DOOM. Find screenshots, online demos, downloadable patches and shareware, and ordering information.

Interplay

http://www.interplay.com/

Interplay Productions is a commercial developer of interactive entertainment software. At its corporate Web site, visitors can learn about the company and demo its popular computer gaming products.

LavaMind Games and Entertainment

http://www.lavamind.com/

LavaMind provides "alternative entertainment with original characters, stories, design, and game-play." Link here for descriptions of the company's unique games and development projects.

MacPlay

http://www.macplay.com/

MacPlay is the Macintosh-only division of Interplay Productions. The company provides entertainment and educational software "for the discriminating Macintosh consumer." Visitors to its promotional site can check out product demos and coming attractions or locate tech support.

Maxis, Inc.

http://www.maxis.com/

An entertainment software company based in Walnut Creek, California, Maxis hosts this home page offering corporate, product, and employment information. Includes technical support and "cheats" for the company's computer games, like SimCity Classic and SimCity 2000.

Nintendo

http://www.nintendo.com/

Nintendo, creators of video game mainstays Mario Brothers and Donkey Kong, presents this promotional home page. Designed for businesspeople and game addicts alike, the site offers corporate information, as well as fun and interesting resources from Nintendo's broad line of games.

Origin Systems, Inc.

http://www.origin.ea.com/origin.html

Origin Systems, Inc. "creates worlds"—*gaming* worlds, that is. And several are available here for download in both demo and final versions. Test drive virtual adventures like Wings of Glory, Cyber-Mange: Darklight Awakening, and Crusader: No Remorse.

Papyrus Design Group

ftp://ftp.std.com/vendors/papyrus

Access the official FTP site of the developers of IndyCar Racing and NASCAR Racing. Find cheats, hints, suggestions, patches, utilities, and more.

Rocket Science Home Page

http://www.rocketsci.com/

Is it advertisement or entertainment? Find out for yourself when you tour Rocket Science and get updates on new games like Space Bar and Ganymede. (If you wander far enough into the Maze you may even discover whether or not it was Obsidian who caused the explosion.)

Small World Software

http://www.smallworld.com/

Small World Software supplies information here about its interactive sports games. The site also details the firm's Web design services, custom-application development, and consulting.

The 3DO Company

http://www.3do.com/

The 3DO Company showcases its games software, hardware, and peripherals at this home page. Visitors will find product information, demos of latest releases, and a corporate overview.

ThrustMaster, Inc.

http://www.thrustmaster.com/

ThrustMaster, Inc., makes and sells interactive control devices used to play computer games. This site showcases the corporation's products, history, and current job opportunities. Also find technical support and customer services, including ordering information.

Total Entertainment Network

http://www.ten.net/

Total Entertainment Network plans to put computer games on the Net. Visitors can read about the company and its plans on this promotional page. Game players can get on the company's notification list here, too.

Wizards of the Coast

http://www.wizards.com/

Wizards of the Coast hosts this commercial site to highlight its fantasy game cards, as well as to provide industry news to players and avid spectators. Overviews and rules of play for popular games include Magic: The Gathering, The Primal Order, and Ars Magica. Hints on tournament play and spellcasting.

FANTASY AND ROLE-PLAYING

The Addventurers!

http://www.addventure.com/

The Addventurers' creator writes that this isn't quite a MUD or an RPG; it's more of a "shared story." Visit here to add thoughts and ideas—in first or third person—to one of three games.

AlphaWorld

http://www.worlds.net/alphaworld

AlphaWorld is a cyber community simulation where participants can acquire and develop property, interact with other people, assume an online character, and live out a virtual life in an unprogrammed and unpredictable world. Includes instructions on becoming a citizen and downloading the latest release.

Gate to Illucia

http://ucsub.colorado.edu/~nakao/fftown.html

A mythical village, Illucia possesses the attributes of a small town: a store, a cafe, and a village inn—all with small town hours of operation. Villagers contribute fantasy fiction and participate in role-playing games. Includes links to other fantasy and fiction sites.

Glorantha

http://www.pensee.com/dunham/glorantha.html

"The magic-rich fantasy world," Glorantha is explored at this resource archive. Find a map, game links, descriptions of creatures and barbarians, a history, and answers to questions.

Internet Resources for Vampire and Other RPGs

http://www.eleves.ens.fr:8080/home/granboul/Vampire/net.html

Web denizens who like to play Vampire and other role-playing games can find tips, tricks, and camaraderie at this site. Links lead to related Web pages, gopher servers, discussion groups, and more.

The MUD Connector

http://www.absi.com/mud/

Jump into the MUD (Multi-User Dimension) via the MUD Connector, a service indexing online games around the Web universe. Search the list of links to locate desired games, or learn about a certain game through descriptions provided by the page.

Shadow Island Games

http://www.pbm.com/

A play-by-e-mail game page, this site offers two choices: an open-ended fantasy called Olympia; and Arena, a gladiatorial combat game. Links to other gaming resources are also available, along with a magazine on the games.

The Sprawl

http://sensemedia.net/sprawl/

The Sprawl is a network that creates a widely expanding, media-rich virtual reality community. Includes connection information, a review of site activities, and services.

Two Towers Multi-User Dungeon

http://www.angband.com/towers/

This page serves as an entrance to the Two Towers Multi-User Dungeon, allowing game players to step into the world of fantasy writer J.R.R. Tolkien. Intrepid visitors can learn about the game or link to Tolkien sites dotting the Net.

Web of Darkness

http://enuxsa.eas.asu.edu/~buckner/wod.html

Enjoy links to over 100 sites dealing with role-playing fun in the land known to gamesters as the World of Darkness. An added bonus includes about a half dozen links to Rage-related sites.

GAMBLING

The Blackjack Server of Universal Access Inc.

http://blackjack.ua.com

Hey, high-roller! Care to play cards for play money? The house will stake all comers to an initial bankroll, but only the skilled will be able to hang on to what they've got and build their pile.

Internet Casinos

http://www.casino.org/

Those who enjoy high and low stakes gaming will find a home at this virtual casino. Play online at theme-oriented gaming venues.

Jackpot

http://www.cs.umu.se/cgi-bin/scripts/jackpot

Visitors can test their luck at the virtual slot machine on the Jackpot page. Play is for fun only.

The UK National Lottery

http://lottery.merseyworld.com/

Get lucky at the UK National Lottery home page, where browsers can play the virtual lottery, peruse winning numbers, bookmark related links, and examine a numerical analysis of previous winners.

INTERNET GAMES

Blow Yer Brains Out

http://www.islandnet.com/~moron/deterrent/roulette.html

The virtually suicidal can play Russian roulette without leaving others to face the messy aftermath of the real thing. Spin the chamber, pull the trigger, and test your fate.

Boston University's Interactive Web Games

http://www.bu.edu/Games/games.html

Boston University's Scientific Computing and Visualization Group provides specialized resources for research and education in high-performance computing environments. Visit this site to play and download samples of its interactive games.

Cindy Crawford Concentration

http://www.facade.com/Fun/concentration/

This online game offers players an excuse to "concentrate" on photographs of supermodel Cindy Crawford.

Connect Four

http://csugrad.cs.vt.edu/htbin/Connect4.perl

This Web site allows visitors to challenge a computer to a game of Connect Four. Rules and a high-score listing await gaming enthusiasts.

Digital Vegas

http://pandarus.usc.edu/ken-bin/digitalvegas.pl

From a University of Southern California student's home page, this site offers visitors a choice of Web Poker, Web Blackjack, and Web Slots. Play is for points only.

Jackpot

http://www.cs.umu.se/cgi-bin/scripts/jackpot

Visitors can test their luck at the virtual slot machine on the Jackpot page. Play is for fun only.

Madlib!

http://www.mit.edu:8001/madlib

Visitors to this site will find an online version of the once popular fill-in-the-blank parlor game Madlib. Play a round by filling in and submitting the form provided, or view an archive of other visitors' creations.

The Maze

http://info.archlab.tuwien.ac.at/~mwuits/maze/maze.html

The second prize winner in an Austrian cyberspace competition, The Maze is an interactive, user-built, question-and-answer challenge. This gateway links to an explanation of and the entrance to The Maze.

Osiris Trivia Quiz

http://osiris.sund.ac.uk/online/quiz/quiztime.html

The University of Sunderland in the United Kingdom offers this offbeat weekly trivia quiz. Visitors can take this 25-question multiple choice test which promises at least one Bob Dylan question per week. Results are e-mailed back.

Outland Home Page

http://www.outland.com/

Outland, an "online destination" for playing graphical, real-time Internet-based games, maintains this site for its Macintosh-only, pay service. Visitors can learn about pricing, read press releases, and link to multiple games simultaneously from this commercial site.

The PBeM News

http://www.pbem.com/pbem-list.html

Find links to play-by-e-mail games from around the globe featured on this page. Information for PBeM newcomers is also included, along with links to online role-playing game tools.

Play-by-Mail Games

http://www.pbm.com/~lindahl/pbm.html

Here is a page of links to information about games played by postal and e-mail. Features include the PBM list of all known play-by-mail games, answers to Frequently Asked Questions (FAQ) and a categorized index to PBM game home pages.

Tic Tac Toe

http://www.bu.edu/Games/tictactoe

The Tic Tac Toe site provides users with an online contest against the computer. Includes background information about the game.

Ultra Cricket

http://diana.ecs.soton.ac.uk/~ta/uc_home.html

"A Play by e-Mail sports simulation," Ultra-Cricket offers "both Test and One-Day Cricket matches." Visitors will find the rules and how to join play, as well as stats, schedules, and scores.

WebMind

http://einstein.et.tudelft.nl/~mvdlaan/WebMind/WM_intro.html

WebMind is an interactive game modeled after the "ever popular family MasterMind game, where the objective is to find the right combination of colors." Visitors to this site can review the rules and play the game.

LIVE-ACTION GAMES

Warpig Paintball Home Page

http://www.warpig.com/

Warpig is a comprehensive information resource on paintball. This site includes specifications on models of paintball guns, safety equipment and camouflage, as well as a picture gallery and links.

---

a2z EDITOR'S CHOICE

Guess the Macromolecule

http://sp1.berkeley.edu/macro.html

Perhaps this game is not for everyone, but even nonscience types can enjoy playing. It does help to know what a *macromolecule* is, however, because the first step in the game requires the player to choose a macromolecule to "pretend to be." The "super-intelligent" computer then asks a series of questions designed to reveal the "silly human" player's macromolecular identity. It's not hard to guess who comes out on top in this contest, so high stakes betting is *not* encouraged. But it is fun to watch the computer "think," eliminating possibilities and narrowing the field of answers.—*Reviewed by Sean McFadden*

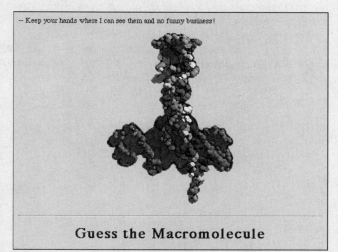

-- Keep your hands where I can see them and no funny business!

Guess the Macromolecule

MISCELLANEOUS GAMES

Guess the Macromolecule
http://sp1.berkeley.edu/macro.html

Play a guessing game with the computer at this site. See Editor's Choice.

Letter R.I.P.
http://www.dtd.com/rip/

Play a black-humored version of Hangman here. See Editor's Choice.

Oh No! It's the Lemmings Games Web Page
http://stud1.tuwien.ac.at/~e8826423/Lemmings.html

Lemming Games? See Editor's Choice.

Railroad Games Home Page
http://ntia.its.bldrdoc.gov/~bing/mayfair.html

Visiting "railroad barons" will find topical tips, news, and other resources to help keep their play on track. Links lead to "Crayons," "Silverton," 18xx, and other rails games information, tournament data and the Train Gamers Association home page.

PUBLICATIONS AND INDUSTRY NEWS

CD-ROM Magazine Online
http://www.widearea.co.uk/cdrom

"CD-ROM Magazine Online" is packed with information on games, movies, references, publishers' sites, game cheats, and software fixes.

Visitors can access back issues, examine the index of the current issue, do a database search for major CD-ROM releases, and offer feedback.

Computer Gaming World
http://www.zdnet.com/~gaming/

The online edition of Computer Gaming World offers previews, reviews, and the occasional cheat code for electronic gaming products. Find the current issue and a searchable archive of past issues at this site

FutureNet: Sega Power
http://www.futurenet.co.uk/games/segapower.html

The online magazine "Sega Power" offers Sega fans product reviews, industry news, hints, and tips. Access to this site requires user registration.

PC Gamer: CD-ROM Computer Gaming
http://www.pcgamer.com/

An electronic edition of the popular PC and CD-ROM games magazine, "PC Gamer" is available at this site from Imagine Publishing. "PC Gamer" covers the latest news, trends, and reviews in the computer gaming industry.

The Web BBS
http://www.swcbbs.com/

The Web BBS, "the home of Apogee and 3D Realms Web sites," maintains this page with information about logging on and a link to the Total Entertainment Network.

PUZZLES

Jumble & Crossword Solver
http://odin.chemistry.uakron.edu/cbower/jumble.html

Those frustrated by a particularly vexing word Jumble or crossword puzzle clue can find relief using these interactive forms. Select puzzle type and fill in the blank; then watch and wait to say, "Oh yeah! I knew that."

The Puzzle Depot
http://iquest.com/~pinnacle/index.html

Hosted by Pinnacle Solutions, this resource "is devoted to puzzles, board games, trivia, related books, and software." Find links to "play for fun" sites, as well as puzzle contests offering cash prizes totaling over $10,000 a month.

The rec.puzzles Archive
http://einstein.et.tudelft.nl/~arlet/puzzles/index.html

Access the puzzle archive of the Usenet newsgroup rec.puzzles. Puzzles are grouped by subject categories which include analogies, arithmetic, cryptology, language equations, probability, riddles, trivia, and more.

 EDITOR'S CHOICE

Letter R.I.P.
http://www.dtd.com/rip/

If hanging stickmen off the "guess-a-word" gallows has lost its appeal, step into Dr. Fellowbug's Lab for a shocking variation on the hangman game that's sure to reanimate most anybody's interest. Chained to the wall of the laboratory, Zeppie the Zombie awaits his fate. For every letter a player misses, Zeppie kisses part of a limb goodbye. At game's end, Zeppie is either disassembled in a bloody heap upon the laboratory floor or miraculously reassembled and signing a thumbs up to the player who successfully guessed the word. Ghoulishly grinning throughout play, the nameless attending nurse goads players with giggles and barbs. All in all, it's a macabre Web loaded with black humor that tickles the funny bone and plays with the head.—*Reviewed by Sean McFadden*

3D riDDle Home Page

http://cvs.anu.edu.au/andy/rid/riddle.html

Game players navigate through this site by solving 3-D riddles. The game relies on single image stereograms; an explanation is provided.

SOFTWARE

Inform Programming

http://www.doggysoft.co.uk/inform

Resources for Inform, a compiler software program for adventure games, can be found at this site. Visit here for example games, library modules, tutorials, and links to related Web sites.

Pueblo Multimedia MUD Client

http://www.chaco.com/pueblo/

From this site, Internet game players and developers can download a free beta version of Pueblo, a multimedia virtual-reality software product from Chaco Communications. The Pueblo software can add realistic 3-D images and sound to text-based MUDs (multi-user domains).

TotWare

http://www.het.brown.edu/people/mende/totware.html

TotWare describes and provides links to selected PC and Macintosh software for kids which is available for downloading. The games and educational applications featured are approved by the compiler's son, Benjamin.

VIDEO AND CD-ROM

Air Havoc Controller

http://com.primenet.com/rainbow

Dozens of planes to guide in and out of the airport, thousands of lives at stake—this is the scenario of Rainbow America's game Air Havoc Controller. Ordering information, sample videos, and images are available at this site.

Air Warrior Web Site

http://cactus.org/AirWarrior/Main.html

Discover the game Air Warrior and find information for online (and stand-alone) play. Site features include a live action demo, flight school tutorial, a library, and links to online host sites.

Angband

http://www.paranoia.com/~jth/angband.html

Find out how to win at the Tolkien-inspired game Angband at this site. It offers a link to download the game for Windows or Macintosh computers, as well as a hintbook full of spoilers to ensure a high score.

Cyberpunk:2020 Web Archive

http://falcon.cc.ukans.edu/~heresy/cyber/

This unofficial Cyberpunk:2020 archive provides information and updates for the computer-based game. Visit here for new rules, tables, essays and dissertations, and more.

DoomGate

http://doomgate.cs.buffalo.edu/

DoomGate is a clearinghouse of information and utilities for the fantasy game DOOM. Links to other DOOM-related resources are also provided.

The DOOM Linux FAQ

http://jcomm.uoregon.edu/~stevev/Linux-DOOM-FAQ.html

What's so great about DOOM? Find out here as you learn where to find a Linux version the game and how to install it. This FAQ site provides a fairly comprehensive review of the equipment needed and some of the problems encountered when playing the Linux version.

The DOOM Page

http://www.cis.ksu.edu/~trm/doom.html

Maintained by a member of The DOOMWeb computer game user group, this site offers a variety of game resources. Visit here for software archives, answers to Frequently Asked Questions (FAQ), game information, and links to topic-related Web sites.

The Game Oasis

http://www.cyberspace.com/acroft/

Computer game players will find hints, cheating tips and Frequently Asked Questions (FAQ) files about an array of games here. The site also includes tips on where to find specific games.

---

a2z   EDITOR'S CHOICE

Oh No! It's the Lemmings Games Web Page

http://stud1.tuwien.ac.at/~e8826423/Lemmings.html

Hosted by Thomas Linder, a computer science student at Vienna University of Technology, this unofficial page began in January 1995 in response to there being "no site for the Lemming games." Since then, Linder has maintained this place for himself and other enthusiasts who enjoy the addictive challenge of moving these anthropomorphic lemmings from a start "Hatch," through a series of hazards, and out through a final "Exit." To assist players, Linder has compiled a keen collection of helpful FAQs, walkthroughs, patches and cheats—plus thrown in downloadable demos, game reviews, and links to newsgroups and fan pages. For fun, lemming graphics and animations are also included. Packed almost as tight as a mass migration of the real-life rodents, this lemmings site is link-laden and otherwise laudably loaded.—*Reviewed by Sean McFadden*

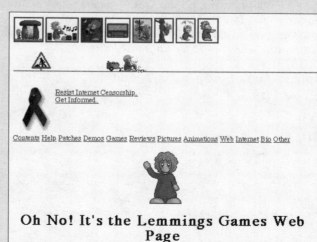

Oh No! It's the Lemmings Games Web Page

Happy Puppy Cheats & Hints

http://happypuppy.com/games/faqcht/
index.html

This "cheats and hints" page from Happy Puppy Games includes answers to Frequently Asked Questions (FAQ) about a large variety of popular computer games. An alphabetical index makes searching for info a breeze.

Myst Hint Guide

http://www.astro.washington.edu/ingram/
myst/index.html

The Myst Hint Guide does exactly what the name says. It offers detailed hints to help players through the labyrinths of this popular CD-ROM game.

VR Slingshot

http://www.cts.com/~vrman/

VR Slingshot, a 3-D virtual reality computer game, is promoted here. Visitors can download a demo and order the title online.

The Wolfenstein 3d Page

http://www.geocities.com/SiliconValley/4825/
wolf.html

This home page provides a link to a download-able demo version of Wolfenstein, a three-dimensional computer game. Includes many utilities that allow players to customize their copies of the adventure game.

The XPilot Page

http://www.cs.uit.no/XPilot/

This site is devoted to XPilot, a multi-player, space-age computer war game. Worldwide rankings, lists of XPilot servers, and an XPilot newsgroup are among the resources players will find here. Also: extensive links to related Internet sites.

XSokoban Home Page

http://clef.lcs.mit.edu/~andru/xsokoban.html

Visitors to this site will find the software and manual for XSokoban, the "spiffiest" version of the game Sokoban. Scoring information and installation notes are also featured.

---

a2z **EDITOR'S CHOICE**

Gothic Gardening

http://www.gsu.edu/~lawjdp/gothgard/index.html

If you are tired of growing the same old thing—ivy, phlox, or petunias—turn to the Gothic Garden and run amok cultivating every noctilucent potion imaginable, perfect for your next witch's brew. Alice and Bob Rosenberg have let their imaginations run wild perfecting a selection of weird and bizarre plants to make the certifiable gardener's dreams come true. For starters, dig into Gardening for Bats, which contains a full description of the various types of *chiroptera* you can lure into your pumpkin patch, including the lowdown on their special taste bud favorites and instructions for building a cozy little bat roost to make the winged creatures comfortable. A visit to "The Little Greenhouse of Horrors" will fill you in on the various species of carnivorous plants which trap little beasties to suck all the vital minerals necessary for their survival. Learn all about VooDoo Lilys and Living Stones, and how to attract snakes to your garden. That being said, get out your hoe and start planting Love Apples, Hemlock and Deadly Nightshade. Even if you're not a dedicated gothic gardener, you'll find this site is filled with fascinating yarns and useful information.—*Reviewed by Eugenia Johnson*

Gothic Gardening by mAlice

Top 5% Award!

The Gothic Gardening pages and all those humans affiliated therewith are proud to have been selected by Point as one of their Top 5% of the Web sites. All hail Pointcom! All Hail Gothic Gardening!

My dear friend mAlice, who's responsible for finding any number of the cool links on my home page, has graciously provided me with her "Gothic Gardening" files, so that I may in turn offer them to you, dear reader. I, of course, take no responsibility for their content, so if something in your garden poisons you or eats your dog or steals your car or something, don't sue me.

Particular thanks are due to Bob Rosenberg of the UK who, for reasons unknown even to himself, took on the task of HTML-izing the Gothic Gardening articles. Thanks, Bob!

Please send all content-related feedback to mAlice, author of the articles. All technical or webmaster-appropriate feedback should be mailed to me, Jason Puckett.

GARDENING

ARCHIVES AND INDICES

The Garden Gate on Prairienet

http://www.prairienet.org/garden-gate/

Gardeners will get their green thumbs dirty here. The extensive site includes regular columns by gardeners, virtual garden tours, growing tips and software reviews devoted to houseplants, greenhouses and outdoor gardens.

ASSOCIATIONS AND ORGANIZATIONS

The Austin Pond Society

http://www.ccsi.com/~sgray/
austin.pond.society/apshome.html

The Austin Pond Society teaches a bit about water gardening and raising Koi fish here. The group also posts its meetings schedule and takes visitors on virtual tours of 19 ponds.

Gothic Gardening

http://www.gsu.edu/~lawjdp/gothgard/
index.html

Visit this site to learn how to make your garden truly unusual. See Editor's Choice.

Ikenobo Ikebana Society of South Florida

http://www.icsi.com/ics/ikenobo/

Learn how Ikenobo, the original form of Ikebana, continues to evolve. Visitors to this site will learn to tell the difference between different styles as well as some of the history of this ancient art form.

International Waterlily Society World Wide Web Server

http://h2olily.rain.com/

The International Waterlily Society is a nonprofit organization of people interested in water gardening. Visitors will find live video images of lily ponds and links to the University of Florida Center for Aquatic Plants, Famous Pete1s Pond Page and similar Web sites

The Pennsylvania Horiticultural Society

http://www.libertynet.org:80/~phs/

The Pennsylvania Horticultural Society aims its programs at all manner of "greening enthusiasts," from the novice gardener to the professional horticulturist. It details its programs and shows here, including the world's largest flower show.

The Tele-Garden

http://www.usc.edu/dept/garden/

Be a virtual gardener in a real garden. See Editor's Choice.

BOTANICAL GARDENS

BG-Map Botanical Garden

http://www.libertynet.org/~bgmap

The BG-Map is a computer based mapping system used by arboreta and botanical gardens to map and catalog collections in a Geographic Information Systems (GIS) format. Visitors here will learn what is needed to run BG-Map and how to order it.

Boyce Thompson Southwestern Arboretum

http://ag.arizona.edu/BTA/

This arboretum invites visitors to take a cyber stroll through its 70-year-old botanical garden. The tour includes a look at the cactus, Wing Memorial, legume and demonstration gardens. The arboretum gives an overview of its work and research here, too.

GardenWeb

http://straylight.tamu.edu/MoBot/welcome.html

GardenWeb is the official home page of the Missouri Botanical Garden. Visitors here can exercise their virtual green thumbs, tour the Garden's diverse plants and flowers, study ongoing botanical research or access "The Learning Network," an educational gallery for kids.

Meerkerk Rhododendron Gardens

http://www.whidbey.net/~kabowers/Meerkerk.html

Take a virtual tour of the Meerkerk Rhododendron Gardens on Whidbey Island near Seattle. Read about the history of the garden and the flowers cultivated there. The site also includes an events calendar and the top 20 rhododendron recommendations for home gardens.

The Royal Botanic Gardens, Kew

http://www.rbgkew.org.uk/

England's Kew gardens are renowned for their beauty. This site offers a virtual tour of the royal gardens and includes information on Kew's scientific research, conservation and heritage

CLUBS

The Internet Bonsai Club

http://141.217.84.167.IBC

The Internet Bonsai Club is devoted to growing and caring for miniature plants. Visitors can learn the art of bonsai here and post pictures of their plants. The site also includes links to related sites.

 EDITOR'S CHOICE

Daylillies Online

http://www.assumption.edu/HTML/daylilies/about.html

Those hardy tough guys, the ones who stick it out through the hottest summers and make your garden glow with orange and yellow, are the honored subjects of Daylilies Online. These old-fashioned trumpets haved graced the gardens of every community in almost every state, and through the years many new hybrids have been developed to make the graceful stems even more appealing. This extensive collection of photographs highlights garden settings of famous growers, and like the Net, virtual tours are available 24 hours a day. For a special treat, stop in and see the lily border at White Flower Farm. If you can't get enough of the vibrant blooms, there are still more links to commercial growers, award-winning daylilies and simply tons of growing information about these robust beauties.—*Reviewed by Eugenia Johnson*

EXHIBITIONS AND SHOWS

Bio-Pictures

http://herb.biol.uregina.ca/liu/bio/bio-ic.html

Marco Bleeker invites viewers into the lush worlds of tropical rainforests and western European garden plants here. Visitors can wander through a gallery of sites and sounds from the rainforest or download photos from Dutch and German gardens.

HORTICULTURE

ARRANGEMENT AND DECORATION

Rittners Floral School

http://www.tiac.net/users/stevrt/index.html

Located in Boston, Rittners School of Floral Design offers courses for the professional and amateur alike. Visit the school's home page to learn more about available courses and careers in floral design, find answers to Frequently Asked Questions (FAQs), or to link to topic-related sites.

BONSAI

The Internet Bonsai Club

http://141.217.84.167.IBC

The Internet Bonsai Club is devoted to growing and caring for miniature plants. Visitors can learn the art of bonsai here and post pictures of their plants. The site also includes links to related sites.

The Online Bonsai Icon Collection

http://www.hav.com/~hav/tobicus.html

A large collection of bonsai tree icons and images is offered at this Web site. Images are available in BMP, GIF, and JPEG format, and browsers can download each of several collections individually. Visitors can also link to the official Bonsai Web site from here.

FLOWERS

Daylilies Online

http://www.assumption.edu/HTML/daylilies/about.html

Daylilies Online claims to provide "the Internet's largest collection of high-resolution daylily photos." The site details which Web browser displays the photos the best (Netscape) and how to adjust your monitor for a good look at the collection. See Editor's Choice.

Friends of the Daylilies Home Page

http://www.primenet.com/~tjfehr/daylily.html

Friends of the Daylilies, a group of the American Hemerocallis Society, works to publicize the perennial flower and its culture. Visit this home page to learn more about the daylily by linking to related organization, publication and event information.

Home Page for Irises

http://aleph0.clarku.edu/~djoyce/iris/

Gardeners with a penchant for irises will find like minds here. This site contains lists of iris societies, a detailed look at the flower and its needs, images and links to online related articles.

The Orchid House

http://sciserv2.uwaterloo.ca/orchids.html

This vast site succeeds in its aim to provide information for the orchid hobbiest. Offerings include details about artificial lighting, plant nutrition, orchid shows and much more about the gorgeous blooms.

Orchid Mall

http://www.netins.net/showcase/novacon/cyphaven/chorcmal.htm

Orchid growers can bolster their operations here. The site includes classifieds with rare varieties for sale, online supply stores and links to orchid groups.

 EDITOR'S CHOICE

The Tele-Garden

http://www.usc.edu/dept/garden/

If you feel you have a fungus thumb, and everything you plant is doomed from the start, this is your opportunity to have all the pleasure of gardening without the pain of loss. The Tele-Garden is a tele-robotic installation that allows you to view and tend a living garden, all from the remote regions of your computer terminal. Garden members plant and cultivate, and their activity is recorded on a log so that progress can be noted and the virtual gardening community can share ideas. This is really a lot of fun! Take the guided tour of the whole enterprise and be a guest just to find out how it all works, or register to be a participating member of the garden. Plant your own seed, see it go into the ground, water it and watch it grow from visit to visit. This is a great activity to do with your children—especially if you don't have access to a real time plot of your own—while both of you learn a little something about gardening. Help is always around if you need it, and zoom and aerial camera views offer both the bird's and the worm's eye view.—*Reviewed by Eugenia Johnson*

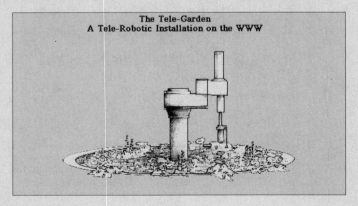

The Tele-Garden
A Tele-Robotic Installation on the WWW

OrchidMania

http://www.orchids.org/

Self-professed "orchid maniacs" have formed a California group that grows and sells orchids to raise money for AIDS relief and prevention efforts. Visitors will learn about the nonprofit's yearly orchid sale here. The site also contains a virtual greenhouse, which is full of information about growing the hot house flowers.

Pete's Pond Page

http://reality.sgi.com/employees/peteo/

In sharing the dazzling pictures of a simple backyard converted to a sophisticated Japanese garden, Pete encourages all of us to attempt this remarkable makeover. Pete has supplied pictures taken in successive years to show how the garden has developed, and provides a comprehensive list of suppliers to help you on your way.

Wild-Flowers

http://www.wild-flowers.com/

As varied as an alpine meadow in full bloom, this wildflower index provides pointers to online catalogs, institutes, identification pages, and much more. A state-by-state directory also provides addresses and phone numbers for public gardens and parks.

FRUITS AND ORCHARD CARE

Strawberries in the Home Garden

http://www.ces.ncsu.edu/hil/hil-8205.html

A pamphlet published by the North Carolina Cooperative Extension Service, this practical brochure guides visitors through planting, tending and harvesting strawberries. It includes a month-by-month chart of tips ("April: remove mulch covering…"), advice on pest control and pointers on selecting varieties.

SUCCULENTS

The Succulent Plant Page

http://www.graylab.ac.uk/usr/hodgkiss/succule.html

The Succulent Plant Page details the abilities of succulent plants—like cacti—which adapted to arid conditions by storing water. Visitors here will find tips about growing and propagating the plants and can download photos of thriving examples.

PUBLICATIONS AND INDUSTRY NEWS

Gardens and Gardening

http://www.cfn.cs.dal.ca/Recreation/Gardening/gg_home.html

Canadian gardeners Peter Henry and Laura Jantek created this informative electronic garden. Visitors can query the couple with gardening questions, read the couple's monthly column, coordinate & swap plants with local gardeners and check local events on a Halifax gardening calendar.

SEED AND BULB CATALOGS

The Gourmet Gardener

http://metroux.metrobbs.com/tgg/catalog.htm

This site is a wishbook for exotic vegetables, heirloom seeds, and edible flowers, all available for ordering.

HOBBIES

Antiques and Collectibles

http://willow.internet-connections.net/web/antiques/

The Antiques and Collectibles site's primary purpose is to provide information and images of antiques to those who are new to collecting. The server deals primarily with items sold at antique shows, auctions and flea markets.

Birding on the Web

http://www-stat.wharton.uenn.edu/~siler/birding.html

Birding on the Web provides links to sites of interest for bird watching enthusiasts. Find pointers to several e-mail sites and home pages for international birding organizations.

Brit-Iron

http://ezinfo.ucs.indiana.edu/~cstringe/brit.html

Visitors to this site will find the home page of Brit-Iron, a mailing list of British motorcycle enthusiasts, from riders and restorers to simple admirers. Links to events calendars, manuals, books, parts suppliers, salvage yards and answers to Frequently Asked Questions (FAQ) are featured.

Clocks and Time

http://glen-ellyn.iit.edu/~clocks/clocks/clocks.html

Webmaster Gordon Uber offers horological pointers both technical—check the Earth's orientation in space—and practical—synchronize your clocks with the world's official timekeepers. For the do-it-yourselfer, interactive instruction for making a sun dial calibrated to specific locations on Earth and how to turn a computer mouse into a stop watch top the list of fun features.

Counted Cross Stitch, Needlework, and Stitchery Page

http://www.wco.com/~kdyer/xstitch.html

A stitchery lover's dream, this site provides links to Net resources for decorative stitching and needlework. Includes pointers to a newsgroup, documents, supplies, conversion charts, fabric care information, historical/cultural references, activities and shipping help.

CraftWeb Home Page

http://www.craftweb.com/

This unusual project hopes to create an online community where "professional crafts people" and artisans "meet, share information and promote fine crafts worldwide." Resources here include real-time chat, an FTP site, links to individual artisans, an online gallery, and access to newsletters and related books.

EuroBirdNet Switzerland

http://cmu.unige.ch/www/ugebn/ugebn_e.html

EuroBirdNet, a network of bird watchers across Europe, maintains this site containing news, ornithology resources and related links. Visit here for rare bird reports, keyword searches, species indices and more.

Galaxy: Leisure and Recreation

http://galaxy.einet.net/galaxy/Leisure-and-Recreation.html

No matter how Web denizens prefer to spend their precious free time, this index of leisure and recreation sites offers up eclectic links to suit most every need. From amateur radio to alternative music to spelunking, like-minded people and organizations are only a mouse-click away.

Harley Owners Group

http://www.magicnet.net/mni/hog.html

The Harley Owners Group maintains this site offering a variety of motorcycling enthusiast resources. Visitors will find chapter listings, stolen vehicle information, Harley Davidson art archives and much more.

Hobbies and Sports

http://euclid.math.fsu.edu/FunStuff/hobbies.html

One person's sport is another person's hobby, and this site has a collection of resources on both. Visitors will find pointers to sites ranging from comics, fishing and climbing to rugby and soccer.

The Internet Textiles and Crafts Site

http://www.textiles.org/index.html

This Web site is sure to delight textile craft hobbyists and professionals alike. See Editor's Choice.

The Magic Page

http://www.daimi.aau.dk/~zytnia/eg.html

Christian Andersen's Magic Page contains a hatful of insights into the world of magic, and hints at the

---

The Plastic Princess Page

http://deepthought.armory.com/~zenugirl/barbie.html

This "on-line 'zine for adult fashion doll collectors" supports a simple formula for successful collecting: 1) define the type of collection desired, whether random or theme-oriented; 2) educate yourself; and 3) enjoy the fun and challenge. The Webmistress, Zoli Nazaari-Uebele, a collector herself, aids the beginner, offering educational resources like a nutshell history of Barbie, a FAQ and a glossary of terms used in the industry. For those preparing to make purchases, a vendors directory and price guides offer online assistance, and a showcase of dolls and doll accessories spotlights items of interest, plus things to look for ... and look out for. In a less serious vein, doll-related humor tickles, a gallery of photos features fashion plates, and a look at tourist spots of interest to doll enthusiasts rounds out the site's "information from collectors for collectors."—*Reviewed by Sean McFadden*

Welcome to the wonderful world of...

The Plastic Princess Page

Established October 1994/Santa Cruz, CA

secrets behind television and movie tricks. Also find links to the Usenet newsgroup alt.magic, a Frequently Asked Questions (FAQ) file, and the home pages of professional and amateur magicians.

Old Postcard Exhibition

http://www.algonet.se/~stenborg/postcard.html

Vintage postal card collector Lars-Olov Stenborg presents selections from his 3,500-piece collection. For those who'd like to see more of the collection, link back to Stenborg's home page for an exhibition of postcards picturing his home town of Karlskrona, Sweden.

The Origami Page

http://www.datt.co.jp/origami

Origami enthusiast Joseph Wu maintains this home page containing a wealth of information and graphics. Visit this site to find out how to make origami, see interesting examples and link to other origami sites.

The Plastic Princess Page

http://deepthought.armory.com/~zenugirl/barbie.html

Zoli Nazaari-Uebele maintains this online 'zine for doll enthusiasts. See Editor's Choice.

RC-Sailing Infocenter

http://honeybee.helsinki.fi/surcp/index.htm

This hobbyists' page is all about the world of Radio Control (RC) sailing. Includes links to classes in RC sailing, boat construction, racing information, rules and sailing events. Also provides pointers to other sailing pages and equipment providers.

Recreation, Sports, and Hobbies

http://www.cs.fsu.edu/projects/group12/title.html

The Recreation, Sports and Hobbies page provides dictionary definitions of all sorts of recreational pursuits. Internet links to related resources are also featured.

Rollercoaster!

http://www.echonyc.com/~dne/Rollercoaster!/

The Rollercoaster! home page is devoted to the quest for the "ultimate ride." It features reviews of new rides and of the most terrifying 'coaster ever.

Secrets of Home Theater and High Fidelity

http://www.sdinfo.com/

This online magazine provides reviews of electronic home entertainment products, geared both to the casual consumer and the electronics buff. Visit here to read articles, contact editorial staff or subscribe to the print version.

The Speaker Building Page

http://bundy.hibo.no/~rpd/Speaker/

Created in 1995 by Roy Viggo Pederson to provide do-it-yourself speaker builders with "amateur designs, some kits, driver info and some design tips," the page has since grown and evolved into a full-fledged online resource.

Treasure Net

http://www.treasurenet.com/

Treasure Net is a collection of resources designed for treasure hunters of every ilk—from gold prospectors to deep-sea divers. Here, "dig up" publications, shops, and treasure links geared to make treasure hunting more successful.

HUMOR

Adrian's Humor Collection

http://gpu.srv.ualberta.ca/~apowell/humor.html

This online humor archive categorizes laugh-inducing material topically. Categories covered include computers, science fiction, religion, and universities as well as men, women, and sex. Includes links to other humorous Internet sites.

AGD Antics and Mayhem Page

http://www.be.com/~dbg/antics

Silicon Graphics, Inc. maintains this employee home page for humorous stories and jokes. Visit the Antics and Mayhem Page for a variety of on-the-job shenanigans.

AirGuitar

http://www.digitalrag.com/mirror/air/air.html

The AirGuitar page takes a light-hearted stab at air-guitar talent with a beginner's lesson—the only lesson—on stage presence. By visiting this site, the visitor also automatically receives an R. Bud Philson air guitar "made from the highest quality oxygen in the United States."

Alt.fan.monty-python: The Official Homepage

http://www.python.com/afmp/

This is the official home page for the Monty Python Usenet newsgroup. Visitors will find an abundance of frequently asked questions about the British comedy troupe, newsgroup information, and "good, silly stuff."

The Amazing Adventures of Bromwyn Bunny

http://leja.cs.utas.edu.au/bromwyn/bromwyn.html

Stuffed animal lovers will enjoy this page, featuring a light-hearted saga of a stuffed bunny's adventures and misadventures. This not-really-for-kids page also contains photos from this renegade rabbit's exploits and encourages other bunny tale submissions.

Anders Mad Scientist Page

http://www.nada.kth.se/~nv91-asa/mad.html

Mad scientists, evil geniuses, and assorted kooks populate this index. Among the resources are sites such as Net Wackiness, The Worldwide Institute for the Preservation of Everything, and Dr. Dookie's Mad Scientist Information Center. Publications, superweapon sites, and events are also listed.

Antics: An Ant Thology Home Page

http://www.ionet.net/~rdavis/antics.shtml

A plug for Richard Davis's book, *Antics: An Ant Thology*, this light-hearted page crawls with visual puns related to picnic-crashing insects. Includes links to a live ant farm and the Squashed Bug Zoo.

The Automatic Complaint Letter Generator

http://www-csag.cs.uiuc.edu/individual/pakin/complaint

Got a bone to pick? Let the complaint letter generator orchestrate a nasty-gram to someone you particularly despise. Just enter the name of the person in question and the generator will instantly compose a verbose and insulting message to them.

Ban Dihydrogen Monoxide

http://www.circus.com/~no_dhmo/

Beware the dangers of dihydrogen monoxide! You can find it everywhere, even leaking from your body on a hot day! Its dangers are detailed on this satirical Web page in a frighteningly realistic manner. To the chemically challenged, this substance is also known as water.

Bastard Operator from Hell

http://www.st.nepean.uws.edu.au/stuff/bofh/

A hostile and intolerant local area administrator from New Zealand maintains this collection of "Bastard Operator from Hell" stories. As the title suggests, this site contains strong language and adult themes.

Bon Mots from the Supermodels

http://www.sils.umich.edu/~sooty/thoughts.html

"I wish my butt did not go sideways, but I guess I have to face that." These profound words are Christie Brinkley's, and many other supermodel quotes are collected here. Visitors will find a host of soon-to-be famous sayings that would make Dan Quayle blush.

Church of the SubGenius

http://sunsite.unc.edu/subgenius

Learn about Bob and his theology. See Editor's Choice.

Citizen Poke

http://www.amherst.edu/~poke/

Oompa doompa doompa dee do, Citizen Poke has another puzzle for you! Visit here for an online humor publication of Amherst College in a variety of viewing formats. Includes a variety of bizarre features, including "Freak of the Week."

Comedy Central

http://comcentral.com

This is a well-designed site, with video clips, contests, news spoofs, and more. See Editor's Choice.

Cool Jargon of the Day

http://www.bitech.com/jargon/cool

Can't keep your floppies straight? Don't know RAM from ROM? Visit this site, featuring an extensive index of hacker slang, with a new term daily. Also includes links to other jargon dictionaries on the Internet.

Daily Muse

http://www.cais.net/aschnedr/muse1.htm

Clever articles and graphics grace this site devoted to ridicule. See Editor's Choice.

Deep Thoughts, by Jack Handy

http://www.umd.umich.edu/~nhughes/htmldocs/deepthoughts.html

"It takes a big man to cry, but it takes a bigger man to laugh at that man." Thoughts like these are available in abundance at this Deep Thoughts collection, based on the humor of NBC's "Saturday Night Live" and maintained by a devoted fan.

The Dysfunctional Family Circus

http://www.thoughtport.com/spinnwebe-cgi-bin/dfc.cgi

The "Dysfunctional Family Circus," part of the SpinnWebe home page, offers visitors a chance to add satirical captions to otherwise benign cartoon panels based on the long-running "Family Circus" strip. Visit here to submit and view winning captions.

Economist Jokes

http://www.etla.fi/pkm/joke.html

"Economists have forecasted nine out of the last five recessions." This and other rib-ticklers about those nutty economists can be found at this humor page, maintained by a very humble economics researcher.

Fun e-Mail

http://www.cco.caltech.edu/~ekrider/FunEMail/funemail.html

The creator of this humor site bothers other Webmasters for "mere entertainment value." Visit this site to read this virtual critic's comments on other people's home pages and project Web sites.

Geek Defined

http://www.circus.com/~omni/geek.html

The Marshmallow Peanut Circus offers this page to define the word "geek." Visit here for the latest definition of this and other derogatory terms describing computer users. Hey, it takes one to know one.

Geek Site of the Day

http://www.owlnet.rice.edu/~indigo/gsotd/

Are we losers? The Webmaster at Geek Site of the Day says we are— and all we did was link to his page! If you enjoy being insulted too, visit this extensive collection of geeky Web resources, updated daily.

Harold Reynold's Humour Collection

http://geog.utoronto.ca/reynolds/humour.html

Pet lovers and pet haters alike will enjoy this collection of animal-related humor sites. Visit here for links to such offerings as the "Bad Horse List," "How to Bathe a Cat," the "Cat Brain Map," and others.

---

a2z **EDITOR'S CHOICE**

Church of the SubGenius

http://sunsite.unc.edu/subgenius/

Born in a cave, raised by zines, and now wired to your brain via the World Wide Web, the anxious followers of J.R. "Bob" Dobbs can control your thoughts (that's right, you there, reading this book) without interference. Dubbed the official home page of the Church of the SubGenius, this site literally reaches into your subconscious, gropes for a conscience, and replaces it with the three-fisted theology of Bob. After beguiling you to click on the face of their fearless leader, Bobites plunge even deeper, first subjecting unsuspecting wayfarers to the "slack fist of retrieval," then the oddly similar "stark fist of removal," then remorselessly crashing browsers with spiky, Java-laden idols—so be careful! Provides full text of nearly every Church-approved rant, downloadable samples from "The Hour of Slack," and a chance to fall prey to a mail order catalog.—*Reviewed by Paul Bacon*

WHICH PATH WILL YOU TAKE?

PINKNESS AND HORROR

OR

WORLD WIDE SLACK?!?

How to Tell If Your Head's About to Blow Up

http://www.mit.edu:8001/people/mkgray/head-explode.html

This page features a 1994 *Weekly World News* report of a chess player's gruesome demise. Visitors can digest the symptoms of hyper-cerebral electrosis and check out preventive tips for avoiding the explosive condition.

Humor Archives at Caltech

http://www.visi.com/~nathan/humor.index.html

This humor archive was set up using material collected from various newsgroups, mailing lists, and other online sources. Includes jokes about Bill Clinton and O.J. Simpson, plus scripts from comedy troupes like Monty Python.

Humorscope

http://www.teleport.com/~ronl/horo.html

"Taurus: Remember what doesn't kill you makes you stronger. Well, except for potato chips." The Humorscope provides laugh-provoking advice like this on a daily basis. Includes e-mail delivery option.

Instrument Jokes

http://www.mit.edu:8001/people/jcb/other-instrument-jokes.html

No matter the orchestra section—strings, woodwinds, brass, or percussion—there's something funny about the instruments found there and this collection of jokes points out the humor. Includes hundreds of jokes for the musically inclined and declined.

Internet Pizza Server Home Page

http://www2.ecst.csuchico.edu/~pizza/

Order pizza over the Web and receive delivery directly to your e-mailbox. The Internet Pizza Server takes your order and fashions a digital pie to your specifications. Strictly for fun, not for nutritional fulfillment.

The Itch

http://holly.colostate.edu/~mumpa

The Itch is the home of Mumpa Itch, a fictional character full of "madness, sadness, and gladness." He likes to "snap those things which snap and find new things which generally don't snap." (Translation: Web silliness and art from the Egg Shell Collective.)

Jonathan Katz' Eclectic Collection

http://www.facade.com/~jonathan/library/

Visitors to this personal assortment of mystical and humorous links will find such offerings as the "Cindy Crawford Concentration Game," the "I Am I in Pi" page, and others. Includes links to "The Tarot Pages" and "The I Ching Pages."

The Kooks Museum

http://www.teleport.com/~dkossy/

The Kooks Museum keeps kookdom under one roof, taking a lighthearted look at the unconventional disciplines of crackpotology, kookology, and psychoosmology. Check out off-the-wall gifts, useless research, and politically incorrect ideas here.

Madlib!

http://www.mit.edu:8001/madlib

...Then she pulled a (blank) out of her (blank). Visitors to this site will find an online version of the once popular fill-in-the-blank parlor game Madlib. Play a round by filling in and submitting the form provided, or view an archive of other visitors' creations.

The Matrix Humor Archive

http://www.marshall.edu/~hartwel1/humor.html

Did you know bad puns, wet dreams, and other humorous offerings make up much of the underbelly of the Web? Check it all out with the links and collected humor articles at this personal humor index.

McChurch Home Page

http://mcchurch.org/

For a fast food approach to religion, hit the drive-up window of McChurch. From this gateway, enter the First Internet McChurch Tabernacle and receive a free "Happy Meal" for the soul. Includes mighty transportable apocryphal links page.

---

a2z EDITOR'S CHOICE

Comedy Central

http://comcentral.com

The cable network that gave the unemployed and bedridden a reason to live hits the Web with a punchy, insulting, and highly interactive presence. Visitors to Comedy Central's home page can enter joke writing contests, get immediate e-therapy from Dr. Katz, and orchestrate hate mail to such celebs as Hugh Grant and Bill Bradley. For those who prefer to veg out completely, the remainder of the site is a powerful one-way stream of comedy. A few clicks around the colorful, well-designed pages turns up spoofy news features, real-time screen shots of the live cablecast and "Web Sites We'd Like to See," a hilarious wish list à la *Mad* magazine. Also offers playable video clips from mainstays "Kids in the Hall" and "Absolutely Fabulous."—*Reviewed by Paul Bacon*

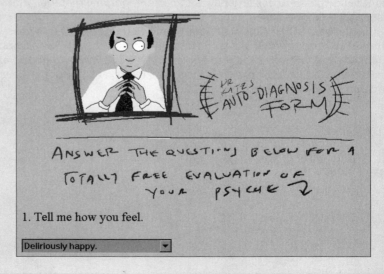

Mr. Smarty Pants Knows

http://www.auschron.com/mrpants/

The Mr. Smarty Pants Knows home page from the *Austin Chronicle* features a weekly column along with pointers to Smarty Pants' favorite Web links and various facts. Visitors can also listen to an audio greeting from Mr. and Mrs. Smarty Pants' dog and cat, or watch video of Mr. Smarty Pants morphing.

Monty Python WWW Homepage

http://www.iia.org/~rosenr1/python/python.html

This site has the series scripts, songs lyrics, film lists, and more. See Editor's Choice.

PhoNETic

http://www.phonetic.com/

If you want a catchy phone number, but can't afford a new phone line, try PhoNETic. This online utility automatically generates possible alpha-equivalents to any given phone number.

PIG Intertainment

http://pigweb.com/PiGWeb_Home.html

For those who view life with an irreverent and off-beat approach, Pig Intertainment offers a collection of bizarre tips for vacationing, politics, and self-help. Learn how to eat at home alone or find out why blue pigs don't oink.

Political Babble Generator

http://www.webcorp.com/polibabble.htm

These randomly generated "speeches" often sound like the real thing. See Editor's Choice.

Private Eye

http://www.intervid.co.uk/eye/

This site serves as a gateway to the online version of the British humor magazine "Private Eye," with cartoons, light poetry, and such features as "Great Bores of Today" and the fictional "John Major's Diary." Subscription and advertising information is also available.

Quotations Home Page

http://www.lexmark.com/data/quote.html

"To be or...how's that go?" A large index of memorable quotations is maintained at this server, along with detailed reference information. Quote collections range from advice, proverbial wisdom, and annoying proverbs to serious sarcasm and poetry.

Radio Free Oz

http://www.rfo.net

This site is the home of Peter Bergman's audio humor shows. See Editor's Choice.

Rainbow Confusion?!

http://www.mps.org/~rainbow/

Self-described "hip young dudes" created this index of online humor and essays, graphics files, and "cheesy software." Visitors can also visit the candy dish, which doles out candy hearts (the kind with the sappy sayings on them) each time you visit.

The Really Big Button That Doesn't Do Anything

http://www.wam.umd.edu/~twoflowr/button.htm

Containing user reactions to pushing the Really Big Button That Doesn't Do Anything, this humor page provides no information, links or help for the individuals who push the button. Includes humorous reflections and deep thoughts.

Roadkills-R-Us News Network

http://www.rru.com/rru/

DisInformation comes to the Internet through the Roadkills-R-Us News Network home page, which contains parodies of Internet mainstays. A discussion of a pending lawsuit brought by the Toys-R-Us toy store is included.

Rodney Dangerfield

http://www.rodney.com/

This site features a multimedia "laugh break" starring the man who gets no respect, Rodney Dangerfield. Video clips, sound bites, photos, and philosophical musings—yes, musings—are featured along with the Joke of the Day, current news, and old annoyances.

Rush Limbaugh's 35 Undeniable Truths

http://www.primenet.com/~triplet/files/35truth.html

Fans of Rush Limbaugh's brand of outspoken conservatism will enjoy this quotation archive. Includes such pearls as "evidence refutes liberalism," "the earth's ecosystem is not fragile," and 33 other provocative statements.

The San Francisco Cacophony Society

http://www.zpub.com/caco

The home page for San Francisco's branch of the Cacophony Society highlights the organization's ongoing campaign of guerilla theater, pointless spectacle, and creative anarchy. Find photos from the annual St. Stupid Day Parade and the Race of Doom, as well as links to kindred dadaists the Museum of Bad Art.

---

a2z EDITOR'S CHOICE

Daily Muse

http://www.cais.net/aschnedr/muse1.htm

If rash political satire and the possibility of watching Hillary Clinton morph into Dennis Rodman don't frighten you, you're gonna love the Daily Muse. Cleverly written articles and goofy graphics greet visitors to this regularly updated site, pandering to the intellectual's favorite pastime: ridicule. A recent visit yielded pages and pages of current, original material, making us suspect this Web-based publication may have something more than a Web server and an HTML jockey going for it. Perhaps a staff of dedicated writers? Anyone in search of a laugh or an example of how to keep a home page fresh and funny will want to bookmark this site. Well-organized and exhaustive, the Muse is a great place to keep tabs on all buffoons, elected and appointed.—*Reviewed by Paul Bacon*

Schwa

http://fringeware.com/SchwaRoot/Schwa.html

Welcome to Schwa, a mysterious corporation set up by an artist who produces hip gear bearing space alien insignias. Visitors here can order products or read tongue-in-cheek press releases, like the Schwa alien invasion survival manual.

Shakespearean Insult Generator

http://alpha.acast.nova.edu/cgi-bin/bard.pl

You *can* raise your vocabulary out of the gutter and still be mean. See Editor's Choice.

The Silly Zone

http://www.wam.umd.edu/~twoflowr/aisle3.htm

The name says it all—if it's here, it's silly. This site from Spatula City includes The Really Big Button That Doesn't Do Anything, CyberStare (the world's first virtual reality staring contest), and similar silliness.

Sole Site of the 1996 Presidential Campaign

http://www.infi.net/jmshoe/

Johnston & Murphy, "maker of fine footwear for every U.S. president since Millard Fillmore," takes a lighthearted look at the 1996 presidential campaign here. It proposes alternate candidates to fill the president's shoes including Princess Di, Oliver Stone, Martha Stewart, and Mr. Potato Head.

Spam Haiku Archive

http://www.naic.edu/~jcho/spam/sha.html

Spam, that mysterious "meat" food product, has spawned a post-modern and cross-cultural literary form: Spam Haiku. Visitors to this humor page can share their poetic epiphanies with the rest of the world and vote for a favorite haiku.

Spatula City

http://www.wam.umd.edu/~twoflowr/

An eccentric and humorous site, Spatula City specializes in offbeat Web links, images, and writings described as "sillyweird and bizzaredisturbing." Includes a teleporter booth for quick access to desired pages.

SpinnWebe

http://spinn.thoughtport.com/spinnwebe/

This site is full of weird images, lists, quizzes, and much more. See Editor's Choice.

Taglines Galore!

http://www.brandonu.ca/~ennsnr/Tags/

"E is for Edible udies!" "Gay means happy...for a reason!" Taglines, riddles, puns, and advice to worms ("Sleep late!") are featured at this humorous site. Visitors will find an index of more than 59,000 amusing and thought-provoking sayings.

Top 10 Ways to Make Your WWW Service a Flop

http://coombs.anu.edu.au/SpecialProj/QLTY/FlopMaker.html

The computer department of the Australian National University provides this page for humorous advice on how to turn a Web-based information system into a failure. Includes links to more conventional instructions on successful Web publishing.

Unofficial Smiley Dictionary

http://www.eff.org/papers/eegtti/eeg_286.html

Smile, it's free! The Electronic Frontier Foundation's Unofficial Smiley Dictionary contains dozens of smiley faces in a variety of forms. Cynics will be tortured and optimists will undoubtedly be delighted here.

Useless World Wide Web Sites

http://www.primus.com/staff/paulp/useless.html

Wacky eclectism is the rule at the Useless World Wide Web Pages site. Using the wide-ranging content of the Web for satirical fodder, this site compiles a humor filled list of hundreds of strange sites deemed to possess no utilitarian value.

Valdosta State University Gopher Menu

gopher://catfish.valdosta.peachnet.edu/11/ccr/subjv/phi

This gopher server from the Georgia college provides a smorgasbörd of links to both serious subjects and fun items—such as humor and puzzles and paradoxes. Visitors can also look at a directory of journals and electronic conferences.

---

a2z EDITOR'S CHOICE

Monty Python WWW Homepage

http://www.iia.org/~rosenr1/python/python.html

A minister quotes the gospel, a professor quotes philosophy, and the rest of us...we quote Monty Python. Those cross-dressing, Bible-thumping British ninnies said more in one sentence than most of us do in a lunchtime. Why, anyone who's ever flicked on the telly can recite the entire dialogue to the dead parrot sketch ("'E's not pinin'! 'E's passed on!"). Can't they? Um, well, for those who still haven't memorized the entire "Flying Circus" series (and for those who have and are just looking for some reassurance), plus dozens of films and song lyrics, this site is for you. A nearly complete collection of writings from the comedy troupe is available at this fan-produced site, reminding you of the digestive risks of wafer-thin mints and how high to count before lobbing the holy hand grenade. Includes links to Python-related people and productions and a whole host of Terry Gilliam films.—*Reviewed by Paul Bacon*

```
A man comes out with a dead-looking old man in a nightshirst slung over
shoulder.  He starts to put the old man on the cart.

Man:          Here's one-
Cart-master:  Ninepence.
Old Man:      (feebly) I'm not dead!
Cart-master:  (suprised) What?
Man:          Nothing!  Here's your ninepence....
Old Man:      I'm not dead!
Cart-master:  'Ere!  'E says 'e's not dead!
Man:          Yes he is.
Old Man:      I'm not!
Cart-master:  'E isn't?
Man:          Well... he will be soon-- he's very ill...
Old Man:      I'm getting better!
Man:          No you're not, you'll be stone dead in a moment.
Cart-master:  I can't take 'im like that!  It's against regulations!
Old Man:      I don't want to go on the cart....
Man:          Oh, don't be such a baby.
Cart-master:  I can't take 'im....
Old Man:      I feel fine!
Man:          Well, do us a favor...
Cart-master:  I can't!
Man:          Can you hang around a couple of minutes?  He won't be long
```

Wall O'Shame

http://www.milk.com/wall-o-shame/

The anarchic and funny Wall O'Shame is not for everyone. It highlights many things that bring us shame, including body odor. To say more would be, well, shameful.

Weird Text and Images

http://www.nada.kth.se/~nv91-asa/weird.html

As the name implies, this is a collection of offbeat and entertaining pages that will appeal to irreverent Web surfers. Page topics run from geekiness to weird religions, from Lovecraftian things to discordian and illuminati stuff.

Zot's Improv Page

http://www.crl.com/~zot/improv.html

Zot's Improv Page serves as a repository for information about improvisational comedy. Visitors can access improv games, books, show listings, and lots of other comedy-related Internet sites.

MOVIES AND VIDEOS

ARCHIVES AND INDICES

alt.sex.movies Home Page

http://www.xmission.com/~legalize/asm/asm.html

This Usenet archive provides movie lists, frequently asked questions files and pointers to places to order adult movies. Other offerings include essays and excerpts from legal briefs concerning pornography.

---

a2z EDITOR'S CHOICE

Political Babble Generator

http://www.webcorp.com/polibabble.htm

Have you ever suspected that political speeches are actually written by a basement full of monolithic, Orwellian machines? Or that the first human to read one of these historical orations is usually doing so from a teleprompter while addressing millions of people? Well, here's your proof! Visit this site to find a state-of-the-art "polibabble" generator, capable of creating an entirely new campaign promise or position statement every five minutes. Using randomly selected phrases from notable speeches, this is a word processor in the strictest sense of the term, producing oddly readable, often hilarious amalgamations with embedded nuggets of wisdom.
—Reviewed by Paul Bacon

GINGOV

A synthetic speech in the style of Newt Gingrich.

Please be sure to select any nuggets of "wisdom" for our Book of Knowledge. Paste or type them into the form at the bottom.

the press coverage, because it had ideas. I am just exaggerating, imagine that you're Senator Chris Dodd, you are conservative or liberal, that is cruel and destroys families.

Its failure is reflected by the information technologies. Tremendous is a simple principle. I am not going to have every kid in a new era. And I think New Partnership is our replacement for the last decade. They cut spending, provided better products, better education and better service for less. But I am just exaggerating, imagine that you're Senator Chris Dodd, you are conservative or liberal, that is cruel and destroys families. Its failure is reflected by the time (laughter). And I, frankly, when the government and balance the budget. That way by genuinely engaging in a one-sided way is I think a despicable comment on how sick this city who would have automatically turned down 4.5 million. (Laughter). They would have automatically turned down 4.5 million dollars, and I would be fine if the newspaper, which after all has the computing power of 3 million vacuum tubes. So today's government operates this way, after we remake it, the Senate passed and the will to do and how we're working to keep their children out of

Best Video

http://www.tagsys.com:80/Ads/BestVideo/index.html

Visitors can search Best Video's thousands of offerings, including many rare and cult films. Other film-related merchandise and film reviews also are provided here. Ordering is available by phone, fax, or surface mail.

The Biz: The Entertainment CyberNetwork

http://www.bizmag.com/

The Biz features multimedia interviews, music videos, and movie trailers, along with news, columns, features and classifieds. Includes the Reuters/Variety Online Entertainment Report and The Source, an entertainment resource guide.

Cinema Sites

http://www.vir.com/VideoFilm/davidaug/Movie_Sites.html

An extensive collection of pointers to online film and television information is maintained at this server. Topics covered range from film festivals and awards updates to screenwriting and film production resources.

CineMedia/Cinema

http://www.gu.edu.au/gwis/cinemedia/CineMedia.cinema.html

CineMedia is an online guide to film and drama resources. Visit this site for links to information about the motion picture industry and acting and directing educational institutions.

CineWEB

http://www.cineweb.com/

This interactive page contains the user registration form for CineWEB, a service designed for the motion picture professional. CineWEB features trade publications, magazines, and specialized, production-oriented databases.

A Clockwork Orange Slang Glossary

http://jake.chem.unsw.edu.au/~michaels/Orange/orange.html

Viddy well my droogies, and fasten your glazzies here. If you're scratching your head, you haven't been doing your required reading of this site's teen-slang glossary based on "A Clockwork Orange." Check images, sound files and more from Stanley Kubrick's film here.

Drew's Script-o-Rama

http://pobox.com/~drew/scripts.htm

This script archive features over 500 screenplays and teleplays. See Editor's Choice.

Early Motion Pictures Home Page

http://lcweb2.loc.gov/papr/mpixhome.html

This U.S. Library of Congress site provides background information and access to collections of motion pictures from 1897–1916. Includes detailed descriptions of the collection and articles on the history and techniques of early filmmakers.

Film.com

http://www.film.com/

Film.com covers such a wide variety of film-related topics, it claims you'll never need to open a movie magazine again. Visit here for reviews, schedules, and movie news as well as a look at many films from a critical perspective.

Flicker

http://www.sirius.com/~sstark/

Billing itself as a "home page for the alternative cinematic experience," Flicker provides visitors with films and videos that "transgress the boundaries of the traditional viewing experience." Budding video and film artists can find listings of alternative venues, images of filmmakers' works, news links, and other resources.

The Guide

http://theguide.gim.de/

The Guide is an online handbook for film, TV, theater, and music production professionals. Visitors will find daily update articles and features available on a subscription basis, with limited fee offerings. In English and German.

Informedia Digital Library

http://fuzine.mt.cs.cmu.edu/im/informedia.html

The Informedia Digital Library, a project of Carnegie-Mellon University, is working to establish an extensive online digital video library for users of desktop computers and metropolitan area networks. Visit this site to learn about the library, its sponsors, and its latest advances.

Internet Movie Database

http://us.imdb.com

This site features a plethora of movie trivia. See Editor's Choice.

Mandy's Film and Television Production Directory

http://www.mandy.com/

Mandy takes her lights, cameras and action seriously with this film and television production directory. Hundreds of international entries contain links to local facilities and professionals in the industry. Includes a searchable index.

The Movie Cliches List

http://www.like.it/vertigo/cliches.html

Hollywood's overused movie cliches are featured here. See Editor's Choice.

MovieWEB

http://movieweb.com/movie/movie.html

Moviegoers can do their homework with MovieWEB. Find movie previews complete with pictures, posters and production notes at this site.

 EDITOR'S CHOICE

Radio Free Oz

http://www.rfo.net

Long before the Internet, and at least a week prior to the invention of television, people used radios to pipe fresh comedy into their homes. Now the one "true" humor medium is just a click away at Radio Free Oz. Visitors will find updated audio shows created by former "Firesign Theater" member Peter Bergman and starring the voices of John Goodman and lesser-known but generally better-liked characters. We love sites like this one, which hint at a coming rennaissance for radio- and album-style humor. Bergman and a handful of other inveterate TV refuseniks have been biding their time with deep, steady breaths for something like the Web to come along. Now, with the freedom of expression available on the Net (we're still crossing out...er, *our* fingers) and an unbridled range of virtual distribution, it's their time to shine. The results are hilarious.—*Reviewed by Paul Bacon*

Shakespearean Insult Generator

http://alpha.acast.nova.edu/cgi-bin/bard.pl

If those infectious, rump-fed dewberries have got you down, don't lower yourself to everyday insults, be eloquent! For help coming up with more than the standard four-letter slap, consult this site for a bit o' the old(e) English(e). Visitors are greeted with a fresh barb upon loading the page, such as this brittle gem, "thou puny, beetle-headed clotpole," or the tart "thou bootless, elf-skinned miscreant." Take a pocketful of screen shots from this site to your next office party and lay into your co-workers. See how their respect for you simply swells as you scream drunkenly from the smoking section, "You dankish, hedge-born whey-faces" and "villainous, tardy-gaited maggot-pies!"—*Reviewed by Paul Bacon*

Each upcoming movie has its own Web page with QuickTime excerpts from the trailers produced by the studios.

The Top Sample Lists

http://www.ee.pdx.edu/~alf/html/samples.html

Ranking the most popular movies, TV series and other sample sources (including serial killers), this relentless resource tracks cultural flotsam and jetsam. Ratings are based on how frequently spoken lines from these sources are sampled and used in songs.

University Art Museum/Pacific Film Archive

http://www.uampfa.berkeley.edu/

Visitors can take a virtual tour of the University of California, Berkeley's University Art Museum/Pacific Film Archive here. The site includes full on-line exhibits from the art museum and an events calendar for the film theater.

ASSOCIATIONS AND ORGANIZATIONS

Alliance Communications Corp.

http://www.alliance.ca

This promotional home page offers links to Alliance's subsidiaries in film and television production and broadcast and cable networks distribution. Also includes information on the company's financial investments in entertainment software syndication.

Entertainment Technology Center

http://cwis.usc.edu/dept/etc/index.html

Here visitors can learn about high-tech projects undertaken by the Entertainment Technology Center, an organization sponsored by entertainment and communications companies and the University of Southern California's schools of cinema-television and engineering.

Film and Video Arts Society

http://valis.worldgate.edmonton.ab.ca/~fava/

Find out what's up with the Film and Video Arts Society of Alberta, Canada. The group's home page features an artist directory of more than 140 members, as well as information about the finished works of member filmmakers.

Lumo: The Magic of Finnish Cinema

http://www.kaapeli.fi/~lumo/English

Visit here for a close look at the Finnish motion picture industry. Includes links to production and history archives, film festivals, director indices, professional contacts, and more. In Finnish, Swedish and English.

Society of Motion Picture and Television Engineers

http://www.smpte.org/

The "preeminent professional society" for motion picture and television engineers, serving 8,500 members worldwide, maintains this site for news, publications and membership information. Visitors will also find conference schedules, officer profiles, employment opportunities, and press releases from the organization.

CREATIVE AND TECHNICAL FILMMAKING RESOURCES

Animation Master Hobbyist

http://www.xmission.com/~gastown/animation/index.html

Users of Animation Master and Playmation software maintain this site to exchange information, ideas, and creations. Visit here to download software reviews and tips files or visit the gallery to see the animation being produced with these software tools.

Arctic Animation

http://www.cs.ubc.ca/spider/edmonds/anime/arctic.html

Arctic Animation is a Vancouver, British Columbia-based group of fans who provide subtitles for Japanese animated films. Anime fans can peruse the Arctic Project Listing and find out how to order tapes and CD-ROMs here. A link to the Fan Subtitling Guide is also provided.

Digital Theater Systems

http://www.dtstech.com/

Cinemas can perfectly reproduce studio master sound recordings with the use of Digital Theater Systems. This promotional site offers detailed information about the system and its design—as well as press releases and answers to Frequently Asked Questions (FAQs).

---

a2z EDITOR'S CHOICE

SpinnWebe

http://spinn.thoughtport.com/spinnwebe/

Forget everything we've told you about the best interactive humor sites on the Web. Okay. Now, the bona fide, official best use of the Web as a medium is...SpinnWebe. We think. Well, if nothing, this multi-tentacled site is breathing heaviest inside your monitor. SpinnWebe is full of bizarre images and engaging, nano-intellectual challenges that actually accept your typed input. Honest. You can submit your own captions for hidden camera shots of random, unattractive people and throw in your two cents on the latest photograph of the Webmaster's left nipple. (Heh, heh.) Visitors are also invited to rewrite comic history in the "Dysfunctional Family Circus." What more do you want, you twisted, thrill-seeking comic adventurers?—*Reviewed by Paul Bacon*

Caption 1 of 38

Turn icons off

Difficult zone: pregnant bride and/or shotgun wedding.

I still say this isn't proof that you're married. These could be prom pictures, fer Chrissakes!
--Capt. phealy

Entertainment Technology

http://www.teleport.com/~moore/
entertech.html

Focusing on the behind-the-scenes technology that creates the magic of film, televison, and theater, this page houses links to information and businesses related to stagecraft, separated into topics such as lighting, sound, or special effects.

Entertainment Technology Center

http://cwis.usc.edu/dept/etc

The Entertainment Technology Center works to ensure the practical application of technological innovation in movie studios and other entertainment-related industries. This support page has information on the center's research, personnel, sponsors, and news.

Lucasfilm THX

http://www.thx.com/thx/

Because "sound is 50 percent of the motion picture experience," Lucasfilm has developed state-of-the-art THX technology for accurate sound reproduction and delivery in theatres and homes. Learn more about the hi-tech audio equipment, its applications and current distribution.

NewTek, Inc.

http://www.newtek.com/

NewTek, Inc. maintains this site to provide information about The Flyer, its "tapeless" video editing system. Visit here to learn about the system's capabilities and configuration.

Screenplay Format

http://www.teleport.com/~cdeemer/
Format.html

Hollywood insider Charles Deemer offers the budding screenwriter tips for getting the margins and tabs just right (which can make or break that million-dollar sale). He also provides links to software designed for computer-literate wordsmiths.

Screenwriters Online

http://screenwriter.com/insider/news.html

Visitors to this site can chat with professional screenwriters or subscribe to the trade journal, "The Screenwriters Insider Report." Registration for new visitors is required.

Screenwriters/Playwrights Page

http://www.teleport.com/~cdeemer/
scrwriter.html

Devoted to the art and craft of screenwriters and playwrights, this informational page offers links to resources professionals and hobbyists will find useful. Visitors can find links to writing tips and courses, film and play databases, reviews, and general information.

Thinking Pictures Web Site

http://www.thinkpix.com/

Thinking Pictures is a multimedia agency that designs video games, Web sites and interactive content for film and television. The company gives an overview of its services on this promotional page and outlines its efforts to establish a premier rock-n-roll network, rock.com.

FESTIVALS AND EVENTS

Atlanta Film and Video Festival

http://www.solutions.ibm.com/multimedia/
festival.html

Winners and nominees from previous and upcoming Atlanta Film and Video Festivals are presented here. Background materials include information on judging criteria, event venues, panel members, and project sponsors.

Festival

http://plaza.interport.net/festival/

The Festival site announces winners and nominees of the awards from the annual Sundance Film Festival held in Park City, Utah. This page also offers up-to-date festival news, interviews, and the "latest buzz."

Film Festivals on the World Wide Web

http://www.laig.com/law/entlaw/filmfes.htm

This index provides a comprehensive listing of film festivals around the world. Includes links to the biggies, like the American Film Institute's shindig in Los Angeles and, of course, Cannes, as well as pointers to lesser known festivals, from student expos to Finland's Espoo Cine.

Film Festivals Server

http://www.filmfestivals.com/

The smell of popcorn, the excited rustling of film fans, the stickiness of the floor under your feet: the true movie lover knows the joy of film festivals. The Film Festivals Server travels around the world to cover events from Cannes to Prague in depth, and they provide an exhaustive list of all worldwide festivals.

San Francisco International Film Festival

http://sfiff.org/

The San Francisco Film Society reels off information about upcoming and previous international film festivals here. Visitors can also download the society's newsletter and join its mailing list on this page.

Stockholm Film Festival

http://www.filmfestivalen.se/

This film festival site provides a slate of new studio releases and separate programs from American and Swedish independent producers. Thumbnail descriptions of the films themselves are also here, with titles that range from "Angel Baby" to "The Young Poisoner's Handbook."

Svjetski Festival of Animated Films

http://animafest.hr/

The 11th World Festival of Animated Films in Zagreb, Croatia, is the focus of this site featuring award winners, daily programs and exhibitions.

 EDITOR'S CHOICE

Drew's Script-o-Rama

http://pobox.com/~drew/scripts.htm

Sprinkled with fabulous photos and covered in juicy trivia, even the heartiest fan pages can lack the one thing true TV and film junkies hunger for: a script. Sure, a carrot-topping of Kenneth Branagh or a hair-teasing of Jennifer Aniston may satisfy the weekend Web warrior, but where's the beef? Dig into this script archive for a menu of more than 500 full-text screenplays and teleplays. Some scripts are even served in rough form, penned by the writers themselves, "not some Cheez Doodle-eating transcriber," as Drew puts it. For a complete meal, try the "Marlon Brando" display mode, featuring all related script info. If you've got to eat and run, try the leaner "Kathleen Turner Style: meaty, but can still move" or "Kate Moss Style: everything you need, but nothin' extra."—*Reviewed by Paul Bacon*

An announcement for the 1996 festival and links to information about Zagreb and Croatia are also included. In Croatian and English.

World Film Festival
http://www.ffm-montreal.org/
Scheduled for August 22 to September 2, 1996, Montreal's World Film Festival previews its event on this home page. Find competition rules, media accreditation regulations and general info. An archive of pages from previous festivals is also included.

FILMMAKERS

Akira Kurosawa: A Tribute to Akira Kurosawa's Dreams
http://www.aisb.org/~ddj/dreams/index.html
This page is a collection of seven JPEG images that comprise a tribute to Japanese filmmaker Akira Kurosawa's most popular works. Visit here for graphics from "Sunshine through the Rain," "The Tunnel," "Crows," and others.

Alfred Hitchcock
http://hitchcock.alienor.fr/
The shower scene in "Psycho" is perhaps the definitive Hitchcock scene. Or is it when Cary Grant is sliding down Mt. Rushmore? No matter which you think it is, if you're a Hitchcock fan, you'll want to visit this French site dedicated to the master of suspense. In French only.

Alfred Hitchcock—The Master of Suspense
http://nextdch.mty.itesm.mx/~plopezg/Kaplan/Hitchcock.html
A reverent rather than critical approach characterizes this collection of facts and musings about Alfred Hitchcock's life and work. At this site, film buffs can explore biographies, essays, and filmographies about the legendary director of classic suspense flicks like "The Birds" and "Vertigo."

The Edward D. Wood Home Page
http://garnet.acns.fsu.edu:80/~lflynn/edwood.html
Ed Wood, a B-movie director known for dressing in angora sweaters, is celebrated here. Fans will find a filmography of the director turned cult figure, along with biographical information, images and tips on which Wood movies to buy.

Kubrick Multimedia Film Guide
http://www.lehigh.edu/~pjl2/kubrick.html
This elaborate fan-produced page has information on the many works of film director Stanley Kubrick. Includes images and sounds from Kubrick's films—including "2001: A Space Oddysey," "A Clockwork Orange," and "Full Metal Jacket."

Mike Jittlov: The Web Page of Speed and Time
http://www.shore.net/~rdl/jittlov/jittlov.html
Animator Mike Jittlov is best known for his work in stop-motion shorts such as "The Wizard of Space in Time," which is the main focus here. Rabid Jittlov fans can find out more about his work, hook up with others of their kind and download a pattern for an origami wizard.

Orson Welles
http://www.voyagerco.com:80/CC/gh/welles/intro.html
The forward-thinking publisher of interactive media, Voyager, presents this glimpse into the life of Orson Welles. Visit here for a look at the underappreciated actor/director/writer who influenced a generation of films with his classic "Citizen Kane."

Quentin Tarantino, A God Among Men
http://www.mind.net/nikko11/QT.html
Quentin Tarantino: a man or a god? Decide for yourself. Read about his professional accomplishments, including the secrets from the film "Pulp Fiction," view selected Tarantino sights, then listen to some soundbites from recent productions.

Quentin Tarantino: Ultimate Quentin Tarantino Links
http://www.idb.hist.no/~kennetha/tarlink.html
Dig him! Fans of black comedy film director Quentin Tarantino, creator of "Pulp Fiction," will enjoy this unofficial disciple page. Visit here for an extensive index of links to Tarantino-inspired Web pages, organized by project, including "Reservoir Dogs" and "True Romance," and "Natural Born Killers."

Tarantino World
http://www.phantom.com/~jbonne/tarantinoworld/
Visit this site to enter the "demented little home for those obsessed by the Big Man of American film," Quentin Tarantino. Features on online homage to the director of "Pulp Fiction," including visions, quotes, sounds, and links.

Woody Allen
http://www.idt.unit.no/~torp/woody/
Admirers of the understated, legendary comedic actor, and film creator Woody Allen can peruse funny lines—and some great soundbites—in this site from a dedicated fan. Explore details of Allen's past career, or check out a complete filmography with photos.

a2z EDITOR'S CHOICE

Internet Movie Database
http://us.imdb.com
Did you ever wonder in what movie Arnold Schwarzenegger uttered the legendary, "I'll be back"? (He said it in eight different flicks, so take your pick.) How about the number of films featuring the song "Unchained Melody"? Only two: "Ghost" and "Naked Gun 2." Visit the Internet Movie Database for tidbits like these, created by a do-it-yourself trivia generator churning through a bank of facts from more than 65,000 films. Everything including film locations is included, offering, for example, all Vietnam warmovies shot in the Philippines (19). Visitors are also encouraged to submit movie-related facts, even continuity mistakes like this from the "Pulp Fiction" file: "Marvin was supposedly shot in the face, yet his intact head can be seen in the trunk of the car."—*Reviewed by Paul Bacon*

Quick Search Form: *(select one area and enter a search string)*

Movie/TV title: ● Substring ○ Exact
Cast/crew name: ○ All ○ Actors ○ Actresses ○ Crew
Character name: ○ Actors ○ Actresses
Word search: ○ Quotes ○ Plots ○ Biographies ○ Soundtracks
Find:

Start search   reset form

FILM SCHOOLS AND INSTITUTES

Chapman University Department of Film & Television

http://www.chapman.edu/comm/ftv/index.html

This Orange County, California-based film education department invites you to tour its facilities and meet its faculty here. It details its graduate and undergraduate programs and posts excerpts from "Animation Journal," a scholarly publication devoted to animation history and theory.

Cyber Film School

http://www.cyberfilmschool.com

Get all the angles on cinematography and movie production here. See Editor's Choice.

George Eastman House

http://www.it.rit.edu/~gehouse/

Stop by this international museum of photography and film page for a biography of George Eastman along with online exhibits and a timeline of his work. It also offers information about courses in motion picture restoration at the Massachusetts Institute of Technology.

London International Film School

http://www.tecc.co.uk/lifs/index.html

The London International Film School offers this page to acquaint potential students with its program and courses. Browsers here can also find school news and events as well as information on some of the better-known graduates.

MacMeckarna

http://www.mm.se/

MacMeckarna, a Swedish multimedia production training company, maintains this promotional site. Subjects taught by the institution include digital sound, video production, graphics and communication technology. Available in Swedish.

The New York Film Academy

http://www.panix.com/~nyfa

The New York Film Academy home page provides information about its eight-week course in film writing, directing, editing, and shooting. This site also offers background on its animation and directing workshops.

Sundance Institute

http://cybermart.com/sundance/institute/institute.html

The Sundance Institute page contains information about the institute's support of independent filmmaking. Includes information about programs, a calendar of events, links to film sites on the Internet and the Sundance catalog.

University of Barcelona Center for Cinematic Research

http://www.swcp.com/~cmora/cine.html

The Center for Cinematic Research at the University of Barcelona provides a general overview of its cinema studies program, course offerings and faculty profiles. Includes information on its home city and links to Spanish servers.

GENRES

Asian Movie Home Page

http://www.seas.upenn.edu/~luwang/lu.html

If you're looking for Jackie Chan or Gong Li, this is the place for films and stars that hail from Hong Kong, "Bollywood," and other film capitals west of the Pacific. Visit the Asian Movie Home Page for actor and actress profiles, photos and film information.

The Cabinet of Dr. Casey Horror Web Page

http://www.cat.pdx.edu/~caseyh/horror/index.html

This ghoulish site is for lovers of the macabre. Visitors will find a multimedia look at horror movies and stories, including an archive of movie posters, a timeline of the popular film genre, and an audio and graphics archive.

Cal-Animage Alpha Chapter

http://server.berkeley.edu/CAA/

The University of California at Berkeley's Japanese Animation Club offers this site, with an on-line art gallery, publications and links to other animation archives around the globe. An image archive of digital animation is also provided here.

Christmas Movies

http://www.auburn.edu/~vestmon/christmas_movie.html

Visitors to this site will info on film productions about everyone's favorite time of year: Christmas. Each entry links visitors to production factoids, starring roles and director profiles. Film critics are asked to submit ratings online.

CowboyPal

http://www.cowboypal.com/

Silver-screen cowboys ride again at this homage to Gene Autry, Roy Rogers and the other Saturday afternoon matinee idols of yesteryear. Shot through with nostalgia, this site offers the chance to hear Hopalong Cassidy's laugh, watch movie clips, shop for memorabilia, and more.

Hindi Movie Songs

http://www.cs.wisc.edu/~navin/india/songs/index.html

Visit this archive site for a collection of Hindi songs from India. Its extensive index provides links to an assortment of poems, film song lyrics,

---

a2z EDITOR'S CHOICE

The Movie Cliches List

http://www.like.it/vertigo/cliches.html

As the evil twin told the balding accountant, shouting over the din of rumbling rednecks, just after narrowly escaping death in a slow-motion explosion, "Movies are full of cliches." These overused stereotypes and nearly every other intellectual shortcut used in Hollywood are exposed at length at this humorous site. Get the lowdown on war: "You're very likely to survive any battle, unless you show someone a picture of your sweetheart back home"; intergalactic travel: "There's a deep humming in space, no doubt about it"; and user-friendly explosive devices: "Evil geniuses are always thoughtful enough to include a visible display (usually LED) of how much time remains before a bomb detonates."—*Reviewed by Paul Bacon*

bhajans, shlokas, and ghazals from the "ITRANS Song Book."

Hong Kong Movies Home Page
http://www.jyu.fi/ntjko/hkmovie/

Hong Kong film buffs can download filmographies and find information on new releases here. The site includes actor profiles and an overview of Hong Kong films, which the Webmaster allows may be cheap—but are never boring.

Horror Haven
http://www.magicnet.net/~tkearns/horror.html

Godzilla will trample your home town if you don't stop by this horror film tribute before your next visit to the video store. One fan has compiled her list of horror favorites from the classics to more recent gore fests at this site.

Jei's Anime Treehouse
http://soyokaze.biosci.ohio-state.edu/~jei/anime/

Jei's Anime Treehouse is one of a growing number of sites that celebrate anime, a Japanese style of animation that often combines innocent imagery and raw brutality. Visitors will find an extensive "turnpike" of anime links and resources, as well as picks and pans.

Silent Movies
http://www.cs.monash.edu.au/~pringle/silent/

Fans of film's earliest days are in for a treat at this silent movie resource index. Visit here for links to sites featuring silent movie classics, stars, accompanying music scores, and preservation societies. Includes links to upcoming screenings.

INDIVIDUAL FILMS a2z

FAN PAGES

Arielholics Anonymous
http://www.csee.usf.edu/~aschenke/tlm/ariel.html

Dedicated to "all things Ariel," the animated superstar of "The Little Mermaid," this fan page is swimming with information on the hit Disney character. Splash into the pool and net image files, sound bites, song lyrics, and more.

Batman: Welcome to Wayne Manor
http://www.books.com/batman/batman1.htm

Welcome to Wayne Manor! Click on "Foyer" to take a virtual tour of Batman's front yard, gallery, library, conservatory, game room, guest rooms, and book stacks. A must for fans of Batman comics, movies or TV series.

Blues Brothers
http://www.nta.no/brukere/kol/bb/

"We'll never get caught. We're on a mission from God." Fans of these two quasi-saints from the windy city will enjoy this unofficial site, featuring an extensive collection of sights, sounds, and film information.

Brazil: Hypermedia Brazil FAQ
http://execpc.com/brazil/

Fans of fantasy film maker Terry Gilliam can learn about the embattled creation of "Brasil," a film that was almost too good for Hollywood. Visit here to learn about Gilliam's controversial project and his struggle to maintain artistic control.

Buckaroo Banzai
http://bbs.annex.com/relayer/bbanzai.htm

Dedicated to the 1984 film and book "Buckaroo Banzai," this offbeat and eclectic Web site serves up background information, sound bites and truly weird delvings into the movie and its online culture. Lots of fun with puzzles, soundbites, and other memorabilia.

Commanders Club/San Francisco: James Bond 007 Home Page
http://www.commanders.com/~bond/

The Commanders Club of San Francisco is a fan club dedicated to the "celebration of the lifestyle of a Scottish peasant named "Bond, James Bond". A plethora of Bond-related information here includes the "essentials" of 007, collectibles, archives, the 007's Day Planner, and club information.

The Crow Home Page
http://pulsar.cs.wku.edu/~nothing/crow.html

Fans of "The Crow" will enjoy this fan-produced site, offering background on the film and its star, Brandon Lee, who was killed during its filming. Bring a fast modem to access graphics-intense pages.

The Gamera Home Page
http://tswww.cc.emory.edu/~kgowen/gamera.html

Awakened by a nuclear explosion, Gamera, the last of his race of prehistoric giant turtles, stars in nine Japanese films and this multimedia Web page. Visitors can find images, sounds and in-depth movie analyses at this site.

The Heathers Home Page...How Very!
http://www.best.com/~sirlou/heathers.shtml

The late 1980s served up a dark satire of high school hijinks in the form of the cult film "Heathers." Join other fans in adulation of the timeless tale of boy meets girl, boy tries to kill girl, boy commits suicide. Complete with images and sounds.

---

a2z EDITOR'S CHOICE

Cyber Film School
http://www.cyberfilmschool.com

If you're preparing for your first shoot or just trying to get into film school, drop by this info-packed site for all the angles on cinematography and movie production. The Cyber Film school posts an amazing amount of film-related instruction and enough Hollywood insider's tips to get even the greenest director or writer lunching with them best of 'em. A virtual classroom provides in-depth coverage of screenwriting, directing and post-production basics. Its "Action!" newsletter provides updates on the latest trends and happenings in filmmaking as well as exclusives on budding players and projects. Other features include an artist-in-residence discussion forum, new screenplay postings and an extensive directory of industry contacts.—*Reviewed by Paul Bacon*

James Bond Agent 007

http://www.mcs.net/~klast/www/bond.html

Visitors can delve into the world of the sophisticated spy and learn about the actors who have played the fictional British spy, from Connery to Brosnan. The site includes clips from the 007 films, a look at Ian Fleming's books and detailed trivia. (It's shaken, not stirred.)

The Official Rocky Horror Picture Show Web Site

http://www.rockyhorror.com

Get the latest "Rocky" info at this site. See Editor's Choice.

Pulp Fiction

http://www.colargol.edb.tih.no/~kennetha/pulp.html

This fan-produced tribute to "Pulp Fiction" contains a wealth of information about the Tarantino film. Includes a gallery of images, sound file, interviews with the actors and director, a copy of the complete script, a filmography, and answers to Frequently Asked Questions (FAQs)..

The Rocky Horror Picture Show

http://chs-web.umdl.umich.edu/odd/RHPS/

The creator of this Rocky Horror resource page explains the popularity of the film from a disciple's perspective. Visitors will also find links to other related sites on the Web, a sound archive, and a collection of images and clips from the film.

The Rocky Horror Picture Show

http://www.cs.wvu.edu/~paulr/rhps/rhps.html

"The Time Warp," "Damnit Janet," "Hot Patootie-Bless My Soul"—this homage to the cult film classic has 'em all. There's even a list of opening credits and an all-important prop list.

The Rocky Horror Picture Show Web Site

http://www.uta.fi/~cstivi/rocky.html

You've seen it a hundred times, but that's still not enough. Fans of the quintessential cult film "Rocky Horror Picture Show" will find memorabilia and fan club news, and virgin newcomers can learn Rocky etiquette and initiate themselves through FAQs. "Enter at your own risk!!"

Spinal Tap Home Page

http://rhino.harvard.edu/elwin/SpinalTap/home.html

"But these go to eleven." Fans of Rob Reiner's spoof rockumentary "This is Spinal Tap" will enjoy this unofficial page, featuring sound clips and digital images. Includes index of other "Spinal Tap" fan pages and reviews of related books and CD-ROMs.

Star Wars Home Page

http://force.stwing.upenn.edu:8001/~jruspini/starwars.html

The legendary sci-fi trilogy lives at this fan-produced site. See Editor's Choice.

The Star Wars Humor Page

http://www.echo.simplenet.com/humor/

A collection of rib-ticklers spoofing the sci-fi classic, the "Star Wars" Humor Page takes on the mother of modern science fiction films with song parodies, graphical humor, merchandising barbs and a "Kill Lando" link. For a chuckle at the expense of the sacred cow of sci-fi flicks, link to this site now.

Star Wars: Jayme's Star Wars Page

http://www.hamline.edu/personal/jstoller/starwars.html

There are tributes to the "Star Wars" trilogy, but this is a Star Wars page with a little extra. In addition to the usual images and links on the Star Wars movies and characters, this site contains complete movie scripts, information on Star Wars toys, poster images, and bloopers for the critical fan.

Star Wars: May The Force Be With You

http://www.mindspring.com/~ejoiner/stwars.html

"Star Wars" fans can launch to dozens of pages devoted to the trilogy from here. This slick index includes graphics and a real audio snippet from Darth Vader.

Star Wars: The Complete Star Wars Listing

http://www.princeton.edu/~nieder/sw/sw.html

This site is determined to index all online resources relating to the "Star Wars" movies. Find hundreds of links to fan-produced tribute sites, company and merchandising home pages, games and collectibles sites, and pictures and multimedia archives.

---

a2z EDITOR'S CHOICE

The Official Rocky Horror Picture Show Web Site

http://www.rockyhorror.com

"Let's do the time warp again!" And again, and again, and again. When will these glove-snapping, water-spurting, toast-throwing heathens quit? "Never" is the prognosis at the long-awaited, official tribute to the quintessential cult classic, "Rocky Horror Picture Show." Now more than 20 years old, this B-grade horror spoof still packs theaters around the world with highly participatory audiences, known for their rituals of dressing like film characters, dancing on stage and screaming like animals. Get the latest "Rocky" info, including updated biographies of cast members, memorabilia catalogs, and in-depth guides on audience etiquette ("Don't throw hot dogs or prunes . . . it attracts rodents and stains the screen").—*Reviewed by Paul Bacon*

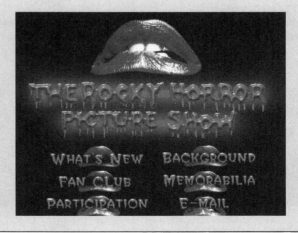

Star Wars: The Rebel Underground Site

http://www.cs.uit.no/~thorr/starwars/starwars.html

May the force be with you as you explore The Rebel Underground, a page that tours the galactic world of "Star Wars." Visit for links to pictures and insights into the popular film trilogy's characters.

Super Catgirl Nuku Nuku

http://www.cs.ubc.ca/spider/edmonds/anime/nuku.html

The Japanese anime Super Catgirl Nuku Nuku, a female android with a cat's brain, is the focus of this fan-produced site. Visitors will find episode summaries and a cast of characters, plus a link to the St. Johns Anime Film Society.

The Terminator Movies Home Page

http://www.ifi.uio.no/~haakonhj/Terminator/

He'll be back! Learn more about the wildly popular science fiction adventure films that turned Ahhnold into a superstar. Links include scripts from the movies, film clips, images, and sound files.

The Tron Home Page

http://www.aquila.com/guy.gordon/tron/tron.htm

What would happen if a computer game player was literally sucked into the game and forced to play for his life? That premise for the movie "Tron" is paid tribute on this fan-produced page. It features images and sounds from the movie, along with a fan list.

PROMO PAGES

Ace Ventura

http://www.aceventura.com/

Just in case you didn't get enough of Ace Ventura from the movie or the animated TV series, visit this official Warner Bros. site. Includes photos, production notes and downloadable "tushy-talking" sounds from the Jim Carrey vehicle.

The American President

http://www.americanpresident.com/

Castle Rock Entertainment plugs its film "The American President" with this elaborate site designed to give the uninitiated a taste of life in the Oval Office. Visitors can face media inquisitors in a virtual press conference or participate in an online poll.

Casper

http://www.mca.com/universal_pictures/casper/

Welcome to Whipstaff Manor and the front gate to a tour of the hit movie "Casper." Don't get spooked when you peek behind the scenes or download the haunting images and scary sounds this promotional home page offers.

Clueless

http://www.paramount.com/Clueless.html

Here, Paramount Pictures promotes "Clueless," a film about Cher Horowitz, a Beverly Hills high school kid who's, like...clueless. The site, which doubles as a spoof on personal pages, details the world of Cher.

Congo

http://voyager.paramount.com/Congo.html

Fans of the blockbuster film based on Michael Crichton's novel "Congo" will enjoy this official Web tribute. Visit here for downloadable images, production notes, and links to animal protection organizations' home pages.

Daughters of the Dust

http://pacificnet.net/geechee/Daughter1.html

Find out about Julie Dash's film "Daughters of the Dust" here—"a tribute to women of color." Visitors can read a biography of the author or link to the home page of Geechee Girls Productions, Inc.

Desperado Spotlight Movie Page

http://www.spe.sony.com/Pictures/SonyMovies/Desperado/index.html

Desperate "Desperado" fans will want to add a bookmark to Sony Online's spotlight of the movie. See clips and stills of the steamy movie—including exclusive pictures of Antonio Banderas and Selma Hayek. In Spanish and English.

First Knight Home Page

http://www.spe.sony.com/Pictures/SonyMovies/16knight.html

The "First Knight" home page summarizes the movie's plot, links to actor and crew information, offers multimedia clips and refers visitors to other King Arthur-related sites. Includes interactive game the Quest and a link to Sony Corp.'s home page.

Goldeneye

http://www.mgmua.com/bond/

Access this dossier for the official MGM/UA briefing on the 1995 James Bond action film, "Goldeneye." Clandestinely capture files on classified film clips, secret images, secured sound bites, and other "for your eyes only" information.

Hackers

http://www.mgmua.com/hackers/index.html

MGM/UA maintains this promotional site for its film "Hackers." Visit here to discover its world be-

hind-the-scenes, from biographies of the cast and filmmakers, to an overview of the production itself.

Johnny Mnemonic

http://www.spe.sony.com/Pictures/
SonyMovies/06jonmnu.html

Peek behind the production scenes of "Johnny Mnemonic"—a big-budget thriller about a man that literally knows too much—on this official page. Visitors can download audio and video and find pictures of heartthrob Keanu Reeves.

Jumanji

http://www.spe.sony.com/Pictures/
SonyMovies/Jumanji/index.html

Hold on to your hat and enter the official "Jumanji" Web site. The film stars Robin Williams as a grown-up little boy who is captured by an enchanted board game. Watch the movie to see if he is set free, but play the game here if you dare.

The Net

http://www.spe.sony.com/Pictures/
SonyMovies/17net.html

This Sony-produced site provides audio, video, and photos taken from "The Net," along with information about the film's star, Sandra Bullock. Visitors also can check out production notes, enter a contest, or buy tickets over the Internet using the MovieLink service.

Phantasm Home Page

http://www.phantasm.com/

One of the scariest movies this reviewer has ever seen, the classic horror flick "Phantasm" is examined and explored on this well-designed fan page. Get background information, sound files, reviews, and a peek behind the scenes.

Showgirls

http://www.mgmua.com/showgirls/index.html

Repackaged as a cult favorite, the film "Showgirls" dances into the spotlight, offering a peak "Behind the Scenes with the Showgirl Queens." Also enjoy the best 25 lines from the film and a trivia quiz, darlin'.

Species

http://www.mgmua.com/species/index.html

Take a journey into a science fiction world where alien and human psychology struggle within the lead character in the MGM/UA movie, "Species." Visitors can read more about the movie or launch into the virtual world through this link.

Strange Days

http://www.strangedays.com/

Viewers can "jack in" to a sleek photo gallery on this promotional page for the film "Strange Days." The 1995 film stars Ralph Fiennes and Angela Bassett and is directed by Kathryn Bigelow.

Virtuosity

http://www.paramount.com/virtuosity/
index.html

Paramount Pictures presents this promotional home page for the film "Virtuosity," starring Denzel Washington. View clips and stills, or read about the behind-the-scenes activities and players.

MOVIE LISTINGS AND THEATERS

Boston Local Movie Listings

http://www.actwin.com/movies/index.html

Active Window Productions Inc., a Boston-based Internet consulting firm, maintains this site offering local movie listings. Visit here to find theater locations and screening times for current films and to link to listings for other cities.

Clamen's Movie Information Collection

http://www.cs.cmu.edu/afs/cs.cmu.edu/user/
clamen/misc/movies/README.html

Silver screen fans in Steeltown can look up cinema schedules, film reviews and the latest industry gossip at Pittsburgh-based Clamen's Movie Information Collection. Film facts, festival news, and commentary abound.

Film Unit

http://www.shef.ac.uk/uni/union/susoc/fu/
home.html

What's playing at the University of Sheffield's student union cinema? Find the current season's program and a proposed program for next season, along with an overview of the student society which produces the showings.

---

a2z EDITOR'S CHOICE

MovieLink

http://www.movielink.com

Some people buy newspapers for news, some for sports, some for the funnies. But many of us buy the paper exclusively for movie listings. For "well-read" movie fans, here's a chance to save a few forests worth of newsprint: an online theater directory. Already available via telephone in several U.S. cities, the popular 777-FILM service is now on the Web. Visitors simply enter a ZIP code and select a film, and MovieLink generates an updated list of all nearby screenings. This free service even remembers where you live, so the next time you check the site—even the following weekend—just pick a movie, and you're off to the theater. Some locations even offer online ticket sales.—*Reviewed by Paul Bacon*

Hello Paul, and welcome to MovieLink. To change your neighborhood from San Francisco, 94109, click here. To change other options, click here.

Local Movie Listings

http://www.actwin.com/movies/other.html

Visitors here will find local movie listings for cities world wide ranging from Dublin to Ljubljana to Iowa City. Seven countries are represented on this site, and the list grows with visitor submissions.

Los Angeles Webstation

http://www.losangeles.com/

Just down the street from Hollywood, but still don't know what's on? Focusing on the Los Angeles area, this online movie guide provides listings of movies appearing on television, available on video and in current theatrical release. Includes film reviews.

MovieLink

http://www.movielink.com

MovieLink provides local movie listings. See Editor's Choice.

Movienet

http://www.movienet.com/

Goldwyn/Landmark Theaters posts a current listing of films showing in the entertainment giant's chain of movie theaters across the United States. Listed by city, you can get the showtimes and features anywhere the company has a theater.

Movies This Weekend

http://www.sai.com/movies/

New Englanders, plan your next trip to the theater or video store with the help of Movies this Weekend. Updated weekly, this page lets visitors search for celluloid entertainment options by movie, location or theater name.

The San Francisco Bay Area Cinema Guide

http://www.movietimes.com/

Moviegoers living in the city by the bay can turn to this movie guide, offering theater schedules, film reviews and links to entertainment-related sites. Visitors will also find pointers to major motion picture studios.

Steps Theatre Programme

http://www.dct.ac.uk/www/steps.html

This page offers synopses of films and the times they will be shown at Steps Theater, located at the University of Abertay Dundee in England. Includes a link to the university's home page.

MOVIE MERCHANDISE AND MEMORABILIA

Blockbuster Entertainment

http://pwr.com/blockbuster/

Find out what's "new and exciting at Blockbuster—but in a whole new way." Drop into Blockbuster Entertainment, Web home for the U.S.-based video store megachain, for news and previews, or catch up on the Blockbuster Entertainment Awards.

Family Home Video

http://www.iea.com/~fhv/

Got a house full of kids, but don't know what movies are fit for consumption? This commercial site features the online catalog of Family Home Video, offering more than 25,000 titles for online ordering.

Movie Madness

http://www.moviemadness.com/

An online store for movie and television memorabilia, the Movie Madness site features an electronic showroom and ordering system. Fans can purchase official t-shirts, mugs and collectibles emblazoned with the title of their favorite film or TV show.

Movie Poster Warehouse

http://www.io.org/~mpw

Movie posters are the focus at this commercial site, but photos and scripts also are available. Shoppers can browse the online catalog of more than 6,500 posters and even get their purchases framed.

The Movie Posters Archive

http://anubis.science.unitn.it/services/movies/index.html

This online resource for movie memorabilia collectors features electronic versions of famous movie posters. All of these collector's items are free and include posters from sci-fi, horror, animation...even Italian movie classics.

The Picture Palace

http://www.ids.net/picpal/

The Picture Palace maintains this promotional site for an enormous catalog of video titles. Visit here for movies and music videos, plus links to a variety movie-related home pages and ordering information.

Star Wars Collectors Archive

http://www.cs.washington.edu/homes/lopez/collectors.html

"Star Wars" memorabilia and collectibles are spotlighted here at this fan-produced site. Visit here for a well-organized listings of toys, cards, costumes, props, autographs, and other items.

Video Disc International

http://www.thesphere.com/VDI/VDI.html

Laserdisc afficionados who don't want to shell out the big bucks for new titles can purchase quality used discs through the online catalog of Video Disc International. Search, review, and order products electronically at this commercial site.

MOVIE STARS

Note: This section is alphabetized by the actor's last name where applicable.

The Sandra Bullock Page

http://weber.u.washington.edu/~louie/sandra.html

You liked her in "Speed." You loved her in "Twice if by Sea." Well, maybe you didn't, but a lot of people did. If you're one of them, stop by this fan-produced site for a wealth of news, press clips and background information on the actress.

The Sandra Bullock Public Information Web Page

http://www.kaiwan.com/~sirfitz/bullock.html

Who is she, where did she come from, what does she think about...things? Hollywood actress Sandra Bullock stands beneath the spotlight at this fan site offering pointers to films, facts, photos, fan fun, and news flashes.

Jim Carrey Web Page

http://www.halcyon.com/browner/

He's got a face of rubber, and a mind of...well, we're not sure. Find out more what goes on inside this super-comedian's head and browse another fan's collection of news, reviews, photos, sound files, and answers to Frequently Asked Questions (FAQs) about Jim Carrey.

Harrison Ford: The Unofficial Harrison Ford Stuff Home Page

http://www.mit.edu:8001/people/lpchao/harrison.ford.html

This multimedia tribute to the ageless hunk Harrison Ford opens with a quick bio and career facts. Browsers can then move on to links, articles and graphics, and for the true fans, audio and video clips.

Jodie Foster Fan Page

http://weber.u.washington.edu/~jnorton/jodie/jodie.html

The woman who started goofing around in Disney films and walking the streets in "Taxi Driver" now has more clout in Hollywood than many film studios. Visit this fan-produced tribute to learn more about actress/director/producer Jodie Foster.

Pamela Franklin: An Appreciation of Pamela Franklin
http://www.webcom.com/~funhaus/pf/

A fan pays tribute here to the actress Pamela Franklin, whose late 1960s and early 70s films include "Flipper's New Adventure" and "The Innocents." Visit for a biography, images and a Java-enhanced filmography. The site also posts a schedule of when Franklin's films rerun on television.

Janeane Garofalo
http://www.crl.com/~rfleming/Janeane/Janeane.html

A fan who boldly states "Janeane Garofalo is my love, my life, my light," shares the object of his adoration with the world. Visitors will find photos of and trivia about the comic actress, plus Garofalo's public appearance schedule.

Anthony Hopkins: Sir Tony
http://www.mit.edu:8001/people/douglas/hopkins.html

From the terribly serious ("Silence of the Lambs") to the terribly silly ("The Road to Wellville") Anthony Hopkins never fails to win the hearts of movie audiences. This fan page, (formatted like a newsletter) pays tribute to the Oscar-winning actor Anthony Hopkins—offering bits of news and other notions.

Laurel & Hardy!
http://www.sirius.com/~sramsey/TheBoys/LandH.html

Back when it was still politically correct to beat up on little guys, Laurel and Hardy were America's favorite comedy duo. Fans of their films will enjoy this site, offering a variety of links to Laurel and Hardy pictures, fan clubs, articles and other funny stuff.

Marilyn Monroe Home Page
http://www.ionet.net/~jellenc/marilyn.html

This multimedia Marilyn page features a biography of the iconic actress, along with information about the films she starred in and scores of photos. Links to memorabilia information and other fan pages are available.

Andie MacDowell—A So-called "Actress"
http://rampages.onramp.net:80/~scottgl/andiemcd.htm

A selection from Scott's Page of Evil, Scott Glazer doesn't pull any punches in tearing apart every movie role Andie MacDowell has ever performed in. And about MacDowell being a supermodel, Scott muses, "First supermodel with a mustache I ever heard of."

Colm Meaney: Miles O'Brien
http://www.astro.umd.edu/~sgeier/obrien.html

"For whatever reason, Miles O'Brien (aka Colm Meaney) seems to be ignored by most people," writes the Webmaster of this site. Not so here. Visitors to this Miles Edward "Chief" O'Brien fan page will find loads of links and adoration regarding the "Star Trek" star.

The Meg Ryan Page
http://web.cs.ualberta.ca/~davidw/MegRyan/meg.cgi

Sweet and funny. Smart and sassy. Fans of diverse comic actress Meg Ryan ("When Harry Met Sally," "Sleepless in Seattle") will enjoy this site featuring a variety of information, images, quotes and an audio archive. There's also a filmography, links to articles about the American actress and a user response form.

Winona Ryder Fan Page
http://www.duc.auburn.edu/~harshec/WWW/Winona.html

Fans of actress Winona Ryder will enjoy this photo-filled, unauthorized fan site, offering info on the actress' life and film roles, from "Beetlejuice" to "Boys." Links to magazine articles, film clips and soundbites also are available.

Elizabeth Shue
http://www.dapence.com/elisabeth.shue

The female star of the award-winning "Leaving Las Vegas" and not-so-award-winning "Cocktail" is the focus of this fan-produced site. Visit here to learn the latest about Elizabeth Shue as well as a biography, images and a list of her work in film and television.

John Travolta Home Page
http://www.execpc.com/~aemog/travolta.html

Can you say "Pulp Fiction saved my career"? John Travolta can, and visitors to this unofficial fan page will find all types of information on the comeback kid from "Welcome Back Kotter." Includes biographies, photos and links to an extensive collection of related sites.

Van Damme: The Shrine to Jean Claude Van Damme
http://www.shef.ac.uk/uni/union/susoc/cass/homes/pm/pm933303/vandamme.html

Biographical information tells his story; action-packed photographs reveal his form. Join fellow fans in paying homage to the martial arts expert and action film star, the man Van Damme.

PUBLICATIONS AND INDUSTRY NEWS

Boxoffice
http://www.boxoff.com

Boxoffice, the business magazine of the motion picture industry for more than 75 years, posts this online offering. Visitors will find a wide variety of article and features, including reviews, interviews, and in-depth reports. Includes back issues and subscription information.

PK Baseline
http://www.pkbaseline.com/baseline.html

Paul Kagen's Baseline is a complete insider's resource for those in the entertainment biz. This fee-based service provides box office information, details about films, biographies, celebrity contact information and online versions of many industry publications, including Daily Variety and The Hollywood Reporter.

Producer's Masterguide Home Page
http://www.producers.masterguide.com/

First published in 1979, "Producer's Masterguide" is billed as the "production bible" for film, television, commercial and video producers. Check out the newest edition of the Masterguide from this site, which features excerpts and the table of contents, and order the book if you like what you see.

REVIEWS AND FILM CRITIQUE

Circle of Critics
http://moviereviews.com/coc-roost.html

Entertaining movie reviews can be found here. See Editor's Choice.

The Dove Foundation
http://www.dove.org

This page provides a listing of wholesome family movies. See Editor's Choice.

Hollywood's Coming!
http://www.c3f.com/hollywoo.html

If Hollywood can't get us right, who can? Visit here to find tongue-in-cheek, satirical capsule descriptions of recent movies about the Internet and its "surfer" culture. Guests can check out summaries of movies like "Hackers" or "Virtuosity," and "save the price of admission."

a2z EDITOR'S CHOICE

Circle of Critics

http://moviereviews.com/coc-roost.html

We had set out to really rip the critics to pieces, being critics ourselves, but this bunch gets two thumbs up! The Circle of Critics, part of the larger Moviereviews.com site, offers articles that are more entertaining than many of the movies they're reviewing. Check out Women's Lip, a female reviewer (who's a dead ringer for Florence Henderson in her fuzzy online photo), trumpeting the merits of "Twister" for its believable portrayal of a woman hero and its ability to create "unsightly stains on the underarms of my sweatshirt. "The Gabby J-man (who's a dead ringer for a female reviewer) also provides some great insight from a British perspective: "I have to say that "Babe" requires the right conditions, and thus watching it after a 'noight 'oot' with the lads getting wired is likely to spoil this just a little bit."—*Reviewed by Paul Bacon*

The Dove Foundation

http://www.dove.org

Here's a resource for anyone who mistakenly took a minivan full of preteens to see "Addams Family Values" only to find out it is a death-worshipping assault on all that is good and right. The Dove Foundation, a non-profit organization aiming to "promote wholesome family entertainment," provides this home page for a listing of more than 1,500 movies deemed worthy of its "Dove Seal of Approval." The reviews have a serious Christian spin, lambasting Disney's "Pocahontas" for depicting frontiersman John Smith as having "succumbed to the influence of Indian nature-centered spiritual beliefs," but more secular audiences may be pleased to find that Dove discourages boycotting Disney entirely for providing "fringe benefit (employment) policies to same-sex partners." Reportedly displayed in more than 800 video stores across the United States, the Dove seal means family-approved entertainment.—*Reviewed by Paul Bacon*

Interactive Movie Reviews

http://batech.com/cgi-bin/showmovie

Interactive Movie Reviews lets you be the judge of the best movies in filmdom, instead of "some overpaid pinhead." Visit here to throw in your two cents so that others may not have to throw in their eight bucks.

Movie Review Query Engine

http://www.cinema.pgh.pa.us/movie/reviews

The Pittsburgh Cinema Project provides this searchable database of movie reviews available on the Web and the Usenet newsgroup rec.arts.movies.reviews. All reviews are indexed by film title.

Moviereviews.com

http://useattle.uspan.com/events/movie-listings.html

Not everyone is born Rex Reed. Not everyone wants to be, either, but if you want an assortment of great movie reviews, check out this elaborate site. Features in-depth reviews of current titles, plus online chat rooms, bulletin boards, and showtimes.

Professor Neon's TV & Movie Mania

http://www.vortex.com/ProfNeon.html

Professor Neon delves into the world of film, television, videos and related topics, with an emphasis on the odd and unusual. Includes are film reviews and an online magazine about the cable television industry. Visitors can also download a full range of audio and video clips.

Teen Movie Critic

http://www.dreamagic.com/roger/teencritic.hyml

"I am 17 years old. I have been fanatically interested in movies since I was very young." Visit this site for some juicy movie reviews from a member of generation Y. Includes current titles and movie classics of the past.

Tucson Weekly's Film Vault

http://desert.net/filmvault/

Tucson Weekly shares terse, smart-alecky reviews of new films here, with hundreds listed alphabetically. Questing film lovers can search for their favorite films or head over to a wealth of other film links.

STUDIOS AND PRODUCTION COMPANIES

Alliance Communications Corp.

http://www.alliance.ca

The Alliance Communications Corp. is a fully integrated supplier of film entertainment. This corporate home page includes links to Alliance's subsidiaries in film and television production and broadcast and cable networks distribution, plus information on the company's financial investments in entertainment software.

Future Pirates

http://www.fpi.co.jp/

The Japanese digital film production company Future Pirates reveals some of its recent productions along with a behind the scenes look at its creator, Takashiro Tsuyoshi. Find out about one of Japan's most outlandish hypermedia creators and his creations. In English and Japanese.

The Lion's Den

http://www.mgmua.com

The Lion's Den is the home lair of MGM/UA productions. Find previews and clips of MGM/UA films and television shows, information on the stars, a glimpse into the proud history of the studio, and a chance to buy merchandise featuring the distinctive trademark lion, Leo.

LucasArts Entertainment Company

http://www.lucasarts.com/

LucasArts Entertainment Company develops and publishes interactive entertainment and educational software. Visit here to learn more about the multifaceted company, comprising Industrial Light & Magic, Skywalker Sound, Lucasfilm Ltd., and THX.

Lucasfilm's THX Home Page

http://www.thx.com/thx/thx.html

George Lucas's production company, Lucasfilm, makes laser discs and THX sound systems for commercial and home theaters. The company gives an overview of its products on this promotional page.

MCA/Universal Cyberwalk

http://www.univstudios.com/

This mammoth commercial Web site gives the lowdown on Universal Pictures' films and MCA Records' artists. Visitors also can check up on other members of the MCA/Universal corporate family, including Universal Studios Hollywood, Putnam Berkley Online, Winterland Productions and Spencer Gifts.

Miramax Cafe

http://www.obs-us.com/obs/english/films/mxframes

Find materials and activities related to select films at this site. See Editor's Choice.

Movies.Com

http://www.wdp.com/

This site serves as the gateway to the Buena Vista MoviePlex, the Buena Vista MoviePlex International and the TVPlex sites. Visit here for information on Buena Vistas' current movies, television programs and promotions.

NoodleHead Network

http://www.together.com/~noodlhed/

The NoodleHead Network is a Vermont-based video company specializing in educational videos by and for children. "Kid-powerd video" subjects range from racism to energy conservation to dealing with grown-ups.

October Films

http://www.octoberfilms.com/user/october/index.html

Founded in 1991, October Films has released such critically-acclaimed independent films as "The Last Seduction" and "Killing Zoe." Visitors to its home page will find a variety of movie-related fun and information.

Pacific Data Images

http://www.pdi.com/

Take a look at the company that made Homer and Bart Simpson three-dimensional in a recent Halloween episode through this page for Pacific Data Images. Visitors can also view animations and clips the digital imaging firm created for such movies as "Batman Forever."

Paramount Pictures Online Studio

http://voyager.paramount.com/Voyager.html

Hollywood entertainment giant Paramount Pictures throws open the studio gates and promotes its latest releases at this official site. Movie-goers can preview what's currently at theaters and television viewers can look behind the scenes of Paramount's TV hits.

Pixar Animation Studios

http://www.pixar.com/

Pixar Animation Studios maintains this site to promote its many multimedia projects, including the Disney film, "Toy Story." Get a glimpse of its animated storybook, link to the company's software customer support site or read reviews of the computer-animated hit film.

Rhythm & Hues Studios

http://www.rhythm.com/

Located in Hollywood, California, Rhythm & Hues Studios produces sophisticated visual effects for feature films, television commercials, theme park rides, and music videos. Visit its home page for

---

a2z EDITOR'S CHOICE

Miramax Cafe

http://www.obs-us.com/obs/english/films/mxframes

Anyone who has been enthralled with a groundbreaking film knows the feeling: you walk out of the theater on a cloud, imagination fired and curiosity peaked. To satisfy that curiosity, pay a visit to the Miramax Cafe, providing an online library of thematic reading materials and multimedia activities for select films. The section for "Cry, the Beloved Country," a film about racial reconciliation, features writings by Nelson Mandela. Fans of "Restoration," based on 17th century England's leap into the Modern Age, are treated to a host of scholarly materials, videos and bibliographies from Cambridge University and other historic archives. Despite its promotional function, this site turns out to be quite an education.—*Reviewed by Paul Bacon*

background information and a look at its latest projects.

Sony Pictures Entertainment
http://www.spe.sony.com/Pictures/
SonyMovies/index.html

Sony Pictures Entertainment's colorful home page offers a virtual screening of the company's current and classic movies. Includes movie news and behind-the-scenes information on films still in the making.

Twentieth Century Fox Home Entertainment
http://www.tcfhe.com/

Hollywood mainstay Twentieth Century Fox invites you to "experience the history of Fox one decade at a time" at this promotional site. Visit here for information on classics such as "Star Wars" and recent blockbusters like "Speed" and "Mighty Morphin Power Rangers."

United International Pictures
http://www.uip.com/

The official site for United International Pictures offers information the latest films it has promoted for MGM/UA, Universal Pictures and Paramount. Visit here for the latest from the distributors of "The Birdcage," "Eye for an Eye," and "The Nutty Professor."

Universal Pictures
http://www.mca.com/universal_pictures/

Preview coming attractions and current releases from Universal Pictures at this official studio site. Enjoy multimedia clips, stills, studio news, star interviews, and other movie magic from the people who brought you "Jaws" and "The 10 Commandments."

MUSIC

ARCHIVES AND INDICES

Acoustic Guitar Song Collection
http://fy.chalmers.se/~jmo/
acoustic.guitar.song.collection.html

This page provides guitar tablatures and musical scores, plus audio and sound files of selected songs by Simon and Garfunkel, Paul Simon, Leonard Cohen, and Serge Gainsbourg. Additional features include links to interviews with the artists and other musical resources.

Ambient Music Information Archive
http://hyperreal.com/ambient/

This repository of information and Web resources is relevant to ambient music. Holdings are organized under the headings of local archives, essential information, and ambient music-related links.

Artist Access
http://www.artistaccess.com/cdaudio/
artistaccess.html

Artist Access introduces the work of independent recording artists by using the Internet and direct mail. Find a list of artists and their CDs, an inexpensive CD sampler, and a calendar of live performances.

Australian Music Charts
http://www.cs.monash.edu.au/~jamies/charts/
index.html

In case you're not satisfied with just knowing who is at the top of the Australian music charts today, use the indices at this site to check chart data dating back to 1989. Links to other Australian and world music charts also are available.

Big Bro Media Home Page
http://www.cyber.nl/bigbro/welcome.html

Big Bro Media of the Netherlands designs and maintains music and entertainment Web sites. This home page includes listings on labels, art-

---

a2z **EDITOR'S CHOICE**

DiscoWeb
http://www.msci.memphis.edu/~ryburnp/discoweb.html

Dust off that polyester suit with the wide lapels for a virtual visit to DiscoWeb, where the bootie shaking is hosted by a professor who claims to be the only University of Memphis faculty member with a fully operational disco ball in his office. Revisit the cringe-worthy dark days of the 1970s by sampling a list of 101 Top Disco Songs; highlights include The Weather Girls' "It's Raining Men," the once ubiquitous "Funkytown," and, of course, the indispensable "I Will Survive," courtesy of Miss Gloria Gaynor.

The wonder and the glory of disco "fashion" is celebrated, catalogued, and dissected here, as is a breathless career retrospective of a younger (less wealthy) John Travolta and the definitive guide to doin' the hustle. Get down, get funky, get a former life in this land where disco never died, but instead got dolled up in platform shoes, a snow-shovel necklace, and a feckless disregard for the inevitable fallout of the party now, pay later years. Do a little dance, make a little love, get down tonight: In cyberspace, no one can hear you scream.—*Reviewed by Julene Snyder*

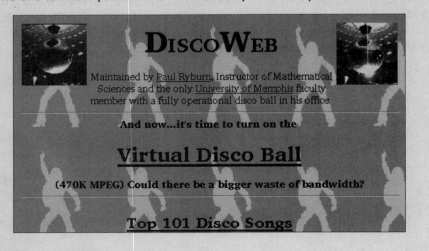

DISCOWEB

Maintained by Paul Ryburn, Instructor of Mathematical Sciences and the only University of Memphis faculty member with a fully operational disco ball in his office

And now...it's time to turn on the

Virtual Disco Ball

(470K MPEG) Could there be a bigger waste of bandwidth?

Top 101 Disco Songs

ists, releases, and raves, as well as news and information on Big Bro and rave/techno music.

CAIRSS Music Database

http://-www.einet.net/hytelnet/FUL064.html

Telnet to CAIRSS—the database of music research literature—from this site, or just use the search screen to find music research information. The contents of 15 relevant journals resides in the database, plus articles from over a thousand additional sources.

Chinese Music Page

http://vizlab.rutgers.edu/~jaray/sounds/chinese_music/chinese_music.html

Lovers of eastern music will find a bounty of Chinese music bytes at this Rutgers University Sound Page. From the traditional and ceremonial to modern melodies, FTP archives provide downloadable .au clips. Political speeches are included, too.

Contemporary Music Info-Junction

http://www.thoughtport.com/thoughtport/gallery/resident/CMIJ/

The Contemporary Music Info-Junction archives information about composition and theory, orchestration and media, institutes, organizations, academic programs, and much more.

CultureFinder: The Internet Address for the Performing Arts

http://www.culturefinder.com/

CultureFinder hosts a wealth of resources for lovers of classical music, dance, opera, and theater. Here browsers can peruse such features as the culture find of the week, news, and interviews, or drop by the online shop and library. In English, French, Spanish, and German.

The Mudcat Cafe

http://www.deltablues.com/dbsearch.html.

Search this cross cultural index for folk songs by title, keyword, or tune. The Digital Tradition Folk Song Database catalogs folk music from around the globe.

DiscoWeb

http://www.msci.memphis.edu/~ryburnp/discoweb.html

Fans of disco music will enjoy this site, maintained by Paul Ryburn, the only University of Memphis faculty member with a fully operational disco ball in his office. Visit here for song lists, historical perspectives, newsgroups, merchandise outlets, and many other disco-related resources. Includes a downloadable disco ball graphic. See Editor's Choice.

European Free Improvisation home

http://www.shef.ac.uk/misc/rec/ps/efi/ehome.html

European Free Improvisation is a comprehensive information source with individual sections ranging from video clips to upcoming concerts.

Ever Expanding Web Music Listing

http://www.columbia.edu/~hauben/music/web-music.html

Here browsers will find the self-proclaimed mother of all hotlists to musical subjects on the Web. A wealth of data concerning musical interests can be found in the subject index, or visitors may sit back and browse the long list of broadly based musical sites.

4AD: The Eyesore Database

http://www.maths.monash.edu.au/people/rjh/music/eyesore/eyesore.html

Influential indie record label 4AD's roster of artists ranges from ethereal mood setters Cocteau Twins to twisted geek rocker Frank Black. This exhaustive archive offers in-depth information about 4AD's releases, including song and performer lists, interviews, and displays of distinctive album art.

The Gigaplex!

http://www.gigaplex.com/

Gigaplex is a vast Web magazine with over 600 pages relating to arts and entertainment. Movies, theater, TV, books, art, and music are among the subject categories. See Editor's Choice.

---

a2z EDITOR'S CHOICE

The Gigaplex

http://www.gigaplex.com

The vast environs of the Gigaplex roam from ArtPlex to YogaPlex to SexPlex, but over at the MusicPlex section, the offerings are succinct, entertaining, and occasionally useful: Dive into a monthly mix tape, check out a list of the top 25 selling albums of all time (hint: think dinosaur rockers), devour dozens of feature interviews with everyone from Annie Lennox to Zubin Mehta to David Byrne to Doc Severinsen (!) and beyond.

Where else can one learn that Dolly Parton writes songs while applying makeup? Or that David Byrne feels sorry for Tony Perkins? Or that even Don Henley cringes when he hears his own songs? Relax, if that's too mind-taxing for you, just look at the pretty pictures of "rock legends of the 1970s" and ponder the axiom that old rockers never die—they just put out career retrospectives and laugh all the way to the bank.
—*Reviewed by Julene Snyder*

Musicplex

GIGAPLEX MIX TAPE NEW!

JUNE 1996

TOP 25 NEW!
BEST-SELLING ALBUMS OF ALL TIME

Global Music Centre

http://www.eunet.fi/womad/

Global Music Centre's Web site puts visitors in touch with an entire planet's worth of world music resources. Included are recordings, educational, and festival information, along with links to related music areas on the World Wide Web. In English and Finnish.

Gothic Image Database

http://www.vamp.org/Gothic/Images/index.html

A gothic rock devotee presents this robust collection of images for fellow fans. Here guests can download a slew of band photos and album artwork, from such infamous musicians as Siouxsie and the Banshees and Christian Death.

Harmony Music List

http://orpheus.ucsd.edu/harmony/

The Harmony Music List, a service of the Music Library of the University of California at San Diego, provides an extensive index of music resources. Visitors will find discographies of selected artists, links to music labels, online publications, and many other music-related Web sites.

The Industrial Page

http://bird.taponline.com/industrial/

A native Chicagoan has compiled an industrial music archive at this site. Wanderers here can find information about the artists, labels, and clubs that make up the bleak, angry landscape of this mechanical music movement.

Internet Music Review Service

http://www.monsterbit.com/IMRS/

Browsers needing a bit more information before hitting the CD aisles will find hundreds of music reviews here. The extensive site is maintained by a team of four writers and includes reviews posted to the newsgroup rec.music.reviews.

Internet Underground Music Archive

http://www.iuma.com/IUMA/

The Internet Underground Music Archive (IUMA) is an online music store offering a searchable directory of bands, both independent and signed, links to online music magazines, and information about events. Online ordering is available. See Editor's Choice.

Internet Underground Music Archive Europe

http://iuma.southern.com/

This London-based site, maintained by Southern Studios, contains links to bands such as the Beastie Boys, labels like Grand Royal, an art gallery, and IUMA itself.

IPEM Multimedia Archive

http://next.rug.ac.be/

Delve into the IPEM Multimedia Archive to immerse yourself in electronic resources relating to new music. Find research articles, musical notation collection, and sound clips here.

Jazz Improvisation

http://hum.lss.wisc.edu/jazz/

Visit this page for a music index featuring links to jazz and blues sites around the world. Also included is a series of articles taken from the syllabus for two jazz classes taught at the University of Wisconsin (Madison).

Jukebox

http://www.sirius.com/~mega/metal/jukebox.html

Mega's Jukebox is a no-frills site offering downloadable audio or .au files of full-length songs. Musical offerings here are geared toward the heavier side of American rock 'n' roll, with such bands as Alice In Chains, Guns 'n' Roses, Jimi Hendrix, Nine Inch Nails, and The Red Hot Chili Peppers.

Latvis' RockData

http://www.sjoki.uta.fi/~latvis/rockdata.html

The latest in Finnish rock is outlined, dissected and hyped here. The site includes information about Finnish record companies, booking agents, bands, venues, and radio stations. In English and Finnish.

The Leo Music Archive

http://www.leo.org/archiv/music

Musicians will find the "Internet's largest charts-collection," a link to the Olga guitar tab archive, and a song lyric archive on this FTP site. The German-based site includes pictures, movies, and information about the Woodstock festivals. In English or German.

Links to Marching Bands

http://seclab.cs.ucdavis.edu/~wetmore/camb/other_bands.html

The Music Man would be thrilled to see this page: He would be able to pick the type of marching band that he wanted to visit next, and he'd discover a list of links to band Web sites. Two members of the Cal Aggie marching band maintain the page.

---

a2z EDITOR'S CHOICE

Internet Underground Music Archive

http://www.iuma.com/IUMA/index_graphic.html

For all the dirt on the indie scene, check out the environs of the Internet Underground Music Archive. Here you'll find the online home of hundreds of independent bands from all over the world, with plenty of details on each. A typical band site includes audio excerpts, an examination of specific songs and recordings, the obligatory bio, and ordering information. Other features include artists indexed by label, links to online music magazines like Gavin and ICE, and "events, experiments, and percolating projects."

Visitors can search by genre, name, or choose a band at random; represented labels include 4AD, Heyday, Metal Blade, TeenBeat Records, and Windham Hill. Impress your friends and dazzle your enemies: Dive into IUMA.—*Reviewed by Julene Snyder*

Welcome to the Net's first, free hi-fi music archive.

It's Fun! It's New!
Sign-In.
Woo Hoo!

Enter
IUMA
at high speed with rich graphics. . .

Enter
IUMA-lite
at low speed with slim graphics. . .

Maestronet

http://www.maestronet.com

Visitors to the Maestronet can browse the Instrument Showroom in search of fine stringed instruments and bows, or stop by the Conservatory and download sheet music. A library of topical materials and a discussion area are also featured.

MIDI Archive FTP Site

ftp://ftp.ucsd.edu/midi

Browsers can download MIDI related software, scores, and documents from this anonymous FTP archive. The archive is maintained by a member of the rec.music.synth Usenet newsgroup.

MIZIK Home Page

http://www.unik.no/~robert/mizik/mizik.html

Dedicated to furthering the musical listening range and education of net users, the MIZIK Home Page connects visitors with sound files of some unusual musical genres—such as African or Brazilian music and folk songs. Visitors can check out an amazing variety of sound files, find out where to order such music, and much more.

Monsterbit Media Home Page

http://monsterbit.com/

Monsterbit Media focuses on today's pop culture and music, providing links to bands, independent labels, music festivals, and more. This page also includes "Pop Culture Press," a 'zine that offers reviews as well as articles about music biz pros.

The MUSIC-Archive

http://www.leo.org/archiv/music/music_e.html

At this music archive, which is available in English and German, visitors can find information such as music charts, song lyrics, tablatures, images, movies, and links. There are also programs, utilities, and information on electronic music, MIDI, and other computer-related music.

Music Education Resource Base

http://www.ffa.ucalgary.ca/merb/

The Music Education Resource Base, which includes the Canadian Music Index, is an archive of more than 27,000 resources in music and music education selected from 27 journals since 1956 to the present. The fully indexed database allows searches by author, journal, title, volume number, and page.

Music Machines

http://www.hyperreal.com/machines/

Some think music that isn't plugged in just isn't worth playing, and Mike Perkowitz, author of this enormous site of electronic music information, is obviously among them. Mike guides synth music lovers through purchasing the right equipment for their needs, with contact information for manufacturers, and specs for many different instruments.

The Music Pages

http://english-www.hss.cmu.edu/music/

Music resources from across the Internet can be accessed via this page, with links to music theory, criticism, and compositions, along with music journals and newsgroups. A part of the English Server project at Carnegie Mellon University.

Music Previews Network

http://www.mpmusic.com/

Hear and read about new music releases from the world of rock, jazz, and country among other genres at the Music Previews Network. Browse an online artists' listing and listen to tunes by downloading clips or using RealAudio software.

Music Resources

http://www.siba.fi/Kulttuuripalvelut/music.html

Finland-based Sibelius Academy presents an exhaustive list of music related resources on the Net, ranging from composers to music libraries to publications. In English and Finnish. See Editor's Choice.

Music Resources on the Internet

http://www.music.indiana.edu/music_resources/

This listing of music resources on the Net is a service of the Indiana University Music Library. Visitors will find links to academic resources, artist-specific sites, and other lists and indices here.

The Numbers: Music

http://web3.starwave.com/showbiz/numbers/music/top250.html

Run down the list of the top 250 albums as compiled by Sound Scan, the company that reports the top sellers to "Billboard" magazine. Find this week's rankings of albums (and artists), their rankings last week and two weeks ago, as well as how many weeks they've been on the charts.

Online Music and Audio References

http://www.art.net/Links/musicref.html

The Online Music and Audio References site is a gateway to various musicians, bands, and online music services. Includes links to record labels, radio station, and related resources.

---

a2z EDITOR'S CHOICE

Music Resources

http://www.siba.fi/Kulttuuripalvelut/music.html

Finland doesn't usually cry out "music!" but this site presented by the Sibelius Academy is one of the most exhaustive lists of music related resources we've found on the Net. It's all just a click away, broken down in categories like music schools, libraries and archives, or by period. If you don't have the time to roam about, the entire site is searchable. In English and Finnish.—*Reviewed by Julene Snyder*

Music Catalogues	Music Magazines
Church Music	Music and Arts Education
Composing	Music Libraries and Archives
Computer Music, MIDI, etc.	Music Schools and Departments
Early Music	Music Theory and Research
Finnish Music	Opera
Folk Music and World Music	Orchestras, etc.
Instruments	

Planet StarChild

http://www.streams.com/starchild/

Starchild Records and MultiMedia presents links, categorized by genre, to musical artists from around the world here. One feature is IndieLink, a searchable directory of bands. Also included are worldwide concert listings and links to online tools and utilities.

Psychedelic Psyberspace

http://cfn.cs.dal.ca/~af678/cyberspace.html

Browsers searching for the eternal long, strange trip will find an index that features "links to various flowerpower sites and a multitude of psychedelic music links" here. In addition to music, links focus on drugs and the culture of the 1960s.

Rastaman

http://www.missouri.edu/~c643267/Rasta.html

Rastaman: The Other Reggae page has links to a number of reggae pages and sites, including the Usenet newsgroup rec.music.reggae, the Jammin' Frequently Asked Questions (FAQs) file, and a Reggae glossary. A link to the Unofficial Bob Marley home page is also included.

RockWeb Interactive

http://www.rock.net/

Silicon Forest provides interactive music resources on the RockWeb. Here browsers will find links to bands, musicians, news, information, image, and sound sources.

San Francisco: Bay Area Underground Music

http://server.berkeley.edu/SFMusic/

This page covers the beat—beginning with the Bay Area underground music scene, then linking club to club and page to page across the country and around the world. Featuring bands, shows, classifieds and comments, the BAUM page rocks, rolls, and reels.

Songs at NVG

http://www.nvg.unit.no/songs/

Vital statistics for selected musical artists can be found at this site, with an open invitation to additional talent.

Sound Wave

http://soundwave.com/

Sound Wave creates and maintains Web pages for people in the music business. Visitors can wander through its clients' pages here, which range from recording studios to artist agencies to bands. The site also includes employment information.

TRAX*USA

http://www.traxusa.com/

TRAX*USA offers guided tours through a collection of music-oriented site collections that compose this "domain where Life, Liberty, and the pursuit of Happiness is paramount." Subject matter is organized together in "villages" such as the New Media Cafe or Fresh Trax.

The Ultimate Band List

http://american.recordings.com/wwwofmusic/ubl/ubl.shtml

The Ultimate Band List is a Web site featuring music and band-related links where visitors can add their favorite links to their own home pages. This site is searchable alphabetically, or by genre, or resource. An online record store is also featured.

VH1 Main Screen

http://vh1.com/

Before you pick up the clicker and dial in the VH1 cable network, check its home page for news about featured artists and highlights from the daily schedule. Stop by to talk with other VH1 viewers in chat areas or let the network know what you think about its play list.

The Vibe: Surf!

http://metaverse.com/vibe/surf.html

Adam Curry, former MTV personality, posts his favorite Web pages at this site. The links compiled are an alphabetical listing of predominantly rock 'n' roll-oriented resources with an emphasis on artist rather than music genre.

Web Wide World of Music

http://american.recordings.com/WWWoM/

Do you want to chat? Then the Web Wide World of Music is the hottest place for that. Check The Ultimate Chat List to locate the best IRC sites, or jump to The Ultimate Band List for an interactive guide to thousands of band Internet resources.

Worldwide Internet Live Music Archive

http://wilma.com/

Keep on top of the live music world at the Worldwide Internet Live Music Archive, or WILMA. This

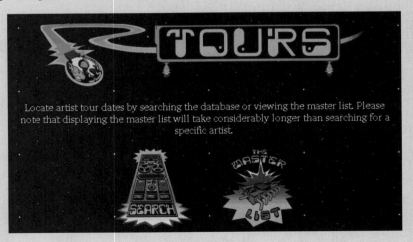

Los Angeles-based company claims a searchable database of more than 5,000 venues and 1,800 artists, providing links to tour information, season schedules, official band Web sites, and more. See Editor's Choice.

World-Wide Web Virtual Library: Music—Artists

http://syy.oulu.fi/artists.html

The author of this page says this is not an exhaustive page for musical artists, but it's a pretty good compendium for musical reference, from the Kronos Quartet to Queen. The author is willing to post pages forwarded by browsers.

ASSOCIATIONS AND ORGANIZATIONS

American Orff-Schulwerk Association

http://www.aosa.org/

The American Orff-Schulwerk Association, an organization of music and movement teachers, explains its school of thought here. Visitors can learn about the technique the group uses to teach children music, developed by Carl Orff, a German composer. Includes an index to music, dance, and arts sites.

Bad Taste Web

http://www.siberia.is/badtaste/badhome.htm

Iceland's Bad Taste, a progressive music organization and main nourishing root of pop band The Sugarcubes, gives visitors a tasty sample of itself here. Sound samples, a virtual gallery, and Quicktime movie are available to the curious.

BMI

http://bmi.com/

BMI is a nonprofit organization representing more than 160,000 songwriters, composers, and music publishers in all areas of music. Visitors can search the royalty-distribution organization's database to find information on songs and weekly music updates.

The Canadian Electroacoustic Community

http://lecaine.music.mcgill.ca:80/~cec/

The Canadian Electroacoustic Community, a Montreal-based nonprofit organization of music composers, performers, education and researchers, maintains this informational site. Visit here for news, publications, membership information, and links to a variety of related Web sites.

Cascade Blues Association

http://www.teleport.com/~boydroid/blues/cba.htm

The Cascade Blues Association, a Portland, Oregon-based blues and roots music preservation organization, outlines its activities at this site. Visit here for news, local blues concerts, and events, band, and musician profiles, blues radio shows, merchandise, and more.

Creative Musicians Coalition

http://spider.lloyd.com/~dragon/cmc.html

The Creative Musicians Coalition is comprised of individuals and institutions devoted to the success of independent musicians and new music. This Web site consists of an overview of the organization, contact information, and CMC members' home pages.

Guild of American Luthiers

http://www.deltanet.com/GAL/index.htm

What's a luthier? A person who makes and repairs stringed instruments and who probably belongs to the guild sponsoring this page. Learn about the organization, review issues of "American Lutherie," the guild's magazine, or find out about becoming a member.

Harmony Central

http://www.harmony-central.com/

An Internet resource for musicians, Harmony Central provides dozens of links to music-related information online. Visitors can also perform a search on all the Harmony Central pages.

JAZZ WEB Dutch Jazz homepage

http://huizen.dds.nl/~toetsie/ukindex.html

A Dutch piano student and semiprofessional musician maintains this site, offering annotated lists of jazz clubs, festivals, and organizations in Holland and Europe. A compilation of links to jazz-related Web sites is also featured.

Los Angeles Music Access

http://com.primenet.com/home/

Los Angeles Music Access (LAMA) maintains this site with a variety of musician and music promoter resources, including artist information, a band gig calendar, sound software, and the LAMA manifesto.

Music Publishers' Association

http://www.mpa.org/

Among the online resources hosted by the Music Publishers' Association, find a directory of member publishers and an index of their imprints. A copyright resource center is also featured as part of the association's continuing mission to disseminate information.

National Online Music Alliance

http://songs.com/noma/

The National Online Music Alliance represents independent American singers and songwriters who have national followings but are not signed with major record labels. Here, browsers can read about the artists, browse through a virtual music store, and order CDs online.

The Plainsong and Mediaeval Music Society

http://www.ncl.ac.uk/~nip2/

The Plainsong and Mediaeval Music Society is a hundred year old English group devoted to the traditions of music and chant before the year 1550. Its membership comprises scholars, clergy, and musicians. It invites new members here and details its small grant program for musicians.

Save The Earth Foundation: ArtRock Auction

http://www.commerce.com/save_earth/

Save The Earth Foundation donates to universities with innovative earth sciences and environmental studies programs. It holds an online ArtRock Auction here to help raise money; browsers can bid on posters and photos signed by famous musicians, or donate directly to the cause. The site also includes an online rock magazine.

Wolverine Antique Music Society

http://www.teleport.com/~rfrederi/

For those who remember when recorded music came on something other than CDs and cassettes, there is the Wolverine Antique Music Society. Information here includes historical articles, images, and recordings.

CITY BEAT

Ann Arbor: Anecdote Productions

http://anecdote.com/

An underground club in Ann Arbor, Michigan, the Anecdote maintains this online mirror of the club's activities. Visitors can check out the art gallery and see who's on stage.

Austin Music

http://www.quadralay.com/www/Austin/AustinMusic/AustinMusic.html

The complete Austin, Texas, music scene is detailed at this site, provided by Quadralay Corporation. Includes listings of clubs and bands, links to other area music servers, and information on classical music performances.

Australia: Next Online

http://www.next.com.au/music

The Music pages of Next Online features music reviews, news, and magazines. Visitors can read issues of the Australian Rolling Stone, download songs, and peruse the latest in industry news.

Australia: Oz-jazz Worldwide

http://magna.com.au/~georgeh/

Oz-jazz Worldwide focuses on Australian jazz music. It includes news, musician profiles, jazz gigs, festivals, radio programs, and sound clips. Links to other music and jazz sites are included.

Australia: Triple J Zone

http://www.abc.net.au/triplej/

Triple J is an Australian youth-culture magazine sponsored by a popular radio station. Browsers on this promotional page can read excerpted features, reviews and comics from the magazine, and give smart-alecky feedback to its editors.

Boston Music Scene

http://www.research.digital.com/CRL/Boston/Music/

Check out what's happening on the music scene in Boston. This enthusiast's page features information on upcoming shows, area clubs, local 'zines, and recording labels—plus links to area band pages.

Britain: Haywire Home Page

http://www.phreak.co.uk/haywire/

Those looking to let loose in the U.K. can check the clubs listed in the Night Haunts section or check out promos of unsigned bands. The ever-shifting, frequently fickle U.K. music scene is the focus here.

British Isles: Christian Gig Guide

http://www.shef.ac.uk/misc/rec/sm/

The Christian Gig Guide serves as a guide to concert information for the British Isles. Webmaster Stephen Mettam posts information about upcoming events as well as pointers to other Christian Web sites of interest.

Chicago Concert Search

http://student-www.uchicago.edu/users/achatche/music/concerts.html

The Chicago Concert Search home page offers visitors a searchable database of classical concerts in the area, including chorales and chamber music. Search by date or series. Also links to a similar search engine for Cleveland, Ohio.

Chicago PsyberView

http://www.chitown.com/

Chicago PsyberView is devoted to the music scene in Chicago. Visitors will find band profiles, concert and club information, and images.

Finland Rave Info

http://www.damicon.fi/fri/

Devoted to providing information about dance raves and other stay-up-late events in the Land of the Midnight Sun, this site links to a rave mailing list, indexes of past events, the club scene, and more. Includes articles on techno (in Finnish only).

France: French Music Database

http://www.sirius.com/~alee/fmusic.html

If it's French and it's concerned with music, you'll find it here. There's an alphabetical index, a French-English concordance chart, a top 50 listing, a directory of composers and lyricists, and links to other music sites. In French.

Los Angeles Club Dates

http://www.primenet.com/~sk8boy/shows.html

Find out who's playing which Los Angeles club and when at this entertainment Web site, which features well-organized listings of alternative, punk, and indie rock around town. Visitors can also link to band home pages or add to the list of club dates.

Los Angeles Music Access

http://com.primenet.com/home/

Los Angeles Music Access (LAMA) maintains this site with a variety of musician and music promoter resources, including artist information, a band gig calendar, sound software. and the LAMA manifesto.

Mountain View: Alberto's Nightclub

http://www.albertos.com/

Latin music and dancing fans can warm up for a night on the town at Alberto's Nightclub. Get salsa lessons online or take down directions to the Mountain View, California club.

New Orleans: William Ransom Hogan Archive of New Orleans Jazz

http://www.tulane.edu/~lmiller/JazzHome.html

This site is the online home of the Hogan Jazz Archive, an "internationally renowned resource for New Orleans Jazz research." Visit here to peruse information on the archive's oral history interviews, sheet music, orchestration, photographs, documentation, and special collections.

New York: The Postcrypt Coffeehouse

http://www.cc.columbia.edu/~crypt/

The Postcrypt Coffeehouse at Columbia University brings its diverse musical background to the Web at this home page. The page includes links to well-known artists who have performed there, including Shawn Colvin, Suzanne Vega, and Patty Larkin.

Prince Edward Island: buzzON

http://www.isn.net/buzzon/index.html

Craving information about the performing arts on Prince Edward Island, Canada? Drop by the Welcome to buzzON page for links to feature stories and images on artists, dancers, and musicians.

San Diego: Zoom Arts & Entertainment News

http://w3.thegroup.net/~zoom/

ZOOM San Diego provides arts and entertainment news for "the City on the Edge." Visit its home page for listings from live theater, concerts, films, museums, and sporting events in the Southern Californian city.

San Francisco: Bay Area Underground Music

http://server.berkeley.edu/SFMusic/

This page covers the beat—beginning with the Bay Area underground music scene, then linking club to club and page to page across the country and around the world. Featuring bands, shows, classifieds, and comments, the BAUM page rocks, rolls, and reels.

San Francisco: Concerts in the Bay Area

http://www.sfbayconcerts.com

The Concerts in the San Francisco Bay Area site provides a listing of concerts, organized by date and venue. Includes an e-mail address for submissions and updates.

San Francisco: Subculture Home Page

http://www.subculture-tv.com/

The Subculture site provides a guide to alternative music and entertainment in the San Francisco Bay area. The page features recent and upcoming happenings in night life, movies, TV, and radio. It also has links to Quicktime video clips, pictures, and multimedia HyperCard and Director files.

The St. Louis Concertweb

http://www.stl-music.com/

Take me to a concert in St. Louis, but check the St. Louis Concert Web before you pick me up. The site offers information about upcoming shows and the local nightlife, as well as tips about concerts elsewhere in the U.S. and the world.

Tokyo Rockin'

http://www.iijnet.or.jp/tko.rockin/

Nippon Television Network in Japan explores the music scene in Tokyo at this graphic-rich site. Visitors will find music charts, monthly party news, and tips on where to find Japanese records in America. In Japanese or English.

Tucson: DesertNet

http://desert.net/

This site features the gateway to the DesertNet, a news and infotainment server originating in Tucson, Arizona. Curiosity seekers won't want to miss the Hall of Heads; audiophiles will enjoy the music bin; movie buffs, the film vault; and for the lonely hearts, personals.

The Underground Point of Pittsburgh

http://info.pitt.edu/~houser/

An "attempt to gather together the Pittsburgh underground and alternative scene" is found here. Browsers will find links to others sites in Western Pennsylvania and information about local radio shows.

COMMUNITY BANDS AND ORCHESTRAS

Boston Chamber Ensemble

http://www.mit.edu:8001/people/jcb/BCE/bce.html

The Boston Chamber Ensemble's home page provides information about this East Coast chamber orchestra and its annual nationwide composition competition. Browsers will also find information about the group's concerts here.

Indianapolis Symphony Orchestra

http://www.in.net/iso/

The Indianapolis Symphony Orchestra unveils its concert schedule and introduces its members through this site. Visitors can also click to the Instrument Petting Zoo with its information about the program that encourages children to pluck and play musical instruments.

Leland Stanford Junior University Marching Band

http://www-leland.stanford.edu/group/lsjumb/

If the hotdog lines at halftime made you miss them live, the Leland Stanford Junior University Marching Band is happy to fill you in on its hijinks and performance highlights here at the band's home page.

Links to Marching Bands

http://seclab.cs.ucdavis.edu/~wetmore/camb/other_bands.html

The Music Man would be so happy to see this page: He would be able to pick the type of marching band that he wanted to visit, and he'd discover a list of links to band Web sites. Two members of the Cal Aggie marching band maintain the page.

Longwood Symphony Orchestra

http://www.ai.mit.edu/people/lethin/longwood.html

Information about the Longwood Symphony Orchestra in Boston hits the Net through this page. Stop in to read about the orchestra's performances in Jordan Hall at the New England Conservatory or to listen to an audio clip of the symphony playing Beethoven's Ninth Symphony.

Marching Owl Band Home Page

http://riceinfo.rice.edu/~lynette/MOB.html

Not your typical marching band with "Q-Tip" hats, Rice University's controversial Marching Owl Band recruits 10 percent of the university's student body to form shapes from "fire hydrants to prophylactics." Visit the MOB's home page for all the news on the band, plus pictures, music, and links to other "scatter" bands.

Melbourne University Choral Society

http://www.cs.mu.oz.au/~winikoff/mucs/mucs.html

The home page of the Melbourne University Choral Society includes biographical details about the choir's conductor, Andrew Wailes, plus information on the group's history, activities, and recent performances.

New England Philharmonic

http://www.mit.edu:8001/people/jcb/NEP/nep.html

Information on the New England Philharmonic of Cambridge, Massachusetts, its music director and its programs are available here. Included is a concert schedule and contact information, as well as music jokes and links to other orchestra sites.

New York Philharmonic Home Page

http://www.nyphilharmon.org/

The home page for the New York Philharmonic Orchestra features information about the current season's schedule along with ticket subscription information and an introduction to the members of the orchestra. Visitors can also take a look back at the esteemed music organization's history.

Princeton University Band Home Page K

http://www.princeton.edu/~puband/

One of less than a dozen "scramble bands" in the country, the Princeton University Band prides itself on getting from one formation to the next by scrambling. This is described as "a highly energetic maneuver that is Random Incarnate."

The Pro Arte Chamber Orchestra of Boston

http://www.proarte.org/

The Pro Arte Chamber Orchestra of Boston is a unique entity; it's organized as a cooperative and the musicians control all aspects of the orchestra. Visitors to the orchestra-sponsored site will learn more about how the musicians operate this special ensemble.

Stanford Symphony Orchestra

http://www-leland.stanford.edu/group/sso/

Visitors to Stanford University's Symphony Orchestra page can find concert information, read about the musicians, and hire the chamber ensemble online.

COMPOSERS

Johan Alkerstedt

http://www.his.se/ida/~a94johal/

Johan Alkerstedt offers pointers to his favorite classical music sites on the Net through this page. It includes sound clips and pages for famous composers—such as Johannes Brahms and Antonin Dvorak.

Johann Sebastian Bach

http://classicalmus.com/composers/bach.html

Visitors to this classical music site can read a concise biography of composer Johann Sebastian Bach and learn about selected Bach recordings from BMG Music.

J.S. Bach Archive and Bibliography

http://www.let.rug.nl/Linguistics/diversen/bach/intro.html

This personal home page offers a look at classical composer Johann Sebastian Bach. Visit the archive and bibliography to learn about his life and work.

The J.S. Bach Home Page

http://www.tile.net/tile/bach/

This home page devoted its electrons to information about the famous composer Johann Sebastian Bach. Visitors can read a biography, look at a list of his complete works, or take a look at a list of recommended recordings.

Ludwig van Beethoven

http://classicalmus.com/composers/beethove.html

Classics World Biography presents this page, which focuses on the life and works of Ludwig van Beethoven. Fans can link to a selection of sound clips, a listing of recommended recordings, and ordering information.

Classical Music

http://weber.u.washington.edu/~sbode/classical.html

The basics of classical music can be picked up at this enthusiast's site, with links to a classical music newsgroup and FAQs as well as biographies of the great composers.

Eric Dolphy Home Page

http://epoch.cs.berkeley.edu:8000/personal/jmh/music/dolphy.html

A multi-instrumentalist and composer, Eric Dolphy gets the star treatment on this fan page. Find links to a discography and sound samples from Dolphy's solo work.

Gilbert and Sullivan Archive Home Page

http://diamond.idbsu.edu/gas/GaS.html

The Gilbert and Sullivan Archive provides historical information on their operettas, access to librettos, and MIDI files of their music. Includes a description of Savoy Operas during the late 19th Century, schedules of Gilbert and Sullivan festivals, and links to related organizations and servers.

GlassPages: Philip Glass on the Web

http://www-lsi.upc.es/~jpetit/pg/

American minimalist composer Philip Glass is the focus here, where browsers will find a discography, articles, scores, images, and more.

The W.A. Mozart Page

http://www.mhrcc.org/mozart/mozart.html

Fans of renowned classical musician Wolfgang Amadeus Mozart can access a slew of resources here. Check out biographies and reviews, or peruse Mozart merchandise.

Wolfgang Amadeus Mozart

http://classicalmus.com/composers/mozart.html

Is Wolfgang Amadeus Mozart the most popular classical composer? If so, this online bio goes a long way to explain why. Part of the Classics World site, this page recommends recordings that present Mozart's music to best effect.

Dmitry Dmitrievich Shostakovich

http://www.cs.umd.edu/~cema/shostakovich.html

Composer Dmitry Shostakovich is the focus of this page, which includes sound files, a "Time" magazine cover story from 1942, and links to other sites containing newsgroup postings, Frequently Asked Questions (FAQs) files, and composition information.

Vangelis: The Man and the Music

http://bau2.uibk.ac.at/perki/Vangelis.html

This multimedia site is devoted to the composer-musician, Evangelos O. Papathanassiou (aka Vangelis). Get all the details here on his solo and collaborative works, plus an introduction from the man himself.

The Really Useful Company Presents Sir Andrew Lloyd Webber

http://www.reallyuseful.com/

Bring musical theater on screen through this official Web page dedicated to the works of Sir Andrew Lloyd Webber. Presented by his company, The Really Useful Company, it features information about shows like "Cats" and "Phantom of the Opera," as well as access to a theater store.

Andrew Lloyd Webber Online

http://www.sas.upenn.edu/~smfriedm/alw.html

British composer Sir Andrew Lloyd Webber steps into the spotlight via this compiled guide to Webber on the Web. Among the featured resources, find links to fan pages dedicated to the man's musical theater successes, biographical sites, a mailing list, and a Usenet newsgroup.

Ralph Vaughan Williams Home Page

http://www.cs.qub.ac.uk/~J.Collis/RVW.html

Classical music lovers can learn about the modern British romantic composer Ralph Vaughan Williams here. A fan, who especially likes Williams' piece "Tallis Fantasia," has established the site with hopes of educating people about the composer's life and works.

Zappa Quote of the Day

http://www.fwi.uva.nl/~heederik/zappa/quote/

Fans of the late rock composer and guitarist Frank Zappa can check into this site for daily words of wisdom. Get a daily quote or browse an archive of Zappa witticisms like "Modern music is a sick puppy" or "In the fight between you and the world, back the world." Visitors are invited to submit new quotes.

FADS AND MEMORABILIA

Steve Clifford's Beatles Page

http://www.islandnet.com/~scliffor/beatles/fabhome.htm

A Beatlemania hobbyist has spent the better part of his life collecting Fab Four information and memorabilia. Find the fruit of his travels right here, presented in a personal narrative; the site includes a forum for other collectors.

Elvis in Latin: Frequently Asked Questions

http://www.cs.uoregon.edu/~bhelm/misc/elvis.html

For those who thought Elvis Presley and Latin were both dead, think again. Here browsers will find details of Presley recordings rendered in Latin, as well as ordering information.

PSYCHEDELIC PSYBERSPACE

http://cfn.cs.dal.ca/~af678/cyberspace.html

Browsers searching for the eternal long, strange trip will find an index that features "links to various flowerpower sites and a multitude of psychedelic music links" here. In addition to music, links focus on drugs and the culture of the 1960s.

Spiral Into the Eighties with Jeff

http://chat.carleton.ca/~jmain/eighties.html

Visitors here will find "Jeff's awesome eighties page" offering links to sites devoted to 1980s entertainers. Find pointers to music, movies, and television pages, plus a miscellany of other sites.

FESTIVALS AND EVENTS

The Bagpipe Web

http://pipes.tico.com/pipes/pipes.html

For experienced pipers and wanna-be blowhards alike, the Bagpipe Web provides a tuneful home. The site features a calendar of bagpipe festivals, reviews of new bagpipe recordings, links to manufacturer pages and clubs worldwide, and a classified section for bargain bagpipes.

European Forum of Worldwide Music Festivals

http://www.eunet.fi/gmc/efwmf/efwmf.html

A schedule of music festivals around the world can be found on the European Forum of Worldwide Music Festivals Web. The page features a number of major festivals in the area of world, ethnic, traditional, and roots music.

Glastonbury Home Page

http://www.crg.cs.nott.ac.uk/~nlc/glast/glast.html

Find maps, photos, performance lineups and more from the 25th annual Glastonbury Festival, held in June 1995. (The festival organizers decided to take a rest in 1996, but promise the show will go on in 1997.) A festival of the performing arts, Glastonbury features "everything from rock and pop to juggling, through performance, fortune telling and standup comedy."

Healing in the Heartland

http://benefit.ionet.net/

Healing in the Heartland offers audio and stills from a July, 1995, benefit concert in Oklahoma for victims of the Oklahoma City bombing. Links to information on the bombing and to Internet software are available here.

JAZZ WEB Dutch Jazz homepage

http://huizen.dds.nl/~toetsie/ukindex.html

A Dutch piano student and semiprofessional musician maintains this site offering annotated lists of jazz clubs, festivals, and organizations in Holland and Europe. A compilation of links to jazz-related Web sites is also featured.

Live Aid—A Celebration

http://www.herald.co.uk/local_info/live_
aid.html

Live Aid, the concert to feed the world that took place on July 13, 1985, is the focus of this page from Herald Information Systems in the UK. Included here are background, a program with links to the artists, and other resources.

The Monterey Jazz Festival

http://www.dnai.com/~lmcohen/montery.html

Begun in 1958, the Monterey Jazz Festival is "the oldest continuous jazz festival in the world and one of the world's most respected jazz festivals." This vibrant site includes details about the upcoming event, ticket ordering information, artist bios, and much more.

Montreux Jazz Festival

http://www.grolier.fr/festival/montreux/

The Montreux Jazz Festival has been in a force in the jazz world since 1967. This site details the festival, which has featured artists like B.B. King, George Benson, and Ice T. Browsers can click on their favorite entertainer and pick up the sounds here or learn about upcoming events.

Musi-Cal

http://concerts.calendar.com/

This site bills itself as "the first online calendar that provides easy access to the most up-to-date worldwide live music information: concerts, festivals, gigs, and other musical events." Visitors using this free service simply plug in the name of the performer and submit their request.

New Orleans Jazz and Heritage Festival

http://www.yatcom.com/neworl/jfest/
jfesttop.html

Before heading down to the world famous New Orleans Jazz Heritage Festival, music lovers can research performance schedules, cultural attractions, and even current weather conditions from this page. The festival is annual event held yearly that rivals Mardi Gras in popularity.

The Unofficial Lollapalooza Page

http://nimitz.mcs.kent.edu/~cstone/lolla.html

The Unofficial Lollapalooza Page contains information on all of the mammoth concerts' events from 1991 to present. Includes details of which band played on which stage, and lists answers to Frequently Asked Questions (FAQs).

Woodstock.com Main Menu

http://metaverse.com/woodstock/

The official Woodstock 1994 Internet site hosts a wealth of information pertaining to that music concert, which was held as a tribute and revival of the original Woodstock. Visitors can browse bulletin boards, read about the artists who headlined the show, or check out radio and television coverage, trivia, and interviews.

Worldwide Internet Live Music Archive

http://wilma.com/

Keep on top of the live music world at the Worldwide Internet Live Music Archive, or WILMA. This Los Angeles-based company claims a searchable database of more than 5,000 venues and 1,800 artists, providing links to tour information, season schedules, official band Web sites, and more.

GENRES

ANCIENT MUSIC

The Plainsong and Mediaeval Music Society

http://www.ncl.ac.uk/~nip2/

The Plainsong and Mediaeval Music Society is a 100-year-old English group devoted to the traditions of music and chant before the year 1550. Its membership comprises scholars, clergy, and musicians. It invites new members here and details its small grant program for musicians.

AVANT-GARDE

Laurie Anderson Info

http://www.netpart.com/phil/laurie.html

Musician, poet and video artist Laurie Anderson is the object of Webmaster Phil Trubey's adoration. Like-minded fans can link to a 1994 WiReD Magazine article, a guide to Anderson's work, and other fan and promotional pages.

The Bonzo Dog Doo-Dah Band

http://bridge.anglia.ac.uk/~systimk/music/
bonzos/

A British "art college band," the Bonzo Dog Doo-Dah Band reached its peak and gained a cult following in the late 1960s—a period which overlaps the group's regular appearances on the United

Kingdom TV show "Do Not Adjust Your Set." Visit this fan tribute to learn more about the group and its legacy of tunes and lunacy.

David Byrne's "Photo Works"

http://www.bart.nl/~francey/byrne.html

Yikes! David Byrne's twisted face is staring at me! A fan of Byrne and the Talking Heads posted these pictures from an exhibition of Byrne's "PhotoWorks." Visitors can also read a biography of the musician/artist and take a tour of the Talking Heads pages.

FSOnLine

http://raft.vmg.co.uk/fsol

FSOnline begins with the sound of brain static; water follows and the future killing sound of London goes on. Colorful graphics accompany these sounds, but as to what it means…well, suffice to say it appears to deal with the group The Future Sounds of London.

Dr. Fiorella Terenzi's Galaxy Spot

http://www.fiorella.com/

Astrophysicist and musician Fiorella Terenzi converts radio waves from galaxies into sound. Listen to her CDs and find out why Dennis Miller calls her "a cross between Carl Sagan and Madonna."

CHANTS

The Gregorian Chant Home Page

http://www.music.princeton.edu/chant_html/

The historical overview of Gregorian chants offered here was written by a Princeton University music professor. This Web page lists chant-related coursework offered by the school and offers links to ecclesiastical sciences and musicology sites.

The Plainsong and Mediaeval Music Society

http://www.ncl.ac.uk/~nip2/

The Plainsong and Mediaeval Music Society is a 100-year-old English group devoted to the traditions of music and chant before the year 1550. Its membership comprises scholars, clergy, and musicians. It invites new members here and details its small grant program for musicians.

CHILDREN'S

The Judy & David Page Judy David
http://www.io.org/~jandd

Children's entertainers Judy and David unleash their musical fun on the Web world through this home page that includes an online songbook, links to a catalog of their music, and information about upcoming shows. The award-winning Canadian duo also introduces itself on the page.

CLASSICAL

Johan Alkerstedt
http://www.his.se/ida/~a94johal/

Johan Alkerstedt offers pointers to his favorite classical music sites on the Net through this page. It includes sound clips and pages for famous composers—such as Johannes Brahms and Antonin Dvorak.

Johann Sebastian Bach
http://www.astro.umd.edu/~sgeier/xB.html

This site is dedicated to Johann Sebastian Bach, who the webmaster maintains is the "least present composer on the Web." The page includes music files, information about various festivals celebrating the baroque composer, a bio, and more.

Johann Sebastian Bach
http://classicalmus.com/composers/bach.html

Visitors to this classical music site can read a concise biography of composer Johann Sebastian Bach and learn about selected Bach recordings from BMG Music.

The J.S. Bach Home Page
http://www.tile.net/tile/bach/

This home page devoted its electrons to information about the famous composer Johann Sebastian Bach. Visitors can read a biography, look at a list of his complete works, or take a look at a list of recommended recordings.

BMG Classical Music
http://www.classicalmus.com/

At this promotional site BMG Music presents its classical music collection, with information about its recordings, selections, music news, and the latest releases.

Chicago Concert Search
http://student-www.uchicago.edu/users/achatche/music/concerts.html

The Chicago Concert Search home page offers visitors a searchable database of classical concerts in the area, including chorales and chamber music. Search by date or series. Also links to a similar search engine for Cleveland, Ohio.

ChoralNet
http://www.sdsmt.edu/choralnet/

ChoralNet asks for donations and offers its "Internet Center for Choral Music" through this site. Stop by for ChoralTalk, access to the ChoralAcademe, and a link to the rec.music.makers.choral Usenet newsgroup.

Classical MIDI Archives
http://www.prs.net/midi.html

A useful site for those building a Web page and wishing to include classical music, this index offers MIDI files of more than 1,500 compositions. Musical interludes and graphics are available for download.

Classical Music
http://weber.u.washington.edu/~sbode/classical.html

The basics of classical music can be picked up at this enthusiast's site, with links to a classical music newsgroup and FAQs, as well as biographies of the great composers.

---

a2z EDITOR'S CHOICE

Classical Net Home Page
http://www.classical.net/music/

If you couldn't tell Beethoven from Bach on a bet and are too embarrassed to admit it out loud, Classical Net provides an easy introduction for the classically challenged listener. A patient Webmaster describes two areas that are "rarely covered comprehensively in conjunction with one another. These two areas are the basic repertoire of works that have, over time, become central to the western tradition of music, and recommended recordings/performances of these works." In other words, bunky, here's the place to figure out what to listen to and how to understand what you hear.

The files offered are organized in four basic categories: a list of basic repertoire, a CD buying guide, recommended CDs, and composer data. Divvied up into historical period, seekers can find baroque, medieval, or modern music, depending on their whim. A searchable index helps locate resources quickly, a moderated classical music mailing list gives novices a place to seek out other like-minded types, and a variety of other resources provide gentle help for those in search of knowledge of all things classical.—*Reviewed by Julene Snyder*

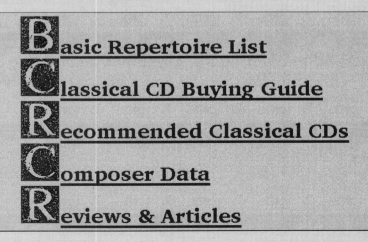

Basic Repertoire List

Classical CD Buying Guide

Recommended Classical CDs

Composer Data

Reviews & Articles

Classical Music: The WWW Virtual Library

http://www.gprep.pvt.k12.md.us/classical/

In the classical music stacks of the Virtual Library users can consult a catalog of electronic resources. Periodicals, reference works, and discussion groups devoted to classical music are indexed here.

Classical Net Home Page

http://www.classical.net/music/

Classical music buffs will find scores of resources here. Classical Net contains information about composers and musicians, a searchable index of CDs, and music reviews. The page also provides links to related newsgroups and mailing lists. See Editor's Choice.

CultureFinder: The Internet Address for the Performing Arts

http://www.culturefinder.com/

CultureFinder hosts a wealth of resources for lovers of classical music, dance, opera, and theatre. Here browsers can peruse such features as the culture find of the week, news, and interviews, or drop by the online shop and library. In English, French, Spanish, and German.

The Guitar Home Page

http://www.guitarist.com/cg/cg.html

The Guitar Page provides an index to Web information and resources concerning classical guitar, with links to the Classical Guitar Beginners' Page, the Portland Guitar Society, the Flamenco Guitar, and other classical guitar pages.

H&B Recordings Direct

http://www.hbdirect.com/

This "online magazine" from H&B Recordings Direct offers classical and jazz recordings on CD. It includes a comprehensive catalog with a search function, ordering information, and links to other music sites.

Internet Resources for Music Teachers

http://www.isd77.k12.mn.us/resources/
staffpages/shirk/music.html

Links to music newsgroups, MIDI pages, and educators resources can be found at this high-volume directory, maintained by a Minnesota school teacher. Visitors can download MacPiano shareware and classic QuickTime compositions by Bach, Chopin, and others.

Kronos Quartet FanWeb

http://www.lochnet.com/client/gs/kq.html

A string ensemble, the Kronos Quartet has built its reputation and repertoire on mostly 20th century music, much of it written specifically for the group. Its multimedia Web page features audio samples, a discography, images, and articles.

Maestronet

http://www.maestronet.com/

Visitors to the Maestronet can browse the Instrument Showroom in search of fine stringed instruments and bows, or stop by the Conservatory and download sheet music. A library of topical materials and a discussion area are also featured.

Melbourne University Choral Society

http://www.cs.mu.oz.au/~winikoff/mucs/
mucs.html

The home page of the Melbourne University Choral Society includes biographical details about the choir's conductor, Andrew Wailes, plus information on the group's history, activities, and recent performances.

The W.A. Mozart Page

http://www.mhrcc.org/mozart/mozart.html

Fans of renowned classical musician Wolfgang Amadeus Mozart can access a slew of resources here. Check out biographies and reviews, or peruse Mozart merchandise.

Gary Stephens' FanWebs

http://www.geocities.com/Vienna/1340/

Meet Gary Stephens, a music fan who lives in the United Kingdom. He has created FanWebs for Cecilia Bartoli, the Kronos Quartet and 3 Mustaphas 3, and invites visitors to take a look.

Ralph Vaughan Williams Home Page

http://www.cs.qub.ac.uk/~J.Collis/RVW.html

Classical music lovers can learn about the modern British romantic composer Ralph Vaughan Williams here. A fan, who especially likes Williams' piece "Tallis Fantasia," has established the site with hopes of educating people about the composer's life and works.

COMPUTER MUSIC

After the Taj Mahal: New music by Christopher Penrose

http://www.music.princeton.edu/TajMahal/

Christopher Penrose's personal home page features a small downloadable collection of his music.

Buddy Project

http://www.buddy.org/

The idea behind the Buddy Project is to provide a clearinghouse for musical creations. It features archives of works by Buddy participants and an area for collaborations. There also are notes and software to assist in the recording of and listening to audio files.

The Canadian Electroacoustic Community

http://lecaine.music.mcgill.ca:80/~cec/

The Canadian Electroacoustic Community, a Montreal-based nonprofit organization of music composers, performers, educators, and researchers, maintains this informational site. Visit here for news, publications, membership information, and links to a variety of related Web sites.

CERL Sound Group

http://datura.cerl.uiuc.edu/

Digital audio signal processing is the focus of the CERL Sound Group's home page, a service of the University of Illinois. Includes computer music and sound computation information, sound-related position papers, and pointers to other sound computation sites.

Computer Music Journal WWW/FTP Archives

http://www-mitpress.mit.edu/
Computer-Music-Journal/

Musicians interested in digitizing their creations should drop by the online home of this journal dedicated to digital audio signal processing and electroacoustic music. In addition to obtaining subscription information, visitors can enjoy sound archives and selected article highlights.

Courses of Study in Sound and Computer Music

http://datura.cerl.uiuc.edu/schools/
courses.html

Prospective music majors with a penchant for computer-produced sounds can review and compare courses of study offered at colleges and universities across the globe at this site. Link to degree programs in computer music using the list of pointers collected here.

Disklavier: New Music for Disklavier and Synthesizer

http://www-crca.ucsd.edu/95_96/bobw/
disklavier.html

The New Music for the Disklavier and Synthesizer site, maintained by a computer researcher at the University of California at San Diego, provides downloadable sound files created by the electronic instrument ensemble. Visit here for MIDI files and concert documentation.

El Camino de Silicio

http://www-crca.ucsd.edu/95_96/bobw/
camino.html

To promote computer music in the Americas, The Silicon Highway page features links to electroacoustic music information and resources on the Web. Links are listed by country and under the categories of research, music production, education, publications, and archives.

IPEM Multimedia Archive

http://next.rug.ac.be/

Delve into the IPEM Multimedia Archive to immerse yourself in electronic resources relating to new music. Find research articles, musical notation collection, and sound clips here.

Kraftwerk unofficial infobahr

http://www.cs.umu.se/~dvlawm/kraftwerk/

The synthesized sounds of Kraftwerk's electronic music are explored through this fan's homage to the band's craft and ground-breaking work. Find a discography, lyrics, and still photos, plus downloadable audio and video clips.

Melodius-Sync

http://www.omix.com/music/hmoore/home.html

Visitors to this promotional site for modern computer-music composer Herb Moore can download tracks from his albums and read general information about his life and work.

Music and Technology at Virginia Tech

http://server.music.vt.edu/technology/technology.html

Hosted by the Department of Music at Virginia Tech, the Music and Technology page explores the department's courses and services focusing on the technical aspects of recording music. An overview of facilities and a look at the future of computers and music is also featured.

Musicware, Inc.

http://www.halcyon.com/musicware/

Musicians looking for ways to use computers as instruments will find Musicware Inc., a swell source of software, publications, demonstrations, and product reviews.

MuSIG Online

http://www.woodwind.com/MuSIG/Home.html

Musicians interested in the blend of music and computers can check this page from MuSIG, a network concerned with computers and music. The MuSIG site includes information about MIDI, hardware, software, education, composition, performance, and programming.

The Stanford Center for Computer Research in Music and Acoustics

http://ccrma-www.stanford.edu/

The Stanford Center for Computer Research in Music and Acoustics houses composers and researchers who use computers as an artistic medium and research tool. Here, the center describes its research, details the software it has created and promotes its summer workshops.

COUNTRY AND FOLK

Note: This section is alphabetized by the musician's last name where applicable.

Heather Alexander

http://www.teleport.com/~seafire/

Dedicated to Celtic musician Heather Alexander, this page features her biography, discography, reviews, photographs, and tour schedule. Find out more about her various bands and where to get her music here.

Archer/Park Home Page

http://www.traveller.com/archpark

RealAudio interviews with the country band Archer/Park are featured at this official home page. Also included: background on Randy Archer, Johnny Park and the rest of the band, along with articles, reviews, photos, video clips, sound clips, concert calendar, and fan club information.

Blucher's Boot Hill

http://www.fn.net/business/boothill/

Boot Hill supplies an index to western, cowboy, and country resources, including sites in areas such as Southwest art, horses, and rodeos. Other listings are provided for cowboys, Indians, and music resources.

Harry Chapin Fan Page

http://www.fn.net/~jmayans/chapin/

At this site devoted to late American folk singer and songwriter Harry Chapin, visitors can listen to his comments and music, as well as peruse biographical information, pictures, poetry, and more.

Country Connection

http://digiserve.com/country/

If you've a hankerin' for some country music news and sound clips, check the pages of the Country Connection. It features links to Web pages devoted to various country artists, along with a collection of tour information.

Cybergrass—The Internet Bluegrass Music Magazine

http://www.banjo.com/BG/

Get the latest on traditional music from this electronic publication. Bluegrass festival and society listings, artist profiles, and other reading matter keep fans current. Classified ads connect pickers and other music makers with banjos, mandolins, and fiddles for sale.

Dirty Linen Magazine

http://www.dirtynelson.com/linen/

Dirty Linen Magazine is a print and online publication devoted to folk, traditional, and world music. This site includes subscription information, back issue archive, articles, reviews, programming guides, and other items of interest.

Bob Dylan: Expecting Rain

http://bob.nbr.no/

Expecting Rain is an encyclopedic site devoted exclusively to the musician Bob Dylan. Visitors will find art, pictures, multimedia, interviews, answers to Frequently Asked Questions (FAQs), news, discography, and links to related sites.

The Flash Girls

http://www.player.org/pub/flash/flash.html

Here's a fan page devoted to the folk music duo: the Flash Girls. Read about the girls, their albums and awards, and check out the group's current ""gig and tour schedule."

Folk Roots

http://www.cityscape.co.uk/froots/

Roots, folk and world music makers headline at Folk Roots, an online magazine. Music lovers can find monthly offerings of articles, interviews, and album reviews at this site.

FolkBook: An Online Acoustic Music Establishment

http://www.cgrg.ohio-state.edu/folkbook/

Offering information about the artists, venues, fans, and festivals, this directory points out folk and acoustic music resources on the Internet. Find the who, what, when, where, and sometimes...the why.

Emmylou Harris

http://www.nashville.net/~kate/

Enthusiasts of "quintessential country music singer" Emmylou Harris will find like-minded fellows at this unofficial fan site. Includes minutia about the singer ranging from award information to fan clubs to recent appearances and much more.

Jackopierce Guitar Chords

http://ccwf.cc.utexas.edu/~arabella/jp/index.html

This page features guitar chords and tablature for the songs of Jack O. Pierce. This page also has contact information, mailing lists, and links to other Pierce-related pages.

The Mudkat Cafe

http://www.deltablues.com/dbsearch.html

Search this cross-cultural index for folk songs by title, keyword, or tune. The Digital Tradition Folk Song Database catalogs folk music from around the globe.

Phil Ochs

http://www.cs.pdx.edu/~trent/ochs/

This site is a memorial to Phil Ochs, a singer/songwriter of the 1960s and a friend of rock icon Bob Dylan. Visit here to learn about the writer of protest songs such as "Draft Dodger Rag." Links are provided to lyrics, discography, and books.

Stan Rogers Page
http://www.math.grin.edu/~schnelle/
stanpages/stan.html

Though the name Stan Rogers may never have shown up on a Billboard chart, in Canadian folk music he was a giant. His powerful songs about the experiences of ordinary Canadians touched many until his career was cut short by an airplane fire in 1983. Learn more about the man and his music on this fan page.

The Original Roughstock Home Page
http://www.roughstock.com/roughstock

Roughstock brings country music to the Web. Find out who the featured artist of the month is or teach your city friends about the history of country music. Visitors will also find the latest music news from industry insiders.

Carly Simon Online
http://www.ziva.com/carly/

Carly Simon is famous for singing such songs as the enigmatic "You're So Vain" and the more self-explanatory "Nobody Does It Better." A fan has devoted a page to the artist's works and life; offerings include interviews, concert information, and a collection of pictures.

Southern Folklife Collection HomePage
http://ils.unc.edu/barba/sfc.html

One of the world's largest collections of Southeastern-tradition derived music is found in the Southern Folklife Collection at the University of North Carolina's Wilson Library. Visitors to this page will find a description of the collection's music and other folk-related memorabilia.

The Story
http://www.cs.umd.edu/users/rager/Story/

Get the latest scoop on Boston-based band The Story at this official home page. A bio, audio samples, performance dates, and record reviews are on file.

Jerry Jeff Walker
http://www.io.com/~ccamden/jjw/

Fans of Jerry Jeff Walker's musical stylings will find bio information, a tour schedule, and much more at this official site.

Dar Williams
http://www.panix.com/~tneff/dar/

The Dar Williams Web Pages are devoted to this popular folk singer from New England. The selections here offer inside glimpses of releases, including sound samples, and provide personal information on the artist herself. Find tour schedules here.

JAZZ AND BLUES

Note: This section is alphabetized by the musician's last name where applicable.

Acid Jazz
http://www.cmd.uu.se/AcidJazz/

Acid jazz lovers can check out clubs, record labels, and magazines catering to the genre at this home page. Includes a listing of groups performing acid jazz, along with searchable archives of informational mailing list postings.

Louis Armstrong
http://www.netspace.org/~haaus/shome.html

Louis "Satchmo" Armstrong, master trumpeter of the Big Band era, is the subject; his life and music is the material. A bio, list of recordings, and related links are among the offerings.

Australia: Oz-jazz Worldwide
http://magna.com.au/~georgeh/

Oz-jazz Worldwide focuses on Australian jazz music. It includes news, musician profiles, jazz gigs, festivals, radio programs, and sound clips. Links to other music and jazz sites are included.

The Belizbeha Home Page
http://www.belizbeha.com

This funkified Web site is filled with the sounds of acid jazz, soul, funk, pop, and hip-hop music. Belizbeha, an eight-piece band out of Burlington, Vermont, offers information on its debut CD, band member bios, and set lists here.

The Blue Highway
http://www.vivanet.com/~blues/

The Blue Highway is music site devoted to the blues, with lists, directories, and guides to that particularly American art form. This page also links to other blues sites and home pages.

Blues Link
http://transport.com/~firm/bluzlink.html

Get the blues in a good way through Randy Haugen's Blues-Link site, which features a comprehensive list of pointers to blues pages from across the Net, as well as periodic reviews of new CDs.

Bluesnet Home Page
http://dragon.acadiau.ca/~rob/blues/

BluesNet is an Internet Blues Resource Center. The Blues fan can learn more about various Blues performers, see pictures of them, and gain access to books and biographies about their favorite artists.

BluesWEB
http://www.island.net/~blues/

The Blues Web presents a wealth of information about that seminal musical genre here, including a collection of blues artists complete with pictures and personal histories. Featured artists like Muddy Waters and Pine Top Perkins are here, as well as a large list of recordings.

Close Enough
http://www.demon.co.uk/blaah/index.html

Close Enough—a "Funky-Blues-Jazz-Dance-Stuff" band from London—gives its fans a chatty monthly update on its whereabouts, photos of the band, merchandise, booking information, and even free beer for Web browsers who request an e-mail voucher and bring it to their shows.

Holly Cole's Web Place
http://www.hollycole.com/

Nightclub/jazz chanteuse Holly Cole, based in Toronto, offers audio clips, Quicktime movies, and photos at her web site. The singer posts messages to her fans here and promises to reply to messages from them.

The Da Capo Press
http://www.jazznet.com/BOOKS/jz_books.htm

Music fans may find something of interest in this large interactive catalog of books about Jazz and Blues, and those who make the music. All titles are indexed alphabetically for quick reference and easy access.

Fly! Music Magazine
http://www.fly.co.uk/index.dhtml

Put some hip in your hop and some jive in your jazz at Fly! The British magazine features articles and reviews of new music—mainly jazz, R & B, and dance. To hear some live grooves, visit the gigs and clubs section for happenings in Great Britain.

InterJazz Home Page
http://www.webcom.com/~ijazz/

InterNet Jazz provides a wide range of resources for Jazz lovers. Visitors to this site can read Jazz articles and news, link to artists on the Net, or browse lists of Jazz clubs. The page also contains the Jazz Yellow pages.

Jazz Clubs Around the World
http://www.acns.nwu.edu/jazz/lists/clubs.html

Here's an index of addresses and telephone numbers for jazz clubs around the globe—from Birdland West in Los Angeles to Jazzclub Karlsruhe in Nuremburg.

Jazz Fan Attic
http://www2.magmacom.com/~rbour/

Somewhat like digging through the jazz bin at a record store, The Jazz Fan Attic links visitors to jazz sites as well as information on jazz styles and artists.

Jazz Improvisation

http://www.hum.lss.wisc.edu/jazz/

Visit this page for a music index featuring links to jazz and blues sites around the world. Also included is a series of articles taken from the syllabus for two jazz classes taught at the University of Wisconsin (Madison).

Jazz Inspiration Records

http://www.hype.com/jazz_inspiration/home.htm

Jazz Inspiration Records, a Toronto-based jazz record label, maintains this site for general information about the company and its products. Visit here to link to artist profiles, order musical CDs, and contact its musicians and staff members.

Jazz Net

http://www.dnai.com/~lmcohen/

An extensive compedium of online news, views and information for Jazz lovers, the Jazz Net site features links to Jazz sites such as "JAZZNow" magazine, The Monterey Jazz festival, KLON's JazzAvenue and Kuumbwa Jazz Center in Santa Cruz, California.

JAZZ Online

http://www.jazzonln.com/JAZZ/

Calling all jazz enthusiasts: This site offers a cool selection of CD reviews, news stories, radio information, and artist features about that most American of musical genres. Ranging from Coltrane to the latest players, there's information here to suit every jazz aficionado's palate.

Jazz: Records & Photography, the 1950s

http://bookweb.cwis.uci.edu:8042/Jazz/JPRA2.html

This jazz site provides a historical perspective on the music and musicians of the 1950s. Includes links to articles, profiles and photo galleries relating to jazz music in the decade after World War II.

Jazzweb

http://huizen.dds.nl/~toetsie/ukindex.html

A Dutch piano student and semiprofessional musician maintains this site offering annotated lists of jazz clubs, festivals, and organizations in Holland and Europe. A compilation of links to jazz-related Web sites is also featured.

MisterLUCKY

http://www.wco.com/~coconutg/

"MisterLUCKY" is not a 'zine, "but a quarterly musical communique celebrating music of a 'jazz-centric' nature." It takes in the whole scene of rhythm and booze, offering reviews and recipes (try the White Lady Cocktail). Subcribe to the hardcopy here.

The Monterey Jazz Festival

http://www.dnai.com/~lmcohen/montery.html

Begun in 1958, the Monterey Jazz Festival is "the oldest continuous jazz festival in the world and one of the world's most respected jazz festivals." This vibrant site includes details about the upcoming event, ticket ordering information, artist bios, and much more.

MusicBase

http://www.musicbase.co.uk/music/

Music fans can follow the news and sounds issuing from European record labels here. The site also includes an online magazine, Blues and Soul, and a sound archive.

New Orleans Jazz and Heritage Festival

http://www.yatcom.com/neworl/jfest/jfesttop.html

Before heading down to the world famous New Orleans Jazz Heritage Festival, music lovers can research performance schedules, cultural attractions, and even current weather conditions from this page. The festival is annual event held yearly that rivals Mardi Gras in popularity.

Ragtime Home Page

http://www.ragtimers.org/~ragtimers/

Ragtime music comes alive through histories, sound clips, and MIDI files on the Ragtime Home Page. View ragtime catalogs, a list of ragtime events around the world, or a list of ragtime CD recordings here.

What is Jazz?

http://town.hall.org/Archives/radio/Kennedy/Taylor/

Dr. Billy Taylor, the noted pianist, historian, and educator, delivered four lectures at the John F. Kennedy Center for the Performing Arts that are reproduced here, with links to artists, styles, discographies, and audio files.

WNUR-FM JazzWeb

http://www.nwu.edu/jazz/

User-built by volunteer energy and creativity, this searchable site serves links that admittedly don't (but definitely try to) answer all questions about jazz. Station programming and local information is also featured.

---

a2z EDITOR'S CHOICE

World Wide Jazz Web

http://www.xs4all.nl/~centrale/jazz.html

For jazz aficionados and neophytes alike, the World Wide Jazz Web offers up sounds for every palate. Jazz musicians from Louis Armstrong to John Zorn are virtually represented here, complete with bios, links, and online interviews. A worldwide listing of jazz clubs, festivals, magazines, management, opportunities, and instruments offers visitors more than a glimpse into America's most original art form.—*Reviewed by Julene Snyder*

WORLD WIDE JAZZ WEB

- Jazz Musicians Worldwide
- Jazz Clubs WorldWide
- Jazz Management
- Labels
- Opportunities
- Fractal Jazz

- Jazz Groups Worldwide
- Jazz Festivals Worldwide
- Jazz Magazines
- More Jazz Sites
- Instruments
- Acid Jazz

19156

3-STAR SITE MAGELLAN

World Wide Jazz Web

http://www.xs4all.nl/~centrale/jazz.html

Jazz fans, you've come to the right place for links to all things important in your world of musical entertainment. Musicians, instruments, festivals, and more make up this comprehensive Jazz-orama. See Editor's Choice.

MIDI

Classical MIDI Archives

http://www.prs.net/midi.html

A useful site for those building a Web page and wishing to include classical music, this index offers MIDI files of more than 1,500 compositions. Musical interludes and graphics are available for download.

Disklavier: New Music for Disklavier and Synthesizer

http://www-crca.ucsd.edu/95_96/bobw/disklavier.html

The New Music for the Disklavier and Synthesizer site, maintained by a computer researcher at the University of California at San Diego, provides downloadable sound files created by the electronic instrument ensemble. Visit here for MIDI files and concert documentation.

Electronic Early Music

http://www.hike.te.chiba-u.ac.jp/eem/

The Electronic Early Music site features downloadable sound files performed by Yasuhiko Higaki using MIDI instruments and mixers. Visitors are invited to listen to the works and then submit their comments to the creator.

Gerd's MIDI Pages: The Collection

http://stud1.tuwien.ac.at/~e8925292/bestmid.htm

The "Very Best of GUS MIDI" Collection features over 650 public domain MIDI music files. Visitors can listen to clips before they download files or packs, and can choose from classical, piano, and pop sections.

M-Cubed—The Macintosh-MIDI-Music User Group

http://coyote.accessnv.com/dhanley/m3/m3.html

The m3 site is a Macintosh user group for musicians. Includes samples of m3 members' work, links to MIDI utilities and other related Web and FTP sites.

MIDI Archive FTP Site

ftp://ftp.ucsd.edu/midi

Browsers can download MIDI related software, scores, and documents from this anonymous FTP archive. The archive is maintained by a member of the rec.music.synth Usenet newsgroup.

MIDI Pal

http://www.music.co.jp/~midipal/

MIDI Pal, a bulletin board of MIDI files, lets you download music or send in your own tunes. See if the selections other music connoisseurs have submitted appeal to your ear. In Japanese and English.

Music and Technology at Virginia Tech

http://server.music.vt.edu/technology/technology.html

Hosted by the Department of Music at Virginia Tech, the Music and Technology page explores the department's courses and services focusing on the technical aspects of recording music. An overview of facilities and a look at the future of computers and music is also featured.

MuSIG Online

http://www.woodwind.com/MuSIG/Home.html

Musicians interested in the blend of music and computers can check this page from MuSIG, a network concerned with computers and music. The MuSIG site includes information about MIDI, hardware, software, education, composition, performance, and programming.

NEW AGE

Miramar

http://www.uspan.com/miramar/

Miramar Images, Inc. sells music and art from a variety of new age artists. Visit here to browse their catalog and stroll through a virtual gallery.

Michael Stearns

http://www.nets.com/stearns

Michael Stearns plays and creates new age, electronic music that weaves together a synthesizer, sounds from nature, and voices from other cultures. Visitors to his page will find information on his solo work and collaborations, a filmography, and details about his latest releases.

α2z EDITOR'S CHOICE

Space Age Bachelor Pad Music

http://www.users.interport.net/~joholmes/index.html

Kool kittens and hepcats will plop another olive in their martini glasses and knock back a cool one for the road upon finding this resource for adventurous musical swingers. From Esquivel to Martin Denney, the cocktail nation is out in full force at this site, whose offerings include a gallery of cheesy album covers, a guide to "lounge culture," and radio show pointers.

The album cover images alone are worth a visit, with "some of the most beautiful and unusual album jackets from the mid-1950s through the early 1960s." Highlights here include "Santa Claus Conquers the Martians," "Music for Bang Baaroom and Harp," and "Riot in Rhythm." Hey, it's a virtual clearinghouse of audio and visual offerings teetering precariously between the groovy and the horrifying. Slinky dresses and fitted jackets advised (but not required) for entry.—*Reviewed by Julene Snyder*

Welcome to...

Space Age Bachelor Pad Music

What, pray tell, is Space Age Bachelor Pad Music???
Read liner notes from The RCA History of Space Age Pop.

Esquivel! | Gallery | Sources | Artists | Pointers

Space Age Bachelor Pad Music on the World Wide Web is not associated with RCA/BMG, Rhino, DCC, or any other record label.

NOVELTY

Awful Music

http://redwood.northcoast.com/~shojo/Awful/
awf.html

One of the curious selections and Web wonders of the world, this collection of awful music can't be found on CD, which is probably just as well.

Blar's Filk Page

http://sundry.hsc.usc.edu/filk.html

Filk music—not to be confused with *folk music*—is the subject of this page. Find descriptions of filk, listings of festivals and artists, and links to merchandise, FTP archives, and related sites.

Elvis in Latin: Frequently Asked Questions

http://www.cs.uoregon.edu/~bhelm/misc/
elvis.html

For those who thought Elvis Presley and Latin were both dead, think again. Here browsers will find details of Presley recordings rendered in Latin, as well as ordering information.

Hands On Music, Inc.

http://www.w2.com/hands.html

Hands On Music, Inc. offers the innovative idea of tunes designed specifically for the driving experience. Find out how to order these series of sounds to make your cruising more enjoyable.

Space Age Bachelor Pad Music

http://www.users.interport.net/~joholmes/
index.html

Squeeze into a blue polyester leisure suit and mix up a shaker of cocktails—now, in living stereo, it's Space Age Bachelor Pad music. Details about all your favorites mingle here, highlighted by the hi-fi magic of Esquivel and Martin Denny. Trivia, track listings, discographies—it's never enough, baby. See Editor's Choice.

Twisted Tunes Home Page

http://www.twistedtunes.com

The Twisted Tunes Web page features links to tons of funny music that can be accessed on the Web. Visitors who have RealAudio Player software loaded can listen to a selection of tunes, including selections from page creator Bob Rivers from his morning radio shows in Seattle.

Yankovic!

http://www.cs.cmu.edu/afs/andrew/usr/sc5x/
www/yankovic.html

Steven Chai features the tunes of musical comedian Weird Al Yankovic while performing a parody of the Yahoo! Web site with his Yankovic! page. Stop by for digitized sounds samples and lyrics to Yankovic classics such as "Eat It."

The Weird Al Yankovic Web Page

http://www.emsphone.com/Al

The grandiose claim is put forth early: this web page vows to "give meaning to your boring miserable life." Offerings include pictures, interviews, sound bytes, and video clips.

OPERA

Cecilia Bartoli Fanweb

http://www.lochnet.com/client/gs/cb.html

Fans of opera virtuoso Cecilia Bartoli can vote for their favorite CD and discuss Bartoli topics here. The fan-produced site also includes sound clips, photos, interviews from print publications, and her appearance schedule.

CultureFinder: The Internet Address for the Performing Arts

http://www.culturefinder.com/

CultureFinder hosts a wealth of resources for lovers of classical music, dance, opera, and theatre. Here browsers can peruse such features as the culture find of the week, news, and interviews, or drop by the online shop and library. In English, French, Spanish, and German.

The Finnish National Opera

http://www.kolumbus.fi/opera/

Founded in Helsinki in 1911, the Finnish National Opera maintains this promotional site for program and membership information. Visit here for tickets and information on its operas, ballets, concerts, and other fine productions.

---

a2z EDITOR'S CHOICE

Beastie Boys Home Page

http://www.southern.com/BeastieBoys/

The irreverent wunderkind of the New York hip-hop scene may be getting older, but that doesn't mean they're getting timid or, to use the vernacular, *wack*. Fans of the Beasties will find a complete discography, Quicktime movies and song lyrics among the wealth of offerings here. But more importantly, they'll learn answers to burning Beastie Boy questions (Q: "Does BEASTIE actually mean something?" A: "According to Mike D, it stands for Boys Entering Anarchistic States Towards Internal Excellence").

Here's the spot to find out everything you ever wanted to know about Michael Diamond (Mike D), Adam Horovitz (the King AdRock) and Adam Yauch (MCA). The fan-produced site does a stellar job of keeping the wealth of Beastie Boys projects (that is, their record label, Grand Royal, shenanigans à la Beastie, a plethora of merchandise, and their commitment to freeing the Tibetan people from genocide) well-organized and easy to access. Check it.—*Reviewed by Julene Snyder*

NEW: The photos you didn't see on Saturday night live (including rare photos of Sir Stewart Wallace), along with **Quicktime video of the Beastie Boys appearance**. **The In Sound From Way Out!**, an instrumental album forthcoming on Grand Royal can now be previewed in the Discography section.

La Scala

http://lascala.milano.it/

Milan's Teatro alla Scala is not only world renowned, it's available on the World Wide Web. This site has sections in both Italian and English where patrons can purchase tickets, read biographies of the principals, and bone up on the history of the opera company. In Italian only.

Libretto Home Page

http://copper.ucs.indiana.edu/~lneff/libretti.html

Browsers will delight in the wealth of links to the raw texts of some public domain operas, songs, and other vocal works of classical music. Contributions are invited in plain ASCII, with other guidelines listed here. Bibliographies, a wishlist, and links to related sites are also featured.

OperaGlass

http://rick.stanford.edu/opera/main.html

OperaGlass explores the many elements of opera entertainment, offering browsers an inside glimpse of composers, companies, and productions. From this page, fans can obtain synopses, libretti, discographies, pictures, and more.

OPERA-L Experimental Server

http://www.physics.su.oz.au/~neilb/operah.html

Opera data online via this resource include A to Z listings of composers and operas, a guide to recorded operas, selected libretto synopses, pictures, and biographies. A collection of links to other opera-related sites is also featured.

The Opera Schedule Server

http://www.fsz.bme.hu/opera/main.html

The Opera Schedule Server lists the programs of opera companies around the world, with information on opera houses, a user help page, opera companies on the Web, and pointers to related resources.

Santa Fe Opera Home Page

http://www.santafeopera.org/

Visit this site to find out all about "something quite extraordinary" celebrated each and every summer, the Santa Fe Opera in northern New Mexico. Local opera lovers can peruse performance schedules and related information here.

Gary Stephens' FanWebs

http://www.geocities.com/Vienna/1340

Meet Gary Stephens, a music fan who lives in the United Kingdom. He has created FanWebs for Cecilia Bartoli, the Kronos Quartet, and 3 Mustaphas 3, and invites visitors to take a look.

Verdi Opera

http://fileroom.aaup.uic.edu/FileRoom/documents/Cases/307verdi.html

This page offers a brief description of Verdi's Opera "Stiffelio" and the conflicts the composer had in the 1850s with the Catholic Church. Includes links to information on politics and society at the time.

POP/ROCK/ALTERNATIVE

Note: This section is alphabetized by the musician's last name where applicable.

Alice in Chains: Into the Flood Again

http://www.proaxis.com/~mcoleman/aliceinchains

This fan page for rock group Alice in Chains includes rumors, fan club information, and audio samples from the band's 1995 self-titled album. Images, song lyrics and guitar tablature are among the site's other offerings.

Alt.Music Home Page

http://www.xmission.com/~adm

Alt.music is a Web page put out by a fan who was afraid of missing something: alternative music. This site features a downloadable song of the day, band information, search tools, and mailing list.

Laurie Anderson: HOMEpage of the Brave

http://www.c3.lanl.gov:8080/cgi/jimmyd/quoter?home

Followers of singer, musician, technical wizard, and performance artist Laurie Anderson can find art of, for, and about their multimedia heroine at the Home Page of the Brave. Explore her discography and performance schedule, or link to the artist's official Web sites.

Bad Taste Web

http://www.siberia.is/badtaste/badhome.htm

Iceland's Bad Taste, a progressive music organization and main nourishing root of pop band The Sugarcubes, gives visitors a tasty sample of itself here. Sound samples, a virtual gallery, and Quicktime movie are available to the curious.

The Band

http://www-ia.hiof.no/~janh/TheBand.html

Enthusiasts for the seminal rock group known as The Band will be in their element at this site, where comprehensive information about Bob Dylan's one-time backup group can be found. Among the data here are history, discography, soundtracks, images, and lyrics.

Beastie Boys Home Page

http://www.southern.com/BeastieBoys/

This is the place to embark on a grand tour of all things Beastie Boys, the hot hiphop/rock group.

Links to a discography, Quicktime videos and audio files, as well as a mail order catalog of Beasties tunes is included. See Editor's Choice.

Better Than Ezra

http://www.ezra.org/

The unofficial home page of the rock band Better than Ezra dishes up a wealth of band-related news, pictures, sound clips, tour dates, concert reviews, and song lyrics. Visitors can also join the mailing list for regular updates.

Blues Traveler Fan Page

http://www.sgi.net/bluestraveler/

The band Blues Traveler (featuring that big guy with the harmonica, John Popper) is the focus of this unofficial fan page. Among the resources are images, lyrics, biographies, articles, tour dates, and links.

The Bobs

http://www.iuma.com/IUMA/band_html/Bobs,_The.html

The Bobs are an *a capella* group composed of three male Bobs and one female Bob whose stage show, lyrical humor, and musical madness have become their trademark. Visitors to their home page can find out how the players garner great reviews.

Boiled in Lead: The Leadheads Web Site

http://www.apocalypse.org/leadheads/home.html

This unofficial Boiled in Lead home page features information about the Minneapolis-based electric and acoustic band. Information here includes tour dates and a discography.

David Bowie File

http://www.etete.com/Bowie/

David Bowie fans, rejoice. This page chronicles the works of the pop icon, exploring lyrics, individual songs, and more details of "one of the most influential songwriters of the modern era."

David Bowie's Outside

http://www.davidbowie.com/

Find out all about David Bowie's album "Outside" at this site. Visitors can check out animations, character information, lyrics, sound bites, tour dates, and photos, or link to other Bowie sites around the globe.

Buzzcocks

http://www.cityscape.co.uk/users/ac46/indbuzz.htm

Song lyrics, sound snippets, and an annotated discography provide insight into the music and history of influential English punkers, the Buzzcocks, as well as band lyricist Pete Shelley's solo work. At our last visit, a Frequently Asked Questions file was under construction.

The Catawampus Universe

http://www.io.com/~catwamps/index.html

This fan-page, devoted to Kentucky-based psychedelic funk band Catawampus, provides article reprints, tour dates, sound clips, and information about the group's recordings. Also included is information about Red Fly Nation—a defunct band that featured members of Catawampus.

Cause & Effect

http://www.cen.uiuc.edu/~wellman/cause_effect/

Fans of rock music group Cause & Effect will enjoy this unofficial fan site, featuring discographies, song lyrics, performance information, and more. Includes graphical and text-based interface.

Chill Web Company

http://www.chapel-hill.nc.us/

"Click 'em and see 'em," the Chill Web Company tells visitors, and users head directly to a series of North Carolina bands like Southern Culture, Zen Frisbee, Red Star Belgrade, and others.

Paula Cole

http://cpcug.org/user/titusb/pcole/

At this fan site, Paula Cole fans will find detailed information about the recording artist with song samples, lyrics, a bio, and tour information.

Consumable Online

http://www.westnet.com/consumable/Consumable.html

Consumable Online, an Internet-based music magazine, provides disc reviews, artist interviews, and tour information on popular, rock and alternative groups. Visitors can read current and back issues here.

Crash Basket Low-rent Home Page

http://www.shadow.net/~proub/basket.html

Crash Basket, a band, takes a light-hearted look at itself here and offers information about its recordings and performance schedule. Fans can download pictures and sound files here and join the band's mailing list.

The Cure

http://gagme.wwa.com/~anaconda/cure2.html

Angst-ridden goth/rock icons, The Cure are celebrated here. Fans of the band can download images, reviews of bootlegs, a Cure fanzine, and a complete discography. The site also serves up a healthy dose of gossip and information on joining the Cure mailing list.

DanceNet

http://www.dance.nl/

The DanceNet Web site is devoted to Dutch dance music. Find out what songs are topping the Dutch charts, read online magazines, and link to information on labels, equipment, DJs, artists, and more.

Dano's Home Page

http://www.magi.com/~dano

Meet Dano, a lead singer in Ottawa-area bands for the past 15 years. Sound clips from his current band, Junkfiend, are featured on his home page, along with pictures and a calendar of club dates.

Dead Angel

http://www.eden.com/zines/deadangel/deadangel.html

Sure the design is ugly, but the writing's not half bad. Dead Angel—"the e-zine with a deeply flawed understanding of HTML"—minces no words in its extended interviews and authoritative reviews of music, movies, and other pop-culture artifacts.

The Dead Milkmen

http://ucunix.san.uc.edu/~hobbscf/milkmen/Milkmen.html

A fan of The Dead Milkmen provides chords (that "are a little messed up"), lyrics and a discography on this page. The site includes the band's newsletter, trivia, and news of the latest album.

The Def Leppard Home Page

http://www.princeton.edu/~nieder/defleppard/def.html

Littered with lyrics and loaded with links, this fan obsession offers it all: FAQs, photos, multimedia, and merchandise. Looking for news and information? That's here, too.

DIGITAL BISCUIT Home Page

http://www.ces.kyutech.ac.jp/student/JapanEdge/DIGIBI/digibi.html

Tokyo's underground monthly, Digital Biscuit, focuses on techno music. Visitors will find information on the paper's aim and history here, along with archives of past issues and techno news flashes. The site is in English; the archives are in Japanese.

DiscoWeb

http://www.msci.memphis.edu/~ryburnp/discoweb.html

Fans of disco music will enjoy this site, maintained by Paul Ryburn, the only University of Memphis faculty member with a fully operational disco ball in his office. Visit here for song lists, historical perspectives, newsgroups, merchandise outlets, and many other disco-related resources. Includes a downloadable disco ball graphic.

Doors Home Page

http://www.vis.colostate.edu/~user1209/doors/

Feast on the lyrics of the Lizard King and company here, or gaze at pictures of this historically famous band. This site, the work of a dedicated fan, includes a complete music guide and what's billed as an "ultimate band list."

The Duranie Connection

http://www.chapman.edu/students/mathur/new/

British pop band, Duran Duran, is the focus of this exhaustive fan page, with articles, a concert guide, lyric index, and much more.

Echo and the Bunnymen Page

http://www.netaxs.com/~jgreshes/echo.html

This page is devoted to the band Echo and the Bunnymen and its new incarnation, Electrafixion. Fans can read a variety of band-related news, articles, and interviews here, and can download sounds and pictures.

The Ecto Home Page

http://www.tela.bc.ca/ecto/

What's an Ectophile and who is Happy Rhodes? Find answers to these questions and pointers to cool music sites through the Ecto Home Page. An offshoot of a mailing list devoted to the music of Happy Rhodes, the page offers information about Rhodes' tunes, as well as the Ectophiles' Guide to Good Music.

The Elastica Connection II

http://www.actwin.com/lineup/

Fans of England-based rock group Elastica will enjoy this unofficial site, featuring discographies, graphics, sound files, lyrics, and more. Includes links to other fan sites.

Elvis: Virtual Voyager

http://www1.chron.com/voyager/elvis/

Browsers can join a virtual search for The King here. While in the neighborhood, why not take an Elvis trivia quiz, download Elvis sounds and software, or wander through a gallery of velvet?

Enigma

http://www.stud.his.no/~joarg/Enigma.html

The musical group Enigma makes monastic chants danceable. For news and reviews, a complete discography, and a picture gallery devoted to the band, visit this fan-produced shrine. Links are also provided to other official and devotee sites offering Enigma-related facts, gossip, and merchandise.

Enya Unofficial Page

http://sunsite.auc.dk/enya/

Delve into the life and music of ethereal pop star Enya on this unofficial, fan-produced page. The extensive site includes guitar tablatures, sound files, pictures, and interviews.

The Evolution Control Committee

http://www.infinet.com/~markg/ecc.html

The Evolution Control Committee makes alternative music that incorporates found sounds. Fans can buy tapes here, read interviews, and download the Committee's sounds.

Finland Rave Info

http://www.damicon.fi/fri/

Devoted to providing information about dance raves and other stay-up-late events in the Land of the Midnight Sun, this site links to a rave mailing list, indexes of past events, the club scene, and more. Includes articles on techno (in Finnish only).

Frankie Say No More—FGTH Fan Pages

http://www.cs.rulimburg.nl/~antal/fgth/fgth-home.html

Fans of Frankie Goes to Hollywood can take a look at photos and listen to sound clips of the British band's works through this fan page. It includes lyrics, a discography, and a history of the band.

Front 242

http://www.waste.org/~terje/front242/

The rock group Front 242 is the focus here, where fans can find general band information, reviews, interviews, and lyrics. Sound clips are also available, as well as an online market that provides a place to buy and sell.

Fugazi

http://www.southern.com/southern/band/FUGAZ/index.html

The Fugazi home page provides information on the band, its musicians, and touring schedules. Includes a discography, links to the group's recording label, and merchandise.

Jerry Garcia: Not Fade Away

http://metaverse.com/vibe/nfa.html

Grateful Dead fans produced this memorial page within days of Jerry Garcia's death. Fans can celebrate Garcia's life here and download songs in Real Audio.

Go! Discs/Portishead

http://www.godiscs.co.uk/godiscs/porthead.html

Here's a multimedia page devoted to the U.K. musical group, Portishead. Find a biography, photos, Quicktime and MPEG movies, plus links to related sites.

God Street Wine

http://www.netspace.org/gsw/

The God Street Wine page plugs fans into a digest of information about this rock group, including tour dates, ordering options, and a few surprising links that interact. Hear sound bites from GSW albums here as well.

Gothic Image Database

http://www.dnx.com/vamp/Gothic/Images/index.html

A gothic rock devotee presents this robust collection of images for fellow fans. Here guests can download a slew of band photos and album art-work, from such infamous musicians as Siouxsie And The Banshees and Christian Death.

The Grateful Dead

http://www.cs.cmu.edu/afs/cs.cmu.edu/user/mleone/web/dead.html

Created by a fan for fans, this comprehensive page devoted to the rock group The Grateful Dead includes graphics, lyrics, concert setlists, Frequently Asked Questions (FAQs) files, merchandise, and links to other Dead sites, including the official one.

Grateful Dead: GD Page

http://sedona.uafphys.alaska.edu/~price/dead.html

This is a collection of links devoted to the Grateful Dead. Visitors will find art and hyperlinks to the many sites on the Web containing information on this legendary band.

Guided By Voices

http://www-dev.lexis-nexis.com/~mikesell/gbv

Guided by Voices, a stubbornly iconoclastic rock band from Dayton, Ohio, is dissected here. Information about individual band members, critics' comments, and other tidbits of interest to fans of the "lo-fi" phenomenon are among the offerings.

Deborah Harry

http://www3.primenet.com/~lab/DHDeborahHarry.html

Fans of rock musician Deborah Harry will enjoy this unofficial fan site. Visit here for information interview reprints, photos, and the like about the artist's life and music, including her participation in the 1970s new wave group Blondie.

PJ Harvey

http://www.polygram.com/polygram/island/artists/harvey_pj/PJBio.html

This official PJ Harvey site from Polygram Records provides a discography of the alternative rock band's work, heralds the new PJ Harvey album, "To Bring You My Love," and explores the charisma of songwriter/chanteuse/lightning-rod Polly Harvey.

Jimi Hendrix

http://gold.spectra.net/jimi/

The legend of rock guitar god Jimi Hendrix lives on via the Internet. Fans will find sounds, sights, and lyrics of the late artist at this unofficial site, which includes dozens of links to Hendrix-related resources.

Shot of Rhythm: The John Hiatt Mailing List Archives

http://www.unicom.com/john-hiatt

Fans can pay homage to musician John Hiatt at the John Hiatt Mailing List archives. Visitors can look up albums in the discography or check out Hiatt pictures here.

Hole: The Drown Soda Pages

http://www.clysmic.com/hole/

Here's a loaded fan shrine to Courtney Love & Co. Visitors are treated to bootleg information, sound and video clips, photos, song lyrics, and more.

Husker Du/Bob Mould/Sugar

http://math.montana.edu/~sanford/sugar.html

This fan page for rock musician Bob Mould—and for his band projects Husker Du and Sugar—contains interviews and articles and a Frequently Asked Questions (FAQs) section. Visitors will also find loads of album information, including song lyrics, guitar tabs, and cover art.

Hyperreal

http://www.hyperreal.com/

Hyperreal is an electronic publication that chronicles the club and rave scene. Visitors will find digital art, rave music resources, and articles on techno culture.

Indie Front by Bystander

http://charlemagne.uwaterloo.ca/

Independent bands are the focus of the Indie Front page and the e-zine it features. Articles about business, music, distribution, personnel, and networking for independent bands are included.

The Industrial Page

http://bird.taponline.com/industrial/

A native Chicagoan has compiled an industrial music archive at this site. Wanderers here can find information about the artists, labels and clubs that make up the bleak, angry landscape of this mechanical music movement.

Innocence Mission Home Page

http://www.huan.com/im/

The band Innocence Mission is celebrated here with a discography, lyrics and a Frequently Asked Questions (FAQs) file about the "shoegazer" band. Also included are articles, reviews, sound files, and touring information.

Japanese Independent Music Archive

http://www.atom.co.jp/INDIES

From the atom Co., Ltd. site, this multimedia page abounds with audio clips featuring Japanese indepedent music. Find sounds from bellissima records and Seance-Room Music, plus artists from other labels. In English and Japanese.

Jartery

http://www.dnai.com/~jar

Jar, a San Francisco-based band, is featured here. Visitors can download video and sound clips, lyrics, interviews, and reviews. The official site also contains gig and merchandise information.

The JAVA Lounge Rolling Stones Page

http://www.stones.com/java_lounge.html

This JAVA Rolling Stones site seems strangely incomplete and devoid of graphics; perhaps it is under construction. Nonetheless, Stones fans can link to song lists and lyrics and answers to FAQs on the dinosaur rock band.

Jazz Improvisation

http://hum.lss.wisc.edu/jazz

Visit this page for a music index featuring links to jazz and blues sites around the world. Also included is a series of articles taken from the syllabus for two jazz classes taught at the University of Wisconsin Madison.

The Jefferson Airplane Home Page

http://grove.ufl.edu/~number6/
Jefferson.Airplane/airplane.html

The home page of rock and roll band Jefferson Airplane contains a wealth of information about the group, their music, achievments, and history. The complete Jefferson Airplane discography, photos, Frequently Asked Questions (FAQs), and concert reviews are among this site's features.

The Jesus and Mary Chain

http://american.recordings.com/American_
Artists/Jesus_And_Mary_Chain/jamc_
home.html

American Recordings' page for alternative rockers The Jesus and Mary Chain contains audio files, album covers, images, and information on the band.

Jukebox

http://www.sirius.com/~mega/metal/
jukebox.html

Mega's Jukebox is a no-frills site offering downloadable audio or .au files of full-length songs. Musical offerings here are geared toward the heavier side of American rock 'n' roll, with such bands as Alice In Chains, Guns 'n' Roses, Jimi Hendrix, Nine Inch Nails, and The Red Hot Chili Peppers.

Kronos Quartet FanWeb

http://www.lochnet.com/client/gs/kq.html

A string ensemble, the Kronos Quartet has built its reputation and repertoire on mostly 20th century music, much of it written specifically for the group. Its multimedia Web page features audio samples, a discography, images, and articles.

Kurdt's Skanking SkaPage

http://www.missouri.edu/~c639772

Kurdt's Skanking SkaPage was created for and by fans of Ska, an infectious musical genre that's big on the club circuit. Visitors can read reviews of Ska recordings and find out when the bands may be appearing at various venues.

The Sandy Lam Home Page

http://www.musicdistrict.com/sandylam/
sandy/

Created by a fan for fans, this page is devoted to Sandy Lam, a female singer from Hong Kong. The singer's discography, biography, list of awards, theme songs, and photo album are featured at this site. In English and Chinese.

Latvis' RockData

http://www.sjoki.uta.fi/~latvis/rockdata.html

The latest in Finnish rock is outlined, dissected and hyped here. The site includes information about Finnish record companies, booking agents, bands, venues, and radio stations. In English and Finnish.

Letters to Cleo

http://www-personal.umich.edu/~hstahl/
letters.html

This home page for the music group Letters to Cleo contains articles, lyrics, pictures, guitar tablature, audio/video clips, tour dates, and a mailing list.

The Levellers Page

http://chem-www.mps.ohio-state.edu/
~pfleming/lvlrs/

This Web page is devoted to the musical band The Levellers, who've been described as "sort of a Celtic Clash." Visitors will find a discography, lyrics, photos, tour dates, and more.

Live From York PA

http://live.cerf.net/

Slavering fans of alternative band Live will want to see the Live from York, PA page, with links to band information, Quicktime videos, audio clips, tour dates, and much more on the group.

Madonna

http://www.buffnet.net/~steve772/maddy.html

Two Madonna fans pay homage to the pop star here. Browsers can download video and audio snippets, read her song lyrics, and shop for hard-to-find merchandise.

MAGiC feet

http://www1.haywire.co.uk/haywire/

Go far beyond Kraftwerk as you explore today's electronic music with MAGiC Feet. Self-described as the UK's "premier underground techno and electronic publication," the zine reviews new releases and takes you to the club scene at this Web edition.

Manic Street Preachers

http://boris.qub.ac.uk/tony/manics

News, a discography and articles on the U.K. band Manic Street Preachers make up the bulk of this home page. Also find information on a Manics mailing list.

The Man or Astro-Man? Web Site of Intergalactic Havoc

http://www.astroman.com/

Man or Astro-Man? is just one of the many bands riding the swelling wave of popularity for guitar-heavy surf music, and fans of the retro sound of Man or Astro-Man? can get all kinds of goodies on the band here. Audio and video clips, the rundown on what the band's done so far, even the Astro newsletter can be had.

Martensville

http://www.islandnet.com/~moron/deterrent/
martensville/marten.html

Martensville is more than just another industrial band, it's a self-described "machine driven unit with three human accomplices." Browsers will find an "atonal soundtrack," an interview, and other details about the group.

Massive Brings

http://www.massive.com/

Massive Brings has got the spin on what's happening in the DJ and club scene from San Francisco to London and beyond. Hip tune reviews and hot news from the dance floor keep DJ hopefuls up to speed.

MC 900 Foot Jesus

http://american.recordings.com/American_
Artists/MC_900FT_Jesus/mc_home.html

Musician/rapper/noisemaker/philosopher Mark Griffin, aka MC 900 Foot Jesus, is the focus of this home page from American Recordings. Among the resources here are a biography, audio clips, video clips, lyrics, and images. Fans also can send e-mail to MC 900 Foot Jesus from here.

Meat Beat Manifesto Home Page

http://www.brainwashed.com/mbm/

Music fans can check the unofficial Meat Beat Manifesto home page for information about the band's discography and a link to a visual Meat Beat page. The simple unofficial page also includes a link to Edge of No Control from the Usenet newsgroup rec.music.misc.

Michael's Music Links

http://www.magick.net/~michael/music.html

Michael loves Sonic Youth. It's his favorite band, and if you visit this page, you'll find articles, interviews, and raves about the band. Also find information about the Minutemen and Glenn Braca.

Midnight Oil: Oilbase Index

http://www.stevens-tech.edu/~dbelson/
oilbase/

OilBase, a fan site devoted to the Australian rock band Midnight Oil, is a group effort of members of a fan mailing list. Visitors will find a discography, song lyrics, audio files, and live-show registries.

Ministry Unofficial Fan Site

http://pulsar.cs.wku.edu/~gizzard/ministry.html

Fans of rock music group Ministry will enjoy this unofficial fan site, featuring discographies, music samples, discussion groups, and links to related music sites. Includes song lyrics and downloadable sound files.

Joni Mitchell Home Page

http://www.well.com/user/wallyb/jonihome.html

A Joni Mitchell fan pays homage to the singer, poet and painter here. Visitors can download her lyrics, artwork, and biography on this extensive site, which also includes a chat room.

The Monkees Home Page

http://www.primenet.com/~flex/monkees.html

Hey, hey, it's the home page of the ragtag band of errant musicians-turned-actors who took American television by storm in the 1960s. Get all the nitty-gritty on a favorite band member, link to other fans online, or tag along on a virtual Monkees romp.

Alanis Morissette

http://www.sgi.net/alanis/

Alanis Morissette, the Canadian pop star, has an unofficial fan page here. Check up on the latest Alanis sightings, gossip, song lyrics, and photos. Links to other Alanis sites provided.

Morphine

http://www.ai.mit.edu/~spraxlo/morphine/Morphine.html

The Boston rock band Morphine is the subject of this multimedia fan page. Find sound clips, movie clips, and details about subscribing to the Morphine newsletter.

"Syl": A Morrissey Fanzine Website

http://www.Morrissey-solo.com/

This online fanzine is devoted to the life and music of Steven Patrick Morrissey. Find out about the ex-Smiths' lead singer, and catch information about upcoming performance dates and locations of his solo act.

My Life with the Thrill Kill Kult: Sanitarium Borderline

http://pulsar.cs.wku.edu/~draven/tkk.html

This My Life with the Thrill Kill Kult fan page contains information on the band, interviews with group members, and a discography. Visitors also will find lyrics, sound samples, and merchandising, and mailing list information.

NegativWorldWideWebLand

http://negativland.com/

Negativland is an alternative rock band concerned with politics and intellectual property issues as well

as music. Visitors can read through a discussion of the U.S. Copyright Act and discover why the band "hates the Information Superhighway," as well as check out its discography, and order music.

New Order

http://www.niagara.edu/New_Order/discography.html

Fans of the British pop rock band New Order can check out an extensive discography here. In addition to information about albums and singles, find the scoop on the band's videos and DJ remixes.

The Nicks Fix: A Homepage Devoted to Stevie Nicks

http://web2.airmail.net/jkinney/

Stevie Nicks is celebrated here. Fans can download photos, videos, and her song lyrics. The extensive site also includes links to other Nicks resources on the Net, including Fleetwood Mac sites, a mailing list, and a forum.

Jeff's Nirvana Archive—The Homepage of the Nirvana FAQ

http://www.oswego.edu/~jmcrae/nindex.html

A Nirvana fan shares articles and interviews that shed light on the life and death of front man Kurt Cobain, as well as the band's music, lyrics, and history. Find out where to trade your bootlegs here.

Nirvana Page

http://www.geffen.com/nirv.html

Live! Tonight! Sold Out! This official Nirvana page is filled with concert and musical information about the short-lived band. At this Geffen site, fans can download photographs, sound samples, and cruise through band information tidbits.

Nirvana Web Archive

http://www.ludd.luth.se/nirvana

Nirvana fans can download photos, deciphered lyrics, and more at this unofficial site. The page also contains information on group leader Kurt Cobain's suicide (including text from the singer/guitarist's final writing) and a link to a Nirvana newsgroup.

Oceans and Garden of Stone List Links

http://www.cs.caltech.edu/~adam/LOCAL/gos.html

Pearl Jam's popularity is evident on this index, where fans can link to dozens of fan-produced sites that celebrate the rock band. Also included are links to a newsgroup and bands that "Pearl Jam fans might like."

Official Grateful Dead Home Page

http://grateful.dead.net/

Check out the long, strange trip of the Grateful Dead on this official site. Band members are no longer touring under the name Grateful Dead, but

tour dates are listed here. The site also hints at future archive releases and details the band's charitable work. Deadheads can order merchandise here, too.

The Orb: Ultraworld Unofficial Page

http://hyperreal.com/music/artists/orb/www/index.html

Ultraworld is the unofficial home page of Orb, an alternative rock band. Includes a discography and information on bootleg live recordings.

Petra

http://www.wam.umd.edu/~lbdavies/music/petra/petrapage.html

Petra, a Christian rock band, get its due on this page, with information about tours, music, and band members. Listen to a 20-second sound byte from one of the group's most popular songs, "Creed."

Tom Petty: Wildflowers

http://www.iuma.com/Warner/html/Petty,_Tom.html

Warner Bros. hosts this site to promote musical maestro Tom Petty's recording, "Wildflowers." An audio clip of "You Don't Know How It Feels" complements liner notes and a Petty bio.

Phreeworld

http://www.art.net/Music/Phreeworld/Phreeworld.html

Pacific Northwest band Phreeworld introduces its music and members to the world through this Web site, which is packed with images and CD soundbytes. The page also includes a Quicktime video of concert clips.

Pink Floyd

http://www.smartdocs.com/~migre.v/floyd/index.html

The Pink Floyd page provides devotees of the seminal rock group with a year-by-year directory of the band's musical accomplishments. Selections provide lyrics and images from all albums produced from 1967 to 1992.

Pink Floyd: All that is Floydian

http://gladstone.uoregon.edu/~stinson/pinkfloyd.html

Pink Floyd isn't so much a rock band as a state of mind, as visitors to this site will discover. Included are lyrics, images, interviews, and articles, as well as links to newsgroups, Frequently Asked Questions, a mailing list, and other resources.

Pizzicato Five fan page

http://www.clark.net/pub/fan/pizz.html

Ty Liotta welcomes fellow Pizzicato Five fans to his page offering "pictures, information, and sounds from this unusual Japanese music group." Among the featured items, find a group history, discography, and links to topical sites.

Poster Children International

http://www.prairienet.org/posterkids/

A Reprise Records group, the Poster Children host this site promoting the band, its music, and its branded merchandise. Check out tour dates, get polled, or linger over lyrics and band news.

The Cheesy Primus Page

http://www.ram.org/music/primus/
primus.html

The Cheesy Primus home page is an unofficial site devoted to the grunge band, Primus. Visitors will find a discography, tour dates, reviews, band member profiles, audio clips, and photos.

Psychedelic Psyberspace

http://cfn.cs.dal.ca/~af678/cyberspace.html

Browsers searching for the eternal long, strange trip will find an index that features "links to various flowerpower sites and a multitude of psychedelic music links" here. In addition to music, links focus on drugs and the culture of the 1960s.

Pop Will Eat Itself: PWEI Nation

http://kzsu.stanford.edu/uwi/pwei/pwei.html

"PWEI Nation" is an unabashed fanzine of the post-punk band Pop Will Eat Itself. This site provides news, rumors, and shopping opportunities to band devotees.

Queen Home Page

http://queen-fip.com/

The official Web site for the legendary rock band Queen is a sophisticated and low-key site. It heralds the release of the band's first new album since the death of singer Freddie Mercury and provides information about Queen's recent videos, television appearances, and philanthropy.

Sheri's Queen/QMS World Wide Web

http://www.rt66.com/unicorn/queen.html

How did an image of lead singer Freddie Mercury appear on the cover of Queen's 1995 album? Find the answer (okay, it's a statue) and delve into minutia about the rock band on this unofficial site. It includes images and the nearly obligatory links to other Queen sites.

radio ethiopia

http://www.nwlink.com/~clr/

Radio Ethiopia: Caryn's Home Page has information about alternative music and bands such as Pearl Jam, R.E.M., and Patti Smith. Also find concert reviews, opinion, and links to a host of other music fan sites.

Rage Against The Machine: The Unofficial Home Page

http://www.cs.man.ac.uk/~gjones/
RageAgainstTheMachine/
RageAgainstTheMachine.html

The fan page for the English band Rage Against The Machine has links to photos, reviews, a discography, and information about world politics.

Chris Rea

http://www.helsinki.fi/~wikgren/chrisrea.html

Chris Rea's Home Page targets fans of the English musical artist, offering biographical sketches and a record of his accomplishments. Other links point to a fanclub, interviews, and touring schedules.

Refreshments

http://rampages.onramp.net/~micheleb/
refresh.html

The Refreshments, a Phoenix, Arizona-based rock music group, maintains this promotional site. Visit here to learn about its members, music, and upcoming performance and recording plans.

R.E.M.: The Chord Archive

http://bubblegum.uark.edu/REM/

An archive of chords and musical compositions of songs by rock band R.E.M. is provided at this Web site. Visitors can jump to pages on individual albums, or conduct searches of various musical information.

R.E.M.—Monster

http://www.iuma.com/Warner/html/
R.E.M..html

R.E.M.'s album, "Monster," is promoted and dissected at this site, with a list of tracks and band member's comments. The page, maintained by the Internet Underground Music Archive, includes 1995 tour dates and a Quicktime video clip.

RzWeb: A Guide to the Works of the Residents

http://www.csd.uwo.ca/~tzoq/Residents/

The fan page of the musical group The Residents contains a history of the band, a discography, and tour information. Includes a lyrics archive, listings of books, and videos and much more.

Rock Online

http://www.rockonline.com/

A mix of promotional material from EMI Records, a New York radio station and rock fans, Rock Online links visitors to information on bands and news in rock, as well as swinging chat rooms and breaking indie bands.

The Rolling Stones Web Site

http://stones.com/

The Voodoo Lounge is the official Rolling Stones Web Site. (Your first clue is that the URL ends in ".com.") This state-of-the-art promo site provides sound and video clips of Mick and the boys in action, interviews with the Stones' extended family, and plenty of the naughty-but-nice imagery for which this raunchy rock band is famous.

Henry Rollins' Stuff

http://www.st.nepean.uws.edu.au/~alf/rollins/

This vast site is devoted to the musician/spoken word performer Henry Rollins. Visitors will find a discography, articles, audio samples, photos, biographical information, and a multitude of links.

The Rush/NMS Home Page

http://syrinx.umd.edu/rush/

A band known for innovative "progressive rock" before Green Day was even out of diapers, Rush is the featured band on this comprehensive fan site. Lyrics, information, interviews, and many more links dot this text-rich page.

Joe Satriani's Home Page

http://www.satriani.com/

One of rock music's most accomplished guitar players is celebrated here. This official site offers biographical information on Joe Satriani, a discography, tour information, photos, and technical notes on his incredible guitar collection. Fans can buy official Satriani merchandise here, too.

Joe Satriani at the Riv

http://www.ncsa.uiuc.edu/SDG/People/rgrant/
riv.html

This personal home page devoted to guitarist Joe Satriani offers browsers vignettes of the author's experiences seeing the artist play live. Check out Joe's autograph here, or link to information about California.

Seefeel

http://hyperreal.com/music/artists/seefeel/
seefeel.html

This home page has information on the band Seefeel, with facts about the band's recordings, links to interviews, and sound files.

Siouxsie And The Banshees Home Page

http://www.dnx.com/vamp/Siouxsie/
index.html

Lyrics, images, and other resources on the band Siouxsie and the Banshees are collected at this fan site. Included are a discography, audio clips, archives of a mailing list, and interviews.

Sister Machine Gun

http://www.smg.org/

Sister Machine Gun, an industrial band from Chicago, provides a new sound on its Web site and a history of how it came to be. Play their music tracks while reading about the band.

A Site for Sore Ears

http://www.mit.edu:8001/people/trellos/
homepage.html

Mixmaster Morris spins audio samples of his (and others') "eclectic electric" music here. The DJ also offers ambient/techno charts and reviews of similar tunes, plus a photo gallery, interview reprints, and some of Morris' fave computer-generated artwork.

Skinny Puppy Central

http://www.cling.gu.se/~cl3polof/central/

Fans of dark electronic soundsmiths Skinny Puppy will enjoy this site, featuring song lyrics, photographs, interviews, trivia and more. Visit here to learn about the band and link to related Web sites.

Eric Agnew's Smashing Pumpkins Site.

http://www.engr.wisc.edu/~agnew/
pumpkin.html

Enjoy Smashing Pumpkins moments with the Webmaster of this electronic tribute to the musical group known for ditties like "1979" and "Tonight Tonight."

The Smashing Pumpkins

http://www.muohio.edu/~carmance/sp.html

Fans of rock music group Smashing Pumpkins will enjoy this unofficial fan site. Visit here for sheet music, song lyrics, recent recording and performance information, press clippings, and more.

Sonic Youth

http://geffen.com/sonic.html

Geffen Records maintains this site to provide information about prototypical indie noise rockers Sonic Youth. Photos and bios are available, as is an opportunity to buy the group's albums.

The Jennys

http://www.thejennys.com/

The Spinning Jenny site contains concert dates, new songs announcements, and general news about the Tempe, Arizona band. Included also are sound clips and a bulletin board to exchange Spinning Jenny comments.

Stone Temple Pilots: Pilots

http://thoth.stetson.edu/music/pilots/
index.html

This is a page dedicated to the rock band Stone Temple Pilots. Check out the group's first two albums, read a bio, and view pictures of the Pilots here.

Stones World

http://www.stonesworld.com/

Catch up on the latest news about the Rolling Stones, including concert news and rumors about new albums. Check into the message board to sound off about Stones topics.

Stutter Home Page

http://www.tsa.net/~lrussink/james

Stutter is the mailing list for fans of James, the British alternative rock band. This page is where fans can share information with others, as well as read back issues of the newsletter One Man Clapping. Find out what the band plans for the future as well.

Matthew Sweet Home Page

http://www.xnet.com/~wakemich/
msweet.shtml

Musician Matthew Sweet's tour dates, tunes, and lyrics are among the offerings at this site. There also are articles and reviews, as well as links to other Matthew Sweet sites.

Talking Head: Francey's Page

http://www.bart.nl/~francey/th.html

This fan page is devoted to the rock group The Talking Heads. Visitors will find a discography, video clips, and biographical information on individual band members here.

Talking Heads

http://129.237.17.3/Heads/Talking_Heads.html

Fans of the punk-turned-"art"-rock band, Talking Heads, have designed this page to supplement their mailing list. This ain't no *disco*, but it is a fair guide to the Byrne-driven quartet, including a discography, cover-ography, lyrics, and "bootleg surveys."

Techno.Net

http://www.techno.net/

Techno.Net is a German-based resource for fans of techno and industrial-style dance music. The site offers nighclub listings, charts, music reviews, and tips on the latest clubwear. In German and English.

Techno Online

http://www.techno.de/

Techno Online provides links to media outlets of interest to aficionados of techno music. Record label and magazine connections can be found here. Some information in German.

ThinWhiteLine

http://www.pitt.edu/~houser/twl.html

The ThinWhiteLine page highlights this Pittsburgh band with art from album covers and sound clips from several releases. Other selections include links to Thin WhiteLine reviews and the Internet Underground Music Archives.

Thought Industry: Web for Insects

http://www.cs.wvu.edu/~deweyg/ti/thought_
industry.html

The band Thought Industry plays a "thrashy kind of progressive rock." This fan page contains information about the group, a discography, song lyrics, a picture gallery, and music samples.

Trade Test Transmission

http://www.cityscape.co.uk/users/ac46/

Trade Test Transmission is devoted to the band Buzzcocks and solo artist Pete Shelley. A discography, lyrics, pictures, and sounds are featured at this fan-produced page.

The Unofficial Jeff Buckley Page

http://www.goodnet.com/~gkelemen/
jeffhome.html

Even though Jeff Buckley's album "Grace" sold very well, he remains a semi-cult musician. Fans of the American songster will find out where they can hear and see Buckley alone reading poetry, or with his band giving a concert.

The Unofficial Lollapalooza Page

http://aegis.mcs.kent.edu/~cstone/lolla/
lolla.html

The Unofficial Lollapalooza Page contains information on all of the mammoth concerts' events from 1991 to present. Includes details of which band played on which stage, and lists answers to Frequently Asked Questions (FAQs).

Unofficial Soundgarden Home Page

http://www.sgi.net/soundgarden/

The sights and sounds of heavyweight Seattle band Soundgarden hit the Web on this unofficial home page. Check in for the latest rumors or to browse the lyrics to some of the band's riff-laden tunes.

Unofficial Tom Petty Fan Site

http://www.ugcs.caltech.edu/~hedlund/tom_
petty/index.shtml

The music of Tom Petty (with and without the Heartbreakers) is featured at this site. Included are albums, lyrics, images and links to other Tom Petty sites and fan e-mail directories.

The Unofficial Violent Femmes Home Page

http://www.gl.umbc.edu/~mmerry2/
femmes.html

Do you really know what the name of the band Violent Femmes means? Visit this site to find out. Then delve even deeper into band trivia and memorabilia with articles, pictures, and bios of the group's members.

Steve Vai's Home on the Web

http://www.vai.com/

Devoted to the music of Steve Vai, browsers will find the obligatory biography and discography along with links to interviews, his current projects, and upcoming concert dates.

Van Halen Home Page

http://carroll1.cc.edu/~rhiggins/vh.html

Rock dinosaur Van Halen, termed "The Greatest Rock & Roll Band on Earth!" here, takes center stage on this page. Visitors will find links to a huge Van Halen bootleg discography, a mailing list, and other fan and promotional Web sites devoted to the arena rockers.

Van Morrison

http://www.harbour.sfu.ca/~hayward/van/van.html

The Van Morrison home page seeks to serve as an informational site for those interested in the man and his music. Biography, reviews, interviews, and more are available here.

Stevie Ray Vaughan

http://www.quadralay.com/www/Austin/AustinMusic/srv/StevieRayVaughan.html

Stevie Ray Vaughan is a legendary rock and blues musician who died in 1990. Visitors can find song lyrics, pictures, and a poster archive at this fan site.

Vergiftung Home Page

http://purgatory.ecn.purdue.edu:20002/JBC/david/vergiftung.html

Browsers can download selected sound clips from the band Vergiftung here. The site also includes a list of upcoming gigs for the Purdue University-based band.

VH1 Main Screen

http://vh1.com/

Before you pick up the clicker and dial in the VH1 cable network, check its home page for news about featured artists and highlights from the daily schedule. Stop by to talk with other VH1 viewers in chat areas or let the network know what you think about its play list.

The Vibe: Surf!

http://metaverse.com/vibe/surf.html

Adam Curry, former MTV personality, posts his favorite Web pages at this site. The links compiled are an alphabetical listing of predominantly rock 'n' roll-oriented resources with an emphasis on artist, rather than music genre.

Violet Arcana

http://www.violet-arcana.com/

Violet Arcana presents a collection of clips, pictures, art, lyrics, multimedia, and reviews of esoteric music here. The band describes itself as providing "dreamy, ethereal, melodic, moody, ambient soundscapes for the surreal music listener."

World Wide Punk

http://www.worldchat.com/vic/wwp

A vast repository of all things of interest to punk rockers includes bands, labels, and zines. A mohawk is not necessary for entrance.

Zappa Quote of the Day

http://www.fwi.uva.nl/~heederik/zappa/quote/

Fans of the late rock composer and guitarist Frank Zappa can check into this site for daily words of wisdom. Check in for a daily quote or browse an archive of Zappa witticisms like "Modern music is a sick puppy" or "In the fight between you and the world, back the world." Visitors also can submit new quotes.

Zappa Tribute Page

http://www.cs.tufts.edu/~stratton/zappa/zappa.html

"If you find factual information here," writes the Webmaster, "don't blame me, I probably didn't mean it." Fans of the late Frank Zappa will enjoy this casual tribute, which includes photos, musings, and links to other Zappa-related sites.

POPULAR STANDARDS

Barbershop Web Server

http://timc.pop.upenn.edu/

The Barbershop Web Server contains information on barbershop music, recordings, and pointers to online resources. Includes links to Frequently Asked Questions (FAQs), organizations around the world, and sheet music.

RAP/HIP-HOP/R&B

Beastie Boys Home Page

http://www.southern.com/BeastieBoys/

This is the place to embark on a grand tour of all things relating to the Beastie Boys, the hot hiphop/rock group. Links to a discography, Quicktime videos, and audio files, as well as a mail order catalog of Beasties tunes is included.

The Belizbeha Home Page

http://www.belizbeha.com

This funkified Web site is filled with the sounds of acid jazz, soul, funk, pop, and hip-hop music. Belizbeha, an eight-piece band out of Burlington, Vermont, offers information on its debut CD, band member bios, and set lists here.

Fly! Music Magazine

http://www.fly.co.uk/

Put some hip in your hop and some jive in your jazz at Fly! The British magazine features articles and reviews of new music—mainly jazz, R&B, and dance. To hear some live grooves and visit the gigs and clubs section for happenings in Great Britain.

HEADz UP!

http://www.public.iastate.edu/~krs_one/HEADzUP/

HEADz UP!, formerly known as HardC.O.R.E., is an e-zine that deals with hip-hop culture. Browsers will find a goodie grab bag, audio files, and reviews.

Hip Hop Reviews

http://www.ai.mit.edu/~isbell/HFh/reviews/000-toc.html

Visitors to this page will find critical reviews of musical recordings from the Hip Hop genre. The reviews are listed alphabetically by artist and many have appeared in "HardC.O.R.E." magazine.

MC 900 Foot Jesus

http://american.recordings.com/American_Artists/MC_900FT_Jesus/mc_home.html

Musician/rapper/noisemaker/philosopher Mark Griffin, aka MC 900 Foot Jesus, is the focus of this home page from American Recordings. Among the resources here are a biography, audio clips, video clips, lyrics, and images. Fans also can send e-mail to MC 900 Foot Jesus from here.

Unofficial Public Enemy Home Page

http://www.louis.ecs.soton.ac.uk/~run95r/public.c/pe/html

This fan's page dedicated to the rap group Public Enemy contains lyrics, a discography, profiles, and a history of the group.

Streetsound e-zine

http://www.streetsound.com/zone/

Visitors to the Streetsound e-zine can check into the music arcade, click to the DJ emporium, or try door number three for entertainment. Dance music of all kinds—techno, hiphop, house, and more—is the focus here, with links to a Red Light District as well as a game room and online gallery.

The Totally Unofficial Rap Dictionary

http://www.sci.kun.nl/thalia/rapdict/

Check out the Rap Dictionary at this site for Rap lingo to standard English translations. Visitors can search the entire site or link to a number of other Rap and Hip Hop related Web pages.

RELIGIOUS

British Isles: Christian Gig Guide

http://www.shef.ac.uk/misc/rec/sm/

The Christian Gig Guide serves as a guide to concert information for the British Isles. Webmaster Stephen Mettam posts information about upcoming events as well as pointers to other Christian Web sites of interest.

Canada: Canadian Christian Concert Page

http://www.interlog.com/~djcl/

Learn who's making a joyful noise unto the Lord in Canada at the CCCP Canadian Christian Music Concert Page. Visitors can read the list of Christian artists performing and link to more information.

ChoralNet

http://www.choralnet.org

ChoralNet asks for donations and offers its "Internet Center for Choral Music" through this site. Stop by for ChoralTalk, access to the ChoralAcademe, and a link to the rec.music.makers.choral Usenet newsgroup.

Christian Music Online Welcome Page

http://www.cmo.com/cmo/index.html

Biographies and photos of Christian music artists are featured here, along with recent news in the genre and concert information. Links to Christian Calendar Magazine and Release Magazine also are included.

Contemporary Christian Music Resource List

http://www.acs.psu.edu/users/jws/ccmpage.html

Onward Christian soldiers to this guide to contemporary Christian music resources on the Web. Visitors will find pointers to and brief descriptions of such resources as a Christian music magazine, an artist index, and more.

The Copenhagen University Choir

http://www.astro.ku.dk/~michael/sang.html

Meet the Copenhagen University Choir, the oldest choir in Denmark, here. The page includes pictures, contact information, and details on upcoming festivals. Also, potential members will learn how the choir recruits singers.

Ari Davidow's Klez Picks

http://www.well.com/user/ari/klez/

Resources on klezmer music are collected at this site, which says "this generation of klezmer musicians reblends jazz and punk and the spirit of an entire Yiddish revival." Included are reviews, band information, and links to any pages related to klezmer or Jewish music.

The Lighthouse Electronic Magazine Home Page

http://tlem.netcentral.net/

Fans of God-approved Christian rock will want to check out "The Lighthouse," an online magazine devoted to Christian music. Check out past or current issues to learn more about featured bands, hear audio files, read up on the music industry, and more.

NetCentral, Inc.

http://www.netcentral.net/

NetCentral, Inc., a Nashville, Tennessee Web marketing company, hosts this site, which includes "A Closer Look," featuring Christian media and entertainment news, NoteStation, a sheet music retail network, and record companies Word and Gotee.

Petra

http://www.wam.umd.edu/~lbdavies/music/petra/petrapage.html

Petra, a Christian rock band, get its due on this page, with information about tours, music, and band members. Listen to a 20-second sound byte from one of the group's most popular songs, "Creed."

The Official Home Page for Promise

http://www.europa.com/~tarie/ccci.html

The Christian music trio Promise is profiled on this official site. The site includes a discography, photos, and links to other Promise sites.

Sonshine Christian Radio

http://www.ozemail.com.au/~cook/sonshine

98.5 Sonshine Radio in Perth, Western Australia, maintains this site to introduce its staff and programming. Visitors will find current playlists, regular program schedules, listener feedback, and more.

SHOWTUNES AND SCORES

Babylon 5 Suite: The Original Soundtrack

http://www.sonicimages.com/b5/b5home.html

The "Babylon 5 Suite: The Original Soundtrack" site contains information about the original soundtrack of the television series. Browsers will find information about the composer, a description of the tracks, critical reviews, and links to other "Babylon 5" pages.

Disney.com

http://www.disney.com/

International entertainment corporation Disney packs its home page with cartoons, games, catalogs, and just plain fun stuff. Includes links to all Disney subsidiaries, including the Disney Channel, Walt Disney Records, and its worldwide network of family theme parks.

Gilbert and Sullivan Archive

http://math.idbsu.edu/gas/GaS.html

Operetta enthusiasts can link to a wide-ranging archive of Gilbert and Sullivan memorabilia, musical scores, plot summaries, and sound files at this home page. Includes access to librettos, organizations, and festivals.

Hindi Movie Songs

http://www.cs.wisc.edu/~navin/india/songs/index.html

This site, produced from the "Itrans Song Book," archives music from Hindi films. Visitors can search for music by title and several other categories.

Jesus Christ Superstar

http://www.webcom.com/~sabata/jcs/welcome.html

Fans of "Jesus Christ Superstar," will enjoy hunting around this page for information about the rock opera. It's still pleasing audiences nationwide, and dates and locations are listed here.

Jesus Christ Superstar: A Resurrection

http://monsterbit.com/daemon/jcs.html

"Jesus Christ Superstar: A Resurrection" is a re-recording of the classic rock opera, with an all-star cast of alternative rockers including the Indigo Girls. This site describes the genesis and intent of the project, offers biographical sketches of the principles, and enables online ordering.

Tower Lyrics Archive

http://www.ccs.neu.edu/home/tower/lyrics.html

This archive offers pointers to sites containing lyrics from various stage musicals. The works of Andrew Lloyd Webber, Boublil and Schoenberg, and Gilbert and Sullivan are featured among others.

Andrew Lloyd Webber Online

http://www.sas.upenn.edu/~smfriedm/alw.html

British composer Sir Andrew Lloyd Webber steps into the spotlight via this compiled guide to Webber on the Web. Among the featured resources, find links to fan pages dedicated to the man's musical theatre successes, biographical sites, a mailing list, and a Usenet newsgroup.

The Really Useful Company Presents Sir Andrew Lloyd Webber

http://www.reallyuseful.com/

Bring musical theater on screen through this official Web page dedicated to the works of Sir Andrew Lloyd Webber. Presented by his company, The Really Useful Company, it features information about shows like "Cats" and "Phantom of the Opera," as well as access to a theater store.

WORLD MUSIC

Ain't Whistlin' Dixie

http://mothra.nts.uci.edu/~dhwalker/dixie/

The Ain't Whistling Dixie home page contains a collection of traditional Celtic music played on the penny whistle and ocarina. Includes a list of downloadable music files and descriptions of the instruments.

Heather Alexander

http://www.teleport.com/~seafire/

Dedicated to Celtic musician Heather Alexander, this page features her biography, discography, reviews, photographs, and tour schedule. Find out more about her various bands and where to get her music here.

Axiom

http://hyperreal.com/music/labels/axiom/

Producer extraordinare Bill Laswell is the focus here, sponsored by the record label Axiom, which bass player Laswell founded. Concerts, new releases, and other details on his collaborative efforts are detailed here, as well as recordings "from the Middle East to funk, from psychedelic trance to jazz."

The Bhangra Page

http://yucc.yorku.ca/home/sanraj/bhangra.html

The Bhangra Page celebrates an East Indian dance and musical style popular among the Punjabi people. The site has general information about the music and instruments used. An audio sample can be downloaded, and there are links to related sites.

Cajun/Zydeco Music & Dance

http://www.bme.jhu.edu/~jrice/cz.html

Cajun/Zydeco music and dance fans can find Cajun music in their area here, or exercise their virtual feet with online dance lessons. The page also posts band schedules, a photo gallery, and links to other spicy dance pages.

Celtic Music on the Internet

http://celtic.stanford.edu/Internet_Sources.html

Celtic Music on the Internet provides a clearinghouse for Celtic music resources. Includes news about bands, discussion sites, concerts, festivals, and Usenet newsgroup connections.

Ceolas Celtic Music Archive

http://celtic.stanford.edu/ceolas.html

Visitors to Ceola's Celtic Music Archive will find "the largest collection of information on celtic music available online." Areas covered here include background on the music, links to topical magazines, fan lists of favorite albums, and a monthly "new releases" newsletter.

Chinese Music Page

http://vizlab.rutgers.edu/~jaray/sounds/chinese_music/chinese_music.html

Lovers of eastern music will find a bounty of Chinese music bytes at this Rutgers University Sound Page. From the traditional and ceremonial to modern melodies, FTP archives provide downloadable .au clips. Political speeches are included, too.

Folk Roots

http://www.cityscape.co.uk/froots/

Roots, folk and world music makers headline at Folk Roots, an online magazine. Music lovers can find monthly offerings of articles, interviews, and album reviews at this site.

Global Music Centre

http://www.eunet.fi/womad/

Global Music Centre's Web site puts visitors in touch with an entire planet's worth of world mu-

sic resources. Included are recordings, educational, and festival information, along with links to related music areas on the World Wide Web. In English and Finnish.

Hindi Movie Songs

http://www.cs.wisc.edu/~navin/india/songs/index.html

This site, produced from the "Itrans Song Book," archives music from Hindi films. Visitors can search for music by title and several other categories.

Jammin' Reggae Archives Home Page

http://orpheus.ucsd.edu/jammin/

Visit Jammin' Reggae Archives for a robust directory of links to Reggae music-related Web sites. Provides links popular lyrics directories, music catalogs, album cover art, answers to Frequently Asked Questions (FAQs), and more.

Kereshmeh Records: Persian Classical, Folk and New Music

http://www.kereshmeh.com

Fans of Iranian music will find a catalog of Persian classical, folk and new music here. Kereshmeh Records offers online ordering and posts a list of stores that carry its label.

Lark In The Morning

http://www.mhs.mendocino.k12.ca.us/MenComNet/Business/Retail/Larknet/larkhp.html

Founded in 1974, Lark In The Morning is a service specializing in hard-to-find musical instruments, sheet music, and instructional materials. This support site includes the service's catalog, online ordering, articles and news, and links to its retail shops in Seattle, Washington and Mendocino, California.

Reggae Ambassadors Worldwide

http://www.xmission.com/~turq/RAW/home.html

The latest news about reggae concerts in the United States and around the world can be found on the Reggae Ambassadors Worldwide page. Join the international network of reggae enthusiasts who are spreading the vibe.

Reggae Down Babylon

http://nyx10.cs.du.edu:8001/~damjohns/reggae.html

The Reggae Down Babylon WWW Home Page, maintained by a music fan, provides links to a variety of online publications and record labels. Visitors to this site will also find song lyrics, downloadable graphics, and access to other music-related sites.

RootsWorld

http://www.rootsworld.com/rw/

RootsWorld covers the world music beat, including reviews of new releases, artist notes, and links to labels like Interra and Temple. The coverage is

eclectic—from a Vietnamese music festival to American jazz to Scottish traditional.

Russian Music

http://mars.uthscsa.edu/Russia/Music/

From a larger site entitled Little Russia in San Antonio, Texas, this page spotlights Russian music. Find romantic and popular song lyrics indexed by artist, with some audio files featured.

Sami's Urdu/Hindi Music Page

http://www.lehigh.edu/sm0e/public/www-data/sami.html

This Hindu film music home page contains information about the sound tracks of Hindu cinema. Includes profiles and articles about composers, singers, and musicians.

Gary Stephens' FanWebs

http://www.geocities.com/Vienna/1340

Meet Gary Stephens, a music fan who lives in the United Kingdom. He has created FanWebs for Cecilia Bartoli, the Kronos Quartet and 3 Mustaphas 3, and invites visitors to take a look.

TuneWeb

http://itpubs.ucdavis.edu/richard/music/tuneweb/

This archive of traditional tunes is indexed by song type. Categories include reels, jigs, slip jigs, slides, hornpipes, polkas, slow airs, O'Carolan, English country dances, waltzes, marches, American, and miscellaneous tunes.

Village Pulse Outpost

http://www.rootsworld.com/rw/villagepulse/outpost.html

Feel the beat through the Village Pulse Web site: This home page features a catalog of Village Pulse recordings of West African style drum music that the site creator says have not been available to the rest of the world.

Wailers Discography

http://www.iea.lth.se/~ielbo/wailers.html

This site links visitors to an extensive number of sites related to reggae greats Bob Marley, Peter Tosh, and more. Includes links to the Reggae Down Babylon home page and other reggae- and Jamaica-related Web sites.

Welcome to Michio's world

http://wsogata.cc.u-tokai.ac.jp/

A Japanese browser has compiled this reggae index. The site includes links to the University of the West Indies, the Reggae Sunsplash, a reggae newsgroup, and The Patois Dictionary.

Yothu Yindi

http://www.yothuyindi.com/

Yothu Yindi, an Australian Aboriginal music group, maintains this site of general information. Visit here to view video clips, listen to song samples, learn about the group's cultural heritage, and more.

HISTORY

The Gregorian Chant Home Page

http://www.music.princeton.edu/chant_html/

The historical overview of Gregorian chants offered here was written by a Princeton University music professor. This Web page lists chant-related coursework offered by the school and offers links to ecclesiastical sciences and musicology sites.

History of Rock 'n' Roll

http://www.hollywood.com/rocknroll/

The History of Rock 'n' Roll is a Web version of the Warner Brothers-produced, ten-hour television series that celebrates the "music we all grew up with." Sound files from the rockumentary, quotes and a video vault are among the offerings.

International Inventory of Musical Sources

http://www.rism.harvard.edu/RISM/

The International Inventory of Musical Sources is the result of a worldwide effort to identify sources of music and music-related writings from the earliest times through 1825. This home page offers news about inventory activities and provides pointers to available online resources.

Jazz: Records & Photography, the 1950s

http://www.book.uci.edu/Jazz/JPRA2.html

This jazz site provides a historical perspective on the music and musicians of the 1950s. Includes links to articles, profiles, and photo galleries relating to jazz music in the decade after World War II.

The Leo Music Archive

http://www.leo.org/archiv/music/

Musicians will find the "Internet's largest charts-collection," a link to the Olga guitar tab archive and a song lyric archive on this FTP site. The German-based site includes pictures, movies, and information about the Woodstock festivals. In English or German.

Ron Smith Oldies Calendar

http://www.oldies.com/index.html

Ron Smith offers a glimpse at This Week in Rock and Roll—including birthdays, deaths and events—as well as a look back at Number One songs from the past through this page. Visitors can also check Smith's résumé.

Styles of Jazz—A Map

http://www.acns.nwu.edu/jazz/styles/style-map.html

Northwestern University takes browsers on a tour here that plots the history and development of various styles of jazz. It's plotted on a large image map; browsers simply click through the decades.

Wolverine Antique Music Society

http://www.teleport.com/~rfrederi/

For those who remember when recorded music came on something other than CDs and cassettes, there is the Wolverine Antique Music Society. Information here includes historical articles, images, and recordings.

INSTITUTES AND SCHOOLS

CalArts School of Music

http://music.calarts.edu/

Aspiring musicians can learn about Valencia, California-based CalArts' various departments here—including academic program details, and an events calendar. Included are links to student and faculty home pages, an e-mail directory, and excerpts from student compositions.

The Center for New Music and Audio

http://www.cnmat.berkeley.edu/

The Music Department of the University of California at Berkeley maintains this information site for its Center for New Music and Audio Technology. Visit here to learn about its people, upcoming events, and musical projects.

The Copenhagen University Choir

http://www.astro.ku.dk/~michael/sang.html

Meet the Copenhagen University Choir, the oldest choir in Denmark, here. The page includes pictures, contact information and details on upcoming festivals. Also, potential members will learn how the choir recruits singers.

Courses of Study in Sound and Computer Music

http://datura.cerl.uiuc.edu/schools/courses.html

Prospective music majors with a penchant for computer-produced sounds can review and compare courses of study offered at colleges and universities across the globe at this site. Link to degree programs in computer music using the list of pointers collected here.

The Csound Front Page

http://www.leeds.ac.uk/music/Man/c_front.html

The Center for New Music and Audio Technologies hosts this site, which features information on the Csound electronic music program. Includes downloading information, access to documentation, and links to other electrosonic resources.

Florida State University School of Music

http://www.music.fsu.edu/

Florida State University presents the home page for its School of Music. Visitors will find information on graduate and undergraduate programs, faculty, events, and news. A special section is offered for alumni.

Furman University Department of Music

http://ns9000.furman.edu/~bschoon/dept/DHome.html

Prospective music students can take a virtual tour of Greenville, S.C.-based Furman University's Music Department at this site. Visitors can download sights and sounds from the department, read its newsletter, and gather general admission information.

The Gregorian Chant Home Page

http://www.music.princeton.edu/chant_html/

The historical overview of Gregorian chants offered here was written by a Princeton University music professor. This Web page lists chant-related coursework offered by the school and offers links to ecclesiastical sciences and musicology sites.

Indiana University School of Music Home Page

http://www.music.indiana.edu/

Indiana University's School of Music describes the school, its departments and libraries at this site. Music theory, archives of African American music, and WFIU Public Radio are among the resources referenced.

IPEM multimedia archive: English Homepage

http://next.rug.ac.be/EnglishHomepage.html

Details about Belgium's Institute for Psychoacoustics and Electronic Music (IPEM) are available here. History, article excerpts, and an index of new musical notation are among the offerings. In English and Dutch.

LaTrobe University Music Department

http://farben.latrobe.edu.au/Music_Docs/MusDeptHomePge.html

Located in Bundoora, Victoria, Australia, La Trobe University's Music Department provides this overview of its courses, staff, and facilities. Also find links to the department's FTP site and other music-related resources.

Leeds University Department of Music

http://www.leeds.ac.uk/music.html

U.K.-based Leeds University provides this home page for the school's Music Department. Here browsers will find information on the department and its musical events, along with a variety of links.

McGill University Music

http://lecaine.music.mcgill.ca/

The Faculty of Music at McGill University in Montreal, Canada maintains this site for general information and music resources. Visit here to learn about the department's programs and people, and to access its music library collections.

Music and Technology at Virginia Tech

http://server.music.vt.edu/technology/technology.html

Hosted by the Department of Music at Virginia Tech, the Music and Technology page explores the department's courses and services focusing on the technical aspects of recording music. An overview of facilities and a look at the future of computers and music is also featured.

The Music Educator's Home Page

http://athena.athenet.net/~wslow/index.html

The Fox Valley Regional Music Technology Center in Kaukauna, Wisconsin maintains this site of music education and curriculum resources with a wide range of information and related materials.

Music Resources

http://www.siba.fi/Kulttuuripalvelut/music.html

Finland-based Sibelius Academy presents an exhaustive list of music related resources on the Net—ranging from composers to music libraries to publications. In English and Finnish.

New York: The Postcrypt Coffeehouse

http://www.cc.columbia.edu/~crypt/

The Postcrypt Coffeehouse at Columbia University brings its diverse musical background to the Web at this home page. The page includes links to well-known artists who have performed there—including Shawn Colvin, Suzanne Vega, and Patty Larkin.

Sibelius Academy

http://www.siba.fi/welcome-eng.html

Through this English-language page, you can introduce yourself to Sibelius Academy—the only music university in Finland. You'll find the standard program information as well as pointers to some of the best music sites on the Net.

Temple Gallery of the Arts

http://betty.music.temple.edu:80/Gallery/

Temple University's Gallery of Arts features student art, music, and film. Sample the works online and link to listings of campus cultural happenings.

University College Salford Music Division

http://www.ucsalf.ac.uk/pa/musdiv/mushome.htm

The Center for Media, Performance, and Communications at the University College Salford offers this Web server with a wealth of information on the center's academics, announcements, associations, and related music schools.

The University of Edinburgh Faculty of Music

http://www.music.ed.ac.uk/

The University of Edinburgh Faculty of Music maintains this page with information about the faculty's programs, postgraduate music courses, research, and a link to the Electroacoustic Music Studios.

University of Oregon Music Resources

http://music1.uoregon.edu/musres.html

The University of Oregon School of Music provides an index to music resources across the Internet here. The page also includes a Frequently Asked Questions (FAQs) file for musicians about tinnitus, and a link the department's main page.

Virginia Tech Music Department

http://server.music.vt.edu/

The home page for the Music Department at Virginia Tech provides a range of information on the school's faculty, students, academics, and music. Visitors can search the music archives or link to the "Electronic Journal of the Virginia Music Educators Association."

INSTRUCTION AND TECHNIQUE

Air Guitar

http://www.digitalrag.com/mirror/air.html

With tongue firmly in cheek, the creators of R. "Bud" Philson's Easy Air Guitar Page discuss the art of air guitar and let visitors leave their tips for better air guitar playing. Links to an eclectic bunch of unusual sites as well as some vibrant images of rockin' air guitar players are among the offerings.

Back Porch Music

http://www.backporchmusic.com/

Back Porch Music Incorporated features tips for beginning musicians as well as information regarding instrument construction and sheet music covering a variety of genres.

The Bottom Line Archive

http://syy.oulu.fi/tbl.html

The Bottom Line, an electronic publication for bass players, maintains this site to provide full text access to its article archives. Also includes photos and newsgroup postings related to bass playing.

Courses of Study in Sound and Computer Music

http://datura.cerl.uiuc.edu/schools/courses.html

Prospective music majors with a penchant for computer-produced sounds can review and compare courses of study offered at colleges and universities across the globe at this site. Link to degree programs in computer music using the list of pointers collected here.

The Leo Music Archive

http://www.leo.org/archiv/music/

Musicians will find the "Internet's largest charts-collection," a link to the Olga guitar tab archive, and a song lyric archive on this FTP site. The German-based site includes pictures, movies, and information about the Woodstock festivals. In English or German.

The Piano Education Page

http://www.unm.edu/~loritaf/pnoedmn.html

Maintained by New Mexico's West Mesa Music Teachers Association, this site offers a one-stop resource page for students, teachers, and fans of the piano. Topics and links include piano teaching software, a kids' section, and related sites, newsgroups, and mailing lists.

Trumpet Player Online

http://www.trb.ayuda.com/~dnote/Trumpet.html

Pick up some tips on playing that trumpet from the pros. This site sponsors online lessons and method workshops with trumpet players, with a new player being featured each month. The site includes trumpet articles and sound files.

INSTRUMENTS

Back Porch Music

http://www.backporchmusic.com/

Back Porch Music Incorporated features tips for beginning musicians as well as information regarding instrument construction and sheet music covering a variety of genres.

Guild of American Luthiers

http://www.deltanet.com/GAL/index.htm

What's a luthier? A person who repairs stringed instruments and who probably belongs to the guild sponsoring this page. Learn about the organization, review issues of "American Lutherie," the guild's magazine, or find out about becoming a member.

Music Machines

http://www.hyperreal.com/music/machines/

Based on contributions from Net-savvy musicians, Music Machines is all about music-making machines: synthesizers, drum machines, effects, and so on. You'll find images, descriptions, reviews, schematics, tips, price lists, and discussions.

INDIVIDUAL INSTRUMENTS

Accordiana
http://www.cs.cmu.edu/afs/cs/user/phoebe/mosaic/accordion.html

The Accumulated Accordion Annotations contains general information about "squeeze boxes," including links to related sites, cartoons, buying advice, band pages, jokes, and other items of note.

Air Guitar
http://www.digitalrag.com/mirror/air.html

With tongue firmly in cheek, the creators of R. "Bud" Philson's Easy Air Guitar Page discuss the art of air guitar and let visitors leave their tips for better air guitar playing. Links to an eclectic bunch of unusual sites as well as some vibrant images of rockin' air guitar players are among the offerings.

The Bagpipe Web
http://pipes.tico.com/pipes/pipes.html

For experienced pipers and wanna-be blowhards alike, the Bagpipe Web provides a tuneful home. The site features a calendar of bagpipe festivals, reviews of new bagpipe recordings, links to manufacturer pages and clubs worldwide, and a classified section for bargain bagpipes.

The Bottom Line Archive
http://syy.oulu.fi/tbl.html

The Bottom Line, an electronic publication for bass players, maintains this site to provide full text access to its article archives. Also includes photos and newsgroup postings related to bass playing.

Ensoniq VFX Home Page
http://www.cs.colorado.edu/~mccreary/vfx/

The Ensoniq VFX home page contains information about its line of VFX and SQ series synthesizers. You'll learn how to find out the current OS version for your synth, what to do if your VFX freezes up, and all about VFX keyboard recalibration errors.

Folk Stuff
http://www.rogo.com/folkstuff/

Folk Stuff provides links offering "how to and where to information" for folk musicians and instrument makers. The autoharp, dulcimer, pennywhistle, theremin, and didjeridu are among the featured instruments.

Guitar: Digital Guitar
http://waynesworld.ucsd.edu/DigitalGuitar/home.html

"Digital Guitar" is an electronic newsletter dedicated to the discussion of musical technology for various stringed instruments. Find the current issue and archive of past issues, plus links to related sites.

Guitar: Harmony Central Guitar Resources
http://www.harmony-central.com/Guitar/

Harmony Central offers a plethora of resources for guitarists and lovers of guitar music. Visitors can join discussion groups, find instruction resources, peruse online classifieds, or link to software sites, archives, and related resources.

The Guitar Page
http://www.guitarist.com/cg/cg.html

The Guitar Page provides an index to Web information and resources concerning classical guitar, with links to the Classical Guitar Beginners' Page, the Portland Guitar Society, the Flamenco Guitar, and other classical guitar pages.

Guitars: Gibson.Net
http://www.gibson.com/

The Gibson USA guitar company maintains this promotional site. Visitors can learn more about the company, which is based in Nashville, Tennessee, and its products, or access Gibson's online services, such as the Gibson Education Collection.

Guitars: Vintage Guitar on the World Wide Web
http://www.vguitar.com/

Vintage Guitar promotes its magazines and books here. Visitors can browse through the tables of contents for the current issues of its magazines, check out its book titles, and buy Vintage Guitar t-shirts and caps. Includes links to guitar dealers.

Hammered Dulcimer
http://tfnet.ils.unc.edu/~gotwals/hd/dulcimer.html

The Hammered Dulcimer page provides learning resources for teachers and enthusiasts of that instrument. Resources for sheet music, sound samples, and links to related Internet news groups are among the services offered.

Lap Steel Guitar: Brad's Page of Steel
http://www.well.com/user/wellvis/steel.html

If you can't get enough of that twangy steel guitar, don't miss The Lap Steel Guitar site. You'll find out about the instrument's origins, plus about great steel guitar players. There's also information on slide guitars and Dobros.

Oboe/Bassoon: International Double Reed Society
http://idrs.colorado.edu/

The International Double Reed Society is composed of 4,000 oboe and bassoon family players, makers, and fans from 45 countries. Its home page offers a newsletter, a survey, and links to other music sites.

The Piano Education Page
http://www.unm.edu/~loritaf/pnoedmn.html

Maintained by New Mexico's West Mesa Music Teachers Association, this site offers a one-stop resource page for students, teachers, and fans of the piano. Topics and links include piano teaching software, a kids' section, and related sites, newsgroups, and mailing lists.

Reed Organs
http://cse.utoledo.edu/userhomes/estell/organs/home.html

Reed organs are most popular today among collectors and museums, but maybe they'll make a comeback if enough people visit this page. Here, you can listen to a reed organ and look inside one. This page has links to reed organ resources galore.

Trombone-L Home Page
http://www.missouri.edu/~cceric/index.html

A trombone information repository, this site includes trombone pictures, articles, song samples, and even mouthpiece specifications. Also here: links to other trombone-and music-related texts and Internet sites.

Trumpet Player Online
http://www.trb.ayuda.com/~dnote/Trumpet.html

Pick up some tips on playing that trumpet from the pros. This site sponsors online lessons and method workshops with trumpet players, with a new player being featured each month. The site includes trumpet articles and sound files.

Windplayer
http://www.windplayer.com/

Windplayer is an online resource for woodwind and brass musical instrument players. Includes information on lessons, classified ads, articles, suppliers, and other resources.

MANUFACTURERS

Ensoniq Corporation
http://www.ensoniq.com/

Ensoniq Corporation, a manufacturer of musical instruments, multimedia sound cards, and integrated circuits, maintains this promotional page. Visitors are invited to learn more about the company and its musical products.

The Fretlight Guitar Page

http://www.optekmusic.com/

Optek Music Systems promotes its leading product, the Fretlight Guitar. Enthusiasts can check out the full product range—along with amps, accessories, and reviews—of this "powerful tool for visualizing hundreds of chord and scale fingering patterns instantly and easily."

Guitars: Gibson.Net

http://www.gibson.com/

The Gibson USA guitar company maintains this promotional site. Visitors can learn more about the company, which is based in Nashville, Tennessee and its products, or access Gibson's online services, such as the Gibson Education Collection.

Modulus Guitars

http://www.dnai.com/~modulus/

Musicians will find useful information about the guitar and bass at Modulus Graphite's home page. The San Francisco-based company introduces its line of musical instruments and necks, along with photos, client list, and price information.

RETAILERS

Lark In The Morning

http://www.mhs.mendocino.k12.ca.us/
MenComNet/Business/Retail/Larknet/
larkhp.html

Founded in 1974, Lark In The Morning is a service specializing in hard-to-find musical instruments, sheet music and instructional materials. This support site includes the service's catalog, online ordering, articles and news, and links to its retail shops in Seattle, Washington and Mendocino, California.

Maestronet

http://www.maestronet.com/

Visitors to the Maestronet can browse the Instrument Showroom in search of fine stringed instruments and bows, or stop by the Conservatory and download sheet music. A library of topical materials and a discussion area are also featured.

SWR Home Page

http://www.primenet.com/~swr/

Hand-crafted bass amplifiers and preamps are the premier offerings of SWR Engineering, manufacturer of premier systems for bass guitarists. View product images, read the company newsletter, or take advantage of product specials.

Upstairs Records Home Page

http://www.upstairs-records.com/

Upstairs Records is a Brooklyn-based retailer of DJ equipment and prerecorded music. Visitors can order CDS, cassettes, and mixing equipment directly from this site. Note, too, that Upstairs Records carries as much vinyl as they can get their hands on.

Washburn International

http://www.washburn.com/

Located in Vernon Hills, Illinois, Washburn International promotes its product catalog of guitars, basses, banjos, and mandolins, plus offers product information from SoundTech, Mapex, and Oscar Schmidt. Check out the instruments online and look into buying one at a dealer near you.

LIBRARIES

Classical Music: The WWW Virtual Library

http://www.gprep.pvt.k12.md.us/classical/

In the classical music stacks of the Virtual Library users can consult a catalog of electronic resources. Periodicals, reference works, and discussion groups devoted to classical music are indexed here.

Music Department of the World Wide Web Virtual Library

http://syy.oulu.fi/music/

The World Wide Web Virtual Library music department contains links to large, music-related information resources on the Internet. Visitors can access lists indexing bands and musical artists home pages, music-related instruments and programs, and more.

Worldwide Internet Music Resources

http://www.music.indiana.edu/music_
resources/

This listing of music resources on the Net is a service of the Indiana University Music Library. Visitors will find links to academic resources, artist-specific sites, and other lists and indices here.

NEWSGROUPS

Celtic Music on the Internet

http://celtic.stanford.edu/Internet_Sources.html

Celtic Music on the Internet provides a clearinghouse for Celtic music resources. Includes news about bands, discussion sites, concerts, festivals, and Usenet newsgroup connections.

OPERA

Cecilia Bartoli Fanweb

http://www.lochnet.com/clients/gs/cb.html

Fans of opera virtuoso Cecilia Bartoli can vote for their favorite CD and discuss Bartoli topics here. The fan-produced site also includes sound clips, photos, interviews from print publications. and her appearance schedule.

ORCHESTRAS

San Francisco Symphony

http://www.sfsymphony.org/

The San Francisco Symphony's home page provides visitors with a wealth of information—including news, ticket prices, and a round-up of this first season under a new conductor.

The San Jose Symphony Home Port

http://www.webcom.com/~sjsympho/

The San Jose Symphony Orchestra offers visitors to its site a preview of upcoming concerts, online ticket, and seating information and biographies of orchestra players. Other features include an audio link to a musical interlude and links to other music-related Web sites.

Stanford Symphony Orchestra

http://www-leland.stanford.edu/group/sso/

Visitors to Stanford University's Symphony Orchestra page can find concert information, read about the musicians, and hire the chamber ensemble online.

POP ARTISTS

GROUPS

Fan Pages

The a-ha World Wide Web Site

http://www.wwiv.com/a-ha/

Fans of the Norwegian rock group a-ha will find the band's latest news, as well as solo efforts by band members, a complete discography and lyrics archive, a list of Frequently Asked Questions (FAQs), and an a-ha mailing list.

Alice in Chains: Into the Flood Again

http://www.proaxis.com/~mcoleman/
aliceinchains/

This fan page for rock group Alice in Chains includes rumors, fan club information, and audio samples from the band's 1995 self-titled album. Images, song lyrics, and guitar tablature are among the site's other offerings.

Asia

http://www.clo.com/~dave/

The officially sanctioned Web home for the rock group Asia highlights the band's past, present, and future, with links to photo pages and album liner notes. It also serves as the home for the Asia Armada newsletter.

The Band

http://thebanc.hiof.no/

Enthusiasts for the seminal rock group known as The Band will be in their element at this site, where comprehensive information about Bob Dylan's one-time backup group can be found. Among the data here are history, discography, soundtracks, images, and lyrics.

Gordon's Place: Barenaked Ladies on the WWW

http://www.cs.mun.ca/~craig/bnl/barenaked.html

If the title to this one doesn't get your attention, nothing will. No, it's not X-rated: The page contains information about an all-male Canadian rock band, Barenaked Ladies, including their musical accomplishments and how they came up with the unusual name.

The Beach Boys-Heroes and Villains Online

http://www.iglou.com/scm/bb/hvo.html

Fans of the Beach Boys can read about the band's history, access lyrics archives, and view photographs of the band. Includes Frequently Asked Questions (FAQs), Brian Wilson sound files and links to other Beach Boys pages.

Beatles Information Page

http://www.cs.rochester.edu/users/grads/jonas/beatles/

This Beatles information page contains a collection of links to various Beatles information resources on the Internet. Includes pointers to music archives, discographies, interviews, sheet music, and other Beatles information sites

Steve Clifford's Beatles Page

http://www.islandnet.com/~scliffor/beatles/fabhome.htm

A Beatlemania hobbyist has spent the better part of his life collecting Fab Four Beatles' and memorabilia. Find the fruit of his travels right here, presented in a personal narrative; the site includes a forum for other collectors.

The Internet Beatles Album

http://www.primenet.com/~dhaber/beatles.html

The Beatles wild popularity also spawned fabulous myths. They are detailed and debunked here with text, sounds, and photos. The fan-produced site also contains "fab facts," a recent radio interview with Yoko Ono, and Beatles trivia.

Mike's Beatles Page

http://www.eecis.udel.edu/~markowsk/beatles/

The Fab Four take center stage on Mike's Beatles Page. Listen to clips from the Beatles' recent "Anthology" release, hear the members say "hello," or read various rumors and factoids about the group.

The rec.music.beatles Home Page

http://kiwi.imgen.bcm.tmc.edu:8088/public/rmb.html

The rec.music.beatles Usenet newsgroup presents its official home page here. Fab Four fans can check out Beatles-related writings, Frequently Asked Questions (FAQs), members' home pages, and links to a plethora of other Beatles resources.

Better Than Ezra

http://www.ezra.org/

The unofficial home page of the rock band Better than Ezra dishes up a wealth of band-related news, pictures, sound clips, tour dates, concert reviews, and song lyrics. Visitors can also join the mailing list for regular updates.

Blues Brothers

http://www.nta.no/brukere/kol/bb/

This page is on a mission from God with sound clips and other information about The Blues Brothers from the 1980 movie of the same name.

Blues Traveler Home Page

http://www.sgi.net/bluestraveler/

The band Blues Traveler (featuring that big guy with the harmonica, John Popper) is the focus of this unofficial fan page. Among the resources are images, lyrics, biographies, articles, tour dates, and links.

Blunt Home Page

http://www.blunt.com/

Fans of new British rock band Blunt will enjoy this site, featuring sound files and discographies. Visitors will also find a roster of band members.

The Bobs Online

http://www.bobs.com/

Get the latest news, concert schedules and fan club information on the Bobs, purveyors of alternative a capella music. Find listings of recordings, multimedia offerings, and contact information on the group's home page.

Boiled in Lead: The Leadheads Web Site

http://www.apocalypse.org/leadheads/home.html

This unofficial Boiled in Lead home page features information about the Minneapolis-based electric and acoustic band. Information here includes tour dates and a discography.

BOKOMARU—In The Spirit of the Grateful Dead

http://www.jam.ca/bokomaru/

The home page for the Montreal-based band Bokomaru explores that group's devotion to the spirit of The Grateful Dead. The band plays a repertoire of more than 70 Dead songs; the site includes sound clips and photos.

The Catawampus Universe

http://www.io.com/~catwamps/index.html

This fan page, devoted to Kentucky-based psychedelic funk band Catawampus, provides article reprints, tour dates, sound clips, and information about the group's recordings. Also included is information about Red Fly Nation—a defunct band that featured members of Catawampus.

Cause & Effect

http://www.cen.uiuc.edu/~wellman/cause_effect/

Fans of rock music group Cause & Effect will enjoy this unofficial fan site, featuring discographies, song lyrics, performance information, and more. Includes graphical and text-based interface.

Coil Homepage

http://ipisun.jpte.hu/coil/coil.html

Fans of underground music makers Coil will find discography, sound bites and interview excerpts at this unofficial home page dedicated to the band.

Collective Soul

http://www.teleport.com/~boerio/cs/

This fan page presents the American rock band Collective Soul. Find tour dates, information on releases, images, and links to related sites.

The Cure

http://gagme.wwa.com/~anaconda/cure2.html

Angst-ridden goth/rock icons The Cure are celebrated here. Fans of the band can download images, reviews of bootlegs, a Cure fanzine, and a complete discography. The site also serves up a healthy dose of gossip and information on joining the Cure mailing list.

Cure Albums

http://www.acpub.duke.edu/~spawn/album.html

Christopher Crosby's personal page contains a short index of his favorite music by the Cure, including the albums "Paris," "Show," and "Disintegration."

The Def Leppard Home Page

http://www.princeton.edu/~nieder/defleppard/def.html

Littered with lyrics and loaded with links, this fan obsession offers it all: FAQs, photos, multimedia, and merchandise. Looking for news and information? That's here, too.

Depeche Mode

http://www.commline.com/

The glamour gloom boys of Depeche Mode are the subject of conversation and adulation at this fan page. Features the band's discography, lyrics, and a collection of images.

Devo: MuteWeb

http://www.nvg.unit.no/~optimus/devo/

The Devo page contains news and rumors about the band Devo, including photos, articles, a discography, and information on bootleg recordings. The page also includes links to other Devo-related sites.

Dire Straits Home Page

http://www.physics.sunysb.edu/~gene/DS/DS.html

This home page is devoted to the rock music band who gets money for nothing, Dire Straits. The page includes a band mailing list, photos, cover art, audio snippets, and links to other band-related sites.

Doors Home Page

http://www.vis.colostate.edu/~user1209/doors/

Feast on the lyrics of the Lizard King and company here, or gaze at pictures of this historically famous band. This site, the work of a dedicated fan, includes a complete music guide, and what's billed as an "ultimate band list."

The Duranie Connection

http://www.chapman.edu/students/mathur/new/

British pop band Duran Duran is the focus of this exhaustive fan page, with articles, a concert guide, lyric index, and much more.

Duran Duran Page

http://carroll1.cc.edu/~kwalker/duranduran.html

The Duran Duran home page contains information about the English band, sounds, a picture gallery, and Frequently Asked Questions (FAQs) file.

The Last Resort: The Eagles Page

http://www.metropolis.nl/~annetted/eagles.html

Onetime mega-rock group The Eagles are the focus at The Last Resort. Browser will find member and group biographies, discographies, quotes, and more.

Echo and the Bunnymen Page

http://www.netaxs.com/~jgreshes/echo.html

This page is devoted to the band Echo and the Bunnyman and its new incarnation, Electrafixion. Fans can read a variety of band-related news, articles, and interviews here and can download sounds and pictures.

Emerson, Lake and Palmer

http://bliss.berkeley.edu/elp/

Fans of the American rock band Emerson, Lake and Palmer will relish this home page. Links to a variety of information about the band are available, including its history and the latest rumors.

The UnOfficial English Beat Home Page

http://www.best.com/~sirlou/ukbeat.html

The unofficial English Beat home page features the music and influencing artists who make up the sound of the band. Visitors can check out the discography of what the Web creator classifies as the greatest ska band of all time among a multitude of other resources.

Enigma

http://www.stud.his.no/~joarg/Enigma.html

The musical group Enigma makes monastic chants danceable. For news and reviews, a complete discography, and a picture gallery devoted to the band, visit this fan-produced shrine. Links are also provided to other official and devotee sites offering Enigma-related facts, gossip, and merchandise.

The Extreme Home Page

http://www.eecs.nwu.edu/~dbleplay/extremeindex.html

Fans of the rock group Extreme will be in their element checking out concert reviews, interviews, pictures of group members, and much more. Guitar tabs, audio clips, and current band news round out the site.

The Flash Girls

http://www.player.org/pub/flash/flash.html

Here's a fan page devoted to the folk music duo, the Flash Girls. Read about the girls, their albums and awards, and check out the group's current "gig and tour schedule."

Future Sound of London

http://hyperreal.com/music/artists/fsol/www/index.html

Fans of British ambient groove band The Future Sound of London will find a slew of band information at this official home page. In addition to the usual artwork, discography, and sound bytes, a smattering of articles includes the band's first Net posting and album reviews.

Jerry Garcia: Not Fade Away

http://metaverse.com/vibe/nfa.html

Grateful Dead fans produced this memorial page within days of Jerry Garcia's death. Fans can celebrate Garcia's life here and download songs in RealAudio.

Bobkirk's Deadhead Family Page

http://www.primenet.com/~bobkirk/index.html

Those still searching for peace and love will find both at this "Deadhead Family" home page. Check in here for a tribute to the late Jerry Garcia, links to other Grateful Dead fan sites, and the keys to being a "happy hippie."

The Grateful Dead

http://www.cs.cmu.edu/afs/cs.cmu.edu/user/mleone/web/dead.html

Created by a fan for fans, this comprehensive page devoted to the rock group The Grateful Dead includes graphics, lyrics, concert setlists, Frequently Asked Questions (FAQs) files, merchandise, and links to other Dead sites, including the official one.

Grateful Dead Almanac

http://www.well.com/user/almanac

The Grateful Dead Almanac is the latest way of keeping in touch with the Deadhead Community. The Almanac reports on individual and collective activities of band members and provides links to The Grateful Dead Mercantile Company's catalog.

Grateful Dead: GD Page

http://sedona.uafphys.alaska.edu/~price/dead.html

This is a collection of links devoted to the Grateful Dead. Visitors will find art and hyperlinks to the many sites on the Web containing information on this legendary band.

Tie-Died: Rock 'n' Roll's Most Deadicated Fans

http://www.tie-died.com/skey.htm

Are you a crunchy Nethead on the bus and hoping for a miracle? If you understood the previous sentence, you're probably not in need of this online glossary of Deadhead terms.

Green Day Home Page

http://pmwww.cs.vu.nl/home/edoe/Green_Day/

Photos, lyrics, articles, tour dates, and a discography are featured on this page about the wildly popular band Green Day. Links to related sites are included.

Guided By Voices

http://www.gbv.com/

Guided by Voices, a stubbornly iconoclastic rock band from Dayton, Ohio, is dissected here. Information about individual band members, critics' comments, and other tidbits of interest to fans of the "lo-fi" phenomenon are among the offerings.

Guns N' Roses Home Page

http://www.teleport.com/~boerio/gnr.html

This unofficial home page for American rock band Guns N' Roses begins with a Frequently Asked Questions (FAQS) file, moves through the discography, songlist, and lyrics, cops some interviews, then slides into tour information. Guitar tabs, bootlegs, and feedback are also featured.

Hole: The Drown Soda Pages

http://www.clysmic.com/hole/

Here's a loaded fan shrine to Courtney Love & Co. Visitors are treated to bootleg information, sound and video clips, photos, song lyrics, and more.

Hootie and the Blowfish

http://weber.u.washington.edu/~jnorton/hootie.html

Find out about the wildly popular band Hootie and the Blowfish at this unofficial, fan-maintained site. Information available here includes lyrics, pictures, and links to other Hootie pages.

The Jefferson Airplane Home Page

http://grove.ufl.edu/~number6/Jefferson.Airplane/airplane.html

The home page of rock and roll band Jefferson Airplane contains a wealth of information about the group, their music, achievements, and history. The complete Jefferson Airplane discography, photos, Frequently Asked Questions (FAQs), and concert reviews are among this site's features.

The Jesus Jones Home Page

http://www.cs.rmit.edu.au/~jbl/jesus.jones/

Photos, sound clips, lyrics, and news on the band Jesus Jones are the focus here. Also included are a discography, magazine, and links.

Jethro Tull Music Archive

http://remus.rutgers.edu/JethroTull/

The venerable English prog-rock band Jethro Tull is celebrated here, where visitors can find general background on the band, a discography, answers to Frequently Asked Questions (FAQs), and a link to a page on progressive rock.

The Kinks

http://hobbes.it.rit.edu/kinks/kinks.html

The Kinks, the English band that hit the music scene in the 1960s, are still going strong, especially at this web site where visitors can listen to their music, watch their videos, read the lyrics, duplicate the chords, check the discography, and keep up on rumors.

KLF Mainpage

http://www.hysator/iu.se/~johol/KLF/index.html

Retired, then reformed, then retired again, KLF (The Kopyright Liberation Front aka in 1993 as The K Foundation) is a hybrid band that is wildly popular among the rave set. Browsers will find lyrics, articles, and much more.

Kronos Quartet FanWeb

http://www.lochnet.com/client/gs/kq.html/

A string ensemble, the Kronos Quartet has built its reputation and repertoire on mostly 20th century music—much of it written specifically for the group. Its multimedia Web page features audio samples, a discography, images, and articles.

Christine Lavin Home Page

http://www.automatrix.com/~lavin/

This site is dedicated to singer/songwriter Christine Lavine and her band, Four Bitchin Babes. Visitors will find band news here, in addition to album release updates and reviews.

Buckeye's Led Zeppelin Page

http://www.dnaco.net/~buckeye/lz.html

This fan-inspired page will send Zeppelin lovers up a virtual stairway to heaven: Download the Kashmir font used for "Houses of the Holy," access set lists and lyrics, peruse "The Led Zeppelin Chronicle," and jump to a host of other Zeppelin resources.

The Legendary Pink Dots

http://www.brainwashed.com/lpd/

The Legendary Pink Dots are an enigmatic rock/performance band. Visitors to this page will find song lyrics and reviews of records and performances.

Letters to Cleo

http://www-personal.umich.edu/~hstahl/letters.html

This home page for the music group Letters to Cleo contains articles, lyrics, pictures, guitar tablature, audio/video clips, tour dates, and a mailing list.

The Levellers Page

http://chem-www.mps.ohio-state.edu/~pfleming/lvlrs/

This Web page is devoted to the musical band The Levellers, who've been described as "sort of a Celtic Clash." Visitors will find a discography, lyrics, photos, tour dates, and more.

Little Feat

http://www.ultranet.com/~amygoode/FEATS.HTML

Here visitors can find news, photos, tour information, recording information, and more on the band Little Feat. Bios, tour information, photos, and links to related site are among the offerings.

Meat Beat Manifesto Home Page

http://www.brainwashed.com/mbm

Music fans can check the unofficial Meat Beat Manifesto home page for information about the band's discography and a link to a visual Meat Beat page. The simple unofficial page also includes a link to Edge of No Control from the Usenet newsgroup rec.music.misc.

DRulz' Metallica Home Page

http://www.dorsai.org/~jkeis/metallic.html

This Metallica fan frenzy offers background information on the group, links to the official fan club, a mailing list, Frequently Asked Questions (FAQs), and bootleg sites. Also find a visitor's survey: Tell DRulz if his site rules or not.

Midnight Oil: Oilbase Index

http://www.stevens-tech.edu/~dbelson/oilbase/

OilBase, a fan site devoted to the Australian rock band Midnight Oil, is a group effort of members of a fan mailing list. Visitors will find a discography, song lyrics, audio files, and live-show registries.

Ministry Unofficial Fan Site

http://pulsar.cs.wku.edu/~gizzard/ministry.html

Fans of rock music group Ministry will enjoy this unofficial fan site, featuring discographies, music samples, discussion groups, and links to related music sites. Includes song lyrics and downloadable sound files.

My Life with the Thrill Kill Kult: Sanitarium Borderline

http://pulsar.cs.wku.edu/~draven/tkk.html

This My Life with the Thrill Kill Kult fan page contains information on the band, interviews with group members, and a discography. Visitors also will find lyrics, sound samples, and merchandising and mailing list information.

New Order

http://www.niagara.edu/New_Order/discography.html

Fans of the British pop rock band New Order can check out an extensive discography here. In addition to information about albums and singles, find the scoop on the band's videos and DJ remixes.

New Order

http://slashmc.rice.edu/ceremony/neworder/neworder.html

Pop supergroup New Order kept club kids of the 1980s dancing all night with monster hits like "Blue Monday" and "Bizarre Love Triangle." If you're feeling in the groove, stop by this New Order fan page to see images and learn about the band which arose from the ashes of gloomy 1970s group Joy Division.

Nine Inch Nails Internet Site List

http://www.engr.orst.edu/~rose/html

Fans of industrial music purveyors Nine Inch Nails, and the group's tortured leader, Trent Reznor, can access audio/video clips and images here. A discography, tablature, bootleg and import listings, lyrics, reviews, and interviews all can be found here—along with links to other NIN home pages and discussion groups.

Nirvana: Smiley's Home Page

http://seds.lpl.arizona.edu/~smiley/nirvana/home.html

A highlight of this page, devoted to the defunct rock group Nirvana, is a response and discussion forum. Other information includes a band history, discography, album list, lyrics, articles, news updates, and links. See Editor's Choice.

NKOTB Home Page

http://www.nkotb.com/

Only true fans can access this page dedicated to the singing group NKOTB, formerly the New Kids on the Block. To get to the guts of the site, visitors need to know the password: the group's original name.

Oingo Boingo: The Boingo Page

http://rhino.harvard.edu/dan/boingo/boingo.html

Fans of Oingo Boingo can indulge in obsessive information collection about the band, its members and its spinoffs at the Boingo Page. Look up lyrics, tour dates, and interviews here. Link to dozens of related Internet resources—from the essential to the tangential—at this unofficial site.

The Unofficial OMD Home Page

http://www.sas.upenn.edu/~plevin/omdpage/omdpage.html

Down-on-their-luck popsters OMD haven't had a hit since 1986, but loyal fans still hang on, God bless 'em! Sights, sounds, song lyrics and other information on OMD (formerly known as Orchestral Maneuvers in the Dark) round out this virtual tribute.

The Orb: Ultraworld Unofficial Page

http://www.theorb.com/net_:index.html

Ultraworld is the unofficial home page of Orb, an alternative rock band. Includes a discography and information on bootleg live recordings.

Ozric Tentacles Home Page

http://www.execpc.com/~mwerning/

Learn more about this European ambient-instrumental band at the Ozric Tentacles Home Page, where visitors can link to articles, discographies, the group's photo album, band merchandise, and more.

Links for Pearl Jam Fans

http://www.cs.caltech.edu/~adam/LOCAL/gos.html

Pearl Jam's popularity is evident on this index, where fans can link to dozens of fan-produced sites that celebrate the rock band. Also included are links to a newsgroup and bands that "Pearl Jam fans might like."

Pearl Jam: The Temple of the Dog

http://www.sccs.swarthmore.edu/~jason/pearl_jam.html

This fan page is a good starting point for Pearl Jam fans on the Web. It consists of pointers to online Pearl Jam resources, including FTP sites. Visitors will even find some Pearl Jam-inspired poetry.

Phish.Net

http://netspace.students.brown.edu/phish/

"Phans" of Phish will find a vast amount of information about the band here. The page includes chords and lyrics of Phish songs, Frequently Asked Questions (FAQs), files from a Phish newsgroup, a tour schedule, and Phish memorabilia for sale.

Phish: Review Net

http://tbone.biol.sc.edu/~dan/review/phishrev.html

Review Net solicits comments about performances of the rock band Phish, archiving them on this page by year and location.

The Pinheads

http://orion.it.luc.edu/~pcrowe/phead.html

The Pinheads are a hardcore punk band from Chicago. Visitors to its page can download music files, lyrics, and pictures. The site also includes a schedule of upcoming shows and links to Chicago record stores.

Pink Floyd

http://www.smartdocs.com/~migre.v/floyd/index.html

The Pink Floyd page provides devotees of the seminal rock group with a year-by-year directory of the band's musical accomplishments. Selections provide lyrics and images from all albums produced from 1967 to 1992.

The Pink Floyd Home Page

http://humper.student.princeton.edu/floyd/

This site is personal shrine to all things Pink. Visitors will find an assortment of interviews, images, discographies, lyrics, and Frequently Asked Questions (FAQs) files here.

---

a2z EDITOR'S CHOICE

Nirvana: Smiley's Home Page

http://seds.lpl.arizona.edu/~smiley/nirvana/home.html

The early exit from this mortal coil by Kurt Cobain hasn't lessened fans' interest in Nirvana one iota in the years since the singer/guitarist took his own life. Here a devotee has put together one of the most well-organized fan sites we've ever come across, celebrating the music and the mystique of the band that put "grunge"" on the map. Smiley's site isn't all slavish devotion though; included are articles about Cobain's drug use, the inability of those close to him to intervene in any meaningful way, and an unflinching look at how addiction destroys lives—famous or not.

Happier offerings include audio files, a complete song list, the "heart-shaped" mailbox, a photo index, and much more. Smiley does a good job of marrying the passion so many feel for Nirvana's music with the ambivalence, grief and anger left by Cobain's shotgun blast. A chat room, bootleg trader's forum, and links to dozens of other sites devoted to Seattle's finest sons are among the many options here. Come as you are.—*Reviewed by Julene Snyder*

Smiley's Nirvana Home Page

By Guy Smiley, 1995

Pizzicato Five fan page

http://www.clark.net/pub/fan/pizz.html

Ty Liotta welcomes fellow Pizzicato Five fans to his page offering "pictures, information and sounds from this unusual Japanese music group." Among the featured items, find a group history, discography, and links to topical sites.

The Police

http://www.dsi.unimi.it/mow/police/

Bone up on trivia regarding defunct rock group the Police. Listen to the band's music, learn to play some of its beloved pop songs, and find out what the three former Police-men are up to these days.

The Cheesy Primus Page

http://www.ram.org/music/primus/primus.html

The Cheesy Primus home page is an unofficial site devoted to wacky music, vision and rabid fan base of the San Francisco-based Primus. Visitors will find a discography, tour dates, reviews, band member profiles, audio clips, and photos.

Unofficial Public Enemy Home Page

http://louis.ecs.soton.ac.uk/~rvn95r/public_e/pe.html

This fan's page dedicated to the rap group Public Enemy contains lyrics, a discography, profiles, and a history of the group.

Pop Will Eat Itself: PWEI Nation

http://kzsu.stanford.edu/uwi/pwei/pwei.html

"PWEI Nation" is an unabashed fanzine of the post-punk band Pop Will Eat Itself. This site provides news, rumors, and shopping opportunities to band devotees.

Queen Page

http://lilly.ping.de/~af/Queen/

Pay homage to the 1970s rock supergroup Queen at this fan-produced site. Pictures of the late Freddie Mercury and his band, along with a complete discography comprise the offerings here.

Sheri's Queen/QMS World Wide Web

http://www.rt66.com/unicorn/queen.html

How did an image of lead singer Freddie Mercury appear on the cover of Queen's 1995 album? Find the answer (okay, it's a statue) and delve into minutia about the rock band on this unofficial site. It includes images and the nearly obligatory links to other Queen sites.

Rage Against The Machine: The Unofficial Home Page

http://www.cs.man.ac.uk/~gjones/RageAgainstTheMachine/RageAgainstTheMachine.html

The fan page for the English band Rage Against The Machine has links to photos, reviews, a discography, and information about world politics.

R.E.M.: The Chord Archive

http://bubblegum.uark.edu/REM/

An archive of chords and musical compositions of songs by rock band R.E.M. is provided at this Web site. Visitors can jump to pages on individual albums or conduct searches of various musical information.

RzWeb: A Guide to the Works of the Residents

http://www.residents.com/

The fan page of the musical group The Residents contains a history of the band, a discography, and tour information. Includes a lyrics archive, listings of books and videos, and much more.

International Roxette Fan Club

http://www.wirehub.nl/~introxfc

The International Roxette Fan Club provides information about the Dutch band here. The page incudes images, news, and guitar tablatures. Visitors can also join the fan club online. In English.

The Rush/NMS Home Page

http://syrinx.umd.edu/rush.html

The Rush/NMS home page lists information about the rock band Rush and the National Midnight Star, an electronic mailing list for fans. Tour dates, articles, and more.

Savatage

http://www.winternet.com/~savaweb/savatage.html

The musical group Savatage is the focus of this fan page. Find news, tour dates, concert reviews, articles, pictures, and sound samples. A discography, plus information on the band members and a fan club are also featured.

The Sex Pistols Unofficial Page

http://www.pi.se/ludde.berntsson/pistols.htm

Die-hard punk rock fans and musicians can delve into The Sex Pistols on this unofficial page that is dedicated to notorious English band. In addition to scrolling through an extensive list of lyrics and guitar tabs, guests can find out the latest information on tour dates.

Siouxsie and the Banshees Home Page

http://www.dnx.com/vamp/Siouxsie/index.html

Lyrics, images, and other resources on the band Siouxsie and the Banshees are collected at this fan site. Included are a discography, audio clips, archives of a mailing list, and interviews.

The Smashing Pumpkins

http://www.muohio.edu/~carmance/sp.html

Fans of rock music group Smashing Pumpkins will enjoy this unofficial fan site. Visit here for sheet music, song lyrics, recent recording and performance information, press clippings, and more.

Eric Agnew's Smashing Pumpkins Site

http://www.engr.wisc.edu/~agnew/pumpkin.html

Enjoy Smashing Pumpkins moments with the Webmaster of this electronic tribute to the musical group known for ditties like "1979" and "Tonight Tonight."

S.P.O.C.K.: STAR PILOT CHANNEL K

http://www.iyu.fi/~enrpena/spock/

Created by a fan for fans of the band, Star Pilot On Channel K (S.P.O.C.K.), this page features links to the group's biography, discography and interviews. Sound clips and photos are also available.

The Steely Dan Internet Resource

http://pages.prodigy.com/S/T/N/steelydan/

Rikki don't lose this URL...it's devoted to the music produced by the studio wizards of Steely Dan. Includes archives of Metal Leg, the original Steely Dan fanzine, plus a verging on obsessive collection of lyrics, artist rosters, and interviews.

Gary Stephens' FanWebs

http://www.geocities.com/Vienna/1340

Meet Gary Stephens, a music fan who lives in the United Kingdom. He has created FanWebs for Cecilia Bartoli, the Kronos Quartet, and 3 Mustaphas 3, and invites visitors to take a look.

Stereolab

http://www.maths.monash.edu.au/people/rjh/stereolab/

This multimedia fan page features the electronic pop music group, Stereolab. Find a discography, lyrics, news, articles, reviews, interviews, photos, sound bites, and video clips.

Stone Temple Pilots: Pilots

http://thoth.stetson.edu/music/pilots/index.html

This is a page dedicated to the rock band Stone Temple Pilots. Check out the group's first two albums, read a bio, and view pictures of the Pilots here.

The Story

http://www.cs.umd.edu/users/rager/Story/

Get the latest scoop on Boston-based band The Story at this official home page. A bio, audio samples, performance dates, and record reviews are on file.

Suede Home Page

http://www.nets.orjp/suede/

The musical group Suede is the focus of this site which includes a discography, photos, lyrics, tour dates, merchandise, and information on fanzines. Also featured is Charlie's Diary from the band's manager.

Talking Head: Francey's Page

http://www.bart.nl/~francey/th.html

This fan page is devoted to the rock group The Talking Heads. Visitors will find a discography, video clips, and biographical information on individual band members here.

Talking Heads

http://129.237.17.3/Heads/Talking_Heads.html

Fans of the punk-turned-"art"-rock band, Talking Heads, have designed this page to supplement their mailing list. This ain't no disco, but it is a fair guide to the Byrne-driven quartet, including a discography, cover-ography, lyrics, and "bootleg surveys."

Talking Heads

http://penguin.cc.ukans.edu/Heads/Talking_Heads.html

The musical group Talking Heads is the focus of this home page, which includes information on a mailing list and images of band members. There also are links to items such as discographies, cover art, lyrics, digitized songs, and more.

Welcome to Therapy?

http://huizen.dds.nl/~whaley/therapy.html

Fans of the band Therapy? can check the group's complete discography on this unofficial fan page. The Netherlands-based band provides fans with concert information and the latest news and rumors.

ThinWhiteLine

http://www.pitt.edu/~houser/twl.html

The ThinWhiteLine page highlights this Pittsburgh band with art from album covers and sound clips from several releases. Other selections include links to Thin WhiteLine reviews and the Internet Underground Music Archives.

Thought Industry: Web for Insects

http://www.cs.wvu.edu/~deweyg/ti/thought_industry.html

The band Thought Industry plays a "thrashy kind of progressive rock." This fan page contains information about the group, a discography, song lyrics, a picture gallery, and music samples.

3 Mustaphas 3 FanWeb

http://lochnet.com/client/gs/3m3.html

The 3 Mustaphas 3 FanWeb is an unofficial fan page of the band known as 3M3. Features include general information about the group, a discography, news, and links to other resources.

Traffic

http://www.fas.harvard.edu/~stribble/sw/traffic.html

This fan page documents the history of Traffic, the popular music group. Find a discography, lyrics to songs, album reviews, and related information.

The Tragically Hip Home Page

http://www.cimtegration.com/tth/thehip.htm

For the word directly from the hipsters' mouth, go to the official Web site of the alternative rock band The Tragically Hip. Get word of the band's adventures on the road, upcoming tour dates, and more at this promotional site.

U2

http://www.cs.cmu.edu/afs/andrew.cmu.edu/usr18/mset/www/U2.html

"I have compiled for your perusal pictures, text, and other information relating to this Irish band," says the author of this fan page. Find U2 FAQs, photos, frank talk, and a concert listing.

JINX U2 Archive

http://www.il.ft.hse.nl/~jinx/u2/

Fans of U2 can link to news about the Irish band, or memorize the lyrics to favorite songs (just in time for that garage rehearsal). Audio samples and a virtual Midi room keep the senses fully engaged.

U2: Guess the Lyric of the Week

http://walden.mo.net/~stheo/

This interactive page features a new selection of lyrics each week from the songs of Irish rock and roll scions, U2. Visitors are encouraged to guess from which song the lyrics come, and are offered links to other U2-related Web sites.

Van Halen Home Page

http://carroll1.cc.edu/~rhiggins/vh.html

Rock dinosaur Van Halen, termed "The Greatest Rock & Roll Band on Earth!" here, takes center stage on this page. Visitors will find links to a huge Van Halen bootleg discography, a mailing list, and other fan and promotional Web sites devoted to the arena rockers.

Vergiftung Home Page

http://purgatory.ecn.purdue.edu:20002/JBC/david/vergiftung.html

Browsers can download selected sound clips from the band Vergiftung here. The site also includes a list of upcoming gigs for the Purdue University-based band.

Veruca Salt

http://www.gordian.com/users/daniel/veruca/

Fans of Chicago-based rock music group Veruca Salt will enjoy this unofficial fan site. Visit here for recent recording and performance information, song lyrics, and links to the band's official Geffen Records home page.

The Unofficial Violent Femmes Page

http://www.gl.umbc.edu/~mmerry2/femmes.html

Do you really know what the name of the band Violent Femmes means? Visit this site to find out. Then delve even deeper into band trivia and

memorabilia with articles, pictures, and bios of the group's members.

True Life Story—the Virgin Prunes pages

http://www.xs4all.nl/~vonb/stuart/vprunes.htm

Mixing punk anger and theatrical surrealism, Ireland's Virgin Prunes has been breaking musical molds since the late 1970s. Examine the duo's continuing impact on the music scene throughout its evolution and the legacy left in its wake.

White Zombie: The PeepShow

http://www.cudenver.edu/~enielsen/zombie/

This home page is devoted to American rock band White Zombie. Visitors will find band member profiles, a discography, audio clips. and links to other White Zombie Web sites.

Widespread Panic: Spreadweb

http://www.netspace.org/Widespread

Widespread Panic, the band that inspires widespread devotion, is the focus of this comprehensive text-only page. Visitors can look at lyric sheets, link to other pages with music files, follow the band tours, and subscribe to a mail list.

Wilson Phillips

http://www.mit.edu:8001/people/jwb/wp.html

This unofficial home page of pop trio Wilson Phillips hosts a collection of photos, along with a handful of links to related pages and lyrics sites.

All Roads Lead to Beatown...XTC

http://www.charm.net/~duke/xtc/beatown.html

Meant to complement the original XTC site, Chalkhills, this site includes details about albums, band news, images, and more.

The Weird Al Yankovic Web Page

http://www.emsphone.com/Al

The grandiose claim is put forth early: This Web page vows to "give meaning to your boring miserable life." Offerings include pictures, interviews, sound bytes, and video clips.

Yes: Notes From the Edge

http://www.wilmington.net/yes/

Notes from the Edge, an unofficial fan site for the veteran rock group Yes, offers tour updates, sound files, song lyrics, and more. Visit here for exclusive interviews and links to other fan sites on the World Wide Web.

GROUPS

Promo Pages

Ace of Base

http://www.dacc.cc.il.us/~mulberry/music/aceofbase/aceofbase.html

Fans of the Swedish band whose catchy ABBA-esque pop songs ruled U.S. airwaves in 1994 can learn more about the group here. Find links to biographical information, discographies, and the usual vital statistics, images, and sounds.

Hittin' the Web with The Allman Brothers Band

http://www.netspace.org/allmans/

The official Allman Brothers Band home page includes interactive access to the sights and sounds of the Allman story, starting with a virtual visit to Macon, Georgia. Places, faces, reviews, and news of the rock group are only a sampling of the on-line offerings here

America

http://www.pacificrim.net/~wahlgren/

The America home page profiles the band's members, albums and special releases. Find a photo album, a concert tour schedule, and fan homages to the soft rock group that hit the top of the charts in the 1970s.

American Gramaphone Records

http://www.amgram.com/

American Gramaphone, a recording company developed by Chip Davis of Mannheim Steamroller, promotes the musical works of Davis and his instrumental band, providing album overviews, press releases, tour dates, and biographical information.

Anomie

http://www.armory.com/~anomie

The online home for the group Anomie features a discography, performance information, art, and "stuff."

Avacost

http://fox.nstn.ca/~warobert

This page from Nudibranch Records introduces Avacost as a cutting-edge rock band outside the mainstream. The group's site features an introduction to the band, profiles of band members, a brief history, photos, and listings of recordings.

Babbalouie Home Page

http://www.frontiernet.net/~babbalou/

The Babbalouie Home Page links, for the most part, to promotional pages for bands such as 10,000 Maniacs, and "Toronto's hottest reggae band the Sattalites." Other other links go to pages for the Rolling Stones and Howard Stern.

The Beastie Boys

http://www.grandroyal.com/BeastieBoys/

For as rowdy as this rap trio is supposed to be, its home page is surprisingly organized. Visitors can access the BB newsgroup, an official record label 'zine, and product information.

The Belizbeha Home Page

http://www.belizbeha.com/

This funkified Web site is filled with the sounds of acid jazz, soul, funk, pop, and hip-hop music. Belizbeha, an eight-piece band out of Burlington, Vermont, offers information on its debut CD, band member bios, and set lists here.

Blur

http://www.parlophone.co.uk/blur/

Fans of Britpop sensation Blur can visit the band's Web site established by EMI Records, Limited. Download sound clips as well song lyrics from each of the albums, or browse through a touring scrapbook.

The Bobs

http://www.iuma.com/IUMA/band_html/Bobs,_The.html

The Bobs are an a capella group composed of three male Bobs and one female Bob whose stage show, lyrical humor, and musical madness have become their trademark. Visitors to their home page can find out how the players garner great reviews.

The Bon Jovi Home Page

http://www.bonjovi.com/bonjovi/

Video clips, concert photos, and handwritten lyric sheets highlight this deluxe page, promoting Mercury Records' pop-metal band Bon Jovi. Visitors can check tour dates and get a behind-the-scenes look at the shooting of the band's "Lie to Me" video.

The Chemlab Home Page

http://www.pitt.edu/~ccast3/chemlab.html

The home page of rock band "ChemLab" includes a wealth of band-related news, images, and information. Includes sound and video clips, a complete discography, interviews, and record label information.

Close Enough

http://www.demon.co.uk/blaah/index.html

Close Enough—a "Funky-Blues-Jazz-Dance-Stuff" band from London—gives its fans a chatty monthly update on its whereabouts, photos of the band, merchandise, booking information, and even free beer for Web browsers who request an e-mail voucher and bring it to their shows.

Crash Basket Low-rent Home Page

http://www.shadow.net/~proub/basket.html

Crash Basket, a band, takes a light-hearted look at itself here and offers information about its recordings and performance schedule. Fans can download pictures and sound files here and join the band's mailing list.

DanceRegina

http://www.fxol.com/regina/

The !DANCeReGINA! page is devoted to the danceable sounds of this Dallas, Texas, band. Fans can read member bios and find out tour dates. Audio samples from five different selections are also available here.

Dano's Home Page

http://www.magi.com/~dano

Meet Dano, a lead singer in Ottawa-area bands for the past 15 years. Sound clips from his current band, Junkfiend, are featured on his home page, along with pictures and a calendar of club dates.

Danzig Home Page

http://american.recordings.com/American_Artists/Danzig/index.shtml

The American Recordings label maintains this site for its recording group, Danzig. Visitors will find photos, bios, video, cover art, promotion schedules, and links to related sites.

D'Cuckoo

http://matisse.net/dcuckoo.html

This page offers concise contact information on D'Cuckoo, the "techno-tribal dance band." Access the D'Cuckoo home page from here for an overview of the troupe, sound clips, and performance history.

Deluxe

http://ultraviolet.com/uvr/deluxe/

San Francisco-based Ultra Violet Recordings promotes the music of Deluxe via this (somewhat) official page. Find a discography featuring audio clips and critical reviews.

The Exceptions

http://www.colby.edu/wmhb/revenge/ex.html

The Exceptions, a Detriot-based ska music group, maintains this site with about the band's latest releases and performance schedules.

Faith No More

http://www.repriserec.com/FaithNoMore

Faith No More fans can read about the band here, find out tour dates, and download a music video. Reprise Records, the band's label, maintains the page and posts a link to its home page.

Fugazi

http://www.southern.com/southern/band/FUGAZ/index.html

The Fugazi home page provides information on the band that invented the DIY ethic, along with details about its musicians and touring schedules. Includes a discography, links to the group's recording label, and merchandise information.

Glass Billies Home Page

http://www.abc.se/~m9503/gb

Swedish band the Glass Billies makes its Web home on this page that includes lyrics to the group's recordings and a photo gallery.

God Street Wine

http://www.netspace.org/gsw/

The God Street Wine page plugs fans into a digest of information about this rock group, including tour dates, ordering options, and a few surprising links that interact. Hear sound bites from GSW albums here as well.

Official Grateful Dead Home Page

http://grateful.dead.net/

Check out the long, strange trip of the Grateful Dead on this official site. Band members are no longer touring under the name Grateful Dead, but tour dates are listed here. The site also hints at future archive releases and details the band's charitable work. Deadheads can order merchandise here, too.

Official Grateful Dead Home Page

http://www.dead.net/

Grateful Dead fans can plug into this official site to fill their eyes with images, their ears with interviews, and their heads with Dead details. A tribute to the late, great Garcia is included, along with music and merchandise ordering.

Hole

http://geffen.com/hole.html

Maintained by Geffen Records, this home page contains a witty bio describing the history and members of histrionic rock band Hole. Includes sound and video clips, plus a link to Geffen's main Web site.

Holler Sisters: Cowgirls

http://www.enteract.com/~cowgal/

Edith Frost, cowgirl singer extraordinaire, has created this downhome Web page with information about herself and her band, The Holler Sisters. There's information here on just about every little thing on the Web that has to do with cowgirls and twangy music, including a link to the official Roy Rogers and Dale Evans Web site.

Indigo Girls

http://www.music.sony.com/Music/ArtistInfo/IndigoGirls.html

Sony's official, multimedia Web presentation starring the Indigo Girls offers the usual photo album, record album information, tour stuff, and fan club facts. But also find audio and video clip highlights, plus an unexpected look at the duo's independent recording label, Daemon Records.

Jartery

http://www.dnai.com/~jar

Jar, a San Francisco-based band, is featured here. Visitors can download video and sound clips, lyrics, interviews, and reviews. The official site also contains gig and merchandise information.

The Jesus and Mary Chain

http://american.recordings.com/American_Artists/Jesus_And_Mary_Chain/jamc_home.html

American Recordings' page for alternative rockers The Jesus and Mary Chain contains audio files, album covers, images, and information on the band.

Letters to Cleo

http://www-personal.umich.edu/~hstahl/letters.html

This home page for the music group Letters to Cleo contains articles, lyrics, pictures, guitar tablature, audio/video clips, tour dates, and a mailing list.

Live Home Page

http://live.cerf.net/live_new/HTML/main_index.html

Find the official scoop on the modern rock band Live at this promotional site. Fans can read interviews, reviews, and touring information, or view publicity photos and QuickTime movies of the band here.

Lords of Acid

http://american.recordings.com/American_Artists/Lords_Of_Acid/lords_home.html

American Recordings sponsors this page to promote the Lords of Acid, a Belgian rock and roll band. Visitors can read the group's bio, see still photos of band members, and find out what makes them the "cause [of] the biggest scene since the year pasties became optional."

Man or Astroman?

http://www.astroman.com/

Man or Astro-Man? is just one of the many bands riding the swelling wave of popularity for guitar-heavy surf music, and fans of the retro sound of Man or Astro-Man? can get all kinds of goodies on the band here. Audio and video clips, the rundown on what the band's done so far, even the Astro newsletter can be had.

Many Hands

http://webservices.comp.vuw.ac.nz/artsLink/ManyHands

Many Hands is a New Zealand percussion band that utilizes a variety of multicultural styles. Visitors to its Web page will find band member profiles and an extensive collection of audio clips.

MARTENSVILLE

http://www.islandnet.com/~moron/deterrent/martensville/marten.html

Martensville is more than just another industrial band, it's a self-described "machine driven unit with three human accomplices." Browsers will find an "atonal soundtrack," an interview, and other details about the group.

NegativWorldWideWebLand

http://www.negativland.com

Negativland is an alternative rock band concerned with politics and intellectual property issues as well as music. Visitors can read through a discussion of the U.S. Copyright Act and discover why the band "hates the Information Superhighway," as well as check out its discography and order music.

Nirvana Page

http://geffen.com/nirv.html

This official Nirvana page is filled with information about the short-lived band that inspired a legion of followers, devotees, and hangers-on. At this Geffen site, fans can download photographs, sound samples, and cruise through band info tidbits.

The Official Oasis Home Page

http://www.oasisinet.com/

Here's the story, morning glory: Britpop sensation Oasis is dissected, celebrated, and examined at this officially sanctioned page. Includes tour news, a "gigography," fan club information and much more.

Phreeworld

http://www.art.net/Music/Phreeworld/Phreeworld.html

Pacific Northwest band Phreeworld introduces its music and members to the world through this Web site, which is packed with images and CD soundbytes. The page also includes a Quicktime video of concert clips.

Go! Discs/Portishead

http://www.godiscs.co.uk/godiscs/porthead.html

Here's a multimedia page devoted to the U.K. musical group, Portishead. Find a biography, photos, Quicktime and MPEG movies, plus links to related sites.

The Poster Children

http://www.prairienet.org/posterkids/

A Reprise Records group, the Poster Children host this site promoting the band, its music, and its branded merchandise. Check out tour dates, get polled, or linger over lyrics and band news.

Pounce International Web Site

http://www.infinet.com/~pounce

Furnace Records recording artist Pounce International is featured at this site, which includes information about new releases and photos. The band is described as "aggro-ambient…kind of like Enigma meets Godzilla."

The Official Home Page for Promise

http://www.europa.com/~tarie/ccci.html

The Christian music trio Promise is profiled on this official site. The site includes a discography, photos, and links to other Promise sites.

Queen Home Page

http://queen-fip.com/

The official Web site for the legendary rock band Queen is a sophisticated and low-key site. It heralds the release of the band's first new album since the death of singer Freddie Mercury and provides information about Queen's recent videos, television appearances, and philanthropy.

Refreshments

http://rampages.onramp.net/~micheleb/refresh.html

The Refreshments, a Phoenix-based rock music group, maintains this promotional site. Visit here to learn about its members, music, and upcoming performance, and recording plans.

R.E.M.—Monster

http://www.iuma.com/Warner/html/R.E.M..html

R.E.M.'s album, "Monster," is promoted and dissected at this site, with a list of tracks and band member's comments. The page, maintained by the Internet Underground Music Archive, includes 1995 tour dates and a QuickTime video clips.

The Rolling Stones: JAVA Lounge

http://www.stones.com/java_lounge.html

This JAVA Rolling Stones site seems strangely incomplete and devoid of graphics; perhaps it is under construction. Nonetheless, Stones fans can link to song lists and lyrics and answers to FAQs on the dinosaur rock band.

The Rolling Stones Web Site

http://stones.com/

The Voodoo Lounge is the official Rolling Stones Web Site. (Your first clue is that the URL ends in ".com.") This state-of-the-art promo site provides sound and video clips of Mick and the boys in action, interviews with the Stones' extended family, and plenty of the naughty-but-nice imagery for which this raunchy rock band is famous.

Stonesworld: The Rolling Stones on the Web

http://www.stonesworld.com/

Catch up on the latest news about the Rolling Stones, including concert news and rumors about new albums. Check into the message board to sound off about Stones topics.

The Rutles Home Page

http://www.primenet.com/~dhaber/rutles.html

Here browsers can find out about the legend of the Rutles, a "legend that will last a lunchtime." Read all about the Prefab Four, also known as Dirk, Nasty, Stig, and Barry. The Rutles.

Seefeel

http://hyperreal.com/music/artists/seefeel/seefeel.html

This home page has information on the band Seefeel, with facts about the band's recordings and links to interviews and sound files.

Simple Minds—Good News From the Web

http://matahari.cv.com/people/Simon.Cornwell/simple_minds/

Simple Minds fans can follow the band on this unofficial fan page. The extensive site includes a discography, lyrics, biographies and tour news. Visitors can link to sites that sell Simple Minds items, too.

Slash's Snakepit

http://geffen.com/slash

Big-haired rocker Slash, taking a break from Guns N' Roses, enlisted some former bandmates plus artists from Alice in Chains and Jellyfish to form Slash's Snakepit. Geffen Records lures listeners here with audio files from Slash's Snakepit's 1995 release: If you like what you hear, click and buy.

Slayer Home Page

http://american.recordings.com/American_Artists/Slayer/slayer_home.html

The Slayer home page contains information about the speed metal band, their music, and a discography. Includes interviews, lyrics archive, and an image gallery of their album covers.

Creation Records: Slowdive

http://www.musicbase.co.uk/music/creation/slowdive/

The British band Slowdive posts its upcoming concert dates, info about the group's recordings and more through this promotional site.

SM Home Page

http://www.ugcs.caltech.edu/~dfarmer/sm.html

The self-described "foremost blues-death band" SM features its hard core lyrics and antics at this home page. Visitors can read lyrics or listen to sound clips.

Sonic Youth

http://geffen.com/sonic.html

Geffen Records maintains this site to provide information about prototypical indie noise rockers Sonic Youth. Photos and bios are available, as is an opportunity to buy the group's albums.

Soul Coughing

http://www.iuma.com/Warner/html/Soul_Coughing.html

Warner Brothers promotes the debut album of the New York band Soul Coughing at this Web page. Find links to sound clips, short biographies of the band members, and a tour schedule.

Stone Roses

http://geffen.com/sroses.html

Read all about British pop band Stone Roses or listen to a few sound clips through this official page from Geffen Records. It features a rare photo as well as an obligatory biography of the band.

Swing Shift Home Page

http://www.pitt.edu/~cxm2/Swingshift.html

The acoustic swing music of the band Swing Shift comes to the Web through this home page. Visitors can meet the band, listen to .au sound samples from their album, learn about upcoming concert appearances, and view pictures of the band in action.

Ten K Maniacs WWW Site

http://www.maniacs.com/

Visit here for discographies, photos and the latest news about the 10,000 Maniacs. Fans can also order t-shirts and signed CDs or jump to Natalie Merchant pages (she left the band in 1993 to pursue a solo career).

This Perfect Day Home Page

http://www.iuma.com/MNW/Soap/html/This_Perfect_Day.html

Music fans can listen to "Headache" from the Swedish popsters This Perfect Day at the group's Web site, located in the Internet Underground Music Archive. This page also contains a photo of the five-member band and the story of the group's development.

The Tragically Hip

http://www.cimtegration.com/tth

Check out the latest from the band The Tragically Hip: where they've been, where they're headed, and what they've sounded like over the years. Links include contact information, .wav sound files, and jumps to a usenet newsgroup devoted to the band.

Violet Arcana

http://www.violet.arcana.com/

Violet Arcana presents a collection of clips, pictures, art, lyrics, multimedia, and reviews of esoteric music here. The band describes itself as providing "dreamy, ethereal, melodic, moody, ambient soundscapes for the surreal music listener."

Weezer Page

http://geffen.com/weezer.html

Geffen Records' Weezer Page celebrates the L.A.-based band that made their mark with a song about sweaters. Photos, sound samples, and bio included.

White Zombie: Planet Zombie

http://geffen.com/planetzombie

Planet Zombie provides standard-issue biographical information along with audio, video, and picture samples of American heavy metal/industrial rockers White Zombie.

Welcome to YELLO on the Net

http://www.yellowch/index_nonjava.html

The Swiss collaboration of Dieter Meier and Doris Blank, YELLO, waves a digital hello to the Internet world through this home page that features QuickTime and MPEG movie clips. The page also has links to sound clips.

Yep! Home Page

http://www.cs.umass.edu/~greene/yep.html

Official information about the music group yeP! can be found at this site, including articles, photos, biographies, sound clips, graphics, and merchandise. Visit here to learn about the band and find performance and recording updates.

SOLO ARTISTS

Note: *This section is alphabetized by the musician's last name where applicable.*

Fan Pages

Church of Tori

http://cctr.umkc.edu/user/cgladish/tori.html

The First International Church of Tori is an online fan shrine devoted to pop musician Tori Amos. Target audience: anyone "despising Men, God, or both." Tori's Prayer: "Our Tori, who art in my CD player, hallowed be thy voice."

The Tori Amos Home Page

http://www.mit.edu:8001/people/nocturne/tori.html

This fan page devoted to pop singer and song writer Tori Amos offers visitors links to concert photos, set lists, song lyrics, articles and a Frequently Asked Questions (FAQs) file about the artist. Features also include links to video and sound clips.

Tori Amos Unofficial Fan Site

http://www.mit.edu:8001/people/jwb/Tori.html

If pop star Tori Amos is the object of your musical affections, visit this unofficial site. Fans will find a discography, artist biography, song lyrics and downloadable graphics.

Tori Links!

http://gto.ncsa.uiuc.edu/khawkins/tori.html

Follow pop star Tori Amos around the Web at the Tori Links! site. This fan-produced homage points to Web sites which are devoted to or mention the hypnotic crooner. Visitors can get directions to pictures, songs and even a Church of Tori here.

Laurie Anderson: HOMEpage of the Brave

http://www.c3.lanl.gov:8080/cgi/jimmyd/quoter?home

Followers of singer, musician, technical wizard and performance artist Laurie Anderson can find art of, for, and about their multimedia heroine at the Home Page of the Brave. Explore her discography and performance schedule, or link to the artist's official Web sites.

Laurie Anderson Info

http://www.netpart.com/phil/laurie.html

Musician, poet and video artist Laurie Anderson is the object of Webmaster Phil Trubey's adoration. Like-minded fans can link to a 1994 WiReD Magazine article, a guide to Anderson's work, and other fan and promotional pages.

Louis Armstrong

http://www.netspace.org/~haaus/shome.html

Louis "Satchmo" Armstrong, master trumpeter of the Big Band era, is the subject; his life and music is the material. A bio, list of recordings and related links are among the offerings.

BILLY BRAGG information World Wide Web Home Page

http://mindspring.com/~usul/billy-bragg.html

Mixing history with trivia, this fan-maintained Web site seemingly answers any question a Billy Bragg fan could harbor. Everything from biographical information to equipment listings and an alternate lyrics roundup provide a detailed portrait of the political pop singer/songwriter.

Bjork WebSense

http://www.centrum.is/bjork/

Fans of ex-Sugarcubes songstress Bjork have created "the Website of the six senses," an homage to the singer with a generous sampling of her music. The "sixth sense" part comes in the form of virtual "extrasensory" traveling while taking an interactive cybertour.

David Bowie File

http://liber.stanford.edu/~torrie/Bowie/BowieFile.html

David Bowie fans, rejoice! This page chronicles the works of the pop icon, exploring lyrics, individual songs and more details of "one of the most influential songwriters of the modern era."

Boy George

http://www-personal.umich.edu/~geena/boygeorge.html

Wonder how Boy George lost his virginity? Get the skinny on the United Kingdom's flamboyant "Boy." With details about his descent into heroine hell to the record that changed his life, this bi-monthly fanzine format digs deep.

The Unofficial Jeff Buckley Page

http://www.goodnet.com/~gkelemen/jeffhome.html

Even though Jeff Buckley's album "Grace" sold very well, he remains a semi-cult musician. Fans of the American songster will find out where they can hear and see Buckley alone reading poetry, or with his band giving a concert.

Jimmy Buffett Parrot(t)head Page

http://www.soasoas.com/

Attention parrotheads! Fans of singer/songwriter Jimmy Buffett will enjoy this unofficial fan site, featuring discographies, biographical information and song lyrics. Includes links to information on the tropical locations on which much of his music is based.

Parrot Heads in Paradise: Jimmy Buffett

http://www.hepcat.com/phip/

Parrot Heads from all over the world can keep up with the latest news and music of Jimmy Buffet. Items on the buffet here include a listing of fan club chapters and their home pages, the Parrot Head Market and the Bank of Bad Habits, an archive of Buffet links.

Nick Cave

http://www.maths.monash.edu.au/people/brett/nick/nick.html

The Nick Cave home page is devoted to the lead singer of the Bad Seeds. Visitors will find interviews, a discography, tour dates and news on future albums and books.

Paula Cole

http://cpcug.org/user/titusb/pcole/

At this fan site, Paula Cole fans will find detailed information about the recording artist with song samples, lyrics, a bio and tour information.

The Unofficial Harry Connick Jr. Home Page

http://www.rcch.com/connick

Fans of pretty-boy crooner Harry Connick Jr. will want to stop by The Unofficial Harry Connick Jr. Home Page for links to his discography, sound bites, interviews, biographical information and more.

Elvis Costello

http://east.isx.com/~schnitzi/elvis.html

Fans of rock musician Elvis Costello will enjoy this unofficial fansite, featuring a variety of information about the man and his legendary music career. Visit here for discographies, concert reviews, interviews with the artist and more.

Bob Dylan: Bringing It All Back Home Page

http://reality.sgi.com/employees/howells/dylan.html

Bob Dylan fans can follow the legendary singer's tour and recording schedule at this unofficial site. For serious Dylan fans, the Webmaster posts a list of bootleg tapes and other unreleased material. Links to other Dylan pages.

Bob Dylan: Expecting Rain

http://bob.nbr.no/

Expecting Rain is an encyclopedic site devoted exclusively to the musician Bob Dylan. Visitors will find art, pictures, multimedia, interviews, answers to Frequently Asked Questions (FAQs), news, discography and links to related sites.

Bob Dylan's 115th Dream

http://www.cen.uiuc.edu/~bdonalds/bob.html

This personal page contains lyrics and musical transcriptions of famed folkie Bob Dylan's songs. Fans can submit reviews of the singer/songwriter's albums, songs, and so forth. Also: links to the Highway 61 Interactive home page and other Dylan-related sites.

Elvis: Virtual Voyager

http://www1.chron.com/voyager/elvis/

Browsers can join a virtual search for The King here. While in the neighborhood, why not take an Elvis trivia quiz, download Elvis sounds and software or wander through a gallery of velvet?

Unofficial Elvis Pages

http://sunsite.unc.edu/elvis/elvishom.html

You ain't nothin' but a hound dog if you're an Elvis fan and don't check out this Web site, dedicated to the American rock 'n' roll icon. Photos, historical information, and other wacky stuff related to the King can be found here, including a Graceland tour, souvenir information, a comic strip and a copy of Presley's last will and testament.

Joe Ely: Letter to Laredo

http://www.ely.com/

Beautifully-designed graphics link visitors to information on little-known but critically-acclaimed Texas country-rock musician Joe Ely. Find links to biographical information, merchandise, tour dates and other Ely info.

Enya Unofficial Home Page

http://www.bath.ac.uk/~ccsdra/enya/homepage.html

Delve into the life and music of ethereal pop star Enya on this unofficial, fan-produced page. The extensive site includes guitar tablatures, sound files, pictures and interviews.

Jerry Garcia

http://www.sfm.com/dawgnet/artists/jerry.html

Explore the acoustic side of deceased Grateful Dead lead singer and musician Jerry Garcia through excerpts from Guitar Player Magazine at this site. Features include info about Garcia's acoustic disc recordings that browsers can purchase.

Jerry Garcia 1942-1995

http://www.rockweb.com/rwi/jerry-tribute/

Maintained by the RockWeb, this page contains a tribute to Jerry Garcia, founder and cornerstone of legendary rock group The Grateful Dead. Visitors can view a musical montage, look through photos, send condolences, read various perspectives on the man and his band, and link to other tributes and related sites.

Jerry Garcia: Not Fade Away

http://metaverse.com/vibe/nfa.html

Grateful Dead fans produced this memorial page within days of Jerry Garcia's death. Fans can celebrate Garcia's life here and download songs in Real Audio.

GlassPages: Philip Glass on the Web

http://www-lsi.upc.es/~jpetit/pg/

American minimalist composer Philip Glass is the focus here, where browsers will find a discography, articles, scores, images and more.

Nanci Griffith

http://www.nvg.unit.no/~paul/nanci/nanci1.html

American folk singer-songwriter Nanci Griffith is given the fan treatment on this home page from Norway. Includes a list of Griffith's recordings, photos, and links to other Griffith-related pages on the Web.

Emmylou Harris

http://www.nashville.net/~kate/

Enthusiasts of "quintessential country music singer" Emmylou Harris will find like-minded fellows at this unofficial fan site. Includes minutia about the singer ranging from award information to fan clubs to recent appearances and much more.

Deborah Harry

http://www3.primenet.com/~lab/DHDeborahHarry.html

Fans of rock musician Deborah Harry will enjoy this unofficial fan site. Visit here for information interview reprints, photos and the like about the artist's life and music, including her participation in the 1970s new wave group Blondie.

Phil's Juliana Hatfield Page

http://www.clark.net/pub/phil/JulianaHatfield.html

Fans of rock musician Juliana Hatfield will enjoy this unofficial fan site. Visit here for a variety of information about the artist, including press clippings, song lyrics, downloadable sound and video files, and more.

Jimi Hendrix

http://www.parks.tas.gov.au/jimi/jimi.html

The legend of rock guitar god Jimi Hendrix lives on via the Internet. Fans will find sounds, sights and lyrics of the late artist at this unofficial site, which includes dozens of links to Hendrix-related resources.

Shot of Rhythm: The John Hiatt Mailing List Archives

http://www.unicom.com/john-hiatt

Fans can pay homage to musician John Hiatt at the John Hiatt Mailing List archives. Visitors can look up albums in the discography or check out Hiatt pictures here.

Don Ho HoHouse Page

http://www.spacestar.com:80/donho/

Aloha from the Don Ho HoHouse! Everybody's favorite Hawaiian singer invites you to download "Tiny Bubbles," win a trip to Hawaii or order CDs online.

Husker Du/Bob Mould/Sugar

http://math.montana.edu/~sanford/sugar.html

This fan page for rock musician Bob Mould—and for his band projects Husker Du, and Sugar—contains interviews and articles and a Frequently Asked Questions (FAQs) section. Visitors will also find loads of album information, including song lyrics, guitar tabs and cover art.

Jackopierce Guitar Chords

http://ccwf.cc.utexas.edu/~arabella/jp/index.html

This page features guitar chords and tablature for the songs of Jack O. Pierce. This page also has contact information, mailing lists and links to other Pierce-related pages.

Jazz Butcher Conspiracy

http://purgatory.ecn.purdue.edu:20002/JBC/jbc.html

This page features a profile on musician Pat Fish, known as "The Jazz Butcher." Features include a discography, lyrics, audio samples, press articles and other information.

The Sandy Lam Home Page

http://www.musicdistrict.com/sandy/am/sandy/

Created by a fan for fans, this page is devoted to Sandy Lam, a female singer from Hong Kong. The singer's discography, biography, list of awards, theme songs and photo album are featured at this site. In English and Chinese.

The Levellers Page

http://chem-www.mps.ohio-state.edu/~pfleming/lvlrs/

This Web page is devoted to the musical band The Levellers, who've been described as "sort of a Celtic Clash." Visitors will find a discography, lyrics, photos, tour dates and more.

Intro to Madonna

http://www.buffnet.net/~steve772/maddy.html

Two Madonna fans pay homage to the pop star here. Browsers can download video and audio snippets, read her song lyrics and shop for hard-to-find merchandise.

The Madonna Home Page

http://www.mit.edu:8001/people/jwb/Madonna.html

This fan-hosted site serves up dish on the all-around American pop star: her hits, her bombs, her contributions to "George" magazine...even the "Top 10 Signs that David Letterman is Obsessed with Madonna."

Yngwie Malmsteen

http://pd.net/yngwie/

The international fan club of Swedish guitar virtuoso Yngwie J. Malmsteen sponsors this site, which includes a biography, touring information, photos, discography and a recorded message from Yngwie.

The Unofficial Aimee Mann Pages

http://songwriting.com/aimeeman/

This unofficial profile of musician Aimee Mann takes a comprehensive look at her music, lyrics and biography. Bend an ear to sound clips, take a peep at photographs or make note of her touring schedule.

The Paul McCartney Home Page

http://home.sprynet.com/sprynet/maireg/paul.htm

The Paul McCartney home page is a valentine for the lad from Liverpool who gave the world Wings. This site concentrates on Paul's music outside of the Fab Four, with a complete solo discography, lyrics and chords to his songs, reviews from the music press and a word or two about Linda.

Sarah McLachlan Home Page

http://www.css.itd.umich.edu/~hubt/sarah/

A home page designed to provide Sarah McLachlan fans with tour schedules, pictures and biographical and discography information about the singer, this Web site also can connect visitors with a link to the official home page run by McLachlan's record label.

SarahSpace—The Sarah McLachlan Pages

http://watt.seas.virginia.edu/~jds5s/music/sarah/sarah.html

Fans of the musical artist, poetess and painter, Sarah McLachlan, can access a plethora of information here. Tour dates, newsletters, catalogs, sound bites and much more are among the offerings.

Steve Sigourney's Sarah McLachlan Pages

http://www.tyrell.net/~vettek/sarah.html

Here browsers will find a truly advanced collection of memorabilia for this young musician, with many other links to other McLachlan pages. Sample her bio, browse books, CDs, tapes, videos, clothing and posters. Pictures and a discography with lyrics to "Fumbling Towards Ecstasy" complete this veritable treasure trove.

Infomas Natalie Merchant Home Page

http://www.primenet.com/~infomas/natalie.html

Natalie Merchant, pop singer and song writer, is the focus of this unofficial fan page for the former frontwoman of 10,000 Maniacs. Concert and tour information are offered, as well as details about her life and articles about her music.

Joni Mitchell Home Page

http://www.well.com/user/wallyb/jonihome.html

A Joni Mitchell fan pays homage to the singer, poet and painter here. Visitors can download her lyrics, artwork and biography on this extensive site, which also includes a chat room.

Alanis Morissette

http://www.sgi.net/alanis/

Alanis Morissette, the Canadian pop star, has an unofficial fan page here. Check up on the latest Alanis sightings, gossip, song lyrics and photos. Links to other Alanis sites provided.

Van Morrison

http://www.harbour.sfu.ca/~hayward/van/van.html

The Van Morrison home page seeks to serve as an informational site for those interested in the man and his music. Biography, reviews, interviews and more are available here.

Morrissey/The Smiths: Cemetry Gates

http://moz.pair.com/

Meet Morrissey at the Cemetry Gates, a fan site devoted to the tragically hip singer/songwriter and his defunct band, The Smiths. Though top-heavy with Morrissey's compelling poetry, plenty of photographs, audio clips and shopping opportunities are worked into the mix.

Morrissey/The Smiths Page

http://www.npl.com/~carvids/Mozpage.html

Big-time fan Christian Arvidson supplies this online shrine for enthusiasts of gloomy rock star Morrissey and his erstwhile band, the Smiths.

Gaia: The Olivia Newton-John Page

http://www-leland.stanford.edu/~clem/

This fan page devoted to the pop songstress, Olivia Newton-John, features current news, career information, and photos. Links to topic-related pages are also featured.

The Nicks Fix: A Homepage Devoted to Stevie Nicks

http://web2.airmail.net/jkinney/

Stevie Nicks is celebrated here. Fans can download photos, videos and her song lyrics. The extensive site also includes links to other Nicks resources on the Net, including Fleetwood Mac sites, a mailing list and a forum.

Phil Ochs

http://www.cs.pdx.edu/~trent/ochs/

This site is a memorial to Phil Ochs, a singer/songwriter of the 1960s and a friend of rock icon Bob Dylan. Visit here to learn about the writer of protest songs such as "Draft Dodger Rag." Links are provided to lyrics, discography and books.

Sinead O'Connor Home Page

http://www.engr.ukans.edu/~jrussell/music/sinead/sinead.html

Sinead O'Connor fans can download her sounds and lyrics from this unofficial page. Browsers here also can read a discography, the Irish musician's poems and magazine interviews here.

Unofficial Tom Petty Fan Site

http://www.ugcs.caltech.edu/~hedlund/tom_petty/index.shtml

The music of Tom Petty, with and without the Heartbreakers, is featured at this site. Included are albums, lyrics, images and links to other Tom Petty sites and fan e-mail directories.

Liz Phair: Little Guyville

http://www.is.co.za/andras/music/lp/

This Liz Phair page contains pictures of the musician, along with a discography, guitar tablatures and an interview. Includes links to other Phair pages.

Liz Phair: Stratford-On-Guy

http://www.nebula.net/~lazlo/liz/

This page, an unofficial shrine to frank-talking alternative rocker Liz Phair, provides biographical and touring information, photographs, lyrics and reviews along with links to other home pages devoted to the singer/songwriter.

Chris Rea

http://www.helsinki.fi/~wikgren/chrisrea.html

Chris Rea's Home Page targets fans of the English musical artist, offering biographical sketches and a record of his accomplishments. Other links point to a fanclub, interviews and touring schedules.

The Reason Why

http://http.bsd.uchicago.edu/~d-hillman/46one/samples.html

In an effort to demonstrate why some consider him the greatest guitar player in the world, this page devoted to Eric Clapton is chock full of audio samples. Ranging from the Yardbirds to Cream to Derek and the Dominos and beyond, there's a sound byte for every fan here.

Lou Reed and The Velvet Underground

http://www.rocknroll.net/loureed/

This is a comprehensive site dedicated to the music of Lou Reed. Visitors will find a discography, lyrics, interviews, a bootleg gallery, guitar tabulature and biographical information.

Happy Rhodes: The Ecto Home Page

http://www.tela.bc.ca/ecto/

What's an Ectophile and who is Happy Rhodes? Find answers to these questions and pointers to cool music sites through the Ecto Home Page. An offshoot of a mailing list devoted to the music of Happy Rhodes, the page offers information about Rhodes' tunes, as well as the Ectophiles' Guide to Good Music.

Henry Rollins' Stuff

http://www.st.nepean.uws.edu.au/~alf/rollins/

This vast site is devoted to the musician/spoken word performer Henry Rollins. Visitors will find a discography, articles, audio samples, photos, biographical information and a multitude of links.

Diana Ross Fan Club

http://www.knoware.nl/music/diana/ross1.htm

From the Netherlands comes this fan page devoted to American pop icon Diana Ross. Find current news, coverage of her career, a biography and a videography, plus information about the fan club and its quarterly magazine, "ROSS."

Todd Rundgren's Freedom Fighters Home Base

http://www.iglou.com/scm/cgi-bin/todd.pl

Todd Rundgren's Freedom Fighter home page offers a huge collection of Runt-related information. Visitors can check out everything from biographical facts about the eclectic musician to quotes, rumors, lyrics and article reprints.

Sade

http://www.diku.dk/~terra/sade/

Fans of the English/Nigerian singer Sade Adu can check out her complete discography, a short biography and a series of sound clips at this page.

Sade's Temple

http://gwis2.circ.gwu.edu/~merlin/sade/sade.html

Sony recording artist Sade receives a fan's attentions at this page. Listen to audio clips of favorite songs or read the lyrics to her entire body of work.

Joe Satriani at the Riv

http://www.ncsa.uiuc.edu/SDG/People/rgrant/riv.html

This personal home page devoted to guitarist Joe Satriani offers browsers vignettes of the author's experiences seeing the artist play live. Check out Joe's autograph here, or link to information about California.

Carly Simon Online

http://www.ziva.com/carly/

Carly Simon is famous for singing such songs as the enigmatic "You're So Vain" and the more self-explanatory "Nobody Does it Better." A fan has devoted a page to the artist's works and life; offerings include interviews, concert information and a collection of pictures.

Frank Sinatra

http://vex.net/~buff/

Stylish songster Frank Sinatra is the subject of adulation here, with a searchable "Frankenindex," mailing list information, and much more.

The Definitive Michael W. Smith Pages

http://www.cs.rose-hulman.edu/~schaefsm/mws/

Wildly popular Christian musician Michael W. Smith is the topic of these fan pages which offer up lyrics to all of Smith's songs as well as Smith images and other information. Smith fans who simply can't get enough can also find contact information for the "Michael's Best Friend" newsletter here.

Unofficial Bruce Springsteen Fan Site

http://e-street.eastlib.ufl.edu/bruce.html

Fans of rock legend Bruce Springsteen will enjoy this unofficial site. Visitors can track his latest performances, guest appearances, recordings, romance and rumors.

Matthew Sweet Home Page

http://www.xnet.com/~wakemich/msweet.shtml

Musician Matthew Sweet's tour dates, tunes and lyrics are among the offerings at this site. There also are articles and reviews, as well as links to other Matthew Sweet sites.

James Taylor Online

http://www.james_taylor.com

JT fans will appreciate this Web page grown out the Usenet newsgroup alt.music.james-taylor. Find articles, interviews, photos, sounds, tour dates and more.

Richard Thompson: Henry The Human Fly Caught In The Web

http://www.alphalink.com.au/~sfy/RT/

The songs and recordings of Richard Thompson are highlighted on the Henry The Human Fly Caught In The Web page. It includes pointers to live performance information as well as bootleg recordings and a photo gallery.

Vangelis: The Man and the Music

http://bau2.uibk.ac.at/perki/Vangelis.html

This multimedia site is devoted to the composer-musician, Evangelos O. Papathanassiou (aka Vangelis). Get all the details here on his solo and collaborative works, plus an introduction from the man himself.

Stevie Ray Vaughan

http://www.quadralay.com/www/Austin/AustinMusic/srv/StevieRayVaughan.html

Stevie Ray Vaughan is a legendary rock and blues musician who died in 1990. Visitors can find song lyrics, pictures and a poster archive at this fan site.

Tom Waits Digest

http://www.nwu.edu/music/waits/

The Tom Waits Digest page features information about the singer's most recent albums as well as a list of taped rare recordings and concert appearances. Fans can also read the extended list of Tom Waits band members sorted by album.

Frank Zappa: St. Alphonzo's Pancake Homepage

http://www.fwi.uva.nl/~heederik/zappa/

A presentation of the world according to Frank Zappa holds center stage at this fan produced site. Tributes to and writings of the American rock star/philosopher/politician dominate this look at his life and work.

Promo Pages

Laurie Anderson's Green Room

http://www.voyagerco.com/LA/VgerLa.html

From the larger Voyager site, this page follows Laurie Anderson as she tours North America and Europe. Find a journal, a schematic of the performer's stage, multimedia online presentations and more.

Big Bamboo

http://www.realitycom.com/bamboo

Big Bamboo is a one-man recording project run by jack-of-all-musical-trades Selwyn Schneider. Visit this site to sample the London-based musician's work. Also here: links to the Internet Music Review Service and the Cerberus Digital Jukebox.

Welcome to David Bowie's "Outside"

http://www.davidbowie.com/

Find out all about David Bowie's album "Outside" at this site. Visitors can check out animations, character information, lyrics, sound bites, tour dates and photos, or link to other Bowie sites around the globe.

Jimmy Buffett's Margaritaville

http://key-west.com/cgibin/var/discover/margaritaville/index.htm

Margaritaville is a state of mind not far from Key West, Florida, where virtual explorers vow to "incorporate the lifestyle portrayed in Jimmy Buffett music into our own."

Mariah Carey

http://www.music.sony.com/Music/ArtistInfo/MariahCarey.html

Fans of American pop idol Mariah Carey will wiggle around in delight while visiting this in-depth site, which is a small slice of entertainment giant Sony Inc.'s "Wiretap" pie. Check out the latest Mariah hype or download sound samples to judge for yourself.

Holly Cole's Web Place

http://www.hollycole.com/

Nightclub/jazz chanteuse Holly Cole, based in Toronto, offers audio clips, QuickTime movies, and photos at her Web site. The singer posts messages to her fans here and promises to reply to messages from them.

Ani DiFranco

http://www.cc.columbia.edu/~marg/ani/

Righteous Babe Records maintains this page for its recording artist, Ani DiFranco. Features include a biography, list of albums, tour schedule, mailing lists, guitar tablatures, song lyrics and photos.

The Peter Gabriel Page

http://www.geffen.com/gabriel.html

The Peter Gabriel Page links visitors to some images and sound files from the popular musician, or to biographical information. Visitors can also link back to the Geffen company home page.

Chris Isaak

http://www.repriserec.com/ChrisIsaak

Featuring audio and a variety of visuals—including video and virtual reality—this interactive multimedia site promotes Reprise Records' artist, Chris Isaak. Fans will find his biography, photo album and some of his cartoon drawings among the many items of interest.

Michael Jackson: Welcome to HIStory!

http://www.music.sony.com/Music/ArtistInfo/MichaelJackson.html

This page acts as a gateway to the official Sony site promoting Michael Jackson's album, "HIStory." Visitors can join a mailing list before moving through this gateway and into the rest of the presentation.

Madonna—Bedtime Stories

http://www.iuma.com/Warner/html/Madonna.html

Promoting Madonna's October 1994 album release "Bedtime Stories," this official site offers a multimedia treat of sight and sound. Stop, look and listen, and find out what the "Material Girl" has to say about the work.

MC 900 Foot Jesus

http://american.recordings.com/American_Artists/MC_900FT_Jesus/mc_home.html

Musician/rapper/noisemaker/philosopher Mark Griffin, aka MC 900 Foot Jesus, is the focus of this home page from American Recordings. Among the resources here are a biography, audio clips, video clips, lyrics and images. Fans also can send e-mail to MC 900 Foot Jesus from here.

Herb Moore: Melodius-Sync

http://www.omix.com/music/hmoore/home.html

Visitors to this promotional site for modern computer-music composer Herb Moore can download tracks from his albums and read general information about his life and work.

Alanis Morissette

http://www.repriserec.com/Alanis

The music of quick-rising Canadian music star Alanis Morissette comes to the Web world through this site from Reprise Records. It features sound clips from her album, "Jagged Little Pill," as well as photos and a complete discography.

Ozzy Osbourne

http://www.music.sony.com/Music/ArtistInfo/OzzyOsbourne.html

Notorious hard-rocker Ozzy Osbourne is profiled on this Sony page. Visit the sleek site for a collection of photos, video clips and a biography of the singer, who formed Black Sabbath in the 1970s and went solo in the 1980s.

Tom Petty: Wildflowers

http://www.iuma.com/Warner/html/Petty,_Tom.html

Warner Bros. hosts this site to promote musical maestro Tom Petty's recording, "Wildflowers." An audio clip of "You Don't Know How It Feels" complements liner notes and a Petty bio.

Joe Satriani's Home Page

http://www.satriani.com/

One of rock music's most accomplished guitar players is celebrated here. This official site offers biographical info on Joe Satriani, a discography, tour information, photos and technical notes on his incredible guitar collection. Fans can buy official Satriani merchandise here, too.

Jerry Jeff Walker

http://www.io.com/~ccamden/jjw/

Fans of Jerry Jeff Walker's musical stylings will find bio information, a tour schedule and much more at this official site.

Dar Williams

http://www.panix.com/~tneff/dar/

The Dar Williams Web Pages are devoted to this popular folk singer from New England. The selections here offer inside glimpses of releases, including sound samples, and provide personal information on the artist herself. Find tour schedules here.

PUBLICATIONS AND INDUSTRY NEWS

Addicted to Noise

http://www.addict.com/

Addicted to Noise unveils the latest music news and rumors in its monthly issues on this page. Stop by for some live conversation in the Talk Talk section or check out a large collection of back issues. See Editor's Choice.

Australia: Next Online

http://www.next.com.au/music/

The Music pages of Next Online features music reviews, news, and magazines. Visitors can read issues of the Australian Rolling Stone, download songs and read the latest in industry news.

Australian Music Charts

http://www.cs.monash.edu.au/~jamies/charts/index.html

In case you're not satisfied with just knowing who is at the top of the Australian music charts today, use the indices at this site to check chart data dating back to 1989. Links to other Australian and world music charts also are available.

Australia: Triple J Zone

http://www.abc.net.au/triplej/

Triple J is an Australian youth-culture magazine sponsored by a popular radio station. Browsers on this promotional page can read excerpted features, reviews and comix from the magazine and give smart-alecky feedback to its editors.

Consumable Online

http://www.westnet.com/consumable/
Consumable.html

Consumable Online, an Internet-based music magazine, provides disc reviews, artist interviews and tour information on popular, rock and alternative groups. Visitors can read current and back issues here.

Cybergrass—The Internet Bluegrass Music Magazine

http://www.banjo.com/BG/

Get the latest on traditional music from this electronic publication. Bluegrass festival and society listings, artist profiles and other reading matter keep fans current. Classified ads connect pickers and other music makers with banjos, mandolins and fiddles for sale.

CyberSleaze

http://metaverse.com/vibe/sleaze/00latest.html

Consult the CyberSleaze page, an offering of The Vibe, an online entertainment magazine, for a daily dose of gossip about pop music stars and the entertainment industry.

Dead Angel

http://www.eden.com/zines/deadangel/
deadangel.html

Sure the design is ugly, but the writing's not half bad. Dead Angel—"the e-zine with a deeply flawed understanding of HTML"—minces no words in its extended interviews and authoritative reviews of music, movies and other pop-culture artifacts.

The Death of Rock 'n' Roll

http://weber.u.washington.edu/~jlks/pike/
DeathRR.html

Fans can explore the roots and manifestations of their attractions to deceased rock icons within the pages of The Death of Rock 'n' Roll: Untimely Demises, Morbid Preoccupations and Premature Forecasts of Doom in Pop Music. Readers will find excerpts of author Jeff Pike's book at this site. See Editor's Choice.

Deterrent Tour Manual

http://www.islandnet.com/~moron/deterrent/
tour_gd.html

Musicians working to book their own tours can download a list of contact names in Canada and the United States from this page. The site also includes a European list, in German only.

DIGITAL BISCUIT Home Page

http://www.ces.kyutech.ac.jp/student/
JapanEdge/DIGIBI/digibi.html

Tokyo's underground monthly, Digital Biscuit, focuses on techno music. Visitors will find information on the paper's aim and history here, along with archives of past issues and techno news flashes. The site is in English; the archives are in Japanese.

Dirty Linen Magazine

http://www.dirtynelson.com/linen/

Dirty Linen Magazine is a print and online publication devoted to folk, traditional and world music. This site includes subscription information, back issue archive, articles, reviews, programming guides and other items of interest.

8-Track Mind

http://virtumall.com/zines/8track/main.html

A quarterly digest for those fascinated by 8-track tapes, this e-zine is produced by a "tracker" who recently completed a documentary about other collectors.

Fly! Music Magazine

http://www.fly.co.uk/index.dhtml

Put some hip in your hop and some jive in your jazz at Fly! The British magazine features articles and reviews of new music—mainly jazz, R&B, and dance. To hear some live grooves visit the gigs and clubs section for happenings in Great Britain.

Folk Roots

http://www.cityscape.co.uk/froots/

Roots, folk and world music makers headline at Folk Roots, an online magazine. Music lovers can find monthly offerings of articles, interviews and album reviews at this site.

Jerry Garcia

http://www.sfm.com/dawgnet/artists/
jerry.html

Explore the acoustic side of deceased Grateful Dead lead singer and musician Jerry Garcia through excerpts from Guitar Player Magazine at this site. Features include information about Garcia's acoustic disc recordings that browsers can purchase.

a2z EDITOR'S CHOICE

Addicted to Noise

http://www.addict.com/

Slaves to the rhythm rejoice! Addicted to Noise is drenched with up-to-the-minute, high-quality writing dealing with all aspects of the music biz. The vast site now has a revamped design—offering both lo- and hi-bandwidth versions—so as not to annoy browsers unnecessarily with oodles of graphics; but if you've got a fast modem, the look of the place is half the fun.

With Real Audio and sound bites galore, there's plenty to listen to in between reading pithy reviews, articles, and columns from a crack team of writers. From Dave Marsh to Sue Cummings, Bill Wyman to Greil Marcus, these scribes are the cream of the crop and they get the interviews to prove it: Patti Smith, Pete Townshend, and Penelope Houston were just a few of the artists explored in a recent issue. The daily "Music News of the World" keeps fans up on the hip and happening dirt. Chock full of attitude and knowledge, Addicted to Noise is top of the pops.—Reviewed by Julene Snyder

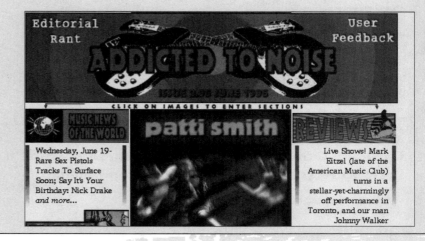

Hot Press

http://www.iol.ie/hotpress/

Recent issues of Hot Press, an Irish music and culture publication, are available online to subscribers only at this site. Issues older than six months are available to all. Subscription information is included.

Hyperreal

http://www.hyperreal.com/

Hyperreal is an electronic publication that chronicles the club and rave scene. Visitors will find digital art, rave music resources and articles on techno culture.

IMMEDIA! P/L

http://www.immedia.com.au/

The Australia-based Immedia electronic magazine unveils the latest news from the industry as well as its 1996 Australian Music Industry Directory here. Visitors in search of a job in the music business can also check for openings on the page.

Inter Dance Web Megazine

http://www.idw.be/

Inter Dance Web Megazine is a Belgian publication devoted to rap, techno, house, ambient, trip hop and other forms of danceable nightclub music. The page features album reviews, sales and airplay charts and links to other dance-music oriented sites.

InterJazz Home Page

http://www.webcom.com/~ijazz/

InterNet Jazz provides a wide range of resources for Jazz lovers. Visitors to this site can read Jazz articles and news, link to artists on the Net, or browse lists of Jazz clubs. The page also contains the Jazz Yellow pages.

The Internet Nightclub

http://www.memcore.com/nightclub/

The Internet Nightclub is a collection of articles on music and nightclub culture. Visitors will find photos, videos, downloadable music, games and contests here.

Internet Rockhouse

http://www.rockhouse.com/

The Internet Rockhouse caters to musicians seeking a presence on the Web. Includes a description of services, pricing information, free classified music listings, music repositories and e-mail service packages. Fans can access images, sounds and bios of listed groups.

Internet Underground Music Archive Home Page

http://www.iuma.com/IUMA/index_graphic.html

A virtual plethora of musical news, information, sound clips and publications are dished up at this site. Visit here to listen to underground bands, explore new music and learn the latest industry dirt.

The Lighthouse Electronic Magazine Home Page

http://tlem.netcentral.net/

Fans of God-approved Christian rock will want to check out "The Lighthouse," an online magazine devoted to Christian music. Check out past or current issues to learn more about featured bands, hear audio files, read up on the music industry and more.

Los Angeles Music Access

http://com.primenet.com/home/

Los Angeles Music Access (LAMA) maintains this site with a variety of musician and music promoter resources, including artist information, a band gig calendar, sound software and the LAMA manifesto.

MAGiC feet

http://www1.haywire.co.uk/haywire/

Go far beyond Kraftwerk as you explore today's electronic music with MAGiC Feet. Self-described as the UK's "premier underground techno and electronic publication," the zine reviews new releases and takes you to the club scene at this Web edition.

MCA Records: AMP

http://www.mca.com/mca_records/

AMP, sponsored by MCA Records, presents information about the label's artists, sound bytes, music news and more.

MisterLUCKY

http://www.mrlucky.com/

"MisterLUCKY" is not a 'zine, "but a quarterly musical communique celebrating music of a 'jazz-centric' nature." It takes in the whole scene of rhythm and booze, offering reviews and recipes (try the White Lady Cocktail). Subcribe to the hardcopy version here.

---

a2z EDITOR'S CHOICE

The Death of Rock 'n' Roll

http://weber.u.washington.edu/~jlks/pike/DeathRR.html

Morbidity is nothing to be ashamed of; better to revel in the grim litany of dead rock stars examined in this online version of Jeff Pike's book, "The Death of Rock n' Roll." Answers to burning questions ("Why do people go to Graceland on their vacations from work? Why is there a section of Central Park, just across from the Dakota Apartments, called Strawberry Fields? Why does Malcolm McLaren consider the Sex Pistols and Sid Vicious to be his literary property?") can be found here, where fans can "explore the roots and manifestations of their attractions to deceased rock icons."

Dead but not forgotten, there's a tidbit for everyone here—from Elvis fans to Janis to Kurt—the only drawback is the long list of those stars impolite enough to die after Pike's book went to press.—*Reviewed by Julene Snyder*

The Death of Rock 'n' Roll:

Untimely Demises, Morbid Preoccupations and Premature Forecasts of Doom in Pop Music

by Jeff Pike (hypertext by Jordan Schwartz and Jeff Pike)

MTV Online

http://mtv.com/index.html

MTV Online features a vast repository of news, music and video reviews, a merchandise site and animation samples. Includes programming schedules and job listings as well as information on how to become further involved with all things MTV.

Music Theory Online

http://boethius.music.ucsb.edu/mto/mtohome.html

Music Theory Online is the electronic version of this scholarly bi-monthly journal that contains articles, job vacancies and dissertation notices. Current and past issues are available here as well as information on discussion groups and details for subscribing.

NetCentral, Inc.

http://www.netcentral.net/

NetCentral, Inc., a Nashville, Tennnessee Web marketing company, hosts this site, which includes "A Closer Look," featuring Christian media and entertainment news, NoteStation, a sheet music retail network, and record companies Word and Gotee.

New Ways to Noise

http://www.maires.co.uk/nw2n/

New Ways to Noise (aka NW2N—oh, and Nigel Wears 2 Nighties) is a British "independent web fanzine" dealing mainly in alternative rock music. Content ranges from feature stories to press releases and concert dates.

The Numbers: Music

http://www.mrshowbiz.com/numbers/music/

Run down the list of the top 250 albums as compiled by Sound Scan, the company that reports the top sellers to "Billboard" magazine. Find this week's rankings of albums (and artists), their rankings last week and two weeks ago, as well as how many weeks they've been on the charts.

Oboe/Bassoon: International Double Reed Society

http://idrs.colorado.edu/

The International Double Reed Society is composed of 4,000 oboe and bassoon family players, makers and fans from 45 countries. Its home page offers a newsletter, a survey and links to other music sites.

Perfomance Concert Tours Database

http://www.quest.net/performance/toursearch

Find out which artists are on tour by using the Performance Concert Tours Database Search Screen, where guests can search the database using the artist name, date and venue. Oddball links include one to an ongoing fictional murder investigation and the "worst of the Web."

POP-i Music Magazine

http://www.popi.com/

Offering reviews (every one with an audio sample), interviews, riff of the day and a "most irritating" sound file, this e-zine leans toward the alternative side of rock.

Anil Prasad's Innerviews

http://www.innerviews.org

Anil Prasad's Innerviews revolve around "the world's most interesting and innovative musicians." Prasad, a Canadian journalist who claims more than 150 musician interviews, provides personal profiles and reviews here.

Progression

http://www.gold.net/users/ex14/

Articles, features, interviews, reviews, images and sounds on culture, music and the arts are featured at Progression, a monthly e-zine. Poetry magazine Tandem and the Ambler art gallery are incorporated into this site.

The Progressive Rock Site

http://prog.ari.net/prog/

Progressive rock is celebrated here. Browsers will find a definition of the nebulous term, concert reviews, interviews, sound samples and discographies. The extensive site also includes resources for musicians, links to newsgroups and upcoming concert information.

QLD Music Magazine

http://www1.design.net.au/qld/

QLD Music Magazine offers this comprehensive list of Australian music-related information. Browsers can check out the QLD's gig guide, music library, news and listings of pubs and clubs in South East Queensland, or link to home pages of Australian musicians here.

Rockweb Interactive

http://www.rockweb.com/rwi/

The Rockweb Interactive site is a comprehensive rock fan page with information on artists and

a2z EDITOR'S CHOICE

SonicNet

http://www.sonicnet.com/

Chat with your favorite rock star or join in a cybercast through the "sonicore" of SonicNet, where a plethora of music-related topics are only as far away as your modem connection. From hip-hop to hard-rock, the offerings are vast and ever-changing. Reviews of records, live shows, and videos are refreshed frequently, as are longer features on bands like the Boredoms, and books like "A Pot Smoker's Guide to Film and Video."

It's a rock 'n' roll virtual circus, what with all the links to bands, labels, magazines and music resources. Concert listings, sound and video clips, and too much more to list round out the site: Plug in, turn up, and check it out.—*Reviewed by Julene Snyder*

bands. Includes music news, musician inter-views, critical reviews of albums, access to audio files, a user survey and much more.

SonicNet

http://www.sonicnet.com/

SonicNet features music reviews, concert listings, sound and video clips, opinion pieces and live chats with rockers and rappers. Visitors also will find features like "action ready singles," travel and photo exhibits. See Editor's Choice.

Sound World

http://www.soundworld.hl.com.au/

Located in Newcastle, Australia, Sound World of-fers its collection of CDs for sale over the Internet and keeps customers informed about develop-ments in the music world at this site. Australian music fans can discover unsigned and local bands as well.

Strobe Magazine

http://www.iuma.com/strobe/

Strobe Magazine, an online rock music publica-tion, features articles, columns and music re-views. An online classified advertisement entry form is also available.

Top Hits Online

http://www.softdisk.com/comp/hits/

See what other "netizens listen to while slaving away at their computers"—Top Hits Online asks people to vote each week for their favorite new song and then posts the results. Visitors can also view other charts such as country and interna-tional charts.

Tokyo Rockin'

http://www.iijnet.or.jp/tko.rockin/

Nippon Television Network in Japan explores the music scene in Tokyo at this graphic-rich site. Vis-itors will find music charts, monthly party news and tips on where to find Japanese records in America. In Japanese or English.

VH1-derland

http://www.vh1.de/

This German page about the music video network VH-1 features music news, interviews, photos, charts and concert dates. Most information is pre-sented in German.

VH1 Main Screen

http://vh1.com/

Before you pick up the clicker and dial in the VH1 cable network, check its home page for news about featured artists and highlights from the dai-ly schedule. Stop by to talk with other VH1 view-ers in chat areas or let the network know what you think about its play list.

XLr8r Magazine

http://www.xlr8r.com/

Get off your couch and dive into the scene—the music and rave scene—with XLr8r magazine. Back issues, including full-text articles, are ar-chived here. Review the culture and news of the techno and house music scene, including feature issues on drag queens and mental abuse.

RECORD LABELS
AND PRODUCTION

INDEPENDENT LABELS

Allegro

http://www.teleport.com/~allegro/

Allegro distributes independent classical music, as well as nostalgia, blues, country, bluegrass, world music, special effects and military march-ing band recordings. This page offers sound bites, catalog listings and new release guides.

American Gramaphone Records

http://www.amgram.com/

American Gramaphone, a recording company de-veloped by Chip Davis of Mannheim Steamroller, promotes the musical works of Davis and his in-strumental band, providing album overviews, press releases, tour dates and biographical infor-mation.

Artist Access

http://www.artistaccess.com/cdaudio/artistaccess.html

Artist Access introduces the work of independent recording artists by using the Internet and direct mail. Find a list of artists and their CDS, an inex-pensive CD sampler and a calendar of live perfor-mances.

Avalanche Records

http://www.bonaire.com/avalanche.html

The Avalanche recording label provides informa-tion here on its artists, including concert tour dates. Visitors will also find an online ordering option for recordings.

Bonaire Communications

http://www.bonaire.com/

This promotional site provides information about Bonaire and Avalanche record labels and their re-spective artists. Visitors can sample and order music by the likes of Saga, Gene Loves Jezebel, Gerry Rafferty and more.

Caulfield Records

http://www.acton.com/bernie/

Caulfield Records specializes in alternative music bands; browsers to the company's page can lis-

ten to some of its bands' songs, read about up-coming releases and review the complete catalog of available music.

DawgNet

http://www.sfm.com/dawgnet/

Unplugged music fans will find a best friend in DawgNet, which begs visitors to click on the Guide Dawg and begin a tour of its "100% Hand-made Acoustic Superhighway." Check out Dawg TV, Dawg Trivia, the Daily Bone, acoustic disc news and more.

Deluxe

http://ultraviolet.com/uvr/deluxe/

San Francisco-based Ultra Violet Recordings pro-motes the music of Deluxe via this (somewhat) of-ficial page. Find a discography featuring audio clips and critical reviews.

Diffusion I Media0000

http://www.cam.org/~dim/index.html

Diffusion I Media provides news and information on composers, festivals and CDS from the empre-intes DIGITALes and SONARt CD labels. An order form is included. In French and English.

ECM Records

http://www.ecmrecords.com/

Independent label ECM Records has been pro-ducing and distributing cutting edge jazz titles for a quarter of a century. Check out their new releas-es, their catalog of titles and tour dates for ECM artists at this site. Select and order music online.

Etiquette Records pages

http://www.w2.com/et.html

Etiquette Records specializes in music of the 1950s from the Northwest. Here, fans can order an anthology of the Fabulous Wailers, a Sonics collection and a Christmas album.

Welcome to Extreme

http://www.xtr.com/extreme/

International label Extreme searches the globe to present "unique and interesting, diverse and ex-citing music." Here browsers will find ordering in-formation, sound samples and artist news.

4AD: The Eyesore Database

http://www.maths.monash.edu.au/people/rjh/music/eyesore/eyesore.html

Influential indie record label 4AD's roster of artists ranges from ethereal mood setters Cocteau Twins to twisted geek rocker Frank Black. This exhaustive archive offers in-depth information about 4AD's releases, including song and performer lists, inter-views and displays of distinctive album art.

Go! Discs Home Page

http://www.godiscs.co.uk/godiscs/

Go! Discs is a British recording label offering a broad spectrum of music. Visit this commercial

Web site to find out about the company and its artists, including Portishead and the Trash Can Sinatras. Includes biographies, photos and downloadable sound files.

Go Kart Records pages
http://www.w2.com/gokart.html

Go Kart Records is an alternative music label, offering titles from bands like Berserk, Buttsteak and Sexpod. Browsers can order CDS online or send a message to various artists.

Heyday Records
http://www.iuma.com/Heyday/

Heyday Records, an independent record label in San Francisco, features artists such as Buck Naked and the Bare Bottom Boys, Steven Yerkey and Connie Champagne. Its site includes liner notes, background on the company and photos and information on the artists.

Indie Front by Bystander
http://charlemagne.uwaterloo.ca/

Independent bands are the focus of the Indie Front page and the e-zine it features. Articles about business, music, distribution, personnel and networking for independent bands are included.

Irdial-Discs
http://www.ibmpcug.co.uk/~irdial/w31.htm

Take a random journey through the site of Irdial-Discs, an English music label, where you're never really sure where you are or how you got there.

Kereshmeh Records: Persian Classical, Folk and New Music
http://www.kereshmeh.com/

Fans of Iranian music will find a catalog of Persian classical, folk and new music here. Kereshmeh Records offers online ordering and posts a list of stores that carry its label.

Matador Records Central
http://www.matador.recs.com/

Thumbing their collective noses at much of the music industry, Matador Records presents a highly irreverent site about its indie label. Oodles of information includes artists like Liz Phair, Pavement and Guided by Voices, as well as other features. See Editor's Choice.

Metalblade Records
http://www.iuma.com/Metal_Blade/

Bands like Mental Hippie Blood, Galactic Cowboys and Skrew are the focus at the Metalblade Records site. Here visitors can learn about new recordings and tour information for a variety of metal bands.

MusicBase
http://www.musicbase.co.uk/music/

Music fans can follow the news and sounds issuing from European record labels here. The site also includes an online magazine, Blues and Soul, and a sound archive.

New Albion Records
http://newalbion.com/

At this promotional site, New Albion Records, based in San Francisco, provides information about the company, new releases, titles, artists, tours and ordering.

Noiz Boiz Production
http://www.gate.net/~noizboiz/

Alternative music fans can download the sounds of Noiz Boiz Production artists here. The south Florida-based label attempts to bring together independent musicians, producers and multimedia artists.

Omnium Recordings
http://www.omnium.com/pub/omnium/

"You could say we like world music that rocks," writes Omnium Recordings here. The Minnesota-based label provides sound samples of its artists here, along with a full catalog of its recordings.

Parasol Records
http://www.cu-online.com/~parasol/

Read about and order indie music from the Parasol Records Home Page, where visitors can link to the main catalog or to offerings from the Urbana, Illinois-based label, order online or link to other musical sites.

Quagmire
http://www.iuma.com/Quagmire/

Quagmire, an independent music label, provides information about its artists and music at this site. Visit here for downloadable sound files, lyrics, discographies, and more.

Racer Records

http://www.racerrecords.com/

The independent record company Racer Records says "we only put out music we truly love." It cuts folk rock, experimental pop and some freeform jazz recordings. Visit for over 70 sound files, information on the label's free sampler and interviews with its artists.

Rage Records Music Catalog

http://www.w2.com/rage.html

Rage Records presents a variety of information about the artists on their label here, including People Without Shoes and Treacherous Human Underdogs. Browsers can order CDS or e-mail artists through this site.

Resonance Records

http://www.netcreations.com/resonance/

Resonance Records offers online ordering from its mega-catalog of new and used recordings. Includes a virtual listening booth, popular label information, and scads of available titles.

Schizophrenic Recordings/Vindaloo Productions Home Page

http://www.rust.net/~vindaloo/

This commercial home page cranks out bios, pictures and sound samples of bands associated with Michigan-based Schizophrenic Recordings and Vindaloo Productions. Includes an online order form visitors can use to purchase recordings by bands like Evolution Noise Slave and Carnival of Souls.

Subpop Wompus Hunt

http://www.subpop.com/

Subpop, the little record label that spawned Nirvana, promotes its artists and recordings here. Visitors can read about bands which might just be the next big thing, download discographies and order online here.

Ultra Violet Recordings

http://ultraviolet.com/uvr/

Ultra Violet Recordings, a San Francisco-based electronic music publisher, maintains this site for artist listings and an online catalog. Visit here for its showcase of groups.

Uprising Records Home Page

http://www.cen.uiuc.edu/~khoury/uprising.html

An independent label based in Ann Arbor, Michigan, Uprising Records markets and distributes new releases from their own and other selected labels. Visit this page to browse the online catalog, find out how to purchase selections, or read about artists and their upcoming tours.

World Anthem Recordings

http://www.worldanthem.com/worldrec/

World Anthem Recordings, a Philadelphia-based, musician-owned recording label, claims to be "the first label built entirely for the Net." Visitors can check out information on the company and its bands, including Witzend.

MAJOR LABELS

BMG Classical Music

http://www.classicalmus.com/

At this promotional site BMG Music presents its classical music collection, with information about its recordings, selections, music news, and the latest releases.

Disney.com

http://www.disney.com/

International entertainment corporation Disney packs its home page with cartoons, games, catalogs and just plain fun stuff. Includes links to all Disney subsidiaries, including the Disney Channel, Walt Disney Records and its worldwide network of family theme parks.

Geffen Records Inc.

http://www.geffen.com/

Rock music fans can wade through promotional copy and publicity photos about their favorite recording artists at the Geffen/DGC home page. Get updated reports on new releases or search for artists' home pages from this site.

MCA Records: AMP

http://www.mca.com/mca_records/

AMP, sponsored by MCA Records, presents information about the label's artists, sound bytes, music news and more.

MCA/Universal

http://www.mca.com/

Entertainment mega-corporation MCA/Universal, parent company of Universal Pictures, Putnam Berkeley Publishing, Winterland Productions and many others, maintains this promotional site. Visitors will find links to subsidiary companies and an online tour of Universal Studios theme park in Southern California.

Philips Media

http://www.polygram.com/

Entertainment giant Philips Media, representing such companies as PolyGram and DefJam Records and such music groups as Bon Jovi and the Cranberries, maintains this promotional site. Visitors will find links to its extensive family of subsidiary media organizations.

PolyGram Online

http://www.polygram.com/index.html

PolyGram Records Inc., a major music recording label with film and video production studios, maintains this multimedia site. Visitors will find audio samples, video clips, release information on new music and films, promotional contests and a basic company profile.

Reprise Records Home Page

http://www.repriserec.com/

Reprise Records offers this enormous collection of pages on its artists, bands and album compilations. Visitors can also read current music industry news and press releases, enter competitions, hear song clips or link to other music sites.

Rhino Records

http://pathfinder.com/
@@OQnHDwUAnOUUmsK@/Rhino/

Rhino Records' online catalog provides categorized listings of the label's offerings. Visitors can access information about recordings from genre and era categories.

Sony Music Online

http://www.sony.com/Music/MusicIndex.html

Sony Music promotes its artists' latest releases and posts tour dates here. The entertainment giant is home to a variety of recording labels, including Columbia, Work, Epic and Legacy. Visitors will find video information, sound and video clips, and a product catalog.

Sony Music Online: Artist Info

http://www.sony.com/Music/ArtistInfo/ArtistInfo.html

Sony Music Online offers plenty of details here on its artists and new releases. Visitors can also take a virtual tour of the label's site.

Sony Music Online: Featured Artists

http://www.sony.com/Music/FeaturedArtists.html

This Sony Music promotional page is loaded with news, sounds and images from the company's pop-music canon. Visitors can check in on such artists as Luther Vandross, Mariah Carey, and the Indigo Girls here, or consult the lineup of scheduled chat sessions.

Sony Music Release Schedule

http://www.sony.com/Music/NewReleases/NewReleases.html

At this Web site you can check out the release dates for all the newest music on the Columbia, Epic, Legacy, and Sony Classical labels, plus artist and tour information.

Sony Online

http://www.sony.com/

Sony Corp.'s Web server provides pointers to the entertainment and electronics giant's many subsidiaries. Visitors can access information about Sony musical artists, movies, television shows, electronic products and more. Includes a link to Sony's Tokyo Web site.

The Vault

http://www.sony.com/Music/TheVault/TheVault.html

Sony Music promotes its artists and new releases on this extensive site. Visitors will also find North American tour schedules, sound files, video clips and an archive of every tape and CD the company still manufactures (although you can't buy them from this site).

Virgin Records

http://www.vmg.co.uk/

The United Kingdom's Virgin Records offers information on new releases and "hot" recording news, links to featured sound and video tracks, and a calendar of gigs.

Artists from Warner Bros. Records

http://www.iuma.com/Warner/html/artists.html

On this promotional site, Warner Brothers Records offers audio files, discographies and information about its artists, including Van Halen, Madonna, Prince, R.E.M., and Neil Young.

Warner Bros. Records

http://www.wbr.com/

Warner Brothers Records Inc. maintains this site for information about its musical artists. Visit here for discographies, biographies and recording information for a variety of contemporary performers.

Warner Bros. Records

http://www.iuma.com/Warner/

The gargantuan Internet Underground Music Archive hosts this taste of Warner Brothers. Get the latest details on Warner artists, as well as interactive promos for bands like Van Halen.

STUDIOS

Omega Productions

http://www.webcom.com/~omegatx/

Based in Dallas, Texas, Omega provides production services for the recording, television and movie industries. Visit the company's Web site to review its 23-year award-studded history, its production capabilities and strengths, and its miscellaneous services.

Paisley Park Studios

http://www.bitstream.net/paisleypark

Take a virtual tour of Paisley Park Studios, the production facility owned by the artist formerly known as Prince. Photos, floor plans and equip-

ment lists are featured along with rental rates for those who need a place to plug in.

SHOPS, SALES, AND SERVICES

A Cappella: Primarily A Cappella

http://www.singers.com/

Primarily A Cappella celebrates and sells vocal music here. Visitors can join an online buying club and browse through a list of over 300 a cappella recordings. The site also includes reviews, news about a cappella competitions, profiles of groups and links to related sites.

AcuTab

http://www.acutab.com/

AcuTab is a small publishing company specializing in banjo and bluegrass tablature books. Visitors will find music news, book descriptions, music files and ordering information.

Allegro

http://www.teleport.com/~allegro/

Allegro distributes independent classical music, as well as nostalgia, blues, country, bluegrass, world music, special effects and military marching band recordings. This page offers sound bites, catalog listings and new release guides.

Audio Related Internet World Wide Web & FTP Sites

http://www.qnx.com/~danh/info.html

Audiophiles cruising the Net can stop by the Audio Related Internet World Wide Web and FTP Sites that is updated monthly. Check in on the activities of the Acoustic Society of America and such sites as the Carver Corporation.

Bargain Finder agent prototype

http://bf.cstar.ac.com/bf/

Andersen Consulting's BargainFinder searches online for the best prices on music albums of your choice. Simply enter artist and title names, and let the search engine provided shop major Web retail outlets to obtain the cheapest price.

Cdworld

http://cdworld.com/

CDworld features over 100,000 compact disc titles and music videos. Visitors can browse through staff recommendations, sale items, or search for select items by artist, title or label—then order online.

Deterrent Tour Manual

http://www.islandnet.com/~moron/deterrent/tour_gd.html

Musicians working to book their own tours can download a list of contact names in Canada and the United States from this page. The site also includes a European list, in German only.

Emusic Home Page

http://www.emusic.com/

Emusic is an online music search and ordering service. Search for music by artist, title, song, or year and order from this site. New release and top seller indexes are also available here.

Guitar: The Holy Grail

http://www.vvg.com/

Guitarists who yearn for vintage guitar may find it at Virtuoso Vintage Guitar. Here, visitors can shop online by downloading sounds and images of classic guitars for sale. The company also posts a stolen instrument list.

H&B Recordings Direct

http://www.hbdirect.com/

This "online magazine" from H&B Recordings Direct offers classical and jazz recordings on CD. It includes a comprehensive catalog with a search function, ordering information and links to other music sites.

Hands On Music, Inc.

http://www.w2.com/hands.html

Hands On Music, Inc. offers the innovative idea of tunes designed specifically for the driving experience. Find out how to order these series of sounds to make your cruising more enjoyable.

Internet Music Review Service

http://www.monsterbit.com/IMRS/

Browsers needing a bit more information before hitting the CD aisles will find hundreds of music reviews here. The extensive site is maintained by a team of four writers and includes reviews posted to the newsgroup rec.music.reviews.

Internet Rockhouse

http://www.rockhouse.com/

The Internet Rockhouse caters to musicians seeking a presence on the Web. Includes a description of services, pricing information, free classified music listings, music repositories and e-mail service packages. Fans can access images, sounds and bios of listed groups.

Lark In The Morning

http://www.mhs.mendocino.k12.ca.us/MenComNet/Business/Retail/Larknet/larkhp.html

Founded in 1974, Lark In The Morning is a service specializing in hard-to-find musical instruments, sheet music and instructional materials. This support site includes the service's catalog, online ordering, articles and news and links to its retail shops in Seattle, Washington and Mendocino, California.

Hal Leonard Online
http://www.halleonard.com/

Music publisher Hal Leonard promotes its publications and products through online catalogs via this site. Find sheet music, instruction books, videos, software and more.

Musi-Cal
http://concerts.calendar.com/

Music comes alive on the Musi-Cal Web site which features up-to-date information about live music around the world. Users can add information or search for concert dates through an online database.

Music Bookstore, University of California
http://www.book.uci.edu/music.html

The University of California at Irvine bookstore presents information on its music products, mostly jazz and classical. The bookstore's product listings are searchable.

Music Boulevard
http://www.musicblvd.com/

Music Boulevard features more than 145,000 CDS and cassettes in every genre—from rock to classical. "Backstage Pass" members receive special discounts and access to additional music resources.

Musicians Network Home Page
http://www.halcyon.com/spotter/mnet.htm

The Musicians Network Mission seeks "to offer a means for networking and mutual support to musicians and people in the music industry." The organization's home page introduces members, points to Internet resources of interest and highlights professional news and events.

Music Machines
http://www.hyperreal.com/machines/

Some think music that isn't plugged in just isn't worth playing, and Mike Perkowitz, author of this enormous site of electronic music information, is obviously among them. Mike guides synth music lovers through purchasing the right equipment for their needs, with contact information for manufacturers and specs for many different instruments.

Music Scene International
http://www.musicscene.com/

Music Scene International is an online shopping service for enthusiasts of all musical genres. Visitors can search by artist or label, previewing audio selections which can then be ordered online.

Oasis Duplication™ Inc.
http://www.oasiscd.com/

Oasis Duplications, a Maryland-based CD and cassette duplication house, posts this guide to music product marketing. Find step-by-step assistance making master recordings, designing graphics, manufacturing saleable dups and promoting the finished product.

On Site Entertainment Inc.
http://custwww.xensei.com/ose/

On Site Entertainment Inc., provides links to entertainment industry information and resources. Visitors can browse through listings and link to record labels, recording studios and other professional service providers.

Onyx Music and Books
http://www.mindspring.com/~onyxpet/onyx.html

Browsers can buy books and music from this online store. Onyx discounts the Billboard Top 100 and titles on The New York Times bestseller list. It is based in Atlanta and provides some links to Atlanta sites.

Opcode Systems
http://www.opcode.com/

The home page of Opcode Systems, Inc. offers browsers a wealth of information about the company's many software products for composing, editing, recording and performing music. Visitors can check out product descriptions, view software demos, read press releases or find out about Opcode employment opportunities.

Pepper Music Archive
http://www.jwpepper.com/

The Pepper Music Network stocks printed music for a wide range of uses, from the home to the classroom to the church. A music resource center here contains a library and links to other music-related sites, including the Pepper National Music Network.

Resonance Records
http://www.netcreations.com/resonance/

Resonance Records offers online ordering from its mega-catalog of new and used recordings. Includes a virtual listening booth, popular label information, and scads of available titles.

Rock Mall
http://www.rockmall.com/

Rock Mall pulls the plug on interactive music, jamming this site with polls and reviews for visitors to participate in. Musically challenged? Try some brain-twister trivia questions or do a little shopping while you're visiting.

Sound Wave
http://soundwave.com/

Sound Wave creates and maintains Web pages for people in the music business. Visitors can wander through its clients' pages here, which range from recording studios to artist agencies to bands. The site also includes employment information.

Sound World
http://www.soundworld.hl.com.au/

Located in Newcastle, Australia, Sound World offers its collection of CDS for sale over the Internet and keeps customers informed about developments in the music world at this site. Australian music fans can discover unsigned and local bands as well.

Starwave Online
http://www.starwave.com/

Stylish electronic publisher Starwave Corp. provides detailed information on its CD-ROM products and wildly popular Web creations here. Visitors can link to such Starwave Web sites as ESPNet SportsZone, Mr. Showbiz, Ticketmaster Online and Outside Online.

SWR Home Page
http://www.primenet.com/~swr/

Hand-crafted bass amplifiers and preamps are the premier offerings of SWR Engineering, manufacturer of premier systems for bass guitarists. View product images, read the company newsletter or take advantage of product specials.

That CD Place
http://www.epix.net/homepage/cdtape

That CD Place, a music store in Binghampton, New York, maintains this site featuring its online catalog. Visit here to browse and order directly from its alphabetical listing of titles. Accepts Visa, Mastercard, and Discover credit cards.

Ticketmaster Online
http://www.ticketmaster.com/

Visit Ticketmaster Online to find out about upcoming concerts and other events or and read news about performers and venues all over the U.S. An online mall provides information about tickets and merchandise users can order by phone.

USA New Gear Price List
http://www.princeton.edu/~casey/newgear.html

This site compiles listings of market prices for electronic musical and professional audio equipment. Also here: links to other Internet locations offering similar musical gear pricing information.

Wa Nui Records

http://planet-hawaii.com/wanui/

Wa Nui Records is a music shopping service that offers records and CDS produced and recorded in Hawaii. Visitors can order from an impressive list covering all genres and musical styles.

Washburn International

http://www.washburn.com/

Located in Vernon Hills, Illinois, Washburn International promotes its product catalog of guitars, basses, banjos and mandolins, plus offers product information from SoundTech, Mapex and Oscar Schmidt. Check out the instruments online and look into buying one at a dealer near you.

SOFTWARE

Cakewalk Music Software

http://www.isvr.soton.ac.uk/People/ccb/Cakewalk/

This unofficial Cakewalk home page presents the company's line of sequencers and other music software packages, with product information, links to support services, demos and pointers to related resources.

The Csound Front Page

http://www.leeds.ac.uk/music/Man/c_front.html

The Center for New Music and Audio Technologies hosts this site, which features information on the Csound electronic music program. Includes downloading information, access to documentation and links to other electrosonic resources.

MIDI Archive FTP Site

ftp://ftp.ucsd.edu/midi/

Browsers can download MIDI related software, scores and documents from this anonymous FTP archive. The archive is maintained by a member of the rec.music.synth Usenet newsgroup.

Opcode Systems

http://www.opcode.com/

The home page of Opcode Systems, Inc. offers browsers a wealth of information about the company's many software products for composing, editing, recording and performing music. Visitors can check out product descriptions, view software demos, read press releases or find out about Opcode employment opportunities.

VIRTUAL MUSIC ARCADES

Bad Habits Music

http://www.w2.com/bad.html

At Bad Habits Music, a shop in The World Square virtual mall, visitors can get more information about and send messages to a label's artists, as well as order CDS online.

Big Bamboo

http://www.realitycom.com/bamboo

Big Bamboo is a one-man recording project run by jack-of-all-musical-trades Selwyn Schneider. Visit this site to sample the London-based musician's work. Also here: links to the Internet Music Review Service and the Cerberus Digital Jukebox.

Big Bro Media Home Page

http://www.cyber.nl/bigbro

Big Bro Media of the Netherlands designs and maintains music and entertainment Web sites. This home page includes listings on labels, artists, releases and raves, as well as news and information on Big Bro and rave/techno music.

Classics World

http://classicalmus.com/

Classics World is a multimedia Internet service providing pictures, information and sound files from its classical music CD catalog. Visit here to enter a free CD contest and listen the music of Bach, Beethoven and other classical composers.

---

a2z EDITOR'S CHOICE

MTV Online

http://www.mtv.com

Slicker than a California freeway after heavy rains, MTV's virtual home lets fans link to text from the "Week in Rock," gaze at images of their favorite VJs and rock stars, learn about Tabitha Soren's hair-coloring secrets (joke!) and generally get their fill of the MTV they so desperately crave. Gossip, tour dates, buzz clip,s and chart listings are among the musical offerings, but (this being MTV), there are plenty more peripheral items to devour as well.

From the "Real World" to "Road Rules," the Beach House to "Squirt TV," there's a whole lot more on the music channel than mere music. Why, heck, you can learn how to vote all by yourself ("Choose or Lose"), join "Yack Live" in order to be publicly humiliated in front of millions of TV viewers, and generally devote yourself to living vicariously through the accomplishments of other, more talented people. There may even be some information about actual bands and real music videos buried in there somewhere.—*Reviewed by Julene Snyder*

The Dark Side

http://www.dnx.com/vamp/

The webmaster of this page describes it as "my area to experiment in HTML and my hobbies and interests." Included are home pages devoted to band Siouxsie and the Banshees and the Gothic scene, an Adobe Photoshop-fueled graphics gallery, and links to various 'zines.

HitsWorld Music Charts Online

http://www.hitsworld.com/

HitsWorld offers access to top music hits from across the United States, around the world and across the Internet. Visitors can play the HitPicks Charts Game or vote for their personal favorites to be included in the Personal Charts section.

Hyperreal

http://hyperreal.com/

The Hyperreal site explores alternative culture, music and expression. Here visitors can access the rave culture archives, duck into music resources on techno and ambient music and link up to some e-zines. Includes a section on alternative drugs.

The Internet Nightclub

http://www.memcore.com/nightclub/

The Internet Nightclub is a collection of articles on music and nightclub culture. Visitors will find photos, videos, downloadable music, games and contests here.

Internet Underground Music Archive

http://www.iuma.com/

The Internet Underground Music Archive (IUMA) provides music fans with various ways to discover new music. IUMA matches listener preferences with search capabilities and allows visitors to download audio clips and read detailed information about all kinds of musical groups.

Jukebox

http://sirius.com/~mega/metal/jukebox.html

Mega's Jukebox is a no-frills site offering downloadable audio or .au files of full-length songs. Musical offerings here are geared toward the heavier side of American rock 'n' roll, with such bands as Alice In Chains, Guns 'n' Roses, Jimi Hendrix, Nine Inch Nails and The Red Hot Chili Peppers.

Kaleidospace

http://www.kspace.com/

Kaleidospace distributes works by independent artists and musicians via the World Wide Web. Among the areas presented are art studio, interactive arena, music kiosk and screening room.

MIZIK Home Page

http://www.unik.no/~robert/mizik/mizik.html

Dedicated to furthering the musical listening range and education of net users, the MIZIK Home Page connects visitors with sound files of some unusual musical genres, such as African or Brazilian music and folk songs. Visitors can check out an amazing variety of sound files, find out where to order such music and much more.

MTV Online

http://mtv.com/index.html

MTV Online features a vast repository of news, music and video reviews, a merchandise site and animation samples. Includes programming schedules and job listings as well as information on how to become further involved with all things MTV. See Editor's Choice.

Musicians On the Internet (MOI)

http://www.oasiscd.com/www/MOIhome.html

This "virtual listening booth" features short descriptions of bands that play a variety of musical styles, from punk rock to world music and jazz. Also here: album cover artwork and song samples from featured bands, plus links to music-related Web sites.

Music Previews Network

http://www.mpmusic.com

Hear and read about new music releases from the world of rock, jazz and country among other genres at the Music Previews Network. Browse an online artists' listing and listen to tunes by downloading clips or using RealAudio software.

Songs FTP Site

ftp://ftp.luth.se/pub/sounds/songs/

Visitors can download popular tunes from a plethora of bands from AC DC to ZZ Top at the Songs FTP Site. Downloads are logged at this European FTP server.

Streetsound e-zine

http://www.streetsound.com/zone/

Visitors to the Streetsound e-zine can check into the music arcade, click to the DJ emporium or try door number three for entertainment. Dance music of all kinds—techno, hiphop, house and more—is the focus here, with links to a Red Light District as well as a game room and online gallery.

TRAX*USA

http://www.traxusa.com/

TRAX*USA offers guided tours through a collection of music-oriented site collections that compose this "domain where Life, Liberty, and the pursuit of Happiness is paramount." Subject matter is organized together in "villages" such as the New Media Cafe or Fresh Trax.

Virtual Radio

http://www.microserve.net/vradio/

Tune in to the Virtual Radio Home page for "user-definable music broadcasts." Browsers can select songs and download radio-quality broadcasts of entire cuts from the band's master DAT. The bands lean toward the obscure side of the indie roster.

PERSONAL HOME PAGES

Note: In this section sites are alphabetized by author's last name where applicable.

Alf-Christian Achilles

http://liinwww.ira.uka.de/~achilles/

An assistant to the Informatics in Science and Engineering chair in the Department of Computer Science at the University of Karlsruhe, Germany, Mr. Achilles' personal home page features his curriculum vita, pointers to university pages and links to computer science resources.

Hans-Martin Adorf

http://ecf.hq.eso.org/staff/hmadorf.html

Meet Hans-Martin Adorf, a data analyst scientist at the European Southern Observatory in Germany. His page features contact information.

Anant Agarwal

http://cag-www.lcs.mit.edu/~agarwal

Anant Agarwal, an associate professor in the MIT Laboratory for Computer Science, provides information on himself and his projects, as well as links to other laboratory pages.

Alpha Moonbog

http://www.unm.edu/~colanut/alpha.html

Landing parties looking for a little lunacy won't be disappointed with this quirky posting. See Editor's Choice.

The Alsop Review

http://www.hooked.net/users/jalsop/

Northern California poet Jaimes Alsop shares his own work and work that inspires him here. Find contemporary poetic offerings, plus a list of links, including pointers to Internet tools, humor and job search resources.

Aaron Anderson's Home Page

http://www.netaxs.com/~aaron/

Aaron Anderson's personal Web page contains links to "Mac Net Journal," Unique Editions and the Bob Marley home page.

Eve Astrid Andersson

http://www.ugcs.caltech.edu/~eveander/

Eve Astrid Andersson proclaims that her dreams have been fulfilled and she has finally made it to The Uselessness of Pi and its irrational friends. A senior at Cal Tech majoring in Mechanical Engineering, Eve links visitors to "interesting places and The E Files."

Arachnaut's Lair

http://www.webcom.com/~hurleyj/home.html

Jim Hurley's personal home page, the Arachnaut's Lair, features samples of his electronic musical compositions, Web page designs and information about breeding tropical fish.

Susan Hayes Archer

http://www.metronet.com/~sarcher

Susan Hayes Archer's personal home page describes her work as a computer consultant. She provides links to various sites useful to Internet wanderers and links to her favorite Internet pages.

The Armory Home Page

http://www.armory.com/

The Armory, a house in Santa Cruz, Calif., with a revolving roster of inhabitants, is managed by a self-admitted geek who runs a Web server and allows users complete freedom in creating their pages. A sampling includes purity tests and deepthought.

Bill Arnett

http://seds.lpl.arizona.edu/billa/arnett.html

The home page of Bill Arnett of San Jose, Calif., provides contact information, personal tidbits and an index to the Web pages he's designed, most of which are related to astronomy.

Michiel B.'s Home Page

http://www.astro.uva.nl/michielb

Meet Michiel B., whose interests include astronomy and photography. Visitors to his home page can follow links to a few of his favorite Web sites.

David A. Bader

http://www.umiacs.umd.edu/~dbader

A computer science student at the University of Maryland posts his technical reports here. He also posts links to related research on the Internet and his department at the university.

Scott Banister's Home on the Web

http://www.cen.uiuc.edu/~banister/scott.html

Libertarian and engineering student, Scott Banister, invites visitors to peruse his personal home page.

Jim Bartlett

http://cdsweb.u-strasbg.fr/people/jb.html

Jim Bartlett of France's Observatoire de Strasbourg maintains this personal page with little more than his contact information.

Oleg Bartunov

http://www.sai.msu.su/~megera/

Visitors to the personal home page of Oleg Bartunov, a researcher at Sternberg Astronomical Institute, Moscow University, can read about his interests, which include yoga, drinking juice and the rock band Genesis.

Jim Baumgardner

http://www.coil.com/~jbaumgar

Jim Baumgardner, a student research assistant in the Physics Department at Ohio State University, maintains this personal home page with information about his interests, work, research and links to various sites.

Joe Baxter

http://lemur.stanford.edu/~jbaxter

An electrical engineering Ph.D. student at Stanford University, Joe Baxter offers his personal home page here. Read about Joe's research and publications, view his results and "ramblings," or link to some of his favorite spots on the Web.

Dave Beckett Home Page

http://www.hensa.ac.uk/parallel/www/djb1.html

Dave Beckett, an editor of "Internet Parallel Computing Archive" based at the University of Kent at Canterbury, England, maintains this personal home page. Visit here for his career highlights, research and publication listings, and favorite World Wide Web links.

---

a2z EDITOR'S CHOICE

Alpha Moonbog

http://www.unm.edu/~colanut/alpha.html

Landing parties looking for a little surface lunacy won't be disappointed with this quirky posting from Garth, better known as Colanut around the University of New Mexico's Department of Medicine. Begin with a look at who is "Running Nek-ked Around the House." Or if streaking is a fad you'd rather forget, check out Schwarzenegger. He's talking to a skull and it's talking back! Those curious about the best drive-through Mexican restaurants in Albuquerque won't be left in the lurch, nor will fans of the musical group Satan's Pilgrims, who headline the Haunted Page of Rock. Given the site's name, of course there's a nod toward sci-fi, but links to Hong Kong movie sites and other Exotic Ports o' Call prove just as alien. Be sure to pick up a souvenir before blasting off — there's a load of free stuff to choose from. Sorry, though, no lunar rocks.—*Reviewed by Sean McFadden*

Contents:

Back by popular demand: Running Nek-ked Around the House. A computer drawn book about a childhood game.

The Colanut Totems I Need art show. Original paintings and gallery

Being Stephen King

http://www.isisw3.com/sking/

Meet Stephen Kings from around the world and enjoy their stories of mistaken identity. See Editor's Choice.

A. Rosina Bignall

http://lal.cs.byu.edu/people/bigna.html

A research assistant at Brigham Young University's Laboratory for Applied Logic, A. Rosina Bignall provides contact info, her resume and pointers to a few of her favorite sites.

Daniel Bleriot

http://elite.calvacom.fr/

Daniel Bleriot, a resident of France, posts links to art, film and computer-related sites which are to his liking. Find announcements of local Paris theater and music events as well.

Boarding House

http://www.ultranet.com/~lynliss/landlord.html

Ol' Lady Lynliss' Boarding House is an elaborate and creative collection of personal pages. House rules are lenient, but everyone must keep beer in the fridge.

Axel Boldt's Home Page

http://math-www.uni-paderborn.de/~axel/

University of California at Santa Barbara (UCSB) mathematics graduate student Axel Boldt dishes up his personal home page here. Visitors can peruse info on Boldt's research, political opinions and thoughts, or check out his index of computer-related links.

Tyler Bourke

http://cfa-www.harvard.edu/~bourke

Tyler Bourke, a predoctoral fellow at the Harvard-Smithsonian Center for Astrophysics, offers links from his personal page to a variety of astronomy, and Australian sites.

Martien Brander

http://huizen.dds.nl/~martienb

An economics researcher at Leidan University, Martien Brander, dishes up his personal home page here. Read all about his education and research interests or link to a large collection of his favorite Web sites, including a link listing employment information for economists.

Jim Browne

http://www.ncsa.uiuc.edu/SDG/People/jbrowne/jbrowne.html

Jim Browne, a Mac programmer at the National Center for Supercomputing Applications, serves up this home page to chronicle his professional projects and personal interests. Find a telnet application, network programming, Mac Traceroute and Led Zeppelin.

Martin Burkhead

http://astrowww.astro.indiana.edu/personnel/burkhead

On this staff bio page, meet Indiana University astronomer Martin Burkhead and review his research interests. Visitors will find the scientist's photo, contact info, and an e-mail link.

Maxime Burzlaff

http://www710.univ-lyon1.fr/~burzlaff/

Maxime Burzlaff's home page includes information about his studies in computer science and artificial intelligence at Lyon University in France. The page includes links to some of his favorite Web sites. In English and French.

Debby Armstrong Buse

http://www.ucalgary.ca/~darmstro

This personal home page provides information and pointers that reflect its maintainer's interests. Includes links to information about Calgary, Alberta, and the surrounding area, skiing information, genealogy tools and links to various women's resource pages.

Robert Calliau

http://www.cern.ch/CERN/People/Robert/PersonalData.html

A Belgian born engineer currently providing hybrid computation expertise to a company in Switzerland, Robert Calliau lays out his life story at this highly personal Web page. Experience his ups and downs from his birth to the present.

William H. Calvin

http://weber.u.washington.edu/~wcalvin/

This personal home page contains listings of the books and articles of William H. Calvin. Includes synopses of the author's works on the human brain and evolution, as well as links to related resources.

Carrie's Crazy Quilt

http://www.mtjeff.com/~bodenst/page1.html

Carrie's Crazy Quilt houses a collection of links to "incredible places to go and things to do on the Net," with an emphasis on Oregon-based Web pages.

Castle Gormenghast

http://manor.york.ac.uk/top.html

Richard G. Clegg dishes up his personal home page here, replete with pages on his work, scribblings and fun, including a wide variety of pointers to interesting places to visit on the Web.

Brian Chaboyer

http://skyc.as.arizona.edu/~chaboyer/

Maintained by a University of Toronto astronomy researcher, this home page provides a variety of personal and academic information links. Visit here to view research papers about galactic globular clusters, dwarf galaxies and other stellar phenomena.

The Chagger

http://www-bios.sph.unc.edu/~chags

The Chagger, a personal home page, offers a variety of "things to stimulate your pineal gland." Visit here for links to sports, cultural and travel tidbits.

Christina's Home Page

http://www.mit.edu:8001/people/cdemello/home.html

Christina DeMello, a technical analyst at Oracle Corp, provides personal and professional information here. Also find a list of colleges and universities worldwide, a list of various airlines' 800 numbers, and a link to the MIT home page.

Nathan Chronister's Home Page

http://www.bucknell.edu/~chronstr/

Nathan Chronister has collected some pictures from his photo album to illustrate one of his unusual hobbies, ornithoptopy—the art of modeling aircraft with flapping wings. Plenty of other topics are also discussed, including religious satire.

Stefano Cobianchi's Home Page

http://www.cs.unibo.it/~cobianch/index.html

This personal home page lists the vital statistics, likes and dislikes of the maintainer of "Know Your Exits," a home page dedicated to the television show "The X-Files."

Matthew Colless

http://msowww.anu.edu.au/~colless/colless.html

This personal home page offers up astronomy-related articles published by the site's creator. Visitors also will find information on contacting the page's author, along with astronomy-related Web links.

John Collier

http://www.astro.washington.edu/collier

John Collier's home page links to other pages detailing his interests. Follow the pointers to John's fantasy baseball league, his personal portrait, and his office at the University of Washington's Astronomy Department.

Daniel W. Connolly's Web Presense

http://www.w3.org/hypertext/WWW/People/Connolly/

Daniel Connolly's personal home page explores his professional life as a staff member of the World Wide Web Consortium. Links to software he has contributed to the Internet community are included.

Deven T. Corzine

http://www.tics.org/deven/

This personal home page, still under construction when we visited, contains a variety of "random" and "really random" links. Visit here to access its "cool" site of the day, read a collection of "Dilbert" cartoons and then go away.

Anne Cowley

http://www.dao.nrc.ca/DAO/STAFF/cowley.html

Meet Professor Anne Cowley of Canada's Dominion Astrophysical Observatory. Her scientific research interests include X-ray astrophysics, variable stars and stellar populations in galaxies. A list of her publications is available here.

Dennis Crabtree

http://cadcwww.dao.nrc.ca/staff/crabtree.html

This home page provides professional information about Dennis Crabtree, an employee of the Canadian Astronomy Data Center. Includes e-mail, phone and fax information.

Jim Croft

http://155.187.10.12/people/croft.jim.html

The personal home page of botanist Jim Croft contains personal and professional information. Includes a detailed summary of his career, publications and projects.

Crossing the Line

http://hamp.hampshire.edu/~jtsF93/

Tabb Sullivan's page has links, entertainment, and more. See Editor's Choice.

Crow's Nest

http://www.cs.dartmouth.edu/~crow

The personal home page of Preston Crow, computer junkie, Lego addict and "Star Trek" fanatic, offers a vast collection of links related to Crow's personal and professional life. Browsers can find information on various educational institutions, technical corporations, and political issues.

Cycle Vietnam

http://www.mindspring.com/~jrolls/cv.html

At Cycle Vietnam, visitors will find a detailed travelogue written by a bicyclist who, with a travel group, rode 1,200 miles from Hanoi to Ho Chi Minh City. The account is enhanced with pictures and maps.

The Dan&Eric Home Page

http://www.danampersanderic.org/

The Dan&Eric page describes itself as "a nebulous, autonomous, continuing, network-facilitated art collective, initiated in 1988 as an independent think-tank." An invitation for browsers to score mass-murderers for style, homemade pizza recipes and poetry are among the offerings.

Dan's Upper Flat

http://www.acsu.buffalo.edu/~tasman

Dan gets aglow over Buffalo, then writes his name in the snow. It's a tradition, he says. Visit this University of Buffalo student's personal page and find out what other traditions he upholds.

Dano's Home Page

http://www.magi.com/~dano

Meet Dano, a lead singer in Ottawa-area bands for the past 15 years. Sound clips from his current band, Junkfiend, are featured on his home page, along with pictures and a calendar of club dates.

Olivier Danvy

http://www.daimi.aau.dk/~danvy

Olivier Danvy features his resume and links to copies of his publications from his personal home page. The site includes information about his current projects along with addresses and phone numbers where he can be reached.

Henry Dardy

http://www.cmf.nrl.navy.mil/CCS/people/dardy.html

This personal home page provides information about a chief scientist at the Naval Research Laboratory in Washington, D.C.

Dazhdbog's Grandchildren

http://sunsite.oit.unc.edu/sergei/Grandsons.html

At his personal home page, this physics grad student posts his postulations on the mythical and historical origins of the Russian people. Additionally, find musings on poetry, music and day to day happenings in the author's life.

John December Index

http://www.december.com/john/

The John December Index tells you more than you thought you needed to know about this Ph.D. candidate and Internet guru. Included in this electronic resume are his doctoral dissertation, his "hyperbio," and details about his work.

Dave DeLaney's Home Page

http://enigma.phys.utk.edu/~dbd

Dave DeLaney, a researcher in theoretical physics, offers background information about the "noticeable phenomena of UseNet." This personal page also includes links to a variety of topical newsgroups.

Lambert Dolphin's Resource Files

http://www.best.com/~dolphin/

Santa Clara, Calif., physicist Lambert Dolphin's home page contains a resume as well as an essay about his "search for purpose and meaning in life." Also included are Web links, adventures, and essays about the Bible.

William C. Donlon

http://www.hooked.net/users/wcd/

At medical professional William Donlon's personal Web page, browsers can check out his family, profession, and link to some of his favorite Web sites.

Bryan Dorland

http://bdc.nrl.navy.mil/

Bryan Dorland, a researcher at the U.S. Naval Research Laboratory, provides personal and professional information. Visit here for a collection of his published articles.

Raymond Doty

http://weber.u.washington.edu/~rtdoty

This home page, maintained by two students at the University of Washington, Seattle, offers personal information, links to online science journals, and a collection of university and local resources. Includes recreation and entertainment links.

Doug's Library

http://www.astro.washington.edu/ingram/books.html

On this personal page, Doug Ingram presents a list of his favorite sci-fi books and links to full-length book reviews. Also find an author index, links to other book-related pages and an e-mail address with user responses.

Tim Doyle Home Page

http://www.doit.com/tdoyle

Tim Doyle's home page features a vast database of genealogy resources along with pointers to some of the best genealogy sites on the Web.

Nikos Drakos

http://cbl.leeds.ac.uk/nikos/personal.html

This page from the staff directory of the Computer Based Learning Unit at the University of Leeds in Great Britain spotlights Nikos Drakos. Find details of his interests, work groups and publications.

Louis-Dominique Dubeau

http://step.polymtl.ca/~ldd

Louis-Dominique Dubeau's personal home page includes social, spiritual, political, and technical features, personal interests and other links. In English with some French.

Geoff Duncan

http://king.tidbits.com/geoff/geoff.html

A self-professed "cyber-geek," Geoff Duncan edits two electronic newsletters. Read the rest of his biographical sketch at this site.

EgOWeB

http://edb518ea.edb.utexas.edu/felipe.html

Felipe Campos' EgOWeB site features—you guessed it—lots of information about Campos. He also posts links to Texan, Latino and multimedia sites.

Guenther Eichhorn Home Page

http://hea-www.harvard.edu/~gei/geichhorn.html

Gunther Eichhorn's personal home page features information about his hobby of flying in aerobatics competitions, as well as details about his work as a project manager on NASA's Astrophysics Data System. The site includes photos of gliders and a Pitts Special S-2A.

---

a2z EDITOR'S CHOICE

Crossing the Line

http://hamp.hampshire.edu/~jtsF93/

Ever wondered what it would take to get you to cross the line? A computer science and biology student at Hampshire College, Tabb Sullivan has "crossed over" and invites all to follow on his heels. Some of Tabb's penetrating probes into the facts of life provide answers to these compelling questions: why fans need only look at Mariah Carey's face to see her bum, who shoots up chicken bouillon, and which are the best uses for a disembodied human head. Those with a scientific bent will enjoy a tutorial on reading DNA gels. Others may prefer the maggots page, Tabb's favorite links, or a dawn-to-dusk timelapse of a cityscape. Entertainment includes a kickline of five dancing monsters and a baked turkey that gets up off its platter for a stroll. None of these features seems so bad? Check out the blasphemy page, starring Beavis.—*Reviewed by Sean McFadden*

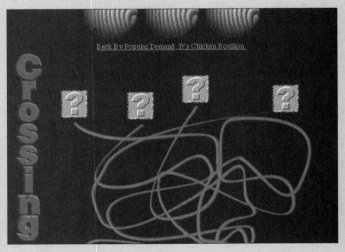

Victor Eijkhout

http://www.math.ucla.edu/~eijkhout

Mathematics professor Victor Eijkhout's home page features his work and play interests. The author of a book about TeX, Eijkhout details his leisure activities and preference for Apple computers, along with applicable links.

Elsewhere

http://werple.mira.net.au/~margaret

Meet Margaret, an Aussie in cyberspace. Find photos of Margaret skiing and scuba diving, and links to some of her favorite sites.

Neil Enns' Home Page

http://www.brandonu.ca/~ennsnr/

The home page for Neil Enns includes details about him and some of the Web pages he has authored.

Lisa Ensman

http://astrowww.astro.indiana.edu/personnel/lisa

Lisa Ensman, a research associate in astronomy at Indiana University, has set up this personal page providing information on herself and her work. This page includes links to the HTML Astronomy Classroom Project (HACP) and the Indiana University Astronomy Department home page.

Eric's SCUBA Page

http://diver.ocean.washington.edu/

Eric's SCUBA Page, a home page from an oceanography student with a serious interest in scuba diving, focuses on Puget Sound, Wash., and the Pacific Northwest. Visitors will find reviews of dive sites, maps, charts, and equipment advice.

Judy Fabian

http://www.uvm.edu/~jfabian/

Judy Fabian, an employee of the University of Vermont, presents personal and professional information at this home page. Visit here to learn about the interests and activities of this cardiology laboratory technician.

Marat Fayzullin

http://www.cs.umd.edu/users/fms/

This home page, set up by a computer science student at the University of Maryland, contains a hypertext copy of the student's resume, plus links to video gaming sites and Russian information repositories on the Internet.

First Brian of 96

http://streams.com/brian/

Visitors can view a movie of Brian, tell him how worthless their lives are, read his bits of wisdom, play his Piercing Mildred game, and otherwise occupy themselves at this personal home page.

Debra Fischer

http://ucowww.ucsc.edu/~fischer/home.html

A University of California graduate student in astronomy details her research interests here. Visitors can also link to her interactive "Ask An Astronomer" site from this page.

Jeff Fox

http://www.dnai.com/~jfox

The owner of Ultra Technology introduces his company and offers tidbits concerning his personal life at this site. Find company info, links to free files and a pointer to the U.S. Aikido Federation.

Robert French

http://suif.stanford.edu/~rfrench

Robert French is the coauthor of the SUIF Compiler System. His home page provides particulars of his curriculum vita as well as his interest in square dancing, amateur radio and hydroponics. The page also links to his academic niche at Stanford University.

Wolfram Freudling

http://ecf.hq.eso.org/staff/wfreudli.html

Wolfram Freudling of the Space Telescope, European Coordinating Facility maintains this personal home page with contact information.

Jack F. Gallimore

http://hethp.mpe-garching.mpg.de/~jfg

This personal Web page for Jack F. Gallimore at the Space Telescope Science Institute includes contact information and links to some of his favorite astronomy-related and recreational Web sites.

Anu Garg's Home on the Web

http://www.wordsmith.org/anu/index.html

On his personal home page, Anu Garg offers links to his pages on word games and words. Visitors can also read about his hobbies and download his resume. In his spare time, Garg answers Web-related questions in "Ask Dr. Web."

Kai Garlipp Personal Home Page

http://wwwdb.informatik.uni-rostock.de/Kai

Published by a computer science student at the University of Rostock, this personal page describes Kai Garlipp's work-related endeavors. Includes links to Perl programs and Web sites maintained by the university and its Computer Science Department.

Amy Goodloe Home Page

http://www.best.com/~agoodloe/home.html

Amy Goodloe, moderator of women-only mailing lists and director of the San Francisco-based Women Online, posts her personal page here. Visit to learn about Ms. Goodloe and access her collection of favorite World Wide Web links.

Mike Grady

http://ewshp2.cso.uiuc.edu/

Here, Mike Grady, a senior research programmer at the University of Illinois Computing and Communications Services Office, chronicles his technical projects.

Lamont Granquist's Home Page

http://www.hyperreal.com/~lamont

Leading off with quotations about freedom and political philosophy, this site provides links to the Webmaster's home page, his test server and a "Hyperreal Drugs Archive."

Carolyn Stern Grant

http://hea-www.harvard.edu/~stern/cgrant.html

Carolyn Stern Grant is a programmer for the Astrophysics Data System project in the Center for Astrophysics at Harvard. Her personal home page includes work and personal information, with links to the ADS abstract service and catalogs.

Philip Greenspun

http://www-swiss.ai.mit.edu/philg/philg.html

Philip Greenspun, a graduate student at the artificial intelligence lab at MIT, provides a personal home page with photos of flowers, one of his hobbies. He also has a photo archive of himself and his friends, his writing samples and travel links.

Patrick Groeneveld

http://olt.et.tudelft.nl/~patrick

Delve into the home and professional lives of a Dutch electronic engineering researcher at this personal home page. Visitors to this site can investigate a range of topics from the author's current work projects to a list of bands he dislikes most.

Robert Gruendl

http://www.astro.uiuc.edu/~gruendl/

Robert Gruendl, a graduate astronomy student at the University of Maryland, stocks his personal home page with contact and personal information, curriculum vitae and a listing of articles he's written. Includes links to the home pages of the university and its Astronomy Department.

Bill Grunfelder

http://acwww.bloomu.edu/~wjgrun

Bill Grunfelder, a Computer Information Systems major at Bloomsburg University, serves up his personal home page here. Check out Grunfelder's resume, job description, and the usual pointers to favorite Web stuff.

Jean-Louis Halbwachs

http://cdsweb.u-strasbg.fr/people/jlh.html

Jean-Louis Halbwachs of France's Observatoire de Strasbourg maintains this page offering contact information.

Howard Harawitz

http://brooknorth.com/welcome4.html

Howard Harawitz, author of the hypertext editors, HTML Assistant and HTML Assistant Pro, is the proprietor of a software firm specializing in Windows programming. His home page has more information about himself and his professional life, as well as contact information.

Michael Hauben's New and Improved Domain

http://www.columbia.edu/~hauben/index.html

Meet Michael Hauben, a computer science graduate from Columbia University in New York. Visitors to his page will find that Hauben enjoys music and works as an editor for the "Amateur Computerist Newsletter."

The Haven

http://www.wordsmith.org/

A.Word.A.Day is featured on this home page, where visitors can check out today's word, yesterday's word, any day's word. The site also includes pages on the rock band Barefoot Serpents and the social group the Zets, as well as the summer movie schedule for Schenley Park in Pittsburgh.

Andre Heck

http://cdsweb.u-strasbg.fr/~heck

A French Observatoire Astronomique employee, Andre Heck serves up this personal home page with a wealth of employment and academic info. Check out Andre's curriculum vita and thematic bibliography, or link to some of his favorite recreational sites.

Frank Hecker

http://access.digex.net/~hecker

This is the personal home page of Frank Hecker, a self-described Internet all-around techie who loves poetry and wants to provide easy access to Web sites. Among other things, visitors here can learn about this systems engineer's professional interests and publications.

Richard M. Heinz

http://astrowww.astro.indiana.edu/personnel/heinz/

Richard M. Heinz, a member of Indiana University's Physics Department, maintains this personal page with professional information and details about his research specialties.

Susan Hill

http://arch-http.hq.eso.org/staff/shill.html

Susan Hill, archive operator at the European Southern Observatory, maintains this personal home page with her contact information.

D.W. Hoard's Personal Home Page

http://www.astro.washington.edu/hoard

Astronomer D. W. Hoard's personal home page includes downloadable songs by Big Dead Fish, original poetry, and links to astronomy-related sites, as well as favorite music, art and film Web pages.

Sake J. Hogeveen

http://stkwww.fys.ruu.nl:8000/~hogeveen/hogeveen.html

Meet "yet another bearded nerd" (his words) at the home page of this Dutch software engineer working at the Astronomical Institute of Utrecht University.

Andras Holl

http://ogyalla.konkoly.hu/staff/holl.html

Andras Holl is a computer systems manager at the Konkoly Observatory in Hungary. His picture, publications and curriculum vita are posted at this site.

Richard Hook

http://ecf.hq.eso.org/staff/rhook.html

Richard Hook is a data analysis scientist at Germany's Southern European Observatory. Find his contact information on this staff profile page.

House of Distraction

http://www.blarg.com/~b/fyard.html

The House of Distraction is an online copy of Brian's and Jeff's house in Seattle. Here, the duo welcomes visitors to tour the basement, bathrooms, kitchen, upstairs landing and other areas, and kindly ask that shoes be removed before entering. A warning: The house is not entirely safe—security of mind and body is not guaranteed.

Howie's Page

http://www.tapr.org/~n2wx/hghome.html

Featured at the home page of Howard Goldstein are resources for people who have lost pets. Also find pointers to Howie's Packet Radio Web Pages and to a selected "weird site."

Peter W. Huber

http://khht.com/huber/home.html

Peter W. Huber's personal home page contains professional information on the attorney's practice in telecommunications markets and antitrust policy. Includes listings of his publications and links to various legal sites related to his specialty.

Lester Ingber's Code and Reprint Archive

http://alumni.caltech.edu/~ingber/

Lester Ingber's Code and Reprint Archive contains computer programming code information and provides visitors with details about the page's author and his commercial consulting work.

Inside Jason's Office

http://george.lbl.gov/cgi-bin/jason/cave-cam

Want to find out why this fellow is transmitting pictures taken inside his office onto the Web? The answer and the current picture are available at this site.

Gerard Jasniewicz

http://cdsweb.u-strasbg.fr/people/gj.html

The home page of astronomer Gerard Jasniewicz contains minimal information: voice, fax and e-mail addresses. In French.

Greg Jones (WD5IVD) Page

http://www.tapr.org/~wd5ivd/gjhome.html

Greg Jones, a doctoral student from the University of Texas, maintains this Web page with links to amateur radio groups and a list of his publications.

Matthew S. Jones

http://www.rit.edu/~msj2134

Matthew S. Jones serves up his resume and links to his favorite Web sites at his personal home page.

Justin's Links from the Underground

http://www.sccs.swarthmore.edu/jahall/

A Swarthmore College student, Justin Hall says this is a home page that shuns the fuddy-duddy. Underground links, a Philly radio station and info on creating your own home page are featured here.

Don K.'s Home Page

http://ucowww.ucsc.edu/~kory/home.html

Visit the personal home page of this astronomer-in-training to check on the progress of his current research projects. Ponder his consideration of a career change, read his resume or link to sites he considers "interesting/fun/worthwhile."

The K Page

http://werbach.com/home.html

Stumble into Kevin Werbach's home page and after sampling some of his herbal tea, turn to the page of stuff where Kevin features wacky, witty and wonderful tidbits he has encountered on the Internet. Check out his "Bare Bones Guide to HTML."

Carl W Kalbfleisch

http://rampages.onramp.net/~cwk

An employee of an Internet provider in Texas posts links to the sites he has created, mostly for Lutheran churches. He also posts links to his favorite sites, which run the gamut from science fiction to Christian. He offers a biographical sketch, too.

Yasusi Kanada

http://www.rwcp.or.jp/people/yk/home-orig.html

This site contains links to various information relating to Yasusi Kanada's research, databases and conference reports. Contact and personal information are also available here. Some pages are in Japanese.

Mikko Karttunen
http://www.physics.mcgill.ca/WWW/karttune

Mikko Karttunen, a student at McGill University in Montreal, Canada, offers visitors a home page with links to McGill, its Department of Physics, various publications, and Mikko's favorite physics servers.

Eugene E. Kashpureff
http://www.halcyon.com/ekashp/eugene.html

A tow operator, Webslinger, bitsmith and Cubmaster, Eugene E. Kashpureff has a lot of talents, including raising a family, whose photo he features on his home page.

Neal Katz
http://www-hpcc.astro.washington.edu/faculty/nsk

Washington University offers information on its Research Assistant Professor Neal Katz here. Visitors can check out some of Nick's research interests or peruse his resume.

William C. Keel Home Page
http://crux.astr.ua.edu/keel/billkeel.html

William C. Keel, a researcher in the Department of Physics and Astronomy at the University of Alabama, maintains this personal home page. Visit here to learn about his research activities and credentials, and find archives of scientific articles and publications.

Dan Kegel
http://www.alumni.caltech.edu/~dank

Dan Kegel's personal home page includes computer-related links and pointers chosen by the author, including an HTML verification service, an ISDN page, an Ethernet page, a guide to publishing product information on the Web and e-mail info.

Ken's Lame Home Page
http://joplin.ahpca.hpc.org/atwell/

A graduate student at Tufts University in Boston posts his "lame" home page with his hobbies, his studies and his favorite links, including his brother's page for chemistry majors.

Abed Khooli's Home Page
http://darkwing.uoregon.edu/~alquds/

Meet Abed Khooli, a Ph.D. student in physics, at the University of Oregon. His home page provides links to a variety of sites, some offering Islamic and Arabic information.

Kitty the Cat
http://www.dao.nrc.ca/DAO/STAFF/kitty.html

Kitty, a resident guard cat, is the subject of this personal home page. Career and contact information for the cat is available here, as well as a list of research interests which include small birds and mice.

Eto Kouichirou's Home Page
http://andro.sfc.keio.ac.jp/eto/

The personal home page of Eto Kouichirou contains a collection of his photographs and essays, along with links to some of his favorite sites on the Web.

Uwe Kunzmann
http://www.cimttz.tu-chemnitz.de/uku/uku.html

This is a personal home page for Uwe Kunzmann, a student at the Technical University of Chemnitz-Zwickau in Germany. Visitors will find a resume, photo, biographical info and links to favorite sites.

Kisho Kurokawa
http://www1.sony.co.jp/KUROKAWA/

Kisho Kurokawa, an architect, details his books, theses, works and projects on his personal home page. A curriculum vita and profile of his company are also included.

Cameron Laird
http://starbase.neosoft.com/~claird/home.html

Professional programmer Cameron Laird invites visitors to his home page for an update on his personal interests, favorite online periodicals, and pointers to a host of daily newspapers with a Web presence.

George Lake
http://www-hpcc.astro.washington.edu/faculty/lake

This page is the Web home of George Lake, an astronomy professor at the University of Washington at Seattle. Visitors will find his resume, publication credits and research information.

Larry's Home Page
http://www.clark.net/pub/lschank/home.html

This librarian's personal home page contains pointers to numerous selected sites and Web guides. Includes Internet learner's pages, links to government document servers, shopping sites and professional librarian resources.

Last Homely House
http://www.bu.edu/~aarondf

Aaron Fuegi's site is a cyber rest stop for the Web traveler. See Editor's Choice.

James Lattimer
http://sbast3.ess.sunysb.edu/~lattimer/plan.html

The personal home page of James Lattimer contains information on his astronomical research pursuits, academic publications and a list of his graduate assistants.

Ron Lawrence's Home Page
http://atlantis.austin.apple.com/people.pages/rlawrence/ron.html

A higher education account rep for Apple computers, Ron Lawrence opens his home page with links to Apple-related sites. Favorite links quickly follow—some fun, some serious.

T. Joseph W. Lazio
http://astrosun.tn.cornell.edu/students/lazio/lazio.html

A student in Cornell University's Astronomy Department hosts this personal home page. Visitors will find research and programming documents.

Brett Lemoine
http://atheist.tamu.edu/~blemoine

More than you ever wanted to know about Brett Lemoine is provided at this personal home page. Read his bio, his personal philosophy and his list of ten reasons why beer is better than Jesus.

Robert Andrew Lentz
http://www.astro.nwu.edu/lentz/plan.html

This personal Web page contains an overview of Robert Lentz's areas of interest, which include astronomy, Macintosh computers, science fiction, and the Internet.

Alan Levine's Personal Home Page
http://www.mcli.dist.maricopa.edu/alan

Stop by and meet Alan Levine, an Instructional Technologist at Arizona's Maricopa Community College. Alan's interests include art, the Internet, and multimedia.

Jim Lippard's Home Page
http://www.primenet.com/~lippard/

At his personal home page, Jim Lippard features information about himself, links to Internet anti-censorship information, and pointers to the latest online issues of "Skeptic" and "The Realist" magazines.

John Lock's Home Page
http://www.mindspring.com/~jlock/home.html

This personal home page acquaints visitors with beer drinker and HTML writer John Lock. This Georgian formed the HTML Writers Guild and edits a heady Frequently Asked Questions (FAQ) listing about his beverage of choice.

David Loundy's E-LAW Web Page
http://www.leepfrog.com/E-Law/

Meet David J. Loundy, an Illinois attorney and author. Read his published work and miscellaneous legal writings, and link to some of his favorite law-related sites

Phyllis M. Lugger

http://astrowww.astro.indiana.edu/personnel/lugger

This page contains the contact data and area of expertise information of Phyllis M. Lugger, a member of the Astronomy Department at Indiana University. A link to the IU Astronomy Department is included.

The Magic Underwater Kingdom of Zooop

http://www.cea.edu/zooop/

The Magic Underwater Kingdom of Zooop features links to Web sites the Webmaster has worked on. Also find links to "favorite movies of all time" and Web art sites.

Jonathan Magid

http://sunsite.unc.edu/jem/

At his personal page, SunSITE administrator Jonathan Magid reveals his fascination with Elvis, as well as his stellar career accomplishments.

Make a Friend on the Web

http://albrecht.ecn.purdue.edu/~jbradfor/homepage/homepage.html

This interactive site spins your Web browser and lands you on some-random-body's home page. While you're there, make a friend.

Malachi's Home Page

http://www-leland.stanford.edu/~deadboy

Malachi's home page, courtesy of Stanford University, offers information about the author and his favorite radio station.

Fabien Malbet

http://gag.observ-gr.fr/~malbet/Fabien_eng.html

Meet Fabien Malbet of the astrophysics laboratory at the Grenoble Observatory in France. He studies star formations and provides links to some of the images he has examined.

James Marcout

http://cdsweb.u-strasbg.fr/people/jm.html

This site contains contact information about James Marcout of the Observatoire de Strasbourg.

Lindsay Marshall Home Page

http://catless.ncl.ac.uk/Lindsay.html

Lindsay Marshall, a lecturer for the Department of Computing Science at England's University of Newcastle upon Tyne, maintains this home page for personal and professional information. Includes links to hobby- and academic-related resources.

Ron Martini's Navy Submarine Base

http://wave.sheridan.wy.us/~rontini/ronpage.html

Unabashed submarine worship is the order of the day at Ron Martini's Navy Submarine Base. This personal home page highlights submarine resources and military news.

Todd Masco's Home Page

http://www.hks.net/~cactus/cactus.html

Visitors to the home page of Todd Masco can read a variety of personal information and link to some of his favorite Web spots. Pointers offered here include science, technology and computer-related Web sites.

Matthew and Jake's Adventures

http://www.mit.edu:8001/mj/mj.html

Matthew and Jake's personal home page details their adventures, with pictures, stories and reader mail. And they also like to surf.

Maxim's Maximal Page

http://www-scf.usc.edu/~khokhlov/

Visitors to this personal page can find out who makes the biggest shows on this planet and why the Semester at Sea program is called a "voyage of discovery." Check it out.

Dr. Robert McClure

http://www.dao.nrc.ca/DAO/STAFF/mcclure.html

Visitors can learn about the research interests and publications of astronomer Dr. Robert McClure from this home page.

Nancy McGough

http://www.magoo.com/nancy

Nancy McGough's personal home page contains personal and professional information. Includes her interests in health, vegetarianism, environmental issues and yoga.

Luis Mendoza's Home Page of Cool

http://www.astro.washington.edu/mendoza

Luis Mendoza, an astronomy student at the University of Washington, maintains his personal home page with astronomy links, his research information and instructions for creating an image map.

---

a2z EDITOR'S CHOICE

Last Homely House

http://www.bu.edu/~aarondf

Proprietor Aaron Douglass Fuegi welcomes visitors to this guest house "which shines in the midst of a beautiful woods ... just in the shade of the tall mountains" and has a history as fantastic as a tale by J.R.R. Tolkien. Offering the amenities of a hideaway retreat, the house is furnished with all the items a weary Web traveler could desire to rest and relax, or to map out exploratory excursions. In the Library and Hall of Fire find reference books, fiction and poetry. The Game Room and Audio/Visual Gallery hold diversions of all nature. The Kitchen offers recipes and other virtual refreshments, while in the Map Room, guests can plot points for future travels on the World Wide Web. Stay as long as you like and come back often. The door is always open.—*Reviewed by Sean McFadden*

Welcome to the Last Homely House

Aaron Fuegi , Proprietor

Click for beautiful full size JPEG (282K) or visit the Rivendell Image Gallery

Merkle's Home Page

http://merkle.com/merkle

Ralph C. Merkle's personal home page details his research in nanotechnology and interest in cryptography, computational chemistry, cryonics and neuroscience. A list of selected academic publications is included here.

Mike Meyer

http://lib.stat.cmu.edu/master/mikem.html

Mike Meyer, a senior research scientist at Carnegie Mellon University, presents a short home page featuring a clickable photo of himself at work. He's the founder of an electronic library of statistical software, datasets, and Internet information.

Georges Michaud

http://www.astro.umontreal.ca/membres/michaud.html

Meet a professor in the Physics Department at the University of Montreal and review his research interests in astronomy. In French and English.

Mkgray's List of Cool Stuff on the Web

http://www.mit.edu:8001/afs/sipb/project/www/html/starting-points.html

Mkgray's List of Cool Stuff on the Web attempts to cover all the bases, boasting of links composed of "everything from sex to cryptography to Star Trek." Category heads include raw information, commercial stuff, weather, audio, books, indices, and online exhibits.

Simon Morris

http://www.dao.nrc.ca/DAO/STAFF/simon.html

This personal home page contains information on Simon Morris' research interests and a list of his astrophysics publications.

Dr. Koji Mukai

http://heasarc.gsfc.nasa.gov/docs/bios/koji.html

Dr. Koji Mukai, an astrophysicist, provides contact and personal information, including his research interests and links to astronomy sites.

George Musser, Jr.

http://astrosun.tn.cornell.edu/students/musser/musser.html

George Musser, Jr. used to be a graduate student in the Department of Astronomy at Cornell University. He is now the editor of "Mercury," an astronomy magazine. His personal home page details his interests, publications, and contact information.

My Sumo Page

http://www.sfc.keio.ac.jp/~s93073no/sumo.html

Like really big guys wearing very little clothes? Then you'll like this home page devoted to Sumo wrestling. Visitors can access images, match results and other online sources of information about the sport from this personal Web page.

Michael Naumann's WWW Page

http://www.eso.org/~mnaumann

A German astronomer outlines his research, music, and travel interests at this personal home page.

Matthias Neeracher

http://www.iis.ee.ethz.ch/~neeri/

Matthias Neeracher, a Swiss integrated systems laboratory researcher, puts his personal views on politics, computers, and sports on the line at this personal home page.

Oscar Nierstrasz

http://iamwww.unibe.ch/~oscar/

Oscar Nierstrasz, a University of Berne, Switzerland, computer science professor, provides a variety of personal and professional information at his home page. Visit here for links to computer programming organizations, related texts, and publications.

Patrick Nolan

http://egret0.stanford.edu/pln

This home page contains personal and professional information about Patrick Nolan, an astronomical researcher. Among the information provided, find a listing of his published papers.

Terje Norderhaug

http://www.ifi.uio.no/~terjen

The home page of Terje Norderhaug, a media systems designer, details the directions of his career and consists of links to various articles and papers he has written for world conferences.

Günther Nowotny

http://tph.tuwien.ac.at/me.html

Ph.D. student Günther Nowotny's home page includes a black and white photo, info about his scientific work and teachings, and a variety of his favorite links.

James J. O'Donnell

http://coat.spas.upend.edu/joy/joy.html

This is a high-brow, elegant site. See Editor's Choice.

---

a2z EDITOR'S CHOICE

James J. O'Donnell

http://coat.spas.upend.edu/joy/joy.html

A professor of Classical Studies at the University of Pennsylvania in Pittsburgh, James J. O'Donnell borrows from the monastic tradition of the scrivener and librarian to post this site of electronically illuminated manuscripts. A Latin scholar who enjoys investigating "the development of Latin Christianity, with a particular emphasis on the interpretation of scripture," the professor welcomes fellow students into his private library, but also posts a public selection of readings he has compiled for past seminars. Find Boethius and Augustine well represented, both in Latin and translation. Perhaps the heady content of this site is not for everyone, but there are lessons to be learned simply in its elegant presentation. —*Reviewed by Sean McFadden*

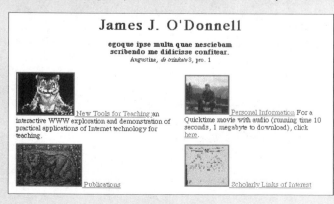

Miles O'Neal's Home Page

http://www.rru.com/~meo/

Modern-day renaissance man Miles O'Neal's personal home page reveals that the computer programmer has somehow found time to pen a number of essays, radio plays and poems. Reams of autobiographical information and favorite links also are available.

Anders Ohlsson's Home Page

http://www.it.kth.se/~ao

Anders Ohlsson posts a home page with Delphi applications, his girlfriend's photo, a PC horror story and more.

Onar's Home Page

http://www.stud.his.no/~onar/

A contemporary classical composer and writer in Norway posts his musings on systems theory and complexity on this personal page. Browsers can download a series of his articles which he is compiling into a book. In English.

Tom Paquin

http://home.netscape.com/people/paquin/index.html

Tom Paquin, creator of MoZilla, answers questions about Web authoring, browsers and his work at Netscape. A link to the Temple 'O' Pacman site heads the page.

Paul's (Extra) Refrigerator Status

http://hamjudo.com/cgi-bin/refrigerator

How do you know if a used refrigerator works? The fridge for sale at Paul Haas' duplex does. Just check out the temperatures automatically recorded on this Web page. He explains how he rigged it, and, because "every refrigerator should have at least one cartoon stuck to the door," rewards visitors with two early "Dilberts."

Paul's Hot Tub Status

http://hamjudo.com/cgi-bin/hottub

Here, you can dip your virtual toe in Paul's hot tub before deciding to take a virtual soak. Paul kindly provides this page with the tub's operational status and temperature, as well as the outside temperature. Wave to his cats and check out his refrigerator, too.

Peacefrog's Lilypad

http://www.netspace.org/~jude/

Jude S. Shabry's home page provides information on the academic and personal life of the Brown University computer science major. Includes links to her journal, lifestyle preferences and pastimes.

Jim Pendleton

http://www.astro.nwu.edu/astro/pendleton

The personal home page of Jim Pendleton, a programmer analyst at the Gamma Ray Observatory, provides a mixture of links and information about his interests. Guests can also view other pages on which Pendleton has worked.

Jacques C. Perrolle

http://www.duke.edu/~h20pipe

This home page from Jacques C. Perrolle points out the various interests of this New England resident's life, including a link to his main passion, the Boston Bruins, an American hockey team.

B. Pirenne

http://ecf.hq.eso.org/staff/bpirenne.html

Find a brief bio and contact information for a European Southern Observatory archive scientist at this site.

Poem of the Day Page

http://www.dataimages.com/poetry/

Mark Fischer makes sure you get your daily poetry fix. See Editor's Choice.

Poor House

http://floydians/ip.com/ph/

The-Apartment-Formerly-Known-As-The-Poor-House is the personal home page of Craig Bailey, former radio man, occasional actor and gainfully employed business writer. Peruse this unusual collage of links for pointers to sites related to music, the Internet, theater and more.

Charles A. Poynton's Home Page

http://www.inforamp.net/~poynton/

A digital video guru posts his articles and Frequently Asked Questions (FAQ) files at this personal home page. Learn about digital video and signal-processing technology, Macintosh computers, typography, graphic design and color theory here.

Baby Pulkka's Home Page

http://red-branch.mit.edu/~tmr/baby.html

Follow the fetal development of Zoie Alandra Pulkka with ultrasound movies and pictures offered at this personal home page. Includes parental commentary and various contests.

---

a2z **EDITOR'S CHOICE**

Poem of the Day Page

http://www.dataimages.com/poetry/

The roses may be blue but the poetry is always read at this interactive site posted by student Mark Fischer. Stop by daily for a dose of simile and metaphor contributed by readers with a touch of the bard. But be careful. You might come down with a touch of the bard yourself. Considering the number of contributors anthologized in the archive, the condition appears to be contagious. Themes explored lean toward love and pain, but pastoral and spiritual allusions receive their share of word play as well. And though most all of the poets presented are virtual unknowns, it's nice to see the career of Anonymous has yet to hit a dry patch.—*Reviewed by Sean McFadden*

The Home of Pulver.Com

http://www.pulver.com/

An Internet professional, (and Wall Street brokerage company employee), Jeff Pulver offers a page of links to his favorite spots: Internet phones, his own web magazine, stock quotes and WCBS radio in New York.

Tom Quinn

http://www-hpcc.astro.washington.edu/faculty/trq

Tom Quinn, an associate professor of astronomy at the University of Washington, Seattle, maintains this page with his personal and professional information. His curriculum vita and publications list is included.

Bo Frese Rasmussens

http://arch-http.hq.eso.org/bfrasmus

Bo Frese Rasmussens maintains this personal page with professional and personal information, as well as a Sybase interface and resources for Web tools and tricks.

David Reiss

http://www.astro.washington.edu/reiss

This page introduces browsers to David Reiss at the University of Washington's Astronomy Department. Selections include his own Internet bookmarks, FTP site listings and a link to the Astronomy Department's home page.

Prentiss Riddle

http://is.rice.edu/~riddle

Prentiss Riddle, Information Administrator at Rice University shares his thoughts on work, school and play. Includes a hotlist of links to his favorite Web pages.

Gill Ritchie

http://www.dcs.qmw.ac.uk/~gillian

Gill Ritchie, a doctoral student in the Computer Science Department at Queen Mary and Westfield College in the United Kingdom, offers a brief bio and a pointer to personal Web pages.

Road to Nowhere

http://sp1.berkeley.edu/nowhere.html

Gene Cutler's site has trivia, games, and more. See Editor's Choice.

Bernadette Rogers

http://www.astro.washington.edu/rodgers

The personal home page of astronomer Bernadette Rogers contains numerous links to astronomy and NASA resources, as well as links to Bernadette's friends' pages and favorite sites.

Eric Carl Rosen

http://www.cse.ucsc.edu/~eric

A computer engineering Ph.D. candidate at the University of California at Santa Cruz subjects visitors to his "boring life" at this personal home page.

Colin Rosenthal

http://bigcat.obs.aau.dk/~rosentha

Dr. Colin Rosenthal, a post-doctoral research fellow at Stanford University, provides his professional information at this personal home page.

Stephen Rothwell

http://www.canb.auug.org.au/~sfr

This personal home page discusses Advanced Power Management issues related to personal computers. Links to technical information, including industry-standard specifications information and a white paper entitled "Standardized Battery Intelligence," can be accessed.

Joe Russin

http://www.cfin.org

Joe Russin likes birding, teaching, and raising goats. He delves into these topics here.

Tony Sanders

http://www.bsdi.com/hyplan/sanders.html

Contact information for Berkeley Software Design, Inc. employee Tony Sanders is presented here along with a brief biography and professional information.

Kevin Savetz's Page o' Stuff

http://www.northcoast.com/savetz/savetz.html

Kevin Savetz's Page o' Stuff contains his collection of recently published articles about the Internet, along with personal and family information. Includes his Frequently Asked Questions (FAQ) lists and links to favorite Web sites.

---

a2Z   EDITOR'S CHOICE

Road to Nowhere

http://sp1.berkeley.edu/nowhere.html

A fourth year graduate student in the Molecular and Cell Biology Department of the University of California at Berkeley, Gene Cutler frequently gets asked the oddest things. An accommodating fellow, he answers inquiries into how many books his friend Bob has read, whether it's raining or not, and if that's a freshly severed head Mary's holding. Don't ask Gene about sheep. Go to the games instead, where you'll have "so much fun it makes you sick." Post a line or two to the collective literary adventures on the mass poetry and fiction pages, stop in to see Juliette the DADA oracle and let her reveal your DADA fortune, or test your skill at finding the Spam. Control freaks will like the site's "select a color" feature and kids of all ages will appreciate the special message posted just for them. If you want to go nowhere fast and have one heck of good time on the way, turn here.—*Reviewed by Sean McFadden*

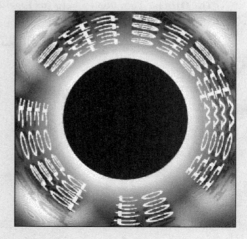

Sean's Home Page

http://www.westol.com/~speck

This personal home page includes a physical description of the author, his likes and dislikes, his resume, his hobbies, and his favorite links.

Tom Shellenberg for President

http://www.sni.net/~tshellen/index.html

Shellenberg shares his political views. See Editor's Choice.

About Pete Shipley

http://remarque.berkeley.edu:8001/~shipley/shipley.html

Visitors to the personal home page of Peter M. Shipley, a Windows system programmer in California, can read an online version of his resume or link to some of his favorite entertainment sites.

Andy Silber

http://www.astro.washington.edu/silber

Andy Silber, a student of astronomy, offers a personal glimpse into his interests—travel, biking, his electronic newsletter—and professional accomplishments.

Luc Simard

http://astrowww.phys.uvic.ca/grads/simard

Luc Simard, a researcher in the Department of Physics and Astronomy at Canada's University of Victoria, profiles his professional pursuits on this page. Research interests, publications, and a few of his favorite links are featured.

Simon's Home Page

http://sunsite.unc.edu/ses

A computer technology guru in California makes a plea for employment in the Chapel Hill, N.C.,

area via his personal home page. Review his resume and check out his progress on current projects here.

Gene Smith's Home Page

http://cassfos01.ucsd.edu:8080/hsmith.html

Gene Smith, of the Center for Astrophysics & Space Sciences/Physics Department at the University of California at San Diego, offers his professional interests and favorite links. Included are his publications, recent work, and educational background in the study of astrophysics.

Chris Smolinski's Home Page

http://www.access.digex.net/~cps

Chris Smolinski produces science and radio-related software for the Macintosh, and visitors can download demos here. This home page also provides shortwave radio pages and lots of links.

Jeff Solof

http://atlantis.austin.apple.com/people.pages/solof/home.html

Jeff Solof, a higher education sales development executive, explains his responsibilities with Apple and his role as a clergyman of the Eastern Orthodox Church. This home page includes religious links and an archive of digitized songs.

Ellen Spertus' Home Page

http://www.ai.mit.edu/people/ellens/ellens.html

Ellen Spertus, a graduate student at the Massachusetts Institute of Technology's Artificial Intelligence Laboratory, provides links to her professional and personal pages from this site.

Stark's Museum of Vacuum Cleaners

http://www.reed.edu/~karl/vacuum/vacuum.html

A part-time janitor and vacuum maintainer at the Stark's Museum of Vacuum Cleaners in Portland, Ore., "smuggled a camera inside" the museum. He posts the virtual results here, which detail one hundred years of vacuum cleaning in pictures and text.

Bob Stein

http://www.pa.msu.edu/~steinr

Bob Stein, professor of physics and astronomy at Michigan State University, provides professional and personal information on this home page. Among the resources he includes are research results, course information and links to astronomy and physics sites.

Doug Stevenson's Home Page

http://www.dougsworld.com/~doug/

Doug Stevenson, a student at Ohio State University, maintains this personal home page with contact information, details about his work, and links to some of his favorite Web sites.

---

a2z   EDITOR'S CHOICE

Tom Shellenberg for President

http://www.sni.net/~tshellen/index.html

A 43-year-old U.S. Army veteran and CPA, Montana's Tom Shellenberg believes in the American Dream and feels that he has the right formula for curing the nation's dis-ease. Author of "Balance the Budget Now & How—The Silver Lining," Shellenberg postulates two rules for helping the government find its economic footing again: 1) cut all waste, and 2) sacrifice. Unfortunately for the Republican candidate who spent the summer of 1995 traveling and speaking in the contiguous United States, his campaign never received the national exposure he needed to become a serious contender. He was forced to withdraw from the race early in 1996. Still politically active, however, and interested in communicating with like-minded citizens, Shellenberg is ever hopeful and helpful, hosting pointers to the White House, the Congress, and THOMAS, the Internet link to federal legislation.—*Reviewed by Sean McFadden*

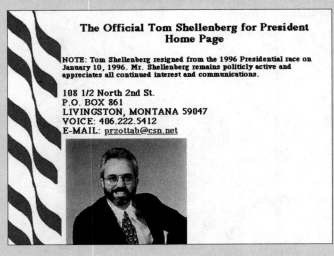

The Official Tom Shellenberg for President Home Page

NOTE: Tom Shellenberg resigned from the 1996 Presidential race on January 10, 1996. Mr. Shellenberg remains politicly active and appreciates all continued interest and communications.

108 1/2 North 2nd St.
P.O. BOX 861
LIVINGSTON, MONTANA 59047
VOICE: 406.222.5412
E-MAIL: przottab@csn.net

James Stilburn

http://www.dao.nrc.ca/DAO/STAFF/
stilburn.html

Visitors to James Stilburn's page will find he's a member of the Dominion Astrophysical Observatory in Canada. His publications and research interests are featured.

Troy C. "Stoney" Stoneking

http://tiger.olivet.edu/~tstone

This home page provides personal and professional information about Professor Troy C. "Stoney" Stoneking, director of Strickler Planetarium in Bourbonnais, Ill. Includes a list of Jungle BBS home pages and a link to the planetarium's home page.

Forrest H. Stroud's Personal Home Page

http://www.tcac.com/~neuroses/

At his personal home page, Forrest H. Stroud provides personal information, a list of favorite Web sites and sports information.

Will Sutherland

http://www-astro.physics.ox.ac.uk/~wjs

Will Sutherland, a graduate student in the Astrophysics Department at Oxford University, maintains this personal home page with information about himself and his research.

Sven's Page

http://www.hypersven.com/svenspage

Sven's Page, created by a student at San Jose State University in California, links pages that Sven (no last name) has created, his favorite sites and pointers for other Web enthusiasts.

Tanju's HomoPage

http://www.geocities.com/WestHollywood/
1068/

Tanju's HomoPage explores the life and dreams of this transplanted Southern leather daddy, who puts his dreams and loves out onto the Internet with photos, links to other gay- and leather-friendly sites and the man's own bio info.

Rachael Taylor's Home Page

http://www.census.gov/~rltaylor

At her home page Rachael Taylor provides a variety of links including business, computer, government and media.

Teen Movie Critic

http://www.skypoint.com/members/magic/
roger/teencritic.html

Roger Davidson shares his take on movies, videos, and directors. See Editor's Choice.

Thalia's Funpage

http://www.sci.kun.nl/thalia/funpage/fun_
en.html

Thalia's Funpage is packed with her favorite links organized into sections that include an art gallery, the Muppets, "Star Trek," and something intended especially for all those cow lovers out there. Also check out "the most visited page in Nijmegen." In Dutch and English.

James "Eric" Tilton

http://www.cs.cmu.edu/~tilt

James Tilton's personal home page features personal and professional information and links to a variety of sites.

Top Ten Cover Page

http://www.winternet.com/~jmg/topten.html

If your site sucks, Jeffrey Glover tells you how to bring it up to par. See Editor's Choice.

Ray Trygstad

http://xtreme2.acc.iit.edu/~trygray

Ray Trygstad, an adjunct assistant professor of computer science at the Illinois Institute of Technology, includes a personal "hot list" and biography on this home page. He also presents his resume and links to other Web sites he maintains.

Utopia: Where Reality and Imagination Coexist

http://www.hu.mtu.edu/~dabrus/

David Allan Brus gives visitors a look at his interests and resume on this sleek personal page. The site includes Brus' hot links and a list of his current projects.

Teuvo Uusitalo

http://turva.me.tut.fi/~tuusital/

Teuvo Uusitalo's home page is more of a professional than personal document. It features contact information, research and his resume. This site also provides an index to occupational safety and health resources.

Stan P. van de Burgt

http://hydra.cs.utwente.nl/~stan

A Ph.D. candidate in the Computer Science Department at the University of Twente in the Netherlands maintains this page offering personal contact information. Topical links are also provided.

Dr. Sidney van den Bergh

http://www.dao.nrc.ca/DAO/STAFF/
vandenbergh.html

Sort of an online resume, this site records the research interests and recent publications of Dr. Sidney van den Bergh, an adjunct professor at the University of Victoria.

Marc VanHeyningen

http://www.cs.indiana.edu/hyplan/
mvanheyn.html

Marc VanHeyningen's personal home page has information about his employment, computer, and Internet interests, as well as a photo.

Michael Vertefeuille

http://sprit.lib.uconn.edu/~mvertefe/

Michael Vertefeuille maintains this personal home page with information about himself, his work, hobbies, and links to his favorite sites.

Virtual Studio and Workshop

http://www.best.com/~ariel/

The Virtual Studio and Workshop is the Web home of Catherine A. Hampton. On her personal page she posts her resume, information about her newly-adopted religious faith, gallery of artwork, and a link to the Human Rights Web.

Philip Wadler

http://www.dcs.glasgow.ac.uk/~wadler

A computing science professor at the University of Glasgow introduces himself to members of the Internet community and shares some of his research interests at this personal Web site.

Carol Wang

http://www.cuug.ab.ca:8001/~wangc/carol.html

Meet Carol Leon-Yun Wang (CLW), a multimedia consultant and programmer. Visitors can read about Carol's friends and hobbies here.

Dave Wang

http://gdbdoc.gdb.org/~djw

Dave Wang's personal home page contains a hot-links page and information on the author's school, Johns Hopkins University.

Archibald Warnock

http://www.clark.net/pub/warnock/archie_
warnock.html

Archibald Warnock, a network information systems consultant in Columbia, Md., offers personal and professional information on his home page. Visitors here will also find resources related to data storage, astrophysics and bluegrass music.

Donald C. Wells

http://fits.cv.nrao.edu/~dwells

A scientist at the National Radio Astronomy Observatory has posted an annotated index of his life's work here. Links are provided to full text versions of his papers and technical reports.

Matt Welsh

http://www.cl.cam.ac.uk/~mdw24/

Monitor the work productivity of a Cornell Robotics and Vision Laboratory research assistant with the help of the live picture feed to his personal home page. Find out what Matt looks like and what he works on at this site.

Matt Westby

http://www.wadham.ox.ac.uk/~mwestby

Matt Westby directs visitors to two Web pages of his own creation. Follow links to his personal home page or to the Oxford University Juggling Club site.

What's Hot and Cool

http://kzsu.stanford.edu/uwi/reviews-m.html

This Web site's creator unveils gold mines discovered during his explorations of the World Wide Web. The page explores weird or otherwise atypical sites, and visitors can choose from a variety of indices.

Beverly R. White

http://www.tezcat.com/~wednsday/

Beverly R. White reveals her writings and Internet obsessions on her creative home page. Visitors can read the BevINTERVIEW, check her religion and spirituality hotlist or look into graphic design work at BobWeb.

---

a2z EDITOR'S CHOICE

Top Ten Cover Page

http://www.winternet.com/~jmg/topten.html

Web weavers posting home pages for pleasure, or for any other purpose, may want to consider the possibility that the sites they've mastered are "sucky." It happens ... a lot; especially if you go by the guidelines in Jeffrey M. Glover's Top Ten Ways to Tell if Your Home Page is Sucky. But don't despair. His Top Ten Ways to Improve Your Home Page offer the wayward Webmaster invaluable advice for bringing wretched postings up to par. "A grand-daddy on the Web" with over two years of authoring and user experience, Glover gives both blinking copy and ticker tape status bars a big yawn. "It was cool the first time we saw it," he explains. And the number one way to improve a home page? Simply put, "BE UNIQUE!" Obvious advice perhaps, but applicable—as are the gems in Glover's latest handout: Top Ten Ways to Improve Your Netscape Browsing Experience. Numbers 10 and one on the list: buy it and be patient.—*Reviewed by Sean McFadden*

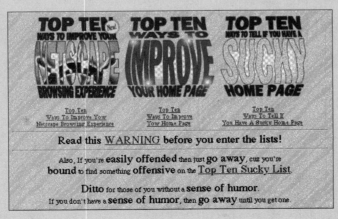

Dr. Nicholas White

http://heasarc.gsfc.nasa.gov/docs/bios/white.html

This home page, maintained by a researcher at the U.S. Goddard Space Flight Center, provides personal and professional information. Visitors will also find links to a variety of astrophysics-related organizations and resources.

Peter D. Wilson

http://astrosun.tn.cornell.edu/students/wilson/wilson.html

A Cornell University astronomy student provides details about his life, ranging from a thesis paper to photos of his pets.

Winter Cycling

http://mudhead.uottawa.ca/~pete/bike.html

This is the personal home page of Pete Hickey, a devotee of winter bicycling. Visitors will find pictures and stories of the Webmaster's experiences riding around in the cold and snow. Also, find out how he thaws his beard.

Mark Winter

http://www.shef.ac.uk/~chem/staff/mjw/mark-winter.html

Dr. Mark Winter, a researcher for the Department of Chemistry at the University of Sheffield, England, maintains this home page for personal and professional information. Visit here for Dr. Winter's career notes, research interests, and collection of links to scientific texts and publications.

Greg D. Wirth

http://astrowww.phys.uvic.ca/rsocs/wirth/home.html

The home page for the University of Victoria's Gregory D. Wirth highlights his interest in studying galaxy clusters. Enjoy his slide gallery, research papers and observation aids.

Jason S. Wiseman

http://www.mcs.net/~wiseman

Jason S. Wiseman presents his resume and background at this personal home page. He also serves up an extensive collection of links with topics ranging from computers to games and gambling to the Vatican.

Patrick Wiseman's Home Page

http://www.mindspring.com/~pwiseman/wiseman.html

Patrick Wiseman's personal page is packed with links to his kind of fun—limericks, Indigo Girls info, "Mother Jones" magazine—and useful resources for the Web-bound.

World Wide Wohlmut

http://www-csli.stanford.edu/users/kyle

Kyle Wohlmut, an administrative associate at Stanford University, serves up his personal home page here. Check out Kyle's background and link to his music, herp and beer pages, or jump to Stanford's Linguistic Department home page.

Heiner Wolf

http://www-vs.informatik.uni-ulm.de/Mitarbeiter/Wolf.html

Meet Heiner Wolf, a computer science faculty member in the Distributed Systems Department at Germany's University of Ulm. Find links related to his research interests which focus on video for the Web.

Meng Weng Wong

http://www.seas.upenn.edu/~mengwong/meng.html

The personal home page of Meng Weng Wong collects his thoughts, accomplishments and jokes for posterity. Find lots of references to student life at the University of Pennsylvania and general computer stuff.

Amos Yahil

http://sbast3.ess.sunysb.edu/~ayahil/plan.html

Amos Yahil, an astronomy researcher at the State University of New York, provides a list of scientific articles at his home page. Visit for a bibliography of reports published in physics and astronomy-related journals.

Yasushi Home Page

http://www.kinoshita.com/index.shtml

A Japanese attorney posts a brief biographical sketch and an index to legal resources on this personal page. Available in English and Japanese.

Frank Younger

http://www.dao.nrc.ca/DAO/STAFF/younger.html

Frank Younger's personal home page contains information on his research interests in astronomical instrumentation, stellar photometry and spectroscopy. Includes contact information and listings of publications.

ZaP!

http://www.armory.com/~zap

Ford's home page features information about the "hacker's" interests and links to miscellaneous sites. Photos included.

Dennis Zaritsky

http://ucowww.ucsc.edu/~dennis/home.html

Dennis Zaritsky of the Lick Observatory at the University of California at Santa Cruz provides images from his research, information on courses he teaches and recent papers. His home page also features a prototype of an educational database.

PETS AND ANIMALS

AquaLink

http://www.aqualink.com/direct/

If the gurgle of an aquarium is music to your ears, tune in to AquaLink, a site dedicated to the aquarium hobbyist. Chat rooms, tropical fish catalogs, aquatic plant catalogs, mailing lists, a help service, clip art, and a BBS make this an all-in-one site.

Aquatic Technology

http://www.actwin.com/AquaticTech/index.html

Aquatic Technology markets aquarium equipment, fish and supplies for the serious hobbyist. Includes an online catalog and ordering instructions.

The Bernese Mountain Dog Home Page

http://www.prairienet.org/~mkleiman/berner.html

Bernese Mountain dog owners and buyers will find information about the breed here. The site includes descriptions of the breed's characteristics, a photo gallery, a link to a mailing list and a Frequently Asked Questions (FAQs) file.

Castalia Llamas

http://www.rockisland.com/~casllama/cllama.html

Castalia Llamas, breeders located in the San Juan islands of Washington State, has set up this promotional page with photographs of its award-winning llamas. Visitors will find company background, and adoption and sale information here.

Cat Fanciers

http://www.fanciers.com

This site is a mecca for cat lovers. See Editor's Choice.

Cats FAQ

http://www.cis.ohio-state.edu/hypertext/faq/usenet/cats-faq/top.html

Just why does kitty do that? Find the answers in this extensive Frequently Asked Questions (FAQs) file posted by the Usenet newsgroup rec.pets.cats. The file can be downloaded in sections.

Chase Tavern Farm Alpacas

http://www.maine.com/ctalpacas

Chase Tavern Farm, an alpaca breeding ranch in Maine, welcomes visitors to its home page and offers information about its operation and animals. Visitors also can shop at its online country store.

a2z EDITOR'S CHOICE

Cat Fanciers

http://www.fanciers.com

Created originally as a private, unmoderated mailing list for announcements and discussion of the breeding and showing of felines, Cat Fanciers' mission has since evolved to include this Web site, along with an expanded purpose and audience. Still linking kitty lovers with breeders, show information, clubs and registries, the page also points to reports, articles and data files offering the basics of responsible cat care. Topics include proper nutrition, illnesses, and the importance of spaying and neutering. Anyone who's thinking of buying a pedigreed puss will appreciate the tutelage here on how to purchase and what to expect from responsible breeders. For folks who fancy felines, and even those just curious about cats, this resource is a real find that has us purring.—*Reviewed by Sean McFadden*

The Virtual Pet Cemetery

http://www.lavamind.com/pet.html

"What to do when a good friend dies?" eulogizes one owner whose pet has passed. "The only thing is to say farewell. Goodbye." And what better way to bid a fond farewell to a loyal and well-loved pet than to post a lasting tribute to his memory and the good times shared. Among the remembered laid to rest in this virtual park, find Emerson, who left behind feathered cagemates Lake and Palmer; Blackie, the Labrador that "might not be dead, but never came back"; and BurrButt, the cat who thought "Life is a Purr." Some poetic, some prosaic, some playful, others sweetly sentimental, all the postings are straight from the heart.—*Reviewed by Sean McFadden*

Cichlid Home Page

http://trans4.neep.wisc.edu/~gracy/fish/opener.html

A freshwater fish popular with aquarium hobbyists, cichlids serve as the unifying subject of this information database. Find details on the origins, care and breeding of the fish species. Links to other sites of topical interest are also featured.

Common Birds of the Australian National Botanic Gardens

http://155.187.10.12/anbg/birds.html

Visitors can do some virtual birding on this site. The Australian National Botanic Gardens in Canberra provides drawings, physical and behavioral descriptions, and calls of birds that visit its gardens. (No fair counting these cyber-spottings toward your life list, though!)

Companion Animal Rescue Effort

http://www.thesphere.com/CARE/CARE.html

The volunteers at the Companion Animal Rescue Effort in Santa Clara County, California place homeless animals into safe and loving homes. Phone support is offered to adopters, along with obedience classes and grooming clinics.

Cows Caught in the Web

http://www.brandonu.ca/~ennsnr/Cows/Welcome.html

"Everything about cows and then some" is available at this site, which asks the poser: "When a cow laughs, does milk come out her nose?" Find a guide to cows, cow trivia, portraits of bovines and links to newsgroups and commercial pages.

Diddi, The Icelandic Horse Network

http://www.centrum.is/diddi/

Diddi, the Icelandic Horse Network, maintains this promotional site to introduce its equestrian sales services. Visitors can learn about its selection of competition or pleasure horses for sale, and find links to related publications, owners associations and equipment dealers.

EE-Link Endangered Species

http://www.nceet.snre.umich.edu/EndSpp/Endangered.html

Learn about endangered species and what you can do to help. See Editor's Choice.

Equinet

http://horses.product.com/

Equine aficionados will find a stable of information on horse products and services here. The site contains listings of horses for sale, horse equipment for sale and job openings. It offers information on riding getaways, too.

Ferret Central

http://www.optics.rochester.edu:8080/users/pgreene/central.html

Ferret Central offers breeding and care information about these domesticated polecats. The site includes a medical Frequently Asked Questions (FAQs) file, a ferret photo gallery and links to many ferret organizations, including the League of Independent Ferret Enthusiasts.

Fish Information Service (FINS) Index

http://www.actwin.com/fish/index.html

FINS is an archive of information about aquariums, both freshwater and marine, tropical and temperate. Visitors will find glossaries, fish catalogs, club listings, and more.

Florida Aquarium

http://www.sptimes.com/aquarium/default.html

Cyber-tourists can explore underwater worlds at the official Florida Aquarium Web site. Find online exhibitions of the aquarium's habitats and inhabitants. The site also posts information about touring the Tampa Bay museum in person.

Harold Reynolds' Humour Collection

http://geog.utoronto.ca/reynolds/humour.html

Get your pet humor fix here. See Editor's Choice.

Horse Country

http://www.horsecountry.com/

The Horse Country site offers resources and information about horses, riding and equestrian events. Visitors will find a riders' library, sounds, images and links to information about horse care, breeds and riding equipment. There are also special links for younger and beginning riders.

Horsemen's Yankee Pedlar

http://www.thepedlar.com

The "Pedlar," based in Massachusetts, is a monthly newspaper covering all aspects and all breeds of horses and riding. The paper's Web site features articles from current and previous issues, as well as classifieds.

Hot Spot for Birds

http://www.lainet.com/hotspot/

Visitors can buy canaries, finches, parrots and other tropical birds on this site, which claims to have the largest collection of birds for sale on the Internet. The site also includes an online guide to the care of feathered friends and articles warning against caffeine and chemicals.

Houssen's Dog World

http://www.houssennet.nb.ca/dogworld.htm

Darr Houssen's Dog Training School in New Brunswick, Canada, provides information and free dog training manuals here. Dog lovers can browse this site for more information about the school, purchase training videos and add their addresses to the school's mailing list.

Kitty the Cat

http://www.dao.nrc.ca/DAO/STAFF/kitty.html

Kitty, a resident guard cat, is the subject of this personal home page. Career and contact information for the cat is available, as well as a list of research interests which include small birds and mice.

LAL Cat Archive

http://imall.com/archives/cats.html

If you're not a cat person, steer clear of this site. Cat people, on the other hand, will enjoy the page's offerings, which include images, trivia, and links to various cat-inspired pages on the Web.

LlamaWeb

http://www.webcom.com/~degraham/

LlamaWeb is designed for people who are interested in these animals for breeding. Includes veterinary information, links to publications, conferences and breed shows.

---

a2z EDITOR'S CHOICE

EE-Link Endangered Species

http://www.nceet.snre.umich.edu/EndSpp/Endangered.html

So what's the difference if another species goes extinct? Well, our own longevity, for starters. The fact is, there are few good reasons why any species should die out, and that so many are threatened suggests the threat may extend to the human race as well. Any disappearing act from a balanced ecosystem means that something or someone will bear the weight of that species' absence somewhere along the food chain. What happens to species and their respective ecosystems when there are no more tuna, tigers, pandas or parrots? What about darters, sculpins and sturgeons? Consider the implications of having no more "natural pest control," or when a species' food supply runs out. Do we really want to face the consequences of breaking the links in Nature's carefully constructed chain? It's a question worth considering and this site offers an excellent place to start. Find out what species are endangered in your area, explore existing laws and review the current political debate. Part of a larger teachers' resource for environmental education, this site welcomes all interested parties to discover more about the delicate balance of the natural world.—*Reviewed by Sean McFadden*

photo (c) John Herron

Please contact ee-link to comment on the content or organization of this page, or to suggest materials we might add.

Many users of this page responded to an on-line survey linked to this page during August. Here are the results!

Table of Contents

What's New on the Endangered Species Page

Endangered and Extinct Species Lists

Marine Fish Catalog

http://www.actwin.com/fish/species.html

The Marine Fish Catalog boasts more than 200 pictures of tropical fish. Visitors can search the entire database, browse pictorial guides to angelfish, butterfly, tangs and clownfish, and link to a freshwater fish catalog.

The National Zoological Park

http://www.si.edu/organiza/museums/zoo/homepage/nzphome.htm

The Smithsonian hosts this digital version of the U.S.'s premiere biopark. See Editor's Choice.

The Online Book of Parrots

http://www.ub.tu-clausthal.de/p_welcome.html

The Online Book of Parrots is devoted to information on parrots and parrot-like birds. Visitors will find photos, databases and descriptions of various parrot breeds.

The Pet Bird Page

http://hookomo.aloha.net/~granty

Visitors to this site will find an online guide to buying and raising pet birds. Browsers can link to pages to learn the usual price, needs and trainability for individual species. Each species page posts e-mail links to owners.

Pigs

http://www.ics.uci.edu/~pazzani/4H/Pigs.html

Visit here to find out "why raising a pig is fun" and to download audio files of pigs. This 4-H site roots around the world of swine, detailing what it takes—logistically and financially—to raise a big, fat, healthy pig.

The Pug Dog Home Page

http://www.camme.ac.be/~cammess/www-pug/home.html

Find a history and general description of Pug dogs here. Visitors can also download pictures and sounds, read health care tips and link to owners clubs.

rec.pets.dogs FAQ Homepage

http://www.zmall.com/pet_talk/dog-faqs/homepage.html

This Usenet site contains a Frequently Asked Questions (FAQs) file about dogs. An index covers veterinary information, behavior and breeding, and lists topical publications.

Reef Science International

http://www.reefscience.com/

Reef Science International distributes marine invertebrates for aquarium hobbyists. Visitors to its promotional site will find out more about the company and its captive-bred creatures.

Running Horse

http://www.webcom.com/~alauck/index.html

The Running Horse home page is a compilation of resources "of interest to horse lovers in general, and particularly those that love to watch horses go fast." Links include the latest U.S. race horse standings, the Texas Thoroughbred Association and a variety of thoroughbred racing directories.

Save-a-Pet Online

http://pasture.ecn.purdue.edu/~laird/Dogs/Rescue/

Save-a-Pet Online, a page at the Purdue Dogs site, provides a list of online organizations and rescue stories.

Sea World/Busch Gardens Animal Information Database

http://www.bev.net/education/SeaWorld/

This info database is more like a virtual activity center. Children and grownups alike can access "fast facts about animals," take an animal quiz, send zoological questions to "Shamu," or learn about building a home aquarium. A topnotch photo index and indices for classroom projects round things out.

Sea World/Busch Gardens Animal Resources

http://www.bev.net/education/SeaWorld/infobook.html

From the Sea World/Busch Gardens site, this page features an index of resources from the theme parks' Education Series. Find in-depth information about whales, manatees, dolphins, turtles, and other animal life. Plus, take a look at biodiversity, endangered species and the possibility of a zoological park career.

Something's Fishy

http://www.webcom.com/~hurleyj/fish.html

This strictly fishy business page provides tropical fish owners with instructions for building a CO_2 injection system, fish humor, a photo gallery and a look at the page's Webmaster. The site includes numerous links to other aquatic sites.

---

a2z   EDITOR'S CHOICE

Harold Reynolds' Humour Collection

http://geog.utoronto.ca/reynolds/humour.html

Pets rule, and Harold Reynolds thinks that's funny. So much so, he has compiled this light-hearted look at life in a household "run" by cats, dogs and other domestic animal lords. Chuckle along as Harold observes the universal frustrations of housebreaking a "Bad Kitty" or "Bad Dog," and nod knowingly as "Cat Rules" and "Dog Rules" examine exactly who has the upper hand in the owner-pet dynamic. Adding to the good humor, reader-contributed offerings include the article "How to Bathe Your Cat" and the Cat Brain Map which diagrams a feline's higher-function centers such as the barf and licking glands, the can opener sonar and the asthmatic person locator. Pet owners from five continents agree, Harold is right: The antics of our "domesticated" animals are funny.—*Reviewed by Sean McFadden*

Harold Reynolds' Humour Collection

If you're reading this, you aren't working! Shame on you! 8-)

Hello, and welcome to my humour collection. This page originated as a way for the net.community to get easy access to my Bad Kitty, Bad Dog, and Cat Rules lists. It has slowly expanded to include other pet humour items, and then other humour lists I've collected, compiled and/or blatantly swiped.

Awarded January 21, 1996. Check out their huge database!

Acme Pet's Cool Pet Site of the Day, June 7, 1996!

Steve's Ant Farm

http://sec.dgsys.com/AntFarm.html

The Ant Movie, a "tour de force that will make your skin crawl," is the lead attraction on Steve's Ant Farm. The site includes links to other ant hills in cyberspace and is maintained by a Washington, D.C. Web designer.

Tennessee Aquarium

http://www.tennis.org/

The Tennessee Aquarium site contains visitor information, press releases and a virtual tour of the aquarium. Includes links to local educational institutions and aquarium merchandise outlets.

Turtle Trax—A Marine Turtle Page

http://www.turtles.org/

Marine turtles star in this advocacy-oriented page devoted to the sea creatures. Find political, zoological and anecdotal information about the ancient animals along with lots of photos.

The Virtual Pet Cemetery

http://www.lavamind.com/pet.html

You can post memorials to pets here. See Editor's Choice.

Weimaraner Club of America

http://www.eskimo.com/~chipper/weim.html

This Web site offers a full kennel of information about Weimaraner dogs. Includes a history of the hounds, the official standard of the breed, a roster of Weimaraner clubs from around the world and a list of dogs available for adoption.

The Weimaraner HomePage

http://www.leitess.com/~jsf/y-me

Devoted to the German-bred hunting dog, this page offers a breed history, photos and links to Weimaraner club events pages. Pointers to breed standards and a list of all U.S. Weimaraner Clubs are also included.

Whales: A Thematic Web Unit

http://curry.edschool.Virginia.EDU/go/whales/

Teachers can use this site's lesson plans, homework suggestions and book reviews to teach a unit on whales. The site, maintained by a graduate student in education, also includes a project gallery and activities for students that involve whales.

Wonderful Canine World

http://www.gae.unican.es/general/dogs/dogs.html

Dogs are kings at The Wonderful Canine World multimedia Web page. Find photos, audio, video and a directory of sites on specific dog breeds. Information on the Canine-L mailing list, various newsgroups, and related commercial sites are also featured. Some information is in Spanish, some in English.

The World-Wide Web Virtual Library: Fish

http://www.actwin.com/WWWVL-Fish.html

Fishing for sport is but one component of the World-Wide Web Virtual Library's site on fish. Visitors also can find links to pages on aquariums, biology and aquatic environmentalism.

The World-Wide Web Virtual Library: Whale Watching

http://www.physics.helsinki.fi/whale/

This whale watching site catalogs physical and cultural sightings of the world's largest mammals. Unabashedly whale friendly, this site addresses whale migration patterns, as well as the role of the whale in world literature. Visit here for a comprehensive index of whale study resources.

PHOTOGRAPHY

Bengt's Photo Page

http://algunet.se/~bengtha/photo/

Bengt's Photo Page contains listings of photographic exhibitions, archives and galleries. Includes links to articles, publications and frequently asked questions about photography.

Black Star Photo and Web Resources

http://www.blackstar.com/

Headquartered in New York City, Black Star represents a network of 350 photographers from around the world. Visitors to this commercial site can browse the organization's photojournalism gallery, check out an online stock photo library, or learn about the company's World Wide Web publishing services.

---

a2z **EDITOR'S CHOICE**

The National Zoological Park

http://www.si.edu/organiza/museums/zoo/homepage/nzphome.htm

Founded in 1889, the Smithsonian Institution's National Zoological Park hosts this "ticketless" wander through the natural wonders on exhibit at what is becoming the United States' premiere biopark. Offering more than just a wildlife menagerie, the park combines the best of natural history museums, botanic gardens, and aquaria to enhance visitors' experiences and better illustrate "the splendor of all living things." Among the offerings housed at this multimedia Web stop, visitors can enjoy a 20-slide presentation on the Amazon rainforest, explore the nature of thinking, and watch a wide selection of animal-specific videos. A map of the park, an events calendar and general facilities information are also available to aid those planning a real-time visit. An impressive display, this site proves for all who would doubt, not all American tax dollars are wasted.—*Reviewed by Sean McFadden*

California Museum of Photography

http://cmp1.ucr.edu/

The California Museum of Photography at the University of California, Riverside, maintains this page with exhibits of contemporary and historical photography and information about upcoming shows. Includes interactive essays and a museum store.

Cloud Gallery

http://www.commerce.digital.com/palo-alto/CloudGallery/home.html

This online gallery offers visitors some ethereal renderings of cloud photography; float through the exhibition or download selected images for your own home page. Includes a photographer's essay on tapping into "angel power," plus contact information.

Department of Photography and Instructional Graphics

http://www.dopig.uab.edu/

This departmental page from the University of Alabama at Birmingham contains information on courses of study, course offerings, admissions and faculty profiles. Includes links to other campus servers and related resources.

Digital Photography '94

http://www.bradley.edu/exhibit/index.html

Sponsored by Illinois' Peoria Art Guild and Bradley University, this online, juried exhibition represents the winners of an annual interstate digital photography competition. Visitors can check out the art on individual "walls" in the virtual galleries, or read about participating artists and organizations.

Digital Photography '95

http://www.bradley.edu/exhibit95/

You don't have to wear black to gain entrance to this virtual gallery reception. Hosted by the Peoria Art Guild and Bradley University, this online exhibit of digital photography includes computer enhanced images originally captured on film, video cameras, still-video, digital cameras and three-dimensional scanners.

Fox Studio Limited

http://www.webcom.com/~foxstu/

Fox Studio Limited of Minneapolis presents selected images from its photographers' portfolios and works-in-progress. The page also has an index of businesses geared toward clients and colleagues.

Fuji Film

http://www.fujifilm.co.jp/

The Fuji Film home page has information on new products, news items and a photo gallery. Available in Japanese and English, the site's product information touts new and emerging Fuji technology, and even takes a shot at its biggest rival (you know, that "other" photo company).

Great Barrier Reef Gallery

http://werple.mira.net.au/~margaret/scuba.htm

Underwater photo enthusiast "Margaret" (who also likes skiing and Pink Floyd), hosts this extensive collection of images taken around the Great Barrier Reef and the waters near Melbourne, Australia. Margaret also likes to use browser frames. Lots and lots of frames.

The Great Smoky Mountains

http://www.mindspring.com/~ahearn/smoky.html

Nature lovers can wander through a virtual photo exhibit of what the Cherokee people called the ' Place of Blue Smoke." Links to other Smoky Mountains sites and technical notes on the photographs are included.

Hoffer School Home Page

http://cmp1.ucr.edu/exhibitions/hoffer/hoffer.homepage.html

Hoffer Elementary School offers information here on its photography and media-related student projects. Check out group pictures, past exhibits from the California Museum of Photography and highlights of the children's other Internet adventures.

Index Stock Photography

http://www.indexstock.com/

A commercial stock photo agency based in New York, Index Stock Photography makes its massive catalog available for online browsing. Reproduction is subject to standard stock purchase fees. Other highlights include company news and a "Help Wanted" section for those seeking work in the stock photo industry.

---

a2z **EDITOR'S CHOICE**

Photo Manipulation

http://aleph0.clarku.edu/~bmarcus/home.html

A fascinating step-by-step guide to manipulating images is found here; the initial shot of a photograph of seven astronauts simultaneously trundling across the moon's surface is a great example of how digital software can enhance and change photographs. Visitors can scrutinize the photo and pick up some handy tips on how to detect similar digital frauds using criteria like "internal inconsistency, "questionable cast shadows," and other flaws that tip off the viewer that a photo has been altered.

On the flip side, the site also gives a good basic introduction for those looking to trick the viewer into believing that montages and other types of hocus-pocus are, in fact, real. The Webmaster asserts that "There's an inherent honesty to photographs. Photographs reveal everything. There's no lying to a camera. Photographs tell a complete story and communicate details." But be sure and take a careful look at what you're assuming is "real"—at least when it comes to digitally enhanced images.

—*Reviewed by Julene Snyder*

Manipulating Images

Digital photomontage of seven astronauts on the surface of the moon was produced from an original photograph made in 1969 by NASA of a single astronaut, Edwin F. Aldrin, Jr. This montage is of high technical quality; it is carefully contrived to seem spatially consistent, and sophisticated digital technology has eliminated any obvious signs of cutting and pasting. SO HOW CAN WE TELL IT IS A FAKE?

Kouichirou's Home Page

http://andro.sfc.keio.ac.jp/eto/

The personal home page of Eto Kouichirou contains a collection of his photographs and essays, along with links to some of his favorite sites on the Web.

The Land of Beauty

http://www.cnd.org/Scenery/

The scenic beauty of China comes to life on this page. Included are high resolution photos of scenic sites in the country, ancient buildings and natural landscapes.

Larry Kanfer Gallery

http://www.prairienet.org/arts/kanfer

A virtual photo gallery, this page highlights the work of photographer Larry Kanfer. Includes a directory of selected portfolios and published collections, as well as a window into the artist's real-time gallery in Champaign, Illinois.

Magical Moments by Randy Wang

http://http.cs.berkeley.edu/~rywang/magic_small.html

A cyber photo tour of California, this site should please nature lovers and landscape enthusiasts equally. Dozens of images from the Golden State's most scenic spots include Big Sur, Yosemite, and the Joshua Tree National Monument.

Michael Major Photography & Publishing

http://www.ozemail.com.au/~mmajor/index.html

The commercial page for Michael Major Publishing & Photography offers information on the Australian company's full range of traditional and digital photography services, as well as links to clients' pages for examples of completed work.

Muslims in the 19th Century Russian Empire

http://www.uoknor.edu/cybermuslim/russia/rus_home.html

This page, maintained by the CyberMuslim Information Collective, features an exhibit of photography and historical information regarding the Turks and Tatars. Part of an interactive history project, this site's growth depends on the contributions of visitors' ideas and memories.

National Museum of Photography, Film and Television

http://www.nmsi.ac.uk/nmpft/

The popular interactive museum located in Bradford, England, serves up a historical perspective on its origins and activities, and details its real-time collections. Some compelling information on early television and cinema, and a schedule of screenings at the museum's popular IMAX theater, but the site is surprisingly text-heavy given the subject matter.

Photo Manipulation

http://aleph0.clarku.edu/~bmarcus/home.html

This photograph of seven astronauts simultaneously trundling across the moon's surface is a great example of image manipulation using digital photo software. Visitors can scrutinize the photo and pick up some handy tips on how to detect similar digital frauds (or…uh…learn how to create their own). See Editor's Choice.

Schwarz Illustrated Photojournalism Site

http://www.michaelschwarz.com/index.html

An Atlanta freelance photojournalist, Michael A. Schwarz, maintains this online gallery of his and other photojournalists' work. Also find photo essays and a portfolio of "favorite images."

Scientific Photography Lab

http://foto.chemie.unibas.ch/

The Scientific Photography Laboratory is operated by the Chemistry Department at the University of Basel, Switzerland. Visitors will find information on research and faculty. Includes numerous scientific pictures.

SciNetPhotos

http://www.scinetphotos.com/

The SciNetPhotos site contains thousands of stock photographic images by photographer Hank Morgan. This page includes an index of images by subject, downloading information and hot links.

Scotland Photos

http://www.cs.ucl.ac.uk/misc/uk/scotland_photos.html

A collection of images from Scotland's countryside includes sweeping vistas and curling lochs (but no monsters that we could see). For those eager to traverse the moors and mountains of the region, links to mountain safety and equipment requirements are provided.

---

a2z EDITOR'S CHOICE

Point Reyes Wild Life

http://users.aimnet.com/~winter/ptreyes.htm

This simple tribute to the beauty of Northern California's Point Reyes National Seashore is an excellent example of what the Web can do best—point visitors to a world they might not otherwise encounter. Here, photographer Greg Gothard describes the land that he loves: "The terrain varies from lush open meadows to beaches to forested hills to the open esteros near Drakes Bay to waterfalls that splash onto the beach." But beyond words, Gothard presents images of mammals, birds and wildlife that awakens the visitors' longing to see these nature-dwellers as up close and personal as the photographer has. Until you can make it to Point Reyes to see for yourself, here bobcats, raccoon, tule elk, and brown pelicans are as close as your computer.—*Reviewed by Julene Snyder*

Greg's Point Reyes Wild Life Page

Stock Solution
http://www.xmission.com/~tssphoto/
The Stock Solution is a photo agency that leases stock images. Visitors can browse through its on-line catalog of more than 200,000 images here.

Storm Chaser
http://www.indirect.com/www/storm5/
Warren Fraidley, a storm photographer, has been struck by lightning, skirted tornadoes, and stood in the eyes of hurricanes to take weather photos for magazines. Visit here to learn more about this death-defying man and look at his photos.

Underwater Photography by Scott Freeman
http://weber.u.washington.edu/~scotfree
Visitors to this Web gallery will come face to face with the colorful creatures lurking underwater in the Pacific Northwest. Includes information about the photographer and his equipment. See Editor's Choice.

Underwater Photography Web Site
http://weber.u.washington.edu/~scotfree
A poem ushers visitors into the Underwater Photography Web, where visitors can view winning photo exhibits, fish around in an art gallery, or subscribe to a mailing list.

Web Voyeur
http://www.eskimo.com/~irving/web-voyeur/
Feel like climbing Pike's Peak? How about a trip to the Taj Mahal? The Web Voyeur whisks visitors away to hundreds of breathtaking views brought to the Internet via electronic images and video.

POP CULTURE

Bodyart
http://www.cis.ohio-state.edu/text/faq/usenet/bodyart/top.html
Tattooing, piercing and other forms of body manipulation are explored and explained at this site, which includes a Frequently Asked Questions (FAQs) file regarding bodyart.

Encyclopedia Brady
http://www.primenet.com/~dbrady/
The Encyclopedia Brady is an information site containing all anyone could ever want to know about "The Brady Bunch" television series. Includes a history of the Brady home and links to numerous Brady Bunch pages.

The Gigaplex!
http://www.gigaplex.com/wow/homepage.htm
Gigaplex is a vast Web magazine with more than 600 pages relating to arts and entertainment. Movies, theater, TV, books, art, and music are among the subject categories.

The Jihad to Destroy Barney
http://www.net/~sheriden/jihad/
Join or simply monitor the nefarious activities of the Jihad to Destroy Barney at this site. Visitors will find propaganda mandating that the popular purple dinosaur who has captured the fancy of U.S. children must die. See Editor's Choice.

The Metaverse
http://metaverse.com/index.html
Check into the Metaverse for a mega-dose of pop culture. Metaverse is the online home for such hefty sites as "Melrose Place" and "Adam Curry's the Vibe." It also hosts regular cybercasts of monumental events.

Spiral into the'80s
http://chat.carleton.ca/~jmain/eighties.html
Visitors here will find "Jeff's awesome eighties page" offering links to sites devoted to 1980s entertainers. Find pointers to music, movies and television pages, plus a miscellany of other sites.

Starwave Online
http://www.starwave.com/
Stylish electronic publisher Starwave Corp. provides detailed information on its CD-ROM products and wildly popular Web creations. Visitors can link to such Starwave Web sites as ESPNet SportsZone, Mr. Showbiz, Ticketmaster Online, and Outside Online.

The Transformers
http://www.vt.edu:10021/other/transformers/
Devoted to Transformers—toy robots that change their appearance—this home page provides an index to online information available. Features include links to games, fan fiction, television show transcripts, and statistics.

a2z EDITOR'S CHOICE

Underwater Photography by Scott Freeman
http://weber.u.washington.edu/~scotfree
Vibrant photos filling several virtual galleries explode in color here, where photographer Scott Freeman reveals the denizens of the Pacific Northwest's deep waters. Under Puget Sound lurk gorgeous beasties like wolf eels and spot prawns; find them at this site, offered up in crisp 16-bit color. It's a dip in the drink that leaves the viewer refreshed...and only slightly damp. A peek at the diver's most dedicated buddy shows that Freeman's interest in wildlife isn't limited to those that lurk beneath the brine.—*Reviewed by Julene Snyder*

The Vibe
http://metaverse.com/vibe/

"The Vibe" is an electronic zine dedicated to all things pop culture. Editorial categories include sights, sounds, sleaze, and surf.

A Visit to Yesterland
http://www.mcs.net/~werner/yester.html

A virtual theme park on the Web, this site features photos and descriptions of discontinued Disneyland rides and attractions. Take a tour through this site's many magical pages, or link to other Disney and theme-park sites on the Web. See Editor's Choice.

RADIO

AMATEUR AND SHORTWAVE

Amateur Radio
http://www.mcc.ac.uk/Radio/

The University of Manchester, England, provides this comprehensive guide to amateur radio. Includes national callbooks and indexes international newsgroups and ham-related Web resources.

Amateur Radio Callsign Search
http://www.mit.edu:8001/callsign

The Amateur Radio Club of the University of Arkansas at Little Rock maintains this site with a searchable index of ham radio user callsigns. Visit here to find name, address and operating license information for any callsign.

Amateur Radio: Galaxy Index
http://galaxy.einet.net/galaxy/Leisure-and-Recreation/Amateur-Radio.html

TradeWave's Galaxy Internet directory maintains this site for its amateur radio index. Visitors will find an extensive collection of related resources provided by private, educational and government organizations

Amateur Radio Information Resources
http://user.itl.net/~equinox/

Devoted to radio enthusiasts, this site offers a wealth of information on amateur stations, world weather, solar information and personal computer software. Links to shortwave radio information, satellite news, and technological data await visitors here. See Editor's Choice.

Amateur Radio Newsline
http://www.acs.ncsu.edu/HamRadio/News.html

Transcripts of "Amateur Radio NewsLine," an audio program for and about ham radio operators, are published at this site. Articles relating to technology, federal regulations and world events are presented in an informal format. Find current and past programs.

Amateur Radio: World Wide Web Virtual Library Index
http://www.meaning.com/pointers/wwwvl-ham.html

Maintained by an amateur radio operator under the auspices of the World Wide Web Virtual Library, this index provides links to related organizations and resources. Includes callbooks, newsgroup listings and amateur radio equipment manufacturer home pages.

Benelux DX-Club
http://promet12.cineca.it/htdx/swls/bdxc.html

Netherlands-based shortwave "radio listening amateur club" Benelux DX maintains this site for news and resources. Visitors will find links to shortwave transmission and radio station listings, related Web links, and downloadable software.

a2z EDITOR'S CHOICE

The Jihad to Destroy Barney
http://www.armory.com/~deadslug/Jihad/jihad.html

The nefarious activities here are perhaps best described by the site's host, who states his predominant goal in life right up front: "This is the Jihad to Destroy Barney on the Worldwide Web, the web page that says, without hesitation, that Barney Must Die, All Else is Irrelevant." Barney, of course, is the treacly, purple TV dinosaur, who's become inexplicably popular among the younger set in the U.S.

Here, the viewer is advised to keep young children "who still cling to the purple menace" from visiting the site, cautioning, "please use discretion in viewing this, including when it's being used as a deprogramming tool." Links to the newsgroup alt.barney.dinosaur.die.die.die are among the offerings, as are graphics, and of course the "Canon of Jihad Literature," which includes a story containing the following charming ditty: "I love you, you love me.....let me have your family.....with a quick stab or kick, we'll set the children free....don't you know you were meant for me.") Brrrr. Die Barney, die.—*Reviewed by Julene Snyder*

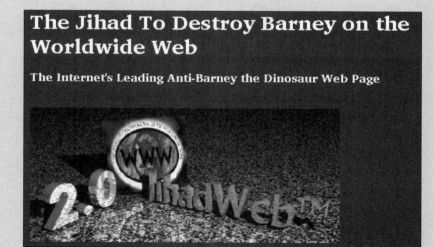

Boston Amateur Radio Club

http://www.acs.oakland.edu/barc.html

Even for those who don't live there, ham jockeys will find plenty of interest at the Boston Amateur Radio Club's home page. The club roster, journal and membership information are available, as well as information about amateur radio exams and various conventions.

Columbia University Amateur Radio Club

http://www.cc.columbia.edu/~fuat/cuarc/

Columbia University in New York City maintains this site for its amateur radio club. Visitors will find news, callsign directories, local license exam listings and membership information.

Com-West Radio Systems

http://www.com-west.com/

Vancouver, British Columbia-based Com-West Radio Systems maintains this site to introduce its selection of amateur, marine and commercial radio equipment. Visitors will also find amateur radio, shortwave, and scanning links.

Naval Postgraduate School Amateur Radio Club

http://www.sp.nps.navy.mil/npsarc/k6ly.html

Amateur radio operators at the U.S. Navy's postgraduate university in Monterey, California maintain this site to introduce this extra-curricular club. Visit here for news, activities listings, public service overviews and technical resources.

OH2BUA WebCluster

http://www.clinet.fi/~jukka/webcluster.html

A Helsinki, Finland-based amateur radio operator maintains this site to provide a variety of broadcasting news and information resources. Visitors will find callbooks, licensing instructions and radio frequency propagation condition forecasts.

The Packet Radio Home Page

http://www.tapr.org/tapr/html/pkthome.html

Arizona-based Tucson Amateur Packet Radio Corporation maintains this site for a variety of amateur radio resources. Visit here for professional journals, technical reports, instructional materials and links to professional digital communications organizations.

QRZ Ham Radio Database

http://www.qrz.com/

Colorado-based QRZ maintains this site for access to its regularly updated U.S. Federal Communications Commission callsign database. Visit here to search for amateur radio operators by name or callsign. Includes information on QRZ's popular CD-ROM database.

QSL Information System

http://www-dx.deis.unibo.it/htlzh/

Visit this Web server to access a searchable database of ham radio operators' callsigns maintained by an amateur operator. Includes a link to the University of Arkansas Little Rock's amateur radio club home page.

Radio Amateur Satellite Corporation

http://www.amsat.org/amsat/
AmsatHome.html

Washington, D.C.-based Radio Amateur Satellite Corporation has directed the launching of more than 30 satellites for use in amateur radio communications. Visitors to its home page will find related publications, membership information and links to Web-based ham resources.

Radio Amateur Telecommunications Society

http://www.rats.org/

The New Jersey-based Radio Amateur Telecommunications Society includes information about its upcoming meetings and a bit of its history on this home page. The nonprofit organization is devoted to the development and application of amateur radio communications technology.

Sveriges Radio

http://www.sr.se/

The shortwave broadcasts of Radio Sweden are available online at this site. Visitors can pick up RealAudio stream through the World Radio Network, or FTP to download listed shortwave frequencies. In Swedish.

U.S. Amateur Radio Club Callsign Lookup Page

http://www.ualr.edu/doc/hamualr/callsign.html

Visit this interactive page for access to the University of Arkansas at Little Rock's database of amateur radio operator callsigns. The database is updated daily and derived from U.S. Federal Communication Commission license data.

VE7TCP: Amateur Radio

http://ve7tcp.ampr.org/

Amateur radio buffs can dial in on two radio clubs in Prince William, British Columbia, here. Browsers will find information on DXing, packet and ham radio, and amateur radio technology.

---

a2z EDITOR'S CHOICE

A Visit to Yesterland

http://www.mcs.net/~werner/yester.html

Most definitely an E-ticket attraction, this site is a virtual trip back in time to the days of an older, gentler Magic Kingdom, one that's long since faded from view amid the glitter and gloss of new Disneyland attractions. Here, Webmaster Werner Weiss invites you to hop aboard a mule-train, revisit Monsanto's "Adventure Thru Inner Space" or take a ride on General Electric's "Carousel of Progress." Find out what attractions are fated to hit Yesterland any minute now (Hint: Captain EO, the Main Street Electrical Parade). Walt Disney once said, "Disneyland will never be completed as long as there is imagination left in the world." In response, Weiss replies, "Yesterland will never be completed as long as there are attractions left to close in Disneyland."—*Reviewed by Julene Snyder*

W3EAX—University of Maryland Amateur Radio Association

http://w3eax.umd.edu/w3eax.html

Providing University of Maryland staff and students with opportunities to participate in amateur radio communications, W3EAX meets on a regular basis during the regular school year. Visitors to its home page will find events, activities and project information.

W5AC Home Page

http://w5ac.tamu.edu/

W5AC is the Texas A&M University ham radio club, founded in 1912 and one of the oldest university radio clubs in the world. W5AC lists information on how to obtain a ham operator's license and links to other amateur radio pages of interest.

W6BHZ

http://www.w6bhz.calpoly.edu/

W6BHZ, the amateur radio club of California Polytechnic State University, maintains this site with club information, member listings, electronic newsletters and meeting minutes archive. Includes resources for the amateur radio community in San Luis Obispo, California.

W6YX Stanford Amateur Radio Club

http://w6yx.stanford.edu/w6yx.html

The Stanford Amateur Radio Club maintains this online newsletter to introduce its programs and membership services. Visit here for news, current activities, staff listings and links to other ham radio resources on the Web.

BROADCAST

ABC RadioNet

http://www.abcradionet.com/

Did you miss Peter Jennings' newscast tonight? You can listen to it here, along with news on the hour, sports, weather and David Brinkley reports. Visitors can also pick a city from a clickable image map for links to more localized news stories and features.

Arrow 93 FM

http://www.arrowfm.com/

Arrow 93 FM, the "all rock and roll oldies" station in Los Angeles, maintains this site for listeners and other music fans. Trivia, artists' biographies, polls and links to other music-related sites are featured.

Bandit 105.5

http://www.bandit.se/

"Better than drugs and safer than sex," is the motto of this Stockholm, Sweden-based FM rock music station. Visit its home page for top 40 song listings, concert calendars, ski reports, and more. Available in Swedish.

Bonneville Broadcast Group

http://www.halcyon.com/kiro/hello.html

Seattle-based Bonneville Broadcast Group maintains this site for access to its member stations and Internet resources. Visit here to find news program schedules, local and community services, and links to other radio station home pages.

Canadian Broadcast Corporation Radio

http://radioworks.cbc.ca/

Canada's news, music and variety radio network maintains this site for an extensive program index. Visitors will find links to news and background information on a wide variety of audio offerings, from jazz to poetry.

CHMA-FM 107

http://aci.mta.ca/TheUmbrella/CHMA/chmastart.html

CHMA-FM 107 is a campus radio station serving Mount Allison University, New Brunswick, Canada, and the surrounding communities. Visitors to the station's home page can link to such items as program schedules, sound clips and recent board meeting minutes.

Digital Radio

http://www.magi.com/~moted/dr

This informational page, maintained by Canada's Task Force on the Introduction of Digital Radio, provides details on the development of digital audio broadcasting. Visitors will find guides, discussions and Internet resources for this new broadcast technology. In English and French.

Hearts of Space

http://www.hos.com/

The producer of nationally syndicated radio program "Hearts of Space," spinning "psychologically stimulating" electronic music, maintains this promotional site. Visitors will find interviews with the show's creator, Stephan Hill, and information on how to submit music to his weekly program of new age music.

---

a2z EDITOR'S CHOICE

Amateur Radio Information Resources

http://user.itl.net/~equinox/

Ham radio operators were connecting to the remote corners of the world long before the Internet age. For decades, this network of enthusiasts has been tapping into shortwave radio frequencies, sending missives and messages around the planet. Sound hauntingly familiar? Well, ham radio is a lot different than the Net. Making a global radio transmission from your living room is easier said than done, and requires not only a basic knowledge of radio spectrum physics, but familiarity with meteorological conditions, including solar activity. To learn more about this fascinating pasttime, tune into the online resources offered here, from cluster newsgroups and antenna manufacturers to a picture of the sun taken 10 minutes before your arrival. Pages and pages of well-indexed and constantly updated links to operators and organizations are guaranteed to satisfy even the most professional amateur —*Reviewed by Paul Bacon*

Learmonth H-Alpha 25 Jun 1996 5:50:57UT

EDITOR'S CHOICE

NPR Online

http://www.npr.org/

One of the world's sanest and most comprehensive news sources now has one of the best-kept sites on the Web. The home page of National Public Radio (NPR), the Washington, D.C.-based provider of progressive radio news, science, and lifestyle programming, offers downloadable sound-files as well as background details on nearly all of its programming. From the daily wrapup of national news offered by "Morning Edition" to the critically-acclaimed issues coverage of "All Things Considered," NPR brings a world of radio alternatives to the Internet. Its well-rounded fare of regular features, many provided here in RealAudio format, cover the gamut from fine arts to car repairs, and from recipes to race relations. NPR listeners will also find biographies of on-air journalists and browsable listings of broadcasters worldwide.—*Reviewed by Paul Bacon*

Original Old Time Radio WWW Pages

http://www.old-time.com/

What sits in your living room, plugs into the wall and was once dubbed "the most stupendous means of entertainment the world has ever witnessed"? No, it's not TV (or the Internet), it's radio! Or at least it was radio, about 50 years ago, and the Webmaster of this nostalgic site promises to take you back to the golden age—to the "thrilling days of yesteryear"— when radio receivers were bigger than ovens. Visitors can listen to historic broadcasts and find online memorabilia for old time favorites from "Burns & Allen" to the "Inner Sanctum." Claiming "nostalgic radio is good for your brain," the site also leads to an endless array of sites offering trivia, transcripts, and annotated histories of some of radio's most memorable moments.—*Reviewed by Paul Bacon*

HSF—Studentenradio

http://www.rz.tu-ilmenau.de/~hsf/hsf.html

The HSF student radio station emanates from Germany, and its Web home page offers a look behind the microphone at what the station plays and the students who play it. In German.

Internet Radio NEXUS

http://www.nexus.org/Internet_Radio/

Visit here to tune in broadcasts from UNESCO Radio, United Nations Radio, Swiss Radio International, and other international radio offerings here. The site is maintained by Internet Radio NEXUS and offers a link to software needed to play the broadcasts.

KJHK University of Kansas Radio

http://www.cc.ukans.edu/~kjhknet

The campus radio station at the University of Kansas presents this home page with links to its worldwide broadcasts and basketball games shown on Internet TV. The radio station is sponsored and maintained as part of the university's journalism and mass communications school.

KKSF and KDFC Radio

http://www.tbo.com/index.html

San Francisco-based jazz and classical radio stations KKSF and KDFC publish programming guides and promotional materials at this site. Visitors will also find corporate information about parent company, The Brown Organization.

KPIG Radio Online

http://www.kpig.com/

Oink, KPIG, oink, is a radio station based in Freedom, California that broadcasts an eclectic mix of rock, blues, country, Hawaiian, cajun, and a whole bunch of other stuff. Visitors to their sty, er, home page will find information on new music, related links and comedy…oink.

KZRR 94 Rock

http://www.94rock.com/kzrr

An Albuquerque, New Mexico rock radio station posts concert and event listings at this promotional site. Visitors can read up on rock history, meet the station's staff (virtually), download clips of songs on KZRR's playlist and rate the programmer's picks.

KZSU Radio

http://kzsu.stanford.edu/

KZSU Radio's home page provides information about Stanford University's all-volunteer, student-run radio station. Programming and news schedules, airplay charts, music reviews and a concert calendar are among the services offered here. Includes links to more than 600 record labels' Web pages.

The Laporte Report

http://www.coville.com/

San Francisco-based technology reporter Leo Laporte maintains this site to supplement his weekly "Laporte on Computers" radio program. Visitors will find daily updated headlines, "hot" Web links and programming notes.

MIT List of Radio Stations on the Internet

http://wmbr.mit.edu/stations/list.html

Anyone working in broadcast radio will want to bookmark this whopper list of international radio stations on the Web. Visit here to find links to hundreds of worldwide stations and add your station's link to the database.

Monitor Radio

http://town.hall.org/radio/Monitor/index.html

The "Christian Science Monitor" maintains this site to introduce its Monitor Radio news broadcast service. Visit here to find program highlights and schedules for the news show, heard on public radio stations around the world.

Nexus—IBA

http://www.nexus.org/

Nexus-International Broadcasting Association, a Milano, Italy-based nonprofit organization of shortwave, FM, and Internet broadcasters, maintains this informational site. Visit here for organizational news, downloadable radio programming from the United Nations and links to member organizations.

NHK (Japan Broadcasting Corporation)

http://www.ntt.co.jp/japan/NHK/

Radio Japan is the international shortwave service run by NHK, Japan's public service broadcaster providing radio programs in 22 languages. Visit here for information about the service and its programming in a variety of languages.

NPR Online

http://www.npr.org/

Washington, D.C.-based National Public Radio, providing commercial-free news and entertainment programming for public broadcasters around the world, maintains this informational site. Visitors will find downloadable audio news stories, special current events features, member station listings and free news transcripts. See Editor's Choice.

Original Old Time Radio WWW Pages

http://www.old-time.com/

You'll find radio show transcripts, trivia, and more here. See Editor's Choice.

Other Non-commercial Radio

http://kzsu.stanford.edu/other-radio.html

In the United States, the FM band between 88 and 92 MHz is allocated for educational and noncommercial use. Stanford University's student-run radio station maintains this list of such broadcasters, promising "you're bound to find eclectic radio." See Editor's Choice.

Q107—Toronto's Best Rock

http://www.q107.com/

Q107, a Toronto, Ontario-based rock music radio station, maintains this site for programming information, concert calendars, listener feedback and more. Visit here for the latest music news and links to local resources and music-related Web sites.

Radio Archive Homepage

http://www.people.memphis.edu/~mbensman/

The University of Memphis, Tennessee, maintains this site for a searchable archive of thousands of historic radio programs. Visitors will also find general broadcasting history notes and an online form for ordering related audio cassettes.

Radio Brume

http://www.brume.org/brume/

The Radio Brume home page provides visitors with background and programming info on this student radio station operating in Lyon and Grenoble, France. Visitors can also link to other student media pages in Europe. Available in French and English.

Radio Canada International

http://radioworks.cbc.ca/radio/rci/rci.html

Montreal, Quebec-based Radio Canada International provides continuous news and features radio programming to the world via satellite. Visitors to its home page will find transmitter frequency updates and schedule information on its English, French, Russian, Ukranian, Arabic, and Spanish programming.

Radio 538—103 FM

http://www.radio538.nl/

This Netherlands-based popular music station peppers its home page with a little Dutch here, a little English there, in presenting what appears to be music news, concert announcements and local resources.

Radio Free Ann Arbor

http://www.umich.edu/~wcbn

88.3 FM Radio Free Ann Arbor, a "free form" radio station based in Ann Arbor, Michigan maintains this promotional site. Visit here to view recent music playlists, event updates, department information and more.

---

a2z EDITOR'S CHOICE

Other Non-commercial Radio

http://kzsu.stanford.edu/other-radio.html

Wander, if you dare, into the lowest frequencies of your FM dial, and you may find something quite unexpected. Turn the knob farther than ever before, leaving behind the familiar screeching of paid advertisements and popular music, into an entirely new realm: noncommercial radio. Visitors to this index page will find an eclectic collection of radio stations that float between 88 and 92MHz, a band allocated in many countries exclusively for nonprofit broadcasters. Maintained by Stanford University's student-

RADIO ONLINE

http://www.radio-online.com

This site provides industry news and much more. See Editor's Choice.

Radio Stations on the Web

http://american.recordings.com/WWWoM/radio/radio.html

A link from American Recording's World Wide Web of Music site, this page provides an extensive index of radio station home pages. Includes dozens of listings for the United States, Canada, Europe, and Oceania.

RealTime

http://realtime.cbcstereo.com/

Canadian Broadcasting Corporation's RealTime live radio variety show maintains this site for programming and content information. Visitors will find contests, downloadable music, and profiles of its guest disk jockeys and in-studio performing artists.

Rock 107—KIK FM

http://www.kikfm.com/

Calgary, Alberta's Rock 107 maintains this promotional site with links to programming and local concert information. Visitors will also find profiles of popular on-air personalities, listener contests, sports news and public service announcements.

Sonshine Christian Radio

http://www.ozemail.com.au/~cook/sonshine

98.5 Sonshine Radio in Perth, Western Australia, maintains this site to introduce its staff and program offerings, including an "adult contemporary mix of mainstream and Christian music.

Visitors will find current playlists, regular program schedules, listener feedback, and more.

Virtual Radio

http://www.microserve.net/vradio/vr.html

Virtual Radio gives new meaning to the term "audience-driven." Tune in here to download radio-quality broadcasts of the songs of your choice. You don't download mere snippets, but rather the entire cut. The site also offers a wealth of recording artist information, including photos.

WBRS-Waltham 100.1 FM

http://www.wbrs.org/

This campus radio station offers an experimental broadcast laboratory for music, ideas and opinions. Find out what sounds and views students are airing at the WBRS Brandeis University Radio home page.

WCBS NewsRadio 88

http://www.newsradio88.com/

The home page of WCBS Newsradio 88, New York, dishes up "all news—all day—all night." Visitors to the site will find the latest top news, sports and weather reports, as well as special technology, science, and lifestyle features.

WEFT Community Radio Page

http://www.prairienet.org/arts/weft/WEFThome.html

The home page of WEFT, a noncommercial, community-oriented radio station in East Central Illinois, provides general information here about the 12-year-old broadcast entity. Includes local music and events listings, show schedules and

descriptions, and the station's monthly publication archives.

WETA-FM

http://soundprint.brandywine.american.edu/~weta

WETA-FM, an independent, nonprofit public radio station, offers news, music and a variety of other audio features. Selections at its home page include programming reviews, a public radio directory, album lists and links to other American public radio broadcasters.

WFMU-FM 91.1 Radio

http://wfmu.org/

East Orange, New Jersey independent radio station WFMU slings music, humor and "multimedia crapola" at this promotional site. Explore the station's wacky offerings at its home page "blunting the cutting edge for your personal safety."

WHSR—Johns Hopkins Student Radio

http://www.jhu.edu/~whsr

Johns Hopkins University's student-run radio station, WHSR, hosts this home page. Find a programming guide, a laudatory article about the station and a few pages of staff musings. Links to a selection of other music pages are also featured.

WKSU-FM RADIO

http://www.wksu.kent.edu/

WKSU radio at Ohio's Kent State University provides an index to its daily program schedule, quarterly newsletters, playlists, music resources, membership benefits, and other information. A link to the National Public Radio home page is also available.

WNUR: Chicago's Sound Experiment

http://www.nwu.edu/WNUR/

This is the home page for Nortwestern University's campus radio, WNUR 89.3, serving the North side of Chicago, and surrounding area. Visitors to its home page will find current program and in-studio performance schedules. The site also hosts JazzWeb, an index to jazz resources on the Net.

WPKNet

http://www.wpkn.org/wpkn

Visitors to this Web page, maintained by Bridgeport, Connecticut jazz and blues station WPKN, will find a program guide and music playlists. Also includes local live music listings and station programmer pages.

WXRT Radio Chicago

http://www.wxrt.com/

At the home page of Chicago Radio Station WXRT, 93.1 FM, visitors can read info on the station's programs and events, browse staff bios or link to band directories and concert lists online. Includes links to local entertainment and community service resources.

---

a2z **EDITOR'S CHOICE**

RADIO ONLINE

http://www.radio-online.com

Anyone in the radio business will want to bookmark this Web-based publication, offering a wealth of industry news, features and contacts. RADIO ONLINE, though primarily a subscriber-only service, still manages to provide more free resources than most other radio pages combined. Nonmember offerings include all known industry player e-mail addresses, extensive job and résumé files, talent agency listings, and show prep files. A 10-day free trial is offered to anyone registering as a radio station employee or a member of the broadcast industry, allowing access to in-depth articles, premium advertising and ratings databases, promotional resources, and enough insider information to make subscribing irresistible.—*Reviewed by Paul Bacon*

RADIO ONLINE™
Radio's Starting Point on the Net

WYLN Radio
http://www.wlyn.com/

Boston-based AM radio station WYLN maintains this site to provide information about the station and its home city. Includes links to a community calendar, a daily journal and a host of other entertaining resources.

Y100 Philadelphia
http://www.y100.com/

Philadelphia rock station Y100 profiles its disc jockeys, lists songs and posts upcoming events on this promotional home page. Visitors can also download RealAudio files of current broadcast offerings.

ROMANCE

Bureau One Personals
http://www.cupidnet.com/cupid/bureau1

Individuals can seek same and opposite sex dates using Bureau One Personals. Voice personals augment print profiles offering potential partners a more complete picture of possible matches.

Chrysalis Counseling Services
http://www.omix.com/sites/drSandy/home.html

This online brochure for Chrysalis Counseling Services in San Francisco provides a brief overview of its approach to counseling and invites clients to contact the service via telephone, FAX or e-mail.

Christian Dating Service
http://www.christiandating.org/

With an eye toward "building Christian families," this world-wide, commercial service boasts of orchestrating hundreds of marriages and thousands of relationships in its 14-year history serving the Christian community. Online testimonials from pastors and couples united through CDS support the service's aims and claims.

Cupid's Woman of the Month
http://www.cupidnet.com/cupid/womnmnth/

Men looking for dates will find the Cupid Network's Woman of the Month profiles here. Each profile contains a photo, a brief description of the woman, and information about how to reach her.

The Cyrano Server
http://www.nando.net/toys/cyrano.html

Operating on the principal of a MadLib, Cyrano asks for a few particulars, beginning with the writing style required: steamy, indecisive, surreal, intellectual, desperate, or poetic. The details determined, Cyrano then pens a passionate epistle tailored to the moment's desires and electronically posts it posthaste. See Editor's Choice.

P.S. I Love You International
http://www.psiloveyou.com/

Here's a '90s version of the mail order bride. Male clients can order a video catalog offering "600+ beautiful, single women," view abbreviated profiles, then order extended profiles of the women who strike their fancies. And to assist those desirous of a face-to-face encounter, a travel service is available, tailoring excursion packages to most any budget's demands.

Single Search National/International
http://nsns.com/single-search/

Offering "old-fashioned romance generated by modern technology," this Tampa, Florida-based commercial matchmaking service invites potential clients to "meet by choice, not by chance." The service is professional, safe (clients decide how they will be contacted), and confidential.

The WebPersonals
http://www.webpersonals.com/

WebPersonals is a free online service for people seeking love and companionship. Browsers can submit personal advertisements or search the WebPersonals archives for that special someone.

The Wedding Source
http://www.pep.com/pep/tws/tws.html

You'll find help with the ceremony, the reception, the honeymoon. There are even resources to help with the "happily ever after." That's the hard part you know, and it's never too soon to think ahead. See Editor's Choice.

---

a2z EDITOR'S CHOICE

The Cyrano Server
http://www.nando.net/toys/cyrano.html

Tongue-tied by the prospect of whispering the right sweet nothing which will endear that special someone to your heart? Fret not a moment longer, timid one. Cyrano is at your service. Operating on the principal of a MadLib, Cyrano asks for a few particulars, beginning with the writing style required: steamy, indecisive, surreal, intellectual, desperate, or poetic. The details determined, Cyrano then pens a passionate epistle tailored to the moment's desires and electronically posts it posthaste. For those who find the point of love's arrow too painful and require separation from that no-longer-special someone, Cyrano can accommodate the need for an electronic "Dear John" (or "Joan") as well. With nothing to lose—but love to gain—come, friend. Cyrano awaits.—*Reviewed by Sean McFadden*

The Cyrano Server

SCIENCE FICTION

alt.cyberpunk FAQ list
http://bush.cs.tamu.edu/~erich/alt.cp.faq.html

This page contains the Frequently Asked Questions (FAQs) file for the Usenet newsgroup alt.cyberpunk. The FAQ discusses cyberpunk as both a literary genre and a subculture. Links to related sites are included.

Arthur C. Clarke Unauthorized Home Page
http://www.lsi.usp.br/~rbianchi/clarke/

Dedicated to science fiction writer Arthur C. Clarke, this unofficial site offers information about the author's biography, awards and filmography. Hypertext versions of interviews are online as well.

Bruce Sterling
http://riceinfo.rice.edu/projects/RDA/VirtualCity/Sterling/index.html

This site contains pointers to Web sites relevant to the career of Bruce Sterling, author, journalist, editor and critic. The themes Mr. Sterling explores are often related to the electronic frontier.

Bubonicon 28
http://www.unm.edu/~lundgren/Bubonicon.html

New Mexico's oldest science fiction convention, Bubonicon 28 is scheduled for August 23 through 25, 1996. Featured events will include the Green Slime Awards for truly awful sci-fi in several categories. Find out more at this site.

Dagobah System: Home of Master Yoda
http://www.li.net/~yoda/dagobah.html

Is it knowledge about The Force you seek, young Jedi. Hmm? Visit the Dagobah System page. It is the home of Jedi master Yoda. Links to "Star Wars" pages, sound files and photos are there for those who seek.

The Darmok Dictionary
http://www.wavefront.com/~raphael/darmok/darmok.html

The Darmok Dictionary, an unofficial "Star Trek: The Next Generation" trivia site,provides definitions of alien phrases used during the "Darmok" episode. Includes analytical discussion and sound files.

Doug's Library
http://www.astro.washington.edu/ingram/books.html

On this personal page, Doug Ingram presents a list of his favorite sci-fi books and links to full-length book reviews. Also find an author index, links to other book-related pages and an e-mail address with user responses.

The Good Reading Guide Index
http://julmara.ce.chalmers.se/SF_archive/SFguide/

Visit this page for reviews of books written in the science fiction and fantasy genres. Authors are listed alphabetically.

The Internet Top 100 Science Fiction Fantasy List
http://www.clark.net/pub/iz/Books/Top100/top100.html

Compiled via a public e-mail voting system, the selected "top" 100 science fiction and fantasy books are listed here. Review the list, or review the list of books that didn't make the top 100.

Irresistible Force
http://paul.spu.edu/~kevnord/starwars/

Fans of the seminal science fiction film trilogy "Star Wars" will find news, trivia, and merchandise of interest at this site. Explore prequels, sequels, and arcade games here.

The Jayhawk Series by Mary K. Kuhner
http://www.klab.caltech.edu/~flowers/jayhawk/

Serialized into 144 postings, the complete text of "Jayhawk" by Mary K. Kuhner is available here. Included is a story background, also written by the author.

The Klingon Language Institute
http://www.kli.org/

Learn Klingon and become the life of the party. See Editor's Choice.

The Linköping Science Fiction & Fantasy Archive
http://sf.www.lysator.liu.se/sf_archive/

Compiled since 1985 from Usenet pages by a science fiction and fantasy fan, this searchable archive offers an author guide, book and movie reviews, and an art gallery. An online science fiction resource guide also is presented.

---

a2z EDITOR'S CHOICE

The Wedding Source
http://www.pep.com/pep/tws/tws.html

Congratulations! So, when's the happy day? Oh, so soon! There's so much to do between now and then. Look, I know someone, her name is LOL, and she has this Web site. Dahling you should stop by. She'll link you up with "what you want, when you want it." I kid her, I say, "LOL, you ain't got what I want!" And she just laughs. But I'm not the one getting married, dahling. You are! Look, stop by. See for yourself. You'll find help with the ceremony, the reception, the hon-ey-moon…you're blushing, dahling. There are even resources to help with the "happily ever after." That's the hard part you know, and it's never too soon to think ahead. Look, go by and see LOL. Go on. It doesn't cost anything to look around. You're beautiful, dahling.—*Reviewed by Sean McFadden*

Macintosh: The Final Frontier

**http://www.astro.nwu.edu/lentz/mac/
software/mac-trek.html**

"Star Trek" related freeware for the Mac is archived at this site. Fans of the seminal science fiction series can download episode guides, Trek sounds and even series-inspired fonts.

Media.Maniacs

**http://www.crawford.com/media.maniacs/
media.html**

Through "strange apocalyptic postings originating from the future" the multimedia fantasy that is "Millennium Fever" unfolds on this page. Other Media.Maniacs creations are also featured.

Mr. Video's Star Trek Vidiot Home Page

http://www.cdsnet.net/vidiot/

The legendary series "Star Trek" occupies a place in the electronic universe too large to be contained in the television set. Trekkies discuss, dissect and disseminate news of and views on the "Voyager," "Deep Space Nine," and "The Next Generation" shows at this fan site.

MIT Science Fiction Library Pinkdex

http://www.mit.edu:8001/pinkdex

Those looking for a simple interface to search the Massachusetts Institute of Technology Science Fiction Library's catalog will appreciate the form on this page. Visitors can search by author or title.

New England Science Fiction Association

http://www.panix.com/NESFA/home.html

One of the oldest such clubs in the northeastern United States, the New England Science Fiction Association posts meeting and convention news to this site. A link to the Lysator Science Fiction & Fantasy Archive is also featured, as are pointers to other topical resources.

The Q Continuum

http://www.europa.com/~mercutio/Q.html

Devoted to the "Q" character from the television series "Star Trek: The Next Generation," this fan page features links to information about the actor who played the part, character quotes, photo,s and sound bites. Definitions of "Q" and the "Q Continuum" are also provided.

Reviews from the Forbidden Planet

**http://www.maths.tcd.ie/mmm/
ReviewsFromTheForbiddenPlanet.html**

Ireland-based comic book retailer Forbidden Planet maintains this site for a variety of title reviews. Visitors will find overviews of dozens of humor, science fiction, fantasy, and horror comic books.

Science Fiction Resources

http://www.arisia.org/sf.html

Science fiction fans can locate like-minded people and topical resources aided by these directional pointers. Included are links to genre-related text archives, gaming sites, film and television references, plus more.

The Science of Star Trek

**http://www.gsfc.nasa.gov/education/just_for_
fun/startrek.html**

A scientist explains what is and isn't scientifically sound in "Star Trek." See Editor's Choice.

The Sci-Fi and Fantasy Dungeon

**http://julmara.ce.chalmers.se/stefan/WWW/
Cyberlinks/saifai.html**

Readers with a developed taste for science fiction, horror and fantasy will appreciate this exhaustive directory of topical resources. Included in the collection are pointers to author biographies and bibliographies, critical reviews and reader polls, Usenet newsgroups, magazines, publishers and commercial vendors. An online search option aids quick reference, as do links to a universe of indices and commercial search engines

Star Trek Conventions

http://www.wwcd.com/shows/strekconv.html

This listing of "Star Trek" Conventions, maintained by the World-Wide Collectors Digest, offers continually updated calendars and event descriptions. Fans will also find a live discussion group, a series newsletter and more.

Star Trek: Points of Interest

**http://www.crc.ricoh.com/~marcush/
startrek.html**

This "points of interest" fan page on all things "Star Trek" includes dozens of links to topical sites. The lineup includes episode guides, movie information, sounds, images and fan club information.

---

a2z EDITOR'S CHOICE

The Klingon Language Institute

http://www.kli.org/

Say it in Klingon, and say it like you mean it! Class is now in session at the only nonprofit corporation in the known universe founded specifically to "promote, foster, and develop the Klingon language…and bring together Klingon language enthusiasts." Opened in 1992 by Dr. Lawrence M. Schoen "with only a few dozen members," the institute's membership now exceeds 1,000. Ongoing projects include translating the Bible's Old and New Testaments, producing a literary journal of original writings and restoring William Shakespeare's classic works back to "the Bard's original language." ("Hamlet" is complete.) Those interested in joining the fun must first complete an 11-lesson mail order course. Visitors don't have to be Klingon scholars, however, to enjoy the many online resources which include visual and aural presentations of the Klingon alphabet and everyday phrases such as the insult, "Hab SoSlI' Quch!" (Translation: Your mother had a smooth forehead!)—*Reviewed by Sean McFadden*

The Klingon Language Institute

Star Trek Usenet FAQs

http://www.cis.ohio-state.edu/hypertext/faq/
usenet/star-trek/top.html

This site contains Frequently Asked Questions
(FAQs) from the Usenet newsgroup hierarchy
rec.arts.startrek about the "Star Trek" television
and movie series.

Star Wars Collectors Archive

http://www.toysrqus.com/

"Star Wars" memorabilia and collectibles are
spotlighted here. Find listings of toys, cards, costumes, props, autographs and other items. Some
items featured may not be for sale.

Star Wars Home Page at UPENN

http://force.stwing.upenn.edu:8001/~jruspini/
starwars.html

This "Star Wars" fan page features a mind-blowing
assortment of files from "a long time ago in a galaxy far, far away." Visitors will find scripts from the
popular science-fiction films, trivia, multimedia
files, and links to such resources as a "Star Wars"
role-playing page and an "insider" magazine.

Tiptree Award

http://www.cs.wisc.edu/wiscon/tiptree/
intro.html

The Tiptree Award page lists the winners of this
sci-fi and fantasy award from 1992 through 1995.
It details the history and process of this recognition and links to a bibliography of feminist sci-fi.

toDaj, AberdeenDaq tlhIngan Duy'a'

http://galaxy.neca.com/~soruk/tlhIngan/

This site is a Klingon fan's dream. See Editor's
Choice.

2019: Off-World

http://kzsu.stanford.edu/uwi/br/off-world.html

Visit this site to learn more about the movie
"Blade Runner." See Editor's Choice.

WARP

http://www.hia.com/hia/pcr/home.html

There's weirdness afoot at the Sarfatti Group's Internet Science Education Project. Let Lt. Alexan-
drova take you on a tour through pages of
science, pseudo-science and "Dilbert" comics.
Visit the Star Force Academy, learn more about
Psi Wars and nanotechnology and ponder the reality of UFOs.

The Web Site of Love

http://fazer.engrs.inf.net/mst3k/

The Web Site of Love is a virtual house of worship
for the underground science fiction television
sensation "Mystery Science Theater 3000." Fans
will find episode summaries, schedules and reviews, as well as links to related discussion
groups and Web pages.

WWW Star Trek Home Page

http://www.chem.ed.ac.uk/adamstar.html

Well organized and extensive, this "Star Trek" index points to games, sounds, articles, pictures,
clubs and organizations, conventions, commercial sites, FAQs, and more.

---

a2z EDITOR'S CHOICE

The Science of Star Trek

http://www.gsfc.nasa.gov/education/just_for_fun/startrek.html

Science fiction fans who have ever wondered where the science ends and
the fiction begins will find this look at the original "Star Trek" and "The
Next Generation" series quite an eye-opener. Dr. David Allen Batchelor, a
NASA Goddard Space Flight Center physicist, examines and ranks in order of decreasing credibility a dozen of the more enterprising pieces of
hardware found on the starships, and a few of those interstellar oddities
encountered by the crews. Most credible is, of course, the ship's computer; most incredible, wormhole interstellar travel and time travel which, according to the good doctor, "stretch Einstein's relativity theory to its
ultimate limits." A fascinating read, the article supports the spirit of the
television series with a commendation for the shows' abilities to uplift
"our vision of what might be possible."—*Reviewed by Sean McFadden*

The Science of Star Trek

Author: David Allen Batchelor

Introduction

Is Star Trek really a science show, or just a lot of "gee, whiz" nonsensical Sci-Fi? Could people
really DO the fantastic things they do on the original Star Trek and Next Generation programs, or is
it all just hi-tech fantasy for people who can't face reality? Will the real world come to resemble the
world of unlimited power for people to travel about the Galaxy in luxurious, gigantic ships, and meet
exotic alien beings as equals?

Well, as for the science in Star Trek, Gene Roddenberry and the writers of the show have started
with science we know and s-t-r-e-t-c-h-e-d it to fit a framework of amazing inventions that support
action-filled and entertaining stories. Roddenberry knew some actual basic astronomy. He knew that
space ships unable to go faster than light would take decades to reach the stars, and that would be too
boring for a one-hour show per week. So he put warp drives into the show -- propulsion by
distorting the space-time continuum that Einstein conceived. With warp drive the ships could reach
far stars in hours or days, and the stories would fit human epic adventures, not stretch out for
lifetimes. Roddenberry tried to keep the stars realistically far, yet imagine human beings with the
power to reach them. Roddenberry and other writers added magic like the transporter and medical
miracles and the holodeck, but they put these in as equipment, as powerful tools built by human
engineers in a future of human progress. They uplifted our vision of what might be possible, and
that's one reason the shows have been so popular.

STYLE

The Bob-Haircut Pages

http://www.informatik.tu-muenchen.de/
cgi-bin/nph-gateway/hphalle9/~kuerten/spec/
bob.html

Asymmetrical bobs, bowl cuts, nice plain
bobs...suffice it to say, if it's a bob and you can
imagine it, you'll probably find a picture of a
woman sporting it here. See Editor's Choice.

Clear Plastic Fashions

http://clearplastic.com/

It's time to toss out that old yellow slicker and
drop by the Clear Plastic Fashions page to find out
about durable plastic rain gear made from shower curtains (what else?). Make your own fantastic
plastic creations by following the on-site instructions.

The Fashion Page

http://www.magna.com.au/~slade/fashion.html

What you wore yesterday—you know, that chic
taupe muumuu—may not be fashionable tomorrow. The Fashion Page strives to help you keep
abreast of the ever-changing trends. Learn to create your own designs at the schools listed, or find
out which agencies are looking to sign the next
supermodel.

in@veda

http://www.aveda.com/

The eco-conscious Aveda Corporation shares specifics on its natural line of hair and skin products. Get the lowdown on such items as Blue Malva shampoo and Flax Seed/Aloe Strong Hold Spray-On Styling Gel. Those interested in cutting-edge social activism will delight in the headlines of Aveda's charitable projects. Our favorite: "Traveling salon serves Midwest poor, homeless."

Kate Moss Photo Archive

http://marlowe.wimsey.com/~jamacht/Kate/Pictures/

Visitors to this fanatically organized fan page in honor of the super(skinny) model will find a tower of JPEGs and GIFs. Click through contact sheets, Cosmo covers and Calvin Klein ads. And, while you're at it, click through more contact sheets, Cosmo covers, and Calvin Klein ads. No doubt, you'll get your Kate kicks here.

Model's Lynk Home Page

http://www.modelslynk.com/

Female models. Male models. Models with swimsuits. Models without. If tracking down hot bodies is your thing, then this is the page for you. A professional talent service for models and actors, Model's Lynk offers a searchable "Talent Quest DataBase," along with information on casting, and a state-to-state listing of relevant services across the U.S. There's also a Webchat facility to talk about...yep, you guessed it.

Ntouch Magazine

http://www.dircon.co.uk/lcf/ntouch.html

Claiming to be the world's first online fashion and style magazine, Ntouch—a product of the students on the B.A. Fashion Promotions course at the London College of FashionFeatures range from men's and women's fashion previews to the "A to Sleaze of London Venues." And don't miss the zine's original photo spreads, which invite visitors to "Go mad stylishly."

Supermodel.com

http://www.supermodel.com/

Dedicated to providing "sensuous pictures, informative editorial, exciting contents, and awesome chat forums," the site features a daily newswire ("Cindy Puckers Up," "Ethan Rocks Out"), snappy party pics, and a Supermodel Shop that's loaded down with calendars and videos for sale. Special features like "Supermodels in the Rainforest" make this nothing short of one-stop glamor shopping.

TELEVISION

ARCHIVES AND INDICES

The Broadcasting Link

http://www.it.kompetens.com/broad.html

Web resources related to television and radio broadcasting are cataloged at this site from the Broadcasting Link. Learn about media around the world by following pointers to European and Asian sites, as well as general journalism links.

Film and Television Reviews

http://english-server.hss.cmu.edu/Film&TV.html

Visitors to this page will find a list of selected film and television Web sites. Dozens are listed in alphabetical order—from the "Activists Put the Public In Public TV" page to the U.S. Media History site.

Satellite Journal International Archives

http://itre.uncecs.edu/misc/sj/sj.html

This site features the searchable archive of Satellite Journal

International, a trade publication for the television and radio industries. Find news and commentary on cable systems, network launches, and related telecommunications legislation.

---

a2z EDITOR'S CHOICE

toDaj, AberdeenDaq tlhIngan Duy'a'

http://galaxy.neca.com/~soruk/tlhIngan/

Obviously a graduate of the Klingon Language Institute's tutorial (see above), "an offbeat Klingon in Aberdeen" who calls himself toDaj posts this Klingon language site offering jokes, poetry, and even a prayer. Can't read "the warrior's tongue" invented by linguist Dr. Marc Okrand? No problem. An English version of the home page reveals an interactive Klingon-to-English dictionary. Other pointers lead to the Klingon Homeworld page, the Klingon Relay Station and the Klingon Educational Virtual Environment. As for the Webmaster, a Human Life Sciences student at Scotland's Aberdeen University who also goes by the name Soruk of Vulcan, he wishes all entering his site "nuqneH" and those leaving, "Qapla'." Better check the dictionary to make sure those aren't fighting words.—*Reviewed by Sean McFadden*

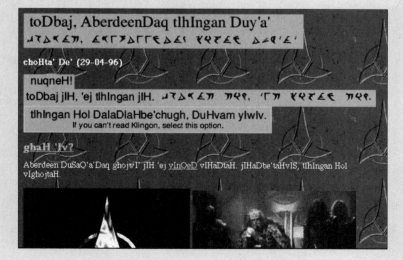

The Satellite TV (and Radio) Page

http://itre.uncecs.edu/misc/sat.html

Satellite watchers will appreciate this page devoted to television and radio dishes. Includes links to illustrated satellite charts, The Satellite Journal International archives and articles that run the gamut of dish issues.

SSatellite TV Images

http://itre.uncecs.edu/misc/images/images.html

The Institute for Transportation Research and Education at North Carolina University posts this collection of satellite television images. The collection includes photos from news broadcasts, cultural programming, station identifications, and more.

CREENsite

http://www.sa.ua.edu/screensite/

SCREENsite provides access to film and television resources on the Web. Information is available about research, education and production, including a reference shelf and mail-order video sources. Available in a variety of languages.

TV1.com

http://www.TV1.com/

TV1.com houses an online guide to broadcast and cable television programming, including a service that provides customized daily TV schedules via e-mail. Visitors can also search for information on television shows and check out products for sale.

TV Net

http://www.tvnet.com

This TV index should satisfy your TV info needs. See Editor's Choice.

ASSOCIATIONS AND ORGANIZATIONS

Academy of Television Arts & Sciences

http://www.emmys.org/tindex.html

The Academy of Television Arts and Sciences multimedia Web page features an online guide to the Emmy Awards, information about the academy, a photo gallery and sound clips. A link to the academy's mailing list is also included.

Association of America's Public Television Stations

http://www.universe.digex.net/~apts/

The Association of America's Public Television Stations is a professional organization of non-commercial television broadcasters. Visitors to its home page will find membership information as well as updates on the latest political developments effecting public broadcasting.

Society for Broadcast Engineers

http://www.sbe.org/

The Society for Broadcast Engineers, an Indianapolis-based professional organization, gives visitors a look at its activities and programs here. The site also includes job listings, conference announcements, and certification information.

Society of Motion Picture and Television Engineers

http://www.smpte.org/

The "preeminent professional society" for motion picture and television engineers maintains this site for news, publications and membership information. Visitors will also find conference schedules, officer profiles, employment opportunities and press releases from the organization.

---

a2z EDITOR'S CHOICE

2019: Off-World

http://kzsu.stanford.edu/uwi/br/off-world.html

A box office failure when originally released in 1982, director Ridley Scott's "Blade Runner" has since become a cult classic. Pitting outlaw artificial life forms Daryl Hannah and Rutger Hauer against police detective Harrison Ford in 2019 Los Angeles, the film's "noir" visual styling coupled with Vangelis's electronic soundtrack conjure a bleak, yet compelling background for this tale of technology gone bad. Explore the film and its various facets at this growing archive. Along with the usual movie site memorabilia such as audio and video files, find essays that examine the symbolism and underlying meanings found in the film, discussion archives of "Blade Runner" issues, and a study guide for Philip K. Dick's short story, "Do Androids Dream of Electric Sheep?," on which the film is loosely based. Visitors with something to contribute are urged to join the discussion forum, City-speak, or to submit their own Off-World documents, articles and essays.—*Reviewed by Sean McFadden*

2019: Off-World (*Blade Runner* Page)

This is a growing archive of All Kinds of Stuff that is related to the movie *Blade Runner*. It is divided into two parts: **material kept on this site**, and **material found elsewhere on the net**. It is provided by the cultural workers of UnderWorld Industries.

Please direct comments and questions ✉ comments to: jon@kzsu.stanford.edu

Material maintained on *Off-World*

Note: If you have documents, articles, etc. about *Blade Runner* and they need a home on the net, please contact me at the address above regarding putting them on Off-World.

- Join in on City-speak, our *Blade Runner* discussion forum!
- Info on the book '*Future Noir: The Making of* Blade Runner', from fellow fan Bill Kolb
- 'Is Blade Runner a Misogynist Text?', essay on *Blade Runner* by Simon Scott

COMPANIES

INTERNATIONAL

The Australian Broadcasting Corporation

http://www.abc.net.au/

The Australian Broadcasting Corporation home page provides an online profile of the noncommercial organization and its network of radio and television stations. Includes details on various program offerings.

BBC Public Access World Wide Web Server

http://www.bbc.co.uk/

This British Broadcasting Corporation site features links to its satellite

broadcasting centers, weather forecasts, national lottery information and selected program pages. Links to the more complete BBC Radio, BBC TV, and BBC Education sites are also featured.

The Box Office

http://www.tbo.nl/index.html

Download sample video clips from The Box Office, a Dutch company that produces and markets television images, text and photographs for electronic and print media. Also includes a company profile, news and links to partner Web design company, Medi@web.

The Broadcasting House

http://www.bbc.co.uk/aberdeen/index.html

The Broadcasting House, a BBC studio facility in Aberdeen, Scotland, expands its production capabilities to accommodate Web publishing. Visitors can review production facilities and sample television and radio programming fare here.

Canadian Broadcasting Corporation

http://www.cbc.ca/

Canada's public broadcasting service offers news, science, education and lifestyle programming in English and French. Visitors to its home page will find a variety of programming notes, national and international news resources, bulletin boards, and much more.

Nippon Television Network Corporation

http://www.ntv.co.jp/

Japan's "top-rated television network" is online here with information about the company, synopses of its shows and a downloadable example of its animation. A link to Japan's largest newspaper is also here.

Rogers World Wide Web Server

http://www.rogers.com/

This corporate home page provides information about Canadian media giant Rogers Communications Inc. Includes information on Rogers' radio and television broadcasting and newspaper and periodical publishing concerns, plus service information for Rogers' cable TV customers.

South African Broadcasting Corporation

http://www.sabc.co.za/

Learn the latest from South Africa from the company that covers its national news on television and radio. Visitors will find links to sport and social clubs, political coverage, marketing and media resources, and much more.

Special Broadcasting Service

http://acslink.net.au/~tomw/sbs.html

The Special Broadcasting Service was established by the Australian Parliament to broadcast multicultural and multilingual radio and television programming. Visitors to its home page will find an explanation of the group's mission and details of its programs and operations.

Television Corporation of Singapore

http://tcs.com.sg/

The Television Corporation of Singapore home page provides daily broadcasting schedules and previews of upcoming programming. Includes browsable "instant TV classifieds" and a "fun page" offering merchandising and celebrity information.

VH1-derland

http://www.vh1.de/

This German language page provides details on the contemporary adult music video network VH-1. Features include music news, interviews, photos, charts, and concert dates.

VPRO Netherlands

http://www.vpro.nl/

Assess the state of public television in the Netherlands at this site. The VPRO Public Broadcasting Organization home page offers programming information almost exclusively in Dutch. Only cursory background information is in English.

---

a2z EDITOR'S CHOICE

The Bob-Haircut Pages

http://www.informatik.tu-muenchen.de/cgi-bin/nph-gateway/hphalle9/~kuerten/spec/bob.html

No one could possibly adore bobbed women more than the "computer-consultings engineer" who maintains these bob-a-licious pages. "This haircut is a timeless, sexy feature which (in my opinion) supports every beautiful woman's face so incredibly," the Webmaster explains. And we learn that the positive feedback on the site has simply "overwhelmed" him. Asymmetrical bobs, bowl cuts, nice plain bobs...suffice it to say, if it's a bob and you can imagine it, you'll probably find a picture of a woman sporting it here.

U.S.

Arkansas Educational Telecommunications Network

http://www.aetn.org/

The Arkansas Educational Telecommunications Network, a member of the Public Broadcasting System, highlights programming and educational services at this site. Visit here to learn about the television network and link to program schedules and profiles.

Cable Television Laboratories, Inc.

http://www.cablelabs.com/

Louisville, Colorado-based research and development consortium Cable Television Laboratories, Inc. maintains this site for member services. Visitors will find public access to a variety of targeted trade publications, industry news reports and current press releases.

The Christian Broadcasting Network

http://the700club.org/

The Christian Broadcasting Network maintains this page with information on the network, a viewer guide, 700 Club information and various press releases. Includes a list of stations carrying Christian programming and access to ministry information.

Corporation for Public Broadcasting

http://www.cpb.org/

The Corporation for Public Broadcasting supports its noncommercial televised programming with this site featuring the "PTV Families" magazine. Also find the Public Broadcasting Directory, the annual report and links to Web-based public broadcast resources.

Discovery Channel Online

http://www.discovery.com

This interactive site is full of information and graphics. See Editor's Choice.

Dominion, the Sci-Fi Channel's Home Page

http://www.scifi.com/

The online home of the Sci-Fi Channel includes program listings and series information. Guests will also find extras like pulp fiction excerpts and reviews and a collection of images and audio and video clips. Includes information for science fiction memorabilia collectors.

Eye on the Net @ CBS

http://cbs-tv.tiac.net/

The CBS Television site features pointers to the home pages of its prime-time and late-night series, as well as "Up to the Minute News" and CBS Sports. Visitors also will find opportunities to buy, download or win CBS merchandise.

KGTV San Diego

http://www.kgtv.com/

KGTV, San Diego's ABC affiliate station, posts its programming schedule and editorial policies at this home page. Find children's resources, news, technological information and more.

KHOU Houston

http://www.khou.com/

This Houston, Texas-based CBS television affiliate, offers information on its programming schedule and local area. Find current news, weather and sports updates, links to network program offerings, and a virtual tour of Houston.

KLAS Las Vegas

http://www.infi.net/vegas/KLAS-TV/

The KLAS-TV Eyewitness News page features information from the Las Vegas television station, including breaking news, weather reports and sports. Includes links to national news stories and the CBS home page.

KPIX San Francisco

http://www.kpix.com/

The home page for San Francisco's CBS affiliate lets visitors peek through a television camera stationed at the top of Nob Hill, read the KPIX station pages, or link to Bay Area weather reports. Also includes background information on shows and news teams.

KVOA Tucson

http://www.kvoa.com/

KVOA-TV in Tucson, Arizona offers news, weather, opinion and stock information here. Visitors can download daily newscast scripts, sports updates, and biographical sketches of the anchors.

---

a2z EDITOR'S CHOICE

TV Net

http://www.tvnet.com

Until the technological breakthrough allowing TV junkies and Web surfers to all huddle around the same box, this site may just get better ratings than the boob tube itself. The self-proclaimed "ultimate" TV index lives up to its boasts, offering more than 5,400 links to 847 series, including official studio home pages, fan-produced tribute sites, newsgroups and the ever-present episode guides. TV Net is also for those who take an active part in television. Almost as numerous as its program links is its directory of international broadcast organizations, production companies, talent agencies and professional contacts. Dozens of letters from people behind the camera—and glued to their screens—attest that this is the new TV guide.—*Reviewed by Paul Bacon*

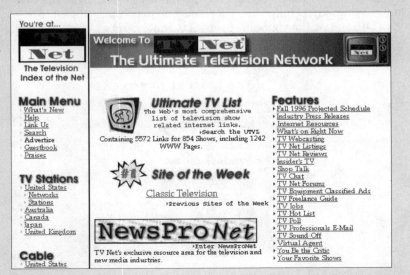

Montana Public Television Visions TV Guide

http://www.kusm.montana.edu/

The Montana Public Broadcast System maintains this online guide to introduce its programming and community offerings. Visitors will also find viewer mail, program schedules and membership information. Links to other interesting sites in Montana are included.

NBC.COM

http://www.nbc.com

NBC's home page has something for everyone. See Editor's Choice.

Paramount Pictures Online Studio

http://voyager.paramount.com/

Visitors to the Paramount Pictures Online Studio can access interactive previews of recently released films from the studio, plot summaries and schedules of popular television series and a look at current television productions. Includes links to online programming and development projects on the Web.

PBS Online

http://www.pbs.org/

The Public Broadcasting System's online guide provides a variety of program-related resources. Visitors will find background information, production credits and talent profiles for many of its current series and specials. See Editor's Choice.

Texas Student Television KVR 9 Austin

http://www.utexas.edu/depts/output/www/tstv.html

Texas Student Television KVR 9 is a student-run facility at the University of Texas, Austin, which broadcasts beyond the campus via KVR-TV (Austin's Channel 9) and KVR-InterneTV. Find information here about the station's operation and programs.

United Paramount Network

http://www.contrib.andrew.cmu.colu/~aaron/upn/upn.html

A television viewer provides this unofficial guide to the United Paramount Network, featuring general information and weekly ratings of its most popular programs. The site also includes schedules, program descriptions and links to home pages for individual shows.

Video Editing Guide

http://www.videonics.com

This site has something for video editors of all levels. See Editor's Choice.

WGN Chicago

http://www.wgntv.com/

Chicago superstation WGN-TV features links to several of its broadcast divisions from this home page, including news, sports and programming, as well as a general information section. Visitors can also access its download library for images, videos and audio files.

WHRO Hampton Roads (Va.)

http://www.whro-pbs.org/

Visitors to this site will find links to the Hampton Roads, Virginia Public Television, National Public Radio and Fine Arts Public Radio broadcasting stations. Also included: WHRO program schedules, and details on learning services and national affiliations.

WISC Madison

http://www.wisctv.com/

WISC-TV3, a Madison, Wisconsin television station, goes online with news, weather, sports, editorials, programming and local links. Visitors to this official site can also search the previous week's worth of news transcripts.

WKBW NewsChannel 7 Buffalo

http://www.wkbw.com/

Buffalo, New York's WKBW Channel 7 promotes its news and talk show lineup at this promotional site. Visitors can e-mail their favorite local television personality or check the station's weekly programming schedule.

WRTV-6 Indianapolis

http://www.wrtv.com/wrtv6/

WRTV-6, the Indianapolis ABC affiliate, maintains this informational site. Visitors will find local news, sports, weather and lottery updates here, as well as extensive links to local career and educational resources.

---

a2z EDITOR'S CHOICE

Discovery Channel Online

http://www.discovery.com

Visit the Discovery Channel home page at your own productive risk. We did and found so much interesting stuff that we almost forgot to come back and tell you about it. Science, animals, sports, sociology—nearly anything that has to do with life on earth is explored at this interactive site, much of it more involving than the award-winning cable TV network that spawned it. Each day of the week is given a different theme, teaching visitors about everything from the life of cicadas to the invention of the headspanner (a caliper-like tool used to measure facial growth). Full-color graphics and bold layouts make the educational articles seem to fly off the page, and it even performs offline research and e-mails you the results.—*Reviewed by Paul Bacon*

SHOWS

Are You Being Served? Homepage!

http://drh.net/jrice/

This fan-produced page is devoted to the BBC comedy series "Are You Being Served?" Visitors will find cast biographies, pictures, an episode list, sound clips, and more.

Beakman's World

http://www.spe.sony.com/Pictures/tv/beakman/beakman.html

Fans of "Beakman's World," a children's science show with a sense of humor, will enjoy this official site from Sony Pictures. Download audio and video clips from the popular series.

Blake's 7

http://hawks.ha.md.us/blake7/index.html

The "Blake's 7" science fiction series, which aired on BBC from 1978 through 1981, is featured on this fan-produced page. Includes information on the cast and characters, as well as episode synopses, scripts, sound bites, photos, and related links.

Charlie's Angels Fan Site

http://www.clever.net/wiley/charliea.htm

The history of ultra-cheesy detective show "Charlie's Angels" comes to life on the Web. This fan site features an episode guide and links to the Angel Trap! zine. Lots of fab photos, too.

Clarissa Explains It All

http://www.ee.surrey.ac.uk/Contrib/Entertainment/Clarissa/

In a quirky Nickelodeon situation comedy, Clarissa, a teenager, describes the things that are happening in her life. This page offers episode guides, cast biographies, recurring characters, interviews, trivia and discussions of character development.

Deus Ex Machina (Mystery Science Theater 3000)

http://sunsite.unc.edu/lunar/mst3k/mst3k.html

Deus Ex Machina is packed with information and links to what appears to be anything and everything on the Web that's related to the television program "Mystery Science Theater 3000." Find QuickTime video segments, a cassette exchange

and answers to Frequently Asked Questions (FAQs).

Dream On

http://www.mca.com/tv/dreamon/

The HBO adult sitcom "Dream On" is the focus of this site, maintained by MCA Television Entertainment. Includes a synopsis of upcoming episodes, animated clips, and a discussion of the show's inspiration by its creators.

Encyclopedia Brady

http://www.primenet.com/~dbrady

If it's not here, it's not Brady. See Editor's Choice.

E.R.

http://src.doc.ic.ac.uk/public/media/tv/collections/tardis/us/drama/ER/

Fans of the hospital drama "ER" can catch up on the latest episode at this unofficial site. Visit for show synopses, publicity photograph archives, answers to frequently asked questions and more.

Forever Knight

http://www.spe.sony.com/Pictures/tv/forever/forever.html

Sony Pictures Entertainment maintains this home page for its syndicated series "Forever Knight," the story of a 13th century vampire living in a modern-day metropolis. Visitors will find cast photos, video and audio clips, and show trivia.

Friends

http://www.friends-tv.org/

This friendly site provides answers to frequently asked questions about *That Show*, an episode guide, articles, images, sound bites, and merchandising. Links to newsgroups, FTP archives and other Web sites on the sitcom phenom.

Friends FTP

ftp://ftp.dartmouth.edu/pub/friends/

Students at Dartmouth College have created this FTP site for fans of the "Friends" comedy series. On file: episode guides, drinking games, cast member trivia and more.

Full House

http://pmwww.cs.vu.nl/service/sitcoms/FullHouse/

"Full House" fans can follow news about the family-oriented sitcom on this unofficial page. Find a worldwide broadcast list, an episode guide, ruminations about the show's future and links to the actors' home pages.

Hawaii Five-O Fan Site

http://web20.mindlink.net/a4369/fiveo.htm

"Hawaii Five-O," the longest continuous-run police series in television history, was popular more for its scenery than its acting. A fan's Web site celebrates the show with links, dialogue and more.

EDITOR'S CHOICE

NBC.COM

http://www.nbc.com

TV ratings king NBC chimes in with the best home page of the commercial networks, offering a well-rounded assortment of news, sports and entertainment features. Its colorful and inviting welcome screen, reminiscent of a "USA Today" front page, has something to offer everyone, from newshounds to the soap opera-addicted. Looking for financial information? The NBC site has you covered, too, offering a wide variety of up-to-the-minute stock market and investing news via its link to the CNBC financial network. Sports fans will find entire sections—many co-developed with publications such as "Golf Digest"—devoted to their game of choice. All this and more is provided at this site, created in part by another fairly well known media entity: Microsoft.—*Reviewed by Paul Bacon*

Highlander

http://mithral.iit.edu:8080/highlander/

Devoted to the Scottish "Highlander" myths and legends, this site explores the popular motion pictures and television series. Includes links to a multimedia gallery and access to an exciting role-playing game.

Jeopardy!

http://www.spe.sony.com/Pictures/tv/jeopardy/jeopardy.html

Check out photographs, video clips, audio clips and more from the American game show mainstay, "Jeopardy!" This official home page also includes background information on the show and details on how to become a contestant.

Late Night with Conan O'Brien Fan Purity Test

http://www.rpi.edu/~nebusj/lnfpt.html

Test your "Late Night with Conan O'Brien" knowledge here. The fan purity test quizzes visitors about the show and its stars and dubs high-scorers "Conan-heads."

Late Show with David Letterman

http://www.cbs.com/lateshow/lateshow.html

The official CBS site for "Late Show with David Letterman" serves up the latest Top 10, cast bios, guest lists and an archive of photos. Amuse yourself with "Dave's lines of the week," or shop for promotional merchandise in the electronic catalog.

Law and Order

http://www.mca.com/tv/laworder/

This "Law and Order" promotional site dishes up a vast assortment of information for the show's fans. Check out the latest episode news, browse production notes, star pages, awards and credit information, or contribute your thoughts to an on-line forum.

MacGyver

http://www.cjnetworks.com/~mkelley/macgyver

Fans of the "MacGyver" television action series will enjoy this site, featuring character and actor biographies, episode guides, and answers to Frequently Asked Questions (FAQs). Includes an index of "MacGyverisms," the clever schemes that the main character seems to pull out of thin air in tight situations.

Mad About You

http://www.spe.sony.com/Pictures/tv/mad/mad.html

This Sony Pictures Entertainment page features a look at NBC's romantic sitcom "Mad About You." Includes photos of the cast, video and audio clips, and a peek backstage.

Married…with Children

http://www.spe.sony.com/Pictures/tv/married/married.html

"Honey, I'm home!" This site promotes everybody's favorite raunchy sitcom, "Married…with Children." Check out photos, video and audio clips, and ticket information for studio tapings.

The Medic ER Web Site

http://www.albany.net/~williamh/welcome.html

Fans of the television hospital drama "ER" can visit the Medic ER site for news, gossip and cast photos. Visit to find the "Emmy watch," or make an appointment to give blood online.

Mr. Video's Star Trek Vidiot Home Page

http://www.cdsnet.net/vidiot/

The legendary series "Star Trek" occupies a place in the universe too large to be contained in the television set. Trekkies discuss, dissect and disseminate news of and views on the "Voyager," "Deep Space Nine" and "The Next Generation" shows at this fan-produced site.

MTV Online

http://www.mtv.com/

MTV's home page is as splashy as you'd expect. Find information on original programming, music news and personalities. Video and audio clips are also available.

The Muppet Page

http://www.sci.kun.nl/thalia/funpage/muppets/muppet_homepage_en.html

Devotees of Jim Henson's snuggly puppets can visit this page to find photo spreads, program transcripts and sound bites from the popular television show. Links are provided to fan pages of such star Muppets as Miss Piggy and Kermit the Frog.

National Talk Show Registry Home Page

http://ourworld.compuserve.com/homepages/ntsgr

Want to be a guest on a talk show? See Editor's Choice.

---

a2z EDITOR'S CHOICE

PBS Online

http://www.pbs.org

For more than 25 years, the Public Broadcasting System has provided quality educational and cultural programming free from commercials and ratings pressures. Visitors to its Web home will find a similar fare of intelligent and informative content, from "Storytime" and "Sesame Street" to its thought-provoking series "The American Experience" and "Masterpiece Theater." Downloadable transcripts and engaging interactive twists on many of the programs are available. Online classroom guides are here to assist educators in relating the content of PBS to students and to suggest learning projects and further reading. A clickable calendar provides full broadcasting schedules, including profiles of the people who make PBS the one network qualified to say "television is a rare medium well done."—*Reviewed by Paul Bacon*

The New Red Green Show Official Fan Site

http://www.redgreen.com/

The producers of "The New Red Green Show," a family-oriented comedy series, maintain this home page for fans. Episode guides, personal appearance schedules and merchandise offers are featured.

The Original Space Ghost Web Page

http://iquest.com/~cshuffle/sghost/

This fan page for "Space Ghost" celebrates the black-hooded interplanetary crusader who has been on television in various incarnations since 1966. The site includes episode guides, sound files and an interview with Space Ghost himself.

P.O.V. Interactive

http://www0.pbs.org/pov

This user-friendly site wants your opinions. See Editor's Choice.

The Q Continuum

http://www.europa.com/~mercutio/Q.html

Devoted to the "Q" character from the television series "Star Trek: The Next Generation," this fan page features links to information about the actor who played the part, character quotes, photos and sound bites.

Ricki Lake Show Official Home Page

http://www.spe.sony.com/Pictures/tv/rickilake/ricki.html

Get online with American daytime talk show hostess Ricki Lake. Receive tickets to a live taping, enter contests, or link to Web sites covering all facets of daytime television.

The Rockford Files Home Page

http://busboy.sped.ukans.edu/~asumner/rockford/

Fans of tongue-in-cheek 1970s detective series "The Rockford Files" will enjoy this unofficial site, which features photographs of James Garner and other actors on the show, an episode guide, answering machine messages and more.

The Save Earth2 Home Page

http://ppsa.com/e2/

The NBC television series "Earth2" is gone but not forgotten. This site provides information on the effort to save the canceled series. Send letters of protest, subscribe to a newsletter, or dig for some information on the show and its cast.

Schoolhouse Rock

http://iquest.com/~bamafan/shr

This site is devoted to those educational animated shorts. See Editor's Choice.

The Science of Star Trek

http://www.gsfc.nasa.gov/education/just_for_fun/startrek.html

An examination of the "Star Trek" series, this site questions the validity of technology presented on the show. The ship's computer, the holodeck, phasers and alien beings are featured subjects.

Seinfeld

http://www.cs.cmu.edu/afs/cs/user/vernon/www/vandelay/index.html/

Visitors to this page will find information about the popular sitcom "Seinfeld" and its cast. Includes episode guides, photos, backstage gossip and links to a variety of other fan-produced sites from around the world.

Seinfeld Official Fan Site

http://www.spe.sony.com/Pictures/tv/seinfeld/seinfeld.html

Sony Pictures Entertainment sponsors this home page dedicated to its sitcom "Seinfeld." Includes photographs of cast members, video and audio clips as well as highlights from the set.

Sliders

http://www.mca.com/tv/sliders/

This official MCA Entertainment page promotes the television series "Sliders," based on the adventures of four pioneers who have discovered how to slide through parallel dimensions of Earth. Find facts about the show, production information and credits, star pages and an online game.

Space Precinct

http://www.neosoft.com/sbanks/sp/SpcPnct.html

The science fiction series "Space Precinct" from British producer Gerry Anderson is the focus of this site. Background information and video from the show are available, along with information on Anderson. Other sci-fi television links are included.

Terminal X

http://www.neosoft.com/sbanks/xfiles/xfiles.html

This is one of the best "X-Files" sites. See Editor's Choice.

---

a2z EDITOR'S CHOICE

Video Editing Guide

http://www.videonics.com

Whether you are a professional video editor, or have just figured out how to make the clock on your VCR read something other than "12:00," this online guide to video editing has something for you. Maintained by a California-based digital video post-production equipment manufacturer, the Video Editing Guide provides a variety of tips and tricks for amateurs and pros alike. The beginner's primer section teaches effective in-camera editing for newbies using only a common camcorder. Intermediate editors are treated to lessons on multi-source video mixing and minimizing generational loss. And for those already in the business, the advanced section compares contemporary video standards, describes the latest advances in special effects, and provides links to a host of professional resources, equipment manufacturers, and upcoming seminars.—*Reviewed by Paul Bacon*

"The difference between an amateur and a professional is that an amateur shows you ALL his pictures."

Theodore Tugboat Online Activity Center

http://www.cochran.com/tt.html

The animated Canadian television series "Theodore Tugboat" provides this online activity center. Features include an interactive story book, an online coloring book, an episode guide and character descriptions.

The Tonight Show

http://www.nbctonightshow.com/

In addition to watching Jay Leno on television's "The Tonight Show," Web surfers can watch clips from the program each day at this official NBC site. The highlights are culled from the previous evening's broadcast and include audio and video clips, guest schedules and jokes galore.

The Top 10 Lists from Late Show with David Letterman

http://www.cbs.com/lateshow/ttlist.html

This page from the larger CBS Web site features a searchable archive of the Top 10 Lists from the "Late Show with David Letterman." Also featured: the Top Ten of the Top Ten as selected by the television show's writers.

TV Nation (Unofficial) Home Page

http://www.xwinds.com/tv/tvnation.html

This fan-produced "TV Nation" site provides information about the award-winning television program and its producer, Michael Moore. Find contact information for Fox Television and the TV show's fan club, plus a link to the show's Usenet newsgroup.

Ultimate TV List

http://tvnet.com/UTVL/utvl.html

From TVNet, a virtual forum hosting discussions on television and the media, comes the "ultimate" guide to TV, offering thousands of links arranged by genre. Real TV junkies can link to related newsgroups and participate in the action by adding their favorite shows to the database.

VR.5 Fan Site

http://daniel.drew.edu/~adebliec/vr5.html

Visit here for an Internet fan page devoted to the now-defunct American television show "VR.5." The page includes show information and television network addresses.

The Wild Wild West Unofficial Episode Guide

http://moose.uvm.edu/~glambert/twww1.html

Western fans and kitsch afficianados alike will enjoy this tribute to 1960s television series "The Wild Wild West." Visitors will find complete episode guides as well as miscellaneous facts about the show and its stars.

---

a2z EDITOR'S CHOICE

Encyclopedia Brady

http://www.primenet.com/~dbrady

"B" is the butterfly poster above Marcia's bed. "R" is the Rockets baseball team, of which Greg is the head. "A" is for Alice, who's scrubbing a plate, and just "DY" is what Jan will do if she can't find a date. Put them all together and you have a Web site so demented, it should be blocked from national online services. Frightening as it may sound, the creator of this "Brady Bunch" tribute has alphabetically cataloged every element from the fanatical '70s sitcom; from Cindy's coveted doll (Kitty Karry-All) down to the license plate on Mr. Brady's convertible (DJF 314). It's all here, from A to Z, along with an episode guide and an exhaustive history of the actual San Fernando Valley house used during the series.—*Reviewed by Paul Bacon*

National Talk Show Registry Home Page

http://ourworld.compuserve.com/homepages/ntsgr

Okay, so you're a recently divorced, chain-smoking, bisexual son of a cross-dressing minister with a penchant for Asian women and Latin men. You have no friends, but you do have a 200-pound cat. What do you do to make sense of your life? Go on a daytime talk show, of course! Touting itself as the "world's first clearinghouse for regular people who want to share their life adventures with a TV audience," the National Talk Show Registry will act as your agent to get you an on-air date with Geraldo, Sally, Ricki—anyone with a mike and a major advertiser. Eager guests-to-be should check the home page of this actual company (it's real, we checked) to find out if they measure up to daytime TV's exacting standards.—*Reviewed by Paul Bacon*

WQED Web of Life

http://www.envirolink.org/orgs/wqed

WQED, of Pittsburgh presents this page on "Web of Life: Exploring Biodiversity," a two-hour public-television special highlighting the diversity of life on earth. A QuickTime preview is available, along with lots of links, descriptions of scenes and home video ordering information.

The X-Files Fan Site

http://www.rutgers.edu/x-files.html

This site is devoted to the popular Fox television program "The X-Files." Visitors creeping around here can hear the theme music, find an extensive episode guide and link to related fan sites.

THEATER

ARCHIVES AND INDICES

Carnegie Mellon University Drama Directory

http://english-www.hss.cmu.edu/drama/

The English Department of Carnegie Mellon University maintains this extensive drama directory. Visitors can link up with plays, motion picture and television scripts, and discussions of drama and dramatic productions.

Guide to Theater Resources on the Internet

http://www-old.ircam.fr/divers/theatre-e.html

This site's title leaves little to the imagination. Among its many theater resources: mailing lists, electronic newsletters, gopher sites, newsgroups, FTP sites, FAQs, and databases.

Home Page of Theatre

http://www.cs.fsu.edu/projects/group4/theatre.html

An extension of the Florida State University Theatre Department, the Home Page of Theatre indexes the playwrights, plays, theater groups, and theater-related miscellany of the Net. Among other things, visitors can do a WAIS search on theater and flip through Ray Bradbury's Theatre Episode Guide here.

The Intuitons College Theatre Guide

http://dolphin.upenn.edu/~intuiton/guide/newguide.html

Intuitons, a student-run experimental theater company at the University of Pennsylvania, compiles this handy guide to college thespianism. Find links to university theater departments, performing arts centers, and other resources.

Joe Geigel's favorite Theatre Related Resources

http://artsnet.heinz.cmu.edu/OnBroadway/links/

Visitors to Joe Geigel's Favorite Theatre Related Resources will undoubtedly have a hard time choosing where to begin. Stagecraft, publications, theatrical groups, shows, and performers pepper the list of coverage here.

Kabuki for Everyone

http://www.fix.co.jp/kabuki/kabuki.html

This site explains Kabuki. See Editor's Choice.

Tower Lyrics Archive

http://www.ccs.neu.edu/home/tower/lyrics.html

Locate the lyrics to your favorite stage musicals at the Tower Lyrics Archive. The works of Andrew Lloyd Webber ("Cats"), Boublil and Schoenberg ("Les Miserables"), and Gilbert and Sullivan ("Pirates of Penzance") are featured prominently, though song lyrics from such titles as "The Little Mermaid" and "Rocky Horror Picture Show" are also spelled out.

---

a2z **EDITOR'S CHOICE**

P.O.V. Interactive

http://www0.pbs.org/pov

If you're tired of the endless, one-way conversation you have with your television every night, throw in your two cents at this interactive site. Claiming that "talking back is as American as watching TV," this page provides an online forum for discussing the myriad social and political issues raised in the PBS documentary series "P.O.V." Developed with the Center for Media Literacy, P.O.V. Interactive leads visitors through a user-friendly process of gathering opinions and viewpoints. And for those who may have missed the documentary on television, important snippets from the shows are available for playback. After eliciting open-ended responses to general questions, the site displays other visitors' comments and provides pointers to other online issues forums such as Cafe Utne and Project Vote Smart.—*Reviewed by Paul Bacon*

A VIEW ADS

B VIEW ADS

PROFILES

After you've 'screened' the ads you can click here to find out additional background information, provided by Project Vote Smart, on the candidates.

SURVEY

P.O.V. and the Center for Media Literacy want to hear your points of view about campaign advertising. Responses will be compiled; come back to review the results.

AD FACTS

A few facts and figures about ads and campaigning.

ASSOCIATIONS AND ORGANIZATIONS

United States Institute for Theater Technology

http://www.ffa.ucalgary.ca/usitt/

Design and production workers in theater can find out about their U.S. trade organization here. Visitors will find information on the institute's structure, publications, grants, events and more.

CITY STAGES a2z

New York: Broadway

http://emall.com/ExploreNY/Broadway/Bway1.html

Get show times, theater addresses, and plot synopses for Broadway and off-Broadway shows at the Broadway page. Links to informative pages of other attractions in the Big Apple are also included.

New York: On Broadway WWW Information Page

http://artsnet.heinz.cmu.edu/OnBroadway/

ArtsNet provides services and information relating to arts management and cultural resources on the Internet. Visit its On Broadway WWW Information Page for a variety of information about Broadway plays and musicals.

COMMUNITY THEATER

Better Bad News - George Coates Performance Works

http://www.georgecoates.org/

George Coats Performance Works is a San Francisco-based theatre group, but its promotional site features much more than performance schedules and ticket information. Visitors can also rifle through a "live web sho" index for interactive entertainment.

COMPANIES

American Conservatory Theater

http://www.act-sfbay.org/

San Francisco's American Conservatory Theater describes itself as an "artist-driven, Tony Award-

winning theater whose mainstage work is energized and informed by a profound commitment to actor training." Read all about it at the home page, along with information on current productions.

Michael Butler Presents

http://www.orlok.com/

Michael Butler Presents is the umbrella page for a Chicago theatrical production company. Included are a link to a retrospective history of "Hair" and a site called the Pope Joan Workshop Web. The latter promotes a Chicago production of a new musical called "Pope Joan," providing excerpts from the script and score, as well as an ongoing behind-the-scenes production diary.

New Heart Company of Artists

http://nyquist.ee.ualberta.ca/~sharma/newheart.html

With its home page, the New Heart Company of Artists, of Edmonton, Alberta, Canada, sheds light on its "cyclic creations through a reactive mix of movement, drama, music, and images."

FESTIVALS AND EVENTS

Bard on the Beach

http://www.faximum.com/bard

Bard on the Beach, a professional Shakespeare Festival in Vancouver, B.C., provides information about its plays, company, and performance schedule. Visitors can access information about the current season as well as ordering information for the festival gift shop.

The California Shakespeare Festival

http://www.via.net:80/~csf/

The California Shakespeare Festival provides schedules and details on festival events along with photos of the previous season's productions. Visitors will also find information on purchasing tickets.

---

a2z EDITOR'S CHOICE

Schoolhouse Rock

http://iquest.com/~bamafan/shr

Every generation or so, a great idea makes its way onto network television. "Schoolhouse Rock" was one of these ideas: a series of animated, educational short subjects from the '70s set to catchy music that showed we learn best when we're having fun. Ask anyone age 20 to 35 how a law is created, and they're likely to sing a few bars of "I'm Just a Bill" to jog their memory. The same applies for grammar ("Conjunction Junction"), civil rights ("Suffrin' Till Suffrage"), and just about everything else taught in school, tested on and immediately forgotten. For full text and sound files of all of the songs, stop by this site, which also provides news about stage productions and rock music remakes of Generation X's most memorable educational experience.—*Reviewed by Paul Bacon*

As your body grows bigger
Your mind will flower
It's great to learn
'Cause knowledge is power!

Renaissance Faire Homepage
http://www.resort.com/~banshee/Faire/index.html

Intended primarily as a reference for Renaissance Faire workers, visitors to this page will find pointers to period information, as well as general resources for faires and reenactments. Featured topics include authentic costuming, language usage and working with the public.

Stratford Festival
http://www.ffa.ucalgary.ca/stratford/

Read about this year's stage schedule for the Stratford Festival in Stratford, Canada. Stop by

the box office to find out how to order tickets, or browse the theater's archives for festival facts.

Utah Shakespearean Festival
http://www.bard.org/

The Utah Shakespearean Festival's site includes a description of various theaters as well as a calendar of events, visitor's guide details on how to order tickets. Links to related sites are also included.

EDITOR'S CHOICE

Terminal X
http://www.neosoft.com/sbanks/xfiles/xfiles.html

With hundreds, possibly thousands, of "X-Files" tributes now lingering in cyberspace, fans of this quirky detective series may count themselves as the largest cult group on the Web. Unfortunately, not all of these homespun fan sites are created equal, most offering little more than a few quips from the show ("Mulder, it's me") and/or the now famous wet t-shirt publicity photo of Gillian Anderson, a k a Agent Sculley. Enter Terminal X, a content-rich guide to Fox's paranormal mystery show. As intelligent as it is intriguing, this independently created site offers links to real-life investigative organizations like the CIA and the FBI, in addition to a plethora of soundbites, related fiction, paranormal testimonies and screen shots of its deadpan co-stars locked in thousand-yard stares.—*Reviewed by Paul Bacon*

FUNDING, ENDOWMENTS, AND GRANTS

The New York Foundation for the Arts
http://www.tmn.com/0h/Artswire/www/nyfa.html

Granting grants and offering support services to artists working throughout the state, the New York Foundation for the Arts works to bring contemporary art to the public. The nonprofit's financial, educational, and advocacy programs are outlined at this site.

IMPROVISATION

Firesign Theatre
http://home.earthlink.net/~ritter/firesign/firesign.html

On its home page, Los Angeles-based comedy troupe Firesign Theatre links to its Usenet newsgroup, sound clips, and a series of FAQ files about its stream-of-consciousness brand of humor.

The Improv Page
http://sunee.uwaterloo.ca/~broehl/improv/index.html

The Improv Page gives would-be comedians and comedy lovers the poop on improvisational theater. The page includes a history of the art form, a list of improv groups, and announcements of upcoming events. It also offers tips on starting an improv group.

MUSICALS

Miss Saigon
http://www.clark.net/pub/rsjdfg/

Check here for info about this blockbuster musical. See Editor's Choice.

10086 Sunset Boulevard
http://www.cen.uiuc.edu/~dd-moore/sunset-blvd.html

Mr. DeMille didn't direct this close-up, but fans of the classic film and musical remake of "Sunset Boulevard" can get up close and personal with the story. Focus in on details of recent productions or pan over to images, sounds, and backstage tours.

Phantom of the Opera
http://phantom.skywalk.com/

This site has graphics and audio bits from the musical. See Editor's Choice.

ONLINE PLAYS

Dramatic Exchange

http://www.dramex.org/

The California Technical Institute puts the show on the Web, so to speak, with the Dramatic Exchange. Dedicated to archiving and distributing scripts of plays, it's not just for the famous—anyone can submit a play here.

PROFESSIONAL RESOURCES

Headquarters Entertainment Corporation Net Links Index

http://www.fleethouse.com/fhcanada/western/bc/van/entertan/hqe/vrhq-lnk.htm

The Headquarters Entertainment Corporation of Vancouver, B.C., presents this guide to professional theater resources. Visitors will find a keyword search, an index of links to Broadway and London theater companies, acting schools, play scripts, and much more.

The Lighting Resource

http://www.webcom.com/~lightsrc/

The Lighting Resource home page offers a variety of information on the theatrical lighting industry. Read press releases, check out the worldwide lighting store at LightNet, or browse features, articles, product information, and archives. Classifieds and employment opportunities within the industry are also listed.

Theatre Central

http://www.theatre-central.com/

Find theater directories, play listings, and much more. See Editor's Choice.

PUBLICATIONS AND INDUSTRY NEWS

Didaskalia Home Page

http://www.warwick.ac.uk/didaskalia/didaskalia.html

Didaskalia is an online journal devoted to works of Greek and Roman drama being performed today. Based at England's University of Warwick, the site also announces topical productions, conferences and other events around the world.

Playbill Online

http://wheat.symgrp.com/playbill/home.cgi

The electrified Playbill accompanies its unwieldy database of newsflashes, features, and photos with a playful user interface and some very nifty search options. Narrow down a hunt for casting notices and jobs, or browse theater listings and road shows the world over.

TRAINS, PLANES, AND AUTOS

American Airlines OnBoard

http://www.amrcorp.com/

Explore the world of American Airlines and its parent company, the AMR Corporation, at this promotional Web site. Check American flights to destinations around the world, learn about the SABRE travel system, and review financial data and business summaries.

Aero.com

http://www.aero.com/

Aero.com aims high with this site that strives to be the most complete online resource for aviation

---

EDITOR'S CHOICE

Theatre Central

http://www.theatre-central.com/

Webmaster Andrew Quixote Kraft's specialties are directing and application of technology to the arts. And he certainly puts technology to good use at Theatre Central, touted as "the hub" of theater on the Net and boasting the most comprehensive listing of theater sites available. The detailed arrangement of Theatre Central's listings is impressive, as well. Served up directory-style, categories are provided for everything from Dinner Theater to Shakespeare festivals; from contact services to the sites of renowned playwrights and composers. Other on-site features include a directory of wired theater professionals, theater listings from around the world, and a home-grown monthly zine for professionals.

THEATRE CENTRAL

DIRECTORIES

RESOURCES
"Directory of Theatre Resources on the 'Net"
Web Sites, FTP Sites and more...

PROFESSIONALS
"Directory of Theatre Professionals on the 'Net"
Names and Contact Information

LISTINGS
"Theatre Listings from Around the World"
Shows and Performances

FEATURES

JOURNAL
"Theatre Central Monthly"
Articles, Editorials and Monthly Columns

BOARD
"Theatre Central's Call Board"
Auditions, Jobs and Other Openings

Listings & Board
Coming Later This Summer

information on the Web. The home page features news, shopping and the Aviation Yellow Pages.

Aero-Web

http://www.brooklyn.cuny.edu/rec/air/air.html

The Brooklyn College Web site for aviation enthusiasts contains links to aviation-related hobbies, museums, airshows and weather information. Users can also access historical information, relevant newsgroups, bulletin boards and contact information.

Air & Space Magazine

http://airspacemag.earthlink.net/

Air & Space magazine's home page features an online table of contents describing stories available in the expanded, electronic version of the publication. Stories are supplemented by photos

and an opportunity to join the National Air and Space Museum or subscribe to the print version of Air & Space.

Aircraft Shopper Online

http://aso.solid.com/

Aircraft Shopper Online posts aircraft, parts and engines for sale, and offers an extensive list of commercial dealers and brokers. Aircraft and pilot services are detailed as well. Ads are free for 30 days.

Air France Web

http://www.airfrance.fr/

Air France maintains this site to introduce its services and aircraft. Visitors will find travel tips and descriptions of passenger accommodations on all

aircraft, including the Concorde supersonic jet. In French and English.

Airlines of the Web

http://w1.itn.net/airlines/

This information page on world airlines was created by a graduate student studying the airline industry. The result provides links to passenger carriers around the world, as well as information on frequent flier programs, airline stock quotes and more.

America's 4x4 4U Video Magazine WWW

http://www.4x44u.com/pub/k2/am4x44u/4x4.html

Fat tires and gunned engines await visitors to America's 4X4 4U Video Magazine. General dirt on trails, events and clubs rides neck-and-neck with technical trucking information and the 4X4 Truck Stop, where gearheads can check out manufacturers and catalogs.

Aristo-Craft Trains Internet Depot

http://com.primenet.com/aristo/

The Aristo-Craft Trains page targets model train hobbyists with news about products and clubs. This is the place to share ideas, get tips from like-minded people and find accessories from online catalogs and shops.

Atlas Model Railroad Company

http://www.atlasrr.com/

Model railroad resources and products are the focus of this site from the Atlas Model Railroad Company. Atlas provides a catalog, newsletter, directory of retailers, forum, and demo of its Right Track Software. Also available are train sounds and general information on model railroading.

Automotive Programs By Bowling

http://devserve.cebaf.gov/~bowling/auto.html

Visitors are greeted by interactive automotive engineering and science resources at Bowling's Automotive Programs site. The mechanically minded will find useful calculation programs such as engine displacement unit conversions here.

Automotive Related Mailing Lists and Pages

http://triumph.cs.utah.edu/othermail.html

Automotive Related Resources is a comprehensive index of car mailing lists—from Alfas to VWs. It also links to car corporation home pages.

Aviation: World Wide Web Virtual Library

http://macwww.db.erau.edu/www_virtual_lib/aviation.html

The World Wide Web Virtual Library maintains a comprehensive index of information on the Inter-

EDITOR'S CHOICE

Kabuki for Everyone

http://www.fix.co.jp/kabuki/kabuki.html

"Japan is being asked by the global community what contributions it can make to the world. I have also wondered what I may do as a Kabuki actor," explains Webmaster and Kabuki master Ichimura Manjiro. His mission to demystify this traditional form of Japanese theater is clear, and drawing from more than 40 years of experience, Manjiro does a swell job of bringing "the fantastic world of Kabuki" to life with his informative Web creation. The actor's odyssey takes visitors back to the early days ("I learned much in my youth just by observing: ways to do make-up, how to wear different kimono…"), and audio files shell out familiar Kabuki sounds, like the beat of a "taiko drum" and the whoop of an enthusiastic fan. The site's showstopper lets observers in on how Manjiro—eyebrow wax and white face cream in hand—"transforms himself into a beautiful woman."

net. Visit here for its aviation page, featuring a variety of related resources from around the world.

Avionics Communications—Avionics Library

http://www.cais.net/avionics/

Avionics Communications provides an online catalog of its books, newsletters, seminars, videos, software, and market reports here. Includes an order form and a request for a print catalog.

The Avion Online Newspaper

http://avion.db.erau.edu/

The Avion Online is touted as "the first aviation/aerospace newspaper on the Internet." Sections in the lively weekly run the gamut—from space technology and "aeronautica" to comics, clubs and diversions. Visitors can hop on the "Current Flight" or peruse back issues in "The Jangar."

AVweb

http://www.avweb.com/

AVweb is an online magazine for aviation enthusiasts. Visitors can take a tour of the site; members can read features and news, and view photos of airplanes, old and new.

Bahnverbindungen in Deutschland

http://www.uni-karlsruhe.de/~rail/

The RailServer allows travelers to query an online database of timetables for trains running across Germany and parts of Europe. Also featured are tips about railroading in Germany. In German and English.

BMW Cars, Bikes & Information

http://www.xs4all.nl/~cbuijs/bmwhome.html

This unofficial BMW site contains information about the well-known automobiles and motorcycles. Includes links to related organizations, events, and design and mechanical specifications.

British Cars Web

http://www.team.net/sol/

Scions of Lucas, a newsgroup dedicated to the discussion of British cars, maintains this Web page. Find e-mail lists, clubs, technical information, and sources for those hard-to-find parts. Links to related sites are also available.

Bugatti Home Page

http://bugatti.vintageweb.net/bugatti.html/

Fans and collectors of the famous Bugatti automobile will enjoy this unofficial but extensive resource site. Find links to pictures, recent news, events notices, information about cars for sale, and more.

Cadillac Home Page

http://www.cadillac.com/index.html

Luxury car lovers can take a cruise through Cadillac's official site. Visit here for new car informa-

tion and the Interactive Design Studio, where customers can create the Cadillac that's perfect for them.

Canadian Airlines

http://www.cdnair.ca/

Stow your baggage, fasten your seat belt and click away on Canadian Airlines' home page for company and flight information. Visitors will also find online access to a variety of travel and car-rental agencies, tourist information, airlines, and hotels.

The Car Place

http://www.cftnet.com/members/rcbowden/

From Mercedes Benz to Chevrolet, the Car Place steers visitors away from the lemons. The page author—a former auto editor and auto book author—gives tips and encourages feedback.

Cathay Pacific Airways

http://www.cathay-usa.com/

Cathay Pacific, an international airline offering service to many Asian destinations, maintains this site to introduce its routes and services. Visitors will find flight schedules, frequent flier program information, route maps, and photos of aircraft.

---

a2z EDITOR'S CHOICE

Miss Saigon

http://www.clark.net/pub/rsjdfg/

A recent medical school graduate who just can't get enough "Miss Saigon" created this page to keep fans like himself abreast of details on the blockbuster musical's various productions around the world. Get all the latest information on open runs and touring companies, and read up on the swelling list of cast members. The site's centerpiece, a musical in pictures, walks viewers through the show's essential moments in two acts; and the complete libretto fills up any remaining plot gaps with dialogue. QuickTime movies and miscellaneous graphics add to the colorful mix. If you're a fan of "Miss," don't miss the fan site.

Center for Advanced Aviation System Development

http://www.caasd.org/

The Center for Advanced Aviation System Development is a federally funded research and development facility focusing on systems engineering. Its site includes descriptions of research programs, access to technical reports, laboratory facilities and links to other aviation servers.

Chinese Military Aviation

http://weber.u.washington.edu/~htong/

Images and information on military aircraft in service or being developed for Chinese armed forces are available at this site. Includes information on fighters, attack aircraft, trainers, and helicopters.

Chrysler Technology Center

http://www.chryslercorp.com/

Here you'll find video clips, a virtual showroom, and more. See Editor's Choice.

Cyberspace World Railroad Home Page

http://www.mcs.net/~dsdawdy/cyberoad.html

The Cyberspace World Railroad page is a virtual switching yard sending browsers down tracks that lead to railroad-related sites around the world. Find images, newsletters, travelogues, transit schedules, computer tools, associations, and more.

Dave Frary's Blue Ribbon Models

http://www.shore.net/~jdf/tswelcome.html

Alternately known as the Blue Ribbon Models and Trackside Modelers home page, this site acts as a central jump station for model railroad enthusiasts. Resources include reference books, kits, video tapes, and links to related Web sites.

DealerNet—The Source for New Car Information

http://www.dealernet.com/

With its virtual showroom, DealerNet wants to sell visitors not only a car, but also a car *dealer*. Use this site to search for a dealer or search for a car (new or used). Visitors can also flip through auto reviews here or download copies of a confidential credit application.

Delaware Valley Association of Railroad Passengers

http://libertynet.org/~dvarp/dvarp.html

The Delaware Valley Association of Railroad Passengers, Inc. invites visitors to join its efforts to improve and expand passenger transit service in the Philadelphia area. Newsletters and information about the group, its meetings, and its projects are available online for review.

Dryden Research Aircraft Photo Archive

http://www.dfrc.nasa.gov/PhotoServer/photoServer.html

The Dryden Flight Research Center, a facility of the U.S. National Aeronautics and Space Administration, maintains this site for digitized photographs of its "unique research aircraft." Visit here to download images in JPEG format.

Embry-Riddle Aeronautics University

http://www.pr.erau.edu/

Embry-Riddle Aeronautics University is an aviation mechanics and flying school in Prescott, Arizona. Its home page features a catalog of courses, admissions information, administrative facts, and links to academic departments.

Experimental Aircraft Association Oshkosh Airshow

http://airspacemag.com/EAA/Oshkosh_Home.html

Air & Space Events and Tours sponsors this online brochure highlighting the Experimental Aircraft Association's Oshkosh Airshow held annually in Oshkosh, Wisconsin. Features include a field guide to Oshkosh, airshow tips, pilots' update, and links to related Web sites.

---

a2z EDITOR'S CHOICE

Phantom of the Opera

http://phantom.skywalk.com/

Gaston Leroux's classic novel and Andrew Lloyd Webber's wildly popular musical stroll hand in hand through this tribute to the creepy guy under the opera house stage. No libretto (yanked down, along with official logos, at the request of Webber's company), but the site makes up for the loss with a story summary, a Phantom FAQ, and a variety of audio files and promotional GIFs from various productions. Other features include a history of the Paris Opera House and a lengthy biographical piece on Leroux, "the man behind the phantom."

Federal Aviation Administration

http://web.fie.com/htdoc/fed/dot/faa/any/menu/any/faaindex.htm

The Federal Aviation Administration offers an overview of regulations, educational programs and FAA employment opportunities on its home page. Also find internal agency information, including general news, administrators' speeches, and procurement notices.

Finnish Railway Timetables

http://www.hut.fi/~ovr/VR.html

Finland's train schedules are posted here in Finnish, Swedish, and English. The site also includes a Finnish railway map and a station-by-station index.

Fly With Us!

http://www.interedu.com/mig29/mig29/

A commercial Moscow flight adventure service offers the ride of a lifetime in a supersonic Soviet-built MiG-29 jet. Visitors to this promotional site can review vacation packages that include a Mach 2 flight over Moscow.

The Frontier Airlines Page

http://www.cuug.ab.ca:8001/~busew/frontier.html

From Bill's Page Of Magnificent Flying Machines comes this glimpse of the more than 40-year history of Frontier Airlines. Visitors can view old flight maps, read historical documents, and find current reservation information.

Galaxy Transportation Index

http://galaxy.einet.net/galaxy/Engineering-and-Technology/Transportation.html

TradeWave's Galaxy information service maintains this site for its transportation resource index. Visitors will find an extensive collection of links to related organizations, publications, government agencies, and events.

Golden Gate Railroad Museum

http://www.ggrm.org/

The Golden Gate Railroad Museum in San Francisco preserves steam and passenger railroad equipment. Visit its home page for news, local railroad history, merchandise offerings, and a chance to rent your own locomotive.

GreenWheels Electric Car Page

http://northshore.shore.net/~kester/

The GreenWheels Electric Car Company maintains this site to spread knowledge and prompt discussion of alternative transportation. Visit here for related images, information, resources, and discussion lists.

GTE Aviation Home Page

http://www.gtefsd.com/aviation/GTEaviation.html

GTE Contel maintains this aviation site for its Direct User Access Terminal Service. Pilots and aviation enthusiasts will find U.S. Federal Aviation Administration weather and flight plan filing services.

Harley Owners Group

http://www.magicnet.net/mni/hog.html

The Harley Owners Group maintains this site offering a variety of motorcycling resources. Visitors will find chapter listings, stolen vehicle information, Harley-Davidson art archives, and much more.

Hot Rods World Wide

http://www.hotrodsworldwide.com/

Hot Rods World Wide is a site for buying and selling street rods, muscle cars, and antique autos. Enthusiasts can place ads and find cars for sale here, or they can check out the links and other hot rod resources.

Interactive Model Railroad

http://rr-vs.informatik.uni-ulm.de/rr/

Operate a virtual model train. See Editor's Choice.

International Aerobatic Club Home Page

http://acro.harvard.edu/IAC/iac_homepg.html

The International Aerobatic Club, a division of the Experimental Aircraft Association, is open to any-

---

a2z EDITOR'S CHOICE

Chrysler Technology Center

http://www.chryslercorp.com/

One of the best perks at this megasite is being able to dream up a wacky name when you check in. Then, when the Chrysler tour begins, the behind-the-scenes Webmasters address you by your new moniker (so be careful with what you dream up). Once inside, bounce through Chrysler's colorful corporate history, scrutinize technical and investor information, or better yet, check out developing concept cars and Chrysler's environmentally minded programs (what major American corporation doesn't want to be thought of as socially responsible these days?). When you've had enough concepts and responsibility, stroll through the real thing: an electronic showroom containing Chrysler, Plymouth, Dodge, Jeep, and Eagle cars. Video clips? They've got those, too. —*Reviewed by Dan Kelly*

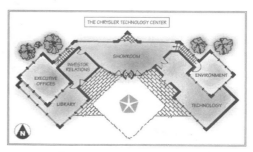

one interested in aviation. Featured on this unofficial page are IAC news, chapter home pages, competition results, and e-mail addresses.

International Wheelchair Aviators

http://www.dsg.cs.tcd.ie/dsg_people/sloubtin/IWA.html

The International Wheelchair Aviators Web site answers the question of whether a disabled person can fly with a resounding "Yes." The site includes contact information for the organization along with an extensive list of hot links.

Jaguar Automobile Enthusiast Site

http://www.oslonett.no/home/nick/jaguar.html

Owners and fans of Jaguar British luxury cars will enjoy this site, featuring Jag archives, photos, and trivia. Visit here for everything from technical information to travelogues.

KLM—Royal Dutch Airlines

http://www.klm.nl/

A profile of KLM Dutch Airlines and details on its worldwide destinations are among the resources at this home page of the "world's first scheduled airline." Includes information on KLM's products and special services.

LAL Aviation Archive

http://imall.com/archives/planes.html

A member of the Computer Science Department at Brigham Young University maintains this large collection of links to aerospace gifs. Airplane enthusiasts and military buffs will surely find a favorite among the many flying machines featured.

Landings

http://www.landings.com/aviation.html

This site is your one-stop aviation info resource. See Editor's Choice.

Los Angeles Freeway Speeds

http://www.scubed.com/caltrans/la/la_big_map.shtml

Check here before you hit the freeway in Los Angeles. This real-time traffic information site, maintained by Maxwell Laboratories, offers freeway speeds and traffic conditions in the Los Angeles area. Includes listings for trouble spots.

Matt's Solar Car Page

http://www-lips.ece.utexas.edu/~delayman/solar.html

Matt's Solar Car Page offers a variety of information about environmentally friendly auto development and the international solar car racing circuit. Visitors will find articles, graphics, and scheduled race postings.

Meadowbrook Invitational Classic Car Auction

http://www.specialcar.com/rm/index.htm

The annual Meadowbrook Invitational Classic Car Auction site contains an auction catalog, sales information, and terms and conditions of purchase. Visitors will find a buyer's guide and links to car-restoration pages.

Mercurio—The European Railway Server

http://mercurio.iet.unipi.it/home.html

Mercurio provides timetables and information on a variety of European rail systems and trains. Visitors will find links to European Railway News magazine and to official and unofficial railway sites.

MG Cars Enthusiasts' Club

http://www.mgcars.org.uk/

The United Kingdom's MG Car Club maintains this page for its members and fellow MG enthusiasts around the world. Site features include club news, a photo gallery, a bulletin board, MG news, a models list, and links to other relevant sites.

MotorCity

http://www.motorcity.com/

MotorCity offers news and information of interest to car shoppers, including new automobile specifications, links to auto dealerships, and a global vehicle locator. Check the Dollars and Sense section for loan and lease information.

New Zealand by Rail

http://www.waikato.ac.nz/nz/rail/timetable.html

Learn how to travel New Zealand by rail through this page that includes complete timetables and tips. Visitors can view a map of New Zealand to see the trains routes.

NS—The Dutch Railways

http://mercurio.iet.unipi.it/ns/ns.html

This guide to rail travel in the Netherlands (part of a personal home page) offers a variety of timetables and destination information. Visitors will also find links to trans-European and local rail systems.

Online Amtrak Schedules

http://www.mcs.net/~dsdawdy/Amtrak/
amtrak.html

The Cyberspace World Railroad maintains this site for official and unofficial Amtrak rail information. Visitors will find timetables, destination listings, and links to other rail-related resources.

Paramotor

http://cyberactive-1.com/paramotor/

Paramotor of Oyster Bay, New York, introduces its unique flying craft that combines a paraglider with a user-mounted propeller engine at this site. Visitors will find an online photo and video gallery, technical specifications, and ordering information.

Paris Metro Maps

http://www.paris.org.:80/Metro/

Paris Metro helps visitors navigate Paris by providing maps and public transportation information. Includes links to other Paris travel and tourism resources.

Penny Bridge

http://bjr.acf.nyu.edu/railinfo/railinfo.html

Penny Bridge provides a large personal collection of train- and railroad-related links. Visit here to connect with train car details, subway maps, railroad schedules, artistic images, literature, and much more.

The Pickup Truck Homepage

http://www.rtd.com/~mlevine/pickup.html

Pickup truck enthusiasts will find profiles, news, and links related to their vehicles of choice at the Pickup Truck Homepage. Catch the latest sport-truck racing standings, or survey pictures of pickup trucks from around the world.

Railroading in France

http://www.eleves.ens.fr:8080/home/cbonnet/
trains/railroad.html

Part of a personal home page, Railroading in France offers a selection of train and travel information resources. Visit here for travel tips, rail maps, and train-related trivia. In French and English.

Railroads, Ships and Aircraft Home Page

http://www.membrane.com/~elmer/

The resources here focus on ships, railroads and aircraft. Includes lots of military-related information, serial number data, and links to related FAQ archives and online commuter rail schedules.

Rails and Transit

http://www.cc.columbia.edu/~brennan/
index-rails.html

A researcher at New York's Columbia University maintains this extensive collection of rail travel-related resources. Visit here for New York City subway and rail maps, trip planners, and links to information on London's Underground rail system.

Railway Technical Research Institute

http://www.rtri.or.jp/index.html

Japan's Railway Technical Research Institute supplies an overview of its projects at this site. Visit here for research and development activity updates, a history of the Japanese rail system, and a look at the structural effects of 1995's Kobe earthquake.

Rec.Motorcycles.Reviews Archives

http://rmr.cecm.sfu.ca/RMR/

Motorcycle enthusiasts will enjoy a visit to Rec.Motorcycles.Reviews archives, featuring a collection of reviews and opinions about motorcycle models and accessories. Visit here for discussion groups, downloadable images, and links to a variety of motorcycle-related resources.

The Saturn Site

http://www.saturncars.com/

At the Saturn Site, visitors can "test drive" the progressive car company's line of automobiles. Visitors also will find Saturn Magazine, retailer information, brochures, and access to the "extended family" database.

Seattle Area Traffic

http://www.wsdot.wa.gov/regions/northwest/
NWFLOW/

Visit here to get the latest Seattle traffic info. See Editor's Choice.

EDITOR'S CHOICE

Landings

http://www.landings.com/aviation.html

Sometimes (albeit rarely) a site covers a topic so thoroughly that it becomes a de facto hub on the Web. Such is the case with Landings. The topic is aviation, and Landings contains resources on aerobatics, hang gliding, helicopters, skydiving, general aviation…and much more, with links to organizations, databases, companies, publications…whew! For aviation insider lowdown, Landings sponsors an aviation forum, hosted by a seasoned pilot. The site also acts as home to NASA's massive First General Aviation Server, one of the first and most comprehensive aviation sites on the Net. As Webmasters proudly assert, they'll "connect you to virtually every lift-generating web site on the net"…and (you guessed it) much more. —*Reviewed by Dan Kelly*

Welcome To The Busiest Aviation Hub in Cyberspace

Aviation Enthusiasts world-wide have made Landings the best Aviation directory / infosource on-line. With its roots in the ACRO.HARVARD GA site and the 'First General Aviation Server' at NASA, Landings is your gateway to the world of on-line Aviation. Bookmark this page for future Landings, and before you go on, please check-in, as we would like to know you better, and feel free to follow this link to learn more about us.

News Briefs:

- Landings is the new home for the information sources of the 'First General Aviation Server' at NASA. We are now in the midst of incorporating this major site into the fabric of Landings.

- We are proud to have 'Joe Benkert' join the Landings effort as the host of The Joe Benkert Forum. Mr. Joe Benkert is a fully rated pilot with a long history in the military, airlines, and corporate flight. He is a published author and is currently on a national tour conducting motivational seminars for flight instructors.

Soaring Information and Sailplane Directory

http://csrp.tamu.edu/Soaring/soaring.html

A wide range of soaring information is maintained at this server. Visitors can view the directory of gliders, towplanes, and flight test reports, or they can link to sailplane clubs, soaring sites around the globe, and related bibliographies.

Special Car Journal

http://www.specialcar.com/

This is the definitive resource for car buffs. See Editor's Choice.

SpeedWay MotorBooks

http://www.primenet.com/~komet/speed/speedway.html

Arizona's SpeedWay MotorBooks sells collectible books, programs, magazines, and videos about cars and racing. Racing cards, models, and slot cars are also available.

Steam Engine Joseph Stalin

http://pavel.physics.sunysb.edu/RR/RailRoads.html

Information about the Joseph Stalin steam engine, which had nothing to do with the political leader, is featured on this page. Train fans can also look at a variety of information about railroads in Russia and the Commonwealth of Independent States.

Steam Locomotive Information

http://www.arc.umn.edu/~wes/steam.html

Need the specifications of a famous steam locomotive? Want to find out which is the biggest and the best? Steam Locomotion Information would be your stop. Visit the B&O Railroad Museum here or check out a family tree of North American Railroads.

The Talyllyn Railway

http://www.aber.ac.uk/~rah94/talyllyn.html

For news and information about Great Britain's Talyllyn Railway, the world's first preserved railway, check into this site. It includes passenger information, a timetable, events listings, and a route description with images.

Targa Tasmania

http://www.tas.gov.au/tourism/targa/index.html

Owners of classic cars who love driving challenges will love Targa Tasmania—a six-day, 2,000-kilometer event on Australia's mountain island of Tasmania. This site supplies information on the race in which 280 drivers try to outwit the ordinary tarmac roads.

Thrust SSC Server

http://thrustssc.digital.co.uk/

Promoters hope Thrust SSC (Super Sonic Car) will break the land speed record and the sound barrier. This page contains documentation on the British car, how it works, and how it was built. Visitors also can download wallpaper and screen savers here or participate in a discussion.

A Towing Company, Inc.

http://www.halcyon.com/ekashp/

A Towing Company, Inc., a Seattle-based company, maintains this promotional site. Visit here for information on tow-truck safety services, a photo gallery, and links to other automotive sites.

Transportation Resources

http://dragon.princeton.edu/~dhb/systems.html

Princeton University's Intelligent Transportation Systems Program provides this extensive collection of transportation-related resources. It includes highway, transit, and rail system information from cities around the world.

Transwede Airways

http://www.transwede.se/

Sweden's Transwede Airways supplies scheduling and flight information at this home page. Visitors will also find an online reservation form. In Swedish only.

Union Pacific

http://www.uprr.com/

Union Pacific Railroad's official page has "something for everyone," including customers, investors, employees, and rail fans. Pull into the station for a daily rail operations report, news releases, history and photo gallery, or buy your own railroading gear at the company store.

---

a2z EDITOR'S CHOICE

Seattle Area Traffic

http://www.wsdot.wa.gov/regions/northwest/NWFLOW/

Okay, so you don't live in Seattle. You don't even live in Tacoma. But that doesn't mean it isn't worth knowing how the traffic is moving on Interstate 405 at Bothell. The Washington State Department of Transportation sponsors this Web-based traffic reporter, complete with graphics-based traffic alerts and continuously updated maps. Timely bulletins, incident reports, and construction information are featured, as well as schedules and information for area airlines, ferries, and trains. Uh oh, we've got a logjam on I-90 at Mercer Island. Gotta run. —*Reviewed by Dan Kelly*

Seattle Metropolitan Area Traffic Condition

TRAVEL

AIRLINE COMPANIES

VIA Rail Canada

http://www.mcs.net/~dsdawdy/Canpass/via/via.html

Destination and scheduling information for VIA Rail Canada, the country's national passenger train service, is available at this site from the Canadian Passenger Rail Home Page. Visit here to find updated intercity and transcontinental rail travel listings.

Vintage Racers Web

http://www.team.net:80/www/vintage-race/

Vintage cars that race on tracks and roads around the world inspired this Web site. Club news, rules, race schedules, and a photo gallery are available here through FTP archives. Includes links to racers' home pages as well as to publications on the sport.

Volkswebbin'

http://www.oroad.com/volkswebbin/

The Volkswagen Bug lives on at this site. Included here are VW images and links, as well as a FAQ with answers to technical questions. Message boards also are provided.

Volvo Cars of North America Inc.

http://www.volvocars.com/

Volvo Cars of North America presents this Web site, which comes fully loaded with detailed descriptions of its cars, dealerships, and services. Includes photographs of the latest models.

Wings America Home Page

http://www.carmelnet.com/Wings/

Products with an aviation theme are available at Wings America. Find models, clothing, books, watches, and more. Aviation links and jokes are also featured.

Wings Over Paradise

http://deeptht.armory.com/~zap/adverts/wop.html

This page, which advertised biplane tours of coastal California, notes that the business has gone belly-up. But the page and its images are maintained in the memory of the antique flying machines used by the defunct company.

WWW Railway Page for Norway

http://www.ifi.uio.no/~terjek/rail/

Ride the rails through Norway (or at least get a glimpse of what you would see if you go there) at this page. The site profiles the national railway and provides timetables. Includes links to railway publications and museums, as well as the Norwegian Railway Club.

Air Canada

http://www.aircanada.ca/

Air Canada's home page provides information on the carrier's routes and connections with other airlines. Also find links to a travel office, the news desk, pictures of aircraft, and frequent flyer information. In French and English.

Air Cruise America: DC-3 Tours

http://www.webcom.com/~aca/

Air Cruise America, an aviation company specializing in nostalgic DC-3 air tours, maintains this promotional page. In addition to learning more about the company and its services, visitors can link to other DC-3 sites.

Canadian Airlines

http://www.cdnair.ca/

Stow your baggage, fasten your seatbelt and click away on Canadian Airlines' home page for reservations, business travel, and flight information. Visitors will also find online access to a variety of travel and car-rental agencies, tourist information, airlines, and hotels.

Frontier Airlines

http://www.cuug.ab.ca:8001/~busew/frontier.html

Denver-based Frontier Airlines maintains this site with a glimpse of its more than 40-year history. Visitors can view old flight maps, read historical documents, and find current reservation information.

---

a2z EDITOR'S CHOICE

Special Car Journal

http://www.specialcar.com/

The classified ads section alone—featuring literally thousands of cars for sale—is enough to make this site worth a visit. Throw in the directory of dealers and the Internet Automotive Yellow Pages, and the Special Car Journal becomes the definitive resource for car buffs. And that's not even taking into account the well-penned articles, reviews, news, and images of classic cars, or the online price guide, or the special Ferrari page. Or an index of out-of-print automotive books (and where to find them). Or the gallery of "automobilia." This is one place where Sunday driving should be required. —*Reviewed by Dan Kelly*

Southwest Airlines

http://www.iflyswa.com/

Billing itself as "the" low-fare airline, Dallas-based Southwest Airlines maintains this promotional site. Visitors will find route and scheduling information, discount fares, and an online version of its in-flight magazine.

AIRPORTS

Norfolk International Airport

http://www.infi.net/orf/

Make your next trip through the Norfolk International Airport easier with the airport facts, maps, flight guide and other information here. The airport serves Norfolk, Virginia Beach, and Williamsburg, Virginia.

ARCHIVES AND INDICES

AMI News

http://www.aminews.com/ami

AMI News is a commercial recreation network providing news and information on skiing, travel, leisure, and the outdoors. Includes destination, reservations, weather, and lodging information.

Asian Travel Industry Index

http://www.pata.org/asia/

The Pacific Asia Travel Association provides this home page for businesses and travelers seeking information on Asian-Pacific countries. Includes links to member country home pages and travel marketing information.

Destinations On-Line

http://dol.meer.net/index.html

Destinations On-Line provides travel information about resorts in popular American vacation spots in California, Florida, and Nevada. Find inspiration and information for planning your next holiday getaway.

GENinc Products and Services

http://www.geninc.com/

Global Exposure Network provides links to travel and real estate services—including access to bed-and-breakfasts, hotels, and a real estate forum. Links to regional community information, and convention and visitors' bureaus.

Leonard's Cam World

http://www.leonardsworlds.com/camera.html

Cam shots from around the world. See Editor's Choice.

NTT Virtual Tourist Northeast Asia Index

http://www.ntt.co.jp/AP/asia-NE.html

Nippon Telephone and Telegraph maintains this Asia guide for resource maps and lists, as well as information about specific countries. Links to other virtual tourist information centers are available.

NTT Virtual Tourist Southwest Asia Index

http://www.ntt.co.jp/AP/asia-SW.html

This guide to Southwest Asian countries, provided by Japan's Nippon Telegraph and Telephone Corporation, offers links to maps, cultural events, local customs, government resources, and more. Includes links to all other world regions.

rec.travel Library

http://www.remcan.ca/rec-travel

Travel the world for information before packing your bags with the help of the Usenet newsgroup rec.travel archive. The site includes links to places to go, with contact information for travel agents and accommodations, and tips from other travelers.

Tourism Offices Worldwide Directory

http://www.mbnet.mb.ca/lucas/travel/

Visitors to this page can search a database of nearly 800 entries to locate tourism offices throughout the world. Also provides listing of offices in specific states or provinces in the United States and Canada.

Travel & Entertainment Network

http://www.ten-io.com/

The Travel and Entertainment Network is a wellspring of information for travelers. The site includes products and services available online, free demonstration software, and the TEN-10 database—for quick location of your specific travel needs.

---

a2z EDITOR'S CHOICE

Leonard's Cam World

http://www.leonardsworlds.com/camera.html

Whoever said a thousand-mile journey begins with one step was *not* a Web junkie. Through the wonders of the Web, you can operate a model train set in Germany, monitor customs activity across the Finnish-Russian border, and check the cloud coverage of the often hidden Mount Fuji. And thanks to Leonard's Cam World, live snapshots like these from around the world are available 24 hours a day. Are you about to catch a plane to London? Don't trust the weather report. The Web cam pointed at Trafalgar Square will show you if you need to pack just an umbrella, or add a trenchcoat and galoshes. You can't get a call through to Los Angeles? Maybe there's been an earthquake. Check the latest Richter scale readings on KNBC's "seismo-cam" to find out. Great fun for actual and virtual travelers alike. —*Reviewed by Paul Bacon*

TravelASSIST

http://travelassist.com/

TravelASSIST, a service of Studio City, California-based ASSIST Information Services, offers a grab bag of online travel information. This commercial site includes a directory of more than 600 inns, small hotels, and bed and breakfasts, along with descriptions of travel-related products and services.

Travelocity

http://www.travelocity.com/

Be your own travel agent. See Editor's Choice.

Travlang's Foreign Languages for Travelers

http://www.travlang.com/languages/

This site has online language lessons. See Editor's Choice.

CURRENCY EXCHANGE

Money Abroad FAQ

http://www.inria.fr/robotvis/personnel/laveau/money-faq/money-abroad.html

The Money Abroad Frequently Asked Questions page contains general information about exchange rates and how to properly convert and handle international currencies. Includes in-depth guides to worldwide policies for use of cash, travelers' checks, and credit cards.

O & A Converter

http://www.olsen.ch/cgi-bin/exmenu

Find out here how the dollar is doing abroad. See Editor's Choice.

DESTINATIONS

The Alaskan Center

http://www.alaskan.com/

Start your Alaskan adventure here! Visitors can shop at the Alaskan Mall, learn about the Iditarod sled dog race, read about local culture, and check the current weather. Travel and tourism information is available to help plan a visit.

Alberta Advantage

http://www.gov.ab.ca/

The Canadian government welcomes visitors to the Province of Alberta at this informational site. Get the official version of events in this government-produced travel brochure and political guide to the Canadian province.

---

a2z EDITOR'S CHOICE

Travelocity

http://www.travelocity.com/

Ever wonder why, in this age of fancy computers 'n' stuff, you still call a travel agent for tickets and reservations? Your travel agents wonder, too, and if they sound a bit nervous next time you call, it's because they know online services like Travelocity may be putting them out of business very quickly. Travelocity, part of the SABRE reservation system, boasts free and instant access to the computers of more than 370 world airlines, automatically providing the lowest prices and most convenient itineraries between any number of cities. Want more? It also offers travel guides to more than 85,000 destinations and services including rental cars, resorts, hotels, restaurants, and shows. If you're still not satisfied, you can always call their toll-free number to talk to a real person—they do that very well, too. —*Reviewed by Paul Bacon*

O & A Converter

http://www.olsen.ch/cgi-bin/exmenu

Sure, anyone can pick up a calculator, check the current exchange rate and convert one currency into another. But do you remember the rate from two months ago? How about last year? No? Well, how are you going to tackle that expense report from your overseas business trip you keep meaning to file? This online converter provided by Swiss financial forecasting company Olsen & Associates (O & A) can help. It provides instant calculations for dozens of world currencies for as far back as January 1, 1990. Whether you're keeping records of past exchanges or planning a vacation abroad, visit O & A for daily updated currency exchange rates—from Albanian leks to Zimbabwe dollars. —*Reviewed by Paul Bacon*

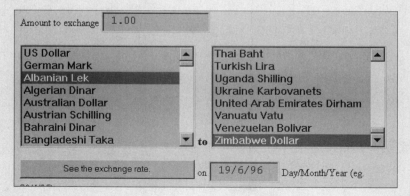

Aloha from Planet Hawaii!

http://planet-hawaii.com/

Hundreds of miles west of California is an island state known at this site as "Planet Hawaii." Visitors to this tourism page will find a variety of local information resources, including culture, business, shopping, and sightseeing.

Arlington County, Virginia Home Page

http://www.co.arlington.va.us/

Visitors heading for the Washington, D.C. area can learn about tourism and business opportunities in nearby Arlington County, Virginia here. The page details Arlington's attractions, including the Pentagon and Iwo Jima Memorial.

Atlanta Conventions & Visitors Bureau

http://www.acvb.com/

Atlanta's Convention and Visitors Bureau Web site contains a variety of informative resources for visitors to the host city of the 1996 Olympics. Includes regular updates of Olympic news and a complete calendar of upcoming city events.

Atlanta Web Guide Home Page

http://www.webguide.com/

This site allows visitors to take a virtual tour of Atlanta and provides an overview of happenings, restaurants, and cultural highlights in the Georgia state capital. Also includes pictures, maps, and a guide to state colleges and universities.

Australian Alpine Information Service

http://www.adfa.oz.au/aais/

The Australian Alpine Information Service maintains this site featuring an interactive guide to the snowfield resorts in Australia and New Zealand. Also offers a photo archive, a listing of clubs and associations, short stories, and links to other related Web-based resources.

Austria: City.Net Index

http://www.city.net/countries/austria/

Excite's City.Net information service maintains this site for its extensive Austria resource index. Visitors will find links to national, regional and local organizations, culture and language guides, tourist information, and much more.

Bali: The Online Travel Guide

http://werple.mira.net.au/~wreid/bali_p1a.html

The Bali Online Travel Guide promises a complete view of the Indonesian island from off the beaten tourist track. Visitors to this site can find cheap accommodations, cultural attractions, and a gourmet restaurant guide.

Big Island of Hawaii

http://bookweb.cwis.uci.edu:8042/Books/Moon/moon.html

The Big Island of Hawaii is a hypertext travel guide leading tourists on a cyberpath through the history, culture, and landscape of the Big Island. Visitors will find background information—plus maps, photos, and audio files from Moon Publications.

California: City.Net Index

http://www.city.net/countries/united_states/california/

Excite's City.Net information service maintains this site for its California resource index. Visitors will find links to state, regional, and local organizations, government and educational listings, tourist information, and much more.

California State Home Page

http://www.ca.gov/

California's official home page offers a variety of information on doing business in the Golden State, including employment opportunities, travel tips, and a guide to official agencies and legislation. Points to a variety of helpful statewide indexes and local Internet providers.

Cape Town

http://www.aztec.co.za/aztec/capetown.html

The Cape Town home page offers information about one of South Africa's favorite tourist destinations. Resources available here include images of Cape Town landscapes, information on the city's flora, a satellite map, weather reports, and links to local Web sites.

---

a2z EDITOR'S CHOICE

Travlang's Foreign Languages for Travelers

http://www.travlang.com/languages/

It's the night before your *trip overseas* ("ryooko" in Japanese) and you don't know enough of your destination country's *language* ("lingua" in Italian) to find a *toilet* ("necesejo" in Esperanto). Well, fear not! The Travlang Company packs this multilingual guide with enough key phrases and interactive lessons to get you to the bathroom, out of the airport and into a deep, philosophical conversation in the tongue of your choice. Just pick your native and target language, and the site leads you through a basic set of online lessons, complete with audio playback to check your pronunciation. Quizzes are administered and scored instantly (no cheating allowed!) and to round out your linguistic journey, each of the site's more than 20 language pages offers external links to advanced lessons, language institute home pages, and online dictionaries. —*Reviewed by Paul Bacon*

Costa Rica Photo Travel Journal

http://swissnet.ai.mit.edu/cr/

Take a look at "the canopy," the community of wildlife and plants living in the treetops of the Costa Rica rainforest. These images and a detailed guide to visiting the Central American country are provided here by a fellow traveler.

Cycle Vietnam

http://www.mindspring.com/~jrolls/cv.html

At Cycle Vietnam, visitors will find a detailed travelogue written by a bicyclist who, with a travel group, rode 1,200 miles from Hanoi to Ho Chi Minh city. The account is enhanced with pictures and maps.

Dallas CityView

http://www.cityview.com/dallas/

New Path Media hosts this comprehensive online guide to Dallas, Texas. A variety of local resources are available here, including information on dining, accommodations, weather, entertainment, real estate, shopping, and sports.

Dallas Entertainment Guide

http://www.wn.com/dallas/

Visit this site for a Texas-sized online guide to Dallas activities. The page links to hundreds of local sites, including events calendars, restaurants, hotels, and shopping districts. Links to Dallas-based businesses and organizations are also available.

Data Wales Country Guide

http://www.data-wales.co.uk/

Data Wales maintains this site for a detailed guide to resources in the British principality. Visitors will find information on local tourism, business, and government resources. Includes links to general United Kingdom-related sites.

Destin*Fort Walton Beach

http://www2.destin-fwb.com/okaloosa/

The home page for Destin*Fort Walton Beach attempts to convince weather-beaten Web surfers to make the northwestern Florida coast a vacation destination. Besides beachy scenery, visitors will find an online accommodation search function here.

Discover Key West

http://discover.key-west.fl.us/

Global Audience Providers, Inc. maintains this site for its index of Key West, Florida tourism resources. Visitors will find extensive information on local accommodations, travel, sport, and recreation activities on the tropical island.

Discover Long Island

http://www.webscope.com/li/info.html

Internet presence provider WebScope maintains this site for a guide to Long Island, New York tourism and business resources. Includes links to local commerce organizations, recreational activities, points of interest, transportation and excursion tour companies, and other local service companies.

El Paso Travel Guide

http://cs.utep.edu/elpaso/main.html

The University of Texas at El Paso maintains this site to introduce the history and culture of its local community. Visitors will also find information on tourism, travel, dining, and accommodations in the "Sun City."

England: City.Net Index

http://www.city.net/countries/united_kingdom/england

Look kids! Big Ben! Parliament! Excite's City.Net information service maintains this site for its England resource index. Visitors will find links to national, regional and local organizations, culture and language guides, tourist information, and much more.

Eugene Business and Travel Guide

http://www.efn.org/~sgazette/eugenehome.html

Oregon's Eugene Free Community Network maintains this guide to local business and tourism resources. Visitors can link to commercial and government organizations, travel and accommodations listings, shopping indexes, and transit maps.

Finnish Travel Reservations

http://www.webtravel.fi

Tourism information service provider WebTravel maintains this site for its Finland resource index. Visitors will find updated reservation listings from travel, accommodations, local events, ski resorts, and other related services.

Hawaii Visitor Bureau

http://www.visit.hawaii.org/

The Hawaii Visitors Bureau invites users to discover the state's tropical paradise at this site. In addition to information about accommodations and local activities, a vacation contest entry is provided. In English and Japanese.

HELLAS Home Page

http://Greece.org/hellas/index.html

The HELLAS home page is designed as a resource for tourists and people of Greek ancestry. Links to subject areas such as travel and news are available, as well as news, pictures, and news of interest to the Greek community.

Helsingborg, Sweden Guide

http://www.helsingborg.se/

The city of Helsingborg, Sweden, presents tourism information and photos on its official home page. Find out what makes the city unique and why more than one million tourists travel there each year. In Swedish, German, and English.

Highland Trail Company

http://www.highlandtrail.co.uk/highlandtrail/

Scotland's business community guides visitors down the Highland Trail, a virtual path through the country's electronic tourist, commercial and cultural sites. Includes links to Scottish producers of traditional goods and services.

Information about Australia

http://www.anu.edu.au/foyer/aus.html

This informational site provides links to Australia tourism guides, government sites, and tourism resources. Visit here for information regarding national parks, territorial governments, railroads, airlines, and the 2000 Olympic games in Sydney.

Introduction to Stillwater, Oklahoma

http://www.okstate.edu/stillwater/introduction.html

The Stillwater Chamber of Commerce maintains this site for an introduction to the city's education, government, and business resources. Includes links to Oklahoma State University and Department of Vocational-Technical Education.

Japanese Information

http://www.ntt.co.jp/japan/

Explore the cultural, physical, and political landscape of Japan with this online travel guide provided by Nippon Telephone and Telegraph. Emphasizing general knowledge about a broad range of social and governmental institutions, this site offers tourist-friendly information in English and Japanese.

Japan National Tourist Organization

http://www.jnto.go.jp/

The Japan National Tourist Organization maintains this informational site for news and travel updates in the East Asian country. Visitors will also find national and local maps, budget travel tips, and suggested itineraries.

Kochi Tourism Information

http://www.kochi-ct.ac.jp/tourism/

The International Affairs division of the Japanese government maintains this site to introduce Kochi prefecture. Visit here to find extensive information and resources on local history, geography, fisheries, forestries, art, and industry. In Japanese and English.

Ljubljana, Slovenia Guide

http://www.ijs.si/slo-ljubljana.html

Slovenian research organization J. Stefan Institute provides information here on its home city of Ljubljana. Visitors will find transportation, sightseeing, and accommodations resources.

The London Guide

http://www.cs.ucl.ac.uk/misc/uk/london.html

The London Guide, an unofficial guide to visiting the British capital city, offers links to hotel, entertainment, and travel resources. Includes links to information on other British destinations.

London, Ontario Guide

http://www.icis.on.ca/homepages/Ralph/London

Same name, different city, eh! London, Ontario's home page immerses visitors in the historic, cultural, and governmental sites of Canada's tenth largest metropolis. Maps, weather statistics, and tourist information fill out the page.

Los Angeles: City.Net Index

http://www.city.net/countries/united_states/california/los_angeles/

Movie Stars! Beaches! Traffic jams! Excite's City.Net international information service maintains this site for its guide to Los Angeles. Visitors will an extensive collection of links to local business, government, tourism, and entertainment resources.

Los Gatos, Calif. Guide

http://www.los-gatos.ca.us/los_gatos/los_gatos.html

Los Gatos-based apparel retailer Nine Lives maintains this site to introduce its home city. Visitors will find information on business, government, and visitors' resources.

Louisiana Guide

http://www.wisdom.com/la/la1.htm

Inter Commerce Corporation, a New Orleans-based Web consulting company, maintains this site for its guide to its home state. Visitors will find an extensive index of tourism, business, and government resources.

Madison Official Web Page

http://www.inmarket.com/madison/

The Greater Madison home page is the official Web site for the city of Madison, Wisconsin. Visitors will find find information about shopping, culture, nightlife, housing ,and local weather. Includes links to other nearby city home pages.

Magnificent Madras

http://comlab1.ee.ufl.edu/~sriraj/madras.html

Travel to the Magnificent Madras home page to find a treasure trove of information about the southern Indian city. Travelers will find pictures and information about interesting places and excursions. Includes links to other Indian cities, international guides, and the Indian Home Page.

Malaysia OnLine

http://www.mol.com/recruit/default.htm

Malayasia Online is a comprehensive storehouse of information about the tropical Southeast Asian country. Job listings, news in several languages, travel information, cultural resources, and much more are provided.

Maui Net

http://maui.net/

Maui Net, offering Internet connectivity to the Hawaiian island community, offers this site with local tourism information, product catalogs, and service descriptions. Visitors will also find publications, real estate listings, online discussion groups, and more.

NetWeb Bermuda

http://www.bermuda.com/

NetWeb Bermuda provides an advertising and information dissemination resource for Bermuda businesses and personal users. Includes Bermuda-related pointers, travel information, and personal home pages.

New Orleans French Quarter

http://www.frenchquarter.com/

Visit here for an introduction to New Orleans's French Quarter, an integral part of the "Big Easy's" nightlife culture. Hear Crescent City sounds from jazz to street noise. Learn what's going on this week and during Mardi Gras next year.

New Zealand

http://www.clearfield.co.nz/mount_cook/

This page offers information about airline travel in New Zealand. For those planning trips within this country, schedules, seat availability, and fee information is provided.

Nova Scotia

http://ttg.sba.dal.ca/nstour/

Nova Scotia, Canada's economic renewal department maintains this site for tourism and cultural information. Includes a virtual visitor's center, an overview of the Halifax G-7 economic summit, a crafts display, and weather reports.

Online Scotland

http://www.ibmpcug.co.uk/~ecs/

Shopping, travel tips, a business information exchange, and accommodations assistance are only a partial list of offerings online at this site. A High-

land welcome and links to other sites of interest are also provided.

Opportunities of Hawaii

http://www.aloha.com/~optunehi

The wonders of life in Hawaii are outlined at the Opportunities of Hawaii site, which lists resources for those looking to vacation, or relocate permanently. Links and software are available, as well as online ordering information.

The Paris Guest Book

http://www.paris.org/Guestsign

Visit this site to register your name in the annals of tourism history. Visitors to the Paris Guest Book Signing Page can leave their name and send remarks to other visitors. Names and e-mail addresses are automatically added to the Paris Guest Book. In French and English.

Paris Page

http://www.paris.org/parisF.html

Whether you're planning a real or virtual trip to the French capital, you'll enjoy a visit to the Paris Pages. "Clique" here for information and graphics covering tourism, entertainment, cultural exhibits, shopping, and many other Parisian resources. In French and English.

Les Pays de Grasse

http://www.aaacom.com/pdg

Explore the French Riviera via this site, which offers 100 ideas for discovering "Le Pays De Grasse." Visitors will find suggestions for accomodations, sporting activities ,and touring opportunities here. In French and English.

Les Pays de Savoie

http://lapphp0.in2p3.fr/maps/pays/pays.html

Visitors to this page will find the Web server for Pays de Savoie, a picturesque region of the French Alps. Photos, maps, tourist and sports information, and links to the home pages of the towns in the area are featured. In French and English.

Salzburg State Board of Tourism

http://www.tcs.co.at/other.html

This tourism page provides potential travelers with information about Salzburg, Austria. Visitors can access information about activities and check out events listings or local countryside regions. Includes a link to the home page of the Austrian National Tourist Office.

San Luis Obispo

http://www.tcs.co.at/other.html

This virtual tour of the California coastal community of San Luis Obispo highlights some of the city's main attractions: resorts and beaches, "Gum Wall Alley," and the Mission San Luis Obispo de Tolusa, erected in 1772. Images and a clickable map guide the visitor.

Santa Cruz Beach Boardwalk

http://www.beachboardwalk.com/

Visitors to this site can take a virtual of California's only seaside amusement park: the Santa Cruz Beach Boardwalk. Discover the classic 1911 Looff Carousel and find other tourist information about the boardwalk and Santa Cruz area attractions on this promotional page.

Sapporo City Guide

http://www.huie.hokudai.ac.jp/hokkaido/eng/sapporo/

The Sapporo Information page lets you navigate through the northern Japanese city of Sapporo, allowing stops at places of interest and pointing out the best accommodations. Get an overview of the city here, along with a little history and a list of annual events.

Scenes of Vermont

http://www.pbpub.com/vermont/

Scenes of Vermont is an "eclectic and independent" online magazine offering a variety of useful info for travelers and residents alike. Check out a guide to the best bed-and-breakfasts and inns in the state, plus history, skiing, events, culture, and more.

South Carolina Welcomes You

http://www.prt.state.sc.us/sc

Cyber-southerners can take a virtual tour of South Carolina's vacation spots here. The page also posts a calendar of events, a listing of hotels, and a guide to golfing in the state.

Tampere, Finland Guide

http://www.tpo.fi/english/tampere/index.html

TPO, Tampere, Finland's telephone company, maintains this site for a guide to its home city. Visitors will find information on Tampere's commerce, government, education, and tourism sectors.

Targa Tasmania

http://www.tas.gov.au/tourism/targa/index.html

Owners of classic cars who love driving challenges will love Targa Tasmania, a six-day, 2,000-kilometer event in autumn on Australia's mountain island of Tasmania, where 280 drivers try to outwit the ordinary tarmac roads to win their class.

Tasmania—Tourism Information for the WWW

http://www.tas.gov.au/tourism/tasman.html

The Department of Tourism, Sport and Recreation in Hobart, Tasmania, provides tourism information for this Australian island province. Includes listings of special events, an image library, and links to an interactive tour and other Tasmanian servers.

Tour in China

http://www.ihep.ac.cn/tour/china_tour.html

Travel to the Tour in China home page for take a virtual trip through Asia's "middle country" and each of its provinces. Also includes a link to the Hong Kong online guide and a map of China.

Traveling to Indonesia

http://www.emp.pdx.edu/htliono/travel.html

Maintained by an Indonesian expatriate in the United States, this guide to the Southeast Asian archipelago offers a variety of cultural, geographic, and tourist resources. Visit here for a one-stop shopping list of information for traveling to Indonesia.

Turkey Travel Guide

http://www.metu.edu.tr/~melih/turkeyhome.html

"All you may need to know traveling Turkey" is promised at the Turkey Travel Guide. From maps to manners, visitors will find factual and cultural resources of use to trip taking and planning.

United States Virgin Islands

http://www.usvi.net/

This Web site offers information on the United States Virgin Islands: St. Croix, St. Thomas, and St. John. Here, visitors will find a guide to shopping, island hot spots, travel agency information, and weather updates.

Vanuatu: A Small Place in the South Pacific

http://www.clark.net/pub/kiaman/vanuatu.html

Vanuatu is a *very* small island nation located in the South Pacific Ocean. Visitors to this page will discover maps, photos, historical notes, and the CIA World Factbook for this tiny but exotic country.

Vegas.COM

http://www.vegas.com/

Potential tourists can strike a jackpot of promotional materials at the home page of Vegas.Com. Find information on gaming, hotels, and entertainment here. For current news and weather, link to Las Vegas radio stations or the local news wire.

Vienna City

http://www.atnet.co.at/Tourism/Vienna/

Take a trip to Vienna via the Web! This site includes historical and background information on the Austrian capital, as well as details on sightseeing, events, accommodations, restaurants, transportation, and useful links.

Virtual Chattanooga

http://www.chattanooga.net/

Virtual Chattanooga, an online guide to resources in the historic Tennessee city, offers information on tourism, government services, educational

materials, and local businesses. Includes keyword search utility.

A Visit to Nepal

http://enigma.phys.utk.edu/~syost/nepal.html

This personal account of a six-week tour of Nepal provides a variety of journal entries, photos, and interactive maps. Includes links to other travel and tourism sites.

Walt Disney World

http://www.travelweb.com/TravelWeb/dw/common/wdw.html

Maintained by the Walt Disney Co., this home page includes information on Magic Kingdom, Epcot, and Disney-MGM Studios. Visitors will find details on tickets, events, and reservations. And for those still in the planning stages, there's the "I'm Going to Disney World" Vacation Planner.

Washington, D.C. Sightseeing Map

http://sc94.ameslab.gov/TOUR/tour.html

Visit this site for information about some of the U.S. capital city's most popular sights and attractions. An interactive map of the city, its museums, monuments, and conference centers are all available here.

The Webfoot's Guide to Spain

http://www.webfoot.com/travel/guides/spain/spain.html

The Webfoot's Guide to Spain provides the prospective traveler with the basic facts of that sunny land, including a cultural overview, maps, currency exchange rates, the latest weather, and excerpts from the handy CIA Factbook on the potential trouble spots for ill-prepared travelers.

The Webfoot's Guide to the British Virgin Islands

http://www.webfoot.com/travel/guides/bvi/bvi.html

The Webfoot's Guide to the British Virgin Islands contains everything you need to know before setting off to visit this tropical paradise. Check out travel advisories, temperature, and precipitation at different times of the year, currency exchange rates, sailing charters, and diving sites.

Welcome Mall

http://www.welcome.com/

The Welcome Mall links visitors to popular tourist destinations in Pennsylvania such as Gettysburg, the Strasburg Rail Road. and Amish Country. Accommodations, shopping, and restaurant information is also featured.

Welcome to Atlanta

http://www.atlantagames.com/atlanta.htm

"The Atlanta Journal-Constitution" maintains this site for information about its home city, host of the 1996 Olympic Games. Visitors will find an extensive index of local business, retail and entertainment resources, and links to the "Journal's" editorial and commercial Web offerings.

Welcome to Bavaria

http://www.bayern.de/

Travelers and businesspeople planning a visit to Bavaria will enjoy this profile of the German state. Includes news and information on local culture, tourism, economics, and international trade relations.

Welcome to Palm Springs Desert Resorts

http://www.desert-resorts.com/

Explore vacation options for Palm Springs, Monterey, and El Paso at this desert resorts travel guide. Visitors will find a number of online publications here, in addition to descriptions of golf facilities, restaurants, and tourist attractions.

Welcome to Quebec, Canada

http://www.iisys.com/www/travel/canada/quebec/quebec.htm

Learn everything about Quebec—from local culture to bankers' holidays—on the Welcome to Quebec page. Links include travel tips and links to universities in Canada's "distinctly different" province.

Welcome to Saudi Arabia

http://darkwing.uoregon.edu/~kbatarfi/saudi.html

An expatriate Saudi journalist studying in the United States maintains this guide to Saudi Arabia and the Arab World. Visitors will find a wealth of cultural, business, and news resources as well as an in-depth guide to understanding Islam.

West Bengal Independent Page

http://www.gl.umbc.edu/~achatt1/wbengal.html

West Bengal is one of the most culturally and ethnically diverse states of India. Travelers to its home page will find a treasure trove of information, including details about local tourism, language, and culture.

What's in San Antonio, Texas

http://www.gadsby.com/

San Antonio, home of the legendary Alamo and Texas Sea World, is the focus of this tourism site. Visitors will find an extensive index of local travel, entertainment, dining, business, and government resources.

GUIDEBOOKS

Bell's Alaska Travel Guide

http://alaskan.com/promos/bells.html

The Alaskan Center, a Web-based content provider covering the northernmost American state, maintains this site to introduce "Bell's Alaska Travel Guide." Visit here to order the most recent edition of this yearly index of local camping, accommodations, sport, and other tourism resources.

Lonely Planet Online

http://www.lonelyplanet.com/

Lonely Planet publishes practical travel guides for the budget-minded wayfarer. Includes links to an interactive world map to access information on destinations, travel journals, tips on transportation, health, and possible political complications. See Editor's Choice.

Moon Publications

http://www.moon.com/

Before you pack your traveling bags, thumb through Moon Travel Handbooks for handy travel tips. The publisher posts an online catalog on this promotional page. Visitors will also find recommended reading lists, online newsletters, and a hypertext travel guide.

Time Out

http://www.timeout.co.uk/

Time Out Net provides city guides along with arts and entertainment listings for international hot spots. Features about Berlin, London, Madrid, New York City, Paris, San Francisco, and other world-class cities can be found here, along with free classified ads.

Tips For Travellers

http://www.webfoot.com/travel/tips/tips.top.html

Wondering how much to take on your next trip? This traveler's help guide (part of a personal

EDITOR'S CHOICE

Lonely Planet Online

http://www.lonelyplanet.com

Anyone who's ever strapped on a backpack in search of the last great place knows the "Lonely Planet" (LP) series of budget travel guides. Published in 1973 in a backstreet Chinese hotel by a Western husband-and-wife team, the first LP book, "Southeast Asia on a Shoestring," has sold more than half a million copies and is now in its eighth printing. LP's softcover guides cover nearly every region in the world, and its home page is quickly surpassing these titles in breadth and depth of coverage. Utilizing the Web's ability to instantaneously update information, the LP site provides current exchange rates, travel advisories, and political conditions, allowing travelers to choose their destination based on a tight budget and/or appetite for adventure. Full text of most LP books is also included, as well as a handy internal search engine. —*Reviewed by Paul Bacon*

home page) offers advice on packing and air travel. Includes links to destination tour guides.

Travel Graphics International Map & Information Center

http://www.tgimaps.com/

Travel Graphics International knows that travelers need maps. The company tries to fill this need digitally through its map and information center on the Web. Currently the site features maps of the Minneapolis/St. Paul area, and plans to have resources available for Dallas and Hawaii in late 1996.

LODGING

Australian Resorts

http://peg.apc.org/~austresorts/home.htm

Australian Resorts promotes its five island resorts off the Great Barrier Reef here. Visitors to take a virtual tour of the resorts and have a look at the flora and fauna of each.

Bed-and-Breakfasts on the WWW

http://www.webcom.com/~neatstuf/bb/home.html

This Web site links travelers to more than 100 reservation service organizations offering access to thousands of bed-and-breakfast accommodations throughout the world. Visitors can view U.S. listings broken out by state, or check out extensive international listings.

Best Western International—Chain Info

http://www.travelweb.com/bw.html

Visit here for the Best Western listing in the larger TravelWeb database. Includes background information about the American motel chain and assistance making reservations and finding accommodations worldwide.

California Bed-and-Breakfasts

http://net101.com/BBCA/

This site contains a region-by-region guide to California's most inviting bed-and-breakfast establishments. Includes a virtual tour of the state of California, plus links to tourist information sites and other local travel resources.

Corporate Rate Hotel Directory

http://www.ios.com/corp_hotels

Corporate Travel Coordinators of America maintains this site to provide international hotel information tailored for business travelers. Visit here to browse lists of hotels participating in corporate pricing programs.

Hawaiian Vacations Brochure

http://hoohana.aloha.net/kahuna

Views of waterfalls are one of the highlights of the Hawaiian resort Hale O' Wailele (House of Leaping Waterfalls) and some are included at this site. Descriptions of the resort, its amenities, and services are featured. Available in Japanese.

Hilton Hotels Internet Travel Center

http://www.hilton.com/

Hilton Hotels has created this virtual concierge to guide users to information about the international hotel chain. Visitors can search for Hilton Hotels worldwide and access reservations and promotions information here.

Holiday Inn Worldwide

http://www.holiday-inn.com/

The Holiday Inn home page offers a complete worldwide guide to its more than 2,000 hotels. From this site, visitors can search for hotel locations according to state, highway location, and local attractions, and then make their reservations. This site also offers a frequently asked questions (FAQ) file.

Hospitality Scotland

http://www.virtual-inn.co.uk/

More than 7,000 inns, hotels, and public houses are listed in the Virtual Inn and First Option Hotel Reservations database. Tourists to the United Kingdom can search for price range, type, or style of accommodation and/or location and then make reservations.

Hostelling International

http://cyber.cclims.com/comp/ayh/ayh.html

Visitors to this site can learn about the inexpensive tourist accommodations available through American Youth Hostels the world over. Also featured are a list of Northern California hostels and reservations information. See Editor's Choice.

Hotel Durant

http://cyber.cclims.com/comp/hdur/hdur.html

The restored Hotel Durant, a landmark luxury hotel in Berkeley, California has provided this Web page with information about room rates and reservations, as well as the hotel's history and location. This page also links to the Pacific Plaza Hotel and CCL Travel sites.

Hotel Net

http://www.u-net.com/hotelnet

This lodging finder service offers links to accommodations in a variety of European countries. Visit here to browse by location for hotels, bed-and-breakfasts, hostels, and more. Also offers links to non-European destinations—including the "U.K. Guide."

---

a2z **EDITOR'S CHOICE**

Hostelling International

http://www.taponline.com/tap/travel/hostels/pages/hostels.html

After a day of traveling in a foreign country with all its strange sights, smells, and toilet configurations, nothing is quite as comforting as seeing the familiar blue triangle of an International Youth Hostel. Founded in Germany in the late 1920s, this worldwide network of inexpensive, clean, and safe accommodations has become the standard for budget travelers of all nationalities. Look to the Hostelling International home page for an annotated listing of its more than 5,000 dormitory-style hotels in 70 countries. Many travelers can lighten their load by replacing their heavy, paperback hostel guides with one strategic copy-and-paste session from these comprehensive pages. The site also provides information on membership benefits—including discounts on entertainment, exhibits, and air, land, and sea transportation. —*Reviewed by Paul Bacon*

Hotel Pendini

http://www.dada.it/pendini/hotel.html

This promotional site for Hotel Pendini, located in downtown Florence, Italy, contains color photographs of rooms, a rate list, and an online reservation service. Visitors will also find location and car maps.

Internet Travel Network

http://www.itn.net/cgi/get?itn/index/

Maintained by the "world's largest professional associations for bed-and-breakfasts and country inns," this site offers a wide variety of proprietor resources. Visit here for industry newsletters, research and marketing resources, conference and events schedules, and links to related Web sites.

Leading Hotels of the World, Ltd.

http://www.interactive.line.com/lead

An "exclusive organization" of international luxury hotels, New York City-based Leading Hotels maintains this site to introduce its network of accommodations in more than 65 countries worldwide. Visit here for hotel descriptions, reservation center listings, and a special e-mail reservation utility.

Marriott International, Inc.

http://www.marriott.com/

Marriot Hotels, providing more than 100,000 rooms in 22 countries, maintains this site to introduce its wide range of accommodations—including Courtyard, Fairfield Inn, and Residence Inn. Check into this home page to peruse corporate information and find lodging at your next destination.

Preferred Hotels & Resorts Worldwide

http://www.travelweb.com/thisco/preferred/common/htllist.html

TravelWeb maintains this site for its index of more than 100 of the "finest hotels and resorts in the world." Visitors can find rates, service descriptions, and reservation information on facilities providing "uncompromising luxury and individual style."

Princeville Resort

http://www.princeville.com/

This promotional site is sponsored by Princeville Resort, a golf resort and community located in Princeville, Hawaii. Visitors are invited to tour the property—including the hotel, golf course, and residential area.

Professional Association of Innkeepers International

http://www.paii.org/paii

Maintained by the "world's largest professional association for bed-and-breakfasts and country inns," this site offers a wide variety of proprietor resources. Visit here for industry newsletters, research and marketing resources, conference and events schedules, and links to related Web sites.

Promus Hotel Corp.

http://www.promus.com/

The Promus Hotel Corp. owns Embassy Suites, Hampton Inns, and Homewood Suites. Visitors to the company's corporate site can find hotel locations and make reservations.

The Register

http://www.travelassist.com/reg/reg_home.html

The Register is a comprehensive directory of more than 600 bed and breakfasts, inns, and small hotels throughout the United States and other parts of the world. Each entry contains photos, descriptions, and rates. See Editor's Choice.

Relais & Chateaux

http://www.travelassist.com/reg/reg_home.html

Relais & Chateaux provides an international online reservation and information service, featuring more than 400 chateaux, country houses, and restaurants. Visit here to plan the perfect vacation.

The Russian Youth Hostel Association

http://www.spb.su/ryh/ryha.html

Staying in a hostel is cheap and it offers a unique way to see a city or country from a nontourist perspective. Russian Youth Hostels offers accommodations in Moscow, Novgorod, Irkutsk, St. Petersburg, and links with other nation's hostels.

---

a2z EDITOR'S CHOICE

The Register

http://www.travelassist.com/reg/reg_home.html

Curl up snug as a bug in a rug at one of the romantic bed-and-breakfasts listed at The Register. More than 600 listings for B&Bs, country inns, and other quaint overnight establishments are nestled within the pages of this charming site, organized by region, with entries for Canada, Europe, Latin America, and the United States. Each of the listings, provided by TravelASSIST and other B&B directories, offers a brilliant color portrait of the location—almost all with smoking chimneys—as well as a warm, fuzzy description of available amenities. Listings also include room rates, dates of business, and directions from the nearest city or airport.—*Reviewed by Paul Bacon*

Mountain-Fare Inn

Campton, New Hampshire, USA

Region: White Mountains of New Hampshire

Lovely 1840's home with the antiques, fabrics and feel of country cottage living. Gardens in summer, foliage in fall, a true skier's lodge in winter. Accessible, peaceful, warm,

St. Petersburg International Hostel

http://www.spb.su/ryh/home.html

Hostel services in Russia provide travelers with an inexpensive way of touring the country. Visit here for comprehensive tourist information on visas, pricing, reservations, Russia traveling tips, and other tourist resources.

TravelWeb

http://www.travelweb.com/

The Hotel Industry Switch Company, Inc. maintains this site for its TravelWeb online reservation system. Visitors can reserve accommodations and facilities at more than 6,000 hotels around the world.

World Wide Travel Exchange

http://www.pope.com/travelex

This site contains lists of homes for exchange, vacation rentals, and bed-and-breakfasts, as well as resort homes and property for sale. Links to the bulletin board and general information are also provided.

NATIONAL PARKS AND OUTDOOR RECREATION

Appalachian Trail Home Page

http://www.fred.net/kathy/at.html

The Appalachian Trail stretches from the mountains of Maine to Georgia. This guide offers extensive resources on the more than 2,000-mile hiking trail. Visit here to learn about the footpath and find maps, hiking tips, news, and much more.

Arizona State Parks

http://www.pr.state.az.us/

The Arizona State Parks' World Wide Web site takes visitors through virtual tours of the southwestern state's 24 natural, cultural and recreational parks. Includes information about the park service's gift shops, featuring a different retailer each month.

Aspen Snowmass OnLine Home Page

http://www.aspenonline.com/aspenonline/

Aspen Snowmass OnLine offers complete information about the Colorado ski resort communities of Aspen and Snowmass. Here visitors can find out about recreational activities, travel, family tips, lodging, nature hikes, and dining suggestions.

The Backcountry Home Page

http://io.datasys.swri.edu/

Dedicated to the outdoor enthusiast, the Back Country Home Page offers visitors maps, gear re-

views, tips, recipes, and a library of other resources for planning outdoor trips. Includes wide variety of links to other outdoor sports home pages.

Colorado Outdoors

http://www.csn.net/~arthurvb/colorado/colorado.html

This guide to Colorado outdoor recreation resources (part of a personal home page) offers information on state and national parks, hiking, camping, climbing, snow sports, and other outdoor activities. Includes links to other Colorado-related Web servers and outdoor sites.

EarthWise Journeys

http://www.teleport.com/~earthwyz/

EarthWise Journeys is an online resource dedicated to environmentally aware travelers. Their site includes a diverse collection of articles on outdoor adventures and spiritual retreats. Highlights include pages on eco-travel, women's travel, and art courses.

GORP Oregon Index

http://www.gorp.com/gorp/location/or/or.htm

The Great Outdoor Recreation Pages service provides this index of Oregon recreation resources. Visitors will find an extensive collection of links to state parks, travel packages, sport equipment retailers, outdoor clubs, health tips, and more.

GORP U.S. National Parks Index

http://www.gorp.com/gorp/resource/US_National_Park/main.htm

The Great Outdoor Recreation Pages service maintains this site for a searchable database of U.S. National Parks and Preserves. Visitors can also access activities information, maps, educational opportunities, and special events.

National Park Service Home Page

http://www.nps.gov/

Before loading up the station wagon for Yosemite or other national parks, contact this electronic visitor center for maps, weather, and camping fees. The site includes a list of all National Parks and an overview of the Park Service's work to "preserve America's heritage."

The Outdoor Network

http://www.outdoornet.com/

The Outdoor Network is a commercial site that intends to be an interactive center for team, extreme, and action sports as well as travel and adventure. Retailers and wholesalers of travel services, gear, and sports equipment are prominently featured.

Rocky Mountain Diving Center and Boulder Scuba Tours

http://www.csn.net/rmdc

A travel agency specializing in dive travel, Colorado's Rocky Mountain Diving Center and Boulder Scuba Tours offers travel packages to dive destinations around the world. Includes information on group diving trips, scuba lessons, and prices.

Rocky Mountain National Park

http://www.csn.net/~arthurvb/rmnp/rmnp.html

Travelers planning a trip to Colorado's picturesque Rocky Mountain National Park can scout attractions, routes, and weather conditions in advance at this official park home page. Peruse the Park Service brochure or review park maps and pictures here.

Shangri La Home Page

http://aleph0.clarku.edu/rajs/Shangri_La.html

Images of the Himalayan mountain range are featured at this site, which includes a clickable map taking visitors to vistas on individual peaks. Includes background material on the legendary Mt. Everest, environmental news, and more.

Skiing at Whistler Resort

http://www.whistler.net/

At this promotional site for Whistler Resort in British Columbia, Canada, visitors can learn about its skiing trails, accommodations, restaurants and activities. Interactive contests and prizes also are featured here.

Sky Adventures

http://www.mainelink.net/SKYADVENTURES/

Gliders can take a look at Sky Adventures' hanggliding and paragliding tours in Maine on this page. The site also includes a photo guide to hang-gliding in Maine and dozens of links to related sites worldwide.

Sports Tours

http://www.travelsource.com/sports/sti

This promotional site is the Web home of Sports Tours, Inc., a company that arranges affordable group outings to sporting events. Vistors can learn more about the company and its services, or link to related sports pages.

Virtual North

http://pcs.mb.ca/~vnorth/vnorth.html

Service provider PCS Internet maintains this site for an overview of travel opportunities in rural and remote areas of Canada. Visit here for links to lodges and resorts, tour companies, travel associations, and many other nature-related tourism resources.

PUBLICATIONS AND INDUSTRY NEWS

Travelmag

http://www.travelmag.co.uk/travelmag/

Travelmag is an online U.K.-based publication targeting people interested in discovering the world around them. It features profiles on vacation spots and invites readers to join a travel club that offers special prices.

RAILWAYS AND ROADWAYS

Amtrak Schedules

http://www.mcs.net/~dsdawdy/Amtrak/amtrak.html

The Cyberspace World Railroad maintains this site for official and unofficial Amtrak rail information. Visitors will find timetables, destination listings, and links to other rail-related resources.

Bahnverbindungen in Deutschland

http://www.uni-karlsruhe.de/~rail/

The RailServer allows travelers to query an online database of timetables for trains running across Germany and parts of Europe. Includes helpful tips for anyone planning to travel through Germany by train. In German and English.

Bay Area Transit Information

http://server.berkeley.edu/Transit/index.html

Northern California commuters can find help getting around without a car at the San Francisco Bay Area Transit Information site. Links to more than 20 transit agencies for access route maps, fare structures, and schedules.

Los Angeles Freeway Speeds

http://www.scubed.com/caltrans/la/la_big_map.shtml

Check here before you hit the freeway in Los Angeles. This real-time traffic information site, maintained by Maxwell Laboratories, Inc., offers freeway speeds and traffic conditions in the greater Los Angeles Area. Includes listings for common trouble spots.

Mercurio—The European Railway Server

http://mercurio.iet.unipi.it/home.html

Mercurio provides timetables and information on a variety of European rail systems and trains. Visitors will find links to "European Railway News" magazine and links to official and unofficial railway sites.

New Zealand by Rail

http://www.waikato.ac.nz/nz/rail/timetable.html

Learn how to travel New Zealand by rail through this page that includes complete timetables and tips. Visitors can view an interactive map of the country to see where the trains connect, or they can link to one of its many New Zealand-related tourism pages.

Train Travel in Finland

http://www.travel.fi/

Finland's train schedules are posted here in Finnish, Swedish, and English. The site also includes a Finnish railway map and a station-by-station index.

VIA Rail Canada

http://www.mcs.net/~dsdawdy/Canpass/via/via.html

VIA Rail Canada, the country's national passenger train service, maintains this site for destination and scheduling information. Visit here to find updated intercity and transcontinental rail travel listings.

Washington State Department of Transportation

http://www.wsdot.wa.gov/

Travelers and commuters in Washington State will find an extensive collection of transportation schedules and related government resources at this informational site. Visit here to learn about transit routes, infrastructure projects, and management commissions.

SHIPS AND CRUISE LINES

BC Ferries

http://bcferries.bc.ca/ferries/

This is a useful transportation page for all ferries running in British Columbia, Canada. Visitors will find ferry services, routes, maps, schedules, news, and fleet information.

CU Cruising WWW Home Page

http://www.cucruising.com/cu/

This commercial site is the travel reservation center maintained by C.U. Cruising of Anaheim, California. Visitors can find out more about the company, review its special tour offers, airfare rates and vacation discounts, or read the company newsletter.

Research Ship Information and Cruise Schedules

http://www.travelassist.com/reg/reg_home.html

Here's a helpful site for ocean travelers, providing detailed ship and cruise schedule information. Local search tools allow visitors to look for ships by name, country of registry, characteristics, and cruise schedules. Links to related databases are also featured.

Royal Caribbean Cruise Line

http://mmink.cts.com/mmink/kiosks/costa/rccl.html

The Royal Caribbean Cruise Line, with destinations around the world, maintains this site to introduce its latest tour packages. Visit here for listings of dates, prices, ports of call, and reservation information.

TOUR AND TRAVEL COMPANIES

Above All Travel

http://www.aboveall.com/

Above All Travel highlights its current trip offerings and information about its business on this commercial page. The Nevada-based agency features adventure travel, cruises, and other "theme" packages.

Architects Abroad

http://www.rahul.net/arctour/

Architects Abroad, a San Francisco-based provider of architecture-oriented travel packages, maintains this site with information on tours, schedules, programs, accommodations, trip costs, and other aspects of the company's service.

Arctic Adventours, Inc.

http://www.oslonett.no/html/adv/AA/AA.html

If you're heading for the North Pole, pay a visit to this site, maintained by a Norwegian tour company specializing in expeditions to the Arctic area. Includes tour package information, online registration, and links to related tour companies and Internet newsgroups.

Around-the-World Airfares & High Adventure Travel

http://www.highadv.com/

High Travel Adventures, Inc., offers a wealth of information here about its around-the-world air fares and travel packages. Visitors to this site can peruse the High Adventures electronic catalog, find out air fare pricings and availability, or read the company's frequently asked questions (FAQs).

ASI-Home Page

http://www.sightseeing.com/

American Sightseeing International is a network of professional, full-service tour companies and transportation operators. This organizational site includes background and membership information, along with links to travel sites detailing destinations in the United States, Canada, and the Caribbean.

Canadian Himalayan Expeditions

http://www.netpart.com/che/brochure.html

Visitors to this site will find the Web home of a Canadian company that arranges Himalayan expeditions and African camping safaris. Summaries of adventure trips to Nepal, India, Pakistan, and Africa are featured along with pricing, flight and weather information, and comments from past participants.

Connections: A Southern Golf & Vacation Guide

http://www.aesir.com/Welcome.html

The Scratch Golf Company invites visitors to take a virtual tour of golf courses in the Southeastern United States at this site. Browsers can also check out company information, resorts and accommodations listings, rental companies, and other tourism resources.

Coral Technologies, Inc.

http://www.coral.net/

The Waterfront/Sunshine Dreams home page has information about vacation destinations, real estate, and scuba diving getaways. Find links to the company's client list, descriptions of clients' products and services, and related Web sites.

Costa Travel

http://mmink.cts.com/mmink/kiosks/costa/costatravel.html

Costa Travel is an online travel agency that specializes in ocean cruises. The company promotes hotel discounts and Club Med specials at its corporate home page.

EcoTravels in Latin America

http://www.txinfinet.com/mader/ecotravel/ecotravel.html

Here you'll find info about environmentally friendly tours. See Editor's Choice.

Harbourside Travel Services

http://www.tagsys.com/Ads/Harbourside

A Florida travel agency that specializes in Disney World resorts and Caribbean cruises offers its services online here.

Kintetsu International Travel Finder for Japan

http://www.kintetsu.com/

The home page of Kintetsu International Express, a Japanese travel company, this promotional site aims to "serve as a reference for all travel to Japan." Features include information about package tours, rail passes, and discounted airline tickets.

Neptune Travel Village

http://www.neptune.com/index.html

Neptune Travel maintains this site for its "automatic reservation service." Visit here for online access to discount hotels, airlines, rental car agencies, and travel packages from around the United States.

PC Travel

http://www.pctravel.com/

Book your flight online with PCTravel. Make airline reservations and purchase tickets at this commercial service provided by American Travel Corporation.

Travel Agents International

http://www.travelagency.com/

Travel Agents International assists travelers with trip planning and reservation confirmations. This commercial home page includes travel tips and special offers. Visitors also can access information about airlines, hotels, rental cars, cruises, and vacation packages.

TravelBase

http://www.travelbase.com/

TravelBase, an Internet travel agency, posts information on U.S. vacation destinations and activities including skiing, scuba diving, and tennis. Includes links to Florida travel guides, and supports a form for making reservations.

Travelogix Flifo Reservation System

http://www.travelogix.com/

Travelogix Online maintains this site for its Flifo airline reservation system. Touted as a "personal travel information grabber," Flifo provides online flight schedule and ticketing services.

Travel Source

http://www.travelsource.com/

Tour the tour providers advertising at this virtual travel mall. Find vacation packages for most every interest: golfing, diving, trekking, boating, eco tours, wine tours, unique tours, and more.

---

a2z EDITOR'S CHOICE

EcoTravels in Latin America

http://www.txinfinet.com/mader/ecotravel/ecotravel.html

Central and South America are host to some of the world's most pristine natural and archeological wonders, and environmentalist Ron Mader wants to keep it that way. The author of two ecology books maintains this site as a "dynamic facilitator" for the awareness of sustainable tourism in Latin America. Visit here for an extensive index of environmentally friendly tour operators and indigenous tribes from Mexico to Chile. Descriptions of facilities and services of each operator is provided, as well as contact information, related reading materials, and nontraditional touring alternatives. Visitors will also find full text archives of his monthly eco-tourism publication "El Planeta Platica" ("The Earth Speaks").—*Reviewed by Paul Bacon*

Center for Disease Control Travel Information Page

http://www.cdc.gov/travel/travel.html

It doesn't take more than one bout with Montezuma's revenge to learn that world health standards vary from region to region. While most people know the caveat "Don't drink the water," few are aware of the myriad health risks associated with travel to unfamiliar countries and climates. Whether you plan to ride an elephant in Thailand or just knock back some brews in Bavaria, stop by this site from the U.S. Center for Disease Control well in advance of your next international trip. A comprehensive, country-by-country guide is provided for travelers, as well as background information and updates on common diseases such as AIDS, cholera, hepatitis, and malaria. A list of recommended vaccinations and prescription drugs is also available. —*Reviewed by Paul Bacon*

U.S. State Department Travel Warnings

http://www.stolaf.edu/network/travel-advisories.html

Western travelers may have the world as their oyster, but it's still a jungle out there. Epidemics, political upheavals, and terrorist attacks are commonplace in many of the world's most fascinating places, making a quick visit to this official U.S. State Department resource a wise precaution. Did you know that Americans need a license to visit Cuba? Or that all Western-ers are advised to stay clear of Egyptian mosques on Fridays? These critical advisories and many more are available here, providing updated warnings on all potential flash points and known health risks. Visitors will also find traveler's safety tips, an index of related resources from other international governments, and a mailing list to receive free, up-to-the-minute official releases via e-mail. —*Reviewed by Paul Bacon*

U.S. State Department Travel Warnings and Consular Information Sheets

http://www.stolaf.edu/network/travel-advisories.html

St. Olaf College in Northfield, MN, USA is the *Internet* and *BITNET* distribution point for United States State Department Travel Warnings and Consular Information Sheets. Click here for general information about the Travel Warnings and Consular Information Sheets.

TRAVELERS' HEALTH AND PREPAREDNESS

Center for Disease Control Travel Information Page

http://www.cdc.gov/travel/travel.html

Protect your health when traveling: This site tells you how. See Editor's Choice.

The Medical College of Wisconsin International Travelers Clinic

http://www.intmed.mcw.edu/travel.html

The International Travelers Clinic provides a fact-filled tip book covering travel-related diseases, immunizations, and environmental hazards. Hot links include the CIA World Factbook and U.S. State Department Travel Warnings.

Stanford Travel Medicine Service

http://www-leland.stanford.edu/~naked/stms-tp.html

The Stanford Travel Medicine Service offers medical advice to travelers here. The site includes information on how to pack a medical kit and what to do if you get ill away from home.

U.S. State Department Travel Warnings

http://www.stolaf.edu/network/travel-advisories.html

Many travel safety tips are here. See Editor's Choice.

ZINES

Alles

http://www.express.co.jp/ALLES/

Alles magazine, a Japan-based online art and multimedia publication, offers feature articles and artist profiles. Read all about Japan's cutting edge multimedia and music creators. Available in Japanese and English.

Beatrice

http://www.beatrice.com/contents/

Beatrice, an online monthly magazine, offers a spread of original fiction, essays, book reviews and interviews.

Bunnyhop Magazine

http://www.bunnyhop.com

Bunnyhop Magazine, published twice annually, covers "alternative music, pop culture, and other soft and fluffy things." Visitors to its Web page will find excerpts from the current and back issues, plus subscription information. See Editor's Choice.

Citizen Poke

http://www.amherst.edu/~poke/

Citizen Poke, an online humor publication of Amherst College, can be accessed from this site. Download the publication in a variety of viewing formats.

CLOCK: London's Culture, News and Views

http://www.clock.co.uk/

Delphi, an Internet access provider in the U.K., maintains this online zine, which includes features on business, entertainment and the latest cultural trends.

Consumable Online

http://www.westnet.com/consumable/
Consumable.html

Consumable Online, an Internet-based music magazine, provides disc reviews, artist interviews and tour information on pop, rock, and alternative groups. Visitors can read current and back issues here.

CyberZine

http://www.cyberzine.com/

Published monthly, CyberZine offers readers sports, comics, chat and much more. Access current and back issues here.

The Daily Bikini

http://www.thedaily.com/bikini.html

The front page photo of The Daily Bikini changes every weekday, but it's always a beautiful bikini-clad babe. Other than that, this zine is full of links to an eclectic resources, from entertainment to news to sports.

Departure from Normal

http://www.xwinds.com/dfn/dfn.html

This electronic arts journal hosts a diverse selection of digitized expressions, from poetry and short fiction to paintings and graphics. Submission guidelines assert, "If we like it, we publish it."

dimFLASH

http://www.well.com/user/futrelle/

dimFLASH features ribald satire, commentary and critique. Visitors will find humorous articles on a variety of topics.

Enterzone

http://ezone.org/ez

This table of contents page for Enterzone links to the zine's various features and articles. Visitors will find poetry, stories, art, essays, criticism, cartoons, music reviews and photography. A subscription form is also available.

Flames

http://www.gold.net/flames/

Flames is a Britain-based zine that features news, interviews and commentary on Internet-related topics. Includes coverage of media, political, economical and technological issues.

FutureNet

http://www.futurenet.co.uk/

FutureNet describes itself as "Europe's leading electronic magazine." Visitors will find world news reports, and features on computing, sports and entertainment. Only registered users are allowed access to its pages, however. To move beyond this point, visitors must either register or enter the correct password.

Heckler Magazine Home Page

http://www.heckler.com

Snowboarding, skateboarding and music come together in the online pages of Heckler. The site contains articles, photos and features found in the print version of the magazine, which is distributed through Tower Books.

Hermenaut

http://www.pwainc.com/hermenaut/1/
herm1.html

A combination of fanzine and philosophy, Hermenaut is "dedicated to the ruthless criticism of all that exists…" Online selections from this print magazine include a Nietzschean interpretation of "Beverly Hills 90210." Subscription and guideline information is also available.

---

a2z **EDITOR'S CHOICE**

Bunnyhop Magazine

http://www.bunnyhop.com/

The brains behind Bunnyhop have got to be at least twice the size of those belonging to the furry beasts for which the achingly well-designed zine is named. With covers that range from a remake of the "Family Circus" (Mom and Dad as "normal" parents instead of drones from another, mythical time of fuzzy family fun) to fisticuffs between a pair of all-too-familiar wabbits, Bunnyhop pledges to present readers with "alternative music, pop culture and other soft and fluffy things." A bevy of witty record reviews, interviews with all manner of folk, provocatively titled articles ("Are Skinny White Women Overrated?" and "A Girl's Guide to Geek Guys") make this one of the most entertaining zines around. Not all copy is available on the Web, but there's enough here to convince you to send in a few bucks and get the whole shebang in hard-copy delivered right to your door-step.—*Reviewed by Julene Snyder*

Hyperreal

http://hyperreal.com/

The Hyperreal site explores alternative culture, music and expression. Here visitors can access the rave culture archives, duck into music resources on techno and ambient music and link up to some topical zines. Includes a section on alternative drugs.

InterText: The Online Fiction Magazine

http://ftp.etext.org/Zines/InterText/intertext.html

InterText features the best of short fiction and art. Readers can opt to view articles online or download them for reading with Adobe Acrobat, as a PostScript file or plain ASCII text.

John Labovitz's e-zine-list

http://www.meer.net/~johnl/e-zine-list/index.html

Search by keyword or access an alphabetical sort of the e-zine list archived at this site. Also find links to topic-related sites and answers to questions like, "What's an 'e-zine' anyway?"

Kulttuurivihkot

http://www.clinet.fi/~lyhty/vihkot.html

Kulttuurivihkot, a Finnish language arts and entertainment journal, calls itself "the coolest journal on the planet." Check out articles on "high and popular" culture from around the world.

Kyosaku Home Page

http://cs.oberlin.edu/students/djacobs/kyo/kyomain.html

Kyosaku is a quarterly zine out of Oberlin College "dedicated to fostering a healthy zeal for poetry, humor, beauty and life." Its current and back issues—filled with poetry, prose and art—are available here.

Madness

http://web1.trenton.edu/~domurat

Horror stories, cutting-edge computer art and revolution manifestos are just a few of the links to be found at Madness. The off-kilter index also posts links to crime archives and anarchist sites.

Media 3

http://www.deakin.edu.au/arts/VPMA/Media3.html

Media 3 offers a diverse collection of hypertext media-related articles; from Japanese animation to women in comics, film and television. Visitors can also obtain contribution information.

Netsurfer Digest Home Page

http://www.netsurf.com/nsd/

Netsurfer Digest is a free online zine featuring "newsbytes," notices and reviews of Internet-related subjects. Visit this site for e-mail subscription information, Web site development tools and the digest's current and back issues. See Editor's Choice.

Netsurfer Focus Home Page

http://www.netsurf.com/nsf/

Netsurfer Focus focuses on one specific "cyberspace" related topic per issue. This site offers readers access to past issues and subscription information.

NWHQ

http://www.knosso.com/NWHQ/

A novel (if less-than-straightforward) Web journal of literature and art, NWHQ is described by its editor as "a labyrinth" where art and text may be links that spin the reader to other areas of the document. This gateway page features an image map offering numerous entry points into the work.

Parallel Gallery

http://www.va.com.au/parallel

This art publication examines cross-disciplinary work from artists and writers, and explores topics ranging from architecture and art to film and fiction. Visitors will find samples of work from a variety of authors and artists.

Pen & Sword Hypersite

http://www.rahul.net/jag/

Find poetry, essays, fiction, graphics and sound bites at Pen N Sword. Along with their works, the artists' bios are featured. See Editor's Choice.

Phrack Magazine

http://www.fc.net/phrack.html

According to its editor, Phrack Magazine speaks to and for the international computer underground. Hackers can look up information in the realms of computer networks, telephony, and operating systems in the long-running zine.

Pop Culture

http://www.melvin.com/Current/PopCulture/PopCulture.html

Visit this page for the latest edition of Pop Culture. Features include film reviews and interviews with popular artists.

---

a2z EDITOR'S CHOICE

Netsurfer Digest Home Page

http://www.netsurf.com/nsd/

Eeek! Between the kids, the dog, the traffic, the ringing phone and the doorbell, who has time to surf the Net? Well, relax, li'l punkin, cause the editors at Netsurfer Digest are happy to do it for you. Here, you'll find all the skinny on the best sites in the "surfing sites" section; recent offerings included mini-reviews of the "Alien Contact" site and a "Bewitched" tribute. Netsurfer Digest has enough hyperlinks to keep you virtually hopping for days as well as "newsbytes," notices and reviews of Internet-related—and more esoteric—subjects. Visitors will find e-mail subscription information, website development tools and the digest's current and back issues. It's big, it's stuffed with stuff, and it changes every dang week. What's not to like?—*Reviewed by Julene Snyder*

NETSURFER DIGEST
More Signal, Less Noise

SUBSCRIBE
MARKETPLACE
SUBMIT
ABOUT
FAQ INFO

Welcome! Netsurfer Digest is a **FREE** e-mail delivered e-zine bringing cyberspace directly to your mailbox since 1994. Subscribe and every week we will bring you a hot-linked gateway to a selection of neat online sites.

Latest Issue: 06/27/96: Vol. 02, #20

Also visit Netsurfer Focus for more in-depth coverage of various topics.

The SenseMedia Surfer

http://www.picosof.com/

A bridge to the "virtual and Pacific rims," Sense-Media Surfer's site features real audio and a wide ranging list of links with an emphasis on arts and entertainment. Music, photography and global trade of the Pacific Rim are explored.

Silly Little Tomte Publications

http://pobox.com/slt/

Sam Johnson's Electronic Revenge, a regularly updated online magazine of essays, opinion, snide remarks, and general wackiness is provided here by Silly Little Tomte Publications. The site also offers access to New Badger Books, which provides full-length electronic publications.

Sober Witness

http://www.sober.com/

Find the current and back issues of Sober Witness, a zine that offers Web navigation tips and tricks, plus links to selected (and reviewed) "worthwhile" sites. See what a "hype-free guide to the Web" looks like.

Spank!

http://www.spankmag.com

More thoughtful than the average online publication aimed at young people, Spank offers the usual roundup of music and film reviews as well as features that range from a report on Middle Eastern strife to the true meaning of daylight saving time. See Editor's Choice.

Strobe Magazine

http://www.iuma.com/strobe/

Strobe Magazine, an online rock music publication, features articles, columns, and music reviews. An online classified advertisement entry form is also available.

Undercurrents

http://darkwing.uoregon.edu/~heroux/home.html

Online e-journal Undercurrents explores the issues behind current events from a cybersmart, Oregonian perspective. Visitors will find alternative viewpoints on issues ranging from the historical to the philosophical in the electronic editions archived here.

Unit Circle

http://www.etext.org/Zines/UnitCircle/

Unit Circle is a Seattle-based paper and electronic zine on alternative culture that also markets books and music. Current and past issues are available, along with information on Unit Circle's other products. See Editor's Choice.

---

a2z EDITOR'S CHOICE

Pen & Sword Hypersite

http://www.rahul.net/jag/

With a bottom line of providing "imaginative, interesting art and writing— poetry, essays, fiction, hypermedia, graphics, video, movies and sounds," Pen and Sword aims to become a sort of Algonquin roundtable for the Internet. It's off to a good start with quality writing that's not overburdened with graphics overloads. This line alone makes me want to take my shoes off and set a spell: "It was a high school graduation present from her father, a man she claimed was actually a figment of her mother's imagination because neither had actually seen him for almost nine years. " Hmm. Not bad. Not bad at all. Then it goes and gets better: "[She] called the car Stanley, which was also the name of her older brother. Both, she claimed, were fond of eating small children and tiny, rat-like dogs that wandered too close to the curb." OK, I'm hooked.—*Reviewed by Julene Snyder*

Pen & Sword logo by the inimitable Daniel Sanchez

Spank!

http://www.cadvision.com/spank/spank.htm

No, no, this is not an online publication aimed at the bondage set. Spank is an e-zine aimed at young people, but don't dismiss it because you're out of the demographic, which seems to hover around the "twentysomething" area. Articles on body image, posing nude and interviews with sports celebrities are among the more serious offerings, while the "tag" area—riddled with inarticulate blather—does, in fact prove that plenty of readers deserve a firm spanking.—*Reviewed by Julene Snyder*

Urban Desires

http://desires.com/issues.html

The monthly electronic magazine Urban Desires features essays, fiction, travel articles, book reviews and digital art. The current issue as well as back issues are available here.

The Vibe

http://metaverse.com/vibe/

The Vibe is an electronic zine dedicated to all things pertaining to popculture. Editorial categories include sights, sounds, sleaze and surf.

(Virtual) Baguette

http://www.mmania.com/

The (Virtual) Baguette is a bilingual French-culture zine "for the pleasure of your five senses." An amusing mix of feature articles and multimedia attractions is provided. In French and English.

Vocal Point

http://bvsd.k12.co.us/cent/Newspaper/Newspaper.html

The Vocal Point, an online monthly newspaper assembled by students at Centennial Middle School in Boulder, Colorado tackles a new topic each issue. Visitors can check out the current and back issues or link to the Boulder Valley School District's home page.

Zines FTP Archive

ftp://etext.org/

This University of Michigan FTP site archives electronic zines on a wide variety of subjects, from cyberculture and humor to science fiction and sex.

---

a2z **EDITOR'S CHOICE**

Unit Circle

http://www.etext.org/Zines/UnitCircle/ Wow.

This Seattle-based paper and electronic zine is a vast repository for articles, reviews and features about (surprise!) alternative culture. Here find pieces and hyperlinks in a dizzying array of subjects, including art, books, comics, fiction, music, non-fiction, opinion and poetry. Whew. The sparse initial design gives way to more graphic-intensive areas the deeper you delve into the Unit Circle. There's so much here that there's pretty sure to be something for everyone—even if you wouldn't know a Nine Inch Nail if it bit you in the butt.—*Julene Snyder*

GOVERNMENT

THE 25 MOST POPULAR GOVERNMENT SITES

Canadian Government Departments
http://192.77.55.3/opengov/departments.html

Congressional Quarterly Gopher
gopher://gopher.cqalert.com/

Federal Communications Law Journal
http://www.law.indiana.edu/fclj/fclj.html

The Federal Register
http://gopher.nara.gov:70/register

The File Room
http://fileroom.aaup.uic.edu/FileRoom/
documents/TofCont.html

INFOMINE
http://lib-www.ucr.edu/govpub/

The Interfaith Alliance
http://www.intr.net/tialliance/

Internal Revenue Service
http://www.irs.ustreas.gov/prod/

The Jefferson Project
http://www.voxpop.org/jefferson/

Legal Information Institute
http://www.law.cornell.edu/

LEGI-SLATE
http://www.legislate.com/

**Library of Congress World Wide Web
Home Page**
http://www.loc.gov/

1990 U.S. Census LOOKUP
http://cedr.lbl.gov/cdrom/doc/lookup_doc.html

O.J. Simpson Trial Court Transcripts
http://www.islandnet.com/~walraven/
simpson.html

PeaceNet
http://www.peacenet.apc.org/peacenet/

PoliticsNow
http://www.politicsnow.com/

The Seamless WebSite
http://seamless.com/

**Statistical Abstract of the United
States**
http://www.census.gov/stat_abstract/

Thomas
http://thomas.loc.gov/

**University of Michigan Economic Data
Gopher**
gopher://una.hh.lib.umich.edu:70/11/ebb

U.S. Department of Veterans Affairs
http://www.va.gov/

**U.S. ZIP Code Lookup and Address
Information**
http://www.usps.gov/ncsc/aq-zip.html

WashLaw WEB
http://lawlib.wuacc.edu/washlaw/
washlaw.html

The White House
http://www.whitehouse.gov/WH/
Welcome.html

The World Factbook 1995
http://www.odci.gov/cia/publications/95fact/

ARCHIVES AND INDICES

CIVIX

http://ibert.org/

The Institute for Better Education Through Resource Technology, a Glendale, California-based nonprofit organization, maintains the CIVIX to explain U.S. federal government spending practices. Find an index of federal agencies and citations of their current budgets.

Galaxy: Government Agencies

http://galaxy.einet.net/galaxy/Government/Government-Agencies.html

Galaxy's comprehensive index to government listings provides links to foreign, international, U.S. and state government agencies. This page also includes user guides, collections of documents and directories to numerous agencies.

Galaxy: Laws and Regulations

http://galaxy.einet.net/galaxy/Government/Laws-and-Regulations.html

This portion of Galaxy's government index connects Web surfers with legal and regulatory information resources. Visitors can also access international governmental home pages or link to academic and nonprofit organizations' home pages.

Government Publications Network Gopher Server

gopher://kraus.com:70/1

Information provided by the U.S. government and various international, intergovernmental organizations is indexed and offered to the online public here. Visitors to this gopher server can read about and search the databases of groups such as the European Community and the United Nations.

INFOMINE

http://lib-www.ucr.edu/govpub/

INFOMINE digs up a collection of government information resources that are available on the Internet. A production of the University of California, Riverside, INFOMINE is a searchable site archive containing hundreds of links. Also provides access to the University of California library system.

World-Wide Government Information Sources

http://www.eff.org/govt.html

This index of international, national, regional and local government servers provides an enormous archive of links and URLs to government-related sites throughout the Internet.

INTERNATIONAL GOVERNMENT

Althingi—The Icelandic Parliament

http://www.althingi.is/

The Althingi's home page contains basic information about the structure, procedures and members of the Icelandic Parliament. Includes links to general information about Iceland. In Icelandic and English.

Association of Finnish Local Authorities

http://www.kuntaliitto.fi/

The Republic of Finland outlines its constitutionally mandated local government system at this informational site. Visitors can research local authorities, municipal boards and other governing bodies. In Finnish and English.

Australian Department of Foreign Affairs and Trade

http://www.dpie.gov.au/dfat/home.html

The Australian Department of Foreign Affairs and Trade provides a directory with information on the department and its ministers, as well as publications and news releases. There's also information about passports, Australia, special events and issues.

Australian Government Home Page

http://gov.info.au/

The Australian government home page features information about the country's political structure as well as links to state department and agency home pages. Links to other Australian sites are offered as well.

Australian Governments on the Net

http://snazzy.anu.edu.au/gov/augov/au.html

Take a scholarly look at online information provided by local, state/territory and commonwealth governmental agencies Down Under. Visitors can link to the resources discussed.

Australian Governments' Entry Point

http://www.nla.gov.au/oz/gov/

An initiative of the National Library of Australia, this link-laden site affords ready access to Australia's government servers—federal, state, and local. Also find pointers to Australian legislation sites and information policy documents.

Australian Parliament

http://www.aph.gov.au

The Parliament of the Commonwealth of Australia home page, an initiative of the Parliamentary Library, provides Internet access to parliamentary information. This page has links to the departments of the Senate, the House of Representatives and the Parliamentary Library.

Belgian Federal Government Online

http://www.belgium.be/belgium/

The Belgian federal government site details the country as both a kingdom and federal state. Links lead to government officials, general information and official publications. Available in Dutch, German, French, and English.

Belgium Embassy

http://www.belgium-emb.org/usa/

Let the Belgium Embassy in Washington, D.C., be your guide to a cybertour of Belgium. Learn about the country's role in world politics or find out about opportunities to study in Belgium.

British Council

http://www.britcoun.org/

Created by Royal Charter, the British Council "promotes educational, cultural, scientific, and technical cooperation between Britain and other countries." Learn about the council, its most recent news and the services it provides.

The Cairo Conference

http://www.iisd.ca/linkages/cairo.html

The United Nations International Conference on Population and Development took place in 1994, but the Cairo Conference Home Page still exists to publish information concerning the preparation for and results of that historic gathering. Find conference documents and media reports at this site.

The Campaign Against Militarism Latin America

http://www.easynet.co.uk/camla/camla.htm

The Campaign Against Militarism Latin America Workgroup was set up "to carry out research and challenge the prevailing prejudices about the region." The London-based group gives an overview of its work here. Visitors can also download two of its reports: "Exploiting the Indians" and "After the Mexican Crash."

Canadian Department of Foreign Affairs and International Trade

http://www.dfait-maeci.gc.ca/

The Canadian Department of Foreign Affairs and International Trade provides information on its staff and services at this site. Visit here for contact information, embassy directories, regional background information, news releases and more.

Canadian Government Departments

http://info.ic.gc.ca/opengov/departments.html

Need to link with a department of the Canadian government? Here's the cyberlink list that will point the way—from the agricultural offices to the treasury. In French and English.

CCTA's U.K. Government Information Service

http://www.open.gov.uk/

The Central Computer and Telecommunications Agency provides this online search tool for accessing British government information sources. Features include links to indexes by organization and function, a what's new file and services information.

Champlain: Canadian Information Explorer

http://info.ic.gc.ca/champlain/champlain.html

Champlain's Canadian Information Explorer site provides information about Canada on the Internet. Search governmental sites—federal, provincial, and municipal—as well as legal sites. In French and English.

Danish Ministry of Research and Information Technology

http://www.fsk.dk/

Denmark's Ministry of Research and Information Technology provides general information, news, online publications and news releases here. In English and Danish.

Edge & Ellison

http://www.edge.co.uk/edge

Edge & Ellison, a worldwide law firm based in England, maintains this site to introduce its staff and services. Visit here to learn about its practice areas, contact international offices, access employment opportunities and more.

The Electronic Embassy

http://www.embassy.org

TeleDiplomacy Inc.'s Electronic Embassy connects visitors to the Washington, D.C., embassy scene and the business, press and government communities with which it overlaps. Visitors can link to the home pages of embassies, businesses and trade organizations, or read Internet status reports.

Estonian Ministry Of Foreign Affairs

http://www.vm.ee/

The Estonian Ministry of Foreign Affairs page provides browsers with information about doing business in or acquiring news about the country. The page also includes consular information and details on Internet opportunities in Estonia.

Europa Homepage

http://europa.eu.int

Europa welcomes visitors to the official party line of the European Union. Check up on the progress of the political integration of the continent, or access the E.U.'s founding documents.

The European Commission Host Organisation (ECHO) Databases

http://www.echo.lu/echo/en/menuecho.html

The European Commission Host Organisation offers free access to more than 20 online databases in all European Community languages. This page includes a FAQ file, manuals, gateway links, and more.

European Union

http://www.chemie.fu-berlin.de/adressen/eu.html

This European Union site promotes political, economical and social cooperation among the 15 independent states and contains information about the various governments' commitment to the European Commission.

European Union Basics FAQ

http://eubasics.allmansland.com/index.html

This FAQ file provides a wealth of information about the European Union. Detailed facts about the E.U. and the European Parliament await the curious.

European Union Home Page

http://s700.uminho.pt/ec.html

This clickable map of the European Union helps visitors find Web servers all over Europe. It also contains links to Information Market, which has details about the European electronic information market, and the EUROPOLE European Forum, a French nonprofit organizer of European events.

Eurostat

http://www.europa.eu.int/en/comm/eurostat/eurostat.html

The mission of EuroStat is to "provide the European Union with a high-quality statistical information service." Visitors to its home page are invited to find out more about the office and its organization, and to access its publications.

Finnish Ministry of the Interior

http://www.intermin.fi/

The Finnish Ministry of the Interior home page contains information about the ministry's mission and responsibilities. A short history of the ministry is also provided. In English, Finnish and Swedish.

Global Security Programme

http://www.gsp.cam.ac.uk/

Cambridge University's Global Security Programme, which focuses on international relations, environmental concerns and other global survival issues, provides information about the program and research activities here.

Government Information in Canada

http://www.usask.ca/library/gic/index.html

This quarterly electronic journal provides federal, regional and local Canadian government information. Find current, topical articles in English and French. Submission guidelines are also featured.

Government of Manitoba Home Page

http://www.gov.mb.ca/

Take a picture tour of the legislature's building, access a guide to provincial departments and agencies, or find out about job postings and other information when you visit this Canadian home page. Tourism information is also available.

Government Policy and the Information Superhighway

http://www.nla.gov.au/lis/govnii.html

The National Library of Australia provides this large collection of online governmental reports and documents pertaining to changing policies resulting from the worldwide construction of the Information Superhighway.

Grundgesetz—Ubersicht

http://www.jura.uni-sb.de/Gesetze/gg.html

The constitution of the Republic of Germany is presented here. Find an index listing the preamble and individual articles. In German.

Her Majesty's Treasury

http://www.hm-treasury.gov.uk/

Visitors to this site will find the official link to the United Kingdom's Department of the Treasury. Budget, economy, and initiative information is featured along with news and guidance.

Information Rosenbad

http://www.sb.gov.se/

The Web pages of the Swedish government are here, in Swedish only. The Webmaster says the information will be available in English in the future.

INTELLEC Information Server

http://slarti.ucd.ie/inttelec/top_level.html

The INTELLEC project at University College Dublin, Ireland, focuses on European Union research and development information. This site is INTELLEC's information service and provides searches of databases, as well as FTP services and other resources.

International Political Economy Network

http://csf.Colorado.EDU:80/ipe/

An information clearinghouse for those concerned with the worldwide political economy, this Web site provides easy access to global resources. Visitors can subscribe to a discussion list, select schools with international political economics programs or access regionally and thematically organized information archives.

International Relations and Security Network

http://www.fsk.ethz.ch/

The International Security Network, an information service covering defense and peace studies, conflict research and international relations, maintains this site. Read activity updates and to connect with member institutions.

Israel Foreign Ministry

http://www.israel.org/

A clearinghouse for official and government information about Israel and the Middle East is found at this site. It includes information of Israel's history, culture, society, education, health, economics, and more.

The Constitution of Japan

http://www.ntt.co.jp/japan/constitution/

An electronic copy of the Constitution of Japan is available at this site. Visitors can read the original Japanese or the English translated version.

Kantei Home Page

http://www.kantei.go.jp/

This official server from the residence of Japan's prime minister supplies a variety of resources. Among them are information on the Asian Women's Fund, a long-range economic plan and details of the 50th anniversary of the close of World War II. In English and Japanese.

Lansstyrelsens Web-server

http://www.lst.se/

Visitors to this site will find general information about Sweden's County Administration and specific information from its 24 counties, including a map with county borders and links to other Web sites. In English and Swedish.

Leiden University's European Documentation Center, U.N. Depository Library and Law Links

http://ruljis.leidenuniv.nl/group/jfbi/www/lawlib.HTM

This collection of Web sites is maintained by the Netherlands' Leiden University. Visit here to link to the United Nations, various human rights organizations and other public and educational institutions.

Treaty on European Union

http://www.europa.eu.int/en/record/mt/top.html

The Maastricht Treaty site contains pointers by title to the full text of the agreement establishing the European Economic Community. Includes an introduction to the signatory nations and a link to the European Union home page.

Mexico Out of Balance

http://www.igc.apc.org/nacla/mexico.html

Mexico Out of Balance chronicles the country's 1995 international debt crisis and the economic course pursued in reaction to it. The page includes essays on elections, rural development and labor.

Moscow Libertarium

http://feast.fe.msk.ru/libertarium/

The Moscow Libertarium is a project aimed at "the information support of social activity and scientific research on the problems of liberalism" in the emerging free-market system in Russia. The site provides articles, research materials, listings of organizations, and details on project management and activities. In Russian with some English.

New Brunswick Government

http://www.gov.nb.ca/

The government of New Brunswick, Canada maintains this site of general information. Visit here to link to government departments and agencies, contact staff members or read updates from its news wire service. Available in French and English.

Northern Ireland Government Server

http://www.nics.gov.uk/

Find links to governmental departments, the Industrial Development Board, regional information and local councils at this searchable site from the government of Northern Ireland. The current issue of Omnibus Magazine is also featured.

ODIN: Norway Documentation Information

http://odin.dep.no/

The Norwegian government page called ODIN (the name is a Norwegian acronym and a reference to the Norse god) allows browsers to download news releases, speeches, and articles by Norwegian ministers, and other government information. Links to the Norwegian embassy in the United States. In English or Norwegian.

Office of the President of the Republic of Croatia

http://www.predsjednik.hr/

The text of news releases, news conferences and the presidential address are available at this site from the office of the president of the Republic of Croatia. Available in English and Croatian.

The Office of the Prime Minister of Hungary

http://www.meh.hu/

Visitors to this Hungarian government site can get information on government meetings and publications or take a virtual tour of the country's parliament. Includes a link to the Office of European Affairs. In English and Hungarian.

Open Government

http://info.ic.gc.ca/opengov/

The Canadian Open Government project is provided by the Network Services Development Group, Industry Canada. Visitors can access the Web sites of nearly every department within the Canadian national government at this vast, searchable site.

Polish Government Server

http://www.urm.gov.pl/

The Republic of Poland's Web server posts English and Polish language versions of government news releases. International affairs, public procurement policy, agriculture and energy are among the topics covered.

Queen's Printer (Province of B.C.)

http://bbs.qp.gov.bc.ca/

The Queen's Printer is the publication arm of the Ministry of Government Services of the Province of British Columbia. Includes links to government agencies and publications.

Romanian Embassy—Washington, D.C.

http://www.embassy.org/romania/

Visitors to the Romanian Embassy on the Web will find a wealth of information about the country and its people. Frequently asked questions are answered, travel and tourism information is offered, and basic facts and images are presented.

Royal Embassy of Saudi Arabia

http://imedl.saudi.net/

Find a profile of Saudi Arabia and its government, travel information and a report on the state of Saudi-U.S. relations at this official embassy site. Publications, news releases and a message from the ambassador are also featured.

The Singapore Government Internet Web Site

http://www.gov.sg/

This official site serves as a clearinghouse of information on the government of Singapore. Visitors will find links to government bodies within the Asian nation, along with news releases and transcripts of speeches.

Social Summit Home Page

http://www.iisd.ca/linkages/wssd.html

This home page presents the history and highlights of the World Summit for Social Development held in 1995 in Copenhagen, Denmark. The page archives information—available in English, French, and Spanish—about the United Nations gathering.

South African Constitutional Assembly

http://www.constitution.org.za/

The South African Constitutional Assembly seeks to "make the constitution-making process accessible to South Africans and the world as it unfolds." Visitors to the site will find initiatives and agendas for the new South African Constitution.

Tasmania

http://info.dpac.tas.gov.au/

The Department of Premier and Cabinet for the Australian state of Tasmania includes an overview of the department here, along with information about the Tasmanian government, parliamentary information and general facts about the region.

UNESCO World Heritage List

http://www.cco.caltech.edu/~salmon/world.heritage.html

The 469 World Heritage Sites, as designated by the United Nations, range from the ancient city of Butrinti in Albania to the sacred city of Kandy in Sri Lanka. Many of these sites are hyperlinked so visitors can learn more about them.

United Kingdom Department of Trade and Industry

http://www.dti.gov.uk/

The United Kingdom's Department of Trade and Industry Internet Service provides visitors with department contacts, as well as information about the organization and its objectives. Visitors will also find information about DTI ministers, their responsibilities and transcripts of their speeches.

United Nations 50th Anniversary

http://www.amdahl.com/internet/events/un50.html

A historical overview of the United Nations on the occasion of its 50th anniversary in 1995 is available here. Includes links to the U.N.'s Web site and other sources of information about the international body.

United Nations Commission on International Trade Law

http://itl.irv.uit.no/trade_law/nav/uncitral.html

Norway's University of Tromso supplies information about the U.N. Commission on International Trade Law at this site. Works carried out by the commission and links to training in international trade law are available, as is access to the founding documents for UNCITRAL.

United Nations Development Programme

http://www.undp.org/

The United Nations Development Programme provides information on sustainable human development issues throughout the world. Visit for news releases, information on program activities and publications, and links to other U.N. servers.

United Nations Fourth World Conference on Women

http://www.undp.org/fwcw/daw1.htm

The home page for the United Nations' Fourth World Conference on Women provides information on the agenda, mission and goals of this international women's event. Includes updates on scheduling, contact information and links to related U.N. organizations. (Of course, even if you could wrangle an invite and a visa to Beijing, you've already missed it.)

United Nations Information Services

http://undcp.or.at/unlinks.html

This Virtual Library Site focuses on United Nations Information Services. It includes links to U.N. divisions, activities and programs, plus non-U.N. sites providing information on human rights, international affairs, activism and similar topics.

United Nations International Drug Control Programme

http://www.undcp.org/index.html

The United Nations International Drug Control Programme provides information here on its illicit-substance monitoring activities. Visit here for news and background resources relating to the international control of drugs. Includes a link to the United Nations main home page.

United Nations Office in Ukraine

http://www.un.kiev.ua/

The United Nation's regional operation for the Ukraine Republic is the focus of this site. Visitors will find reports on infrastructure projects and human rights issues. This Web page can be accessed in English, Ukrainian, and Russian.

United Nations Scholars' Workstation

http://www.library.yale.edu/un/unhome.htm

The United Nations Scholars' Workstation collects texts, data sets, maps and electronic information about disarmament, economic and social development, environment, human rights, international relations, and population and demography.

United Nations System Internet Servers

http://www.unicc.org/

This site, maintained by the International Computing Centre, lists the United Nations' Internet servers, including Web pages and gopher sites. Organizations here are listed in alphabetical order.

Virtual Embassy of Finland Main Page

http://www.mofile.fi/fennia/um/

The Finland Ministry of Foreign Affairs maintains its Virtual Embassy home page to provide general embassy and contact information. Visit here to learn about its activities, perform a keyword search of its database and contact staff members at diplomatic posts around the world.

WarZone

http://mediafilter.org/MFF/WarZone.html

Yugoslavs dedicated to free expression, despite government attempts at censorship, established the Sarajevo Pipeline for communication between anti-war activists and human rights groups. Links to independent media, artists and activists are posted.

World Citizen Web

http://www.worldcitizen.org/

Those who define themselves as humans first and geographical citizens second will be interested in the World Citizen Web. World government documents, news, descriptions of related activities and projects are available, as well as an opportunity to register as a world citizen for a $20 fee. See Editor's Choice.

The WWW Virtual Library: United Nations Information Services

http://www.undcp.org/unlinks.html

Visitors to this site will find a general directory pointing to United Nations information servers. Find access to U.N. gopher sites, Web pages and search engines. Links to sites of related interest are also featured.

LAW

INTERNATIONAL

Canadian Law Resources on the Internet
http://mindlink.net/drew_jackson/mdj.html

Canadian law resources on the Internet fill this page that is compiled and maintained by Art of Research Communications Incorporated. It contains a comprehensive list of links to legal eagles, government resources, law schools, discussion groups, and more.

Canadian Legal Resources on the WWW
http://www.mbnet.mb.ca/~psim/can_law.html

Barrister and solicitor Peter Sim supplies this extensive collection of pointers to Canadian legal resources. Link to specific sites ranging from accounting and tax law to universities and colleges. An online search offers quick reference.

Constitutional Law Repository, Wits Law School
http://pc72.law.wits.ac.za/

The University of Witwatersrand in Johannesburg, South Africa, presents this Web page for its Constitutional Law Repository. Visitors will find court judgments, cases under consideration, constitutional documents and discussions.

Copyright Law in Japan
http://www.ntt.co.jp/japan/misc/copyright.html

This page contains an index of sites relevant to copyright law in Japan. Information available in Japanese only.

The Copyright Website
http://www.benedict.com/

Focused on untangling Web-related copyright issues, The Copyright Website looks at copyright law and registration, public domain and "bleeding edge" Internet issues. Also find links to source documents and related resources.

Intellectual Property Law Primer for Multimedia Developers
http://www.eff.org/pub/CAF/law/ip-primer

Posted at this site is an intellectual property law primer for multimedia developers written by J. Dianne Brinson and Mark F. Radcliffe. Visitors can read the full text of this legal outline online.

InterNet Bankruptcy Library: Worldwide Troubled Company Resources
http://bankrupt.com/

Posted by Bankruptcy Creditor's Service, Inc., this site offers a virtual library dealing with bankruptcy. Includes news items and publications, directories of bankruptcy professionals, and a variety of data sites dealing with various aspects of insolvency.

The Journal of Online Law
http://www.law.cornell.edu/jol/jol.table.html

The Journal of Online Law publishes scholarly essays about online-communications law and cyberspace. Find current articles and general journal information at this site.

Law Reform Commission of British Columbia
http://bbs.qp.gov.bc.ca/lrc/lrchome.htm

The Law Reform Commission of British Columbia is an independent advisory agency under the auspices of the Ministry of the Attorney General. The commission reviews the laws of the Canadian province to suggest changes and development. Included are academic and judicial comment on recommendations and reports.

Law Reform Commission of Nova Scotia
http://www.cfn.cs.dal.ca/Law/LRC/LRC-Home.html

The Law Reform Commission of Nova Scotia site describes the purpose of the organization, its op-

a2z EDITOR'S CHOICE

World Citizen Web
http://www.worldcitizen.org/home.html

Merely living in the world doesn't qualify one for world citizenship. At least not according to the World Citizen Web, which brings its international movement for peace and harmony to the Internet. From the WC credo: "A World Citizen accepts the dynamic fact that the planetary human community is interdependent and whole, that humankind is essentially one." Wannabe WCs will find plenty of movement rhetoric here, and, if they can cough up $20 U.S., can even sign up to become a member, er, a Citizen. The site also contains loads of World Citizen news, reference materials, project information and cartoons (with a message, of course). Learn all about the World Syntegrity Project and about Mundialization, "The declaration of specified territory—a city, town, or state, for example—as world territory, with responsibilities and rights on a world scale." Those who shimmy for Pat Buchanan may be offended.—*Reviewed by Dan Kelly*

eration and methods. There are also reports and summaries in English, French and Mi'kmaq.

The Law Society
http://www.lawsoc.org.uk/

The Law Society of England and Wales provides information and services to solicitors, legal practitioners and the public here. Includes details on services and links to other legal organizations.

Office of Data Protection
http://www.open.gov.uk/dpr/dprhome.htm

At this site, the U.K. government explains the British Data Protection Act of 1984 and defines key terms in the law. Links to more information on the Office of Data Protection are available.

Paul Teale/Karla Homolka Information Site
http://www.cs.indiana.edu/canada/karla.html

This home page is devoted to information about convicted thrill killer Paul Bernardo (aka Paul Teale), whose trial was kept secret by Canadian authorities. Includes news clips from trial coverage and information pulled from the Usenet newsgroups alt.pub-ban.homolka and alt.fan.karla-homolka.

Republic of Slovenia Constitutional Court
http://www.sigov.si/us/eus-ds.html

The Constitutional Court of the Republic of Slovenia is described here. The page also contains the 1991 Constitution of the country, information on cases the court is considering and an overview of the Legal Information Center.

Roman Law
http://www.jura.uni-sb.de/Rechtsgeschichte/Ius.Romanum/origo.html

The original version of this Latin server may have browsers scrambling for their high school primers. But for speakers of English, Italian, or German, an alternative exists. In the language of your choice, access a collection of detailed information on ancient Roman law, or peruse biographical data on Roman and medieval lawyers.

The Supreme Court of Canada
http://www.droit.umontreal.ca/SCC.html

This is the central server for the Supreme Court of Canada. Visitors will find recent Supreme Court rulings and a searchable database of legal documents.

United Nations Commission on International Trade Law
http://itl.irv.uit.no/trade_law/

Norway's University of Tromso hosts this site, which contains info about the United Nations Commission on International Trade Law. Works carried out by the commission and links to training in international trade law are available, as is access to the founding documents for UNCITRAL.

University of Auckland School of Law
http://130.216.73.108/

Academic and staffing information about the law school at the University of Auckland in New Zealand is featured here. Visitors also can access online legal resources or browse through a listing of New Zealand lawyers' e-mail addresses.

University of Bristol Law Faculty
http://www.bris.ac.uk/Depts/Law/

The Department of Law at Great Britain's University of Bristol maintains this page with links to information about the department, its faculty and legal research centers. Links to topic-related sites on and off campus are also provided.

Web Journal of Current Legal Issues
http://www.ncl.ac.uk/~nlawwww/

The Web Journal of Current Legal Issues is published by the University of Newcastle in England. An online bimonthly, it covers judicial decisions, law reform, legislation, legal research, information technology and more. Visit here to read current and back issues.

World Intellectual Property Organization
http://www.uspto.gov/wipo.html

An arm of the U.S. Patent and Trademark Office, the World Intellectual Property Organization maintains this site offering a list of information, most of which is restricted for the use of USPTO personnel. A link to the WIPO Arbitration Center and the Patent Cooperation Treaty are accessible, however.

The World Wide Web Virtual Library: Law
http://www.law.indiana.edu/law/v-lib/lawindex.html

The WWW Virtual Library's law index from the Indiana University School of Law provides access to hundreds of law-related documents and resources online. Includes alphabetical listings of U.S. law schools, legal firms, U.S. government servers and international law sites.

The World Wide Web Virtual Library: Law: Law Firms
http://www.law.indiana.edu/law/v-lib/lawfirms.html

An extensive index of links to the home pages of law firms worldwide is provided here by the World Wide Web Virtual Library. The list is alphabetized for quick reference.

Yasushi Home Page
http://www.kinoshita.com/

A Japanese attorney posts a brief biographical sketch and an index to legal resources on this personal page. Available in English and Japanese.

UNITED STATES

ARCHIVES AND INDICES

Chicago-Kent College of Law: Lawlinks Index
http://www.kentlaw.edu/lawlinks/index.html

Chicago-Kent College of Law posts a searchable database of legal resources here. The page also contains a link to the college's pick for law site of the week.

Electronic Freedom Foundation Church of Scientology Archive
http://www.eff.org/pub/Censorship/CoS_v_the_Net/

Find out the latest information regarding legal cases involving the Church of Scientology at this Web archive. The site, maintained by the Electronic Frontier Foundation, includes files and articles indexed by date.

Feminist Curricular Resources Clearinghouse
http://www.law.indiana.edu/fcrc/fcrc.html

In an effort to prove that feminist law is not an oxymoron, scholars at Indiana University and other institutions have compiled a Feminist Curricular Resources Clearinghouse to facilitate the teaching of the feminist perspective in law schools across the country.

The File Room Censorship Archive
http://fileroom.aaup.uic.edu/FileRoom/documents/homepage.html

The File Room offers detailed information and updates on censorship cases worldwide. Visitors can browse the illustrated archive of cases or submit their own tales of oppression.

The Freedom Forum First Amendment Center
http://www.fac.org/

The Freedom Forum First Amendment Center at Vanderbilt University offers an overview of the freedoms of speech, religion and assembly guaranteed by the U.S. Constitutional. Also find names, addresses, phone numbers and e-mail stops for the 535 members of Congress.

Galaxy: Laws and Regulations

http://galaxy.einet.net/galaxy/Government/
Laws-and-Regulations.html

This portion of Galaxy's government index connects Web surfers with legal and regulatory information resources. Visitors can also access international governmental home pages or link to academic and non-profit organizations' home pages.

JOSHUA, the Judicial Online Super-Highway User Access System

http://justice.courts.state.fl.us/

The main server for Florida's State Supreme Court judicial information system offers electronic access to judicial news and documentation for civil and criminal courts at all levels. Includes opinions, proceedings and legislative documents.

Law and Economics

http://www-leland.stanford.edu/~tstanley/
lawecon.html

Maintained by a Ph.D. candidate in the Engineering-Economic Systems program of Stanford University's engineering school, this page contains economics- and law-related links and references. Visitors will find pointers to university departments, bibliographies, working papers and journals.

Law Student Web

http://darkwing.uoregon.edu/~ddunn/l_
schl.htm

The Law Student Web, a personal collection of law school research and networking resources, offers links to journals, law schools and humorous, law-related anecdotes. Includes a growing index of student home pages from around the United States. LawLinks: The Internet Legal Resource Center http://lawlinks.com/ Billing itself as "the Internet's most comprehensive legal resource site for both attorneys and consumers," LawLinks lives up to its name. Visitors will find such resources as a virtual law library, a consumer center and links to bar associations.

LawTalk

http://www.law.indiana.edu/law/lawtalk.html

A service of Indiana University, LawTalk features briefs on various aspects of the law written by I.U. School of Law faculty members. Subjects covered include amendments to the U.S. Constitution, criminal law, personal law, and business and personal finance law.

The Legal Domain Network

http://www.kentlaw.edu/lawnet/lawnet.html

The Legal Domain Network, a service of Chicago-Kent College of Law, provides access to legal mailing lists and Internet discussion groups. Visit here to link with a variety of online reference sources, a keyword search and details about participation.

Legal dot Net: The Legal Network for Everyone

http://www.legal.net/

Legal dot Net is a database of professional law resources and information. Visitors can find home pages for attorneys and information on legal services available on the Internet.

LEGI-SLATE Inc. Gopher Service

http://gopher.legislate.com/

The LEGI-SLATE gopher offers "timely" access to U.S. Congressional and regulatory information. Although many areas offer free browsing, subscriptions are required for unrestricted server access.

The National Law Net

http://www.lawsites.com/

The National Law Net presents itself as a "comprehensive, quality controlled legal resource." Authored by a Florida attorney who represents computer and high technology firms, the page provides links to selected Web sites offering legal resources and information.

Neopolis Law Resource Center

http://www.neosoft.com/neopolis/library/law/
default.html

The Neopolis Law Resource Center provides an extensive index of legal resources available on the Internet. Browsers can link to the sites of legal publishers, law schools, law-related mailing lists and other related Web servers.

P-Law Legal Resource Locator

http://www.dorsai.org/p-law/

This is a starting point for legal research. Find numerous links to legislative and governmental information sites, multicategory reference sites, specialized topics, statistical information, journal services and New York state and federal cases.

The Practicing Attorney's Home Page

http://www.legalethics.com/pa/main.html

Internet Legal Services provides this page, which is loaded with U.S. and California state resources of interest to those in the legal profession. Links in the searchable database range from the California Bar Business Law Section to the Library of Congress gopher server.

RefLaw: The Virtual Law Library Reference Desk

http://lawlib.wuacc.edu/washlaw/reflaw/
refhotkeys.html

The law library at Washburn University in Topeka, Kansas presents this extensive collection of legal information. Resources available range from general reference and government law material to news and political reports. Visitors may link to other legal sites from here or search the entire site for specific information.

Rutgers University School of Law— Newark: Ackerson Law Library

http://www.rutgers.edu/lawschool.html

Rutgers University's law library offers a selection of its holdings online. Access virtual reference desks linking to nationwide archives from Boston to Berkeley, or peruse a selection of law-related gopher sites. Restricted access applies to certain materials.

The Seamless WebSite

http://seamless.com/

The Seamless WebSite is a commercial legal resource. Find news, legal writings, and access to lawyers and legal service providers. Chat rooms and job listings are also available.

ASSOCIATIONS AND ORGANIZATIONS

The Center for Democracy and Technology

http://www.cdt.org/

The Center for Democracy and Technology, based in Washington, D.C., addresses censorship and other civil liberties issues as they apply to today's forms of communication. Visitors to its home page will find publications and full details on current issues.

Colorado Bar Association

http://www.usa.net/cobar/index.htm

The Colorado Bar Association offers details here on its committees, forums, events, and membership benefits. Visit this site to learn about the association and link to a variety of public and educational legal resources.

Copyright Clearance Center

http://www.copyright.com/

The Copyright Clearance Center is a nonprofit organization that helps companies comply with U.S. copyright law. Nonmember visitors to this site can learn more about the organization, demo its services, and link to related Web sites.

League for Programming Freedom

http://www.lpf.org/

The League for Programming Freedom sponsors this page to promote its opposition to software patents and interface copyrights. Site features include the organization's history and newsletter, legal resources and links to related sites.

Legal Information Institute

http://www.law.cornell.edu/

Cornell Law School's Legal Information Institute offers access to hypertext versions of such primary resources as U.S. Supreme Court, U.S. Circuit Court and New York Court of Appeals decisions and the full U.S. Code. Also find an online version of the Cornell Law Review and access to the Cornell Law Library.

National Center for State Courts

http://www.ncsc.dni.us/

A Virginia-based nonprofit organization, the National Center for State Courts outlines its mission to improve the U.S. justice system. Find articles and briefs about the use of technology in courts and information about the center.

National Federation of Paralegal Associations Home Page

http://www.paralegals.org/

News, career resources, publications and membership information are included at this site from the National Federation of Paralegal Associations. Visitors will also find a calendar of events, networking groups listings and legal resources.

State Bar of Georgia IP Law Section Home Page

http://www.kuesterlaw.com/ip.html

Past issues of A Novel Expression of Confusion, the newsletter of the Intellectual Property Law Section of the State Bar of Georgia, are featured at this site. Also find section officers and events, plus information on technology-related bills in the Georgia Assembly.

Tennessee Bar Association: TBALink

http://www.tba.org/

The Tennessee Bar Association and the University of Tennessee College of Law have teamed up to create the TBALink Web page. This site features information about how to join TBA and opinions on selected court cases.

Texas Law Librarians Home Page

http://ccwf.cc.utexas.edu/~suefaw/

An all-in-one resource for legal research and legal reference information, the State of Texas Law Librarians' home page focuses on Texas but is useful for those from other states as well. Guests can link to federal or state legislative, judicial or regulatory information, to reference sources for such information or to related sites.

United Citizens for Legal Reform

http://www.usa.net/uclr/

United Citizens for Legal Reform purports to be grass-roots effort to retool the judicial system in America. The enemy? "Lawyer self-regulation," the "lawyer monopoly, and the lack of a strong jury-based system to compensate victims and keep criminals behind bars." The site offers an overview, tracts on divorce and bankruptcy, links to legal-reform groups around the country and a petition aimed at the U.S. Congress.

ATTORNEYS ONLINE

AttorneyNet

http://www.attorneynet.com/

A service of Attorney Internet Marketing of Mountain View, California, AttorneyNet offers an easy-to-use resource for finding legal counsel. Just enter a location and the type of attorney desired; the site does the rest. Includes index of legal resources.

Bailey, Harring and Peterson, P.C.

http://www.aescon.com/bhplaw/index.htm

Bailey, Harring and Peterson, a law firm based in Denver, maintains this site of general information. Visit here to learn about its practice areas, view staff biographies and find contact information.

Bricker & Eckler

http://benet-np1.bricker.com/welcome.htm

The Bricker & Eckler home page contains background information on the Columbus, Ohio law firm. Includes staff profiles, descriptions of services and links to other legal resources on the Web.

Brobeck, Phleger & Harrison

http://www.brobeck.com/

Law firm Brobeck, Phleger & Harrison offers online legal services and information here. Clients of the firm can contact their attorney or submit electronic filings to the U.S. Securities and Exchange Commission from this site.

Collier & Associates

http://rampages.onramp.net/~collier/

The Texas-based law firm of Collier & Associates provides information here about its practice, which covers the areas of employment law, intellectual property, commercial litigation and creditors' rights in bankruptcy.

David Loundy's E-LAW Web Page

http://www.leepfrog.com/E-Law/

Meet David J. Loundy, an Illinois attorney and author. Read his published work and miscellaneous legal writings, and link to some of his favorite law-related sites.

Faegre & Benson

http://www.faegre.com/

Minneapolis legal powerhouse Faegre & Benson weigh in on current legal rulings, issues and topics at this corporate site. Review the firm's areas of practice and inspect its stable of attorneys here.

Fenwick & West Home Page

http://www.batnet.com/oikoumene/FWHome.html

Fenwick & West is a law firm, located in Silicon Valley, that specializes in new media technologies. The firm gives an overview of its work and

posts articles on electronic commerce and the computer industry here. Also included are guides and reports for businesses and investors.

Foley & Lardner Biotechnology Law Web Server

http://biotechlaw.ari.net/

Foley & Lardner, a Washington, D.C.-based law firm, maintains this site for its biotechnology law Web server. Visitors can access its patent primer, intellectual property resource center, ag-biotech page and related resources.

Franklin, Cardwell & Jones

http://www.fcj.com/

Franklin, Cardwell & Jones, a Houston-based law firm, maintains this site for legal resources, contact information and Internet tutorials. Visit here to learn about the firm's commercial, tort and professional malpractice law expertise and to link to the American Bar Association.

Hale and Dorr, Counsellors at Law

http://www.haledorr.com/

Hale and Dorr, one of the largest law firms in New England, has offices in Boston, Washington, D.C., and Manchester, New Hampshire. Visit this site to find out about the firm, read its publications or access its online law resources.

Ice Miller Donadio & Ryan

http://www.imdr.com/imdr/

The law firm of Ice Miller Donadio and Ryan of Indianapolis provides information on its services and personnel at this home page. Also included at this site are legal updates, legislative updates, and legal and government resources from Indiana and the United States.

John P. Weil & Co.

Http://seamless.com/jpw

John P. Weil & Co., a management consulting firm based in Orinda, California, maintains this site to promote law-related services. Visit here to learn about its planning capabilities, marketing programs, client services and more.

Ladas & Parry Home Page

http://www.ladas.com/

Ladas & Parry, a New York-based intellectual property rights consulting firm, supplies a variety of informational links here. Visit here for resources covering trademark and patent laws from around the world.

Law Offices of C. Matthew Schulz

http://www.schulzlaw.com/~mschulz

The home page of a San Francisco law firm that specializes in immigration issues, this Web site offers a wealth of visa and immigration information. Also find links to topic-related Internet resources.

Peter W. Huber

http://khht.com/huber/home.html

Peter W. Huber's personal home page contains professional information on the attorney's practice in telecommunications markets and antitrust policy. Includes listings of his publications and links to legal sites related to his specialty.

The Skornia Law Firm

http://www.internet-is.com/skornia/index.html

This virtual law firm claims to have the expertise to escort clients onto the information superhighway. "The law in this area is fast-paced and constantly changing," this site says. "We know where the speed traps are."

Venable, Baetjer, Howard & Civiletti

http://venable.com/

Venable, Baetjer, Howard & Civiletti, LLP, a business law firm in the Washington/Baltimore area, provides this Web server with more than 150 articles on legal topics. Visitors can also find out more about the firm and its clients.

Vorys, Sater, Seymour and Pease

http://www.vssp.com/

An Ohio law partnership, advertised as one of the nation's 100 largest law firms, provides this page with law links, case reviews, law news from Washington, D.C., and its own poll of the presidential race. Contact information for the firm's offices is also included.

BUSINESS LAW AND CRIMINAL LAW

Advertising Law

http://www.webcom.com/~lewrose/home.html

A law firm based in Washington, D.C., posts this primer on advertising law. The site also includes pointers to other marketing and consumer law sites on the Net.

Center for Corporate Law, University of Cincinnati

http://www.law.uc.edu/CCL/

The College of Law at the University of Cincinnati serves up a collection of business law resources here. Visitors can access the texts of securities acts, read rules and regulations promulgated under them, and check out additional info on trust and investment laws.

The Consumer Law Page

http://seamless.com/alexanderlaw/txt/intro.html

Hosted by the Alexander, Rapazzani, and Graham law firm, this page offers a variety of consumer law resources and information. Visitors can read topical articles, peruse more than 100 brochures of general interest to consumers and business people, and link to related sites.

Cornell Law School Trademark Law Materials Page

http://www.law.cornell.edu/topics/trademark.html

The Legal Information Institute at Cornell Law School maintains this collection of trademark law materials. Visitors will find text of legal cases and Supreme Court decisions, international law references, professional publications and other related resources.

Crime Scene Evidence File

http://www.crimescene.com/

On April 2, 1995, Valerie Wilson, 26, was found murdered in her Oxford, Mississippi apartment. With this online investigation, law enforcement encourages observations, questions and, possibly...some leads. A suspect, Wilson's boyfriend, who nearly surrendered on an Undernet chat server, was recently found dead as well.

Cryptography Export Control Archives

ftp://ftp.cygnus.com/pub/export/export.html

The U.S. government's policies toward cryptography and encryption are deciphered at this site. Read about legal efforts to keep technology in the hands of the users and the changing status of computer export regulations.

---

a2z EDITOR'S CHOICE

Simpson Court Transcripts

http://www.islandnet.com/~walraven/simpson.html

Now showing at a Web site near you— "O.J. and the Magic Knife." This action-packed thriller stars Hall of Fame football player O.J. Simpson as himself. Watch as O.J. is drawn into a web of jealousy and hate, provoked by the pain of divorce and victimized by a jurisprudence system that would rather prosecute a guilty man than give an innocent bystander an even break. Follow the efforts of the family of O.J.'s murdered ex-wife to bring our hero to justice when all about them have given up interest. Immerse yourself in this compelling drama of police incompetence and legal bumbling, where a pair of ill-fitting gloves play a larger role than truth, justice and the American way. Enjoy it all from the comfort of your computer, where every word of testimony, every piece of evidence and every judge's decision is presented in a browsable index and downloadable files. Don't miss the spectacle of this ongoing tragedy. It can't last forever. Can it?—*Reviewed by Dan Kelly*

The O.J. Simpson Trial Court Transcripts

This site is maintained by Jack Walraven and has been rated among the top 5% of all sites on the Internet by Point Survey.

Status as at 4:00pm PDT on Friday, June 28th.
Latest upload(s): A.C. Cowlings deposition of April 26th.

Why does it take so long to get the civil trial depositions?
Unlike the trial transcripts which were released in electronic form, the depositions are "selectively" distributed by the plaintiffs' lawyers to various news organizations as hard copy (often poor-quality fax or photocopies). Before they can be put on line, they need to be scanned, proofed and corrected - a laborious process even with the latest technology. Only Court TV has made an effort to do so and I thank them for their work. ---JW

Why don't I respond to your email?
I know many of you get tired of checking this site for updates and have sent me email to ask what's going on. Unfortunately, I don't have the time at the moment to respond to all of you. You may wish to utilize a "robot" that automatically checks whether this site has been updated. ---JW

The Civil Trial

- Simpson's statement to the LAPD.
- Simpson's "suicide" letter.
- Civil suit filed by the Brown family. (source: Court TV)
- Civil suit filed by the Goldman family. (source: Court TV)
- Full text of Simpson's interview with Black Entertainment Television (BET).

Dennis Erlich Copyright Violation Case: Amended Complaint

http://www.eff.org/pub/Censorship/CoS_v_the_Net/amend_cos_030395.complaint

Visitors to this page will find the amended complaint of the Religious Technology Center and Bridge Publications, Inc. against Dennis Erlich. The infringement in question: copyright violation and misappropriation of trade secrets.

Dmitri's O.J. Simpson Trial Center

http://www.cs.indiana.edu/hyplan/dmiguse/oj.html

The O.J. Simpson trial is the focus of this site, which traces events from the pre-murder stage through the jury verdict. There is much information here and many links to other topic-related pages.

Forensic Web Home Page

http://www.eskimo.com/~spban/forensic.html

This index to resources in forensics includes pointers to sites such as the Metro-Dade Police Department Crime Lab, the Legal Research Network and the FBI. Also find links to mailing lists, ftp sites, organizations and resources in forensics education.

Galaxy: Intellectual Property—Law

http://www.einet.net/galaxy/Law/Intellectual-Property.html

Intellectual property law and its relationship to new media are examined here. Links to a variety of related information archives, periodicals and directories can help visitors grasp the concept.

KuesterLaw—Jeff Kuester's Technology Law Resource

http://www.kuesterlaw.com/

Jeff Kuester, a patent, copyright and trademark attorney in Atlanta, provides browsers with a substantial collection of information relating to technology and intellectual property law.

Oppedahl and Larson Patent Law Web Server

http://www.patents.com/

Maintained by Oppedahl & Larson, a law firm offering patent, copyright, trade secret and other intellectual property rights services, this page contains a variety of information on intellectual property law. Also find FAQs and back issues of the Oppedahl & Larson News.

Police Resource List

http://www.sas.ab.ca/profess/police/police.html

This police resource page contains links to information on police techniques, law enforcement education, and Internet resources. It includes links to local, state, and federal law enforcement servers.

Simpson Court Transcripts

http://www.islandnet.com/~walraven/simpson.html

This page contains transcripts from the O.J. Simpson murder trial. Also featured are transcripts from interviews with jurors, motions and court orders, and text items introduced into evidence. See Editor's Choice, page 507.

Ten Big Myths About Copyright Explained

http://www.clari.net/brad/copymyths.html

The 10 Big Copyright Myths page covers issues of intellectual property rights as they relate to the Internet and the World Wide Web. Visitors can read about the facts and common misconceptions concerning copyright law on the Internet.

U.S. Patent and Trademark Office, General Information on Patents

http://www.uspto.gov/web/patinfo/toc.html

From the U.S. Patent and Trademark Office site, this page offers ready answers to pertinent questions such as, "What is a patent?" Review patent laws, find out what can be patented and discover the purpose of the Patent and Trademark Office.

U.S. Patent Law

http://www.law.cornell.edu/topics/patent.html

Cornell Law School's Legal Information Institute offers comprehensive patent law information at this Web site. Find details on recent Supreme Court rulings, a link to the U.S. Patent and Trademark Office and a patent database.

U.S. Patent Related Network Resources

http://town.hall.org/patent/patent.html

Maintained by the Internet Multicasting Service, this site points to patent search services, the U.S. Patent and Trademark Office and the Copyright Office gopher server. Also find links to the Global Network Navigator, the Legal Information Institute at Cornell Law School and more.

Villanova Center for Information Law and Policy

http://www.law.vill.edu/

The Villanova Center for Information Law and Policy maintains this Web site offering links to electronic state and federal law resources. Also find an index of U.S. federal government sites, a virtual library and conference room, and information about the Villanova University School of Law.

LAW SCHOOLS

Chicago-Kent College of Law

http://www.kentlaw.edu/

The Chicago-Kent College of Law and the Illinois Institute of Technology maintain this site for general information and Internet resources. Visit here to learn about the schools, their programs, faculty and students. Links to related sites and Internet search tools are also available.

Cleveland-Marshall College of Law

http://www.law.csuohio.edu/

Located on the campus of Cleveland State University, the Cleveland-Marshall College of Law offers prospective students this overview of its programs and faculty. The page also contains links to legal sites on the Net.

Emory University School of Law

http://www.law.emory.edu/

Visitors to this site can access information on the law program at Emory University of Atlanta, discover a variety of law-related search tools and visit the Emory law library. Links to other Emory University sites are also available.

Florida State University College of Law

http://www.law.fsu.edu/

Florida State University's College of Law provides information on costs, placement services, student organizations, admissions and computing services at this site. A link to ResearchNet, an index of Net research resources, is also provided.

Franklin Pierce Law Center Home Page

http://www.fplc.edu/fplchome.htm

The Franklin Pierce Law Center site offers information about the New Hampshire center's curriculum, staff and events, plus links to general law resources on the Web and special areas of interest.

Hastings College of the Law

http://www.uchastings.edu/

This Web site offers information about the University of California's Hastings College of the Law in San Francisco, plus links to the Public Law Research Institute's index of reports and other legal resources.

Georgia State University College of Law

http://www.gsulaw.gsu.edu/

Provided for the benefit of the professors and students at the College of Law, this site boasts a "meta-index" for legal research and links to other law-related resources. Includes discussions of governmental checks and balances, the Bill of Rights and pointers to online legal publications.

Indiana University School of Law, Bloomington

http://www.law.indiana.edu/

Indiana University's law school in Bloomington gives prospective students a look at its courses, faculty and admissions policies here. The site also contains online legal journals and links to other legal sites on the Web.

John Marshall Law School

http://www.jmls.edu/

Chicago's John Marshall Law School provides this page, with information about the school, libraries and links to other law schools.

Law School Web and Gopher Server Index

http://www.usc.edu/dept/law-lib/librarys/locators.html

Maintained by the assistant director for information technology at the University of Southern California Law Center, this site indexes law school Web and gopher servers. Links to legal organizations, directories and other indices also can be found here.

Ohio Northern University College of Law

http://www.law.onu.edu/

The Pettit College of Law home page features electronic resources for the students and faculty of Ohio Northern University's law school in Ada, Ohio. The page links to faculty articles, course review materials and related sites.

Rutgers University, School of Law— Camden

http://www-camlaw.rutgers.edu/

Prospective law students can get an overview of Rutgers School of Law—Camden and request an application here. School announcements, access to the law library, law links, and pointers to other sites of related interest are also featured.

Saint Louis University School of Law

http://lawlib.slu.edu/home.htm

The Saint Louis University School of Law guides the user to employment, health and human rights law resources on the Internet. Find pointers to law-related Web sites and the school's information services at this site.

Temple University School of Law

http://www.temple.edu/departments/lawschool/index.html

The Temple University School of Law offers a general overview of its educational facilities and academic programs. Visit here to learn about the campus, faculty and student body.

Tulane Law School WWW Site

http://www.law.tulane.edu/

Tulane Law School, located in New Orleans, has put together a comprehensive page of information about its facility. Among other things, there's information about admissions, career services, the academic calendar and the law library. Includes links to other law-related sites and the Tulane University central server.

University of Arkansas School of Law

http://law.uark.edu/

Information on the University of Arkansas' law school is available at this home page. Includes a library catalog, faculty profiles, course materials and a student handbook.

University of Colorado Law Library

http://www.colorado.edu/Law/lawlib/

The University of Colorado at Boulder presents this informative page describing its law library. Visitors will find information on facilities, hours of operation and library staff. Access to this library's card catalog is also provided.

University of Houston Law Center

http://www.lawlib.uh.edu/

The University of Houston Law Center provides access to its law library here. Also included are publications from the Houston Law Center and a link to the Internet Reference Desk.

University of Illinois College of Law

http://www.law.uiuc.edu/

The College of Law at the University of Illinois offers a wealth of information here about its academic programs, faculty, students, admissions, publications and events. The site includes a virtual tour of the college library and links to further information about the university and surrounding area.

---

a2z EDITOR'S CHOICE

WashLaw

WEB http://lawlib.wuacc.edu/washlaw/washlaw.html

Washburn is a public university in Topeka, Kan., with an enrollment of 6,000 and an athletic mascot called the Ichabod. Ivy League it ain't, but suffice it to say that, if the Ichabods were the sports equivalent of the WashLaw WEB, they'd be NCAA champions almost every year. The Net is just crawling with comprehensive law directories, and this one, with its excellent organization, takes the prize. The welcome page contains a chart with categories ranging from bar associations and law firms to professional journals and state law. Other features include video-conferencing rooms and a page of full-text search resources such as the Federal Register, the U.S. Tax Code and circuit court decisions. The site also incorporates RefLaw, which focuses on legal reference material found on the Net. Chalk one up for the Ichabods.—*Reviewed by Dan Kelly*

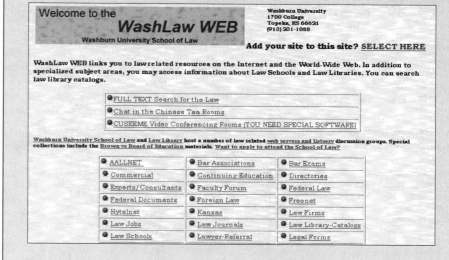

University of Southern California Law Center

http://www.usc.edu/dept/law-lib/index.html

The University of Southern California Law Center offers comprehensive information about its services. Access legal and government resources, journals, lists of law schools, career services and more. Includes links to virtual law libraries and the USC main home page.

University of Texas at Austin School of Law Homepage

http://www.law.utexas.edu/

This keyword-searchable site for the Tarlton Law Library at the University of Texas at Austin features a link to the Internet Reference Desk along with details about the school. Visitors can also check out legal journals and organizations.

University of Washington Law School Home Page

http://felix.law.washington.edu/
CondonHome.html

The University of Washington School of Law allows visitors to take a virtual tour through school facilities and services. Legal links provide professionals with directories and resources, as well.

WashLaw Web at Washburn University School of Law

http://lawlib.wuacc.edu/washlaw/
washlaw.html

Maintained by the staff of Washburn Law Library, the searchable WashLaw Web affords access to law-related resources around the world. Grouped into categories, offerings include law schools, journals, firms, libraries and books, plus state, federal and foreign law. See Editor's Choice, page XX.

Whittier College and Law School Home Page

http://www.whittier.edu/

This gateway page directs visitors to the home pages of Whittier College and Whittier Law School. Information featured here includes academic program and faculty listings. Visitors also can access the parent institution's libraries and computing resources.

LEGAL ADVICE

Advice & Counsel Incorporated

http://seamless.com/adviceco/willpage.html

Baffled by the complex legal requirements of wills or estate plans? Stop by the free advice and counsel page of Advice & Counsel Inc., a law firm with offices in San Francisco and San Diego. The page offers help understanding wills, trusts, and estate planning.

Divorce Page

http://www.primenet.com/~dean/

The Divorce Page offers resources to anyone who is going through a divorce or ending a relationship. Visitors will find articles on recovery, legal options and romance self-help. Find diverse offerings ranging from an index of lawyers to the "Love Boat" theme song.

PUBLICATIONS AND INDUSTRY NEWS

Federal Communications Law Journal

http://www.law.indiana.edu/fclj/fclj.html

This online library holds electronic copies of the Federal Communications Law Journal, which is co-published by the Federal Communications Bar Association and the Indiana University School of Law-Bloomington. Includes articles pertaining to U.S. and international communications issues.

Groups: law.listserv

http://www.kentlaw.edu/cgi-bin/ldn_news/-
G+law.listserv

If you're looking for a mailing list on law, this is the place to find one. Listings here range from law.listserv.ar-news, the Animal Rights Public News Wire, to law.listserv.telecomreg, which is about telecommunications regulations and cable discussions.

High Technology Law Journal

http://server.berkeley.edu/BTLJ/index.html

Delve into the ethical and political issues specific to the information age at the online edition of the High Technology Law Journal. The University of California at Berkeley's School of Law publishes this legal investigation of technology here.

How Our Laws Are Made

http://thomas.loc.gov/home/
lawsmade.toc.html

This page from the Thomas site contains an article detailing how proposed legislation becomes law in the U.S. Congress. The article can be reviewed in total or by chapter.

Indiana Journal of Global Legal Studies Home Page

http://www.law.indiana.edu/glsj/glsj.html

The Indiana Journal of Global Legal Studies offers online issues of this publication. Also included here is subscription and publication information, as well as profiles of the journal's editorial boards.

iway hyperdocs, ltd.

http://www.aescon.com/iway/index.htm

Colorado-based iway hyperdocs specializes in providing legal hypertext documents to business professionals. Visit here to learn about its online

offerings, including a comprehensive listing of Colorado statutes in a variety of downloadable formats.

Language in the Judicial Process

http://hamlet.la.utk.edu/

Language in the Judicial Process, an online newsletter devoted to language and law, provides a wealth of articles on related legal topics. There are archives of abstracts, current citations in the field and links to related sites and resources.

Law Office Technology

http://seamless.com/ds/

The Law Office Technology site features information about the use of law office technology and its associated issues, negotiating computer contracts, management perspectives, and links to related sites. The site is provided by Dana Shultz & Associates, a technology consulting firm.

LawTech

http://www.well.com/user/lawtech

The LawTech home page supplies information about software and hardware solutions for law offices. In addition to a monthly technology update, LawTech also provides links to other law office technology resources.

Lawyers Cooperative Publishing

http://www.lcp.com/

This legal publishing company presents information on products, company history and contact points. Includes a legal list, news items and user feedback.

The Legal List

http://www.lcp.com/The-Legal-List/
TLL-home.html

Visitors to this site will find download and search options for the e-text edition of the book, "The Legal List, Fall 1995 Internet Desk Reference, Law-Related References on the Internet and Elsewhere."

Litigation Video

http://www.winternet.com/~lv/

The Litigation Video home page suggests ways in which video can be further utilized in U.S. courts. The company claims its services can make clients' cases more convincing through such things as video reenactments and taped depositions.

The National Journal of Sexual Orientation Law

http://sunsite.unc.edu/gaylaw

Lesbians, gays and bisexuals can monitor the legal fight for equal rights with the scholarly articles and analyses appearing in The National Journal of Sexual Orientation Law. Visit here to read current and back issues online.

The New York Law Publishing Company

http://public.ljextra.com/catstart.html

The New York Law Publishing Company supplies its catalog of books, newsletters, CD-ROMs and audiotapes for the legal community here. The company also conducts also online legal seminars and provides links to law-related resources on the Internet.

Prison Legal News

http://www.synapse.net/~arrakis/pln/pln.html

Prison Legal News is a monthly newsletter published by two Washington State convicts. Directed toward prisoners, their friends and families, PLN aims to help prisoners vindicate their rights and be progressive forces in developing a public policy debate on issues of crime and punishment.

Richmond Journal of Law & Technology

http://www.urich.edu/~jolt/

Visitors to this site will find the Richmond Journal of Law & Technology, one of a coalition of online law journals working to develop standards for the electronic medium. Site features include the current issue, archives of past issues and links to other online law journals.

Stanford Journal of Law, Business & Finance

http://www-leland.stanford.edu/group/sjlbf

Stanford University provides this home page for the Stanford Journal of Law, Business & Finance. Visitors will find writers' guidelines, subscription information and an archive of past issues and articles. This journal specializes in emerging legal issues affecting the business and finance communities.

STATE AND FEDERAL

California's Legal Code

http://seamless.com/alawyer/criminal.html

Would-be lawyers in California will find information on changes and quirks in the state's legal code on this page sponsored by lawyer Jerome P. Mullins. Fledgling court junkies might be particularly interested in the glossary of legal terms.

Decisions of the U.S. Supreme Court

http://www.law.cornell.edu/supct/

Cornell University's Legal Information Institute maintains this comprehensive list of U.S. Supreme Court decisions. Visit here to browse and search by keyword for decisions from 1990 to the present.

Federal Rules of Evidence

http://www.law.cornell.edu/rules/fre/overview.html

The Legal Information Institute presents a complete hypertext version of the U.S. Federal Rules of Evidence. The document includes a full-text search capability.

Project Hermes

ftp://ftp.cwru.edu/hermes/

Can't remember whether flag-burning is outlawed or medicinal pot is legal? Through the Project Hermes gopher index at Case Western Reserve University, visitors can download official opinions of the U.S. Supreme Court. Both binding and dissenting opinions are available, dating back to the project's beginnings in 1990. Files are offered in ASCII and WordPerfect formats.

Uniform Commercial Code—Articles 1–9

http://www.law.cornell.edu/ucc/ucc.table.html

Published by Cornell Law School's Legal Information Institute, this hypertext document offers access to Articles 1-9 of the Uniform Commercial Code. Articles are presented individually "for the limited purposes of study, teaching and academic research."

Uniform Law Commission

http://www.kentlaw.edu/ulc/

Drafts of Uniform and Model Acts are available at this site maintained by the National Conference of Commissioners on Uniform State Laws and the Chicago-Kent College of Law. Drafts are available through the Web, gopher, FTP, and electronic mail. Comments to the posted drafts may be submitted by postal mail via the address provided.

U.S. Code

http://www.law.cornell.edu/uscode/

Text files of all U.S. federal laws and codes are contained at this site. Visitors can read the law and find resources for legal research.

U.S. Court of Appeals, 11th Circuit

http://www.mindspring.com/~wmundy/opinions.html

The past three months' decisions from the 11th U.S. Circuit Court of Appeals are provided here in compressed files. A daily log tells visitors what is available. The opinions are in WordPerfect 5.1/5.2 format.

U.S. Court of Appeals, 4th Circuit

http://www.law.emory.edu/4circuit/

Law students and practitioners can scour the decisions of the 4th U.S. Circuit Court of Appeals at this site. Emory University's law library has provided full texts of these opinions since January 1995 as part of its Courts Publishing Project.

U.S. Court of Appeals, 9th Circuit

http://www.law.vill.edu/Fed-Ct/ca09.html

Visitors here will find archived opinions handed down by the 9th U.S. Court Circuit of Appeals. The past year's decisions are listed by month and by the names of involved parties. A keyword search function was promised.

U.S. House of Representatives: Internet Law Library

http://law.house.gov

The U.S. House of Representatives Internet Law Library offers access to U.S. state, federal and territorial law information. Also includes indices of international laws and treaties, along with links to legal library catalogs and attorney directories.

U.S. Supreme Court Decisions Archive

http://www.law.cornell.edu/supct/supct.table.html

This Web site, maintained by Cornell Law School's Legal Information Institute, archives U.S. Supreme Court decisions from 1990 to 1995. Visitors can perform keyword searches or make use of topical and party name indices. Includes topically indexed information on key pre-1990 decisions.

U.S. Tax Code On-Line

http://www.fourmilab.ch/ustax/ustax.html

Though not sponsored by the U.S. government, this page allows access to the complete text of the U.S. Internal Revenue Title 26 of the Code (26 U.S.C). For ease of cross-referencing, hyperlinks have been embedded in the text.

MILITARY

INTERNATIONAL

The Australian Defence Force Academy

http://www.adfa.oz.au/

The Australian Defence Force Academy home page contains information on academic departments, programs of study and military training courses. Includes background on the academy, info on student life, faculty profiles, and details on the officer leadership programs.

Canadian Department of National Defence

http://www.dnd.ca/

The Department of National Defence Home Page provides all the pertinent facts about Canada's national defense: its structure, functions, finances, latest news and more. In English and French.

Chinese Military Aviation

http://weber.u.washington.edu/~htong/

Images and information on military aircraft in service or being developed for Chinese armed forces are available at this site. Includes information on fighters, attack aircraft, trainers and helicopters.

E-Hawk

http://www.e-hawk.com/

De re militari Association is a society devoted to the study of classical and medieval military history. Visitors to its site will find newsletters, archives of articles, writing guidelines and membership information.

The High Energy Weapons Archive

http://www.pal.xgw.fi/hew/

The High Energy Weapons Archive offers a sobering look at the Nuclear Age and the proliferation of nuclear weapons across the world. The Web site features essays, articles and news reports, plus eyewitness accounts provided by survivors of the Hiroshima and Nagasaki bombings.

NATO—Allied Command Atlantic

http://www.saclant.nato.int/

Allied Command Atlantic is the North Atlantic Treaty Organization's major military command in North America. Find news, facts, biographies and other information on the command, as well as links to other NATO sites.

NATO Gopher

gopher://gopher.nato.int/

The North Atlantic Treaty Organization supplies this gopher server with a collection of info on European-American political and military cooperation. Visitors can link to gopher servers around the globe, including a number of international peace-initiative organizations.

NATO—Supreme Allied Commander Atlantic, Undersea Research Centre

http://www.saclantc.nato.int/

NATO's Supreme Allied Commander Atlantic (SACLANT) Undersea Research Centre concentrates on improving methods and technology for the detection, classification, and localization of submarines and mines. Visitors to its home page can review the organization's research activities, assets, publications, and recruitment programs.

Swedish Armed Forces

http://www.mil.se/FM/

Visitors can inspect the Swedish armed forces on this official page, which profiles the Army, Navy, and Air Force. The site also offers a clickable map of the peace-loving nation and its military bases. In English and Swedish.

Therion's Armor and Weapons Page

http://www.io.com/~therion1/armor.html

Not nearly as menacing as the title would imply, this enthusiast's informational page contains a clanking collection of photographs and descriptions of European and Asian arms and armor.

UNITED STATES

Aberdeen Test Center

http://dale.apg.army.mil/

In the field at the Aberdeen Test Center, the U.S. Army tests its weapons to ensure they work properly. Visit this page to read a history of the facility and review its testing procedures.

ACQWeb—Office of the Undersecretary of Defense for Acquisition & Technology

http://www.acq.osd.mil/HomePage.html

ACQWeb serves as a public access service for information pertaining to the Undersecretary of Defense for Acquisition and Technology's unclassified activities. Read publicly accessible documents from the U.S. military's tech heads.

Air Force Materiel Command

http://www.afmc.wpafb.af.mil/

Materiel is the nuts and bolts and bullets that keep the military running. At this site, visitors will find links to the organizations within the Air Force Materiel Command, including air logistics centers, product centers and laboratories. AFMC news, programs, projects and publications are also featured. Some areas are restricted to military access.

The Air Force Reserve

http://www.afres.af.mil/

The Headquarters Air Force Reserve Web site provides information to the Defense Department and public. Defense Department information is confidential and requires passwords, but the public informaton is free for everyone. This includes news releases as well as enlistment information.

AirForceLINK

http://www.dtic.dla.mil/airforcelink/

AirForceLINK is the home page of the U.S. Department of the Air Force. Find fact sheets, links to the commands, photo galleries and a search tool for the numerous Air Force databanks and servers. Users can also access the latest edition of Airman Magazine.

Army Link—The Fort Bliss HomePage

http://bliss-www.army.mil/

Visit the U.S. Army Air Defense Artillery School at the Fort Bliss, Texas home page. Visitors are allowed to tour the base and follow links to local and Web-wide U.S. Army servers.

Arnold Engineering Development Center

http://info.arnold.af.mil/

Located at Arnold Air Force Base in Tennessee, the Arnold Engineering Development Center is the world's largest flight-simulation test facility. Links include the EPA/AEDC Spectral Database, AEDC technical reports and the AEDC newsletter.

Backgrounds Data Center Home Page

http://bdc.nrl.navy.mil/

The Backgrounds Data Center is a major archive site for the Ballistic Missile Defense Organization. The home page describes the center's mission and software development efforts, and provides links to other sites in the Space Sciences Division of the Naval Research Laboratory.

Brooks Air Force Base World Wide Web Server

http://www.brooks.af.mil/

The Brooks Air Force Base site profiles the facilities and activities of the U.S. military installation as well as offering links to other Air Force servers accessible via the Internet.

Capt. Richard M. Cassidy, U.S.N.

http://www.nrl.navy.mil/nrl/cassidy.html

This Web page provides a personal biography of U.S. Navy Capt. Richard M. Cassidy. It explains Cassidy's background and his work as a commanding officer at the Naval Research Laboratory and includes a link to the NRL home page.

The Center for Army Lessons Learned

http://call.army.mil:1100/call.html

The Center for Army Lessons Learned, a project of the U.S. Army, maintains this site for its history-based instructional program. Visit here to learn about the program, browse its index of military publications, contact staff members, subscribe to its news update service and more.

China Lake Research and Technology Division

http://peewee.chinalake.navy.mil/

Located in China Lake, California, the Research and Technology Division supports the Naval Air Warfare Center Weapons Division through its weapon systems research and development work. Visit this site to access RTD's research branches, technology programs and information resources.

Cooperative Monitoring Center

http://www.cmc.sandia.gov/

The Cooperative Monitoring Center at Sandia National Laboratories in Albuquerque, New Mexico helps political and technical experts acquire the technology-based tools they need to implement nonproliferation and arms control. The center provides an overview of its work and information on security technology here.

Defense Acquisition University

http://www.acq.osd.mil/dau/dau.html

The U.S. Defense Acquisition University offers overviews of its courses and event schedule at this site. Created by Congress in 1990 to consolidate training for the Defense Acquisition Workforce, the DAU offers links to the Acquisition Reform Communications Center and other related sites.

Defense Advanced Research Projects Agency

http://www.arpa.mil/

The Defense Advanced Research Projects Agency is the central research and development organization for the U.S. Department of Defense. Visit this site to learn about DARPA's mission, organizational structure and contract activities.

Defense Advanced Research Projects Agency Electronics Technology Office

http://esto.sysplan.com/ESTO/

Find up-to-date information on the electronics research being sponsored by the Electronics Technology Office of the Department of Defense's Defense Advanced Research Projects Agency. An overview of programs and contact information are featured.

Defense Information Systems Agency

http://www.disa.mil/

The Defense Information Systems Agency's mission is to develop, operate and maintain information systems for the Department of Defense. Site features include links to DISA services, software programs and related organizations.

Defense Information Systems Agency, Information Technology Standards

Document Library

http://www.itsi.disa.mil/cfs/itsi_lib.html

The Information Technology Standards Document Library serves as a central online clearinghouse for "policies, guidance, standards and other references related to building affordable, maintainable and interoperable standards-based information systems" for the Department of Defense.

Defense Information Systems Agency, WESTHEM Server

http://198.49.191.26/

This central server offers links to Army Installation Support Modules, the DISA WESTHEM Systems Management Center, Defense Megacenters and the DISA WESTHEM Home Page.

Defense Logistics Services Center

http://www.dlsc.dla.mil/

The mission of the Defense Logistics Services Center is to support the Department of Defense "through the collection, processing, storage and dissemination of data." Find information on DLSC training and workshops, profiles of its products and services, and links to related sites.

Defense Standardization Program Division

http://www.acq.osd.mil/es/std/stdhome.html

The Defense Standardization Program Office of the U.S. Department of Defense maintains this site featuring updates on military specifications and reform. FAQs, links to newsletters and memos, and contact information are featured.

The Defense Technical Information Center

http://www.dtic.dla.mil/

The Defense Technical Information Center contributes to the management of defense research for the U.S. Department of Defense. Visit this site to learn about the center and access many of its resources, including a gopher site, help desk, user services and more.

Defense Technical Information Web

http://www.dtic.dla.mil/dtiw/

A service of the U.S. Defense Technical Information Center, this site acts as an electronic clearinghouse of information about, and of interest to, the U.S. Department of Defense. Visitors can access reports chronicling related news, acquisition announcements and research activities. Includes links to other military-related resources.

Department of Veterans Affairs

http://www.va.gov/

This is the official Web site for the U.S. Department of Veterans Affairs. Visitors will find profiles of veterans, details of veteran benefits, and descriptions of facilities and research programs.

Dr. Timothy Coffey

http://www.nrl.navy.mil/nrl/coffey.html

This page from the Naval Research Laboratory's directory profiles Dr. Timothy Coffey, the director of research. The doctor is recognized as an authority on the theory of nonlinear oscillations and has played a major role in the national program on high-altitude nuclear effects.

Fort Monmouth

http://www.monmouth.army.mil/

At the Fort Monmouth U.S. Army base in New Jersey soldiers are preparing for war with computers, communications, intelligence and the electronic warfare project book. Take a look at how the military is preparing for the future with the public information offered here.

Fort McPherson

http://www.mcphersn.army.mil/

The Web site for Fort McPherson in Atlanta provides information on available computer courses, a link to government Web servers and information about Atlanta.

Global Positioning System Time Series

http://sideshow.jpl.nasa.gov/mbh/series.html

Curious visitors can finger the U.S. Department of Defense's electric eyes in the sky at this home page, which records the locations of the 24 satellites that make up the DoD's Global Positioning System. Includes information about the GPS.

GulfLINK: Persian Gulf War Veterans Illnesses Home Page

http://www.dtic.dla.mil/gulflink/

GulfLINK, a service of the U.S. Defense Technical Information Center, provides access to the Persian Gulf War Veterans Illnesses Task Force. Visit here for reported illness cases, declassified documents, news releases and other information resources.

James Madison University Reserve Officer Training Corps

http://www.jmu.edu/rotc/rotc.html

James Madison University presents this Web site devoted to its Reserve Officers Training Corps program. Visitors can read pages offering general information about the ROTC program and its cadet resources, or link to related sites of interest.

Jane's Electronic Information System

http://www.btg.com/janes/

Jane's Electronic Information System is a collaboration between Jane's Information Group and BTG, Inc. The site is a defense and aerospace information center. Includes a demonstration, overview and FAQs.

Jane's Online

http://www.janes.com/janes.html

Jane's Online offers information about defense, weaponry, civil aviation and transportation. Visitors to this page will find Jane's interview of the week, free screen savers, photos, combat simulations, a resource center and a product catalog.

LabLINK—Department of Defense Laboratory Community System

http://www.dtic.dla.mil/lablink/

LabLINK provides a vehicle for coordination and interaction among Department of Defense laboratories. Find links to specific lab sites, policy issues, legislation and other resources.

List of 81 DoD Lab Activities

http://www.dtic.dla.mil/labman/projects/list.html

Featured at this site is an index of 81 Department of Defense laboratories, grouped by service branch. Laboratory activity information is also included with each entry.

Materials Science and Component Technology Directorate

http://www.nrl.navy.mil/nrl/direct/code.6000.html

Looking for new materials, developing new uses for old materials and studying material behavior lies behind the U.S. Navy's Web site on materials science and component technology. The directorate concentrates on fluid mechanics and hydrodynamics, nuclear weapons effect simulations and interaction of materials with radiation.

Military Family Institute

http://mfi.marywood.edu/

Located at Marywood College in Scranton, Pennsylvania, the Military Family Institute is a Department of Defense research facility focusing on families. Find a general overview of the institute and its current research.

National Defense University

http://www.ndu.edu/

The National Defense University in Washington, D.C., presents a site filled with information on its institutes and colleges, including the National War College and the Institute for National Strategic Studies. A searchable index of research and publications is provided.

Naval Aviation Systems TEAM

http://www.navair.navy.mil/

The Naval Aviation Systems TEAM develops and supports sea-based systems for aircraft. Visit this site to learn more about the TEAM, its mission and vision. Also find links to other Navy sites.

Naval In-Service Engineering West Coast Division

http://mork.nosc.mil/

Serving the Naval Command, Control and Ocean Surveillance Center (one of four major warfare centers) the In-Service Engineering West Coast Division (NISE West) performs diverse electronic systems support functions. Visit this page for a profile of the San Diego-based unit and contact information.

Naval Postgraduate School

http://www.nps.navy.mil/

The Naval Postgraduate School provides an overview of the U.S. Navy's advanced training institution, information on academic departments and programs of study. Includes links to administrative departments, research groups and campus-wide information systems.

The Naval Research Laboratory

http://www.nrl.navy.mil/

The Naval Research Laboratory is the Navy's corporate research and development laboratory. This site has information about the laboratory, its directorates, special projects, publications, announcements and more.

Naval Research Laboratory Information Technology Division

http://www.itd.nrl.navy.mil/

In an effort to improve military operations, the Information Technology Division of the Naval Research Laboratory studies and develops programs for the collection, transmission and processing of information. Find out more about the ITD and the NRL, plus find links to related sites.

Naval Surface Warfare Center, Coastal Systems Station

http://www.ncsc.navy.mil/

Located in Panama City, Florida, the Naval Surface Warfare Center's Coastal Systems Station serves as the lead center of technical direction and development for sea- and land-mine countermeasures, special warfare programs, strategic sealift capabilities and amphibious assault techniques.

Naval Surface Warfare Center, Dahlgren Division

http://www.nswc.navy.mil/

The Naval Surface Warfare Center's Dahlgren Division site features an overview of the division, its facilities, events and publications. Also find links to local servers such as the Signal Processing and Electro-Optics Groups, and the Coastal Systems Station.

Naval Surface Warfare Center Dahlgren Division, Advanced Computation Technology Group

http://irisd.nswc.navy.mil/

The Advanced Computation Technology Group at the Naval Surface Warfare Center's Dahlgren Division maintains this site outlining its mission to apply pattern recognition and image-processing techniques to naval operations. Find out more about the group and its current research.

Naval Surface Warfare Center, Louisville Site

http://www.nosl.sea06.navy.mil/

The Naval Surface Warfare Center's Louisville Site links visitors to military Web servers containing information on weapons (big and small) and testing equipment. Includes links to NavyOnLine and the Navy News Service.

Naval Surface Warfare Center, Hydromechanics Directorate

http://www50.dt.navy.mil

The Hydromechanics Directorate is the U.S. Navy lab "responsible for the research, development, testing, and evaluation of ships, submarines and other marine technologies." Visit this site for a multimedia project gallery, technical reports and an organizational overview.

Navy Center for Applied Research in Artificial Intelligence

http://www.aic.nrl.navy.mil/

Involved in the field since 1982, the Navy Center for Applied Research in Artificial Intelligence reviews its mission and presents an overview of its projects at this site. Also find general information about the center and its operation.

Navy Environmental Programs

http://enviro.navy.mil/

The Department of the Navy's Environmental Program educates visitors about the program's latest conservation techniques and applications. The site includes a directory of key names, phone numbers and addresses for more information.

Navy News Service

http://www.ncts.navy.mil/navpalib/news/navnews/.www/navnews.html

Located at the Navy Public Affairs Library, the Navy News Service is the primary news organ of the Department of Navy. Visitors to this page are invited to learn more about the NAVPALIB and NAVNEWS, and to download current and past news reports.

Navy Jobs Home Page

http://www.navyjobs.com/

This U.S. Navy career page offers information on job opportunities in the fleet and in medicine. Find job descriptions and information on the benefits of the military life, including college savings plans and travel.

Navy Public Affairs Library

http://www.ncts.navy.mil/navpalib/.www/welcome.html

The U.S. Navy maintains NavyOnLine to provide access to its external communications resources. Visit this segment, the Navy Public Affairs Library, to learn about Navy departments and worldwide activities, view its large collection of documents and publications, and download graphic images.

NavyOnLine Home Page

http://www.ncts.navy.mil/

This is a gateway to the U.S. Department of the Navy's online resources. Visitors will find dozens of links here to such locations as the Navy News Service, the Public Affairs Library and Recruiting Command.

Nellis Air Force Base

http://www.nellis.af.mil/

Located in Las Vegas, Nellis Air Force Base, "Home of the Fighter Pilot," maintains this site outlining the units that support the base's Air Warfare Center. Find information on the 57th Wing and the 99th Air Base Wing, as well as an aircraft gallery.

The Northrop Grumman SC W3 Server

http://axon.scra.org/

Grumman Data Systems, a division of Northrop Grumman Corporation, develops software systems for military and industrial manufacturing. GDS promotes its products and services at this commercial Web site.

Office of Naval Research

http://www.onr.navy.mil/

The Office of Naval Research, promoting the science and technology programs of the U.S. Navy and Marine Corps, maintains this informational site for an overview of its missions and activities. Visit here to learn about the office and its technical advice programs.

Office of the Secretary of Defense for Command, Control, Communications, and Intelligence

http://www.dtic.dla.mil/c3i/

Delve deep into the U.S. federal bureaucracy with a trip to the Office of the Assistant Secretary of Defense for Command, Control, Communications and Intelligence. Visitors are invited to inspect staff photos and bios, and review official policy directives.

Patch American High School

http://192.253.114.31/

Located at Patch Barracks, headquarters for the U.S. European Command in Stuttgart, Germany, Patch American High School welcomes visitors to the site of the first high school Web server in Europe. The school's academics and extracurricular activities are highlighted.

Pentagon Home Page

http://www.dtic.dla.mil/defenselink/pubs/pentagon/index.html

Visitors to this Web site can learn about the Pentagon, the enormous, five-sided building that headquarters the U.S. Department of Defense. Includes tour and historical information about the structure, plus statistics and a schedule of operating hours.

PERSCOM Online

http://www-perscom.army.mil/

PERSCOM Online is the gateway to U.S. Army Personnel Command resources. Site features include information on selection boards and promotions, and an online index arranged by subject.

Phillips Laboratory

http://www.plk.af.mil/

Phillips Laboratory on Kirtland Air Force Base in Albuquerque, New Mexico describes itself as "a world-class research center for national defense in space and missile systems, geophysics, directed energy and advanced weapons concepts." Find research reports, facility descriptions and links to the lab's staff

Reliability Analysis Center

http://rome.iitri.com/rac/

A Department of Defense facility, the Reliability Analysis Center improves the "reliability and maintainability of components and systems" through the collection, analysis and dissemination of pertinent data. Visitors to this page can find out more about the center, its information products and engineering services.

Rome Laboratory Reliability Science Publications Directory

http://erd.rl.af.mil/ER-News/Newsletter.html

This Web site is home to reliability sciences publications produced by the U.S. Air Force's "Super Lab for C4I technology." Includes divisional status reports, newsletters and information about Rome Laboratory's Directorate of Electromagnetics and Reliability.

Ron Martini's Navy Submarine Base

http://wave.sheridan.wy.us/~rontini/ronpage.html

Unabashed submarine worship is the order of the day at Ron Martini's Navy Submarine Base. This personal home page highlights submarine resources and military news.

Sandia National Laboratories California

http://www.ca.sandia.gov/

This Sandia National Laboratories site offers information on weapons

systems and energy research activities at Sandia's California location. Visitors also can access publications, reports and facts about conducting business with Sandia.

SHAPE Technical Centre

http://www.stc.nato.int/

General information, projects and publications from the SHAPE Technical Centre are the focus here. STC, which conducts research and provides technical assistance for Allied Command Europe, also offers links to other NATO organizations.

Software Technology Support Center

http://stsc.hill.af.mil/

Located at the Ogden Air Logistics Center at Hill Air Force Base in Utah, the Software Technology Support Center helps Air Force software organizations create and produce better products. This site explains the STSC's adoption and evaluation

services, and provides links to technical documents and other related sites.

Soldiers Online

http://www.redstone.army.mil/soldiers/home.html

Soldiers, the official U.S. Army magazine, is published to provide personnel with information about people, politics, operations, technical developments and trends. Find the current and past issues here, plus contact and submission information.

Team Redstone

http://www.redstone.army.mil/

Team Redstone from Redstone Arsenal in Alabama furnishes U.S. Army Missile Command directives, information and news here. The site also offers historical information on the arsenal and pointers to centers, offices and projects.

U.S. Air Force Academy

http://www.usafa.af.mil/

The U.S. Air Force Academy in Colorado Springs, Colorado maintains this site for general information and Internet resources. Browsers can learn about the school's campus, programs, faculty and students. Links to related sites and a keyword search of Internet tools are also available.

U.S. Air Force Rome Laboratory

http://www.rl.af.mil/

The U.S. Air Force's Rome Laboratory works to advance communications technology for the Air Force and assist in the creation of related applications for private industry. Visit this site for current events, information on technology transfers and Internet resources.

U.S. Army

http://www.army.mil/

The home page of the U.S. Army opens with greetings from the Army's Chief of Staff, then marches on to present the Army's military vision, a performance review, recruitment information and a personnel location directory. More than 300 Army-related pages are on the Web, all of which can be reached from here.

U.S. Army Construction Engineering Research Laboratories

http://www.cecer.army.mil/

The home page for the U.S. Army Corps of Engineers' Construction Engineering Research Laboratories in Champaign, Illinois features an overview of the facility and its mission. Links also provide visitors with details on the laboratories' operations, personnel and research projects.

U.S. Army Corps of Engineers Information Network

http://www.usace.army.mil/

The U.S. Army Corps of Engineers serves to "manage and execute engineering, construction and real estate programs for the U.S. Army and Air Force and for other federal agencies." The US-ACE Information Network provides news, information on programs and links to resources inside and outside USACE.

U.S. Army Intelligence Center at Fort Huachuca

http://huachuca-usaic.army.mil/

The U.S. Army Intelligence Center at Fort Huachuca sponsors this Web site in an attempt "to create an interactive educational environment." Visitors can read information on the center's school, the garrison and its forces, or they can link to other military resources on the Web.

U.S. Army Research Laboratory

http://info.arl.army.mil/

A mission statement for the Army Research Laboratory, research directorates and publications are available at this site. Includes news releases, information on business opportunities, technology transfers and links to related government servers.

U.S. Army Training and Doctrine Command

http://www-tradoc.army.mil/

The U.S. Army Training and Doctrine Command is the official training program for new recruits. Visitors will find information on the organization's history, nationwide facilities, staff and programs.

U.S. Coast Guard Navigation Center

http://www.navcen.uscg.mil/

Located in Alexandria, Virginia, the U.S. Coast Guard Navigation Center collects and disseminates information from, to and about radio navigation systems. Visit this site to obtain system updates, charts and local mariner notices.

U.S. Marine Corps Headquarters

http://www.hqmc.usmc.mil/

Visitors to the Marine Corps Headquarters page will find links to the offices of the commandant, Personnel Management Division, Human Resources Division, and Administration and Resource Division. Pointers to other governmental and military pages are also included.

U.S. Naval Academy

http://www.nadn.navy.mil/

The U.S. Naval Academy in Annapolis, Maryland maintains this site offering general information about the undergraduate college for officer training. Links to the school's information resources and an index of U.S. Navy Web pages are featured.

U.S. Naval Observatory

http://www.usno.navy.mil/

One of the oldest scientific agencies in the country, the U.S. Naval Observatory provides astronomical data and determines precise time—both of which are imperative for successful navigation. Visit here to link with its public affairs office, library collection and research directorates.

Vietnam Veterans Home Page

http://grunt.space.swri.edu/

The Vietnam Veterans Home Page honors "...Vietnam vets, living and dead, who served their country on either side of the conflict." Toward that end, the site includes information about upcoming events, support groups and organizations of interest to veterans.

White Sands Missile Range

http://www-wsmr.army.mil/

The U.S. Army's White Sands Missile Range in New Mexico maintains this Web site offering information on the installation's general mission, location, personnel and facilities. Links to maps, Internet search tools and other federal government sites are also available.

Wright Laboratory

http://www.wl.wpafb.af.mil/

Wright Laboratory, located at the Wright-Patterson Air Force Base in Ohio, conducts research on Air Force weapon systems. This site offers information on aero propulsion, armaments, avionics, flight dynamics, manufacturing technology and solid-state electronics.

Wright Laboratory Armament Directorate

http://www.wlmn.eglin.af.mil/

The Wright Laboratory Armament Directorate is a munitions development facility at Eglin Air Force Base in Florida. Visitors to this site will find descriptions of test programs, research projects, links to facilities and a directory of employees.

Wright-Patterson Air Force Base

http://www.wpafb.af.mil/

Located near Dayton, Ohio, Wright-Patterson Air Force Base is the largest, most complex base in the USAF and is home to the Air Force Materiel Command, the Aeronautical Systems Center and the U.S. Air Force Museum. Visit this site to tour the base and its many facilities.

POLITICS

ANARCHY AND REVOLUTION

Anarchy List

http://www.cwi.nl/cwi/people/Jack.Jansen/anarchy/anarchy.html

The Anarchy List site maintains a mailing list for people interested in topics related to nonviolent anarchism. Also find information on current topics of interest to the group, an archive and a link to the Spunk anarchist contact list.

Bosnia

http://www.cco.caltech.edu/~bosnia/bosnia.html

The Campus Computing Organization of the California Technical University maintains this site for information about the war in the former Yugoslavia. Visit the Bosnia home page for news updates, article archives, official Bosnian government news releases and much more.

Fascist New World Order

http://www.calyx.com/fascist.html

You may have heard whispers about the New World Order. Consider modernity from another viewpoint through the Fascist New World Order site. It offers a glimpse of the dark side of the Web as well as information about how often the FBI visits this page.

Free Burma

http://freeburma.org/

The Free Burma site provides information about the current political situation, military dictatorship, and the efforts for change and reform. Find links here to archives and news.

The Seed

http://web.cs.city.ac.uk/homes/louise/seed2.html

The Seed is an archive of anarchist information located at the School of Informatics, City University, London. The page contains information about presses, journals, and associations.

Spunk Press Home

http://www.cwi.nl/cwi/people/Jack.Jansen/spunk/Spunk_Home.html

Spunk Press publishes books and newsletters on anarchism and related issues. Visitors to its site can read political action alerts and order books.

Spunk Press—Anarchist Contacts

http://www.cwi.nl/cwi/people/Jack.Jansen/
spunk/Spunk_Resources.html

Spunk Press presents a series of anarchist contacts and resources from around the Internet. Visitors can download a text file containing the entire document or follow links to Internet sources including mailing lists and newsgroups.

Utah Anarchism and Revolution

http://www.cs.utah.edu/~galt/revolt.html

The Utah Anarchism and Revolution page offers pointers to progressive political-action groups and anarchy-related information. Links to an activist calendar, historical anarchist information, texts and contacts are among this site's features.

ARCHIVES AND INDICES

All Things Political

http://dolphin.gulf.net/Political.html

Provided by the Washington Weekly, the All Things Political site offers "an alternative look at Washington from the citizen's perspective." Visitors can peruse a wide variety of political news, views and information, including portraits of candidates, political speeches and opinion polls.

File Room

http://fileroom.aaup.uic.edu/FileRoom/
documents/TofCont.html

Muntadas and Randolph Street Gallery in Chicago maintains this site to provide information about the issue of censorship. Visit The File Room to learn about the past, present and possible future of censorship.

The Grand Old Page Directory of Political Sites

http://www.berkeleyic.com/gop/sites.html

The Grand Old Page Directory of Political Sites is a list of political sites—many with a right-wing slant. Find links to the Whitewater page, libertarian resources, firearms, and pro-life sites, as well as personal political pages, organizations, articles and essays.

Interactive Democracy

http://www.cgx.com/id.html

The Interactive Democracy page provides a directory of government and media e-mail addresses in the United States that can be searched to provide users the contact information they need to voice their concerns. The service is free.

The Jefferson Project

http://www.stardot.com/jefferson/

Myriad online political resources in the United States are collected at this site from Stardot Consulting. The searchable index features categories such as The Left, Political Humor, Magazines and News, Campaign '96 and many more. See Editor's Choice, page 518.

Karl Marx/Friedrich Engels Archives

http://csf.colorado.edu/psn/marx/

"There's no way to monetarily profit from this project" of putting the Karl Marx/Friedrich Engels archives online, the archivist of this site says, but he hopes the material will be pleasurable and enlightening. The works are accompanied by photos of the two thinkers.

---

a2z EDITOR'S CHOICE

The Jefferson Project

http://www.voxpop.org/jefferson/

We were a little wary at first of a product from Stardot Consulting Ltd., trumpeting the assertion that it's "The Comprehensive Guide to On-Line Politics." After all, who *isn't* the comprehensive guide to online (insert your favorite subject) these days. But then we started fiddling with the thing and fell prey to its Zipper, which, when fed a ZIP code, spits out the names of corresponding senators and representatives along with addresses (street and e-mail) and numbers for phone and fax. Next we discovered Netgrams, which, for a small fee, allow you to blast a red-hot message to Congress via fax or Western Union. Of course, the same service is free via e-mail, but most of these guys are far too busy trying to regulate the Internet to actually get on it, so Netgrams turn out to be quite the bargain. Finally, we couldn't resist casting our five free presidential votes in the site's Vox Pop Strawpoll. As for that guide, well, we won't go so far as to say that it's the comprehensive guide to online politics; simply that it is a comprehensive guide to politics and that it is arranged in delightfully user-friendly categories such as "personalities," "do-it-yourself politics" and "political humor." And it is definitely online, which makes this baby well worth the price of admission.—*Reviewed by Dan Kelly*

The Marxism/Leninism Project

http://www.idbsu.edu/surveyrc/Staff/jaynes/marxism/marxism.htm

Hoping to correct historical misimpressions, the Marxism/Leninism Project aims to be an objective and authoritative resource on communism. The site provides biographical and historical information on Marx, Lenin, and Engels, as well as archives of their writings.

National Election Studies

http://www.umich.edu/~nes/

The National Election Studies produces data on voting, public opinion and political participation. This site contains an overview of NES, along with links to the organization's data collections and resources. Visitors can also order NES data and documentation from this location.

Political Methodology Section of the American Political Science Association

http://wizard.ucr.edu/polmeth/polmeth.html

Read papers here on campaign strategy, communications, spin-doctoring and other political-methodology issues. Visitors are invited to add to this site from the American Political Science Association by submitting their own papers. Back issues of The Political Methodologist journal are also available, as is poli-sci and demographic research software.

Political Science Resources

http://www.keele.ac.uk/depts/po/psr.htm

Political Sciences Resources is an extensive index to political sites on the Web. Visitors can link to government pages worldwide, political theory sites, local government pages and much more.

The Texas Political Resource Page

http://www.political.com/

Browsers interested in Texas and U.S. politics can access a wealth of information here, courtesy of George Strong & Associates. Check out the latest political gossip and political analysis, browse an index of related Web sites and directories, or link to other political sites on the Web.

United Nations Scholars' Workstation

http://www.library.yale.edu/un/unhome.htm

The United Nations Scholars' Workstation collects texts, data sets, maps, and electronic information about disarmament, economic and social development, environment, human rights, international relations, and population and demography.

The World-Wide Web Virtual Library: Politics and Economics

http://www.w3.org/hypertext/DataSources/bySubject/politics/Overview.html

This Virtual Library site contains links to information on politics and economics. Information is categorized by subject and includes pointers to resources in political science, economics research, sociological issues and governmental pages.

---

a2z EDITOR'S CHOICE

Bob Dole for President (Unofficial)

http://www.dole96.org/

The presidential race is over? Doesn't matter, they're still going bananas for Bob Dole at this "official World Wide Web Internet site." Title and URL aside, this one's just for yuks. If the line at the top of the page—"Bob Dole for president, the ripe man for the job"—doesn't tip it off for you, the first paragraph certainly will: "Bob Dole, of course, is the founder of the Dole Fruit Company and a popular senator. Bob Dole loves tropical fruits, especially slightly over-ripe bananas which are just starting to turn black and mushy, but not so black and mushy as to be inedible." The site has plenty of other laughs, most of them at the expense of everybody's favorite aging, esteemed former senator from Kansas. Check out his "courageous stands" on issues like war, terrorism and peace. Read about the "disrespectful weenies" who dared to challenge him. And, before you go, check out an assortment of links to other fruit and vegetable lovers. Hey, we know it's not polite to make fun of our elders, but funny is as funny does.—*Reviewed by Dan Kelly*

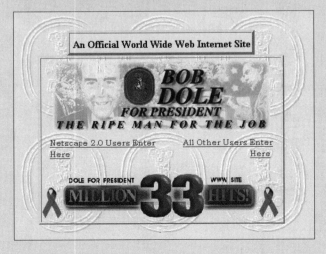

POLITICS

CAMPAIGN '96

Alan Keyes Network

http://sandh.com/keyes/index.html

The Alan Keyes Network contains an archive of pronouncements from this former Republican presidential candidate. It also links to background information, along with campaign events and contact people.

California Election Server

http://www.election.ca.gov/

The California Voter Foundation and Digital Equipment Corporation have joined forces to create the Election Servers Web site. Monitor California statewide and San Francisco local election results. In English, Spanish, Tagalog, Vietnamese, Japanese, and Chinese.

Campaign Central Home Page

http://www.clark.net/ccentral/

Pundits and the general populace alike can retrieve election information at the Campaign Central Home Page. Top political stories, weekly updates and election results are a few of the services offered. Links to campaigns, candidates and voter education sites are also available.

Clinton, Yes!
http://www.av.qnet.com/~yes

An "unofficial home page in support of the president" and the first lady, this pro-Clinton page spotlights positive aspects of the Clinton presidency. Find opinion and praise, plus attacks on Clinton foes. Links to news and related pages provide support and additional commentary.

CyberCaucus: Iowa's First-in-the-Nation Caucus
http://www.drake.edu/public/caucus.html

CyberCaucus profiles Iowa's first-in-the-nation presidential caucus, with a history of the importance of the caucus since its inception. Includes political party information, candidate profiles and links to related Web sites.

Election '96 Homepage
http://dodo.crown.net/~mpg/election/96.html

The Election '96 Homepage is intended to be the starting point to other Internet resources related to the U.S. elections of 1996. It covers issues, the parties and their candidates, with links to other related pages.

Harry Browne for President
http://www.rahul.net/browne/

Harry Browne was a Libertarian Party candidate in the 1996 U.S. presidential campaign. Visitors to this site will find a biography, position papers, transcripts of speeches and debates, a contributions form and other campaign materials.

LaRouche Exploratory Committee
http://www.clark.net/larouche/welcome.html

Presidential candidate Lyndon H. LaRouche Jr. promotes himself, his ideas and his qualifications at this official campaign home page. Find a biography of the candidate, information about the campaign and briefings on topic such as Justice Department corruption and how Newt Gingrich is destroying the country.

A Libertarian Review of the 1996 U.S. Presidential Candidates
http://www.libertarian.com/96/

Take a look at the U.S. presidential field for the 1996 elections through the perspective of the limited-government Libertarian Party. Each of the major candidates (and a few of the minor ones) is reviewed, with pointers to official campaign home pages.

Majority 96
http://www.cais.com/majority96/

Billed as a grassroots effort, Majority 96 is dedicated to the promotion of "New Candidates and New Ideas for a Democratic Majority in 1996." Find out

more about the group and its efforts, learn about targeted races and link to topic-related sites.

Powell for President
http://www.powell2000.org/index.htm

The optimistic Powell for President site proposes Gen. Colin Powell as the answer to America's problems and the Republican Party's gridlock. The site offers a Powell bio, his presumptive political platform and a petition to draft the recalcitrant Powell into the presidential fray.

Presidential Campaign Tour and Opinion Page
http://www.ipt.com/vote/

Browsers can brush up on the 1996 presidential slate of candidates here. The page provides an index to candidate and party sites, from the Greens to the GOP. The page also contains a virtual voting booth, where browsers can cast opinions.

Rick Tompkins for President
http://www.nguworld.com/rick96/

Tired of traditional politics? Then stop by the Rick Tompkins for President page for news about this Libertarian's road to the White House. (And no, he was not the only Libertarian running.) Hear what Tompkins has to say about government tyranny and read his unconventional campaign platform.

Russell for President 1996
http://www.magnet.com/russ4pres/

Russell Hirshon is a 34-year-old bartender in Washington, D.C., who describes himself as politically left of Ronald Reagan and right of Jerry Brown. If elected to the presidency, Hirshon promises to "furlough Congress without pay."

Sole Site of the 1996 Presidential Campaign
http://www.infi.net/jmshoe/

Johnston & Murphy, "maker of fine footwear for every U.S. president since Millard Fillmore," takes a lighthearted look at the 1996 presidential campaign here. It proposes alternate candidates to fill the president's shoes, including Princess Di, Oliver Stone, Martha Stewart, and Mr. Potato Head.

INSTITUTES AND THINK TANKS

Acton Institute Online
http://www.acton.org/

The Acton Institute for the Study of Religion and Liberty is a nonprofit educational center in Grand Rapids, Michigan that promotes religious pluralism, individual liberty and governmental conservatism. This Web site states the institution's history and purpose, and presents news, publications and opinions.

The Brookings Institution
http://www.brook.edu/

Find out what's on the minds of some of the most influential thinkers in American politics at the Brookings Institution home page. Find out about its research programs, meet the Brookings scholars and read excerpts from The Brookings Review here.

Cato Institute
http://www.cato.org/

The Cato Institute is a think tank that promotes limited government, free markets, individual liberty and peace. Visitors to this site will find research areas, news releases, congressional testimony, job and internship opportunities, and the Cato Policy Report.

Democratic Leadership Council and Progressive Policy Institute
http://www.dlcppi.org/

The Democratic Leadership Council and its affiliated think tank, the Progressive Policy Institute, jointly sponsor this page to promote and build a new generation of Democratic leadership. Learn more about both organizations, access the online library and find information on hot issues.

The Heritage Foundation
http://www.heritage.org/

Beef up your political IQ and dig into the commentaries and forums presented at this home page for the conservative Heritage Institute. The site offers lecture and article excerpts, links to a speakers bureau, a directory of like-minded organizations and back issues of the institute's publications.

Kansai Institute of Information Systems
http://www.kiis.or.jp/kiis/kiis_eng.html

The Kansai Institute of Information Systems is a nonprofit think tank in Japan devoted to public policy on information technology. It promotes technological innovation (particularly in western Japan) and advises industry and government on the role of computers in an evolving society.

RAND Home Page
http://www.rand.org/

RAND is a nonprofit research and analysis institution aimed at improving public policy. Visitors to this site can read up on the organization's activities and publications or link to RAND's specialty research centers.

Vera Institute Of Justice
http://broadway.vera.org/

The Vera Institute of Justice is a public policy group devoted to helping produce humane public policies and practices in the United States. Read about its efforts to provide legal services for the poor, secure employment for parolees and people with disabilities, and its other social activist projects.

World Game Institute

http://www.worldgame.org/~wgi

The World Game Institute is a nonprofit research institution devoted to furthering the work of Buckminster Fuller, specifically Fuller's World Game, which simulates and prioritizes global development. Read about the organization's mission as well as its plans for "creating a positive vision of the future and empowering participants to build it."

JOURNALS AND PERIODICALS

All Things Political

http://dolphin.gulf.net/Political.html

Provided by the Washington Weekly, the All Things Political site offers "an alternative look at Washington from the citizen's perspective." Visitors can peruse a wide variety of political news, views and information, including portraits of candidates, political speeches and opinion polls.

Bad Subjects

http://english.hss.cmu.edu/BS/BadSubjects.html

The English Server at Carnegie Mellon University presents the online version of Bad Subjects, a fearless journal of progressive thought that encourages its readers "to think hard about the political dimension to all aspects of everyday life."

The Consortium

http://www.delve.com/consort.html

The Consortium home page provides links to investigative articles on government misdeeds. At the time of this review, the feature story was a well-documented piece exposing the machinations behind Saddam Hussein's rise to power.

Cornell Political Forum

http://cpf.slife.cornell.edu/

This is the Web site for a political journal published by Cornell University. Visitors will find the current issue, a call for submissions and a statement of the forum's philosophy.

Le Monde Diplomatique

http://www.ina.fr/CP/MondeDiplo/mondediplo.fr.html

Le Monde Diplomatique is a French monthly magazine that covers politics. Visitors can read an online version here or subscribe to the print version. In English and French.

Slate

http://www.slate.com/

See Editor's Choice for a look at this new zine.

The Socialist Worker

http://www.anu.edu.au/polsci/marx/contemp/swuk/swuk.html

Workers of the world, go surfing! The site offers an online version of the twice-monthly organ of the Socialist Workers Party of Great Britain. The proletariat (and infiltrators) will find archived back issues that cover progressive politics, the union movement and the crimes of industry.

The Washington Weekly

http://www.federal.com/

The Washington Weekly claims to be an alternative to the much-alluded-to "liberal media." The electronic newsmagazine surveys the week's political events and offers conservative commentary.

Women & Politics

http://www.westga.edu/~wandp/w+p.html

Women & Politics, an academic journal, encourages research and theory development on women's political participation and role in society, and the impact of public policy upon women's lives. Here, researchers and contributors will find abstracts, submission guidelines and more.

 **EDITOR'S CHOICE**

Slate

http://www.slate.com/

This socio-political zine was brand-spankin' new when we compiled our list of top government-related sites. We felt compelled to include it here if for no other reason than the fact that we so thoroughly enjoyed the greeting audio clip of Fats Waller music. Make no mistake, Slate isn't about music; it's the pet project of Microsoft's Bill Gates, who really needed a pet project, we're sure. Actually, Gates did a good thing by enlisting esteemed journalist Michael Kinsley to run the show, available free when it debuted, although the once-you're-hooked yearly subscription rate of $19.95 was creeping. Based on what we saw of the weekly—magazine-style articles, analyses and commentary from, in Kinsley's words, "various perspectives"—that's a pretty good deal. Owner considered, we were impressed that the first issue featured a Committee of Correspondence discussion on "Does Microsoft play fair?" Political cartoons and a daily diary by David O. Russell round out the mix, and the tasteful visual presentation makes reading lengthy articles online seem almost palatable.—*Reviewed by Dan Kelly*

Go to the Table of Contents
Hear Music

June 28-30, 1996

Slate

New on Friday, June 28:
Early e-mail from readers ...
Robert Wright on hearing it through the Internet grapevine.

■ When Jews Play Second Fiddle

■ Miss Manners Gets Forked

■ The Temptation of Bob Dole

ILLUSTRATION: PHILIP BURKE
© 1996 Microsoft and/or its suppliers. All rights

POLITICAL ACTION AND PUBLIC POLICY

Acquisition Reform Net

http://www-far.npr.gov

The Acquisition Reform Network wants to improve how the U.S. government buys goods and services from the private sector. (No more $1,000 toilet seats.) This government Web site informs visitors of opportunities to sell to the government, how to make best use of the options (without gouging the taxpayer) and where to get training.

The Action Coalition

http://action.org/

Human rights activists and organizations unite at The Action Coalition, a nonprofit organization dedicated to a more peaceful, healthier, sustainable world. Visitors here will find links to sites concerned with social justice and peaceful activism.

Adam Rifkin's Lead...or Leave Page

http://www.cs.caltech.edu/~adam/lead.html

Lead...or Leave was a large youth political organization in the United States that lobbied to put generational issues on the national political map. This page has links to political and youth-oriented sites and will be maintained, for now, as if the group still existed.

Brian's Progressive Pages

http://paul.spu.edu/~sinnfein/progressive.html

Formerly known as The Left Side of the Web, this page features pointers to sites of potential interest to the political left. Features include a section on secret paramilitary groups, activist-related newsgroups, and various articles, news reports and interviews.

Carter Center

http://www.emory.edu/CARTER_CENTER/homepage.htm

The home page of Jimmy and Rosalynn Carter's progressive public policy institute offers an overview of the center's efforts in fighting disease, hunger, poverty and oppression worldwide. Access details of programs such as the Carters' much-publicized urban revitalization initiatives.

The Concord Coalition

http://www.concordcoalition.org/

Posted by "a nonpartisan, grassroots movement," this site describes the Concord Coalition's hopes to "eliminate the deficit and bring entitlements down to a level that's fair to all generations." Peruse U.S. budget news and read the coalition's Zero Deficit Plan.

D.C. Metro Prolife News/Events Line

http://www.clark.net/pub/jeffd/plnel.html

This page provides anti-abortion news and events information. Includes a database of Biblical and medical quotes and a Hall of Shame profiling pro-choice activists and government leaders.

The Electronic Activist

http://www.berkshire.net/~ifas/activist/

The Institute for First Amendment Studies, a non-profit organization focusing on the perceived misdeeds of the radical right, provides this contact directory of legislators, the White House and the media. Rush Limbaugh, you have been warned!

The Electronic Policy Network

http://epn.org/

Stay abreast of the latest developments in national policy and politics through this site. It offers access to the virtual magazine called Idea Central, with news about civic participation, health policy and economics.

The Electronic TownHall

http://www.phoenix.net/~townhall/

Easier than snail-mailing government representatives, the Electronic TownHall Home Page links browsers to information on U.S. laws and ordinances, allows users to register their feelings about the information and sends compiled comments to representatives. The site also lists upcoming elections and provides links to related sites.

Freedom From Religion Foundation

http://freethought.tamu.edu/org/ffrf

Find out how to preserve the U.S. constitutional firewall between church and state at the Freedom from Religion Foundation home page. Visitors can review the foundation's publications or sign up for membership here.

The Interfaith Alliance

http://www.intr.net/tialliance/

Founded by a minister, the Interfaith Alliance works to counteract the Christian Coalition's political agenda. Visitors here can download the alliance's report on the religious right and a how-to manual on stopping the Christian Coalition.

Legislative Analyst's Office

http://www.lao.ca.gov/

The California Legislative Analyst's Office Home Page showcases the office's "analysis and non-partisan advice to the legislature on fiscal and policy issues." The page's contents are specific to California state politics and reference pertinent state government sites.

Multilaterals Project

http://www.tufts.edu/fletcher/multilaterals.html

The text of multilateral agreements and treaties, especially environmental treaties, can be found on links at the Multilaterals Project Home Page. Guests can link to treaties on topics such as cultural protection or arms control, search the database for information or link to the FTP site to download text.

National Lawn Care Now!

http://www.athenet.net/~jlindsay/NLCN.shtml

Arguing that better lawns make better neighborhoods, this tongue-in-cheek (albeit tax-exempt) organization is agitating for a national campaign of urban renewal through federally supported lawn care. See Editor's Choice, page 524.

The National Organization for Women

http://www.now.org/

Find general information, an organizational history and current issues concerning the National Organization for Women here. Site features also include a newsletter and listings of Internet feminist resources.

National Rifle Association

http://www.nra.org

Sponsored by the National Rifle Association's Institute for Legislative Action, this page invites visitors to learn more about its membership benefits and its programs. News, research and a firearms law review are also featured.

The Natural Resources Defense Council

http://www.igc.apc.org/nrdc/

The Natural Resources Defense Council fights for the environment in the courts and the halls of Congress. It dispenses environmental news, opinion and mobilization information here, where browsers can keep up with the status of the clean air campaign, pending legislation and other issues. The site also includes a list of NRDC's books and magazines and information on how to become a member.

PeaceNet

http://www.peacenet.apc.org/peacenet/

PeaceNet is dedicated to peace, social justice, human rights and the struggle against racism. The organization's home page explains its goals and posts news items of topical interest. Also find listings of related organizations such as Amnesty International and the Center for Third World Organizing.

Policy.Net

http://policy.net/

Policy.Net is a project of Issue Dynamics, Inc., an electronic advocacy organization that specializes in public affairs monitoring. This server points to an array of public policy groups in areas ranging from education and health to telecommunications. Also access information on political campaigns and publications, and link to CapWeb, a guide to the U.S. Congress.

The Political Participation Project

http://www.ai.mit.edu/people/msb/ppp/home.html

Part of the Massachusetts Institute of Technology's Intelligent Information Infrastructure Project, the Political Participation Project examines how computer networks affect U.S.politics. This Web site explains the project's goals and research, and serves up a working paper titled "Grassroots in Cyberspace: Using Computer Networks to Facilitate Political Participation."

Republican Contract With America

http://www.house.gov/CONTRACT.html

Remember that Contract With America thing from a couple years back? See if the Republicans have fulfilled their pact with the people at this site that provides the full text of the document.

Votelink

http://www.votelink.com/

Votelink, an interactive electronic democracy site, is a forum for Internet citizens to make their voices heard on a variety of issues, from the end of a popular cartoon strip to the future of a old-line civil rights organization.

POLITICAL PARTIES

Advocates for Self-Government

http://www.self-gov.org/

Take the world's smallest political quiz and find a FAQ about Libertarianism. Links to other Libertarian and related political sites are also featured.

Democratic National Committee

http://www.democrats.org/

This searchable site is the Web home of the Democratic National Committee. Find an overview of the Democratic Party structure with links to elected officials' pages, a look at what's "new," "cool" and "hot," and links to documents with national and party significance.

Digital Democrats

http://www.digitals.org/digitals/

Devoted to educating the online public about the Democratic Party, the Digital Democrats page offers a look at the party's candidates, elected officials and positions on the issues. Find links to federal and state sites, media pages and a variety of information on the Digital Democrats group.

The Grand Old Page

http://www.berkeleyic.com/conservative/

The Grand Old Page is the official Web site of the U.S. Republican Party. Visitors will find a political multimedia archive, links to services, gateways to media and pointers to related sites.

Green Parties of North America

http://www.greens.org/

The Green Parties of North America espouse global responsibility toward all living things. Get your daily dose of greens here, at least in the way of political food for thought, and learn about Green presidential nominee Ralph Nader.

Homepage Dutch Labour Party

http://www.pvda.nl/indexgb.html

The Dutch Labour Party maintains this Web site containing current information on party news and politics. Drop by the virtual pub for a political dialog, or check out the party's library and digital world sections for a wealth of Internet resources. In English and Dutch.

Libertarian Party

http://www.lp.org/lp/

The official site of the U.S. Libertarian Party provides an overview of the party's platform, information on membership and access to member directories across the country. Official documents include By-Laws and Convention Rules, and Libertarian Programs from 1989 to the present.

---

a2z EDITOR'S CHOICE

National Lawn Care Now!

http://www.athenet.net/~jlindsay/NLCN.shtml

If you love puns ("We are a grassroots organization …"), plays on words ("… staking out new turf in the field of social justice …") and downright silliness ("… plant seeds of reform by telling your friends and neighbors about us, and by writing congressmen to demand nationalized lawn care now!"), you probably will find this site amusing. However, if you are a serious sort of person who objects to the ribbing of conservatives ("Picture a home surrounded by dry, yellow weeds that haven't been mowed or watered ever since the era of hate and greed began under Reagan/Bush …") and corporate America ("…the greed of the money-hungry Big Lawn Care Companies, which act like vacuums sucking up money like loose grass clippings …"), you'll definitely want to weed this one out of your virtual garden. Libertarians who oppose more government ("Our charter calls for nationalization of all lawn care industries into a single provider run by the U.S. Department of Agriculture and funded through a revitalized House Bank") are most likely to be offended. But, hey, the grass is always greener …—*Reviewed by Dan Kelly*

National Lawn Care Now!

The Official NLCN! Home Page

Welcome to the home page for National Lawn Care Now! We are a grassroots organization working for an equitable program of nationalized lawn care in the United States. NLCN! is also an environmental group - indeed, we are the ultimate expression of Green politics, staking out new turf in the field of social justice. However, we need your help to maintain our growth in this cutting-edge area! How can you help?

- First, get informed by reading the information below.
- Second, plant seeds of reform by telling your friends and neighbors about us, and by writing Congressmen to demand nationalized lawn care now!

Libertarian Party of California

http://www.lp.org/lp/ca/lpc.html

The Libertarian Party of California provides information here on its political viewpoints and election activities. Visit here to learn about the party, find out how to join, contact Libertarian elected officials and candidates, and link with related Internet-based resources.

Libertarian Party of Canada

http://clipper.uvic.ca/GVLA/lpcan.html

This home page describes the nature and purpose of the Libertarian Party of Canada. Includes information about the party's history, politics and an explanation of party philosophy.

MIT Libertarians

http://www.mit.edu:8001/activities/libertarians/home.html

The home page for the Libertarian Party at the Massachusetts Institute of Technology provides an overview of the mission and agenda of the party, a calendar of upcoming events and local contact information. Visitors can also link to the national party's home page or fill out a membership application.

New Democrats Party of Canada

http://www.bc.ndp.ca/

The New Democrats political party in British Columbia uses this home page to proffer the archives of its newspaper and provide Canadian government links and a calendar of events.

The New Party

http://www.newparty.org

Find out more about third-party politics at the New Party Web site. Read about the New York-based organization's founding principles and goals, and find essays from party members.

Quebecois Party

http://www.itr.qc.ca/PQ/

Will Quebec keep trying to split from the rest of Canada? Go straight to the source on this French-language page for the Quebecois Party. Visitors can check recent publications and news about the latest never-say-die political initiatives.

Republican National Committee

http://www.rnc.org/

The Republican National Committee offers this virtual city where visitors can take a stroll down a Republican-themed Main Street, visiting the café (for conversation), the newsstand (for the latest scuttlebutt), the post office (for contact information), and the gift shop (for quality merchandise) along the way.

Republicans Web Central

http://republicans.vt.com/

Republicans Web Central offers visitors a chance to mingle with other conservatives on the Net. If

you're of that ilk, you can search for information on your state's party or find out about rightward-leaning student organizations.

The Robot Wisdom Pages

http://www.mcs.net/~jorn/home.html

"Home of the new, conservative-left Responsible Party," Robot Wisdom proposes creating a computer model of the human predicament. This will help clear the path for a new political paradigm, where "cynical predators" can no longer feed. Visitors here will find political, philosophical and social looks at the plan.

Socialist Party USA Cybercenter

http://sunsite.unc.edu/spc/spc.html

The Socialist Party USA defines the principles of socialism, explains how to be a Socialist and profiles what the Socialist Party USA is. Also find links to membership information, publications and socialist organizations around the world.

POLITICAL PHILOSOPHY

Common Sense Revisited

http://www.america.net/com/liberty/commonsense.html

The Common Sense Revisited page touts the wisdom of Thomas Paine, whose Revolutionary-era tract still resonates with freedom-loving peoples everywhere. The site also offers a menu of political-action links, articles, poems and interviews.

DSA Home Page

http://www.dsausa.org

The Democratic Socialists of America, the Chicago-based affiliate organization of Socialist International, maintains this informational site. Visit here for news, activities updates, future projects and links to related subjects on the World Wide Web.

Internet Conservative Resource Network

http://www.townhall.com/cnews

Right wingers have at least one place to go on the Net, the Internet Conservative Resource Network. If it's a conservative link, you'll find it here—grouped into sections such as conservative personalities, conservative news, conservative organizations and publications, and more.

Open Society Insitute

http://www.soros.org/

George Soros is a philanthropist who supports institutions that share a goal of developing democratic societies around the world. The Open Society page explains the Soros philosophy as well as the society's programs and philanthropic

endeavors, and it provides links to Soros organizations worldwide.

Political Methodology Section of the American Political Science

http://wizard.ucr.edu/polmeth/polmeth.html

Read papers here on campaign strategy, communications, spin-doctoring and other political-methodology issues. Visitors are invited to add to this site from the American Political Science Association by submitting their own papers. Back issues of The Political Methodologist journal are also available, as is poli-sci and demographic research software.

The Right Side of the Web

http://www.clark.net/pub/jeffd/index.html

According to Wired magazine, this popular page is an "online haven to all manner of dittoheads, gun nuts, and religious wackos." Visitors may want to make their own decisions after glancing at such features as the Rush Limbaugh Info Page, the comic strip Demockracy, and philosophical nuggets from Pat Buchanan.

Sovereign WWW Page

http://Syninfo.Com/Sov

This site is devoted to libertarian, conspiracy and militia issues. Visitors here will find opinions on U.S. elections, articles critical of government actions and a list of scheduled protests.

World Liberalism

http://www.worldlib.org/

Liberals in need of a cyperspace safe house will find this page a wellspring of like-minded folks. Liberal news and links to political hot spots worldwide are available at this site maintained by Liberal International, a union of liberal parties worldwide.

The World's Smallest Political Quiz

http://lydia.bradley.edu/campusorg/libertarian/wspform.html

The College Libertarians at Bradley University provide this online quiz, which focuses on libertarian and economic issues. Visitors can take the quiz then compare their sentiments with previous results.

POLITICIANS

Gov. Lowell P. Weicker Jr.

http://www.competition96.com/

This page touts the political philosophy and presidential aspirations of former Connecticut governor Lowell Weicker, who, until recently, offered a nonpartisan alternative for American voters who were dissatisfied with the two major parties but still wanted a name-brand chief executive.

KlugWatch

http://emporium.turnpike.net/J/jking/kw/index.html

U.S. Rep. Scott Klug of Wisconsin is labeled a "Newt wanna-be" at this unflattering site, which trumpets the Republican's alleged misdeeds on behalf of big-money special interests.

Senator Bob Dole

http://www.umr.edu/~sears/primary/dole.html

This unofficial home page provides information about former Sen. Bob Dole. Visitors can peruse Dole's resume, listen to speech sound clips, view photos, video clips and voting records, or link to related sites.

Smart Politics for the 21st Century

http://www.webcom.com/~smartpol/

John Vasconcellos, state assemblyman and state senate candidate in California, presents his views on politics at this site. Read his program for change and listen to reasons to support his campaign.

The Speaker's Corner...The Newt Gingrich WWW FanPage

http://www.clark.net/pub/jeffd/mr_newt.html

From the cutting-edge political site called the Right Side of the Web comes this page devoted to the Speaker of House Newt Gingrich. Visitors can read excerpts from his writings, hear sound bites from his speeches, connect to related home pages and visit other Republican sites of interest.

PUNDITRY AND SPIN DOCTORING

The Anti-Rush Limbaugh Page

http://www.cjnetworks.com/~cubsfan/rush/antirush.html

The Anti-Rush Limbaugh Page is a scathing look at the conservative pundit. Includes meticulous and humorous critiques of his writings and on-air commentaries, links to related reviews, jokes and reproductions of anti-Rush bumper stickers.

A Basic Citizen's Definitive Electronic Freedom Guide

http://www.winn.com/abcdefg/

Phillip Winn, the irascible author of ABCDEFG, does not expect you to agree with everything he says. This site is simply his way of bringing political discourse to the Web. Read what he has to say about everything from conspiracies to gun control to the Christian right to talk radio.

The Punch Rush Limbaugh Page

http://www.indirect.com/www/beetle87/rush/index.html

A fellow named Jason invites visitors to take a virtual swing at the king of conservative talk radio

via this largely apolitical site, saying, "I don't strongly oppose conservative views, I just don't like Rush."

Rush Limbaugh Articles and Resources on the 'Net

http://www.well.com/user/srhodes/rush.html

This page links to articles and resources dealing with controversial talk-radio star Rush Limbaugh. The Webmaster compiled information for the site while working on a PBS documentary, "Rush Limbaugh's America."

Unofficial Rush

http://www.rtis.com/nat/pol/rush/

The talk may be conservative but the amount of Limbaugh dogma, diatribe and devotion compiled into this collection is quite, umm, liberal. Among the featured items, find Rush's theme music and info on his swell new tie collection.

The Unofficial Rush Limbaugh Home Page

http://www.eskimo.com/~jeremyps/rush/

At the Unofficial Rush Limbaugh Home Page, visitors can learn more about the talk show host's philosophies, including why the only way to get rid of nuclear weapons is to use them.

SCHOOLS AND INSTITUTES

Carnegie-Mellon School of Public Policy and Management

http://info.heinz.cmu.edu/

The H. John Heinz III School of Public Policy and Management at Carnegie Mellon University provides information about the school and its academic and research programs here. Visitors also will find links to public policy and management resources, including ArtsNet, an index to arts management and cultural resources.

Defense Acquisition University

http://www.acq.osd.mil/dau/dau.html

The U.S. Defense Acquisition University offers overviews of its courses and event schedule at this site. Created by Congress in 1990 to consolidate training for the Defense Acquisition Workforce, the DAU offers links to the Acquisition Reform Communications Center and other related sites.

The Hoover Institute

http://WWW-Hoover.Stanford.EDU/

The Hoover Institute is a conservative think tank located at Stanford University in Palo Alto, California. Visitors to its War, Revolution and Peace page will find essays, indexes, research and multimedia presentations on international relations and politics.

Institute for the Study of Civic Values

http://libertynet.org/~edcivic/iscvhome.html

The Institute for the Study of Civic Values promotes civic involvement through a series of online project examples and explanations to help strengthen communities and citizen participation in government.

Inter-University Consortium for Political and Social Research

http://www.icpsr.umich.edu/

This consortium based at the University of Michigan gives an overview of its services here. The site also contains vast files about politics and social change. American election studies, census data, studies of conflict and war, organizational behavior and social indicators are a few of the topics indexed.

John F. Kennedy School of Government

http://ksgwww.harvard.edu/

The John F. Kennedy School of Government at Harvard University offers a graduate program for would-be idealists who are entering the political arena. Visitors to this home page can link to departmental information, check out lists of classes, peruse KSG publications, negotiate their way around campus maps and more.

K9 Academy For Law Enforcement: The Police Dog Home Pages

http://www.best.com/~policek9/k9home.htm

The K9 Academy For Law Enforcement, an Anaheim, California-based police training center, seeks to provide education in effective and ethical canine law enforcement and protection. Visit here for general information, online police and business resources, dog owner associations, and more.

Keio University Graduate School of Media and Governance

http://www.mag.keio.ac.jp/

Keio University's Graduate School of Media and Governance offers details about lectures and current projects at the school through this Web page. Most texts are in Japanese, with some in English.

Uniformed Services University of the Health Sciences

http://www.usuhs.mil/

The Uniformed Services University of the Health Sciences is the nation's federal health sciences university. Visitors to its home page will find its mission statement, admissions requirements and general program information.

University of North Carolina Institute of Government Home Page

http://ncinfo.iog.unc.edu/

The server of the Institute of Government at the University of North Carolina in Chapel Hill offers resources for governmental training and research. Find North Carolina state government directories as well as U.S. government information source indices.

U.S. GOVERNMENT

AGENCIES AND DEPARTMENTS

BISNIS Online

http://www.itaiep.doc.gov/bisnis/bisnis.html

BISNIS Online is the home page for the U.S. Department of Commerce's Business Information Service for the Newly Independent States. Visit here to find resources for doing business in Russia and other countries of the former Soviet Union.

Brookhaven National Laboratory

http://suntid.bnl.gov:8080/bnl.html

The Brookhaven National Laboratory, part of the U.S. Department of Energy, provides information here on its laboratory research, user facilities, departments and administrative offices. Includes database access and employment opportunity listings.

Bureau of Alcohol, Tobacco and Firearms

http://www.ustreas.gov/treasury/bureaus/atf/atf.html

Visitors to the home page of the U.S. Bureau of Alcohol, Tobacco and Firearms can examine its mission statement and bureau news releases. Included here are bureau publications and news about the agency's activities, plus a link to the Treasury Department's home page.

Bureau of Indian Affairs, Division of Energy and Mineral Resources

http://snake2.cr.usgs.gov/

The Bureau of Indian Affairs' Division of Energy and Mineral Resources outlines the services it provides for Indians with mineral rights here. The

page includes databases of mineral exploration and extraction by reservation, as well as bureau publications.

Bureau of Reclamation

http://www.usbr.gov/

The U.S. Bureau of Reclamation manages water west of the Mississippi River. It is the largest wholesale supplier of water in the country, and it also sells hydroelectric power. It provides an overview of its work here and posts news releases, project updates and job openings.

Bureau of Transportation Statistics

http://www.bts.gov/

The U.S. Department of Transportation's Bureau of Transportation Statistics offers access to resources related to pedestrians, transit, safety, design and other transportation issues at this informational site. Link to the National Transportation Library, Office of Airline Information or Geographical Information Services.

Center for Information Technology Accommodation

http://www.gsa.gov/coca/cocamain.htm

Maintained by the U.S. Center for Information Technology Accommodation, this server acts as a "clearinghouse of information on making Information Systems accessible to all users." Topics featured include legislation and policies, information resources, and Web page design guidelines.

Centers for Disease Control

http://www.cdc.gov/

The home page for the Centers for Disease Control includes general information and current news about the CDC, discussions of diseases, health risks and injuries, and a link to the CDC Wonder system, a database of CDC reports, guidelines and public health data. Visitors can also link to CDC internal centers such as Environmental Health, Infectious Diseases and the National Immunization Program.

Central Intelligence Agency

http://www.odci.gov/cia/

Explore publicly available information from and about the U.S. "spy" service, the Central Intelligence Agency. At this official home page, access CIA publications, news releases and an agency-generated fact sheet.

Central Intelligence Agency, Office of the Director

http://www.odci.gov/

This is the official Web site for the Office of the Director of the Central Intelligence Agency. Visitors can link to the CIA's central Web server or to the U.S. Intelligence Community Web server.

Defense Mapping Agency

http://www.dma.gov/

Working to "provide global geospatial mapping information and services to support and advance national security objectives," the Defense Mapping Agency serves "the unified commands, military services, DoD and other federal agencies." Learn more about this U.S. government agency, its mission and its products.

Defense Reutilization and Marketing Service

http://www.drms.dla.mil/

Welcome to the discount warehouse of surplus U.S. Defense Department government supplies. Public shoppers can eyeball the wares here—everything from automobiles and aircraft parts to clothing, computers, furniture, scrap metal and more.

Defense Supply Center, Columbus

http://www.dscc.dla.mil/

Located in Ohio, the Defense Supply Center, Columbus—a building procurement operation of the U.S. government—maintains this site detailing its activities and services. Links to DSCC software is also available.

Department of Commerce

http://www.doc.gov/

The U.S. Department of Commerce maintains this site for news, news releases and an extensive index of information services. Includes links to other federal departments and resources:

Department of Education

http://www.ed.gov/

The U.S. Department of Education home page contains loads of links to education-related resources and institutions throughout the world. Visitors will find information on department programs and services here, as well as access to publications, grant information and more.

Department of Education, Office of Inspector General

http://www.ed.gov/offices/OIG/edoig.html

The home page of the Office of the Inspector General presents the Education Department's goal to assure the continued improvement of the national education program. Find links to regional offices and related education sites.

Department of Energy Home Page

http://www.doe.gov/

The Department of Energy's Home Page includes information about services, hot topics such as new laser programs and related people, places and organizations. Includes links to other energy sites.

Department of Energy Office of Energy Research

http://www.er.doe.gov/

This U.S. Department of Energy site provides information on basic research and the development of new techniques in energy sciences. Find information on magnetic fusion energy, high energy nuclear physics and other alternatives to traditional energy production.

Department of Energy Office of Human Radiation Experiments

http://www.ohre.doe.gov/

Read recently declassified federal documents on the U.S. government's radiation tests on humans during the Cold War. This Department of Energy site is part of an attempt to make public a dark chapter in U.S. history.

Department of Energy Technology Information Network

http://www.dtin.doe.gov/

This electronic network is designed to promote technology-based

partnerships between American industry and the U.S. Department of Energy's scientific facilities. Selections allow visitors to gather information pertaining to the department's laboratories and programs.

Department of Housing and Urban Development

http://www.hud.gov/

The home page of the U.S. Department of Housing and Urban Development provides general information, HUD research findings, profiles of selected cities and neighborhoods, and a guide to housing.

Department of the Interior

http://www.usgs.gov/doi/

The U.S. Department of the Interior's home page offers daily news updates along with general departmental information. Find employment listings and links to the natural resources management agency's bureaus, offices and committees.

Department of State Diplomatic Security Service

http://www.heroes.net/

This U.S. Department of State page details the nation's counter-terrorism and counter-narcotics rewards programs. Also find information on the passport and visa fraud investigations program.

Department of Transportation

http://ww.dot.gov/

The U.S. Department of Transportation maintains this site for general information. Visit to learn about DOT programs, activities and personnel. Links to sites of related interest are also featured.

Department of the Treasury

http://www.ustreas.gov/

Information on the U.S. Treasury Department's services is available here, along with details on its bureaus, special events and projects. Includes tax help from the Internal Revenue Service, sanctions and embargo information, and seized-property auction listings.

The Department of the Treasury, Financial Crimes Enforcement Network

http://www.ustreas.gov/treasury/bureaus/fincen/fincen.html

The Department of the Treasury's Financial Crimes Enforcement Network investigates money laundering. Visit here for an overview of the agency and its efforts. The site includes news releases and the department's Suspicious Activity Report.

The Department of the Treasury, United States Mint

http://www.ustreas.gov/treasury/bureaus/mint/mint.html

This is the U.S. Department of the Treasury's home page for the U.S. Mint system. Visitors will find an organizational overview and information on special commemorative mints.

Department of Veterans Affairs

http://www.va.gov/

This is the official Web site for the U.S. Department of Veterans Affairs. Visitors will find profiles of veterans, details of veteran benefits, and descriptions of facilities and research programs.

Drug Enforcement Administration

http://www.usdoj.gov/dea/deahome.htm

The U.S. Drug Enforcement Administration serves up a wealth of organizational info here. Check out the DEA mission statement, news releases, publications and employment opportunities, or link to the home page of the U.S. Department of Justice.

Energy Information Administration

http://www.eia.doe.gov/

The Energy Information Administration is the "U.S. government's statistical agency with responsibility for the collection and dissemination of energy data and analysis." Visit this searchable Web site to find energy market analyses, consumption and price data, and other related items and links.

Environmental Protection Agency

http://www.epa.gov/

The U.S. Environmental Protection Agency's Web server offers browsers a substantial index of information about the federal agency. Areas of interest featured include EPA offices, laboratories, grants, contracts, legislation and publications.

FDA News

http://www.fda.gov/opacom/hpnews.html

The U.S. Food and Drug Administration maintains this site to provide regularly updated information about a variety of national health concerns. Visit here for information about FDA activities, programs, publications and more, or link to the FDA home page.

Federal Aviation Administration

http://www.faa.gov/

The U.S. Federal Aviation Administration maintains this site to introduce its programs and services. Visit here for news, aviation-related World Wide Web sites and links to other online government resources.

Federal Aviation Administration, Technical Center

http://www.tc.faa.gov/

The Federal Aviation Administration's Technical Center home page links users to aviation research, development and engineering information. For the technically inclined rather than policy wonks, a typical link takes the browser to the Reconfigurable Cockpit Simulator Laboratory Home Page.

Federal Bureau of Investigation

http://www.fbi.gov/

The FBI home page offers news from the crime front, contact information, investigation overviews and updates, public notices, official statements and links to related government departments. But of particular interest is the online version of the FBI's Ten Most Wanted list of fugitives.

Federal Communications Commission

http://www.fcc.gov/

The Federal Communications Commission is charged with regulating interstate and international communications by radio, television, wire, satellite and cable. Visitors to its site will find general information, consumer alerts, auction schedules and other items of interest.

Federal Deposit Insurance Corporation

http://www.fdic.gov/

Founded in 1933 by the U.S. Congress, the Federal Deposit Insurance Corporation "promotes the safety and soundness" of the nation's banking system. Visit its home page for current assets sales and information on financial institutions across the United States.

Federal Emergency Management Agency

http://www.fema.gov/

The Federal Emergency Management Agency has a broad range of responsibilities: disaster education, assisting in local and state emergency preparedness, coordinating the federal response to disasters, training emergency managers and more. Here, it provides an overview of its work, news of recent natural disasters and information on how to seek federal relief.

Federal Information Exchange, Inc.
http://web.fie.com/fedix/index.html

The Federal Information Exchange oversees the transfer and flow of information among other federal agencies in reference to minority affairs. This searchable site features information on FEDIX and minorities, cross-agency lists and downloadable files.

Federal Trade Commission
http://www.ftc.gov/

The U.S. Federal Trade Commission's home page provides information about the agency's regulations, enforcement powers and consumer services. Includes news releases, public notices and access to the FTC ConsumerLine.

Food and Drug Administration
http://www.fda.gov/fdahomepage.html

The U.S. Food and Drug Administration regulates the production and distribution of more than $1 trillion worth of food, cosmetics and medical products every year. Visit its home page to learn about its programs, facilities and administrators. Links to related agencies, including the Department of Health and Human Services, are also available here.

Food and Drug Administration, Center for Food Safety & Applied Nutrition
http://vm.cfsan.fda.gov/index.html

This is a gateway to the U.S. Food and Drug Administration's main page and to its Center for Food Safety & Applied Nutrition. Links to other sites of topical interest are also featured.

General Accounting Office
http://www.gao.gov/

The investigative arm of Congress, the General Accounting Office is "charged with examining matters relating to the receipt and disbursement of public funds." Visit here to link to the GAO Daybook and monthly Reports and Testimony archives.

General Services Administration
http://www.gsa.gov/

This government site provides information about the U.S. General Services Administration's organization, policies and regional offices. Visitors can access federal purchasing and travel facts aimed at government workers and agencies, or link to GSA publications and training center home pages.

IGnet—Inspectors General Network
http://www.sbaonline.sba.gov/ignet/ig.html

IGnet links more than 60 federal offices of inspectors general and provides public access to I.G. information. The site includes reports, hot line numbers to report fraud and a list of the inspectors general.

Institute for Telecommunication Sciences
http://www.its.bldrdoc.gov/its.html

The National Telecommunications & Information Administration is a U.S. federal organization that oversees telecommunications policy. Included here are links to sites about telecommunications research and technology, public safety, grants, and NTIA activities and organizations.

The Intelligence Community
http://www.odci.gov/ic

The Intelligence Community is a group of 13 U.S. government agencies, headed by the CIA, involved in what is politely called "intelligence gathering activities." Find out who they are what they do (sort of) at this Web site from the Office of the Director of Central Intelligence.

Lawrence Livermore National Laboratory
http://www.llnl.gov/

The Lawrence Livermore National Laboratory home page contains background on the research facility, links to research groups and staff personal home pages. Visitors can also access listings of publications, news items and pointers to related resources.

NASA Dryden Flight Research Center
http://www.dfrc.nasa.gov/dryden.html

Located in Edwards, California, Dryden Flight Research Center is an aeronautic research facility and space-shuttle landing site. The center's home page provides information about its research projects—current and historic—and details on a free tour available to visitors.

NASA Network Information Center
http://naic.nasa.gov/naic

NASA's Network Information Center assists the public in accessing NASA resources. Visitors to the center's home page can learn more about it, or they can directly access NASA's information and photo files.

The National Archives and Research Administration
http://www.nara.gov/

The National Archives and Records Administration is the arm of the U.S. government responsible for preserving and maintaining official records since 1774. The archives here are massive

and include everything from genealogical and biographical data to official petitions and legislative records.

National Coordination Office for High Performance Computing and Communications
http://www.hpcc.gov/

This office coordinates High Performance Computing and Communication activities and acts as a liaison for the program's participants. Vistors to this site can learn more about the NCO and HPCC, read publications, find grants and awards information, and link to related sites.

National Endowment for the Humanities
http://ns1.neh.fed.us/

The National Endowment for the Humanities, a government agency that funds projects in history, philosophy and other areas of the humanities, details its organization, background and aims here. The site includes application guidelines, an overview of recent awards and a list of current grantees.

National Estuary Program
http://www.epa.gov/nep/nep.html

The Environmental Protection Agency's Office of Water (wetlands, oceans and watersheds) maintains this site detailing the agency's National Estuary Program. Features include a map-based interface and a keyword search for accessing data, as well as a categorized index of links.

National Institute of Standards and Technology
http://www.nist.gov/

The Commerce Department's National Institute of Standards and Technology works to promote economic growth through technology, measurements and standards. Visitors will get an overview of NIST and its programs here, and can search an online database of its documents.

National Institutes of Health
http://www.nih.gov/index.html

This gateway site provides links to servers and offices at the National Institutes of Health. The federal government agency offers information on news and events listings, health initiatives, scientific resources, grants and contracts.

National Nuclear Data Center
http://www.nndc.bnl.gov

Funded by the Department of Energy, the National Nuclear Data Center provides "information services in the fields of low and medium energy nuclear physics." Visit this site for nuclear structure and decay data, and nuclear reaction data.

National Ocean Service

http://www.nos.noaa.gov/

The U.S. government monitors and maintains its coastal and oceanic environments with the help of the National Ocean Service. Visitors who hear the call of the sea can review agency fact sheets, newsletters and news releases at this site.

National Renewable Energy Laboratory

http://nrelinfo.nrel.gov/

The U.S. Department of Energy's National Renewal Energy Laboratory conducts efficiency research to develop new clean technologies for heating, lighting and powering U.S. buildings and vehicles. Access the lab's research areas, program activities and information resources here.

National Science Foundation

http://www.nsf.gov/

An independent agency of the federal government, the National Science Foundation "promotes the progress of science and engineering." Visitors to this site will find an overview of the NSF and its areas of focus, current news and information on grants.

National Security Agency

http://www.nsa.gov:8080/

An agency within the Department of Defense, the National Security Agency provides specialized services "to protect U.S. communications and produce foreign intelligence." Find an overview of the agency, its mission and employment opportunities at this site. Also find the National Cryptologic Museum.

National Technology Transfer Center

http://iridium.nttc.edu/nttc.html

Considered "the hub of a national network linking U.S. companies with federal technologies," the National Technology Transfer Center posts this overview of its activities, projects and available information. Find out about the center's free technical assistance by phone or link to technology gateways.

National Telecommunications and Information Administration

http://www.ntia.doc.gov/

The National Telecommunications and Information Administration is a U.S. federal agency that oversees telecommunications policy. Included here are links to sites about telecommunications research and technology, public safety, grants, NTIA activities and related organizations.

Natural Resources Conservation Service

http://www.ncg.nrcs.usda.gov/

An agency of the Department of Agriculture, the Natural Resources Conservation Service "works with landowners on private lands to conserve nat-ural resources." Visit this site to learn more about the NRCS and its conservation partners. Also find technical resources and links to topical sites.

NOAA National Oceanographic Data Center

http://www.nodc.noaa.gov/index.html

This home page for the U.S. National Oceanographic Data Center provides ocean data management and ocean data services to researchers and other users around the world. The NODC is one of the environmental data centers operated by the National Oceanic and Atmospheric Administration.

Nuclear Regulatory Commission

http://www.nrc.gov/

Nonmilitary uses of nuclear energy span the commercial, academic and medical realms. The U.S. Nuclear Regulatory Commission keeps an eye on peaceful uses of nuclear energy to ensure public health. Review NRC programs and policies at its home page.

Occupational Safety and Health Act Regulations

http://www.osha-slc.gov/OshStd_toc/OSHA_Std_toc.html

Visitors to this page will find a table of pointers to Department of Labor OSHA regulations. Links to standard interpretations of the regulations are also provided.

Occupational Safety and Health Administration

http://www.osha.gov/

The Occupational Safety and Health Administration maintains this informational site. Visit here for news releases, publications, compliance assistance information and other resources for "saving lives, preventing injuries and protecting the health of America's workers."

Office of Civilian Radioactive Waste Management

http://www.rw.doe.gov/

This Department of Energy page on the Office of Civilian Radioactive Waste Management features an introduction to its mission as well as details about plans for nuclear waste storage at facilities around the country. It includes links to recent testimony and speeches.

Office of Surface Mining Reclamation and Enforcement

http://www.osmre.gov/

The U.S. Department of the Interior presents the home page for its Office of Surface Mining Reclamation and Enforcement. Visitors will find links to related legislation, policy, projects, maps and budgets. There are also links to related mining and environmental sites and resources.

Peace Corps

http://www.peacecorps.gov/

The U.S. Peace Corps sends 4,000 citizens every year overseas to help interested nations train their own citizens. This page recruits volunteers and donors, and provides a history of the organization, a list of countries it serves, information on "stuff you'll do overseas" and publications.

U.S. Agency for International Development

http://www.info.usaid.gov/

The Agency for International Development, an independent federal government agency providing foreign assistance and humanitarian aid, maintains this informational site. Visitors will find news and overviews from a variety of its programs.

U.S. Census Bureau

http://www.census.gov/

The Census Bureau, the federal agency that tracks demographic trends and population statistics in the country, offers access to its databases on population and housing, the economy and geography here. The site includes a search tool.

U.S. Census Bureau Tiger Map Service

http://tiger.census.gov/

Cartography buffs should check out the home page for the Tiger Map Service, sponsored by the Bureau of the Census. TMS's goal is to provide a public resource for generating high-quality, detailed maps of anywhere in the United States, using public geographic data.

U.S. Customs Service

http://www.ustreas.gov/treasury/bureaus/customs/customs.html

The Department of the Treasury posts this page to outline the mission of the Customs Service. Also find information on Customs public auctions and links to other Treasury bureaus.

U.S. Department of Agriculture

http://www.usda.gov/

The Department of Agriculture offers current news, an overview of its seven program mission areas and a message from the secretary to those who visit this home page. Links to the department's agencies, a topical guide to its programs and an online visitors center are also featured.

U.S. Department of Energy

http://apollo.osti.gov/

The Department of Energy provides an overview of its work here, along with updates on it projects. Visit for news of upcoming public meetings, text of the Secretary of Energy's speeches and correspondence, and an archive of declassified information.

U.S. Department of Energy Office of Environmental Management

http://www.em.doe.gov/

The Department of Energy's Office of Environmental Management provides regulatory and environmental information here. The office also gives visitors an overview of its mission to protect human health and the environment.

U.S. Department of Justice

http://www.usdoj.gov/

The Department of Justice maintains this site for access to its internal organizations, issues-related materials and information resources. Includes links to other federal government and criminal justice departments.

U.S. Department of Labor

http://www.dol.gov/

The Department of Labor provides an overview of the federal bureau, its agencies and mission. Includes information about America's Job Bank, relevant statutes and regulations, programs, activities and grants.

U.S. Department of State Home Page

http://www.state.gov/index.html

This server provides access to the State Department's Foreign Affairs Network gopher and other resources. Visitors are invited to take a photographic tour of the department or review reports of interest on current events.

U.S. Fish and Wildlife Service

http://www.fws.gov/

The Fish and Wildlife Service stocks this Web site with a wealth of U.S. wildlife information. Learn about coastal ecosytems, conservation programs, federal aid, fisheries and more. Visitors can also read about employment opportunities.

U.S. Geological Survey EROS Data Center

http://sun1.cr.usgs.gov/

Find a variety of cartographic, earth science, satellite topographic and other data at this U.S. Geological Survey facility. Also find links to current research projects, EROS Data Center affiliates and the USGS home page.

U.S. Information Agency Home Page

http://www.usia.gov/

An independent foreign affairs agency, the U.S. Information Agency maintains this site to introduce its services and programs. Visitors will find links to educational and cultural exchange resources, history collections, staff profiles and the agency's international affairs activities.

U.S. International Trade Commission

http://www.usitc.gov/

Among other duties, the U.S. International Trade Commission provides trade expertise to the executive and legislative branches of the federal government. Visit the commission's home page to find trade reports, information on current investigations into unfair trade practices and links to related resources.

U.S. Patent and Trademark Office

http://www.uspto.gov/

The Patent and Trademark office provides general information at this home page. Visitors will find announcements, details on pending public hearings and explanations of office services.

U.S. Postal Service Consumer Information

http://www.usps.gov/consumer/

Step up to the Web window of the Postal Service, offering the kinds of information that keeps Internet-savvy consumers from waiting in line. Rate and delivery guides are included, as well as tips on fraud and how to acquire unclaimed parcels.

U.S. Postal Service Internet Branch

http://www.usps.gov/

The Postal Service has opened this "branch" on the Internet to offer customers information about zip codes, stamps, and other USPS products and services. The site also features a business-oriented section the postmaster promises could prove profitable to businesses that depend heavily on the mail.

ARCHIVES AND INDICES

CCER National Budget Simulation

http://garnet.berkeley.edu:3333/budget/budget.html

The National Budget Simulation is a vibrant visual aid for browsers to see the tradeoffs necessary to balance the U.S. budget. For purposes of clarity, the simulation asks that the 1995 fiscal deficit be cut all in one year.

---

a2z **EDITOR'S CHOICE**

The Directorate of Time, U.S. Naval Observatory

http://tycho.usno.navy.mil/time.html

Does anybody really ever know what time it is? Why, yes. As a matter of fact, someone does—right down to the nanosecond. Big deal, you say? When you take a little time to consider how few certainties life has to offer, this nifty little Web gadget may begin to take on a certain allure. The main feature, of course, is the USNO Master Clock, which visitors can adjust to various time zones and which is updated each time the page is refreshed. As a little bonus, the U.S. Naval Observatory clockmasters explain how the time is determined (it involves an ensemble of 55 clocks, no less) and further captivate time gazers with calculations for sunrise, moonset and everything in between. One thing's for certain: You'll never have to guess again.—*Reviewed by Dan Kelly*

The Directorate of Time U.S. Naval Observatory

The Directorate of Time, U.S. Naval Observatory is the official source of time used in the United States.

USNO MASTER CLOCK 18:11:41 UTC

Consumer Information Center Commercials

http://www.gsa.gov/staff/pa/cic/multimed.htm

Nostalgic visitors can download examples of the Consumer Information Center's award-winning (and much beloved) television commercials and print ads here. Each of these gems once advertised the free Consumer Information Catalog—you know, the one you get from Pueblo, Colorado.

Declassified Satellite Photographs

http://edcwww.cr.usgs.gov/dclass/dclass.html

This sampling of recently declassified intelligence satellite photographs from the 1960s is an offering of the U.S. Geological Survey. Images on display here include Soviet Airfield, Aral Sea and Klyuchevskaya Volcano.

The Directorate of Time, U.S. Naval Observatory

http://tycho.usno.navy.mil/time.html

Find out the exact time down to the nanosecond and much more at this site. See Editor's Choice.

Federal Acquisition Jumpstation

http://procure.msfc.nasa.gov/fedproc/home.html

The Federal Acquisition Jumpstation provides a gateway to information on federal procurement offices, procedures and business opportunities for government contractors. Includes pointers to small business assistance, aquisition regulations and instructions for electronic commerce in the federal arena.

Federal Information Center— United States Government

http://www.gsa.gov/et/fic-firs/fichome.htm

A function of the General Services Administration, the Federal Information Center provides citizens with answers to questions about the government. Visit here to learn about the center and access its directory of telephone numbers to call.

Federal Information Exchange Home Page

http://web.fie.com/

The Federal Information Exchange indexes a broad array of employment, equipment exchange and grant opportunities for educators and researchers looking for a piece of the federal pie. Find listings from minority colleges and universities, a used equipment network, and general research and employment initiatives.

The Federal Web Locator

http://www.law.vill.edu/Fed-Agency/fedwebloc.html

Maintained "to bring the cyber citizen to the federal government's doorstep," this locator intends to provide one-stop shopping for links to federal government and related sites. Link to anything from the Library of Congress to tax analysts here.

FedWorld Home Page

http://www.fedworld.gov/

The National Technical Information Service provides FedWorld "to help with the challenge of accessing U.S. government information online." The goal of this site is to help the public locate and order government information. Visitors will find links to government information servers and recent government reports here.

Government Databases

http://town.hall.org/govt/govt.html

This listing of government databases provides links to the Congressional Record, United Nations, the Joint Economic Committee and other U.S. government information resources.

Government Information

http://www.lib.utexas.edu/Libs/PCL/Government.html

Find an extensive index of U.S. government resources on this server. Databases, reference works and documents of every description from the House, Senate and the executive branch are featured. Links to information on Texas are also included.

Government Information Locator Service

http://info.er.usgs.gov/gils/index.html

The Government Information Locator Service aims to identify and provide access to government information resources. Visitors to this Web site can access information about GILS and technical topics related to the service, or search U.S. Government Printing Office resources.

Government Information Sharing Project

http://govinfo.kerr.orst.edu/

The goal of the Government Information Sharing Project at Oregon State University is to demonstrate how technology can be used to create a user-friendly system for accessing U.S. federal government information.

Government Information Xchange

http://www.info.gov/

The federal government's General Services Administration provides an extensive index to federal, state and local government sites here. It also includes a federal yellow pages and links to foreign government sites.

Independent Federal Agencies and Commissions

http://www.whitehouse.gov/WH/Independent_Agencies/html/independent_links.html

This page from the White House's Interactive Citizen's Handbook features a list of governmental agency seals. The seals act as hot links to the agencies and commissions they represent.

Interactive Citizen's Handbook

http://www.whitehouse.gov/WH/html/handbook.html

The Interactive Citizen's Handbook offers visitors a variety of tools for learning about the government. Search for specific items of interest on the White House database and all the federal government's Web sites, access the Government Information Locator Service, or follow the links provided and take a leisurely tour.

Jobs, Labor, and Management

http://www.fedworld.gov/jobs.htm

Visitors to this site from the FedWorld Information Network will find an annotated index of links to job-, labor-, and management-related U.S. government servers. Employment opportunities listings, labor statistics and pointers to other government information servers also are offered.

LEGI-SLATE Inc. Gopher

http://gopher.legislate.com/

LEGI-SLATE's gopher service offers access to U.S. congressional and regulatory information. Although many areas offer free browsing, subscriptions are required for unrestricted server access.

Marshall Space Flight Center Procurement Home Page

http://procure.msfc.nasa.gov/

This NASA procurement office site contains information about business opportunities, procurement tools and links to other related NASA sites. Includes informtion on small-business programs and receiving solicitation packages.

NASA Langley Research Center— Other Government Laboratories

http://mosaic.larc.nasa.gov/nasaonline/gov.html

NASA's Langley Research Center presents this detailed collection of pointers to U.S. government research laboratories. Find links to national laboratories, National Science Foundation centers, Department of Defense centers, consortiums and other federal government sites.

NASA Office of Procurement

http://www.hq.nasa.gov/office/procurement/

The U.S. National Aeronautics and Space Administration maintains this site to offer information to businesses competing for upcoming contracts. Visitors will find an acquisition forecast, procurement initiatives, the Procurement Countdown newsletter and links to facilities' procurement home pages.

NASA Shuttle Web Archives

http://shuttle.nasa.gov/

Scientists and space buffs can follow the latest U.S. space exploration and experimentation at NASA's Shuttle Web Archives. Visitors can monitor current—and review past—Space Shuttle missions from countdown to landing.

National Technology Transfer Center

http://iridium.nttc.edu/nttc.html

Considered "the hub of a national network linking U.S. companies with federal technologies," the National Technology Transfer Center posts this overview of its activities, projects and available information. Find out about the center's free technical assistance by phone or link to technology gateways.

Occupational Safety and Health Act Regulations

http://www.osha-slc.gov/OshStd_toc/OSHA_Std_toc.html

Visitors to this page will find a table of pointers to U.S. Department of Labor OSHA regulations. Links to standard interpretations of the regulations are also provided.

Occupational Safety and Health Administration Computerized Information System

http://www.osha-slc.gov/

Housed in Salt Lake City, Utah, OSHA's Computerized Information System provides access to an extensive safety health database. Federal regulations, documents, technical data and training information are featured, along with links to other servers of topic-related information.

Shadow Patent Office Patent Services

http://www.spo.eds.com/patent.html

Electronic Data Systems' Shadow Patent Office provides free, cursory search options and reports of U.S. patents issued since 1972. The company's commercial patentability and infringement search services are also detailed at this site.

STAT-USA/Internet Information System

http://sunny.stat-usa.gov/

STAT-USA, a service of the U.S. Department of Commerce, claims to be the world's largest source of federally sponsored trade, business and economic information. Visit here for a comprehensive index of resources from more than 50 federal agencies.

State and Local Governments

http://lcweb.loc.gov/global/state/stategov.html

The Library of Congress posts these indexes for state and local governments. Along with legislative info and issues, visitors can access regional economic data and links to hundreds of cities and state maps.

The Student Guide

http://www.ed.gov/prog_info/SFA/StudentGuide/

This Student Guide details financial aid programs available from the U.S. Department of Education. Includes a general overview of programs, descriptions of specific grants, work-study opportunities and loans.

Thomas: Legislative Information on the Internet

http://thomas.loc.gov/

Legislative information on the Internet, "in the spirit of Thomas Jefferson," is provided here. Pages on Congressional bills and records, legislative documents, the U.S. Constitution, the lawmaking process and U.S. House of Representatives audit reports are included.

U.S. Census Data at Lawrence Berkeley National Laboratory

http://cedr.lbl.gov/mdocs/LBL_census.html

Visitors can download Census data from 1970, 1980 and 1990 here. The site is maintained by the Lawrence Berkeley National Laboratory and is believed to be the largest collection of census information on the Internet.

U.S. Census LOOKUP 1990

http://cedr.lbl.gov/cdrom/doc/lookup_doc.html

This online database maintained by the University of California retrieves information from the 1990 U.S. Census. Visitors can view examples of search results and browse the U.C. CD-ROM Information System.

U.S. Department of Agriculture Research Database

http://medoc.gdb.org/best/stc/usda-best.html

The U.S. Department of Agriculture maintains this site for its research database. Visit here to search the department's research documentation, access related foreign country resources and link to sites covering specific research disciplines.

U.S. Department of Education Publications

http://www.ed.gov/pubs/index.html

The U.S. Department of Education provides a list of publications through this Web page, including educational newsletters, publications for parents and statistical abstracts.

U.S. Federal Government World Wide Web Servers

http://www.fie.com/www/us_gov.htm

This gateway page contains a detailed listing of U.S. government Web servers. Includes links to multiple and single federal agency sites and a listing of government-sponsored consortia.

U.S. Geological Survey Global Land Information System

http://edcwww.cr.usgs.gov/glis/glis.html

The U.S. Geological Survey provides this interactive database for researchers looking for information about the earth's land surfaces. Visitors can telnet or FTP to the full services of the Global Land Information System.

U.S. Geological Survey Internet Resources

http://www.usgs.gov/network/index.html

The U.S. Geological Survey provides this index to sites containing scientific research and databases.

U.S. Geological Survey Mapping Information

http://www-nmd.usgs.gov/

Visit this U.S. Geological Survey site for up-to-date cartographic data and information on the United States. Find resources for geography teachers and students, learn about new discoveries in cartography, and get USGS product and service information.

U.S. Geological Survey Server Index

http://info.er.usgs.gov/network/science/earth/usgs.html

The U.S. Geological Survey maintains this site for its index of computer servers and regional and state Web sites. Visitors can link to geology-related information resources across the United States.

U.S. Geological Survey State Representatives

http://h2o.er.usgs.gov/public/wrd011.html

Visitors to this site will find a complete list of Geological Survey representatives in each of the 50 states. The listing features names and contact information.

U.S. Government Printing Office

http://www.access.gpo.gov/su_docs/aces/aaces001.html

The home page of the Government Printing Office allows electronic access to online databases as well as issues of the Federal Register, Congressional Record and Congressional Bills.

U.S. Library of Congress Indices

http://lcweb.loc.gov/global/globalhp.html

The U.S. Library of Congress offers a guide to its indices of World Wide Web services at this site. This particular catalog emphasizes governmental agency information and news periodicals.

U.S. Postal Service Address and ZIP Code Information

http://www.usps.gov/ncsc/

The U.S. Postal Service maintains this site for address and zip code information. Visit here for a keyword-searchable zip code database and other Postal Service resources.

Washington, D.C., and the Federal Government (Planet Earth)

http://www.nosc.mil/planet_earth/washington.html

The District of Columbia info found on the Planet Earth Home Page contains links to extensive data about U.S. government branches, departments, bureaus and agencies, as well as local information about the District. Features also include lists of servers in the District, Maryland and Virginia.

World Wide Web Virtual Library: U.S. Government Information Sources

http://iridium.nttc.edu/gov_res.html

The National Technology Transfer Center maintains this index of U.S. government Web pages. Users can link to sites established by federal branches, executive departments and independent agencies, or search the database by keyword.

CONGRESS

Congressional Black Caucus Information

http://drum.ncsc.org/~carter/CBC.html

Review a history of the Congressional Black Caucus and examine its position papers through this unofficial page. It features members' reports and offers e-mail directories for Congress and the national media.

U.S. House of Representatives Democratic Caucus

http://decaucusweb.house.gov

For the official word on party politics in the House of Representatives, visit the House Democratic Caucus site. The history, membership and objectives of the House's Democratic bloc are online here. The site also provides links to other Congressional resources and individual members.

BILLS AND LEGISLATION

The 104th Congress—Full Text of Legislation

http://thomas.loc.gov/home/c104query.html

From the Thomas site, this page offers an interactive form for searching the legislation of the 104th Congress. Search by keyword, bill sponsor or bill number. Online help and links to topical sites offer assistance.

Voter Information Services

http://www.vis.org/

Voter Information Services tracks the voting records of the members of the U.S. Congress and posts them here. The site also details the votes on bills from the Republican effort dubbed the Contract With America.

CONGRESSIONAL RECORDS

Congressional Record—104th Congress

http://thomas.loc.gov/home/r104query.html

Search the full text of the Congressional Record for the 104th Congress at this site. Find a variety of query options, including searches by keyword, speaker and a range of dates.

HOUSE OF REPRESENTATIVES

Congressional E-Mail Addresses

http://www.webcom.com/~leavitt/cong.html

Send e-mail to a congressional representative of your choice. This page offers a directory of elected national leaders' public e-mail addresses.

Congressman Jim Talent's Second District of Missouri Home Page

http://www.house.gov/talent/welcome.html

A good source of information on Missouri politics and its players, Congressman Jim Talent's Second District of Missouri Home Page has links to personal information, as well as links to other political sites for Missouri and the nation.

Congressman John Joseph Moakley

http://www.house.gov/moakley/welcome.html

This Web site provides information about Massachusetts Congressman Joe Moakley and his work. Includes information about the 9th Congressional District and legislative topics Moakley tackles, along with links to federal and state government resources.

Congressman Peter DeFazio

http://www.house.gov/defazio/index.htm

Peter DeFazio is a U.S. congressman from Oregon's 4th District. Visitors to this Democrat's home page will find biographical information, legislative position papers, voting records and contact information. Links are also provided to sites discussing issues facing the government.

Congressman Richard K. Armey's Home Page

http://www.house.gov/armey/

Congressman Richard K. Armey's page includes personal information about the representative and facts and figures about his district in Texas. The site also includes a plug for the flat tax, pointers to U.S. House of Representatives pages and recent op-eds published by the Republican.

Congressman Robert Dornan

http://www.umr.edu/~sears/primary/dornan.html

Project Vote Smart is the sponsor of this site that provides information about Republican Congressman Robert Dornan of California. In addition to reading a bare-bones résumé, browsers can listen to an audio clip and examine Dornan's ratings of special-interest groups. Search capabilities are also provided.

Representative Newt Gingrich

http://clerkweb.house.gov/members/house.htm

This subpage of the official U.S. House of Representatives membership directory will virtually connect you to Newt Gingrich, the Republican congressman from Georgia's 6th District and the Speaker of the House. Visitors can check out Gingrich's service history, link to his legislative records and send him fan mail.

U.S. House of Representatives Democratic Leadership

http://www.house.gov/democrats/

This is the spot to learn what is happening in U.S. government. There are updates on current legislation, news releases from House Democrats and links to federal programs and agencies. Includes a link to the U.S. House of Representatives Home Page.

U.S. House of Representatives Home Page

http://www.house.gov/

Keep an eye on the legislative process at the U.S. House of Representatives World Wide Web service. Follow bills and resolutions on their way to the House floor. House members and committees can be contacted, and the body's history and rules can be researched at this site. Hundreds of links to government information resources are listed.

U.S. House of Representatives—Member Directory

http://clerkweb.house.gov/members/house.htm

This directory of the U.S. House of Representatives' members offers telephone numbers and postal addresses organized alphabetically and by state.

U.S. House of Representatives—Who's Who

http://www.house.gov/Whoswho.html

The U.S. House of Representatives publishes its member and committee directories at this informational site. Visit here to view contact information indexed by members, committees and house leadership offices.

U.S. House of Representatives—Your Comments Please

http://www.house.gov/Comments.html

This site maintained by the U.S. House of Representatives provides an e-mail-based feedback form. Visit here to send your comments to the legislative organization, and to find links to staff directories, educational resources and other informational pages.

Will T. Bill

http://www.unipress.com/will-t-bill.html

A service of Unipress World Wide Web, this site provides free, searchable access to full-text versions of the bills and resolutions of the U.S. House of Representatives. Includes e-mail access to elected officials.

SENATE

Jesse Helms Speaks

http://www.nando.net/sproject/jesse/helms.html

The World According to Helms is devoted to North Carolina Sen. Jesse Helms. The majority of the site consists of quotes by Helms, but visitors also will find newspaper articles about his controversial stances on several issues. Includes cartoons and a pictorial tour of his career.

Sen. Edward M. Kennedy

http://www.senate.gov/member/ma/kennedy/general/

Sen. Edward Kennedy's home page contains background on the politician, his voting record and contact information. Includes links to U.S. government servers, Massachusetts on the Web and pointers to political activist pages.

Sen. John Breaux, Louisiana

ftp://www.senate.gov/~breaux/

Democratic Sen. John Breaux's home page presents his biography and legislative accomplishments and introduces visitors to "Jambalaya," theLouisiana senator's hot-and-spicy monthly cable TV show. Includes Cajun recipes and information for Louisiana-bound tourists.

Sen. Richard Lugar

http://www.umr.edu/~sears/primary/lugar.html

Compiled by Project Vote Smart, this page features a fact sheet on Sen. Richard Lugar, candidate in the 1996 presidential election. Site features include a search mechanism for accessing the senator's voting record.

Sen. Richard Lugar for Indiana

http://www.iquest.net/lugar/lugar.html

Here is the online headquarters for the (now-dissolved) presidential campaign of Indiana Sen. Richard Lugar. Read about Lugar's positions on issues and link to a forum to offer your own thoughts.

U.S. Senate Members

http://policy.net/capweb/Senate/Senate.html

This U.S. Senate directory from CapWeb provides links to individual senators. Search by name, state, political party and committee assignment, or link to the rest of CapWeb, a guide to the U.S. Congress.

U.S. Senator Patrick Leahy's Home Page

ftp://ftp.senate.gov/member/vt/leahy/general/pjl.html

Sen. Patrick Leahy posts biographical and contact information here and details his committee assignments. The Vermont Democrat also provides information on the environment and protecting rights on the Internet. The page also includes links to Vermont sites.

DOCUMENTS

Constitution of the United States of America

http://pobox.com/~whig/Constitution.html

An indexed, hypertext version of the U.S. Constitution (on a faux parchment background, no less) ensures every cybercitizen easy access to the United States' most vital document. Includes links to constitutional amendments and to the Bill of Rights.

Constitution of the United States of America

http://www.law.cornell.edu/constitution/constitution.overview.html

This site contains the complete text of the Constitution of the United States. The text is presented in sections—preamble, individual articles, signers and amendments, respectively.

Declaration of Independence

http://www.cs.indiana.edu/statecraft/decl.html

Read the background and full text of the Declaration of Independence of the 13 American colonies at this site. Adopted by the Continental Congress on July 4, 1776, the document is an explanation of why the colonies (now states) declared their independence.

Drell Subpanel Executive Report

http://www.hep.net/documents/drell/full_report.html

The U.S. Department of Energy's Division of High Energy Physics takes a look at the future of the field in this report. Find an executive summary, as well as the full text of the Drell Panel report. Figures, tables and appendices are attached.

National Information Infrastructure: Agenda for Action

http://sunsite.unc.edu/nii/NII-Table-of-Contents.html

The National Coordination Office for the U.S. Federal High Performance Computing and Communications Program maintains this site to outline its National Information Infrastructure agenda. Visit here to learn about the NII and its proponents.

Occupational Safety and Health Act of 1970

http://www.osha-slc.gov/OshAct_toc/OshAct_toc_by_sect.html

Workers and employers alike can brush up on the fine points of state-mandated workplace wellness at the U.S. Occupational Safety and Health Act site. Find the full text of the 1970 legislation and amendments passed in 1990.

Political Documents

http://www.cs.indiana.edu/inds/politics.html

This political documents page, provided courtesy of Indiana University, offers the texts of historical and modern political documents, from the Magna Carta to the Gettysburg Address to the U.N. charter.

Securities Act of 1933

http://www.law.uc.edu/CCL/33Act/index.html

This site, maintained by the University of Cincinnati College of Law's Center for Corporate Law, contains the text of the U.S. Securities Act of 1933. Visitors can read each of the act's 26 sections.

Statistical Abstract of the United States

http://www.census.gov/stat_abstract/

The Statistical Abstract site offers a collection of tables and graphs on social, economic and international subjects. This site features frequently requested tables, state rankings, and state and county data. See Editor's Choice.

Technology for the National Information Infrastructure

http://www.hpcc.gov/blue95

The Federal High Performance Computing and Communications Program produced a report titled, "Technology for the National Information Infrastructure." Read it here and discover how the U.S. government plans to bolster the country's economy through the development of advanced information systems.

United States Constitution

http://www.house.gov/Constitution/Constitution.html

An electronic print of the complete U.S. Constitution is available at this Web site. Topic-related notes are also included.

U.S. Government Hypertexts

http://sunsite.unc.edu/govdocs.html

This site contains U.S. government hypertexts focusing on current policies and proposals as evidenced through speeches and other presentations. Features include links to the White House and other government-related sites.

U.S. House of Representatives: Internet Law Library—Code of Federal Regulations

http://law.house.gov/cfr.htm

Need help understanding U.S. federal regulations? The U.S. House of Representatives and Personal Library Software Inc. maintain this site, which contains a text-based, searchable database, to make accessing and understanding the federal code easier.

EXECUTIVE BRANCH

The Council on Environmental Quality

http://ceq.eh.doe.gov/

The Council on Environmental Quality, which operates from the executive office, features its annual reports and a list of regulations here. Also access the Environmental Protection Agency Review and an extensive bibliography.

Federal Government: Executive Branch

http://lcweb.loc.gov/global/executive/fed.html

This Library of Congress page offers links to executive branch resources, the White House and executive branch agencies. Links to independent agencies, quasi-governmental agencies and other Library of Congress sites are also featured.

The National Performance Review

http://sunsite.unc.edu/npr/nptoc.html

The National Performance Review, "From Red Tape to Results," is a special report from Vice President Gore. Visitors to this page can read the report on government efficiency and listen to audio messages from Gore and President Clinton.

Vice President Al Gore

http://www.whitehouse.gov/WH/EOP/OVP/html/GORE_Home.html

Vice President Gore can be seen, heard and read about on this government page. The site includes Gore's environmental links, information about the National Performance Review and his other areas of political expertise.

The White House

http://www.whitehouse.gov/

Tour the White House and learn about its history, visit the first family and find out what's new with the president, or search the virtual library for documents, speeches and photos. Also find the Interactive Citizen's Handbook and a special area for the children.

White House Electronic Publications

http://www.whitehouse.gov/WH/Publications/html/Publications.html

The White House Electronic Publications home page archives White House news releases, policy briefings, speeches, executive orders and other governmental documents. Includes a FAQ and user surveys.

White House Information

http://english-server.hss.cmu.edu/WhiteHouse.html

Maintained at Carnegie Mellon University, this page provides information about the executive branch. Find domestic and international affairs

EDITOR'S CHOICE

Statistical Abstract of the United States

http://www.census.gov/stat_abstract/

What's the largest city in the United States? Wrong! The "largest" city is Anchorage, AK—and it's not even close. Geography buffs, demographic fans and statistical nuts could spend all day perusing the charts and graphs from the Statistical Abstract of the United States. It's a hefty chunk off of the U.S. Census Bureau site, which has plenty of factoids to offer on its own. But the ratio of good stuff to fluff is much better here than at the parent site. Amuse yourself for hours with population tables, budget summaries, crime rates, sales figures, weather statistics, etc. Okay, okay: New York is No. 1 in population, but the Big Apple rates a sorry 13th in land area. Anchorage, at 1,697.6 square miles, is tops in that category; nearly 1,000 square miles ahead of the second-largest city. Which is ... ?—*Reviewed by Dan Kelly*

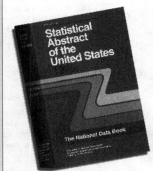

overviews, examine presidential appointments or run a gopher-based search of White House information.

White House Web: Executive Branch

http://www.whitehouse.gov/WH/EOP/html/3_parts.html

The White House Web server offers its virtual visitors access to the offices of the president and vice president, the cabinet, the independent federal agencies and commissions under the executive branch, and even the mysterious catacombs of White House itself. Visitors can use a clickable map or search by subject.

INTERNAL REVENUE SERVICE

Internal Revenue Service

http://www.irs.ustreas.gov/prod/

Whether Uncle Sam is dipping into your pockets, or you're dipping into his, you'll find all you need to complete the deal at this U.S. Treasury Department-sponsored server: downloadable tax forms and instructions, information on where to get help with taxes, and where and when to file. Still have questions? Browse the online FAQs.

The Tax Prophet

http://www.taxprophet.com/

The Tax Prophet "deciphers the Internal Revenue Code for U.S. and foreign taxpayers, and professionals alike" on this cyberjourney through the indecipherable labyrinth that is the IRS.

JUDICIAL BRANCH

Americans With Disabilities Act & Disability Information

http://www.public.iastate.edu/~sbilling/ada.html

The U.S. Department of Justice provides links to information on the Americans with Disabilities Act and the full text of the ADA. Includes links to ADA accessibility guidelines and legal resources.

Department of Justice Civil Rights Division

http://gopher.usdoj.gov/crt/crt-home.html

The Civil Rights Division of the U.S. Attorney General's Office trumpets the news about affirmative-action policies and civil-rights case law through this page.

Federal Judicial Center

http://www.fjc.gov/

The Federal Judicial Center is the federal courts' agency for research and continuing education.

Here visitors can find detailed information about the center, read publications, get telephone numbers and link to other Web servers.

Immigration and Naturalization Service

http://www.ins.usdoj.gov/

An arm of the Department of Justice, the Immigration and Naturalization Service outlines its mission and duties on this page. A link to the INS information on the Justice gopher is also included.

Justices of the Supreme Court

http://www.law.cornell.edu/supct/justices/fullcourt.html

This unofficial page is devoted to the nine august individuals who constitute the highest legal authority in the nation. Visitors will find photos and biographical information for all current Supreme Court justices.

LIBRARIES

Digital Library Technology Home Page

http://dlt.gsfc.nasa.gov/

The Digital Library Technology Project is a U.S. government program aimed at developing the technology to put National Aeronautics and Space Administration electronic archives online. Software and hardware systems are in the works to make NASA information systems accessible to the public via computers.

---

a2z EDITOR'S CHOICE

Library of Congress World Wide Web Home Page

http://www.loc.gov/

It's easy to be overwhelmed by the amount of information available at the Library of Congress Web site, which, frankly, needs a better librarian. But with THOMAS, LOCIS, MARVEL and the Law Library of Congress all under one roof, this has to be the ultimate stop-off for all of that messy government stuff you'll inevitably have to dig up someday. Big bad THOMAS supplies full-text legislative info, including the Congressional Record and the status and summary of each bill. LOCIS (Library of Congress Information System) contains legislative databases available via telnet. MARVEL (Machine-Assisted Realization of the Virtual Electronic Library) is a gopher-based system that provides access to still more resources over the Net. And the Law Library packs a database with the national laws of more than 35 countries. Plenty more where all that came from, too, but do yourself a favor and get acquainted with the site's search mechanism first. You'll need it.—*Reviewed by Dan Kelly*

The Library of Congress
Founded in 1800

Choose a topic below, see what's new, or search our Web pages and Gopher menus.

General Information and Publications
Find out about the Library and its mission, special programs and services, information for visitors, publications (including Library Associates and *Civilization Magazine*), employment opportunities, and other general information.

Government, Congress, and Law
Search THOMAS (legislative information), access services of the Law Library of Congress (including the Global Legal Information Network), or locate government information.

Research and Collections Services
Browse historical collections for the National Digital Library (American Memory), visit Library Reading Rooms, access special services for persons with disabilities, and read about Library of Congress cataloging, acquisitions, and preservation operations, policies, and related standards.

Library of Congress

http://www.loc.gov/

This site contains a guide to the U.S. Library of Congress materials available online. Featured categories include exhibits and events, services and publications, digital collections, online systems, and Congress and government.See Editor's Choice.

Library of Congress Online Systems

http://lcweb.loc.gov/homepage/online.html

This page offers Web-searching tools for the Library of Congress. Included are links to Marvel, the gopher-based information system; LOCIS telnet; and anonymous FTP. Search guides, library hours and a link to the Vietnam Prisoner of War/Missing in Action Database are included.

Library of Congress Soviet Archives Exhibit

http://www.ncsa.uiuc.edu/SDG/Experimental/soviet.exhibit/soviet.archive.html

The U.S. Library of Congress presents its Soviet archives exhibit online. Visit here to explore its collection of documents from the "previously top secret archives of the Central Committee of the Communist Party."

Library of Congress Z39.50 Database Search Site

http://lcweb.loc.gov/z3950/gateway.html

The Library of Congress' Z39.50 site explains this retrieval protocol and its usage. The page links to other Z39.50 resources and servers on the Internet.

Library of Congress Special Collections

http://lcweb.loc.gov/spcoll/spclhome.html

The Library of Congress presents this index to the institution's many special collections. The collections' descriptions can be viewed by subject, geographical location, format or chronological division.

National Library of Medicine

http://www.nlm.nih.gov/

The National Institutes of Health National Library of Medicine gives an overview of its services, publications and databases. Also find details on research projects and upcoming conferences.

U.S. Copyright Office

http://lcweb.loc.gov/copyright/

The U.S. Copyright Office of the Library of Congress has prepared this Web site to provide general information about copyright registration and other basic questions. Also included are links to other copyright-related resources on the Internet.

U.S. House of Representatives Internet Law Library

http://law.house.gov

This interactive site offers a form to perform keyword searches of the U.S. Code and federal regulations. Online help assists users, and a feedback option encourages comments on this experimental server.

PUBLIC UTILITIES

U.S. Geological Survey Water Resources in California

http://water.wr.usgs.gov

The U.S. Geologic Survey provides information about water resources in California on this page. Visitors will find current stream flow conditions in the state and bulletins about floods and earthquakes. The extensive site also includes information on water-quality programs and hydrological data.

STATE AND LOCAL GOVERNMENTS

Alaska Department of Transportation and Public Facilities

http://www.dot.state.ak.us/

The State of Alaska Department of Transportation and Public Facilities home page offers system overviews of the state's highways and airports. Find design specifications and facility plans here.

Arizona Department of Transportation

http://www.dot.state.az.us/

The highways and byways of Arizona are traversed online via the Arizona Department of Transportation's site. Includes information on computer-aided engineering, roadway design and the online version of Arizona Highways magazine.

Arizona Government Home Page

http://www.state.az.us/

The State of Arizona maintains this site to provide its state agencies and residents with access to services traditionally available only during business hours. Visit here to connect with federal and state government resources and educational institutions.

Boulder County, Colorado USA

http://www.boco.co.gov/

From the home page for Boulder County, visitors can learn about the government and business activities in a locale that ranges from lush national forests and mountain peaks to one of the most dynamic university and research communities in the United States.

California Department of Forestry and Fire Protection

http://spp-www.cdf.ca.gov/

The California Department of Forestry and Fire Protection supplies information about its Strategic Planning Program on this home page. Among the resources featured are a map-making facility and various publications.

California Department of Industrial Relations

http://www.dir.ca.gov/

Created to advance employment conditions and opportunities, California's Office of Industrial Relations maintains this site offering information on workers' compensation, occupational safety and health, and labor law. Also find statistics, research, news and departmental bulletins.

California Department of Water Resources

http://www.water.ca.gov/

The California Department of Water Resources posts a gateway to its sites here. Visitors can access the department's main page, as well as the California Cooperative Snow Surveys, the Division of Planning and other related official sites.

California Election Results

http://www.election.ca.gov/home.html

Results for 1996, 1995, and 1994 elections in San Francisco and throughout California are available in English and Spanish on the Election Server, sponsored by the Digital Corporation and the California Voter Foundation. Other links include news stories and campaign finance information. (News flash: Californians have voted in favor of mountain lions and against trial lawyers.)

California Energy Commission

http://www.energy.ca.gov/energy/

The California Energy Commission is charged with establishing energy policy and planning to ensure a reliable and affordable energy supply. The agency's home page details the commission's major responsibilities, describes its divisions and programs, provides a topical index to commission information and posts an Internet site for educational resources.

California State Assembly

http://www.assembly.ca.gov/

The California State Assembly home page provides information on the state's government. Visitors can take a virtual tour of the state capital or access information on elected officials and legislation. Includes links to other government agencies.

California State Lands Commission

http://diablo.slc.ca.gov/

The California State Lands Commission maintains this site for public notices, environmental impact reports and geographic information system data. Visit here for commission resources and links to other state agencies.

California State Senate

http://www.sen.ca.gov/

Find direct access to California's Senate members, committees and offices at this state-sponsored site. A user's guide and tutorial on how to find legislative information, Senate Internet resources and links to other California state sites are also featured.

Council of State Governments

http://www.csg.org/

The Council of State Governments is an organization aiming to foster cooperation among U.S. states and territories. Visit this site for links to general information, gopher servers and related organizations.

Florida Communities Network

http://www.state.fl.us/

The Florida Communities Network is a shared resource network for Florida communities. Individual sites statewide can be accessed through a series of image maps. Included are trade associations, economic-development organizations, chambers of commerce and more. This site also has information about the network's mission, services and projects.

Florida Department of State

http://www.dos.state.fl.us/

The home page for Florida's Department of State offers election information as well as details about its responsibilities and mission. The page also includes links to state historical documents.

Georgia Online Network

http://www.state.ga.us/

The Georgia Online Network offers a collection of links to government departments and agencies in the state, as well as some other Georgia-specific sites.

Georgia State Department of Transportation

http://www.dot.state.ga.us/

See what the Department of Transportation is doing to make travel in Georgia safe and easy. Visitors can read the Statewide Transportation Improvement Plan or find out how to contact various offices. DOT staff can use the Web to post information or communicate with coworkers.

Hawaiian Affairs Office

http://hoohana.aloha.net/~oha/

The Office of Hawaiian Affairs provides access to information about the organization's work. Includes articles from the office's monthly newspaper, a collection of statistical data about aboriginal Hawaiians, and links to relevant cultural and informational Web sites.

Home Page Washington

http://www.wa.gov/

Home Page Washington operates as an online information guide to the official working of Washington's state government. The executive,

legislative and judicial branches are represented, complete with document indices, staff directories and the latest news releases.

Houston City Government

http://www.ci.houston.tx.us/

Residents of Houston can find out whom to yell at when roads spout geysers or whom to praise for the well-groomed parks. The city has established this page to provide information about city government and events.

Los Angeles City Fire Department

http://www.ci.la.ca.us/department/LAFD/index.html

Residents of the southern California tinderbox zone can get official advice for protecting their homes from brush fires at the Los Angeles City Fire Department home page. Find 9-1-1 instructions and special season safety tips here.

Louisiana State Legislature

http://www.house.state.la.us/

Visitors to this interactive site need only select Louisiana's Seal for the Senate or Seal for the House to access information about members, committees and selected topics. Online tutorials on the Louisiana legislative process are also provided.

Maine State Government

http://www.state.me.us/

This official state government site provides information on Maine's governor, state agencies, cities and towns. It also includes tourist and weather information.

Massachusetts State Government

http://www.state.ma.us/

Learn all you ever wanted to know but were afraid to ask about Massachusetts' state government through this page. Find out how the government is organized and what the responsibilities of different sections are.

Michigan Department of Management and Budget

http://mic1.dmb.state.mi.us/

Audit the Michigan Department of Management and Budget at this page. See how the folks in Lansing are spending the public's dough, or link to the Michigan Information Center, Michigan Environmental Science Board or Michigan Aging Services System.

Michigan Department of State

http://www.sos.state.mi.us/

The Michigan Department of State home page features resources and information concerning the state government. Visitors here can get information about license-tag renewal, state museums, elections and laws. There are also links to the state historical center, traffic quizzes, pamphlets and related sites.

Mississippi State Government Home Pages

http://www.state.ms.us/

Mississippi invites visitors to explore its Department of Economic and Community Development, Department of Education, Department of Information Technology Services, Department of Insurance and other state offices through this mix-and-match Web site.

National Conference of State Legislatures

http://www.ncsl.org/

The National Conference of State Legislatures provides this electronic clearinghouse for information from and about U.S. lawmakers on the state level. It offers articles on legislative developments, budgetary trends and putting state government information online. It also provides a springboard to individual state-government sites.

Nebraska State Government

http://www.state.ne.us/

The gateway to information about Nebraska's state government, this Web site offers links to state agencies, state-funded colleges and universities, and other Nebraska resources. Includes a searchable list of state agency personnel.

New York City Public Advocate

http://www.pubadvocate.nyc.gov/~advocate

The New York City Public Advocate's home page aims to enhance citizen involvement in city government. Included in this cyber hall are New York City municipal publications, a list of representatives, green resources, voter registration information, and more.

North Dakota's State Government

http://www.state.nd.us/

North Dakota's state government home page offers visitors a variety of information about the Peace Garden State. Included here are government resources (road reports, job opportunities, and agency home pages), educational information, and more.

Official California Legislative Information

http://www.leginfo.ca.gov/

Is it legal to marry your fish? Who the heck is the California state comptroller? Just how does a bill become a law? Find out answers to these questions and more on California law, the legislative process and legislators at the Official California Legislative Information Home Page.

Ohio Government Front Page

http://www.ohio.gov/

The State of Ohio Front Page is an introduction to Ohio state government. Visitors can link to bureaucratic departments or access personnel directories. Includes pointers to related Internet sites.

Online Sunshine

http://www.leg.state.fl.us/

Online Sunshine, a service of the Florida Legislature, contains information on current statutes and bills, lobbyist information and the legislative calendar. Includes a link to additional information.

Oregon Web Sites

http://www.oda.state.or.us/

This official Web page contains governmental links for Oregon. Visitors will find the governor's office, the Department of Agriculture and the Oregon Legislature all linked here.

Pima County Internet Information

http://www.pima.gov/

Arizona's Pima County maintains this information server for its citizens and visitors. Links to the county's Board of Supervisors, courts and Development Service Center are provided.

Portland Office, Housing and Urban Development Multifamily Division

http://www.teleport.com/~mrtom/

Those working in the field of government-subsidized multifamily housing will find that this Portland, Oregon site could save many hours of research. It provides e-mail access to U.S. Housing and Urban Development staff in Portland, training opportunities, market and economic information, application information and related links.

State and Local Governments

http://www.loc.gov/global/state/stategov.html

The Library of Congress posts these indexes for state and local governments. Along with legislative information and issues, visitors can access

regional economic data and links to hundreds of cities and state maps.

State and Local Government on the Net

http://www.webcom.com/~piper/state/states.html

This index of state and local government Internet sites allows users to run quick keyword searches. Includes a FAQ and state-specific links.

StateLaw: State Government & Legislative Info

http://lawlib.wuacc.edu/washlaw/uslaw/statelaw.html

The Washburn University School of Law, located in Topeka, Kansas maintains this page packed with links to the nation's state governments and their legislative information. Also, find links for court opinions and statutes, as well as general legislative information affecting all the states.

State of California, Office of the Governor

http://www.ca.gov/gov/governor.html

This page includes general information from the office of California Gov. Pete Wilson. Visitors will find biographical information on Wilson (the former mayor of San Diego) and his wife, as well as a selection of government documents. There also are instructions for dropping Pete a postcard.

State of North Carolina

http://www.sips.state.nc.us/

North Carolina provides this entry point into its collection of information. Visitors will find details on state agencies and related projects—including links to such places as the State Courier Service and Department of Agriculture. Links to national government resources are featured as well.

StateSearch—Sponsored by NASIRE

http://www.nasire.org/

Visitors can access online government resources across the nation with the aid of StateSearch. Use the topical index to locate links to state agencies and information sources for categories as specific as "criminal justice" and "lieutenant governors."

Texas Comptroller's Window on State Government

http://www.window.texas.gov/

This window on state government looks in on the Texas Comptroller of Public Accountants. Visitors can look over the comptroller's shoulder to see what's on the official's desk and mind.

Texas Senate

http://www.senate.state.tx.us/

Nuts-and-bolts information about Texas lawmakers and their activities is available here. Visitors will find agendas, committee schedules and pending-legislation updates. Includes a nifty ignorance-relief device that allows Texans to enter their zip code and learn who represents them.

Virginia Institute of Government

http://www.institute.virginia.edu/

Find out what makes the government agencies of Virginia tick by checking the Virginia Institute of Government site. It offers information about a growing number of cities in the state with Web resources as well as access to the Local Government Technology Electronic Mailing List.

Washington Policy and Regulation Division

http://www.wa.gov/DIS/OITO/index.html

The Washington State government provides a clearinghouse of information here on the state's technology and computing policies. Residents can access a wealth of information about how the state is spending its techno dollars and supporting home-grown computer research.

Washington State Department of Transportation

http://www.wsdot.wa.gov/

Travelers and commuters in Washington State will find an extensive collection of transportation schedules and related government resources at this informational site. Visit here to learn about transit routes, infrastructure projects and management commissions.

Washington State Legislature

http://leginfo.leg.wa.gov/

Some of the greatest minds in the Pacific Northwest display their civic smarts at the home page of Washington State legislature. Visitors can check on the status of bills, download reports of House and Senate members and follow the work of legislative committees.

Washington State Legislature Public Access System

ftp://leginfo.leg.wa.gov/pub

The Washington State Legislature's Public Access System FTP site provides access to information from the Washington State legislature. The /pub index contains a calendar, legislative process information and more.

World Wide Web Virtual Library: State Government Servers

http://www.law.indiana.edu/law/v-lib/

HEALTH AND MEDICINE

THE 25 MOST POPULAR HEALTH AND MEDICINE SITES

Action on Smoking and Health
http://www.ash.org/ash/

Alternative Medicine Home Page
http://www.pitt.edu/~cbw/altm.html

American Academy of Pediatrics
http://www.aap.org/

The Bad Bug Book
http://vm.cfsan.fda.gov/~mow/intro.html

Centers for Disease Control
http://www.cdc.gov/

The Complete Internet Sex Resource Guide
http://www.best.com/~craig/netsex.htm

Computer Related Repetitive Strain Injury
http://engr-www.unl.edu/ee/eeshop/rsi.html

Dental Related Internet Resources
http://www.nyu.edu/Dental/intres.html

Drug Database
http://pharminfo.com/drugdb/db_mnu.html

Emergency—A Guide to the Emergency Services of the World
http://www.catt.citri.edu.au/emergency/

FDA Center for Food Safety & Applied Nutrition
http://vm.cfsan.fda.gov/

First Aid Online
http://www2.vivid.net/~cicely/safety/

Images from the Visible Human Project
http://www.nlm.nih.gov/research/visible/visible_gallery.html

The Integral Yoga Web Site
http://www.webcom.com/~miraura/

Johns Hopkins Medical Institutions InfoNet: Patient Advocacy Groups
http://infonet.welch.jhu.edu/advocacy.html

MedSearch America's Physician Finder Online
http://msa2.medsearch.com/pfo/

The Medical College of Wisconsin International Travelers Clinic
http://www.intmed.mcw.edu/travel.html

Medicine
http://galaxy.einet.net/galaxy/Medicine.html

MedWeb: Disabilities
http://www.gen.emory.edu/medweb/medweb.disabled.html

The Nando Times Health & Science
http://www.nando.net/nt/health/

The Obituary Page
http://catless.ncl.ac.uk/Obituary/

Quick Information about Cancer for Patients and Their Families
http://asa.ugl.lib.umich.edu/chdocs/cancer/CANCERGUIDE.HTML

Rice Health-Info Gopher Menu
gopher://riceinfo.rice.edu/11/Safety/HealthInfo

Toxicology and Environmental Health Information Program
http://tamas.nlm.nih.gov/~boyda/htdocs/

The Urbana Atlas of Pathology
http://www.med.uiuc.edu/PathAtlasf/titlePage.html

ALTERNATIVE MEDICINE

Acupuncture.com
http://www.acupuncture.com/

The information on this page gets right to the point—the acupuncture needle point, that is. It covers other types of Eastern remedies as well, such as Qi Gong, Chinese nutrition, and herbology. Both patients and professionals will find resources here.

The Alternative Medicine Homepage
http://www.pitt.edu/~cbw/altm.html

Visitors to this site can link up for information on such alternative practices as herbal treatments, acupuncture, and chiropractic therapy. See Editor's Choice.

Celestia
http://www.celestia.com/alpha

Providing links to a variety of spirituality- and health-related Web sites, this page points visitors toward Sterling Rose Press, the Spiritual Rights Foundation and other related resources on the Internet.

Connecting with Nature
http://www.pacificrim.net/~nature/

This site explores ways to re-integrate nature into our lives. See Editor's Choice.

Global on the Web
http://www.islandnet.com/~global/

Interested in learning more about the world of spiritual techniques such as pranic and sound healing from a perspective "rooted in love, caring for all life, humanity and planet?" Drop by the nonprofit Global for a tour of its research, training, products and studies.

Holistic Internet Community
http://www.holistic.com/%7Eholistic/

The Holistic Internet Community promotes the exchange of information concerning the understanding of healing as it relates to human relationships. This page provides holistic resources, tools and links to related sites.

The People's Place on the Web
http://peopleplace.com/

Browsers interested in nutrition and alternative health can shop in this cyber marketplace for personal growth services, yoga classes and health food. The page also contains cancer information.

ARCHIVES AND INDICES

Dr. Bower's Complementary Medicine Home Page
http://galen.med.virginia.edu/~pjb3s/ComplementaryHomePage.html

Compiled by a medical doctor, this site contains a wealth of information on alternative and complementary medicine. Find out about everything from acupuncture and alternative cancer therapies to Native American healing traditions. Link to the American Complementary Practice Registry.

Homeopathic Internet Resources List
http://antenna.nl/homeoweb/resource.html

Fans of alternative healing techniques can access a medley of informative reading materials via this handy map of homeopathic Internet resources. Conveniently categorized by resource type, guests can browse through dozens of links ranging from medical databases and publications to manufacturers of pharmaceutical products.

a2z EDITOR'S CHOICE

The Alternative Medicine Homepage
http://www.pitt.edu/~cbw/altm.html

Not surprisingly, university library staffs prepare some of the best collections of electronic reference materials. The Alternative Medicine Homepage (assembled by the Falk Library of the Health Sciences at the University of Pittsburgh) is a salubrious example. These links explore the world of unorthodox therapeutic practices such as folk medicine, herbal treatments, faith healing, chiropractic, acupuncture, massage, and music therapy. Long scorned by the medical establishment as mere quackery, alternative medicine practices have slowly begun to shed their back-alley reputation and reach wider acceptance among patients dissatisfied with the assembly-line practices at many doctors' offices. In 1992, the Office of Alternative Medicine was established at the National Institutes of Health with the purpose of evaluating the efficacy of alternative treatments and helping to integrate them into mainstream medical practice. While there are indisputably some snake oil peddlers in the bunch, an overwhelming body of evidence shows that many of these "outmoded" treatments work for many patients, especially the modalities that take a holistic, mind-body interaction approach to wellness. The Alternative Medicine Homepage includes links to the significant sites and collections on the Internet so that interested wellness explorers can learn more about this fascinating field.
—*Reviewed by Kathleen McFadden*

The Alternative Medicine Homepage
Falk Library of the Health Sciences
University of Pittsburgh

This page is a jumpstation for sources of information on unconventional, unorthodox, unproven, or alternative, complementary, innovative, integrative therapies.

Homeopathy Home Page

http://www.dungeon.com/~cam/homeo.html

The Homeopathy Home Page is a meta-index of homeopathic resources for both practitioners and patients. Access databases, libraries, organizations and other homeopathy sites. Explore Homeopathy Frequently Asked Questions (FAQs), subscribe to a mailing list, or locate homeopathic practitioners worldwide.

Internet Medical and Health Care Resources

http://www.teleport.com/~amrta/iway.html

The Internet Medical and Health Care Resources page features pointers to health care, nutrition and alternative medicine resources. From acupuncture to yoga, with the Family Health and Medical Matrix pages in between, these resources cover a wide range of issues.

Mind & Body Links and Articles

http://www.stud.unit.no/~olavb/mindbody.html

Part of a personal home page, this extensive directory of mind and body resources provides links to information about meditation, yoga, vegetarian recipes, psychology and self-help. There are also instructions for joining the Wellness mailing list.

WorldWide Wellness

http://www.doubleclickd.com/wwwellness.html

Visit the WorldWide Wellness site for resources and information devoted to holistic living. This site features a women's section and contains a directory of holistic health care professionals, health fair conference schedules, and a linked index to related alternative health sites.

---

a2z EDITOR'S CHOICE

Connecting with Nature

http://www.pacificrim.net/~nature/

Long before the Industrial Revolution, long before agribusiness, long before the Computer Revolution, our ancestors knew that we were inextricably bound to the energies of the Earth—that our spiritual and mental health depended in great measure on our integration into the natural order. At our current spot on the historical timeline, the traffic, cell phones, grocery stores, and cities have cut us off from the natural world. We see the effects everyday, from personal unhappiness to vague feelings of dislocation to a yearning for something that actually matters. Project Nature-Connect seeks to bridge the gap between the modern and the ancient, by providing psychological insights and tranquility through ecological activities and a free online course. Here's a restorative for the modern soul "that lets thoughtful sensory contacts with Earth catalyze wellness, spirit and responsibility." —*Reviewed by Kathleen McFadden*

CONNECTING WITH NATURE

Eric S. Chen --LINE AROUND THE WORLD-- Bob Park

TOP 5% OF ALL WEB SITES POINT This site has been selected as being in the top 5% of all web pages. For more information see Point's homepage.

Are you discouraged by the growing violence, mental illness and hatred in our society? Does the destruction of our forests, wildlife and oceans cause you distress? Help heal the wounds inflicted on our planet and ourselves. Project NatureConnect is a fun and innovative program offering books, email courses, workshops and a mailing list that reconnect us with personal and global sanity.

-Net Happenings Digest, MIDnet October, 1995

The University of Global Education

ASSOCIATIONS AND ORGANIZATIONS

The Health Action Network Society (HANS)

http://www.hans.org/

This Canadian nonprofit organization, dedicated to providing "information on alternative health," solicits members at this site. Nonmember browsers are treated to a page sampler covering subjects from acupuncture and chiropractic to pesticides and practitioners.

International Network for Interfaith Health Practices

http://www.interaccess.com/ihpnet/

A joint project of The Interfaith Health Program and the Congregational Nurse Program of Saint Francis Hospital, this forum welcomes people of all religions to explore the relationship between spirituality and health. Health surveys and a sampling of health-promotion models are featured.

The Life Extension Foundation

http://www.lef.org/lef/index.html/

The ultimate goal of this nonprofit organization is "physical immortality." In the meantime, the Life Extension Foundation is dedicated to helping its members live longer by sharing information about the latest life extension research, offering "the most advanced life extension products in the world at discount prices," and keeping members up to date on relevant legal and political developments.

BIRTH METHODS

The Homebirth Choice

http://www.efn.org/~djz/birth/homebirth.html

Pregnant women making decisions about where and how to have their babies can consult the Homebirth Choice site for information on midwifery. Visitors can also find guidelines on how to select a midwife.

CHIROPRACTIC

Chiropractic Online Today

http://www.panix.com/~tonto1/dc.html

This resource for chiropractic professionals is home to a referral directory, a "chiro discussion page," and links to news of interest to the professional community, as well as non-pros interested in the field.

The Chiropractic Page

http://www.mbnet.mb.ca/~jwiens/chiro.html

The Chiropractic Page corrals electronic resources for professional practitioners, students, prospective patients, and the health care provider community. Educational programs are outlined and research data is made available here.

CHIROWEB

http://www.chiroweb.com/

A chiropractor's delight, CHIROWEB serves up an all-inclusive medley of resources for both medical professionals and patients alike. Drop by the domicile of Dr. Brett for personal answers and info-packages such as "a comprehensive history of chiropractic" and "glossary of chiropractic terms" or indulge yourself at the "Feel Better Store." CHIROWEB also helps guests locate the chiropractor nearest them and track down special promotion offers.

HERBS

Legalize It!

http://www.mojones.com/mother_jones/ND94/castleman.html

The goal of "Legalize It!" is to urge the FDA to allow herbal remedy labels to state that they are effective treatments. Read about how herbs can help fight high cholesterol, motion sickness, infection, and more.

UW Medicinal Herb Garden Home Page

http://www.nnlm.nlm.nih.gov/pnr/uwmhg/index.html

The University of Washington Medicinal Herb Garden offers maps, walking tours and garden news at this site. Herbalists and health care workers can consult the garden's index by botanical or common name.

INSTITUTES AND SCHOOLS

New York Open Center

http://www.panix.com/~openctr/

The New York Open Center is the largest urban holistic learning center in the United States, and this site contains information about courses and workshops on topics such as alternative health and bodywork disciplines, depth psychologies, sociocultural issues, spiritual and meditative teachings and multicultural arts.

Southwest School of Botanical Medicine

http://www.rt66.com/hrbmoore/HOMEPAGE/HomePage.html

The Southwest School of Botanical Medicine in Albuquerque, New Mexico offers a five-month residency program and weekend workshops. Access the school's catalog here, along with a database of around 700 JPEG images of medicinal plants and a collection of manuals, folios, and classic texts.

MASSAGE AND STRESS THERAPY

The Integral Yoga Web Site

http://www.webcom.com/~miraura/

Read a general introduction to yoga and browse information about the spiritual path of Integral Yoga through this site. It features biographies of the founders of Integral Yoga along with published works and information about upcoming events around the world.

Noodles' Panic-Anxiety Page

http://www.algy.com/anxiety/anxiety.html

Combat your stress with the relaxation techniques provided here. Find all kinds of methods for controlling panic attacks, from Eastern techniques to nutrition. With any luck, you'll have those shaking hands steady in no time.

Rolfing

http://www.bnt.com/~rolfer/

This promotional page for a Virginia-based Rolfer explores Rolfing massage therapy and explains the benefits of a ten-session program. General background information on the Rolf Institute and its founder, Ida Rolf, is also featured.

Sedona Center for the Alexander Technique

http://wizard.sedona.net/life/alex/

The Arizona-based Sedona Center for the Alexander Technique provides this overview of the technique, a method for reducing stress and obtaining greater relaxation. Information on classes and books for sale is also included.

PUBLISHERS AND PUBLICATIONS

Aesclepian Chronicles

http://www.forthrt.com/~chronicl/homepage.html

Maintained by the Synergistic Health Center in Chapel Hill, North Carolina, this online journal contains book reviews, informational articles and information related to the holistic, mind-and-body-in-balance approach to medical care. The site includes indexes of complementary and allopathic links, and you can *even* find out who Aesclepius was.

Good Medicine Magazine

http://none.coolware.com/health/good_med/ThisIssue.html

This electronic version of Good Medicine magazine provides articles on preventive medicine and the integration of traditional and holistic healing.

Wellspring Media

http://wellmedia.com/

Wellspring Media backs the notion of "total wellness" of mind, body and spirit with a collection of articles and presentations that include information on physical and spiritual health. The company also sells videotapes, and online ordering is available.

DEATH AND DYING

DeathNET

http://www.islandnet.com/~deathnet/

"Ask not for whom the bell tolls" is the greeting at DeathNET, "where the surfin' stops." This international archive specializes in all aspects of death, with a "sincere respect for every point of view."

The Obituary Page

http://catless.ncl.ac.uk/Obituary/

As the title implies, this page lists the names and dates of dead notables and not-so-notables, categorized by occupational field. Some of the more famous persons have links to biographical or related sites. Features include a virtual memory garden in which anyone's death can be recorded, instructions for registering a death and links to other death-related sites.

DENTISTRY

Amalgam-Related Illness FAQ
http://www.algonet.se/~leif/AmFAQigr.html
Visitors to this page can read online or download a Frequently Asked Questions (FAQs) file concerning mercury poisoning from amalgam dental fillings. The site also features an annotated list of related articles.

DentalAssist
http://www.dentistry.com/
Aesthetic Dentistry Associates' (ADA) DentalAssist offers advice for personal dental care and information about new advances in dentistry. This page also showcases articles presented by the ADA and links to the California Dental Association.

Dental-Telecommunications-Network
http://www.onramp.net/Den-Tel-Net/
Den-Tel-Net is designed to "further the knowledge and understanding of dentistry for the 21st century." It is sponsored by dental specialists throughout North America and provides links to a large team of physicians.

Dentistry On-Line
http://www.cityscape.co.uk/users/ad88/dent.htm
Dentists and patients alike will find information in this international forum for dentistry. Papers cover topics that range from what kind of toothbrush to buy to restorative dentistry. Browse the dentistry bookshop, submit an article, link to other dentistry sites or check out the German version.

ARCHIVES AND INDICES

Dental Education Resources on the Web
http://www.derweb.ac.uk/derweb.html
The University of Sheffield offers this online library of dental images for use in teaching and research. The library contains more than 600 images, and visitors can view a complete index of documents with brief descriptions. Links are provided to additional teaching resources and dentistry information.

Dental Related Internet Resources
http://www.ddental-resources.com
New York University's College of Dentistry maintains this site of dental-related Internet resources. Dozens of links include educational sites, bulletin boards, dental associations and commercial home pages.

Internet Dentistry Resources
http://indy.radiology.uiowa.edu/Beyond/Dentistry/sites.html
The Internet Dentistry Resources site contains links to dental schools, bulletin boards and newsgroups. Includes listings of related organizations and associations, as well as commercial and personal home pages for dentists.

ASSOCIATIONS AND ORGANIZATIONS

The American Dental Association
http://www.ada.org/
Visitors who sink their teeth into this Web site can view professional and consumer information provided by the American Dental Association (ADA). Electronic publications of interest to the organization's members reside here, along with dental society directories and listings of ADA products and services.

INSTITUTES AND SCHOOLS

Columbia-Presbyterian Medical Center: School of Dental and Oral Surgery
http://cait.cpmc.columbia.edu/health.sci/dental.toc/
The School of Dental and Oral Surgery at Columbia-Presbyterian Medical Center in New York City provides an overview of the school, its programs of study and faculty listings. Includes descriptions of facilities, educational resources and admissions guidelines.

Humboldt University: Department of Periodontology and Synoptic Dentistry
http://www2.rz.hu-berlin.de/inside/paro/
Humboldt University in Berlin presents information about its dental school, with staff publications, academic program overviews, directory information, and a list of dentistry links.

PROFESSIONAL RESOURCES

The DENTalTRAUMA Server
http://www.unige.ch/smd/orthotr.html
Sponsored by the University of Geneva School of Dentistry, this site is "dedicated to the dissemination of basic and therapeutic knowledge on dentofacial trauma" and describes the information collected during a 520-patient study of dentoalveolar traumas.

DISABILITIES

Archimedes Project
http://kanpai.stanford.edu/arch/arch.html
The Archimedes Project at Stanford University aims to give people with disabilities access to the world via information technology. The project is profiled on this page.

Blind Children's Center
http://www1.primenet.com/bcc/
This California-based nonprofit organization outlines its programs for blind and visually impaired children—including an educational preschool, family services and infant stimulation. Contact information and related links are provided.

Canine Companions for Independence
http://caninecompanions.org/
Canine Companions for Independence is a nonprofit organization serving people with disabilities by providing trained service, hearing and social dogs. Get detailed information on the organization at this home page or link to other service dog and related organization sites.

Center for Independent Living
http://www.wenet.net/~cil/
The Center for Independent Living is a Berkeley, California organization devoted to helping disabled persons lead active and productive lives. Visitors to its Web site will find an overview of the mission and activities of this group.

The Other Side of the Web: Ed Arnold's Home Page
http://www.csn.net/~era/
Digress with Ed as he talks about himself, then attend Ed's intercession on behalf of Aul Pedajas, an Estonian suffering from spinal muscular atrophy. Ed seeks to form a virtual "Joshua Committee," a group committed to help a disabled person do what the person cannot do alone.

Royal National Institute for the Blind

http://www.rnib.org.uk/

London's Royal National Institute for the Blind provides a straightforward, nontechnical discussion of the eye and how it works, the causes and prevention of visual impairment, and the symptoms and treatment of eye diseases. The site includes a guide to the Institute's services, a reference library and links to related sites.

University Affiliated Program for Developmental Disabilities

http://www.lsi.ukans.edu/uap/uap.htm

The University of Kansas unveils information about its University Affiliated Program on Developmental Disabilities through this page. Program director Steve Schroeder offers a history of the interdepartmental cooperative that "develops alternatives to institutional care" for people with developmental disabilities.

ARCHIVES AND INDICES

American Foundation for the Blind Gopher Menu

http://www.afb.org/afb/

The American Foundation for the Blind maintains this informational gopher server. Visitors will find links to its information and technology centers, government affairs groups, public policy materials, and other helpful resources.

Americans with Disabilities Act Document Center

http://janweb.icdi.wvu.edu/kinder/

The Americans with Disabilities Act (ADA) Document Center offers extensive information about the ADA statute and regulations here. Visitors can download various forms and find out what is covered by the act. The site also includes job information and an index to disability resources on the Net.

Blind Links

http://www.seidata.com/~marriage/rblind.html

Blind Links, a comprehensive index of resources for the visually impaired, offers links to related adaptive technologies, training programs, publications, employment services and much more. Includes government and commercial resources.

Cornucopia of Disability Information Gopher Server

http://cod.buffalo.edu/

Cornucopia of Disability Information (CODI) maintains this gopher server as a community resource for those seeking information about disability issues. The selections here lead visitors to various institutions, organizations and databases

that offer the latest in research and rights for many different types of disabilities.

Deaf Gopher

gopher://burrow.cl.msu.edu:70/11/msu/dept/deaf

Michigan State University offers this gopher server as a resource for the deaf and hearing impaired. Browsers can access university information, deaf resources in the state of Michigan and more.

MedWeb: Disabilities

http://www.gen.emory.edu/medweb/medweb.disabled.html

This index to disability information on the Web is maintained by Emory University. The site contains a long list of links to disability-related guides, documents, databases, bibliographies and more.

National Library Service for the Blind and Physically Handicapped

http://lcweb.loc.gov/nls/nls.html

The Library of Congress provides a page for the National Library Service for the Blind and Physically Handicapped. Among the resources are an audio clip from a talking book and a listing of state and regional libraries for the blind and handicapped.

National Rehabilitation Information

http://disability.com/

Link to information on disabilities at the National Rehabilitation Information Center home page, where guests can check out information on and publications from the center, link to a disability database or check out other resources.

WebABLE

http://www.yuri.org/webable/

Computer users with disabilities can search a directory of accessibility resources, read about new products and participate in online conferences at this site.

ASSOCIATIONS AND ORGANIZATIONS

Audies Web

http://www.tsi.it/contrib/audies/home.html

This home page for the Audies Association, a national association in Italy dedicated to the fight against deafness, assembles a number of deaf-related links—including news and clinical reports. The page also hosts a variety of unrelated links chosen by the president of the association, in-

cluding an extensive section on finance and stock trading. In Italian and English.

Deaf World Web

http://deafworldweb.org/dww/

Deaf World Web serves as a meeting point for the global deaf community. The deaf-owned, deaf-run service offers its content in English and French. Users can join the directory and search for info on research covering everything from living with hearing loss to sociocultural resources.

COMMERCIAL PRODUCTS AND SERVICES

Apple Computers: The Disability Connection

http://www2.apple.com/disability/welcome.html

Computer users with disabilities can learn methods for entering information commands into their computers at this site. Expanded keyboards, voice input and screens for braille readers are among the many options available. Links to other disability resources are provided.

Disability Resources from Evan Kemp Associates

http://disability.com/

Evan Kemp Associates provides information, products and services to people with disabilities. Visit this site to access its article and speech archive, and browse its online Disability Mall. Includes links to related Internet resources.

Equal Access to Software and Information (EASI)

http://www.rit.edu/~easi/

People with disabilities can locate news and discussion about accessible computing technologies thanks to EASI, Equal Access to Software and Information. Look here for hardware and software products, as well as services for users with specialized needs.

Gus Communications Inc.

http://www.gusinc.com/

Visitors to this promotional page can learn about Gus Communications Inc., a company that produces computer-based communication augmentation systems for people with disabilities. Includes descriptions of the company's products, customer testimonials, and ordering information.

Kokoro Web

http://www.ibm.co.jp/kokoroweb/

People with disabilities can find information about adapting computers to fit their needs via this page from IBM of Japan. Visitors can also find information about the Kokoro Resource Book for computer users with disabilities. In Japanese; top page in English.

RESEARCH

Adaptive Technology Resource Centre

http://www.utoronto.ca/artc/

Find out about alternative keyboards and mouse systems, screen magnifiers, voice recognition systems and braille displays from the Adaptive Technology Resource Centre at the University of Toronto. Research focus at the Center is on developing solutions to the challenges faced by users of adaptive technology.

Center for Assessment and Demographic Studies

http://gri.gallaudet.edu/

The Center for Assessment and Demographic Studies at Gallaudet University researches the deaf and hearing impaired in the United States. The site includes a look at the center, its articles and statistical data.

Trace Research and Development Center

http://www.trace.wisc.edu/

The Trace Research and Development Center in Madison, Wis., offers information on its research, resources, design guidelines, training and direct services that make access to computer information systems easier for the disabled.

ENVIRONMENTAL MEDICINE

Information Ventures, Inc. (IVI) Online

http://infoventures.com/

IVI is a scientific information service. Here visitors will find EMF-Link, which addresses the health effects of electric and magnetic fields (EMF), current literature on occupational safety and health, the Environmental Health Clearinghouse, and CancerWeb. Some documents can be accessed for free; fees are charged for others.

The Lead Tester

http://www.branch.com/epa/

The Lead Tester is a kit that tests for high levels of lead in the home. This site has information about the element itself, lead poisoning, and the testing kit. Online ordering is available.

National Institute of Environmental Health Sciences

http://www.niehs.nih.gov/

The National Institute of Environmental Health Sciences provides access to a number of its resource servers. Visitors will find journals, research programs, databases and statistics for several environmental disciplines.

National Institute of Environmental Health Sciences Gopher Menu

gopher://gopher.niehs.nih.gov:70/1

The National Institute of Health Sciences (NIHS) offers this gopher server, with a variety of organizational and environmental health sciences information. Library and technical resources, program and research grant information, and links to other servers can be found here.

Poison Control Centre Database

http://medweb.nus.sg/PID/PCC/centre.html

Locate poison control centers around the globe using the Poison Control Center Database. Whether you've ingested lethal toxins in Algeria or stumbled across a poisonous substance in Zimbabwe, an A to Z listing of worldwide facilities leaves few bases uncovered.

HUMAN-MADE TOXINS

Agency for Toxic Substances and Disease Registry

http://atsdr1.atsdr.cdc.gov:8080/atsdrhome.html

The Agency for Toxic Substances and Disease Registry (ATSDR) of the U.S. Department of Health and Human Services provides this searchable site. Find ATSDR news, links to related agencies and departments, and a database of information on hazardous substances and their health effects.

Agency for Toxic Substances and Disease Registry (ATSDR) Science Corner

http://atsdr1.atsdr.cdc.gov:8080/cx.html

The Agency for Toxic Substances and Disease Registry maintains this online guide to environmental health information on the Web. Use the search tool, access information about the Agency, find out about hazardous waste conferences and more.

Agency for Toxic Substances and Disease Registry—EPA's Top 20 Hazardous Substances

http://atsdr1.atsdr.cdc.gov:8080/cxcx3.html

The U.S. Environmental Protection Agency is required by law to update a list of the world's most hazardous substances each year. This list, from 1993, ranks lead as the number one offender, followed by arsenic (with the dreaded DDT coming in at number 12). Includes links to toxicologic profiles and public health statements.

Hazardous Substance Release/Health Effects Database

http://atsdr1.atsdr.cdc.gov:8080/hazdat.html

The Hazardous Substance Release/Health Effects (HazDat) database provides access to information on the release of hazardous substance from Superfund sites, other emergency events and documentation of substance effects on human health. The database is searchable by site, toxicological profile or by public health statements.

Medical Management Guidelines for Acute Chemical Exposures: Patient Information

http://atsdr1.atsdr.cdc.gov:8080/mmg.html

The Agency for Toxic Substances and Disease Registry developed this user-friendly guide of Frequently Asked Questions (FAQs) concerning acute chemical exposure. Visitors can find information on chemicals—from ammonia to xylene.

National Library of Medicine TOXNET Search Interfaces

http://tamas.nlm.nih.gov/~boyda/htdocs/TOXNET/experimental-forms.html

The Specialized Information Services Division of the National Library of Medicine maintains this informational site. Visitors will find a variety of TOXNET search interfaces and experimental databases.

Pesticide Poisoning Handbook

http://gnv.ifas.ufl.edu/~fairsweb/text/pp/19729.html

This site features an index to pesticide poisonings by symptoms and signs, with comprehensive information on specific pesticides and their uses, toxicology and treatment regimens.

Toxicology and Environmental Health Information Program

http://tamas.nlm.nih.gov/~boyda/htdocs/

The Toxicology and Environmental Health Information Program provides information here on environmental and occupational health. This site links to TOXNET fact sheets, databases, the National Library of Medicine Web site and other related sites.

PLANT AND ANIMAL TOXINS

Poisons Information Database

http://vhp.nus.sg/PID/PID.html

The Poisons Information Database includes a catalog of natural toxins and poisons found in animals, snakes, and plants of the Asia-Pacific region and provides directories of antivenoms, toxinologists and poison control centers around the world. Information is available in English and Chinese.

Poisons Information Database— Antivenoms

http://medweb.nus.sg/PID/AV/antivenom.html

The Antivenom Database contains recipes and formulas for combating the effects of the poison from venomous creatures. Visitors will find an extensive collection of databases that includes antidotes for scorpion, spider, snake, and tick bites and stings.

ETHICS AND LEGAL ISSUES

Forensic Science Reference List

http://ash.lab.r1.fws.gov/

The Forensic Science Web Server provides pointers to information sources on the application of natural and physical sciences to legal matters. Includes links to medical, educational and governmental sites.

Institute for Jewish Medical Ethics

http://www.hia.com/hia/medethic/

The Institute For Jewish Medical Ethics of the Hebrew Academy of San Francisco seeks to identify underlying principles of Jewish law as they relate to medicine and analyze the efficacy of these principles as they apply to specific medical problems. Visitors can learn more about the Institute and access information about its annual conferences at this site.

The Journal of Biblical Ethics in Medicine

http://www.usit.net/public/CAPO/jbem.html

The Center for the Advancement of Paleo Orthodoxy (CAPO), a biblical and historic consortium, provides articles on a variety of topics, including ethical and religious conflicts in medical practice and teen sexuality. Visitors can link to CAPO's home page, the Augustine Institute (Ethics) or the Calvin Institute (Theology).

MacLean Center for Clinical Medical Ethics

http://ccme-mac4.bsd.uchicago.edu/CCMEHomePage.html

The MacLean Center for Clinical Medical Ethics at the University of Chicago posts course and faculty information here. The site advises that "Ethics is Easy...Life is Hard" and lists an index to medical and bioethics sites on the Net.

Medical College of Wisconsin Bioethics Online Service

http://www.mcw.edu/bioethics/

The Bioethics Center at the Medical College of Wisconsin maintains this informational site, featuring news and announcements, academic texts and periodicals, database resources, and more. Includes keyword searches for internal documents and links to major Internet search engines.

Psychiatry & the Law

http://ua1vm.ua.edu/~jhooper/

Psychiatry & the Law, the forensic psychiatry resource page of the University of Alabama, offers information about legal issues surrounding mental illness. Visit here for landmark cases, U.S. Supreme Court Rulings, links to psychiatry and law databases and more.

FAMILY MEDICAL ALMANAC

EMERGENCY MEDICINE

Emergency Medical Services

http://galaxy.tradewave.com/editors/fritz-nordengren/ems.html

At the Emergency Medical Services (EMS) site find resources ranging from step-by-step medical emergency instructions to home pages of medical dramas on television. Link to other EMS sites, online medical 'zines and related emergency organizations.

First Aid Online

http://www.prairienet.org/~autumn/firstaid/

First Aid Online presents instructions for basic first aid, with an emphasis on accidents that occur in the home. Information is provided on shock, poisoning, breathing difficulties and more. The site also features links to online medical resources.

University of Texas Health Science Center at San Antonio Trauma Home Page

http://rmstewart.uthscsa.edu/

The University of Texas Health Science Center at San Antonio maintains this site focusing on injury, injury prevention and surgical critical care. Visitors will find news, activities updates, patient presentations, physician contact information, and an index of related links.

GENERAL WELLNESS

Canadian Health Network

http://www.hwc.ca/

The Canadian Health Network has one mission: "to help the people of Canada maintain and improve their health." But everyone can benefit from the family medicine information provided here, which includes research and health topics. In French and English.

Dr. Bil's Cool Medical Site of the Week

http://www.hooked.net/users/wcd/cmsotw.html

Dr. Bil's Cool Medical Site of the Week points Web surfers toward interesting sites—some serious, some hilarious, all medically oriented. Includes a link to the home page of this site's creator.

Duke Community and Family Medicine Home Page

http://dmi-www.mc.duke.edu/cfm/cfmhome.html

This guide to community and family medicine resources, maintained by the Duke University Medical Center, offer links to its health-related divisions. Visit here for information on biometry, diet and fitness, family medicine, medical informatics, occupational and environmental medicine and other medical disciplines.

Healthwise

http://www.columbia.edu/cu/healthwise

The Columbia University Health Service provides a very useful and engaging interactive question and answer service for health here, See Editor's Choice.

Institute of HeartMath (IHM)

http://www.heartmath.org/welcome.html

IHM, a nonprofit corporation located in Boulder Creek, California, seeks to study the effects of stress on the body and apply the findings to proactive measures for improving the quality of life. Visitors to this page can access information about the work of the institute and its outreach programs, or link to Planetary Publications for topical literature.

NicNet: The Arizona Nicotine and Tobacco Network

http://ahsc.arizona.edu/nicnet

Get the impetus and support at this page to quit that tobacco habit! From information on tobacco company manipulation to the effects of second-hand smoke on kids, the news and research updates at this site are grim. Nonsmoker wannabes can access a variety of help sheets and support groups.

Stretching and Flexibility

http://www.cs.huji.ac.il/papers/rma/stretching_toc.html

This page features "everything you *never* wanted to know" about stretching and flexibility. This primer, which is organized into links, has information on the physiology of stretching, types of stretches, and detailed instructions on how to stretch properly.

Worldguide: Health & Fitness Forum Welcome Page

http://www.worldguide.com/Fitness/hf.html

Does an apple a day keep the doctor away? What are the best types of cardiovascular exercise? Find out at the Worldguide: Health & Fitness Forum Welcome Page, where visitors can link to health and fitness information of all sorts, or check out related software and publications.

WorldWide Wellness

http://www.doubleclickd.com/wwwellness.html

Visit the WorldWide Wellness site for resources and information devoted to holistic living. This site features a women's section and contains a directory of holistic health care professionals, health fair conference schedules and a linked index to related alternative health sites.

JOURNALS AND NEWSLETTERS

International Health News

http://vvv.com/HealthNews/

Visitors to this page will learn how to subscribe to International Health News. The publication tries to provide information that will help individuals take responsibility for their own health. Visitors can read subscription information and comments from readers.

The Medical Reporter

http://www.dash.com/netro/nwx/tmr/tmr.html

This online magazine provides health articles of both breadth and depth. See Editor's Choice.

The Nando Times Health & Science

http://www.nando.net/nt/health/

Check the day's top medical and science stories courtesy of the Nando Times.

LIBRARIES, DATABASES, AND INDICES

GeroWeb

http://www.iog.wayne.edu/GeroWeb.html

The Gero-informatics workgroup at Wayne State University offers this online resource for students, educators and practitioners. Check out the virtual library for a wealth of information on aging and links to educational facilities, government agencies, organizations and related archival material.

---

a2z EDITOR'S CHOICE

Healthwise

http://www.columbia.edu/cu/healthwise/

The Columbia University Health Service presents Go Ask Alice, an interactive health question and answer service. Alice isn't afraid of your questions, no matter how difficult or potentially embarrassing. There's no obfuscation or half answers here. Alice responds authoritatively and engagingly, but never in a condescending way. She treats all questions seriously and provides facts, comfort, and suggestions for sources of additional help. Fortunately for Netizens, all of Alice's past questions and answers are archived and readers can search or browse through discussions of sex, relationships, drugs and alcohol, fitness and nutrition, emotional well-being, and general health. Alice gets her share of bizarre questions, such as whether nose picking is a health hazard, but she also deals with a variety of serious, real-world issues such as the emotional fallout following abortion, obsessive-compulsive disorders, cervical cancer, alcoholic binges, sexually transmitted diseases, exercise problems, dietary guidelines, and more. Even if you don't have a specific question, the Alice archives are a good read and a marvelous source of information.
—*Reviewed by Kathleen McFadden*

Healthwise is the Health Education and Wellness program of Columbia University Health Service. We are committed to helping you make choices that will contribute to your personal health and happiness, the well-being of others, and to the planet we share.

An Interactive Health Question & Answer Service

HealthGate

http://www.healthgate.com/

HealthGate is the Internet source for news and information on health issues. The searchable database contains a vast storehouse of medical information for professionals and patients alike.

Internet Health Resources Home Page

http://www.ihr.com/

With the goal of helping individuals take more personal responsibility for their health care and wellness, this site features pointers to online health information, arranged in alphabetical order by topic. Featured topics range from allergies and attention deficit disorder to vegetarian recipes and women's health. The site also includes lists of state and national health care organizations, relevant publications and more.

Internet Medical and Health Care Resources

http://www.teleport.com/~amrta/iway.html

The Internet Medical and Health Care Resources page features pointers to health care, nutrition and alternative medicine resources. From acupuncture to yoga, with the Family Health and Medical Matrix pages in between, these resources cover a wide range of issues.

Med Help

http://medhlp.netusa.net/

Med Help, a nonprofit organization, offers subscriptions to its online medical libraries and resources. Subscribers can download thousands of articles from this site or Telnet to its searchable archive. The site also hosts links to other health-related sites such as the Pain Institute in Chicago.

Medicine

http://galaxy.einet.net/galaxy/Medicine.html

Galaxy's hyperguide to medicine provides access to information on a range of topics, from chiropractic care to nuclear medicine. The references provided are oriented to both consumers and professionals.

TRAVEL MEDICINE

Global Emergency Medical Services

http://www.globalmed.com/

Global Emergency Medical Services helps travelers and expatriates find medical assistance in foreign countries. With a global base of providers, this service offers membership to "MEDPASS," a program that directs emergency phone calls, links patients with professionals and maintains individual medical records for physician reference.

The Medical College of Wisconsin International Travelers Clinic (ITC)

http://www.intmed.mcw.edu/travel.html

The International Travelers Clinic (ITC) provides a fact-filled tip book covering general information, diseases and immunizations, and environmental hazards. Hot links include the CIA World Factbook and U.S. State Department Travel Warnings.

Stanford Travel Medicine Service

http://www-leland.stanford.edu/~naked/stms.html

Get information on vaccinations, travel advice, and prevention at this site. See Editor's Choice.

---

a2z EDITOR'S CHOICE

The Medical Reporter

http://www.dash.com/netro/nwx/tmr/tmr.html

The Medical Reporter's masthead states that this free online journal emphasizes "preventive medicine, primary care, patient advocacy, education, and support, as well as topics in sub-specialty medicine of interest to men and women." That's a dauntingly *wide* scope, but this monthly electronic publication lives up to its promise. Readers will find a combination of reprints and original material covering up-to-the-minute news on a broad spectrum of health issues and recent research findings. Subjects of the full-text articles in a recent issue include depression, the HIV home test system, chlamydia screening, and the AMA's recommendations for preventing summer recreation injuries. Published solely in cyberspace since April 1995, the journal's past issues are archived and can be read online. The May 1996 edition contains a superb article on pap smears and cervical cancer, as well as a frightening discussion of "mad cow disease" and a report on the incidence and treatment of rosacea. Want to know more about antibiotic treatment for ulcers, infertility, cerebral palsy research, or the use of black tea for stroke prevention? How about impotence, long-term hormone treatment, endometriosis, or antioxidants? With its broad range and wide target audience, The Medical Reporter truly has something for everyone. —*Reviewed by Kathleen McFadden*

 The Medical Reporter   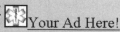Your Ad Here!

The Medical Reporter, June 1996 Vol II, No 3

Past Issues of The Medical Reporter (Apr.1995–May.1996)

Masthead

Write to the Editor

Sites Linked to TMR

HOSPITALS AND CLINICS

Brigham & Women's Hospital Home Page

http://bustoff.bwh.harvard.edu/

Harvard University's Brigham & Women's Hospital puts its divisions and departments online here.

Explore the hospital's research, education and treatment resources or link to its gopher to access the hospital's information systems.

Brighton Health Care National Health Service Trust Home Page

http://www.pavilion.co.uk/HealthServices/BrightonHealthCare/

The Brighton Health Care National Health Service Trust features facts and figures about the medical services it provides to residents of England's south coast. Includes contact information for the trust's regional hospitals.

---

a2z EDITOR'S CHOICE

Stanford Travel Medicine Service

http://www-leland.stanford.edu/~naked/stms.html

If you're planning an international excursion or a wilderness adventure, the trip won't be much fun if you snag a case of yellow fever, so add the Stanford Travel Medicine Service to your itinerary. The site provides a good overview of the vaccinations required for overseas travel, along with creepy disease descriptions and vaccination contra-indications. Find valuable travel alerts and information on malaria, diarrhea, and gastrointestinal problems (known in less polite circles as Montezuma's Revenge), acute mountain sickness, and HIV. The general travel advice and suggestions on medical kits, travel insurance, and traveling with children can all help prepare travelers for those unexpected twists in the trail. Particularly useful is the section on how to treat diarrhea in children and preventive measures for avoiding parasitic infection. A world of reference links are provided, including the Centers for Disease Control, National Institutes of Health, and World Health Organization. The CDC site in particular contains a suitcase full of useful travel information. Another excellent link is The International Travelers Clinic from the Medical College of Wisconsin. And for the indecisive traveler, the U.S. State Department Travel Warnings will advise you where *not* to go. —*Reviewed by Kathleen McFadden*

Comprehensive Healthcare For International and Wilderness Travelers

Stanford Travel Medicine Service

Eric L. Weiss, MD, DTM & H
Director, Stanford Travel Medicine Service

Cedars-Sinai Medical Center Home Page

http://www.csmc.edu/

A visitor's information booth for Cedars-Sinai Medical Center (CSMC) operates at this site. Examine hospital services and get help negotiating health care plans. This site caters to the health care consumer.

Children's Hospital at Stanford

http://www-med.stanford.edu/MedCenter/LPCH/

The Lucille Salter Packard Children's Hospital is located on the campus of Stanford University. Visitors to this site will find a general overview of the hospital and its resources, including research and education.

Children's Medical Center Home Page

http://galen.med.virginia.edu/~smb4v/cmchome.html

Located at the University of Virginia, the Children's Medical Center maintains this page detailing its medical services and educational programs. Includes links to related sites.

Cleveland Clinic Foundation

http://www.ccf.org/

The Cleveland Clinic Foundation gives an overview of its patient care and research activities here. Visitors can request an appointment online and take a virtual tour or follow the latest research issuing from the clinic.

CPMCnet: Columbia-Presbyterian Medical Center

http://cpmcnet.columbia.edu/

This site serves as the home page for the Columbia University Health Sciences Division and Presbyterian Medical Center. Among other choices, visitors can link to departments and organizations, news and information files, and clinical resource files.

Home Page for the Department of Medicine—St. Vincent's and Geelong Hospitals

http://www.medstv.unimelb.edu.au/

Australia's University of Melbourne, Department of Medicine provides a home page for these two hospitals in Melbourne. Links include research activities, job vacancies and medical resources.

Index to Health Services

http://www.stjosephs.london.on.ca/

The St. Joseph's Health Centre in Ontario, Canada, maintains this site for links to related health institutions. Visit here to connect with University Hospital, Victoria Hospital, the Lawson Research Institute and other local health centers.

The Massachusetts General Hospital WWW Server

http://www.mgh.harvard.edu/

The Massachusetts General Hospital home page features policies and procedures, plus a directory of doctors, staff and departments. Also find links to databases, library services and other health-related resources.

M.D. Anderson Cancer Center

http://utmdacc.mda.uth.tmc.edu/

Along with facts about the Center, job openings and an online magazine, the M.D. Anderson Cancer Center in Houston provides cancer and patient information, library resources for medical and science professionals and training program details.

New England Medical Center

http://www.nemc.org/

The New England Medical Center in Boston serves as both a medical and an educational institution. On this page, find an overview of the facility with information about its many areas of medical expertise. A physician referral guide is also featured.

University of Texas at Austin Student Health Center

http://www.utexas.edu/student/health/

Students at UT Austin can find out what health services and programs are available and access info about the bicycle safety diversion program.

DEPARTMENT HOME PAGES

Cleveland Clinic Foundation Department of Neurological Surgery

http://www.neus.ccf.org/

The Department of Neurological Surgery at the Cleveland Clinic Foundation provides information about its clinical, educational and research programs. Includes Frequently Asked Questions (FAQs) about neurological disorders and pointers to other online resources.

Massachusetts General Hospital Department of Emergency Medicine

http://emergency.mgh.harvard.edu/

The Massachusetts General Hospital Department of Emergency Medicine maintains this page with information about staff, continuing education courses and emergency medicine. Information for medical students and about the emergency medical residency program is also available here, along with links to related sites.

Massachusetts General Hospital Neurosurgical Service

http://neurosurgery.mgh.harvard.edu/

The Neurosurgical Service of Massachusetts General Hospital/Harvard Medical School offers pointers to its clinical specialty units, with additional links to information on conditions treated by neurosurgeons. Visitors can also meet the staff via their personal home pages, access medical school information and check out the conference schedule.

HUMAN SEXUALITY

The Complete Internet Sex Resource Guide

http://www.best.com/~craig/netsex.htm

The Complete Internet Sex Resource Guide links to everything you always wanted to know about sex (but were afraid to click on). Links include Usenet newsgroups, FTP sites, questions and answers, chat groups, and more.

ILLNESSES AND DISORDERS

AIDS/HIV

AIDS Information Newsletter

http://www.cmpharm.ucsf.edu/~troyer/safesex/vanews/

The AIDS Information Newsletter, a service of the U.S. Department of Veterans Affairs, offers biweekly updates on the critical health care issue. Visit here for important information about the prevention and treatment of AIDS.

AIDS Patents Project

http://app.cnidr.org/

The AIDS Patents Project offers access to databases of U.S. patents relating to Acquired Immune Deficiency Syndrome (AIDS). Boolean searches as well as browsing are allowed.

The Body

http://www.thebody.com/

The Body offers straightforward information about what AIDS is (and isn't), news on the latest treatment options, links to support groups, advice on mental well-being, and much more.

Centers for Disease Control National AIDS Clearinghouse Web Server

http://www.cdcnac.org/

Maintained by the Centers for Disease Control and Prevention (CDC), this informative page provides pointers to sites relevant to Acquired Immune Deficiency Syndrome (AIDS) research, education, prevention and trend analysis. Free AIDS-related publications can also be ordered via an online order form.

Computerized AIDS Ministries (CAM)

http://198.139.157.121/

The Computerized AIDS Ministries Home Page provides a variety of AIDS-related resources. Visit here to find educational information about the disease, Methodist ministry-sponsored support services and a bulletin board service. Links to other AIDS-related sites are also available.

Joint United Nations Programme on HIV/AIDS

http://www.unaids.org/

Read the latest analysis of the global AIDS crisis, access pages devoted to World AIDS Day, consult the Frequently Asked Questions (FAQs) file, and learn about sexually transmitted diseases, women and AIDS, and related subjects. Link to other United Nations projects, including UNICEF, UNESCO and the World Health Organization.

Marty Howard's HIV/AIDS HomePage

http://www.smartlink.net/~martinjh/

Marty Howard keps up with the vast flow of AIDS/HIV information and presents it here. See Editor's Choice.

The Names Project Foundation

http://www.aidsquilt.org/

The Names Project Foundation leads the AIDS memorial quilt effort to "help bring an end to the AIDS epidemic." Here, visitors can learn about the quilt and how to contribute to it. The site also includes information on the quilt's travels to communities around the world and information about its upcoming display in Washington, D.C.

Stop AIDS Shirt

http://www.infomall.org/sohodesign/aids.html

Keith Haring Designs in New York offers this "Stop AIDS" print t-shirt to benefit AMFAR, an AIDS research group. Browsers can obtain ordering information here.

The World-Wide Web Virtual Library: AIDS

http://www.planetq.com/aidsvl/index.html

Investigate AIDS- and HIV-related issues from political, social and medical points of view using the extensive collection of pointers offered at this vast online resource. The list of links emphasizes access to community resources and medical publications.

ARTHRITIS

The Pediatric Rheumatology Home Page

http://www.wp.com/pedsrheum/

Parents of children with arthritis and the doctors who care for them can learn more about this disease and other childhood rheumatic diseases courtesy of the Hospital for Special Surgery in New York. Find out about the symptoms and onset of different types of arthritis and get the latest medical advice on alternative medical treatments.

BIRTH DEFECTS AND GENETIC DISORDERS

Autism Resources

http://web.syr.edu/~jmwobus/autism/

The Autism Resources page is an index of information and resources currently available online about this developmental disability. This page includes personal accounts, general information, methods, research programs, libraries and links to online publications.

CF-WEB, Online Information about Cystic Fibrosis

http://www.ai.mit.edu/people/mernst/cf/

This Web site offers medical information, support group contacts, Frequently Asked Questions (FAQs), archives, and more related to cystic fibrosis. Both doctors and lay readers will find useful resources concerning this genetic disorder.

Intellectual Disability Information

http://www.monash.edu.au/informatics/idcn.html

Find out about the diagnosis and treatment of Down's syndrome, autism, cerebral palsy and other brain and severe psychiatric disorders at this site, along with special medical concerns, legal issues, vocational development, educational programs and more.

Tidewater Down Syndrome Association Home Page

http://www.infi.net/~jwheaton/tdsahome.html

Serving Hampton Roads, Virginia, this nonprofit organization provides support, information and opportunities to persons with Downs Syndrome and their families. Visit this page to learn more about the group, its meetings and activities, plus find an online newsletter and archive of recent articles.

Von Hippel-Lindau (VHL) Disease Family Alliance

http://neurosurgery.mgh.harvard.edu/vhl-fa/

Sponsored by Massachusetts General Hospital, this informational site for physicians and those affected by this genetic blood vessel disorder includes a comprehensive reference handbook and a variety of additional resources. Information is available in English, French and Spanish.

❋2❋ EDITOR'S CHOICE

Marty Howard's HIV/AIDS HomePage

http://www.smartlink.net/~martinjh/

There may be AIDS/HIV pages on the Web with more information than Marty Howard's, but you'd be hard-pressed to find them and Marty's is definitely the place for the most current news. HIV-positive Marty Howard loads this page with links to articles, product information, mailing lists, support groups, clinical trials reports, and medication data. The link to Dr. Tim France's text list contains descriptions and URLs for 43 AIDS/HIV sites, including indexes from Yahoo! and the World Wide Web Virtual Library, along with government sites from the CDC and National Library of Medicine. But what's more important, Marty puts a face on this disease; he personalizes it the way government databases and CDC updates and World Health Organization reports never can. And Marty is so polite. He closes every explanatory paragraph by thanking the reader. No, thank you, Marty, for devoting so much time and effort to this vital source of information. —*Reviewed by Kathleen McFadden*

Marty Howard's HIV/AIDS HomePage

The graphic "Aids Ribbon Under Latex" is provided through the courtesy of Mark W. Claunch. Mark can be reached at mwc@primenet.com, while I can be reached via the e-mail buttons near the bottom of this page. Thank you, Marty

---

Message of the day. - June 14, 1996

The Message of the day will be changed as appropriate and the date changed at that time.

12:30 Pacific - I have just posted this past weeks CDC News and ATN #248. Thank you, Marty

CANCER

American Cancer Society

http://www.cancer.org/

The American Cancer Society "investigates conditions under which cancer is found," educating the public to decrease the frequency of the disease. Find an overview of the organization and information on various kinds of cancer.

The Anthony Nolan Bone Marrow Trust

http://wombat.doc.ic.ac.uk/bone-marrow/index.html

This site contains an online registration form allowing United Kingdom residents to add their names to the Anthony Nolan Bone Marrow Trust donor database. Links to the U.S. registry and those of other countries are also provided.

Avon's Breast Cancer Awareness Crusade

http://www.avon.com/about/awareness/frame.html

Avon provides facts, links and phone numbers to various breast cancer resources with this "awareness crusade" site. Visitors can take Avon's "Pledge for Better Breast Health" here, and read transcripts of Awareness Online conferences.

Cancer—Medical Specialties

http://galaxy.einet.net/galaxy/Medicine/Medical-Specialties/Cancer.html

The TradeWave Galaxy index for cancer lists books, guides, directories and organizations. Visitors can also link to other medical specialties.

Cancer Patient Resources Available Via WWW

http://www.charm.net/~kkdk/

Providing information for cancer patients from a cancer patient is the focus of this page. Dr. Darrel Kilius of Baltimore, a cancer survivor, catalogs links to conventional and alternative treatment resources and provides a comprehensive list of associations, labs, institutes, and documents.

CANSEARCH: A Guide to Cancer Resources

http://www.access.digex.net/~mkragen/cansearch.html

Sponsored by the National Coalition for Cancer Survivorship, this site provides a guided tour of an extensive list of cancer-related resources, including educational sites, research centers, organizations, support groups, and more.

Community Breast Health Project

http://www-med.stanford.edu/CBHP/

Sponsored by the Stanford Medical Center, the Community Breast Health Project is a public ser-vice dedicated to providing information and support for those with breast cancer and their loved ones. A fixed feature of the page is a section of links to relevant Web sites.

Gynecologic Oncology

http://gynoncology.obgyn.washington.edu/

The Gynecologic Oncology server at the University of Washington offers tutorials and references to cancer researchers and health care professionals. It also offers links to other sites on cervical cancer, uterine cancer, endometrial cancer and related illnesses.

The Human Lymphocyte Antigen (HLA) Registry Foundation, Inc.

http://www.register.com/hla/

The recruitment site for this nonprofit organization is an emotional appeal for contributions and potential bone marrow donors "for transplantation into a little boy or girl, or an adult, in the United States, or anywhere in the world." The FAQs file addresses 20 common questions about bone marrow donations, including costs, pain, procedures, and risks.

Medicine On Line

http://www.meds.com/mol/welcome.html

UltiTech, Inc., a communications development company, provides a page that links visitors to

a2z EDITOR'S CHOICE

The Prostate Cancer InfoLink

http://www.comed.com/Prostate/index.html

Prostate cancer is a high-profile disease these days, having lately claimed the lives of such notables as Frank Zappa and Timothy Leary. Approximately 317,100 American men are expected to be diagnosed with prostate cancer in 1996, and early detection is complicated by the fact that the disease has no definitive set of symptoms; all the early signs can be caused by other illnesses or normal aging. The Prostate Cancer InfoLink arms its readers with the facts. Written in simple, understandable language, the page carefully lays out the risk factors and symptoms, along with information on screening and early detection. Men who have the disease can benefit from the extensive information on how to understand and interpret their diagnosis and treatment. The discussion includes the "grades" of the disease and its clinical stages, definitions of related medical abbreviations and acronyms, and treatment options. Finally, the site includes a number of additional resources, including pointers to support organizations, tips on choosing a physician, a FAQ, and the Ask Arthur feature—an interactive question and answer forum.—*Reviewed by Kathleen McFadden*

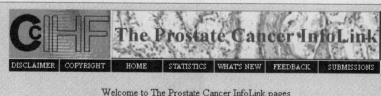

Welcome to The Prostate Cancer InfoLink pages at The CoMed Communications Internet Health Forum

Contents

What's Hot?
Where to Begin?
Can You Avoid It?/Should You Be Screened?
Understanding Diagnosis
Understanding Treatment
Help and Support

cancer resources, including research institutions and forums. Access to CancerNet puts visitors in touch with support groups and associations.

OncoLink, The University of Pennsylvania Cancer Center Resource

http://cancer.med.upenn.edu/

The University of Pennsylvania Cancer Center presents this "first multimedia oncology information resource" on the Net. Visitors will find cancer news and statistics here, as well as information on meetings and access to journals.

Prostate Cancer Home Page

http://www.cancer.med.umich.edu/prostcan/prostcan.html

The University of Michigan creates an online information center for news and research related to prostate cancer. From medical articles to drug trials announcements, all aspects of this form of cancer are covered from the disease itself to current and future treatment options.

The Prostate Cancer InfoLink

http://www.comed.com/Prostate/index.html

This important site provides detailed information on prostate cancer written in clear and understandable language. See Editor's Choice.

---

a2z EDITOR'S CHOICE

The Heart: An Online Exploration

http://sln2.fi.edu/biosci/heart.html

Take a guided tour of the human heart courtesy of the Franklin Institute Science Museum and the Unisys Corporation. Virtual travelers can start with The Heart Preview Gallery, a detailed, hyperlinked introduction to the full exhibit. The preview highlights the interactive activities, images and movies, educational materials, and audio files folded into the virtual tour. Travel on to the table of contents to customize your tour and pick your destinations. Choose from presentations covering healthy hearts, the artery-vein-capillary connection, the oxygen-carbon dioxide tradeoff, and the "fascinating fluid of life." Test your blood I.Q. Listen to the difference between a healthy heart and a heart murmur. Look at a comparison of two heart x-ray images. Watch a video of heart bypass surgery—if you dare. Besides all the medical and scientific stuff, the exhibit doesn't neglect the popular images of the heart in movies, books and songs. How many novels with the word "heart" in the title can you name? Check your answers against the list and add any that aren't there. Heartened visitors are even invited to submit original poems. If it's heart-related, it's here—from the purely scientific to the purely whimsical. —*Reviewed by Kathleen McFadden*

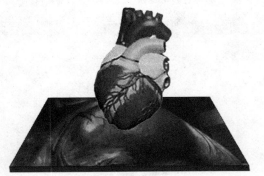

The Heart: An Online Exploration

From the moment it begins beating until the moment it stops, the human heart works

---

Roxane Pain Institute

http://www.roxane.com/

Ohio's Roxanne Laboratories, a pain management product manufacturer, provides online promotional and educational information on their products and services for AIDS and cancer patients. Features include a pain slide show, drug prescription information and a list of upcoming lectures and seminars.

CARDIOLOGY-RELATED DISORDERS

American Heart Association

http://www.amhrt.org/

Dedicated to fighting cardiovascular disease, the American Heart Association provides links to AHA information and resources on its page, as well as consumer literature on heart disease prevention. The AHA home page also connects visitors to the latest in cardiovascular research.

American Heart Association Gopher Menu

gopher://gopher.amhrt.org/

The American Heart Association supplies information about its mission and activities at this gopher site, along with information on conferences, programs, biostatistical facts and research. Also included here are news releases, publications, patient support and Heart Healthy information.

Audio Heart Sounds

http://synapse.uah.ualberta.ca/synapse/00b10000.htm

Heart Sounds contains a variety of sound files with recordings of healthy and diseased hearts.

The Heart: An Online Exploration

http://sln2.fi.edu/biosci/heart.html

Take a guided tour of the human heart. See Editor's Choice.

DERMATOLOGICAL DISORDERS

The Body Electric

http://www.surgery.com/body/

Are you tired of what you see in the mirror? Find how to form or reform your body through The Body Electric. It features information about breast implants, laser surgery, and hair transplants.

Introduction to Skin Cancer

http://www.maui.net/~southsky/introto.html

Maybe that glowing suntan isn't *exactly* a sign of good health. An Introduction to Skin Cancer helps visitors become acquainted with various kinds of skin cancer as well as ways to avoid becoming a victim.

National Skin Centre, Singapore

http://medweb.nus.sg/nsc/nsc.html

Look here for nontechnical discussions of the causes, symptoms, and treatments for all types of skin disorders—from acne to warts. Read about how the environment affects your skin and how to protect yourself from deleterious effects of the sun, cosmetics and occupational hazards. The site also includes news, announcements and services offered by the Center and links to other medical servers in Singapore.

Plink: The Plastic Surgery Link

http://www.nvpc.nl/plink/

Claiming to collect "everything related to plastic surgery available on the net," this Dutch site provides information about reconstructive, cosmetic and other forms of plastic surgery. Surgeons looking for the latest news and consumers contemplating a little tuck or an overall makeover are accommodated here.

GASTROINTESTINAL AND GENITOURINARY DISORDERS

Crohns Disease Ulcerative Colitis Inflammatory Bowel Disease Pages

http://qurlyjoe.bu.edu/cduchome.html

This site provides an extensive index of medical resources. Visit here for links to Frequently Asked Questions (FAQs) files, medical institutions, clinical trial information, personal histories, patient services, government agencies, commercial health providers, newsgroups, and more.

Diseases of the Liver

http://cpmcnet.columbia.edu/dept/gi/disliv.html

Columbia-Presbyterian Medical Center presents an alphabetical list of liver diseases and conditions with links to files, current papers in the field, a multimedia textbook of liver pathology and other liver-related sites.

Hernia Information Home Page

http://www.demon.co.uk/herniainfo/

The Hernia Information Home Page, sponsored by the British Hernia Centre in London, explains how hernias develop, defines the different types of hernias and describes hernia repair techniques, all in straightforward, easy-to-understand language. The site also features upcoming conference information for surgeons.

National Institute of Diabetes and Digestive and Kidney Disease (NIDDK)

http://www.niddk.nih.gov/

The NIDDK of the National Institutes of Health maintains this educational site. Visitors will find information about diabetes and about digestive, endocrine, kidney, nutrition and urologic disorders. Research and professional info, as well as diverse patient resources, are also featured.

LIBRARIES, DATABASES, AND INDICES

CDC Immunization Information Page

http://www.cdc.gov/diseases/immun.html

The Centers for Disease Control offers information about illnesses for which immunizations are available. Visitors can read descriptions of disease progression and treatment as well as find out about possible side effects of the serums.

Centers for Disease Control

http://www.cdc.gov/

The home page for the Centers for Disease Control (CDC) includes general information and current news about the CDC, discussions of diseases, health risks and injuries, and a link to the CDC Wonder system, a database of CDC reports, guidelines and numeric public health data. Visitors can also link to any of the 11 CDC internal centers such as Environmental Health, Infectious Diseases, and the National Immunization Program.

Centers for Disease Control Wonder System

http://wonder.cdc.gov/

Use the Wonder system to search the databases of the Centers for Disease Control through this page. Visitors can retrieve guidelines and reports on a wide range of topics or check the latest statistics about AIDS, cancer or other diseases.

Communicable Disease Fact Sheets Gopher Menu

gopher://gopher.health.state.ny.us/11/.consumer/.factsheets

This New York State Department of Health gopher contains alphabetized fact sheets on common communicable diseases such as chickenpox and the flu, along with diseases you may never have heard of such as Kawasaki Syndrome and tularemia. Each fact sheet presents a description of the disease, symptoms, methods of communi-

cability, treatment protocols, and prevention techniques.

Medscape

http://www.medscape.com/

Medscape features peer-reviewed articles, graphics, literature searches and annotated links to Internet resources. Health care professionals and consumers can access articles in categories such as infectious diseases, AIDS, urology, surgery and managed care. Access is free, but you must register as a user.

MedWeb: Biomedical Internet Resources

http://www.cc.emory.edu/WHSCL/medweb.html

MedWeb is an authoritative, up-to-date and easy to use health and medical resource. See Editor's Choice.

National Institute for Allergy and Infectious Diseases (NIAID)

http://www.niaid.nih.gov/

Access both technical and nontechnical information on a variety of illnesses and disorders, from allergies and HIV/AIDS to rabies and tuberculosis, at this site. Read about research activities, technology transfer resources and current news. Link to the NIAID gopher server or to other related Web sites.

National Institute for Allergy and Infectious Diseases (NIAID) Gopher Menu

gopher://gopher.niaid.nih.gov:70/1

The National Institute for Allergy and Infectious Diseases maintains this gopher server for access to its scientific data collection. Visit here for disease-specific research, useful search tools and links to related gophers.

University of California, Irvine Medical Education Software Repository

ftp://ftp.uci.edu/med-ed/

The University of California, Irvine, hosts this FTP site. Visitors will gain access to a medical newsletter, information on multiple sclerosis and chronic fatigue syndrome, software for Macintosh and MS-DOS users, and various Internet guides.

MUSCULOSKELETAL DISORDERS

Southern California Orthopedic Institute Home Page

http://www.scoi.com/

Southern California Orthopedic Institute's page teaches visitors about sports injuries, orthopedic procedures and basic anatomy in plain language.

Those who want to become intimate with knee surgery can view a QuickTime movie of the inside of a knee here.

USA Fibrositis Association
http://www.w2.com/fibro1.html
This advocacy group for fibromyalgia, also called fibrositis, provides information on the musculoskeletal disease, pertinent contacts and a call to membership.

NEUROLOGICAL DISORDERS

The Alzheimer Page
http://www.biostat.wustl.edu/alzheimer/
Washington University in St. Louis, Missouri, presents a collection of Alzheimer's Disease information and links here. Visitors can search and browse the Alzheimer archive, join the mailing list and link to a variety of aging and dementia sites.

EDITOR'S CHOICE

MedWeb: Biomedical Internet Resources
http://www.cc.emory.edu/WHSCL/medweb.html
For sheer volume of information, you can't beat Emory University's MedWeb, a meta-index to medicine, medical science, and health resources on the Internet. What do you want to know today? How to handle suspected health fraud? The source of the name of the Ebola virus? The fat content of fast food restaurant offerings? The answer to just about any medical or health question can be found somewhere in the MedWeb pages. The home page table of contents lists over 70 primary categories in alphabetical order—from Aerospace Medicine to Virtual Reality. Secondary pages are also categorized, some containing a few and some a few dozen subcategories. For extra help, some links are followed by brief explanatory text. Forget all those print-based medical almanacs and encyclopedias. MedWeb is far more complete and up-to-date. It is an authoritative, easy-to-use, and comprehensive index to health and medicine targeted equally to clinical professionals and health consumers.—*Reviewed by Kathleen McFadden*

> **MedWeb: Biomedical Internet Resources**
>
> MedWeb
> Emory University Health Sciences Center Library
>
> Search MedWeb
>
> **Table of Contents**
> Lists of Internet Resources
> News and What's New
> Conferences and Calendars
> Directories
> Aerospace Medicine
> AIDS and HIV
> Alternative Medicine

Alzheimer Web
http://werple.mira.net.au/~dhs/ad.html
At this site, researchers and others interested in Alzheimer's Disease can link to the Alzheimer's Association, join a discussion group or subscribe to a mailing list devoted to advice for care givers.

Alzheimer's Disease Web Page
http://med-amsa.bu.edu/Alzheimer/home.html
Maintained at Massachusetts' Bedford Geriatric Research Education Clinical Center, this page is "dedicated to the distribution of information" on Alzheimer's disease. Find resources for care givers and families, a course on the molecular basis of neurologic disease and related offerings.

Alzheimer's Association
http://www.alz.org/
The Alzheimer's Association, a Chicago-based public advocacy and service group, maintains this site for its information and research resources. Visit here for medical community news, local chapter listings, care giver brochures, public policy activity updates and links to related Web sites and information services.

Aneurysm Information Project
http://www.columbia.edu/~mdt1/
The Aneurysm Information Project home page presents resources—answers to Frequently Asked Questions (FAQs), papers, a victim's support page, and more—related to cerebral and other types of aneurysms. Visitors also can link to related research and reference resources.

Department of Neurosurgery at New York University
http://mcns10.med.nyu.edu/
New York University's Department of Neurosurgery Web site is intended for patients, their families and health care professionals. Nonprofessionals will find a straightforward introduction to neurosurgery that answers questions about brain tumors, aneurysms and spinal disorders. Professionals can learn from the case presentations and the diagnostic challenge of the month.

Hydrocephalus Association Homepage
http://neurosurgery.mgh.harvard.edu/ha/
The latest research about hydrocephalus—a medical condition that causes an abnormal accumulation of fluid within cavities inside the brain—comes to the Web through this site. Read about the disease, family support services, upcoming conferences and recent research papers.

Institute For Brain Aging and Dementia
http://www.alz.uci.edu
The Institute for Brain Aging and Dementia home page provides information about Alzheimer's disease and other senile dementia conditions along

with links to clinical resources. Visitors can jump to the AlzNet discussion group from this site.

The Journal of Cognitive Rehabilitation
http://www.inetdirect.net/nsp/

Targeting therapists, families and patients, this online journal focuses on the treatment and rehabilitation of head injuries. Broad in scope, the journal includes trauma, stroke, attention deficit disorder and learning disabilities in its purview.

The Parkinson's Web
http://neuro-chief-e.mgh.harvard.edu/parkinsonsweb/Main/PDmain.html

This reference page contains information about Parkinson's Disease, support groups and available medical treatments. Visitors can access news bulletins, publications, research updates, related neurological sites and more.

Polio Survivors Page
http://www.eskimo.com/~dempt/polio.html

The Polio Survivors Page is a compilation of topical information and reports for polio survivors. The pages include such items as a "post-polio information packet," remembrances, newsletters and links to medical articles and related sites.

The Rehabilitation Learning Center
http://weber.u.washington.edu/~rlc/

The Rehabilitation Learning Center at the University of Washington in Seattle provides support for people with acute or chronic spinal cord injuries. This site contains information about the Center, as well as links to resources for people with disabilities.

PULMONARY DISORDERS

Asthma—General Information
http://www.cco.caltech.edu/~wrean/asthma-gen.html

Asthma sufferers looking for treatments for their symptoms and answers to common questions about the condition can check this page, the FAQs for the alt.support.asthma newsgroup. The page creators warn that the FAQs are for discussion only and not meant to be a source of medical advice.

Comprehensive Lung Center
http://www.clc.upmc.edu/

The University of Pittsburgh's Comprehensive Lung Center site provides information about its eight core programs, from sleep-disordered breathing to occupational lung disease. Includes links to its faculty and patient referral services.

Tuberculosis Resources
http://www.cpmc.columbia.edu/tbcpp/

This index of tuberculosis treatment resources, maintained by the New York City Department of Health, offers information for patients and health care providers. Visit to learn about the disease, its prevention, and its treatment. Available in English and Spanish.

SLEEP DISORDERS

The Sleep Medicine Home Page
http://www.cloud9.net/~thorpy/

This site provides a compendium of material related to sleep. See Editor's Choice.

SNORE: Sleep apNoea Online Resource for Education
http://www.access.digex.net/~faust/sldord/

Check this site for the causes, symptoms, consequences and treatment of sleep apnea, a condition characterized by the cessation of breathing during sleep. Browse the Frequently Asked Questions (FAQs), read the bed-buying tips, explore the wonders of snoring and link to other sleep disorder sites.

---

a2z EDITOR'S CHOICE

The Sleep Medicine Home Page
http://www.cloud9.net/~thorpy/

Snoozing isn't always a soothing balm: Some of us sleep too much, some of us sleep too little, some of us make noises, and some of us have bad dreams. All are accommodated at The Sleep Medicine Home Page, a vast compendium of links to all things drowsy. If it's true that "about 40 million Americans suffer from sleep disorders such as narcolepsy, sleep apnea, restless legs syndrome, and the insomnias," a lot of people out there are dragging through their days. Help is here in the form of information, treatment options, and links to worldwide sleep centers and discussion groups. Check these somnolent facts: Narcolepsy may be a genetic autoimmune disease. Snoring is not necessarily an indication of sleep apnea. Still can't snooze? Insomniacs can take the restless legs' quiz, find out about sleep disorders caused by prescription drugs, and read Aristotle's musings on the nature of sleep. If Aristotle's tedious recitation of the obvious ("Sleep is evidently a privation of waking") doesn't help you close your eyes, it may be time to check into a sleep center. —*Reviewed by Kathleen McFadden*

The **Sleep Medicine** Home Page

Welcome to the Sleep Medicine Home Page

Last Updated June 14, 1996

This home page lists resources regarding all aspects of sleep including, the physiology of sleep, clinical sleep medicine, sleep research, federal and state information, patient information, and

VIRAL DISORDERS

Ebola Interview
http://outcast.gene.com/ae/WN/NM/interview_murphy.html

A former director of the National Center for Infectious Diseases at the Centers for Disease Control is interviewed about new and emerging killer viruses. Read about the Ebola Virus in plain language, consult the bibliography, or look at electron micrographs of three viruses.

OTHER BODY SYSTEMS

Chronic Fatigue Syndrome
http://www.ncf.carleton.ca/ip/social.services/cfseir/CFSEIR.HP.html

Asserting that chronic fatigue syndrome (CFS) is a "real" disease, this page provides background, symptom and treatment information, along with tips on finding good medical care, descriptions of current research projects and an index to emotional support resources.

Lupus Home Page
http://www.hamline.edu/lupus/index.html

Hamline University in St. Paul, Minnesota gives visitors the "ins and outs" of lupus, an autoimmune disease that affects millions. Find out what it is and how it affects the body. Information on treatment accompanies links to support groups.

National Lymphedema Network
http://www.hooked.net/users/lymphnet/

The National Lymphedema Network provides information for patients and health care professionals on the prevention and management of primary and secondary lymphedema. Visitors can access news, a resource guide, course information, support groups and more.

The On-Line Allergy Center
http://www.sig.net/~allergy/welcome.html

Visit this site to learn about the causes, prevention, and treatment of allergies. See Editor's Choice.

Tinnitus Frequently Answered Questions
http://www.cccd.edu/faq/tinnitus.html

Find out the symptoms and available treatments for this auditory nerve ailment that causes "ringing" ears and other head noises. Visitors to this fact-packed site can also access newsgroups, prevention information, and the American Tinnitus Association.

UNOS Transplantation Information Site
http://www.ew3.att.net/unos

UNOS, which administers the National Organ Procurement and Transplantation Network, provides information, resources and statistics on organ transplantation. Included here is an FTP site with UNOS documents, along with news releases and links to related sites.

Vestibular Disorders Association (VEDA)
http://www.teleport.com/~veda/

This nonprofit organization offers information for sufferers of inner ear problems and the related symptoms of dizziness, vertigo, nausea, and impaired vision. Visitors can learn about the causes, symptoms and treatment for a variety of disorders, access information about VEDA and link to related sites.

---

a2z EDITOR'S CHOICE

The On-Line Allergy Center
http://www.sig.net/~allergy/welcome.html

Many of us have experienced the nasal drips, red eyes, and sneezing, but did you know that hyperactivity, depression, and loss of short-term memory are also allergy symptoms? Dr. Russell Roby of Austin, Texas knows and has authored this page "to provide helpful allergy tips and information to allergy sufferers worldwide." Dr. Roby explains the allergic reaction so simply and clearly that a child can understand it. Follow along with the good doctor as he enumerates the vexing manifestations of allergies, read his tips for keeping symptoms at bay, and find out how ultraviolet light can eliminate mold spores. The site also boasts three interactive newsgroups devoted to allergy, asthma, and migraine. For those who suspect food allergies, Dr. Roby includes a program and specific schedule for assessing reactions to certain types of food, along with remedies for food reactions and a form for monitoring food intake. Dr. Roby can't write you an online prescription, but he does share a sizeable snort of allergy how-comes and how-tos. —*Reviewed by Kathleen McFadden*

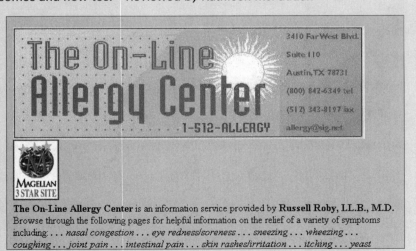

The On-Line Allergy Center is an information service provided by **Russell Roby, LL.B., M.D.** Browse through the following pages for helpful information on the relief of a variety of symptoms including: . . . *nasal congestion . . . eye redness/soreness . . . sneezing . . . wheezing . . . coughing . . . joint pain . . . intestinal pain . . . skin rashes/irritation . . . itching . . . yeast*

JOBS ONLINE AND PHYSICIAN FINDERS

MedSearch America

http://www.medsearch.com/

MedSearch America provides a venue for U.S. medical professionals to submit and search résumés, view current job listings and access employer profiles. Job seekers can search for jobs and post résumés for free. Employers must subscribe to gain full access to the résumé database and post an organization profile. Links to health care forums and the Recruiter's Net also are featured.

MEDICAL HISTORY

Michigan Digital Historical Initiative in the Health Sciences

http://www.med.umich.edu/HCHS/

The Michigan Digital Historical Initiative in the Health Sciences (MDHI) serves as a guide to Web-based repositories of museum materials, photographs, artifacts and online galleries, all containing objects of interest to medical historians. Visitors here can view historical information about African-Americans' experiences with health care.

Scientific and Medical Antiques

http://www.duke.edu/~tj/sci.ant.html

The Scientific and Medical Antiques site provides information for enthusiasts and collectors of science and medicine antiques, including old telescopes, scales and surgical equipment. Visitors can find out about online auctions and learn about rare and antiquarian books, among other services.

MEDICAL IMAGING, INFORMATICS, AND TELEMEDICINE

American Medical Informatics Association

http://amia2.amia.org/

Health care professionals can keep up with new developments in the application of computer technology to medical care at the online service of the American Medical Informatics Association (AMIA). Visitors can find membership information and a calendar of AMIA events.

DoD Telemedicine Home Page

http://www.matmo.org/

The Department of Defense presents a directory of its telemedicine projects here. Also here are a calendar and a library of downloadable telemedicine-related documents. Includes a link to the Radiological Society of North America.

Health Information Research Unit (HIRU)

http://hiru.mcmaster.ca/

Physicians interested in using computers for more effective diagnosis, treatment and teaching will be interested in the projects and services explained at this site. HIRU's activities focus on the "development of new information resources to support evidence-based health care."

Image List

http://130.219.15.246/imageList.html

The Laurie Imaging Center, which serves hospitals in New Jersey, presents a long list of images from interesting medical cases.

Image Processing Group Home Page

http://www-ipg.umds.ac.uk/IPG/

The Imaging Process Group of the United Medical & Dental Schools of Guy's and St. Thomas' Hospitals in London, England, maintains this informational site. Visitors can access its staff and project directories, teaching files, employment listings, and other scientific and medical resources.

Images from the Visible Human Project

http://www.nlm.nih.gov/research/visible/visible_gallery.html

The National Library of Medicine presents these images from the Visible Human Project featuring cryosections and computer-aided tomography (CAT) scans of cadavers. Also included are magnetic resonance imaging (MRI) scans.

Marching Through the Visible Man

http://www.crd.ge.com/esl/cgsp/projects/vm/

A project of the National Library of Medicine, the Visible Human is an ongoing attempt to create a digital atlas of the human body. The document at this site "describes a methodology and results for extracting surfaces from the Visible Male's CT data." Images are included.

Medical Imaging Internet Resources

http://agora.leeds.ac.uk/comir/resources/links.html

This is a collection of worldwide links to medical imaging resources on the Internet. Visitors will find information on medical schools, hospitals and research facilities.

Physiological Imaging

http://everest.radiology.uiowa.edu/

Watch movies of the heart, lung, brain and airway courtesy of the University of Iowa College of Medicine's Division of Physiological Imaging. Find out about current research projects in the use and development of imaging techniques.

The Radiological Society of North America (RSNA) Link

http://www.rsna.org/

Click the hyperlink to access the RSNA home page. Visitors will find info on the group, research, educational and practice resources, plus notes from the annual meeting. A radiologic technology marketplace is also featured.

Telemedicine Information Exchange

http://tie.telemed.org/

Telemedicine is the practice of health care over phone lines or satellites. Visitors here will learn how doctors can examine patients through teleconferencing, for example. The site is maintained by the Telemedicine Research Center and also includes related product information and a legal and ethical discussion of the practice.

TeleSCAN: Telematics Services In Cancer

http://telescan.nki.nl/

TeleSCAN is a European Internet service for cancer research designed for both the general public and medical professionals. Visitors will find relevant medical databases and links for cancer-related research.

3D Reconstruction Home Page

http://biocomp.arc.nasa.gov/3dreconstruction/

The 3D Reconstruction home page is dedicated to providing information and results pertaining to 3-D reconstruction work for medical and life science research. Browsers can find out what reconstruction is, get software, data, reconstruction images, and link up to the NASA Ames Biocomputation Center.

Virtual Anatomy Image Browser

http://www.vis.colostate.edu/cgi-bin/gva/gvaview

This image browser site provides several human body animation sequences that can be viewed online.

Virtual Anatomy Project

http://www.vis.colostate.edu/library/gva/gva.html

This multimedia project aims to generate a three-dimensional database of the human body. The site contains links to information on the researchers at Colorado State University, the software they're using, and to anatomical MPEGS of the human body.

Visible Human Project

http://www.nlm.nih.gov/research/visible/visible_human.html

The Visible Human Project is working to create complete, anatomically detailed, three-dimensional representations of the human body. Visit this National Library of Medicine site to learn more about the project, view images, read articles and review related materials.

COMMERCIAL PRODUCTS AND SERVICES

Molecular Structure Corporation Home Page

http://www.msc.com/msc.html

The Texas-based Molecular Structure Corporation maintains a home page providing information about its commercial x-ray services and software for radiology technology. Link to other sites devoted to x rays.

INSTITUTES AND SCHOOLS

Center for Advanced Medical Informatics at Stanford

http://www-camis.stanford.edu/

Stanford University School of Medicine's academic, research, and administrative computing services are linked by way of the Center for Advanced Medical Informatics at Stanford (CAMIS). Find academic programs, publications and research relating to biomedical informatics.

Centre for Health Informatics, Aberystwyth

http://www.ihi.aber.ac.uk/index.html

The Centre for Health Informatics in Aberystwyth, Wales, provides information here on its faculty, educational programs, publications, and research resources. Visit here to learn about the center and link to its parent site at the University of Wales.

Duke University Medical Center: Division of Medical Informatics

http://dmi-www.mc.duke.edu/

The Division of Medical Informatics at Duke University Medical Center provides information about its training program, its history, requirements for admission and course descriptions. Includes links to faculty, research groups and other Medical Center servers.

Johns Hopkins University School of Medicine: Medical Imaging Lab

http://prospero.bme-mri.jhu.edu/

Johns Hopkins University School of Medicine's Medical Imaging Lab invites visitors to review its projects, read its papers, and meet the faculty and students associated with the facility. Links to related resources are also featured.

Laurie Imaging Center

http://130.219.15.246/

Sponsored by a collective of New Jersey-based hospitals and the Robert Wood Johnson Medical School, the Laurie Imaging Center offers magnetic resonance imaging cases to physicians and virtual anatomy teaching files to students. Full explanations and examples of the Center's work are provided.

The Levit Radiologic-Pathologic Institute

http://rpisun1.mda.uth.tmc.edu/

Check out the multimedia learning centers—human anatomy, 3-D foot and ankle and scientific exhibits—provided at this site, along with information about the Institute and links to cancer and general medicine sites.

Mallinckrodt Institute of Radiology

http://www.mir.wustl.edu/

Located in St. Louis, Missouri at Washington University Medical Center, the Mallinckrodt Institute of Radiology presents this overview of its facilities and educational programs. Links to its departmental servers and electronic publications are also featured.

Massachusetts General Hospital Positron Emission Tomography Laboratory

http://neurosurgery.mgh.harvard.edu/pet-hp.htm

Click to the Positron Emission Tomography Laboratory at Massachusetts General Hospital to see how the technology is being applied to studying neurological disorders. The page offers sample images with accompanying explanations.

McConnell Brain Imaging Centre

http://www.mni.mcgill.ca/

The Montreal Neurological Institute at McGill University maintains this site for its McConnell Brain Imaging Centre. Visitors will find information about academic programs and links to research groups.

Medical Image Processing Group

http://mipgsun.mipg.upenn.edu/

Maintained by the Department of Radiology at the University of Pennsylvania Medical Center, this site serves as the Medical Image Processing Group's (MIPG) home page. Features include links to information about this research group, its personnel, publications and seminars.

Medical Informatics at Stanford University School of Medicine

http://camis.stanford.edu/

Medical informatics is the scientific field that researches the use of information technology to solve medical problems. Learn more about this area of research by accessing the FAQs and publications at this site or link to information about the university and medical school.

Medical School of Rennes Multimedia Laboratory

http://www.med.univ-rennes1.fr/

This French medical school welcomes visitors to its multimedia laboratory in three languages: French, English, and Italian. Demos and presentations on medical Web servers, the medical informatics lab projects and the radiology server are presented only in French.

National Center for Macromolecular Imaging

http://ncmi.bcm.tmc.edu/

The National Center for Macromolecular Imaging at Baylor College of Medicine is a national facility for intermediate electron cryomicroscopy and image reconstruction. Descriptions of current core and collaborated research projects are offered on this page along with a look at the NCMI's online resources.

Oklahoma State University TeleMedicine Center

http://telemed1.ocom.okstate.edu/

The College of Osteopathic Medicine at OSU in Tulsa presents the TeleMedicine Center—"the physician's other black bag." Visit here to learn how combining telecommunications with medical practice can result in better and more effective health care.

Penn State University: Department of Radiology

http://www.xray.hmc.psu.edu/home.html

The Penn State University Department of Radiology maintains this home page with information about its faculty, residency program and the Pennsylvania Radiological Society, as well as links to practice guidelines, journals, medical image databases and more.

State University of New York, Buffalo: Department of Nuclear Medicine

http://www.nucmed.buffalo.edu/

The State University of New York (SUNY) at Buffalo posts its career and educational opportunities in nuclear medicine on this page. Prospective students and visitors also can check the staff directory and follow links to some of the department's research groups.

SUMMIT—Stanford University Medical Media and Information Technologies Group

http://summit.stanford.edu/

SUMMIT specializes in applying computer technologies to enhance medical education. Visit this site for images from the Visible Human Project, an interactive guide to neuroanatomy, a patient case presentation program and more.

University of Illinois: Biomedical Visualization

http://www.bvis.uic.edu/

The University of Illinois, Chicago, offers a Master of Associated Medical Sciences degree in Biomedical Visualization, which combines visual problem-solving skills with knowledge of science, education, communication and media. Visitors to this page will find details on the profession and admissions information.

University of Leeds: Centre of Medical Imaging Research (CoMIR)

http://agora.leeds.ac.uk/comir/comir.html

Research at CoMIR focuses on the development of new, superior methods for imaging data acquisition and interpretation. Visit this site for publica-

tions (some with image galleries), a guide to personnel, descriptions of research activities and lists of upcoming events.

University of Manchester Medical Informatics Group Home page

http://www.cs.man.ac.uk/mig/index.html

The Medical Informatics Group in the Computer Science department of the University of Manchester provides information here on its projects in the design and implementation of health care information systems. Details on personnel and teaching programs are included, along with related links.

University of Minnesota: Health Computer Sciences

http://www.nmsr.labmed.umn.edu/

Health Computer Sciences, University of Minnesota, features information about its graduate program in health informatics and provides several links, including the National Micropopulation Simulation Resource, the biocatalysis/biodegradation database, and the university's medical school.

University of Pavia: The Medical Informatics Laboratory

http://ipvaimed9.unipv.it/

The Medical Informatics Laboratory at the University of Pavia, Italy, is involved in the fields of artificial intelligence in medicine and hospital information systems. This site contains information about the lab, its research, staff, documents, statistics and links to software.

University of Pennsylvania Medical Center: Department of Radiology

http://www.rad.upenn.edu/

The University of Pennsylvania Medical Center offers a general overview of its Department of Radiology's resources and programs. Visitors will find faculty profiles, fellowship applications and links to related Web sites.

University of Washington Radiology Webserver

http://www.rad.washington.edu/

Attempt to diagnose the case of the week at the University of Washington's Department of Radiology site. Cases, textbooks and teaching files are posted here for medical students and physicians interested in continuing education.

Yale Center for Medical Informatics

http://paella.med.yale.edu/

This home page for Yale University's Center for Medical Informatics in New Haven, Connecticut contains information on the center's people, postdoctoral fellowship programs, projects, and computing resources.

RESEARCH

Biomedical Information Communication Center

http://www.ohsu.edu/

The Biomedical Information Communication Center (BICC) at Oregon Health Sciences University conducts research into the field of medical informatics, the study of the use of information technology (such as computers) in the teaching and practice of health care. At the BICC Web site, visitors can read about the Center's educational and research activities or link to other biological and medical resources.

The Center for Imaging and Pharmaceutical Research Home Page

http://cipr-diva.mgh.harvard.edu/

The Massachusetts General Hospital Center for Imaging and Pharmaceutical Research, exploring the relationship between imaging technology and drug development, maintains this informational site. Visitors will find multidisciplinary research information, program overviews, project updates and other scientific resources.

CSIRO Ultrasonics Laboratory

http://www.ul.rp.csiro.au/

A facility of Australia's Commonwealth Scientific and Industrial Research Organization's Division of Radiophysics, the Ultrasonics Laboratory maintains this page. Visitors can review the lab's research work in ultrasonic imaging, medical ultrasound and related health services.

Dalhousie University Division of Oral and Maxillofacial Radiology Home Page

http://bpass.dentistry.dal.ca/

This Web page houses a collection of links to medical research sites relating to dentistry and radiology. Resources listed—including scholarly societies, medical journals and newsgroups, and teaching files—focus on issues of interest to medical students and researchers.

Decision Systems Group

http://dsg.harvard.edu/

The Decision System Group is a medical informatics research and development laboratory operated by Harvard Medical School and Brigham and Women's Hospital. The group's home site focuses on the development of software environments, as well as tools that support the work of health care professionals.

The Magnetic Resonance Imaging Group

http://www-mri.uta.edu/

The Magnetic Resonance Imaging Group at the University of Texas, Arlington, researches technologies for the acquisition, processing, and visualization of medical images. Visit this site to learn about its latest breakthroughs and link to related sites.

Medical Data Analysis Projects

http://www.c3.lanl.gov/cic3/projects/Medical/main.html

The Computer Research and Applications Group at Los Alamos National Laboratory and the National Jewish Center for Immunology and Respiratory Medicine in Denver provide information on their research in medical imaging and their development efforts in multimedia data management telemedicine.

Physical Biochemistry Division

http://npbsn41.nimr.mrc.ac.uk/

The Physical Biochemistry Division of England's National Institute for Medical Research offers up detailed information on its work with x-ray diffraction here. The page also posts a listing of the division's seminars in London.

Yale Image Processing and Analysis Group Home Page

http://noodle.med.yale.edu/

Find graphics, research summaries and online publications at the Yale Image Processing and Analysis Group home page. A joint project of the Departments of Diagnostic Radiology and Electrical Engineering, the site provides multimedia demonstrations and visual examples of current research.

Yale Nuclear Magnetic Resonance Research Group

http://mri.med.yale.edu/

Check this page for an overview of biomedical imaging techniques and research conducted by this group at Yale University. Potential students can find out about educational opportunities and admissions requirements; professionals can link to related publications and organizations.

MEDICAL INSURANCE

Families USA Foundation

http://epn.org/families.html

The Electronic Policy Network houses this Web site, showcasing the efforts of a nonprofit advocacy group calling for affordable health care for Americans. News article reprints, press releases and other reports address issues like insurance and Medicare.

FHP Health Care Home Page

http://www.fhp.com/

This corporate Web site offers information about FHP Health Care, an Arizona-based, health-maintenance organization (HMO). Includes information about FHP's products and services, a fitness quiz and details about FHP's Fit Kids Club.

MEDICAL RESEARCH

Artificial Heart and Lung Program

http://info.pitt.edu/~gwb1/

Visitors to the University of Pittsburgh Medical Center's Artificial Heart and Lung Program home page will learn all they need to know about the UPMC artificial heart and how it works, as well as information on the program itself.

Auditory Perception: Demonstrations and Experiments

http://www.music.mcgill.ca/auditory/Auditory.html

When a sound is heard how does the brain make sense of the noise and fit it into a pattern of understanding? That question is at the center of the Auditory Perception: Demonstrations and Experiments, part of a graduate research project which tests auditory theories or lets visitors find out more about the auditory process.

Clinical Trials and Noteworthy Treatments for Brain Tumors

http://www.lanminds.com/local/brain/trial.html

Check on the latest research into treatments for brain tumors through this site. It offers links to information about clinical trials and experimental treatments, along with selected journal abstracts.

Neuromuscular Physiology Home Page

http://ortho84-13.ucsd.edu/

Read all about how muscles work in the introduction to muscle physiology presented by The Neuromuscular Physiology Lab at the University of California at San Diego. Strengthened with this basic knowledge, visitors can then delve into the details of current research activities and meet the professionals involved.

RadEFX: Radiation Health Effects Research Resource

http://radefx.bcm.tmc.edu/

Research into the effects of radiation is the thrust of this page from the Center for Cancer Control

Research at Baylor College of Medicine, with support resources from various institutions and agencies. The information targets professionals by providing a full range of registries, documents, and guidelines, as well as conference dates and software.

ASSOCIATIONS AND ORGANIZATIONS

Cognitive Science Society Information

http://www.pitt.edu/~cogsci95/

Membership in the Cognitive Science Society is open to professionals in cognitive science and to full-time students. The Society's home page includes information about annual meetings, news, and a searchable index of titles, authors and abstracts.

Dana Foundation

http://www.dana.org/

The philanthropic Charles A. Dana Foundation provides grants for programs in health and education. Its activist arm—the Dana Alliance for Brain Initiatives—advocates brain research. Here, visitors will find an overview of the two groups, which are looking for partners to broaden the Foundation's impact.

International Federation for Medical and Biological Engineering Home Page

http://vub.vub.ac.be/~ifmbe/ifmbe.html

Visitors can download the meeting minutes, speeches and constitution of the International Federation for Medical and Biological Engineering here. The page also posts information on conferences and biographical sketches of the Federation's council members.

North American Primary Care Research Group

http://views.vcu.edu/views/fap/napcrg.html

This Kansas City, Missouri-based membership organization focuses on primary care research. Family practice physicians and researchers will be interested in the group's work in developing practice-based research networks and primary care classification taxonomies.

Society of Nuclear Medicine: Computer and Instrumentation Council Home Page

http://gamma.wustl.edu/tf/caic.html

Interested researchers can consult this site for a calendar of events, mailing list and an archive of newsletters. Visitors can also review meeting summaries and council bylaws, or link to nuclear medicine sites of interest.

COMMERCIAL PRODUCTS AND SERVICES

Novagen Home Page

http://www.novagen.com/

This promotional site is the Web home of Novagen, a company that markets molecular markers, cloning kits and other bio-related tools. Find the product catalog, product support literature and the newsletter among the information at this site.

PanVera Corporation Home Page

http://www.panvera.com/

Wisconsin's PanVera Corporation supplies biological products, particularly human recombinant proteins, for health care and life science researchers. Visitors to this corporate home page will find company news along with ordering and technical information.

GRANTS AND FUNDING

National Institutes of Health (NIH) Guide to Grants and Contracts Database

http://www.med.nyu.edu/nih-guide.html

The NIH publishes a weekly guide to its available grants and contracts. Visitors can have this publication e-mailed to them or read all the past issues online.

INSTITUTES & SCHOOLS

Abbott Northwestern Hospital Cancer Research Laboratory

http://www.msi.umn.edu/Projects/mg90601/anwhome.html

Northwestern Hospital in Minneapolis hosts this Web site. Peruse an index of laboratory papers and journal articles, many of them focused on research connected with the mouse mammary tumor virus.

The Aging Research Center (ARC)

http://www.hookup.net/mall/aging/agesit59.html

The Aging Research Center page provides information for researchers in the field. Visitors will find archives of scientific papers, aging theory documentation and links to scheduled seminars, workshops, and conferences.

Albert Einstein Cancer Center

http://www.ca.aecom.yu.edu/

Finding the cure for cancer is one of the goals of the Albert Einstein Cancer Center, located at the Albert Einstein College of Medicine in New York. The page offers a look at the people behind the microscopes, and links to the Center's newsletter and other research information.

Applied Science and Engineering Laboratories

http://www.asel.udel.edu/

Dedicated to the "research development and dissemination of new technologies for people with disabilities," the Applied Science and Engineering Laboratories addresses needs in five major areas: rehabilitation robotics, speech, system structure, natural language interfaces, and opportunities for students with disabilities.

The Biomedical Engineering Center at the University of Minnesota

http://pro.med.umn.edu/bmec/bmec.html

The programs and resources of the Biomedical Engineering Center at the University of Minnesota are featured at this site. Visitors will also find links to topical images, sounds, movies, and other biomedical engineering resources.

Boston University NeuroMuscular Research Center

http://nmrc.bu.edu/

The Boston University NeuroMuscular Research Center has set up this home page with links to information about each of its specialized research labs.

Brain Information Processing Group

http://www.bip.riken.go.jp/

Meet the researchers at the Brain Information Processing Group, an affiliate of the Institute of Physical and Chemical Research in Japan, who are using mathematics and information science to try to determine how the brain processes information. The application of their research is the replication of brain functions in computers.

Cardiovascular Development Research Group

http://www.cvdev.rochester.edu/

The Cardiovascular Development Research Group at the University of Rochester, New York offers information here on its interdisciplinary research into human congenital cardiac defects. Visitors can peruse project abstracts or link to a number of related organizations and Web sites.

Center for Complex Infectious Diseases

http://www.ccid.org/

The Stealth Virus Research Program at the University of Southern California Infectious Disease Laboratory is outlined on this page. It contains links to current research and publications, as well as a questions and comments area.

Centre for Visual Sciences

http://cvs.anu.edu.au/

Research at the Centre for Visual Sciences of the Australian National University focuses on how visual images are processed by the brain. Visitors to this site can view the world through the eyes of a honeybee and enjoy some lively commentary from the researcher, attempt to solve a 3-D riddle and view a collection of single-image stereograms.

Claude Bernard University Department of Experimental Medicine

http://ura1195-6.univ-lyon1.fr/

Join these French researchers to explore the function and facility of sleep and dreaming. Find research themes, selected articles, images and videos, a bibliography and more. In French and English.

Comprehensive Cancer Center

http://www.cancer.med.umich.edu/

Associated with the University of Michigan, the Comprehensive Cancer Center research staff pursues both basic and clinical cancer research. This site offers news of its active protocols, links to related information and research groups and the Center's toll-free cancer information line.

Dana-Farber Cancer Institute

http://www.dfci.harvard.edu/

The Dana-Farber Cancer Institute is a medical research facility located in the Boston area. This page offers links to its various divisions of study, including biostatistics, molecular biology and core flow cytometry. Visitors will also find additional cancer-related resources here.

Fred Hutchinson Cancer Research Center

http://www.fhcrc.org/

Located in Seattle, the Fred Hutchinson Cancer Research Center maintains this overview of the medical facility, current research projects, events, newsgroups and links to related sites.

German Cancer Research Center

http://www.dkfz-heidelberg.de/

The German Cancer Research Center offers a direct link to its eight fields of research. Areas of study range from cancer risk factors and prevention to tumor immunology. Available in English and German.

H. Lee Moffitt Cancer Center & Research Institute

http://daisy.moffitt.usf.edu/

The Moffitt Cancer Center at the University of South Florida maintains this site to provide cancer education and information on the Center's programs in basic cancer research, clinical trials and cancer control studies.

Haskins Laboratories

http://www.haskins.yale.edu/

Research at Haskins Laboratories, a private, non-profit research laboratory in New Haven, Connecticut, focuses on speech perception, synthesis and analysis, speech production and cognitive science. Among other items of related interest, find current lab news, an overview of current projects and a history of the facility.

Institut Pasteur

http://www.pasteur.fr/welcome-uk.html

The Pasteur Institute features its yearly calendar and overviews of its scientific research projects at this home page. Visitors can read a profile of the Institute or recent publications in French. Contains partial English translations.

International Agency for Research on Cancer

http://www.iarc.fr/

The International Agency for Research on Cancer (IARC) is based in Lyon, France and is affiliated with the World Health Organization. IARC describes its mission as being "to coordinate and conduct research on the causes of human cancer and to develop scientific strategies for cancer control." The site describes research projects, goals and staff.

International Myeloma Foundation

http://www.comed.com/IMF/imf.html

The International Myeloma Foundation is a non-profit medical research group dedicated to finding a cure and improving living conditions for myeloma patients. Visitors will find information on patients, research and publications.

The Low Temperature Laboratory Home Page

http://boojum.hut.fi/

Bundle up warmly when you stop by the Low Temperature Laboratory to learn about this program and its work or its parent university in Finland. Visitors can also link to other low-temperature resources on the Web.

National Jewish Center for Immunology and Respiratory Medicine Home Page

http://www.njc.org/

The National Jewish Center for Immunology and Respiratory Medicine is a research and treatment center located in Denver, Colo. Visitors to the organization's Web site will find information on staff members, research projects and treatment programs.

Nelson Institute of Environmental Medicine

http://charlotte.med.nyu.edu/HomePage.html

The Nelson Institute of Environmental Medicine at New York University maintains this informational site. Visit here to learn about the Institute and access its research into the health effects of environmental pollution.

Positron Emission Tomography (PET) Program

http://pss023.psi.ch/

The Positron Emission Tomography (PET) Program at the Paul Scherrer Institute in Switzerland lists its staff and projects in oncology and neuroscience here.

Radiation Effects Research Foundation

http://www.rerf.or.jp/

To support the health and welfare of atomic bomb survivors and enhance the health of all mankind, Japan's Radiation Effects Research Foundation (RERF) examines the medical effects of radiation on man. Find information about RERF, technical reports and publications, and data on past uses of the A-bomb.

Rehabilitation Engineering and Prosthetics Orthotic Center (REPOC)

http://www.repoc.nwu.edu/

Jump from this welcome page to the REPOC home page at Northwestern University and find out about current research in computer-assisted design and development of prosthetics and orthotics. The researchers present a number of QuickTime movies demonstrating socket and tissue stresses, imaging techniques, and the Squirt-Shape socket.

Research Triangle Institute

http://www.rti.org/home.html

Research Triangle Institute—a multidisciplinary research facility concerned with public health, medicine, environmental protection, advanced technologies and public policy—offers corporate, technical, software, publication and research information at this Web site.

Scripps Research Institute

http://www.scripps.edu/

The Scripps Research Institute, a La Jolla, California-based medical and chemistry research organization, maintains this site to provide access to its wide range of scientific resources. Visit here to connect to its specialized research Web pages and find contact information for its many related organizations.

Sloan-Kettering Institute

http://www.mskcc.org/

The Memorial Sloan-Kettering Cancer Center sponsors this site to provide information about the institution and its services, basic information on cancer prevention and early detection, a physician referral guide and an overview of ongoing research projects.

TB/HIV Research Laboratory

http://www.brown.edu/Research/TB-HIV_Lab/

The TB/HIV Research Laboratory, located at Brown University in Providence, Rhode Island, conducts research on the prevention and treatment of the human immunodeficiency virus (HIV) and tuberculosis (TB). This site provides background information on the lab and its projects. Links to lab personnel, resources and e-mail addresses are included.

University of Arkansas, Little Rock: Biologic Fluid Dynamics Home Page

http://giles.ualr.edu/

Located at the University of Arkansas at Little Rock, the Biologic Fluid Dynamics Group researches flow patterns in the human vascular and airway systems. Visitors to its site can access the group's documents, reports and other online resources.

The Vision Group at NASA Ames Research Center

http://vision.arc.nasa.gov/

This team of scientists and engineers conducts research on human vision and visual technology for NASA missions. Its site includes news, personnel information, projects and publications.

The Walter and Eliza Hall Institute Web Service

http://www.wehi.edu.au/

This research facility in Melbourne, Australia showcases its projects in immunology, cancer, molecular biology. and related biomedical topics here for visitors and prospective students. Find out about the lab's history, check out available job opportunities and access numerous biological databases and scientific resources.

Walter Reed Army Institute of Research Home Page

http://160.151.240.59/wrair.htm

This site, hosted by Walter Reed Army Hospital, offers links to its research facilities and programs. Bioscience types can get the skinny on the Institute's Information Resources Center and Library, Behavioral Biology Sleep and Performance project, and the Department of Membrane Biochemistry.

Worcester Foundation for Biomedical Research

http://sci.wfeb.edu/

The Worcester Foundation, a Massachusetts-based biomedical research institution, maintains this site for Internet resource access. Visit here to link with other medical institutions, computer programming help files and local information, including the Worcester MetroPages.

JOURNALS AND NEWSLETTERS

Behavioral & Brain Sciences Target Article Preprints

http://cogsci.ecs.soton.ac.uk/~harnad/bbs.html

This interdisciplinary journal, published by the Cambridge University Press, focuses on neuroscience, cognitive science, artificial intelligence, behavioral biology and psychology. Site features include an archive of articles, search tool, instructions for authors and commentators, and a link to the Open Journal Project.

Journal of the Experimental Analysis of Behavior

http://www.envmed.rochester.edu/wwwrap/behavior/jeab/jeabhome.htm

Sample the most recent issue of this journal and read about experiments relevant to the behavior of individual organisms. Visitors can also access subscription or search the abstracts database.

On the Brain

http://www.med.harvard.edu/publications/On_The_Brain/.index.html

The Harvard Mahoney Neuroscience Institute's newsletter offers brainy articles aimed at medical professionals. Visitors to the Harvard Medical School online publication will find search-oriented pieces discussing issues and the latest discoveries in neuroscience.

LIBRARIES, DATABASES, AND INDICES

Annual Reviews: Entire Index for Jan 1984 - Feb 1996

http://www-lmmb.ncifcrf.gov/annRev.html

The mission of this nonprofit scientific publisher is "to provide systematic, periodic examinations of scholarly advances in a number of fields of science." Each of the 26 Annual Review publications is dedicated to a specific research area. Search the tables of contents from the past 12 years or

find a particular topic, article or author by searching the online abstract database.

APStracts

http://www.uth.tmc.edu/apstracts/

A weekly electronic notice published by the American Physiological Society, APStracts features abstracts of research articles scheduled to appear in the society's journals. Visitors to this page can access the archives.

BioMed Web Server

http://biomed.nus.sg/

Visit Singapore's Cyberspace Hospital or check out the university's biotechnology databases. Research-oriented links to other Singapore servers and foreign biomedical sites are also included.

BMEnet Biomedical Engineering Resource

http://fairway.ecn.purdue.edu/bme/

BMEnet is a biomedical engineering resource maintained at Purdue University in West Lafayette, Indiana. Search BMEnet for health-care publications, job listings, conference and meeting schedules and academic program details.

The Carcinogenic Potency Database Project (CPDB)

http://potency.berkeley.edu/cpdb.html

Researchers searching for a repository of test results of how different carcinogens affect animals in long-term experiments can check this page. It offers qualitative and quantitative information on positive and negative experiments, all through a standardized database.

Department of Energy Research Involving Human Subjects

http://www.gdb.org/HTB/htb.html

This Department of Energy site contains a database of report summaries on all research projects involving human subjects that are currently funded by DoE. (For information on giant radioactive Gila monsters, you will have to look elsewhere.)

Sapporo Local Area Medical Network (LAMeN)

http://www.sapmed.ac.jp/

LAMeN, a medical network in Japan, maintains this page with links to sites specializing in medical information sources, experimental science, histology, and medical databases. Includes links to Japanese and international medical servers. In Japanese and English.

The World-Wide Web Virtual Library: Vision Science

http://vision.arc.nasa.gov/VisionScience/VisionScience.html

This Virtual Library site provides pointers to information on vision research in humans and other

organisms. Includes instructions for adding related materials to the index.

MENTAL HEALTH

Navy Psychiatry Home Page

http://164.167.49.31/psych/npsyhom.htm

Navy Psychiatry Home Page outline its psychiatric care to U.S. sailors and marines. Visitors can learn about training programs, research and operations.

ADDICTION

Canadian Centre on Substance Abuse

http://www.ccsa.ca/

This Canadian substance abuse site is dedicated to minimizing the ravages of alcohol, tobacco and drug addiction. Site features include information about the center, its publications, activities and information resources. In English and French.

HabitSmart

http://www.cts.com/~habtsmrt/

HabitSmart provides information on addictive behaviors and models for change. Primary topics are alcohol and substance abuse, with links to several addiction-related Web sites.

Web of Addictions

http://www.well.com/user/woa/

This site provides the facts about an array of drugs. See Editor's Choice.

ASSOCIATIONS AND ORGANIZATIONS

American Psychological Society

http://www.hanover.edu/psych/APS/aps.html

Maintained as a member service of the American Psychological Society, this site offers a mix of APS news and professional resources. Find general membership and conference information, as well as links to Internet discussion groups, software resources, related sites and more.

APA Division of Psychopharmacology and Substance Abuse

http://charlotte.med.nyu.edu/woodr/div28.html

The Division of Psychopharmacology and Substance Abuse of the American Psychological Association maintains this overview of its purpose and activities. Among other items of interest, find access to archives, a newsletter, links to various advisory groups and info on funding opportunities.

Christians in Recovery

http://www.goshen.net/cir/

This page from Christians in Recovery is devoted to explorations of the 12-step process in a Christian context. The group's intent is to provide support and guidance for those recovering from "abuse, family dysfunction, depression, anxiety, grief, or addictions."

PsychNET

http://www.apa.org/

The American Psychological Association maintains this searchable site offering its members and the public information related to psychology, science, medical practice and education. Also find links to APA books, journals, conferences and the PsychINFO database.

CHILDREN AND TEENS

Attention Deficit Disorder WWW Archive

http://homepage.seas.upenn.edu/~mengwong/add/

Browsers interested in learning more about Attention Deficit Disorder (ADD) can access an index of online resources at this site. Here you will find links to conferences, criteria for ADD, articles, papers, news, and more.

School Psychology Resources Online

http://mail.bcpl.lib.md.us/~sandyste/school_psych.html

The National Association of School Psychologists in Bethesda, Md., maintains this site to provide information on a variety of specific mental and psychological problems of interest to school guidance counselors and psychologists. Includes links to hundreds of professional and research organizations and psych-related home pages.

COMMERCIAL PRODUCTS AND SERVICES

Center for Anxiety & Stress Treatment

http://www.cts.com/~health/

Focusing on stress and anxiety-related problems, this clinic site promotes self-help books and audiotapes that can be ordered online. The site includes pointers to counseling services and workshops.

Chrysalis Home Page

http://www.omix.com/sites/drSandy/home.html

This online brochure for Chrysalis Counseling Services in San Francisco provides a brief overview of their approach to counseling and invites clients to contact them via telephone, fax, or e-mail.

The Option Institute

http://www.option.org/index.html

The nonprofit Option Institute in Sheffield, Massachusetts offers personal growth and self-improvement programs. Browse the program calendar, read background information about the Institute, and access the publications, and videos list.

Psychology.Com

http://www.psychology.com/

Hosted by Integrated EAP, Inc., a professional employee assistance program, this promotional page offers a variety of psychology-related services. Visitors can order online tests to measure their entrepreneurial quotient or reveal their personality profile, browse a list of therapists or link to other psychological resources.

---

a2z EDITOR'S CHOICE

Web of Addictions

http://www.well.com/user/woa/

Don't look for smirks or tacit approvals at Web of Addictions (WOA), just cold hard facts about the ravages of drug and alcohol abuse. Part activist site, part stern taskmaster, and part educator, the WOA was developed to counteract pro-drug messages, correct misinformation about abused drugs and provide the global community with an educational resource. And educate they do, with a series of public-domain fact sheets that cover every conceivable abused drug. The fact sheets provide a brief history and the pharmacological value (or nonvalue) of the drug, followed by its current use, physical symptoms, short-term and long-term effects, and any possible complications (if you can call death a complication) of drug-drug interactions. Another feature of potential benefit to parents and teachers is the list of slang terms for street drugs. Everybody knows that amphetamines are called speed, but did you know that they're also called "jellybeans" or that crack cocaine is called "Conan"? There's a lot to learn at WOA, and the authors include a selection of articles that help evaluate a person's risk for substance abuse, target teens and their exposures, and discuss treatment options and benefits. WOA is a must-read for all parents and their children. —*Reviewed by Kathleen McFadden*

Web of Addictions

Welcome to the *Web of Addictions*.

The *Web of Addictions* is dedicated to providing accurate information about alcohol and other drug addictions. We developed the Web of Addictions for several reasons. We are concerned about the pro drug use messages in some Web sites and in some use groups. We are concerned about the appalling extent of misinformation about abused drugs on the internet, particularly on some usenet news groups. Finally, we wanted to provide a resource for teachers, students and others who needed factual information about abused drugs.

EMOTIONAL AND PSYCHIATRIC DISORDERS

Collected Writings of Ivan K. Goldberg

http://avocado.pc.helsinki.fi/~janne/ikg/

Search the writings of "maybe the most active psychopharmacologist on the Internet" here. Goldberg's words previously appeared on the Walkers-in-Darkness mailing list, an online resource for people suffering from various depressive disorders. Includes a link to the Mood Disorders Page.

David Baldwin's Trauma Info Pages

http://gladstone.uoregon.edu/~dvb/trauma.htm

Compiled and maintained by a Ph.D., this site focuses on the research and clinical aspects of emotional trauma and traumatic stress. Featuring a mix of information and resources, the presentation reaches out to victims and survivors, as well as clinicians, researchers and students.

False Memory Syndrome Foundation

http://iquest.com/~fitz/fmsf/

The FMS Foundation maintains this educational page to explore False Memory Syndrome, a condition characterized by the memory of a traumatic experience that did not actually occur but that negatively affects a person's identity and interpersonal relationships. The focus is on identification, prevention and help for victims. Visitors can join related mailing lists, link to related sites or read Frequently Asked Questions (FAQs).

Mood Disorders

http://avocado.pc.helsinki.fi/~janne/mood/mood.html

Find links to Frequently Asked Questions (FAQs), articles, Web pages, mailing lists, and other resources dealing with depression and similar mood disorders. Also access information about commonly prescribed mood-altering drugs.

INSTITUTES AND SCHOOLS

Center for Mental Health Policy and Services Research

http://www.med.upenn.edu/~cmhpsr/

The Department of Psychiatry at the University of Pennsylvania Medical School maintains this page with information about current and completed research activities, seminars and staff members. Link to medical centers, mental health sites and related Web pages.

Florida Mental Health Institute Home Page

http://hal.fmhi.usf.edu/

The Florida Mental Health Institute, part of the University of South Florida's Tampa campus, maintains this site to introduce its programs and services. Visit here to search its text and publication collection, read about recent grant awards and employment opportunities, and find access to a variety of other mental health education and administration resources.

National Institute of Mental Health (NIMH) Home Page

http://www.nimh.nih.gov/

This Web site includes general information about the Institute, current clinical studies and patient referral guidelines, grant information and online brochures on a variety of mental health topics.

New York University: Psychiatry Department

http://www.med.nyu.edu/Psych/NYUPsych.Homepage.html

New York University's Psychiatry Department page contains general information about the department and its academic and residency programs. Includes links to a reference desk, textbooks, interactive testing and the Bellevue Hospital Psychiatry Department.

Psychiatry Star Home Page

http://www.psych.med.umich.edu/

Maintained by the University of Michigan's psychiatry department, this web site also houses the American Academy of Child & Adolescent Psychiatry, the University of Michigan Psychiatric Informatics Program and the Psychiatric Society for Informatics. Includes information on study programs, announcements, and a variety of psychiatric and medical references.

JOURNALS AND NEWSLETTERS

Journal of Mind and Behavior

http://kramer.ume.maine.edu/~jmb/welcome.html

An interdisciplinary approach to psychology is investigated and showcased in the Journal of Mind and Behavior. Find abstracts of articles from back issues, submission guidelines and subscription information. Link to other psych sites and publishers.

Psychiatry On-Line

http://www.cityscape.co.uk/users/ad88/psych.htm

Psychiatry On-Line is a medical journal that examines issues relevant to the professional psychiatric community. Visitors can access an extensive list of articles published in current and past issues, browse the bookshop, link to worldwide psychiatry resources or check out geographic-specific sections from the Caribbean, Italy, and France.

Psychiatry On-Line: Italia

http://www.cityscape.co.uk/users/ad88/ital.htm

Psychiatry On-Line: Italia is an Italian-only peer-reviewed journal that includes papers, regular features, and archives. This site is one of the geographically specific editions of the English-language international publication Psychiatry On-Line.

Psycoloquy

http://cogsci.ecs.soton.ac.uk/~harnad/psyc.html

This online journal, sponsored by the American Psychological Association, publishes articles in all areas of psychology and in cognitive science, neuroscience, behavioral biology, artificial intelligence, robotics/vision, linguistics and philosophy. Visit this site for recent articles, archived issues, subscription information and submission guidelines.

LIBRARIES, DATABASES, AND INDICES

Behavior Online

http://www.behavior.net/

Behavior Online offers access to conversations addressing a wide range of topics in mental health and behavioral science. The site also features pointers to books, an online forum, and continuing education opportunities.

Dr. Bob's Mental Health Links

http://uhs.bsd.uchicago.edu/~bhsiung/mental.html

Originally Dr. Bob designed this index for other mental health professionals, but he invites anyone to use it. The Chicago psychologist provides a wide range of mental health links including institutes, journals and disease-specific sites.

Galaxy: Psychology

http://galaxy.einet.net/galaxy/Social-Sciences/Psychology.html

TradeWaves' Galaxy online service serves up Internet psychology resources at this site. From self-help to science, a range of psychology-related links is organized and presented in this index.

MedWeb: Mental Health, Psychiatry, Psychology

http://www.gen.emory.edu/medweb/
medweb.mentalhealth.html

MedWeb provides a seemingly endless list of links here for mental health, psychiatry and psychology resources on the Net. Pointers range from Web of Addiction to the World Federation of Sleep Research Societies newsletter.

Mental Health InfoSource

http://www.mhsource.com/

Mental health professionals are targeted by this hefty database, with diagnosis and treatment information, publications, links to advocacy groups, continuing education opportunities, FAQs, job postings and more. The "Ask the Expert" feature is an interactive question and answer column covering all aspects of mental health and drug therapy.

Metuchen Psychological Services

http://www.castle.net/~tbogen/mps.html

Family practice psychologists located in Metuchen, New Jersey, have developed this index of mental health resources for the layperson rather than the psychologist. Visit here for links to pages focusing on addiction, obsessive-compulsive disorder, anxiety, depression, trauma, and other mental health topics.

Psych Web

http://www.gasou.edu/psychweb/
psychweb.htm

The Psych Web gateway links the user to comprehensive listings of information on psychology. Includes pointers to educational resources and programs, tip sheets for students, commercial counseling services and products, scientific and research sites, self-help pages and a wealth of other resources.

Specifica

http://www.realtime.net/~mmjw/

An Austin, Texas-based psychologist offers an index to medical and mental health resources. The index is organized by category and includes a section on resources available for psychology professionals.

NEWSGROUPS

Personality Typing Systems Newsgroup

http://sunsite.unc.edu/personality/

Information from and about the Usenet newsgroup, alt.psychology.personality, is provided here with archives, a Frequently Asked Questions (FAQs) file, a directory of personality type profiles, the Keirsey Temperament Sorter and other resources.

NUTRITION AND WELLNESS

CyberNutrition Online

http://chd.syr.edu/chd/CyberNutrition2.html

Justify all that beer and pizza (yes...it's actually good for you) by accessing CyberNutrition On-Line. From Syracuse University's College for Human Development, this page provides answers to questions about food you may (or may not) want to know.

Food and Nutrition Information Center

http://www.nalusda.gov/fnic/

The Food and Nutrition Information Center, located in Beltsville, Maryland., targets professionals with dietary guidelines, food service management materials, labeling information and other resources for those searching for a healthy diet.

International Food Information Council

http://ificinfo.health.org/

"Anyone interested in food issues" can find a pantry full of information here. Parents who need help with their kids' eating habits, consumers worried about the effects of aspartame, reporters researching pesticides and teachers looking for food safety curriculum materials are just a sampling of the questioners served at this site.

The Nutrition Pages

http://deja-vu.oldiron.cornell.edu/~jabbo/

The Nutrition Pages serves up a collection of colorful and informative pages on nutrition, health and wellness. Read a diverse collection of articles, browse the FAQs covering basic definitions, lifestyle and sports nutrition, or click on the smiling head to access related links.

The Recipes Folder

http://english-server.hss.cmu.edu/Recipes.html

Favoring the vegetarian flavors, recipes in this folder feature garden variety dishes—beans, eggplant, berries, and the like. For meat eaters, a sampling of recipes for "dead cow," "dead bunny," and "dead chicken" are sure to whet the appetite. Visitors are invited to submit their own kitchen-tested works.

World Guide to Vegetarianism

http://catless.ncl.ac.uk/veg/Guide/

A special link found on the Vegetarian Pages, "this is a hypertext list of restaurants, organizations and other interesting information around the world, separated into regions and subregions."

COMMERCIAL PRODUCTS AND SERVICES

PR Nutrition Home Page

http://www.thegroup.net/prbar/prhome.htm

Fastburn Nutrition Technology presents this promotional site for its Personal Record Bar, a dietary supplement for body-fat reduction. Bar nutritional information is provided, as are "tips by athletes."

Welcome to Uptime's Web Site

http://www.up-time.com/

Uptime distributes Natural Cellular Nutrition, a high-energy vitamin supplement. Read the ingredients list, order a free sample and check out their other products.

Whole Foods Market

http://www.wholefoods.com/wf.html

This promotional site is the Web home of Whole Foods Market, Inc., a Texas-based national chain of 40 natural food supermarkets. Visitors can read about the company's quality standards, pick up some recipe tips, review the company's potential as an investment and find out how to contact its distribution centers.

FOOD SAFETY

The Bad Bug Book

http://vm.cfsan.fda.gov/~mow/intro.html

Presented by the Food and Drug Administration, this hypertext handbook provides information about foodborne pathogenic microorganisms and natural toxins. Get the skinny on *Salmonella*, *Listeria*, red kidney bean poisoning, and other "bad bugs." Selected technical terms are linked to the National Library of Medicine's Entrez glossary and recent articles are appended to keep the handbook current.

Food and Drug Administration Center for Food Safety & Applied Nutrition

http://vm.cfsan.fda.gov/

This site focuses on safety issues in food consumption and preparation. See Editor's Choice.

FOOD SCIENCE

Caffeinated Home Page

http://net-abuse.org/~lizardo/caffeine.html

This page sporting the "Mr. Coffee" logo (but no indication that it's official) concerns itself with all things caffeinated. Picture collections, textual musings on the drug, and pointers to "caffeinated stuff" complement a caffeine chemical data sheet.

Food Science, Purdue University

http://www.foodsci.purdue.edu/

Visit the Food Science Department at Purdue, meet the staff and read about current research programs in computer-integrated food manufacturing, carbohydrate research and a NASA-affiliated project involved with the development of a sustainable food supply for future manned missions to Mars. The site includes a publications listing, student information, and more.

Krispin Komments on Nutrition and Health

http://www.krispin.com/

Digest this essential information for your innards, courtesy of a clinical nutritionist. Use Krispin's tables and formulas to calculate your ideal potassium and protein daily requirements. Krispin also provides food for thought with his komments on the body-mind interaction in abuse recovery.

LIBRARIES, DATABASES, AND INDICES

Arizona Health Sciences Library Nutrition Guide

http://www.medlib.arizona.edu/educ/nutrition.html

The Arizona Health Sciences Center provides this guide to selected nutrition resources on the Net. The site is specifically aimed at the educational, research and health care needs of the center's community.

OCCUPATIONAL MEDICINE

Brookhaven National Laboratory— Safety and Environmental Protection Division

http://sun10.sep.bnl.gov/seproot.html

The Brookhaven National Laboratory—Safety and Environmental Protection Division establishes standards and policies for employees working in high-risk environments in the course of Lab research projects. Includes training schedules, a cal-

endar of major activities, material safety data sheets and an employee safety handbook.

Carpal Tunnel Syndrome

http://www.sechrest.com/mmg/cts/ctsintro.html

This guide to carpal tunnel syndrome, a repetitive-motion injury to the hand and wrist, supplies information on anatomy, diagnosis and treatment. It is presented by the Medical Multimedia Group.

Computer Related Repetitive Strain Injury

http://engr-www.unl.edu/ee/eeshop/rsi.html

Written and maintained by a sufferer of repetitive strain injury (RSI), this page offers a guide to the symptoms, diagnosis, prevention and treatment of the condition, with diagrams and photographs of correct and incorrect typing techniques and postures. Visitors will also find summaries of useful books and links to related Web sites.

---

a2z EDITOR'S CHOICE

Food and Drug Administration Center for Food Safety & Applied Nutrition

http://vm.cfsan.fda.gov/

Do your food-handling practices send a hearty "all aboard" to bacteria and invite them to take a ride into your intestinal tract? Don't get indignant; take the Food Safety Quiz prepared by the FDA. If you've ever tasted raw cookie dough, eaten a rare hamburger or chopped the onions on the same board you used to cut up the chicken, you have put yourself at risk of pathogenic infection. The FDA does a fine job of highlighting important safety issues in food selection, storage, preparation, and food-drug interactions. Find out why pregnant women should not eat soft cheeses, check your raw egg savvy, read raw oyster facts, and more. Special online brochures address food safety issues for persons with AIDS and those with liver disease, diabetes, and gastrointestinal disorders. Link to the FDA's Bad Bug Book, a hypertext handbook that provides information about Salmonella, listeria, red kidney bean poisoning, and other "bad bugs" you've never even heard of. They're all out there…lurking…waiting for you to drop your guard. You'll never look at food the same way again.—*Reviewed by Kathleen McFadden*

FDA/CFSAN Home Page

Center for Food Safety & Applied Nutrition - Food & Consumer Information

Food and Drug Administration WWW Server
Department of Health and Human Services or go to the White House
NTIS/FedWorld or other US Government INTERNET Sources
All US Government Web Servers via Federal Information Exchange
Thomas US Congress Legislative Information

Other World Wide Web Resources:
A Reference Shelf (Dictionary, Travel Info., Zip Codes, Fed. Register, etc.)
Biological Collections, Chemistry, or Computer, PC & Network info.
Index at NCSA home of Mosaic, or W3 Consortium on the WEB

Cornell Theory Center

http://www.tc.cornell.edu/~hedge/

Cornell research shows that there really are "sick" buildings and "healthy buildings." Read about the symptoms prominent among workers in "sick" buildings and access other ergonomic studies on carpal tunnel syndrome, new carpet emissions, back injury, and more.

Finnish Institute of Occupational Health

http://www.occuphealth.fi/

The Finnish Institute of Occupational Health site contains information about the departments, functions, personnel, research and finances of this institute dedicated to the promotion of safe working environments. Includes links to related servers. In Finnish and English.

Occupational Safety and Health Administration Computerized Information System

http://www.osha-slc.gov/

Housed in Salt Lake City, Utah, OSHA's Computerized Information System provides access to an extensive safety health database. Federal regulations, documents, technical data and training information are featured along with links to other servers of topic-related information.

SafetyLine

http://sage.wt.com.au/~dohswa/

Australians will learn about workplace safety laws here at SafetyLine. The page also contains manuals on creating a safe working environment and solutions to specific workplace hazards.

Swedish Association for the Electrically and VDT Injured

http://www.feb.se/

This site describes the symptoms of electrical oversensitivity and explains that the first signs often occur as a result of working with video display terminals (VDT). The reference database includes The Electrical Sensitivity Handbook, research articles and press releases. Information is available in English and Swedish.

Typing Injuries

http://alumni.caltech.edu/~dank/typing-archive.html

Learn how your poor posture and bent wrists can cause debilitating repetitive strain injury and how you can straighten up now to prevent these problems. Sift through the reviews of ergonomic products, read the Frequently Asked Questions (FAQs) files, and access dozens of other information sources.

U.S. Army Center for Health Promotion and Preventative Medicine

http://chppm-www.apgea.army.mil/

The U.S. Army Center for Health Promotion and Preventative Medicine introduces servers addressing industrial hygiene, environmental noise and hazardous waste disposal instructions. Read about the Center's mission and goals, or link to related electronic resources here.

COMMERCIAL PRODUCTS AND SERVICES

Relax the Back Store Home Page

http://www.relaxtheback.com/

Visitors to the Relax the Back Store can find all kinds of products for their aching backs. Besides providing information and help for back pain sufferers, this store also sells items such as office chairs, cervical pillows, and massagers. Related links, along with contact and ordering information, are provided.

Safety Related Internet Resources

http://www.ccohs.ca/Resources/hshome.htm

The Canadian Centre for Occupational Health and Safety supplies this index of safety-related resources. Link to various environmental health and labor-related agencies, and to businesses selling everything from ergonomically correct chairs to radiation-detection instrumentation.

PARENTING

American Academy of Pediatrics

http://www.aap.org/

Parents and pediatricians can visit this site to find out about the resources and services offered by the American Academy of Pediatrics. Parents can find out how to get a pediatrician recommended by the organization as well as review a list of books.

Hints for Divorcing Parents

http://www.realtime.net/~mmjw/jw.htm

Find out how to make divorce easier on your children and yourself at Hints for Divorcing Parents, a page of information and advice supplied by a psychologist as part of a database of informational articles.

Interesting Places for Parents

http://www.crc.ricoh.com/people/steve/parents.html

Interesting Places for Parents is an index of links that parents may find useful, including educational resources, kids' software, articles, a shopping link and information about Internet safety and censorship.

KidSource

http://www.kidsource.com/

KidSource is an online source for kid-related education, health care, and product information. Whether it's for newborns or teens, visitors will find books, articles, organizations, software and forums to assist in making the best choices for their families.

MECC Home Page

http://www.mecc.com/

MECC, a leading producer of children's software, posts a company overview and product list on this promotional page. It includes a software primer for parents and links to dozens of child advocacy groups on the Web.

ParentsPlace.com

http://www.parentsplace.com/

ParentsPlace.com provides an online index of parenting resources on the Internet. Visitors can read articles and books, chat with other parents, or perform a keyword search of its databases. Links to a variety of parenting centers and related businesses are also available.

PEDINFO: A Pediatrics WebServer

http://www.uab.edu/pedinfo/

Not just for doctors, this index to children's health includes a directory of children's hospitals, descriptions of pediatric specialty education programs, information on conditions and diseases, and a parenting section.

Sexual Assault Information Page

http://www.cs.utk.edu/~bartley/saInfoPage.html

This site presents a wealth of information about sexual assault. Broad categories covered include statistics, counseling directories, domestic violence, child abuse, legal issues and prevention.

CHILD SAFETY

Child Safety Forum

http://www.xmission.com/~gastown/safe/

The Child Safety Forum is a resource for parents who wish to protect their young children from typical household hazards. Articles and tips are provided to educate parents on the hidden dangers that exist in all households.

JOURNALS AND NEWSLETTERS

The Family Explorer
http://www.parentsplace.com/readroom/explorer/index.html

The Family Explorer is a monthly print newsletter focused on science and nature activities that parents can do with their children. This Web page includes activities from the newsletter and offers information about how to subscribe.

Family Planet
http://family.starwave.com/

Family Planet is a publication by Starwave Corporation that covers "what's happening on the family front nationally and internationally." Stories revolve around medicine, education, child care and other topics indispensable to parents.

Family World Home Page
http://family.com/

Family World online magazine is a collaborative effort of more than 40 regional parenting magazines. Visit here for activity calendars, articles on education, and links to Internet resources for parents, children and schools.

PERSONAL HOME PAGES

Baby Pulkka's Home Page
http://red-branch.mit.edu/~tmr/baby.html

Follow the fetal development of Zoie Alandra Pulkka with ultrasound movies and pictures offered at this personal home page. Includes parental commentary and various contests.

PHARMACEUTICALS

Larry's Pharmacy, Inc.
http://www.liberty.com/home/foxfire/

Larry C. Beierle looks like a friendly guy, so visit him here. Larry's Pharmacy in San Clemente, California provides information on its mail-order business, plus links to pharmacy-related sites, pharmaceutical companies and other resources.

CORPORATE HOME PAGES

Eli Lilly and Company
http://www.lilly.com/

Eli Lilly and Company, a pharmaceutical corporation headquartered in Indianapolis, provides information on the company and its mission. Also featured here are news releases, financial information, employment information, an annual report and an Environmental, Health, and Safety Report.

Genentech, Inc.
http://www.gene.com/

The pharmaceutical company Genentech provides product information here but also an invaluable science education resource. See Editor's Choice.

a2z EDITOR'S CHOICE

Genentech, Inc.
http://www.gene.com/

Genentech manufactures and markets six protein-based pharmaceuticals. Their corporate home page contains the usual self-promotion and product descriptions, but here's a drug company that gives something back. The Science, Science, Science section provides a remarkably clear and interesting explanation of the drug discovery, testing, and approval process, a virtual mystery to the health care consumer who only knows that prescription drugs are outrageously expensive but has no idea why. Best of all is the Access Excellence program, Genentech's online resource for high school biology teachers. Access Excellence is full of ideas, activities, networking opportunities, and news, all geared toward biotechnology and life sciences education. The monthly seminar feature includes a background paper on the selected topic, focus discussions, related Internet resources, and a suggestion box for feedback and ideas. Previous seminars are archived and cover such kid-friendly topics as fishkeeping, leeches, and allergies. The resource center is crammed with life science links to use in the classroom. Genentech deserves a hearty round of applause for its commitment to biology education and the obvious care and preparation that have gone into Access Excellence. With well-designed graphics and engaging text, the Genentech site is a real find.—*Reviewed by Kathleen McFadden*

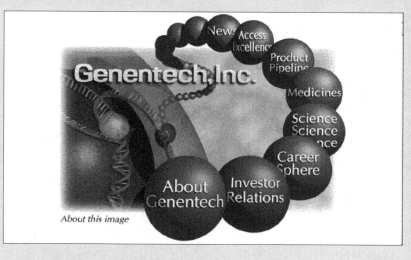

About this image

Merck & Co., Inc.

http://www.merck.com/!!q_TqO3ghTq_
TqO3ghT/

Merck & Co., an international marketer of animal and human health products and services, maintains this promotional site. Visitors will find in-depth research overviews, health services publications and product information.

Novo Nordisk

http://www.novo.dk/

Diabetics will be particularly interested in the health care info offered by this Denmark-based "world leader" in the field of diabetes care and pharmaceutical manufacturing. In addition to the usual company news and promotional material, Novo Nordisk offers extensive information on their environmental policies and practices.

PharmaSoft Welcome Page

http://www.pharmasoft.se/

PharmaSoft, located in Uppsala, Sweden, supplies software, systems, solutions and information services to the pharmaceutical industry, health care services and pharmacies. Visitors to this promotional site will find general information on the company, its employees and its products and services.

Sparta Pharmaceuticals, Inc.

http://www2.interpath.net/interweb/cato/
sparta/sparta.html

Sparta Pharmaceuticals develops drugs and technologies for cancer treatment. Included are a company profile, financial reports, descriptions of anticancer agents and drug delivery technologies.

INSTITUTES AND SCHOOLS

Charles University: Faculty of Pharmacy

http://www.faf.cuni.cz/

Check out the five-year academic study plan at this Czech University and access information on tuition fees for foreign students taking courses taught in English or Czech. The pharmacy faculty posts their journal, Folia Pharmaceutica, online here and provides details of research activities at the university.

The University of Arizona, College of Pharmacy

http://www.pharm.arizona.edu/

The University of Arizona's College of Pharmacy maintains this home page with admissions information, as well as details about available courses and degree programs. Prospective students can also check the electronic student handbook.

University of Arkansas: College of Pharmacy

http://amanda.uams.edu/CoP.html

Find academic program information and links to pharmaceutical and biomedical resources on the College of Pharmacy page from the University of Arkansas. Access to the Arkansas Poison & Drug Control center is also available here.

University of Cambridge: Department of Pharmacology

http://www.phar.cam.ac.uk/

Access this page for information about teaching programs, research groups and departmental seminars in pharmacology at Cambridge. Links to worldwide pharmacology sites are also provided.

The University of Texas: College of Pharmacy

http://saklad.uthscsa.edu/

The University of Texas College of Pharmacy sounds a recruiting call for the profession and outlines its educational opportunities here. Visitors can explore research facilities and academic programs.

JOURNALS AND NEWSLETTERS

Transgenica: Topics in Clinical Biotechnology

http://pharminfo.com/pubs/transgen/tg_
hp.html

Published by Pharmaceutical Information Associates, Ltd., the focus of this online journal is to promote communication among medical researchers working in biotechnology, particularly in the field of new drug development. Visitors can access current articles and contact the editorial staff.

LIBRARIES, DATABASES, AND INDICES

Drug Database

http://pharminfo.com/drugdb/db_mnu.html

This interactive site contains the search tool to access drug information in the PharmInfoNet database. Related links are also featured.

INTELIFEST

http://www.medical.net.au/

Registration is free at Australia's INTELIFEST to gain full access to MIMS Australia, a searchable online pharmaceuticals reference, and to an A to Z listing of pharmaceutical companies. The site also includes product information announcements and product recalls. General medical information geared toward the professional community in Australia is also included.

Pharmacokinetic and Pharmacodynamic Resources

http://www.cpb.uokhsc.edu/pkin/pkin.html

Researchers studying drug level time courses in the human body can find pointers to related Internet sites at the Pharmacokinetic and Pharmacodynamic Resources page. Includes pointers to pharmacy-related software, journals, and discussions.

PharmInfoNet: Pharmaceutical Information Network

http://pharminfo.com/pin_hp.html

This site offers a wealth of information on pharmaceuticals. Access drug FAQ, numerous journals, links to home pages and a searchable database on drug names. Meeting and conference information is also posted here.

Smart Drug/Nootropic Info

http://www.damicon.fi/sd/

Nootropics, or "smart drugs," are a class of drugs that act as cognitive enhancers, with no side effects or toxicity. Visitors can browse reports, discussions and debates about various smart drugs at this site.

World Wide Drugs

http://community.net/~neils/new.html

Neil Sandow provides a compendium of up-to-date drug facts here along with links to several other related sites. See Editor's Choice.

The World-Wide Web Virtual Library: Pharmacy

http://157.142.72.77/pharmacy/pharmint.html

The World Wide Web Virtual Library sponsors this stack of pharmacy-related Net resources. Links to pharmacy schools at universities around the globe are complemented by pointers to professional organizations, a pharmaceutical job bank, as well as related chemistry and drug servers.

RESEARCH AND DEVELOPMENT

CenterWatch: Clinical Trials Listing Service

http://www.centerwatch.com/

New drugs and old drugs for new indications are constantly being tested through clinical patient trials. Find out who's testing, where they're located and how to contact them in this international index. Pick a disease category and read a brief summary of the study or the clinical site, get an overview of clinical research or browse through the latest drugs approved by the FDA.

Centre for Drug Design and Development

http://www.uq.oz.au/ddd/index.html

Current research at the Centre for Drug Design and Development in Australia focuses on drugs for AIDS, cancer, arthritis, central nervous system disorders, and antivirals. Read about the Centre's research, access its annual report, and check the list of upcoming conferences.

Cohen Group Welcome Page

http://www.cmpharm.ucsf.edu/

Fred Cohen's pharmacology laboratory at the University of California at San Francisco conducts research primarily in protein structure modeling and drug discovery. Read abstracts from the Cohen group and access other science resources from this site.

University of Southern California: Laboratory of Applied Pharmacokinetics

http://www.usc.edu/hsc/lab_apk/

Research projects at the Laboratory of Applied Pharmacokinetics include work in dosage regimens and drug delivery systems. Read about software used in research protocols, browse the bibliography and check out the upcoming workshops.

PROFESSIONAL MEDICINE

ALLIED HEALTH

World Wide Web of Emergency Services

http://dumbo.isc.rit.edu/ems/index.html

This resource provides information for those in the emergency services professions. Includes fire, police and emergency medical services resources, along with training and conference information.

ASSOCIATIONS AND ORGANIZATIONS

The Alliance for Fire and Emergency Management

http://internet.roadrunner.com/afem/

The Alliance for Fire and Emergency Management is a network of eight professional associations whose members serve the needs of the fire, life safety and emergency management community. Visitors will find access to a resource center, training calendar and the associations' publications here.

American Association of Physicists in Medicine

http://www.aapm.org/

The American Association of Physicists in Medicine provides online journals and resources geared specifically to the professional medical community. Includes future meeting dates, past meeting minutes and membership information.

The Medical Library Association Home Page

http://www.kumc.edu/MLA/

The Medical Library Association is an organization "of more than 5,000 individuals and institutions in the health information field." Explore

---

a2z EDITOR'S CHOICE

World Wide Drugs

http://community.net/~neils/new.html

Neil Sandow, a Pharm.D., is a person you'd like to see behind the counter at your local drug store. Here's a guy who has all the answers to drug-related questions or knows where to find them. Neil may not compound your prescriptions, but he has made his knowledge accessible by compiling this impressive catalog of pharmaceutical sites. The first entry on the prescription pad is the Rx List: a cross-referenced index of over 4,000 prescription and over-the-counter drugs. Next, take a dose of Martindale's Virtual Pharmacy Center. Martindale's is packed with drug databases, medical dictionaries, online pharmacy journals, and scary facts about drug interactions and reactions. Want more? Check out the World-Wide Web Virtual Library Pharmacy. Neil also includes several universities and general medical sites with their own databases, research updates, and drug news. For those who don't hold with chemical remedies, the alternative medicine and homeopathic links provide some natural options. So the next time you want drug facts, don't consult the 1989 Physicians' Desk Reference you picked up at the last library book sale, log on to Neil's site for the best drug sites on the Internet. —*Reviewed by Kathleen McFadden*

WORLD WIDE DRUGS

MAGELLAN 4 STAR SITE

Neil Sandow, Pharm.D.

- RXLIST A cross index of over 4,000 prescription and 'otc' products
- Known Links to RxList
  Pharmacy/Medical/University/Hospital/Commercial/Personal/Search

- The Internet Sleuth ....Medical Database Search Forms

membership options and association benefits at this site.

COMMERCIAL PRODUCTS AND SERVICES

Tecfen Corporation HomePage

http://www.tecfen.com/

Rescue teams can increase their preparedness levels by ordering medical products and emergency equipment from California's Tecfen Corporation. Shop for products online at this promotional site.

NURSING

JOURNALS AND NEWSLETTERS

American Journal of Nursing Company Online Services

http://www.ajn.org/

The American Journal of Nursing (AJN) specializes in publications for the nursing profession. Visitors will find descriptions and ordering info for trade and research publications, books and multimedia products. Practicing nurses may want to check into AJN Online, an interactive forum for discussions of practice, research, and ideas.

LIBRARIES, DATABASES, AND INDICES

Nursing (Medicine)

http://galaxy.einet.net/galaxy/Medicine/Nursing.html

This page from the Galaxy collection contains an index to sites relevant to medical nursing. Resources featured include articles, guides, collections, directories, and academic organizations.

PHYSICIANS

Audiology Forum: Video Otoscopy

http://www.li.net/~sullivan/ears.htm

This resource for audiologists who use video otoscopy in clinical practice is a detailed technical presentation, with dozens of image files and some motion video. Clinical commentary, an extensive list of references and viewing information FAQs are among the additional features.

The Australasian Anaesthesia Web Site

http://www.usyd.edu.au/su/anaes/anaes.html

Maintained by the Royal Prince Alfred Hospital in Camperdown, Australia, topical discussions at this site include anaphylaxis and the treatment of stings and bites from venomous creatures in Australia. Visitors can also access upcoming meeting schedules, link to anesthesia departments worldwide and download a Mac program that teaches recognition of common major arrhythmias.

Clinician's Handbook of Preventive Services

http://indy.radiology.uiowa.edu/Providers/ClinGuide/PreventionPractice/TableOfContents.html

This page, from the Virtual Hospital, offers access to a searchable e-text edition of the Clinician's Handbook of Preventive Services. Links to national health service sites are also featured.

GASNet Anesthesiology Home Page

http://gasnet.med.yale.edu/

This Global Anesthesiology Server Network (GASNet) page provides resources for anesthesiologists. Visitors can stay awake, however, by browsing through clip art, a newsletter, book reviews, discussion group digests and a hypermedia anesthesiology textbook.

The Home (page) for Clinical Psychophysiologists and Biofeedback Therapists

http://freud.tau.ac.il/~biosee/

Learn about biofeedback and how it "is an established non-experimental treatment" for diagnoses ranging from asthma to neuromuscular disorders. This site also includes information about its electronic forum for clinicians, conferences, studies and links to related organizations and resources.

Johns Hopkins Vestibular Laboratory Home Page

http://www.bme.jhu.edu/labs/chb/index.html

Clinicians who need to bone up on the red lens test and Wallenberg's Syndrome can get in-depth explanations of these terms and many more at this site. A comprehensive resource on hearing and balance disorders is available here, including case studies, research results and a quiz to test clinical diagnosis skills.

MEDIC: What's New!

http://medic.med.uth.tmc.edu/publ/00000885.htm

Professionals and laypersons alike will find useful news and information about what's new in medicine at the MEDIC: What's New! page. Part of a

larger medical education information resource, this page highlights news in medicine around the world.

Neuro-oncology Resources

http://neurosurgery.mgh.harvard.edu/nonc-hp.htm

Massachusetts General Hospital and Harvard's Neuro-oncology Resources site is a repository of information relating to brain tumors. Among the many info services are treatment protocols and gene therapy. Bios of attending staff and lists of the pros and cons of various therapies are also included.

Perfusion Pages

http://eja.anes.hscsyr.edu/perf/ect.html

"Get into the flow of perfusion information" courtesy of The State University of New York Health Science Center in Syracuse. The site includes chat rooms, a quiz generator, forms and charts to help out on the job, commercial products, education and many other topics of interest to professional perfusionists.

Talaria: Hypermedia Clinical Practice Guidelines for Cancer Pain

http://www.stat.washington.edu/TALARIA/TALARIA.html

Targeted to health care professionals, Talaria is a prototype hypermedia version of the Agency for Health Care Policy and Research Guidelines on Cancer Pain. Visitors can click through this edition just as if they were paging through a book. The home page table of contents makes it easy to find and access such features as the Guidelines text, figures, QuickTime movies, and index.

TraumAID Home Page

http://www.cis.upenn.edu/~traumaid/home.html

The TraumAID software program is designed to assist physicians during the critical period after the patient enters the hospital and has stabilized. This site provides information about the program, the project personnel, recent publications and links to related sites.

University of Texas Health Science Center at San Antonio Trauma Home Page

http://rmstewart.uthscsa.edu/

The University of Texas Health Science Center at San Antonio maintains this site focusing on injury, injury prevention and surgical critical care. Visitors will find news, activities updates, patient presentations, physician contact information, and an index of related links.

ASSOCIATIONS AND ORGANIZATIONS

American College of Cardiology

http://www.acc.org/

Find out what it takes to be elected to the American College of Cardiology (ACC) at this site. In the meantime, download guidelines covering medical practices from AMI management to pacemaker implants, check out continuing education programs and tutorials, and keep abreast of cardiac issues via the news updates.

Association of Reproductive Health Professionals

http://policy.net/arhp/

Dedicated to supporting and educating those who make a living in reproductive health, the Association of Reproductive Health Professionals presents info here on the pro-choice organization as well as a well-reasoned diatribe against an FDA action to block over-the-counter contraceptives.

Internet World Congress on Biomedical Science

http://www.medic.mie-u.ac.jp/ANNO/ANNO.html

The secretariat of the Internet World Congress on Biomedical Science at Mie University School of Medicine in Mie, Japan, maintains this site for medical conference announcements and administrative support. Visit here to learn about upcoming events and contact conference support staff.

Society for Neuroscience

http://www.sfn.org/

The Society for Neuroscience is a professional organization of scientists and physicians dedicated to understanding the brain, spinal cord and associated nervous systems. Visitors will find journals, news, job listings and events schedules.

Society of Nuclear Medicine: Computer and Instrumentation Council Home Page

http://gamma.wustl.edu/tf/caic.html

Interested researchers can consult this site for a calendar of events, mailing list and an archive of newsletters. Visitors can also review meeting summaries and council bylaws, or link to nuclear medicine sites of interest.

COMMERCIAL PRODUCTS AND SERVICES

FIRSTMARK

http://www.firstmark.com/

The FIRSTMARK home page offers dozens of databases and directories of medical business companies and resources. Visitors can use these resources to research business issues, medical information, health care and high technology companies.

Intelitool

http://www.com/intelitool/index.html

Intelitool's promotional site offers information on its "cutting-edge computerized physiology" tools. Visitors will find descriptions of products such as Flexicomp, a computerized reflex hammer, and Spirocomp, a respiratory measurement and graphing tool.

DISCUSSION GROUPS AND FORUMS

CBR-MED: An Internet Mailing List for Discussion of Case-Based Reasoning in Medicine

http://www.cs.uchicago.edu/cbr-med/

Case-based reasoning (CBR) is a diagnostic tool that uses information and lessons learned from past cases to solve new problems. This moderated mailing list provides a forum for the discussion of CBR in medicine, particularly with regard to computer technology application and medical informatics.

Fam-Med

http://apollo.gac.edu/

Fam-Med is an e-mail discussion group for family physicians to help them stay current and obtain information that may not be available locally. Includes subscription and background information, descriptions of services and instructions for obtaining files.

Gateway to Neurology at Massachusetts General Hospital

http://132.183.145.103/

Participate in the Neurology Web-Forum's online discussions at this site or access departmental and hospital information along with a collection of medical links.

JOURNALS AND NEWSLETTERS

British Medical Journal

http://www.bmj.com/bmj/

Medical researchers can download the British Medical Journal (BMJ), here. The site also includes archives of past issues, medical conference updates, and links to other BMJ online publications.

Digital Journal of Ophthalmology

http://www.meei.harvard.edu/meei/DJOhome.html

Eye specialists can keep up with recent developments in ophthalmology with the articles and resources in this online journal from the Massachusetts Eye & Ear Infirmary and Harvard Medical School.

Health Info-Com Network Medical Newsletters

http://biomed.nus.sg/MEDNEWS/welcome.html

Health Info-Com's Network Medical Newsletter site is the home of Mednews, a biweekly news digest with articles of interest to the medical community.

Hospital News

http://www.hospital-news.com/

This electronic version of "Florida's Newspaper for Healthcare Professionals" offers articles and features on topics such as managed care, risk management and liability, and current medical news. The site includes subscription information for the complete print version.

The Journal of Immunology

http://journals.at-home.com/JI/

The Journal of Immunology provides "rapid communication of novel research and current issues in immunology" online. Visitors can read current issues, or browse the archive of past issues. Information is also included on submission of manuscripts.

The Medical Reporter

http://www.dash.com/netro/nwx/tmr/tmr.html

This online journal will appeal to pros and families alike. It features articles on a diverse array of health-related issues, from nutrition for kids to advice for seniors. Both current issues and past-issue archives are featured.

Medical Sciences Bulletin

http://pharminfo.com/pubs/msb/msbmnu.html

The Medical Sciences Bulletin features articles and information on pharmaceuticals, diseases and general health. Includes links to PharmInfo-Net and the DrugDB databases.

LIBRARIES, DATABASES, AND INDICES

Biomedical Information Resources & Services By Subject

http://www.mic.ki.se/Other.html#history

Find a plethora of medical resources at this index site, categorized for easy access. Professionals and nonprofessionals alike will find information of interest here, ranging from chemistry to neuroscience to telemedicine.

CommonHealthNet

http://griffin.vcu.edu/html/biomede/imednet.html

This international information exchange for the medical and scientific communities provides access to libraries and databases, distance learning and online courses, messaging and communication services, and more. Sponsored by an international consortium, this nonprofit organization offers most of it services for free. Currently in English, future versions will be available in nine other languages.

Emory University Health Sciences Center Library

http://www.cc.emory.edu/WHSCL/WHSCLhome1.html

The Health Sciences Center Library of Emory University in Atlanta, Georgia provides this site for library and Internet resources. Visit here for links to its text and periodical collections, computer information tools, and other university departments.

HealthWeb

http://www.ghsl.nwu.edu/healthweb/

HealthWeb connects a variety of medical and health science libraries to create a specialized, comprehensive health information resource. Includes information about the network, listings by subject, member libraries and search features.

HyperDOC: U.S. National Library of Medicine

http://www.nlm.nih.gov/

HyperDOC, the National Library of Medicine's (NLM) home page, provides information about the world's largest biomedical library's significant programs, from medical history to biotechnology. Visitors here will find links to NLM databases, publications and information about its grants, contracts and research activities.

Internet/Bitnet Health Science Resources

http://kufacts.cc.ukans.edu/cwis/units/medcntr/menu.html

The University of Kansas Medical Center posts a list of links to Web, gopher and Usenet health science resources at this site. Consult this list of pointers for access to special interest groups, research databases, online medical libraries and publications, and more.

Medicine

http://galaxy.einet.net/galaxy/Medicine.html

Galaxy's hyperguide to medicine provides access to information on a range of topics, from chiropractic care to nuclear medicine. The references provided are oriented to both consumers and professionals.

Medicine Links

http://www.hooked.net/users/wcd/listmed.htm

This index page contains a hyperlinked listing of medical, dental, pharmacological and psychiatric organizations and journals. Includes links to related educational institutions, science foundations and related governmental agencies.

Medscape

http://www.medscape.com/

Medscape features peer-reviewed articles, graphics, literature searches and annotated links to Internet resources. Health care professionals and consumers can access articles in categories such as infectious diseases, AIDS, urology, surgery and managed care. Access is free, but you must register as a user.

MedWeb: Biomedical Internet Resources

http://www.cc.emory.edu/WHSCL/medweb.html

The Emory University Health Sciences Center Library maintains this colossal index of all things medical. Medical schools, specialized areas of medicine and medical science, journals, employment, illustrations, libraries, and more—it's all here.

National Network of Libraries of Medicine (NN/LM)

http://www.nnlm.nlm.nih.gov/

Administered by the National Library of Medicine, the NN/LM provides health science practitioners, investigators, educators, and administrators in the United States with access to biomedical and health care information resources. Visit here to connect to the libraries in its network and to the vast resources within.

PaperChase

http://enterprise.bih.harvard.edu/paperchase/

PaperChase is a commercial service for finding medical and health databases on the Web. Visitors can read the PaperChase Frequently Asked Questions (FAQs) file and obtain detailed pricing and service information here.

PATHY

http://www.med.nagoya-u.ac.jp/pathy/pathy.html

The medical school at Nagoya University in Japan maintains this site for access to its pathology database. Visit PATHY WWW for links to Japanese and English language medical resources.

Physicians' Online

http://www.po.com/

Maintained by doctors for doctors, Physicians' Online provides links to the most current medical knowledge, diagnosis and treatment information available. A sampling of links includes MEDLINE, GenRX and Foreign GenRX, CANCERLIT, AIDSLINE, Medical News, and Disease Centers.

The Virtual Hospital

http://vh.radiology.uiowa.edu/

The multimedia laboratory at the University of Iowa College of Medicine presents The Virtual Hospital, a continuously updated health sciences library. Health care providers and consumers

alike can explore the resources and publications offered here.

Virus Databases On-Line

http://life.anu.edu.au/viruses/welcome.html

This directory of online viral information connects visitors with databases maintained by Australian National University's Bioinformatics Facility. Find information on classification and nomenclature of viruses, reference collections, electron micrographs and tutorials in virology.

World Wide Web Server for Virology

http://www.bocklabs.wisc.edu/Welcome.html

The Institute for Molecular Virology at the University of Wisconsin maintains this site for its virology information service. Visit here for an extensive index of texts, publications, government agencies, nonprofit organizations, and educational institutions.

The World-Wide Web Virtual Library: Biosciences

http://www.ohsu.edu/cliniweb/wwwvl/

The WWW Virtual Library presents this comprehensive list of links to medical biosciences resources and information. Information is categorized by provider and subject.

The World-Wide Web Virtual Library: Epidemiology

http://chanane.ucsf.edu/epidem/epidem.html

The Epidemiology Page is maintained by the Department of Epidemiology and Biostatistics at the University of California, San Francisco. It has links to a wide variety of medical and bioscience resources, including governmental and academic sites.

The World-Wide Web Virtual Library: Immunology (Biosciences)

http://golgi.harvard.edu/biopages/immuno.html

From the Virtual Library, this page features a comprehensive collection of links to information and resources relevant to immunology. Find an alphabetical index pointing to associations, institutions, journals, databases and various scientific disciplines.

The World-Wide Web Virtual Library: Microbiology and Virology (Biosciences)

http://golgi.harvard.edu/biopages/micro.html

The World Wide Web Virtual Library's microbiology and virology page lists links to Web, FTP and gopher sites containing bioscience resources. Access to extensive lists of protocols and databases is provided in a format geared toward academic researchers.

PROFESSIONAL MEDICINE

SCHOOLS AND INSTITUTES

ALLIED HEALTH

Boston University School of Medicine: Department of Biophysics

http://med-biophd.bu.edu/

Find out what it takes to get an M.A. or Ph.D. in biophysics at Boston University. The site contains information on graduate courses, research, faculty, and students.

Boston University School of Public Health

http://www-busph.bu.edu/

The Boston University School of Public Health site provides information on courses of study, research projects and faculty listings. Includes departmental listings, a library catalog and access to the university Web server.

Harvard School of Public Health

http://www.hsph.harvard.edu/

The Harvard School of Public Health site contains information about the department, courses, research, news and publications. Includes links to Yahoo! and Lycos Web search engines and the Harvard University home page.

University of California, San Francisco

http://www.ucsf.edu/

The University of California, San Francisco presents overviews of its graduate programs in health sciences at this site. Includes information on courses of study, student activities, research projects, clinical programs and more.

University of Texas-Houston: School of Public Health

http://utsph.sph.uth.tmc.edu/

The best place to get details about an academic program is from a college catalog, and the online version posted by the School of Public Health at UT-Houston lives up to its promise. Browsers can get information on the four graduate degree programs available, the six public health modules/disciplines, research activities and admission requirements.

NURSING

Ohio State University: College of Nursing

http://utsph.sph.uth.tmc.edu/

Considering a career or graduate work in nursing? Check out the Online U.S. News ranking of nursing colleges provided courtesy of the OSU College of Nursing. Meet the faculty and staff at OSU, get the details of the undergrad and graduate programs, and browse the nursing and medical resources.

University of California, San Francisco Nurseweb Home Page

http://nurseweb.ucsf.edu/www/ucsfson.htm

The University of California, San Francisco, presents this promotional site on its School of Nursing, and for general information on the "science of caring." Visitors will also find "news bytes" and details on employment opportunities here.

PHYSICIANS

Akademii Medycznej w Gdansku

http://www.amg.gda.pl/

This site contains the Web information server home page located at the Academy of Medicine in Gdansk, Poland. Visitors are invited to link to the academy's home page and learn more about its offerings or to the academy's computer center. In Polish only.

Albert Einstein School of Medicine at Yeshiva University

http://www.aecom.yu.edu/

The Albert Einstein School of Medicine at Yeshiva University provides information on its academic programs, courses of study and biomedical research projects. Includes an online course catalog, information on admissions, faculty profiles and links to affiliated servers.

Baylor College of Medicine: Neonatology Section

http://l.neo.tch.tmc.edu/neo.html

The Neonatology Section at the Baylor College of Medicine outlines academic programs and projects for incoming students, as well as in-house information specifically for the campus.

Case Western Reserve University School of Medicine

http://mediswww.meds.cwru.edu/

The Case Western Reserve University School of Medicine contains information on programs of study, admissions, research projects and faculty.

Charles University: Faculty of Medicine

http://dante.lfp.cuni.cz/

This university in Pilsen, Czech Republic, provides information on the medical faculty, courses of study and navigation help. Includes links to other university servers, medical resources and search features by subject.

Columbia University: Gastroenterology Web

http://cpmcnet.columbia.edu/dept/gi/

Columbia University's gastroenterology department home page provides information about faculty and fellows, as well as general departmental information and details about specific gastroenterologic interests and diseases. Includes links to related Internet sites.

Cornell University Medical College Gopher Menu

gopher://gopher.med.cornell.edu:70/1

This is the Cornell University Medical College gopher. Visitors will find a calendar of events and phone books on file here, in addition to research, medical and student information.

Duke University Medical Center

http://www.mc.duke.edu/

Duke University Medical Center offers general information about its administration, academic departments and research at this site, as well as links to University Information Services and other campus servers.

Harvard Medical Web Home Page

http://www.med.harvard.edu/

The Harvard Medical Web serves Harvard Medical School, Harvard School of Dental Medicine and Harvard School of Public Health. Features of this site include access to Countway Library, various departments in the medical schools, publications, and other related sites and resources.

The Hebrew University of Jerusalem, Hadassah Medical School

http://www1.huji.ac.il/md/

The Hadassah Medical School at the Hebrew University of Jerusalem maintains this informational site. Visit here for an overview of the university and its programs, research, people and resources.

Indiana University: School of Optometry

http://www.opt.indiana.edu/

Indiana University School of Optometry home page provides an overview of the department, with information on programs, continuing education and faculty members. Other links point to university eye-care services and resources.

The Johns Hopkins Medical Institutions

http://www.jhu.edu/jhmi.html

Reach out to the individual departments of world-renowned Johns Hopkins Medical Institutions at this central Web site. Doctors and medical researchers can link to the information and library services maintained by Johns Hopkins here.

Johns Hopkins Medical Institutions Information Network

http://cwis.welch.jhu.edu/

Both students and patients will find useful information at this site. From research opportunities and medical zines to campus maps and nearby restaurants, all of Johns Hopkins is here for browsing.

Louisiana State University Medical Center Campus Information System

http://www.lsumc.edu/

Aspiring doctors can explore educational and professional opportunities at the LSU Medical Center site. Tours of the New Orleans campus, academic course catalogs and research facilities are open for public inspection here.

Loyola University Medical Education Network (LUMEN)

http://www.meddean.luc.edu/lumen/

Find the answers to questions about Loyola University in Chicago at this site. Visit the Stitch School of Medicine, evaluate the library and check out the curriculum.

Ludwig-Maximilians-University: Faculty of Medicine

http://www.med.uni-muenchen.de/

Check out the academic program at this medical school in Munich, Germany. Information and links to resources about melanoma and breast cancer are also included. Text in German and English.

Marshall University School of Medicine

http://musom.marshall.edu/

West Virginia's Marshall University School of Medicine provides information about its academic and residency programs, rural health care initiatives, affiliated hospital and health science library.

Medical College of Ohio at Toledo

http://www.mco.edu/

The Medical College of Ohio maintains this index of information about its schools and academic departments. Also find links to the institution's available health care services, resources and technology.

Medical College of Wisconsin InfoScope

http://www.mcw.edu/

This private medical school in Milwaukee welcomes prospective students and provides information about research, departments, references and curriculum. Visitors can also access information about the Integrated Advanced Information Management System and its applications to lifelong learning and information exchange.

Medical University of Lubeck

http://www.mu-luebeck.de/

The Web site for the Medical University of Lubeck, Germany, features general information about the school and current research. Although it was under construction when last visited, the Webmasters promise links to Usenet news related to medical issues and profiles of the university faculty. This page is offered in German only.

MedWeb: Medical Centers and Medical Schools

http://www.gen.emory.edu/medweb/medweb.schools.html

The Emory University MedWeb site contains an index of medical centers and medical schools in the United States and countries around the world.

The Milton S. Hershey Medical Center

http://www.hmc.psu.edu/

Profiles of the Pennsylvania State University College of Medicine and University Hospital are included at this site, along with general information on Penn State and other hospital affiliations.

Morehouse School of Medicine

http://www.msm.edu/

Atlanta, Georgia's Morehouse School of Medicine provides browsers with info about students, faculty and staff as well as admissions and library access.

National University of Singapore's Medical Web Site

http://ch.nus.sg/

Visitors to this gateway page can access Cyberspace Hospital or Cybermed, two professional medical Web sites maintained by the National University of Singapore. Includes medical news and journals, educational information for med students, and indices listing Internet resources for professional care givers.

New England Medical Center

http://www.msm.edu/

The New England Medical Center in Boston serves as both a medical and an educational institution. On this page, find an overview of the facility with information about its many areas of medical expertise. A physician referral guide is also featured.

New York University: Department of Neurosurgery

http://mcns10.med.nyu.edu/

New York University's Department of Neurosurgery Web site is intended for patients, their families and health care professionals. Nonprofessionals will find a straightforward introduction to neurosurgery that answers questions about brain tumors, aneurysms and spinal disorders. Professionals can learn from the case presentations and the diagnostic challenge of the month.

New York University Medical Center

http://www.med.nyu.edu/HomePage.html

The New York University Medical Center provides an introduction to its academic departments, research facilities and hospital operations here. Browsers will also find directories of administrative, medical and academic staff.

Osaka Medical College

http://www.osaka-med.ac.jp/

The home page for Osaka Medical College in Japan links to the college gopher server, library, and the electronic version of the Japan Journal of Medical Informatics. General information on the college, its departments and research programs is available in English and Japanese.

Osaka University Medical School

http://www.med.osaka-u.ac.jp/

Osaka University Medical School in Osaka, Japan provides information here on its departments and online services. Visit here to learn about the school and link to related research centers and health science services. Available in Japanese and English.

Penn State University: Anesthesia

http://www.anes.hmc.psu.edu/AnesthHome.html

The Pennsylvania State University Anesthesia site features information about residencies, employment, faculty, academics, as well as links to publications and related sites.

PulseWeb

http://www.kumc.edu/Pulse/

The Pulse Web page from the University of Kansas Medical Center serves as an online information center for education and training materials on medical issues. Visitors to the site can check breaking news from the medical center or click for information about the faculty, current research, and a host of other topics.

The Queen's University of Belfast: Department of Orthopaedic Surgery

http://brigit.os.qub.ac.uk/

The Department of Orthopedic Surgery at Musgrave Park Hospital in Belfast, Ireland maintains this informational site. Visit here for an overview of the department, contact information and links to other medicine-related Web sites.

St. Francis Medical Center

http://www.sfhs.edu/

This Pittsburgh-based hospital explains its health care services and graduate medical education programs at this site. Visit here to learn about residency and fellowship programs and to link to the University of Pittsburg Medical Center.

Shimane Medical University

http://www.shimane-med.ac.jp

Prospective students can take a virtual tour of the Shimane Medical University in Japan here. Visitors can also download samples from the university's 3-D medical imaging library. In Japanese, with an English home page.

Southern Illinois University School of Medicine

http://www.siumed.edu/

The Southern Illinois University School of Medicine page maps out the six major medical programs the institution has to offer, as well as specific information about curriculum and faculty. Find links to other medical facilities here.

Southwestern MedInfo

http://www.swmed.edu/

Southwestern MedInfo is the home page of the University of Texas Southwestern Medical Center, Dallas. A university overview is available, along with research, library and publication-related topics.

Stanford University Medical Center

http://med-www.stanford.edu/MedCenter/welcome.html

The Stanford University Medical Center provides information on medical education, health care and treatment facilities. Includes pointers to research groups, information on medical technology, staff and faculty listings.

State University of New York: Department of Anesthesiology

http://eja.anes.hscsyr.edu/anes/home.html

The SUNY Health Science Center in Syracuse, New York maintains this page to provide links to the Anesthesiology Discussion List, the Medical Professionals Internet Registry and an anesthesia mailing list database.

Tulane Medical Center

http://www.mcl.tulane.edu/

What's it like to go to medical school in New Orleans? The home page for Tulane University Medical Center offers information about the school's programs in clinical and tropical medicine, admissions guidelines and a broad selection of New Orleans links.

Uniformed Services University of the Health Sciences: Department of Pathology

http://wwwpath.usuf2.usuhs.mil/

The Department of Pathology at the Uniformed Services University of the Health Sciences in Bethesda, Maryland maintains this overview of its programs, faculty and resources. An exam archive and links to related sites on and off campus are also featured.

United Medical and Dental Schools

http://www.umds.ac.uk/

The United Medical and Dental Schools of Guy's and St Thomas's Hospitals has two main campuses in London. The UMDS home page provides information about its departments, library services, publications and more. Features links to biomedical servers, including one maintained by the British Medical Journal.

University of Bergen: Department of Public Health and Primary Health Care

http://www.uib.no/isf/Welcome.html

This Web site, maintained by the Department of Public Health and Primary Health Care at the University of Bergen in Norway, offers information on the department's projects and resources. Most information is in Norwegian, with some pages in English.

University of Bonn Medical Center

http://www.meb.uni-bonn.de/welcome.en.html

The MedNews site at the University of Bonn Medical Center provides information on medical standards, the Center's Poison Information Center and the German Institute of Medical Documentation and Information. Includes numerous links to other medical resources such as HealthWeb, several medical Newsgroups, institutes and clinical hospitals as well as listings of Medical Center staff members and physicians.

University of California, Davis Health System

http://edison.ucdmc.ucdavis.edu/

This Web site provides information about the medical center and med school at the University of California, Davis. Visitors will find information on academics, admissions, faculty and more, plus links to the center's departments, from anesthesiology to urology.

University of California, Irvine: College of Medicine

http://meded.com.uci.edu/

Choose your interest, from medical school to residencies to graduate programs, and click over to detailed information about the department, academic curriculum and faculty.

University of Cambridge: Department of Pathology

http://www.path.cam.ac.uk/

The UK's Cambridge University Department of Pathology offers biology-related information services here. Drop in on the Molecular Genetics Club or look at the schedule for the lively discussions held by the Department of Pathology Tea Club Programme.

University of Chicago: Anesthesia & Critical Care

http://airway.bsd.uchicago.edu/

Access information about the university, educational programs, residency, research projects and faculty. Includes links to the city of Chicago and other sites of interest.

University of Connecticut Health Center

http://www.uchc.edu/

The University of Connecticut in Farmington maintains this site to inform visitors about its educational programs in medicine, dentistry and the biomedical sciences. Browsers can also link to research facilities, library resources and administrative departments.

University of Florida College of Medicine: Department of Anesthesiology

http://www.anest.ufl.edu/

The Department of Anesthesiology at the University of Florida's College of Medicine provides an index to general information, personnel, residencies, programs and research. The site includes links to other anesthesiology resources.

University of Illinois at Urbana-Champaign: College of Medicine

http://www.med.uiuc.edu/

The College of Medicine at the University of Illinois at Urbana-Champaign offers program overviews and access to biomedical resources. Visitors will find information on residency programs, internal medicine and family practice as well as a pathology atlas here.

University of Maryland at Baltimore: Anesthesiology Labs Home Page

http://audio.ab.umd.edu/

The University of Maryland at Baltimore's Anesthesiology Labs home page features a QuickTime movie about the department and labs. Also included are links to street maps and local weather.

University of Medicine & Dentistry of New Jersey

http://njmsa.umdnj.edu/umdnj.html

Visit this site to learn about academic programs, information resources, health care facilities, library-based academic materials and more.

University of Miami School of Medicine

http://www.med.miami.edu/

The School of Medicine at the University of Miami maintains this home page with information concerning research, health care providers and clinical care. This page also links to the campus library and has a searchable database.

University of Michigan Medical Center: Department of Pathology

http://zapruder.pds.med.umich.edu/

There's not a lot about the academic program at this Ann Arbor, Michigan university here, but visitors can check out the online Pathology Laboratories Handbook of Tests, link to home pages of organizations within the department and access a catalog of pathology-related links.

University of North Dakota School of Medicine Home Page

http://www.med.und.nodak.edu/

This Web site contains academic and events information related to the University of North Dakota's med school. Visitors will find departmental, staff and faculty directories, plus research information and links to the school's pathology, sports medicine, pharmacology and other departments.

The University of Oklahoma Health Sciences Center Cardiovascular Section

http://wailer.vahsc.uokhsc.edu/

The Department of Medicine at the University of Oklahoma Health Sciences Center in Oklahoma City maintains this page of Cardiovascular Section resources. Find the Cardiac Arrhythmia Advisory System, an introductory module to the EINTHOVEN System, papers and other related items.

University of Queensland: Anaesthesiology & Intensive Care

http://gasbone.herston.uq.edu.au/home.html

Check out the Global Anaesthesiology Textbook at this site for an index of relevant tutorials or join Gasbone, an online educational project that will include "on demand video and other technological wonders as appropriate." Sponsored by the Medical School faculty at the University of Queensland in Brisbane, Australia, this site also includes intensive care links and lecture notes.

University of Texas Health Science Center at San Antonio

http://www.uthscsa.edu/

Prospective and current students in medicine, dentistry, nursing and allied health fields at UT, San Antonio can access virtually the entire campus at this site, along with medical resources, online publications and research info.

University of Texas-Houston Medical School

http://www.med.uth.tmc.edu/

The Dean welcomes visitors to this site and invites prospective students to check the catalog and sample the student resources. Current students will find lots of need-to-know information on the Medical Student Home Page, including a Medical Student Private Zone for checking grades and evaluating courses.

University of Texas-Houston Medical School: Department of Obstetrics, Gynecology & Reproductive Sciences

http://obg.med.uth.tmc.edu/

Visitors to this site can learn about the OB/GYN programs and subspecialties available at UT-Houston, link to the medical school home page and access a file of patient-asked questions with answers.

University of Texas Medical Branch at Galveston

http://www.utmb.edu/

The University of Texas Medical Branch at Galveston gives an overview of its departments, research and patient care here. The site also includes campus maps, newsletters and online directories.

The University of Vermont: College of Medicine

http://salus.uvm.edu/

The College of Medicine at the University of Vermont provides information here on its campus, programs, faculty and students. Visit here to learn about the university and access its collection of Internet search resources.

University of Virginia: Health Sciences Center

http://www.med.virginia.edu/

Visitors can jump from this page into descriptions of the UVA School of Medicine, the School of Nursing and the graduate sciences programs. Information about the medical center/hospital and health sciences library is also included.

The University of Wales: College of Medicine

http://www.uwcm.ac.uk/

The University of Wales College of Medicine maintains this site with information about the school, its facilities, departments, student organizations, as well as links to related sites.

University of Washington: Department of Orthopaedics

http://www.orthop.washington.edu/

The University of Washington Department of Orthopaedics home page provides facility information for incoming students and links to numerous medical resource sites for medical professionals, including the home page of the Arthritis Foundation.

University of Washington: Department of Pathology

http://www.pathology.washington.edu/

The Pathology Department at the University of Washington presents its own vital statistics here: details on graduate and residency programs, seminar information and a link to the UW cytogenetics and genome project related tools. Visitors can also link to pathology journals and related Web sites.

University of Washington Health Sciences Center

http://www.hslib.washington.edu/

HealthLinks, a project of the University of Washington Health Sciences Center, provides this site for health and medical resources. Visit here for links to reference materials, professional journals, library collections, university information listings and more.

University of Wisconsin: Anesthesiology Department

http://www.anesthesia.wisc.edu/

This home page for the University of Wisconsin Department of Anesthesiology contains such features as a study-guide for clinical anesthesia and an online residency brochure. Visitors will also find information on research, affiliated hospitals, and support facilities.

University of Wisconsin-Madison: Medical School InfoLink

http://www.biostat.wisc.edu/

The University of Wisconsin-Madison's Medical School site provides excellent resources for biomedical and academic research as well as links within the university and to other university medical schools.

Vanderbilt University Medical Center Information System

http://www.mc.vanderbilt.edu/

The Vanderbilt University Medical Center home page contains information about the health care facility, its educational departments and biomedical resources. This page includes guidelines for admission to the schools of medicine and nursing and links to other Vanderbilt servers.

Victorian Institute of Forensic Medicine Home Page

http://www.vifp.monash.edu.au/

The Victorian Institute of Forensic Medicine site provides full text medical publications and protocols at this site. Produced by the Department of Forensic Medicine at Australia's Monash University, the site provides research materials for the practicing and academic communities.

Washington University School of Medicine

http://medinfo.wustl.edu/

The Becker Medical Library at Washington University in St. Louis, offers this Web site with a variety of medical and scientific resources. Visitors can read about the school's departments and programs, check out its health care, science and molecular biology resources, or link to the reference shelf to view a range of useful scientific documents.

West Virginia University: Robert C. Byrd Health Sciences Center

http://www.hsc.wvu.edu/

West Virginia University's Health Sciences Center provides an index to its schools, events, departments and directories. There are also links to information about the university and the state.

Yale University School of Medicine

http://info.med.yale.edu/medical/

The school of medicine at Yale University in New Haven, Connecticut invites visitors to its home page to learn more about the school, its curriculum, research projects and resources. Includes campus information and a shuttle bus schedule.

STUDENT RESOURCES

American Medical Association (AMA) — Medical Student Section

http://www2.umdnj.edu/~ama/ama.html

The AMA sponsors this site for would-be doctors to introduce them to the Association, post news on meetings and legislative items of interest, and provide a list of medical education-related links.

The Medical Education Page

http://www.scomm.net/~greg/med-ed/

A second-year medical student has assembled this compendium of information resources targeted to students, but practicing physicians and other interested persons will find plenty to look at here too. Features include a medical specialties page, medical indexes and links to medical schools on the Internet.

TEACHING TOOLS

Anatomy Index

http://130.219.15.246/MyMapTest.html

These anatomy teaching files, with images and descriptions, can help students and clinicians update their bodily expertise on clavicles, scapulae, rotator cuffs, and beyond. Visitors can click on the body map or select entries from the index.

Cornell University Medical College Education Center

http://edcenter.med.cornell.edu/

Visitors to this site will find general information about the facility, courseware (such as case studies, images, and notes), and links to other medical Web servers of interest.

Dermatology WWW-Server

http://www.rrze.uni-erlangen.de/docs/FAU/fakultaet/med/kli/derma/

Study dermatology online with these case reports and course materials from the University of Erlangen's School of Medicine. A dermatologic image atlas, along with links to dermatology-related Internet sites, round out the offerings. Some materials are provided only in German.

Glossary

http://pharminfo.com/pia_glos.html

This glossary page contains terms and definitions related to medicine and pharmacology.

The Interactive Patient

http://medicus.marshall.edu/medicus.htm

Sponsored by the Marshall University School of Medicine, this teaching tool allows visitors to "simulate an actual patient encounter." Designed for physicians, residents and medical students, the site presents a case and the "doctor" has to request the patient's history, perform a physical, review lab data and then submit a diagnosis and treatment plan.

The Internet Pathology Laboratory for Medical Education

http://www-medlib.med.utah.edu/WebPath/webpath.html

The University of Utah maintains this electronic laboratory that includes "over 1,800 archived

images demonstrating gross and microscopic pathologic findings associated with human disease states." In addition, this multimedia educational site includes case-based laboratory exercises, mini-tutorials and an examination database with over 1,500 questions.

Joint Program in Nuclear Medicine Teaching File

http://count51.med.harvard.edu/JPNM/TF.html

Sponsored by several Harvard Medical School teaching hospitals, this site provides health care professionals and educators with teaching files, case studies and a long list of nuclear medicine-related Internet resources.

Medical Microbiology Home Page

http://biomed.nus.sg/microbio/home.html

The National University of Singapore's (NUS) Medical Microbiology home page links to medical and clinical microbiology resources and information of use to doctors, medical students and microbiologists. This page also offers information on medical microbiologists practicing in Singapore and lecture notes for students at NUS.

The Microbial Underground!

http://www.ch.ic.ac.uk/medbact/

The Microbiological Underground is a compilation of Web pages containing microbiological, medical and molecular biology information and pointers to related material available on the Internet. The primary feature of this site is the author's online course in medical bacteriology.

Pathology 703 Home Page

http://www.biostat.wisc.edu/educ/path/path703.html

The University of Wisconsin-Madison's med school pathology department offers material to complement its Pathology 703 course. Besides a general introduction to pathology, students may access lecture and laboratory schedules and view lab slides.

Pathology Cases of the Month

http://dpalm2.med.uth.tmc.edu/path/tocpath.htm

The Pathology Cases of the Month Web page from the University of Texas-Houston Pathology and Laboratory Medicine features a graphically intense online examination of individual cases. The page also has links to clinical pathology resources.

Recombinant DNA Technology Class

http://lenti.med.umn.edu/recombinant_dna/recombinant_flowchart.html

The Recombinant DNA Technology Course offered by the University of Minnesota Medical School provides a clickable map interface to navigate major issues and information covered in the course lecture.

Special Topics in Virology

http://www.bocklabs.wisc.edu/Tutorial.html

Students will want to check out the introduction to molecular virology in this online tutorial and read about emerging viral diseases in farm animals, the detailed information on Ebola and hantaviruses, and the critical scientific questions for AIDS research.

Virtual Brain

http://lenti.med.umn.edu/NEURON_BRAIN/
BRAIN.html

The Department of Cell Biology Neuroanatomy at the University of Minnesota offers this graphics archive. Visit here to find images of anatomical structures including the ventricles, cortex and overlying soft tissues of the brain. An MPEG movie is also featured.

The Urbana Atlas of Pathology

http://www.meddean.luc.edu/lumen/MedEd/
GrossAnatomy/GA.html

Sponsored by the University of Illinois College of Medicine, this atlas includes an extensive library of pathologic images with explanatory text. Visitors can see everything from atherosclerosis in the aorta to uterine cancer.

The Whole Brain Atlas

http://www.med.harvard.edu/AANLIB/
home.html

Can you name the top 100 brain structures? Find out what they are in The Whole Brain Atlas and learn about the normal functions of the brain, the process of aging and brain diseases. The Atlas is illustrated by an extensive image gallery and some entries include guided tours.

PUBLIC HEALTH

COMMUNITY LEVEL

Health Information Resources and Services Inc. Community Profiling Workstation

http://www.hirs.com/

Local assessment teams developing community health improvement plans can find tools and strategies at this site. Access health surveys, community surveys, tips on compiling a profile of community resources and step-by-step development and implementation guidelines.

INTERNATIONAL

Action Programme on Essential Drugs (DAP) - World Health Organization

http://www.who.ch/programmes/dap/DAP_
Homepage.html

The World Health Organization's (WHO) Drug Action Program site is filled with information about drug use and control. This site, available in both Spanish and English, details WHO projects, activities, history, publications and much more.

Communicable Disease Surveillance Centre (CDSC) Home Page

http://www.open.gov.uk/cdsc/cdschome.htm

The Communicable Disease Surveillance Center, a national resource for communicable disease research in England and Wales, maintains this informational site. Visit here for its reports, reviews and pointers to other sites of interest.

Emergency—A Guide to the Emergency Services of the World

http://www.catt.citri.edu.au/emergency/

Help before, during and after a crisis is available at this site. The World Wide Web Guide to Emergency Services puts visitors in touch with information resources from around the world.

The Global Health Network

http://info.pitt.edu/HOME/GHNet/GHNet.html

The Global Health Network of the University of Pittsburgh maintains this site for general information and resource access. Visit here to glean information about global health issues, contact related organizations and view employment opportunities.

Health-Related Web Servers

http://www.who.ch/others/
OtherHealthWeb.html

The World Health Organization presents this collection of pointers to health-related Web servers around the world. The list, though not comprehensive, is fairly complete and broad-based in its scope.

HealthNet

http://debra.dgbt.doc.ca/~mike/home.html

The HealthNet project focuses on applying communications technologies toward the development of a health-care information infrastructure for Canada. One feature here is HealthNet to GO!, a software package that helps users access health sites on the Internet. There also is information on a Web Demonstration Project and a HealthNet listserv.

HealthNet WWW Demonstration Project: Health Resource List in Hypertext

http://debra.dgbt.doc.ca/~mike/healthnet/
lhlist/hancock.html

The HealthNet WWW Demonstration Project demonstrates the electronic communications that can be applied in the development of a Canadian health information infrastructure. This project page is an alphabetical listing of health resources by type, including links to databases, gopher, WAIS, and Web resources.

Ministry of Health

http://www.mzcr.cz/

The Czech Republic's Ministry of Health maintains this Web site with information about government and medical resources. Most pages here are in Czech, with a few in English.

World Health Organization Division of Child Health and Development

http://cdrwww.who.ch/default.htm

This site contains information on some of the world's most lethal diseases (particularly in developing countries), considered by WHO officials to be leading child killers. Integrated management techniques, research papers and more are offered.

World Health Organization WWW Home Page

http://www.who.ch/

The home page for the World Health Organization provides the "World Health Report," press releases and newsletters for public consumption. Among the site's many features, visitors will find news of virus outbreaks, vaccination requirements, and general health advice.

UNITED STATES

Comprehensive Epidemiologic Data Resource WWW Home Page

http://cedr.lbl.gov/CEDRhomepage.html

The Comprehensive Epidemiologic Data Resource at Lawrence Berkeley National Laboratory invites you to browse its accumulated data related to humans exposed to radiation. Visitors can search the data by keyword or link to related sites, like the Department of Energy home page.

Food and Drug Administration

http://www.fda.gov/fdahomepage.html

The U.S. Food and Drug Administration regulates the production and distribution of more than $1 trillion worth of food, cosmetics and medical products every year. Visit its home page to learn about its programs, facilities and administrators. Links to related agencies, including the Department of Health and Human Services, are also available here.

Food and Drug Administration News

http://www.fda.gov/opacom/hpnews.html

The U.S. Food and Drug Administration (FDA) maintains this site to provide regularly updated information about a variety of national health concerns. Visit here for information about FDA activities, programs, publications and more or link to the FDA home page.

Harvard School of Public Health Biostatistics

http://biosun1.harvard.edu/

The Harvard School of Public Health Biostatistics home page contains departmental information and events, faculty members, faculty publications and technical papers. Includes links to other Harvard Web servers and related sites.

Health Care Financing Administration

http://www.hcfa.gov/

The Health Care Financing Administration, the agency which administers Medicare and Medicaid, maintains this site offering an overview of its mission and its programs. Statistics, data rates, reports, regulations, laws, manuals and research are available for review.

Morbidity and Mortality Weekly Report

http://www.cdc.gov/epo/mmwr/mmwr.html

This site contains the electronic version of the Morbidity and Mortality Weekly Report. Prepared by the Centers for Disease Control and Prevention, it summarizes the weekly reports submitted by state health departments across the nation. Links to these health departments and other related resources are also featured.

National Center for Health Statistics Home Page

http://www.cdc.gov/nchswww/nchshome.htm

This site presents U.S. National Center for Health Statistics (NCHS) background information and health data gleaned from surveys. Includes access to NCHS publications, news releases and fact sheets, plus job opportunities listings.

National Center for Infectious Diseases

http://www.cdc.gov/ncidod/ncid.htm

The National Center for Infectious Diseases in the United States maintains this server with a wealth of information about public health research, pro-

grams, publications and divisions. Visitors will also find the Center's online journal, Emerging Infectious Diseases.

National Institutes of Health

http://www.nih.gov/index.html

This gateway site provides links to various servers and offices at the National Institutes of Health. The U.S. Federal Government agency offers info on news and events listings, health initiatives, scientific resources, grants and contracts.

National Institutes of Health: Division of Computer Research and Technology

http://www.nih.gov/dcrt/

The NIH Division of Computer Research and Technology page provides scientific and technological resources for the Public Health Service and other Federal organizations needing biomedical and statistical computing. Includes information on services, research projects, training programs, job opportunities and publications.

Public Health Information Guide

http://128.196.106.42/ph-hp.html

The Arizona Health Sciences Center sponsors this guide to public health resources. Choose from a diverse collection of links covering topics from environmental safety to communicable diseases.

Put Prevention into Practice (PPIP)

http://www.os.dhhs.gov:81/PPIP/

Under the aegis of the U.S. Public Health Service, the PPIP program advocates the aggressive delivery of clinical preventive services with the goal of preventing disease or detecting it in its earliest stages. Guidelines for clinicians and patients are featured, along with FAQs and general resources. The site includes a link to the National Health Information Center—a vast repository health-related information.

TB Clinical Policies and Protocols

http://www.cpmc.columbia.edu/tbcpp/cover.html

The Department of Medical Informatics at Columbia University in New York City maintains this site for New York City Department of Health information. Visit here to read about clinical policies and protocols for chest clinics and resources from the city's Bureau of Tuberculosis Control.

U.S. Department of Energy Environment, Safety and Health Technical Information Services

http://tis.eh.doe.gov/

Visitors can download technical reports from the U.S. Department of Energy's Technical Information Service here. The site also includes access to

software, Occupational Safety and Health Administration (OSHA) regulations and documents, and general federal government information.

U.S. Department of Health and Human Services

http://www.os.dhhs.gov/

The U.S. Department of Health and Human Services home page links to listings of HHS agencies, research and databases, consumer information, and news and public affairs releases. The GrantsNet and a topic index are also featured.

PUBLIC POLICY ISSUES

Action on Smoking and Health

http://www.ash.org/ash/

Action on Smoking and Health is a national nonprofit that fights for nonsmokers' rights. Visitors to this feisty page will learn about the group's "war on smoking" in the courts and in legislative bodies. The 30-year-old group traces its history here and posts its publications.

Bicycle Helmet Safety Institute Home Page

http://www.bhsi.org/

Advocates of bicycle helmet laws promote their public policy agenda from the Bicycle Helmet Safety Institute Home Page. Read up on helmet laws, standards and compliance efforts at this site.

Johns Hopkins Medical Institution InfoNet: Patient Advocacy Groups

http://infonet.welch.jhu.edu/advocacy.html

The Johns Hopkins Medical Institution's Information Network provides patient advocacy phone numbers in various subject areas; dozens of organizations are listed.

The Nicotine & Tobacco Network

http://www.ahsc.arizona.edu/nicnet/

Get the impetus and support at this page to quit that tobacco habit. From information on tobacco company manipulation to the effects of secondhand smoke on kids, the news and research updates at this site are grim. Nonsmoker wannabes can access a variety of help sheets and support groups.

The Tobacco Control Archives

http://galen.library.ucsf.edu/tobacco/

Tobacco policy researchers hit the mother lode here, a central source of information about to-bacco control issues, with an emphasis on initi 41atives in California. The site also includes links to information on court cases, a newspaper clip-ping service by the Advocacy Institute, and ex-poses of tobacco companies.

World Health Organization Helmet Initiative

http://www.emory.edu/WHI/home.html

The World Health Organization Helmet Initiative maintains this site for information about its ef-forts to promote proper use of motorcycle and bi-cycle helmets. Visit here for related updates, worldwide helmet law listings, links to helmet manufacturers, and more.

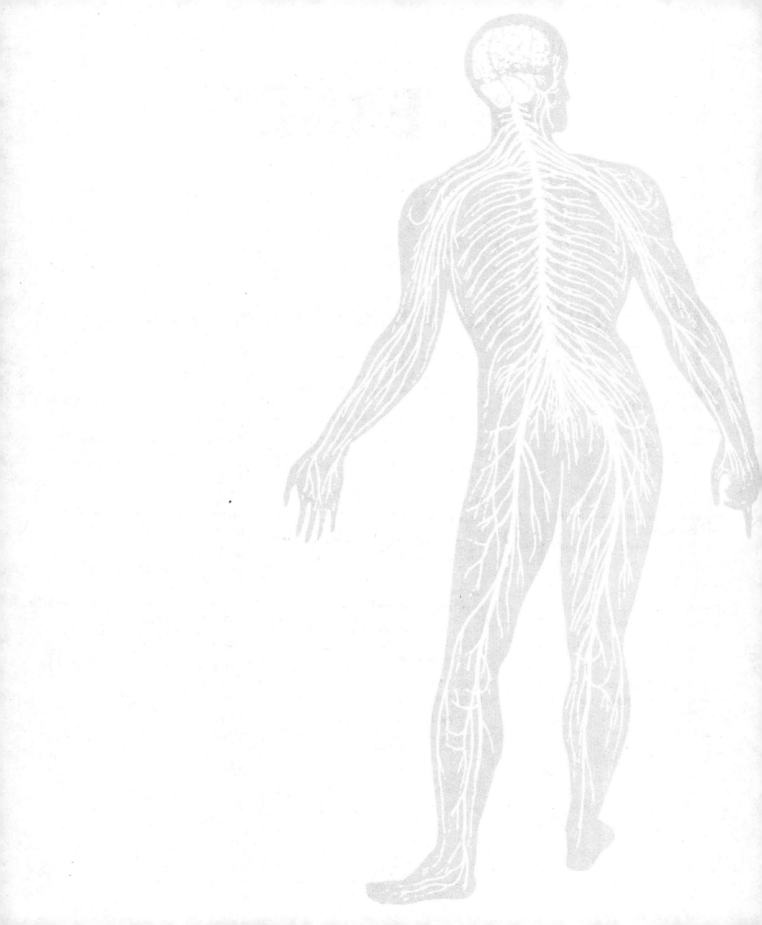

INTERNET

THE 25 MOST POPULAR INTERNET SITES

America Online FTP
ftp://mirror.aol.com/

Apple and the Internet
http://www2.apple.com/documents/
internet.html

BBN Planet
http://www.BBN.com/

**bsy's List of Internet Accessible
Machines**
http://www-cse.ucsd.edu/users/bsy/iam.html

c|net
http://www.cnet.com/

Cornell University CU-SeeMe
http://cu-seeme.cornell.edu/

Electronic Frontier Foundation
http://www.eff.org/

Freedom of Expression Censor-Bait
http://www.mit.edu:8001/activities/safe/
notsee.html

GeoCities
www.geocities.com

**Grafica Obscura, Collected Computer
Graphics Hacks**
http://www.sgi.com/grafica/

**GVU Center's World Wide Web User
Survey**
http://www.cc.gatech.edu/gvu/user_surveys/
User_Survey_Home.html

JavaSoft
http://java.sun.com

Internet Relay Chat Information (IRC)
http://www2.undernet.org:8080/~cs93jtl/
IRC.html

Lycos
http://www.lycos.com/

**National Center for Supercomputing
Applications**
http://www.ncsa.uiuc.edu

Netscape
http://home.netscape.com/

PGP Frequently Asked Questions
http://www.cis.ohio-state.edu/hypertext/faq/
usenet/pgp-faq/top.html

Progressive Networks
http://www.realaudio.com/prognet/index.html

Project 2000
http://www2000.ogsm.vanderbilt.edu/

**Stroud's Consummate Winsock
AppsList**
http://www.cwsapps.com

The Web Developer's Virtual Library
http://www.stars.com/

What's Cool?
http://home.netscape.com/home/whats-
cool.html

**World Wide Web Consortium (W3C):
A Short Prospectus**
http://www.w3.org/hypertext/WWW/
Consortium/Prospectus/Overview.html

**World Wide Web FAQ
(With Answers, of Course!)**
http://www.boutell.com/faq/

Yahoo
htttp://www.yahoo.com

ACCESS PROVIDERS

COMMERCIAL SERVICES

America Online Inc.
http://www.aol.com/

Enter the world of the uber-online service provider: America Online Inc. Visitors to the home page of the self-described "largest provider of online services in the world" can learn about AOL service options and rates. Includes information about signing up for a free trial of the company's services.

America Online FTP
ftp://mirror.aol.com/

The America Online FTP site welcomes AOL members and anonymous users alike. The array of archives housed at this site include such popular download selections as the AOL Web browser and the AOL online service interface, plus Mac and PC software collections, games, musical resources, and more.

CompuServe
http://www.compuserve.com/index1.htm

The promotional page for CompuServe acts as the Web home for the subscriber-based commercial online service. Includes CompuServe's corporate basics, daily news reports and membership information.

Delphi Internet
http://www.delphi.com

The commercial online provider Delphi Internet describes its service as "the world's first online encyclopedia" which eventually evolved into a "meeting place of hundreds of online communities." Find out how to become a subscriber, and tap into the company's online discussion forums, customized content, and Web access services.

GEnie Services
http://www.genie.com/

General Electric's entrant among the commercial online services introduces its products and rates at the GEnie Services home page. Check out its Internet guide, or request further information about its special content and online forums.

MSN
http://www.msn.com/

Microsoft Corporation, having conquered operating systems, moves on to the Internet with the Microsoft Network, an online service and Web exploration starting point that can be customized with sports scores, stock quotes, comics...whatever content the customer prefers. Includes information about Microsoft's products and services.

Prodigy
http://www.prodigy.com/

Prodigy is a subscriber-based commercial online service offering original online content and news services, as well as Internet access. Visitors to the Prodigy home page will get a full tour of the popular online service, including a review of membership benefits, account options, and available information resources.

DOMAIN REGISTRATION SERVICES

Japan Network Information Center
http://www.nic.ad.jp/index.html

The Japan Network Information Center offers a general overview of its domain registration functions and information provider services at this promotional site. Link to its corporate profile, or peruse company publications. In Japanese with limited English translations.

RIPE Network Coordination Centre
http://www.ripe.net/

RIPE provides support to Internet access providers in Europe. Visit this page to learn about the company and its support services, plus find practical how-to information of interest to current and would-be Internet hosts.

Staking Your Claim on Cyberspace
http://www.links.net/webpub/domains.html

One of the young old men of the Web, Justin Hall, outlines domain name registration procedures in this corner of his gigantic Web guide, Justin's Links from the Underground. Find easy instructions and links to InterNIC forms.

FREENETS AND COMMUNITY COMPUTING

Australian Public Access Network Association
http://www.apana.org.au/

The Australian Public Access Network Association is a nonprofit Internet access provider. Visitors will find an application form, usage rules, and an overview of the organization's mission and goals.

Austria Public Netbase
http://www.t0.or.at/

A project of the Austrian Ministry for Science, Research, and Arts, Public Netbase provides Internet access to the general public and to the research communities of Vienna. In German and English.

The Blacksburg Electronic Village (BEV)
http://www.bev.net/

The Blacksburg Electronic Village serves citizens and visitors of Blacksburg, Virginia as a central information site. Local indexes, directories, and pointers are provided offering information on government, education, business, and health care.

Buffalo Free-Net
http://freenet.buffalo.edu/

The Buffalo Free-Net is an Internet community information service for western New York state. Includes links to governmental, cultural, professional, business, social, and educational information centers.

Central Virginia Free-Net
http://freenet.vcu.edu/cvanet.html

Central Virginia Free-Net offers regionally-focused information services about organizations, people, and events in the community. Access services, news and information at this site.

Charlotte's Web
http://www.charweb.org/

Charlotte's Web is a community network in Charlotte, North Carolina. The searchable site includes categories such as jobs and business, government, culture, religion, and arts, and entertainment.

Colorado's SuperNet Inc.
http://www.csn.net/

Colorado's SuperNet Inc. is a nonprofit organization providing Internet access to a number of businesses, schools, and government agencies in the United States.

Community Computer Networks and Free-Net Web Sites

http://freenet.victoria.bc.ca/freenets.html

A Victoria Free-Net member posts his index of community computer networks and Free-Net Web sites around the globe. The list features gateways in Canada and throughout the world.

Dorsai Embassy

http://www.dorsai.org/

Explorers and would-be explorers of the Internet can stop by the Dorsai Embassy Web page for links to Internet software tools and pointers to landmark sites from around the world. The New York-based nonprofit organization offers public Web access and specializes in helping other non-profits make use of the Internet.

Ebone

http://www.ebone.net/

Ebone is a nonprofit European organization that connects over 40 regional networks in more than 20 countries to each other and the Internet. It gives an overview of its mission and work here, and lists what researchers and groups are part of its network.

The FREEnet Center of the Ural Region

http://www.urc.ac.ru/

The FREEnet Center of the Ural Region provides its customers with e-mail, Usenet news, and access to FTP archives and the World Wide Web. This home page describes the organization's services and provides information on the city of Chelyabinsk. In English and Russian.

FREEnet Web (EN)

http://www.free.net/

FREEnet Web provides information about Russian academic and research networks. Most documents are in Russian.

Global Info-Links

http://infoservice.gil.com.au/

Global Info-Links is an Australian Internet access provider maintained by an initiative of the Ipswich City Council in Queensland. Visitors are invited to sample GIL connectivity packages and information services geared to the local community.

Grand Rapids Freenet

http://www.grfn.org/

Grand Rapids Freenet makes local community news and reference directories available online. Visitors to the Michigan organization's home page can search its document archives or browse postings on the bulletin board.

Great Plains Free-Net Inc.

http://www.gpfn.sk.ca/

Great Plains Free-Net Inc. offers free, text-based Internet access to residents of the Regina, Saskatchewan local calling region. This site explains the organization's services and policies. Includes a link to the Regina Public Library home page.

Grex

http://www.cyberspace.org/

Participate in conferencing on the Internet using the Ann Arbor, Michigan public access system: Grex. Find out how to join Grex and who is currently logged onto the "electronic town hall."

The Institute for Global Communications

http://www.igc.apc.org/igc/igcinfo.html

This organization emphasises special activism and community networking. See Editor's Choice.

The Institute for Global Communications

http://www.igc.apc.org/igc/igcinfo.html

The Institute for Global Communications was formed in 1987 to coordinate PeaceNet and EcoNet, networks composed of activists and organizations united by their commitment to social issues. IGC was quick to seize upon the online revolution's potential for the creation of low-cost, worldwide communication systems, immediately setting out to harness the new technology to build additional community networks. Today, IGC is an Internet service provider under whose tutelage the above networks—as well as ConflictNet, LaborNet and WomensNet—thrive, matching concerned progressives with resources and each other via high-speed communications technology and access to digital publishing forums. Through the efforts of these networks and the activists who use them, the Web is utilized as a tool for bringing people together and for calling attention to events and opinions largely ignored by other, less accessible media outlets. IGC is a founding member of the Association for Progressive Computing, an international coalition of progressive computer networks that aims to reduce "the gap between the information-poor and the information-rich." It is through APC that IGC works around the world to help indigenous organizations establish local networks by making available technology and the expertise required to use it. —*Reviewed by Becky Bond*

Institute for Global Communications **@igc**

The Institute of Global Communications, through its IGC Networks -- PeaceNet, EcoNet, ConflictNet, LaborNet and now, WomensNet -- serve individuals and organizations working toward peace, environmental protection, human rights, social and economic justice, sustainable and equitable development, health, and nonviolent conflict resolution.

- Serving the environmental and progressive movements since 1986, IGC currently links over 13,000 members and an additional 30,000 activists and organizations via our membership in the Association for Progressive Communications, with local access in over 133 countries.

- The IGC Networks are directly connected with the Internet and its vast range services, including ftp, telnet, gopher, SLIP/PPP, e-mail and news.

- As a member of any one of the IGC Networks, you have access to the resources of all of them. In addition to the services available to members only, the IGC Networks also have a presence on the Internet's World Wide Web through the IGC Progressive Directory, and in speedy, text-only format via the IGC Gopher.

The Knot at the Cable

http://www.kaapeli.fi/

The Helsinki City Library in Finland provides free public access to the Internet. The site also acts as a publishing house and is linked to the Cable Factory, a collective of Finnish artists. In Finnish and English.

Michiana Free-Net

http://michiana.org

The Michiana Free-Net provides St. Joseph and Elkhart counties in Indiana dialup access to the Internet for free. Visitors will learn about the nonprofit provider, as well as general topics of public interest government, health, employment, and culture.

National Capital FreeNet

http://www.ncf.carleton.ca/

The home page of the National Capital FreeNet of Carleton, California offers online guides and instructional pages for its users. In English and Spanish.

The National Public Telecomputing Network

http://www.nptn.org/

This nonprofit corporation in Cleveland helps communities start online computing network systems and provides professional support thereafter. Read about the organization's programs and services.

Nyx

www.nyx.net

This site provides information about Nyx, a free, open-to-the-public Internet access provider based in Denver. Includes a FAQ about the organization, an essay describing the philosophy behind the service, and links to home pages created by Nyx users.

Phrantic's Public Housing Project

http://phrantic.com/phrantic/index.html

Phrantic's Public Housing Project leads the fight for squatters' rights in cyberspace. The nonprofit organization seeks to provide an e-mail address and personal home page to people in need. Sign up for a home page or offer your services as a landlord here.

RAIN

http://www.rain.org/

The Regional Alliance for Information Networking is a nonprofit Internet access provider in California. Visitors here will learn about its services, training opportunities, and organizational philosophy.

The River Project

http://www.mtn.org/

The River Project is an effort of the Minneapolis Telecommunications Network that aims to provide Internet access to nonprofit and government agencies. It gives an overview of its services and posts links to its clients' pages.

St. John's InfoNET

http://www.infonet.st-johns.nf.ca/

The FreeNet in St. John's, Newfoundland, Canada, maintains this page for users and community members. Find an overview of services and Internet navigation aids, as well as links to other FreeNets.

Three Rivers Freenet

http://trfn.pgh.pa.us/

Resources from the Pittsburgh, Pennsylvania area are featured at the Three Rivers Freenet home page. Categories include cultural activities, social services, and government. Three Rivers Freenet is a local Internet access provider.

Twin Cities Freenet

http://freenet.msp.mn.us/

Twin Cities Freenet brings public Internet access to the Minneapolis-St. Paul community. The nonprofit organization's free services further its mission of electronically enfranchising traditionally technology-poor communities.

Vancouver Community Net

http://www.vcn.bc.ca/welcome.html

The Vancouver Regional FreeNet Web page include information about how the FreeNet system works and how people can join, along with an index of community news for the Canadian city. The page also includes links to discussions of local issues.

Victoria Telecommunity Network

http://freenet.victoria.bc.ca/vifa.html

Victoria Free-net is the home of a community computing information system made available as a free service to the city of Victoria, British Columbia, Canada. Find information regarding services and resources at this introductory site.

INTERNATIONAL

BBN Planet

http://www.BBN.com/

"We helped build the Internet" is one of the many bona fides claimed by Internetworking broker and managed access provider BBN Planet. The company (whose clients include the likes of Harvard University, the U.S. Senate, and Silicon Graphics)

offers Internet access, site maintenance, and network infrastructure development for businesses and organizations worldwide.

GES Internet

http://www.jvnc.net/

Global Enterprise Services provides Internet access and network services to commercial, academic, and government organizations worldwide. This site provides links to company directories, client lists, and more.

IBM Internet Connection

http://www.ibm.net/

Visitors to this corporate site will find IBM's collection of links to corporate news, customer service information, computer resources, and an index of IBM servers worldwide. Includes information about Big Blue's Global Network dialup Internet access service, plus an online help desk. In English and Japanese.

PIPEX Worldserver Business Park

http://www.worldserver.pipex.com/

The European Internet access service offers Web presence design, maintenance and FTP archive services to the world business community. Find an outline of the company's services at this promotional site, as well as client links organized by "market."

Pronet Global Interactive Business Centre

http://www.pronett.com/

British Columbia-based Pronet Enterprises Ltd. provides Internet access and Web page development for businesses around the world. This commercial page contains pricing and contact information for the company.

PSINet

http://www.psi.net/

PSINet, a major commercial Internet access provider, provides an overview of the company, descriptions of services, and pricing information. Includes an analysis of the company's stock performance, corporate services, and a listing of international and domestic business affiliates.

AFRICA

Zambian National World Wide Web Server

http://www.zamnet.zm/

Zambia's national Internet provider pitches its services and connectivity packages. Features links to Zambian sites, including government, university, and newspaper pages.

ASIA

Global Link

http://www.glink.net.hk/

Global Link, an Internet service provider in Hong Kong, provides the usual Web reference information, search engine links, and rate schedules. Check out access offerings and Internet beginners guides.

HA Telecom

http://www.hatelecom.or.jp/

HA Telecom, an Internet access provider and telecommunications products retailer in Japan, promotes its services and products. The site includes links to the company's home page and a customized search tool. In Japanese and English.

IIJ

http://www.iij.ad.jp/

Internet access provider Interactive Initiative Japan loads its home page with company information and a menu of access and design services for business. In Japanese.

INDOnet

http://www.indo.net.id/

INDOnet, an Indonesia-based Internet service provider, maintains this promotional site. Includes individual and business account information, customer service contacts, and links to client Web sites.

InterSpin

http://www.attjens.co.jp/ *or, if you have a better system:* http://www.attnet.or.jp/

InterSpin, a service in partnership with AT&T Jens, offers Internet access, news, and support. Claiming to be Japan's first commercial Internet service provider, Interspin details its hosting, design, and Web gateway options. In Japanese and English.

JETON

http://www.jeton.or.jp/

JETON, a Japanese Internet access provider, presents information about its services and pricing. Links to user home pages and other sites of interest are featured. In Japanese and English.

Korean Telecom

http://nac.kotel.co.kr/

The Korean Telecom CO-LAN site presents a glossary of the company's products and services—plus links to related sites. In Korean.

The Kuki Tower

http://www.kuki.co.jp/

The Kuki Tower provides Internet access service organized into multiple tiers of "rooms," starting with the Internet Cafe, a public arena designed for expression and communication. Jump on the "elevator" and move on to Web graphics support, a teens' fan club, Internet stores and adult-only services. In Japanese and English.

Mesh

http://www.meshnet.or.jp/

C&C Internet, a Japan-based Internet access provider and Web designer for commercial accounts, introduces Mesh, its global Internet service. Includes company background, service index, and links to client sites. In Japanese and English.

Pacific Surf

http://www.technet.sg/

Maintained by Pacific Internet, a Singapore-based Internet service provider for individuals and businesses, this Web site offers visitors service and fee information, guides for surfing the Web, and downloadable software.

ParkPlace

http://www.cet.co.jp/

ParkPlace, an Internet access provider in Japan, presents information on its products and services. Includes links to corporate clients who entrust their Web presence maintenance to the company.

Pristine Communications

http://www.pristine.com.tw/

Pristine Communications serves as a Taiwanese language consultant for the online community and an Internet access provider for Taiwan. The company's Web site features links to subsidiaries in Hong Kong and the United States. In English, German, French, and Spanish.

Rahajasa Media Internet (RADNET)

http://www.rad.net.id/

Rahajasa Media Internet (RADNET), an Indonesian Internet service and online information provider, explains its offerings. Includes company information, along with links to commercial Web sites and regional data sources.

SingNet

http://www.singnet.com.sg/

SingNet, a public database access and Internet access service of Singapore Telecom, maintains this promotional site. Includes news, commercial and individual service rates, technical support, and a look at current customer Web sites.

TWICS

http://www.twics.com/

TWICS, an Internet service provider in Japan, presents information on its services and outlines its corporate background. Includes indexes of client home pages and service options.

Vision Online

http://www.vol.net/

Vision Online, a Hong Kong-based Internet service provider, presents online service information and customer support. Learn about the company's business and personal connectivity accounts, link to client Web pages, and browse its index of interesting and informative Internet sites.

World-Wide Information Network: WIN

http://www.win.or.jp/

The World-Wide Information Network, an Internet provider in Japan, introduces its services along with links to online shopping resources and WIN member sites at its home page. In Japanese and English.

AUSTRALIA/ OCEANIA

Access One

http://www.aone.net.au/

Access One is a full-service Internet provider offering connections across Australia. Includes descriptions of services and pricing, as well as introductory Web guides and software packages.

Australia On Line

http://www.ozonline.com.au/

Australia On Line, an Australian Internet service provider, details its subscriber account options and online publishing services.

Australian Public Access Network Association

http://www.apana.org.au/

The Australian Public Access Network Association is a nonprofit Internet access provider. Visitors will find an application form, usage rules, and an overview of the organization's mission and goals.

Ballarat NetConnect Pty Ltd.

http://www.bnc.com.au/

Australian Internet access provider Ballarat NetConnect Pty Ltd. offers information about its networking products and services. Visitors can also dish up the Internet Entree for a beginner's introduction to the online world, or go surfing at Ballarat's World Wide Web beach.

connect.com.au pty ltd.

http://www.connect.com.au/

The Web home of connect.com.au pty ltd., an Australian Internet access provider, features extensive corporate information, along with pointers to associated companies, Internet surveys, and selected Web links.

Global Info-Links

http://infoservice.gil.com.au/

Global Info-Links is an Australian Internet access provider maintained by an initiative of the Ipswich City Council in Queensland. Visitors are invited to sample GIL connectivity packages and information services geared to the local community.

HunterLink

http://www.hunterlink.net.au/

HunterLink is an Internet service provider based in New South Wales, Australia. The company outlines its customer services and offers the usual pointers to Internet starter resources and Australia-related sites.

Internet Directory Australia

http://www.ida.com.au/

Internet Directory Australia, an Internet access provider and Web publishing company, offers information on Australian travel, tourism, and commerce. Includes details about company services and pricing.

Microplex

http://www.mpx.com.au/

An Internet access provider in Australia gives an overview of its pricing and services. Includes links to basic Internet connectivity software tools, as well as pointers to Usenet sources of local news.

Mid North Coast Internet

http://www.midcoast.com.au/

The Australian Internet access provider details its services and provides directories of business, professional, and educational Web sites. Includes free classified ads, tourist information about Australia's Holiday Coast, and links to regional government home pages.

Mira Networking

http://www.mira.net.au/

Mira Networking is a Melbourne, Australia-based access provider that originated as a nonprofit public site. It offers an archive of Australian arts, technology, and law resources, plus links to search engines and user home pages.

1990 Multiline BBS

http://www.multiline.com.au/

The Perth Internet access provider is the home to multiplayer networked gaming and what the company claims is Australia's largest online game collection. Subscribers can learn how to set up a home page or access the company's help desk.

Open Net Pty Ltd.

http://www.opennet.net.au/

Australia's Educational Internet Services promises "online delivery of flexible learning, using Internet technologies to make available quality educational opportunities." Features include edu-cational news, partnering opportunities, and details on upcoming conferences and exhibitions.

Spirit Networks

http://www.spirit.com.au/

Spirit Networks prides itself on bringing the magic of the Web to subscribers in Canberra, Australia. Review the Internet access provider's products and services, or link to home pages of the company's commercial clients.

Telstra Internet

http://www.telstra.net

Telstra is an Australian Internet service provider offering connection packages promising national coverage. This home page includes corporate background information, plus pointers to user comments and the company's other online services.

CANADA

Disc Scribe

http://www.discribe.ca/home.html

A Canadian Internet access provider outlines its services and rates here. The site also includes a newbies guide to the Internet. In English and French.

EarthLink Network

http://www.earthlink.net/

The EarthLink Network provides full Internet access to users across the United States and Canada. In addition to dialup services, EarthLink offers Web storage space for businesses and individuals, as well as domain name registration.

Magic Online Services Winnipeg

http://www.magic.mb.ca/

Magic Online provides Internet connectivity services to a wide range of corporations, nonprofits, research institutions, small businesses, and individuals in Canada. Read about Magic Online's services, documentation and software.

UUNET Canada

http://www.uunet.ca/

UUNET Canada, a Canadian Internet service provider, offers complete Internet access and custom network options to its clients. Order access or consulting services at the company's home page.

ALBERTA

Alberta Supernet

http://www.supernet.ab.ca/

Alberta Supernet provides Canadian users with a variety of services, including an Internet search capability, links to local businesses, and more.

Review rates and connectivity options at the company's home page.

BRITISH COLUMBIA

auroraNet

http://www.aurora.net/

The Canadian Internet service provider located in Vancouver, British Columbia, offers visitors information about its fees for individual and business accounts. Find out how to get online in the western Canadian province.

AWINC Network

http://www.awinc.com/

AWINC is an Internet connectivity company based in Canada. At the AWINC Web site visitors can read tips for Windows 95 installation, or delve deeper into AWINC's products, services, business. and leisure pages.

Axion

http://www.axionet.com/

Axion, an Internet service provider in Vancouver, British Columbia, offers a wide range of information about its Internet services. Visitors can read about Axion's fully digital connectivity offerings, including software information, business directories, and technical support.

Infomatch

http://infomatch.com/

Infomatch is an Internet access provider in coastal British Columbia. Includes descriptions of services and pricing, as well as links to client home pages, interesting Web sites and business listings.

Island Net

http://www.islandnet.com/

Island Net, an Internet access provider in Vancouver Island, British Columbia, presents information about the company's customers, products, and services. Visitors can also search Island Net's archives for pointers to interesting places to visit on the Web.

MIND LINK

http://www.mindlink.net/

MIND LINK, an Internet access provider for western Canada, offers visitors information about its Web-related services. Links to articles and information on Web products and technology are also featured.

Okanagan Internet Junction

http://www.junction.net/

The Okanagan Internet Junction, a Vernon, Canada-based Internet service provider, maintains this promotional site. Visit the company's home page to learn about its personal and business dialup accounts, leased-line connections, and Web site hosting services.

Ottawa.Net

http://www.ottawa.net/index.html

This home page, maintained by Ottawa-based Internet Access Inc., details the Internet service provider's offerings. Includes pricing and training information, plus links to the home pages of companies and individuals who have chosen to spin their Web sites on Ottawa.Net.

UNIServe

http://www.uniserve.com/

UNIServe Online, an online service provider in southwestern British Columbia, outlines its Internet connectivity products and services at its home page. The site details service options and offers online classified pages.

Vancouver CommunityNet

http://www.vcn.bc.ca/welcome.html

The Vancouver CommunityNet Web site includes information about how the FreeNet system works and how people can join, along with an index of community news for the Canadian city. The page also includes links to discussions of local issues.

Victoria Telecommunity Network

http://freenet.victoria.bc.ca/vifa.html

Victoria Telecommunity Network is the home of a community computing information system made available as a free service to the city of Victoria, British Columbia. Find information regarding services and resources at this introductory site.

MANITOBA

Astra Network Inc.

http://www.man.net/

This promotional site is the Web home of Astra Network Inc., an Internet access provider in Winnipeg, Manitoba. Visitors are invited to review the company's services, customer support, and rates, or access its online Internet search and navigation tools.

MBnet

http://www.mbnet.mb.ca/

MBnet, an Internet service provider in Manitoba, maintains this Web site for its users. Instructions for accessing account information, general navigation tips, and system news are featured.

NEWFOUNDLAND

St. John's InfoNET

http://www.infonet.st-johns.nf.ca/

The FreeNet in St. John's, Newfoundland, maintains this page for users and community members. Find an overview of services and Internet navigation aids, as well as links to other FreeNets.

NOVA SCOTIA/P.E.I.

Atlantic Connect

http://www.atcon.com/

Atlantic Connect is a full-service Internet provider in Halifax, Nova Scotia. Includes information on Internet access services, Web development, training, and technical support.

PEINet

http://bud.peinet.pe.ca/

PEINet, a Prince Edward Island-based Internet service provider, offers company and service information. The company also features Canada-specific resources such as government and business news, local community information, and educational materials.

ONTARIO

HookUp Communications

http://www.hookup.net/

HookUp Communications is a Toronto-based Internet access provider. The company's home page details products and services, as well as items of general Web wisdom.

Inforamp

http://www.inforamp.net/

Inforamp is a Toronto-based Internet service provider, boasting easy-to-use software packages, high-speed connections, and a low subscriber to telephone line ratio. Review products and services, and find out how to subscribe at the company's home page.

Information Gateway Services—IGS

http://www.igs.net/

Information Gateway Systems is an Internet service provider offering coverage in eastern and southern Ontario and western Quebec. Includes descriptions of products, services, prices, and links to commercial sites.

Inter*Com Information Services

http://www.icis.on.ca/

Inter*Com Information Services is a full-service Internet provider in the Ontario area. Includes descriptions of services, training, pricing, and links to client home pages.

Interlog

http://www.interlog.com/

Toronto's Interlog Internet Services provides descriptions of access services and pricing structures. Includes links to client pages and other Canadian and international Web pages of interest.

Internet Connectivity Services Inc.

http://www.icons.net/

Internet Connectivity Services is an Internet service provider in Ontario, Canada. Visitors to its site will find information on the company's services and fees.

Internet Connect Niagara

http://www.niagara.com/

Internet Connect Niagara is an access provider in St. Catharines, Ontario. Visitors to its home page can learn about the company, products, and services.

Internex Online

http://www.io.org/

Internex Online is a Toronto-based Internet service provider. The Canadian company promotes its connectivity products and services, and points to general sites explaining the ins and outs of getting on the Web.

IOSphere Internet Services

http://www.sonetis.com/

Iosphere, an Ottawa-based Internet access provider, details its products and services. Ontario residents can find out how to get online with information including rates, services, and navigation guides.

MGL Systems, Internet Division

http://www.mgl.ca/

MGL Systems Computer Technologies Inc. is an Ontario-based company peddling Internet access services. The company's home page offers system, subscription, and policy details, along with a collection of recommended Web links.

Onramp Network Services Inc.

http://www.onramp.ca/

Onramp Network Services' home page explains its Web managing and Internet connectivity options for the people of Markham, Ontario. Includes information on Canadian real estate offerings, with listings for Calgary, Barrie, Halifax, and Oakville-Milton.

Trytel Internet Inc.

http://www.trytel.com/

Ottawa-based Trytel Internet Inc. provides Internet access, Web page design, software sales, and connection setup services. This site includes information about the company's services and prices, along with links to customer home pages.

UUNET Canada

http://www.uunet.ca/

UUNET Canada, a Canadian Internet service provider, offers complete Internet access and custom network installation and maintenance to its clients. Order access or consulting services in the province of Ontario at the company's home page.

ViaNet

http://www.vianet.on.ca/

ViaNet, an Ontario-based Internet service provider, maintains this promotional site. Find out about the company's individual and business accounts, Web site hosting capabilities, and customer support services.

The Wire

http://www.the-wire.com/

The Wire is an Internet access provider in the Toronto area. The company's home page contains information about subscribing, a list of Toronto pages of interest, and details on its Internet training classes.

QUEBEC

CiteNet Telecom Inc.

http://www.citenet.net/

CiteNet Telecom Inc. in Montreal introduces its Internet access services and products. Visitors are invited to take a look at the service provider's business center and local resource links. In French and English.

Information Gateway Services—IGS

http://www.igs.net/

Information Gateway Systems is an Internet service provider covering eastern and southern Ontario and western Quebec. Includes descriptions of products, services, prices and links to commercial sites.

Métrix Interlink

http://www.interlink.net/

This promotional site is the Web home of Métrix Interlink, an Internet access provider in Montreal. Visitors will find information about the company and the range of services it provides. In French and English.

Reseau Internet Quebec Inc.

http://www.riq.qc.ca/

Reseau Internet Quebec Inc., the official Internet server of the government of Quebec, maintains this site for access to a variety government and business resources. In French.

TotalNet

http://www.infobahnos.com/

A Montreal Internet access provider outlines its services at this promotional site. In addition to rates and connection options, the page includes the company's picks for Internet hot spots.

SASKATCHEWAN

Northern Lights Internet Solutions

http://www.lights.com/

Northern Lights Internet Solutions, based in Saskatoon, Saskatchewan, offers Internet marketing strategies and access services for companies diving into cyberspace. Its clients include a safety audit firm, a wheat pool, and a local Mexican restaurant.

SaskTel

http://www.sasknet.com/

Internet service provider SaskTel offers information about its services for the Saskatchewan region of Canada. Visitors can check the Agribition camera image, AgriCan index, or browse a directory of local government resources.

EUROPE

Cistron Internet Services

http://www.cistron.nl/

Cistron Internet Services introduces details about its Europe-based Internet access service for individuals and businesses. The site includes recent news, descriptions of services, and links to CIS customers. In Dutch and English.

Ebone

http://www.ebone.net/

Ebone is a nonprofit European organization that connects over 40 regional networks in more than 20 countries to each other and the Internet. It gives an overview of its mission and work, and lists member researchers and institutions.

EUnet Communications Services

http://www.eu.net/

EUnet boasts that it is Europe's largest Internet provider. The company's home page provides detailed descriptions of services offered and the countries in which they are available.

AUSTRIA

Austria Public Netbase

http://www.t0.or.at/

A project of the Austrian Ministry for Science, Research, and Arts, Public Netbase provides Internet access to the general public and to the research communities of Vienna. In German and English.

Tech Consult Salzburg

http://www.tcs.co.at/

Tech Consult, an Internet resources company based in Austria, offers an electronic gateway to the city of Salzburg at its corporate home page. Visitors will find a company overview along with

tourist information, global market updates, and links to related Internet Relay Chat pages.

BELGIUM

The Belgian Research Network

http://www.belnet.be/

The Belgian Research Network seeks to connect the country's researchers with each other and with the global scientific community. BELNET provides an overview of its mission and the Internet services it offers.

EUnet Belgium

http://www.eunet.be/

EUnet Belgium, claiming to be the country's oldest and largest Internet provider, highlights its products and services. A variety of resources are available, including company information, search engines, and a list of customers.

INnet BENELUX Internet Service Provider

http://www.innet.net/

The INnet home page outlines the company's Internet access services and pricing options for residents of Belgium, the Netherlands, and Luxembourg. Includes links to the INnet marketplace, directory services, and a user help desk.

PING Belgium

http://www.ping.be/

PING, a spin-off of EUnet Belgium, is an Internet service provider offering cheap access to the consumer market "before and after working hours." Visit this site to obtain service information, download browsing software, and visit client Web sites. Available in Dutch, French, and English.

CZECH REPUBLIC

EUnet Czech Republic

http://www.eunet.cz/

EUnet Czechia, a commercial Internet access provider located in the Czech Republic, introduces its business and individual service options. Includes files discussing computer and network security, along with other information resources. In Czech and English.

Network Resources in Czech Republic

http://www.cesnet.cz/html/cesnet/map.html

This directory of Internet resources available in the Czech Republic covers topics including local Internet providers, plus Web, FTP, gopher, and Usenet news services. Visitors can use either a text directory or a clickable image map to obtain information.

ESTONIA

EENet
http://www.eenet.ee/english.html

EENet is an Internet access provider in Estonia. Find a description of services, as well as links to Estonian Web servers and related Internet resources at this site. In English and Estonian.

FINLAND

EUnet Finland
http://info.eunet.fi/

EUnet Finland, an Internet access provider, details its online connection services and makes its online home at this site. In Finnish.

FUNET
http://www.funet.fi/resources/
kotimaisia-palvelimia.html

FUNET provides an index to Finnish Internet access providers and information resources. Other selections point to international services and databases. In Finnish and English.

The Knot at the Cable
http://www.kaapeli.fi/

The Helsinki City Library in Finland provides free public access to the Internet. The site also acts as a publishing house and is linked to the Cable Factory, a collective of Finnish artists. In Finnish and English.

Metropoli BBS
http://www.mpoli.fi/

Finland's Metropoli BBS, an Internet service provider in Helsinki, features links to member home pages and a gateway to downloadable files. The page also includes links to information about Finland. In Finnish with limited English translations.

Net People Oy
http://www.netppl.fi/

Finland's Net People Web site features information about its own Internet access services, as well as links to popular Internet resources about investing and other topics. In Finnish with limited English translations.

Scifi Communications International Oy
http://www.sci.fi/

This promotional site is maintained by Scifi Communications International, an Internet access provider in Tampere, Finland. Visitors are invited to learn about the company and its services. In Finnish and English.

Tervetuloa Nexor System Service Oy
http://www.nexor.fi/

Access Internet service provider Nexor at the company's home page. Features pointers to to other Finnish servers. In Finnish.

Xgateway Finland Oy
http://www.xgw.fi/

Finland's Xgateway Web site features a variety of regularly updated links including the Declaration of Independence of the People of Internet and public access Linux information. In Finnish with limited English translations.

FRANCE

FranceNet
http://www.francenet.fr/

The commercial home page of FranceNet, an Internet service provider, features FranceWeb, an index to the Web. The site also presents information on FranceNet's services and links to personal home pages of the company's customers. In French.

Internet Way
http://www.iway.fr/

This promotional site is the Web home of Internet Way, an access provider in France. Visitors are invited to learn about the company, its products and customer services, or access the Web search assistance it offers. In French and English.

World-Net
http://www.sct.fr/

World-Net, an Internet access provider in France, maintains this information exchange both as a service to its customers and as a promotional site for business. Visitors can find out about World-Net, access its users guide, or utilize the news link. In French and English.

GERMANY

EUnet Deutschland GmbH
http://www.germany.eu.net/

EUnet, offering Internet access to 34 European and North African countries, maintains this site for its index of German information resources. Visitors can learn about its business and individual access accounts and link to a variety of commercial Web-based services. In German and English.

MAZ-Internet Services
http://www.maz.net/

MAZ-Internet Services of Hamburg, Germany, presents a marketplace, descriptions of its services and links to interesting Web sites. In German.

Mittweida, HTWM, MiNIC
http://www.htwm.de/

The Mittweida Network Information Center provides Internet access and hosts personal home pages for the rural district of Mittweida in Saxony, Germany. Links are provided to the Mittweida University of Technology and Economics. In German.

Netplace
http://www.netplace.com/

Netplace provides Internet access, consulting, and Web page design services in Munich, Germany. Its promotional page details its services and rates. In German.

NTG/Xlink
http://www.xlink.net/

NTG/Xlink provides Internet access services in Germany. Find a list of the company's products and services at this site. In English, French, and German.

Ping
http://www.ping.de/

Ping is an Internet service provider in Dortmund, Germany. Includes descriptions of services, pricing information, training programs, and background on the company. In German and English.

GREECE

Hellas On Line
http://www.hol.gr/

This Greek online information service and Internet access provider offers company information, plus facts about Greece, business news, and an online magazine. Links to mirror sites are also available.

ICELAND

ISnet Information
http://www.isnet.is/

ISnet, the Icelandic arm of Internet service providers NORDUnet and EUnet, maintains this site to introduce its services and information resources. Includes an index of all Web and gopher servers in Iceland.

IRELAND

Cork Internet Services
http://www.cis.ie/

Cork Internet Services offers a full range of Internet connectivity options to communities in the south of Ireland. Find company information, plus links to Irish and international sites on this promotional page.

Ireland On-Line
http://www.iol.ie/

The Web home of Ireland On-Line, an Internet access provider based in the Emerald Isle, offers information about products and services. Includes pointers to business, cultural, and political news and resources.

University of Limerick's Irish Computer Server Index
http://itdsrv1.ul.ie/Information/IrishServerList.html

The University of Limerick, Ireland, maintains this list of Irish Internet servers. Features an extensive index of computer services from commercial, educational, and government organizations.

ITALY

GARR Network Information Service
http://www.nis.garr.it/

The GARR Network Information Service provides links to Italy-based Internet service providers as well as other electronic information resources. In Italian.

Inrete
http://www.inrete.it/

Inrete is an Italian Internet on-ramp. Jump from here to Italian information servers, or check out Inrete's online magazine.

Italia Online
http://www.iol.it/

Italia Online, an Italian information service and access provider, offers a variety of news and lifestyle electronic resources. Visitors will find links to the latest in cinema, music, news, travel, and the Internet. In Italian.

ITnet
http://www.it.net/

ITnet, an Italian Internet access provider, offers company information and customer services, including the DOit Index Page which answers the question, "What's new?" In Italian with limited English translations.

LATVIA

VERnet
http://www.vernet.lv/

Latvia's commercial Internet access provider, VERnet, features information about its computer resources and service options on its home page. Includes a link to price lists and access to Latvia OnLine. In Russian and English.

MONACO

Magma Communications Ltd.
http://www.magmacom.com/

Magma Communications Ltd. is an Internet access provider in Monaco. This promotional site includes information on services and pricing, as well as access to company-sponsored chat rooms.

NETHERLANDS

Cistron Internet Services
http://www.cistron.nl/

Cistron Internet Services introduces details about its Europe-based Internet access service for individuals and businesses. The site includes recent news, descriptions of services, and links to CIS customers. In Dutch and English.

EuroNet
http://www.euro.net/

EuroNet, based in Amsterdam, offers Internet connection services across Europe. This page boasts information about software and services, plus links to commercial and personal home pages. In Dutch and English.

INnet BENELUX Internet Service Provider
http://www.innet.net/

The INnet home page outlines the company's Internet access services and pricing options for residents of Belgium, the Netherlands, and Luxembourg. Includes links to the INnet marketplace, directory services, and a user help desk.

NLnet
http://www.nl.net/

NLnet is a Dutch Internet service provider offering connectivity options to corporations and individuals. Visitors will find information about services, fees, and an extensive database of Web servers in the Netherlands. In Dutch with limited English translations.

PublishNET
http://www.publishnet.nl/

Netherlands-based Internet provider PublishNET outlines its services and includes links to magazines and software at its home page. In Dutch with limited English translations.

SupportNET
http://www.publishnet.nl/

The Netherlands' Amsterdam-based SupportNET offers a variety of Internet access services and Web site maintenance options. In Dutch and English.

SURFnet InfoServices
http://www.nic.surfnet.nl/

InfoServices, a service of SURFnet bv, offers links to Netherlands-based commercial and educational Internet information providers. In Dutch and English.

World Access
http://www.worldaccess.nl/

A commercial service with the slogan, "the easy way to Internet," Netherlands-based World Access restricts entry to some areas of its site to members. Links include shopping, culture, and sports pages. In Dutch with limited English translations.

xxLINK Internet Services
http://www.xxlink.nl/

Amsterdam-based xxLINK Internet Services claims to be the "first Dutch commercial information provider on the Internet." Information available at this site covers Dutch business, tourism, research, and education. In Dutch and English.

ZeelandNet
http://www.zeelandnet.nl/

The ZeelandNet is an Internet access provider for the Netherlands. Features include details of service options and network resources. In Dutch.

NORWAY

InterLink— Norway
http://www.interlink.no/

The InterLink home page outlines the service's connectivity options and its availability in Norway. The page includes links to Internet starting points. In Norwegian.

RUSSIA

Elvis+
http://www.elvis.ru/

The Russian company Elvis+ publicizes its computer networking business at its home page. The company also describes its Internet access and software products. In Russian and English.

The FREEnet Center of the Ural Region
http://www.urc.ac.ru/

The FREEnet Center of the Ural Region provides its customers with e-mail, Usenet news, and access to FTP archives, and the Web. This home page describes the organization's services and provides information on the city of Chelyabinsk. In English and Russian.

GlasNet

http://www.glasnet.ru/

Russian Internet service provider GlasNet touts its services and history as the first nonprofit, nongovernmental telecommunications network in the former Soviet Union. Visitors can find out what it takes to get connected to the Internet in Moscow.

Middle Volga Communications

http://www.stc.simbirsk.su/

Middle Volga Communications outlines its Internet services and highlights the wonders of the Web at its home page. The site also includes information about Russian politics and government structures. In Russian and English.

NEVAlink, St. Petersburg

http://www.arcom.spb.su/

NEVAlink is a Russian Internet service provider and Web publishing firm. In addition to a description of services and prices, the company provides a tour of St. Petersburg, exploring its business climate, culture, and people.

Stack Ltd.

http://www.stack.serpukhov.su/

Stack Ltd. is an Internet access and support provider for Russia's south Moscow region. Find company information, links to the usual Internet tools, and access to scientific databases.

SLOVAKIA

EUnet's Slovakia Document Store, Slovak Republic

http://www.eunet.sk/

EUnet Slovakia describes its Internet access services, complete with account overviews and pricing structures. Includes links to an online technology magazine, commercial sites, and an Internet teaching guide.

SLOVENIA

ARNES-Academic and Research Network of Slovenia

http://www.arnes.si/

The Academic and Research Network of Slovenia provides Internet services to the Slovenian educational community. Read about news and events from the region, as well as local research initiatives.

SPAIN

Dónde?

http://donde.uji.es/

This Spanish Internet resources directory provides pointers to Internet servers and access pro-

viders in Spain. Also included is a search engine for e-mail addresses and general information on the country.

SWEDEN

AlgoNet

http://www.algonet.se/

Algonet AB of Stockholm, Sweden, makes its Web home at this site. Link to the Internet service provider's online information, support, and communication resources. In Swedish.

NetGuide

http://www.netg.se/

NetGuide is an Internet service provider based in Gothenburg, Sweden. Visitors can learn about the services provided by the company and access indexes of Swedish information servers. In Swedish and English.

Personal Internet

http://www.pi.se/

Swedish Internet service provider @pi.se outlines its connectivity products and services. Includes company profile, Internet introduction guide, and service details. In Swedish.

SWITZERLAND

EUnet Switzerland

http://www.eunet.ch/

EUnet, the European Internet access provider, offers information about its services and specials in Switzerland. News and Web links are also featured. In German, English, and French.

Fastnet

http://www.fastnet.ch/

Fastnet, an Internet provider in Switzerland, presents a virtual gallery, information on its services, and business listings. Also featured are a guided tour of the French-speaking part of Switzerland and Geneva's International Car Museum.

Internet Access AG

http://www.access.ch/

Internet Access SA offers its introductory message in both German and French, with links to music, shopping, and technical links. Includes a basic run down of Internet connection options and networking services.

Internet ProLink SA

http://www.fastnet.ch/

Internet ProLink, an Internet provider in Switzerland, offers company information, customer support, local news, and Internet tools. In French and English.

Switch

http://www.switch.ch/

The Swiss Internet access provider Switch details its connectivity products and services. Includes catalogs and indexes, pointers to Web gateways, and FAQs.

TINET

http://www.tinet.ch/

TINET is an Internet access provider for the Italian-speaking regions of Switzerland. Find information about the company, its products and services, plus links to selected sites of local area residents.

UKRAINE

Dcnet: Donbass Communications Network

http://www.aladon.donetsk.ua/

An Internet access provider in Ukraine offers an overview of its services. Find a look at the Donetsk region of Ukraine, along with rates and connectivity information. In Russian and English.

Global Ukraine Inc.

http://www.gu.kiev.ua/

Explore bandwidth options in eastern Europe with Global Ukraine. Providing Internet access services to Ukrainians, the company offers a corporate profile and product listings at this promotional site.

Monolit Internet Service Provider

http://www.cs.kiev.ua/

CS/Monolit Online Hypermedia Services boasts that it is Ukraine's largest provider of network services, open systems, and client/server technology for the Unix platform. The company's home page offers the usual corporate information, plus instructions for configuring computers to display Cyrillic characters.

UNITED KINGDOM

Aladdin

http://www.aladdin.co.uk/

Aladdin, an Internet provider in England, supplies information on its dialup and leased-line services for individuals and businesses. Includes links to regional resources on the Web.

BT Let's Talk

http://www.bt.net/

British Telecom, the United Kingdom's telephone and communications giant, introduces users to its new online services which include BTnet, an Internet access provider. Corporate news and the latest U.K. telecom regulations and developments are provided.

C'Lock

http://www.clock.co.uk/

Delphi, an Internet access provider in the United Kingdom, publishes this online e-zine that includes features on business, entertainment and the latest cultural trends.

Demon Internet

http://www.demon.net/

Advertising itself as Britain's largest Internet access provider with over 60,000 customers, Demon Internet pitches its dialup and leased-line connection packages at its corporate home page. Find information about the company, its products, and Web consulting services.

Direct Connection

http://www.dircon.co.uk/

The United Kingdom-based Internet service provider offers individual accounts and Web publishing services. Survey the company's products and rates at this promotional site.

Frontier Internet Services

http://www.ftech.co.uk/

London's Frontier Internet Services presents news and detailed information about its rates and high-speed connection services. Includes links to client home pages and London-area resources.

Genesis Project Ltd.: Northern Ireland's Premier Internet Service Provider

http://www.gpl.net/

The Genesis Project, an Internet service provider for Northern Ireland, maintains this home page with a description of subscriber services, a client list, and local information pages.

innotts.co.uk

http://www.innotts.co.uk/

Internet access provider innotts.co.uk presents information on its services and a directory to resources on and from Nottingham, England. Includes listings of commercial, educational, sports, entertainment, and tourism sites.

Pavilion Internet

http://www.pavilion.co.uk/

Pavilion Internet is a British Internet access provider offering dialup and ISDN Internet connections and networking services. Features include the Pavilion Internet resource index, community pages, hot sites, and a Web directory.

Tardis Public-Access Computing

http://www.tardis.ed.ac.uk/

Scotland's University of Edinburgh makes Unix service available to the community through Tardis. Log on to the Tardis project's public access computing services at this site.

Total Connectivity Providers

http://www.tcp.co.uk/

United Kingdom-based Total Connectivity Providers introduces its networking services and technical support along with links to customer Web sites at its home page. The company offers services ranging from simple e-mail access to full Internet connections.

Unipalm PIPEX

http://www.unipalm.pipex.com/

Unipalm PIPEX, a company specializing in Internet access and networking products, offers online access to product, service, and company information. Visitors can read the latest news, press releases and promotion updates, or peruse the PIPEX pricing list.

Zynet Internet Services

http://www.zynet.co.uk/

The English Internet access provider Zynet Internet Services offers the scoop on its connectivity products. Visitors will find Internet tips and Zynet product and service information, as well as tourist resources about South West England and Torbay Borough.

LATIN AMERICA/ CARIBBEAN

Cable & Wireless plc.

http://www.candw.ag/

The eastern Caribbean islands of Antigua and Barbuda have been wired by Cable & Wireless plc., a company which seeks to provide a global network from this tropical base. Browsers can find Caribbean postcards plus files for getting started on the Web.

Datacom Caribe

http://www.coqui.com/

Datacom Caribe, which provides networking products and services in Puerto Rico and the Caribbean, presents general information on the company, its products, and services. Includes links to a business center and an index of Puerto Rican links. In Spanish and English.

MEXICO

SPIN-Internet Mexico, D.F.

http://www.spin.com.mx/

SPIN is an Internet access provider serving Guadalajara, Monterey, Tijuana, and surrounding areas in Mexico. Find information on the company, its services and support, subscriber home pages, and Internet tools. In Spanish.

UNITED STATES

ANS CO+RE Systems Inc.

http://www.ans.net/

ANS CO+RE Systems Inc. is a national Internet service provider offering high-speed connections and dedicated Internet access to businesses and individuals. Review services and prices at this promotional site.

BBN Planet

http://www.BBN.com/

"We helped build the Internet" is one of the many bona fides claimed by Internetworking broker and managed access provider BBN Planet. The company (whose clients include the likes of Harvard University, the U.S. Senate, and Silicon Graphics) offers Internet access, site maintenance, and network infrastructure development for businesses and organizations worldwide.

CERFnet

http://www.cerf.net/

This promotional site is the home of CERFnet, an Internet access provider for businesses. Visitors to its home page can read about the company, review its services. and find out about its special projects.

CRL Network Services

http://www.crl.com/

CRL Network Services is a nationwide, business-oriented Internet service provider based in San Francisco. This page provides details about the company's products and services, technical support information, employment opportunities, and a list of CRL's dialup locations.

EarthLink Network

http://www.earthlink.net/

The EarthLink Network provides full Internet access to users across the United States and Canada. In addition to dialup services, EarthLink offers Web storage space for businesses and individuals, as well as domain name registration.

FreeMark Communications

http://www.freemark.com/

FreeMark Mail offers free e-mail service to all PC users in the continental United States, with the fees for the service picked up by "discreetly placed" advertisements. Check out a demo at the FreeMark home page.

GES Internet

http://www.jvnc.net/

Global Enterprise Services provides Internet access and network services to commercial, academic, and government organizations worldwide. This site provides links to company directories, client lists, and more.

IBM Internet Connection

http://www.ibm.net/

Visitors to this corporate site will find IBM's collection of links to corporate news, customer service information, computer resources, and an index of IBM servers worldwide. Includes information about Big Blue's Global Network dialup Internet access service, plus an online help desk. In English and Japanese.

I-Link

http://www.i-link.net/

This United States-based Internet access provider offering nationwide dialup services details its products and pricing. Register for a free trial run, or become a subscriber online.

InfiNet

http://www.infi.net/

Internet access provider InfiNet is owned by newspaper publishing heavy hitters, Gannett Co. Inc. and Knight-Ridder Inc. and, not surprisingly, specializes in bringing newspapers online. The site includes service descriptions, a 4-1-1 directory, and an electronic newsstand.

INFO.Net

http://www.infonet.com/

INFO.Net, part of the Infonet Services Corporation, is a provider of Internet access. This site presents corporate information and details on products and services, as well as tools and resources.

Intercon: Internet Information and Resources

http://www.intercon.net/

Intercon is a nationwide Internet access provider offering Web starting points and basic guides to the Internet at its home page. The site offers a listing of what's new on the Internet, as well as links to downloadable software.

LDS iAmerica

http://www.iamerica.net/

Internet service provider LDS iAmerica, an affiliate of Long Distance Savers Inc., pitches its access options in the local Texas and Oklahoma area and in the rest of the continental United States. The page includes links to customer pages and technical support.

MCI

http://www.mci.com/

Telecommunications giant MCI, providing long distance, wireless, local access, paging and Internet services, offers this corporate home page. Visitors can learn about its latest connectivity promotions and find detailed information about its products for business and home.

NETCOM

http://www.netcom.com/

NETCOM On-line Communication Services Inc. is a national provider of Internet access. At the NETCOM site learn about products and services, subscribe electronically, and download the company's custom interface, NetCruiser.

Network-USA's ISP Catalog

http://www.netusa.net/ISP/

This Internet access provider catalog indexes countries, complete with links to individual area codes, allowing users to find available Internet services in any desired region. Internet service providers can add themselves to the list via e-mail.

The NFIC MultiHost Server

http://www.nfic.com/Multi/Host

The New Frontiers Information Corporation MultiHost Server provides a demonstration of the firm's services here. Includes answers to Frequently Asked Questions, tech specifications and pricing information.

Pilot Network Services Inc.

http://www.pilot.net/

Pilot Network Services Inc., headquartered in San Francisco with offices in Los Angeles, Chicago, and New York, provides secure Internet services for commercial use. Visitors to its home page can learn more about the company and its services.

Pronet Global Interactive Business Centre

http://www.pronett.com/

British Columbia-based Pronet Enterprises Ltd. provides Internet access and Web page development for businesses around the world. This commercial page contains pricing and contact information for the company.

PSINet

http://www.psi.net/

PSINet, a major mainstream commercial Internet access provider, provides an overview of the company, descriptions of services and pricing information. Includes an analysis of the company's stock performance, corporate services, and a listing of international and domestic business affiliates.

Random Access

http://www.randomc.com/

An Internet access provider posts its services and rates here along with a catalog of hardware. The page also contains links to the server's user pages.

Real/Time Communications

http://www.realtime.net/

Real/Time Communications provides Internet access to individuals and business users, supporting terminal-based access and SLIP/PPP accounts attached directly to the global network. Contact and account information are provided, as well as a help desk.

Source Internet Services, North America

http://www.sisna.com/

Source Internet Services offers Internet access and Web page development services nationwide. Review SIS product offerings and connectivity options at this promotional site.

SprintLink

http://www.sprintlink.net/

Information on SprintLink, the wide area network service of the major U.S. telecommunications company, Sprint Corporation, is available at this site. Visitors will find its customer handbook, contact information, and links to the main Sprint home page. Includes index of Internet-related career opportunities.

USA.NET

http://www.usa.net/

USA.NET offers Web hosting services which include domain registration, Web site design, and other commercial presence options. The Internet service provider serves up company information, along with a newsstand and glossary of Web resources.

UUNET Technologies

http://www.uu.net/

UUNET Technologies, a commercial Internet service provider, promotes itself and its products here. The company describes the services it markets to the business community and offers a corporate profile.

West Coast Online Inc.

http://www.wco.com/

The home page of this Internet access provider explains the company's business and personal service offerings. The company's online newspaper, available here, provides coverage of telecommunication and technology issues. Site includes links to the Jumbo Software Archive and similar resources.

WinNET Communications Inc.

http://www.win.net/

WinNET hawks its international Internet access services through this corporate home page. The site explains who WinNET is, describes its services, and includes links to customer Web sites.

ALABAMA

Datasync

http://www.datasync.com/

People in southern Mississippi and southern Alabama can "git online" using the services of Datasync, a local Internet access provider. The company details its services and rates at this promotional site.

Di's Online Cafe, Mobile

http://www.dibbs.net/cafe/

For "information à la carte," amble into Di's Online Cafe. Di offers dialup Internet access to Mobile-area users, a direct link to the Mobile Register, and pointers to Alabama and Internet-wide hot spots.

HiWAAY Information Services and Nuance Network Services

http://www.nuance.com/

A directory of Huntsville-area Internet service providers and BBSs is available for perusal at this site. Locate access servers and purveyors of connectivity products in northern Alabama.

interQuest

http://www.iquest.com/

This promotional site is sponsored by interQuest, an Alabama Internet access provider. Visitors are invited to learn about the company, its products and services, or to thumb through the pages of a virtual Huntsville daily newspaper.

Traveller Information Services Master Index

http://www.traveller.com/

The master index for Traveller Information Services, an Internet provider in Alabama, presents company information, links to its networks in several cities and price structures.

WSNetwork Communications Services

http://www.wsnet.com/

WSNetwork Communications Services of Montgomery provides information on its Internet access services. It also posts a local business directory, help pages and links to Montgomery-area sites.

ALASKA

Internet Alaska Inc.

http://www.alaska.net/

Internet Alaska Inc. is a full-service Internet provider. Includes descriptions of connectivity products, pricing information, training programs, and links to Alaska resources and commercial pages.

PolarNet Inc.

http://www.polarnet.com

Alaskan Internet access provider PolarNet Incorporated offers details about its service plans and prices. Links to Web sites across Alaska are also featured.

ARIZONA

ACES Research Inc.

http://www.aces.com/

ACES Research Inc. is an Internet provider and network consulting firm in Tucson. The company's home page includes descriptions of services and pricing information.

AzTeC Computing

http://aztec.asu.edu

AzTeC Computing is a FreeNet Internet access provider and bulletin board serving the Phoenix metropolitan area. Visitors to its home page can learn about the services AzTeC provides and access a number of local cultural, arts, and entertainment information servers.

Crossroads Communications

http://www.xroads.com/

Crossroads Communications provides Internet access for residential and business customers in the metro-Phoenix area. Its home page offers information on available services and links to customer Web sites.

GetNet

http://www.getnet.com/

Visitors to this Arizona-based company's home page can read about its Internet connectivity services or link to regional resources. Includes Internet education information, the GetNet Boutique for cybershoppers, and links to various Arizona recreation and government sites.

Internet Direct Inc.

http://www.direct.net/

Internet Direct Inc., based in Phoenix provides Internet access and network maintenance services for area business customers. Product and services info, demonstrations, support, and a company overview flesh out the offerings of this commercial site.

Opus One

http://www.opus1.com/

Arizona-based Internet service provider and consulting firm Opus One highlights client home pages and service options at its home page. The site includes information about how to contact the company.

Primenet

http://www.ramp.com/

Primenet, an Arizona Internet access provider, supplies service details, technical information, links to user pages and announcements. Also featured are links, downloadable software, and Web page creation help.

RTD Systems & Networking Inc.

http://www.rtd.com/index.html

RTD Systems & Networking, an Internet service provider located in Tucson tells about its access offerings for businesses and individuals at this corporate site. Includes details about RTD's networking services and products.

ARKANSAS

IntelliNet, the Internet Specialists

http://www.intellinet.com/

Arkansas' "first and largest" Internet service provider, IntelliNet, provides information on company and client services. Includes links to IntelliMall, business storefronts, and ArkWeb— the Arkansas Web White Pages. Visitors can also peruse listings of events in Arkansas and customer home pages.

World Lynx

http://www.cei.net/

The home page of Arkansas-based Internet access provider World Lynx Inc. connects users with news, government, and entertainment links. Includes a listing of the corporation's Arkansas office locations.

CALIFORNIA

Arasmith Engineering

http://www.arasmith.com/

Arasmith Engineering, a Sunnyvale-based computer consulting company, maintains this promotional site to introduce its Internet connectivity services and amateur radio enthusiast resources. Includes link to the Bay Area Communications Society.

Berkeley Internet Link

http://bilink.berkeley.edu:8000/net.html

Maintained by the University of California at Berkeley for its faculty, staff and students, this online forum allows visitors to open an Internet account. UC Berkeley ID is required.

Best Internet Communications Inc.

http://www.best.com/

An Internet access provider in Mountain View gives an overview of its services and prices here. The company also posts a company FAQ and its picks for top Web pages.

Brainstorm Networks

http://www.brainstorm.net/

Brainstorm Networks' promotional site provides details on Internet connection, consulting and equipment offered by the San Francisco Bay Area company. Includes price listings for high-speed Internet connections for business and personal use.

Castles Information Network

http://www.castles.com/

Castles Information Network is a full-service Internet connection provider based in California. Includes links to downloadable software, products, and services.

CCnet Communications

http://www.ccnet.com/

CCnet, an Internet access provider in the San Francisco Bay Area, presents information about its services and the pages of its clients here. Features include a site maintained by Leo Laporte, the host of a television talk show about computers.

CERFnet

http://www.cerf.net/

This promotional site is the home of CERFnet, a California-wide Internet access provider for business. Visitors to its home page can read about the company, review its services, and find out about its special projects.

Community ConneXion

http://www.c2.org/

The Community ConneXion is a Berkeley-based Internet access provider. Prices, policies, and the scoop on the company's parties are provided.

Connect Inc.

http://www.connectinc.com/

Connect Inc., a Mountain View-based company, establishes online services for public and private networks by providing software and services to create interactive online marketplaces.

Connectnet Internet Services

http://www.connectnet.com/

Connectnet Internet Services is an Internet access provider located in San Diego. Visitors will find information on individual and business accounts at this commercial home page.

The Cyberg8t

http://www.cyberg8t.com/

Cyberg8t is an Internet access and service provider based in Claremont. Customers can utilize the Web, e-mail, Usenet newsgroups, Internet Relay Chat, and telnet via the company's services. Its main site offers search functions and community Web pages.

Cybergate Information Services

http://www.cybergate.com/

Cybergate Information Services is an Internet service provider based in Fresno. The company offers online tutoring, local news and weather, and advertising services, plus links to search engines and software.

Delta Internet Services-DeltaNet

http://www.deltanet.com/

Delta Internet Services, a Southern California Internet service provider, presents a general company overview at its corporate home page. Review Internet connection options and rate schedules.

Diamond Lane

http://www.tdl.com/

The Diamond Lane, a California-based Internet access provider, offers a variety of accounts and Web publishing resources for its customers and visitors to the site. Includes details of services and rates.

DigiLink Network Services

http://www.digilink.net/

DigiLink Network Services is an Internet access provider serving the Orange County and greater Los Angeles area. Visitors to its home page will find information on the company and its ISDN/PPP, frame relay, and HiCap telephone services.

Direct Network Access

http://www.dnai.com/

DNAI provides Internet access to the San Francisco Bay Area. Visitors to this promotional page will find information on the company's products and services, a business center, and access to user Web pages.

ElectriCiti

http://www.electriciti.com/

ElectriCiti is a full-service Internet access provider located in San Diego. Visitors will find information on the company's Web consulting services and Internet accounts, along with an online gallery of member artwork.

emf.net

http://www.emf.net/

Internet access provider, emf.net, offers service to the San Francisco and Berkeley communities. Visitors will find information on a variety of business and individual accounts.

Exodus Communications

http://www.exodus.net/

Exodus Communications is an Internet access provider for businesses. The Sunnyvale-based company is also an Internet consulting firm and provides details of its Web presence design and maintenance services.

GeoNet Communications Inc.

http://www.geo.net/

Palo Alto-based GeoNet Communications Inc., a provider of turnkey Internet and Web services, details its corporate outlook. Includes information about products and current clients.

Global Internet

http://www.mid.net/

Global Internet provides Internet access and consulting services to commercial, educational and scientific organizations in Palo Alto. This page has information on the company's products, services and resources.

Grapevine Networking

http://www.gvn.com/

An Internet service provider and marketing consultant in Anaheim, provides information on its services for area businesses. The site includes a list of the company's clients.

Great Basin Internet Services

http://www.greatbasin.net/

Great Basin Internet Services provides Internet access to northern Nevada and eastern California. Visitors to its home page can find out about the company and the services it provides.

HLC Internet

http://www.hlc.net/index.html

HLC Internet provides Internet access to corporations and organizations. Visitors here can get information about products, services and marketing. A company FAQ and links to client home pages are also provided.

HoloNet

http://www.holonet.net/

HoloNet, a Berkeley-based Internet service provider, maintains this promotional site. Visit here to learn about its dialup and dedicated account rates, custom domain name services, and high-speed connections.

Hooked.Net

http://www.hooked.net/

Hooked is a full-service Internet provider in the San Francisco Bay Area. This site includes descriptions of services for individual and commercial accounts, software information, links to client home pages, and pricing details.

The Human Factor

http://www.human.com/

The Santa Cruz-based company The Human Factor is an Internet service provider. Visit this site to learn about its Web page creation and hosting services.

ICOnetworks

http://www.ico.net/

ICOnetworks is a full-service Internet provider in the Monterey Bay area. Includes descriptions of products, services, and pricing.

Idiom Consulting

http://www.idiom.com/

Idiom Consulting pitches its Internet access and training services at this promotional site where visitors are invited to review the company's product offerings. Includes catalogs listing free software, database systems, compilers, and interpreters.

INFO.Net

http://www.infonet.com/

INFO.Net, part of the Infonet Services Corporation, is a provider of Internet access. This site presents corporate information and details on products and services.

Internet International

http://interinc.com/

This site, maintained by Internet access provider and Web page designer, SSP International Inc., features information for businesses interested in leasing space for commercial Web sites. Visitors also will find a list of current Internet International customers.

The Internet MainStreet

http://www.mainstreet.net/

The Internet MainStreet, a Los Altos-based Internet service provider, maintains this site for general information. Visit the company's home page to learn about its subscriber accounts, Web site hosting services, and other Internet resources.

InterNex Information Services

http://www.internex.com/

InterNex Information Services Inc. is an Internet access provider located in Santa Clara. Visitors will find information on services and fees.

JovaNet Communications

http://www.jovanet.com/

JovaNet Communications, an Internet access provider based in Marina Del Rey, introduces its connectivity products and services. Visitors are invited to find out about the company and the services it provides.

Kaiwan Internet

http://www.kaiwan.com/

Kaiwan Internet is a California-based access provider. Visitors to its site will find service and fee information for individual and business accounts.

Leonardo Internet

http://www.leonardo.net/

Leonardo Internet, an Internet service provider in Santa Monica, maintains this home page with information about its products and services, which include computer graphics, programming, and Web site storage. Includes links to its online Leonardo Da Vinci museum and customer pages.

Lightside Inc.

http://www.lightside.com/

Los Angeles-based Internet access provider and Web marketing firm, Lightside, gives an overview of its services. The site also contains links to client pages.

LineX Communications

http://linex.com/

The LineX Communications home page introduces visitors to the San Francisco Bay Area-based Internet access provider and the world of the Web. This site explains Web navigation and information retrieval, links explorers to popular Internet destinations, and provides information for clients.

Maximized Online

http://maxonline.com/

Maximized Online is an Internet service provider in California's Orange County. The company's home page tells about its offerings, including an interactive greeting card service and links to information on Web-related seminars.

MediaCity

http://www.mediacity.com/

Palo Alto-based Internet access provider Media City offers a wealth of online resources and information. Not just an ISP, the company also runs Media City University and an online mall hosting electronic commerce. Scope out services and price schedules, or link to the usual Internet tips and tricks files.

MeerNet

http://www.meer.net/

MeerNet, an Internet access provider located in "warm, but somewhat ugly, Mountain View," offers ISDN and direct access accounts to the Northern California region. Read about services and rates at this promotional site.

NetConnect

http://www.tcd.net/

NetConnect boasts that it was the first commercial Internet provider to bring Internet services to the residents of Wyoming. Today it continues to serve Wyoming (as well as Utah and portions of California) with high-speed dialup Internet connections. Services and rate structures are outlined.

NetGate Communications

http://www.netgate.net/

This site holds the gateway to the Web home of NetGate Communications, an Internet access provider based in San Jose. Visitors who access the company's home page can learn about its services, access its user utilities, or visit the online mall.

NetUSA Inc.

http://www.netusa.com/

NetUSA ambitiously calls itself "The Gateway to the World." An Internet access provider based in Mountain View, the company provides this promotional page as a customer service. Find links to shopping and Internet starting points.

Network Intensive

http://www.ni.net/

An Internet access provider in Irvine details its rates and services for businesses and individuals.

North Bay Network

http://www.nbn.com/

The North Bay Network offers Internet connectivity to the regions just north of San Francisco. Visit this site to learn about its Internet tools and resources, or to link to customer Web sites.

Pacific Internet

http://www.pacific.net/

An Internet access provider and Web page designer based in Mendocino details its services and rates here. The company also posts links to customer home pages and other Internet resources.

Quakenet Internet Services

http://www.quake.net/

Quakenet Internet Services aims to provide value-added connectivity and information services to businesses and individuals by crafting custom network options to serve customer needs. Includes descriptions of services, pricing information, and links to Web pages of interest to the company's clients.

Quantum Networking Solutions Inc.

http://www.av.qnet.com/

Quantum Networking Solutions is an Internet service provider offering service to Antelope Valley, Simi Valley, and Thousand Oaks in California. Visitors will find information on individual and business accounts.

RAIN

http://www.rain.org/

The Regional Alliance for Information Networking is a nonprofit Internet access provider in California. Visitors here will learn about its services, training opportunities, and organizational philosophy.

Scruz-Net

http://www.scruz.net/

Scruz-Net is an Internet service provider for individuals and businesses in the southern part of California's San Francisco Bay Area. View information about its connection options, including regular and high-speed leased-lines, and learn how to register a domain name.

Sierra-Net

http://www.sierra.net/

Sierra-Net, an Internet access provider for the Lake Tahoe/northern Nevada area and selected California cities, invites visitors to its home page to find out about its services. Features include the Sierra Electronic Mall, Ski Web, and news and weather updates.

Sirius Connections

http://www.sirius.com/

Sirius Connections is an Internet service provider in the San Francisco Bay Area. The company details its services and rates, as well as offering an online registration option and company newsletter.

Slip.Net

http://www.slip.net/

San Francisco-based Internet access provider Slip.Net offers information about its dialup, leased-line, and ISDN services—in addition to Web development tips and Internet navigational tools. A directory of Slip.Net's business users is provided.

SNA

http://www.sna.com/

SNA is an direct-connection Internet provider based in Sacramento. At its home page, visitors can get information about its Internet and Web access services, including links to personal and business home pages. Company contact information and other links are located here as well.

Tahoe Online

http://www.tol.net/

A Lake Tahoe Internet access provider lists its rates and services here, along with a virtual tour of the local area. The site also posts local news, weather, and road conditions.

TLGnet

http://www.tlg.net/

The Little Garden, or TLGnet, is a San Francisco-based Internet service provider specializing in services for businesses and technical users. This page has information about its services, hardware and company policies, including manuals and links to customer home pages.

Universal Access Inc.

http://www.ua.com/

Santa Barbara-based Universal Access provides fax-on-demand information about its direct connections to the Internet, along with traditional Web development and design products and services. Visit this site to learn about the company's software offerings, including standard Internet connections and Web marketing strategies.

ValleyNet

http://www.valleynet.com/

ValleyNet Communications of Fresno is an Internet access provider that doubles as a commercial Web page designer. This promotional site provides links to client home pages, a tutorial on creating a Web presence, and a directory of local businesses.

ViaNet Communications

http://www.via.net/

ViaNet Communications specializes in providing Internet connectivity for businesses and home users in California's Los Angeles and San Francisco metropolitan areas. Visitors can peruse a range of company information here, including service area availability, pricing, and the ViaNet FAQ.

Web Communications

http://www.webcom.com/

Web Communications, a Santa Cruz-based Internet presence provider, creates and maintains Web sites. Visit here to send e-mail to its San Francisco Bay Area customer service department.

West.Net

http://www.west.net/

West.Net, a California-based Internet access provider for the counties of Santa Barbara and Ventura, maintains this server. Visitors will find information on the provider's clients, products, and services.

WombatNet

http://www.batnet.com/

WombatNet is a San Francisco Bay Area Internet service provider dedicated to putting Macintosh users and small businesses on the Internet. Visit this site to learn about the company's Mac-friendly products and services.

Z Net

http://www.znet.com/

Z Net is an Internet access provider offering connectivity services across California. Find details its products and rates here.

Zocalo Internet Services

http://www.zocalo.com/

Zocalo Internet Services of Berkeley supplies information about its MultiPoint Access and services for businesses at this promotional site.

Zoom.com

http://www.zoom.com/

Zoom.com Information Services is a service provider located in Fremont. Visitors to this promotional site will get details on its access options, as well as its custom consulting and software development services.

COLORADO

Brecknet

http://www.brecknet.com/

Brecknet Inc. is an Internet service provider offering access products like Colorado.Net—a ski resort and weather conditions information source. Find a list of information products and corporate information at the company's home page.

eSoft Inc.

http://www.esoft.com/

Colorado-based eSoft Inc. trumpets the technological virtues of its Internet connectivity services and bulletin board software at its corporate home page. Includes company information, an archive of educational articles about the Internet, and a bimonthly newsletter for eSoft customers.

Indra's Net

http://www.indra.com/

Indra's Net Inc. is a Boulder-based Internet access provider boasting low-cost services for individuals, businesses and organizations. Review the corporation's newsletter, products and services.

Infosphere

http://www.infosphere.com/

Infosphere is an Internet service provider in Aspen that offers commercial access accounts. Visitors can link to client pages ranging from High Country News to Aspen Snowmass OnLine.

CONNECTICUT

Connix

http://www.connix.com/

Connix, an Internet service provider in Connecticut, provides information about its services at this promotional site. Visitors will find registration instructions, index search tools, and FAQ files for Usenet newsgroups. Includes links to Web and gopher servers, commercial services, electronic media, and job listings.

I-2000

http://www.i-2000.com/

I-2000 is an Internet access provider offering coverage in New York, New Jersey, Connecticut, and Pennsylvania. Visitors will find information on setting up individual and business accounts.

NETAXIS

http://www.netaxis.com/

Connecticut-based NETAXIS links businesses and individuals to the information superhighway with its Internet access and Web publishing services. Review products and prices at this promotional site.

NETPLEX

http://www.ntplx.net/

Connecticut-based Internet access provider NETPLEX shows off its services and pricing options here. The commercial home page includes links to user home pages and a list of Internet starting points.

New England Service Providers Directory

http://www.pn.com/neci/providers.html

New Englanders can locate regional and local Internet access services using the listing of providers offered at this site. Includes a brief list of national companies.

The Internet Access Company Inc. (TIAC)

http://www.tiac.net/

The Internet Access Company Inc. is an Internet access provider offering service to several New England states. Visitors will find information on services and fees for individual and business accounts.

U.S. Miracle Communications Inc.

http://www.miracle.net/

Miracle Net, a Hartford-based Internet service provider, offers a small virtual mall and entertainment center. Explore the company's connectivity products, including its ISDN access option.

DELAWARE

DelMarVa Online

http://www.dmv.com/

DelMarVa Online is provided by WBOC-TV 16 in Salisbury, Maryland and serves the Delaware peninsula, joining Delaware, Maryland, and Virginia. The online service advertises itself as the gateway to the Eastern Shore, with news, weather, and area sports.

iNet Communications

http://www.inetcom.net/

Delaware residents can hook into the Internet using the dialup and leased-line connections offered by iNet Communications. The company's products, services and prices are outlined, along with customer support options and employment.

InterNet Delaware

http://www.delnet.com/

Internet Delaware, the self-proclaimed "Delaware's High Speed Connection to the World," offers pricing information on its products and news about its home state. Link to a restaurant guide, Delaware government pages, and other related state sites.

The Magnetic Page

http://www.magpage.com/

The Magnetic Page is an Internet access provider for northern Delaware and southeastern Pennsylvania, providing dialup accounts, shell access, ISDN access, Unix consulting, and leased-line Internet connections.

FLORIDA

Acquired Knowledge Systems Inc.

http://www.aksi.net/

Acquired Knowledge Systems Inc. is a Florida-based Internet service provider. Visit the company's home page to learn about its individual and corporate accounts, Web site hosting capabilities, and technical support services.

Amaranth Communications

http://www.amaranth.com/

Amaranth Communications of Pensacola provides information on its Internet access, Web advertising, and Web design services. Includes an online marketplace and a guide to Pensacola.

CyberGate Internet Connections

http://www.gate.net/

CyberGate Internet Connections maintains this commercial site to provide information about its services. The Florida-based company's customers can contact its technical support staff or learn about planned service interruptions.

EmiNet Domain

http://www.emi.net/

The EmiNet Domain is an Internet service provider in Palm Beach County. Includes information on services and pricing.

Florida Communities Network

http://fcn.state.fl.us/

The Florida Community Network is an Internet access provider for the state's residents. Visitors are offered an opportunity to search Web information by category, location, or keyword. Subscription information is also available.

Florida Online Internet Surf Team

http://digital.net/

The Florida Online Internet Surf Team site contains information about this central Florida Internet access provider, including links to support staff pages.

Internet Access Group Inc.

http://www.iag.net/

The Internet Access Group, a service provider in central Florida, offers services to help business, government, educators and individuals access the Internet.

MAG Information Services Inc.

http://www.magg.net/

Magg Information Services provides Palm Beach County with Internet access. This promotional page details the company's services, including SLIP/PPP and shell accounts.

Neptune Internet Express

http://www.neptune.com/

Neptune Internet Express is an Internet service provider in Miami. Discover the company's Web design services, utilities for users, and tips on where to start exploring.

NetPoint Communications

http://www.netpoint.net/

Netpoint Communications is a Miami-based Internet access provider offering both regular phone line hookups and high-speed digital connections. Includes information on the company's Internet marketing and consulting services.

Polaris

http://www.polaris.net/

Polaris, a Tallahassee-based Internet service provider, maintains this promotional site. Visit here for service descriptions, user home pages, and a variety of commercial and informational Web resources.

SatelNET Communications

http://www.satelnet.org/

SatelNET Communications Inc. is an Internet access provider in Davie. It details its services and rates, and provides links to user home pages.

Shadow Information Services Inc.

http://www.shadow.net/

Shadow Information Services, an Internet access provider in Miami, offers access to news and weather reports, a resource directory, and software archives.

GEORGIA

America.Net

http://www.america.net/

Georgia-based America.Net supplies information on its Internet access and Web site design services. Featured is an index with a variety of Internet resources, including references and search engines, plus member business sites and home pages.

CyberNet Communications Corporation

http://www.atlwin.com/

CyberNet Communications Corporation is an Internet access provider located in Atlanta. Visitors to its promotional site will find details on the company's full range of services for individuals and businesses.

Digital Landlords

http://clever.net/self

The Digital Landlords is an Internet service provider based in Atlanta. At its home page, visitors can get service details about its services, news, and access to the company's FAQ file.

Info Avenue

http://www.sunbelt.net/

This home page features info about the regional Internet provider, servicing North and South Carolina, as well as portions of Georgia, Louisiana, Tennessee, and Texas. Includes links to Internet starting points, FTP access, and the company gopher server.

MindSpring Enterprises

http://www.mindspring.com/

The home page for MindSpring, an Internet service provider based in Atlanta contains extensive company product and service information, as well as links to helpful starter pages for those unfamiliar with the Web.

Navigator Communications

http://www.nav.com/

Navigator Communications is a full-service Internet provider. Services include links to "cool" pages, as well as areas exploring finance, health, politics, and Internet navigation.

HAWAII

Data Plus Systems

http://www.dps.net/

Data Plus Systems Internet is a Hawaiian Internet service provider. The company's home page lets visitors check out what its clients are up to, or access information about Internet telephones, coffee crops, and computer magazines.

Hawaii Online

http://www.aloha.net/

Hawaii Online, an Internet service provider for Hawaii, introduces company rates and services at its home page. Visit here for company news, account applications, user home pages, and local information resources.

Maui Net

http://maui.net/

Maui Net, offering Internet connectivity to the Hawaiian Islands, offers this site for local tourism information, product catalogs, and service descriptions. Visitors will also find publications, real estate listings, online discussion groups, and more.

Pacific Information eXchange Inc. NETwork

http://www.pixi.com/

Pacific Information eXchange is an Internet service provider for the Hawaiian Islands. Browsers can link to home pages in Hawaii, read news items, or search the online Hawaiian marketplace.

IDAHO

First Step Research

http://www.fsr.com/

Idaho's First Step Research is a Web consulting and Internet access company. At this promotional page visitors can check out the company and its services.

Micron Internet Services

http://www.micron.net/

Micron Internet Services, a "direct-access" Internet service provider based in Idaho, maintains its support page with information about products, services, sales, technical support, and Internet tools.

RMC Internet Services

http://www.rmci.net/

RMC Internet Services of Boise sells Internet access to businesses and individuals, as well as Web development, consulting services, and domain name registration. This site has information on customer utilities, Internet licensing, and a showcase of model Web pages.

ILLINOIS

Allied Access Inc.

http://www.intrnet.net/

This promotional page is the Web home of Allied Access Inc., a commercial Internet service provider in Illinois. Find descriptions of connectivity products and services, along with local tourist and business resources.

American Information Systems Inc.

http://www.ais.net/

An Internet access provider and consulting firm in Chicago gives an overview of its services on this promotional page. The company also describes its work with Java here.

Dave's World Inc.

http://www.dave-world.net/

Dave's World Inc., an Internet access provider in central Illinois, stocks this site with information about its services, pricing, and online resources for business.

I Connection

http://www.iconnect.net/

I Connection, a Waukegan-based Internet service provider, offers individual and business account information, links to online services, and an index of customer Web sites.

InterAccess

http://infoweb.interaccess.com/

InterAccess is an Internet service provider for the greater Chicago area. The company's home page delivers service information, information on employment opportunities and instructional programs, and InterAccess subscription details.

ICEnet of Normal-Bloomington

http://www.ice.net/

Interactive Communications and Explorations, or ICEnet, is an Internet service provider peddling connectivity products in the Bloomington area. Find a summary of rates and services, along with links to local community resources.

MCSNet

http://www.mcs.net/

MCSNet is a full-service Internet provider located in Chicago. At the company's Web site, visitors can read about MCS products, services and history, or read the MCS FAQ.

Midwest Internet

http://www.midwest.net/

Midwest Internet provides information on its Internet access services in southern Illinois, as well as pointers to its client Web pages and subscriber home pages. Includes rates and services and details on connection speed options.

netILLINOIS

http://infoserv.illinois.net/

A nonprofit corporation, netILLINOIS serves the educational communities of the state by providing electronic support and services including Internet access. Visitors to this page can find out more about how netILLINOIS is connecting the state to the World Wide Web.

Sol Tec

http://www.soltec.com/

Sol Tec Incorporated claims to be "a mirror image of the real world…only better." The Internet service provider introduces visitors to its virtual world via the company's home page.

Sun Valley SoftWare Ltd.

http://www.svs.com/

Sun Valley SoftWare is a computer consulting and software development company which provides Chicago suburbs with dialup access to the Internet. Review rates and services, or visit the Web homes of company clients.

Tezcatlipoca Inc. DBA Tezcat Communications

http://www.tezcat.com/

Tezcat Communications, a Chicago-based Internet access provider and consulting firm, maintains this site for general information, pricing, and resource access. Visit here to learn about its consulting services and Internet search tools.

WorldWide Access (SM)

http://www.wwa.com/

Chicago-based WorldWide Access provides dialup Internet connections. This site contains information about the company, customer service access, and commercial connection options.

XNet Information Systems

http://www.xnet.com/

XNet Information Systems, a Lisle-based Internet service provider, maintains this promotional site to introduce its dialup and leased-line services. Visit this site for current modem speeds, local access numbers, downloadable software, and links to client Web sites.

INDIANA

B.C.Web

http://bcpub.com/

This index for B.C. Web, an Indiana-based Internet service provider and Web publishing company, contains information on rental prices for pages, tours of client sites, and a link to the company's home page. The site also includes listings of Internet tool kits and Windows95 resources on the Internet.

Commercial Information and Order Express Corp.

http://www.cioe.com/

Commercial Information and Order Express Corp. provides information on the services it offers in Indiana at this Web site. Includes information on the corporation's Internet access options, hardware and software offerings, and online services.

Crown.Net

http://www.crown.net/

Indiana Internet access provider Crown.Net Incorporated highlights its services and pricing options along with links to user home pages. Businesses and real estate companies in the area are featured as well.

HolliCom Internet Services

http://www.holli.com/

HolliCom Internet Services, an Internet access provider in north-central Indiana, maintains this promotional page. Visitors are invited to learn about the company, read its newsletter, and review its connection services.

Michiana Free-Net

http://michiana.org

The Michiana Free-Net provides St. Joseph and Elkhart counties in Indiana dialup access to the Internet for free. Visitors will learn about the nonprofit provider, as well as general topics of public interest government, health, employment, and culture.

Net Direct

http://www.inetdirect.net/

Net Direct, an Indianapolis access provider, offers an overview of its services and links to other Indianapolis-related sites. Consult this site for a rundown of the company's connection options and rate ranges.

University of Indiana's Computing Services Support Center

http://www.indiana.edu/~ucshelp

The University of Indiana's Computing Services Support Center maintains this online help site. Students can request account services and appointments here, or download a questions file and other online computing publications.

IOWA

INS Info Services

http://www.netins.net/

An Iowa server goes online with an overview of its services, technical support, and links to other Iowa resources. The page also promotes Iowan Network Services—a telecommunications firm in Des Moines.

MidWest Communications Inc.

http://www.mwci.net/

MidWest Communications Inc. is an Internet access provider located in Dubuque. Visitors will find information on PPP, 1-800 access, T-1, and ISDN accounts for individuals and corporations. MidWest also offers Web page development and marketing services.

Sioux City—SiouxLAN Information Services

http://www.siouxlan.com/

Business and news information about Sioux City comes to the Internet through the SiouxLAN home page. Visitors can check out general information about the city and the surrounding area, read about local government, or check into Internet service options through SiouxLAN.

KANSAS

SouthWind Internet Access Inc.

http://www.southwind.net/

This promotional site is the Web home of SouthWind Internet Access Inc., a provider serving lower Kansas. Find information about the company and its services, plus a link to the Kansas Heritage Server.

Tyrell Corporation

http://www.tyrell.net/

Tyrell Corporation is a full-service Internet access provider in Kansas. Visitors can read about Tyrell's products, services, news and support here, or browse the master list of user home pages.

KENTUCKY

BluegrassNet

http://www.bluegrass.net/

BluegrassNet, an Internet service provider based in Louisville offers information about its services. Includes employment and investment opportunities listings, links to employee Web pages, and a company FAQ.

Kentucky Network Servers

http://www.uky.edu/kentucky-network-services.html

World Wide Web servers residing in the State of Kentucky are cataloged at this site, provided by the University of Kentucky at Lexington. Follow the alphabetical listing of links to Internet resources—from bluegrass to education.

MISNet

http://www.mis.net/

Kentucky's MISNet—a commercial Internet access provider and consulting company—sponsors this home page featuring links to a variety of state and local information servers. In deference to the Kentucky Derby, a special feature of the site is the International Museum of the Horse.

LOUISIANA

AccessCom—New Orleans Internet Provider

http://www.accesscom.net/

Providing Internet services to New Orleans, AccessCom offers this instructional page which explains how to get on the Web and how to retrieve relevant information once online. Find company information along with an Internet tutorial.

Communiqué Inc.

http://www.communique.net/

Communiqué Inc. provides Internet access to southeast Louisiana. Visitors to its home page can learn about company services, view client Web sites, and access customer support.

Info Avenue

http://www.sunbelt.net/

This home page features information about the regional Internet provider, servicing North and South Carolina, as well as portions of Georgia, Louisiana, Tennessee, and Texas. Includes links to Internet starting points, FTP access, and the company gopher server.

Net-Connect

http://www.net-connect.net/

This promotional site is the Web home of Net-Connect, an Internet access provided located in Lafayette. Find company information and services, plus links to local sites and Internet tools. Includes a Cajun culture tutorial.

MAINE

Biddeford Internet Corp.

http://www.biddeford.com/

Biddeford Internet is an Internet access provider in Maine. Its site includes information on its services, as well as links to its business, community, and online information resources.

MaineStreet Communications

http://www.maine.com/

MaineStreet Communications offers Internet access, publishing and electronic commerce services to Maine residents. Includes information on the company's products and pricing, plus links to client advertising sites.

New England Service Providers Directory

http://www.pn.com/neci/providers.html

New Englanders can locate regional and local Internet access services using the listing of providers offered at this site. Includes a brief list of national companies.

The Internet Access Company Inc. (TIAC)

http://www.tiac.net/

The Internet Access Company Inc. is an Internet service provider offering services in several New England states. Visitors will find information on services and fees for individual and business accounts.

MARYLAND

Aspen Systems Corporation

http://www.aspensys.com/

Rockville-based Aspen Systems Corporation provides corporate and government information management services. Visitors to its home page will find company news, product and service descriptions, and employment opportunity listings.

DelMarVa Online

http://www.dmv.com/

DelMarVa Online is provided by WBOC-TV 16 in Salisbury and serves the Delaware peninsula, joining Delaware, Maryland, and Virginia. The online service advertises itself as the gateway to the Eastern Shore, with news, weather, and area sports.

Internet Access Group Inc.

http://www.iagi.net/

Located in Bethesda, this Web site publisher and Internet access provider maintains a home page providing information about its services and prices. Includes the Hub, a collection of home pages constructed for the company's clients.

jaguNET

http://www.jagunet.com/

An Internet provider and Web publisher for northern and central Maryland, jaguNET's site features promotional information as well as a variety of links. Includes links to Maryland-related resources, including sports, education, and media pages.

Microserve Information Systems

http://www.microserve.net/

Microserve Information Systems offers high-speed Internet access services to businesses and individuals in Pennsylvania, Virginia, Maryland, and New Jersey. Find out about services, products, and price structures at this promotional site.

Monumental Network Systems

http://www.mnsinc.com/

Monumental Network Systems is an Internet access provider for both businesses and individuals in the Maryland/Virginia area. Visitors here can find out about the company's high-speed connection services and contact information.

MASSACHUSETTS

Crocker Communications

http://www.crocker.com/

Crocker Communications is an Internet access provider in Massachusetts. This site offers information about starting up an account, dialup rates, and technical support. Includes links to corporate and user pages.

cyways

http://www.cyways.com/

Massachusetts-based cyways is a full-service Internet provider for commercial and individual users. Includes a description of services and pricing information.

HarvardNet

http://www.harvardnet.com/

HarvardNet, a dedicated Internet access provider, sponsors this promotional page with information about the company's products and services. A mix of utility, entertainment, and information links are also provided.

Pioneer Global

http://www.pn.com/

Pioneer Global, an Internet service provider in Boston, maintains this site with descriptions of products and services, pricing information, and links to client Web pages.

TerraNet Internet Services

http://www.terra.net/

Internet access provider TerraNet presents an online shopping arcade of its clients' products and services. From art online to orchid nurseries, visitors will find full details of TerraNet's Internet products and services.

The Internet Access Company Inc.

http://www.tiac.net/

The Internet Access Company Inc. is an Internet service provider offering services in several New England states. Visitors will find information on services and fees for individual and business accounts.

UltraNet

http://www.ultranet.com/

UltraNet is a Massachusetts-based Internet access provider. Visitors to its home page will find information on its services, pricing, and areas of coverage.

The Xensei Corporation

http://www.xensei.com/

The Xensei Corporation brings Internet connectivity to Boston's South Shore. Review the Internet access provider's products and services at this promotional site.

MICHIGAN

Alliance Network Inc.

http://www.alliance.net/

This promotional site is the Web home of Alliance Network Inc., a Michigan-based Internet access provider. Visitors can learn about the company, its products, services and staff.

ICNet

http://www.ic.net/

ICNet is an Internet access provider offering service to the State of Michigan. Includes company information and descriptions of products and services.

Iserve

http://www.iserv.net/

Michigan-based Iserv presents its Internet services and pricing information at its home page. The site contains links to Grand Rapids-area resources along with pointers to places to visit on the Internet.

Isthmus Corporation

http://www.izzy.net/

The Isthmus Corporation, an Ann Arbor-based Internet service provider, maintains this promotional site. Visit here to learn about its connectivity and Web site creation services.

Merit Network Inc.

http://nic.merit.edu/

The nonprofit Merit Network operates MichNet, an Internet access provider, and provides electronic communications development services to a variety of agencies and organizations. This site includes information about the company's projects, research and development, and staff profiles.

mich.com

http://www.mich.com/

A Detroit Internet provider posts its prices and services at this site. Visitors can link to mich.com's service guide or access Macintosh help files.

Michigan Internet Cooperative Association

http://www.mica.net/

The Michigan Internet Cooperative Association provides its members with Internet access according to a cooperative model of cost sharing. Services offered by MICA include dialup, leased-line, and concentrator hub with shared or dedicated ethernet ports.

Msen

http://www.msen.com/

Based in Ann Arbor, Msen Inc. offers Internet connectivity, presence, and consulting services. Its corporate Web site outlines these services and offers links to home pages maintained by Msen clients.

Rust Net

http://www.rust.net/

Rust Net, an Internet service provider based in southeastern Michigan, offers general company and service information. Visit this site to learn about its connection plans and options, or contact its customer service department.

Traverse Communication Co.

http://www.traverse.com/

An Internet provider that serves the Grand Traverse Bay area of Michigan details its services and rates. The page includes online tips for newcomers to the Internet and extensive links to Michigan-related sites.

MINNESOTA

Bitstream Undernet

http://www.bitstream.net/

Bitstream Underground Inc. is an Internet access service in the Minneapolis area. Find a company profile, details of services, and links to selected Web resources.

CloudNet

http://www.cloudnet.com/

CloudNet is a full-service Internet provider in central Minnesota. Includes descriptions of products, services, and pricing programs.

ComputerPro

http://www.cp.duluth.mn.us/

ComputerPro, an Internet access service based in Duluth, provides links to news, weather, sports, and entertainment resources, as well information about its services.

Fentonnet

http://fentonnet.com/

Fentonnet, a Minneapolis Internet service provider catering to business customers, offers career- and commercial-related links, information about the Twin Cities, and the usual Internet search guide.

gofast.net

http://gofast.net/

ISDN access for the metro area of Minneapolis/St. Paul, can be obtained from gofast.net. The company's home page has information about the its connectivity services, LAN access, and more.

MRNet

http://www.mr.net/

MRNet is an Internet access provider based in Minneapolis. This site provides information about products, services and company policies, with links to gopher and FTP servers. Links to other Minnesota pages and Twin Cities weather reports are also available from this site.

Network Systems Corporation

http://www.network.com/

Network Systems Corporation, a corporate Internet access provider, offers information about products, clients and sales support, plus a link to the Network Systems FTP site.

pclink.com

http://www.pclink.com/

This home page is maintained by pclink.com, an Internet access provider based Minneapolis/St. Paul. Includes a description of individual and commercial accounts offered by the company, a software library, and pricing information.

SkyPoint Communications Inc.

http://www.skypoint.com/

Internet access provider SkyPoint Communications Inc., located in Minneapolis/St. Paul, explains its pricing and services. Includes links to SkyPoint's commercial customer home pages and instructions for creating Web documents.

Twin Cities Freenet

http://freenet.msp.mn.us/

Twin Cities Freenet brings public Internet access to the Minneapolis/St. Paul community. The nonprofit organization's free services further its mission of electronically enfranchising traditionally technology-poor communities.

MISSISSIPPI

Datasync

http://www.datasync.com/

People in southern Mississippi and southern Alabama can "git online" using the services of Datasync, a local Internet access provider. The company details its services and rates at this promotional site.

MISSOURI

MVP-Net

http://www.mo.net/

MVP-Net is a full-service Internet provider in the St. Louis area. Site features include information on services, pricing, an account application form, and links to area commercial and informational sites.

MONTANA

Internet Services Montana

http://www.ism.net/

Internet Services Montana Inc. provides Internet access and connectivity products to the Missoula area. ISM's home page features links to pricing information, Missoula and Montana tourism information, and Web search tools.

NEBRASKA

Novia Internetworking

http://www.novia.net/

Novia is an Internet service provider and consulting firm based in Nebraska. The company's home page contains information about its connectivity products, publications, and consulting services. Includes pricing information and links to customer sites.

Probe Technology

http://www.probe.net/

Probe Technology Internet Services is an access provider for Omaha. Visit here for company information, including pricing and services. Visitors will also find Usenet newsgroups, a local FTP site, online stock quotes, and headline news.

NEVADA

Access Nevada: Las Vegas

http://www.accessnv.com/

Access Nevada, a Las Vegas Internet access provider, offers information on the company, its products, and services. Visitors can read the latest company news, or check out the Vegas-related pages indexed here.

Great Basin Internet Services

http://www.greatbasin.net/

Great Basin Internet Services provides Internet access to northern Nevada and eastern California. Visitors to its home page can find out about the company and the services it provides.

Sierra-Net

http://www.sierra.net/

Sierra-Net, an Internet access provider for the Lake Tahoe/Northern Nevada area and selected California cities, invites visitors to its home page to find out about its services. Features include the Sierra Electronic Mall, Ski Web, news and weather updates.

Tahoe Online

http://www.tol.net/

A Lake Tahoe Internet access provider lists its rates and services here, where visitors can also take a virtual tour of the local area. The site also posts reports on local news, weather, and road conditions.

NEW HAMPSHIRE

Cabletron

http://www.ctron.com/

This corporate Web site offers an overview of Cabletron Systems Inc.'s activities and products. Includes service and support information, corporate news, and a rate rundown.

NETIS Public Access Internet

http://www.netis.com/

NETIS Public Access Internet in Londonderry is an Internet service provider serving the local community and its members. Check out the site's Internet guide, area business directories, and an online auction.

New England Service Providers Directory

http://www.pn.com/neci/providers.html

New Englanders can locate regional and local Internet access services using the listing of providers offered at this site. Includes a brief list of national companies.

The Internet Access Company Inc. (TIAC)

http://www.tiac.net/

The Internet Access Company Inc. is an Internet service provider offering services in several New England states. Visitors will find information on services and fees for individual and business accounts.

NEW JERSEY

Castle Network

http://www.castle.net/

Castle Network is an Internet service provider for the central New Jersey area. Visitors to the company's gateway page will find a collection of Internet search engines, information on accounts and fees, and links to online games.

Computer Network Services

http://www.cns-nj.com/

Computer Network Services is an Internet service provider located in Denville. Visitors will find an accounting of fees and services for New Jersey-area individuals and businesses.

CyberENET

http://www.cyberenet.net/

An Internet access provider in New Jersey details its services and rates. The site includes an outline of the company's plans to provide access in India by the end of 1996.

E-dezign Group

http://www.ezweb.com/

New Jersey Internet service provider E-dezign checks in with the facts on rates and services, plus links to entertainment and current events news from the Garden State.

GTI GlobalNet

http://www.gti.net/

Global Telecom Inc. is an Internet service provider serving the New Jersey area. Learn about the company's many Internet products and services, or review client and user home pages.

IBS Interactive

http://emerald.interactive.net/index.html

IBS Interactive is an Internet access provider serving New York City and northern New Jersey. The company specializes in providing "one-stop shopping" for software, hardware, and connectivity needs.

I-2000

http://www.i-2000.com/

I-2000 is an Internet access provider offering service in New York, New Jersey, Connecticut, and Pennsylvania. Visitors will find information on setting up individual and business accounts.

Microserve Information Systems

http://www.microserve.net/

Microserve Information Systems offers high-speed Internet access solutions to businesses and individuals in Pennsylvania, Virginia, Maryland, and New Jersey. Find out about services, products, and price structures at this promotional site.

Panix—Public Access Networks Corporation

http://www.panix.com/

Panix is an Internet provider offering Web access to residents of New York and New Jersey. Visitors will find service and fee descriptions at this promotional site.

Planet Access

http://www.planet.net/

Internet explorers can get started with the how and where advice posted by New Jersey Internet service provider Planet Access Networks. Begin with search engines such as Lycos and Yahoo, or access connectivity software with the links provided. Includes Planet Access Networks rates and service information.

The Internet Access Company Inc. (TIAC)

http://www.tiac.net/

The Internet Access Company Inc. is an Internet service provider offering services in several New England states. Visitors will find information on services and fees for individual and business accounts.

NEW MEXICO

New Mexico Internet Access

http://www.nmia.com/

New Mexico Internet Access, an Albuquerque-based Internet service provider, details its individual and commercial account offerings, describes its customer service capabilities, and offers links to providers in surrounding areas.

Rt66.COM

http://www.rt66.com/

Rt66.COM, an Albuquerque-based Internet service posts general information about its individual and business accounts. Includes links to a variety of local community- and commerce-related Web sites.

Southwest Cyberport

http://www.swcp.com/

Southwest Cyberport is an Internet access provider located in Albuquerque. Visitors will find information on services and fees for individual and business accounts at the company's home page.

Studio X

http://www.nets.com/

Located in Santa Fe, Studio X is an experimental media company and Internet access provider. It gives an overview of its services, including Web site design and storage, and posts a gallery of its work here.

NEW YORK

Adirondack NET

http://www.adirondack.net/

Internet service provider Adirondack NET serves up this online "gateway to the Adirondacks and New York State." A slew of pointers guides users through the site featuring links ranging from the arts to retailers and tourism.

America's Suggestion Box

http://www.asb.com/

America's Suggestion Box of Ronkonkoma provides BBS and Internet services. Its site presents company information, as well as details on its connection options. Links to commercial and member home pages are included.

Buffalo Free-Net

http://freenet.buffalo.edu/

The Buffalo Free-Net is an Internet community information service for western New York state. Includes links to government, cultural, professional, business, social, and educational information centers.

Cloud 9 Consulting Inc.

http://www.cloud9.net/

Cloud 9 Consulting, based in White Plains, is an Internet access provider. Services, pricing, and rules are explained here at this support page. Visitors can also link to customer home pages from this site.

D&D Consulting Ltd.

http://www.disaster.com/

At this commercial site, New York's D&D Consulting Ltd. presents information on its Web authoring, computer network setup and Internet connection services for business. A company history and client list also are featured.

EMI Communications Online

http://www.emi.com/

EMI Communications, a Syracuse-based Internet product and service provider, creates leased-line and dialup online systems for its clients. Visit this site for company, product and service information, technical support, and more.

fly.net @Cafe/

http://www.fly.net/

Fly.net hosts @Cafe, a cybercafe and Internet access provider serving up a variety of digital dishes. Read a history of the cafe, link to user home pages, or find out how to become a fly.net member.

The Global One

http://www.globalone.net/

The Global One, an Internet access provider based in Albany, stocks this Web site with company and service information, customer support resources, and a Global One subscriber page.

Internet Connection

http://cnct.com/

The Internet Connection, a New York-based Internet access provider, presents information on its services and pricing. Subscription information is included—as are details on the Connection's Renegade Outpost MUD.

Interport Communications

http://www.interport.net/

Interport Communications, a New York City-based Internet access provider, maintains this site to introduce its staff and services. Visit here to learn about its dialup accounts, dedicated connections, high-speed access, and other connectivity offerings.

I-2000

http://www.i-2000.com/

I-2000 is an Internet access provider offering service in New York, New Jersey, Connecticut, and Pennsylvania. Visitors will find information on setting up individual and business accounts.

KeithNet

http://www.keithnet.com/

KeithNet is an Internet access provider in West Nyack. On this page, the company posts its picks for favorite Web sites and offers a glossary of services and prices.

Long Island Information Inc.

http://www.liii.com/

Long Island Information Inc. claims to be one of the East Coast's largest Internet providers. This page acts as a springboard to the Web and gives browsers information about products, pricing, and services.

MindVox

http://www.phantom.com/

MindVox, an Internet service provider, offers a variety of online services to its members, including discussion forums, special content features, and a software library. Visitors can meet community members here, check out who's online, and find out how to become a subscriber.

Net Technologies Inc.

http://www.nette.com/

Net Technologies, a New York City-based Internet service provider, offers a rundown of its business accounts, Web-based marketing strategies, employee training services, and other Internet information.

Network-USA

http://www.netusa.net/

Network-USA is an Internet access provider on Long Island. Visitors can read about the company's services and contributions to the Internet, or link to client home pages.

NY WEBB Inc.

http://www.webb.com/

NY WEBB, a New York City-based Internet service provider, offers general company information at its home page. Visit the site to learn about its dialup accounts, Web site hosting services, and system design capabilities.

NYSERNet
http://nysernet.org/

This promotional site for NYSERNet, a New York-based Internet service provider, offers visitors information about the organization, its projects, and its services. Features also include information on its commercial directories, public service projects, and employment opportunities.

Panix—Public Access Networks Corporation
http://www.panix.com/

Panix is an Internet provider offering Web access to residents of New York and New Jersey. Visitors will find service and fee descriptions at this promotional site.

The Internet Access Company Inc. (TIAC)
http://www.tiac.net/

The Internet Access Company Inc. is an Internet service provider offering services in several New England states. Visitors will find information on services and fees for individual and business accounts.

WebScope
http://www.webscope.com/

WebScope is a Long Island-based Internet access provider that offers complete Web services—from page design to publicity. The company's home page provides an overview of its products, services and pricing information.

The World Wide Web LI Net Style
http://www.li.net/

LI Net connects New York's Long Island to the world via the Web. Preprepared packages of shareware connectivity applications are ready for Windows users with Mac kits reportedly in the works. Read about the company's Internet access rates and services, and take a tour of clients' Web sites.

NORTH CAROLINA

Charlotte's Web
http://www.charweb.org/

Charlotte's Web is a community network in Charlotte. The searchable site includes categories such as jobs and business, government, culture, religion, and arts and entertainment.

gateway.com inc.—Apex, NC
http://www.gateway.com/

An Internet access provider and consultant in North Carolina gives a brief overview of its services here. Potential clients can fill out an online form to query the company, which will in turn customize a rate and service package for the client.

Info Avenue
http://www.sunbelt.net/

This home page features info about the regional Internet provider, servicing North and South Carolina, as well as portions of Georgia, Louisiana, Tennessee, and Texas. Includes links to Internet starting points, FTP access, and the company gopher server.

The Tri-Cities Connection
http://www.tricon.net/

An Internet access provider for eastern Tennessee, southwestern Virginia, and western North Carolina makes its Web home at this site—complete with service and pricing information. Long distance visitors can learn about the tri-state area as well.

Vnet Internet Access Inc.
http://www.vnet.net/

Based in Charlotte, Internet service provider Vnet opened its doors in April 1993. The company's home page offers information about services offered, along with a company profile, and an index of advertisers.

Wilmington Internet Service Enterprises Inc.
http://www.wilmington.net/

Wilmington Internet Service Enterprises Inc. is a North Carolina company offering promotional Internet services to area businesses. WISE's home page serves up contact and service information, plus Wilmington Online—an interactive magazine about the greater Wilmington area.

OHIO

A Little Cupid's Note About APK...
http://www.cupidnet.com/cupid/apk.html

Daniel Bender, president of Cupid's Network Inc., posts a business love letter singing the praises of its service bureau and server provider, APK.

EriNet Online Communications
http://www.erinet.com/

EriNet Online Communications, an Internet service provider based in Dayton, offers a variety of PPP connections. This Web site allows visitors to sign up for the company's services and includes links to several computer resource sites of interest to Internet wanderers.

Exchange Network Services Inc.
http://www.en.com/

Exchange Network Services is a full-service Internet access provider in the Cleveland area. Includes description of services and pricing information.

Internet Access Cincinnati
http://www.iac.net/

Internet Access Cincinnati is an Internet access provider located in Ohio. Visitors will find complete details on setting up an account with the company, in addition to links to interesting sites on the Web.

Morning Star Technologies
http://www.morningstar.com/

Morning Star Technologies, a Columbus-based Internet service provider and networking applications developer, maintains this site for product information and technology overviews. Includes career opportunity listings.

OARnet
http://www.oar.net/

OARnet offers a variety of Internet services in the State of Ohio. Visitors to this site will find complete organizational information, including online help for dialup clients, as well as links to service plan options and rate structures.

OneNet Communications
http://www.one.net/

OneNet Communications wires the Cincinnati, Ohio, and Tri-State area with Internet access and Web publishing services. Explore the company's connectivity offerings at this promotional site.

OKLAHOMA

Galaxy Star Systems
http://www.galstar.com/

This promotional site is the Web home of Galaxy Star Systems, an Internet access provider based in northeastern Oklahoma. Visitors can find out about the company and its services, or link to user pages.

ioNET
http://www.ionet.net/

Oklahoma Internet service provider ioNET pitches its connectivity and Web site creation services at this promotional site. Includes links to community resources and tips for home page creation.

LDS iAmerica
http://www.iamerica.net/

Internet service provider LDS iAmerica, an affiliate of Long Distance Savers Inc., introduces its services and access options for the local Texas and Oklahoma areas and the rest of the United States. The page includes links to customer pages and technical support.

OREGON

Empire Net

http://www.empnet.com/

Empire Net wires central Oregon to the Web and beyond with Internet access services and other connectivity products. Includes an electronic business directory for easy access of local travel, real estate, and insurance companies' online offices.

Hevanet Communications

http://www.hevanet.com/

Hevanet Communications is an Internet access provider in Portland. Its site contains information on the company and its services, plus a list of Internet starting points and other links.

Mind.Net

http://www.mind.net/

Mind.Net, based in Ashland, is an Internet service provider and host to individual and business Web pages. Its home page has information about its services, Internet training classes, a help desk, and links to the company's favorite sites.

PDN Internet

http://www.chatlink.com/

PDN Internet provides Internet access, Web site development, and a BBS service in southern Oregon. This commercial site offers information on rates, services and links to its 20 most-visited customer sites.

PSGnet Guest System

http://www.psg.com/

PSGnet, a subscriber group of Oregon-based Internet access provider RAINet, offers links to member home pages at this site. Includes a pointer to RAINet, where an overview of pricing and services accompanies links to other client sites.

RainDrop Laboratories

http://www.rdrop.com/

RainDrop Laboratories is an Internet access provider in Portland. This page provides service information and links to search engines, HTML documentation, and Internet navigation aids.

Structured Network Systems

http://www.structured.net/

Structured Network Systems Inc., an Internet access service provider in Oregon, offers detailed information about its products and services. Visitors can visit the home pages of SNS clients or link to other Oregon Web sites.

Teleport

http://www.teleport.com/

Teleport is an Internet provider in Oregon. It details its services and rates here and provides local news, discussion forums, and online training classes.

PENNSYLVANIA

I-2000

http://www.i-2000.com/

I-2000 is an Internet access provider offering service in New York, New Jersey, Connecticut, and Pennsylvania. Visitors will find information on setting up individual and business accounts.

The Magnetic Page

http://www.magpage.com/

The Magnetic Page is an Internet access provider for northern Delaware and southeastern Pennsylvania, providing dialup accounts, shell access, ISDN access, Unix consulting, and leased-line Internet connections.

Microserve Information Systems

http://www.microserve.net/

Microserve Information Systems offers high-speed Internet access solutions to businesses and individuals in Pennsylvania, Virginia, Maryland, and New Jersey. Find out about services, products, and price structures at this promotional site.

Net Access

http://www.netaxs.com/

This promotional site is the Web home of Net Access, an Internet connection provider in the Philadelphia area. Find a list of services and fees, plus links to user home pages and access to user guides.

Philadelphia LibertyNet

http://www.libertynet.org/

LibertyNet describes itself as the home page of the Philadelphia region and offers a complete index of local Internet service providers. With movies, photos, and maps, this page contains links to information on local community groups, government bodies, and commercial entities.

PREPnet

http://www.prep.net/

PREPnet provides commercial Internet access in the state of Pennsylvania. Check out the company, its services and resources at this site. Links are provided to Pennsylvania government, business, and educational sites.

Telerama Public Access Internet

http://www.lm.com/

Telerama Public Access, a Pittsburgh Internet access provider, lists its services and provides customer support information here. Visitors will also find links to customer home pages and information about Pittsburgh events, culture, and business opportunities.

Three Rivers Freenet

http://trfn.pgh.pa.us/

Resources from the Pittsburgh area are featured at the Three Rivers Freenet home page. Categories include cultural activities, social services, and government. Three Rivers Freenet is a local Internet access provider.

VoiceNet

http://www.voicenet.com/

VoiceNet is an Internet service provider located near Philadelphia. The company's Web site offers links to informational resources—from arts and business to government and science—as well as providing facts about Philadelphia and surrounding areas.

RHODE ISLAND

Brainiac Services

http://www.brainiac.com/

The Brainiac Services home page offers information about subscribing to its Internet services, including price structures for individuals and businesses. The access provider aims to make the Internet inexpensive and easy to access for the people of Rhode Island.

NetSpace Project

http://www.netspace.org/

The Brown University NetSpace Project is a student-run initiative providing Unix accounts and access to information technology to the Brown community.

New England Service Providers Directory

http://www.pn.com/neci/providers.html

New Englanders can locate regional and local Internet access services using the listing of providers offered at this site. Includes a brief list of national companies.

SOUTH CAROLINA

Info Avenue

http://www.sunbelt.net/

This home page features information about the regional Internet provider, servicing North and South Carolina, as well as portions of Georgia, Louisiana, Tennessee, and Texas. Includes links to Internet starting points, FTP access, and the company gopher server.

South Carolina SuperNet Inc.

http://www.scsn.net/

South Carolina SuperNet Inc., a full-access Internet provider, offers its customers connections, plus Web publishing and design services. Find out about the company and its products at this promotional site.

A World Of Difference Inc.

http://www.awod.com/

A World Of Difference Inc. is an Internet access provider for the Charleston area. This page has information about customer services, events, news updates and sales. Find also links to sites about local sports teams.

TENNESSEE

ARIS Technology Inc.

http://www.aris.com/

ARIS Technology Inc. is an Internet service provider located in Starkville, Mississippi. Visitors will find information on the company's services and fees for Mississippi and western Tennessee.

Edge Internet Services—Nashville, Tennessee

http://www.edge.net/

This aid to Web navigation is provided by Edge Internet Services, an access provider for middle Tennessee. Visitors are invited to follow the links for the services and sites listed.

Info Avenue

http://www.sunbelt.net/

This home page features information about the regional Internet provider, servicing North and South Carolina, as well as portions of Georgia, Louisiana, Tennessee, and Texas. Includes links to Internet starting points, FTP access, and the company gopher server.

ISDN-Net Inc.

http://www.isdn.net/

ISDN-Net Inc. tailors Internet access services to business customers in the southeastern region of the United States. A commercial provider for Internetworking giant, BBN Planet, the company describes its networking solutions for workgroups, as well as its general rates and services.

The Tri-Cities Connection

http://www.tricon.net/

An Internet access provider for eastern Tennessee, southwestern Virginia, and western North Carolina is online here, with service and pricing information. Long distance visitors are invited to learn about the tri-state area as well.

U.S. Internet

http://www.usit.net/

U.S. Internet takes the information superhighway metaphor to its extreme by offering potential customers "on ramps," "road service and assistance," and "the best grade petrol on the Internet." Check out the Internet access provider's services and products at this promotional site.

TEXAS

BTR Communications Company

http://www.einet.net/hytelnet/FEE069.html

TradeWave's Galaxy offers a short summary of the fee-based Internet access services hawked by BTR Communications. Learn about BTR's public access Unix accounts, e-mail and Usenet offerings, or link back to the Galaxy online information service's home page.

Commuter Communication Systems

http://www.ccsi.com/

Commuter Communication Systems, a Internet access provider in Austin, offers an assortment of services and links on its business-oriented home page.

Computek Net

http://www.computek.net/

An Internet access provider in Texas posts its prices and services here. The company also provides an online hardware catalog and digital media archives of movies, images, and sounds files.

Connection Technologies

http://www.connect.net/

Connection Technologies, an Internet provider in Dallas, supplies information on its services along with listings of its clients' personal and business home pages. Also provided is an index with links in categories such as news, business, government, education, and community.

CyberTects

http://einstein.ssz.com/

CyberTects is an Internet service provider located in Austin. Visitors can find out about the company's consulting schemes, Internet services, and rate structures.

The Eden Matrix

http://www.eden.com/

The Eden Matrix, maintained by an Internet access provider in Austin, serves up information about the company's services alongside a decidedly hip collection of links focusing on popular and underground media. Visitors can jump to Web sites devoted to music, comics, and films.

Electrotex

http://www.electrotex.com/

Electrotex calls itself the "Electronics Parts and Information Highway Connection." Find out about the company's Internet access products that include service to the Texas communities of Houston, Austin, San Antonio, Beaumont, and Corpus Christi. Electrotex also sells and distributes electronic components.

Freeside Communications Inc.

http://www.fc.net/

Freeside Communications Inc. introduces its Internet services for individual and commercial dialup clients in Austin. Includes descriptions of and rates for SLIP/PPP access, along with Austin-area information and general Internet pointers.

Info Avenue

http://www.sunbelt.net/

This home page features information about the regional Internet provider, servicing North and South Carolina, as well as portions of Georgia, Louisiana, Tennessee, and Texas. Includes links to Internet starting points, FTP access, and the company gopher server.

Internet Connect Services Inc.

http://www.icsi.net/

This promotional site is sponsored by Internet Connect Services Inc., a full-service Internet access provider in south Texas. Visitors are invited to learn about the company, to review its products and services, and to access the information servers it hosts.

Internet Direct Incorporated

http://www.txdirect.net/

Internet Direct Inc.'s home page features information about the San Antonio-based Internet service provider and the Web at large. Find also Virtual City San Antonio and Inter-Rent, an electronic apartment locator with listings for several states.

LDS iAmerica

http://www.iamerica.net/

Internet service provider LDS iAmerica, an affiliate of Long Distance Savers Inc., introduces its services and access options for the local Texas and Oklahoma areas and the rest of the United States. The page includes links to customer pages and technical support.

NETCOM Interactive

http://www.pic.net/

NETCOM Interactive, a Dallas-based Internet service provider, presents local community resources at its home page. Visitors will find links to news, weather, sports, and tourism sites related to the Dallas/Fort Worth area. Includes link to online account information.

NeoSoft Inc.

http://www.neosoft.com/

NeoSoft Inc., based in Houston, is an Internet access provider. Visitors here can get information about the company's services, products, and link to commercial home pages.

Onramp Access

http://www.onr.com/

Residents of Austin can merge onto the information highway via Onramp Access. The Internet access provider outlines its products and services at this promotional site. Includes a variety of pointers to interesting starting points for Web newbies.

OnRamp Technologies

http://www.onramp.net/

Texas Internet service provider, Onramp Technologies, presents its catalog of services and pricing at this promotional site. Visitors can also check out pages created by Onramp users.

OuterNet Connections Strategies

http://www.outer.net/

OuterNet is an Austin-based Internet access provider and consulting firm. The company gives an overview of its services and rates and posts links to its user pages.

Phoenix DataNET Inc.

http://www.phoenix.net/pdn/

This corporate home page, maintained by Phoenix DataNET Inc., describes the Houston-based Internet access provider's services and prices. Includes technical support information, software archives, and indexes of Phoenix's business clients.

Real/Time Communications

http://kaleidoscope.bga.com/

Real/Time Communications is an Internet provider based in Austin. The company's support page includes information on services, pricing, and links to local commercial sites.

sig.net

http://www.sig.net/

Based in Austin, Internet access provider Signet Partners Inc. maintains this page to promote its online services. Visitors will find an entertainment section among the information options on this page.

South Coast Computing Services

http://www.sccsi.com/

South Coast Computing Services is a Texas-based Internet access provider and networking consultant. Visitors can read about its services and download tips for HTML programming.

Tab Net Internet Services

http://www.tab.com/

Tab Net Internet Services hosts the Austin Minority Business Journal and the Home Business Review on its Web server. Find out about the business-oriented connectivity products offered by the Texas-based access provider and Web site designer.

Texas Metronet

http://www.metronet.com/

Texas Metronet Inc. is a Dallas-based Internet service provider for area individuals and businesses. Includes descriptions of services, job listings, and links to client pages.

Texas Networking Inc.

http://www.texas.net/

TexasNetworking Inc., a San Antonio-based Internet service provider, maintains this site for service information and customer support. Learn about its personal and group accounts, receive technical support, and link to its collection of interesting and informative Web sites.

Turning Point Information Services

http://www.tpoint.net/

The Turning Point is an Internet access provider for businesses in the Austin area. The company's home page lists its subscriber plans and prices, community resource pages, and related items of interest.

Valley Tech

http://www.vt.com/

McAllen-based Valley Tech is an Internet service provider patting itself on the back for being "South Texas' first and finest Internet on-ramp." Read about the company's rates and services, or link to client home pages.

Zilker Internet Park

http://www.zilker.net/

Zilker Internet Park, an Internet access provider located in Austin, maintains this promotional site with information about the company, its products, and services. Features also include links to unrelated but interesting sites on the Web.

UTAH

ArosNet

http://www.aros.net/

ArosNet, a Salt Lake City-based Internet service provider, plugs company products and connection rates at this promotional site. Learn about the company and its rates for dialup and dedicated Internet accounts.

DirecTell

http://www.ditell.com/

DirecTell offers Internet access services to residents of Park City, Heber Valley, Brighton, and Solitude. Visitors can review the company's connectivity products at this promotional site.

Fibernet

http://www.fiber.net/

Fibernet is an Internet access provider and consulting firm in Utah. It details its full range of servic-

es—from dialup connections to T-1 lines. The page also includes the company's picks for hot links.

The Friendly Net

http://www.utw.com/

The Friendly Net is an Internet provider offering information on its services and prices at this site. Visitors can link to client business pages and the staff's favorite sites from this page.

NetConnect

http://www.tcd.net/

NetConnect boasts that it was the first commercial Internet provider to bring Internet services to the residents of Wyoming. Today it continues to serve Wyoming, as well as Utah and portions of California, with high-speed dialup Internet connections. Services and rate structures are outlined.

VERMONT

The Internet Access Company Inc. (TIAC)

http://www.tiac.net/

The Internet Access Company Inc. is an Internet service provider offering services in several New England states. Visitors will find information on services and fees for individual and business accounts.

New England Service Providers Directory

http://www.pn.com/neci/providers.html

New Englanders can locate regional and local Internet access services using the listing of providers offered at this site. Includes a brief list of national companies.

Sovernet

http://www.sover.net/

Southern Vermont's unlimited access to the Internet is aided by Sovernet, a provider who offers computer and navigation help to its customers.

VIRGINIA

The Blacksburg Electronic Village (BEV)

http://www.bev.net/

The Blacksburg Electronic Village serves citizens and visitors of Blacksburg as a central information site. Local indexes, directories, and pointers are provided offering information on government, education, business, and health care.

Central Virginia Free-Net

http://freenet.vcu.edu/cvanet.html

Central Virginia Free-Net offers regionally-focused information services about organizations, people, and events in the community. Access services, news, and information at this site.

CIX Association

http://www.cix.org/

CIX Association is a membership organization for "Public Data Internetwork service providers" in the Sterling area. Read documentation about the association's mission, or link to area Internet service providers.

DelMarVa Online

http://www.dmv.com/

DelMarVa Online is provided by WBOC-TV 16 in Salisbury, Maryland, and serves the Delaware peninsula, joining Delaware, Maryland, and Virginia. The online service advertises itself as the gateway to the Eastern Shore, with news, weather, and area sports.

Global Connect Inc.

http://www.gc.net/

Global Connect Inc. is a business-oriented Internet provider and electronic publishing service agency based in Willamsburg. Visitors to its home page will find links to information about the company, its services, and other resources.

i2020

http://www.i2020.net/

An Internet service provider in central Virginia details its services and rates here. It also posts links to Richmond sites, local classifieds, and sports and entertainment news.

InterRamp Support

http://www.interramp.com/support/support.html

The support page for the far-flung customers of InterRamp Internet includes downloadable software, account information, and reports of technical glitches along the Internet service provider's network. Includes documents about Internet abuse and "appropriate" postings to the Usenet domain.

Microserve Information Systems

http://www.microserve.net/

Microserve Information Systems offers high-speed Internet access services to businesses and individuals in Pennsylvania, Virginia, Maryland, and New Jersey. Find out about services, products and price structures at this promotional site.

Monumental Network Systems

http://www.mnsinc.com/

Monumental Network Systems is an Internet access provider for both businesses and individuals in the Maryland/Virginia area. Visitors here can find out about the high-speed connection services the company offers and how it can be contacted.

The Tri-Cities Connection

http://www.tricon.net/

An Internet access provider for eastern Tennessee, southwestern Virginia, and western North Carolina makes its online home at this site, offering service and pricing information. Long distance visitors are invited to learn about the tri-state area.

WASHINGTON

AccessOne

http://www.accessone.com/

Washington-based Internet access provider AccessOne serves up a variety of company information here. Read about AccessOne's high-speed dialup services, browse client and user home pages, or link to some of the company's favorite Web sites.

Cortland Electronics

http://www.cortland.com/

This promotional page is the Web home of Cortland Electronics, an Internet host and service provider based in Seattle. Visitors can learn about the company, its products, and services.

Interconnected Associates

http://www.ixa.com/

Interconnected Associates is an Internet access provider located in Seattle. Visitors will find information on accounts and fees with a focus on high-speed business connections.

Internet On-Ramp Inc.

http://www.ior.com/

Internet On-Ramp offers Spokane residents commercial access to the information superhighway. Evaluate the company's products and services, or review its corporate profile at this promotional site.

Network Access Services

http://www.nas.com/

The Network Access Services home page provides information about company services, Internet guides and listings of customer home pages. Includes a price list and index of Internet tools and techniques.

Pacific Rim Network Inc.

http://www.pacificrim.net/

The Pacific Northwest's Pacific Rim Enterprises presents information on its Internet services, including pricing and customer assistance. One enterprise in Bellingham is Tony's Internet Cafe, where you can eat at a workstation (or work at an eating station).

Seanet

http://www.seanet.com/

Seattle denizens can connect to the Internet via Seanet Online Services. Link to user home pages, Seattle information and other regional resources at this site.

Semaphore Corp.

http://www.semaphore.com/

Semaphore Corporation, a Seattle-based Internet service and presence provider, maintains this promotional site. Visit here to learn about its individual and business connections, Web site hosting capabilities, and customer support services.

WLN

http://wln.com/

WLN is a nonprofit Internet service provider and technology consultant located in Lacey. Visitors will find information on services for individual and business accounts at this home page.

WASHINGTON D.C.

Alexandria: World Web

http://www.worldweb.net/

World Web, an Internet provider and new media publishing firm in the Washington, D.C. area, supplies information on its services and provides user support at this site. Find also the World Web client portfolio.

Clark Internet Service

http://www.clark.net/

ClarkNet is an Internet access provider for the Metro Baltimore-Washington, D.C. area. The provider's resources and range of services for business and private use are detailed here. Includes a user directory.

The Internet Access Company Inc. (TIAC)

http://www.tiac.net/

The Internet Access Company Inc. is an Internet service provider offering services in several New England states. Visitors will find information on services and fees for individual and business accounts.

WEST VIRGINIA

Mountain Net

http://www.mountain.net/

A West Virginia Internet access provider details its services and rates here. Information is power, the company says, and so it provides libraries, markets, and a digital photo gallery at its site.

WISCONSIN

AthEnet

http://www.athenet.net/

AthEnet wires Appleton and its surrounding environs into the Internet. Visitors can review service plan options or link to client Web sites at the Internet access provider's home page.

Berbee Information Networks Corp.

http://www.binc.net/

This site serves as an electronic welcome mat for clients of the Berbee Information Networks Corp., a Wisconsin-based provider of Internet services for businesses. Visitors can find out about the company, link to client home pages, or follow the general-interest pointers provided.

Entercom

http://www.entercom.net/

Wisconsin-based Internet access provider and Web site developer Entercom introduces itself to the Web community and pitches its service plans and options at its home page. The company specializes in Web document design, consulting, and Internet training.

FullFeed Communications

http://www.fullfeed.com/

FullFeed Communications is a Wisconsin-based Internet access provider. Browsers can search through file archives, link to Internet exploration starting pages, or read all about FullFeed's products and services.

GlobalDialog Internet

http://www.globaldialog.com/

GlobalDialog Internet is an information service provider for the Wisconsin communities of Dane, Jefferson, Milwaukee and Waukesha Counties. A wide variety of state information is also available—including entertainment resources and indexes of Wisconsin home pages.

IntraNet Inc.

http://www.itis.com/

Located in Madison, IntraNet is a full-service Internet access provider. Its home page provides details on the company's FTP and gopher resources, plus information about its Web consulting and publishing business. Includes a "virtual Madison" tour.

NetNet Inc. Green Bay

http://www.netnet.net/

Green Bay residents can hook up to NetNet Inc. for high-speed Internet connections. Products and services of the Internet access provider are outlined, as well as regional news and weather.

SupraNet Communications Inc.

http://www.supranet.com/

SupraNet, a Madison Internet access provider, maintains this site with information about its products, services, and links to client Web pages.

WYOMING

NetConnect

http://www.tcd.net/

NetConnect boasts that it was the first commercial Internet provider to bring Internet services to the residents of Wyoming. Today it continues to serve Wyoming, as well as Utah and portions of California, with high-speed dialup Internet connections. Services and rate structures are outlined.

OCCUPATION-SPECIFIC PROVIDERS

ARInternet: Knowledge on Demand

http://www.ari.net/

ARInternet is a national Internet access provider catering to students and professionals in the fields of science, medicine, engineering, and education. Descriptions of the company's services, along with pricing details and a subscription form, are provided.

BELNET: The Belgian Research Network

http://www.belnet.be/

The Belgian Research Network seeks to connect the country's researchers with each other as well as with the global scientific community. The organization provides an overview of its mission and Internet access services.

Cinenet Communications

http://www.cinenet.net/

Internet access provider, Cinenet Communications, specializes in serving up information for the entertainment industry. Check out Cinenet's business clients' home pages, read feature articles and news, or link to related spots of interest on the Web.

ConflictNet

http://www.igc.apc.org/conflictnet/

The Institute for Global Communication's ConflictNet is a network for mediators "dedicated to promoting the constructive resolution of conflict." Learn how to join the network, which also provides Internet access service, and read about its member professionals and organizations.

Convergence Systems Inc.

http://www.convergence.com/

Networking consultant firm Convergence Systems assists cable providers in connecting to the "Fast Internet." Visit its home page for service descriptions, client lists, and a variety of cable industry-related information resources.

HandsNet

http://www.igc.apc.org/handsnet/

HandsNet is a network of 5,000 public interest and human services groups across the United States. It offers visitors membership information, as well as a sample of typical services provided to its members. The site contains daily updates on various public policy issues, opinions, nonprofit news, and online forums.

ASSOCIATIONS AND ORGANIZATIONS

Bandwidth Conservation Society

http://www.infohiway.com/faster/index.html

This group of developers seeks to streamline the network and cut waiting time. See Editor's Choice.

The Center for Democracy and Technology

http://www.cdt.org/

The Center for Democracy and Technology, based in Washington D.C., addresses civil liberties issues as they apply to today's communication media—primarily the Internet. Visitors to its home page will find publications on the subject and full details of its stands on current issues.

Center for Information Technology Accommodation

http://www.gsa.gov/coca/cocamain.htm

This organization wants to expand technology to include culture and politics and to reach the physically impaired and disabled. See Editor's Choice.

CNIDR

http://www.cnidr.org/

The Center for Networked Information Discovery and Retrieval offers access to its education servers, papers, presentations, and research. The organization which sets standards and develops applications for online document retrieval is funded by the National Science Foundation.

Communications Policy Project

http://cdinet.com/Benton/

The Benton Foundation's Communications Policy Project is devoted to furthering the interest of "public interest values and noncommercial services for the National Information Infrastructure" through research, analysis, and publishing. Read about the nonprofit organization's mission statement and program implementation notes at this site.

Communications for a Sustainable Future

http://csf.colorado.edu/

Professing a belief that "computer networking should be used to enhance communications with the objective of working through disparate views and ideologies to secure a more promising future," this site tackles many of today's current political and economic issues as they relate to the Internet.

Computer Professionals for Social Responsibility

http://www.cpsr.org/dox/home.html

The Computer Professionals for Social Responsibility home page is geared toward those "interested in the impact of computer technology on society." The site includes information on the organization itself, membership, programs, and upcoming events.

Electronic Frontier Foundation

http://www.eff.org/

The Electronic Frontier Foundation, an organization dedicated to the preservation of civil liberties in cyberspace, has been fighting for online rights since the inception of the Web. Focusing on the battles against censorship, the political advocacy group posts updates on legislation actions and alerts against bills designed to curb freedom of speech on the Internet.

Electronic Privacy Information Center

http://epic.org/

The Electronic Privacy Information Center works to focus public attention on civil liberties issues arising from the increasing use of information technology. Review EPIC stands on Internet political litmus tests, take a look at its current listing of "hot topics," or do background research on is-sues of interest by accessing the organization's policy archives.

Information Infrastructure Task Force

http://iitf.doc.gov

The mission of the White House's Information Infrastructure Task Force is to articulate and implement the government's vision for the "Information Superhighway." In support of the effort, this site offers an overview of IITF committees and working groups, speeches, testimony, and documents, and a link to the task force's public education campaign.

HTML Writers Guild

http://www.hwg.org/

The HTML Writers Guild site details the guild's activities, resources for Web page creation, conference,s and online journals. The organization representing the people who construct the Web's public face offers membership information, FAQs, and access to utilities and tools.

The HTML Writers Guild Mirror Sites

http://www.hwg.org/mirror.html

The HTML Writers Guild is designed to serve the informational, educational and support needs of its members. As the guild's site has grown, it has provided this page with links to site mirrors around the world so visitors can choose the nearest page for quick access.

Information Market-Europe

http://www2.echo.lu/home.html

Information Market-Europe "acts as a medium for supporting...the European Commission in stimulating the European electronic information services market and multimedia content industries." Find updates and information on organizations like the Multilingual Information Society and pointers to EU-wide activities—including the Information and Communications Technologies Partnership.

International Engineering Task Force

http://www.ietf.cnri.reston.va.us/home.html

The International Engineering Task Force is an open organization of network designers, operators, vendors, and researchers concerned with the evolution and smooth operation of the Internet. Concerned visitors can join the discussion and add their own two cents.

Internet Society

http://www.isoc.org/

Internauts are welcomed to the Internet Society's list of local chapters, standards and policies. The organization which describes itself as dedicated to the advancement of "global cooperation and coordination for the Internet and its internetworking technologies and applications" archives papers and presentations at this site.

---

a2z   EDITOR'S CHOICE

Bandwidth Conservation Society

http://www.infohiway.com/faster/index.html

Cyberspace might be infinite, but the hardware on-ramps that connect clients to servers on the Information Superhighway have definite limits. The Bandwidth Conservation Society is a group of Internet developers committed to sharing tips, techniques, and tutorials aimed at producing sleek, efficient online presentations with the fastest possible Internet delivery speeds. While the average Internet user might think a 28.8 modem and a phone line should be a large enough artery for her information circulation needs, there's a lot of digital cholesterol out there to clog the pipe and slow the flow. Developers can suck the fat out of a Web site by making GIFs smaller in byte size, using distributed processing technologies and compressing images with methods such as Consecutive Run Length Insertion. (Whew!) The end result for Web surfers means less time to pick your nose while waiting for a page to download (you've been meaning to cut back anyway). The reward for Webmasters is a streamlined site boasting browser-friendly load times. —*Reviewed by Becky Bond*

bcs
the bandwidth conservation society

Welcome to the Bandwidth Conservation Society

Last June, a loosely knit group of web developers put up a couple of pages about making gif files smaller in bytesize (hence, faster web delivery). The mail was phenomenal, we were even able to answer some of it (but, having day-jobs, spouses, spawn, etc., the BCS was pretty static.) Here is v2 of the Bandwidth Conservation Society.

The goal is that this site becomes a resource for web developers with an interest in optimizing performance, but still maintaining an appropriate graphic standard. The conviction (or perhaps hallucination) that there is a balance between a pleasing page and an economical, low-bandwidth delivery of that page.

National Center for Supercomputing Applications

http://www.ncsa.uiuc.edu

The National Center for Supercomputing Applications, operated by the University of Illinois at Urbana-Champaign, first parted the Web waters for the masses with its Mosaic browser. The NCSA remains a developer of and repository for an exhaustive supply of multimedia exhibits and Internet tools which appeal to both the industry experts and at-home neophytes.

The Novell Smithsonian Innovation Network

http://innovate.si.edu/

The Innovation Network is a joint project of Novell, Computerworld and the Smithsonian in a united effort to promote information technology for the purpose of improving society. The concerned computing public are invited to read about the Innovation Network's goals and the Computerworld Smithsonian Awards.

The National Public Telecomputing Network

http://www.nptn.org/

This nonprofit corporation in Cleveland, Ohio, helps communities start online computing network systems and provides professional support thereafter. Read about the organization's programs and services.

Polska Spolecznosc Internetu

http://www.psi.org.pl/

Polish chapter of the Internet Society explains itself at this informational site. Includes links to the international parent organization's home page. In Polish.

SGML Open

http://www.sgmlopen.org/

The Standard Generalized Markup Language Open home page provides information on the organization's technical activities, member listings, and upcoming events. Includes access to a library and related news items.

Student Association for Freedom of Expression

http://www.mit.edu:8001/activities/safe/home.html

A page from the Massachusetts Institute of Technology Student Association for Freedom of Expression includes discussion of recent topics in freedom of expression at MIT and elsewhere. Includes an archive of literature on freedom of expression.

The Web Society

http://info.websoc.at/

Learn about the activities and membership benefits of The Web Society. The organization which exhorts visitors "when you get stuck on the Net you call the Web Society" offers upcoming conference announcements, a membership directory, and online columns.

Webaholics Home Page v2.1

http://www.cns-web.cns.ohiou.edu/~rbarrett/webaholics/ver2/

People with World Wide Web monkeys on their backs can vote for their favorite home pages and read testimonials from like-minded Internet addicts. Includes links to support group pages.

Wireless Opportunities Coalition

http://wireless.policy.net/wireless/wireless.html

The Wireless Opportunities Coalition maintains this site to detail Federal Communications Commission regulations on wireless technologies and communications. The coalition also gives visitors an overview of its work and urges support for its efforts.

 EDITOR'S CHOICE

Center for Information Technology Accommodation

http://www.gsa.gov/coca/cocamain.htm

In light of the rapid proliferation of Internet publishing and communication tools, Web literacy becomes a question not merely of access to information and technology but of political, cultural, and economic enfranchisement. The Center for Information Technology Accommodation, a division of the U.S. government's General Services Administration, positions itself as a "clearinghouse of information on making Information Systems accessible to all users," including the blind, hearing impaired persons, and the physically challenged. To some users, computers are simply another piece of consumer electronics, no different than television, Sega Genesis, or a booming stereo system. To users with special needs, the computer becomes a prosthetic device that can act as eyes, ears, or vocal chords, providing enhanced access—and in some cases, the only access—to previously inaccessible experiences. To aid that end, CITA Webmasters show you how to create disabled-friendly Web sites. Did you know that Netscape's <BLINK> tag renders Braille and speech display systems inoperable? Do you include text transcriptions of audio clips used at your site? The electronic ramps and guides suggested in the accessible HTML tutorial offer step-by-step instructions for retrofitting your Web page with universally accessible features and content to accommodate most any visitor's special needs. —*Reviewed by Becky Bond*

Welcome to the Center on Information Technology Accommodation (CITA)

This server is a clearinghouse of information on making Information Systems accessible to all users.

Select your area of interest:

- National Information Infrastructure (NII)
- Legislation and policies
- Resources
- WWW design Guidelines
- Access Technologies

World Wide Web Consortium (W3C): A Short Prospectus

http://www.w3.org/hypertext/WWW/
Consortium/Prospectus/Overview.html

The World Wide Web Consortium is an entity composed of companies united in the aim to "maintain the stability of the World Wide Web." W3C provides free reference software, news and updates, and technical information on Web architecture. Members share access to software development resources, develop workshops, and host brainstorming sessions.

ETHICS, NETIQUETTE, AND LEGISLATION

CYBERMANNERS

Blacklist of Internet Advertisers

http://www.cco.caltech.edu/~cbrown/BL/

A straightforward document, the Blacklist of Internet Advertisers serves as a big wanted poster of Internet denizens deemed obnoxious in their online capitalistic quest. Offenders and solutions are discussed, as is the Internet significance of a certain pink, canned lunch meat.

net.acceptable

http://arganet.tenagra.com/Tenagra/
net-acceptable.html

The net.acceptable site contains links to documents which detail acceptable behavior for using the Internet, specifically in the areas of advertising and marketing.

The Net: User Guidelines and Netiquette

http://www.fau.edu/rinaldi/netiquette.html

Visitors can be sure to dot their Internet i's and cross your Usenet t's by brushing up on the instructions outlined in The Net: User Guidelines and Netiquette. The mannerly tome is available electronically in English, German, Italian, French, Portuguese, and Spanish.

Phish Net

http://www.phish.net/

The Phish home page offers a collection of resources that range from a course on netiquette to an Internet chess game. Take the bait, and find out what's prescribed for successful and well-mannered Internet navigation.

Unofficial Smiley Dictionary

http://www.eff.org/papers/eegtti/eeg_286.html

The Electronic Frontier Foundation's Unofficial Smiley Dictionary contains dozens of smiley faces in a variety of forms. Cynics will be tortured and optimists will be delighted by the collection of emotion-betraying character sets.

POLITICS AND SOCIAL CONCERNS

The Center for Democracy and Technology

http://www.cdt.org/

The Center for Democracy and Technology, based in Washington D.C., addresses civil liberties issues as they apply to today's communication media, primarily the Internet. Visitors to its home page will find publications on the subject and full details of its stands on current issues.

Child Safety on the Information Highway

http://www.4j.lane.edu/InternetResources/
Safety/Safety.html

Parents can learn how to regulate and evaluate what their children see on the Internet at this site, focusing on child safety on the Information Highway. The site offers the pros and cons of letting kids roam the online realm without supervision.

Church of Scientology vs. the Internet

http://www.cybercom.net/~rnewman/
scientology/home.html

This personal home page rounds up reports on the Church of Scientology's alleged attempts to quash free speech on the Internet. Includes summaries of the most current news stories on this topic, plus a comprehensive listing of newspaper and magazine articles available online.

Communications Policy Project

http://cdinet.com/Benton/

The Benton Foundation's Communications Policy Project is devoted to furthering the interest of "public interest values and noncommercial services for the National Information Infrastructure" through research, analysis and publishing. Read about the nonprofit organization's mission statement and program implementation notes at this site.

Communications for a Sustainable Future

http://csf.colorado.edu/

Professing a belief that "computer networking should be used to enhance communications with the objective of working through disparate views and ideologies to secure a more promising future," this site tackles many of today's current political and economic issues as they relate to the Internet.

Computer Access of Obscene Material

http://www.pitt.edu/DOC/94/271/42590/
policies/10/10-02-99.html

This site contains the text of the University of Pittsburgh's ad hoc policy on Computer Access to Obscene Material, dated January 1995.

Congress Is Attempting to Censor the Internet

http://www.zilker.net/senate/s314.html

Zilker Internet Park's Web page explores Senate Bill S. 134—the infamous Communications Decency Act of 1995. Find a collection of articles about the bill and documentation on the effects of its implementation.

The Copyright Website

http://www.benedict.com/index.html

The free-spirited Copyright Website describes its online contribution as "real world, practical and relevant copyright information of interest to infonauts, netsurfers, webspinners, content providers, musicians, appropriationists, activists, infringers, outlaws, and law abiding citizens." Find fundamentals, registration information and even a section on famous infringement cases.

A Crime By Any Other Name

http://www.theta.com/goodman/crime.htm

Freedom, a division of the Religious Technology Center, presents this document on Internet crime, covering the field from hackers to copyright violators.

Cryptography Export Control Archives

ftp://ftp.cygnus.com/pub/export/export.html

Visitors interested in cryptography-export news and opinions will find an index of available resources at this site. Link to info on relevant court cases, political moves and technical updates.

Cyber-Rights

http://www.cpsr.org/cpsr/nii/cyber-rights/
cyber-rights.html

Cyber-Rights seeks to raise awareness about the commercial development of the Internet and to promote support for the right to privacy online. This site offers topical links and mailing-list information.

Electronic Frontier Foundation

http://www.eff.org/

The Electronic Frontier Foundation, an organization dedicated to the preservation of civil liberties in cyberspace, has been fighting for online rights since the inception of the Web. Focusing on the battles against censorship, the political advocacy group posts updates on legislation actions and alerts against bills designed to curb freedom of speech on the Internet.

Electronic Privacy Information Center

http://epic.org/

The Electronic Privacy Information Center works to focus public attention on civil liberties issues arising from the increasing use of information technology. Review EPIC stands on Internet political litmus tests, take a look at its current listing of "hot topics," or do background research on issues of interest by accessing the organization's policy archives.

Freedom of Expression Censor-Bait

http://www.mit.edu:8001/activities/safe/notsee.html

The Freedom of Expression Censor-Bait page contains an index to sites with "items the censors don't want you to see." Among other treacheries, topics include sex, drugs, and rock 'n' roll. Be titillated or forewarned, depending on your predisposition, for the Webmaster insures that "there's S-E-X here. And rebellion. And subversion."

Government Policy and the Information Superhighway

http://www.nla.gov.au/lis/govnii.html

The National Library of Australia provides this large collection of online governmental reports and documents pertaining to changing policies resulting from the worldwide construction of the "Information Superhighway."

The Great GIF Licensing Controversy

http://www.xmission.com/~mgm/gif/

An attempt to explain the "great GIF licensing controversy" is made at this site which outlines the Web-wide ramifications of CompuServe and Unisys' dissension about the use of graphic interfaces. Includes relevant articles as well as a discussion of alternate graphic formats.

Information Infrastructure Task Force

http://iitf.doc.gov

The mission of the White House's Information Infrastructure Task Force is to articulate and implement the government's vision for the "Information Superhighway." In support of the effort, this site offers an overview of IITF committees and working groups, speeches, testimony and documents, and a link to the task force's public education campaign.

Letter to Judge Whyte

http://www.eff.org/pub/Censorship/CoS_v_the_Net/kobrin_whyte_022795.letter

This letter was sent to a U.S. District Judge by a Netcom Online representative, in the matter of Religious Technology Center, et al. v. Netcom Online Communications Services, Inc., et al. Netcom seeks to enforce a restraining order against the Religious Technology Center for repeated postings which they claim violate the Fair Use act in appropriating materials authored by others.

Jim Lippard's Home Page

http://www.primenet.com/~lippard/

At his personal home page Jim Lippard features information about himself, links to Internet anti-censorship information, and pointers to the latest online issues of Skeptic and The Realist magazines.

MIT Program on Communications Policy

http://farnsworth.mit.edu/

The Massachusetts Institute of Technology Program on Communications Policy posts its Digital Information Infrastructure Guide and other reports and publications at this site. Find discussions about the social, political and economic implications of the electronic information revolution.

Netizens: On the History and Impact of Usenet and the Internet

http://www.columbia.edu/~hauben/project_book.html

The visitor to this site can read a full-text version of Michael and Ronda Hauben's online book "Netizens: On the History and Impact of Usenet and the Internet."

The Network Observer

http://communication.ucsd.edu/pagre/tno.html

The Network Observer, a free, online publication of the Department of Communications at the University of California at San Diego, provides a look at "networks and democracy." Visit this site for current and back issues, answers to Frequently Asked Questions, and links to related publications and institutions.

Pornography Debate

http://www2000.ogsm.vanderbilt.edu/cyberporn.debate.cgi

Visitors will find a discussion about the Cyberporn debate here. The page contains links to research papers and articles, including work by Martin Rimm, the controversial researcher whose work has popularized the debate.

Scientology v. the Internet

http://www.skeptic.com/03.3.jl-jj-scientology.html

This page contains an article presented by the Skeptics Society entitled Scientology v. the Internet: Free Speech & Copyright Infringement on the Information Super-Highway. Information on the group and its magazine, Skeptic, is also featured.

Sex, Censorship, and the Internet

http://www.eff.org/CAF/cafuiuc.html

This scholarly document delves into academic freedom and censorship issues as they relate to today's hard-wired society. Includes information on library policies regarding freedom of expression.

State Bar of Georgia Computer Law Section

http://www.computerbar.org/

The State Bar of Georgia presents this Web page on computer law. Visitors will find sections on Internet ethics, pertinent newsletters, technology-related bills in the Georgia legislature and links to lawyers who specialize in the field.

Student Association for Freedom of Expression

http://www.mit.edu:8001/activities/safe/home.html

A page from the Massachusetts Institute of Technology Student Association for Freedom of Expression includes discussion of recent topics in freedom of expression at MIT and elsewhere. Includes an archive of literature on freedom of expression.

Why AOL Sucks

http://www.aolsucks.org/

The one-sided site argues that America Online is the worst commercial online service provider extant in the electronic universe. The author's support for this argument includes charges of censorship, claims of poor software, and allegations of questionable billing practices.

Wireless Opportunities Coalition

http://wireless.policy.net/wireless/wireless.html

The Wireless Opportunities Coalition maintains this site to detail Federal Communications Commission regulations on wireless technologies and communications. The coalition also gives visitors an overview of its work and urges support for its efforts.

XS4ALL Internet Scientology Press Release

http://www.xs4all.nl/~felipe/cos/pers.eng.html

This Web site offers a press release regarding a copyright-infringement lawsuit filed by the Church of Scientology against an Amsterdam-based Internet service provider, XS4ALL. Includes information on a police visit to the XS4ALL offices and links to censorship and Scientology-related Web sites. In English and Dutch.

INTERNET NEWS

BUSINESS AND TECHNOLOGY NEWS AND REPORTS

BIX the Byte Information eXchange

http://www.mcs.com/~jvwater/bix.html

The Byte Information eXchange offers links to full-text archives of back issues of Byte magazine, chat facilities and online conferencing services.

c|net

http://www.cnet.com/

Online chronicler c|net exemplifies mixed interactive media, wearing hats in both the broadcast and online publishing realms. With a television show, constantly updated online content, discussion forums and links to well-maintained electronic information depositories, the company has the capability to pin down Web trends and happenings as they occur.

CommunicationsWeek Interactive

http://techweb.cmp.com/techweb/cw/current/default.html

Networking and telecommunications professionals can track industry trends with CommunicationsWeek Interactive magazine. Readers will find industry news, product reviews and links to related Internet resources.

Cyberspace Today

http://www.cybertoday.com/cybertoday/

Cyberspace Today is the online version of the monthly newspaper about life on the Internet from the Northern California perspective. Visitors will find chat facilities, government news and an advertising section. Subscription information is also available.

Economic Consequences of the World Wide Web

http://www.homefair.com/homefair/webeconc.html

Presented at the Second International WWW Conference in 1994, this white paper attempts to project the economic benefits of marketing on the Web. Find visions of how the Web will change the world economy in "some unusual ways."

Interactive Age

http://techweb.cmp.com/ia/current/

This online version of the magazine tackling electronic commerce features a daily media and marketing report, plus syndicated computer news from The New York Times. Devoted to the business of Web tools and page content, the publication delivers the latest information about commercial Internet operations.

Internet Professional

http://www.netline.com/

Internet users and professionals will find subscription information on trade publications, as well as listings of suggestions for topical online reading. A collection of Internet career resources is also available.

Internet Talk Radio

http://www.ncsa.uiuc.edu/radio/radio.html

Meet the "Geek of the Week," or read an overview of Internet Talk Radio's Internet Town Hall feature. Although not a complete archive of the program's audio files, this site provides an annotated, informative look at ITR interviews revolving around technology and politics.

iWorld

http://www.iworld.com

Mecklermedia, a Westport, Connecticut-based publisher and Internet trade show sponsor, posts company news and Internet headlines on its home page. Includes access to discussion groups, online publications and a schedule of Internet World trade shows.

Journal of Electronic Publishing

http://www.press.umich.edu/jep/

The Journal of Electronic Publishing anthologizes electronic works related to virtual libraries and publishing on the Internet. Works chosen for the archive concentrate on the policies and issues facing the electronic publishing industry.

KFH Publications Incorporated

http://www.pscu.com/

Puget Sound computer users can keep abreast of computer and telecommunications news with the links provided by KFH Publications. Electronic versions of Cybernautics Digest and Puget Sound Computer User are available, along with a link to the Computer User Information eXchange BBS.

La Jornada en Internet

http://serpiente.dgsca.unam.mx/jornada/index.html

La Jornada en Internet is a journal about the Internet published by a Mexican university. Visitors can read current and past issues. In Spanish.

Net Online

http://www.thenet-usa.com/

Net Online is the electronic version of a colorful new magazine that marries cartoon graphics, innovative storytelling techniques and solid Internet news. Readers will find pointers to shareware and instructions for subscribing to a print version.

Netsurfer Digest

http://www.netsurf.com/nsd/index.html

Published weekly by a Silicon Valley-based team of Web wanderers, Netsurfer Digest offers Internet news plus tips on new and interesting Web sites. Visitors can access e-mail subscription information, Web site development tools, and an archive of current and back issues.

Netsurfer Focus

http://www.netsurf.com/nsf/

Netsurfer Focus is an e-zine which focuses on a single cyberspace-related topic per edition, for in-depth treatment of a pressing issue. Readers are offered subscription information and access to back issues.

Netsurfer Tools

http://www.netsurf.com/nst/

Netsurfer Tools is a free e-zine about online technology delivered via e-mail. This site offers background information on the electronic publication which is aimed at Webmasters, system administrators and other tech types.

NetWatch

http://www.pulver.com/netwatch/

NetWatch represents the sum effort of two individuals' attempt to bring the Internet's latest technologies to the average browser. Visitors will find links to demo versions of software as well as Internet news updates.

Newsbytes Pacifica

http://www.nb-pacifica.com/welcome.shtml

Newsbytes Pacifica is an electronic publication and wire service which provides daily coverage of the computer and telecommunications industries. Headquartered in Minneapolis, Newsbytes boasts correspondents throughout the world. Features include headline news, a daily summary of happenings and a weekly info index.

Online World Monitor Newsletter

http://login.eunet.no/~presno/monitor.html

The Online World Monitor Newsletter, a bimonthly publication, tracks worldwide Internet trends. Read the periodical's online edition to learn how the Web and other networks are evolving around the world.

Seidman's Online Insider
http://www.clark.net/pub/robert/current.html
Seidman's Online Insider is a Web newsletter covering computer- and Internet-related industries. Features include stock reports and subscription information.

WEBster, the Cyberspace Surfer
http://www.tgc.com/webster.html
The business of the Web provides fodder for the reports and columns of WEBster, the Cyberspace Surfer. An online magazine devoted to news about the Web, this commercial site offers business-oriented information and commentary about the electronic marketplace and the industries that drive it.

World Wide Web News
http://www.w3.org/pub/WWW/News/9305.html
Visitors to this site will find Web-related news and reviews posted by Internet authority World Wide Web Consortium. Search back issues of the electronic newsletter or sign up for mailing list distribution.

CONFERENCE ANNOUNCEMENTS AND PROCEEDINGS

Asia-Pacific World Wide Web Conference & Exhibition
http://www.csu.edu.au/special/conference/WWWWW.html
This Web conference and exhibition site details the programs, tutorials and supporting organizations that comprise the event. Includes links to related meetings, conference organizers, and attendee home pages.

Conferences in Hypertext, Networking and IR
http://www.w3.org/hypertext/Conferences/Overview.html
Check out details about upcoming hypertext and networking conferences, or read reports about past events at this site. Includes links to other resources offering information about Web conferences.

Electronic Proceedings of the Second World Wide Web Conference
http://www.ncsa.uiuc.edu/SDG/IT94/Proceedings/WWW2_Proceedings.html
The archive contains papers presented at the Second World Wide Web Conference '94: Mosaic and the Web. The reports, which are abstracted and topically categorized, focus on subjects ranging from arts and humanities to commercialization of the Web.

The Third International World-Wide Web Conference
http://www.igd.fhg.de/www95.html
Organizers of the Third International World-Wide Web Conference, held in Darmstadt, Germany, in April 1995, deliver post-mortem event information. Find out about conference events, notable attendees and future conference plans.

CULTURE CHRONICLES

Computer-Mediated Communication Magazine
http://www.rpi.edu/~decemj/cmc/mag/index.html
This industry magazine, produced in New York City, reports on the people, technology, culture and events related to communication over the Internet. Visitors are treated to articles such as "Thoreau Takes to the Internet" and numerous book reviews.

Computer Underground Digest
http://sun.soci.niu.edu/~cudigest/
A weekly (or so) electronic journal, Cu Digest features news, research and discussion on topics germane to computing culture. Visitors to publication's home page will find the current edition, an archive of back issues and FAQ files.

Cyberspace Report
http://www.ics.uci.edu/~ejw/csr/cyber.html
Cyberspace Report is a public-affairs radio show broadcast out of Irvine, California Visitors can access .au format copies of recent shows on themes touching upon the Internet and society.

CyberWire Dispatch, by Brock N. Meeks
http://cyberwerks.com/cyberwire
Brock N. Meeks, author of Inter@ctive Week's CyberWire Dispatch, delivers commentary, investigations and hard news to and about the Internet community. Visit this site for articles and features, subscription information, and links to communications policy organizations.

Flames
http://www.gold.net/flames/
Flames is a British e-zine featuring news, interviews and commentary on Internet-related topics. Includes coverage of political, economic and technological issues.

FutureCulture
http://www.uio.no/~mwatz/futurec/
FutureCulture describes itself as a cyberpunk community forum which serves as a venue for discussions on a broad range of topics related to digital society. Past mailing list discussions have revolved around issues such as virtual reality, rave culture, and the computer underground.

geekgirl
http://www.next.com.au/spyfood/geekgirl/
Australian print and online publication shows that girls want to have fun on the Internet, too! See Editor's Choice.

Planète Internet
http://www.netpress.fr/
Visitors to this page will find the gateway to the Web site of Planète Internet, a French magazine devoted to the subject of cyberspace. In French.

The Red Rock Eater
http://communication.ucsd.edu/pagre/rre.html
The editor of the Red Rock Eater News Service e-mails subscribers a summary of the varied bits of cyberstuff which have caught his eye. Appears roughly five times per week.

ThesisNet FAQ
http://www.seas.upenn.edu/~mengwong/thesisfaq.html
ThesisNet is a mailing list which analyzes and criticizes works-in-progress related to human interaction and cyberspace. Visit here for an introduction to the service and answers to Frequently Asked Questions.

Wherefore Web
http://www.river.org/~isaac/wweb/
Wherefore Web is an online publication focusing on issues about the Internet, Web and other forms of new media. Includes links to current and back issues, listings of related resources, and profiles of staff members.

HISTORIES

First WWW Conference
http://www1.cern.ch/WWW94/Welcome.html
The first international conference on the Web was held in Geneva, Switzerland, in May 1994. This document offers proceedings from the momentous occasion and includes announcements of the dates of upcoming Web conferences.

From Grass Roots to Corporate Image—The Maturation of the Web
http://www.ncsa.uiuc.edu/SDG/IT94/Proceedings/Campus.Infosys/quinn/quinn.html
A Stanford University electrical engineer explores Web presence development "from the bottom up." Includes an explanation of how universities have taken advantage of the information superhighway from the outset, and continues with a de-

scription of what contemporary access means to the "this high tech playground" called the Web.

From Webspace to Cyberspace

http://www.eit.com/~kevinh/cspace

"From Webspace to Cyberspace" is an online book which provides a brief history of the Web and analyzes the future of cyberspace. Visitors can download the 254 page document at this site.

Hobbes' Internet Timeline

http://www.umd.umich.edu/~nhughes/
htmldocs/timeline.html

This chronological rundown of Internet history provides details about the paving of the Information Superhighway—from the 1960s to 1994. Includes a chart summarizing the Internet's growth and a short FAQ file about the document and its creator.

The Internet 25th Anniversary

http://www.amdahl.com/internet/events/
inet25.html

The 25th anniversary of the Internet is celebrated on this page with a brief historical overview, including listings of Internet history texts and related resources.

Netizens: On the History and Impact of Usenet and the Internet

http://www.columbia.edu/~hauben/project_
book.html

The visitor to this site can read the full text of Michael and Ronda Hauben's online Netbook "Netizens: On the History and Impact of Usenet and the Internet."

People Who Have Contributed to the World Wide Web Project

http://www.w3.org/hypertext/WWW/
People.html

The World Wide Web Consortium presents an online salute to some of the people who have contributed to the Web project since its creation at CERN. The site includes brief biographical information and links to further details about selected individuals.

---

a2z EDITOR'S CHOICE

geekgirl

http://www.next.com.au/spyfood/geekgirl/

Even if the Web is still a boy's world after all, can we girls help it if we mature faster and our content is more interesting? An "e-ticket" Internet ride, geekgirl dazzles readers with its riotous mission and design aesthetic. The Australian print and online publication calls itself "the world's first cyberfeminist zine" and proves it deserves its bitchy credentials issue after issue. Count on its intrepid writers and editors to tackle the tough issues you care so much about, like the recent feature on "Babes, BluBlockers & Broncos" and the Internet service provider guide titled "The Buggers are Everywhere." Chronicling grrrls' adventures in the virtual world shares bandwidth with plenty of how-to resources designed to get readers elbow deep in the mechanics of computer hardware and HTML code. Don't miss the Friendly Grrrls Guide to the Internet, and it goes without out saying, don't mess with geekgirl. —*Reviewed by Becky Bond*

geekgirl tm

NEW
issue six - high flyers

issue five - hysteria

issue four - mermaids and myths

issue three - broadband

issue two - m@gic, m@nga and m@yhem!

issue one - stick!

subscriptions

SURVEYS

Browser Statistics for the Random Yahoo Link

http://www.cen.uiuc.edu/~ejk/bryl.html

The tables found on this page summarize which browsers were used to access the Random Yahoo Link—a page that indiscriminately spins browsers to Web sites. The survey records data in three week intervals.

GVU Center's World Wide Web User Survey

http://www.cc.gatech.edu/gvu/user_surveys/
User_Survey_Home.html

Who uses the Web, how, and why are the subjects of the Graphics, Visualization and Usability Center's World Wide Web annual user surveys. The seminal surveys are conducted by the Georgia Institute of Technology's College of Computing and have been endorsed by the World Wide Web Consortium as well as the NCSA's Software Development Group.

Internet Domain Survey, July 1995

http://www.nw.com/zone/WWW/report.html

This 1995 Network Wizards survey of hosts, domains and networks attempts to count every domain on the Internet. The survey reports that "WWW is by far the most popular host name," but "…no one has any clue how many users there are." Find detailed survey data at this site.

Internet Growth Graphs by MIDS

http://www2.mids.org/growth/internet/
index.html

Matrix Information and Directory Services graphically illustrates the growth of the Internet. The result of surveys conducted by MIDS, the graphs illustrate the number of Internet hosts and the presents Internet activity in terms of bytes, packets, and other criteria.

Maloff Company

http://www.trinet.com/maloff

The Maloff Company, an Internet business consulting firm, released a survey in February 1995 finding that annual sales in the Internet marketplace have topped the $1 billion mark. Visitors to the site can read excerpts of the survey and find out how to order the full-text version.

The Mysterious Netizen

http://www.cc.columbia.edu/~hauben/text/
WhatIsNetizen.html

The Mysterious Netizen is a research project that attempts to describe the habits and activities of the often elusive Internet user. Visitors will find statistics and analysis of "Netizen" behavior conducted by Columbia University's Michael Hauben.

Project 2000

http://www2000.ogsm.vanderbilt.edu/

Project 2000 is Vanderbilt University's five-year sponsored research effort into the marketing implications of commercializing hypermedia environments like the Web. The Project 2000 home page hosts an index of articles and resources on the theory and practice of marketing in computer-mediated environments.

Web100

http://www.w100.com/

The Web100 rates and reports the 100 U.S. companies conducting the greatest amount of business on the Web. Take stock of big-time corporate Internet presences at this site.

MAKING THE CONNECTION

BROWSERS, E-MAILERS, AND OTHER CLIENTS

About Lynx

http://kufacts.cc.ukans.edu/about_lynx/about_
lynx.html

This informational page devoted to Lynx, the text-only Web browser for the Unix and VMS platform, offers documentation and news about the latest version of the software.

Accessing Japanese World Wide Web Sites with Netscape and Other Browsers

http://condor.stcloud.msus.edu:20020/
netscape.html

Access Japanese Web sites using Netscape and other browsers with the aid of information resources collected at this site. Links offer support, browsers and code.

Browsers, Viewers and HTML Preparation Resources

http://www.utoronto.ca/webdocs/HTMLdocs/
intro_tools.html

The University of Toronto's Information Commons provides an overview of Web navigation and HTML tools for Macintosh, PC, and Unix users. Visitors can download guides and Web-publishing software packages.

Eudora Mail Package Guide

http://www.soc.staffs.ac.uk/eudora/
contents.html

This guide to the popular shareware e-mail application, Eudora, offers instructions for both its Windows and Macintosh versions. Among the topics covered are creating a message, forwarding messages and creating a signature file.

Exploring The Internet Using XMosaic

http://www.leeds.ac.uk/ucs/docs/papers/
exploring_internet.html

Computer scientists can download a University of Leeds research paper that describes how the school's various departments use XMosaic. It also calls for the academic community in England to start Web development.

Figlet

http://www.inf.utfsm.cl/cgi-bin/figlet

The Figlet program is a stylized text generator that uses 103 different fonts to create signature files for attachment to e-mail messages or personal home pages.

Innosoft International Inc.

http://www.innosoft.com/

Innosoft International, Inc., of West Covina, California promotes its PMDF e-mail software at this site. Find program documentation, technical support and general company information.

Lynx Users Guide v2.3

http://www.cc.ukans.edu/lynx_help/Lynx_
users_guide.html

The University of Kansas provides information on the Lynx Web client. Find a help guide for the text-only browser, and examine a comprehensive index of pointers to related resources.

Mosaic-TueV

http://ftp.uni-tuebingen.de/pub/WWW/Mosaic-
TueV

The distribution directory for Mosaic-TueV, the University of Tübingen's upgrade of NCSA's Mosaic 2.4, is accessible at this FTP site. Includes useful helper applications and binaries.

Mosaic and External Viewers

http://www.ncsa.uiuc.edu/SDG/Software/
WinMosaic/viewers.html

The NCSA provides a rundown on Mosaic and external viewers at this informational site. Multiple Internet Mail Extension, better known as MIME, file type determinants are explained, and external viewer and file compatibilities are charted.

NCSA Mosaic Demo Document

http://www.ncsa.uiuc.edu/SDG/Experimental/
demoweb/demo.html

Visitors are invited to take an interactive tour demonstrating the capabilities of the well-known browser software developed by the NCSA at the University of Illinois at Urbana-Champaign. Visitors running Mosaic can check out the bells and whistles of the experimental hypermedia shows presented.

NCSA Mosaic Frequently Asked Questions

http://www.ncsa.uiuc.edu/SDG/Software/
Mosaic/Docs/mosaic-faq.html

The NCSA keeps users up to date and up to speed on its Mosaic Internet browsing software at this site. A comprehensive FAQ file is available, as well as links to a variety of communications software help resources.

Netscape

http://home.netscape.com/

Netscape Communications Corporation has built a business out of outfitting Internet explorers with free handouts of first-rate navigational software. The company's popular Internet browsing software, Netscape Navigator, plus a wealth of utilities and add-on applications, are available for download at Netscape's home page.

Netscape FTP Archive

ftp://ftp.netscape.com/

Netscape's FTP site archives its chat and browser software for anonymous download.

Netscape Latest News

http://www.mcom.com/

Netscape Communications Corp. posts the latest news about its products, upgrades and services. The site also provides pointers to other Netscape pages, plus access to search engines and Internet directories.

Netscape Navigator Handbook

http://home.netscape.com/eng/mozilla/1.1/handbook/

Netscape Communications Corporation, developer of popular Internet browsing applications, maintains this tutorial site to demonstrate its Navigator software. Find explanations of basic Internet concepts and an alphabetized index of instructional resources.

Netscape Navigator Helper Applications

http://home.netscape.com/assist/helper_apps/index.html

This Netscape site provides access to helper applications that improve performance and broaden the capabilities of Netscape Navigator Internet browsing software. Provides links to shareware and freeware sites where the helper applications can be downloaded.

A Note About Web Browsers and Privacy

http://www.uiuc.edu/~ejk/WWW-privacy.html

No graphics, just straight talk on the etiquette of browsing and privacy. See Editor's Choice.

Popular Navigational Aids

http://wings.buffalo.edu/contest/awards/navigators.html

The Popular Navigational Aids page gives Internet explorers a resource for finding servers and services for effective operation on the Web. The page includes a briefly annotated directory of Internet client software.

Post Office

http://www.cis.ksu.edu/~novak/po.html

Post Office, a background e-mail checking program, is available for download at this site. Find news on version updates and an archive containing versions of application in a variety of formats.

RealAudio

http://www.realaudio.com/

From this page, visitors can download RealAudio client software for instantaneous Web audio playback. Find also links to ABC-TV, National Public Radio news, and other sites with live and archival audio feeds. In English, French, German, Japanese, and Korean.

SlideShow Instructions

http://www.eit.com/software/slideshow/ss.html

Enterprise Integration Technologies maintains this page about SlideShow, a utility used to control NCSA's X11-based Mosaic Web browser from the command line. The page details the syntax for command line access.

---

a2z   EDITOR'S CHOICE

A Note About Web Browsers and Privacy

http://www.uiuc.edu/~ejk/WWW-privacy.html

A Note About Web Browsers and Privacy delivers what the Web does best. Expect no graphics, just unadulterated 12-point, Geneva type. It's an engineer's page that simultaneously tells a story and demonstrates its active principle. An alert is issued describing how Web browsers transparently pass off user names, e-mail addresses and who knows what else when visiting HTTP servers. Think of it in terms of the age old conflict between marketing executives and child safety experts. One founded the oldest profession while the other was, well, the first mom. The marketeer boasts the slick come-on, "What's your name, little girl," while the mother barks stern warnings: "Don't talk to strangers, especially the ones with candy." Within the electronic marketplace is a dimly lit ghetto of content products that serve to distract a visitor's attention while she is virtually felt up by the mechanical claws of the site's host. When the client/server relationship reaches the danger zone, A Note About Web Browsers and Privacy clears the air. Does your browser tell the server who you are, where you've been, what hardware company you're in bed with? Follow a link to find out what your navigational software has to say to strange computers when you surf the Web. —*Reviewed by Becky Bond*

A Note About Web Browsers & Privacy

Ed Kubaitis - ejk@uiuc.edu - 8 November 1994
Updated 20 November 1994

Some users may have noticed that some WWW browsers allow configuring an email address. We have recently discovered that some browsers use this information not only for mail or news posting purposes, but also provide it to every http server you visit. Further, some Unix browsers provide your username even if an email address is not configured.

Since even experienced WWW users here were surprised to learn this, we decided to pass the information on. Silent delivery of a user's email address or username (other than for email or news posting purposes which most users would expect) seems to open a door to potential abuse -- junk email, for example.

Note: we are alerting you to *potential*-- not actual -- abuse. At this time we know of no sites that abuse this information. Indeed, the NCSA httpd server, used by many sites on the web, does not even record email or account information in its logs.

TradeWave MacWeb

http://www.einet.net/EINet/MacWeb/
MacWebHome.html

TradeWave's MacWeb 1.1 is a freeware browser for navigating the Web on a Macintosh. Visitors can read info on installing, configuring and downloading MacWeb, or link to the home page of the TradeWave Galaxy Internet search engine.

TradeWave winWeb

http://www.einet.net/EINet/WinWeb/
WinWebHome.html

Texas-based TradeWave Corporation, known for its Galaxy online service, deals in software and consulting for electronic commerce. Download winWeb, the company's Web browser for Windows, or link to the Galaxy search engine from this site.

World Wide Web Software for Windows PCs

http://www.utoronto.ca/webdocs/HTMLdocs/
pc_tools.html

Browsers, viewers and HTML preparation software for PCs head up the bill of fare at this easy-to-follow directory of tools. Find software for browsing the Web, complete with download instructions and documentation.

World Wide Web Viewer Test

http://www-dsed.llnl.gov/documents/
WWWtest.html

The World Wide Web Viewer Test is a series of exercises designed to evaluate browser performance. Visitors can run their Web browser through a battery of tests.

WorldView Version 0.9g Pre Beta

http://www.webmaster.com/vrml/

The informational site for the VRML browser, WorldView, offers documentation, release information and customer support. Use this program to navigate virtual reality spaces on the Web.

Usenet 1.0.2

http://www.netimages.com/~snowhare/
utilities/usenet-web/

Usenet 1.0.2 is a combination Usenet newsgroup archiver and Web presentation system. Users can download the program along with documentation about system requirements and unique features.

CHAT SOFTWARE AND CHANNEL GUIDES

CyberPark

http://www.cyberpark.com/

CyberPark is a collection of chat lines that cover many topics and categories. Visitors are asked to sign the guest book before venturing off to the various chat rooms.

The Electronic Conferencing Co.

http://www.tecc.co.uk/

This corporate site provides information about the Electronic Conferencing Co. and its services and products, including software designed to assist the exchange of information via the Internet. TECC also is the Web home for businesses such as Top Gear Magazine and Illuminations.

Global Stage Live Chat Software

http://www.prospero.com/globalstage/

Prospero Systems Research Inc. brings live, commercial chat to the Internet via its Global Chat software. Visitors to the company's Web site can check out various versions of the product and download a copy for evaluation.

Internet Relay Chat Information (IRC)

http://www2.undernet.org:8080/~cs93jtl/
IRC.html

The Web is not just a publishing medium, it is a communication medium as well. Comprehensive explanations and instructions related to Internet Relay Chat, a programming method that allows real-time, text-based online conversations, are indexed at this site.

Internet Relay Chat (IRC) Frequently Asked Questions

http://www.kei.com/irc.html

In this FAQs for Internet Relay Chat systems visitors can find the answers to common questions and answers related to conducting text-based, online exchange via IRCs.

Internet Roundtable Society

http://www.irsociety.com/

The Internet Roundtable Society hosts the Internet Roundtable interviews and the WebChat Broadcasting System. The site also promotes an Internet consulting service for businesses.

IRC Related Resources on the Internet

http://urth.acsu.buffalo.edu/irc/WWW/
ircdocs.html

Visitors will find an index of Internet resources related to Internet Relay Chat compiled at this site. Listed links include documents, stats, newsgroups, mailing lists, and FTP sites.

Maroc

http://www.mines.u-nancy.fr/~mhamdi/
maroc.html

This page supports the Moroccan IRC channel. It contains a list of channel regulars and links to Moroccan-related Web pages, as well as a general explanation of IRC and how to participate.

The River

http://www.river.org/

The River, an uncensored, commercial conferencing system, maintains this site containing background and membership information. Visit here to learn about upcoming group discussions and to browse its index of current members.

Talker

http://www2.infi.net/talker/

Visitors to this page can select an identity and enter Talker, a site for online chat. Public chat rooms include a bar, gallery, kitchen, beach, lawn, and pool. Visitors are free to "listen" or "talk" here.

WebChat

http://www.irsociety.com/webchat/
webchat.html

WebChat, a real-time, multimedia chat application, allows Web site visitors to converse as well as trade still and moving images, sounds, and links. A free version of the software which works as an add-on to standard browsers is available at this site, as well as an order form for a fully supported version.

WebChat Broadcasting System

http://www.irsociety.com/wbs.html

The WebChat Broadcasting System enables users to dial in and talk with each other at the company's "stations" which are based on Usenet groups, Web sites and general topics. Scan the channels offered to locate chat opportunities across the Internet.

Zircon, an X11 Client for IRC—Release 1.16

http://catless.ncl.ac.uk/Programs/Zircon/

Information about the Zircon client for Internet Relay Chat under the X Window System is provided. The site includes instructions for installing Zircon and using its interface.

HOW-TO GUIDES AND INSTRUCTION KITS

Access Authorization in World Wide Web

http://www.w3.org/hypertext/WWW/
AccessAuthorization/Overview.html

The World Wide Web Consortium (also known as W3C) offers documentation from its library concerned with telnet access and authorization on the Web. Visitors will find links to official protocols and access procedures.

Charm Net Personal Internet Provider

http://www.charm.net/ppp.html

The Charm Net Personal Internet Provider offers an exhaustive index of resources for connecting to the Internet. Visitors are invited to learn about a variety of tools including Winsock, PPP and SLIP software.

E-Mail Web Resources

http://andrew2.andrew.cmu.edu/cyrus/email/
email.html

Anyone interested in finding out how to use and locate e-mail accounts via the Internet will find instructional resources at this site, courtesy of Ohio State University. Check out mail-related FAQs, and learn how to access the Internet with e-mail software.

Internet and Computer-Mediated Communication Information Sources

http://www.december.com/cmc/info/
index.html

For Web denizens who seek to understand how the technologies that drive the Internet work and how to use them, noted online educator, John December, provides this primer. The guide offers introductions to Internet communication technologies, supplemented by explanations that span technical, cultural and social aspects of cyberspace.

Internet Connections

http://tbone.biol.scarolina.edu/~dean/kit/
kit.html

This document provides contact information for two Internet connectivity packages. Internet in a Box and the DOS/Windows Internet Kit are featured.

Internet Starter Kit for Macintosh Modem Page

http://www.mcp.com/hayden/iskm/
modems.html

Mac users who are having trouble hooking up to the Web and suspect their modem is the guilty culprit can consult this site for modem connection strings and instructions.

ISDN for Linux

http://www.ix.de/ix/linux/linux-isdn.html

ISDN for Linux is a collection of documents and links to information on high-speed Internet connections for the Linux platform. Visitors will find complete information on setting up and maintaining Linux ISDN connections.

Russification

http://www.orst.edu/dept/is/ruslit/

The Sviaz site contains software designed to "Russify" computers and prepare them for interfacing with Russian Internet sites. Includes links to relevant software sites and Russian newsgroups.

SLiRP/TIA and Trumpet Winsock Setup Menu

http://www.webcom.com/~llarrow/tiarefg.html

This reference resource is designed to ease people's Internet travels by offering configuration assistance for users of the TCP/IP emulator SLiRP. Find detailed technical information about The Internet Adapter and the TCP/IP stack Trumpet Winsock, plus links to similar sites.

Software Ventures Corporation

http://www.svcdudes.com/

Software Ventures Corporation, maker of Internet Valet and Microphone, claims it sells an "instant, hassle-free, complete, affordable, fun and risk-free way to explore the Internet." The company pitches its Internet connection software and offers technical support at its home page.

Texas ISDN Users Group (TIUG)

http://www.crimson.com/isdn/

Internet users who connect using ISDN modems have a friend in the Texas ISDN Users Group. Visitors to the TIUG home page can check out its schedule of upcoming meetings or click through an educational series of links that explains what ISDN is and how it works.

Windows and TCP/IP for Internet Access

http://learning.lib.vt.edu/wintcpip/
wintcpip.html

Harry M. Kriz of Virginia Polytechnic Institute and State University presents this paper describing principal functions and services available via the Internet. The treatise "outlines the technical background and terminology needed by the beginner who wants to make his or her PC a host on the Internet."

ELF Communications' WinTalk

http://www.elf.com/elf/wintalk.html

Find out what WinTalk is, how to get it and where to find it. An introduction to WinTalk, a free software enabling "two-way, text-based conversation," and online FAQs is available.

World Wide Web Software

http://www.w3.org/hypertext/WWW/
Status.html

The World Wide Web Software site provides a general overview of background information and updates concerning Web software products and news. Features links to databases, libraries, gateways, and other archives.

INTERNET TELEPHONY

CyberPhone

http://magenta.com/cyberphone/

This commercial site promotes CyberPhone, a real-time phone system utilizing the Internet. Visitors can learn about the product, its history and equipment requirements, plus cost and ordering information.

INTERNET TOOLS

Andrew's MacTCP Drive-Thru

http://www.echonyc.com/~andrewj/
drive-thru.html

Andrew's MacTCP Drive-Thru serves up a menu offering an array of Mac and Web programs available for download from public FTP sites. Browsers can choose from the latest versions of Macintosh connectivity applications.

Apple and the Internet

http://applenet.apple.com/

Apple Computer Inc. supplies the computing community with innovative hardware and software offerings for its easy-to-use, graphics-friendly operating system. Macintosh users have hit the Internet early and in full force, and Apple obliges its devotees with the host of navigational and development applications and utilities available for download at this site.

Brad.Net Apple Internet Server 6150

http://www.ape.com/

Apple enthusiast Brad Schrick has a list of over 1700 Macintosh Internet Servers. See Editor's Choice.

Corporation for Research and Educational Networking

http://www.cren.net/

The Corporation for Research and Educational Networking provides educators, researchers and the rest of the Internet community with software and services. Includes descriptions of applications and details of services.

CyberWISE

http://www.cyberwise.com/

The Saratoga Group presents CyberWISE, computer-based learning software. The company promises its products will make "learning about the Internet quick, easy and fun." Download free sample software at this promotional site.

CuteFTP

http://papa.indstate.edu:8888/CuteFTP/

The CuteFTP page is dedicated to an FTP program that allows novice users to utilize the capabilities of FTP without having to know all the details. Visitors can download the shareware or contact its author here.

Frontier Technologies

http://www.frontiertech.com/

This promotional site is the Web home of Frontier Technologies Corporation, a developer and marketer of Internet connection software headquartered in Wisconsin. Visitors to its home page can read about the company, its products and services.

FTP Software Inc.

http://www.ftp.com/

FTP Software Inc. is a commercial producer of TCP/IP networking products for Internet connection. Visitors to the company's site will find product information, technical support, sales contacts and press releases.

IBM Internet Connection Family

http://www.ibm.com/Internet

Computer industry giant IBM promotes an Internet access service complete with servers, Web tools and client software aimed at the business customer. Links to information on these and other IBM products are featured.

InterCon Systems

http://www.intercon.com/

InterCon, a manufacturer of cross-platform Internet connectivity software, maintains this Web site. Find information about the company, its products, technical support and an index of free software demos.

Internaut

http://www.zilker.net/users/internaut/update.html

PC users of TCP/IP Internet software can access documentation and help files for various connectivity applications at this site. Visitors will find answers to Frequently Asked Questions (FAQs), links to relevant newsgroups and software updates.

Internet Goodies

http://www.ensta.fr/internet/

Internet Goodies provides information and software for hooking up to the Internet. Visitors to this site are able to download freeware and shareware for all major computing platforms.

Internet Software & Services

http://wwwhost.ots.utexas.edu/mac/internet.html

An archive of Macintosh software and miscellaneous TCP/IP applications begins the list of resources available here. Find a variety of FTP, gopher, mail, news and Web-editing applications.

Internet Tools Summary

http://www.december.com/net/tools/index.html

John December's Internet Tools Summary provides an overview of applications and utilities commonly used for information retrieval and computer-mediated communication. Visitors will find instructional information, searchable databases and links to related resources.

John A. Junod Winsock

http://www.csra.net/junodj/

This collection of Winsock Internet connectivity software is made available by a U.S. Army computer programmer. Visitors will find downloadable utilities for a variety of computer platforms. Includes links to Windows 95 software archives.

---

a2z **EDITOR'S CHOICE**

Brad.Net Apple Internet Server 6150

http://www.ape.com/

Brad Schrick is a poster boy for everything that's good and true about Apple devotees and Internet nuts. I even forgive him for using frames on his Web page. Appealing to geeky do-gooders and earth-tone-clad technology enthusiasts (you know who you are), it's not surprising that he named his site after his server. One look at Brad's bearded mug and you are lost forever in the arms of his unadulterated love of Internet-serving software and hardware. Brad.Net debuted in 1994, running MacHTTP on a Mac Plus for five full months before experiencing its first crash—yes, Brad boasts, while using the Mac OS. Now Brad maintains a list of Macintosh Internet servers that tops out at over 1,700 entries. Read about Brad's Macintosh-only Web design services for commercial entities and public service organizations, or see what he likes and dislikes about businesses in the Apple market in the Heroes and Zeroes section. The page's short FAQ reads in its entirety: "FAQ: Why is Brad's head on all of these pages?!...A: Brad needs a scanner, a digital camera, a high-end Mac, and high-end software...until he gets them, this is all you get...!"—*Reviewed by Becky Bond*

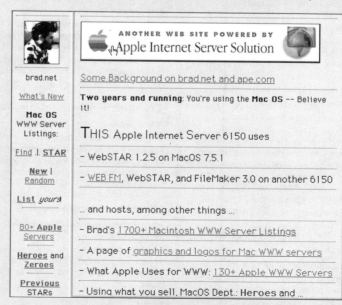

brad.net

What's New

Mac OS
WWW Server
Listings:

Find | STAR

New |
Random

List *yours*

80+ Apple
Servers

Heroes and
Zeroes

Previous
STARs

ANOTHER WEB SITE POWERED BY
Apple Internet Server Solution

Some Background on brad.net and ape.com

Two years and running: You're using the **Mac OS** -- Believe it!

THIS Apple Internet Server 6150 uses

- WebSTAR 1.2.5 on MacOS 7.5.1

- WEB FM, WebSTAR, and FileMaker 3.0 on another 6150

... and hosts, among other things ...

- Brad's 1700+ Macintosh WWW Server Listings

- A page of graphics and logos for Mac WWW servers

- What Apple Uses for WWW: 130+ Apple WWW Servers

- Using what you sell. MacOS Dept.: Heroes and ...

Mac Internet Applications

http://community.net/~csamir/macapp.html

The Mac Internet Applications site contains listings of Internet-related applications for the Macintosh. Includes an annotated index software available for download.

Mailcap Files

http://www.ncsa.uiuc.edu/SDG/Software/Mosaic/Docs/mailcap.html

Mailcap Files maps a file format for multiple mail reading programs. It outlines in specific detail the mechanisms designed to work with mail systems.

McGill Systems Inc.

http://musicm.mcgill.ca/

McGill Systems Inc. offers details about networking and Internet software products at its corporate home page. Texts of recent company presentations regarding the Internet are included.

NetDial

http://www.enterprise.net/netdial

The NetDial home page provides information and specifications about the Internet dialer for Microsoft Windows users. Visitors can download the software and learn how it can be customized to fit a variety of systems.

IBM: The Internet Connection Family

http://www.networking.ibm.com/icf/icfprod.html

IBM offers a wide variety of networking services, including design consultation, secure servers and Web access clients. Demos and previews are available at the Internet Connection home page.

OS/2 Internet Apps

http://www.phoenix.net/~vccubed/os2apps.html

PC users running OS/2 can download Internet connectivity software here. The extensive collection of software includes freeware and shareware versions of e-mailers, IRC clients, and Web browsers.

An Overview of Hypertext and IR Systems and Applications

http://www.w3.org/hypertext/Products/Overview.html

The gloss of hypertext and information retrieval systems and applications offers a quick fix for Web junkies, with its index of resources, definitions and news on state-of-the-art systems. The page includes dozens of links, from Essence, an indexing prototype, to Doorway, an hypertext system with annotation and mixed graphics.

The PC-Mac TCP/IP and NFS FAQ list by Rawn Shah

http://www.rtd.com/pcnfsfaq/faq.html

This FAQ site helps visitors choose TCP/IP and NFS products for PC and Macintosh systems. Includes basic information on connectivity options such as TCP/IP, NFS, ethernet, SLIP, and PPP.

PPP Frequently Asked Questions

http://www.cis.ohio-state.edu/hypertext/faq/usenet/ppp-faq/top.html

This Usenet FAQ file anticipates common questions about PPP, a software tool for connecting to the Internet. Includes information on PPP installation and configuration.

Stroud's Consummate Winsock AppsList

http://cws.internet.com/

Stroud's Consummate Winsock AppsList is a comprehensive listing of Internet software sites and up-to-date collections of Winsock applications for Windows users. Well organized and exhaustive in scope, the site serves up a healthy menu of Internet applications including utilities, HTML editors, news readers, graphics viewers, and browsers.

Stroud's Consummate Winsock AppsList Mirror Site—Finland

http://www.cws.internet.com/

The widely-used archive of Internet software for Windows users, the Consummate Winsock AppsList is mirrored in Finland for easier European access.

Sybase Inc.

http://www.sybase.com/

Sybase, Inc. markets client/server software and services for building online, enterprise-wide information systems. This site provides comprehensive company information and a searchable index.

Talent Communications, Inc.

http://www.talentcom.com/

At Talent Communications' corporate home page, potential customers can examine its Internet browsing and search engine utilities and services online. Demo software packages, or download beta versions of the company's Internet tools at this site.

Trumpet Software International

http://www.trumpet.com.au/

Trumpet Software International develops and markets Winsock software, Internet connectivity applications and utilities for PCs. Visit the company's home page for product updates and downloadable software.

WebCopy Documentation

http://www.inf.utfsm.cl/~vparada/webcopy.html

The beta 2.0 version of WebCopy and its documentation are available at this site. The perl program retrieves URLs, specific HTML files and file trees.

Web Technology

http://www.base.com/gordoni/webtech.html

This personal home page indexes general Web technology resources on the Internet. Pointers include an Internet tools summary, TCP/IP communications, an HTML development jumpstation and links to popular browsers.

The Winsock Client Listing

http://www.mbnet.mb.ca/winter/index.html

Winsock applications are used by Windows users to make possible connections to the Internet. Visitors will find descriptions, technical documentation and download instructions for Winsock freeware, shareware and commercial demo packages.

WinZip

http://www.winzip.com/

Nico Mak Computing Inc. is a software company located in Bristol, Conn. Visitors to its home page can learn about the company's WinZip software product, a Windows Internet compression utility.

World Wide Web Tools/Utilities

http://hplyot.obspm.fr/~dl/wwwtools.html

This directory of Web tools and utilities is maintained by a member of the Observatoire de Paris-Meudon. Among the offerings are an anonymous HTTP proxy and e-cash gambling software.

VIRTUAL COMMUNITIES

AlphaWorld

http://www.worlds.net/alphaworld

AlphaWorld is an online community simulation where participants can acquire and develop property, interact with other people, assume an online character, and live out a virtual life in an unprogrammed and unpredictable world. Includes instructions on becoming a citizen and downloading the latest release.

Atlantis Cyberspace

http://vr-atlantis.com/

To get a taste of virtual reality, browsers are invited to download pictures and movies from the Atlantis Cyberspace, a proposed "virtual theme park." Complete details are available about the project, as are links related to corresponding virtual reality Web destinations.

Connection—E-Mail Key Pals

http://www.comenius.com/keypal/index.html

For a fee, visitors to this site can sign up to be matched with e-mail pen pals from around the world. General info about the service and the company that provides it is featured.

Cyborganic

http://www.cyborganic.com/welcome.html

A virtual community with a botanical theme. See Editor's Choice.

Digital Communities: Urban Design and Planning in Cyberspace

http://alberti.mit.edu/arch/4.207/homepage.html

This Massachusetts Institute of Technology site describes a graduate seminar in urban planning and design in cyberspace. Includes a course description, prerequisites for registration and profiles of course instructors.

Electric Communities

http://www.communities.com/

Electric Communities, a software company in Los Altos, California, is developing software technology called the Cyberspace Operating System, or COS, which supports social communities. The site features information about the company, its research and its available software products.

GeoCities

http://www.geocities.com

The wide-open Web is a natural frontier for homesteading. GeoCities answers cybersettlers' needs with free personal home pages for noncommercial content. With more than 25 neighborhoods to choose from, create your own ghetto or start squatting in posh Beverly Hills. GeoCities even supplies video cameras in the "actual" locations of its neighborhoods to import users with "a feeling of 'really being someplace.'"

Internet Multicasting Service

http://www.town.hall.org/

The Internet Town Hall, a site sponsored by 20 corporations, is as varied and contentious as a real town hall. Visitors will find links to U.S. government databases, Internet radio sites, and a look at new and trendy Internet protocols.

More about MOOs

http://www.itp.berkeley.edu/~thorne/MOO.html

Visitors to this page can follow links to MUDs, MOOs, and MUSHs across the Internet. It includes links to Multi-User Domains, object-oriented MUDs and Multi-User Shared Hallucinations, along with explanations of what they are.

The MUD Connector

http://www.absi.com/mud/

Jump into the Multi-User Dimension via the MUD Connector, a commercial service linking online games around the Web universe. Search the list of links to locate desired games, or learn about a certain game using descriptions provided by the page.

The MUD Resource Collection

http://www.godlike.com/muds/

The MUD Resource Collection is a list of links to MUD FAQs and information sources. Visitors will find Web game interfaces, FTP archives and MUSH lists. The links are of interest to MUD users and researchers alike.

MUDs @ Lysator

http://www.lysator.liu.se:7500/mud/main.html

This page contains pointers to sites dealing with MUDS, that is, Multi-User Dialog or Dungeon online gaming systems. A MUD FAQs is included.

soho.net

http://www.soho.net/

Media Access Systems presents soho.net, which it pitches as a "virtual community based on the geographical location of Soho, yet not limited within these boundaries." Explore its Web resources and BBS access service.

Telecommuting, Teleworking and Alternative Officing

http://www.gilgordon.com/

Extensive documentation and links of interest to anyone with a professional interest in telecom-

---

a2z EDITOR'S CHOICE

Cyborganic

http://www.cyborganic.com/welcome.html

Cyborganic has firmly planted the roots of a new type of community on the Web, accomplishing its dual mission of establishing a "virtual home" and a "realtime hangout." In the company's own words, "Cyborganic Gardens is the first step in our grand plan to build a funky, friendly place that exists on both sides of the screen—just like we do." The botanical theme is adhered to religiously with personal home pages in the forest, commercial sites in the orchard and Web publishing tools in the garden shed. Particularly well-tended and exotic sites swelter in the hothouse, where you'll find the likes of Justin's Links to the Underground, the collage art of Winston Smith and commentary by Howard Rheingold. Less virtual Cyborganic plots include the Space Bar, which is part chat room and part online salon, and the service's famed flesh and blood Thursday night dinner gatherings. Future plans also predict a Cyborganic café, a permanent physical space to complement the company's preexisting online condition. Get online with Cyborganic while you can. With their ambition and "techno-how," its hard to tell if Cyborganic emulates life, or if life will end up emulating Cyborganic.—*Reviewed by Becky Bond*

muting are presented at this site. Visitors will find news, conference schedules, publications, and links to resources on telecommuting and the virtual office.

WEBCASTING AND ONLINE VIDEO CONFERENCING

AudioNet

http://www.audionet.com/

AudioNet describes itself as "the first audio network on the Internet." Check out this page for the schedule of real-time and near-time broadcasts, plus links to live audio feeds.

Cornell University CU-SeeMe

http://cu-seeme.cornell.edu/

Cornell University's CU-SeeMe project aims to advance the technology of Internet telecommunications with quick and dirty video conferencing freeware. With accessories such as an inexpensive digital camera and a modem, CU-SeeMe allows people with computers to interact face to face via the Internet.

Desktop Video Conferencing

http://www.visc.vt.edu/succeed/videoconf.html

An exhaustive discussion of desktop video conferencing is available at this site, including information about products to enhance connectivity, an explanation of bandwidth, and opinions about the virtues and drawbacks of ISDN and ethernet.

INRIA Videoconferencing System

http://zenon.inria.fr:8003/rodeo/personnel/Thierry.Turletti/ivs.html

The INRIA Videoconferencing System is a software that transmits video and audio signals over the Internet. Featured information includes platform compatibility, an installation guide and user tutorials.

MBONE

http://www.cs.ucl.ac.uk/mice/mbone_review.html

MBONE, the Multicast BackbONE, is a resource for "developing protocols and applications for group communication." Read about its network delivery services for video conferencing and audio needs.

Multicast backBONE (MBONE) Frequently Asked Questions

http://www.mediadesign.co.at/newmedia/more/mbone-faq.html

MBONE is a virtual network used to facilitate live audio and video transmissions over the Internet.

Featured here are files describing the what, where, and how of the network.

Tenet Group

http://tenet.berkeley.edu/

The Tenet Group conducts research on real-time and high performance computer networks. Take a look at tomorrow's media applications such as video conferencing at this research and development-oriented site.

STANDARDS AND SECURITY

DIGITAL CASH AND ELECTRONIC COMMERCE

Case Study: Electronic Commerce on The World Wide Web

http://www.cox.smu.edu/mis/cases/webcase/home.html

Teaching materials and case studies concerning electronic commerce on the Web can be found at this site. Includes discussion questions, abstracts and marketing strategies related to the conduct of monetary transactions online.

CommerceNet

http://www.commerce.net/

CommerceNet, a nonprofit corporation, is conducting a large-scale study of electronic Internet commerce. Read about the company's mission, or tap into the CommerceNet directory services rounding out the site's offerings.

CyberCash

http://www.cybercash.com/

Find something you want to buy online? Visit CyberCash to learn about its "secure purchase" services for consumers and merchants on the Web.

DigiCash

http://www.digicash.com/

A payment technology product provider oversees monetary transactions via the Internet. See Editor's Choice.

The Digital REST Area at SUNY Plattsburgh DigiCash College Store

http://137.142.42.95/DigiCash/eStore/EStore.html

The State University of New York, Plattsburgh, DigiCash College eStore is a fictional place where participants in the beta testing of the Ecash project can spend their Cyberbucks.

Ecash

http://www.digicash.com/ecash/ecash-home.html

Ecash, a service of payment technology product provider DigiCash, is a secure online payment software package. Visit here to learn about the software and its Cyberbucks currency.

Electronic Commerce Association

http://www.globalx.net/eca/

Ottawa, Ontario-based Electronic Commerce Association provides networking and educational opportunities for members of high-technology industries. Visitors to its home page will find events calendars, membership information and professional resources.

Enterprise Integration Technologies

http://www.eit.com/

The home page for Enterprise Integration Technologies provides information on the company's software products and services. EIT develops strategies and products which make possible electronic commerce on the Internet. Includes a search engine.

Net1

http://www.netchex.com/

Net1 is the online home of NetChex, a virtual checking account that facilitates online transactions. The page presents company information and provides a virtual marketplace in which to exercise the company's technology.

The NetBill Project

http://www.ini.cmu.edu/netbill/

The NetBill Project site offers an electronic goods and services purchasing system on the Internet. This site provides information about the system, including research goals, publications and development tools.

NetCash

http://www.netbank.com/~netcash/

NetCash, a service of NetBank, allows online vendors and their customers to conduct "virtual" cash transactions over the Internet. At this home page, visitors can withdraw information about the system and how it works.

Network Payment Mechanisms and Digital Cash

http://ganges.cs.tcd.ie/mepeirce/project.html

This informational site, maintained by a researcher at Trinity College in Dublin, Ireland, provides information about Internet-based payment mechanisms and digital cash services. Visit here for links to existing systems, news about upcoming technologies and various articles on the subject of network security.

Open Market, Inc.

http://www.openmarket.com/

This site is the home page for Open Market Inc. located in Boston. The company is a software developer focusing on the production of enterprise-wide applications for electronic commerce.

Stefan Brands

http://www.cwi.nl/~brands/

Stefan Brands' personal home page provides information about his research in "untraceable offline electronic cash and privacy-protecting mechanisms for digital credentials."

ENCRYPTION

Applied Cryptography

http://www.openmarket.com/techinfo/applied.htm

"Applied Cryptography," a 1994 book by Bruce Schneier, offers documents and software packages related to the discipline of encryption and decoding. Find information on obtaining the book, plus an extensive collection of links to cryptography resources available on the Internet.

Computer Privacy Handbook

http://www.well.com/user/abacard

Maintained by Andre Bacard, author of the "Computer Privacy Handbook," this site answers Frequently Asked Questions (FAQs) concerning e-mail privacy, anonymous remailers, and PGP. Links to topically relevant sites are featured along with details for ordering the book.

Cryptography Export Control Archives

ftp://ftp.cygnus.com/pub/export/export.html

Visitors interested in cryptography-export news and opinions will find an index of available resources at this site. Includes links to information on relevant court cases, political developments and technical updates.

DELTA

http://muse.bio.cornell.edu/delta/

DELTA is an encoding process for taxonomic descriptions used in computer processing. This site describes and illustrates DELTA, offers availability information, and points to Web homes of DELTA USA and DELTA Australia.

I Broke Hal's SSL Challenge

http://pauillac.inria.fr/~doligez/ssl/

At this site, Damien Doligez, a computer whiz who cracked Netscape's encryption code in the summer of 1995, offers his account of the feat. This page includes his virtual press conference and links to encryption information.

Internet Commerce Group

http://www.sun.com/security/

Sun Microsystem's Internet Commerce Group sells products and services to corporations and Internet service providers. This page highlights its cryptography, protocol and security products.

NetPartners

http://www.netpart.com/

NetPartners is a software developer located in San Diego, Calif. Visitors to its site can learn about NetPartners Internet security and encryption programs and services.

---

a2z EDITOR'S CHOICE

DigiCash

http://www.digicash.com/

If you thought it was a big mistake when the United States abandoned the gold standard, you'd better bury the family silver in the backyard. If, by now, you are convinced that paper money will not wreck the republic, read on to prepare for the future of currency as it exists today. The Web is a field of dreams desperately staked on the principle, "If you build it, they will come." If the hordes do come and they come ready to shop, DigiCash will be ready with electronic currencies promising the safe conduct of monetary transactions via the Internet. Ironically, the company's first trials of digital money were conducted not on the Infobahn, but on the freeways of Japan, as an automatic road toll payment system. A secure software client that withdraws value from an online bank, Ecash can be exchanged via e-mail for Internet goods and services. What does the future hold? Purchasing by pointing and clicking, making the Web a viable venue for software requisition and delivery, as well as a host of other faceless transactions. Whether it delights or scares the bejesus out of you, it's the future, so get online at the Internet cash register.—*Reviewed by Becky Bond*

PGP Distribution Authorization Form

http://bs.mit.edu:8001/pgp-form.html

Visitors to this page will find an authorization form which must be completed prior to downloading Pretty Good Privacy, the high-security cryptographic software distributed by MIT. Includes details about PGP and licensing information.

PGP Frequently Asked Questions

http://www.cis.ohio-state.edu/hypertext/faq/usenet/pgp-faq/top.html

Pretty Good Privacy, or PGP as it is better known, is a widely-used Web encryption program. As security coding software should be indecipherable but not unfathomable, a collection of Usenet FAQs covering the PGP basics is indexed at this site.

Portland Software

http://www.portsoft.com/

Portland Software makes ZipLock, an application enabling digital encryption for Internet file transfers. Find information about company's products and services at this site, along with press clippings, and a link to a biography of Harpo Marx.

Pretty Good Privacy

http://www.thegate.gamers.org/~tony/pgp.html

Ensure secure communication over the Internet with PGP 2, the cryptosystem popularly known as Pretty Good Privacy. Visit this site to find out how to obtain, install and use the freely-distributed cryptographic software.

Pretty Good Privacy Encryption FAQs

http://www.quadralay.com/www/Crypt/PGP/pgp00.html/

This site contains a list of FAQs serving up basic background info and advanced user instructions for the Pretty Good Privacy encryption program. It is one of two FAQs on PGP offered by the newsgroup alt.security.pgp.

Pretty Good Privacy: MIT Distribution Site

http://web.mit.edu/network/pgp.html

The Massachusetts Institute of Technology provides access to the Pretty Good Privacy cryptographic security software at this site. Visitors can learn about PGP and download necessary software.

Privacy Forum

http://www.vortex.com/privacy.htm

Vortex Technology hosts this online discussion forum dedicated to issues of privacy in the information age. Peruse the forum's archives, or link to the Vortex Technology home page.

Recent www-security Messages

http://192.187.146.100/www-security.html/

The e-mail messages and alerts posted to a Web security issues mailing list are sorted here by date. Topics include encryption, legislative initiatives, passwords and FTP security.

RIPEM

http://www.cs.indiana.edu/ripem/dir.html

This guide to Riordan's Internet Privacy Enhanced Mail, a public key e-mail encryption application, is maintained by the University of Indiana's computer science department. Find a user guide, a list of vulnerabilities and defenses, and answers to Frequently Asked Questions (FAQs).

Ronald L. Rivest: Cryptography and Security

http://theory.lcs.mit.edu/~rivest/crypto-security.html

This indexed gateway site provides links to pages dealing with cryptography and security issues. Includes pointers to bibliographies, related government resources, commercial enterprises and nonprofit organizations.

RSA Data Security Inc.

http://www.rsa.com/

The California-based computer company produces cryptography and security software. Visitors to its home page will find detailed product information, company news, and security FAQs.

VeriSign Inc.

http://www.verisign.com/

VeriSign Inc. markets digital authentication services, as well as electronic commerce and communications security products. Includes news about the digital ID industry.

NETWORK SECURITY AND FIREWALLS

Bellcore Security Products

http://www.bellcore.com/

The Bellcore (Bell Communications Research) site features information on the company's computer and network security products. Links to individual product lines and a host of other Bellcore sites are featured.

CheckPoint Software Technologies Ltd.: Home of FireWall-I

http://www.checkpoint.com/

CheckPoint Software Technologies is a developer of Internet computer network security applications. This page includes background information on the company, product descriptions and ordering instructions.

COAST

http://www.cs.purdue.edu/coast/coast.html

The Computer Operations, Audit and Security Technology project of Purdue University in Lafayette, Indiana, makes its Web home at this site. Visitors are invited to learn about the project, read newsletters and reports, contact faculty and staff, and link additional security-related Internet resources.

CSTC Security

http://ciac.llnl.gov/cstc/CSTCHome.html

The Computation Security Technology Center, a division of the Lawrence Livermore National Laboratory, outlines its consulting services at this site. Get a rundown of its information technology capabilities, which include computer incident advisories, product development and secure systems services.

Great Circle Associates

http://www.greatcircle.com/

Great Circle Associates is a California-based company that specializes in Internet training and consulting. Visitors are encouraged to read promotional information about the company's Internet Security Firewalls Tutorial, as well as its other products and services.

McAfee Network Security and Management

http://www.mcafee.com/

McAfee Network Security and Management provides company news at this corporate home page. Visitors will find press releases, information on products and services, and access to files at the McAfee FTP site.

Microsystems Software on the Web

http://www.microsys.com/

Microsystems Software Inc. pitches CyberPatrol, an Internet filter utility for shielding innocent Internet denizens from perceived Web dangers. Find company information along with ordering instructions.

NCSA Access Configuration Tutorial

http://hoohoo.ncsa.uiuc.edu/docs/setup/access/Overview.html

The NCSA presents an access configuration tutorial to instruct Internet users on the finer points of computer server security and access control.

NIST Computer Security Resource Clearinghouse

http://csrc.ncsl.nist.gov/

The Computer Security Resource Clearinghouse, a service of the National Institute of Standards and Technology, provides access to information regarding general computer security risks, viruses, and privacy and legal issues.

Raptor Systems Inc.

http://www.raptor.com/

Raptor Systems Inc. is a Waltham, Mass.-based software developer that specializes in computer security products. The company's home page features information on its integrated and modular firewall security management software, and services.

Rutgers World Wide Web-Security Index

http://www-ns.rutgers.edu/www-security/

The World Wide Web Security site, maintained by Rutgers University, indexes security information for the Web, HTTP, HTML, and related software and protocol research. Links to references, issues, mailing lists and working groups are available.

SATAN Release Information

http://www.cs.ruu.nl/cert-uu/satan.html

Release information is available for Satan 1.1, a tool to help system administrators recognize network-related security problems. A comprehensive index of FTP mirror sites where Satan can be downloaded is provided.

Secure Computing Corporation

http://www.sctc.com/

Secure Computing Corporation is an information security services company that develops and markets encryption programs, security firewalls and digital security systems. Find product and services summaries at this promotional page.

Trove Investment Corporation and Net Nanny

http://www.netnanny.com/netnanny/

Net Nanny, a product of Trove Investment Corporation, acts as "an invisible monitor between the Internet and your family," screening out what it deems "potentially harmful" or "inappropriate" information.

Unix Network Monitoring Tools

http://ciac.llnl.gov/ciac/ToolsUnixNetMon.html

This U.S. Department of Energy site supplies descriptions and downloading instructions for network monitoring tools. Includes programs for detecting SATAN probes and attacks, network management, traffic logging, and other network tools.

V-ONE Corporation

http://www.v-one.com/

Get the lowdown on smartcard technologies at this site from software and hardware developer, Virtual Open Network Environment Corporation. Technologies featured include V-ONE's Cyber Wallet and SmartCAT, the company's smartcard-based user authentication client.

The World Wide Web Security FAQ

http://www-genome.wi.mit.edu/WWW/faqs/www-security-faq.html

Visitors to this site will find a document containing answers to Frequently Asked Questions regarding security on the Web. A bibliography is attached.

STANDARDS, SPECIFICATIONS, AND PROTOCOLS

Bibliography for the World Wide Web

http://www.w3.org/hypertext/WWW/Bibliography.html

This site archives standards information about the World Wide Web. Includes manuals and primers on HTML and URLs, along with academic and research papers discussing the Web.

IAB Internet Architecture Board Meetings Minutes

http://info.internet.isi.edu:80/IAB

This virtual filing cabinet archives the minutes of Internet Architecture Board meetings. Includes links to the IAB's home page, the Internet Society gopher server and related resources.

IETF

http://www.ietf.cnri.reston.va.us/

The Internet Engineering Task Force an organization dedicated to the architecture and operation of the Internet, particularly in the areas of protocols and standards. Participation is open to all interested parties. Includes links to Internet-related groups and societies.

IETF—Hypertext Transfer Protocol (HTTP) Working Group

http://www.ics.uci.edu/pub/ietf/http/

The Hypertext Transfer Protocol Working Group is a part of the Internet Engineering Task Force. This Web page summarizes issues and discussions currently or recently taking place within the group. Links to specific meeting notes, conference papers, and working drafts of proposals may be accessed here.

Information Highway Advisory Council of Canada

http://strategis.ic.gc.ca/IHAC

The Canadian Information Highway Advisory Council, established by the Ministry of Industry, archives Internet development resources. Visit this site for research results, reports, news releases and other related documents from the government-sponsored organization. In English and French.

Internet Documentation and IETF Information

http://ds.internic.net/ds/dspg0intdoc.html

The InterNIC Internet Documentation site is an online resource of the Internet Engineering Task Force, a group concerned with architecture and operation of the Internet. IETF reports, schedules and organizational news are provided.

Internet Drafts Overview

http://web.nexor.co.uk/public/internet-drafts/id.html

The Nexor company provides this overview of the Internet Engineering Task Force working groups, which handle the technical tasks of the protocol engineering and development arm of the Internet. Visitors to this site will find a searchable database of working groups currently publishing drafts.

Internet Request For Comments (RFC)

http://www.cis.ohio-state.edu/hypertext/information/rfc.html

This site contains a listing of the written protocols and policies of the Internet. Site features include entry points for retrieving listed documents.

InterNIC Internet Documentation (RFC's, FYI's, etc.)

http://ds.internic.net/ds/dspg1intdoc.html

The Internet Engineering Task Force maintains this site for its Request for Comments file. Visit here for a browsable index and keyword search utility covering Internet topics and TCP/IP protocol-related subjects.

ISO 9000 Forum

http://www.iso.ch/9000e/forum.html

Straight from the International Standardization Organization, this page contains the facts on ISO 9000. Site features also include links to the ISO 9000 newsletter and complete documentation of the program's goals and ongoing projects.

Mime FAQ

http://www.cis.ohio-state.edu/hypertext/faq/usenet/mail/mime-faq/top.html

This Usenet FAQ archive provides online enlightenment regarding Internet mail standard MIME. Includes MIME product listings and advanced technical information.

Names and Addresses, URIs, URLs, URNs, URCs

http://www.w3.org/hypertext/WWW/Addressing/Addressing.html

The World Wide Web Names and Addresses, URIs, URLs, URNs, URCs site explains the ins and outs of addressing technologies for the Web. Discussions of the general topics are peppered with handy definitions and specifications.

Organizations—Standards

http://www.december.com/cmc/info/
index.html

If you wonder who sets the technical standards for worldwide telecommunications and networking systems, consult the directory offered by this page to find out who the groups are and what they do. For the few entities without a Web site, addresses or phone numbers are provided.

SSL Version 3.0

http://home.netscape.com/newsref/std/
SSL.html

This page explains Secure Sockets Layer, a proposed security standard for the Internet. This lengthy document details technical information about the SSL protocol.

Standards

http://cuiwww.unige.ch/OSG/MultimediaInfo/
mmsurvey/standards.html

Internet-related and other proprietary standards for audio and visual files are outlined at this site. Find detailed standard specifications, explanations and hot lists.

Status codes in HTTP

http://www.w3.org/hypertext/WWW/
Protocols/HTTP/HTRESP.html

If you're frustrated with the mysterious error codes on the Internet, turn to the status codes in HTTP page. Visitors to this site will find the values for the numeric error messages which appear on the screen when something goes wrong.

Technical Aspects of the World-Wide Web

http://www.w3.org/pub/WWW/Technical.html

This technical site offers visitors information, advice and guidance for placing a site on the Web. Features include discussions of HTTP protocol, CGI, and recent technical developments.

Technical Information and Specifications

http://www.ncsa.uiuc.edu/SDG/Software/
Mosaic/Docs/d2-tech.html

The NCSA, a high-performance computing and communications research center, makes available Internet programming resources. Visit this site for detailed information about HTML, the primary programming language of the Web.

Uniform Resource Identifiers (URI) Charter

http://www.ietf.cnri.reston.va.us/html.charters/
uri-charter.html

The Uniform Resource Identifiers Working Group is responsible for setting standards and protocol for Internet URL addresses. Visitors to the organization's Web site will find a history of how the Internet address system came to be, along with

working drafts of proposals. Visitors are encouraged to leave their comments.

URI Mail Archives

http://www.acl.lanl.gov/URI/archive/
archives.html

This is an archive of the mailing list for the Internet Engineering Task Force's working group on Uniform Resource Identifiers. The archive is divided into sections, designated by year, dating back to 1992.

WAIS Overview

http://www.w3.org/pub/Products/WAIS/
Overview.html/

The World Wide Web Consortium, or W3C, offers information on systems and applications that are used on the Internet, including the Wide Area Information System.

World Wide Web Consortium (W3C): A Short Prospectus

http://www.w3.org/hypertext/WWW/
Consortium/Prospectus/Overview.html

The World Wide Web Consortium is an entity composed of companies who have joined together to "maintain the stability of the World Wide Web." W3C provides free reference software, news and updates, as well as technical blueprints for Web architecture. Take a look at the people, technology and institutions that make the Web work.

WEB GADGETS AND ODDITIES

The Amazing Bull Creek Cam

http://bigmac.bullcreek.austin.tx.us/realtime/
realtime.html

The Bull Creek Cam offers regularly updated images of Mark Bryant's office in Austin, Texas. Visitors also can peruse a QuickTime movie of KXAN-TV's coverage of the Cam, or link to a number of other Internet cameras.

Anonymous Message Server

http://www.smalltime.com/nowhere/

Sort of like an online bathroom wall, this Web server allows visitors to submit a message anonymously, with no holds barred. Submit your special witticism, and for an added bonus read the previous visitor's electronic graffiti.

Automated QuickCam in an Elementary School Classroom

http://buckman.pps.k12.or.us/picturecam.html

Buckman School, an arts magnet school in Portland, Oregon, decorates its Room 100 page with images from a camera overlooking the surrounding area, and includes pictures from its video microscope.

Automatic Talking Machine—Speak to Rob Hansen

http://www.inference.com/~hansen/talk.html

Rob Hansen of Inference Corporation in Los Angeles operates the Automatic Talking Machine, where visitors can type words into a screen and which are then spoken out loud in his office. Guests can also eavesdrop on recent comments to Rob.

Autopilot

http://www.mit.edu:8001/people/mkgray/
mkgray.html

On this promotional page, net.Genesis demonstrates Autopilot, which takes visitors on a mouseless tour of the Web. The company describes other products, including forms that do not require CGI programming.

Barcode Server

http://www.milk.com/barcode/

The Barcode Server, a unique utility provided on a personal home page, generates a barcode based on any 12-digit product code. Includes links to parent site MILK Kommunikations Ko-Op, "your lactose pipeline along the information hypeway."

Boston Camera View

http://www.openmarket.com/boscam/
index.html

Open Market Incorporated opens a window to the outside world through two live camera shots taken from the windows of offices in Palo Alto, California and Boston. Both images are updated once a minute.

bsy's List of Internet Accessible Machines

http://www-cse.ucsd.edu/users/bsy/iam.html

Webheads bitten by the gadget bug bring the wide world to the World Wide Web via the remote-controlled appliances and live camera feeds. This laundry list of Internet-accessible machines prods visitors to talk to a cat, give instructions to Xavier the robot, and provides an eye on Steve's Ant Farm for an online reality check.

CICA News Spy

http://www.extreme.indiana.edu/spy/

Spy on executives of the Center for Innovative Computer Applications via cameras mounted to their workstations, providing browsers with real-time images.

Confession Booth

http://anther.learning.cs.cmu.edu/priest.html

This online confession booth claims to have been "bringing the Net to its knees since 1994." Visitors can confess to a "digital priest," who then delivers a penance. A "public confession" section displays the submissions of others.

The Electric Postcard

http://postcards.www.media.mit.edu/Postcards/

The Electric Postcard allows the user to select from a wide variety of postcards, write a message and send it via e-mail. Includes a pick-up window, instructions, browser eccentricities and references.

e-minder

http://www.netmind.com/e-minder/e-minder.html

The E-Minder Free Reminder-By-Email Service will send automated e-mail messages to remind users of important occasions. A free service provided by NetMind.

Foam Bath Fish Time

http://redwood.northcoast.com/cgi-bin/fishtime

The Foam Bath Fish Time page is nothing to carp about. The famous fish sponge bath toys have gone to school and learned how to tell the time in your area and the major time zones of the world, "magically" arranging themselves in 24-hour notation.

Fractal Explorer

http://www.vis.colostate.edu/~user1209/fractals/index.html

The Fractal Explorer provides background information about the computer-generated images, plus two fractal sets for visitors to enjoy: the Mandelbrot and Julia sets. Includes a link to the home page of the site's author.

Fun e-Mail

http://www.cco.caltech.edu/~ekrider/FunEMail/funemail.html

The creator of this humor site bothers other Webmasters for "mere entertainment value." Visit this site to read the virtual critic's comments on other people's home pages and project Web sites.

Iguana Images' IguanaCam

http://iguana.images.com/dupecam.html

Live images of an iguana can be found here, along with links to iguana-related sites.

The Informant

http://informant.dartmouth.edu/

Enter the cloak and dagger world of stool pigeons and snitches. See Editor's Choice.

Inside Jason's Office

http://george.lbl.gov/cgi-bin/jason/cave-cam

Want to find out why this fellow is transmitting pictures taken inside his office onto the Web? The answer and the current picture are available at this site.

Internet Pizza Server

http://www2.ecst.csuchico.edu/~pizza/

Order pizza over the Web and receive delivery directly to your e-mailbox. The Internet Pizza Server takes your order and fashions a digital pie to your specifications. Strictly for fun, not fulfillment.

Internet Reminder Service

http://www.novator.com/Remind/Remind.html

The Internet Reminder Service sends its clients free e-mail reminders of important calendar dates. This page offers information about the service and includes an online registration form.

---

a2z EDITOR'S CHOICE

The Informant

http://informant.dartmouth.edu/

It hurts me to heap praise upon an Internet service that models itself after a snitch. However, the personal Internet search agent developed by the smart computer scientists at Dartmouth College is a canary I can't help liking. Imagine a world in which you never have to face the disappointment of visiting your favorite site only to discover that there is no new content to bring light and edification into your life. With The Informant, this imaginary world can be your reality. Register your favorite URLs and any necessary passwords, and the service notifies you via e-mail when changes to content are detected. Specify keywords associated with subjects of interest, and The Informant will periodically sweep the Lycos Catalog of the Internet for corresponding resources. E-mail reports are dispatched on the findings at intervals you request. Think of it as short order information delivered directly to your e-mail box for free. You can't beat that with a stick, even with a name like The Informant. —*Reviewed by Becky Bond*

Image © Brian Brewington 1996

The Informant is a program that will save your favorite keywords and URLs, check them periodically, and send you email to tell you whether they have been updated. Your personal agent on the Web. Get more information about the Informant.

NEW! Learn about advertising on the Informant and licensing Informant technology for your **IntraNet** or **Service Provider**.
NEW! Look Who's Talking about the Informant !

NEW! **The Informant has a *NEW* structure ! Registered users can view their new results immediately !! See for yourself...**
NEW! In the spirit of comntinuous improvement, the Informant will now drastically reduce the number of unreachable pages !

Best of all, the Informant is currently a **FREE !!** service of its developers at the Computer Engineering Program at Dartmouth College.

Internet Tele-operation

http://www.eia.brad.ac.uk/mark/fave-inter.html

Internet Tele-operation is a list of sites which have remote equipment connected and directly controllable by visitors, such as garden tools, a model railroad, an interactive Christmas tree and video cameras.

KPIX Online: Live San Francisco View

http://www.kpix.com/live/

Keep your eye on the San Francisco, landscape from atop Nob Hill. Local television station KPIX feeds an image to this page every five minutes as its camera pans across the city from the Golden Gate to the Bay Bridge.

Make a Friend on the Web

http://albrecht.ecn.purdue.edu/~jbradfor/homepage/homepage.html

This interactive site spins your Web browser and lands you on some-random-body's home page. While you're there, the page exhorts: Make a friend.

Paul's Hot Tub Status

http://hamjudo.com/cgi-bin/hottub

Here, you can dip your virtual toe in Paul's hot tub before deciding to take a virtual soak. Paul kindly provides this page with the tub's operational status and temperature as well as the outside mercury level. Wave to his cats, and check out his refrigerator, too.

Progressive Networks

http://www.realaudio.com/prognet/index.html

Enables users to send and receive audio and audio-based multimedia services. See Editor's Choice.

Remailers

http://electron.rutgers.edu/~gambino/anon_servers/anon.html

Looking for a little anonymity on the Internet? Browsers can find out all about anonymous remailers who provide free computer services that privatize e-mail. Includes a FAQ and contact information.

Snapshots from around the UMBC Computer Science Department

http://www.cs.umbc.edu/video_snapshots/

This video snapshot site is provided by the Computer Science Department at the University of Maryland at Baltimore. Visit this site for current images from cameras located in graduate labs and faculty offices.

Status of Paul's (Extra) Refrigerator

http://hamjudo.com/cgi-bin/refrigerator

How do you know if a used refrigerator works? The fridge for sale at Paul Haas' duplex does. Just check out the temperatures automatically recorded on this Web page. He explains how he rigged it, and…because "every refrigerator should have at least one cartoon stuck to the door"…rewards visitors with two early Dilberts.

Strange Things Out There On The Web

http://darkwing.uoregon.edu/~joe/strange-things.html

A resource for those interested in Strange Things Out There on the Web, this site roams from alt.usenet.kooks to Mr. Potato Head to Oliver North.

The Surrealist Compliment Generator

http://pharmdec.wustl.edu/cgi-bin/jardin_scripts/SCG

Certainly your trout are more prosperous to vacuum than the flying coachmen of Czar Nicholai! If this made you blush, check out the other "surreal" compliments instantly created at this site. Features a new compliment upon each visit.

 **EDITOR'S CHOICE**

Progressive Networks

http://www.realaudio.com/prognet/index.html

The first time I used Progressive Network's RealAudio player, I felt a bit like Nipper listening to his masters voice in the old RCA Victor advertisements. The company's popular interactive audio clients and servers enable instantaneous playback of audio files via the Internet. While not a cultural milestone on the order of the phonograph, the "instantaneous" component of the technology is quite revolutionary when users are accustomed to waiting 20 minutes to download a four-minute audio file. Faster is better in the Web world, and Progressive Networks has sprinted to the front of the line in bringing tools of true interactivity to average Web explorers. While the server costs a bundle, RealAudio players, like almost all Web clients, are freely distributed on the Web. It's worth noting that Progressive Networks doesn't just pay lip service to the political ideals that inspired the Seattle-based company's name. The company hosts WebActive, an online guide to progressive politics and activism resources online.

—Reviewed by Becky Bond

Progressive Networks, based in Seattle, develops and markets software products and services designed to enable users of personal computers and other digital devices to send and receive audio and audio-based multimedia services using the existing infrastructure.

Progressive Networks' RealAudio client-server software system enables Internet and on-line users equipped with conventional multimedia personal computers and voice-grade telephone lines to browse, select, and play back audio or audio-based multimedia content on demand, in real time. This is a real breakthrough compared to typical download times encountered with delivery of audio over conventional on-line methods, in which audio is downloaded at a rate that is five times longer than the actual program; the listener must wait 25 minutes before listening to just five minutes of audio.

Progressive Networks offers the RealAudio Server product for major media content providers to distribute audio or audio-based multimedia streams over the Internet to a broad base of consumers and end users.

SYNERGY:PANIC

http://sunsite.unc.edu/otis/synergy/panic.html

A virtual graphics forum that brings you the joys of uploading. See Editor's Choice.

Telerobot

http://telerobot.mech.uwa.edu.au/

Visitors can mix it up with an online robot. The site, maintained by University of Western Australia's Department of Mechanical and Material Engineering, includes a robot tutorial and links to other robotics sites.

TommyCam

http://www.usc.edu/dept/TommyCam/

Prospective students looking at the University of Southern California can watch student life go by from this campus camera located in the student union. Visitors can also take a virtual tour of the campus.

Trojan Room Coffee Machine

http://www.cl.cam.ac.uk/coffee/coffee.html

From England's University of Cambridge Computer Laboratory, witness the group's first successful application of an RPC mechanism: the online coffee pot. See the pot, hear what BBC radio has to say about it, and visit the lab where it was born.

Tung Nan Junior College of Technology's Hypermedia Server

http://peacock.tnjc.edu.tw/

Visitors to this Taipei junior college site will find a live camera link and information on simulcast radio broadcasts over the Internet. A link to the college's home page is also featured. In Chinese and English.

The URL-minder

http://www.netmind.com/URL-minder/URL-minder.html

The URL-minder, "your own personal Web robot," delivers e-mail messages indicating when a favorite URL has changed. Visitors can sign up for the service at this page.

The Virtual Memorial Garden

http://catless.ncl.ac.uk/Obituary/memorial.html

The Virtual Memory Garden is a site that lists online obituaries. Includes instructions on adding a memorial.

Web Voyeur

http://www.eskimo.com/~irving/web-voyeur/

Feel like climbing Pike's Peak? How about a trip to the Taj Mahal? The Web Voyeur whisks visitors away to hundreds of breathtaking views brought to the Internet via electronic still images and video.

Weird Places On The Net

http://www.euronet.nl/users/deiman/index.html

Webmasters warn visitors to explore this site "at your own risk, some links are very extreme." Pointers to "weird" sites in such common categories as art, television, and weather abound.

WWW Calendar Generator

http://www.intellinet.com/CoolTools/CalendarMaker/

WWW Calendar Generator v2 offers a service which allows visitors to log in using Netscape and to save and print a personal calendar agenda. Entry windows allow browsers to tag dates and headings.

---

a2z EDITOR'S CHOICE

SYNERGY:PANIC

http://sunsite.unc.edu/otis/synergy/panic.html

If you merely read or surf the Web, you miss out on one of its primary joys: uploading. To participate fully in Web culture it is not enough to author your own home page, you must join the fray of the two-way information exchange. PANIC is a virtual graphics forum that bills itself as an "ongoing live image exchange and manipulation gathering." In an online event that began at a Minneapolis nightclub, people download GIFs and JPEGs from a central FTP site, manipulate them "in odd and stimulating ways," and then upload them for general viewing and discussion. An IRC channel is dedicated to the proceedings, enabling PANIC participants to talk and collaborate freely in real time. Make new friends with which to play Exquisite Corpse, based on the Dada parlor game which assigns the design of the head to one person, the torso to another and the legs to still another. Frankenstein wannabes band together to invent entirely new creatures called "bio-collages" out of a hodgepodge of human and animal body parts. Think of it as an Internet quilting circle or a pictorial version of the telephone. If you want to push the collaborative potential of Internet technology and community, SYNERGY:PANIC is a great place to start.—*Reviewed by Becky Bond*

SYNERGY:PANIC

The On-Going Live Image Exchange and Manipulation Gathering

(initiated January 28, 1994)

Your options....

- This week's PANIC images. (FTP directory)
- Last week's PANIC images. (FTP directory)
- The PANIC Image Archives (FTP directory)
- Catalog images from first PANIC. (FTP directory)
- Images from RoboFest (Mar 26, 1994)
- BUZZfest weekend mega-PANIC (April 1-2, 1994)
- The GRID page, intense multi-artist collaboratives.
- The List of SYNERGY IDs, do you have one?

What is PANIC, anyway?

WEB PUBLISHING AND SITE CONSTRUCTION

CGI

Common Gateway Interface
http://hoohoo.ncsa.uiuc.edu/cgi/overview.html
This overview of CGI is provided courtesy of the NCSA. Visitors can explore intricacies of the interface which is designed for using external applications with information servers.

CGI Environment Variables
http://hoohoo.ncsa.uiuc.edu/cgi/env.html
The NCSA defines CGI environment variables at this informational site. The page, which is part of a larger site filled with official specifications for CGI scripting, presents examples as well as information.

cgi-lib.pl
http://www.bio.cam.ac.uk/cgi-lib/
This site provides technical information for Web site publishers regarding use of the Perl programming language in conjunction with CGI forms. Includes a Perl library, along with other scripting resources.

CGI.pm—a Perl5 CGI Library
http://www-genome.wi.mit.edu/ftp/pub/software/WWW/cgi_docs.html
Perl5 is an HTML tool that allows users to create CGI forms in Web pages. Visitors will find installation guidelines, documentation , and a users guide.

The CGI Specification
http://hoohoo.ncsa.uiuc.edu/cgi/interface.html
A technical page for users of CGI version 1.1, the CGI Specification site features protocol information.

CGI Test Cases
http://hoohoo.ncsa.uiuc.edu/cgi/examples.html
Web site authors can use a CGI test server to gain an understanding of how the language works. The page, maintained by the NCSA, also provides a link to a full tutorial on CGI scripting.

Critical Mass Communications
http://criticalmass.com/
Critical Mass Communications provides a variety of services including site hosting, Web design,

and CGI programming. The company also hosts a Usenet newsgroup archive.

Decoding Forms with CGI
http://hoohoo.ncsa.uiuc.edu/docs/cgi/forms.html
NCSA offers this guide to decoding and demystifying forms using CGI. For Web authors unfamiliar with forms, beginners instructions are available.More savvy visitors can access detailed programming info.

Directory of /Web/httpd/Unix/ncsa_httpd/cgi
ftp://ftp.ncsa.uiuc.edu/Web/httpd/Unix/ncsa_httpd/cgi
CGI is an interface allowing external programs to interact with information servers such as HTTP servers. This directory contains CGI-based programs submitted by their authors for distribution.

Felipe's AppleScript CGI Examples
http://edb518ea.edb.utexas.edu/scripts/cgix/cgix.html
Download the AppleScript CGIs Felipe uses on his Web server, or link to other people's CGIs and related AppleScript stuff.

An Instantaneous Introduction to CGI Scripts and HTML Forms
http://kuhttp.cc.ukans.edu/info/forms/forms-intro.html
CGI and HTML are scripting programs for creating pages and hyperlinks on the Web. Those visiting this site will find detailed lessons and tips for using the scripting tools.

Matt's Script Archive
http://worldwidemart.com/scripts/
This home page, maintained by a Hewlett-Packard employee and admitted Webhead, contains a CGI script archive, a listing of searchable indexes, and a random link generator.

Un-CGI version 1.7
http://www.hyperion.com/~koreth/uncgi.html
Un-CGI, a Web-related software package, is a front end for processing queries and forms on Unix systems. This informational site includes a general introduction, information on obtaining the program, installation instructions, and a users guide.

Windows CGI 1.1 Description
http://www.city.net/win-httpd/httpddoc/wincgi.htm
Windows programmers who are aching to bite into the Web with a CGI interface can explore the capabilities of Windows CGI 1.1. Materials include a general introduction to the program along with instructions for putting Windows CGI 1.1 to work.

DEVELOPERS RESOURCES

HyperAct Inc.
http://www.hyperact.com/
HyperAct Inc. markets Web publishing software tools to online developers. The company's home page sports product demos, "new age" authoring tools, and an electronic software catalog.

HTML Developer's Tool Library
http://www.awa.com/nct/software/webtools.html
This HTML Developer's Tool Library from The Web Developer's Journal includes Web authoring tools, browsers, graphics editors, and other utilities such as mail and news readers.

Institute for Integrated Publication and Information Systems
http://www.darmstadt.gmd.de/IPSI/index1.html
Maintained by the German National Research Center for Information Technology, this Web site explains the activities of the Institute for Integrated Publication and Information Systems. Visitors can learn about the institute's development of hypermedia systems, multimedia protocols, and cognitive user interfaces.

MAGIC
http://www.magic.net/
The MAGIC Gigabit Testbed provides information on the development of the "information superhighway" and is sponsored by the Advanced Research Projects Agency and the National Science Foundation. Visitors will find overviews and documentation for several major Internet research projects.

MOMspider—Distribution Information
http://www.ics.uci.edu/WebSoft/MOMspider/
MOMspider is a Web-roaming robot program written in Perl script that performs maintenance on wide-area Webs. The site includes MOMspider documentation, distribution directions, and availability info.

Quadralay
http://www.quadralay.com/
Quadralay Corp. produces software for creating and managing commercial Web sites. Company background and product information are available, including details about WebWorks Publisher.

SG-Scout
http://www-swiss.ai.mit.edu/~ptbb/SG-Scout/SG-Scout.html
This Web page reports the activities of the SG-Scout Robot running at Xerox PARC in Palo Alto,

Calif. Like most Web robots, this wanderer roves through the Internet and retrieves linked pages.

Sunnyside Computing Inc.

http://www.cpsr.org/

Sunnyside Computing is a fully secure Netsite server in Palo Alto, Calif., offering Quartermaster, a Web cataloging system. Includes links to a travel agency network, restaurant delivery service, and medical technology products.

Tcl/Tk Project At Sun Microsystems Laboratories

http://www.sunlabs.com/research/tcl/

Sun Microsystems Laboratories, a Mountain View, Calif.-based computing concern, maintains this site for programming information. Visitors are presented with info about Tcl/Tk, a future universal scripting platform for the Internet.

WebTech's Web Developer Directory

http://www.webtechs.com/cgi-bin/ htmlscript?webdir.hts

Almost everything there is to know about building a place in cyberspace can be found within the WebTech's Web Developer Directory. The searchable database links to resources ranging from HTML editors to languages, and from graphics tools to turnkey Web server solutions.

W3Kit 2.2, An Object-Oriented Toolkit for Interactive World Wide Web Applications

http://www.geom.umn.edu/docs/W3Kit/ W3Kit.html

W3Kit 2.2 is an object-oriented software package for building Web sites and applications. Visitors can download the software with its accompanying technical documentation.

EDITORS AND CONVERTERS

All About LaTeX2HTML

http://cbl.leeds.ac.uk/nikos/tex2html/doc/ latex2html/latex2html.html

LaTeX2HTML is a Unix system tool that helps convert documents written in LaTeX into HTML. Visit this page to discover where to get the software and how to use it.

ARTA Media Group

http://www.halcyon.com/artamedia/ webwizard/arta.html

Windows users can find Web design and server software at the ARTA Media Group company home page. The company invites visitors to review products such as WEB Wizard: The Duke of URL and Windows HTTP servers.

CU_HTML.DOT (Version 1.5.3)

http://www.cuhk.hk/csc/cu_html/cu_html.htm

With the aid of the document template provided at this site, Microsoft Word for Windows users can create HTML documents from within the word processing program. Find the CU_HTML.DOT application along with installation information and documentation.

Dave: The PageMaker to HTML Conversion Utility

http://www.bucknell.edu/bucknellian/dave/

The DAVE home page contains information on the PageMaker to HTML conversion utility. Browsers can download the latest version, read about system requirements, or link to the site for downloading PageMaker Websucker, another PageMaker to HTML converter.

A Filter to Translate RTF to HTML

http://www.sunpack.com/RTF/rtftohtml_ overview.html

This Web site is devoted to rtftohtml, a document converter that translates existing word processing documents into HTML. Visitors can download companion software or peruse a users guide.

Futplex System

http://gewis.win.tue.nl/applications/futplex/

The Futplex Unix software package creates documents with read/write access on the Web. Visitors can read about the software's features and check out a demo at this site, which also offers a users guide and FTP file access.

GT_HTML.DOT (Version 6.0d)

http://www.gatech.edu/word_html/release.htm

The Georgia Institute of Technology's Research Institute announces the release of GT_HTML.DOT (Ver 6.0a). Visitors can download the Microsoft Word macro that facilitates HTML document authoring at this site.

Howard Harawitz

http://www.brooknorth.com

Howard Harawitz, author of the hypertext editors HTML Assistant and HTML Assistant Pro, is the proprietor of a software firm specializing in the development of Windows programming tools. His home page details his professional life and provides contact data.

The HotDog Web Editor

http://www.sausage.com/

HotDog is an HTML Web editor produced by Sausage Software. Visitors to this site will find demonstrations, ordering information, and articles about HotDog.

HoTMetaL

ftp://ftp.ncsa.uiuc.edu/Web/html/hotmetal/ Windows/hotm1new.exe

The latest version of the HoTMetaL home page construction tool can be downloaded at NCSA's FTP site. Follow this link to download HotMetaL shareware for Windows.

HTML Assistant Frequently Asked Questions (FAQ)

http://www.brooknorth.com/

This FAQ file provides information about the hypertext editor HTML Assistant. Includes access to downloadable copies of the freeware, plus information about the program's capabilities.

HTML Assistant Pro

http://www.brooknorth.com/

This commercial site advertises the commercial version of the Web-publishing program HTML Assistant Pro 2. Includes details on new features incorporated into the product's latest version, plus ordering information, and FAQ.

HTML Assistant Pro FTP Index

ftp://ftp.cs.dal.ca/htmlasst/

This FTP site archives HTML Assistant Pro, a freeware hypertext editor for MS Windows, and URL Grabber, a URL collector, and general Web tool. The software and its documentation are available for anonymous download.

HTMLed(tm)—An HTML Editor for Microsoft Windows

http://www.ist.ca/htmled/

HTMLed is an HTML editor for use with Microsoft Windows-based systems. Download the unregistered shareware version at this site, or use the order form to obtain a registered copy. Detailed information about the editor is provided.

HTML Editor for the Macintosh

http://dragon.acadiau.ca/~giles/HTML_Editor/ Documentation.html

A downloadable copy of HTML Editor for the Macintosh is available at this Web site. Find detailed information on using the editor to create hypertext documents for the Web.

html-helper-mode

http://www.santafe.edu/~nelson/tools/

This site contains the beta version of html-helper-mode, a software application designed to ease the editing of HTML files. Features include information concerning download availability, as well as program specifications, and documentation.

HTML Markup

http://www.printerport.com/klephacks/ markup.html

HTML Markup 1.1 is a text-to-HTML software application. This site includes instructions for downloading the program, a users manual, and mailing list.

HTML Widget

http://www.ncsa.uiuc.edu/SDG/Software/ Mosaic/Docs/htmlwidget.html

The HTML Widget takes an ASCII string of text in HTML and formats it for display in an X window. Read about the software program, and obtain download information at this site.

HTML Writer

http://www.public.asu.edu/~bottger/

Visitors to this home page can obtain ordering information and a users guide for the Web document editor HTML Writer. The application is compatible with Windows-based systems.

Hypermail 1.02

http://www.eit.com/goodies/software/ hypermail/hypermail.html

This site features information on a freeware "e-mail to HTML" compiler which converts e-mail to hypertext. The utility is of particular interest to mail list maintainers' and sysops' hosting a Web site. Includes ordering info.

Interleaf's Cyberleaf Online Publishing Application

http://www.ileaf.com/ip.html

Interleaf, a publishing software company, maintains this site for information about its Cyberleaf application. Visit here for product information, online publishing tips, and FAQ index.

Quark to HTML

http://the-tech.mit.edu/~jeremy/qt2www.html

Web authors who want to put desktop publishing files online can get tips and tricks from this Quark to HTML conversion site. Find out how to translate documents authored in the popular layout program QuarkXPress into Web-readable documents.

Salvo

http://www.simware.com/salvo/

Simware's Salvo is a "plug-and-play" application that allows PC users to integrate "enterprise applications through a Web Browser, by translating 3270 datastreams into HTML and vice versa." A demo version is available at the Salvo home page.

Silcot's Nisus HTML Janus Macros

http://www.unimelb.edu.au/~ssilcot/docs/ SilcotsHTMLMacrosReadMe.html

Silcot's Nisus HTML Janus Macros home page provides just that: macros to be used with Nisus Writer, a word processor created to work especially well with HTML. This site includes lists of bugs, as well as news on features to be added in future versions.

Simple HTML Editor (SHE)

http://dewey.lib.ncsu.edu/staff/morgan/ simple.html

The Simple HTML Editor for the Macintosh is available for downloading at this site, along with information on usage, system requirements, help texts, and release notes. SHE requires HyperCard or HyperCard Player.

SoftQuad: HoTMetaL PRO 3.0

http://www.sq.com/products/hotmetal/hmp-org.htm

This Web site details the commercial version of the multimedia Web publishing program HoTMetaL PRO. Visitors to the site can place an order, download software or learn about the HTML editor.

WebDoor

http://www.opendoor.com/webdoor

WebDoor is an automatic Web publishing system developed by Open Door Networks. Visitors can find out how to obtain a WebDoor account, view sample pages, and download WebDoor Publisher software.

WebSite Central

http://website.ora.com/

O'Reilly & Associates pitches its WebSite authoring software as "The Web Publisher for Everyone." WebSite Central is host to a company FAQ as well as a downloadable demo of the HTML and Web publishing application for Windows and Windows NT. An on-site software library houses a collection Web gadgets and gizmos.

Windows HTML Editing Tools

http://www.ncsa.uiuc.edu/SDG/Software/ WinMosaic/HTMLEdit.htm

Visitors to this page will find descriptions and pointers to HTML editing tools for Windows users. Featured tools include editors, templates, an imagemap editor and general HTML references.

GENERAL TOOL COLLECTIONS

Browsers, Viewers and HTML Preparation Resources

http://www.utoronto.ca/webdocs/HTMLdocs/ intro_tools.html

Presented by the University of Toronto's Information Commons, this site provides an overview of Web navigation and HTML tools for Macintosh, PC and Unix users. Visitors can download guides and various Web-publishing software packages.

HTML Tools Library

http://www.awa.com/nct/software/ webtools.html

This HTML Developer's Tool Library from The Web Developer's Journal includes Web authoring tools, browsers, graphics-editing utilities, and mail and news readers.

OneWorld/SingNet WWW & HTML Developer's JumpStation—ver 2.0 (21 Oct 1994)

http://oneworld.wa.com/htmldev/devpage/ dev-page.html

Discover the tools and language of the Web here, where visitors will find HTML editors, server software and Web directory services.

The Web Developer's Virtual Library

http://www.stars.com/

One of the Web's primary charms remains the realization that one does not have to be an architect to construct a home, storefront or gallery online. The Web Developer's Virtual Library offers software tools and advice to individuals who build or wish to learn to build Web sites.

Web Technology

http://www.base.com/gordoni/webtech.html

This personal home page indexes general Web technology resources on the Internet. Pointers include an Internet tools summary, TCP/IP communications, an HTML development jumpstation and links to popular browsers.

WebTools

http://king.syr.edu:2006/Misc/HPDC4/Foils/ WebTools.html

This index of pointers to Web development tools includes an online HTML editor, navigation applications and documentation, as well as spell, edit and search functions. Accessible in PostScript, ASCII or GIF formats.

World Wide Web and HTMLTools

http://www.w3.org/pub/WWW/Tools/

Find software to manage Web servers and generate hypertext at the World Wide Web and HTML Tools page. Primers on CGI extension scripts, writing HTML, troubleshooting and analyzing log files lay a nice foundation for both beginners and seasoned builders.

World Wide Web Tools/Utilities

http://hplyot.obspm.fr/~dl/wwwtools.html

This directory of Web tools and utilities is maintained by a member of the Observatoire de Paris-Meudon. Among the offerings are an anonymous HTTP proxy and e-cash gambling software.

GRAPHICS, ICON, AND WALL PAPER ARCHIVES

Aaron's Graphic Archive
http://hoohoo.ncsa.uiuc.edu/Public/AGA/

Aaron's Graphic Archive contains files organized in a variety of subject areas, including 3-D, television, art, music and animals. The size of each graphic is given and, where appropriate, a link to the site from which the graphic came.

Anthony's World Wide Web Images
http://www.cit.gu.edu.au/images/Images.html

This site offers access to Anthony's library of downloadable Web icons. Links to mirror sites are also featured, along with a readme file containing information about the images available.

The Background Sampler
http://home.mcom.com/assist/net_sites/bg/backgrounds.html

Go behind the scenes of your Web site to spruce up its appearance. The Background Sampler provides the instructions and materials to implement a variety backgrounds , keeping in mind fast loading and easy viewing using Netscape Navigator.

CMU ECE Icon Repository
http://www.ece.cmu.edu/misc/icons.html

This site houses hundreds of icons suitable for inclusion in Web pages. Includes instructions on adding the symbols to HTML documents.

DTP Internet Jumplist—Clipart
http://www.teleport.com/~eidos/dtpij/dtpij.html

An extensive list of pointers is offered to clip art resources on the Internet. Link to a wide range of clip art archives, varying from agricultural and architectural collections to medical and Greek packages.

Fractal Design Corp. FTP Archive
ftp://ftp.fractal.com/

The anonymous FTP server maintained by graphics software developer Fractal Design provides a place for visitors to pick up images, files and tips of use in computer design work.

GIFs Directory
http://www.acm.uiuc.edu/rml/Gifs/

The GIFs Directory is devoted to digital pictures. An extensive image guide indexed by subject and date, this site contains thousands of GIFs—sit back and enjoy the view, or download selections for use with your own Web creations.

Grafica Obscura, Collected Computer Graphics Hacks
http://www.sgi.com/grafica/

Provides the user with the ins and outs of computer graphics. See Editor's Choice.

Graphics for Your Pages
http://www-pcd.stanford.edu/gifs/

Courtesy of the folks at Stanford University, this site offers a compressed 50K file featuring graphic elements and instructions for recreating them in Web pages.

---

a2z EDITOR'S CHOICE

Grafica Obscura, Collected Computer Graphics Hacks
http://www.sgi.com/grafica/

The Web's best conflation of computing know-how and compositional craft is presented with joy, grace, and technical finesse in the form of Grafica Obscura: Collected Computer Graphics Hacks. Imagine a technical manual in the form of an art gallery, complete with instructions, examples and works of art presented by a computer graphics researcher at Silicon Graphics. Image extrapolation, texture mapping, production for the Web, and paperfolding sculpture are explained and demonstrated with a marriage of depth and elegance rarely found in online publishing. Java-savvy designers will be delighted by The Impressionist, a paint program that creates painted representations of photographs. Soul food seekers can read an inspirational quotation about the properties of shadows, or review the stated mission of the Futurist Programming movement. You won't find advertising, 200K page downloads, or gratuitous eye candy here, just unadulterated visual pleasure and idea-inspiring tools. For this fresh breath of ether, we can thank Grafica Obscura's curator, Paul Haeberli, who finds beauty in advertising slogans, photos, typefaces and light.—*Reviewed by Becky Bond*

GRAFICA *Obscura*
Collected Computer Graphics Hacks

Curated by Paul Haeberli

Welcome to Alpha 0.45 of GRAFICA Obscura, my evolving computer graphics notebook. This is a compilation of technical notes, pictures and essays that I've accumulated over the years. For maximum enjoyment, check the viewing notes provided.

Contents

A Paper Folding Project
Here are step by step instructions on how to make a folded paper sculpture.

Japanese English Advertising Slogans
Beautiful and poetic word combinations from Japan.

The Impressionist NEW!
If you have a JAVA enabled browser, try *The Impressionist.* This is a paint program that lets you create a painted representation of a photograph.

Portfolio
A collection of digital pictures. This includes photographic and synthetic images.

H's Seamless Background Archive

http://www.whitenoise.com/champ/
backgrounds

H's backgrounds page features Netscape-compatible backgrounds for Web page creators. The black and white and color background tiles can be easily downloaded and pasted into pages.

The HYPE Background Selector for Netscape 1.1

http://www.phantom.com/~giant/HYPE_BACK/
hypeback.html

HYPE Electrazine supplies an index of backgrounds for use with Netscape 1.1. The site offers a small sample of the backgrounds available for download.

Icons

http://ivory.nosc.mil/html/trancv/html/
icons-hcc.html

This page contains assorted icons collected from sites around the globe. Webmasters are invited to use the icons for enhancing their own sites. Instructions for copying are included.

Icons and Images for Use in HTML Documents

http://www.uncg.edu/~bucknall/uncg/icons/

Graphics for use in HTML documents are presented at this site. Includes an index to the archive and pointers to other Web icon collections.

Images, Icons, and Sounds

http://members.aol.com/htmlguru/images.html

This personal page provides a large collection of images, icons and sounds for use in Web page design.

Index of /hypertext/WWW/Icons

http://www.w3.org/pub/WWW/Icons

An extensive index covering icons and image collections on the Web is maintained at this site. Find pointers to similar graphics archive indexing sites.

Jon's Image Archive

http://lynx.uio.no/jon/gif/

The images at Jon's Image Archive run the gamut of topics from art to comics to boys and girls. Pictures are available for download for use by individuals. Some images contain depictions of nudity.

LAL Images for Buttons

http://lal.cs.byu.edu/buttons/gifs.html

This index of free, downloadable graphic icons is provided by the Laboratory for Applied Logic at Brigham Young University. Visit here for icons, buttons and inline images for use in creating Web sites.

The Online Bonsai Icon Collection

http://www.hav.com/~hav/tobicus.html

A large collection of bonsai tree icons and images is offered at this Web site. Images are available in BMP, GIF and JPEG format, and browsers can download each of several collections individually. Visitors can also link to the official Bonsai Web site.

Pattern Land

http://www.netcreations.com/patternland/
index.html

Put bumps, tartans or splotches beneath the text on your Web page. Pattern Land is a collection of background GIFs for HTML design. Search the archive by image or pattern name. Links to other background libraries are provided.

Resources for Icons, Images, and Graphics

http://osiris.colorado.edu/~brumbaug/
graphics.html

Building a Web page, brightening up a report or just looking for a desktop icon? Visit the Resources for Icons, Images, and Graphics page for links to image sources of all kinds.

Rutgers University Network Services World Wide Web Icons and Logos

http://ns2.rutgers.edu/doc-images/

Rutgers University Network Services offers access to this archive of publicly accessible icons and logos for use on Web pages. The images are collected under these categories: icons, buttons, small buttons and logos.

Textures for HTML 3.0 Clients

http://www.baylor.edu/textures/

Baylor University in Texas maintains this site for Internet publishing resources. Visit here for graphic elements for use in assembling Web sites and home pages.

Virtual Image Archive

http://imagiware.com/via.cgi

This extensive index to digital arts images is organized by topic and ranges in content from fractals to animals to movie stars.

World Wide Web Icons at BSDI

http://www.bsdi.com/icons/

Visitors are invited to download artwork from this collection of public domain Web icons for use in the design of their own Web pages.

The World Wide Web Power Index— Icons

http://www.webcom.com/webcom/html/
icons.html

Geared toward Webmasters, this site is full of icon and graphics indexes. Listings include symbols, "realm" graphics, virtual icons, a bonsai collection, and pointers to dozens of other sites and pages.

GRAPHICS VIEWERS AND UTILITIES

Background Colors

http://www.infi.net/wwwimages/
colorindex2.html

Webmasters can choose a new color scheme for their site by visiting this home page from Infi.Net. Includes Netscape 1.1 and higher color codes for backgrounds, text, links and visited links.

ColorEditor for CGI V1.01

http://www.infocom.net/~bbs/cgi-bin/
colorEditor.cgi

ColorEditor for CGI V1.01 uses Netscape extensions to HTML 3.0 to set background colors, pictures and link hues. The site includes instructions for downloading the software and an application FAQ.

ColorMaker

http://www.missouri.edu/~wwwtools/
colormaker/

Constructing Web documents including colors in HTML requires authors to use a hex number system. ColorMaker automates this process, allowing designers to pick out colors which the application automatically translates into HTML-friendly terms.

The Color Specifier For Netscape

http://www.users.interport.net/~giant/COLOR/
hype_color.html

The Color Specifier is a utility for creating and viewing color backgrounds for the Netscape Web browser. Includes dozens of codes for creating colorful Web pages.

Colors and Their Hex Equivalents

http://www.ohiou.edu/~rbarrett/webaholics/
ver2/colors.html

The Colors and Hex Equivalents site contains a color conversion table as implemented in Netscape version 1.1. Includes a link to the Webaholics home page.

Colour Selector Page

http://catless.ncl.ac.uk/Lindsay/colours.html

From a series of menus Web site publishers can pick page colors for background, text, and visited and active links. The result is a page that demonstrates the Netscape-specific HTML coding needed to produce the colors chosen. Includes an electronic color swatch page to ease selection.

Controlling Document Backgrounds

http://home.netscape.com/assist/net_sites/bg/index.html

Netscape offers a guide to controlling HTML document backgrounds. The site outlines programming tips for color and texture manipulation.

Graphics

http://www.cis.ohio-state.edu/hypertext/faq/usenet/graphics/top.html

A Usenet resource, this site provides a categorized compilation of FAQs concerned with graphics. Info about animation, file formats and related topics can be found, along with a detailed resources list.

Graphics Viewers, Editors, Utilities and Info

http://www2.ncsu.edu/bae/people/faculty/walker/hotlist/graphics.html

Find graphics viewers, editors and utilities via this catalog of links to Internet software resources. From 3-D modeling to morphing, locate software tools for most graphics tasks.

How To Do Imagemaps

http://www2.ncsu.edu/bae/people/faculty/walker/hotlist/imagemap.html

Web authors will find instructions and software for creating imagemaps. The page also includes links to information on transparent images and general graphics pages.

Interactive Graphics Renderer

http://www.eece.ksu.edu/IGR/

Sponsored by the Department of Electrical Engineering at Kansas State University, this page contains a tool to generate graphics for use in home page design. Features include the graphics generator, samples of its output, instructions for its use, and related documentation and files.

Kai's Power Tips and Tricks for Photoshop

http://the-tech.mit.edu/KPT/

Adobe Photoshop users will learn some of the tricks of the trade. Kai's Power Tips and Tricks was originally published on America Online and contains 23 tips on using Photoshop. The page also includes pointers to other tutorials for Web page designers.

Lines For Use In Mosaic

http://www.eecs.wsu.edu/~rkinion/lines/lines.html

This guide to Mosaic rulers, part of a personal home page, offers advice for adding transparent lines to Web sites. Find HTML programming code and downloadable graphic elements.

Mac-ImageMap

http://weyl.zib-berlin.de/imagemap/Mac-ImageMap.html

Give a Web site graphic depth with the imagemap utility offered here. The Mac-ImageMap freeware application enables Macintosh users to install clickable maps served by MacHTTP servers. Mac users can download the free software at this site.

Pixelsite

http://www.pixelsight.com/PS/pixelsite/pixelsite.html

Visitors to this page, part of a larger Web site maintained by an altruistic graphic designer, can use the Pixelsite application and clip art archives to design custom icons. Includes examples, instructions and FAQ file.

RGB Hex Triplet Color Chart

http://www.phoenix.net/~jacobson/rgb.html

This personal home page provides a useful RGB Hex Triplet Color Chart for Web publishing. Visitors can find out about handy tools for working with Internet e-mail and Web forms, or sign the author's guest book.

Thalia: Guide: The Background FAQ

http://www.sci.kun.nl/thalia/guide/color/faq.html

The Background FAQ site offers answers to common inquiries about Web site backgrounds and the browsers that support them.

Transparent Background Images

http://members.aol.com/htmlguru/transparent_images.html

Transparent Background Images contains instructions for creating images which make graphics float in browser windows. Features include examples and how-to advice.

Transparent/Interlaced GIF Resources

http://dragon.jpl.nasa.gov/~adam/transparent.html

The Transparent/Interlaced GIF Resource page, part of a personal home page, offers a variety of advanced graphics programming tools. Visitors will find helpful resources for use with DOS, Windows, Macintosh and Unix platforms.

VRL's Imaging Machine

http://www.vrl.com/Imaging/

VRL's Imaging Machine is a software program designed to make image processing in Web page design hassle-free. Visitors will find a description of the application, users manual and services index.

Web Sites with Cool PDF

http://www.adobe.com/Acrobat/

Adobe Systems Inc. provides numerous links to sites with downloadable PDF-formatted graphics.

Includes pointers to instructions for obtaining, configuring and using Adobe Acrobat software to view listed PDF files.

GIZMOS, THINGAMAJIGS, AND AD HOC APPLICATIONS

Dataflight Software

http://concord.lax.primenet.com/

Dataflight Software promotes Concordance, a database that can retrieve information on a variety of levels and that can be used in Web publishing. PC users can download a demo, or read software reviews and documentation.

GLOCOM

http://www.glocom.ac.jp/

The Center for Global Communications is operated by the International University of Japan. Visitors to this site will learn about incorporating the Japanese language into Web and HTML applications. In English and Japanese.

HTGREP Frequently Asked Questions List

http://iamwww.unibe.ch/~scg/Src/Doc/htgrep.html

HTGREP is a software utility designed to facilitate construction of simple search engines for the Web. This FAQ details software and product info, and addresses general questions on searching, querying, and installation.

HTML Access Counter 4.0

http://www.webtools.org/counter/

Counter 4.0 is a software tool that adds counters to Web pages. Visitors will find fast facts about this latest version, as well as a "quick start" installation guide.

HTML Grinder

http://www.matterform.com/grinder/

HTML Grinder is a software utility that helps Web designers build trouble-free hyperlinks. Visitors can download the software along with a copy of its users guide.

Internet Audit Bureau

http://stats.internet-audit.com/cgi-bin/

The Internet Audit Bureau is an independent provider of visitor counts for Web pages. Its home page includes detailed descriptions of services, company information and instructions on participation.

ssd's counter page

http://www-mae.engr.ucf.edu/~ssd/
counter.html

This page contains a Web site traffic counter for export and use at other sites. Additional features include documentation, use registration forms and news.

Voyager CDLink

http://www.voyagerco.com/cdlink/cdlink.html

Voyager CDLink is a Web browser helper application that allows Web page designers to incorporate music into their sites via CD-ROM. Download the shareware, or obtain help and background info, including press releases and a feature-length article.

WebNexus

http://sunsite.unc.edu/lunarbin/webnexus.cgi

Here's a site dedicated to "true interconnectivity." WebNexus automatically generates a return link to the page a visitor has left to land on the WebNexus page. The "return" links compiled by WebNexus are listed at this site.

World Wide Web Access Counter and Clock

http://www.fccc.edu/users/muquit/

The World Wide Web Access Counter and Clock lets Webmasters meter hits to Web sites. Find out who peeks at your pages and when with this handy shareware utility for Unix, Microsoft NT and IBM OS/2 platforms.

How-To Guides

The Basics

The Bare Bones Guide to HTML

http://werbach.com/barebones/

The Bare Bones Guide to HTML is a list of virtually every official HTML 2.0 tag, plus the Netscape extensions and several HTML 3.0 tags, arranged in a concise, organized manner. In English, Japanese, Spanish, German, French, Portuguese, Dutch and Italian.

A Beginner's Guide to HTML

http://www.ncsa.uiuc.edu/General/Internet/
WWW/HTMLPrimer.html

The Beginner's Guide to HTML is a primer for producing Web documents using HTML. Information about creating documents, linking and formatting can be found.

Composing Good HTML

http://www.cs.cmu.edu/~tilt/cgh/

Composing Good HTML, maintained by an HTML programmer, provides a platform for learning the page description language of the Web. Visit this site to find helpful tips on programming and learn how to avoid common errors.

Crash Course on Writing Documents for the Web

http://www.pcweek.com/eamonn/crash_
course.html

Prospective Web authors can get their pages up and running quickly with the tips and tricks offered at the Crash Course on Writing Documents for the Web. Visitors will find plain English explanations and instructions for HTML authoring and editing.

Creating HTML Documents

http://www.ncsa.uiuc.edu/SDG/Software/
Mosaic/Docs/d2-htmlinfo.html

The Creating HTML Documents page provides links to three sites which offer aids for Web page authors. Includes two beginners guides.

Creating Net Sites

http://home.mcom.com/assist/net_sites/
index.html

This educational page, maintained by Netscape Communications Corp., provides technical information for Web site creators. Includes guides for beginners, stylistic pointers and links to a variety of developer's tools for advanced Web publishers.

Elements of HTML Style

http://www.book.uci.edu/Staff/StyleGuide.html

Like the Strunk and White classic reference work which serves as this site's "ostensible model," this guide states "a number of very simple things, over and over again." While these elements of style for HTML mostly date back to early 1994, the site's Webmaster asserts, "most of them still hold true."

Guides to Writing Style for HTML Documents

http://union.ncsa.uiuc.edu/HyperNews/get/
www/html/guides.html

Web authoring students will find a collection of pointers to electronic HTML writers guides. Also included are various style guides for Web site construction, such as the Bad Style Page.

Homepage Creation

http://the-inter.net/www/future21/html.html

The Home Page Creation Center offers one-stop shopping for Web authors seeking the tools and know-how to construct their own pages. Visitors can download shareware browsers, and HTML and graphics editors.

The Homepage Creator System

http://the-inter.net/www/future21/create1.html

Paint by numbers and, voila, create your own home page. This idiot-proof method creates HTML documents with little effort. Just pull down the title bars and fill in the blanks. Sample documents are provided.

The Home Page Maker

http://www.wizard.com/~fifi/pagemake.html

The Home Page Maker creates home pages for visitors to download and post on their servers. Simply fill in the form with your information and choice of colors, and follow the detailed instructions.

How Do They Do That With HTML?

http://www.nashville.net/~carl/htmlguide/
index.html

Web authors will find simple tips on writing basic HTML documents. The site boasts dozens of links to HTML and Web-authoring resources.

How to Change Your Home Page

http://www.ncsa.uiuc.edu/SDG/Software/
Mosaic/Docs/specifying-home.html

The NCSA maintains this how-to page, dishing out instructions and code for improving personal, educational, and corporate home pages.

How to Put Information on the Web

http://www.w3.org/pub/WWW/Provider/
Overview.html

This site explains how to put content up on the Web. Visitors can choose to place material online as either an author, a Webmaster or a system administrator. Find reference materials about HTML telnet server setup.

How to Write HTML files

http://www.ucc.ie/info/net/htmladv.html

University College in Cork, Ireland, maintains this site for Internet programming resources. Visit here to learn about HTML, the primary language of the Web.

Introduction to HTML

http://www.utoronto.ca/webdocs/HTMLdocs/
NewHTML/htmlindex.html

This educational document explains how to use the various coding elements employed in HTML and offers tips on creating well-designed Web documents. Includes information on the sites author, Ian Graham, and his book credits.

Introduction to HTML

http://members.aol.com/htmlguru/about_
html.html

With this introduction to HTML, visitors can learn how to write HTML and how to manage their own server. Includes access to a collection of images for free use on Web pages.

Macintosh World Wide Web Resources

http://www.comvista.com/net/www/
WWWDirectory.html

Beginners and experts alike can pick up tips for creating and maintaining a Web site at the World Wide Web Developer Resources page. From a history of the Internet to HyperText HTML writing guides, find what is needed to distribute information online.

Macmillan's HTML Workshop

http://www.mcp.com/general/workshop/

Macmillan Publishing provides resources and information on HTML and on Macmillan's HTML-related books and products. Included are listings for beginning, intermediate, and advanced users.

Revised Introduction to HTML: 1995 Edition

http://scholar.lib.vt.edu/reports/soasis-slides/HTML-Intro.html

Beginners can find out how to speak the language of the Web at the Revised Introduction to HTML: 1995 Edition site. HTML is demystified in plain prose allowing visitors to learn how to create Web documents with ease.

Style Guide for Online Hypertext

http://www.w3.org/hypertext/WWW/Provider/Style/Overview.html

This style guide for online hypertext is designed to help create a Web hypertext database. It includes a table of contents which quickly links the user directly to desired information.

Templates for Homepages.

http://www-pcd.stanford.edu/mogens/intro/templates.html

Internet neophytes who want to create their own Web sites but can't be bothered with HTML can instead use the prefabricated blank pages offered at Templates for Homepages. For the more adventurous, an HTML tutorial is offered.

Thalia: Tips & Tricks for WWW-providers

http://www.sci.kun.nl/thalia/guide/

The guide to creating Web documents is well-stocked with tips, demonstrations and pointers to a wide-ranging collection of resources touching on all aspects of page design.

Tools for Aspiring Web Weavers

http://www.nas.nasa.gov/NAS/WebWeavers/

The Web Weavers Page offers detailed help in setting up Web sites on the Internet. Visitors will find tutorials for several different Web authoring tools, as well as general HTML tips and techniques.

Top 10 Ways to Make Your World Wide Web Service a Flop

http://coombs.anu.edu.au/SpecialProj/QLTY/FlopMaker.html

The Coombs Computing Unit of the Australian National University provides this page for humorous advice on how to turn a Web-based information

system into a failure. Includes links to conventional instructions on successful Web publishing.

Top Ten Ways to Tell if You Have a Sucky Home Page

http://www.winternet.com/~jmg/TopTenF.html

Make your own website more aesthetically pleasing. See Editor's Choice.

Web Designer

http://web.canlink.com/webdesign/

The Web Designer page contains instructions for designing and developing home pages. Includes detailed information on Netiquette, HTML editors, authoring tools, graphics, and general publishing info.

---

a2z EDITOR'S CHOICE

Top Ten Ways to Tell if You Have a Sucky Home Page

http://www.winternet.com/~jmg/TopTenF.html

There's a reason why most forms of media have institutionalized editorial filters: In general, we're not interested in everything everyone has to say. On the Web, we are called upon to employ our own critical capacities to sort through massive amounts of raw information. While this sharpens the brain muscles, it also wastes time. More bandwidth or a bigger pipe may in the end simply mean that more sewage goes in and more sewage goes out, to paraphrase an old adage. Head off potential complaints about the contents and style of your personal Web presence with the tips and tsk-tsks offered at this site. Personal faves are the rants against header pictures over 50K, admonitions to avoid ticker tape status bars, and an expressed annoyance with "under construction" graphics—"I think we all know that pages are always under construction," the author complains. I might add Top Ten Lists to Top Ten Ways to tell if You Have a Sucky Home Page. Do you ever get the idea that too much of the time, too many people are too easily influenced by David Letterman? —*Reviewed by Becky Bond*

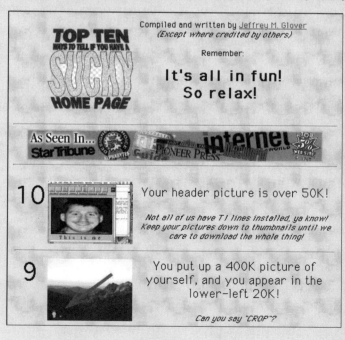

World Wide Web FAQs and Guides

http://cuiwww.unige.ch/OSG/FAQ/www.html

This site contains a listing of electronically accessible guides on Web surfing and publishing topics. Includes pointers to HTML tutorials, FAQs and guides to Web indexes.

The WorldWideWeb Handbook

http://www.ucc.ie/~pflynn/books/wwwbook.html

Peter Flynn promotes his book "The WorldWideWeb Handbook" here. Visitors can download a selection from the book and an HTML reference card. The page also provides a link to the publisher's home page.

World Wide Web Locator Guide

http://groucho.gsfc.nasa.gov/Code_520/locator/locator.html

The Locator Guide seeks to provide pointers to everything a person could want to know about the Web. The site includes links to Web primers and guides, HTML info and general authoring FAQs.

Writing HTML Documents

http://oneworld.wa.com/htmldev/devpage/dev-page1.html

The Developer's JumpStation provides links to sites that detail creation of Web pages. Includes guides for both the rank beginners and the Internet-savvy Webmasters.

Writing HTML, SGML, TEI, etc.

http://www.speakeasy.org/~dbrick/Hot/html.html

The comprehensive index at this site points to information and resources relevant to writing HTML, SGML and TEI. With a primary focus on guides, editors and other tools for creating Web documents, visitors will find HTML resources for beginners and old hands alike.

WWW: Background Information

http://www.ncsa.uiuc.edu/SDG/Software/Mosaic/Docs/www-info.html

WWW: Background Information provides basic information on the Web, HTTP and HTML. The site consists of an annotated bibliography of and links to electronic instructional texts.

ADVANCED TECHNIQUES

Carlos' Forms Tutorial I

http://robot0.ge.uiuc.edu/~carlosp/cs317/cft.html

Budding Webmasters can learn how to make forms work on their Web sites. Clever and accessible, the tutorial proves a good starting place for the novice interested in tackling advanced Web techniques.

Complex Features for Information Providers

http://www.ncsa.uiuc.edu/SDG/Software/Mosaic/Docs/d2-complex.html

The NCSA offers tips for professionalizing Web site design at its Complex Features for Information Providers page. Find step-by-step instructions for designing graphical maps, access control devices and forms creation.

Dynamic Documents

http://home.netscape.com/assist/net_sites/dynamic_docs.html

Netscape Communications publishes info on mechanisms for dealing with dynamic documents, or Web files that are updated frequently. Read about server push and client pull, as well as the Mozilla animation demo.

Evaluation of the Sun Microsystems Web Site

http://www.sun.com/sun-on-net/uidesign/

The designers of Sun's internal Web site offer advice to Web authors on usability, readability and elegance of construction. View successful Web page and icon designs, and examine the fundamental concepts on which they are based.

How to Do a Searchable Database

http://www2.ncsu.edu/bae/people/faculty/walker/hotlist/isindex.html

Webmasters looking for examples and hints for building a searchable database online will find instructional files, sample code and other tips.

HTML Form-Testing

http://www.research.digital.com/nsl/formtest/home.html

Digital Equipment Corporation maintains this site for its HTML Form-Testing home page. Visitors will find news, test results, online documentation and links to related resources.

MHonArc

http://www.oac.uci.edu/indiv/ehood/mhonarc.html

MHonArc is Perl mail-to-HTML converter application which acts as an archiving and mail thread linking utility. Find out how to use the program to maintain e-mail archives for a Web server and to allow users to read MIME messages.

NCSA Imagemap Tutorial

http://hoohoo.ncsa.uiuc.edu/docs/tutorials/imagemapping.html

This NCSA site offers a step-by-step tutorial for designing and developing informational graphic maps using the latest release version of Imagemap.

net.presence

http://arganet.tenagra.com/Tenagra/net-presence.html

Delve into the onus placed upon Web publishers to play "a significant role in enhancing the Internet." The site's sponsor, Tenagra Corp., presents links and instructions which inform businesses and individuals about creating and maintaining a quality Internet presence.

Netscape Enhancement Index Intro

http://www.ibic.com/Program/NScapeHome.html

The Netscape Enhancement Index includes examples of some of the innovative ways users have pushed their browser to the limits. Visitors can look at examples of server push animations, background creations and tables.

Omnibus Eye at Northwestern University

http://www.rtvf.nwu.edu/

The Department of Radio/TV/Film at Northwestern University details its Omnibus: Eye project. The project which studies the production of digital media on the Web uses this site to share links to what it deems exemplary pages.

The Rationale of Hypertext

http://jefferson.village.virginia.edu/public/jjm2f/rationale.html

Author Jerome McGann expounds his thoughts on the topic The Rationale of HyperText at this text-heavy Web page. The essay explains the necessity for hypermedia and its applications.

The Table Sampler

http://home.netscape.com/assist/net_sites/table_sample.html

Netscape provides a tutorial on creating tables in HTML. The document offers examples of the tags necessary to list information on Web pages.

Web/Genera

http://gdbdoc.gdb.org/letovsky/genera/genera.html

Web/Genera is a software tool set that simplifies the integration of Sybase databases into the Web. This page includes information on obtaining and using the software.

World Wide Web Mail Gateway

http://www-bprc.mps.ohio-state.edu/mailto/mailto_info.html

World Wide Web Mail Gateway is a self-contained software program that allows users to put mail gateways in HTML documents. Visitors can download the application and find full documentation and support at this site.

World Wide Web Authoring Information

http://www.netspace.org/users/dwb/www-authoring.html

Netscape's authoring information site for Web developers offers up-to-date guides and tutorials on a comprehensive list of relevant subjects. Among them: HTML forms, clickable images, HTTP servers, Usenet newsgroups, and CGI scripts.

W3.COM

http://w3.com/

W3.COM develops software tools that enable detailed site tracking and real-time Web page customization. Visit this site to register as a guest on the company's server.

HTML

Extensions to HTML

http://home.netscape.com/assist/net_sites/html_extensions.html

This online primer explains extensions to the HTML 2.0 specification, with information about adding tables, backgrounds and dynamic updating to documents.

HTML analyzer 0.30 Readme

http://www.gatech.edu/pitkow/html_analyzer/README.html

This Web site contains the readme file accompanying HTML analyzer 0.30. Information is available on the program's availability, motivation, processing, rationale, version changes and copyright.

HyperText Markup Language Charter

http://www.ietf.cnri.reston.va.us/html.charters/html-charter.html

This is the online version of the HTML Working Group's Charter, a project launched to develop a universal description of the HTML and ultimately to develop an Internet-wide standard for its use. This site details the group's goals and milestones, and houses archive addresses for working files and mailing lists.

HTML Design Notebook

http://www.w3.org/pub/WWW/People/Connolly/drafts/html-design.html

HTML is the primary authoring code of the Web. The HTML Design Notebook site provides background, specifications, documentation, tools, and publications related to the creation of HTML documents.

HyperText Markup Language (HTML)

http://union.ncsa.uiuc.edu/HyperNews/get/www/html.html

This site explores the ins and outs of HTML. Included are links to directories full of documents discussing HTML style guides, editors, and learning tools.

The HTML Language

http://union.ncsa.uiuc.edu/HyperNews/get/www/html/lang.html

A meta-index of HTML resources, this site showcases pointers to Web pages on the HTML language itself. Listed by category, classifications include: quick reference, full specification and research, and related topics.

HTML-opas

http://www.helsinki.fi/~jpackale/html-opas.html

At Helsinki, Finland's HTML-opas site, find the Finnish take on Web authoring and navigation. In Finnish.

HTML+ (Hypertext Markup Format)

http://www.w3.org/pub/WWW/MarkUp/HTMLPlus/htmlplus_1.html

This is a detailed educational site dedicated to providing information for Web page designers using HTML+.

HTML Publication History

http://www.w3.org/pub/WWW/MarkUp/HTML.html

The publication history of the early development HTML is detailed in this archive site. HTML facts and documents are presented in timeline form.

HTML Quick Reference

http://www.cc.ukans.edu/info/HTML_quick.html

The HTML Quick Reference is a listing of elements used in the development of HTML documents. Includes an index of elements and examples of proper use.

HTML Reference Manual

http://www.sandia.gov/sci_compute/html_ref.html

Sandia National Laboratories provides this online HTML reference manual, with extensive information on all aspects of Web page design and production.

---

a2z EDITOR'S CHOICE

HTML Writers Guild List of HTML Resources

http://www.hwg.org/resources/html/

Looking for HTML tools on the Internet is like hiring middle managers from the ranks of the unemployed. There are a lot to choose from, and they all look the same. If you seek a trustworthy gloss of the Web's seemingly endless supply of HTML software and how-to guides, look no further than the HTML Writers Guild List of HTML Resources. HTML is a simple programming language for creating Web-readable documents. A working knowledge of its basic elements is so simple to acquire, even an adult can learn the finer points. Whether your needs require introductory materials or advanced specifications, the best shareware available is thoughtfully collected and reviewed by guild members. Resources range from style guides to standards to validators, everything required to write, preview and test HTML code. What is conspicuously absent from the collection are editors and converters, but I suppose we can't ask the guild to build a site that puts its writers out of work. —*Reviewed by Becky Bond*

THE HTML WRITERS GUILD

HTML Resources

This is the HTML Writers Guild's list of HTML resources. The scope of this document has been limited to ``documents that help you write HTML,'' and purposely excludes some other areas of creating Web services such as Server Administration and CGI Programming. For links to other information sources, please see the Guild's Home Page.

HTML Style Guide and Test Suite
http://www.charm.net/~lejeune/styles.html
The HTML Style Guide and Test Suite is a document designed to demonstrate that one example is more effective than 1,000 words.

The HTML 3.0 Hypertext Document Format
http://www.w3.org/pub/WWW/Arena/tour/start.html
This page provides information about the HTML 3.0 hypertext document format. The site provides a discussion of updated capabilities offered in version 3.0 of the primary architectural language of the Web.

HTML 2.0 DTD: All elements
http://www.oac.uci.edu/indiv/ehood/html2.0/ALL-ELEM.html
Web authors can get thorough explanations of all coding elements in HTML 2.0 DTD at this site. Includes complete descriptions of HTML coding language.

HTML-WG Mail Archives
http://www.acl.lanl.gov/HTML_WG/archives.html
Visitors can download the mailing list archive of an HTML working group. The archive dates back to 1994.

HTML Writers Guild List of HTML Resources
http://www.hwg.org/resources/html/
A comprehensive guide to all the resources of HTML. See Editor's Choice.

HyperText Mark-up Language Quick Reference, December 1994; April 1995
http://uts.cc.utexas.edu/~churchh/htmlqref.html
This HyperText Mark-up Language Quick Reference site has advice and instructions for writing correct HTML, the most common code for Web pages. The site offers an index of handy tips and basic instructions.

HyperText Markup Language Specification 3.0
http://www.w3.org/pub/WWW/MarkUp/html3/Contents.html
This site contains the Table of Contents for a document addressing the process of refining HTML 3.0. Understanding HTML and working with the various text elements of a document are covered.

HyperText Markup Language: Working and Background Materials
http://www.w3.org/hypertext/WWW/MarkUp/MarkUp.html
The World Wide Web Consortium develops computer software that produces common standards for the Internet. Visit this site to learn about HTML, the most widely-used programming language of the Web.

Otmar's List of HTML Tags
http://www.cosy.sbg.ac.at/~lendl/tags.html
Beginning Web page authors can find help editing HTML documents at this site. Otmar's List of HTML Tags offers a guide to character codes used in basic document editing. Find links to other HTML instructional resources.

Searching the HTML 2.0 Specification
http://hopf.math.nwu.edu/html2.0/dosearch.html
Visitors can perform keyword searches on Northwestern University's WN Web server for specific information about the HTML version 2.0 specification. Links to the server's main page and software sections are available

Weblint
http://www.khoral.com/staff/neilb/weblint.html
The Weblint home page helps Perl scripters "pick the lint off" HTML pages with Weblint's minimal style checker. Download this capability via FTP.

JAVA

Java
http://king.syr.edu:2006/Misc/HPDC4/Foils/Java.html
The Northeast Parallel Architectures Center at Syracuse University in Syracuse, N.Y., offers Java programming resources. Visit here for links to PostScript, ASCII, and GIF formatted documents about the interactive Internet language.

JavaSoft
http://www.december.com/works/java.html
Java is a programming environment from Sun Microsystems which is taking over animation of Web sites faster than a magic GIF can inspire a hard drive crash. Developers can embed Web sites with applets which allow visitors to experience interactive displays without possessing the driving application on their desktop. Find FAQs, examples and access to the Java Developer's kit at Sun's official Java home page.

Presenting Java
http://www.december.com/works/java.html
"Presenting Java" is an instructional book for the computer programming language, Java, which creates animations and simulations for the Web. This promotional page has information about the book along with language demos and source code.

SERVER SOFTWARE

Analog
http://www.statslab.cam.ac.uk/~sret1/analog/
Analog is a program that analyzes log files from Web servers on any Unix-based system. This informational page provides a description, source code, links to other programs and statistical reports.

The Apache HTTP Server Project
http://www.apache.org/
Apache is a public domain server based on NCSA HTTPd 1.3. Visitors can download the latest version of Apache and choose from several links providing information about the software.

ARTA Media Group
http://www.halcyon.com/artamedia/webwizard/arta.html
Windows users can find Web design and server software at the ARTA Media Group company home page. Review products and services at this promotional site.

Getstats Documentation
http://www.eit.com/software/getstats/getstats.html
Getstats (formerly called Getsites) is a versatile Web server log analyzer which takes log files from individual servers and creates reports on volume of hits and domain activity.

GlimpseHTTP Overview
http://glimpse.cs.arizona.edu/ghttp/
This site provides information on capabilities, components, documentation and software associated with GlimpseHTTP. Includes links to related servers, contributed software and the server's authors.

GoServe
http://www2.hursley.ibm.com/goserve/
GoServe is a multipurpose computer server at IBM's Hursley Park, England, laboratories offering visitors instructional information about for creating Web server systems.

Gwstat Web Server Utility
http://dis.cs.umass.edu/stats/gwstat.html
The Distributed Artificial Intelligence Laboratory at the University of Massachusetts maintains this site for its Gwstat Web server utility. Visitors can learn how to obtain and use the application which generates graphs illustrating the amount of server traffic.

The Harvest Cache and Httpd-Accelerator

http://excalibur.usc.edu/

Soup up normal Web servers with the Harvest Cache and Httpd-Accelerator offered at this site. Mosaic, Netscape, and Lynx Web clients can increase server performance (up to a factor of 10, the site's authors claim) by downloading and installing this free software.

The Internet Factory

http://www.aristosoft.com/ifact/inet.htm

The Internet Factory, which develops Web servers for the Windows NT and Windows 95 platforms, provides product and ordering information. Also included are a developer's corner and software documentation.

MacHTTP FAQ Documentation

http://arpp1.carleton.ca/machttp/doc/

The MacHTTP FAQ is an informational site for those searching for information about HTTP programming in the Macintosh environment. Visitors to this site will find information on HTTP troubleshooting, software and utilities.

NCSA HTTPd

http://hoohoo.ncsa.uiuc.edu/

The NCSA demonstrates its HTTP software at this site. Includes information on online security and links to NCSA and the University of Chicago main home pages.

NCSA HTTPd Overview

http://hoohoo.ncsa.uiuc.edu/docs/

This server provides documentation on NCSA HTTPd, an HTTP/1.0 compatible application for making hypertext and other documents available to Web browsers. Includes installation instructions and in-depth tutorials on configuration.

NCSA HTTPd Tutorials

http://hoohoo.ncsa.uiuc.edu/docs/tutorials/

NCSA provides tutorials on setting up HTTPd servers. Visitors will also find a variety of lessons on Web designing and configuration.

NCSA HTTPd Tutorial: CGI Configuration

http://hoohoo.ncsa.uiuc.edu/docs/tutorials/cgi.html

Learning CGI scripting for computerized documents is a good way to create documents quickly. NCSA's tutorial on CGI configuration brings would-be Webmasters up to speed.

NCSA HTTPd Tutorial: Server Side Includes (SSI)

http://hoohoo.ncsa.uiuc.edu/docs/tutorials/includes.html

This NCSA HTTPd Tutorial about Server Side Includes features information about server side issues, setup, conversion, format, and environment variables.

Overview of HTTP

http://www.w3.org/pub/WWW/Protocols/Overview.html

Visitors to this page will find an overview of HTTP prepared by the World Wide Web Consortium. Links supplement issues presented in the text.

Plexus

http://bsdi.com/server/doc/plexus.html

The information provided about Plexus, a public domain HTTP server, includes an introduction, overview and availability report, as well as details on installation, configuration, and administration. Link from this site to an FTP archive containing the software.

Proxy Gateway Support in NCSA Mosaic for the X Windowing System

http://www.ncsa.uiuc.edu/SDG/Software/Mosaic/Docs/proxy-gateways.html

This electronic document explains how to set up NCSA Mosaic (version 2.2 and later) for the X Windowing system to enable the use of proxy gateways. A description of the proxy gateway and its implementation are provided.

Silicon Graphics' WebFORCE

http://www.sgi.com/Products/WebFORCE/

This commercial site provides news and information about Silicon Graphics' WebFORCE product line, designed to enable "media-rich Web authoring and high-performance Web serving." Visitors can locate the high-tech company's distributors, read success stories, or learn about Club WebFORCE.

Spinning the Web: Setting Up World Wide Web Servers

http://scholar.lib.vt.edu/reports/Servers-web.html

At the Spinning the Web: Setting Up World Wide Web Servers home page, visitors and Webmasters-to-be can get detailed instructions for setting up Web-functional servers and software.

WebSTAR

http://www.starnine.com/webstar/webstar.html

WebSTAR is a Macintosh-based, desktop Web publisher. This page hosts information about obtaining evaluation copies, pricing strategies, and ordering procedures, along with links to press releases and documentation.

Wide Area Networked Environment Information

http://www-wane.scri.fsu.edu/

This site features information on Wide Area Networked Environment, a comprehensive service package for clients wishing to connect a server to the Internet. Includes information about the Supercomputer Computations Research Institute, the software's developer, plus details on the hardware required for WANE use.

Willow Glen Graphics

http://wgg.com/

Willow Glen Graphics is a San Jose, Calif.-based producer of Web server utilities and applications. Visitors will find product information and release news.

Windows HTTPd 1.4

http://www.city.net/win-httpd/

This promotional site for the server, Windows HTTPd 1.4, offers documentation, technical support and download instructions for the popular, public-use software. The application is free to personal and educational users, but commercial and governmental concerns must register after a 30-day free trial.

W3C HTTPd

http://www.w3.org/pub/WWW/Daemon/Overview.html/

Find information for obtaining and installing the shareware hypertext server W3C HTTPd at this site. Link to discussion forums for Unix Web servers, or look up the current version's source code.

W3C HTTPd as a Proxy

http://www.w3.org/pub/WWW/Daemon/User/Proxies/Proxies.html

Find an explanation of a proxy, defined as "a HTTP server typically running on a firewall machine," at this site. Includes configuration specifications for running W3C HTTPd as a proxy, general server setup instruction data and other technical info.

World Wide Web Server Software

http://www.w3.org/pub/WWW/Servers.html

This compilation of links to sites dedicated to Web server software offers resources ranging from Apache to WN.

XFree 86 Project

http://www.xfree86.org/

The XFree 86 Project Inc. is a nonprofit producer of X Window servers for PC-based Unix and Unix-like systems. Visitors can find out where to get their free copy of XFree 86 and how to make donations to the project.

ZBServer

http://www.zbserver.com/

ZBServer is a Windows-based freeware application that allows nonprofessionals to publish Web documents using a PC. Includes documentation, downloading info, and installation instructions.

SGML

Fred: The SGML Grammar Builder

http://www.oclc.org/fred/

Fred: The SGML Grammar Builder is a project of the Online Computer Library Center and focuses on the manipulation of tagged text. A look at current research is available, including attention to automatic DTD creation and grammar reduction services.

sgml directory

ftp://ftp.th-darmstadt.de/pub/text/sgml

This FTP server hosts a variety of Structured Graphical Markup Language-related software and files. Directories pertaining to SGML grammar, format and parsers are among the resources offered.

SGML on the Web

http://www.ncsa.uiuc.edu/SDG/Software/Mosaic/WebSGML.html

The SGML site offers a wide variety of resources, including info on SGML events, user notes, and links to online tutorials and demonstrations. Visitors can also link to a number of related Web servers and sample SGML chapters.

VRML

Emerson—On The Net: Internet Resources in Virtual Reality

http://www.hitl.washington.edu/projects/knowledge_base/onthenet.html

Researchers will find an extensive, annotated index to Virtual Reality-related sites. References are organized into the categories of applications, publications, and resources.

WHY SEARCH WHEN YOU CAN FIND

COMMERCIAL DIRECTORIES AND INTERNET YELLOW PAGES

BizWeb

http://www.bizweb.com/

Atlanta, Ga.-based BizWeb promises links to more than 3,000 national products and services at this index site. Visitors will find everything from computer software to flower delivery here, organized by industry and area.

Business and Commerce

http://galaxy.einet.net/galaxy/Business-and-Commerce.html

The TradeWave Galaxy offers a selective index of business and commerce resources online. Tap these listings for commercial directories, periodicals, and news.

The Business of the Internet

http://www.rtd.com/people/rawn/business.html

The Business of the Internet offers visitors a large collection of links to information about the Internet. Geared to the commercial Web denizen, the site offers plain talk on Internet issues of importance to the business community.

CommerceNet

http://www.commerce.net/

CommerceNet, a nonprofit corporation, is conducting a large-scale study of electronic Internet commerce. Read about the company's mission, or tap into the CommerceNet directory services that round out the site's offerings.

Commercial Sites Index

http://www.directory.net/dir/directory.html

This index site contains a directory of over 17,000 listings of commercial services, products and information available on the Internet. Includes access to a keyword search tool, category index, and instructions for submitting new listings.

Electronic Storefronts

http://www.cs.colorado.edu/homes/mcbryan/public_html/bb/15/summary.html

Electronic Storefronts is a comprehensive index of Web vendor sites. Product and service categories are listed alphabetically and indicate how many entries each subject area contains.

The Global On-Line Directory

http://www.gold.net/gold/gold2.html

Commercial Web service provider GoldSite Europe maintains this site for its Global On-Line Directory user input page. Visitors can enter their business' vital information for inclusion in this Internet commercial directory.

infoMarket

http://www.infomkt.ibm.com/

IBM's infoMarket is a free service which allows users to search Web and commercial online resources simultaneously. Receive results from news and information sources like Business Wire and Usenet newsgroups with a single search.

ISP Internet Yellow Pages

http://supepages.gte.net

The Internet Yellow Pages is a free electronic search service that finds pages on the Web. This page, offered by a consortium of Internet service providers, lets users make selections by using word searches and category options.

Japanese Open Yellowpage

http://www.st.rim.or.jp/~saito/JOY/JOY.html

The Japanese Open Yellowpage Web site boasts a directory of links that showcases commercial Internet pages. In Japanese and English.

NetPages

http://www.aldea.com/

NetPages serves up individual and business listings, classified advertising, and an Internet survival guide. Visitors can add their own listings or check out ordering information for paperback editions of NetPages.

New Riders' Official World Wide Web Yellow Pages

http://www.mcp.com/nrp/wwwyp/

The World Wide Web Yellow Pages site provides keyword and category search capabilities. Find instructions for submitting new servers and a text-only version of the search engine.

Professionals Online

http://www.prosonline.com/

Professionals Online presents a directory of Web resources categorized by profession. Among the areas covered are business, finance, accounting, law, computers and technology, and government. Includes a job finder service.

Trade Point USA

http://www.tpusa.com/

International trade creates a need for international data. Trade Point USA offers an online trade information service, where users can search a 250,000-company database and catalog center. Free services include a road map for exporting and tips on doing business under NAFTA.

University of Houston College of Business Administration World Wide Web Yellow Pages

http://www.cba.uh.edu/ylowpges/ylowpges.html

The business college at the University of Houston has compiled this massive index to sites on the Web. The site also gives a brief overview of the school's online courses.

World Wide Yellow Pages

http://www.yellow.com/

The World Wide Yellow Pages is a commercial site offering an array of business listings and services on a fee basis. Search the directory's entries, or find out how to have your company's site included.

TheYellowPages.com(tm)

http://theyellowpages.com/

TheYellowPages.com is a commercial Internet directory cataloging Web resources by subject. Find links to subject indexes ranging from architecture to zoology.

ECLECTIC LINK COLLECTIONS

Addicted To Stuff

http://www.morestuff.com

Addicted to Stuff, a wacky index to decidedly hip sites, sends visitors to sites about drinking, cars, good words, bad words and the like.

The Bureau of Atomic Tourism

http://www.oz.net/~chrisp/atomic.html

The Bureau of Atomic Tourism promotes tourism to places where there have been atomic explosions, where atomic research occurred or where weapons are displayed. Visitors here will find an index to atomic hot spots on the Internet.

finest materials

gopher://gopher.well.sf.ca.us/1

An online refuge for writers, educators, activists and the overly educated, the WELL, also known as Whole Earth Lectronic Link, opens up its gopher gateway to the general population of the Internet. The index of resident resources and links includes topics such as communications and media, cyberpunk and postmodern culture, K-12 education, and science.

The Funky Times

http://www.realitycom.com/Funky.html

The Funky Times features links to daily stuff—news, weather, comics, etc. Included are newspapers, magazines, current satellite images, Dilbert, zodiac forecasts, Cool Site of the Day and NASA Today.

NETLiNkS

http://www.netlinks.net/

NETLiNkS is an online guide that provides links to offbeat Web pages. Includes a help site, fan mail, pointers to interesting pages and entrepreneurial ethnic advertising.

RZAPP

http://www.mindspring.com/~rzapp/rzapp.html

The matriarch Granny dispenses links on genealogy, HTML, financial planning and education. The well-rounded site, based in Atlanta, also offers an electronic look at the 1996 Olympics.

UWI's Web's Edge

http://kzsu.stanford.edu/uwi.html

UnderWorld Industries is a low-volume e-mail list that encourages free thinking. It dubs this Web page its cultural playground. Find plenty of links to materials from the electronic underground.

Webaholics Top 50 Links List

http://cns-web.cns.ohiou.edu/~rbarrett/webaholics/favlinks/entries.html

The Webaholics Top 50 Links list is somewhat self-explanatory. An eclectic list of links has been compiled with a heavy emphasis on sites of pop cultural significance. Other sites qualify by reaching heights of obscurity or absurdity.

Wiretap Electronic Text Archive

http://wiretap.spies.com/

The Wiretap Electronic Text Archive opens with a recitation of First Amendment to the U.S. Constitution. With this in mind, visitors are invited to peruse Wiretap's various text, software and BBS archives.

GOPHER DIRECTORIES

All Gopher Sites

gopher://liberty.uc.wlu.edu:70/11/gophers/other

The Washington and Lee gopher server hosts an extensive menu of gopher indexes around the globe. Visitors can access the University of Minnesota's index of registered gophers, search gophers by name or subject, or browse indexes by geographic location.

Bulletin Boards—Telnet-Accessible (via Texas A&M)

gopher://gopher.tamu.edu:70/11/.dir/bbs.dir

Bulletin Board Systems provided electronic forums for message and file exchange long before the Web existed. Texas A&M maintains a gopher menu of BBSs and offers telnet links to each system listed in its index.

Connecting to Minnesota Univ. Server for Other Gopher Connections

gopher://gopher2.tc.umn.edu:70/1

The University of Minnesota, developer of gopher Internet technology, posts information about the retrieval system. Its Computing and Consulting Service offers the latest gopher news as well as access to discussion groups.

Global Electronic Library Gopher Server

gopher://marvel.loc.gov/11/global

The Global Electronic Library Gopher Server offers access to a large collection of Internet resources. Visitors will find a wealth of free network services, texts, databases, organizations and electronic journals.

Gopher

gopher://rs.internic.net:70/11/rs

Archives and WHOIS searches are available at this InterNIC Registration Services gopher where network information, policies and templates are among the directories. At this site browsers can find out what domain names (e.g., www.superbowl.com, www.itchy-scratchy.com) are taken and which ones are still free for the pickin'.

Gopher Tree of Internet-Accessible Libraries

gopher://libgopher.yale.edu:70/1

This searchable gopher index connects Web wanderers with online information resources at universities around the world. Includes instructions for accessing the different catalog types.

Guides to the Internet

gopher://dewey.lib.ncsu.edu:70/11/library/ reference/guides

The North Carolina State University Libraries gopher presents this index of gopher directories and guides, with a strong focus on locating Internet resources. Other areas covered include agriculture, electronic academic journals and health sciences.

Iceland Gopher

gopher://gopher.isnet.is:70/

ISnet features information from the Icelandic portions of NORDUnet and EUnet. This gopher index features pointers to general information about ISnet and a list of gopher servers in Iceland.

Internet Resources (Michigan State U)

gopher://gopher.msu.edu:70/11/internet

Michigan State University puts its local file resources online, serving up text files containing info ranging from political polls to census data to crime statistics. The gopher menu is organized by field of study and type of access.

North Carolina State University Library (Without Walls) Gopher

gopher://dewey.lib.ncsu.edu:70/1

North Carolina State University's Library Services offers this gopher server where browsers can access a wealth of library info and links to related points of interest on the Internet. Newsletters, government documents and campus resources are among this server's features.

Searchable Veronica Indexes

gopher://liberty.uc.wlu.edu:70/11/gophers/ veronica

This gopher server links browsers to text info contained in the files of the Universidad Nacional Autonoma de Mexico, and the searchable indexes of New York's NYSERNet and Virginia's PSINet.

Selected Gopher Servers

gopher://liberty.uc.wlu.edu:70/11/gophers/ other/new_gophers

Offerings through this service include science, education, and preservation sites from around the world. Explore the Institute of Chemical Technology in Prague, the Central China Regional Network Center, the NEA Resource Center for Higher Education and the Sierra Club, to name only a few.

University of Michigan Library Services Gopher Site

gopher://una.hh.lib.umich.edu:70/11/inetdirs

Library services at the University of Michigan offers this gopher site, a clearinghouse for subject-oriented Internet resource guides. Visitors can access a complete list of the guides, with help on using them, or search the archive for specific topics.

Veronica

gopher://veronica.scs.unr.edu:11/veronica

Veronica is a resource-discovery system providing access to information resources held on most of the world's gophers. At this gopher site, browsers can read the Veronica FAQ, find out how to compose queries, or search for information.

Veronica Frequently Asked Questions File

gopher://gopher.unr.edu:70/00/veronica/ veronica-faq

Those thirsting for information about Veronica, a resource-discovery system providing access to info contained on most of the Internet's gopher servers, will find a multitude of data here. Includes instructions for composing Veronica queries and getting servers into the Veronica database.

Veronica Information Gopher Menu

gopher://gopher.scs.unr.edu:70/11/veronica

This gopher server is dedicated to providing helpful information about Veronica, a constantly updated database of the names of menus on thousands of gopher servers. Visitors can access a FAQ, plus info on Veronica software, directories and search capabilities.

INTERNET FAQS AND GUIDES

About The Internet

http://home.mcom.com/home/ about-the-internet.html

Netscape's introduction to the Internet links Web surfers with information on dipping their toes in the digital waters. Includes links to EFF's (Extended) Guide to the Internet and the Internet Society's home page.

Ask Dr. Internet Index

http://promo.net/drnet/

Find answers to a variety of questions about the Information Superhighway. Ask Dr. Internet covers topics ranging from bandwidth to Netiquette to viruses.

Canadian Internet Handbook

http://www.csi.nb.ca/handbook/handbook.html

The home page of The Canadian Internet Handbook is a quick study of how-to resources relating to the Canadian Internet world. In addition to info on the handbook, browsers can find other publications to help navigate Internet and Canadian hinterlands.

Crispen's Homepage

http://ua1vm.ua.edu/~crispen/crispen.html

Patrick Douglas Crispen, an undergraduate student at the University of Alabama, provides Inter-

net training and consulting in his spare time. Some of his projects, such as the Roadmap (a 27-lesson Internet workshop) and the Atlas Web Workshop, are featured here, along with personal stuff.

EFF's (Extended) Guide to the Internet

http://www.eff.org/papers/bdgtti/eegtti.html

Visitors can download the Electronic Frontier Foundation's (Extended) Guide to the Internet. The 300-page Web site includes a detailed table of contents.

ESHNAV.COM

http://eshnav.com/

The ESHNAV.COM index site provides a weekly review of useful sites on the Web, pages from a surfer's diary, access to over 30 search engines and a subscriber service.

An Executive Summary of the World-Wide Web Initiative

http://www.w3.org/pub/WWW/Summary.html

Newcomers to the Internet seeking a short, understandable explanation of the theory, mechanics and techniques comprising the global information network will find simple answers to their questions at this Web summary site.

Exploring the Internet

http://www.ci.berkeley.ca.us/bpl/

Explore the Internet with the Berkeley Public Library. The library explains guidelines for using the Internet, offers classes and tutoring, and provides links to San Francisco Bay Area Internet service providers.

Exploring the Internet

http://www.cen.uiuc.edu/exploring.html

Visitors will find an index to the Internet here, compiled by the College of Engineering at the University of Illinois at Urbana-Champaign. It includes pointers to tutorials, games, multimedia sites, weather resources, and much more.

Global Internet Access

http://www.global.co.za/

Global Internet Access offers an indexed guide to Internet resources to help explorers find their way in online world. Topics include astrology, business, magazines, Netiquette, Web directories, software, travel, and more.

Global Network Navigator

http://www.gnn.com/

This opening screen for the Global Network Navigator site—which claims to offer up the "best of the Web"—provides a splashy glimpse at what is available inside. Visitors can choose between GNN News, the Whole Internet Catalog and a variety of popular Internet directories, plus such features as a Story Cafe and the latest issue of Web Review.

Glosario de Internet

http://www.uco.es/ccc/glosario/glosario.html

This glossary offers links to explanatory sites providing definitions and documentation on Internet acronyms and terminology. In Spanish.

Guide to Cyberspace 6.1: Contents

http://www.eit.com/web/www.guide/

This Guide to Cyberspace, a lesson on exploring and understanding the structure of the Web, includes a hyperlink table of contents covering all aspects of the Web and tools to enable its exploration.

Guides to the Internet

gopher://dewey.lib.ncsu.edu:70/11/library/reference/guides

The North Carolina State University Libraries gopher presents this index of directories and guides, with a strong focus on locating Internet resources. Other areas covered include agriculture, electronic academic journals, and health sciences.

Help for USGS World Wide Web Services

http://h2o.usgs.gov/public/help.html

The U.S. Geological Survey maintains this site for explanations of basic Internet-related concepts. Visit this site to learn how to navigate the Web and other global information networks.

IETF/TERENA Training Materials Catalogue

http://www.trainmat.ietf.org/catalogue.html

This text-only catalog provides pointers to educational materials for use by Internet sysops and tech personnel in training users. Resources include a Netiquette primer, guides to e-mail and other Internet applications, and introductions to gopher and WAIS.

ILC Glossary of Internet Terms

http://www.matisse.net/files/glossary.html

If you feel like an illiterate on the Web you're not alone. A company called Internet Literacy Consultants has compiled a list of Internet-specific terminology and coupled it with easy to understand definitions. The ILC Glossary of Internet Terms tackles everything from obscure acronyms to the indecipherable argot of the programming set.

Information SuperLibrary

http://www.mcp.com/index.html

A service of Viacom, the Information SuperLibrary hosts online homes for publishing heavy hitters such as Macmillan, Simon and Schuster, and SSI Distribution Services. Visitors are invited to browse reference works, resource directories, software libraries, the Internet Starter Kit, and more.

INTAC FAQ Index

http://www.intac.com/FAQ.html

The INTAC FAQ Index is a form-based Glimpse gateway for the Web. Every imaginable FAQ directory and file is accessible (as well as many you would never imagine). Allows the user to browse or search.

Internet in a Baby

http://www.wideweb.com/baby/

This guide to the Web features an interface that uses the image of a baby as its map. To reach different Web sites, just point to various parts of the baby's body and click.

Internet Information and Resources

http://www.intercon.net/

Intercon is an Internet access provider offering Web starting points and basic guides at this home page. The site offers a listing of what's new on the Internet, as well as links to downloadable software.

Internet: La Toile d'Araignee

http://www.loria.fr/~charoy/ToileInternet/text.html

Internet Web is an index to the Internet, offering links to basic overviews of the Web and Netiquette, search engines, and Usenet newsgroups, among others. In English and French.

Internet Resources

http://www.brandonu.ca/~ennsnr/Resources/

Internet Resources represents a collection of resources useful to Internet trainers, as well as just about anyone else who uses the Internet. Includes links to Internet guides, FTP archives, an index of Usenet newsgroups and a catalog of online courses.

Internet Resources for Institutional Research

http://apollo.gmu.edu/~jmilam/air95.html

Visitors to this page will find a collection of annotated links selected to assist users in navigating the Internet. A categorical index to the material listed and hot button links are offered for quick reference.

Internet Resources: Internet Guides

http://www.brandonu.ca/~ennsnr/Resources/guides.html

Brandon University in Manitoba, Canada, maintains this site to list helpful Internet resources. Visit here for an index of guides to Internet programming, information search engines and Web site design.

Internet Resources List

http://www.eit.com/web/netservices.html

A wide-ranging list of pointers to Internet resources populates this index. Includes links to publications, services, tools, and legal resources.

Internet Resources on the Web

http://www.brandonu.ca/~ennsnr/Resources/resources.html

This collection of resources is specially geared towards Internet trainers. Guides are included, as are mailing lists, gopher sites, and FTP archives.

Internet Web Text

http://www.december.com/web/text/index.html

If you are confused by the Internet, this is the place to be. This site offers an extensive guide to understanding the Internet and the Web. Visit to obtain a variety of instructional materials covering the basics along with advanced skills and resources.

The Jargon File

http://www.denken.or.jp/cgi-bin/JARGON

The Jargon File is a compendium of hacker slang illuminating aspects of hacker tradition, folklore and humor. Using the searchable index visitors can enter words and receive full definitions of hacker lingo.

1996 World Wide Web Ultimate Home Page

http://hoohana.aloha.net/~billpeay/ulthome.html

A laundry list of search engines, cool sites and philosophical musings about the Internet compose the contents of the 1996 World Wide Web Ulimate Home Page. The text-based site packs the screen with loads of links ranging from archival materials to today's news.

NSTN True North

http://www.nstn.ns.ca/nstn.html

NSTN, a Canadian Internet access provider, introduces its True North Web navigation guide. Claiming to be "your navigational constant," True North uses iconic symbols based on Inuit figurative art to orient users to the Internet. The Dangerous Bear leads to commercial sites, while the Owl leads to a "cybrary," and so on.

Online World

http://login.eunet.no/~presno/index.html

The Online World resources handbook provides general information on the Internet. The site offers articles about subjects such as effective use of the Internet, online services, how to search databases and how to save money.

Overview of the Web

http://www.w3.org/pub/DataSources/Top.html

This virtual library organizes information by subject matter. It's a loosely organized, one-stop gathering place for Internet resources. Includes a list of registered servers indexed by country.

PC/Computing's Web Map

http://www.zdnet.com/pccomp/webmap/

PC/Computing magazine offers its own map of the Web. Tour the virtual world courtesy of the pundits' pointers using the navigational tips offered.

Planet Internet

http://www.pi.net/

This site contains links to the three Planet Internet information products: the Daily Planet, Planet News and Planet Multimedia. Includes a graphical index of links to a variety of educational, news and entertainment sites.

Rescue Island

http://www.comcomsystems.com/

Rescue Island calls itself a "safe haven" amidst the Internet's "stormy seas." The site which seeks to entertain and inform Web-weary visitors is a promotional service from ComCom Systems, purveyor of forms-processing and image-archiving network services.

Roadmap Workshop

http://www.mobiusweb.com~mobius/
Roadmap/

The Roadmap Workshop is an Internet training site designed to teach new users how to navigate the rapidly expanding Information Superhighway. The live lectures of Internet personality Patrick Crispen are reproduced in text format online. Includes a syllabus and links to registration sites for lecture events.

A Short, Semi-Guided Tour of the Internet

http://www.kei.com/internet-tour.html

New browsers can navigate a short tour of the Web by following the hypertext links embedded in this narrative description of the Internet. A smattering of sites are sampled from the nonprofit to commercial and from the educational to the just plain silly.

Starting Point

http://www.stpt.com/welcome.html

Starting Point introduces visitors to the wonders of the Web with its keyword search engine and preset hot buttons. Explore the Internet by querying your interests or following the Webmaster's suggestions.

Starting Points for Internet Exploration

http://www.ncsa.uiuc.edu/SDG/Software/
Mosaic/StartingPoints/
NetworkStartingPoints.html

Maintained by the NCSA, the developers of the Mosaic Web browser, this page offers access to download the most recent version of Mosaic. Also find an overview of the Web, instructions for using Mosaic, and numerous links to major info gateways.

SunSITE

http://sunsite.unc.edu/

Maintained by the University of North Carolina at Chapel Hill, find at this site the home page for the SunSITE Web server. A general Internet resource clearinghouse and guide, SunSITE features Internet search access, links to Sun information and statistics, and access to free software, government hypertexts, and multimedia exhibits.

SunSITE Japan

http://sunsite.sut.ac.jp/

The Science University of Tokyo maintains the Japanese SunSITE which hosts a wealth of info on the Internet, Asia, and technology. Visitors can search the Web or link to other SunSITE pages. In English and Japanese.

TradeWave Galaxy

http://www.einet.net/galaxy.html

TradeWave Galaxy describes itself as "a guide to worldwide information and services" and offers visitors access to wide-ranging listings of merchandise, information and services available on the Web. Includes information on TradeWave's business policies, instructions for listing with the service, search tools, and access to the company's online monthly newsletter.

Virtual Tourist World Map

http://wings.buffalo.edu/world/index.html

The Campus-Wide Information Service for the State University of New York at Buffalo maintains this site for Internet search resources. Visit its Virtual Tourist site for a geographic guide of Web resources around the globe.

The Web as a Learning Tool

http://www.cs.uidaho.edu/~connie/
interests.html

The Web as a Learning Tool serves as an educationally-oriented guide to using the Web. Created by an employee at the University of Idaho, this site links to information on designing Web pages, humanities, entertainment, world news, and schools.

Web Documentation/Resources

http://www.astro.nwu.edu/html-www/
html-docs.html

This Web documentation and resources site contains an overview of and comprehensive information on Web tools, navigation instructions, manuals, and related resources.

Web Information Guide

http://www.bsdi.com/server/doc/web-info.html

This guide is chock full of pointers to Web information sites, including a glossary of hypertext terms, multimedia demos, a Web primer, and a list of starting points for Internet neophytes.

Web Publishing Paradigms

http://hoshi.cic.sfu.ca/~guay/Paradigm/
Paradigm.html

This document examines the paradigms involved in the birth of a new medium—the Web. It provides an overview of the history of the Web, with discussions of print, multimedia, hypertext, documverse and interactive approaches to the online world.

The Web Wanderer Directory

http://www.xnet.com/~blatura/wanderer.shtml

The Web Wanderer suggests a path through the Web which is characterized by amusement and informality. Look through the Webmaster's picks for diversions, people, computers, the Web and an electronic newsstand for starters.

Whole Internet Catalog

http://nearnet.gnn.com/wic/index.html

The Whole Internet Catalog, brought to the Web as a service of Global Network Navigator, boasts a discriminating and thoughtful survey of the online universe. Browsers can link to Internet search engines Yahoo and WebCrawler, or view the catalog's Best of the Net picks.

World Wide Web

http://www.ncsa.uiuc.edu/General/Internet/
WWW/WebIntro.html

The NCSA provides this introductory primer for the World Wide Web, featuring FAQs, how-to instructions, and links to software archives.

World Wide Web FAQ

http://www.io.org/faq/www/index.html

This site contains a Web FAQ in several languages and formats. The explanations of key Web and Internet concepts and can be downloaded from this site or one of several mirrors listed. An introduction and contents listing are included.

World Wide Web FAQs and Guides

http://cuiwww.unige.ch/OSG/FAQ/www.html

This site contains an index to guides on Web surfing and publishing. It includes pointers to HTML tutorials, FAQs, and guides to Web indexes.

World Wide Web FAQ (With Answers, of Course!)

http://www.boutell.com/faq/

Thomas Boutwell's seminal Frequently Asked Questions file introduces the uninitiated to the wonders of the Web. Designed to answer the most common questions about the Web, the informational site acts as a crash course in browsers and servers, Web page authoring tools and techniques, image use, and basic scripting.

The World Wide Web Unleashed

http://www.december.com/works/wwwu.html

Find a table of contents and excerpted chapters from the book, "The World Wide Web Unleashed," at this site. Web facts and figures are presented along with a navigational guide. Includes ordering info.

Zen and the Art of the Internet—Table of Contents

http://sundance.cso.uiuc.edu/Publications/Other/Zen/zen-1.0_toc.html

Here's the complete text for Brendan P. Kehoe's famed beginner's guide to the Internet, "Zen and the Art of the Internet."

MAILING LIST DIRECTORIES

Mailing List World Wide Web Gateway

http://www.netspace.org/cgi-bin/lwgate

The Mailing List World Wide Web Gateway presents information about mailing lists. Find a hypertext interface for listing archives on the NetSpace server, and learn how to use mailing list commands with ease.

Publicly Accessible Mailing Lists (PAML)

http://www.neosoft.com/internet/paml/

This is a list of Internet mailing lists—different from a newsgroup because users don't receive anything unless they actually request it. Lists listed here include descriptions and subscription information.

tile.net/lists

http://www.tile.net/tile/listserv/index.html

To discover what's being talked about on the Internet, consult the tile.net/listserv site. A reference source for Internet discussion, find groups listed according to name, host country and subject.

World Wide Web Mailing Lists

http://www.leeds.ac.uk/ucs/WWW/WWW_mailing_lists.html

This Web page from the University of Leeds, England, features information about mailing lists and Usenet groups devoted to topics related to the World Wide Web.

NEWSGROUP DIRECTORIES

Anchorman

http://www.ph.tn.tudelft.nl/People/pierre/anchorman/Amn..html

Access Anchorman, a hierarchical newsreader, contains a search utility to help users find various

newsgroups. Includes an index of links to thousands of newsgroups listed by category.

DejaNews Research Service

http://www.dejanews.com/

DejaNews Research Service maintains this site for its index of Usenet search tools. Visit here for archives, how-to guides and online help for getting the most out of Usenet.

Digital America

http://www.community.net

Community Net, by Digital America, puts all its newsgroups on a dedicated server for greater storage space. The idea of the net is to "improve education, government, business, and personal communications, by connecting them all through the Internet."

Discuss

http://www.mit.edu:8008/

Discuss is a networked electronic conferencing system at the Massachusetts Institute of Technology which operates in a manner similar to bulletin boards. Visitors can use this gateway to join electronic meetings that probe issues of academic and political interest.

The Forum News Gateway

http://forum.swarthmore.edu/forum.news.gateway.html

Forum News Gateway is a utility for reading Usenet news, but it adds the twist of allowing reading and posting of hypertext articles in HTML. Visitors can test demo versions of the product, or link to Forum's home page.

Free Agent Newsreader

http://www.forteinc.com/forte/agent/freagent.htm

The Free Agent Newsreader from Forte is a device designed as a "guide to news, fun and info in Usenet newsgroups." Visitors can read descriptions and reviews of the freeware product at this Web site.

HyperNews

http://union.ncsa.uiuc.edu/HyperNews/get/hypernews.html

HyperNews is a cross between the Web and Usenet that allows readers to respond to articles or responses they read in the HyperNews web. This page provides complete information on HyperNews and links to many topical resources.

Index of /ftparchive/WWW/utils/hyperactive

http://www.york.ac.uk/ftparchive/WWW/utils/hyperactive

This software archive, maintained by computer science researchers at the University of York, England, offers access to a Usenet conversion program. Visit this site to download the utility.

Index to Archives of Newsgroup Postings

http://starbase.neosoft.com/~claird/news.lists/newsgroup_archives.html

This document provides links to newsgroup archives throughout the Internet. Includes instructions for use, formatting information, indexes of sites, and archive construction.

Internet Newsgroups

http://www.w3.org/pub/DataSources/News/Groups/Overview.html

The Internet Newsgroups site provides an alphabetical index of newsgroups arranged by group name.

List of Usenet FAQs

http://www.cis.ohio-state.edu/hypertext/faq/usenet/FAQ-List.html

This document claims to contain a list of all Usenet FAQs found in news.answers. Additional features include options for limited keyword searches and listings by newsgroup.

Newsgroups Available (ANU) Under aus

http://coombs.anu.edu.au/CoombswebPages/Newsreader/aus.html

The Australian National University provides this comprehensive list of newsgroups on Australia-related topics. Visitors will find links to newsgroups in all categories.

rn KILL file FAQ

http://www.cis.ohio-state.edu/hypertext/faq/usenet/killfile-faq/faq.html

The FAQ for rn KILL files describes its subject, the KILL file, as "a way of recording what articles you want to kill (skip over)." This detailed, highly technical site includes answers to the most common questions about the subject, as well as instructions for utilizing the newsgroup utility.

Search List of Discussion Groups

http://alpha.acast.nova.edu/cgi-bin/lists

Maintained at Dartmouth College, the site hosts a database of over 5,900 Bitnet and Internet interest groups. The page provides a keyword search form to aid list access.

tile.net/news

http://www.tile.net/tile/news/index.html

"The complete reference to Usenet Newsgroups" is how tile.net/news trumpets its services. Links include database sources listed by description or newsgroup hierarchy.

Usenet Frequently Asked Questions (FAQ) Files Search

http://www.cis.ohio-state.edu/htbin/search-usenet-faqs/form

This site provides a searchable index of Usenet FAQs. Incapable of providing a full search of the postings' texts, this index allows visitors to search by newsgroup and archive names, subjects, and keywords.

Usenet Info Center Launch Pad

http://sunsite.unc.edu/usenet-i/home.html

The Usenet Info Center Launch Pad offers how-to advice along with a history of Usenet newsgroups. Visitors can search for sites through a comprehensive newsgroup database.

Usenet News Finder

http://www.nova.edu/Inter-Links/cgi-bin/news.pl

The Usenet News Finder offers visitors an electronic query form for ease in locating Internet newsgroups of particular interest.

Utrecht CS News.Answers Frequently Asked Questions Access Methods

http://www.cs.ruu.nl/cgi-bin/faqwais

The Department of Computer Science at the Netherlands' University of Utrecht has collected FAQ files from the Usenet newsgroup, news.answers at this site.

NEW SITE INDEXES

comp.infosystems.www.announce Archive

http://sunsite.unc.edu/gerald/ciwa/

The Usenet newsgroup comp.infosystems.www .announce is archived at this site. Visitors can search for specific Web site announcements, or read about the newsgroup which announces new Web pages and URL address changes.

FAQ: How To Announce Your New Web Site

http://ep.com/faq/webannounce.html

This FAQ, from EPage Internet Classifieds, explains how and where to publicize new Web sites.

NCSA What's New

http://www.ncsa.uiuc.edu/SDG/Software/Mosaic/Docs/whats-new.html

The NCSA Mosaic What's New page gets 1,500 submissions per week, and the page itself is updated three times per week. The site, which catalogs new Web offerings, includes a subject search, an alphabetical listing of new sites and a pick of the week.

NCSA What's New Submission Form

http://www.ncsa.uiuc.edu/SDG/Software/Mosaic/Docs/whats-new-form.html

This interactive site aids visitors in submitting entries to What's New. Only select submissions are encouraged.

Recently Announced World Wide Web Sites

http://www.csci.csusb.edu/doc/www.sites.html

This page lists recently announced Web sites. Links to the new pages (and the designated Web site of the week) provide easy access to Internet current events.

What's New

http://www.netscape.com/home/whats-new.html

What's New is Netscape's offering to the promotion of new sites popping up on the Web. Constantly updated, this page not only connects visitors with the latest sites, but it also allows them to submit new URLs via an online submission form.

What's New for Commercial Sites Index

http://www.directory.net/dir/whats-new.html

This page, maintained by Open Market Inc., alphabetically indexes new commercial sites on the Internet. Includes keyword searching capability and a link to the software corporation's main Web site.

What's New on the Internet?

http://www.clark.net/pub/global/new.html

Visit this page for an index of sites answering the question, "What's new?" Included in the list, are What's New at Yahoo and What's New on the Web.

What's New Too

http://newtoo.manifest.com/WhatsNewToo/index.html

What's New Too posts over 500 new Web sites everyday. Search for worldwide postings by subject or view its exhaustive index. Submissions accepted and posted within 36 hours.

What's New Too Submit Page

http://newtoo.manifest.com/WhatsNewToo/submit.html

What's New Too is a searchable index of new offerings on the Web. People with Web pages can fill out the forms to have their site listed. Visitors can search the databases to find the newest sites on the Web.

PEOPLE DIRECTORIES

Carnegie Mellon University White Pages Query

http://c.gp.cs.cmu.edu:5103/prog/name?

Pittsburgh's Carnegie Mellon University White Pages Query site offers searchable Internet white pages for obtaining online addresses.

Culture—People—Lists—Directories, Home Pages

http://www.december.com/cmc/info/culture-people-lists.html

Thumb through an index of home page directories and Who's Who on the Internet collections at this site. An index of indexes, this site points to ways to locate Web denizens.

E-Mail Web Resources

http://andrew2.andrew.cmu.edu/cyrus/email/email.html

Anyone interested in finding out how to track down the e-mail address of someone can benefit from checking this site from Ohio State University. Check out mail-related FAQs and learn how to access the entire Internet via e-mail only.

ETHZ Phone Book

http://www.ethz.ch/cgi-bin/csoq

The Swiss Federal Institute of Technology, with 5,000 employees, 320 professors and 11,000 students, offers a searchable phone book, updated daily, for its staff members. Visitors can search by name, institute, department, e-mail address or phone number. In English and German.

Four11 White Page Directory

http://www.four11.com/

Four11 claims to be the Internet's largest White Page Directory with over 1.5 million listings and 300,000 registered users. Free listing and searching is supported by Web Page Services and PGP Services.

Hunting for E-Mail Addresses

http://twod.med.harvard.edu/labgc/roth/Emailsearch.html

Trying to find that old college roommate who still owes you for the phone bill? Browsers will find an index to e-mail address-finding resources here. The page includes links to online white pages, WHOIS services and finger gateways.

Inter-Links' Finding People on the Internet Index

http://www.nova.edu/Inter-Links/phone.html

Inter-Links Internet Access, a service of Nova Southeastern University, maintains this site for its Finding People on the Internet Index. Visitors can select from a variety of methods to locate organizations and individuals with an Internet presence.

Internet White Pages

http://home.netscape.com/home/internet-white-pages.html

Browsers looking for individuals in cyberspace can use Netscape's Internet White Pages to link to directories and e-mail address databases to locate people and places across the Web.

LookUP!

http://www.lookup.com/

LookUP! boasts an Internet search engine for locating Web denizens by name or e-mail address. Personal home page services are offered in addition to the e-mail search utility.

Netscape's People and Places

http://home.mcom.com/home/internet-white-pages.html

If you're looking for someone with an e-mail or Web address, Netscape's People and Places provides a hyperlinked list of directory services such as Four 11, Netfind, Knowbot, home page directories, and MIT and Yale's white pages.

SEARCH ENGINES AND GENERAL INDEXES

ALIWEB

http://web.nexor.co.uk/public/aliweb/aliweb.html

ALIWEB is Internet search engine maintained as a public service by the British-based company, NEXOR. Visitors can search the database or read about its history at this site.

ALIWEB Indiana University Mirror

http://www.cs.indiana.edu/aliweb/form.html

Visitors to this Indiana University mirror site can access the British-based Internet search engine, ALIWEB.

All-in-One Search

http://www.albany.net/allinone/

Visitors can conduct multiple searches of the Internet's vast array of contents from a single site. Find access to major Internet search engines, and conduct multiple searches using topic-specific query tools.

AltaVista

http://www.altavista.digital.com/

Digital Equipment Corporation combined a Web crawler with fast scalable indexing software to form an Internet search engine that culls information from over 30 million Web pages. Look for information in the far-reaches of the Internet by calling on the exhaustive searching capabilities of AltaVista.

ArchiePlex Form

http://pubweb.nexor.co.uk/public/archie/archieplex/doc/form.html

This ArchiePlex Form allows users to locate files on anonymous FTP servers anywhere on the Internet. Conduct searches with ease using the electronic form provided, or link to other Archie gateways.

Archie Request Form

http://hoohoo.ncsa.uiuc.edu/archie.html

Archie, a database of anonymous FTP sites, is a useful search tool for finding computer software on the Internet. This form-based Archie gateway for the Web includes a link to the Monster FTP Sites List and a simple, formless search option.

a2z

http://a2z.lycos.com/

Lycos combines its time-tested spider technologies with an effective dose of editorial input to present the a2z directory, a virtual encyclopedia of the Internet's most popular sites. The directory is searchable and browsable by topic. Original descriptions and editorial content supplement an exhaustive database of URLs to help you find what you're looking for.

Australian National University Register of World Wide Web Search Engines

http://coombs.anu.edu.au/CoombswebPages/SearchEngines.html

The Australian National University Register of Web search engines keeps track of information retrieval facilities important to social science and humanities researchers. The site currently boasts links to nearly 50 search engines.

BUBL Information Service Web Server

http://www.bubl.bath.ac.uk/BUBL/Tree.html

Search the Internet by topic with the help of this subject tree index of Internet sites, a service of the Bulletin Board for Libraries at Scotland's University of Strathclyde.

Clearinghouse for Subject-Oriented Internet Resource Guides

http://www.clearinghouse.net/

This site contains a topically-indexed guide that attempts to "identify, describe, and evaluate" Internet resources. Guides are rated according to level of resource, design, and organization. Features a "guide of the month" listing.

CUI Search Engines

http://cuiwww.unige.ch/search-form.html

This Web site, maintained by the University of Geneva's Centre Universitaire d'Informatique, houses several Internet search engines. Visitors can use the tools provided, or link to information about the Swiss school's computer science department.

CUSI at Internet Direct

http://abyss.idirect.com/cusi.html

The Configurable Unified Search Interface allows visitors to search the databases of a collection of Web indexes using keyword queries. Search the contents of online catalogs such as TradeWave's Galaxy, WebCrawler and Lycos from a single jumpstation. This site is a secondary mirror to the primary CUSI server in the United Kingdom.

Experimental Meta-Index

http://www.ncsa.uiuc.edu/SDG/Software/Mosaic/Demo/metaindex.html

This online resource allows visitors to demo various keyword search tools. Choices include the CUI World Wide Web Catalog, the Whole Internet Catalog, Veronica, Jughead and the WAIS directory of servers index.

Find-It

http://www.cam.org/~psarena/find-it.html

Visit Find-It for direct access to several Internet search engines. A browser that supports forms is necessary to utilize the directories.

French Internet Index

http://www.uqat.uquebec.ca/~wwweduc/franc.html

This topical index of Internet resources, maintained by the University of Quebec, provides Web surfers with links to a wide-ranging variety of resources. In French.

Glossary-of-Servers Server

http://gloss.stanford.edu/

GIOSS, the Glossary-of-Servers Server, was developed by Stanford University to locate data sources via query. This site allows browsers to search for a variety of documents.

Harvest Information Discovery and Access System

http://harvest.cs.colorado.edu/

The Harvest Information Discovery and Access System is an "integrated set of tools to gather, extract, organize, search, cache, and replicate relevant information across the Internet." This informational site instructs visitors on how to the configure and use the system in order to increase network efficiency.

Hytelnet Information

http://www.lights.com/hytelnet/

Hytelnet is a utility that gives IBM PC users access to telnet-accessible catalogs, such as gopher and WAIS sites. This guide details proper use of Hytelnet and provides a link to an FTP archive where it can be downloaded.

IBM's Query By Image Content

http://wwwqbic.almaden.ibm.com/~qbic/qbic.html

IBM's Query By Image Content site contains a search engine for large image databases, serving as a demo for QBIC technology. Find links to other QBIC resources and info on IBM products which incorporate the technology.

Indexing a Web Site for ALIWEB

http://www.ai.mit.edu/tools/site-index.html

Learn how to index Web sites for inclusion in the ALIWEB index service. Step-by-step instructions walk Webmasters through the preparation of local and multiple indexes.

Infoseek

http://www.infoseek.com/

Infoseek Corporation's "roadmap to the Internet" is an Internet search service that draws on data from both free and commercial electronic information services. Users can search the Internet index by topic or keyword. Includes tips for formulating successful searches.

InterCAT WebZ

http://www.oclc.org:6990/

InterCAT boasts a searchable index of bibliographic records for Internet resources, courtesy of library catalog services around the world. Access resources by keyword search or by browsing topically-organized categories.

Inter-Links

http://www.nova.edu/Inter-Links/

The public service utility assists Web navigators in finding sought after information and resources. Visitors can take tutorials, read scholarly journals or operate Inter-Links' 12 original search engines.

Internet Cataloging Project: Call for Participation

http://www.oclc.org/oclc/man/catproj/catcall.htm

The Online Computer Library Center strives to secure better access to the world's information via Internet cataloging. The project provides an overview of its growing database of specially formatted bibliographic records and seeks participants to help further its goals.

Internet Directory

http://home.netscape.com/home/internet-directory.html

The Netscape Internet directory exposes visitors to a variety of searching tools, from biggies like Yahoo to more specialized databases like the Environmental Organization Web Directory. Provides descriptions and links to each index.

An Internet Hypertext List (6/16/93)

http://www.cs.indiana.edu/internet/internet.html

This alphabetized laundry list of links circles the globe with a broad band of topics. From Africa Web Servers to the List of Lists, visitors can search by category or keyword.

Internet Resources Indexed by Type of Service

http://www.w3.org/pub/DataSources/ByAccess.html

This page offers a briefly annotated index of other annotated Internet indexes. The site is organized by protocol rather than by subject.

Internet Resources Meta-Index

http://www.ncsa.uiuc.edu/SDG/Software/Mosaic/MetaIndex.html

The Internet Resource Meta-Index is list of indexes to Internet resources. This collection of directories is usefully organized into searchable, subject-ordered and server-cataloging lists. Resources can be navigated in text list or graphical map form.

Internet Resources Metamap

http://www.ncsa.uiuc.edu/SDG/Software/Mosaic/Demo/metamap.html

The Internet Resources Metamap, provided by the NCSA, offers a graphical format for locating information on the Internet. Visit here for a virtual map of resources on the Web, plus pointers to gopher servers, WAIS directories and government agencies.

Internet Search

http://home.netscape.com/home/internet-search.html

Web surfers can find the needle in the virtual haystack with the help of this Netscape Communications Corp. page. Visitors will find a variety of Internet search engines here, including offerings from Lycos, AltaVista, WebCrawler and Infoseek.

The Internet Services List

http://slacvx.slac.stanford.edu/misc/internet-services.html

The Internet Services List is a discriminating index of sites organized topically and presented alphabetically. The online reference features frequent updates to content and a what's cool listing.

InterNIC Directory and Database Services

http://www.internic.net/

AT&T provides this directory and database service, partially supported through a cooperative agreement with the National Science Foundation. Visitors will find an index of pointers to general resources, products and services accessible to the Internet. The site also includes a collection of public-access databases containing information of interest to the Internet community.

IS Workgroup, Search Page

http://www_is.cs.utwente.nl:8080/cgi-bin/local/nph-susi1.pl

Find a collection of search engines at the IS Workgroup Search Page. Searchable guides to information servers, software libraries, people, publications and news are all accessible from this site.

A List of Various Subject Matter Guides

gopher://una.hh.lib.umich.edu/11/inetdirsstacks

The University of Minnesota's library posts Internet directories on a full range of topics, from Africa to women's studies. Within its area of stated expertise, each directory provides links to sites of interest from the far-flung corners of the Internet.

A List of Virtual Libraries on the Web

http://www.w3.org/pub/DataSources/bySubject/Virtual_libraries/Overview.html

This Web site connects visitors with various tools for finding information on the Internet. Links to many virtual and searchable libraries, including CyberSight and the Whole Internet Catalog, are featured.

LLNL List of Lists

http://www.llnl.gov/llnl/lists/listsl.html

The LLNL List of Lists is a comprehensive collection of Internet search engines and locators. Visitors can search by detailed categories or utilize other query options to pinpoint the location of resources on the Internet. Includes a detailed catalog of scientific and research resources

Lycos

http://www.lycos.com/

Lycos, the self-proclaimed "catalog of the Internet," offers a powerful search engine developed by the smart computer science types at Carnegie Mellon University. The company integrates encyclopedic directory services into its exhaustive indexing and search capabilities, bringing the Web world to your virtual doorstep and explaining it to boot.

Magellan

http://www.mckinley.com/

The McKinley Group develops Internet searching tools and informational directories. Visitors here can use the company's search engine, Magellan, and get an overview of the company's other services.

Monster FTP Sites List

http://hoohoo.ncsa.uiuc.edu/ftp/

Visitors can download the Monster FTP Sites List, a 21-part index to FTP archives across the Internet. The page also includes an introduction to the list and FAQs about anonymous FTP sites.

Mother-of-all BBS

http://wwwmbb.cs.colorado.edu/~mcbryan/bb/summary.html

From the American Disabilities Act to zoos, the Mother of All BBS serves up an extensive list of links to subject-oriented bulletin boards and Web sites. Find other BBS indexing resources and a form for submitting sites to the list.

NEXOR's Public Services

http://pubweb.nexor.co.uk/

NEXOR details the public services it offers to the Internet community at this page. Focusing on searches, standards and directories, the page contains such items as links to the RFC Index, the ArchiePlex Archie Service and the ALIWEB distributed cooperative catalog.

Oldenburg Archie Gateway

http://marvin.physik.uni-oldenburg.de/Docs/net-serv/archie-gate.html

Looking for an FTP site from which to download software or text files? Visit this site for access to the Archie tool which locates FTP sites by using a variety of search types.

The Otis Index—Searching the Internet

http://www.interlog.com/~gordo/otis_pubsearch.html

This interactive page from the Otis Index provides access to over a half-dozen Web search engines. Among those tools featured are Lycos, Yahoo, Infoseek, and WebCrawler.

Outils de Recherche World Wide Web

http://www.risq.net/outilwww.html

This interactive page contains a variety of online Internet search tools. In French.

Planet Earth

http://www.nosc.mil/planet_earth/info.html

This virtual library provides a host of links to information on science, world regions, and governmental and educational institutions. Also includes reference and multimedia resources and a search engine collection.

Point

http://www.pointcom.com/

Point Communications has compiled a comprehensive collection of Web site reviews to aid discriminating users in locating quality information and entertainment resources on the Internet. Search the entire survey of reviews, or browse through a database of sites receiving "Top 5% of the Web" honors from the company.

Quarterdeck: Net Search

http://www.qdeck.com/cusi.html

Visitors to the Quarterdeck: Net Search site will find a full complement of Web search engines. Categories of tools featured include Web indexes, software, directories and dictionaries.

RBSE's URL database

http://rbse.jsc.nasa.gov/eichmann/urlsearch.html

A searchable index, this site allows visitors to sift through a collection of URLs by entering keywords. Includes pointers to other Web spiders and several papers on Internet search devices.

Recyclinx

http://www.amsmain.com/cgi-amsmain/recyclinx

Recyclinx offers a searchable list of Web links. Visitors can view random links, search for whatever suits their interests, or opt to add a new link to the recycling bin.

RiceInfo: Internet Navigation Tools

http://riceinfo.rice.edu/Internet/

This guide to Internet navigation, provided by Rice University, provides a comprehensive index of search resources. Visit here to find the best tools for searching for information by subject, keyword, location and other criteria.

SavvySearch

http://www.cs.colostate.edu/~dreiling/smartform.html

SaavySearch does electronic research for browsers. A smart Internet query tool, SaavySearch takes keyword queries and feeds them through a group of Internet search engines. The responses are compiled and returned to the requester as a single list of linked results.

Search Engines

http://oneworld.wa.com/htmldev/devpage/search.html

Having all of the information in the world on the Web can be of little use unless you have an effective method for sifting through it. Look to this site for a convenient collection of major Internet search engines, plus directories, catalogs and software libraries.

Search Engines on Internet

http://www.cwi.nl/cusi.html

Finding people, files or Web pages is not a problem with the search engines and indexes at this site. Visitors can use the electronic forms provided to search a number of comprehensive Internet indexes and databases.

Searching the Web

http://mosaic.larc.nasa.gov/facts/search.html

Most Web users know about search engines, but not everyone is familiar with the full breadth of the Internet query tools available. This list from NASA provides links to both big and small search engines, and expounds upon the differences between FTP, gopher, WWW and WAIS.

Searching the Web

http://union.ncsa.uiuc.edu/HyperNews/get/www/searching.html

The prosaically named Searching the Web site offers what you would expect, references to searching services and software. Additionally find Web tutorials and explanations of Internet terms and standards.

Search the IBM Planetwide Web

http://www.ibm.com/Search/

IBM, the U.S. computing powerhouse, specializes in computer systems and business machines. This site is a service provided by IBM for visitors to search for information on the Internet. Included is a link to IBM's home page.

Search The Internet with The Internet Sleuth

http://www.isleuth.com/

Featuring a collection of over 750 searchable databases, this site offers keyword access to the Web. For those who prefer to browse, an index of topics is also featured.

Senrigan Search

http://www.info.waseda.ac.jp/search.html

An Internet search engine helps Japanese speakers navigate the Web. In Japanese.

SenseMedia Surfer

http://sensemedia.net/

The SenseMedia Surfer is a resource for effective Web surfing. Visitors will find an entertaining mix of original news and entertainment content, as well as links to a vast number of Web sites.

Sok BIBSYS

http://www.bibsys.no/search/pubn.html

Learn about BIBSYS search tools at this site. In Norwegian.

Super Searcher

http://www.iquest.net/iq/reference.html

IQuest Network Services presents Super Search-er, a site that unites popular and useful Web searchers on a single page.

Surf-N-Search Engine

http://www.infohiway.com/index.html

This page presents an alternative approach to search engines called "surf engines." Includes a virtual tour of home pages, geographical listings on international Web sites, as well as surfers for Web, gopher and FTP servers.

SWISH Documentation

http://www.eit.com/software/swish/swish.html

The Simple Web Indexing System for Humans is explained and documented at this site. Includes instructions for downloading the program and a tutorial.

The-Inter.net

http://the-inter.net/www/future21/

The-Inter.net is a free, public-access information server, with a broad collection of information and online resources. The subject matter covers a wide range of topics, including links to sporting news, personal home pages, love connections, modem information and virtual reality demos.

University of Texas at Austin Internet Search

http://www.utexas.edu/search

The University of Texas at Austin groups local and Web-wide search engines at the handy Searching the Internet page. Query the school's own Web servers for info, or conduct keyword searches of other university libraries, e-mail ad-dress directories and general Internet indexes.

Verity Virtual Library

http://www.verity.com/vlibsearch.html

The Verity Virtual Library site contains a full-text search engine for the Web. Options include a search refinement tool. Helpful tips assist first-time users.

WAIS Content Router

http://www-psrg.lcs.mit.edu/Projects/CRS/content-router.html

If you're looking for information on WAIS servers, this content router provides query refinement and routing to over 500 sites. Includes tips for ef-fective searching.

WAIS Inc.

http://www.wais.com/

WAIS Inc., a supplier of online publishing sys-tems, maintains this home page offering informa-tion about the company, its products and services. Features include a demonstration of the company's keyword search tool.

WebCrawler Lightning Fast Web Search

http://webcrawler.com/WebCrawler/WebQuery.html

The WebCrawler search mechanism allows users to search the Internet by keyword. Includes help files to demystify the process, a listing of 25 fa-vored Web sites and a random link generator for agenda-free Web surfers.

WebCrawler Searching

http://webcrawler.com/

WebCrawler is an Internet search engine owned by America Online. Find Internet resources by en-tering keywords into the form provided, or sub-mit URLs to WebCrawler's database.

WebCrawler URL Registry

http://webcrawler.com/WebCrawler/SubmitURLS.html

America Online's WebCrawler Internet search en-gine maintains this site for URL registration. Visit here to register your Web site or home page for inclusion in the information retrieval service.

Where.Com Index

http://where.com/ls/LinkSearch.html

Browsers can choose from dozens of search en-gines at the Where.Com Index. The site includes Web, software and document search tools.

World Internet Technologies

http://www.wit.com/

Providing free access to information sources on the Internet is the mission of World Internet Tech-nologies. Electronically reproduced art, books and music compose the public offerings at this site. Includes public domain software collected and developed by WIT.

The World Wide Web Power Index from Web Communications

http://www.webcom.com/~webcom/power/index.html

Covering a wide area of interests, this categorical index links visitors to topic-specific indexes. Move from art to weather with the click of a mouse.

World-Wide Web Search Engines

http://www.amdahl.com/internet/meta-index.html

The Amdahl Corporation's Search Engine site aims to meet the challenge of finding an info nee-dle in the Web haystack. Among the many resourc-es included are Web catalogs, software, and search engines for people, publications and news.

W3 Search Engines

http://www.lib.ncsu.edu/meta-index.html

An extensive index of search engines on the Web is provided at this site. Visitors can link to engines to track down information servers, software, people, publications, news and documentation on the Web.

World Wide Web Servers Index

http://cuiwww.unige.ch/meta-index.html

The Centre Universitaire d'Informatique of the University of Geneva maintains this site for its in-dex of Web search engines. Visitors can select from a comprehensive collection of information retrieval tools, organized by search topic.

Yahoo

http://www.yahoo.com

The granddaddy of Internet directories, Yahoo was started as procrastination fodder for a couple of prospective engineers at Stanford University but has ended up as a multimillion dollar Goliath in the race to cash in on catalogs of the Internet. Find a topically-organized index of the Web com-plete with search functions, reviews, and infor-mation accessories.

Scott Yanoff's Internet Services List

http://www.spectracom.com/islist

Scott Yanoff's Internet Services List contains a long list of resources organized into categories such as agriculture, aviation, games, literature, software and travel. Find an alphabetical list of links supporting the range of topics indexed.

SERVER DIRECTORIES BY GEOGRAPHIC LOCATION

Alabama World Wide Web Server List

http://www.eng.auburn.edu/alabama/web.html

"Git online" could be the battle cry of the Ala-bama World Wide Web Server List. Locate links to information servers in the southern state using the index compiled by Auburn University.

Arizona Destinations World Wide Web Server

http://www.amdest.com/

The Arizona Internet Yellow Pages connects visi-tors with attractions, services and an online shop-ping mall, among other Arizona-based Internet servers. This large document includes links to Ar-izona Kids Net, photo galleries and more.

Arizona World-Wide Web Servers

http://www.eas.asu.edu/az/servers.html

This site, a public service of the University of Ari-zona, features an alphabetical list of Arizona Web servers.

Aussie Index

http://www.aussie.com.au/

The Aussie Index catalogs all that is Australian on the Web. Divided into commercial and noncommercial databases, visitors can search or browse this enormous offering of the country's electronic resources.

Australian Internet Directories

http://www.sofcom.com.au/WWW.AU/

This collection of Australian Internet directories provides online tourists with tools to search Aussie Web sites, Usenet newsgroups and e-mail address listings. Includes a link to the home page of Sofcom, this directory's maintainer.

Australian Web Servers

http://www.csu.edu.au/links/ozmap.html

Charles Stuart University maintains this interactive map providing information about Web servers in Australia. Visitors also can access a geographically categorized listing of Australian servers or indexes offering links to tourist, weather and governmental resources.

Boston Area Map of World Wide Web Resources

http://donald.phast.umass.edu/misc/boston.html

This interactive map, created by the University of Massachusetts' Astronomy Department, shows locations of Web servers in the Boston area. Visitors can select a listed name or symbol near the site's location to link to that server.

British Columbia World Wide Web Servers

http://freenet.victoria.bc.ca/bcw3list.html

Map the electronic landscape of western Canada using this list of British Columbia's Web servers. Visitors will find an extensive collection of links to servers and selected home pages in the region.

Charles University Czech Servers Gopher

gopher://gopher.cuni.cz:70/1

The Computer Centre for Charles University in Prague, Czech Republic, features links to other gophers in the country and public information services. Highlights include links to the Czech Educational and Scientific Network and the Prague Academic and Scientific Network.

China World Wide Web Server List

http://www.ihep.ac.cn/china_www.html

This index provides a listing of Web servers in China. Includes links to the China Home Page, Chinese education-related servers, ChinaNet, and GlobalNet.

Czech Republic World Wide Web Server List

http://www.cesnet.cz/cesnet/wwwservers.html

This site provides a lengthy list of Web servers in the Czech Republic. Visitors can link to governmental, commercial, and educational resources.

DENet Web

http://info.denet.dk/

The home page for DENet, the Danish Research Network, offers links to its Denmark centers and services (in Danish), and links to Denmark-related resources (in English). Includes a clickable map of the country and pointers to Danish e-mail directories and servers.

Dónde?

http://www.uji.es/spain_www.html

This Spanish Internet resource directory provides pointers to Internet servers and access providers in Spain. Also included is a search engine for e-mail addresses and general information on the country.

EENeti

http://www.eenet.ee/

EENeti World Wide Web server connects browsers to the Estonian Educational and Research Network. Visitors can link to all Internet sites in Estonia. The service is provided in English and Estonian.

Freie University, Berlin World Wide Web Server Index

http://www.chemie.fu-berlin.de/outerspace/www-german.html

The Department of Chemistry at the Freie University in Berlin, Germany, maintains this site for an index of German Web servers. Visitors can browse by server location or search by keyword.

Germany World Wide Web Server Registry

http://www.chemie.fu-berlin.de/outerspace/www-register.html

The World Wide Web Register Service for Germany offers pointers to sites across the country. In German.

H.I.T. World Wide Web Server

http://www.hi-tech.ac.jp/

This Japanese server provides links to other servers in Japan and around the world. In Japanese.

Hong Kong World Wide Web Sites and Pages

http://www.hk.super.net/~johnb/hkmap.html

Navigate Hong Kong's online landscape with the maps provided at the Hong Kong World Wide Web Server and Pages site. Visitors can browse Internet offerings using the pointers provided.

Icelandic World Wide Web Servers

http://www.rfisk.is/english/sites.html

A comprehensive index of virtually all Web servers in Iceland is featured at this site. Servers are listed according to the categories of education, government, networks and communications. Specific

servers run the gamut from the Icelandic Fisheries Laboratories to Hewlett-Packard in Iceland.

Illinois World Wide Web Servers

http://cs-www.uchicago.edu/html/external/illinois/illinois-text.html

The University of Chicago maintains this site to provide an index of Web servers in the Illinois area. Includes links to a variety of business, government, and institutional Web sites.

Information Resource Map of Finland

http://www.funet.fi/resources/clickable-Suomi.html

This map allows users to plot the Information Superhighway's route across the country of Finland. Use the map to link to Finnish information servers, or look up general statistics about the regions depicted. In English and Finnish.

Irish National Information Server

http://www.hea.ie/

This Irish information server provides links to universities, research groups and business resources located on the Emerald Isle. Includes pointers to government and media sites, arts and music information, and educational resources.

Japan World Wide Web Server List

http://www.ntt.co.jp/SQUARE/www-in-JP-j.html

A catalog of Japanese Web information servers is available, as well as details about the major links offered at each site. In Japanese and English.

Jubii

http://www.jubii.dk/

Jubii offers a comprehensive listing of all that is Danish on the Internet. In Danish

Kvasir

http://kvasir.oslonett.no/kvasir/

This site contains the home page of Kvasir, the OsloNett information server. Visitors are presented a variety of information options including a keyword search tool and access to Norway-based Internet sites and tools. In Norwegian.

Liste des Serveurs W3 en France

http://www.urec.fr/cgi-bin/list

This page provides a list of 1,246 Web servers in France. The list is alphabetized for easy access. In French.

List of Multimedia Servers in Poland

http://info.fuw.edu.pl/pl/servers-list.html

The List of Multimedia Servers in Poland provides an exhaustive collection of Polish technical university computer resources. Visit here to browse its alphabetical listing of Polish Web servers.

Luxembourg World Wide Web Server List

http://www.restena.lu/other/luxservers.html

Visitors can link to a variety of Web sites through this topically-indexed listing of servers located in the Grand Duchy of Luxembourg. Includes a link to the home page of Luxembourg's National Network for Education and Research, the maintainer of this directory.

Macom Networking Ltd.

http://www.macom.co.il/

Located in Jerusalem, the Macom Networking Ltd. server is a gateway to Israeli online resources and Web sites.

Maryland World Wide Web Servers

http://www.fie.com/www/maryland.htm

The Federal Information Exchange Inc. has compiled this list of servers in Maryland. An annotated list of servers, the alphabetized index entries range in style from the super corporate the grungy underground.

Massachusetts Map of World Wide Web Resources

http://www-astro.phast.umass.edu/misc/mass.html

Located at this site is an interactive map detailing the locations of Web servers in Massachusetts. Created by the University of Massachusetts' astronomy department, the site includes separate maps for the Boston and Amherst areas.

MO Media Email List

http://www.crl.com/~becnel/momedia.html

For a list of Missouri media entities that have electronic addresses, turn to the MO Media Email List home page. Print, television, and radio resources—and a whole lot mo'—are available here.

Netherlands Index

http://www.nic.surfnet.nl/nlmenu.eng/w3all.html

This site contains an extensive A to Z index of sites located in the Netherlands. In English and Dutch.

Netherlands World Wide Web Server Map

http://www.eeb.ele.tue.nl/map/netherlands.html

The Netherlands' W4 Internet Consultancy maintains this site for its Dutch Home Page Internet directory. Visitors will find an extensive index of Dutch commercial, government, and educational resources.

Network Resources in Czech Republic

http://www.cesnet.cz/html/cesnet/map.html

This site features a directory of Internet resources available in the Czech Republic, including Web,

FTP, gopher and Usenet news services. Visitors can use either a text directory or a clickable imagemap to obtain information.

Nordic W4 Project, Automatic Indexing and Classification of WAIS databases

http://www.ub2.lu.se/auto_new/UDC.html

This site is the Web subject tree of WAIS databases. It contains a stable of subject categories within which to search, including applied sciences, medicine, linguistics, literature, religion, and sports.

Northern Nevada Web Server

http://www.scs.unr.edu/index.html

The Northern Nevada Web is a service of the University and Community College System of Nevada, which is comprised of seven schools. This site features links to the schools' servers as well as an index of Nevada Internet resources.

Norwegian Web Sites

http://www.service.uit.no/homepage-no

If you're looking to reach Norway via the Web, consult this list of links to Norwegian Web servers and Internet resources. Find both English and Norwegian language sites listed.

Poland World Wide Web Server Map

http://info.fuw.edu.pl/pl/PolandResourceMap.html

The Poland World Wide Web Server Map consists of an overview of multimedia servers in Poland. Browsers can select sites by clicking on a provided map or search through a text-only index categorized by location.

Portugal WWW Servers.

http://s700.uminho.pt/Portugal/all-pt.html

This Portugal Web server contains links to the countries Web servers. Includes links to universities, businesses and government sites.

Russian World Wide Web Servers

http://www.ac.msk.su/map_list.html

This index presents a listing of Russian servers arranged alphabetically by city. Includes a link to an interactive map of Russian sites.

Slovak World Wide Web Servers

http://www.tuzvo.sk/list.html

A comprehensive index of Slovak World Wide Web servers is maintained at this site.

South Africa World Wide Web Server List

http://www.is.co.za/www-za.html

The visitor to this page will find an annotated listing of Web servers in South Africa arranged by geographic location. Includes links to other South African Web indexes.

SUNET—Swedish University Network

http://www.sunet.se/

SUNET, the Swedish University Network, provides information about Swedish Internet resources. Visitors will also find software archives and a variety of Internet search and information services.

Thailand World Wide Web Server Map

http://www.chiangmai.ac.th/Servers-th.html

This index of Thailand Web servers includes pointers to the Asian Institute of Technology, Bangkok University and Cockatoo Press Online. E-mail instructions for Thai server submissions are included.

UNINETT's Meta Indeks

http://www.service.uit.no/uninett/index.html

UNINETT's Meta Indeks page furnishes browsers with a directory of Norway's Web resources. In Norwegian.

United Kingdom Based World Wide Web Servers

http://src.doc.ic.ac.uk/all-uk.html

This site attempts to group together all Web servers in the United Kingdom. Visitors can use a search engine or a sensitive map of the U.K.

U.K. Directory

http://www.ukdirectory.com/

U.K. Directory, a comprehensive guide to everything on the Web in the United Kingdom, offers a huge, searchable index. Subject categories range from business and employment information to entertainment, sports and travel news.

URL Square

http://www.ntt.co.jp/SQUARE/

URL Square offers a virtual library of links to directories of Internet resources, primarily in Japan. Visitors can link to a wide range of topics from publishing and business news to online shopping malls and multimedia. In English and Japanese.

Vermont/New Hampshire Map of WWW Resources

http://www.destek.net/Maps/VT-NH.html

This map-based interface links visitors to info servers in Vermont and New Hampshire. The servers of colleges and medical facilities are featured, along with home pages of towns and cities.

Virginia World Wide Web Servers

http://www.fie.com/www/virginia.htm

This site provides detailed descriptions of and access to an array of servers throughout the state of Virginia. Visitors will find links ranging from activist organizations to corporate home pages.

Web Texas

http://www.utexas.edu/texas/

Web Texas is the official University of Texas registration site for servers operating in that state. The Austin-based page has links to registered servers, with the Texas sites arranged in categories according to type.

West Virginia World Wide Web Servers

http://www.marshall.edu/wvweb/

Discover West Virginia with the aid of this map-based interface. Click a city, and find links to the Web servers in that area. General state information is also available.

World Wide Web Servers: Massachusetts

http://sturtevant.com/wwwlist/mas.html

This alphabetical listing of Massachusetts-based Web servers provides an annotated index of the state's online resources.

The World Wide Web List of Servers: Server Registration

http://www.w3.org/pub/DataSources/WWW/Geographical_generation/new.html

The World Wide Web Consortium produces computer software to develop common standards for the Internet. Visit this site to register a Web server on its world list.

World Wide Web Servers: South Africa (Map)

http://www.is.co.za/www-za/www-za-map.html

Consult this list of servers to research Internet offerings from South Africa. Use the map provided to navigate a wide range of electronic resources originating in the African country.

World-Wide Web Servers: Summary

http://www.w3.org/pub/DataSources/WWW/Servers.html

This page offers a comprehensive list of Web servers, arranged alphabetically by continent, country and state. Includes instructions on how to send announcements of new servers.

SITE OF THE DAY AND COOL PAGE PICKS

All-Internet Shopping Directory: All-In-One Cool Sites

http://www.webcom.com/~tbrown/coolsite.html

The All-In-One Cool Sites page wants to eliminate bookmark list clutter forever by providing top

Web picks organized by subject category. Peruse what the Webmasters believe to the cream of the online crop.

Amdahl's World Wide Web Hot Topics

http://www.amdahl.com/internet/hot.html

This "hot topics" index offers a collection of links to various Web sites of current interest. Visitors will find links to sites on politics, engineering, sports and news. "This day in history" information is available here as well.

The Awesome Lists

http://www.clark.net/pub/journalism/awesome.html

An Internet consultant and columnist offers an index to his picks for the top 100 sites on the Internet. The page also includes Web and Usenet search engines.

Barbara's Best Bookmark of the Day

http://www.shsu.edu/users/std/stdkco/pub2/best.html

This personal home page promises to link visitors to an interesting Web site each day. Includes an archive of past picks, the content of which ranges from chat areas to digital birdhouses.

Bat's Catch of the Day

http://batech.com/catch.html

Bat's Catch of the Day features a daily link to different Web sites favored by the author. Browsers can view past daily picks, and are invited to submit their comments and suggestions.

Best of the Web Contest

http://wings.buffalo.edu/contest/

The online home of the Best of the Web Awards posts rules for the contest which allows Web users to nominate and cast ballots for outstanding sites. Review past winners, and link to information about the current competition.

Best of the Web '94 Recipients

http://wings.buffalo.edu/contest/awards/

Link to the winners in the Best of the Web '94 competition. Over a dozen categories are featured, including the Best Overall Site.

Cool Jargon of the Day

http://www.bitech.com/jargon/cool

Browsers can keep hip here. The site defines hacker slang, adding a new term daily. It also includes links to jargon dictionaries on the Internet.

Cool Site of the Day

http://cool.infi.net/

Cool Site of the Day, a service of Norfolk, Va.-based Internet service provider Infi.Net, provides links to interesting and informative Web sites. Visit here for its daily updates in a variety of subject categories.

Dynamite Site of the Nite

http://www.netzone.com/~tti/dsotn.html

Every day, the Dynamite Site of the Nite page posts its oddball pick for Web browser fodder. Find current and past picks archived, with a heavy emphasis on the counter culture, conspiracy theories and entertainment news.

Geek Site of the Day

http://www.owlnet.rice.edu/~indigo/gsotd/

Are we losers? The Webmaster at Geek Site of the Day says we are—and all we did was link to his page. If you enjoy being insulted too, visit this extensive collection of "geeky" Web resources, updated daily.

Hot Hot List

http://www.ccsf.caltech.edu/~roy/others.html

The Hot Hot List indexes a large collection of Web sites and documents. Burning categories include the likes of cities, multimedia, food and literature.

Fred Langa's Web HotSpots

http://www.winmag.com/flanga/hotspots.htm

CMP Publishing's WinWebMag editorial director posts his daily pick of hot Web sites. See what unusual reaches of the Internet that Fred has chosen for his visitors, or link to the company's commercial magazine online offerings.

MagicURL Mystery Trip

http://www.netcreations.com/magicurl/index.html

Sometimes the site's host says it all: "Imagine a place where every random link goes somewhere cool ... No college home pages, no MAKE MONEY FAST, no 'hi, I'm Biff, and I'm into TV!' Every link is hand selected by me, and I'm picky. Feel free to submit a link to me!" Who is he? Ryan Scott at NetCreations Inc.

Mkgray's List of Cool Stuff on the Web

http://www.mit.edu:8001/afs/sipb/project/www/html/starting-points.html

Mkgray's List of Cool Stuff on the Web attempts to cover all the bases, boasting of links composed of "everything from sex to cryptography to Star Trek." Category heads include raw information, commercial stuff, weather, books and online exhibits.

NetWatch Top Ten

http://www.pulver.com/netwatch/topten/tt13.htm

The NetWatch Top Ten is a regular feature in the monthly e-zine, NetWatch, which is devoted to the emerging technologies and content of the Web. Find the editors' picks which can run the gamut from the top ten women's sites on the Web to the top ten Internet tools and applications.

Random URLs from the WebCrawler

http://webcrawler.com/cgi-bin/random

America Online-owned search engine, Web-Crawler, spices up your online exploration with a ten-link dose of randomly selected URLs. New adventure picks are posted every day.

Toadsearch

http://sodom.mt.cs.cmu.edu/htbin/toadsearch

Visitors to this interactive site will find a keyword search engine that looks for URLs whose page content contains the search string. From "Toad's Hotlist."

Web Site of the Week

http://www.duke-net.com/wsw/

The Web Site of the Week highlights a new site weekly that the authors deem worthy of viewing. All previously selected sites are listed, along with a brief description of their content.

What's Cool?

http://home.netscape.com/home/whats-cool.html

Netscape Communications Corporation, makers of popular Web navigational software, periodically posts pointers to "what's cool" in the eyes of the mainstream Internet juggernaut's team of sage surfers. Links lead explorers to interesting, adventurous, and sometimes useful Web pages.

What's Hot and Cool

http://kzsu.stanford.edu/cgi-bin/uwi/reviews.pl?3

This index provides descriptions of and links to oddball and interesting sites on Web. Visitors with a taste for high weirdness can sift through a heady brew of anarchy, sarcasm, music, roadkill and art. Bring your bookmarks and check out cyberspace's sickly white underbelly.

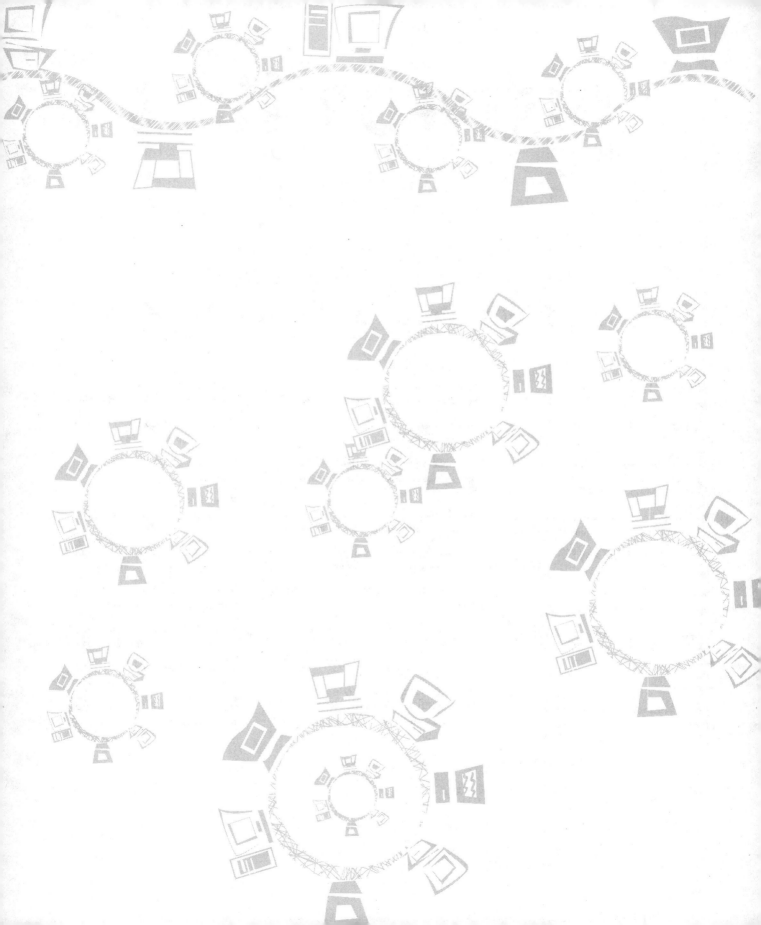

JUST FOR KIDS

THE 25 MOST POPULAR SITES JUST FOR KIDS

Aunt Annie's Craft Page
http://www.auntannie.com/

BHI Teens 90210
http://www.asiaconnect.com.my/90210/

The Big Busy House: HarperCollins Children's Books
http://www.harpercollins.com/kids/

The Canadian Kids Home Page
http://www.onramp.ca/~lowens/107kids.htm

Dole 5 A Day Home Page
http://www.dole5aday.com/

The Dove Foundation
http://www.dove.org/

Encyclopedia of Women's History— Written by and for the K–12 Community
http://www.teleport.com/~megaines/women.html

Global Show-n-Tell Museum Wings
http://www.manymedia.com/show-n-tell/

Horse Country
http://www.pathology.washington.edu/Horse/

Hyperman
http://www.hyperman.com/

Interesting Places for Kids
http://www.crc.ricoh.com/people/steve/kids.html

KID List
http://www.clark.net/pub/journalism/kid.html

Kiddin' Around
http://alexia.lis.uiuc.edu/~watts/kiddin.html

Kidlink: Global Networking for Youth 10–15
http://www.kidlink.org/

Kids on Campus
http://www.tc.cornell.edu/cgi-bin/Kids.on.Campus/top.pl

Kids Web—A World Wide Web Digital Library for Schoolkids
http://www.npac.syr.edu/textbook/kidsweb/

Latitude28 Schoolhouse
http://www2.opennet.com/schoolhouse/

North Pole Web
http://north.pole.org/santa/

Nye Labs Online
http://nyelabs.kcts.org/

Press Return
http://199.95.184.10/public/Network/PressReturn/Press-Return.html

The Realist Wonder Society
http://www.wondersociety.com/

School House Rock Page
http://iquest.com/~bamafan/shr/

Uncle Bob's Kids' Page
http://gagme.wwa.com/~boba/kidslinks.html

Virtual Jack-O-Lantern
http://www.chaco.com/~glenn/jack/

You Can with Beakman & Jax
http://www.nbn.com:80/youcan/

Aunt Annie's Craft Page

http://www.auntannie.com/

Aunt Annie's Craft Page is chock-full of creative learning projects—including papercraft, puppetry, .gif images for stickers, fabric angels, cardboard tapestry dolls, personalized lunch bags, and much more.

Beakman's Electric Motor

http://fly.hiwaay.net:80/~palmer/motor.html

Here, kids can learn how to build a simple electric motor like the one on television's "Beakman's World" using just a few household items. Diagrams are included. See Editor's Choice.

Berit's Best Sites for Children

http://www.cochran.com/theosite/ksites.html

Berit's Best Sites for Children indexes, annotates and rates selected children's pages on the Web. Featured topics include activity centers, pages by kids for kids, family and kids' home pages, games and toys, world travel and more.

BHI Teens 90210

http://www.cochran.com/theosite/ksites.html

Beverly Hills Internet's Teens 90210 site is a virtual hangout any kid can call home. Here, kids under 18 can submit their own home pages.

The Big Busy House

http://www.harpercollins.com/kids/

The Big Busy House, the Web home for Harper-Collins Children's Books, features interviews with authors and illustrators and explains how a book is made.

Canadian Kids Home Page

http://www.onramp.ca/~lowens/107kids.htm

The Canadian Kids page is a Web "starting place for both the young and the young at heart." Pointers are provided to "great Canadian pages" ranging from Theodore Tugboat and SchoolNet to Street Cents Online and Women in Canadian History. See Editor's Choice, page 690.

Children's Literature Web Guide

http://www.ucalgary.ca/~dkbrown/index.html

The Children's Literature Web Guide contains a huge searchable archive of Internet resources related to books for children. Visitors will find lists of recommended books, discussion groups, online stories and much more. See Editor's Choice, page 691.

The Children's Page

http://www.comlab.ox.ac.uk/oucl/users/jonathan.bowen/children.html

The Children's Page is a family project where everyone has a home page: Mommy and Daddy, Emma and Alice. Children's joke pages, calendars, sound clips, games, museums, movie clips and other family-oriented links are included.

A Christmas Toy Trek

http://www.dash.com/netro/fun/ttrek/ttrek.html

Join Tillie, Dusty and Barbie for "A Christmas Toy Trek." This Apple QuickTime-enhanced virtual visit to the North Pole includes Santa's home, sleigh, and toy workshop.

Crayola

http://www.crayola.com/crayola/

Check out the Crayola home page for all the news and information about the world's favorite crayons. Find details on such Crayola developments as changeable crayons, mini-stampers and sunlight prints.

 EDITOR'S CHOICE

Beakman's Electric Motor

http://fly.hiwaay.net:80/~palmer/motor.html

A fan of the television show "Beakman's World" created this page with instructions for building the simple electric motor featured on the show. Perfect for children, only a few materials are required, most of them common household items. The step-by-step instructions and diagrams are clear, so this would make a good science project for an older child or a fun experiment for adults to try with younger children. The author also provides tips for further experiments with the motor and advice in case the motor is used as a school project. For those using text-only browsers, the diagrams can be downloaded as .gif files. —*Reviewed by Amy Hembree*

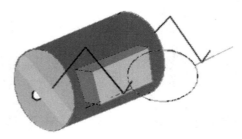

Figure: Motor.gif

*I saw this on the TV show **Beakman's World** and I was very impressed that you could actually build a working electric motor with so few parts. I built one and brought it to work and it was a big hit with all the engineers around here. This writeup was for a friend of mine who wanted instructions that his son could follow for a science fair project. So, if you missed the show, here's how to build one. If you are using a text only browser, you can click on the "Figure" links to download the drawing s (GIF files). BTW, my friend's son won second place in the school's science fair. BTW, I am not Beakman, nor do I have anything to do with the show. I am just a fan...*

Crayola Kids

http://www.crayola.com/crayola/crayolakids/2_4/home.html

Here, kids will find an electronic version of Crayola's magazine, "Crayola Kids" with games, contests and details about new toys.

CyberKids Home

http://www.cyberkids.com/

Mountain Lake Software's CyberKids Web site features a free online magazine and games galore as part of its effort to help kids learn about the Internet while having fun. Visitors can enter a writing contest or explore the world at the CyberLaunchpad.

Doug and Lisa's Disney Home Page

http://www.lido.com/disney/

At this unofficial Disney page, visitors will find loads of trivia and information about Disney theme parks, movie art and animated films. A Frequently Asked Questions (FAQs) file is included, as are links to other Disney resources.

Dole 5 A Day Home Page

http://www.dole5aday.com/

The Dole 5 A Day home page reminds visitors to get five servings a day of fruits and vegetables. The "Fun with Fruits and Vegetables Kids Cookbook" makes the concept more appealing to kids.

Ear Mountain Radio

http://www.nettiradio.fi/test/santa/saneng.htm

Ear Mountain Radio, the official Santa Claus radio station, broadcasts from Finland, close to the North Pole. Santa is off-duty until next December (the Webmaster tells us), so tune in then with your letters to Santa.

Edge

http://www.jayi.com/jayi/Fishnet/Edge/

"Edge" is the bimonthly cyberzine for high-performance students. It's filled with provocative, cutting-edge stories, reviews and insights for teens who want to go the extra mile.

FishNet

http://www.jayi.com/jayi/Open.html

FishNet is a Web space for academically talented teens. It features a college guide, a conversation forum and a huge database of articles and details about educational opportunities. See Editor's Choice, page 692.

Global Show-n-Tell Museum Wings

http://www.telenaut.com/gst/

Global Show-n-Tell, a virtual exhibition space for children, provides this forum for kids to show off their favorite possessions, projects, accomplishments and collections. Visit the free exhibition and submit your own entry.

Gordon's Entomological Home Page

http://www.ex.ac.uk/~gjlramel/welcome.html

This kid-friendly page is a terrific introduction to the world of bugs and insects. It offers a primer on bug anatomy, links to bug collector clubs and bug-enthusiast home pages, a lesson in proper bug classification and a section on "odd beliefs and ideas associated with insects." See Editor's Choice, page 693.

Halloween-o-Webbery

http://www.primenet.com/~trix/hallo.htm

Halloween-o-Webbery features a year-round look at Halloween scariness and trickery. It includes links to sound and movie files, Halloween poems, and other sites devoted to the holiday.

Headbone Interactive

http://www.headbone.com/home.html

Headbone Interactive is the electronic home of the Headbone multimedia projects, from "The Gigglebone Gang" to "What the Heck Will Elroy Do Next?" Visitors will also find demos and product information.

---

a2z EDITOR'S CHOICE

The Canadian Kid's Page

http://www.onramp.ca/cankids

The Canadian Kid's Page is a great jumping-off point to sites designed for the younger set. Although this site does have corporate sponsorship, there are no links to commercial sites or advertisements, so parents won't have to worry about a barrage of toy and junk food ads. Easy to navigate and understand, links are annotated and feature symbols giving hints to special contents on each page, including warnings for lengthy download times: Canadian sites feature the nation's flag, a camera stands for a plethora of pictures, and a speaker alerts visitors to sites with sound. A link to a collection of software required to run sound and movie files is also provided. Kids can find pen pals here or submit their own pen pal requests with descriptions of their personal hobbies and interests. Not for Canadian kids only, the site is a fun resource for parents and children all over the world who wish to learn more about other countries. —*Reviewed by Amy Hembree*

Welcome to the **Canadian Kids Home Page**! This page is provided as a starting place for both the young and the young at heart. It is meant as a jumping in point for parents and children exploring the World-Wide Web together. The Internet and the World-Wide Web have lots of fun and interesting things for you to do and see. This page will lead you to some of these great things that we have found.

Horse Country
http://www.horse-country.com/

Trot on over to Horse Country for a comprehensive look at horse history, science, stories, images, art and more. Visitors will find more than 400 horse-loving e-pals here, and such features as an interactive dream stable game.

Hyperman
http://www.hyperman.com/

Fans of television's Hyperman won't want to miss this chance to go on a mission with him. Along the way, they can check out Emma's cool links, or take the agent test at mission control with the Comptroller.

Interesting Places for Kids
http://www.crc.ricoh.com/people/steve/kids.html

Compiled by the parent of a 10-year-old daughter, this page points to a wide variety of sites of potential interest to children. Indexed by topic, categories include art and literature, music, museums and other exhibits, science and math, toys and games, arts and crafts, and more.

International Kids' Space
http://www.kids-space.org/

The International Kids' Space page is maintained especially for children, with links to the kids' gallery, a story book section and a chat area for kids. In Japanese and English.

Kiddin' Around
http://alexia.lis.uiuc.edu/~watts/kiddin.html

Kiddin' Around contains a vast collection of links for teens. Subjects covered range from movies and music to libraries and museums to fantasy and outer space.

Kidlink: Global Networking for Youth 10-15
http://www.kidlink.org/

The goal of Kidlink is to involve as many children around the world as possible in a global electronic dialogue. Join the more than 50,000 kids from 80 countries who are already participating.

Kids on Campus
http://www.tc.cornell.edu/Kids.on.Campus/

Kids On Campus, a project of the Cornell Theory Center, is dedicated to increasing computer awareness and scientific interest among third, fourth, and fifth graders via activities, videos and demos.

Kids on the Web
http://www.zen.org/~brendan/kids.html

Kids on the Web contains an extensive listing of children's resources. Visitors will find fun stuff, educational sites, children's books and information for parents, too.

Kids Web—A World Wide Web Digital Library for Schoolkids
http://www.npac.syr.edu/textbook/kidsweb/

The Kids Web is a library of links to kid-friendly arts, science and sports resources on the Web. Guests will also find such fun items as games, comics, and crafts pages.

Kids' Space
http://www.kids-space.org/

The Kids' Space is a showcase for children's art, stories, music and letters. Kids can communicate with one another via e-mail and bulletin boards, and the site includes a page of links to other kid-friendly sites on the Web.

a2z EDITOR'S CHOICE

The Children's Literature Web Guide
http://www.ucalgary.ca/~dkbrown/index.html

According to the author, this online children's guide "is an attempt to gather together and categorize the growing number of Internet resources related to books for children and young adults." More than a mere list of links, however, the guide also presents book award lists from print and Internet sources. Information about children's movies and television programs based on popular books is also collected here, including "Jumanji," "Tom and Huck," "The Secret Garden," and "Tall Tale: The Unbelievable Adventures of Pecos Bill." The wide selection of online literature includes myths and legends, contemporary stories, and—one of the most interesting sections—a collection of links to sites that feature stories written by children. Well-researched by its author, a University of Calgary librarian who explores and describes each link and feature, The Children's Literature Web Guide is an exhaustive resource for parents, educators, and children who can never get enough stories and literature.—*Reviewed by Amy Hembree*

Children's Literature Web Guide
Internet Resources Related to Books for Children and Young Adults

WHAT'S NEW ~ SEARCH ~ INTRODUCTION ~ EMAIL

Movies and Television Based on Children's Books	Online Children's Stories:	General Children's Literature Resources
Children's Book Awards	Collections	Children's Literature Journals and Book Reviews Online
Best Books Lists	Classics	Internet Discussion Groups
	Folklore, Myth and Legend	
	Contemporary Stories	
Children's Bestsellers:	Children's Songs and Poetry	
Resource Links Canadian	Readers' Theatre	Conferences and Book Events

Kids' Window

http://jw.stanford.edu/KIDS/kids_home.html

Kids' Window is a service of Japan Window, a U.S.-Japan collaboration for Internet-based Japan information. It provides many resources for education about Japanese culture, including a picture dictionary.

KidsCom Home Page

http://www.kidscom.com/

KidsCom is a "communication playground" on which kids can find an e-pal, write on a graffiti wall, play games, talk about their favorite things and write stories, all in French, German, Spanish, or English.

North Pole Web

http://north.pole.org/santa/

It's Christmas year 'round at the North Pole Web site. Visitors can talk to Santa, Rudolph, and the elves, decorate a digital tree, or listen to Handel's "Messiah."

Nye Labs Online

http://nyelabs.kcts.org/

Fans of PBS's Bill Nye, "the Science Guy," can enter his online laboratory and explore the world of science. Be sure to check out the Demo of the Day and the Nyestore's home videos.

Pocahontas

http://www.disney.com/DisneyPictures/Pocahontas/?GL=H&referer=^DisneyPicture

Images and clips from Disney's "Pocahontas" are featured here, and visitors are also treated to a behind-the-scenes look at the making of the movie.

Press Return

http://199.95.184.10/public/Network/PressReturn/Press-Return.html

"Press Return" is the online teen magazine from the people at Scholastic. Each theme-based issue represents a collaboration between young writers and professional editors.

Questacon

http://sunsite.anu.edu.au/Questacon/

Take a virtual tour of Questacon, Australia's national science and technology center. The Questacon home page features a "KidSpace" full of exhibits, games, and activities.

The Realist Wonder Society

http://www.wondersociety.com/

The Realist Wonder Society is a "whistle-stop of imaginzation between way stations of reality." It features kid-oriented fantasy stories, art and poetry.

Santa's Home Page

http://www.netm.com/eh/christma/santa.htm

This Santa home page features humor and history of the Jolly Old Elf as well as a "Merry Virtual Christmas" greeting. Visitors can jot down recipes from Mrs. Claus' kitchen or send e-mail to Santa.

Time for Kids

http://pathfinder.com/TFK/index.html

"Time" magazine's kid-friendly news site contains feature stories, reports and lots of color. Headlines include "Kids Design a Space City."

Virtual Jack-O-Lantern

http://www.chaco.com/~glenn/jack/

Who says Jack-O-Lanterns are only for Halloween? Here children can carve virtual pumpkins in 3-D by choosing from various eyes, nose, mouth and stem options on a checklist. Submit the design and, voila, an artistic pumpkin appears. The program displays VRML files only, but provides a link to download VR Scout.

Virtually React

http://www.react.com/

The electronic version of the teen mag "react" is appropriately titled "virtually react." Actually, it's brimming with news, sports, entertainment, photos, jokes, contests and, of course, a cybermall (without the food court).

FishNet

http://www.jayi.com/sbi/Open.html

FishNet is the Web hangout for teens who like to think not only about where they've been or where they are, but where they're going. Academically-oriented, FishNet features guides to colleges and other educational opportunities, as well as "Edge" magazine, the electronic continuation of "Young Scholar," which covers teen and academic issues in depth. Topics there include life in high school, hot issues in education, and the travails of choosing—and getting into—a college. FishNet also realizes that all work and no play makes for a dull teen. Street Speak follows the ever-changing linguistic habits of teenagers with a healthy library of (clean) slang, including the old stand-bys (cool) and words that someone's best friend submitted last week (wooshie, meep). FishNet also features a chat area, and the self-explanatory Weird Fact of the Day. Those who register with FishNet receive regular updates and a birthday surprise by e-mail. There's lots to do and learn here, perfect for teens who never stop thinking. —*Reviewed by Amy Hembree*

a2z EDITOR'S CHOICE

Gordon's Entomological Home Page
http://www.ex.ac.uk/~gjlramel/welcome.html

So what is a bug, anyway? Some people might think it's anything that's small and gross and careens with unbelievable speed through the air or across the kitchen floor—or slowly and creepily down the sidewalk—a monstrosity generally subject to the frenzied ministrations of either a fly-swatter or stamping feet. Entomologists, however, have narrowed bugs down to the insect order *Hemiptera*. And *Hempitera*-obsessed children—and adults—will find Gordon's Entomological Home Page a delightful Web stop. The mysteries of a multitude of insect identities and anatomies are explained here, with links to buggy details about each insect order, including *Hemiptera* or "true bugs." The famous and gorgeous Death's Head Hawkmoth greets visitors in living color, and pages of links—both on the Insects Home Page and the links page—buzz bug-fans to even more creepy-crawly sites. Colorful, well-organized and easy to navigate, this site is a fitting and fascinating tour—not bad for creatures that make up 99.99 percent of all the animals on Earth. —*Reviewed by Amy Hembree*

Welcome to Gordon's Entomological Home Page

I hope this new front page is quicker to download, if you have too many problems do let me know. The old home Page is still here, you can find it with all its links and imagery behind both the Death's Head Hawkmoth and the Links symbol.

NEWS AND INFORMATION

THE 25 MOST POPULAR NEWS AND INFORMATION SITES

Calendar
http://www.cmf.nrl.navy.mil/calendar

CNN Interactive
http://www.dsu.edu/projects/word_of_day/
word.html

Commercial News Services on the Internet
http://www.jou.ufl.edu/commres/webjou.htm

Consumer Products Safety Commission Gopher
gopher://cpsc.gov/1

Create Your Own Newspaper (CRAYON)
http://crayon.net/

Dictionaries, etc.
http://galaxy.einet.net/galaxy/
Reference-and-Interdisciplinary-Information/
Dictionaries-etc.html

FAIR—Fairness & Accuracy in Reporting
http://www.fair.org/fair/

Federtal Trade Commission Consumer Brochures
http://www.webcom.com/~lewrose/
brochures.html

HomeArts
http://homearts.com/depts/fresh/
newhome.htm

HotWired
http://www.hotwired.com/frontdoor/
index.html

The Lighthouse Weather Server
http://the-tech.mit.edu/Weather/

Macworld Online
http://www.macworld.com/

The Media and Communications Studies Site
http://www.aber.ac.uk/~dgc/media.html

Nando.net
http://www.nando.net/welcome.html

The Newsroom
http://www.auburn.edu/~vestmon/news.html

The New York Times Information Services Group
http://nytinfoserv.com/

Online Magazines
http://www.physik.unizh.ch/zines.html

Pulitzer Prizes
http://www.pulitzer.org/

The Quotations Page
http://www.starlingtech.com/quotes/

Smash! magazine
http://smash.cs.com/

Starving Shirley's Savings Page
http://www.shirl.com/

Survival Bible 2001
http://www.io.org/~richard/

USA Today
http://www.usatoday.com/

Weather World
http://www.atmos.uiuc.edu/wxworld/html/
top.html

The WWW Virtual Library: Electronic Journals
http://www.edoc.com/ejournal/

CONSUMER INFORMATION

The Better Business Bureau

http://www.igc.apc.org/cbbb/

Visit this site to learn more about this nonprofit organization and the affiliate serving your community. See Editor's Choice, page 696.

Chemical Industry Institute of Toxicology

http://www.ciit.org/

The Chemical Industry Institute of Toxicology, supported by industrial groups, aims to improve understanding and assessment of the adverse effects of chemicals, pharmaceuticals and consumer products on humans. Information about the organization's activities and summaries of its reports are online here.

Consumer Information Center

http://www.pueblo.gsa.gov/

This page features a catalog of consumer information, provided by the Consumer Information Center in Pueblo, Colorado. Categories include cars, health, children, small businesses, employment and money. Also available are links to related sites, media listings and the Consumer Centers' Top 20.

CouponNet Home Page

http://coupon.com/coupon.html

CouponNet is a service pointing visitors to products sold on the Internet for which money saving coupons are available. The exchange area allows visitors to trade coupons and rebate offers with one another.

Federal Trade Commission Consumer Brochures

http://www.webcom.com/~lewrose/
brochures.html

Browsers interested in educating themselves about consumer problems and rights will find more than 100 brochures published by the Federal Trade Commission's Office of Consumer and Business Education. Topics run the gamut, from credit card fraud to buying over the phone and telemarketing scams.

Home Recording Rights Coalition

http://www.hrrc.org/

The Home Recording Rights Coalition is a nonprofit information and lobbying group dedicated to preserving consumers' rights "to purchase and use audio and video recording products for noncommercial purposes." Read the organization's latest news and calls to action here.

Starving Shirley's Savings Page

http://www.shirl.com/

This information-packed and fun site provides many tips on saving money. See Editor's Choice.

Street Cents Online

http://www.screen.com/streetcents.html

This online companion to the Canadian television series is all about money—"how to get it and how not to get ripped off when you spend it." Join the show's street-smart team of young correspondents online as they reveal what's a deal and what's not.

---

a2z EDITOR'S CHOICE

Starving Shirley's Savings Page

http://www.shirl.com/

The only untruth to be found on this playful consumer-tips page is the implication that its gray matter, Shirley, "the viscontess of discount," is somehow going hungry. Far from it. One pictures this thrifty online dervish, a crown of coupons worn proudly upon her shopping smarts, surrounded by a gusty swirl of circulars. By oath, Shirley takes coupons wherever she goes, keeps an eagle eye open for free stuff, and packs rubber gloves for those irresistible bouts of "dumpster diving." And she shares all of her tricks of the trade here. Follow Shirley's mindful footsteps down the consumer path of life, from establishing a budget to purchasing a dream car. She'll also point you to a goldmine of online goodies, like shareware that will help you track your coupons and rebates. Shirley may be a thrifty downloader, but she's definitely not a freeloader: "Pay your shareware fee!" she demands. —*Reviewed by James Fitch*

$tarving $hirley

Table of Contents:

$ Buy Low, Sell High at Thrift and Consignment Stores

$ Cheap Eats

$ A Gold Mine in the Sunday Paper

$ Starving Shirley's Download Goodies!

$ Great savings links, including links to free STUFF!

$ Send your own personal hints and tips to Shirl!

$ Place a classified ad on $tarving $hirley's $avings $pecials!

U.S. Consumer Product Safety Commission Gopher

gopher://cpsc.gov/1

Since 1972, the U.S. Consumer Product Safety Commission has kept a watchful eye on products to protect the safety of consumers. Visit this gopher menu for the commission's publications, product hazard reports and press releases.

U.S. National Debt Clock

http://www.brillig.com/debt_clock/

Find up-to-date, up-to-the-minute information on the national debt of the United States government. Stalwart visitors can also link to a variety of topic-related sites.

DAILY NEWS

ARCHIVES AND INDICES

Local News Sources

http://www.trib.com/news/local.html

Visitors will find links to news servers from around the U.S. and the world. Find out what's happening in St. Petersburg—Florida or Russia.

The Newsroom

http://www.auburn.edu/~vestmon/news.html

The comprehensive Newsroom site contains links to various news- and business-related Internet re-

sources, including newspapers and radio and television stations.

Online Newspapers

http://www.mediainfo.com/ephome/npaper/nphtm/online.htm

This document, part of the Editor & Publisher magazine site, contains links to hundreds of newspapers on the Web. You can search by country, state or university. Whether it's the Bingo Bugle or the Wall Street Journal, you'll find it here.

Taxi's Electronic Newspapers

http://www.deltanet.com/users/taxicat/e_papers.html

Taxi's Newspaper List is an international index to online newspapers. The extensive list is organized by country and state.

Web News Index

http://recycle.green.ri.cmu.edu/~speck/

Web News Index is an up-to-the-minute searchable index of news articles available on the Web. Users can find out the latest on any breaking story.

BROADCASTING COMPANIES

ABC News Reports

http://www.prognet.com/contentp/abc.html

Users of the RealAudio Player software can check the ABC News Web site for hourly news updates, along with sports reports and the Peter Jennings Journal. The service is free.

ABC Radio Net

http://www.abcradionet.com/

Did you miss Peter Jennings' newscast tonight? You can listen to it here, along with news on the hour, sports, weather and David Brinkley. You can also pick a city from an image map for local news. And this site includes plenty more nifty features.

Canadian Broadcasting Corporation Headline News

http://www.radio.cbc.ca/radio/programs/news/news.html

The Canadian Broadcasting Corporation provides a headline news service at this site. Includes links to international mirror sites, a subject search index and pointers to other sites of interest.

CBS News Up To The Minute

http://uttm.com/

Snippets of overnight news coverage from CBS television can be found at this site, embellished with audio and video features. In addition to general news, the site promises the latest Internet news, movie reviews, women's health reports, parenting tips and science stories. A reporter's re-

---

a2z EDITOR'S CHOICE

The Better Business Bureau

http://www.igc.apc.org/cbbb/

From the mission statement, the Council of Better Business Bureaus promotes and fosters "the highest ethical relationship between business and the public." By way of its many regional bureaus, the nonprofit organization is perhaps best known for collecting complaints from fuming consumers and providing reliability reports for the cautious ones. This information page lets business owners find out whether or not they stack up to BBB membership standards. It also allows users to file their complaints online, and educates them as to what exactly happens throughout the complaint process. On our last visit, only one bureau was distributing reliability reports over the Net. But its searchable database, with more than 63,000 reports, updated daily, was an encouraging harbinger. Follow the links here to find the BBB serving your community.—*Reviewed by James Fitch*

source section and a link to the main CBS site fill out the page.

CNN Interactive

http://www.cnn.com/

Visit this creatively designed site to explore the latest news. See Editor's Choice.

Internet Radio Nexus

http://www.nexus.org/Internet_Radio/

Visit this site to tune in broadcasts from UNESCO Radio, United Nations Radio, Swiss Radio International and other international airwave offerings. The site includes the software needed to play the broadcasts.

KVOA-TV Tucson—Eyewitness News Online

http://www.kvoa.com/

KVOA-TV in Tucson, Arizona offers news, weather, opinion and stock information here. Visitors can download daily newscast scripts, biographical sketches of the anchors and sports updates. WCBS

NewsRadio 88

http://www.newsradio88.com/

The home page of WCBS NewsRadio 88, New York, dishes up "all news, all day, all night." Visitors to the site will find the latest top news, sports and weather reports.

INTERNATIONAL

Asahi.com

http://www.asahi.com/english/english.html

Visitors to this Web site can glean breaking news from Japanese newspaper Asahi Shimbun or link to the home pages of *The New York Times* and the *San Jose Mercury News*. Includes photos and editorials. Available in English and Japanese.

AsiaOne

http://www.asia1.com.sg/

AsiaOne is a service providing links to Asian newspapers and business publications. Visitors can read the news from a variety of sources in Singapore and Thailand.

Canadian Press and Broadcast News

http://www.canpress.ca/canpress/

Find Canada's top news stories (updated each weekday) and award-winning photos on file at this site. The page also provides an online style-book, media links for journalists, and reference resources. In English and French.

China News Digest

http://www.cnd.org/

The China News Digest is an electronic information center that provides access to online publications and databases focusing on news from China. Includes picture galleries, technical support, guides and links to related resources.

ClariNet Tearsheet: World News

http://www.clarinet.com/Samples/reutworld.html

The ClariNet Tearsheet World News home page is a segment of the company's e.News Internet newspaper, with world news-bites by country available courtesy of Reuters.

Czech Republic News Digest

http://www.columbia.edu/~js322/czech.html

This Web site provides news, from various sources and in various languages, regarding the Czech Re-

---

a2z EDITOR'S CHOICE

CNN Interactive

http://www.cnn.com/

There's little for Wolf Blitzer and Bobbie Battista to do at CNN Interactive—and Larry King only lives through show transcripts—but their on-the-air spirits resonate through hypertext newsflashes that will have online info-junkies reloading the screen in loops. "Book says Hillary talks to dead" and "Shuttle crew asks, if a tree bends in space…" are but a few provocative moments in the fast-paced world of "always accurate and unbiased" Headline News. And who better to deliver this service online than the network which practically coined the phrase offline? Along with digestible news, expanded coverage and topical sections for everything from style to politics, this sensibly designed site throws out such extra bones as an interactive news quiz and an ominously titled "Big Brother Cam," which relays live shots of the newsroom for all you folks at home.—*Reviewed by James Fitch*

public. Includes Radio Praha news and schedules, and a link to the PragueFinancial Monitor. Visitors will also find tourist, public transit, exchange rate and government directory information.

Daily News from Iceland

http://www.centrum.is/icerev/daily1.html

The Daily News from Iceland site offers a selection of articles from domestic news and publishing services. Visit here to read recent news reports, browse back issues and link with other Iceland consumer and trade publications.

Der Standard Online—Austria

http://www.DerStandard.at/

Visitors with a hankering for the sights and sounds of old Vienna will find the current online edition of Austria's Der Standard newspaper here. In German only.

Der Tagesspiegel—Germany

http://www.tagesspiegel-berlin.de/

The Berlin daily Der Tagesspiegel has a colorful and technologically savvy online version. It offers news, reviews, features, sports, commentary and more. In German.

Electronic Telegraph—England

http://www.telegraph.co.uk/

The Electronic Telegraph is a technologically sophisticated online daily from merry olde England. It provides comprehensive news, features and erudite opinion pieces, free of charge to registered members.

FutureNet

http://www.futurenet.co.uk/

Updated daily, "FutureNet" describes itself as "Europe's leading electronic magazine." Visitors will find world news reports, and features on computing, sports and entertainment. Only registered users are allowed access to its pages, however. To move beyond this point, visitors must either register or enter the correct password.

GlobeNet

http://www.globeandmail.ca/

This Web site complements the Toronto newspaper The Globe and Mail. Visitors to this site can get a variety of business and political news from Canada and the world.

Halifax Daily News Online—Canada

http://www.hfxnews.com/media/daily

Get some perspective on what's happening in the Canadian city of Halifax via the virtual pages of the Daily News. Strong emphasis on local events (fishing, anyone?), plus online personals and classifieds.

Halifax Herald Limited—Canada

http://www.herald.ns.ca/

This Canadian site offers headline news, an electronic edition of The Halifax Chronicle-Herald and an index of newspaper services. Other features include a kids' section, links to regional servers and a tour of the Canadian Maritime provinces.

Hindu Newspaper Online

http://www.webpage.com/hindu/

The Hindu is an online edition of India's national newspaper, updated weekly with news from India and the world. Visitors can read the current issue and search back issues of the paper here.

The Irish Times

http://www.irish-times.ie/

Ieunet, an Irish Internet service provider, offers access here to The Irish Times, a daily newspaper covering the Emerald Isle and the world. Visitors can read the current edition or browse an archive of back issues. The site also offers an online store of Irish-made goods.

Jerusalem Post

http://www.jpost.com/

The online version of the highly respected Jerusalem Post keeps its readers abreast of events in Israel and throughout the Middle East. It also provides balanced and influential editorial commentary on the ongoing troubles in the region, and a lively roundup of lifestyle features.

La Vanguardia—Spain

http://vangu.ese.es/

This is the gateway to the electronic edition of La Vanguardia, a daily newspaper published in Barcelona, Spain. In Spanish only.

News From Around the World

http://www.funet.fi/pub/sounds/news.html

Sift through the latest international news at the News From Around the World site. Broadcasts from the Canadian Broadcasting Corporation and U.S. government-run Voice of America are presented in English, Russian and Chinese.

Polish Press Agency

http://www.pap.waw.pl/

The Polish Press Agency has been churning out state-funded news reports since 1945 on events in Poland. You'll find short summaries about everything from politics to sports. The agency includes a photo service consisting of 25 snap-happy photographers.

The Star—Malaysia

http://www.jaring.my/~star/

The Star claims to be Malaysia's most widely read English-language daily. Visitors to this site will find daily news and features, readership information, and a brief history of the publication.

The StarPhoenix Online—Canada

http://www.saskstar.sk.ca/index.html

The StarPhoenix newspaper in sunny Saskatoon, Canada, maintains this online outlet for news, sports, comics, editorials and advertising.

Sydney Morning Herald—Australia

http://www.smh.com.au/

This site contains an online version of the Australian daily. It offers news, sports, weather, feature stories, election previews and a generous sampling of computer news for the techno-literate Aussie.

NEWS SERVICES AND DIRECTORIES

Associated Press Wire Stories on Trib.com

http://www1.trib.com/NEWS/APwire.html

Information junkies can browse breaking news hot off the Associated Press wire at this Web site, maintained by the Casper, Wyoming Star-Tribune and Howard Publications. Stories, updated every five minutes, are indexed both topically and regionally.

ClariNet Home Page

http://www.clarinet.com/

This subscription-based electronic news service offers a broad array of features—general and international news, sports, technology, entertainment and financial items, and U.S. government information. Visitors will find ordering information, as well as details on related newsgroups.

Commercial News Services on the Internet

http://www.jou.ufl.edu/commres/webjou.htm

The Commercial News Services on the Internet page provides links to news services categorized by type and frequency. Also includes gopher and telnet listings.

CRAYON—Create Your Own Newspaper

http://crayon.net/

This is the home page for CRAYON, as in CReAte Your Own Newspaper. The service is "a tool for managing (U.S.) news sources on the Net...a news page customized for you with the daily information that you are most interested in." Visitors can check out a sample newspaper here, or start one of their own.

The Daily News—Free Internet Sources

http://www.helsinki.fi/~lsaarine/news.html

This catalog service lists sites on the Net that provide "significant news on a daily basis without charge." It also provides a link to the free inet-news mailing list, where new online information services can declare themselves for all the world to judge.

The Daily News—Just the Links

http://www.cs.vu.nl/%7Egerben/news.html

A boon for newshounds, this site connects info-junkies with online daily news sources from around the world. Visitors can link to dozens of geographically indexed home pages maintained by newsgathering organizations or check out special current events sections providing details on specific newsworthy subjects.

E.W. Scripps Co.

http://www.scripps.com/

The Scripps Howard corporation owns newspapers, television stations and cable systems nationwide. Visitors to its home page can link to dozens of these holdings.

Internet Disaster Information Center

http://www.disaster.net/

This site offers a detailed document of the Oklahoma City bombing, as well as keeping up with other disasters. See Editor's Choice, page 701.

Nando.net

http://www2.nando.net/nt/nando.cgi

Nando.net delivers piping hot news, sports and entertainment information to visitors in a variety of packages. Visit here to link to the Nando Times, Nando Next, and other cutting-edge information sites.

NewsPage

http://www.newspage.com/

NewsPage boasts a comprehensive listing of more than 500 online business news resources and 25,000 pages of related information. Browsers can register to access articles, organized by industry. Topics covered range from multimedia and banking to insurance and environmental services.

The New York Times Information Services Group

http://nytinfoserv.com/

The New York Times Information Services Group's best-known product is TimesFax (a daily fax digest of the newspaper), and you can access it here. This site also has information on other divisions within the group and provides pointers to other NYT sites, such as *Computer News Daily* and *Your Health Daily*.

New York Times' TimesFax Service

http://nytimesfax.com/

TimesFax provides highlights and excerpts from *The New York Times* daily newspaper (America's "newspaper of record"), including political, business, sports and editorial coverage. Visitors can register for the free service from this information page.

The Omnivore

http://way.net/omnivore/index.html

News junkies won't go wanting when they explore the bounty of news, weather, economics, sports and culture links offered here. Regional, national, international and topical links are featured along with pointers to search engines for quick reference.

The Online Intelligence Project

http://kahn.interaccess.com/intelweb/index.html

People interested in international news and commerce can get the up-to-date news through the Online Intelligence Project home page. It features news, security information and reference materials for regions around the world. It also includes a Bosnia update.

Pathfinder

http://pathfinder.com/welcome/

Visit Pathfinder to get quick news excerpts, entertainment gossip, and the like. See Editor's Choice.

Point Now

http://www.pointcom.com/now/

Self-described as "your daily connection to the pulse of the Web," Point Now delivers a concise, timely guide to news stories posted on servers around the World. It's a service of Point Communication, the folks who rate the Web's "Top 5%."

 EDITOR'S CHOICE

Pathfinder

http://pathfinder.com/welcome/

At best it's a guilty pleasure; at worst it's a convoluted jumble of blocks, icons and color. Confused? Just click on a logo. With Pathfinder, the Time Warner Empire attempts the ultimate online newsstand and ends up contributing a shelf full of current events Cliff's Notes. No complaints here: You don't have to buy a copy of Money anymore to learn "The Best Places to Live," and you don't have to track down a copy of Life to pinpoint "The 50 Most Influential Boomers." More than anything, though, it's the conglomerate's People/Entertainment Weekly brand of "sleez and cheez" that will keep you glomming on for more. (Remember, this is the monster that gave birth to O.J. Central and Susan Smith On Trial.) Even the covert ad gimmicks are a hoot. Rhino Records hosts "Rocky's Pad," where you can "drop a nickel in the juke, flip on the tube," or thumb through a catalog, conveniently located on a virtual coffee table. Hey, when you're busy filling out forms to get the extended weather forecast for your zip code (courtesy of the Weather Channel), it's easy to forget that life here is just one big happy promotion. —*Reviewed by James Fitch*

U.S. NEWSPAPERS

Beloit Daily News Home Page

http://www.bossnt.com/bdn.html

The Beloit (Wisconsin) *Daily News* home page supplies the day's top local stories, as well as article archives, special sections, comic strips, columns and a schedule of local government meetings. Visitors will also find information on subscribing and submitting letters to the editors.

Birmingham Post-Herald

http://www.postherald.com

The online edition of Alabama's *Birmingham Post-Herald* provides daily headlines, a roundup of local and national news, sports, commentary and religion, and "best bets" for entertainment activities in the Birmingham area.

The Capital

http://www.infi.net/capital/

The Capital Online is an electronic version of the Annapolis, Maryland daily newspaper. With a focus on local news and a columnar format, this site almost feels like newsprint.

The Dallas Morning News Opinions

http://www.dallasnews.com/

The Dallas Morning News provides a sampling of its editorials and analytical reporting at this site. Examples include the series "Whither the Cities," "The We Decade," and the complete text of the newspaper's coverage of the 1993 siege at the Branch Davidian compound in Waco. The site also provides an opportunity for instant reader response.

Detroit Journal

http://www.rust.net/~workers/strike.html

This online version of *The Detroit Free Press,* produced by striking workers, offers standard newspaper fare—daily, business and sports news, columns, editorials and letters—without the newsprint. Visitors also can access union news.

Detroit News

http://www.detnews.com/

The Detroit News maintains this site for its online edition. Visit here for local, national and international news, business and sports features, and links to local Internet resources.

The Gate—San Francisco

http://www.sfgate.com/

A joint venture of the *San Francisco Chronicle* and *San Francisco Examiner* newspapers, The Gate is a full-service and technologically sophisticated daily newspaper that offers regional and national news, sports, commentary and classifieds.

Houston Chronicle Interactive

http://www.chron.com/

Houston Chronicle Interactive is the online version of the Texas daily. It includes excerpts from the day's newsstand edition, up-to-the-minute headlines and links to community resources. Requires registration.

Maui News

http://www.maui.net/~mauinews/news.html

The Maui News, covering local and international issues for the laid-back populace of the Hawaiian island, maintains this online site to supplement its daily print edition. Visit to read current articles, browse an index of sun-struck tourism information and link to other "hot" Internet sites.

Mercury Center

http://www.sjmercury.com/

The San Jose Mercury News provides up-to-the-minute news and features—including its much-lauded coverage of Silicon Valley and the technology biz—at this pioneering online site. Some portions are available by subscription only.

The Nando Times

http://www2.nando.net/nt/nando.cgi

The Nando Times online news service (from the Charlotte, North Carolina *News and Observer*) provides daily updates on top stories from the world, the nation, the playing fields and and the political arena. A classified-ad service targets users from North Carolina. Additional links to online travel and financial services are available.

Newshare

http://www.newshare.com:9999/moved.html

Newshare is the online home for the American Reporter, offering daily news, editorials, humor and other scribblings. The enterprise is owned by the reporters themselves, who appreciate your patronage.

RWorld From The Orange County Register

http://www.ocregister.com/

RWorld is a limited Web version of the Orange County *California Register*. This page features selected stories and images from the newspaper.

St. Petersburg Times

http://www.times.st-pete.fl.us/

Visitors can read daily news and sports features from the Tampa Bay, Florida area here. When we

---

a2z EDITOR'S CHOICE

Internet Disaster Information Center

http://www.disaster.net/

Dedicated to the memory of those killed in the bombing of the Oklahoma City Federal Building, and to the men and women of that city's emergency services, this offering from two disaster buffs aims to keep the Internet community abreast of the ongoing and historical disasters of the world. On our last visit, the historical segment was limited to information on the Oklahoma City bombing; but what a thorough collection it is. From preserved Internet Relay Chat logs to phone numbers providing family counseling and disaster relief, the events and emotions surrounding the bombing are painstakingly documented here. Additionally, the site serves as a link-a-thon to organizations typically bound to disaster (GriefNet, American Red Cross, the Bureau of Alcohol, Tobacco & Firearms). When disaster strikes, direct your browser accordingly. —*Reviewed by James Fitch*

visited, this online newspaper said it would soon add classifieds.

San Francisco Chronicle

http://www.sfgate.com/

A complete index to the *San Francisco Chronicle* newspaper, this site archives articles that are a year old or less. Also links to related news-feature pages.

The San Francisco Free Press

http://www.ccnet.com/SF_Free_Press/welcome.html

The San Francisco Free Press was published electronically for almost two weeks in November 1994 by striking employees of the *San Francisco Chronicle*, *The San Francisco Examiner* and the San Francisco Newspaper Agency. The online editions from those days are archived here.

San Jose Mercury News Breaking News

http://www.sjmercury.com/whatsnew.htm

This is the older, text-based version of the Silicon Valley's main newspaper's breaking news page. *The San Jose Mercury News* offers hyperlinked headlines to a short version of the day's latest news.

Standard-Times Home Page

http://www.s-t.com/

The Standard-Times, an electronic newspaper based in southern Massachusetts, presents link-laden coverage of state, national and international news. Features and information of local interest, comics and various online search tools complete the page.

Tacoma News Tribune

http://www.tribnet.com/

The Tacoma News Tribune presents TRIBweb, an online version of the Northwest daily. Visitors can read news, sports and weather reports from the last 10 days, search the classified ads or link to a variety of entertaining and informative Web sites.

Trib.com—The Internet Newspaper

http://www.trib.com/

Trib.com, "the Internet newspaper," offers readers general news reports, sports, weather and feature stories. Additional attractions include an online Web search tool and links to reference and shopping sites.

USA Today Online

http://www.usatoday.com/

The online version of "the nation's newspaper" offers easily digestible sections on news, sports, money, lifestyles and weather. Regular readers of the paper will note that *USA Today* offers extensive coverage of the Internet and emerging technologies.

Washington Free Press

http://www.speakeasy.org/wfp/

From this gateway, visitors can access the free-thinking Seattle newspaper's coverage of news, politics, the arts and special events in Washington State.

Worldwide News

http://www.worldwidenews.net/

The online Worldwide News offers coverage of politics, sports, entertainment and general-interest news. Includes an online shopping mall and a link to the InterList, an online reference library.

JOURNALISM AND WRITING RESOURCES

ASSOCIATIONS AND ORGANIZATIONS

The Canadian Press

http://www.xe.com/canpress/

At the Canadian Press site find today's top stories, award-winning photos, stylebooks and information on press, broadcast and photo services in Canada. Some information is in French, though most is provided in English.

Michigan Press Photographers Association Home Page

http://www.cris.com/~mppa/

The Michigan Press Photographers Association Home Page lists links to journalistic issues and achievements. Get locations and dates for upcoming seminars.

The National Press Club

http://town.hall.org/places/npc/

The National Press Club home page provides an information center and newsroom, as well as details on the club and its facilities, services and programs.

National Press Photographers Association

http://sunsite.unc.edu/nppa/

The National Press Photographers Association maintains this site to provide general information. Visit here to learn about its programs, conferences and other resources. Also find a digital gallery and short course.

New World Media / Digital Alternative Media

http://www.worldmedia.com/

This nonprofit organization seeks to build "a digital infrastructure for global social transformation and information sharing." The service is inspired by the works of intellectual-scientist-dissident Noam Chomsky, and this site boasts one of the world's most comprehensive archives of his works. Visitors will find resources here from alternative media organizations from around the world, in addition to online conferencing and chat capabilities, and a weekly current affairs section.

Society for the History of Authorship, Reading & Publishing

http://www.indiana.edu/~sharp/

The Society for the History of Authorship, Reading and Publishing is a network aimed at scholars, librarians, publishing professionals and authors interested in the history of print. Visit here to learn how to join the society, track down publishers' archives and link to historical sites.

PROFESSIONAL RESOURCES

Airwaves Media Resource

http://www.airwaves.com/

The Airwaves Media Resource home page is devoted to discussions and news on radio and television broadcasting. Visitors will find publications, newsgroups and links to sites relating to the U.S. broadcasting industry.

Hot News/Hot Research

http://www.poynter.org/hr/hr_intro.htm

Journalists chasing the latest information brush-fire can stop by the Hot News/Hot Research page (from The Poynter Institute for Media Studies) for links to potential interview subjects on breaking news stories. New links to qualified "talking heads" are added as events unfold around the world.

The Internet Newsroom

http://www.dgsys.com/~editors/index.html

The Internet Newsroom is a gateway to key resources for journalists and researchers. Includes links to international news sources, the National Press Club, article archives and journalism education pages.

Media and Communication Studies

http://www.aber.ac.uk/~dgc/media.html

Media and communications studies come to the Web via this page of links to academic papers. Maintained by a faculty member at the University of Wales, Aberystwyth, this site points to publications covering topics such as semiotics, news media, advertising, film studies, media influence and more.

Media Online Yellow Pages

http://www.webcom.com/~nlnnet/yellowp.html

The Media Online Yellow Pages is an index of broadcast media Web sites and e-mail addresses around the world. It is heavy on television and

light on radio listings. Regulatory and research databases are included, as well as an index search.

A Reporter's Internet Survival Guide

http://www.qns.com/~casey/

An Oklahoma journalist provides this list of Web resources for reporters. Find government-spon-

sored sites, reference materials and links to general online search engines.

Survey.Net

http://www.survey.net/

A product of the Louisiana-based Internet Commerce Corporation, Survey.Net takes the pulse of users through its online polls dealing with today's topical issues. Also find featured columns and letters from readers.

WWW Virtual Library: Journalism

http://www.cais.com/makulow/vlj.html

This segment of the WWW Virtual Library is devoted to journalism and provides numerous links to journalism-related sites. Associations, clubs, universities, grants and news bureaus are in the mix.

---

a2z EDITOR'S CHOICE

FAIR—Fairness & Accuracy in Reporting

http://www.fair.org/fair/

Watchdogs can be fun to watch, and the Web offers an excellent public forum for American media group Fairness & Accuracy in Reporting (FAIR). In its drive to "correct media bias and imbalance"—no doubt one of the most unwieldy of undertakings these days—FAIR zeroes in, specifically, on "corporate ownership of the press, the media's allegiance to official agendas and their insensitivity to women, labor, minorities, and other public interest constituencies." Whether it's putting an allegedly racist radio host on the hot seat or chronicling a popular politician's decades of bigotry, FAIR puts a new spin on the journalism most people heedlessly digest as truth. The organization's no-nonsense site showcases "Counter-Spin," the weekly FAIR radio show (for which partial transcripts are provided), and EXTRA!, the organization's bimonthly newsletter. In the face of information overload, FAIR might just help you to get the balance right.
—*Reviewed by James Fitch*

FAIR
Fairness & Accuracy In Reporting

FAIR (Fairness & Accuracy In Reporting) is the national media watch group offering well-documented criticism in an effort to correct media bias and imbalance. FAIR focusses public awareness on the narrow corporate ownership of the press, the media's allegiance to official agendas and their insensitivity to women, labor, minorities, and other public interest constituencies. FAIR seeks to invigorate the First Amendment by advocating for greater media pluralism and the inclusion of public interest voices in national debates. More information about FAIR.

What's new on the FAIR WWW pages (updated June 5, 1996).

Contents:

- Of special interest
- *EXTRA!* magazine
- *CounterSpin* radio show
- "Media Beat" syndicated column
- FAIR reports and miscellaneous
- *In Fact* magazine historical articles
- How to help FAIR
- Additional online resources
- FAIR contact information

PUBLICATIONS AND INDUSTRY NEWS

American Journalism Review NewsLink

http://www.newslink.org/menu.html

Advertising itself as "the most comprehensive news resource on the World Wide Web," the American Journalism Review NewsLink offers visitors free access to "all" newspaper, magazine, broadcasting and news service sites. Find links to selected sites of the week and the NewsLink Top 25, plus surveys, research and more.

FAIR—Fairness & Accuracy in Reporting

http://www.fair.org/fair/

The organization FAIR is a careful watcher of the media. Visit this site to get their perspective on "media bias and imbalance." See Editor's Choice.

Global Student News

http://www.jou.ufl.edu/forums/gsn/

Global Student News seeks to provide a forum for sharing ideas useful to students and educators involved in news media. Using Internet distribution as a springboard, the site offers learning tools to get student online publications up and running.

Media Watchdog

http://theory.lcs.mit.edu/~mernst/media/

Media Watchdog is a collection of online resources with specific media criticism and information about media watchgroups. Emphasis is on critiquing the accuracy and exposing biases of the mainstream media. Links to related organizations.

Pulitzer Prizes

http://www.pulitzer.org/

The Pulitzer Prizes are among the highest awards bestowed upon newspaper reporters, authors, playwrights and composers in America. Features here include a current list of winners, audio excerpts, full texts of selected news articles and synopses of honored books.

STUDENT NEWSPAPERS

Arizona Daily Wildcat

http://wacky.ccit.arizona.edu/~wildcat

The Arizona Daily Wildcat, the student print newspaper at the University of Arizona, is published on weekdays during the fall and spring semesters. This page contains the paper's editorial and advertising information as well as an archive of back issues.

Bucknellian

http://www.bucknell.edu/publications/bucknellian/index.html

The Bucknellian, the student newspaper of Bucknell University in Lewisburg, Pennsylvania, maintains this site to supplement its regular print edition. Visit here for articles on campus activities, sports, world news and opinions from a decidedly Bucknell perspective.

Campus Press

http://bcn.boulder.co.us/campuspress/Presshome.html

The Campus Press student newspaper of the University of Colorado, Boulder, maintains this site to supplement its biweekly print edition. Visit here for campus and community news, opinion columns and a vicarious whiff of the Rockies.

Carolina

http://www.cuni.cz/cucc/carolina/carolina.html

Carolina is an e-mail news service covering the Czech Republic. It is published weekly by journalism students at the Faculty of Social Sciences, Charles University, Prague. In Czech and English.

The Chronicle Online

http://www.chronicle.duke.edu/

Duke University's student newspaper, the *Chronicle* offers this suitably brainy online version with current campus news and editorials, a sports databank, and an archive of back issues.

The Daily Beacon

http://beacon-www.asa.utk.edu/

The Daily Beacon is an independent student newspaper at the University of Tennessee, Knoxville. This site features the contents of the current and previous issues, and links to campus information as well as other student papers on the Internet.

Digital Cardinal

http://www.cardinal.wisc.edu/

The Digital Cardinal is the online version of the daily newspaper of the University of Wisconsin, Madison. The site offers articles, feature stories and opinions that cover campus and city news, the arts, and the exploits of the mighty Badger sports teams. The site also offers an archive of past issues and links to other student-journalism pages.

Fishwrap

http://fishwrap.mit.edu/

Fishwrap is an experimental personalized newspaper project designed to help integrate first year students into the Massachusetts Institute of Technology community. Provides links to hometown media services, MIT news servers, feature articles and other selections.

Netcomtalk

http://web.bu.edu/COM/communication.html

Netcomtalk, an online multimedia publication presented by Boston University's college of communication, posts daily news reports and showcases student work. Feature stories, photo-essays and information about the college's faculty and alumni can be found in this spiffy cyberspace product.

Oklahoma Daily Online

http://www.daily.ou.edu/

The Oklahoma Daily Online from the University of Oklahoma provides weekday editions during the school year and archives of recent editions. Read special coverage of events such as the Oklahoma City bombing as well as previews of Sooner football games. Daily features include news, opinion, sports coverage, and arts and entertainment listings.

Old Gold and Black

http://ogb.wfu.edu/

The Old Gold and Black is the campus newspaper of Wake Forest University, Winston-Salem, North Carolina. The newspaper's electronic edition features university news, editorials, sports and entertainment, and also offers an archive of its back issues.

Omnibus: Eye at Northwestern University

http://www.rtvf.nwu.edu/

The Department of Radio, Television and Film at Northwestern University details its Omnibus: Eye project here. The project studies the production of digital media on the Web; this page contains links to exemplary pages.

The Orion Online

http://orion.csuchico.edu/

Check out what's happening this week on the campus of California's Chico State University.

Orion Online, an electronic edition of the student newspaper, includes news articles, sports, entertainment, opinion, a photo index and more.

The Tech

http://the-tech.mit.edu//

The Tech (the oldest and largest campus newspaper) at Massachusetts Institute of Technology maintains this online edition. Visitors can read the twice-weekly issues, search the archives, access general MIT information or link to related technology sites.

The Technician

http://www2.ncsu.edu/ncsu/stud_pubs/Technician/

The electronic edition of the *Technician,* North Carolina State University's thrice-weekly newspaper, features daily news, campus information and an archive of back issues.

Trincoll Journal

http://www.trincoll.edu/tj/trincolljournal.html

The Trincoll Journal, of Connecticut's Trinity College, is an online weekly of student writing that bills itself as the Internet's original Web zine. Incorporating video, sounds and graphics in its articles, the Trincoll Journal is free and open to reader submissions.

University Daily Kansan

http://www.kansan.com/

The University Daily Kansan is the student-produced campus newspaper for the University of Kansas. This online edition features daily campus and sports news, weather and entertainment.

University Newspaper Index

http://beacon-www.asa.utk.edu/resources/papers.html

The Daily Beacon at the University of Tennessee maintains this index of online university newspapers around the world. The site also includes pointers to professional and student journalism organizations and related education resources.

University Publications Gopher

gopher://gopher.tc.umn.edu:70/11/News

This gopher server provides access to a wide range of electronic publications from American universities. Visitors will find newspapers, magazines, journals, reviews and radio news bulletins.

Washington Square News

http://www.nyu.edu/pages/wsn

Washington Square News, the daily student newspaper of New York University, is available here in electronic form. Read its most recent articles, browse an index of back issues, link to other university newspapers, and get a vicarious taste of Greenwich Village.

MAGAZINES AND PERIODICALS

ARCHIVES AND INDICES

Chapman & Hall Electronic Journals

http://www.thomsonscience.com/

Chapman & Hall publishes dozens of highly specialized academic and professional journals, from *Tumor Targeting* to *Leisure Studies*. The company promotes its electronic editions at this site, where visitors can order sample issues or full subscriptions.

CMP Publications

http://www.techweb.com/info/publications

CMP Publications maintains this site for its computer and technology-related publications. Link to a variety of online magazines and periodicals, including *CommunicationsWeek, Home PC, InteractiveAge* and others.

Electronic Newsstand

http://www.enews.com/

The Electronic Newsstand gathers together a collection of published articles from various magazines, newspapers, newsletters and more. A commercial service, the site also links to business information providers.

Fanzine Media

http://www.fanzine.se/

This "media experiment" from a Scandinavian publishing conglomerate creates magazines whose content can be distributed in various media, including the online world. Magazine topics range from snowboarding to horseback riding. Find out more about the company and its publications here.

Journals and Newspapers

http://english-www.hss.cmu.edu/journals/

This online index provides a large alphabetical listing of journals, periodicals and newspapers. Includes a separate new journal index, links to other journal collections and a submission form for new listings.

MagNet

http://www.cris.com/~milewski/magnet.html

MagNet is a listing of computer and Internet magazines. Part of the Milewski Index, it includes links

to *Computer Currents, HotWired,* the *Cybernautics Digest* and many other publications.

Mir—Editoria in Rete

http://www.mir.it/

Visit this site for an index of rabble-rousing Italian periodicals, including the political broadsheets, il *Manifesto* and *Manifestolibri*. In Italian only.

Newsletter Library

http://pub.savvy.com/

The Internet Newsletter Library contains a categorized list of more than 11,000 newsletters covering every topic imaginable—from alcoholism to fly fishing to pharmaceutical developments. Visitors can use the online order form to request free copies of newsletters.

Taxi International Newsstand

http://www.deltanet.com/users/taxicat/newsstand.html

The home page for California-based newsstand *Taxi International News* contains links to Web sites for numerous magazines and newspapers, both electronic and print. A search engine is also provided.

The WWW Virtual Library Electronic Journals Catalog

http://www.edoc.com/ejournal/

The WWW Virtual Library maintains the Electronic Journals Catalog with online search resources, academic journals, magazines and newspapers, a keyword search and more.

POPULAR TITLES

The American Prospect Home Page

http://epn.org/prospect.html

American Prospect Online is the electronic version of that magazine of liberal politics. Here you can read current and back issues, subscribe to the paper edition and contact the editors.

The Biz: The Entertainment Cybernetwork

http://www.bizmag.com/

The Biz features multimedia interviews, music videos and movie trailers, along with news, columns, features and classifieds. Included are the Reuters/Variety Online Entertainment Report and The Source, an entertainment resource guide.

c|net online

http://www.cnet.com

c|net online, a magazine-style spin-off of a cable-TV technology showcase, is a hip yet authoritative guide to cyber culture. It offers interviews with industry kingpins, breaking news from the computer-biz boardroom, software tips, copious

product reviews, game cheats, offbeat links and more.

Coloquio Magazine

http://www.clark.net/pub/jgbustam/coloquio/coloquio.html

Hispanic culture hits the Internet through the Coloquio home page. Visitors can browse back issues of the award-winning magazine, which, in print form, circulates in the Washington, D.C., and Baltimore metropolitan areas.

Computer Gaming World

http://www.zdnet.com/gaming/

The online edition of *Computer Gaming World* offers previews, reviews and the occasional cheat code for electronic gaming products. Find the current issue and a searchable archive of past issues at this site.

Computer Shopper

http://www.zdnet.com/cshopper/

This online version of *Computer Shopper* magazine includes feature stories, pundits and "review nuggets." Visitors can read the latest issue, or review past selections.

Cyberwest Magazine

http://www.cyberwest.com/

Cyberwest is an online magazine featuring a virtual feast of travel adventure and sports information from the American West. Visitors to this site can peruse feature articles, news, views and images or link on to other sites of interest.

Fortean Times

http://alpha.mic.dundee.ac.uk/ft/ft.html

From the United Kingdom, Fortean Times is a cheeky bimonthly magazine that covers "all manner of strange phenomena and experiences, curiosities, prodigies and portents." Visitors will find links to current and past issues, special reports and articles, and subscription information here.

HomeArts

http://homearts.com/meta/mirror/meta7.htm

HomeArts compiles articles and features from the popular Hearst magazines *Redbook, Good Housekeeping, Country Living* and *Popular Mechanics*. The menu is heavy on food, relationships, health, home and garden.

HotWired

http://www.hotwired.com/frontdoor/

HotWired, the techno-savvy online offspring of *Wired* magazine, delivers news, reviews, commentary and features from the cutting edge of online society. Expect nothing short of the cattiest chat, the hippest links and the hottest graphics.

HyperJournal

http://www.gold.ac.uk/history/hyperjournal/hyperj.htm

HyperJournal is a discussion list devoted to electronic journals; those publishing on the Web, in particular. The HyperJournal site has information concerning all aspects of production and publishing.

Interactive Week Online

http://www.zdnet.com/intweek/

Browsers can keep up with the latest in interactive technology here. Interactive Week Online covers the telecommunications industry and contains features from the print magazine plus frequently updated online sections.

The Internet Herald Home Page

http://www.iherald.com/

The Internet Herald, a monthly "journal of news and commentary by Generation X," is an online entertainment, news and opinion magazine. Visit here to read the publication and to find out how to contribute articles, jokes and poetry that speak for a generation.

MacUser Web

http://www.zdnet.com/macuser/

MacUser Web is the online version of *MacUser,* the magazine of hands-on Macintosh and Apple computing. Visitors can download software, read product reviews and browse through back issues of the magazine.

Macworld Online

http://www.macworld.com/

Taking the global perspective, the online version of *Macworld* magazine provides the latest Mac news for the Internet community. Mac fans can read articles, browse the software library, post a note on a message board, or loiter in the site's Technocultural Cafe.

The MoJo Wire

http://www.mojones.com/

Visit MoJo for a scathing look at current political issues. See Editor's Choice.

NetGuide

http://techweb.cmp.com/techweb/ng/current/

NetGuide—one of the many new Internet magazines on the racks—also publishes this online version with much of the material found in print. It features a calendar of online events, reviews, articles and a site of the day.

The Net Online

http://www.thenet-usa.com/

The Net is an online version of a colorful new magazine that marries cartoon graphics, innovative storytelling technique and solid Net news. Readers will also find pointers to shareware here and instructions for subscribing to the print version.

NewsPage

http://www.newspage.com/NEWSPAGE/newspagehome.html

NewsPage, an online trade magazine published by Burlington, Massachusetts-based Individual Inc., offers news and features on a variety of topics. Visit for the latest from the worlds of business, high technology, defense, environmental conservation, media and many others. Updated daily.

Out.com

http://www.out.com/

Visit the Web version of the magazine *Out*. See Editor's Choice.

PC Computing

http://www.zdnet.com/~pccomp/

PC Computing, Ziff-Davis' monthly magazine for the anti-Apple corps, is available in online form at this site. Visit here for industry dirt, product reviews, sneak previews of new software, and even a little humor ("Woody Allen's Hotlist").

PC Gamer: CD-ROM Computer Gaming

http://www.pcgamer.com/

An electronic edition of the popular PC and CD-ROM games magazine, PC Gamer online covers the latest news, trends and reviews in the computer gaming industry.

---

a2z EDITOR'S CHOICE

The MoJo Wire

http://www.mojones.com/

The tagline at Mother Jones Interactive says it's "like punk rock, except it's a Web site." Make no mistake: MoJo is comparing itself to the punk rock of the 1970s; but it's talking about the issues of the 1990s. So...if examining the phenomenon of corporate "downsizing" (and its positive correlation to bloated CEO salaries) makes you sweat; if a sneak peak at "Bob Dole's marriage with Big Tobacco" makes you blush; if the thought of "a case study of the enigmatic first lady" makes you want to go to the gym, perhaps you'd better back up and clear your cache. The rest of you are in for a righteous feast of interactive exposés and politics. And when you're finished reading, queue up all of your good thoughts and head over to Live Wire, MoJo's "interactive ideological battleground." —*Reviewed by James Fitch*

Like punk rock, except it's a web site.

Ebert & Sayles
Roger Ebert and John Sayles list their top 20 political flicks of the past 20 years.

The Axmen Cometh
CEOs say "downsizing" is a bitter pill we must swallow to make American business globally competitive. But does downsizing extend up the ladder? See what you think.

Who's Hillary?
As a Senate committee zeroes in on Hillary's role in Whitewater, we explore the First Lady's past.

Election '96
Field Reports: Bob Dole quits his day job, but he still has to pick a running mate to play in his garage band.

Who's on Board:
MoJo exposes extremist NRA board members, from rock star Ted Nugent to *Soldier of Fortune* publisher Robert K. Brown.

Tobacco Strikes Back
Our series of exposés about the tobacco industry: Bob Dole's marriage with Big Tobacco, the Christian Coalition's unholy compromise, and video clips from the tobacco exposé ABC wouldn't air.

The MoJo 400
The MoJo Wire's list of America's biggest political donors and who they gave to. Investigate on your own with our searchable database of the Fat Cats' itemized contributions.

PC Magazine

http://www.zdnet.com/~pcmag/

PC Magazine delivers the latest dope from the desktop. This online edition provides up-to-the-minute computer-industry news, downloadable software, feature articles such as "How To Be Hip in the Cyberscene" and reviews of the latest hardware and software.

PC Week Online

http://www.pcweek.com/

Find breaking computer-biz news, columns, special reports and rumors at this searchable site archiving the online edition of *PC Week* magazine. Highfalutin' opinions, Internet news and software downloads are also featured along with links to other Ziff-Davis publishing sites.

PC World Online

http://www.pcworld.com/

Consumers and industry denizens alike will find informative news and reviews in the current edition of *PC World Online*. The electronic version of the major computer monthly offers the latest info on hardware, software and PC-related enterprises.

Penthouse on the Internet

http://www.penthousemag.com/

Adults-only publication *Penthouse* magazine unveils its online version here. Visitors will find sexually oriented stories, cartoons and jokes, along with photos of women without clothes. Includes an erotic toy store.

Popular Mechanics PM Zone

http://popularmechanics.com/

The tinkerer's bible, *Popular Mechanics,* is available online at the PM Zone. From hard drives to drive trains, this site traverses both the real and the virtual superhighways of the world. Search back issues here or sign up for a subscription to the newsstand version.

Smithsonian

http://www.smithsonianmag.si.edu/

The online version of *Smithsonian* magazine features columns and articles about the arts, environment, culture and entertainment, history and "America's attic." Online subscription ordering is also available, as well as a gift shop.

Spiegel Online

http://www.spiegel.de/

Spiegel Online is the electronic version of the popular German news magazine, *Der Spiegel.* Visit here to find national and international news, photos, and sports coverage. Available in German and English.

TexasMonthly WWW Ranch

http://www.texasmonthly.com/

Mosey on over to a site that bills itself as the ultimate Texas resource, the TexasMonthly WWW Ranch. The online version of the free-thinking regional magazine wrestles with such topics as whether executions should be public, and offers a roundup of offbeat feature stories on life in the Lone Star State. Visitors will also find entertainment listings, Texas-sized classifieds and cooking tips.

Time Magazine

http://pathfinder.com/@@0wENugUAJOjDIki7/time/

This home page for the venerable newsmagazine *Time* contains a bevy of topical news stories, analysis and interactive options. Visitors can check out the current week's edition or browse back issues. Includes a daily news service and international editions for Asia and Europe.

---

a2z EDITOR'S CHOICE

Out.com

http://www.out.com/

Neither "out there" nor particularly outrageous, Out.com turns the Web inside out with subtle, stylish aplomb; a piece of cake when you're already sailing with a wildly popular print version. Out's electronic baby sister, which is claiming to be the number one gay and lesbian Web site, delivers an excellent sampling each month of the magazine's authoritative look at gay culture, news and politics. The site's frames-based interface may make navigation a bit perplexing, but what you'll eventually unearth is well worth the effort. Pros like Liz Smith and Michelangelo Signorile lend their distinctive points of view while the usual brood of frontline reporters and leisurely reviewers keeps us abreast of everything from Internet censorship to the latest Tori Amos opus. Tongue planted firmly in cheek, Out.com also serves up a few "gratuitous boy, girl" shots, updated regularly, "just to keep you interested." —*Reviewed by James Fitch*

Time Out

http://www.timeout.co.uk/

Time Out Net provides city guides and arts and entertainment listings for international hot spots. Features about Berlin, London, Madrid, New York, Paris, San Francisco, and other world-class cities can be found here, along with free classified ads.

The Utne Lens

http://www.utne.com/

The Utne Reader is an unabashedly "progressive" magazine that collects and publishes articles and excerpts from alternative media sources. Cyber folk can visit its online persona, the Utne Lens, for left-of-center news and commentary.

The Village Voice WorldWide

http://www.villagevoice.com/

New York's legendary weekly newspaper sounds its distinctive voice via the Web with electronic exclusives and a generous sampling of the weekly print version. Besides the trademark cutting-edge news, views and criticism (not to mention those great personals), visitors to this site will find nightlife listings for New York, and a link to the Voice's West Coast cousin, LA Weekly.

Webster's Weekly

http://www.awa.com/w2/

Webster's Weekly is an esoteric online digest offering a liberal mix of arts, entertainment and serious thought from a "humanist" perspective. Features range from a guide to safe sex to movie reviews to a gun-owner's column. Features include a handy sampler for first-time browsers, an index to current issues and links to the archives.

WinMagWeb

http://www.winmag.com/

For a comprehensive source of Windows information, visit the Internet home of *Windows* magazine. This site complements the print version with articles on systems, software and other Windows-related topics.

REFERENCE INFORMATION

ARCHIVES AND INDICES

Information SuperLibrary

http://www.mcp.com/index.html

The Information SuperLibrary hosts online homes for publishing heavy hitters such as Macmillan, Simon and Schuster, and SSI Distribution Services. Visitors are invited to browse reference works, resource directories, software libraries, the Internet Starter Kit and more.

The Internet Services List

http://www.spectracom.com/islist/

Special Internet Connections, a collection of online resources, provides links to information on a variety of topics. Visit here to browse its extensive index of subjects, from business and biology to space and sports.

Library Catalog Index

gopher://libgopher.yale.edu:70/11/

Yale University posts an extensive index of online library catalogs on this gopher menu. The index is arranged by country.

Media Research Laboratory Home Page

http://found.cs.nyu.edu/MRL/

The Media Research Laboratory, a New York-based interdisciplinary communications technology research organization, maintains this site for general information, research resources and links to related institutions. Includes contact information and feedback forms.

National Institutes of Health Desk Reference

gopher://odie.niaid.nih.gov/11/deskref

The National Institutes of Health has created this virtual desk reference to provide quick access to a variety of online dictionaries, directories, guides and almanacs. Read articles from the Voice of America or find out how much vitamin C a peach contains.

Online Reference Works

http://www.cs.cmu.edu/Web/references.html

This site provides an index to reference books, databases and other media found online. Among the reference sources featured are dictionaries, encyclopedias, maps and catalogs.

RiceInfo gopher

gopher://chico.rice.edu:70/11/Subject

Gopher to the RiceInfo Information collection and find an alphabetized menu of academic subject categories. Use RiceInfo to locate electronic resources related to subjects such as aerospace, sociology or women's studies.

THOR+: The Virtual Reference Desk

http://thorplus.lib.purdue.edu/reference/index.html

Maintained by the Libraries of Purdue University, this site offers access to a virtual library of reference books and materials. Among the resources are dictionaries, selected documents concerning information technology, maps, U.S. documents, phone books, weather data and more.

TheYellowPages.com

http://theyellowpages.com/

TheYellowPages.com is an Internet directory cataloging Web resources by subject. Find links to subject sites ranging from Architecture to Zoology.

ASSORTED FACTS AND FIGURES

Britannica Online

http://www.eb.com/eb.htm

Britannica Online bills itself as "the first encyclopedia on the Internet." A subscriber service, the page won't permit searching but will allow users to sign up for a free trial or purchase an annual subscription.

Britannica's Lives

http://www.eb.com/calendar/calendar.html

Britannica's Lives is a collection of all the biographies listed in the Encyclopedia Britannica. Visitors can enter a birthdate and age range, and Britannica will then provide all the biographies that fit that description.

Bureau of Transportation Statistics

http://www.bts.gov/

The U.S. Department of Transportation's Bureau of Transportation Statistics offers access to resources related to pedestrians, transit, safety, design and other transportation issues at this information site. Link to the National Transportation Library, Office of Airline Information or Geographical Information Services.

Earth View

http://www.fourmilab.ch/cgi-bin/uncgi/Earth/action?opt=-p

A current global topographic map of Earth is offered at this site. Visitors can manipulate various controls (latitude, longitude, satellite source and the like) to access the precise information they desire.

Emergency Preparedness Information Exchange Gopher

gopher://hoshi.cic.sfu.ca:5555/

The Emergency Preparedness Information Exchange posts information on emergency preparedness and dealing with the results of natural disasters. The site is maintained by the Center for Policy Research on Science and Technology at Simon Fraser University in Toronto.

Flags

http://155.187.10.12/flags/flags.html

This site contains a representative collection of links to images and information about flags and their use. Motor racing flags, selected national flags, maritime signal flags, and semaphore are featured.

POPClock Projection

http://www.census.gov/cgi-bin/popclock

The projected population of the U.S. at the current date and time is calculated and displayed upon access to the POPClock Projection site. Link to the documentation page for background information.

The Quotations Page

http://www.starlingtech.com/quotes/

This site provides a complex reference resource for quotes. It will also translate unknown acronyms and abbreviations. See Editor's Choice, page 709.

Survival Bible 2001

http://www.io.org/~richard

Whether you fear revolutions or earthquakes, you'll find handy advice for filling your basement with provisions in the Survival Bible. With research drawing on events from "2001 B.C. to 2001 A.D.," you'll find one-stop information shopping for surviving in all climates and conditions.

Today's Fun Fact

http://www.dreamsville.com/CSN/Wardo/fact.html

Today's Fun Fact delivers just what the title promises, each and every day. Includes links to previous factoids, subscription information and the Webmaster's home page.

U.S. Census Bureau

http://www.census.gov/

The U.S. Census Bureau, the nitpicking federal agency that tracks demographics trends and population statistics across the country, offers access to its databases on population and housing, the economy and geography. Includes a search tool.

World of Maps

http://www.worldofmaps.com/

Now there is no excuse for getting lost. World of Maps comes to the rescue with literally thousands of travel maps and books from every country in the world. Maps for streets, topo areas, nautical terrain—you name it—are accessible from this page.

Xerox PARC Map Viewer: world 0.00N 0.00E

http://mapweb.parc.xerox.com/map/

The Xerox Palo Alto, California lab presents the PARC Map Viewer. This global map allows viewers to pinpoint longitude and latitude readings, as well as other earthly details.

DATE AND TIME

Date and Time Gateway

http://www.bsdi.com/date

This index provides the time and date for cities around the world in Greenwich Mean Time. City listings are arranged alphabetically within continental categories.

Directorate of Time

http://tycho.usno.navy.mil/time.html

The U.S. Naval Observatory in Washington, D.C., uses this site to provide the time of day according to its highly accurate atomic clock. Visit here to find the time anywhere in the world, learn how the clock works and link to its time services, including telephone and modem connections.

---

a2z EDITOR'S CHOICE

The Quotations Page

http://www.starlingtech.com/quotes/

Equal parts Web gizmo and desktop reference, the Quotations Page and the World Wide Web Acronym and Abbreviation Server are the ultimate bookmarks for those who find themselves tapping the keyboard at a loss for words (or for those staring blankly at nine capital letters in a row). If—as the quote that opens the Quotations Page states—"Language exists to conceal true thought," you'll find 10 distinctive closets full of funky and formal shrouds for any occasion here (from the Webmaster's own collection to Dave Barry's to the Devil's Dictionary). Check out the site's quotes of the day, roll the dice for quotes at random, or type in a keyword for an assortment of topical sayings. We typed in "bored" and found that "The cure for boredom is curiosity." Then we typed in "curiosity," only to find that "Curiosity killed the cat." Life is confusing…and so are those pesky acronyms and abbreviations. Like a gift from the cybergods, the Acronym and Abbreviation Server demystifies such wretched combos as ROTFLASTC (rolling on the floor laughing and scaring the cat) and LTBFYPW (learn to be funny, you pathetic wanker). The nifty gadget not only allows you to you punch in an acronym to see its expansion, but to search for a word in the expansion, and to submit your favorite acronym for inclusion in the database. Rated VG. (Look it up.) —*Reviewed by James Fitch*

Local Times Around the World

http://www.hilink.com.au/times/

Want to know the time in Bora Bora or Beijing? This page provides the local times in all the world's countries and most of the islands.

U.S. Naval Observatory Master Clock

http://tycho.usno.navy.mil/what.html

With this interactive site, the U.S. Naval Observatory answers the eternal question, "What time is it?" Eastern, Central, Mountain, Pacific, Universal. Whatever's your pleasure.

DICTIONARIES AND TRANSLATORS

Cool Word of the Day

http://www.edu.yorku.ca/~wotd

This educational site features a new word each day along with its definition. Visitors can also review past words and nominate cool words they think should be chosen in the future.

English-German Dictionary

http://www.tu-chemnitz.de/urz/netz/forms/dict.html

This interactive site allows visitors to find German equivalents for English words, and vice versa. Simply enter a word, German or English, and search (or *suche*). Instructions are in German only.

The Eurodicautom

http://www.public.iastate.edu/~pedro/pt_all/pt_dict.html

The Eurodicautom is a program that translates technical and official terms. Visitors can translate terms between eight different major European languages. Presented in English and Portuguese.

Hypertext Webster Interface

http://c.gp.cs.cmu.edu:5103/prog/webster/

The Hypertext Webster Interface provides a point-and-click service for accessing the famous dictionary publisher's services on the Net. Included is a word search function that links the browser to a variety of hypertext definition pages.

The University of Tromso Dictionaries Page

http://www.ub.uit.no/dictionaries.html

This Norwegian site contains a variety of translation dictionaries including English-French, English-Japanese, and English-Italian. An online *Roget's Thesaurus* and other references manuals are here, too. The page itself is in Norwegian.

Webster's Hypertext Interface Search

http://c.gp.cs.cmu.edu:5103/prog/webster?/

This online resource offers visitors a hypertext interface with the *Webster's Dictionary* services on the Internet. Features include apoint-and-click keyword search.

INFORMATION RETRIEVAL SERVICES

DataStar

http://www.krinfo.ch/

The DataStar Information Retrieval Service, a news and information search engine, offers access to hundreds of databases worldwide. Visit to browse its index of resources or perform a keyword search.

LEXIS-NEXIS Communication Center

http://www.lexis-nexis.com/

The LEXIS-NEXIS Communications Center introduces the company's widely used online legal, news and business information services. Full-text archival and current publication searches and reference access are the hallmark of this commercial information provider.

PHONE AND POSTAL DIRECTORIES

AmeriCom Long Distance Area Decoder

http://www.xmission.com/~americom/aclookup.html

Need to reach that ol' college chum from across the sea? This handy device will spit out the appropriate country and area code for dialing locales around the world. It will also quote you a per-minute connection charge. Thus we learn that for Glasgow, Scotland, the country code is 44, the area code is 141, and it will cost 35 pence a minute to chat with McDougal.

AT&T Toll-Free 800 Directory

http://www.tollfree.att.net/dir800/

The AT&T Toll-Free 800 Directory provides listings of all 800 telephone numbers carried by the long distance phone company. The database can be searched by category or keyword. User help is available.

National Address Server

http://www.cedar.buffalo.edu/adserv.html

Visitors to this Web site, set up by the Center of Excellence for Document Analysis and Recognition, can enter an address in hopes of retrieving a PostScript file containing a printable barcode for speed delivery of their mail.

TODAY'S WEATHER

INTERNATIONAL

Australian Weather Forecasts

http://atmos.es.mq.edu.au/weather/ausweather.html

For current and forecasted meteorological conditions down under, consult the Australian Weather Forecasts site. A graphical interface to data from the Australian Bureau of Meteorology greets weather-curious visitors.

Canada Public Weather Forecasts

http://www.on.doe.ca/text/

The Public Weather Forecasts site provides up-to-the-minute weather predictions for cities and regions across Canada. The forecasts are sorted by province. (Northern Territories: chilly.) In English and French.

CRS4 Meteo Satellite Images for Italy

http://www.crs4.it/~luigi/METEO/meteo.html

Take a look at the weather in Europe as it develops each day through the CRS4 Meteo home page. The site features weather movies produced from a series of regularly updated satellite images focused on Italy.

The Geosynchronous Operational Environmental Satellite (GOES) Project

http://climate.gsfc.nasa.gov/~chesters/goesproject.html

Look at tonight's weather satellite image before you watch the news to get a jump on the newscasters. (The GOES satellite provides images for news broadcasts.) Visitors to this site can also look through the archived images or learn about field experiments.

German Climate Computing Center

http://www.dkrz.de/

The German Climate Computing Center monitors and researches weather conditions in Germany. This site provides research data, various software, and tools for viewing the data. In English and German.

Hurricane Watch

http://www.netcreations.com/hurricane

This Web site tracks hurricanes and provides interested parties with radar, satellite and infrared images of tropical storms. Includes links to public and marine advisories, the Disaster Information Network and the National Weather Service's severe weather warnings.

INTELLiCast Home Page

http://www.intellicast.com/

NBC News presents this online guide to weather and skiing information. Visitors can check out U.S. and International conditions here (enhanced with maps and photos) or link back to the news source for headlines.

Interactive Weather Browser

http://rs560.cl.msu.edu/weather/interactive.html

Here is a site that allows visitors to type in a geographical location and find out current weather conditions.

Kochi University, Weather Index

http://www.is.kochi-u.ac.jp/weather/index.html

This world weather information server, maintained by the Department of Information Science of Japan's Kochi University, offers weather forecasts, updates, satellite images and more. Visit here for meteorological data from around the globe.

Live Access to Climate Data

http://ferret.wrc.noaa.gov/fbin/climate_server

Live Access to Climate Data provides current information on climate and meteorological conditions worldwide. Includes a data entry form for specific geographic locations.

Macquarie University Atmospheric Science Program

http://atmos.es.mq.edu.au/

The School of Earth Sciences at Australia's Macquarie University in Sydney presents this overview of its Atmospheric Science program. Also find a searchable database of atmospheric science servers such as the Automatic Weather Station.

South African Weather Bureau

http://cirrus.sawb.gov.za/

The South African Weather Bureau maintains this online weather information server. Find forecasts, current weather, radar images, charts, dawn and dusk timetables, and more.

StormCast at the University of Tromso

http://www.cs.uit.no/~ken/images/big/weather.gif

The StormCast Project at the University of Tromso (in sunny Norway) provides a short local weather forecast and a great big photo of present conditions in the scenic Tromso valley.

Tropical Weather

http://asp1.sbs.ohio-state.edu/tropicaltext.html

Ohio State's Tropical Weather site combines information on the general conditions of tropical weather patterns with specific updates about storms and other meteorological features of the tropics.

Weather & Climate Images

http://grads.iges.org/pix/head.html

Get a current and accurate picture of today's weather in the United States and around the world. Get a look at tomorrow's weather, while you're at it.

Weather Machine Gopher Menu

gopher://wx.atmos.uiuc.edu:70/1

The Weather Machine Gopher Server is located in the Department of Atmospheric Sciences at the University of Illinois. Visitors will find easy access to weather information for locations around the world.

Weather Maps to Go

http://rs560.cl.msu.edu/weather/getmegif.html

Customize Weather Maps to Go at this site by the Michigan State University Unix Computing Group. Online help assists users to specify rendering options and station IDs.

WeatherNet: Tropical Weather Products

http://cirrus.sprl.umich.edu/wxnet/tropical.html

If you're fascinated by hurricanes, WeatherNet's Tropical Weather page offers access to related advisories, complete with tracking maps, satellite photos and storm progress reports.

WeatherNet: Weather Cams

http://cirrus.sprl.umich.edu/wxnet/wxcam.html

Seeing is believing is the predication upon which WeatherCam is founded. Meteorologists' prognostications aside, skeptical weather buffs can visit this site to get an almost live picture of the weather conditions in the city of their choosing.

U.S.

California Snow Page

http://snow.water.ca.gov/

California Cooperative Snow Surveys releases data relating to California water supplies through the monitoring of mountain snowpack levels and local water sources. It contains updated information valuable to travelers, such as road conditions and avalanche reports.

Chicago Weather from INTELLiCast

http://www.intellicast.com/weather/ord/

This page offers weather-related information about Chicago. Visitors will find a four-day forecast, along with satellite images, Chicago weather history and more.

Current U.S. Weather

http://www.mit.edu:8001/usa.html

This map-based site delivers current U.S. weather conditions. For forecasts, simply click on the corresponding area of the map. Links to other weather resources are also provided.

Current Weather Maps/Movies

http://rs560.cl.msu.edu/weather/

Michigan State University's Unix computing group plays meteorologist at this site, providing weather news and forecasts for the Lansing, Michigan area. Also here: satellite shots of Earth and a national weather summary.

Daily Planet: Weather and Climate

http://www.atmos.uiuc.edu/weather/weather.html

From the Daily Planet site, this page features a list of links to popular weather and climate resources. Find the Weather World Web Server, the Weather Machine Gopher Server, the United States Climate Page, instructional materials in climatology, text-based model forecast tools and more.

Dykki's Custom Weather Service

http://sunsite.unc.edu/dykki/ncweather.html

Statewide and regional weather forecasts for North Carolina are posted here. Visitors can read text reports on current conditions or download the latest satellite images.

Florida Institute of Technology School of Aeronautics

http://sci-ed.fit.edu/soa/soa.html

The highlights of this site from the Florida Institute of Technology's School of Aeronautics include an updated Florida radar image, a Central Florida four-day forecast and the national weather outlook. Also included is information about the school's programs and facilities.

Hawaii Meteorology

http://www.hawaii.edu/News/weather.html

The latest weather information for the Hawaiian Islands can be accessed at this page. Includes satellite photos, along with infrared images and weather forecasts.

Hawaii Weather and Surf

http://www.hawaii.edu/News/weather.html

This informational site, maintained by the University of Hawaii, is for those who surf the ocean—as well as the Internet. Visit here for local surf and weather conditions, satellite photos and links to other weather-related Web sites.

High Plains Climate Center

http://hpccsun.unl.edu/

At this site, meteorologists can download satellite maps of North America and maps with updated information from the Automated Weather Data Network. Nebraskans can download weather forecasts for the Cornhusker State and maps related to drought and crop moisture.

Hurricane Home Page

http://www.hurricane.com/

A service of Coral Technologies Inc., this page provides information on hurricanes and tropical storms for Florida's Broward, Dade, Monroe and Palm Beach Counties. At this site, visitors can check out radar and satellite images of storms or link to the National Hurricane Center's home page.

The Lighthouse Weather Server

http://the-tech.mit.edu/Weather/

This interactive site provides up-to-the-minute weather reports and forecasts for most U.S. cities. Includes links to the U.S. National Weather Summary and the International Weather Summary.

National Weather Service

http://www.nws.noaa.gov/

An agency of the National Oceanic and Atmospheric Administration, the National Weather Service offers visitors to its page an operations overview, answers to Frequently Asked Questions (FAQs), and links to weather data, including forecasts and warnings, charts, and climate information.

New Jersey Weather

http://www.nj.com/weather/

The New Jersey Online weather page focuses on the local region, but also features forms with which visitors can check the five-day forecasts for their cities. Other almanac-type information is included.

North Carolina State University Meteorology

http://meawx1.nrrc.ncsu.edu/

North Carolina State University's meteorology server provides up-to-date weather information for the Raleigh area, plus regional and national weather maps and various satellite images. Includes links to servers providing tropical storm updates and National Weather Service data.

Northeast Regional Climate Center

http://met-www.cit.cornell.edu/

From the Northeast Regional Climate Center page, find a database collected by Cornell University containing useful information for climatologists who need up-to-date weather info and climate conditions.

Oregon Climate Service

http://ocs.ats.orst.edu/

The Oregon Climate Service is the state repository for weather and climate information. Its home page provides the latest Oregon weather forecasts and images, as well as publications, data archives and precipitation mapping.

Unidata Integrated Earth Information Servers

http://atm.geo.nsf.gov/ieis/weather.html

This site provides the latest weather data and forecasts for the Washington, D.C., metropolitan area. It also has links to other U.S. weather sites, ski reports and polar data.

University of Washington Department of Atmospheric Sciences

http://www.atmos.washington.edu/

The Department of Atmospheric Sciences of the University of Washington offers departmental information and news, plus Seattle area weather data and links to other weather-related servers. Visit here for satellite images, forecasts, and weather information from across the U.S.

Virginia State Climatology Office

http://faraday.clas.virginia.edu/~climate

Weather and climate information for the State of Virginia can be viewed on this page from the Virginia State Climatology Office. Visitors can read current weather conditions and zoned forecasts, as well as view Doppler radar images.

WeatherNet: Travel Cities Weather

http://cirrus.sprl.umich.edu/wxnet/wsi.html

WeatherNet provides this server with current weather information for more than 20 cities across the U.S. Browers can read weather forecasts, conditions and climate reports or view satellite images here.

THE ROAD LESS TRAVELED

THE 25 MOST POPULAR SITES ON THE ROAD LESS TRAVELED

Adze Mixxe: Astrologist Extraordinaire
http://www.adze.com/

Alien Information
http://www.iinet.com.au/~bertino/alien.html

Anders Magick Page
http://www.nada.kth.se/~nv91-asa/magick.html

Astral Projection Home Page
http://www.lava.net/~goodin/astral.html

Celestia
http://www.celestia.com/alpha/

CoGweb
http://www.cog.org/cog/

The Crossroads
http://www.io.com/~mjg/

Dr. Bruce Cornet: A Special Presentation
http://www.cee.hw.ac.uk/~ceewb/fsr/fsrhome.htm

The Dream and The Interpretation—Dream Analysis
http://www-edin.easynet.co.uk/douglas/

50 Greatest Conspiracies of All Time
http://www.webcom.com/~conspire/

Fortean Times
http://alpha.mic.dundee.ac.uk/ft/ft.html

FringeWare Inc.
http://www.fringeware.com/

Graphology Club Home Page
http://www.ntu.ac.sg/~tjlow/gclub.html

Harry Harrison's New AgeWWW Home Page
http://pages.prodigy.com/psychics/psychicplay.html

Horoscopes / Astrology : Weekly Cyber-Stars from John James
http://www.bubble.com/cybstars/stars.html

Hypnosis.com
http://www.hypnosis.com/

Lifestyles International Astrological Foundation
http://oeonline.com/~lifeintl/

Mysticism in the World's Religions
http://www.realtime.net/~rlp/dwp/mystic/

The Pronoia Page
http://myhouse.com/pronoia/

Shamanistic Healing-Energies on the Internet
http://www.prgone.com/bus/dpedro/

StrangeMag
http://www.cais.com/strangemag/home.html

Tarot Resources
http://www.iii.net/users/dtking/tarot.html

Tribal Voice
http://www.tribal.com/

Vodoun (or Voodoo) Information Pages
http://www.vmedia.com/shannon/voodoo/voodoo.html

White Mountain Education Association
http://www.primenet.com/~wtmtn/

CONSPIRACIES AND HOAXES

ARCHIVES AND INDICES

50 Greatest Conspiracies of All Time
http://www.webcom.com/~conspire/
The 50 Greatest Conspiracies of All Time home page delivers exactly what it promises: theories on aliens and UFOs, JFK's assassination, AIDS as a U.S. biological warfare operation — if you suspect it, it's here. Includes a tool allowing visitors to search the site by key word.

Gonzo Links
http://www.capcon.net/users/lbenedet/
Gonzo Links is your guide to fringe Web sites unlikely to be tampered with by McCarthy's America. Link to sites dealing with conspiracy theories, UFOs, cults and other esoteric material that bends the outer limits of mainstream conservatism.

New Paradigms Project
http://gopher.a-albionic.com:9006/
A virtual library of conspiracy theories, the New Paradigms Project catalogs bibliographic information and links regarding assassination conspiracies, secret societies and more.

Psychedelic Tabby Cabal
http://www.paranoia.com/~fraterk/
Psychedelic Tabby Cabal links conspiracy theoreticians, drug enthusiasts and the just plain curious to dozens of commentaries, pages, and discussion groups dealing with off-the-wall topics.

Real History Archives and Links
http://www.webcom.com/~lpease/
The Real History Archives and Links page is packed full of conspiracy theories on everything from Waco to the Kennedy asassination to the Iran-Contra scandal. Some investigative pieces ferreting out the "hidden truth" behind the government's official version of events also are featured.

Skeptic Annotated Bibliography
http://www.public.iastate.edu/~edis/skeptic_biblio.html
This site provides visitors with an annotated index of resources offering skeptical treatments of fringe science issues such as UFOs, ESP and paranormal

events. Features include links to other Internet resources, including newsgroups and FTP sites.

The Skeptic's Dictionary
http://wheel.dcn.davis.ca.us/~btcarrol/skeptic/dictcont.html
Don't fall for all that paranormal baloney, huh? Neither does Bob Carroll, philosophy professor from the University of California. He put together this Skeptic's Dictionary that almost debunks the elements of "self-deception," from aliens to Yeti.

Survival Bible 2001
http://www.io.org/~richard/
Whether you fear revolutions or earthquakes, you'll find handy advice for filling your basement with provisions in the Survival Bible. With research drawing on events from "2001 B.C. to 2001 A.D.," you'll find one-stop information shopping for surviving in all climates and conditions.

ASSOCIATIONS AND ORGANIZATIONS

Skeptics Society Web
http://www.skeptic.com/
The Skeptics Society promotes science and critical thinking, and disseminates information on pseudoscience, pseudohistory, the paranormal, etc. This site highlights skeptical resources, including an electronic version of "Skeptic" magazine.

GOVERNMENT COVER-UPS AND ABUSES

Abuses of the Bureau of Alcohol, Tobacco, and Firearms
http://www.access.digex.net/~croaker/batfabus.html
This page provides an "unofficial collection" of anecdotes relating to alleged abuses of power by the U.S. Bureau of Alcohol, Tobacco, and Firearms. Includes article reprints and a section entitled "Strange Things BATF Agents Do."

Real History Archives and Links
http://www.webcom.com/~lpease/
The Real History Archives and Links page is packed full of conspiracy theories on everything from Waco to the Kennedy asassination to the Iran-Contra scandal. Some investigative pieces ferreting out the "hidden truth" behind the government's official version of events also are featured.

Silo
http://www.xvt.com/users/kevink/silo/silo.html
Explore the subterranean missile sites of a bygone era. See Editor's Choice.

The Unabomber's Manifesto
http://www.panix.com/~clays/Una/index.html
Maybe the Feds bagged the Unabomber, maybe not. But the terrorist's manifesto, "Industrial Society And Its Future," lives on in its full-length, hyperlinked glory here. A table of contents and footnotes are provided

HOAXES AND CONSPIRACY THEORIES

The Lisa Marie Home Page
http://www.docs.uu.se/~y89hbo/presley/lisa.html
Lisa Marie Presley may not be who you think. See Editor's Choice.

The Pronoia Page
http://myhouse.com/pronoia/
Browsers here can delve into the world of "pronoia," the suspicion that others are conspiring to help you—that is, the opposite of paranoia. Includes links to religious, musical and political sites that the webmaster believes foster pronoia.

Real History Archives and Links
http://www.webcom.com/~lpease/
The Real History Archives and Links page is packed full of conspiracy theories on everything from Waco to the Kennedy asassination to the Iran-Contra scandal. Some investigative pieces ferreting out the "hidden truth" behind the government's official version of events also are featured.

The War On Drugs Is a Scam
http://www.paranoia.com/~fraterk/wod.html
The War on Drugs is "a fraudulent waste of taxpayer's money fighting a battle which cannot be won," says this page. Arguments against criminalization of drugs, the uses of hemp and drug information resources can be found here.

Yoknapatawpha County, Law Enforcement Division Evidence File
http://www.quest.net/crime/crime.html
The Sheriff's Office lets you peruse evidence in hopes that you will uncover helpful clues. Not for the squeamish.

a2z **EDITOR'S CHOICE**

Silo

http://www.xvt.com/users/kevink/silo/silo.html

Watch your footing here as you ease your way down the creepy corridor to the control room. If you fall and are injured, there may not be a way out! The total emptiness of this abandoned underground missle site exudes a lonely eeriness. Using detailed photographs of the rooms, corridors and entrances to these underground tunnels, Webmasters take you on a tour of a labyrinth relic of the Cold War, but you're off-site, out of danger—radioactive or otherwise. Entering an abandoned missile site is against Federal trespassing laws, and these Webmasters got caught (but not before they could process the film). "Do not try to enter one of these sites yourself," they warn. "Felony charges will haunt you the rest of your life! Even in the middle of nowhere, they're watching." But you don't have to take that risk on this virtual tour. Careful coming out, though; make sure there's no rancher standing over you with a loaded shotgun.—*Reviewed by Eugenia Johnson*

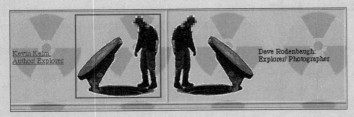

Kevin Kelm
Author/ Explorer

Dave Rodenbaugh
Explorer/ Photographer

The Lisa Marie Home Page

http://www.docs.uu.se/~y89hbo/presley/lisa.html

Michael Jackson may believe that the Lisa Marie he married is Elvis Presley's daughter, but the folks here claim they have evidence that the public figure known as Lisa Marie is NOT Elvis's daughter, but a ringer. They maintain that the real Lisa Marie disappeared in 1977 and has not been seen since. Evidence presented includes "scientific" reports, recorded conversations and "exclusive" photographs. Study the purported fake signature of Vernon Presley on a dubious will ("experts ... have indicated that the signature ... is forged"), or marvel at the words of Lisa Marie's cousin Jimmy Velvet: "This ... girl could have taken Lisa's place and Lisa could be over in Europe ... I know the snake that Priscilla is ... Lisa Marie hasn't been around for years ...." Also find an analysis of vertical facial proportion based on facial growth studies, and an age progression carried out by digital imaging specialists showing a very different Lisa Marie. We dare the National Enquirer to top this one.—*Reviewed by Eugenia Johnson*

The Lisa Marie Home Page

World Power Systems

http://www.wps.com/

At World Power Systems visitors can find out about propane as a motor fuel, the toilet camera hoax and scads more fascinating stuff. Tom Jennings' personal home page also features a photo of an "early, miserable attempt at a VR helmet" and a travelogue of the southwest U.S.

JOURNALS AND PERIODICALS

Skeptic Magazine

http://www.skeptic.com/ss-skeptic.html

The journal of the Skeptics Society maintains this page offering access to current and back issues. Guidelines for subscribing, advertising and submitting articles also are featured.

CRYSTAL BALL

ARCHIVES AND INDICES

The Crossroads

http://www.io.com/~mjg/

Have your fortune told or relive popular myths and legends at the Crossroads. The site offers pointers to Vision Quest Online, an art gallery and Strange Fire, a journal of unorthodox spirituality.

ASTROLOGY

Astrology—The Metalog Yellow Pages

http://www.astrologer.com/

If you're wondering what the stars have to say about your astrological forecast, Metalog may have the answer. Connect with international astrologers and get a listing of popular books.

AstroMatch Hotline

http://www.xiisigns.com/xiisigns

Find out how compatible you are with your date or loved ones using the astrological system developed by the AstroMatch Hotline. This page includes information about how people can reach the hotline and how to order a self-harmony report.

Bantam Doubleday's Daily Horoscopes

http://www.bdd.com/horo1/bddhoro1.cgi/horo1

Will you find romance? Money? Success? See what the stars have in store for you at Bantam Doubleday Dell's (BDD) Daily Horoscopes. BDD uses this page for more than just cosmic connections; it includes a full range of book titles and featured authors.

Barbara Schermer's Astrology Page

http://www.lightworks.com/Astrology/Alive/

Barbara Schermer, professional astrologer and author of several books on the subject, maintains this page with information about her services, which include astrological reports by e-mail. Book chapters, articles and appearances by guest astrologers are also featured here.

Cosmopolis's High-Tech Horoscopes

http://www.xmission.com/~mustard/cosmo.html

Get a technologically advanced horoscope from Cosmopolis Panopolus, part-time astrologer, full-time fat content manager at a sausage factory. Be warned, however: You may not receive the news you desire. One horoscope cautioned that Cancers "will discover that you really like country music."

Destiny Starworks

http://www.tq.com/destiny_starworks/destiny_starworks_home.html

Astrology for the 21st century to explaining the unexplainable. See Editor's Choice.

Lifestyles International Astrological Foundation

http://www.lifeintl.com

Find out what's in the stars for you at the Lifestyles International Astrological Foundation. Guests can link to articles and information from astrologers, read celebrity profiles, or check out the foundation's offer to custom-write astrological profiles for clients and celebrities.

Metalog Yellow Pages

http://www.astrologer.com:80/

Search for an astrologer in your neck of the woods through the Metalog Yellow Pages. It offers country-by-country listings as well as a utility allowing astrologers to register for inclusion in the list.

Adze Mixxe: Astrologist Extraordinaire

http://www.adze.com/

AdZe MiXXe bills himself as an "astrologist extraordinaire." Here on his home page, visitors can evaluate that claim for themselves by checking out his 'zine, celebrity astrology profiles, astrology news and more. Visitors can also order MiXXe's books here.

Your Personal Horoscope

http://www.realitycom.com/webstars/order/personal.html

True believers can buy a personal horoscope reading here that contains aspect, element and quality charts. The British-based site takes orders over the Internet or via fax.

Your Year Ahead

http://www.realitycom.com/webstars/order/yahd.html

Guests at this page can purchase personal horoscopes by Jonathan Cainer when visiting this site. Included in the price: astrological information such as chart wheels, planetary positions and a look at important transits affecting the individual.

Weekly Cyber-Stars from John James

http://www.bubble.com/cybstars/stars.html

Visitors to this page can check out their horoscopes for the week. Links to some astrological/New Age links are also featured.

PREDICTIONS AND PROPHESIES

Magic Infinity-Ball

http://www.jaked.org/8ball.html

The Magic Infinity-ball answers questions about love, money, health or whatever is on the mind. Simply ask a yes or no question to receive prophetic answers such as "outlook not so good" and "it is decidedly so."

---

a2z   EDITOR'S CHOICE

Destiny Starworks

http://www.tq.com/destiny_starworks/destiny_starworks_home.html

This startling astrological interpretation of O.J. Simpson's natal chart describes the former football icon as a powerful athlete, beloved hero and fallen star. It's matched against a natal interpretation for Nicole Brown Simpson, described as a woman who lived a dazzling life colored by glamour and violence (well, duh). Despite what seems obvious to us in hindsight, the frank discussion of this star-crossed relationship makes you wonder why more people didn't predict the outcome of this desperate union. And as science proves that the universe is more cohesive than we could have believed, astrology becomes harder to ignore. Once a tool of the ancients, the stars were sought for advice on many things: wars, marriage and daily tribulations. Cleopatra used astrology to plan her campaigns against the Roman Empire, and rumor has it that Ronald Reagan wouldn't make a single state decision before consulting with his personal astrologer. If you're ready to take the plunge, Destiny Starworks offers a detailed approach to reading the stars, proving a powerful connection between your life and the solar system, and perhaps giving answers to burning questions like, "Am I going to win the lottery this year?" Natal chart interpretations, relationship overviews and transits are offered at moderate prices.—*Reviewed by Eugenia Johnson*

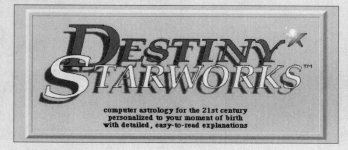

computer astrology for the 21st century
personalized to your moment of birth
with detailed, easy-to-read explanations

Maranatha

http://www.infi.net/~stegner/

Sponsored by the Gospel Baptist Church of Richmond, Va., this page cites Biblical prophesies and relates them to current events. Personal testimonies and links to other Christian resources on the Web also are featured.

Pray Before the Head of "Bob"

http://www.resort.com/~banshee/Misc/8ball/index.html

Formerly the Ultimate Oracle's Magic 8-Ball site, this page now allows visitors to ask a "yes" or "no" question of "Bob," a mystical figure much revered by the Church of the Subgenius. Slack visitors can type in questions and see answers in seconds. Thank Bob!

The Rapture Index

http://www.novia.net/~todd/

The Christian prophecy of the Rapture, found in the Bible's last book of Revelation, states that sometime in the future, after a series of signs, believers will be taken bodily into heaven. At the Rapture Index, learn more about this prophecy and read news items and world indicators purported to be signs of its imminence.

Your Lucky Fortune Cookie

http://hci.ise.vt.edu/~kelso/fortune.html

John Kelso's Your Lucky Fortune Cookie delivers a lengthy fortune with a lottery number to boot. It generates a new fortune and number on each visit to the page.

PSYCHICS AND CLAIRVOYANTS a2z

Internet Psychics

http://www.infohaus.com/access/by-seller/INTERNET_PSYCHICS

Web denizens seeking information of a clairvoyant sort can turn to the commercial services of Internet Psychics. Visitors can peruse customer testimonials before forking over the dough in order to delve into past lives and catch a glimpse of future paths.

TAROT

I-Tarot

http://manor.york.ac.uk/cgi-bin/cards.sh

The I-Tarot are described by the Web author as, "so mystical that it is in fact dangerous to see the face sides of them." With this in mind, visitors can reload the page as many times as needed to achieve the desired fortune from cards such as "The Life Insurance Salesman" and "the six of traffic cones."

The Original Tarot Web Page

http://www.facade.com/Occult/tarot/

These age-old cards will reveal all. See Editor's Choice.

MISCELLANEOUS MARVELS

BIZARRE, ODD AND UNUSUAL PURSUITS

How to Tell if Your Head's About to Blow Up

http://www.mit.edu:8001/people/mkgray/head-explode.html

This page features a 1994 "Weekly World News" report of a chess player's gruesome demise. Visitors can digest the symptoms of hyper-cerebral electrosis and check out preventive tips for avoiding the condition.

Hyper-Weirdness by World Wide Web

http://www.physics.wisc.edu/~shalizi/hyper-weird/

Link to the weirdest sites on the Web with Hyper-Weirdness by World Wide Web, the electronic version of popular book "High Weirdness by Mail." Surreal, wacky sites on religion, conspiracy theories, Elvis worship and other pages from the freakier sites of the Web.

---

a2z EDITOR'S CHOICE

The Original Tarot Web Page

http://www.facade.com/Occult/tarot/

Unbutton your bookmarks and make a space for The Original Tarot Web Page. This site has been giving free Tarot card readings since the beginning of Webtime, and they're not chintzy either. Offering several different decks and layouts, choose your personal favorites and get ready to enter a mystical world of prediction that is centuries old. Concentrate on a question and in moments, a deck of beautiful cards is dealt, and a reading performed which relates to the question you have posed. All layouts are prepared with descriptive text so that you can better understand where and why the cards are positioned as they are. See The Emperor in your past? Chances are you've been dominated by a patriarchal, oppressive presence (or perhaps you have been the oppressor); dealt The World as your final card? Then perhaps it's destined to be your oyster, after all. Good fun for believers and non-believers alike.—*Reviewed by Eugenia Johnson*

What does the future hold?

The Kooks Museum
http://www.teleport.com/~dkossy/

Take a stroll into the world of the weird and bizarre. See Editor's Choice.

News of the Weird
http://www.nine.org/notw/latest

The online version of Chuck Shepherd's popular "News of the Weird" newspaper column is a periodic collection of offbeat-but-verified news reports from various publications. The stories tend toward the salacious and verge on the incredible, proving once again that truth is weirder than fiction.

Skeptics Society
http://www.skeptic.com/skeptics-society.html

The Skeptics Society, an "organization of scholars, scientists, historians, magicians and the intellectually curious," provides society information and resources here. The site also contains tables of contents and selected articles from "Skeptic Magazine."

JOURNALS AND PERIODICALS

Fortean Times
http://www.forteantimes.com

From the United Kingdom, Fortean Times is a cheeky bi-monthly magazine that covers "all manner of strange phenomena and experiences, curiosities, prodigies, and portents." Visitors will find links to current and past issues, special reports, and articles, and subscription information here.

HotAir
http://www.improb.com/

Hot AIR features information on and from "The Annals of Improbable Research." The site includes articles from AIR, submissions from readers (such as "Fun with Grapes" and the secret formula for guk), posters, a schedule of events, information on special projects and subscription info.

Real Stories for Real People
http://www.io.com/~mjg/visionary/

The Visionary Publishing site contains games, fiction and a journal designed to showcase new talent and to focus on the interaction of myth, legend, roleplaying and storytelling. Includes information on conferences, contacts and links to related sites, newsgroups, and writers' home pages.

StrangeMag
http://www.strangemag.com/

StrangeMag: This is the Strangest Mag! How Strange? Strange enough to make the Top 10 Strangest list! Clogged with a host of peculiar people, monsters and mystery animals, Promis-

ing "an objective, level-headed approach to strange phenomena," this Web site offers a peek inside the covers of Strange Magazine. Selected article reprints and first-person accounts of bizarre occurrences deal with UFOs, the Loch Ness monster and other paranormal perennials.

Will of Nature
http://erg.ucd.ie/won.html

"Para-natural" organization Will of Nature publishes its eponymously titled magazine here. Visitors will find articles exploring virtual reality, "magick," body art and drugs, plus music samples and pictures, presented by a neopagan group that aims to "fight the techno/Christian materialism."

---

a2z EDITOR'S CHOICE

The Kooks Museum
http://www.teleport.com/~dkossy/

With your map in hand, get set to take a tour of the Kooks Museum, a repository for all things strange and unusual, right here under one virtual roof. Join "noted authority" Dr. Ahmed Fishmonger on an exciting cyberseas journey to the Seven Wonders of Kookdom and visit S.P. Dinsmoor's Garden of Eden, a concrete paradise and mausoleum somewhere in Kansas. Along the way take a look at Houston postal worker Jack McKissack's monument to good health and nutrition, the "Orange Show," an effort that took him 25 years to build (and no, to the best of our knowledge, he's not disgruntled). After dropping in on the Hall of Quackery and the Hall of Hate, stop by for a souvenir at the Gift Shoppe, where there's a sale every day. No trip to paradise would be complete, however, without a glimpse of Honolulu's Kookmobile or a peek at virtual stacks in the Library of Questionable Scholarship. A kook salute to Donna Kossy, who developed and maintains this site and who writes with unbridled enthusiasm about kooks, crackpots and possible visionaries, while still maintaining high weirdness and a healthy mistrust of the status quo. —*Reviewed by Eugenia Johnson*

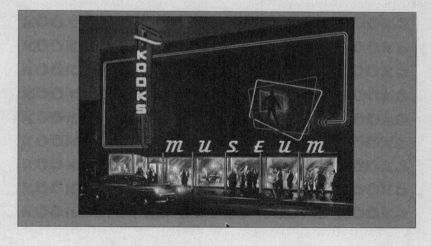

SPIRUALITY AND MYSTICISM

ANCIENT BELIEFS AND RELIGION

Spirit-WWW

http://zeta.cs.adfa.oz.au/Spirit.html

Spirit-WWW is dedicated to providing a forum for the expression of ancient teachings and religious belief systems in a modern context. Visit here for links to informational sites covering metaphysics, UFOs, alternative healing and more.

10 Bulls

http://fas.sfu.ca/cs/people/ResearchStaff/jamie/personal/10_Bulls/Title_Page.html

In the 12th century, Chinese master Kakuan drew pictures of "10 Bulls." As this site asserts, those drawings purely represent the compromises and progressive steps made in the Zen follower's journey toward enlightenment. The illustrations are reproduced here, with comments.

ARCHIVES AND INDICES

Celestia

http://www.celestia.com/alpha/

Providing links to a variety of spirituality- and health-related Web sites, this page points visitors toward Sterling Rose Press, the Spiritual Rights Foundation and other related resources on the Internet.

INSTITUTES AND SCHOOLS

Chinmaya Mission

http://www.tezcat.com/~bnaik/chinmiss.html

Visitors will find a religious roadmap leading to vedantic truths at the Chinmaya Mission home page. Centers across the world are listed here, along with links to study groups, religious texts and a biography of founder Swami Chinmayananda.

INTERFAITH SPIRITUALITY

Celebrating the Spirit

http://www.crc.ricoh.com/~rowanf/CTS/cts.html

A spiritual revival is envisioned by authors of the Berkeley Area Interfaith Council's Web site. The council's Global Ethic project beckons browsers to explore the page; the council promises updates on its interfaith project.

The Fourth Way

http://www.geocities.com/Tokyo/1236/

Books and background on George Gurdjieff's "Fourth Way" philosophy of higher states of consciousness are featured at this site. Visitors are invited to browse the Fourth Way newsgroup and search its archives.

Look Within: Inspirations of Love

http://users.aimnet.com/~amidaprs/

This page promotes a spiritual book written by an Indian mystic offering to guide readers to a relationship with God. The page offers a glimpse of the book's message, bios of the author and editor, and information on ordering.

Rainbow Family of Living Light Home Page

http://welcomehome.org/rainbow.html

Visitors to this unofficial page can trace the history of the Rainbow Family movement in words and pictures. Among the varied items here, visitors will find calendars of events, online photo scrapbooks, regional news and links to Rainbow camps and kitchens.

The Way

http://www.webcom.com/~way/the-way.html

The Way is a New Age spiritual group subscribing to the tenet that mankind was created by a number of human and alien races. Visitors can read a complete philosophical guide to this group's teachings and beliefs.

MAGIC, MYSTICISM AND THE OCCULT

Anders Magick Page

http://www.nada.kth.se/~nv91-asa/magick.html

The Anders Magick Page lists links to Internet sites devoted to magick, mysticism and related topics. Includes subpages featuring both traditional and modern groups, hermetica, books and magickal philosophy texts.

Demon Possession Handbook

http://www.opendoor.com/higher.ground/hs.html

Here, DiskBooks presents the full text of the "Demon Possession Handbook" by J. F. Cogan. Written for "human service workers," the handbook covers deliverance from possession, the origin of Satan, rock music and spiritual warfare. A link to Cogan's other book, "Bible Sex Facts," is also available.

Gothic Gardening

http://www.arches.uga.edu/~malice/gothgard/index.html

Even Goths garden. Turn to this site for plant lore about "Black Plants," "The Witches' Garden" and "The Garden of Ill Omens," among other dark topics.

Hell: The Online Guide to Satanism

http://webpages.marshall.edu/~allen12/index.html

This page is devoted to providing information about Satanic organizations and belief systems. Links to organizations, the Church of Satan, the Temple of Set and related groups are provided, along with pointers to devilish news and publications.

The Skeptic's Dictionary

http://wheel.ucdavis.edu/~btcarrol/skeptic/dictcont.html

The Skeptic's Dictionary, part of a philosophy professor's personal home page, offers a critical look at supernatural, mystical, psychic and paranormal subjects. Visit here for an extensive index of articles about the occult.

Will of Nature

http://erg.ucd.ie/won.html

"Para-natural" organization Will of Nature publishes its eponymously titled magazine here. Visitors will find articles exploring virtual reality, "magick," body art and drugs, plus music samples and pictures, presented by a neopagan group that aims to "fight the techno/Christian materialism."

MEDITATION AND CONTEMPLATIVE PURSUITS

The Foundation for Meditation and Spiritual Unfoldment

http://www.cityscape.co.uk/users/ea80/fisu.htm

The Foundation for Meditation and Spiritual Unfoldment initiates visitors into the teachings of Gururaj Ananda Yogi and promotes the general benefits of meditation. Seekers of enlightenment and information may submit questions or register for courses online.

Independent Research on the Transcendental Meditation Technique

http://www.trancenet.org/

Not necessarily for skeptics only, this comprehensive site contains a survey of independent research conducted on transcendental meditation as promoted by the Maharishi Mahesh Yogi. A list of answers to Frequently Asked Questions (FAQ) also is provided.

Interlude

http://www.teleport.com/~interlud/

Withdraw from the stressful world and find meditative peace. See Editor's Choice.

Spirits Evolving

http://www.webcom.com/~spirits/

Visitors can get a spiritual forecast at Spirits Evolving, which deals in spiritual consultations and publications. The site also offers inspirational essays, a spiritual advice column, and instructions for visualization, relaxation and meditation.

NATIVE AMERICANS

Tribal Voice

http://www.tribal.com/

A group of Native Americans hosts this site, which explores traditional culture and history from a contemporary point of view. Includes opportunities for online "powwows" using the group's downloadable chat application and a gallery of digital tribal art.

NEW AGE

ConsciousNet

http://www.consciousnet.com/

ConsciousNet offers one-stop New Age shopping for products, ideas and information. Astrology, meditation and personal healing techniques are among theconsciousness-raising resources that can be accessed from this site.

Earth Portals

http://www.earthportals.com/Earthportals/

Earth Portals' home page offers New Age information and "transformational products and services." Visitors can read visions of the future, browse the words of various New Age sages or link to environmental and spiritual Internet resources from this site.

JLA Enterprises

http://www.jla.com/

JLA Enterprises provides this collection of New Age art and music resources. Visitors will find articles, clip art and links to related pages and resources, including the Stop Smoking Program and the Massage Practitioner's Directory.

New Civilization Network Server One

http://www.newciv.org/

Visitors out to change the world will find links to groups aiming to do the same here. The server is dedicated to "new concepts, inspirations and visions." Visitors will find links to Millennium Matters, New Civilization Network and more.

Paper Ships, Books & Crystals

http://www.nbn.com/jacob/ship.html

A clearinghouse for information about angels, UFOs, indigenous cultures, personal healing, sacred geometry and other elements of the mystical brew, this site features book reviews and listings of sightings.

SHAMANISM

Shamanistic Healing-Energies on the Internet

http://www.prgone.com/bus/dpedro/

A shaman instructs visitors on absorbing healing energy here. The process involves watching an image on the computer screen for 10 minutes at specific times. The page includes testimonials from the energized and information on the guru himself, Don Pedro.

SPITITUAL LEADERS a2z

Avatar Meher Baba Ki Jai

http://www.oslonett.no/home/erics/index.html

Avatar Meher Baba Ki Jai is a Hindu spiritual leader with a large following in Norway. Visitors to his

---

a2z EDITOR'S CHOICE

Interlude

http://www.teleport.com/~interlud/

If you know that burn-out is just around the corner, or work has stressed you out to the max, place Interlude on your desktop, where every day just a couple of clicks could renew your spirit. This site, maintained by the Cybermonks, brings you the Thought of The Day, Meditation of the Week and other contemplative pursuits. Give yourself the gift of a few moments of peace, composure and renewal, like this gem culled from a recent visit: "Through our senses the world appears. Through our reactions we create delusions. Without reactions the world becomes clear." For those days when you just have to get away from the computer and out into the sunshine, the monks offer a suggested reading list for meditative reading on the go.—*Reviewed by Eugenia Johnson*

INTERLUDE

An Internet Retreat
A place to renew the spirit

home page will find related news articles and descriptions of his teachings.

Krishnamurti Foundation of America

http://rain.org/~kfa

The Krishnamurti Foundation of America is committed to the belief that "emptiness itself brings about a complete revolution in consciousness." Visitors to its home page can learn about the foundation and read excerpts from "The Book of Life: Daily Meditations with J. Krishnamurti."

Terence McKenna Land

http://www.deoxy.org/index.htm

Visitors can get a dose of druggie/philosopher Terence McKenna's consciousness-altering studies of ethnopharmacology and shamanism here. Includes an indexed quote collection, interviews, book reviews, and McKenna's travel schedule, along with information on hallucinogenic drugs and flying saucer theories.

Summum

http://www.summum.org/

In 1975, Claude "Corky" Nowell, now known as Summum Bonum Amen Ra—he goes by Corky Ra—met the Summa Individuals, beings who instructed him in the principles of the universe. At the Summum page learn more about this philosophy, comprehend creation and "receive the keys to understanding."

White Mountain Education Association

http://www.primenet.com/~wtmtn/

The White Mountain Education Association's Ageless Wisdom page disseminates the teachings of seers from religious writings, including the Vedas, Upanishads, Vishnu Puruna, Bhagavad Gita, Book of Moses, Kaballa, New Testament, Mahabarata, Koran and Yoga studies.

VOODOO AND SANTARIA

Vodoun (or Voodoo) Information Pages

http://www.vmedia.com/shannon/voodoo/voodoo.html

Learn about the origins of voodoo at this comprehensive informational site. The page features descriptions of basic rituals, a discussion of the role of black magic and a calendar of Vodoun ceremonies.

WICCA AND PAGANISM

CoGweb

http://www.cog.org/cog/

The Covenant of the Goddess Web site explains the activities of the international organization of cooperating, autonomous Wiccan congregations and practitioners. This site offers information on witchcraft and answers to commonly asked questions. It also posts events and offers links to various covens.

Covenant of the Goddess, Northern California Local Council

http://www.crc.ricoh.com/~rowanf/COG/cog.html

The home page for the Northern California affiliate of the Covenant of the Goddess contains general information on the council, which practices a religion known as Wicca. The page also includes information on other Wiccan and pagan resources.

Dark Side of the Net Home Page

http://www.gothic.net/darkside/index.html

The Dark Side of the Net page is a list of gothic, wiccan, pagan, vampire, occult and other dark resources available on the Internet. The list also includes IRC channels, mailing lists, FTP sites, newsgroups, gophers and e-zines.

The Green Pages

http://www.oakgrove.org/GreenPages

These pages contain links to resources for pagans, including listings of gatherings, covens and groups. Visitors also will find general information submitted by participating organizations, along with links to pagan publications and Web sites.

THE MIND

ASTRAL PROJECTION

Astral Projection Home Page

http://www.lava.net/~goodin/astral.html

This home page provides links to Internet resources related to astral projection, out-of-body experiences and lucid dreams. The Astral Library located here supports key-word searches.

CHAOS AND CONSCIOUSNESS

Anders Transhuman Page

http://www.nada.kth.se/~nv91-asa/trans.html

Transhumanism is a philosophy which asserts that humankind can surpass its current physical, mental and social levels. Visit here for information concerning intelligence amplification, bionics, artificial intelligence, cryonics and immortality.

Deoxyribonucleic Hyperdimension

http://www.intac.com/~dimitri/dh/deoxy.html

The contemporary philosophers represented on this page "peer into bits and zones of Chaos," exploring alternate realities and expanded levels of consciousness. Contemplate the writings of Alan Watts, Timothy Leary, Terrence McKenna and Robert Anton Wilson.

The Internet Science Education Project

http://www.hia.com/hia/pcr/

Those who wander into this mind-bending site will encounter fiction, scholarly essays and "a Web forum for critical and poetical inquiry into controversial ideas in the post-modern physics of time travel and consciousness research."

Laboratory for Consciousness Studies

http://hrcweb.lv-hrc.nevada.edu/cogno/cogno.html

The Consciousness Research Laboratory "conducts scientific research on anomalies of human consciousness" with studies on the correlates of mind-matter interaction, extended perceptual capabilities and physical correlates of mental states. Take a virtual tour of the lab, read descriptions of its mission and research or participate in its investigation of luck.

Mind Uploading

http://sunsite.unc.edu/jstrout/uploading/MUHomePage.html

Science fiction is fact at the Mind Uploading home page where "the putative future process of copying one's mind from the natural substrate of the brain into an artificial one manufactured by humans" is explored. Subjects include technology, timelines, philosophy and policy.

The Monroe Institute

http://www.monroe-inst.com/

A non-profit organization based in Lovingston, Va., the Monroe Institute fosters the understanding of human consciousness through a variety of methods, including out-of-body and other exploratory experiences. Visit the institute's home page for information about its programs and instructional materials.

Terence McKenna Land
http://www.deoxy.org/index.htm
Visitors can get a dose of druggie/philosopher Terence McKenna's consciousness-altering studies of ethnopharmacology and shamanism here. Includes an indexed quote collection, interviews, book reviews, and McKenna's travel schedule, along with information on hallucinogenic drugs and flying saucer theories.

DREAMS AND DREAM THERAPY

DreamLink
http://www.iag.net:80/~hutchib/.dream/
Have your dreams interpreted or learn to translate dreams at DreamLink. Visitors also can find tips on controlling and remembering dreams in the Technique a Week department or participate in the DreamLink roundtable talk sessions.

dreamMosaic
http://www.itp.tsoa.nyu.edu/~windeatr/dreamMosaic.html
Web dreamers can post their latest mental meanderings at the dreamMosaic site. Visitors will find a collection of dreams indexed and cross-referenced for browsing ease and pleasure.

The Dream Page
http://www.cs.washington.edu/homes/raj/dream.html
Webmasters explore the dynamics of dream messages, asking for submissions that will be published and interpreted. An index of current dreams allows visitors to make their own evaluations. From this page, dream weavers also can link to psychological and literary resources.

The Lucidity Institute Inc.
http://www.lucidity.com/
The Lucidity Institute conducts research on the nature and potential of consciousness during the dream state. This page includes a catalog of high-tech products to help users develop lucid dreaming abilities and listings of related publications.

HYPNOSIS

Hypnosis.com
http://www.hypnosis.com/
Sort of a hypnosis mall, this site links visitors to book and tape vendors selling hypnosis-related materials. Includes information on related educational resources and a Frequently Asked Questions (FAQ) file.

Hypnotica
http://www.servtech.com/public/hypnotica/
Self-hypnosis as a tool in personal development. See Editor's Choice.

INSTITUTES AND SCHOOLS

Association for Research and Enlightenment Inc.
http://www.ip.net/are/
This association disseminates the teachings of Edgar Cayce. See Editor's Choice.

Koestler Parapsychology Unit
http://www.ed.ac.uk/~parapsi/kpu.html
The Koestler Parapsychology Chair at the University of Edinburgh was established to study ESP and similar phenomena. This page has information about the unit's participants, research and methodologies, with a reading list and links to related sites.

The Option Institute
http://www.option.org/
The Option Institute offers self-help counseling programs to those who seek happiness and success in life. The institute's site offers electronic print resources as well as information for ordering books, videos and tapes.

---

a2z EDITOR'S CHOICE

Hypnotica
http://www.servtech.com/public/hypnotica/
Get that weight off! Unload those cigarettes! You can, through self-hypnosis. Long used in psychotherapy and to combat an abundance of ills, some practitioners believe that your own efforts—rather than those of an analyst or counselor —can be a more effective means to eradicate smoking, control weight, improve concentration and memory, and to act as a barrier to pain. Dr. Chuck Henderson, a psychologist and author of several books and autosuggestion tapes on the subject, explains how you can use this effective science to gain better control over your own life. But he warns that while hypnosis is a powerful tool for personal development, it must be used correctly. Here, he takes you through the proper steps from beginner to expert. Learn to experiment with age and past life regression, control jealousy, sleep more soundly, and develop a better attitude. All that is necessary is a little faith and a lot of determination. "I will not eat the hot fudge sundae, I will not eat the hot fudge sundae, I will not eat ..." uh, sorry! Just practicing.—*Reviewed by Eugenia Johnson*

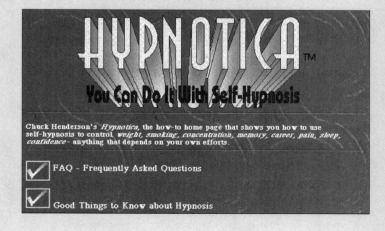

JOURNALS AND PERIODICALS

Collected Writings of Ivan K. Goldberg
http://avocado.pc.helsinki.fi/~janne/ikg/
Search the writings of "maybe the most active psychopharmacologist on the Internet" here. Goldberg's words previously appeared on the Walkers-in-Darkness mailing list, an online re-source for people suffering from various depres-sive disorders. Includes a link to the Mood Disorders Page.

SMART DRUGS

Better Thinking Through Chemistry
http://www.uta.fi/~samu/SMARTS2.html
Visitors to this page will find an article on smart drugs originally written for a Belgian rave zine. A bibiliography is attached, but links are limited.

Smart Drug/Nootropic Info
http://www.damicon.fi/sd/
Nootropics, or "smart drugs," are a class of drugs that act as cognitive enhancers, with no side ef-fects or toxicity. Visitors can browse reports, dis-cussions and debates about various smart drugs at this site.

---

a2z EDITOR'S CHOICE

Association for Research and Enlightenment Inc.
http://www.ip.net/are/
Edgar Cayce is probably the best known and most documented psychic of all time. Also a prolific writer, his many prophetic experiences are pre-served in a way no other psychic's have ever been. The Association for Re-search and Enlightment, Inc. (A.R.E.) is the international headquarters dedicated to studying Cayce's work, and to archiving these psychic read-ings which cover more than 10,000 subjects. A.R.E.'s mission and activities are detailed here. The organization offers seminars, publications and con-ferences across the country exploring health and healing, meditation and psychic development, reincarnation, dream interpretation and interperson-al relationships. A.R.E. is housed at Virginia Beach, Va., in the same build-ing that was once home to Cayce's own hospital, and is committed to preserving and applying the wisdom and heritage that the psychic felt would enable human beings to experience a better life.—*Reviewed by Eu-genia Johnson*

A.R.E.®
ASSOCIATION FOR
RESEARCH AND ENLIGHTENMENT, INC.

UFOS AND MYSTERIOUS CREATURES

ALIEN VISITS AND ABDUCTIONS

The Alberta UFO Research Association (AUFORA)
http://ume.med.ucalgary.ca/~watanabe/ufo.html
The Alberta UFO Research Association presents this home page exploring alien visitations to our humble planet, Earth. Visitors will discover the latest UFO news, journals, first-hand accounts of sightings and links to related Internet sites.

"Alien Autopsy"—Faked or Fiction?
http://www.trudang.com/autopsy.html#CONTENTS
You be the judge in this classic film. See Editor's Choice.

The Contact Project
http://sunsite.unc.edu/lunar/alien.html
This page, maintained by the fanciful Lunar Insti-tute of Technology, presents a puzzle: Visitors are invited to try their hands at decoding a fictional message from an alien intelligence. Explorers who find this site are provided with a history of the project and links to sites of interest to science fiction fans.

ARCHIVES AND INDICES

Galaxy: Unidentified Flying Objects
http://galaxy.einet.net/galaxy/Community/Parascience/Unidentified-Flying-Objects.html
From the larger Galaxy collection, this index points to resources and information on UFOs. Vis-itors will find articles and publications, sights and sounds, collections and directories.

Protree
http://galaxy.einet.net/galaxy/Community/Parascience/Unidentified-Flying-Objects.html
Browsers here can download "alternative/mind expansion information." The site includes point-ers to facts on metaphysics, UFOs, spiritualism and ecological issues, along with a commercial page that offers private investigation services.

UFO, Paranormal & Skeptic links

http://weikko.tky.hut.fi/ufo.html

If you believe in extraterrestrials (and even if you don't), you can land at this site and find links to UFO and paranormal events pages. Visitors also can access otherworldly newsgroups and a section where skeptics can find like-minded pages.

UFOs

http://ernie.bgsu.edu/~jzawodn/ufo/

These electronic aisles of the World Wide Web Virtual Library house resources regarding extraterrestrials and their preferred mode of travel, flying saucers. Visitors can link to a variety of interesting sites offering UFO-related goldmines like an overhead photo of Area 51, Operation Right to Know, and "The Desert Rat Newsletter.

AREA 51

Area 51/Groom Lake

http://www.ufomind.com/area51/

Individuals who think we're not alone will find scientific fuel for the fire at this site, maintained by the Area 51 Research Center. Visitors can look up current news stories and testimonials concerning UFOs allegedly housed at the U.S. military's mysterious installation.

Area 51 Research Center Guide to Knowledge

http://www.ufomind.com

Rumors and realities about a secret U.S. military base in Nevada—known as Area 51 or Groom Lake—can be viewed at this site. It includes links to the Groom Lake Desert Rat newsletter and UFO news related to the area.

EXTRA-TERRESTRIAL RESEARCH

Dr. Bruce Cornet: A Special Presentation

http://orion.adp.wisc.edu/bcornet1/

Earth inhabitants may not be alone in the universe, and Dr. Bruce Cornet knows something about it. Find out more about this lecturer who believes he has hard evidence of UFO activity and take a good squint at the photographs he took to prove his claims.

Search for Extra-Terrestrial Intelligence League Inc.

http://seti1.setileague.org/homepg.html

This group, dedicated to the electromagnetic Search for Extra-Terrestrial Intelligence, offers up

general information about itself here. Linked pages offer related articles, membership information, press releases and meeting schedules.

Search for Extra-Terrestrial Intelligence Institute

http://www.seti-inst.edu/

Scientists engaged in the Search for Extra-Terrestrial Intelligence project publish their research strategies, goals and findings here on the SETI Insitute's home page. Visitors can link to researchers, investigators and summaries of current projects from his site.

JOURNALS AND PERIODICALS

SETIQuest

http://www.setiquest.com/

SETIQuest is a magazine that covers the continuing search for extraterrestrial intelligence. Here, a promotion for the magazine lists the contents of the current issue. Visitors can request previous issues via e-mail or read brief, online updates on extraterrestrial research around the world.

 EDITOR'S CHOICE

"Alien Autopsy"—Faked or Fiction?

http://www.trudang.com/autopsy.html#CONTENTS

A 17 minute film, silent and in fuzzy black and white, has been the subject of controversy ever since its release. On a morgue table in a small white room lies a naked alien (?) creature, with six fingers, bulbous belly and a long gash in it's leg. Surrounding the creature are humans in contamination suits, circling the body, slicing the chest and skull in half and removing the internal organs. Some people hope that this creature may be genuine, an alien life form on earth, evidence of the report of a UFO crash near Roswell, N.M., in 1947 and allegedly covered up by the US Government. But skeptics believe that this film is just a clumsy hoax. The video tape has become the hot property of the year and is a staple on Fox TV which doles out new clues on every episode of "The X Files." Selling in video stores like hot cakes, it will soon be offered by mail in 35 catalogs. "The Truly Dangerous Company" attempts to prove that the "alien" is a deception, by illustrating how you too can make an alien, using makeup books and mail order supply houses. The most convincing proof, however, is the grisly comparison to a human autopsy, illustrating blatant goofs in the video's production. Fascinating stuff, but not for the faint at heart.—*Reviewed by Eugenia Johnson*

"Alien Autopsy" - Faked Or Fiction?

Contents:

How To Make An Alien

Autopsy Bleeps and Blunders
Rent the video, read along as you watch, and play *Spot The Goof !*

FX Artist Poll
Our ongoing tally of other FX artists' opinions.

"Alien Autopsy" Face-Off
Dueling Alien Autopsies !

Autopsy Face-Off, Part Two!
A few selected comparisons with authentic human autopsies.
Warning ! Not for the squeamish!

PARANORMAL PHENOMENA

Archive X

http://www.crown.net/X/

Part of the WWW Virtual Library, Archive X contains links to Web pages related to paranormal phenomena. Visitors are invited to submit their own stories of experiences with ghosts, whether hauntings or single encounters, angels and channeling.

PICTURE ARCHIVES

Dr. Bruce Cornet: A Special Presentation

http://orion.adp.wisc.edu/bcornet1/

Earth inhabitants may not be alone in the universe, and Dr. Bruce Cornet knows something about it. Find out more about this lecturer who believes he has hard evidence of UFO activity and take a good squint at the photographs he took to prove his claims.

PLANETARY ACTIVITY

The Face on Mars

http://barsoom.msss.com/education/facepage/
face.html

Elaborating on images some believe show an artificially shaped, face-like landform on the surface of Mars, Malin Space Science Systems Inc. presents this educational page discussing the raw images that sparked the controversy and providing a brief lesson on image-processing techniques.

VAMPIRES

Guide to the Children of Darkness

http://www.maths.tcd.ie/pub/vampire/
intro.html

The Guide to the Children of Darkness, a personal collection of vampire lore, offers links to information about related films and literature. Naturally, it includes in-depth coverage of the work of Anne Rice. Join the "Vorld Vide Veb" at this home page. Visitors can learn about bloodsuckers and test their chances of becoming one, or follow links to other Web sites of "similar veins of interest."

SCIENCE AND TECHNOLOGY

THE 25 MOST POPULAR SCIENCE AND TECHNOLOGY SITES

The American Institute of Physics Press
http://www.aip.org/aippress/

Bio-wURLd
http://www.ebi.ac.uk/htbin/bwurld.pl

ChemEd: Chemistry Education Resources
http://www-hpcc.astro.washington.edu/scied/chemistry.html

Comprehensive Conceptual Curriculum for Physics
http://phys.udallas.edu/

The Daily Planet
http://wx3.atmos.uiuc.edu/

Dante II Frame Walking Robot
http://maas-neotek.arc.nasa.gov/dante/

Electronic Visualization Laboratory
http://www.ncsa.uiuc.edu/EVL/docs/html/homePage.html

European Space Agency
http://www.esrin.esa.it/htdocs/esa/esa.html

ForestNet
http://www.forestnet.com/

Geometry Forum
http://forum.swarthmore.edu/

Institute of Social and Cultural Anthropology
http://www.rsl.ox.ac.uk/isca/index.html

The Interactive Frog Dissection
http://curry.edschool.Virginia.EDU/go/frog/home.html

JPL Robotics
http://robotics.jpl.nasa.gov/

Keirsey Temperament Sorter—Jungian Personality Test
http://sunsite.unc.edu/jembin/mb.pl

Mathart.com
http://mathart.com/

The Mercury Project at USC
http://www.usc.edu/dept/raiders/story/mercury-story.html

National Plant Data Center
http://plants.usda.gov:80/npdc/

Nine Planets: A Multimedia Tour of the Solar System
http://seds.lpl.arizona.edu/nineplanets/nineplanets/nineplanets.html

Reconstruction of Ancient Egyptian Mummy
http://www.pavilion.co.uk/HealthServices/BrightonHealthCare/mummy.htm

Resources for Psychology and Cognitive Sciences
http://sasuke.shinshu-u.ac.jp/psych/

The Science Museum London
http://www.nmsi.ac.uk/Welcome.html

Sierra Club Home Page
http://www.sierraclub.org/

Social Sciences & Humanities INFOMINE
http://lib-www.ucr.edu/rivera/

Topex/Poseidon Home Page
http://topex-www.jpl.nasa.gov/

The Weather Underground at the University of Michigan
http://groundhog.sprl.umich.edu/

AGRICULTURE

ANIMAL CULTURE

AGEN Home Page

http://www.agen.com.au/

AGEN Biomedical, a biotechnology company from Brisbane, Australia, features its products and corporate objectives through its Medical and Veterinary Diagnostics Web page. Visitors can talk with the scientists, or check other biotechnology links from the page.

American Society of Animal Science

http://www.asas.org/

The American Society of Animal Science hosts a vast repository of information and resources on animal science research, agriculture, public policy, and education. There are also links to publications, news, and membership services.

Auburn University College of Veterinary Medicine

http://www.agen.com.au/

This site contains an interactive tour of the College of Veterinary Medicine at Auburn University in Alabama. Other features include information on admissions and courses, departments and organizations, and people at the college. Access to other Auburn sites is also available.

Cornell University College of Veterinary Medicine

http://zoo.vet.cornell.edu/

The Cornell Vet Web offers visitors an overview of the university's veterinary college and its programs. Find links to facilities, departments, and online resources. Read newsletters, review the workings of CONSULTANT for computer-aided diagnosis, and access the college's gopher.

Domestic Animal Endocrinology

http://www.ag.auburn.edu/dae/dae.html

This quarterly, peer-reviewed journal explores the endocrine systems of domestic animals. This page contains subscription information, author guidelines, and an online manuscript form for reviewers.

FDA Approved Animal Drug Data Base

http://borg.lib.vt.edu/ejournals/vetfda.html

U.S. Food and Drug Administration regulations mandate that a list of all approved veterinary drugs be released as public information. Here's the list in electronic form. Visitors can use the search tool to access drug data from the online database.

Free University of Berlin Faculty of Veterinary Medicine

http://www.vetmed.fu-berlin.de/

This Web site familiarizes visitors with the Free University of Berlin's program in veterinary medicine. Find information on academics, faculty and personnel, research, and facilities. In German and English.

The Global Entomology Agriculture Research Server (GEARS)

http://gears.tucson.ars.ag.gov/

This vast entomology Web resource explores the world of bugs, bees, and planted things—and how they relate to each other. There are dozens of hand-picked links to related entomological pages, including a virtual classroom, a research area, and a U.S. Department of Agriculture software site.

Institute for Genetic Disease Control in Animals

http://mendel.berkeley.edu/dogs/gdc.html

This Berkeley, California-based institute hosts an informative site about dog genetics. Visitors can study genetic history and learn how to register dogs' genetic profiles.

Journal of Veterinary Medical Education

http://www.vetmed.fu-berlin.de/

An official publication of the Association of American Veterinary Medical Colleges, the "Journal of Veterinary Medical Education" contains full-text articles, features, and book reviews.

LlamaWeb

http://www.webcom.com/~degraham/

LlamaWeb is directed primarily to the breeder. Includes veterinary information, links to publications, conferences, and breed shows.

MARC Table of Contents

http://www.ag.auburn.edu/dae/dae.html

The USDA's U.S. Meat Animal Research Center in Clay Center, Nebraska maintains this data access site. Links to swine and cattle genome maps, and a genome database are provided.

Michigan State University College of Veterinary Medicine

http://www.vetmed.fu-berlin.de/

The College of Veterinary Medicine at Michigan State University offers a trio of links from this gateway. Visitors can opt to enter the graphical interface for the college, jump to the main university page, or follow links to other veterinary Web sites.

Mississippi State University College of Veterinary Medicine

http://www.vetmed.fu-berlin.de/

This site from the College of Veterinary Medicine at Mississippi State University contains informa-

tion on the school's programs of study, research projects, and faculty. Includes a personnel directory and an online tour of the school's facilities.

National Institute of Animal Health, Japan

http://ss.niah.affrc.go.jp/

Japan's National Institute of Animal Health provides this informational site with links to veterinary science and animal health Web sites around the world. Visit here to connect with libraries, universities, professional journals, and more.

The National Pork Producers Council

http://www.nppc.org/

Pig out on information about the pork industry through this official page of the National Pork Producers Council. Visitors can stop by for cooking ideas or details about the status of the pork industry.

NetVet

http://netvet.wustl.edu/vet.htm

This site is a comprehensive veterinary resource. See Editor's Choice.

NetVet: Bird Page

http://netvet.wustl.edu/birds.htm

This section of the NetVet Index covers poultry, pet birds, exotic birds and commercial concerns. Link to pages offering general information and specific data—plus a pointer to The Electronic Zoo.

NetVet: Cow

http://netvet.wustl.edu/cows.htm

The NetVet Cow page is filled with valuable links leading to Web resources relevant to the world of bovine husbandry. Explore the areas of dairy and beef production, as well as a variety of miscellaneous topics.

NetVet: Electronic Zoo Animal Information & Archives Home Page

http://netvet.wustl.edu/ssi.htm

The Electronic Zoo hosts this index of links to a multitude of resources relating to animals of all descriptions, from cats and dogs to exotic and fictional species. Visitors can also link NetVet server providing a variety of Internet resources for veterinary medical professionals.

North Carolina State University College of Veterinary Medicine

http://www2.ncsu.edu/ncsu/cvm/cvmhome.html

NCSU's Veterinary School maintains this page containing information about its programs, research, faculty, veterinary teaching hospital, and a link to general information about "pets and vets."

Oklahoma State University College of Veterinary Medicine

http://www2.ncsu.edu/ncsu/cvm/cvmhome.html

Find an overview of the College of Veterinary Medicine at Oklahoma State University. Features include a look at the college's academic programs, online resources and journals, and links to other veterinary medicine schools.

Pigs

http://www.ics.uci.edu/~pazzani/4H/Pigs.html

Visit here to find out "why raising a pig is fun" and to download audio files of pigs. This 4-H site roots around the world of swine, detailing what it takes—logistically and financially—to raise a big, fat, healthy pig.

Purdue University School of Veterinary Medicine

http://www.vet.purdue.edu/

Indiana's Purdue University School of Veterinary Medicine maintains this overview of its academic programs, faculty, and resources. A calendar, administrative information, and links to related sites on and off campus are also featured.

The Queen's University of Belfast Veterinary Science Department

http://boris.qub.ac.uk/vsd/index.html

The Veterinary Science Department at The Queen's University of Belfast, Northern Ireland, maintains this site containing information about the department, its research, publications, archives, and electron micrographs of animal viruses.

Royal Veterinary Agricultural University Department of Dairy and Food Service

http://www.foodsci.kvl.dk/

The Department of Dairy and Food Service at the RVAU in Copenhagen, Denmark, provides information about its current activities in research and teaching. Available in Danish and English.

U.S. Food and Drug Administration's Approved Animal Drug Database

http://boris.qub.ac.uk/vsd/index.html

The United States Food and Drug Administration satisfies the requirements of the Generic Animal Drug and Patent Restoration Act of 1988 by maintaining this searchable database. The database is a list of all animal drugs approved by the FDA for safety and effectiveness.

University of California-Davis School of Veterinary Medicine

http://www.cvm.uiuc.edu/

The Veterinary School of the University of California at Davis describes its program of study, admissions guidelines and academic departments. Includes information on faculty, administration and research groups.

University of Edinburgh Faculty of Veterinary Medicine

http://www.vet.ed.ac.uk/

The Faculty of Veterinary Medicine at the University of Edinburgh posts this page featuring the Dick Vet Web, "the first veterinary Web server in the European Union." Find links to the academic divisions in the school, online directories, and other resources.

University of Florida College of Veterinary Medicine

http://www.vetmed.ufl.edu/

The College of Veterinary Medicine at the University of Florida in Gainesville maintains this overview of its academic programs and facilities. The Wildlife Department, Department of Pathobiology, Department of Small Animal Clinical Sciences, and the teaching hospital are featured.

University of Illinois College of Veterinary Medicine

http://www.cvm.uiuc.edu/

Future dog docs can find out everything they need to know about the vet curriculum, graduate study programs and general college information at this site. Visitors can also access NetVet, a gateway to professional veterinary resources.

University of Pennsylvania School of Veterinary Medicine

http://www.vet.upenn.edu/

The University of Pennsylvania's veterinary medicine school provides information about its de-

partments here. Look in on the Center for Medical Genetics or Comparative Oncology and Critical Care. Links to the Philadelphia university's veterinary hospital and the George D. Widener Hospital for Large Animals can be found here.

Veterinary Studies Home Page

http://numbat.murdoch.edu.au/home.html

Murdock University's School of Veterinary Studies maintains this Web server with a wealth of information on the School's two divisions of study: Veterinary Biology and Veterinary Medicine. Visitors can peruse information on academics, research, and administration, view images of the school, or read course study material.

Virginia-Maryland Regional College of Veterinary Medicine

http://www.vetmed.vt.edu/

This is the central Web server for the Virginia-Maryland Regional College of Veterinary Medicine. Visitors will find an overview of the college, academics, research, faculty, and admissions information.

Zootecnica International

http://194.184.5.15/Zootecnica/International/

Hatched monthly, Zootecnica International provides the poultry industry with news on the latest scientific breakthroughs, business reports, and product reviews. The online edition boasts special stories, company profiles, and article reprints—along with a listing of upcoming industry events.

HYDROPONICS

Hydroponic Society of America

http://www.intercom.net/user/aquaedu/hsa/index.html

The Hydroponic Society of America gives an organizational overview and solicits memberships here. The page also contains information on growing plants without soil, as well as hydroponic conferences and seminars.

ARCHIVES AND INDICES

Ag-Links - Links for the Agriculture Industry

http://www.gennis.com/aglinks.html

A service of the Gennis Agency, this page points the way to agricultural Web resources around the world. Find general ag information, farms and companies, associations, magazines and newsletters, government pages, research and education, and weather.

Agricomm

http://agricomm.com/agricomm

A virtual agri-mall, this page links browsers to educational, commercial and legislative sites relevant to agriculture. Pointers include equipment and machinery pages, crops and livestock pages, newsgroups and information sources, export and markets pages, plus more.

Agricultural Biotechnology Resources

http://www.lights.com/gaba/

This collection of agricultural biotechnology resources includes links to agricultural colleges and institutes, bibliographic databases and libraries, newsletters and journals, plant and animal information, and more.

Agricultural Genome Information Server (AGIS)

http://www.lights.com/gaba/

From the Genome Informatics Group at the National Agricultural Library, this site features links to databases, documents, newsletters, and journals. Also find links to biological servers.

Agricultural Info Index

http://www.cs.indiana.edu/internet/agri.html

Visitors will find an index to agricultural information on the Internet here. The index includes telnet links to current livestock market prices and gopher links to the Department of Agriculture's extension service.

Agriculture

http://www.cs.fsu.edu/projects/group3/agri.html

Visit this page for a compilation of selected directories and indices pointing to ag-stuff on the Net. Find Web pages, Usenet newsgroups and Wide Area Information Server (WAIS) databases.

Agriculture Online

http://www.agriculture.com/

At Agriculture Online, find news, weather and shopping services aimed at the rural citizen. From homesteads to soil maps, this site chronicles the farmer's life and provides the media he or she needs to conduct the business of everyday life.

AgriGator: Agricultural and Related Information Index

http://gnv.ifas.ufl.edu/www/agator/htm/ag.htm

A service of the University of Florida, the massive AgriGator index points to Web, gopher, FTP, WAIS, and Telnet sites offering ag-data. Sources include U.S. government, state, commercial and international sites, almanacs, publications, list servers, and marketing services.

The Alabama Extension System Gopher

gopher://gopher.acenet.auburn.edu/1

The Alabama Extension System gopher server brings agricultural resources to the Net along with details about educational programs for families and youths. Get information on gardening and agriculture, weather, local extension programs, and more.

CSIRO Division of Food Science and Technology

http://www.dfst.csiro.au/

A deliciously thorough list of food-science links and more general links are available at the Division of Food Science and Technology Web Server welcome page. Users can link to DFST information, consumer information on food science topics, newsletters, other databases and search engines, and even a DFST FTP site.

Florida Agricultural Information Retrieval System (FAIRS)

http://hammock.ifas.ufl.edu/

Handbooks for agriculture-related activities are archived on the Florida Agricultural Information Retrieval System. Peruse the collection of online how-to guides—covering a range of topics, including beneficial insects, alternative crops, and dairy science—courtesy of the University of Florida.

The Food and Agriculture Organization

http://www.dfst.csiro.au/

The FAO is dedicated to facilitating access to information about food, agriculture, fisheries and forestry. At this gopher site, browsers can access a collection of files, including information on the United Nations and links to related gopher servers and information sources.

INFOMINE Biological, Agricultural & Medical Resources

http://lib-www.ucr.edu/bioag/

Maintained by the Bio-Agricultural Library at the University of California, Riverside, INFOMINE offers visitors a "comprehensive biological, agricultural, and medical Internet resource collection." Search by subject, keyword or title, view the table of contents or check out the "What's New" page.

Maize Genome Database World Wide Web Server

http://lib-www.ucr.edu/bioag/

Access to the Maize Genome Database—part of the Plant Genome Database sponsored by the USDA—allows biologists to view abstracts and full texts of online journals. Also links to other sites of interest to maize experts.

Purdue Cooperative Extension

gopher://hermes.ecn.purdue.edu:70/1

Purdue University's Cooperative Extension gopher provides much of the information that you'd expect from an agriculture extension service: lawn and garden tips, rural development, ag news, state fair results, and water quality data. The site also provides cybernews—with searchable databases and links to other information servers.

USDA Economics and Statistics System

gopher://usda.mannlib.cornell.edu/

The United States Department of Agriculture (USDA) Economics and Statistics System gopher server offers access to agriculture reports and data sets produced by its agencies.

The U.S. Department of Agriculture's National Agricultural Statistics Service

http://www.usda.gov/nass

The U.S. Department of Agriculture's National Agricultural Statistics Service provides links to ag-related information, statistics and databases. Visit for updated economic stats, the service's publications, color graphs, and the 1992 Census of Agriculture.

Virginia Cooperative Extension Gopher

gopher://gopher.ext.vt.edu:70/1

The VCE Gopher Service includes detailed info on agricultural topics, animal and poultry science, dairy science, horticulture, and more.

WWW Virtual Library: Agricultural Economics

http://www.ttu.edu/~aecovl/

This page from the World Wide Web Virtual Library features information about agricultural economics. Visit here for a one-stop resource of agricultural information including mailing lists, universities, and market analysis.

WWW Virtual Library: Agriculture

http://ipm_www.ncsu.edu/cernag/cern.html

This Virtual Library site focuses on agricultural resources on the Internet. Includes links to research programs, pest management information, relevant software, Usenet groups, texts, and commercial sites.

ASSOCIATIONS AND ORGANIZATIONS

Agronet—Ministry of Agriculture and Forestry

http://www.mtt.fi/

Agronet, the Internet service of Finland's Ministry of Agriculture and Forestry, provides access to the ministry's primary information centers. Visit here for news and links to national agriculture and rural advisory departments. Available in Finnish and English.

American Society of Agricultural Engineers

http://www.mtt.fi/

The activities and goals of the American Society of Agricultural Engineers are highlighted on this page. Visitors can read recent announcements or apply for membership. Includes employment opportunity listings, industry standards information, events listings, and a publications directory.

CGIAR Home Page

http://www.worldbank.org/html/cgiar/HomePage.html

Visitors to this site can learn how the Consultative Group on International Agricultural Research helps developing countries implement modern technologies for more efficient production in the areas of agriculture, forestry, and fisheries.

The Christmas Tree Association

http://www.christree.org/

Christmas comes but once a year, but the Christmas Tree Association works year-round. Included here are articles on Christmas tree farming, selecting a tree, recycling trees, and much more. Also available is a listing of state and regional tree-association contacts.

The Cooperative State Research, Education and Extension Service

gopher://esusda.gov/

CSREES is a division of the U.S. Department of Agriculture and describes itself as "a dynamic change agent and international research and education network." Visit this gopher for an overview of the agency, Farm Bill information, and the latest on disaster relief.

Council for Agricultural Science and Technology

http://www.netins.net/showcase/cast/

The Council for Agricultural Science and Technology interprets scientific research data regarding food and fiber, as well as environmental and agricultural issues for governmental bodies and policy decision makers. This Web site explores the mission of CAST and offers links to its publications, news releases, and services.

The Institute for Agriculture and Trade Policy

gopher://gopher.igc.apc.org:70/11/trade/iatp

The Institute for Agriculture and Trade Policy's goal is "to create environmentally and economically sustainable communities and regions through sound agriculture and trade policy." The Minneapolis-based group provides information on agriculture, chlorine, and biodiversity, among other topics. In English and Spanish.

Ministry of Agriculture, Fisheries and Food, British Columbia

http://bbs.qp.gov.bc.ca/bcmaff/bcagweb.htm

The Ministry of Agriculture, Fisheries and Food for Canada's province of British Columbia supplies information on its office and profiles provincial industries and commodities. Other topics featured include technology, education, and history. Links to many publications are also provided.

Ministry of Agriculture, Fisheries and Food, United Kingdom

http://www.open.gov.uk/maff/maffhome.htm

The United Kingdom's Ministry of Agriculture, Fisheries and Food maintains this searchable information server offering background on the ministry and its aims. United Kingdom food and farming statistics are also online.

North Carolina Cooperative Extension Service

http://www.ces.ncsu.edu/

Find educational resources, agricultural weather forecasts, and a calendar of events at the North Carolina Cooperative Extension Service site. Links to related resources and the NCCES administration are also featured.

North Carolina Department of Agriculture

http://www.agr.state.nc.us/

The North Carolina Department of Agriculture offers a wealth of information on its divisions, services, and administration here. Also available at this site are current press releases, market news, and a brief history of agriculture.

U.S. Department of Agriculture

http://www.usda.gov/

The USDA offers current news, an overview of its seven-program mission and a message from the Secretary. Links to the department's agencies, a topical guide to its programs, and an online visitors center are also featured.

Wageningen NMR Centre

http://gcg.tran.wau.nl/wnmrc/wnmrc.html

The NMR Centre at Wageningen Agricultural University in the Netherlands provides access to

NMR spectrometers and training in their use. This site includes news and organizational information, as well as specifics on the center's spectrometers and projects.

CONSERVATION AND LAND USE

Canadian Soil Information System

http://res.agr.ca/PUB/CANSIS/_overview.html

The Canadian Soil Information System describes the location and characteristics of Canadian soil types and how they relate to biological productivity. The site includes descriptions of landscape attributes such as slope, surface form, and rock outcroppings. Includes links to related resources.

Edwards Aquifer Research and Data Center

http://eardc.swt.edu/

This research facility provides information on the underground reservoir that supplies water for more than 1.5 million people in the San Marcos, Texas area. The site includes information on endangered species of the region.

Geographic Resources Analysis Support System (GRASS)

http://www.cecer.army.mil/grass/GRASS.main.html

Geographic Resources Analysis Support System (GRASS), a service of the U.S. Army Corps of Engineers, provides land- and environmental-management tools here. Visit this site to learn about GRASS and access its computer-based support system.

Indiana WETnet Home Page

http://ingis.acn.purdue.edu:9999/wetnet.html

Researchers in Indiana can access a wealth of water information here. WETnet contains a huge database of water and crop information, a look at water projects in the state, and links to agencies and professionals dealing with water.

Sustainable Agriculture Research and Education Program

http://www.sarep.ucdavis.edu/

With an eye to the effects of commercial farming on the environment and society, the Sustainable Agriculture Research and Education Program at the University of California researches new methods of farming. Learn more on SAREP here and in its publication, or link to other agricultural sites.

Universities Water Information Network Home Page

http://www.uwin.siu.edu/

The Universities Council on Water Resources is a professional organization of universities "united

to encourage education and research in water resources." Included are a water resources update, graduate programs directory, career opportunities in water resources, and a hydrology brochure.

FARMING

Farmer to Farmer

http://www.organic.com/Non.profits/F2F/

"Farmer to Farmer," a monthly publication dedicated to the interests of professional farming, offers news, profiles, and how-to articles. Find out the latest news and opinions on issues such as organic farming, soil building, and more.

ASSOCIATIONS AND ORGANIZATIONS

International Sugar Organization

http://www.sugarinfo.co.uk/

Got a sweet-tooth for the sugar business? This site offers a wealth of information about the International Sugar Organization (ISO), an intergovernmental association dedicated to "improving conditions on the world sugar market through debate, analysis, special studies, and transparent statistics." Includes the latest sugar prices and links to sugar importer-exporters.

CROPS

CROP SCIENCE

The CSIRO Grapevine Server

http://cgswww.adl.hort.csiro.au/

"A developmental research site focused on grapevine research cultivar identification," the CSIRO Grapevine Server feeds information to the worldwide vinticulture research community. Among the primary resources, find grapevine identification by DNA profile or ampelography, a bibliography, and a cultivar names and synonyms database.

GrainGenes Gopher Server

gopher://greengenes.cit.cornell.edu:70/1

The USDA Plant Genome Research project hosts the GrainGenes gopher site, offering access to the Triticeae Genome Database of molecular and phenotypic information about wheat, barley, oats, and other small grains.

Maize Genetics Cooperation—Stock Center

http://www.uiuc.edu/ph/www/maize

Use the Maize Genetics Cooperation—Stock Center's Web site to investigate, review, and order genetic stocks online. Find specialty maize germplasm here or link to the Maize Genome Database for additional information.

Maize Genome Database World Wide Web Server

http://www.agron.missouri.edu/

Access to the Maize Genome Database—part of the Plant Genome Database sponsored by the USDA—allows biologists to view abstracts and full texts of online journals. Also links to other sites of interest to maize experts.

National Plants Data Center

http://plants.usda.gov:80/npdc/

The National Plants Data Center, a facility of the U.S. Department of Agriculture, provides information here on its programs and resources. Visit this site to learn about the center, read about current activities and access its plants database.

Plant Genome Databases

http://probe.nalusda.gov:8300/plant/index.html

The Agriculture Genome Information Server's Plant Genome Database, a service of the U.S. Department of Agriculture, provides genetic information on a variety of plant species. Visit here to search the database, view publications, and link with related Internet-based resources.

Rice Genome Research Program (RGB) Home Page

http://www.staff.or.jp/

This is the home page of the Rice Genome Project at STAFF Institute in Tskuba, a division of the Japanese Ministry of Agriculture, Forestry, and Fisheries Genome Project. Visitors can access a variety of project materials here, including the semiannual newsletter, RGP data, and paper abstracts.

USDA Maize Genome Database Gopher

gopher://teosinte.agron.missouri.edu/1

Access the USDA's Maize Genome Database Gopher for information about the project and access to the database and a repository of maize newsletters.

FARMING

FIELD CROPS

The Corn Growers Guidebook

http://www.agry.purdue.edu/agronomy/ext/com/cornguid.htm

Corn, the king of American crops, reigns on this page from Purdue University. The Corn Growers Guidebook harvests information from multiple resources, and includes forums and newsletters to help enhance production techniques. Besides an earful of bona fide how-tos, find some "corny" trivia and related Web sites.

StratSoy Home Page

http://www.ag.uiuc.edu/stratsoy.html

StratSoy, a service of The University of Illinois and the United Soybean Board, offers resources for the U.S. soybean industry. Visit here for links to Strat-Soy experts, databases, and related organizations.

DISEASES AND PESTS

National Integrated Pest Management Network

http://ipm_www.ncsu.edu/

Integrated Pest Management uses insects, mechanical means, and limited chemicals to control noxious weeds and pests. Visitors here will learn about the national network that promotes this form of management and can read the latest information for home garden, agricultural, and forest applications.

FARM MACHINERY AND ENGINEERING

82nd Annual International Plowing Match & Farm Machinery Show

http://www.sentex.net/ipm95

Winners from Canada's 82nd Annual International Plowing Match & Farm Machinery Show are listed here, along with the program schedule and exhibitor information for the September 1995 event.

FOOD SAFETY

Agriculture and Agri-Food Canada's Electronic Information Service

http://aceis.agr.ca/

Maintained by the Canadian government, this site provides farming, environmental, regulatory, research, nutrition, food inspection, labeling, and related information. Available in English and French.

CSIRO Division of Food Science and Technology

http://www.dfst.csiro.au/

A deliciously thorough list of food-science links and more general links are available at the Division of Food Science and Technology Web Server welcome page. Users can link to DFST information, consumer information on food science topics, newsletters, other databases and search engines, and even a DFST FTP site.

Food Science, Purdue University

http://www.foodsci.purdue.edu/

Visit the Food Science Department at Purdue, meet the staff and read about current research programs in computer-integrated food manufacturing, carbohydrate research and a NASA-affiliated project involved with the development of a sustainable food supply for future manned missions to Mars. The site includes a publications listing, student information, and more.

USDA Animal and Plant Health Inspection Service

http://www.aphis.usda.gov/

The U.S. Department of Agriculture's Animal and Plant Health Inspection Service works to ensure the health and safety of livestock and produce, and to improve national agricultural output. This site provides an index of the service's resources, including staff directories, publications, gopher sites, and more.

FORESTS AND FORESTRY

Bonanza Creek/Caribou, Poker Creek Research Watershed

http://www.lter.alaska.edu/

The Bonanza Creek Experimental Forest in interior Alaska is home to a long term ecological research project that studies the boreal forest. Visitors here can learn about the project and download site maps, data, and climate reports.

California Department of Forestry and Fire Protection

http://spp-www.cdf.ca.gov/

The California Department of Forestry and Fire Protection supplies information about its Strategic Planning Program on this home page. Among the SPP resources featured are a map-making facility and various publications.

Forest Research Institute

http://www.metla.fi/

Finland's Ministry of Agriculture and Forestry maintains this informational site for its Forest Research Institute. Visit here for research activity

and service overviews, professional publications, staff directories, and an online keyword search utility.

OSU Forestry Sciences Laboratory Gopher Menu

gopher://gopher.fsl.orst.edu/

The Forestry Sciences Laboratory at Oregon State University maintains this gopher to allow visitors access to Geographic Information System files. Links to other databases and sources of information are also featured.

Pacific Forestry Centre Home Page

http://www.pfc.forestry.ca/

The Pacific Forestry Center on Canada's Vancouver Island maintains this informational site. Visit here to learn about the center, read its recent publications, and link to current research programs.

Rovaniemi Research Station

http://www.roi.metla.fi/welcome.html

The Rovaniemi Research Station (ROI)—a facility of the Finnish Forestry Research Institute (MET-LA) located near the Arctic Circle—invites visitors to its home page to explore the station and review its projects. Links to topic-related sites are also provided. In English.

South Africa Institute for Commercial Forestry Research

http://www.icfrnet.unp.ac.za/

South Africa's Institute for Commercial Forestry Research advises the country's forest products producers on matters of sustainable development. Visit its home page to find organizational news, publications, and links to other forestry-related Web servers.

Steve Shook's Directory of Forest Products, Wood Science and Marketing

http://weber.u.washington.edu/~esw/fpm.htm

Do you need a giant lathe? Do you want to learn how to use a giant lathe? Ready to give up and let a pro make that plywood? For any of these needs, look at Steve Shook's page of links related to forest products.

The World-Wide Web Virtual Library: Forestry

http://www.metla.fi/info/vlib/Forestry/

The Virtual Library's Forestry page is provided by the EMIT-laboratory at the Finnish Forest Research Institute. The library contains a vast range of forestry-related electronic resources: newsgroups, networks, journals, mailing lists, publishers, legislative issues, software, and databases.

INSTITUTES AND UNIVERSITIES

Agricultural Biotechnology Center

http://www.abc.hu/

A research institute located in Hungary, the Agricultural Biotechnology Center maintains this searchable overview of its facility and research services. Site features also include access to the ABC gopher server, as well as links to topical sites around the world.

Agriculture University of Poznan

http://swan.au.poznan.pl/

Poland's Agriculture University of Poznan's Web site is still under construction, but what exists on its English language page points to a series of black-and-white photographs of Polish mountains, its local address, and links to other university and national servers.

Dina KVL

http://www.dina.kvl.dk/

The Danish Informatics Network in the Agricultural Sciences at the Royal Veterinary and Agricultural University in Copenhagen features information about its academics, personnel, and current research projects. Links to related sites on and off campus are also featured.

Institut National de la Recherche Agronomique

http://www.jouy.inra.fr/

France's National Institute of Agricultural Research makes its online home at this site. Look here for descriptions of courses, academic programs, faculty and research projects. In French.

New Zealand Institute for Crop and Food Research Ltd.

http://www.crop.cri.nz/

Working to improve food production through innovative practices and technology, this Crown Research Institute maintains research groups throughout New Zealand. Find a mission statement and an organizational overview posted to this informational page.

North Carolina State University Department of Biological and Agricultural Engineering

http://www.bae.ncsu.edu/bae/

North Carolina State University Department of Biological and Agricultural Engineering provides information to potential students about the department, its history and its application of engineering.

Nova Scotia Agricultural College

http://www.nsac.ns.ca/

Brush up on Canadian farming techniques at the Nova Scotia Agricultural College home page. Review research reports or look into the activities of their Department of Agriculture and Marketing here.

Purdue University Agricultural Administration

http://www.agad.purdue.edu/

The School of Agriculture at Indiana's Purdue University offers this look at its academic, research, and outreach programs. Links to international programs, related ag sites, and other topical pages are also featured

Purdue University: Agricultural Communication Service

http://hermes.ecn.purdue.edu:8001/

Purdue University combines information from all its agricultural programs at the Agricultural Communication page. Categories include academics, libraries, and student and community information.

Purdue University Agricultural Computer Network

http://www.acn.purdue.edu/

The Agricultural Computer Network of Purdue University in West Lafayette, Indiana maintains this site to support the computing and communications needs of the state's Cooperative Extension service. Visit here for a variety of local and international computing resources, staff profiles, and links to other university Web sites and servers.

Purdue University Horticulture Department

http://www.hort.purdue.edu/hort/hort.html

The Horticulture Department at Purdue University details its academic and research focus as one of the top horticultural resources in the U.S. Also featured, find information about the NASA Center for Research and Training in Bioregenerative Life Support Systems.

Radioecology, Swedish University of Agricultural Sciences

http://www.radek.slu.se/

Radioecology deals with ecological problems caused by radioactivity. The Swedish University of Agricultural Sciences (SLU) provides specialized courses in this field as a result of the Chernobyl disaster. Includes links to other resources in this field.

Scottish Agricultural College

http://www.sac.ac.uk/

The Scottish Agricultural College in Edinburgh offers advanced education and training, as well as research and consultancy work. Visitors to this site will find descriptions of the school and its services, including veterinary and commercial services.

South Dakota State University Plant Science Department

http://www.sdstate.edu/~wpls/http/pscihome.html

The Plant Science Department at South Dakota State University maintains this look at its instructional programs and faculty. Links to departmental outreach programs and useful Internet resources are also featured.

Texas A&M University Department of Agricultural Engineering

http://ageninfo.tamu.edu/

Visit this overview of Texas A&M's Department of Agricultural Engineering for a look at its academic and research programs. Links to Texas Agricultural Extension Service resources are also featured.

Texas A&M's Department of Rangeland Ecology and Management

http://ranch.tamu.edu/rlem/

The Department of Rangeland Ecology and Management lets potential students know what to expect at this home on the range within Texas A&M University. Program descriptions and faculty introductions ride with campus research projects and academic details.

Texas A&M University: Institute of Biosciences and Technology

http://keck.tamu.edu/ibt.html

Research at The Institute of Biosciences and Technology is focused on molecular aspects of agriculture and medicine. Visit this site to learn about its mission, research facilities, technology transfers, faculty positions, and more.

Texas Aggie Horticulture

http://aggie-horticulture.tamu.edu/

Visit the server of the Texas Horticulture Program at Texas A&M University for program information and links to related Internet resources. Find crop, garden, and plant tissue-oriented databases and discussions at this site.

UF Food and Resource Economics

http://www.fred.ifas.ufl.edu/

Located in the College of Agriculture at the University of Florida, the Food and Resource Economics Department offers this overview of its academic programs, faculty's interests, administration, and resources. Links to topic-related pages on and off campus are also included.

UMN Soil Science Web Server

http://www.soils.umn.edu/

The University of Minnesota's Soil, Water, and Climate Department provides the dirt on its graduate program here. Visitors can dig through academic, landscape, and agriculture information, or access the department's gopher server.

University of Arizona College of Agriculture

http://ag.arizona.edu/

AgInfo, the Web server for the University of Arizona's College of Agriculture, offers links to information on the department's academic programs, research projects, and extension units. Faculty, staff, and student home pages are also available.

University of Arizona Department of Agricultural Resources Economics

http://ag.arizona.edu/AREC/arechome.html

The Agricultural and Resource Economics Department at the University of Arizona invites visitors to review its undergraduate and graduate programs, access its Range Cow Culling and Fuzzy Expert System tutorials, and visit the Farm Bill Forum. Links to online resources and marketing guides are also available.

University of Delaware College of Agricultural Sciences

http://bluehen.ags.udel.edu/

In addition to reviewing the departments and academic programs in the College of Agricultural Sciences, visitors to this University of Delaware page can also tour the botanical gardens. Links to the insect database and other related resources are also featured.

University of Florida—Institute of Food and Agricultural Sciences

http://gnv.ifas.ufl.edu/

At the University of Florida Institute of Food and Agricultural Sciences (IFAS) find electronic resources relating to food, agriculture, and the environment. Includes dozens of links to local Florida research centers as well as to related academic departments at the University.

University of Helsinki Faculty of Agriculture and Forestry

http://honeybee.helsinki.fi/

The Faculty of Agriculture and Forestry at Finland's University of Helsinki provides general departmental and academic information at this site. Review the current faculty roster and their research projects, visit the library, or link to other topical sites. Available in Finnish, Swedish, and English.

University of Illinois College of Agricultural, Consumer and Environmental Sciences

http://w3.ag.uiuc.edu/

The College of Agricultural, Consumer and Environmental Sciences at the University of Illinois Urbana-Champaign maintains this overview. Links to the college's administration offices, academic units, computer and information units, online class resources, and related sites are provided.

University of Illinois Department of Agricultural Engineering

http://www.age.uiuc.edu/

The agricultural engineers at the University of Illinois place department course descriptions, research programs, and career opportunities online.

University of Nebraska Institute of Agriculture & Natural Resources

http://ianrwww.unl.edu/

You'd *expect* the University of Nebraska to have a strong ag program and they do. Read about the Institute, the divisions, colleges and departments, the special programs, and more.

Utah State University Extension Home Page

http://ext.usu.edu/

The Extension Office at Utah State University maintains this site with links to information and resources concerning agriculture, nutrition, community development, publications, and telecommunications. Access to an extension office gopher is also featured, along with quick links to related sites.

LAW AND LEGISLATION

Council for Agricultural Science and Technology

http://www.netins.net/showcase/cast/

The Council for Agricultural Science and Technology interprets scientific research data regarding food and fiber, as well as environmental and agricultural issues for governmental bodies and policy decision makers. This Web site explores the mission of CAST and offers links to its publications, news releases, and services.

LIBRARIES

Databases at the National Agricultural Library

http://probe.nalusda.gov:8300/

The National Agricultural Library databases offer detailed information about genomes and proteins. Visitors will find databases for plants, livestock animals, and other biological life forms.

National Agriculture Library

http://www.nalusda.gov/

Find a general introduction to the services of the U.S. Department of Agriculture's National Agricultural Library at this site. Visit before accessing the library's public resources and find answers to Frequently Asked Questions (FAQ), along with an outline of the NAL's collections, products, and services.

National Agricultural Library Gopher

gopher://gopher.nalusda.gov:70/1

The National Agricultural Library (NAL) gopher server provides information on NAL activities and offers links to publications and resources. Other selections include agricultural-related data, software, and libraries.

PROFESSIONAL PRODUCTS AND SERVICES

Agribiz

http://www.agribiz.com/

Those in the business of agriculture or related professions will want to visit the Agribiz Home Page for links to all the financial, horticultural, and weather information the agricultural business person needs. Guests can also link to search help.

PUBLICATIONS AND INDUSTRY NEWS

Farmer to Farmer

http://www.organic.com/Non.profits/F2F/

"Farmer to Farmer," a monthly publication dedicated to the interests of professional farming, offers news, profiles, and how-to articles. Find out the latest news and opinions on issues such as organic farming, soil building, and more.

The Western Producer Online

http://www.producer.com/

The Western Producer is a Canadian site compiled by and for ranchers and farmers. Visit for classifieds, news from the industry, livestock sale information, and the FarmFax newsletter.

RESEARCH AND DEVELOPMENT (GENERAL)

Agricultural Genome Information Server

http://probe.nalusda.gov:8000/

Sponsored by the U.S. Department of Agriculture, the Agricultural Genome Information Server provides access to databases, documents, and software tools pertinent to the study of plant and livestock animal genomes. FTP and gopher access are provided along with links to related servers.

Agriculture, Forestry and Fisheries Research Council, Japan

http://www.affrc.go.jp/

Access to Japan's Ministry of Agriculture, Forestry and Fisheries' 29 research organizations is offered via this Web server. Find a server map and list—plus a link to the ministry's home page. In Japanese and English.

The Genome Informatics Group

gopher://probe.nalusda.gov:70/1

The Genome Informatics Group at the National Agricultural Library packs this gopher with genome information relative to plants, insects, and animals, a documents database, an FTP archive, and links to other biological gophers.

U.S. Deptartment of Agriculture ARS GRIN National Genetic Resources Program

gopher://gopher.ars-grin.gov:70/1

Researchers will find germplasm information on plants, animals, microbes, and insects at this gopher hole. The site is provided by the U.S. Department of Agriculture's Research Service.

SUSTAINABILITY

Sustainable Agriculture Research and Education Program

http://www.sarep.ucdavis.edu/

With an eye to the effects of commercial farming on the environment and society, the Sustainable Agriculture Research and Education Program at the University of California researches new methods of farming. Learn more on SAREP here and in its publication or link to other agricultural sites.

URBAN AGRICULTURE

Master Gardener Information

http://leviathan.tamu.edu:70/1s/mg

Maintained by the Texas Agricultural Extension Service at Texas A&M University, this interactive site provides access to the Master Gardener Information database.

WILDLIFE MANAGEMENT

ODFW Home Page

http://www.dfw.state.or.us/

The Oregon Department of Fish & Wildlife "works to protect and enhance Oregon's fish and wildlife and their habitats for use and enjoyment by present and future generations." This site continues this mission by offering general information on the department, data about fish and wildlife, and links to other Oregon-related sites.

Resource Development and Wildlife

http://www.rr.ualberta.ca/~lmorgant/index.html

An adjunct professor at the University of Alberta created this site for land managers. It contains research on the impacts on wildlife from logging, industrial development, recreation, and agriculture. It includes bibliographies and links to other relevant sites.

U.S. Fish and Wildlife Service

http://www.fws.gov/

The U.S. Fish and Wildlife Service stocks this Web site full of U.S. wildlife information. Learn about coastal ecosystems, conservation programs, federal aid, fisheries, and more. Visitors can also read about current employment opportunities.

ANTHROPOLOGY

ANTHROPOLOGICAL THEORY (EVOLUTION)

More Aquatic Ape Theory

http://huizen.dds.nl/~seismo/aat.html

This unique site explores the notion that humans may have evolved from marsh creatures. (No, not the "my in-laws are swamp monsters" kind.) Visit here to read bona-fide documentation from researchers. See Editor's Choice.

WWW Virtual Library: Evolution

http://golgi.harvard.edu/biopages/evolution.html

The World Wide Web Virtual Library hosts this site containing an index to Internet resources on evolution. Visitors will find extensive links to educational and institutional information servers, software archives, science libraries, and related references.

ANTHROPOLOGISTS

The Worldwide Email Directory of Anthropologists

http://wings.buffalo.edu/academic/department/anthropology/weda

This volunteer project aims to facilitate communications between scholars of anthropology throughout the world. Visitors can search the WEDA database using keywords or by browsing through a series of directories.

APPLIED ANTHROPOLOGY

Applied Anthropology Computer Network

gopher://gopher.acs.oakland.edu/1ftp%3avela.acs.oakland.edu%40/pub/anthap/

This computerized network serves members of the Society for Applied Anthropology and the National Association for the Practice of Anthropology. The gopher hole here links to files that cover relevant issues, news, and methodologies.

ARCHIVES AND INDICES

The Anthropology Corner

gopher://rsl.ox.ac.uk/11/anthro-corn

This archive from Oxford University provides students and professionals with access to worldwide field resources, including information about specific cultural groups and a directory of anthropologists.

University of Kent Anthropology Resources

http://lucy.ukc.ac.uk/index.html

The University of Kent at Canterbury provides a listing of research projects conducted by the Centre for Social Anthropology and Computing. Highlights include the study of the Cook Island population and its response to nuclear testing.

WWW Virtual Library: Anthropology

http://www.usc.edu/dept/v-lib/anthropology.html

This Virtual Library site houses a comprehensive, classified index of anthropology information. Includes links to related specialized fields, institutions, virtual libraries, and more. An index of employment opportunities in related disciplines is also available.

CULTURAL ANTHROPOLOGY

EtnoLab

http://cc.joensuu.fi/HumanistineuTDK/Kalevala/

The Ethnographic Media Laboratory (EtnoLab) is part of Finland's University of Joensuu. It uses the latest media technologies to examine and research cultural studies in new ways, and offers a demonstration here. In Finnish, with a smaller site in English.

International Society for Human Ethology

http://evolution.humb.univie.ac.at/

This professional organization promotes recognition of diverse views of ethology in the sciences. Visitors will find a membership application, event schedules, archives of ethnographic studies, and links to related sites on the Internet.

University of Oxford Institute of Social and Cultural Anthropology

http://www.rsl.ox.ac.uk/isca/index.html

Read C.K. Meek's classic 1931 study on the tribes of Northern Nigeria or examine the thesis abstracts of Oxford's social anthropologists since 1989. Here, Oxford's Institute of Social and Cultural Anthropology posts local and world resources in the study of people and cultures.

INSTITUTES AND UNIVERSITIES

University of California, Santa Barbara Department of Anthropology

http://www.sscf.ucsb.edu/anth/

The University of California at Santa Barbara's Department of Anthropology provides information about its graduate and undergraduate programs and projects here. This site also introduces the department's faculty and students.

The University of Geneva Department of Anthropology and Ecology

http://anthropologie.unige.ch/

The University of Geneva's Department of Anthropology and Ecology outlines general information about its programs and faculty here. The site includes information about the laboratories and a course catalog for the current academic year.

---

a2z EDITOR'S CHOICE

More Aquatic Ape Theory

http://huizen.dds.nl/~seismo/aat.html

It's dangerous to monkey around with evolutionary theory. Scope out the State of Tennessee's attempt to—again—ban Darwinian concepts from the classroom. The legislation failed, but a relatively new concept has again raised the banners of outrage in anthropological circles: the theory that man is descended from an aquatic hominid whose human characteristics predated the savanna bipeds, like Austalopithicus and his descendents. The aquatic ape theory postulates that human features can "only be explained in the light of an aquatic, or more likely semi-aquatic stage that our ancestors underwent in the past." Citing such adaptive characteristics in homo sapiens as the skin-bonded subcutaneous fat usually found in aquatic species, conscious breath control, the hairlessness common to sea-going mammals, large sebaceous glands needed for waterproofing skin or fur, and the excretion of minerals and salt in human tears and sweat, this site poses some fascinating questions for the professional anthropologist and amateur Darwinian. Next time you feel the need to ape a dolphin while monkeying around in the local swimming hole, ask yourself if it is more than coincidence.—*Reviewed by Steve Ellis*

More Aquatic Ape Theory

AAT

More Aquatic Ape Theory

Welcome to these Aquatic Ape Theory pages, maintained by Maarten.Fornerod@stjude.org. Last updated: April 21, 1996.

The times they are a-changing! Not only do we see a beautiful brand new color-logo, also the prestigious Top 5% emblem of PointCommunications has appeared. Thanks to Jesper Storinggaard (vipdk@image.dk) who created this composition! Still I wish to appologize to Lynx users, and comfort them with the thought that the 45 rpm record, the Levi's 501 and the Datsun Sunbird once were out of fashion too. Many thanks to Dewi Morgan, Dewi Jonker and everybody else who contributed to these pages.

PRIMATES AND PRIMATOLOGY

Wisconsin Regional Primate Research Center

http://www.primate.wisc.edu/

This primate research center site contains information about current projects, staff, and software archives. Includes links to the Primate InfoNet and university servers conducting similar research.

URBAN ANTHROPOLOGY

Pompeii Forum Project

http://jefferson.village.virginia.edu/pompeii/page-1.html

This site archives data from the Pompeii Forum Project—a project designed to examine the ruins of Pompeii as an urban center. Visitors can view images of the site and link to discussions of the data gathered.

ARCHAEOLOGY

Abzu

http://www-oi.uchicago.edu/OI/DEPT/RA/ABZU/ABZU.HTML

Abzu, provided by the Oriental Institute in Chicago, offers an online guide to resources for studying the ancient Near East. Visitors to this site will find an extensive index of publications, museums, and archaeological sites.

Abzu Regional Index: Egypt

http://www-oi.uchicago.edu/OI/DEPT/RA/ABZU/ABZU_REGINDX_EGYPT.HTML

Access this extensive index for resources and info on Egypt. Research can be conducted by exploring subject categories such as archaeology, art, museums, and philology, or by searching available databases alphabetically by author.

Annual Egyptological Bibliography Home Page

http://www.leidenuniv.nl/nino/aeb.html

The Annual Egyptological Bibliography, a service of The Netherlands' International Association of Egyptologists, provides an index of books and reports submitted to the association's review board. Visit here for information about the latest Egypt-related research publications.

Archaeological Research at Oslonki, Poland

http://www.princeton.edu/~bogucki/oslonki.html

This archeological research page contains information about a dig at one of the earliest farm sites on the Northern European Plain near Oslonki, Poland. A detailed description of the project and photos are included.

ArchWEB, The Netherlands

http://archweb.leidenuniv.nl/archweb_gb.html

This site provides information about archaeological projects in The Netherlands, related organizations, and upcoming conferences. Includes links to Leiden University and other archaeological servers. Presented in English and Dutch.

Ashmolean Museum of Art & Archaeology

http://www.ashmol.ox.ac.uk/

The home page of the Ashmolean Museum of Art & Archeology provides information about this venerable University of Oxford institution. Listings of current and upcoming temporary exhibitions, plus historical information and descriptions of the museum's permanent collection.

The Dinosauria: Truth Is Stranger Than Fiction

http://www.ucmp.berkeley.edu/diapsids/dinosaur.html

The Dinosauria examines the historical and scientific background of dinosaurs. Visitors will find discussions defining dinosaurs, dispelling dinosaur myths and detailing dinosaur diversity. Links to related Web sites are also featured. See Editor's Choice.

Phylogeny of the Mammals

http://ucmp1.berkeley.edu/exhibittext/mammal.html

The University of California Museum of Paleontology takes visitors on a virtual tour of hairy animals throughout the ages at its Hall of Mammals home page.

Honolulu Community College Dinsosaur Exhibit

http://www.hcc.hawaii.edu/dinos/dinos.1.html

Dinosaurs in Hawaii? You betcha. Honolulu Community College presents its permanent collection of "fossils"—actually replicas from the American Museum of Natural History, New York City. Visitors can browse fossil pictures and explanations or take the narrated tour.

Introduction to Dilophosaurus

http://www.ucmp.berkeley.edu/dilophosaur/intro.html

Dinosaurs return to life on the Internet at the Dilophosaurus: A Narrated Exhibition page. Find out how the dinosaur was discovered and learn about its habits. The tour is led by Sam Welles, the man who discovered the Dilophosaurus.

The Kelsey On-Line: The Roman Site of Karanis, Egypt

http://www.umich.edu/~kelseydb/

The "Kelsey On-Line" archaeological guide, provided by researchers at the University of Michigan, catalogs Egyptian and Roman artifacts recovered at the Karanis site from 1926 to 1935. Coins, sculptures, and clay and glass containers are featured.

Mary Rose Virtual Maritime Museum

http://www.maryrose.org/

Nautical archaeology buffs can tour wreckage of the "Mary Rose," a warship built in 1510 and sunk in 1545. Visit this virtual maritime museum to discover how the ship was originally operated and recently excavated.

Material Culture of the Ancient Canaanites, Israelites and Related Peoples

http://staff.feldberg.brandeis.edu/~jacka/ANEP/ANEP.html

This electronic resource for the University of Pennsylvania course, Introduction to Biblical Archaeology, details materials from "excavations at Beth Shan, Gibeon, Sarepta and Tell es-Sa'idiyeh as well as Haverford College's excavation at Beth Shemesh." Review articles from the Iron Age through the Persian Period.

The Mercury Project at USC

http://www.usc.edu/dept/raiders/story/mercury-story.html

The mystery of several apparently non-natural formations in the Nevada Test Site nuclear testing grounds in the U.S. is posted here for research, informed speculation, and consideration of paleontologists. Some of the information of the original investigation is classified, but the government agreed to let this portion be published on the Web.

The Museum of Antiquities

http://www.ncl.ac.uk/~nantiq/

The Museum of Antiquities, an archaeological museum in northeast England, specializes in the region's history, especially Hadrian's Wall. Features here include an exhibition centered around Stone Age European hunter-gatherers, object of the month, and general museum information.

The Ohio State University Excavations at Isthmia

http://www.acs.ohio-state.edu/history/isthmia/isthmia.html

Find out what archaeologists are digging up at the Sanctuary of Poseidon, an Ohio State University excavation site at Isthmia. Consult this page to access the program's reports and fieldwork opportunities.

Online Archaeology—An Electronic Journal Of Archaeological Theory

http://avebury.arch.soton.ac.uk/Journal/journal.html

"Online Archaeology" is an experimental first copy of an electronic publication with the aim of 'promoting rapid dissemination of speculative ideas about archaeology." Includes a reader response form.

Pompeii Forum Project

http://jefferson.village.virginia.edu/pompeii/page-1.html

This site archives data from the Pompeii Forum Project, a project designed to examine the ruins of Pompeii as an urban center. Visitors can view images of the site and link to discussions of the data gathered.

Radiocarbon Home Page

http://packrat.aml.arizona.edu/

"Radiocarbon" is the international journal of record for research relating to Carbon14 dating. The journal posts abstracts of its most recent issue here, along with announcements of interest to the C14 community. It also offers links to other radiocarbon-related information on the Net.

The Royal Tyrrell Museum of Palaeontology

http://tyrrell.magtech.ab.ca/

Visitors to this page will find an introduction to the Royal Tyrrell Museum of Palaeontology, located outside Drumheller, Canada. Links to the museum's home page and related sites are featured.

Runer

http://gonzo.hd.uib.no/NCCH-docs/runes.html

Developments in the computer-based study of runes, as well as ancient and medieval inscriptions, are published and linked at this Norwegian site. Mac users can download rune fonts here. In Norwegian and English.

Scrolls from the Dead Sea: The Ancient Library of Qumran and Modern Scholarship

http://sunsite.unc.edu/expo/deadsea.scrolls.exhibit/intro.html

Examine the Dead Sea Scrolls at an exhibit curated by the U.S. Library of Congress. Delve into the scholarly controversy surrounding the ancient religious texts or view scroll fragments and other objects comprising the exhibit.

University of California Museum of Paleontology

http://ucmp1.berkeley.edu/

Here's an online version of the Museum of Paleontology at the University of California at Berkeley. Visitors are invited to navigate through online exhibits using phylogeny, geology, or evolutionary theory as a paradigm. The site also includes general museum information and online catalogs. See Editor's Choice.

UC Museum of Paleontology Public Exhibits

http://www.ucmp.berkeley.edu/

The University of California, Berkeley's Museum of Paleontology aims to show that there is more to paleontology than the study of fossils. The site offers strolls through several virtual exhibits and lessons in geology and evolutionary theory.

UCMP Subway

http://www.berkeley.edu/subway/subway.html

Berkeley's University of California Museum of Paleontology (UCMP) maintains this site to provide access to its research and academic resources. Visit the UCMP Subway to link to related organizations on the Berkeley campus and around the world. An index of Internet resources is also available.

University of Melbourne Classics and Archaeology Department

http://www.arts.unimelb.edu.au/Dept/ClassArch/

The Department of Classics and Archaeology at the University of Melbourne, Australia, provides information here on its undergraduate studies and projects—which include ancient Greek, Latin, and medieval studies.

---

a2z   EDITOR'S CHOICE

The Dinosauria: Truth Is Stranger than Fiction

http://ucmp.berkeley.edu/diapsids/dinosaur.html

Not everything big and dead is a dinosaur. But what do we know about the "thunder lizards?" How did they evolve? And, perhaps most importantly to humanity, what led to their extinction? The answers are found in the Dinosauria, a colorful and comprehensive Web site devoted to topics in "the paleontological investigation of dinosaurs." The site is filled with interesting facts and myth-busting information, like the fact that pterosaurs were not true dinosaurs, but only a sub-genus of archosaurs. The well-known sail-backed Dimetrodon was "neither a reptile nor a mammal, " but "an early relative of the ancestors of mammals." The aquatic ichthyosaurs and marine plesiosaurs were neither fish nor fowl, nor were they true dinosaurs; they enjoy a unique taxonomy all their own. While the site may be somewhat technical for smaller children, it should prove an invaluable resource for elementary students working on those dino-projects, complete with plenty of illustrations. The higher education set can use a search tool to dig through the impressive online vertebrate catalog, link from the collection of pointers to other dinosaur resources on the Web, or dig deeper into their studies with the impressive bibliography.—*Reviewed by Steve Ellis*

(courtesy of Saurian Studios)

The Dinosauria:
Truth is Stranger than Fiction

University of Michigan Department of Classics and Mediterranean Archaeology

http://rome.classics.lsa.umich.edu/welcome.html

The Department of Classics and Mediterranean Archaeology at the University of Michigan maintains this site for related literature and academic resources. Visitors can link to texts, journals, bibliographies, image files, and World Wide Web sites.

University of Southampton Archaeology Department

http://avebury.arch.soton.ac.uk/

The University of Southampton in Great Britain presents the Web server for its Archaeology Department. Visitors will find an overview of departments, academics and links to downloadable software.

University of Waikato Radiocarbon Dating Laboratory

http://www2.waikato.ac.nz/c14/

The Radiocarbon Dating Laboratory at New Zealand's University of Waikato is an independent, commercial department within the School of Science and Technology. Visitors can find out about its services and price list, review its staff and research projects, or access the archaeological database.

WWW Virtual Library: ArchNet

http://www.lib.uconn.edu/ArchNet/

Affiliated with the University of Connecticut, this virtual archaeology library houses vast resources for pros, academes, and the generally curious. Visitors can browse by subject area—from archeometry to cartography—and region, or tour a host of museums, newsgroups, and publications.

BIOLOGY AND BOTANY

ARCHIVES AND INDICES

Anderson's Timesaving Comparative Guides: Restriction Enzyme Edition

http://www.atcg.com/

Anderson's Timesaving Comparative Guides on the Web presents this page with information about biological reagents. Several editions are featured, including restriction enzyme, premade commercial libraries, modifying enzymes, and filters and membranes. A link to protocols on the Web is also featured.

Australian National University Biology Gopher Menu

gopher://life.anu.edu.au:70/1

The Australian National University provides a biology gopher menu ranging from complex systems to medical information to landscape ecology to bioviruses. Essential software resources can be snagged here, too.

BBRC: Brazilian Bioinformatics Resource Center

gopher://asparagin.cenargen.embrapa.br:70/1

This gopher menu lists many of the online biology references and resources in Brazil. Included are the Biosafety Database (BINAS), Brazilian Bio Net (BBNET), Brazilian Enterprise for Research in Agriculture (EMBRAPA) and many, many more. Don't forget to check out the Entomopathogenic Fungi Databank when you visit.

---

a2z EDITOR'S CHOICE

University of California Museum of Paleontology

http://ucmp1.berkeley.edu/

Housing the fourth largest collection of fossilized protists, plants, invertebrates and vertebrates in America, the University of California Museum of Paleontology (UCMP) offers an unusually well-developed and designed Web site. While not as graphically pleasing as some of the eye candy common to many other online natural science museums, the UCMP more than fulfills its stated mission of "the conservation of paleontological materials, collections development, and research and instructional support." For example, the publications section of the site offers a comprehensive indexed archive of papers published by staff, graduate students and faculty affiliated with the museum, along with issues of the peer reviewed museum publication "Paleobios." Visitors to these pages can also enjoy a virtual tour of the museum's state-of-the-art research facilities, like the Environmental Scanning Electron Microscope Laboratory, or schedule their attendance at one of the UCMP's acclaimed Public Outreach programs. And if all these possibilities don't get your paleontological juices flowing, navigate your way through the "extensive online exhibits using phylogeny, geology or evolutionary theory as your paradigm."—*Reviewed by Steve Ellis*

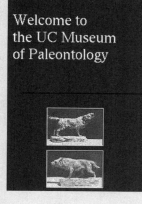

Welcome to the UC Museum of Paleontology

About This Museum
Find out the mission, history, publications and public outreach activities at UCMP

On-line Exhibits
Navigate through our extensive on-line exhibits using phylogeny, geology or evolutionary theory as your paradigm

BIODIDAC

http://biodidac.bio.uottawa.ca/

The fiercely Francophone BIODIDAC site aims to rescue the Canadian biology curriculum from the clutches of English-only textbooks. It is a digital repository of French-language biology texts and audio-video material. In French and English.

Biodiversity and Biological Collections Gopher Menu

http://muse.bio.cornell.edu/

Biologists studying systems and organisms will find collection catalogs and taxonomic archives at this gopher server. The server is maintained as a collaboration between the MUSE Project of Cornell University and the Museum Informatics Project at the University of California, Berkeley.

BioEd: Biological Sciences Education Resources

http://www-hpcc.astro.washington.edu/scied/biology.html

Whether you are looking for a FAQ on the theory of evolution or you want to start diving into genetics materials, the BioEd site has what you need. Jump to a zoology site that features an interactive frog dissection or check out The Visible Human Project.

Biological Data Transport

http://www.data-transport.com/

The Biological Data Transport bills itself as the "first source for biological science & product information integration." This index site covers the spectrum of biological data and services, including links to a lab full of announcements, libraries, databases, conferences and more. Also find customized search tools, a biotech registry, vendor services and the AuctionLink.

Biologist's Control Panel

http://gc.bcm.tmc.edu:8088/bio/

The Baylor College of Medicine's Genome Center posts an extensive index of genome and protein databases, articles, and biology-related libraries here. The site also contains links to human genome centers and funding agencies.

Biology

http://info.er.usgs.gov/network/science/biology/index.html

The U.S. Geological Survey maintains this index as a service to researchers. Visit here for links to laboratories, universities, botanical museums and a host of other biology-related sites.

Biology (Science)

http://galaxy.einet.net/galaxy/Science/Biology.html

Galaxy provides this extensive index of biology resources and information with subtopics that include botany, entomology, medicine, microbiolo-gy, paleontology and zoology. Links to publications, guides, software, periodicals, directories and online organizations are available.

Bio-wURLd

http://www.ebi.ac.uk/htbin/bwurld.pl

Bio-wURLd provides an extensive collection of resources and tools for biological study and research. Includes links to databases, tools, institutions, journals, software, commercial sites and tutorials, along with search tools for locating specific info resources.

California State University Bioweb

http://arnica.csustan.edu/

Housed at California State University, Stanislaus, this biological sciences server includes a "fruit image map" and numerous links to Internet biological sciences resources such as plant images, evolution, and virology.

Collection of WWW Sites of Biological Interest

http://www.abc.hu/biosites.html

The Agricultural Biotechnology Center in Godol-lo, Hungary, maintains this site for its collection of biology-related World Wide Web links. Visit here to connect with catalogs, tutorials, conferences, databases and many other scientific and academic resources.

The ESG Biology Hypertextbook Home Page

http://esg-www.mit.edu:8001/esgbio/7001main.html

Learn biology over the Web with this hypertext-book developed by the Massachusetts Institute of Technology. Find instructional text, practice problems and self-administered quizzes. Virtual students can even contact tutors online from this site.

Harvard University Biological Collections Gopher Menu

gopher://huh.harvard.edu/

Harvard University's Biological Collections gopher contains data and documents, as well as links to other biological, botanical and biodiversity resources.

Hotlist - Joe Walker

http://www.bae.ncsu.edu/bae/people/faculty/walker/hotlist.html

This collection of Internet links provided by an American soil and water management researcher offers access to a variety of biology and high-technology resources. Visit here for links to dozens of Web sites around the world.

Indiana University Bio Archive for Biology Data and Software

http://iubio.bio.indiana.edu/

The Indiana University Bio Archive offers visitors access to a wide variety of BioTech info. Software tools, databases, demonstrations and topical news items are featured.

Indiana University Biological Sciences Gopher Menu

gopher://ftp.bio.indiana.edu:70/11/Other-Bio-Gophers

An extensive index to biology and medical research-related gopher menus is offered by this FTP server, courtesy of Indiana University. From forestry references to human genome maps, search for servers filled with biological and general science resources.

Indiana University Biology Gopher Menu

gopher://ftp.bio.indiana.edu:70/1

Indiana University offers this gopher server, dedicated to providing biology-related news and information. Visitors can peruse a variety of network news, databases, software and data, or link to other information sources.

Indiana University's BioTech Information Server

http://biotech.chem.indiana.edu/

BioTech, a "hybrid biology/chemistry educational resource and research tool," is provided here by Indiana University. Visitors will find science resources, educational guides, reference databases, publication and many other information services.

INFOMINE Biological, Agricultural & Medical Resources

http://lib-www.ucr.edu/bioag/

Maintained by the Bio-Agricultural Library at the University of California, Riverside, INFOMINE offers visitors a "comprehensive biological, agricultural and medical Internet resource collection." Search by subject, keyword or title, view the table of contents or check out the What's New page.

Life Sciences Research in the European Union

http://www.cryst.bbk.ac.uk/CEC/eupage.html

Visitors to this site will find links to European research databases and archives dealing with the life sciences. An online search form (with a special link to Lycos) allows for quick reference.

List of WWW Sites of Interest to Ecologists

http://biomserv.univ-lyon1.fr/Ecology-WWW.html

This alphabetized and searchable index of ecology sites on the Web is maintained by the University of Lyon, France. A mirror site is located in North America. Links to literally thousands of sites include entries like the Agriculture WWW Virtual Library and PlanetKeepers. Extensive and regularly updated.

Montana Natural Heritage Program Directory

http://nris.mt.gov/mtnhp/

The Montana Natural Heritage Program collects information on Montana's biological features, noting threatened, endangered or sensitive plants and animals. Visitors here can download species lists by county or browse through its many databases.

Music and Brain Information Database

http://galaxy.einet.net/hytelnet/FUL063.html

This Galaxy link points to a searchable database of scientific references and abstracts on music as related to the brain and behavior. Maintained at the University of California, Irvine, the wide focus of the database includes human and animal behavior, creativity, neuropsychology of music, medicine and more.

National Biological Service

http://www.its.nbs.gov/nbs/

The U.S. Department of the Interior's National Biological Service provides technologies for the management of natural resources. The NBS seeks to balance ecosystem protection with economic progress by making biological inventories and research data accessible to the scientific community.

National Genetics Research Program Gopher Menu

gopher://gopher.ars-grin.gov:70/

The National Genetics Research Program (NGRP) of the U.S. Department of Agriculture maintains this gopher server, which offers information about plants, animals, microbes and insects. A wealth of resources is available here, including databases and links to other global biological information servers.

National Institute of Environmental Health Sciences (NIEHS) Scientific Database

http://lmb.niehs.nih.gov/home.html

Still under construction, this site offers links to a magnetic resonance database, the Laboratory of Reproductive and Developmental Toxicology, the Laboratory of Molecular Biophysics, and limited access to a human cDNA database.

The New Biodiversity and Biological Collections Gopher Menu

gopher://muse.bio.cornell.edu/

Cornell University's gopher for biodiversity and biology information resources offers images,

software, data models and links to other biological sites.

NPFauna and NPFlora for the U.S. National Park Service

http://ice.ucdavis.edu/US_National_Park_Service/

The U.S. National Park Service lists vertebrates and vascular plants found in the nation's parks at this site. Visit to browse a flora and fauna list and to search for species information via a Wide Area Information Server (WAIS) interface.

100+ Global Biological Information Servers by Topic

gopher://genome-gopher.stanford.edu:70/11/topic

This gopher menu is devoted to biology and science resources ranging from the botanical to the zoological with a genome or two in between. The list of links to life science topics is organized alphabetically.

Research Funding Agencies

http://www.cs.virginia.edu/~seas/resdev/sponsors.html

Grant seekers will find a lists of agencies that offer funding opportunities in all fields of science and technology on this page. This considerable database includes links to such entities as the National Science Foundation, U.S. Department of Education, the Rotary Foundation and more.

Rice University Biology Gopher Menu

gopher://riceinfo.rice.edu/11/Subject/Biology

This gopher from Rice University features a comprehensive set of links to biology sites across the Internet. Visitors can start with the link to A Biologist's Guide to the Internet and take off to hundreds of sites from there.

Smithsonian Institution Museum of Natural History Gopher Menu

gopher://nmnhgoph.si.edu/

Leave it to the Smithsonian to pack a gopher with so diverse a biological selection. Find info on botany, zoology, paleobiology, anthropology, entomology, biodiversity and biological conservation. Newsletters, projects, specimen catalogs, announcements and more reflect the vast resources of this national museum.

Stanford Gopher Menu

gopher://genome-gopher.stanford.edu/11/topic

This gopher server offers a wealth of biological and earth sciences information, including publications, links to organizations, departments and institutes, and more.

ASSOCIATIONS AND ORGANIZATIONS

American Association of Plant Taxonomists Gopher Menu

gopher://nmnhgoph.si.edu/11/.botany/.aspt

The American Association of Plant Taxonomists (ASPT) publishes a quarterly newsletter that contains news, funding, job opportunities and other information related to the field. Find current and back issues at this gopher site.

American Phytopathological Society: APSnet

http://www.scisoc.org/

The American Phytopathological Society boasts nearly a century of plant disease research and an array of international members. Some of its publications are available to the public; to get the meaty stuff, subscribe here.

American Society for Horticultural Science Home Page

http://www.ashs.org/

Individuals with both green thumbs and Ph.D.s compare notes, share data and post publications at the American Society for Horticultural Science home page.

American Society of Ichthyologists and Herpetologists

http://www.utexas.edu/depts/asih/

Background information, news and membership details are featured on the home page of the American Society of Ichthyologists and Herpetologists. Also find a directory of members, meeting information and a listing of related organizations such as the Society for the Study of Amphibians and Reptiles.

The Australian Commonwealth Scientific and Industrial Research Organisation

http://www.csiro.au/

The Australian Commonwealth Scientific and Industrial Research Organisation provides resources to the country's corporate, industrial and scientific communities. Visit here to learn about its research programs and projects, browse its staff directory and link to its index of reference materials.

Federation of American Societies for Experimental Biology Information Services

http://www.faseb.org/

The Federation of American Societies for Experimental Biology is the largest coalition of life science societies in the United States. Visitors here will find an overview of the federation along with information on careers in experimental biology, the latest news from the field and a list of members.

Harvard Undergraduate Society for Neuroscience

http://hcs.HARVARD.EDU/~husn/

The Harvard Undergraduate Society for Neuroscience provides information here about its mission, seminars and special events. Visit here for society publications and links to related neuroscience home pages.

Hydroponic Society of America

http://www.intercom.net/user/aquaedu/hsa/index.html

The Hydroponic Society of America gives an overview of itself and solicits memberships on this page. The page also contains information on growing plants without soil, hydroponic conferences and seminars.

International Centre for Genetic Engineering and Biotechnology

http://base.icgeb.trieste.it/

This United Nations organization promotes the safe use of biotechnology. Visitors can learn about the Biodiversity Information Network, refer to Bioline Publications, and read about biosafety and environment.

International Federation for Medical and Biological Engineering Home Page

http://vub.vub.ac.be/~ifmbe/ifmbe.html

Visitors can download the meeting minutes, speeches and constitution of the International Federation for Medical and Biological Engineering here. The page also posts information on conferences and biographical sketches of the Federation's council members.

National Institutes of Health Campus Yeast Interest Group

http://www.nih.gov/sigs/yeast/index.html

Scientists who study yeast will want to check out the NIH Campus Yeast Interest Group Home Page, with links to information about the group and meeting times, as well as a roster of members with linked pages showing their scientific interests and publications.

Natural Heritage Network

http://www.abi.org/

A joint effort of the Nature Conservancy and the National Biological Service, the Central National Heritage and Conservation Data Centre home page has links to publications, jobs and a program overview.

Physiology Online

http://physiology.cup.cam.ac.uk/

This electronic information service of The Physiological Society provides membership info, news, publications, conference announcements and more.

Society for Mathematical Biology Gopher Menu

gopher://gopher.nih.gov:70/11/res/SMBdigest

The Society for Mathematical Biology provides a searchable archive of its SMB Digest at this gopher site. Also find information about the society and a membership application.

Society for the Study of Amphibians and Reptiles

http://falcon.cc.ukans.edu/~gpisani/SSAR.html

The Society for the Study of Amphibians and Reptiles, a nonprofit herpetological society founded in 1958, maintains this informational site for scientific resources. Visit here to learn about the society and its efforts to promote research, conservation and education about amphibians and reptiles.

The World-Wide Web Virtual Library: Biology Societies and Organizations

http://golgi.harvard.edu/afagen/depts/orgs.html

This page from the much larger World Wide Web Virtual Library collection features a links to biology societies and organizations with Web pages. Search by country and alphabetically, or link to other databases and search tools.

BIOCHEMISTRY

ARCHIVES AND INDICES

The Aberystwyth Quantitative Biology and Analytical Biotechnology Group

http://gepasi.dbs.aber.ac.uk/home.htm

Online biochemistry and microbiology resources abound at this site maintained by the Institute of Biological Sciences at the University of Wales at Aberystwyth. Includes information on members of the research group as well.

Amino Acids

http://www.chemie.fu-berlin.de/chemistry/bio/amino-acids.html

An extensive index of amino acids is provided at this Web site. Browsers can read a summary of each molecule's chemical makeup and view a molecular diagram. In German and English.

Amino Acid Substrate/Product Names

http://www.mcs.anl.gov/home/compbio/pathways/compounds.html

The Mathematics and Computer Science Division of Argonne National Laboratory offers this page from the Enzyme and Metabolic Pathways Project with information about the pathways of 630 compounds. Compounds are listed by product/substrate name, and a graphic of each compound is included.

Entrez Browser

http://atlas.nlm.nih.gov:5700/Entrez/index.html

Provided by the National Center for Biotechnology Information, Entrez offers access to online databases specifically geared toward medicine and biomedical research. A straightforward search form allows the user to specify the field, search mode and keyword.

MHC Binding Peptides Gopher Menu

gopher://gopher.wehi.edu.au:70/1

This gopher server is a database listing for MHC-binding peptides, with entries compiled from published reports and experimental data submissions at the Walter and Eliza Hall Institute of Medical Research in Melbourne, Australia. Additional resources from related discussion groups and other research facilities can also be found at this site.

NetBiochem Welcome Page

http://www-medlib.med.utah.edu/NetBiochem/NetWelco.htm

NetBiochem is a multimedia educational presentation of biochemistry topics. Visitors will find animations, graphs and audio, a search engine and links to other biochemistry sites.

INSTITUTES AND UNIVERSITIES

Institute of Biology and Chemistry Proteins

http://www.ibcp.fr/

The Institute of Biology and Chemistry Proteins in Lyons, France, provides an overview here, in French. In English, researchers will find a protein sequence analysis database and an index to biology sites on the Net.

Martinsried Institute for Protein Sequences (MIPS)

http://www.mips.biochem.mpg.de/

Researchers who need yet another tool for identifying protein sequences can visit this site maintained by Martinsried Institute for Protein Sequences. Users can search seven databases for matches and can access information about the European Commission genome projects.

Purdue University: Biochemistry Department

http://www.biochem.purdue.edu/

The department of biochemistry at Purdue University in West Lafayette, Ind., maintains this information site. Visitors can link to its graduate and undergraduate departments, faculty listings, laboratory facilities, personal home pages and other administrative and academic resources.

Royal Institute of Technology: Department of Biochemistry and Biotechnology

http://kiev.physchem.kth.se/

This is the home page for the department of biochemistry and biotechnology at the Royal Institute of Technology in Stockholm, Sweden. Visitors will find information on the department, its programs of study, research projects and access to a variety of biology databases.

University College London: Biochemistry Department Home Page

http://www.biochem.ucl.ac.uk/

The department of biochemistry and molecular biology at University College London presents this departmental overview. Find links to academic programs, staff and research projects, plus links to affiliated academic institutions.

University of Toronto: Bioinfo Home Page

http://bioinfo.med.utoronto.ca/biochemistry.html

The University of Toronto's department of biochemistry hosts this site, with links to biochemistry resources, files and related links.

JOURNALS, PERIODICALS, AND ABSTRACTS

Bio/Chemical Journals and Newsletters

http://www.public.iastate.edu/~pedro/rt_journals.html

This page offers an extensive collection of links to chemical and biological journals and newsletters, arranged in alphabetical order. Visitors can also link to a number of other general chemistry-related resources.

Journal of Biological Chemistry

http://www-jbc.stanford.edu/jbc/

The electronic edition of the Journal of Biological Chemistry, published by the American Society for Biochemistry, sponsors this page. Of primary interest to biomedical and chemical professionals, visitors can search here for current and back issues, get a sneak preview of upcoming publications and sign the JBC guest book.

Protein Science

http://www.prosci.uci.edu/

Visitors can download or search the journal Protein Science, published by Cambridge University Press, here. The site also includes ProTeach, a database of resources for teaching protein science, and other relevant links.

PROTEINS

Basic Local Alignment Search Tool (BLAST)

http://www.ncbi.nlm.nih.gov/BLAST/

The National Center for Biotechnology Information (NCBI), Bethesda, Md., explains BLAST here and provides available documentation about the programs, searchable databases, and NCBI servers. Visitors will find such items as BLAST news, a bibliography and an e-mail server.

Blocks WWW Server

http://www.blocks.fhcrc.org/

The Blocks WWW Server site is produced by the Fred Hutchison Cancer Research Center. Geared to the scientific and medical research community, the site provides access to resources for the "detection and verification of protein sequence homology."

The Brookhaven PDB Gopher Hole

gopher://pdb.pdb.bnl.gov/

This gopher hole for the Brookhaven protein data bank (PDB) provides search functions and information on files available electronically. Browsers will also find newsletters and a link to the PDB's anonymous file transfer protocol (FTP) site.

Centre for Protein Engineering, Cambridge, UK

http://www.mrc-cpe.cam.ac.uk/predict/

Biomedical researchers working on protein structure prediction will want to access this site for current news on attempts to solve "the folding problem" and for information on upcoming symposia, prediction competitions and online prediction services.

EC Enzyme

http://www.gdb.org/Dan/proteins/ec-enzyme.html

This site contains a tool for searching the EC Enzyme database. Features include hot links within entries and an online user's manual.

Enzyme Search by Enzyme Class

http://expasy.hcuge.ch/cgi-bin/enzyme-search-cl

The ExPASy molecular biology server provides the Enzyme Data Bank, a list of definitions of enzyme classes, subclasses and sub-subclasses. Visitors can get a list of all enzymes in the corresponding classes here.

European Bioinformatics Institute Sequences Data Submission Form

http://www.ebi.ac.uk/subs/emblsubs.html

The European Bioinformatics Institute provides this form for submission of nucleic acid sequences data to its Web server. Instructions are provided for the new user, as well as a Frequently Asked Questions (FAQ) file about the service.

ExPASy

http://expasy.hcuge.ch/

ExPASy, the molecular biology server of the Geneva University Hospital and the university of Geneva in Switzerland, is dedicated to the analysis of protein and nucleic acid sequences. Find a variety of database entry points and links to other molecular biology sites.

ExPASy - Compute pI/Mw Tool

http://expasy.hcuge.ch/ch2d/pi_tool.html

From the ExPASy molecular biology Web server of the Geneva University Hospital and the University of Geneva, the interactive form on this page computes the theoretical isoelectric point and molecular weight for one or more SWISS-PROT protein identifiers or for user-entered sequences.

ExPASy - Enzyme Nomenclature Database

http://expasy.hcuge.ch/sprot/enzyme.html

Featuring six search options including EC number, enzyme class and chemical compound, this online repository stores the ENZYME database, along with user documentation and related links.

The G-Protein-Coupled Receptor DataBase

http://receptor.mgh.harvard.edu/GCRDBHOME.html

This site contains pointers to sites relevant to G-proteins and coupled receptors (GCR). Motif and alignment resources, diseases caused, and other basic information about GCRs are included.

Molecules R Us

http://molbio.info.nih.gov/cgi-bin/pdb

If you're looking for access to the protein data bank, this search tool from the National Institutes of Health is the place to start. Enter your keywords into the Molecules R Us utility and receive a text or image response (your choice).

NNPredict

http://www.cmpharm.ucsf.edu/~nomi/nnpredict.html

Biologists looking for a way to find out the secondary structure of a protein sequence can plug the known sequence into the interactive form on the NNPredict page and watch it spit out the resulting prediction. Maintained by the University of California at San Francisco, the site includes online help.

NRL3D-Web

http://www.gdb.org/Dan/proteins/nrl3d.html

NRL3D is a sequence-structure database derived from three-dimensional structures of proteins, deposited with the Brookhaven National Laboratory's protein data bank. This site details ongoing research and resources.

OWL Web

http://www.gdb.org/Dan/proteins/owl.html

The OWL Web site is a search engine for protein sequences from a number of large databases. Aside from the search feature, there are links to other databases providing information on proteins, enzymes and DNA.

Prediction of Protein Sorting Signals and Localization Sites in Amino Acid Sequences (PSORT)

http://psort.nibb.ac.jp/

Visit the PSORT server home page for more information on this program which attempts to predict protein sorting signals and localization sites in amino acid sequences. Page users can access the program manual, bibliography or predictions.

PredictProtein Server

http://www.embl-heidelberg.de/predictprotein/predictprotein.html

Visitors to this site will find an "automatic service for the prediction of protein structure." Simply send an amino acid sequence and the server returns a multiple sequence alignment and predictions of secondary structure, residue solvent accessibility, and helical transmembrane regions.

Protein Data Bank World Wide Web Server

http://www.pdb.bnl.gov/

Scientists seeking three-dimensional structures of biological macromolecules can search the Protein Data Bank World Wide Web Server. Newsletters, documentation and Frequently Asked Questions (FAQ) files are also available here.

The Protein Identification Resource (PIR)

http://www.gdb.org/Dan/proteins/pir.html

Supported by the National Library of Medicine, the Protein Identification Resource is a searchable database of protein and nucleic acid sequences. Researchers can use this tool to identify specific proteins and their corresponding coding sequences.

Protein Information Retrieval Online World Wide Web Lab (PROWL)

http://chait-sgi.rockefeller.edu/

The Laboratory for Mass Spectrometry and Gaseous Ion Chemistry offers a smorgasbord of protein databases and mass spectrometry software at its home page. Find recipes for protein and

peptide cleavage as well as lists of common protein solution contaminants here.

Protein Interactions / Brent Lab Information

http://xanadu.mgh.harvard.edu/

The Department of Genetics from Harvard Medical Center and the Department of Molecular Biology at Massachusetts General Hospital offer information from the Brent Lab regarding protein interactions through this scientific Web site.

Protein Sequence Analysis

http://www.ibcp.fr/predict.html

Find sequence analysis and secondary structure predictions of proteins on this server from the Institute of Biology and Chemistry of Proteins from Lyons, France. Visitors can also use three different databases to search for multiple alignments.

Protein Sequence Analysis (PSA) E-mail Server

http://bmerc-www.bu.edu/psa/

Boston University's BioMolecular Engineering Research Center (BMEC) allows visitors to order protein sequence analysis services via e-mail from this Web site.

Protein Structure Group

http://www.yorvic.york.ac.uk/

The chemistry department at the University of York offers this Web site with information on its Protein Structure Group. Browsers can read about the group's labs, members and courses, or view the yearly lab report.

REBASE - The Restriction Enzyme Database

http://www.gdb.org/Dan/rebase/rebase.html

REBASE is a restriction enzyme database containing information including recognition sequences, cleavage sites and commercial availability. Also includes references to published and unpublished observations of the documented enzymes.

The Sander Group

http://www.sander.embl-heidelberg.de/

The European Molecular Biology Laboratory (EMBL) Sander Group designs software and protein databases. At the group's home page link to database search functions, learn more about the group's members and get details about the software they design.

The SBASE Page

http://base.icgeb.trieste.it/sbase/

Biologists can look up annotated protein domain sequences at the SBASE page. Search the comprehensive database offered here, or link to other sources of protein sequence data.

Sequence Analysis Bibliographic Reference Database

http://expasy.hcuge.ch/sprot/seqanalr.html

Visit this site to find a fully searchable data bank of research and technical papers from mathematical and computer analyses of biomolecular sequences. Link to other protein and enzyme databases.

Structural Classification of Proteins

http://scop.mrc-lmb.cam.ac.uk/scop/

Structural Classification of Proteins contains detailed descriptions of the structural and evolutionary relationships of all proteins, as well as sources for further research and classification. Visitors can run sequence similarity and keyword searches on the database.

Swiss-Model: Automated Protein Modeling Server

http://expasy.hcuge.ch/swissmod/
SWISS-MODEL.html

Swiss Model, an automated protein modeling server at the Glaxo Institute for Molecular Biology in Geneva, Switzerland, is available at this site. Visit here to access the server and link with a variety of related Web sites and scientific resources.

BIOLOGY (NONHUMAN)

BIOENGINEERING

Artificial Life Online

http://alife.santafe.edu/

Artificial Life is the name given to a new discipline that studies natural life by attempting to recreate biological phenomena from scratch within computers and other artificial media. Alife complements the traditional analytic approach to biology by attempting to put together systems that behave like living organisms rather than dissecting organisms to see how they work.

Artificial Life Online Software

http://alife.santafe.edu/alife/software/

Artificial Life Online, from MIT Press, provides this page of downloadable programs that simulate complex systems and evolutionary changes. Programs for Unix, Macintosh, and Windows-based machines are listed from Tierra to Starlogo.

North Carolina State University: Department of Biological and Agricultural Engineering

http://www.bae.ncsu.edu/bae/

The North Carolina State University Department of Biological and Agricultural Engineering provides information to potential students about the department, its history and its application of engineering.

BIOINFORMATICS

Australian National University Bioinformatics

http://life.anu.edu.au/

The Australian National University Bioinformatics Hypermedia Service provides a collection of pointers to biology-related resources available on the Internet.

Australian National University Bioinformatics Gopher

gopher://life.anu.edu.au/

The Australian National University maintains this gopher server for its bioinformatics facility. Visitors will find links to news, publications, downloadable software and related academic resources. Includes events updates and conference listings.

European Bioinformatics Institute (EBI) Home Page

http://www.ebi.ac.uk/

The European Bioinformatics Institute, Hinxton Hall, England, maintains this site to provide access to its research database. Visit here to link to information about protein and nucleotide sequences, submit data and perform keyword searches.

Johns Hopkins University BioInformatics Web Server

http://www.gdb.org/

The Johns Hopkins University BioInformatics Web Server provides access to biological databases and electronic publications for biology. Included is Prot-Web, a massive collection of protein databases.

Université Aix-Marseille: L' Atelier Bioinformatique de Marseille

http://www-biol.univ-mrs.fr/

The School of Bioinformatics provides information about its academic programs and research on this page. It includes links to seminar schedules as well as other biology-related links. In French and partial English.

COMPUTATIONAL BIOLOGY

Center for Computational Biology Home Page

http://www.compbio.caltech.edu/

The Center for Computational Biology at the California Institute of Technology maintains this site for general information and resource access. Visit here to find information about programming languages, networking systems and computational biology applications.

NASA Ames Biocomputation Center

http://biocomp.arc.nasa.gov/

Ames Biocomputation Center, a research facility of the U.S. National Aeronautics and Space Administration, develops three-dimensional computer visualization technology for biology applications. Visit here for news, staff and facilities profiles, and links to sample programs.

University of Minnesota: Computational Biology Centers Medical School

http://www.cbc.med.umn.edu/

Visitors to the Computational Biology Centers Medical School at the University of Minnesota can read descriptions of the school's research projects which delve into molecular biology and genetics. The site also includes selected online papers.

W.M. Keck Center For Advanced Training in Computational Biology

http://www.cs.pitt.edu/keck/Welcome.html/

The W.M. Keck Center for Advanced Training in Computational Biology, Pittsburgh, Pa., provides information on its graduate and postdoctoral training programs. Other resources include a list of faculty and fellows and links to the center's collaborators.

ENTOMOLOGY

B-EYE: The World Through the Eyes of a Bee

http://cvs.anu.edu.au/andy/beye/beyehome.html

This page allows visitors to see the world through the eyes of a honey bee. Presented by a neuroscientist studying bee vision, this unusual site presents a gallery of preprocessed, downloadable images and allows visitors to choose an image, set parameters and run the B-EYE program.

Entomology at Colorado State University

http://www.colostate.edu/Depts/Entomology/ent.html

Visitors to the Colorado State University Department of Entomology home page will find downloadable images, movies and newsletters, as well as general staff, faculty and student information. Job opportunities are also posted here.

Entomology Image Gallery

http://www.ent.iastate.edu/imagegallery.html

Iowa State's Entomology Image Gallery features still images and movie clips of beetles, ticks, mosquitoes and lice on its Web page. The page also has links to images at the Smithsonian Institution and other insect resources on the Internet.

Entomology Index of Internet Resources

http://www.public.iastate.edu/~entomology/ResourceList.html

All that is insect on the Internet is cataloged here. Entomologists will find an alphabetical list of links to related electronic resources and archives using the index provided.

Flea News

http://www.ent.iastate.edu/FleaNews/AboutFleaNews.html

Entomologists can catch up on the latest news about fleas and other insects belonging to the order Siphonaptera through the biannual Flea News newsletter. The newsletter can be read in full on this page.

FlyBase

gopher://fly.bio.indiana.edu:70/11/Flybase

Visitors to this site will find FlyBase, a database of genetic and molecular data for Drosophila, a species of fruit fly. Find an extensive bibliography, a directory of researchers, genetic map info, listings of nucleic and protein sequence accession numbers, genomic clones and more.

Flybrain

http://flybrain.uni-freiburg.de/

Flybrain is an online atlas and database of the Drosophila (fruit fly) nervous system. It includes a glossary of terms, a searchable index, information on gene expression and immunocytochemisty, and links to related sites.

FlyView: A Drosophila Image Database

http://pbio07.uni-muenster.de/

FlyView lets scientists take a closer look at Drosophila, the guinea pig of genetic research. Includes fruit fly images and related databases.

Forensic Entomology

http://www.uio.no/~mostarke/forens_ent/forensic_entomology.html

Learn about entomology's place in forensic studies. See Editor's Choice.

The Global Entomology Agriculture Research Server

http://gears.tucson.ars.ag.gov/

The Global Entomology Agriculture Research Server talks about bugs, bees and planted things, and how they relate to each other. Lots of hand-picked links to related topics can be found here.

Harvard University Entomology Gopher Menu

gopher://huh.harvard.edu/11/collections_info/mcz

This Harvard University gopher contains searchable catalogs for microlepidoptera, general entomology, spiders and fish specimens, and collections.

Illinois Entomology

http://www.life.uiuc.edu/Entomology/
home.html

The entomology department at the University of Illinois at Urbana-Champaign provides information on its courses, faculty and research here. Visitors can also download over 30 drawings of insects and find out about the offerings at this year's Insect Fear Film Festival.

Mississippi State University: Entoplath

http://www.msstate.edu/Entomology/
ENTPLP.html

Mississippi State University's Department of Entomology and Plant Pathology invites visitors to its home page to explore the department, review its educational programs and meet the faculty. Links to sites of interest on and off campus are provided.

Mosquito Genomics WWW Server

http://klab.agsci.colostate.edu/

Access genomic databases of various mosquito species or link to the MacArthur Foundation Research Network to research the biology of parasite vectors. Includes pointers to the Vector-Biology Usenet newsgroup, other genomic information sites and mosquito image galleries.

Ohio State University Insect Collection

http://iris.biosci.ohio-state.edu/inscoll.html

Maintained at the Ohio State University College of Biological Sciences Department of Entymology, the Insect Collection is just one of six units in the university's Museum of Biological Diversity. Visitors to its home page are invited to learn about the collection or link to related sites of interest on and off campus.

University of Delaware Entomology Home Page

gopher://bluehen.ags.udel.edu:71/hh/.insects/
.descriptions/entohome.html

The University of Delaware Department of Entomology and Applied Ecology presents this online insect database with information and images on a variety of insect orders, such as Collembola and Hemiptera.

Virtual FlyLab

http://vflylab.calstatela.edu/edesktop/VirtApps/
VflyLab/IntroVflyLab.html

Scientists at California State University have devised the Virtual FlyLab to enable viewers to "play the role of a research geneticist." Custom design fruit fly matings to create personalized mutations, learning the correct rules of genetic inheritance as you go.

Wonderful World of Insects

http://www.ex.ac.uk/~gjlramel/six.html

The Wonderful World of Insects provides a lively page full of insect trivia. Visitors can link to an Internet search of Gordon's Entomological Pages or browse the eclectic collection of other insect pointers.

The World-Wide Web Virtual Library: Drosophila Index

http://www-leland.stanford.edu/~ger/
drosophila.html

The World Wide Web Virtual Library maintains this site for the Drosophila index of its biosciences area. Visitors will find extensive information about the uses of Drosophila melanogaster for research and genetics and developmental biology.

The World-Wide Web Virtual Library: Entomology (Biosciences)

http://www.colostate.edu/Depts/Entomology/
WWWVL-Entomology.html

Visitors to the Virtual Library section for Entomology will find links to universities, job information, images, movies, and topical publications.

EXPERIMENTAL BIOLOGY

Federation of American Societies for Experimental Biology Information Services

http://www.faseb.org/

The Federation of American Societies for Experimental Biology is the largest coalition of life science societies in the United States. Visitors here will find an overview of the Federation along with information on careers in experimental biology, the latest news from the field and a list of members.

---

a2z EDITOR'S CHOICE

Forensic Entomology

http://www.uio.no/~mostarke/forens_ent/forensic_entomology.html

One of the wonders of the Web is stumbling across a subject you never even knew existed, like forensic entomology. Entomologists all over the world assist police departments by analyzing the insects present on a dead body to help determine or corroborate the time, place and cause of death. That's right, bugs on dead people. Webmaster Morten Stærkebyan, an entomology student at the University of Oslo, Norway, wants to tell you all about it. He warns off the squeamish, but don't expect gruesome pictures or lurid details; this site avoids sensationalism and concentrates on facts and technique. Moving from the causes of rigor mortis and the five stages of bodily decay, Stærkebyan then discusses the life cycle of the blowfly and how the age of the insects can be used to estimate the time of death. He includes a catalog of insects occurring on dead bodies, from the common to the rare, with descriptions and effects, and explains the methods of forensic entomology examination and specimen collection. The facts come together in the selection of fascinating case histories. Despite the somewhat fractured English and misspelled words, this site provides an intriguing glimpse into a precise and painstaking aspect of scientific criminology.—*Reviewed by Steve Ellis*

Forensic Entomology

Drawing by E.P. Catts

GENETICS AND HEREDITY

The Alces WWW Server

http://alces.med.umn.edu/start.html

This page hosts the Virtual Genome Center, a resource for molecular biologists that features tools and databases useful in research activities.

Animal Genome Database in Japan

http://ws4.niai.affrc.go.jp/

Biologists can search for and view genetic information including cytogenetic and linkage maps about pigs, cattle, horses, mice and humans here. Includes DNA and sericultural information and links to the Japanese Dairy Cattle Improvement Program and the National Institute of Animal Industry.

The Arabidopsis thaliana Genome Center at the University of Pennsylvania

http://cbil.humgen.upenn.edu/~atgc/ATGCUP.html

The Arabidopsis thaliana Genome Center of the University of Pennsylvania, Philadelphia, maintains this site for resource access. Visit here for genetic and physical map information, data submission information and related resource links.

Avida

http://www.krl.caltech.edu/avida/

The Avida Group at the California Institute of Technology serves up information here about its research into the fields of genetic evolution and auto-adaptive genetic systems (AAGS). Visitors to this site can peruse the group's progress reports, scientific papers and images.

The Boston BioMolecular Engineering Research Center

http://bmerc-www.bu.edu/

The Boston BioMolecular Engineering Research Center researches DNA, RNA and protein sequences. In addition to providing specifics about its ongoing research, the site features links to its papers, journals, staff listings and related sites.

Caenorhabditis elegans WWW Server

http://eatworms.swmed.edu/

The University of Texas Southwestern Medical Center devotes an entire server to a soil nematode used extensively in the study of genetics and neurobiology. Find Caenorhabditis elegans worm-related facts and research here.

Caenorhabditis Genetics Center (CGC) Gopher Menu

gopher://elegans.cbs.umn.edu:70/1

The Caenorhabditis Genetics Center (CGC) maintains and distributes genetic stocks of Caenorhabditis elegans, a nematode. Researchers can access information on the Center's services and stocks, search past issues of the Worm Breeder's Gazette and link to other biological or worm-related gophers.

E. coli Genetic Stock Center

gopher://cgsc.biology.yale.edu:70/1

Visitors to this Yale server will find information about strains, mutations, genes and references taken from the public areas of the CGSC database. Links to other biology and general gophers are also featured.

Fungal Genetics Gopher Menu

gopher://utmmg20.med.uth.tmc.edu:70/1

The searchable Fungal Genetics gopher is maintained by the University of Kansas Fungal Genetics Stock Center and the University of Texas Medical School, Houston, Department of Microbiology and Molecular Genetics. Databases include mitochondrial mutants, plasmid, sordaria and chromosomal aberrations.

Genestream

http://genome.eerie.fr/home.html

The Ecole pour les Etudes et la Recherche en Informatique et Electronique hosts this page with four sequence database search tools, along with genome data and a link to the Frontiers in Bioscience journal.

Généthon

http://www.genethon.fr/

This information server provides access to biogenetic science-related resources including software, databases, indexes and libraries. Additional features include links to other information servers. Information is available in French and English.

The Genetic Algorithms Research and Applications Group (GARAGe) Home Page

http://isl.msu.edu/GA/

Michigan State University's Genetic Algorithms Research and Applications Group (GARAGe) applies genetic algorithms and genetic programming to real-life problems. Visitors will find basic information on GARAGe, upcoming conferences, the researchers and the software the group uses.

A Genome Database for Forest Trees

http://s27w007.pswfs.gov/

The Institute of Forest Genetics Dendrome Project's genome database for forest trees provides an electronic resource for molecular genetic research. Links to topic-related sites are also available.

Globin Gene Server Home Page

http://globin.cse.psu.edu/

The regulation of the beta-like globin gene cluster is the focus of the Globin Gene Server. The site provides information and images of genetic models, gene sequence analyses and a database of experimental results.

Harvard Biological Laboratories - Genome Research

http://golgi.harvard.edu/

A wealth of biology-related Internet resources can be found here. Visit this site to link to research laboratories, databases and directories from around the world.

The Institute for Genomic Research

http://www.tigr.org/

The Institute for Genomic Research presents a collection of databases containing DNA and protein sequences, gene expression, taxonomy and sample collection data for a variety of biological species. Visitors can access databases, find information about genetic conferences and speeches, and learn about job opportunities at TIGR.

International Institute of Genetics and Biophysics

http://sun01.iigb.na.cnr.it/

The Italy-based International Institute of Genetics and Biophysics offers information here about its research activities in animal and human genetics and molecular biology. It also posts seminar information, press releases, journals and the stress proteins database, along with newsgroup listings, national news and links to related sites.

Maize Genetic Database

http://teosinte.agron.missouri.edu/query.html

The maize database offers biologists a searchable source of general genetic and plant genome mapping information.

Maize Genetics Cooperation - Stock Center

http://w3.ag.uiuc.edu/maize-coop/

Use the Maize Genetics Cooperation - Stock Center's Web site to investigate, review and order genetic stocks online. Find specialty maize germplasm here or link to the maize genome database for additional info.

Maize Genome Database World Wide Web Server

http://www.agron.missouri.edu/

Access to the Maize Genome Database—part of the Plant Genome Database sponsored by the USDA—is available here, along with abstracts and full texts of online journals. The site also links to other sites of interest to maize experts.

MendelWeb Homepage

http://www.netspace.org/MendelWeb/

MendelWeb, an online resource for the study of classical genetics, maintains this site for access to the findings of 19th century researcher Gregor Mendel. Visit here for glossaries, introductory tutorials, biographical information and much more. Available in German and English.

Mosquito Genomics WWW Server

http://klab.agsci.colostate.edu/

Access genomic databases of various mosquito species or link to the MacArthur Foundation Research Network to research the biology of parasite vectors. Includes pointers to the Vector-Biology Usenet newsgroup, other genomic information sites and mosquito image galleries.

Mouse Genome Informatics

http://www.informatics.jax.org/mgd.html

The Jackson Laboratory's Mouse Genome database site offers access to empirical data on lab mice. Available searches include probes, genetic markers, PCR primers and mammalian homologs. Related links are also available.

National Center for Biotechnology Information dbEST

http://www.ncbi.nlm.nih.gov/dbEST/index.html

The dbEST contains sequence data and other information on single-pass cDNA sequences or expressed sequence tags from a number of organisms.

National Center for Genome Resources Home Page

http://www.ncgr.org/

The National Center for Genome Resources is a not-for-profit organization created to design, develop, support, and deliver resources in support of genome research. This site provides links to its databases, small business resources, job opportunities listings and more.

Pig Cytogenetic Map Image

http://ws4.niai.affrc.go.jp/dbsearch2/pmap/pmap.html

The Animal Genome Database in Japan offers a Pig Cytogenic Map Image at this site. Browsers can also link to the database home page here.

Plant Genome Databases

http://probe.nalusda.gov:8300/plant/index.html

The Agriculture Genome Information Server's Plant Genome Database, a service of the U.S. Department of Agriculture, provides genetic information on a variety of plant species. Visit here to search the database, view publications and link with related Internet-based resources.

Quantitative Genetics Resources

http://nitro.biosci.arizona.edu/zbook/book.html

This is an electronic supplement to a two-volume text, Fundamentals of Quantitative Genetics. The site include useful quantitative genetics links to programs, FTP sites and PostScript files.

RiceGenes, a Rice Genome Database

gopher://gopher.ars-grin.gov/1

The RiceGenes gopher presents a genome database where visitors will find molecular and phenotypic information about rice. It's a searchable database, with downloadable images and maps.

Rice Genome Research Program Home Page

http://www.staff.or.jp/

This is the home page of the Rice Genome Project at STAFF Institute in Tskuba, a division of the Japanese Ministry of Agriculture, Forestry and Fisheries Genome Project. Visitors can read a wealth of project material here, including the semiannual newsletter, program data, and paper abstracts.

RNA Secondary Structures

http://pundit.colorado.edu:8080/RNA/GRPI/about.html

This list of RNA secondary structures from the University of Colorado includes a Group I Intron Database and 16S rRNA Secondary Structures. There are also links to biology-related sites.

State University of New York, Stony Brook: Department of Molecular Genetics and Microbiology

http://asterix.bio.sunysb.edu/

The State University of New York (SUNY) in Stony Brook provides information on its faculty, staff and programs of study in molecular genetics and microbiology at this site. Visitors can also take a look at the department's research, computing and library facilities.

T&t Research

http://www.io.org/~tmaler/

This company site exposes visitors to T&t Research's family of high-tech products, including DNA Parrot, a talking DNA sequence reader, and CourseBuilder a cross-platform multimedia authoring and testing tool.

U.S. Poultry Gene Mapping

http://poultry.mph.msu.edu/

The Chicken Mapper's Message Board is among the resources at the U.S. Poultry Gene Mapping site. Also find a searchable list of members of the international gene mapping community, as well as newsletters, databases and genetic maps.

University of Montreal MegaGopher

gopher://megasun.bch.umontreal.ca/

The University of Montreal MegaGopher provides support for the MegaSequencing project and data for organellar genome and molecular evolution research. Also available are the Genetic Data Environment package and other biological resources.

Virtual FlyLab

http://vflylab.calstatela.edu/edesktop/VirtApps/VflyLab/IntroVflyLab.html

Scientists at California State University have devised the Virtual FlyLab to enable viewers to play the role of a research geneticist. Custom design fruit fly matings to create personalized mutations, learning the correct rules of genetic inheritance as you go.

LIFE

WQED Web of Life

http://www.envirolink.org/orgs/wqed/

WQED of Pittsburgh presents this page on "Web of Life: Exploring Biodiversity," a two-hour, public-television special that celebrates the diversity of life on earth. A QuickTime preview is available, along with lots of links, descriptions of scenes and home video info.

MARINE BIOLOGY

Bamfield Marine Station

http://bms.bc.ca/

Canada's Bamfield Marine Station, located at Barkley Sound, British Columbia, is a research facility that offers courses in marine sciences. Get general information about all courses, including public education programs, here.

British Columbia Creature Page

http://clever.net/kerry/creature/creature.htm

An index to images, names and descriptions of the fascinating animals that live in British Columbia's ocean waters is presented here. Among the collected creatures are rockfish, nudibranchs, crabs, sponges, echinoderms and more.

Cephalopod Page

http://is.dal.ca/~ceph/wood.html

Biologists and fans of cephalopods can get their fill of information at the Cephalopod Page from Dalhousie University in Canada. The page includes an introduction to cephalopods, as well as links to photos and additional information.

The DEEPSEA Research Newsgroup

http://www.bio.net:80/hypermail/DEEPSEA

This newsgroup exists to "serve as an electronic forum for the world's community of deep-sea and hydrothermal vent/seep biologists, oceanographers, and geologists." Find links to access discussion and topical Web sites.

The Fish Net

http://zfish.uoregon.edu/index.html

Zebrafish researchers will find an online guide to using the fish in the lab, genetic maps and information on various mutant strains here. The page is maintained by the Institute of Neuroscience at the University of Oregon.

Icelandic Fisheries Laboratories

http://www.rfisk.is/

The Icelandic Fisheries Laboratories site contains information about laboratories and institutions researching fisheries and aquaculture in the Northern Atlantic. Includes links to mailing lists and other related servers.

Inter-Institutional Database of Fish Biodiversity in the Neotropics

gopher://fowler.acnatsci.org/

The Inter-Institutional Database of Fish Biodiversity in the Neotropics (NEODAT) Project is a cooperative effort to provide systematic and geographic data on neotropical freshwater fish in various collections in the Americas and Europe. Browsers can search the database here, download NEODAT documents and find out who's who in neotropical ichthyology.

Inter-Research Science Publisher

http://www.int-res.com/int-res/

Inter-Research Science Publisher, a journal from Germany, includes its publications schedule along with recent tables of contents. Links to other journals and pages about marine ecology, aquatic microbial ecology and climate research are included.

The Marine Biological Laboratory

http://www.mbl.edu/

The Marine Biological Laboratory in Massachusetts outlines its research and educational projects, and provides access to library information through this graphically rich Web site. Visitors can read about upcoming events and link to related information.

Marine Biology Database

http://www.calpoly.edu/delta.html

The biological sciences database of marine biology from California Polytechnic State University offers faculty and students access to digital instructional materials for self-tutoring. The searchable database is available for nonprofit use.

Marine Fish Catalog

http://www.actwin.com/fish/species.cgi

The Marine Fish Catalog boasts more than 200 pictures of tropical fish. Visitors can search the entire database, browse pictorial guides to angelfish, butterfly, tangs and clownfish, and link to a freshwater fish catalog.

Monterey Bay Aquarium

http://www.mbayaq.org/

The Monterey Bay Aquarium home page features pointers to various parts of this amazing bayside facility, including details about exhibits and information about the gift and bookstore. Visitors can also check out the kinds of research underway at the aquarium.

NASA SeaWiFS Project

http://seawifs.gsfc.nasa.gov/SEAWIFS.html

SeaWiFS is a global ocean color monitoring project of the National Aeronautics and Space Administration (NASA). Through the observation of ocean color, scientists can determine the concentration of marine plants which remove carbon from the atmosphere. Find research updates at this site.

National Marine Fisheries Service NEFSC Headquarters

http://www.wh.whoi.edu/noaa.html

From the Northeast Fisheries Science Center (NEFSC) Headquarters in Woods Hole, Mass., the National Marine Fisheries Service provides historical photos and data on ocean conservation in the northeast United States. Fish gathering techniques, fish facts, stock assessments and links to related sites are also featured.

Northwest Fisheries Science Center

http://listeria.nwfsc.noaa.gov/

The Northwest Fisheries Science Center is a research facility responsible for providing scientific and technical support for the management, conservation and development of the Pacific Northwest's marine fishery resources. Visit this site to review coastal zone and estuarine studies, learn more about the center or access its other resources.

Ocean Color Data and Resources

http://daac.gsfc.nasa.gov/CAMPAIGN_DOCS/OCDST/OB_main.html

NASA's Goddard Space Flight Center describes how scientists use ocean color data to determine the concentration of marine plants, which are important players in the planet's carbon cycle. Visitors to the site will find newsletters, educational materials, descriptions of related software, documentation and professional journals.

Office of Protected Resource

http://kingfish.ssp.nmfs.gov/tmcintyr/prot_res.html

A chapter-by-chapter presentation of the Marine Mammal Protection Agency Annual Report 1990-1991 is featured at this site of the Office of Protected Resources from the National Marine Fisheries Service. The Marine Mammal Protection Act Bulletin and other publications are included.

Sea World/Busch Gardens

http://www.bev.net/education/SeaWorld/homepage.html

The Animal Information Database, provided by Sea World/Busch Gardens, is intended to educate visitors about worldwide species preservation efforts. Visit here for instructional materials, video classrooms, and other means of learning how to help the marine and terrestrial animal worlds.

Stanford University Hopkins Marine Station

http://www-marine.stanford.edu/

The Hopkins Marine Station of Stanford University reveals its history and academic programs at this site. Visitors can view pictures of the station, read about seminars and check out the latest research projects.

University of South Carolina Marine Biology and Coastal Research

http://inlet.geol.scarolina.edu/

The University of South Carolina gives visitors a look at its Baruch Institute of Marine Biology and Coastal Research here. The page includes general information and documentation for field and laboratory research.

WhaleNet

http://whale.wheelock.edu/

A combined project of Wheelock and Simmons Colleges and the U.S. National Science Foundation, WhaleNet is a interdisciplinary effort to foster learning about the natural environment for schools around the world. Visit its home page to find a variety of fun and informative resources, including whale tracking and marine mammal slide shows.

Zebrafish

http://golgi.harvard.edu/zebra.html

The zebrafish is a small aquarium dweller commonly used in biological research. This Web site provides resources for biologists and others who might find themselves using zebrafish in their work. Links include such sites as the Harvard Biolabs home page and Fish Net.

MOLECULAR BIOLOGY

Baylor College of Medicine Search Launcher

http://kiwi.imgen.bcm.tmc.edu:8088/search-launcher/launcher.html/

The Baylor College of Medicine has compiled database and analysis services on the Web as a service to molecular biologists. Here researchers can search many sequence databases with a single query.

BioCatalog Software Directory

http://www.ebi.ac.uk/biocat/biocat.html

The European Bioinformatics Institute provides this directory containing software of interest to geneticists and molecular biologists. Visitors to the site can download programs and access biological databases.

Biocomputing & Molecular Modeling

http://www-bio.unizh.ch/home.html

The University of Zurich provides an overview and database of biocomputing and molecular modeling. Includes search features, visualizations and links to related resources.

Cell & Molecular Biology Online

http://www.tiac.net/users/pmgannon/

Cell and Molecular Biology Online serves as a general resource for the biology community. It features picks of the best Internet resources for cell and molecular biology along with pointers to electronic publications and career resources.

Collaborative BioMolecular Tools (CBMT) Home Page

http://www.dl.ac.uk/CBMT/HOME.html

The United Kingdom's Collaborative BioMolecular Tools home page features the latest research and development news regarding protein structures. Check for the latest biomolecular research tools.

European Molecular Biology Laboratory

http://www.embl-heidelberg.de/

Founded in 1974, this cooperative effort by a group of molecular biologists is an international training and research center for the European community. Visitors can read about the laboratory's history and major projects here, including the development of synchrotron radiation and developmental genetics. Maps, press releases and contact info are also here.

The ExPASy Molecular Biology Server

http://expasy.hcuge.ch/cgi-bin/listdoc

The ExPASy Molecular Biology Server provides a listing of documents focusing on molecular biology services, software, e-mail servers, FTP sites and more. Includes links to related research groups, teams of scientists and an index of related databases.

GenoBase at the National Institutes of Health

http://specter.dcrt.nih.gov:8004/

The GenoBase server at the National Institutes of Health (NIH) provides access to an NIH copy of GenoBase, an object-oriented molecular biology database. This site provides access to the database, Selkov Metabolic Pathway diagrams, GenBank and molecular biology database.

Image Library of Biological Macromolecules

http://www.imb-jena.de/IMAGE.html

The Image Library of Biological Macromolecules offers a broad collection of VRML files pertaining to biological materials. Browsers can access files on building blocks, macromolecule structures and protein data, or link to other related image archives available on the Web.

Journal of Molecular Biology

http://www.hbuk.co.uk/jmb/

The online version of the Journal of Molecular Biology includes the table of contents from this week's and past issues, a searchable abstracts database and a list of the papers that have been accepted for publication in the current week's issue.

Meeting on Interconnection of Molecular Biology Databases

http://www.ai.sri.com/people/pkarp/mimbd.html

This page offers a synopsis of the Meeting on Interconnection of Molecular Biology Databases held at Cambridge University in 1995. Included are resources of interest to molecular biologists and an announcement regarding the 1996 meeting.

MidasPlus

http://cgl.ucsf.edu/midasplus.html

The University of California, San Francisco, maintains this page to offer a demonstration of Midas-Plus, an advanced molecular modeling system used to display and manipulate macromolecules. A tutorial and FAQ help answer questions about the system, along with links to related news.

Molecular Biology Computational Resource

http://condor.bcm.tmc.edu/home.html

The Molecular Biology Computational Resource at Baylor College of Medicine provides computational support for molecular biology via commercial software and programs developed by researchers. Only university employees with an account can access the system. Other visitors to the site can use the collection of links to locate information.

Molecular Biology Gopher Menu

gopher://gopher.nih.gov/11/molbio

Visitors to this molecular biology gopher from the U.S. National Institutes of Health (NIH) can query the Genbank database as well as the Swiss-Prot database, or read information about the Standard Genetic Code.

Molecular Biology Resources

http://biology.anu.edu.au/internal/other.sites/BiolSites.html

Maintained at the Australian National University, this page offers links to molecular biology resources on the Web. Find databases, bibliographies, tutorials, software, newsgroups and miscellaneous sites.

Molecular Biology Vector Sequence Database

http://www.atcg.com/vectordb/

Molecular biologists can look up vector sequence data to their hearts' content with this online database. Search for over 2500 vector sequences that have been organized and annotated by biologists at Canada's Queens University.

Network Browser for Databanks in Molecular Biology

http://www.embl-heidelberg.de/srs5/

A service of the European Molecular Biology Laboratory, this page assists visitors in searching for and browsing databanks in molecular biology. Search options include sequence and bibliographic libraries, and libraries with protein structure information.

Northwest Fisheries Science Center (NWFSC) Molecular Biology Protocols

http://research.nwfsc.noaa.gov/protocols.html

The Microbial Pathogenesis/Utilization Research Division of the Northwest Fisheries Science Center presents its Molecular Biology Protocols on this page. Find info on the division's methods, plus links to its manuals and resources.

The O WWW Home Page

http://kaktus.kemi.aau.dk/

Users of O, the molecular modeling computer environment, will find a variety of resources at this site. Visit here to find keyword searches, O user manuals and more.

The Oxford Center for Molecular Sciences (OCMS) Home Page

http://nmra.ocms.ox.ac.uk/

Scientists find biophysics resources and protein structure models at the Oxford Centre for Molecular Sciences (OCMS) Home Page. Access databases and OCMS news and events schedule at this site.

Survey of Molecular Biology Databases and Servers

http://www.ai.sri.com/people/pkarp/mimbd/rsmith.html

This survey of molecular biology databases and servers is hosted by the Human Genome Center and the W.M. Keck Center for Computational Biology. Users can link to Harvard University's biological laboratories, the Johns Hopkins bioinformatics page, and more.

Theory of Molecular Machines

http://www-lmmb.ncifcrf.gov/~toms/

Explore molecular information theory at this site, which provides online papers, Delila software and documentation from a lab in Fredericks, Md.

Unite de Conformation de Macromolecules Biologiques

http://www.ucmb.ulb.ac.be/

The University of Brussels highlights its research in molecular dynamics, molecular modeling and other molecular studies through this educational Web site. The page features the people and projects underway at the university.

University of California, Davis: Section of Molecular and Cellular Biology

http://www-mcb.ucdavis.edu/

Prospective students can check out cellular and molecular biology studies at the Division of Biological Sciences at the University of California, Davis. The site posts a departmental overview, program descriptions, faculty listings and links to the university's main page.

The World-Wide Web Virtual Library: Biomolecules

http://golgi.harvard.edu/sequences.html

This Virtual Library site, maintained by Harvard Biolabs, contains a complete index of sites related to biomolecular studies. Links include sequence databases categorized by type, cordon usage tables and metabolic compound databases.

PHYLOGENY

The Tree of Life Home Page

http://phylogeny.arizona.edu/tree/phylogeny.html

This is the home page for the Tree of Life, a project containing information about the phylogenetic relationships of organisms. Visitors can read all about the Tree of Life's goals, news, plans and participants. Links to related sites are included here.

STRUCTURAL BIOLOGY

Center for Structural Biology

http://csbnmr.health.ufl.edu/

The Center for Structural Biology at the University of Florida aims to increase understanding of biological function by determining the structures of large biological molecules, supramolecular assemblies and whole organisms. Explore its research techniques and data findings at this site.

Stanford Structural Biology

http://hyper.stanford.edu/

The department of structural biology at the Stanford University Medical Center maintains this page with information about the department and its graduate program, faculty and research. There also are other Stanford medical links.

BIOPHYSICS

Axel Brunger's Research Group and the X-PLOR Home Page

http://xplor.csb.yale.edu/

This page features the research of a group of students in Yale University's Department of Biophys-

ics and Biochemistry and the software program, X-PLOR, developed by the group's head professor. Recent papers and reviews, plus quick links are also included.

Biophys Uni-Düsseldorf - New Welcome Page

http://www.biophys.uni-duesseldorf.de/

The home page for the department of biophysics at Heinrich Heine University in Dusseldorf (Germany) contains information about its lab, research projects and links to other bio-information and bio-computing resources on the Web.

Boston University School of Medicine: Department of Biophysics

http://med-biophd.bu.edu/

Find out what it takes to get an M.A. or Ph.D. in biophysics at Boston University. The site contains information on graduate courses, research, faculty and students.

International Institute of Genetics and Biophysics

http://sun01.iigb.na.cnr.it/

The Italy-based International Institute of Genetics and Biophysics offers information here about its research activities in animal and human genetics and molecular biology. It also posts seminar information, press releases, journals and the stress proteins database, along with newsgroup listings, national news and links to related sites.

Oxford University Laboratory of Molecular Biophysics Home Page

http://biop.ox.ac.uk/www/welcome.html

Oxford University's Laboratory of Molecular Biophysics maintains this site for its index of related resources. Visit here for links covering biochemistry, crystallography, synchrotrons and a variety of other university information services.

University of Aberdeen: Department of Bio-Medical Physics and Bio-Engineering

http://info.biomed.abdn.ac.uk/

This university in Scotland provides information on its graduate courses of study and major research groups. Visitors can link to the computing group and general departmental information.

University of Genoa School of Medicine Institute of Biophysics

http://citbb.unige.it/

The Institute of Biophysics maintains this server to provide easy access to network facilities for local researchers. Links to selected databases, such as protein databases, and an archive of scientific software are also provided.

Washington University: Molecular Biophysics and Biochemistry

http://bmb.wustl.edu/

Washington University, St. Louis, Mo., provides this Web site with information about its graduate studies programs in molecular biophysics and biochemistry. Visitors can read detailed program info here or search the entire site.

BIOTECHNOLOGY

ARCHIVES AND INDICES

Biomechanics World Wide

http://dragon.acadiau.ca/~pbaudin/biomch.html

Biomechanics World Wide is a vast collection of databases meant to assist biomechanists, and includes discussion forums and access to multiple research institutes. Societies and journals are also listed here along with career opportunities and conference information.

The World-Wide Web Virtual Library: Biotechnology

http://www.cato.com/interweb/cato/biotech/

The World Wide Web Virtual Library maintains a comprehensive, classified index of information on the Internet. Visit this site for its biotechnology index with links to educational, theoretical and professional resources.

ASSOCIATIONS AND ORGANIZATIONS

International Center for Genetic Engineering and Biotechnology

http://base.icgeb.trieste.it/

This United Nations organization promotes the safe use of biotechnology. Visitors can learn about the Biodiversity Information Network, refer to Bioline Publications, and read about biosafety and the environment.

International Center for Genetic Engineering and Biotechnology (ICGEB) Gopher Menu

gopher://genes.icgeb.trieste.it:70/1

The International Center for Genetic Engineering and Biotechnology (ICGEB) is an organization of the United Nations that promotes the safe use of biotechnology, especially in developing countries. Visitors here will get an overview of ICGEB and can search its molecular biology databases, download software or link to related gopher servers.

666 SCIENCE AND TECHNOLOGY

BIOMEDICAL ENGINEERING

BMEnet
http://fairway.ecn.purdue.edu/bme/

Search BMEnet for professional and research resources in the biomedical engineering field. Administered by Purdue University, the BMEnet site concentrates on services to the professional academic community.

International Federation for Medical and Biological Engineering Home Page
http://vub.vub.ac.be/~ifmbe/ifmbe.html

Visitors can download the meeting minutes, speeches and constitution of the International Federation for Medical and Biological Engineering here. The page also posts information on conferences and biographical sketches of the Federation's council members.

Nuclear Medicine Group
http://www.biomed.abdn.ac.uk/~mph469/nm.html

Read about the physics of the "Gamma Camera" courtesy of a doctoral student in the Department of Medical Physics and Bio-engineering at the University of Aberdeen. Links are provided to nuclear medicine teaching files and other imaging resources.

COMPANIES

BioSpace
http://www.biospace.com/

Synergistic Designs Inc. promotes biotechnology companies through art and interactive media. Visit its BioSpace Web site to learn about the San Francisco, Calif.-based company's industry events, access its publication and resource library, and link to partner organizations.

Interactive Simulations
http://www.intsim.com/~isigen/

Biotechnology companies can employ Interactive Simulations to create molecular modeling and drug design software. Review the company's products and services at this promotional site.

INSTITUTES AND UNIVERSITIES

Advanced Biotechnology Center (ABC) Biotech Department WWW Server
http://www.biotech.ist.unige.it/Welcome.html

Affiliated with the University of Genoa, Italy, the ABC has six basic research laboratories working in fields including bioengineering, developmental biology and immunology. Visitors to this site will find databases, gopher links and related sites.

The Biomedical Engineering Center at the University of Minnesota
http://pro.med.umn.edu/bmec/bmec.html

The programs and resources of the Biomedical Engineering Center at the University of Minnesota are featured at this site. Visitors will also find links to topical images, sounds, movies, and other biomedical engineering resources.

Instituto de Biotecnologia, UNAM
http://www.ibt.unam.mx/

The Biotechnology Institute from the Universidad Nacional Autonoma de Mexico unveils its graduate study programs and highlights campus resources at its home page. Visitors can read recent publications from the school in Spanish and English.

Maurice E. Muller Institute for Biomechanics
http://cranium.unibe.ch/

The Orthopaedic Biomechanics Division of the M.E. Muller Institute for Biomechanics in Berne, Switzerland, maintains this informational site. Visit here for events, staff listings, programs and links to research-related Web servers around the world.

The Norwegian EMBnet node
http://biomaster.uio.no/

Sweden's University of Oslo Biotechnology Centre offers historical, research and administrative resources at its server home page. Visitors can access information on courses, services and electronic library holdings.

University of Washington: Molecular Biotechnology Department
http://www.biotech.washington.edu/

This page is a gateway to groups at the University of Washington's Biotechnology Department that are working on flow karyotyping and chromosome mapping.

JOURNALS, PERIODICALS, AND ABSTRACTS

The Scientist Newsletter Gopher Menu
gopher://ds.internic.net:70/11/pub/the-scientist

This gopher server archives articles and job files from The Scientist Newsletter, a journal that addresses issues in biotechnology, education, National Science Foundation Funding and medical research.

Transgenica: Topics in Clinical Biotechnology
http://pharminfo.com/pubs/transgen/tg_hp.html

Published by Pharmaceutical Information Associates, Ltd., the focus of this online journal is to promote communication among medical researchers working in biotechnology, particularly in the field of new drug development. Visitors can access current articles and contact the editorial staff.

BOTANICAL GARDENS

BG-Map Botanical Garden
http://www.libertynet.org:80/~bgmap/

The BG-Map is a computer-based mapping system used by arboreta and botanical gardens to map and catalog collections in a Geographic Information Systems (GIS) format. Visitors here will learn what is needed to run BG-Map and how to order it.

Missouri Botanical Garden Home Page
http://www.mobot.org/welcome.html

The plant-filled grounds of the Missouri Botanical Garden come to life via a virtual tour of the institution and color photographs of flora found there. Includes historical facts about the garden, information on educational programs and a special section offering activities for kids.

Niagara Parks Botanical Gardens and School of Horticulture
http://www.npbg.org/

This Web site provides information about Canada's Niagara Parks Botanical Gardens and School of Horticulture. Here visitors will find a photo archive, a listing of upcoming events and academic information for prospective students. Includes links to botanical Web resources.

Nichols Arboretum
http://www.umich.edu/~snrewww/arb/

Stroll through the 123-acre Nichols Arboretum virtual exhibits and view its plant collections or read about current news, special events and research projects. Visitors can link to educational materials, shop for gifts or study ecology and effective use of renewable resources.

University of Delaware Botanic Garden Home Page
http://bluehen.ags.udel.edu/udgarden.html

The College of Agriculture at the University of Delaware maintains this site for online tours of its botanical gardens facility. Visit here for graphic images and detailed information from its large collection of plant species.

BOTANY

ALGOLOGY

Protist Image Data Archive

http://megasun.bch.umontreal.ca/protists/protists.html

This archive, maintained by the University of Montreal's Molecular Evolution and Organelle Genomics program, provides access to pictures of and information about various algae and protozoa. Visitors can learn, for instance, about the life history of Chlamydomonas.

Seaweed

http://seaweed.ucg.ie/seaweed.html

The Seaweed Information page from Ireland includes facts about different varieties of seaweed and algae. The page also includes links to a checklist of seaweeds found in Britain, Ireland and Europe.

ARCHIVES AND INDICES

Botanical Glossaries

http://155.187.10.12/glossary/glossary.html

Stumped by a botanical word? This glossary lists terms found in The Flora of Australia and The Flora of New South Wales, from adaxial to zygomorphic.

A Checklist of the Vascular Plants of Texas

http://straylight.tamu.edu/tamu/tracy/chklcon.html

This checklist from the S.M. Tracy Herbarium at Texas A&M University is a continuation of previous taxonomic efforts with the vascular plants of Texas and is an experimental effort to convert published biodiversity information to electronic form. The site also includes an ecological summary of Texas plants.

Chez Marco's Botany & Fieldwork Pages

http://www.euronet.nl/users/mbleeker/

Support tools for botanists and ecology fieldworkers are available at Chez Marco's, including a fieldwork software checklist, pictures of plants native to Surinam and Europe, botanical links and more.

CSU Bioweb - Botany

http://arnica.csustan.edu/BT.html

This area of the California State University Bioweb indexes botany sites from around the world. Find BUGNET, Chile Heads, Garden Gate and other sites with equally interesting names and content.

The Farlow Herbarium Diatom Catalog and Harvard Herbaria Type Specimen

gopher://huh.harvard.edu/11/collections_info/huh

The searchable Farlow Herbarium Diatom Catalog and Harvard Herbaria Type Specimen Catalog gopher features general information about the catalogs and a types index bulletin board.

Flora of Europe: A Photographic Herbarium

http://www.knoware.nl/flora/

A vast selection of flora families—from Aponcynaceae to Euphorbiaceae to Violaceae—are indexed here. Descriptions and images are featured for each genus.

Harvard University Biological Collections Gopher Menu

gopher://huh.harvard.edu/1

Harvard University posts a variety of its biological collections on this gopher. Visit for texts and collection catalogs for its biodiversity collections and the Harvard Gray Herbarium.

Harvard University Herbarium

gopher://www.herbaria.harvard.edu/

The Gray Herbarium at Harvard University has compiled a database that includes nearly 300,000 records of New World vascular plant taxa. Botanists can access the database from this gopher menu.

Internet Directory for Botany - Alphabetical List

http://herb.biol.uregina.ca/liu/bio/botany.shtm

Botany fanatics can access a slew of links conveniently organized by subject at this site. The work of three botanists from the United States, Finland and Canada, this robust index offers some two thousand links and is available through several mirror sites in a variety of European languages.

Lichen Herbarium at the Swedish Museum of Natural History

http://www.nrm.se/kbo/saml/lichen.html

A list of all lichen species in the museum's lichen herbarium is available via FTP. Access this site for a description of the list and a link to the FTP server.

Missouri Botanical Garden Gopher Menu

gopher://gopher.mobot.org/1

The Missouri Botanical Garden gopher server features a wide variety of horticultural information for not only the state of Missouri but all of North America. It also contains information about the flora of Mesoamericana and the flora of China.

National Plants Data Center

http://plants.usda.gov:80/npdc/

The National Plants Data Center, a facility of the U.S. Department of Agriculture, provides information here on its programs and resources. Visit this site to learn about the center, read about current activities and access its plants database.

Plant Genome Databases

http://probe.nalusda.gov:8300/plant/index.html

The Agriculture Genome Information Server's Plant Genome Database, a service of the U.S. Department of Agriculture, provides genetic information on a variety of plant species. Visit here to search the database, view publications and link with related Internet-based resources.

SMASCH Project

http://www.calacademy.org/smasch.html

The Specimen Management System for California Herbaria (SMASCH) Project is a collaborative effort to develop and implement a distributed database offering information about the state's vascular plants. Access to the SMASCH query form for collecting data is available at this site.

Smithsonian Department of Botany Gopher Menu

gopher://nmnhgoph.si.edu/11/.botany

Visitors to this page will find the Smithsonian Department of Botany gopher. Site features include databases and newsletters compiled, maintained or edited by the Smithsonian or U.S. National Herbarium staff.

U.S. National Herbarium Gopher Menu

gopher://nmnhgoph.si.edu/11/.botany/.types

All 88,000 specimens at the U.S. National Herbarium have been compiled into a botanical type specimen register that is available on this gopher. Visit for searchable indices about ferns, flowering plants, mosses and other classifications.

Wild-Flowers

http://www.wild-flowers.com/

As varied as an alpine meadow in full bloom, this wildflower index provides pointers to online catalogs, institutes, identification pages, and much more. A state-by-state directory also provides addresses and phone numbers for public gardens and parks.

The World-Wide Web Virtual Library: Plant Biology (Biosciences)

http://www.uoknor.edu/cas/botany-micro/www-vl/

Visit the World-Wide Web Virtual Library's plant biology stacks using the catalog of links provided at this site. Find an extensive list of pointers to agriculture, biosciences and forestry resources here.

ASSOCIATIONS AND ORGANIZATIONS

American Association of Plant Taxonomists Gopher Menu

gopher://nmnhgoph.si.edu/11/.botany/.aspt

The American Association of Plant Taxonomists (ASPT) publishes a quarterly newsletter that contains news, funding, job opportunities and other information related to the field. Find current and back issues at this gopher site.

American Phytopathological Society: APSnet

http://www.scisoc.org/

The American Phytopathological Society boasts nearly a century of plant disease research and an array of international members. Some of its publications are available to the public; to get the meaty stuff, subscribe here.

American Society for Horticultural Science Home Page

http://www.ashs.org/

Individuals with both green thumbs and Ph.D.s compare notes, share data and post publications at the American Society for Horticultural Science home page.

Hydroponic Society of America

http://www.intercom.net/user/aquaedu/hsa/index.html

The Hydroponic Society of America gives an overview of itself and solicits memberships on this page. The page also contains information on growing plants without soil, hydroponic conferences and seminars.

INSTITUTES AND UNIVERSITIES

Botanical Museum, Finnish Museum of Natural History

http://www.helsinki.fi/kmus/index.html

The Botanical Museum provides a discussion of its collections, databases and archives, as well as an overview of the European Flower Atlas project and a list of museum publications. Visitors will also find information on the vascular plants in Finland.

Botany at the Smithsonian Institution

gopher://nmnhgoph.si.edu:70/11/.botany

Information on the Smithsonian Department of Botany and the U.S. National Herbarium is available through this gopher site. Includes links to bibliographies, newsletters, specimen collection catalogs, type specimen registers and biological conservation information.

Boyce Thompson Institute's Environmental Biology Program

http://birch.cit.cornell.edu/

The Boyce Thompson Institute for Plant Research's Environmental Biology Program explores the interaction of plants and the environment. The institute, which is housed at Cornell University, gives an overview of its research and staff here.

Cornell University: Floriculture and Ornamental Horticulture Department

http://www.cals.cornell.edu/cals/dept/flori/

The floriculture and ornamental horticulture department at Cornell University serves up information here on its academics, faculty, students, events and research. Visitors can also peruse online tutorials created by students and faculty, or link to a number of horticultural sites on the Web.

National Museum of Natural History Botany Page

http://nmnhwww.si.edu/departments/botany.html

The Department of Botany at the Smithsonian Institution's National Museum of Natural History provides details on its collections, programs, publications and staff. One highlight is the United States National Herbarium. Includes numerous botany links.

National Wildflower Research Center Home Page

http://www.wildflower.org/

Visitors to this Web site can learn about the 42-acre wildflower research center located in Austin, Texas. Includes essays written by staff members, directions to the center and a guided tour of the institution.

Niagara Parks Botanical Gardens and School of Horticulture

http://www.npbg.org/

This Web site provides information about Canada's Niagara Parks Botanical Gardens and School of Horticulture. Here visitors will find a photo archive, a listing of upcoming events and academic information for prospective students. Includes links to botanical Web resources.

Purdue University: Horticulture Department

http://www.hort.purdue.edu/hort/hort.html

The horticulture department at Purdue University details its academic and research focus as one of the top horticultural resources in the United States. Also featured, find information about the NASA Center for Research and Training in Bioregenerative Life Support Systems.

South Dakota State University: Plant Science Department

http://www.sdstate.edu/~wpls/http/pscihome.html

The plant science department at South Dakota State University maintains this look at its instructional programs and faculty. Links to departmental outreach programs and useful Internet resources are also featured.

University of Georgia: Botany Department Greenhouses

http://dogwood.botany.uga.edu/greenhouse/greenhouse.html

This site features a collection of photographs taken throughout six botanical greenhouses. Visitors will also find information about relationships among the major land plant groups.

University of Guelph: Department of Botany

http://www.uoguelph.ca/botany/index.htm

The botany department at the University of Guelph in Ontario supplies information here about its faculty, programs, courses and research. Visitors can also take a virtual tour of its greenhouse.

University of Oxford: Department of Plant Sciences

http://ifs.plants.ox.ac.uk/

The department of plant sciences at Oxford provides access to publications, research reports and databases produced by the department. Includes an overview of the department, its educational and research programs, faculty and staff listings, and links to numerous related plant science resources.

University of Texas, Austin: Department of Botany

http://www.botany.utexas.edu/

The botany department at the University of Texas, Austin, maintains this page with information about the department, faculty and degrees. Course descriptions and links to departmental resources, such as the UTEX Algae Culture Collection, are also provided.

University of Toronto: Department of Botany

http://www.botany.utoronto.ca/

The department of botany at the University of Toronto, Canada, offers a site where visitors can learn about the faculty and courses offered. There's a link to the university home page, as well as information on the city of Toronto.

Wageningen Nuclear Magnetic Resonance (NMR) Centre

http://gcg.tran.wau.nl/wnmrc/wnmrc.html

This research facility in the Netherlands provides access to NMR spectrometers and training in their use. Read about cooperative botanical research projects, including the study of the mechanisms of plant virus infection, metabolism and bioenergy conversion in plants, and the effects of environmental factors.

JOURNALS, PERIODICALS, AND ABSTRACTS

Weeds World

http://nasc.nott.ac.uk:8300/home.html

Weeds World is the International Electronic Arabidopsis Newsletter. Browsers will find abstracts, full-text articles, protocols, meetings and more.

MYCOLOGY

Fungal Genetics Gopher Menu

gopher://utmmg20.med.uth.tmc.edu:70/1

The searchable Fungal Genetics gopher is maintained by the University of Kansas Fungal Genetics Stock Center and the University of Texas Medical School, Houston, Department of Microbiology and Molecular Genetics. Databases include mitochondrial mutants, plasmid, sordaria and chromosomal aberrations.

Fungal Genetics Stock Center

http://www.kumc.edu/research/fgsc/main.html

The Fungal Genetics Stock Center provides an online catalog to the genes and fungi it has for sale from the University of Kansas Medical Center's microbiology department.

Mycelium

http://www.hcds.net/mushroom/welco.html

This page welcomes visitors into "the fascinating world of mushrooms, fungus and fungi." Webmaster Wayne serves up recipes, reports, tips on finding mushrooms in the woods and mushroom enthusiasts online, articles, book reviews, photos and charts.

The MycoPage

http://www.inf.unitn.it/~mflorian/mycology/

An Italian browser posts his archive of fungi images here. The site also includes abstracts from Italian mycological reviews, a link to a newsgroup and an index to other mycological sites on the Net.

The World-Wide Web Virtual Library: Mycological Resources on the Internet

http://muse.bio.cornell.edu/~fungi/

Here are the offerings of the World-Wide Web Virtual Library from the wonderful world of fungi. Links to the BIOSCI Electronic Newsgroup Network, Usenet newsgroups and specific mycological sites around the world are featured.

PALEOBOTANY

Palynology and Palaeoclimatology

http://www.csu.edu.au/landscape_ecology/pollen.html

Scientists can study pollen over the ages thanks to the Australian National University. From the Palynology and Palaeoclimatology site visitors can follow links to archaeology and palaeontology collections. Special emphasis is placed on palaeoclimates and palaeoenvironments.

Plant Fossil Record

http://sunrae.uel.ac.uk/palaeo/pfr2/pfr.htm

The Plant Fossil Record, provided by the University of East London, England, includes descriptions and occurrences of thousands of extinct plant species. Names, dates and ages can be searched and occurrences instantly plotted on a global map.

PLANT MORPHOLOGY

Visual Models of Morphogenesis: A Guided Tour

http://www.cpsc.ucalgary.ca/projects/bmv/vmm/title.html

Visual Models of Morphogenesis shows off the latest advances in the simulation and visualization of biological phenomena via computer modeling. The site provides detailed computer renderings of biomolecular structures and evolution from the plant and animal kingdoms.

PLANT PATHOLOGY

American Phytopathological Society: APSnet

http://www.scisoc.org/

The American Phytopathological Society boasts nearly a century of plant disease research and an array of international members. Some of its publications are available to the public; to get the meaty stuff, subscribe here.

Texas A&M University: Department of Plant Pathology

http://cygnus.tamu.edu/

At Texas A&M University's Department of Plant Pathology page, visitors can learn about the department and its academic programs. The Texas Plant Disease Handbook is also featured along with links to the Texas Plant Disease Diagnostic Laboratory and related sites.

TREES

British Trees

http://www.u-net.com/trees/

The trees of Great Britain come to life on the Web through this page that features an introductory guide as well as links to magazines and publications with information about trees. Visitors can check the pointers to conservation and other botanical resources in Britain.

CSIRO Tropical Forest Research Centre

http://www.tfrc.csiro.au/

Australia's Commonwealth Scientific and Industrial Research Organization (CSIRO) hosts the online Tropical Forest Research Center, which provides information on the condition of tropical rain forests, including access to the center's Division of Wildlife and Ecology, Division of Soils and Division of Entomology.

European Forest Institute

http://www.efi.joensuu.fi/

The European Forest Institute is an independent, non-governmental research body that conducts problem-oriented and multidisciplinary forest research. The EFI site includes a mission statement, info about staff, projects, databases and more.

A Genome Database for Forest Trees

http://s27w007.pswfs.gov/

The Institute of Forest Genetics Dendrome Project's genome database for forest trees provides an electronic resource for molecular genetic research. Links to topic-related sites are also available.

University of Minnesota Forestry Library Gopher Menu

gopher://minerva.forestry.umn.edu/1

Tree huggers, students, forestry professionals and others will find links to useful sites and information on forestry here. Visitors can search for information in several different forestry disciplines, such as urban forestry or trail planning.

TYPES OF PLANTS

Arabidopsis Information Management System

http://aims.cps.msu.edu/aims/

The Arabidopsis Information Management System, a project of Michigan State University, maintains this site of general project information and resources. Visitors here can learn about the project, its directors and database resources.

Arabidopsis Research Companion Gopher Menu

gopher://weeds.mgh.harvard.edu/

Provided by the department of molecular biology at Massachusetts General Hospital, the Arabidopsis Research Companion provides access to information about the small flowering plant (Arabidopsis thaliana) used as a model system for plant biological research. Links to data of related interest are also featured.

The Arabidopsis thaliana Genome Center at the University of Pennsylvania

http://cbil.humgen.upenn.edu/~atgc/ ATGCUP.html

The Arabidopsis thaliana Genome Center of the University of Pennsylvania, Philadelphia, maintains this site for resource access. Visit here for genetic and physical map information, data submission information and related resource links.

BOTN 201 Taxonomy of Flowering Plants

http://www.isc.tamu.edu/FLORA/ tfphome1.html

Presented by Texas A&M University's biology department, this page contains the current semester's course information for Botany 201, entitled Taxonomy of Flowering Plants. Lecture and lab syllabi, student information and the class archive are featured here.

Maize Genetic Database

http://teosinte.agron.missouri.edu/query.html

The maize database offers biologists a searchable source of general genetic and plant genome mapping information.

Maize Genetics Cooperation - Stock Center

http://w3.ag.uiuc.edu/maize-coop/

Use the Maize Genetics Cooperation - Stock Center's Web site to investigate, review and order genetic stocks online. Find specialty maize germplasm here or link to the maize genome database for additional info.

Maize Genome Database World Wide Web Server

http://www.agron.missouri.edu/

Access to the Maize Genome Database—part of the Plant Genome Database sponsored by the USDA—is available here, along with abstracts and full texts of online journals. The site also links to other sites of interest to maize experts.

Nottingham Arabidopsis Stock Centre

http://nasc.nott.ac.uk/

The Nottingham Arabidopsis Stock Centre at England's Nottingham University stocks 8000 lines of Arabidopsis thaliana to support molecular plant research. Scientists can order from its seed list and download the latest genetic map of Arabidopsis here.

Orchids of Wisconsin: An Interactive Key

http://www.wisc.edu/botany/Orchids/Orchids_ of_Wisconsin.html

The Orchids of Wisconsin page provides images, taxonomic information and range maps for the state's native and naturalized orchid populations.

RiceGenes, a Rice Genome Database

gopher://gopher.ars-grin.gov/1

The RiceGenes gopher presents a genome database where visitors will find molecular and phenotypic information about rice. It's a searchable database, with downloadable images and maps.

Rice Genome Research Program Home Page

http://www.staff.or.jp/

This is the home page of the Rice Genome Project at STAFF Institute in Tskuba, a division of the Japanese Ministry of Agriculture, Forestry and Fisheries Genome Project. Visitors can read a wealth of project material here, including the semiannual newsletter, program data, and paper abstracts.

EVOLUTION (NONHUMAN)

Charles Darwin - The Origin of Species

http://www.literature.org/Works/ Charles-Darwin/origin/

Naturalist Charles Darwin's seminal work on evolution is provided here in its entirety, courtesy of the Online Literature Library.

IlliGAL Home Page

http://gal4.ge.uiuc.edu/illigal.home.html

The Illinois Genetic Algorithms Laboratory at the University of Illinois maintains this informational site. Visit here to learn about its evolution-based computing research, view scientific publications and link to a variety of related Web sites.

The Talk.Origins Archive

http://www.talk.origins.org/

Find a searchable archive, a virtual university and fossil images at this site devoted to the discussion of biological and physical origins. Answers to Frequently Asked Questions (FAQ), updates, and links to related sites are also featured.

University of Connecticut: Department of Ecology and Evolutionary Biology

http://florawww.eeb.uconn.edu/ homepage.html

The department of ecology and evolutionary biology (EEB) at the University of Connecticut provides information about its resources. Find links to the EEB greenhouse collections, the Center for Conservation and Biodiversity and the Bartlett Arboretum.

The World-Wide Web Virtual Library: Evolution

http://golgi.harvard.edu/biopages/ evolution.html

The World-Wide Web Virtual Library maintains this site with an index to Internet resources concerning evolution. Visitors will find extensive links to educational and institutional information servers, software archives, science libraries and related resources.

HABITATS

Bio-Pictures

http://herb.biol.uregina.ca/liu/bio/bio-pic.html

Marco Bleeker invites viewers into the lush worlds of tropical rainforests and western European garden plants here. Visitors can wander through a gallery of sites and sounds from the rainforest or download photos from Dutch and German gardens.

Flynn Bogs System Tour

http://csdl.tamu.edu/FLORA/flynnbog/ FB1.HTML

A Tour of the Flynn Bogs System guides botanists and environmentally minded browsers through a unique system of bogs located in Leon County, Texas. Visuals complement text in this comprehensive package on southern wetlands.

International Arid Lands Consortium (IALC)

http://ag.arizona.edu/OALS/IALC/Home.html

The International Arid Lands Consortium is an independent, nonprofit research organization supporting ecological sustainability in arid and semiarid lands. This page contains information on the organization and its mission, a newsletter, strategic plan and links to information on topical workshops and conferences.

HUMAN BIOLOGY

ANATOMY

Marching Through the Visible Man
http://www.crd.ge.com/esl/cgsp/projects/vm/

A project of the National Library of Medicine, the Visible Human is an ongoing attempt to create a digital atlas of the human body. The document at this site "describes a methodology and results for extracting surfaces from the Visible Male's CT data." Images are included.

Visible Human Cross Sections
http://www.meddean.luc.edu/lumen/MedEd/GrossAnatomy/cross_section/index.html

Visitors to this site can simply point and click to view cross-sectional, anatomical images of a body. An explanation of the Visible Human Project's purpose also is provided.

GENETICS

Baylor College of Medicine Gene Finder
http://dot.imgen.bcm.tmc.edu:9331/gene-finder/gf.html

If only solving the mysteries of life were as simple as this cut-and-paste DNA sequence gene finder provided by the Baylor University College of Medicine.

Baylor College of Medicine Human Genome Center
http://gc.bcm.tmc.edu:8088/home.html

The Human Genome Center at the Baylor College of Medicine presents information about its publications, academics, research and resources. Visitors can read the Center's newsletter or search the site for specific info.

The Biological Mass Spectrometry Lab
http://thompson.mbt.washington.edu/

The Biological Mass Spectrometry Lab at the University of Washington gives an overview of its role in the huge undertaking to sequence the humane genome here. It provides a description of its method for performing protein identification using mass spectrometry. The page also contains links to related sites.

Canadian Genome Analysis & Technology (CGAT) Program Bioinformatics Support Services (CGATBSS)
http://cgat.bch.umontreal.ca/

The Canadian Genome Analysis and Technology Program is an information resource and communication nexus for genomics research in Canada. Visitors to this searchable database will find such items as "genomics calendars," a software archive, and information on researchers and projects. In English and French.

Chromosome 12 Genome Center
http://paella.med.yale.edu/chr12/Home.html

The Chromosome 12 Genome Center is a research facility formed from the collaboration of the Albert Einstein College of Medicine and the Yale University School of Medicine. Visitors will find abstracts, reports and technical data about the mapping of human chromosome 12.

Cold Spring Harbor Laboratory Online
http://www.cshl.org/

The Cold Spring Harbor Laboratory (CSHL) is an independent biological research facility chartered by the University of the State of New York. Visitors here can get general information, learn about the human genome project and order books from CSHL Press.

Cooperative Human Linkage Center
http://www.chlc.org/

Genetic maps and markers populate the Cooperative Human Linkage Center. Highly technical in content, this site seeks to make available the Center's detailed genetic maps and other contributions to the Human Genome Project.

DNA Data Bank of Japan
http://www.nig.ac.jp/

The highly technical site of the DNA Data Bank of Japan is available in both Japanese and English, and includes links to the National Institute of Genetics and documentation about collaborations with other databanks.

Emory University: Department of Genetics & Molecular Medicine
http://infinity.gen.emory.edu/

Drop in on Emory University School of Medicine researchers at the department of genetics and molecular medicine home page. Find access to library catalogs, medical journals and human genome databases.

Genes & Development
http://207.22.83.2:443/cshl/journals/gnd/

This genetics journal, published in association with the Genetical Society of Great Britain, solicits subscriptions here. Visitors will find indexes of recent issues, information on the editorial board and subscription details.

Genetics Computer Group
http://www.gcg.com/

This promotional site is the Web home of the Genetics Computer Group, a Wisconsin-based developer of genetic sequencing and analysis software. Visitors are invited to learn more about the company, its history and its products.

GenLink
http://www.genlink.wustl.edu/

GenLink is a multimedia database resource for human genetics. Visitors can access mapping information and software tools for genetic linkage data here, or link to related sites of interest on the Web.

Genome Data Base
http://gdbwww.gdb.org/

Johns Hopkins University School of Medicine maintains this site for its genome database. Visit here for a collection of genomic mapping data submitted by researchers from around the world. Includes an online index and keyword search functions.

Genome Data Base -- Ideogram Interface
http://gdbwww.gdb.org/gdb/ideo/docs/ideogram.html

In support of the Human Genome Project, software specialists in the University of Washington Pathology Department developed this tool for exploring and studying chromosomes. Searches are assisted by a graphical interface.

The Genome Sequence DataBase
http://www.ncgr.org/gsdb/gsdb.html

This site presents an archive of DNA sequence data and related information. It includes data retrieval and submission links as well as pointers to software and documentation.

Genome Sequencing Center Home Page
http://genome.wustl.edu/gsc/gschmpg.html

The Washington University in St. Louis Medical School Genome Sequencing Center Home Page contains information about current genetic research and databases, along with links to related sites.

GenQuest - The Q Server
http://www.gdb.org/Dan/gq/gq.form.html

This is the "front end" to GenQuest(Q), an integrated sequence comparison server. The system provides for "rapid and sensitive comparison of DNA and protein sequence to existing DNA and protein sequence databases and the rapid retrieval of the full database entries of any sequence found in the course of a search."

Helen Donis-Keller Lab
http://hdklab.wustl.edu/

Research at this St. Louis, Mo.-based university lab focuses on genome mapping, the molecular genetics of human disease and database development. Visitors can read research summaries, access physical and linkage genome maps, and search the GenLink databases.

HPV Sequence Database

http://hpv-web.lanl.gov/

The Human Papillomaviruses Database, located at the Los Alamos National Laboratory, collects, curates, analyzes and publishes genetic sequences of Papillomaviruses and related cellular proteins. Take a guided tour of the site and access volumes of data, including medical and public health aspects.

Human Genome Program

http://www.er.doe.gov/production/oher/hug_top.html

The Human Genome Program spearheads the U.S. Department of Energy's efforts to characterize the genomes of humans and other model organisms. Includes detailed specifications for its research program, as well as links to related databases and other electronic bioinformation resources.

Human Genome Project Information

http://www.ornl.gov/TechResources/Human_Genome/home.html

Oak Ridge Laboratory's Human Genome Information site offers a complete listing of genome-related events and informatics. It provides links to other subject-related URLs of interest.

Human Population Genetics Lab (Cavalli Lab)

http://lotka.stanford.edu/

The Cavalli Lab at Stanford University processes and archives human genetic data. Visitors to the site will find descriptions of research projects, manuscript preprints and abstracts, staff information and links to related sites.

Infobiogen

http://www.infobiogen.fr/

Infobiogen, a French genetic research company, maintains general information about the company's activities and resources at this site. Visitors can learn about its projects, contact staff members and link to related Web sites. In French and English.

The Jackson Laboratory Home Page

http://www.jax.org/

The Jackson Laboratory offers information on its genetic research and the resources it makes available to scientists. Included is a price list for Jackson's genetically defined mice, neurology news and a description of its training and education programs.

Lawrence Berkeley National Laboratory Human Genome Center

http://www-hgc.lbl.gov/

The Human Genome Center at the Lawrence Berkeley National Labs looks for ways to accurately and effectively study DNA sequences in humans. Biologist will find links to other genome resources here.

Lawrence Livermore National Laboratory Human Genome Center

http://www-bio.llnl.gov/bbrp/genome/genome.html

Lawrence Livermore National Laboratory's Human Genome Center home page provides highly technical information dealing with biology and genetics. Visitors can learn about the lab's projects and access chromosome maps, DNA sequencing information and a link to the National Laboratory Gene Library Project.

MITOMAP: A Mitochondrial DNA Database

http://infinity.gen.emory.edu/mitomap.html

Based on the report of an international committee of doctors and scientists, the link-laden document on this page acts as a database which maps human mitochondrial DNA. An index of topics, tables and references in or supporting the presentation precedes the text.

Primer on Molecular Genetics (Department of Energy)

http://www.gdb.org/Dan/DOE/intro.html

The U.S. Human Genome Project presents this primer on molecular genetics. Includes in-depth information on DNA, mapping and sequencing the human genome, and related technology.

Program in Molecular and Genetic Medicine

http://pmgm-www.stanford.edu/

The Program in Molecular and Genetic Medicine brings together a variety of researchers from the Beckman Center for Molecular and Genetic Medicine, the Stanford School of Medicine and the Departments of Biology and Chemistry. Visitors to this page will find full details on the program and pointers to topical resources.

Resource Center/Primary Database of the German Human Genome Project

http://rzpd.rz-berlin.mpg.de/

The Genome Analysis Laboratory at London's Imperial Cancer Research Fund maintains this bio-data server. Visitors will find access to the Reference Library DataBase (RLDB2) and other biological databases.

Ribosomal Database Project

http://rdp.life.uiuc.edu/

The University of Illinois at Urbana-Champaign hosts this Ribosomal Database Project. Microbiologists can access the project to find over 3000 ribosomal sequences that have been collected from around the world. Visit this page to find out more about the project and how to access the databases.

Ribosomal Database Project Gopher Menu

gopher://rdpgopher.life.uiuc.edu/

The Ribosomal Database Project (RDP) gopher from the University of Illinois features information about how to use the recent releases of the database as well as programming pointers for ribosomal sequence analysis and display.

San Antonio Genome Center

http://mars.uthscsa.edu/

The San Antonio Genome Center provides detailed physical and genetic maps of polymorphic and expressed markers for human chromosome 3. Find links to human chromosome 3 databases, sensitive chromosome 3 maps and listings of recent publications from the project.

SIGMA: Home Page

http://www.ncgr.org/sigma/home.html

The National Center for Genome Resources in Santa, Fe, N.M., maintains this site for its System for Integrated Genome Map Assembly database tool. Visit this site for access to the application, designed for building and viewing integrated genome maps. Includes downloadable software and online documentation.

Stanford Human Genome Center

http://shgc.stanford.edu/

The Stanford Human Genome Center (SHGC), an education and research facility, endeavors to construct high resolution radiation hybrid maps of the human genome and sequence genomic regions. Visitors to its home page are invited to learn more about the center's research projects and education programs, and review available data.

UK Medical Research Council (MRC) Human Genome Mapping Project Resource Centre

http://www.hgmp.mrc.ac.uk/

The UK MRC provides access to the Human Genome Project searchable database here. Visitors can find genetic and protein sequences archived in this comprehensive biology database.

University of Michigan Genetics Gopher Menu

gopher://una.hh.lib.umich.edu/11/science/lifesci/genetics

Genetics researchers will find an index loaded with genetics information on this gopher, provided by the University of Michigan. Includes genetic databases, Human Genome Project reports and protein databanks.

University of Washington Pathology Cytogenetics Resources & Genome Project Related Tools

http://www.pathology.washington.edu/cyto_page.html

Human genomes exist in real space, and the University of Washington's pathology department has compiled some tools for scientists who need to look at karotypes and map chromosomes.

The World-Wide Web Virtual Library: Genetics

http://www.ornl.gov/TechResources/Human_Genome/genetics.html

Part of the World Wide Web Virtual Library, this exhaustive and well-linked bioscience resource offers a full index of organism genome information from cellular slime molds to human beings.

INSTITUTES AND UNIVERSITIES

Aarhus University: Biological Sciences

http://www.pop.bio.aau.dk/geneco.html

"This page is out of date," warns the powers that be at the departments of microbial ecology and genetics and ecology at this Denmark university, but what the heck, the few links on the page still point to an overview of the departments and e-mail addresses for departmental staff and students. Some addresses are linked to home pages or pictures of the addressees.

Australian National University Biology Gopher

gopher://life.anu.edu.au:70/11

Visit this gopher for a mix of databases, molecular biology resources, software, bioinformatics, publications and university info.

Biometrie und Populationsgenetik

http://www.uni-giessen.de/~gh43/biometrie.html

The Biometrie und Populationsgenetik department of the Justus-Liebig Universitat serves up info about its course offerings and degree programs. In German.

Biophys Uni-Düsseldorf

http://www.biophys.uni-duesseldorf.de/

The home page for the department of biophysics at Heinrich Heine University in Dusseldorf (Germany) contains information about its lab, research projects and links to other bio-information and bio-computing resources on the Web.

Boston University: Department of Cognitive and Neural Systems

http://cns-web.bu.edu/

The Center for Adaptive Systems and the Department of Cognitive and Neural Systems at Boston University provide information here on their people, programs and resources. Visit here to learn about the organizations and access publications, directories and staff profiles.

Boston University School of Medicine: Department of Biophysics

http://med-biophd.bu.edu/

Find out what it takes to get an M.A. or Ph.D. in biophysics at Boston University. The site contains information on graduate courses, research, faculty and students.

Boyce Thompson Institute's Environmental Biology Program

http://birch.cit.cornell.edu/

The Boyce Thompson Institute for Plant Research's Environmental Biology Program explores the interaction of plants and the environment. The institute, which is housed at Cornell University, gives an overview of its research and staff here.

Brown University: Division of Biology and Medicine

http://biomedcs.biomed.brown.edu/

Brown University's Division of Biology and Medicine maintains this site, which includes info about graduate study and research in ecology and evolutionary biology, neuroscience, pathology, laboratory medicine, obstetrics and gynecology. Topic-related links are available at this site.

California Institute of Technology: Computation & Neural Systems Home Page

http://www.cns.caltech.edu/

Visitors to this page will find an overview of the Computational & Neural Systems Program at the California Institute of Technology. Information about lab resources, faculty and classes are featured along with links to related sites.

Carnegie Institution of Washington

http://www.ciwemb.edu/

Check this site for information about the five departments in this Baltimore, Md.-based Institution: The Observatories, Geophysical Laboratory, Department of Embryology, Department of Plant Biology and Department of Terrestrial Magnetism.

Cornell University: Division of Biological Sciences

http://www.bio.cornell.edu/

Find detailed info about the departments, faculty and students of Cornell's Division of Biological Sciences here. Marvel at the images and animations generated in Division labs; applaud the recent accomplishments of faculty members; and exclaim over the special programs in biotechnology, chemical ecology, macromolecular crystallography and more.

Cornell University: Floriculture and Ornamental Horticulture Department

http://www.cals.cornell.edu/cals/dept/flori/

The floriculture and ornamental horticulture department at Cornell University serves up information here on its academics, faculty, students, events and research. Visitors can also peruse online tutorials created by students and faculty, or link to a number of horticultural sites on the Web.

Cornell University: Neurobiology and Behavior Program

http://www.bio.cornell.edu/neurobio/sofneurobio.html

The Neurobiology and Behavior Program at Cornell University profiles its courses and faculty here. Housed in the school's Division of Biological Sciences, the program also posts a "crawdad" page and a page on insect sound and vibration.

CTI Biology

http://www.liv.ac.uk/ctibiol.html

The CTI Centre for Biology promotes using learning technologies in the United Kingdom's higher education system. Visitors here will find publications and information on its services and projects. Links are provided to various CTI-related sites.

Desert Research Institute

http://www.dri.edu/

The Desert Research Institute, appropriately located in Nevada, has some 400 scientists that research humanity's struggle to adapt to harsh environments, global change and water issues, among other topics. Visit for an overview of the institute and access to its library.

Duke University: Department of Neurobiology

http://www.neuro.duke.edu/

The brain and its function are under the microscope at Duke, with research going on in molecular, cellular, developmental and systems neurobiology. Read about the scientists performing this work and about graduate study programs at this premiere North Carolina university.

Emory University: Department of Genetics & Molecular Medicine

http://infinity.gen.emory.edu/

Drop in on Emory University School of Medicine researchers at the Department of Genetics & Molecular Medicine home page. Find access to library catalogs, medical journals and human genome databases.

Entomology at Colorado State University

http://www.colostate.edu/Depts/Entomology/ent.html

Visitors to the Colorado State University Department of Entomology home page will find downloadable images, movies and newsletters, as well as general staff, faculty and student information. Job opportunities are also posted here.

European Forest Institute

http://www.efi.joensuu.fi/

The European Forest Institute is an independent, non-governmental research body that conducts problem-oriented and multidisciplinary forest research. The EFI site includes a mission statement, info about staff, projects, databases and more.

Graduate Programs in Biological/Biomedical Sciences

http://www.faseb.org/graduate.html

Scientists will find a helpful collection of links to graduate programs in the biological and biomedical sciences at this site.

Humboldt-Universität zu Berlin, Institut Biologie

http://www.biologie.hu-berlin.de/

The Humboldt University Department of Biology, Berlin, presents information on its research activities and courses, as well as general information such as addresses. Some information is in English.

Illinois Entomology

http://www.life.uiuc.edu/Entomology/home.html

The entomology department at the University of Illinois at Urbana-Champaign provides information on its courses, faculty and research here. Visitors can also download over 30 drawings of insects and find out about the offerings at this year's Insect Fear Film Festival.

Indiana and Purdue Universities Biology

http://www.biology.iupui.edu/

The biology home page at Indiana and Purdue Universities (IUPUI) has information about the department, faculty and programs. The page also links to FTP and gopher sites, as well as other miscellaneous directories and Web pages.

Indiana State University: Department of Life Sciences

http://mama.indstate.edu/dls/

Indiana State University's Department of Life Sciences maintains this multimedia home page. Visitors can find out about the department's graduate and undergraduate programs, its facilities and its faculty.

Indiana University: Program in Animal Behavior

http://loris.cisab.indiana.edu/

Indiana University's Center for the Integrative Study of Animal Behavior provides information on its program, faculty and Research Training Group in Animal Behavior here. The page also contains an archive of computer software used in the field and links to animal behavior-related sites.

The Institute for Genomic Research

http://www.tigr.org/

The Institute for Genomic Research presents a collection of databases containing DNA and protein sequences, gene expression, taxonomy and sample collection data for a variety of biological species. Visitors can access databases, find information about genetic conferences and speeches, and learn about job opportunities at TIGR.

Institute of Biology and Chemistry Proteins

http://www.ibcp.fr/

The Institute of Biology and Chemistry Proteins in Lyons, France, provides an overview here, in French. In English, researchers will find a protein sequence analysis database and an index to biology sites on the Net.

Institut für Genetik und Allgemeine Biologie der Universität Salzburg

http://www.gen.sbg.ac.at/home.html

The genetics and general biology program at the University of Salzburg, Austria, profiles its current research and staff here. Molecular biologists will also find databases, an online library, a software archive and an index of biofirms selling wares. In English or German.

Instituto de Biotecnologia, UNAM

http://www.ibt.unam.mx/

The Biotechnology Institute from the Universidad Nacional Autonoma de Mexico unveils its graduate study programs and highlights campus resources at its home page. Visitors can read recent publications from the school in Spanish and English.

Macquarie University: School of Biological Sciences

http://www.bio.mq.edu.au/Default.html

Studies at the School of Biological Sciences at Macquarie University, Australia "unite plant biology, animal biology, genetics, biochemistry, ecology and molecular biology." If any of that captures your interest, you can read all about courses, faculty and students here.

Maurice E. Muller Institute for Biomechanics

http://cranium.unibe.ch/

The Orthopaedic Biomechanics Division of the M.E. Muller Institute for Biomechanics in Berne, Switzerland maintains this informational site. Visit here for events, staff listings, programs and links to research-related Web servers around the world.

Max-Planck-Institute

http://wwweb.mpib-tuebingen.mpg.de/

The research focus at the Max-Planck-Institute near Stuttgart, Germany, is developmental biology. Visitors to the Institute's home page will learn more about the staff of scientists and the work they do. Links to the other scientific institutes include information about joint seminars. Some links are in English; most are in German.

Mississippi State University: Entoplath

http://www.msstate.edu/Entomology/ENTPLP.html

Mississippi State University's Department of Entomology and Plant Pathology invites visitors to its home page to explore the department, review its educational programs and meet the faculty. Links to sites of interest on and off campus are provided.

National Institute for Basic Biology Home Page

http://www.nibb.ac.jp/index.html

The National Institute for Basic Biology is a Japanese research facility focusing on basic biological research. This page includes information on administration, mission and listings of laboratory and research group links.

Niagara Parks Botanical Gardens and School of Horticulture

http://www.npbg.org/

This Web site provides information about Canada's Niagara Parks Botanical Gardens and School of Horticulture. Here visitors will find a photo archive, a listing of upcoming events and academic information for prospective students. Includes links to botanical Web resources.

North Carolina State University: Department of Biological and Agricultural Engineering

http://www.bae.ncsu.edu/bae/

The North Carolina State University Department of Biological and Agricultural Engineering provides information to potential students about the department, its history and its application of engineering.

The Norwegian EMBnet node

http://biomaster.uio.no/

Sweden's University of Oslo Biotechnology Centre offers historical, research and administrative resources at its server home page. Visitors can access information on courses, services and electronic library holdings.

Pagina Principal de INBio

http://www.inbio.ac.cr/

Costa Rica's National Institute of Biodiversity (INBio) is a nonprofit institution charged with planning, researching, sustainably developing and marketing the country's diverse landscape and natural resources. Visitors here can learn more about INBio and its programs. In Spanish and English.

Purdue Neuroscience Web Server

http://bieber.bio.purdue.edu/

Find courses, organizations, journals and biotech links among the worldwide resources featured on Purdue University's Neuroscience home page. Links to universities, medical centers and veterinary medical centers are also featured.

Purdue University: Biochemistry Department

http://www.biochem.purdue.edu/

The department of biochemistry at Purdue University in West Lafayette, Ind., maintains this information site. Visitors can link to its graduate and undergraduate departments, faculty listings, laboratory facilities, personal home pages and other administrative and academic resources.

Purdue University: Horticulture Department

http://www.hort.purdue.edu/hort/hort.html

The horticulture department at Purdue University details its academic and research focus as one of the top horticultural resources in the United States. Also featured, find information about the NASA Center for Research and Training in Bioregenerative Life Support Systems.

Royal Institute of Technology: Department of Biochemistry and Biotechnology

http://kiev.physchem.kth.se/

This is the home page for the department of biochemistry and biotechnology at the Royal Institute of Technology in Stockholm, Sweden. Visitors will find information on the department, its programs of study, research projects and access to a variety of biology databases.

Rutgers University: Center for Molecular & Behavioral Neuroscience

http://www.cmbn.rutgers.edu/cmbn.html

Rutgers University's Center for Molecular and Behavioral Neuroscience (CMBN) maintains this page. Visitors will find information on the CMBN, its study programs, personnel, research projects and events.

The Santa Fe Institute

http://www.santafe.edu/

Santa Fe Institute is a multidisciplinary research and education center devoted to creating a "new kind of scientific research community." Visit here

for general institute information, computing resources, employment opportunities and more.

Simon Fraser University: Biological Sciences

http://mendel.mbb.sfu.ca/

From the Simon Fraser University in British Columbia, comes a site devoted to its biological sciences department. Here's information on the department, faculty and staff, research groups and surfing the Net. Includes link to the university's home page.

South Dakota State University: Plant Science Department

http://www.sdstate.edu/~wpls/http/pscihome.html

The plant science department at South Dakota State University maintains this look at its instructional programs and faculty. Links to departmental outreach programs and useful Internet resources are also featured.

Stanford Structural Biology

http://hyper.stanford.edu/

The department of structural biology at the Stanford University Medical Center maintains this page with information about the department and its graduate program, faculty and research. There also are other Stanford medical links.

State University of New York, Stony Brook: Department of Molecular Genetics and Microbiology

http://asterix.bio.sunysb.edu/

The State University of New York (SUNY) in Stony Brook provides information on its faculty, staff and programs of study in molecular genetics and microbiology at this site. Visitors can also take a look at the department's research, computing and library facilities.

Texas A&M University: Department of Plant Pathology

http://cygnus.tamu.edu/

At Texas A&M University's Department of Plant Pathology and Microbiology page, visitors can learn about the department and its academic programs. The Texas Plant Disease Handbook is also featured along with links to the Texas Plant Disease Diagnostic Laboratory and related sites.

Unite de Conformation de Macromolecules Biologiques

http://www.ucmb.ulb.ac.be/

The University of Brussels highlights its research in molecular dynamics, molecular modeling and other molecular studies through this educational Web site. The page features the people and projects underway at the university.

Université Aix-Marseille: L' Atelier Bioinformatique de Marseille

http://www.biol.univ-mrs.fr/

The school of bioinformatics provides information about its academic programs and research on this page. It includes links to seminar schedules as well as other biology-related links. In French and partial English.

University College London: Biochemistry Department Home Page

http://www.biochem.ucl.ac.uk/

The department of biochemistry and molecular biology at University College London presents this departmental overview. Find links to academic programs, staff and research projects, plus links to affiliated academic institutions.

University of Aberdeen: Department of Bio-Medical Physics and Bio-Engineering

http://info.biomed.abdn.ac.uk/

This university in Scotland provides information on its graduate courses of study and major research groups. Visitors can link to the computing group and general departmental information.

University of Alaska, Fairbanks: Biology

http://zorba.uafadm.alaska.edu/iab/index.html

This University of Alaska, Fairbanks, home page connects visitors with the school's Institute of Arctic Biology, its biology and wildlife department, and the Alaska Cooperative Fish & Wildlife Research Unit. Information regarding programs of study, admissions, research projects and faculty listings can be found here.

University of California, Davis: Section of Molecular and Cellular Biology

http://www-mcb.ucdavis.edu/

Prospective students can check out cellular and molecular biology studies at the division of biological sciences at the University of California, Davis. The site posts a departmental overview, program descriptions, faculty listings and links to the university's main page.

University of Cambridge: School of Biological Sciences

http://www.bio.cam.ac.uk/

The School of Biological Sciences site offers course and department information. Include are reference materials, software and links to various databases. Access to Cambridge University main home page.

University of Cape Town: Department of Medical Microbiology

http://www.uct.ac.za/depts/mmi/index.html

The department of medical microbiology at the University of Cape Town, South Africa, includes profiles of its faculty and postgraduate students along with links to current research projects and programs of study. Includes a search tool.

University of Cape Town: Microbiology Department

http://www.uct.ac.za/microbiology/

Retrieve the usual bits of "this is us; this is what we do; you can, too," but also find Virus News and Views, featuring updated Ebola reports and links to info on other viral diseases. A linkable list of microbiology resources is also featured.

University of Connecticut: Department of Ecology and Evolutionary Biology

http://florawww.eeb.uconn.edu/homepage.html

The department of ecology and evolutionary biology (EEB) at the University of Connecticut provides information about its resources. Find links to the EEB greenhouse collections, the Center for Conservation and Biodiversity and the Bartlett Arboretum.

University of Delaware: Entomology Home Page

gopher://bluehen.ags.udel.edu:71/hh/.insects/.descriptions/entohome.html

The University of Delaware Department of Entomology and Applied Ecology presents this online insect database with information and images on a variety of insect orders, such as Collembola and Hemiptera.

University of Freiburg: WWW-Server Faculty for Biology

http://www.biologie.uni-freiburg.de/

The University of Freiburg in Germany presents the faculty page for its biology department. Visitors will find biography and research information for faculty in all disciplines of biology.

University of Georgia: Botany Department Greenhouses

http://dogwood.botany.uga.edu/greenhouse/greenhouse.html

This site features a collection of photographs taken throughout six botanical greenhouses. Visitors will also find information about relationships among the major land plant groups.

University of Guelph: Department of Botany

http://www.uoguelph.ca/botany/index.htm

The botany department at the University of Guelph in Ontario supplies information here about its faculty, programs, courses and research. Visitors can also take a virtual tour of its greenhouse.

University of Illinois, Urbana-Champaign: Life Sciences

http://www.life.uiuc.edu/

The University of Illinois at Urbana-Champaign provides information about its life sciences programs here. Visitors will find departmental information, course descriptions and a look at the program's labs.

The University of Kansas: Microbiology Department

http://ukanaix.cc.ukans.edu/~micro

The department of microbiology at the University of Kansas offers a wealth of information about its faculty, staff, research, academics and alumni here. Visitors can also link to the home page of Division of Biological Sciences, University of Kansas online resources and other related sites.

University of Maine: Department of Wildlife Ecology

http://wlm13.umenfa.maine.edu/w4v1.html

The department of wildlife ecology at the University of Maine offers a wealth of information here about its faculty, students, programs, research, events and resources. Visitors can also link here to related sites of interest, such as biological and U.S. federal government agencies.

University of Maine: Microbiology Homepage

http://icarus.ume.maine.edu/~bmmb/

The department of biochemistry, microbiology and molecular biology at the University of Maine outlines its graduate and undergraduate programs of study. Explore overviews of the department's academic offerings, students and faculty.

University of Manchester: Biological Sciences Graduate School Home Page

http://mbisg2.sbc.man.ac.uk/

The department of biological sciences of The University of Manchester, England, maintains this site for general information. Visit here to learn about its graduate and undergraduate programs, research projects and link to related university Web sites.

University of Minnesota: Computational Biology Centers Medical School

http://www.cbc.med.umn.edu/

Visitors to the Computational Biology Centers Medical School at the University of Minnesota can read descriptions of the school's research projects which delve into molecular biology and genetics. The site also includes selected online papers.

University of Missouri, St. Louis: The International Center for Tropical Ecology

http://ecology.umsl.edu/

The International Center for Tropical Ecology at the University of Missouri in St. Louis, promotes research in the study of tropical ecosystems. It details its mission, faculty and program here. The site includes the center's newsletter, a look at tropical ecology courses and information about the center's reprints request service.

University of Oklahoma Health Sciences Center: Microbiology & Immunology

http://www.microbiology.uokhsc.edu/

Jump from this welcome page to details about the graduate program and academic requirements of the microbiology and immunology department, or look at the library and computing resources provided by the OU Health Sciences Center. The page also includes links to a number of useful science databases for DNA searching and more.

University of Oxford: Department of Plant Sciences

http://ifs.plants.ox.ac.uk/

The department of plant sciences at Oxford provides access to publications, research reports and databases produced by the department. Includes an overview of the department, its educational and research programs, faculty and staff listings, and links to numerous related plant science resources.

University of South Carolina: Department of Biological Sciences Gopher

gopher://marine.geol.sc.edu/

The department of biological science at the University of South Carolina offers this gopher server with a collection of information about the department and links to biology-related resources on the Net. Visitors can also access the school's Computer Sciences Division gopher server from here.

University of South Carolina: Marine Biology and Coastal Research

http://inlet.geol.scarolina.edu/

The University of South Carolina gives visitors a look at its Baruch Institute of Marine Biology and Coastal Research here. The page includes general information and documentation for field and laboratory research.

University of Texas, Austin: Department of Botany

http://www.botany.utexas.edu/

The botany department at the University of Texas, Austin, maintains this page with information about the department, faculty and degrees. Course descriptions and links to departmental resources, such as the UTEX Algae Culture Collection, are also provided.

University of Toledo: Biology

http://131.183.61.190/

The department of biology at Ohio's University of Toledo invites visitors to its home page to learn about the department, its educational programs and research projects. Links to sites of interest on and off campus are provided.

University of Toronto: Bioinfo Home Page

http://bioinfo.med.utoronto.ca/
biochemistry.html

The University of Toronto's department of biochemistry hosts this site, with links to biochemistry resources, files and related links.

University of Toronto: Department of Botany

http://www.botany.utoronto.ca/

The department of botany at the University of Toronto, Canada, offers a site where visitors can learn about the faculty and courses offered. There's a link to the university home page, as well as information on the city of Toronto.

University of Washington: Molecular Biotechnology Department

http://www.biotech.washington.edu/

This page is a gateway to groups at the University of Washington's biotechnology department that are working on flow karyotyping and chromosome mapping.

University of Washington: Neurosciences

http://weber.u.washington.edu/wcalvin/
neuro-uw.html

The department of neurosciences at the University of Washington provides details about its graduate program in behavioral neurosciences here. The site includes details on the department's molecular and cellular Ph.D. program.

University of Wisconsin-Madison: Department of Neurophysiology

http://www.neurophys.wisc.edu/

Check out the Comparative Mammalian Brain Collection courtesy of the department of neurophysiology and find the answer to the question, "Why study brains?" Additional offerings at this eclectic site include links to neurophysiology resources and auditory sites, and a reference shelf of phone books, dictionaries, weather info and more.

Washington University: Institute for Biomedical Computing

http://www.ibc.wustl.edu/

Researchers who have been longing for a nucleic to amino acid conversion utility can find it and

many more biochemical research tools at this site. This St. Louis, Mo., university research facility packs its page with graduate course info, research opportunities, and descriptions of its three labs, each addressing a specific area of computer-assisted biomedical and biological research.

Washington University: Molecular Biophysics and Biochemistry

http://bmb.wustl.edu/

Washington University, St. Louis, Mo., provides this Web site with information about its graduate studies programs in molecular biophysics and biochemistry. Visitors can read detailed program info here or search the entire site.

The World-Wide Web Virtual Library: International Biology Departments and Institutes

http://golgi.harvard.edu/afagen/depts/
deptintl.html

The World-Wide Web Virtual Library's international biology departments and institutions index provides comprehensive links to biological research facilities around the world. Visitors will find links to academic and professional biology sites indexed by home country.

Yale University - Department of Biology

http://www.biology.yale.edu/

The department of biology at Yale University provides detailed departmental and application information for prospective students here. The site includes a course listing and information on living in New Haven.

INSTRUMENTS AND EQUIPMENT

IMAGING SYSTEMS

Beckman Institute Visualization Facility Home Page

http://delphi.beckman.uiuc.edu/

The Beckman Institute Visualization Facility at the University of Illinois maintains this site to introduce its scientific visualization and advanced microscopy services. Visitors will find news, staff listings, facilities overviews and links to related resources.

MICROSCOPES

Argonne National Laboratory Microscopy and Microanalysis

http://www.amc.anl.gov/

The Microscopy and Microanalysis site from the Material Sciences Division at Argonne National

Laboratory includes information about microscopy and microanalysis and links to information services, national and international societies, and related Web sites.

CIME—Electron Microscopy, Lausanne

http://cimewww.epfl.ch/

CIME, the central facility and research center in electron microscopy at the Ecole Polytechnique Federale de Lausanne, Switzerland, includes links to general program information, a who's who and listings of recent publications.

Integrated Microscopy Resource

http://www.bocklabs.wisc.edu/imr/imr.html

This site is the Web home of Integrated Microscopy Resources, a biological research service funded by the National Institutes of Health. Information about the organization's instruments and facilities, a user database, publications, and a directory of microscopists on the Net are among the features.

Microscopy Page

http://www.ou.edu/research/electron/mirror/

The Microscopy Page collects related resources from all over the Internet into a convenient, topically organized catalog of pointers. Find courses, discussion groups and meeting schedules concerned with the study and use of microscopes.

MicroVision Home Page

http://www.pbrc.hawaii.edu/~kunkel/

Intriguing images of ants and aphids loom larger than life in this colorful electronic gallery maintained by photomicrographer Dennis Kunkel. Here, cat fleas frighten and polio viruses entice. Kunkel also advertises his microscopy services and his book, *MicroAliens*.

Multidimensional Microscopies and Maize Structures

http://128.205.21.24/

The Advanced Microscopy and Imaging Laboratory at the State University of New York, Buffalo, presents this online study of multidimensional microscopies. The site provides documentation on topical publications and meetings, as well as movies and images, including a Maize Structure Atlas.

Park Instruments

http://www.park.com/

Researchers in the market for a new scanning probe microscope and those who want to learn more about the technology will want to check out this promotional site. Find out how the 'scope works, marvel at its versatility and see actual color images. Contact info for the company is provided.

3-D Confocal Microscopy Home Page

http://www.cs.ubc.ca/spider/ladic/
confocal.html

Brought to the Net by the University of British Columbia's computer science department, this Web site presents information and resources about a three-dimensional imaging technique called Laser Scanning Confocal Microscopy (LSCM). Visitors can read about this tool for examining biological specimens, get source code tips, or check out pages on graphics and recent announcements.

SOFTWARE

BioCatalog Software Directory

http://www.ebi.ac.uk/biocat/biocat.html

The European Bioinformatics Institute provides this directory containing software of interest to geneticists and molecular biologists. Visitors to the site can download programs and access biological databases.

BioNet Teaching and Learning Technology Programme Project

http://www.leeds.ac.uk/bionet.html

BioNet is a project at Leeds University in England to move computer-based teaching into mainstream biology and preclinical medicine instruction. Visitors can learn about the program, browse through an animation gallery and download related software.

Genetics Computer Group

http://www.gcg.com/

This promotional site is the Web home of the Genetics Computer Group, a Wisconsin-based developer of genetic sequencing and analysis software. Visitors are invited to learn more about the company, its history and its products.

Oxford Molecular Group

http://www.oxmol.co.uk/

Oxford Molecular Group PLC, a company that develops and markets computer-aided chemistry and bioinformatics software, introduces its products and services at this promotional site.

VENDORS

BioSupplyNet: The Lab Manual Source Book

http://www.biosupplynet.com

This database of biomedical research products contains information on thousands of products from hundreds of suppliers. Search by product name, supplier name or category. Additional features include links to product user groups, special offers and info on new products.

The Nest Group Home Page

http://world.std.com/~nestgrp

People and institutions engaged in DNA work will want to take a look at The Nest Group Inc.'s home page. The company specializes in electrophoretic and chromatographic separation and scale-up of proteins, peptides and nucleic acids.

New England Biolabs

http://www.neb.com/

New England Biolabs Inc., which produces restriction endonucleases and other products for molecular and cell biology research, provides information about the 20-year-old company, its products and ordering information here.

Novagen Home Page

http://www.novagen.com/

This promotional site is the Web home of Novagen, a company that markets molecular markers, cloning kits and other bio-related tools. Find the product catalog, product support literature and the newsletter among the items at this site.

On Line Ordering for Biologists and Biochemists

http://condor.bcm.tmc.edu/buying.html

Biologists and biochemists can access links to over 50 online catalogs for laboratory supply companies.

Promega Corporation Home Page

http://www.promega.com/

Headquartered in Madison, Wis., Promega Corp. produces biochemistry and molecular biology products. Visitors will find information on the Promega's products, technical support and documentation, and background information on the company.

T&t Research

http://www.io.org/~tmaler/

This company site exposes visitors to T&t Research's family of high-tech products, including DNA Parrot, a talking DNA sequence reader, and CourseBuilder, a cross-platform multimedia authoring and testing tool.

JOURNALS, PERIODICALS, AND ABSTRACTS

APStracts

http://www.uth.tmc.edu/apstracts/

A weekly electronic notice published by the American Physiological Society, APStracts features abstracts of research articles scheduled to appear in the society's journals. Visitors to this page can access the archives.

Bio/Chemical Journals and Newsletters

http://www.public.iastate.edu/~pedro/rt_journals.html

Pedro's BioMolecular Research Tools page offers an extensive collection of links to chemical and biological journals and newsletters, arranged in al-

phabetical order. Visitors can also link to a number of other general chemistry-related resources.

BIOSIS Welcome

http://www.biosis.org/

Biological and zoological abstract publisher BIOSIS provides information about its printed and compact disc reference products here. Visitors also can access support and training resources at this site.

Genes & Development

http://207.22.83.2:443/cshl/journals/gnd/

This genetics journal, published in association with the Genetical Society of Great Britain, solicits subscriptions here. Visitors will find indexes of recent issues, information on the editorial board and subscription details.

Inter-Research Science Publisher

http://www.int-res.com/int-res/

Inter-Research Science Publisher, a journal from Germany, includes its publications schedule along with recent tables of contents. Links to other journals and pages about marine ecology, aquatic microbial ecology and climate research are included.

Journal of Biological Chemistry

http://www-jbc.stanford.edu/jbc/

The electronic edition of the Journal of Biological Chemistry, published by the American Society for Biochemistry, sponsors this page. Of primary interest to biomedical and chemical professionals, visitors can search here for current and back issues, get a sneak preview of upcoming publications and sign the JBC guest book.

Journal of Molecular Biology

http://www.hbuk.co.uk/jmb/

The online version of the Journal of Molecular Biology includes the table of contents from this week's and past issues, a searchable abstracts database and a list of the papers that have been accepted for publication in the current week's issue.

Journal of Neurophysiology Gopher Menu

gopher://oac.hsc.uth.tmc.edu:3300/11/publications/jn

The Journal of Neurophysiology, a monthly scientific journal, covers electrophysiology, experimental neuroanatomy, electron microscopy and tissue culture. Visitors to this gopher site can find tables of contents for journal issues, as well as ordering information and a submission form.

Learning & Memory

http://207.22.83.2:443/cshl/journals/lnm/

This journal from the Cold Spring Harbor Laboratory Press focuses on neurobiological research into learning and memory. Visitors to the site can read an overview of the journal, access the tables of contents and article abstracts for recent issues, and locate subscription info.

Network Science

http://edisto.awod.com/netsci/

The Network Science Corporation, a nonprofit, provides its monthly publication, NetSci, here. It uses "the power of the Web to explore and discuss science and technology." Visit for features, literature reviews, software and a biotechnology focus section.

Protein Science

http://www.prosci.uci.edu/

Visitors can download or search the journal Protein Science, published by Cambridge University Press, here. The site also includes ProTeach, a database of resources for teaching protein science, and other relevant links.

The Scientist Newsletter Gopher Menu

gopher://ds.internic.net:70/11/pub/the-scientist

This gopher server archives articles and job files from The Scientist Newsletter, a journal that addresses issues in biotechnology, education, National Science Foundation Funding and medical research.

Transgenica: Topics in Clinical Biotechnology

http://pharminfo.com/pubs/transgen/tg_hp.html

Published by Pharmaceutical Information Associates, Ltd., the focus of this online journal is to promote communication among medical researchers working in biotechnology, particularly in the field of new drug development. Visitors can access current articles and contact the editorial staff.

Weeds World

http://nasc.nott.ac.uk:8300/home.html

Weeds World is the International Electronic Arabidopsis Newsletter. Browsers will find abstracts, full-text articles, protocols, meetings and more.

The World-Wide Web Virtual Library: Bioscience Journals, Conferences and Current Awareness Services

http://golgi.harvard.edu/journals.html

This World-Wide Web Virtual Library page lists bioscience Web sites, biology Internet resources, electronic news, biologists' addresses and links to search engines for bioscience information.

LABORATORIES

Advanced Biotechnology Center (ABC) Biotech Department WWW Server

http://www.biotech.ist.unige.it/Welcome.html

Affiliated with the University of Genoa, Italy, the ABC has six basic research laboratories working in fields including bioengineering, developmental biology and immunology. Visitors to this site will find databases, gopher links and related sites.

Argonne National Laboratory, Advanced Photon Source

http://epics.aps.anl.gov/welcome.html

Built by the U.S. Department of Energy as a national user facility, the Argonne National Laboratory's Advanced Photon Source (APS) creates super-intense x rays for scientific research. Visit this site to access an overview, the APS information services, the Collaborative Access Team members' pages and a calender of meetings and conferences.

Avida

http://www.krl.caltech.edu/avida/

The Avida Group at the California Institute of Technology serves up information here about its research into the fields of genetic evolution and auto-adaptive genetic systems (AAGS). Visitors to this site can peruse the group's progress reports, scientific papers and images.

Axel Brunger's Research Group and the X-PLOR Home Page

http://xplor.csb.yale.edu/

This page features the research of a group of students in Yale University's Department of Biophysics and Biochemistry and the software program, X-PLOR, developed by the group's head professor. Recent papers and reviews, plus quick links, are also included.

Bamfield Marine Station

http://bms.bc.ca/

Canada's Bamfield Marine Station, located at Barkley Sound, British Columbia, is a research facility that offers courses in marine sciences. Get general information about all courses, including public education programs, here.

The Barton Group Home Page

http://geoff.biop.ox.ac.uk/

The Laboratory of Molecular Biophysics at the University of Oxford predicts and annotates protein structures with the aid of powerful computers. Here, browsers can download the lab's publications, run samples of its in-house software or check out job openings.

Bermuda Biological Station for Research, Inc.

http://www.bbsr.edu/

The Bermuda Biological Station for Research, Inc. offers a variety of information about its educational and scientific projects. Check out the latest facility news or read pages with detailed info on educational research, scientific and risk prediction projects and initiatives. Visitors can also link to related sites about the local area.

The Biological Mass Spectrometry Lab

http://thompson.mbt.washington.edu/

The Biological Mass Spectrometry Lab at the University of Washington gives an overview of its role in the huge undertaking to sequence the humane genome here. It provides a description of its method for performing protein identification using mass spectrometry. The page also contains link to related sites.

The Biomedical Engineering Center at the University of Minnesota

http://pro.med.umn.edu/bmec/bmec.html

The programs and resources of the Biomedical Engineering Center at the University of Minnesota are featured at this site. Visitors will also find links to topical images, sounds, movies, and other biomedical engineering resources.

BITMed: Laboratory for Bioinformatics & Theoretical Medicine

http://bitmed.ucsd.edu/

Explore "true complex systems simulations of biological, chemical and physical systems" at the BITMed Simulation Server of the University of California, San Diego. The current simulators are tools for teaching neuroimmunology and HIV-induced disease to students at both the high school and university level.

Bock Laboratories at the University of Wisconsin-Madison

http://www.bocklabs.wisc.edu/

The Robert M. Bock Laboratories at the University of Wisconsin-Madison maintains this site to provide links to its affiliated institutes. Visit here to learn about the Institute for Molecular Virology, the Laboratory of Molecular Biology and the Integrated Microscopy Resource.

The Boston BioMolecular Engineering Research Center

http://bmerc-www.bu.edu/

The Boston BioMolecular Engineering Research Center researches DNA, RNA and protein sequences. In addition to providing specifics about its ongoing research, the site features links to its papers, journals, staff listings and related sites.

The Bower Lab WWW Home Page

http://www.bbb.caltech.edu:80/bowerlab/

The Bower Laboratory at Cal Tech provides information on its research projects, publications and educational initiatives. Includes a staff directory and descriptions of facilities and departments.

Brookhaven National Laboratory Biology Department Web Server

http://bnlstb.bio.bnl.gov:8000/

The biology department at this Long Island laboratory presents research programs in the department and structural biology user facilities. There also are contacts, biology links and corporate links.

Center for Biological and Computational Learning

http://www.ai.mit.edu/projects/cbcl/web-homepage/web-homepage.html

Learning is at the core of intelligence, the Center for Biological and Computational Learning at the Massachusetts Institute of Technology notes, and it seeks to learn how the brain works and how to make intelligent machines. Courses, seminars, projects, brochures and links are found here.

The Center for Complex Systems

http://www.ccs.fau.edu/ccs.html

The Center for Complex Systems at Florida Atlantic University provides information about its activities and resources. Visit here for news, scientific publications, faculty biographies, links to related Web sites and more.

Center for Computational Biology Home Page

http://www.compbio.caltech.edu/

The Center for Computational Biology at the California Institute of Technology maintains this site for general information and resource access. Visit here to find information about programming languages, networking systems and computational biology applications.

Center for Innovative Computer Applications

http://www.cica.indiana.edu/projects/Biology/index.html

The Center for Innovative Computer Applications (CICA) is a multidisciplinary support center at Indiana University. This CICA site offers an overview of its biology research projects. Visitors can view images and MPEG movies from the research here.

Center for Structural Biology

http://csbnmr.health.ufl.edu/

The Center for Structural Biology at the University of Florida aims to increase understanding of biological function by determining the structures of large biological molecules, supramolecular assemblies and whole organisms. Explore its research techniques and data findings at this site.

Center for the Neural Processes in Cognition

http://neurocog.lrdc.pitt.edu/npc/

A joint program of the University of Pittsburgh and Carnegie Mellon University, the Center for the Neural Processes in Cognition supports an interdisciplinary research program in pre- and postdoctoral training. Visitors to its home page can find out more about the training program and other center activities.

Centre for Neural Systems

http://www.cns.ed.ac.uk/

The Centre for Neural Systems (CNS) is a University of Edinburgh group dedicated to computational neuroscience and neural network research. This home page provides updates on current CNS projects and profiles of the people behind the research.

Centre for Population Biology

http://forest.bio.ic.ac.uk/cpb/cpb/cpbintro.html

An affiliate of the University of London, the Centre for Population Biology studies ecological processes in the key areas of food webs and community assembly, biodiversity and population genetics. Visitors to this site can access information on current research projects and staff members.

Centre for Visual Sciences

http://cvs.anu.edu.au/

Research at the Centre for Visual Sciences of the Australian National University focuses on how visual images are processed by the brain. Visitors to this site can view the world through the eyes of a honeybee and enjoy some lively commentary from the researcher, attempt to solve a 3D riddle and view a collection of single image stereograms.

Chromosome 12 Genome Center

http://paella.med.yale.edu/chr12/Home.html

The Chromosome 12 Genome Center is a research facility formed from the collaboration of the Albert Einstein College of Medicine and the Yale University School of Medicine. Visitors will find abstracts, reports and technical data about the mapping of human chromosome 12.

Church Lab WWW Server

http://twod.med.harvard.edu/

The George M. Church Lab, Harvard, provides documents, data, publications and programs here. Links include a guide to sequence searching, the 100Kb Club (DNA sequences longer than 100,000 bp), a sequence assembly program and Andy Link's Protein Sequence from 2D Gels. Visitors can check out the personnel behind this stuff, too.

Cold Spring Harbor Laboratory Online (CLIO)

http://www.cshl.org/

The Cold Spring Harbor Laboratory (CSHL) is an independent biological research facility chartered by the University of the State of New York. Visitors here can get general information, learn about the human genome project and order books from CSHL Press.

Computational Neurobiology Laboratory

http://dirac.bcm.tmc.edu/

The Computational Neurobiology Laboratory at the Baylor College of Medicine in Houston, Texas, maintains this informational site. Visit here for information on its faculty members, publications and research facilities.

CSIRO Tropical Forest Research Centre

http://www.tfrc.csiro.au/

Australia's Commonwealth Scientific and Industrial Research Organization (CSIRO) hosts the online Tropical Forest Research Centre, which provides information on the condition of tropical rain forests, including access to the center's Division of Wildlife and Ecology, Division of Soils and Division of Entomology.

European Molecular Biology Laboratory

http://www.embl-heidelberg.de/

Founded in 1974, this cooperative effort by a group of molecular biologists is an international training and research center for the European community. Visitors can read about the laboratory's history and major projects here, including the development of synchrotron radiation and developmental genetics. Maps, press releases and contact info are also here.

The Genetic Algorithms Research and Applications Group (GARAGe) Home Page

http://isl.msu.edu/GA/

Michigan State University's Genetic Algorithms Research and Applications Group (GARAGe) applies genetic algorithms and genetic programming to real-life problems. Visitors will find basic information on GARAGe, upcoming conferences, the researchers and the software the group uses.

Genome Sequencing Center Home Page

http://genome.wustl.edu/gsc/gschmpg.html

The Washington University in St. Louis Medical School Genome Sequencing Center Home Page contains information about current genetic research and databases, along with links to related sites.

Harvard Biological Laboratories

http://golgi.harvard.edu/genome.html

Harvard University posts general and research information from its various labs in the Department of Molecular and Cellular Biology here. The extensive page also includes dozens of biological databases and links to other biology sites of note on the Net.

Helen Donis-Keller Lab

http://hdklab.wustl.edu/

Research at this St. Louis, Mo.-based university lab focuses on genome mapping, the molecular genetics of human disease and database development. Visitors can read research summaries, access physical and linkage genome maps, and search the GenLink databases.

Human Population Genetics Lab (Cavalli Lab)

http://lotka.stanford.edu/

The Cavalli Lab at Stanford University processes and archives human genetic data. Visitors to the site will find descriptions of research projects, manuscript preprints and abstracts, staff information and links to related sites.

Icelandic Fisheries Laboratories

http://www.rfisk.is/

The Icelandic Fisheries Laboratories site contains information about laboratories and institutions researching fisheries and aquaculture in the Northern Atlantic. Includes links to mailing lists and other related servers.

IlliGAL Home Page

http://gal4.ge.uiuc.edu/illigal.home.html

The Illinois Genetic Algorithms Laboratory at the University of Illinois maintains this informational site. Visit here to learn about its evolution-based computing research, view scientific publications and link to a variety of related Web sites.

The Jackson Laboratory Home Page

http://www.jax.org/

The Jackson Laboratory offers information on its genetic research and the resources it makes available to scientists. Included is a price list for Jackson's genetically defined mice, neurology news and a description of its training and education programs.

Jay Ponder Lab

http://dasher.wustl.edu/

The Jay Ponder Lab Web server from the Department of Molecular Biophysics and Biochemistry at the Washington University School of Medicine includes details about its current research and links to anonymous FTP packages.

Laboratoire de Biometrie, Genetique et Biologie des Populations

http://biom1.univ-lyon1.fr:8080/

The Laboratoire de Biometrie, Genetique et Biologie des Populations conducts research studies at the intersection of biology and methodology. Review the lab's population-based research activities at this site.

Laboratory of Neuro Imaging Web Server

http://www.loni.ucla.edu/

The Laboratory of Neuro Imaging at the University of California, Los Angeles, provides general information about its resources and activities here. Visitors can access online data sets, including the Rat Atlas, and various publications.

Lawrence Berkeley National Laboratory Human Genome Center

http://www-hgc.lbl.gov/

The Human Genome Center at the Lawrence Berkeley National Labs looks for ways to accurately and effectively study DNA sequences in humans. Biologist will find links to other genome resources here.

Lawrence Livermore National Laboratory: Biology and Biotechnology Research Program

http://www-bio.llnl.gov/bbrp/bbrp.homepage.html

This is the home page of the Biology and Biotechnology Research Program at the Lawrence Livermore National Laboratory. Visitors will find a general overview of the program, research areas and centers, and current educational opportunities.

Lawrence Livermore National Laboratory: Human Genome Center

http://www-bio.llnl.gov/bbrp/genome/genome.html

Lawrence Livermore National Laboratory's Human Genome Center home page provides highly technical information dealing with biology and genetics. Visitors can learn about the lab's projects and access chromosome maps, DNA sequencing information and a link to the National Laboratory Gene Library Project.

The Marine Biological Laboratory

http://www.mbl.edu/

The Marine Biological Laboratory in Massachusetts outlines its research and educational projects, and provides access to library information through this graphically rich Web site. Visitors can read about upcoming events and link to related information.

Meister Lab Home Page

http://rhino.harvard.edu/

How what we see becomes something we can understand is the topic of research for a team at Harvard University's department of cellular and molecular Biology. People interested in the problem can examine the lab's methodology and take a look at photos of the researchers.

NASA Ames Biocomputation Center

http://biocomp.arc.nasa.gov/

Ames Biocomputation Center, a research facility of the U.S. National Aeronautics and Space Administration, develops three-dimensional computer visualization technology for biology applications. Visit here for news, staff and facilities profiles, and links to sample programs.

Nebraska Behavioral Biology Group

http://cricket.unl.edu/nbbg.html

The Nebraska Behavioral Biology Group combines the resources of three universities in eastern Nebraska at this page. Find academic program information, faculty and staff listings, and publications and databases.

Neural Systems Group

http://york37.ncl.ac.uk/www/neural_systems_group.html

The Neural Systems Group site explains its mission as "exploring interdisciplinary research for experimental and computational neuroscience." Based at the UK's University of Newcastle, the site includes a list of members and contact info.

Northwest Fisheries Science Center

http://listeria.nwfsc.noaa.gov/

The Northwest Fisheries Science Center is a research facility responsible for providing scientific and technical support for the management, conservation and development of the Pacific Northwest's marine fishery resources. Visit this site to review coastal zone and estuarine studies, learn more about the center or access its other resources.

Okazaki National Research Institutes

http://ccinfo.ims.ac.jp/map/index.html

The Okazaki National Research Institutes in Okazaki, Japan, maintains this site for general information about its three biological research facilities: the Institute for Molecular Science, the National Institute for Basic Biology and the National Institute for Physiological Sciences. Visit here for current research news and staff info.

The Oxford Center for Molecular Sciences (OCMS) Home Page

http://nmra.ocms.ox.ac.uk/

Scientists find biophysics resources and protein structure models at the Oxford Centre for Molecular Sciences (OCMS) Home Page. Access databases and OCMS news and events schedule at this site.

Oxford University Laboratory of Molecular Biophysics Home Page

http://biop.ox.ac.uk/www/welcome.html

Oxford University's Laboratory of Molecular Biophysics maintains this site for its index of related resources. Visit here for links covering biochemistry, crystallography, synchrotrons and a variety of other university information services.

Protein Structure Group

http://www.yorvic.york.ac.uk/

The chemistry department at the University of York offers this Web site with information on its Protein Structure Group. Browsers can read about the group's labs, members and courses, or view the yearly lab report.

The Sander Group

http://www.sander.embl-heidelberg.de/

The European Molecular Biology Laboratory (EMBL) Sander Group designs software and protein databases. At the group's home page link to database search functions, learn more about the group's members and get details about the software they design.

Stanford University Hopkins Marine Station

http://www.marine.stanford.edu/

The Hopkins Marine Station of Stanford University reveals its history and academic programs at this site. Visitors can view pictures of the station, read about seminars and check out the latest research projects.

Wageningen Nuclear Magnetic Resonance (NMR) Centre

http://gcg.tran.wau.nl/wnmrc/wnmrc.html

This research facility in the Netherlands provides access to NMR spectrometers and training in their use. Read about cooperative botanical research projects, including the study of the mechanisms of plant virus infection, metabolism and bioenergy conversion in plants, and the effects of environmental factors.

W.M. Keck Center for Advanced Training in Computational Biology

http://www.cs.pitt.edu/keck/Welcome.html

The W.M. Keck Center for Advanced Training in Computational Biology, Pittsburgh, Pa., provides information on its graduate and postdoctoral training programs. Other resources include a list of faculty and fellows and links to the center's collaborators.

W.M. Keck Center for Integrative Neuroscience

http://keck.ucsf.edu/

The W.M. Keck Center for Integrative Neuroscience at the University of California, San Francisco, posts links to various neuroscience and language learning sites on campus here. The page also includes seminar announcements and pointers to technical information on neuroscience and neural networks.

Wolf Park Home Page

http://tigerden.com/Wolf-park/Welcome.html

Located in Battle Ground, Ind., Wolf Park is a research facility studying the interpack and reproductive behavior of the wolf. Links to the park's educational programs, photo album and operating information are featured here.

Wormworld

http://wormworld.ucsf.edu/

Ilan Zipkin's Wormworld Web page features information about worm labs around the world. The site is located at the University of California at San Francisco's Kenyon Lab. It includes pointers to other science links.

LIBRARIES

The World-Wide Web Virtual Library: Biology Societies and Organizations

http://golgi.harvard.edu/afagen/depts/orgs.html

This page from the much larger World-Wide Web Virtual Library collection features a links to biology societies and organizations with Web pages. Search by country and alphabetically, or link to other databases and search tools.

The World-Wide Web Virtual Library: Biomolecules

http://golgi.harvard.edu/sequences.html

This Virtual Library site, maintained by Harvard Biolabs, contains a complete index of sites related to biomolecular studies. Links include sequence databases categorized by type, cordon usage tables and metabolic compound databases.

The World-Wide Web Virtual Library: Bioscience Journals, Conferences and Current Awareness Services

http://golgi.harvard.edu/journals.html

This World-Wide Web Virtual Library page lists bioscience Web sites, biology Internet resources, electronic news, biologists' addresses and links to search engines for bioscience information.

The World-Wide Web Virtual Library: Biosciences

http://golgi.harvard.edu/biopages.list

This Virtual Library site focuses on resources related to the biosciences. Includes links to a wide variety of biological journals, software, specialized archives and indexes.

The World-Wide Web Virtual Library: Biotechnology

http://www.cato.com/interweb/cato/biotech/

The World-Wide Web Virtual Library maintains a comprehensive, classified index of information on the Internet. Visit this site for its biotechnology index with links to educational, theoretical and professional resources.

The World-Wide Web Virtual Library: Caenorhabditis elegans

http://eatworms.swmed.edu/VLhome.shtml

Caenorhabditis elegans is a tiny soil nematode that scientists use to study the genetics of development and neurobiology. Visitors not familiar with the nematode will find an introduction and pictures here. The site also includes genetic maps, related newsletters and recent papers for researchers.

The World-Wide Web Virtual Library: Drosophila Index

http://www-leland.stanford.edu/~ger/drosophila.html

The World Wide Web Virtual Library maintains this site for the Drosophila index of its biosciences area. Visitors will find extensive information about the uses of Drosophila melanogaster for research and genetics and developmental biology.

The World-Wide Web Virtual Library: Entomology (Biosciences)

http://www.colostate.edu/Depts/Entomology/WWWVL-Entomology.html

Visitors to the Virtual Library section for Entomology will find links to universities, job information, images, movies, and topical publications.

The World-Wide Web Virtual Library: Evolution

http://golgi.harvard.edu/biopages/evolution.html

The World-Wide Web Virtual Library maintains this site with an index to Internet resources concerning evolution. Visitors will find extensive links to educational and institutional information servers, software archives, science libraries and related resources.

The World-Wide Web Virtual Library: Genetics

http://www.ornl.gov/TechResources/Human_Genome/genetics.html

Part of the World-Wide Web Virtual Library, this exhaustive and well-linked bioscience resource offers a full index of organism genome information from cellular slime molds to human beings.

The World-Wide Web Virtual Library: Immunology (Biosciences)

http://golgi.harvard.edu/biopages/immuno.html

From the Virtual Library site, this page features a comprehensive collection of links to information and resources relevant to immunology. Find an alphabetical index pointing to associations, institutions, journals, databases and various scientific disciplines.

The World-Wide Web Virtual Library: International Biology Departments and Institutes

http://golgi.harvard.edu/afagen/depts/deptintl.html

The World-Wide Web Virtual Library's international biology departments and institutions index provides comprehensive links to biological research facilities around the world. Visitors will find links to academic and professional biology sites indexed by home country.

The World-Wide Web Virtual Library: Mycological Resources on the Internet

http://muse.bio.cornell.edu/~fungi/

Here are the offerings of the World-Wide Web Virtual Library from the wonderful world of fungi. Links to the BIOSCI Electronic Newsgroup Network, Usenet newsgroups and specific mycological sites around the world are featured.

The World-Wide Web Virtual Library: Plant Biology (Biosciences)

http://www.uoknor.edu/cas/botany-micro/www-vl/

Visit the World-Wide Web Virtual Library's plant biology stacks using the catalog of links provided at this site. Find an extensive list of pointers to agriculture, biosciences and forestry resources here.

The World-Wide Web Virtual Library: Vision Science

http://vision.arc.nasa.gov/VisionScience/VisionScience.html

This Virtual Library site provides pointers to information on vision research in humans and other organisms. Includes instructions for adding related materials to the index.

The World-Wide Web Virtual Library: Yeast

http://genome-www.stanford.edu/Saccharomyces/VL-yeast.html

Biologists will find a wealth of information on three yeast organisms here. The site also lists dozens of pointers to yeast databases, Usenet newsgroups and mailing list archives. For the nonscientific visitor, the page answers the question "What are yeast?"

The World-Wide Web Virtual Library: Zoos

http://www.mindspring.com/~zoonet/www_virtual_lib/zoos.html

Make a virtual visit to the zoo through this page that includes information about zoos around the world. Visitors can click through animal-related links full of pictures and sounds or opt to check out specific institutions from an extensive list of commercial and public zoos.

MICROBIOLOGY

ARCHIVES AND INDICES

The Malaria Database

http://www.wehi.edu.au/biology/malaria/who.html

Under the aegis of the United Nations, this site includes FTP text files of nucleotide and protein sequence data, malaria genome and strain information, a bibliography of references about malaria antigens, a discussion group link, employment information, software and more.

Medical Microbiology Home Page

http://biomed.nus.sg/microbio/home.html

Sponsored by the National University of Singapore, the Medical Microbiology home page links to a variety of medical and clinical microbiology resources and information of use to doctors, medical students and microbiologists. This page also offers information on medical microbiologists practicing in Singapore.

The Microbial Underground!

http://www.ch.ic.ac.uk/medbact/

The Microbiological Underground is a compilation of Web pages containing microbiological, medical and molecular biology information and pointers to related material available on the Internet. The primary feature of this site is the author's online course in medical bacteriology.

Pedro's BioMolecular Research Tools

http://www.public.iastate.edu/~pedro/research_tools.html

This gateway provides links to information and services related to microbiology. Features include search engines, bibliographies, tutorials, help tools, and access to related journals and newsletters.

The World Federation for Culture Collections (WFCC) World Data Center for Microorganisms

http://wdcm.nig.ac.jp/

The WFCC World Data Center for Microorganisms provides a complete directory listing of microbial databases, cell lines and culture collections. It

also serves as a gateway to molecular biology, genome projects and biodiversity information.

BACTERIA

EcoCyc: Encyclopedia of E. coli Genes and Metabolism

http://www.ai.sri.com/ecocyc/ecocyc.html

E. coli, that nasty bacterium that can cause illness and death, is the focus of the EcoCyc project: a compilation of a large knowledge base describing the genes and intermediary metabolism of the bacterium.

E. coli Genetic Stock Center

http://cgsc.biology.yale.edu/top.html

The E.coli Genetic Stock Center maintains this site for its database of E.coli genetic information. Visitors to this public database will find genotypes and reference information for thousands of strains, a gene list with map and gene product information.

The E. coli Index

http://sun1.bham.ac.uk/bcm4ght6/res.html

This information guide to the Escherichia coli bacterium, provided by the University of Birmingham, England, offers links to related societies, publishers, companies and researchers. Visit here for a comprehensive index of professional and educational resources.

IMMUNOLOGY

The World-Wide Web Virtual Library: Immunology (Biosciences)

http://golgi.harvard.edu/biopages/immuno.html

From the Virtual Library site, this page features a comprehensive collection of links to information and resources relevant to immunology. Find an alphabetical index pointing to associations, institutions, journals, databases and various scientific disciplines.

INSTITUTES AND UNIVERSITIES

State University of New York, Stony Brook: Department of Molecular Genetics and Microbiology

http://asterix.bio.sunysb.edu/

The State University of New York (SUNY) in Stony Brook provides information on its faculty, staff and programs of study in molecular genetics and microbiology at this site. Visitors can also take a look at the department's research, computing and library facilities.

University of Cape Town: Department of Medical Microbiology

http://www.uct.ac.za/depts/mmi/index.html

The department of medical microbiology at the University of Cape Town, South Africa, includes profiles of its faculty and postgraduate students along with links to current research projects and programs of study. Includes a search tool.

University of Cape Town: Microbiology Department

http://www.uct.ac.za/microbiology/

Retrieve the usual bits of "this is us; this is what we do; you can, too," but also find Virus News and Views, featuring updated Ebola reports and links to info on other viral diseases. A linkable list of microbiology resources is also featured.

The University of Kansas: Microbiology Department

http://ukanaix.cc.ukans.edu/~micro/

The department of microbiology at the University of Kansas offers a wealth of information about its faculty, staff, research, academics and alumni here. Visitors can also link to the home page of Division of Biological Sciences, University of Kansas online resources and other related sites.

University of Maine: Microbiology Homepage

http://icarus.ume.maine.edu/~bmmb/

The department of biochemistry, microbiology and molecular biology at the University of Maine outlines its graduate and undergraduate programs of study. Explore overviews of the department's academic offerings, students and faculty.

University of Oklahoma Health Sciences Center: Microbiology & Immunology

http://www.microbiology.uokhsc.edu/

Jump from this welcome page to details about the graduate program and academic requirements of the microbiology and immunology department, or look at the library and computing resources provided by the OU Health Sciences Center. The page also includes links to a number of useful science databases for DNA searching and more.

VIROLOGY

Australian National University Bioinformatics Facility Virus Gopher Menu

gopher://life.anu.edu.au:70/11/viruses

The Australian National University Bioinformatics Facility virus gopher contains two sets of databases: the approved names of virus families/groups and members and viruses of plants in Australia. Publications, news and animal virus information are also available.

Emerging and Re-Emerging Viruses

http://www.uct.ac.za/microbiology/ebola.html

Researchers can download a short or long version of a report on the Ebola virus called Emerging and Re-emerging Viruses: An Essay, 2 here. The page is authored by the microbiology department at the University of Cape Town and links to it.

Virus Databases On-Line

http://life.anu.edu.au/viruses/welcome.html

This directory of online viral information connects visitors with databases maintained by Australian National University's Bioinformatics Facility. Find information on classification and nomenclature of viruses, reference collections, electron micrographs and tutorials in virology.

NEUROPHYSIOLOGY

APLYSIA Hometank

http://ganglion.med.cornell.edu/Hometank.html

An online information resource for the molluscan neuroscience community, the APLYSIA Hometank site features an overview of the molluscan database project, the community questionnaire database, meeting reports, prototype database client tools, and related Web links.

Boston University: Department of Cognitive and Neural Systems

http://cns-web.bu.edu/

The Center for Adaptive Systems and the Department of Cognitive and Neural Systems at Boston University provide information here on their people, programs and resources. Visit here to learn about the organizations and access publications, directories and staff profiles.

The Center for Complex Systems

http://www.ccs.fau.edu/ccs.html

The Center for Complex Systems at Florida Atlantic University provides information about its activities and resources. Visit here for news, scientific publications, faculty biographies, links to related Web sites and more.

Center for the Neural Processes in Cognition

http://neurocog.lrdc.pitt.edu/npc/

A joint program of the University of Pittsburgh and Carnegie Mellon University, the Center for the Neural Processes in Cognition supports an interdisciplinary research program in pre- and postdoctoral training. Visitors to its home page can find out more about the training program and other center activities.

Centre for Neural Systems

http://www.cns.ed.ac.uk/

The Centre for Neural Systems (CNS) is a University of Edinburgh group dedicated to computational neuroscience and neural network research. This home page provides updates on current CNS projects and profiles of the people behind the research.

Centre for Visual Sciences

http://cvs.anu.edu.au/

Research at the Centre for Visual Sciences of the Australian National University focuses on how visual images are processed by the brain. Visitors to this site can view the world through the eyes of a honeybee and enjoy some lively commentary from the researcher, attempt to solve a 3D riddle and view a collection of single image stereograms.

Cognitive Neuroscience Resources

http://www.cs.cmu.edu/Web/Groups/CNBC/other/other-neuro.html

This neuroscience information server hosts a wealth of resources from the Center for the Neural Basis of Cognition (CNBC) and the Neural Processes in Cognition (NPC) graduate training program. Hundreds of links are provided here, including university department pages, publications, archives, Usenet newsgroups and organizations.

Computational Neurobiology Laboratory

http://dirac.bcm.tmc.edu/

The Computational Neurobiology Laboratory at the Baylor College of Medicine in Houston, Texas, maintains this informational site. Visit here for information on its faculty members, publications and research facilities.

Duke University: Department of Neurobiology

http://www.neuro.duke.edu

The brain and its function are under the microscope at Duke, with research going on in molecular, cellular, developmental and systems neurobiology. Read about the scientists performing this work and about graduate study programs at this premiere North Carolina university.

Foundation for Neural Networks

http://www.mbfys.kun.nl/SNN/

The Foundation for Neural Networks stimulates basic and applied research in neural information processing in behavior, vision and cognitive systems. Includes links to publications and related resources.

Harvard Undergraduate Society for Neuroscience

http://hcs.HARVARD.EDU/~husn/

The Harvard Undergraduate Society for Neuroscience provides information here about its mission, seminars and special events. Visit here for society publications and links to related neuroscience home pages.

Journal of Neurophysiology Gopher Menu

gopher://oac.hsc.uth.tmc.edu:3300/11/publications/jn

The Journal of Neurophysiology, a monthly scientific journal, covers electrophysiology, experimental neuroanatomy, electron microscopy and tissue culture. Visitors to this gopher site can find tables of contents for journal issues, as well as ordering information and a submission form.

Laboratory of Neuro Imaging Web Server

http://www.loni.ucla.edu/

The Laboratory of Neuro Imaging at the University of California, Los Angeles, provides general information about its resources and activities here. Visitors can access online data sets, including the Rat Atlas, and various publications.

Learning & Memory

http://207.22.83.2:443/cshl/journals/lnm/

This journal from the Cold Spring Harbor Laboratory Press focuses on neurobiological research into learning and memory. Visitors to the site can read an overview of the journal, access the tables of contents and article abstracts for recent issues, and locate subscription info.

Neural Systems Group

http://york37.ncl.ac.uk/www/neural_systems_group.html

The Neural Systems Group site explains its mission as "exploring interdisciplinary research for experimental and computational neuroscience." Based at the UK's University of Newcastle, the site includes a list of members and contact info.

Neurosciences on the Internet

http://www.neuroguide.com

The Neurosciences on the Internet site, maintained by Pittsburgh, Penn.-based service provider, Telerama, offers a searchable index of basic science and clinical resources. Visit here for information on neurobiology, neurology, neurosurgery, psychiatry, psychology and cognitive sciences.

Purdue Neuroscience Web Server

http://bieber.bio.purdue.edu/

Find courses, organizations, journals and biotech links among the worldwide resources featured on Purdue University's Neuroscience home page. Links to universities, medical centers and veterinary medical centers are also featured.

University of Wisconsin-Madison: Department of Neurophysiology

http://www.neurophys.wisc.edu/

Check out the Comparative Mammalian Brain Collection courtesy of the department of neurophysiology and find the answer to the question, "Why study brains?" Additional offerings at this eclectic site include links to neurophysiology resources and auditory sites, and a reference shelf of phone books, dictionaries, weather info and more.

Virtual Brain

http://lenti.med.umn.edu/NEURON_BRAIN/BRAIN.html

The department of cell biology and neuroanatomy at the University of Minnesota offers this graphics archive. Visit here to find images of anatomical structures including the ventricles, cortex and overlying soft tissues of the brain. An MPEG movie is also featured.

Virtual Neuron

http://lenti.med.umn.edu/NEURON_BRAIN/NEURON.html

From the University of Minnesota department of cell biology and neuroanatomy comes this collection of images of a dorsal root ganglia neuron from an embryonic chick. Interested researchers can read about the preparation and processing techniques.

W.M. Keck Foundation Center for Integrative Neuroscience

http://keck.ucsf.edu/

The W.M. Keck Foundation Center for Integrative Neuroscience at the University of California, San Francisco, posts links to various neuroscience and language learning sites on campus here. The page also includes seminar announcements and pointers to technical information on neuroscience and neural networks.

The World-Wide Web Virtual Library: Vision Science

http://vision.arc.nasa.gov/VisionScience/VisionScience.html

This Vitual Library site provides pointers to information on vision research in humans and other organisms. Includes instructions for adding related materials to the index.

NEUROPSYCHOLOGY

Neuropsychology Central

http://www.premier.net/~cogito/neuropsy.html

Neuropsychology, which concentrates on the link between brain activity and psychology, is the focus of Neuropsychology Central. Visit here for links to neuropsychology information, programs,

publications, newsgroups and more, as well as general neuroscience links.

NEWSGROUPS

BioNet

http://www.w3.org/pub/DataSources/News/Groups/bionet.html

Maintained by the World Wide Web Consortium, this annotated index of biology-related Internet newsgroups places visitors within a click of online discussions among biologists about everything from computational biology to immunology.

BIOSCI/bionet Electronic Newsgroup Network for Biology

http://www.bio.net/

The BIOSCI/bionet Electronic Newsgroup Network for Biology connects biologists across the globe via Usenet newsgroups and parallel e-mail lists. Links to archives, databases, and topic-related sites are featured.

The DEEPSEA Research Newsgroup

http://www.bio.net:80/hypermail/DEEPSEA/

This newsgroup exists to "serve as an electronic forum for the world's community of deep-sea and hydrothermal vent/seep biologists, oceanographers, and geologists." Find links to access discussion and topical Web sites.

PHYSIOLOGY

Physiology Online

http://physiology.cup.cam.ac.uk/

This electronic information service of The Physiological Society provides membership info, news, publications, conference announcements and more.

PROFESSIONAL RESOURCES AND CONFERENCES

APNet: Academic Press

http://www.apnet.com/

Academic Press features its newest textbooks and journals on this page. Stop by to read special offerings in the areas of life and biomedical sciences and neuropsychology.

Catalogue of Books available from CSHL Press

http://www.cshl.org/books/

Cold Spring Harbor Laboratory Press, a publisher of biology-related materials, displays its online catalog here. Visitors can browse its index of titles pertaining to plant and molecular biology, laboratory manuals, neurobiology and more.

Positions in Bioscience and Medicine

http://www.informatik.uni-rostock.de/
HUM-MOLGEN/anno/position.html

Sponsored by HUM-MOLGEN, the Internet communication program for the Human Genome Project, this list of worldwide academic and clinical positions can be searched by subject or by continent. The list is updated regularly and includes pre- and post-doctoral opportunities.

The World-Wide Web Virtual Library: Bioscience Journals, Conferences and Current Awareness Services

http://golgi.harvard.edu/journals.html

This World-Wide Web Virtual Library page lists bioscience Web sites, biology Internet resources, electronic news, biologists' addresses and links to search engines for bioscience information.

RESEARCH AND DEVELOPMENT (GENERAL)

Department of Energy Biological and Environmental Research

http://www.er.doe.gov/production/oher/oher_
top.html

The U.S. Department of Energy provides this Web server with extensive information about its Biological and Environmental Research Program. Visitors can read numerous pages provided by the project's three divisions: Environmental Science, Health Effects and Life Sciences, and Medical Applications and Biophysical Research.

Mouse and Rat Research Home Page

http://www.cco.caltech.edu/~mercer/htmls/
rodent_page.html

This site contains a comprehensive list of Internet information and resources related to the use of rodents in research. Features include information arranged by subject area, including a what's new file, conference schedules, ethical guides and protocols, and more.

Niwot Ridge Long-Term Ecological Research Home Page

http://culter.colorado.edu:1030/

The Niwot Ridge Long-Term Ecological Research program, part of the U.S. National Science Foundation, provides information here on its ecological phenomena research. Visit here for news, geography and wildlife data, employment opportunities and staff listings.

Sevilleta Long-Term Ecological Research Project

http://sevilleta.unm.edu/

The Sevilleta Long-Term Ecological Research Project at the University of New Mexico outlines its research at the Sevilleta National Wildlife Refuge on this page. Visitors will get an overview of the work and can search for related documents.

TAXONOMY

Taxacom Listserv Archives

http://muse.bio.cornell.edu/archive/
taxacom.html

Taxonomists will find archives of the Taxacom Listserv here that date back to 1993. Taxacom discusses botanical and biological taxonomy and specimen storage. It is managed through the University of Kansas Natural History Museums.

Web Lift to Any Taxon

http://www.ucmp.berkeley.edu/help/
taxaform.html

Biologists can take the Web Lift to any major taxa, or simply view a complete listing of taxa, through this site from the University of California Museum of Paleontology at Berkeley. The list shows each taxa's scientific name with its corresponding common name.

ZOOLOGY

ANATOMY

The Interactive Frog Dissection

http://curry.edschool.Virginia.EDU/go/frog/
home.html

This interactive, online tutorial leads visitors through the dissection of a frog. Designed for high school biology labs, this electronic frog can be used over and over.

Virtual Frog Dissection Kit

http://george.lbl.gov/vfrog/

Part of the Whole Frog project, this program allows interactive dissection of a frog and includes the capability to make movies. A tutorial, overview and FAQ are available to help students with the project.

Whole Frog Project

http://george.lbl.gov/ITG.hm.pg.docs/
Whole.Frog/Whole.Frog.html

The Lawrence Berkeley Laboratory Whole Frog Project is designed to introduce concepts of computer-based three-dimensional visualization and demonstrate 3D imaging of a frog's anatomy as a high school biology teaching aid. This site provides step-by-step information on using computers to create 3D images. Also includes numerous links to related sites and to the Lawrence Berkeley Laboratory.

ANIMAL BEHAVIOR AND PSYCHOLOGY

Indiana University: Program in Animal Behavior

http://loris.cisab.indiana.edu/

Indiana University's Center for the Integrative Study of Animal Behavior provides information on its program, faculty and the Research Training Group in Animal Behavior. The page also contains an archive of computer software used in the field and links to animal behavior-related sites.

Nebraska Behavioral Biology Group

http://cricket.unl.edu/nbbg.html

The Nebraska Behavioral Biology Group combines the resources of three universities in eastern Nebraska at this page. Find academic program information, faculty and staff listings, and publications and databases.

Wolf Park Home Page

http://tigerden.com/Wolf-park/Welcome.html

Located in Battle Ground, Ind., Wolf Park is a research facility studying the interpack and reproductive behavior of the wolf. Links to the park's educational programs, photo album and operating information are featured here.

ARCHIVES AND INDICES

Sea World Animal Information Database

http://www.bev.net/education/SeaWorld/

Sponsored by Sea World and Busch Gardens, this info database received the Significant Achievement in Education Award from the American Zoo and Aquarium Association. Kids and grownups alike can access facts about animals, take an animal quiz, send their zoological questions to "Shamu," or learn about building a home aquarium. A photo index and indices for classroom projects round things out.

GENETICS

Animal Genome Database in Japan

http://ws4.niai.affrc.go.jp/

Biologists can search for and view genetic information including cytogenetic and linkage maps about pigs, cattle, horses, mice and humans here. Includes DNA and sericultural information and links to the Japanese Dairy Cattle Improvement Program and the National Institute of Animal Industry.

The Jackson Laboratory: Mouse Genome Informatics

http://www.informatics.jax.org/

This page from the Jackson Laboratory in Bar Harbor, Maine, features access to the mouse genome database along with recent news and announcements from biological research. The page also has an encyclopedia of the mouse genome.

Mouse Cytogenetic Map Image

http://ws4.niai.affrc.go.jp/dbsearch2/mmap/mmap.html

Researchers can select a chromosome from the Mouse Cytogenetic Image Map on this page from the Animal Genome Database in Japan. The experimental site will then yield information about that part of the genetic structure of a mouse.

Mouse Genome Informatics

http://www.informatics.jax.org/mgd.html

The Jackson Laboratory's Mouse Genome database site offers access to empirical data on lab mice. Available searches include probes, genetic markers, PCR primers and mammalian homologs. Related links are also available.

Pig Cytogenetic Map Image

http://ws4.niai.affrc.go.jp/dbsearch2/pmap/pmap.html

The Animal Genome Database in Japan offers a Pig Cytogenic Map Image at this site. Browsers can also link to the database home page here.

Transgenic/Targeted Mutation Database (TBASE)

http://www.gdb.org/Dan/tbase/tbase.html

Visitors to TBASE can search this database for information on genetic engineering and transgenic animals.

U.S. Poultry Gene Mapping

http://poultry.mph.msu.edu/

The Chicken Mapper's Message Board is among the resources at the U.S. Poultry Gene Mapping site. Also find a searchable list of members of the international gene mapping community, as well as newsletters, databases and genetic maps.

HERPETOLOGY

American Society of Ichthyologists and Herpetologists

http://www.utexas.edu/depts/asih/

Background information, news and membership details are featured on the home page of the American Society of Ichthyologists and Herpetologists. Also find a directory of members, meeting information and a listing of related organizations such as the Society for the Study of Amphibians and Reptiles.

Australian Herpetological Directory

http://www.jcu.edu.au/dept/Zoology/herp/herp2.html

Australian reptiles and amphibians take center stage at this repository for herpetological research. Among other items of related interest, find recent publications, studies and an e-mail directory of Australian herpetologists.

Herp Pictures, Galleries 1 through 17

http://gto.ncsa.uiuc.edu/pingleto/lobby.html

Lovers of the cold and scaly can check out pretty pictures of frogs, turtles, snakes and other species which fall under the category of herpetology. Vis-

---

a2z EDITOR'S CHOICE

The Raptor Center

http://www.raptor.cvm.umn.edu/

Don't look for the Jurassic Park experience here; the raptors at this Center are predatory birds like eagles, hawks, falcons and owls. The Raptor Center at the University of Minnesota is an international medical facility that has treated thousands of sick and injured birds since it was founded in 1972, and is committed to preserving biological diversity in the face of human environmental depredation. Although some of these birds sustain natural injuries, many have been shot, poisoned or injured by contact with human-made structures or equipment. The site details the medical care these birds receive, explains the rehabilitation process and provides valuable tips on handling injured raptors. One indicator of the importance of the Center's work is the fact that over one-tenth of the bald eagles now flying in the wild were treated there. Additional features of this excellent educational resource include classroom activities, a diary of an eagle's nest site, general info about predatory birds and photographs of peregrine falcon nests (one on the 32nd floor of Montreal's Stock Exchange!). You don't have to be an eco-warrior to appreciate the magnificence of these birds and to be moved by the description of a once-injured bird's release into the skies.—*Reviewed by Steve Ellis*

THE RAPTOR CENTER: MAIN MENU

- Overview, mission and history
- Building hours and tours
- Census of birds now in treatment
- Announcements, events and bird releases
- Midwest U.S. & Canada Peregrine Falcon Nest Updates
- TRC's Freedom Gift Store

- Membership information
- Volunteer information
- Internships, job postings and exchange programs
- Educational presentations and projects
  - The Minnesota Electronic Environmental Education Network (Highway To The Tropics)
  - Track Osprey Migration from Minnesota (Data Page)

itors who find the pictures whet their thirst for herpetological knowledge can jump to the author's Herpocultural big links page.

HerpMed

http://www.xmission.com/~gastown/herpmed/

HerpMed is dedicated to exchanging information related to the medical aspects of herpetology (both the dangers and the potentials). Visit this index for links to a wealth of reptilian sites—from wilderness medicine pages to conservation sites—and to find Reptile and Amphibian Magazine.

Lisko

http://stekt.oulu.fi/~suopanki/lisko.html

Fans of lizards will want to dart to this page, presuming they can read the Scandinavian language.

Society for the Study of Amphibians and Reptiles

http://falcon.cc.ukans.edu/~gpisani/SSAR.html

The Society for the Study of Amphibians and Reptiles, a nonprofit herpetological society founded in 1958, maintains this informational site for scientific resources. Visit here to learn about the society and its efforts to promote research, conservation and education about amphibians and reptiles.

INSTITUTES AND UNIVERSITIES

University of Maine: Department of Wildlife Ecology

http://wlm13.umenfa.maine.edu/w4v1.html

The department of wildlife ecology at the University of Maine offers a wealth of information here about its faculty, students, programs, research, events and resources. Visitors can also link here to related sites of interest, such as biological and U.S. federal government agencies.

NEMATOLOGY

Caenorhabditis elegans WWW Server

http://eatworms.swmed.edu/

The University of Texas Southwestern Medical Center devotes an entire server to a soil nematode used extensively in the study of genetics and neurobiology. Find Caenorhabditis elegans worm-related facts and research here.

Caenorhabditis Genetics Center (CGC) Gopher Menu

gopher://elegans.cbs.umn.edu:70/1

The Caenorhabditis Genetics Center (CGC) maintains and distributes genetic stocks of Caenorhabditis elegans, a nematode. Researchers can access information on the Center's services and stocks, search past issues of the Worm Breeder's Gazette and link to other biological or worm-related gophers.

The World-Wide Web Virtual Library: Caenorhabditis elegans

http://eatworms.swmed.edu/VLhome.shtml

Caenorhabditis elegans is a tiny soil nematode that scientists use to study the genetics of development and neurobiology. Visitors not familiar with the nematode will find an introduction and pictures here. The site also includes genetic maps, related newsletters and recent papers for researchers.

Wormworld

http://wormworld.ucsf.edu/

Ilan Zipkin's Wormworld Web page features information about worm labs around the world. The site is located at the University of California at San Francisco's Kenyon Lab. It includes pointers to other science links.

ORNITHOLOGY

Common Birds of the Australian National Botanic Gardens

http://155.187.10.12/anbg/birds.html

Visitors can do some virtual birding on this site. The Australian National Botanic Gardens in Canberra provides drawings, physical and behavioral descriptions, and calls of birds that visit its gardens. (There's no counting these cyber-spottings toward your life list, though.)

EuroBirdNet Switzerland

http://cmu.unige.ch/www/ugebn/ugebn_e.html

EuroBirdNet, a network of bird watchers across Europe, maintains this site for news, ornithology resources and related links. Visit here for rare bird reports, keyword searches, species indexes and more.

The Online Book of Parrots

http://www.ub.tu-clausthal.de/p_welcome.html

The Online Book of Parrots is devoted to information on parrots and parrot-like birds. Visitors will find photos, databases and descriptions of various breeds of parrots.

Raptor Center

http://www.raptor.cvm.umn.edu/

The Raptor Center of the University of Minnesota in St. Paul, Minn. works to preserve biological diversity among the many species of birds of prey. Visit this site to find membership information, program updates, educational and career opportunities. Information about providing emergency care for injured birds is also available here. See Editor's Choice.

Takern Fieldstation Homepage

http://www.lysator.liu.se/~ngn/tfhome.html

Bird watchers can live vicariously by visiting the Takern Fieldstation Homepage. See what birds live at Lake Takern and how the members of the field station monitor their activities. Some links in English, most in Swedish.

Tweeters

http://weber.u.washington.edu/~dvictor/

Tweeters is the name of a mailing list for birders of all feather located in the northwest United States and British Columbia, Canada. Find links to the Tweeters archives and subscription information, plus pointers to a nest of birding sites on the Web.

The Virtual Emu

http://www.vicnet.net.au/~raou/raou.html

The Virtual Emu is the home page of the Royal Australasian Ornithologists Union (RAOU) which is dedicated to the preservation of avian biodiversity in Australasia and Antarctica through the study of birds, their habitats and public education. Includes information on indigenous species, an Australasian bird image gallery and links to other ornithological servers.

ZOOS

The American Association of Zoo Keepers

http://aazk.ind.net/

The American Association of Zoo Keepers (AAZK) is a nonprofit organization for professional zoologists dedicated to animal care and conservation. A range of information on AAZK services is available here, as well as links to zoological and ecological resources.

The World-Wide Web Virtual Library: Zoos

http://www.mindspring.com/~zoonet/www_virtual_lib/zoos.html

Make a virtual visit to the zoo through this page that includes information about zoos around the world. Visitors can click through animal-related links full of pictures and sounds or opt to check out specific institutions from an extensive list of commercial and public zoos.

CHEMISTRY

ARCHIVES AND INDICES

Chemistry

http://galaxy.einet.net/galaxy/Science/Chemistry.html

This page from the larger Galaxy site contains pointers to all manner of chemistry-related information and resources on the Web. Find chemistry guides, software, discussion groups, organizations and directories from around the world.

Chemistry Gopher Menu
gopher://argon.ch.ic.ac.uk:70/1

This gopher server maintained by the Imperial College of London Department of Chemistry provides a storehouse of chemistry resources, including demos, software, links to related servers and publications.

Chemistry Gopher Menu
gopher://gopher.csc.fi:70/11/tiede/kemia

This chemistry gopher from Finland provides links to computational and general chemistry servers around the world. WAIS and FTP archives are also here, as is a file on conferences.

Chemistry Information on the Internet
http://hackberry.chem.niu.edu:70/cheminf.html

The Chemistry Information on the Internet site provides reference material about chemical databases, journals, textbooks and conferences. Includes links to a protein database, chemists' address/phone book and an online chemistry employment center.

Chemistry on the Internet: The Best of the Web 1995
http://www.ch.ic.ac.uk/infobahn/boc.html

Each year, chemistry professionals select outstanding chemistry-related Internet sites. The1995 winners are posted here and include an online address book of celebrity chemists, a paper on the chemical composition of Jamaican coffee with pimento and a Web presentation of chemical art.

Fundamental Physical Constants
http://physics.nist.gov/PhysRefData/codata86/codata86.html

Look up physics and chemistry constants and conversion factors in the index provided here. The National Institute of Standards and Technology publishes this helpful 1986 document, plus offers a link to the NIST Physics Laboratory Server.

Index of Chemical Names
http://gnv.ifas.ufl.edu/~fairsweb/text/pp/15578.html

This no-frills index of chemical names features an alpha search function: find definitions and uses for HalizanHalocarbon Fumigants, Neguvon, Bactospeine, and more.

Index of Material Safety Data Sheets
http://physchem.ox.ac.uk/MSDS/

This index site provides links to pages relating to physical and theoretical chemistry. Descriptions of chemicals and chem lab equipment can be found here.

RiceInfo Gopher Menu
gopher://riceinfo.rice.edu/11/Subject/Chemistry

The RiceInfo gopher is an information-by-subject directory that links to international chemistry resources, including research institutions, publications and software. The site is maintained by Rice University in Houston, Texas.

Some Chemistry Resources on the Internet
http://www.uq.oz.au/ddd/staff_folder/MStoermer/chemres.html

Compiled at the Indiana University Chemistry Library and mirrored on this Australian site, the index of chemistry resources provides pointers to databases, gophers, online search services, periodicals and other documents. Query services are provided on the welcome page.

World-Wide Web Virtual Library: Chemistry
http://www.chem.ucla.edu/chempointers.html

This vast site provides extensive links to chemistry pages, including worldwide lists of university departments, organizations and resources relating to that discipline.

ASSOCIATIONS AND ORGANIZATIONS

The ACSWeb from the American Chemical Society
http://www.acs.org/

The American Chemical Society, the world's largest scientific society, provides information on its products and services. ACSWeb, which is searchable, features a link to the organization's Chemical Abstracts Service.

American Chemical Society: Division of Analytical Chemistry
http://nexus.chemistry.duq.edu/analytical/analytical.html

The activities of the American Chemical Society's Division of Analytical Chemistry are outlined and updated on this site. Access databases and find out about grant and fellowship opportunities through the page.

American Chemical Society: Division of Inorganic Chemistry
http://infoeagle.bc.edu/chemistry/Inorganic/Inorganic.html

Chemists visiting the home page for the American Chemical Society's Division of Inorganic Chemistry will find information about national and international meetings, newsletters, journals, and awards in inorganic chemistry.

American Chemical Society: Division of Organic Chemistry
http://www.organic.emory.edu/acsorg/index.html

Visitors to this site will find membership info for the American Chemical Society Organic Chemistry Division. A link to the ChemKey search database, conference info and the Society's newsletter are also featured.

American Chemical Society: Division of Polymer Chemistry
http://www.chem.umr.edu/~poly/

The American Chemical Society's Division of Polymer Chemistry provides information about its conferences, meetings and membership benefits here. The page also includes preprints from The Polymer, the division's journal.

American Crystallographic Association
http://nexus.hwi.buffalo.edu/ACA/

The American Crystallographic Association provides links to its special interest groups (SIGs), conference, meeting and workshop schedules, and listings of job openings. Links to topic-related associations and other sites are also featured.

AOAC Home Page
http://www.aoac.org/

AOAC International's webmaster describes this Gaithersburg, Maryland organization as an association of scientists "devoted to the validation of analytical chemical and microbiological methods and promotion of quality measurements in the analytical sciences." Visitors will find complete information on programs, membership, courses and regular events.

Beilstein Informationssysteme GmbH
http://www.beilstein.com/

Beilstein is an association of chemists dedicated to advancing the practice of chemical research and information dissemination. Visitors can find news, press releases and new product information on chemical breakthroughs.

Canadian Society for Chemistry: Organic Division
http://www.chemistry.mcmaster.ca/csc/orgdiv/orgdiv.html

Members of the Canadian Society for Chemistry, Organic Division, can keep up on the division's news and events by stopping by this home page. Visitors can also check out other sites of interest to organic chemists.

The Electrochemical Society Home Page
http://www.electrochem.org/ecs/

The Electrochemical Society's home page features information about its membership and publications. Visitors can also check the abstracts of the society's meetings.

International Society of Heterocyclic Chemists

http://euch6f.chem.emory.edu/ishc.html

The home page for the International Society of Heterocyclic Chemistry and the Royal Society of Chemistry Perking Division Heterocyclic Group features profiles of its research focus and a links to a related mailing list.

The Royal Society of Chemistry

http://chemistry.rsc.org/rsc/

The Royal Society of Chemistry is a British institution for the advanced study of chemistry. Visitors will find news and announcements, membership information and carefully selected links to other chemistry sites.

U.K. Computational Chemistry Working Party

http://www.ccwp.ac.uk/ccwp

The U.K. Computational Chemistry Working Party consists of researchers at university chemistry departments who use computational techniques. Its searchable home page features membership information, computer programs, conferences and publications.

World Association of Theoretically Oriented Chemists (WATOC)

http://www.ch.ic.ac.uk/watoc.html

The World Association of Theoretically Oriented Chemists (WATOC) highlights the benefits of membership and upcoming conferences at its home page. Visitors can learn how to join WATOC and sign up for its online mailing list.

CHEMISTS

Chemical On-Line Presentations, Talks and Workshops

http://www.ch.ic.ac.uk/talks/

Chemistry presentations made before audiences around the world (past, present and future) are announced and recorded on this hyperlinked calendar dating back to 1994. Entries include presentation date and title, plus the presenter's name and e-mail address.

Chemistry on the Internet: The Best of the Web 1995

http://www.ch.ic.ac.uk/infobahn/boc.html

Each year, chemistry professionals select outstanding chemistry-related Internet sites. The 1995 winners are posted here and include an online address book of celebrity chemists, a paper on the chemical composition of Jamaican coffee with pimento and a Web presentation of chemical art.

Henry Rzepa

http://www.ch.ic.ac.uk/rzepa.html

This is the personal home page of Henry S. Rzepa, a reader in the Chemistry Department at the Imperial College of Science in London, England. Visitors to his site will find biographical information and details of recent research projects.

Nick's Place

http://www.chem.ucla.edu/~nick/

Nicholas C. DeMello, a self-professed molecular sculptor and binary poet, posts his personal page here with a bit of personal background and links to dozens of Macintosh sites.

T. Daniel Crawford

http://zopyros.ccqc.uga.edu/~crawdad/Daniel.html

Fourth-year graduate student T. Daniel Crawford highlights his academic studies and whimsical interests in this personal home page. The site includes papers written by the Department of Defense graduate fellow, along with his current research projects.

COMPANIES

Calgon Corporation Home Page

http://www.calgon.com/

Calgon Corporation, a Pittsburgh-based specialty chemical and water treatment company, provides information here on its products and services. Visitors will also find corporate news, technical support resources and world-wide staff directories.

Catalytica

http://www.catalytica-inc.com/

Catalytica develops and markets chemical catalysts and related products. This home page for the California company links to information on the corporation and its products.

Hoechst Internet Forum

http://www.hoechst.com/

This corporate home page provides information on Hoechst, a company that supplies materials for industrial chemistry, pharmaceutical and agricultural businesses. Includes press releases, annual reports, and research and development information. In English and German.

Kumho Chemical Laboratories

http://camd1.kkpcr.re.kr/

Kumho Chemical Laboratories, a Korea-based chemistry research company, maintains this promotional site. Visit here for links to departmental resources and a collection of Internet-based search and information tools.

Molecular Simulations Inc.

http://www.msi.com/

Molecular Simulations Inc.'s home page details its chemical-computing products for the materials and life sciences. Includes information on the company's educational and consultancy offerings as well as its software for molecular designers.

Replas Inc. Home Page

http://www.replas.com/

Replas manufactures performance resins and compounds, such as polypropylenes and impact-modified resins. The promotional home page of this Indiana-based company includes a technical data notebook with full product information.

Silicon Graphics: Chemistry and Biological Sciences

http://www.sgi.com/ChemBio/

This promotional site presents Silicon Graphics, Inc.'s supercomputing offerings to the scientific community. Review the company's computer systems especially equipped for scientific research, as well as a company overview, product information and event announcements.

CRYSTALLOGRAPHY

Advanced Liquid Crystalline Optical Materials (ALCOM)

http://alcom.kent.edu/ALCOM/ALCOM.html

This site provides information about the National Science Foundation Center for Advanced Liquid Crystalline Optical Materials (ALCOM) and the International Liquid Crystal Society (ILCS). Seminar information, preprints and a link to the Liquid Crystal Institute's gopher server can be found here.

Cambridge Crystallographic Data Centre

http://www.ccdc.cam.ac.uk/

The Cambridge Crystallographic Data Centre maintains the Cambridge Structural Database, including its search functions, visual analysis and molecule display. This page has information on the center, its research and links to related sites.

International Union of Crystallography

http://www.iucr.ac.uk/

The International Union of Crystallography supplies a wealth of crystallography resources here. Resources include a world database, journals, the Crystallographic Information File (CIF), reports, newsletters, information on upcoming meetings, and pointers to related sites.

ELEMENTS

PERIODIC TABLE

Interactive Periodic Table
http://hawserv80.tamu.edu/HawHomePage/NMRPerTab/NMRPerTab.html

This interactive periodic table of the elements is presented by the Laboratory for Magnetic Resonance and Molecular Science at Texas A&M University. Visitors can click on an element's symbol to learn detailed information about the substance.

Periodic Table of the Elements Gopher Menu
gopher://ucsbuxa.ucsb.edu:3001/11/.Sciences/.Chemistry/.periodic.table

This periodic table of the elements gopher server presents a complete alphabetical listing of all the elements with individual descriptions of each element's characteristics.

INSTITUTES AND UNIVERSITIES

Australian National University: Department of Chemistry
http://rsc.anu.edu.au/DEPT/ChemDept.html

The Department of Chemistry at the Australian National University provides information here on its people and programs. Visit here for a researcher's index, honors course materials, computer software, academic texts, publications, links to related Web sites, and more.

Australian National University: Research School of Chemistry
http://rsc.anu.edu.au/Default.html

The Research School of Chemistry at the Australian National University provides information here on its programs and research facilities. Visit here for news, events, staff directories, software, research resources and more.

Binghamton University: Chemistry Department
http://chemiris.chem.binghamton.edu:8080/

Prospective students hoping to pursue graduate studies in chemistry at the State University of New York (SUNY) can begin their research at this site. Investigate academic programs, research facilities and admission information here.

Boston University: Department of Chemistry
http://chem.bu.edu/

The Chemistry Department at Boston University provides information on graduate and undergrad-

uate programs of study, course information and faculty. The Department also provides an indexed FTP server, an online periodic table and a good listing of chemistry-related Internet resources.

Brown University: Chemistry Department
http://www.chem.brown.edu/index.html

Prospective students visiting Brown University's Chemistry Department page will find an overview of its facilities and research, faculty profiles, and course listings.

California State University, Stanislaus: Chemistry Home Page
http://wwwchem.csustan.edu/

California State University Stanislaus uses this site to provide information about its chemistry department and academic program. Refrain from smoking while here—the page links to a whole pack of tobacco news to satisfy your nicotine needs.

Caltech: Division of Chemistry and Chemical Engineering
http://www.caltech.edu/caltech/Chemistry.html

The Division of Chemistry and Chemical Engineering at the California Technical University provides information here on its graduate and undergraduate programs. Visit here to learn about its faculty, research projects and laboratory facilities.

Carnegie Mellon University: Department of Chemistry
http://www.chem.cmu.edu/

This home page for Carnegie Mellon University's Chemistry Department features graduate and undergraduate program information. Visitors will also discover faculty research interests, and a collection of current course home pages.

EDITOR'S CHOICE

WebElements
http://www.shef.ac.uk/uni/academic/A-C/chem/web-elements/web-elements-home.html

Throw away those dusty chemistry reference books; they're probably outdated anyway. WebElements serves up a hypertext version of the periodic table here and turns the intimidating chart on the chemistry classroom wall into an interactive, user-friendly tool. Created by Mark Winter at the University of Sheffield in England, the chart lists 117 elements and provides the atomic weight, atomic number, and group number for each element. That's the usual stuff you'd expect from a periodic table, but there's more! Specify the type of information you want—general, chemical, physical, electronic, biological, geological or crystallographic properties—or find reduction potentials, isotope abundances, electronic configurations and ionization enthalpies. WebElements is the hottest thing to happen to chemistry since the Bunsen burner. The site is virtually an online chemistry tutor. Along with the elemental facts, WebElements includes links to the Sheffield ChemPuter, a set of interactive calculators for chemistry, and to the Sheffield ChemDex, a list of over 1600 Internet chemistry sites. Continually updated, plans are to add definitions, sound files and additional information to WebElements' already-extensive resources. Mirrored all over the world, this site is an alchemist's dream.—*Reviewed by Steve Ellis*

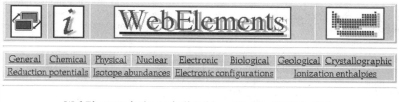

WebElements is the periodic table on the World-Wide Web by Mark Winter, University of Sheffield, England.

Chemical Laboratory at Cambridge University

http://www.ch.cam.ac.uk/

The Chemical Laboratory at Cambridge University provides information on its colloquia, courses and research projects. Includes access to the library, introductions to academic staff and links to other chemical resources.

Chemistry at the Center for Scientific Computing

http://www.csc.fi/lul/csc_chem.html

The Center for Scientific Computing (CSC) in Finland maintains this site offering visitors an index to information about the Center's chemistry programs. Features also include links to other fields of interest at CSC.

Chemistry UK—an Internet Resource

http://www.u-net.com/ukchem/

Chemistry UK is a comprehensive collection of university chemistry departments at major educational facilities in the United Kingdom. Visitors can link directly to these sites, which include Bristol University and the Cambridge chemical lab.

The CTI Centre for Chemistry WWW Home Page

http://www.liv.ac.uk/ctichem.html

Located in the Chemistry Department of England's University of Liverpool, the CTI Centre for Chemistry is "one of 23 subject-based centres working to encourage the use of learning technologies in UK higher education." Visit this page to learn more about the center and its projects.

Drago Research Group

http://inorganic1.chem.ufl.edu/

The Drago Research Group from the Department of Chemistry at the University of Florida profiles its leader, Dr. Russell S. Drago, along with its current research here.

Duke University: Department of Chemistry

http://www.chem.duke.edu/

The Department of Chemistry at North Carolina's Duke University maintains this overview of its department and program. Review online course materials, visit the chemistry library, browse the departmental photo album or link to related sites.

Freie University: Department of Chemistry

http://www.chemie.fu-berlin.de/index.html

This site contains the home page of the Department of Chemistry at Freie University in Berlin (FU Berlin). It provides access to the CHEMnet, the department, the university, and other Web servers in Germany. In German and English.

Fritz-Haber-Institut, Berlin

http://www.rz-berlin.mpg.de/

The Fritz-Haber-Institut in Berlin presents an index featuring its departments of Inorganic Chemistry, Surface Reactions, Surface Physics, Physical Chemistry and Theory. In English and German.

Georgetown University: Department of Chemistry

http://www.georgetown.edu/departments/chemistry/chemistry.html

Read back issues of Hoya Chimica, the newsletter from the chemistry department at Georgetown University. Visitors can also view a brochure for graduate students that highlights the faculty and their projects.

Harvard Chemistry Department Home Page

http://www-chem.harvard.edu/

Find out about the state of the study of chemistry at Harvard University here. The university's Department of Chemistry provides a departmental overview, course information, faculty notes, and links to related resources—on campus and off.

Homepage des Institutes für Chemie an der Humboldt Universität

http://www.chemie.hu-berlin.de/index.html

This page provides pointers to the four chemistry institutes at Humboldt University in Germany. Links to other chemistry servers and to the home page of the university are included. In German, with English and French versions available soon.

Ian Wark Laboratory Home Page

http://www.chem.csiro.au/

The Australian Commonwealth Scientific and Industrial Research Organization (CSIRO) welcomes visitors to its Ian Wark Laboratory on this page. Visitors can learn about the lab and learn about its research involving various chemical and forest products.

Indiana University Purdue University Indianapolis (IUPUI): Department of Chemistry

http://chem.iupui.edu/

The graduate brochure at this university site provides a good overview of the programs available, financial support, housing and the city of Indianapolis. The site also features a schedule of seminars, faculty and research information, and photographs.

Institute of Chemical Process Fundamentals, Academy of Sciences

http://www.icpf.cas.cz/

The Institute of Chemical Process Fundamentals, Academy of Sciences, Czech Republic, Prague, maintains this site with information about upcoming conferences and details about the institute. In Czech and English.

The Institute of Physical and Chemical Research (RIKEN)

http://www.riken.go.jp/

The Institute of Physical and Chemical Research (RIKEN) located in Japan provides this overview of its organizational structure and research. Also find links to the RIKEN Accelerator Research Facility (RARF), the RIKEN Computation Center and a number of other related sites.

Interdisciplinary Research Center in Polymer Science and Technology

http://irc.leeds.ac.uk/

The Interdisciplinary Research Center in Polymer Science and Technology is a department at the University of Leeds, England. Visitors to the site can view chemical models and learn about theoretical modeling in chemistry.

Korea University: Department of Chemistry

http://jschem.korea.ac.kr/

The Department of Chemistry, Korea University, maintains this site with information about the department, research, chemistry software manuals, seminar schedules and links to related sites on and off campus.

Latvian Institute of Organic Synthesis

http://www.osi.lanet.lv/

The research focus at the Latvian Institute of Organic Synthesis is on organic, bioorganic and physical organic chemistry and on the investigation of biological and pharmacological properties of synthesized compounds. Read about current research at the Institute and their scientific partnerships.

Louisiana State University Department of Chemistry

http://chrs1.chem.lsu.edu/

The Chemistry Department from Louisiana State University features current research projects and weekly news bulletins on its Web page. Visitors to the site can learn about graduate programs and local organizations within the department.

Michigan State University: Department of Chemistry Home Page

http://www.cem.msu.edu/

The Michigan State University (MSU) Department of Chemistry maintains this page to provide information about its facilities and academic offerings, including contact directories. Other selections point to additional MSU resources and Internet chemistry sites.

North Carolina State University: Department of Chemistry X-ray Structural Facility

http://laue.chem.ncsu.edu/web/xray.welcome.html

The North Carolina State University Department of Chemistry's X-ray Structural Facility maintains this overview. Find information on the unit's equipment and resources, plus links to related sites on and off campus.

Northern Illinois University Chemistry WWW Home Page

http://hackberry.chem.niu.edu/webpage.html

A pilot project funded by the Camille and Henry Dreyfus Chemical Informatics Program, this site provides NIU chemistry departmental data, plus offers a collection of topical resources. Find conference information, software, stock prices, an employment clearinghouse and journal submission guidelines.

Okanagan University College: Department of Chemistry

http://oksw01.okanagan.bc.ca/chem/home.html

If you thought hyperactive kids were bad, try hyperactive *molecules*. The Chemistry Department page from Okanagan University College in Canada features tutorials on hyperactive molecules along with a department profile, descriptions of academic programs and research facilities.

Oklahoma State University: Department of Chemistry

http://bubba.ucc.okstate.edu/jgelder/Main.html

The Department of Chemistry at Oklahoma State University, Stillwater, maintains this home page with information about organic chemistry, the periodic tables, and solid state and introductory chemistry. The gopher link offers information about the department, academic programs, faculty and resources.

Pennsylvania State University: Department of Chemistry

http://www.chem.psu.edu/

Pennsylvania State University's Department of Chemistry maintains this informational site. Visit here to learn about graduate study opportunities and link with its many research group home pages.

Purdue University: Biochemistry Department

http://www.biochem.purdue.edu/

The Department of Biochemistry at Purdue University in West Lafayette, Indiana maintains this information site. Visitors can link to its graduate and undergraduate departments, faculty listings, laboratory facilities, personal home pages and other administrative and academic resources.

Purdue University: Department of Chemistry

http://www.chem.purdue.edu/

The Department of Chemistry at Purdue University provides information on programs of study, course offerings and research projects. Includes faculty listings, descriptions of departmental facilities and contact information.

Queen's University: Department of Chemistry

http://www.chem.queensu.ca/

The chemistry department at Queens University in Ontario, Canada, maintains this server, providing information on the department's academics, research, faculty, students and resources. Browsers can read the department's weekly and annual newsletters here.

Rensselaer Polytechnic Institute: Chemistry Department

http://www.rpi.edu/dept/chem/rpichem/chemhome.html

Prospective students of New York's Rensselaer Polytechnic Institute (RPI) can get an overview of its chemistry department here. The site also posts a virtual classroom that gives visitors online access to course materials.

Rice University: Department of Chemistry

http://pchem1.rice.edu/RiceChem.html

Visit the Rice University Chemistry Department and sign up online for a graduate study application. Learn about the latest chemistry-related seminars and peek into the Chemistry Stockroom and the Electronics Shop. Other links tell about Rice University and other interesting programs.

Salford University: Department of Chemistry

http://www.salford.ac.uk/docs/depts/chemist/homepage.html

The UK's Salford University introduces the educational programs of its Department of Chemistry here. Investigate degree requirements, research facilities and academic offerings at this site.

Slovak Academy of Sciences

http://savba.savba.sk/

The Slovak Academy of Sciences home page offers info on its various institutes and conferences, plus a phone directory and a link to a still-under-construction crystallography page.

State University of New York, Stony Brook: Molecular Structure Laboratory

http://sbchem.sunysb.edu/msl/homepage.html

The chemistry department of State University of New York at Stony Brook introduces visitors to its molecular structure laboratory at this site. Browsers also can link to crystallographic Internet resources like the International Union of Crystallography.

Swiss Federal Institute of Technology, Lausanne: Chemistry Department

http://dcwww.epfl.ch/

The chemistry department of the Swiss Federal Institute of Technology at Lausanne presents this overview of its programs in physical chemistry and chemical engineering. Links to chemistry students' home pages and departmental directories are also featured. In French, with some English.

Swiss Federal Institute of Technology, Zurich: Department of Chemistry

http://www.chem.ethz.ch/

The department of chemistry of the Swiss Federal Institute of Technology at Zurich maintains this informational site. Visit here to learn about its departments, faculty, and related institutes.

TH Darmstadt—Fachbereich Chemie

http://tutor.oc.chemie.th-darmstadt.de/

The Technical University of Darmstadt, Germany, provides interactive teaching materials and information from all areas of chemistry. The site includes information on the university's chemistry department. In German and English.

University Erlangen: Computer Chemistry Center

http://derioc1.organik.uni-erlangen.de/

This affiliate of the inorganic chemistry department at University Erlangen in Germany provides information on its research resources, upcoming events and cooperative projects. Visitors can also download abstracts and examples of papers from the Journal of Molecular Modeling. In English or German.

University of Bayreuth: Institute of Structure and Chemistry of Biopolymers

http://btcpxc.che.uni-bayreuth.de/

The University of Bayreuth in Germany presents the home page for its Institute of Structure and Chemistry of Biopolymers here. Visitors will get an overview of the institution's programs, along with information on events and software. In English and German.

University of California, Berkeley: College of Chemistry

http://www.cchem.berkeley.edu/index.html

The College of Chemistry of the University of California, Berkeley, offers a general overview of its educational and research opportunities. Access its academic resources and learn about the campus, programs, faculty and students.

University of California, Davis: Department of Chemistry

http://www-chem.ucdavis.edu/

The University of California at Davis posts information about its chemistry department here. Find out what's happening in areas of research and development, and in the U.C. Davis labs. E-mail addresses and electronic resources are also accessible.

University of California, Los Angeles: Chemistry

http://www.chem.ucla.edu/dept/Chemistry.html

Learn about the current state of the study of chemistry and biochemistry at the University of California, Los Angeles. Access faculty research projects, descriptions of study programs and departmental information resources at this site.

University of California, San Diego: Chemistry and Biochemistry Departments

http://checfs1.ucsd.edu/

The University of California at San Diego's chemistry and biochemistry departments maintain this server for departmental information. Visitors to this site can read about the department's faculty, programs, seminars and administration.

University of California, Santa Barbara: Chemistry

http://128.111.114.72/

The chemistry department at the University of California at Santa Barbara provides extensive information on courses, administration, research and students, and includes a host of links to related Web servers.

University of Chicago: Department of Chemistry

http://rainbow.uchicago.edu/chemistry/

The University of Chicago's department of chemistry provides information about its programs and faculty here. Visitors can check out the graduate class offerings or take a peek into The Virtual Chemistry Library.

University of Durham: Department of Chemistry

http://www.dur.ac.uk/~dch0www/index.html

The chemistry department at University of Durham in the United Kingdom outlines its undergraduate and postgraduate course offerings at this straightforward site. Includes a list of academic and research staff members and a rundown of their specific research interests.

University of Fribourg: Section of Chemistry

http://sgich1.unifr.ch/

The chemistry department at this Swiss university fills its page with information about its four chemistry divisions and research groups.

University of Groningen: Chemistry Department

http://www.chem.rug.nl/

Providing access to the numerous research laboratories at the university, this gateway also includes pointers to chemistry-related information, a local search engine, Frequently Asked Questions (FAQs), and access to a virtual library.

University of Idaho: Department of Chemistry

http://www.chem.uidaho.edu/

The department of chemistry at the University of Idaho provides information about its courses, faculty, staff and students here. The page also contains information on the department's K-8 science teacher outreach program.

University of Illinois: School of Chemical Sciences

http://www.scs.uiuc.edu/

The School of Chemical Sciences at the University of Illinois provides information about its department, interdisciplinary programs and service facilities. The chemistry, chemical engineering and biochemistry departments each have their own pages.

University of Illinois, Chicago: Chemistry Department

http://gopher.chem.uic.edu/

The University of Illinois at Chicago presents this home page for its chemistry department. Visitors will find information on academics, admissions, faculty and research.

University of Kentucky, Lexington: Department of Chemistry

http://www.chem.uky.edu/

The department of chemistry at the University of Kentucky, Lexington, maintains this site of general information and resource access. Visit here to learn about its faculty and programs, and link to a variety of chemistry resources and downloadable software.

University of Leeds: School of Chemistry

http://chem.leeds.ac.uk/default.html

The School of Chemistry at this British university provides information on its faculty, programs, research and resources.

University of Manchester: Institute of Science and Technology

http://uchsg11.ch.umist.ac.uk/

The chemistry department at this British university offers a slew of academic information here. Find out about the research currently being conducted, or check out scholarship information.

University of Minnesota: Department of Chemistry Home Page

http://www.chem.umn.edu/

The department of chemistry at the University of Minnesota maintains this informational site. Visit here to learn about its faculty members, scientific programs and research facilities.

University of Nijmegen: Laboratory for Analytic Chemistry

http://www-sci.sci.kun.nl/cac/

The Laboratory for Analytic Chemistry at the Netherlands' University of Nijmegen maintains this overview of its academic programs, faculty, facilities and research projects. Includes publications and job listings.

University of Oklahoma: Department of Chemistry and Biochemistry

http://cheminfo.chem.uoknor.edu/

The department of chemistry and biochemistry at the University of Oklahoma provides information about its faculty, curriculum and courses. Links to related sites on and off campus are also featured.

University of Oklahoma: School of Chemical Engineering and Materials Science

http://www.uoknor.edu/cems/

This site provides departmental information about graduate and research programs at the University of Oklahoma's School of Chemical Engineering and Materials Science. Visitors can browse through categorical listings or access information via a keyword search.

University of Oxford: Physical & Theoretical Chemistry Laboratory

http://joule.pcl.ox.ac.uk/

The home page for the Physical & Theoretical Chemistry Laboratory presents a general overview of the facility and its faculty, along with links to other Oxford Web servers.

University of Pavia: Chemistry Departments

http://chifis1.unipv.it/

Learn more about the curriculum and programs of the departments highlighted in this Italian university's chemistry page. Visitors can link to program information about the school.

University of Pennsylvania: Department of Chemistry

http://www.chem.upenn.edu/

The department of chemistry at the University of Pennsylvania maintains this site for information about its people, programs and facilities. Visit here to learn about the department and enter its gallery of selected research projects.

University of Reading: Chemistry Department

http://www.chem.rdg.ac.uk/

The chemistry department of the University of Reading, England, maintains this site for dissemination of general information. Visit here to learn about the department's facilities, programs, faculty and students. Links to information about the local area also are available here.

University of Rhode Island: Department of Chemistry

http://www.chm.uri.edu/index.html

The chemistry department at the University of Rhode Island offers a peek at its graduate and undergraduate curricula, faculty research projects and general program information. Link to other University of Rhode Island servers from this site.

University of Sussex: School of Chemistry & Molecular Sciences

http://tc.cpes.susx.ac.uk/

The School of Chemistry & Molecular Sciences at the University of Sussex outlines general information of interest to incoming students. Learn about undergraduate and postgraduate coursework, as well as research programs.

University of Toronto: Department of Chemistry Home Page

http://www.chem.utoronto.ca/

Aspiring chemists can explore undergraduate and graduate level educational opportunities at the University of Toronto here. The department of chemistry enumerates research programs and course offerings at this home page.

University of Uruguay: Faculty of Chemistry

http://bilbo.edu.uy/

The University of Uruguay's Faculty of Chemistry features a "molecular modeling e-conference" along with profiles of the department's academic program and current research. Also includes links to other servers in Uruguay.

University of the West Indies: Department of Chemistry

http://wwwchem.uwimona.edu.jm:1104/

The department of chemistry at the University of the West Indies in Jamaica provides this Web site with information on departmental academics, staff and facilities.

Vienna University of Technology

http://www.iac.tuwien.ac.at/

The Vienna Institute of Technology devotes its material and human resources to research in analytical chemistry. Explore educational opportunities and laboratory research projects at this introductory site.

Washington University: Department of Chemistry

http://wunmr.wustl.edu/

The department of chemistry at Washington University in St. Louis provides a general departmental overview, as well as details on courses, resources and faculty. A department directory is also included.

INSTRUMENTS AND EQUIPMENT

MASS SPECTROMETERS

Murray's Mass Spectrometry Page

http://tswww.cc.emory.edu/~kmurray/mslist.html

This Web site provides a number of pointers to mass spectrometry resources on the Web—including companies and downloadable software. Browsers can also access the home pages of Emory University and its chemistry department.

North Carolina State University Mass Spectrometry Facility

http://ch9000.chem.ncsu.edu/MS_Home.html

The Mass Spectrometry Facility at North Carolina State University provides information here on its staff, facilities and funding. Visit here to learn about the scientific laboratory and link to a sample program demonstrating its methods of exact mass calculation.

Nicolet

http://www.nicolet.com/

Nicolet manufactures and sells Fourier transform infrared and Fourier transform Raman spectrometers. These instruments are used to identify and quantify unknown chemical compounds. Visitors can find out more about the company, its products and applications, and its participation in upcoming seminars and trade shows.

NEWSGROUPS

Chemistry News Groups

http://www.chem.ucla.edu/chem_news.html

The department of chemistry at the University of California, Los Angeles, maintains this index of chemistry, biochemistry, biology, and other science newsgroups.

ONLINE COURSES

Australian Computational Chemistry Project

http://www.chem.swin.edu.au/

The Australian Computational Chemistry Project has developed Web-based educational modules in topics such as basic molecular modeling, basic quantitative structure activity relationships, and molecular mechanics and dynamics. The site includes links to related course materials and conference papers.

ChemCAI: Instructional Software for Chemistry

http://www.sfu.ca/chemed/

Simon Frasier University in British Columbia, Canada, features resources for chemistry educators through its Web site. Digital textbook chapters and other materials can serve as alternatives to traditional teaching methods. The pages also include downloadable software.

Chemical Separations

http://odin.chemistry.uakron.edu/chemsep/

Visitors to this page will find a University of Akron lecture series for the course in Chemical Separations. The course stresses the theory and application of modern chromatographic methods.

Chemistry Teaching Resources

http://www.anachem.umu.se/eks/pointers.htm

Hundreds of chemistry resources are easily available here for questing chemistry teachers: from lesson plans to reference guides to experiments. Enough resources are provided here for the chemistry teacher to toss out the textbook and use this site instead.

Electronic Textbook for PFP 95

http://dept.physics.upenn.edu/courses/gladney/mathphys/Contents.html

The University of Pennsylvania offers this colorful interactive textbook for its interdisciplinary course in chemistry, mathematics and physics. This well-designed e-textbook includes instruction, problems and solutions.

Global Instructional Chemistry

http://www.ch.ic.ac.uk/GIC/

Distributed education with a chemistry focus is the subject of this page. Link here for chemical problems suitable for tutorial and classes, case histories illustrating modern chemistry in action and "hyperactive" molecules. The site is searchable and submissions are encouraged.

ORGANIC CHEMISTRY

The Alchemist's Den

http://gpu.srv.ualberta.ca/~psgarbi/psgarbi.html

The Alchemist's Den is a collection of Internet resources for organic chemists. Includes pointers to a number of related journals, mailing lists, companies, conferences, organizations and newsgroups.

The Electronic Conference on Trends in Organic Chemistry

http://www.ch.ic.ac.uk/ectoc/

The Electronic Conference on Trends in Organic Chemistry site contains news from the most recent conference, along with pointers to older materials. The conferences are conducted online, via e-mail.

PHYSICAL CHEMISTRY

ATOMS AND ATOMIC STRUCTURE

Table of the Nuclides

http://necs01.dne.bnl.gov/CoN/index.html

This page has a graphic, interactive chart of all known nuclides along with help and explanations.

CHEMICAL COMPOUNDS

Element Percentage Calculator

http://www.shef.ac.uk/~chem/chemputer/

This Web site allows visitors to calculate the percentage of particular elements in chemical compounds. From here, browsers can link to this page's mother document: an online chemistry resource called WebElements.

Material Safety Data Sheets Gopher Menu

gopher://gopher.chem.utah.edu/11/MSDS

The material safety data sheets for thousands of chemical products rest here in this archive from the University of Utah chemistry department. What it is, what it does, how to protect yourself from it, and many more questions are answered for each chemical compound.

CHEMICAL REACTIONS

Corrosion Information Server

http://www.cp.umist.ac.uk/

The Corrosion Information Server is provided by the chemistry department of UMIST, Great Britain. Visitors will find journals, classes, job opportunities and related material on corrosion.

COMPUTATIONAL CHEMISTRY

Center for Computational Quantum Chemistry

http://zopyros.ccqc.uga.edu/

The Center for Computational Quantum Chemistry at the University of Georgia displays its efforts in the development of computational methods through mathematical models for understanding the movement of electrons in molecules.

Computational Chemistry List

http://www.osc.edu/chemistry.html

The Computational Chemistry List, provided by The Ohio Supercomputer Center, offers a remailer service for computational chemists. Visitors will find its archive menu, e-mail search utility and related links.

Computer Center Institute for Molecular Science

http://ccinfo.ims.ac.jp/

The Computer Center Institute for Molecular Science (CCIMS) home page offers quantum chemistry-related search resources and links to online journals and Web sites. Also available in Japanese.

MOLECULES AND MOLECULAR STRUCTURE

Centre Europeen de Calcul Atomique et Moleculaire

http://www.cecam.fr/

CECAM is a European research center for atomic and molecular calculations which aims to improve international cooperation in the areas in computational science about atomic, molecular and condensed-matter physics and chemistry. Its multinational Web site, based in Lyon, France, offers researchers a wide variety of resources.

Chemist's Art Gallery

http://www.csc.fi/lul/chem/graphics.html

Proving that chemistry can be beautiful and chemists can be artistic, this site offers works of art from the Visualization and Animation Laboratory. Visitors can view visualizations and animations of small molecule diffusion and proteins here.

Index of /pub/Graphics/

http://expasy.hcuge.ch/pub/Graphics/

Download molecular models and other science-related 3-D images from this gopher site. Image views for various formats are available for downloading.

Nanotechnology

http://nano.xerox.com/nano

Nanotechnology is concerned with manufacture at the atomic level. Find pointers to Internet resources related to the scientific field at this site.

The Representation of Molecular Models and Rendering Techniques

http://scsg9.unige.ch/fln/eng/toc.html

From the department of physical chemistry at the University of Geneva comes this hypertext on molecular modeling and shading techniques. Learn about four molecular structural models and their applications in biochemistry and crystallography, types of surfaces and their properties, and animated models.

University of Veszprem: Molecular Modeling Group

http://indy.mars.vein.hu:8000/molmod.html

The University of Veszprem in Hungary maintains this home page for its Molecular Modeling Group. Visitors can check up on activities, research programs and staff.

University of Wisconsin: Molecular Modelling Laboratory

http://www.pharmacy.wisc.edu/

Here's a resource for all the chemical molecular modelers in the crowd. Asserting that "molecular modeling is art," this site includes links to chemistry art galleries, along with a list of links to virtual reality sites and information on a number of modelling programs. Crystallography and 3-D resources are also covered.

POLYMER CHEMISTRY

Interdisciplinary Research Centre in Polymer Science and Technology

http://www.dur.ac.uk/~dch0www2/

The Interdisciplinary Research Centre in Polymer Science and Technology is a consortium of plastics professionals from U.K. universities at Durham, Leeds, and Bradford. The group's home page describes its facilities, personnel and ongoing research, plus provides links to other polymer chemistry sites.

THEORETICAL CHEMISTRY

University of Lund: Department of Theoretical Chemistry

http://garm.teokem.lu.se/index.html

The Department of Theoretical Chemistry at Sweden's University of Lund gives an overview of its program and posts abstracts of Ph.D. theses here. The site includes a hypertext staff directory, information about MOLCAS quantum chemistry software and a totally unscientific world championship ice hockey betting pool.

PUBLICATIONS AND INDUSTRY NEWS

American Chemical Society Publications Catalog Gopher Menu

gopher://infx.infor.com:4500/

Finding chemical publications is easy on this gopher because it allows searching by author's name, title, or keyword. Browsers can also take a look at new titles or access subject-specific lists of books, journals and software. This handy gopher also includes fax order forms.

American Chemical Society (ACS) Publications Division

http://pubs.acs.org/

ACS Publications, a division of the American Chemical Society, maintains this site with information about its books, annual directories and 29 scientific periodicals. Information about ACS electronic editions and ACS software are also featured.

Bio/Chemical Journals and Newsletters

http://www.public.iastate.edu/~pedro/rt_journals.html

Pedro's BioMolecular Research Tools page offers an extensive collection of links to chemical and biological journals and newsletters, arranged in alphabetical order. Visitors can also link to a number of other general chemistry-related resources.

Chemical Abstracts Service Home Page

http://info.cas.org/welcome.html

The American Chemical Society's Chemical Abstracts Service (CAS) offers specialized scientific information products, including books, online resources and more. Visitors to the organization's Web site can learn about CAS, its wares, and its support and training programs.

Chemical Applications of the World Wide Web System

http://www.ch.ic.ac.uk/rzepa/RSC/CC/4_02963A.html

Chemical Applications of the World Wide Web System describes how the Web can be used for "efficient and intuitive delivery of chemical information in a wide variety of formats."

Chemical On-Line Presentations, Talks and Workshops

http://www.ch.ic.ac.uk/talks/

Chemistry presentations made before audiences around the world (past, present and future) are announced and recorded on this hyperlinked calendar dating back to 1994. Entries include presentation date and title, plus the presenter's name and e-mail address.

ChemTech Publishing

http://www.io.org/~chemtec/

Peruse offerings of chemistry-related journals, books and software from ChemTech Publishing at this commercial site. Includes listings of publications and ordering information.

Journal of Chemical Physics Express Gopher Menu

gopher://jcp.uchicago.edu/

The Journal of Chemical Physics Express distributes preprints of manuscripts bound for the journal through this gopher site. Visitors can download the manuscripts, indexed by author.

SOFTWARE

CAOS/CAMM Center in the Netherlands

gopher://camms1.caos.kun.nl:70/1

A Netherlands expert's center for computer-assisted work in chemistry, the Computer Assisted Organic Synthesis and Computer Assisted Molecular Modelling Center (CAOS/CAMM) provides software tools for chemists to use on a central computer system. Other chemistry resources are linked to this gopher menu.

Chemical Concepts

http://www.vchgroup.de/cc/

Germany-based Chemical Concepts introduces its spectroscopy software on this promotional page. Product descriptions and applications to chemistry research are provided, along with contact information.

ChemKey Search Database

http://euch6f.chem.emory.edu/

Download a free demo of the ChemKey Search Database software for both Mac and PC plat-

forms. This program contains thousands of references for organic chemists, with yearly updates available. Find out how to order here. From Heterodata, Inc.

Daylight Chemical Information Systems

http://www.daylight.com/

Daylight Chemical Information Systems produces chemical information software, tools and databases. Visitors will get an overview of the company's wares as well as an opportunity to download demos of its software offerings. Includes manuals and tutorials.

Falcon Software

http://www.falconsoftware.com/falconweb/products.html

Falcon Software creates computer products for college students learning chemistry, environmental science, and electronics. Some of Falcon's products include a chemistry review series, an electronics lab simulator and an environmental science field lab. Falcon products are searchable at this Web site by subject area or by author/school.

General Atomic and Molecular Electronic Structure System Home Page

http://www.msg.ameslab.gov/GAMESS/GAMESS.html

Information on the General Atomic and Molecular Electronic Structure System, a chemistry software package maintained at Iowa State University, is featured at this site. Along with a summary of the program, there is information on how to obtain it and graphics programs for it.

MDL Information Systems, Inc.

http://www.mdli.com/

MDL's home page features information about its chemical information management software, databases and related services. ISIS, a client-server system; Project Library, a drug design tool; and MACCS-II and REACCS are also profiled.

Prode

http://www.prode.milano.it/prode.html

This Italian commercial Web site provides information about its software for chemical engineering. Documents include newsletters, abstracts and other chemical engineering resources.

SoftShell

http://www.softshell.com/

SoftShell produces chemistry software, including the ChemWeb drawing program featured at this site. Includes technical support for SoftShell products, reviews and resources. In English, French, Japanese and German.

WindowChem Software

http://www.windowchem.com/

WindowChem Software describes itself as the "Number One source for Windows-based chemistry/laboratory software." Located in Fairfield, California, the company lets you see what virtual vials and more have to offer. You can also order their products from this page.

COMPUTER SCIENCE

ACADEMIC RESEARCH FACILITIES

Alabama Research and Education Network

http://sgisrvr.asc.edu/index.html

The Alabama Research and Education Network presents the Alabama Supercomputer Network through its home page. The site includes facts about the program and the latest news and research.

The Arcadia Project

http://www.ics.uci.edu/Arcadia/

Maintained at the University of California Irvine, this page provides an overview of the Arcadia Project and its research into improving the software engineering process. Also find links to papers, software and the program's sponsors.

BoWeb 94 - Best Educational Service

http://wings.buffalo.edu/contest/awards/educate.html

The best educational resources on the Internet receive their just rewards at this page that presents awards to services teaching the basics of technical subjects. It includes links to the hottest sites.

Center for Information Technology

http://logic.stanford.edu/cit/cit.html

Stanford University presents this information page for its Center for Information Technology. Visitors will find an overview of current research projects like CommerceNet, a system connecting Silicon Valley manufacturers and distributors.

CITI

http://www.citi.umich.edu/

The University of Michigan's Center for Information Technology Integration (CITI) works to develop new computing technologies and integrate them into the college learning milieu. This site documents and explains CITI's work.

Cold Soldered is DOWN!

http://yar.cs.wisc.edu/

A showcase of personal work done by undergraduate programmers at the University of Wisconsin-Madison's Computer Science Department, Cold Soldered displays code, graphics and music/sound projects. Also find links to students' personal home pages.

Flux Project

http://www.cs.utah.edu/projects/flexmach/

The Flux Operating System Project is an effort to develop a "nanokernel-based decomposed operating system that achieves high performance while retaining inter-component protection and rich functionality." Includes project-related papers, access to software and job listings.

FUNET Network Services, CSC Finland

http://www.funet.fi/

The Finnish University and Research Network (FUNET) is housed at the Centre for Scientific Computing. Visitors to its home page are invited to learn more about the network, its member organizations and the services it provides. In Finnish and English.

Georgia State University Mathematics and Computer Science Department

http://www.cs.gsu.edu/

Georgia State University's Mathematics and Computer Science Department posts this page offering a wealth of information about the department's academics, research, faculty and resources. Links to sites of topical interest on and off campus are also included.

IC DoC Theory and Formal Methods

http://theory.doc.ic.ac.uk/

The Theory and Formal Methods Section of the Department of Computing at the Imperial College of Science, Technology and Medicine in London maintains this overview of its programs. Find information on seminars, research projects and publications featured.

Indiana University's Center for Innovative Computer Applications

http://www.cica.indiana.edu/

This site presents information on Indiana University's Center for Innovative Computer Applications. Includes info on research projects, staff

publications, a graphics gallery, high performance computing, instructional resources and access points to related resources.

Indiana University Visual Inference Laboratory

http://www-vil.cs.indiana.edu/

The Visual Inference Laboratory (VIL) at Indiana University is devoted to the study of the visual aspects of reasoning and the development of computer technology to support this type of reasoning. The VIL page provides details on current research, publications, software and its members.

Information Mechanics Group - MIT

http://www-im.lcs.mit.edu/

The Information Mechanics Group at the Massachusetts Institute of Technology's (MIT) Laboratory of Computer Science gives visitors here a look at its research into the physics of computation. The page also contains a variety of related links.

Institute of Computer Science and Applied Mathematics

http://www.informatik.uni-kiel.de/

The Institute of Computer Science and Applied Mathematics at the Christian-Albrechts-University of Kiel in Germany provides an index with general information and details on research groups and topics, technical reports, publications and more. In English and German.

Institute of Technology

http://www.tele.pw.edu.pl/

The Institute of Telecommunications at the Warsaw University of Technology gives an overview of its departments, programs and research here. The site includes information for post doctoral candidates. In Polish and English.

International Computer Science Institute

http://http.icsi.berkeley.edu/

Affiliated with the Electrical Engineering and Computer Science departments at UC Berkeley, the International Computer Science Institute is engaged in "fundamental research in the field of computer science." Find information on the institute's services and projects at this home page.

Iowa State University Vislab

http://www.icemt.iastate.edu/about.html

The Iowa State University Visualization Laboratory page contains information on current work related to visualization and virtual reality applications. Includes sample movies and images from past projects along with biographies of Vislab staff. Includes links to other related resources.

IST Indiana University

http://education.indiana.edu/isthome.html

This home page connects Web searchers with the instructional systems technology department of Indiana University. Program and coursework descriptions, faculty and student information and employment opportunities can be located here.

Kestrel Institute

http://kestrel.edu/

The Kestrel Institute is a computer science research institute, focusing on "knowledge-based methods for incremental automation of the software process." Read about its aim to construct intelligent software and support all activities in the software life-cycle.

Laboratory for Computer Science Research WWW Server

http://athos.rutgers.edu/

The Rutgers University Laboratory for Computer Science outlines its programs and resources at this site. Armchair scientists can check up on current research projects or access technical reports online.

Mississippi Center for Supercomputing Research

http://www.mcsr.olemiss.edu/

The Mississippi Center for Supercomputing Research, offering computer support to state educational and medical institutions, provides information on its activities and resources. Visit here for online and computing services, texts and publications, technical documentation, and links to related resources on the World Wide Web.

MIT Alewife Project

http://cag-www.lcs.mit.edu/alewife/

The Webmaster of MIT's Alewife project describes it as a "large-scale multiprocessor that integrates both cache-coherent, distributed shared memory and user-level message-passing in a single integrated hardware framework." Visitors will find technical documents and specifications for Alewife.

Northeast Parallel Architectures Center

http://www.npac.syr.edu/

The Northeast Parallel Architecture Center at New York's Syracuse University is a computer center specializing in high-performance computing and communications. Find links to research projects, papers and publications, academic programs and more.

NSWCPC

http://server.srcpc.unsw.edu.au/

The Sydney Regional Centre for Parallel Computing (SRCPC) provides information on research projects in parallel computing in New South Wales. Visitors can also learn about the computa-

tional science classes at area universities, access the center's resources or link to related resources on the Web.

NYU Ultracomputer Project

http://cs.nyu.edu/cs/projects/ultra

Conducted at New York University's Ultracomputer Lab, this project is designed to research parallel computer architecture and software design. Visitors to this page will find the project proposal, technical reports, information on the staff and students and related theses.

Overview of the Cornell Theory Center

http://www.tc.cornell.edu/ctctour.html

The Cornell Theory Center, one of four national Advanced Scientific Computing Centers, offers expertise in software, visualization and parallel processing. Visitors to this page will find links to technical information, supporting scientific research and related material.

Oxford University Computing Laboratory

http://www.comlab.ox.ac.uk/

The Computing Laboratory at England's Oxford University provides information here on its history and structure, instructional courses, seminars and employment opportunities. Visitors will also find links to research groups and staff, publications and other computer-related Web sites.

Oxford University Formal Methods Group

http://www.comlab.ox.ac.uk/archive/formal-methods.html

The Formal Methods Group at England's Oxford University maintains this site for research and academic resources. Visitors will find a variety of formal methods information by following the sites links to articles, notations, publications, projects, who's who indexes and more.

La Page D'Accueil du CERCA

http://www.cerca.umontreal.ca/Welcome.html

The Centre de Recherche en Calcul Aplique (CERCA) in Montreal, Canada explains its services and scientific purpose through this home page. The site also has links to computer science texts and the CERCA phone book. In French and English.

PARADIGM Project

http://www.crhc.uiuc.edu/Paradigm

The University of Illinois Center for Reliable and High-Performance Computing presents a report on its PARADIGM Project. Visitors will find an overview of the parallelizing compiler research initiative as well as access to the group's publications.

Parallel Architecture Research Laboratory (PARL)

http://tracebase.nmsu.edu/

New Mexico University's Parallel Architecture Research Laboratory site describes research in parallel computing. This page includes details on current projects, a trace database for information sharing and profiles of the staff.

Parallel Programming Laboratory

http://charm.cs.uiuc.edu/

The University of Illinois Department of Computer Science maintains this site with information on its Parallel Programming Laboratory. Here, visitors will find information about research, projects and group members, as well as links to papers, manuals and binaries.

Pittsburgh Supercomputing Center

http://pscinfo.psc.edu/

The Pittsburgh Supercomputing Center (PSC) is one of four national computing hubs funded by the National Science Foundation. Dedicated to developing research techniques based on high performance computing capabilities the PSC offers program and facility information at this site.

Program of Computer Graphics

http://www.graphics.cornell.edu/

The Cornell University Program of Computer Graphics conducts research and development projects for application in mechanical engineering, medical imaging, perception psychology, architecture, art and animation. Information about the program, its faculty and research is available at this site. Other links include academic papers, newsletters and other resources around the Internet.

Project Mach

http://www.cs.cmu.edu/afs/cs.cmu.edu/project/mach/public/www/mach.html/

Project Mach, a computer operating systems research project of Carnegie Mellon University, maintains this informational site. Visit here for project updates and instructional materials, including online publications, user manuals and tutorials.

The Purdue University Computing Center

http://www.cc.purdue.edu/PUCC

Purdue University's Computing Center (PUCC) offers this home page, with information about its various divisions. Visitors can read about the Center's facilities, services, operations, computing and networking.

Purdue University—Department of Computer Sciences

http://www.cs.purdue.edu/

Purdue University's Department of Computer Sciences gives an overview of its programs, research and faculty here. The site also includes information on the department's K-12 outreach program.

Rhodes University Computer Science

http://cs.ru.ac.za/

The Department of Computer Science at Rhodes University provides a wealth of information about the department's faculty, students, research, academics and conferences. Special features of this site include technical documents, a picture gallery, links to personal home pages and the department's Virtual Reality Special Interest Group.

Sakamura Laboratory Web Server

http://tron.is.s.u-tokyo.ac.jp/

The University of Tokyo's information sciences department maintains this home page, which provides information about its Sakamura Laboratory. Visitors will learn of the latest news and research in the department. Includes information on The Real-time Operating system Nucleus (TRON) project.

San Diego Supercomputer Center

http://www.sdsc.edu/

The San Diego Supercomputer Center researches computational science and engineering. Its site provides information on the center's research, services and publications. Includes detailed images and a link to the National Science Foundation's site.

SCIT at Wolverhampton

http://scitsc.wlv.ac.uk/

The University of Wolverhampton's School of Computing and Information Technology home page provides information about the university and its surrounding areas, plus pointers to plenty of Web highlights. Also find info about SCIT's coursework, research and publications.

Stanford Research Institute Computer Science Laboratory

http://www.csl.sri.com/

The Stanford Research Institute Computer Science Laboratory provides information here on its current research activities. Includes information on staff, a history of important accomplishments and links to other lab activities and documention resources.

The Stanford SUIF Compiler Group

http://suif.stanford.edu/index.html

At this site provided by the SUIF Compiler Group at Stanford University, Calif., visitors can read an overview of the group's research projects, papers, download software and link to related Web sites.

The Stanford University Database Group

http://www-db.stanford.edu/

Stanford University's Computer Science Department maintains this home page for its Database Group. Visitors will find information on research projects, staff profiles, group activities and publications.

Stanford Vision and Imaging Science and Technology

http://white.stanford.edu/

Stanford Vision and Imaging Science and Technology, located within the Department of Psychology, maintains this page with information about its staff and links to information about its software, including demos.

TCD Computer Science Department

http://www.cs.tcd.ie/

The Computer Science Department at the Trinity College Dublin provides information about its research, courses and publications here. Some of its technical papers are available online here, too.

Texas A&M University Department of Computer Science

http://www.cs.tamu.edu/

The Computer Science Department at Texas A&M, College Station, Texas, supplies its home page with information about faculty, courses and research.

UC Irvine, Information and Computer Science

http://www.ics.uci.edu/

This is the University of California's site for its Information and Computer Science Department. Visitors can find out about doctoral and undergraduate studies, research areas, technical reports and download maps and pictures of the campus.

UCL Department of Computer Science

http://www.cs.ucl.ac.uk/

The home page of the University of London's Department of Computer Science offers course guides and degree program overviews. Link to info on the department's research projects, or peruse past lecture notes.

University Centre for Computer Corpus Research on Language

http://www.comp.lancs.ac.uk/computing/research/ucrel/

Information on the University Centre for Computer Corpus Research on Language at Lancaster University in the U.K. is provided here. Also available are research overviews, technical papers, reference and event information and links to related resources.

University of Birmingham School of Computer Science

http://www.cs.bham.ac.uk/

This home page for the School of Computer Science at the University of Birmingham, U.K., provides information on admissions, courses, research and seminars. Other features include a "technical report" archive and online course material.

The University of Dublin's Distributed Systems Research Group

http://www.dsg.cs.tcd.ie/

The Distributed Systems Research Group at the University of Dublin provides information here on its research projects. The group also posts papers, technical reports, theses and personnel information on this site.

Univeristy of Haifa Department of Mathematics and Computer Science

http://mathcs11.haifa.ac.il/

The Department of Mathematics and Computer Science at Israel's University of Haifa offers a wealth of information about its events, academics, programs, Internet resources and students. Browse the library catalog, view software sources, documentation and course materials or link to a number of math and computer science resources.

University of Manchester Computer Science Publications

http://www.cs.man.ac.uk/csonly/cstechrep/index.html

The Computer Science Department at the University of Manchester offers this index of its technical report series, a collection of publications by Department members. Visitors can browse the archives by year, find out how to obtain hard copies or link to other technical report indices on the Web.

University of Rochester CS Dept.

http://www.cs.rochester.edu/

Flip through the department brochure at the University of Rochester's computer science department home page. Research projects and course information are outlined here. Visitors can access technical reports, as well as the department's software archive, at this site.

University of Texas High Performance Computing and Software Lab

http://rabbit.cs.utsa.edu/Welcome.html

The High Performance Computing and Software Lab of the University of Texas at San Antonio maintains this site to introduce its people, programs and services. Visit here to learn about its major research activities, read member profiles, view professional publications and find monitoring and visualization software.

University of Washington Computer Science and Engineering
http://www.cs.washington.edu/

The University of Washington Computer Science and Engineering department supplies its site with general program information, course descriptions and access to technical reports and abstracts. Includes a local search tool.

U of Colorado at Boulder, Computer Science
http://www.cs.colorado.edu/

The University of Colorado at Boulder's Department of Computer Science maintains this overview of is academic program. Meet faculty and students, review course requirements, learn about the department's ongoing research projects, read its publications or link to related sites.

U Penn's Center for Human Modeling and Simulation
http://www.cis.upenn.edu/~hms

The Center for Human Modeling and Simulation gives visitors a detailed look at its research and equipment here. Its research includes computer graphics modeling and elaborate software named Jack. Visitors here can download the center's reports and link to a page on Jack.

The UTS Computing Sciences
http://www.socs.uts.edu.au/

The School of Computing Sciences at the University of Technology, Sydney, presents general information, as well as details about its centers and laboratories. The Centre for Object Technology and Research and the Distributed Multimedia Laboratory are also housed here.

UW-Madison Machine Learning Research Group
http://www.cs.wisc.edu/~shavlik/uwml.html

The Machine Learning Research Group (MLRG) at the University of Madison provides information about the research projects and staff. Browsers can check out MLRG's archives of papers, datasets and domain theories, or link to a number of local and international related resources.

Warsaw University of Technology Institute of Control and Computational Engineering
http://www.ia.pw.edu.pl/

The Institute of Control and Computational Engineering at Poland's Warsaw University of Technology maintains this site to introduce its people and programs. Visit here for staff and student home pages, computer networking services, publications and other academic and administrative resources. In Polish and English.

WPI Computer Science Department
http://cs.wpi.edu/

The Worcester Polytechnic Institute Computer Science Department contains informaton about undergraduate and graduate programs of study, course offerings and research groups. Includes faculty listings, FAQs and links to related resources.

Yale Linda Group
http://www.cs.yale.edu/HTML/YALE/CS/Linda/linda.html

The Linda Group at Yale University's Department of Computer Science explores research topics in parallel and distributed computing, adaptive computation and parallel programming languages—often based on the Linda programming language. Find the group's research projects and publications at this site.

Yale University Computer Science Department Overview
http://www.cs.yale.edu/HTML/YALE/CS/FrontDoor.html

The Computer Science Department at Yale University in New Haven, Conn., provides information on faculty, academic courses and research groups. Visitors will also find technical support services, free software archives and links to other computer science resources.

Yonezawa Lab
http://web.yl.is.s.u-tokyo.ac.jp/

The Yonezawa Laboratory of the University of Tokyo, maintains this informational site. Visit here to learn about its facilities, projects, research groups, publications and people. Available in Japanese and English.

ARTIFICIAL INTELLIGENCE AND NEURAL NETWORKS

Binghamton University Philosophy, Computers and Cognitive Sciences
http://turing.pacss.binghamton.edu/index.html

This Web site provides information on an interdisciplinary program combining coursework in philosophy, computers and cognitive sciences at New York's Binghamton University. Visitors can read recent publications or link to The Journal for Experimental and Theoretical Artificial Intelligence.

Computational Intelligence
http://calypso.cs.uregina.ca/

Computational Intelligence, a journal from the University of Regina in Canada, features research

on artificial intelligence. This site provides information about the journal, as well as on submissions and subscriptions. Tables of contents are available, as are author and title searches.

Computation & Neural Systems
http://www.cns.caltech.edu/

Visitors to this page will find an overview of the Computational & Neural Systems Program at the California Institute of Technology. Information about lab resources, faculty and classes are featured along with links to related sites.

DFKI
http://www.dfki.uni-kl.de/

The German Research Center for Artificial Intelligence provides information about the Center's research projects and facilities. Browsers can read information from the library, link to services or the home page of related divisions and other affiliations.

DFKI Computational Linguistics Lab
http://cl-www.dfki.uni-sb.de/

The Computational Linguistics Lab at the German Research Center for Artificial Intelligence provides information on its projects and staff. Links to publications, an FTP repository and other related resources are also featured.

Distributed Artificial Intelligence at QMW
http://www.elec.qmw.ac.uk/dai/

A program of the Department of Electronic Engineering at London's Queen Mary and Wesfield College, the Distributed Artificial Intelligence Research Unit's site offers a look at its research projects. Also find links to publications, unit members' home pages and related books.

The Distributed Artificial Intelligence Laboratory
http://dis.cs.umass.edu/

The Distributed Artificial Intelligence Laboratory is a part of the Computer Science Department at UMass. Find specific information about its research, publications, presentations and personnel, plus numerous links to topic-related sites.

Edinburgh Department of Artificial Intelligence
http://www.dai.ed.ac.uk/

The University of Edinburgh's Department of Artificial Intelligence hosts this server detailing its programs and services. Browse through an index of degree courses, research efforts and teaching documentation.

Georgia Institute of Technology Cognitive Science
http://www.cc.gatech.edu/cogsci/

This Web site provides information about cognitive science research undertaken at Georgia Tech.

Includes standard departmental details along with research reports in the areas of artificial intelligence, cognitive psychology and engineering and computer science.

German Research Center for Artificial Intelligence

http://www.dfki.uni-sb.de/

The German Research Center for Artificial Intelligence contains a collection of information on the center's research, facilities, programming systems, systems support and associated Web sites.

IJCAI

http://ijcai.org/

The International Joint Conference on Artificial Intelligence (AI) is a professional organization for AI researchers. Visitors will find databases, indexes and information on events in this field.

IMKAI's and OFAI

http://www.ai.univie.ac.at/

The Department of Medical Cybernetics and Artificial Intelligence at the University of Vienna and the Austrian Research Institute for Artificial Intelligence present general overviews of their programs and facilities at this site. Visitors are invited to learn about current research in the field of artificial intelligence. In English and German.

Informatics Group

http://avalon.epm.ornl.gov/

The Informatics Group constructs high-performance computing and artificial intelligence-based analysis systems, as well as database access tools. Visitors to this site can learn more about the group and the tools it has developed.

Institut Dalle Molle d'Intelligence Artificelle Perceptive (IDIAP)

http://www.idiap.ch/

Applied research in artificial intelligence is the focus of this French institute, covering research topics ranging from artificial neural networks to optical character recognition. Get the lowdown on current projects as well as a list of available IDIAP publications and technical reports. In French and English.

ISSCO - A Research Institute for Natural Language Processing

http://issco-www.unige.ch/

This Web site provides historical and organizational information about a University of Geneva research laboratory that studies artificial intelligence and computational linguistics. This page also features links to related sites.

Julia's

http://fuzine.mt.cs.cmu.edu/mlm/julia.html

This home page introduces visitors to Julia, a "chatterbot" robot program that can participate in multi-player computer games. Visitors can talk to Julia or follow links to artificial intelligence resources.

Knowledge Systems Laboratory

http://www-ksl.stanford.edu/

The Knowledge Systems Lab (KSL), an artificial intelligence research laboratory within the Department of Computer Science, Stanford University, focuses on knowledge sharing technologies and adaptive intelligence systems. This site provides more information about the lab, including technical reports.

LSI - Laboratorio de Sistemas Integraveis

http://www.lsi.usp.br/

The Laboratory of Integrated Systems at the University of Sao Paulo in Brazil presents general information and a directory of its divisions, which include artificial intelligence and digital systems. Examples of animation and art projects are included.

Machine Learning Information Services

http://www.lsi.usp.br/

People who have given up on the real thing can consult the Austrian Research Institute for Artificial Intelligence's Machine Learning Information Group for Internet resources pertaining to applied machine learning. Find an extensive list of pointers maintained by the group at this site.

MIT Clinical Decision Making Group

http://medg.lcs.mit.edu/

Located in MIT's Laboratory for Computer Science, the Clinical Decision Making Group researches and develops computer science and artificial intelligence medical applications. Visitors can find out more about its research projects and access its publications, resources and demos.

MIT Computer Architecture Group

http://cag-www.lcs.mit.edu/

The Computer Architecture Group of the Massachusetts Institute of Technology maintains this site for network access. Visit here to link with related research groups, download software, find programming resources and more.

ML & CBR Folks

http://www.aic.nrl.navy.mil/~aha/people.html

This page connects visitors with researchers working on machine learning and case-based reasoning projects. The index is organized alphabetically and by the researchers' geographic locations.

Neural Adaptive Control Technology (NACT)

http://www.mech.gla.ac.uk/~nactftp/nact.html

The Neural Adaptive Control Technology (NACT) research project is an undertaking of Daimler-Benz and Glasgow University. The site hopes to deliver "transparent, constructive and engineering orientated design methods resulting from the consistent and consolidated theory of NACT." A project description is available at the site.

Neural Computing Research Group

http://neural-server.aston.ac.uk/

The Neural Computing Research Group in the Department of Computer Science and Mathematics at Great Britain's Aston University offers visitors to its page a look at its research, courses, seminars and publications. Links to related resources on and off campus are also included.

Neural Networks at Pacific Northwest National Laboratory

http://www.emsl.pnl.gov:2080/docs/cie/neural/neural.homepage.html

The Neural Networks home page describes research activities at the Pacific Northwest National Laboratory (PNNL) in organic and artificial neural networks. Includes information on workshops, specific areas of research and access to related publications from the PNNL.

Neural Networks Group at OFAI

http://www.ai.univie.ac.at/oefai/nn/nngroup.html

The Neural Networks Group at the Austrian Research Institute for Artificial Intelligence introduces its staff of five scientists and explains its research activities through its home page. Visitors can read the group's publications and link to related resources.

Programming Systems Lab at DFKI

http://ps-www.dfki.uni-sb.de/

The Programming Systems Lab at the German Research Center for Artificial Intelligence provides information on its research projects here, with details on the lab's mission, staff, systems and current and future projects.

SRI International

http://www.ai.sri.com/

SRI International maintains this page for its Artificial Intelligence Center (AIC), with information about its research programs, staff, publications and more.

University of Maryland's Laboratory for Advanced Information Technology

http://www.cs.umbc.edu/

This site is the gateway to the University of Maryland's Laboratory for Advanced Information Technology. Located in Catonsville, Md., the lab's home page features information and resources about intelligent information agents, software agents, softbots, knowbots, infobots and more.

University of Michigan AI Lab
http://ai.eecs.umich.edu/

The University of Michigan's Artificial Intelligence Laboratory home page offers an overview of its research projects, educational programs, and research staff. Includes a calendar of events and links to related resources

University of Pavia: The Medical Informatics Laboratory
http://ipvaimed9.unipv.it/

The Medical Informatics Laboratory at the University of Pavia, Italy, is involved in the fields of artificial intelligence in medicine and hospital information systems. This site contains information about the lab, its research, staff, documents, statistics and links to free software.

UTCS Neural Nets Research Group
http://www.cs.utexas.edu/

The Neural Nets Research group at the University of Texas offers information here about its members, alumni, publications, software and research into the fields of artificial intelligence and cognitive science. Visitors can view research demos and virtual posters, or link to a wealth of related Web sites.

BOOKS, INDICES, AND GUIDES

CERN STING Information Service
http://dxsting.cern.ch/sting/sting.html

The Software Technology Interest Group provides visitors to its page pointers to programming resources and computer science archives on the Web. Site features also include STING organizational data and contact information.

Chicago Journal of Theoretical Computer Science
http://cs-www.uchicago.edu/publications/cjtcs/

The "Chicago Journal of Theoretical Computer Science" is a peer-reviewed scholarly journal distributed over the Internet. This site features journal articles, news, editorial information and submission guidelines.

Cognitive Science at Birmingham
http://www.bham.ac.uk/cogsci/home_page.html

The University of Birmingham, U.K., Cognitive Science Program, a cross-disciplinary program supported by the psychology, computer science and philosophy departments, maintains this page with information about departmental research, facilities, courses and more.

The Collection of Computer Science Bibliographies
ftp://ftp.cs.umanitoba.ca/pub/bibliographies/index.html

This site hosts a collection of more than 600 computer science bibliographies. Visitors can browse the archive by subject, link to other computer science resources on the Net, or search the entire collection for specific information.

Comp.human-factors FAQ
http://www.dgp.toronto.edu/people/ematias/faq/contents.html

This page lists FAQs relating to the comp.human-factors newsgroup. The group concerns itself with human characteristics and how they apply to computer design.

comp.speech WWW site
http://www.speech.su.oz.au/comp.speech/

The Speech Technology Group at the University of Sydney, Australia maintains this site for resource access. Visit here for a FAQ index of human and computer speech topics, downloadable software, and group contact information.

Computational Science Education Project
http://www.ccs.uky.edu/csep/csep.html

Sponsored the U.S. Department of Education and aimed at college students, this electronic publication provides an introduction to high-performance computing for would-be computer scientists and engineers. This Web site also offers events listings and a primer on Hypertext Markup Language (HTML).

Computer Almanac - Numbers About Computers
http://www.cs.cmu.edu/afs/cs.cmu.edu/user/bam/www/numbers.html

From the Computer Science Department at Carnegie Mellon University, this page features statistics and other numbers related to computers and computer usage. A table of contents allows quick access into the document.

Computer Architecture
http://www.cs.wisc.edu/~arch/www/

This index of computer architecture resources, maintained by researchers at the University of Wisconsin, provides a wealth of Internet links. Visit here to connect with professional organizations, technical materials, employment opportunities and more.

Computer Science Bibliography Glimpse Server
http://glimpse.cs.arizona.edu:1994/bib/

Glimpse, a computer science bibliographic database maintained at the University of Arizona, offers search facilities for more than 300,000 citations. Topics covered range from artificial intelligence to parallel processing. Search form included.

Computer Science Technical Report Project
http://cs-tr.cs.cornell.edu/Info/cstr.html

The Computer Science Technical Report Project is sponsored by ARPA and seeks to make accessible technical reports from the nation's top computer science departments.

Computer Science Technical Reports Archive Sites
http://daneel.rdt.monash.edu.au/tr/siteslist.html

This lengthy, personally maintained home page indexes Internet sites archiving computer science technical reports. Includes e-mail addresses for the sites' webmasters.

Computing Online Learning Center
http://www-ts.cs.oberlin.edu/

Oberlin College has created a virtual computer learning center for non-computer science students and offers it here. Visitors will learn about the world of computers, multimedia and software development in this online classroom.

The Crossroads Homepage
http://info.acm.org/crossroads/index.html

"Crossroads" is the student magazine of the Association for Computing Machinery, Inc., a scientific and educational organization dedicated to advancing the applications of information technology. Find current and back issues, plus links to indexes and other information.

Digital Libraries and Xerox
http://www.parc.xerox.com/parc-go.html

Xerox's Palo Alto Research Center site posts overviews and bibliographies of digital library research. Includes a prospectus of digital library research it may carry out with Stanford, the University of California (UC), Berkeley or UC Santa Barbara.

Houston Advanced Research Center
http://www.harc.edu/

The Houston Advanced Research Center's home page offers visitors a status report on the HARC-C image compression technology under development. "Corollary," HARC's news magazine, is also available online.

Human-Computer Interaction
http://hydra.bgsu.edu/HCI/

This index to Human-Computer Interaction resources represents a collection of links to everything on the Web the Webmaster could find concerning the interface between humans and computers. Find a gateway to related Web-wide sites using the categorized index offered here.

Information Systems Meta-List

http://www.cait.wustl.edu/cait/infosys.html

This meta-list site provides a comprehensive index of pointers to information systems resources on the Internet.

Information Technology Division of the University of Michigan

http://www.us.itd.umich.edu/itddoc

The Information Technology Division of the University of Michigan maintains this site for a documentation search engine. Visit here to perform a keyword search its instructional and reference materials and link with additional resource locator services.

Interesting Hacks To Fascinate People: The MIT Gallery of Hacks

http://fishwrap.mit.edu/Hacks/Gallery.html

The merry pranksters at the Massachusetts Institute of Technology shed light on the "hack"—the prototypical "clever, benign, and 'ethical' prank or practical joke, which is both challenging for the perpetrators and amusing to the MIT community"—at this site. Includes a "best of" listing and a tool for reporting hacks "in progress."

The Jargon File 3.0.0

http://www.phil.uni-sb.de/fun/jargon/index.html

The document in this site features an index of links related to hacker jargon, slang and techspeak. A jargon lexicon is also featured.

Journal of Artificial Intelligence Research

http://www.cs.washington.edu/research/jair/home.html

This electronic journal covers all aspects of artificial intelligence research. Visitors can browse online editions, search the articles' texts, order bound copies or learn about the publication's editorial staff.

KMi at The Open University, UK

http://kmi.open.ac.uk/

The Knowledge Media Institute at the Open University of London, England provides information on academic programs and research projects in informational sciences and technology. Visitors can read about conferences, admissions guidelines and access the newsletter.

Madison Department of Computer Science Library

http://www.cs.wisc.edu/trs.html

Search for technical reports at any of the participating sites at the University of Wisconsin, Madison Department of Computer Science library. Fielded searches requires HTML forms only. Sorted by subject and authors, these reports are linked to a document name that will allow visitors

to view the document's abstract. Also links the user to a list of other documents by that author.

Michael Trick's Operations Research Page

http://mat.gsia.cmu.edu/

A professor at Carnegie Mellon University's Graduate School of Industrial Administration maintains this site devoted to all aspects of operations research. Includes FAQs along with links to related organizations and resources.

New Hacker's Dictionary

http://www.ccil.org/jargon/jargon_toc.html

Visitors to the New Hacker's Dictionary can get hip to hackers' jargon with the pronunciations, writing and speech styles, definitions and origins included here.

OFAI Library Information System Biblio

http://www.ai.univie.ac.at/biblio.html

The Austrian Research Institute for Artificial Intelligence makes its database of bibliographic information available here. Visitors can query the database for information on research papers, conference papers and journal articles pertaining to the field.

OFAI Library Information System Biblio - Neural Networks

http://www.ai.univie.ac.at/oefai/nn/conn_biblio.html

This reference site indexes more than 5,000 books, research papers and journal articles relating to neural networks. Researchers can search the database by title, author or subject.

Parallel I/O Archive

http://www.cs.dartmouth.edu/pario/

The Parallel I/O Archive contains research reports, bibliographies and other technical resources of interest to the computing research community.

Pattern Recognition Information

http://www.ph.tn.tudelft.nl/PRInfo.html

Pattern recognition research is the study of the operation and design of systems that recognize patterns in data. Information about research, publications and bibliographies is presented at this site, with info about conferences, professional organizations, news and research groups.

PDS: The Performance Database Server

http://netlib2.cs.utk.edu/performance/html/PDStop.html

The Performance Database Server (PDS) archives reports and data related to benchmark- and performance-related testing of various high-tech computers and programs. Related papers and bibliographic information also can be found here.

Robotics Internet Resources

http://piglet.cs.umass.edu:4321/robotics.html

The Laboratory for Perceptual Robotics at the University of Massachusetts hosts this index of robotics resources on the Net. The page contains pointers to FTP sites, robot demos, FAQs and much more.

Scientific Web Resources

http://boris.qub.ac.uk/edward/index.html

Scientists and mathematicians will find a collection of pointers to World Wide Web resources of technical interest here. Ireland's Queens University outlines its own scientific sites and offers links to other resources worldwide.

Signal Processing Information Base (SPIB)

http://softlib.rice.edu/spib.html

A project sponsored by the Signal Processing Society and the National Science Foundation, the Signal Processing Information Base acts as a repository of links and pointers to sites with information or resources relevant to signal processing development and research.

SPLIB: Signal Processing URL Library

http://www-dsp.rice.edu/splib/

Searching for signal processing-related URLs is made easy at this site from the Digital Signal Processing group at Rice University. The library is searchable, but resources are also grouped in categories such as audio, multimedia, robotics and software.

Technology for the National Information Infrastructure

http://www.hpcc.gov/blue95

The Federal High Performance Computing and Communications Program produced a report titled, "Technology for the National Information Infrastructure." Read it here and discover how the U.S. government plans to bolster the country's economy through the development of advanced information systems.

Virtual Museum of Computing

http://www.comlab.ox.ac.uk/archive/other/museums/computing.html

The Virtual Museum of Computing is a compilation of Internet links to places offering exhibits and displays on the history of computers and technology.

VLSI Index

http://www.mrc.uidaho.edu/vlsi/vlsi.html

The Microelectronics Research Center at the University of Idaho posts an index to VLSI-related sites here.

Why Are There So Few Female Computer Scientists

http://www.ai.mit.edu/people/ellens/Gender/pap/pap.html

Read this report to find out. The page contains an abstract and index to the 1991 Massachusetts Institute of Technology technical report, "Why are There so Few Female Computer Scientists," by Ellen Spertus. Societal, environmental and language factors are explored in the report.

Women and Computer Science

http://www.ai.mit.edu/people/ellens/gender.html

Visitors to this site will find an abundance of writings—from the Webmaster and others—on the topic of women and computer science. Other topical resources and info-sites are linked as well.

World Wide Web Virtual Library: Computing, Programming Languages

http://src.doc.ic.ac.uk/bySubject/Computing/Overview.html

Programmers visiting this site will find numerous pointers to online reference materials about computer languages and software development tools.

WWW VL: Human-Computer Interaction

http://www.cs.bgsu.edu/HCI/

Maintained at the Computer Science Department of Bowling Green State University, this page from the WWW Virtual Library contains pointers to Web sites featuring info or resources relevant to human-computer interaction. Includes links to FAQs, software, people, organizations and more.

CONSORTIUMS, PRIVATE INSTITUTES, AND PUBLIC ORGANIZATIONS

Berlin Center for Scientific Computing

http://www.zib-berlin.de/

Germany's Berlin Center for Scientific Computing maintains this site devoted to application-oriented algorithmic mathematics. Find info about the center's research and development programs, its special projects, publications and software and the use of supercomputers in math research.

Center for Advanced Studies, Research and Development (CRS4)

http://www.crs4.it/HTML/homecrs4.html

CRS4, a Sardinia, Italy-based computing research center, develops advanced simulation techniques for the solution of large-scale computational problems. Visit this site for general information, computing resources, Internet search tools and more.

The Center for Nonlinear Studies

http://cnls-www.lanl.gov/

The Center for Nonlinear Studies (CNLS) located at the Los Alamos National Laboratory offers a guide to its facilities and nonlinear science research. Visitors can review the CNLS mission statement, current happenings and workshop programs. Find also access to the Nonlinear Science e-Print archive.

Centre de Recherche Informatitique de Montreal (CRIM)

http://www.crim.ca/

The Centre de Recherche Informatitique de Montreal (CRIM) Web site features current research into parallel computing architectures and software engineering underway at the institution. Includes profiles of speech recognition and human-computer interface research. In French and English.

Computer Professionals for Social Responsibility

http://www.cpsr.org/home

Computer Professionals for Social Responsibility is a public-interest alliance which focuses on the impact of computer technology on society. Visit this page to find info about the group, its members, events and publications, how to get involved, current "hot topics" and CPSR programs.

Computer Science and Mathematics Division at the Oak Ridge National Laboratories

http://www.epm.ornl.gov/

The Computer Science and Mathematics Division at the Oak Ridge National Laboratories provides links to its sections, programs and facilities. Find nuclear, engineering, cognitive and computational sciences employed in the US national interest at this site.

Computing Research Association

http://cra.org/

More than 150 North American academic departments of computer science and engineering, professional societies and industrial laboratories make up the Computing Research Association. You'll find congressional testimony, job listings, academic rankings and a call for more and better research at this site.

Datorforeningen vid Lunds Universitet och Lunds Tekniska Hogskola (DF)

http://www.df.lth.se/

The Computer Society of Sweden's Lund University offers its charter, newsletter, application for membership, library, server stats and links to members' pages. Mostly in Swedish, with some English.

Digital Corporation's Systems Research Center

http://www.research.digital.com/

Digital Corporation's Systems Research Center jumps on emerging technology developments and creates status reports for the enlightment of the people back at Digital's home office. Check out their current research report series at this site.

ECCC - The Electronic Colloquium on Computational Complexity

http://www.eccc.uni-trier.de/eccc/

The Electronic Colloquium on Computational Complexity is an online arena for professionals in this field. Visitors to this site will find reports, books, bibliographies, conference schedules and other related events of interest.

ECRC GmbH

http://www.ecrc.de/

The European Computer-Industry Research Centre (ECRC), located in Munich, Germany, hosts this site providing info on its research in information technologies. In addition, access general info and press releases, staff profiles and an overview of Net services.

ECVNet

http://afrodite.lira.dist.unige.it/

The European Computer Vision Network Relay Server provides news, info and research to the European science and industrial communities working toward technological advances in automation. Visitors to its home page are invited to learn more about the ECVNet, its services and parent organization, and to review available resources.

FORTHnet

http://www.forthnet.gr/

The Foundation for Research and Technology is a computer science research facility located on the island of Crete. Visitors will find information about research projects, descriptions of facilities, links to the Athens News Agency and related resources.

Fourth IEEE International Symposium on High Performance Distributed Computing

http://uvacs.cs.virginia.edu/~hpdc95

The Fourth IEEE International Symposium on High Performance Distributed Computing, held in Virginia in August 1995, provided its program and demonstrations at this Web site along with other conference-related information.

GI-Online: GI im WWW und Internet
http://www.iig.uni-freiburg.de/gi/gi-online.html

The German Computer Society was founded in 1969 in Bonn with the objective of supporting the field of computer science through the sponsorship and development of many types of academic resources including the organization of events and the promotion of university computer science classes. Among other things, this site contains information about the board and its management, departments and special interest groups and ethical guidelines. Most pages here available only in German.

GMD Darmstadt
http://www.darmstadt.gmd.de/

The German National Research Center for Information Technology is a government-supported research institute. Find out how it gathers, analyzes and synthesizes data pertaining to telecommunications and information systems at its home page.

Goddard Space Flight Center Space Data and Computing Division
http://sdcd.gsfc.nasa.gov/SDCD.html

The Space Data and Computing Division at NASA's Goddard Space Flight Center in Greenbelt, Md., maintains this overview of its activities. Find pointers to the Digital Library Technology Project, the Digital Technical Resource Center and other SDCD projects and divisions.

High Performance Computing & Communications: Toward a National Information Infrastructure
http://www.hpcc.gov/blue94/index.html

This is an index to information on the High Performance Computing and Communications Program, which conducts research in computer and network communications, national networks and high-performance computing centers. The site includes illustrations, contacts and a glossary.

ICM
http://www.icm.edu.pl/

Poland's Interdisciplinary Centre for Mathematical and Computational Modelling provides supercomputing technology and resources to the Polish scientific community. Visit this page for details about the center's program. In Polish and English.

InteractiveSISU
http://ernie.sisu.se/

The Swedish Institute for Systems Development (SISU) assists the development of improved competence in information systems development throughout the public and private sectors of the Swedish economy. This support site includes news, services, research, agenda and index information.

International Association for Cryptologic Research
http://www.iacr.org/~iacr/

The home page of the International Association for Cryptologic Research provides information about cryptology conferences and publications. Visit here to learn about its activities, contact its directors and find membership information.ss

International Conference on Software Engineering
http://www.gmd.de/Events/ICSE18/

Germany's International Conference on Software Engineering provides a forum for the dissemination of ideas and research in software engineering. A wealth of info about the March 1996 conference is available here, including a call for papers, guidelines, members and mailing list.

International Federation for Information Processing
http://www.ifip.or.at/

This site contains the home page for the International Federation for Information Processing, an association of professional and technical organizations concerned with information management. Features include the group's mission statement, organizational structure, standing technical committees and affiliations.

ISWorld Net: Text Version
http://www.isworld.org/isworld/isworldtext.html

ISWorld Net assists information scholars locate and use resources related to information technologies and the management of information. This site provides info about the organization, discussion lists, how to contribute and its governance.

KIIS
http://www.kiis.or.jp/

This is the home page for the Kansai Institute of Information Systems, a nonprofit organization devoted to promoting information technologies in the Osaka, Japan area. Visitors will find background information and the home pages of 270 participating businesses. Available in English and Japanese.

LANL ACL
http://www.acl.lanl.gov/Home.html

A collection of organizations that do research in high performance computing.

Linc
http://www.linc.or.jp/

Linc is a wide-area networking independent research club in Japan. This page provides information on the group as well as a roster of its members and their home pages. In English and Japanese.

Los Alamos National Laboratory Advanced Computing Lab
http://www.acl.lanl.gov/

Explore current programs and projects of the Los Alamos National Laboratory's Advanced Computing Lab at this site. High performance computing and parallel computation research resources can be accessed.

Maui High Performance Computing Center
http://www.mhpcc.edu/mhpcc.html

Managed by a consortium led by the University of New Mexico, this center provides research and development supercomputing resources for Air Force and Department of Defense labs. Site visitors will find technical documentation, information on current research and project development, and more.

NASA/WVU Software Research Laboratory
http://atlantis.ivv.nasa.gov/

The Software Research Laboratory, a joint program of the U.S. National Aeronautics and Space Administration and West Virginia University, maintains this informational site. Visitors here for news, project and technical documentation, lecture and events information, staff profiles and more.

Naval Research Laboratory Information Technology Division
http://www.itd.nrl.navy.mil/

In an effort to improve military operations, the Information Technology Division of the Naval Research Laboratory studies and develops programs for the collection, transmission and processing of information. Find out more about the ITD and the NRL, plus find links to related sites.

NCSA BLANCA Testbed
http://www.ncsa.uiuc.edu/General/CC/CCBLANCA.html

Computer scientists can read a brief description of the BLANCA Testbed, a gigabyte-per-second network research program at the University of Illinois at Urbana-Champaign. The site provides links to all the program's partners and supporters.

Norwegian Computing Center
http://www.nr.no/

The Norwegian Computing Center is a research institute for information technology and applied statistics. Information about the center's various departments and its faculty members' research endeavors can be found here, in both English and Norwegian.

NSF Scientific Computing Division
http://http.ucar.edu/scd.html

The Scientific Computing Division, a part of the National Science Foundation, supports supercomputing in atmospheric, oceanic and related research fields. This page provides links to related sites and resources.

Object Management Group

http://www.omg.org/

The Object Management Group is a nonprofit organization that promotes the theory and practice of "object technology" for computing systems. This site includes detailed information on OMG, plus access to its publications and staff. Also find links to other object technology Web sites.

Olivetti Research Laboratory (ORL)

http://www.cam-orl.co.uk/

Olivetti Research Laboratory (ORL), part of the research and development organization of Ing. C. Olivetti & C., S.p.A., is located in Cambridge, England. This site has information about ORL's research, searchable technical reports and papers and links to related sites.

Research Center

http://www.arc.nasa.gov/

The U.S. National Aeronautics and Space Administration's Ames Research Center specializes in the fields of information systems technologies, supercomputing and artificial intelligence. Visit this site for links to information about its mission, projects and related resources.

Richo California Research Center

http://www.crc.ricoh.com/

The California Research Center concerns itself with the science of information, "from basic science through applied research to advanced prototyping." This center, owned by the Japanese firm Ricoh, uses its page to introduce CREW, what the webmaster calls "a completely new type of image compression system."

Robotics and Control-Related Conferences

http://www.cee.hw.ac.uk/~acc/conf-list.html

Scientists and engineers can block out time for professional events using the information provided at the Robotics and Control Related Conferences site. Find links to upcoming conferences, symposia and workshops listed here in date order.

RXRC Cambridge Laboratory (EuroPARC)

http://www.rxrc.xerox.com/home.html

The RXRC Cambridge Laboratory, formerly known as EuroPARC, is profiled on this page. Visitors can read about members of the laboratory, check an overview of the laboratory and read about current research on such things as context-based information systems.

SIGART Electronic Information Service

http://sigart.acm.org/

This site contains the home page of the Association for Computing Machinery's (ACM) Special Interest Group (SIG) for Artificial Intelligence. Features include links to information about SIGART and ACM, conference and workshop notices, bulletins and other related Web sites.

Sony Computer Science Laboratory Inc.

http://www.csl.sony.co.jp/

Dedicated to promoting technical and social development through original research, Sony's Computer Science Lab gives info on its research in distributed operating systems and computer networks. Also find a clickable guide to the lab, FAQs and links to other sites.

Special Interest Group on Management of Data

http://bunny.cs.uiuc.edu/

SIGMOND is the information server of the Association for Computing Machinery's Special Interest Group on Management of Data. Includes access to record archives, databases, software, publications and other resources.

Swedish Institute of Computer Science

http://www.sics.se/

Visitors to this nonprofit research foundation's home page can learn about the institute's research, read its publications, download software or access its electronic library. Includes job opportunities listings.

UK Simulation Interoperability Working Group

http://siwg.dra.hmg.gb/

The UK Simulation Interoperability Working Group provides information on its systems, organizations, research activities, events and employment opportunities. Includes links to other simulation-related Web sites.

Usenix Association

http://www.usenix.org/

This home page for Usenix, the advanced computing systems professional and technical association, also provides information on SAGE, the System Administrators Guild. Designed for members, options include links to the calendar of events, the membership directory and publications.

THE CUTTING EDGE

Agent Info

http://www.cs.bham.ac.uk/~amw/agents/index.html

The Agent Info page concerns, "the use of autonomous agents in the fields of HCI and CSCW - commonly referred to as Interface Agents." Resources here include papers, links to projects and technology pages, and information about conferences, mailing lists and more.

Autonomous Agents Group

http://agents.www.media.mit.edu/groups/agents/

The Media Laboratory of the Massachusetts Institute of Technology maintains this informational site for its Agents Group projects and members. Visit here for a index of researchers, current projects and scientific papers.

Basel University Biocomputing

http://www.ch.embnet.org/

The Swiss national EMBnet node is featured at Basel University's biocomputing site. There are biocomputing research resources, including newsletters and archives.

Biomedical Information Communication Center

http://www.ohsu.edu/

The Biomedical Information Communication Center (BICC) at Oregon Health Sciences University conducts research into the field of medical informatics, the study of the use of information technology (such as computers) in the teaching and practice of health care. At the BICC Web site, visitors can read about the Center's educational and research activities or link to other biological and medical resources.

Carnegie Mellon University Vision and Autonomous Systems Center

http://www.cs.cmu.edu/~vaschelp/

The Vision and Autonomous Systems Center at the Carnegie Mellon University Robotics Institute provides this help page for researchers to learn about VASC software and access documentation. Includes search tools and links to other university servers and related resources.

Center for Computational Biology

http://www.compbio.caltech.edu/

The Center for Computational Biology at the California Institute of Technology maintains this site for general information and resource access. Visit here to find information about programming languages, networking systems and computational biology applications.

The Center for Spoken Language Understanding

http://www.cse.ogi.edu/CSLU/

The Center for Spoken Language Understanding at the Oregon Graduate Institute of Science and Technology aims to develop state-of-the-art spoken language systems. Browsers will get an overview of its research here and can download journals, theses and conference proceedings.

Computational Phonology

http://www.cogsci.ed.ac.uk/phonology/CompPhon.html

The Center for Cognitive Science at the University of Edinburgh, Scotland, provides this information server about computational phonology. Visit here for reference resources, published articles and links to the main university home page.

Computer Supported Cooperative Work Research Group

http://orgwis.gmd.de/

The Research Group on Computer Supported Cooperative Work in Germany studies the problems of working groups distributed in time and space and develops support systems. The site presents information on research, projects and publications.

Computer Vision Lab

http://vision.ce.pusan.ac.kr/

Prospective computer engineering students will get an overview of the Computer Vision Lab in Korea's Pusan National University here. The page details some of the lab's work and provides links to the Department of Computer Engineering and the university home pages.

Document Image Understanding Information Server

http://documents.cfar.umd.edu/

This home page, maintained by the University of Maryland at College Park's document-processing group, offers technological information, data sets, source code and access to online publications related to optical character recognition (OCR) and document understanding theory.

Duke University Medical Center: Division of Medical Informatics

http://dmi-www.mc.duke.edu/

The Division of Medical Informatics at Duke University Medical Center provides information about its training program, its history, requirements for admission and course descriptions. Includes links to faculty, research groups and other Medical Center servers.

Face Recognition

http://www.cs.rug.nl/~peterkr/FACE/face.html

The Face Recognition home page has information on technology, hardware and software research of human face recognition technology. This page includes links to research groups, commercial and free software, publications and information on conferences worldwide.

Genetic Programming

http://www.salford.ac.uk/docs/depts/eee/genetic.html

The Genetic Programming home page contains listings of software, related publications and research personnel. It also includes information on genetically programmed art, music and a FAQ.

GMD Institut FIT

http://zeus.gmd.de/

One of eight research institutes located near Bonn, the GMD Institute for Applied Information Technology researches artificial intelligence in computers, human interaction with computers and cooperation systems. Its recent publications are online here.

Graphics, Visualization and Usability (GVU) Center

http://www.cc.gatech.edu/gvu/

The Graphics, Visualization & Usability Center at the Georgia Institute of Technology works to develop technologies which make computers accessible to the masses. Find a searchable database of technical reports as well as links to newsgroups and other resources.

Harvard Robotics Laboratory

http://hrl.harvard.edu/

Links to people, projects, reports and events at the Harvard Robotics Laboratory are provided here. Also featured are pointers to related resources.

Human-Computer Interaction at Stanford

http://www-pcd.stanford.edu/hci.html

Stanford University's Program in Human-Computer Interaction features information about its 1995-96 programs on this home page. It includes details about the faculty, HCI-related degree programs and information about current research.

Human Computer Interaction Laboratory

http://is.twi.tudelft.nl/hci/

The Human Computer Interaction Laboratory home page contains information on research in extending computer sensory boundaries. Includes research into interfaces between computers and vision, hearing and touch. Entries include conferences and workshops, publications, reviews, research groups and links to relevant resources.

Human Interface Technology Laboratory

http://www.hitl.washington.edu/

The Human Interface Technology Laboratory page contains general information about the Laboratory, its research projects and staff. Includes site update info, links to publications and the Virtual Worlds Consortium.

Information Science Research Institute

http://www.isri.unlv.edu/

The Information Science Research Institute at the University of Nevada sets out to "foster the improvement of automated technologies for understanding machine-printed documents" in the advancement towards a "paperless society." This home page provides information on the organization, its people, publications, and activities.

Institute for Integrated Publication and Information Systems

http://www.darmstadt.gmd.de/IPSI/index1.html

Maintained by the German National Research Center for Information Technology, this Web site explains the activities of the Institute for Integrated Publication and Information Systems. Visitors can learn about the institute's development of hypermedia systems, multimedia protocols and cognitive user interfaces.

Laboratory for Molecular Robotics

http://www-lmr.usc.edu/~/mr

The University of Southern California's Laboratory for Molecular Robotics peers into the world of nanotechnology. Meet the scientists trying to create nanorobots—machines built on atomic scale—at this site.

Laboratory for Perceptual Robotics

http://piglet.cs.umass.edu:4321/lpr.html

The Laboratory for Perceptual Robotics (LPR) of the University of Massachusetts' computer science department researches a variety of subjects, from mobile robot navigation to assembly planning. Included at this site are movies of robotics lab demos, a virtual tour and faculty information.

Machine Listening Group at MIT

http://sound.media.mit.edu/

The Machine Listening Group engages in research to create machines that can understand and simulate sound cues in natural acoustic environments. Find information on the group's projects and publications, plus links to related resources.

MIT's Spoken Language Systems Group

http://sls-www.lcs.mit.edu/

The Spoken Language Systems Group at the Massachusets Institute of Technology is working to develop interactive conversational systems. Visitors here will get an overview of the group's members, projects and research.

NASA Ames Biocomputation Center

http://biocomp.arc.nasa.gov/

Ames Biocomputation Center, a research facility of the U.S. National Aeronautics and Space Administration, develops three-dimensional computer visualization technology for biology applications. Visit here for news, staff and facilities profiles, and links to sample programs.

NASA Ames Intelligent Mechanisms Group

http://maas-neotek.arc.nasa.gov/

The Intelligent Mechanisms Group at NASA's Ames Research Center focuses on developing and building intelligent mechanisms without bias toward any platform or application. Visitors to its home page can learn more about the group and its work, as well as link to other topic-related sites.

NASA Space Telerobotics Program

http://ranier.oact.hq.nasa.gov/telerobotics.html

The NASA Space Telerobotics Program develops telerobotics for remote manipulation. Learn more about about the program here and link to hands-on resources such as Xavier, an Internet-guided robot wandering around Carnegie Mellon University or an interactive model railroad set in Germany.

People, Computers and Design

http://www-pcd.stanford.edu/

The interaction between humans and computers is examined at the Project on People, Computers and Design site. A program of Stanford University, the project encourages research and education in the field of human computer interaction and software design.

University of Southampton VSSP Group

http://www.cs.rochester.edu/

The Vision Speech Signal Processing page of the University of Southhampton includes information about research projects in speech processing, intelligent systems, computer vision and image processing. Includes links to history trivia, movie reviews, a multimedia lab and Unix software descriptions.

Xerox User Interface Research

http://www.msi.umn.edu/

The University of Minnesota, in conjunction with the Minnesota Supercomputer Center Inc., offers information about this interdisciplinary academic institution. Visitors will find details on seminars, workshops, grants and internships in the field of supercomputing.

The Yale Vision and Robotics Group

http://www.cs.yale.edu/HTML/YALE/VISION/GroupPR.html

The Yale University Robotics Group practices cross-disciplinary projects in robotics. The group researches the junctures of computer science, neuroscience, psychology and engineering. Associated faculty members' home pages are linked to this site.

EARTH SCIENCES AND THE ENVIRONMENT

ARCHIVES AND INDICES (GENERAL)

Central European Environmental Data Request Facility

http://pan.cedar.univie.ac.at/

The Central European Environmental Data Request (CEDAR) Facility provides access to relevant databases, research groups and institutions dealing with ecological research and study.

Crustal Dynamics Data Information System

http://cddis.gsfc.nasa.gov/cddis.html

Find geodesy and geodynamics related data archived at this NASA information storage site. Links to current program and activity information, related NASA resources and programs, and related international resources and programs are featured.

Earth and Environmental Science

http://info.er.usgs.gov/network/science/earth/index.html

Maintained by the U.S. Geological Survey (USGS), this site offers visitors an index of non-USGS resources by topic. Categories include climate, earth science, earthquake, environment, hydrology, oceanography and volcanology.

Earth Science Related Pointers

http://www.ems.psu.edu/RelatedWebSites.html

Maintained by Penn State's College of Earth and Mineral Sciences, this page provides links to sites relevant to earth sciences. Find environment, weather and geography sites, plus teacher resources and pages for kids.

Earthwatch Radio Gopher

gopher://gopher.adp.wisc.edu/11/.news/.special/.sea/.ew/

Search this archive for the scripts from Earthwatch Radio programs, which are sponsored by the Sea Grant Institute and the Institute for Environmental Studies at the University of Wisconsin-Madison. Each program is a two-minute segment on science and the environment.

EnviroLink Network

http://www.envirolink.org

The EnviroLink Network is a nonprofit organization that operates as a resource for environmental information. This page includes an environmental library, the Internet Green marketplace and search tools.

Environmental and Environment-related Acronyms

http://kaos.erin.gov.au/general/acronyms.html

This list of environment-related acronyms has been drawn up for use in the Environment, Sport and Territories Portfolio of the Australian government. For quick reference, a search form is attached to the page.

Environmental Measurements

http://globe.fsl.noaa.gov/input/input.html

GLOBE maintains this page of online environmental resources. Links to information and resources about the earth's atmosphere and climate, hydrology, biology and geology are available here.

Galaxy Geosciences

http://galaxy.einet.net/galaxy/Science/Geosciences.html

Read information on the earth sciences at this library of articles, directories and collections courtesy of TradeWave's online service, Galaxy. Find a comprehensive listing of links to Web sites focused on geochemistry, geology, geophysics and meteorology.

The Global Land Information System

http://sun1.cr.usgs.gov/glis/glis.html

The Global Land Information System is an interactive computer system designed by the U.S. Geological Survey to provide scientists information about the Earth's land surfaces. Visitors to this site can access the database of files.

The HAPEX-Sahel Information System

http://www.orstom.fr/hapex

The HAPEX-Sahel Information System offers an interdisciplinary database with "contributed studies in hydrology, soil moisture, surface fluxes and vegetation, remote sensing science and meteorology." Anyone can browse, but only registered investigators can download data.

Lamont-Doherty Earth Observatory Geology Resource Index

http://www.ldeo.columbia.edu/

The Lamont-Doherty Earth Observatory of Columbia University maintains this informational site for its index of geology and earth sciences resources. Visit this site for an extensive collection of links to educational, government and commercial organizations. Includes staff and departmental information.

Long Term Ecological Research (LTER) Gopher

gopher://lternet.edu:70/1

Learn about the U.S. Long-Term Ecological Research Network (LTER) through this gopher site that includes basic information along with a world of publications and general links for ecologists. Visitors can even check out software tools designed especially for ecologists.

National Environmental Information Resources Center

http://www.gwu.edu/~greenu/

The National Environmental Information Resources Center site contains general info about the Center and pointers to numerous environmental sites. Includes links to educational programs, Usenet news groups and Web search engines.

Other Environmental Information Servers

http://kaos.erin.gov.au/other_servers/other_servers.html

At this site browsers will find servers of environmental information, collected by the Environmental Resources Information Network. Sorted by world region and category, the index is searchable.

The Progressive Directory @igc

http://www.igc.apc.org/index.html

The Institute for Global Communications present its Progressive Directory, a gateway to environmental and progressive resources around the globe, through this home page. Among the links are pointers to PeaceNet, EcoNet, ConflictNet, LaborNet and WomensNet.

REINAS Home Page

http://csl.cse.ucsc.edu/reinas.html

The Real-time Environmental Information Network and Analysis System (REINAS) is a database supporting real-time and retrospective regional environmental science maintained by the Baskin Center at the University of California, Santa Cruz. Demonstrations of REINAS are available at this site, along with information on the systems components and related projects.

Rockhounds Information Page

http://www.rahul.net/infodyn/rockhounds/rockhounds.html

Dedicated to rock collectors, this site offers a plethora of links to topical resources and materials. Find mailing lists, software, clubs, commercial sites, articles, images, and sites related to the study of Earth Sciences.

U.S. Geological Survey Internet Resources

http://www.usgs.gov/network/index.html

The U.S. Geological Survey provides this index to sites containing scientific research and databases related to earth sciences, cartography and environmental issues.

ASSOCIATIONS AND ORGANIZATIONS

The American Geophysical Union

http://earth.agu.org/kosmos/homepage.html

The American Geophysical Union is an international society with over 32,000 members and a motto that reads "unselfish cooperation in research." The union profiles its work here and posts articles on science and society, meeting schedules and information on its publications.

Earth and Environmental Sciences Center

http://terrassa.pnl.gov:2080/

The Earth and Environmental Sciences Center of The Pacific Northwest Laboratory in Richland, Wash. maintains this site containing general information and resources. Visit here to learn about the center, view technical reports, connect with related Web sites and more.

Earthwatch International

http://gaia.earthwatch.org/

Earthwatch International is a nonprofit organization that sponsors scientific field research. It aims to improve human understanding of the planet and our impact on it. Visit for a look at the group and to learn about how to join research efforts in

the field. The site includes pointers to the group's international offices.

Finnish Association for Nature Conservation

http://www.sll.fi/

The Finnish Association for Nature Conservation maintains this informational site for its environmental interest group. Visit here to learn what Finlandians are doing to protect their forests, water and air. Available in a mix of Finnish and English.

International Geothermal Association

http://www.demon.co.uk/geosci/igahome.html

The International Geothermal Association provides information here about geothermal energy. The page also contains details about the organization's scope, mission and members.

COMMERCIAL

COMPANIES

Alpha Analytical Labs

http://world.std.com/~alphalab

Alpha Analytical Labs, a New England-based environmental analysis laboratory, gives an overview of its services, pricing and facilities on this promotional page.

The Cygnus Group

http://www.cygnus-group.com:9011/

The Cygnus Group helps businesses implement environmentally sound planning, marketing and communications programs. The Michigan-based firm gives an overview of its services on this promotional page.

Eco-Rating International

http://www.eco-rating.com/

Eco-Rating International is an environmental agency that determines if a company passes the "green" litmus test. A panel of professionals judges performances, awarding leaves of approval to qualifying firms. Read about the process and take a look at the company scores.

Eikon Group Inc.

http://www.worldweb.com/Eikon

Eikon Group, a Canada-based oil and gas consulting group, provides an overview of its work here. It pitches its principles, strengths, services, abilities and resources on this promotional page.

Khem Products

http://www.khem.com/home.html

Khem Products provides information on its environmental systems software products for the U.S. and world markets. One such product is a regulatory compliance chemical-tracking and inventory-management system. A company profile is included.

A Program for Aquifer Data Evaluation

http://www.us.net/adept/welcome.html

Download a demo copy of ADEPT, a program for aquifer data evaluation, or look at a slide show about the program on this promotional page for Consulting Hydrogeology & Environmental Software Services Inc. Visitors can also access information about the corporation's scientific and Web-development services.

Serveur WWW du BRGM

http://www.brgm.fr/

Environmentalists and miners will find common ground at BRGM, a French firm combining scientific research with a commitment to public service and a clean earth. Find out more about the company's research and international activities here.

NEW TECHNOLOGIES/ SOFTWARE

Datasurge Geotechnical Engineering Software Development

http://www.usa1.com/datasurg

Datasurge is a software company offering titles that deal with geological data intensive tasks such as soil testing, rock mechanics and boring logs. Get a list of software packages, download a demo and peruse a partial list of clients at this site.

The Global Network of Environment and Technology

http://www.gnet.org/

The Global Network of Environment and Technology (GNET) offers this presentation as a gateway to environmental technology business news. Find institutions and organizations that deal with marketing, products and opportunities.

Grid Analysis and Display System

http://grads.iges.org/grads/head.html

The Grid Analysis and Display System (GrADS), an Unix and DOS application used for displaying earth sciences data, is explained and available here. It is freeware.

RockWare Incorporated Earth Science Software

http://www.aescon.com/rockware/index.htm

Products such as RockWorks and MacGeoPak from RockWare's collection of earth science software are featured here. Company information, a dealer listing, a catalog, demos and free software are provided.

CONSERVATION AND RESOURCE MANAGEMENT

ENERGY CONSERVATION

E&E Web Page

http://eande.lbl.gov/EE.html

The Lawrence Berkeley National Laboratory's Energy and Environment Division hosts scientists, economists and architects pursuing multidisciplinary research into environment-friendly energy uses. Visitors to this page can monitor the progress of ongoing research projects.

Economic Forum (Communications for a Sustainable Future)

gopher://csf.colorado.edu:70/11/eforum

Communications for a Sustainable Future sponsors several forums. Visitors will find the energy forum here and can download interviews, book reviews and discussion on the topic.

Energy and the Environment

http://zebu.uoregon.edu/energy.html

The University of Oregon's Energy and the Environment site contains links to the school's online classes, an animated wind farm and a fossil fuel primer. Includes information about energy resources and fusion.

Energy Efficiency and Renewable Energy Program

http://www.ornl.gov/ORNL/Energy_Eff/Energy_Eff.html

The Energy Efficiency and Renewable Energy Program, part of the Oak Ridge National Laboratory, features its research and development program through its home page. Visitors can read detailed descriptions about the program and its achievements.

Energy Information Administration

http://www.eia.doe.gov/

The Energy Information Administration is the "U.S. government's statistical agency with responsibility for the collection and dissemination of energy data and analysis." Visit this searchable Web site to find answers to Frequently Asked Questions (FAQ), energy market analyses, consumption and price data, and other related items and links.

Hanford Home Page

http://www.hanford.gov/

The Hanford Nuclear Reservation is located near Richland, in southeast Washington. Its plutonium reactors have been mothballed; now it supports research in waste management, environmental restoration and energy. Visitors will learn about its work here.

International Geothermal Association

http://www.demon.co.uk/geosci/igahome.html

The International Geothermal Association provides information here about geothermal energy. Includes details about the organization's scope, mission and members.

National Energy Authority of Iceland

http://www.os.is/

Visitors to this Web server will find an organizational overview of Iceland's National Energy Authority and information on its employees. Information about the country and links to other Internet servers are also featured. In Icelandic with some English.

National Renewable Energy Laboratory

http://info.nrel.gov/

The Department of Energy's National Renewable Energy Laboratory researches energy efficiency. Visitors here can read about its programs in alternative fuels, photovoltaics, wind technology and hybrid vehicles.

National Supercomputing Center for Energy and the Environment

http://www.nscee.edu/

Located at the University of Nevada, Las Vegas, the National Supercomputing Center for Energy and the Environment offers supercomputer training and services to various public and private institutions conducting research on energy and the environment. The NSCEE home page offers a virtual tour of the facility and info on current research projects.

Oak Ridge National Laboratory

http://www.ornl.gov/

Oak Ridge National Laboratory, a facility of the Department of Energy, conducts research on energy resources and the environment. Visitors to its Web page can access an overview of the lab, review its research projects and publications, learn the latest lab news and link to related sites.

The Rocky Mountain Institute

http://www.rmi.org/

Rocky Mountain Institute in Snowmass, Colo., is a nonprofit research foundation headed by energy gurus Amory and Hunter Lovins. Its goal is to "foster the efficient and sustainable use of resources as a path to global security." Visit for a look at its work in energy, water, green development and much more.

Solstice: Sustainable Energy and Development Online!

http://solstice.crest.org/

Maintained by the Center for Renewable Energy and Sustainable Technology, Solstice provides visitors information and links to resources concerning energy efficiency, renewable energy and sustainable living technologies. Visitors are encouraged to register and leave comments.

Texas A&M University Energy Systems Lab

http://www-esl.tamu.edu/

Texas A&M University demonstrates its commitment to energy conservation by sponsoring environmental engineering research at the Energy Systems Lab. Read about the lab's work in the Texas LoanSTAR Program, a state project designed to monitor energy use and recommend energy-saving retrofits. Site visitors can also access papers on energy audits and conservation and download software that analyzes energy consumption data.

United Nations Environment Programme Collaborating Centre

http://www.risoe.dk/sys/ucc

The home page of this United Nations Environment Programme (UNEP) center tells about its efforts to incorporate environmental considerations into world-wide energy planning. Visitors can learn about the research and other efforts of the organization's team of scientists, engineers and economists.

U.S. Department of Energy's Energy Efficiency and Renewable Energy Network

http://www.eren.doe.gov/

The goal of the Department of Energy's Office of Energy Efficiency and Renewable Energy is to develop efficient technologies that are affordable. The office gives a detailed look at its various projects and partnerships here and provides extensive information about energy efficient and renewable technologies.

INSTITUTES AND UNIVERSITIES

Biodiversity and Ecosystems Network (BENE)

http://straylight.tamu.edu/bene/bene.html

The EPA, the National Performance Review, the Smithsonian and the W.M. Keck Center have teamed up to create this network, which exchanges ideas on the emerging discipline of ecosystem management. Visit here for a look at the network's projects and to access its mailing list and FTP archives.

Center for Coastal and Land-Margin Research

http://amb1.ccalmr.ogi.edu/

The Center for Coastal and Land-Margin Research is housed at the Oregon Graduate Institute of Science and Technology. It provides information on its research, programs, faculty and students here.

Finnish Forest Research Institute Gopher Menu

gopher://gopher.metla.fi:70/11

The Finnish Forest Research Institute provides access to forestry databases and archives here. The site also contains information on services in forestry and natural resources. In English and Finnish.

Germinal

http://dgrwww.epfl.ch/GERMINAL/Germinal.html

The GERMINAL Project, established by the Swiss Federal Institute of Technology, develops high-technology environmental management systems. Visit this site to learn about the project and its applications.

Resources for the Future

http://www.rff.org/

Resources for the Future is a natural resources think tank that aims to help people make better decisions about conservation. Visitors to its site can read its discussion papers and articles and order its books.

The Rocky Mountain Institute

http://www.rmi.org/

Rocky Mountain Institute in Snowmass, Colo., is a nonprofit research foundation headed by energy gurus Amory and Hunter Lovins. Its goal is to "foster the efficient and sustainable use of resources as a path to global security." Visit for a look at its work in energy, water, green development and much more.

School of Forest Resources and Conservation Home Page

http://aris.sfrc.ufl.edu/Welcome.html

The home page for this program at the University of Florida, Miami, provides general information about academic programs in forest study and conservation, research projects and faculty. This page includes links to other university servers.

School of Natural Resources and Environment

http://www.snre.umich.edu/

The University of Michigan's School of Natural Resources and Environment undertakes a scientific interrogation of environmental management, policy and advocacy. Explore the school's academic programs and related information resources at this site.

Solstice: CREST Information

http://solstice.crest.org/common/crestinfo.html

The Center for Renewable Energy and Sustainable Technology in Washington, D.C., presents its quarterly newsletters and introduces its staff through this home page provided by Solstice Internet Services.

The Stockholm Environment Institute

http://www.channel1.com/users/tellus/seib.html

The Stockholm Environment Institute presents information about its global environmental studies and software resources here. Read about how the institute is establishing methods of sustainable development and "assessing alternative futures in order to guide policy today."

University of Alberta Department of Renewable Resources

http://www.rr.ualberta.ca/

The Department of Renewable Resources is home to University of Alberta programs in environmental and conservation sciences and forestry, as well as the land resources (soil science) major within the Agriculture program. Details on the department, its people and activities are available here.

Worldwatch Institute

gopher://gopher.igc.apc.org/11/orgs/worldwatch

The Worldwatch Institute, an ecological organization dedicated to "fostering a sustainable society," conducts interdisciplinary research on emerging global issues. This gopher includes tables of contents from past issues of World Watch Magazine, state-of-the-world reports, topic-specific studies and more.

LAND

The Blue Goose Server

http://bluegoose.arw.r9.fws.gov/

The Blue Goose Server provides information on the National Wildlife Refuge System and subjects relevant to wildlife and natural resources management. This site includes links to the U.S. Fish and Wildlife Service, related resources and tools to search the Internet.

SOIL

Canadian Soil Information System

http://res.agr.ca/PUB/CANSIS/_overview.html

The Canadian Soil Information System describes the location and characteristics of Canadian soil types and how they relate to biological productivity. The site includes descriptions of landscape attributes such as slope, surface form and rock outcroppings. Includes links to related resources.

WATER

American River/Folsom Dam Update by CERES

http://ceres.ca.gov/topic/American.html

The California Department of Water Resources and CERES, a program of the California Resources Agency, maintain this site to provide project updates. Visit here to learn about the American River/Folsom Dam project and link to related departments and agencies.

Barwon Water Authority

http://www.barwonwater.vic.gov.au/

The Water Authority of Australia's Barwon Region details its mission and water quality policies here. The site includes a look at the authority's staff and an archive of press releases.

California Department of Water Resources

http://www.water.ca.gov/

The California Department of Water Resources posts a gateway to its various sites here. Visitors can access the department's main page, as well as the California Cooperative Snow Surveys, the Division of Planning and other related official sites.

Canada Centre for Inland Waters, Burlington

http://www.cciw.ca/

The Canadian National Water Research Institute presents this page on inland waters. Visitors will find research information, program descriptions and discussions of ecological issues here. In English and French.

The Cooperative Research Centre for Freshwater Ecology

http://lake.canberra.edu.au/crcfe/crchome.html

The Cooperative Research Centre for Freshwater Ecology (CRCFE) focuses on improving the management of Australian water resources. The site includes information on the center and its programs, as well as a directory, an online newsletter and other publications. Links to CRCFE partners and related sites are included.

Dutch Ministry of Transport, Public Works and Water Management

http://www.minvenw.nl/

The Netherlands' Ministry of Transport, Public Works and Water Management posts directives from and descriptions of its divisions here. In Dutch, French and English.

The Edwards Aquifer

http://www.txdirect.net/users/eckhardt

Hardly a watered-down page of information, the description of Edwards Aquifer, a massive underground water system in Texas, includes maps and charts that point out drainage and recharge.

Find out its significance to natural resources and how it's managed here.

Edwards Aquifer Information Page

http://eardc.swt.edu/Edwards-info.html

Journey through the Edwards Aquifer via a series of movie clips at this informational Web site. The aquifer spans from north of Austin, Tex., under San Antonio and on to Bracketville; it is critical habitat for a number of endangered species.

Edwards Aquifer Research and Data Center

http://eardc.swt.edu/

The Edwards Aquifer Research and Data Center provides information here on the underground reservoir that supplies water for more than 1.5 million people in the San Marcos, Texas, area. The site includes information on endangered species of the region.

The Groundwater Remediation Project

http://gwrp.cciw.ca/

The Groundwater Remediation Project, part of Environment Canada, focuses on groundwater issues and education. This site has research, publications, software and other resources. In French and English.

Middle East Water Information Network Home Page

http://www.ssc.upenn.edu/~mewin/

The Middle East Water Information Network, working to improve water resource management in the Middle East, maintains this informational site. Visitors can learn about the University of Pennsylvania-based organization and find out how to join its membership of scientists and legal professionals.

U.S. Geological Survey Water Resources in California

http://water.wr.usgs.gov/

The U.S. Geologic Survey provides information about water resources in California on this page. Visitors will find current stream flow conditions in the state and bulletins about floods and earthquakes. The extensive site also includes information on water quality programs and various hydrological data.

Water Resource Research Center

http://ag.arizona.edu/AZWATER

This page, from Arizona State University's Water Resources Research Center, provides issue summaries, stream-gauge maps, a directory for the Southwest and a searchable database for the state's universities.

Water Resources Home Page

http://www.dwr.csiro.au/

Australia's Institute of National Resources and Environment presents the home page for its Divi-

sion of Water Resources. Visitors will find publications and research documentation of the division's programs.

Water Resource Systems Research Unit

http://wrsru7.ncl.ac.uk/

The Water Resource Systems Research Unit is a group within the Department of Civil Engineering at England's Newcastle-upon-Tyne University. Find a general overview of the program as well as specific research project reports at this site.

WETLANDS & MARSHES

Great Lakes Regional Environmental Information System

http://epawww.ciesin.org/

Visit this site to watch the recovery taking place in the North's massive wetland areas. The Great Lakes Regional Environmental Information System page highlights initiatives and recovery programs currently underway.

ENVIRONMENTAL ADVOCACY

ASSOCIATIONS AND ORGANIZATIONS

The Audubon Society

http://www.audubon.org/

The National Audubon Society, a New York, N.Y.-based nonprofit wildlife and environmental conservation organization, maintains this informational site. Visit here for news and activity updates, project profiles, government affairs resources, links to local chapters, membership information, and more.

Conservation Volunteers Northern Ireland!

http://www.btcv.org.uk/

Irish environmentalists join forces online with the organizing help of the Conservation Volunteers of Northern Ireland. Irish initiatives to save the planet are outlined here, and environmental troops are marshaled.

Earth Pledge Foundation Home

http://www.earthpledge.org/

The Earth Pledge Foundation was created at the 1992 Earth Summit in Rio de Janeiro to promote sustainable development. It gives an overview of its projects here, posts books reviews and details its essay and kids art contests.

Environmental Organizations

http://envirolink.org/orgs/index.html

Green activists can stay in cyber touch here. This site includes a directory of environmental organizations and resources, as well as general pointers to nonprofits.

Environmental Working Group

http://www.ewg.org/

The Environmental Working Group researches a wide range of environmental issues. Visit here for scientific, political and economic looks at farming, pesticides, drinking water and much more.

The European Centre for Nature Conservation

http://www.ecnc.nl/

Europe's many environmental groups are linked through the ECNC, the European Centre for Nature Conservation. The pan-European group researches environmental issues and advocates governmental policies based on their findings. Find out all about the ECNC or check out other earth-friendly European organizations and information on the ECNC Home Page.

Finnish Association for Nature Conservation

http://envirolink.org/orgs/index.html

The Finnish Association for Nature Conservation maintains this informational site for its environmental interest group. Visit here to learn what Finlandians are doing to protect their forests, water and air. Available in a mix of Finnish and English.

Friends of the Santa Clara River

http://envirolink.org/FSCR/FSCR.html

The Friends of the Santa Clara River, an organization dedicated to the proper management of one of two remaining natural river systems in southern California, maintains this informational site. Visit here for news, publications, background information and activity updates.

Greenpeace: French Nuclear Testing

http://www.greenpeace.org/~comms/rw/rw.html

Greenpeace, an environmental advocacy organization, has designed a Web page to inform the public on France and China's nuclear testing. Here you will find reference material and video clips on nuclear testing, as well as an electronic anti-testing petition to fill out.

Greenpeace International (Amsterdam)

http://www.greenpeace.org/

Greenpeace is an organization devoted to identifying and proposing solutions to global environmental problems. Visitors to the Amsterdam chapter's home page will find membership information, descriptions of current campaigns and a searchable index of Greenpeace articles and publications.

Greenpeace International Gopher Menu

gopher://gopher.greenpeace.org/

Greenpeace International hosts this gopher directory providing a wealth of information for members and interested browsers. Check out Greenpeace addresses, phone numbers, job opportunities, newsletters, press releases and more here.

Greenpeace's Index to Non-Greenpeace Environmental Sites

http://www.greenpeace.org/others.html

Greenpeace points browsers to other international environmental organizations, anti-nuclear testing pages and political sites from this index, which also includes links to environmentally friendly media.

Headwaters Forest

http://www.impactonline.org/baa/rallycry/index.html

This advocacy page focuses on the effort to save Northern California's Headwaters Forest, the world's largest unprotected old-growth redwood forest. Pacific Lumber Company has other ideas for the forest. Visitors will find photos of the massive trees and action alerts here.

The Natural Resources Defense Council

http://www.igc.apc.org/nrdc/

The Natural Resources Defense Council fights for the environment in the courts and the halls of Congress. It dispenses environmental news, opinion and mobilization information here, where browsers can keep up with the current status of the clean air campaign, pending legislation and other issues. The site also includes a list of NRDC's books and magazines and information on how to become a member.

The Progressive Directory @igc

http://www.igc.apc.org/index.html

The Institute for Global Communications present its Progressive Directory, a gateway to environmental and progressive resources around the globe, through this home page. Among the links are pointers to PeaceNet, EcoNet, ConflictNet, LaborNet and WomensNet.

The Rainforest Action Network Home Page

http://www.igc.apc.org/ran/

Rainforest Action Network posts alerts about its campaigns to save the planet's rainforests on this sleek activist-oriented site. Visitors can e-mail appropriate officials from here or find out about nearby demonstrations. The page also includes membership information.

The Research into Artifacts Center for Engineering

http://www.race.u-tokyo.ac.jp/

The Research into Artifacts Center for Engineering (RACE) at the University of Tokyo both conducts artifact research and assesses the problems and opportunities facing modern culture. The site includes information about RACE's research and information about the protests against French nuclear testing. In English and Japanese.

Sierra Club Home Page

http://www.sierraclub.org/

The Sierra Club is a nonprofit group that works for the environment by influencing public policy decisions. Visit this site to learn about its activities, apply for membership, access local chapters and more. Links to related Internet resources are also available.

JOURNALS AND PERIODICALS

South Florida Environmental Reader

http://www.envirolink.org/florida/

The South Florida Environmental Reader is an electronic monthly newsletter for and by environmental activists. Visit for updates on local and national issues that affect the Everglades and other areas in South Florida.

ENVIRONMENTAL EDUCATION AND AWARENESS

EE-Link Endangered Species

http://www.nceet.snre.umich.edu/EndSpp/Endangered.html

Environmental Educators teach about endangered species here. Visitors will find a list of animals hanging in the balance and can read historical and legal information about the Endangered Species Act. The site also includes classroom materials and photos.

The Environmental Education Network

http://envirolink.org/enviroed

The Environmental Education Network is a collaborative effort of educators, private industry and the environmental community to bring environmental education online. Includes links to libraries, databases, marketplaces and user participation sites.

The Environmental News Network Inc., (ENN)

http://www.enn.com/

The Environmental News Network (ENN) is a fee-based environmental news service that compiles news from wire services, government agencies, industry, special interest groups and environmental professionals. At this site find daily news, the ENN library, an events calendar and membership information.

Global Rivers Environmental Education Network (GREEN)

http://www.igc.apc.org/green/green.html

Global Rivers Environmental Education Network (GREEN) is a Michigan organization dedicated to saving U.S. watersheds and rivers. Visitors will find an online conference and discussion area, extensive educational resources and schedules for workshops and classes.

GLOBE Educational Materials

http://globe.fsl.noaa.gov/edu/edu.html

A variety of earth science-related educational resources are provided here by Global Learning and Observations to Benefit the Environment (GLOBE), an international network of science and educators that work to increase environmental awareness. Visitors can read pages on earth atmosphere and climate, hydrology, biology and geology.

The GLOBE Program

http://www.globe.gov/

The GLOBE Program unites students, teachers and scientists for the study of the environment. At its home page, GLOBE explains its organizational philosophy, describes current projects and programs.

GLOBE Visualizations

http://rsd.gsfc.nasa.gov/globe

This NASA-sponsored site features graphical representations of conditions on Earth based on current environmental data. Other site features include a lesson on how the images are created.

ENVIRONMENTAL POLICY AND LEGISLATION

Environmental Law World Wide Web Site

http://www.webcom.com/~staber/welcome.html

Lawyers and environmental professionals can keep up with the latest in environmental law here. Offered by Chicago lawyer Steven M. Taber, this page features links to state and federal agency re-

sources along with a host of information about U.S. environmental law.

100 Day Scorecard

http://www.lcv.org/

The 100 Day Scorecard, compiled by the League of Conservation Voters, documents the environmental impact of the Republican party's Contract With America. Browsers here can also review the environmental voting records of Congressman in the first 100 days of the 104th Congress.

The Stockholm Environment Institute

http://nn.apc.org/sei/

The Stockholm Environment Institute researches environmental and development issues, focusing in the global and regional policy arena. Visitors to its home page will find background and research information, a publications catalog and more.

ENVIRONMENTAL POLLUTION AND REMEDIATION

ACID RAIN

EcoNet's Acid Rain Resources

http://www.igc.apc.org/acidrain/

EcoNet has compiled publications, articles and educational activities about acid rain and offers links to them here. The site also includes conference information and proceedings.

ARCHIVES AND INDICES

The Agency for Toxic Substances and Disease Registry -- EPA's Top 20 Hazardous Substances

http://atsdr1.atsdr.cdc.gov:8080/cxcx3.html

The U.S. Environmental Protection Agency is required by law to update a list of the world's most hazardous substances each year. This list, from 1993, ranks lead as the number one offender, followed by arsenic, with the dreaded DDT coming in at number 12. Includes links to toxicologic profiles and public health statements.

The Agency for Toxic Substances and Disease Registry -- Science Corner

http://atsdr1.atsdr.cdc.gov:8080/popdocs.html

The Agency for Toxic Substances and Disease Registry (ATSDR) provides this annotated index of its key science and Web-navigating links. Visitors can follow pointers to a large collection of sites here, with an emphasis on hazardous substances, environmental data and public health issues.

Chemical Safety Fact Sheets

gopher://ecosys.drdr.virginia.edu:70/11/library/gen/toxics

This gopher menu contains an alphabetical listing of toxic entities (the nonhuman kind), complete with identifying characteristics and a description of the hazards they present. Advice on protective handling and first aid is also provided for each substance.

Solvent Alternatives Guide (SAGE)

http://clean.rti.org/

Visitors to this site will find general info on solvents and environmentally-preferred alternative methods for cleaning and degreasing. The SAGE page provides a search form and hypertext index to access data, plus links to related sites.

CONTROL AND REMEDIATION

The Environmental Molecular Sciences Laboratory

http://www.emsl.pnl.gov:2080/

The government's Pacific Northwest Lab is constructing a new building to house its Environmental Molecular Sciences Laboratory, which researches environmental cleanup efforts. This site gives an overview of the new building and contains dozens of technical reports, a Gaussian Basis Set Library, and a look at the lab's work in theoretical and experimental research.

RADIATION POLLUTION

Chernobyl and Its Consequences: Project Polyn

http://polyn.net.kiae.su/polyn/manifest.html

This site provides a hypertext database on the accident at the Chernobyl Nuclear Power Plant. This site includes official Soviet reports, materials from the Chernobyl Kurchatov Institute Expedition, articles from scientific publications and more.

Office of Civilian Radioactive Waste Management

http://www.rw.doe.gov/

Learn about this agency's research, engineering and more. See Editor's Choice.

Radioecology, Swedish University of Agricultural Sciences

http://www.radek.slu.se/

Radioecology deals with ecological problems caused by radioactivity. The Swedish University of Agricultural Sciences (SLU) provides specialized courses in this field as a result of the Chernobyl disaster. Includes links to other resources in this field.

TECHNOLOGIES

The Global Network of Environment and Technology

http://www.gnet.org/

The Global Network of Environment and Technology (GNET) offers this presentation as a gateway to environmental technology business news. Find institutions and organizations that deal with marketing, products and opportunities.

UCLA CCT Home Page

http://cct.seas.ucla.edu/

This site provides information about current activity at the Center for Clean Technology at the University of California, Los Angeles. Visitors will find an overview of the center, information on research programs, and a listing by subject of all files on the server.

WATER QUALITY AND POLLUTION

EMILY

ftp://www.ccwr.ac.za/emily/

The Electronic Membrane-Information Library (EMILY) is a project of the Water Research Commission of South Africa. Visitors here can access membrane modeling software, newsletters, online publications and databases. Information on researchers and conferences, plus links to related sites are also featured.

The Great Lakes Environmental Research Laboratory

http://www.glerl.noaa.gov/

The Great Lakes Environmental Research Laboratory (GLERL) in Ann Arbor, Mich., explains its mission and current research here. The laboratory, part of the National Oceanic and Atmospheric Administration, researches toxicants, natural hazards, invasive species and local effects from global change, all with emphasis on the Great Lakes.

The Water Treatment FAQ

http://www.siouxlan.com/water/faq.html

The Water Treatment FAQ is drowning in information about hard water, soft water, smelly water and even slimy water. Tips from Culligan offer advice on how to manage hard-to-get-along-with H20.

ENVIRONMENTAL PROTECTION

ARCHIVES AND INDICES

Chemical Safety Fact Sheets

gopher://ecosys.drdr.virginia.edu:70/11/library/gen/toxics

This gopher menu contains an alphabetical listing of toxic entities (the nonhuman kind), complete with identifying characteristics and a description of the hazard it presents. Advice on protective handling and first aid is also provided for each substance.

Florida Dept. of Environmental Protection

gopher://gopher.dep.state.fl.us:70/1

This Department of Environmental Protection gopher features various environmental and earth science resources. From here, access the Environmental Protection Agency, the Forest Science Laboratory in Oregon and other agencies that focus on management and conservation.

 EDITOR'S CHOICE

Office of Civilian Radioactive Waste Management

http://www.rw.doe.gov/

"Our mission is to manage and dispose of the Nation's spent nuclear fuel and high-level waste." This daunting task is the responsibility of the Office of Civilian Radioactive Waste Management (OCRWM), whose Web site describes its research, engineering, administrative and lobbying efforts to accomplish this job while protecting the environment, winning public confidence, and assuring public and worker health and safety within the confines of today's budgetary constraints. Sound like a daunting task? It is: read the texts of congressional testimony and public speeches delivered by program officials, or review current events and ongoing activities within this burdened government agency. You can also reference publications, reports, educational materials and facts about the agency's programs. One of the more compelling projects under the aegis of the OCRWM is the Yucca Mountain Project, an attempt to establish a national central waste repository in Southwestern Nevada, where radioactive wastes can be safely and securely stored for the next 10,000 years. But until such a site can be established—if ever—discover what temporary measures are being taken by the agency to process, transport and house the nation's fissionable byproducts.—*Reviewed by Steve Ellis*

Gaia Forest Conservation Archives

http://www.forests.org/gaia.html

This site provides links to more than 2,000 rainforest- and biodiversity-related articles, studies and news items. Includes Rainforest Action Network alerts and links to an image gallery and ecological- and political-action organizations.

ASSOCIATIONS AND ORGANIZATIONS

About the Information Center for the Environment (ICE)

http://ice.ucdavis.edu/about_ICE.html

A collaborative effort of university, government and research environmental scientists, the Information Center for the Environment seeks to provide a central repository of data, information and current research in environmental protection and regulation. Includes an overview of the Center, its services and staff.

The Communications for a Sustainable Future Gopher

gopher://csf.colorado.edu/

The Communications for a Sustainable Future gopher features information about economics, the environment and foreign policy and how they relate to a reasonable future for humans and the planet. Visitors can also read information about peace and conflict resolution.

Environmental Resources Information Network Database Gateway

http://kaos.erin.gov.au/database/db.html

A service of the Australian Department of the Environment, Sport and Territories, the Environmental Resources Information Network Database offers searchable access to information about Australian public lands and protected areas. Also find biological data, ERIN's data dictionary and catalog, species lists and overviews of government projects.

Friends of the Environment

http://www.fef.ca/

Canada's Friends of the Environment Foundation funds community environmental projects across the country. Visit here for an overview of the foundation, application guidelines and online press releases.

CONSERVATION

The European Centre for Nature Conservation

http://www.ecnc.nl/

Europe's many environmental groups are linked through the ECNC, the European Centre for Nature Conservation. The pan-European group researches environmental issues and advocates

governmental policies based on their findings. Find out all about the ECNC or check out other earth-friendly European organizations and information on the ECNC Home Page.

Gap Analysis Home Page

http://www.nr.usu.edu/gap

The Gap Analysis assesses the current biological resources at the landscape level to prevent additional species from being listed as threatened or endangered. Links lead browsers to online data, a bulletin board and more at this site.

Global Futures

http://www.quiknet.com/globalff/globalfu.html

Global Futures Foundation is a nonprofit environmental foundation specializing in promoting environmentally beneficial programs and publications. It posts feature articles, program descriptions and links to other foundations here.

Information Center for the Environment (ICE), University of California, Davis

http://ice.ucdavis.edu/

Environmental scientists at the University of California, Davis have formed the Information Center for the Environment (ICE) in order to provide access to information about ongoing environmental protection projects. More project than policy oriented, the ICE site focuses on what's currently happening in the field of environmental protection.

Mark Sheehan's Nature Conservancy Page

http://copper.ucs.indiana.edu/~sheehan/conservancy.html

An officer of the Indiana chapter maintains this page on The Nature Conservancy as "a convenience to Web users looking for TNC-related materials." Links to chapters nationwide and an overview of projects and programs are provided.

National Parks and Conservation Association

http://www.npca.org/home/npca/

The National Parks and Conservation Association is a private, nonprofit watchdog of the nation's parks. Visitors here will learn about the association's park preservation and maintenance efforts at both the grassroots and national levels.

Natural Resources Conservation Service

http://www.ncg.nrcs.usda.gov/

An agency of the U.S. Department of Agriculture, the Natural Resources Conservation Service "works with landowners on private lands to conserve natural resources." Visit this site to learn more about the NRCS and its conservation partners. Also find technical resources and links to topical sites.

ENVIRONMENTAL PROTECTION AGENCY

The Environmental Protection Agency

http://earth1.epa.gov/

The United States Environmental Protection Agency's (EPA) informational server offers a wealth of information about its regulatory work. In addition info about its programs, initiatives, and grants, it provides a variety of helpful documentation and publications.

Gulf of Mexico Program Information Network

http://pelican.gmpo.gov

The U.S. Environmental Protection Agency maintains this informational site on the environmental challenges in the Gulf of Mexico. Visit here for progress reports on the project and a variety of related environmental links.

JOURNALS AND PERIODICALS

Our Environment

http://maui.net/~jstark/ournvmag.html

Visitors to this page can read the current issue of Our Environment, an electronic magazine devoted to exposing environmental concerns and promoting solutions to the problems. Also find links to topic-related sites.

Worldwatch Institute

gopher://gopher.igc.apc.org/11/orgs/worldwatch

The Worldwatch Institute, an ecological organization dedicated to fostering a sustainable society, conducts interdisciplinary research on emerging global issues. This gopher includes tables of contents from past issues of "World Watch Magazine," state-of-the-world reports, topic-specific studies and more.

GEOGRAPHY

ANCIENT GEOGRAPHY

History of Cartography

http://feature.geography.wisc.edu/histcart/

The University of Wisconsin's History of Cartography project works to understand the cultural context and historical functions of maps, as well as how they were made. Geographers can get an extensive overview of the project here.

ARCHIVES AND INDICES

The Association of Geographic Information GIS Dictionary

http://www.geo.ed.ac.uk/root/agidict/html/welcome.html

The AGI GIS Dictionary is an online dictionary of more than 300 Geographical Information Systems (GIS) terms provided by the Department of Geography at the University of Edinburgh, Scotland, and the Association of Geographic Information.

The Australian Surveying and Land Information Group

http://www.auslig.gov.au/welcome.htm

The Australian Surveying and Land Information Group provides organizational facts and a full range of land information services at this home page. Includes a search engine.

GIS Resource List

http://www.geo.ed.ac.uk/home/giswww.html

The Department of Geography at the University of Edinburgh, Scotland, provides this index of geographic information systems (GIS) sites. It includes links to government, commercial and educational pages.

The National Geospatial Data Clearinghouse

http://nsdi.usgs.gov/nsdi/

This Web document is presented by the National Geospatial Data Clearinghouse as a guide to finding online information about geospatial data available from USGS.

Nice Geography and GIS Servers

http://www.frw.ruu.nl/nicegeo.html

Geography resources from around the world are collected at this site, which features links to dozens of schools and university departments of geography. Also included here are geographic information systems (GIS) servers, remote-sensing servers and related newsgroups.

Topographical Pictures

http://www.softsource.com/softsource/topo.html

This U.S. Geological Survey (USGS) site contains topographical pictures created from USGS databases using a custom program. Includes instructions for downloading images of topographically prominent locations (like the Grand Canyon or Mount Rainier) and raw digital elevation model data.

U.S. Geographic Names

gopher://gopher.peabody.yale.edu:71/1

Located at Yale University's Peabody Museum of Natural History, this gopher supports the Geographic Names Information System. Here you will find searchable records on the nearly 2 million geographical features (both natural and man-made) found on the U.S. Geological Survey's topographical maps.

University at Buffalo Geographic Information and Analysis Lab

http://ncgia.geog.buffalo.edu/GIAL/netgeog.html

Geographers take note: This site from the University at Buffalo Geographic Information and Analysis Lab offers an exhaustive list of links to Internet-based geographical resources. Visitors can access U.S. government and commercial sites and global information repositories or make use of searchable, online indices like the CIA World Factbook.

ASSOCIATIONS, ORGANIZATIONS, AND AGENCIES

Canada Centre for Remote Sensing

http://www.ccrs.nrcan.gc.ca

The Canada Centre for Remote Sensing acquires remotely sensed data and develops remote sensing applications. Information on the center, its activities and its resources is included, as are data, images and products. In English and French.

PIENet - Home Page

http://www.dpie.gov.au/

PIENet -- a service of the Australian Department of Primary Industries and Energy -- provides information on agriculture, energy, the environment, fisheries, forestry, geoscience and details of PIENet's publications and training center.

ATLASES, GLOBES, AND MAPS

America's Roof

http://www.inch.com/~dipper/highpoints.html

Climbers and geologists will find maps and graphs of the highest peak in each state on this site. A page is devoted to each peak and includes elevation information, weather, directions and links to U.S. Geological Survey quadrangle maps of each.

Area Accurate Map / The Peters Projection

http://www.webcom.com/~bright/petermap.html

In 1974, Arno Peters created a geographically accurate area map of the world called The Peters Projection. This support page has information about the map and a downloadable tutorial.

California Geographical Survey

http://geogdata.csun.edu/

The Department of Geography at California State University Northridge provides an Internet library here that contains an electronic map collection, census data archive, digital map bases and more.

Digital Relief Map of the U.S.

http://www.zilker.net/~hal/apl-us/

Visitors will find a relief map of the United States here that is divided into interactive grid cells—click on a cell and you'll find images and descriptions of the selected region. The site includes an elevation key and an index map. It was created by the Applied Physics Lab at Johns Hopkins University.

Gateway to Canadian Geography

http://www-nais.ccm.emr.ca/

Canada's geographical, social and political landscapes are mapped here by the National Atlas Information Service. Examine digital and conventional cartographic products and services here. In English and French.

Geomatics Canada

http://www.ccrs.emr.ca/linc

Geomatics Canada, a department within Natural Resources Canada, surveys and maps the country. Visitors will learn of its surveying, remote sensing and mapping services here. In French and English.

How Far Is It?

http://www.indo.com/distance/

This service finds the latitude and longitude of two requested locations, and then calculates the distance between them. A map displaying the two locations is also provided. U.S. and many world cities included.

Map Maker

http://www.pcug.co.uk/~MapMaker/

The freeware Map Maker is designed for people in developing countries who need to create and manipulate maps on basic personal computers. This page allows browsers to download the software, a simple Geographical Information System.

Maps of the Americas

http://www.lib.utexas.edu/Libs/PCL/Map_collection/americas.html

Visitors can download CIA maps of each country in the Americas here, from Antigua to Venezuela. The site is maintained by a library at the University of Texas at Austin.

The National Land Survey of Finland

http://www.nls.fi/

The National Land Survey of Finland outlines its mapping services here. Visitors will learn about its various departments, its use of geographic information systems and its satellite image center. In Finnish and English.

U.S. Geological Survey Mapping Information

http://www-nmd.usgs.gov/

Visit this U.S. Geological Survey site for up-to-date cartographic data and information on the United States. Find resources for geography teachers and students, learn about new discoveries in cartography, and get USGS product and service information.

University of California, San Diego, Maps and Spatial Data Home Page

http://gort.ucsd.edu/mw/maps.html

The University of San Diego's Map and Spatial Data site features a description of the school's map room, San Diego census data, land and ocean info systems, atmosphere and planetary data, and much more.

Xerox PARC Map Viewer

http://pubweb.parc.xerox.com/map/

The Xerox Corporation's Palo Alto Research Center presents this site containing its map viewer creation. The map viewer is a Web HTTP server that accepts requests for a World or U.S. map and returns an HTML document including an image of the requested map. Each map image is created on demand from a geographic database.

INSTITUTES AND UNIVERSITIES

Edinburgh Geographical Information Systems (GIS) Server Home Page

http://www.geo.ed.ac.uk/home/gishome.html

The GIS (Geographical Information Systems) Web server delivers information about the University of Edinburgh's Department of Geography. Visitors will learn about programs and research as well as meet the staff.

GeoData Institute WWW Home Page

http://www.geodata.soton.ac.uk/

The GeoData Institute, a research organization at the University of Southampton, England, specializes in geographical information systems. This page describes the products and services available from GeoData.

The Geographical Survey Institute

http://www.gsi-mc.go.jp/

The Geographical Survey Institute in Japan provides a look at its geodetic and geographic departments here. The site also includes links to earthquake predictions and information concerning major disasters.

The National Center for Geographic Information and Analysis

http://www.ncgia.ucsb.edu/

The National Center for Geographic Information and Analysis (NCGIA) is a research consortium funded by the National Science Foundation to conduct research in geographic data analysis. Visitors to the NCGIA home page can access information about the group's publications, meetings, research and personnel.

NIS Cartography

http://www.iko.unit.no/gis/gisen.html

The Norwegian Institute of Technology's surveying and mapping department home page directs visitors to Internet geographic resources. Visitors will find related software, map archives and conference schedules. In English and Norwegian.

Research Program in Environmental Planning and Geographic Information

Systems

http://www.regis.berkeley.edu/

The Research Program in Environmental Planning and Geographic Information Systems (REGIS) of the University of California, Berkeley develops information systems tools for application in environmental planning, management, research and teaching. Visit here for publications and software related to the research group.

University of Edinburgh Geography Server

http://www.geo.ed.ac.uk/

Scotland's University of Edinburgh provides information about its academic programs and staff in its Departments of Geography and Archaeology here. It also details its Geographical Information Systems (GIS) research.

University of Victoria Department of Geography

http://geography.geog.uvic.ca/dept/homepage.html

The Geography Department at the University of Victoria in Canada provides information about its programs, research and faculty here. The site also includes announcements of upcoming conferences and links to graduate student home pages.

UW-Madison Geography Home Page

http://feature.geography.wisc.edu/

The Geography Department at the University of Wisconsin, Madison maintains this informational site. Visit here to learn about its facilities, programs, faculty and students.

JOURNALS AND PERIODICALS

GIS World

http://www.gisworld.com/

GIS World publishes magazines related to geographic information systems (GIS) and related books. It also organizes conferences on the topic. Visitors to this promotional page are encouraged to learn more about the company, its products and the market it serves.

PHYSICAL GEOGRAPHY

Earth

http://seds.lpl.arizona.edu/nineplanets/nineplanets/earth.html

Part of the Nine Planets series from the University of Arizona, this rich site offers a hypertext look at our planet. Visit here to learn about the physical facts of Earth, from mass to composition to plate tectonics. It includes statistics, photos and maps.

Geodetic Survey of Canada

http://www.geod.emr.ca/

The Geodetic Survey of Canada page is provided by Geomatics Canada, a sector of the Natural Resources department of the Federal Canadian Government. This page contains a wealth of information about GES products and services, geoscience resources, personal home pages and links to related sites and services. Available in French and English.

Great Lakes Forecasting System

http://superior.eng.ohio-state.edu

The Great Lakes Forecasting System allows access to "regularly scheduled predictions of the physical and related variables of the Great Lakes." Visitors can review readings of water surface temperature, elevation, currents and more. Also find topical reports and pointers.

Land Surveying and Geomatics

http://homepage.interaccess.com/~maynard/

Get linked to what page creators term the second-oldest profession at the Land Surveying and Geomatics page. Visitors can link to news, information, servers, newsgroups, software and much more.

The National Geophysical Data Center

gopher://gopher.ngdc.noaa.gov/1

The National Geophysical Data Center (NDGC) in Boulder, Colo., manages data from the upper atmosphere, space environment and the sun, along with data from the land, sea, and earth's interior. The results of the NGDC's data management efforts are accessible via this gopher, which includes a massive archive of earth, climate and space info.

Current data holdings include more than 300 digital and analog geophysical databases.

U.S. National Geodetic Survey Home Page

http://www.ngs.noaa.gov/

The U.S. National Geodetic Survey (NGS) is charged with the development and maintenance of the National Spatial Reference System (NSRS), a network of precise locations used "to correlate longitude, latitude, height, scale, and orientation" in the United States. NGS's home page explains the NSRS' function and provides information about NGS products and services.

POLAR REGIONS

British Antarctic Survey Home Page

http://www.nerc-bas.ac.uk/

The British Antarctic Survey represents the scientific interests of the United Kingdom at the research facilities of the South Pole. Find general info about BAS, the Antarctic and current research projects on the group's home page.

The Cooperative Research Centre for the Antarctic and Southern Ocean Environment

http://www.antcrc.utas.edu.au/antcrc.html

The Cooperative Research Centre for the Antarctic and Southern Ocean Environment page describes the organization's research on the relationship between polar regions and global climate change.

TECHNOLOGY

ARC-INFO Geographical Imaging System

http://boris.qub.ac.uk/shane/arc/ARChome.html

Providing a comprehensive introduction to the basic commands in the ARC-INFO Geographical Imaging System (GIS) , this online tutorial is designed to help new users grasp the fundamentals of the cartographic application with practical exercises and links to related help files.

ESRI - Home of The GIS People

http://www.esri.com/

Environmental Systems Research Institute, Inc., produces geographic information system (GIS) software and databases. Visitors will get an overview of its products and services here and will find details on its K-12 library program. Online ordering is available.

Geographic Information Systems - GIS

http://info.er.usgs.gov/research/gis/title.html

This site from the U.S. Geological Survey explains Geographical Information Systems (GIS) mapping, which uses layers of databases to create digital maps. The site also offers links to related mapping sites and an FTP software archive.

Geographic Resources Analysis Support System GIS

http://www.cecer.army.mil/grass/viz/VIZ.html

Geographic Resources Analysis Support System, a service of the U.S. Army Corps of Engineers, provides land and environmental management tools. Visit here to download examples of its environmental models and visualizations made with geographic information systems (GIS) databases.

GEOLOGY

GENERAL

What Is Geology?

http://www.sci.sdsu.edu/geology/text/whatis.html

San Diego State University (SDSU) answers the question, "What is geology?" in general terms, using a career-day-type approach to interest prospective students in the field. Visitors who want to know more can link back to the SDSU Department of Geological Sciences home page.

ASSOCIATIONS, ORGANIZATIONS, AND AGENCIES

The American Association of Stratigraphic Palynologists Inc., (AASP)

http://www.geology.utoronto.ca/AASP

The American Association of Stratigraphic Palynologists is a worldwide professional association that gathers yearly to exchange information about the field. Visitors will get an overview of the group here and can download its quarterly newsletter in full, or abstracts from its annual journal.

British Geological Survey

http://www.nkw.ac.uk/bgs/home.html

Geological information for the United Kingdom and details about the British Geological Survey (BGS) are featured on the Survey's home page. Visitors can browse BGS publications and databases, or find out how to get advice from the BGS.

EROS-Alaska Field Office

http://www-eros-afo.wr.usgs.gov/welcome.html

An arm of the U.S. Geological Survey's EROS Data Center, the Alaskan Field Office provides information here about its ongoing projects. The site also includes pointers to related resources.

Geological Society of America

http://www.aescon.com/geosociety/index.html

Billing itself as "The Professional Resource for Earth Scientists," The Geological Society of America site offers educational resources to the geology profession. Focusing on publications, meetings and professional directories, the site has a strong academic and scientific bent.

Geoscience Information Group

http://www.bris.ac.uk/Depts/Geol/gig/gig.html

The Geoscience Information Group of The Geological Society supplies details on past and future meetings along with a newsletter, committee member listings and committee minutes. Includes information on joining the group's mailing list.

Iowa Geological Survey Bureau Home Page

http://www.igsb.uiowa.edu/

Iowa's Geological Survey Bureau (GSB) is part of the state's Department of Natural Resources. Here it provides access to its publications, an online catalog of its Geographic Information System (GIS) library and detailed information about Iowa's geology.

Maryland Geological Survey

http://mgs.dnr.md.gov/

The Maryland branch of the U.S. Geological Survey offers program descriptions and research overviews at this official site. Visitors can investigate regional and statewide survey data here. An online pamphlet series explores the possibilities of experiencing an earthquake or finding gold in the state.

U.S. Geological Survey

http://www.usgs.gov/index.html

This is the home page of the U.S. Geological Survey, a division of the Department of the Interior that serves as a science research and information agency. A wealth of geological information is available here, including pages on mapping, water resources, environmental research, publications, data products and links to related Internet resources.

U.S. Geological Survey Fact Sheets

http://h2o.usgs.gov/public/wid/indexlist.html

This United States Geological Survey page provides a directory of links to information categorized by state. This site also includes links to special topics and the USGS home page.

U.S. Geological Survey Geo Data

http://sun1.cr.usgs.gov/doc/edchome/ndcdb/ndcdb.html

This site provides file transfer profile (FTP) access to a variety of U.S. Geological Survey digital data sets. Includes public domain software and a link to the USGS EROS Data Center home page.

U.S. Geological Survey Global Land Information System

http://edcwww.cr.usgs.gov/glis/glis.html

The U.S. Geological Survey provides this interactive database for researchers looking for information about the earth's land surfaces. Visitors can telnet or FTP to the full services of the Global Land Information System.

U.S. Geological Survey Index

http://geology.usgs.gov/

The U.S. Geological Survey provides an index to various geologic sites here. Visitors can jump to Ask-A-Geologist where browsers can query geologists about the planet, a site about geologic hazards research and various earthquake centers, volcano observatories and marine geology research centers.

U.S. Geological Survey Server

http://info.er.usgs.gov/network/science/earth/usgs.html

The U.S. Geological Survey maintains this site for its index of computer servers and regional and state World Wide Web sites. Visitors can link to geology-related information resources across the United States.

U.S. Geological Survey State Representatives

http://h2o.er.usgs.gov/public/wrd011.html

Visitors to this site will find a complete list of U.S. Geological Survey representatives in each of the fifty states. The listing features names and contact information.

INSTITUTES AND UNIVERSITIES

American Geological Institute

http://agi.umd.edu/agi/agi.html

Visitors can find information on what the American Geological Institute is and what it does here. The site features information on the GeoRef Database, but it is not searchable at this site. Links to other earth sciences resources on the Web also are provided.

Birkbeck Crystallography Homepage

http://www.cryst.bbk.ac.uk/

The Department of Crystallography at Birkbeck College in London, England, maintains

this site for student and faculty resources, departmental overviews and host links to related institutional home pages. Includes a keyword search and a departmental notice board.

The Consortium for Research in Elastic Wave Exploration Seismology Project

http://www-crewes.geo.ucalgary.ca/

The Consortium for Research in Elastic Wave Exploration Seismology at the University of Calgary researches high-tech ways to find natural resources. Visit here to read profiles of the consortium and its industry partners and to read an overview of its research.

The Department of Geological Sciences at the University of British Columbia

http://www.geology.ubc.ca/

The Department of Geological Sciences at the University of British Columbia, Canada, links visitors with information about the department, people and research. It offers a look at courseware, materials used for online education, as well as upcoming events.

Department of Geology Home Page, Duke University

http://www.geo.duke.edu/

Duke University's geology department describes its graduate studies program, research facilities and Marine Laboratory at this site. Visitors can peruse abstracts and publications or check out a departmental calendar.

Department of Geology, University of Illinois at Urbana-Champaign

http://www.geology.uiuc.edu/

The Department of Geology of The University of Illinois at Urbana-Champaign provides a look at its various research projects here. The page also contains an online course catalog and information for prospective undergraduate and graduate students.

Geophysical Institute, University of Alaska Fairbanks

http://www.gi.alaska.edu/

This is the home page of the Geophysical Institute at the University of Alaska, Fairbanks. Visitors will find institute news and services here, in addition to information on administration and research disciplines.

Geotechnology LTH

http://lthgt.tg.lth.se/

Get a Swedish perspective on Geotechnology at this Lund University site. Engineering geology and soil mechanics are among related topics to which visitors will find links. In Swedish and English.

Institute for Mineralogy Home Page

http://www.immr.tu-clausthal.de/

The Institute for Mineralogy and Mineral Resources in Clausthal, Germany, maintains this site for general information. Visit here to connect to its departments, academic materials and related Internet resources.

The Newcastle Research Group

http://nrg.ncl.ac.uk/

The Newcastle Research Group (NRG) is an postgraduate and research institution in the United Kingdom that focuses on fossil fuels and environmental geochemistry. Visitors can learn about NRG's staff, programs and facilities here.

New Mexico Tech E&ES Department Homepage

http://griffy.nmt.edu/

The New Mexico Institute of Mining & Technology earth and environmental science home page provides visitors with departmental information about the school. Includes links to home pages maintained by the school's faculty members and geology/geochemistry, geophysics and hydrology programs.

Purdue Geophysics Home Page

http://www.geo.purdue.edu/

Purdue University's earth and atmospheric sciences department home page offers information about departmental research and publications. Includes links to home pages maintained by the Indiana school and by the Geological Society of America.

RHBNC Geology Department

http://glsun2.gl.rhbnc.ac.uk/

London's Royal Holloway's Department of Geology maintains this site, which includes info about the department, staff and research.

Rice University Department of Geology and Geophysics - Intro

http://zephyr.rice.edu/department/dept_intro.html

The Rice University Department of Geology and Geophysics maintains this page with information about its faculty, research programs, graduate and undergraduate education, facilities and links to various earth science sites.

Stanford University Geophysics Department

http://pangea.stanford.edu/~sjm/geophysics.html

Visitors to the Stanford Geophysics Department home page will find information about the academic programs, research groups, faculty and project seminars. Links to sites of related interest are also featured.

Statistical Analysis of Natural Resource Data (SAND)

http://www.nr.no/home/SAND/index.html

Scientific Analysis of Natural Resource Data (SAND), a Norwegian nonprofit research entity, provides research to the petroleum industry. Its site contains profiles of the geoscientists and their research.

University of Chicago Department of the Geophysical Sciences

http://geosci.uchicago.edu/

The home page for the Department of Geophysical Sciences at the University of Chicago offers links to information about the department and its faculty, as well as current research in the fields of atmospheres, oceans, geochemistry, paleontology and evolution.

University of Edinburgh Department of Geology and Geophysics

http://www.glg.ed.ac.uk/

The Department of Geology and Geophysics at Scotland's University of Edinburgh provides information on its programs of study, course offerings and faculty. The site includes descriptions of research projects, a picture gallery, campus maps, a brief department history and links to other geological resources.

University of Oulu Department of Geophysics

http://babel.oulu.fi/

The Department of Geophysics at Finland's University of Oulu maintains this site offering general information. Visit here to learn about the department's teaching staff and academic degrees. Available in Finnish and English.

University of Texas Austin, Institute for Geophysics

gopher://gopher.ig.utexas.edu:70/1

The University of Texas at Austin's Institute for Geophysics gopher provides information about graduate and doctoral studies here. It also gives an overview of its ongoing research, calendars of events and link to its library.

UW - Madison Geology and Geophysics Home Page

http://geology.wisc.edu/

This University of Wisconsin-Madison site contains information on programs of study offered by its geology and geophysics faculty. Includes general info on the department, admissions, faculty and research projects.

Yale University, Dept. of Geology and Geophysics

http://stormy.geology.yale.edu/kgl.html

Yale University's geology and geophysics home page outlines departmental research interests and activities. Also included here are lists of the department's members and a link to the university's Center for Earth Observation.

MINERALS

Bob's Rock Shop

http://www.rockhounds.com/

Rock hounds can mine the contents of Bob's Rock Shop for choice images of rocks and minerals. Includes info about geology events and links to other rock, fossil and mineral sites.

MineNet

http://www.microserve.net/~doug/

MineNet, "the ultimate gateway to world wide mining Information" from Tensor Technologies, maintains this page offering mining information from government agencies, universities and societies. Publications, business resources and the Conference Connection are also available.

U.S. Geological Survey Mineral Resource Surveys Program

http://minerals.er.usgs.gov/

This U.S. Geological Survey site offers a mine of information concerning the mineral deposits in the country. Visitors will find data on mineral quality, quantity and present availability.

ORIGIN AND EVOLUTION OF THE EARTH

Geology Entrance

http://www.ucmp.berkeley.edu/exhibit/geology.ntml

Here's a site detailing the earth's geologic changes and formations through the ages. Read the Webmaster's introduction to the study, then review the exhibits in order or scan for specifics using the search tools provided.

UCMP Web Time Machine

http://www.ucmp.berkeley.edu/help/timeform.html

The Web Lift for Geologic Time takes visitors on a detailed tour of the earth's geologic history from the Hadean to the Holocene. Provided by the Museum of Paleontology at the University of California, Berkeley, this site features photographs, visual aids, and links to the taxonomy Web Lift.

Virtual Geomorphology

http://hum.amu.edu.pl/~sgp/gw/gw1.htm

Have you ever wondered how a desert is created? Visit this electronic textbook, issuing from a Polish university, to see how different elements of our world are formed. Neophytes can cull a good introduction to geomorphology while the pros can collect more information for research. In English or Polish.

PETROLEUM AND NATURAL GAS

The Australian Petroleum Cooperative Research Centre

http://www.dpr.csiro.au/apcrc/apcrc.html

The Australian Petroleum Research Centre, a consortium of private industry and educational institutions working to develop the country's oil resources, maintains this site to outline objectives and current progress. Visit here to learn about the organization, read annual reports and update news sheets, link to research proposals, and more.

Caltech Experimental Petrology

http://expet.gps.caltech.edu/

Researchers at Caltech provide information about the Hawaii Scientific Drilling Project here. The site includes lithologic core log data from Mauna Loa and Mauna Kealook, photographs and links to the participants' home pages.

The Geotechnology Research Institute (GTRI)

http://gtri.harc.edu/

The Geotechnology Research Institute is a private, nonprofit center working on high-tech solutions to geophysics issues facing the oil and gas industry. The institute's home page details its research projects, staff and facilities.

GO-TECH Base Page

http://baervan.nmt.edu/

The Gas & Oil Technology Exchange and Communication Highway, a joint project of New Mexican oil industrial organizations, provides information here about its local petroleum industry. Visit here for directories, publications, contact information and more.

National Indian Oil and Gas Evaluation and Management System

http://snake2.cr.usgs.gov/overview.html

The Division of Energy and Mineral Resources is developing an automated oil and gas information system that will help tribes to monitor, verify, and report on the status of production on tribal lands. It details the system here.

The Petroleum Recovery Institute

http://www.pri.ab.ca/

The Petroleum Recovery Institute in Alberta, Canada maintains this server featuring info about the research organization's staff, membership services, courses and resources. Visitors can read project and annual reports, or link to related sites.

Sci.Geo.Petroleum Internet Resources

http://www.slb.com/petr.dir/.guthery.html

The newsgroup sci.geo.petroleum offers an extensive index to geology and petroleum sites here. Geologists can use this index to find maps, stock information, libraries labs and more.

SEISMOLOGY

ABAG Earthquake Maps and Information

http://www.abag.ca.gov/bayarea/eqmaps/eqmaps.html

The Association of Bay Area Governments provides a wealth of earthquake-related information here. Visitors can view earthquake hazard maps, find out about quake proof retrofit wood-frame homes, link to FEMA disaster resources and more. Don't be shakin' when the ground's a-quakin'. Be ready!

Access to Current Seismicity

http://quake.wr.usgs.gov/QUAKES/CURRENT/current.html

The U.S. Geological Survey provides maps of the earthquakes in California and Hawaii here, along with weekly seismicity reports from around the globe and other related data.

Caltech Seismological Laboratory

http://www.seismo.unr.edu/

The Caltech Seismological Laboratory, a division of Geological and Planetary Sciences at Caltech University, offers information on its research activities and facilities at this server. Includes links to data on southern California seismic activity.

The Consortium for Research in Elastic Wave Exploration Seismology Project

http://www-crewes.geo.ucalgary.ca/

The Consortium for Research in Elastic Wave Exploration Seismology at the University of Calgary researches high-tech ways to find natural resources. Visit here to read profiles of the consor-

tium and its industry partners and to read an overview of its research.

Depto. de Sismologia Home Page

http://tlacaelel.igeofcu.unam.mx/Sismo.html

Earth scientists can follow seismic activity in Mexico on this site from the Institute of Geophysics at the Universidad Nacional Autonoma de Mexico. The institute profiles its research projects and faculty and posts weekly seismic news and graphs. In English and Spanish.

Earthquake Data

http://www.geophys.washington.edu/seismosurfing.html

This is a detailed collection of links to seismology resources on the Internet. Visitors will find maps, articles and Web sites devoted to the study of geology and earthquakes.

Earthquake Engineering Research Center UC Berkeley

gopher://www.eerc.berkeley.edu/

A wealth of information for scientists and professionals who deal with earthquakes is available at this gopher site from the Earthquake Engineering Research Center at the University of California at Berkeley. The offerings range from recent quake information to the Insurance Institute for Property Loss Reduction.

Earthquake Info from the USGS

http://quake.wr.usgs.gov/

The official earthquake-news site of the U.S. Geological Survey proves that tracking temblors is a 24-hour job. This massive site features current data, a weekly review of quake activity worldwide, measurements from notorious quake hot spots and information on quake preparedness.

Earthquake Information - Current Seismicity Plots

http://www-geology.ucdavis.edu/eqmandr.html

Maintained by the Geology Department at the University of California Davis, this page features pointers to institutions, information, images and indexes relevant to earthquakes and seismology. Featured sites include the Northern and the Southern California Earthquake Data Centers and the U.S. Geological Survey National Earthquake Information Center.

The IRIS Data Management System

http://www.iris.washington.edu/

The Incorporated Research Institutions for Seismology (IRIS) provides information about its Data Management Center in Seattle, Washington, here. Visitors can access the center's earthquake data, find out more about its services or link to related Web sites.

Los Angeles Current Earthquake Map

http://quake.wr.usgs.gov/QUAKES/CURRENT/los_angeles.html

This site from the Caltech Southern California Seismic Network provides current data on earthquake activity in the Los Angeles area. It features a clickable map.

National Center for Earthquake Engineering Research

http://nceer.eng.buffalo.edu/

Will your house or office building crumble if The Big One hits? People at the National Center for Earthquake Engineering Research are working to ensure that new buildings and bridges will survive earthquakes. Stop by to read quake basics, download the center's publications and software and read about a monthly featured topic.

Nevada Seismological Laboratory Home Page

http://www.seismo.unr.edu/

This page, maintained by the Nevada Seismological Laboratory at the University of Nevada, Reno spreads the word on shakers. Visitors can access earthquake information and details about the lab's staffers and resources. Includes job listings.

Northern California Earthquake Data Center

http://quake.geo.berkeley.edu/

The Northern California Earthquake Data Center (NCEDC) is a long-term archive and distribution center for seismological and geodetic data for Northern and Central California. Visitors are welcome to browse, search or retrieve data from the NCEDC database. Links to related sites are also available.

Pacific Northwest Seismograph Network Recent Earthquakes

gopher://geophys.washington.edu:79/0quake

The Pacific Northwest Seismograph Network's list of recent earthquakes for Washington and Oregon can be reached through this link. The quake list includes the location, magnitude and quality of each earthquake registered at magnitude 2.0 and higher.

San Francisco Bay Area Current Earthquake Map

http://quake.wr.usgs.gov/QUAKES/CURRENT/san_francisco_bay.html

The shaky future of the San Francisco Bay area is mapped out here in exquisite detail by the U.S. Geological Survey. The current earthquake map shows the major faults and the past 72 hours of activity in an interactive downloadable map.

Seismo Lab Home Page: The World-Wide Earthquake Locator

http://www.geo.ed.ac.uk/quakexe/quakes

The World-Wide Earthquake Locator, from the Department of Geography, University of Edinburgh, offers access to earthquake analysis material. The interface enables users to view data in a Xerox PARC Map Viewer format, replete with zoom-in features. An report index available.

The Seismology Group at the University of Zaragoza

http://zar.unizar.es/

The Seismology Group at the University of Zaragoza in Spain provides general information about seismology and geophysics here. The group also posts news from its latest research efforts. In English.

Southern Arizona Seismic Observatory

http://www.geo.arizona.edu/saso/

The Department of Geosciences at the University of Arizona supplies information about its Southern Arizona Seismic Observatory. Featured are details on programs and research, current and past seismograms, maps of global and Western U.S. seismicity, and resources on earthquakes.

The Southern California Earthquake Center @ UCLA

http://scec.ess.ucla.edu/

The UCLA Southern California Earthquake Center researches crustal deformation structure and does theoretical work on fault behavior and motion. This home page provides links to the center itself, the UCLA Department of Earth and Space Sciences and a lot of quake and geology information.

Southern California Integrated GPS Networks

http://milhouse.jpl.nasa.gov/

NASA's Jet Propulsion Laboratory (JPL) examines the cause and effect dynamics of earthquakes via satellite technology. View selected maps and link to related laboratories at this Southern California Integrated GPS Network page.

Spyder System for Rapid Earthquake Data

http://www.cs.indiana.edu/finger/
dmc.iris.washington.edu/spyder/w

This site contains specific instructions for using the the IRIS DMC 'Spyder' application to access "wave-form data from recent large earthquakes.'" This seismic page was generated by the Indiana University finger gateway.

Stanford Exploration Project

http://sepwww.stanford.edu/

The Stanford Exploration Project (SEP) conducts research in reflection seismology. The result: images of the earth's interior. This site houses reports, Ph.D. theses and other information related to this industry-funded project at Stanford University.

The World Earthquake Bulletin Gopher

gopher://gldfs.cr.usgs.gov:79/0quake

The World Earthquake Bulletin gopher maintains a complete list of temblors from around the world via the National Earthquake Information Service (NEIS) of the U.S. Geological Survey. The list includes all major earthquake activity and is updated frequently.

TECHNOLOGY

Landmark Graphics

http://www.lgc.com/

Computer-aided oil exploration takes center stage on the Landmark Graphics page. Geologists, geophysicists and engineers who analyze the earth's subsurface for petroleum reserves can check out available software here.

MultiSpectral Scanner Landsat Data

http://sun1.cr.usgs.gov/glis/hyper/guide/landsat

MultiSpectral Scanner Landsat Data is an overview of the U.S. Geological Survey's Landsat program, which provides information about the Earth's surface, including the effects of deforestation, pollution and volcanic activity. Learn more about Landsat data acquisition and management here.

U.S. Geological Survey SPOT

http://sun1.cr.usgs.gov/glis/hyper/guide/spot

The U.S. Geological Survey maintains this site for access to its SPOT High Resolution Visible Data collection. Visit here for data characteristics, organization and availability notes and information on applications and related data sets.

VOLCANOES

Cascades Volcano Observatory

http://vulcan.wr.usgs.gov/

Visitors to this site can learn about the research activities underway at the U.S. Geological Survey's Cascades Volcano Observatory in Vancouver, Wash. Facts, photos and history about Mt. St. Helens and other domestic volcanoes can be accessed here.

The Dante II Frame Walking Robot

http://maas-neotek.arc.nasa.gov/dante/

Dante II is a tethered walking robot designed to remotely conduct research and gather samples for volcanologists engaged in monitoring volcanoes. Read descriptions of current projects, technical readouts or view images from its visual simulation tools.

The Electronic Volcano

http://www.dartmouth.edu/~volcano/

Get the latest volcanic activity information from around the world at the Electronic Volcano page. Links to a volcano mailing list as well as catalogs of active volcanoes and articles from scientific journals are available here.

Global Volcanism

gopher://nmnhgoph.si.edu/11/.gvp

The Smithsonian's Natural History Museum documents volcano eruptions that have occurred in the last 10,000 years to better understand the geologic phenomenon. Its gopher menu posts an overview of its volcanism program, its newsletter and proceedings from a listserv.

Hawaii Scientific Drilling Project

http://expet.gps.caltech.edu/Hawaii_
project.html

Visitors here can explore core samples and related data retrieved from a drilling in Hilo, Hawaii. The information provides a glimpse at the geology of the Mauna Loa and Mauna Kea volcanoes. A press release explains the National Science Foundation-funded project's goals.

Michigan Technological University's Volcanoes, Rabaul Caldera

http://www.geo.mtu.edu/volcanoes/rabaul

The Michigan Technological University details September 1994 eruptions and current volcanic activity in Rabaul Caldera, Papua New Guinea, here. Visitors will find maps, aerial and satellite images, data and links to topic-related sites.

Remote Sensing of Volcanoes

http://www.geo.mtu.edu/eos/

Dive into the study of active volcanoes at the National Aeronautics and Space Administration's Volcanology site. A plain-spoken approach characterizes this explanation of volcanic phenomena (as observed from space) and the technology used to analyze it.

U.S. Geological Survey Hawaiian Volcano Observatory

http://www.soest.hawaii.edu/hvo/

Check the weekly status of volcanic activity in Hawaii here. The U.S. Geological Survey's Hawaiian Volcano Observatory posts photos, seismic maps and research articles on this page.

The Volcano Systems Center at the University of Washington

http://www.vsc.washington.edu/

The Volcano Systems Center at the University of Washington provides information about its faculty and current research efforts here. The page also includes an index to volcano-related sites elsewhere on the Net.

Volcano Watch

http://www.soest.hawaii.edu/hvo/index.html

Here, the United States Geological Survey presents Volcano Watch, a weekly newsletter for the general public and published by the Hawaiian Volcano Observatory. Issues are theme oriented, focusing on specific areas of geological interest. The site includes an archive of back issues.

GLOBAL WARMING

Carbon Dioxide Information Center

http://cdiac.ESD.ORNL.GOV/cdiac/

A facility of the Environmental Sciences Division at Oak Ridge National Laboratory in Tennessee, the Carbon Dioxide Information Analysis Center assists global researchers, policy makers and educators evaluate complex environmental issues such as potential climate changes. Visit this site to access the database and other CDIAC resources.

The Centre for Climate and Global Change Research

http://www.meteo.mcgill.ca/welcome.html

The Centre for Climate and Global Change Research at McGill University in Montreal provides an overview of its work here. Visitors can download abstracts of its recent publications on global change, look at a full list of its publications and browse through a calendar of upcoming seminars. In English and French.

Genie Casual User Interface

http://www-genie.mrrl.lut.ac.uk/

The Casual User Interface to the Genie global environmental change data network allows Web users to search the database by a number of criteria, including topics, places, organizations, data centers and people. The page also includes links to other Genie projects on the Web.

Global Change Master Directory

http://gcmd.gsfc.nasa.gov/

This NASA site serves as a comprehensive source offering Earth science, biosphere, climate and environmental systems information. Also find Global Change Master Directory news and documentation, plus links to other related servers.

Global Warming Update

http://www.ncdc.noaa.gov/gblwrmupd/global.html

Earth scientists can download a paper on global warming presented by Thomas R. Karl, a senior scientist at the National Climactic Data Center, at the 74th Annual Meeting of the American Meteorological Society. Research data and conclusions of decades of global temperature studies are available here.

The Goddard Distributed Active Archive Center

http://daac.gsfc.nasa.gov/

The Goddard Distributed Active Archive Center stores data about global change. Visitors can access its FTP archive from here, or learn how to order data for free. The site includes an online newsletter and an overview of the center's work.

The Potsdam Institute for Climate Impact Research

http://www.pik-potsdam.de/

The Potsdam Institute for Climate Impact Research is dedicated to investigating global climate change and its potential impact on the ecosphere and human society. Visitors can access various departments, research groups, projects and databases here.

U.S. Geological Survey Global Change Research Program

http://geochange.er.usgs.gov/gch.html

The U.S. Geological Survey provides an overview of its global change research program here. It posts results of climatic change studies along with data sets, article abstracts and a searchable index on this page.

University of Iowa CGRER Home Page

http://www.cgrer.uiowa.edu/

The Iowa Center for Global and Regional Environmental Research provides details on its interdisciplinary approach to the research of global environmental change here. The center also supplies news, a calendar, contacts and links to topical resources.

---

a2z EDITOR'S CHOICE

VolcanoWorld

http://volcano.und.nodak.edu/

Think you're ready to blow your stack? Well, you have nothing on this Web site. VolcanoWorld brings you real-time information and images drawn extensively from remote sensing equipment around the globe. The pages "add value to these data by relating each image to geologic processes, and by encouraging users to analyze images with provided algorithms." Explore volcanic regions, dive into submarine volcanoes or warp to other planetary volcanoes through the provided hyperlinks. Maps provide an intuitive interface for navigating to further information, and online interactive experiments stimulate learning for students of all ages. Take a tour of volcanic parks and monuments, or enter through the Kids' Door for elementary-level educational materials. Visitors to these pages can read the latest related news items, search through an online terminology dictionary or query the scientific database. If you are feeling competitive, you can even participate in an online quiz to match wits with other enthusiasts. So let the lava flow along with the abundant resources available at these pages ... but watch your ash.—*Reviewed by Steve Ellis*

HOWDY! MY NAME IS ROCKY AND I WANT TO WELCOME YOU TO...

Supported by NASA's Program:
Public Use of Earth and Space Science Data Over the Internet

GOVERNMENT AGENCIES

INTERNATIONAL

Agriculture, Forestry and Fisheries Research Council, Japan

http://www.affrc.go.jp/

Access to Japan's Ministry of Agriculture, Forestry and Fisheries' twenty-nine research organizations is offered via this Web server. Find a server map and list, plus a link to the ministry's home page. In Japanese and English.

Australian Antarctic Division

http://www.antdiv.gov.au/

The Antarctic Division of Australia's Department of Environment, Sport and Territories provides information here on its science programs, expeditions, employment opportunities and more. Includes division news and links to other related Web sites.

Australian Environmental Resources Information Network

http://kaos.erin.gov.au/erin.html

The Australian government puts its finger on the pulse of the nation's environment here. Visitors will find reports on topics ranging from land and water use issues to biodiversity and the state of environmental reporting.

Australian Environment Online

http://www.erin.gov.au/erin.html

Stop here for the Australian government's assessment of the country's environmental health. The site includes dozens of online reports on air, water, land and sustainable development. The country's conservation efforts are also sized up.

Barwon Water Authority

http://www.barwonwater.vic.gov.au/

The Water Authority of Australia's Barwon Region details its mission and water quality policies here. The site includes a look at the authority's staff and an archive of press releases.

Denmark Ministry of Environment and Energy

http://www.mem.dk/

Denmark's Ministry of Environment and Energy unveils information about its functions and current projects here, including reports about the state of Denmark's environment. In Danish with limited English.

Great Lakes Information Management Resource

http://www.cciw.ca/glimr/intro.html

This Web resource, maintained by Environment Canada, allows visitors to search the Great Lakes Information Management Resource (GLIMR) database for press releases, weather reports and details about regional environmental projects. Includes a link to Ontario's "Green Lane" environmental page. In English and French.

Ministry of Environment, Lands & Parks MELP

http://www.env.gov.bc.ca/

Visitors to this searchable site can read about environmental protection policies and programs, water management and the national parks of British Columbia. A ministry phone book and links to related sites are also featured.

Natural Environment Research Council

http://www.nerc.ac.uk/

This home page describes environmental research and monitoring work done by the United Kingdom's Natural Environment Research Council. Includes a variety of links to related resources and organizations, including the Institute of Freshwater Ecology.

Natural Resources Canada / Ressources Naturelles Canada

http://www.emr.ca/

Natural Resources Canada is a department of Canada's federal government. At this site, find data regarding Canada's interior land mass, including energy, mineral and timber resources. In English and French.

PIENet - Home Page

http://www.dpie.gov.au/

PIENet -- a service of the Australian Department of Primary Industries and Energy -- provides information on agriculture, energy, the environment, fisheries, forestry, geoscience and details of PIENet's publications and training center.

Tasmanian Parks and Wildlife Service

http://www.parks.tas.gov.au/tpws.html

The Tasmanian Parks and Wildlife Service maintains this site with information about the local fauna and flora, bio-environmental regionalization, archaeology and the park's library services. Links to related sites are offered here as well.

THERMIE Home Page

http://erg.ucd.ie/thermie.html

The European Union's THERMIE project directs funds to energy projects in order to decrease the federation's dependence on outside sources for energy. This site provides information on THERMIE as well as links to other European energy resources found on the Internet.

United Nations & Related Gophers

gopher://gopher.undp.org:70/11/ungophers

This gopher server, set up by the Central Europe Environmental Data Request Facility, links visitors to major international environmental organizations and groups that further the noble cause of global communication and cooperation on environmental issues.

The United Nations Environmental Program in Kenya

gopher://unep.unep.no/

The United Nations Environmental Program in Kenya maintains this gopher server. Visitors can access news, U.N. info and pointers to other environmental information servers around the globe.

United Nations Environment Programme (UNEP) Home Page

http://unep.unep.no/

The United Nations presents the home page for its environmental programs. Visitors will find information on research projects, events, organizations and related directories.

The United Nations Geneva Executive Center

http://www.unep.ch/

The Geneva Executive Center is the hub of United Nations programs and treaties dealing with the environment and sustainable development. Visitors can download information about U.N. conventions, trade programs and policy here.

UNITED STATES

AVHRR Pathfinder Home Page

http://xtreme.gsfc.nasa.gov/

This NASA site contains descriptions of the land data gathered by the Advanced Very High Resolution Radiometers (AVHRR) on the NOAA/TIROS meteorological satellites. Visitors can access the data set descriptions, view movie loops showing the "greening up" of the northern hemisphere, run a keyword search on the database or link to other NASA and topic-related sites.

California Department of Conservation

http://www.consrv.ca.gov/

The California Department of Conservation is chartered to protect and conserve California's natural resources. Visitors here can link to its recycling, geology and geothermal resources divisions.

California State Lands Commission

http://diablo.slc.ca.gov/

The California State Lands Commission maintains this site for public notices, environmental impact reports and geographic information system data. Visit here for commission resources and links to other state agencies.

The Council on Environmental Quality

http://ceq.eh.doe.gov

The Council on Environmental Quality, which operates from the Executive Office of the President of the United States, features its annual reports and a list of regulations here. Also access the Environmental Protection Agency Review and an extensive bibliography.

The Environmental Management Technical Center

http://www.emtc.nbs.gov/

The Environmental Management Technical Center of the National Biological Service maintains this site featuring biological, physical, spatial and technical data relating to the Upper Mississippi River System. Visitors can learn more about the EMTC and NBS, and access the data on file.

Geographic Resources Analysis Support System (GRASS)

http://www.cecer.army.mil/grass/GRASS.main.html

Geographic Resources Analysis Support System (GRASS), a service of the U.S. Army Corps of Engineers, provides land- and environmental-management tools here. Visit this site to learn about GRASS and access its computer-based support system.

Goddard Space Flight Center Earth Sciences Directorate

http://sdcd.gsfc.nasa.gov/ESD/

The Earth Sciences Directorate at the National Aeronautics and Space Administration's Goddard Space Flight Center posts information about its official mission and key projects at this site.

Illinois Department of Natural Resources

http://dnr.state.il.us/

The Illinois Department of Natural Resources offers information about its stewardship mission and current activities through this home page. The site offers links to the various offices within the department and details about the state's natural areas and outdoor recreation resources.

Michigan Department of Natural Resources

http://www.dnr.state.mi.us/

The Michigan Department of Natural Resources provides an introduction and history of the department, its current management plan, the DNR calendar and press releases. Links to its three divisions and related topical sites are also featured.

Montana Natural Resource Information System

http://nris.msl.mt.gov/

The Montana Natural Resources Information System offers data on the natural resources and people of the state of Montana. Visitors will find databases for natural heritage, water information and geography. Maps and general statistics for the state are provided.

The Oak Ridge National Laboratory Environmental Sciences Division

http://www.esd.ornl.gov/

The Oak Ridge National Laboratory sponsors this page from its Environmental Sciences Division. Visitors can read about the division's projects, including the Carbon Dioxide Information Analysis Center and the Biofuels Information Network. Feature articles, research news and annual reports are also available.

Office of Surface Mining

http://info.er.usgs.gov/doi/office-of-surface-mining.html

The Office of Surface Mining is the regulatory agency that oversees surface mining. Its charge is to protect citizens and the environment around active mines and to pursue reclamation of abandoned coal mines. This page has more information about the agency, its mission and vision.

The Pacific Northwest National Laboratory

http://www.pnl.gov:2080/

The Pacific Northwest National Laboratory is part of the U.S. Department of Energy. It provides information here on its multi-disciplinary research that aims to solve environmental, energy, health and national security problems.

Sandia National Laboratories

http://www.sandia.gov/

The Department of Energy's Sandia National Laboratories describes its programs and research here. The site includes a search tool.

Terrestrial Ecosystems Regional Research and Analysis Laboratory

http://www.terra.colostate.edu/

Terrestrial Ecosystems Regional Research and Analysis Laboratory (TERRA), an interagency group of U.S. government earth scientists, incorporates knowledge of the ecosystem into earth system modeling. Links here lead primarily to U.S. government sites and TERRA information.

USDA Forest Service Home Page

http://www.fs.fed.us/

The U.S. Forest Service is mandated to provide multiple uses on the nation's public forests. It provides information on its various programs -- from cutting trees to maintaining camp sites.

U.S. Department of Energy

http://apollo.osti.gov/

The Department of Energy provides an overview of its work here along with current updates on it various projects. Visit for news of upcoming public meetings, text of the Secretary of Energy's speeches and correspondence, and an archive of declassified information.

"GREEN" COMPANIES

The Consortium on Green Design and Manufacturing

http://pan.cedar.univie.ac.at/

The Consortium on Green Design and Manufacturing, an initiative sponsored by the University of California at Berkeley, researches environmentally conscious manufacturing. It outlines its projects here and posts synopses of its papers.

The Direct Alternatives

http://www.sofcom.com.au/DA

Australia-based Direct Alternatives presents information about its mail-order business that sells environmentally and socially responsible products and services. Visitors can view clothing, toys, paper products and more, and can place orders online.

Eco-Rating International

http://www.eco-rating.com/

Eco-Rating International is an environmental agency that determines if a company passes the "green" litmus test. A panel of professionals judges performances, awarding leaves of approval to qualifying firms. Read about the process and take a look at the company scores.

Serveur WWW du BRGM

http://www.brgm.fr/

Environmentalists and miners will find common ground at BRGM, a French firm combining scientific research with a commitment to public service and a clean earth. Find out more about the company's research and international activities here.

HYDROLOGY

The California Rivers Assessment

http://ice.ucdavis.edu/California_Rivers_Assessment/

The California Rivers Assessment (CARA) program's home page provides details about and explains the project. A map shows the rivers involved, and visitors can access data about each river basin separately.

Edwards Aquifer Research and Data Center

http://eardc.swt.edu/

The Edwards Aquifer Research and Data Center provides information here on the underground reservoir that supplies water for more than 1.5 million people in the San Marcos, Texas, area. The site includes information on endangered species of the region.

The Great Lakes Environmental Research Laboratory

http://www.glerl.noaa.gov/

The Great Lakes Environmental Research Laboratory (GLERL) in Ann Arbor, Mich., explains its mission and current research here. The laboratory, part of the National Oceanic and Atmospheric Administration, researches toxicants, natural hazards, invasive species and local effects from global change, all with emphasis on the Great Lakes.

The HAPEX-Sahel Information System

http://www.orstom.fr/hapex

The HAPEX-Sahel Information System offers an interdisciplinary database with "contributed studies in hydrology, soil moisture, surface fluxes and vegetation, remote sensing science and meteorology." Anyone can browse, but only registered investigators can download data.

Hydrology-Related Internet Resources

http://terrassa.pnl.gov:2080/EESC/resourcelist/hydrology.html

Hydrology Web is maintained by the Pacific Northwest Laboratory's Earth and Environmental Sciences Center. Among other hydrology-related features, the site contains a keyword search for items in its extensive resources list. Visitors are invited to submit entries.

Navigation Information Connection (NIC) - Inland River Home Page

http://www.ncr.usace.army.mil/nic.htm

Developed to serve the needs of the inland navigation industry, the Army Corps of Engineers, the Coast Guard and others concerned with rivers and transport, this page offers an index to related information and resources found on the Internet.

Visitors will find access to photos, charts, maps, reports, notices and books.

Universities Water Information Network Home Page

http://www.uwin.siu.edu/

The Universities Council on Water Resources is a professional organization of universities "united to encourage education and research in water resources." Included are a water resources update, graduate programs directory, career opportunities in water resources and a hydrology brochure.

INSTITUTES AND UNIVERSITIES

Australian National University Research School of Earth Sciences

http://wwwrses.anu.edu.au/

The Research School of Earth Sciences at the Australian National University offers information about its program and introduces its staff on this page. The department's research groups also detail their latest projects.

BC Research Inc.

http://www.bcr.bc.ca/

BC Research, Inc. is a technology development corporation based in Vancouver, Canada. Visitors can learn about forest biotechnology, transportation systems and ergonomic projects. Employment opportunity listings and aerial photos of the facilities are available.

The Cecil H. and Ida M. Green Institute of Geophysics and Planetary Physics

http://igpp.ucsd.edu/

The Cecil H. and Ida M. Green Institute of Geophysics and Planetary Physics provides access to its server and various research units here. Find general information about the institute, as well as specific information about its programs and projects.

Cooperative Institute for Research in Environmental Sciences

http://cires.colorado.edu/

The Cooperative Institute for Research in Environmental Sciences at the University of Colorado, Boulder, maintains this home page with information about the institute, faculty and academic programs. Research and employment information, and links to related sites are offered.

Cornell University Center for the Environment

http://www.cfe.cornell.edu/

The Cornell Center for the Environment focuses on research, education and outreach programs,

with detailed information on research programs, seminars and numerous educational resources.

Earth Sciences and Resources Institute Home Page

http://www.esri.utah.edu/

The Earth Sciences and Resources Institute site contains background information on the Institute, descriptions of research projects in fossil fuels, mineral, geothermal and environmental assessments. Includes listings of publications, educational programs and facilities descriptions.

Ecological Modelling

http://dino.wiz.uni-kassel.de/ecobas.html

The University of Kassel, Germany, provides simulation models of ecological processes, information about simulation software and online related literature here. Visitors can also submit their own ecological models to the site. In English.

Environmental Research Institute of Michigan Home Page

http://www.erim.org/

The Environmental Research Institute of Michigan details its activities, facilities and programs here. Visitors can learn about the nonprofit's imaging technology research, access an image catalog or read conference and job vacancy listings.

Institute for Computational Earth System Science

http://skua.crseo.ucsb.edu/

The Institute for Computational Earth System Science at the University of California, Santa Barbara, couples earth and computer sciences. It details its research here, including a look at its long term ecological research in the Antarctic and a bio-optics project in Bermuda.

The Institute for Space and Terrestrial Science

http://www.ists.ca/Welcome.html

The Institute for Space and Terrestrial Science, a member of Canada's Ontario Centre of Excellence, maintains this informational site. Visit here to learn about the institute and link to its multidisciplinary research groups and related resources.

McGill University Earth and Planetary Sciences Department

http://stoner.eps.mcgill.ca/

The Earth and Planetary Sciences Department at Canada's McGill University maintains this site to introduce its people and programs. Visitors will find user home pages, graphic images, and other academic and administrative resources.

MIT Earth Resources Laboratory

http://www-erl.mit.edu/

The Earth, Atmospheric and Planetary Science division at Massachusetts Institute of Technology sponsors this page. Visitors can read about the relationships between applied geophysics and tectonophysics, seismology, environmental engineering and parallel computing.

National Geophysical Data Center

http://web.ngdc.noaa.gov/

The National Geophysical Data Center (NGDC) home page provides information about the organization and the fields with which it concerns itself: solar-terrestrial physics, solid earth geophysics, marine geology and geophysics, paleoclimatology and glaciology. Links are also provided to related Internet resources.

Oregon Graduate Institute of Science & Technology Environmental Science and Engineering Department

http://www.ese.ogi.edu/

The Department of Environmental Science and Engineering at the Oregon Graduate Institute of Science & Technology maintains this look at its research centers and facilities, faculty, course listings and admissions requirements. Links to related sites on and off campus are also featured.

Oxford University Department of Earth Sciences

http://www.earth.ox.ac.uk/

The Department of Earth Sciences at the University of Oxford, England offers a site with information about the department, access to research data, publications, an anonymous FTP service and links to related sites.

Stanford University School of Earth Sciences

http://pangea.stanford.edu/

The School of Earth Sciences at Stanford University offers information about its programs as well as links to other earth sciences resources. Visitors will find faculty directories and general information here.

SUNY Stony Brook - Earth and Space Sciences

http://sbast3.ess.sunysb.edu/home.html

At this site, the Department of Earth and Space Sciences at the State University of New York, Stony Brook, provides academic information for future geologists, astronomers, physicists and other scientists.

UCAR/OFPS

http://www.ofps.ucar.edu/

The University Corporation for Atmospheric Research in Boulder, Colo., maintains this site for its Office of Field Project Support. Visitors will find its mission statement, activity updates, project overviews and links to affiliated organizations.

University of Arizona Geosciences

http://www.geo.arizona.edu/

Explore academic and research opportunities at the University of Arizona's Department of Geosciences site. Educational outreach programs and seismic observatory facilities are also outlined here.

University of Chicago Department of the Geophysical Sciences

http://geosci.uchicago.edu/

The home page for the Department of Geophysical Sciences at the University of Chicago offers links to information about the department and its faculty, as well as current research in the fields of atmospheres, oceans, geochemistry, paleontology and evolution.

University of Hong Kong Department of Earth Sciences

http://www.hku.hk/earthsci/rock.html

The Department of Earth Sciences at the University of Hong Kong maintains this overview of its academic programs. An introduction to the university, plus links to the libraries and service centers are also featured.

University of Illinois College of Agricultural, Consumer and Environmental Sciences

http://w3.ag.uiuc.edu/

The College of Agricultural, Consumer and Environmental Sciences at the University of Illinois Urbana-Champaign maintains this overview. Links to the college's administration offices, academic units, computer and information units, online class resources and related sites are provided.

The University of Illinois Imaging Systems Laboratory

http://imlab9.landarch.uiuc.edu/

The University of Illinois Imaging Systems Laboratory uses computer visualization to evaluate large scale environmental changes. Visitors here will get an overview of its research and can access software and databases.

University of Kuopio

http://www.uku.fi/

The University of Kuopio is an institute in Finland for the study of natural, health and social sciences. Visitors to this site will find information on degree programs, research projects and faculty. In English and Finnish.

University of Maine Department of Wildlife Ecology

http://wlm13.umenfa.maine.edu/w4v1.html

The Department of Wildlife Ecology at the University of Maine offers a wealth of information here

about its faculty, students, programs, research, events and resources. Visitors can also link here to related sites of interest, such as biological and U.S. federal government agencies.

The University of Oklahoma College of Geosciences

http://geowww.gcn.uoknor.edu/

The College of Geosciences at the University of Oklahoma provides academic links, links to weather sites and geoscience research organizations. Newsletters on atmospheric electricity are provided as is information about the energy center.

The University of Oregon Environmental Studies Department

http://zebu.uoregon.edu/~ambiente/enviro/

The University of Oregon Environmental Studies Department maintains this page with information about its faculty, links to student resources, and details about the department and its programs.

The World Conservation Monitoring Centre

http://www.wcmc.org.uk/

The World Conservation Monitoring Centre keeps a finger on the pulse of sustainable development world wide. The Cambridge, England-based organization posts data and published materials here and provides links to related sites.

Worldwatch Institute

gopher://gopher.igc.apc.org:70/11/orgs/worldwatch

The Worldwatch Institute researches sustainable growth options and takes the pulse of the planet on a yearly basis. Visitors will get an overview of the widely respected institute and its publications here.

York University Geophysics Group

http://aurora.york.ac.uk/

York University's Geophysics Group is the base for the U.K. Sub-Auroral Magnetometer Network. The group maintains this page as a guide to its projects, data and personnel, and as a gateway to related sites of interest.

JOURNALS AND PERIODICALS

The Arid Lands Newsletter

http://ag.arizona.edu/OALS/ALN/ALNHome.html

This University of Arizona publication offers ecological perspectives on topics related to desert lands. Issue titles have included "Conserving

Biodiversity" and "The Deserts in Literature." Access to the electronic archive is available here.

CRC Press, Inc. - Home Page

http://www.crcpress.com/

CRC Press of Boca Raton, Fla., supplies information on its journals (such as Critical Reviews in Analytical Chemistry), newsletters and other offerings. Included are product catalogs and information on environmental short-courses and seminars.

Ecosystem

http://www.gold.net/ecosystem/

The Ecosystem home page from the Conservation Foundation serves as an environmental information service on the Web, with links to The Environment Digest as well as Tomorrow Magazine and The Ecologist. It also provides information on environmentally responsible businesses and various organizations that are working to keep our planet healthy.

LIBRARIES

EcoDirectory

gopher://poniecki.berkeley.edu:570/1

This gopher menu is the electronic version of the "EcoDirectory." It contains an extensive listing of libraries and environmental information centers in Poland, Hungary, the Czech and Slovak Republics, Bulgaria and Romania.

Electronic Membrane-Information Library

ftp://www.ccwr.ac.za/emily/

The Electronic Membrane-Information Library (EMILY) is a project of the Water Research Commission of South Africa. Visitors here can access membrane modeling software, newsletters, online publications and databases. Information on researchers and conferences, plus links to related sites are also featured.

Internet Environmental Library

http://www.envirolink.org/EnviroLink_Library/

The Internet Environmental Library, a project of the EnviroLink Network, is a clearinghouse of all environmental information on the the Internet. Links to info on how to protect the planet, Enviro-Events, the Educational Network for Environmentalists and Green Business and Government Resources.

Lamont-Doherty Earth Observatory Climate Group's Data Library

http://rainbow.ldgo.columbia.edu/datacatalog.html

The LDEO Climate Library provides users with a powerful database of information in climatology, oceanography and earth sciences. In addition to a general introduction and users' guide, researchers can conduct database searches, access relevant electronic magazines and utilize interactive learning materials.

University of Michigan Digital Library Project

http://http2.sils.umich.edu/UMDL/HomePage.html

Located at the University of Michigan in Ann Arbor, the Digital Library Project represents an interdisciplinary collaboration to assemble and provide a diverse collection of earth and space sciences resource materials. Visitors are invited to learn more about the project and those working on it. This page also links to related sites.

Virtual Library: Geophysics

http://www-crewes.geo.ucalgary.ca/VL-Geophysics.html

This Virtual Library Geophysics page is maintained by the University of Calgary. Visitors can find links to resources, software and physics-related references.

The World-Wide Web Virtual Library: Environment

http://ecosys.drdr.virginia.edu/Environment.html

The WWW Virtual Library environment index provides links to sites specializing in biodiversity and ecology, earth sciences, energy, environmental law, forestry, landscape architecture and oceanography.

RECYCLING

EcoWeb

http://ecosys.drdr.virginia.edu/

The University of Virginia's EcoWeb page contains data about the school's environmental information systems, the school recycling program, links of interest and a keyword search.

The Home Page of Global Recycling Network

http://grn.com/grn/ora.html

The Global Recycling Network provides volumes of paperless information about the recycling industry here. The site contains up-to-date commodity and stock information, links to organizations, links to businesses selling recycling and recycled wares, and online directories for companies in the recycling industry.

SOLID WASTE DISPOSAL COMPANIES

WMX Technologies

http://www.wmx.com/

Illinois-based environmental-services company WMX Technologies explains its waste-management and related services at this home page. The main feature here is a link to the company's most recent annual report.

ENGINEERING

ACOUSTICAL ENGINEERING

Audio Engineering Society

http://www.aes.org

This page provides information on educational and career opportunities in audio engineering. Includes links to audio products, a Web index, interactive career forum and related resources.

Department of Speech Communication & Music Acoustics, KTH

http://www.speech.kth.se/

The Department of Speech Communication and Music Acoustics at the Royal Institute of Technology maintains this server, which provides information about the department's education and research. Browsers can listen to demonstrations of the departments speech synthesizers in 12 languages and link to other online campus resources here.

AERONAUTIC AND AEROSPACE ENGINEERING

COMPANIES

Malin Space Science Systems

http://barsoom.msss.com/

Malin Space Science Systems designs, develops and operates spacecraft instrumentation. This site provides links to information about its projects, educational activities and flight project participation.

DESIGN AND DEVELOPMENT

The Aircraft Aerodynamics and Design Group

http://aero.stanford.edu/ADG.html

The Aircraft Aerodynamics and Design Group from Stanford University is profiled through this page. Visitors can read about the people in the group, as well as their projects and technical reports. The group's work is supported by a number of aerospace firms.

Arnold Engineering Development Center

http://info.arnold.af.mil/

Located at Arnold Air Force Base in Tennessee, the Arnold Engineering Development Center is the world's largest flight simulation test facility. Links include the EPA/AEDC Spectral Database, AEDC technical reports and the AEDC newsletter.

Center for Advanced Aviation System Development

http://www.caasd.org/

The Center for Advanced Aviation System Development is a federally funded research and development facility focusing on systems engineering. Includes descriptions of research programs, access to technical reports, laboratory facilities and links to other aviation servers.

Desktop Aeronautics Index Page

http://www.desktopaero.com/index.html

This Web site connects visitors with information about Desktop Aeronautics, Inc., a company which offers software products used in aerodynamic design and analysis. Included here are catalog and software information, sample source code, program demos, related links and an order form.

Glenn L. Martin Wind Tunnel

http://windvane.umd.edu/

Seeking to advance aerodynamic design of vehicles and aircraft as well as develop cutting-edge testing methods, the Glenn L. Martin Wind Tunnel incorporates state-of-the-art modeling methodologies, instrumentation and integration of computing capabilities to enhance design technologies and techniques in aerospace engineering.

Numerical Aerodynamic Simulation

http://www.nas.nasa.gov/

Maintained by NASA and the U.S. Department of Defense, the Numerical Aerodynamic Simulation facility allows engineers to test the aerodynamics of various machinery models. Find out more about the facility, search the NAS data and information archive or link to sites of related interest.

The Wisconsin Wind Tunnel Project

http://www.cs.wisc.edu/~wwt/

The Wisconsin Wind Tunnel Project of the University of Wisconsin at Madison maintains this informational site. Visit here to learn about the project, download graphics and technical documents, link to related programs, and more.

INDICES

NASA Scientific and Technical Information Server

http://www.sti.nasa.gov/STI-homepage.html

NASA's Scientific and Technical Information Server provides easy access to more than three million aerospace-related information sources, both current and historical.

INSTITUTES AND UNIVERSITIES

Advanced Computational Engineering (ACE) Lab

http://diana.ae.utexas.edu/

The Advanced Computational Engineering (ACE) Laboratory invites visitors to its home page to learn about the lab and its work. Publications, images, staff profiles and general information are offered for review.

Department of Aerospace Engineering

http://www.aero.gla.ac.uk/

The Department of Aerospace Engineering at Scotland's University of Glasgow maintains this overview of its academic program. Meet faculty and students, review course requirements, learn about upcoming seminars or link to related sites.

Information Infrastructure Technology and Applications

http://iita.ivv.nasa.gov/iita1.html

This page explains NASA's Information Infrastructure Technology and Applications (IITA) project, which was designed to speed up the development and implementation of the United States' information infrastructure. Visitors can learn about this multi-faceted program and link to a listing of IITA projects here.

Institute of Fluid Mechanics at the German Aerospace Research Establishment

http://www.ts.go.dlr.de/

The Institute of Fluid Mechanics is part of the German Aerospace Research Establishment (DLR). Its site contains general information, as well as information on research activities and links to other DLR sites. In English and German.

CAD (COMPUTER AIDED DESIGN)

COMPANIES

Ashlar

http://www.ashlar.com/

CAD software developer, Ashlar, Inc., pitches its newest version of Ashlar-Vellum 3D at this promotional site. Visitors can review new product offerings and access technical support.

AspenTech

http://www.aspentec.com/

This promotional site is the corporate home page of AspenTech, an international supplier of process modeling technology. Visitors are invited to learn more about the company, its software products, customer support, services and university programs.

Bentley MAINline - The MicroStation Automated Information Network

http://www.bentley.com/

Bentley Systems, Inc., located in Exton, Pa., manufactures computer-aided design products for engineers, architects and drafters. Visit this site to learn about its CAD products, services and related resources. Includes keyword search.

Elan GMK

http://elan-gmk.com/elan.htm

Elan GMK, an electronic scanning, drafting and data storage company based in Moorpark, Calif., outlines its services at this promotional site. Visit here to learn about its capabilities, including engineering document scanning, vector conversion and re-drafting, CD-ROM recording, and Internet marketing.

Pathtrace Systems Inc.

http://mfginfo.com/cadcam/edgecam/pathtrace.htm

Manufacturers searching for solutions to engineering problems can check Pathtrace System Inc., for news about its CAD CAM-based manufacturing software. Visitors can also use the search engine to find information about manufacturers, suppliers and more.

Welcome to Silicon Engineering

http://www.sei.com/

Silicon Engineering, Inc., a Scott Valley, Calif.-based engineering services company, maintains this promotional site. Visit here to learn about its corporate client base, design services and product offerings. Includes employment opportunities and contact information.

INSTITUTES AND UNIVERSITIES

The CAD Centre at the University of Strathclyde

http://www.cad.strath.ac.uk/Home.html

The CAD Centre at the University of Strathclyde, Glasgow, Scotland, is a postgraduate center researching design methods for engineering applications. This page has information on courses, research, facilities and publications.

Center for Design Research Home Page

http://gummo.stanford.edu/

The Center for Design Research (CDR), Stanford University, facilitates research on design process and design tool development for engineering. A range of information on the center's staff, laboratories and projects is available at this site.

Tri-Service CADD/GIS Technology Center

http://mr2.wes.army.mil/

Computer-Aided Design and Drafting and Geographic Information Services resources are available from the Tri-Service CADD/GIS Technology Center in Vicksburg, Miss. Visitors can learn about the center's organization and mission or link to a variety of technical and Department of Defense resources.

NEWS

Journal of Computer-Aided Molecular Design

http://www.ibc.wustl.edu/jcamd/jcamd.html

A product of ESCOM Science Publishers, the "Journal of Computer-Aided Molecular Design" is archived at this site. Find back issues of the journal, subscription data, submission guidelines and information about the editor and editorial board.

CHEMICAL ENGINEERING

ASSOCIATIONS AND ORGANIZATIONS

The Ecosse Group

http://www.chemeng.ed.ac.uk/ecosse/

The home page of the Ecosse Group -- an organization dedicated to constructing better designs for chemical process -- provides directories, technical reports and information on the design engineering environment and support system.

Society of Petroleum Engineers - Gulf Coast Area

http://www.neosoft.com/spegcs

The Society of Petroleum Engineers presents information on the Gulf Coast Section of the organization, its newsletter, member home pages and career search tools. Includes info on related conferences and seminars.

INDICES

Petroleum Pages Index

http://www.pe.utexas.edu/Dept/Reading/petroleum.html

This page contains an index of resources all relating to the petroleum industry. Among some of the destinations offered here are publications, jobs, government agencies, educational institutions and software.

Petroleum Technology Research Information System

http://www.pteris.co.uk/psti.html

The Petroleum Technology Research Information System (PTERIS) Web page features information about online conferences on the oil and gas industry and provides links to oil and gas resources on the Web. The non-profit company is dedicated to improving oil and gas exploration and production efficiency.

The WWW Virtual Library Chemical Engineering

http://www.che.ufl.edu/WWW-CHE/index.html

The WWW Virtual Library Chemical Engineering site offers links to organizations, electronic publications, listings of various chemical engineering-related events and information on submitting items to be included at this site.

INSTITUTES AND UNIVERSITIES

Caltech: Division of Chemistry and Chemical Engineering

http://www.caltech.edu/caltech/Chemistry.html

The Division of Chemistry and Chemical Engineering at the California Technical University provides information here on its graduate and undergraduate programs. Visit here to learn about its faculty, research projects and laboratory facilities.

Chemical Engineering

http://che.www.ecn.purdue.edu/

This site is the home page of the Chemical Engineering Department of Purdue University in West Lafayette, Ind. Visitors can learn more about the department's undergraduate and graduate programs, its research projects, facilities, student organizations, faculty and staff.

Chemical Engineering, Carnegie Mellon University

http://www.cheme.cmu.edu/

The Department of Chemical Engineering at Carnegie Mellon University outlines its undergraduate and graduate study programs on this home page. The site also includes a who's who among the faculty and descriptions of the facilities.

The Department of Chemical Engineering at Edinburgh University

http://www.chemeng.ed.ac.uk/

Edinburgh University's Department of Chemical Engineering posts information on its courses, faculty and students here. The site also contains course materials and a link to the department's FTP archive.

Department of Chemical Engineering Princeton University

http://www.princeton.edu/~chemical

Princeton University's Department of Chemical Engineering maintains this site featuring information on its academic programs, personnel and research projects. Links to online resources and related sites outside the department are also included.

Fraunhofer IAO - Home Page

http://www.iao.fhg.de/

The Fraunhofer Institute of the University of Stuttgart, Germany, maintains this site for general information. Visit here to learn about its engineering projects and consulting centers, access its database archives, find employment opportunities and more.

The Petroleum Recovery Institute

http://www.pri.ab.ca/

The Petroleum Recovery Institute in Alberta, Canada maintains this server featuring info about the research organization's staff, membership services, courses and resources. Visitors can read project and annual reports, or link to related sites.

CIVIL ENGINEERING

GENERAL

ASCE Journal of Infrastructure Systems

http://ce.ecn.purdue.edu/jis.html

"The Journal of Infrastructure Systems" is published by the American Society of Civil Engineers and contains articles and resources pertinent to the profession. Visitors can learn about the journal, check author and subject indices or browse abstracts of published papers here. Includes guidelines for authors.

Civil Engineering at Carleton University

http://www.civeng.carleton.ca/

Faculty and staff at Carleton University's Civil and Environmental Engineering department outline general professional information, course offerings and describe ongoing research projects here. A few completed theses and abstracts are also available.

Department of Civil and Mechanical Engineering - University of Tasmania

http://info.utas.edu.au/docs/beasley/civenghp.htm

The Civil Engineering Department at the University of Tasmania in Australia features its programs and faculty on this home page. Visitors can check out the department or click to the college home page for more general information.

Faculty of Civil Engineering Home Page

http://www.fce.vutbr.cz/

The Faculty of Civil Engineering at Czech Technical University of Brno provides information on its academic programs and research projects at this site. Review educational resources and opportunities in English and Czech.

Fakultät Bauwesen - Universität Bochum

http://www.bi.ruhr-uni-bochum.de/

The Civil Engineering Department at the University of Bochum in Germany provides information about its offices and departments. Only partial information is available in English.

Infrastructure Technology Institute (ITI)

http://iti.acns.nwu.edu/

Here, Northwestern University's Infrastructure Technology Institute (ITI) features the latest research and technology related to infrastructure development. The page covers current research projects concerning roads, bridges and high-speed telecommunications.

RMIT Civil & Geological Engineering

http://www.civgeo.rmit.edu.au/

The Royal Melbourne Institute of Technology introduces its academic programs and research in geological, environmental and civil engineering. Read descriptions of the various graduate and undergraduate programs of study, access the department's computer network or meet with the faculty and staff.

University of Manitoba Department of Civil and Geological Engineering

http://www.ce.umanitoba.ca/

Engineers or wannabes will find information about the University of Manitoba's Civil and Geological Engineering Department, as well as a list of the department's current activities and outside links.

Upside Engineering

http://www.worldweb.com/Upside

Services provided by Upside Engineering are detailed here, including development engineering, project management, design engineering and operations engineering. Examples of the company's latest innovations, projects and clients are provided. The company is based in Calgary, Canada.

World-Wide Web Virtual Library: Civil Engineering

http://www.ce.gatech.edu/WWW-CE/home.html

Visitors to the Virtual Library Civil Engineering page are provided with a comprehensive list of links to information about Civil Engineering, including gopher servers and FTP archives. This list also includes links to universities, organizations, government agencies and commercial sites from around the world.

ASSOCIATIONS AND ORGANIZATIONS

Building Research Establishment

http://www.bre.co.uk/

Building Research Establishment offers advice and information to building engineers and the construction industry. Visitors can review the British government agency's consulting services and online resources.

U.S. Army Corps of Engineers Information Network

http://www.usace.army.mil/

The U.S. Army Corps of Engineers serves to "manage and execute engineering, construction and real estate programs for the U.S. Army and Air Force and for other federal agencies." The USACE Information Network provides USACE news, information on its programs, and links to resources inside and outside of the USACE.

CONSTRUCTION AND EXCAVATION

AceNet

http://www.aecnet.com/

This home page provides resources for architects, engineers and those in the construction trades.

Visitors will find industry and building product news, plus various reference materials and a job mart here.

InterPRO Resources Inc.

http://www.ipr.com/

This Orlando, Fla.-based company offers a wide variety of information and services for architects, engineers and contractors. Visitors will find publications and lists of construction industry firms and professional organizations.

U.S. Army Construction Engineering Research Laboratories

http://www.cecer.army.mil/

This site contains the home page for the U.S. Army Corps of Engineers' Construction Engineering Research Laboratories located in Champaign, Ill. Links provide visitors an overview of the facility, its mission, operations and personnel, and current research projects.

U. S. Army Corps of Engineers: Seattle District

http://www.nps.usace.army.mil/cenps.html

The Seattle district of the U.S. Army Corps of Engineers maintains this site for general information and resource access. Visit here for construction specifications, historical structures preservation programs, upcoming contract information and links to other Army Corps districts.

HYDRAULIC ENGINEERING

California Water Page

http://wwwdwr.water.ca.gov/

The California Department of Water Resources is online with descriptions of its research and administrative programs, current water conditions throughout the state and the latest press releases. Users can get an overview of the government agency or read about the mammoth State Water Project.

Cold Region Engineering

http://www.usace.army.mil/crrel

The U.S. Army Corps of Engineers introduces its Cold Regions Research and Engineering Laboratory in Hanover, N.H., here. The site includes online publications, information about CRREL's research programs -- like the Ice Engineering Research Division and the Icejam Database-- and news of upcoming conferences.

Institute of Hydraulics and Automation

http://www.tut.fi/~ihatut/index.html/

Learn about hydraulics and fluid power without getting wet at this Web site, maintained by the Institute of Hydraulics and Automation at the Tampere University of Technology. This site features the latest research as well as course information.

Water Resource Systems Research Unit

http://wrsru7.ncl.ac.uk/

The Water Resource Systems Research Unit is a group within the Department of Civil Engineering at England's Newcastle-upon-Tyne University. Find a general overview of the program as well as specific research project reports at this site.

MUNICIPAL ENGINEERING

Alaska Department of Transportation and Public Facilities

http://www.dot.state.ak.us/

The State of Alaska Department of Transportation and Public Facilities home page offers system overviews of the state's highways and airports. Find design specifications and facility plans here.

California Partners for Advanced Transit and Highways

http://www-path.eecs.berkeley.edu/

California Partners for Advanced Transit and Highways (PATH) — a collaboration involving the University of California, the California Department of Transportation and private industry players — aims to unsnarl traffic congestion while decreasing smog and fuel consumption. This Web site explains PATH's goals and various research projects.

Galaxy Transportation Index

http://galaxy.einet.net/galaxy/Engineering-and-Technology/Transportation.html

TradeWave's Galaxy information service maintains this site for its transportation resource index. Visitors will find an extensive collection of links to related organizations, publications, government agencies and events.

Railway Technical Research Institute

http://www.rtri.or.jp/index.html

Japan's Railway Technical Research Institute maintains this site for an overview of its projects and various rail-related subjects. Visit here for research and development activity updates, a history of the Japanese rail system, and a look at the structural effects of 1995's Kobe earthquake.

York Traffic Web

http://gridlock.york.ac.uk/

The York Network Control Group is an organization dedicated to designing new ways of reducing urban traffic congestion. Visitors to this site can read about the group's research, members and programs, or access online versions of its papers.

STRUCTURAL ENGINEERING

Bridge Engineering Home Page

http://www.best.com/~solvers/bridge.html

The Bridge Engineering home page, maintained by Mountain View, Calif.-based SC Solutions, Inc., provides links to government agencies, research and educational institutions, companies and other organizations in the civil/structural bridge engineering community. Includes news and upcoming events.

The Bridges of Portland, Oregon

http://www.teleport.com/~bizave/portland/bridges/

Probably recreational reading to civil engineers, the Bridges of Portland, Oregon, makes clear the ingenuity behind bridge building. Maps and information are included at this photo-rich site, proving that a picture is worth a thousand words.

ELECTRICAL ENGINEERING

GENERAL

Electrical Engineering on the World Wide Web

http://www.e2w3.com/

E2W3 -- Electrical Engineering on the World Wide Web -- provides a searchable index of links to companies that manufacture semiconductors, computer hardware and software. Includes links to publications and information on conferences, educational programs and associations.

General Electric Co.

http://www.ge.com/

General Electric, a U.S.-based technology, manufacturing and services company, maintains this promotional site. Visitors will find news, products and services descriptions, worldwide operations overviews, and departmental/divisional information resources.

Lexicon of Semiconductor Terms

http://rel.semi.harris.com/docs/lexicon/preface.html

An exhaustive lexicon of semiconductor terms, abbreviations and acronyms is maintained at this Web site by industry giant, Harris Semiconductor.

Mitre Corp.

http://www.mitre.org/

MITRE specializes in the development and acquisition of large-scale electronic information systems for such clients as the U.S. Department of Defense and Federal Aviation Administration. Visitors to its home page will find corporate news, resource and capability overviews, and employment opportunities.

ASSOCIATIONS AND ORGANIZATIONS

ASEE Clearinghouse for Engineering Education

http://www.asee.org/

The American Society for Engineering Education is a professional organization of electrical engineers and educators. Visitors to its site will find databases of engineering associations and education programs. Links to electrical engineering sources on the Internet are also provided.

The Electronics Research Group

http://www.erg.abdn.ac.uk/

The Electronics Research Group site contains information about research activities, satellite link-up programs, neural Web service and archives of the group's publications. Includes information about software reengineering services and background material.

European Association for Education in Electrical and Information Engineering

http://cran.esstin.u-nancy.fr/PresEAEEIE.html

The European Association for Education in Electrical and Information Engineering works to foster communication and improve educational practices throughout the European community. Visit here for conference information, activity bulletins and links to related resources.

EXACT Home Page

http://exact.fmv.se/

EXACT, an international technical association, seeks to facilitate communication about electronic component technology. This site gives background information on the organization and provides access to reports as well as a directory of test equipment.

The Georgia Center for Advanced Telecommunications Technology

http://www.gcatt.gatech.edu/

The Georgia Center for Advanced Telecommunications Technology works to develop the growth of Georgia's telecommunications industry through collaborative research, education, health care and public policy programs. This site explains the organization's activities and lists its corporate sponsors.

IEEE Communications Society

http://www.comsoc.org

The IEEE Communications Society offers registration for Broadband Workshop '96. The society's scope of interest encompasses all aspects of communications with machines.

IEEE: The Institute of Electrical and Electronics Engineers, Inc. Student Activities

http://fiddle.ee.vt.edu/ieee/home.html

The Institute of Electrical and Electronics Engineers, Inc., (IEEE) Student Activities Committee page provides links to the regional activities board, membership information, technical standards information, and a list of sections, chapters, areas and councils.

The Institute of Electrical and Electronics Engineers

http://www.ieee.org/i3e_hp.html

The Institute of Electrical and Electronic Engineers site contains information about the organization, its member services and affiliated technical societies. Includes a student activities section, bookstore, listings of publications and links to related local events.

Institute of Electrical and Electronics Engineers Societies

http://www.ieee.org/society.html

At this site is a directory of the dozens of technical societies from the Institute of Electrical and Electronics Engineers. Among them are the Broadcast Technology, Communications and Information Theory societies.

Institution of Electrical Engineers Home Page

http://www.iee.org.uk/

The Institution of Electrical Engineers is a professional organization for European engineers. Visitors here will find information about conferences, events and guidelines.

International Commission on Illumination

http://www.hike.te.chiba-u.ac.jp/ikeda/CIE/home.html

The International Commission on Illumination is composed of a world-wide group of member nations committed to the cooperation "on all matters relating to the science and art of lighting." Find publications and standards relating to light and lighting from vision to photometry at this site.

International Electrotechnical Commission,IEC

http://www.hike.te.chiba-u.ac.jp/ikeda/IEC/home.html

This site details aspects of the International Electrotechnical Commission, located in Geneva, Swit-

zerland, and founded in 1906. The commission promotes international cooperation on all questions of standardization and related matters in the fields of electrical and electronic engineering.

Lasers and Electro Optics Society

http://msrc.wvu.edu/leos/

Applying itself to research, development, design and manufacture of "lasers, optical devices, optical fibers, and associated lightwave technology," this Institute of Electrical and Electronics Engineers professional society posts its publications here, along with events and job opportunities listings.

Professional Organizations and Government Labs for Electrical Engineers

http://www.ee.umr.edu/orgs/

Electrical Engineers can link to professional organizations and government labs at this site. Find a laundry list of scientific acronyms and their corresponding associations and facilities here.

SPAsystem

http://stdsbbs.ieee.org/

"A loosely connected set of information technologies," SPAsystem is "intended to streamline IEEE (Institute of Electrical and Electronic Engineers) standards development process." Visit this site to access announcements, Frequently Asked Questions (FAQ) and working groups or read about IEEE products and publications.

Student Branches of the Institute of Electrical and Electronic Engineering

http://sandbox.ieee.org/lists/branches.html

The Institute of Electrical and Electronic Engineering (IEEE) provides this large collection of links to its student branches with Web pages. Links are arranged by region.

Yale IEEE Chapter

http://joyce.eng.yale.edu/

The Yale University chapter of the Institute of Electrical and Electronics Engineers (IEEE) maintains this WWW Server & Student Lab/Lounge. Find the minutes from past meetings, restaurant recommendations, chapter news flashes and links to selected Web and FTP sites.

CIRCUITRY

The Berkeley Sensor & Actuator Center Homepage

http://bsac.eecs.berkeley.edu/

The Berkeley Sensor and Actuator Center (BSAC) focuses on sensors and miniature moving mechanical elements that take advantage of the progress in integrated circuit technology. This Web site discusses BSAC's personnel and

research projects and archives the center's publications.

The Center for Compound Semiconductor Microelectronics

http://www.ccsm.uiuc.edu/ccsm/

Here, engineers and prospective students can get an overview of the Center for Compound Semiconductor Microelectronics at the University of Illinois-Urbana. The center posts information about its research, a seminar schedule and a call for papers.

Circuit Theory Laboratory

http://www.aplac.hut.fi/

The Circuit Theory Laboratory at Finland's Helsinki University of Technology maintains this site for general information. Visit here to learn about its research activities in analog components, review its courses and browse its publications. In English and Finnish.

Com21, Inc.

http://www.com21.com/

Com21 is a Mountain View, Calif.-based telecommunication company that develops integrated products for cable television and regional telephone service infrastructures. Visit this site to link with corporate background information, product descriptions and employment opportunities.

Cypress Semiconductor - Welcome

http://www.cypress.com/

Cypress Semiconductor Corporation supplies integrated circuits to the telecommunications, computer and military industries. Visitors to this California company's Web site will find a corporate profile, product information and technical support.

Electronic Circuit Design Home Page

http://www.eeb.ele.tue.nl/

Visitors to the Electronic Circuit Design Home Page can find information on neural networks, digital signal processing, ProRISC and electrical engineering.

FTP Interface for Motorola Archives

http://nyquist.ee.ualberta.ca/html/motorola.html

This online archive provides working tools for engineers working on Motorola microprocessor development. Included here are links to the site's provider, the University of Alberta's electrical engineering department, and to Motorola's home page and freeware services.

IBM Microelectronics

http://www.chips.ibm.com/

The Microelectronics Division of IBM sponsors this page. Check out the latest developments in the industry, browse product information, access employment opportunities or link to the IBM main server.

Microelectronics Research Center at the University of Idaho

http://www.mrc.uidaho.edu/

This site for the Microelectronics Research Center at the University of Idaho includes information on the center, its research staff and current projects related to high-performance integrated circuits. Includes links to NASA and other related Internet resources.

MIT Microsystems Technology Laboratories

http://www-mtl.mit.edu/

The Massachusetts Institute of Technology (MIT) Microsystems Technology Laboratories supports education and research in microsystems engineering through its programs, publications and seminars. Link to the lab's bulletins and research abstracts at this site.

Semiconductor Subway

http://www-mtl.mit.edu/semisubway.html

Maintained by the MIT Microsystems Technology Lab, this page is designed to promote education and disperse info on microsystems and semiconductor technology. Topics include fabrication, technology computer aided design, manufacturing research, microelectromechanical systems and more.

INSTITUTES AND UNIVERSITIES

Applied Science and Engineering Laboratories

http://www.asel.udel.edu/

Dedicated to the "research development and dissemination of new technologies for people with disabilities," the Applied Science and Engineering Laboratories addresses needs in five major areas: rehabilitation robotics, speech, system structure, natural language interfaces, and opportunities for students with disabilities.

The Argonne National Laboratory

http://www.anl.gov/

The Argonne National Laboratory is a Department of Energy research group with sites in Illinois and Idaho. Visitors will find detailed information on Argonne's projects, staff, facilities and activities.

The Berkeley Sensor & Actuator Center Homepage

http://bsac.eecs.berkeley.edu/

The Berkeley Sensor and Actuator Center (BSAC) focuses on sensors and miniature moving mechanical elements that take advantage of the progress in integrated circuit technology. This Web site discusses BSAC's personnel and research projects and archives the center's publications.

Chiba University—Ikeda Lab

http://www.hike.te.chiba-u.ac.jp/

The Ikeda Lab at the Department of Electrical Engineering at Chiba University in Japan gives a detailed look at its research here. The page also contains calls for papers and an extensive index to related sites on the Web. In English.

The Computational Neuroengineering Laboratory

http://www.hike.te.chiba-u.ac.jp/

Located in the Electrical Engineering Department at the University of Florida, the Computational Neuroengineering Laboratory provides this virtual tour. Visitors will find an overview of the lab with information on personnel, research projects, publications and seminars. Neural network resources are also included.

Czech Technical University Faculty of Electrical Engineering

http://www.feld.cvut.cz/

The Faculty of Electrical Engineering from the Czech Technical University, Praha, highlights its current research activities and available courses here. Visitors can also see an image of the main campus building and peruse a history of its studies. In English.

Department of Communication and Electronic Engineering

http://www.co.rmit.edu.au/

The Department of Communication and Electronic Engineering at the Royal Melbourne Institute of Technology in Australia, maintains this Web site to provide information on the Department's academics, awards, students and research.

Department of Electrical and Computer Engineering at Johns Hopkins University

http://www.ece.jhu.edu/

The Department of Electrical and Computer Engineering at Johns Hopkins University maintains this site offering information on its academic programs, teaching personnel and research facilities. Links to associated research centers, conference information and campus maps are also provided.

Department of Electrical and Computing Engineering at Mississippi State

http://www.ee.msstate.edu/

The Department of Electrical and Computing Engineering at Mississippi State University provides details on its faculty, programs and courses. Links to the High Voltage Laboratory and the Microsystems Prototyping Laboratory are included. The department also maintains a newsgroup, msu.ece.

Department of Electrical Engineering

http://electra.micro.caltech.edu/

The California Institute of Technology Department of Electrical Engineering home page offers an overview of its graduate and undergraduate curriculum. Faculty profiles, research information and pointers to related Web resources are provided as well.

The Department of Electronic Engineering at Hanyang University

http://venus.hanyang.ac.kr/

The Department of Electronic Engineering at Hanyang University in Korea was under construction when we last checked it. The Webmasters promise the site will contain information about the department as well as links to other Web servers in Korea.

The Department of Electronics at Carleton University

http://www.doe.carleton.ca/

The Department of Electronics at Carleton University gives potential students a first-class tour of this Canadian campus, providing information on academic programs, research activities and seminar series. This page also offers links to additional Ottawa Web servers and supporting software.

DIBE - Università di Genova

http://dibemail.dibe.unige.it/Welcome.html

The Department of Biophysical and Electronic Engineering at the University of Genova, Italy, provides information here on its academic departments and learning initiatives. Visit here to learn about the department and link to a variety of Internet starter pages.

Duke University Department of Electrical and Computer Engineering

http://www.ee.duke.edu/

Visitors to the Duke University Department of Electrical and Computer Engineering will find information about the department, research project, staff and facilities. Links to other engineering sites and publications are available.

ECE Department, UCSB

http://www.ece.ucsb.edu/

The Electrical and Computer Engineering Department at the University of California, Santa Barbara, provides details on research activities, programs of study and faculty accomplishments. Includes links to student information, campus resources and job listings.

EECS Department at Lehigh University

http://www.eecs.lehigh.edu/

General information on the people, resources and organizations that comprise Lehigh University's Electrical Engineering and Computer Science Department is provided here.

The EECS Department Home Page

http://www.eecs.umich.edu/

The University of Michigan at Ann Arbor presents the home page for its Electrical Engineering and Computer Sciences Department. Visitors will find information on academic programs, faculty, students, research and related organizations.

EHTZ: Department of Electrical Engineering

http://www.ee.ethz.ch/

The Department of Electrical Engineering at the Swiss Federal Institute of Technology in Zurich provides information on its research laboratories and academic departments. Links to the library, Computing Support Group and Microelectronics Design Center are also featured.

Electrical and Computer Engineering, Rice University

http://www-ece.rice.edu/

Here, prospective engineering students can learn about the program and faculty at Rice University's Department of Electrical and Computer Engineering. Researchers can also access the department's research archives here.

Electrical Engineering Department University of Maryland at College Park

http://www.ee.umd.edu/

Information on faculty, staff, programs, organizations and research are supplied here by the Department of Electrical Engineering at the University of Maryland. Among the institutes and centers located here are the Center for Automation Research and the Institute for Systems Research.

Electrical Engineering University of Edinburgh

http://www.ee.ed.ac.uk/

The University of Edinburgh's Department of Electrical Engineering provides information about its course offerings, programs of study and research projects. Includes faculty profiles, students' personal home pages, online documentation and links to other campus info servers.

Electrical and Computer Engineering - Carnegie Mellon University

http://www.ece.cmu.edu/Home-Page.html

The Electrical and Computer Engineering Department of Carnegie Mellon University maintains this informational site. Visit here to learn about the department's facilities, programs, faculty and students.

Electrical and Computer Engineering Department at Aristotle University of Thessalonika

http://uranus.eng.auth.gr/

The Electrical and Computer Engineering Department at Greece's Aristotle University of Thessalonika maintains this page. Visitors are invited explore the department, its resources, academic programs and course listings. In English and Greek.

Electrical and Computer Engineering Department of George Mason University

http://bass.gmu.edu/

The electrical and computer engineering department of George Mason University provides departmental announcements, seminar details and course offering information here. Includes an overview of programs offered.

Electrical Engineering and Computer Science Contributed Web, Northwestern University

http://www.eecs.nwu.edu/

This site is an in-house service providing access to Web publishing for the Northwestern University's electrical engineering and computer science department. This server offers departmental research information, plus links to university programs and information as well as local notices.

The ElectroScience Laboratory Home Page

http://hertz.eng.ohio-state.edu/

The ElectroScience Laboratory site describes its research projects in electromagnets. Includes descriptions of services, procedures and links to news items about the Ohio State University College of Engineering.

GTE Laboratories

http://info.gte.com/

GTE Laboratories in Waltham, Mass. is the central research and development arm of electrical product supplier GTE. Visit this site to learn about its products, research facilities, community services and more.

Hacettepe University Department of Electrical Engineering

http://www.ee.hun.edu.tr/

Hacettepe University's Department of Electrical Engineering provides this home page with information about the Turkey-based school's academics, faculty and students.

Institute of Electrical and Electronics Engineers Gopher Menu

gopher://gopher.ieee.org/

This is the gopher menu for the Institute of Electrical and Electronics Engineers (IEEE). Files are provided for general IEEE information, societies, products and services.

Institute of Microtechnology, University of Neuchâtel, Switzerland

http://www-imt.unine.ch/

The Institute of Microtechnology at Switzerland's University of Neuchatel offers information on its electronics and optics research projects and academic courses of study.

Istituto Ellettrotecnico Nazionale Galileo Ferraris

http://www.ien.it/

The study of robotics, metrology and the physics of matter are a few of the areas covered in a home page for the Istituto Ellettrotecnico Nazionale Galileo Ferraris in Torino, Italy. The page includes a history of the institute and a museum along with general information about its programs.

MIT Department of Electrical Engineering and Computer Science

http://www-eecs.mit.edu/

The Department of Electrical Engineering and Computer Science at Massachusetts Institute of Technology (MIT) gives a detailed look at its program, courses and faculty here. The site also includes links to student groups and the university's related research labs.

Mitsubishi Electric Research Laboratories

http://www.merl.com/

Mitsubishi Electric Research Laboratories in Cambridge, Mass., provides this informational site featuring a general overview, technical reports and research updates. Includes links to the Japanese parent company's home page.

New Mexico Institute of Mining and Technology Electrical Engineering and Physics Department

http://www.ee.nmt.edu/

The Electrical Engineering and Physics Departments of the New Mexico Institute of Mining and Technology maintains this site for general information on the department and and its academic resources. Visit here to learn about programs of study, faculty and course offerings.

Politechnika Gdanska, Electronics

http://www.gumbeers.elka.pg.gda.pl/

The Technical University of Gdansk's electronics department maintains this Web site from which visitors can access information about electrical engineering and computing, as well as details about the department. Includes links to Polish, Unix and Internet resources.

Portland State University: Department of Electrical and Computer Engineering

http://www.ee.pdx.edu/

Consider living up to your scientific potential at the Portland State University Department of Electrical Engineering home page. Explore educational opportunities, academic programs and research facilities.

Purdue School of Electrical and Computer Engineering

http://dynamo.ecn.purdue.edu/

The Department of Electrical and Computer Engineering at Purdue University, West Lafayette, Ind., has set up this home page with information about the department, faculty and research programs. Includes links to related engineering sites and the university's home page.

The Research and Development Center of Electrical Engineering

http://www.cpdee.ufmg.br/

The Research and Development Center of Electrical Engineering at Brazil's Universidade Federal de Minas Gerias provides departmental, research and faculty information at this site. In English and Portuguese.

Research Laboratory of Electronics

http://rleweb.mit.edu/

The Research Laboratory of Electronics provides an overview of the research facility, its history and research projects. The home page contains links to publications, staff members, descriptions of facilities and services.

School of Electrical and Computer Engineering

http://www.ee.gatech.edu/

The home page for the School of Electrical and Computer Engineering at the Georgia Institute of Technology presents information about research projects, course offerings and campus organizations. Includes academic program overviews and faculty profiles.

School of Electrical Engineering at the State University of Campinas

http://www.fee.unicamp.br/

The School of Electrical Engineering at the State University of Campinas in Brazil gives an overview of its research, courses and labs here. In English and a bit of Portuguese.

Stanford University - Electrical Engineering

http://www-ee.stanford.edu/ee.html

Stanford University's Electrical Engineering Department maintains this site to provide information about their faculty and facilities. Including are links to information on their programs, laboratories and research centers.

Temple Electrical Engineering Home Page

http://www.eng.temple.edu

The College of Engineering at Temple University offers this site devoted to its Electrical Engineering Department. Visitors can read about the departmental mission and faculty members here.

Tufts Electrical Engineering and Computer Science

http://www.cs.tufts.edu/

The Electrical Engineering and Computer Science department at Tufts University provides an overview of its degree programs here. The page also includes faculty and student home pages and the course catalog.

UC Davis: Electrical and Computer Engineering

http://www.ece.ucdavis.edu/

The University of California at Davis Department of Electrical and Computer Engineering (ECE) home page offers departmental news and listings of undergraduate and graduate student resources. Also included are links to ECE online research and computer lab information resources.

University of Alberta Electrical Engineering

http://nyquist.ee.ualberta.ca/index.html

Here, the University of Alberta Electrical Engineering Department features its Electronic Cookbook with circuit schematic fun, including the Blue Clipper fuzz box, switch debouncer and RC Relaxation oscillator. The page also has staff, research and graduate/undergraduate course details.

The University of California, Berkeley, Electrical Engineering and Computer

http://www.eecs.berkeley.edu/

The University of California, Berkeley, presents the Web server for its Electrical Engineering and Computer Sciences Department. Visitors will find information on research, classes, faculty and students here.

The University of Delaware Electrical Engineering and Computer and Information

http://www.eecis.udel.edu/

The University of Delaware's Electrical Engineering (EE) and Computer and Information Sciences

(CIS) departments maintain this site with information about course work, research and Internet services.

University of Illinois at Chicago Electrical Engineering and Computer Science Department

http://www.eecs.uic.edu/

Prospective students will learn about the University of Illinois at Chicago Electrical Engineering and Computer Science Department at this site. Visitors can read course descriptions and check out faculty and student profiles.

University of Illinois Department of Electrical and Computer Engineering

http://www.ece.uiuc.edu/

A Web site provided Department of Electrical and Computer Engineering at the University of Illinois at Urbana-Champaign is found here. The page includes faculty position announcements and links to other World Wide Web sites of interest.

University of Kansas EECS Home Page

http://www.eecs.ukans.edu/

The University of Kansas Electrical Engineering and Computer Science Department maintains this page with information about the department, graduate and undergraduate programs, and links to staff profiles. Links to research activities and instructional labs are also available.

University Of Oulu, Department Of Electrical Engineering

http://ee.oulu.fi/

Finland's University of Oulu celebrates the 30th birthday of its Department of Electrical Engineering. Tour the laboratories, review the courses and evaluate current research activities. Finnish speakers can take an online Unix course as well. Some English available.

University of Reeding Electronic Engineering

http://www.elec.rdg.ac.uk/

The University of Reeding in the United Kingdom presents the home page for its Engineering Department. Visitors will find information on academics, courses, admissions, faculty and research.

University of Washington Electrical Engineering

http://www.ee.washington.edu/

Research projects and faculty come to life on the Web through this site from the University of Washington's electrical engineering department. Visitors can see an overview of the programs offered and time schedules for upcoming seminars.

Washington State University, School of EE/CS

http://www.eecs.wsu.edu/

Washington State University's School of Electrical Engineering and Computer Science provides this overview. Find links to faculty and students as well as research groups and descriptions of department resources.

SPAsystem

http://stdsbbs.ieee.org/

"A loosely connected set of information technologies," SPAsystem is "intended to streamline IEEE (Institute of Electrical and Electronic Engineers) standards development process." Visit this site to access announcements, Frequently Asked Questions (FAQ) and working groups or read about IEEE products and publications.

POWER ENGINEERING

Ames Laboratory Home Page

http://www.ameslab.gov/

A U.S. Department of Energy laboratory operated by Iowa State University, Ames Laboratory explores the chemical, engineering, materials, mathematical and physical sciences in search of solutions to energy-related problems. Site features include an overview of the lab, its research programs and data.

Department of Energy, Office of Energy Research

http://www.er.doe.gov/

This U.S. Department of Energy site provides information on basic research and the development of new techniques in energy sciences. Find information on magnetic fusion energy, high energy nuclear physics and other alternatives to traditional energy production. Links to energy research offices and related servers.

Electric Power Research Institute

http://www.epri.com/

The Electric Power Research Institute (EPRI) encourages the development of technology within the electricity industry. The EPRI Web site displays a slick interface linking users to publications, databases and business groups related to the advancement of electrical power.

Hanford Home Page

http://www.hanford.gov/

The Hanford Nuclear Reservation is located near Richland, in southeast Washington. Its plutonium reactors have been moth balled; now it supports research in waste management, environmental restoration and energy. Visitors will learn about its work here.

Lockheed Martin Energy Systems

http://www.ornl.gov/mmes.html

Lockheed Martin Energy Systems manages energy-related facilities for the U.S. Department of Energy. Visitors can browse through general company-related information, as well as information on specific technologies, products and facilities.

National Renewable Energy Laboratory

http://nrelinfo.nrel.gov/

The U.S. Department of Energy's National Renewal Energy Laboratory conducts efficiency research to develop new clean technologies for heating, lighting and powering U.S. buildings and vehicles. Access the labs research areas, program activities and information resources.

Nonintrusive Appliance Load Monitoring

http://www.i.net/~george/research/nalm.html

This technical document explains nonintrusive appliance load monitoring and provides references and links to related Internet resources. Visitors can read the text here or investigate a book published by this Web site's maintainer.

The Salt River Project

http://www.srp.gov/

Power production and water resources are the focus of the Salt River Project, which unveils information about its vast holdings that serve more than 1 million electric customers and water shareholders. Stop by for customer info or to check out employment opportunities.

Solar Energy Laboratory

http://sel.me.wisc.edu/

The College of Engineering Solar Energy Laboratory, University of Wisconsin, Madison, maintains this home page with information about the lab, its research of practical solar applications, faculty and computer programs. This page also links to related sites.

Student Solar Information Network

http://www.neosoft.com/internet/paml/groups.S/ssin.html

This is the listing for the Student Solar Information Network (SSIN) from the index of Publicly Accessible Mailing Lists of NeoSoft. SSIN provides information and resources to people studying solar and renewable energy.

U.S. Department of Energy's Energy Efficiency and Renewable Energy Network

http://www.eren.doe.gov/

The goal of the Department of Energy's Office of Energy Efficiency and Renewable Energy is to develop efficient technologies that are affordable.

The office gives a detailed look at its various projects and partnerships here and provides extensive information about energy efficient and renewable technologies.

University of California - Department of Energy National Laboratories

http://labs.ucop.edu/

Three Department of Energy National Laboratories operated by the University of California are profiled on this Web site. Read about the organization, management and research projects in this unique system, or download a copy of the newsletter and selected publications from the documents library.

World Power Technologies

http://www.webpage.com/wpt

World Power Technologies is a manufacturer of wind-powered generators. Includes product descriptions, technical specifications and instructions on planning individual electrical systems.

SIGNALS AND IMAGES

Digital Signal Processing FAQ

http://www.cis.ohio-state.edu/hypertext/faq/usenet/dsp-faq/top.html

This index from Ohio State University consists of pointers to Frequently Asked Questions (FAQ) files on digital signal processing.

Electronic Imaging Systems Lab (EISL) Home Page

http://duotone.ecn.purdue.edu/

The Electronic Imaging Systems Lab of Purdue University in West Lafayette, Ind., maintains this site to introduce its faculty and graduate students. Still under construction when we visited, the site features photographs and brief personal profiles.

Electronic Visualization Laboratory

http://evlweb.eecs.uic.edu/

Engineering, science and art come together at the Electronic Visualization Laboratory's site, which offers browsers info about its interactive computer graphics research programs. Virtual reality, multimedia and televisualization tools are explored here.

Entertainment Technology Center

http://cwis.usc.edu/dept/etc/index.html

Here visitors can learn about high-tech projects undertaken by the Entertainment Technology Center (ETC), an organization sponsored by entertainment and communications companies and the University of Southern California's schools of cinema-television and engineering.

Micronet MD DSP Group Home Page - Calgary Centre

http://www-mddsp.enel.ucalgary.ca/

The Micronet Multidimensional (MD) Signal Processing Research Group is concerned with the engineering applications of multidimensional signals and digital images. The research group maintains this home page with information about its research, personnel and links to online publications, technical information and related sites.

1995 IEEE International Conference on Image Processing

http://www.ee.princeton.edu/~icip95

The Institute of Electrical and Electronics Engineers Signal Processing Society's 1995 International Conference on Image Processing is documented here. Includes tutorials, an authors' kit offering information on preparing camera-ready publications, and a listing of accepted papers.

Signal Processing Information Base (SPIB)

http://softlib.rice.edu/spib.html

A project sponsored by the Signal Processing Society and the National Science Foundation, the Signal Processing Information Base acts as a repository of links and pointers to sites with information or resources relevant to signal processing development and research.

Technology Service Corporation

http://www.tsc.com/

Technology Service Corporation (TSC) is "a team of experts involved in the research and development of advanced radars and related technologies." Visit this site to read about the company's products, services and research programs, or check out the listings of career opportunities with TSC.

UCT Digital Image Processing

http://www.dip.ee.uct.ac.za/

The home page of the Digital Image Processing Laboratory of the Electrical Engineering Department at the University of Cape Town provides information about the lab's work. Visitors can view pages on image processing, staff home pages and link to sites of related interest.

ENGINEERING MANAGEMENT

COMPANIES

Calgon Corporation Home Page

http://www.calgon.com/

Calgon Corporation, a Pittsburgh, Penn.-based specialty chemical and water treatment company, provides information here on its products and services. Visitors will also find corporate news, technical support resources and world-wide staff directories.

Energy Federation, Inc.

http://www.tiac.net/users/efi/

EFI provides information to commercial contractors interested in the sustainable use of our planet's water and energy resources. Besides a list of contractors, link to organizations and institutional end-users.

ENERGY CONSERVATION AND MANAGEMENT

The Argonne National Laboratory

http://www.anl.gov/

The Argonne National Laboratory is a Department of Energy research group with sites in Illinois and Idaho. Visitors will find detailed information on Argonne's projects, staff, facilities and activities.

Brookhaven National Laboratory

http://suntid.bnl.gov:8080/bnl.html

The Brookhaven National Laboratory, part of the U.S. Department of Energy, provides information here on its laboratory research, user facilities, departments and administrative offices. Includes database access and employment opportunity listings.

Energy and the Environment

http://zebu.uoregon.edu/energy.html

The University of Oregon's Energy and the Environment site contains links to the school's online classes, an animated wind farm and a fossil fuel primer. Includes information about energy resources and fusion.

Energy Efficiency and Renewable Energy Program

http://www.ornl.gov/ORNL/Energy_Eff/Energy_Eff.html

The Energy Efficiency and Renewable Energy Program, part of the Oak Ridge National Laboratory, features its research and development program through its home page. Visitors can read detailed descriptions about the program and its achievements.

THERMIE Home Page

http://erg.ucd.ie/thermie.html

The European Union's THERMIE project directs funds to energy projects in order to decrease the federation's dependence on outside sources for energy. This site provides information on THERMIE as well as links to other European energy resources found on the Internet.

United Nations Environment Programme Collaborating Centre

http://www.risoe.dk/sys/ucc/

The home page of this United Nations Environment Programme (UNEP) center tells about its efforts to incorporate environmental considerations into world-wide energy planning. Visitors can learn about the research and other efforts of the organization's team of scientists, engineers and economists.

ENVIRONMENTAL ENGINEERING

Yucca Mountain Project

http://www.ymp.gov/

Yucca Mountain, Nevada is a proposed Department of Energy radioactive waste repository site. Read the environmental impact statement, download details on the implementation plan, contact the movers and shakers on the project or use the searchable index to find the information you are looking for.

INSTITUTES AND ORGANIZATIONS

Advanced Research Projects Agency, Electronics Technology Office

http://esto.sysplan.com/ESTO/

Find up-to-date information on the electronics research being sponsored by the Electronics technology Office of the Department of Defense's Advanced Research Projects Agency. An overview of programs and contact information are featured.

Argonne National Laboratory, Technology Development Division

http://www.td.anl.gov/

The Technology Development Division at Argonne National Laboratory supports a number of Department of Energy programs "in environmental restoration and waste management, nonproliferation, and arms control." Find an overview of projects, current news and links to related sites.

Bienvenue a Supelec-Rennes

http://hydromail.supelec-rennes.fr/

L'Ecole Superieure d'Electricite offers electrical engineers a chance to brush up on some of their skills and potential students a chance to check out this 100-year-old school.

The Consortium on Green Design and Manufacturing

http://euler.berkeley.edu/green/cgdm.html

The Consortium on Green Design and Manufacturing, an initiative sponsored by the University of California at Berkeley, researches environmentally conscious manufacturing. It outlines its projects here and posts synopses of its papers.

The Environmental Molecular Sciences Laboratory

http://www.emsl.pnl.gov:2080/

The government's Pacific Northwest Lab is constructing a new building to house its Environmental Molecular Sciences Laboratory, which researches environmental cleanup efforts. This site gives an overview of the new building and contains dozens of technical reports, a Gaussian Basis Set Library, and a look at the lab's work in theoretical and experimental research.

The Environmental Technology Laboratory

http://www.etl.noaa.gov/

The Environmental Technology Laboratory (ETL) in Boulder, Colo., assists the geophysical research community by developing remote sensing systems. Features on its home page include an overview of ETL, lab information, publications and access to research data.

GENERAL ENGINEERING INDICES

Advanced Research Corp.

http://info.arc.com/

Advanced Research Corp. offers engineering and consulting services to commercial industry. Review the company's services and check up on the status of research projects in the works at this promotional site.

Applied Research Laboratories, The University of Texas at Austin

gopher://gopher.arlut.utexas.edu:70/1

Applied Research Laboratories at the University of Texas provide this gopher server for organizational directories and electronic resources. The site hasn't been updated since 1993.

The Engineers' Club

http://www.engineers.com/

Descriptions of software libraries and a downloadable catalog of files are featured at The Engineers' Club, a service for the engineering and technical community. An order form for the libraries and other products is included. Also available here are a newsletter and members' home pages.

Internet Connections for Engineering Index

http://www.englib.cornell.edu/ice/ice-index.html

The ICE Index page -- the Internet Connections for Engineering -- is a comprehensive catalog of engineering resources collected by Cornell University. Professionals and students can use this index to find engineering-related information organized alphabetically, or link to the Cornell Engineering Library for additional resources.

GENERAL ENGINEERING INSTITUTES AND UNIVERSITY DEPARTMENTS

About the Design Research Institute

http://dri.cornell.edu/Info/DRI.html

The Design Research Instititute is collaboration between industry, academic scientists and engineers focusing on using computation technology to solve problems in engineering design. Includes descriptions of three major areas of research and development.

Alberta Research Council Home Page

http://www.arc.ab.ca/

Canada's Alberta Research Council, committed to "advancing the economy of Alberta through the application of science, engineering and technology," maintains this site for its strategic business area index. Visitors will find news, staff overviews and a keyword search utility.

The American Indian Science and Engineering Department

http://bioc02.uthscsa.edu/aisesnet.html

The University of Montana, Missoula, maintains AISENET, the Web site for the American Indian Science and Engineering department. Visitors to the site will find papers, research subjects, announcements, seminar schedules and job openings.

Anna University, Madras, India

http://www.annauniv.org/

Anna University, popularly known as the Guindy Engineering College, supplies images and sound on its home page to accompany information about the Madras, India, school. Featured are listings of alumni, along with Guindy news and links to other engineering schools in India.

The Asian Institute of Technology

http://emailhost.ait.ac.th/

The Asian Institute of Technology, Thailand, maintains this site with admissions information, technical papers and access to its libraries.

Asian Institute of Technology Gopher Menu

gopher://emailhost.ait.ac.th:70/1

The Asian Institute of Technology, a postgraduate technological institute near Bangkok, provides campus, Asian and news information at this gopher server. Its research work and library are online, and there's now a Web page as well.

Beckman Institute for Advanced Science and Technology

http://www.beckman.uiuc.edu/

This site provides information on research, faculty and facilities at the University of Illinois at Urbana-Champaign's Beckman Institute for Advanced Science and Technology. The school exists to perform research in engineering and the life, physical and behavioral sciences.

Board of European Students of Technology

http://www.nada.kth.se/~ovidiu/best/

The Board of European Students of Technology (BEST) wants engineering students in Europe to work together and exchange information and education. Find out these Europeans' current activities and their whereabouts, but click lightly around the BEST private area.

Brookhaven National Laboratory

http://www.bnl.gov/

The Brookhaven National Laboratory in Upton, NY is a U.S. Department of Energy laboratory dedicated to basic and applied investigation in a multitude of scientific disciplines. Visit this site for access to its facilities and information about its departments, divisions and offices.

Cambridge University Engineering Department Control Group Home Page

http://www-control.eng.cam.ac.uk/

Visitors to this site will find papers, publications and research relating to control engineering, courtesy of Cambridge University's engineering department. Includes information on seminars and a control engineering virtual library.

The Canada Institute for Scientific and Technical Information

http://www.cisti.nrc.ca/cisti/cisti.html

The Canada Institute for Scientific and Technical Information, a service of the National Research Council of Canada, maintains this site for resource access. Visit here to connect with its electronic document delivery services, informational databases, educational programs and more.

The Centre for Systems and Control

http://www.mech.gla.ac.uk/Control/

The Center for Systems and Control is not a political training ground but an interdisciplinary research center affiliated with the engineering department at Scotland's Glasgow University. Review program information and electronic information resources at this site.

Clausthal Technical University

http://www.tu-clausthal.de/

The University of Clausthal is a technical school located in Germany. Visitors to their site will find information about faculty, courses of study and library access. This service is offered in English and German.

Clemson's College of Engineering and Science

http://www.eng.clemson.edu/

The College of Engineering and Science at South Carolina's Clemson University provides information here on its people and programs. Visit here for an overview of academic departments, student and public services, research centers and more.

College of Engineering

http://www.cit.cmu.edu/

Carnegie Mellon's engineering college page provides departmental and facility information for incoming graduate and undergraduate students. Includes links to faculty and research centers.

College of Engineering and Applied Sciences, ASU

http://www.eas.asu.edu/

Arizona State University's College of Engineering and Applied Sciences provides information on courses, departments and upcoming events on this graphically pleasing site. It includes an index of student pages and other Arizona pages.

The College of Engineering at Kansas State University

http://www.engg.ksu.edu/

The College of Engineering at Kansas State University maintains this site with information about the college's programs in engineering and computer science and engineering support service organizations.

The College of Engineering at North Carolina State University

http://www.eos.ncsu.edu/coe/coe.html

The College of Engineering at North Carolina State University provides a directory to information on academic affairs, departments, programs, news, research and other areas.

The College of Engineering at the University of Texas

http://www.eng.auburn.edu/

The College of Engineering at the University of Auburn, Texas provides information on its departments and research here. The site also contains information for prospective students and an online address book.

The College of Engineering at the University of Wisconsin-Madison

http://www.engr.wisc.edu/

The College of Engineering at the University of Wisconsin-Madison provides information for prospective undergraduate and graduate students here. The page includes online directories and a calendar of upcoming events.

Computational Engineering International

http://www.ceintl.com/

Computational Engineering International develops, supports and markets advanced visualization tools for computational analysis. Its Web site features publications, press releases, activity updates and an introduction to EnSight, its visualization software package.

Computer and Information Science and Engineering at the University of Florida

http://www.cis.ufl.edu/

The Computer and Information Science and Engineering Department at the University of Florida offers information about its academic programs and research activities at this site. Access course catalogs and technical reports.

Concurrent Engineering or Share

http://cdr.stanford.edu/html/SHARE/share.html

The SHARE Project provides "enabling technology to support design engineers by allowing them to access helpful information over a network not typically available to a single user environment" and by providing computation and information services. Includes links to SHARE sites and subprojects.

Council for the Central Laboratory of the Research Councils

http://www.cclrc.ac.uk/

The Council for the Central Laboratory of the Research Councils (CCLRC) is a European organization supporting the research of over twelve thousand scientists and engineers. Browsers can read about CCLRC's research facilities, annual and technical reports or find out how to gain access to CCLRC facilities.

The David Sarnoff Research Center

http://www.sarnoff.com/

The David Sarnoff Research Center, a subsidiary of SRI International, works on commercial and government projects. This home page highlights the institution's high-tech strong suits and provides information about its various divisions and spinoffs.

Defense Sciences Engineering Division at Lawrence Livermore National Laboratory

http://www-dsed.llnl.gov/

The Defense Sciences Engineering Division (DSED), located at Lawrence Livermore National Laboratory near San Francisco, works with electromagnetics, pulsed power, optics and material science. The division's home page has information about its facilities, programs, projects and research.

Department of Engineering Science and Mechanics at Penn State University

http://www.esm.psu.edu/

The Department of Engineering Science and Mechanics at Penn State University provides a page with academic and administrative information about the school, conference news, and statistics for the numerically-minded.

L'Ecole Supérieure d'Ingénieurs en Electrotechnique et Electronique

http://www.esiee.fr/

The French Center for Advanced Engineering Education provides info on its educational programs, seminars and conferences in the various engineering disciplines. Includes e-mail addresses and links to related servers. In French and English.

The Electronic Visualization Laboratory

http://evlweb.eecs.uic.edu/

The University of Illinois at Chicago Electronic Visualization Laboratory (EVL) introduces visitors to its laboratory, degree programs and ongoing projects. An electronic gallery, links to student home pages and library of published papers are available for review.

Elektronica en Informatiesystemen Universiteit Gent

http://www.elis.rug.ac.be/

Belgium's University of Ghent presents an online brochure for its Department of Applied Sciences. Visitors can access research, publications, library holdings and job listings.

The Engineering High School for Electrotechnic, Electronic, Computing and Hydraulics

http://www.enseeiht.fr/

The home page of the Engineering High School for Electrotechnic, Electronic, Computing and Hydraulics (EHSEECH) provides a wealth of pages on the school's courses, research, organizations and associations. Most pages are in French only.

The Engineering Society at Queen's University

http://engsoc.queensu.ca/

The Engineering Society at Queen's University in Canada posts organizational info here. Included is information on services, events and academics, as well as images from entries in design competitions.

Engineering Workstations

http://www.cen.uiuc.edu/

Look up info about the University of Illinois, Urbana-Champaign engineering department at the Engineering Workstation Server. Find course descriptions and timetables as well as access to student engineering organizations here.

Fachhochschule Aachen

http://www.fh.aachen.de/

The Fachhochschule Aachen offers higher education and post-graduate degrees in the applied sciences. The large staff of teachers and researchers also places emphasis on continued research in engineering and technology. This site hosts test document and personal pages of teachers and students. In German, limited English.

The Faculdade de Engenharia da Universidade do Porto

http://www.fe.up.pt/

The Faculdade de Engenharia da Universidade do Porto maintains this page with information about its courses and departments in engineering, as well as information about its staff, students and degree programs. In Portuguese and English.

Faculteit Toegepaste Wetenschappen, WWW Home Page

http://info1.vub.ac.be:8080/index.html

Students, assistants, faculty and others in the Division of Applied Sciences at the University of Brussels use this Web server to offer internal news and a link to the Internet. Outsiders will an insider's view of the school.

Faculty of Engineering

http://www.fen.bris.ac.uk/

The University of Bristol Faculty of Engineering page profiles the UK school's professors and research facilities. Includes links to Web pages for each department within the school.

Faculty of Engineering, University of Waterloo

http://sail.uwaterloo.ca/

The Faculty of Engineering at the University of Waterloo, Canada provides information about its various engineering departments. Included are descriptions of programs and lists of faculty.

GMI Engineering and Management Institute Home Page

http://www.gmi.edu/

GMI Engineering and Management Institute in Flint, Mich., maintains this site to introduce its people and programs. Visit here for undergraduate course catalogs, admissions information, staff and student listings, library services, and other computing and academic resources.

Graduate School of Engineering

http://www.gse.rmit.edu.au/

Researchers at this Australian university detail their projects in engineering systems management here. Visitors can also access the Computer Systems, Aerospace, and Civil and Geological Engineering departments for academic and admissions info.

Grainger Engineering Library Information Center

http://www.grainger.uiuc.edu/grainger.htm

The Grainger Engineering Library Information Center is the hub of online info for students in the engineering department at the University of Illinois. This site offers direct access to the Grainger Library's card catalog as well as links to the academic departments, the main university library and other campus facilities.

Helsinki University of Technology

http://www.hut.fi/

The Helsinki University of Technology's home page offers general information on the Finnish school's research and academic activities. Provided in English and Finnish.

The Idaho National Engineering Laboratory Home Page

http://www.inel.gov/

The Idaho National Engineering Laboratory, a multi-purpose applied engineering research facility, provides this site to introduce its capabilities,

partnerships and programs. Visitors will also find organizational news and events calendars.

Institute for Commercial Engineering

http://www.fe.msk.ru/

Russia's Institute for Commercial Engineering is a private scientific research institution that works to reduce the costs of engineering projects. This page offers links to Web sites that relate to the Russian economy, businesses, scientific developments and investment and brokerage houses.

The Institute of Occupational Safety Engineering, Tampere University of Technology, Finland

http://turva.me.tut.fi/

The Institute of Occupational Safety Engineering, part of the Department of Mechanical Engineering at the Tampere University of Technology, Finland, offers courses in mechanical and electrical engineering, biomechanics, and occupational safety. In English and Finnish.

Interstaatliche Ingenieurschule Neu-Technikum Buchs

http://www.ntb.ch/

Prospective students will get an overview of the Interstate School of Engineering in Buchs, Switzerland here. The page contains course information, a list of publications and a look at Buchs. In English or German.

Kogakuin University

http://www.kogakuin.ac.jp/

With campuses in midtown Tokyo and the Tama Hills area 35 kilometers west of the city, Japan's century old Kogakuin University is a four-year engineering and technology institution. Visit this home page to learn about its programs and campuses.

Memorial University of Newfoundland Faculty of Engineering and Applied Science Home Page

http://www.engr.mun.ca/

This Memorial University of Newfoundland site contains information about its faulty of engineering and applied science department. Includes an academic calendar, a student orientation handbook, conference information and info on research groups.

Musashi Institute of Technology

http://www.musashi-tech.ac.jp/

The Musashi Institute of Technology home page contains information on the various schools of engineering, programs of study and research centers. Includes info on admissions, faculty and links to other Japanese servers. Japanese and English.

New Mexico Engineering Research Institute (NMERI)

http://nmeri.unm.edu/

The New Mexico Engineering Research Institute introduces its research divisions and development activities at this home page. Includes staff directory and job listings.

NIST Boulder

http://www.boulder.nist.gov/

The National Institute of Standards and Technology provides information about research at its Boulder Labs site. The page also provides information on public tours at the lab and links to other U.S. Department of Commerce labs housed in the same complex, including the National Oceanic and Atmospheric Administration (NOAA) and National Telecommunications and Information Administration (NTIA).

Notre Dame Computer Science and Engineering

http://www.cse.nd.edu/

The Department of Computer Science and Engineering at the University of Notre Dame offers an electronic brochure for its degree programs and educational opportunities here. Prospective students can link to research projects, publications and faculty profiles.

Penn School of Engineering and Applied Science

http://www.seas.upenn.edu/

The home page for the School of Engineering and Applied Science at the University of Pennsylvania, provides information on the schools departments, programs, student activities, and links to class and student home pages.

Physical Sciences, Engineering, Computing & Math

http://lib-www.ucr.edu/physci/

A mine of Internet physical science, engineering, computing and mathematics resources can be found at this University of California site. It is searchable by keyword, title or author, and contains a table of contents and a subject list.

Prairie View A&M University College of Engineering and Architecture

http://www.pvamu.edu/

Information, services and departments at Prairie View A&M University's College of Engineering and Architecture are featured here. An index includes pointers to the High Energy Physics Department, the Texas Space Grant Consortium Home Page and the Student Organizations Home Page.

Project Eos Computing Environment

http://www.eos.ncsu.edu/

This North Carolina State University College of Engineering Web server offers instructions for working on the Eos network of high-end UNIX workstations, information about hardware and software, and answers to Frequently Asked Questions (FAQ).

Purdue University Schools of Engineering

http://www.ecn.purdue.edu/

Indiana's Purdue University School of Engineering provides program information and access to the school's Engineering Computer Network here. Links to Purdue's main home page.

The Research into Artifacts Center for Engineering

http://www.race.u-tokyo.ac.jp/

The Research into Artifacts Center for Engineering (RACE) at the University of Tokyo both conducts artifact research and assesses the problems and opportunities facing modern culture. The site includes information about RACE's research and information about the protests against French nuclear testing. In English and Japanese.

The Royal Swedish Academy of Engineering Sciences

http://www.iva.se/

The Royal Swedish Academy of Engineering Sciences introduces its programs of study, research projects, publications and faculty on this home page. Includes descriptions of courses and links to other engineering sites. In Swedish.

Sandia National Laboratories California

http://www.ca.sandia.gov/

This Sandia National Laboratories site offers information on weapons systems and energy research activities at Sandia's California location. Visitors also can access publications, reports and facts about conducting business with Sandia.

School of Engineering at Interkantonales Technikum Rapperswil

http://www.itr.ch/

The School of Engineering at Interkantonales Technikum Rapperswil in Switzerland provides information on its departments, people, graduate studies, services and research. The home page is in English but most information is in German.

Singapore Polytechnic

http://www.sp.ac.sg/home.html

Singapore Polytechnic presents visitors with a clickable map to access information about the engineering technology institute. A campus map is provided as are selected press clippings about the school and its graduates.

Stanford University Departments of Engineering, Economic Systems and Operations Research

http://www-soe.stanford.edu/soe.html

The Stanford University departments of Engineering- Economic Systems and Operations Research maintains this page describing its merger into a single department. Learn more about the newly formed department's purpose here.

Stanford University - School of Engineering

http://www-soe.stanford.edu/soe.html

The second largest school on the Stanford University campus, the School of Engineering maintains this informational page. Visitors can learn more about the school, its academic departments and programs, and its many areas of research.

The Southeastern University and College Coalition for Engineering Education

http://succeed.engr.vt.edu/

The Southeastern University and College Coalition for Engineering Education (SUCCEED) works to revitalize undergraduate engineering education. The coalition promotes its agenda, offers links to its databases, and posts online papers and its annual report here.

Toyohashi University of Technology

http://www.tut.ac.jp/

The Toyohashi University of Technology, Japan, maintains this site with information about the school, departments, and student and staff information. In Japanese and English.

U.S. Army Research Laboratory

http://info.arl.army.mil/

This site contains a mission statement for the Army Research Laboratory (ARL), along with research directorates and publications. Includes press releases, information on business opportunities, technology transfers and links to related government servers.

United Technologies Research Center

http://utrcwww.utc.com/

United Technologies Research Center conducts research in fluid mechanics, chemical sciences (including combustion and environmental sciences), embedded electronic systems, materials and structures, product development and manufacturing. The high-tech center details its work at four labs across the world and provides online reports here.

UC College of Engineering

http://decon.coe.uc.edu/

The University of Cincinnatti's College of Engineering inducts neophytes into its academic programs and general campus culture at this introductory site. Find a history of the school, admissions information and a college tour here.

UC San Diego School of Engineering

http://www-soe.ucsd.edu/

The School of Engineering at the University of California, San Diego provides information here on its academic departments, course offerings, research groups and faculty members. Includes admissions information, links to other campus servers and engineering resource pages.

University of California at Irvine School of Engineering

http://www.eng.uci.edu/

The School of Engineering at the University of California, Irvine, invites visitors to its home page to learn more about its departments, academic programs and research groups. Links to sites of interest on and off campus are provided.

University of Kansas School of Engineering

http://www.engr.ukans.edu/

The University of Kansas School of Engineering provides an index to its departments, news, organizations, resources, and information servers.

University of Michigan College of Engineering

http://www.engin.umich.edu/college/

The home page for the University of Michigan College of Engineering provides information on programs, courses, research, student societies and the college's Computer Aided Engineering Network. There is also information about creating personal home pages.

University of Portland School of Engineering

http://www.up.edu/

The University of Portland School of Engineering in Oregon takes browsers on a video tour of the school here. The site also contains links to the department's gopher server and FTP archive.

University of Washington Computer Science and Engineering

http://www.cs.washington.edu/

The University of Washington Computer Science and Engineering department supplies its site with general program information, course descriptions and access to technical reports and abstracts. Includes search capabilities.

Victoria Jubilee Technical Institute

http://www.ece.iit.edu/~hchhaya/vjti/vjti.html

A directory of alumni from the Victoria Jubilee Technical Institute in Bombay, India, is featured here, along with a job listings page. There also are indexes of VJTI news and links, plus information on the VJTI Alumni Association.

Warsaw University of Technology Institute of Control and Computational Engineering Home Page

http://www.ia.pw.edu.pl/

The Institute of Control and Computational Engineering at Poland's Warsaw University of Technology maintains this site to introduce its people and programs. Visit here for staff and student home pages, computer networking services, publications and other academic and administrative resources. In Polish and English.

Washington Technology Center, University of Washington

http://www.ia.pw.edu.pl/

The Washington Technology Center, a Seattle-based technology development organization, maintains this site for program information and requests for proposals. Visit here to learn about its work in advanced materials, computer systems, environmental technology and other fields.

Washington University in St. Louis School of Engineering and Applied Science

http://www.ecl.wustl.edu/seas/

This page, maintained by Washington University in St. Louis, provides information about the institution's School of Engineering and Applied Science (SEAS). Includes academic and organizational information, staff and student directories, an events calendar and campus maps.

INDUSTRIAL ENGINEERING

GENERAL

Cornell Injection Molding Program

http://xenoy.mae.cornell.edu/

The Cornell Injection Molding Program (CIMP) profiles its 20-year history, along with its staff and research projects, through this home page. Visitors also can read "Molding the Future," the Cornell Theory Center newsletter.

ASSOCIATIONS AND ORGANIZATIONS

International Ergonomics Association

http://turva.me.tut.fi/iea97

The International Ergonomics Association (IEA) sponsors this informational page concerning IEA's 13th Triennial Congress to be held June 29 - July 4, 1997 in Tampere, Finland. Visitors to this site can find out more about the association and the upcoming conference.

Society of Manufacturing Engineers

http://www.sme.org/

The Society of Manufacturing Engineering is the "premier source of learning and knowledge for the manufacturing community." Visit this site for information on professional certification, conferences, expositions and other society activities.

INSTITUTES AND UNIVERSITIES

Department of Computer Engineering and Industrial Automation Home Page

http://www.dca.fee.unicamp.br/

This Web site, maintained by the computer engineering and industrial automation department at the State University of Campinas in Sao Paulo, Brazil, provides information about departmental projects, students and faculty and staff members. Includes a link to the university's home page.

Department of Industrial Engineering

http://www.ie.utoronto.ca/

The University of Toronto's department of industrial engineering offers academic and technical information at this site. Links include other engineering resources found on the Internet.

Department of Manufacturing Engineering at Nottingham University

http://marg.ntu.ac.uk/

The Department of Manufacturing Engineering at the U.K.'s Nottingham University provides information about the school's various programs here. Browsers will find details of courses, related links and more.

The Ergonomics in Teleoperation and Control Laboratory Augmented and Virtual Reality Home Page

http://vered.rose.utoronto.ca/

Researching "human factors/ergonomic issues related to telerobotics, stereoscopic displays, virtual reality and augmented reality," the ETC-Lab details its research projects, workshops and publications. Visitors less inclined to reading text can view MPEG demonstration videos.

The Institute of Industrial Science Home Page

http://www.iis.u-tokyo.ac.jp/

Visitors can investigate research projects and electronic services of the Institute of Industrial Science at this site. The department, a part of the University of Tokyo, offers access to general program information and publications here. In English and Japanese.

Manufacturing Automation and Design Engineering Home Page

http://elib.cme.nist.gov/made/made.html

The Manufacturing Automation and Design Engineering program of the U.S. Advanced Research Projects Agency maintains this site for project descriptions, proposal information and program history. Includes links to key events and related resources.

University of Hannover, Germany

http://www.ifw.uni-hannover.de/

The Institute of Production Engineering and Machine Tools at the University of Hannover, Germany, provides information here on its research subjects and related departments. Visit here for maps, technical materials and general institute information in German and English.

PRODUCTION AND QUALITY MANAGEMENT

The American Society for Quality Control

http://www.asqc.org/

The American Society for Quality Control is a non-profit quality improvement organization located in Milwaukee, Wis. Visitor to its site will find product and service details, publications and membership guidelines.

Continuous Quality Improvement Server

http://deming.eng.clemson.edu/

This is the Continuous Quality Improvement Server located at the Department of Industrial Engineering at Clemson University. It contains links to local items of interest, access to related files, and links to other related sites of interest.

Japanese Industrial Standards

http://www.hike.te.chiba-u.ac.jp/ikeda/JIS/index.html

This index of industrial standards in Japan as of 1994 includes a general outlook for the standardization process, an overview of the quality-systems registration scheme, and a list of items covered by the standardization procedure, which include medicines, certain agricultural chemicals, silk yarn and some foodstuffs. (But you already knew that, didn't you?)

JOURNALS

International Journal for Numerical Methods in Engineering and Communications in Numerical Methods in Engineering

http://www.ep.cs.nott.ac.uk/wiley/numeng.html

The cumulative index of two Wiley publications focusing on numerical methods in engineering provides a complete collection of the articles published in these two professional journals. Browse the index of titles or probe into the documents archive with the flexible search tool.

International Journal of Small Satellite Engineering

http://www.ee.surrey.ac.uk/EE/CSER/UOSAT/IJSSE/ijsse.html

Small satellite engineers, take note of this electronic version of the International Journal of Small Satellite Engineering, a technical publication that covers all aspects of professional interest. The page extends a call for scholarly papers and provides subscription information.

Journal of Mechanical Design

http://www-jmd.engr.ucdavis.edu/jmd/

The American Society of Mechanical Engineers publishes this quarterly journal. Visitors will find scholarly articles on all areas and aspects of mechanical engineering and design in this online edition.

New Review of Applied Expert Systems

http://www.abdn.ac.uk/~acc025/ijaes.html

The "New Review of Applied Expert Systems" is a journal focusing on the development of expert systems for "organizations and in all branches of industry, commerce, the professions, education and government." The journal provides information that can help system managers apply proven approaches and techniques to solve their own system problems.

Scientific Computing & Automation

http://www.scamag.com/

Are you a scientific computing professional looking for a zine with the latest product announcements, company profiles, news and special events listings? Then click on the title to link to a dynamic and detailed online publication designed for the cutting-edge pro.

LIBRARIES

Control Engineering Virtual Library

http://www-control.eng.cam.ac.uk/extras/Virtual_Library/Control_VL.html

The Cambridge University Engineering Department Control Group maintains the Control Engineering Virtual Library site. Find an extensive collection of pointers to control groups around the world, conferences and related online resources.

Cornell University Engineering Library Gopher Menu

gopher://gopher.englib.cornell.edu:70/1

The Cornell University Engineering Library maintains this gopher site, which offers a Frequently Asked Questions (FAQ) file, library service information, instructional materials and information on electronic library projects. Includes a collection of engineering jokes.

The Engineering Library of Cornell University

http://www.englib.cornell.edu/

The Engineering Library of Cornell University in Ithaca, N.Y. maintains this site to provide access to its educational and Internet resources. Visit here for university academic program information and links to a variety of library materials.

Grainger Engineering Library Information Center

http://www.grainger.uiuc.edu/grainger.htm

The Grainger Engineering Library Information Center is the hub of online info for students in the engineering department at the University of Illinois. This site offers direct access to the Grainger Library's card catalog as well as links to the academic departments, the main university library and other campus facilities.

The World-Wide Web Virtual Library: Chemical Engineering

http://www.che.ufl.edu/WWW-CHE/index.html

The WWW Virtual Library Chemical Engineering site offers links to organizations, electronic publications, listings of various chemical engineering-related events and information on submitting items to be included at this site.

The World-Wide Web Virtual Library: Civil Engineering

http://www.ce.gatech.edu/WWW-CE/home.html

Visitors to the Virtual Library Civil Engineering page are provided with a comprehensive list of links to information about Civil Engineering, including gopher servers and FTP archives. This list also includes links to universities, organizations, government agencies and commercial sites from around the world.

The World-Wide Web Virtual Library: Mechanical Engineering

http://cdr.stanford.edu/html/WWW-ME/home.html

Part of the massive Virtual Library, this cyberstack for mechanical engineers is a gateway to university ME departments, institutes and societies, and subject vendor pages. Online catalogs, research and technical reports.

The World-Wide Web Virtual Library: Technical Ceramics

http://www.ikts.fhg.de/ceramics.html

This index of technical ceramics resources is provided by the World Wide Web Virtual Library. Visit here to link to related journals, societies, conferences and other sites around the world.

MATERIALS AND METALLURGY

GENERAL

Bekaert

http://www.bekaert.com/

Bekaert, a Zwevegem, Belgium-based steel wire manufacturer, provides comprehensive corporate information at this promotional site. Visitors will find product descriptions, employment opportunities for Bekaert and subsidiary company, Delaware Computing.

CLI International, Inc.

http://www.clihouston.com/

CLI International provides contract services for materials evaluation, corrosion testing, consulting and failure analysis to industry. Includes detailed information on the company's activities, services and programs.

DuPont Lubricants Web

http://www.lubricants.dupont.com/

Visitors can learn about DuPont's many lubricating products — including advanced coatings for use in the aerospace, automotive and semiconductor industries — on this corporate home page. Technical information, customer service and support details and a link to the corporation's main home page can be found here.

GRC International, Inc.

http://www.grci.com/

GRC International Inc., based in Vienna, Va., is an information technology and materials testing company that works for defense, space, intelli-

gence and civil organizations. Its Web site features its products and services, financial results (including quarterly reports) and modeling/simulation services.

Rohm and Haas Co.

http://www.rohmhaas.com/

This page presents an overview of Rohm and Haas, a producer of specialty polymers and bioactive compounds. Site features include company and product information, a user feedback page and links to related Web sites.

Stanislaw Staszic University of Mining and Metallurgy, Cracow

http://www.uci.agh.edu.pl/

The Stanislaw Staszic University of Mining and Metallurgy in Cracow, Poland maintains this home page with information about its research and organizations. Links to related home pages, archives, documents and other resources are available. In English and Polish.

The World-Wide Web Virtual Library: Materials Engineering

http://m_struct.mie.clarkson.edu/VLmae.html

This Virtual Library site contains links to information on materials engineering and dozens of universities.

ASSOCIATIONS AND ORGANIZATIONS

ASM International Home Page

http://www.asm-intl.org/

ASM International fosters the application of engineered materials and their research, design, manufacture and proper use. This site has information about the society, its products, and links to materials sites, suppliers and the ASM BBS.

The Minerals, Metals & Materials Society

http://www.tms.org/

The Mineral, Metals and Materials Society is a professional organization for members of the materials science and engineering field. This page has information about membership, publications, meetings and student services, as well as links to society division home pages.

CERAMICS

The World-Wide Web Virtual Library: Technical Ceramics

http://www.ikts.fhg.de/ceramics.html

This index of technical ceramics resources is provided by the World Wide Web Virtual Library. Visit here to link to related journals, societies, conferences and other sites around the world.

INSTITUTES AND UNIVERSITIES

The Materials Laboratory of Technology of Helsinki University

http://focus.hut.fi/

The Materials Laboratory at Helsinki University of Technology is outlined here. Researchers and prospective students can read up on the lab's research projects and find a listing of its recent publications. In Finnish and English.

Materials Research Society

http://dns.mrs.org/

The Materials Research Society home page provides info about that organization, which conducts research on materials of technological importance. Publications, courses and corporate participation program are detailed.

Materials Science and Component Technology Directorate

http://www.nrl.navy.mil/nrl/direct/code.6000.html

Looking for new materials, developing new uses for old materials and studying material behavior lies behind the U.S. Navy's Web site on materials science and component technology. The directorate concentrates on fluid mechanics and hydrodynamics, nuclear weapons effect simulations and interaction of materials with radiation.

MIT Department of Materials Science and Engineering

http://tantalum.mit.edu/

The Department of Materials Science and Engineering at the Massachusetts Institute of Technology defines "materials science" and offers a departmental overview at this site. Find links to news, research and academic programs, student groups, courseware and more.

National Research Institute for Metals Home Page

http://www.nrim.go.jp/

Japan's National Research Institute for Metals describes the institute's research activities here. The site includes information on computer modeling workshops and a link to the institute's anonymous FTP archive. In English.

NCSU College of Textiles

http://www.tx.ncsu.edu/

The College of Textiles at the North Carolina State University maintains this site to introduce its academic program, one of two accredited textile engineering programs in the United States. Visit here for project overviews and course offerings.

Purdue's Materials Engineering Home Page

http://mse.www.ecn.purdue.edu/MSE/

The School of Materials Engineering at Purdue University maintains this home page. Visitors are invited to find out more about the school and its programs.

University of Queensland's Mining and Metallurgical Engineering

http://www.minmet.uq.oz.au/

Students thinking about a career in mining may want to visit the University of Queensland's Mining and Metallurgical Engineering department. In addition to finding out about the Australian program requirements, visitors may review the department's facilities and see students at work.

University of Tokyo's Concrete Materials and Structures

http://concrete.t.u-tokyo.ac.jp/

The University of Tokyo's Concrete Materials and Structures Laboratory is devoted to the study of concrete-based construction. To find out what happens to concrete structures over time, consult the research reports and review study curricula offered at this site.

PLASTICS

General Electric Plastics Page

http://www.ge.com/plastics/index.html

This page provides general information and news on General Electric's engineered plastics. This site also offers online technical help, product information, news and announcements, a polymers database and more.

Plastics Technology Center

http://www.lexmark.com/ptc/ptc.html

The Plastics Technology Center develops and manufactures engineered plastic parts and assemblies for other companies. The company home page details products and services provides an online corporate brochure, client references and a collection of images.

MECHANICAL ENGINEERING

GENERAL

Azure's AutomationNET

http://www.automationnet.com/

AutomationNET is a huge directory of automation products, systems integrators and automation

engineering consultants. An alphabetical "company phonebook" is also provided.

WWW Virtual Library: Mechanical Engineering

http://cdr.stanford.edu/html/WWW-ME/home.html

Part of the massive Virtual Library, this cyber-stack for mechanical engineers is a gateway to university ME departments, institutes and societies, and subject vendor pages. Online catalogs, research and technical reports.

ASSOCIATIONS AND ORGANIZATIONS

The International Human-Powered Vehicle Association

http://www.ihpva.org/

The International Human-Powered Vehicle Association provides a wealth of information about human-powered bicycles, submarines and other modes of transport here. Visit to read how-to articles like "How I Made A Carbon Fiber/Epoxy Composite Bike in My Garage" and announcements of upcoming races.

Society for the Advancement of Autodynamics

http://www.webcom.com/~saa

The Society for the Advancement of Autodynamics, a Long Beach, Calif.-based research association, maintains this site as a general information resource. Visit here to learn about its directors and activities, view instructional materials·about the field of autodynamics and link to related organizations around the world.

COMPANIES

Automotive Programs By Bowling

http://devserve.cebaf.gov/~bowling/auto.html

Visitors are greeted by a staggering array of interactive automotive engineering and science resources at Bowling's Automotive Programs site. From fuel injector sizing programs to engine displacement unit conversions, the mechanically minded will find useful calculations here.

AZtech

http://cosmos.ot.buffalo.edu/aztech.html

AZtech Inc. is a non-profit enterprise, operated by the Rehabilitation Engineering Research Center on Technology Evaluation and Transfer, that adopts inventors' products for the disabled, then handles the manufacturing and distribution. Its site features background on the company, contact info for inventors, and descriptions of services for inventors and clients.

FLUID DYNAMICS

ICEM CFD Engineering

http://icemcfd.com/

ICEM CFD Engineering develops products for use in computational fluid dynamics. Visitors will get an overview of the company and its products on this promotional page.

The Institute for Computer Applications in Science and Engineering

http://www.icase.edu/

The Institute for Computer Applications in Science and Engineering (ICASE) conducts research in applied mathematics, numerical analysis, fluid dynamics and computer science. This page provides information about research, events and the ICASE organization and staff.

United Technologies Research Center

http://utrcwww.utc.com/

United Technologies Research Center conducts research in fluid mechanics, chemical sciences (including combustion and environmental sciences), embedded electronic systems, materials and structures, product development and manufacturing. The high-tech center details its work at four labs across the world and provides online reports here.

INSTITUTES AND UNIVERSITIES

The Berkeley Sensor and Actuator Center

http://www-bsac.eecs.berkeley.edu/

The Berkeley Sensor and Actuator Center researches sensors and miniature moving mechanical elements. Take a short course on surface micromachining or visit the microfabrication laboratory. Grad students can also find out how to become a researcher there.

California Institute of Technology - Mechanical Engineering

http://avalon.caltech.edu/me

As home to the mechanical engineering department at the California Institute of Technology, this site includes information on the school's faculty, students and courses. Application information also is included.

Center for Design Research Home Page

http://cdr.stanford.edu/

Stanford University's Center for Design Research, a division of the Department of Mechanical Engineering, hosts this page detailing Center events, projects and technical information. A keyword search engine allows browsers to locate more specific Center news and reports. Profiles of Center staff and faculty.

Department of Internal Combustion Engines and Thermodynamics at Technical University Graz

http://fvkma.tu-graz.ac.at/

This is the home page of the Department of Internal Combustion Engines and Thermodynamics at Technical University Graz. The site includes information on several projects, as well as symposium information and links to faculty personal home pages. In German and English.

Department of Mechanical Engineering

http://cdr.stanford.edu/html/ME/home.html

The Mechanical Engineering Department at Stanford University maintains this look at its academic program divisions, faculty and course offerings. Links to related sites on campus are featured.

Department of Mechanical Engineering - The University of Edinburgh

http://ouse.mech.ed.ac.uk/

The Department of Mechanical Engineering at the University of Edinburgh provides information here on its people and programs. Visit here for links to research projects, staff and student listings, seminars and other university web sites. Faculty member photographs and a campus map are also available.

Faculty of Mechanical Engineering Czech Technical University

http://www.fsid.cvut.cz/

Czech Technical University's Department of Mechanical Engineering presents technical reports, research archives and conference proceedings. In Czech and English.

Firefox Home Page

http://firefox.postech.ac.kr/

Korea's Pohang University of Science and Technology hosts this site for its Department of Mechanical Engineering. Visitors will find information about the program, faculty and staff, public services, and a virtual library here.

Jyvaskyla Institute of Technology

http://www.jytol.fi/

The Jyvaskyla Institute of Technology in Finland unveils its Department of Mechanical Engineering and logistics programs through this home page. Visitors to the site can search the site or follow links to the University of Jyvaskyla. In Finnish and English.

MIT Mechanical Engineering Department

http://me.mit.edu/

MIT's Mechanical Engineering Department maintains a well-designed site with info about that school. Links to news, people, labs, resources, administration and courses are among the areas available to browsers.

Tampere University of Technology Department of Mechanical Engineering

http://www.me.tut.fi/

Visitors to this home page are invited to tour the Department of Mechanical Engineering at Finland's Tampere University of Technology. Links to other sites of interest both on and off campus are also provided. In Finnish and English.

MANUFACTURING

Stong Nice Enterprise Co.

http://www.transend.com.tw/~parkerch

Taiwan-based Strong Nice Enterprise Co., Ltd. maintains this site to outline its "tooling & OEM" parts and components. Visit here for a rundown of its capabilities and guidelines on how to submit inquiries with "maximum confidentiality and minimum turn-around time."

MINING

Commonwealth Scientific and Industrial Research Organization Division of Minerals

http://www.per.dmp.csiro.au/

Australia's Commonwealth Scientific and Industrial Research Organization (CSIRO) provides a mine of information about its work and its Division of Minerals on this page. Find mission statements, organizational and project overviews, contact information and related links.

School of Mineral Engineering

http://mineral.uafsme.alaska.edu/

The University of Alaska's page for the School of Mineral Engineering contains a short history of the school and information about its academic departments and programs. Links to the school's research and outreach programs are also featured.

University of Queensland's Mining and Metallurgical Engineering

http://www.minmet.uq.oz.au/

Students thinking about a career in mining may want to visit the University of Queensland's Mining and Metallurgical Engineering department. In

addition to finding out about the Australian program requirements, visitors may review the department's facilities and see students at work.

NAVAL ENGINEERING

Decavitator Human-Powered Hydrofoil

http://lancet.mit.edu/decavitator/

It's a boat. It's a plane. It's the Decavitator human-powered hydrofoil that set a world speed record for the fastest human-powered water craft in 1991. Find out about the project and get a glimpse of the machine through this Web site.

The Naval Research Laboratory

http://www.nrl.navy.mil/home.html

Focusing its efforts on basic research related to the U.S. Navy's environments of sea, sky and space, the Naval Research Laboratory investigates a broad range of scientific disciplines from oceanography and sonar to state-of-the-art communications systems and materials science. Read breakdowns of the Laboratory's research directorates, descriptions of current research or access its numerous public servers.

NUCLEAR ENGINEERING

GENERAL

AlliedSignal

http://www.os.kcp.com/

AlliedSignal, which operates the Kansas City Plant for the U. S. Department of Energy, provides information about the company and the plant. Samples of the technologies here include multichip modules and simulation samples. Resources on technology transfer mechanisms also are included.

INSTITUTES AND UNIVERSITIES

The Radiation Shielding Information Center

http://epicws.epm.ornl.gov/

The Oak Ridge National Laboratory maintains this Web site for its Radiation Shielding Information Center. Visitors will find an organizational overview, historical notes, RSIC newsletters and software information among other items of related interest.

trans4.neep.wisc.edu

http://trans4.neep.wisc.edu/

The trans4 page at the Nuclear Engineering Department of the University of Wisconsin contains links to the Nuclear Safety Research Center and the Fusion Technology Institute, which are located at the university, and other sites, including the Cichlid home page, which is a database for the popular freshwater fish.

The University of California Department of Nuclear Engineering

http://neutrino.nuc.berkeley.edu/ucbne.html

The University of California, Berkeley, Department of Nuclear Engineering presents research, technical papers and resources in areas such as fusion and thermal hydraulics. In addition, there's information on faculty, courses, advanced designs and more.

NEWS

Chernobyl and Its Consequences: Project Polyn

http://polyn.net.kiae.su/polyn/manifest.html

This site provides a hypertext database on the accident at the Chernobyl Nuclear Power Plant. This site includes official Soviet reports, materials from the Chernobyl Kurchatov Institute Expedition, articles from scientific publications and more.

STANDARDS AND SAFETY

The Center for Nondestructive Evaluation

http://www.cnde.iastate.edu/cnde.html

The Center for Nondestructive Evaluation (CNDE) focuses on the development of new theories and techniques used in quantitative NDE. This page includes faculty contact information, conference updates, links to related organizations and professional publications, and more.

Yucca Mountain Project

http://www.ymp.gov/

Yucca Mountain, Nevada is a proposed Department of Energy radioactive waste repository site. Read the environmental impact statement, download details on the implementation plan, contact the movers and shakers on the project or use the searchable index to find the information you are looking for.

PROFESSIONAL ISSUES

GENERAL

Ethics in Science

http://www.chem.vt.edu/ethics/ethics.html

Maintained by the chemistry department at Virginia Polytechnic Institute, this Web site houses essays related to scientific ethics. Includes a bibliography of publications pertaining to ethics and misconduct in science, plus a link to the Virginia Tech chemistry department home page.

The SPIE Employment Service

http://butler.spie.org/employment/employmentforum.qry

SPIE, an international, non-profit society for optical engineering professionals, maintains this free job search resource page. Includes regularly updated listings and resume posting service.

PROFESSIONAL ASSOCIATIONS

Engineering and Physical Sciences Research Council

http://www.epsrc.ac.uk/

The U.K.'s Engineering and Physical Sciences Research Council hosts this site featuring information about its mission, people, research and contact points. Visitors can read annual reports, program info, press releases and the online magazine, or link to sites of related interest.

The Engineering Coalition of Schools for Excellence in Education and Leadership

http://echo.umd.edu/

A professional educational association, the Engineering Coalition of Schools for Excellence in Education and Leadership (ECSEL) seeks to influence undergraduate curricula through emphasis on teaching design techniques. Explore ECSEL program initiatives and member schools at this site.

Federation of American Scientists

http://www.fas.org/

The Federation of American Scientists was founded by members of the Manhattan Project to address the implications and dangers of the nuclear age. This page has information about peace and security issues, governance and global security projects.

Gateway to New Zealand Science

http://www.rsnz.govt.nz/

The Royal Society of New Zealand is a national academy of science and technology. Review governmental programs for the advancement of the sciences at this site, or check out the group's scientific publications and events listings. Includes a searchable database of science professionals.

The International Organization for Standardization

http://www.iso.ch/welcome.html

The International Organization for Standardization seeks to assure that products, materials, processes and services are subject to common worldwide rules and regulations. Visitors can learn about the organization's various programs and specifications at this site.

Lasers and Electro Optics Society

http://msrc.wvu.edu/leos/

Applying itself to research, development, design and manufacture of "lasers, optical devices, optical fibers, and associated lightwave technology," this Institute of Electrical and Electronics Engineers professional society posts its publications here, along with events and job opportunities listings.

Photonics Information Gateway

http://www.spie.org/gateway.html

This page, maintained by the International Society for Optical Engineering (SPIE), indexes Internet resources of interest to those in the optics industry. Includes topically indexed technological resources and links to professional groups, universities, businesses and government organizations.

Sigma Phi Delta at the University of Illinois

http://stimpy.cen.uiuc.edu/soc/spd

At this site, the University of Illinois chapter of Sigma Phi Delta, a professional fraternity of engineers, presents a code of ethics, chapters around the nation and a pointer to the national home page.

Society for Technical Communication Regional and Chapter Information Index

http://stc.org/

The Society for Technical Communication, a Virginia-based professional organization, maintains this site for its regional and chapter information index. Visitors will find news, publications, events calendars, and links to local chapters.

Society of Women Engineers

http://www.swe.org/

Find an overview of the organization, info about its member services and national committee reports at the Society of Women Engineers home page. Links to the organization's regional offices' home pages are also featured.

GENERAL SCIENCE

ACADEMIES, ASSOCIATIONS, AND ORGANIZATIONS

Academy of Sciences of the Czech Republic

http://www.site.cas.cz/

The Czech Republic welcomes visitors to its Academy of Sciences. Link to the academy office, check out an organizational chart, or peruse an alphabetical list of academic institutes here. In English.

American Association for the Advancement of Science

http://www.aaas.org/

This Web site offers varied information about this non-profit, cross-discipline, professional scientific organization. Visitors can learn about forums, science-based careers and access educational resources, including "Science," the association's flagship journal.

Canadian National Research Council

http://www.corpserv.nrc.ca/corpserv/nrc.html

The home page of Canada's National Research Council (NRC) offers contact information and details about its service as the principal science and technology research agency of the Canadian government. Visitors can learn about current research projects in a wide range of disciplines from biotechnology to astronomy.

Classification Society of North America

http://www.pitt.edu/~csna/

The CSNA is a nonprofit interdisciplinary organization that promotes the scientific study of classification and clustering. This Web site offers a wealth of information about its meetings, publications, laboratories, services and researchers. Browsers can also peruse CSNA newsletter, search the bibliography archives or link to a handful of related servers and home pages.

C.N.R. Bologna Research Area

http://www.bo.cnr.it/

Researchers will find an index to research institutes and centers in Bologna, Italy here. The page is maintained by the National Research Council (CNR) Bologna Research Area and is available in English and Italian.

Council for the Central Laboratory of the Research Councils

http://www.clrc.ac.uk/index.html

Read about the facilities at "one of Europe's largest multidisciplinary research support" centers and about the latest projects undertaken by this United Kingdom-based organization. The council's technology-transfer efforts also are explored here, and various publications are made available.

Engineering and Physical Sciences Research Council

http://www.epsrc.ac.uk/

The U.K.'s Engineering and Physical Sciences Research Council hosts this site featuring information about its mission, people, research and contact points. Visitors can read annual reports, program info, press releases and the online magazine, or link to sites of related interest.

European Science Foundation

http://www.esf.c-strasbourg.fr/

The European Science Foundation is a professional organization for scientists and professors. Visitors will find information on committees, research programs and symposiums.

Federation of American Scientists

http://www.fas.org/

The Federation of American Scientists was founded by members of the Manhattan Project to address the implications and dangers of the nuclear age. This page has information about peace and security issues, governance and global security projects.

Irish Research Scientists' Association Home Page

http://www.physics.dcu.ie/irsa.html

The Irish Research Scientists' Association is a volunteer organization that works to promote scientific research in Ireland. Visitors here will get an overview of the group and can download its electronic newsletter and results from a survey it conducted.

The KBN Home Page

http://www.kbn.gov.pl/

KBN, the Polish State Committee for Scientific Research, is the authority on state policy in science and technology. This site has more information about the committee, research projects and institutions, including links to other Polish sites. In English and Polish.

MIT Center for Coordination Science

http://ccs.mit.edu

The Center for Coordination Sciences at the Massachusetts Institute of Technology offers information here about its research, members and industry participation. Browsers can read a variety of working papers, take a virtual tour of the center's offices or link to CCS associated organizations.

National Science Foundation World Wide Web Server

http://stis.nsf.gov/

The National Science Foundation is an independent agency of the U.S. government that fosters scientific research through grants and fellowships. It gives an overview of its mission and organization here. The site also contains research results, online publications and grant information.

The Nobel Foundation

http://www.nobel.se/

The Nobel Foundation, in Stockholm, Sweden, presents a page full of information about the organization and the prizes it awards. Ever wondered who picks the winners? Find out here.

Royal Swedish Academy of Sciences

http://www.kva.se/

The venerable Royal Swedish Academy of Sciences gives an overview of its work, including its administering of the Nobel Prizes, here. Featured is information on the selection process for the awards and a look at the academy's environmental work, polar research and scientific institutes. In English or Swedish.

ARCHIVES AND INDICES

Annotated Scientific Visualization Web Site Bibliography

http://www.nas.nasa.gov/RNR/Visualization/annotatedURLs.html

Scientific Visualization Sites, provided by the Numerical Aerodynamic Simulation program, is an annotated bibliography of links categorized by university, government laboratories, commercial and military resources. [Find Related Sites]

BABEL: A Glossary of Computer Related Abbreviations and Acronyms

http://www.access.digex.net/~ikind/babel96b.html

BABEL is for people who don't know a bit from a BAT. Visit here for an alphabetized glossary of acronyms and abbreviations used in computing, electronics, mathematics and other disciplines. Updated three times a year.

Cambridge Information Servers

http://www.cl.cam.ac.uk/ext/Cambridge.html

Cambridge Information Servers is an alphabetized collection of links to various mathematical and scientific Web, gopher and FTP resources.

These servers are located mostly within Cambridge University.

Community of Science Inventions Search Screen

http://medoc.gdb.org/work/invent.html

Working on building a better mousetrap and want to find out who's already done it? Use the Community of Science Inventions Search Screen to search the community's database for global inventions, using the inventor's name, the invention's name, the inventing facility or other fields.

The Community of Science Web Server

http://medoc.gdb.org/

The Community of Science Web Server helps browsers identify and locate researchers with interests and expertise similar to their own. A comprehensive inventory of researchers, inventions and facilities across the U.S. and Canada is maintained and searchable. Also included are pages regarding funding opportunities and the "Commerce Business Daily."

Help for xxx E-Print Archive (index)

http://xxx.lanl.gov/help

This is an automated e-mail archive of scientific research papers and electronic preprints. Visitors can select their fields of interest and have documents sent to their e-mail.

Instructions for Searching the Community of Science Databases

http://cos.gdb.org/work/help/cos.help.html

Detailed instructions here are provided for searching the Community of Science Databases, an online inventory of researchers, inventions and facilities in leading North American universities and R & D organizations.

The Millipore On-line Catalog

http://www.gdb.org/Dan/catal/milli-intro.html

The Millipore Online Catalog was created at Johns Hopkins University to make accessible different types of data that are valuable to scientists. Visit the bioinformatics server via this introductory gateway.

Science on the Internet

http://info.er.usgs.gov/network/science/index.html

The U.S. Geological Survey hosts this research service, providing access to a variety of science resources available on the Internet. Links to astronomy, earth science, computer science, biology and physics sources are accessible here.

Science's Next Wave

http://sci.aaas.org/nextwave/

Sponsored by Science magazine and the American Association for the Advancement of Science, this site offers career-planning tips and electronic article reprints. Features informational and inspirational reports from young scientists working in the trenches.

ScienceWeb

http://scienceweb.dao.nrc.ca/

Canada-based ScienceWeb aims to "present the spectrum of scientific and technological activities in Canada in a comprehensive way." Services include a resource guide, press releases, links to clubs and other topical sites. In French and English.

Scientific Web Resources

http://boris.qub.ac.uk/edward/index.html

Scientists and mathematicians will find a collection of pointers to World Wide Web resources of technical interest here. Ireland's Queens University outlines its own scientific sites and offers links to other resources worldwide.

Tradewave Galaxy Index for Science

http://www.einet.net/galaxy/Science.html

The Tradewave Galaxy index for Science resources provides hyperlinks to categories such as Astronomy, Biology, Chemistry, Geosciences, Mathematics and Physics, each with multiple subcategories to choose from. There also are entries for Articles, Collections, Periodicals, Organizations and more.

Weird Research, Anomalous Physics

http://www.eskimo.com/~billb/weird.html

Visitors will learn about out-of-the-ordinary construction projects, bizarre theories and "weird science" research institutions on this personal home page. The site also provides links to two unconventional science mailing lists.

WWW Virtual Library History of Science, Technology and Medicine

http://www.asap.unimelb.edu.au/hstm/hstm_ove.htm

The World Wide Web Virtual Library offers this index of sites related to the history of science, technology and medicine. Included are pointers to organizations, specialized subjects and biographies of famous people.

EDUCATION

GENERAL

Bibliography of Organizational Computer-Mediated Communication

http://shum.cc.huji.ac.il/jcmc/rudybib.html

The Bibliography of Organizational Computer-Mediated Communication includes a list to be used for educational, non-commercial purposes.

The site includes various laboratory experiments, surveys and papers are presented here.

Colorado Space Grant Consortium

http://www-sgc.colorado.edu/

NASA established the Colorado Space Grant Consortium to help strengthen the educational base for science, math and technology, enlisting the participation of 14 colleges throughout the state. Link to schools, people and projects associated with the Consortium.

Program on Science, Technology and Society

http://www2.ncsu.edu/ncsu/chass/mds/psts.html

The Program on Science, Technology and Society comes from North Carolina State University and links you to more than 100 science, technology and society (STS) information sources. Includes information on joining the program, details about various university STS programs, events listings and a link to the Science Shops home page.

Sargent-Welch

http://www.sargentwelch.com/

Sargent-Welch is a supplier of science education supplies and materials for in-service workshops and seminars. The Sargent-Welch home page includes an indexed catalog and order form.

Science Hobbyist

http://www.eskimo.com/~billb/

Amateur scientists will find this Web site a hot temptation. It's chock-full of demos and exhibits, "weird science" experiments, and contains loads of links to science-related resources all over the Web.

PRIMARY

Activities Integrating Mathematics and Science Educational Foundation

http://204.161.33.100/AIMS.html

The AIMS Education Foundation -- Activities Integrating Mathematics and Science -- maintains this site as a resource for its K-9 educational program. Primarily for educators, browsers can access an AIMS discussion forum, a puzzle corner, and an extensive activity archive containing classroom exercises.

UT Science Bytes

http://loki.ur.utk.edu/ut2kids/

Visit here to find the University of Tennessee's electronic magazine for the K-12 crowd, "Science Bytes." Each issue seeks to educate and inspire young minds by describing current research at the university.

SCIENCE FAIRS

Information Booth

http://www.educ.wsu.edu/fair_95/announcement.html

A virtual science fair, complete with registration, judging and prizes is held annually at this site. Browse the sample exhibits or obtain entry information at this educational site.

SECONDARY

Learning in Motion Home Page

http://www.learn.motion.com/

Learning in Motion is a corporate producer of K-12 educational software. Visitors will find information and demos of the company's math, science and multimedia note-taking programs. Includes a list of "top 10 educational sites" on the Web.

UCI Science Education Programs Office

http://www-sci.lib.uci.edu/SEP/SEP.html

The K-16 Science Education page provides teachers and students a place to link to science and mathematics information on the Internet. Resources are sorted by grade level and category. Contains pointers to other educational sources.

UT Science Bytes

http://loki.ur.utk.edu/ut2kids/

Visit here to find the University of Tennessee's electronic magazine for the K-12 crowd, "Science Bytes." Each issue seeks to educate and inspire young minds by describing current research at the university.

TELEVISION PROGRAMS

Beakman's World Fan Site

http://www.spe.sony.com/Pictures/tv/beakman/beakman.html

Visitors can download audio and video clips from the television show "Beakman's World" here. The kids television show teaches science with humor.

Nextstep

http://www.nextstep.com/

Information about the Discovery Channel's science and technology show "nextstep" right here, offering a peek at schedules and people behind the scenes. Explore the program's topics or ask the research staff questions.

Science Television

http://www.service.com/stv/home.html

Science Television is a production company specializing in programming for the professional and educational scientific community. Visitors will find product and ordering information for titles on videotape.

ETHICS AND SOCIAL IMPLICATIONS

Crew System Ergonomics Information Analysis Center (CSERIAC)

http://www.dtic.dla.mil/iac/cseriac/cseriac.html

CSERIAC provides up-to-date human factors information to promote ergonomic considerations in the design of human-operated equipment. This page contains the gateway designers, engineers and researchers enter to access the CSERIAC datafiles.

Department of Energy Research Involving Human Subjects

http://www.gdb.org/HTB/htb.html

This Department of Energy site contains a database of report summaries on all research projects involving human subjects that are currently funded by DoE. (For information on giant radioactive Gila monsters, you will have to look elsewhere.)

HISTORY OF SCIENCE

Great Canadian Scientists

http://fas.sfu.ca/css/gcs/main.html

Visitors here can download short biographies of important Canadian scientists. The authors of the page hope to create a book with these biographies, and they ask for contributions here.

INFORMATION THEORY

Nordinfo

http://www.hut.fi/Palvelut/Kirjastopalvelut/NORDINFO/index.html

NORDINFO is dedicated to the timely, efficient dissemination of scientific information and documentation. This home page describes its activities and its role as a coordinator for both Nordic and international information. In English and Swedish.

INSTITUTES AND UNIVERSITIES

Applied Research Lab

http://www.arl.psu.edu/

The Applied Research Lab at Pennsylvania State University is dedicated to "advancing the U.S. Navy's technology base through basic and applied research, and through exploratory and advanced development." Includes descriptions of facilities, research programs and contracting opportunities.

The Australian Commonwealth Scientific and Industrial Research Organisation

http://www.csiro.au/

he Australian Commonwealth Scientific and Industrial Research Organisation provides resources to the country's corporate, industrial and scientific communities. Visit here to learn about its research programs and projects, browse its staff directory and link to its index of reference materials.

Brookhaven National Laboratory

http://www.bnl.gov/bnl.html

This Long Island laboratory, one of several operated for the U.S. Department of Energy, is dedicated to basic and applied non-defense investigation in physics, medicine, chemistry, biology, engineering and environmental research. You can take a virtual tour, visit its science museum, listen to its radio shows and consider the technology transfers stemming from its work.

The Center for Complex Systems

http://bambi.ccs.fau.edu/ccs.html

The Center for Complex Systems at Florida's Atlantic University provides information about its activities and resources. Visit here for news, scientific publications, faculty biographies, links to related Web sites and more.

The Central Science Laboratory at the University of Tasmania

http://lab.csl.utas.edu.au/

The Central Science Laboratory at the University of Tasmania provides info here on its facilities. Visitors can also link to other University and science lab servers on the Web.

Centre National De La Recherche Scientifique

http://www.auteuil.cnrs-dir.fr/

France's National Center for Scientific Research outlines its priorities and multidisciplinary programs here. All pages are in French, with some in English.

Christopher Newport University College of Science and Technology

http://www.pcs.cnu.edu/

Prospective science students can visit this page to learn about the College of Science and Technology at Virginia's Christopher Newport University. Link to official servers for the school's Mathematics, Physics, Computer Science, Biology, Chemistry and Environmental Science Departments.

Daresbury Laboratory

http://www.dl.ac.uk/

The Daresbury Laboratory in Northern Chesire, England, maintains this informational site. Visit here to learn about its facilities and contact staff members.

Department of Facilities Management

http://www.abs.uci.edu/depts/facil

The Department of Facilities Management hosts an online tour of the University of California's campus at Irvine. Also find information on renovation projects and energy consumption.

Department of Science and Technology

http://www.dost.gov.ph/

The Department of Science and Technology in the Philippines guides the national development of the islands' technological infrastructure. Visitors can access staff directories, research project descriptions and information on scholarships, grants and other forms of public funding.

The Ernest Orlando Lawrence Berkeley National Laboratory

http://www.lbl.gov/

The Ernest Orlando Lawrence Berkeley National Laboratory is "a multiprogram lab where research in advanced materials, biosciences, energy efficiency, detectors and accelerators focuses on national needs in technology and the environment." Read up on research highlights, the laboratory's nine Novel Prize winners or use the search tool to access detailed lab information.

Faculteit Toegepaste Wetenschappen, WWW Home Page

http://info1.vub.ac.be:8080/index.html

Students, assistants, faculty and others in the Division of Applied Sciences at the University of Brussels use this Web server to offer internal news and a link to the Internet. Outsiders will an insider's view of the school.

Faculty of Applied Sciences at Simon Fraser University

http://fas.sfu.ca/

This site provides information about Simon Fraser University's (SFU) applied sciences school. Details about the school's research center and academic departments -- including its schools of

communication, computing science, engineering science and kinesiology -- can be found here.

The Faculty of Science

http://dinf.vub.ac.be/sciences/scienceshome.html

The faculty of sciences at the University of Brussels offers a Web page in both English and Dutch. It offers Internet help, administrative and academic information, and details on the school's various scientific departments.

Faculty of Sciences Base Page

http://turing.upjs.sk/

The Faculty of Sciences at Safarik University in Kocise, Slovakia maintains this site for general information and resource access. Visit here to connect with its many academic departments and access a variety of computer-based resources.

Fukuoka Junior College of Technology

http://www.fjct.fit.ac.jp/index.html

The Fukuoka Junior College of Technology of Japan presents information on academics and departmental events at this home page. Offered in English and Japanese.

Harvard University Division of Applied Sciences

http://das-www.harvard.edu/

The highly-esteemed Harvard University's Division of Applied Sciences provides information here on its departments of engineering, computer science, applied mathematics, physics and atmospheres and oceans. Prospective students will find admissions and course information while enrolled students will find online journals and computing help.

Hawaii Research and Technology Home Page

http://www.hawaii.org/

Maybe a virtual trip to Hawaii isn't as quite as good as the real thing, but the Hawaiian Research and Technology site come close with a real-time image of the Manoa Valley. Other features include information on university research projects and an oceanographic expedition. This page also links to the Hawaii state home page.

Imaging Research Center Welcome

http://www.tno.nl/

The Imaging Research Center at the University of Maryland's Baltimore campus provides information here about its staff, research, services and images. Visitors can also link to related graphics sites.

Indian Institute of Science

http://ece.iisc.ernet.in/iisc.html

The Indian Institute of Science, located in Bangalore, India, offers graduate study programs and

research in science and engineering. Includes information about academics, research projects, laboratory facilities and campus life.

JTEC/WTEC Page

http://itri.loyola.edu/

Get the latest U.S. reviews of foreign research and development from the Japanese Technology Evaluation Center (JTEC) and the World Technology Evaluation Center (WTEC) at Loyola College. Included is a studies in progress list and links to reports.

The Korean Basic Science Institute

http://comp.kbsc.re.kr/KBSC_home.html

The Korean Basic Science Institute provides information on the joint use of advanced equipment between Korean scientific department branches. This page also includes links to related sites, search engines and anonymous FTP archives.

Lawrence Livermore National Laboratory

http://www.llnl.gov/

The Lawrence Livermore National Laboratory (LLNL) home page contains general background on the research facility, links to research groups and staff personal home pages. Visitors can also access listings of publications, news items and pointers to related resources.

The Loka Institute

http://www.amherst.edu/~loka

The Loka Institute is an Amherst, Mass.-based research organization concerned with the social, political and environmental repercussions of science and technology. Visitors can download its recent alerts and publications here and e-mail subscription information.

Microworlds

http://www.lbl.gov/MicroWorlds/

Microworlds presents an interactive tour of materials science research performed at Lawrence Berkeley National Laboratory at the University of California. This educational site includes images and information on electrons, Kevlar, wetlands and more.

Ministry of Science and Technology Policy

http://www.mnts.msk.su/

RD MNTS-Service provides a broad discussion of scientific and technological research taking place in Russia. Visitors will learn about institutions and scientists in Russia.

National Center for Science Information Systems

http://www.nacsis.ac.jp/

The National Center for Science Information Systems, a government division in Japan, provides information on its departments and services. Visit this site to learn about the center and link to research and development-related resources. Available in Japanese and English.

The National Institute of Applied Sciences at Toulouse

http://www.insa-tlse.fr/

The National Institute of Applied Sciences at Toulouse, France maintains this overview of its academic programs and facilities. Find a clickable campus map, links to the laboratories and students' pages among other items of interest. In French and English.

National Renewable Energy Laboratory

http://www.nrel.gov/

Focusing on research on renewable fuels and energy efficiency, this laboratory page offers details on research projects and program activities. Includes links to other information resources.

The National Research Council

http://www.nas.edu/

This site combines information on and resources from three subdivisions of the National Academy of Sciences: the National Academy of Engineering, the Institute of Medicine, and the National Research Council.

National Science Foundation

http://www.nsf.gov/

An independent agency of the federal government, the National Science Foundation "promotes the progress of science and engineering." Visitors to this site will find an overview of the NSF and its areas of focus, current news, and information on grants.

Netherland Organization for Applied Scientific Research

http://www.tno.nl/

The Netherland Organization for Applied Scientific Research home page provides background information on the organization, its research projects and staff. Includes facility descriptions, news releases and links to a central Infodesk.

The Oregon Graduate Institute of Science and Technology

http://www.ogi.edu/

The Oregon Graduate Institute of Science and Technology graduate level academic facility dedicated to research and education in the physical and technological sciences. Visit the institute's home page for information about its programs and departments.

Paul Scherrer Institute

http://www.psi.ch/

The Paul Scherrer Institute is a multidisciplinary research institute for the natural sciences and technology. It's active in elementary particle physics, life sciences, solid-state physics, material sciences, nuclear and non-nuclear energy research and energy-related ecology. Its site links to its research, its directories and an events calendar. In English, French and German.

Physical Sciences, Engineering, Computing & Math

http://lib-www.ucr.edu/physci/

A mine of Internet physical science, engineering, computing and mathematics resources can be found at this University of California site. It is searchable by keyword, title or author, and contains a table of contents and a subject list.

Rutherford Appleton Laboratory

http://www.rl.ac.uk/

Great Britain's Rutherford Appleton Laboratory is a broadly based scientific research institute conducting studies in the fields of biology, chemistry, physics, astronomy, and more. Visitors are invited to learn about the laboratory, its facilities and professional affiliations.

The Santa Fe Institute

http://santafe.edu/

The Santa Fe Institute is a multidisciplinary research center dedicated to exploring emerging sciences. Visitors to its page will find a general overview, profiles of people, publications and a calendar of events.

Scientific Photography Lab

http://foto.chemie.unibas.ch/

The Scientific Photography Laboratory is operated by the Chemistry Department at the University of Basel, Switzerland. Visitors will find information on research and faculty. Includes numerous scientific pictures.

SINTEF World Wide Web Server

http://www.sintef.no/

The Foundation for Scientific and Industrial Research at the Norwegian Institute of Technology hosts this Web server for the Scandinavian SINTEF Group. A guide to the group and its operational units is provided, as are links to individual department servers.

Stanford Research Institute

http://www.sri.com/

Stanford Research Institute (SRI) at Stanford University, Palo Alto, Calif., maintains this site with an overview of the institute and information on its main operating groups in engineering, science and technology and business. A search engine is

included, as well as a link to Stanford University's home page.

STEP Home Page

http://sparc1k.images.alaska.edu/

The Alaska SAR Facility of the Geophysical Institute provides information here about its science technology and education programs. Pages devoted to facility history, research bibliographies, staff, software, hardware and research tools are among this site's features. Browsers can also view sample image products and animations.

Tampere

http://www.hermia.fi/

Tampere, Finland's Technology Centre presents a colorful Web site emphasizing its development efforts with industry, health care and research firms. The site is still under construction, with limited English content. Mostly in Finnish.

Technical Research Centre of Finland

http://www.vtt.fi/

The Technical Research Centre of Finland is a contract research firm for industry and the public in Nordic countries. Visit here to learn read about its research in a wide array of fields, including electronics, information technology, biotechnology and food research.

Unité RÉseaux du CNRS

http://www.urec.fr/

The National Center for Scientific Research (CNRS) in Paris hosts this collection of research documentation prepared by the center. The site also links to related information on the mission, personnel and projects of the CNRS, and to World Wide Web servers throughout France. In French only.

University of California - Department of Energy National Laboratories

http://labs.ucop.edu/

Three Department of Energy National Laboratories operated by the University of California are profiled on this Web site. Read about the organization, management and research projects in this unique system, or download a copy of the newsletter and selected publications from the documents library.

University of Florida College of Liberal Arts and Sciences

http://www.clas.ufl.edu/

In addition to a course catalog and program overviews, the University of Florida's College of Liberal Arts and Sciences home page offers details on its computing and networking facilities. Pointers to related campus departments and Web search tools are also provided.

University of Nijmegen Science Departments

http://www.sci.kun.nl/

The Science Departments at the University of Nijmegen, The Netherlands, maintain this site with a link to each department, and information about students and facilities.

University of Pennsylvania School of Arts and Sciences

http://www.sas.upenn.edu/

The School of Arts and Sciences at the University of Pennsylvania provides descriptions of its graduate and undergraduate programs, academic departments and admissions guidelines. Includes info on computing facilities, alumni services, publications and links to other campus servers.

UTS - Faculty of Science - Web Index

http://www.bio.uts.edu.au/

At the faculty home page for the Science Department at the University of Technology in Sydney, Australia, visitors will find research, conference schedules and grant information. Links to the university's main Web servers are provided.

Westinghouse Science and Technology Center

http://www.stc.westinghouse.com/

The Westinghouse Science and Technology Center describes the systems, processes, research and technologies utilized by the corporation in the development and manufacture of a wide variety of products. Includes links to laboratories, projects and other company resources.

Yuan Ze Institute of Technology

http://www.yzit.edu.tw/

Presented in English and Chinese, the Yuan-Ze Institute of Technology home page offers an overview of its academic programs and campus life. Pointers are also provided to the student clubs, library resources and Chinese literature.

INSTRUMENTS AND EQUIPMENT

IMAGING SYSTEMS

CSIRO Ultrasonics Laboratory

http://www.ul.rp.csiro.au/

A facility of Australia's Commonwealth Scientific and Industrial Research Organization's Division of Radiophysics, the Ultrasonics Laboratory maintains this page. Visitors can review the lab's research work in ultrasonic imaging, medical ultrasound and related health services.

Laboratory for Perception Systems

http://www.etca.fr/

France's Laboratory for Perception Systems details its research here in perception science, with links to information on image processing and robotics. Visitors can find research reports, articles and information about projects. In French and English.

SOFTWARE

LOGAL Software

http://www.logal.com/

LOGAL Software's specialty is science and mathematics programs for students of middle-school age and older. Get the facts on LOGAL and their software products, whose aim is to make science and math concepts less abstract.

PGPLOT Graphics Subroutine Library

http://astro.caltech.edu/~tjp/pgplot/

To quote the Webmaster, the "PGPLOT Graphics Subroutine Library is a Fortran-callable, device-independent graphics package for making simple scientific graphs." Visit this site to learn more about the package, download the software and read its documentation.

Software Support Laboratory

http://sslab.colorado.edu:2222/ssl_homepage.html

The Software Support Laboratory, located in Colorado, provides software to earth and space scientists. Data systems and centers, software developers, and software titles can be found here.

VENDORS

Mandalay Scientific

http://www.fred.net/mandalay

Mandalay Scientific bills itself as "THE Internet one-stop shop for scientific and industrial data models of every kind." A wealth of information is provided about Mandalay's free models and how to obtain them.

LIBRARIES

Technology Access Resources

http://www.larc.nasa.gov/org/library/larc-lib.html

Technology Access Resources is a scientific library administered by NASA. Visitors can find documentation on optics, aerospace engineering, computing, astronomy, physics and other scientific disciplines.

UCSD Science and Engineering Library Homepage

http://scilib.ucsd.edu/

The Science & Engineering Library at the University of California, San Diego maintains this site for general information and resource access. Visit here to learn about its reference services, electronic classrooms, Internet resources and more.

World Wide Web Virtual Library Standards and Standardization Bodies Index

http://www.iso.ch/VL/Standards.html

The World Wide Web Virtual Library maintains this site for its index of standards and standardization bodies. Visit here to browse its regional, national and international listings. The World Wide Web Virtual Library maintains this site for its index of standards and standardization bodies. Visit here to browse its regional, national and international listings.

MUSEUMS

Boston Museum of Science

http://www.mos.org/

The Museum of Science in Boston, Mass., provides information here on current exhibits and programs, hours and dates of operation, and visitor services. Visit here to take a virtual tour of the museum and link to its many educational offerings.

ExploraNet

http://www.exploratorium.edu/

San Francisco's Exploratorium houses a collection of interactive exhibits for teachers, students and science enthusiasts. ExploraNet, its online museum, offers electronic tours and demonstrations.

Field Museum of Natural History

http://www.bvis.uic.edu/museum/

The Field Museum of Natural History in Chicago offers information on worldwide nature and cultures. Visitors will enjoy imaginative exhibits, essays and related references to topics as diverse as ethnography, archaeology and nature conservation.

Franklin Institute Science Museum

http://sln.fi.edu/tfi/welcome.html

Philadelphia's Franklin Science Museum maintains this collection of exhibits and program information concerning astronomy, the earth, mathematics and much more. Exhibits incorporate animation, video and sound.

Hands-On Science Centers Worldwide

http://www.cs.cmu.edu/~mwm/sci.html

This is an extensive list of worldwide museums offering interactive science exhibits. Visitors can link directly to the museums to find information about available offerings.

Houston Museum of Natural Science

http://www.hmns.mus.tx.us/

Take a trip to the outer reaches of the universe or come face to face with an Edmontosaurus at the Houston Museum of Natural Science. The museum's home page lets you take a virtual tour of the museum and tells you about the special programs it offers.

Israel National Museum of Science

http://www.elron.net/n_sci_museum/

The Israel National Museum Of Science, Haifa, Israel, maintains this site with information about its exhibits, both special and permanent, and historical details about the museum itself. Permanent exhibit topics include magnetism, acoustics, wave phenomena and light.

Lawrence Hall of Science

http://www.lhs.berkeley.edu/

Located at the University of California at Berkeley, the Lawrence Hall of Science is a public science center for the schools and citizens in the Berkeley community. Visitors to its home page are invited to view the online exhibits, review the center's programs and read its publications.

The Lost Museum of Sciences

http://www.netaxs.com/people/aca3/
ATRIUM.HTM

Pour yourself a cup of java and pull up the chair for some serious museum browsing through the Lost Museum of Sciences. Jump to more than 300 museum Web pages in the Hall of Antiquity, the Hall of Physical Science or the Natural History Rotunda. Remember: the idea here is to get lost.

Montshire Museum of Science

http://www.valley.net/~mms/

The Montshire Museum of Science, an educational gallery in Norwich, Vt., maintains this informational site. Visit here to learn about the museum and its school programs, membership benefits, volunteer opportunities and more.

Ontario Science Center Home Page

http://www.osc.on.ca/

Canada's Ontario Science Center maintains this site for its hands-on science and technology museum. Visit here to take a virtual tour of the facility, offering more than 800 exhibits, educational programs, demonstrations and public events. Includes annual report, upcoming events and media contact information.

The St. Louis Science Center

http://www.slsc.org/

The St. Louis Science Center gives browsers a well-defined hint of what to expect in the event they visit the actual Missouri site. Museum information accompanied by virtual exhibits make this page a learning experience.

The Science Museum London

http://www.nmsi.ac.uk/Welcome.html

Wander through the galleries and collections of the online Science Museum of London and see exhibits on agriculture, chemistry, space and other science-oriented subjects. The museum also provides links to resources for researchers, schedules of special events and news releases.

Science Museum of Minnesota

http://www.ties.k12.mn.us/~smm/

The Science Museum of Minnesota presents this front door to two of its science learning resources. Maya Adventure includes images from the museum's anthropological collections and details about its exhibits. Thinking Fountain is a "living card file full of ideas and activities," including toucans and fake mold.

Science World

http://www.scienceworld.bc.ca/

An exploreum located in Vancouver, Canada, Science World is dedicated to "inspiring a greater appreciation of science and technology." Visit here to learn more about the attraction, its history, programs, events, school trips, science fairs and more.

---

a2z EDITOR'S CHOICE

The Exploratorium Home Page

http://www.exploratorium.edu/

Comprised of 650 interactive exhibits in the areas of science, art, and human perception, the Exploratorium provides a unique educational experience for students of all grade levels through "maximum exposure to the phenomena of science in an environment with a minimum of apparent structure." The unconventional approach to the learning experience goes beyond a standard "hands-on" science museum: With active use of visual and performing artists to expand students' focus and perception, museum curators include the full range of cognition, "using the mind to understand the very workings of the mind itself" as an integral part of the learning process. Educators and students can sample special projects or visit the digital library to jump into a few of the Exploratorium's famous interactive exhibits, view still images or listen to sound files. Perform your own dissection at the interactive online Cow's Eye Dissection page, take part in film and lecture series, or catch up on the latest news and events from the world of science. This vibrant, creative Web site offers an unusual and memorable learning experience for students and teachers alike by making full use of the potential of interactive technology.—*Reviewed by Steve Ellis*

The Exploratorium is located in the Palace Of Fine Arts in the Marina district of San Francisco.

Electronic exhibits, news and resources. New LANDSAT image resource, plus a brand new exhibit!
Click here to visit The Learning Studio

New Issue! Aurora photos, wetlands breakthrough, and where to order a free CD-ROM!
What's New in the World of Science

PUBLICATIONS AND INDUSTRY NEWS

Annual Reviews Inc.

http://www.annurev.org/

Annual Reviews Inc., is a nonprofit organization providing critical summaries of recent research advances in a variety of scientific fields. Users can search reviews online or order volumes of past publications at this site.

Baltzer Science Publishers

http://www.nl.net/~baltzer/

Baltzer Science Publishers maintains this site for its ordering information and submission guidelines. Visit here to browse its index of scientific titles, view its upcoming publication schedule and find manuscript submission details.

Bugs in the News!

http://falcon.cc.ukans.edu/~jbrown/bugs.html

A science professor offers scientific news and knowledge to information seekers in understandable, interesting language. As the title of the page implies, many of the science lessons here are inspired by yesterday's headlines.

Cambridge Scientific Abstracts (CSA)

http://www.csa.com/csa-home.html

Cambridge Scientific Abstracts lists their publications by subject and offers copies of its abstracts in print, tape, CD-ROM or by downloading. Includes descriptions of services, pricing and ordering info.

Cold Spring Harbor Laboratory Press

http://www.cshl.org/about_cshl_press.html

This site features the home page of the Cold Spring Harbor Laboratory (CSHL) Press, a publisher of scientific books and other media. Visitors can access the online catalog of book and journal titles as well as the home pages of staff members.

Complexity

http://www.journals.wiley.com/1076-2787/

Complexity is a journal that delves into the science of complex adaptive systems. The papers in each issue offer recent research results and discussion of controversial theories. Visit this promotional page for a glimpse at the table of contents for past issues and submission and subscription information.

Computer Science Technical Reports Archive Sites

http://www.rdt.monash.edu.au/tr/siteslist.html

Maintained at Australia's Monash University, this page contains a list of pointers to sites around the world which archive technical reports. Sites are presented in alphabetical order.

Discover Magazine

http://www.enews.com:80/magazines/discover/

The popular and lay-friendly science publication Discover Magazine makes its online home on this Web page that includes selected articles from the current issue, an educators' forum, a schedule for TV's Discovery Channel and an archive of back issues. The editors of the magazine also provide pointers to their favorite science sites.

Elsevier Science Gopher

gopher://gopher.elsevier.nl/

Elsevier Science publishes books, research monographs, technical dictionaries, handbooks, reference works and more than 1100 English-language journals in core scientific research areas. This gopher includes an online catalog of all the Elsevier Science books and journals in print and announcements of forthcoming article publications.

Elsevier Science - Home Page

http://www.elsevier.nl/

Elsevier Science publishes scientific journals online in disciplines such as computational molecular biology, life sciences and astrophysics. Access these periodicals or the company's complete catalog of publications at this promotional site.

InterJournal

http://dynamics.bu.edu/InterJournal

"InterJournal," a refereed online journal of the sciences, features a database of abstracts, comments and manuscript information. Here, visitors can perform searches, find instructions for manuscript submission and get details about author/referee correspondence.

Ion Science

http://www.INJersey.com/Media/IonSci/

Visit ION Science if you can't make much sense of the complicated science-speak in most journals but still want to keep up on the news. This journal tries to translate complex science news into articles for the lay person. Articles span all topics from hurricanes to pandas.

National Academy Press

http://www.nas.edu/nap

The National Academy Press (NAP) publishes reports from the National Academy of Sciences, National Academy of Engineering, Institute of Medicine and the National Research Council. Visitors to this site can search catalogs and order publications online. News and information on the NAP and the four bodies also are available.

Nature Magazine

http://www.nature.com/

"Nature," a weekly international academic journal of science, is a "rich store" of articles that brings readers up to snuff on news and policy. Readers will also find events and employment information here as well as back issues. Visitors can subscribe here, too.

ORNL Review - The Lab's Research and Development Magazine

http://www.ornl.gov/ORNLReview/rev26-2/text/home.html

Visitors to this multimedia site will find the Oak Ridge National Laboratory's online copy of its research and development magazine, "ORNL Review." Current and past issues are featured, as are links to related sites.

Preprints by Author

http://theory.doc.ic.ac.uk/tfm/papers.html

The Theory and Formal Methods Section of the Department of Computing at Great Britain's Imperial College of Science, Technology and Medicine maintains this archive of authors writing about theoretical science and related subjects. The archive is indexed by collections, countries, individuals, institutions and departments.

Quebec Science

http://www.quebecscience.qc.ca/QuebecScience/index.html

Quebec's "Science" magazine is available online exclusively in French. Events of interest and the magazine's history are available as well as texts of 1995 articles.

Science Magazine

http://www.aaas.org/science/science.html

Science, a lay-friendly publication of the American Association for the Advancement of Science, maintains this site for news and features, programs and projects, and links to related publications and institutions. Includes online shopping area, featuring science and research-related projects and texts.

Science On-Line

http://science-mag.aaas.org/science/

Visitors will find online versions of the weekly magazine "Science," here. The extensive science site also contains an electronic marketplace, a job vacancy listing and Science's Next Wave, an electronic network for tomorrow's scientists. See Editor's Choice.

Science's Next Wave

http://sci.aaas.org/nextwave/

Sponsored by Science magazine and the American Association for the Advancement of Science, this site offers career-planning tips and electronic article reprints. Features informational and inspirational reports from young scientists working in the trenches.

The Scientific Data Format Information

http://fits.cv.nrao.edu/traffic/scidataformats/faq.html

The Scientific Data Format Information FAQ (Frequently Asked Questions) is the FAQ for the Usenet newsgroup sci.data.formats. The document is presented here with instructions on its use and other locations.

Specialist Science Books Home Page

http://www.demon.co.uk/ssb

Information on more than 3,000 books ranging from botany to zoology is provided here by Specialist Science Books. Included are listings of featured books, details about planned publications and ordering information.

Telos Home Page

http://www.telospub.com/

Telos is a scientific books imprint located in New York City. Visitors to this corporate Web site can read reviews of Telos publications, wade through an online file archive or browse the company's catalog of titles.

VCH Publishing Group

http://www.vchgroup.de/

VCH Publishing Group is an international firm that deals in scientific books and texts. Visitors to its promotional page will learn about its print and electronic offerings.

SCIENTIFIC COMMUNICATION

The Belgian Research Network

http://www.belnet.be/

The Belgian Research Network seeks to connect the country's researchers with each other as well as with the global scientific community. The organization provides an overview of its mission and Internet services here.

Community of Science Web Server

http://cos.gdb.org/

The Community of Science Web Server is designed to help users identify and locate researchers with similar interests and expertise. It contains an on-line directory of researchers, inventions and facilities located in North America at universities and research centers. Other links of interest to the research community are also featured.

Community Research and Development Information Service

http://www.cordis.lu/

Member states of the European Union share research and technology resources via CORDIS, the Community Research and Development Information Service. Access CORDIS databases, publications and policies here.

Institute for Operations Research and the Management Sciences

http://www.informs.org/

INFORMS Online is a service of the Institute for Operations Research and the Management Sciences. A professional management organization, INFORMS provides networking opportunities and resources to the people who administer science facilities.

Instructions for Searching the Community of Science Databases

http://cos.gdb.org/work/help/cos.help.html

Detailed instructions here are provided for searching the Community of Science Databases, an online inventory of researchers, inventions and facilities in leading North American universities and R & D organizations.

---

a2Z **EDITOR'S CHOICE**

Science On-Line

http://science-mag.aaas.org/science/

Page through current and back issues of the online version of Science magazine, one of the most notable publications on the World Wide Web. Going far beyond selective reproduction of the print version, Science On-line offers a wealth of educational materials, interactive experiences, databases and information on the latest scientific news and projects. The publication itself provides both full-text and summary versions of the articles covering the whole of current research in medicine, biology, climatology, oceanography, physics and every other imaginable scientific discipline. Readers can browse through the issues or elect to use the search tool basing queries on subject, keyword, title or author. Go beyond the printed page and participate in the interactive Web projects designed exclusively for readers of this fine online publication. View an STS-based map of the human genome, explore genetic clues to Alzheimer's Disease, or grasp the subtleties of fluid dynamics. If all this seems beyond the comprehension of younger readers, proceed through the gateway to Science's Next Wave, "an electronic network for the next generation of scientists." Everyone from researcher to layman interested in current trends in science need look no further than this Web site to satisfy their curiosity.—*Reviewed by Steve Ellis*

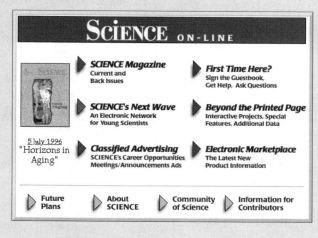

Multimedia European Research Conferencing Integration

http://www.cs.ucl.ac.uk/mice/mice.html

Scientific collaboration across Europe is aided and encouraged by Multimedia European Research Conferencing Integration, allowing researchers to share their opinions and data across vast distances in real time. Review project publications, or contact national support centers from this site.

Network for Engineering and Research in Orgeon

http://www.nero.net/

The NERO project, aimed at fostering cooperation among Oregon engineering institutions and U.S. federal agencies, maintains this informational site. Visit here to learn about the project, its goals, participants, resources and more.

MATHEMATICS

ACADEMIES, ASSOCIATIONS, AND ORGANIZATIONS

American Mathematical Society

http://www.ams.org/

In support of its mission "to further mathematical research and scholarship," the American Mathematical Society offers its members and the public this site called, "e-MATH." Find society news and information, links to math resources on the Web, events notices, professional services, publications and more.

CAMEL: The Information Services of the Canadian Mathematical Community

http://camel.cecm.sfu.ca/

The Canadian Mathematical Society, a focus of activity and resources for the mathematical community in Canada, maintains this server. CAMEL offers links to bulletins, societies and other mathematical information sources. Pages are offered in French and English

Edinburgh Mathematical Society

http://www.maths.ed.ac.uk/~chris/ems/

Dedicated to the improvement of scientists in pure and applied mathematics, the Edinburgh

Mathematical Society is a network of mathematicians from Scottish universities and other educational institutions. Includes details on meetings, colloquia, the Society's library and membership.

Mathematical Association of America

http://www.maa.org/

"The world's largest organization devoted to the promotion of collegiate mathematics," the Mathematical Association of America maintains this page as a service to its membership. Find general organizational info, meeting announcements, publications and links to related sites, including MAA sections around the country.

Russian Academy of Sciences Mathematical Branch Information and Publishing

http://www.ac.msk.su/

This informational page offers details about the Russian Academy of Sciences' Mathematical Branch, its departments, projects and staff. Includes a list of other Russian servers, science-related resources, picture galleries and a publications listing.

Society for Industrial and Applied Mathematics

http://www.siam.org/

Dedicated to advancing the application of mathematics to science and industry through research and information exchange, the Society for Industrial and Applied Mathematics promotes its goals on this page. Find information about SIAM membership, publications, conferences, and SIAM News, as well as other activities, products and services.

Society of Industrial and Applied Mathematics' Undergraduate Page

http://www.math.unh.edu/~siamug/

As part of the Society of Industrial and Applied Mathematics' "efforts to serve the mathematics and industrial communities," the society sponsors this page to promote the work of its undergraduate members. Find papers, announcements and a list of student chapters.

Space Mechanics Group at the University of Pisa

http://adams.dm.unipi.it/

The Space Mechanics Group in the Mathematics Department at Italy's University of Pisa offers information on its members, research projects and publications. Browsers can also link to the European Asteroid Research Node and other related Web sites.

Young Mathematicians Network

http://www.ms.uky.edu/~cyeomans

The Young Mathematicians Network home page provides a variety of information on this organization for junior mathematicians. Visitors will find pictures, reports and details on topical newsgroups. Links are provided to a number of job- and math-related sites as well.

ALGEBRA

Algebraic Topology Discussion List

http://www.lehigh.edu/~dmd1/algtop.html

If you know what algebraic topology is, you'll be in good company with the discussion group on this page. Messages and addresses of participants are featured here, as well as information about upcoming conferences.

Multidimensional Analysis

http://www.i.net/~george/research/multanal.html

Prof. George Hart of Hofstra University provides this primer on multidimensional analysis, which is defined as a "generalization of linear algebra which incorporates ideas from dimensional analysis. The central idea is that vectors and matrices as used in science and engineering can be thought of as having elements which are not just real (or complex) numbers, but formally have different types, such as length or voltage."

ANALYSIS

CALCULUS

Interactive Learning in Calculus and Differential Equations with Applications

http://www.ma.iup.edu/MathDept/Projects/CalcDEMma/Summary.html

Utilizing cutting-edge educational technology, the Mathematics Department at Indiana University of Pennsylvania has implemented an interactive calculus and differential equations educational program. This site describes the methodology, course objectives and the topics covered in the graduated study environment.

Xmorphia

http://www.ccsf.caltech.edu/ismap/image.html

Xmorphia is a process intended to "show the variety of patterns that may be exhibited by a relatively simple parabolic partial differential equation." This site explains xmorphia and provides links to several relevant sites.

VECTOR ANALYSIS

Multidimensional Analysis

http://www.i.net/~george/research/multanal.html

Prof. George Hart of Hofstra University provides this primer on multidimensional analysis, which is defined thusly: "a generalization of linear algebra which incorporates ideas from dimensional analysis. The central idea is that vectors and matrices as used in science and engineering can be thought of as having elements which are not just real (or complex) numbers, but formally have different types, such as length or voltage." Indeed.

APPLIED MATHEMATICS

Complex Systems Information Network

http://complex.csu.edu.au/complex/

Visitors to this page will find an index to sites with information or resources relevant to complex systems. Links to a public domain repository of information and its mailing list are featured.

LAPACK Users' Guide

http://www.netlib.org/lapack/lug/lapack_lug.html

The LAPACK Users' Guide, Second Edition, is published by the Society for Industrial and Applied Mathematics (SIAM). the entire text is available online and can also be ordered in printed form directly from SIAM.

ARCHIVES AND INDICES

The Algebraic Methodology And Software Technology (AMAST) Newsletter

http://www.cs.utwente.nl/data/amast/Index.html

The Algebraic Methodology And Software Technology (AMAST) newsletter from the computer science faculty at the University of Twente features access to its current and back issues through this page. It also contains details about upcoming workshops.

Algebraic Number Theory Archives

http://www.math.uiuc.edu/Algebraic-Number-Theory/

Mathematicians can search for preprint papers in algebraic number theory and arithmetic geometry here. This preprint archive stores papers until they are published and accepts submissions online.

Center for Scientific Computing - Mathematical Topics

http://www.csc.fi/math_topics/

Finland's Center for Scientific Computing is a government organization for high performance computing and networking. This page provides links to mathematical resources and information, including gophers, Usenet newsgroups, software, books and journals. Finnish and English.

CompactMATH

http://www.zblmath.fiz-karlsruhe.de/cgi-bin/CompactMATH-freeWAIS

This home page, maintained at Germany's Karlsruhe University, allows limited access to the Berlin-based school's CompactMATH CD-ROM database. Visitors can use the online freeWAIS retrieval form to access mathematics abstracts.

Danish Electronic Mathematical Information Retrieval

http://dan-emir.euromath.dk/dan-emir.html

Search for information from mathematical institutes throughout Denmark at the Dan-EMIR server. Find links to university departments and mathematical journals, as well as information about courses, people, publications and employment.

Electronic Journal of Combinatorics and World Combinatorics Exchange

http://ejc.math.gatech.edu:8080/Journal/ejc-wce.html

This gateway page points visitors to "The Electronic Journal of Combinatorics" and to the World Combinatorics Exchange. Together, they offer articles, databases, events announcements, and links to people and groups relevant to advanced mathematics research.

Electronic Sources for Mathematics

http://www.math.upenn.edu/MathSources.html

The University of Pennsylvania provides students and visitors with this collection of mathematics resources found on the Web. Categories include preprint archives and an alphabetic list of mathematics department servers.

E-Print Archive

http://www.msri.org/preprints/archive.html

The E-Print Archive offers access to online mathematical preprints covering topics such as differential geometry and global analysis, quantum algebra and topology, functional analysis, and more. Search by author and title, or follow links to sites of related topical interest.

The European Mathematical Information Service

http://www.maths.soton.ac.uk/EMIS/index.html

Watch this Web page for news about upcoming mathematics conferences in Europe. The European Mathematical Information Service site also offers an electronic library of mathematics as well as regularly published newsletters.

The European Mathematical Information Service Home Page

http://cirm.univ-mrs.fr/EMIS/

Links to mathematics servers, societies, conferences, publications and more information from all over Europe can be found at the European Mathematical Information Service Home Page. Visitors can also link to mirror sites to access the multitude of European mathematics links.

Frequently Asked Questions in Mathematics

http://daisy.uwaterloo.ca/~alopez-o/math-faq/math-faq.html

Those curious about the "Monty Hall problem," the names of large numbers, and how to calculate the day of the week given the month, date and year will find answers to these and other Frequently Asked Questions (FAQ) about mathematics at this site. Topics range from basics to advanced theory.

Galaxy: Mathematics - Science

http://galaxy.einet.net/galaxy/Science/Mathematics.html

This page from the Galaxy collection contains an index of links to mathematics sites, articles, guides, software, periodicals and much more. A search engine is also available here.

Henry Baker's Archive of Research Papers

ftp://ftp.netcom.com/pub/hb/hbaker/home.html

The documents in Henry Baker's FTP archive of research papers "are included by the contributing authors as a means to ensure timely dissemination of scholarly and technical work on a noncommercial basis." Papers from a variety of academic aspects, especially math, computer science and physics, are included.

Mathematical Resources on the Web

http://www.math.ufl.edu/math/math-web.html

This site compiles an extensive listing of mathematical resources on the Web. Visitors will find links to conference and lecture announcements, organizational servers, electronic journals, software archives and much more.

Mathematics Archives

http://archives.math.utk.edu/index.html

The Mathematics Archives provides organized access to the wealth of educational mathematics resources on the Internet. Links to software, databases, journals, graphing calculators, images, tutorials and a host of other resources are featured by category.

Mathematics Department Web Servers

http://euclid.math.fsu.edu/Science/Servers.html

Part of the Virtual Library, this page features an exhaustive directory of mathematics department servers located at universities around the globe. The directory is organized geographically by nation.

Mathematics Information Servers

http://www.math.psu.edu/OtherMath.html

The Mathematics Information Servers site lists mathematics department Web servers from around the world, as well as providing a plethora of other mathematics-related information. Several mirrors of this site exist and are linked to this page.

Math Forum Internet Resources Collection

http://forum.swarthmore.edu/~steve/

The Math Forum at Swarthmore College compiled this collection of Internet math resources for researchers and teachers. The collection is offered as a list or as an annotated version.

MathSearch

http://www.maths.usyd.edu.au:8000/MathSearch.html

MathSearch, provided by the School of Mathematics and Statistics at the University of Sydney, Australia, offers access to more than 40,000 mathematics documents. Visit here to perform a keyword search of mathematics and statistics computer servers around the world.

Mid-West Mathematics

http://www.math.niu.edu/mwmath/

Collegiate-level mathematics studies in the U.S. Midwest are profiled at this Web page. It features links to colleges in Illinois, Indiana, Iowa, Kentucky, Michigan, Minnesota, Ohio and Wisconsin. Each site includes information about mathematics seminars that are on the schedule.

Netlib Repository

http://www.netlib.org/index.html

The Netlib Repository contains software, documents and databases of interest to the mathematics community. It is maintained by AT&T Bell Laboratories, the University of Tennessee and Oak Ridge National Laboratory.

Wavelet Resources

http://www.mathsoft.com/wavelets.html

Hosted by a Massachusetts-based software developer, this page offers "one-stop shopping for wavelet papers." Visit here for a comprehensive index of research reports and articles available on the Internet.

Wavelets: Internet Sources

http://www.mat.sbg.ac.at/~uhl/wav.html

Visit this page for an index of sources offering wavelet information. Sources are categorized by server type: Web pages, FTP and gopher. Also find a section of Bibtex bibliographies.

ARITHMETIC AND COMPUTATION

Googolplex

http://www.uni-frankfurt.de/~fp/Tools/Googool.html

It's 10 times bigger than a googol, and it's a number you better never see on your phone bill. Download software here that will let you create and print your own "handy" (according to its computer science author) googolplex.

Interval Computations

http://cs.utep.edu/interval-comp/main.html

In order to make numbers and data processed by computers even more accurate, mathematicians and scientists are working on applications for interval computations. Visit this site to learn more about the science and for lists of related software and books. Maintained by the University of Texas, El Paso.

Pi

http://cad.ucla.edu/repository/useful/PI.txt

Does pi equal 3.14? Find out in exhaustive detail through this page from the University of California at Los Angeles.

NUMBER THEORY

The Magma System for Algebra, Number Theory and Geometry

http://www.maths.usyd.edu.au:8000/comp/magma/Overview.html

Number aficionados can employ a new system to solve computationally difficult problems. Mathematicians will find the Magma system for algebra, number theory and geometry explained and explored here.

PRIME NUMBERS

The Largest Known Primes

http://www.utm.edu/research/primes/largest.html

Integers greater than one and divisible only by one and themselves are the focus on the Largest Known Primes page. Scan lists of record-breaking prime numbers and jump to other mathematics sites.

EDUCATION

Shell Centre Publications

http://acorn.educ.nottingham.ac.uk/ShellCent/PubList/

Located in the Education Department of Great Britain's University of Nottingham, the Shell Centre for Mathematical Education maintains this annotated list of materials available for ordering. Find classroom resources, software, books, reports and other publications.

CLASSROOM ACTIVITIES

Appetizers and Lessons for Math and Reason

http://www.cam.org/~aselby/lesson.html

The Appetizers and Lessons for Math and Reason site is an online math and logic classroom. Grade school students learn how to use rules and patterns or click math lessons covering everything from basic arithmetic to calculus.

Calculus Graphics

http://www.math.psu.edu/dna/graphics.html

The Department of Mathematics at Pennsylvania State University maintains this site for resource access. Visitors will find graphics for calculus instruction in a variety of dowloadable formats.

MathMagic

http://forum.swarthmore.edu/mathmagic/

MathMagic is a project for K-12 students to solve math problems while using the Internet. The challenges are split into grade groupings, with current and past puzzles available. Teachers can use this site to prompt discussions and carry on what kids learn. Registration costs, but unregistered visitors can work the problems, too.

Mega Mathematics

http://www.c3.lanl.gov/mega-math/

MegaMath brings unusual and important mathematical ideas to elementary school children and their teachers so they can think about them together. MegaMath provides games, a "usual day at unusual school," the Hotel Infinity, a glossary and stories.

Transitional Mathematics Project at the Imperial College of London

http://othello.ma.ic.ac.uk/

The Imperial College of London Transitional Mathematics Project server, Othello, has created modules in mathematics for the Project. Students and visitors alike can learn more about the Project and view a list of modules available. There are also links to several math-related sites.

ONLINE COURSES

Interactive Learning in Calculus and Differential Equations with Applications

http://www.ma.iup.edu/MathDept/Projects/CalcDEMma/Summary.html

Utilizing cutting-edge educational technology, the Mathematics Department at Indiana University of Pennsylvania has implemented an interactive calculus and differential equations educational program. This site describes the methodology, course objectives and the topics covered in the graduated study environment.

Mathematics Experiences Through Image Processing (METIP)

http://www.cs.washington.edu/research/metip/metip.html

The Mathematics Experiences Through Image Processing (METIP) site describes the project and its goal to maintain student interest in science and mathematics through the use of digital image processing. Includes descriptions of programs and recruitment information for K-12 teachers who would like to participate.

SOFTWARE

Mathematical MacTutor

http://www-groups.dcs.st-and.ac.uk:80/~history/Mathematical_MacTutor.html

Mathematical MacTutor, an award-winning program designed by two math professors from the University of St. Andrews in Scotland, illustrates complex mathematical functions from calculus to geometry to group theory. Visitors are invited to download a sample of the program before purchasing it.

Transmath - A CBL Mathematics Tutor

http://caliban.leeds.ac.uk/

This home page acquaints users with Transmath, a Windows-based math tutor employed by the University of Leeds' applied mathematics department. Information about the project and a listing of lesson modules can be accessed here.

Waterloo Maple Inc.

http://www.maplesoft.com/

Waterloo Maple Inc., a Waterloo, Canada-based technical and educational mathematics software developer, maintains this promotional site. Visit here for news, product descriptions, demonstration software and ordering information.

GAMES, PUZZLES, AND RECREATIONS

Mathematical Visualizations and Animations

http://www.csc.fi/math_topics/Movies

The Mathematical Visualizations and Animations page contains visual representations of mathematics processes and equations created at Finland's Center for Scientific Computing. Includes links to similar sites on the Web.

RECREATIONAL MATHEMATICS

Space-Time Travel Machine

http://blanche.polytechnique.fr/lactamme/Mosaic/descripteurs/demo_14.html

In the Space-Time Travel Machine, computers, mathematics and art collide. View the results at this online exhibit. The artist also offers his philosophical perspective on the work and its implications for the future.

GEOMETRY

Gallery of Interactive On-Line Geometry

http://www.geom.umn.edu/apps/gallery.html

An offering of the University of Michigan's Geometry Center site, this gallery hosts an assortment of interactive programs for experimenting with geometry. Features allow visitors to "explore the effects of negatively curved space" in a pinball-style game, or "build a rainbow" by examining a mathematical model of light passing through a water droplet. See Editor's Choice.

Geometry Center Graphics Archive

http://www.geom.umn.edu/graphics/

The Geometry Center Graphics Archive offers special and general-interest images created at the University of Minnesota. Fractals and objects habiting more than four dimensions can be found here.

Geometry Literature Database

http://www.cs.ruu.nl/people/rene/

A collective work by members of the computational geometry community, the Geometry Literature Database allows visitors to search its annals by author, title, keywords, journal, year and other parameters. The database currently contains over 6,000 entries.

Synergetics on the Web

http://www.teleport.com/~pdx4d/synhome.html

Euler discovered a relationship between edges, faces and vertices; synergetics connects to the visual arts via Euler's Law. At Synergetics on the Web, visitors can learn more about this law, as well as explore geodesic domes, design science and Fuller projection.

FRACTAL GEOMETRY

Fractal Microscope

http://www.ncsa.uiuc.edu/Edu/Fractal/Fractal_Home.html

The Fractal Microscope allows visitors to explore the Mandelbrot set and other fractal patterns. Includes information on fractals and a related bibliography, along with a discussion of the use of supercomputers in the study of these mathematical wonders.

Fractals

http://www.vis.colostate.edu/~user1209/fractals/

Neal Kettler's Fractals home page at the University of Colorado features the Fractal Explorer program which allows visitors to dynamically examine specific fractal images, as well as background information on what fractals are and how images are made using them. It also includes links to a number of sample fractal images and a cgi program called Background Explorer that enables visitors to generate their own fractal images.

SOLID GEOMETRY

Pavilion of Polyhedreality

http://www.li.net/~george/pavilion.html

The Pavilion of Polyhedreality page provides a preview of the work by George W. Hart in preparation for the 1996 World's Fair in Cyberspace. The page features links to selected projects by Hart and related sites.

HISTORY OF MATHEMATICS

History of Mathematics

http://aleph0.clarku.edu/~djoyce/mathhist/mathhist.html

Maintained at the Department of Mathematics and Computer Science of Clark University, this site features a look at the history of mathematics. Find historical accounts by regions of the world, timelines, a chronology, an index of files, and a list of books and other resources.

MacTutor History of Mathematics Archive

http://www-groups.dcs.st-andrews.ac.uk/~history

MacTutor History of Mathematics archive from St. Andrews University, Scotland, offers search forms, suggestions, and historical and biographical information. The common subject, of course, is math.

Mathematical Quotations Server

http://math.furman.edu/~mwoodard/mquot.html

From South Carolina's Furman University, this site offers visitors quotations about math. Fea-

tures include a keyword search engine and links to the sponsoring university.

EASTERN MATHEMATICS

History of Mathematics: China

http://aleph0.clarku.edu/~djoyce/mathhist/china.html

The Department of Mathematics and Computer Science at Clark University in Worcester, Mass., maintains this site to outline the history of mathematics in China. Visit here to view a chronology of Chinese math studies, read profiles of noted mathematicians, and link to other Chinese historic and cultural resources.

a2z EDITOR'S CHOICE

Gallery of Interactive On-Line Geometry

http://www.geom.umn.edu/apps/gallery.html

Looking for a new angle on understanding geometric concepts? Go no further than this Web site which features fascinating graphically-oriented exercises that illustrate fundamental and advanced theorems in geometry. Even the most mathematically challenged can get the point of these exercises and gain an understanding of the "plane" facts illustrated in these interactive exercises. While the terminology and nomenclature can be intimidating to many visitors, diving into the offerings will enlighten even the dimmest of mathematical corners in the mind. Take Projective Conics; once you grasp the fundamentals of the construct, the interactive exercise illustrates it beautifully and in full color. Ever wonder how rainbows are formed? Build a Rainbow examines a mathematical model of light passing through a water droplet and demonstrates why rainbows occur only when the sun is behind the observer. And if a discrete symmetry group of the hyperbolic plane leaves you cowering in the corner, the Lafite program will create Escher-like patterns by replicating a motif through the action of a user-selected group, clearing up any questions you may have. If this all sound too intimidating, forget the words and let the visual interactions guide you to geometric enlightenment. You won't be disappointed.—*Reviewed by Steve Ellis*

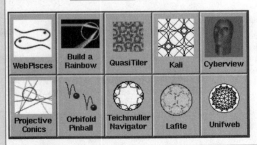

Gallery of Interactive Geometry:

In order to enjoy this exhibit, you will need a Web browser that understands graphical Fill-Out Forms. See our list of browsers for more information.

INSTITUTES AND UNIVERSITIES

Basic Research Institute in the Mathematical Sciences

http://www-uk.hpl.hp.com/brims/

The Basic Research Institute in the Mathematical Sciences in Bristol, England, is part of a Hewlett-Packard research lab. Visit this page for a look at the institute's research, a description of its post-doctoral fellowships, and a schedule of its conferences and seminars.

Ben Gurion University Department of Mathematics and Computer Science

http://www.cs.bgu.ac.il/

The Department of Mathematics and Computer Science of Israel's Ben Gurion University offers visitors to its home page an overview of its undergraduate and graduate programs, current research and academic courses. Information on the faculty and links to sites of topical interest on and off campus are also featured.

Biomathematics at Marquette University

http://hachiman.mscs.mu.edu/

The Biomathematics at Marquette University page lists information about the program's faculty, research and courses. Other links point to various departments and resources within the university, as well as related mathematics and science sites.

Boston University Mathematics Department

http://math.bu.edu/

Boston University presents the home page for its Mathematics Department at this site. Visitors will find a class catalog, databases and information on faculty, research and job opportunities.

Bowling Green University Department of Mathematics and Statistics

http://www.bgsu.edu/departments/math/

Visit the Bowling Green University Department of Mathematics and Statistics home page for information on academic programs, planned events, departmental faculty, class schedules and financial aid programs. Guests can also link to other mathematical Web sites.

Brigham Young University Department of Mathematics

http://www.math.byu.edu/

The Department of Mathematics at Utah's Brigham Young University maintains this overview. Visitors can review academic programs, tour the facilities, and meet the faculty, staff and students. Online materials for selected classes are also featured.

California State University-Hayward Department of Mathematics and Computer Science

http://www.mcs.csuhayward.edu/

The Department of Mathematics and Computer Science at California State University at Hayward, provides this informational site. Visit here to learn about its programs and people, access departmental and university computer resources, and link with related information servers around the United States.

Cambridge Information Servers

http://www.cl.cam.ac.uk/ext/Cambridge.html

Cambridge Information Servers is an alphabetized collection of links to various mathematical and scientific Web, gopher and FTP resources. These servers are located mostly within Cambridge University.

Catholic University of the West Institute of Applied Mathematics

http://www.math-appli-uco.fr/

The Institute of Applied Mathematics at France's Catholic University of the West provides information here on its campus, programs, faculty and students. In French only.

Centre for Experimental and Constructive Mathematics

http://www.cecm.sfu.ca/

The Centre for Experimental and Constructive Mathematics, Simon Fraser University, Canada, specializes in conventional mathematics and modern computation. Visitors here can find out more about the center, its members, research projects, publications and more.

Charles University Faculty of Mathematics and Physics

http://www.karlin.mff.cuni.cz/

The Faculty of Mathematics and Physics, Charles University, Czech Republic, maintains this page with information about the faculty, study programs, general Internet information and links to related sites. In Czech and English.

The Citadel Department of Mathematics and Computer Science

http://macs01.mathcs.citadel.edu/

The Department of Mathematics and Computer Science at The Citadel provides information about the department and its academic programs. Links to the school's online mathematics, computer science and education resources are also featured.

Clark University Department of Mathematics and Computer Science

http://aleph0.clarku.edu/

The Department of Mathematics and Computer Science at Clark University maintains this over-view of its program. Find a variety of information about the department's faculty, students, alumni, academics and resources.

Computer Science and Mathematics Division at the Oak Ridge National Laboratories

http://www.epm.ornl.gov/

The Computer Science and Mathematics Division at the Oak Ridge National Laboratories provides links to its sections, programs and facilities. Find nuclear, engineering, cognitive and computational sciences employed in the US national interest at this site.

Courant Institute of Mathematical Sciences

http://www.cims.nyu.edu/

Courant Institute of Mathematical Sciences, a division of New York University, is "a center for research and advanced training in mathematics and computer science." The page offers in-depth information about the departments as well as the Graduate School of Arts and Science.

Dalhousie University Department of Mathematics, Statistics and Computer Science

http://www.cs.dal.ca/www-home.html

The Dalhousie University Department of Mathematics, Statistics and Computer Science page contains information about academic programs, courses of study and research projects. Includes faculty profiles, pointers to university services and other campus servers.

Delft University of Technology Faculty of Technical Mathematics and Informatics

http://www.twi.tudelft.nl/

This home page provides information about the technical mathematics and informatics school at the Delft University of Technology in the Netherlands. Includes information on the school's various departments and services, plus technical reports and theses.

De Montfort University Department of Mathematical Sciences

http://www.cms.dmu.ac.uk/People/maths-people.html

The Department of Mathematical Sciences at the United Kingdom's De Montfort University offers this gateway to information about current research and researchers. A link to the university's home page is also featured.

Departamento de Matemática

http://www.mat.uc.pt/

The Mathematics Department at the University of Conimbri features recent papers and research conducted by students and faculty. Includes details on academic programs, course offerings and a department overview. Portuguese with limited English.

Department of Mathematics and Statistics at McMaster University

http://www.science.mcmaster.ca/MathStat/Dept.html

The Department of Mathematics and Statistics at McMaster University in Ontario, Canada, pulls together information about its program and a directory of students and faculty. Find info on post-doctoral fellowship opportunities.

Department of Mathematics and Statistics at York University

http://math.yorku.ca/

The Department of Mathematics and Statistics at York University, Canada, maintains this page with information about its programs, courses, seminars and colloquia. Also featured is its statistical consulting service, which assists university students and faculty with statistical methods used in research.

Department of Mathematics & Statistics Home Page

http://www.math.mun.ca/

The Memorial University of Newfoundland Department of Mathematics & Statistics home page offers undergraduate and graduate curriculum overviews, faculty and staff profiles, plus pointers to related resources, including their online courses.

Department of Mathematics at the University of Illinois at Urbana-Champaign

http://www.math.uiuc.edu/

This site contains the home page for the Department of Mathematics at the University of Illinois at Urbana-Champaign and offers visitors an overview of both the undergraduate and graduate programs, as well as a schedule of current semester course offerings and seminars. Features include links to faculty and facilities, with online maps of buildings.

Department of Mathematics at the University of South Carolina

http://www.math.scarolina.edu/

The Department of Mathematics at the University of South Carolina lets visitors browse through a comprehensive guide of its academic and campus information on this page. It includes descriptions of course work, research activities and faculty job search.

Duke University Department of Mathematics

http://www.math.duke.edu/

The Duke University Department of Mathematics provides course and degree information, a faculty profile and an academic calendar here. Visit also for conference information and selected pre-prints.

ETH Zurich Mathematics Department
http://www.math.ethz.ch/

The Mathematics Department of ETH Zurich maintains this online overview. Visit research units, meet the staff or review the academic programs and resources.

Fachbereich Mathematik
http://www.math.uni-hamburg.de/math/

The Department of Mathematics at Germany's University of Hamburg invites visitors to explore the scientific units in the department, review academic programs and projects, and visit the libraries. In German and English.

Florida State University Department of Mathematics
http://euclid.math.fsu.edu/

Visit this site to learn about the academic programs in mathematics at Florida State University. A general department guide is featured along with guides for applied, pure and actuarial math students. Also find links to topical and not-so-topical sites on and off campus.

Free University of Berlin Department of Mathematics and Computer Science
http://www.math.fu-berlin.de/

The Department of Mathematics and Computer Science at Germany's Free University of Berlin maintains this overview of its organization, academic programs, and research and development projects. Find links to publications, services, events and other sites of related interest.

Furman University Mathematics Department
http://math.furman.edu/

The Mathematics Department at Furman University in South Carolina details its courses, schedules and faculty here. The site includes a profile of visiting mathematicians and an online journal of undergraduate math.

FWI Home Page
http://www.fwi.uva.nl/

The University of Amsterdam profiles its Department of Mathematics, Computer Science, Physics and Astronomy here. The page includes a look at the department's faculty, research and courses. It also contains an online phone book.

Georgia Institute of Technology School of Mathematics
http://www.math.gatech.edu/

The School of Mathematics at Georgia Tech supplies general information and details on its degrees and courses. Also available are preprints, the "Electronic Journal of Combinatorics" and an FTP site.

Georgia State University Mathematics and Computer Science Department
http://www.cs.gsu.edu/

Georgia State University's Mathematics and Computer Science Department posts this page offering a wealth of information about the department's academics, research, faculty and resources. Links to sites of topical interest on and off campus are also included.

Harvard University Department of Mathematics
http://www.math.harvard.edu/

The Harvard University Department of Mathematics supplies information about faculty, courses and computing help, as well as an FTP site and reference materials. The page also has a listing of mathematical talks and math-related Web sites.

Heriot-Watt University Mathematics Department
http://www.ma.hw.ac.uk/maths.html

The Mathematics Department at Heriot-Watt University provides an overview of the mathematics program, its courses, faculty and research on this home page. Includes job listings for professors and researchers as well as links to related math and science servers.

Indiana University-Bloomington Program in Pure and Applied Logic
http://www.phil.indiana.edu/~iulg/iulg.html

The Program in Pure and Applied Logic at Indiana University-Bloomington maintains this page profiling its multidisciplinary course of study. Find information on the faculty, seminar schedules, abstracts of publications and class offerings.

Indiana University Mathematics Department
http://www.math.indiana.edu/

Information on the faculty, courses, research and seminars from the Indiana University Mathematics Department is provided here. Visitors can also link to a few other math sites or to the university's home page.

The Institute for Computer Applications in Science and Engineering
http://www.icase.edu/

The Institute for Computer Applications in Science and Engineering (ICASE) conducts research in applied mathematics, numerical analysis, fluid dynamics and computer science. This page provides information about research, events and the ICASE organization and staff.

Institute of Advanced Mathematical Research
http://galois.u-strasbg.fr/

Located in Strasbourg, France, the Institute of Advanced Mathematical Research's page spotlights its mathematicians. Also find links to electronic preprints, the library, a calendar of meetings and seminars, and links to topical sites. In French and English.

Institute of Applied and Computational Mathematics
http://www.iacm.forth.gr/

Detailing research projects in marine acoustics, wave propagation and software development, the Institute of Applied and Computational Mathematics presents an overview of projects and educational activities on this home page.

Institute of Applied Mathematics of the University of Erlangen-Nuremberg
http://www.am.uni-erlangen.de/

Two chairs in applied mathematics at the Friedrich Alexander University of Erlangen-Nuerenberg are described here. Visitors will get a look at the staff, research and publications of each chair at this site. In English.

Institut für Mathematik, Humboldt Universität zu Berlin
http://www.mathematik.hu-berlin.de/

Humbolt University in Berlin, Germany offers the home page for its Institute for Mathematics. Visitors will find information on academics, faculty, research and departmental publications. Available in German only.

Isaac Newton Institute for Mathematical Sciences
http://www.newton.cam.ac.uk/

A national institute located at Great Britain's Cambridge University, the Isaac Newton Institute for Mathematical Sciences offers this overview of its history, ongoing scientific work and services. Also find access to its FTP and gopher servers.

Kuwait University Mathematics Department
http://www.sci.kuniv.edu.kw/

Kuwait University's Mathematics Department maintains this site for general information and Internet resources. Visit here to learn about the department's facilities, programs, faculty and students. Links to mathematics and computer science Internet servers are also available.

The Laboratoire Bordelais de Recherche en Informatique
http://www.labri.u-bordeaux.fr/

The Laboratoire Bordelais de Recherche en Informatique in France features its research activities and publications at this home page. The site also includes profiles of the staff. In French.

Laboratory for Computer Aided Mathematics

http://sophie.helsinki.fi/

Located in the Department of Mathematics at the University of Helsinki, Finland, the Laboratory for Computer Aided Mathematics (CAM) maintains this page offering information about its current seminars and research projects. Site features also include links to CAM publications and preprints, the Euromath Bulletin and the Annales Academiase Scientiarum Fennicae.

Lancaster University Mathematics and Statistics Department

http://mathssun5.lancs.ac.uk:2080/

The home page for the Department of Mathematics and Statistics at Great Britain's Lancaster University provides information on academic programs, course offerings and research projects. Includes an overview of the department, its facilities and faculty.

Luleå University: Department of Mathematics

http://www.sm.luth.se/math/

This Swedish university puts its course catalog online here, which includes descriptions of its undergraduate math courses. Contact information for members of the math faculty are also provided, along with a presentation of Magma, a new system designed to solve difficult problems in algebra, number theory and geometry. In Swedish and English.

Lund University Mathematics Department

http://www.maths.lth.se/

The Mathematics Department at Sweden's Lund University maintains this home page with information about the department and its academic programs. A link to the main university site is also featured.

Macquarie University School of Mathematics, Physics, Computing and Electronics

http://www.mpce.mq.edu.au/

Located in Sydney, Australia's Macquarie University posts this home page for its School of Mathematics, Physics, Computing and Electronics. Find information on the various departments, their courses of study, admissions policies and faculty.

The Mathematical Institute of the Hungarian Academy of Sciences

http://www.math-inst.hu/

The Mathematical Institute of the Hungarian Academy of Sciences in Budapest maintains this overview of its academics and research. Find links to its primary research groups, the library and an archive of preprints.

Mathematical Sciences

http://www.bath.ac.uk/Departments/maths.html

The School of Mathematical Sciences at the University of Bath in England offers information here on its mathematics, statistics and computing departments. Visitors can check out course information, groups, reports and publications or link to related sites on the Web.

Mathematical Sciences Research Institute

http://www.msri.org/

Located in Berkeley, Calif., the Mathematical Sciences Research Institute provides program information, schedules, events and seminar postings at this site. Visitors will also find library information and a search catalog.

Mathematics Department IUP

http://www.ma.iup.edu/

The Mathematics Department from Indiana University of Pennsylvania announces current faculty openings and unveils its study programs through this home page. Visitors and prospective students can check out the department's computer labs along with links to the area around Pittsburgh, Pa.

Mathematics Department, Universitaet Halle

http://www.mathematik.uni-halle.de/

The Department of Mathematics and Computer Science at Martin-Luther University, Germany, maintains this home page with information about department organization, activities, course materials, examinations, university regulations and technical reports.

Mathematics, University of Toronto

http://www.math.toronto.edu/

The Department of Mathematics at the University of Toronto details its programs, courses and research for undergraduates and graduates here. The department also posts seminar information and portraits of two famous mathematicians.

Michigan State University Mathematics Department

http://www.mth.msu.edu/

The Michigan State University Mathematics Department introduces future students to academic programs, faculty and the Cyber-Math online help service. Visitors can also find colloquia and seminar calendars and faculty employment details.

Mid-West Mathematics

http://www.math.niu.edu/mwmath/

Collegiate-level mathematics studies in the U.S. Midwest are profiled at this Web page. It features links to colleges in Illinois, Indiana, Iowa, Kentucky, Michigan, Minnesota, Ohio and Wisconsin. Each site includes information about mathematics seminars that are on the schedule.

Mississippi School for Mathematics and Science

http://www.msms.doe.k12.ms.us/

Located in Columbus, the Mississippi School for Mathematics and Science is a high school for academically talented students. Visitors to this home page will find information about the campus and the school's disciplinary approaches, news, and publications.

MIT LCS Theory of Computation

http://theory.lcs.mit.edu/

The Theory of Computation Group at the Massachusetts Institute of Technology provides information about its various research projects here. The site also includes links to MIT's departments of mathematics and computer science.

National University of Singapore: Department of Mathematics

http://www.math.nus.sg/

The Department of Mathematics from the National University of Singapore maintains this page to introduce academic and admission details to new students and to provide in-house information for department personnel.

Northwestern University Department of Mathematics

http://www.math.nwu.edu/

Northwestern University presents the central server for its Department of Mathematics. Visitors will find information on departmental activities, programs of study, courses, faculty and research.

Odense University Department of Mathematics and Computer Science

http://www.imada.ou.dk/

The Department of Mathematics and Computer Science at Denmark's Odense University provides this departmental overview. Find information on educational and research activities, the faculty, staff and available resources. Links to sites of topical interest are also included.

Ohio State University College of Mathematical and Physical Sciences

http://www.mps.ohio-state.edu/

The Ohio State University College of Mathematical and Physical Sciences site contains information on academic programs, course offerings and faculty. Includes links to other campus servers, admissions info and research projects.

Old Dominion University Department of Mathematics and Statistics

http://claymore.math.odu.edu/~web/home.html

The Department of Mathematics and Statistics at Old Dominion University maintains this look at its graduate and undergraduate degree programs. Meet the faculty and staff, review the courses and find out about computer-based instruction.

Penn State Department of Mathematics

http://www.math.psu.edu/

The Penn State Department of Mathematics walks visitors through its programs and facilities at this introductory site. Find simple explanations of the who, what and why of the department along with links to more complex departmental resources.

Purdue Mathematics Department

http://www.math.purdue.edu/

Both graduate and undergraduate programs are detailed on the Purdue Mathematics Department page. Potential students can access class schedule info, meet the faculty and correspond with current math majors at the school. Tackle the math problem of the week to see if you've got what it takes.

Rensselaer Polytechnic Institute Math Home Page

http://www.math.rpi.edu/index.html

The Department of Mathematical Science at New York's Rensselaer Polytechnic Institute focuses on applied mathematics through an interdisciplinary approach. Visitors to the department's home page can find out about current research programs as well as review course materials and general info about degree options.

Royal Institute of Technology Department of Numerical Analysis and Computing Science

http://www.nada.kth.se/

Located in Stockholm, Sweden, the Royal Institute of Technology presents this home page for its Department of Numerical Analysis and Computing Science. Visitors will find an overview of its academics, research areas, faculty and students. In Swedish and English.

Rutgers University Mathematics Department

http://www.math.rutgers.edu/

The home page for the Mathematics Department at Rutgers University offers information about the department's courses, faculty and facilities. Includes descriptions of research projects and the computing center, plus links to other campus information servers.

St. Patrick's College Department of Mathematics

http://www.maths.may.ie/

The Mathematics Department at Ireland's St. Patrick's College in Maynooth posts this page offering information on its students, staff, academics and facilities. Browsers can download a version of the student handbook, browse the math library or link to other mathematics and Irish sites on the Web.

School of Mathematics

http://www.amsta.leeds.ac.uk/

The School of Mathematics at the University of Leeds provides an overview of the department, its programs in pure and applied mathematics and statistics. Includes faculty profiles, course descriptions and links to other mathematical servers on the Web.

The Shell Centre for Mathematical Education

http://acorn.educ.nottingham.ac.uk/Maths/

The Shell Centre for Mathematical Education at the University of Nottingham, England, researches and develops methods for teaching math. It gives an overview of its program and research degrees here.

Stetson University Unofficial Web Home

http://thoth.stetson.edu/

Maintained by a small group of students as an outlet for expression, this "(Very Unofficial!)" site offers general information about the Stetson University Department of Math and Computer Science. Also find e-texts, event information, music and entertainment pages, and works from area writers and artists.

Stockholm University Department of Mathematics

http://www.matematik.su.se/

The Department of Mathematics at Stockholm University maintains this online directory of the department's personnel. In English and Swedish.

SUNY at Stony Brook Department of Applied Mathematics and Statistics

http://ams.sunysb.edu/ams.html

The Department of Applied Mathematics and Statistics of the State University of New York at Stony Brook posts this home page with an overview of its undergraduate and graduate programs. Also find faculty profiles, links to research groups, descriptions of facilities and more.

SUNY at Stony Brook Mathematics Department

http://math.sunysb.edu/home.html

The home page of the Mathematics Department at the State University of New York at Stony Brook contains links to academic and departmental resources, including class schedules, people associated with the department and descriptions of degree programs offered. Also here: links to computer resources at the school, including a Unix tutorial.

Texas A&M University Department of Mathematics

http://www.math.tamu.edu/

Texas A&M University's Department of Mathematics provides information for its staff and students as well as prospective students here. Visit for teaching schedules, course home pages and an online software archive. The site also includes a general overview of the program.

Texas Institute for Computational and Applied Mathematics

http://www.ticam.utexas.edu/

The Texas Institute for Computational and Applied Mathematics (TICAM) is a research institute affiliated with the University of Texas, Austin. Visitors here can learn more about the institute's research and graduate program and link to its publications and seminar information.

Trinity College Dublin Department of Pure and Applied Mathematics

http://www.maths.tcd.ie/

The Department of Pure and Applied Mathematics at Trinity College in Dublin, Ireland, maintains this site for general information and resources. Visit this page for departmental details, graduate and undergraduate course requirements, and entertaining diversions.

Tulane University Mathematics Department

http://bach.math.tulane.edu/

The Tulane University Mathematics Department home page offers faculty bios, graduate student profiles and descriptions of research projects. Also find a program overview and links to online resources.

Universidade do Minho: Departamento de Matemática

http://www.math.uminho.pt/

Delve into the world of sine and cosine at the University of Minho in Braga, Portugal. Degree requirements and a staff list are posted here as well as an overview of the areas of specialization. Visitors can also see what conferences the department is sponsoring.

Universität Bern Institut für Informatik und angewandte Mathematik

http://iamwww.unibe.ch/index.html

The University of Bern's Institute of Computer Science and Applied Mathematics offers this site with a host of information about its research groups, academics, students, personnel and computing resources. In German, English, French and Italian.

University College Cork Department of Mathematical Physics

http://symphony.ucc.ie/

The Department of Mathematical Physics of Ireland's University College Cork maintains this informational site. Visit here to learn about the department's people and programs, link to user home pages, and access departmental Internet search resources.

University of Beyreuth Mathematics Department Home Page

http://btm2xd.mat.uni-bayreuth.de/

The Mathematics Department at the University of Beyreuth, Germany, maintains this site to introduce its people and programs. Visit here for staff listings, research topics, publications, and other academic and administrative resources.

University of Bielefeld Mathematics

http://www.mathematik.uni-bielefeld.de/

German students interested in studying mathematics at the University of Bielefeld can visit this page to see what the program offers and who teaches there. Students may want to visit the site for the resource and journal links offered. In German only.

University of Bonn Mathematics Institute

http://rhein.iam.uni-bonn.de:1025/

The Mathematics Institute presents information on its undergraduate and graduate programs of study, faculty listings and research projects. Includes links to other University of Bonn servers, related publications and documentation.

University of California-Davis Department of Mathematics

http://math.ucdavis.edu/

The University of California-Davis presents this home page for its Mathematics Department. Visitors will find information on research programs, faculty and classes, plus job openings and a link to the university's home page.

University of California-Los Angeles Department of Mathematics

http://www.math.ucla.edu/

The University of California at Los Angeles Department of Mathematics outlines its academic degree programs and research activities on this home page. Link to descriptions of the department's facilities, faculty and student majors.

University of Cambridge Faculty of Mathematics

http://www.maths.cam.ac.uk/

Prospective math students can learn about the University of Cambridge Faculty of Mathematics

and the course and research options it offers. Find links to the Isaac Newton Institute for Mathematical Sciences and the two departments that fall under the faculty.

University of Colorado at Denver Department of Mathematics

http://www-math.cudenver.edu/Home.html

This university mathematics site describes course offerings, programs of studies and research. Includes information on faculty, publications, colloquia and seminars.

University of Delaware Mathematical Sciences Department

http://www.math.udel.edu/

Visitors to this unofficial Web page can learn about the University of Delaware's Mathematical Sciences Department. The site highlights undergraduate and graduate programs, research activities, special projects and course materials.

University of Durham Department of Mathematical Sciences

http://fourier.dur.ac.uk:8000/

The Department of Mathematical Sciences at Great Britain's University of Durham offers this overview. Find information about the department's programs, projects and personnel, as well as a link to the university's home page.

University of Exeter Department of Mathematics

http://www.maths.ex.ac.uk/

The Department of Mathematics from England's University of Exeter provides a look at its undergraduate programs and this term's seminars. The page also introduces staff and students and offers a pictorial tour of the university, which is in Devon.

University of Florida Department of Mathematics

http://www.math.ufl.edu/

Local resources on the University of Florida Department of Mathematics home page include mathematics course home pages, Math Department colloquium and weekly events schedules, various directories and e-print archives. Also find links to selected campus servers and Web resources.

University of Glasgow Department of Mathematics

http://www.maths.gla.ac.uk/

Information on staff, research, programs and seminars are included at this site of the Department of Mathematics at the University of Glasgow, Scotland. Also featured are preprints and other publications, along with links.

University of Haifa Department of Mathematics and Computer Science

http://mathcs11.haifa.ac.il/

The Department of Mathematics and Computer Science at Israel's University of Haifa offers a wealth of information about its events, academics, programs, Internet resources and students. Browse the library catalog, view software sources, documentation and course materials, or link to a number of math and computer science resources.

University of Illinois at Chicago Department of Mathematics, Statistics & Computer Science

http://www.math.uic.edu/

Find course catalogs, an overview of academic programs and current research, plus a tour of the facilities featured on the home page of the Department of Mathematics, Statistics & Computer Science of the University of Illinois at Chicago. Links to topical sites on and off campus are also included.

University of Iowa Department of Mathematics

http://www.math.uiowa.edu/

The University of Iowa's Department of Mathematics provides links to its Mathematics Sciences Library and Mathematics/Statistics Educational Laboratory. A general guide to computing facilities is also included.

University of Jyväskylä Department of Mathematics

http://www.math.jyu.fi/

The Department of Mathematics at the University of Jyvaskyla in Finland features its academic programs and research projects in this home page. Visitors can click through an image map of classrooms in the department or take a look at a map of Jyvaskyla. In Finnish and English.

University of Kansas Mathematics Department

http://www.math.ukans.edu/index.html

Visit this page to review the program of the Mathematics Department at the University of Kansas in Lawrence. Find links to faculty, staff and student directories, departmental information, research groups and the local ftp site.

University of Konstanz Department of Mathematics and Computing Sciences

http://www.mathe.uni-konstanz.de/

The Department of Mathematics and Computing Sciences at Germany's University of Konstanz provides general departmental information at this home page. In German only.

University of Kuopio Department of Computer Science

http://www.cs.uku.fi/

The Department of Computer Science and Applied Mathematics at the University of Kuopio in Finland outlines its research program on this page. Visit to find out what it takes to be one of 25 students admitted to the program annually.

University of Liverpool's Statistics & Computational Mathematics

ftp://ftp.liv.ac.uk/pub/Stats+Comp_Maths/intro.html

The Department of Statistics and Computational Mathematics at the University of Liverpool in England disseminates information on departmental research activities, seminars and undergraduate course offerings here. Includes links to staff members and other university sites.

University of Massachusetts-Amherst Department of Mathematics and Statistics

http://www.math.umass.edu/

This home page for the Department of Mathematics and Statistics at the University of Massachusetts at Amherst contains information on programs of study, course offerings and areas of research. Includes information about admissions, departmental resources and links to related resources.

University of Newcastle Department of Mathematics

http://maths.newcastle.edu.au/

The Department of Mathematics at Australia's University of Newcastle provides information on its programs of study, course offerings and faculty. Site features also include links to other campus and mathematical servers.

University of New Hampshire Department of Mathematics

http://www.math.unh.edu/

The Department of Mathematics of the University of New Hampshire maintains this site for general information. Visit here to learn about its programs, faculty, resources and courses.

University of Notre Dame Department of Mathematics

http://www.science.nd.edu/math/math.html

Check on upcoming seminars and study opportunities at the Notre Dame's Department of Mathematics. Users can meet the faculty via their home pages or get down to business by browsing course offerings.

University of Nottingham Mathematics Department

http://www.maths.nott.ac.uk/

The Mathematics Department at Great Britain's University of Nottingham gives an overview of its programs here. The site also includes a list of seminars and a look at the faculty.

University of Paderborn Mathematics Department

http://math-www.uni-paderborn.de/

The Mathematics Department at Germany's University of Paderborn offers visitors to its home page a chance to learn about faculty and course offerings. Also find math journals and other math documents. In German and English.

University of Pennsylvania Mathematics Department

http://www.math.upenn.edu/

The University of Pennsylvania Mathematics Department offers a general program overview. Visit here to learn about its facilities, degree opportunities, faculty and students.

University of Puget Sound: Department of Mathematics and Computer Science

http://www.math.ups.edu/

The University of Puget Sound, in Tacoma, Wash., provides information about its Department of Mathematics and Computer Science, linking visitors to academics, events and student life. There's something for alumni, too, including job-hunting resources.

University of St. Andrews School of Mathematical & Computational Sciences

http://www.dcs.st-and.ac.uk/

The School of Mathematical and Computational Sciences at the University of St. Andrews posts this page offering information about its academic programs, course offerings and research projects. Includes job listings and links to other campus servers.

University of Salford Department of Mathematics and Computer Science

http://www.salford.ac.uk/docs/depts/mcs/homepage.html

The Department of Mathematics and Computer Science at the United Kingdom's University of Salford offers information on its five undergraduate programs. Information on contacting and visiting the department is also featured.

University of South Florida, Tampa Department of Mathematics

http://www.math.usf.edu/

The Department of Mathematics at the University of South Florida, Tampa provides the browser with information on current research projects, access to department journals and details of the industrial mathematics seminar. Includes links to preprints, reports and graduate study programs.

University of Sterling Department of Computing Science and Mathematics

http://www.cs.stir.ac.uk/

This gateway page of the Department of Computing Science and Mathematics at the United Kingdom's University of Stirling points visitors to descriptions of the department's academic programs and to the university's electronic information system. Includes a demonstration of NCSA Mosaic.

University of Sydney Mathematics and Statistics

http://www.maths.usyd.edu.au:8000/

The home page for the University of Sydney's Mathematics and Statistics Department contains an overview of the department, its programs of study and course offerings. Visitors can link to research groups, publications, departmental news, calendars and links to other math and statistics servers on the Internet.

University of Tasmania Department of Mathematics

http://euler.maths.utas.edu.au/

The University of Tasmania's Department of Mathematics unveils its programs and research for students and prospective students at its home page. Also, read about the faculty and campus here.

University of Trento Department of Mathematics

http://www-math.science.unitn.it/

Italy's University of Trento presents this home page for its Mathematics Department, offering course descriptions, general news and information on the faculty. Also find a university phone book, MIDI facts for electronic music makers and information on computer science activities at the school. In Italian and English.

University of Utah Department of Mathematics

http://www.math.utah.edu/

Prospective and current students can visit this site for the latest about the Department of Mathematics at the University of Utah. The site outlines the programs available and details the department's faculty, computer resources and research projects.

University of Warwick Mathematics Institute

http://www.maths.warwick.ac.uk/

The home page of the Mathematics Institute at England's University of Warwick in Coventry contains information on the institute's research, administration and services. Also find maps of the school and directions for getting there.

University of Washington Department of Applied Mathematics

http://www.amath.washington.edu/

University of Washington Department of Applied Mathematics introduces the staff, faculty, students and alumni and gives descriptions of department seminars, The Mathematical Biology Journal Club, Numerical analysis Reading club and related class materials. Links to the University, the Graduate school and Libraries are also listed.

University of Waterloo Faculty of Mathematics

http://math.uwaterloo.ca/

The Faculty of Mathematics at Canada's University of Waterloo provides this home page with information on its graduate and undergraduate programs, admissions guidelines and department facilities. Links to research groups, student organizations and the university home page are also featured.

University of Wisconsin-Madison Mathematics Department

http://math.wisc.edu/

The University of Wisconsin-Madison Mathematics Department page features the Mathematics Talent Search to test the aptitude of high school and middle school students. There are also Frequently Asked Question (FAQ) files and assorted helpful links.

University of Wuppertal Department of Mathematics

http://wmwap1.math.uni-wuppertal.de/pub/Mosaic/Mathematics_WWW.html

The Department of Mathematics at Germany's University of Wuppertal maintains this overview of its academic program, faculty and facilities. Links to resources on and off campus are featured. In German only.

Vanderbilt University Mathematics Department

http://math.vanderbilt.edu/

The Mathematics Department at Tennessee's Vanderbilt University provides this departmental overview with info on its academic programs, faculty and scheduled events. Links to related sites on and off campus are also featured.

Vassar College Department of Mathematics

http://math.vassar.edu/

The Department of Mathematics at Vassar College in Poughkeepsie, N.Y., provides information about its faculty and academic offerings. Visit this page to learn about the department and link to related Web sites.

Vrije University Faculty of Mathematics and Computer Science

http://www.cs.vu.nl/

The Faculty of Mathematics and Computer Science at Amsterdam's Vrije University provides an overview of its departments and programs here. Foreign students will also find exchange program information on this page. In Dutch and English.

Warsaw University Faculty of Mathematics, Informatics and Mechanics

http://hydra.mimuw.edu.pl/

The gateway to the facilities and research of Warsaw University's Faculty of Mathematics, Informatics and Mechanics can be found here. Explore the electronic resources of the department or link to other scientific faculties and servers across Poland. In English and Polish.

Yale University Mathematics Department

http://www.math.yale.edu/

The Department of Mathematics at Yale University maintains this overview. Visitors can check out seminars and preprints, plus find a list of senior faculty and their research projects.

INSTRUMENTS AND EQUIPMENT

The Slide Rule Home Page

http://photobooks.atdc.gatech.edu/~slipstick/slipstik.html

Turn back the clock to the days when slide rules were high tech. This page offers an explanation of what a slide rule is, how it's used and what distinguishes different types of slide rules. The author also provides an online exhibit of his own slide rule collection.

CALCULATORS

Hewlett-Packard HP28 Calculator Archive

http://www.ccl.kuleuven.ac.be/~luc/HP28/

This site is dedicated to Hewlett-Packard HP28 calculator family. Visitors can peruse an archive of postings relating to the products or submit their own additions.

JOBS

Jobs in Mathematics

http://www.cs.dartmouth.edu/~gdavis/policy/jobmarket.html

The market for PhDs in Mathematics is not exactly brimming with opportunities; just take a look at the market statistics on this career page. But all is not lost. Find information on marketable skills in the field, listings of job openings, solutions to the problems in job hunting and documentation of labor policies. Mathematicians unite! You have only your unemployment to lose.

LIBRARIES

Electronic SCV Library Gopher

ftp://iu-math.math.indiana.edu/pub/scv/

Abstracts of mathematical papers and other topics are unveiled through the Electronic SCV Library gopher from Indiana University. The downloadable files from this File Transfer Protocol (FTP) directory are formatted as hypertext, TeX and PostScript files.

MatheMatrix Out-Of-Core Matrix Algebra Library

http://www.primenet.com/~bolster/mmatrix.html

MatheMatrix, Inc. provides high performance out-of-core, dense, direct solve matrix algebra Fortran libraries for both real skyline and complex full matrices. Includes a description of company services, technical documentation and Frequently Asked Questions

MathWorks Library

ftp://ftp.mathworks.com/

The MathWorks Library is an anonymous FTP archive for MATLAB users. It contains user-contributed M-files, product announcements and information, digests, documentation, and bug fixes.

SUNY Stonybrook Math FTP Archive

ftp://math.sunysb.edu/preprints/

The Stony Brook Institute for Mathematical Sciences makes preprints from its extensive library of Math publications available for anonymous download at this ftp site. Complete instructions on file types and downloading procedure are also provided.

MATHEMATICAL/ SYMBOLIC LOGIC

Logic Eprints

http://www.math.ufl.edu/~logic/

Logic Eprints provides an archive of mathematical logic preprints and articles from scholarly journals around the world. Visit here to read the tutorial on searching the database, retrieving documents and accessing the list of e-mail addresses.

MATHEMATICIANS

Alphabetical Index of Mathematicians

http://www-groups.dcs.st-and.ac.uk/~history/ Alphabetical.html

This alphabetical index of mathematicians links to their detailed biographies. A chronological index, a short biographies index and a history topics index are also available.

Charles S. Peirce (1839-1914)

http://www.peirce.org/

Read the works of philosopher, scientist and mathematician Charles Sanders (Santiago) Peirce. Peirce wrote such works as "The Fixation of Belief" (an article on logic), and gave philosophical speeches like "On a New List of Categories." Visitors can also access the Pierce Telecommunity Project.

Douglas N. Arnold

http://www.math.psu.edu/dna/

Meet mathematician Douglas N. Arnold, Distinguished Professor in Penn State's Math Department. He includes pointers to his online publications and other work-related sites.

1996 WHO's On-line: Mathematicians

http://www.math.psu.edu/WHO/math.html

Lonely mathematicians will find a directory of peers at this site. The page also has links to other professional directories online.

Women Mathematicians

http://www.scottlan.edu/lriddle/women/ women.htm

The Agnes Scott College Mathematics Department hosts this collection of biographies of women mathematicians. Browse the biographies by alphabetical or chronological order, read the photo credits or link to related resources on the Web.

NUMERICAL ANALYSIS

ETNA Home Page

http://etna.mcs.kent.edu/

Browsers can download Electronic Transactions on Numerical Analysis, a journal published by Kent State University, here. The journal publishes significant new and important developments in numerical analysis and scientific computing.

PROFESSIONAL RESOURCES AND CONFERENCES

CAMEL: The Information Services of the Canadian Mathematical Community

http://camel.cecm.sfu.ca/

The Canadian Mathematical Society, a focus of activity and resources for the mathematical community in Canada, maintains this server. CAMEL offers links to bulletins, societies and other mathematical information sources. Pages are offered in French and English.

Chaos Network Sign-In

http://www.prairienet.org/business/ptech/

Once an online registration form for a complexity theory convention held in 1995, this site now posts the conference brochure, which explains key ideas of the conference and describes its workshops and featured speakers.

The European Mathematical Information Service

http://www.maths.soton.ac.uk/EMIS/ index.html

Watch this Web page for news about upcoming mathematics conferences in Europe. The European Mathematical Information Service site also offers an electronic library of mathematics as well as regularly published newsletters.

Math Forum Internet Resources Collection

http://forum.swarthmore.edu/~steve/

The Math Forum at Swarthmore College compiled this collection of Internet math resources for researchers and teachers. The collection is offered as a list or as an annotated version.

PUBLICATIONS AND INDUSTRY NEWS

ACM Transactions on Mathematical Software

http://gams.nist.gov/toms/Overview.html

A quarterly journal, "Transactions on Mathematical Software" belongs to a family of journals produced by ACM, "the First Society in Computing." The TOMS page provides access to articles, information for authors, and an outline of ACM's vision of the future of electronic publishing.

BIT

http://math.liu.se/BIT

"BIT," is an academic journal that "emphasizes numerical methods in approximation, linear algebra, and ordinary and partial differential equations." Subscription and contributors' information can be found here, as well as the journal itself and forthcoming papers.

Electronic Journal of Differential Equations

http://ejde.math.swt.edu/

The "Electronic Journal of Differential Equations" is an online publication dealing with all aspects of equations and their applications. Visitors can browse volumes, make submissions and link to other math servers. Mirror sites available.

Electronic Research Announcements-American Mathematical Society Home Page

http://www.ams.org/era/

Electronic Research Announcements, an online journal of the American Mathematical Society, posts "high quality research announcements . . . of significant advances in all branches of mathematics." The site includes a search tool and submission information.

ETNA Home Page

http://etna.mcs.kent.edu/

Browsers can download Electronic Transactions on Numerical Analysis, a journal published by Kent State University, here. The journal publishes significant new and important developments in numerical analysis and scientific computing.

Evolutionary Computation

http://www-mitpress.mit.edu/jrnls-catalog/ evolution.html

"Evolutionary Computation" is a quarterly publication covering the theoretical and practical aspects of evolutionary computational systems. Visitors to this page will find subscription information and links to past issues.

Institute for Mathematical Sciences Preprint Server

http://math.sunysb.edu/preprints.html

The Institute for Mathematical Sciences at Stony Brook Preprint Server offers access to abstracts and complete preprints online. An online form offers a keyword search of authors, titles and abstracts.

Le Journal de maths des eleves

http://www.ens-lyon.fr/JME/JME.html

The server for the the "Journal of Math" at L'ecole normale superieure de Lyon offers articles written by students at the school. In French.

Journal of Statistics Education

http://www2.ncsu.edu/ncsu/pams/stat/info/jse/homepage.html

Educators will find academic studies on the post-secondary teaching of statistics at the "Journal of Statistics Education" home page. Search current and past issues for articles, bibliographies and data sets.

LAPACK Users' Guide

http://www.netlib.org/lapack/lug/lapack_lug.html

The LAPACK Users' Guide, Second Edition, is published by the Society for Industrial and Applied Mathematics (SIAM). the entire text is available online and can also be ordered in printed form directly from SIAM.

Los Alamos Combinatorics E-print Server

http://www.c3.lanl.gov/laces

Visitors to the Los Alamos Combinatorics E-print Server will find ready access to current combinatorics research. Search the LACES archive, or learn more about the repository and how to submit material.

Missouri Journal of Mathematics Sciences

http://www.mathpro.com/math/mjmsJournal/mjms.html

The "Missouri Journal of Mathematics Sciences," a refereed publication of the Central Missouri State University, maintains this online version with publication information, a list of referees, subscription form and more. The journal publishes articles covering mathematics elementary and advanced, applied and pure.

New York Journal of Mathematics

http://nyjm.albany.edu:8000/

"The New York Journal of Mathematics" is promoted as "the first electronic general mathematics journal." Visitors to its home page can search the journal's archive, learn how to submit papers for consideration or link to other electronic math journals.

Nonlinear Science e-Print Archive

http://xyz.lanl.gov/

The Nonlinear Science e-Print Archive is a searchable index maintained by Los Alamos National Laboratories. Visit here to locate and download documents on chaos theory, fuzzy logic and other areas of advanced physics.

Nonlinear Science Today

http://www.springer-ny.com/nst/

Back issues of Nonlinear Science Today: An Electronic Adjunct to the Journal of Nonlinear Science are available here. The journal is from Springer-Verlag, which does scientific, technical and medical publishing. A directory to Springer-Verlag is provided.

Theory and Applications of Categories

http://www.tac.mta.ca/tac/

Visitors to this page will find "Theory and Applications of Categories," an "all-electronic, refereed journal on Category Theory, categorical methods and their applications in the mathematical sciences." Site features include articles, subscription information and submissions guidelines.

U.K. Nonlinear News

http://www.amsta.leeds.ac.uk/Applied/news.dir/index.html

The mission of the U.K. Nonlinear News newsletter is to "allow researchers in the applied and theoretical sides of nonlinear mathematics to keep abreast of the wide variety of nonlinear activities throughout the UK." Visit this site to read current and back issues, subscribe, or link to similar publications.

The Wavelet Digest

http://www.wavelet.org/wavelet/index.html

Produced by the Department of Mathematics at the University of South Carolina, "The Wavelet Digest" is archived at this site. Find recent and back issues, papers, events calendars and more.

SOFTWARE

Googolplex

http://www.uni-frankfurt.de/~fp/Tools/Googool.html

It's 10 times bigger than a googol, and it's a number you better never see on your phone bill. Download software here that will let you create and print your own "handy" (according to its computer science author) googolplex.

GRTensor

http://astro.queensu.ca/~grtensor/GRHome.html

Maintained at Queen's University in Ontario, Canada, this Web site offers information about GRTensor, a computer algebra package for "doing

calculations primarily of interest to relativists." Visitors can read documentation including reports, updates and benchmark calculation times.

Interval Computations

http://cs.utep.edu/interval-comp/main.html

In order to make numbers and data processed by computers even more accurate, mathematicians and scientists are working on applications for interval computations. Visit this site to learn more about the science and for lists of related software and books. Maintained by the University of Texas, El Paso.

Isabelle

http://www.cl.cam.ac.uk/Research/HVG/isabelle.html

Here, Isabelle, a generic theorem prover, is described and explained. The program can be downloaded, complete with manuals, from the FTP links provided. Research information includes the Isabelle Users Workshop and projects done with Isabelle.

Mathbrowser Home Page

http://www.mathsoft.com/browser/index.html

Mathcad is a program which allows mathematics to be computed and displayed in a unique electronic form. To fully use Mathcad, visitors can drop by the Mathbrowser Home Page to find out more about and download this Net browser formulated for Mathcad users.

MathSoft, Inc.

http://www.mathsoft.com/

The MathSoft, Inc., home page showcases the company's technical calculation applications, Web browser and other tools for computers. Company info and links to other sites are also featured.

Mathsource FTP

ftp://mathsource.wri.com/

This "electronic resource for Mathematica materials" includes FTP resources for algebra, calculus, discrete math and more. Visitors should be prepared to browse the lists; documentation is provided for many applications.

MathType

http://www.mathtype.com/mathtype/

MathType is a mathematical equation editor for Macintosh and Windows-based platforms. It interfaces with most word processors, graphics programs and desktop publishing packages.

The MathWorks Inc.

http://144.212.100.10/

Mathematicians looking for the latest software for complex computing tasks can check the pages of MathWorks Incorporated. The company presents product information, publications and technical support at this promotional site.

MicroMath Scientific Software

http://www.MicroMath.com/

Engineers and scientists working on the Windows/DOS platform can obtain software for solving equation systems from Micromath. The company provides links to downloadable demo versions of its most popular software titles at this promotional site.

The Muti Processing Algebra Data Tool

http://math-www.uni-paderborn.de/~cube/

The Department of Mathematics and Science at the University of Paderborn in Germany maintains this server with information on its Muti-Processing Algebra Data Tool (MuPAD). MuPAD is a computer algebra system which is available for free downloading through FTP and on CD for commercial purchase. Visitors can read a wealth of info on MuPAD including Frequently Asked Questions (FAQs), papers and journals, development info, conferences and discussion forums.

NonEuclid: Geometry Software

http://riceinfo.rice.edu/projects/NonEuclid/NonEuclid.html

Visit this page to learn about a Rice University software package that offers "an interactive simulation of the Poincare Model of Hyperbolic Geometry for use in high school and undergraduate education." Find an introduction to the software and a discussion of the model it presents.

The Numerical Algorithms Group Ltd

http://www.nag.co.uk/

The Numerical Algorithms Group Ltd. in Oxford, England, provides information on its products, services and activities at this site. Visitors can explore numerical and statistical software offerings.

The REDUCE Computer Algebra System

http://www.rrz.uni-koeln.de/REDUCE/

The REDUCE Computer Algebra System site details a new version of an interactive program for use by scientists, engineers and mathematicians in general algebraic computations. The page also includes information on similar packages offered by other sources, along with a REDUCE network library.

Wolfram Research

http://mathsource.wri.com/

Wolfram Research, the makers of the software program Mathematica, promotes its products and services at this site. Review math related books, newsletters and software here. Technical support for Wolfram Research products is also available.

STATISTICS

American Statistical Association Home Page

http://www.amstat.org/

The American Statistical Association fosters the use of statistics in the biological, physical, social and economic sciences. Visitors here will find news from its chapters, an online directory of its members and a schedule of upcoming meetings and conferences.

International Association for Statistical Computing

http://www.stat.unipg.it/iasc

The Department of Statistics at Italy's University of Perugia sponsors this home page for the International Association for Statistical Computing. Browsers can access an overview of the organization, IASC meeting info, minutes and software archives.

The Statistical Society of Australia

http://www.mathstat.flinders.edu.au/stats/stat_soc.html

Statisticians of Australia invite you to learn more about statistical science and its applications. Information about the Statistical Society of Australia Inc. conferences and state branches is also available.

BIOSTATISTICS

A Guide to Biostatistics Information Sources

http://www.biostat.washington.edu/~arossini/stat-services/

Looking for a solid and comprehensive collection of resources relating to statistical support for medicine, environmental science and related fields? This page includes online publications, software packages, course offerings and more.

INSTITUTES AND UNIVERSITIES

Bowling Green University Department of Mathematics and Statistics

http://www.bgsu.edu/departments/math/

Visit the Bowling Green University Department of Mathematics and Statistics home page for information on academic programs, planned events, departmental faculty, class schedules and financial aid programs. Guests can also link to other mathematical Web sites.

Dalhousie University Department of Mathematics, Statistics and Computer Science

http://www.cs.dal.ca/www-home.html

The Department of Mathematics, Statistics and Computer Science at Dalhousie University in Canada offers a collection of general information about available programs through this page. The entryway into the site also features pointers to help documents for using the Web.

Department of Mathematics and Statistics at York University

http://math.yorku.ca/

The Department of Mathematics and Statistics at York University, Canada, maintains this page with information about its programs, courses, seminars and colloquia. Also featured is its statistical consulting service, which assists university students and faculty with statistical methods used in research.

Duke University: Institute of Statistics & Decision Sciences

http://www.isds.duke.edu/

There's a high probability that your questions about graduate study in statistics at Duke will be answered here. In addition to general information about the department, courses and conferences, visitors can access the Working Paper Series and read the schedules and abstracts for the Institute's research seminar.

Penn State Department of Statistics

http://www.stat.psu.edu/

Penn State University presents the home page for its Department of Statistics. Visitors will find research information, class schedules and internship opportunities.

Purdue University Department of Statistics

http://www.stat.purdue.edu/

The Purdue University Department of Statistics offers a general overview of its academic programs and educational opportunities at this site. Access the department's admissions, research and computing information here.

Stanford University Department of Statistics

http://playfair.stanford.edu/

In its own words, the Stanford University Department of Statistics "provides information on department members, a fledgling collection of Technical Reports, and some exciting statistical software by department members." Also find information on the undergraduate minor in statistics program.

The Statistical Consulting Center for Astronomy

http://www.stat.psu.edu/scca/homepage.html

The Statistical Consulting Center for Astronomy at Pennsylvania State University, University Park, maintains this site of general information. Visit here to learn about its programs and people and to peruse its Frequently Asked Questions (FAQ) file.

Statistics Finland

http://www.stat.fi/

Statistics Finland, the national statistical institute, calculates most of the official statistics for the country. Visit this page to learn more about the institute, review the most recent statistical news and link to topic-related sites. Available in Finnish and English.

University of Cambridge Statistical Laboratory

http://www.statslab.cam.ac.uk/

The University of Cambridge Statistical Laboratory posts departmental and postgraduate information here. Visitors to this page will also learn about the university's preprint services and job vacancies.

University of Florida, Department of Statistics

http://stat.ufl.edu/

The University of Florida Department of Statistics provides information on undergraduate programs and graduate course offerings. Links to the statistics Virtual Library and the Statlib at Carnegie Mellon.

University of Glasgow Department of Statistics

http://www.stats.gla.ac.uk/home.html

The Department of Statistics at Scotland's University of Glasgow maintains this home page with information about the department's courses, faculty and research. Links to statistics-related sites—such as AT&T Bell Lab's statistics archive, Netlib—can also be found here.

University of Minnesota School of Statistics

http://www.stat.umn.edu/

The University of Minnesota's School of Statistics points browsers to its ongoing projects and research, faculty and students, classes, and general info about the school's programs.

PROBABILITY

The Probability Web

http://www.maths.uq.oz.au/~pkp/probweb/probweb.html

It would be simply illogical to pass up the links on the Probability Web. Logicians can link to people in the probability field, get helpful software, find out about conferences and happenings or link to other probability sites on the Web.

SOFTWARE

Completed, Ongoing, or Contemplated Projects in Lisp-Stat

http://euler.bd.psu.edu/lispstat/lispstat.html

Here's a periodically updated list of projects using Lisp-Stat. Reader submissions are encouraged and additional links point to the program page for the Statistical Computing in Lisp session held in 1995 and to the Linux Journal.

Journal of Statistical Software

http://www.stat.ucla.edu/journals/jss/

Statisticians can find out which programs work the best and download programs at this online journal from the Statistics Department at the University of California, Los Angeles. Author's instructions are available for readers who want to submit a software review.

StatLib Index

http://lib.stat.cmu.edu/

The home page for StatLib—a system for electronic distribution of statistical software and data sets—provides an annotated summary of contents. Visitors can search the database for information they need

StatLib: Other Places Index

http://lib.stat.cmu.edu/www/otherplaces/

StatLib is an Internet-based distribution system for statistical software, datasets and related information. This StatLib page provides an index of statistics departments around the world.

StatSci

http://www.mathsoft.com/

StatSci develops statistical and data analysis software for scientific users. Find product information and technical support at this promotional site.

STATISTICAL ANALYSIS

The CHANCE Database

http://www.geom.umn.edu/docs/snell/chance/welcome.html

CHANCE is a quantitative literacy course drawing on statistics reported in daily newspapers and journals to improve the statistics knowledge and critical analysis capabilities of students. The CHANCE database contains course syllabi, reference materials and teaching aids.

STATISTICIANS

Allstat

http://www.stats.gla.ac.uk/allstat/introduction.html

The Computers in Teaching Initiative's Centre for Statistics offers several e-mail lists for subscribers. Visitors can sign up to have newsletters from this English organization sent automatically.

THEORIES AND RESEARCH

Argonne National Laboratory Mathematics and Computer Science Division

http://www.mcs.anl.gov/

The Argonne National Laboratory's Mathematics and Computer Science Division extends an audio and text welcome to visitors at its home page. General introductions to the facility and to the division's research projects are provided.

The Center for Nonlinear Studies

http://cnls-www.lanl.gov/

The Center for Nonlinear Studies (CNLS) located at the Los Alamos National Laboratory offers a guide to its facilities and nonlinear science research. Visitors can review the CNLS mission statement, current happenings and workshop programs. Find also access to the Nonlinear Science e-Print archive.

The Computing and Applied Mathematics Laboratory

http://www.cam.nist.gov/

The Computing and Applied Mathematics Laboratory at the National Institute of Standards and Technology provides this overview. It presents information on its mission, units and services and posts the CAML Guide to Available Mathematical Software.

European Research Consortium for Informatics and Mathematics

http://www.ercim.inria.fr/

With a membership spanning 13 nations, the European Research Consortium for Informatics and Mathematics works to foster collaboration and cooperation within Europe's research community and with its industries. Visit this page to learn about the group's activities, publications and members.

Frequently Asked Questions About Cellular Automata

http://alife.santafe.edu/alife/topics/cas/ca-faq/ca-faq.html

Visitors to this site will find a Frequently Asked Questions (FAQ) index concerning Cellular Automata (CA). Questions and answers were contributed by members of the CA community.

MIT LCS Theory of Computation

http://theory.lcs.mit.edu/

The Theory of Computation Group at the Massachusetts Institute of Technology provides information about its various research projects here. The site also includes links to MIT's departments of mathematics and computer science.

The Nonlinear and Complex Systems Laboratory

http://www-ncsl.postech.ac.kr/

The Nonlinear and Complex Systems Laboratory at Pohang University in Pohang, Korea, maintains this site for general information. Visit here to learn about its research focus, view scientific publications and contact staff members.

Stanford University Metaphysics Research Lab

http://mally.stanford.edu/

The Metaphysics Research Lab of Stanford University in Palo Alto, Calif., studies abstract mathematical objects, concepts and literature. Visit this site to view its published research resources, contact staff members, and link to a variety of related departments and organizations around the world.

CHAOS THEORY

Chaos Group at the University of Maryland-College Park

http://www-chaos.umd.edu/

This site spotlights the University of Maryland Chaos Group, a multidisciplinary scientific study coalition focusing on the field of nonlinear chaotic dynamics. Features include general information about the group, listings of publications and links to related sites.

Visual Math Institute

http://hypatia.ucsc.edu/

The Visual Math Institute is a Santa Cruz, California organization dedicated to chaos theory and its applications in the sciences and arts. Visitors will find information on projects and CD-ROM products that are in production.

METEOROLOGY

ARCHIVES AND INDICES

Daily Planet: Weather and Climate

http://www.atmos.uiuc.edu/weather/weather.html

From the University of Illinois' Daily Planet site, this page features a list of links to popular weather and climate resources. Find the Weather World Web Server, the Weather Machine Gopher Server, the United States Climate Page, instructional materials in climatology, text-based model forecast tools and more.

Defense Meteorological Satellite Program Data Archive

http://www.ngdc.noaa.gov/dmsp/dmsp.html

Information for this site comes from "a two-satellite constellation of near-polar orbiting, sun synchronous satellites monitoring meteorological, oceanographic and solar-terrestrial physics environments." Items of interest include hurricane images and a tropical cyclone summary.

The Dundee Satellite Receiving Station

http://www.sat.dundee.ac.uk/

Since 1978, the satellite receiving station at Dundee University has been recording data from National Oceanic and Atmospheric Administration satellites. Visitors can check out reduced resolution "quick look" images from the past six months and order high resolution pictures. The site includes a brief weather movie.

Free University of Berlin Institute of Meteorology Weather Information

http://www.met.fu-berlin.de/english/Wetter/index.html

Visit this German page for weather reports from around the world. Links to a meteorology newsgroup, a conference calendar, the International Geosphere-Biosphere Program, and the Virtual Library: Meteorology are also featured.

Ionospheric Data Archive

http://www.ngdc.noaa.gov/stp/IONO/ionohome.html

The Ionospheric Physics Group at the National Geophysical Data Center offers access to its data archive here. Find an overview of the group's work and data collection efforts, as well as an index of its publicly accessible holdings.

Lamont-Doherty Earth Observatory Climate Group's Data Library

http://rainbow.ldgo.columbia.edu/datacatalog.html

The LDEO Climate Library provides users with a powerful database of information in climatology, oceanography and earth sciences. In addition to a general introduction and user's guide, researchers can conduct database searches, access relevant electronic magazines and utilize interactive educational materials.

Meteorological Sources on the Internet

http://www.atmos.uiuc.edu/kemp/wefaq.html

Visit this page to find an index of meteorological Internet resources from around the world. Links lead to Web pages, gopher servers and FTP sites offering weather maps, reports, satellite images and other data.

National Oceanic and Atmospheric Administration Weather Page

http://www.esdim.noaa.gov/weather_page.html

Visit this page for a directory of NOAA sources of weather information on the Net. Also find links to other organizational and institutional weather servers grouped by type: Web servers, gophers, telnet, finger, FTP and WAIS.

NOAA National Geophysical Data Center Gopher

gopher://gopher.ngdc.noaa.gov:70/1

The National Oceanic and Atmospheric Administration (NOAA) provides information about its National Geophysical Data Center in Boulder, Colo. Visitors can also access a variety of data on topics ranging from paleoclimatology to snow and ice.

Unidata Program Center's Integrated Earth Information Server

http://atm.geo.nsf.gov/

The Unidata Program Center, part of the U.S. National Science Foundation, maintains this site for its Integrated Earth Information Server. Visitors will find current electronic weather maps and bulletins, environmental information, and meteorological instructional materials from institutes across the United States.

Weather & Global Monitoring

http://www.csu.edu.au/weather.html

The Australian National University Bioinformatics Hypermedia Service posts this page offering a directory of links to international weather sites. Find satellite images, movies, maps, reports and forecasts, plus frequently asked questions and links to organizations and centers around the world.

WeatherNet

http://cirrus.sprl.umich.edu/wxnet/

WeatherNet asserts it is "the most comprehensive and up-to-date onramp to the world of weather data." Budding meteorologists will find more than 200 links to weather-related sites, radar info and maps worldwide.

WeatherNet: Radar & Satellite Menu

http://cirrus.sprl.umich.edu/wxnet/radsat.html

On this WeatherNet page, visitors can access satellite imagery of U.S. cities and regions by clicking on the map-based interface. Satellite images from around the world are also available.

WeatherNet: Weather Cams

http://cirrus.sprl.umich.edu/wxnet/wxcam.html

Seeing is believing is the predication upon which WeatherCam is founded. Meteorologists' prognostications aside, skeptical weather buffs can visit this site to get an almost live picture of the weather conditions in the city of their choosing.

Weather Station IDs

http://rs560.cl.msu.edu/weather/wids.html

Michigan State University's Unix Computing Group sponsors this simple Web site listing U.S. weather station IDs and locations, including latitude and longitude.

The WWW Virtual Library: Meteorology

http://www.ugems.psu.edu/~owens/www_Virtual_Library/

The WWW Virtual Library provides pointers to international meteorology resources on the Net. Visit for links to maps, forecasts, satellite images, movies and more.

ASSOCIATIONS, ORGANIZATIONS, AND AGENCIES

Fleet Numerical Meteorology and Oceanography Center

http://www.fnoc.navy.mil/

The U.S. Navy's Fleet Numerical METOC Center is a California-based organization specializing in meteorology, oceanography and satellite imagery. Visitors to this site can read detailed information on the center's research and resources, or view the gallery of satellite images.

Institute for Meteorology of the Free University of Berlin

http://www.met.fu-berlin.de/konferenzen/index.html

Information about upcoming conferences at the Free University of Berlin's Meteorological Institute can be found on this page, which also includes information taken from the bulletins of the German and American Meteorological societies. In English and German.

National Operational Hydrological Remote Sensing Center

http://www.nohrsc.nws.gov/

The National Operational Hydrologic Remote Sensing Center, operating under the National Weather Service, creates and distributes products using remotely sensed data. This site provides more information about the center, its products and technology.

National Weather Service

http://www.nws.noaa.gov/

An agency of the National Oceanic and Atmospheric Administration, the The National Weather Service offers visitors an operations overview, answers to frequently asked questions, and links to weather data, including forecasts and warnings, charts, and climate information.

National Weather Service Office Descriptions

http://www.noaa.gov/nws/nws_intro.html

This National Weather Service site outlines the organizational structure of the national meteorological service. Visitors will find links to all National Oceanic and Atmospheric Administration and NWS regional sites.

NOAA Network Information Center

http://www.nnic.noaa.gov/

The National Oceanic and Atmospheric Administration's Network Information Center provides a gateway into the agency's vast online resources. The page includes links to agency information, weather sites, an FTP site and NOAA data centers.

World Meteorological Organization

http://www.wmo.ch:80/

This United Nations agency paves the way for international cooperation in the field of meteorology and provides detailed data about global climate and change. Visitors can learn about the organization's various programs and link to its members' sites. In English, French and Spanish.

THE ATMOSPHERE

Cambridge University Centre for Atmospheric Science

http://www.atm.ch.cam.ac.uk/

Visitors to this site can take a multimedia tour of the ozone hole. The site is maintained by the Centre for Atmospheric Science at the University of Cambridge, which also provides details on its atmospheric research here.

CSIO Division of Atmospheric Research

http://www.dar.csiro.au/

Australia's Commonwealth Scientific and Industrial Organization's Division of Atmospheric Research seeks to find answers to problems "concerning the physics and chemistry of the atmosphere." Visit this site for descriptions of the division and its research projects, plus links to topical resources.

Environment Canada

http://www.ec.gc.ca

Browsers can download reports on stratospheric ozone depletion and Pacific Herring fish stocks here. The reports are part of Canada's National Environmental Indicator Series and are available in English and French.

Meteorological Dynamics Laboratory at the National Center for Scientific Research

http://www.lmd.ens.fr/

France's National Center for Scientific Research Meteorological Dynamics Laboratory hosts this overview of its facilities and programs. Also find links to the library, information about the lab's collaborations, and selected sites of topical interest.

National Center for Atmospheric Research

http://www.ucar.edu/

Located in Boulder, Colo., the National Center for Atmospheric Research hosts this overview offering information on the center's divisions, programs, facilities and services, plus access to its research data archives. A weather section contains links to satellite images and realtime forecasts.

NOAA Environmental Information Services

http://www.esdim.noaa.gov/

Visit this site to discover what data products are available from the National Oceanic and Atmospheric Administration, how they can be used and where they can be found. Links to NOAA National Data Centers and to information on NOAA's national and international affiliations are also featured.

NOAA National Data Buoy Center

http://seaboard.ndbc.noaa.gov/

The National Data Buoy Center's home page provides access to "buoy-measured environmental data" as published by the National Oceanic and Atmospheric Administration. Includes meteorological and oceanographic data, as well as information about the NDBC.

NOAA Nitrous Oxide and Halocompounds Division

http://www.cmdl.noaa.gov/noah/noah.html

The National Oceanic and Atmospheric Administration's Nitrous Oxide and Halocompounds Division is studying the depletion of the ozone layer and aims to quantify the sources and sinks of chlorofluorocarbons. Check out graphics, reports and an overview of the staff.

Ozone Depletion FAQ

http://www.cis.ohio-state.edu/hypertext/faq/usenet/ozone-depletion/top.html

This Ohio State University page contains a four-part frequently asked questions file concerning ozone depletion.

Total Ozone Mapping Spectrometer

http://jwocky.gsfc.nasa.gov/

The Total Ozone Mapping Spectrometer page offers continually updated information about the Earth's ozone, including satellite retrieval data, press releases, images of the ozone hole and QuickTime movies.

CLIMATOLOGY

Climate Action Network Online

http://www.igc.apc.org/climate/Eco.html

Climate Action Network's newsletter, Eco, is published from the United Nations Climate Talks and from the Geneva sessions of the Ad Hoc Group on the Berlin Mandate. Visitors can download current and back issues of the newsletter here.

Climate and Radiation Branch at NASA

http://climate.gsfc.nasa.gov/

The Climate and Radiation Branch at NASA conducts research with the goal of improving the understanding of Earth's climate. This searchable site features information on aerosols, clouds and rainfall, as well as information on the branch's projects, personnel and publications.

Climate Prediction Center

http://nic.fb4.noaa.gov/

This page presents information on climate prediction, analysis of climate anomalies and monitoring of climate systems. Includes links to databases, products and an overview of the Climate Prediction Center, a facility of the National Centers for Environmental Prediction.

CLIMVIS

http://www.ncdc.noaa.gov/onlineprod/drought/xmgr.html

The National Climactic Data Center designed CLIMVIS, a graphing tool for displaying climate data. Visitors can use the tool to create graphs for U.S. climate and drought data from 1895 to the present. The center's database also includes current global climate summaries.

Geophysical Fluid Dynamics Laboratory

http://www.gfdl.gov/

The Geophysical Fluid Dynamics Laboratory studies oceanic circulation and climate dynamics. Find climatological datasets, technical reports and research papers at this site. A freely distributed ocean model is made available for public access.

Global Climate Perspectives System

http://www.ncdc.noaa.gov/gcps/gcps.html

The Global Climate Perspectives System is a research project of the National Oceanic and Atmospheric Administration that focuses on global climate changes. The site includes data, research descriptions and papers on the project.

Global Energy and Water Cycle Experiment

http://www.cais.com/gewex/gewex.html

Conducted by the World Climate Research Program, the Global Energy and Water Cycle Experiment is a project designed to "observe and model the hydraulic cycle and energy fluxes in the atmosphere." Visitors can read an overview of GEWEX and numerous pages featuring news, reports, meetings, documents and Web resources.

GLOBE Visualizations

http://rsd.gsfc.nasa.gov/globe

This NASA-sponsored site features graphical representations of conditions on Earth based on current environmental data. Other site features include a lesson on how the images are created.

NOAA Climate Diagnostics Center

http://www.cdc.noaa.gov/

The National Oceanic and Atmospheric Administration's Climate Diagnostics Center provides data on climate conditions around the world. Access satellite data, browse through archives or link to relevant organizations, people, publications and other home pages.

NOAA Climate Monitoring and Diagnostic Laboratory

http://www.cmdl.noaa.gov/

The National Oceanic and Atmospheric Administration's Climate Monitoring and Diagnostic Laboratory, located in Boulder, Colo., presents this overview of its mission and research programs. Find links to data on aerosols, ozone and water vapor, solar and thermal radiation, meteorology and more.

NOAA National Climatic Data Center

http://www.ncdc.noaa.gov/

A facility of the National Oceanic and Atmospheric Administration, the National Climatic Data Center posts this online weather update service with access to more than 5,000 weather stations and an "Interactive Visualization of Climate Data." Also find a link to the World Data Center for Meteorology.

NOAA Paleoclimatology Program

http://www.ngdc.noaa.gov/paleo/paleo.html

The NOAA Paleoclimatology Program presents a variety of data resources and program features here, with a number of paleoclimatology datasets and a search engine. Visitors can also read about the program's funded research, download software and link to related sites.

Northeast Regional Climate Center

http://met-www.cit.cornell.edu/nrcc_home.html

Weather conditions and forecasts are the focus of the Northeast Regional Climate Center at Cornell University. Visit the center's home page for access to databases, research, impact reports and climate summaries. Links to other regional climate centers are also featured.

Oregon Climate Service

http://ocs.ats.orst.edu/

The Oregon Climate Service is the state repository for weather and climate information. Its home page provides the latest Oregon weather forecasts and images, as well as publications, data archives and precipitation mapping.

Scripps Institution of Oceanography Climate Research Division

http://meteora.ucsd.edu/

For a scientific examination of the weather, consult the Climate Research Division of the Scripps Institution of Oceanography. Find data, forecasts and predictions related to weather and climate at this site.

United Nations Framework Convention on Climate Change

http://www.unep.ch/iucc.html

Earth Scientists can download official documents from the United Nations Framework Convention on Climate Change. Visitors can also read general information about the convention on this page and link to organizations working on global warming.

University of East Anglia Climatic Research Unit

http://www.cru.uea.ac.uk/

The Climatic Research Unit at the University of East Anglia, Norwich, England, maintains this page. Visitors can read a wide range of info about the school's people, publications, research and weather reports. Links are also provided to other climate research facilities on the Web.

COMPUTERS AND METEOROLOGY

NCSA Atmospheric and Oceanic Group

http://redrock.ncsa.uiuc.edu/AOS/home.html

Learn about the University of Illinois National Center for Supercomputing Applications project to link atmospheric/oceanic studies and technology. Access information on the project, its members and related publications.

The Program for Climate Model Diagnosis and Intercomparison

http://www-pcmdi.llnl.gov/

The Program for Climate Model Diagnosis and Intercomparison, which researches global climate models and develops associated software products, provides information about its projects, publications, research and software.

UCARweb

http://www.ucar.edu

Weather forecasts and radar imagery are among the many items you can access here. See Editor's Choice.

FORECASTING

Australian Weather Forecasts

http://atmos.es.mq.edu.au/weather/ausweather.html

For current and forecasted meteorological conditions down under, consult the Australian Weather Forecasts site. A graphical interface to data from the Australian Bureau of Meteorology greets weather-curious guests.

Bermuda Weather Page

http://www.bbsr.edu/Weather/

This weather page from the Bermuda Biological Station for Research (BBSR) contains numerous links to weather-related resources on the Net, particularly those dealing with Bermuda and the North Atlantic. You'll find satellite images and a tropical storm corner (in season, of course), but nothing about mysterious plane disappearances.

Great Lakes Forecasting System

http://superior.eng.ohio-state.edu/

The Great Lakes Forecasting System allows access to "regularly scheduled predictions of the physical and related variables of the Great Lakes." Visitors can review readings of water surface temperature, elevation, currents and more. Also find topical reports and pointers.

NOAA Forecast Systems Laboratory

http://www.fsl.noaa.gov/

A National Oceanic and Atmospheric Administration facility located in Colorado, the Forecast Systems Laboratory's main mission is "to transfer technological developments ... to the nation's operational atmospheric and oceanic services." Find an operations overview, meteorology publications, research data and forecasts on the lab's home page.

a2z EDITOR'S CHOICE

UCARweb

http://www.ucar.edu

The University Corporation for Atmospheric Research (UCAR) meets the demands of a program "encompassing the Earth's atmosphere, land masses and oceans, and the interaction between our planet and the Sun" by use of computer modeling, theoretical study and direct observation. The coordination of these interdisciplinary investigations and the synthesis of the data are the most challenging aspects of the laboratory's goal of developing viable climate models and meteorological prediction paradigms. UCAR's Web pages provide links to its numerous laboratories, research centers, field units and satellite monitoring stations that work in such diverse scientific disciplines as atmospheric chemistry, scientific computing, climatology, remote sensing and solar physics. UCAR also provides one of the most comprehensive sets of weather-related links on the Internet which "includes dozens of sites with global weather and research data, CD-ROMs, education resources" and image archives. Weather forecasts and conditions are available along with real-time radar imagery and accurate weather maps by region and city across the United States. The severe weather pages contain datasets and information about hurricanes, tornadoes and other dangerous weather systems as well as satellite imagery, reconnaissance data and background. In short, UCAR is a one-stop resource for virtually every aspect of climatology and meteorology.—*Reviewed by Steve Ellis*

Tropical Atmosphere Ocean Array

http://www.pmel.noaa.gov/toga-tao/
realtime.html

The Tropical Atmosphere Ocean Array measures ocean and meteorological variables that help the National Oceanic and Atmospheric Administration predict weather patterns from the tropics—especially El Nino. Visit here to chart realtime data from the TAO Array, including sea surface temperatures and wind.

The Weather Machine

gopher://wx.atmos.uiuc.edu/

The University of Illinois Weather Machine, known as "WX" in cyberspace, provides international weather maps, posted here. The gopher server also contains hurricane warnings and images.

INSTITUTES AND UNIVERSITIES

Colorado State University Department of Atmospheric Science

http://www.atmos.colostate.edu/

The Department of Atmospheric Science at Colorado State University presents general information about the department, its academic programs and faculty. Includes a gallery of aerial photographs, staff home pages, e-mail directories, links to campus servers and related resources.

Cooperative Institute For Meteorological Satellite Studies at the University of Wisconsin-Madison

http://cimss.ssec.wisc.edu/

Located at the University of Wisconsin-Madison, the Cooperative Institute for Meteorological Satellite Studies outlines its educational and research programs at this site. Find data on numerical modeling, tropical cyclones and research instruments such as the Geostationary Operational Environmental Satellite.

Finnish Meteorological Institute Department of Geophysics

http://www.geo.fmi.fi/

The Department of Geophysics of the Finnish Meteorological Institute maintains this site offering information about its programs. Also find news, publications, events schedules and related links. Includes downloadable software and local weather information.

Florida State University Center for Ocean-Atmospheric Prediction Studies

http://www.coaps.fsu.edu/

Florida State University's Center for Ocean-Atmospheric Prediction Studies performs research in air-sea interactions. Find links to the center's mis-

sion statement, research data and personnel, plus sites of related topical interest.

Florida State University Meteorology

http://thunder.met.fsu.edu/

Florida State University's Meteorology site provides general information on the department's undergraduate and graduate programs. Also find Signals, the departmental alumni newsletter, and a list of the requirements for receiving a certificate in meteorology.

Free University of Berlin Institute for Meteorology

http://www.met.fu-berlin.de/

Located in the Department of Geosciences at Germany's Free University of Berlin, the Institute for Meteorology provides this look at its programs, current research and research groups. Links to weather resources and sites of topical interest are also featured.

Lyndon State College Meteorology Department

http://apollo.lsc.vsc.edu/

Hosted by the Meteorology Department at Vermont's Lyndon State College, this site offers links to an overview of the department, the college's home page and main server, and weather information.

Macquarie University Atmospheric Science Program

http://atmos.es.mq.edu.au/

The School of Earth Sciences at Australia's Macquarie University in Sydney presents this overview of its Atmospheric Science program. Also find a searchable database of atmospheric science servers such as the Automatic Weather Station.

Ohio State University Atmospheric Science Program

http://asp1.sbs.ohio-state.edu/

Weather is more than small talk at Ohio State University's Atmospheric Science Program. Weather text, images and the meteorological curricula are available here.

Pennsylvania State University Department of Meteorology

http://chaos7.met.psu.edu/welcome.htm

Find out what the weatherperson of the future is learning today at the Penn State Meteorology home page. Course descriptions, research projects and faculty biographies are provided, along with a look at current weather conditions on campus.

Purdue University Atmospheric Sciences Department

http://meteor.atms.purdue.edu/

Purdue University presents the home page for its Atmospheric Sciences Department. Visitors will

find a departmental overview, news and announcements, weather data, maps and photos.

Texas A&M University Department of Meteorology

http://www.met.tamu.edu/

The Department of Meteorology at Texas A&M University provides information about its research and academic facilities. Visit for satellite and radar data, realtime weather, and weather analyses and forecasts.

University of Albany Department of Atmospheric Science

http://www.atmos.albany.edu/

The Department of Atmospheric Science at the University of Albany, N.Y., maintains this site to introduce its people and programs. Visit here for staff and student listings, course offerings, publications and meteorology resources.

University of Hawaii Meteorology

http://lumahai.soest.hawaii.edu/

The Meteorology Department at University of Hawaii maintains this weather information service. Get department information, up-to-the-minute weather from around the world, regional forecasts, and links to other weather-related Web sites.

University of Maryland Department of Meteorology

http://www.metolab3.umd.edu/
meteorology.html

The Department of Meteorology at the University of Maryland provides information here on its people and programs. Visitors will also find local meteorological data and links to other university departments.

University of Reading Department of Meteorology

http://typhoon.reading.ac.uk/typhoon.html

The Department of Meteorology at the University of Reading, England, provides an overview of the department, its programs of study and course offerings. Includes information on seminars, faculty and job openings. Links to related Internet search tools are also available.

University of Washington Department of Atmospheric Sciences

http://www.atmos.washington.edu/

The Department of Atmospheric Sciences at the University of Washington offers departmental information and news, plus Seattle area weather data and links to other weather-related servers. Find satellite images, forecasts and other weather information from across the United States.

The Weather Underground at the University of Michigan

http://groundhog.sprl.umich.edu/

Find links to World of Weather, WeatherNet and curriculum activities targeted for K-12 at the University of Michigan Weather Underground. Imagery, current conditions and forecasts are featured among these "weather watch" pages.

STORMS

Hurricane Home Page

http://www.hurricane.com/

A service of Coral Technologies Inc., this page provides information on hurricanes and tropical storms for Florida's Broward, Dade, Monroe and Palm Beach Counties. At this site, visitors can check out radar and satellite images of storms or link to the National Hurricane Center's home page.

Hurricane Watch

http://www.netcreations.com/hurricane

This Web site tracks hurricanes and provides interested parties with radar, satellite and infrared images of tropical storms. Includes links to public and marine advisories, the Disaster Information Network and the National Weather Service's severe weather warnings.

National Severe Storms Laboratory

http://www.nssl.uoknor.edu/

The National Severe Storms Laboratory defines its mission and describes current programs and research projects here. The federal agency also posts staff profiles, employment information and links to related resources.

Storm Chaser Home Page

http://taiga.geog.niu.edu/chaser/chaser2.html

Tornado chasers from the U.S. Midwest take the Web by storm at this page with close-up photos of twisters as well as details about tracking and studying storms. The page also features current weather information and eyewitness accounts from the chasers.

Tropical Prediction Center

http://www.nhc.noaa.gov/

The Tropical Prediction Center is the home page of the National Hurricane Center. Follow the tracks of the 1995 hurricanes in the Atlantic, watch the public advisories on upcoming stories, and mosey through meteorological information, statistics and products. There's also a link to Florida International University, where the center is located.

WeatherNet: Tropical Weather Products

http://cirrus.sprl.umich.edu/wxnet/tropical.html

If you're fascinated by hurricanes, WeatherNet's Tropical Weather page offers access to related advisories, complete with tracking maps, satellite photos and storm progress reports.

WEATHER PATTERNS

El Nino

http://www.pmel.noaa.gov/toga-tao/el-nino-story.html

The National Oceanic and Atmospheric Administration provides this informative page on the El Nino weather system. Visitors will find animations, satellite and infrared images, articles and theories about this recurring weather pattern off the coast of Peru.

El Nino Theme Page

http://www.pmel.noaa.gov/toga-tao/el-nino/home.html

The National Oceanic and Atmospheric Administration posts these pointers to pages answering questions about El Nino: what is it, what is its impact, what is its current forecast and what are its latest measurements? Find a variety of data and answers to other frequently asked questions.

ARCHIVES AND INDICES

List of Oceanography Resources

http://www.esdim.noaa.gov/ocean_page.html

The National Oceanic and Atmospheric Administration (NOAA), a division of the U.S. Department of Commerce, maintains this collection of pointers to online oceanography resources. Featured sites include databases and project reports of the NOAA and of research institutions around the world.

OCEANIC—Ocean Information Center

http://www.cms.udel.edu/

Maintained by the University of Delaware's Graduate College of Marine Studies, this home page offers a sea of information—publication abstracts, data sets, research vessel information, and much more—related to oceanography. Includes an ocean area map.

South African Data Centre for Oceanography

http://fred.csir.co.za/ematek/sadco/sadco.html

The South African Data Centre for Oceanography "stores, retrieves, and manipulates multidisciplinary marine information from the areas around Southern Africa." Visit the centre's page to review its services, inventories, charges, and contacts.

ASSOCIATIONS

ORGANIZATIONS AND AGENCIES

CSIRO Marine Laboratories Home Page, Australia

http://www.ml.csiro.au/

Australia's largest government scientific research agency, CSIRO hosts this page for its marine laboratories. Find links to the division's remote sensing project, the library, and seminar announcements.

Geological Survey of Canada (Atlantic) Home Page

http://agcwww.bio.ns.ca/

The Geological Survey of Canada is the principal marine geoscience facility in the country with a team of more than 100 specialists. Visit this site to learn more about the organization and to access its extensive information resources.

National Oceanic and Atmospheric Administration

http://www.noaa.gov/

The U.S. National Oceanic and Atmospheric Administration (NOAA) provides an agency overview, mission statement and list of its responsibilities here. The site includes a Frequently Asked Questions (FAQ) file, links to research sites, and information on pending legislation related to the agency's work.

National Ocean Service—Sanctuaries and Reserves Division

http://www.nos.noaa.gov/ocrm/srd

The Sanctuaries and Reserves Division (SRD) is a part of the National Ocean Service Office. This page provides a directory of SRD sites categorized by name, state and region. There are also links to SRD Publications and the Biodiversity Initiative.

NOAA Environmental Information Services

http://www.esdim.noaa.gov/

Visit this site to discover what data products are available from the National Oceanic and Atmospheric Administration, how they can be used, and where they can be found. Links to NOAA National Data Centers, to information on NOAA's national, and international affiliations are also featured.

NOAA National Oceanographic Data Center

http://www.nodc.noaa.gov/index.html

This home page for the U.S. National Oceanographic Data Center provides ocean data management and ocean data services to researchers and other users around the world. The NODC is one of the environmental data centers operated by the U.S. National Oceanic and Atmospheric Administration.

The Oceanography Society

http://www.tos.org/

The Oceanography Society is a Washington, D.C.-based nonprofit organization that is dedicated to fostering knowledge of the planet's oceans. Browsers can read information about the group and its raison d'être here.

CHARTS, MAPS, AND PHOTOGRAPHS

SatLab Server

http://satftp.soest.hawaii.edu/

Hosted by the University of Hawaii, the SatLab Server offers access to satellite images of Hawaii and the Central Pacific. Also enjoy links to the Ocean Atlas of Hawaii and Maui Weather Today.

Sea Surface Temperature Satellite Images

http://dcz.gso.uri.edu/avhrr-archive/archive.html

Maintained by the University of Rhode Island Graduate School of Oceanography, the archive accessed via this page features sea surface temperature satellite images. An online classroom lesson plan provides teachers ideas for uses of the images.

Topex/Poseidon Home Page

http://topex-www.jpl.nasa.gov/

A joint U.S./French experiment aimed at using satellite images to map Earth's oceans, Topex/Poseidon maintains this Web site to display documentation of the project, including a collection of images and data. Also available are pointers to other sources of information about Topex/Poseidon at university campuses, astrodynamics laboratories, and NASA. See Editor's Choice.

EDUCATION

Oceanographic Gateway: Education Projects for School-Agers

http://seawifs.gsfc.nasa.gov/

Link through this gateway to NASA's SeaWiFS Project, the JASON Project, the Smithsonian's Ocean Planet home page, or In Search of Giant Squid.

GEOLOGICAL OCEANOGRAPHY

COASTAL GEOGRAPHY

USGS Marine and Coastal Geology Program

http://marine.usgs.gov/

This U.S. Geological Survey program investigates "geologic issues of marine and coastal ar-

---

a2z EDITOR'S CHOICE

TOPEX/Poseidon Home Page

http://topex-www.jpl.nasa.gov/

The Ocean Topography Experiment (TOPEX/Poseidon) is a cooperative project between the United States and France to develop and operate an advanced satellite system dedicated to observing the Earth's oceans. The satellite was launched in summer of 1992, and is used to track changes in ocean currents and to chart the height of the seas across ocean basins. Combining these data with measurements from other resources such as the NASA Microwave Radiometer, which estimates total atmospheric water vapor content, the project provides a dataset that relates the changes in these environmental conditions to atmospheric and climate patterns. This site includes a collection of impressive images prepared specifically for public release and publication, continuously updated by the TOPEX/Poseidon team. Visitors to these Web pages can read papers and reports prepared by the team's principal investigators, or order an information CD-ROM produced by the scientific computing group affiliated with the project.—*Reviewed by Steve Ellis*

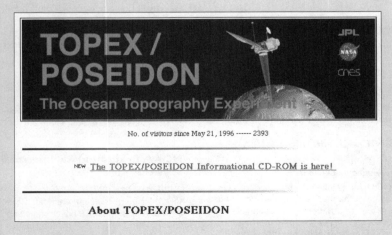

No. of visitors since May 21, 1996 ------ 2393

NEW The TOPEX/POSEIDON Informational CD-ROM is here!

About TOPEX/POSEIDON

eas under the themes of Environmental Quality and Preservation, Natural Hazards and Public Safety, Natural Resources, and Earth-Sciences Information, and Technology." Look into the specifics here.

THE OCEAN FLOOR

Ocean Floor Datasets

http://imager.ldeo.columbia.edu/

Maintained by the Lamont-Doherty Earth Observatory (LDEO) at Columbia University, this page contains links to the RIDGE Multibeam Synthesis Project, the East Pacific Rise Petrology Database, and movies of the Pacific/Antarctic Ridge. A link to the LDEO home page is also included.

World Data Center-A for Marine Geology & Geophysics

http://www.ngdc.noaa.gov/mgg/aboutmgg/wdcamgg.html

The World Data Center-A for Marine Geology and Geophysics sees the ocean floor as a map leading to key information about the physical evolution of the earth. Researchers can follow pointers to the center's seafloor environment research reports and datasets at this site.

GULFS, BAYS, AND ESTUARIES

Gulf of Mexico Program Information Network

http://www.epa.gov/docs/gumpo/gulf_index.html

The U.S. Environmental Protection Agency maintains this informational site on the environmental challenges in the Gulf of Mexico. Visit here for progress reports on the project and a variety of related environmental links.

INSTITUTES AND UNIVERSITIES

Dalhousie University Department of Oceanography

http://www.phys.ocean.dal.ca/

The Department of Oceanography at Dalhousie University in Halifax, Nova Scotia, provides a directory that includes general information and oceanographic resources—plus two live views from the roof.

Florida State University Department of Oceanography

http://ocean.fsu.edu/

The Department of Oceanography at Florida State University is a small, research-oriented department in Tallahassee, Florida. An interesting, in-depth definition of oceanography, links to the FSU Marine Lab and Center for Ocean-Atmosphere Prediction Studies and "Not the Main Menu" round out the site.

French Institute of Research and Exploitation of the Sea

http://www.ifremer.fr/

The French Institute of Research and Exploitation of the Sea (IFREMER) does research in geology, physical oceanography, biology, and chemistry, and monitors aquacultural resources, fisheries, and the environment. Learn more about IFREMER and browse its photographic library here. In French and English.

The Japan Marine Science and Technology Center

http://www.jamstec.go.jp/

The Japan Marine Science and Technology Center conducts ocean and coastal research. Find Japanese oceanographic exploration and observational data at this site.

Mississippi State University Center for Air Sea Technology

http://www.cast.msstate.edu/

Although the center's "emphasis is on application of numerical ocean models and modeling techniques toward realistic simulation of ocean conditions...CAST has expanded its efforts to coupled air-ocean modeling." Review projects, meet staff, and look into academic programs at the center's home page.

Old Dominion University Department of Oceanography

http://www.ocean.odu.edu/

Old Dominion University's Department of Oceanography features information about its research facilities, a link to "Wavelengths," the department's semiannual report, and details about the department's courses, seminars and faculty.

Old Dominion University's Center for Coastal Physical Oceanography

http://www.ccpo.odu.edu/

The Center for Coastal Physical Oceanography's hypertext information system offers a listing of the center's activities, research facilities, projects and educational information. Includes a user's guide and help.

Polish Academy of Sciences Institute of Oceanology

http://www.iopan.gda.pl/

The Institute of Oceanology at the Polish Academy of Sciences provides information about its programs of study, course offerings, and publications here. Includes links to research groups and a directory of oceanography resources on the Internet.

Scripps Institution of Oceanography

http://sio.ucsd.edu/

The Scripps Institution of Oceanography (SIO) conducts research of the earth's marine environment. Based at the University of California, San Diego, SIO offers graduate study in oceanography, marine biology, and earth sciences. Find an introduction to SIO's facility, programs, and research resources at this site. See Editor's Choice.

Scripps Institution of Oceanography Center for Coastal Studies

http://coast.ucsd.edu/

The University of California at San Diego researches the coastal environment through its Center for Coastal Studies. Visit its home page to explore the study of waves, sediment transport, and marine archaeology.

Skidaway Institute of Oceanography

http://minnow.skio.peachnet.edu/

Georgia's Skidaway Institute of Oceanography invites visitors to its home page to learn about its projects and programs. Links to the library and Skidaway Marine Science Foundation are also provided.

Stanford University Hopkins Marine Station

http://www-marine.stanford.edu/

The Hopkins Marine Station of Stanford University reveals its history and academic programs through this higher education site. Visitors can view pictures of the station, read about seminars, and check out the latest research projects.

Texas A&M University Oceanography Department

http://www-ocean.tamu.edu/

The Texas A&M University oceanography department keeps tabs on El Nino here. Visitors can also take virtual tours of the department's research ship and the Smithsonian Institution's exhibit on the Ocean Planet. The page also includes information about the department.

University of British Columbia Oceanography Department

http://www.ocgy.ubc.ca/

Prospective students will find information about courses of study, course descriptions and faculty in the Oceanography Department at the University of British Columbia, Canada, on this site. It includes links to other oceanographic servers, departmental publications, and related resources.

University of Cape Town Oceanography Department

http://emma.sea.uct.ac.za/

The Oceanography Department at the University of Cape Town, South Africa, provides information here on its Centre for Marine Studies, the Association of South African Women in Science and En-

gineering, and the Sea-Viewing Wide Field-of-View Sensor.

University of Colorado Program in Atmospheric and Oceanic Sciences

http://marigold.colorado.edu/

This site at the University of Colorado, Boulder, offers information about the Program in Atmospheric and Oceanic Sciences, with course descriptions, faculty listings, and links to other campus servers.

---

a2z EDITOR'S CHOICE

Scripps Institution of Oceanography

http://sio.ucsd.edu/index4.html

Recognized worldwide as one of the finest oceanographic research and educational institutions, Scripps Institution of Oceanography comes alive on these Web pages. From its state-of-the-art research vessels and laboratories to its renowned graduate programs in all spheres of oceanography and marine biology, visitors to its site are treated to well-designed tours and comprehensive information servers. Click on the interactive map of Scripp's Stephen Birch Aquarium Museum for a description of the giant kelp forest display, or wade through the tide pool and learn all about the crustaceans and small fish who inhabit these incredibly productive and environmentally sensitive ecosystems. For those interested in graduate study at this prestigious institution, read about admissions guidelines and the programs of study available for the select few who are accepted into the school. Ride the high seas with the high-tech vessels who roam the ocean blue studying environmental conditions, weather patterns and underwater mountain ranges. For the student or researcher, dive into the numerous databases of raw and collated data on coastal geophysics, hydrographic observations, cetacean migratory patterns and behavior, marine biomedicine, fish collections and literally dozens of other areas of study undertaken by this venerable Institution.—*Reviewed by Steve Ellis*

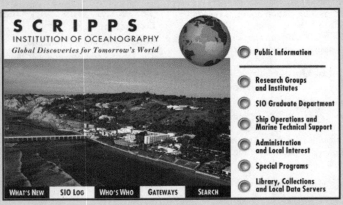

University of East Anglia Oceanography

http://www.mth.uea.ac.uk/climateinfo.html

The Oceanography page from the University of East Anglia, U.K., features various multidisciplinary projects undertaken by the school's physical oceanographers. Access to a virtual oceanography library as well as an in-depth look at the schools of mathematics and environmental sciences is offered.

University of Hawaii School of Ocean and Earth Science and Technology

http://www.soest.hawaii.edu/

The University of Hawaii's School of Ocean and Earth Science and Technology introduces itself at this site. Find academic program, faculty, and research facility information here, as well as links to the school's weather server and virtual Hawaii site.

University of Rhode Island Graduate School of Oceanography

http://www.gso.uri.edu/

The University of Rhode Island Graduate School of Oceanography supplies information about its programs, faculty, research and facilities. Research at the school's Ocean Technology Center—a featured link—includes environmental monitoring systems and underwater acoustics.

University of Washington College of Ocean and Fishery Sciences

http://www.cofs.washington.edu/

The College of Ocean and Fishery Sciences at the University of Washington in Seattle maintains this Web server, providing a wealth of information about the school's departments, academics, research, publications, faculty, students, and facilities.

University of Washington School of Oceanography

http://www.ocean.washington.edu/

The University of Washington School of Oceanography provides information on its programs of study, course offerings and faculty here. Site features include a look at the school's research vessels, ongoing research projects, and publications.

Woods Hole Oceanographic Institution

http://www.whoi.edu/index.html

Hit the virtual high seas through the Woods Hole Oceanographic Institution (WHOI) home page. The site includes general information about the largest independent marine science research facility in the U.S. and links to other oceanographic sites.

INSTRUMENTS AND EQUIPMENT

NOAA National Data Buoy Center

http://seaboard.ndbc.noaa.gov/

The National Data Buoy Center's home page provides access to "buoy-measured environmental data" as published by the National Oceanic and Atmospheric Administration. Includes meteorological and oceanographic data, as well as information about the NDBC.

Polar Science Center International Arctic Buoy Program

http://iabp.apl.washington.edu/

The Polar Sciences Center at the University of Washington, Seattle, has floated this home page about the International Arctic Buoy Program. Researchers and students can get program specifics, plus images and datasets collected via buoys released in the Arctic Basin to "monitor synoptic-scale fields of pressure, temperature, and ice motion."

COMPUTER SYSTEMS AND SOFTWARE

University of Hawaii School of Ocean and Earth Science and Technology FTP

http://www.soest.hawaii.edu/soest/about.ftp.html

A listing of FTP offerings from the School of Ocean and Earth Science and Technology at the University of Hawaii is provided here. Among the items available are generic mapping tools software and satellite images.

LIBRARIES

Scripps Institution of Oceanography Library

http://scilib.ucsd.edu/sio/

The Scripps Institution of Oceanography Library presents an index to watery Web resources, including bibliographies, periodicals, guides, and institution home pages. Oceanic conditions, data, and predictions for the San Diego area are featured.

SIO Library: Oceanographic & Earth Science Institutions Directory

http://orpheus.ucsd.edu/sio/inst/

The Scripps Institution of Oceanography Library maintains this site to provide access to a long list of related resources. Its Oceanographic & Earth Science Institutions directory has links to hundreds of government, private, and nonprofit organizations.

The World-Wide Web Virtual Library: Oceanography

http://www.mth.uea.ac.uk/ocean/oceanography.html

Maintained at the School of Mathematics of Great Britain's University of East Anglia in Norwich, this Virtual Library page provides an index of resources relevant to oceanography. Find subject and geographical search options, plus links to societies, conferences, publications, and more.

MUSEUMS AND AQUARIUMS

Stephen Birch Aquarium-Museum

http://aqua.ucsd.edu/

The Stephen Birch Aquarium-Museum site features an overview of the University of San Diego, California facility and its programs. This page includes background and general information, as well as links to research groups and institutes at the affiliated Scripps Institution of Oceanography.

NEWSGROUPS AND LISTSERVS

The DEEPSEA Research Newsgroup

http://www.geocities.com/capeCanaveral/8431/deepsea.html

This newsgroup exists to "serve as an electronic forum for the world's community of deep-sea and hydrothermal vent/seep biologists, oceanographers, and geologists." Find links to access discussion and topical Web sites.

PHYSICAL OCEANOGRAPHY

OGS Department of Oceanology and Environmental Geophysics

http://oce715a.ogs.trieste.it/

The Department of Oceanology and Environmental Geophysics at Trieste's Observatory for Experimental Geophysics performs research in physical oceanography as it pertains to the seas surrounding Italy. Access current research projects via this home page.

Fleet Numerical Meteorology and Oceanography Center

http://www.fnoc.navy.mil/

The U.S. Navy's Fleet Numerical METOC Center is a California-based organization specializing in meteorology, oceanography, and satellite imagery. Visitors to this site can read detailed information on the center's research and resources, or view the gallery of satellite images.

Pacific Marine Environmental Lab Home Page

http://www.pmel.noaa.gov/pmelhome.html

The Pacific Marine Environmental Lab conducts scientific investigations in physical oceanography, marine meteorology, geochemistry, and related subjects. Browsers will find a lab overview, research projects, and PMEL software (among other offerings).

U.S. Geological Survey Coastal Ocean Modeling

http://crusty.er.usgs.gov/

The U.S. Geological Survey, a program of the Department of the Interior, provides access to its coastal ocean modeling images here. Visitors will find downloadable video demonstrating the circulation of selected bodies of water, among other extensive resources.

The U.S. Joint Ocean Flux Page

http://www1.whoi.edu/jgofs.html

The U.S. Joint Ocean Flux page is an integral part of global climate-change research in the United States and abroad. This site offers links to a global carbon dioxide survey and time-series measurements in Bermuda and Hawaii. Visitors can view satellite images showing the oceans' colors.

PHYSICAL OCEANOGRAPHY

OCEAN DYNAMICS

Florida State University Center for Ocean-Atmospheric Prediction Studies

http://www.coaps.fsu.edu/

Florida State University's Center for Ocean-Atmospheric Prediction Studies performs research in air-sea interactions. Find links to the center's mission statement, research data, and personnel, plus sites of related topical interest.

Geophysical Fluid Dynamics Laboratory

http://www.gfdl.gov/

The Geophysical Fluid Dynamics Laboratory studies oceanic circulation and climate dynamics. Find climatological datasets, technical reports, and research papers at this site. A freely distributed ocean model is made available for public access.

Mississippi State University Center for Air Sea Technology

http://www.cast.msstate.edu/

Although the center's "emphasis is on application of numerical ocean models and modeling techniques toward realistic simulation of ocean conditions...CAST has expanded its efforts to coupled air-ocean modeling." Review projects, meet staff, and look into academic programs at the center's home page.

Scripps Institution of Oceanography Center for Coastal Studies

http://coast.ucsd.edu/

The University of California at San Diego researches the coastal environment through its Center for Coastal Studies. Visit its home page to explore the study of waves, sediment transport, and marine archaeology.

PUBLICATIONS AND INDUSTRY NEWS

Supplements to Atmospheric & Oceanic Publications

http://www-cmpo.mit.edu/met_links/index.html

This service contains full-text versions of and supplements to published or submitted papers in the atmospheric and ocean sciences. Entries are arranged by author and by journal, and visitors are encouraged to submit their own work.

PHYSICS

ARCHIVES AND INDICES

Brown University High Energy Physics Group

http://www.het.brown.edu/

The Brown High Energy Physics Group presents this user-friendly resource for "physics around the Web." Visitors will find links to physics news and high-energy physics labs here, in addition to resources provided by the Brown University research community.

Cold Fusion Technologies

http://www.mit.edu:8001/people/rei/CFdir/CFhome.html

The Cold Fusion Technologies home page provides up-to-date information on this emerging science. Visitors will find news, articles and frequently asked questions files on cold fusion here.

The Computational Fluid Dynamics (CFD) Codes List

http://icemcfd.com/cfd/CFD_codes.html

The CFD Codes List features a definition of CFD, a category of commercial, public domain and shareware software, and a link to the newsgroup sci.physics.computational.fluid-dynamics.

FreeHEP

http://heplibw3.slac.stanford.edu/FIND/FHMAIN.HTML

Visitors can find software used in the study of high-energy physics and related fields at the searchable FreeHEP site. Software archives, tutorials and a discussion group are featured.

Galaxy—Physics

http://www.einet.net/galaxy/Science/Physics.html

Tradewave's Galaxy indexes electronically available physics resources at this site. Find pointers to books, collections, directories and organizations on the Web that fall within or reference the scientific discipline.

Gismo: a Package for Particle Transport and Detector Simulation

http://www.phys.washington.edu/%7Eburnett/gismo/

Maintained by the Department of Physics at the University of Washington, the Gismo page provides access to "a library of C++ classes from which one can build applications that allow simulation of particle detectors."

Graduate Programs in Physics

http://www.phy.duke.edu/Graduate/GradPrograms.html

Duke University maintains this list of U.S. colleges with graduate programs in physics. Visitors can link to the physics department of their choice to find information on that school's graduate program in physics.

HEPDATA Index

http://cpt1.dur.ac.uk/HEPDATA

Visitors to this page will find access to the HEPDATA databases located at Durham University in the United Kingdom. Offerings include the Reaction Data, Particle Properties, Experiments, and SLAC Preprints Databases. Also find the HEPDATA User Guide.

High Energy Physics (HEP) Database

http://www-spires.slac.stanford.edu/find/hep

The Stanford Public Information Retrieval System—SPIRES—hosts this search page to find bibliographic summaries of more than 300,000 particle physics papers." Users create their own search machine by entering search terms and then selecting the output format.

High Energy Physics (HEP) Database—Make Your Own Search

http://heplibw3.slac.stanford.edu/FIND/hep

A service of the Stanford University library, this interactive page offers a form for users to search the High Energy Physics Database. a link to other forms pages for the search of HEP preprints is also featured and online help is available.

High Energy Physics (HEP) Virtual Phonebook

http://www.hep.net/sites/directories.html

The HEP Virtual Phonebook is an index of pointers to phonebooks and directories of high-energy physics sites around the world, provided by HEP Network Resource Center. Includes links to other e-mail address databases.

High Energy Theory Page

http://www.hepth.cornell.edu/

The High Energy Theory Page, from Cornell University's Laboratory of Nuclear Studies, links to people, publications, seminars and special events. The local links, which include course information, are joined by worldwide links.

Lattice High Energy Physics

http://info.desy.de/user/projects/Lattice.html

The Lattice High Energy Physics page presents and explains theories on high-energy physics, featuring academic preprints and databases. Also provides users with a keyword search function.

Nanotechnology

http://nano.xerox.com/nano

Nanotechnology is concerned with manufacture at the atomic level. Find pointers to Internet resources related to the scientific field at this site.

Nonlinear Dynamics and Topological Time Series Analysis Archive

http://cnls-www.lanl.gov/nbt/intro.html

Find an extensive collection of nonlinear dynamics and topological time information and resources, including publications, papers in postscript format, meeting information, data sets and software archives. Also, find information about the author, his research and favorite Web sites.

Plasma on the Internet

http://plasma-gate.weizmann.ac.il/Plasma1.html

A reference resource for the research community working in plasma physics, Plasma on the Internet links to universities and research groups from Austria to New Zealand and beyond. The site is provided primarily for those interested in the academic and technical aspects of plasma physics research.

Plasma Science and Technology

http://www-plasma.umd.edu/

Devoted to the study of plasma, the fourth state of matter behind solids, liquids and gases, this site provides visitors with links to topical areas and resources related to plasma science and technology. Features include links to reference materials, societies, forums, journals and education outreach programs.

Physical Science Resources on the Web

http://www.aip.org/aip/physres.html

The natural sciences that deal with the properties and interactions of matter and energy are the focus of this site from the American Institute of Physics. The long list of links here to science Net resources is organized by topics like geophysics, lasers and volcanism.

Physics Hypertext Home Page

http://web.phys.washington.edu/

Visit this page to find a gateway to documentation, help and tutorial systems for selected physics-related projects. Links to other Web servers at the physics department of the University of Washington are also featured.

Physics Internet Resources

http://www.het.brown.edu/physics/index.html

Maintained by Brown University's High-Energy Physics Group, this index to online physics resources offers visitors access to publications, job and conference listings, and topically arranged information. Includes links to FTP sites maintained by the American Institute of Physics and others.

Physics Lecture Demonstrations

http://www.mip.berkeley.edu/physics/physics.html

Physics professors at the University of California, Berkeley, can refer to this online list of lecture aids (from film strips to videotapes) when preparing course materials. The collection is only available to UC Berkeley professors and teaching assistants, but the links to other physics sites are available to all.

Sean Morgan's Nanotechnology Page

http://www.lucifer.com/~sean/Nano.html

Ever been curious about the field of nanotechnology? Wonder no longer. At this site you can access dozens of links to molecular nanotechnology, scanning probe microscopy, molecular modeling and nanoelectronics. Resources available include mailing lists, e-magazines, journals and book reviews.

Theoretical Physics HyperText Archives

http://dftuz.unizar.es/

The Department of Theoretical Physics from the University of Zaragoza in Spain offers pointers to physics resources across the Internet from this page. The page includes downloadable information and a link to a university gopher server.

The Wonders of Physics

http://sprott.physics.wisc.edu/wop.htm

The Wonders of Physics, provided courtesy of the University of Wisconsin, Madision, is aimed at generating a public interest in physics with physics demonstrations that are both entertaining and educational. This site has information on shows, videotapes and demonstration software, as well as additional information on the program.

The WWW Virtual Library: Beam Physics and Accelerator Technology

http://beam.slac.stanford.edu/www/library/w3/alab.htmlx

This Virtual Library site features links to news, periodicals, discussion groups and job listings related to beam physics and accelerator technology.

The WWW Virtual Library: High-Energy Physics

http://www.cern.ch/Physics/HEP.html

This index of high-energy physics resources, provided by the European Laboratory for Particle Physics' Virtual Library service, offers links to research institutions around the world. Includes separate listings for research abstracts, conferences, societies, software and more.

The WWW Virtual Library: Nuclear Physics

http://www.rarf.riken.go.jp/rarf/np/nplab.html

The Virtual Library provides an alphabetical listing of nuclear physics research institutes and accelerator facilities with a presence on the Internet. Links to other topic-related sites are also available.

The WWW Virtual Library: Physics

http://www.w3.org/pub/DataSources/bySubject/Physics/Overview.html

The World Wide Web Virtual Library of Physics site provides a comprehensive list of physics resources, including specialized fields, university departments and more.

The X-Ray World Wide Web Server

http://xray.uu.se/

The Department of Physics at Uppsala University in Sweden posts x-ray information here. X-ray spectroscopists can search the COREX bibliography and database and the Henke atomic scattering factors. The site also provides links to conference information and other x-ray sites.

ASSOCIATIONS AND ORGANIZATIONS

Academia Sinica, Beijing: Institute of High Energy Physics

http://www.ihep.ac.cn/ihep.html

The Institute of High Energy Physics is a research organization located in Beijing, China. Visitors will find information about the organization, its seminars, conferences and scientific work at this site.

Academia Sinica, Taiwan: High Energy Physics Group

http://hep3.phys.sinica.edu.tw/

The High Energy Physics Group in the Institute of Physics at Taiwan's Academia Sinica maintains this overview of its current experiments. Also find links to the group's members and announcements, plus pointers to HEP sites around the globe.

Academy of Science: Nuclear Physics Institute

http://hp.ujf.cas.cz/

The Nuclear Physics Institute at the Academy of Sciences in the Czech Republic presents this Web site with extensive information on the institute's divisions, groups and activities. Browsers will also find pointers to other institutes conducting research into high-energy physics.

American Association of Physicists in Medicine

http://www.aapm.org/

The American Association of Physicists in Medicine provides online journals and resources geared specifically to the professional medical community. Includes future meeting dates, past meeting minutes and membership information.

American Institute of Physics

http://www.aip.org/

Chartered to promote the advancement and diffusion of physics knowledge and its application, the American Institute of Physics works to meet that challenge at this home page. Find the AIP gopher and FTP sites, a variety of publications and information on AIP programs.

The American Nuclear Society

http://www.ans.org/

The American Nuclear Society is an international organization with more than 17,000 engineers, scientists, educators and students in nuclear-related fields. Conferences, events and local organizations are highlighted.

American Physical Society

http://hq.aps.org/

The American Physical Society site presents information on the physics organization and its membership, journals, meetings, awards and programs. APS News Online is available to members only, but What's New is available to all. Listings of scientific societies and physics links are included.

American Vacuum Society

http://www.vacuum.org/

The American Vacuum Society is a member society of the American Institute of Physics. This site features information about the science of working with vacuums, thin films and plasmas. Check in to read journals such as Surface Science Spectra or to find out about upcoming conferences.

Christian-Albrechts-University, Kiel: Institute for Applied Physics

http://www.ang-physik.uni-kiel.de/

Located in Kiel, Germany, at the Christian-Albrechts-University, the Institute for Applied Physics hosts this home page in both English and German. Find links to the institute's various research groups and technical publications.

Comprehensive Conceptual Curriculum for Physics

http://phys.udallas.edu/

The Comprehensive Conceptual Curriculum for Physics (C3P) is a project supported by the National Science Foundation for the revision of high school physics programs. Find out how it works and who is behind it.

The Croatian Physical Society

http://www.hfd.hr/hfd/

The Croatian Physical Society's Web server includes a profile of the group that promotes scientific, educational and cultural activities in the fields of physics and related scientific fields. Visitors can learn how to join or read about upcoming meetings.

Deutsches Elektronen-Synchrotron: Institute for High Energy Physics

http://sgi.ifh.de/

Physicists can follow the work of the Deutsches Elektronen-Synchrotron Institute for High Energy Physics from this page. Visitors can read about the Hamburg-based institute's multiple research projects and link to related newsgroups.

European Physical Society

http://www.nikhef.nl/www/pub/eps/europa.html

Link to information on physics societies from Austria to Yugoslavia at the European Physical Society home page. Visitors can link to the server sites for each country's group to find out more about the societies or related information.

Finnish Physical Society Home Page

http://www.physics.helsinki.fi/~sfs/

The Finnish Physical Society Home Page provides a general overview of the organization, contact information and details on meetings. Visitors will also find a spread of topical articles and links.

Friedrich-Alexander-Universität Erlangen-Nürnberg: Institut für Theoretische Physik III

http://theorie3.physik.uni-erlangen.de/

This site features the home page of the Institute of Theoretical Physics at the Friedrich-Alexander-Universität Erlangen-Nürnberg in Germany. Visitors are invited to learn more about the institute, its publications and projects, and are welcome to access its physics information servers.

The General Atomics Fusion Group

http://fusioned.gat.com/

The General Atomics Fusion Group targets high school physics students with links to fusion technology information and related organizations.

Hangyang University Theoretical Physics Group

http://hepth.hanyang.ac.kr/

The Theoretical Physics Group of Hangyang University provides information about its research and the university's physics department here. The page also contains links to physics labs worldwide and Korean research facilities in other disciplines. In English.

HEPiX

http://wwwcn.cern.ch/hepix/www/Overview.html

HEPix is a group of Unix users in the high-energy physics community. This site offers access to the group's archived materials and documentation files stored at different HEPix sites.

Imperial College of Science, Technology and Medicine: Condensed Matter Theory Group

http://www.sst.ph.ic.ac.uk/

The Condensed Matter Theory Group at the U.K.'s Imperial College of Science, Technology and Medicine offers faculty and research fellow contact information here. Also find a program prospectus, library catalog, and links to related sites around the world.

Imperial College of Science, Technology and Medicine: Theoretical Physics Group

http://euclid.tp.ph.ic.ac.uk/

The theoretical physics group at the U.K.'s Imperial College of Science, Technology and Medicine makes information about its research, coursework and publications available on this site. Visitors also can learn about the department's students.

IN2P3: Nuclear Research in France

http://info.in2p3.fr/

IN2P3 is an institute of the CNRS, the French National Center for Scientific Research. Its mission is to promote research activities in nuclear and particle physics. Visitors will find animations of nuclear reactions, news, conferences and seminars relating to the field. In French and English.

Institute for Atomic and Molecular Physics

http://www.amolf.nl/

Supported by the FOM Foundation, the largest government-supported organization in the field of physics in the Netherlands, the Institute for Atomic and Molecular Physics provides this overview of its facilities and services. Link to departments, publications, an events calendar and more.

Institute for High Energy Physics

http://www.ifh.de/

Learn more about the experiments and projects being conducted at the Institute for High Energy Physics, Zeuthen, Germany, a national research center for particle and synchrotron radiation research. Links include projects, theory and various databases.

Institute for High Energy Physics: Department of Electronics and Automatization

http://www.oea.ihep.su/

The Institute for High Energy Physics Department of Electronics and Automatization in the former Soviet Union maintains this basic page with links to references, including world-sensitive maps, academic papers, FTP archives and an Archie server.

Institute of Fluid Mechanics

http://www.ts.go.dlr.de/

The Institute of Fluid Mechanics is part of the German Aerospace Research Establishment (DLR). Its site contains general information, as well as information on research activities and links to other DLR sites. In English and German.

Institute of Nuclear Physics

http://www.ifj.edu.pl/

The Institute of Nuclear Physics in Cracow, Poland, provides general information as well as details on its divisions, experiments and conferences. Among the links are conferences, laboratories and other physics sites.

The Institute of Physical and Chemical Research (RIKEN)

http://www.riken.go.jp/

The Japanese Institute of Physical and Chemical Research (RIKEN) provides this overview of its organizational structure and research. Also find links to the RIKEN Accelerator Research Facility (RARF), the RIKEN Computation Center and a number of other related sites.

Institute of Physics

http://www.ioppublishing.com/

The Institute of Physics is a professional society for physicists in Great Britain and Ireland. Visitors to this site will find links to physics-related journals, reference works, magazines, newsletters and conferences.

International Institute of Theoretical and Applied Physics

http://www.physics.iastate.edu/

The International Institute of Theoretical and Applied Physics throws U.S. scientists together with their counterparts in developing countries to facilitate international communication and information exchange. Review the organization's many projects and events at this site.

The International Union of Crystallography

http://www.iucr.ac.uk/welcome.html

The International Union of Crystallography promotes crystallographic research and facilitates the standards of methods, nomenclatures and symbols in the field. It details its work here and posts its journals.

Introduction to the SLD Collaboration

http://www-sld.slac.stanford.edu/sldwww/sld.html

The SLD collaboration consists of about 150 physicists from many universities and laboratories who have built, maintain and analyze data from the SLD detector at the Stanford Linear Accelerator Center (SLAC). Find out more about their work here.

Italian National Institute for Nuclear Physics (INFnet)

http://www.infn.it/

INFNet is the central server for the Italian National Institute for Nuclear Physics. Visitors can locate projects, research, a phone book and related documentation here.

Jagiellonian University Institute of Physics

http://www.if.uj.edu.pl/

The Institute of Physics at Poland's Jagiellonian University maintains this gateway leading to a general overview of the institute's programs, faculty and events. Also find links to the university's home page and other related sites.

Joint Institute for Laboratory Astrophysics

http://www.boulder.nist.gov/jila/jilahome.html

The Joint Institute for Laboratory Astrophysics, a Boulder, Colorado-based scientific research organization, maintains this site to introduce its facilities and staff. Visit here to learn about its many research disciplines, including atomic interactions, chemical physics, geophysical measurements and more.

J. Stefan Institute Information System

http://www.ijs.si/

Get up to speed on the state of physics research in Slovenia with a trip to the J. Stefan Institute Information System page. Also find announcements, events and activities, plus links to other Slovenian Internet servers.

Kernfysisch Versneller Instituut

http://kviexp.kvi.nl/

Review the physics research projects and facilities of the Kernfysisch Versneller Instituut at its home page. Information about this and other particle accelerators can be accessed from this site.

Korea Atomic Energy Research Institute: Nuclear Data Team

http://hpngp01.kaeri.re.kr/

The Nuclear Data Evaluation Team at Korea Atomic Energy Research Institute (KAERI) presents results of its research here. Included is a link to atomic nuclides and a bulletin board of current projects.

Kyoto University: Yukawa Institute for Theoretical Physics

http://www.yukawa.kyoto-u.ac.jp/

Kyoto University's Yukawa Institute for Theoretical Physics Web site houses e-print archives and allows visitors to search through the collection. There are also links to other physics-related Internet resources here.

Lasers and Electro Optics Society

http://msrc.wvu.edu/leos/

Applying itself to research, development, design and manufacture of "lasers, optical devices, optical fibers, and associated lightwave technology," this Institute of Electrical and Electronics Engineers professional society posts its publications here, along with events and job opportunities listings.

Lawrence Livermore National Laboratory High Energy Physics Group Home Page

http://www-hep.llnl.gov/

The Lawrence Livermore National High Energy Physics Group Home Page links visitors to all they need to know about the program, including projects, participants, how to contact the program and more. Links to software programs for download and similar physics sites are also given.

Lyon Institute of Nuclear Physics

http://lyoinfo.in2p3.fr/

The Lyon Institute of Nuclear Physics concentrates on postgraduate teaching and fundamental research. Its Web site provides conference and seminar transcripts, preprints and research project reports. In French and English.

Max-Born-Institut, Berlin

http://www.mbi.fta-berlin.de/

The Max-Born-Institute for Nonlinear Optics and Ultrafast Spectroscopy, located in Berlin, provides information here on its activities and staff members. Available in German and English.

Max-Planck-Institut Fur Plasmaphysik

http://www.ipp.mpg.de/

The Max-Planck Institute of Plasma Physics located near Munich, Germany, studies the physical principles of nuclear fusion power plants. Stop by this site to see what study programs are offered and explore the research projects.

Max-Planck-Institut, Stuttgart

http://www.mpi-stuttgart.mpg.de/

The Max-Planck-Institute in Stuttgart, Germany, highlights details about upcoming seminars along with information about its research. In English and German.

National Institute for Nuclear Physics and High-Energy Physics

http://www.nikhef.nl/

The National Institute for Nuclear Physics and High-Energy Physics in Amsterdam, handles all subatomic physics experiments in the Netherlands (and probably doesn't have many businesses located nearby). Get the skinny on the institute and the physics work it does.

The National Institute of Standards and Technology Physics Laboratory

http://physics.nist.gov/

The National Institute of Standards and Technology Physics Laboratory supports U.S. industry by providing measurement services and research for electronic, optical and radiation technologies. Includes information on technical activities, research facilities, publications and more.

New South Wales (NSW) Branch of the Australian Institute of Physics

http://www.physics.usyd.edu.au/naip/index.html

The NSW Branch of the Australian Institute of Physics features information about its upcoming meetings as well as links to physics-related mailing lists and conferences. The NSW Branch seeks to "promote all aspects of physics to the wider community as well as providing support to physicists."

Nordic Institute for Theoretical Physics

http://www.nordita.dk/

The home page of NORDITA, the Nordic Institute for Theoretical Physics, provides information about the organization, theoretical astrophysics and condensed-matter, high-energy and nuclear physics. Also find listings of staff members and fellows, along with seminar information, the institute's bimonthly newsletter and the links to related sites.

Nuclear Regulatory Commission

http://www.nrc.gov/

Nonmilitary uses of nuclear energy span the commercial, academic and medical realms. The U.S. Nuclear Regulatory Commission (NRC) keeps an eye on peaceful uses of nuclear energy to ensure public health. Review NRC programs and policies at its home page.

OpticsNet

http://www.osa.org/

The Optical Society of America, a professional organization, is online here with links to its publications, academic papers and membership information. Visitors can also find out how Washington is effecting the optics industry and what jobs are available.

Particle Data Group

http://www.cad.ornl.gov/

The Particle Data Group (PDG) is an international collaboration for the

review of particle physics research and related areas of astrophysics. The PDG review is available at this Web site along with further information about PDG publications, educational materials, experiments and laboratories.

The Pattern Recognition Group: Delft University of Technology

http://www.ph.tn.tudelft.nl/

The Pattern Recognition Group at the Netherlands' Delft University of Technology researches image processing and robotics. This page provides information about the projects and coursework along with links to publications and software.

Russian Academy of Sciences: Lebedev Physical Institute

http://www.lpi.msk.su/

The P.N. Lebedev Physical Institute at the Russian Academy of Sciences provides information on its academic divisions, student clubs and research resources. Visit this site to learn about the institute and link to a variety of Internet search tools.

Tata Institute of Fundamental Research: Theoretical Physics Group

http://theory.tifr.res.in/

Part of Bombay's Tata Institute of Fundamental Research, the Theoretical Physics Group offers general information about itself and its research in physics and quantum mechanics. Links to other sites in India are also included.

Ukrainian National Academy of Sciences: Institute of Physics and Mechanics

http://www.ipm.lviv.ua/

Part of the Ukrainian National Academy of Sciences, The Institute of Physics and Mechanics maintains this page to outline its organization and detail its work in materials science. Visitors will also find links to other Ukrainian science institutes and information servers.

University of Aarhus: Institute of Physics and Astronomy

http://www.dfi.aau.dk/

The University of Aarhus Institute of Physics and Astronomy provides research and education opportunities to the Danish scientific community. Includes descriptions of educational programs, research groups and faculty.

University of Adelaide Institute for Theoretical Physics

http://www.physics.adelaide.edu.au:80/itp/

This home page for the Institute for Theoretical Physics at the University of Adelaide in Australia features information about research and educational programs. The site also offers links to university maps and services, as well as travel and weather information for Australia.

University of Augsburg Institute for Physics

http://www.physik.uni-augsburg.de/

The Institute for Physics at the University of Augsburg, Germany, gives an overview of its courses and faculty here. In German and some English.

University of Bonn Electron Stretcher Accelerator Group

http://elsar1.physik.uni-bonn.de/

Welcome to the Electron Stretcher Accelerator Group of the University of Bonn, Germany. the site provides descriptions of accelerator facilities, activities, experimental groups, publications, links to related servers and more.

University of Bonn Physics Institute

http://WWW.PHYSIK.UNI-BONN.DE/

Information about intermediate and high-energy physics research at the Physics Institute at the University of Bonn hits the Web on this page. It features links to information about atmospheric

physics, experimental activities, theoretical physics and departmental news.

University of California, San Diego, Institute for Nonlinear Science

http://inls.ucsd.edu/

This site contains the home page of the Institute for Nonlinear Science (INLS) at the University of California at San Diego. Visitors can learn about the research at INLS, read papers and publications, access the reference library and link to topic-related sites.

University of California, San Diego, Wilson Group Home Page

http://www-wilson.ucsd.edu/

The Webmaster of the University of California at San Diego's Wilson Group describes the group's goal as an effort to "combine theoretical and numerical quantum and classical dynamics with ultrashort light pulse experiments to learn how to control the quantum time evolution of molecules." Visitors to this site will learn about this research and related programs.

University of Glasgow Experimental Particle Physics Group

http://ppewww.ph.gla.ac.uk/

The department of physics and astronomy at the University of Glasgow offers information here on its Experimental Particle Physics Group. Visitors can access loads of information about the group's research, members and publications, read about department conferences or check out a running commentary and update on ATLAS software.

University of Hawaii Material Physics Group

http://mpg.phys.hawaii.edu/

The home page for the University of Hawaii Material Physics Group consists of links to related Internet resources. Find also general program information provided here.

University of Helsinki: Research Institute for Theoretical Physics

http://www.physics.helsinki.fi/tft/tft.html

The Research Institute for Theoretical Physics at the University of Helsinki, Finland, lets browsers tour the department of physics and learn about the rest of the university through this site.

University of Mainz: Condensed Matter Theory Group

http://www.cond-mat.physik.uni-mainz.de/

Physicists can download publications from the Condensed Matter Theory Group at the Institute of Physics at the University of Mainz here. The page also profiles the group's scientists and projects. Links to conference information and publications from other sites. In English.

University of Manchester High Energy Physics Group

http://mphh2.ph.man.ac.uk/

The High Energy Physics Group at England's University of Manchester sponsors this server containing a variety of group and physics-related information. Visitors can read about ongoing research, conferences, seminars and events, along with extensive experiment documentation. Also find links to other university Web resources.

University of Maryland, College Park, Chaos Group

http://www-chaos.umd.edu/

This site spotlights the University of Maryland Chaos Group, a multidisciplinary scientific study coalition focusing on the field of nonlinear chaotic dynamics. Features include general information about the group, listings of publications and links to related sites.

University of Minnesota Society of Physics Students

http://cedar.spa.umn.edu/

The University of Minnesota Society of Physics hosts a World Wide Web server for students. Links to the school's physics- and astronomy-related resources, as well as to general university information services, are included.

University of Newcastle Theory of Condensed Matter Group

http://bragg.ncl.ac.uk/index.html

The Theory of Condensed Matter Group at Britain's University of Newcastle provides an elegant interface at its Web server, with accessible research, papers and other academic information.

University of Notre Dame High Energy Physics Group

http://undhe6.hep.nd.edu/

The University of Notre Dame High Energy Physics Group maintains this overview of its research and academic programs. Link to online resources and related sites...or cue up the Notre Dame fight song.

University of Oulu Space Physics Group

http://www.oulu.fi/~spaceweb/

The Space Physics Group, University of Oulu, Finland, carries on active research in ionospheric and magnetospheric physics. Detailed information about the group's research is available, as are links to the Space Institute of Oulu and the Space Physics textbook.

University of Texas, Austin, Center for Relativity

http://godel.ph.utexas.edu/

The Center for Relativity at the University of Texas, Austin, has set up this home page with infor-

mation about personnel and research. There are also links to academic papers and preprints, and downloadable software.

University of York Nuclear Structure Group

http://yksc.york.ac.uk/

The University of York in the United Kingdom brings the Nuclear Structure Group home page to the Web. The site features research activities and pointers to physics information on the Internet.

Vienna University of Technology Institute for Theoretical Physics

http://tph.tuwien.ac.at/

The Institute for Theoretical Physics at the Vienna University of Technology provides information about its organization, research groups and academic programs. A wealth of Austria-related resources are also provided, including a virtual "no clicks needed" tour of the country.

Yale University Condensed Matter Theory Group

http://sachdev.physics.yale.edu/

Get a glimpse behind the scenes at the Yale Condensed Matter Theory Group via its home page. The site includes profiles of the group's researchers and links to other condensed matter theory groups on the Internet.

CONFERENCES

Computing in High-Energy Physics '95 Conference

http://www.hep.net/conferences/chep95/welcome.htm

The Computing in High-Energy Physics '95 Conference is over, but this site remains to let visitors know what went on there. Guests can link to conference schedules, papers and transparencies, vendor information, and more.

Physics Announcements Forum

http://xxx.lanl.gov/Announce/

This page, maintained by the U.S. Department of Energy's Los Alamos National Laboratory (LANL), lists physics job and conference announcements. Visitors can browse the listings, submit their own announcements with the example HTML form, or link to LANL's main Web site.

Physics Conference Announcements By Thread

http://xxx.lanl.gov/Announce/Conference/

Announcements about upcoming meetings of interest to physicists are posted at this site, which visitors can search by date, subject or author. Individual entries offer details (including contact information) on the conferences.

INSTRUMENTS AND EQUIPMENT

Nanothinc

http://nanothinc.com/

Nanothinc provides information, services and products to businesses specializing in nanotechnology, the manipulation of matter at the atomic level. Via video and sound, Nanothinc's page provides company information, including a list of nanotechnology-related scientific disciplines.

Smooth

http://hermes.astro.washington.edu:80/tools/SMOOTH/

Smooth is a program that calculates several mean quantities for all particles in an N-body simulation output file. This page has more information about Smooth, including new features and changes. The program is available from an anonymous FTP site linked to this page.

Spectrocell, Inc.

http://spectrocell.com

Spectrocell, Inc. manufactures cells and civettes for spectroscopists to use in research. It posts an online catalog here, along with instructions on caring for spectrophotometer cells.

JOBS

American Institute of Physics Careers Bulletin Board

http://www.aip.org

The American Institute of Physics Careers Bulletin Board is here to guide aspiring young physicists to the laboratory of their dreams. It points students and newcomers to juicy career options and puts them in touch with working professionals.

Physics Announcements Forum

http://xxx.lanl.gov/Announce/

This page, maintained by the U.S. Department of Energy's Los Alamos National Laboratory (LANL), lists physics job and conference announcements. Visitors can browse the listings, submit their own announcements with the example HTML form, or link to LANL's main Web site.

Physics Job Announcements by Thread

http://xxx.lanl.gov/Announce/Jobs/

Physicists who are out of work or on the move can consult the high tech job openings listed here. It includes a long list of links to worldwide research, teaching and publishing opportunities.

LABS, RESEARCH CENTERS, AND EXPERIMENTS

The Accelerator Laboratory in Munich

http://www.bl.physik.tu-muenchen.de/

The Accelerator Laboratory is jointly operated by two German universities in Munich. Visitors here will get an overview of its research. The welcome page is in English, but most links are in German.

The ALEPH Experiment

http://alephwww.cern.ch/WWW/

This Web site provides information about ALEPH, a high-energy physics experiment undertaken at CERN's large electron-positron collider. Visitors can access research results, publications, meeting schedules and job opportunity information.

Ames Laboratory Home Page

http://www.ameslab.gov/

A U.S. Department of Energy laboratory operated by Iowa State University, Ames Laboratory explores the chemical, engineering, materials, mathematical and physical sciences in search of solutions to energy-related problems. Site features include an overview of the lab, its research programs and data.

Applied Physics Center

http://apc.pnl.gov:2080/

Located in Richland, Washington at the Pacific Northwest Laboratory, the Applied Physics Center performs research in the areas of energy, transportation, medical technologies, national security and the environment. Visit this site to learn more about the center, its work and personnel.

Argonne National Laboratory: Advanced Photon Source

http://epics.aps.anl.gov/welcome.html

Built by the U.S. Department of Energy as a national user facility, the Argonne National Laboratory's Advanced Photon Source (APS) creates super-intense x-rays for scientific research. Visit this site to access an overview, the APS information services, the Collaborative Access Team members' pages and a calender of meetings and conferences.

Argonne National Laboratory: The Intense Pulsed Neutron Source

http://pnsjph.pns.anl.gov/ipns.htm

Operated by the University of Chicago for the U.S. Department of Energy, the Intense Pulsed Neutron Source at Argonne National Laboratory is a national facility for neutron scattering research. Find an IPNS map, instrument information, staff directory and proposal submission guidelines among other information and links.

Artificial Neural Networks in High Energy Physics Home Page

http://www1.cern.ch/NeuralNets/nnwInHep.html

Meet scientists who are applying artificial neural network techniques to experimental high-energy physics. Visitors can link to specific experiments, conferences and workshops organized around this line of inquiry. Includes information on software and hardware used in the field.

ATLAS: a Toroidal LHC Apparatus

http://atlasinfo.cern.ch/Atlas/Welcome.html

Find experiments, notes, software documents and engineering data pertaining to ATLAS, a toroidal large hadron collider (LHC) apparatus, at this site. Also find links to newsgroups, meeting information, other ATLAS pages, and the LHC site.

Australian National University Laser Physics Centre

http://laserspark.anu.edu.au/

The home page of the Australian National University's Laser Physics Centre highlights ongoing research projects. Also find an online brochure about ANU Photonics.

Beijing Spectrometer (BES) Information

http://www-bes.slac.stanford.edu/beswww/bes.html

Stanford University provides information here about the Beijing Spectrometer located at the Institute of High Energy Physics in the People's Republic of China. The site includes pictures, a subway map to the institute and a list of collaborators and institutes.

Caltech W.K. Kellogg Radiation Lab

http://www.krl.caltech.edu/

The California Institute of Technology presents this home page for its W.K. Kellogg Radiation Laboratory. Visitors will find information on symposia, projects and publications in theoretical and experimental nuclear physics research. An extensive collection of links to related Internet resources is provided.

Center for Atomic-Scale Materials Physics

http://www.fysik.dtu.dk/

Denmark's Center for Atomic-Scale Materials Physics examines the nanoworld of materials and the chemical properties of surfaces. Here, visitors can access related publications, research and scientific staff information.

Center for Electromagnetic Materials and Optical Systems

http://www.uml.edu/Dept/EE/RCs/CEMOS/index.html

The Center for Electromagnetic Materials and Optical Systems conducts research "focusing on the interaction of electromagnetic fields with materials and devices of importance in optical information processing and optical communications." The site details research projects, personnel and short online courses.

Center for Particle Physics at Marseille

http://marwww.in2p3.fr/

France's Center for Particle Physics at Marseille offers this overview of its mission, facilities and research. In French.

Centre EuropÈen de Calcul Atomique et Molèculaire (CECAM)

http://www.cecam.fr/

CECAM is a European research center for atomic and molecular calculations which aims to improve international cooperation in the areas of computational science about atomic, molecular and condensed-matter physics and chemistry. Its multinational Web site, based in Lyons, France, offers researchers a wide variety of resources.

College of France Physics Laboratory

http://cdfinfo.in2p3.fr/

The Physics Laboratory at the College of France maintains this site. Visitors are invited to learn more about the lab, its technical groups, publications and experiments. Related links are also available. In French and English.

Cornell University Laboratory of Atomic and Solid State Physics

http://www.lassp.cornell.edu/

This is the home page for Cornell University's Laboratory of Atomic and Solid State Physics. Visitors will find technical notes and documentation, information on students and graduate programs, maps and models of physics properties.

The DELPHI Experiment

http://delinfo.cern.ch/Delphi/Welcome.html

This page gives an overview of the Delphi Detector for the Lepton, Photon and Hadron Identification (DELPHI) Project, an international effort to detect what happens in the world's largest particle accelerator, LEP. Physicists visiting here can watch for the latest news on the project.

Deutsches Elektronen-Synchrotron

http://www.desy.de/

DESY—the Deutsches Elektronen-Synchrotron— is a Hamburg laboratory conducting high-energy and particle physics research. Its server features the latest news, research developments and program information.

Deutsches Elektronen-Synchrotron: H1 Particle Collider Project

http://dice2.desy.de/

Deutsches Elektronen-Synchrotron, a physics research institution in Hamburg, Germany, maintains this site to provide information about its H1 particle collider project. Visit here to learn about the project and its researchers, or to link to related Web sites from around the world.

ENSLAPP Laboratory for Theoretical Physics

http://enslapp.ens-lyon.fr/

The ENSLAPP Laboratory for Theoretical Physics presents information about its two research groups—the Lyon Group and the Annecy Group—at this home page. Visitors can jump to either site, or search for phone numbers and e-mail addresses of researchers. In French and English.

European Laboratory for Particle Physics (CERN)

http://www.cern.ch/

The European Laboratory for Particle Physics, also known as CERN, is located in Geneva, Switzerland. Visitors to its site will find related databases, news, activities and research information.

European Laboratory for Particle Physics (CERN): SL Division

http://www.cern.ch/CERN/Divisions/SL/welcome.html

This CERN site contains information on the laboratory's super proton synchrotron and large electron positron particle accelerators. Includes details on research projects, seminars, publications, history and background.

European Synchrotron Radiation Facility

http://www.esrf.fr/

The European Synchrotron Radiation Facility (ESRF), an institution that is "the most intense source of synchrotron x-ray radiation in the world," posts a web page with a broad collection of links about the facilities administration, computing, job announcements, conferences, experiments and news.

Experiments Online: Home Pages of HEP Experiments

http://www-spires.slac.stanford.edu/find/explist.html

Follow the links indexed here to get the latest on high-energy physics experiments at various institutes around the world. Includes research details, article preprints and more. The site also includes a list of laboratories that have particle accelerators.

Fermilab Collider Detector

http://www-cdf.fnal.gov/

This Website is intended primarily as a venue for the internal exchange of information within Fermilab, a U.S. Department of Energy accelerator lab. Visitors can browse information about the collider detector experiment at Fermilab, access lab data pages or link to the Fermilab home page.

Fermilab Education Office

http://www-ed.fnal.gov/

Here's a friendly way to learn about nuclear physics. See Editor's Choice.

Fermi National Accelerator Laboratory Home Page

http://www.fnal.gov/fermilab_home.html

The U.S. Department of Energy's Fermi National Accelerator Laboratory unveils information about what it is and the kinds of research that are underway at the facility on this page. Visitors can read through sections about such things as the discovery of the top quark.

Gesellschaft für Schwerionenforschung

http://www.gsi.de/

Gesellschaft für Schwerionenforschung (GSI) conducts heavy ion research in Darmstadt, Germany. Workshop schedules, topics of research and a facility tour are available at GSI's home page. The adventurous can even apply for beam time at the accelerator facility.

Georgia Institute of Technology: Applied Chaos Laboratory

http://ac2.physics.gatech.edu/

The mandate of Georgia Tech's Applied Chaos Laboratory "is to apply the latest concepts from nonlinear dynamics and chaos to real world applications and devices." Visit this site for an overview of the lab, its research, personnel and publications.

---

a2z EDITOR'S CHOICE

Fermilab Education Office

http://www-ed.fnal.gov/

If you think a quark is related to a Klingon and a lepton is a type of lizard, you've got a lot to learn about nuclear physics. Despair not! The Fermilab Education Office, a division of the Fermi National Accelerator Laboratory outside of Chicago, stands ready with the facts on these smallest of small particles. Fermilab is the home of Tevatron, a gigantic, four-mile ring that sends protons whizzing around at nearly the speed of light. To find out why and explore this subatomic world, start with the Phantastic Physix essay in the QuarkQuest newsletter. It may be targeted to middle school students, but it's written at a perfect level for most non-quarkians. Along with this basic intro to particle physics, find discussions of high-energy physics and the discovery of the top quark. The teachers' resource section includes info about the role of accelerators and computers in subatomic research, and articles that explain particle properties and current theories. This crash course may set your head to spinning like the Tevatron, but you'll leave the Fermilab site with a greater appreciation for the most basic particles and forces in nature, not to mention the scientists who probe these mysteries of the universe.—*Reviewed by Steve Ellis*

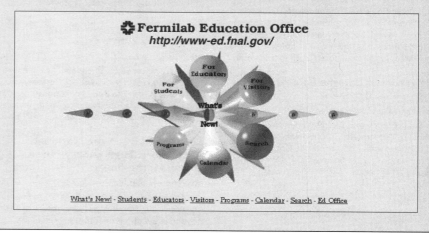

Fermilab Education Office
http://www-ed.fnal.gov/

What's New! - Students - Educators - Visitors - Programs - Calendar - Search - Ed Office

The HERMES Experiment

http://dxhra1.desy.de/

The HERMES experiment on the HERA electron beam is intended to measure the spin distributions of the quarks in protons and neutrons. At the HERMES home page visitors can view the project's library, newsgroups, documentation and pictures.

High Speed Interconnect at CERN

http://www.cern.ch/HSI/Welcome.html

The High Speed Interconnect (HSI) project page includes information about and links to high performance data acquisition systems for high-energy physics experiments. Also find HSI meeting and conference schedules.

Hiroshima University: Photon Physics Laboratory

http://photon.hepl.hiroshima-u.ac.jp/

The Photon Physics Laboratory at Hiroshima University maintains this collection of pointers to research groups, staff and student home pages, and information about the department's academic programs. Available in Japanese and English.

Joint European Torus Project

http://www.jet.uk/

Attempting to make nuclear fusion a reality, the Joint European Torus project is a large-scale magnetic confinement fusion experiment. Visitors to this site can learn the basics of fusion as an energy source or explore the specifics of the JET project.

KEK Home Page

http://www.kek.jp/

KEK, a Japan-based high-energy physics research laboratory, maintains this site to introduce its projects and facilities. Visitors can learn about research, computer and networking services, and employment opportunities.

Kyoto University Cosmic-Ray Group

http://www-cr.scphys.kyoto-u.ac.jp/

The Cosmic-Ray Group in the Kyoto University Department of Physics maintains this page with directions to its laboratory, an anonymous FTP link and a link to the department of physics home page. In Japanese with some English translation.

Laboratoire d'Energie Solaire et de Physique du Batiment

http://lesowww.epfl.ch/index.html

The Solar Energy and Building Physics Laboratory provides information about research activities and software under development. Continuing education programs are taken up and links are provided to other servers with similar topics.

Laboratory for Electromagnetic Field Theory and Microwave Electronics

http://www.ifh.ee.ethz.ch/

Zurich's Laboratory for Electromagnetic Fields and Microwave Electronics at the Swiss Federal Institute of Technology provides information on research projects, meetings, colloquiums and publications at the institute and around the world.

The Laboratory for Space Astrophysics and Theoretical Physics

http://www.laeff.esa.es/

The Laboratory for Space Astrophysics and Theoretical Physics was created by the Spanish National Institute for Aerospace Technology in 1990. Visit for an overview of the lab's research. In English.

Laboratory for Terrestrial Physics

http://ltpwww.gsfc.nasa.gov/

The National Aeronautics and Space Administration (NASA) uses the Laboratory for Terrestrial Physics to find out information about the surface and interior of the Earth and other planets. Visit each of the various laboratory branches from this site for a review of technical facilities and research projects.

The Large Electron Positron Collider L3 Experiment

http://hpl3sn02.cern.ch/

The L3 Experiment is a high-energy physics experiment at the Large Electron Positron Collider operated by the European Organisation for Nuclear Research (CERN) in Geneva. Here, visitors can learn more about the experiment via pictures, publications and documentation.

The Large Hadron Collider

http://www.cern.ch/CERN/LHC/LHCwelcome.html

The Large Hadron Collider is an accelerator that will cause protons to collide at higher energies than before, allowing scientists to investigate the structure of matter and recreate the conditions in the universe seconds after the Big Bang. Find out more about the Swiss collider here.

Lawrence Berkeley National Laboratory Home Page

http://www.lbl.gov/

Children and research scientists alike can find items of interest at the Lawrence Berkeley Laboratory home page. The Berkeley Laboratory offers in-depth investigations into its particle physics research and educational programs.

Lawrence Livermore National Laboratory: High Energy Physics Group Home Page

http://www-hep.llnl.gov/

The Lawrence Livermore National High Energy Physics Group Home Page links visitors to all they need to know about the program, including

projects, participants, how to contact the program and more. Links to software programs for download and similar physics sites are also given.

Lawrence Livermore National Laboratory: Physics and Space Technology Directorate

http://www-phys.llnl.gov/

The Physics and Space Technology Directorate covers the highly technical topics of photonics, microelectronics and optoelectronics. This site allows professionals to find information and research updates in the fields of condensed matter physics, atomic, nuclear, and particle physics and high-temperature physics and astrophysics.

Louisiana State University Center for Advanced Microstructures and Devices

http://www.camd.lsu.edu/

The Center for Advanced Microstructures and Devices (CAMD) home page defines this physics research facility run by Louisiana State University. Includes technical information about the facility, employment opportunity listings and links to home pages maintained by other radiation laboratories.

Louisiana State University Gravitational Wave Experiment

http://phwave.phys.lsu.edu/

The home page of Louisiana State University's Gravitational Wave Experiment provides a wealth of information about the project's personnel, history, publications and associated organizations. Browsers can also link a number of physics-related sites at the university and worldwide.

Lund University MAX-Lab

http://www.maxlab.lu.se/

This is the home page for the National Electron Accelerator Laboratory for Nuclear Physics and Synchrotron Radiation Research. Visitors will find an overview of the facility and its work, current news, publications, a personnel directory and links to sites of related topical interest.

The Nanoworld Home Page

http://www.uq.oz.au/nanoworld/nanohome.html

A major research institution looking at the smallest materials, the Centre for Microscopy and Microanalysis introduces itself and its work at the Nanoworld Home Page. Images, abstracts and program information relating to the study of atoms, molecules and cells are obtainable online.

National Meson Research Facility

http://www.triumf.ca/

The National Meson Research Facility in Canada is located on the University of British Columbia campus and provides facilities for experiments in subatomic research. This page contains general information about the facility, its research groups, staff home pages, sponsored conferences, links to related sites and useful reference material.

National Physical Laboratory, United Kingdom

http://www.npl.co.uk/

The National Physical Laboratory of the United Kingdom is the center of research into the physics of metrology and measurements. Includes links to laboratories, conference information and staff profiles.

National Synchrotron Light Source

http://www.nsls.bnl.gov/

The National Synchrotron Light Source is a research facility funded by the U.S. Department of Energy. Site features include a description and map of the facility, overview of programs and services, links to the beamline research and development group, access to publications and more.

Neutrino Oscillation Magnetic Detector

http://nomadinfo.cern.ch/

The Neutrino Oscillation Magnetic Detector (Nomad) is a detector used in a physics experiment at CERN. Visitors to this extensive site will find an overview of Nomad and can download experiment data, images and computing notes.

Next Linear Collider

http://nlc.physics.upenn.edu/nlc/nlc.html

View the latest plans for the Next Linear Collider. The site features include illustrations and descriptions of what physicists hope they can discover with such a tool. Links to related study groups, software and general information sites are also included.

Next Linear Collider Test Accelerator

http://beam.slac.stanford.edu/www/library/nlcta/nlcta.htmlx

Visit here for information about the Next Linear Collider Test Accelerator, a project of Stanford University to test key components of the Next Linear Collider. An overview of the project, staff profiles, hardware information and more are available.

Oak Ridge National Laboratory Computational Physics and Engineering Division

http://www.cad.ornl.gov/

Oak Ridge National Laboratory's Computational Physics and Engineering Division provides technical, problem solving and consulting services supporting engineering computing systems. The site includes links to sections such as engineering, physics and integrated computer applications.

Pennsylvania State University Center for Gravitational Physics and Geometry

http://vishnu.nirvana.phys.psu.edu/

The Center for Gravitational Physics and Geometry of the physics department at Penn State University provides information here on its personnel, research, publications, seminars, conferences, journals and physicists.

Relativistic Heavy Ion Collider

http://www.rhic.bnl.gov/

Complete in 1999, the Relativistic Heavy Ion Collider (RHIC) will collide subatomic particles at energies of 100 GeV to create a hot, dense plasma of quarks and gluons. Learn more about the RHIC accelerator complex and experiments—and check out an aerial view of the thing.

The Relativistic Heavy Ion Collider Detector Group

http://rsgi01.rhic.bnl.gov/html/home.html

Information on the Relativistic Heavy Ion Collider (RHIC) Detector Group of the Brookhaven National Laboratory (BNL) is contained on this page. Computing documents and project information is included, along with pointers to other RHIC groups and BNL resources.

Rutherford Appleton Laboratory: ISIS

http://www.nd.rl.ac.uk/

Rutherford Appleton Laboratory in the United Kingdom gives visitors to this site a detailed look at ISIS, its neutron beam facility for probing condensed matter. The page includes news about the neutron beam and the lab's latest scientific research.

Rutherford Appleton Laboratory: Particle Physics Department

http://hepwww.rl.ac.uk/

The Particle Physics Department at Rutherford Appleton Laboratory, England, conducts experiments at accelerator and nonaccelerator sites worldwide. Its Web site provides general information resources and links to other high-energy physics pages.

Sandia National Laboratories

http://www.sandia.gov/

The Department of Energy's Sandia National Laboratories describes its programs and research here. The site includes a search tool.

Stanford Linear Accelerator Center

http://beam.slac.stanford.edu/www/welcome.htmlx

Information about the Stanford Linear Accelerator Center (SLAC) comes to the Web through this home page. It features details about research being conducted at the center as well as the Accelerator Theory and Special Projects Department at the university.

Stanford Linear Accelerator Center (SLAC) BABAR Detector Home Page

http://www.slac.stanford.edu/BF/doc/www/bfHome.html

BABAR refers to the B/B-bar system of mesons to be produced by the Stanford Linear Accelerator Center's (SLAC) PEP-II collider in 1999. This page explains more about the project, particles and collider system, and offers reports, a newsletter and BABAR database access (along with BABAR t-shirts and calendars).

The Stanford Synchrotron Radiation Laboratory Home Page

http://ssrl01.slac.stanford.edu/welcome.html

The Stanford Synchrotron Radiation Laboratory provides synchrotron radiation, x-rays or light produced by electrons circulating at nearly the speed of light. The focus of this site is current research in that area.

Triangle Universities Nuclear Laboratory

http://www.tunl.duke.edu/

Triangle Universities Nuclear Laboratory is a Department of Energy laboratory located at Duke University, Durham, North Carolina. Its home page has information about the lab, its research, announcements and links to lab member institution sites.

Underground Laboratory for Particle Physics and Astrophysics

http://www.lngs.infn.it/

The Underground Laboratory for Particle Physics and Astrophysics in Italy comes to the Web through this page that includes a description of the lab and details about some of its current research.

University of Cambridge Department of Physics: Cavendish Laboratory

http://www.phy.cam.ac.uk/www/physics.html

The University of Cambridge Department of Physics highlights its teaching resources and research through this home page. Links to the history of the department and the Cavendish Laboratory are included.

University of Colorado Gravitational Fluid Mechanics Laboratory

http://iml.colorado.edu/gflhome.htm

Study the effects of gravity on fluid physics at the University of Colorado's Gravitational Fluid Mechanics Laboratory. Visitors can view descriptions of current research or review the lab's mission and goals here.

University of Helsinki Accelerator Laboratory

http://beam.helsinki.fi/

The department of physics at the University of Helsinki, Finland, provides information here on its

Accelerator Laboratory. Learn about the laboratory's staff, facilities and scientific programs. Available in Finnish and English.

University of Missouri Physics Laboratory

http://www.phlab.missouri.edu/

The University of Missouri Physics Laboratory site contains information on ongoing research projects and current policies at the lab. Includes links to other university servers and a Web guide.

University of Tennessee High Energy Physics Laboratory

http://enigma.phys.utk.edu/

The High Energy Physics Laboratory at Knoxville's University of Tennessee offers this Web site with a collection of physics-related resources. Pages here include electronic papers, a bulletin board, an FTP directory and software documentation.

University of Texas, Austin, Fusion Research

http://w3fusion.ph.utexas.edu/

This University of Texas site, dedicated to fusion research, provides details on research and studies at the Institute for Fusion Studies and the Fusion Research Center. The site includes a staff directory and links to other university-related sites.

University of Washington Applied Physics Laboratory

http://www.apl.washington.edu/

The Applied Physics Laboratory at the University of Washington in Seattle has set up this home page with links to information about faculty and personnel, seminar schedules, research, contact information and employment opportunities.

University of Washington Applied Physics Laboratory: Polar Science Center

http://psc.apl.washington.edu/

The Applied Physics Laboratory of the University of Washington at Seattle maintains this site for its Polar Science Center. Visit here for staff contact information and details about the physical processes that shape the earth's polar regions.

University of Washington High Energy Physics Laboratory

http://www.phys.washington.edu/groups/hepl

The department of physics at the University of Washington gives prospective students and physicists a look at its High Energy Physics Laboratory. Includes information on research projects, staff and educational opportunities. It also posts links to information about linear accelerators on the Web.

University of Washington Nuclear Physics Laboratory

http://mist.npl.washington.edu/home.html

The nuclear physics department at the University of Washington is involved in basic physics research using accelerators and in nonaccelerator research on solar neutrino physics. Read all about it here in the lab's annual reports and internal reports, or access the ultra-relativistic heavy ion experiments.

University of Western Ontario: Surface Science Western

http://www.uwo.ca/ssw/

Canada's University of Western Ontario surface science lab provides consulting services to industry regarding aspects of material surface development and analysis. Read about the facility's mission and research activities at this home page.

Weizmann Institute of Science (WIS): Plasma Laboratory

http://plasma-gate.weizmann.ac.il/

The WIS Plasma Laboratory page details research projects, staff, publications and general information about the laboratory. Includes links to related physics resources.

Wilson Synchrotron Laboratory Home Page

http://w4.lns.cornell.edu/

The Wilson Synchrotron Laboratory, a high-energy physics laboratory on the Cornell University campus, provides information on its current activities, scientific publications and research facilities. Includes a link to the National Science Foundation.

MUSEUMS

Museum of Physics Department

http://hpl33.na.infn.it/Museum/Museum.html

Historical instruments and other scientific relics from the venerable Naples Institute of Physics are exhibited at the Museum of Physics Department. Examine JPEG files of scientific instruments from 1645 to 1900. In Italian and English.

Physics Museum at the University of Queensland

http://www.physics.uq.oz.au:8001/physics_museum/homepage.html

Visitors to this page can take a virtual tour of the physics department museum at Australia's University of Queensland. The museum library, the museum catalog and the "Pitch Drop" experiment are also featured.

PHYSICISTS

Note: This section is alphabetized by scientist's last name where applicable.

Claude Carignan

http://www.astro.umontreal.ca/membres/claude.html

University of Montreal physics professor Claude Carignan includes general contact information and a brief description of his work on this home page. The page can be read in French and English.

Vassilis Charmandaris

http://www.public.iastate.edu/~vassilis/

Vassilis Charmandaris, a graduate student in the Department of Physics and Astronomy at Iowa State University, supplies contact information, along with details on his education, work, areas of interest and hobbies.

Dr. Timothy Coffey

http://www.nrl.navy.mil/nrl/coffey.html

This page from the Naval Research Laboratory's directory profiles Dr. Timothy Coffey, the Director of Research. The doctor is recognized as an authority on the theory of nonlinear oscillations and has played a major role in the national program on high-altitude nuclear effects.

Serge Demers

http://www.astro.umontreal.ca/membres/demers.html

Serge Demers, a professor in the Department of Physics at the University of Montreal in Canada, features his contact information on this simple home page. It contains his e-mail and snail-mail addresses along with phone and fax numbers.

Severin Gaudet

http://www.dao.nrc.ca/DAO/STAFF/gaudet.html

This simple page gives contact information for Severin Gaudet, a software developer and researcher at the Hertzberg Institute of Astrophysics in Canada. It contains Gaudet's phone number and e-mail address.

Helmut Gratl

http://ast7.uibk.ac.at/innsbruck/staff/hg.html

The home page of Helmut Gratl at Austria's University of Innsbruck contains information on his research interests in data image processing, physics and quantum optics. Includes contact points.

Prof. Dr. Gregor Herten

http://hpfrs6.physik.uni-freiburg.de/

From the directory of the physics department at Germany's Freiburg University, this page features Prof. Dr. Gregor Herten, a research group leader in high-energy physics. Find contact information, a list of group members, research projects and links to topical sites.

Mikko Karttunen

http://www.physics.mcgill.ca:80/WWW/karttune/

Mikko Karttunen, a student at McGill University in Montreal, Canada, offers visitors a home page with links to McGill, its physics department, various publications and Mikko's favorite physics servers.

Anthony F.J. Moffat

http://www.astro.umontreal.ca/membres/moffat.html

Anthony F.J. Moffat, professor of physics at the University of Montreal, maintains his personal home page with contact information and a list of his interests. This page also links to related sites. In English and French.

Nobel Laureates in Physics 1995–1901

http://www.slac.stanford.edu/library/nobel.html

This index of winners of The Nobel Prize in Physics is provided by a researcher at the Stanford University Linear Accelerator Center. Visit here for biographical and background information for prize winners dating back to 1901.

Martin Perl Wins Nobel Prize in Physics

http://www.slac.stanford.edu/slac/hottopic/mperl95/mperl95.html

The Stanford Linear Accelerator Center, which conducts research in physics and radiation, proudly trumpets the achievements of Martin Perl, who won the 1995 Nobel Prize in physics for the discovery of the tau lepton particle. Information on his discovery and life's work shares space with announcements about his prize.

Scott C. Smith

http://einstein.drexel.edu/pages/associated/Smith/scott.html

This page, from the Physics and Atmospheric Science directory at Drexel University, spotlights Dr. Scott C. Smith. Find information on the doctor's research group and projects, as well as his available e-prints.

Leo Szilard Home Page

http://www.peak.org/~danneng/szilard.html

Leo Szilard was an atomic physicist who worked on early U.S. atomic programs. Visitors to this page will find biographical information, research papers and extensive links to related sites.

PUBLICATIONS AND INDUSTRY NEWS

American Institute of Physics (AIP) Press

http://www.aip.org/aippress/

Hard-to-find physics books are easier to find and order here. The AIP Press offers more than 200 titles, including reference volumes, general interest books, texts, research monographs, conference reports and directories.

American Physical Society E-Print Archive Forum

http://publish.aps.org/EPRINT/eprthome.html

The American Physical Society is devoted to the advancement of physics knowledge and education. For years, the society has been concentrating on electronic publishing and dissemination of knowledge. This archive forum has more information about e-prints, or academic papers preprinted on the Web for reading and discussion.

American Physical Society: What's New

http://hq.aps.org/WN/wn95gen.html

To find out what's new at the American Physical Society, check out the archived issues of its newsletter, What's New. Items of interest to scientists include editorials about federal funding, physics research and a look at Biosphere II.

Astrophysics Abstracts, Publications and Preprints

http://babbage.sissa.it/

The SISSA E-Print Server provides this index of electronic astrophysics-related abstracts and publications available online. Preprints are also available here dating from 1992.

Computers in Physics

http://www.aip.org/cip/ciphome.html

A bimonthly American Institute of Physics publication, Computers in Physics, is edited by scientists whose columns provide "hands-on tutorials on physics-related themes." The journal's home page features answers to Frequently Asked Questions (FAQs), news regarding interactive products and links to related sites.

Drell Panel Full Report

http://www.hep.net/documents/drell/full_report.html

The U.S. Department of Energy's Division of High Energy Physics takes a look at the future of the field in this report. Find an executive summary, as well as the full text of the Drell Panel report. Figures, tables and appendices are attached.

Energy Sciences Network

http://www.es.net/

The Energy Sciences Network (ESnet), funded by the U.S. Department of Energy, Office of Energy Research, is a nationwide computer data network connecting members of the energy research community. ESnet provides links to research groups, related archives, laboratories and participating government agencies.

European Laboratory for Particle Physics (CERN): Public News Groups

http://crnvmc.cern.ch/NEWS/?

This hypertext index lists and briefly describes public newsgroups at the CERN scientific research facility.

EurophysNet

http://www.nikhef.nl/www/pub/eps/eps.html

EurophysNet is a physics information and service network created and maintained by the European Physical Society. Includes links to databases, conference schedules, job listings and related news items.

High Energy Physics (HEP) Articles Posted on Various E-print Archives Today

http://www-spires.slac.stanford.edu/FIND/bull0.html

The Stanford Linear Accelerator Center posts links to newly posted articles and preprints related to high-energy physics. Use this index to locate the most current reports found in archives across the Web.

High Energy Physics (HEP) Articles Posted on Various E-print Archives Yesterday

http://www-spires.slac.stanford.edu/FIND/bull1.html

Find links to high-energy physics articles that were posted to various archives the previous day. Select by archive and choose brief or full article descriptions.

High Energy Physics (HEP) Newsletters and Periodicals

http://www.hep.net/documents/newsletters/newsletters.html

Physicists will find pointers to a dozen high-energy physics newsletters and periodicals here. The site posts the title of the publication, a brief description and a link.

Imperial College Theory Group Preprint List

http://euclid.tp.ph.ic.ac.uk/Papers/

The Theoretical Physics Group at the Imperial College of Science, Technology and Medicine in London provides preprints at this site. Visitors can download papers dating back to 1993.

Journal of Chemical Physics

http://jcp.uchicago.edu/

Dive into the latest theories in the fields of chemistry and physics through the pages of the Journal of Chemical Physics. The Web edition that is provided by the American Institute of Physics offers manuscripts from top scientists as well as access to a pair of mailing lists.

Mathematical Physics Electronic Journal

http://www.ma.utexas.edu/mpej/MPEJ.html

Visitors to the Mathematical Physics Electronic Journal can view past or present issues, learn how to submit papers, or send an e-mail request for more information.

National Nuclear Data Center

http://necs01.dne.bnl.gov/html/nndc.html

Funded by the Department of Energy, the National Nuclear Data Center provides "information services in the fields of low and medium energy nuclear physics." Visit this site for nuclear structure and decay data, and nuclear reaction data.

Nonlinear Science e-Print Archive

http://xyz.lanl.gov/

The Nonlinear Science e-Print Archive is a searchable index maintained by Los Alamos National Laboratories. Visit here to locate and download documents on chaos theory, fuzzy logic, and other areas of advanced physics.

Nuclear Physics Electronic

http://www.nucphys.nl/

Elsevier Science offers this experimental online service for subscribers to the scientific journal Nuclear Physics. Includes listings of articles featured in back issues.

Particle Data Group

http://www.cad.ornl.gov/

The Particle Data Group (PDG) is an international collaboration for the review of particle physics research and related areas of astrophysics. The PDG review is available at this Web site along with further information about PDG publications, educational materials, experiments and laboratories.

Physical Review Online Archives

http://www.c3.lanl.gov:8080/apswelcome

Maintained by the Los Alamos National Laboratory, this site features articles from back issues of Physical Review, the journal of the American Physical Society.

Physicists Discover Top Quark

http://www.fnal.gov/pub/top95/top_news_release.html

Fermilab physicists' discovery of the top quark in early 1995 eventually prompted this press release, which explains the discovery's significance. If you're not sure what a quark is or why it's important, research papers, background material and links to related sites are available.

Physics e-Print Archive

http://babbage.sissa.it/

Visitors to this site will find an automated index to the physics-related articles archived here. Features include selections by category, an index to the authors and links to related sites.

Physics News

http://www.het.brown.edu/news/index.html

The High Energy Physics Group at Brown University maintains site for physics-related news. Visitors will find current and archived news items from major media and science organizations around the world.

Physics News Update Newsletter

http://www.w3.org/pub/DataSources/bySubject/Physics/Overview.html

The American Institute of Physics' technically oriented Physics News Update Newsletter, published biweekly online by the Physics Publication Information Department, presents both recent issues and back issue archives here.

PREP

http://www.ccsnet.com:80/prep/

PREP, the Psychology Preprint Server, is an academic preprint archive and distribution system augmenting the current practice of circulating papers prior to actual publication. Here, academics can learn how to submit papers to PREP, browse the current collection and check the editorial comments.

Stanford Linear Accelerator Center (SLAC) Abstracts Database

http://www-spires.slac.stanford.edu/FIND/abstracts

The Stanford Linear Accelerator Center, a laboratory operated by Stanford University for the U.S. Department of Energy, maintains an abstracts database here. Find a keyword search of abstracts and full texts of high-energy physics e-prints, collected and stored daily.

The Virtual Review

http://www.het.brown.edu/physics/review/index.html

The Virtual Review is an online magazine of physics and astronomy academic research papers.

UNIVERSITY DEPARTMENTS

Australian National University Physics

http://www.anu.edu.au/Physics/Welcome.html

The Australian National University (ANU) presents an index with general information on the physics program at ANU. Includes information on courses, research projects and faculty as well as links to other departments, schools and facilities. The site includes links to journals and archives.

Bayreuth University Department of Physics

http://www.uni-bayreuth.de/departments/physik/institut.html

The department of physics at Beyreuth University displays its course of study in experimental and theoretical physics. Other physics resources are linked.

Boston University Physics Department

http://buphy.bu.edu/

The Physics Department at Boston University presents a department overview, plus information about events, courses, research projects and support facilities. A listing of current announcements is included.

Brock University Department of Physics

http://www.physics.brocku.ca/

The physics home page maintained by this Ontario, Canada, institution features departmental news and details on research programs underway. Visitors can meet the physics faculty, check a list of upcoming seminars and run through physics career options.

Brookhaven National Laboratory Physics Department

http://www.phy.bnl.gov/

The Physics Department of Brookhaven National Laboratory in Long Island, New York provides information here on its programs, resources, workshops and seminars. Learn about the U.S. Department of Energy facility.

Brown University Physics Department

http://www.physics.brown.edu/

Brown University's Physics Department home page offers up seminar schedules, research and academic information, and links to the Rhode Island university's computer resources. Includes maps of the campus and the surrounding area, plus a departmental computing guide.

Caltech High Energy Physics

http://www.cithep.caltech.edu/

The high-energy physics department at the California Institute of Technology provides information about its programs, ongoing research and weekly seminars. The site also contains accommodations information for visitors.

Caltech Physics of Computation Group

http://house.pcmp.caltech.edu/

The Physics of Computation Group at Caltech in Pasadena, California designs and evaluates neuromorphic analog chips that emulate the functions of pieces of the human nervous system. This page tells more about the group's work, its members and resources. Includes links to other related sites.

Carleton University Physics

http://www.physics.carleton.ca/

Canada's Carleton University Physics Department provides information about the physics program at this site. Course offerings, program news, research project updates and faculty contact information are available. Links include the university home page and other physics and Canadian sites.

Centenary College Department of Physics

http://alpha.centenary.edu/

The Centenary College Department of Physics provides information about academic courses, students, faculty and publications. In addition, browsers can follow pointers to other physics-related educational sites on the Web.

Florida Tech Physics and Space Sciences

http://pss.fit.edu/

The Florida Tech Physics and Space Sciences Department home page contains information on programs of study, admissions guidelines and faculty profiles. Includes links to research groups, other campus servers and related resources.

Friedrich-Schiller-Universität, Jena: Faculty of Physics, Astronomy and Technical Sciences

http://www.physik.uni-jena.de/

The Faculty of Physics, Astronomy and Technical Sciences at the Friedrich-Schiller-University in Jena, Germany, offers a wealth of information about its institutes, research, education and administration. Also find topic-related links. In English and German.

Freien Universitat, Berlin, Physics Department

http://www.physik.fu-berlin.de/

The Freien Universitat, Berlin, presents the Web server for its physics department here. Visitors will find departmental news regarding academics, research, admissions and faculty. Links to a variety of physics newsgroups can be found as well. In German and English.

Georgia Institute of Technology School of Physics

http://www.gatech.edu/physics/PhysicsTech.html

The Georgia Tech School of Physics site contains information about degree programs and research projects, course descriptions and faculty profiles. Information on joint opportunities with other institutions and links to campus servers are also provided.

Hong Kong University of Science & Technology Physics Department

http://physics.ust.hk/

The physics department at Hong Kong University of Science & Technology maintains this server offering departmental information and links to online physics resources. Visitors can read about the department's faculty or visit course home pages.

Imperial College of Science, Technology and Medicine Department of Physics

http://www.ph.ic.ac.uk/

The physics department of the U.K.'s Imperial College of Science, Technology and Medicine features audio clips, maps and general school information through this Web site. The department's various research activities are described here.

Kansas State University Physics Department

http://bluegiant.phys.ksu.edu/

The physics department of Kansas State University in Manhattan maintains this site for its physics education research group. Visit here to connect with many of its current projects, view class listings and link to other physics groups at different universities.

King's College London: Image Processing Group

http://physig.ph.kcl.ac.uk/ipg/Welcome.html

The Image Processing Group, part of the King's College Department of Physics, provides a brief overview of current research projects, faculty and course information, computing resources and a collection of local links.

Linkoping University Department of Physics and Measurement Technology, Biology and Chemistry

http://www.ifm.liu.se/

The Department of Physics and Measurement Technology, Biology and Chemistry at Linkoping University in Sweden provides general information here. Visit also for an overview of its various research divisions—ranging from applied physics to environmental science. In English.

Louisiana State University Department of Physics and Astronomy

http://mleesun.phys.lsu.edu/

The Physics and Astronomy Web from Louisiana State University includes recent news and information from the department, along with details about current research. The site includes a jobs resource and information for graduate and undergraduate students.

McGill University Department of Physics

http://physics.mcgill.ca/

The department of physics at McGill University offers general information about programs and course offerings, as well as details about ongoing research projects. It also includes links to other college information.

McMaster University Department of Physics and Astronomy

http://www.physics.mcmaster.ca/

The department of physics at McMaster University, Ontario, Canada, provides links to various departmental research areas such as astrophysics and condensed matter theory. The home page also provides information on the graduate program, an area map, and links to other physics-related databases and institutions.

Michigan State University Physics and Astronomy Department

http://pads1.pa.msu.edu/

This home page provides visitors with information about Michigan State University's Physics and Astronomy Department. Includes details about MSU's National Superconducting Cyclotron Laboratory and Abrams Planetarium, plus research information and online scientific publications.

National Central University Department of Physics

http://www.phy.ncu.edu.tw/

The department of physics at National Central University, located in the Republic of China, introduces visitors to its programs in physics and astronomy. It offers information about coursework as well as a look at campus life.

New Mexico Institute of Mining and Technology: Electrical Engineering and Physics Department

http://www.ee.nmt.edu/

The Electrical Engineering and Physics Departments of the New Mexico Institute of Mining and Technology maintains this site for general information on the department and its academic resources. Visit here to learn about programs of study, faculty and course offerings.

Northwestern University Graduate Programs

http://www.astro.nwu.edu/astro/grad/intro.html

Northwestern University's graduate programs in physics and astronomy are detailed on this page. Features include outlines of academic programs, descriptions of research facilities and highlights of current research projects.

Northwestern University Undergraduate Physics and Astronomy

http://www.astro.nwu.edu/astro/undergrad/intro.html

The Department of Physics and Astronomy at Northwestern University maintains this overview of its undergraduate programs. Site features include information on courses, degree requirements, the honors programs, advanced placement and teaching certification.

Open University Physics Department

http://yan.open.ac.uk/

Open University's Physics Department server provides information on the U.K. institution's research and teaching. Includes staff listings for the entire university.

Oregon State University Department of Physics

http://www.physics.orst.edu/

Oregon State University's Department of Physics presents information about the department's academic programs, people and areas of research. Links to related resources and other sites on campus are included.

Pohang University of Science and Technology Department of Physics

http://sol.postech.ac.kr/

The Department of Physics at Korea's Pohang University of Science and Technology offers an introduction to its academic courses and programs. Visitors can explore the university's research initiatives and facilities, as well as links to its local directories.

Prague Academy of Sciences Institute of Physics Elementary Particle Physics Department

http://www-hep.fzu.cz/Welcome.html

The Elementary Particle Physics Department at Prague's Institute of Physics provides links to its current and past research programs. A list of Czechs and Slovaks working in elementary particle physics is also featured.

Queen's University at Kingston: Subatomic Physics (SNO)

http://snodaq.phy.queensu.ca/

This Canadian site contains the home page of the Sudbury Neutrino Observatory Data Acquisition (SNODAQ) system at the physics department, Queen's University. Visitors can learn more about the observatory and the astronomical research group.

Rice University Center for Nanoscale Science and Technology

http://cnst.rice.edu/

Rice University's Web page for the Center for Nanoscale Science and Technology introduces an interdisciplinary program dedicated to the study of nanoscience.

Rome University La Sapienza Physics Department: Chimera

http://chimera.roma1.infn.it/

Chimera is a Web server located in the physics department of the Rome University La Sapienza. Visitors can link to the department and the university here, or check out images of artwork depicting mythological entities.

Simon Frasier University Physics Department

http://www.phys.sfu.ca/

The physics department at Simon Frasier University in Burnaby, British Columbia, maintains this site featuring current seminar and colloquia schedules, access to undergraduate class materials and information about graduate studies. Includes links to the Retrocomputing Museum and Exploranet.

State University of New York, Stony Brook: Buckyball Home Page

http://buckminster.physics.sunysb.edu/

The Fullerene research groups in the physics department at the State University of New York, Stony Brook, maintains this overview of its research and team members. A list of publications, a movie and links to related sites are featured.

State University of New York, Stony Brook: Department of Physics

http://insti.physics.sunysb.edu/Physics/

The State University of New York at Stony Brook presents this home page for its department of physics. Visitors will find information on the department and research groups, in addition to resources for such concentrations as theoretical physics and experimental high-energy physics.

Stockholm University Department of Physics

http://www.physto.se/

Information on courses, projects and research groups are featured at the home page of the department of physics at Stockholm University. In Swedish and English.

Tata Institute of Fundamental Research: Theoretical Physics Group

http://theory.tifr.res.in/

Part of Bombay's Tata Institute of Fundamental Research, the Theoretical Physics Group offers general information about itself and its research in physics and quantum mechanics. Links to other sites in India are also included.

Technische Hochschule Darmstadt Department of Physics

http://www.physik.th-darmstadt.de/

The department of physics at the Technische Hochschule Darmstadt page contains information on research projects, programs of study and student organizations. Includes links to research groups, library resources and course descriptions. In English and German.

Tel Aviv University School of Physics and Astronomy

http://star.tau.ac.il/

The home page of the School of Physics and Astronomy at Tel Aviv University offers visitors information on the school's research, seminars and personnel. Also find links to other departments at this Israeli institution.

University of California, Berkeley, Physics Department

http://www.physics.berkeley.edu/

The physics department at the University of California, Berkeley, maintains this site with information about the department, faculty, research and courses. There's also information about departmental facilities and events.

University of California, Irvine, Department of Physics and Astronomy

http://www.ps.uci.edu/physics/

This home page from the University of California, Irvine, Department of Physics and Astronomy features details on the 1995 Nobel Prize won by Prof. Frederick Reines. Also included here are newsletters, course Web sites, other university sites and information on faculty, graduate programs and the department observatory.

University of California, Santa Barbara, Physics Department

http://www.physics.ucsb.edu/

The physics department of the University of California, Santa Barbara, offers information about its faculty, students, publications and research. Visitors can also link to a number of interesting sites, including a list of American universities and the Santa Barbara County home page.

University of Chicago Astronomy and Astrophysics Department

http://astro.uchicago.edu/

This departmental home page links visitors to home pages created by faculty members and students at the University of Chicago's astronomy and astrophysics department. Includes staff and faculty listings, an online copy of the department's graduate brochure and departmental news.

University College Cork Department of Mathematical Physics

http://symphony.ucc.ie/

The Department of Mathematical Physics at Ireland's University College Cork maintains this informational site. Visit here to learn about the department's people and programs, link to user home pages and access departmental Internet search resources.

University of Delaware Department of Physics and Astronomy

http://www.physics.udel.edu/

The University of Delaware presents this home page for its Department of Physics and Astronomy. Visitors will find details on upcoming colloquia and seminars here, in addition to course listings and an online brochure for the graduate program.

University of Duisburg: Theoretical Low-Temperature Physics

http://www.thp.uni-duisburg.de/

This is the home page of theoretical low-temperature physics studies at the University of Duisburg, Germany. This site includes information regarding publications and seminars, with links to the university's home page and a physics archive. In English and German.

University of Hawaii, Hilo, Department of Physics and Astronomy

http://maxwell.uhh.hawaii.edu/

The Department of Physics and Astronomy at the University of Hawaii at Hilo provides departmental updates, news and notes here. Links are also included to local resources, such as Online Hawaii.

University of Illinois at Urbana-Champaign Department of Physics

http://www.physics.uiuc.edu/

The Department of Physics at the University of Illinois at Urbana-Champaign provides information about undergraduate and graduate courses of study, faculty profiles and research projects here. The page also includes career information, seminar schedules and links to related resources.

University of Innsbruck Physics Department

http://physik.uibk.ac.at/

The physics department at the University of Innsbruck, Austria, offers information about its teaching programs and institutes, with links to other university departments. In German, with some English.

University of Iowa Physics and Astronomy

http://www.physics.uiowa.edu/

This site contains course offerings, profiles of faculty and a listing of their areas of research. Site features also include links to the physics library, specific research sites and access to research group Web pages.

University of Iowa: WWW Nonlinear Optics Resource

http://marv.eng.uiowa.edu/

The University of Iowa provides information on research on nonlinear optics at the university. Visitors will find technical information, publication and links to related resources.

University of Kansas Department of Physics and Astronomy

http://www.phsx.ukans.edu/index.html

The Department of Physics and Astronomy of the University of Kansas provides information here on its student groups, research programs and academic materials. Visit this site to learn about the department and its research and career resources.

University of Leeds Department of Physics

http://www.leeds.ac.uk/physics

The Department of Physics at England's University of Leeds provides this page of links to its research groups in astronomy, astrophysics and polymer physics. A link to the university's home page is also included.

University of London Queen Mary & Westfield College Physics Department

http://www-star.qmw.ac.uk/physics/Physics.html

The physics department at the Queen Mary and Westfield College, University of London, offers information about its various research areas and divisions. Visitors can peruse pages of the astrophysics, organic, engineering and experimental research groups.

University of Maryland Department of Physics Home Page

http://delphi.umd.edu/

The Department of Physics at the University of Maryland maintains this site for student and departmental information, research group listings and faculty profiles. Links to its science and engineering award program.

University of Nevada, Las Vegas, Department of Physics

http://www.physics.unlv.edu/

The University of Nevada, Las Vegas, physics department not only provides details about its courses, research and admissions here, it also posts pointers to dozens of physics-related sites on the Net. Visit for links to government agencies, professional societies and an online periodic table.

University of New Hampshire Department of Physics

http://www.physics.unh.edu/

The University of New Hampshire's physics department home page provides information on coursework, research groups and faculty. The site includes a link to the Physics Round Table, an undergraduate discussion group.

University of Oregon Physics Department

http://zebu.uoregon.edu/

This physics department server at the University of Oregon provides information on courses of study, faculty listings and research projects presented in multimedia and text formats.

University of Oregon Physics Students Page

http://zebu.uoregon.edu/~probs

If you're taking a physics class at the U of O, or are just someone who's interested in the subject, stop by this collection of Web documents that are "at least vaguely useful" to someone in your situation. The site's main attraction: interactive physics problems.

University of Oxford: Atmospheric, Oceanic and Planetary Physics

http://www-atm.atm.ox.ac.uk/index.html

The Atmospheric, Oceanic and Planetary Physics page from University of Oxford, England, features information about its research, seminars and meetings, undergraduate courses and the department of physics.

University of Oxford Department of Physics

http://www.physics.ox.ac.uk/

The physics department at the University of Oxford, England, provides information here on its facilities, programs, faculty and students. Visitors to this site will also find links to campus sports clubs and related scientific resources from around the world.

University of Pennsylvania Department of Physics and Astronomy

http://dept.physics.upenn.edu/

The University of Pennsylvania Physics and Astronomy Department presents recent announcements pertaining to its educational programs and research projects. Includes access to research papers and links to related sites.

University of St. Andrews School of Physics and Astronomy

http://star-www.st-and.ac.uk/physics/

The home page for the School of Physics and Astronomy at the United Kingdom's University of St. Andrews contains information on the undergraduate and graduate programs and departmental research groups. Also find a handful of pages with additional topical information.

University of Stockholm: Field and Particle Theory

http://vanosf.physto.se/

Find out about the research into field and particle theory by the University of Stockholm's department of physics. Visitors can peruse pages on faculty and students, find out about seminars and activities or read a collection of related documents.

University of Surrey Physics Web Server

http://www.ph.surrey.ac.uk/

The University of Surrey Physics Department gives visitors information about its program, course descriptions and computing facilities. The site includes links to other university servers and related research groups.

University of Sydney School of Physics

http://www.physics.usyd.edu.au/

The School of Physics at Australia's University of Sydney provides visitors with information on the school's undergraduate and graduate programs, research projects, faculty and physics society. There are also links to other Australian Web servers.

University of Technology, Aachen, Department of Physics

http://www.physik.rwth-aachen.de/

The Department of Physics at the University of Technology in Aachen, Germany, invites visitors to learn more about its academic program and re-

search projects. Links to topic-related sites on and off campus are provided. In English and German.

University of Tokyo Department of Physics

http://www.phys.s.u-tokyo.ac.jp/

The physics department at the University of Tokyo presents general program and facility overviews at its home page. Visitors will find activity reports and departmental information for several areas of physics studies. Extensive links to physics sites on the Internet are provided.

University of Wales, Swansea Department of Physics

http://python.swan.ac.uk/

You can find information on courses and teaching staff in the physics department at the Swansea campus of the University of Wales. The site also has links to research in physics, as well as computing and entertainment. In Welsh and English.

University of Washington Department of Physics

http://www.phys.washington.edu/

The Department of Physics at the University of Washington provides departmental information, details on research groups and graduate studies, and a selection of campus images at this home page.

Utrecht University Department of Nuclear Magnetic Resonance Spectroscopy

http://www-nmr.chem.ruu.nl/

The Department of NMR Spectroscopy from Utrecht University in the Netherlands features information about its current research projects and includes a complete Frequently Asked Questions (FAQs) file on this page. Browsers can also read about academic programs, faculty and facilities.

Utrecht University Faculty of Physics and Astronomy

http://www.fys.ruu.nl/Home_eng.html

Would-be physicists and astronomers can consider their options for studying in the Netherlands at the University of Utrecht after digesting the information presented here. Visitors can review the school's courses, departments and research facilities. In Dutch and English.

Vassar College Physics and Astronomy

http://noether.vassar.edu/

The Department of Physics and Astronomy at Vassar College provides this overview of its academic programs. Links to faculty and staff, course requirements and listings, resources and related sites are featured.

Warsaw University Physics Department

http://info.fuw.edu.pl/

The physics department at Warsaw University gives visitors an overview of its programs here. The site also includes pages about Poland, Warsaw and the university's flea market. In English.

Wayne State University Physics and Astronomy Department

http://www.physics.wayne.edu/

Wayne State University's Physics and Astronomy Department offers this Web site, providing a wealth of departmental information and pointers to other interesting online resources. A departmental newsletter, journals, and links to home pages of faculty and students are among this site's features.

PSYCHOLOGY

ARCHIVES AND INDICES

Cognitive and Psychological Sciences on the Internet

http://www-psych.stanford.edu/cogsci/

Discover cognitive and psychological sciences on the Internet, courtesy of the Stanford psychology department. Use the index provided to link to professional journals, academic departments and relevant newsgroups. Resources referenced are oriented to research rather than practical needs.

Dr. Bob's Mental Health Links

http://uhs.bsd.uchicago.edu/~bhsiung/mental.html

Originally Dr. Bob designed this index for other mental health professionals, but he invites anyone to use it. The Chicago psychologist provides a wide range of mental health links including institutes, journals and disease-specific sites.

Galaxy: Psychology

http://galaxy.einet.net/galaxy/Social-Sciences/Psychology.html

TradeWaves' Galaxy online service serves up Internet psychology resources at this site. From self-help to science, a range of psychology-related links are organized and presented in this index.

Mental Health InfoSource

http://www.mhsource.com/

Mental health professionals are targeted by this hefty database, with diagnosis and treatment information, publications, links to advocacy groups, continuing education opportunities, FAQs, job postings and more. The "Ask the Expert" feature is an interactive question and answer column covering all aspects of mental health and drug therapy.

PsychNET

http://www.apa.org/

This searchable site from the American Psychological Association (APA) covers a broad spectrum of issues targeted to professionals and interested consumers. From children to aged parents, from panic disorders to federal legislation, APA's PsychNET informs and educates.

Psych Web

http://www.gasou.edu/psychweb/psychweb.htm

The Psych Web gateway links the user to comprehensive listings of information on psychology. Includes pointers to educational resources and programs, tip sheets for students, commercial counseling services and products, scientific and research sites, self-help pages and a wealth of other resources.

Resources for Psychology and Cognitive Sciences

http://sasuke.shinshu-u.ac.jp/psych/

This site contains comprehensive indexes of university and research Internet sites related to the mind and the behavioral sciences. Visitors can search the psychology database by keyword or access electronic publications, software archives, and online bookstores from this location.

Specifica

http://www.realtime.net/~mmjw/

An Austin, Texas-based psychologist offers an index to medical and mental health resources. The index is organized by category and includes a section on resources available for psychology professionals.

ASSOCIATIONS AND ORGANIZATIONS

American Psychological Society

http://www.hanover.edu/psych/APS/aps.html

Maintained as a member service of the American Psychological Society, this site offers a mix of APS news and professional resources. Find general membership and conference information, as well as links to Internet discussion groups, software resources, related sites and more.

APA Division of Psychopharmacology and Substance Abuse

http://charlotte.med.nyu.edu/woodr/div28.html

The Division of Psychopharmacology and Substance Abuse of the American Psychological Association maintains this overview of its purpose and activities. Among other items of interest, find access to archives, a newsletter, links to various advisory groups and information on funding opportunities.

Milton's InterPsych Page

http://www.psych.med.umich.edu/web/intpsych/

InterPsych is a nonprofit, 8,000-member organization dedicated to interdisciplinary work in psychopathology. Academics and clinicians can subscribe to an online journal and participate in e-mail and real-time conferences.

Organizations & Conferences

http://matia.stanford.edu/cogsci/org.html

This comprehensive list of cognitive and psychological science organizations and conferences will keep users abreast of international events in the field. Visitors can link directly to worldwide organizations and chronological calendars of events here.

Society for Computers in Psychology

http://www.lafayette.edu/allanr/scip.html

The department of psychology at Lafayette College in Easton, Pennsylvania maintains this site for its Society for Computers in Psychology. Visit here to learn about the society's activities and membership, view research publications and find the latest news on upcoming conferences.

BEHAVIORAL PSYCHOLOGY AND ANALYSIS

Behavior Analysis Resources

http://www.coedu.usf.edu/behavior/behavior.html

The Behavior Analysis page from the University of South Florida features a collection of links to Internet resources in the field. The site includes links to FTP sites, the journal Behavior Analysis and Therapy, mailing list information, and university pages.

Behavior Online

http://www.behavior.net/

Behavior Online offers access to conversations addressing a wide range of topics in mental health and behavioral science. The site also fea-

tures pointers to books, an online forum, and continuing education opportunities.

Institute for Behavioral Genetics

http://ibgwww.colorado.edu/

How do you study twins and families? What effects do environment and genetics have on individual behavior? You'll find some answers at the University of Colorado's interdisciplinary Institute of Behavioral Genetics home page.

Institute for Mathematical Behavioral Sciences

http://www.socsci.uci.edu/mbs/

The Institute for Mathematical Behavioral Sciences at the University of California, Irvine, features profiles of its faculty and an introduction to current studies on its home page. It also includes links to technical reports and updates on upcoming presentations in a colloquium series.

SouthEastern Behavior Analysis Center

http://jsucc.jsu.edu/psychology/sebac.html

Located at Alabama's Jackson State University, the SouthEastern Behavior Analysis Center posts this overview of its lab facilities and residents. Site features include information about research projects and other university resources.

CLINICAL PSYCHOLOGY

American Academy of Child & Adolescent Psychiatry Home Page

http://www.aacap.org/web/aacap/

Visitors to this page can research child and adolescent mental disorders. Find 46 fact sheets in English, Spanish and French covering topics from adoption and autism to teenage problems. The site includes a directory of psychiatric resources available on the Internet.

David Baldwin's Trauma Info Pages

http://gladstone.uoregon.edu/~dvb/trauma.htm

Compiled and maintained by a Ph.D., this site focuses on the research and clinical aspects of emotional trauma and traumatic stress. Featuring a mix of information and resources, the presentation reaches out to victims and survivors, as well as clinicians, researchers and students.

The Home (page) for Clinical Psychophysiologists and Biofeedback Therapists

http://freud.tau.ac.il/~biosee/

Learn about biofeedback and how it "is an established non-experimental treatment" for diagnoses ranging from asthma to neuromuscular disorders. This site also includes information about its electronic forum for clinicians, conferences, studies, and links to related organizations and resources.

COGNITIVE PSYCHOLOGY

ARCHIVES AND INDICES

Cognitive Neuroscience Resources

http://www.cs.cmu.edu/Web/Groups/CNBC/other/other-neuro.html

This neuroscience information server hosts a wealth of resources from the Center for the Neural Basis of Cognition (CNBC) and the Neural Processes in Cognition (NPC) graduate training program. Hundreds of links are provided here—including university department pages, publications, archives, Usenet newsgroups and organizations.

Psycho Hackers at the University of Helsinki

http://avocado.pc.helsinki.fi/

The Psycho Hackers page could be described as a collection of scattered pick-up sticks targeting the psychophysical and cognitive world. Find out the latest in mood disorder studies, download clip art and follow the research of visual processing.

ASSOCIATIONS AND ORGANIZATIONS

Cognitive Science Society Information

http://www.pitt.edu/~cogsci95/

Membership in the Cognitive Science Society is open to professionals in cognitive science and to full-time students. The Society's home page includes information about annual meetings, news, and a searchable index of titles, authors, and abstracts.

NEURO-LINGUISTIC PROGRAMMING

Computational Phonology

http://ftp.cogsci.ed.ac.uk/phonology/CompPhon.html

The Computational Phonology service at the Centre for Cognitive Science, University of Edinburgh, maintains this page with information and links to resources concerning this field and details about SIGPHON, a group from the Association for Computational Linguistics.

NEUROSCIENCES

Georgia Institute of Technology: Cognitive Science

http://www.cc.gatech.edu/cogsci/

This Web site provides information about cognitive science research undertaken at Georgia Tech. Includes standard departmental details along with research reports in the areas of artificial intelligence, cognitive psychology and engineering, and computer science.

Indiana University: Cognitive Science Program

http://www.psych.indiana.edu/

Indiana University's Cognitive Science Program maintains this page with information about the program, its labs and research groups, a list of its Web publications, and more.

Indiana University: Visual Inference Laboratory

http://www-vil.cs.indiana.edu/

The Visual Inference Laboratory (VIL) at Indiana University is devoted to the study of the visual aspects of reasoning and the development of computer technology to support this type of reasoning. The VIL page provides details on current research, publications, software and its members.

The Johns Hopkins Department of Cognitive Science

http://www.cogsci.jhu.edu/

Johns Hopkins University uses this page as an introduction to its department of cognitive science, the faculty and students. Other selections include directories that link to related facilities and resources.

Stanford Vision and Imaging Science and Technology

http://white.stanford.edu/

Stanford Vision and Imaging Science and Technology, located within the department of psychology, maintains this page with information about its staff and links to information about its software, including demos.

Swiss Group for Artificial Intelligence and Cognitive Science

http://expasy.hcuge.ch/sgaico/

The home page of the Swiss Group for Artificial Intelligence and Cognitive Science provides extensive information on the group's history, executive board, conferences, activities and contact information.

University of California, Irvine: Cognitive Sciences

http://www.socsci.uci.edu/cogsci/

Research at the University of California, Irvine, focuses on visual and auditory perception, experi-

mental psychology and mathematical psychology. Visitors to this page can read research overviews, access psychology course materials, meet the faculty and evaluate the academic program.

University of California, Santa Cruz: Perceptual Science Laboratory

http://mambo.ucsc.edu/index.html

The Perceptual Science Laboratory at the University of California, Santa Cruz, conducts research on perception and cognition. Find experimental data and theoretical musings on these and related subjects at the lab's home page.

University of Edinburgh: Joint Centre for Cognitive Science and the Human Communication Research Centre Server

http://www.cogsci.ed.ac.uk/

This central server links to the Centre for Cognitive Science and the Human Communication Research Centre at Scotland's University of Edinburgh. General information about the university—online publications, academic programs, student information, and news—can also be accessed from this point.

DREAMING AND SLEEPING

ANALYSIS

The Dream Page

http://www.cs.washington.edu/homes/raj/dream.html

Webmasters explore the dynamics of dream messages, asking for submissions that will be published and interpreted. An index of current dreams allows visitors to make their own evaluations. From this page, dream weavers also can link to psychological and literary resources.

EXPERIMENTAL PSYCHOLOGY

Medical Research Council (MRC) Research Centre in Brain and Behaviour

http://www.mrc-bbc.ox.ac.uk/

The MRC Research Centre in Brain and Behaviour at the University of Oxford posts this page on its department of experimental psychology. The site includes descriptions of research programs, along with listings of recent publications and the research staff.

PSYCHOLOGY 805

HISTORY OF PSYCHOLOGY

Carl Jung: Anthology
http://www.enteract.com/~jwalz/Jung/

Selected quotations from Carl Jung are posted here for the enlightenment of lay and academic psychology enthusiasts. In addition to the brief text selections, find biographic and bibliographic notes on the famous psychologist. Related links are collected here as well.

INSTITUTES AND UNIVERSITIES

Georgia Institute of Technology: Cognitive Science
http://www.cc.gatech.edu/cogsci/

This Web site provides information about cognitive science research undertaken at Georgia Tech. Includes standard departmental details along with research reports in the areas of artificial intelligence, cognitive psychology and engineering, and computer science.

Hanover College: Psychology Department
http://psych.hanover.edu/

The psychology department at Indiana's Hanover College provides departmental, student and course information, along with links to psychology-related Internet sites and electronic journals. Visitors can participate in online psychological experiments or run through psychological tutorials on various subjects.

Indiana University: Cognitive Science Program
http://www.psych.indiana.edu/

Indiana University's Cognitive Science Program maintains this page with information about the program, its labs and research groups, a list of its Web publications and more.

Indiana University: Visual Inference Laboratory
http://www-vil.cs.indiana.edu/

The Visual Inference Laboratory (VIL) at Indiana University is devoted to the study of the visual aspects of reasoning and the development of computer technology to support this type of reasoning. The VIL page provides details on current research, publications, software and its members.

Institute for Behavioral Genetics
http://ibgwww.colorado.edu/

How do you study twins and families? What effects do environment and genetics have on individual behavior? You'll find some answers at the University of Colorado's interdisciplinary Institute of Behavioral Genetics home page.

Institute for Mathematical Behavioral Sciences
http://www.socsci.uci.edu/mbs/

The Institute for Mathematical Behavioral Sciences at the University of California, Irvine, features profiles of its faculty and an introduction to current studies on its home page. It also includes links to technical reports and updates on upcoming presentations in a colloquium series.

The Institute of Psychology
http://www.glasnet.ru/~vega/ipras/index.html

The Institute of Psychology at the Russian Academy of Sciences outlines its history and current research projects at its home page. Links to each of its laboratories are also included, along with publishing information and conference announcements.

The Johns Hopkins Department of Cognitive Science
http://www.cogsci.jhu.edu/

Johns Hopkins University uses this page as an introduction to its department of cognitive science, the faculty and students. Other selections include directories that link to related facilities and resources.

Medical Research Council (MRC) Applied Psychology Unit
http://www.mrc-apu.cam.ac.uk/

Located at Cambridge University, the MRC's Applied Psychology Unit posts this home page. Find an overview of the unit, the scientists undertaking this line of academic inquiry and the scientific models guiding their work.

Medical Research Council (MRC) Research Centre in Brain and Behaviour
http://www.mrc-bbc.ox.ac.uk/

The MRC Research Centre in Brain and Behaviour at the University of Oxford posts this page on its department of experimental psychology. Includes descriptions of research programs, listings of recent publications and research staff.

National Institute of Mental Health (NIMH) Home Page
http://www.nimh.nih.gov/

This Web site includes general information about the Institute, current clinical studies and patient referral guidelines, grant information and online brochures on a variety of mental health topics.

New York University: Psychiatry Department
http://www.med.nyu.edu/Psych/NYUPsych.Homepage.html

New York University's Psychiatry Department page contains general information about the department and its academic and residency programs. Includes links to a reference desk, textbooks, interactive testing and the Bellevue Hospital Psychiatry Department.

Northwestern University: Psychology Department
http://www.psych.nwu.edu/

This Northwestern University site profiles the psychology department's academic programs, faculty and research staff, course information and lecture schedules. Includes an "informal" departmental library and a link to the university's home page. Students can access personal academic information as well.

Psychiatry Star Home Page
http://www.psych.med.umich.edu/

Maintained by the University of Michigan's psychiatry department, this web site also houses the American Academy of Child & Adolescent Psychiatry, the University of Michigan Psychiatric Informatics Program and the Psychiatric Society for Informatics. Includes information on study programs, announcements, and a variety of psychiatric and medical references.

Psychology Web
http://psy.ucsd.edu/otherpsy.html

The Psychology Web contains links to university psychology departments around the world. An alphabetical search offers quick reference.

SouthEastern Behavior Analysis Center
http://jsucc.jsu.edu/psychology/sebac.html

Located at Alabama's Jackson State University, the SouthEastern Behavior Analysis Center posts this overview of its lab facilities and residents. Site features include information about research projects and other university resources.

Stanford Psychology
http://matia.stanford.edu/

Stanford University's Department of Psychology gives browsers an overview of the department through this site. Facts and figures, graduate admissions, faculty, staff and students are among the links offered.

Stanford Vision and Imaging Science and Technology
http://white.stanford.edu/

Stanford Vision and Imaging Science and Technology, located within the department of psychology, maintains this page with information about its staff and links to information about its software, including demos.

University of California, Irvine: Cognitive Sciences

http://www.socsci.uci.edu/cogsci/

Research at the University of California, Irvine, focuses on visual and auditory perception, experimental psychology and mathematical psychology. Visitors to this page can read research overviews, access psychology course materials, meet the faculty and evaluate the academic program.

University of California, Santa Cruz: Psychology Department

http://www.ucsc.edu:80/ucsc/catalog/psyc/

The psychology department of the University of California at Santa Cruz maintains this overview of its academic program, course offerings and faculty. Links to related sites on and off campus are also featured.

University of Edinburgh: Joint Centre for Cognitive Science and the Human Communication Research Centre Server

http://www.cogsci.ed.ac.uk/

This central server links to the Centre for Cognitive Science and the Human Communication Research Centre at Scotland's University of Edinburgh. General information about the university—online publications, academic programs, student information, and news—can also be accessed from this point.

University of Freiburg: Institute of Psychology

http://www.psychologie.uni-freiburg.de/

The home page for the Institute of Psychology at the University of Freiburg, Germany, provides access to services and local information, plus a link to the university's home page. In English and German.

The University of Geneva: School of Psychology and Education

http://tecfa.unige.ch/

The University of Geneva's School of Psychology and Education gives an overview of its Learning and Training Technologies program at this site. Visitors can download its publications and take a look at its courses and faculty. In English with some materials in French.

University of Leeds: Department of Psychology

http://lethe.leeds.ac.uk/psychology.html

The Department of Psychology at Great Britain's University of Leeds maintains this site for general

information. Find a profile of the department's facilities, academic programs and faculty.

University of Plymouth: Faculty of Human Sciences

http://tin.ssc.plym.ac.uk/

The Faculty of Human Sciences at the United Kingdom's University of Plymouth maintains this gateway to the servers of its politics, psychology, sociology, and social policy and social work departments. Links to related sites on and off campus are also included.

The University of Wales: Department of Psychology

http://www.psych.bangor.ac.uk/

The department of psychology at the University of Wales gives a departmental overview here. Visit for undergraduate and graduate program information, staff publication lists and job announcements.

University of Waterloo: Psychology Department

http://watarts.uwaterloo.ca:80/PSYC/bee/

The psychology department home page for the University of Waterloo in Ontario, Canada, contains information about the department, its study programs, faculty, and employment opportunities. Includes links to other campus servers and psychology resources on the Internet.

Washington University: Philosophy/Neuroscience/Psychology

http://www.artsci.wustl.edu/~philos/pnp.html

This site presents information about the doctoral program in a multidisciplinary program focusing on cognitive neuroscience and psychology. The site includes access to the electronic archives, faculty listings, admissions information and links to related resources.

PERSONALITY

NEWSGROUPS AND LISTSERVS

Personality Typing Systems Newsgroup

http://sunsite.unc.edu/personality/

Information from and about the Usenet newsgroup, alt.psychology.personality, is provided here with archives, a Frequently Asked Questions (FAQs) file, a directory of personality type profiles, the Keirsey Temperament Sorter, and other resources.

PERSONALITY TESTS

Keirsey Temperament Sorter—Jungian Personality Test

http://sunsite.unc.edu/jembin/mb.pl

Extrovert or introvert? Feeling or thinking? At the Keirsey Temperament Sorter site take a Jungian personality test and expose yourself to the world of personality typing systems. It feels like a pop quiz but, never fear—it's multiple choice.

PROFESSIONAL RESOURCES AND CONFERENCES

Organizations & Conferences

http://matia.stanford.edu/cogsci/org.html

This comprehensive list of cognitive and psychological science organizations and conferences will keep users abreast of international events in the field. Visitors can link directly to worldwide organizations and chronological calendars of events.

PSYCHOLOGISTS, PSYCHOTHERAPISTS, AND COUNSELORS

PSYCHOLOGISTS AND COUNSELORS

Center for Anxiety & Stress Treatment

http://www.cts.com/~health/

Focusing on stress and anxiety-related problems, this clinic site promotes self-help books and audiotapes that can be ordered online. The site includes pointers to counseling services and workshops.

Chrysalis Home Page

http://www.omix.com/sites/drSandy/home.html

This online brochure for Chrysalis Counseling Services in San Francisco provides a brief overview of their approach to counseling and invites clients to contact them via telephone, FAX or e-mail.

Navy Psychiatry Home Page

http://164.167.49.31/psych/npsyhom.htm

Navy Psychiatry Home Page outline its psychiatric care to U.S. sailors and marines. Visitors can learn about training programs, research and operations.

Psychology.Com

http://www.psychology.com/

Hosted by Integrated EAP, Inc., a professional employee assistance program, this promotional page offers a variety of psychology-related services. Visitors can order online tests to measure their entrepreneurial quotient or reveal their personality profile, browse a list of therapists or link to other psychological resources.

PUBLICATIONS AND INDUSTRY NEWS

JOURNALS AND ARTICLES

Behavioral & Brain Sciences Target Article Preprints

http://cogsci.ecs.soton.ac.uk/~harnad/bbs.html

This interdisciplinary journal, published by the Cambridge University Press, focuses on neuroscience, cognitive science, artificial intelligence, behavioral biology and psychology. Site features include an archive of articles, search tool, instructions for authors and commentators, and a link to the Open Journal Project.

Harnad E-Print Archive and Psycoloquy and BBS Journal Archives

http://cogsci.ecs.soton.ac.uk/~harnad/

The University of Southampton, England, maintains this site for program information. Visit here to learn about its cognitive sciences or behavioral and brain science programs or link to the Psycoloquy journal archive.

The Journal of Applied Behavior Analysis

http://www.envmed.rochester.edu/wwwrap/behavior/jaba/jabahome.htm

The Journal of Applied Behavior Analysis (JABA) site features the latest research and abstracts from the pages of the print publication. Visitors can search JABA abstracts, read the latest table of contents and view hypertext reprints of selected articles.

Journal of Mind and Behavior

http://kramer.ume.maine.edu/~jmb/welcome.html

An interdisciplinary approach to psychology is investigated and showcased in the Journal of Mind and Behavior. Find abstracts of articles from back issues, submission guidelines and subscription information. Link to other psych sites and publishers.

Psyche: An Online Journal

http://psyche.cs.monash.edu.au/

Psyche, a journal covering the interdisciplinary exploration of consciousness and its relation to the brain, is available online here. Find articles, symposium information, materials archives and submission guidelines.

Psychiatry On-Line

http://www.cityscape.co.uk/users/ad88/psych.htm

Psychiatry On-Line is a medical journal that examines issues relevant to the professional psychiatric community. Visitors can access an extensive list of articles published in current and past issues, browse the bookshop, link to worldwide psychiatry resources or check out geographic-specific sections from the Caribbean, Italy, and France.

Psycoloquy

http://cogsci.ecs.soton.ac.uk/~harnad/psyc.html

This online journal, sponsored by the American Psychological Association, publishes articles in all areas of psychology and in cognitive science, neuroscience, behavioral biology, artificial intelligence, robotics/vision, linguistics and philosophy. Visit this site for recent articles, archived issues, subscription information and submission guidelines.

SCHOOL COUNSELING

School Psychology Resources Online

http://mail.bcpl.lib.md.us/~sandyste/school_psych.html

The National Association of School Psychologists in Bethesda, Maryland maintains this site to provide information on a variety of specific mental and psychological problems of interest to school guidance counselors and psychologists. Includes links to hundreds of professional and research organizations and psych-related home pages.

THEORIES AND RESEARCH

Genetic Linkage Analysis Web Server

http://linkage.cpmc.columbia.edu/

The link between psychiatric disorders and genetics is explored by the institutions sponsoring this page. Includes contact points, newsletter, linkage software, access to other genetics research pages, and pointers to articles in related scientific journals.

SOCIOLOGY

ARCHIVES AND INDICES

Economic and Social Research Council Data Archive

http://dawww.essex.ac.uk/

The Economic and Social Research Council Data Archive, hosted by the University of Essex, England, claims to house "the largest collection of accessible computer-readable data in the social sciences and humanities in the United Kingdom." Scan a broad sampling of subject holdings, from agriculture and rural life to population studies and censuses.

Galaxy: Social Sciences and History

http://galaxy.einet.net/galaxy/Social-Sciences/History.html

Galaxy, an Internet directory, provides this index to historical pages that relate to the social sciences.

Social Science Data Archives at the Australian National University

http://ssda.anu.edu.au/

The Australian National University's Research School of Social Sciences maintains this gateway to its Social Science Data Archives. Links to the Australian Consortium for Social and Political Research Inc. and the university's home page are also provided.

The Social Science Data Collection

http://ssdc.ucsd.edu/

The Social Science Data Collection is a large numeric datafile with a set of computer programs that are being designed to provide easy access to the databases. Still in development, data retrieval is not yet implemented. Visitors can browse the site and study descriptions.

Social Science Information Gateway

http://sosig.esrc.bris.ac.uk/Welcome.html

Plug into a worldwide academic information network using the pointers provided at the Social Science Information Gateway (SOSIG). At this site, researchers can make the scholarly rounds from anthropology to sociology, with economics, government, psychology and other subjects popping up in between.

University of Virginia Social Sciences Data Center

http://www.lib.virginia.edu/socsci/

This site is a demographer's wonderland. See Editor's Choice.

The World-Wide Web Virtual Library: Clearinghouse for Social Sciences Subject-Oriented Bibliographies

http://coombs.anu.edu.au/CoombswebPages/BiblioClear.html

Social scientists will find a bibliography of titles in the social sciences, humanities and Asian-Pacific studies here. This page of the Virtual Library provides links to an extensive collection of digital indices and archives.

The World-Wide Web Virtual Library: Social Sciences

http://coombs.anu.edu.au/WWWVL-SocSci.html

This segment of the Virtual Library offers links to sites dealing with the social sciences. Visitors to this searchable database will find pointers to subjects ranging from Aboriginal Studies to United Nations Information Services.

World-Wide Web Virtual Library: Sociology

http://www.w3.org/pub/DataSources/bySubject/Sociology/Overview.html

The Sociology segment of the Virtual Library offers pointers to centers for research, electronic journals, newsletters, organizations and other resources.

ASSOCIATIONS AND ORGANIZATIONS

National Council for the Social Studies

http://www.ncss.org/online/

The National Council for the Social Studies (NCSS) serves as an umbrella organization for elementary, secondary and college teachers of the social sciences. Find out about the publications, members, resources, meetings and programs of this network of over 100 affiliated groups.

COMMUNITIES

UTOPIAS AND EXPERIMENTAL

Center for Utopian/Dystopian Studies

http://oak.cats.ohiou.edu/~aw148888/

The best of all possible worlds—maybe—is the subject of the Center for Utopian/Dystopian Studies home page at Ohio University. Scan a library of literature depicting great (and not-so-great) worlds. Visit a gallery of utopian art and architecture, or browse other utopian links.

The Island Group

http://www.island.org/

The Island Group is a California-based organization dedicated to the creation of a psychedelic culture. The group, inspired by Aldous Huxley's novel, "Island," discusses the book here.

DEMOGRAPHY

Penn State Population Research Institute

http://www.pop.psu.edu/

The Penn State Population Research Institute page provides general information about the facility and its demographic research. The site includes links to various sources offering national and international vital statistics.

---

a2z EDITOR'S CHOICE

University of Virginia Social Sciences Data Center

http://www.lib.virginia.edu/socsci/

Who says population statistics are boring? Well, lots of people, but you may change your tune after visiting The University of Virginia's Social Sciences Data Center. This demographer's wonderland includes mountains of data accessible through an impeccably organized home page. Select Data Collections to browse a well-annotated, alphabetized catalog of studies and data sets. Okay, so that section of the Data Center is targeted primarily to students and researchers. But here's the fun part: back on the home page, select Interactive Data Resources. The County and City Data Books let you select geographic locations and search parameters, and then choose to have the results displayed on your browser or prepared for FTP. Want to know the net population change from 1980 through 1992 in Phoenix? How about the number of males per 100 females in Alaska? The percentage of the Miami Beach population over 75 years old? The permutations are practically endless. Go back to the home page and select Hypertext Documents for yet another library of info, including the Government Reference Shelf. To embellish your next letter to Congressman Blowhard with a few facts, or just to satisfy your curiosity, the UVA collection provides one-stop browsing.—*Reviewed by Steve Ellis*

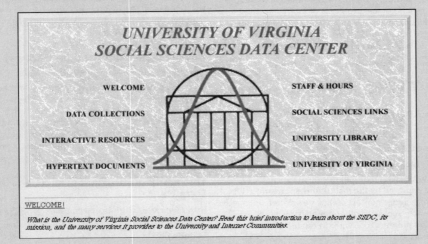

UNIVERSITY OF VIRGINIA
SOCIAL SCIENCES DATA CENTER

WELCOME   STAFF & HOURS
DATA COLLECTIONS   SOCIAL SCIENCES LINKS
INTERACTIVE RESOURCES   UNIVERSITY LIBRARY
HYPERTEXT DOCUMENTS   UNIVERSITY OF VIRGINIA

WELCOME!

What is the University of Virginia Social Sciences Data Center? Read this brief introduction to learn about the SSDC, its mission, and the many services it provides to the University and Internet Communities.

Princeton University Population Research

http://opr.princeton.edu/

Fertility, mortality, population size, migration, projections versus predictions, demography and the effects of population on world resources are all subjects found on the Princeton University Office of Population Research Web pages.

INSTITUTES AND UNIVERSITIES

Center for Social Science Computation and Research

http://augustus.csscr.washington.edu/

Located at Seattle's University of Washington (U of WA), the Center for Social Science Computation and Research (CSSCR) provides support services for the university's social science departments. Much of the center's data is only available to U of WA students, faculty and staff, but some data—particularly census data housed at the center—is available to all.

European Research Centre on Migration and Ethnic Relations

http://www.ruu.nl/ercomer/

Situated at the Netherlands' University of Utrecht, the European Research Centre on Migration and Ethnic Relations is the only university-based center of its kind focused on Eurocentric issues. Visitors to its home page can learn more about the center and its research.

The International Development Research Centre (IDRC)

http://www.idrc.ca/

The International Development Research Centre supports research focusing on developing countries and the world's poor. Its site provides general information, news items, publications and research resources. In French and English.

The International Political Economy Network

http://csf.colorado.edu/ipe/

The International Political Economy Network (IP-ENet) is a research site focusing on the global political economy. Includes an overview of the organization, discussion groups, access to IP-ENet archives, publications and links to related resources.

University of California, Irvine: School of Social Sciences

http://www.socsci.uci.edu/

The School of Social Sciences at the University of California-Irvine provides information about its courses, faculty, students and resources here.

Visitors can link to the home pages of individual departments for more detailed information.

University of Oulu: Department of Information Studies and Sociology

http://syy.oulu.fi/

The department of information studies and sociology at Finland's University of Oulu is online here. Links to its women's studies, political studies, information studies and sociology curriculum servers are featured.

University of Plymouth: Faculty of Human Sciences

http://tin.ssc.plym.ac.uk/

The Faculty of Human Sciences at the United Kingdom's University of Plymouth maintains this gateway to the servers of its politics, psychology, sociology, and social policy and social work departments. Links to related sites on and off campus are also included.

Youth Affairs Research Network Server

http://yarn.insted.unimelb.edu.au/

Visit this site to access a variety of information about youth-related research in Australia. Find links to the University of Melbourne's Youth Research Centre and its Youth Affairs Research Network. Conference listings and abstracts describing research projects are also featured.

LIBRARIES

Data and Program Library Service (DPLS) Home Page

http://dpls.dacc.wisc.edu/

Located at the University of Wisconsin-Madison, the DPLS "provides access to machine readable data files to the social science community" on campus and disseminates locally published papers to scholars at other institutions. Visitors to its page can learn more about DPLS and access its archival repository, catalog of holdings, and publications.

METHODS, TECHNIQUES, AND TOOLS

The Gallup Organization

http://www.gallup.com/

For decades, the Gallup Organization has been providing industry and government with comprehensive information about consumer and political trends. This site provides links to employment

opportunities, general information and even a chance to participate in a poll.

PUBLICATIONS AND INDUSTRY NEWS

Cultural Dynamics

http://dynamics.rug.ac.be/

Cultural Dynamics is an online scholarly journal dedicated to providing a forum for the study of cultural diversity. Visitors to this page can read current and past issues, plus find instructions for contributing.

What's New in World Wide Web Social Sciences Newsletter

http://coombs.anu.edu.au/WWWVLPages/WhatsNewWWW/socsci-www-news.html

The online newsletter, What's New in World Wide Web Social Sciences, is provided as a service of the Australian National University. Read current and past issues of the newsletter for pointers to related Web resources.

SPACE AND ASTRONOMY

ASSOCIATIONS AND ORGANIZATIONS

American Astronomical Society

http://www.aas.org/

The American Astronomical Society (AAS) is an organization for both professional and amateur astronomers. Its home page has information about the organization, its activities and committees. Also features a job registry.

American Astronomical Society Job Register

http://www.aas.org/JobRegister/aasjobs.html

Out of work or on the move astronomers can peruse job openings at the American Astronomical Society Job Register. Find a comprehensive listing of academic professional faculty and research positions at this site.

American Geophysical Union Space Physics and Aeronomy Division

http://igpp.ucla.edu/spa/Welcome.html

The Space Physics and Aeronomy (SPA) division of the American Geophysical Union offers information here about its subsections, members and research. Visitors can peruse special events info, meeting schedules and the U.S. National Report to IUGG, or link to a number of related sites.

Ames Area Amateur Astronomers

http://www.cnde.iastate.edu/aaaa.html

Iowa's Ames Area Amateur Astronomers group maintains this home page with information about celestial bodies and events, newsletters, educational materials, conferences and more. Links to image resources are also available here.

Astronomical Society, Denmark

http://www.dsri.dk/AS/

Visitors here will find information about the Astronomical Society, a Danish group open to anyone interested in astronomy. News and membership information is available, and visitors can submit their own text, figures and images to the society. In English and Danish.

Astronomical Society of the Pacific

http://www.aspsky.org/

The Astronomical Society of the Pacific provides this information page on its members, events, news, work and activities. Visit here for articles, product catalogs, membership directories and links to image archives.

Astronomy and Astrophysics in Jena

http://www.astro.uni-jena.de/

The Astronomy & Astrophysics in Jena page lets browsers select between information about the Max Plank Society or the Institute for Astrophysics/University Observatory. The page provides links to star-related workshops, publications and other related resources.

Berkeley Illinois Maryland Association

http://bima.astro.umd.edu/bima

The Berkeley Illinois Maryland Association (BIMA) comprises the Berkeley Radio Astronomy Laboratory, the University of Illinois' Laboratory for Astronomical Imaging and the University of Maryland's Laboratory for Millimeter-Wave Astronomy. This starry site includes links to BIMA research, data, guides and references.

Converging Computing Methodologies in Astronomy

http://www.hq.eso.org/conv-comp.html

Converging Computing Methodologies in Astronomy, a European Science Foundation Scientific Network, maintains this informational site. Visit here for background materials, network activities and links to related resources.

Eugene Astronomical Society

http://www.efn.org/~bsackett/

The Eugene Astronomical Society supplies general group information and links to past and current newsletters at its club page. Pointers to astronomy resources on the Web are also featured.

European Southern Observatory Online Information System

http://http.hq.eso.org/eso-homepage.html

The European Southern Observatory (ESO) is an organization of eight European member states, with astronomical observatories in Chile. This support page has news and events, information about ESO facilities and meetings, and links to publications, observation schedules and related sites.

European Space Agency

http://www.esrin.esa.it/htdocs/esa/esa.html

The European Space Agency provides information here about its efforts to promote cooperative space research for peaceful purposes. It also gives an overview of its member states, posts press releases and lists its publications on this page.

European Space Agency/European Space Research Institute

http://www.esrin.esa.it/htdocs/esrin/esrin.html

The European Space Research Institute (ESRIN), an Italian research establishment that collects and distributes data from Earth-observation missions, maintains this site in conjunction with its parent organization, the European Space Agency (ESA). Visitors here can learn details about ESA's many labs and research projects.

Imperial College Space and Atmospheric Physics Group

http://www.sp.ph.ic.ac.uk/

The Space and Atmospheric Physics Group at Imperial College in London, England maintains a Web site with information about the university and research activities. Includes links to space-related resources and information about the city of London.

Institute of Astronomy Radio Astronomy Group Directory

http://mimas.ethz.ch/people.html

This page contains a directory of the Radio Astronomy Group members at the Institute of Astronomy in Zurich, Switzerland. The area of expertise, phone number and e-mail address are given for each member listed.

International Astronomical Union

http://www.lsw.uni-heidelberg.de/iau.html

The International Astronomical Union's site provides information on IAU services, announcements, bulletins and members. An overview of the organization and a brief description of the World Wide Web are also featured.

International Astronomical Union Minor Planet Center

http://cfa-www.harvard.edu/cfa/ps/mpc.html

The Minor Planet Center, a Smithsonian Astrophysical Observatory research group, maintains this site for general information and resource access. Visit here to learn about the center, and link to a variety of scientific publications and reports.

The Interstellar Propulsion Society

http://www.tyrian.com/IPS/

The Interstellar Propulsion Society (IPS) offers this organizational site, loaded with information on its goals, structure, membership, services and events. Visitors can access the IPS Digital Research Library for articles and entire publications.

Lockheed Martin Corp.

http://www.lockheed.com/

Lockheed Martin, the result of a merger of the Lockheed and Martin Marietta corporations, is a world leader in the manufacture of space systems, missiles, aeronautics and electronics. Its Web site offers a video tour of the giant corporation, as well as fast facts, financia reports and a list of its operating units and subsidiaries.

Manchester Astronomical Society Home Page

http://www.u-net.com/ph/mas/

The Manchester Astronomical Society claims to have the longest continuous history of any provincial astronomical society in England. Browsers can take a guided tour of the Godlee Observatory, among a wealth of other options.

NASA Headquarters

http://www.hq.nasa.gov/

Located in Washington, D.C., the headquarters of the National Aeronautics and Space Administration posts this operational overview. Find information on NASA's structure, budget, personnel and policies. Links to other NASA sites are also featured.

The NASA Homepage

http://www.nasa.gov/

The home page of the National Aeronautics and Space Administration (NASA) serves as a guide to NASA's specific online resources and to general information about the U.S. space program. Geared to the lay visitor more than the research scientist, prepared exhibits, histories and graphic demonstrations illuminate the role of NASA in the area of space exploration. See Editor's Choice.

National Council for Scientific and Technologic Development, Brazil

http://obsn.on.br/

This is the home page for the National Council for Scientific and Technologic Development facility, of Rio de Janiero, concerned with the study of astronomy, astrophysics, and geophysics.

Peoria Astronomical Society

http://bradley.bradley.edu/~dware/

An independent, educational hobbyist's group, the Peoria Astronomical Society maintains this page to provide information about its star-gazing activities. Visitors will find links to astronomical resources, data and images, including various newsgroups and the Abrams Sky Watcher Diary.

Planetary Society

http://planetary.org/tps/

The Planetary Society, "...the largest non-governmental space organization on Earth," promotes solar system exploration and the search for extraterrestrial life. Visitors here will find essays like, "Dead Dinosaurs Or, It Came From Outer Space," as well as image archives, the Space Stuff Store and membership infomation.

Publications of the Astronomical Society of the Pacific

http://www-pasp.stsci.edu/PASP-top.html

The Astronomical Society of the Pacific's journal has been published continuously since 1889 "except for one issue which was lost in the 1906 San Francisco earthquake and had to be reprinted." Visitors will find submission guidelines, ordering forms for indices, links to FTP files for conference books and an abstracts search.

Salford Astronomical Society: Home Page

http://axp2.ast.man.ac.uk:8000/~salfordac/sashome.htm

The Salford Astronomical Society, of England, provides information on its observatory and events with this home page. Visitors will also find an assortment of links and images for The Great comet of 96!

Space Mechanics Group at the University of Pisa

http://adams.dm.unipi.it/

The Space Mechanics Group in the Mathematics Department at Italy's University of Pisa offers information on its members, research projects and publications. Browsers can also link to the European Asteroid Research Node and other related Web sites.

Students for the Exploration and Development of Space

http://seds.lpl.arizona.edu/seds/seds.html

Students for the Exploration and Development of Space gives visitors to this site a look at its mission. Also find chapter information, news on upcoming conferences, discussion forums and the group's top ten reasons to explore space.

Students for the Exploration and Development of Space, Purdue Chapter

http://roger.ecn.purdue.edu/~seds/

The Purdue University chapter of Students for the Exploration and Development of Space (SEDS) is an organization dedicated to promoting interest in and education about space. At its home page, visitors will find more information about the chapter, area space-related events and a link to the "Virtual Moon Base," as well as links to other related sites.

Theoretical Astrophysics Center / TAC Copenhagen Homepage

http://www.tac.dk/

The Theoretical Astrophysics Center in Denmark maintains this site for local scientific community information, computing documentation, and links to astronomy resources and affiliated institutions. Extensive international listings are available.

---

a2z EDITOR'S CHOICE

The NASA Homepage

http://www.nasa.gov/

If you think space, you probably think NASA, and this is the gateway to the largest repository of space-related information on the Internet. For all of its problems, the accomplishments of this agency defy belief. Think about it: NASA landed men on the moon who drove around in a buggy! Vehicles launched from the Kennedy Space Center have explored the surface of Mars; the Hubble Space Telescope has photographed the outer limits of our galaxy with unprecedented clarity and detail; the Space Shuttle has positioned and recovered satellites using a robotic arm; and countless revolutionary advances in aeronautics, computer science and technology development can be directly attributed to NASA. The Mission to Planet Earth alone has led to radical advances in environmental science, meteorology, geology, cartography, navigational systems and a host of applied and theoretical disciplines. The agency's Web presence is quite possibly the single largest entity on the Internet, and this gateway takes you to the incredible array of information, images and databases it offers. It would be impossible to list the possibilities for research, study and entertainment. Just link from this home page and launch yourself into a galaxy of resources that quite possibly encompass the whole of modern science and technology.—*Reviewed by Steve Ellis*

Universities Space Research Association

http://www.usra.edu/

The Universities Space Research Association is a nonprofit that fosters cooperation among various universities, the U.S. government and other organizations involved in space and technology research. It gives an overview of its programs and member institutions here.

ASTRONOMERS

Note: This section is alphabetized by scientist's last name where applicable.

Rudolf Albrecht

http://ecf.hq.eso.org/staff/ralbrech.html

Rudolf Albrecht's home page includes his photo and information about how to contact him in Germany. He is employed at the Space Telescope European Coordinating Facility.

Ant's Page

http://axp2.ast.man.ac.uk:8000/~ajh/mypage.html

Visitors to Anthony Holloway's personal home page will find online versions of the PhD student's Astronomy-related academic papers and photography.

Bill Arnett

http://seds.lpl.arizona.edu/billa/arnett.html

The home page of Bill Arnett of San Jose, Calif., provides contact information, personal tidbits and an index to the Web pages he's designed, most of which are related to astronomy.

Astronomical Information System

http://ezinfo.ethz.ch/ezinfo/astro/astro.html

The Astronomical Information System provides research details on a wide range of topics from a team of eight amateur astronomers. It includes links to amateur astronomy resources, as well as recent news and a calendar of events.

Long-Term Guest Workers—Dr. Alan Batten

http://www.dao.nrc.ca/DAO/STAFF/batten.html

This personal home page lists Dr. Alan Batten's research interests in astronomy and his recent publications. Dr. Batten is on the staff of the Dominion Astrophysical Observatory.

Piero Benvenuti

http://ecf.hq.eso.org/staff/pbenvenu.html

Piero Benvenuti, a project scientist at the European Southern Laboratory, has posted his contact information on this personal page.

Francois Bonnarel

http://cdsweb.u-strasbg.fr/people/fb.html

This simple page contains addresses and phone numbers where Francois Bonnarel can be reached in France. It is part of the Strasbourg Observatory Web site.

Martin Burkhead

http://www.astro.indiana.edu:80/personnel/burkhead/

On this staff bio page, meet Indiana University astronomer Martin Burkhead and review his research interests. Visitors will find the scientist's photo, contact info and an e-mail link.

Sherri Chasin Calvo

http://heasarc.gsfc.nasa.gov/docs/bios/sherri.html

This is a personal home page for an employee of NASA's Laboratory for High Energy Astrophysics. It includes her short biographical sketch along with links to the lab and general astronomy sites.

Adeline Caulet

http://ecf.hq.eso.org/staff/acaulet.html

The European Coordinating Facility of the Space Telescope provides contact information here for instrument scientist Adeline Caulet. Includes telephone, surface and electronic mail information.

Matthew Colless

http://msowww.anu.edu.au/~colless/colless.html

This personal home page offers up astronomy-related articles published by the site's creator. Visitors also will find information on contacting the page's author, along with astronomy-related Web links.

Anne Cowley

http://www.dao.nrc.ca/DAO/STAFF/cowley.html

Meet Professor Anne Cowley of Canada's Dominion Astrophysical Observatory. Her scientific research interests include X-ray astrophysics, variable stars and stellar populations in galaxies. A list of her recent publications is also available here.

Dr. Tim Davidge

http://www.dao.nrc.ca/DAO/STAFF/davidge.html

Dr. Tim Davidge, an astronomer affiliated with Canada's Gemini Project, has posted his resume at this site. Also find a recent list of published articles.

Eric Deutsch

http://www.astro.washington.edu/deutsch/

This home page, maintained by a researcher at the Department of Astronomy at the University of Washington in Seattle, offers personal and professional information. Visit here to find out what's in this "ratty shoebox of miscellaneous links."

Daniel Egret

http://cdsweb.u-strasbg.fr/people/de.html

The director of the Strasbourg Observatory in France posts a brief personal page here with address, phone and email information.

Lisa Ensman

http://www.astro.indiana.edu:80/personnel/lisa/

Lisa Ensman, research associate in astronomy at Indiana University, has set up this personal page providing information on herself and her work. This page includes links to the HTML Astronomy Classroom Project (HACP) and the Indiana University Astronomy Department home page.

Manuel Forestini

http://gag.observ-gr.fr:80/~forestin/

Astrophysicists can download the research of Manuel Forestini, a scientist at the University of Grenoble, from this page. In English.

Pascal Fouque

http://denisexg.obspm.fr/people/fouque.html

Pascal Fouque's personal home page contains professional information about the research astronomer. Includes descriptions of research areas of interest.

Wolfram Freudling

http://ecf.hq.eso.org/staff/wfreudli.html

Wolfram Freudling of the Space Telescope, European Coordinating Facility maintains this personal home page with contact information.

Galileo in the Institute and Museum of the History of Science of Florence, Italy

http://galileo.imss.firenze.it/museo/4/index.html

This segment of the Institute and Museum multimedia catalogue chronicles its collection of artifacts pertaining to the life and work of 17th century astronomer Galileo. Find biological info, early observation instruments and "the middle finger of Galileo's right hand" at this site.

Jack F. Gallimore

http://hethp.mpe-garching.mpg.de/~jfg/

This personal Web page for Jack F. Gallimore at the Space Telescope Science Institute includes contact information and links to some of his favorite astronomy-related and recreational Web sites.

Karen Gloria

http://www.apo.nmsu.edu/site/directory/kgloria/kgloria.html

Karen Gloria, a staff member of Apache Point Observatory at New Mexico State University, offers this personal home page featuring details of her work experience and links to various astronomy resources. Visitors can also find listings of other interests and family background information.

David F. Gray

http://phobos.astro.uwo.ca/~dfgray/

An astronomer at the University of Western Ontario posts his research interests and reference listings at this site.

Caryl Gronwall

http://ucowww.ucsc.edu/~caryl/home.html

Caryl Gronwall, a graduate student researcher at the Lick Observatory, University of California, Santa Cruz, presents a research home page with papers, abstracts and conference proceedings.

Robert Gruendl

http://www.astro.uiuc.edu/~gruendl/

Robert Gruendl, a graduate astronomy student at the University of Maryland, stocks his personal home page with contact and personal information, curriculum vitae and a listing of articles he's written. Includes links to the home pages of the university and the astronomy department.

Francois Guglielmo

http://denisexg.obspm.fr/people/gugli.html

A member of the Observatory of Paris at Meudon, Francois Guglielmo provides his personal contact information on this page. A link to the observatory's home page is also featured.

Jean-Louis Halbwachs

http://cdsweb.u-strasbg.fr/people/jlh.html

Jean-Louis Halbwachs of France's Observatoire de Strasbourg maintains this page offering contact information.

Hamilton Amateur Astronomers

http://www.science.mcmaster.ca/HAA/

The Hamilton Amateur Astronomers page provides members and visitors with information on the group's activities and astronomy. A newsletter and a list of predicted starry nights are also available. Links include other astronomy sites.

Andre Heck

http://cdsarc.u-strasbg.fr:80/~heck/

French Observatoire Astonomique employee Andre Heck, serves up his personal home page here, with a wealth of employment and academic info. Check out Andre's curriculum vitae and thematic bibliography, or link to some of his favorite recreational sites.

Richard M. Heinz

http://astrowww.astro.indiana.edu/personnel/heinz/

Richard M. Heinz, a member of Indiana University's Physics Department, maintains this personal page with professional information and details about his research specialties.

Graham Hill

http://www.dao.nrc.ca/DAO/STAFF/hill.html

This document provides professional information on Dr. Graham Hill, an astronomer. His research interests and recent publications are listed.

Susan Hill

http://arch-http.hq.eso.org/staff/shill.html

Susan Hill, archive operator at the European Southern Observatory, maintains this personal home page with her contact information.

D.W. Hoard's Personal Home Page

http://www.astro.washington.edu/hoard/

Astronomer D. W. Hoard's personal home page includes downloadablesongs by Big Dead Fish, original poetry, and links to astronomy-related sites as well as favorite music, art and film Web pages.

R. Kent Honeycutt

http://www.astro.indiana.edu:80/personnel/honey/

This Web page provides professional information about R. Kent Honeycutt, a member of Indiana University's Astronomy Department. Includes information on his research specialties and a link to the department's home page. [Find Related Sites]

Hollis R. Johnson

http://www.astro.indiana.edu:80/personnel/johnsonh/

This Web site provides contact and area-of-expertise information on Hollis R. Johnson, a member of Indiana University's Astronomy Department. A hyperlink to the department's home page is provided.

James Lattimer

http://sbast3.ess.sunysb.edu/~lattimer/plan.html

The personal home page of James Lattimer contains information on his astronomical research pursuits, academic publications and a list of his graduate assistants.

Scientific Staff—Brian Leckie

http://www.dao.nrc.ca/DAO/STAFF/leckie.html

This page contains contact information for a researcher at the Dominion Astrophysical Observatory at Canada's Herzberg Institute of Astrophysics.

Soizick Lesteven

http://cdsweb.u-strasbg.fr/people/sl.html

This personal home page provides contact information for French astronomer Soizick Lesteven at the Observatoire de Strasbourg. In French.

Leon Lucy

http://ecf.hq.eso.org/staff/llucy.html

An instrument scientist at the European Southern Observatory provides professional contact information at this site.

Phyllis M. Lugger

http://www.astro.indiana.edu:80/personnel/lugger/

This page contains the contact data and area of expertise information of Phyllis M. Lugger, a member of the Astronomy Department at Indiana University. A link to the IU Astronomy Department is included.

Bruce Margon

http://www.astro.washington.edu/margon/

Meet Bruce Margon and share his interest in astronomy. Bruce presents his curriculum vita and publication list, and provides a photo tour of his stomping grounds in and around the University of Washington.

Dr. Robert McClure

http://www.dao.nrc.ca/DAO/STAFF/mcclure.html

Visitors can learn about the research interests and recent publications of astronomer Dr. Robert McClure from this home page.

Georges Michaud

http://www.astro.umontreal.ca/membres/michaud.html

Meet a professor in the Physics Department at the University of Montreal and review his research interests in astronomy. In French and English.

Dirk Muders

http://ctiot6.ctio.noao.edu/~dm/dm.html

The Southern Columbia Millimeter Telescope, a facility of the Cerro Tololo Interamerican Observatory in Chile, provides contact information here for Dirk Muders. Includes telephone numbers and address listing.

Edward M. Murphy

http://www.cv.nrao.edu/~emurphy/

A researcher at the National Radio Astronomy Observatory, Edward M. Murphy presents info about his master's thesis and research interests. A number of astronomy-related links are also included.

James A. Musser

http://www.astro.indiana.edu:80/personnel/musser/

James A. Musser of the University of Indiana Physics Department posts this personal page. Find his contact information and research specialties listed.

Daniel Nadeau
http://www.astro.umontreal.ca/membres/nadeau.html

A lecturer in astrophysics at the University of Montreal posts his contact information here. The page links to the university's Physics Department and other Montreal sites. In English or French.

Northwestern Astronomy Personnel
http://www.astro.nwu.edu/astro/who.html

The Northwestern Astronomy Personnel page is a directory of those involved in the Dearborn Observatory at Northwestern University's Department of Physics and Astronomy.

Pascal Dubois
http://cdsweb.u-strasbg.fr/people/du.html

This site provides contact information on Pascal Dubois of the Observatoire de Strasbourg in France.

Bruce A. Peterson
http://msowww.anu.edu.au/~peterson/bapeterson.html

Dr. Bruce A. Peterson of the Mount Stromlo Observatory in Australia supplies contact information, research interests, recent publications, current work and links to other astronomical resources.

B. Pirenne
http://ecf.hq.eso.org/staff/bpirenne.html

Find a brief bio and contact information for a European Southern Observatory archive scientist at this site.

Prairie Astronomy Club
http://www.infoanalytic.com/pac/index.html

The Prairie Astronomy Club from Lincoln, Neb., wants to tell you about its amateur astronomy activities. Read about upcoming star parties or browse the pages of the club newsletter.

Tom Quinn
http://hermes.astro.washington.edu:80/faculty/trq/

Tom Quinn, an associate professor of astronomy at the University of Washington, Seattle, maintains this page with his personal and professional information. His curriculum vita and publications list is included.

Bo Frese Rasmussen
http://www.dtv.dk/~bfr/

Find contact information for a software engineer at Germany's Space Telescope European Southern Observatory on this page.

Bernadette Rogers
http://www.astro.washington.edu/rodgers/

The personal home page of astronomer Bernadette Rogers contains numerous links to astronomy and NASA resources, as well as links to Bernadette's friends' pages and favorite sites.

Anurag Shankar
http://chandra.cis.brown.edu/personal/

Anurag Shankar, an Indiana University computing services/astronomy research associate, describes his current work here. His page also includes a short movie, "Convection on a White Dwarf Surface."

Walter Siegmund
http://www.apo.nmsu.edu/site/directory/wsiegmund/wsiegmund.html

Walter Siegmund, a project engineer for the Sloan Digital Sky Survey at the Department of Astronomy, University of Washington, maintains his page with his vitae, publication list and professional interests.

Andy Silber
http://www.astro.washington.edu/silber/

Andy Silber, a student of astronomy, offers a personal glimpse into his interests—travel, biking, his electronic newsletter—and professional accomplishments

Michal Simon
http://sbast3.ess.sunysb.edu/~msimon/plan.html

A member of the Department of Earth and Space Sciences at the State University of New York at Stony Brook, Michal Simon posts to this page his research interests and a list of his recent publications.

Gene Smith's Home Page
http://cassfos01.ucsd.edu:8080/hsmith.html

Gene Smith's Home Page from the Center for Astrophysics & Space Sciences/Physics Department at the University of California at San Diego offers his professional interests and favorite links. Included are his publications, recent work and educational background in the study of astrophysics.

Bob Stein
http://www.pa.msu.edu:80/~steinr/

Bob Stein, professor of physics and astronomy at Michigan State University, provides professional and personal information on this home page. Among the resources he includes are research results, course information and links to astronomy and physics sites.

Will Sutherland
http://www-astro.physics.ox.ac.uk/~wjs/

Will Sutherland, a graduate student in the Astrophysics Department at Oxford University, maintains this personal home page with information about himself and his research.

Peter Teuben
http://www.astro.umd.edu/~teuben/index.html

The personal home page of Peter Teuben of the Astronomy Department at the University of Maryland provides information on his research pursuits. Also find phone and e-mail contact points, as well as links to the home pages of the university and the Astronomy Department.

Stephen Thorsett
http://pulsar.princeton.edu/~steve/Home.shtml

Stephen Thorsett, a faculty member of the Princeton University Physics Department, says his home page is really "more a hot list" than anything else. Thorsett works on gamma-ray burst astronomy, and visitors will find links to his favorite astronomy pages, as well as dozens of other physics and general science sites.

J. Kelly Truelove
http://astro.berkeley.edu/truelove/home.html

Meet J. Kelly Truelove, a graduate student in Theoretical Interstellar Astrophysics at the University of California, Berkeley. Some of his favorite links include the NASA home page and the AstroWeb.

Jeremy Walsh
http://ecf.hq.eso.org/staff/jwalsh.html

Meet Jeremy Walsh, an instrument scientist at the European Southern Observatory in Germany. Contact information is provided.

Washington Area Astronomers' Home Page
http://aa.usno.navy.mil/waa

The Washington Area Astonomer's Meetings page defines the purpose of the regular forums in the Washington/Baltimore vicinity, which is to allow professionals to share research results and exchange knowledge. A synopsis of the next scheduled meeting, as well as registration and location information, is available here.

Douglas L. Welch
http://www.physics.mcmaster.ca/Faculty/DLWelch.html

This person page contains contact information and research interests of Douglas L. Welch, a faculty member of the Department of Physics and Astronomy at McMaster University, Hamilton, Ontario, Canada. There are also details about some of his publications.

Donald C. Wells
http://fits.cv.nrao.edu:80/~dwells/

A scientist at the National Radio Astronomy Oservatory has posted an annotated index of his life's work here. Links are provided to full text versions of his papers and technical reports.

Marc Wenger

http://cdsweb.u-strasbg.fr/people/mw.html

Marc Wenger's personal home page provides his contact information at the Observatoire de Strasbourg, France.

Dr. Nicholas White

http://heasarc.gsfc.nasa.gov/docs/bios/white.html

This home page, maintained by a researcher at the U.S. Goddard Space Flight Center, provides personal and professional information. Visitors will also find links to a variety of astrophysics-related organizations and resources.

Richard White

http://sundog.stsci.edu/first/rick.html

Richard White's UMass Graduate Brochure page details his research in interstellar matter near the Pleiades star cluster, as well as including listings of his academic publications.

Frank Younger

http://www.dao.nrc.ca/DAO/STAFF/younger.html

Frank Younger's personal home page contains information on his research interests in astronomical instrumentation, stellar photometry and spectroscopy. Includes contact information and listings of recent publications.

Dennis Zaritsky

http://ucowww.ucsc.edu/~dennis/home.html

Dennis Zaritsky of the Lick Observatory at the University of California at Santa Cruz provides images from his research, information on courses he teaches and recent papers. His home page also features a prototype of an educational database.

Dan Zucker

http://www.astro.washington.edu/zucker/

College graduate student Dan Zucker highlights his studies in astrophysics and astronomy through his home page. The site includes links to the stock market quote server and Le WebLouvre.

ASTROPHYSICS

Note: This section is alphabetized by scientist's last name where applicable.

Advanced Satellite for Cosmology and Astrophysics

http://heasarc.gsfc.nasa.gov/docs/asca/asca2.html

This site documents the progress and history of the Advanced Satellite for Cosmology and Astrophysics (ASCA), a Japanese cosmic x-ray astronomy mission. Includes an overview of the research project, descriptions of instrumentation and links to related resources.

Advanced Satellite for Cosmology and Astrophysics Guest Observer Facility

http://heasarc.gsfc.nasa.gov/docs/asca/ascagof.html

The Advanced Satellite for Cosmology and Astrophysics (ASCA) Guest Observer Facility Web page includes information on the Japanese cosmic x-ray astronomy mission, plus an archive of images and data observations. Also featured are ASCA news updates, publications and meeting schedules.

American Geophysical Union Space Physics and Aeronomy Division

http://igpp.ucla.edu/spa/Welcome.html

The Space Physics and Aeronomy (SPA) division of the American Geophysical Union offers information here about its subsections, members and research. Visitors can peruse special events info, meeting schedules and the U.S. National Report to IUGG, or link to a number of related sites.

Astronomy and Astrophysics at the National Space and Science Data Center

http://nssdc.gsfc.nasa.gov/astro/astro_home.html

Astronomy and Astrophysics at the National Space and Science Data Center (NSSDC) offers a site that provides access to lots of data in the NSSDC archives about these two fields. Find a photo gallery, a CD-ROM catalog, information on planetary science, observatories, satellites and links to numerous related sites.

Astronomy and Astrophysics in Jena

http://www.astro.uni-jena.de/

The Astronomy & Astrophysics in Jena page lets browsers select between information about the Max Plank Society or the Institute for Astrophysics/University Observatory. The page provides links to star-related workshops, publications and other related resources.

Astronomy and Astrophysics Research at QMW

http://starsun7.ph.qmw.ac.uk/physics/

Astronomy and astrophysics research at Queen Mary and Westfield College at the University of London is explained in detail on this home page. The site includes pictures and data from recent observations along with information on post-graduate research opportunities.

The Astrophysical Journal Letters

http://www.noao.edu/apjl/apjl.html

The American Astronomical Society publishes The Astrophysical Journal three times a month. Visit here for the electronic letters from the journal, an index of papers submitted, and titles and abstracts of letters accepted but not yet published.

Astrophysics

http://xxx.lanl.gov/archive/astro-ph

Astrophysics abstracts and preprints for the years 1992-1996 are available here, posted by the Los Alamos National Laboratory.

Astrophysics Abstracts, Publications and Preprints

http://babbage.sissa.it/

The SISSA E-Print Server provides this index of electronic astrophysics-related abstracts and publications available online. Preprints are also available here dating from 1992.

Astrophysics and Space Plasma Physics Laboratory

http://www.rosat.mpe-garching.mpg.de/

The Astrophysics and Space Plasma Physics Laboratory site provides information on related databases, seminars and abstract services. Includes software descriptions and documentation as well as links to ROSAT group members.

Astrophysics Data Facility at the Goddard Space Research Center

http://hypatia.gsfc.nasa.gov/adf/adf.html

Located at the Goddard Space Research Center, the Astrophysics Data Facility supports "the processing, management, archiving and distribution of NASA mission data." Links to the specific data archives of NASA missions and projects with ADF participation are featured.

Astrophysics Data System Abstract Service NASA

http://adswww.harvard.edu/

NASA's Astrophysics Data System Abstract Service hosts this interactive site allowing visitors to search for abstracts of articles on astrophysics, space instrumentation, physics and geophysics by author, title, object names, keywords or abstract words.

Astrophysics Data System Article Service NASA

http://adscat.harvard.edu/catalog_service.html

This service from NASA's Astrophysics Data System provides access to "scanned images of journal articles since 1975." Three access options assist in searches.

Astrophysics Data System Data Services NASA

http://adswww.harvard.edu/ads_services.html

The Astophysics Data System (ADS) provides access to several data services on the World Wide Web. Available resources at this site include the abstract service, article service, catalog access service and the Einstein archive service.

Astrophysics Data System Einstein Archive NASA

http://adsarc.harvard.edu/einstein_service.html

NASA's Astrophysics Data System provides access and search capabilities to the Einstein Observatory Database, including the 29 CD-ROMs released by the Einstein Observatory project at the Smithsonian Astrophysical Observatory.

Astrophysics Group Home Page

http://www.ph.unimelb.edu.au/astro/home.html

The Astrophysics Group at the University of Melbourne, Australia, provides information about its faculty and research here. The page also includes images, online publications from the group and undergraduate information.

Astrophysics Preprints

http://www.physics.mcmaster.ca/AstroPreprints.html

The Astrophysics Preprint page offers full text and tables from research abstracts. Typical titles include

Astrophysics Web

http://xxx.lanl.gov/archive/astro-ph

Astrophysics abstracts and preprints for the years 1992-1996 are available here, posted by the Los Alamos National Laboratory.

The AXAF Science Center

http://hea-www.harvard.edu/asc/axaf-welcome.html

This page from NASA details information on the Advanced X-Ray Astrophysics Facility (AXAF), an advanced x-ray astronomy satellite to be launched in 1998. Includes a project overview, newsletters and schedule of events.

Bristol University's Astrophysics Group

http://nike.phy.bris.ac.uk:80/~phwjl/

Bristol University's Astrophysics Group includes regular news updates and information about current research on its home page. Visitors can also check out the group's personnel. Although it was under construction when we last checked, it promises links to other astronomy sites as well.

California Institute of Technology Space Radiation Laboratory

http://www.srl.caltech.edu/

The California Institute of Technology's Space Radiation Laboratory offers visitors a look at its research projects in high energy and computational astrophysics. Links to departmental publications, seminar and personnel information, and related sites are also featured.

Canadian Institute for Theoretical Astrophysics

http://www.cita.utoronto.ca/

The Canadian Institute for Theoretical Astrophysics' site contains general information about the institute, its personnel and current projects. Includes pointers to publications, job listings and other CITA programs.

Canary Islands Institute of Astrophysics

http://www.iac.es/

Tour of the Canary Islands Institute of Astrophysics: its headquarters, research center and observatory in Tenerife, and the observatory in La Palma. Links to weather, photos, software, events and other topic-related information can also be found. In Spanish and English.

Center for Astrophysics and Space Sciences at the University of California-San Diego

http://cassfos01.ucsd.edu:8080/ghrs.html

The Center for Astrophysics and Space Sciences at the University of California at San Diego features its work with the Hubble Space Telescope and multi-channel Digicon photon detectors. The page includes links to developers and researchers.

Center for EUV Astrophysics at the University of California-Berkeley

http://www.cea.berkeley.edu/

The Center for EUV Astrophysics at the University of California, Berkeley is the scientific base for NASA's extreme ultraviolet explorer (EUVE). Its Web site offers a searchable index of info related to the CEA.

Center for Particle Astrophysics

http://physics7.berkeley.edu/home.html

This "gateway" to the Center for Particle Astrophysics, an NSF Science and Technology Center, provides general information and such features as a Frequently Asked Questions (FAQ) file on black holes.

Anne Cowley

http://www.dao.nrc.ca/DAO/STAFF/cowley.html

Meet Professor Anne Cowley of Canada's Dominion Astrophysical Observatory. Her scientific research interests include X-ray astrophysics, variable stars and stellar populations in galaxies. A list of her recent publications is also available here.

The Department of Extragalactic Astrophysics and Cosmology at the Observatoire de Paris-Meudon

http://gin.obspm.fr/

The Department of Extragalactic Astrophysics and Cosmology at the Observatoire de Paris-Meudon provides an index of home pages and a directory of DAEC members and other Web servers at the observatory. In French, English, Portuguese, Italian and Spanish.

European Space Agency Astrophysics Division

http://astro.estec.esa.nl/

The European Space Agency presents the home page for its Astrophysics Division. Visitors will find descriptions of programs and research, as well as access to databases and archives.

Murray Fletcher

http://www.dao.nrc.ca/DAO/STAFF/fletcher.html

Canada's Herzberg Institute of Astrophysics maintains this contact page for research Murray Fletcher. Visit here for telephone and e-mail contact information and a list of professional publications.

Manuel Forestini

http://gag.observ-gr.fr:80/~forestin/

Astrophysicists can download the research of Manuel Forestini, a scientist at the University of Grenoble, from this page. In English.

Carolyn Stern Grant

http://hea-www.harvard.edu/~stern/cgrant.html

Carolyn Stern Grant is a programmer for the Astrophysics Data System project in the Center for Astrophysics at Harvard. Her personal home page includes work and personal information, with links to the ADS abstract service and catalogs.

Harvard-Smithsonian Center for Astrophysics

http://cfa-www.harvard.edu/cfa-home

The Harvard-Smithsonian Center for Astrophysics combines the resources and research facilities of the Smithsonian Astrophysical Observatory and the Harvard College Observatory. The center studies the processes that determine the nature and evolution of the universe. Visit this site for information about the center's facilities and staff.

Harvard-Smithsonian Center for Astrophysics Library

html http://cfa-www.harvard.edu/library/

The Harvard-Smithsonian Center for Astrophysics (CfA) presents this information page. Visitors will find publications and abstract services here, in addition to an online catalog containing information about the holdings of the CfA Library.

High Energy Astrophysics Division FTP Archive

ftp://sao-ftp.harvard.edu/

Astronomers can download files regarding various projects at the Smithsonian Astrophysical Observatory from its High Energy Astrophysics Division anonymous FTP archive. Users can also retrieve related software here.

Implementation of an Astrophysics Information System on the World-Wide Web

http://www.ncsa.uiuc.edu/SDG/IT94/ Proceedings/Astronomy/richmond/ richmond.html

The High Energy Astrophysics Science Archive Research Center at Goddard Space Center wants at this site to let astrophysicists get to catalogues and astronomical data now scattered all over the Web and from high-energy satellites. It contains tools as well as data.

Johann Wolfgang Goethe-University Frankfurt Astrophysics Program

http://earth.astro.uni-frankfurt.de/

Maintained at Germany's Johann Wolfgang Goethe-University Frankfurt, this page focuses on the astrophysics program, offering links to research, lectures and seminars. The page also serves as a springboard to other stargazer resources on the Internet.

Joint Institute for Laboratory Astrophysics

http://www.boulder.nist.gov/jila/jilahome.html

The Joint Institute for Laboratory Astrophysics, a Boulder, Colo.-based scientific research organization, maintains this site to introduce its facilities and staff. Visit here to learn about its many research disciplines, including atomic interactions, chemical physics, geophysical measurements and more.

Journal Query Form for ADS Articles

http://adsabs.harvard.edu/article_service.html

This interactive page contains a form to query astrophysical journals for articles. An online help option aids first time users.

Laboratoire d'Astrophysique de l'Observatoire de Grenoble

http://gag.observ-gr.fr/

The Laboratoire d'Astrophysique at the Observatoire des Sciences de l'Univers de Grenoble offers dozens of links to astrophysics and astronomy-related Internet resources. In French.

Laboratory for Computational Astrophysics

http://zeus.ncsa.uiuc.edu:8080/lca_home_ page.html

The National Center for Supercomputer Applications and the Department of Astronomy at the University of Illinois at Urbana-Champaign develop and disseminate theoretical modeling software for astrophysics research. Visitors can read about their ongoing projects, including documentation and performance data.

Leeds University Astrophysics

http://ast.leeds.ac.uk/

Visitors to the Astrophysics at Leeds University site will find links to three research groups at the university, as well as to other related pages.

The MACHO Dark Matter Search Project

http://wwwmacho.anu.edu.au/

Find out what MACHO means to the Australian-American astronomic research team that maintains this page. Review the project data, inspect the equipment systems and access the online resources.

Fabien Malbet

http://gag.observ-gr.fr/~malbet/Fabien_ eng.html

Meet Fabien Malbet of the astrophysics laboratory at the Grenoble Observatory in France. He studies star formations and provides links to some of the images he has examined

Max Planck Institute for Astrophysics

http://www.mpa-garching.mpg.de/

This German astrophysics institute provides its research on cosmology, gravitational lensing, molecular physics, comets, the formation of galaxies, hydrodynamics and how stars are formed.

McMaster Cepheid Photometry and Radial Velocity DataArchive

http://www.physics.mcmaster.ca/Cepheid/ HomePage.html

A collection of data files and tables of photometric data for galactic and extragalactic Cepheid variables are maintained at this server. Reference papers are cited for those interested in reading full descriptions of the original data.

Simon Morris

http://www.dao.nrc.ca/DAO/STAFF/simon.html

This personal home page contains information on Simon Morris' research interests and a list of his astrophysics publications.

Dr. Koji Mukai

http://heasarc.gsfc.nasa.gov/docs/bios/ koji.html

Dr. Koji Mukai, an astrophysicist, provides contact and personal information, including his research interests and links to astronomy sites.

Daniel Nadeau

http://www.astro.umontreal.ca/membres/ nadeau.html

A lecturer in astrophysics at the University of Montreal posts his contact information here. The page links to the university's Physics Department and other Montreal sites. In English or French.

NASA Space Physics Data System

http://spds.nasa.gov/spds.html

NASA's Space Physics Data System preserves historical data and provides access to space physics information. Site features include a directory of services, indexed databases and an overview of the system. [Find Related Sites]

National Institute of Astrophysics, Mexico

http://www.inaoep.mx/

Mexico's National Institute of Astrophysics (INAOE) maintains this home page. The INAOE is a training and research institution founded at the site of the old Tonantzintla Observatory. Areas covered include astrophysics, optics and electronics.

Robert J. Nemiroff

http://cossc.gsfc.nasa.gov/htmltest/rjn.html

NASA astrophysicist Robert J. Nemiroff offers a list of his favorite links, his biography and a link to RJN's Comedy of Science Page here. The page also contains links to MPEG movie trips featuring black holes and neutron stars.

Oxford University Astrophysics Department

http://www-astro.physics.ox.ac.uk/

The Astrophysics Department at England's Oxford University sponsors this informational and educational home page. Visitors can pick up a map of the stars, view photos of space, see the first light images from the Infra-Red camera installed at WHT, find out about ongoing research projects and upcoming colloquia or retire from the observatory and visit other sites on campus.

Dr. Robert Petre

http://heasarc.gsfc.nasa.gov/docs/bios/ petre.html

This personnel page provides contact and professional information about astrophysicist Dr. Robert Petre. Includes details about his research and other activities.

Frank P. Pijpers

http://www.astro.uu.se/~frank/FPP_ perpag.html

Meet Dr. Frank P. Pijpers, an astrophysicist at the Theoretical Astrophysics Center in Aarhus, Denmark. His research interests include waves, convection and turbulence.

Princeton University Observatory

http://astro.princeton.edu/

The Princeton University Observatory maintains this astrophysical sciences Web server. Visit here for academic course descriptions, student and faculty listings, and a variety of scientific resources and publications.

RAL Astrophysics Starlink Node

http://ast.star.rl.ac.uk/

The Astrophysics Starlink Node is part of the UK-based Central Laboratory of Research Councils. This home page details projects of the Astrophysics Division and Space Science Department, as well as info on related conferences, job openings and software developments.

Ritter Astrophysical Research Center

http://www.physics.utoledo.edu/www/ritter/ritter.html

Operated by the Department of Physics and Astronomy at the University of Toledo, the Ritter Astrophysical Research Center serves as the subject of this page. Find info on the center's research and research groups, meet the faculty and staff, and read

Scientific Staff—Gerald Justice

http://www.dao.nrc.ca/DAO/STAFF/justice.html

This page from the staff directory at Canada's Dominion Astrophysical Observatory spotlights the UNIX System Manager, Gerald Justice. Find his contact information and research interests.

Smithsonian Astrophysical Observatory

http://cfa-www.harvard.edu/sao-home.html

The Smithsonian Astrophysical Observatory is a research bureau of the Smithsonian Institution in Washington, D.C. Browsers can visit the Central Bureau for Astronomical Telegrams and the Minor Planet Center. Also, find several archives of software, images and documentation relating to Smithsonian projects.

Will Sutherland

http://www-astro.physics.ox.ac.uk/~wjs/

Will Sutherland, a graduate student in the Astrophysics Department at Oxford University, maintains this personal home page with information about himself and his research.

Swedish Institute of Space Physics

http://www.tp.umu.se/Space

The Swedish Institute of Space Physics provides information on its people, projects and publications. Visit here for divisional resources and links to related institutions.

Theoretical Astrophysics Group - Los Alamos

http://qso.lanl.gov/

The Theoretical Astrophysics Group at the Los Alamos National Laboratory in California maintains this page. Find information on research projects, a directory of personnel, publications and links to other astrophysics Web sites.

Underground Laboratory for Particle Physics and Astrophysics

http://www.lngs.infn.it/

The Underground laboratory for Particle Physics and Astrophysics in Italy comes to the Web through this page that includes a description of the lab and details about some of its current research.

WebStars

http://www.stars.com/WebStars/

Go star gazing online through the WebStars site. Dedicated to astronomy and astrophysics, the page offers a starting point for scientists and the general astronomy community. Visitors can also download software.

Dr. Nicholas White

http://heasarc.gsfc.nasa.gov/docs/bios/white.html

This home page, maintained by a researcher at the U.S. Goddard Space Flight Center, provides personal and professional information. Visitors will also find links to a variety of astrophysics-related organizations and resources.

COMETS, METEORS, AND ASTEROIDS

Comet Hale-Bopp Home Page (JPL)

http://newproducts.jpl.nasa.gov/comet/

The comet officially designated C/1995 O1, but more commonly known by the last names of its discoverors, Alan Hale and Thomas Bopp, is the subject of this home page maintained by the NASA Jet Propulsion Laboratories. Visitors will find news, data and images of the comet, among other items of interest.

Comet Images

http://encke.jpl.nasa.gov/images.html

Take a look at images of dozens of periodic and long-period comets as well as news and info on other orbital heavenly bodies.

Comet Observation NASA

http://encke.jpl.nasa.gov/

NASA's Comet Observation home page is filled with comet images and information for both the professional and amateur astronomer. There are also links to related sites, including the NASA and JPL home pages.

Comet P/Shoemaker-Levy 9 Impact Home Page

http://seds.lpl.arizona.edu/sl9/sl9.html

View the 1994 Comet P/Shoemaker-Levy 9 Collision with Jupiter. Visitors to this page will find Frequently Asked Question (FAQ) files, fact sheets and images of the astronomical event.

Comets and Meteor Showers

http://medicine.wustl.edu/~kronkg/

Gary Kronk's labor of love brings expertise about comets and meteor showers to the Web world through this page. Stop by for reports about upcoming events and news about how best to see approaching objects from the depths of space.

Comet Shoemaker-Levy Collision with Jupiter

http://www.jpl.nasa.gov/sl9/

Information about the collision of Comet Shoemaker - Levy with Jupiter in the month of July, 1994 is available at this Web site. Visitors can read information relating to the collision including background information, television coverage, spacecraft observations of the impact, ground observations or link to other related sites.

Comet Shoemaker-Levy 9 FAQ

http://www.isc.tamu.edu/~astro/sl9.html

This Texas A&M Observatory page is devoted to the collision of comet Shoemaker-Levy 9 with Jupiter—an event of enormous importance to astronomers. Browsers can view pictures of the collision, read pre- and post-collision questions and link to other observatory pages.

Giotto Information

http://nssdc.gsfc.nasa.gov/planetary/giotto.html

Comet Halley is the subject of Giotto, a site named for the spacecraft that photographed Halley in 1986. Photos and text recreate the event in detail. There are also links to related sites.

NASA Near Earth Asteroid Rendezvous

http://nssdc.gsfc.nasa.gov/planetary/near.html

NASA's Near Earth Asteroid Rendezvous mission scheduled for February and March 1996 is detailed on this page. Learn what the mission is supposed to accomplish, how it will be done and what it will cost—less than $150 million. Links to other NASA and space research sites are provided.

National Space Science Data Center

http://nssdc.gsfc.nasa.gov/planetary/planetfact.html

The National Space Science Data Center sets up a page full of fact sheets about planets, asteroids and other heavenly bodies, targeting those with more than a little understanding of the universe.

SL9 Observations in Massachusetts

http://scruffy.phast.umass.edu/Whately/sl9.html

This astronomy site, maintained by the University of Massachusetts' Whately Telescope, provides a detailed look at the 1994 collision of comet SL-9 and the planet Jupiter. Visit here for images and documentation of the event and links to "a plethora of general information about comet impacts."

COMPANIES AND SERVICES

Astromart
http://www.astromart.com/
Astromart, an online marketplace for astronomers, provides easy access to products and services. Visit here to shop for telescopes, photography equipment, maps and more. Links to user groups, classified advertisements and other services are available.

AstroWeb Resource Entry Form
http://fits.cv.nrao.edu/www/astroweb/aref.html
This interactive site allows visitors to add URLs to the AstroWeb database. An option to check recent additions to the database is also featured.

International Astronomical Union: Central Bureau for Astronomical Telegrams
http://cfa-www.harvard.edu/cfa/ps/cbat.html
The Central Bureau for Astronomical Telegrams is a subscription service operated by the International Astronomical Union. Members receive the latest information on discoveries of new stars, comets and other transient astronomical phenomena.

Jane's Electronic Information System
http://www.btg.com/janes/
Jane's Electronic Information System is a collaboration between Jane's Information Group and BTG, Inc. The site is a defense and aerospace information center. Includes a demonstration, overview and Frequently Asked Questions (FAQ).

Lockheed Martin Missiles & Space
http://www.lmsc.lockheed.com/
Lockheed Martin Missiles and Space, a major aerospace and defense enterprise, provides press reports, photos, a corporate newsletter and job openings online. Visitors can also look at some of the technical work the firm is doing on various peacekeeping projects.

Malin Space Science Systems
http://barsoom.msss.com/
Malin Space Science Systems designs, develops and operates spacecraft instrumentation. This site provides links to information about its projects, educational activities and flight project participation.

NASA Commercial Technology Network
http://fits.cv.nrao.edu/www/astroweb/aref.html
Here, the National Aeronautical and Space Administration (NASA) provides information about its technological advances that may benefit the U.S. industrial community. The site contains access to NASA publications, announcements of upcoming events, advice on partnerships and a catalogue of opportunities for private companies.

NASA Small Business Innovation Research Program
http://sbir.hq.nasa.gov/SBIR.html
The Small Business Innovation Research Program of the U.S. National Aeronautics and Space Administration offers seed funding for the development of innovative technologies. Visit this site to learn how to apply for funding and read previous solicitations.

Radio Amateur Satellite Corporation
http://www.amsat.org/
The Radio Amateur Satellite Corporation (AMSAT) offers information about the amateur space program here. Enthusiasts can browse its catalogs and news briefs, join its mailing list and download software.

Rutherford Appleton Laboratory's Starlink Project
http://star-www.rl.ac.uk/
This home page provides information on Rutherford Appleton Laboratory's Starlink Project, which is aimed at enabling astronomers' use of computers for data analysis. Includes information on hardware, software and support available through the organization.

SatPasses Home Page
http://ssl.berkeley.edu/isi_www/satpasses.html
SatPasses predicts when spacecraft will pass over 63 cities in North America . Browsers here will learn when they will be able to see the Atmosphere Research Satellite, the Space Shuttle, the Russian Space Station Mir and the Hubble Telescope.

SpaceCom
http://www.spacecom.com/
SpaceCom markets satellite audio and data broadcasting services. Visitors to this site will learn more about the company's services, its corporate profile and its latest news. The site also posts its current job openings.

Swedish Space Corporation Home Page
http://www.ssc.se/
The Swedish Space Corporation is a government owned company that covers the full range of space-related work. This extensive overview of its efforts includes a look at its scientific and telecommunication satellites, its satellite mapping work and its global positioning tools.

World Wide Web Aerospace Business Development Center
http://arganet.tenagra.com/Tenagra/aero_bd.html
Aerospace business professionals are the target audience for this online business development center. Visitors will find a multitude of links, including dozens of procurement centers, Department of Defense information sources, and related news articles and press releases.

CONFERENCES AND CONVENTIONS

Astronomical Data Analysis Software and Systems Conference Information
http://cadcwww.dao.nrc.ca/ADASS/adass.html
Detailed information is available at this site regarding the Astronomical Data Analysis Software and Systems (ADASS) Conference. ADASS is a discussion forum for scientists and programmers working with astronomical data. The conference consists of paper presentations, talks and poster sessions.

Astronomical Data Analysis Software and Systems 1994
http://ra.stsci.edu/ADASS.html
Review the program of speakers and events for 1994's Conference on Astronomical Data Analysis Software and Systems. Link to abstracts of academic papers presented at the conference or contact organizers from this site.

Center for Advanced Space Studies Online
http://cass.jsc.nasa.gov/CASS_home.html
Visitors to this home page can learn about the Universities Space Research Association's (USRA) Houston-based research and conference facility. Includes online publications, links to the center's three divisions and astronomy-related conference listings.

International Astronomical Union's Symposium
http://cass.jsc.nasa.gov/CASS_home.html
This page provides information on the International Astronomical Union's symposium on astrophysical applications of gravitational lensing. Includes an outline of conference proceedings and a conference program.

International Astronomy Meetings
http://cadcwww.dao.nrc.ca/meetings/meetings.html
Astronomers can keep track of professional happenings with the aid of the International Astrono-

my Meetings site. Academic conferences and workshops for physicists and astronomers are listed here.

Nicolaus Copernicus Astronomical Center

http://www.ncac.torun.pl/

This page provides information on the Nicolaus Copernicus Astronomical Center, its projects, staff and upcoming seminars. Includes links to other Polish and international astronomy home pages .

1995 Young European Radio Astronomers Conference

http://www.cup.cam.ac.uk/onlinepubs/YERAC/YERACtop.html

This cover page provides an introduction to the electronic publication of the papers presented at the 1995 Young European Radio Astronomers Conference. A link to the publisher, Cambridge University Press, is included.

Science with the Hubble Space Telescope II

chttp://www.ncac.torun.pl/

Maintained by the European Southern Observatory, this site contains information on Science with the Hubble Space Telescope, a scientific conference co-sponsored by the Space Telescope Institute in Baltimore, Md. Links to program notes, a participants list and related topical sites are featured.

Solar Workshops

http://www.oat.ts.astro.it/isps/sworkshops.html

Astronomers will find a listing of solar conferences and international astronomy meetings on the Solar Workshops page.

Third Huntsville Symposium on Gamma-Ray Bursts

http://cossc.gsfc.nasa.gov/grb3.html

The home page for the Third Huntsville Symposium on Gamma-Ray Bursts provides information on the program schedule, invited speakers, the banquet, hotel and travel guides. The conference was held Oct. 25-27, 1995 and produced by the Gamma-Ray Astronomy Group at the NASA Marshall Space Flight Center.

Weaving the Astronomy Web

http://cdsweb.u-strasbg.fr/waw.html

Weaving the Astronomy Web is a conference organized by the Strausbourg Astronomical Observatory in France offering event information. Visit here for conference proceedings, listings of participants and associated programs, and links to the observatory's home page

COSMIC RAYS AND RADIATION

California Institute of Technology Space Radiation Laboratory

http://www.srl.caltech.edu/

The California Institute of Technology's Space Radiation Laboratory offers visitors a look at its research projects in high energy and computational astrophysics. Links to departmental publications, seminar and personnel information, and related sites are also featured.

Gamma Ray Burst Index at Northwestern University

http://www.astro.nwu.edu/astro/osse/bursts/index.html

Physicists will find a collection of gamma ray burst images here. The Department of Physics and Astronomy at Northwestern University, which collects the images as part of an ongoing experiment, explains its research here.

Solar and Upper Atmospheric Data Services Home Page

http://www.ngdc.noaa.gov/stp/SOLAR/solar.html

The Solar and Upper Atmospheric Data Services site of the U.S. National Geographical Data Center provides updates and scientific research results. Visit here for the latest findings from its studies of solar and interplanetary phenomena, flare-associated events and cosmic rays.

Solar Radio Emissions

http://www.oa.uj.edu.pl:80/sol/

Providing daily values of solar radio emissions, Cracow University's Solar Radio Emission page contains an archive of readings from July 1994 to current date.

Third Huntsville Symposium on Gamma-Ray Bursts

http://cossc.gsfc.nasa.gov/grb3.html

The home page for the Third Huntsville Symposium on Gamma-Ray Bursts provides information on the program schedule, invited speakers, the banquet, hotel and travel guides. The conference was held Oct. 25-27, 1995 and produced by the Gamma-Ray Astronomy Group at the NASA Marshall Space Flight Center.

X-Ray Timing Explorer (XTE)

http://heasarc.gsfc.nasa.gov/docs/xte/XTE.html

The X-Ray Timing Explorer is a Goddard mission intended to further the study of time variability in the emission of X-ray sources. Visitors to this site can read information about the mission's instrumentation, scientific planning and data processing being conducted by the Guest Observer

Facility, the Science Operations Facility and the XTE Science Data Center.

COSMOLOGY

Advanced Satellite for Cosmology and Astrophysics

http://heasarc.gsfc.nasa.gov/docs/asca/asca2.html

This site documents the progress and history of the Advanced Satellite for Cosmology and Astrophysics (ASCA), a Japanese cosmic x-ray astronomy mission. Includes an overview of the research project, descriptions of instrumentation and links to related resources.

Advanced Satellite for Cosmology and Astrophysics Guest Observer Facility

http://heasarc.gsfc.nasa.gov/docs/asca/ascagof.html

The Advanced Satellite for Cosmology and Astrophysics (ASCA) Guest Observer Facility Web page includes information on the Japanese cosmic x-ray astronomy mission, plus an archive of images and data observations. Also featured are ASCA news updates, publications and meeting schedules.

The Department of Extragalactic Astrophysics and Cosmology at the Observatoire de Paris-Meudon

http://gin.obspm.fr/

The Department of Extragalactic Astrophysics and Cosmology at the Observatoire de Paris-Meudon provides an index of home pages and a directory of DAEC members and other Web servers at the observatory. In French, English, Portuguese, Italian and Spanish.

The InfraRed Army

http://www.cco.caltech.edu/~btsoifer/ira.html

Based in Caltech's Downs Laboratory of Physics, the InfraRed Army research group works in the "near infrared" range of the electromagnetic spectrum. The group's Web site offers an image gallery featuring its research and team members.

Low Surface Brightness Galaxy Gallery

http://zebu.uoregon.edu/sb2.html

This site provides a gallery of images of "low surface brightness galaxies." Visitors can also read about galaxy structures and surface brightness, or peruse a detailed reference list for additional info.

Radio Pulsar Resources

http://pulsar.princeton.edu/rpr.shtml

Radio Pulsar Resources is a collection of home pages of interest to specialists in the field of radio pulsar. Visitors will find links to institutions, as well as personal home pages of researchers.

Relativity Group at the National Center for Supercomputing Applications

http://jean-luc.ncsa.uiuc.edu/

The National Center for Supercomputing Applications' Relativity Group studies black holes and gravitational waves. The research organization's home page outlines its projects, papers and members. Movies and exhibits are also available here.

Virtual Trips to Black Holes and Neutron Stars Page

http://antwrp.gsfc.nasa.gov/htmltest/rjn_bht.html

Astronomy enthusiasts will enjoy this site, featuring "visual trips" to astronomical phenomena such as black holes and neutron stars. Links to an assortment of MPEG movies and downloadable MPEG players are available.

FAQs, Guides, and Reference

ADS Abstract Service

http://adswww.harvard.edu/abs_doc/abs_help.html

ADS Abstract Service helps scientists sift through scientific astronomy papers by providing summaries of published works in a searchable database. Astronomy related publications from the past 20 years are indexed here.

Astronomer's Bazaar

http://cdsweb.u-strasbg.fr/Cats.html

Located and maintained at France's University of Strasbourg Data Center, this page offers keyword access to an annotated list of astronomical data catalogs. Also find the Dictionary of Nomenclature of Celestial Objects, tables from "Astronomy & Astrophysics" and other topical links.

Astronomical Information System

http://ezinfo.ethz.ch/ezinfo/astro/astro.html

The Astronomical Information System provides research details on wide range of topics from a team of eight amateur astronomers. It includes links to amateur astronomy resources, as well as recent news and a calendar of events.

The Astronomy Cafe

http://www2.ari.net/home/odenwald/cafe.html

The Astronomy Cafe allows young, future astronomers an easy-to-follow and colorful look at the skies and what it is like to be a professional stargazer. Visitors can ask the resident astronomer questions or learn the "anatomy of a research paper."

Astronomy HyperText Book

http://zebu.uoregon.edu/text.html

From the Electronic Universe Project at the University of Oregon, this site contains a hypertext textbook dealing with astronomy. Visitors can select a subject from the table of contents, then view an animated presentation illustrating the principle chosen.

Astronomy Notes

http://www.astro.washington.edu/strobel/lecturenotes.html

Educator Nick Strobel posted the lecture notes from his University of Washington introductory astronomy courses at this site. Visitors will find an annotated content directory along with the full text version of Strobel's courses. Includes links to the Backyard Astronomer, the Morehead Planetarium Sky Calendar and related resources

Astrophysics Preprints

http://www.physics.mcmaster.ca/AstroPreprints.html

The Astrophysics Preprint page offers full text and tables from research abstracts. Typical titles include

Astrotext

http://uu-gna.mit.edu:8001/uu-gna/text/astro/index.html

Stargazers seeking formal instruction can learn the galaxies online with the help of Astrotext. This introductory textbook uses Internet resources along with traditional instructional writings to compose an accessible but rigorous course of electronic study.

Backyard Astronomy: Choosing Binoculars

http://www.skypub.com/backyard/choosbin.html#top

Alan MacRobert, Associate Editor of Sky & Telescope magazine, helps visitors sort through the bewildering array of binoculars on the market today. Find out about power, aperture, focusing, and quality versus price.

CDSBull

http://cdsweb.u-strasbg.fr/Bull.html

The Data Center at the University of Strasbourg's observatory maintains this page featuring an electronic edition of its bulletin. Links to the center and its SIMBAD database are also included.

Commonly Used Acronyms

http://heasarc.gsfc.nasa.gov/docs/acronyms.html

The folks at NASA's Goddard Space Flight Center explain their acronyms in this online glossary.

The Daily Martian Weather Report

http://nova.stanford.edu/projects/mgs/dmwr.html

The Daily Martian Weather Report is brought to you by the Mars Global Surveyor Radio Science Team at the Jet Propulsion Laboratory. Visitors will find weather maps, temperature and pressure readings as well as other planetary data.

Digital Library Technology Home Page

http://dlt.gsfc.nasa.gov/

The Digital Library Technology Project is a U.S. government program aimed at developing the technology to put National Aeronautics and Space Administration electronic archives online. Software and hardware systems are in the works to make NASA information systems accessible to the public via computers.

European Space Information System

http://www.esrin.esa.it/htdocs/esis/esis.html

Located at Frascati, Italy, the European Space Information System provides access to scientific information collected on European Space Agency (ESA) and non-ESA space missions. At this Web site, visitors will find the ESIS for Astronomers catalog, a browser and related documentation.

Goddard Space Flight Center Space Science Data Operations Office

http://www.gsfc.nasa.gov/c630/ssdoo_main.html

The Space Science Data Operations Office at the National Aeronautics and Space Administration's Goddard Space Flight Center "serves various space science missions in processing, archiving, and disseminating data" and is the home of the National Space Science Data Center and the World Data Center-A for Rockets & Satellites.

High Energy Astrophysics Science Archive Research Center

http://heasarc.gsfc.nasa.gov/

This science archive research center is intended to "support a multi-mission archive facility in high energy astrophysics for scientists around the world." It's a joint effort between the National Space Science Data Center and the Laboratory for High Energy Astrophysics. Visitors will find data, images and videos here.

IDL Astronomy User's Library

http://idlastro.gsfc.nasa.gov/homepage.html

This central repository for astronomical procedures provides researchers with a collection of astronomical methodologies. Includes a users' guide, instructions for submitting procedures to the library and links to related resources.

Implementation of an Astrophysics Information System on the World-Wide Web

http://www.ncsa.uiuc.edu/SDG/IT94/
Proceedings/Astronomy/richmond/
richmond.html

The High Energy Astrophysics Science Archive Research Center at Goddard Space Center wants at this site to let astrophysicists get to catalogues and astronomical data now scattered all over the Web and from high-energy satellites. It contains tools as well as data.

Index of /pub

ftp://ftp.sunspot.noao.edu/pub/

Index of /pub an FTP archive from the National Solar Observatory/ Sacramento Peak at Sunspot, New Mexico, USA—contains NSO/SP software and data products-coronal maps, solar images, active region lists, sunspot numbers, NSO/SP Workshop paper templates, Radiative Inputs of the Sun to the Earth (RISE) and Sunspotter Newsletters.

The Internet Science Education Project

http://www.hia.com/hia/pcr/

Those who wander into this mind-bending site will encounter fiction, scholarly essays and "a Web forum for critical and poetical inquiry into controversial ideas in the post-modern physics of time travel and consciousness research." [Find Related Sites]

Introductory Astronomy Notes

http://www.astro.washington.edu/strobel/
index.html

Take a virtual Introductory to Astronomy course here. Nick Strobel teaches the course at Bakersfield College and posts an entire quarter's worth of lecture notes on this site, which also details the astronomer's research.

IUCAA PRE-PRINTS

http://iucaa.iucaa.ernet.in/publications/
preprints.html

The Inter-University Centre for Astronomy & Astrophysics, Pune University, India, maintains this archive for access to its scientific document and preprints concerning various astronomical phenomena.

Langley Distributed Active Archive Center

http://eosdis.larc.nasa.gov/

The National Aeronautics and Space Administration stores scientific data on radiation, clouds, aerosols and tropospheric chemistry at the Langley Distributed Active Archive Center. Researchers can freely download data sets from this NASA site.

Mount Wilson Observatory Online Stargazer Map

http://www.mtwilson.edu/Services/StarMap/

The Stargazer Map, provided by California's Mount Wilson Observatory, will create a map of any astronomical location a visitor may choose. Visit here for a PostScript file of any favorite place in the heavens.

NASA AESP Home Page

http://www.okstate.edu/aesp/AESP.html

The NASA Aerospace Education Services Program provides information here on its workshops and seminars designed to increase public awareness of airborne scientific research and technological development. Also included are links to space-image libraries and other educational resources.

NASA Public Affairs

http://www.sel.noaa.gov/

This site provides a wide variety of NASA information, news, history and current events. Includes the Spacelink (especially designed for educators and students), a gallery of photo, movie and audio archives, and links to other NASA pages.

NASA Space Calendar

http://newproducts.jpl.nasa.gov/calendar/

Maintained by a U.S. National Aeronautics and Space Administrationn astronomer, the Space Calendar provides information about space-related activities and anniversaries for the coming year. Visit this site to find out about past, present and future celestial happenings, such as meteor showers, satellite launches, and other events.

National Radio Astronomy Observatory Library

http://www.cv.nrao.edu/html/library/
library.html

The library of the National Radio Astronomy Observatory supplies an online catalog as well as a searchable index of preprints and published papers. There also is information on future and past meetings, conferences and workshops, plus pointers to other preprint services, published papers and other astronomy resources.

National Space Science Data Center

http://nssdc.gsfc.nasa.gov/nssdc/nssdc_
home.html

The National Space Science Data Center is a NASA facility located in Greenbelt, Md. Visitors to its home page will find links to discipline-specific scientific resources, research data archives and general program overviews.

Network Resources for Astronomers

http://www.hq.eso.org/online-resources-paper/
rrn.html

A document prepared by the Astronomical Society of the Pacific, this page promises an overview of astronomical resources available on the Web and basic descriptions of each. Paper preprints, astronomical archives and related software are among the resources indexed here.

The Observatorium - NASA Remote Sensing Public Access Center

http://www.rspac.ivv.nasa.gov/

NASA provides public access to its earth and space data at this site. Features include an exhibit hall filled with images and data about Earth and the universe, as well as a technology park, offering an in-depth look at science, remote sensing and information technology.

On-Line Glossary of Solar-Terrestrial Terms

http://www.ngdc.noaa.gov/stp/GLOSSARY/
glossary.html

What is an angstrom? Flux? A penumbra? Researchers and students can look up definitions of solar-terrestrial terms on this online glossary and learn a bit about the mighty sun in the process.

Sky Online

http://www.skypub.com/

The Sky Publishing Corporation offers a wide variety of astronomy-related books and software. Visit this site to learn more about the company's products and to access its collection of astronomy pages, including Tips for Backyard Astronomers and the Comet Page.

Space Calendar

http://newproducts.jpl.nasa.gov/calendar/
calendar.html

Astronomy enthusiasts can mark time with the Jet Propulsion Laboratory's Space Calendar. Know when and where to look for astronomical events, or celebrate important dates in the history of space exploration with the help of this site.

Space Science Education Home Page

http://www.gsfc.nasa.gov/education/
education_home.html

NASA's Space Science Education home page provides learning opportunities and details about the aerospace organization's missions. Student activities, lessons and curricula materials can be accessed here.

The StarChild Project: Connecting NASA and the K12 Classroom

http://heasarc.gsfc.nasa.gov/docs/StarChild/
StarChild.html

The StarChild Project is a NASA educational initiative aimed at providing learning experiences to K-12 students. Find astronomy-related topics discussed and demonstrated in fun and easy terms at this site.

Star*s Family StarBits

http://www.gsfc.nasa.gov/education/
education_home.html

The Star*s Family StarBits site offers a searchable dictionary of over 100,000 astronomy-related abbreviations, acronyms, symbols, contractions and other related entries of interest.

Strasbourg Astronomical Data Center

http://cdsweb.u-strasbg.fr/

The Strasbourg Astronomical Data Center (CDS) is a gathering point for astronomical data. Located at the Strasbourg Astronomical Observatory in France, the page includes links to databases and abstracts. In French, Spanish, German, Italian and English.

Sunrise/Sunset Computation

http://tycho.usno.navy.mil/srss.html

Browsers can find out local sunrise, sunset, moonrise and moonset times for anywhere in the United States here. The site is maintained by the U.S. Naval Observatory in Washington, D.C., and covers the years 1975 through 2025.

Theoretical Isochrones

http://www.pd.astro.it/evolution/

Astronomers and astrophysicists may visit this page to download files of isochrones discussed in the paper. The tables are sorted by composition.

Todays Space Weather

http://www.sel.bldrdoc.gov/today.html

This site provides weather updates for space, which includes geomagnetic fields, storms, solar activity and updates on satellite environments.

The Virtual Library: Aerospace

http://macwww.db.erau.edu/www_virtual_lib/
aerospace.html

An extensive index of aerospace information and resources available online is provided here by the World Wide Web Virtual Library. Visitors can link to listings of images, museums, publications, NASA space centers and more from this comprehensive site.

Amos Yahil

http://sbast3.ess.sunysb.edu/~ayahil/plan.html

Amos Yahil, an astronomy researcher at the State University of New York, provides a list of scientific articles at his home page. Visit here for a bibliography of reports published in physics and astronomy-related journals.

HISTORY OF ASTRONOMY

History of Space Exploration Archive

http://www.ksc.nasa.gov/history/history.html

Presented by NASA, this historical archive details the history of U.S. space exploration. Includes rocket history, manned missions and mission patches.

The Maya Astronomy Page

http://www.astro.uva.nl/michielb/maya/
astro.html

Intrepid explorers hacking through the Web jungle shouldn't miss the Maya Astronomy page. Packed with graphics, visitors can learn about Mayan mathematics, calendar, writing and their talent for astronomy, including their special interest in the sun.

NASA History

http://www.gsfc.nasa.gov/hqpao/history.html

Students and interested browsers will learn about the history of the National Aeronautics and Space Administration here. The page offers up timelines, statistics and sketches of the men and women who have participated in the space program.

75th Anniversary Astronomical Debate

http://antwrp.gsfc.nasa.gov/diamond_jubilee/
debate.html

Great astronomical debates held in the early 20th century and commemorated 75 years later are chronicled here. Visitors will be greeted by historical background and content reports on the 1920 "The Scale of the Universe" discussion and its 1995 reprise "The Distance Scale to Gamma-Ray Bursts."

IMAGE FILES AND ARCHIVES

Adonis Adaptive Optics project WWW Server

http://hplyot.obspm.fr/

This is Adonis, the Adaptive Optics system with nightly mirrors of the great Nine Planets, the Web Nebulae and Planetary Nebulae. Includes an image gallery and project descriptions.

Ames Imaging Library System NASA

http://ails.arc.nasa.gov/

Access the National Aeronautics and Space Administration's (NASA) Ames Imaging Library System here. Visitors can search the imaging archives for space, spacecraft and NASA facility photographs.

Ames Research Center Images Archive

ftp://explorer.arc.nasa.gov/pub/SPACE/GIF/

Hosted by the NASA Ames Research Center, this archive offers an extensive collection of images and explanatory text.

Astro directory

ftp://ftp.cnam.fr/pub/Astro/

Here, visitors will find an FTP index of astronomical images, part of a larger archive at Rennes University, France.

Astronomical Images Archive

http://force.stwing.upenn.edu:8001/~jparker/
astronomy/index.shtml

Get a new view of the universe right from your screen with these online images of galaxies, planets and other heavenly bodies. If these images don't satisfy your celestial cravings, maybe the list of links to other astronomy sites will.

Astronomical Pictures

http://www.univ-rennes1.fr/ASTRO/astro.html

This picture gallery site provides links to astronomical images, animation, sounds and more. Among the offerings are planets, eclipses and visuals from the Hubble Space Telescope. In French and English.

Astronomy Newsgroup Image Files

http://web.cnam.fr/Images/Usenet/abpa/
summaries/index.html

Astronomical pictures that have made recent news are archived here. Find what everyone has been discussing in the astronomy Usenet newsgroup by viewing the contact sheets of images at this site.

AstroWeb Image Index

http://fits.cv.nrao.edu/www/yp_pictures.html

This AstroWeb page features an annotated index of sites offering access to astronomical images. Also find information on the Mediterranean Association of Environmental and Space Sciences and its projects, plus links to other astronomical projects.

Big Bear Solar Observatory FTP Server

ftp://suncub.bbso.caltech.edu/

California's Big Bear Solar Observatory's anonymous FTP server provides its visitors with jpeg images of the skies. Daily observation summaries, weather data and polar magnetograms are also available.

Canadian Astronomy Data Centre HST Science Archive

http://cadcwww.dao.nrc.ca/hst.html

At this site maintained by the Canadian Astronomy Data Centre, scientists can access data gathered by the the Hubble Space Telescope. Search the database and preview images here.

CCD Images of Galaxies

http://zebu.uoregon.edu/galaxy.html

This page from the University of Oregon's Electronic Universe Project features a wealth of astronomical images taken with charge-coupled devices (CCDs). Also find information on the project and other resource material.

Chesley Bonestell Gallery

http://www.secapl.com/bonestell/Top.html

Paintings of space and planetary scenes are featured at the Chesley Bonestell Interactive Art Gallery. Each work by Bonestell is accompanied by a brief narrative; familiar subjects include Earth, Jupiter, Mars and Saturn.

Clementine

http://www.nrl.navy.mil/clementine/clementine.html

Details of Clementine Deep Space Program Science Experiment, sponsored by the U.S. National Aeronautics and Space Administration and other organizations, are available here. Visit this site for images, data and mission information.

Comet Images

http://encke.jpl.nasa.gov/images.html

Take a look at images of dozens of periodic and long-period comets as well as news and info on other orbital heavenly bodies.

The Data Center Home Page

http://hea-www.harvard.edu/einstein/Ein_home/ein_welcome.html

The Smithsonian Astrophysical Observatory houses the Einstein Observatory Data Archive. View images and data gathered by the satellite-based X-ray telescope at this site.

Different Categories of Pictures

http://crux.astr.ua.edu/choosepic.html

The University of Alabama offers a Web album of astronomical images. Choose from the collections of galaxies and star clusters, each with an explanation to point out interesting features.

Dryden Research Aircraft Photo Archive

http://www.dfrf.nasa.gov/PhotoServer/photoServer.html

This photo archive contains digitized images of the many unique research aircraft flown at what is now known as NASA Dryden Flight Research Center from the 1940s to the present. Includes links to the research projects overviews and fact sheets.

DSN Solar System Menu

http://esther.la.asu.edu/asu_tes/TES_Editor/dsn_solarsyst.html

Providing a virtual travelogue of the solar system, this page features images of planets, asteroids, spacecraft, the sun and the moon. Includes links to three other space tours.

Earth and Universe

http://www.eia.brad.ac.uk/btl/

Visit this site for a comprehensive multimedia guide to the stars and galaxies taken from the "Earth and Universe" PC CD-ROM from BTL Publishing Limited. Find sound, video, text and still photos.

Earth Observation Images

http://images.jsc.nasa.gov/html/earth.htm

This substantial collection of Earth images is sponsored by NASA. Link to the NASA home page or Imagery Services for more planetary observations.

Earth Observatorium CD-ROM

http://www.csn.net/malls/rmdp/ee.html

The Earth Observatorium CD-ROM contains nearly 13,000 color photographs from Space Shuttle Flight 59. Includes annotations for each image, and a description of the NASA mission through interactive text, sound and movies.

Earth Viewer

http://www.fourmilab.ch/earthview/vplanet.html

At the Earth Viewer site, visitors can view the earth from the sun or the moon, or can look at a map of the earth showing the regions in day and night. The earth can also be modeled from topographical maps and satellite photos. Other sites of astronomical interest are also listed.

Einstein Observatory Data Archive

http://adswww.harvard.edu/einstein_service.html

Part of NASA1s Astrophysics Data System (ADS), this Web site offers astronomers access to image files, photon event lists and other data gathered by the Einstein Observatory. Visitors can search the databases, review documentation, or link to other ADS sites.

ESIS Image Files

http://ecf.hq.eso.org/ESIS-GIF.html

The European Space Information System maintains this list of astronomical and related image files. A description of each GIF is provided.

The Face on Mars

http://barsoom.msss.com/education/facepage/face.html

Elaborating on images some believe show an artificially shaped, face-like landform on the surface of Mars, Malin Space Science Systems Inc. presents this educational page discussing the raw images that sparked the controversy and providing a brief lesson on image-processing techniques.

The Faint Images of the Radio Sky at Twenty Centimeters (FIRST) Survey

http://sundog.stsci.edu/

The Faint Images of the Radio Sky at Twenty Centimeters (FIRST) survey outlines the project designed to produce a radio equivalent of the Palomar Observatory Sky Survey over 10,000 square degrees of the North Galactic Cap. Visitors can view recent images here.

Galaxy: Astronomy Science

http://galaxy.einet.net/galaxy/Science/Astronomy.html

This extensive index covers amateur astronomy, astronautics, astrophysics and observatories. Find articles, journals, image collections, databases, directories, institutions and more.

Galileo Messenger Issue 34

http://www.jpl.nasa.gov/gllmess/Mess34TOC.html

Take a look at the latest electronic version of the Galileo Messenger for articles on astronomers, comets, satellites and everything cosmic. Readers can view and download images or catch up on the back issues of the publication at the archive site.

HST Greatest Hits 1990-1995 Gallery

http://www.stsci.edu/pubinfo/BestOfHST95.html

Shots taken by the Hubble Space Telescope offer unprecedented birdseye views of Orion, a storm on the planet Saturn, a comet impact and black holes, to name but a few. A cosmophile's delight.

HST News

http://cdsweb.u-strasbg.fr/HST.html

This site compares a space image shot with the Wide-Field and Planetary Camera-II to one of the same region shot with a Wide-Field and Planetary Camera-I. Along with the images, visitors will find a caption provided by the Space Telescope Science Institute.

Hubble Space Telescope Public Images

http://www.stsci.edu/pubinfo/Pictures.html

Naysayers predicted failure for the Hubble Space Telescope, the giant craft sent deep into space to return images and info on places no man has seen, but six years after HST was released, the telescope is still going strong and sending back information. Marvel at HST images here with accompanying text, such as an image of the rings of Saturn, the atmosphere of Jupiter and Uranus, and documentation of a dying star.

Ionia Global Land Data Set Net-Browser

http://shark1.esrin.esa.it/

Take a look at images and datasets from the European Space Agency's (ESA) orbiting satellite Ionia. Access a variety of images of individual orbital passes, query the ESA server for specific information or simply browse the large data collection.

Jet Propulsion Laboratory Image/ Information Archive

http://www.jpl.nasa.gov/archive/

The U.S. National Aeronautics and Space Administration's Jet Propulsion Laboratory maintains this site for its image and information archives. Visitors will find graphic images in a variety of downloadable formats, online video catalogs and access to informational databases.

Jet Propulsion Laboratory Public Image Archive

http://www.jpl.nasa.gov/archive/images.html

View celestial objects without leaving your home at this image archive from NASA and the Jet Propulsion Laboratory. Full-color photos of comets, planets and spacecraft—gleaned from a variety of space agency missions—are available to the public via this site.

Johnson Space Center Digital Images Archive

http://images.jsc.nasa.gov/

Here, NASA displays an out-of-this-world collection of Johnson Space Center (JSC) digital images from yesterday and today, linking browsers to a large selection of photos from specific programs and missions. Includes links to both NASA and JSC.

Low Surface Brightness Galaxy Gallery

http://zebu.uoregon.edu/sb2.html

This site provides a gallery of images of "low surface brightness galaxies." Visitors can also read about galaxy structures and surface brightness, or peruse a detailed reference list for additional info.

Mariner 4

http://esther.la.asu.edu/asu_tes/TES_Editor/ IMAGES/SOL_SYST/MARS/OLD_SPACECRAFT/ marin4.gif

View an image of Mariner 4 from the Mars Thermal Emission Spectrometer Project at Arizona State Unversity.

Mars Images Menu

http://esther.la.asu.edu/asu_tes/TES_Editor/ SOLAR_SYST_TOUR/Mars.html

This Mars Images site contains links to photographic galleries of Mars and its moons, Phobos and Deimos.

Mars MPEG

http://www.stsci.edu/ftp/stsci/epa/mpeg/ Mars.mpg

This link leads to an MPEG movie clip of Mars. It's taken from the Space Telescope Electronic Information Service site, which features information about the Hubble Space Telescope.

Mars Multi-Scale Map

http://www.c3.lanl.gov/~cjhamil/Browse/ mars.html

Visitors to this planetary mapping site can zoom into a selected area of the planet Mars for detailed viewing of the surface. Options for this interesting online tool include varying resolutions in pixels per degree and different sizes in pixels. Users can also specify latitude and longidtude.

Mars Thermal Emission Spectrometer Project Image

http://esther.la.asu.edu/asu_tes/TES_Editor/ IMAGES/SOL_SYST/MARS/CRATERS/ mar6crat.gif

This is an image of Mars from the Mars Thermal Emission Spectrometer Project at Arizona State University.

MSSS Viking Image Archive

http://barsoom.msss.com/http/vikingdb.html

This searchable archive, maintained by Malin Space Science Systems (MSSS), houses over 30,000 images of Mars collected by Viking orbiters between 1976 and 1980. The page includes a link to the MSSS home page.

The National Space Science Data Center Photo Gallery

http://nssdc.gsfc.nasa.gov/photo_gallery/ PhotoGallery.html

The National Space Science Data Center, part of NASA, provides this immense photo gallery. Visit to download photos of the planets, astronomical objects, the sun and various spacecraft.

NCSA Astronomy Digital Image Library

http://imagelib.ncsa.uiuc.edu/imagelib.html

Search the universe from your computer desktop using the National Center for Supercomputing Applications (NCSA) Astronomy Digital Image Library. The growing site offers hundreds of images, including VRML 3D visualizations.

Planet Earth Home Page - Images, Icons, Flags

http://www.nosc.mil/planet_earth/images.html

This visually oriented personal home page links visitors to archives of icons, space- and travel-related images, and flags. Includes links to the Internet Museum of Holography and an online fractal art gallery.

Planetary Probes FTP

http://spacelink.msfc.nasa.gov:80/ NASA.Projects/Planetary.Probes/

Planetary Probes is a File Transfer Protocol (FTP) archive containing details and images of planetary space probes launched by NASA. Missions include the Cassini Mission to Saturn and the Comet Rendezvous/Asteroid Flyby.

Regional Planetary Facility

http://ceps.nasm.edu:2020/rpif.html

The Regional Planetary Image Facility points professional andamateur astonomers to images and research sites in a comprehensive planetary library.

Saturn Ring Plane Crossings of 1995-1996

http://newproducts.jpl.nasa.gov/saturn/

Maintained by a U.S. National Aeronautical and Space Administration engineer, this site offers images from the Hubble Space Telescope's view of Saturn. Visit here for a variety of Saturn images, including a rare look at its rings.

SkyView

http://skyview.gsfc.nasa.gov/skyview.html

An online "virtual observatory on the Net," SkyView can generate "images of any part of the sky at wavelengths in all regimes from radio to gamma-ray." Explore the various interfaces, execute a batch query or access the SkyView FTP connection.

SkyView Virtual Observatory

http://skyview.gsfc.nasa.gov/

A virtual observatory, SkyView allows visitors to view images of the sky at various wavelengths. Find also links to other astronomy-related Internet resources.

Smithsonian Aviation Images Archive

http://www.landings.com/aviation.html

Maintained by the Smithsonian Astrophysical Observatory, this site offers a variety of aviation image archives. Visit here to view and download images of the U.S. Space Shuttle, military aircraft, satellites and more.

Solar Images at SDAC

http://umbra.gsfc.nasa.gov/images/latest.html

This page contains high-resolution pictures of current (or at least recent) solar activity. It is also possible to submit requests for data at a certain date and time. There are several other links dealing with solar-terrestrial observations.

Solar System Live

http://www.fourmilab.ch/solar/solar.html

Viewing the entire solar system or perhaps just the inner planets is made possible at the Solar System Live site. Set the time, date and observing location to track planets, satellites or asteroids in real time. The site is accessible to amateur stargazers and professional astronomers alike.

Space Movie Archive

http://www.univ-rennes1.fr/ASTRO/ anim-e.html

The Space Movie Archive contains real-time video footage of astronomical and meteorological phenomena, NASA and Russian space mission events, launches and still images of solar system bodies. Includes some science fiction animations and links to other space resources.

Space Radar Images of Earth

http://www.jpl.nasa.gov/sircxsar/

A joint U.S.-German-Italian satellite project, the Spaceborne Imaging Radar-C/X-Band Synthetic Aperture Radar has been flown twice over the earth to capture images useful across a wide range of scientific disciplines. Visit this archive to learn more about the project and review the image files.

Space Science and Engineering Center Real Time Data

http://www.ssec.wisc.edu/data/index.html

this site for its real-time data server. Visit here to view images from a variety of geostationary satellites, showing atmospheric conditions, sea temperatures, and composite imagery.

Space Shuttle Photographs Repository

http://ceps.nasm.edu:2020/RPIF/SSPR.html

The Center for Earth and Planetary Studies (CEPS) in cooperation with NASA, maintains an extensive collection of space shuttle photographs at this site. Browsers can view current images taken by astronauts, browse the archive of previous pictures or link to other sources of earth observation photography on the Web.

Triton Image

http://stardust.jpl.nasa.gov/planets/jpeg/nep/trtnpnk.jpg

The U.S. National Aeronautics and Space Administration's Planetary Data System maintains this site for its "trtnpnk" JPEG graphic file. Visit here to view the image and link to an extensive index of astronomy-related graphics.

Vesta Image

http://www.stsci.edu/ftp/pubinfo/gif/Vesta24.gif

This page contains a GIF image of the asteroid Vesta. It is one of 24 images showing the rotation of the 325-mile diameter asteroid and was taken by the Hubble Space Telescope.

Vesta MPEG Movie

http://www.stsci.edu/ftp/stsci/epa/mpeg/Vesta.mpg

This page contains a MPEG movie of Vesta as viewed from the Hubble Space Telescope. It is part of a larger site maintained by the Space Telescope Electronic Information Service.

Virtually Hawaii!

http://www.satlab.hawaii.edu/space/hawaii/

Virtually Hawaii!, maintained by the University of Hawaii, NASA and TerraSystems, Inc., provides an electronic archive of Earth and space science data focused on the Pacific island chain. Visitors

will find satellite images, weather maps and remote sensing images.

Virtual Trips to Black Holes and Neutron Stars Page

http://antwrp.gsfc.nasa.gov/htmltest/rjn_bht.html

Astronomy enthusiasts will enjoy this site, featuring "visual trips" to astronomical phenomena such as black holes and neutron stars. Links to an assortment of MPEG movies and downloadable MPEG players are available.

IMAGING SYSTEMS AND SOFTWARE

AASTeX Author Package

http://www.aas.org/publications/aastex/

AASTeX, a text preparation utility for submissions to American Astronomical Society journals, can be accessed at this site. Visit here to download software and learn how to prepare articles, graphics and tables for the society's family of scientific publications.

Advanced Spaceborne Thermal Emission and Reflection Radiometer

http://asterweb.jpl.nasa.gov/

The Advanced Spaceborne Thermal Emission and Reflection Radiometer is an imaging instrument used by NASA's Earth Observing System. Peruse detailed info about ASTER here, including documentation, data products architecture, the ASTER Directory, simulated images and databases.

Astronomical Data Analysis Software and Systems Conference Information

http://cadcwww.dao.nrc.ca/ADASS/adass.html

Detailed information is available at this site regarding the Astronomical Data Analysis Software and Systems (ADASS) Conference. ADASS is a discussion forum for scientists and programmers working with astronomical data. The conference consists of paper presentations, talks and poster sessions.

Astronomical Software on Linux

http://bima.astro.umd.edu/nemo/linuxastro/

A collection of pointers to astronomical software resources for Linux platforms, this server links to the linuxastro mailing list, as well as FTP archives containing software updates and releases

Canada-France-Hawaii Telescope Archive MOS Users' Manual

http://www.cfht.hawaii.edu/manuals/mos/mos_man.html

This site houses a users' manual for the CFHT Multi-Object Imaging Spectrograph (MOS). Technical and specific information is presented here,

including discussions of optical and mechanical layout, environment and performance, and control and data acquisition.

The Center for Advanced Spatial Technologies

http://www.cast.uark.edu/

The Center for Advanced Spatial Technologies of the University of Arkansas, Fayetteville develops Geographic Information Systems applications. Visit here to access its general information files, scientific databases and links to related organizations.

COMPTEL

http://cossc.gsfc.nasa.gov/cossc/COMPTEL.html

NASA operates COMPTEL, an Imaging Compton Telescope, at its Laboratory for High Energy Astrophysics. Visitors can learn about the instrument and access the data it collects at this site.

Computer Management Software Information Center

http://www.cosmic.uga.edu/

This site explains COSMIC, NASA's technology transfer center. Visitors will find a catalog of COSMIC's software offerings, plus program demos and technical support information.

European Southern Observatory-Munich Image Data Analysis System

http://www.hq.eso.org/midas-info/midas.html

The European Southern Observatory-Munich Image Data Analysis System provides general tools that facilitate image processing and data reduction for astronomical applications at this site.

Flexible Image Transport System Support Office

http://www.gsfc.nasa.gov/astro/fits/fits_home.html

The Flexible Image Transport System (FITS) Support Office home page provides general information, documents and software for use by astronomers for data interchange and archival storage. Includes a link to the Astrophysics Data Facility at NASA's Goddard Space Flight Center.

High Performance Computing Group Software Tools

http://hermes.astro.washington.edu:80/tools/

Software tools developed by the High Performance Computing and Communications Group at the University of Washington's Astronomy Department are available here. Among them are TIPSY (Theoretical Image Processing System) and FOF (``a friends-of-friends group finder for N-body simulations'').

Image Meteo

http://www.unige.ch/gap-e/met-inln.html

An image chart from the GAP-Energie in Switzerland is provided at this site, which is in French. A link to current conditions recorded by an Eppley solar tracker on the roof of the Atmospheric Sciences Research Center in Albany, New York, is also provided.

Image Reduction and Analysis Facility

http://iraf.noao.edu/

The Image Reduction and Analysis Facility is a software system that reduces and analyzes astronomical data. Visitors to this site will find an overview of the software created by the National Optical Astronomical Observatories.

Image Reduction and Analysis Facility Support Services

http://iraf.noao.edu/iraf-homepage.html

This site explains the National Optical Astronomy Observatories' general-purpose software system, which is used to analyze astronomical data. Includes IRAF documentation, newsletters and tutorials, along with a link to the National Science Foundation.

Infrared Processing and Analysis Center

http://iraf.noao.edu/iraf-homepage.html

This NASA site enlightens visitors by explaining the functions of the Infrared Processing and Analysis Center (IPAC), which carries out large-scale processing tasks for the infrared astronomy program. Included here are news items, information on projects and access to a science support center.

Laboratory for Computational Astrophysics

http://zeus.ncsa.uiuc.edu:8080/lca_home_page.html

The National Center for Supercomputer Applications and the Department of Astronomy at the University of Illinois at Urbana-Champaign develop and disseminate theoretical modeling software for astrophysics research. Visitors can read about their ongoing projects, including documentation and performance data.

Near Infra-Red Camera and Multi-Object Spectrometer

http://nicmosis.as.arizona.edu:8000/NICMOS.html

Astronomers and researchers can learn about the Near Infra-Red Camera and Multi-Object Spectrometer (NICMOS) at the University of Arizona through this site. It features a breakdown of the instrument, profiles the staff that runs the program and describes current research projects.

NEMO - A Stellar Dynamics Toolbox

http://bima.astro.umd.edu/nemo/

NEMO is described here as a "stellar dynamics toolbox" with "programs to create, integrate, analyze and visualize N-body and SPH like systems." Among the resources here are guides, tutorials, images, papers, installation information and other software.

Rutherford Appleton Laboratory's Starlink Project

http://star-www.rl.ac.uk/

This home page provides information on Rutherford Appleton Laboratory's Starlink Project, which is aimed at enabling astronomers' use of computers for data analysis. Includes information on hardware, software and support available through the organization.

RVSAO Radial Velocity Package for IRAF

http://tdc-www.harvard.edu/iraf/rvsao/rvsao.html

According to this page, the RVSAO Radial Velocity Package "is an IRAF add-on package developed at the Smithsonian Astrophysical Observatory Telescope Data Center to obtain radial velocities from spectra using cross-correlation and emission line fitting techniques." Find more information about the package at this site.

SKYMAP Astronomical Mapping Program

http://tdc-www.harvard.edu/software/skymap.html

The Smithsonian Astrophysical Observatory Telescope Data Center maintains this site for its SKYMAP astronomical mapping program. Visit here to plot and view maps of the heavens in a variety of formats.

Smithsonian Astrophysical Observatory Telescope Data Center

http://tdc-www.harvard.edu/TDC.html

The Smithsonian Astrophysical Observatory Telescope Data Center develops software to process and store data from several optical telescopes. Includes descriptions of software, as well as access to data sites and image galleries.

Smooth

http://hermes.astro.washington.edu:80/tools/SMOOTH/

Smooth is a program that calculates several mean quantities for all particles in an N-body simulation output file. This page has more information about Smooth, including new features and changes. The program is available from an anonymous FTP site linked to this page.

Space Telescope Science Data Analysis System

http://ra.stsci.edu/STSDAS.html

The Space Telescope Science Data Analysis System site contains information about this software for processing data from the Hubble Space Telescope. Includes downloading instructions, documentation and help.

WFPC 2 Home Page

http://www.stsci.edu/ftp/instrument_news/WFPC2/wfpc2_top.html

The Space Telescope Science Institute Web site contains instrument-specific information about the Wide Field and Planetary Camera 2, the projects involving the satellite astronomical device and a Frequently Asked Questions (FAQ) file. Includes links to images, documentation, software and other astronomical resources.

Richard L. White

http://sundog.stsci.edu/first/rick.html

Richard L. White of the Space Telescope Science Institute in Baltimore, Md., maintains his personal page with a pointer to the VLA FIRST Survey and resources on image compression and image restoration.

Xephem: An Astronomy Program for X Windows/Motif

http://iraf.noao.edu/~ecdowney/xephem.html

The home page of Xephem, an interactive astronomy program for Windows, provides detailed software documentation, descriptions of computational capabilities and specifications of graphics displays.

INDICES

ADS Abstract Service

http://adswww.harvard.edu/abs_doc/abs_help.html

ADS Abstract Service helps scientists sift through scientific astronomy papers by providing summaries of published works in a searchable database. Astronomy related publications from the past 20 years are indexed here.

Astro-FTP List

http://seds.lpl.arizona.edu/pub/faq/astroftp.html

The Astro-FTP List offers a collection of anonymous FTP file servers containing astronomy and space research materials. Find images and text files among the resources featured.

Astronomer's Bazaar

http://cdsweb.u-strasbg.fr/Cats.html

Located and maintained at France's University of Strasbourg Data Center, this page offers keyword access to an annotated list of astronomical data catalogs. Also find the Dictionary of Nomenclature of Celestial Objects, tables from "Astronomy & Astrophysics" and other topical links.

Astronomical Data Center

http://adc.gsfc.nasa.gov/

For access to astronomical data, visit the Astronomical Data Center, where guests can link to data in computer-readable form, download software, read ADC publications and information, or link to other space or astronomy sites.

Astronomy & Astrophysics on the Web

http://heasarc.gsfc.nasa.gov/docs/www_info/Webstars.html

Visitors to this page will find an extensive index of astronomy and astrophysics sites on the Internet. Links include the NASA home page and Hubble Space Telescope resources.

Astronomy and Space Science

http://info.er.usgs.gov/network/science/astronomy/index.html

As a service to the research community, the U.S. Geological Survey maintains this compiled registry of astronomy and space science pointers. Listed alphabetically, links lead to resources at institutions around the world.

Astronomy World Wide

http://www.strw.leidenuniv.nl/astroww.html

Initiated by astronomical institutions around the world, the AstroWeb provides a general index to astronomical information and resources on the Web. Also here are links to the Virtual Library and the U.S. Geological Survey general index.

Astrophysics and Space Plasma Physics Laboratory

http://www.rosat.mpe-garching.mpg.de/

The Astrophysics and Space Plasma Physics Laboratory site provides information on related databases, seminars and abstract services. Includes software descriptions and documentation as well as links to ROSAT group members.

Astrophysics Preprints

http://www.physics.mcmaster.ca/AstroPreprints.html

The Astrophysics Preprint page offers full text and tables from research abstracts. Typical titles include

Canadian Astronomy Data Centre

http://cadcwww.dao.nrc.ca/

The Herzberg Institute of Astrophysics houses the Canadian Astronomy Data Centre. From the CADC site, access a collection of astronomical data archives and observation catalogs. The CADC distributes data from the Hubble Space Telescope and the Canada France Hawaii Telescope.

Centre ISO, IAS, ORSAY

http://iscam1.ias.fr/

The home page of the Centre ISO Francais of the Insitute d'Astorphysique in Spatiale, Orsay, France is a French language site providing links to Internet astronomy resources.

Departement d'Astrophysique Extragalactique et de Cosmologie

http://gin.obspm.fr/e-index.html

The Departement d'Astrophysique Extragalactique et de Cosmologie, in Paris, France, offers access to its servers and information systems at this site. Find astronomical observation data presented in French, Portugese, Italian and English.

European Southern Observatory and the Space Telescope-European Coordinating Facility Archive

http://arch-http.hq.eso.org/ESO-ECF-Archive.html

The European Southern Observatory and the Space Telescope-European Coordinating Facility Archive page offers access to a large collection of astronomical resources. Find the ESO databases and the Hubble Space Telescope databases, plus astronomical catalogs and sky surveys.

Galactic Cepheid Database

http://ddo.astro.utoronto.ca/cepheids.html

Toronto's Galactic Cepheid Database contains four tables listing data on 504 cepheids. Hypertext links include an abstract, introduction, description of tables and references.

Galactic PNe Database Innsbruck

http://ast2.uibk.ac.at/

The Galactic PNe Database from the Institute of Astronomy at the University of Innsbruck includes the latest information about planetary nebulae. Visitors can search the database by name and link to the institute's home page.

Galaxy: Astronomy Science

http://galaxy.einet.net/galaxy/Science/Astronomy.html

This extensive index covers amateur astronomy, astronautics, astrophysics and observatories. Find articles, journals, image collections, databases, directories, institutions and more.

General Relativity Around the World

http://jean-luc.ncsa.uiuc.edu/World/world.html

The GR World home page is maintained by the NCSA Relativity Group and lists relativity sites around the world. Find pointers to relativity groups, plus physics, astronomy and supercomputing servers.

Goddard Institute for Space Studies

http://www.giss.nasa.gov/

This index site provides access to preprints and articles from an astronomical institute affiliated with the University of Virginia.

Guide to NASA Online Resources Web

http://nic.nasa.gov/nic/guide/

The National Aeronautics and Space Administration (NASA) posts an index of NASA and space related sites here. The page also includes a search tool.

High Energy Astrophysics Division FTP Archive

ftp://sao-ftp.harvard.edu/

Astronomers can download files regarding various projects at the Smithsonian Astrophysical Observatory from its High Energy Astrophysics Division anonymous FTP archive. Users can also retrieve related software here.

IPS Radio & Space Services

http://www.ips.oz.au/

IPS Radio & Space Services is a unit of the Australian Government Department of Administrative Services. Visitors to this site will find links to various observatories, consulting services, and educational material. There is also a multimedia tour of nine planets and a glossary of solar-terrestrial terms.

Langley Distributed Active Archive Center

http://eosdis.larc.nasa.gov/

The National Aeronautics and Space Administration stores scientific data on radiation, clouds, aerosols and tropospheric chemistry at the Langley Distributed Active Archive Center. Researchers can freely download data sets from this NASA site.

Langley Technical Report Server

http://techreports.larc.nasa.gov/ltrs/ltrs.html

The Langley Research Center of the U.S. National Aeronautics and Space Administration posts technical reports at this site. Browse its index of abstracts and citations from the past 10 years or search by keyword.

Leicester Database and Archives Service

http://ledas-www.star.le.ac.uk/

The home page of the Leicester Database and Archives Service, located in the Department of Physics and Astronomy at the University of Leicester in the U.K. features an online user guide and links to related databases and services.

Mike Boschat's Astronomy Page

http://www.atm.dal.ca/~andromed/

Astronomer Michael Boschat of the John F. Kennedy Astronomy Observatory provides an extensive alphabetical index of links to hundreds of astronomical sites and resources on the Internet.

NASA Astrophysics Data System Abstract Service

http://adswww.harvard.edu/abstract_service.html

NASA's Astrophysics Data System Abstract Service hosts this interactive site allowing visitors to search for abstracts of articles on astrophysics, space instrumentation, physics and geophysics by author, title, object names, keywords or abstract words.

NASA Hot Topics

http://www.nasa.gov/nasa/nasa_hottopics.html

NASA's Hot Topics page is a selection of the best links for any particular day's events at NASA. Visitors can link to an interesting array of NASA projects and sites here.

NASA Information by Subject

http://www.nasa.gov/nasa/nasa_subjects/nasa_subjectpage.html

This is the home page for NASA Web information and links organized by subject. This page is most likely incomplete and is subject to frequent changes and updates.

NASA International Space Agencies Index

http://www.nasa.gov/nasa/other_agencies.html

This National Aeronautics and Space Administration (NASA) site provides links to other space agencies around the world.

NASA Network Applications and Information Center

http://nic.nasa.gov/nic/

The challenge of NASA's Network Applications and Information Center is to assist the public in accessing NASA resources. Visitors to the center's home page can learn more about NAIC, or they move to the services area and directly access NASA's information and photo files.

NASA Office of Procurement

http://www.dfrc.nasa.gov/Procure/NPSE/

The Office of Procurement for the U.S. National Aeronautics and Space Administration maintains this site for its synopses search engine. Visit here to perform a keyword search of procurement synopses, including a variety of query options to tailor your information request.

NASA Online Information

http://mosaic.larc.nasa.gov/nasaonline/nasaonline.html

The National Aeronautics and Space Administration posts volumes of data online at different Internet sites. The NASA Online Information page provides a directory to the maze of electronically accessible resources provided by the government's space research and development arm.

Network Resources for Astronomers

http://www.hq.eso.org/online-resources-paper/rrn.html

A document prepared by the Astronomical Society of the Pacific, this page promises an overview of astronomical resources available on the Web and basic descriptions of each. Paper preprints, astronomical archives and related software are among the resources indexed here.

Nicolaus Copernicus Astronomical Center

http://www.ncac.torun.pl/

This page provides information on the Nicolaus Copernicus Astronomical Center, its projects, staff and upcoming seminars. Includes links to other Polish and international astronomy home pages .

Observatories and Astronomical Institutions

http://sousun1.phys.soton.ac.uk/Institutions.html

A comprehensive index of astronomy institutions and observatories on the World Wide Web is provided at this site. Visitors may also follow links to related Web sites and resources.

The Observatorium - NASA Remote Sensing Public Access Center

http://www.rspac.ivv.nasa.gov/

NASA provides public access to its earth and space data at this site. Features include an exhibit hall filled with images and data about Earth and the universe, as well as a technology park, offering an in-depth look at science, remote sensing and information technology.

The Planetary Rings Node

http://ringside.arc.nasa.gov/

This NASA site is dedicated to archiving and disseminating information on planetary ring systems. Includes links to animations, images and scientific data sets.

Resources on Astronomy, World Wide Web

http://heasarc.gsfc.nasa.gov/docs/www_info/genastro.html

This index of online astronomy information provides a comprehensive listing of astronomical re-

sources. This gateway links the user to textbooks, images and info on comets, meteors, the solar system and observatories, including WebStars and the Royal Greenwich Observatory.

Southampton University Astronomy Group

http://sousun1.phys.soton.ac.uk/

Discover a diverse collection of astronomy-related resources at the Southampton University Astronomy Group home page. The sampling emphasizes UK-based sites and pages of academic interest.

The Space Digest FTP

ftp://isu.isunet.edu/pub/space/policy

The Space Digest mailing list posts archives of its messages here.. Once a mailing list for all space-related topics, it has split into several lists dealing with space policy, the space shuttle, space news and more.

Space Mission Acronym List and Hyperlink Guide

http://ranier.oact.hq.nasa.gov/Sensors_page/MissionLinks.html

Visitors to this Web site can get the lowdown on NASA acronyms and the missions for which they stand. Browse an alphabetical listing of NASA projects, with a special emphasis on robotic science missions. Includes links to numerous NASA pages.

University College London Starlink

http://www.star.ucl.ac.uk/

The University College London presents a collection of links to Internet accessible astronomical information, tools and research sites. Find pointers to preprint archives, observatory home pages and software applications here.

The Virtual Library: Aerospace

http://macwww.db.erau.edu/www_virtual_lib/aerospace.html

An extensive index of aerospace information and resources available online is provided here by the World Wide Web Virtual Library. Visitors can link to listings of images, museums, publications, NASA space centers and more from this comprehensive site.

The World-Wide Web Virtual Library: Aerospace

http://macwww.db.erau.edu/www_virtual_lib/aeronautics.html

The Aerospace section of the World Wide Web Virtual Library provides a comprehensive guide to aeronautics and space information resources on the Internet. From electronic museums to research databases, this site compiles links and organizes them into easily navigable subject categories for lay users and scientists alike.

The WWW Virtual Library: Astronomy and Astrophysics

http://www.w3.org/pub/DataSources/
bySubject/astro/Overview.html

The Worldwide Web Virtual Library provides this index to astronomy and astrophysics sites. The index was compiled from the popular AstroWeb collection.

INDUSTRY NEWS

American Astronomical Society Job Register

http://www.aas.org/JobRegister/aasjobs.html

Out of work or on the move astronomers can peruse job openings at the American Astronomical Society Job Register. Find a comprehensive listing of academic professional faculty and research positions at this site.

NASA News

http://www.cs.indiana.edu:800/finger/
space.mit.edu/nasanews/w

This NASA news service, sponsored by MIT's Center for Space Research, offers bulletins and current news from the American space center, updated daily. Visitors can get the latest info on NASA projects from mission status reports to launch forecasts.

NASA Newsletters Gopher Menu

http://cass.jsc.nasa.gov/newsletters/lpib/

Maintained by NASA's Lunar and Planetary Institute (LPI), this Web site offers access to archived newsletters. Visitors can follow links back to the LPI home page.

NASA Newsroom

http://www.gsfc.nasa.gov/hqpao/
newsroom.html

Keep up with current U.S. space activity, policies and research at the National Aeronautics and Space Administration (NASA) Newsroom. Monitor current missions, press releases and daily internal news.

NASA Space Calendar

http://newproducts.jpl.nasa.gov/calendar/

Maintained by a U.S. National Aeronautics and Space Administration astronomer, the Space Calendar provides information about space-related activities and anniversaries for the coming year. Visit this site to find out about past, present and future celestial happenings, such as meteor showers, satellite launches, and other events.

NASA Television on CU-SeeMe

http://btree.lerc.nasa.gov/NASA_TV/NASA_
TV.html

The U.S. National Aeronautics and Space Administration rebroadcasts television coverage using

CU-SeeMe, a point to point, multiplatform videoconferencing software. Visitors can view a demo of NASA television, locate pointers to video reflectors in Europe and the U.S., or link to pretaped images.

New Space Network

http://www.newspace.com/

The New Space Network is "an information clearinghouse for anyone interested in small and low cost space programs." If you didn't know there was such a thing as a low cost space program, you haven't been following the latest developments in satellite technology, the European and Japanese space programs, and domestic rocketry. This tech-heavy site has links to many contractors, publications, and research organizations.

Solar Forecast

http://www.sel.noaa.gov/forecast.html

The Current Solar Forecast, a collaborative effort of the U.S. Department of Commerce, NOAA, Space Environment Center and the U.S. Air Force, provides a day-by-day report and forecast of solar and geophysical activity.

SPACEWARN Bulletin

http://nssdc.gsfc.nasa.gov/spacewarn/
spacewarn.html

Providing up-to-date info on satellites and space probes, the monthly bulletins archived at this official NASA site—maintained by the agency1s National Space Science Data Center—list launch dates and describe missions undertaken by international organizations

Today @ NASA

ttp://www.hq.nasa.gov/office/pao/NewsRoom/
today.html

Visitors can follow the latest NASA efforts here. The extensive site includes images from the Hubble Telescope, the latest news from Galileo's probe into Jupiter's atmosphere and an index to archived images and movies. Browsers can track space shuttle missions here, too.

INSTITUTES AND UNIVERSITY DEPARTMENTS

Alaska Space Grant Program

http://asgp.uafsoe.alaska.edu/

The Alaska Space Grant Program (ASGP) sponsors programs related to teaching, research and educational outreach in aerospace-related disciplines. Its site includes information on the program and research projects. Includes links to the Alaska Teachers Resource Manual and the International Space University.

APS Home Page

http://isis.spa.umn.edu/homepage.aps.html

The University of Minnesota maintains this online astronomical catalog. Visitors can learn about the collection of automated plate scanner-digitized images derived from the Palomar Observatory Sky Survey or read online science papers at this site.

Astronomical Observatory at the University of Copenhagen

http://www.astro.ku.dk/

The Astronomical Observatory is part of the Niels Bohr Institute at the University of Copenhagen, Denmark. Explore academic programs and research opportunities in instrument construction, observational astronomy and theoretical astrophysics here.

Astronomy and Astrophysics in Jena

http://www.astro.uni-jena.de/

The Astronomy & Astrophysics in Jena page lets browsers select between information about the Max Plank Society or the Institute for Astrophysics/University Observatory. The page provides links to star-related workshops, publications and other related resources.

Astronomy and Astrophysics Research at QMW

http://starsun7.ph.qmw.ac.uk/physics/

Astronomy and astrophysics research at Queen Mary and Westfield College at the University of London is explained in detail on this home page. The site includes pictures and data from recent observations along with information on postgraduate research opportunities.

Astronomy at the University of Texas, Austin

http://www.as.utexas.edu/

The University of Texas offers both general astronomy information and specific facts about its astronomy degree program at the Department of Astronomy home page. Review research programs and educational resources here.

Astronomy Department of Bologna University

http://www.bo.astro.it/dip/DepHome.html

The Astronomy Department at Universita Di Bologna maintains its home page with access to library documentation, archives, the departmental phone book and astrophysical preprints. Information on the school's observatory and links to personal home pages are also available. In Italian and English.

Astronomy Department Home Page

http://www.astro.lsa.umich.edu/

The University of Michigan Astronomy Department Home Page contains descriptions of course and degree programs at the university as well as links to astronomy-related resources and campus observatories.

Astronomy Faculty and Research

http://astrosun.tn.cornell.edu/faculty/faculty.html

Cornell University provides a complete listing of faculty and research staff in the Astronomy Department. Includes links to research projects and faculty publications.

Astronomy-VUB

http://www.vub.ac.be/STER/ster.html

The Astronomy Server of the Vrije Universiteit Brussel features information about the Astronomy Department's staff and research, as well as links to observatories, newsletters, journals and more.

Bradford University Engineering in Astronomy

http://www.eia.brad.ac.uk/

Bradford University in England presents the home page for its Engineering in Astronomy (EIA) Department. Visitors can operate an interactive telescope via the Web, link to other remote hardware that can be controlled over the Web or read descriptions of research projects within the EIA Department.

Bristol University's Astrophysics Group

http://nike.phy.bris.ac.uk:80/~phwjl/

Bristol University's Astrophysics Group includes regular news updates and information about current research on its home page. Visitors can also check out the group's personnel. Although it was under construction when we last checked, it promises links to other astronomy sites as well.

Brown University Astronomy Group

http://www.physics.brown.edu/astro/

The Astronomy Group at Brown University provides information on course offerings, faculty profiles and observatories here. The site also includes a collection of images from Brown's observatories.

California Institute of Technology Space Radiation Laboratory

http://www.srl.caltech.edu/

The California Institute of Technology's Space Radiation Laboratory offers visitors a look at its research projects in high energy and computational astrophysics. Links to departmental publications, seminar and personnel information, and related sites are also featured.

Cambridge Astronomy

http://www.ast.cam.ac.uk/

The astronomy department at England's Cambridge University maintains this informational site. Visit here to link to its astronomy facilities

and related projects and organizations. Includes information about the university as well.

Canary Islands Institute of Astrophysics

http://www.iac.es/

Tour of the Canary Islands Institute of Astrophysics: its headquarters, research center and observatory in Tenerife, and the observatory in La Palma. Links to weather, photos, software, events and other topic-related information can also be found. In Spanish and English.

Center for Advanced Space Studies Online

http://cass.jsc.nasa.gov/CASS_home.html

Visitors to this home page can learn about the Universities Space Research Association's (USRA) Houston-based research and conference facility. Includes online publications, links to the center's three divisions and astronomy-related conference listings.

Center for Atmospheric and Space Sciences

http://www.cass.usu.edu/

Utah State University presents the home page for its Center for Atmospheric and Space Sciences. Visitors will find an overview of academic programs, research and faculty.

Cornell University Department of Astronomy

http://astrosun.tn.cornell.edu/Home.html

The Cornell University Department of Astronomy Web site contains information about Cornell's undergraduate and graduate programs of study, research projects and journals. Visitors here can also hook up with astronomical organizations and link up to several observatories.

Delft University of Technology Space Research and Technology Section

http://dutlru8.lr.tudelft.nl/

The Space Research and Technology Section at the Netherlands' Delft University of Technology does orbit computation, gravity field modeling and GPS processing. This site features more information about the section's research.

Faint Object Spectrograph Group at the University of California-San Diego

http://cassfos01.ucsd.edu:8080/fos.html

The University of California at San Diego offers an overview of the Hubble Space Telescope's Faint Object Spectrograph (FOS) here, including a history of its development and the UCSD FOS Team involvement. Access the team's scientific papers and notes, and view images which "prove the existence of [a] massive black hole."

Five College Astronomy Department

http://www-astro.phast.umass.edu/

The Astronomy Program at the University of Massachusetts, Amherst, maintains this home page with information about its graduate program, faculty and research. A link to its scientific data archives with departmental preprints is available.

Florida Institute of Technology School of Aeronautics

http://sci-ed.fit.edu/soa/soa.html

The highlights of this site from the Florida Institute of Technology's School of Aeronautics include an updated Florida radar image, a Central Florida four-day forecast and the national weather outlook. Also included is information about the school's programs and facilities.

Florida Tech Physics and Space Sciences

http://pss.fit.edu/

The Florida Tech Physics and Space Sciences Department home page contains information on programs of study, admissions guidelines and faculty profiles. Includes links to research groups, other campus servers and related resources.

Friedrich-Schiller-University Jena Faculty of Physics, Astronomy and Technical Sciences

http://www.physik.uni-jena.de/

The Faculty of Physics, Astronomy and Technical Sciences at the Friedrich-Schiller-University Jena offers a wealth of information about its institutes, research, education and administration. Also find topic-related links. In English and German.

Galactic PNe Database Innsbruck

http://ast2.uibk.ac.at/

The Galactic PNe Database from the Institute of Astronomy at the University of Innsbruck includes the latest information about planetary nebulae. Visitors can search the database by name and link to the institute's home page.

Georgia State University Astronomy Department

http://www.chara.gsu.edu/

Atlanta's Georgia State University Astronomy Department offers an online tour of its research facilities and library of publications here. At this site, Stargazers can explore galaxies or opportunities for graduate study.

Herzberg Institute of Astrophysics

http://www.dao.nrc.ca/

The National Research Council of Canada's Herzberg Institute of Astrophysics operates and administers astronomical observatories maintained by the government of Canada. Visit this site for information about HI subdivisions and related facilities.

Imperial College Space and Atmospheric Physics Group

http://www.sp.ph.ic.ac.uk

The Space and Atmospheric Physics Group at Imperial College in London, England maintains a Web site with information about the university and research activities. Includes links to space-related resources and information about the city of London.

Indiana University Astronomy Department

http://astrowww.astro.indiana.edu/

Indiana University's Astronomy Department page offers information on the faculty, courses of study and facilities. This site also features a multimedia solar system tour, as well as links to other topical sites.

Institut de Radio Astronomie Millimetrique

http://iram.fr/

Research in millimeter astronomy is performed by IRAM, the Institut de Radio Astronomie Millimetrique. Link to IRAM sites in Germany, France and Spain or download astronomical software here.

Institute for Astronomy at the University of Hawaii

http://www.ifa.hawaii.edu/

The University of Hawaii's Institute for Astronomy performs research in astrophysics and planetary science, and maintains a number of local observatory facilities. Visit this site for information about its programs, observatories, faculty and st

Institute for Astronomy Innsbruck On-Line Information System

http://ast7.uibk.ac.at/

The University of Innsbruck, Austria, presents the home page for its Institute for Astronomy. Visitors will find information on the facility's faculty, research and astronomical imaging activities. Available in English and German.

Institute of Geophysics and Planetary Physics at the University of California-Los Angeles

http://www.igpp.ucla.edu/

The Institute of Geophysics and Planetary Physics at the University of California in Los Angeles gives an overview of its research and the four centers it houses. Visitors can also download IGPP publications from this site.

Instituto de Astrofísica de Canarias Home Page

http://www.iac.es/home.html

Spain's Instituto Astrofisica de Canarias shares the view from its Canary Islands observatory at this site. can share the view with Canary Islands, at this site. Stargazers can link to reports of the facility's latest news, discoveries and publications here.

Inter-University Centre for Astronomy and Astrophysics

http://iucaa.iucaa.ernet.in/

India's Inter-University Centre for Astronomy and Astrophysics pools the intellectual and technical resources of the country's universities in order to improve research efforts in the field. Visitors can access publications, research groups and degree program info.

Iowa State University Department of Physics and Astronomy

http://www.public.iastate.edu/~astro/

Stargazers looking to make astronomy their profession may review the academic degree programs and research opportunities at the Iowa State University Department of Physics and Astronomy. Visitors will find a general overview of the department, its faculty and recent publications.

Istituto di Tecnologie e Studio delle Radiazioni Extraterrestri

http://www.tesre.bo.cnr.it/

Bologna's Consiglio Nazionale delle Ricerche Istituto di Tecnologie e Studie delle Radiazioni Extraterrestri maintains this overview of its facilities and activities. The site also features Internet and local links. In Italian and English.

The Kapteyn Institute Information Server

http://kapteyn.astro.rug.nl/

The Kapteyn Institute encompasses the Department of Astronomy of Groningen University, the Kapteyn Observatory and the Laboratory of the Space Research Organization Netherlands. This site provides information about the institute and links to its astronomical software.

Leeds University Astrophysics

http://ast.leeds.ac.uk/

Visitors to the Astrophysics at Leeds University site will find links to three research groups at the university, as well as to other related pages.

Leonardo Bronfman

http://ctiot6.ctio.noao.edu/~rtel/lbronfman.html

This page from the faculty directory of the University of Chile's Astronomy Department spotlights Leonardo Bronfman.

Lunar and Planetary Institute

http://cass.jsc.nasa.gov/lpi.html

Located in Houston at the USRA Center for Advanced Space Studies, the Lunar and Planetary Institute maintains this page for general information and data access. Visitors can learn about the institute, review its schedule of meetings and conferences, or search its catalogs and collections.

Max-Planck Institute for Astronomy

http://www.mpia-hd.mpg.de/

The Max-Planck Institute for Astronomy in Heidelberg is one of 68 Max-Planck Institutes in Germany. Visitors here will find a link to the institute, which specializes in astronomical research at optical and infrared wavelengths. The page also provides a link to the institute's observatory in Spain.

McGill University Earth and Planetary Sciences Department

http://stoner.eps.mcgill.ca/

The Earth and Planetary Sciences Department at Canada's McGill University maintains this site to introduce its people and programs. Visitors will find user home pages, graphic images, and other academic and administrative resources.

Michigan State University Physics and Astronomy Department

http://pads1.pa.msu.edu/

This home page provides visitors information about Michigan State University's Physics and Astronomy Department. Includes details about MSU's National Superconducting Cyclotron Laboratory and Abrams Planetarium, plus research information and online scientific publications.

Mississippi State University Department of Physics and Astronomy

http://www.msstate.edu/Dept/Physics/

Mississippi State University introduces the degree programs and research facilities offered by its Department of Physics and Astronomy at this site.

MIT Center for Space Research

http://space.mit.edu/

This is the Massachusetts Institute of Technolgy's Center for Space Research Web site. Visitors can learn about the many space-related research projects conducted by MIT faculty and students.

MIT EAPS Home Page

http://www-eaps.mit.edu/

This departmental site at the Massachusetts Institute of Technology focuses on earth, atmospheric and planetary academic disciplines, research groups, courses of study and faculty. Includes course descriptions, electronic class materials and links to related Web sites.

National Institute of Astrophysics, Mexico

http://www.inaoep.mx/

Mexico's National Institute of Astrophysics (IN-AOE) maintains this home page. The INAOE is a training and research institution founded at the site of the old Tonantzintla Observatory. Areas covered include astrophysics, optics and electronics.

National Undergraduate Research Observatory

http://nuro.phy.nau.edu/

The National Undergraduate Research Observatory is a consortium of undergraduate universities united to provide hands-on training and research work for students in order to encourage scientific careers. This page includes descriptions of research projects, an mage gallery and links to AstroWeb and other related sites.

Northern Arizona University Department of Physics and Astronomy

http://www.phy.nau.edu/

The Department of Physics and Astronomy at Northern Arizona University provides information here about its graduate and undergraduate programs. Links to related facilities and research organizations are also available here.

Northwestern University Graduate Programs

http://www.astro.nwu.edu/astro/grad/intro.html

Northwestern University's graduate programs in physics and astronomy are detailed on this page. Features include outlines of academic programs, descriptions of research facilities and highlights of current research projects.

Northwestern University Physics & Astronomy

http://www.astro.nwu.edu/

The Physics & Astronomy Department at Northwestern University, Evanston Ill., maintains this home page with information about the department, its research, courses and students. Links to related sites are available.

Northwestern University Undergraduate Physics and Astronomy

http://www.astro.nwu.edu/astro/undergrad/intro.html

The Department of Physics and Astronomy at Northwestern University maintains this overview of its undergraduate programs. Site features include info on courses, degree requirements, the honors programs, advanced placement and teaching certification

OSU Department of Astronomy Homepage

http://www-astronomy.mps.ohio-state.edu/

Ohio State University's Department of Astronomy home page connects visitors with information about the department's staff, events and the school's Astrophysics Theory Group. Also included: links to astronomy Internet sites and department faculty members' and graduate students' home pages.

Oxford University Astrophysics Department

http://www-astro.physics.ox.ac.uk/

The Astrophysics Department at England's Oxford University sponsors this informational and educational home page. Visitors can pick up a map of the stars, view photos of space, see the first light images from the Infra-Red camera installed at WHT, find out about ongoing research projects and upcoming colloquia or retire from the observatory and visit other sites on campus.

Penn State Astronomy and Astrophysics

http://www.astro.psu.edu/

The Department of Astronomy and Astrophysics at Pennsylvania State University maintains this home page with information about faculty, programs, research and students. Visitors can also link to the FTP archives, university services and astronomy-related Web sites.

Queen Mary & Westfield College Astronomy Unit Home Page

http://www.maths.qmw.ac.uk/~www/astro/home.html

The astronomy unit at Queen Mary & Westfield College at the University of London provides information on its research and postgraduate programs here. Also included are details on seminars, personnel, preprints and publications.

Rice University Space Physics and Astronomy

http://spacsun.rice.edu/

Rice University's Space Physics and Astronomy page introduces visitors to related academic departments and research facilities. Find general school information, check out courses offered, and get the latest scoop on current research.

Richard H. Durisen

http://www.astro.indiana.edu:80/personnel/durisen/

Providing contact and specialty information about a member of the Astronomy Department at Indiana University (IU) in Bloomington, this Web site also allows visitors to link to the department's home page.

Royal Melbourne Institute of Technology Aerospace Engineering Department

http://www.aero.rmit.edu.au/

The Aerospace Engineering Department of Australia's Royal Melbourne Institute of Technology (RMIT) maintains this page featuring a site map, facilities description and information on its postgraduate degree. Links to related sites on and off campus are also provided.

Saint Mary's University Astronomy and Physics

http://mnbsun.stmarys.ca/WWW/smu_home.html

The Astronomy and Astrophysics Department at St. Mary's University in Halifax, Nova Scotia maintains this overview of its department, academic programs and research. A calendar of events and links to related sites on and off campus are included.

Search for Extra-Terrestrial Intelligence Institute

http://www.seti-inst.edu/

Scientists engaged in the Search for Extra-Terrestrial Intelligence project publish their research strategies, goals and findings here on the SETI Insitute's home page. Visitors can link to researchers, investigators and summaries of current projects from this site.

SEDS Internet Party House

http://seds.lpl.arizona.edu/

Students for the Exploration and Development of Space, part of the Lunar and Planetary Laboratory at the University of Arizona, maintains this informational site. Visit here for club news, publications and an extensive collection of astronomy images and educational materials.

The Statistical Consulting Center for Astronomy

http://www.stat.psu.edu/scca/homepage.html

The Statistical Consulting Center for Astronomy at Pennsylvania State University, University Park, maintains this site of general information. Visit here to learn about its programs and people and to peruse its Frequently Asked Questions (FAQ) file.

The Sterrenkundig Institute

http://www.fys.ruu.nl/~wwwstk/

University, Holland. Visitors to this site will find research topics and resources, bibliographies, announcements and faculty information. Provided in English and Dutch.

SUNY Stony Brook - Earth and Space Sciences

http://sbast3.ess.sunysb.edu/home.html

At this site, the Department of Earth and Space Sciences at the State University of New York,

Stony Brook, provides academic information for future geologists, astronomers, physicists and other scientists.

Tel Aviv University School of Physics and Astronomy

http://star.tau.ac.il/

The home page of the School of Physics and Astronomy at Tel Aviv University offers visitors information on the school's research, seminars and personnel. Also find links to other departments at this Israeli institution.

Theoretical Astrophysics Program

http://lepton.physics.arizona.edu:8000/

Access the resources of the University of Arizona's theoretical astrophysics program at this site. Visit here to learn about the program and its people, view publications and related graphic images, and read about upcoming events.

University of Aarhus Institute of Physics and Astronomy

http://www.dfi.aau.dk/

The University of Aarhus Institute of Physics and Astronomy provides research and education opportunities to the Danish scientific community. Includes descriptions of educational programs, research groups and faculty.

University of Alabama Department of Physics and Astronomy

http://crux.astr.ua.edu/AstroHome.html

The Department of Physics and Astronomy at the University of Alabama, Tuscaloosa, maintains this home page with information about its astronomy program, faculty and research. Links to related sites are also available.

University of Arizona Department of Planetary Sciences

http://crux.astr.ua.edu/AstroHome.html

The University of Arizona's Department of Planetary Sciences and Lunar and Planetary Laboratory packs its home page with departmental information and various astronomy-related resources.

University of British Columbia Department of Geophysics and Astronomy

http://www.astro.ubc.ca/

The Department of Geophysics and Astronomy at the University of British Columbia, Canada, offers information about its courses, faculty and graduate program here. The page also contains links to related resources.

University of California-Berkeley Astronomy and Astrophysics

http://astro.berkeley.edu/home.html

This site introduces the University of California, Berkeley's astronomy and astrophysics programs

and research facilities. Academic department information, job listings and event schedules provided.

University of California-Irvine Department of Physics and Astronomy

http://www.ps.uci.edu/physics/

This home page from the University of California at Irvine Department of Physics and Astronomy features details on the 1995 Nobel Prize won by Prof. Frederick Reines. Also included here are newsletters, course Web sites, other university sites and information on faculty, graduate programs and the department observatory.

University of Chicago Astronomy and Astrophysics Department

http://astro.uchicago.edu/

This departmental home page links visitors to home pages created by faculty members and students at the University of Chicago's astronomy and astrophysics department. Includes staff and faculty listings, an online copy of the department's graduate brochure, and departmental news.

University of Colorado Department of Astrophysical, Planetary and Atmospheric Sciences

http://apas.colorado.edu/homepage.html

The Department of Astrophysical, Planetary and Atmospheric Sciences at the University of Colorado provides information on undergraduate and graduate courses of study, course descriptions and faculty profiles. Includes info on research, colloquia schedules and links to other campus servers.

University of Delaware Department of Physics and Astronomy

http://www.physics.udel.edu/

The University of Delaware presents this home page for its Department of Physics and Astronomy. Visitors will find details on upcoming colloquia and seminars here, in addition to course listings and an online brochure for the graduate program.

University of Hawaii Physics and Astronomy

http://www.phys.hawaii.edu/

This University of Hawaii physics and astronomy home page provides departmental information on coursework, financial aid and research specialties. Includes links to the school's Institute for Astronomy and main home pages.

University of Iowa Automated Telescope Facility

http://inferno.physics.uiowa.edu/

The Automated Telescope Facility at the University of Iowa maintains this site for general information about and access to its space images.

University of Iowa Physics and Astronomy

http://www.physics.uiowa.edu/

This site contains course offerings, profiles of faculty and a listing of their areas of research. Site features also include links to the physics library, specific research sites and access to research group Web pages.

University of Kansas Physics and Astronomy Department

http://www.phsx.ukans.edu/index.html

The Department of Physics and Astronomy of the University of Kansas provides information here on its student groups, research programs and academic materials. Visit this site to learn about the department and its research and career resources.

University of Manchester Astronomy Group

http://axp2.ast.man.ac.uk:8000/

The University of Manchester Astronomy Group details its graduate study and research programs, describes special educational projects and seminars, and provides links to its publications, journals and newsletters. Users can link to the univery's Astronomy Department, access staff home pages and zoom in on the facilties and other astronomical resources.

University of Manchester Astronomy Group Preprints

http://axp2.ast.man.ac.uk:8000/Preprints.html

The University of Manchester, England, presents these preprints of departmental research for its Astronomy Group. Here, visitors will find preliminary versions of astronomy articles before they go to press.

University of Manchester Department of Physics and Astronomy

http://mphhpc.ph.man.ac.uk:4321/

The Department of Physics and Astronomy at Britain's University of Manchester offers links to its undergraduate and post graduate program information as well as descriptions of its ongoing research projects. Links to other science and British servers are also available.

University of Massachusetts Astronomy Department

http://donald.phast.umass.edu/

Explore options for study at the University of Massachusetts Astronomy Department, or review current research facilities and projects at this site. Department Ph.D. theses are available for perusal, along with access to Internet-wide electronic astronomy resources.

University of Minnesota Astronomy Department

http://ast1.spa.umn.edu/

This is the home page for the University of Minnesota's Department of Astronomy. Visitors will find a department directory, undergraduate degree requirements, and an introduction to the Astronomy Graduate Program here.

University of Pennsylvania Department of Physics and Astronomy

http://dept.physics.upenn.edu/

The University of Pennsylvania Physics and Astronomy Department presents recent announcements pertaining to its educational programs and research projects. Includes access to research papers and links to related sites.

University of Pisa Astronomy and Astrophysics Section

http://astrpi.difi.unipi.it/

The Department of Physics at the University of Pisa, Italy, provides information here on its people and programs. Visit here for an overview of the department, scientific publication archives, links to other university departments and more.

University of St. Andrews School of Physics and Astronomy

http://star-www.st-and.ac.uk/physics/

The home page for the School of Physics and Astronomy at the United Kingdom's University of St. Andrews contains information on the undergraduate and graduate programs and departmental research groups. Also find a handful of pages with additional topical information.

University of Southampton Astronomy Group

http://sousun1.phys.soton.ac.uk/

Discover a diverse collection of astronomy-related resources at the Southampton University Astronomy Group home page. The sampling emphasizes UK-based sites and pages of academic interest.

University of Sussex Astronomy Center

http://star-www.maps.susx.ac.uk/index.html

This site provides information on research groups, staff, publications and other items of interest from the University of Sussex Astronomy Center. Includes links to other Sussex University sites and astronomical resources.

University of Thessaloniki Section of Astrophysics, Astronomy and Mechanics

http://www.astro.auth.gr/

The Section of Astrophysics, Astronomy and Mechanics at the Aristotle University of Thessaloniki, Greece, maintains this home page with information about its faculty, research, students and seminars. General astronomical information is also available here.

University of Toledo Department of Physics and Astronomy Homepage

http://www.physics.utoledo.edu/www/homepage.html

The Department of Physics and Astronomy at the University of Toledo provides information about the department, its academic programs, research projects and faculty. Includes hypertext links to related academic and research resources.

University of Toronto Department of Astronomy

http://www.astro.auth.gr/

For a view of the universe from western Canada, consult the University of Toronto Department of Astronomy home page. Explore scientific facilities, research activities and educational opportunities at this site.

University of Victoria Astronomy Home Page

http://info.phys.uvic.ca/uvphys_welcome.html

The Department of Physics and Astronomy of the University of Victoria, Canada, maintains this informational page about its astronomy program. Visit here to learn about current events, access educational resources and link to related Internet search resources.

University of Vienna Institute for Astronomy

http://venus.ast.univie.ac.at/

Visit this page to find AstroNetVienna, the Web server of the Institute for Astronomy at Austria's University of Vienna. Find a link to information about the institute's programs, activities and facilities. Also find links to a variety of astronomical resources. Some pages are in German.

University of Virginia Astronomy Home Page

http://venus.ast.univie.ac.at/

The University of Virginia's astronomy department home page allows visitors to take virtual tours of the McCormick and Fan Mountain Observatories. This site also includes details on the department's research activities, undergraduate and graduate coursework and programs, and contact information.

University of Washington Astronomy Department

http://www.astro.washington.edu/

The University of Washington introduces its Department of Astronomy's degree programs, research facilities and faculty accomplishments at this site. Find images of the department and campus as well as Pacific Northwest-related links.

University of Wisconsin - Madison Astronomy Department Home Page

http://www.astro.wisc.edu/

The University of Wisconsin-Madison Astronomy Department allows potential students to peruse graduate and undergraduate program information. There are also links to preprint, project and facility pages.

University of Wisconsin-Madison Space Science and Engineering Center

http://www.ssec.wisc.edu/

The University of Wisconsin-Madison's Space Science and Engineering Center offers a multidisciplinary approach to the study of space and science. Visitors will find data, research, library access and an excellent collection of space-related photos and films.

Utrecht University Faculty of Physics and Astronomy

http://www.fys.ruu.nl/Home_eng.html

Would-be physicists and astronomers can consider their options for studying in the Netherlands at the University of Utrecht after digesting the information presented here. Visitors can review the school's courses, departments and research facilities here. In Dutch and English.

Vassar College Physics and Astronomy

http://noether.vassar.edu/

The Department of Physics and Astronomy at Vassar College provides this overview of its academic programs. Links to faculty and staff, course requirements and listings, resources and related sites are featured.

Warsaw University Astronomical Observatory

http://www.astrouw.edu.pl/

Warsaw University's Astronomical Observatory maintains this site to provide access to its research network. Visit here for links to the Polish school's resources and related institutions.

Wayne State University Physics and Astronomy Department

http://www.physics.wayne.edu/

Wayne State University's Physics and Astronomy Department offers this Web site, providing a wealth of departmental info and pointers to other interesting online resources. A departmental newsletter, journals and links to home pages of faculty and students are among this site's features.

Wesleyan University Astronomy Department

http://sun.astro.wesleyan.edu/astro.html

The Wesleyan University Astronomy Department home page contains information on graduate and undergraduate courses of study, research projects and faculty profiles. Includes listings of publications and links to other campus servers.

Williams Astronomy and Astrophysics

http://albert.astro.williams.edu/

The Williams College (Massachusetts) Astronomy Department site contains an assortment of links covering various aspects of the department. Visitors will find information on faculty and staff, research projects, an online course catalog, and more.

JOURNALS AND PERIODICALS

AASTeX Author Package

http://www.aas.org/publications/aastex/

AASTeX, a text preparation utility for submissions to American Astronomical Society journals, can be accessed at this site. Visit here to download software and learn how to prepare articles, graphics and tables for the society's family of scientific publications.

Andrea Milani

http://adams.dm.unipi.it/~milani/homemilani.html

This home page, set up by an associate editor of "Celestial Mechanics and Dynamical Astronomy," lists his research interests and recent publications. Serious browsers can read scholarly papers about asteroids; not-so-serious visitors can link to science fiction sites.

Anton Pannekoek Preprints and Articles

http://www.astro.uva.nl/preprints/preprints.html

This index site provides access to preprints and articles from an astronomical institute affiliated with the University of Virginia.

The Astronomer Magazine

http://www.demon.co.uk/astronomer/

This online astronomy publication contains articles on a variety of astronomical subjects. Includes information on related software, images and subscription details.

The Astronomical Journal

http://www.astro.washington.edu/astroj/index.html

"The Astronomical Journal" is published by the American Institute of Physics in Woodbury, New York. Its site provides information on publication and contributor's guidelines, as well as preprint information.

Astronomy and Astrophysics Abstracts Service

http://cdsweb.u-strasbg.fr/Abstract.html

This interactive site features keyword search access to the abstracts from the "Astronomy and Astrophysics" main journal and supplemental series. This service is provided by the Strasbourg astronomical Data Center (CDS) in France.

The Astrophysical Journal

http://www.journals.uchicago.edu/Apj/

The Astrophysical Journal is published three times a month for the American Astronomical Society. It posts its latest issue online here, as well as submissions directions. The page also contains titles and abstracts of submissions accepted but not yet published.

The Astrophysical Journal Letters

http://www.noao.edu/apjl/apjl.html

The American Astronomical Society publishes The Astrophysical Journal three times a month. Visit here for the electronic letters from the journal, an index of papers submitted, and titles and abstracts of letters accepted but not yet published.

The Astrophysical Journal Supplement Series

http://www.noao.edu/apjsup/apjsup.html

Extensive astronomical data collections and articles are published monthly in the form of the Astrophysical Journal Supplement Series. Review online editions of these complete reports of scientific investigations and calculations at this site.

The Be Star Newsletter

http://www.chara.gsu.edu/BeNews/intro.html

The "Be Star" newsletter is a "non-refereed" electronic and paper journal, published about twice a year. Articles include observations, theory and news concerning "early-type stars ... especially hot, near main-sequence stars." The goal is "to foster communication between researchers interested in this field of stellar astronomy."

Earth and Sky

http://www.neosoft.com/internet/paml/groups.E/earth_and_sky.html

This online publication, available by mailing list, deals weekly with earth science and astronomy.

Galileo Messenger Issue 34

http://www.jpl.nasa.gov/gllmess/Mess34TOC.html

Take a look at the latest electronic version of the Galileo Messenger for articles on astronomers, comets, satellites and everything cosmic. Readers can view and download images or catch up on the back issues of the publication at the archive site.

George Musser, Jr.

http://astrosun.tn.cornell.edu/students/musser/musser.html

George Musser, Jr. used to be a graduate student in the Department of Astronomy at Cornell University. He is now the editor of "Mercury," an astronomy magazine. His personal home page details his interests, publications and contact information.

Journal Query Form for ADS Articles

http://adsabs.harvard.edu/article_service.html

This interactive page contains a form to query astrophysical journals for articles. An online help option aids first time users.

Langley Technical Report Server

http://techreports.larc.nasa.gov/ltrs/ltrs.html

The Langley Research Center of the U.S. National Aeronautics and Space Administration posts technical reports at this site. Browse its index of abstracts and citations from the past 10 years or search by keyword.

Leeds University Optical Astronomy Group Publications

http://ast.leeds.ac.uk/papers/papers.html

Publications of the Optical Astronomy Group (OAG) at Leeds University in the United Kingdom are available at this site. Visitors can request preprints, read abstracts and link to

Mount Stromlo and Siding Spring Observatories - Preprints

http://msowww.anu.edu.au/preprints/preprints.html

The observatory at Australian National University makes preprints of scientific papers available through this Web site. The index is organized by author.

National Radio Astronomy Observatory Library

http://a2z.lycos.com/Science_and_Technology/Space_and_Astronomy/Journals_and_Periodicals/#J

The library of the National Radio Astronomy Observatory supplies an online catalog as well as a searchable index of preprints and published papers. There also is information on future and past meetings, conferences and workshops, plus pointers to other preprint services, published papers and other astronomy resources.

1995 Young European Radio Astronomers Conference

http://www.cup.cam.ac.uk/onlinepubs/YERAC/YERACtop.html

This cover page provides an introduction to the electronic publication of the papers presented at the 1995 Young European Radio Astronomers Conference. A link to the publisher, Cambridge University Press, is included.

Papers Submitted to North American Astronomical Publications

http://www.noao.edu/apj/ypages/yp.html

This searchable site contains listings of papers submitted to North American astronomical journals. Listings include titles, authors and dates of submission, plus information on obtaining preprints.

Princeton Observatory Preprints

http://astro.princeton.edu/~library/prep.html

This Web site archives preprints of Princeton Observatory publications. Visitors can read abstracts or download PostScript versions of the documents here.

Sacramento Peak Observatory Preprint Library

http://www.sunspot.noao.edu/index.html

The Sacramento Peak Observatory offers online access to its preprints here. On our last visit, preprint topics included "Probing the Depths of Sunspots," and "Observations of Active Region Dynamics: Preflare Flows and Field Observations."

Space Telescope Science Institute Library

http://sesame.stsci.edu/library.html

Researchers can check out published papers and preprints at the Space Telescope Science Institute Library. Physicists and astronomers will find academic journals, data sets and links to other online libraries.

Stephen Morris

http://www.dao.nrc.ca/DAO/STAFF/morris.html

Dr. Stephen Morris is one of the staffers at the Dominion Astrophysical Observatory, part of the Canadian Hertzberg Institute of Astrphysics. His personal home page lists his recent publications, research interests and contact information.

University of Wisconsin, Madison Astronomy Department Preprints

http://www.astro.wisc.edu/~astrolib/Preprints.html

Visitors to this site will find access to preprints from the Astronomy Department at the University of Wisconsin, Madison.

The Virtual Review

http://www.het.brown.edu/physics/review/index.html

The Virtual Review is an online magazine of physics and astronomy academic research papers.

NEWSGROUPS

Usenet Newsgroup sci.astro.research

http://xanth.msfc.nasa.gov/xray/sar.html

This is the Web page for the Usenet newsgroup sci.astro.research. Visitors will discover discussions concerning the astronomical sciences, NASA projects and missions as well as a link to the FTP archive.

OBSERVATORIES

AFRICA

South African Astronomical Observatory

http://da.saao.ac.za/

The South African Astronomical Observatory is a research facility located at the Cape of Good Hope, South Africa. Visitors will find an overview of the organization, research projects and facilities.

ASIA

Earth Observation Center, Japan

http://hdsn.eoc.nasda.go.jp/

Japan's Earth Observation Center offers this overview of its activities and resources. Access information on the center's satellites and operations, plus other items of related interest. In Japanese and English.

Korea Astronomy Laboratory

http://hanul.issa.re.kr/

Information about the Korea Astronomy Observatory's research members is featured here. There also are pointers to two other observatories that are divisions of KAO, as well as to newsgroups, FTP servers, gopher servers, weather charts and newsletters.

AUSTRALIA/OCEANIA

A.A.O. Home Page

http://www.aao.gov.au/

The Anglo-Australian Observatory (AAO) in northwest New South Wales, Australia, operates two telescopes at the edge of Warrumbungle National Park. Visitors can view images from the telescope, read further information about AAO, or link to other astronomy-related sites on the Web.

Grove Creek Observatory

http://www.netsys.com/-steven/index.html

This site is a virtual tour of the Grove Creek Observatory in Australia. Features include introductory information, an image gallery, news groups and links to other astronomy-related Web sites.

Mount Stromlo and Siding Spring Observatories

http://meteor.anu.edu.au/home.html

This site features Australia's Mount Stromlo and Siding Spring Observatories. Visitors are welcome to access the astronomy database, as well as learn more about the observatory, its people, publications and projects.

Parkes Observatory and Parkes Radiotelescope Home Page

http://wwwpks.atnf.csiro.au/

Australia's Parkes Observatory welcomes 55,000 visitors a year to "the world's most beautiful radiotelescope" and that's not counting virtual visitors. Its Web site offers photos, updates on research projects, and surveys and databases.

EUROPE

Arcetri Astronomical Observatory

http://www.arcetri.astro.it/Inglese/index.html

The Arcetri Astronomical Observatory in Italy provides general information about the observatory's facilities, its research and educational programs. Includes links to technical reports, libraries and related resources.

Armagh Observatory Welcome Page

http://star.arm.ac.uk/

Northern Ireland's Armagh Observatory posts planetarium news and the observatory's preprint series at this site. There are also links to other Irish sites of interest to astronomers.

Astronomical Observatory at the University of Copenhagen

http://www.astro.ku.dk/

The Astronomical Observatory is part of the Niels Bohr Institute at the University of Copenhagen, Denmark. Explore academic programs and research opportunities in instrument construction, observational astronomy and theoretical astrophysics here.

Astronomical Observatory, Jagiellonian University

http://www.oa.uj.edu.pl/

Jagiellonian University's Cracow Observatory page contains general information about the facility, departments and research groups. Includes a history of the observatory, publications and personnel directory.

Bologna Astronomical Observatory

http://www.bo.astro.it/

Bologna Astronomical Observatory in Italy maintains this home page offering general astronomy info, as well as details on the BAO observatories and facilities.

CDS, Strasbourg

http://cdsweb.u-strasbg.fr/CDS-f.html

Located at France's Strasbourg Astronomical Observatory, the Data Center collects and distributes astronomical and related data. Visitors to its Web site can access the SIMBAD astronomical database, the recognized reference database for identifying astronomical objects. In French, English, German, Spanish and Italian.

Deep Near Infrared Survey of the Southern Sky (DENIS)

http://denisexg.obspm.fr/

DENIS will be a deep, complete survey of the astronomical sources of the southern sky in two near-infrared bands and one optical band simultaneously, using a 1-meter, ground-based telescope. This page from Observatoire de Paris-Meudon features papers, pictures and instrument gallery and more.

ESO On-Line Information System

http://www.hq.eso.org/

The European Southern Observatory (ESO) home page contains descriptions of facilities at ESO, links to observatory archives, information of educational programs and press releases. Includes listings of publications, observation schedules and details of past and current research projects.

Haute-Provence Astronomical Observatory

http://www.obs-hp.fr/

France's Haute-Provence Observatory maintains this site to introduce its facilities and programs. Visit here to learn about its instrumentation and capabilities, read related publications and find events schedules. In French.

Institute of Radio Astronomy of Bologna: NOTO VLBI Station

http://akrai.ira.noto.cnr.it/

This observatory site contains information on research activities, staff and technical descriptions of the facility. Includes listings of Italian servers and related astronomy sites.

Konkoly Observatory

http://ogyalla.konkoly.hu/

The Hungarian Academy of Sciences' Konkoly Observatory home page offers information about the astronomical center's history, facilities and research projects. Visitors also can access the "Information Bulletin on Variable Stars" and observatory publications.

The Loiano Telescopes

http://www.bo.astro.it/loiano/LoianoHome.html

The Loiana Telescopes site provides information on the educational programs, research and staff of the astronomical research facility and its equipment. Includes detailed descriptions of the telescopes, observations and links to relevant publications.

Lund Observatory

http://nastol.astro.lu.se/Html/home.html

Sweden's Lund Observatory maintains this site with information on the facility, staff and projects, and astronomy. Visitors can learn more about the Nordic Optical Telescope, view images and peruse scientific and research data. In English and Swedish.

Mullard Radio Astronomy Observatory

http://www.mrao.cam.ac.uk/

The Mullard Radio Astronomy Observatory at the University of Cambridge, England, maintains this Web site with updates on current projects. There is also information on the observatory's telescopes and reports from astronomy conferences.

Onsala Space Observatory

http://www.oso.chalmers.se/

This is the home page of the Onsala Space Observatory, a national observer facility for Radio Astronomy at the Chalmers University of Technology. Read about telescope observations, space geodesy, geodynamics and satellites here or link to the home pages of associated institutions.

Osservatorio Astronomico di Torino

http://otoxd2.to.astro.it/

The Osservatorio Astonomico Di Torino in Italy offers information here about its research, staff, projects, services, and network resources. Links are also available to astronomical preprints and the Window on Italy page.

Roque de Los Muchachos Observatory

http://www.iac.es/folleto/orm.html

The Roque de Los Muchachos Observatory on the Island of La Palma hosts this site highlighting its William Herschel Telescope. Learn more about the observatory's projects and research, as well as the Instituto de Astrofisica de Canarias, its parent organization.

ROSAT GOF

http://heasarc.gsfc.nasa.gov/docs/rosat/rosgof.html

The Roentgen Satellite (ROSAT) is an X-ray observatory developed by Germany, the U.K. and the U.S. Visitors to this page will get an overview of its mission and its related research. The page also includes guidelines for using its Guest Observer Facility.

Royal Greenwich Observatory

http://www.ast.cam.ac.uk/RGO/RGO.html

The Royal Greenwich Observatory operates and supports telescopes and astronomy-related projects. This site details the observatory's research, archives, services and libraries. There are also several astronomy-related links, including the main Cambridge University site in England.

Solar and Heliospheric Observatory

http://sohowww.nascom.nasa.gov/

The ESA/NASA Solar and Heliospheric Observatory (SOHO) home page provides information on international solar physics and the experimental SOHO observatory. The presentations here include artwork and animation.

Teide Observatory

http://www.iac.es/folleto/teide.html

This home page for the Teide Observatory in the Canary Islands touts the observatory's significance as a key site for solar research and home for some of the best solar telescopes in the world. The Web site features photos of the telescopes and descriptions of research projects.

Uppsala Astronomical Observatory

http://www.astro.uu.se/

The Swedish observatory offers information on its recent sightings, staff and seminars. Find the planetary system and galaxies explained here, or link to other Swedish observatories and universities.

Warsaw University Astronomical Observatory

http://www.astrouw.edu.pl/

Warsaw University's Astronomical Observatory maintains this site to provide access to its research network. Visit here for links to the Polish school's resources and related institutions.

XMM Science Operations Centre

http://astro.estec.esa.nl/XMM/xmm.html

The High-Throughput X-Ray Spectroscopy Mission (XMM) is an "X-ray astrophysics observatory under development by the European Space Agency ... to conduct sensitive X-ray spectroscopic observations." Visitors to the operations center site can review documentation, data, software, the image gallery and newsletter.

LATIN AMERICA/ SOUTH AMERICA

Cerro Tololo Interamerican Observatory
http://ctios2.ctio.noao.edu/ctio.html

The home page of the Cerro Tololo Interamerican Observatory serves up an overview of its facilities in La Serena, Chile, as well as its press releases and a "What's New" file. Also find information on the observatory's telescopes and other instruments.

Fortaleza, Brazil VLBI Antenna
ftp://ray.grdl.noaa.gov/dist/vlbi/.HTML/ FORTALEZA.html

The VLBI observatory at Fortaleza, Brazil, is a radio astronomy research facility. The observatory's vital statistics as well as reports on its research activities and data collections can be found at this informational site.

NORTH AMERICA

Apache Point Observatory
http://www.apo.nmsu.edu/

The Apache Point Observatory home page contains information about staff, projects, observation scheduling and position announcements. Includes an image library, user's guide and observatory documentation.

Bucknell Observatory
http://www.bucknell.edu/map/ Observatory.html

A page from Bucknell University's map-based campus tour, this page shows a picture of the Bucknell Observatory and pinpoints its location on a campus map. A pointer to the Physics Department (which runs the observatory) is also featured.

Climenhaga Observatory
http://astrowww.phys.uvic.ca/climenhaga/obs/ telescope.html

Canada's Climenhaga Observatory presents this information page on its telescope system and research interests. One highlight is a graph of the

Compton Observatory Science Support Center
http://cossc.gsfc.nasa.gov/cossc/cossc.html

The Compton Observatory Science Suport Center is a NASA facility dedicated to space exploration instrumentation. Visitors to the site will find announcements, news bulletins and information on various missions and related instruments programs.

Harvard College Observatory
http://cfa-www.harvard.edu/hco-home.html

The Harvard College Observatory in Cambridge, Mass., maintains this site of links to related departments and staff members. Visit here to connect with Harvard University, the Harvard-Smithsonian Center for Astrophysics, graduate student home pages and more.

Haystack Observatory
http://www.haystack.edu/haystack/ haystack.html

The Haystack Observatory at the Massachusetts Institute of Technology is an interdisciplinary research center engaged in radio astronomy, geodesic study, atmospheric sciences and radar applications. Includes links to other institutions and government agencies engaged in this work.

Kirkwood Observatory
http://www.astro.indiana.edu:80/facilities/ observatories/kirkwood/

A facility of the Indiana University Astronomy Department, Kirkwood Observatory maintains this site to introduce its refracting and solar telescopes. Visit here to learn about the observatory and its astronomy research staff.

The Kuiper Airborne Observatory
http://www.exploratorium.edu/learning_ studios/link/

Based in California, NASA's Kuiper Airborne Observatory is a modified C-141A jet transport aircraft which supports research in infrared astronomy. Visit this site to learn more about the craft and its mission, read the newsletter and review the online gallery of photos and graphics.

The Laser Interferometer Gravitational-Wave Observatory
http://www.ligo.caltech.edu/

An attempt to develop new observational technology, the Laser Interferometer Gravitiational Wave Observatory seeks to open a new paradigm on the universe by utilizing advances in gravitational theory and technology. Includes links to technical overviews, publications and staff.

The Lick Observatory
http://ucowww.ucsc.edu/

Visitors to this site will find observing information and preprints from the Lick Observatory at the University of California, Santa Cruz. The page also includes an astronomical catalog and press packets on the planets discovered by the observatory's astronomers.

Mauna Kea Observatories
http://www.ifa.hawaii.edu/mko/mko.html

This is the home page of Mauna Kea Observatories, a facility based near the summit of Mauna Kea in Hawaii. Visitors can read more about the observatory's work, view images, and link to re-

lated sites, including the telescope at the University of Hawaii.

Mount Laguna Observatory
http://mintaka.sdsu.edu/

San Diego State University's Mount Laguna Observatory home page includes links to the astronomy department images of the Comet Hyakutake. Stargazers can also take a virtual tour of the observatory.

National Astronomy and Ionosphere Center Arecibo Observatory
http://aosun.naic.edu/

The Arecibo Observatory site contains statistics about the 305 meter telescope, descriptions of research projects and staff profiles. Includes general information for tourists and visiting scientists.

National Optical Astronomy Observatories
http://www.noao.edu/noao.html

The National Optical Astronomy Observatories (NOAO) gives visitors a look at its various observatories and research projects here. The extensive site also includes online newsletters and forums, updates on the Shoemaker-Levy comet and a video of a nearby asteroid.

National Radio Astronomy Observatory
http://www.cv.nrao.edu/nrao-hq.html

The National Radio Astronomy Observatory in Charlottesville, Va., presents information on its Astronomical Image Processing System, Central Development Lab and other resources. Included here are preprints and papers from the NRAO library, back issues of the NRAO newsletter and more.

National Solar Observatory
http://argo.tuc.noao.edu/

The National Solar Observatory is an astronomical observation site located in New Mexico. Visitors to the site can find out about the mission, agenda, staff and research taking place at this observatory.

National Undergraduate Research Observatory
http://nuro.phy.nau.edu/

The National Undergraduate Research Observatory is a consortium of undergraduate universities united to provide hands-on training and research work for students in order to encourage scientific careers. This page includes descriptions of research projects, an image gallery and links to AstroWeb and other related sites.

NRAO Socorro Home Page
http://info.aoc.nrao.edu/doc/Socorro.html

The National Radio Astronomy Observatory in New Mexico Web access for visitors is somewhat restricted, but users can browse through the library, schedule time on the observatory computers and retrieve some astronomy programs. Includes a nifty real-time map of the weather.

NRAO Very Long Baseline Array

http://zia.aoc.nrao.edu/doc/vlba/html/VLBA.html

Astronomers will find details here on how to apply for observing time on the Very Long Baseline Array at the National Radio Astronomy Observatory.

Owens Valley Radio Observatory

http://www.ovro.caltech.edu/

The California Institute of Technology's Owens Valley Radio Observatory gives visitors a close look at its instruments and resources here. The site also includes links to Caltech and other astronomical sites on the Internet.

Pacific Space Center

http://pacific-space-centre.bc.ca/

The Pacific Space Center, a joint facility of Canada's H.R. MacMillan Planetarium and Gordon Southam Observatory, maintains this site to introduce its programs and services. Visitors can learn about the center's events and educational courses, link to online membership forms, and track the progress of its astronomy research activities.

Queen's Subatomic Physics (SNO)

http://snodaq.phy.queensu.ca/

This Canadian site contains the home page of the Sudbury Neutrino Observatory Data Acquisition (SNODAQ) system at the Physics Department, Queen's University. Visitors here can learn more about the observatory and the astronomical research group.

The Robinson Lunar & Planetary Observatory

http://www.sky.net/~robinson/

The Robinson Lunar & Planetary Observatory, located in Bonner Springs, Kan., invites visitors to browse the observation sites, check out the equipment and learn about the current projects. Links to related sites are also featured.

Royal Observatories' Joint Astronomy Centre

http://www.jach.hawaii.edu/

This home page links visitors to information about the twin telescopes that comprise the Royal Observatories' Joint Astronomy Centre (JAC). Visitors to this Web site also will find information about JAC's software and computing services, along with technical support details for users of Unix and general-interest astronomical software.

Solar and Heliospheric Observatory

http://sohowww.nascom.nasa.gov/

The ESA/NASA Solar and Heliospheric Observatory (SOHO) home page provides information on international solar physics and the experimental

SOHO observatory. The presentations here include artwork and animation.

Submillimeter Telescope Observatory

http://hannen.as.arizona.edu/smt.html

Get information on the Submillimeter Telescope Observatory located at Steward Observatory on the University of Arizona campus. Includes specifications of the facility, a staff directory, user information and descriptions of research projects.

Sudbury Neutrino Observatory

http://www.physics.uoguelph.ca/sno/Sno.html

Sudbury Neutrino Observatory, which is being built in Canada by a coalition of five universities and two national laboratories, is profiled here. Included is a drawing of the site and links to information about neutrinos.

U.S. Naval Observatory

http://www.usno.navy.mil/

One of the oldest scientific agencies in the country, the U.S. Naval Observatory provides astronomical data and determines precise time—both of which are imperative for successful navigation. Visit here to link with its public affairs office, library collection and research directorates.

The U.S. Spectrum-X-Gamma Coordination Facility

http://hea-www.harvard.edu/SXG/sxg.html

The U.S. Spectrum-X-Gamma Coordination Facility is a high-energy astrophysics observatory. Visitors can learn about research and programs, as well as find out about software and proposal preparation and submission.

Whipple Observatory

http://cfa-www.harvard.edu/cfa/whipple.html

Whipple Observatory in Amado, Arizona, provides information here on its optical and electromagnetic telescope equipment. Visit this site for details on the sizes and types of equipment used at the facility.

The Wisconsin, Indiana, Yale and NAOA 3.5 Meter Telescope

http://www.astro.indiana.edu:80/facilities/observatories/wiyn/

An image of the Wisconsin, Indiana, Yale and NAOA (WIYN) 3.5 meter telescope on Kitt Peak in Arizona can be downloaded from this page. There are also links to the WIYN observatory home page and Indiana University's astronomy resources.

Wyoming Infrared Observatory

http://faraday.uwyo.edu/physics.astronomy/brochures/wiro.html

The Wyoming Infrared Observatory (WIRO) home page contains information on research projects and staff. Includes descriptions of facilities, technical info and educational programs.

PLANETARIUMS AND MUSEUMS

Adler Planetarium and Museum

http://astro.uchicago.edu/adler/

The first planetarium in the Western Hemisphere, Chicago's Adler Planetarium and Museum maintains this information server as part of its tradition for bringing the universe and its exploration to the widest possible audience. Visitors can preview exhibits and shows, learn about special events and courses, and link to the online resources.

Armagh Planetarium

http://star.arm.ac.uk/planet/planet.html

Ireland's Armagh Planetarium maintains this site with a tour of the planetarium, as well as Armagh City and surrounding countryside. See the stars as seen from Armagh, browse the gift catalog or link to other planetarium sites.

Astronomical Museum, Bologna

http://boas3.bo.astro.it/dip/Museum/MuseumHome.html

This site contains the home page of the Astronomical Museum and Observatory, part of the Department of Astronomy at the University of Bologna, Italy.

Henrietta Leavitt Flat Screen Space Theater

http://ucsu.colorado.edu/~peterscc/Home.html

The Henrietta Leavitt Flat Screen Space Theater features a virtual planetarium on this page. Visitors can watch The Planetarium Show That Never Ends, check the space image gallery or stop by the gift shop.

National Air and Space Museum

http://ceps.nasm.edu:2020/NASMpage.html

Located at the Smithsonian Institution in Washington, D.C., the National Air and Space Museum specializes in aeronautics and planetary studies. This site enables visitors to explore the museum via an interactive map and learn about its events.

Northern Lights Planetarium

http://www.uit.no/npt/homepage-npt.en.html

The Northern Lights Planetarium is a public planetarium located in Norway. Visitors to its Web site can learn about its exhibits, performances and schedules.

Pacific Space Center

http://pacific-space-centre.bc.ca/

The Pacific Space Center, a joint facility of Canada's H.R. MacMillan Planetarium and Gordon Southam Observatory, maintains this site to introduce its programs and services. Visitors can learn about the center's events and educational courses, link to online membership forms, and track the progress of its astronomy research activities.

Tycho Brahe Planetarium

http://www.astro.ku.dk/tycho.html

Located in Copenhagen, Denmark, the Tycho Brahe Planetarium and Omnimax Theater provides information about its shows and activities here. The site also includes pointers to a few astrolinks. In English and Danish.

PLANETS AND THE SOLAR SYSTEM

Adonis Adaptive Optics project WWW Server

http://hplyot.obspm.fr/

This is Adonis, the Adaptive Optics system with nightly mirrors of the great Nine Planets, the Web Nebulae and Planetary Nebulae. Includes an image gallery and project descriptions.

Center for Earth and Planetary Studies of the Smithsonian Institution's National Air and Space Museum

http://ceps.nasm.edu:2020/homepage.html

The Center for Earth and Planetary Studies (CEPS) is a research arm of the Smithsonian Institution's National Air and Space Museum. Primarily concentrating on the geology of planets, photos and research conducted by the U.S. space program is presented at this site.

Chesley Bonestell Gallery

http://www.secapl.com/bonestell/Top.html

Paintings of space and planetary scenes are featured at the Chesley Bonestell Interactive Art Gallery. Each work by Bonestell is accompanied by a brief narrative; familiar subjects include Earth, Jupiter, Mars and Saturn.

Comet Shoemaker-Levy Home Page (JPL)

http://www.jpl.nasa.gov/sl9/

In July 1994, professional and amateur astronomers observed the collision of two solar system objects: the fragments known as Comet Shoemaker-Levy and the planet Jupiter. This home page features information, images, links and resources about the astronomical event.

Comet Shoemaker-Levy 9 FAQ

http://www-erl.mit.edu/flolab/csl9press/csl9hj.html

This Texas A&M Observatory page is devoted to the collision of comet Shoemaker-Levy 9 with Jupiter—an event of enormous importance to astronomers. Browsers can view pictures of the collision, read pre- and post-collision questions and link to other observatory pages.

Earth

http://seds.lpl.arizona.edu/nineplanets/nineplanets/earth.html

Part of the Nine Planets series from the University of Arizona, this rich site offers a hypertext look at our planet. Visit here to learn about the physical facts of Earth, from mass to composition to plate tectonics. It includes statistics, photos and maps.

Earth and Universe

http://www.eia.brad.ac.uk/btl/

Visit this site for a comprehensive multimedia guide to the stars and galaxies taken from the "Earth and Universe" PC CD-ROM from BTL Publishing Limited. Find sound, video, text and still photos.

Earth Science and Solar System Exploration Division Home Page

http://exploration.jsc.nasa.gov/

This site provides information about various planetary and space science research projects conducted by NASA's Earth Science and Solar System Exploration Division .Includes newsletters and images of planets and other extraterrestrial objects.

The Face of Venus (FOV) Home Page

http://stoner.eps.mcgill.ca/bud/first.html

Browsers can explore Venus here. Visit for information on the surface of the planet, including databases of its craters and corona and an introduction to its volcanic, tectonic and impact structures. The site was crafted by a two men in Canada, at Kimana Software and McGill University.

GPS Division Home Page

http://www.gps.caltech.edu/

The California Institute of Technology has set up this home page for its Division of Geological and Planetary Sciences. This academic division specializes in earth and other planetary body research. The division's academic programs are also detailed.

Global Oscillation Network Group

http://helios.tuc.noao.edu/gonghome.html

Global Oscillation Network Group's home page dwells on helioseismology and documents a study of the sun's internal structure and dynamics. Contains images, references and in-depth info about the group's project.

The Goddard Distributed Active Archive Center

http://daac.gsfc.nasa.gov/

The Goddard Distributed Active Archive Center stores data about global change. Visitors can access its FTP archive from here, or learn how to order data for free. The site includes an online newsletter and an overview of the center's work.

Jupiter's Ring System

http://ringside.arc.nasa.gov/www/jupiter/jupiter.html

This NASA-maintained site brings into view information on the planet Jupiter's ring system. Animations, images and reference materials can be accessed here, along with information on the Shoemaker-Levy 9 comet's effects on the Jovian rings.

Laboratory for Terrestrial Physics

http://ltpwww.gsfc.nasa.gov/

The National Aeronautics and Space Administration (NASA) uses the Laboratory for Terrestrial Physics to find out information about the surface and interior of the Earth and other planets. Visit each of the various laboratory branches from this site for a review of technical facilities and research projects.

The MACHO Dark Matter Search Project

http://wwwmacho.anu.edu.au/

The MACHO project aims to determine if dark matter in the halo of the Milky Way is made up of objects like brown dwarfs or planets. Here, astronomers can read about this collaboration between an Australian observatory, American universities and the Lawrence Livermore National Lab.

Mars Exploration Program

http://www.jpl.nasa.gov/mars/

This information site on the Mars Exploration Program of the Jet Propulsion Laboratory at the California Institute of Technology offers such features as a

Mars Global Surveyor Project Home Page

http://mgs-www.jpl.nasa.gov/

The Mars Global Surveyor Project Home Page provides an overview of the MGS project, it staff and research focus. Includes a slide show on the MGS Mission, links to fact sheets and descriptions of technical innovations.

Mars Images Menu

http://esther.la.asu.edu/asu_tes/TES_Editor/SOLAR_SYST_TOUR/Mars.html

This Mars Images site contains links to photographic galleries of Mars and its moons, Phobos and Deimos.

Mars Multi-Scale Map

http://www.c3.lanl.gov/~cjhamil/Browse/mars.html

Visitors to this planetary mapping site can zoom into a selected area of the planet Mars for detailed viewing of the surface. Options for this interesting online tool include varying resolutions in pixels per degree and different sizes in pixels. Users can also specify latitude and longidtude.

The Moon, Should We Return to?

http://www.ari.net/back2moon.html

The National Space Society and ARInternet Corporation sponsor this site, addressing the issue of further missions to the moon. Visit here to weigh the pros and cons and learn how to add your opinion to the topical forum.

National Earth Orientation Service

http://maia.usno.navy.mil/

The National Earth Orientation Service (NEOS) is administered by the U.S. Naval Observatory, the Geosciences Laboratory and the National Oceanic and Atmospheric Administration. Visitors to the site will find extensive documentation and publications on Earth orientation and positioning.

National Space Science Data Center

http://nssdc.gsfc.nasa.gov/planetary/ planetfact.html

The National Space Science Data Center sets up a page full of fact sheets about planets, asteroids and other heavenly bodies, targeting those with more than a little understanding of the universe.

The Nine Planets

http://seds.lpl.arizona.edu/billa/tnp/

Tour the nine planets of the solar system in text, pictures and sound. Visitors to this site will be introduced to the the sun, the planets and the major moons. NASA spacecraft photos provide up-close looks at our nearest neighbors.

Nine Planets: A Multimedia Tour of the Solar System

http://seds.lpl.arizona.edu/nineplanets/ nineplanets.html

This online essay, which is supplemented by images and sounds, introduces visitors to the many worlds within our solar system. Includes historical information and statistics about the planets and their satellites.

Planetary Data System

http://pds.jpl.nasa.gov/

The Planetary Data System serves as a digital archive of data collected by NASA through its missions and operations. Visitors to its home page are invited to learn more about PDS and access the astronomical data available in its extensive archives.

The Planetary Rings Node

http://ringside.arc.nasa.gov/

This NASA site is dedicated to archiving and disseminating information on planetary ring systems. Includes links to animations, images and scientific data sets.

Planetary Sciences at the NSSDC

http://nssdc.gsfc.nasa.gov/planetary/planetary_ home.html

The National Space Science Data Center, the archive for NASA planetary and lunar data, maintains this site offering visitors links to its holdings and resources. Features include NASA's Master Directory as well as a teacher's resource center.

Planetary Society

http://planetary.org/tps/

This site presents an overview of the Planetary Society, related news items and NASA mission details. Includes links to an online resource center, articles, image archives and membership information.

Pluto a Planet?

http://dosxx.colorado.edu/plutohome.html

Perhaps you were thinking Pluto is a cartoon dog? Anyway, find an answer to the "planet" question presented in words, pictures and graphs by Prof. Fran Bagenal of the APAS Department at the University of Colorado, Boulder.

Saturn Events

http://www.isc.tamu.edu/~astro/saturn.html

The Saturn Events page details observations of phases, moon and ring activities and ring plane crossings. There are also diagrams, images, reports and links to related Saturn resources.

Saturn Ring Plane Crossing Information

http://ringside.arc.nasa.gov/www/rpx/rpx.html

During 1995 and 1996, the sun and Earth will be passing through Saturn's ring plane. Find general information on the scientific study of these events, theoretical predictions and links to the Saturn Viewer, the Saturn Moon Tracker and related sites.

Solar and Upper Atmospheric Data Services Home Page

http://dosxx.colorado.edu/plutohome.html

The Solar and Upper Atmospheric Data Services site of the U.S. National Geographical Data Center provides updates and scientific research results. Visit here for the latest findings from its studies of solar and interplanetary phenomena, flare-associated events and cosmic rays.

Solar Data Analysis Center

http://umbra.gsfc.nasa.gov/sdac.html

The NASA Solar Data Analysis Center, located in Greenbelt, Md., maintains this site with extensive information on solar eclipses, NASA missions and studies. Pictures of recent eclipses can be downloaded here.

Solar Exhibit

http://www.sunspot.noao.edu/index.html.

This solar exhibit site provides an overview of general solar information. This site includes data on flares, prominences, solar activity, telescopes used in research and some photographs.

Solar Forecast

http://www.sel.noaa.gov/forecast.html

The Current Solar Forecast, a collaborative effort of the U.S. Department of Commerce, NOAA, Space Environment Center and the U.S. Air Force, provides a day-by-day report and forecast of solar and geophysical activity.

Solar System Live

http://www.fourmilab.ch/solar/solar.html

Viewing the entire solar system or perhaps just the inner planets is made possible at the Solar System Live site. Set the time, date and observing location to track planets, satellites or asteroids in real time. The site is accessible to amateur stargazers and professional astronomers alike.

Solar Terrestrial Physics

http://www.ngdc.noaa.gov/stp/stp.html

Scientists staring at the sun can rest their eyes at the Solar Terrestrial Physics site. Links to data archives and related Internet resources are provided here. Research-oriented materials include daily solar data reports.

Spacelink: Our Solar System

http://spacelink.msfc.nasa.gov/ Instructional.Materials/Curriculum.Materials/ Sciences/Astronomy/Our.Solar.System/

Science and astronomy teachers can get cosmic help from the text, images and classroom activities available at this gopher. Features include a rocket-sized portfolio of planet-specific info, the Basics of Spaceflight Workbook, Galileo educational materials, a solar system puzzle kit, and a link to the SpaceLink Web site

Space Radar Images of Earth

http://www.jpl.nasa.gov/sircxsar/

A joint U.S.-German-Italian satellite project, the Spaceborne Imaging Radar-C/X-Band Synthetic Aperture Radar has been flown twice over the earth to capture images useful across a wide range of scientific disciplines. Visit this archive to learn more about the project and review the image files.

The StarChild Project: Connecting NASA and the K12 Classroom

http://heasarc.gsfc.nasa.gov/docs/StarChild/ StarChild.html

The StarChild Project is a NASA educational initiative aimed at providing learning experiences to K-12 students. Find astronomy-related topics discussed and demonstrated in fun and easy terms at this site.

Total Ozone Mapping Spectrometer

http://jwocky.gsfc.nasa.gov/

The Total Ozone Mapping Spectrometer page offers continually updated information about the Earth's ozone, including satellite retrieval data, press releases, images of the ozone hole and QuickTime movies.

Views of the Solar System

http://bang.lanl.gov/solarsys/

An educational tour of the solar system, Views of the Solar System provides visitors with images and information on the Sun, planets, asteroids, moons, comets and meteroids throughout our corner of the universe. Use hypertext links to get more detailed info on a desired planet or other heavenly body.

Viking Lander Images

http://barsoom.msss.com/mars/pictures/
viking_lander/viking_lander.html

Visitors to this page will find an explanation of color discrepancies in images from the surface of the planet Mars, as recorded by the Viking Lander. The discussion is accompanied by an image of the planet's surface.

Welcome to the Planets

http://pds.jpl.nasa.gov/planets/

This National Aeronautics and Space Administration (NASA) page provides images of the planets in Earth's solar system at the Welcome to the Planets site. Pictures of the space exploration craft which provided these planetary images are also available.

RADIO ASTRONOMY

Catalogue of Galactic Supernova Remnants

http://www.mrao.cam.ac.uk/surveys/snrs/.

A researcher at Cambridge University's astronomy observatory offers his catalog of galactic supernova remnants on this page. Includes detailed listings for the supernovas and links to the school's Department of Physics.

The Daily Martian Weather Report

http://nova.stanford.edu/projects/mgs/
dmwr.html

The Daily Martian Weather Report is brought to you by the Mars Global Surveyor Radio Science Team at the Jet Propulsion Laboratory. Visitors will find weather maps, temperature and pressure readings as well as other planetary data.

Dominion Radio Astrophysical Observatory 10cm Solar Radio Noise Patrol

http://www.drao.nrc.ca/icarus/www/sol_
home.shtml

The Solar Radio Group of the Canadian National Research Group maintains this site for data access. Visit here for results of solar radio noise flux experiments, daily and monthly reports, staff contact names, and more.

Effelsberg 100-m telescope (MPIfR)

http://www.mpifr-bonn.mpg.de/effberg.html

The Effelsberg 100-m Radio Telescope is the world's largest movable radio telescope, belonging to the Max-Planck-Institute for Radioastronomy in Germany. Visit here for descriptions of the telescope, an image gallery, proposal request forms and staff profiles.

The Faint Images of the Radio Sky at Twenty Centimeters (FIRST) Survey

http://sundog.stsci.edu/

The Faint Images of the Radio Sky at Twenty Centimeters (FIRST) survey outlines the project designed to produce a radio equivalent of the Palomar Observatory Sky Survey over 10,000 square degrees of the North Galactic Cap. Visitors can view recent images here.

Hat Creek Radio Observatory

http://www.astro.uiuc.edu:80/-bima/proposal/
technical.html

The BIMA Millimeter Array is a six-antenna interferometer array suitable for planning astronomical observations. The document on this page examines various technical aspects of the array and its abilities.

Institute of Astronomy Radio Astronomy Group Directory

http://mimas.ethz.ch/people.html

This page contains a directory of the Radio Astronomy Group members at the Institute of Astronomy in Zurich, Switzerland. The area of expertise, phone number and e-mail address are given for each member listed.

Max Planck Institute for Radio Astronomy

http://www.mpifr-bonn.mpg.de/

Located in Bonn, Germany, the Max Planck Institute for Radio Astronomy is home to the world's largest moveable radio telescope. Visitors to this site can download observation data from the telescope, bibliographies, databases and statistical models.

Mullard Radio Astronomy Observatory

http://www.mrao.cam.ac.uk/

The Mullard Radio Astronomy Observatory at the University of Cambridge, England, maintains this Web site with updates on current projects. There is also information on the observatory's telescopes and reports from astronomy conferences.

National Astronomy and Ionosphere Center Arecibo Observatory

http://aosun.naic.edu/

The Arecibo Observatory site contains statistics about the 305 meter telescope, descriptions of research projects and staff profiles. Includes general information for tourists and visiting scientists.

The National Radio Astronomy Observatory Library

http://info.cv.nrao.edu/html/library/library.html

The National Radio Astronomy Observatory, maintaining four scientific facilities across the United States, maintains this site for its library collection. Visitors will find preprint services, published papers and other astronomy-related publications and texts.

1995 Young European Radio Astronomers Conference

http://www.cup.cam.ac.uk/onlinepubs/YERAC/
YERACtop.html

This cover page provides an introduction to the electronic publication of the papers presented at the 1995 Young European Radio Astronomers Conference. A link to the publisher, Cambridge University Press, is included.

NRAO Green Bank

http://info.gb.nrao.edu/

The National Radio Astronomy Observatory's home page provides visitors with information about the facility and its telescopes. The site features links to public education programs, announcements and events schedules, the resource library and the NRAO master home page.

NRAO Headquarters

http://www.cv.nrao.edu/nrao-hq.html

Located in Charlotte, Va., the National Radio Astronomy Observatory maintains this overview of its educational programs. Also find guidelines for submitting observing proposals, software development sites and links to the business administration and personnel offices.

The Princeton Pulsar Group

http://pulsar.princeton.edu/

The folks at The Princeton Pulsar Group direct this page to heavy users of large radio telescopes. Part of the Gravity Group at Princeton University's Department of Physics, they have prepared a catalog of over 700 pulsars, including pictures of some of the largest radio telescopes in the world. Queries welcome.

Radio Amateur Satellite Corporation

http://www.amsat.org/

The Radio Amateur Satellite Corporation (AM-SAT) offers information about the amateur space program here. Enthusiasts can browse its catalogs and news briefs, join its mailing list and download software.

The Radiophysics Laboratory Home Page

http://www.rp.csiro.au/

Part of Australia's Commonwealth Scientific and Industrial Research Organisation, the Radiophysics Laboratory houses two divisions: the Australia Telescope National Facility and the Division of Radiophysics. Browsers can link to both divisions from this site.

Radio Pulsar Resources

http://pulsar.princeton.edu/rpr.shtml

Radio Pulsar Resources is a collection of home pages of interest to specialists in the field of radio pulsar. Visitors will find links to institutions, as well as personal home pages of researchers.

University of Manchester Radio Astronomy Group

http://mphhpc.ph.man.ac.uk:4321/rad_astron.html

Find out who's who in the Manchester Radio Astronomy Group, review information on current research or access local computing documents. A link to the University of Manchester home page is also featured.

The Westerbork Radio Synthesis Telescope

http://kapteyn.astro.rug.nl/UserDoc.html

The Netherlands Foundation for Research in Astronomy supplies documentation for the Westerbork Radio Synthesis Telescope. The files are provided in six parts. Also, there are aids to submitting project proposals.

REMOTE SENSING

AVHRR

http://edcwww.cr.usgs.gov/glis/hyper/guide/avhrr

The Advanced Very High Resolution Radiometer is an orbiting sensor aboard a National Oceanic and Atmospheric Administration satellite. Visitors here can take a detailed look at the abilities of the sensor and get information on how to obtain data from it.

The Center for Advanced Spatial Technologies

http://www.cast.uark.edu/

The Center for Advanced Spatial Technologies of the University of Arkansas, Fayetteville develops Geographic Information Systems applications. Visit here to access its general information files, scientific databases and links to related organizations.

Earth Observing System

http://eospso.gsfc.nasa.gov/

The Earth Observing System is being developed by NASA to find insights about the natural processes that govern the planet. Browsers here will find news about the program, which is part of the planet Earth mission.

Earth Observing System Data and Information System

http://spsosun.gsfc.nasa.gov/ESDIShome.html

NASA's Mission to Planet Earth is gathering information about our planet's natural systems and how humans are affecting them. Its Earth Observing System Data and Information System manages the data collected by the mission. Visitors here will get an overview of the project and can download its publications.

The Environmental Technology Laboratory

http://www.etl.noaa.gov/

The Environmental Technology Laboratory (ETL) in Boulder, Colorado, assists the geophysical research community by developing remote sensing systems. Features on its home page include an overview of ETL, lab information, publications and access to research data.

Laboratory for Telecommunication and Remote Sensing Technology

http://tudedv.et.tudelft.nl/www/ttt/index.html

The Laboratory for Telecommunication and Remote Sensing Technology, part of the Netherlands' University of Delft, is working on airborne imaging radar projects. Images of this device, attached beneath a small plane, are available at the site, with accompanying research reports.

NASA Space Instrument and Sensing Technology

http://ranier.oact.hq.nasa.gov/Sensors_page/InstHP.html

NASA's official Instrument and Sensing Technology page offers an overview of its technology and latest accomplishments, including details of space-related experiments and infrared astronomy. General background on space sensors also provided.

The Observatorium - NASA Remote Sensing Public Access Center

http://camille.gsfc.nasa.gov/rsd/

NASA provides public access to its earth and space data at this site. Features include an exhibit hall filled with images and data about Earth and the universe, as well as a technology park, offering an in-depth look at science, remote sensing and information technology.

World-Wide Web Virtual Library: Remote Sensing

http://www.vtt.fi/aut/ava/rs/virtual/

Visit the Remote Sensing stacks of the World Wide Web Virtual Library to find resources concentrating on this area of study within the astronomy and space research disciplines. Locate remote sensing organizations by country or access satellite data and related technical reports.

RESEARCH AND STUDIES

Advanced Satellite for Cosmology and Astrophysics

http://heasarc.gsfc.nasa.gov/docs/asca/asca2.html

This site documents the progress and history of the Advanced Satellite for Cosmology and Astrophysics (ASCA), a Japanese cosmic x-ray astronomy mission. Includes an overview of the research project, descriptions of instrumentation and links to related resources.

Ames Research Center

http://www.arc.nasa.gov/

The U.S. National Aeronautics and Space Administration's Ames Research Center specializes in the fields of information systems technologies, supercomputing, artificial intelligence, and other NASA-related disciplines. Visit this site for links to information about its mission, projects and related resources.

Amos Yahil

http://sbast3.ess.sunysb.edu/~ayahil/plan.html

Amos Yahil, an astronomy researcher at the State University of New York, provides a list of scientific articles at his home page. Visit here for a bibliography of reports published in physics and astronomy-related journals.

Andrea Milani

http://adams.dm.unipi.it/~milani/homemilani.html

This home page, set up by an associate editor of "Celestial Mechanics and Dynamical Astronomy," lists his research interests and recent publications. Serious browsers can read scholarly papers about asteroids; not-so-serious visitors can link to science fiction sites.

Bristol University's Astrophysics Group

http://nike.phy.bris.ac.uk/~phwjl

Bristol University's Astrophysics Group includes regular news updates and information about current research on its home page. Visitors can also check out the group's personnel.

Center for Advanced Space Studies Online

http://cass.jsc.nasa.gov/CASS_home.html

Visitors to this home page can learn about the Universities Space Research Association's (US-RA) Houston-based research and conference facility. Includes online publications, links to the center's three divisions and astronomy-related conference listings.

Debra Fischer

http://ucowww.ucsc.edu/~fischer/home.html

A University of California graduate student in astronomy details her research interests here. Visitors can also link to her interactive "Ask An Astronomer" site from this page.

Deep Near Infrared Survey of the Southern Sky (DENIS)

http://denisxg.obspm.fr/

DENIS will be a deep, complete survey of the astronomical sources of the southern sky in two near-infrared bands and one optical band simultaneously, using a one-meter, ground-based telescope. This page from Observatoire de Paris-Meudon features papers, pictures, an instrument gallery and more.

Dr. Andrew Woodsworth

http://www.dao.nrc.ca/DAO/STAFF/woodsworth.html

Maintained by an astronomy researcher, this home page provides personal and professional information. Find a description of the researcher's interests and recently published articles.

Dr. Bev Oke

http://www.dao.nrc.ca/DAO/STAFF/oke.html

Dr. Bev Oke at the Dominion Astrophysical Observatory of the Herzberg Institute of Astrophysics in Victoria, B.C., presents directory information, research interests and recent publications here.

Educational Space Simulations Project

http://chico.rice.edu/armadillo/Simulations/simserver.html

The Educational Space Simulations Project is sponsored by the Houston Independent School District and Rice University. Visitors to this page will find information on projects that combine technological simulations with educational programs for children.

European Astronaut Centre

http://www.esrin.esa.it/htdocs/esa/eac.html

This info page from the European Astronaut Centre describes the mission of the German-based facility that selects and trains the flyboys and flygirls of the European space initiative.

European Space Research and Technology Centre

http://www.estec.esa.nl/

This external site contains technical information and news items from the Center. Links to internal servers are restricted to authorized users.

Global Oscillation Network Group

http://www.dlr.de/

Global Oscillation Network Group's home page dwells on helioseismology and documents a study of the sun's internal structure and dynamics. Contains images, references and in-depth info about the group's project.

International GPS Service for Geodynamics

http://igscb.jpl.nasa.gov/

The International GPS Service for Geodynamics is part of the National Aeronautical and Space Administration (NASA). It supports researchers who use satellites in the U.S. Defense Department's Global Positioning System (GPS) for studies in geodynamics. Visitors here will learn

---

a2z EDITOR'S CHOICE

International Space Station

http://issa-www.jsc.nasa.gov/

Ever wonder what it would be like to live in outer space? How would it be to sleep floating in zero gravity? These questions and more are addressed at NASA's International Space Station site. The Technical Data Book page provides a frequently updated database of current station design, where you can view schematics of the design in progress or click on an interactive drawing of the proposed homestead in space. Visitors to this site can view animations of the orbiting habitat or link to an archive of images proposed by the design team. If you are looking for information on how future denizens of the ISS will prepare for their adventure, link to the Mockup & Trainer section for a description of the habitable portions of the space station; or link to the Business Opportunities section for descriptions of proposed on-board research and development facilities which will play an integral role in the financial viability of the ISS. A weightless dream is but a click away.—*Reviewed by Steve Ellis*

INTERNATIONAL SPACE STATION

PUBLIC ACCESS

- Program Overview
- Newsletter
- Movies
- Policies
- Pictures
- Factsheets
- Acronyms
- Bulletin Board Access Request
- Comments & Questions
- Technical Data Book
- Mockup & Trainer
- MSFC Space Station page
- Space Station as an Engineering Center
- Space Station Business Opportunities

ISS Team Access
- Program Team In-Process Information
- IS Applications
- 7:30 Stand up Meeting Minutes

about the service and staff and get an overview of GPS satellites.

Introductory Astronomy Notes

http://www.astro.washington.edu/strobel/index.html

Take a virtual Introductory to Astronomy course here. Nick Strobel teaches the course at Bakersfield College and posts an entire quarter's worth of lecture notes on this site, which also details the astronomer's research.

James Stilburn

http://www.dao.nrc.ca/DAO/STAFF/stilburn.html

Visitors to James Stilburn's page will find he's a member of the Dominion Astrophysical Observatory in Canada. His recent publications and research interests are featured.

Jet Propulsion Laboratory, NASA

http://www.jpl.nasa.gov/

Noted worldwide as "the lead U.S. center for robotic exploration of the solar system," NASA's Jet Propulsion Laboratory (JPL) provides information on its missions, instrumentation development and research programs. Download images and data from the detailed archives, read the latest press releases or check out the JPL Web Index to access the laboratoy's extensive resources.

Laboratory for Astronomy and Solar Physics, NASA

http://stars.gsfc.nasa.gov/www/welcome.html

Dedicated to the study of solar physics as well as UV/optical and infrared/submillimeter/radio astronomy, this NASA laboratory takes part in a variety of the space agency's missions. Learn about the lab's current, future and proposed endeavors at this official government site.

Langley Research Center

http://www.larc.nasa.gov/

NASA's Langley Research Center in Hampton, Va., conducts basic research in aeronatics and space technology. Take a graphical tour of the facility, find out about the Center's current and past cutting-edge research activities and read about Langley's economic impact in Virginia and the United States.

Lewis Research Center

http://www.lerc.nasa.gov/LeRC_homepage.html

NASA's Lewis Research Center in Cleveland, Ohio, maintains this look at its facilities and programs. Visitors can access Lewis by subject area, organization, project and information resource, or run a search query.

Los Alamos Theoretical Astrophysics Group

http://qso.lanl.gov/

The Theoretical Astrophysics Group at the Los Alamos National Laboratory in California maintains this page. Find information on research projects, a directory of personnel, publications and links to other astrophysics Web sites.

Luis Mendoza's Home Page of Cool

http://www.astro.washington.edu/mendoza

Luis Mendoza, an astronomy student at the University of Washington, maintains his personal home page with astronomy links, his research information and instructions for creating an image map.

Manuel Forestini

http://gag.observ-gr.fr/~forestin

Astrophysicists can download the research of Manuel Forestini, a scientist at the University of Grenoble, from this page. In English.

NASA Aerospace Education Services Program

http://www.okstate.edu/aesp/AESP.html

The NASA Aerospace Education Services Program provides information here on its workshops and seminars designed to increase public awareness of airborne scientific research and technological development. Also included are links to space-image libraries and other educational resources.

NASA Office Of Aeronautics: Human Factors

http://olias.arc.nasa.gov/

NASA's Human Factors site contains information on aviation systems/human interaction research. Includes descriptions of research programs, personnel, facilities and publications.

National Institute for Space Research, Brazil

http://www.inpe.br/

The National Institute for Space Research of the Brazilian Ministry of Science and Technology presents information about the institute, meetings and conferences, and announcements of job opportunities/internships. Includes links to the institute's technical divisions and information about research projects.

The National Radio Atronomy Observatory

http://www.cv.nrao.edu/html/library/intro_preprints.html

Astronomers will find an index to published papers and preprints written by staffers and visiting observers at National Radio Astronomy Observatory. Includes a link to the observatory.

National Research LaborSpace Science Division

http://bdc.nrl.navy.mil/SSD/

The Space Science Division (SSD) of the Naval Research Laboratory Web site provides a lot of information here about atmospheric, solar, and astronomical research aboard NASA, DoD, and other space projects.

National Undergraduate Research Observatory

http://nuro.phy.nau.edu/

The National Undergraduate Research Observatory is a consortium of undergraduate universities united to provide hands-on training and research work for students in order to encourage scientific careers. This page includes descriptions of research projects, an image gallery and links to AstroWeb and other related sites.

Search for Extra-Terrestrial Intelligence Module

http://albert.ssl.berkeley.edu/serendip/

Syracuse University's physics department teaches an interdisciplinary course which explores astronomy, biology and communications technology through the study of SETI, the Search for Extra-Terrestrial Intelligence. Visit here to learn about scientific, literary and historical aspects of the search for life beyond the Earth.

Space Telescope Science Institute Library

http://sesame.stsci.edu/library.html

Researchers can check out published papers and preprints at the Space Telescope Science Institute Library. Physicists and astronomers will find academic journals, data sets and links to other online libraries.

Stephen Morris

http://www.dao.nrc.ca/DAO/STAFF/morris.html

Dr. Stephen Morris is one of the staffers at the Dominion Astrophysical Observatory, part of the Canadian Hertzberg Institute of Astrophysics. His personal home page lists his recent publications, research interests and contact information.

The Strasbourg Astronomical Data Center (CDS)

http://cdsweb.u-strasbg.fr/CDS.html

The Strasbourg Astronomical Data Center (CDS) is dedicated to the collection and distribution of astronomical data. It is located at the Strasbourg Astronomical Observatory, France. This site provides catalogs and tables, abstracts, databases and more. In French, English, Spanish, German and Italian.

Universities Space Research Association

http://www.usra.edu/

The Universities Space Research Association is a nonprofit organization that fosters cooperation among various universities, the U.S. government and other organizations involved in space and technology research. It gives an overview of its programs and member institutions here.

University of California, Berkeley, Space Sciences Laboratory

http://ssl.berkeley.edu/

The Space Sciences Laboratory furthers its goal of educating the next generation of space scientists with this Web site. It features recent findings from major study projects at the University of California at Berkeley. Visitors will also find a personnel directory and a personal message from the director.

University of California, San Diego, Center for Astrophysics and Space Sciences

http://cassfos01.ucsd.edu:8080/ghrs.html

The Center for Astrophysics and Space Sciences at the University of California at San Diego, features its work with the Hubble Space Telescope and multi-channel Digicon photon detectors. The page includes links to developers and researchers.

University of Maryland Space Systems Laboratory

http://www.ssl.umd.edu/

Zoom in on information about the Space Systems Laboratory at the University of Maryland, including current projects and experiments related to space operations, staff profiles, copies of papers and publications, instructions for reaching the university and a detailed campus map. Includes links to related resources.

University of Melbourne Astrophysics Group

http://www.ph.unimelb.edu.au/astro/home.html

The Astrophysics Group at the University of Melbourne, Australia, provides information about its faculty and research here. The page also includes images, online publications from the group, and undergraduate information.

Utah State University Center for Atmospheric and Space Sciences

http://www.cass.usu.edu/

Utah State University presents the home page for its Center for Atmospheric and Space Sciences. Visitors will find an overview of academic programs, research and faculty.

The Vision Group at NASA Ames Research Center

http://vision.arc.nasa.gov/

This team of scientists and engineers conducts research on human vision and visual technology for NASA missions. Its site includes news, personnel info, projects and publications.

Vitaly G. Promislov

http://diogen.asc.rssi.ru/Vitaly.html

Vitaly G. Promislov, of the Astro Space Center in Moscow, provides information on his research and a personal QuickTime greeting.

PLANETARY

Armagh Observatory Preprint Series

http://star.arm.ac.uk/~ambn/preprints.html

Astronomers can view abstracts from the Armagh Observatory Preprint Series at this site. From analyses of stellar coronas to the modeling of main sequence star chromospheres, users can access scientists' reports on their observations.

Astronomy and Astrophysics Research at QMW

http://starsun7.ph.qmw.ac.uk/physics/

Astronomy and astrophysics research at Queen Mary and Westfield College at the University of London is explained in detail on this home page. The site includes pictures and data from recent observations, along with information on postgraduate research opportunities.

Astronomy at the University of Texas, Austin

http://www.as.utexas.edu/

The University of Texas offers both general astronomy information and specific facts about its astronomy degree program at the Department of Astronomy home page. Review research programs and educational resources here.

Bruce A. Peterson

http://msowww.anu.edu.au/~peterson/bapeterson.html

Dr. Bruce A. Peterson of the Mount Stromlo Observatory in Australia, supplies contact information, research interests, recent publications, current work and links to other astronomical resources.

CANSPACE Archive

http://degaulle.hil.unb.ca/Geodesy/CANSPACE.html

The Canadian Space Geodesy Forum is an online information dissemination tool and discussion group area for scientists and engineers. Participants can exchange news, comments, questions and answers here.

CDS, Strasbourg

http://cdsweb.u-strasbg.fr/CDS-f.html

Located at France's Strasbourg Astronomical Observatory, the Data Center collects and distributes astronomical and related data. Visitors to its Web site can access the SIMBAD astronomical database, the recognized reference database for identifying astronomical objects. In French, English, German, Spanish and Italian.

Center for Earth and Planetary Studies of the Smithsonian Institution's National Air and Space Museum

http://ceps.nasm.edu:2020/homepage.html

The Center for Earth and Planetary Studies (CEPS) is a research arm of the Smithsonian Institution's National Air and Space Museum. Visitors to this site will find information on the geology of planets, photos, and research conducted by the U.S. space program.

Center for Earth Observation

http://ceo-www.jrc.it/

The European Earth Observation System (EEOS) is a joint initiative of the European Space Agency (ESA), the European Community and its member states to streamline space research. The European Community's contribution to the system is the Center for Earth Observation, which is detailed here.

Douglas L. Welch

http://www.physics.mcmaster.ca/Faculty/DLWelch.html

This personal home page contains contact information and research interests of Douglas L. Welch, a faculty member of the Department of Physics and Astronomy at McMaster University, Hamilton, Ontario, Canada. There are also details about some of his publications.

Earth

http://seds.lpl.arizona.edu/nineplanets/nineplanets/earth.html

Part of the Nine Planets series from the University of Arizona, this rich site offers a hypertext look at our planet. Learn about the physical facts of Earth, from mass to composition to plate tectonics. It includes statistics, photos and maps.

Earth Observing System Data and Information System

http://eospso.gsfc.nasa.gov/

NASA's Mission to Planet Earth is gathering information about our planet's natural systems and how humans are affecting them. Its Earth Observing System Data and Information System manages the data collected by the mission. Visitors here will get an overview of the project and can download its publications.

Earth Observing System Project Science Office

http://spso.gsfc.nasa.gov/spso_homepage.html

Serving as the principal component in NASA's Mission to Planet Earth (a project to observe the natural processes that govern the planet), the Earth Observing System is detailed on this home page. Find mission profiles, publications, educational materials, research data and more.

European Space Agency/European Space Research Institute

http://www.esrin.esa.it/htdocs/esrin/esrin.html

The European Space Research Institute (ESRIN), an Italian research establishment that collects and distributes data from Earth-observation missions, maintains this site in conjunction with its parent organization, the European Space Agency (ESA). Visitors here can learn details about ESA's many labs and research projects.

Gamma Ray Burst Index at Northwestern University

http://www.astro.nwu.edu/astro/osse/bursts/index.html

Physicists will find a collection of gamma ray burst images here. The Department of Physics and Astronomy at Northwestern University, which collects the images as part of an ongoing experiment, explains its research here.

The Goddard Distributed Active Archive Center

http://daac.gsfc.nasa.gov/

The Goddard Distributed Active Archive Center stores data about global change. Visitors can access its FTP archive from here, or learn how to order data for free. The site includes an online newsletter and an overview of the center's work.

The Hiraiso Solar Terrestrial Research Center/CRL

http://hiraiso.crl.go.jp/

The Hiraiso Solar Terrestrial Research Center/CRL administers the Space Environment Information Service for the Internet. The online real-time data service provides glossaries, weather services, solar activity charts and other information related to space environment.

IDL Astronomy User's Library

http://idlastro.gsfc.nasa.gov/homepage.html

This central repository for astronomical procedures provides researchers with a collection of astronomical methodologies. Includes a users' guide, instructions for submitting procedures to the library and links to related resources.

ISTP Home Page

http://www-istp.gsfc.nasa.gov/

The International Solar-Terrestrial Physics Science Initiative is a NASA project researching the Sun-Earth space environment. Visitors can sur-vey programs and facilities or link to physics-related Internet resources.

Laboratory for Extraterrestrial Physics

http://lep694.gsfc.nasa.gov/code690.html

Located at NASA's Goddard Space Flight Center in Greenbelt, Md., the Laboratory for Extraterrestrial Physics (LEP) invites visitors to its home page to learn more about the lab, its offices and branches, and its ongoing work. Links to the lab's research tools and flight programs are provided.

Laboratory for Terrestrial Physics, NASA

http://ltpwww.gsfc.nasa.gov/

The National Aeronautics and Space Administration (NASA) uses the Laboratory for Terrestrial Physics to find out information about the surface and interior of the Earth and other planets. Visit each of the various laboratory branches from this site for a review of technical facilities and research projects.

The Laser Interferometer Gravitational-Wave Observatory

http://www.ligo.caltech.edu/

An attempt to develop new observational technology, the Laser Interferometer Gravitational Wave Observatory seeks to open a new paradigm on the universe by utilizing advances in gravitational theory and technology. Includes links to technical overviews, publications and staff.

Marslink Project Essays

http://barsoom.msss.com/http/ps/intro.html

Find a growing collection of essays on Mars-related topics by Mike Caplinger of Malin Space Science Systems. These essays arose from the author's participation in The Planetary Society's Marslink Project, a program designed to stimulate students' interests in space.

Mars Thermal Emission Spectrometer Project

http://esther.la.asu.edu/asu_tes/

Join the Arizona State University Department of Geology in the Mars Thermal Emission Spectrometer Project. The results of the Mars experiments are accessible in a K-12 educational format, as well as a data sharing format for research scientists.

Mission to Planet Earth

http://www.hq.nasa.gov/office/mtpe/

NASA keeps an eye on what's happening on earth with the unique perspective available to space travelers, and it spits the information back out for Net travelers here. The Mission to Planet Earth's function is to monitor global environmental changes and human activity and provide this info worldwide for environmental planning. Link to mission info here or to a variety of NASA or NASA-related organizations.

MIT Microwave Subnode

http://delcano.mit.edu/

The Planetary Data System Microwave Subnode, a research group of the Massachusetts Institute of Technology, archives and distributes digital data related to the study of planetary bodies. Visit here for access to its latest findings and images, and link to a variety of related organizations. A comprehensive frequently asked questions index is also available.

NASA Planetary Data System

http://pds.jpl.nasa.gov/

The Planetary Data System (PDS) archives and distributes digital data from past and present NASA planetary missions, astronomical observations and laboratory measurements. Visit this site to browse its topics list, contact its many organizations and view its catalogs and online data. Links to related sites are also available here.

National Radio Astronomy Observatory Library

http://www.cv.nrao.edu/html/library/library.html

The library of the National Radio Astronomy Observatory supplies an online catalog as well as a searchable index of preprints and published papers. Also included: information on future and past meetings, conferences and workshops, and pointers to other preprint services, published papers and astronomy resources.

Open University Astronomy Group

http://yan.open.ac.uk/~ajnorton/astro/

Located in the Physics Department of the United Kingdom's Open University, the Astronomy Group maintains this overview of its research activities and academic programs. An index of astronomical resources on the Web is also featured.

The Planetary Data System Small Bodies Node

http://pdssbn.astro.umd.edu/

Located in the Astronomy Department of the University of Maryland at College Park, the Planetary Data System Small Bodies Node gathers and archives data related to comets, asteroids, and interplanetary dust. Visitors are welcome to learn more about the facility and its staff, access the SBN data files, or link to topic-related sites.

The Planetary Rings Node

http://ringside.arc.nasa.gov/

This NASA site is dedicated to archiving and disseminating information on planetary ring systems. Includes links to animations, images and scientific data sets.

Princeton Observatory Preprints

http://astro.princeton.edu/~library/prep.html

This Web site archives preprints of Princeton Observatory publications. Visitors can read abstracts or download PostScript versions of the documents here.

Queen's University Astronomy Research Group

http://astro.queensu.ca/

The Queen's University Astronomy Research Group posts information describing itself and its research programs here. Also find links to astronomy services at this site.

Relativity Group at the National Center for Supercomputing Applications

http://jean-luc.ncsa.uiuc.edu/

The National Center for Supercomputing Applications' Relativity Group studies black holes and gravitational waves. The research organization's home page outlines its projects, papers and members. Movies and exhibits are also available here.

Rob Seaman

http://iraf.noao.edu/~seaman/seaman.html

A programmer at the National Optical Astronomy Observatories posts his projects, publications and interests on this staff profile page.

Saturn Ring Plane Crossing Information

http://ringside.arc.nasa.gov/www/rpx/rpx.html

Find general information on the scientific study of the Earth passing through Saturn's ring plane, theoretical predictions and links to the Saturn Viewer, the Saturn Moon Tracker and related sites.

Smithsonian Astrophysical Observatory

http://cfa-www.harvard.edu/sao-home.html

The Smithsonian Astrophysical Observatory is a research bureau of the Smithsonian Institution in Washington, D.C. Visit the Central Bureau for Astronomical Telegrams and the Minor Planet Center. Also, find several archives of software, images and documentation relating to Smithsonian projects.

Solar and Upper Atmospheric Data Services Home Page

http://www.ngdc.noaa.gov/stp/SOLAR/solar.html

The Solar and Upper Atmospheric Data Services site of the U.S. National Geographical Data Center provides updates and scientific research results. Visit here for the latest findings from its studies of solar and interplanetary phenomena, flare-associated events and cosmic rays.

Solar Data Analysis Center—NASA

http://umbra.gsfc.nasa.gov/sdac.html

The NASA Solar Data Analysis Center, located in Greenbelt, Md., maintains this site with extensive information on solar eclipses, NASA missions

and studies. Pictures of recent eclipses can be downloaded here.

Space and Geophysics Group at the University of Texas at Austin

http://www.arlut.utexas.edu/~sggwww/index.html

The Space and Geophysics Group from the University of Texas at Austin features presentations and papers on its Web site. The page also includes links to the divisions within the SGG, along with details about current research projects.

Space Environment Center Home

http://www.sel.bldrdoc.gov/

The Space Environment Center, a facility of the U.S. National Oceanic and Atmospheric Administration, maintains this site to introduce its programs and services. Visitors will find solar terrestrial data and a variety of tailored space weather products.

Space Telescope Science Institute: Office of Public Outreach

http://www.stsci.edu/public.html

The Space Telescope Science Institute offers up a tasty site about astronomy and space exploration. Included here is information of interest to educators, students, the news media and the general public. Images captured by the Hubble Space Telescope also are available.

Theses from the Five College Astronomy Departments

http://decoy.phast.umass.edu/

The result of the scientific toils of budding astronomers are posted online here. Visitors can read Ph.D. theses from students in the Amherst, Massachusetts' Five College Astronomy Department.

Ulysses Mission

http://ulysses.jpl.nasa.gov/

The National Aeronautic and Space Administration (NASA) gives visitors here a close look at its Ulysses spacecraft, which studies the heliosphere around the sun. Browsers can download images, animations and a bibliography of Ulysses publications from this site.

University of Glasgow Astronomy and Astrophysics Group

http://www.astro.gla.ac.uk/

The Astronomy and Astrophysics Group at the University of Glasgow provides information about its involvement in the U.K.-wide Starlink project and other research activities. Visitors can browse the group's seminar and preprint list or link to other Astronomy resources on the Web.

Virgo Home Page

http://www.pi.infn.it/virgo/virgoHome.html

The Virgo interferometer program is a collaboration by international astronomical institutions to

detect gravitational waves reaching the earth from outer space. Visitors to this page will find info on participating institutes and the people involved.

Wake Shield Facility Information Center

http://www.svec.uh.edu/

The Wake Shield Facility (WSF) is a research and development facility designed to use the "pure vacuum of space to conduct scientific research in the development of new materials." Read press releases and descriptions of past and future projects, or access the control center for updates on mission results and view images and video from the mission vehicle.

SPACE FLIGHT

Aerospace Research Center

http://enws229.eas.asu.edu/

The Aerospace Research Center at Arizona State University provides information about its projects, director and program manager here. Prospective students can also request information via e-mail on this page.

Burst and Trasient Source Experiment

http://cossc.gsfc.nasa.gov/cossc/BATSE.html

The Goddard Space Flight Center details the Burst and Transient Source Experiment (BATSE) here. Visitors can browse through a Burst Catalog, access FTP archives with public data and software related to the project, and gather detailed burst data.

Delft Institute for Earth-Oriented Space Research

http://dutlru8.lr.tudelft.nl/

The Space Research and Technology Section at the Netherlands' Delft University of Technology does orbit computation, gravity field modeling and GPS processing. This site features more information about the section's research.

Delta Clipper/SSRT Program

http://gargravarr.cc.utexas.edu/ssrt/index.html

The Ballistic Missile Defense Organization's Single Stage Rocket Technology program was created to demonstrate the practicality of reusable launch vehicles. Read about the program's technologies and systems, and its flight testing and funding. Link to related NASA sites.

Dryden Flight Research Center

http://www.dfrf.nasa.gov/

The NASA Dryden Flight Research Center page contains general information on projects and operations. Includes links to educational resources, historical info, research facilities and other information services.

850 SCIENCE AND TECHNOLOGY

European Space Agency

http://www.esrin.esa.it/htdocs/esa/esa.html

The European Space Agency provides information here about its efforts to promote cooperative space research for peaceful purposes. It also gives an overview of its member states, posts press releases and lists its publications on this page.

Goddard Space Flight Center Home Page

http://pao.gsfc.nasa.gov/

The Goddard Space Flight Center, a facility of the U.S. National Aeronautics and Space Administration, maintains this site to introduce its departments and programs. Visit here for mission overviews, scientific publications, research materials, public information services and departmental resources.

Goddard Space Flight Center Space Data and Computing Division

http://sdcd.gsfc.nasa.gov/SDCD.html

The Space Data and Computing Division at NASA's Goddard Space Flight Center in Greenbelt, Md., maintains this overview of its activities. Find pointers to the Digital Library Technology Project, the Digital Technical Resource Center and other SDCD projects and divisions.

Johnson Space Center

http://www.jsc.nasa.gov/

The Johnson Space Center, a division of the National Aeronautics and Space Administration, maintains this overview of its mission. Find links to JSC facilities and labs, projects, programs and groups, and general NASA services. A keyword search option offers quick reference.

Kennedy Space Center

http://www.ksc.nasa.gov/ksc.html

This NASA-maintained page provides information about the Kennedy Space Center's facilities and various space shuttle missions. Includes a shuttle reference manual, a frequently asked questions file and a KSC phone book.

Life Sciences Data Archive at the National Space Science Data Center

http://nssdc.gsfc.nasa.gov/life/lsdahome.html

Scientists, educators and students interested in space life sciences can go out of this world on this page. Scientists can search the master catalog and order data from human and nonhuman space-flight experiments. Teachers and students can read summaries of these missions and browse the digital image library.

Malin Space Science Systems

http://barsoom.msss.com/

Malin Space Science Systems designs, develops and operates spacecraft instrumentation. This site provides links to information about its

projects, educational activities and flight project participation.

Marshall Space Flight Center

http://www.msfc.nasa.gov/

NASA develops and maintains space transportation and propulsion systems at its Marshall Space Flight Center in Huntsville, Ala. Visitors to the center's Web site will find updates on the institution's activities and current missions. Includes technical information and a link to NASA's home page.

Microgravity Science and Applications Division—NASA

http://microgravity.msad.hq.nasa.gov/

NASA's Microgravity Science and Applications Division supports research in Biotechnology, Combustion Science, Fluid Physics and Materials Science. Visitors to this page will find innumerable links to programs and experiments, plus access to the searchable database, newsletter and a virtual reality presentation of Spacelab.

MIT Center for Space Research

http://space.mit.edu/

This is the Massachusetts Institute of Technolgy's Center for Space Research Web site. Visitors can learn about the many space-related research projects conducted by MIT faculty and students.

NASA Newsroom

http://www.gsfc.nasa.gov/hqpao/newsroom.html

Keep up with current U.S. space activity, policies and research at the National Aeronautics and Space Administration (NASA) Newsroom. Monitor current missions, press releases and daily internal news.

Poker Flat Research Range

http://dac3.gi.alaska.edu/

The University of Alaska is the only school to own a rocket launching facility. Explore the Poker Flat Research Range and the Geophysical Institute which operates it.

Space Environment Effects Branch

http://satori2.lerc.nasa.gov/

The Space Environment Effects Branch page examines and investigates GEO spacecraft anomalies. Read about its findings and objectives, or link to other NASA-supported programs.

Spacelab Home Page

http://hvsun21.mdc.com:8000/~mosaic/spacelab.html

The Spacelab home page provides information on the joint European Space Agency (ESA)/NASA project to establish a viable microgravity orbiting research facility. Includes details of Spacelab resources, descriptions of previous and future missions as well as links to related aerospace topics.

Space Physics Data System—NASA

http://spds.nasa.gov/spds.html

NASA's Space Physics Data System preserves historical data and provides access to space physics information. Site features include a directory of services, indexed databases and an overview of the system.

Space Shuttle Publications—NASA

ftp://explorer.arc.nasa.gov/pub/SPACE/SHUTTLE

This NASA gopher menu contains publications regarding the space shuttle. It includes briefs, reviews and shuttle status reports from September 1988 through September 1994. The menu's parent directory contains a wealth of NASA and space-related information.

Wake Shield Facility Information Center

http://www.svec.uh.edu/

The Wake Shield Facility (WSF) is a research and development facility designed to use the "pure vacuum of space to conduct scientific research in the development of new materials." Read press releases and descriptions of past and future projects, or access the control center for updates on mission results. View images and video from the mission vehicle.

SATELLITES

Advanced Communications Technology Satellite

http://kronos.lerc.nasa.gov/acts/acts.html

This NASA page is devoted to its Advanced Communications Technology Satellite program. Visitors can read about the program's launches, earth stations and experiments in investigating new ways to communicate.

The Global Positioning System (GPS)

http://www.utexas.edu/depts/grg/gcraft/notes/gps/gps.html

The Department of Geography at the University of Texas provides this overview of the Global Positioning System (GPS). Featured are information on the U.S. Department of Defense Satellite Navigation System, GPS data, documents relating to GPS and links to related resources.

The GOES Satellite

http://www.ngdc.noaa.gov/stp/GOES/goes.html

Monthly Data for the GOES satellites (6,7) is available from NGDC in both the 5.0 minute and 3.0 sec resolutions at the GOES site. For information on how to order the satellite transmission data, follow the pointers offered here.

International GPS Service for Geodynamics

http://igscb.jpl.nasa.gov/

The International GPS Service for Geodynamics is part of the National Aeronautical and Space Administration (NASA). It supports researchers who use satellites in the U.S. Defense Department's Global Positioning System (GPS) for studies in geodynamics. Visitors here will learn about the service and staff and get an overview of GPS satellites.

International Ultraviolet Explorer Satellite Data Analysis Center

http://iuewww.gsfc.nasa.gov/iuedac/iuedac_homepage.html

NASA's Data Analysis Center is the operator of the International Ultraviolet Explorer Satellite. Visitors to this site will find IUE images, analysis tools and data sets.

NRAO Orbiting VLBI Home Page

http://info.gb.nrao.edu/ovlbi/OVLBI.html

The NRAO OVLBI Home Page details NASA's orbiting tracking station in Green Bank, W.V., and links to a series of documentation that describes the activities of various satellite projects, operation groups and research.

Pioneer Home Page

http://pyroeis.arc.nasa.gov/pioneer/PNhome.html

The Centrifuge Facility Project of the U.S. National Aeronautics and Space Administration maintains this site for its Pioneer 10 and 11 satellites information index. Visitors will find mission status reports, downloadable images, flight paths, and scientific instrument descriptions.

ROSAT GOF

http://heasarc.gsfc.nasa.gov/docs/rosat/rosgof.html

The Roentgen Satellite (ROSAT) is an X-ray observatory developed by Germany, the U.K. and the U.S. Visitors to this page will get an overview of its mission and its related research. The page also includes guidelines for using its Guest Observer Facility.

Satellite Imagery FAQ 1/5

http://www.geog.nottingham.ac.uk/remote/satfaq.html

Get the big picture by reading the Satellite Imagery FAQ (frequently asked questions) page. From there you can jump to sites all over the Internet featuring satellite images of the earth.

Space Radar Images of Earth

http://www.jpl.nasa.gov/sircxsar/

A joint U.S.-German-Italian satellite project, the Spaceborne Imaging Radar-C/X-Band Synthetic Aperture Radar has been flown twice over the earth to capture images useful across a wide range of scientific disciplines. Visit this archive to learn more about the project and review the image files.

University of California, Berkeley, Center for EUV Astrophysics at the

http://www.cea.berkeley.edu/

The Center for EUV Astrophysics at the University of California, Berkeley, is the scientific base for NASA's extreme ultraviolet explorer (EUVE). Its Web site offers a searchable index of info related to the CEA.

Villafranca Satellite Tracking Station

http://www.vilspa.esa.es/

The European Space Agency (ESA) operates the Villafranca Satellite Tracking Station, which is located near Madrid, Spain. Follow satellite projects currently based at the station or check into other astronomical pursuits of the ESA.

The XMM Project

http://astro.estec.esa.nl/XMM/about/xmm.html

The High-Throughput X-Ray Spectroscopy Mission is an astrophysics observatory that conducts sensitive X-ray observations of a wide variety of cosmic sources. Includes descriptons of scientific objectives, the XMM spacecraft, its payload and staff profiles.

The Yohkoh Spacecraft

http://mssla3.mssl.ucl.ac.uk/www_solar/yohkoh.html

The Yohkoh Spacecraft page is devoted to the satellite being operated by the Japanese Institute of Space and Astronautical Science.

SPACE COLONIES

Orbital Space Settlements

The National Aeronautics and Space Administration (NASA) posits the who,

what, where and why of space settlement at this site. Find studies on the design, feasibility and desirability of creating permanent human settlements in space.

SPACE MISSIONS AND PROBES

ISO-IRAS Support

http://ast.star.rl.ac.uk/isouk/isouk.html

Visitors to this site will find launch and orbit information on the Infrared Space Observatory. Orbit-by-orbit summaries are provided, in addition to movies and links to other topical sites.

Planetary Probes FTP

http://spacelink.msfc.nasa.gov/NASA.Projects/Planetary.Probes

Planetary Probes is an archive containing details and images of planetary space probes launched by NASA. Missions include the Cassini Mission to Saturn and the Comet Rendezvous/Asteroid Flyby.

Space Mission Acronym List and Hyperlink Guide

http://ranier.oact.hq.nasa.gov/Sensors_page/MissionLinks.html

Visitors to this Web site can get the lowdown on NASA acronyms and the missions for which they stand. Browse an alphabetical listing of NASA projects, with a special emphasis on robotic science missions. Includes links to numerous NASA pages.

The XMM Project

http://astro.estec.esa.nl/XMM/about/xmm.html

The High-Throughput X-Ray Spectroscopy Mission is an astrophysics observatory that conducts sensitive X-ray observations of a wide variety of cosmic sources. Includes descriptons of scientific objectives, the XMM spacecraft, its payload and staff profiles.

X-Ray Timing Explorer (XTE)

http://heasarc.gsfc.nasa.gov/docs/xte/XTE.html

The X-Ray Timing Explorer is a Goddard mission intended to further the study of time variability in the emission of X-ray sources. Visitors to this site can read information about the mission's instrumentation, scientific planning and data processing being conducted by the Guest Observer Facility, the Science Operations Facility and the XTE Science Data Center.

APOLLO

Project Apollo

http://www.ksc.nasa.gov/history/apollo/apollo.html

Visitors to this NASA page will find a program overview of the Apollo project. Features include a description of the spacecraft, a flight summary and access to the image directory.

JUPITER

Comet Shoemaker-Levy 9 Encounters Jupiter

http://marvel.stsci.edu/EPA/Comet.html

View the 1994 encounter between the Comet Shoemaker-Levy 9 and the planet Jupiter. Animation of the collision is available along with images of the impact site and resulting fragments. Images are provided by the Hubble Space Telescope and other observatories.

Galileo Mission to Jupiter Online Resources

http://www.jpl.nasa.gov/galileo

This page contains a list of resources relevant to the Galileo Mission to Jupiter and is intended to be helpful to both the scientific community and general public. Among the materials are images and photographs, data files, documentation and press releases.

Project Galileo

http://www.jpl.nasa.gov/galileo/

As the Galileo spacecraft's orbiter spends its time studying Jupiter and its moons, the Project Galileo Home Page keeps earthlings abreast of the situation. Check out images, FAQ files and, of course, the latest in Galileo news here.

Project Galileo: Bringing Jupiter to Earth

http://www.jpl.nasa.gov/galileo/index.html

NASA offers this page dedicated to Project Galileo's mission to Jupiter. Visitors can check out the Galileo Probe team's science results and peruse the latest news, background information and frequently asked questions.

Ulysses Mission

http://ulysses.jpl.nasa.gov/ULSHOME.html

The home page of the Ulysses space craft, this site offers information on the craft's mission to explore the solar poles. Featured here are a description of the mission, science results, a movie, articles and bibliographies, as well as links to topic-related sites.

MAGELLAN

Magellan Mission to Venus—Online Resources

http://www.jpl.nasa.gov/magellan/

In words and photographs, this site details the Magellan trip to Venus. Visitors will find a variety Venus- and Magellan-related facts here.

MARS

Center for Mars Exploration

http://cmex-www.arc.nasa.gov/

The NASA Ames Home Page hosts this educational site about the planet Mars. Visitors will find space images, information on Mars missions and links to other topical organizations. Details are also provided on Mars-related software.

Mars Mission Research Center (M2RC) at N.C. State University

http://www.mmrc.ncsu.edu/

The Mars Mission Research Center at North Carolina University was established by NASA in 1988 and researches technology needed for expeditions to Mars. Visit for undergraduate and graduate information, online technical papers and an update of the center's current research.

Mars Surveyor MENU

http://esther.la.asu.edu/asu_tes/TES_Editor/MsurveyorMENU.html

MENU provides background about the Mars Surveyor Program, which begins with the launch of an orbiter in 1996. The site consists of news and updates on the program and links to other Mars resources.

MSSS Viking Image Archive

http://barsoom.msss.com/http/vikingdb.html

This searchable archive, maintained by Malin Space Science Systems (MSSS), houses more than 30,000 images of Mars collected by Viking orbiters between 1976 and 1980. The page includes a link to the MSSS home page.

Viking Mission to Mars—Online Resources

http://www.jpl.nasa.gov/planets/welcome/viking.htm

An index of online resources relating to the Viking Mission to Mars is provided here by NASA. Includes a short summary of the mission, descriptions of the Red Planet, technical information and resources specific to Viking Landers.

Viking Project Information

http://nssdc.gsfc.nasa.gov/planetary/viking.html

NASA's Viking Mission to Mars is described and illustrated at this Web site, which also contains information on spacecraft, experiments, and data available from the National Space Science Data Center Master Catalog. Visitors can view images sent back by the spacecraft.

THE MOON

Clementine

http://www.nrl.navy.mil/clementine/clementine.html

Details of Clementine Deep Space Program Science Experiment, sponsored by the U.S. National Aeronautics and Space Administration and other organizations, are available here. Visit this site for images, data and mission information.

Should We Return to the Moon?

http://www.ari.net/back2moon.html

The National Space Society and ARInternet Corporation sponsor this site, addressing the issue of further missions to the moon. Visit here to weigh the pros and cons and learn how to add your opinion to the topical forum.

NASA

Goddard Space Flight Center Home Page

http://pao.gsfc.nasa.gov/gsfc.html

The Goddard Space Flight Center, a facility of the U.S. National Aeronautics and Space Administration, maintains this site to introduce its departments and programs. Visit for mission overviews, scientific publications, research materials, public information services and departmental resources.

Goddard Space Flight Center Projects and Organizations

http://ssdoo.gsfc.nasa.gov/GSFC_orgpage.html

NASA's Goddard Space Flight Center posts a directory of projects and events here. Organized by directorate, the general administrative info mixes with research data relating to space observation.

Goddard Space Flight Center Space Science Data Operations Office

http://www.gsfc.nasa.gov/c630/ssdoo_main.html

The Space Science Data Operations Office at the National Aeronautics and Space Administration's Goddard Space Flight Center "serves various space science missions in processing, archiving, and disseminating data" and is the home of the National Space Science Data Center and the World Data Center-A for Rockets & Satellites.

John C. Stennis Space Center

http://www.ssc.nasa.gov/

A visit to the John C. Stennis Space Center site will inform users of the center's current and historical role in U.S. space exploration. A facility of the National Aeronautics and Space Administration (NASA), the center primarily tests rocket propulsion systems for the Space Shuttle.

Johnson Space Center

http://www.jsc.nasa.gov/

The Johnson Space Center, a division of the National Aeronautics and Space Administration, maintains this overview of its mission. Find links to JSC facilities and labs, projects, programs and groups, and general NASA services. A keyword search option offers quick reference.

The Kuiper Airborne Observatory

http://jean-luc.arc.nasa.gov/KAO/homepage.html

Based in California, NASA's Kuiper Airborne Observatory is a modified C-141A jet transport aircraft which supports research in infrared astronomy. Visit this site to learn more about the craft and its mission, read the newsletter and review the online gallery of photos and graphics.

Mission Operations and Data Systems Directorate

http://ddwilson.gsfc.nasa.gov/

NASA's Mission Operations and Data Systems Directorate is responsible for management of mission operations faciltiies, command and control, computer network configuration, communications and data processing. Includes links to directorate offices, divisions and the online information server.

NASA Kennedy Space Center

http://www.ksc.nasa.gov/

The home page for the NASA Kennedy Space Center tells visitors when the next space shuttle launch is planned and who will be on board. Historic archive info, programs and general U.S. space policies can also be accessed.

NASA Near Earth Asteroid Rendezvous

http://nssdc.gsfc.nasa.gov/planetary/near.html

NASA's Near Earth Asteroid Rendezvous mission scheduled for February and March 1996 is detailed on this page. Learn what the mission is supposed to accomplish, how it will be achieved and what it will cost—less than $150 million. Links to other NASA and space research sites are provided.

Voyager Mission Fact Sheet

http://vraptor.jpl.nasa.gov/voyager/voyager_fs.html

From NASA's larger Voyager Mission site, this page contains a text-only document offering a history of the Voyager mission and details of Voyager operations. Facts about the four planets surveyed are also featured.

SATURN

Cassini Information

http://nssdc.gsfc.nasa.gov/planetary/cassini.html

NASA serves up detailed information about the planned Cassini Oribiter mission here. The mission, scheduled for a 1997 launch, will deliver a probe to Titan and remain in orbit around Saturn to collect information on the planet. Astronomers and space buffs can also link to other planetary pages and related data.

Cassini Mission to Saturn

http://www.jpl.nasa.gov/cassini

The NASA Cassini Mission home page describes the upcoming mission to Saturn scheduled for launch in October 1997. Includes information about the spacecraft, a Saturn database and details on the flybys of Venus, Earth and Jupiter prior to the arrival at Saturn in 2004.

Cassini Mission to Saturn - Online Resources

http://cdwings.jpl.nasa.gov/PDS/public/cassini/cassini.html

In October 1997, the Cassini Orbiter will be launched on a mission to deliver the Huygens probe to Saturn and its moon, Titan. This home page is packed with information about the mission and launch, along with fact sheets, images and a universe of related links to explore.

Saturn Ring Plane Crossings of 1995-1996

http://newproducts.jpl.nasa.gov/saturn/

Maintained by a U.S. National Aeronautical and Space Administration engineer, this site offers images from the Hubble Space Telescope's view of Saturn. Visit here for a variety of Saturn images, including a rare look at its rings.

SPACE SHUTTLE

John C. Stennis Space Center

http://www.ssc.nasa.gov/

A visit to the John C. Stennis Space Center site will inform users of the center's current and historical role in U.S. space exploration. A facility of the National Aeronautics and Space Administration, the center primarily tests rocket propulsion systems for the Space Shuttle.

NASA Shuttle Web Archives

http://shuttle.nasa.gov/

Scientists and space buffs can follow the latest U.S. space exploration and experimentation at NASA's Shuttle Web Archives. Visitors can monitor current—and review past—Space Shuttle missions from countdown to landing.

SAREX - Shuttle Amateur Radio Experiment

http://hypatia.gsfc.nasa.gov/sarex_mainpage.html

Teachers who visit this NASA page can find out how their students can talk with Space Shuttle astronauts while they're in orbit. The agency's Shuttle Amateur Radio Experiment is detailed here and includes voice excerpts from space missions.

Shuttle Launch Countdown Home Page

http://www.ksc.nasa.gov/shuttle/countdown/

An official site maintained by NASA, this page describes the agency's space shuttle program. Photos and movies from recent missions are offered for public consumption, along with details on the spacecraft's construction and capabilities. A countdown clock ticks as launch times approach.

Space Shuttle Launches

http://www.ksc.nasa.gov/shuttle/missions/missions.html

Visitors to this site will learn about current and past Space Shuttle launches from the Kennedy Space Center. The site includes photos, shuttle details and the current shuttle manifest.

TELESCOPES

Adonis Adaptive Optics project WWW Server

http://hplyot.obspm.fr/

This is Adonis, the Adaptive Optics system with nightly mirrors of the great Nine Planets, the Web Nebulae and Planetary Nebulae. Includes an image gallery and project descriptions.

Broad Band X-ray Telescope Program

http://heasarc.gsfc.nasa.gov/docs/bbxrt/bbxrt_menu.html

The U.S. National Aeronautics and Space Administration's Goddard Space Flight Center maintains this site for its Broad Band X-ray Telescope Program. Visitors will find project overviews, facility descriptions, database access and discussions of related issues.

Caltech Millimeter Array

http://www.ovro.caltech.edu/~sls/cma

Visitors to this practical page will find in-house observatory instructions for utilizing the Caltech Millimeter Array of telescopes. Links to technical documents and online demos are also featured.

Cambridge Low-Frequency Synthesis Telescope

http://www.mrao.cam.ac.uk/

The Low-Frequency Synthesis Telescope facility at England's Cambridge University maintains this informational site. Visit here for an overview of the facility and links to current survey data records.

Cambridge Optical Aperture Synthesis Telescope

http://www.mrao.cam.ac.uk/

The Cambridge Optical Aperture Synthesis Telescope (COAST) "is planned as a coherent array of four telescopes operating in the red and infrared." Visitors to this site can learn more about the instrument and the objectives of the project.

Canada-France-Hawaii Telescope Archive

http://cadcwww.dao.nrc.ca/cfht/cfht.html

The Canada-France-Hawaii Telescope Archive (CFHT) is a compilation of data based on observations through a telescope atop the summit of Mauna Kea, a dormant volcano in Hawaii. This data is catagorized into departments such as REDEYE (infra-red camera) and MOS (MultiObject Spectrograph) to name a few. Data is public, but acknowledgement to CFHT is requested.

Canada-France-Hawaii Telescope Archive MOS Users' Manual

http://www.cfht.hawaii.edu/manuals/mos/mos_man.html

This site houses a users' manual for the CFHT Multi-Object Imaging Spectrograph (MOS). Technical and specific information is presented here, including discussions of optical and mechanical layout, environment and performance, and control and data acquisition.

COMPTEL

http://cossc.gsfc.nasa.gov/cossc/COMPTEL.html

NASA operates COMPTEL, an Imaging Compton Telescope, at its Laboratory for High Energy Astrophysics. Visitors can learn about the instrument and access the data it collects at this site.

CSIRO Australia Telescope National Facility FTP Archive

ftp://ftp.atnf.csiro.au/pub/software/karma

Karma is the anonymous FTP software archive operated by CSIRO Australia Telescope National Facility in Sydney. Look here for data and utilities useful for radiophysics work. It's also available by e-mail.

Danish Telescopes

http://www.astro.ku.dk/~michael/dantel.html

This is a collection of descriptions and photos of Danish astronomical telescopes. Visitors can find information on professional and student astronomical instruments.

Deep Undersea Muon and Neutrino Detection

http://web.phys.washington.edu/local_web/dumand/aaa_dumand_home.html

DUMAND—Deep Undersea Muon and Neutrino Detection—is a special telescope sensitive to neutrinos rather than light. This home page covers the project with information, related links and several layers of explanation provided for laymen, amateurs and scientists.

Effelsberg 100-m telescope (MPIfR)

http://www.mpifr-bonn.mpg.de/effberg.html

The Effelsberg 100-m Radio Telescope is the world's largest movable radio telescope, belonging to the Max-Planck-Institute for Radioastronomy in Germany. Find descriptions of the telescope, an image gallery, proposal request forms and staff profiles.

Energetic Gamma Ray Experiment Telescope

http://cossc.gsfc.nasa.gov/cossc/EGRET.html

Information about NASA's Energetic Gamma Ray Experiment Telescope (EGRET) project can be accessed via this home page. Visitors can read descriptions of the telescope and view images.

The Gemini 8m Telescopes Project

http://www.gemini.edu/

The Gemini 8m Telescopes Project is an international astronomy partnership between the U.S., England, Canada, Chile, Argentina and Brazil. Visitors to the site will find photos, announcements, a newsletter and documentation among the available data.

HEAT Experiment Page

http://tigger.physics.lsa.umich.edu/www/heat/heat.html

The HEAT Home page is a site devoted to the High-Energy, Antimatter Telescope Experiment being conducted by NASA. Schematics and descriptions of the research are included.

Hopkins Ultraviolet Telescope Project

http://praxis.pha.jhu.edu/hut.html

Johns Hopkins University maintains this site for its Ultraviolet Telescope, designed and built by astronomers and engineers at Johns Hopkins to perform observations in the far-ultraviolet portion of the electromagnetic spectrum. Visitors will find an introduction to the telescope, its creators and a wide range of scientific observations.

Infrared Telescope Facility—NASA

http://irtf.ifa.hawaii.edu/

This Web site features general facility information and electronic reprints of documents associated with NASA's Infrared Telescope Facility. Includes a gallery of images obtained by the telescope, plus information for use by the facility's community.

The Isaac Newton Group of Telescopes

http://www.ast.cam.ac.uk/ING

Investigate the Royal Observatories' Canary Islands-based telescope trio—three eyepieces aimed at the sky from their home on La Palma—at this site. Visitors here will spot details about the astronomical equipment, along with scheduling information, observation logs and more.

The Loiano Telescopes

http://www.bo.astro.it/loiano/LoianoHome.html

The Loiano Telescopes site provides information on the educational programs, research and staff of the astronomical research facility and its equipment. Includes detailed descriptions of the telescopes, observations and links to relevant publications.

Lund Observatory

http://nastol.astro.lu.se/Html/home.html

Sweden's Lund Observatory maintains this site with information on the facility, staff and projects, and astronomy. Visitors can learn more about the Nordic Optical Telescope, view images and peruse scientific and research data. In English and Swedish.

National Optical Astronomy Observatories (NOAO)

ftp://gemini.tuc.noao.edu/pub/wiyn

The National Optical Astronomy Observatories maintains this FTP site with information about the United States Gemini Program, the liaison between the United States Astronomical Community and the international Gemini Telescopes. Find out more about the telescopes and link to the IR Weather Pictures Directory.

Nordic Optical Telescope

http://nastol.astro.lu.se/Html/not.html

The Nordic Optical Telescope is a 2.6 meter telescope located at La Palma, Canary Islands, and is jointly operated by the Nordic Countries. Observation schedules and forms for observing time applications are available.

Osservatorio Astronomico di Padova.

http://www.pd.astro.it/

The Astronomical Observatory of Padova is a major node in the Italian network of astronomical research facilities. Visitors to its site will find an organizational overview, project and telescope descriptions, news, and job announcements for post-doctorate positions.

Parkes Observatory and Parkes Radiotelescope Home Page

http://wwwpks.atnf.csiro.au/

Australia's Parkes Observatory welcomes 55,000 visitors a year to "the world's most beautiful radiotelescope," and that's not counting virtual visitors. Its Web site offers photos, updates on research projects, and surveys and databases.

RGSC HST Guide Star Catalog Search Program

http://tdc-www.harvard.edu/software/rgsc.html

The Telescope Data Center presents instructions, examples, history and an FTP directory for rgsc software, which extracts entries of the Space Telescope Guide Star Catalog and saves the results to a disk file.

Sloan Digital Sky Survey

http://www-sdss.fnal.gov:8000/

Sloan Digital Sky Survey (SDSS) is a National Foundation of Science project seeking to build a telescope for wide-angle sky surveys. Find general information and operations specifications for the SDSS astronomical research project on this server.

Smithsonian Astrophysical Observatory Telescope Data Center

http://tdc-www.harvard.edu/TDC.html

The Smithsonian Astrophysical Observatory Telescope Data Center develops software to process and store data from several optical telescopes. Includes descriptions of software, as well as access to data sites and image galleries.

Soft X-Ray Telescope

http://pore1.space.lockheed.com/SXT/homepage.html

Lockheed's Solar and Astrophysics Laboratory presents the home page for its Soft X-Ray Telescope program. Visitors can view pictures of the sun taken with this instrument and obtain information about the lab's research projects and other programs.

Space InfraRed Telescope Facility

http://sirtf.jpl.nasa.gov/sirtf

Currently under development by NASA, the Space InfraRed Telescope Facility (SIRTF) will be a space-based astronomical workhorse. This Web site provides detailed information about the planned telescope, including news, overviews and pictures.

Stratospheric Observatory For Infrared Astronomy

http://sofia.arc.nasa.gov/

The Stratospheric Observatory For Infrared Astronomy (SOFIA) is a long name for a short telescope mounted in a Boeing 747. SOFIA is used for performing observations at stratospheric altitudes. Find program information and data here.

Teide Observatory

http://www.iac.es/folleto/teide.html

This home page for the Teide Observatory in the Canary Islands touts the observatory's significance as a key site for solar research and home for some of the best solar telescopes in the world. The Web site features photos of the telescopes and descriptions of research projects.

The United Kingdom InfraRed Telescope

http://www.jach.hawaii.edu/UKIRT/home.html

The Joint Astronomy Center (JAC) provides information on the United Kingdom InfraRed Telescope (UKIRT). Visitors can learn more about the telecope, affiliated research projects and its observations, or follow links to topic-related sites.

University of Iowa Automated Telescope Facility

http://inferno.physics.uiowa.edu/

The Automated Telescope Facility at the University of Iowa maintains this site for general information about and access to its space images.

Very Large Telescope (VLT) Project

http://http.hq.eso.org/vlt.html

The Very Large Telescope Project at the European Southern Observatory serves as the subject of this page. Find news releases, preprints and other publications, plus links to topic-related sites.

The Westerbork Radio Synthesis Telescope

http://kapteyn.astro.rug.nl/UserDoc.html

The Netherlands Foundation for Research in Astronomy supplies documentation for the Westerbork Radio Synthesis Telescope. The files are provided in six parts. Also find aids for submitting project proposals.

Whately Page

http://scruffy.phast.umass.edu/Whately/whately.html

The Whately Telescope is a part of Amherst's University of Massachusetts Department of Astronomy. This site provides images, research notes and specifications for this student research instrument.

Whipple Observatory

http://cfa-www.harvard.edu/cfa/whipple.html

Whipple Observatory in Amado, Arizona, provides information here on its optical and electromagnetic telescope equipment. Visit this site for details on the sizes and types of equipment used at the facility.

The Wisconsin, Indiana, Yale and NAOA 3.5 Meter Telescope

http://www.astro.indiana.edu/facilities/observatories/wiyn

An image of the Wisconsin, Indiana, Yale and NAOA (WIYN) 3.5 meter telescope on Kitt Peak in Arizona, can be downloaded from this page. There are also links to the WIYN observatory home page and Indiana University astronomy resources.

Wyoming Infrared Observatory

http://faraday.uwyo.edu/physics.astronomy/brochures/wiro.html

The Wyoming Infrared Observatory (WIRO) home page contains information on research projects and staff. Includes descriptions of facilities, technical info and educational programs.

HUBBLE SPACE TELESCOPE

Astronomical Pictures

http://www.univ-rennes1.fr/ASTRO/astro.html

This picture gallery provides links to astronomical images, animation, sounds and more. Among the offerings are planets, eclipses and visuals from the Hubble Space Telescope. In French and English.

Astronomical Pictures

http://web.cnam.fr/astro.english.html

France's National Conservatory of Arts and Crafts maintains this site an index of astronomy-related graphics. Visit here for images from the Hubble Space Telescope and other international space exploration activities. In French and English.

Canadian Astronomy Data Centre

http://cadcwww.dao.nrc.ca/

The Herzberg Institute of Astrophysics houses the Canadian Astronomy Data Centre. From the CADC site, access a collection of astronomical data archives and observation catalogs. The CADC distributes data from the Hubble Space Telescope and the Canada-France-Hawaii Telescope.

Canadian Astronomy Data Centre HST Science Archive

http://cadcwww.dao.nrc.ca/hst.html

At this site, maintained by the Canadian Astronomy Data Centre, scientists can access data gathered by the the Hubble Space Telescope. Search the database and preview images here.

Center for Astrophysics and Space Sciences at the University of California, San Diego

http://cassfos01.ucsd.edu:8080/ghrs.html

The Center for Astrophysics and Space Sciences at the University of California at San Diego features its work with the Hubble Space Telescope and multi-channel Digicon photon detectors. The page includes links to developers and researchers.

Comet Shoemaker-Levy 9

http://nssdc.gsfc.nasa.gov/planetary/comet.html

Watch the 1994 Comet Shoemaker-Levy 9 collide with the planet Jupiter. Observations of this astronomical event and its aftermath were recorded by the Hubble Space Telescope and other spacecraft and observatories. View these images or link to related Internet sites here.

Faint Object Spectrograph Group at the University of California-San Diego

http://cassfos01.ucsd.edu:8080/fos.html

The University of California at San Diego offers an overview of the Hubble Space Telescope's Faint Object Spectrograph (FOS) here, including a history of its development and the UCSD FOS Team involvement. Access the team's scientific papers and notes, and view images which "prove the existence of [a] massive black hole."

Hubble Space Telescope

http://ecf.hq.eso.org/HST.html

The European Coordinating Facility of the Hubble Space Telescope maintains this site to outline the satellite's observation capabilities. Visit here to learn about its optical and electromagnetic telescope equipment.

Hubble Space Telescope: Latest Releases

http://www.stsci.edu/EPA/Latest.html

The National Aeronautics and Space Administration's (NASA) Space Telescope Science Institute posts data from its latest look at the stars. View globular clusters and star births at this site.

Hubble Space Telescope Public Images

http://ecf.hq.eso.org/stecf-pubrel.html

Naysayers predicted failure for the Hubble Space Telescope, the giant craft sent deep into space to return images and info on places no man has seen, but six years after HST was released, the telescope is still going strong and sending back information. Marvel at HST images here with accompanying text, such as an image of the rings of Saturn, the atmosphere of Jupiter and Uranus, and documentation of a dying star.

Latest Hubble Space Telescope Observations

http://www.stsci.edu/pubinfo/Latest.html

Take a peek at the distant reaches of the galaxy by viewing the pictures exhibited here. The Space Telescope Science Institute offers the latest press releases about and photos from the Hubble Space Telescope, along with archives of older images.

Saturn Ring Plane Crossing

http://www.stsci.edu/EPA/PR/95/25.html

Maintained by a U.S. National Aeronautical and Space Administration engineer, this site offers images from the Hubble Space Telescope's view of Saturn. Visit here for a variety of Saturn images, including a rare look at its rings.

Science with the Hubble Space Telescope II

http://http.hq.eso.org/hst2.html

Maintained by the European Southern Observatory, this site contains information on Science with the Hubble Space Telescope, a scientific conference co-sponsored by the Space Telescope Institute in Baltimore, Md. Links to program notes, a participants list and related topical sites are featured.

Space Telescope-European Coordinating Facility

http://arch-http.hq.eso.org/
ESO-ECF-Archive.html

The European Coordinating Facility (ECF) helps the European astronomy community fully develop the research opportunities provided by NASA's Hubble Space Telescope. Astronomers can take a detailed look at ECF here and can link to sites that contain Hubble's observing guidelines and images.

Space Telescope Science Data Analysis System

http://ra.stsci.edu/STSDAS.html

The Space Telescope Science Data Analysis System site contains information about this software for processing data from the Hubble Space Telescope. Includes downloading instructions, documentation and help.

Space Telescope Science Data Analysis System–Help System Top Level

http://ra.stsci.edu/HelpSys.html

The Space Telescope Science Data Analysis System is a calibration and analysis software tool for Hubble Space Telescope data. This highly technical site provides pointers to help files.

Usenet Newsgroup sci.astro.hubble

http://wfpc3.la.asu.edu/sah.html

Arizona State University maintains this archive of material for the Usenet newsgroup sci.astro.hubble, which is devoted to the Hubble Space Telescope. Visitors here will find frequently asked questions files, images, and various interfaces and access points for both the archive and newsgroup.

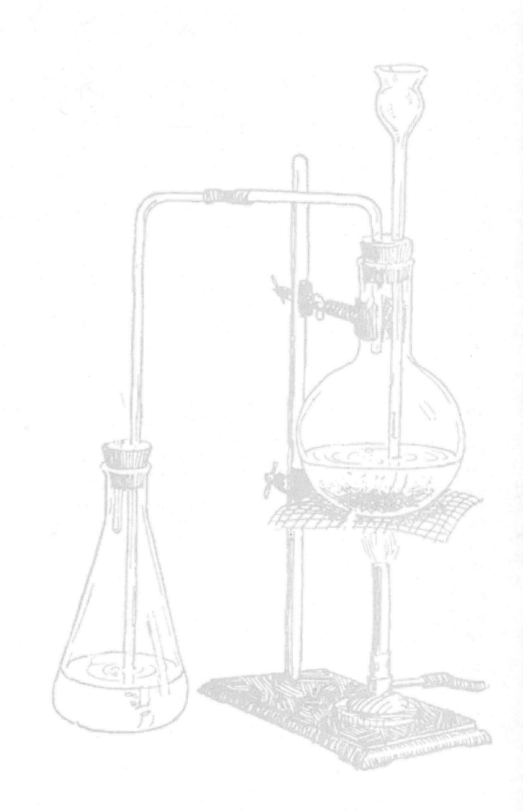

SHOPPING THE NET

THE 25 MOST POPULAR SHOPPING SITES

All-Internet Shopping Directory
http://www.webcom.com/~tbrown/

Ashly Audio Inc. Home Page
http://www.ashly.com/

Chic Paris
http://www.inetbiz.com/chic/

Chile Today - Hot Tamale
http://emall.com/Chile/Chile1.html

CouponNet Home Page
http://coupon.com/coupon.html

The Dragonfly Toy Company
http://www.magic.mb.ca/~dragon/

Electronic Gun Shop
http://www.xmission.com/~chad/egs/egs.html

Emergency Preparedness Information Center
http://TheEpicenter.com/

Enter FAO Schwarz
http://faoschwarz.com/

First Virtual InfoHaus
http://www.infohaus.com/

The Flower Link
http://go.flowerlink.com/html/menu1.html

Flower Stop Storefront
http://www.flowerstop.com/fstop/fstopmain.html

Gallery of American Artisans
http://www.usa.net/gallery/

Guitar: The Holy Grail
http://www.vvg.com/

The Home Team
http://www.hometeam.com/

Internet Village
http://www.internet.village.com/

Kinesava Geographics
http://www.insv.com/kinesava/

Namark Cap & Emblem
http://www.accessnv.com/namark/

Naturally Yours
http://www.america.com/mall/store/naturally.html

Northwest River Supplies
http://www.gorp.com/nrs.htm

Residential Designs
http://www.atlwin.com/resdes/resdes.htm

Spectrum Trading
http://www.spectrum-t.com/

Star Trek: The Next Generation Holographic T-Shirt
http://www.icw.com/global/startrek.html

Sweet Seductions
http://connexion.parallax.co.uk/seduct/

Uncommon Connections
http://www.mps.org/~uncommon/

APPAREL

America's (Genius) T-Shirt Order Form

http://branch.com/amshirt/ordshirt.htm

Like your T-shirts with a scholarly bent? The company offers over 40 designs, including the visages Einstein, Lincoln and the Bard himself. This page is the order form, but a link to the main page is offered.

Burlington Coat Factory

http://www.coat.com/

The Burlington Coat Factory brings its venerable business to the Internet. This home page incorporates a clickable-map store locator, a "Baby Depot" browser, and links to such destinations as the current "savings flyer," the luxury linens division, and the personnel department.

Chic Paris

http://www.inetbiz.com/chic/

The Chic Paris site is an online fashion catalog and shopping site for selected Paris fashions, with browsing and search features, instructions on ordering and a return policy.

Earrings by Lisa!

http://mmink.cts.com/mmink/kiosks/earrings/earrings.html

If your earlobes are full of empty holes, or if you just can't get enough of bangles, french hooks, hoops and studs, stop by Earrings by Lisa for handmade earrings. Visitors can browse images of the earrings and reserve them online. Payment is made through the mail. Sorry, no virtual piercing available (yet).

Express Online

http://express.style.com/

The Internet Plaza hosts Express, a French Internet club for "fashion-forward" women. Includes a tour for visitors that includes fashion tips. Registrants can receive discounts and special shopping opportunities.

Fashion World International

http://www.quiknet.com/fashion/fwi.html

This shopping site offers erotic fashions from mild to wild. Visitors are invited to browse a selection of Victorian corsets, maid's dresses and more. No nudity.

Hot Deals Deadwear

http://www.hotdeal.com/deadwear/

Exclusive deals on Deadwear ranging from tie-dyed shirts to brief cases can be purchased online or via a toll-free number at Hot Deals Deadwear.

Visitors will also find links to additional Grateful Dead resources.

The Jewelers of Las Vegas

http://www.manifest.com/Jewelers/index.html

The Jewelers of Las Vegas specializes in the manufacture, import and distribution of fine jewelry. Visitors can peruse details about the store's 10 U.S. locations, browse an online catalog or read about jewelry manufacturing.

Mighty Dog Designs

http://sashimi.wwa.com/~notime/mdd/mddhome.html

Mighty Dog Designs of Clemson, S.C., supplies vibrant images and information on its T-shirts and coffee mugs. An online ordering form is included.

The Milne Jewelry Company

http://branch.com/milne/Milne01.html

The Milne Jewelry Company offers an online catalog of its southwestern jewelry here. Visitors can browse the catalog, obtain company contact information or link to the Branch Mall, the host of this page. In Japanese and English.

Namark Cap & Emblem

http://www.accessnv.com/namark

Namark Cap & Emblem custom prints T-shirts, mugs and caps. Shoppers can fax or email designs and place orders online here.

Netscape General Store

http://merchant.netscape.com/netstore/index.html

The Netscape General Store allows online purchasing of Netscape's logo-intensive clothing. Shoppers can use credit cards to consummate the deal electronically.

Nine Lives Clothing Consignment Store

http://chezhal.slip.netcom.com/index.html

Nine Lives Clothing Consignment Store is a consignment clothing shop based in Los Gatos, Calif. Visitors can browse the inventories of men's and women's clothing or fill out a personal profile and hire a personal shopping assistant.

Pegasus Printing

http://www.teleport.com/~codpiece/index.html

Here, Pegasus Printing presents descriptions and ordering information about its clothing lines from Codpiece International and Bridal Casuals. Includes background on the company and contact information.

Preziosi Jewelry Online Catalog

http://www.italnet.it/italweb/preziosi/homepage.html

Preziosi, an Italian jeweler, posts an online catalog of its 18-karat gold handmade jewelry here. Visitors can shop online, read a background of the

company or send an e-mail request for a catalog via postal mail.

Sophisticated Shirts

http://www.a1.com/shirt/t-shirt.html

Sophisticated Shirts, an online shop that sells artistic T-shirts and sweatshirts, maintains this promotional site with shirt previews and ordering information.

X-Large Inte[r]network

http://www.cinenet.net/XLarge/

Hipster clothiers X-Large posts the current collection complete with a statement from its spokesmodel at the X-Large Inte[r]network. Find the outlet nearest you.

AUTOS

Auto-By-Tel

http://www.autobytel.com/

Web surfers who'd rather be driving can buy or lease a new car or truck online from Auto-By-Tel. The company claims to offer the lowest prices for the purchaser's area.

The Automobile Buyers' Network

http://www.dmssoft.com/

Kick tires online at the Automobile Buyers' Network. Visitors can peruse classified listings complete with color photos or link directly to a list of dealers via this service.

The Automobile Home Page

http://ganglion.anes.med.umich.edu/NSX/misc/other-pages.html

The Automobile Home Page is a collection of links to various automobile resources on the Internet. Visitors will find links to car manufacturer pages and auto care resources.

Automobiles2

http://www.w2.com/pacepub.html

Pace Publications pitches its automotive price and buying guides at this site, a segment of the World Square online mall. Visitors will find prices and ordering information for such items as new- and used-car buying guides and an "Auto Price Almanac."

AutoNetwork

http://www.autonetwork.com/

Take some of the mystery out of buying a car at AutoNetwork. Visit its Interactive Purchasing Agent site for preferred service and updated price listings that will get you the best deal possible on a new or used automobile.

AutoWeb Interactive

http://www.autoweb.com/

AutoWeb Interactive, a Cupertino, Calif.-based online guide for car buyers, offers detailed information and listings from dealers around the United States. Visit here to find the best deal on a new or used car.

Cadillac Hard Drive

http://www.cadillac.com/

Luxury car-lovers will enjoy a cruise this Cadillac enthusiast site. Visit here for new and classic car information, top-rated automotive service centers and links to related sites.

Chevrolet-Online

http://www.chevrolet-online.com/

Chevrolet-Online offers 24-hour showroom shopping for car and truck buyers in the northeast. Browse the makes, models, and money matters, then e-mail or visit the nearest dealership to close the deal.

Criswell Chevrolet

http://www.clark.net/pub/networx/autopage/dealers/de002.html

Criswell Chevrolet, a Maryland-based car dealer, features its current sales stock of used and new vehicles at this promotional site. Visitors can access photos and descriptions of the cars, along with retail prices.

DealerNet: The Source for New Car Information

http://www.dealernet.com/

With its "virtual showroom," DealerNet wants to sell you not only a car, but a car dealer. Use this site to search for a dealer or a car. isitors can also flip through auto reviews or download a copy of a confidential credit application.

Hot Rods World Wide

http://www.america.net/com/hotrods/hrhome.html

HotRods World Wide is a site for buying and selling street rods, muscle cars and antique autos. Enthusiasts can place ads and find their dream cars for sale here.

MotorCity

http://www.motorcity.com/

MotorCity offers news and information of interest to car shoppers, including new automobile specifications, links to auto dealerships and a global vehicle locator. Visitors can check the Dollars and Sense section for loan and leasing information.

Universal City Nissan

http://www.deltanet.com/nissan1

Universal City Nissan, a southern California dealership, maintains this promotional site with sales and repair information. Visit here for a virtual tour of its new car showroom, price and availability information, parts listings and more.

FLOWERS

Absolutely Fresh Flowers

http://www.cts.com/~flowers/

At Absolutely Fresh Flowers, shoppers can have flower arrangements shipped via Federal Express from the southern California flower grower to any location within the United States. Electronic orders accepted.

The Flower Link

http://go.flowerlink.com/html/menu1.html

This digital flower and gift shop, set up by a group of U.S. and Canadian florists, allows visitors easy access to directories of participating florists, categorized by ZIP code and region. Cut flower and plant care information is also available here.

Flower Stop Storefront

http://www.flowerstop.com/fstop/fstopmain.html

Flower Stop, a Colorado Springs, Colo.-based retail florist, maintains this promotional site and online ordering form. Visit here to select and send floral arrangements across town or around the globe.

FlowersUSA

http://flowersusa.com/flowers2.html

Sure, FlowersUSA offers a huge selection of plants and flower arrangements ... but they also carry a full line of fruit and gourmet baskets, candy, balloons, etc. Same-day service is offered for U.S. deliveries.

FOOD AND DRINK

Chile Today–Hot Tamale

http://emall.com/Chile/Chile1.html

Chile Today–Hot Tamale is a company offering personal gift memberships for monthly deliveries of chile or hot sauces. Visitors to this site can obtain ordering info, read a variety of factoids about chile, or browse numerous chile and hot sauce recipes.

The Chocolate Lovers' Page

http://bc.emanon.net/chocolate/

The Chocolate Lovers' Page presents a comprehensive list of shops and companies that sell chocolate on the Internet, as well as links to recipes and other chocolate goodies.

Godiva Online Home Page

http://www.godiva.com/

At the Godiva Chocolatier's site, shop online, browse the recipe file or read the current issue of "Chocolatier" magazine. Also find contests, company news and chocolate resources featured.

Kosher Express

http://www.marketnet.com/mktnet/kosher

Stumped for the holiday feast? The Matzah Market offers kosher culinary delights including recipes for the essential kugel, potato knish and mandelbrot. You can fax in an order for bagels, kisha mix or gefilte fish using the online catalog provided.

Michigan Marketing Association Earthy Delights Home Page

http://earthy.com/index.htm

The Michigan Marketing Association (MMA) Earthy Delights distributes specialty produce to restaurants, clubs, hotels and the "adventurous gourmet." Sample MMA's top-shelf products including hot chiles and Southwest cuisine, baby vegetables, edible flowers and purple sticky rice.

Naturally Yours

http://www.america.com/mall/store/naturally.html

Based in Daytona Beach, Fla., Naturally Yours promotes health and better eating through its varied selections of natural organic grains, berries, sprouts and uncooked honey. Visit this electronic storefront to shop or link to pages offering recipes, health guides and more.

Pizza Hut

http://www.pizzahut.com/

The Pizza Hut home page invites visitors to peruse its menu and order pizza online. If you so desire, you can also submit comments to the restaurant chain.

Spice Merchant

http://emall.com/Spice/Spice1.html

Cooks and spice specialists can harvest those hard-to-find spices at this online source. Find Chinese condiments, Thai and Indonesian specialties, and Indian spices and teas. Online ordering.

Sweet Seductions

http://www.parallax.co.uk/seduct/

Sweet Seductions presents some of the finest chocolates available on the Internet for virtual sweet tooths. Visitors can browse the shop's selection of chocolate confections or follow links to information about cocoa, its history and uses.

Virtual Vineyards

http://www.virtualvin.com/

Virtual Vineyards gives advice on how to buy the gourmet foods and fine wines recommended by renowned wine expert, Peter Granoff. Visit this site to use Peter's trademarked tasting chart and to order food and wine selections online.

Wines on the Internet

http://www.wines.com/

Lovers of the grape will find a "cyberspace guide to wine and wineries" at Wines on the Internet. Explore "virtual wine country" or check out the "tasting room." Those seeking "unique or exceptional values" can even order selections online.

YCC Wineline—Wine Online

http://www.interaccess.com/wineline/

This commercial page is the Web home of Your Country Cellar, an online wine shop offering selection assistance and guidance. Learn about the company, subscribe to the free newsletter or browse the shop for gifts and wines from around the world.

GIFTS

Archie McPhee

http://www.mcphee.com/

Archie McPhee boasts a broad selection of popular culture artifacts available for sale online. Visitors can browse this eclectic collection of objects, ranging from rubber chickens to voodoo dolls and bizarre candy.

Auntie Q's Antiques & Collectibles

http://www.teleport.com/~auntyq/

Auntie Q's Antiques & Collectibles lets you browse an online catalog of gifts and books, complete with ordering information. Find out what's "new" among the "old" in a weekly special offering.

Celtic Cultures

http://www.sover.net/~celtic/

Celtic Cultures, an online market of Celtic goods, offers books, clothing, jewelry and more. This page also features links to other Celtic sites on the Internet.

Chosen Reflections

http://www.primenet.com/~magazin

Commemorate a birthday with a magazine printed on the date of the recipient's birth. Chosen Reflections serves up information on over 1,000 available magazines for collectors or original gift givers. Order magazines or browse a catalog of available products at this promotional site.

Classique Structure

http://www.netaxs.com/~vlad/cs

Need a gargoyle? How about a cherub? The Pennsylvannia-based Classique Structure sells gift items and home furnishings over the Internet. Online ordering is available.

Crafter's Showcase

http://www.northcoast.com/unlimited/product_directory/cs/cs.html

California-based artisans offer photographs and descriptions of their homey crafts at this site. Visitors who wish to purchase angel dolls, cat plaques, or miniature redwood carousels will find ordering information here.

Danner Studios

http://www.dannerstudios.com/

This online exhibition of wildlife sculptures from Danner Studios of Roanoke, Va., showcases the work of artist Dennis Danner. Danner's handiwork includes owls, rabbits, chipmunks, and other woodland creatures. Ordering details included.

Dewey Trading Company

http://www.nets.com/dewey

The Dewey Trading Company offers southwestern trail blankets designed by Native American weaver Ramona Sakiestewa. Sales of these blankets support charitable organizations dedicated to history, education, and environmental preservation.

5-D Stereograms Home Page

http://www.ais.net/netmall/bma/

Here's an ad for 5-D Stereograms from Blue Mountain Arts. Stereograms hide two different views of a scene within a single piece of artwork. Visitors to this page can preview these 5-D graphics and obtain ordering information.

FolkArt & Craft Exchange

http://www.folkart.com/

The FolkArt & Craft Exchange, a service of Sunnyvale, Calif.-based arts promoter Latitude International, provides a forum for buying and selling hand-made crafts by American indigenous peoples. Visit here for an index of resources in English, Japanese and Spanish.

Gallery of American Artisans

http://www.usa.net/gallery/

The Gallery of American Artisans offers a collection of handcrafted gifts and accessories for sale online. Includes an electronic catalog, ordering information and artisans' bios.

Jan's Custom Knits

http://www.puffin.com/puffin

If you've got a hankering to knit your niece or nephew a personalized baby blanket, you might consider this option. You can order a custom made blanket (or other item) at this site, and let the recipient think you made it yourself. Many designs are available in a variety of languages.

Khazana-India Arts Online

http://www.winternet.com/~khazana/index.html

Khazana, a Minneapolis, Minn.-based retailer of collectibles from India and Nepal, maintains this site with general information. Visit here to view its wide range of handmade ornaments, statues, and more.

Spencer Gifts

http://www.btg.com/spencer/

In search of a letter from Elvis? How about Kurt Cobain's face? It's all available at the Spencer Gifts site. Other products include signs, wall fixtures and phones.

Uncommon Connections

http://www.mps.org/~uncommon

Uncommon Connections, an online shopping service of Winona, Minn.-based Vanguard Technology Group, offers links to unique gift merchants. Visit here to find "extra special gifts you're not going to find at the local mall," including gourmet coffees, environmentally friendly electronics, designer checks, and more.

GRAB BAG

Catalog Mart Home Page

http://catalog.savvy.com/

Catalog Mart offers a "direct way to receive just about any catalog offered in the U.S." The site's list includes more than 10,000 titles. Visitors can browse the list and order catalogs; vendors can add titles to the list.

Classified Advertising

http://www.imall.com/ads/ads.shtml

The iMALL, an Internet shopping venue, maintains this site offering classified advertising. Visitors can perform a keyword search, browse ads or link to other iMALL areas of interest.

CouponNet

http://coupon.com/coupon.html

CouponNet is a service pointing visitors to products sold on the Internet for which money saving coupons are available. The exchange area allows visitors to trade coupons and rebate offers with one another.

Defense Reutilization and Marketing Service

http://www.drms.dla.mil/

Welcome to the discount warehouse of surplus U.S. Defense Department government supplies. Public shoppers can eyeball the wares here—everything from automobiles and aircraft parts to clothing, computers, furniture, scrap metal and more.

EPages Internet Classifieds

http://ep.com/

The EPages Internet Classifieds provides free classified advertising for Internet users. Classifieds are divided by subject and region. Includes instructions for placing an ad.

FinanceNet

http://www.financenet.gov/

FinanceNet provides listings of government asset sales to the general public. Visitors can access document libraries, mailing lists and discussion forums devoted to government auctions and sales.

Flea Market @ FUW

http://info.fuw.edu.pl/market/market.html

Warsaw University's Physics Department sponsors an online flea market. Services include ad placement and search forms.

Future Endeavors

http://www.lsi.net/Business/Future

Future Endeavors markets consumer services, including grocery coupon books for brand-name products, mortgage purchases, telephone check verification and a long distance service. Site features include price and ordering information.

Hypnosis.com

http://www.hypnosis.com/

Sort of a hypnosis mall, this site links visitors to book and tape vendors selling hypnosis-related materials. Includes information on related educational resources and a Frequently Asked Questions (FAQ) file.

Ingrid O'Neil—Olympic Games Memorabilia

http://www.infopost.com/olympics/index.html

Shoppers can order a catalog of Olympic memorabilia here. The page contains a look at some of the merchandise such as porcelain plates and participation medals. Includes a phone number for ordering, pricing and catalog information.

Iron Rod, Inc.

http://www.xmission.com/~ironrod

Iron Rod presents a menu of religious products: books, scriptures software, music, videos, pictures, statuary, toys, and more. An order form is included.

Lamp Technology, Inc.

http://www.webscope.com/lamptech/info.html

Lamp Technology, Inc., Bohemia, N.Y., offers over 10,000 types of light bulbs at discounted prices, with product and price information, interesting facts about lighting, and an order/catalog request form.

Netsurfer Marketplace

http://www.netsurf.com/nsm/latest.mktplace.html

Netsurfer Marketplace is the commercial supplement to Netsurfer Digest, available on the Web and by e-mail. The Marketplace provides information on companies, services and products, with links to those home pages and, when appropriate, ordering information.

NETWorld MarketPlace

http://www.networldmkt.com/networld

NETWorld MarketPlace is a commercial service offering an index of products and services. Among the products are watches and nylons; among the services are classifed ads and job opportunities.

Oxystat

http://www.oxystat.com/diabetes

Diabetics can order medical supplies and accessories online at the Oxystat commercial site. Promoting a complete and fully stocked inventory, automatic delivery and insurance billing, plus bilingual customer service, the company urges visitors to become Oxystat clients.

The People's Place on the Web

http://peopleplace.com/

Shoppers interested in nutrition and alternative health can shop in this cyber marketplace for personal growth services, yoga classes and health food. The page also contains cancer information.

Price Costco

http://www.pricecostco.com/

This promotional site is the Web home of Price-Costco, a national, members-only retail "warehouse" chain. Visitors can learn about the company, read its online newsletter or access its product forum.

Steamed Heat of California

http://steamedheat.com/

"Steamed Heat," an online catalog of erotic art and fashion, hawks its sexually charged products here. Visitors can view and order products and link with Web sites offering body jewelry and information for "outgoing, social couples."

Street Cents Online

http://www.screen.com/streetcents.html

"Street Cents Online is about your money—how to get it and how not to get ripped off when you spend it." These money-conscious Canadian correspondents operate a kind of "Consumer Reports" for the Web, evaluating products and offering seasonal money-saving tips throughout the year.

The Sunday Paper

http://www.sundaypaper.com/

A presentation of Bulkin Enterprises Inc., "The Sunday Paper" is an online classified ad network. Visitors can find out how to receive free monthly deliveries and place ads.

Tecfen Corporation

http://www.tecfen.com/

Rescue teams can increase their preparedness levels by ordering medical products and emergency equipment from California's Tecfen Corporation. Shop for products online at this promotional site.

TradeSafe Online

http://www.brainiac.com/tradesafe

A flea market in cyberspace? You bet! Buy, sell or trade with people from around the world. Hosted by the TradeSafe Online Corporation, this site features company information and fee schedule.

UFO Trading
http://www.ufo.com.au/UFO
UFO Trading, a company based in Melbourne, Australia, offers a range of funky products available for ordering online; from condom vases to SmileyWear T-shirts.

Ultimate Weapons Systems Home Page
http://www.uws.com/
At this site, the public can check out the stash of tactical weapons and accessories used by law enforcement. Included on the Ultimat Weapons Systems' index of products are binoculars, holsters, rifle stocks, heat shields and more. Ordering is available by e-mail.

Virtual Toy Store
http://www.halcyon.com/uncomyn/home.html
Step into the Virtual Toy Store from Uncomyn Gifts at this page. It features hard-to-find and obnoxious gift items, toys, T-shirts an jewelry for the science fiction, anime and fantasy enthusiast. Includes "Star Trek" and "Babylon 5" paraphernalia.

Wings America Home Page
http://www.carmelnet.com/Wings
Products with an aviation theme are available at Wings America. Find models, clothing, books, watches, and more. Aviation links and jokes are also featured.

World Wide Collectors Digest
http://www.wwcd.com/
The World-Wide Collectors Digest is an online haven for buying or selling trading cards, comic books, memorabilia, figurines and toy trains and planes. This site includes a free classifieds section, a business section with ads, live "auctions," and trade show listings.

HOME

Carpeteria Store Listing
http://carpeteria.com/
Ventura, Calif.'s "Carpeteria" maintains this promotional page advertising its products and services. Southern Californians will find an online shop-at-home service, as well as links to industry manufacturers like DuPont and Monsanto.

Classique Structure
http://www.netaxs.com/~vlad/cs
Need a gargoyle? How about a cherub? The Pennsylvannia-based Classique Structure sells gift

items and home furnishings over the Internet. Online ordering is available.

Energy Efficient Environments.
http://www.mcs.net/~energy/home.html
Energy Efficient Environments, Inc., is a retailer of "environmentally friendly" products. Visitors are invited to browse the company's online catalogs of cleaners, energy saving goods and household items.

Faucet Outlet Online Home Page
http://www.faucet.com/faucet/
This is the online pipeline to kitchen and bathroom faucets. Faucet Outlet makes its catalog of faucets and other plumbing accessories, complete with prices, available at this site. A toll-free number is provided for ordering. Also available here is information on plumbing basics and tips on choosing a faucet.

The Home Team
http://www.hometeam.com/
The Home Team is a collection of articles and links for designing intelligent homes. Visitors will find information and product descriptions of home security and lighting systems, communications, and entertainment, to name a few.

Indesign
http://www.intergate.bc.ca/business/indesign/
Indesign creates drapery hardware and accessories, including finials, rods, rings and supports, all available in a variety of materials and finishes. Online ordering is available.

KK Tech & International Water Guard
http://www.hk.linkage.net/~kkt/
International Water Guard Industries, Inc., in Vancouver, Canada, maintains this site to provide information about its ultraviolet air and water purification systems. Visit here to learn about its complete line of sterilization equipment for residential, commercial, municipal, and industrial uses.

The Lead Tester
http://branch.com/epa
The Lead Tester is a kit that tests for high levels of lead in the home. This site has information about the element lead, poisoning and the testing kit itself. Online ordering is available.

Pacific Coast
http://www.pacificcoast.com/
The Seattle-based Pacific Coast company offers a full line of high-quality goose down products (pillows, comforters, feather beds, etc.) for comfortable sleeping. Check it out at this home page.

Philips DAP
http://www.dap.philips.com/
Philips, a Netherlands-based electrical products company, maintains this promotional site for its Domestic Appliances and Personal Care division. Visit here to learn about the division and its products, sold in more than 60 countries.

PoolWizard for Windows
http://www.getnet.com/~microw/poolwiz.html
PoolWizard 1.0 for Windows allows users to determine the proper chemical needs of their swimming pools. Visitors to this promotional site can download a demo, review the application's literature and press, and find out how to order.

Sweeps Vacuum & Repair Center, Inc. Miele Product Line
http://www.vacuums.com/
Sweeps Vacuum & Repair Center, Inc. in Hudson, N.Y., maintains this site to introduce its selection of its highly-acclamied, German-made Miele vacuum cleaners. Visitors will find extensive descriptions of its product line and an online ordering utility.

KID STUFF

Concertina: Books on the Internet
http://www.digimark.net/iatech/books/intro.htm
Concertina is a Canadian children's print and online book publisher that emphasizes Jewish and Biblical themes. Visitors will find book and ordering information at this promotional site.

The Dragonfly Toy Company
http://www.magic.mb.ca/~dragon/
The Dragonfly Toy Company offers more than 2,000 products for children with special needs, including musical instruments, puzzles, board games and books. Dragonfly also provides a search service for any product that they don't stock.

Enter FAO Schwarz
http://faoschwarz.com/
FAO Schwarz guides the young (and the young at heart) through an online store full of fantasy, playthings and specialty toys. Find real FAO Schwarz stores at a directory of locations.

Flix Productions Animated Shareware
http://www.eden.com/~flixprod
At this site, find shareware from Flix Productions, a company that specializes in animated educa-

tional software. Descriptions, screenshots and download options are featured for such titles as Animated Old Testament, Animated Mother Goose and Animated Alphabet.

OFFICE AND TECHNOLOGY

Branch Business Center
http://branch.com/business.htm
Branch Business Center links visitors to merchandisers offering electronics, computer furniture, hardware and software and various business services. Visitors to this site can link to other businesses' Web pages and check out the goods. Includes a link to the Branch Mall.

Combo Directory
http://www.combo.com/
Calgary's Allscan Distributors, Inc., maintains the Combo directory containing links to office furniture manufacturers worldwide. Information about office-wide ergonomics is also available, as well as details about ergonomically designed furnishings.

Government Technology Services Inc. Online
http://www.gtsi.com/
This catalog outlining products available from Government Technology Services Inc. (GTSI) allows government customers to shop for computers and other high-tech products online. Includes corporate information about GTSI and technical support services for customers.

Lexmark International, Inc.
http://www.lexmark.com/index.html
Lexmark, a Lexington, Ky.-based business and printing products company, maintains this promotional site. Visit here for news, press releases, technical support and information about its printers, typewriters, keyboards and other products.

Maxtor Corporation
http://www.maxtor.com/
Maxtor Corporation, a San Jose, Calif.-based data storage products company, maintains this site for a corporate overview, news, technical support and product descriptions. Includes a bulletin board service and employment listings.

Metamorphosis Design & Development, Inc.
http://www.com/metamorphosis
Metamorphosis Design & Development, Inc., an Atlanta, Ga.-based ergonomic office furniture

maker, maintains this site to display its line of user-friendly products. Visit here to find out how a comfortable workplace can improve your health and productivity.

Metricom, Inc.
http://www.metricom.com/
Metricom, Inc., a Los Gatos, Calif.-based wireless communications products company, maintains this site for news and product and service information. Visit here to learn about the company and link to a collection of wireless-related resources.

National Instruments
http://www.natinst.com/
The National Instruments page provides an overview of its science and engineering-related PC products and workstations. Laboratory applications, instrument control interfaces and numerical analysis software are among the company's major product lines.

Network Buyer's Guide–Strategic Research Corp.
http://www.sresearch.com/
A central buying guide for communications and connectivity, visitors will find pointers to everything from hardware and peripherals to industry publications here. Search storage, networking and general communications products using an online "expert guide," or, for the savvier buyer, a keyword search.

Network Marketing Solutions, Inc.
http://www.netmark.com/
Netmark, an online federal-government products and services shopping guide, provides access to major brand names. Visit here for information about federal buying programs and assistance.

Office Techniques
http://www.otisnet.com/oti
Office Techniques supplies furniture, accessories and ergonomic information for computer users and businesses. The company's home page has information about new products, projects, and a link to its online catalog.

OnSale
http://www.onsale.com/
OnSale is a real-time interactive auction house that sells new, refurbished and closeout computers. Visitors can read a description of the sale item and place bids online here.

PartNet
http://part.net/
PartNet provides an interactive catalog that allows visitors to search for mechanical and electronic components from numerous vendors simultaneously. The site also offers general information about PartNet and plenty of help for would-be searchers.

Pro CD, Inc.–Phonebooks on CD-ROM
http://www.procd.com/
This promotional site is sponsored by Pro CD, Inc., a manufacturer of phonebooks on CD-ROM. Visitors can learn more about the company and its services, demo its products, and register for current contests and giveaways.

Sony Drive
http://www.sony.co.jp/
If you want to buy a Sony Corp. product, this home page is for you. It offers graphics-laced and text-based information on the electronics manufacturer's products, plus technical support tips and links to other Sony Web sites. In Japanese and English.

Sony Deutschland Online
http://www.sony.de/
Sony's German corporate page can be found here, in German only.

Syracuse University InfoMall Program of NPAC
http://www.infomall.org/
This "virtual corporation" is designed to help American business and society take advantage of emerging information technologies, high performance computing applications, and high speed networking. Visitors can shop for software, books, and journals here.

U.Vision.Inc Home Page
http://www.uvision.com/
The Computer ESP Electronic Search Page helps visitors find deals on the latest in hardware and software. ESP's "Browse Engine" learns and remembers the most frequented vendor sites and steers users toward "better" purchase decisions.

Vive Synergies, Inc.
http://www.vive.com/
The Vive Synergies Inc. page promotes the specialty telephony products and services the company offers. Visitors also will find information on the Canadian company's international call-back and prepaid calling card services.

Voice Recognition Systems
http://www.voice-recognition.com/
DragonDictate is the most powerful PC dictation program yet from Voice Recognition Systems. A downloadable demo is available at the VRS home page.

WAIS, Inc.
http://www.wais.com/
WAIS, Inc., a supplier of online publishing systems, maintains this home page offering information about the company, its products and services. Features include a demonstration of the company's keyword search tool.

Xerox Small Office/Home Office Home Page

http://www.xerox.com/soho.html

Xerox's corporate page contains information about the company's products, supplies, and services. Includes links to Xerox's customer support center, training programs and various business services.

XSoft, A Division of Xerox Corporation

http://www.xerox.com/XSoft/XSoftHome.htmlv

XSoft, a division of Xerox, sells software designed to improve the way documents are created and captured, aiming to manage and communicate ideas and information. Its Web site offers an animated demonstration, tech support and product news.

SPORTING GOODS

Century Martial Arts Supply Online

http://www.centuryma.com/

Century Martial Arts Supply Online sells the tools of the trade via this electronic catalog. Curious visitors can link to an event calendar, articles on the sport or related Internet resources.

The Classic Angler

http://www.gorp.com/bamboo.htm

The Classic Angler home page provides information and products for tackle collectors and fly fishermen alike. The "Fly Fishing Mini-Mall" link takes anglers shopping for everything from modern fly reels to specialty products for rod builders.

Cobra Golf

http://www.cobragolf.com/

"Become a believer" with Cobra Golf's oversized woods and irons in both men's and ladies' models. The Cobra home page also features a "Pro Shop Locator" and a chance to win a free driver.

Decathlon

http://www.decathlon.com/

Decathlon is a French company that sells sporting goods and outdoor clothing. This page features an online catalog in French (with an English version promised), as well as information about the company in both languages.

Diving Masks

http://www.seavisionusa.com/

SeaVision USA, Inc., specializes in producing underwater viewing devices such as gauge readers and masks. This site offers product and ordering information. Visitors will also find links to related scuba and optical Web sites.

Electronic Gun Shop

http://www.xmission.com/~chad/egs/egs.html

Gun owners can buy and sell their weapons here. The site includes classifieds, gun news, commercial pages, and links to gun organizations.

Gibraltar Internet Bikes

http://www.gibikes.com/home.cgi

Gibraltar Internet Bikes is an Internet catalog shop with an online ordering system. This site also provides information about payment, shipping, the company's return policy and links to related cycling sites.

Kitty Hawk Sports

http://www.khsports.com/khs/

This promotional page is the Web home of Kitty Hawk Sports. Features include information about windsurfing and kayaking, plus the company's guided tours, merchandise and rentals.

K2 Sports On-line

http://www.k2sports.com/

Check out the latest skis, snowboards and in-line skating gear in the K2 store at the manufacturer's Web site, or run your skiing questions by the K2 Mom. Snow conditions and RealAudio ski reports also are available.

Northwest River Supplies

http://www.gorp.com/nrs.htm

Order rafting, kayaking and canoeing supplies here and browse the online catalog of Northwest River Supplies. The page also offers a photo gallery, river information and environmental news.

Online Sports

http://www.onlinesports.com/

Online Sports is a collection of sports-related products and services available via the Internet, including a sports career job file and resume bank, links to various sports resources on the Web and the Online Sports business center.

The Outdoor Network

http://www.outdoornet.com/

The Outdoor Network is a commercial site that intends to be an interactive center for team, extreme and action sports as well as travel and adventure. Retailers and wholesalers of travel services, gear and sports equipment are prominently featured.

Pacific Offshore Divers Inc.

http://www.thesphere.com/PODI/

Pacific Offshore Divers of San Jose, Calif., provides information here on its SCUBA adventures and instructional classes. Visit here to read about its underwater excursions and browse its index of "favorite" diving-related Web sites, including weather forecasts, safety tips and more.

Ray's Tennis Shop

http://www.cts.com/~tennisa1

Ray's Tennis Shop specializes in volume close-out merchandise. Visitors here can browse its on-line catalog and order via fax, phone or mail.

Reebok International

http://www.planetreebok.com/

The Planet Reebok home page provides a gateway to information on sports and fitness, outdoor adventure and company-sponsored special events. Visitors also will find Reebok corporate and product information.

Saucony

http://www.saucony.com/

Saucony is a manufacturer of athletic shoes. Visitors to its Web site will find information about products, ordering and company history.

Springfield InterActive

http://www.springfield-armory.com/

Springfield InterActive is the home page for Springfield Armory, which manufactures firearms. In addition to finding product information, visitors can order a catalog and can find firearms links.

Yachtlink

http://www.vossnet.co.uk/yacht/

Used yachts for sale are listed at Yachtlink by country and new yachts by manufacturer. Information on charters, holidays, accessories, equipment and services is also available here.

VIRTUAL MALLS

The Access Market Square Internet Shopping Mall

http://www.icw.com/ams.html

Access Market Square describes itself as a Web Multi-Mall. Online consumers can shop for art, alternative medical treatment and Internet novelties, along with traditional offerings of food, clothing and accessories for your place of shelter.

All-Internet Shopping Directory

http://www.webcom.com/~tbrown/

The All-Internet Shopping Directory is a gateway to malls, products and shopping services across the World Wide Web. Features include a tour of the directory, links to dozens of merchandise and service outlets, and a search tool for locating desired stores and products.

American Shopping Mall

http://www.greenearth.com/

The American Shopping Mall aims to provide an electronic town center for consumers across the globe. Shop for goods and services here, or link to announcements about your own community's local events to achieve that home town feeling online.

Asia Trade

http://www.asiatrade.com/

Asia Trade features searchable Asian business directories. Travel and leisure, investments, duty-free shopping, real estate and insurance are only a sampling of the goods and services represented here.

Austrian HomeShop

http://www.austrian-homeshop.co.at/homeshop/

Austria's HomeShop, a virtual mall, hosts a dozen shopping venues offering goods and services from books to photography to toys. Some information is in English, with most in German.

Branch Mall

http://branch.com:1080/

This online shopping site provides links to a wide variety of products and services. Includes quick references for retail and business items, detailed product listings by category, and pointers to other mall sites and business centers.

Cybershop

http://www2.cybershop.com/Cybershop/Online

You can shop till you drop at the Cybershop virtual mall. It's all here, from gourmet food to fashion accessories to electronics. Cybershop provides free shipping and guarantees the lowest prices.

Cyberspace Malls International

http://chili.rt66.com/cyspacemalls

Cyberspace Malls International is a gateway to a number of virtual malls around the world. Includes a store directory, product descriptions, ordering information and links to a frequent buyer's club.

Downtown Anywhere

http://www.awa.com/

Describing itself as "the virtual city with a real economy," Downtown Anywhere offers its clients a prime slice of cyberspace in which to set up businesses. To its online visitors it offers access to shopping and business services, news, museums and galleries, ideas and education.

Electronic Mall Bodensee

http://www.bodan.net/

The Electronic Mall Bodensee, an open forum for electronic commerce in the region around the Lake of Constance, includes links to commercial, educational and technological information. In German and English.

Evergreen Internet

http://www.cybermart.com/

At Evergreen Internet, you can find shopping, entertainment services, travel services, healthy living features and the Women's Web site. It also includes an index to several popular shopping catalogs.

Fido the Shopping Doggie!

http://www.continuumsi.com/cgi-bin/Fido/Welcome

Continuum Software, Inc. offers a search engine here dubbed Fido the Shopping Doggie to help online shoppers find products. Visitors can enter a brief product description and Fido will fetch some options.

First Virtual InfoHaus

http://www.infohaus.com/

This mall allows clients to post their commercial information services. Includes listings of information shops, along with instructions for establishing a site and uploading information.

The Futuris Internet Business Center

http://www.futuris.net/

Futuris is an Internet shopping service located in Hartford, Conn. Businesses can learn about becoming a member here, while visitors can shop for a variety of company services and products.

Gui n' da Hood.

http://www.dnai.com/~gui/index.html

Gui n' da Hood features the "best from neighborhoods around the world." Handicrafts, software, rollerblades, urban fashions, and coffee are only a sampling of the products and merchants visitors will find at this mall.

Hall of Malls

http://nsns.com/MouseTracks/HallofMalls.html

The Hall of Malls is a directory of online malls from around the globe. Electronic shoppers can connect with dozens of commercial Web locations offering everything under the digital sun.

iMall

http://www.imall.com/

iMall offers a directory of products and services that can be purchased on the Internet. Free classified advertising is available to users.

Internet Avenue

http://www.iads.com

Internet Advertising of San Antonio, Texas, maintains this site for its Internet Avenue online shopping directory, featuring commercial and career resources from around the United States. Visitors can link to retailers, employers, recreation and tourism companies, local chambers of commerce, and many other organizations doing business on the Web.

The Internet Forum

http://www.forum.net/TheInternetForum

The Internet Forum is an index of sites that conduct business on the Internet and are likely to be of interest to the average consumer. The directory is organized alphabetically, but visitors can access randomly selected sites. A form for nominating sites for inclusion is provided.

Internet Mall Home Page

http://www.internet-mall.com/

The Internet Mall features access to scores of businesses and shops peddling a wide range of goods that can be ordered electronically. Visitors can search the mall for specific goods and services or even set up their own storefront.

The Internet Plaza

http://internet-plaza.net/

This online shopping and information center includes greeting card, gift, fashion, book, computer, and children's stores, along with information on travel, skiing and windsurfing, careers, and finance. Includes a link to a featured "Site of the Month."

Internet Shopping Network

http://www.internet.net/stores/infoworld/index.html

Browse the stores of the Internet Shopping Network for a wide variety of merchandise including a large selection of computer goods and home electronics. Process orders, make payments, and returns online at this commercial site.

Internet Village

http://www.internet.village.com/

This virtual mall lists its stores by state, category, or alphabetically. Shoppers can vote for their favorite online store here, too.

The London Mall

http://www.londonmall.co.uk/

The London Mall is England's largest commercial Web page, with links to banks, shopping, travel agents, publications, insurance, and other related pages.

Mall 2000 Home Page

http://www.mall2000.com/

Mall 2000 is an Internet shopping service based in Dayton, Ohio. Online visitors can browse and order a variety of products and services.

New City Global Mall

http://ngwwmall.com/

New City Global World Wide Mall offers online shoppers links to commercial home pages all over the Web. Also includes bulletin boards, links to online weather and graphics resources, a collection of Internet search engines and a categorized listing of Web sites.

New South Showcase

http://www.newsouth.com/

The New South Showcase is a mall of mainly commercial sites with links to shopping, movie and restaurant information. Other links include education, finance and health areas.

Online Computer Market, Inc.

http://www.ocm.com/default.htm

Visitors to this technology mall will find hardware and software companies, resellers, research companies and consulting firms. Forums, trade show info and industry news are also featured.

Phrantic's Flea Market

http://207.49.108.51/

Phrantic's Flea Market offers affordable Web advertising to small businesses. Includes client listings, descriptions of services, and price information.

Rocky Mountain Cyber Mall

http://www.hardiman.com/malls/rmcm

The Rocky Mountain Cyber Mall hosts a plethora of virtual shops. Visitors can browse a wide variety of consumer goods available for online ordering, including beauty and cleaning products, entertainment goods, maps, videos, gourmet food, and sportswear.

Spiegel

http://www.spiegel.com/spiegel/

Spiegel's Web site allows shoppers to browse its online catalog, exchange advice with others or solicit "expert" opinions from the company's panel of sages. Visitors can check out shopping tips or order clothing, toys, gourmet foods, and more.

The Tarheel Mall

http://netmar.com/mall/

The Tarheel Mall offers online advertising for businesses in the Durham, N.C., area. Visitors can browse and order services and products, while businesses can lease virtual storefronts.

UK Business on the Web

http://www.u-net.com/ukcom/

U-Net Ltd., provides this comprehensive index of United Kingdom business pages on the Web. Visitors here can view the listings by subject category or alphabetical listing. The business pages here include retail, food and drink, and travel

Village Potpourri Mall

http://www.vpm.com/

The Village Potpourri Mall hosts a wide variety of shops for nearly every imaginable consumer good. Check out the latest mall news and products, or link to search engines and the Internet Directory for further exploration of the Internet.

WebStore Product Home Pages

http://www.webstore.com/

At the WebStore Product home page find links to sites selling products that will soup up your motorcycle engine or PC microprocessor. Find sales pitches from a random assortment of product and service vendors here.

World Kiosk

http://www.std.com/

The World Kiosk is a cybermall indexed by products, services and business. You'll find photo restoration experts here as well as computer expertise.

World Square

http://www.w2.com/

The World Square, a service of the World Square Corporation, is described as a "one-stop shopping place for information and goods." Visit this site for product and ordering information. al service offering an index of products and services.

SOCIAL AND COMMUNITY AFFAIRS

THE 25 MOST POPULAR SOCIAL AND COMMUNITY AFFAIRS SITES

Adoption Network Home Page
http://www.adoption.org/adopt/

Amnesty International
http://www.io.org/amnesty/

Artists Against Racism
http://www.vrx.net/aar/

Canadian Wildlife Federation
http://www.igc.apc.org/green/green.html

Children's Defense Fund
http://www.tmn.com/cdf/index.html

CLNET Home Page
http://latino.sscnet.ucla.edu/

Cyber-Rights
http://www.cpsr.org/cpsr/nii/cyber-rights/

Defenders of Wildlife
http://www.defenders.org/

Femina
http://www.femina.com/

Food For The Hungry: Virtual Learning Center
http://www.fh.org/

Free Tibet Home Page
http://www.manymedia.com/tibet/

Greenpeace International
http://www.greenpeace.org/

Human Rights Web
http://www.traveller.com/~hrweb/hrweb.html

James Daugherty's New Paradigms Project
http://a-albionic.com/a-albionic/gopher/about

LaborWEB
http://www.aflcio.org/

Lesbian and Gay New York Home Page
http://gravity.fly.net/~lgny/

The National Coalition of Free Men
http://www.ncfm.org/

One World Online
http://www.oneworld.org/

Out.com
http://www.out.com/

Peace Corps
http://www.peacecorps.gov/

PeaceWire Home Page
http://www.peacewire.org/pw

RabbitRat
http://www.razorfish.com/bluedot/rabbitrat/

The Sea Shepherd Conservation Society
http://www.envirolink.org/orgs/seashep/

Wolf Haven International
http://www.teleport.com/~wnorton/wolf.shtml

The World ORT Union
http://www.ort.org/ortnet.htm

ADVOCACY AND ACTIVISM

ANIMAL RIGHTS

Connecticut Cat Rescue Web

http://www.pcnet.com/~stenor/catweb

Forlorn felines can find solace at the Connecticut Cat Rescue Web site, whose mission is to help homeless cats find homes. Toward that end, here are lists of cats available for adoption, links to shelters and humane societies, a picture gallery and pointers to related sites.

Defenders of Wildlife

http://www.defenders.org/

Defenders of Wildlife led the charge to return the wolf to Yellowstone. The organization also fights to keep the Endangered Species Act intact, and champions other wildlife issues. Visitors to this home page can become keyboard activists by reading action alerts and firing off e-mail to officials.

EcoNet

http://www.econet.apc.org/endangered/

This page will get visitors up to speed on the Endangered Species Act and various Congressional plans to reauthorize it (and gut it in the process). Visit here for analyses, position papers and testimony from the Center for Marine Conservation. The site also provides background on the Act from the National Wildlife Federation.

RabbitRat

http://www.razorfish.com/bluedot/rabbitrat/

Rabbit Rat "is a freedom fighter, part cockroach, part rat, part unruly squirrel and sneaky cat." Visit Melanie Einzig's page of "documentary fantasies" and images to follow the continuing adventures of Museum of Natural History escapee Rabbit Rat.

The Sea Shepherd Conservation Society

http://www.seashepherd.org/

This well-known activist group takes to the high seas to defend marine mammals. Visitors will learn about the radical organization and its campaigns through news releases, alerts and information on how to get involved.

Turtle Trax

http://www.io.org/~bunrab/

This site is about marine turtles, with many wonderful photos and graphics of these huge creatures. See Editor's Choice.

Whale Adoption Project

http://www.webcom.com/~iwcwww/whale_adoption/waphome.html

Visit this site to learn more about humpback whales and how to help them. See Editor's Choice.

Wolf Haven International

http://www.teleport.com/~wnorton/wolf.shtml

Wolf Haven International is sanctuary for wolves in the small town of Tenino, Wash., that also teaches about wolves and promotes wolf restoration. Visitors can download photos of the organization's wolves, wolf fact sheets and information on the group's wolf adoption program.

World Parott Trust USA

http://www.mecca.org/~rporter/PARROTS/wptindex.html

The World Parrot Trust, an international organization dedicated to the survival of parrots worldwide, explains its goals and projects here. Bird lovers can obtain membership information and peek at a parrot portfolio.

The World-Wide Web Virtual Library: Animal Health, Well Being and Rights

http://www.tiac.net/users/sbr/animals.html

The World Wide Web Virtual Library maintains this site for its index of animal health, well being, and rights resources. Visit here for links to animal-related Web sites from commercial and non-profit organizations around the world.

---

a2z EDITOR'S CHOICE

Turtle Trax

http://www.io.org/~bunrab/

No, Bobby, you can't take this turtle home in a shoebox. (It would probably take a moving van.) Turtle Trax is devoted to marine turtles—the enormous, prehistoric, endangered type—and is dedicated in particular to the memory of Clothahump, a young Hawaiian green sea-turtle whose unfortunate home was wedged between a sewage treatment plant and a concrete channel. Befriended by the Turtle Trax Webmasters in 1988, Clothahump eventually developed fibropapilloma tumors, an obvious result of "wastewater" contamination to her habitat. Soon after, she disappeared, never to be seen again. Turtle Trax tells her story and illustrates the plight of these remarkable creatures in their daily fight for life. The site is a true adventure, with glorious photographs and assertive graphics that take visitors to faraway places. The romance of the marine turtle is bound to capture you as you read the stories, both tragic and comic. Learn of bills brought before the U.S. Congress that endanger all marine life here, and find out what you can do to can help.—*Reviewed by Eugenia Johnson*

©UKB & PAB

A Page Devoted to Marine Turtles

ARCHIVES AND INDICES

EcoNet Gopher

gopher://gopher.econet.apc.org/

Part of the Institute for Global Communications Progressive Directory, visitors here can learn about the work of groups EcoNet, ConflictNet, LaborNet and WomensNet. The extensive site also includes information on law and the United Nations.

Emily's Social, Political and Environmental Links

http://www.fearless.net/~spamily/

This site features a wide range of resources about social issues, politics and the environment. Visitors will find an index of information on human rights, child care, privacy and free expression, environmental conservation, and more.

Encyclopedia of Direct Action

http://envirolink.org/action/eda.html

The Encyclopedia of Direct Action contains information on progressive direct action groups, their campaigns and tactics. Includes instructions on demonstration techniques and maintaining secrecy.

Fourth World Documentation Project Home Page

http://www.halcyon.com/FWDP/fwdp.html

The Fourth World Indigenous Documentation Project provides the online community with access to Fourth World resources. This site includes archives, internship information and an archive search. Links to related sites are also offered.

Links for Those with Conscience And Consciousness

http://artitude.com/links.htm

Links for Those with Conscience and Consciousness describes itself as "a '60s trading post for the '90s." The page includes links to a variety of progressive pages, from Greenpeace International to the Electronic Frontier Foundation.

Macrocosm USA

http://www.macronet.org/macronet/

Macrocosm USA describes itself as a "clearinghouse for progressives." The nonprofit group promotes its handbook of grassroots political information and commentary here and offers links to over 6,000 progressive and liberal organizations, publications, businesses and media contacts.

CHILD AND FAMILY ADVOCACY

Administration for Children and Families

http://www.acf.dhhs.gov/

The U.S. Department of Health and Human Services Administration For Children and Families promotes the economic and social safety of families, children, individuals and communities. Visitors to this site can explore the structure, programs and services of the ACF.

Bethany Christian Services

http://www.bethany.org/

The protection of the lives of children and families is the goal of this Christian organization. The site describes the group's mission and provides links to related Internet sites.

Child Relief and You

http://www.wnx.com/~cry/

Child Relief and You (CRY), a children's rights and relief organization based in Bombay, India, maintains this site to describe its activities. Visit here to find educational literature, view press clippings or donate to the cause.

Children Now

http://www.dnai.com/~children/

Children Now speaks for children in the halls of Congress, on the editorial pages of newspapers and in local communities. It gives an overview of its work here and posts current news and action alerts. Visitors can learn how to get involved, too.

Children's Defense Fund

http://www.tmn.com/cdf/index.html

The Children's Defense Fund is a nonprofit organization dedicated to protecting the needs of children in the United States, particularly those who are poor, in a minority group or disabled. Visitors here will find out about the group's efforts and can read its publications.

The Family Research Council

http://www.frc.org/

Promoting and protecting family values is the focus of the Family Research Council, a nonprofit advocacy organization that operates within Christian

a2z EDITOR'S CHOICE

Whale Adoption Project

http://www.webcom.com/~iwcwww/whale_adoption/waphome.html

Over the centuries, humankind has had an insatiable fascination for these mysterious behemoths of the sea. Books have extolled their rare characteristics, and science has discovered an abundance of interesting facts about their lifestyle and hunting preserves, and the fertilization, birth and care of their young. It has been firmly established that whales do talk, at least to one another, and that they have well-organized communities that they aim to protect. This online adoption project gives participants a chance both to satisfy their curiosity and to become instrumental in helping the humpback whale preserve its right to ocean habitat. The extensive site, loaded with photos and reports, also features the online version of "Whalewatch," a quarterly newsletter that examines the horrors and the beauty of the global marine community.—*Reviewed by Eugenia Johnson*

belief systems. It updates its site daily with current events and radio commentary and provides online articles that keep an eye on Washington.

The Future of Children

http://www.futureofchildren.org/

The Future of Children, a contemporary issues publication of The David and Lucile Packard Foundation, offers information on trends and public policies related to child development. Visit here to learn how low birth weight, violence, HIV/AIDS, sexual abuse, divorce and other forces will impact our children's future.

Idea Central—Welfare and Families

http://epn.org/idea/welfare.html

Often the motives and truths behind a national debate are buried in rhetoric. The Welfare and Families Page attempts to cut through it, with articles and reports about welfare reform and the minimum wage. The page is part of the Electronic Policy Network.

Infact's Tobacco Industry's Campaign

http://www.boutell.com/infact/

Almost as many kids recognize Joe Camel as Mickey Mouse and INFACT is steamed about it. Here, the group exposes the tobacco companies that target kids, calls for a boycott against them and asks visitors to fire off e-mail letters to them.

Saf.T.Child Online

http://yellodino.safe-t-child.com/

Parents and child advocates will find information here about preventing child abduction and child abuse. The site includes a "child's street smarts" quiz, online newsletters and promotions for Safe-T-Child products.

CIVIL LIBERTIES

Action on Smoking and Health

http://www.ash.org/ash/

Action on Smoking and Health is a national non-profit that fights for nonsmokers' rights. Visitors to this feisty page will learn about the group's "war on smoking" in the courts and in legislative bodies. The 30-year-old group traces its history here and posts its publications.

The Boston Coalition for Freedom of Expression

http://world.std.com/~kip/bcfe.html

Fighting for the free-speech rights of artists, the Boston Coalition for Freedom of Expression opposes local, state and national laws that gag artists. An informal affiliate of the National Campaign for Freedom of Expression, it overviews its battles and posts its "heroes and villains list" here.

The Electronic Privacy Information Center

http://www.digicash.com/epic/

The Electronic Privacy Information Center is a public interest research center in Washington, D.C. established to address the issues of civil liberties relating to national ID cards, medical record privacy and the sale of consumer data. Includes links to Privacy International.

The Fight Against Coercive Tactics Networks

http://www.lightlink.com/factnet1/pages/index.html

The Fight Against Coercive Tactics Network is embroiled in the Scientology controversy on the Net. The Webmasters say that since they began working on this anti-Scientology site, they've been raided by the Church, which took their computer equipment. They explain their call for help and ask for donations here.

File Room

http://fileroom.aaup.uic.edu/FileRoom/documents/TofCont.html

Muntadas and Randolph Street Gallery in Chicago, Ill., maintains this site to provide information about the issue of censorship. Visit the File Room to learn about the past, present and possible future of censorship.

The Institute for First Amendment Studies

http://apocalypse.berkshire.net/~ifas/

The Institute for First Amendment Studies tracks the radical religious right and publishes its findings. Here, find the institute's monthly magazine, a state-by-state e-mail directory of legislators and media, and advice for ex-fundamentalists.

Progress Freedom Foundation

http://www.pff.org/

The Progress Freedom Foundation is a nonprofit think tank devoted to rescuing American civilization from "cultural nihilism" and to securing a future based upon "core values of the American Creed." Access information about PFF publications and programs at its home page.

Protest Rally and Demonstration/First Amendment Rights

http://www.hotwired.com/staff/digaman/

RealAudio and Hot Wired held a joint rally in December 1995 to protest the House of Representatives' vote on the telecommunications bill. This page advertises the rally and gives some background on the bill, which has since passed into law.

National Committee for Public Education and Religious Liberty Home Page

http://www.tiac.net:80/users/doyle/PEARL.html

The National Committee for Public Education and Religious Liberty champions the First Amendment guarantee of a separation between church and state. Visitors will get an overview of the group on this page, which includes litigation updates and activist alerts.

Seperation of School and State Alliance

http://www.sepschool.org/

Calling for a competitive marketplace for education, the maintainers of this site describe their anti-government views about schooling. Background on the alliance and starting points for those wishing to join the cause are offered, along with news and opinion on educational issues.

Voters Telecommunications Watch

http://www.vtw.org/

A nonprofit watchdog follows legislation on telecommunications and civil liberties here. Browsers can watch the progress of bills, learn the details of the Communications Decency Act and join the group's efforts to sway the 1996 election.

DRUGS AND DRUG USE

Cannabis Canada Online

http://www.hempbc.com/

"Cannabis Canada," a magazine about Canadian marijuana laws and decriminalization efforts, offers an online version here. The site also includes a hemp library and a variety of links to related sites.

Drug Education Page

http://www.magic.mb.ca/~lampi/new_drugs.html

This annotated index offers pointers to articles and papers on drug laws and policy. It also provides information on specific topics, such as addiction, nicotine and alcohol.

Drugs Paranoia

http://www.paranoia.com/drugs/

Paranoia.Com avers that its drug page is not maintained "to glorify drug use, though many of the files here do exactly that." The site includes articles about the war on drugs, browsers' drug stories and price reports.

ecstasy.org

http://ecstasy.org/

Offering hypertext reference works and other scientific and cultural resources related to MDMA (also known as "ecstasy"), this site provides pointers to related subjects ranging from dance culture to the drug's dangers.

Hyperreal Drugs Archive

http://www.hyperreal.com/drugs/

Find a library of informational sites dedicated to recreational pharmaceuticals and their use at this drug information archive. It is maintained by "Hyperreal," a counterculture online magazine, and includes pointers to pricing guidelines and postings on topics ranging from hemp cultivation to heroin purification.

Life Education International Home Page

http://www.lec.org/

Life Education International is a nonprofit organization "dedicated to the prevention of drug abuse, violence, AIDS, and all forms of personal harm-related behavior." This home page describes the organization's activities and links visitors to sites related to preventing alcoholism and drug abuse.

Marijuana Archive

http://www.calyx.com/~olsen/

Iowa resident Carl E. Olsen details information about his legal battles with the U.S. Drug Enforcement Administration (DEA) over the use of marijuana as a medicine and as part of religious practices at this archive. He also details the facts about hemp as an industrial and food resource.

Marijuana Policy Project

http://www.mpp.org/

Visitors to this Web site can learn about the Marijuana Policy Project's efforts to reform federal laws concerning the drug. Articles concerning the medical uses of and legal issues surrounding pot can be perused at this politically active group's site.

The Tobacco Control Archives

http://galen.library.ucsf.edu/tobacco/

Tobacco policy researchers hit the mother lode here, a central source of information about tobacco control issues, with an emphasis on initiatives in California. The site also includes links to info on court cases, a newspaper clipping service by the Advocacy Institute and exposes of tobacco companies.

ENVIRONMENT

American Waterworks Association

http://www.awwa.org/

Hey, you don't want to anger the American Water Works Association: The 3,700 member utility companies in this group serve as watchdogs over safe drinking water supplies which supply water to around 170 million people. Learn more about the AWWA and their efforts to make water safer, or link to water-related goods and services.

Blackfoot River Threatened by Gold Mine

http://www.montana.com/cfpoc/

Montana's Blackfoot River—of the "A River Runs Through It" fame—is the proposed site for a massive gold mine. Here, a group fighting the mine provides a thorough look at the proposal and the environmental effects of gold mining. Visitors can fire off opinions to the state's governor, too.

The Cairo Conference

http://www.iisd.ca/linkages/cairo.html

The United Nations International Conference on Population and Development took place in 1994, but the Cairo Conference Home Page still exists to publish information concerning the preparation for and results of that historic gathering. Find conference documents and media reports at this site.

The Chesapeake Bay Trust

http://www2.ari.net/home/cbt/

The Chesapeake Bay Trust gives grants to civic and community organizations in Maryland that are working to clean up and protect the bay. The Trust details its program here and provides information on the state's "Treasure the Chesapeake" license plates, which generate money for the Trust.

Creating Land Trusts

http://www.possibility.com/LandTrust/

Quietly and without fanfare, some 900 land trusts have protected—forever—nearly 3 million acres of land in America. This page explains how to form a land trust and details a trust's basic preservation tools: conservation easements and land donations.

The Earth Pledge Foundation

http://www.earthpledge.org

The Earth Pledge Foundation was born at the Earth Summit in Rio de Janeiro in 1992. It works to promote sustainable development, "the most important concept to emerge from the Conference." Visit here to read background and to take the pledge to help keep the planet healthy.

EcoNet

http://www.econet.apc.org/econet/en.issues.html

EcoNet is a non-profit computer network hosted by the Institute for Global Communications (IGC). Check out a variety of environmental resources here, covering issues of health, frugal living, wildlife, sustainable development or link to IGC's other progressive networks.

EcoNet's Acid Rain Resources

http://www.igc.apc.org/acidrain/

EcoNet has compiled publications, articles and educational activities about acid rain and offers links to them here. The site also includes conference information and proceedings.

EnviroLink Network

http://www.envirolink.org

The EnviroLink Network is a nonprofit organization that operates as a source of environmental information. This page includes an environmental library, the Internet Green marketplace and search tool.

Environmental Information Services on the Internet

http://www.foe.co.uk/pubsinfo/infosyst/other_services.html

Environmental Information Services, part of the larger Friends of the Earth site, presents a collection of links to Internet resources that include biodiversity and habitats, economics, energy and, of course, pollution.

Environmental Working Group

http://www.ewg.org/

The Environmental Working Group researches a wide range of environmental issues. Visit here for scientific, political and economic looks at farming, pesticides, drinking water and much more.

Friends of the Earth Home Page

http://www.foe.co.uk/

The Friends of the Earth is an environmental group that aims to alert the public about known chemical releases. Visitors can gather information and view maps of chemical release sites, learn about the group's worldwide chapters and join Friends of the Earth here.

Friends of the Environment

http://www.fef.ca/

Canada's Friends of the Environment Foundation funds community environmental projects across the country. Visit here for an overview of the foundation, application guidelines and online press releases.

Friends of the Red Road

http://planet-hawaii.com/redroad/

A group that lives close to the land in Hawaii is challenging an electric company's plans to lay down a power grid. The group reports on its efforts and lawsuit on this page, which was produced solely with solar power.

Friends of the Santa Clara River

http://envirolink.org/FSCR/FSCR.html

The Friends of the Santa Clara River, an organization dedicated to the proper management of one of two remaining natural river systems in southern California, maintains this informational site. Visit here for news, publications, background information and activity updates.

Global Recycling Network

http://grn.com/grn/

The Global Recycling Network (GRN) dubs itself the "Internet's Number One Recycling Information Resource." Includes lists of recycling companies, a reference library, links to related publications and stock quotes of recycling companies.

Global Rivers Environmental Education Network (GREEN)

http://www.igc.apc.org/green/green.html

Global Rivers Environmental Education Network (GREEN) is a Michigan organization dedicated to saving U.S. watersheds and rivers. Visitors will find an online conference and discussion area, extensive educational resources and schedules for workshops and classes.

Greenpeace International (Amsterdam)

http://www.greenpeace.org/

Greenpeace is an organization devoted to identifying and proposing solutions to global environmental problems. Visitors to the Amsterdam chapter's home page will find membership information, descriptions of current campaigns and a searchable index of Greenpeace articles and publications.

Greenpeace's Index to Non-Greenpeace Environmental Sites

http://www.greenpeace.org/others.html

Greenpeace points browsers to other international environmental organizations, anti-nuclear testing pages and political sites from this index, which also includes links to environmentally friendly media.

IISDnet Home Page

http://iisd1.iisd.ca/

The International Institute for Sustainable Development's site is devoted to balancing environmental integrity, economic efficiency, and the well-being of people. This Canadian organization's home page offers links to organizations that work to end poverty and ensure global security.

International Arid Lands Consortium (IALC)

http://ag.arizona.edu/OALS/IALC/Home.html

The International Arid Lands Consortium is an independent, nonprofit research organization supporting ecological sustainability in arid and semi-arid lands. This page contains information on the organization and its mission, a newsletter, strategic plan and links to information on topical workshops and conferences.

International Council for Local Enviornmental Initiatives

http://www.iclei.org/

The International Council for Local Environmental Initiatives (ICLEI) takes thinking globally and acting locally to heart. Visitors here will learn about the group, which promotes local actions that can make a global impact on the environment. Its extensive site outlines its various programs, which have a bent toward sustainable development.

---

a2z EDITOR'S CHOICE

The Mountaineers Home Page

http://www.cyberspace.com/mtneers/

Lavishly illustrated with exceptional photographs of the mountains, forests and water courses of the U.S. Pacific Northwest, the Mountaineers Home Page speaks for the third largest outdoor recreational organization in America. Founded in 1906, and currently 15,000 members strong, the group has been instrumental in developing several national parks, and safeguarding the history and tradition of the Pacific Northwest area. Mountaineers promotes good fellowship among those who love and respect the great outdoors, and offers training courses in climbing, skiing, kayaking and nature study. The organization also holds seminars on wilderness etiquette and environmental activism. Fiercely protective of the wilderness that surrounds them, the Mountaineers Conservation Division acts as a watchdog for wildlife in the Cascade and Olympic mountains. Learn all about the dynamic organization here, then turn to the on-site bookstore for mountain-climbing instructions and a list of the 100 best hikes with children.—*Reviewed by Eugenia Johnson*

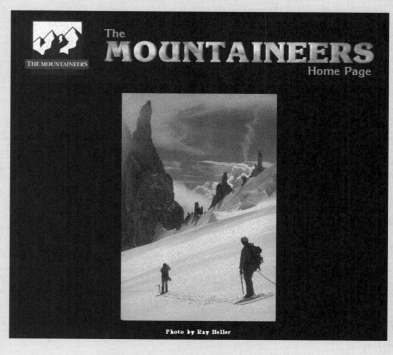

Photo by Ray Heller

James Daugherty's New Paradigms Project

http://a-albionic.com/a-albionic/gopher/about

James Daugherty has gathered reports, journals and books about crafting a new world view here. Visitors can download reports and order books online.

Linkages

http://www.iisd.ca/linkages/

Linkages, provided by the International Institute for Sustainable Development (IISD), is designed to be an electronic clearinghouse for information on past and upcoming international meetings related to environment and development. Includes a photo and image gallery.

The Mountaineers Home Page

http://www.cyberspace.com/mtneers/

Visit this site to learn more about the ecology, history, and traditions of the mountains of the Pacific Northwest region. See Editor's Choice .

National Parks and Conservation Association

http://www.npca.org/home/npca/

The National Parks and Conservation Association is a private, nonprofit watchdog of the nation's parks. Visitors here will learn about the association's park preservation and maintenance efforts at both the grassroots and national levels.

The Natural Resource Directory

http://www.npca.org/home/npca/

The Natural Resource Directory provides "environmentally and socially responsible resources" for those lucky folks living in the vicinity of California's Orange County. Visitors can either find or list products and services here. From ITL America Inc., a multimedia company.

The Natural Resources Defense Council

http://www.npca.org/home/npca/

The Natural Resources Defense Council fights for the environment in the courts and the halls of Congress. It dispenses environmental news, opinion and mobilization information here, where browsers can keep up with the current status of the clean air campaign, pending legislation and other issues. The site also includes a list of NRDC's books and magazines and information on how to become a member.

The New England Light Pollution Advisory Group

http://cfa-www.harvard.edu/~graff/nelpag.html

The New England Light Pollution Advisory Group is dedicated to educating the public about glare-free outdoor lighting that doesn't light up the night sky. Visitors can download its educational circulars here.

OceanVoice International

http://www.conveyor.com/oceanvoice.html

The Canada-based conservation and environmental organization Ocean Voice International unveils information about its aim to promote harmony between people, marine life and the environment on this page. Find out how to get involved or review the group's history.

One Hundred Day Scorecard

http://www.lcv.org/

The 100 Day Scorecard, compiled by the League of Conservation Voters, documents the environmental impact of the Republican party's Contract With America. Visitors can also review the environmental voting records of Congressman in the first 100 days of the 104th Congress.

Patagonia

http://www.patagonia.com/

"What's a rag seller doing on the environmental soapbox?," Patagonia asks here. Besides detailing its tithing program and giving a corporate overview, the outdoor gear company gives the basics on critical environmental issues and asks visitors to sign digital petitions.

The Rainforest Action Network

http://www.igc.apc.org/ran/

Rainforest Action Network posts alerts about its campaigns to save the planet's rainforests on this sleek activist-oriented site. Visitors can e-mail appropriate officials from here or find out about nearby demonstrations. The page also includes membership information.

Recycler's World

http://www.sentex.net/recycle/

Recycler's World offers everyone a chance to learn more about and participate in recycling programs of all types. This site features a database of regional recycling programs, product exchange information and details on green publications and associations.

South Carolina Ducks Unlimited

http://www.netside.com/~scdu/scdu1.html

South Carolina Ducks Unlimited is a group of duck hunters committed to protecting waterfowl habitat. Visit here for descriptions of the group's programs and news of its latest efforts.

South Florida Environmental Reader

http://www.envirolink.org/florida/

The South Florida Environmental Reader is an electronic monthly newsletter for and by environmental activists. Visit for updates on local and national issues that affect the Everglades and other areas in South Florida.

United Nations Development Programme

http://www.undp.org/

The United Nations Development Project provides information on sustainable human development issues throughout the world here. Visit for press releases, information on program activities and publications and links to other UN servers.

Welcome to Environment Canada's Pacific & Yukon Green Lane

http://www.pwc.bc.doe.ca/

Put your finger on Canada's environmental pulse here. Environment Canada posts online environmental reports, weather-related information, a market place and a pointer to a site that includes online text of the country's environmental laws. In English and French.

The World Conservation Monitoring Centre

http://www.wcmc.org.uk/

The World Conservation Monitoring Centre keeps a finger on the pulse of sustainable development world wide. The Cambridge, England-based organization posts data and published materials here and provides links to related sites.

FIREARMS AND GUN CONTROL

National Rifle Association

http://www.nra.org/

Sponsored by the National Rifle Association's (NRA) Institute for Legislative Action, this page invites visitors to learn more about its membership benefits and its programs. News, research, and a firearms law review are also featured.

GLOBAL ARMAMENT AND WEAPONRY

Cooperative Monitoring Center

http://www.cmc.sandia.gov/

The Cooperative Monitoring Center at Sandia National Laboratories in Albuquerque, N.M., helps political and technical experts acquire the technology-based tools they need to implement nonproliferation and arms control. The center provides an overview of its work and information on security technology here.

Greenpeace: French Nuclear Testing

http://www.greenpeace.org/~comms/rw/rw.html

Greenpeace, an environmental advocacy organization, has designed a Web page to inform the public on France and China's nuclear testing practices. Here you will find reference material and video clips on nuclear testing, as well as an electronic anti-testing petition to fill out.

International Security Network

http://www.fsk.ethz.ch/d-reok/fsk/defs_hom.html

The International Security Network, an information service covering defense and peace studies, conflict research and international relations, maintains this site for resource access. Visit here to read activity updates, connect with member institutions and use its collection of Internet search tools.

Peace and Security WWW Server

http://www.cfcsc.dnd.ca/

The Peace and Security Web server from Canada features access to the Canadian Forces College Information Resource Centre and the Peace and Security Integrated Internet Resources Guide. The page can be accessed in English or French.

PeaceWire Home Page

http://www.peacewire.org/pw

Canadian or international peace activists can get news and information from links on the PeaceWire Home Page. Primarily focused on Canadian issues and activists, this page offers links to anti-war projects and the latest peace news as well as other peace-mongering sites on the Web.

The Stanford Center for International Security and Arms Control

http://www-leland.stanford.edu/group/CISAC/

The Stanford Center for International Security and Arms Control is a multidisciplinary research organization dedicated to the issues of international security. Visitors here will get an overview of its research and recent publications and can download selected publications.

Your Say—French Nuclear Testing

http://www.world.net/yoursay/home.html

Here, visitors are asked to speak out on international political and security issues. The site contains a background on a given issue (when we visited, it was French nuclear testing) and provides a form to e-mail world leaders with your comments. The page also includes sample letters.

HUMAN RIGHTS

Amnesty International

http://www.io.org/amnesty/

The high profile human rights activist organization, Amnesty International (AI), highlights rights violations and abuses here. Three new cases are featured here each month. Visit this site to become a member of AI or to contribute to the organizations current campaigns.

The Amnesty International Page

http://www.igc.apc.org/amnesty/

This Amnesty International information guide describes the mission and activities of the "grandfather of human rights organizations." Visit here to learn about the organization's efforts to promote awareness and adherence to universally accepted rights and freedoms.

Artists Against Racism

http://www.vrx.net/aar/

Artists Against Racism, a Canadian group, uses public service announcements, posters, this Web page and a star-studded speakers bureau to hammer home its message that "we are all one people." Visit to learn more about the group's efforts and how to get involved.

Carter Center

http://www.emory.edu/CARTER_CENTER/homepage.htm

The home page of Jimmy and Rosalynn Carter's progressive public policy institute offers an overview of the center's efforts in fighting disease, hunger, poverty and oppression world-wide. Access details of the African Governance Program, a child survival and development task force, and the Carters' much-publicized urban revitalization initiatives.

Euthanasia Research and Guidance Organization

http://www.efn.org/~ergo/

Oregon-based Euthanasia Research and Guidance Organization puts visitors in touch with resources that support assisted suicide for terminally ill patients. Find links to publications, law and even to Dr. Jack Kevorkian.

Execution of Ken Saro Wiwa

http://www.gem.co.za/ELA/ken.html

Both a memorial to Ken Saro Wiwa and a call to boycott Shell Oil Co., this site provides background information on the Nigerian author/activist who was put to death for "leading the protest against the exploitation of Ogonilands and Ogoni people."

Free Burma

http://sunsite.unc.edu/freeburma/freeburma.html

The Free Burma site provides information about the current political situation, military dictatorship and the efforts for change and reform. Find links here to archives, news, reports and the press statement concerning Aung San Suu Kyi's release from house arrest.

Free Tibet Home Page

http://www.manymedia.com/tibet/

Since 1959, Tibet has been controlled by the Chinese. This activist site calls for political action to free Tibet from Chinese rule. Visitors will find historical background, ways to support and participate in the freedom movement, and links to other Tibetan sites.

GlobalVision:The Other Network...

http://www.igc.apc.org/globalvision/

Visit the Rights & Wrongs Home Page to learn more about this television newsmagazine series on human rights. Find out when and where this show, which uses mini-cameras to covertly document human rights abuses, airs in your community and read comments from both viewers and critics.

The Golan Heights Information Server

http://www.golan.org.il/

Browsers can get news updates from the Golan Heights here. The extensive site includes cultural and geographic information, updates from Golan Residents Committee and a slide show. The site also calls for campaign help to retain Israeli sovereignty in the contested region.

Human Rights

http://www.intac.com/PubService/human_rights/

A depository for Human Rights resources is offered here by a student at Essex University in the U.K. A large collection of files available here cover topics ranging from war and peace resources to enviornmental issues and human rights.

Human Rights Information

http://www.idt.unit.no/~isfit/human.rights.html

Human Rights Information is posted by the International Student Festival in Trondheim at this site. Find government-based gopher servers and Web sites containing reports on the state of human rights across the globe. Predominated by United States and United Nations documents.

Human Rights Web

http://www.hrweb.org/

The Human Rights Web Home Page introduces the human rights movement from historical, political and philsophical perspectives. The site addresses how and why to to get involved in the international fight for human rights.

Multinational Monitor Archives

http://www.essential.org/monitor/monitor.html

Activists can keep tabs on environmental and human rights records of international companies from Multinational Monitor's archives. The site also includes back issues of the Monitor's magazine, which tracks corporate activity in the Third World, focusing on labor and environmental issues.

One World Online

http://www.oneworld.org/

OneWorld Online, a member of the British Broadcast Company's Networking Club, provides this forum for global justice, education, human rights and other social change issues. The site includes in-depth news features, guides to human rights issues, an online gallery and much more. Updated every weekday.

Peace Corps

http://www.peacecorps.gov/

The U.S. Peace Corps sends 4,000 citizens every year overseas to help interested nations train their own citizens. This page recruits volunteers and donors, provides a history of the 35-year-old organization, a list of countries it serves, information on "stuff you'll do overseas" and publications.

PeaceNet

http://www.peacenet.apc.org/peacenet/

PeaceNet is a resource dedicated to peace, social justice, human rights and the struggle against racism. The organization's home page explains its goals and posts news items of topical interest. Also find listings of related organizations like Amnesty International and the Center for Third World Organizing.

Planet Peace

http://www.teleport.com/~amt/planetpeace/

Planet Peace aims to give voice to Native American and environmental activists. Visit here for action alerts and discussion on defense of homelands, human rights, AIDS and prison issues. Turn here for art and poetry, too.

PRIVACY Forum

http://www.vortex.com/privacy.html

Netizens concerned about privacy on the Internet and in the world in general may want to subscribe to PRIVACY Forum, a moderated exchange of ideas and analysis related to privacy for individuals and groups. The archive of past issues can also be accessed from this site.

Refuse & Resist

http://www.calyx.com/~refuse/

Activists fighting conservative politics publish their political views and strategies here. Refuse & Resist! supports the political rights of the poor, marginalized and disenfranchised segments of the global community. Find current campaigns as well as tracts tracing philosophical underpinnings.

Refuse & Resist: Stop the Legal Lynching of Mumia Abu-Jamal

http://www.calyx.com/~refuse/mumia/index.html

Mumia Abu-Jamal is an African-American journalist who, at the time of publication, was on death row in Pennsylvania, convicted of murdering a policeman. This page is dedicated to an international effort to free him from what many consider a wrongful conviction based on his political beliefs.

The Rutherford Institute

http://www.rutherford.org/

The Rutherford Institute is a non-profit legal and educational organization involved in the defense of religious liberty and human rights. The institute home page provides links to its education, legal and international departments, as well as its publications.

Social Summit Home Page

http://www.iisd.ca/linkages/wssd.html

This home page unveils the history and highlights of the World Summit for Social Development held in 1995 in Copenhagen, Denmark. The page archives information —available in English, French and Spanish — about the United Nations gathering.

Support Democracy in China

http://www.christusrex.org/www1/sdc/sdchome.html

Support Democracy in China is a volunteer group based in Silicon Valley that promotes human rights in China. Visitors here will find up-to-date news, a pictorial history of 1989's uprising in Tiananmen Square and an overview of the group.

United Nations Related Links

http://www.undp.org/unso_www.html

Visitors can link to every United Nations Development Program site on the Net from this page or link to similar human rights and peacekeeping organizations.

Vera Institute Of Justice

http://broadway.vera.org/

The Vera Institute of Justice is a public policy group devoted to helping produce humane public policies and practices in the U.S. Read about its efforts to provide legal services for the poor, secure employment for parolees and people with disabilities, and its other social activist projects.

VISTA Home Page

http://libertynet.org/~zelson/vweb.html

Volunteers in Service to America (VISTA) is to America what the Peace Corps is to the developing world. Visitors here will learn about its volunteer programs that help the country's urban and rural poor. The site also includes news, local chapter listings and links to other service-related resources.

World Neighbors

http://www.halcyon.com/fkroger/wn.html

World Neighbors, a non-profit organization working to eliminate hunger, disease and poverty in Asia, Latin America and Africa, maintains this site with information about the organization, its projects, publications and links to related sites.

LABOR

LaborNet

http://www.igc.apc.org/labornet/

LaborNet@igc is a community of labor unions, activists, and organizations using computer networks for information-sharing and collaboration with the intent of "increasing the human rights and economic justice of workers." This site links to information about new items, unions and organizations, action alerts and more.

Resource Directory/The Industrial Workers of the World

http://iww.org/

Follow the labor movement here. The Industrial Workers of the World (IWW) provides information about strikes around the country, posts links to its member organizations and keeps visitors abreast of international union news.

MEN'S MOVEMENT

Bioenergetics Press Home Page

http://www.msn.fullfeed.com/~rschenk/bioecat.html

Bioenergetics Press markets books and videos on men's and gender issues. Product and ordering information is available here, as is a men's opinion page and details on a speakers' bureau.

Divorce Online

http://www.divorce-online.com/index.html

Divorce Online, a service for people considering or in the midst of divorce, outlines basic legal facts and tips for surviving a divorce, psychologically and financially. Visitors here will also find an online directory to lawyers, therapists and financial planners.

"M.E.N. Magazine"

http://www.vix.com/menmag/

"M.E.N Magazine" offers a full menu of male-related issues and services, sponsored in part by the

Seattle Men's Evolvement Network. The magazine features articles, poetry, audiotapes and more.

Men's Issues Page

http://www.vix.com/pub/men/index.html

This section of the World Wide Web Virtual Library links visitors to Internet resources related to the male of the species. Includes indexed links to Web sites providing insight on such hot-button topics as domestic violence, anti-male attitudes, sexual abuse and harassment, romance, fatherhood and more.

The National Coalition of Free Men

http://www.ncfm.org/

The National Coalition of Free Men turns the table on sexual discrimination. It aims to raise awareness about the "male experience" and champions individual cases. Here it details the case of a man who claims innocence but was nonetheless sentenced to jail for ten years for raping his wife. The site also includes the group's publications, a look at its current projects and a call for help.

Sexual Assault Information Page

http://www.cs.utk.edu/~bartley/
saInfoPage.html

This site presents a wealth of information about sexual assault. Broad categories covered include statistics, counseling directories, domestic violence, child abuse, legal issues and prevention.

Worldwide Web Virtual Library: Men's Issues

http://www.vix.com/men/

The World Wide Web Virtual Library posts this index of men's issues. Visitors will find links to discussions, writings and references about child support, sexual harassment, veterans' matters and social attitudes.

PARAMILITARY

The EZLN Page

http://www.peak.org/~justin/ezln/ezln.html

Mexican anti-government rebels known as Zapatistas are the focus here, with info on the cause and its founder, Emiliano Zapata. In English and Spanish.

Sovereign WWW Page

http://Syninfo.COM/Sov/index.htmlx

This site is devoted to libertarian, conspiracy and militia issues. Visitors here will find opinion on U.S. elections, articles critical of government actions and a list of scheduled protests.

Stormfront

http://stormfront.wat.com/stormfront/

White supremacists and their critics can keep current with the supremacy movement here. Visitors can download articles on white nationalism, Waco, Ruby Ridge and the NRA; join mailing lists and newsgroups, or link to other supremacist sites.

PORNOGRAPHY

American Family Association

http://www.gocin.com/afa/home.htm

This is the Web home for the Donald Wildmon-led organization, famous for organizing controversial boycotts against Circle K stores and other purveyors of what AFA views as family-destroying pornography. Many links here seem to be out of order but curious visitors can still find out more on the AFA, whom they're boycotting and why.

Breaking the Cycle

http://www.stolaf.edu/people/bierlein/noxxx/
noxxx.html

Breaking the Cycle is dedicated to providing "a nonjudgmental, accepting, and supportive place for people struggling with pornography in all its various forms." Its author posts personal essays, book excerpts and links to mailing lists here.

PRISONER'S RIGHTS

Kentucky Department of Public Advocacy—Criminal Law Links

http://dpa.state.ky.us/~rwheeler/

The Kentucky Department of Public Advocacy offers an extensive index to criminal law-related sites on the Net here. Part of the index is annotated and offers a discussion on the death penalty and criminal justice issues.

Prison Legal News

http://www.synapse.net/~arrakis/pln/pln.html

"Prison Legal News" (PLN) is a monthly newsletter published by two Washington State convicts. Directed towards prisoners, their friends and families, PLN aims to help prisoners vindicate their rights and be a progressive force in developing a public policy debate on issues of crime and punishment.

Prison-Related Resources

http://www.cs.oberlin.edu/students/pjaques/
prison/home.html

For articles, postings and resources on prison-related topics, visitors can check out this site's index. Topics include the death penalty and polit-

ical prisoners as well as a listing of recent news and links to activist groups.

Stop Prisoner Rape

http://www.igc.apc.org/spr/

The Stop Prisoner Rape page "necessarily includes sexually-explicit language that some may want to avoid." Essays, reports and an account of the most "outrageous case SPR knows of" is included.

Yellow Ribbon Home Page

http://www.swaninc.com/yellowribbon/

Originally "used in the cause to gain (the) freedom" of the two United States citizens arrested and imprisoned in Iraq on March 13, 1995, this site now "has a new mission: The full, uncensored telling of the myriad untold stories behind the scenes at the Yellow Ribbon Home Page."

REPRODUCTIVE RIGHTS

Abortion & Reproductive Rights Web Sites

http://www.caral.org/abortion.html

This well-balanced site, maintained and sponsored by the California Abortion and Reproductive Rights Action League, offers links for everyone on every side of this controversial issue. From Papal position papers to pro-choice activist handbooks, this index goes a long way toward illustrating just how complex the abortion discussion has become.

The Abortion Rights Activist

http://www.cais.com/agm/index.html

Webmaster Adam Guasch-Melendez independently hosts this site in order to " provide information to the pro-choice community, to women seeking an abortion, or to anyone with an interest in abortion and abortion-related issues." Offered here is a reference library, updates on clinic violence, tips for activists and related news links.

Catholics United for Life

http://www.mich.com/~buffalo/

Catholics United for Life is a "pro-life" organization. It offers an endorsement for presidential hopeful Pat Buchanan here, as well as a weighty selection of photographs and documents that back the pro-life platform.

D.C. Metro Prolife News/Events Line

http://www.clark.net/pub/jeffd/plnel.html

This page provides anti-abortion news and events information. Includes a database of Biblical and medical quotes and a "Hall of Shame" profiling pro-choice activists and government leaders.

Online Reproductive Health Library

http://www.choice.org/library.html

Breaking news and reproductive health issues are examined here, from acts of violence against women's clinics and health care providers, to efforts to dispel myths that breast cancer and abortion are linked. An extensive reference section provides valuable information on sexuality education, contraception, pregnancy, abortion and birth.

Stop Fetal Tissue Research

http://user.mc.net/dougp/stopftr.html

Maintained by a McHenry, Ill.-based activist group, this site tends more toward invective than information. With its "enemies list, "startling expose" of Margaret Sanger, and "stories to make you cry," the focus is on the emotional side of the anti-abortion debate. Visitors are urged to call the President and print and send the online petition to the U.S. Congress.

TECHNOLOGY AND SOCIETY

America Online—Why Not?

http://www.en.com/users/tfinley/

"Their marketing practices are disgusting. Their software is poorly constructed. Their billing system is, by anyone's definition, fraudulent." So begins the beating administered to America Online at this site. Visit to read the feisty tirade and to find out why the Webmaster is urging people to leave AOL.

AusNet Services

http://www.world.net/yoursay

Ausnet, an Internet service provider in Melbourne, Australia, asks explorers to speak their minds here. It posts background information on a couple of issues, followed by an online survey. When we last visited, Internet regulation and French nuclear testing were featured.

Electronic Frontier Foundadtion Home Page

http://www.eff.org/

The blue ribbons decorating pages across the Net all point to the Electronic Frontier Foundation, a group that works to protect free speech and privacy online. Visitors will find out about its efforts here and can download its publications. The page also includes an extensive index of related sources.

The Loka Institute

http://www.amherst.edu/~loka/

The Loka Institute is an Amherst, Mass.-based research organization concerned with the social, political and environmental repercussions of science and technology. Visitors can download its

recent alerts and publications here and e-mail subscription information.

The Research Libraries Group, Inc.

http://www-rlg.stanford.edu/welcome.html

The RLG is a not-for-profit coalition of universities, archives, historical societies, museums, and other institutions devoted to improving access to information. This site details the group's objectives, collaborative activities and user services.

Wireless Opportunities Coalition

http://wireless.policy.net/wireless/wireless.html

The Wireless Opportunities Coalition maintains this site to detail Federal Communications Commission regulations on wireless technologies and communications. The coalition also gives browsers an overview of its work and urges support for its efforts.

UNSOLVED CRIMES AND MISSING PERSONS

Abducted from Mason City, Iowa

http://www.netins.net/showcase/keithh/missing.htm

The disappearance of a small-town television anchorwoman in middle America has puzzled her co-workers and family. They have taken their search into cyberspace; here, browsers are urged to download a color picture of the broadcaster to aid in the search for her.

The National Center for Missing or Exploited Children

http://www.missingkids.org/

The National Center for Missing and Exploited Children (NCMEC) is a non-profit organization working in conjunction with the U.S. Department of Justice. This site offers a database of missing children, a description for children at risk, and links to topical publications and resources.

COMMUNITY ORGANIZATIONS

The George Lucas Educational Foundation

http://glef.org/

The George Lucas Educational Foundation, a San Rafael, Calif.-based teaching technology organi-

zation, aims to "improve education so all students will be prepared to live and work in an increasingly complex world." Visit here to learn about the foundation, view it's "Edutopia" newsletter and find contact information.

Who Cares: A Journal of Service and Action

http://www.whocares.org/

The goal of "Who Cares" is to inspire and enlist an army of community servants and volunteers. This online journal explores ways to solve society's problems through activism.

Worldwide Cemetery

http://www.cemetory.org/

This site may be the ideal place to share the biography and sccomplishments of a cherished friend with the rest of the world. You can even leave flowers.

The World-Wide Web Virtual Library: Community Networks

http://www.rmsd.com/comnet/wwwvl_commnet.html

Here, the World Wide Web Virtual Library supplies an international listing of community computer networks—information services provided by and for local communities. The index here is categorized by continent, country and state.

ADOPTION AND FOSTER CARE

AdoptioNetwork Home Page

http://www.adoption.org/

"A volunteer-operated information resource," the AdoptioNetwork offers a multitude of links to serve as a starting point in exploring the issues and procedures of adoption. Topics covered include agencies, birthparents, adoptees, adoptive parents, international resources and more.

adoptionHELP!

http://www.webcom.com/~nfediac/

The adoptionHELP! site contains information and resources for adopting a child and for putting a child up for adoption.

CHARITABLE ORGANIZATIONS

American Red Cross Home Page

http://www.crossnet.org/

Visitors to the home page of the American Red Cross will find an overview of the relief organization, including a list of its offices and facilities. Information on how volunteers can become involved is also provided.

Bay Area Volunteer Information Center

http://www.meer.net/users/taylor/

This site provides an extensive list of nonprofit organizations offering volunteer opportunities in the San Francisco Bay Area. Visitors can link directly to these organizations to find out about their volunteer programs.

The Contact Center Network Home Page

http://www.contact.org/

The Contact Center Network facilitates interaction and networking for individuals and organizations who work for a better world. This page includes information about the group, its services and how others can get involved. This page also links to nonprofit-oriented sites on the Internet.

Easter Seals Online

http://www.cyberplex.com/CyberPlex/EasterSeals.html

The Ontario-based Easter Seal Society presents an index to information on its programs, services, events and research, as well as details on donating and volunteering.

HandsNet

http://www.igc.apc.org/handsnet/

HandsNet is a network of 5,000 public interest and human services groups across the United States. It gives browsers membership information, as well as a sample of the kind of information it provides to its members. The site contains daily updates on various public policy issues, opinions, nonprofit news and online forums.

The International Committee of the Red Cross

http://www.icrc.ch/

The International Committee of the Red Cross in Geneva, Switzerland, provides this informational site. Visit here for news, press releases, publications and information about worldwide operations and international humanitarian law.

IFRC Home Page

http://www.ifrc.org/

The International Federation of Red Cross and Red Crescent Societies provides relief to disaster and war-stricken areas around the world. Discover the principles of the international aid movement and learn the basics of disaster preparedness and response.

The Millennium Report to the Rockefeller Foundation

http://www.cdinet.com/Millennium/

This 1994 report, commissioned by the Rockefeller Foundation, is a key component of the foundation's initiative, The Common Enterprise, which focuses on community revitalization.

Peace Corps

http://www.peacecorps.gov/

The U.S. Peace Corps sends 4,000 citizens every year overseas to help interested nations train their own citizens. This page recruits volunteers and donors, provides a history of the 35-year-old organization, a list of countries it serves, information on "stuff you'll do overseas" and publications.

River of Hope Home Page

http://www.riverhope.org/

Take a charitable dip in the waters of nonprofit organizations at this River of Hope Coalition site. It provides dozens of links to community organizations with a range of services, from feeding the hungry to treating eating disorders.

Rotaract

http://www.mcs.net/~dhartung/rotaract.html

Rotaract is associated with Rotary, but is aimed at people 18–30 years old. Here, the community service group details its activities around the world, posts recent news, promotes upcoming events and invites browsers to subscribe to its mailing list.

VISTA Home Page

http://libertynet.org/~zelson/vweb.html

Volunteers in Service to America (VISTA) is to America what the Peace Corps is to the developing world. Visitors here will learn about its volunteer programs to help the country's urban and rural poor. The site also includes news, local chapter listings and links to other service-related resources.

CIVIC AWARENESS

The Civic Network (civic.net)

gopher://gopher.civic.net:2400/1

The Civic Network gopher hosts a collection of Internet resources aimed at improving civic life and public participation in local government. Includes information from the Communitarian and Sustainable Development Information networks.

Hands On Atlanta

http://www.mindspring.com/~rtbrain/hands.html

Hands On Atlanta is a nonprofit organization dedicated to promoting community action and involvement in Atlanta, Ga. Visit here for information on the organization's services and how to pitch in as a volunteer.

Houston Proud

http://houston.proud.org/

Houston Proud is a nonprofit volunteer organization that promotes community-oriented service projects and general boosterism. Visit for information on the group and the Texas city to which it is devoted.

Institute for the Study of Civic Values

http://libertynet.org/~edcivic/iscvhome.html

Institute for the Study of Civic Values promotes civic involvement through a series of online project examples and explanations to help strengthen communities and citizen participation in government.

National Civic League

http://www.ncl.org/ncl/

"Creating communities that work for everyone" is the aim of the National Civic League. Founded by Theodore Roosevelt, the nonprofit outlines its initiatives to revitalize communities here. It also posts a list of its publications, which include "Model City Charter" and "Measuring City Hall Performance."

EMERGENCY AND DISASTER RELIEF

The Alliance for Fire and Emergency Management

http://internet.roadrunner.com/afem/

The Alliance for Fire and Emergency Management is a network of eight professional associations whose members serve the needs of the fire, life safety and emergency management community. Visitors will find access to a resource center, training calendar and the associations' publications here.

American Red Cross Home Page

http://www.crossnet.org/

Visitors to the home page of the American Red Cross will find an overview of the relief organization, including a list of its offices and facilities. Information on how volunteers can become involved is also provided.

Emergency Preparedness Information Center

http://nwlink.com/epicenter/

Epicenter, a disaster assistance product supplier based in Seattle, Wash., maintains this site for its Emergency Preparedness Information Center. Visit here to learn how to prepare for natural disasters such as earthquakes, tornadoes and hurricanes. Also find products to aid in preparations.

Federal Emergency Management Agency

http://www.fema.gov/

This searchable site offers an overview of the mission and assistance programs of the Federal Emergency Management Agency. Also find emergency preparedness tips, FEMA news, a library and a look at the Floods of '96.

Healing in the Heartland

http://benefit.ionet.net/

Healing in the Heartland offers audio and stills from a July, 1995, benefit concert in Oklahoma for victims of the Oklahoma City bombing. Links to information on the bombing and to Internet software are available here.

IFRC Home Page

http://www.ifrc.org/

The International Federation of Red Cross and Red Crescent Societies provides relief to disaster and war-stricken areas around the world. Discover the principles of the international aid movement and learn the basics of disaster preparedness and response.

The International Committee of the Red Cross

http://www.icrc.ch/

The International Committee of the Red Cross in Geneva, Switzerland, provides this informational site. Visit here for news, press releases, publications and information about worldwide operations and international humanitarian law.

Mennonite Central Committee

http://www.mennonitecc.ca/mcc/

The Webmaster of the Mennonite Central Committee describes this organization as the "relief and development arm of the North American Mennonite and Brethren in Christ churches." Visitors will find background and volunteer information on programs for disaster relief and third world development.

FOOD AND HUNGER RELIEF

Food For The Hungry: Virtual Learning Center

http://www.fh.org/

Hunger-relief programs worldwide are described on the Arizona-based charity Food for the Hungry home page. Also here are links to famine statistics and information on how to sponsor a child in the Third World.

Greater Horn Information Exchange

http://gaia.info.usaid.gov/HORN/

Visitors here will learn about the US Agency for International Development (USAID) effort to address hunger in the horn of Africa. This informational page includes a clickable map that offers reports, fact sheets, activity summaries, data sets, scientific papers and analysis for each country in the region.

Hunger Resources Gopher

gopher://gopher.brown.edu:70/11/brown/
departs/worldhun/hungerne

This gopher server contains a collection of hunger-related information on theInternet. Visitors can link to organizations, speeches, articles and other informationhere.

HOMELESS SERVICES

Covington's Homeless: A Documentary

http://www.iia.org/~deckerj/profiles.html

Visit this moving site protraying the lives of the homeless population of Covington, Kentucky. See Editor's Choice6.

The International Union of Gospel Missions (IUGM)

http://www.iugm.org/

The International Union of Gospel Missions (IUGM) is an association of rescue missions and Christian organizations serving the homeless across the U.S. Read about IUGM's news, events, services, programs and history, or link to related resources on the Internet.

National Coalition for the Homeless

http://www2.ari.net/home/nch/

Visitors to the National Coalition for the Homeless site can learn abouthomelessness, read about individual cases and find out how to become involved. Thepage includes a directory of state and national housing advocacy organizations.

LITERACY PROJECTS

National Center on Adult Literacy

http://litserver.literacy.upenn.edu/

The National Center on Adult Literacy researches and aims to improve adult literacy programs nationwide. Visitors will get an overview of the center's efforts and can download its technical reports from this home page.

NEIGHBORHOOD/ REGIONAL CRIME WATCH

Rate Your Risk

http://www.nashville.net/~police/risk/

The Rate Your Risk site provides threat assessment tests for users to determine theirchances of becoming victims of crimes. Includes links to a multimedia violence reduction game, self-defense tips and other crime prevention pages.

VETERAN'S GROUPS

Vietnam Veterans Home Page

http://grunt.space.swri.edu/

The Vietnam Veterans Home Page honors "...Vietnam Vets, living and dead, who served their country on either side of the conflict." Toward that end, the siteincludes information about upcoming events, support groups and organizations of interest to veterans.

YOUTH CLUBS AND ASSOCIATIONS

Berkeley Boy Scout Troop 24

http://www.emf.net/~troop24/t24.html

The home page of the Berkeley Boy Scout Troop 24 provides profiles of the troop's scouts and leaders, plus info on the group's activities and programs. Pointers to other Scouting and recreational sites are also featured.

The MacScouter

http://www.macscouter.com/

The folks at MacScouter ought to get a badge for their efforts to compile this index for Scouts and Scout leaders. The large collection of activities, ceremonies and organizations defines the nature of scouting and points to valuable helpmates for every troop.

Mount Diablo Silverado Council

http://www.emf.net/~troop24/council/
mdsc.html

The Mount Diablo Silverado Council 23 of the Boy Scouts of America is profiledhere. Visitors can read a memo from the Chief Scout Executive, find out about the troop or obtain division contact information.

Tidewater Council BSA

http://www.infi.net/~sipe/scouts/

The Tidewater Council of the Boy Scouts of America serves parts of Virginia and North Carolina. Review the council's history, find news from the districts and link to the home pages of the packs, troops and posts. Also find camping info and links totopic-related sites.

55+

AARP—American Association of Retired Persons

http://www.aarp.org/

The grandaddy of senior resources is personified on this Web page. Its stated mission is to help seniors develop independent lifestyles with dignity and purpose. Described here are the volunteer and community programs that are available, the benefits to members and where this group stands on issues and advocacy.

Administration on Aging

http://www.aoa.dhhs.gov/

Coming from the goverment agency of Health and Human Services, this site is dedicated to contributing information useful to older persons and their families. One feature, the Eldercare Locator, is a repository of information detailing resources for older persons needing special care. The National Aging Information Center, a huge resource of helpful information can be found here as well.

Blacksburg Electronic Village Seniors Information Page

http://northcoast.com/unlimited/news/srnews/srnews.html

Seniors are encouraged to represent their special interests and hobbies here. Get your Senior group or program included. Special interests include grandparenting and senior activities, or check out the member index that includes e-mail addresses.

Elderhostel

http://www.elderhostel.org/

Visit this site to find out more about the wonderful educational-travel opportunities offered through Elderhostel. See Editor's Choice.

The Florida Department of Elder Affairs

http://fcn.state.fl.us/doea/doea.html

The mission of this department is to maximize opportunities for self sufficiency and personal independence for the elder population of Florida. This agency acts an as advocate and coordinates with other state agencies to ensure that services are accessible and responsive. A list of recent legislation is available, along with with health insurance information. Help is provided to those interested in retirement to Florida and the site links to the Elder Helpline.

Grand Times

http://www.grandtimes.com/

Grand Times is a sprightly publication, designed for active older adults. Articles are timely, entertaining and sometimes controversial, with an emphasis on the particular challenges adults face as they grow older. Visitors may want to check out the Senior Friendship Connection to meet new friends.

The Kansas Elder Law Network (KELN)

http://www.ink.org/public/keln/

This network is maintained as a public service to the state and national community of senior citizens, and claims to be the nation's most comprehensive electronic resource dedicated to elder law. This site is affiliated with the University of Kansas Elder Law Clinic and is maintained by Kansas University Law Professor Kim Dayton.

Los Angeles Seniors

http://www.laseniors.com/

Hosted by the YWCA Intervale Senior Services, this site outlines Intervale meal locations, delivery and menus, discusses aging issues and senior news, and hosts 55 Alive Classes for the mature driver. Job opportunities are posted.

---

a2z **EDITOR'S CHOICE**

Covington's Homeless: A Documentary

http://www.iia.org/~deckerj/profiles.html

John Decker has captured the despair and humiliation, as well as the toughness, of the homeless population living in Covington, Kentucky. His poignant online photo-documentary extols the dignity of those who must live without proper shelter, sometimes without food and always without humanity. The presentation tells the stories of a few people living along the Ohio riverbank in a "hootch" community of makeshift homes—like the one "Backpack Bill" has constructed from scraps and debris he collected on the roadside. You'll also meet Patty and Art, whose story embodies the strength of the human spirit and its ability to overcome the most desperate circumstances. Having met on a freight train while riding the rails, the two fell in love and now make their home together in the hootch. Take some time to visit these residents of Covington, and let this site be a reminder that when things get tough, they can always be tougher for someone else.—*Reviewed by Eugenia Johnson*

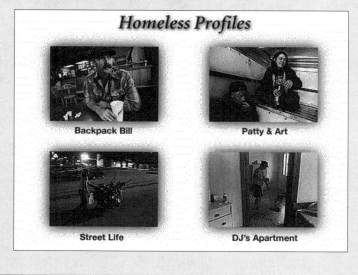

Homeless Profiles

Backpack Bill   Patty & Art

Street Life   DJ's Apartment

Mid-Florida Area Agency on Aging

http://seniors-site.com/

Sponsored by the State of Florida Department of Elder Affairs, this site is directed to senior residents of that state. It provides information on legal matters, disaster info, special programs and services, plus reference material and an Elder Helpline.

National Aging Information Center

http://www.ageinfo.org/

The Administration on Aging provides searchable databases for senior information needs. Forums for discussion of aging issues are available, as well as many publications for download and offline reading. NAIC specialists will also respond to inquiries and provide statistical data and materials, as well as pointers to referral sources.

Selected Sites of Interest

http://www.mbnet.mb.ca/crm/other/genworld/sources.html

This is a grab bag of sites for senior citizens. Included are pointers to software and gopher holes, news and magazines, reference and research, as well as the expected links to Gerontology. Seniors will find links to museums, freenets and specific links to other elder resources on the Web.

Senior.Com

http://www.senior.com/

Senior.Com states that it is a complete resource for the online senior user, providing information on lifestyles, travel services, on-line shopping, legal and financial services, and much, much more. The site comes complete with information on government programs and non-profit organizations of particular interest to oldsters. Participate in online chats on a variety of topics.

Senior Internet Project

http://www.rmwest.com/sip/

This eight-week pilot project to provide an educational initiative for seniors is hosted by Mesa County, Colo. The project aims to give senior citizens a special opportunity to participate in the technological revolution by acquiring a working knowledge of software tools used on the Internet. Curriculum is broken into three courses of eight two-hour classes.

Senior Japan

http://www.mki.co.jp/senior/seni.html

This electronic magazine is dedicated to the enrichment of life for all retirees. The publication offers topics on driving safety tips, studying at the University of Japan, introduces seniors home pages, and then throws in a dollop of senior wisdom. In English and Japanese.

SeniorNet

http://www.seniornet.org/

This international organization composed of 19,000 dues-paying seniors mission is to make today's computer technology accessible to seniors through teaching and information. The group has 88 physical sites worldwide, where seniors can learn the latest in computer technology, socialize, and attend real-time seminars on various subjects. All sites are staffed by volunteers, who claim that they may be the largest volunteer staff in the universe. This site has a library and a variety of chat features, including "Squabble," a public bulletin board where seniors' opinions really count.

Seniors Computer Information Project

http://www.mbnet.mb.ca/crm/

SCIP is a world-wide information guide to resources and services aimed at seniors in Manitoba, Canada. Information is listed by category, geography, features and selected sites of interest. The site provides a searchable index and a one-minute survey with online results.

Seniors-Site

http://seniors-site.com/

This lively site is dedicated to providing interesting and unique information to older adults, and also for younger folks who must look after parents, grandparents or friends. Offered is a free book, "The Second 50 Years," a reference resource for Seniors. Special sections provide information on pets, physical disorders, fun activities, plus much more on varied topics.

Shepherd's Centers of America

http://www.qni.com/~shepherd/

Shepherd's Centers is an interfaith, non-profit organization that maintains 100 independent centers throughout the United States and Canada. Holding to the philosophy that senior citizens are not frail, lonely or dependent, the centers attempt to enrich the later years with opportunities for service to others, self expression and meaningful work. Sustaining close friendships and remaining independent are other goals the centers strive to fulfill for oldsters.

SR.News

http://northcoast.com/unlimited/news/srnews/srnews.html

What a bargain! News and features by and about the senior community are sponsored by the Humboldt Senior Resource Center, operating in Cali-

---

a2z EDITOR'S CHOICE

Elderhostel

http://www.elderhostel.org/

If you are 55 or older, expand your horizons, unbutton your mind, sharpen those scholastic skills and stand in line to experience an exceptional educational adventure. This organization, hosted by educational institutions around the world, offers a vast array of inexpensive mind-expanding challenges for seniors. Elderhostel has grown from tiny groups in New England colleges to a quarter of a million people enrolled on campuses in every American state, Canada and 45 countries around the world. The motto: "Studying there is half the fun." As a participant, you might find yourself in the old city of Jerusalem studying aspects of the Torah, or knee-deep in a desert experience in secluded foothills of the Superstition Mountains. If sampling Acadian cuisine is your current crave, try a class held at "Le Village" on Prince Edward Island, Canada. Registration information is only a click away.—*Reviewed by Eugenia Johnson*

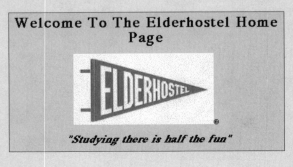

Welcome To The Elderhostel Home Page

ELDERHOSTEL

"Studying there is half the fun"

fornia since 1981. This is the online version of their monthly 20-page newspaper, which currently reaches 7,500 subscribers along the north coast.

GAY AND LESBIAN RESOURCES

Adventuring/IGLOO Welcome Page

http://access.digex.net/~erewhon/

Gays and Lesbians who prefer the great outdoors to cityscapes come together at Adventuring and IGLOO, two gay and lesbian outdoor-oriented organizations. Visitors to this site can find out about upcoming events and local meetings.

Allies

http://www.contrib.andrew.cmu.edu/org/allies/

Visitors to this Carnegie Mellon University site will learn more about Allies, a campus group for people who support gays, bisexuals and lesbians. Here, the group posts its minutes, an online resource library and links to other resources on the Web.

GALAXe

http://www.servtech.com/public/racer/galaxe/

Written by and for gays and lesbians employed by Xerox, this page details the Xerox workplace, including policy and benefit information. It also provides pertinent news and links to related resources.

GaySource

http://www.gaysource.com/

An electronic magazine for the gay and lesbian community, GaySource serves up a solid mix of information, entertainment and insight. An online chat service and links to topic-related sites are also featured.

Gerber/Hart Library & Archives

http://www.gerberhart.org/

Chicago's Gerber/Hart Library & Archives is the Midwest's largest gay, lesbian and bisexual circulation library. Visitors to the institution's home page can access information aimed at the Midwest's gay and bisexual community. Includes links to pages like Digital Queers Chicago and similar sites.

High-Tech Gays

http://www.htg.org/

High Tech Gays is an organization of gays and lesbians working in the computer industry and related high-tech fields in Northern California. The group's site contains a calendar of events, including guest speakers, and archives of past issues of the group's newsletter.

Home Pages of Queer People Out on the Net

http://www.infoqueer.org/queer/qis/homepages.html

This site provides links to the home pages of individuals in the gay community around the world. Home page links are arranged by country, and for those in the U.S., by state.

LBG Student Association of Helsinki University

http://www.helsinki.fi/jarj/oho/engindex.html

The "sexually non-normative" students of Helsinki University formed OHO to spread news of gay and lesbian life in Finland. The women's group is called OLE. Its web site links to other lesbian/bisexual/gay sites around the world.

The Lesbian, Gay and Bisexual Sports Page

http://www.kwic.net/lgb-sports/

The Lesbian, Gay, Bisexual (LGB) Sports Home Page surveys gay men's perspectives on sports, offers a home for LGB sports organizations and events, and highlights out elite athletes. It also provides a list of related books and notes on LGB sports in the media.

The National Journal of Sexual Orientation Law

http://sunsite.unc.edu/gaylaw/

Lesbians, gays and bisexuals can monitor the legal fight for equal rights with the scholarly articles and analyses appearing in "The National Journal of Sexual Orientation Law." Visit here to read current and back issues online.

Out.com

http://www.out.com/

The controversial and increasingly popular Out magazine posts its current issue here. While reaching out to a general-interest urban readership, the magazine surveys political, social and entertainment matters that reflect and affect the lesbian and gay community.

OutNow!

http://www.outnow.com/

OutNOW! is an online newspaper serving the gay and lesbian community that contains feature articles, news, arts coverage and classified ads. It devotes special coverage to Northern California and the San Francisco Bay Area.

Q San Francisco Online

http://www.qsanfrancisco.com/

Q San Francisco provides information for the gay and lesbian community. Includes shopping info, events listings, tourism, cyberlife and an index.

Queer Resources Directory

http://www.qrd.org/QRD/

The Queer Resources Directory offers a wealth of information of interest to the lesbian, gay, bisexual and transgender communities. Visitors will find information about queer families, youth, religion and HIV/AIDS. Special sections are devoted to media, events and history.

QueerAmerica Database

http://www.queer.com/queeramerica/

This searchable database of lesbian and gay resources is sponsored by !OutProud!, "the national coalition for gay, lesbian and bisexual youth." Visitors will find pointers to community centers, support groups and more, all organized by age and region.

Same-sex Marriage Home Page

http://nether.net/~rod/html/sub/marriage.html

Visitors can keep up to date about legal issues surrounding same-sex marriages here. The page contains updates from across the country, a general resolution in support of same-sex unions and a chart of same-sex marriage rights. The page is the Web home of the marriage@abacus.oxy.edu mailing list.

Soc.support.youth.gay-lesbian-bi Home Page

http://www.youth.org/ssyglb/

At this page, information on the Usenet newsgroup soc.support.youth.gay-lesbian-bi is provided, including instructions for posting, information about the moderators and a Frequently Asked Questions (FAQ) file.

Transgender Forum

http://www.cdspub.com/

Crossdressers, transvestites and transsexuals can find a blend of resources on this index, which provides pointers to support groups, events, chats, newsletters, shops and publications.

Unity: A Celebration of Gay Games IV and Stonewall

http://www.prowillen.com/Unity.html

Net users who attended Gay Games IV or have memories of the Stonewall riot in New York may want to check out the home page for the book "Unity: A Celebration of Gay Games IV and Stonewall." Visitors can take a look at a book review and order the book, leave their memories and thoughts on the Gay Games, or read what others have written.

WebCastro

http://www.webcastro.com/

The online magazine WebCastro highlights the business, culture and people of San Francisco's Castro district. The site is hosted by two area residents and includes their personal reporting on the arts, history and computing.

MINORITY AFFAIRS

CLNET Home Page

http://latino.sscnet.ucla.edu/

Supported by the computers at the University of California, CLNET is a Latino-focused Internet information server and part of California's Chicano/Latino Electronic Network. Among the areas of interest presented are jobs, minority institutes, calendars and research. In English and Spanish.

Equal Access to Software and Information

http://www.rit.edu/~easi/

People with disabilities can locate news and discussion about accessible computing technologies thanks to EASI, Equal Access to Software and Information. Look here for hardware and software products, as well as services for users with specialized needs.

The ERaM (Ethnicity, Racism and the Media)

http://www.brad.ac.uk/bradinfo/research/eram/eram.html

The ERaM Program facilitates the exchange and dissemination of information, research, policy statements and news in the areas of ethnicity, rac-

ism and the media. Visitors to its home page are invited to learn more about the project, its mission and subscribe to its mailing lists.

Federal Information Exchange, Inc.

http://web.fie.com/fedix/index.html

The Federal Information Exchange, Inc. oversees the transfer and flow of information between other federal agencies in reference to minority affairs. This searchable site features information on FEDIX and minorities, cross agency lists and downloadable files.

Great Lakes Regional American Indian Network

http://www.glrain.net/glrain/

The purpose of GLRAIN is to help introduce the native American peoples to the Internet and introduce non-native Americans to the aboriginal peoples of the Great Lakes area. Visitors to its home page can access information on the Great Lakes Indians' culture, events and crafts.

Index of Native American Resources on the Internet

http://hanksville.phast.umass.edu/misc/NAresources.html

The Index of Native American Resources on the Internet provides an exhaustive collection of links to government, commercial and nonprofit organizations. Visit here to find information on art, culture, history and contemporary Native American issues

Kwanzaa Information Center

http://www.melanet.com/melanet/kwanzaa/kwanzaa.html

Visit this site to learn about the African-American festival Kwanzaa. See Editor's Choice.

LatinoWeb

http://www.catalog.com/favision/latnoweb.htm

LatinoWeb is an information center serving the needs of the Latin American commuity with links to cultural, government and educational servers. Includes pointers to publications, historical sites and Latino business resources.

MELANET: Your Commerce & Information Center

http://www.melanet.com/melanet/

A service for African American business people, MELANET provides an index of online African American owned businesses and services. Visit here to search for companies, browse informational links and download graphics and Quicktime movies.

Minority On-Line Information Service

http://web.fie.com/web/mol/

MOLIS, the Minority On-Line Information Service, gathers and dispenses information about federal

---

a2z EDITOR'S CHOICE

Kwanzaa Information Center

http://www.melanet.com/melanet/kwanzaa/kwanzaa.html

A seven-day festival which strikes up each year on the day after Christmas, Kwanzaa is a unique celebration of African-American heritage. The holiday was established to provide African-Americans with a greater understanding of and connection to their cultural roots, and its rituals recall a way of life once lived by the ancestors of present day celebrants. It's a festival of the spirit, a joyous occasion that magnifies the goodness of life, using clearly defined principles, practices and symbols to reinforce unity in the black community. This informative site outlines those principles and symbols, and lists schedules for various celebrations and activities. The Internet Living Swahili Dictionary is on hand for those who want to delve into the language, and the site's virtual bazaar hosts a gallery of Kwanzaa ceremonial items.—*Reviewed by Eugenia Johnson*

The African Holocaust Film from Haile Gerima

Welcome to your Kwanzaa Information Center provided by the MELANET Information and Communications Network. Please utilize this on-line guide as you celebrate this African American Holiday. While the Kwanzaa celebration is a seasonal event, the principles used in celebrating are meant to be a year-round way-of-life. The Kwanzaa Information Center will remain year-round and will contain additional information as we strive to strengthen our families and communities.

Please also visit:

- The MELANET On-line Kwanzaa Bazaar
- The National Kwanzaa Activities Calendar

scholarships, contracts and other opportunities for minority communities. Access hundreds of related minority service organizations via MOLIS.

Native Web
http://web.fie.com/web/mol/
Native Web links to the Oklahoma Native Voices Project, Native American Languages and other Native Language Resources on the Internet. Visit here to hear a variety of sound files.

Saludos Web
http://www.saludos.com/
Saludos Web promotes Hispanic careers and education with links to job listings, internships and scholarships. Includes articles from "Saludos Hispanos" magazine, resume postings and a variety of Hispanic-related Web links.

Tribal Voice Search
http://www.tribal.com/search.htm
This Web site provides users with a tool for searching the database of Tribal Voice, an online resource full of information about Native American culture and related issues. Includes a link back to the Tribal Voice home page.

UEweb
http://eric-web.tc.columbia.edu
The Urban Education Web is dedicated to assisting urban students and those who teach, guide and mentor them. Among other items, site features include urban and minority family resources, topical publications, education materials, and links to ERIC (library) databases.

The Universal Black Pages
http://www.gatech.edu/bgsa/blackpages.html
This site offers visitors an index to African diaspora-related Web sites. Categories featured include schools and student organizations, music, art, professional organizations and businesses, to name only a few.

WOMEN'S RESOURCES

The Ada Project
http://www.cs.yale.edu/HTML/YALE/CS/HyPlans/tap/tap.html
Connecting conferences, projects and discussion groups, The Ada Project creates an electronic networking space for women involved in computing. A clearinghouse of information by, for, and about computing, this service offers women their own gateway for learning from and about the Internet.

Amy Goodloe Home Page
http://www.best.com/~agoodloe/home.html
Amy Goodloe, moderator of women-only mailing lists and director of San Francisco, Calif.-based Women Online, posts her personal page here. Visit here to learn about Ms. Goodloe and access her collection of favorite World Wide Web links

Avon's Breast Cancer Awareness Crusade
http://www.avon.com/about/awareness/frame.html
Avon Products Incorporated brings its Breast Cancer Awareness Crusade to the Web through this site that features a history of the effort along with details about how people can get involved.

The Breast Cancer Information Clearinghouse
http://nysernet.org/bcic/
The Breast Cancer Information Clearinghouse is produced by the New York State Educational and Research Network. Visitors will find diverse information for breast cancer patients and their families here.

CMU Women's Center
http://english-server.hss.cmu.edu/WomensCenter.html
The Women's Center at Carnegie Mellon University provides general information about its library and weekly discussion—coffee talk—here. The site includes an online catalog of the center's books.

a2z EDITOR'S CHOICE

Water Birth Information
http://www.path.net/user/karil/
If it's good enough for your friendly neighborhood porpoise, then it could work for you. The concept of birthing babies underwater may be a new one for 20th century moms, but from all accounts it may be more comfortable—and certainly more peaceful—than the tortuous way we humans have been going about it for the past several centuries. And that's what many enlightened physicians, humanist psychologists and parents-to-be are excited about. San Francisco filmmaker Karil Daniels has produced an award-winning video, "Water Baby," which examines the practice of water birth, and the sensitive and illuminating film is highlighted here. It's a remarkale narration of a gentle birth in water, and a must-see for health care practitioners and those awaiting delivery of a new baby. Along with information on the video, Daniels' site provides an assortment of facts and photos that, if your birthing days are history, may make you wish you had the chance to do it all over again.—*Reviewed by Eugenia Johnson*

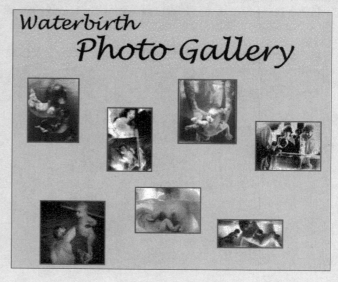
Waterbirth Photo Gallery

Creating A Celebration of Women Writers

http://www.cs.cmu.edu/Web/People/mmbt/women/celebration.html

Creating a Celebration of Women Writers is an effort to post public-domain or copyright-authorized works of female authors. The evolving site lists women writers and instructions for submitting work at this web site.

Divorce Online

http://www.divorce-online.com/index.html

Divorce Online, a service for people considering or in the midst of divorce, outlines basic legal facts and tips for surviving a divorce, psychologically and financially. Visitors here will also find an online directory to lawyers, therapists and financial planners.

Femina

http://www.femina.com/

Women and girls will find an index to sites by, about and for females here. The page is indexed by topic and provides a search function. Topics cover a wide range of interests, including Health and Well-being, Shopping, Motherhood and Women Writers.

Feminism and Women's Resources

http://www.ibd.nrc.ca/~mansfield/feminism/

The Feminism and Women's Resources site provides listings on feminism, women's studies and links to other women-related sources on the Internet. Includes instructions for posting new URLs that deal with women's issues.

Feminist Activist Resources on the Net

http://www.igc.apc.org/women/feminist.html

Feminist Activist Resources on the Net provides a comprehensive index of resources, including links to indexes concerning reproductive rights, domestic violence, economic issues and women's organizations.

Feminist Curricular Resources Clearinghouse

http://www.law.indiana.edu/fcrc/fcrc.html

In an effort to prove that feminist law is not an oxymoron, scholars at Indiana University and other institutions have compiled a Feminist Curricular Resources Clearinghouse to facilitate the teaching of the feminist perspective in law schools across the country.

The Global Fund for Women

http://www.igc.apc.org/gfw/

The Global Fund for Women (GFW) is an international grantmaking organization that supports groups working to ensure the political and social enfranchisement of women. Visitors can read about the GFW's programs here, as well as projects completed by grant recipients.

Guide to Women's Health Issues

http://asa.ugl.lib.umich.edu/chdocs/womenhealth/womens_health.html

Links to information on women's emotional, physical and sexual health are included in this online guide.

Kassandra Project

http://www.reed.edu/~ccampbel/tkp/

The "kassandra project" offers a series of web pages which feature German women writers, artists and thinkers from the second half of the 1800s to the first decades of the 1900s. The project seeks to "clear the cultural shadows" cast by Goethe, Schiller and Kant.

Letter to Women

http://listserv.american.edu/catholic/church/papal/jp.ii/jp2wom95.html

Here, browsers can read the papal letter written to women on the eve of the Fourth World Conference on Women in Beijing, China. The letter was issued by the Vatican in July, 1995.

The National Organization for Women

http://now.org/now/home.html

Find general information, an organizational history and current issues concerning the National Organization for Women. Site features also include a newsletter and listings of Internet feminist resources.

---

a2z   EDITOR'S CHOICE

Wombats on the Web: Women's Mountain Bike and Tea Society

http://www.wombats.org/

Ever since the turn of the century, women have fought to take their rightful place alongside men, both in the workplace and as social equals. But nowhere could the fight have been more "uphill" than breaking into the testosterone laden, gnarly sport of cycling. Mountain biking, with its macho lingo and emphasis on techno-junk, can be especially unnerving for women. But since 1984, Jacquie Phelen has worked tirelessly to help other women get involved in the sport, targeting gals who can't keep up with their menfolk on a two-wheeler, and those who put on their helmets backwards, but who don't mind looking a little foolish while learning the techniques and the trails. This cycling network encourages women's interest in cycling, proving to them that they don't need a Y-chromosome to "manhandle" a mountain bike. Stop in for some virtual tea and enjoy the whimsical graphics and pithy articles. For women who love mud, Camp Winna Wombat awaits.—*Reviewed by Eugenia Johnson*

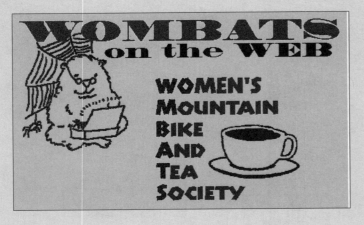

Point of View

http://www.path.net/user/karil/

Point of View Productions provides information here on water birthing techniques. The page includes descriptions of the delivery process and links to related obstetrical resources.

Sexual Assault Information Page

http://www.cs.utk.edu/~bartley/saInfoPage.html

This site presents a wealth of information about sexual assault. Broad categories covered include statistics, counseling directories, domestic violence, child abuse, legal issues and prevention.

United Nations Development Fund for Women (Unifem)

http://iron.ingenia.com/unifem/

Details about the United Nations Development Fund for Women (Unifem) are presented on this page. Find links to Unifem's international projects, its chapters and its news organs.

VOWworld: Voices of Women

http://www.voiceofwomen.com/

Visitors to this page will find the electronic home of the "Voices of Women Journal," a magazine described by its editors as "the most comprehensive women's resource on the Internet." Articles, a calendar of events, a directory of professional women and subscription info are featured.

Water Birth Information

http://www.path.net/user/karil/

Visit this site and learn about the rediscovered practice of water birth See Editor's Choice3.

Wombats on the Web: Women's Mountain Bike and Tea Society

http://www.wombats.org/

Visit this site to learn about the Wombats. See Editor's Choice.

Women & Politics

http://www.westga.edu/~wandp/w+p.html

"Women & Politics," an academic journal, encourages research and theory development on women's political participation and role in society, and the impact of public policy upon women's lives. Here, researchers and contributors will find abstracts, submission guidelines and more.

Women in Film and Television

http://www.deakin.edu.au/arts/VPMA/wift.html

Women in Film and Television is an Australian professional organization that encourages mentoring and networking traditions among women in the field. Read about the group's mission and goals here, along with information on WIFT's advocacy and information services.

Women's Health Interactive

http://www.entertain.com/

Women's Health Interactive provides links to information and educational resources for women, their health and health-related issues. Includes links to relevant organizations, services and consumer resources.

Women's Home Page

http://www.mit.edu:8001/people/sorokin/women/index.html

This extensive listing of online resources by, for and about women features topics that include women in computer science and engineering, women's studies programs, women in academia, and gender and sexuality references.

Women's Resources

http://sunsite.unc.edu/cheryb/women/wresources.html

Women's Resources on the Internet maps feminine, feminist and just plain female outposts in cyberspace. Topics covered include news, art and music, biographies, bisexual and lesbian resources, the law, and health issues, plus electronic discussion forums, sports info, women's college indices and much more.

WWW Women's Sports Page by Amy Lewis

http://fiat.gslis.utexas.edu/~lewisa/womsprt.html

The World Wide Web Women's Sports Page houses an extensive index of women's sports pages around the Net. From flying and gliding to soccer, "iron" sports and volleyball, there is something here for everyone. Also includes links to issues in women's sports.

SPORTS

THE 25 MOST POPULAR SPORTS SITES

Aero.com
http://www.aero.com/

The Classic Angler
http://www.gorp.com/bamboo.htm

CNN Interactive Sports
http://www.cnn.com/SPORTS/index.html

College Nicknames
http://grove.ufl.edu/~recycler/sports.html

The Consummate Skiing
http://ski.websmith.ca/ski/

ESPNET SportsZone
http://espnet.sportszone.com/

GolfWeb
http://www.golfweb.com/

Horse Country
http://www.pathology.washington.edu/Horse/
index.html

Instant Baseball
http://www.instantsports.com/baseball.html

MLB@BAT
http://www.majorleaguebaseball.com/

The Nando Sports Server
http://www.nando.net/SportServer/

NBA.com
http://www.nba.com/

Nerd World: Sports
http://www.nerdworld.com/cgi-bin/
page.cgi?SPORTS/26

NHL Open Net
http://www.nhl.com/

Official 1996 Olympic Web Site
http://www.atlanta.olympic.org/

RaceWeb
http://www.alpenglow.com/~cj/raceweb/
raceweb.html

RaceZine
http://www.primenet.com/~bobwest/
index.html

Rico's Martial Arts Page
http://www.update.uu.se/~rico/martial_arts/

SI Online
http://pathfinder.com/@@F7AkEQUAut8a3H3q/
si/welcome.html

SoccerNet
http://soccernet.com/

The Sports Network
http://www.sportsnetwork.com:80/filter/
filter.cgi/home.html

Sports Schedules As You Like 'Em
http://www.cs.rochester.edu:80/u/ferguson/
schedules/

Team NFL
http://nflhome.com/

Tennis Worldwide
http://www.xmission.com/~gastown/tennis/
index.html

YachtNet/Intersail
http://www.yachtnet.com/

AEROBICS AND STEP

Planet Reebok
http://planetreebok.com/
At Planet Reebok, the shoe manufacturer provides much more than promotional propaganda. Its smorgasbörd of resources includes live chat, bulletin boards, training tips, and pages for the Women's Sports Foundation and National Standards for Athletic Coaches. See Editor's Choice.

ASSOCIATIONS AND ORGANIZATIONS

Amateur Athletic Foundation
http://www.aafla.com/
The Amateur Athletic Foundation is a nonprofit institution that supports youth sports in Southern California and manages the largest sports research library in North America. This site provides a newsletter, research reports, and information on the sports library, among other resources.

The Centre
http://www.cdnsport.ca/
Many sports organizations in Canada call The Centre "home," including Baseball Canada, the Canadian Hockey Association, and the Canadian Amateur Wrestling Association. This site also features listings of active-living associations, as well as an FTP site and related links.

Pac-10 Conference
http://www.pac-10.org/
The Pacific 10 Conference is a U.S. athletic league composed of major universities on the West Coast and in Arizona. Visitors can link to pages on every Pac-10 school and every Pac-10 sport through this site.

United States Sports Academy
http://www.sport.ussa.edu/
The United States Sports Academy of Daphne, Alabama offers graduate programs in all areas of sports—including sports medicine, sports science, and just plain playing sports. Take a jog around this page to learn about the academy's

offerings or to check out pages on U.S.A. team handball and beach handball.

BASEBALL

The Baseball Server
http://www2.nando.net/SportServer/baseball/
Nando.net's Baseball Server serves up a host of baseball information. Baseball fans can read daily updates, check out game statistics, read sketches of players, and delve into baseball news from the early years of baseball. Links to Nando's other sports servers are available.

The Baseball Statistics Page
http://www.cloud9.net/~jcg
This site has all the statistics a baseball fan could ever want. See Editor's Choice.

Baseball Weekly
http://www.usatoday.com/bbwfront.htm
Based merely on its coverage of the college game, Baseball Weekly from USA Today is worth checking out. But this site also supplies articles and team notes on the major leagues, as well as a minor-league report. Current and past issues are available.

---

a2z EDITOR'S CHOICE

Planet Reebok
http://planetreebok.com/
What do you get when you cross a healthy planet with a healthy body? Find out at Planet Reebok, where the shoe manufacturer provides promotional propaganda—but plenty of other stuff, too. Among the items that caught our eye were a page on human rights activists, journals by world-class athletes (who happen to be sponsored by Reebok) and several areas focusing on women in sports. Training tips and information on community projects are among resources that include audio, video, live chat, and bulletin boards, plus pages for the Women's Sports Foundation and the National Standards for Athletic Coaches. There are also contests and information about the online Reebok Fitness Conference. Of course, if you're looking for information on athletic shoes and equipment, that's available here, too. —*Reviewed by Dan Kelly*

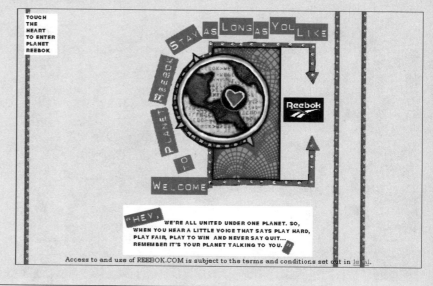

The Carl Michael Yastrzemski Page

http://www.epix.net/~brett/yaz.html

A fan page on former Boston Red Sox player Carl Yastrzemski, the Yaz Page houses information on Yastrzemski's career, images of Yastrzemski collectibles, the text of his Hall of Fame speech, and more. A link to Virtual Fenway Park is available.

Cleveland Indians Home Page

http://www.indians.com

Cleveland Indian fans can interact with each other and with players from the 1995 American League champions at this page. The official site of the Indians also supplies game coverage, contests, statistics, video clips, and a merchandise shop.

Cosmic Baseball Association—Home Plate

http://www.clark.net/pub/cosmic/cba1.html

The Cosmic Baseball Association raises America's pastime to a different level, metaphorically speaking. Where else would you find an outfield of Euclid, Comte de Buffon, and Galileo? Or memorials to both Mickey Mantle and Jerry Garcia? Just check it out. See Editor's Choice.

Crawdads Home Page

http://www.hickory.nc.us/ncnetworks/crawdads.html

The Hickory Crawdads, a minor-league baseball team in Hickory, N.C., maintains this promotional

site. It features a schedule, game reports, and player information, as well as merchandise and team photographs.

David's Unofficial Page for the Baltimore Orioles

http://pluto.njcc.com/~nieporen/oriole.html

Organizational reports by position and other minor-league information are among the features at this unofficial page on the Baltimore Orioles. News, schedules, standings, and other information help Orioles fans keep up on their favorite team.

ESPNET SportsZone: Major League Baseball

http://espnet.sportszone.com/mlb/

The ESPNET SportsZone baseball site delivers up-to-the-minute results, news, stats, and schedules, plus features and columns—even after the season. As on any sports page, photos, facts, and figures abound.

Fastball

http://www.fastball.com/

Team-by-team news and discussion areas—maintained year-round—are the focus of this site from Cox Newspapers. Baseball fans can also find current team rosters, recent transactions, audio clips, insightful quotes, and more.

Home of the Braves

http://www.atlantabraves.com/

If you didn't know the Atlanta Braves won the 1995 World Series, you don't know baseball. This official page is heavy with fan pride, offering information about the team and players, as well as game reports and lots of merchandise for sale. A fan forum is included.

Instant Baseball

http://www.instantsports.com

A service of Instant Sports, Instant Baseball provides near-live animated renditions of major-league games. Look at what's happening today or what happened yesterday, review the standings and statistics, or check out schedules. See Editor's Choice.

John Skilton's Baseball Links

http://www.baseball-links.com

Major league, minor league, college, youth and international—John Skilton's page is the "mother of all baseball links pages." It boasts hundreds of links to baseball-related sites on the Internet—including pages on stadiums, newsgroups, and collectibles.

MLB@BAT

http://www.majorleaguebaseball.com

This site follows league play from the opening day through the postseason. With this site's news and notes, box scores, statistics, and even

---

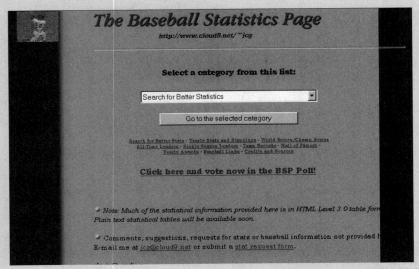

a2z EDITOR'S CHOICE

The Baseball Statistics Page

http://www.cloud9.net/~jcg

Baseball is the quintessential American sport, and statistics are its lifeblood. Ergo, this site is a vital component in the fabric of our society. (Drumroll, please.) That might be overstating the situation just a tad, but the fact remains that this is about as close to heaven on the Web as a baseball fan can get. Compiled by a fan in New York state, the Baseball Statistics Page contains team records, individual season leaders, World Series statistics, award winners, a batters database…and that's just for starters. The package is attractive and well organized, which makes it easy to find whatever information you're seeking. Simply select from several categories of statistics (single-season leaders, all-time leaders, and so on), then choose the more specific information you seek (doubles, earned-run average) from drop-down menus. The only problem here is that the statistics are unofficial; the Webmaster says he has collected them from "several sources," so you might not want to write a baseball master's thesis based on them, but they're good enough to settle bar bets. —*Reviewed by Dan Kelly*

a photo gallery, if you can't get to the park, you don't have to miss the game.

Negro Baseball Leagues
http://www.blackbaseball.com

All baseball fans have heard of Satchel Paige and Josh Gibson, but what about Mules Suttles and Bingo DeMoss? They are among the players from the Negro Baseball Leagues featured at this site, which focuses on the stories of the teams and players.

New York Yankees Home Plate
http://www.yankees.com/

The New York Yankees Home Plate, a promotional site for the American League team, supplies Yankees fans with the basics. Provided here are a roster, schedule, ticket information, details on publications, and, of course, a George Steinbrenner bio.

The New York Yankees Page—KAT
http://grove.ufl.edu/~kat152/nyy.html

Team news and game reports are featured on this New York Yankees fan page. Information about players, an e-mail discussion list, and links to other Yankee sites are provided.

The Oakland Athletics
http://www.oaklandathletics.com/

The Oakland Athletics provide a plethora of information at this site. Visitors can find the roster of the American League baseball club here, along with ticket information, a schedule, statistics, news releases, and much more. Sites on all of the A's minor-league teams are provided.

Overview of the National Baseball Hall of Fame and Museum
http://www.enews.com/bas_hall_fame/overview.html

Plan your trip to Cooperstown at this site from the Electronic Newsstand. It provides information on all the basics of the Baseball Hall of Fame, including exhibits, directions, and rates. Online shopping also is available here.

Philadelphia Phillies Unofficial Home Page
http://storm.cadcam.iupui.edu/phils/phils.html

Fans of the Philadelphia Phillies will find plenty of information at this unofficial site, including standings, a schedule, player statistics, and more. News, ticket information, and links to other Phillies pages are provided.

Professional Baseball (Japan)
http://www.inter.co.jp:80/Baseball/

Looking for Clete Boyer's batting average with the Taiyo Whales of the Japanese professional league in the early 1970s? This English-language site has the scoop in its registry of players. Also

provided here are Japanese standings dating to 1936, statistics, and more.

Seattle Mariners
http://www.mariners.org/

This official home page of the Seattle Mariners offers resources that include a media library with downloadable images, audio, and video. Also find team and player information, schedules, merchandise information, and more on the American League team.

Tornado Boy
http://www.st.rim.or.jp/~k_ono/tornado/

Dedicated to the National League 1995 Rookie of the Year, Hideo Nomo (nicknamed Tornado Boy), this Japanese page features reports, columns, profiles, and fan notices. Fans can also learn how to write posters with messages such as "Blow Them Over Tornado" in Japanese.

The Toronto Blue Jays
http://fas.sfu.ca/cs/people/GradStudents/niguma/personal/jays.html

At this unofficial Toronto Blue Jays site, baseball fans will find player profiles, SkyDome information, statistics, and news. Take the Blue Jays quiz and vote for your favorite players here.

The Toronto Blue Jays
http://www.bluejays.ca

This official page for the Toronto Blue Jays baseball team contains stats, interviews, photos, fan surveys, and ticket information. There's also a special area for the kids here.

---

a2z EDITOR'S CHOICE

Cosmic Baseball Association—Home Plate
http://www.clark.net/pub/cosmic/cba1.html

The Cosmic Baseball Association "is dedicated to the notion that the great game of the quadrature is really just a metaphor for the life of the mind." If you understand what that means, you're a natural for membership in the CBA. The activity here involves standings and statistics, but don't confuse it with fantasy baseball or real baseball. The CBA simply raises the science of baseball to a different level, metaphorically speaking. To get an idea of what this site is like, consider that Beethoven is one of the top hitters here, that one outfield consists of Euclid, Comte de Buffon, and Galileo, and that the teams include the Nirvanaville Yogis and the Vestal Virgins. There also are tributes to both Mickey Mantle and Jerry Garcia. Don't bother visiting if you're looking for serious baseball analysis. But if you're of the belief that baseball is more a spiritual pastime than a national one, check it out. —*Reviewed by Dan Kelly*

The World Wide Web Virtual Library: Sport—Baseball

http://www.atm.ch.cam.ac.uk/sports/baseball.html

The World Wide Web Virtual Library boasts an extensive baseball collection within its sports listings. Available here are links to other baseball servers, leagues, organizations, teams, and more.

World Youth Baseball 1994

http://www.brandonu.ca/~ennsnr/WYB/

World Youth Baseball 1994 is an unofficial site that provides scores, standings, and participating teams from the 1994 championships for 16 to 18-year-olds in Brandon, Canada. Results from previous championships and a listing of World Youth players who made it to the major leagues are included.

---

a2z EDITOR'S CHOICE

Instant Baseball

http://www.instantsports.com/baseball.html

Truth be told, we probably lack the patience to sit through an entire baseball game on Instant Baseball. Or, for that matter, an entire inning. But even for a batter or two, this is a pretty exhilarating experience. Instant Baseball is part video game and part VCR...and very popular among baseball fans on the Web. The Java applet allows visitors with Windows 95 or Windows NT to watch the action of major league games through animated coverage as they happen, live, in virtual realtime (if you're confused, you won't be after a couple of hitters). Meanwhile, continuously updated scores of other big league games scroll across the screen. If you're an insatiable baseball junkie, replays of games already completed are also available (and you can skip through the boring parts), as are standings, statistics, game recaps and box scores. The entire season schedule is available, and fans can use it to select any past game for instant replay...in Instant Baseball. So next time your TV's on the fritz (or you're arguing with your spouse about whether to watch the game or the Movie of the Week), tune into Instant Baseball. Although the graphics and the site's popularity make for some long waits, this is fun stuff. —*Reviewed by Dan Kelly*

| Instant Ballpark | Today's Games | Yesterday's Games | Standings | Statistics | Schedule |

Instant Baseball

Instant Baseball is designed to provide entertaining, virtual-realtime coverage of Major League Baseball for fans around the world. Follow your favorite team and players, in any game, anytime, from anywhere with Internet access. Whether you want to keep up with today's game, relive the highlights of past games, or get up-to-the-minute statistics for your favorite players, Instant Baseball is the place. And there are no user fees.

Instant Ballpark - The award-winning Java-animated ballfield allows Netscape 2.0 users running on Windows 95 or Windows NT to watch, in virtual-realtime, nearly everything of interest in a Major League Game. Instant Ballpark provides animation, lineups and status of all current games and personalized replay of any play of any game for the season. Recent winner in the Interact '96 Java Applet Contest

Today's Games - Up-to-the-pitch game situations, statistics, and scores for all the Major League games scheduled for the day. The data is typically updated within a minute or two of the action on the field, so you can stay in the game, even when you can't get the broadcast. Works with any browser.

Yesterday's Games - Play-by-play recaps of all the games let you create your own scouting reports. Detailed box scores with the details you want. Replay the action in the game with Instant Ballpark.

Standings - Current standings in all the division races. Updated at the end of every game.

Statistics - Every team, every player, and up to the minute. No need to wait for the morning paper, our records are updated at the end of each game.

BASKETBALL

Blazers Home Page

http://www.blazers.com/

Word is they now prefer plain, old Blazers to Trail Blazers. In any case, the National Basketball Association's Portland franchise is making a name for itself on the Web with this site. In addition to finding news, a schedule, and the like at this official team page, fans can join a Blazers mailing list.

Boston Celtics WWW Server

http://www.ics.com/~drisko/celtics.html

Boston Celtics fans can grade the performance of Coach M.L. Carr at this fan page. The site also has everything fans need to know about the National Basketball Association team, including ticket information, player statistics, scores, game summaries, pictures, and links.

Chicago Bulls

http://www.nando.net/SportServer/basketball/nba/chi.html

A section of Nando.net's Sports Server, this Chicago Bulls page links fans to current news and information about the National Basketball Association team. Stories and summaries on the Bulls' most recent games are available, as are photos, a team history, and an archive of stories from throughout the season.

College Basketball

http://www.cs.cmu.edu/afs/cs.cmu.edu/user/wsr/Web/bball/bball.html

Rankings, schedules, news, and game results are among the resources available at this comprehensive index of college basketball sites. Links also are provided to conferences, individual teams, rules changes, recruiting information, and more.

ESPNET SportsZone: Men's College Basketball

http://espnet.sportszone.com/ncb/

College basketball news and scores come to the Web through this page from the popular ESPNET SportsZone. Visitors will find regularly updated scores and standings, as well as features about the top men's basketball teams in the U.S.

ESPNET SportsZone: NBA

http://espnet.sportszone.com/nba/

Current news and results from the National Basketball Association are featured at this ESPNET SportsZone site. Among the other resources are columns, standings, statistics, player profiles, and even a roster of referees.

ESPNET SportsZone: Women's College Basketball

http://espnet.sportszone.com/ncw/

Women's college basketball takes center stage on this page from ESPNET SportsZone. Find daily updates, including scores, standings and statistics, as well as chat, feature stories, and more.

In The Paint

http://www.primenet.com/~shannon/index.html

This is a fan-created page for the Phoenix Suns, providing NBA box scores and standings, along with the latest news on Charles Barkley and Co.

Nando.net 1994-95 NBA Archive

http://www.nando.net/newsroom/basketball/1994/nba/archive/game

For the most dogged of basketball fans, Nando.net provides an archive of National Basketball Association game articles from the 1994–95 season. The articles are listed game by game, day by day, starting from January 3, 1995.

NBA Leaders

http://www.nando.net/newsroom/basketball/1994/nba/stat/nbalead.html

Nando.net offers final 1994–95 statistics from the National Basketball Association on this page. Visit here for the final leaders in scoring, free-throw percentage, rebounding, assists, and other statistics.

NBA Standings

http://www.nando.net/newsroom/basketball/1994/nba/stat/standings.html

Sports fans can check the final National Basketball Association standings from the 1994–95 season at this site from Nando.net.

North Carolina Tar Heels Web Page

http://www.cs.unc.edu/~chen/tarheels/tarheels.html

Nothing but basketball matters at this fan page dedicated to the North Carolina Tar Heels. Visitors will find information on tournaments and tickets, as well as schedules, stats from 1981 to the present, and plenty of topical links.

On Hoops

http://www.onhoops.com/

This is an unofficial site with commentary and gossip. See Editor's Choice.

'BLADING AND 'BOARDING

INLINE SKATING

Hardcore Inline Skating

http://www.aggressive.com/inline

Aggressive inline skaters will find 16 megs worth of memory in photos, videos, poetry, tour information, and tips here. The site includes a health and injuries section, manufacturers' lists, and product reviews. The Webmaster aims to "give inline skating the positive exposure it deserves."

Inline Online

http://bird.taponline.com/inline/

Same name, different site. This Inline Online features everything from an overview of inline skating to opinions on particular skates. Readers can check out where to skate and who's who in inline skating, or they can follow links to publications and organizations.

---

a2z EDITOR'S CHOICE

On Hoops

http://www.onhoops.com/

On Hoops introduces itself by saying it "is not affiliated with the NBA in any way. We have the utmost admiration for the Game and the League and hope not to conflict with any of the League's Internet plans, no matter how boring they may be." Needless to say, this is an NBA site with an attitude. Assembled and maintained by two basketball fans, it largely reflects their peculiar point of view, which is considerably less serious than, say, *The New York Times*. Most of the stuff here consists of commentaries and offbeat ideas like the Chump Register and the Golden Chuck Awards. They aren't afraid to share unsubstantiated rumors or to bad-mouth the NBA's overpaid crybabies, either. The grammar, spelling, and syntax might cause the more learned among us occasionally to cringe, but we have to admit most of their offerings are entertaining. If mainstream information is what you're after, On Hoops also provides links to team sites, statistics, and more. —*Reviewed by Dan Kelly*

On Hoops is a service brought to you by Los Chucks of Vidya Media Ventures, Inc. **On Hoops** is not affiliated with the N.B.A in any way. We have the utmost admiration for the Game and the League and hope not to conflict with any of the League's internet plans, no matter how boring they may be.

As for us "aspiring to be the center for thoughtful and opinionated N.B.A. discussion"- what are they smoking over there at YAHOO (and where can we get some?)? We suppose that's a nice mission statement, but mostly we're just speaking our mind, cracking jokes and just plain have too much time on our hands. Our thanks to the folks at YAHOO anyway.

Think maybe you're a Chuck too? We just love submissions, so email articles ya' write to On Hoops. If it "chucks" we will post it.

On Hoops

New York City Inline Skating Guide

http://www.skatecity.com/NYC/

The New York City Inline Skating Guide serves as a one-stop information source about places to skate and upcoming events in the Big Apple. The page also gives skaters tips on the law, pointers to skate merchants, and a heads-up on skate-unfriendly businesses.

Skating the Infobahn

http://www.skatecity.com/Index/

Calling itself "the most comprehensive inline skating index on the Web," this site provides a searchable collection of links. It also contains an index with categories such as Aggressive Skating, Events, Traditional Rollerskating, and Where to Skate.

SKATEBOARDING

DansWorld Skateboarding

http://web.cps.msu.edu/~dunhamda/dw/dansworld.html

Visitors to this online skateboarding journal will find photos and a "Net skater showcase" profiling people who spend time surfing the information highway as well as the sidewalks. Links include FAQ files and newsgroups.

Enternet Communications

http://www.enternet.com/

Influx, a digital journal on skateboarding, and a skateboard chat site are featured at the home page of Enternet Communications. The site also contains skateboarding links, as well as the home pages of Platt College in San Francisco and of WinClassic training software.

SNOWBOARDING

Board? The European Snowboarding Network

http://www.earth.ox.ac.uk/~andyc/

The European Snowboarding Network focuses on the latest snowboarding news. It includes addresses of European snowboarding contacts, a link to the European Championships in Finland, and more.

Burton Snowboards

http://www.burton.com/

Check out the latest product lines from Burton Snowboards, along with news releases, photos, and more at this home page. If you have something to say, spit it out on Electronic Spit.

Killington Vermont

http://www.killington.com/

Claiming to be the "East's largest Ski and Snowboard Resort," Killington offers skiers a heated gondola in the winter and mountain bikers a place to play in the summer. Check the resort's home page for trail conditions and year-round events.

Ocean & Snow Surfer Home Page

http://www.cts.com/browse/scwindan/

South Coast Surf Shops of San Diego present resources here geared toward surfers and snowboarders. In addition to photos, links to companies, and information on merchandise, this site has video reviews and a directory of surf clubs.

Snowboarding

http://www.nyx.net/~mwallace/sb_faq.html

The rec.skiing.snowboarding newsgroup posts its FAQ at this site. The rules of the road and a glossary of snowboarders' jargon are among the topics covered.

BODYBUILDING

Faith Sloan's Bodybuilding Site

http://www.frsa.com/bbpage.shtml

Faith Sloan, professional bodybuilder, has some strong ideas on pumping up at this site, including articles on strengthening techniques and nutrition. Here, get the rundown on upcoming competitions and link to like-minded people.

The Training-Nutrition Home Page

http://www.dgsys.com/~trnutr/index.html

This is the home page for the Training-Nutrition mailing list, dedicated to hard-core natural bodybuilders who are interested in how nutrition affects their training. Everything you need to know is in the FAQ.

BOOMERANG

Colorado Boomerangs

http://pd.net/colorado/

Okay, so this is largely a promotional site for a manufacturer of boomerangs. Still, we have this odd urge to keep coming back. At the very least, this site is worth checking out because it provides detailed instructions on throwing a boomerang.

BOWLING

Bowling Page

http://www.rpi.edu/~miller3/bowling.html

Schedules and results from the men's and women's professional bowling tours in the United States are featured on the Bowling Page. It includes national and regional events, as well as links to other resources such as the Bowling Hall of Achievement.

Dream Team Bowling Club

http://www.bowling.it/

The Dream Team boasts of being the "first Italian bowling club on Internet." It introduces itself to visitors and provides details on when and where it plays. There also is information on the Italian Bowling Federation and its events.

Professional Bowlers Association

http://www.pba.org/

Bowlers and bowling fans will find information from and about the PBA Tour here, including tournament results and schedules. The site also offers message boards and online chats with bowling pros.

BROOMBALL

Broomball, What the HELL is Broomball, Home Page

http://www.ozemail.com.au/~kshapley/index.html

Take a look at broomball information from around the world at this page. It contains details on equipment for playing the game— a "sport similar to ice hockey" except for "a number of significant details"—along with official rules and results.

CRICKET

Australian Cricket Page

http://www.ida.com.au/sport/cricket/

Although this page concentrates on Australian and New Zealand cricket—offering news, schedules and match reports—a link to the Oregon-based CricInfo Database provides international information about the sport as well. Visitors also can find cricket rules here.

CricInfo

http://cricinfo.cse.ogi.edu/

CricInfo provides up-to-date information on the sport of cricket. Visitors will find news, scores, statistics, player profiles, and league standings for English and international cricket.

The Wonderful World of Cricket

http://www.dcs.ed.ac.uk/home/sma/HTML/cricket.html

Take a look at top cricket teams and home pages from around the world at this collection of links. Visitors can learn the rules of the game, or find out how cricket strategies vary from Sri Lanka to Zimbabwe.

CURLING

The Brown University Curling Club

http://www.brown.edu/Students/Brown_Curling_Club/

The Brown University Curling Club offers information here on its members, ice schedule, and events. A variety of curling information is also provided, including articles, a history and explanation of curling, and links to related Web sites.

CYCLING

Beetle's Bike Page

http://www.beetle.com/mtb.html

Get ready to push the envelope and shred the single-track. Beetle's Bike Page features Chris Bailey's reviews of tires, bike stuff for sale, biking tips, and more. The mountain bike racer also offers racing photos.

Backcountry Bicycle Trails Club

http://www.compumedia.com/~agb/bbtc/

Mountain biking enthusiasts will learn about the Seattle-based Backcountry Bicycle Trails Club here. Visitors can download the club's newsletter, map out great rides, and link to other biking sites from this page.

Bicycle Helmet Safety Institute Home Page

http://www.bhsi.org/

Advocates of bicycle helmet laws promote their public policy agenda from the Bicycle Helmet Safety Institute home page. Read up on helmet laws, standards, and compliance efforts at this site.

Bike Culture & EnCYCLEopedia

http://cyclery.com/open_road/

Read selected articles, commentaries and essays from the magazine *Bike Culture Quarterly* at this site. Along with the current and back issues, the page offers partial access to the EnCYCLEopedia, with its bicycle art, and merchandise information.

B.I.K.E.S.

http://www.eskimo.com/~gorts/bikes.html

B.I.K.E.S., a bicycle club in Snohomish County, Washington, supplies club information and details on club events and area trails. Among the Web bicycling resources here are several newsgroups.

Boulder Community Network Bicycle Center

http://bcn.boulder.co.us/transportation/bike.page.html

Bicycling is serious business in colorful Colorado—so serious that the Boulder Community Network offers a cycling resources page packed with everything from information on races and clubs to trail guides and magazines. It's enough to get cyclists heading to the high country.

Cascade Bicycle Club Home Page

http://cascade.org/cbc.html

The Cascade Bicycle Club home page provides riding calendars, lists of upcoming events, and general cycling information. Stories, pictures, and recommended routes are supplemented by Washington state cycling laws and links to related sites.

Coghead Corner

http://www.teleport.com/~bazzle/coghead.shtml

Coghead Corner is devoted to mountain biking in Portland, Oregon and the surrounding area. Visitors will find information on biking trails and conditions, along with links and a trail of the month.

College Park Bicycle Club

http://www.glue.umd.edu/~naru/cpbc.html

Competitive cycling hits the Web through the College Park Bicycle Club's home page from the Washington, D.C. area. Visitors here can read about the club's activities and members, or follow links to cycling resources.

Cyber Cyclery: An Internet Bicycling Resource

http://cyclery.com/

Visitors to Cyber Cyclery can check out *Cycling Times* magazine (among many other publications), join in chats, or link to almost any club, company, product, or event related to cycling. Users also can post bicycling events to the page. See Editor's Choice.

The Cyberider Cycling WWW

http://blueridge.infomkt.ibm.com/bikes/

A hub site for cycling enthusiasts, Cyberider Cycling links visitors to an amazing amount of information. Learn the best places to ride, check out cycling news and newsgroup postings, download bike images, or link to other Web cycling sites.

Dirt Camp Home

http://www.dirtcamp.com/mtb

Although the name might be misleading, mountain bike enthusiasts will probably know where this page is going. Dirt Camp is a series of instructional workshops held at the world's top riding destinations. This site contains information on these instructional bike vacations, including schedules and locations.

Dirt Rag

http://cyclery.com/dirt_rag/

Dirt Rag, an alternative to mainstream print mountain-bike magazines, prides itself on being for "real" bikers. Tables of contents, selected articles, and features are provided at this site.

800-BIKE-PRO

http://www.bikepro.com/

Bike-Pro of Santa Rosa, California supplies thousands of pages of cycling parts and equipment at this Web site. Potential customers can search for just the part they need, then order by phone or e-mail.

GearGrinder.com

http://www.geargrinder.com/

The focus here is on off-road bicycle racing in Colorado, but this site also provides news on World Cup cross country racing and the American Mountain Bike Challenge series. A schedule and results of Colorado races are available.

GORP—Biking

http://www.gorp.com/gorp/activity/biking.htm

Pedal pushers and armchair cycling enthusiasts can check out biking information from around the world at this page, which includes an extensive list of bike trails. The comprehensive resource is part of the Great Outdoor Recreation Pages site.

The International Human-Powered Vehicle Association

http://www.ihpva.org/

The International Human-Powered Vehicle Association provides a wealth of information about human-powered bicycles, submarines, and other modes of transport. Visit here to read how-to articles such as "How I Made a Carbon Fiber/Epoxy Composite Bike in My Garage" and announcements of upcoming races.

Internet Bicycling

http://cyclery.com/links.html

The Cyber Cyclery, created by individuals, clubs, and nonprofit organizations, provides this index of bicycling resources. Visit here to browse categories such as clubs, tours, racing, a cool link of the week and more.

Iron Horse Bicycle Classic

http://www.creativelinks.com/ironhorse/

Get the rundown on the annual Iron Horse Bicycle Classic in Durango, Colorado at this page. Would-be racers can even register online here. This page also points out other race schedules and information about local trails.

MassBike: Bicycling in Massachusetts

http://www.massbike.org/

MassBike's Web site is a gateway to cycling resources in the state of Massachusetts. Maintained by the Bicycle Coalition of Massachusetts, the page includes links to mailing lists, biking events, and bike laws.

Mini FAQ on Bicycle Lights

http://www.bath.ac.uk/~bspahh/bikelights/lights.html

Do not go gently into that dark night—especially on a bicycle. Visit this FAQ to find out which lights are recommended for night rides and how to make them work.

The Mountain Bike Pages

http://catless.ncl.ac.uk/mtb/

With a focus on Britain, this site contains information on mountain biking, related newsgroups, publications, and race schedules. Includes links to Olympic information and to manufacturers, as well as biking routes in the U.K. and mailing lists.

Mountain Bike Resources Online

http://www.mbronline.com/

MBR Online presents information on trails, details on tours, and other resources on mountain biking, primarily in the United States. The MBR Newsletter supplies news from competitions, and there are links to bike shops, bike clubs, hostels, and more.

Mountain Biking Austin

http://actlab.rtf.utexas.edu/~captain/mt.bike.html

Austin, Texas mountain biker Captain urges lazy drivers to kick the car habit and get out on a bike—for their health and the planet's. Read Captain's enthusiastic bike tales, find out more on biking in Austin or join the Campaign for Clean Air and Exercise.

New Jersey Biking

http://www.nj.com/bike/

Strap on that helmet and ride over to the biking page from New Jersey Online. Visitors can link to bike tour maps in the Garden State, racing results and commuter tips, as well as a discussion forum and the home page of the U.S. Bicycling Hall of Fame.

Ottawa Bicycle Club

http://www.sce.carleton.ca/rads/greg/obc/

Ottawans who enjoy viewing the world from behind a set of handlebars can visit the Ottawa Bicycle Club page for information on the Canadian club. Included here are details on the club's competitive events, social events, and touring events.

Peloton Online

http://www.eskimo.com/~cycling/

For those who bike in the northwest U.S., tips on riding in the rain are invaluable. Cyclists can find them at Peloton Online, along with a Northwest racing calendar, race results, home pages of racing teams, classified ads, and more.

---

a2z EDITOR'S CHOICE

Cyber Cyclery: An Internet Bicycling Resource

http://cyclery.com/

This is one of about a billion indexes that catalog the 10 zillion cycling sites on the Web. So what sets it apart from the rest? Well, in addition to providing those zillions of links, it is the home of Cycling Times, Bike Culture Quarterly, Dirt Rag, and a few other great biking publications, along with countless links to commercial cycling sites. Visitors can join in chats, plan a cycling vacation, read racing news, and shop for bikes and accessories. Users also can post upcoming bicycling events and check out racing calendars. Its sister site, VeloNet, contains a worldwide directory of organizations and hundreds of cycling mailing lists. The entire site is searchable, plus there are some pretty neat graphics here. In short, it's much more than an index of links; it's a virtual pedalist's dream come true. —*Reviewed by Dan Kelly*

The (Pittsburgh) Bicycling Home Page

http://www.cs.cmu.edu/afs/cs.cmu.edu/user/jdg/www/bike/

Pedalers from Pittsburgh will find useful information on this page that includes lists of organizations, events, and even tips on buying a bicycle. Get the scoop on where to ride in Pennsylvania and how to do it safely.

Sacramento Valley Cycling

http://www.mother.com/saccycle/

The Sacramento Valley Cycling page covers cycling in northern California. Information about events, cycling routes, and more is provided, as are the home pages of several clubs.

San Diego Bicycling

http://www.qualcomm.com/users/srram/biking/sdbike.html

Pedal pushers can get the scoop on San Diego-area biking clubs through this page. Check out on-line maps and bike commuting advice, as well as pointers to cycling resources from elsewhere in the world.

Specialized

http://www.specialized.com/

Specialized Bicycle Components Inc. supplies a dealer directory and e-mail access to Specialized engineers and pros at this promotional site. Cyclists also can find racing news and tips about how to take their cycling to a new level.

Stanford Cardinal Coed Club Cycling

http://www-leland.stanford.edu/group/cycling/

No, this isn't one of those joke "Co-ed Naked..." deals. Stanford University's co-ed cycling club posts photos, meeting information, and race results here. The site includes access to the club's newsletter and links to newsgroups such as rec.bicycles.racing and rec.bicycles.rides.

The Stolen Bike Registry

http://www.nashville.net/cycling/stolen.html

This interactive site features a registry for bike owners to document ownership of their bikes in the event they get stolen. A registry of bikes that have been reported stolen is also included.

Trek Home Page

http://www.trekbikes.com

Visit the Trek Home Page for information on the company and its bikes. Guests can look at a catalog of Trek bikes and accessories, check out the Trek riders' group, get technical information on Trek bikes, and more.

Unicycling Home Page

http://www.unicycling.org

Here's a comprehensive roundup of facts and tips on the sport of unicycling. Learn how to ride and what kind of 'cycle to buy. Includes a "trading post" for buying and selling.

VeloNet

http://www.cycling.org/

VeloNet is a clearinghouse for cycling resources on the Internet. Network with fellow athletes across the globe by using the mailing lists and directories provided here. This site also features the VeloWeb, a directory of cycling links under categories ranging from Advocacy to Traveling with Your Bicycle.

VeloNews

http://www.velonews.com/VeloNews/

Regional listings of cycling events are featured at the site of *VeloNews*, a print magazine that also provides a table of contents and selected articles. The magazine covers the racing scene, cycling culture, and bike products. Visitors here can request a free copy of the print version.

Westy's Cycling Page

http://eksl-www.cs.umass.edu/~westy/cycling.html

Westy's Cycling Page provides a range of information for cyclists in the Amherst, Massachusetts area. Visitors can check out the image gallery, read about local rides, trails, and tours, or link to other cycling pages.

Winning Online

http://www.winningmag.com/

The online home of *Winning Bicycling Illustrated* magazine provides cycling news and more. In addition to articles, results, and photos from current and past issues, this site contains a buyer's guide and a marketplace.

WOMBATS on the Web

http://www.wombats.org/

WOMBATS on the Web is the home page of the Women's Mountain Bike and Tea Society. Visitors to this site can read news relevant to female bikers, browse the WOMBAT online art gallery, or link to other bike-related sites on the Web.

WSDOT Bicycling

http://www.wsdot.wa.gov/ppsc/bike/

The Washington State Department of Transportation highlights two-wheeled travel on this page, with links to a broad assortment of bicycling resources. Here, steer your way through trails, clubs, and events from throughout the northwest region.

WWW Bicycle Lane

http://www.cs.purdue.edu/homes/dole/bikelane.html

The World Wide Web Bicycle Lane, a personal collection of bicycling-related Internet resources, offers an extensive index of news, publications, and commercial sites. Includes links to cycling clubs, bike shops, trade publications, online discussion groups, and more.

DARTS

Anything Goes Darts

http://www.darts.com/anything_goes_darts/

Anything Goes Darts, a North American dart equipment retailer, maintains this promotional site for product information and sporting resources. Visit here to link with dart enthusiast Web sites and virtual pubs from England, Ireland, and the United States.

EQUESTRIAN SPORTS

GENERAL

Aberdeen University Riding Club World Equestrian Information

http://www.abdn.ac.uk/~src011/equine.html

The World Equine Resource List sets out to catalog links to the wide world of horses and the humans who watch, ride, and love them. Equestrians can follow pointers to clubs, photos, and even a kid's pony page.

American Quarter Horse Association On-Line

http://www.aqha.com/

From Amarillo, Texas the American Quarter Horse Association presents a page full of information about the horse with a "colorful history." It gallops from online racing and performance publications to show schedules and AQHA rules. Also, find the AQH museum here.

Hay.net

http://www.freerein.com/haynet/

Horse people are known to be a bit snobbish about their breeding—a Paso Fino person wouldn't be caught dead on a Morgan, and vice versa. At Hay.net, however, the breeds come together in a show of unity. Resources on all horses are collected here, right down to model horses. Included is a listing of veterinary links.

Horse Country

http://www.horse-country.com

The Horse Country site offers resources and information about horses, riding, and equestrian events. Visitors will find a riders library, sounds, images, and links to information about horse care, breeds, and riding equipment. There are also special links for younger and beginning riders.

Horsemen's Yankee Pedlar

http://www.thepedlar.com

The Pedlar, based in Massachusetts, is a monthly newspaper covering all aspects and all breeds of horses and riding. The paper's Web site features articles from current and previous issues, as well as classifieds.

Horse Previews Magazine

http://www.iea.com/~adlinkex/HP/index.html

Horse Previews, a monthly magazine from Spokane, Washington presents articles and information on horses, horse organizations and horse people, with a focus on the Pacific Northwest. Includes classifieds, a calendar of events, and a listing of horses for sale.

United States Dressage Federation Home

http://www.usdf.org/

For those who don't know what dressage is, this site supplies the basics on the sport of classical horsemanship. For those familiar with dressage, the United States Dressage Federation provides information on competitions, programs, merchandise, and more.

RODEO

New Mexico Gay Rodeo Association

http://www.swcp.com/~rkmartin/nmgra.html

Meet the board members of the New Mexico Gay Rodeo Association here and find out where and when it holds events. Calendars of regional and national gay rodeo events are available at this site, which also includes details about the national finals in Albuquerque.

Sarah's Rodeo Page

http://mama.indstate.edu/prentice/sarah

This rodeo resource page offers a wealth of information for rodeo lovers. Check out upcoming events, related news articles, and lists of rodeo links, or join the rodeo discussion group.

EXTREME SPORTS

AdventureTime

http://www.nauticom.net/adventuretime/

Visit here to view articles, features, and columns about skiing, scuba diving, snow skating, street luge, and other adventurous sports. This site also provides a trip of the month and an online product catalog.

FENCING

Harvard Fencing

http://hcs.harvard.edu/~fencing/

Visit this site for details of Harvard University's fencing program: the people, schedules, and results. A FAQ, a history of the sport, and links to related Web sites are also featured.

FLYING

AVIATION

Aero.com

http://www.aero.com/

Aero.com aims high with this site that strives to be the most complete online resource for aviation information on the Web. The home page features news, shopping, and the Aviation Yellow Pages.

Colorado Soaring Association

http://www.csn.org/~rjc/csa_intro.html

Where eagles fly is where you'll find members of the Colorado Soaring Association, a club of glider pilots located in Fort Collins. Learn about the organization here and get information about this sport.

International Aerobatic Club Home Page

http://acro.harvard.edu/IAC/iac_homepg.html

The International Aerobatic Club, a division of the Experimental Aircraft Association, is open to anyone interested in aviation. Featured on this unofficial page are IAC news, chapter home pages, competition results, and e-mail addresses.

MIT Soaring Association

http://acro.harvard.edu/MITSA/mitsa_homepg.html

This Massachusetts-based soaring society introduces itself at this site and provides links to gliding- and aerobatics-related information. Also here, visitors will find links to aviation archives and weather information.

Soaring Information and Sailplane Directory

http://csrp.tamu.edu/Soaring/soaring.html

A wide range of soaring information is maintained at this server. Visitors can view the directory of gliders, towplanes, and flight test reports, or they can link to sail plane clubs, soaring sites around the globe, and related bibliographies.

Soaring Society of America

http://acro.harvard.edu/SSA/ssa_homepg.html

The Soaring Society of America is devoted to providing information on flying using motorless aircraft. A FAQ file answers questions about equipment, safety, and even proper diet. Link to a list of soaring and gliding events, or find like-minded aviators in a city near you.

HANGLIDING

Directory of Hang Gliding and Paragliding Home Pages

http://www.mainelink.net/SKYADVENTURES/myhom13.html

The hang gliding and paragliding resources here feature home pages from around the world and an index of image galleries. An extensive listing of classified ads is included.

Hang Gliding Site Guide

http://www.vii.com/hang

Hang out at this site to find the best spots in the world to launch a hang glider. Sensitive maps also take visitors to schools and associations, and the page is full of photos and personal narratives.

Skywings on the Web

http://test.ebrd.com/SkyWings/Home.html

The British Hang Gliding and Paragliding Association presents an abridged version of its monthly magazine at this site. Included here are news of national and international competitions and profiles of pilots. Back issues are available.

SKYDIVING

Canadian Sport Parachuting Association

http://www.islandnet.com/~murrays/cspa/

The Canadian Sport Parachuting Association is a nonprofit organization that promotes sport parachuting. It provides news about upcoming events here and posts rules and regulations. The page also includes links to clubs that can help with your first dive through the skies. Available in English and French.

skydive.net

http://www.skydive.net/

Competition Formation Skydiving, Skydive Switzerland and other related groups have sites at skydive.net. Visitors who are ready to take the plunge can order proper equipment or contact publishers of skydiving-related books.

Skydive UK!—The Clubs

http://www.cityscape.co.uk/users/cg90/skydive.html

Thrill-seeking Net users who get their jollies jumping out of planes can find places to do it in the United Kingdom here. This site features a listing of clubs and centers affiliated with the British Parachute Association.

FOOTBAG

Footbag WorldWide

http://www.footbag.org/

Sponsored by the San Francisco Bay Area Footbag Foundation, this page is dedicated to the sport of footbag, the competitive version of what is commonly referred to as "hacky sack." Visitors will find information on clubs and leagues, events, newsletters, and related links. See Editor's Choice.

Stanford University Footbag Club

http://gregorio.stanford.edu/footbag/SUFC.html

Forget soccer, football, and water polo. Get outside and play footbag with the Stanford University Footbag Club. Visit the club's page to learn about local events, national competitions, and worldwide resources.

FOOTBALL

Al's American Football Page

http://fiachra.ucd.ie/~alan/american_football.html

Learn about the Dublin Tornadoes and the Shamrock Bowl at this page about the Irish American Football League. Yes, American football in Ireland. Visitors can read about the four-team league, take a look at the rules of the game and review results.

"The Boys" Unofficial Dallas Cowboys Fan Site

http://theboys.com/

Fans of the Dallas Cowboys will flock to this site for news, commentaries, statistics, and player information. During the National Football League season, previews and results of games are available.

The Buccaneer Net-Zine (Tampa Bay Buccaneers Home Page)

http://www.tampabaybucs.com

Tampa Bay Buccaneers fans can get all the vital statistics for their favorite football team here. Find league standings, post-game summaries, and general expressions of adulation at this fan-produced site.

Canadian Football League

http://www.cfl.ca/

For those who don't follow the Canadian Football League closely, this official CFL site provides rules and history in addition to news and statistics. Links to the home pages of CFL teams are listed.

Chicago Bears

http://nflhome.com/teams/bears/bears.html

The Chicago Bears take center stage on this page from the National Football League's Team NFL site. Along with news, information on games, statistics, a roster, and more, there are links to the rest of Team NFL.

Dallas Cowboys

http://www.nflhome.com/teams/cowboys/cowboys.html

From the Team NFL site, this page presents news and information on the Cowboys. In addition to statistics, a roster and a schedule, visitors can find a listing of links on their hometown heroes.

Dallas Cowboys Home Page

http://www.nando.net/SportServer/football/nfl/dal.html

From the Nando.net Sports Server comes a page on America's Team. This page spotlights the Dallas Cowboys of the National Football League, with news articles, statistics, schedule, photos, and daily notes and quotes.

Dallas Cowboys Training Camp Page

http://www.eden.com/~fgoodwin/cowboys.htm

From Austin, Texas, home of the Dallas Cowboys' training camp, comes a fan site with a depth of information on the five-time world champions that only a diehard Cowboys fan could truly appreciate. From training-camp details to salary-cap figures, this site covers the team from sideline to sideline. It even has Dallas Cowboys Cheerleaders links.

ESPNET SportsZone: College Football

http://espnet.sportszone.com/ncf/

College football fans will find a wealth of information on ESPNET's page, which is updated daily and includes features, scores, and analysis. Links to live football audio are included.

ESPNET SportsZone: NFL

http://espnet.sportszone.com/nfl/

ESPNET's site offers up-to-date information on the National Football League. Here, football lovers can read articles about players and games or view standings and schedules. There also are a chat and a question-and-answer area.

Football Server

http://www.nando.net/SportServer/football/

The Football Server from Nando.net presents news and information on college and professional football. Current news headlines, standings, statistics, and columns are available, as well as conference-by-conference or team-by-team listings.

Miami Dolphins

http://nflhome.com/teams/dolphins/dolphins.html

The National Football League's Team NFL site supplies this page on the Miami Dolphins. Game results, statistics, a roster, and other information are available here.

Miami Dolphins WWW Page

http://www.cybercom.net/~cfennell/Dolphins/

Fans of the Miami Dolphins can keep up with their favorite National Football League team year-round at this unofficial home page. Visitors here can read the Dolphins' latest news and roster moves or peruse game information, schedules, and statistics.

The Ohio State University Football WWW Site

http://www.erinet.com/kralicd/osufoot.html

How seriously does this fan take his Ohio State football? Well, this site had summaries of Coach John Cooper's radio shows (until the school complained). Among many other resources here are statistics, a roster, profiles, Big Ten statistics, and previous years' results.

San Francisco 49ers

http://nflhome.com/teams/49ers/49ers.html

Virtual 49ers can keep track of their team at this official page from the National Football League's Team NFL site. Visitors can learn not only about draft picks and scores, but also can look back at archived records and statistics.

Sainternet

http://ccwf.cc.utexas.edu/~serpas/saints.html

Sainternet is the unofficial New Orleans Saints football team fan page. Catch team information, schedules, and rosters, or link to other Saints sites and other football sites.

Sports Network: College Football

http://www.sportsnetwork.com:80/filter/filter.cgi/collegefootball/index.html

The Sports Network's College Football Page is a sports fan's link to news, standings, statistics and schedules. It includes odds, bowl information, and pages on every major conference.

Team NFL

http://nflhome.com/

Visit the National Football League's home page for the latest news headlines, statistics and information from U.S. professional football. A kids page, merchandise, and keyword search are also available.

The Unofficial Buffalo Bills Home Page

http://www.gobills.com/

Buffalonians could read into the next football season at this unofficial Bills page. Get the news and history on the NFL team here, as well as editorials, gossip and more.

USA Football Center Online

http://cybergsi.com/foot2.htm

USA Football Center is an extensive resource for fans of college and professional football. Fans can tune in for scores, betting lines, predictions, articles, and player profiles.

The World-Wide Web Virtual Library: Sport—American Football

http://www.atm.ch.cam.ac.uk/sports/gridiron.html

This Virtual Library site focuses on American football, providing links to numerous football servers. This page also includes information on football leagues, organizations, and teams on the professional and collegiate level.

---

a2z **EDITOR'S CHOICE**

Footbag WorldWide

http://www.footbag.org/

"So dude, wanna do some footbag, wanna kick it around for a while?"

"Naw dude, got this thing to go to this afternoon."

"What thing's that, dude?"

"I dunno, but I think it's kinda important."

"Yeah, sure man, maybe some other time."

Footbag. Does it conjure up an image of kids in tie-dyed t-shirts on the corner of Haight and Ashbury Streets, kicking a soft ball back and forth, stumbling into tourists and into the street? Well if it does, think again, dude. This is a serious sport and the Board of Directors for The Bay Area Footbag Foundation are all big wigs in the computer industry. So there. This former city park fad has been recognized as a competitive sport since the late 1970s, and the setup for play is similar to tennis and volleyball. What's more, it's not limited to the wealthy elite—you don't need admittance to a fancy country club, all you need is a footbag, a pair of shoes, and a net. Choosing the "right" equipment is a little more tricky (joke!), but all you need to know is within the pages of Footbag WorldWide.—*Reviewed by Paul Wood*

FRISBEE

The Frisbee Page
http://www.sccs.swarthmore.edu/~dalewis/frisbee.html

The Frisbee Page, part of a personal home page, offers links to newsgroups, how-to sites, graphics, and more from the world of Ultimate Frisbee. Visit here to get involved in the unique competitive sport.

Thomas Griesbaum's International Frisbeesport
http://www.ira.uka.de/~thgries/disc

In addition to being the official home of the World Flying Disc Federation, Thomas Griesbaum's International Frisbeesport page contains a collection of links to associations and teams in Ultimate Frisbee and disc golf. Other links lead to tournament results.

The Ultimate Page
http://www.access.digex.net/~cdl/ultimate.html

The Ultimate Page offers a low-impact introduction to Ultimate Frisbee, which combines elements of soccer, football, and basketball. The site provides a history of the game, the rules, information about tournament play, and links.

Ultimate Players Association Home Page
http://radon.gas.uug.arizona.edu/~hko/upa/home.html

The UPA home page contains news from the organization's governing body, tournament schedules, and general information about the Frisbee sport, Ultimate. Includes pointers FAQs, disc golf sites, and other Frisbee sporting events.

GOLF

The Arizona Golf Guide
http://www.getnet.com/azgolf

The Arizona Golf Guide offers information about courses, associations, and tournaments in the sunny state. It also includes links to Web pages devoted to major tournaments played in Arizona.

BellSouth Senior Classic
http://www.datatek.com/BellSouth/SrClassic.html

The BellSouth Senior Classic golf tournament in Nashville, Tennessee provides a schedule, results, player information, and more at this site. It is possible to e-mail players on the PGA senior tour from here.

Golf Archives
http://dunkin.princeton.edu/.golf/

Visitors to the Golf Archives can check out images, club makers, course descriptions, and loads of links. Access also is available via anonymous FTP and gopher.

Golf Scorecard Archives
http://www.traveller.com/golf/scorecards/

Scorecards from golf courses such as the Pebble Beach Golf Links in California, the Pinehurst-Plantation in North Carolina, the Inverness Club in Ohio, and dozens more around the world are collected in this archive. The images are arranged by state and country.

GolfWeb—Everything Golf on the World Wide Web
http://www.golfweb.com/

If you can't be out on the fairways and greens, at least you can read about them on this page. GolfWeb "offers something for everyone with an interest in golf," including news, product information, and more.

GolfWeb—What's New
http://www.golfweb.com/gwwn.htm

GolfWeb, an online guide to international golf news and resources, maintains this listing of upcoming events and recent results. Visit here to search for golf news and events from around the world.

Hawaii Golf Courses
http://www2.hawaii.edu/golfstuff/golf_courses.html

Visitors to this page will find a list of Hawaii's golf courses. Information about greens fees for each course is included here.

iGOLF: The Players' Exchange
http://www.igolf.com/indexlycos.html

The Players' Exchange is an electronic golf zine filled with news and feature articles. Golf tips ("iGOLFOLOGY") and many more resources for the avid golfer are provided.

InterGolf
http://www.golf.com/travel/packages/InterGolf/

Golf nuts can make plans to take their swings around the globe at InterGolf, which features golf-oriented travel packages. Stop by for information on the Tour of the Month and read about custom packages that take golfers to several courses in scenic regions.

Traveller Golf Information Center
http://www.traveller.com/golf/

The Traveller Golf Information Center contains a golf course database, listings of golf associations and links to other golf Web sites. This page includes a gallery of pictures from the Masters tournament.

The Virtual Golfer
http://www.golfball.com/

Check out course reviews, shop for a 9-iron or read the articles at this golf site from Toronto, Canada. Duffers will find tips to improve their games, along with pro tour news and a golf zine called Greenside.

THE GREAT OUTDOORS

CAMPING

GORP U.S. National Parks Index
http://www.gorp.com/gorp/resource/US_National_Park/main.htm

The Great Outdoor Recreation Pages (GORP) provide this searchable database of U.S. National Parks and Preserves. Visitors can also access activities information, maps, educational opportunities, and special events.

CANOEING

Manitoba Recreational Canoeing Association Home Page
http://kohlrabi.cs.umanitoba.ca/mrca/mrca.html

The Manitoba Recreational Canoeing Association Home Page contains links to canoeing and kayaking courses offered by the group, as well as membership information, descriptions of Manitoba canoeing locations, and links.

CLIMBING

Big Wall Climbing Home Page

http://www.primenet.com/~midds/

Information on the largest rock faces in the world is the focus of the Big Wall Climbing Home Page. Among the resources here are ratings, pictures, equipment, and stories. This is also the home of A5 Adventures of Flagstaff, Arizona, complete with a catalog of climbing gear.

Climbing Archive!

http://www.dtek.chalmers.se/Climbing/

Rock and mountain climbing enthusiasts will enjoy the Climbing Archive, featuring articles and resources related to the outdoor sport. Visit here to view its guidebooks, link with equipment providers, learn new climbing techniques, and more.

DOG SLEDDING

Iditarod SuperSite

http://www.dogsled.com/

Results, photos, and other details on the famous Alaskan dog sled race are included here. Find information about participating mushers, race reports, news releases, and audio files, as well as a pointer to the 1995 Iditarod page.

FISHING

Alaska Department of Fish and Game

http://www.state.ak.us/local/akpages/FISH.GAME/adfghome.htm

The Alaska Department of Fish and Game's home page reports on commercial and sport fishing in the state. Visitors to the site will also find details on regulations and photos of the sought-after fish.

The Anadromous Page

http://www.peak.org/~robertr/fishing.html

"Anadromous" means "running upward," and at this site the fishing resources are constantly on the rise. It features regional and local fishing reports from around the world, along with tips, techniques, and recipes, all contributed by volunteers.

Anglers Online

http://www.inetmkt.com/fishpage/index.html

Anglers Online provides everything a fisherman could want. Visitors can hook into classified ads, current fishing reports, online equipment catalogs, outfitter and guide listings, and even a fish photo archive. Includes a variety of categorized links to Web fishing holes.

Bass Fishing Home Page

http://wmi.cais.com/bassfish/index.htm

Co-sponsored by a professional guide service and a custom rod designer, this page contains bass fishing reports from around the world, as well as tips on lures, tactical advice, and equipment guides. Also provided is a message board for bass fishermen.

The Classic Angler

http://www.gorp.com/bamboo.htm

The Classic Angler home page provides information and products for tackle collectors and fly fishermen alike. The Fly Fishing Mini-Mall link takes anglers shopping for everything from modern fly reels to specialty products for rod builders.

Creekside Fly Fishing Shop—Salem, Oregon

http://www.halcyon.com/flyshop/

Creekside Fly Fishing of Salem, Oregon brings its virtual fly fishing shop to the Web with an online catalog, along with a listing of fishing guides in the Northwest. The page includes tips on fly fishing in Washington and Oregon.

Fishing Fool's World

http://www.webcom.com/~towns/fish/fish.html

The Fishing Fool's World contains fishing resources from all over the United States and Europe. Included are extensive links to fly fishing and sport fishing opportunities.

Fly Fishers of Davis

http://www.davis.com/flyfish/

Find out where the fish are biting at this page from the Fly Fishers of Davis, who provide reports from northern California, the eastern Sierra, and Oregon. The site also contains a club newsletter and other Davis, California fishing resources.

Fly Fishing in Arizona

http://www.azlink.com/~jshannon/

Current fishing reports are featured at this site, which hooks up visitors with fly fishing information, from fly-tying tips to mail-order businesses. Emphasis is on Arizona fishing destinations and news.

Fly Fishing Online

http://www.flyfishing-online.com/

Whether they want to spin yarns or cast lures, anglers will find conversation, information, and merchandise at Fly Fishing Online. The interactive fly shop offers fly fishing gear and the opportunity to talk about it at this commercial site.

Illinois Fishing Page

http://www.cba.uiuc.edu/~rtaylor/fish/fish.htm

Anglers can find weather and water reports on the Illinois Fishing Page. Read tales of spectacular catches or link to fish locators, guide and accommodation recommendations, and articles about steelhead, crappie, and more here.

Internet Bass Magazine

http://www.harvestman.com/onochan/

Internet Bass Magazine, for the consummate bass fisherman, contains reader's reports and discussions, plus a beginner's page and much more. In Japanese and English.

Missouri Flyfishing Page

http://www.agron.missouri.edu/flyfishing/

The who, what, when, where, and how of fly fishing in Missouri are examined on this page. Read reviews of equipment such as waders, tackle boxes, and vests. Information on fishing spots, licenses, and organizations are provided.

New Mexico Fly Fishing

http://www.unm.edu/~datkins/flyfish/flyfish.html

Visitors to this page will find descriptions of the fly fishing available in each of four regions of New Mexico, as well as a listing of fly fishing stores in the state. Newsgroups and other items of general interest also are provided, including fly-tying information.

North Georgia Trout On-Line

http://www.mindspring.com/~ngtrout/gofish.html

Fisherfolks will delight in North Georgia Trout On-Line, which includes a listing of year-round streams, events, and reviews of fishing spots in the area.

Saltwater Fishing Home Page

http://wmi.cais.com/saltfish/index.html

Saltwater fishermen and women will learn what's running where by reading these personal accounts. Browsers can post fishing tales of their own, get tips about tactics, and research sport fishing quotas here. Includes links to other angling resources on the Internet.

Steve B Hill's Fishing Page

http://sbh.cse.bris.ac.uk/fishing.html

Steve Hill's Fishing Page features links to U.K. Fishing World, the Carp Corner, Fly Fishing in Arizona, and more. There are also links to Usenet newsgroups alt.fishing and rec.outdoors.fishing.

Women's Fishing Partnership Home Page

http://www.eskimo.com/~baubo/wfp.html

A resource for women who wish to fish, this Web site offers links to the U.S. Fish and Wildlife Service's Web site and to state-specific fishing resource pages. Includes a directory of Women's Fishing Partnership coordinators, indexed by state.

The World-Wide Web Virtual Library: Sport Fishing

http://wmi.cais.com/www/sportfsh/index.html

Charter fishing businesses, fishing home pages, and other sport fishing resources can be reached at this page. Included here are links to fishing guides, magazines, associations, and more.

HIKING

The Bushwalking Page

http://www.anatomy.su.oz.au/danny/bushwalking/index.html

The Bushwalking Page provides hikers ("bushwalkers" in Aussie lingo) with everything they need to know to get out into the bush—weather reports, maps, environmental information, gear, books, and advice. Links are made to U.S. back-country Web sites, but this is mostly an Australian page.

Colorado Mountain Club Home Page

http://www.entertain.com/cmc/

The Colorado Mountain Club's home page offers an overview of the organization's mission—to promote hiking and conservation in the state—and provides information on how to join the club. Includes links to other alpine enthusiast sites.

Georgia Appalachian Trail Club, Inc

http://www.atl.mindspring.com/~vhill

The Georgia Appalachian Trail Club, Inc. maintains this informational site for a variety of online hiking resources. Visit here for maps, hiking tips, facilities descriptions, and links to favorite hiking destinations.

GORP Hiking

http://www.gorp.com/gorp/activity/hiking.htm

One of the most comprehensive hiking and backpacking pages on the Web comes to life through this link. Part of the Great Outdoors Recreation Pages (GORP), this site features annotated listings of international, national, and regional trails. Other resources here include details about hiking books and magazines.

Hiking and Walking Homepage

http://www.teleport.com/~walking/hiking.html

Looking for a place to hike? This is a good place to find it. In addition to listings of hiking areas, in-

formation on vacations and walking tours is available here. There are plenty of other resources, including organizations, newsgroups, and a chat page.

Huachuca Hiking Club—Sierra Vista, Arizona

http://www.primenet.com/~tomheld/hhc.htm

The Huachuca Hiking Club of Sierra Vista, Arizona promotes its mission to explore and conserve natural wilderness heritage through hiking, camping, and volunteer trail maintenance at this home page. Included here are club information, details about special events, trail directions, and hiking resources.

Outside Online

http://outside.starwave.com/index.html

This site is a great resource for information about outdoor activities. See Editor's Choice.

Potomac Appalachian Trail Club Home Page

http://patc.simplenet.com/

The Potomac Appalachian Trail Club is a nonprofit organization dedicated to providing information on hiking trails, shelters, and cabins in Virginia, Maryland, West Virginia, Pennsylvania, and the District of Columbia. Includes safety tips and information about related books and maps.

Smoky Mountain Field School

http://web.ce.utk.edu/Smoky/

The Great Smoky Mountains National Park and the University of Tennessee teach outdoor courses in backpacking, landscape photography, and more through the Smoky Mountain Field School. Visitors will find the school's full program schedule and registration information here.

Volksmarch and Walking Index

http://www.teleport.com/~walking

The Volksmarch and Walking Index is provided by the American Volkssport Association in Universal City, Texas. Visitors will find comprehensive links to resources of interest to individuals who walk for fitness, enjoyment, and sport.

HUNTING

Rec.guns on the Web!

http://www.recguns.com

Self-described as "the most complete gun resource on the Net," this site points to the answers of FAQs, gun safety tips, movie mishaps, firearm links, firearm sounds, and targets. Also find commercial links and an NRA promotion.

KAYAKING

California Kayak Friends

http://www.intelenet.com/clubs/ckf/

Members of California Kayak Friends, a paddle sports club in Irvine, California, share adventures and information at this site. Club resources, including a monthly newsletter, are available, along with resources such as kayaking magazines on the Internet and mailing lists.

Kitty Hawk Sports

http://www.khsports.com/khs/

This promotional page is the Web home of Kitty Hawk Sports. Features include information about windsurfing and kayaking, plus the company's guided tours, merchandise, and rentals.

NEWS AND INFORMATION

Adventure Sports Online

http://www.adventuresports.com/

Looking for tasty recipes to try while camping? Adventure Sports Online has them—and just about anything else to do with outdoor sports. From canoeing and mountain biking to horse packing and fly fishing, this site has them covered. Among the resources are shopping, publications, sound clips, news groups, and much more.

AMI News

http://www.aminews.com/ami

AMI News is a commercial recreation network providing news and information on skiing, travel, leisure, and the outdoors. Includes destination, reservations, weather, and lodging information.

Colorado Outdoors

http://www.csn.net/~arthurvb/colorado/colorado.html

This guide to Colorado outdoor recreation resources, part of a personal home page, offers information on state and national parks, hiking, camping, climbing, snow sports, and other outdoor activities. Includes links to other Colorado-related Web servers and outdoor sites.

GORP—Great Outdoor Recreation Pages

http://www.gorp.com/

Bringing the great outdoors onto a computer screen is no easy task, but GORP does it. With resources on everything from biking and backpacking to rafting and hangliding to birding and boating, GORP covers it all. Visitors can spend all day hiking around this site.

Sagi's Outdoor News

http://www.infop.com/outdoor/

Visitors can bag news of interest to hunters and fishermen at the home page of Sagi's Outdoor News. Articles and features from the print publication (which has an Arizona emphasis) cover freshwater and saltwater fishing, hunting, shooting, camping, and conservation.

White Mountains

http://www.cs.dartmouth.edu/whites/

Provided by Dartmouth College in Hanover, New Hampshire, this guide to this state's White Mountains offers a look at the geology, wildlife, and recreational offerings of the mountain range. Includes links to the U.S. Forest Service and hiking-related Web sites.

SPELUNKING

The Cave Page

http://rschp2.anu.edu.au:8080/cave/cave.html

The Cave Page provides links to cave exploration sites around the globe. Features here include notes on techniques, a cave rescue guide, a cave songbook, and a cookbook.

Caves and Caving in the UK

http://www.sat.dundee.ac.uk/~arb/speleo.html

The Caves and Caving in the UK site gets down and dirty for the benefit of British spelunkers. The site offers a survey of the British caving districts, links to caving clubs and interest groups, conservation information, and even tips on what to eat for breakfast.

GYMNASTICS

Gymn Forum

http://gym.digiweb.com/gym/

Flip through a wealth of gymnastics information here, including magazine articles and reports on international competitions. The page also presents videos for sale and posts links to dozens of gymnastics sites.

HORSE AND DOG RACING

American Quarter Horse Association On-Line

http://www.aqha.com/

From Amarillo, Texas, the American Quarter Horse Association presents a page full of information about the horse with a "colorful history." It gallops from online racing and performance publications to show schedules and AQHA rules. Also, find the AQH museum here.

Churchill Downs

http://www.churchilldowns.com/

Horse racing buffs who can't make it to Kentucky can still visit Churchill Downs, home of the Kentucky Derby. This site features historical information, the track's schedule, and anything a fan wants to know about the Derby.

Cyberspace Racing Team

http://www.crt-stable.com

The Cyberspace Racing Team is an Internet-based horse racing partnership. The site features pages on each of the group's horses, with video clips, audio clips of race calls, workout histories, and more. Racing fans interested in joining this innovative venture can get further details.

Equine Online

http://www.equineonline.com/

The Equine Online Exchange classified section and other horse-industry resources are the focus of this commercial site, which includes a thorough list of equine links. Among the home pages featured here are the Breeders' Cup and Equibase Company, a database of racing and pedigree information.

---

a2z EDITOR'S CHOICE

Outside Online

http://outside.starwave.com/index.html

Got a question about backpacking or hiking? The Interactive Gear Guy has the answers at Outside Online, which comes from the folks who bring us ESPNET SportsZone. The Gear Guy is one small part of an amazing array of information covering virtually every activity that takes place outside, including water sports, snow sports, climbing, and cycling. Visitors also can find environmental news, as well as articles and features from the current and past issues of *Outside Magazine*. The publication's archives are searchable, and a vacation guide, buyer's guide, and travel guide are available. When we last visited, other features ranged from the Tour de France to trekking the Himalayas to crime on the trails, as well as a review of Invasion Pants. Content is updated every day.—*Reviewed by Dan Kelly*

Friday, June 14, 1996

Java Front Page | Non-Java Front Page | Mostly Text Front Page

Tour de Suisse
Outside Online Euro-cycles on

► Summit Journal '96

► McRorys provisioned for a fast West Indies run
And Dad's sailing around, sporting a crazed new buzz cut

► Words of lust fill the air over Florida's swamps
The throaty chorus of frogs sending out amphib-amore

► Gear Guy pinned as readers pine for more
Michael has Gear Guy envy; Lori just wants a drink

► Mine trails and singletrack around Telluride
Knob heaven in the summer: the San Juan Mountains

TABLE OF CONTENTS ►

Hastings Park Racecourse

http://www.hastingspark.com/

Not only can racing fans find almost everything they could possibly want to know about the horses that run at Hastings Park on this home page, but they also can check out the menu (the roast prime rib with Yorkshire pudding is $22.95). This site from the Vancouver, British Columbia, racecourse also provides audio clips of race calls and links to other tracks with Web sites.

Horsehead Lines

http://www.cyberspace.com/rmyers

Get the scoop on the Pacific Northwest horse racing scene at the Horsehead Lines site. Go to the virtual tracks to find the latest race results, surface conditions, and favorite picks. Cigar smoking is optional.

The 1996 Iditarod Home Page

http://www.alaska.net/~Iditarod

Results, photos, and other details on the famous Alaskan dog sled race are included here. Find information about participating mushers, race reports, news releases, and audio files, as well as a pointer to the 1995 Iditarod page.

Performance Index & Systems, Inc. Homepage

http://www.pindex.com/

Horse racing handicappers trying to beat the odds can consult the Performance Index, a "provider of horse racing analytics." One-week trials of the subscription service are available. Nonsubscribers can check results from tracks around the country.

The Running Horse

http://www.webcom.com/

The Running Horse home page is a compilation of resources "of interest to horse lovers in general, and particularly those that love to watch horses go fast." Links include the latest U.S. race horse standings, the Texas Thoroughbred Association, and a variety of thoroughbred racing directories.

Thoroughbred Times On-Line

http://www.thoroughbredtimes.com/

Thoroughbred Times is a weekly magazine, but it presents daily news from the world of horse racing at this site. Features and international coverage from the print publication also are available, as are classifieds.

ICE HOCKEY

Atlanta Knights Sports Center

http://www.newsouth.com/029/029.html

The Atlanta Knights of the International Hockey League provide fans with information about the minor-league team, including news updates, a roster, a schedule, and statistics. Visitors might want to check out the merchandise catalog, complete with sale items.

The Blue Line

http://www.mcs.net/~blueline/home.html

Electronic editions of The Blue Line, an alternative program sold at Chicago Blackhawks' home games, are posted at this site. Also available here is information about the Blackhawks mailing list and links to other hockey sites.

Boston Bruins WWW

http://www.clever.net/bruins/

Here is a fan's multimedia devotion to the Boston Bruins of the National Hockey League. Find statistics, schedules, profiles, images, sounds, history, and memories, plus links to related sites.

Chicago Blackhawks Home Page

http://www.enteract.com/~zabolots/blkhawks.htm

Diehard hockey fan Scott Zabolotzky unveils his tribute to the Chicago Blackhawks on this page. It includes a schedule and results, as well as ticket information, images of the team in action, and links to daily news stories.

Le Coq Sportif

http://www.canadas.net/sports/Sportif/

From daily news to historical archives, Le Coq Sportif has the NHL covered. A chat forum and features from the weekly print magazine also are available, but the collection of current and past statistics is the centerpiece here.

The Cup Stops Here

http://www.bergen.com/devils95/

Relive the triumph of the 1995 National Hockey League champions, the New Jersey Devils. This page from the *Bergen Record* newspaper features statistics, trivia, photos, and an audio clip from the conclusion of the final game of the Devils' four-game sweep of the Detroit Red Wings.

The Edmonton Oilers Homepage

http://gpu.srv.ualberta.ca/~flood/oilers/oilers.html

Wayne Gretzky is long gone, but the Edmonton Oilers live on at this fan page. Visitors can read about the Gretzky years and the history of this National Hockey League team, or they can check out photos, a schedule, and statistics.

ESPNET SportsZone: NHL

http://espnet.sportszone.com/nhl/

The National Hockey League is showcased on this page from ESPNET SportsZone. Fans can find news on players and teams, as well as schedules, salaries, a listing of top prospects, a Q&A with Gordie Howe, and more.

Hartford Whalers Home Page

http://www.access.digex.net/~kayleigh/whalers.html

With an unofficial site such as this, who needs an official site? Certainly not the National Hockey League's Hartford Whalers, who are the beneficiary of this page that includes results, history, information on prospects in the system, and even a team merchandise store.

Hockey Hall of Fame

http://www.hype.com/hhof/

The Hockey Hall of Fame in Toronto, Canada supplies basic information here on its contents, hours, admission fees, and location. This site also provides links to other Toronto attractions.

Igloo Report

http://www.iglooreport.com/

Catch the latest news about the Pittsburgh Penguins of the NHL through the Igloo Report, an unofficial page for team information and statistics. The site also offers pointers to a slew of other Penguin resources.

Informationen zur Deutschen Eishockey Liga

http://www.math.uni-augsburg.de/~zahn/DEL/

At this home page of the German Ice Hockey League, visitors will find player profiles, game schedules, statistics, and scores. Available in German only.

Liam Maguire's NHL Hockey Trivia

http://infoweb.magi.com/~liam/hockey.html

Ice hockey fans can test their knowledge at this personal home page, which runs weekly trivia contests. The author's hockey trivia book and links to other hockey resources also are available here.

National Hockey League Players' Association —NHLPA

http://www.nhlpa.com/

Hockey fans can get news and views right from the horse's mouth at the official Web site of the National Hockey League Players' Association. Meet the player of the day, take the trivia test, or listen to audio sound bites from the pros.

NHL Individual Scoring Leaders

http://www.nando.net/newsroom/sports/hkn/1995/nhl/nhl/stat/leaders.html

Current individual scoring leaders in the National Hockey League are posted at this page from Nando.net. In addition to goals, assists, and total points for each player, the statistics include plusminus ratings and more.

NHL Open Net

http://www.nhl.com

To get an idea of the depth of this official National Hockey League site, consider that it contains standings and award winners dating to 1917. Also available here are news, schedules, statistics, rosters, news releases, rules, and more—including live cybercasts of games.

NHL Pages

http://www.wpi.edu/~defronzo/

From standings, statistics and schedules to injuries, rosters and rules, this unofficial National Hockey League site has it all. Included here is a listing of team pages (unofficial and official) for every NHL franchise.

NHL Wreckroom

http://amadeus.ccs.queensu.ca/Hockey/Hockey.html

A collection of images of National Hockey League players, arranged by team, is the main attraction at this fan site. Among the other features here are standings, statistics, schedules, and rumors.

Professional Hockey Server

http://maxwell.uhh.hawaii.edu/hockey/hockey.html

A Canadian-gone-Hawaiian maintains this fan page on the National Hockey League. Visitors can take in statistics, schedules, team standings, and lots of action photos here, or link to a handful of other hockey sites.

San Jose Shark Bytes

http://hockey.plaidworks.com/sharks/

An unofficial home page for the San Jose Sharks of the National Hockey League, this site supplies a team roster, schedule, and results. Links to other Sharks sites, including the official team site, are listed, as is information on a Sharks e-mail list.

San Jose Sharks

http://www.sj-sharks.com/

The San Jose Sharks provide fans with a chat room and forms to send messages to players at this official site. Along with detailed information about the National Hockey League team and its players, fans can find trivia, video clips, audio clips, and loads of statistics here.

Stanley Cup Finals

http://www.usatoday.com/sports/hockey/shn/shn.htm

This National Hockey League results and standings page is provided by USA Today. It contains the latest scores, standings, and summaries, plus previews of today's games and pointers to other USA Today hockey pages.

Winnipeg Jets Home Page

http://www.ee.umanitoba.ca/~ddueck/jets/jets.html

The Jets have played their final game in Winnipeg, but this site from Manitoba treats them as the home team. The unofficial home page offers news, scores, and a glimpse at the history of the National Hockey League team, which moves to Phoenix for the 1996–97 season.

WWW Hockey Guide

http://www.hockeyguide.com/

The World Wide Web Hockey Guide serves up its index of more than 1,100 hockey links through this page. It includes information about the National Hockey League, amateur hockey, and hockey from around the world. The site also features awards for the best pages.

ICE SKATING

Figure Skating Page

http://frog.simplenet.com/skateweb/

At the Figure Skating Page, maintained by an enthusiast at Yale University, darlings of the sport get praised, ribbed, and profiled. Visitors can find links to skating news, humor archives, and fan-produced pages devoted to favorite athletes.

KORFBALL

Korfball

http://www.earth.ox.ac.uk/~geoff/

Visit this home page to korf…er…learn something new about Korfball, the world's only mixed team sport. Browsers can peruse photos, read championship news, or link to Korfball contacts.

LAND YACHTING

O'Neill European Championships Land Yachting

http://www.tbo.nl/ekstrand/home.htm

Pictures and news from the O'Neill European Championships Land Yachting event are featured at this site. An explanation of land yachting is included, along with ordering information for the official event video.

MARTIAL ARTS

Aikido at Stanford

http://www-leland.stanford.edu/group/aikido/

Information on Stanford University's Aikido class is the focus of this site, which includes a class schedule and requirements for two tests in this martial art. There are links to other Aikido sites on the Web and to other martial arts at Stanford.

The Aikido FAQ

http://www.ii.uib.no/~kjartan/aikidofaq/aikido.html

Everything a beginner (or an advanced practitioner) could want to know about the Japanese martial art of Aikido is available at this FAQ site. Topics covered include the principles of Aikido, training, and organizations. Visitors can also peruse a glossary, a bibliography, and periodicals.

Aikido Information

http://www-cse.ucsd.edu/users/paloma/Aikido/

Aikido is a Japanese martial art that centers its teaching on defensive moves. Visitors to this index can link to dozens of Aikido resources, including an FTP site, mailing list, publications, organizations, and a state-by-state listing of clubs.

American Black Belt Academy

http://nall.com/abba/

Martial arts enthusiasts looking for a training resource in Austin, Texas, can check the American Black Belt Academy page. The academy specializes in Tae Kwon Do and Hapkido. A few martial arts Web resources also are available here.

Bay Area Wing Chun Association

http://www.thesphere.com/SJWC/SJWC.html

Wing Chun is a Chinese martial arts discipline founded 300 years ago. The Bay Area Wing Chun Association provides pages here on associations in San Jose, San Francisco, and Menlo Park, California. It also gives a brief description of the discipline.

Black Belt Home Page

http://www.blackbeltmag.com/

Selected feature articles from *Black Belt Magazine* and other martial arts magazines are provided at this site, which markets magazines, books, videos, and other products. A page for kids is available, along with listings of martial arts schools and events.

Eclipse's Martial Arts Page

http://www.ultranet.com/~eclipse/ma.html

A collection of self-defense resources, including links to Kung Fu, Aikido, Judo, and Taekwon Do sites, is featured here. Also provided are tips on schooling and equipment, and even some fencing links.

ISU Karate Club

http://www.public.iastate.edu/~scc/karate/karate.homepage.html

The Iowa State University Karate Club has assembled this site to help visitors learn more about the club and Taekwon Do. Members can find out about upcoming events and club news.

Japanese Sword Arts FAQ

http://www.ii.uib.no/~kjartan/swordfaq/

Kendo is the way of the sword, or Japanese fencing, which is one of many facts visitors to this page can learn. Find out how to swing a Kendo stick like a master by consulting this FAQ file, or consult the page to ensure that the sword you're considering buying is worth its weight.

Judo Information Site

http://www.rain.org/~ssa/judo.htm

The Judo Information Site boasts that it is the "world's biggest virtual Judo club." Learn the finer points of the history and practice of the martial art using the pointers and resources collected here.

LFowler's Martial Arts Home Page

http://www.afternet.com/~lfowler/home2.html

Explore the quieter, philosophical side of the martial arts at this home page. Among links to other martial arts sites, the author has placed poems and pictures relating to the spiritual path of the martial artist. There also are a lot of resources such as martial arts dictionaries and bibliographies here.

Martial Arts

http://www.middlebury.edu/~jswan/martial.arts/ma.html

This enthusiast's page boasts hundreds of links related to martial arts resources on the Web. Featured topics in the index include self defense, Judo, Karate, Japanese sword arts, and Aikido.

Martial Arts Page

http://www.update.uu.se/~rico/martial_arts/

Does Aikido take longer to master than other martial arts? Yes. Find out that fact and everything else you'll ever want to know about the martial arts at this site full of links. In addition to Aikido, this page has resources on Jujitsu, Judo, Karate, Taekwon Do, and other disciplines.

Martial Arts Resource Site

http://www.floor6.com/MARS/MARS.html

This Web document presents an organized collection of links to martial arts-related Internet sites. An extensive list itemizes literature, histories, biographies, and glossaries available in hypertext form. Includes archives of newsletters, mailing list postings, and FAQ files.

National Taekwon-Do Federation Home Page

http://www.ntf.CA:8082/

The home page of the National Taekwon-Do Federation offers a guide for those interested in pursuing this Korean form of karate. Includes membership information and links to FAQ files on stretching and martial arts, plus a searchable index of the rec.martial-arts newsgroup.

Palo Alto Judo Club

http://www.svi.org/~nates/judo.html

The Palo Alto Judo Club offers information about its role in hosting the 1996 Senior National Championships. Includes links to club information, practice times, and other Judo sites.

Planet Wing Chun

http://www.wingchun.com/

The Bay Area Wing Chun Association, a northern California-based Chinese martial arts organization, maintains this site for general information. Visit here to learn about the history and practice of the art of Wing Chun, contact member chapters, and link to related resources.

Tae Kwon Do Reporter

http://www.taekwondoreporter.com//

A bi-monthly magazine focusing on the martial arts, the Tae Kwon Do Reporter provides articles and features here from its print publication, as well training tips and more. A readers forum, Taekwon Do calendar, and directory of schools are other online features.

UCMAP—U.C. Martial Arts Program

http://server.berkeley.edu/ucmap/

The University of California at Berkeley's Martial Arts Program is the topic of this server featuring an introduction to and overview of the program, club schedules, and related biodynamics course listings. Information on upcoming demonstrations and self-defense classes are also featured.

Wing Lam Enterprises

http://www.wle.com/

Wing Lam Enterprises provides martial arts instruction and materials from its headquarters in Sunnyvale, California. This home page describes the Kung Fu subdisciplines it teaches, provides an overview of the benefits of martial arts training, and includes pictures of happy students in action.

MOTOR SPORTS

GENERAL

The Dakar Official Site

http://www.dakar.com/

Cars, trucks, and motorcycles race from France to Dakar in the annual Dakar Rally. At this official site of the race, visitors can check out results, videos, photos, and a map of the race, or subscribe to a daily postcard with Dakar facts. In English and French.

Motorsport News International

http://www.motorsport.com/

Motorsport News International serves as an online source for news, race results, and feature articles on motor sports of all levels—from Indy cars to regional midget races. Site features include a searchable archive of articles and links to related Web, FTP, and Usenet newsgroup sites.

rec.autos.sport FAQ

http://www.bath.ac.uk/~bspahh/rasfaq.html

Find answers to FAQs about motorsports in an article taken from the Usenet newsgroup rec.autos.sport. To access the file, visitors can choose from the two sites listed: Bath, Great Britain, and Mississippi.

SpeedWay MotorBooks

http://www.primenet.com/~komet/speed/speedway.html

Arizona's SpeedWay MotorBooks sells collectible books, programs, magazines, and videos about cars and racing. Racing cards, models, and slot cars are also available.

AUTO RACING

American Racing Scene

http://www.racecar.com/

NASCAR and Indy car fans can turn to the American Racing Scene for the latest standings and happenings. Dig into photographs and articles about racing personalities and a calendar of events.

Detroit Grand Prix Page

http://detroit.freenet.org/grandprix

The official home page of the 15th Detroit Grand Prix, an auto racing event held June 7 through 9, 1996, supplies fast facts, news features, a schedule of events, and a map of the track. Other racing-related links are provided.

Dutch Racing Scene

http://www.euro.net/TDRS

The Dutch Racing Scene celebrates the thrills of auto racing in the Netherlands. Information about 1995 events, various Dutch tracks, and racing/training schools are some of the areas explored.

ESPNET SportsZone: Auto Racing

http://espnet.sportszone.com/car/

The auto racing page from ESPNET SportsZone features the latest news and features about the world's fastest sport. Visitors can check current series standings or find out what racing is scheduled for coming weeks.

Laguna Seca Raceway

http://www.laguna-seca.com/

Located east of Monterey, California, the Laguna Seca Raceway sponsors this promotional site. Visitors will find track, event, and ticket information, details of the track's corporate hospitality programs, and a link to SCRAMP, the Sports Car Racing Association of the Monterey Peninsula.

Lebanon Valley Dragway

http://www.dragway.com/

Hold onto your mouse and get ready for a fast-paced ride down the track and the world of drag racing. Visitors will find a variety of racing-related information and a chance to subscribe to the Lebanon Valley Dragway News.

Matt's Solar Car Page

http://www-lips.ece.utexas.edu/~delayman/solar.html

Matt's Solar Car Page offers a variety of information about environmentally friendly auto development and the international solar car racing circuit. Visitors will find articles, graphics, and scheduled race postings.

McLaren International

http://www.mclaren.co.uk/

The McLaren International Formula One auto racing team supplies news updates and photos, as well as information on the car and drivers. Details from each grand prix race are included, as are statistics and world championship tables.

Medic Drug Grand Prix of Cleveland

http://www.grandprix.com/

Get information here about the Grand Prix of Cleveland—a PPG Indy Car World Series race. Here, you can find news, photos, schedules, and information about the people behind the wheels and in the pit. Includes ticket information.

Mild Seven F1 WWW Server

http://www.jtnet.ad.jp/WWW/MILDSEVEN/F1/Welcome.html

Japan Tobacco maintains this promotional site for its Mild Seven Formula One Racing Team. Visitors will find team news, international rankings, race calendars, and links to other corporate racing team home pages.

Mobil 1 Racing

http://www.mobil.com/mobil_1/racing.html

Al Unser Jr. and Rusty Wallace are two stars of Mobil 1 Racing, which sponsors drivers in NASCAR, Indy car, and Formula One. This site contains areas featuring information on the Mobil 1 drivers in all three styles of racing. A Mobil 1 Racing merchandise catalog is available.

The Monaco Grand Prix

http://www.monaco.mc/monaco/gprix/index.html

Auto racing fans can motor around this site that features results of the Grand Prix of Monaco, along with a history of the race and photos from past races. The page also includes links to other Formula One racing information on the Internet.

NHRA Online

http://www.goracing.com/nhra/

News, results, statistics, and other drag-racing information are available at the National Hot Rod Association site. Included are articles from the NHRA weekly magazine National DRAGSTER and the monthly Jr. Drag Racer, plus a photo gallery, racing schedule, and track directory.

Opel Team Rosberg

http://honeybee.helsinki.fi/mmkat/matti/dtm/opeleng.htm

Car racing fans can follow the Finnish Team Rosberg, which drives Opels, at this unofficial site. It supplies information on team members, race results and schedules, and links to other racing sites.

RaceZine

http://www.primenet.com/~bobwest/index.html

RaceZine shifts into high gear by offering visitors images, trivia, sound bites, and news about auto racing. Includes links to Sandman's MotorSports page and other online racing resources.

SpeedNet

http://www.starnews.com/speednet/

SpeedNet features auto racing news from the Indianapolis Star and News, as well as profiles, schedules, and more. Visitors can ask questions of drivers and discuss issues with other fans. Access to the rest of Star/News Online is available.

Tracks Around the World

http://www.bath.ac.uk/~py3dlg/tracks.html

Automotive racetrack information from around the world is organized here by country and continent. Click on one of the listed countries to get track locations and contact information.

Unofficial Sports Car Club of America Pages

http://www.wizvax.net/rwelty/scca/

The Unofficial Sports Car Club of America Pages provide an overview of the organization's sanctioned races, rallies, and autocross events. Visitors will find news, race schedules, event descriptions, membership information, and more.

The World Rally Championship Infosystem

http://www.travelnet.fi/wrc/

The World Rally Championship Infosystem is devoted to this annual auto racing series. Visitors can find standings and detailed information on each of the circuit's races.

MOTORCYCLING

Canadian Biker Homepage
http://www.islandnet.com/~canbike/canbike.html

Motorcycle enthusiasts will find selected columns and articles from *Canadian Biker* magazine here, along with subscription information. In addition, links take visitors to a bikers mall and to motorcycle-related resources.

Cope Racing Intro
http://www.coperacing.com/home.htm

If you don't believe Cope motorcycle racing engines are "the fastest anywhere in the world," this promotional site will try to convince you of that fact. It features an advice forum and technical tips for racers, as well as a listing of performance records and a catalog.

Dorna TWP
http://www.dorna.com/

The "Official Information Service of the World Motorcycle Championship" supplies results and rider information on the motorcycle road-racing series that goes from Malaysia to Australia, with plenty of stops along the way. Current news also is provided here.

Federation of European Motorcyclists
http://dredd.meng.ucl.ac.uk/www/mag/fem.html

Based in Brussels, Belgium, this bikers' advocacy group fights for motorcyclists' rights. Cruise this site for information on the organization and its activities. Includes news stories of interest to riders, along with information about the group's member organizations.

Let's Go Roadracing
http://www.afmracing.org/

Let's Go Roadracing takes you to the home of the American Federation of Motorcyclists, a site that stays on track with roadracing news, competition results, and membership information. Never tried motorcycle roadracing? Doesn't matter. AFM has a school for rookies.

Motorcycle Online Magazine
http://motorcycle.com/motorcycle.html

In addition to daily news, Motorcycle Online Magazine provides features, columns, classifieds, and more. Among the resources here are product reviews, a new-model database, an advice column, and a multimedia archive.

Motorcycling—the Honda V4 Files and More
http://math.uwaterloo.ca/~rblander/moto.html

Born to be wild, eh? Then ride with the Denizens of Doom, the rec.motorcycles "non-club" accessible here. But there's a lot more rolling: Most information is about Honda's performance motorcycles, including all the technical goodies.

Rec.Motorcycles.Reviews Archives
http://rmr.cecm.sfu.ca/RMR/

Rec.Motorcycles.Reviews Archives feature a collection of reviews and opinions about motorcycle models and accessories. Visit here for discussion groups, downloadable images, and links to a variety of motorcyle-related Web sites and information resources. Reader feedback and participation is encouraged.

Speedway Home Page
http://amed01.amg.gda.pl/speedway/speedway.html

Speedway motorcycle racers are not afraid to get dirty. Learn all about speedway racing worldwide on this page, which offers event listings and news. Includes a photo gallery and information on ice, long track, and grass track racing.

The Thumper Page
http://www.ionet.net/~jhanna/THUMPER.HTML

Fans of the four-stroke, single-cylinder Thumper motorcycle will find a plethora of postings to peruse at this site. Check out the Thumper Owners Page, a photo album, and messages from riders around the globe. Also find links to newsgroups, mailing lists, organizations, and more.

NEWS AND INFORMATION

adidas WebZine
http://www.adidas.de/

The monthly adidas WebZine contains articles as well as information on adidas sporting goods products. Athletes who endorse adidas products are the focus of the news and features.

America's Sports Headquarters
http://www.sport-hq.com/

The thousands of sites contained in this directory cover the full gamut of sports, although the listings under the major U.S. sports of baseball, football, basketball, and hockey are the most impressive. Sites are grouped by sport as well as by type, such as team sites, information services, and fantasy.

Australian Sport World Wide Web
http://www.ausport.gov.au/

This information server provides links to sports organizations in Australia, information on international sporting events, and profiles of Australian athletes. The National Sport Information Center, which maintains this page, also provides information about itself and its publications.

CNN Interactive Sports Main Page
http://www.cnn.com/SPORTS/index.html

News and scores are the focus of this searchable sports site from the Cable News Network. What separates CNN from most other sports sites are its pages on international sports such as cricket, rugby, and soccer. Also featured here is the WWW National Football Recruiting Center.

College Sports Internet Channel
http://www.xcscx.com/colsport/

College Sports Communications ferrets out individual resources on the Web and repackages the information as the CSC College Sports Internet Channel. Link to Web and gopher sites chronicling and relating to college sports teams.

ESPNET SportsZone
http://espnet.sportszone.com/

With this site available, who needs a newspaper sports section? ESPNET SportsZone presents up-to-the-minute sports news, as well as features, columns, and statistics. Paid subscribers get even more including video highlights.

Fox Sports Cyber Scoreboard
http://www.iguide.com/sports/

Fox supplies sports headlines, team-by-team notes and up-to-date results on U.S. professional sports at this site. Live chat and active discussion areas are other draws here.

The Global Bearcat
http://ucunix.san.uc.edu/~zureick/bearcat.html

Fans of the University of Cincinnati's Bearcats sports teams can check out a wealth of information here, including news, history, and season results. Links to fan organizations and newsgroups also are provided.

Hobbies and Sports
http://euclid.math.fsu.edu/FunStuff/hobbies.html

One person's sport is another person's hobby, and this site has a collection of resources on both. Visitors will find pointers to sites ranging from comics, fishing, and climbing to rugby and soccer.

Interactive Internet Sports
http://www.iis-sports.com/

Visitors can register for free memberships to play the games and contests featured at Interactive Internet Sports. This site also provides news and columns, and fans can get further involved through the bulletin boards here.

Kids Sports Network

http://www.texas.net/user/kidsport/

Kids who play sports and adults who coach kids can find useful resources on the Kids Sports Network, which focuses on youth sports in San Antonio and Texas but includes items of national interest. Articles, commentaries, advice, and links are among the resources here.

Leonard's Trivia World

http://www.leonardsworlds.com/trivia.html

Sports fans can spend hours testing their knowledge here. Visitors have a selection of sports, each of which provides a trivia question, followed by the answer, followed by another question, *ad infinitum*.

The Nando Sports Server

http://www.nando.net/SportServer/

Sports fans can check the latest scores and read feature stories, or simply join in online discussions about their teams through the Nando Sports Server Web page. The site includes links to pages for each major team sport.

Online Sports

http://www.onlinesports.com/

Online Sports is a collection of sports-related products and services available via the Internet, including a sports career job file and résumé bank, links to various sports resources on the Web, and the Online Sports business center.

Physical Activity & Disability

http://info.lut.ac.uk/research/paad/home.html

Loughborough University in the United Kingdom disseminates information on sports, physical education, recreation, and rehabilitation to people with disabilities. Visitors here will find resources on wheelchair sports and the International Paralympics Committee.

Planet Reebok

http://planetreebok.com/

At Planet Reebok, the shoe manufacturer provides much more than promotional propaganda. Its smorgasbörd of resources includes live chat, bulletin boards, training tips, and pages for the Women's Sports Foundation and National Standards for Athletic Coaches.

Purdue Sports Mailing List Information

http://meteor.atms.purdue.edu/sports/

The Purdue Sports Mailing List Information is an unofficial home page that passes along scores, standings, and news related to the school's athletic programs. Includes men's and women's sports.

SI Online

http://pathfinder.com/si/

Sports Illustrated magazine presents far more than its print product online at this site. In addition to articles, features, and photos from the magazine, visitors will find daily news, scores, and statistics, as well as bulletin boards, special reports, and a site for SI For Kids.

SportsLine USA

http://www.sportsline.com/

Fans who enjoy reading sports columns from around the country will want to consider a paid membership to SportsLine USA. There is plenty of free stuff here, too, including news, statistics, and loads of interactive features. Free 30-day trial memberships are available.

The Sports Page

http://www.premrad.com/sports/sports.html

Sports fans who would rather listen than read will enjoy The Sports Page, where the content is limited but the audio clips are numerous. The features here, all with audio components, include a quiz, interviews, and the day in sports.

Sports Schedules As You Like 'Em

http://www.cs.rochester.edu:80/u/ferguson/schedules/

Sometimes the best ideas are simple. At this page, sports fans can use forms to generate precisely the professional sports schedules they desire. For example, it is possible to produce a schedule consisting of the home games in November 1996 for the National Football League's Houston Oilers. The leagues covered here range from the NFL to Roller Hockey International.

Stadiums and Arenas

http://www.wwcd.com/stadiums.html

Why go to the stadium when World-Wide Collectors Digest brings the stadium to the Web? All professional stadiums and arenas in North America are listed at this site, with information such as address, phone number, and capacity; most also have photos. Some racetracks and college stadiums also are included.

Stanford Athletics

http://www-athletics.stanford.edu/

The athletic department at Stanford University maintains this look at the school's sports programs. News and information on varsity teams, club teams, and general recreation are featured.

Sydney Cricket Ground/Football Stadium

http://www.scgt.oz.au/

Straight from Australia, land of the oval football field, comes the Sydney Cricket Ground/Football Stadium page. Learn more about this facility and the events it hosts, with links to the Sydney International Aquatic Centre and the Australian Football League.

University of Arizona Wildcats

http://www.hacks.arizona.edu/sports/

This unofficial University of Arizona athletics site provides information on intercollegiate and club teams, with indexes on sports, players, and coaches. Included are a listing of events, season highlights, opinions, and chat, as well as a page on former U.A. athletes.

USA Today Sports

http://www.usatoday.com/sports/sfront.htm

Up-to-the-minute news and team-by-team reports in every major sport help make this site even more thorough than *USA Today*'s daily print product. Among the many other features here are columns, high school rankings, Olympic pages, gaming odds, lottery results, and computer rankings.

The World-Wide Web Virtual Library: Sport

http://www.just~right.com/sports/

The sports section from the World-Wide Web Virtual Library features a host of sports links, ranging from youth soccer to professional football. Visitors can search the site or browse the listings that are sorted by topic.

WWW Women's Sports Page by Amy Lewis

http://fiat.gslis.utexas.edu/~lewisa/womsprt.html

The World Wide Web Women's Sports Page houses an extensive index of women's sports pages around the Net. From flying and gliding to soccer, "iron" sports and volleyball, there is something here for everyone. Also includes links to issues in women's sports.

THE OLYMPICS

Atlanta Games

http://www.atlantagames.com/index.htm

With the *Atlanta Journal-Constitution* supplying the news, this Olympics site provides a depth of coverage that isn't available elsewhere. When we visited, there was an article on demonstrators protesting a lack of public toilets. Standing offers here include details on lodging, tickets, entertainment, and more.

Authentic Olympic Games Collection

http://www.sportsnetusa.com/olympics/

Even fans who get no closer to the Olympic Games than their television screens can look like they were in Atlanta. Shoppers can order officially licensed products of the Atlanta Committee for the

Olympic Games at this site, which also provides pages on Olympic history and Olympic trivia.

It's Atlanta!—The Olympic Web Page

http://www.com-stock.com/dave/

This personal 1996 Olympics hotlist points sports fans in all the right directions. It includes links to Olympic organizations, guides to Atlanta, ticket information, event specifics, and even to corporate sponsors' home pages.

Latest Olympic News

http://167.8.29.13/olympics/oly.htm

USA Today presents a page of resources on the 1996 Summer Olympics that begins with news on every sport but goes much further. Features include an event-by-event schedule, information on venues, and a diary by track star Michael Johnson.

Nagano Olympic Winter Games

http://www.linc.or.jp/Nagano/

Information on the 1998 Winter Olympic Games to be held in Nagano, Japan is the focus of this page. Included here are details on events and venues, directions on getting to Nagano and a drawing of the official mascot, Snowlets. In English and Japanese

1996 Centennial Olympic Games Home Page

http://www.atlanta.olympic.org/

Visitors to the official site for the 1996 Atlanta Committee for the Olympic Games will find Olympic sports and venues, ticket information, official products, travel information, and the official program of the 1996 Summer Olympics.

The Olympic Movement

http://www.olympic.org/

Get Olympic news directly from the source at the site of the International Olympic Committee, which provides news releases, information on the IOC, and much more. The resources here include lots of historical details on the Olympic movement. See Editor's Choice.

Results from The 1994 Winter Olympics at Lillehammer

http://briskeby.sn.no/OL/OL94.html

Visit this site for results from the 1994 Winter Olympics at Lillehammer, Norway. Find a chronological list of events, an image archive, audio clips, and a searchable results database.

Salt Lake Olympic Organizing Committee for the Olympic Winter Games of 2002

http://www.SLC2002.org/

The dates are set: February 9 through 24, 2002. That's when Salt Lake City, Utah will play host to

the XIX Winter Olympic Games. This site supplies details on the city and its successful effort to gain the Games, and it promises more extensive information in the future.

Sydney 2000

http://www.sydney.olympic.org/

While the rest of the world focuses on Atlanta '96, Sydney 2000 is planning ahead. Visitors will be overwhelmed by the details available here on the 2000 Summer Olympics. Check out the elaborate environmental guidelines covering areas such as ozone depletion and waste management.

ORIENTEERING

Orienteering and Rogaining Home Page

http://www2.aos.princeton.edu/rdslater/orienteering/

The Orienteering and Rogaining Home Page provides information on these two sports that rely on navigational skills to conquer unfamiliar terrain. Here, visitors can learn more about these sports, link to related pages, learn about equipment and see a map-view of orienteering clubs in the United States.

---

a2z   EDITOR'S CHOICE

The Olympic Movement

http://www.olympic.org/

Maybe it's because 1996 is an Olympic year, but this site from the International Olympic Committee has us sitting at attention. Visitors can get Olympic news straight from the source here, and they can see how the nearly 100-year-old Games got to where they are today. Among the resources are news releases, background on the IOC, and historical details on the Olympic movement. One highlight is a chart showing how the Olympics have grown from 13 nations, 43 events, and 280 athletes at the 1896 Athens Games to 169 nations, 284 events, and 9,368 athletes at the 1992 Barcelona Games. Day-by-day countdowns to the 1998 Winter Games in Nagano, 2000 Summer Games in Sydney, and 2002 Winter Games in Salt Lake City also are provided, with links to more information on each of those events. It's all done to promote the Olympics, but hey…it's educational. —*Reviewed by Dan Kelly*

Orienteering Federation of Australia

http://www-personal.usyd.edu.au/~markz/oz-o/ofa.html

Orienteering—finding your way across unfamiliar territory using a map and a compass—is the topic of the Orienteering Federation of Australia site. Learn about the sport and the association here, or link to orienteering societies in Australia or to related pages.

PAINTBALL

Warpig Paintball Home Page

http://www.warpig.com/

Warpig is a comprehensive information resource on paintball. This site includes specifications on models of paintball guns, safety equipment, and camouflage, as well as a picture gallery and links. See Editor's Choice.

POOL/ BILLIARDS

WWW Snooker

http://www.ifi.uio.no/~hermunda/Snooker/

What do you call a person who plays snooker? No, not a *snookie*—just a snooker player. Learn about snooker, a variation of pool, at this home page, which features the rules of the game as well as information on top players and tournaments.

RACQUET SPORTS

Badminton

http://mid1.external.hp.com/stanb/badminton.html

The Badminton home page dishes up a wealth of information for badminton lovers around the globe. Read a variety of background information, check out current events and tournaments, or link to organizations and other badminton-related Web sites.

Internet Squash Federation

http://www.ncl.ac.uk/~npb/

The World Squash Federation provides information here on its activities, tournaments, coaching, Olympics 2000, and more. An index of links includes player profiles, publications, and online mail order.

RUGBY

RugbyInfo

http://rugby.phys.uidaho.edu/rugby.html

Video clips of rugby action are among the many resources at the RugbyInfo page. This comprehensive listing of rugby links also includes the basics and rules of the game, coaching information, and trivia.

RUNNING

Cambuslang Harriers Page

http://www.chem.gla.ac.uk/~david/harriers.html

The Cambuslang Harriers are a Scottish cross-country racing team. Visitors to their home page will find profiles of team members, race schedules, results, photos, and descriptions of training programs.

Cross-Country Analysis

http://www.cs.uml.edu/~phoffman/xc.html

For those who know what a Purdy Point is, this site supplies calculators that predict performances in cross country and track running events. Among the other resources here for coaches and athletes is information on college track and cross country programs.

Dead Runners Society

http://storm.cadcam.iupui.edu/drs/drs.html

The Dead Runners Society is a listserv discussion group for folks who love running. At its Web site, browsers will find instructions on joining the mailing list, as well as forum and publication archives and links to all things afoot.

Dr. Pribut Sports Page

http://www.clark.net/pub/pribut/spsport.html

Dr. Stephen Pribut offers this site dedicated to running injuries and what you can do about them. Visitors can peruse a wide selection of information, including books, shoe-buying tips, track records, and links to related Web sites.

The Running Page

http://sunsite.unc.edu/drears/running/running.html

Want to find out if there is a marathon next month in Sweden? A pit stop at The Running Page will provide information on upcoming races worldwide and much more, including listings of running clubs and race results.

Ultramarathon World

http://fox.nstn.ca/~dblaikie/

Ultra-athletes who run ultra-distances can find international news and archives here at Ultramarathon World. Access information on major races, buy gear at the Ultra Shop, locate run-related organizations, and keep up with the news about other marathoners.

WebRunner Running Page

http://www.catalog.com/webrun/running/running.html

The WebRunner Running Page is an online guide to race and fitness running, with an emphasis on the southeastern United States. Visit here for race updates and schedules, links to running clubs, downloadable software, and more.

SHOOTING

Rec.guns FAQ Home Page

http://www.recguns.com/

Self-described as "the most complete gun resource on the Net," this site points to the answers of FAQs, gun safety tips, movie mishaps, firearm links, firearm sounds, and targets. Also find commercial links and an NRA promotion.

SKIING

Alpine World

http://www.alpworld.com/

The world of alpine skiing comes to the Web through Alpine World Magazine's site. If this page's graphics, complete with animation, aren't enough to satisfy visitors, then the resort guide and ski reports from around the globe will be.

Aspen Snowmass OnLine Home

http://www.aspenonline.com/aspenonline/

Aspen Snowmass OnLine offers complete information about the Colorado ski resort communities of Aspen and Snowmass. Here, visitors can find out about recreational activities, travel, family tips, lodging, nature hikes, and dining.

Global Snow and Surf Report

http://www.geezer.com/

The Geezer presents this site, which is not for geezers. It contains daily snow reports from North American ski resorts, as well as sports-oriented

EDITOR'S CHOICE

GoSKI

http://www.goski.com/

You've got to like the philosophy here: "Quit the day job. Call in sick. Go Ski." And if you need help deciding where to "go ski," GoSKI Webmasters will point you to skiing resources worldwide. And we do mean *worldwide*. The site's centerpiece is a searchable database of more than 1,500 ski resorts, with pertinent details and user-contributed reviews covering resorts from Andorra to New Zealand. For example, visitors might discover that the Muju resort in the Mt. Togyusan National Park of South Korea has 23 trails, nine lifts, and one hotel. In St. Moritz, Switzerland, a contributor writes: "There is no way to ski the whole mountain with less than a week's stay." (As if we can all afford two weeks in St. Moritz.) Among the other resources here are racing news, equipment reviews, and a listing of clubs and organizations, as well as a job-hunting service. For those who love to ski, this site is a year-round resource. Remember, "It's snowing somewhere right now." —*Reviewed by Dan Kelly*

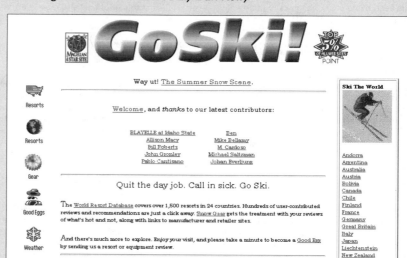

shopping opportunities. When we last visited, surf reports and X-rated links were in the works.

GORP—Snowsports

http://www.gorp.com/gorp/activity/skiing.htm

At the Snowsports page from the Great Outdoor Recreation Pages (GORP), find links to resources related to nordic and alpine skiing as well as other outdoor winter activities. Pointers are worldwide in scope and organized according to geographic region.

GoSKI

http://www.goski.com/

GoSKI is a guide to skiing worldwide. Skiers, snowboarders, and other snow sliders will find feature articles, a database of resorts, product reviews, and condition reports here. See Editor's Choice.

Killington Vermont

http://www.killington.com/

Claiming to be the "East's largest ski and snowboard resort," Killington offers skiers a heated gondola in the winter and mountain bikers a place to play in the summer. Check the resort's home page for trail conditions and year-round events.

rec.skiing FAQ

http://skiing.geo.ucalgary.ca/skiing/faq.html

The rec.skiing newsgroup posts a FAQ file here to answer questions browsers might have about alpine and nordic skiing. Find tips on equipment, clothing, and technique that enable you to safely (and comfortably) hit the powder.

SkiCentral

http://skicentral.com/

Check ski conditions at resorts around the world or link to skiing magazines and news from this site. This searchable index has links to nearly 2,000 ski-related pages, and it includes contests, a photo gallery, and other goodies.

Ski Colorado

http://www.aescon.com/ski/

Aspen, Vail, Steamboat Springs. Colorado lures skiers to its mountains here, with information on ski areas, plus details on lodging and tours. Among the other resources available are maps, snowboarding information, and cross country ski information. In English, German, French, and Spanish.

Ski IN

http://www.idnet.fr/ski/

Ski IN, The Global Ski Guide, reviews ski resorts and offer tips for excursions—on and off the slopes. The emphasis here is on Europe, although details on a few North American resorts are available. In English, French, and German.

Skiing at Whistler Resort

http://www.whistler.net/

At this promotional site for Whistler Resort in British Columbia, Canada, visitors can learn about its skiing trails, accommodations, restaurants, and activities. Interactive contests and prizes also are featured here.

Southland Ski Server

http://www.cccd.edu/ski.html

Southland Ski Server features information on ski resorts in southern California and the eastern Sierras. Find an extensive collection of resort information (trail maps, rate sheets, and so on), road reports, weather reports, ski reports, and general skiing resources.

Steamboat

http://www.steamboat-ski.com/ski

Steamboat Springs, the western-themed Colorado ski resort, provides information on its mountain, with maps, condition reports, and a daily photo from the trails. Off-mountain links include resources on dining, shopping, lodging, transportation, rates, equipment rentals, and other activities.

SOCCER

Arsenal Supporters' WWW Page

http://www-ipg.umds.ac.uk/~rw/arsenal.html

ArseWEB can turn your computer into a "Gooner" with its images, sound clips, and video clips of the Arsenal soccer team from the English Premier League. Fans also can get news, scores, and player profiles at this unofficial site. See Editor's Choice.

Belgian Soccer Archive

http://www.wi.leidenuniv.nl/home/andries/belgian_soccer.html

Soccer junkies can find nearly everything they want to know about Belgian soccer and the game in general at the Belgian Soccer Archive. This page contains links to Belgian team schedules, Belgian Supercup information, the Usenet newsgroup rec.sport.soccer, and its main Web archive, the Rec.Sports.Soccer Statistics Foundation.

Besiktas Home Page

http://www.bjk.com/

Followers of Turkish soccer will find results from the Turkish Professional Premier League here as well as complete information on the Besiktas team. Read about the team's 85-year history and follow its every move in daily news reports. Some links in English.

Campionato Italiano di Calcio

http://www.crs4.it/~meola/football/schedina.html

The Campionato Italiano di Calcio page posts the latest Italina soccer scores and standings. Link to other sports results here. In Italian.

CarlingNet—Football's No 1 Web Site

http://www.fa-premier.com/

For fans of British soccer, CarlingNet is the first place to stop for news and information. It provides in-depth pages on each club in the FA Carling Premiership, as well as results, statistics, standings, discussion groups, merchandise, and more.

Continental Indoor Soccer League Homepage

http://www.cec.wustl.edu/~krm1/cislmain.html

The Continental Indoor Soccer League is a U.S.-Mexican professional league that has played since 1993. This page keeps fans current on standings, stats, and schedules. Link to news and to CISL team home pages.

Coventry City Football Club

http://www.warwick.ac.uk/~cudbu/SkyBlues.html

News and standings on the Coventry City Football Club of the English Premier League are featured on this page. Meet team members and follow their exploits, or review past glories. See Editor's Choice.

Danmarksturneringen

http://www.daimi.aau.dk/~rorschak/sl/dmtur.html

For fans of Danish soccer, the Danmarksturneringen site is an indispensable resource. It provides the latest results and standings from Danish leagues, information about a fantasy league, and more.

DC United Supporters Page

http://www.screaming-eagles.com/

The DC United Supporters Page is designed for fans of the Major League Soccer team based in Washington, D.C. Read up on the latest news, team statistics, and scores.

Derby County Football Club

http://lard.sel.cam.ac.uk/derby_county/

Fans of the Derby County Rams Football Club can review match results and see what's next for the soccer team, which plays in Britain's Endsleigh League, at this unofficial site. Visitors also can join the RamsNet mailing list here.

The Dutch Soccer-Competition

http://soccer.boa.nl/

A smorgasbörd of results, schedules, and team information is available at this Dutch soccer site. Links to pages on Dutch teams and Dutch players can be found, along with archives of team and individual performances from previous seasons.

England '96 Qualification

http://www.daimi.aau.dk/~rorschak/sl/ecfix.html

Find out how teams from around the world qualified for the England '96 soccer tournament at this page. It features results from all qualifying groups, as well as a schedule for the tournament.

English Premiership Pages

http://www.cs.rochester.edu/users/grads/oriain/premier.html

Links to sites on the English Premier League, including several from foreign countries, are provided here. Visitors to this page can locate results, standings, and much more on the top English soccer league.

ESPNET SportsZone: Soccer

http://espnet.sportszone.com/soccer/

The ESPNET SportsZone soccer page has news and information on national, international, and college teams, with stats, scores, and standings. Includes English, German, and Scottish league tables and results.

FC Kaiserslautern

http://www.uni-kl.de/FCK/

Follow the FC Kaiserlautern of the German Bundesliga at this site, which also provides complete Bundesliga results. A detailed history of the nearly 100-year-old soccer team from Kaiserlautern, Germany, is included. In English and German.

Ferencvaros

http://ogyalla.konkoly.hu/staff/zsoldos/fradi.html

The Ferencvaros home page features information about the history and traditions of the soccer club in Budapest, Hungary. This unofficial page also includes pictures and up-to-date information about the current season. The women's handball and basketball teams are also featured.

French Soccer Web server

http://www.cc.columbia.edu/~yn25/soccer.html

Soccer fans can follow the sport in France here. The site contains team descriptions, division results, league predictions, and calendars for the French and World Cups. Browsers will also find information about the France-Foot mailing list, a soccer dictionary, and links to European soccer servers.

Futebol em Portugal

http://shiva.di.uminho.pt/~miguel/FUTEBOL/pt/portugal.html

In English, "Futebol em Portugal" means "Soccer in Portugal." This page—offered in both languages—has information on the national sport, with standings, results and related links, as well as team histories and information.

Hypertext Hibs

http://duke.usask.ca/~macpherc/hibs/hibs.html

Hypertext Hibs is an fanzine providing news and information about the Hibernian Football Club of the Scottish Premier League. Visitors can learn about the soccer team's history or check out photos, club news, and a mailing list.

International Soccer Server

http://sigwww.cs.tut.fi/riku/soccer.html

Fans of European soccer can find data on their favorite teams here. Visitors can contribute information to the Webmaster or link to other international soccer servers.

Jesper Lauridsen's Football Page

http://www.daimi.aau.dk/~rorschak/fodbold.html

Soccer information from Denmark and Europe is the focus here, although results from around the world are available. Visitors can link to pages on the European Cup, the World Cup, and more.

J. League Home Page

http://www.dentsu.co.jp/J-LEAGUE/

J. League promotes the popularization and proliferation of soccer in Japan. Here visitors can familiarize themselves with the teams, the towns they represent, and the schedules they play. Also find updates of Japan's bid to host the 2002 World Cup.

Manchester City F.C. Supporters Home Page

http://www.uit.no/mancity/

The Manchester City F.C., an English professional soccer team, boasts an international roster and an international following, both of which are evident at this page maintained by a fan in Norway. Visitors can vote for a player of the month and check out photos, player profiles, statistics, and league standings.

---

a2z EDITOR'S CHOICE

Arsenal Supporters' WWW page

http://www-ipg.umds.ac.uk/~rw/arsenal.html

What do Johnny Rotten, the Queen Mother, Elvis Presley, Ronny Biggs (the great train robber), Buster Bloodvessel, and God all have in common? If you guessed they're all "Gooners" (supporters of England's Arsenal football club), then you'd be right.

As full as Highbury Park on a Saturday afternoon, this site offers the usual fixtures and results, stats and photos of the team, but with some suprises along the way. Stop by the multimedia section, where you'll find plenty of soundbites and QuickTime movies, live updates of the day's game, and a photo of John (Rotten) Lydon sporting the latest Arsenal football kit in his own inimitable way. It's all more than enough to satisfy even the neediest of Arse surfers. And last but not least, "The Cybury Gooners," a football team made up of people on the Arsenal mailing list, encourage you to challenge them to a match (preferably in the London area). So if you've just started your new soccer team in Bald Knob, Arkansas and you're looking for a challenge, you'd better start saving for the air fare now. —*Reviewed by Paul Wood*

The Arsenal Supporters'

WWW page

Welcome to the *Internet* home of football.

𝕬𝖗𝖘𝖊𝖜𝖊𝖇

Mondo CALCIO

http://www.vol.it/raitgs/mcalciio/msoccer.htm

Mondo CALCIO (the Italian Soccer Hypermedia Information Service) features the latest scores and standings from the Italian soccer scene. Historical information also is available. Most pages are in Italian.

N.A.C. Breda Homepage

http://www.xs4all.nl/~cjrdboer/nac2.htm

The soccer team N.A.C. Breda is called here "one of the oldest and most beloved professional football clubs in the Netherlands." Get the facts here on N.A.C. Breda, including game results, a player roster, and more, along with Dutch soccer links. In English and some Dutch.

Nando Soccer Features

http://www.nando.net/newsroom/sports/oth/1995/oth/soc/feat/soc.html

The Soccer Features section of the Nando Sports Server contains an enormous collection of information about the worlds's most popular sport. You'll find British, French, German, Italian, and Spanish standings, as well as NCAA men's and women's soccer updates.

The 1995 America Cup

http://cypress.mcsr.olemiss.edu/

The Argentine Soccer WWW Server supplies articles, results and statistics on the 1995 America Cup tournament. This site also provides America Cup results dating to 1916.

---

a2z EDITOR'S CHOICE

Coventry City Football Club

http://www.warwick.ac.uk/~cudbu/SkyBlues.html

Much to my surprise, Coventry City Football Club's home page is the fifth most popular soccer sight in the A2Z directory; this must be the most recognition Coventry has received since Lady Godiva rode naked through its streets nearly 1,000 years ago. Coventry City F.C. is the equivalent of a woman's underwear nightmare—it has only one cup and little support. It's no wonder they haven't become very fashionable.

Visiting "The Home of Big Fat Ron's Sky Blue Army" (sorry, no JPEGs of this one) is about as uninspiring as the team itself. Although you won't find any great art direction here, team stats and information are delivered with all the devotion and accuracy of the proudest of Coventry's fans, Rory Donovan. Log in for the mandatory pre- and post-game local pub crawls (virtual, of course), and if that isn't enough to whet your appetite, then peruse the business wizardry of Coventry's buying and selling tactics. Notice how team owners buy players' contracts for one and two million pounds, then can't even give them away. One player was traded for free, but Coventry's owners had to throw in 10,000 meat pies just to make sure he wasn't coming back.

The Webmaster says, "If Coventry City were a member of the Royal family they would probably be Princess Anne." I think they are more closely related to the corgis of Buckingham Palace: They're small, no trouble, and kind of nice to have around. —*Reviewed by Paul Wood*

Coventry City F.C.

The Home Page of Big Fat Ron's Sky Blue Army

That's your lot for this season. Don't expect much more than today's tidying up. Thanks to all the contributors to the City match reports. Hope you've all enjoyed the offerings. Here's to another 30 years at the top. Wa-hey!!

Norwegian Football

http://www.unik.no/~larsa/football.html

Results and standings, past and present, for Norwegian soccer leagues are featured at this site. Recent news and reports on the national team also are provided, along with links to other Norwegian soccer sites and to international sites.

Official FC Den Haag Home Page

http://ado.denhaag.org/

Soccer from The Hague in Holland comes to the Web through the FC Den Haag home page that is officially recognized by the club. It includes recent news, scores, and standings as well as a history archive and soccer-related comics. In English and Dutch.

Official F.C. Twente Page

http://www.trimm.nl/fctwente/

Check the standings and statistics of the F.C. Twente soccer team here. This Dutch site offers information on the team's history, schedule, and stadium, and visitors can download a photo of the team. In Dutch and English.

Qualifying of the European Championship 1996 in England

http://iamwww.unibe.ch/~ftiwww/Sonstiges/Tabellen/EM/em1996.html

Group standings and game results from qualifying for the 1996 European soccer championships are provided at this site. Results of previous championships, held every four years, are available dating to 1960. In German and English.

Rec.Sport.Soccer—The Web Page

http://www.just~right.com/rss/

Information from the rec.sport.soccer newsgroup's FAQ is available at this page, along with a link to the newsgroup. Computer soccer games, an index of soccer mailing lists, and World Cup links are among the other resources.

Rete!

http://www.tin.it/rete/

Soccer fans can search the database at this site for photos, video clips, and information on more than 1,500 teams worldwide. The site updates news on competitions and matches daily. In English and Italian. See Editor's Choice.

Rosenborg BK

http://home.sn.no/~terjerix/rbk/

News, results dating back several decades, statistics, and other information on the Rosenborg Ballklub—a Norwegian soccer team—are supplied at this site. Available in English and Norwegian.

The Russian Football Homepage

http://www.quark.lu.se/~oxana/football.html

Soccer fans can follow Russian teams and leagues here. The page includes a look at the national team, the leagues, a history of the teams, and transfers of players. In English and Russian.

Seattle Pitch

http://www.halcyon.com/zipgun/sounders/sounders.html

Soccer fans can follow the professional Seattle Sounders, 1995 champions of the A-League, at this site. The latest news, schedules, statistics, and player information are provided.

SE London & Kent Soccer Pages

http://www.ibmpcug.co.uk/~pollaxed/index.html

A virtual league is among the resources at this site about all levels of soccer in southeast London and Kent. Visit here for tournament results, player profiles, photographs, and other information.

Shamrock Rovers F.C. Fan Site

http://paul.maths.may.ie:8000/Rovers.html

Fans of the Irish soccer team, the Shamrock Rovers F.C., can check out the latest results and take in a bit of the club's history through this unofficial home page. It also includes the words to Rovers songs and chants, along with interviews with legendary players.

The Soccer Home Page

http://www.distrib.com/soccer/homepage.html

The Soccer Home Page, sponsored by The Soccer Store, contains a comprehensive listing of soccer links. Included are kids' sites, professional scores, Olympic links, equipment makers, World Cup facts, and more. Visitors can listen to audio clips or check out the women's soccer scene here.

Soccer Is Life Page

http://nextdch.mty.itesm.mx/~rlopez/SOCCER.html

Soccer is Life gives a shot in the arm to fans inflicted with *socceritis*. The page provides links to rules, mailing lists, and other Web sites, as well as to a soccer dictionary.

SoccerNet

http://soccernet.com/

SoccerNet, a guide to English soccer leagues, provides links to team and tournament information. Visit here to look up your favorite team and find facts and figures from games around the United Kingdom.

Soccer-Tables

http://www.marwin.ch/sport/fb/index.e.html

For soccer information from around the globe, this is the place to start. The site includes pointers, grouped by country, to sites posting standings, club information, competition news, and more. In English and German.

Sporting Clube de Portugal

http://jupiter.di.uminho.pt/~rui/futebol/sporting/

News, results and player information are available at this site from Sporting Clube de Portugal, a soccer team in Lisbon. Other features here include the team's results and standings in the Portuguese League.

SportStats Soccer

http://www.islandnet.com/~agcur/soccer1.html

SportStats Soccer is an online magazine chronicling the English football scene. Find schedules, scores, and a who's who of the field, as well as plenty of statistics and sports-oriented banter.

The Strange Soccer Story Collection

http://www.i-way.co.uk/~readingfc/story.html

The Strange Soccer Stories site contains...well...strange stories about unusual events at soccer games. Includes instructions for submissions of users' tales of soccer weirdness.

Tampa Bay Mutiny Homepage

http://www.unix.oit.umass.edu/~litterer/mls/mutiny.html

A Mutiny fan posts this unofficial page promoting Tampa Bay's Major League Soccer team. Get the who, what, when, and where...and then some.

TSI Soccer

http://www.tsisoccer.com/tsi/

Soccer players and fans can purchase apparel and merchandise from the TSI Soccer catalog at this site, which also contains the official mail-order catalog of Major League Soccer. Information on youth soccer camps and tournaments also is available.

Turkish League

http://sigwww.cs.tut.fi/riku/soccer_html/tur0.html

Soccer fans can keep up with the status of the Turkish League on this page with results, league tables, and past performance archives. Direct access to Turkish soccer clubs also can be found here.

---

a2z EDITOR'S CHOICE

The Leicester City Football Club WWW Page

http://www.dur.ac.uk/~d3g2w4/lcfc.html

Feel like stormin' the Web with Leicester City, feel in a fighting mood, and want to get into the spirit of English soccer? If the answers to these questions are yes, then this is the page for you. Go immediately to the song page and learn the words to the beautifully poetic "Tip Toe through the Trent End," and the soon-to-be classic, chart-topping hit, "If I Had the A*se of a Cow." Then download the Wembly audio file (which is actually very good) and you're all set...well almost. There are match reports from each of Leicester City's games over the past two seasons here. Whether you're a fan or not, you can relive past victories and untimely losses and feel proud to be a part of it all. So go for it—nothing is stopping you; you can scream and shout profanities, jump up and down, be a virtual hooligan for a day, and upset no one (except the next door neighbor).—*Reviewed by Paul Wood*

United Systems of Independent Soccer Leagues

http://www.jump.net/~netminder/quitameehu/usisl/

The United Systems of Independent Soccer Leagues consist of teams from across the United States that play in a Select League, a Pro League and an amateur Premier League. This unofficial home page for the USISL, based in Tampa, Florida, supplies schedules, media guides, standings, and scores.

The Unofficial Ajax Homepage

http://pmwww.cs.vu.nl/home/edoe/Ajax/

Fans of Ajax, a top professional Dutch soccer team, can find game reports, complete with photos and video clips, at this fan page. Statistics, ticket information, player profiles, and more round out the resources here. Information varies from English to Dutch.

ValeWeb—The Port Vale F.C. Web Pages

http://web.dcs.hull.ac.uk/people/pjp/PortVale/PortVale.html

Results from current and past seasons are among the resources at this fan page on the Port Vale soccer team of the English First Division. Visitors also can find league standings, a roster, ticket prices, club honors, and more.

Washington Mustangs Home Page

http://pie.org/E19612T3575

Check out the Washington Mustangs soccer club, a professional feeder team for Major League Soccer's DC United, through this page. It offers a schedule, statistics, news from the team, and more.

Women's Soccer World

http://www.womensoccer.com/index.html

Featuring news, views and action from the amateur, college, and professional ranks, Women's Soccer World magazine covers the sport around the globe. Commentaries, rosters, schedules, and classifieds are among the resources at this site.

World Cup USA '94

http://sunsite.sut.ac.jp/wc94

Relive the thrills and spills that were the World Cup '94 competition. Soccer fans can revisit the tournament held in the United States at this page, which contains photos, information on the teams, and a description of the final showdown between Brazil and Italy.

World Cup USA '94 Preview

http://www.wmart.com/soccer

Extensive details previewing the 1994 World Cup soccer championships in the United States are available here. History, schedules, player information, and more are presented, but you'll have to go elsewhere for results.

TABLE TENNIS

Home Page of Table Tennis Pro

http://earth.execpc.com/~donw/

Pro Table Tennis Supplies markets table tennis equipment and services, including training and exhibitions. This site includes biographical information about company owner and coach Donald Winze, details on equipment, ordering information, and more.

TENNIS

ATP Tour Home Page

http://atptour.com/

Fans can stay up to date on the men's professional tennis tour at the ATP's official site. Although bios are provided only for the top players, the site includes rankings, results, and a calendar—along with plenty of promotional material.

ESPNET SportsZone: Tennis

http://espnet.sportszone.com/ten/

ESPNET SportsZone's tennis site offers pro rankings, major tournament wrap-up information, a tour for subscribers, and late-breaking developments.

The Official Corel WTA Site

http://www.corelwtatour.com/

Women's tennis fans can get the latest tournament information from the Corel WTA Tour at this official site. Review past events or check out news, statistics, and player biographies.

OverTheNet

http://www.efrei.fr/~dicesare/OverTheNet

Find the latest results and rankings from the professional tours at OverTheNet, The Tennis Stats Server. Visit here to follow the men's ATP tour and the women's WTA tour. Statistical overviews of players are provided.

The Sports Network: Women's Tennis Page

http://www.sportsnetwork.com:80/tennis-w/index.html

Current and recent news on professional women's tennis is provided at this site from The Sports Network. Statistics, a forum and a link to the men's tennis page also are available, as is a search option.

Tennis—Frequently Asked Questions

http://www.mindspring.com/~csmith/TennisFAQ.html

What's a Grand Slam tournament? Stop by this tennis page to answer that simple question and to review player rankings. It also offers information on players and media, as well as tips about tennis equipment.

Tennis Information

http://www.mindspring.com/~csmith/TennisNews.html

Tennis fans can keep tabs on international events here. The site includes tournament news, rankings, and statistics. It also contains archives of Women's Tennis Association results and rankings.

The Tennis Server Homepage

http://www.tennisserver.com/

The Tennis Server serves up tennis. Lots of it. In addition to news, rules, club listings, equipment tips, and the like, this site presents contests, original columns, and information on an e-mail newsletter.

Tennis Warehouse

http://www.tennis-warehouse.com

This commercial site displays a wide range of tennis-related products for sale. Items include tennis shoes, racquets, strings, replacement grips, bags, hats, caps, and visors. Includes a toll-free number for ordering and links to tennis-related home pages.

Tennis Web

http://www.tennisw.com/tweb/

Tennis anyone? This Web site contains dozens of links to tennis-related resources on the Internet, including camps, schools, newsgroups, clubs, resorts, tournaments, and FAQs.

Tennis Worldwide

http://www.tennisw.com/

Home to Tennis Worldwide magazine and a Web page devoted to junior tennis, this site also offers amusements such as contests and a fantasy tennis league. Classified ads and the site's Tennis Mall point visitors toward a smashing array of equipment and services.

TRACK AND FIELD

Athletics Canada

http://www.canoe.ca/Athcan

Track Canada, an unofficial site from a competitor-turned-doctor, offers a variety of Canadian track and field information. Included are athlete profiles and a database of records, clubs, and rankings.

VOLLEYBALL

Association of Volleyball Professionals (AVP)

http://www.volleyball.org/avp

Spikes and bumps are commonplace on the Association of Volleyball Professionals' Web site. The page includes information about the group and schedules for the AVP tours, as well as profiles of the players.

4-Person Pro Beach

http://www.volleyball.org/4person

Players and fans stop here for game results, rosters, player profiles, and news from the four-person professional beach volleyball circuit.

San Jose/San Francisco Area Volleyball

http://www.volleyball.org/bay_area

San Jose and San Francisco volleyball resources and specialty stores are highlighted on this Web page. Read about adult and high school leagues, or check into the status of the Storm women's pro indoor team.

Schneid's Volleyball Page

http://www.xnet.com/~schneid/vball.shtml

Mike Schneider is a volleyball coach, referee and player, so perhaps it's not surprising that his volleyball page covers every imaginable aspect of the game—from rules, strategy, and drills to training and equipment. The page also contains copious resources on general conditioning, sports medicine, and nutrition.

USA Volleyball Home Page

http://www.volleyball.org/usav/

USA Volleyball, the national governing body for the sport, supplies information on its operation and organization at this home page. Also available here are schedules and rosters of national teams, information on Junior Olympic, youth and adult programs, and other resources.

Volleyball Sites on the WWW

http://www.volleyball.org/www_sites

Volleyball enthusiasts will find an extensive worldwide index to volleyball sites on the Internet on this page from Volleyball WorldWide. It is arranged by country but also has listings under Olympics, colleges, professional, and others.

Volleyball WorldWide

http://www.volleyball.org/

Volleyball WorldWide, a personal collection of volleyball-related resources, offers links to collegiate, professional, national, and international associations, and teams. Includes an extensive index of playing rules and instructional materials.

Women's Professional Volleyball Association (WPVA)

http://www.volleyball.org/wpva

Volleyball Worldwide's page on the Women's Professional Volleyball Association provides information on this organization, which governs women's pro beach volleyball. Schedules, results, and player bios are included.

WATER SPORTS

ARCHIVES AND INDICES

MarineNet
http://www.gsn.com/

MarineNet offers a boatload of links related to boats, scuba-diving, cruises, fishing, and other moist diversions. Includes classifieds, manufacturers' sites, calendars of events, clubs, schools, and more.

NauticalNet
http://www.nauticalnet.com/

Boats and fishing are the mainstays of NauticalNet, which contains information on the tackle, charters, and electronics required in recreational water sports. Boaters can also get marine weather reports here.

BOATING

Decavitator
http://lancet.mit.edu:80/decavitator/Decavitator.html

The Decavitator was a human-powered hydrofoil watercraft that set a world speed record in a 100-meter race across the Charles River (Boston) in 1991. Find resources on the Decavitator project here, including videos, images, and text, as well as specifications on the boat itself.

United States Power Squadrons
http://www.usps.org/

The United States Power Squadrons home page has information about this private, nonprofit organization of boating aficionados. Included are listings of USPS educational programs and a collection of USPS and other nautical flags, as well as links to other boating resources on the Internet.

ROWING

Montgomery Rowing Club
http://wsnet.com/~jiml/mrc/mrc.html

The Montgomery Rowing Club in Alabama is a new "and enthusiastic club of, well, about ten rowers." Meet the crew here and learn how to catch up with them on the river.

UC Davis Crew
http://asucd.ucdavis.edu/sports/crew/

The University of California at Davis Rowing home page highlights information about the men's and women's crew teams. Visitors can read about the history of UC Davis crew, check out rosters, schedules, and results, or click into a photo gallery. Links to UC Davis sites and to rowing sites are provided.

World Rowing Championships 1995
http://dmiwww.cs.tut.fi/row95/

Visitors to this page will find results from the World Rowing Championships held August 20 through 27, 1995, in Tampere, Finland. Also find a program from the event, an image gallery, and media coverage.

SAILING

Ade's Sailing Page
http://www.helsinki.fi/~avnurmin/sail.html

Sailing links are the focus on this page, which features an index of resources on One Design classes such as Flying Scot, Lightning, and International 14's. Also included are listings of commercial services, FTP archives, newsgroups, and Finnish yacht clubs.

Ade's Soling Page
http://www.helsinki.fi/~avnurmin/soling.html

This enthusiast's page is devoted to soling, the only Olympic-class keelboat for a crew of three. A history of the sport, boat specifications, results from competitions, and images are featured.

America's Cup Online
http://www.ac95.org

America's Cup Online offers stem to stern coverage of the major sailing sporting event. Visitors will find text and graphics chronicling the 1995 race, along with links to other Internet sites containing related sea-sailing content.

Angelo Mascaro's Sailing Page
http://www.inrete.it/vela/sail.html

Angelo Mascaro's Sailing Page is a reference guide for anyone planning on—or even fantasizing about—sailing the Mediterranean. Topics on this page include classification of boats, tips on where to sail, and recommendations of related movies and books. In Italian, with some English translations.

BoatNet
http://www.boatnet.com/boatnet/

Shopping for a yacht or sailing accessories? You might want to check the boats and marine products for sale here. The site also offers news of interest to boaters—weather information, race

listings, and so on—and diversionary photos and maritime stories.

48° North—The Northwest Sailing Magazine
http://www.gosailing.com/

In addition to articles and editorials on sailing, this magazine from Seattle, Washington provides listings of sailboats for sale and classified ads. This is also home to The Sailing Site, which features a comprehensive list of sailing links.

Hoofer Sailing Club Home Page
http://rso.union.wisc.edu/Hoofers/sailing/sailhome.html

The Hoofer Sailing Club of Madison, Wisconsin maintains this informational site for news, racing event updates, weather reports, safety rules, sailing tips, and more. Includes administrative and contact listings.

Iowa Sailing Club
http://panda.uiowa.edu/sail

The Iowa Sailing Club from the University of Iowa posts regatta results and other club information at this home page. Visitors can also browse the photo gallery or check the classified ads for sailing equipment.

Monterey Bay Sailing
http://www.armory.com/~lew/sports/sailing/sail.html

Sailing in Monterey Bay is only a small piece of this page's broad focus. Sailing and sailing conditions around the world is the true topic, with site features that include links to photos, weather information, race schedules, and other Web servers.

North Isle Sailing's San Juan Islands Home Page
http://islander.whidbey.net/~nis

This page presents information about the San Juan Islands, located off the coast of Washington state. Maintained by North Isle Sailing, a sailboat chartering company, this page offers lists of links to boating, environmental, and regional Web sites of related interest.

Page d'accueil de Brest '96
http://www.enst-bretagne.fr:3000/

Brest '96 is an "international rendez-vous for boats and mariners and of all seafaring enthusiasts." This French site supplies information on the sailing, and it includes information on the region of Brest, France. In French and English.

Sailboats Inc.
http://www.sailboats-inc.com/

Looking for a yacht to charter? Sailboats Inc. is the place on the Web to come. The company's site also provides information on its sailing courses and marina operations, as well as a listing of sailing events.

Sail4U

http://www.sail4u.be/

Make sure you know port from starboard when you visit Sail4U. Find out where to buy or rent boats, then plot a trip with Sail4U's recommendations. Race results, classified ads, and other boating resources are included.

SailNet

http://www.sailnet.com/

SailNet features The Sailing Directory, a listing of commercial sites related to sailing that includes builders, magazines, and more. Other resources available here include weather reports and software archives.

The Sailing Source—The Internet Sailing Magazine

http://www.paw.com/sail/

Articles, book excerpts, and information on new boats and gear are included here, as well as a wealth of event coverage. This is also the online home of the International Yacht Racing Union and many sailing-related businesses.

Sail Training Association

http://www.soton.ac.uk/~sta1

With this home page from its Southampton and Salisbury chapter in England, the Sail Training Association presents general information on the association and on sailing. Browsers can check out upcoming STA events, such as the annual Tall Ships Race, at this site.

University of Florida Sail Club

http://grove.ufl.edu/~ufsail

Check out the sailing information at this site, courtesy of the University of Florida Sail Club. Visitors can read club information, drop by the image gallery, or link to a multitude of related sites, with a focus on college sailing clubs.

The West Wight Potter Web Page

http://euler.sfasu.edu/

Follow the voyages of the West Wight Potter sailboat at this tribute page. Sailors and boat enthusiasts will find a wide variety of nautical offerings, including an introduction to the craft and its crew, background information on the sport of sailing, and a full complement of related Web links.

Windjammer Sails

http://fox.nstn.ca/~windjamm/

Windjammer Sails is a company specializing in sail making and furling, rigging, and yacht brokerage. This site includes background information on the company, descriptions of products and services, and links to other boating sites.

SCUBA AND SNORKELING

Aquanaut

http://www.aquanaut.com/

Aquanaut has a treasure trove of scuba resources. Included at this site are a wreck database and listings of other dive sites worldwide, as well as an image gallery and dive gear reviews.

Divers Alert Network

http://www.dan.ycg.org/

The Divers Alert Network is a membership association that emphasizes safety, education and research in recreational scuba diving. It provides a dive safety center here, with an interactive medical Q&A, information on courses, and more.

Diving in Australia

http://www.uq.edu.au/underwater/diving/

Scuba divers testing the waters around Australia will find an interactive map of dive sites here, with Australian weather reports, club information, a collection of underwater images, and more.

Eric's SCUBA Page!

http://diver.ocean.washington.edu/

This home page from an oceanography student with a serious interest in scuba diving focuses on Puget Sound, Washington, and the Pacific Northwest. Visitors will find reviews of dive sites, maps, charts, and equipment advice.

Mad Dog Expeditions

http://www.mad-dog.net/

Adventure travel fans can check the Mad Dog Expeditions page for a schedule of its sport diving outings to the Amazon, the Arctic, and other areas. The site features one expedition and includes information about training classes and staff.

Pacific Offshore Divers Inc.

http://www.thesphere.com/PODI/

Pacific Offshore Divers of San Jose, California provides information here on its scuba adventures and instructional classes. Visit here to read about its underwater excursions and browse its index of diving-related Web sites, including weather forecasts, safety tips, and more.

PADI World Wide Web Site

http://www.padi.com/PADIToday/default.asp

The Professional Association of Diving Instructors presents information on its courses in scuba, snorkeling, open water diving, and more at this home page. Visitors also can check out PADI products and a travel network.

Rocky Mountain Diving Center and Boulder Scuba Tours

http://www.csn.net/rmdc

A travel agency specializing in dive travel, Colorado's Rocky Mountain Diving Center and Boulder Scuba Tours offers travel packages to dive destinations around the world. Includes information on group diving trips, scuba lessons, and prices.

Scuba Central

http://www.evansville.net/~mmd/rscuba.html

At this collection of links and resources for scuba divers, visitors will find scuba shops, equipment talk, travel information, magazines, clubs, newsgroups, how-to articles, and much more.

Scuba Dudes

http://www.primenet.com/~trog/SCUBADUDE.html

From the folks who brought us the defunct Phoenix public-access television show "Scuba Dudes" comes the Web site of the same name. The Dudes talk about scuba stuff, and they provide photos, tips, and links.

Scuba.Net

http://www.scuba.net/

Divers can gather information on dive sites, weather conditions, dive shops, and local instructors at this site, which has a northern California emphasis. Also featured here are information on scuba mailing lists and links to other scuba sites.

South Florida Dive Journal

http://www.sfdj.com/

The South Florida Dive Journal is an online magazine focusing on scuba diving in south Florida. Visitors can view back issues with underwater photos, download videos, and visit the virtual storefronts of dive stores.

UK Diving

http://www.cru.uea.ac.uk/ukdiving/index.htm

European divers will want to visit this index of online resources on scuba diving in the United Kingdom. Included are links to diving news, a wreck database, trip reports, and more.

Underwater Sports World

http://www.uwsports.ycg.com/

Self-described as "the premiere interactive resource for divers," Underwater Sports World posts the current issue of its interactive magazine on this page. Also find an archive of back issues, a virtual dive shop, forums, a bulletin board, industry listings, and more.

SURFING

Hawaii Weather and Surf

http://www.hawaii.edu/News/weather.html

This informational site, maintained by the University of Hawaii, is for those who surf the ocean as well as the Internet. Visit here for local surf and weather conditions, satellite photos, and links to other weather-related Web sites.

The London Surf Club

http://www.unl.ac.uk/surfing/lsc.html

The London Surf Club maintains this enthusiasts site for a variety of resources. Visit here for club membership information, weather and wave reports from around the world, surfing tournament schedules, and more.

Ocean & Snow Surfer Home

http://www.cts.com/browse/scwindan/

South Coast Surf Shops of San Diego present resources here geared toward surfers and snowboarders. In addition to photos, links to companies, and information on merchandise, this site has video reviews and a directory of surf clubs.

Surfin' Holland Home Page

http://www.xs4all.nl/~edwardl/

Surfin' Holland, a guide to resources for the European surfing community, offers visitors links to related Web sites, folklore, graphics, and e-mail addresses of enthusiasts. Includes a variety of articles and sports association links.

SWIMMING AND DIVING

Austin Swimming

http://www.realtime.net/~dhbrown

If it makes a splash in Austin, Texas, it is covered here. This site serves as the home page of the University of Texas Longhorn swim teams, Texas Aquatics, and the Texas Swimming Center, with meet results and schedules for all levels of competition.

Harvard Men's Swimming and Diving

http://hcs.harvard.edu/~menswim/

The Harvard University men's swimming and diving team posts its season schedule and roster here, along with school records and top performances. A link to the Harvard women's swimming team site is provided.

WATER POLO

H2O Polo

http://www.h2opolo.com/

With links to information about water polo and its players, H2O Polo Web Site gives water polo players the chance to learn more about all levels of their sport as well as hook up with other players worldwide.

WINDSURFING

Adirondack Boardsailing Club Home Page

http://www.rpi.edu/~guidom/adirondack.html

The Adirondack Boardsailing Club is located in northeastern New York state. Visitors here will find events and classes for boardsailing in the area, as well as links to the Northeastern Windsurfing Site Guide, weather information, and resources categorized by U.S. region.

Jo 90's Windsurfing Home Page

http://faraday.ucd.ie/~joseph/windsurf/windsurf.html

Those curious about windsurfing—or more specifically, windsurfing in *Ireland*—will find answers to questions and links likely to satisfy. Equipment, association gossip, and sailing hot spots are featured topics.

Kitty Hawk Sports

http://www.khsports.com/khs/

This promotional page is the Web home of Kitty Hawk Sports. Features include information about windsurfing and kayaking, plus the company's guided tours, merchandise, and rentals.

The Maui Windsurfing Report

http://maui.net/~mauiwind/MWR/mwr.html

At the Maui Windsurfing Report, wind junkies will find Maui weather information, sailing reports, pictorials, and interviews with celebrity windsurfers. Links to shops and schools, as well as information about the Hawaiian island, also are provided.

Stig Johansen's Windsurfing Home Page

http://www.cs.uit.no/~stig/windsurfing.html

Windsurfing enthusiasts will enjoy this home page featuring links to a variety of information. Visit here to learn about the sport, find helpful tips, review travel information, and weather updates, and browse an index of windsurfing events around the world.

windsurfer.com

http://www.windsurfer.com/

If it's related to windsurfing, it's probably linked to this page. Commercial resources, travel information, weather forecasts, and regional guides are featured, along with location reviews, tips, and how-to guides. An online calculator to convert windspeeds, weights, and lengths also is provided.

Windsurfing Paradise

http://www.dvsystems.com/scruz

Complete information on windsurfing in the Santa Cruz, California area is offered at this site. Visitors will find details on local weather, surf shops, safety tips, and conditions at favorite surf sites.

The World-Wide Web Virtual Library: Windsurfing

http://wmi.cais.com/www/windsurf/index.html

The World-Wide Web Virtual Library hosts this page devoted to windsurfing. A large collection of windsurfing-related resources here includes magazines, associations, catalogs, and wind-condition pages.

WEIGHT LIFTING

Weight Training Page

http://www.cs.unc.edu/~kyle/weights.html

Weightlifting enthusiasts will enjoy this personal home page, featuring a variety of weight training and fitness resources. Visit here for links to professional and amateur associations, fitness clubs, nutrition publications, and more.

WRESTLING

Ivan Koloff Home Page

http://www.singnet.com.sg/~ckliew/first.html

Meet tough guy Ivan Koloff, a Russian-born professional wrestler called "The Russian Bear" who retired after 34 years. A Singapore fan supplies this collection of information about Koloff, including photos that depict all sides of his personality—which isn't always so tough.

Jerry Yang's Sumo Information Page

http://akebono.stanford.edu/users/jerry/sumo/

This Sumo wrestling site contains general information about the sport, tournament results, news items, and a picture gallery. Includes links to other Sumo sites and Japan-related servers.

The Mat

http://www.coe.uncc.edu:80/~jrlareau/

From The Mat, visitors can get a grip on the latest developments in collegiate, high school, and international wrestling. This site includes up-to-the-minute wrestling news, an e-mail directory, a newsgroup, and a discussion forum.

My Sumo Page

http://www.sfc.keio.ac.jp/~s93073no/
sumo.html

Like really big guys wearing very little clothes? Then you'll like this home page devoted to Sumo wrestling. Visitors can access images, match results, and other online sources of information about the sport from this personal Web page.

Sumo Images and Information

http://www.hal.com/~nathan/Sumo/

This is a collection of Web sites featuring images and information on the Japanese sport of Sumo wrestling. Visitors can link to sites containing news, photos, videos, and match results. Most sites are available in English and Japanese.

THE WORLD

THE 25 MOST POPULAR WORLD SITES

Asian Studies World Wide Web Virtual Library
http://coombs.anu.edu.au/
WWWVL-AsianStudies.html

Chinese-Language-Related Information Page
http://www.webcom.com/~bamboo/chinese/
chinese.html

City.Net's Countries and Territories Index
http://www.city.net/countries/

City.Net Search
http://www.city.net/search.html

The Computation and Language E-Print Archive
http://xxx.lanl.gov/cmp-lg/

Date and Time Gateway
http://www.bsdi.com/date

Dunya: CyberMuslim Information Collective
http://www.uoknor.edu:80/cybermuslim/

East Asian Libraries Cooperative World Wide Web
http://pears.lib.ohio-state.edu/

EFL (English as a Foreign Language) Web Home Page
http://www.u-net.com/eflweb/

The Gumbo Pages
http://www.webcom.com/~gumbo/
welcome.html

Hostels Europe
http://www.tardis.ed.ac.uk/~og/hostels.html

Indian Pueblo Cultural Center
http://hanksville.phast.umass.edu/defs/
independent/PCC/PCC.html

New York Subway Finder
http://www.krusch.com/nysf.html

Official California Legislative Information
http://www.leginfo.ca.gov/

Oriental Institute, University of Chicago
http://www-oi.uchicago.edu/OI/default.html

Timezone Converter
http://poisson.ecse.rpi.edu/cgi-bin/tzconvert

The Translator's Home Companion
http://www.rahul.net/lai/companion.html

UNESCO World Heritage List
http://www.cco.caltech.edu/~salmon/
world.heritage.html

US Gazetteer at University of Buffalo
http://wings.buffalo.edu/geogw/

Vietnam VietGATE
http://www.saigon.com/

Virtual Tourist—North America
http://www.vtourist.com/webmap/na.htm

Voodoo Information Pages
http://www.vmedia.com/shannon/voodoo/
voodoo.html

World Factbook Gopher Index by SunSITE
gopher://sunsite.unc.edu:70/7waissrc%3a/ref.d/
indexes.d/world-factbook.src

The World Wide Web Virtual Library: Latin America
http://www-oi.uchicago.edu/OI/default.html

Yucatan Gateway
http://www.netaxs.com/~jduncan/
Yucatan.html

CITIES, STATES, AND REGIONS

WORLD CITIES AND STATES

AFRICA

Cape Town

http://www.ctcc.gov.za/

Cape Town, South Africa presents its city and the surrounding region at this Web site. Browse through a collection of paintings, business information, and the latest area news. The page includes resources for tourists.

Cape Town Welcome

http://www.aztec.co.za/aztec/capetown.html

Cape Town, billed here as the "Fairest Cape," is famed for its stunning flower-strewn landscapes. Aztec, a local Internet service provider, hosts this site in the hope that potential tourists will find the brief descriptions of Cape Town's weather, landscape and hotspots alluring enough to check out both the city and Aztec's services.

ASIA

Gifu Prefecture

http://milky.info.gifu-u.ac.jp/places/gifu.html

Web surfers can take a cyber tour of Gifu Prefecture, located in the center of the Japanese archipelago. Take a virtual stroll through its districts, study traditional crafts or check a sightseeing calendar. In English.

Hong Kong: City.Net

http://www.city.net/countries/hong_kong/

City.Net offers a gloss of information about Hong Kong available through the Internet. Visitors can stop by to obtain city guides and maps or to check out educational, entertainment, and government resources in Hong Kong.

Hyogo Prefecture

http://www.kobe-u.ac.jp/hyogo/hyogo_index.html

Travel around the world to the Hyogo Prefecture in Japan for a glimpse of its arts, climate, and history. The page includes facts about the Akashi-Kaikyo Bridge and prefecture government.

Ibaraki, Japan

http://www.pref.ibaraki.jp/

Citizens living in the Ibaraki, Japan prefecture invite you to explore their home and see what's being offered for businesses moving to the area. Visitors can also learn about international exchange projects.

Internetwork Kyoto

http://www.kyoto-inet.or.jp/

The Kyoto, Okoshiyasu, home page features information about the Japanese city in both English and Japanese. Visitors and travelers can learn about local art, sightseeing, conventions, industry, and education. Links to city office information are also available.

Kanazawa, Japan

http://www.iia.or.jp/kanazawa/

Meet the mayor of Kanazawa, take a virtual tour of the Japanese city's sights and review its history. Find out what the Yowaku Hot Spring and Tentokuin Temple are like before visiting the city in real-time. In Japanese with some English.

Kato Lab

http://ks001.kj.utsunomiya-u.ac.jp/

The Kato Lab home page features information about the city of Utsunomiya, Japan, a Tochigi prefecture museum guide, and a link to the Kegon Net Web server. In Japanese and English.

Kyoto, Japan

http://www.kyoto-np.co.jp/

Get to know the city of Kyoto and glimpse its history through this home page for the Kyoto Shimbun. The local newspaper introduces the city and region, with pointers to interesting tourist destinations in the area. In Japanese and English.

Magnificent Madras

http://comlab1.ee.ufl.edu/~sriraj/madras.html

Travel to the Magnificent Madras home page to find a treasure trove of information about the southern Indian city. Travelers will find pictures and information about interesting places and excursions. Includes links to other Indian cities, international guides, and the Indian Home Page.

---

a2z EDITOR'S CHOICE

City.Net

http://www.city.net/

So where do you want to go today? With thousands of cities online, City.Net can probably get you there. This massive repository houses thousands of indices of countries, states and regions, and connects instantly to hot destinations like Tokyo and New York. The service digs up resources from arts and entertainment listings to government sites; from hotel guidebooks to local weather. Scale the lofty heights of San Francisco's Coit Tower and peer down at an amazing view. Or gawk at wacky travelers courtesy of the editors of Monk Magazine, the online/on-the-road zine that lends new meaning to the great American road trip. Whether you want to sip tequila on a beach in Cancun or navigate the maze of Prague's subway system, you're best bet is going to be City.Net.—*Reviewed by Joyce Slaton*

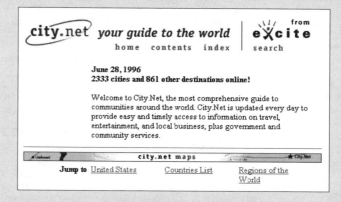

city.net *your guide to the world* | home contents index | from eXcite search

June 28, 1996
2333 cities and 861 other destinations online!

Welcome to City.Net, the most comprehensive guide to communities around the world. City.Net is updated every day to provide easy and timely access to information on travel, entertainment, and local business, plus government and community services.

city.net maps

Jump to United States   Countries List   Regions of the World

Singapore InfoMap

http://www.sg/

Visit this page for links to sites offering information about Singapore. Links are grouped by category and include media, arts and culture, sports and leisure, government, community, business, and finance.

Teleparc

http://teleparc.com/index.htm

Teleparc, an electronic magazine from Fujitsu, features articles on culture and entertainment in Tokyo. It also follows the latest news in the auto industry. Access to some areas requires registration and a password. In Japanese and English.

Toyama Prefecture

http://www.pref.toyama.jp/

The prefecture of Toyama on the western side of the Japanese home islands introduces its history, location, people, industry, education, culture, and nature. In Japanese and English.

World Wide Web Servers in Hong Kong

http://www.cuhk.hk/hkwww.html

The Chinese University of Hong Kong maintains this index to sites based in Hong Kong. Organized by subject, it includes links to government organizations, music and entertainment sites, commercial and academic sites, and news outlets.

AUSTRALIA AND OCEANIA

Spectrum Citycam

http://spectrum.com.au/citycam.html

See the sunrise or the night sky in Sydney, Australia without venturing from your workstation. Pictures taken through a Down Under living room window are posted every two hours. (If you want a view of the other side of the city, access a series of shots taken from the bedroom window.)

Sydney, Australia Olympics

http://www.sydney.olympic.org/

While the rest of the world focuses on Atlanta '96, Sydney 2000 is planning ahead. Visitors will be overwhelmed by the details available here on the 2000 Summer Olympics. Check out the elaborate environmental guidelines covering areas such as ozone depletion and waste management.

Victoria Guide

http://www.csu.edu.au/australia/vic/vic.html

If you're headed Down Under to southern Australia, and Victoria in particular, prep for your trip with a visit to this page. Here you can examine maps, climate data and weather forecasts, air and rail timetables, holidays, and fact sheets on the local government.

Wellington, New Zealand

http://www.wcc.govt.nz/

Visitors can find out all about the capital city of New Zealand at this site. Check out a plethora of information on tourism, community affairs, news, business, nightlife, and more.

Western Australia

http://www.csu.edu.au/australia/wa/wa.html

Charles Stuart University in Western Australia maintains this site for local information. Visit the Guide to Western Australia for government, business, travel, and computing resources.

EUROPE

Welcome to Bavaria

http://www.bayern.de/

Travelers and business people planning a visit to Bavaria will enjoy this profile of the German state. Includes news and information on tourism, economics, and trade relations.

Bavaria Alpine Net Guide

http://www.bavaria.com/

Look into the culture and businesses of the area around Munich, Germany, through the Bavaria Alpine Net Guide. It includes information about travel resources, entertainment, and sports. In English, German, and French.

Berlin

http://www.chemie.fu-berlin.de/adressen/berlin.html

The Berlin site includes the city's history and vital statistics in English, French, and German. Complete and concise, the site supplies hundreds of links to fill in any missing details for an excursion—mental or physical—into the historic German city.

Berlin Bear Home Page

http://www.berlin-bear.de/

This resource focuses on the cities of Berlin and Brandenburg. Includes listings for tourism, governmental services, entertainment, and business. In English and German.

Bern

http://www.vptt.ch/bern-page.html

From the Swiss Telecom site, this page treats browsers to a multimedia tour of Switzerland's political and diplomatic capital. Enjoy photos, maps, music, videos, and text.

Birmingham, UK: ASSIST Project

http://birmingham.gov.uk/

ASSIST, maintained by the University of Birmingham, is a service for both local and international communities that provides information about Birmingham and the surrounding area of central En-

gland. This page covers local attractions, municipal news, and business opportunities.

Brighton, England

http://www.pavilion.co.uk/vbrighton/

Pop into virtual Brighton and Hove, the South Coast, and Sussex, in England. They offer 24-hour tourist information, history, pubs, clubs, and a map. Fancy going to the cinema? The films are listed here. A Brighton screen saver is in the works.

Brussels, Belgium

http://pespmc1.vub.ac.be/BRUSSEL.html

Take a look at things to do and see in Brussels, Belgium, through this page from the Principia Cybernetica Web site. Visitors can read the text or follow a link to information about the Free University of Brussels. In English.

Cambridge Area Information

http://www.cam.ac.uk/CambArea/index.html

Where can you go in Cambridge, England to buy a book, see some paintings, or pay a parking ticket? Find out at the Cambridge Area Information page, where visitors can link to tourist and general information about the city.

Cambridge, England City Guide

http://www.cs.ucl.ac.uk/misc/uk/cambridge.html

The Department of Computer Science at University College in London, England, maintains this site for its Cambridge local resources index. Visitors can link to local merchants and organizations, browse an index of available Web servers, and take a virtual tour of pubs in the university town.

City.Net Paris Index

http://www.city.net/countries/france/paris/

City.Net packs this Web site with a wealth of information about the French capital. Visitors can peruse tons of Paris-related links here—from dining, entertainment and accomodations, to maps, photos, and subway navigators. In French, English, and Spanish.

Croatia and Bosnia-Herzegovina

http://www.helsinki.fi/~tervio/info.html

Browsers interested in the political and social climate of Croatia and Bosnia-Herzegovina can visit here for an exhaustive index of links to online resources, pertinent facts, and maps detailing vital demographic statistics. Among the external resources cataloged here are news sources, personal stories, and virtual city tours.

Data Wales Country Guide

http://www.data-wales.co.uk/

Data Wales maintains this site as a detailed guide to resources in the British principality. Visitors will find information on local tourism, business, and government resources. Includes links to general United Kingdom references.

Dortmund, Germany

http://www.dortmund.de/

This page offers an introduction to Dortmund, the seventh largest city in Germany. It provides a well-rounded look at the culture, business climate and activities of this 1,100-year-old community. Selections targeting the tourist are also available. In German and English.

Edinburgh—Scotland's Capital City

http://www.efr.hw.ac.uk/EDC/Edinburgh.html

The City of Edinburgh District Council maintains this site as an introduction to the Scottish city. Visit here for an official online tour, a list of famous residents, and an index of notable facts and figures. Links to the local and national tourist boards are also available here.

Electronic Mall Bodensee

http://www.bodan.net/

The Electronic Mall Bodensee (EMB), an open forum for electronic commerce in the region around the Lake of Constance (sandwiched in between Switzerland, Austria, and Germany), includes links to commercial, educational, and technological information. Browsers choose from English and German versions.

Helsinki

http://www.hel.fi/

The city of Helsinki comes to the Web in Finnish, Russian, and English. Visitors to the site can view a map of the city, look at a calendar of events, and check out the arts and cultural happenings.

Joensuu, Finland

http://www.jns.fi/

The city of Joensuu, Finland fills this Web page with information about its culture, travel, and tourism. Visitors can link to city maps as well as other Joensuu Internet sites. In Finnish and English.

Jyvaskyla City

http://www.jkl.fi/

The Jyvaskyla City page presents information on tourism in the region, the city's science park, and congresses. Includes links to museums, the university, water sports, and related Finnish resources. English and Finnish.

Kuopio

http://www.kuopio.fi/

Browsers can read about Kuopio, Finland's eighth largest city, download a photo, glean information about the urban hamlet, and learn about its growing market. In English and Finnish.

Ljubljana, Slovenia Guide

http://www.ijs.si/slo/ljubljana/

Slovenian research organization J. Stefan Institute provides information here on its home city of Ljubljana. Visitors will find transportation, sightseeing, and accommodations resources.

London Calling

http://www.london-calling.co.uk/

This hipster site (eponymously named for The Clash hit single) offers comprehensive travel and entertainment information about London and the United Kingdom. Readers can access in-depth travel articles, take an interactive tour, or avail themselves of online shopping opportunities.

The London Guide

http://www.cs.ucl.ac.uk/misc/uk/london.html

This unofficial guide to the British capital city offers links to hotel, entertainment, and travel resources. Includes links to information on other British culture, and tour and travel sites.

London Pubs

http://www.cs.ucl.ac.uk/misc/uk/london/pubs/index.html

Visitors to this site can almost smell the ale. London pubs are listed by area with information such as addresses, featured beers, and special attractions. Most pubs are graded on a one-to-four rating scale.

Lublin

http://www.umcs.lublin.pl/

This city home page for Lublin, Poland, provides information about the town, a city map, and descriptions of its seven local universities. Includes links to related sites of interest. In Polish and English.

Lutherstadt Wittenberg, Germany

http://www.wittenberg.de/

Information about the German city of Lutherstadt Wittenberg comes to life on the Web through this page—featuring photos and historical details about the city known as the birthplace of the Reformation. In German and English.

---

a2z EDITOR'S CHOICE

Hell Home Page

http://www.666hell.com/hell/

Welcome to Hell. Hell, Norway, that is; a small region in the icy land with a population of 352, including Miss Universe 1990. Rock along with Hell's Top 10 (yes, that includes "Sympathy for the Devil") or get straight-faced info on Hell's history, which dates back to 4000 B.C. Money burning a hole in your pocket? Blow it at the Hellmart, where a hunk of "666% solid rock" will set you back $36. This site will even tell you how to send postcards from Hell, postmarked and stamped by real Hellions. Before you leave, be sure to apply for a special credit card, which, according to the Webmasters, you can use to pay "the devil's dues." Truly the information highway to Hell, this page may have you making regular visits. Just tell 'em that the devil made you do it.—*Reviewed by Joyce Slaton*

928 THE WORLD

Monaco
http://www.monaco.mc/
The first things that come to mind when many people think of Monaco are Grand Prix auto racing and Princess Grace. Both are represented here, along with businesses, tourist information, Internet services, and more.

Nîmes Guided Tour
http://www.eerie.fr/Nimes/Nimes.html
As you know, there's more to France than Paris. The School of Engineering and Research in Computer Science invites you to take a guided tour of Nîmes. Learn the history and look at the ancient artifacts preserved in this city known as the "French Roma."

Oleane, Opérateur Internet
http://www.oleane.net/
This is the official Web site for the city of Orleans, France. Visitors will find information on business, culture, and regional events. In French.

Oxford
http://www.cs.ucl.ac.uk/misc/uk/oxford.html
Anglophiles will enjoy this site, which contains photos and tourist information for the English city of Oxford: "how to get there, how to leave, and what to do in between."

Paris Links
http://www.paris.org/Links/
Got a passion for Paris? Satisfy it with this generous offering of pointers that lead the way to a siteseeing Web tour of the capital city and surrounding French countryside. Find it all (or a lot of it, anyway), from art to transportation services, and most everything in between.

The Paris Page E-Mail
http://www.paris.org.:80/Mailparis/
The Paris Page provides listings for the French city's art and cultural events. Send e-mail to the maintainers of the information service using the electronic form offered at this site.

Les Pages de Paris/The Paris Pages
http://www.paris.org/
Whether you're planning a real or virtual trip to the French capital, you'll enjoy a visit to the Paris Pages. "Clique" here for information and graphics covering tourism, entertainment, cultural exhibits, shopping, and many other Parisian resources. In French and English.

Paris Pages: Richard Erickson's Paris Journal
http://www.paris.org/Ric/
This electronic editors of the Paris Pages, a nonprofit French information project, have dispatched freelance correspondent Richard Erickson to cover the city. His collection of eclectic features will make nonresident Francophiles yearn for plane tickets.

Les Pays de Grasse
http://www.aaacom.com/pdg/
Explore the French Riviera via this site, which offers 100 ideas for discovering "Le Pays De Grasse." Visitors will find suggestions for accomodations, sporting activities, and touring opportunities here. In French and English.

Les Pays de Savoie
http://lapphp0.in2p3.fr/maps/pays/pays.html
Visitors to this page will find the Web server for Pays de Savoie, a region in the French Alps. Photos, maps, tourist and sports information, and links to the home pages of the towns in the area are featured. In French and English.

Salzburg State Board of Tourism
http://www.tcs.co.at/other.html
This tourism page provides potential travelers with information about Salzburg, Austria. Visitors can access information about activities and check out events listings or the local countryside. Includes a link to the home page of the Austrian National Tourist Office.

Salzburg Tourism Information
http://www.tcs.co.at/fvp.html
The Salzburg State Board of Tourism offers this online guide to holidays in Salzburg, Austria. Peruse a wealth of information on sports, accomodations, news, and more.

Stockholm Public Transit
http://www.sunet.se/stockholm/SL/SL.html
If you're sitting in your office in London or Seattle, you won't care about the Stockholm subway system. If you're a student in Stockholm, however, you will want to visit this site to see which train to take to go from the university to the Grand Hotel and just about anywhere else in Stockholm.

St. Petersburg Times
http://www.spb.su/times/index.html
"The St. Petersburg Press" is the Web version of the Russian city's English-language weekly newspaper. This site includes the current issue, back issue archives, culture and lifestyle guides, and information about print subscriptions and mirror sites.

St. Petersburg Web
http://www.spb.su/index.html
The historic Russian city of St. Petersburg provides a virtual welcome at this page, where you can browse a newsstand, stroll through a gallery of photos and cartoons, check out accommodations, and investigate business opportunities. In English.

Trier
http://www.uni-trier.de/trier/trier_eng.html
Germany's oldest city is explored here, including its colorful history and a number of map and image files. Visitors can view Roman ruins in the area, like the Porta Nigra and the Amphitheatre. In German and English.

Tampere, Finland Guide
http://www.tpo.fi/english/tampere/index.html
TPO, Tampere, Finland's telephone company, maintains this site as a guide to its home city. Visitors will find information on Tampere's commerce, government, education, and tourism sectors.

Tampereen Kaupunki
http://www.tampere.fi/
The city of Tampere and the Tampere region of Finland welcome visitors to its home page. Information about the area and its university are provided, as are links to topic-related sites. In Finnish and English.

Torino, Italy
http://www.comune.torino.it/
This northwestern Italian city serves up a site chock full of historical and current information. Includes cultural events listings and notes on a research and development park for environmental technology organizations. In English and Italian.

Turun Kaupunki
http://www.tku.fi/
The home page for the city of Turku, Finland, provides a calendar of current events, tourist resources, and a wealth of information about schools and health services. In Finnish, Swedish, English, German, and Greek.

Vienna City
http://www.atnet.co.at/Tourism/Vienna/
Take a virtual trip to the Austrian capital of Vienna. This site includes historical information on the city, as well as details on sightseeing, events, accommodations, restaurants, and transportation.

Vienna: City.Net
http://www.city.net/countries/austria/vienna/
City.Net provides a guide to online resources in Vienna, Austria. Includes pointers to everything from arts and entertainment to government pages, maps and transportation. Visitors can also utilize a search tool for finding specific information.

Virtual Manchester
http://www.manchester.com/
The sights, sounds and shopping of the city of Manchester, England, are among the features offered here. Resources from and about Manchester include businesses, education, events, hotels, maps, music, organizations, sports, and media.

Zagreb

http://tjev.tel.etf.hr/hrvatska/HRgradovi/
Zagreb/Zagreb.html

Zagreb, the capital city of the Republic of Croatia, serves as the focus of this page featuring maps, photos, historical accounts, and descriptive text. Visit museums and galleries, the Zagreb Cathedral, and the Croatian National Theatre.

Zurich Guide

http://www.zurich.ch/

This online guide to Zurich, Switzerland, features tourist information and an interactive map of places of interest. Browsers can take a look at Zurich by night, or read about the events of the month. In English and German.

NORTH AMERICA

ABAG Homepage

http://www.abag.ca.gov/

The governments of the communities surrounding California's San Francisco Bay have formed a collaborative information service called Access to Bay Area Governments Online (ABAG Online). A key to transit schedules, earthquake information, and local government news, ABAG Online covers these and other items of regional interest.

Alabama Department of Archives and History Home Page

http://sgisrvr.asc.edu/archives/agis.html

The encyclopedic Alabama Department of Archives and History page keeps the Camellia State online with reference services, museum tours, the state history, genealogy links, publications, and a state agency directory.

Alabama World Wide Web Server Map

http://www.eng.auburn.edu/alabama/map.html

This clickable maps allows visitors to locate all the World Wide Web servers in Alabama. Additionally, some sites include local and business information.

Alaska Official Home Page

http://www.state.ak.us/

At Alaska's official Web site, visitors can search for information from state agencies, find out what's new in Alaska and access a Frequently Asked Questions (FAQ) file.

The Alaskan Center

http://alaskan.com/

The Alaskan Center highlights information about America's largest state, along with Alaskan adventures and the Alaskan Mall. Visitors can check a calendar of events throughout the state as well as read about travel and tourist information.

Alaskan Independence Party

http://www.polarnet.fnsb.ak.us/End_of_Road/
soapbox.dir/aip.dir/

Should Alaska be a state, a territory, or a sovereign nation? Although it seems that debate is long over, Joe Vogler and the Alaskan Independence Party offer their spin on the topic through this page.

Alberta Advantage

http://www.gov.ab.ca/

The Canadian regional government welcomes visitors to Alberta here. Get the official version of events in this government-produced travel brochure/political guide to the Canadian province.

Alberta WWW Server Index

http://www.tcel.com/albertawww/index.html

The Alberta WWW server index lists many of the WWW servers in Alberta. It also contains an index to business, government, tourism, education, and other Alberta resources on the Internet. Includes a form to submit server information for indexing.

Ann Arbor, Michigan (U.S.A.)

http://http2.sils.umich.edu/AnnArbor/
AnnArbor.html

This unofficial Ann Arbor page gives visitors a friendly look at the Great Lakes city and the University of Michigan's campuses. The author of this page also contributes a little information about himself, as well as the technologies he used to create the site.

Ann Arbor, Michigan, USA

http://ann-arbor.com/

This info-Web serving Ann Arbor, provides a guide to the area and its resources. Links lead to the Chamber of Commerce, the University of Michigan, commercial and industrial sites, cultural venues, and other interesting spots.

Arizona Central

http://www.azcentral.com/

Planning on visiting Arizona? Before you go, drop by Arizona Central, where visitors can find out where to eat, shop, play, and stay in the state, as well as some Arizona facts and history.

Arizona: City.Net

http://www.city.net/countries/united_states/
arizona/

City.Net is an online guide to travel, entertainment, business, and government information for communities around the world. Visit this site for its Arizona index, featuring a keyword search and indices to a variety of local resources from the Southwest American state.

Arizona Destinations World Wide Web Server

http://www.amdest.com/

The Arizona Internet Yellow Pages connects visitors with attractions, services, and an online shopping mall. This large document includes links to Arizona Kids Net, photo galleries, and much more.

Arizona State Parks

http://www.pr.state.az.us/

The Arizona State Parks' World Wide Web site takes visitors through virtual tours of the Southwestern state's 24 natural, cultural, and recreational parks. Includes information about the park service's gift shops, featuring a different retailer each month.

Arlington, Texas

http://www.arlington.org/

Get the lowdown on Arlington at this official gateway. Users will find visitor and tourist information about the city, as well as a quarterly newsletter and contact information for local businesses.

Atlanta Conventions & Visitors Bureau

http://www.acvb.com/

Atlanta's Convention & Visitors Bureau Web provides general information about the region, along with regular updates of Olympic news and a complete calendar of upcoming city events.

Atlanta Web Guide Home Page

http://www.webguide.com/

This site hosts a virtual tour of Atlanta and provides an overview of happenings, restaurants and cultural highlights in the Georgia city. Included here are pictures, maps and a guide to Georgia colleges and universities.

Atlanta: City.Net

http://www.city.net/countries/united_states/
georgia/atlanta/

The City.Net Atlanta, Georgia, USA page furnishes browsers with a directory of informational sites about this city. The page offers a full menu of art, entertainment, city guides, community organizations, and events, as well as links to the logistics of visiting Atlanta.

Atlantic Canada Opportunities Agency

http://www.acoa.ca/

The Atlantic Canada Opportunities Agency's aim is to give a boost to the economy of Atlantic Canadian communities like Newfoundland and Nova Scotia by encouraging business growth. Read some O.C.O.A. success stories here and learn more on what the agency does.

Austin City Connection

http://www.ci.austin.tx.us/

The City of Austin, Texas, maintains this site to connect users to business, government and public information. Visit the City Connection for business news, city services, public safety services, and educational resources.

Austin Information Center

http://www.tech.net/austin/

TECH.NET's Austin Information Center contains facts about the Texas city, ranging from public service listings to links for businesses in the region. Prospective visitors can check the Austin Dining Guide.

Austin MAIN Community Pages

http://www.main.org/

The Metropolitan Austin Interactive Network presents community information about the Austin, Texas area. Includes law, medicine, education, performing arts, social services, science, and government resources.

Bay Area Transit Information

http://server.berkeley.edu/Transit/index.html

Northern California residents can find help getting around without a car at the San Francisco Bay Area Transit Information site. Link to over 20 transit agencies to access route maps, fare structures, and schedules.

Bellingham Chamber of Commerce

http://www.pacificrim.net/~chamber/

Bellingham, Washington is located on the Northwest coast's scene Puget Sound, near Seattle. Visitors to this site will find information on local business, culture, and events.

The Berkshire Connection

http://berkcon.com/

Information about Massachusetts' Berkshire County is provided here for tourists and residents alike. Events listings, feature articles and lists of local services, attractions, and accommodations can be found here—along with a link to the Berkshire Visitors' Bureau.

The Big Easy

http://www.big-easy.com/

New Orleans is more than just Mardi Gras, and you can find out more about the city's culture, music, and geography right here. (Plenty of poop on the bacchanalian revelry that is Fat Tuesday, too.)

Big Island of Hawaii—Moon Publications

http://www.book.uci.edu/Books/Moon/moon.html

The Big Island of Hawaii is a hypertext travel guide leading tourists on a cyberpath through the history, culture, and landscape of the Big Island. Find text, maps, photos, and audio files.

Blacksburg Electronic Village

http://crusher.bev.net/index.html

Devoted to the city of Blacksburg, Virginia, this site offers visitors a look at the city's history and photo album. Also find links to the village mall, community news and events, education and health care centers, government offices, the library, and more.

Block Island

http://www.ids.net/flybi/

Make a virtual visit to New England at the Block Island and More page from Rhode Island. Users can learn about the area and its businesses, religious services, weather, and real estate.

Boca Raton

http://bocaraton.com/

Get a business-oriented view of a Florida city at the Boca Raton Home Page. The Greater Boca Raton Chamber of Commerce sponsors this look at the companies and industries that drive this coastal Florida community.

Boston Area Map of WWW Resources

http://donald.phast.umass.edu/misc/boston.shtml

The Boston Area Map of World Wide Web Resources contains an interactive map showing the locations of servers in the Boston area. Includes commercial, government, educational, tourist, and entertainment sites.

Boston: City.Net

http://www.city.net/countries/united_states/massachusetts/boston/

This CityNet guide features the city of Boston with its abundant entertainment, tourist, and arts resources. Includes links to city services, government, online guide books, museums, and other visitor information.

Boston Online

http://ftp.std.com/NE/boston.html

Boston Online boasts a treasure trove of links to electronic resources from and about the capital of the Commonwealth of Massachusetts. From commercial to cultural to educational sites, this list of pointers serves as a virtual tour of the historic city's online offerings.

Boston.Com Welcome Page

http://www.boston.com

Visit this site for information on all things Boston. Areas covered include the media, arts, sports, real estate, and employment opportunities. Highlights include the "Globe" Business Forum and links to popular radio stations.

The Birmingham Web Project

http://www.the-matrix.com/

Visitors to the Birmingham Web will find listings of events, attractions, schools, governments, churches, sports, and more from the Alabama city. Links to new or updated pages are featured, as is information on the Birmingham Web Project.

Branson Net

http://www.branson.net/

BransonNet—an information server for the Branson, Missouri area—provides details on and access to local attractions. Visitors will learn about Branson's business, government, and popular entertainment resources here.

British Columbia Government

http://www.gov.bc.ca/

The government of British Columbia provides this general information site for residents and tourists. Visitors will find such feature items as legislative and constituency information, links to government ministries and organizations, and a tourism guide.

British Columbia Ministry of Small Business, Tourism, and Culture

http://www.tbc.gov.bc.ca/

The British Colombia Ministry of Small Business, Tourism, and Culture provides easy access to Internet sites regarding the territory, its government, and its people. Includes tourism information, examination of aboriginal issues, and small business startup information.

B.C. Tourism

http://www.tbc.gov.bc.ca/tourism/tourismhome.html

Tourism information for British Columbia makes its home here. Visitors can click through an interactive map that leads to tourist information on the area, check current and extended weather forecasts, or take a look at downloadable video clips.

British Columbia Yellow Pages

http://www.bcyellow.com/

Let your mouse do the walking at this searchable directory of British Columbia business sites. Includes news, weather, and traffic updates for info-junkies; stock quotes and lottery results should satiate the money-minded masses. Classifieds list cars, jobs, personals, and more.

Bryan/College Station, Texas

http://www.ipt.com/

This Bryan/College Station "virtual community" provides commercial, organizational, and city government listings. Classified ads, a local weather report, a community calendar, and an entertainment guide all can be found at this Web site. Also here: a visitors guide to the area, designed for virtual tourists.

Buffalo Free-Net
http://freenet.buffalo.edu/

The Buffalo Free-Net is an Internet community information service for western New York state. Includes links to governmental, cultural, professional, business, social, and educational information centers.

California (Planet Earth)
http://www.nosc.mil/planet_earth/california.html

Planet Earth provides this home page with a vast range of information about California. Resources available here include the Super Bowl pages, an index of state servers, and pointers to government pages. Browsers can also link to pages dedicated to other cities and countries around the globe.

California: City.Net
http://www.city.net/countries/united_states/california/

The City.Net information service maintains this page as its California resource index. Visitors will find links to state, regional and local organizations, government and educational listings, tourist information, and much more.

California State Home Page
http://www.ca.gov/

The State of California's official home page offers a variety of information on doing business in the Golden State, employment opportunities, travel tips, and a guide to official agencies and legislation. Pointers to a variety of helpful statewide indexes, including area Internet providers.

California World Wide Web Servers
http://www.calif.com/ca/servers.html

Here's the California segment of the W3 Consortium's list of Web servers. It features maps, academic organizations, commercial entities, and general information about the state. Includes a search engine.

California Yellow Pages
http://www.research.digital.com/SRC/virtual-tourist/CaliforniaYP.html

The California Yellow Pages feature hundreds of businesses, media outlets, and tourist organizations accessible by topic. Visitors can submit additions or corrections to the Webmaster.

Cambridge and Boston Activities
http://web.mit.edu/outandabout.html

This index of activities comes from the Massachusetts Institute of Technology (MIT). It includes campus activities such as club events, arts and sports, as well as guides to happenings in Cambridge, Boston, and New England. There's also a subway map.

Cape Cod Information Center
http://www.allcapecod.com/

The Cape Cod Information Center, sponsored by Maxm Consulting, is an information resource for residents of and visitors to the Cape Cod area of Massachusetts. Check out the daily updates on public service and community announcements, or link to a multitude of Cape-related links.

Carmel.Net
http://www.carmelnet.com/

Visitors will find a collection of Carmel-based businesses here. The California seaside town caters to high tastes; visitors here will find businesses that include Gallery 21, Laguna Seca Raceway, Wings America, Indian Creek Ranch, and the La Boheme Restaurant. Carmel Internet also provides information about its Web marketing services here.

Centre Square
http://www.csquare.com/

People looking for local services on the Internet should plan a stop at Centre Square. Select your city or locality to find an extensive index of local commercial, community, and education resources. Currently this service is only available for Pennsylvania.

Carmel-by-the-Sea Home Page
http://www.carmelnet.com/bythec/

The Carmel-by-the-Sea, California home page features information about the city for travelers and tourists, including events, restaurants, and wineries. There also local government and community information and resources.

The CedarNet Community
http://www.cedarnet.org/

Iowans in the Cedar Valley area can stay abreast of community events here. The page includes information on local arts, the farmers' market and local government.

Charlotte
http://www.hickory.nc.us/ncnetworks/clt-intr.html

If this site on the city of Charlotte, North Carolina doesn't have enough information for you, you can always send a message to get some more. Included here are a map and calendar of events, details on art, culture, history, and information on shopping, lodging, and dining.

Charlottesville and Albemarle, Virginia
http://www.virginia.edu/cville.html

The University of Virginia maintains this site with information about the cities of Charlottesville and Albemarle as well as the State of Virginia. Links include Central Virginia's Free-Net, the Commonwealth of Virginia NetServer, Albemarle County Schools, public radio station pages, and local government sites.

Charlottesville Online
http://atlantic.evsc.virginia.edu/julia/cville.html

Charlottesville Online has general information about the Virginia City. This page includes links to Monticello Avenue, a page with information about property taxes, neighborhoods, and the police department. Other links include a "virtual walking tour" of Charlottesville, a Virginia atlas, Amtrack schedules, and the local weather.

Charm Net Baltimore Page
http://www.baltimore.com/

Baltimore calls itself "Charm City," and the Web page dedicated to this Maryland community is a charming collection of links to businesses, sports teams, congressional offices, a local television show, the state lottery, and tourist information.

Chebucto Community Net Home Page
http://cfn.cs.dal.ca/

The Chebucto Community Net of Canada contains information on culture, education, government, and recreation in metropolitan Halifax, Nova Scotia. Includes links to business, environmental issues, professional offices, and technological enterprises.

Chicago—Sunnysite
http://www.mcs.net/~tgermann/site2.html

Sunnysite is a collection of Web exploration resources considerably compiled by advertising designer and systems administrator, Todd German. This portion of Sunnysite dishes up a blossoming guide to resources in the Chicago area. Here guests can peruse a vast array of links, spanning the spectrum from arts and commercial services, to publications, technology, and city guides.

Chicago!
http://www.tezcat.com/web/chicago.html

Check out the Chicago skyline or look up information about entertainment and other interests through the Chicago! Web page. The site, provided by Internet consulting agency Tezcat Communications, includes an index of general information about the city, as well as Web-related highlights.

Chicago Home Page
http://www.webcore.com:80/chicago/

Need to know how to get to Comiskey Park to see the White Sox play? Chicago's Home Page can help you do that and answer many other visitor-related queries. Links to dining, lodging, and spectator events are provided.

Chicago Information System
http://reagan.eecs.uic.edu/

The Chicago Information System provides detailed statistics and information on the city here. Visitors will find complete demographic data on the Windy City, as well as information on events, tourism, transportation, schools, and government.

Chicago Mosaic
http://www.ci.chi.il.us/
This well-rounded page offers an electronic guided tour of the Windy City, information about urban services, and the police department (an important contact for any urban dweller or traveler). Even a profile of the mayor is included.

Chicago World Wide Web Server
http://www.cs.uchicago.edu/vt/chicago.html
Sponsored by the Illinois Virtual Tourist, this page highlighting Chicago offers an extensive index of Web servers throughout the metro area. It also provides pointers to the Chicago home page, a Virtual Tourist world map, maps of North America and the state of Illinois, and a guide to the Chicago suburbs.

Chicago!
http://www.uchicago.edu/chicago.html
This is a community and information service for the city of Chicago. Visitors will find transportation schedules, cultural events, movie times, government information, and more.

City of Cambridge, Massachusetts
http://www.ci.cambridge.ma.us/
A wealth of useful governmental, recreational, and educational information about the city of Cambridge can be found here. Includes links to federal and state government resources and to City.Net, a listing of international cities' Web sites.

City of Halifax Home Page
http://www.ccn.cs.dal.ca/Government/HfxCity/HalifaxHome.html
Halifax, the capital city of Nova Scotia on Canada's Atlantic coast, posts a virtual city hall on the World Wide Web, with a community profile, business profile, lists of neighbors, weather, and links to the real-time city hall.

City of South San Francisco
http://www.ci.ssf.ca.us
The official home page of the city of South San Francisco, California has sections for the police department (including a mission statement and access to public records), and much more official information on the area.

Clear Lake, Texas, Information
http://www.crl.com/~akmathes/clearlake.html
The community of Clear Lake has compiled an index of general information for those visiting this site, including links to area churches, public schools, and marinas.

Cleveland, Ohio
http://www.cleveland.oh.us/
Goings-on in the city of Cleveland take center stage on this site. It features highlights of shows at such places as the Cleveland Museum of Natural History and the Rock and Roll Hall of Fame. Visitors will also find government information.

Cleveland.Net
http://www.cleveland.net/cleveland/
An electronic information guide to the city of Cleveland is presented at this site. Visitors can choose from news, entertainment, dining, business, and lifestyle subjects.

Colorado: City.Net
http://www.city.net/countries/united_states/colorado/
Here is your guide to "colorful" Colorado from City.Net, a page that will take you to specific cities, counties, education, and all the activities in this outdoor playground. State government is also part of the offering along with weather information.

Colorado's Home Page
http://www.state.co.us/
The Centennial State invites visitors to discover Colorado—from the capital building in Denver to the remotest valley in the Rocky Mountain Range. Information is organized in categories which include education, government, groups, and organizations. A tourism guide is also at hand.

Columbia River Gorge
http://www.gorge.net/
This page contains comprehensive information on Columbia River Gorge businesses, communities, government agencies, and recreational activities. Includes an event calendar, historical information, maps, and links to area Web servers.

Columbus, Ohio
http://www.columbuspages.com/
Visit lovely Columbus or take a peek at Columbus resources here, with information from Columbus businesses, community organizations, and other groups.

Concord, Massachusetts
http://www.concordma.com/
Concord Webworks, Inc., hosts this page about the fair city of Concord. The community boasts a rich history and a wealth of resources for today's visitors and residents, providing links to all facets of life, government, and education.

Connecticut Interactive Map
http://www.cs.yale.edu/HTML/YALE/MAPS/connecticut.html
Virtual visitors to the State of Connecticut can locate tourism information and related Internet resources at this site. In addition to the "Virtual Connecticut Map" find tourist agency phone numbers, links to local Internet service providers, gopher servers, and more.

The Connecticut Library Home Page
http://www.scsu-cs.ctstateu.edu/lib/ct_library.html
If you are planning a trip to Connecticut, check out this clickable map and tourism guide sponsored by the Connecticut Library Home page. The page is dedicated to providing an educational and entertaining introduction to the Constitution State.

Connecticut State Information
http://www.state.ct.us/
The Connecticut State Information Server links interested parties to the state's university system and library, in addition to offering economic, educational, governmental, and recreational information. Visitors can access vacation guides and the state's social service agencies as well.

Connecticut, USA
http://www.connecticut.com/
The Connecticut, USA page is chock full of local and statewide resources, including skiing conditions, business directories and tourist information. Take virtual tours of the state's major cities, or experience 3-D views of Hartford using Quick-Time VR.

County of San Bernardino
http://www.co.san-bernardino.ca.us/
Access history, demographics and maps of San Bernardino County, California. Also find information on county services, government agencies, and local elections, as well as special events.

Crested Butte Online
http://www.cbinteractive.com/cbws/index.html
This is a community home page for the city of Crested Butte, Colorado. Visitors will find information on local culture, business, government, education, skiing, news, and more.

Dallas CityView
http://www.cityview.com/dallas/
New Path Media hosts this comprehensive guide to Dallas, Texas. A variety of local resources are available, including information on dining, accomodations, weather, entertainment, real estate, shopping, and sports.

Dallas Entertainment Guide
http://www.wn.com/dallas/
Visit this site for a Texas-sized online guide to Dallas. The page links to hundreds of local sites, including events calendars, restaurants, hotels, and shopping districts. Links to Dallas-based businesses and organizations are also available.

Dane County, Wisconsin
http://danenet.wicip.org/
Provided as a public service from Dane County in Wisconsin, DANEnet connects Dane County residents to the Net and to community information.

Find out about DANEnet's Net access program, available for a nominal fee, or link to information on Dane County government, education, and events.

Davis Community Network Welcome Page

http://www.dcn.davis.ca.us/

The Davis Community Network, a collection of online resources, offers visitors a variety of government, business, and community information about this northern California city.

Delaware WWW Map

http://www.udel.edu/delaware/map.html

The Delaware Interactive Map, maintained by the University of Delaware, provides easy access to local resources. Click anywhere on the map to link to government, business, and tourism information from that area.

Delaware State Page

http://www.state.de.us/

The home page for the State of Delaware features comprehensive information on tourism, government, economic development, and education. Fast facts are provided, as are links to numerous Delaware-related Web sites.

Denver Chamber of Commerce Home Page

http://www.aescon.com/denver/index.htm

The Information Store isn't selling you a bill of goods—the straight dope on the Denver metropolitan area is here, with publications that specialize in relocation, employment, and demographics. Potential Denver-bound emigrants can also find advice and money-saving specials to help with their move.

Des Moines, Iowa

http://www.dsmnet.com/

Take a virtual trip to Des Moines. Here you can find information on the city, a calendar of events, local weather, sports teams and businesses. There also is a directory of Iowa Web servers.

Discover Arizona State Parks

http://www.webcom.com/~borchers/azparks.html

Tour Arizona's state-owned natural resources at this Web site. Potential state visitors can find links to historical, educational and recreational facilities, and outdoorsy retreats here. Includes a clickable map of park locations.

Discover Long Island

http://www.webscope.com/li/info.html

Internet service provider WebScope maintains this site as a guide to Long Island, New York. Includes links to local commerce organizations, recreational activities, points of interest, transportation and ex-cursion tour companies, and other local service companies.

Discover Key West

http://discover.key-west.fl.us/

Global Audience Providers, Inc. maintains this site for its index of Key West, Florida tourism resources. Visitors will find extensive information on local accommodations, travel, sport, and recreation activities.

East Maui Watershed Management and Research

http://ice.ucdavis.edu/~robyn/eastmaui.html

The East Maui watershed is the largest source of surface water in Hawaii; one-third of the state's rare species live on the island and some of the most intact native forests are found there. The home page of the watershed partnership working to protect it provides geological maps, photos, descriptions of research, and historic information on the area.

El Paso, Texas Travel Guide

http://cs.utep.edu/elpaso/main.html

The University of Texas at El Paso maintains this site to introduce the history and culture of its local community. Visitors will also find information on tourism, travel, dining, and accomodations in the "Sun City."

Emerald Web—Seattle, Washington

http://www.cyberspace.com/bobk/

The Emerald Web is a collection of sites devoted to the city of Seattle and the Puget Sound region. Visitors will find sections on business, government, technology, people, recreation, and more.

ErieNet

http://www.erie.net

ErieNet provides information on the city's business climate, educational facilities, news, and entertainment. Includes links to other Pennsylvania resources, virtual malls, and personal pages.

Eugene Free Community Network

http://www.efn.org/

Oregon Public Networking, "using advanced technology to build an informed democratic community," maintains this site for its index of Eugene, Oregon-based resources. Visitors will find an extensive collection of links—including community events, local businesses and Web search tools.

Eugene, Oregon

http://www.ci.eugene.or.us/

The city of Eugene maintains this site to provide tourist, cultural, and business information about the state's second largest city. Visit to learn about Eugene's government organizations, major investors, recreational events, and more. A City.Net site.

The Express Systems Needle Cam

http://www.express-systems.com/expsys/needlecam/spacendl.htm

The Needle Cam provides a view from Seattle's Space Needle that is updated every minute. The site also contains a detailed description and history of the Space Needle.

Flagstaff, Arizona

http://usacitylink.com//flagstaf/default.html

Welcome to sunny Flagstaff, where high elevation, pleasant climate, and rich Native American history has won many fans. Find out what to do, where to eat, where to stay, and even more stuff on Flagstaff.

Florida: City.Net Index

http://www.city.net/countries/united_states/florida/

This site is packed with information on the Florida cities, counties, islands, and regions. A wide variety of links to state business, government, education, and tourism resources are also available.

Florida Communities Network

http://www.state.fl.us/fcn/lite/

The Florida Communities Network is a shared resource network for Florida communities. Individual sites statewide can be accessed through a series of image maps. Included are trade associations, economic-development organizations, chambers of commerce, and more. This site also has information about FCN's mission, services and projects.

Florida Facts and History

http://www.dos.state.fl.us/flafacts/

The Florida Facts and History page serves as a reference point for those seeking information about the State of Florida. Topics here include history, state symbols, and name origins.

Fort Myers

http://www.coconet.com/fortmyers/info.html

The Greater Fort Myers Chamber of Commerce provides information about the Florida city here. A wealth of information related to "The City of Palms" is available—from accomodations and restaurants listings, to fine arts and real estate.

Fort Lauderdale

http://ft-lauderdale.info-access.com/

The city of Fort Lauderdale, long known for spring break partying and stunning beaches, comes to the Web through its Information Access home page. The site serves as an online town center for the community, and visitors to the page will find links to local businesses, as well as children's resources.

Gainesville, Florida

http://www.cis.ufl.edu/cis/grad/
gainesville.html

If you're interested in Gainesville, either as a traveler or prospective student at the University of Florida or other school, then you'll want to visit this site for general information about the city, its history, and surrounding area.

Geographic Nameserver

http://www.mit.edu:8001/geo/

The Massachusetts Institute of Technology maintains this site for keyword searches of its North American geography database. Visit here to find vital statistics on American cities, including latitude and longitude, elevation, zip codes, and more.

Gold Canyon

http://www.goldcanyon.com/

Here visitors can read the history of Gold Canyon, located in Arizona southwest of the Superstition Mountains. This site also tells how to survive in the desert, provides local images, and gives details on trails and other area attractions.

Great Outdoor Recreation Page Oregon Index

http://www.gorp.com/gorp/location/or/or.htm

The Great Outdoor Recreation Pages service maintains this site for its index of Oregon recreation resources. Visitors will find an extensive collection of links to state parks, travel packages, sport equipment retailers, outdoor clubs, health tips, and more.

Greater Minneapolis Convention and Visitors Association

http://www.minneapolis.org/

The Greater Minneapolis Convention and Visitors Association hopes the bait in this trap will lure visitors (especially convention-goers) to the "City of a Thousand Lakes." Learn a bit about Minneapolis and visiting the area here.

The Gumbo Pages

http://www.gumbopages.com/index.html/

The Gumbo Pages focus on life in New Orleans and Acadiana (Cajun country). Among the offerings are recipes, tourist information, and musical information—including an Uncle Tupelo home page.

H4, Hawaii's Data Superhighway

http://www.hotspots.hawaii.com/

With a hearty "Aloha!" H4 welcomes visitors to this site absolutely packed with Hawaiian links. Brought to the Web by a self-confessed Hawaiianophile with a predilection for radio, the site's main draw are the many RealAudio files of Hawaiian music, news, and even comedy routines from the Aloha State. Links to commercial sites, Hawaii news, and weather reports round out the site.

Hampton Roads, Virginia

http://www.abel-info.com/regguide/

Visit Hampton Roads, the Virginia harbor where the Newport News shipbuilders and the Norfolk Navy base share water space. This resource for newcomers, tourists, and locals includes information on area history, museums, outdoor recreation, and the local business climate. Visitors will find lots of maps, demographics, and a searchable index of area resources.

Hanover

http://www.valley.net/~hanover/

The city of Hanover, New Hampshire makes its home on this Web site featuring a calendar of upcoming civic meetings, a look at local programs, and links to town offices, the police, and the fire department. Also find access to the local libraries, the Chamber of Commerce, and more.

Hawaii: City.Net

http://www.city.net/countries/united_states/
hawaii/

What state other than Texas was a nation before it joined the U.S.? Where can six distinct regions be found within one state? Find answers to these and other questions on this page exploring the Hawaiian islands' culture and language, government, education, sports, recreation, and more.

Hawaii Visitor Bureau

http://www.visit.hawaii.org/

The Hawaii Visitors Bureau invites users to discover the state's tropical paradise at this site. In addition to information about accomodations and local activities, a vacation contest entry is provided. In English and Japanese.

Howard County WebColumbia

http://catalog.com/columbia/

WebColumbia puts Maryland's Howard County online. Access community news and information including entertainment, business, and calendar listings.

Houston Metropolitan Page

http://www2.utsi.com/metro/index.html

Visit virtual Houston. Find links to Web sites from across the metro area grouped by topic and listed alphabetically. Arts, business, education, government, and sports only highlight the list of categories covered.

Houston Real-Time Traffic Report

http://herman.tamu.edu/traffic.html

Don't leave your house or office before you check this Houston Real-Time Traffic Report. The map of surrounding freeways will let you know which routes to avoid. Current average speed for each direction is updated at least every half hour.

Houston, Texas

http://www.academ.com/houston/

An online information source for Houston can be found at this page with facts about area, a link to chambers of commerce, and information about local arts, government, and businesses.

Idaho, the Gem State

http://www.cs.uidaho.edu/~beers/Idaho/

Idaho is known for potatoes, pristine mountains, and its isolationist bent. Visitors to this extensive, unofficial page will find information on these traits and more. The page also contains pointers to businesses and tourist spots throughout the state.

Illinois Official Home Page

http://www.state.il.us/

Illinois puts its best foot forward in this online publicity brochure. Explore the state's political system—notable tourist sites and educational offerings here.

Illinois World Wide Web Servers

http://www.cs.uchicago.edu/vt/illinois-
text.html

The University of Chicago maintains this site to provide an index of World Wide Web servers in the Illinois area. Includes links to a variety of business, government, and institutional Web sites.

In and Around Kingston, Ontario, Canada

http://info.queensu.ca/kingston.html

Information about the region around Kingston, Ontario, can be found on this page. Find facts about the area's businesses and festivals, as well as links to tourism resources, government services, educational organizations, and more.

InBerkeley Civic Network

http://www.ci.berkeley.ca.us/

InBerkeley, the City of Berkeley, California's civic network, provides links to pages including city government and services, arts and entertainment, business, and community. There's also information about the city's special projects.

Info Louisiana

http://www.state.la.us/

Visit Louisiana's governor's office, the legislature, and the state departments at this searchable site. Education, tourism, and employment information are also featured.

Information Network of Kansas (INK)

http://www.ink.org/

INK was established by the state legislature in order to give all state residents equal access to state and local information. Here visitors will find information on everything from insurance to legal issues to local government sites.

InteliSys Technologica

http://www.intelinet.net/

Visitors to this hodgepodge site will find a high school basketball guide for teams in the Georgia–South Carolina region. Browsers can also wander through an online photo gallery, read about the local funk band "Mother of 2," and learn about bed-and-breakfast accomodations.

InterLink Hawaii

http://www.ilhawaii.net/

InterLink Hawaii welcomes you to the Aloha State with an online brochure of things to do, places to visit, and where to stay. If you're thinking of investing, check out the real estate link or get annoyed with InterLink's latest reports on Internet outrages.

Internet Alaska Inc.

http://alaska.net/

Internet Alaska, Inc. provides a detailed directory of statewide services and information. Visit here to link with local and state governments, businesses, education, and computer resources.

Introduction to Stillwater, Oklahoma

http://www.okstate.edu/stillwater/introduction.html

The Stillwater Chamber of Commerce maintains this site for an introduction to the city's education, government and business resources. Includes links to Oklahoma State University and Department of Vocational-Technical Education.

Ithaca, New York

http://www.cornell.edu/Ithaca.html

Find out what's happening in Ithaca. Part of Cornell University's web site, this page shows visitors how to get around town and what to do for fun—from bowling to giving blood.

IthacaNet

http://www.ithaca.ny.us/

IthacaNet provides detailed information about the city of Ithaca, New York. Visitors will find resources on Ithaca community events, government, education, libraries, arts, entertainment, and sports.

Iowa City and Coralville, Iowa

http://www.biz.uiowa.edu/iapages/iowacity/index.html

Are you thinking of traveling to Iowa City? Before you head out the door, stop by this page to get a preview of what to see and do in the Iowa City and Coralville, Iowa, area. The City.Net page offers a community guide and pointers to online businesses in the region.

Iowa PROfiles

http://www.profiles.iastate.edu/

Iowa PROfiles is a catch-all site for information relevant to education, business, and agriculture in

the Hawkeye state. It offers a statistical profile of the population, calendars and event notices, a software library, and links to Iowa organizations and agencies.

Kansas State Historical Society

http://history.cc.ukans.edu/heritage/kshs/kshs1.html

Join the Kansas State Historical Society for links to historical information and images highlighting Kansas history. Includes links to remote sites relevant to Kansas and its past.

Kentucky

http://www.state.ky.us/

The official Web server of the U.S. Commonwealth of Kentucky welcomes visitors with a virtual tour of the state and access to selected government documents and servers.

Kentucky Network Servers

http://www.uky.edu/kentucky-network-services.html

World Wide Web servers residing in the state of Kentucky are cataloged at this site, provided by the University of Kentucky at Lexington. Follow the alphabetical listing of links to Internet resources from bluegrass to education.

King County

http://www.metrokc.gov/

The government of King County, Washington, maintains this home page with information about voting, the stadium, recycling, transit, and environmental concerns in the Seattle area.

---

a2z · **EDITOR'S CHOICE**

Kansas Sights

http://falcon.cc.ukans.edu/~nsween/europa.html

It's right in the middle, but we probably don't have to tell you that Kansas isn't known for being a hip, happening epicenter. If everyone there has a sense of history and drama as keen as these Webmasters, however, the Midwestern state's boring reputation will soon be shattered. An interactive map guides visitors through the wheatlands, with notorious speed traps identified for the driver hell-bent on finding Oz. Along the way, stop by the Kansas Bigfoot Center, or fill your tank with handy sightseeing tips and lodging info. Beyond the typical tourist pap offered by most state information sites, this one digs deep into history, taking an excursion through the Old West and introducing famous Kansans like Laura Ingalls Wilder (of "Little House on the Prairie" fame) and gunfighter Wild Bill Hickock. Take an exciting ride with the Pony Express mail service, or follow the trails which brought settlers to the Western frontier. Take note, these savvy Webmasters see all sides of the great plains expansion, making sure to balance the picture of the rugged pioneer against the impact these settlers had on Native American culture. First-rate stuff from the heartland.—*Reviewed by Joyce Slaton*

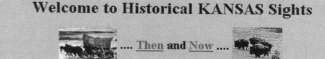

Welcome to Historical KANSAS Sights

.... Then and Now ....

- How did Kansas get it's name?
- Native Americans - The People
- Come back to Kansas soon! Or explore even more on
  □ Savvy Search | Alta Vista | Procomp's Virtual USA | A 2 Z | InfoSeek | Inktomi | Kan-I-Srch? | Lycos | Yahoo | Americasbest |
- Thanks for thinking of Kansas with us, reader # 10974 (lynx readers). And thanks for making this one of those Hope to see you again real soon.

Historical Kansas, by the Sweens, at nsween@kuhub.cc.ukans.edu

Knoxville

http://www.korrnet.org/

A prototype server for the city of Knoxville, Tennessee, this site includes cultural and historical highlights, weather, and city government information. Link directly to the Knoxville Museum of Art and the local newspaper.

Las Vegas, Nevada

http://www.infi.net/vegas/vlv/

Visitors to this site can find all the information they need to plan a trip to Las Vegas, including details on entertainment, gaming, tourism, and shopping.

Lawrence County

http://www.usit.net/lawrence/

Lawrence County, Tennessee, touts its qualities here: 60 miles south of metropolitan Nashville; just north of the biggest energy producer in the nation; good schools; a willing workforce; and home of the historic explorer Davy Crockett. It invites visitors and new businesses to take a virtual look on this page.

Lexington, Massachusetts

http://link.ci.lexington.ma.us/

The community of Lexington directs visitors to selected resources, including public schools and the Massachusetts Institute of Technology's Lincoln Laboratory. Access the gopher site provided here for more on this historical city.

London Page One

http://www.page1.org/london/

London Page One is a virtual guide to the city of London, Ontario in Canada. Visitors to the site can take a tour of the city, with highlighted businesses and entertainment resources.

Los Angeles

http://www.ci.la.ca.us/

Cities all over the world are using the Internet to distribute governmental, tourism and cultural information, and Los Angeles is in the thick of that trend. In addition to those links, L.A. offers traffic and weather reports, museum and entertainment links, sister city information, and civic events.

Los Angeles Superstation

http://www.fountainhead.com/super.html

Is the earth quaking in Los Angeles? Find out at the earthquake link from Fountainhead's Los Angeles Superstation site. The page offers real-time traffic reports and images of the sprawling town.

Los Angeles Traffic Report

http://www.scubed.com/caltrans/la/la_transnet.html

Check here before you hit the freeway in Los Angeles. This RealTime traffic information site, maintained by Maxwell Laboratories, Inc. and the California State Department of Transportation, offers freeway speeds and traffic conditions in the greater Los Angeles Area. Includes listings for trouble spots.

Los Angeles: City.Net Index

http://www.city.net/countries/united_states/california/los_angeles/

Excite's City.Net international information service maintains this site for its guide to Los Angeles. Visitors will an extensive collection of links to local business, government, tourism, and entertainment resources.

Los Gatos, California Guide

http://www.los-gatos.ca.us/los_gatos/los_gatos.html

Los Gatos-based apparel retailer Nine Lives maintains this site to introduce its home city. Visitors will find information on business, government, and visitors' resources.

Louisiana Guide

http://www.wisdom.com/la/la1.htm

Inter Commerce Corporation, a New Orleans-based Web consulting company, maintains this site for its guide to Louisiana. Visitors will find an extensive index of tourism, business and government resources.

Louisville, Kentucky

http://www.iglou.com/lou/

Louisville, one of Kentucky's largest cities, offers a friendly welcome to visitors with useful information for both short or long stays. Where to get comfortable, how to find good things to eat, and when to have fun are all part of the page.

Low Bullsh*t Guide to St. Louis

http://www.inlink.com/~jbhicks/stlguide.html

Sharply different than most city guides, the informative tongue-in-cheek Low Bullsh*t Guide to St. Louis attempts to explain what it's really like to live in St. Louis. With topics like "White Trash Cuisine" or "Tourist Attractions to Skip," the guide's creator links guests to amusing (yet useful) St. Louis information. See Editor's Choice.

Madison Official Web Page

http://www.visitmadison.com/

The Greater Madison home page is the official Web site for the city of Madison, Wisconsin. Visitors to the site can find information about shopping, culture, night life, housing, and local weather. Includes links to other city sites.

Maine Index, BonAire Communications

http://www.mbeacon.com/

Head East for news and views from Maine, sponsored by publishing company BonAire Communications. BonAire's weekly newspaper, The Coastal Beacon, is online for Maine lovers, or jump to the Maine Index for Net links.

Maine Tour

http://www.visitmaine.com/

Tons of information on the farthest north New England state of Maine crowds this page, with plenty of photos and text to tempt the tourist northeast. Regional information, listings of special attractions, and outdoor activities share space here.

Marin Information and Data Access System

http://marin.org/

Marin Information and Data Access System guides you through California's Marin County, with information useful to both vacationers and potential immigrants. Here learn about the people and projects of Marin County, as well as employment opportunities.

Maryland Eastern Shore and Chesapeake Bay

http://www.covesoft.com/Eastern/

This is the place to visit to discover things to do and places to see in the Maryland Eastern Shore and Chesapeake Bay area. Included are historic towns, area attractions, a fishing report, and real estate, as well as photo tours and a map of the region. There also are home pages of cities, businesses, and organizations.

Maryland State Archives

http://www.mdarchives.state.md.us/

The Maryland State Archives houses records dating back to its founding in 1634. The archives contain governmental, church and business records, maps, photographs, and newspapers. Dig through indices, exhibits, and preservation news here.

Massachusetts: City.Net

http://www.city.net/countries/united_states/massachusetts/

The City.Net guide to the state of Massachusetts offers information on business, entertainment, education, and government resources in the Bay State, as well as a town-by-town directory.

Massachusetts Map of WWW Resources

http://donald.phast.umass.edu/misc/mass.shtml

This clickable map from the University of Massachusetts escorts browsers on a virtual tour of the New England state. Visit corporate, educational, and cultural organizations from Boston to Great Barrington, and link to home pages where provided.

Maui Net

http://www.maui.net/

Web surfers and surf surfers can check out the Hawaiian scene here. Includes Maui events and business listings, accommodations and activities information for tourists, real estate links for those interested in buying a piece of The Valley Island," and recreational, health, and lifestyle pages.

Mendocino Community Network

http://www.mcn.org/

The Mendocino Community Network features information about this scenic region of California, including pointers to education, business, and arts and entertainment resources. Visitors can also peruse community resources through the page.

Miami Information Access

http://miami.info-access.com/

Miami Information Access is an online guide to multiple resources in the Miami area, for either vacation or relocation. From here, access information about recreation, real estate, organizations, discussions groups, and more.

Michigan Electronic Library

http://mel.lib.mi.us/

This electronic library from the University of Michigan's MLink Program and the Library of Michigan provides resources from and about the state. The searchable collection is topically arranged in categories such as business, education, government, humanities, science, and social issues.

Michigan House of Representatives

http://www.house.state.mi.us/

Michigan residents can check in with their state representatives on this page or learn more about Michigan's House of Representatives. The page also links to other state and national government sites.

Michigan State Government

http://www.migov.state.mi.us/

Michigan provides this comprehensive overview of its state government system. Visitors will find detailed information and links to Michigan's executive, legislative, and judicial branches.

Northern Michigan Wineries

http://www.michiweb.com/wine/wineries.html

Wineries from across Northern Michigan are featured on this page. Visitors can read about current activities in the vineyards, follow links to a number of wineries or click to other wine sites on the Net.

Minnesota Government Information and Services—North Star

http://www.state.mn.us/

North Star, a service of Minnesota state government, maintains this site to provide tourist and governmental information. Visit here for a state history, a list of government offices, tourism, community information, and more.

Minnesota Regional Network

http://www.mr.net/MRNet.html

Visitors can access academic, research, and economic information when they drop by the Minnesota Regional Network Corp. home page. The documents here can be searched by keyword. Also available are links to MRNet's gopher and FTP servers and regional Web resources.

Minnesota State Fair

http://www.statefair.gen.mn.us/

The Minnesota State Fair provides information about phone contacts, special days, entry deadlines, performances, and exhibitions. This page was designed as a preview to the 1995 fair.

Missouri Web—Show-Me Missouri, the Cyberspace Tradeshow

http://www.ecodev.state.mo.us/

"Show Me Missouri," provided by the Missouri Department of Economic Development, is the state's official online information source. Visit here for an index of travel, government, and economic development resources.

Montana Maps

http://nris.msl.mt.gov/gis/mtmaps.html

The Montana Natural Resource Information System presents dozens of downloadable maps viewable as GIFs. The maps are in categories; find counties, cities, lakes and streams, highways, railroads, population density, and legislative districts.

Montana Natural Resource Information System

http://nris.msl.mt.gov/

The Montana Natural Resources Information System offers data on the natural resources and people of the state of Montana. Visitors will find databases for natural heritage, water information, and geography. Maps and general statistics for the state are provided.

---

a2z EDITOR'S CHOICE

Low Bullsh*t Guide to St. Louis

http://www.inlink.com/~jbhicks/stlguide.html

Straight-from-the-hip author J. Brad Hicks wanted a guide to St. Louis that he wouldn't be embarrassed to show his out-of-town friends. Well, Hicks must have some pretty interesting friends. Sharply different from most city guides, the informative tongue-in-cheek Low Bullsh*t Guide to St. Louis attempts to explain what it's really like to live in the "gateway to the west." The ins and outs of getting around on public transit are explained, with Hicks' admonition that St. Louis buses are dirty, ramshackle and "filled with crazies ... some of whom drive them." Hicks also gives the rundown on what St. Louis attractions are worthwhile and which ones are losers, and gives the real story behind the city's crime rate, including a list of crime-heavy neighborhoods to avoid. Many more links to real life in St. Louis round out the site, including an explanation of strange St. Louis native customs, a cost-savvy guide to living and working in the city, and advice on ferreting out the offbeat stuff.—*Reviewed by Joyce Slaton*

The Low Bullshit Guide to St. Louis

Voted 3rd Place, Best of the St. Louis Web

This guide was conceived (and so far, written) by me, J. Brad Hicks. I wanted something that I wouldn't be embarrassed to show an out-of-town friend. I wanted a guide to St. Louis that gave a better idea of what St. Louis looked like, and what it felt like to be in St. Louis. I wanted a guide that gave practical advice on getting around (and getting along) in St. Louis.

Update: Back when I started this guide, the "other" St. Louis guide was nothing but a bunch of business ads and reprints of Regional Commerce and Growth Association pamphlets. Joe Haspiel's done a much better job lately, especially linking in personal pages from other St. Louisans (including mine). I cross-reference his pages, too.

Moscow

http://www.moscow.com/

This site is an entry point for the Palouse region of northern Idaho and northeastern Washington. Includes links to Moscow municipal and commercial resources, regional information, news, and weather.

Nashville.Net

http://www.nashville.net/

The goal of this server is to "provide a starting point for Internet services in Nashville." It's a colorful jump-station to local government, media, education, entertainment and shopping servers. If it's about Nashville and on the Net, you'll probably be able to access it from here.

New Brunswick, Canada

http://www.csi.nb.ca/

Open the Tool Bench at Cybersmith Inc. and tour New Brunswick, Canada, checking out what's new and cool along the way. This Internet index also offers business and municipal links for the area and general-purpose surf aids.

Newfoundland and Labrador Home Page

http://www.compusult.nf.ca/nfld/nfld.html

Visit the Newfoundland and Labrador home page to access historical, cultural, and governmental resources on the region. Travelers and information seekers will find business directories, shopping guides, tourists attractions, and local weather details here.

Newfoundland Emporium—Wordplay

http://www.wordplay.com/

This eclectic site contains links to a bookstore, art gallery, television station, and the Newfoundland Arts Council. Site features also include a Newfoundland directory and tourist information.

New Hampshire

http://newww.com/

Visitors can tour the covered bridges of New Hampshire and much more at this site. Information and events calendars are provided for each of six regions in the Granite State, and the entire database is searchable by keyword. Submissions are invited.

New Orleans

http://www.neworleans.com

Lurking in the heart of every potential romantic is the dream of seeing New Orleans at Mardi Gras (or at any other time). At the New Orleans home page, find a city map and Jazz Festival schedule as well as other city information.

New Orleans and Louisiana Virtual Library

http://www.satchmo.com/nolavl/

Take a virtual trip to Louisiana to see what's going on over the airwaves, on the sports courts, and on the Net through the New Orleans and Louisiana Virtual Library. Users can stop by for news about the area or check out a hot list of music links.

New Orleans Cemeteries

http://www.webcorp.com/images/nocemtnt.htm

Tour the New Orleans cities of the dead in this demonstration of what Webcorp's multimedia Web sites can look like. The photos, originally from the American Memory Home Page, have been electronically hand-tinted and present the diverse architecture of the old tombs and crypts.

New Orleans Free-Net

http://www.gnofn.org/

The Greater New Orleans FreeNet site contains information about the city, community organizations, educational institutions, and entertainment.

The New Orleans Times and Directory

http://www.gna.com/

The New Orleans Times and Directory provides a searchable directory of addresses and phone numbers for businesses in the area plus detailed listings in areas such as automotive, entertainment, real estate, and finance.

New Mexico Viva!

http://www.viva.com/nm/

VIVA New Mexico! covers all aspects of life in this southwestern state. Visitors will find community events, arts and culture information, travel guides, almanacs, and business directories. Links to government agencies, schools, and libraries are also included.

New Mexico: America's Land of Enchantment

http://www.nets.com/newmextourism/

Get all the facts on New Mexico from links on the Bienvenidos a Nuevo Mexico page. Visitors can look at New Mexico maps, get tourism information, access New Mexico ski reports, and more.

New York City: City.Net

http://www.city.net/countries/united_states/new_york/new_york/

City.Net's guide to the Big Apple is everything you'd expect—and then some! For tourists and denizens alike, this site features information about where to go, what to do, and when to do it (which is, of course, *anytime* in New York).

New York City Explorations

http://emall.com/exploreny/ny1.html

At the Explore New York site, visitors can learn the city's history and take a virtual tour of its attractions, including Broadway, Madison Square Garden, the Empire State Building, and, of course, the Statue of Liberty.

New York City Useful References and Guides

http://www.columbia.edu/~hauben/nyc-guides.html

This home page provides a variety of Internet-based references and guides to New York City. Visit here for information on government, business, tourism, transportation and entertainment resources.

New York State

http://www.state.ny.us/

Are you thinking of a trip to the Big Apple? Before you go, stop by the New York State Web page. It features tourism information helpful for travelers as well as details about statewide organizations and the state government.

New York Subway Finder

http://www.krusch.com/nysf.html

Don't get lost in the maze of New York City on your next visit. Instead, check out this nifty New York Subway finder offered by The Paperless Guide to New York Web site. This in-depth resource enables users to obtain subway directions "to any Manhattan street in minutes." If that doesn't sort you out, check out online subway maps and the "street locator" for further help.

The New York Web Home Page

http://www.nyweb.com/

Check out the night life, the club scene and the must-see and must-do places in the Big Apple at the New York Web page. It contains such gems as A Social Climber's Guide to Manhattan.

Niagara FallsCam Home Page

http://fallscam.niagara.com/

Another great live cam page, this one offers ten-second MPEG videos of North America's wettest natural wonder (or one of them, anyway). The page also includes a link to Internet Connect Niagara, where visitors can get still more info about the Niagara Falls area.

North Carolina Encyclopedia

http://hal.dcr.state.nc.us/nc/cover.htm

The North Carolina Encyclopedia offers a state profile by category. Select from topics that give overviews of government, education, history and local vital statistics.

North Carolina Home Page— University of North Carolina

http://sunsite.unc.edu/nc/nchome.html

Maintained at the University of North Carolina, Chapel Hill, this site serves as the state's home page with links to universities and colleges, governmental departments, media, and cultural and civic groups. Features include a custom weather server and links to other related Web sites.

North Carolina Public Information

http://www.sips.state.nc.us/nchome.html

The North Carolina state government maintains this site to provide general state-wide information. Visit here for links to governmental and educational departments, agencies and resources. A Frequently Asked Questions (FAQ) index is also available.

North Carolina: The Tar Heel State

http://www.webpress.net/ncnetworks/

The cities of North Carolina are featured at this info-page on the Tar Heel State. Visitors will also find listings for professional sports, furniture showrooms, businesses, weather, tourist attractions, and the interstate system.

Northern Nevada Web

http://www.scs.unr.edu/

The University and Community College System of Nevada maintains this site containing state and general Internet resources. Visitors will find links to state government, commercial and educational Web servers, Internet directories, and World Wide Web search engines.

Nova Scotia

http://ttg.sba.dal.ca/nstour/

Nova Scotia's economic renewal department offers tourism information. Includes a visitor center, news on the G7 Halifax summit, a crafts display, and weather reports.

Nunatsiaq News Home Page

http://www.nunanet.com/~nunat/index.html

The Nunavut community newspaper provides an online version of its weekly here. Browsers can download features, news and photos from Canada's Inuit Territory and link to information about the Arctic. The page also contains links to online books, magazines and reference material.

Official Arlington County, Virginia Home Page

http://www.co.arlington.va.us/

Visitors heading for the Washington D.C. area can learn about tourist activities in nearby Arlington County, Virginia here. The page details Arlington's attractions, including the Iwo Jima Memorial and the Pentagon.

Oklahoma, Native America

http://www.oklaosf.state.ok.us/

This site contains the state of Oklahoma's informational home page. Visitors can read the latest in the current events file, check in on the state government, access tourism information, arts and recreation listings, and more.

Old West Kansas Home Page

http://history.cc.ukans.edu/heritage/kshs/kshs1.html

Net browsers wanting to feel a little of the old American frontier spirit may want to visit the Old West Kansas Home Page, with links to historical information on the Kansas of the Old West. Links to maps, images, biographies, and historical essays on Kansas are all found here.

Olympic Peninsula

http://www.olympus.net/

Visitors to this page will find Washington State's Olympic Peninsula information server. From how to get around to what to get around to, the information offered covers all aspects of life, leisure (and emergency) on the peninsula.

Olympus Welcome

http://olympus.dis.wa.gov/

The Washington State government maintains this site for its Internet public access server. Visit here for links to state programs and projects such as Doing Business with Washington State, Home Page Washington, InfoX, and others.

Ontario, Canada

http://www.gov.on.ca/

Discover what's happening in the Canadian province of Ontario from the government's point of view. Get Ontario's vital statistics, order government publications, and link to related sites from here. In English and French.

Orange County

http://www.oc.ca.gov/

This is the official community page for Orange County, California. Visitors to this site will find county press releases, government agencies, Board of Supervisors information, and tax guidelines.

Orange County Traffic Report

http://www.scubed.com/caltrans/oc/oc_transnet.html

From the California Department of Transportation, the Orange County Traffic Report Web features information about road closures and real-time maps depicting traffic speeds, and areas of congestion. The data is updated about once a minute to aid commuters.

Oregon Area Information

http://city.net/countries/united_states/oregon/

Oregonians and cybertourists can link to dozens of Oregon cities from the city.net Oregon index. The page also posts links to state government pages, an Oregon events site, and a page devoted to the state's weather and road conditions.

Oregon, Galaxy

http://galaxy.einet.net/galaxy/Community/US-States/Oregon.html

This page from the larger Galaxy site provides visitors links to Web sites around the State of Oregon. Features include links to directories, government and nonprofit organizations, and event information.

Oregon Online

http://www.or.gov/

Oregon Online is an information resource on the state's economy, government and educational system. Includes listings of individual community resources and research materials.

Oregon State Archives

http://159.121.28.251/

The State of Oregon maintains this site to preserve and provide access to its permanent document collection. Visit the Oregon State Archives to perform keyword searches, submit research requests, and view a variety of publications and art collections.

Oregon World Wide Web Server List

http://darkwing.uoregon.edu/~llynch/or-text.html

Maintained at the University of Oregon, this page serves up a directory of sites online in that Northwestern state. Find links to governmental, educational, commercial, and nonprofit organizations.

Ozarks Online

http://www.ozarksol.com/

Ozarks Online offers Web consulting and hosting services in the scenic hill country of southwest Missouri. This page contains a collection of businesses within the area as well as some travel and recreational tips for visitors. (That means Branson, y'all.)

Palo Alto Historical Association

http://www.commerce.digital.com/palo-alto/historical-assoc/home.html

The home page for the Palo Alto Historical Association describes how the city of Palo Alto, California got its name and provides a list of its publications.

Pasadena, California

http://www.ci.pasadena.ca.us/

Sunny Pasadena contains more than just the little old lady of whom the Beach Boys sang. Find out more on Pasadena's home page, which offers basic information on the city—along with tourist-friendly links. Includes links to city government sites, a calendar of events, and business information.

Pennsylvania State Data Center

http://howard.hbg.psu.edu/psdc/psdchome1.1.html

The Pennsylvania State Data Center compiles economic and demographic information for the state. It offers its files, maps, and databases online here. The page also includes an overview of the center's products and services.

Philadelphia History

http://www.libertynet.org/iha/

The Independence Hall Association celebrates and promotes Philadelphia here. Visitors will find tourist tips for the city and can take a virtual walking tour of Philadelphia's historic mile.

Philadelphia Neighborhoods Online

http://libertynet.org/community/phila/nol.html

Bolstering communities through online interaction is a focus of the City of Philadelphia Neighborhoods Online project. Visitors can access information here about city services and common city application forms, or find out how to contact city council members.

Philadelphia Online

http://www.phillynews.com/

Yo, Adrian! Here's Philadelphia Online, from Philadelphia Newspapers, Inc., offering a truckload of news, features, sports, weather, visitor information and entertainment from the City of Brotherly Love *and* hoagies. Includes subscription information for the city's daily newspapers: the Inquirer and the Daily News.

PICnet Dallas Directory

http://www.pic.net/

PICnet, a Dallas, Texas-based Internet service provider, maintains this site offering pointers to local resources. Visitors will find links to news, weather, sports, tourism, and commercial organizations in the Dallas/Fort Worth area. Includes link to online account information.

Pittsburgh: The Links

http://www.maya.com/Local/mazur/daBurgh.html

The City of Pittsburgh springs to life through at this home page, which contains dozens of links to resources in the city, including art, restaurants, sports, music, and more.

PittsburghNet

http://www.pittsburgh.net/

Check out the famed Golden Triangle, interesting neighborhoods and fun things to do in Pittsburgh. Includes links to dozens of local resources.

Planet Hawaii Hawaiian Eye

http://planet-hawaii.com/ph/he.html

If the view from your own window isn't so hot, try the view at the Planet Hawaii Hawaiian Eye page, where the Hawaiian Eye camera is trained on the Aloha tower in Oahu. Visitors can enjoy the view, access stock photos or link to other viewing camera sites.

Point Reyes Light

http://www.ptreyeslight.com/prl/

The "Point Reyes Light," a weekly newspaper from Marin County, California, provides news articles, columns, an activities calendar, and a business directory. Also find a cartoon, tourist information, and topical links.

Portland, Oregon Community, Visitor and Business Information

http://www.teleport.com/~peekpa/pdx.home.html

A cyber-gateway into the "City of Roses," this page showcases Portland entertainment: restaurants, museums, and outdoor recreation areas. More thorough Portland guides are also linked for the insatiably curious.

Prince William County, Virginia

http://www.pwcweb.com/

Divided neatly into four categories—commerce, government, recreation and nonprofit—this informational offering introduces visitors to Prince William County, Virginia. Includes details on a fundraising effort to benefit children of the area's "working uninsured" and links to other regional resources.

Provincetown Village, Massachusetts

http://www.provincetown.com/

Residents of Provincetown Village on Cape Cod introduce their seaside community at this Web site. Read about tourist attractions and the country's oldest continuous art colony, or check out a blizzard slide show from 1996.

Pullman, Washington

http://www.pullman.com/

Visit the home of Washington State University and the Cougars. Or if you're a local, meet your neighbors and find out how to make a bigger impact on your community by visiting the information center.

Quebec

http://www.gouv.qc.ca/

The Canadian province of Quebec's home page is in French, with links to English and Spanish language versions. A thorough encyclopedia of the area, topics include Quebec's government, culture, and society.

Quebec, Canada

http://www.iisys.com/www/travel/canada/quebec/quebec.htm

Learn everything about Quebec—from how to get to there to bankers' holidays—at this welcome page. Links include travel tips and links to universities in Canada's "distinctly different" province.

Rancho Cucamonga

http://www.citivu.com/index.html

Is Rancho Cucamonga the definition of suburban utopia? Located about 40 miles east of Los Angeles, the city offers site surfers a glimpse of the many attractions and daily activities available to tourists and residents.

Red Rock State Park

http://www.pr.state.az.us/parkhtml/redrock.html

Peruse an informative description of Red Rock State Park in Arizona or link to the Arizona State Parks (ASP) home page for further reviews, news, and virtual park tours.

Redwood Country Unlimited

http://www.northcoast.com/unlimited/unlimited.html

Redwood Country Unlimited maintains this site to introduce products and services from the Northcoast region of California. Visitors will find business and tourism resources from Del Norte, Humboldt, Trinity, and Mendocino counties.

Redwoods Country: Leggett Valley California

http://redwoods.com/~ebarnett/leggett.ca.html

Take an online to trip California's Leggett Valley, better known as the Grand Canyon of the Redwoods. This page includes a photo tour of the valley, maps, and information about old-growth redwood forests and the Eel River.

Rocky Mountain National Park

http://www.csn.net/~arthurvb/rmnp/rmnp.html

Travelers planning a trip to Colorado's Rocky Mountain National Park can scout attractions, routes and weather conditions ahead of time at this official park home page. Peruse the Park Service brochure or review park maps and pictures at this online information station.

Roseville Police Department

http://www.sna.com/rosepd/

The police department of Roseville, California reaches out to the community with this home page. Information on various police services as well as links to other criminal justice sites are provided.

RuralNet

http://ruralnet.mu.wvnet.edu/

The RuralNet home page provides information on available health care services throughout rural

West Virginia. Includes listings of community resources, interactive public access medical servers, search tools, medical education resources, grant and funding opportunities, and more.

Saint Pierre et Miquelon

http://www.io.org/~socrates/

Saint Pierre and Miquelon are France's oldest and last remaining colonial sites in North America. These islands' home page provides a virtual tour of the colony, and information on tourism, history, social sciences, language, and culture. Available in French and English.

San Antonio, Texas

http://www.electrotex.com/sa.html

Welcome to sunny San Antonio, Texas, home of the Alamo and the 45th National Square Dance Convention. For more on what to do and see, not to mention where to eat and where to go to school in San Antonio, visit here.

San Diego

http://www.sannet.gov/

The home page for the city of San Diego, California includes a wealth of government information and city services. Link to the mayor's office, the city council, or browse current public policy issues.

San Diego

http://www.nosc.mil/planet_earth/sandiego.html

Take a close-up look at the City of San Diego on this page that includes a comprehensive list of links to a smorgasbörd of city information. Travelers can read about hotels and entertainment, and locals can check weather forecasts and festivals along with a slew of other links.

San Diego infoPost

http://www.infopost.com/sandiego/index.html

This directory provides links to information and resources in the San Diego area. Visitors to this site will find listings on local entertainment, cultural events, dining, sports, news, shopping, government agencies, emergency telephone numbers, and other resources.

San Diego Online

http://www.sandiego-online.com/

San Diego Online, "a great place to find out what's what and who's who," provides a few extras on top of entertainment and activity information in the area, including profiles and features.

San Diego Traffic Report

http://www.scubed.com/caltrans/sd/sd_transnet.html

This public service provides real-time traffic information on San Diego's freeways and roads including incidence and flow reports and construction closures.

San Diego: Zoom Arts & Entertainment News

http://w3.thegroup.net/~zoom/

ZOOM San Diego provides arts and entertainment news for "the City on the Edge." Visit its home page for listings from live theater, concerts, films, museums, and sporting events in the Southern Californian city.

San Francisco Municipal Railway

http://server.berkeley.edu/Transit/Carriers/MUNI/

The San Francisco Municipal Railway offers updates about transit news as well as access to current bus, streetcar, and cable car schedules through this page. Visitors can also check out the fares for specific routes before heading out the door.

San Luis Obispo

http://baretta.calpoly.edu/htmlpages/slo.html

This virtual tour of the California coastal community of San Luis Obispo highlights some of the city's main attractions: resorts and beaches, "Gum Wall Alle" and the Mission San Luis Obispo de Tolusa, erected in 1772. Images and a clickable map guide the browser.

Santa Cruz County Electronic Guide

http://www.cruzio.com/

Cruzio, a Santa Cruz, California-based Internet service provider, provides general information about this seaside city and county. Visit here to connect to the city's arts, business and government resources.

Santa Monica, California

http://pen.ci.santa-monica.ca.us/

This is a community page for the city of Santa Monica, California. Visitors will find tourist information, local government pages, and links to related sites on the Internet.

Sarasota Online

http://www.insarasota.com/sarasota/default.asp

Sarasota Online offers an official tour of the Florida city, along with links to local news and government resources. The site is meant to help empower the city and provide an information resource, with Yellow Pages and tourism pointers.

Saskatoon Free-Net

http://www.sfn.saskatoon.sk.ca/

Saskatoon Free-Net is a community information service for this city in Saskatchewan, Canada. Visitors will find community news, event listings, and information on volunteering for local social organizations.

SCESCAPE: Experience South Carolina

http://www.scescape.com/

The acronym says it all: SCESCAPE = South Carolina Experiences, State/Local Government, Commerce, Arts/Sports/Entertainment, People, and Education. Those areas are covered in a searchable index. There's also a gallery of South Carolina images.

Seattle

http://www.ci.seattle.wa.us/

The official Web site of the City of Seattle hits like a strong cup o' joe beside the Puget Sound. It offers pages on Seattle education, the environment, local government, news, entertainment, and more.

Seattle Area Traffic Flow

http://198.238.212.10/regions/northwest/NWFLOW/

Washington State's Department of Transportation provides this Web site, with bulletins about Washington traffic updated every two minutes. Visitors can check out a highway map, access public transportation information, or link to the department's home page here.

Seattle Caustic Compendium

http://www.oz.net/~evad/

Billed as "an unflinching urban guide to Seattle living," the Caustic Companion gives the real lowdown on the Seattle scene, devoid of touristy soft pedaling. Check out this description of a Seattle club: "Dirty, smelly, gross, noisy….. You'll want to take a shower after drinking a cheap pitcher of Brew 66 and watching some of Seattle's best not-so-famous rock stars." More pithy descriptions of restaurants, coffee houses, and galleries follow. See Editor's Choice.

Seattle Chamber of Commerce

http://www.wolfe.net/~seattle/

The Greater Seattle Chamber of Commerce site contains information about the various programs and services the business organization provides. Includes membership and relocation information and access to publications.

Seattle Hometown News

http://www.halcyon.com/normg/snews.html

This site provides news coverage of the Seattle area as reported by two "long-time local media observers." A lengthy list of reports under "What we're talkin' about in Seattle" is accompanied by links to numerous Seattle-specific resources on the Web.

Seattle, Washington

http://useattle.uspan.com

Links to Seattle area travel and entertainment resources comprise this site. Includes information on films, hotels, music, dining, sports, and shopping.

Seattle, Washington

http://weber.u.washington.edu/~mosaic/
seattle.html

Take a virtual trip to the birthplace of grunge. Unlike city pages which present dry recitations of civic facts, links here connect guests to all sorts of fun spots, with special touches like city guides written by lighthearted natives. If text here intrigues you, a virtual Seattle tour can also be had for the clicking.

Sequim's Home Page

http://www.sequim.com/

The Sequim home page contains information about Northwestern Washington and the Olympic Peninsula. Information is included on local government, business, education, outdoor recreation, and other resources.

ShastaLink Home Page

http://www.shasta-co.k12.ca.us/

California's Shasta County Office of Education sponsors this extensive compendium of Shasta County information and resources. Visit educational facilities, browse the news and government hotlink pages, or jump to online directories and lists for exploring the Internet.

Shreveport, Louisiana

http://www.softdisk.com/shreve/

Make a stop in lovely Louisiana by way of Shreveport and the abundant links here. Pointers for tourists and residents spell out what to do, where to stay, and much more info on local attractions.

Silicon Valley

http://www.netview.com/svg/

Planning on taking a job in Silicon Valley? Stop here first for information on culture, weather, accommodations, health care, real estate, and more. Job-seekers will find an extensive employment index.

Silicon Valley, California

http://www.netview.com/svg/

NETView Communications presents this comprehensive guide to Silicon Valley in California—an area considered to be both a major hub of wired culture and a "model of diversity." Here you'll find the scoop on everything from local businesses and educational facilities to famous tourist hot spots.

Smart Valley, Inc.

http://www.svi.org/

Smart Valley attempts at this site to create an electronic community for the San Francisco Bay area. Includes links to an overview of the network, listings of new sites, and pointers to a wide variety of business, government, and entertainment listings.

The Smoky Mountains

http://www.nando.net/smokies/smokies.html

Visit North Carolina's Smoky Mountain National Park at this site for a peek at the state's natural beauty and land resources. Nando.net provides maps, history, images, audio clips, and more about the Smokies.

South Carolina-Public Information Home Page

http://www.state.sc.us/

The official Web site for the State of South Carolina offers access to a wealth of state government resources as well as providing information on this southern state's history, commerce, educational opportunities, and tourist industry. Allows state residents to electronically communicate with and participate in their government.

South Coast Air Quality Management

http://www.aqmd.gov/

Southern Californians who can't go outside because of smog and dirty air can stay inside and read *why* at the South Coast Air Quality Management District page. Learn more about the AQMD, its regulations, and air quality here.

South Dakota Official Home Page

http://www.state.sd.us/

This official site, run by the State of South Dakota, provides information about the state's government, cities, tourism possibilities, and educational and Internet resources. Includes an on-site search mechanism.

Southeastern Pennsylvania Transportation Authority

http://www.libertynet.org/~septa/

The Southeastern Pennsylvania Transportation Authority maintains this site to introduce its regional service divisions. Visit here for news, events, service overviews, maps, and more.

Southwest Colorado Access Network (SCAN)

http://www.scan.org/

Browsers can flip through an online guide to Southwest Colorado here. Find government, business, and entertainment links featured.

---

a2z EDITOR'S CHOICE

Seattle Caustic Compendium

http://www.oz.net/~evad/

Billed as "an unflinching urban guide to Seattle living," the Caustic Companion delivers the real lowdown on the Grunge capital of the world, devoid of touristy soft-pedaling. Check out this description of a typical club: "Dirty, smelly, gross, noisy ... You'll want to take a shower after drinking a cheap pitcher of Brew 66 and watching some of Seattle's best not-so-famous rock stars." (Can't wait!) Restaurant reviews from various Seattle neighborhoods like Capitol Hill or Ballard are skewed towards the vegetarian muncher with an adventurous palate and not many dollars in the pocket. And the listing of shopping spots zeroes in on the stomping grounds of slackers: record stores and thrift shops. Plenty of info on where to find double lattes and microbreweries, too.—*Reviewed by Joyce Slaton*

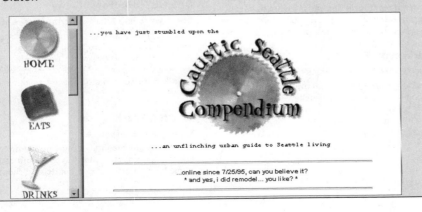

Spokane, Washington...the Inland Empire
http://www.eznet.com/personal/solomon/3depg2.html

This site devoted to the Washington City of Spokane features a photo album, business center, links to universities, weather, traffic and government information, and more.

The State of Montana
http://www.mt.gov/

The State of Montana provides visitors with information about the "Big Sky" state here. The site includes tourist information, job listings, an index to governmental sites, and links to state universities.

Surf Conditions, Oahu's North Coast
http://www.soest.hawaii.edu/soest/surf/caldwell.html

Surfers in Hawaii can glom the latest information about the winds and expected surf conditions off the North Coast of Oahu through this Web page. It includes handy details about wave directions and swell heights.

Tempe in Touch
http://www.tempe.gov

Tempe in Touch, maintained by the City of Tempe, Arizona, offers a variety of local information resources. Visit here for city service listings, events calendars, recreation and education indexes, employment opportunities, and more. Includes message from Mayor Neil Giuliano.

Tennessee's Home Page
http://www.state.tn.us/

This Web document offers information about Tennessee. Find links to many of the Volunteer State's governmental bodies, including its Supreme Court, Secretary of State, and Departments of Employment Security and Education. Visitors can also check out tourist and weather information.

Texas: City.Net
http://www.city.net/countries/united_states/texas/

Take a look at all the cities in Texas that have an Internet presence through this page, part of the city.net project. Each city listing leads to a separate home page. The page also has a list of Texas resources sorted by topic.

Texas Department of Transportation
http://www.dot.state.tx.us/

Run the roads of the "Lone Star State" with the department that runs the roads. Find out how revenues are spent, contracts won, and daily business done. Plus find vehicle registration and legislation information, as well as tourism and sightseeing links.

Texas Government Information Server
http://www.texas.gov/tih.html

The Texas Department of Information Resources provides this page of links for the state's citizens and visitors. Searchable access to information on tourism, employment, business, and government agencies is featured, as are links to special collections of Texas maps and Internet case studies.

Three Shields Hawaii
http://www.aloha.com/~curran/

Just like taking a trip to the islands, except without the crystal water, gorgeous weather and ever-flowing tropical drinks. Okay, maybe it's just like visiting a *page* on the islands, but this page has tons of Hawaiian links. Music, food, Hawaiian culture—the links go on and on. You're even invited to Aunty Leilani's luau.

La Toile du Quebec
http://www.toile.qc.ca/englqc.htm

Providing a virtual guide to the Canadian province of Quebec, Webmasters have cataloged a host of government, arts and culture, tourism, news, and leisure pages here. Information on Canadian newsgroups, too. Available in both French and English.

Toledo, Ohio Home Page
http://www.toledolink.com/~matgerke/toledo/toledo.html

The Toledo, home page offers an overview of the city, information on businesses, educational institutions, and cultural attractions. Includes press releases, travel tips, a history of the city, and a statistical database.

Toronto Life
http://www.tor-lifeline.com/

Here is "advice for the urban explorer" from Toronto Life magazine, pointing out some things to do with your time while visiting this Canadian metropolis. Guides take you restaurants, night spots and cultural events to help you "get a life."

Toronto, Ontario, Canada
http://www.math.toronto.edu/toronto/

The Toronto, Ontario, Canada page provides a wealth of tourist and visitor information about the vibrant metropolis that the United Nations has designated as the most ethnically diverse city on earth. This unofficial site offers sections on Toronto entertainment, recreation, dining, shopping, business, media, weather, computing, and much more.

Traverse City FreePort Web Server
http://leo.nmc.edu/

This site provides information about Traverse City, Michigan. Find a link to Northwestern Michigan College, plus a recreation page and information on local schools and the Communications Decency Act.

Tucson: DesertNet
http://desert.net/

This site features the gateway to the DesertNet, a news and infotainment server originating in Tucson, Arizona. Curiosity seekers won't want to miss the Hall of Heads; audiophiles will enjoy the music bin; movie buffs, the film vault; and for the lonely hearts, personals.

The Twin Cities Web
http://www.fentonnet.com/tcweb.html

The Twin Cities (those cold northern metropolises of Minneapolis and St. Paul) have thriving businesses and lively entertainment, many churches and an activist government. Leave your parka and mukluks behind, and virtually visit here.

The Unofficial Missouri Page
http://www.missouri.edu/~c675032/index.htm

The Unofficial Missouri Page has links to general information about the state as well as a list of famous Missourians. Also included here is information on events, history, government, and weather.

USA CityLink Project Overview
http://usacitylink.com//

USA CityLink claims to be the "most comprehensive United States city and state listing on the Web." Access information about select U.S. cities and communities, or take a look at the "Internet's first Java-powered American flag."

Utah State Archives
http://utstdpwww.state.ut.us/~archives/

The Utah State Archives serve as a repository for historical records derived from official government business. County, court, and statewide resources are available and searchable, and there are sections on Utah state history and on using the Web for genealogical research.

Utah WWW Sites Map and List
http://www.vtourist.com/web-ut/

This list of Utah WWW sites is a collection of links to Web pages and resources about the State of Utah. Links include government and military, university and college, commercial, tourism, cities, and neighboring states.

Vancouver Online
http://www.vancouver-online.com

Link to a wide variety of Web pages from the Vancouver area at the Vancouver Online Home Page. Visitors can search the database by keyword or click on categories such as business or entertainment to call up lists of links.

Vancouver Welcomes You
http://www.city.vancouver.bc.ca/

Maintained by the city of Vancouver's municipal government, this site offers visitors information on services this Canadian city provides its resi-

dents. Areas covered include police, fire and rescue, libraries, parks and cultural centers, garbage
collection, recycling, and transportation.

Vermont Official Home Page

http://www.cit.state.vt.us

Discover what makes the Green Mountain State
unique by a visit to the Vermont home page. Access to state sites for every interest begins here:
tourism, culture, education, and government.

Victoria, B.C.

http://www.tbc.gov.bc.ca/tourism/Victoria/
victoria.html

Cybertravelers will get a taste of Victoria, British
Columbia, at this site. Visitors can wander
through some of the city's attractions here and
link to pages about Vancouver Island and tourism
in the province.

Victoria, Canada

http://www.city.victoria.bc.ca/

Canada's City of Victoria considers itself "the premiere tourist spot in the Pacific Northwest," and is
here to tell you all about its attractions and events.
But it also supplies a good dose of background and
includes links to municipal government.

Virginia: City.Net

http://www.city.net/countries/united_states/
virginia/

City.Net's guide to Virginia provides a thumbnail
visitors' guide to the Tidewater State and its many
tourist attractions. This site has special sections
for dozens of Virginia cities as well as information
on statewide special events, education, and news.

Virginia World Wide Web Servers

http://www.fie.com/www/virginia.htm

This site provides detailed descriptions of and access to an array of servers throughout the State of
Virginia. Visitors will find links ranging from activist organizations to corporate home pages here.

Virtual Chattanooga

http://www.chattanooga.net/

Virtual Chattanooga—an online guide to resources in the Tennessee town—offers information on
tourism, government services, educational materials, and local businesses. Includes keyword
search utility.

Virtual Lake Tahoe

http://www.virtualtahoe.com/

Virtual Lake Tahoe is a vacationer's guide to this
Nevada tourist destination spot. This page helps
visitors of all ages find accommodations, restaurants, entertainment, and shopping. General information about the area and real estate listings
are also included.

Virtually California

http://www.virtually.com/

Sample the food, shopping, sights and entertainment at Virtually California. This site provides indexes of online resources on San Francisco, Los
Angeles, San Diego, and Mexico, including local
community information.

Virtually Hawaii!

http://www.satlab.hawaii.edu/space/hawaii/

Virtually Hawaii!, maintained by the University of
Hawaii, NASA and TerraSystems, Inc., provides
an electronic archive of Earth and space science
data focused on the Pacific island chain. Visitors
will find satellite images, weather maps, and remote sensing images.

Washington: City.Net

http://city.net/countries/united_states/
washington/

City.Net hosts this comprehensive index of Washington *State* Web sites, browsable by city. Visitors
can find a wealth of links here to Washington
businesses, entertainment, sights, dining, media,
transportation, and more.

Washington, DC: City.Net

http://www.city.net/countries/united_states/
district_of_columbia/washington/

This CityNet page provides information on historic buildings, museums, entertainment, and subway directions in Washington, D.C. Includes links
to government resources, city guides, places of
worship, sporting events, and more.

Washington Web

http://www.washweb.net/

Internet provider Internet Interstate presents
Washington Web, with resources on and from the
Washington, D.C. area. Includes the arts, business, education, news, travel, and more. A demonstration page shows features that clients can
include on their own Web pages.

WebCastro

http://www.webcastro.com/

The online magazine WebCastro highlights the
business, culture, and people of San Francisco's
Castro District—an internationally recognized gay
and lesbian mecca. The site is hosted by two area
residents and includes their personal reporting on
the arts, history, and computing.

Welcome to Atlanta

http://www.atlantagames.com/atlanta.htm

"The Atlanta Journal-Constitution" maintains
this site for information about its home city, host
of the 1996 Olympic Games. Visitors will find an
extensive index of local business, retail and entertainment resources, and links to the "Journal's"
editorial and commercial Web sites.

Welcome to Rochester, New York USA

http://www.rochester.ny.us/

The home page for Rochester provides information on local businesses' Web sites, a professional directory, online classified ads, local Internet
access providers, business resources, legal, financial and economic information, and more.

West Virginia World Wide Web Servers

http://www.marshall.edu/wvweb/

Discover West Virginia with the aid of this map-
based interface. Click a city and find links to the
Web servers in that area. General state information is also available.

What's in San Antonio, Texas

http://www.gadsby.com/

San Antonio, Texas, home of the legendary Alamo and Texas Sea World, is the focus of this tourism site. Visitors will find an extensive index of
travel, entertainment, dining, business, and government resources.

Wichita, Kansas

http://www.southwind.net/ict/index.html

Read about the businesses, communities, and
people that make up the City of Wichita. It contains tourism information, along with obligatory
outlines of the area's government and educational resources

Winnepeg, Manitoba, Canada

http://www.freenet.mb.ca/

Local weather, daily headlines, public discussion
groups, and police radar locations are but a few of
the public services that the Blue Sky Community
Networks group provides for the people of Winnipeg with this site.

Winston-Salem Online

http://www.greensboro.nc.us/frontier/wsol/

Maintained by Triad Internet Services, Winston-
Salem Online provides a directory of sites found
in that North Carolina community and links to selected places beyond.

Wisconsin Information and Web Sites

http://infomad.com/wisconsin/

The Wisconsin Pages provide loads of links of and
relating to—you guessed it!—Wisconsin. Visitors
will find access to commercial sites, community
resources, government, entertainment guides,
and general information about the state.

Wisconsin Web Page

http://www.state.wi.us/

Burrow through official information from Wisconsin with Badger, Wisconsin's state information
server. Governmental servers, state directories,

and general information pages fill the page with links to satisfy the questing surfer.

Wisconsin—World Wide Web Consortium

http://www.inmarket.com/wisconsin/

Here is the World Wide Web Consortium's geographic listing for Wisconsin. It features annotated entries in categories such as commercial organizations, cities and communities, education, the University of Wisconsin, government, and other nonprofits.

Wolfe County Schools & Community

http://wolfen.wolfe.k12.ky.us/

Wolfe County, Kentucky provides residents and visitors with information about its schools, civic groups, and businesses, as well as links to "everything on the Net related to Kentucky."

WorcesterWeb

http://worcester.lm.com/

This site covers "the heart of Massachusetts," the Worcester area. Restaurants, schools, museums, businesses, hospitals, and media outlets are among the topics indexed. Includes links to many Worcester-area institutions' home pages.

World-Wide Web Servers: Connecticut

http://ctguide.atlantic.com/sites/servers.html

The Connecticut Guide to Web Sites is a comprehensive list of hundreds of sites maintained for CERN by Atlantic Computing Technology Corporation. The page also includes links to a list of the state's Internet resources at Southern Connecticut State University.

POLAR

Antarctic Support Associates Home Page

http://www.asa.org/

Antarctic Support Associates, based in Englewood, Colorado, features video clips and news about Antarctica. Visitors can check out the latest Antarctic infrared satellite weather images or click to information about the company's mission to serve research facilities in the U.S. Antarctic Program.

Australian Antarctic Division

http://www.antdiv.gov.au/

The Antarctic Division of Australia's Department of Environment, Sport and Territories, provides information here on its science programs, expeditions, employment opportunities, and more. Includes division news and links to other related Web sites.

U.S. MIDDLE ATLANTIC

Atlantic Ocean and Caribbean Sea Images

http://www.hawaii.edu/News/localweather/atl.latest.gif

This link takes visitors to a recent GIF image of the eastern United States and the Atlantic Ocean. During the hurricane season, such images can be used to track storms in the Atlantic. The page is part of a weather Web site at the University of Hawaii.

U.S. SOUTH AND SOUTHEAST

The American South

http://sunsite.unc.edu/doug_m/pages/south/south.html

Electronic resources for southern regional studies are consolidated at the American South Home Page. Access two major academic centers: the University of North Carolina's Center for the Study of the American South, and the University of Mississippi's Center for the Study of Southern Culture. See Editor's Choice.

---

a2z **EDITOR'S CHOICE**

The American South

http://sunsite.unc.edu/doug_m/pages/south/south.html

The American South is loaded with Elvis photos and greets its guests with some "mood music" from "Deliverance." Not an Olympics logo in sight, so we figure this is a trip to the Old South. But hey, y'all: grab a sweet tea, pull up a chair and see what the heck's goin' on down there. Start your anthropologic journey with something different—a look at the funerals of Southern heroes, perhaps. Got an ear for music? You're in luck with a multimedia exhibit for flat-picking guitar wiz Doc Watson. The hopelessly devoted can get the word on the latest International Conference on Elvis, and real live Southerners can click around by state to see what the weather's holding in store for places like Selma and Chattanooga. Everything but the grits.—*Reviewed by Joyce Slaton*

-----------The American South-------------

-----------Internet Resource Center-----------

COUNTRIES AND CONTINENTS

AFRICA

Abyssinia Cyberspace Gateway

http://www.cs.indiana.edu/hyplan/dmulholl/acg.html

The Abyssinia Cyberspace Gateway is a site devoted to celebrating the collective cultures of people from the African nations Djibouti, Eritrea, Ethiopia, Somalia and Somaliland. This site is available for viewers to add their own art, literature, comments and complaints as long as they are nonpolitical in nature.

Jambo Home Page

http://www.africa.kyoto-u.ac.jp/

The Center for African Area Studies at Japan's Kyoto University maintains this overview of the center and its programs. Links to Internet resources on Africa and Japan are also featured. In English and Japanese.

K-12 Africa Guide

http://www.sas.upenn.edu/African_Studies/Home_Page/AFR_GIDE.html

Teachers will find African resources meant for elementary and high school students here. Visitors can download information about specific countries or resources for teaching specific topics, including languages and the environment.

Systems Inter@ctive

http://www.systems.co.za/

The Inter@ct page puts browsers in touch with Web resources in Africa. The page provides info on new site additions and changes, and lays down general facts about the continent.

Times Around the World: Africa

http://www.hilink.com.au/times/africa.html

This Local Times Around the World page features the time of day in each country in Africa. There's also information about African time zones and daylight savings time.

Travel Southern Africa—The Complete Travel Guide

http://rapidttp.com

Travel & Trade Publishing of Johannesburg, South Africa, maintains this online guide to the southern portion of the African continent. Visitors will find links to tourist news, tour companies, travel and accommodation providers, and various cultural resources.

The Universal Black Pages

http://www.gatech.edu/bgsa/blackpages.html

This site offers visitors an index to African diaspora-related Web sites. Categories featured include schools and student organizations, music, art, professional organizations and businesses, to name only a few.

Virtual Tourist—Africa

http://www.vtourist.com/webmap/africa.htm

The Virtual Tourist page provides a clickable map that allows visitors to link to Web servers in Africa. Includes a link to the Virtual Tourist II clickable map, which offers pointers to general information about the continent's countries.

BOTSWANA

African Travel Gateway Botswana

http://cy.co.za/atg/stbrob.html

An online publication designed to promote African tourism, the African Travel Gateway links guests to tourism info for the Wild Continent, including facts, images and maps of the Botswana region.

CAMEROON

Home Page of The Republic of Cameroon

http://www.compufix.demon.co.uk/camweb/

Explore the triangle-shaped region which bridges Western and Central Africa on this home page, with plenty of facts on the history and culture of this agricultural area formerly owned by the French and British.

MADAGASCAR

Madagasikara Home Page

http://www.cable.com/madagas/madagas.htm

Flash cards for learning Malagasy (the language of Madagascar), a Malagasy music guide, lemur photo archives and news from Madagascar are all found on this web site, which is also an online meeting place for the expatriate Malagasy community.

SOUTH AFRICA

THE Home Page 2.0

http://mickey.iafrica.com/~intech/

Tagging itself as "South Africa's premiere Netainment site" THE Home Page 2.0's purpose is to hook visitors up with well-presented and entertaining sites from South Africa. Link to THE's list of "WebPerfect" outstanding South African sites or to THE's list of entertainment links.

Link 2 South Africa

http://link2southafrica.com/

The office of the South African Consulate-General in Los Angeles hopes the updated links on South Africa here may convince tourists and businesses to come hither. Feeling susceptible? Check out info on South African visits here or just find out more on the country and its breaking news.

Virtual Africa Home Page

http://africa.com/

Virtual Africa is an online service providing information on South African business, trade, travel, tourism and real estate. Includes an overview of the people and cultures of South Africa.

Welcome to the Marques Systems South African Net List

http://minotaur.marques.co.za/index.htm

Browsers will find pointers to South African sites on this page. The page posts links to news, entertainment, academic and business information. Visitors can download tips on polishing Web sites here, too.

ANTARCTIC AND ARCTIC

ANTARCTICA

Live From Antarctica

http://quest.arc.nasa.gov/antarctica/index.html

This site is an educational resource for teachers and students interested in Antarctic studies. Find teacher guides and classroom activities, field journals, archives of FrequentlyAsked Questions (FAQ), images, newsletters, and other resources.

A Tourist Expedition to Antarctica

http://http2.sils.umich.edu/Antarctica/Story.html

A tourist aboard an expeditionary cruise to the Antarctic documents his journey here. The trip included famous explorers and experts on Antarctic biology and geology. Visitors can follow his travels and absorb what he learned through photos, journal entries, and sound files on this site.

ARCTIC REGIONS

The Arctic Circle

http://www.lib.uconn.edu/ArcticCircle/

Take an educational trip to one of the coldest spots on Earth, the Arctic Circle. Though icy and harsh, the area still retains a rich cultural history in its native people, a history explored here with a special focus on environmentally-friendly info.

Polar Regions Home Page

http://www.stud.unit.no/~sveinw/arctic/

This home page offers facts and information about the world's polar regions, both North and South. Features include the history of the polar regions, wildlife files and tips on tourism.

ASIA

Asiaville

http://www.asiaville.com/

Information seekers curious about Eastern regions can access "the best of Asian resources" here. Primarily business-focused, this jam-packed site offers classifieds, travel updates, and much more.

Local Times Around the World—Asia and Australasia

http://www.hilink.com.au/times/asia.html

What time is it in Kookaburra or Tokyo? Like an international clock, this Web site answers that question by ticking off local times for Asian and Australasian locales. Visitors can click on a country or region's name to learn the current time there.

ASIA/CENTRAL

Mongolia

http://www.bluemarble.net/~mitch/mongolia.html

The Mongolia page is a study of laws that affect trade and democracy in Mongolia. An overall picture of the country's political and economic structure, including its constitution, is available along with information on the country's people, culture and history.

Uzbekistan Images

Webcorp presents this gallery of photos taken on a wild trip through this South-Central Asian country, which formerly belonged to the Soviet Union. The images are complemented by textual descriptions of the sites and optional audio insights, courtesy of the photographer.

ASIA/EAST

Active Map for WWW Servers in Korea

http://firefox.postech.ac.kr/map/korea_map.html

The interactive map and database at this site allows visitors to find Web servers in cities all over Korea. The Web servers are primarily located at universities, companies and government institutions.

The Anti-Japanophile Japan Page

http://www.iac.co.jp/~reed/japan.html

Access to "almost anything and everything Japanese" is what this server promises to provide. Start with the "latest news" from Japan, then jump to official government pages, from consulates and embassies to the Prime Minister. Cultural info includes links to Sumo pages, as well as Kabuki and "Outrageous Tokyo." See Editor's Choice.

The Center for Global Communications

http://www.glocom.ac.jp/index.html

The Center for Global Communications (GLOCOM), located in Tokyo, Japan, has set up this site to provide information about Japanese society, politics and industry. Links to GLOCOM's text archives, research, news and projects are included. Pages are available in English and Japanese, with Japanese predominating.

China—World Wide Web Virtual Library

http://coombs.anu.edu.au/WWWVLAsian/China.html

The Asian Studies—China branch of the World Wide Web Virtual Library contains China-related links. The Web sites listed discuss everything about China from the democracy movement to ancient astrology and divinations techniques.

China Guide Web Page

http://groupweb.com/chinagc/index.htm

The China Guide Web page touts itself as "the gateway to Chinese culture." It contains links to information about various Chinese medicines and medicinal methods as well as import and export details for the country.

China Home Page

http://www.ihep.ac.cn/china.html

Infused by the spirit of cross-cultural exchange, this site seeks to educate visitors about China's cultural, commercial and scientific resources. Published by Bejing's Institute of High Energy Physics.

China/Chinese-Related Home Page Index

http://www.cnd.org/Other/Chinese.html

The China/Chinese Related Home Pages Index links users to pages from or about China. Guests can link to information on the country, Chinese newsgroups, Chinese associations, servers from China and more from the mysterious East.

ChinaNet

http://www.bta.net.cn/

Visit China and its people through ChinaNet, the service which offers an introduction to the country as well as details about selected cities. Users who can read Chinese can also check the Chinese Information Supermarket for the links they need. In English and Chinese.

Chinascape

http://harmony.wit.com/chinascape/

If you don't leave this page with a better than fair understanding of China and her people, you didn't take the time. It's all here—culture, travel, government, society—including a special section for Chinese living overseas.

East Asian Libraries Cooperative WWW

http://pears.lib.ohio-state.edu/

The East Asian Libraries Cooperative World Wide Web promotes access to research materials on East Asia and the sharing of those materials. The site breaks down the subject areas into Asian, Chinese, Japanese and Korean studies.

---

a2z EDITOR'S CHOICE

The Anti-Japanophile Japan Page

http://www.sas.upenn.edu/~stevenso/japan.html

Though this site claims not to be aimed at the growing population of Japanophiles (those obsessed with anything and everything Japanese), it links directly to anything and everything a true blue Japanophile could possibly want from the Net. Borrowing two of the "underlying tropes of Japanese civilization," the Webmaster asserts, "nothing is as it seems at first glance, and you are only transient." Whatever. Transiting around the Anti-Japanophile Japan Page turns up some fascinating finds, whether you're a 'phile or not. Start with the latest news, professional and street-wise, then jump to official government pages from the prime minister, including the Keidanren, the organization which rules the Japanese economy with an iron fist. Lighter fare offers sumo enthusiasts an opportunity to cheer on their favorite wrestlers. And music fans can locate a headbanging refuge for Japanese heavy metal. As for the Japanese reggae scene ... well, you'll just have to see that one for yourself.—*Reviewed by Joyce Slaton*

The Anti-Japanophile Japan Page

This is not a page for the Japanophile. Yet, it provides exactly what the Japanophile needs most: access to almost anything and everything Japanese. In most cases, the insatiable appetite of this species is only satisfied by the establishment of a relationship with a member of the Japanese race. And sometimes, even this is not enough. The insulted Japanophile may find fault, understandably, by the apparently non-Japanese names of the authors of this page. For those insulted, may I remind you of two of the underlying tropes of Japanese civilization: nothing is as it seems at first glance, and you are only transient.

Gateway to Japan

http://condor.stcloud.msus.edu:20020/tojpn.html

The St. Cloud State University Gateway to Japan site offers links to Japanese home pages and servers from governmental bodies, universities and other groups with Eastern interests. Visitors can also download Kanji-capable Web browsers here.

Hong Kong Terminal

http://zero.com.hk/

Hong Kong Central serves up a mix of cultural information about the city and the whole of China, from Hong Kong stock reports and the China News Digest to a restaurant database and virtual dim sum. One page provides links to Internet sources of political, social and economic news about China. In English.

Hong Kong Trade Development Council

http://www.tdc.org.hk/

For more than thirty years the Hong Kong Trade Development Council has promoted Hong Kong and Asian businesses, and this home page allows visitors to enter the HKTDC site and access the wealth of information and news on business and the business market in both Hong Kong and China.

Japan: City.Net

http://www.city.net/countries/japan/

City.Net lists the major cities of Japan and their characteristics. For example, the city guide for Sapporo, a city to the North known for good skiing, provides a history of the city and tourist information. Information on Japan as a whole is also included.

Japan Information Network

http://jin.jcic.or.jp/

Maintained by the Japan Center for Intercultural Communications, the Japan Information Network presents a wealth of up-to-date info on all aspects of Japan. Current events, regional nd statistical data, plus a Japan Web navigator are featured.

Japan International Cooperation Agency—Institute For International Cooperation Home Page

http://jica.ific.or.jp/

Visitors will learn about the history and future prospects of the Japanese economic juggernaut at this page from the Japan International Cooperation Agency and the Institute for International Cooperation. Links to the World Bank and other economic development resources are provided.

Japanese Open Yellowpage

http://www.st.rim.or.jp/~saito/JOY/JOY.html

Let your fingers do the walking through the Japanese Open Yellowpage Web site, which boasts a directory of links that showcase music, the Internet, graphics, games and computers. In Japanese and English.

Japanese Window

http://jw.nttam.com/

Stanford University hosts the Japanese Window project, a large collection of information about Japanese technology, government, business, travel, culture and children's entertainment. Check out the project's Japan Directory and Events Calendar, or search the entire site for specific info.

The Kaleidoscope of Japan

http://www.aist.go.jp/Htmls/JPIHome.html

Learn a bit about the geography, trade and economy of Japan at this site, with links to brief and kinda odd English-language summaries obviously translated from Japanese. An example: "Doyo is a general term for Japanese traditional songs for children. It is as the Mother Goose's Melodies such as Old King Cole."

Kochi Guide Book, Tourism Information

http://www.kochi-ct.ac.jp/tourism/

The International Affairs division of the Japanese government offers this Web site with extensive information and resources on Japanese history, geography, fisheries, forestries, art and industry. In English and Japanese.

The Land of Beauty

http://www.cnd.org/Scenery/

The scenic beauty of China comes to life on this page. Included are high resolution photos of scenic sites in the country, ancient buildings and natural landscapes.

National Pages

http://info.fuw.edu.pl/national.html

This reference page contains links to the home pages of selected European nations and Japan. Visitors can just click a flag and go.

The Republic of China

http://peacock.tnjc.edu.tw/ROC.HTML

The Republic of China (Taiwan) provides information about the branches of its government here. The site includes an audio file of the country's national anthem, details about political parties and information about unification with mainland China.

SunSITE Japan

http://sunsite.sut.ac.jp/

The Science University of Tokyo offers this SunSITE page with a wealth of info on Asia, multimedia, computers, technology and a collection of archives. Visitors can also link to other SunSITE pages. In English and Japanese.

Taiwan: City.Net

http://www.city.net/countries/taiwan/

Find the gateway to Taiwan, its culture and its vital statistics from this page provided by City.Net. Here visitors get the flavor of Asia while perusing information about languages, regions, education and government. Maps and tourism guides are included.

Taiwan World Wide Web Master Index

http://peacock.tnjc.edu.tw/ROC_sites.html

The Taiwanese index provides listings of over 180 Web servers searchable by alphabetical order, geographical order or date of entry. Includes a form for submitting new listings.

Tour in China

http://www.ihep.ac.cn/tour/china_tour.html

Travel to the Tour in China home page and take a virtual tour of the country through links to each of its provinces. Tour in China also includes a link to the Hong Kong online guide and a map of China.

U.S.-Japan Technology Management Center

http://fuji.stanford.edu/

Stanford University introduces its U.S.-Japan Technology Management Center here. Visitors to the site will find information and course details regarding Japan's unique business and technology culture. A guide to Japanese information resources also is included.

Window on China

http://china-window.com/

Go ahead, take a peek. Look into this window to catch a glimpse of modern Chinese culture and life. Business and political news reports from several Chinese news service are gathered here. Visitors can also explore world entertainment and travel.

ASIA/SOUTH

Bangladesh Home Pages

http://www.asel.udel.edu/~kazi/bangladesh/bd.html

The encyclopedic Bangladesh Home Pages site features information about the South Asian country whose name means "Land of Bengals." Bursting at the seams with facts, the page points the guest to enough info on the country to transform the ignorant into Bangladesh experts.

India

http://www.ic.gov/94fact/country/112.html

The vital stats on India, such as population, climate, religions, etc., plus some pretty darned strange stats. Anyone need to know about India's illicit drug trade or how many total kilometers of paved highway have been laid in India?

India Home Page

http://mathlab.sunysb.edu/~cpandya/india.html

Though under construction at the time of review and with many links inoperable, the India Home Page still connects users to eclectic and interesting info on India. Indians looking for old friends can fill out an online form here to post their name or browse through lists of already-registered Indian people. Other highlights include links to immigration info, Indian holidays, currency exchange rates.

India Online

http://www.indiaonline.com/

India Online aims to provide current info pertaining to India and countries of the Indian subcontinent. Resources include links to businesses, telecommunication services, politics, travel and more.

India World

http://indiaworld.com/open/index.html

A world of information on India is available at the IndiaWorld—India on the Internet page. Browsers can link to daily news from India, company profiles of Indian businesses, film reviews, Indian airline schedules and much more on the country.

INDOlink

http://www.genius.net/indolink/

INDOlink is an information server dedicated to India and Indian communities around the globe. A diverse collection of Indian resource pages here include news, film reviews, legal info, travel, poetry and recipes.

Maharashtra, India

http://wwwvms.utexas.edu/~savkar/rashtra.html

The Western Indian state of Maharashtra is the focus here, with the standard general information on the area plus the finer points of the area's cultural interests, historical perspective and local population.

Some Indian Stuff

http://www.cs.wisc.edu/~navin/india/india.html

Unlike most dry pages meant to electronically explore a country for the benefit of tourists, the maintainer of this page describes it as "a collection of random links" on India. The mostly-entertainment links include sites on films, music, photographs, movies, travel, humor, and more.

Tamil Nadu, India

http://tamil.math.utk.edu/cgi-bin/tamilnadu

Tamil Nadu, the southernmost state of India, is examined and unveiled on this page. It offers images of the region along with information about the Tamil language and the culture of the 55 million people who speak it.

A Visit to Nepal

http://enigma.phys.utk.edu/~syost/nepal.html

This personal account of a six-week tour of Nepal provides a variety of journal entries, photos and interactive maps. Includes links to other travel and tourism sites.

West Bengal Independent Page

http://www.gl.umbc.edu/~achatt1/wbengal.html

West Bengal is one of the most culturally and ethnically diverse states of India. Travelers to its home page will find a treasure trove of information, including details about tourism, language, and culture.

World Wide Web Virtual Library—India

http://webhead.com/WWWVL/India/

The ever-comprehensive World Wide Web Virtual Library dishes up this index of information pertaining to India online. From here visitors can access just about everything, from culture and economics to political updates.

ASIA/SOUTHEAST

Bali

http://www.indo.com/

Watch the beautiful Balinese dancers as you let the waves gently washing ashore lull you into an unbelievable peace. Well, at least you can dream about it when you look at this page full of information about where to go and what to do in Bali.

Bali FastFacts

http://www.hk.super.net/~rlowe/bali/bali.html

Maps and images of Bali are among the many resources available on the island nation's home page. The site features information on hotels, restaurants, cultural events, tourist attractions and tips on bargaining with local shopkeepers.

Bali: The Online Travel Guide

http://werple.mira.net.au/~wreid/bali_p1a.html

The Bali Online Travel Guide promises a complete view of the Indonesian island from off the beaten tourist track. Visitors here can find cheap accomodations, cultural attractions and a gourmet restaurant guide.

Bimasakti: Indonesian WWW Galaxy

http://www.cs.utexas.edu/users/adison/cgi/bimasakti

Bimasakti is a user-maintained Indonesian home page, complete with a database and site navigator, which showcases the Indonesian Internet community. Visitors can start with art and browse straight through to travel on this informative home page.

Chiang Mai University and Northern Thailand

http://www.chiangmai.ac.th/

Chiang Mai University (CMU) offers this Web site with a variety of CMU and Northern Thailand information. Visitors can also check out a collection of pages on SEA games. In English and Thai.

East Timor

http://amadeus.inesc.pt/~jota/Timor

Information about the political and social turmoil in East Timor, a former Portuguese colony under the control of Indonesia since 1975, can be found here. Visitors can read archives of political information and hair-raising accounts of torture.

East Timor—TimorNet

http://www.uc.pt/Timor/TimorNet.html

Maintained at Portugal's University of Coimbra, the TimorNet archives information about the people of East Timor, a Portuguese colony in Southeast Asia annexed in the mid-1970s by Indonesia. Links to an introductory course on the subject, a guide to Internet resources and an in-depth treatment of the history are featured.

Holiday in Cambodia

http://none.coolware.com/entmt/cambodia/cambodia.html

"Holiday in Cambodia" is a multimedia CD-ROM conveying in text and images a tourist's eye view of the Southeast Asian country. Visitors can preview elements of BlackBird software's upcoming title at this site.

Indonesia FTP Archives

ftp://ftp.ee.umanitoba.ca/pub/indonesian/

This University of Manitoba FTP archive contains useful and eclectic Indonesian files, including embassy addresses, song lyrics and an English-Indonesian dictionary, all downloadable and available for the clicking.

Indonesian Home Page

http://www.umanitoba.ca/indonesian/homepage.html

University of Manitoba's all-encompassing home page for Indonesia serves up a wealth of information on the Asian country. Visitors will find a travel guide, recipes and details about Indonesian music, arts, publications and businesses here.

Journey to Vietnam

http://maingate.net/vn/

This page offers complete information on traveling and doing business in Vietnam. Visitors can click cities on an interactive map to obtain historical notes, geography, cultural events, photos and business opportunities.

Malaysia

http://www.jaring.my/

The Malaysia home page provides data about information servers and gives background information on the region, with specifics on education and tourism, government, the economy and research and development.

Malaysian Information Sources

http://st-www.cs.uiuc.edu/users/chai/malaysia.html

Malaysian Information Sources is a directory that can link browsers up with nearly everything related to Malaysia. From here, find news services, personal home pages, maps, organizations and more from the Southeast Asian country.

Malaysia Online, WWW HomePage

http://www.mol.com

Malaysia Online is a comprehensive storehouse of information about the Asian country. Job listings, news in several languages, travel information and more are provided.

Picturesque Philippines

http://www.europa.com/~ria/pinoy.html

The Picturesque Philippines Page offers traditional touristy resources along with 'zines, literary journals and other cultural fare. Experience island life online courtesy of the intimate historical and cultural introduction afforded at this site.

Siam.NET Welcome

http://www.siam.net/

Take a virtual tour of Thailand using the links found at Welcome to Siam.NET. Link to information on Thai cities, travel, tourism, business and much more or download Thai video and audio clips.

Soc.Culture.Filipino the Philippine Cyberbayan—What's New?

http://www.mozcom.com/SCF/Body.html

This colorful site from the Filipino-interest newsgroup is filled with information on the Phillipines, including a business directory, many personal pages with pictures, news and Philippines-related groups.

Southeast Asia

http://sunsite.nus.sg/asiasvc.html

This information server guides visitors to a wealth of resources relating to the 10 countries within Southeast Asia. Selections here include historical and infrastructure information, as well as travel material and shopping destinations.

SunSITE Singapore

http://sunsite.nus.sg/

SunSITE Singapore offers information on the country and its various information providers, with an emphasis on Asian Web sites. Links to software and information archives are also available.

The Thai Heritage Page

http://www.cs.ait.ac.th/~wutt/wutt.html

The Thai Heritage Page offers cultural backgrounders on Thailand and the historical Kingdom of Siam. Visitors will find information on language, music, customs, history, Buddhism and tourism.

Thailand World Wide Web Information

http://www.chiangmai.ac.th/thmap.html

From the Chiang Mai University site, this interactive page features a map-based interface encouraging visitors to explore Thailand. The cities indicated support their own Web information servers.

Traveling to Indonesia

http://www.emp.pdx.edu/htliono/travel.html

Maintained by an Indonesian expatriate living in the United States, this guide to the Southeast Asian archipelago offers a variety of cultural, geographic and tourist resources. Visit here for a one-stop shopping list of information for traveling to Indonesia.

Vietnam—Vannevar New Media, Inc.

http://vannevar.com/vn/

Texas-based Internet publishing and applications company Vannevar New Media, Inc. presents business home pages for the Vietnam Trading Corporation's generous map of Vietnamese Internet resources. Boasting "over fifteen hundred pages"—when last we checked—this in-depth resource covers the national spectrum of this "dynamic economic region," from cultural pondering to banking, travel tips and nifty road maps.

AUSTRALIA & OCEANIA

Local Times Around the World—Asia and Australasia

http://www.hilink.com.au/times/asia.html

What time is it in Kookaburra or Tokyo? Like an international clock, this Web site answers that question by ticking off local times for Asian and Australasian locales. Visitors can click on a country or region's name to learn the current time there.

AUSTRALIA

Aussie Index

http://www.aussie.com.au/

The Aussie Index catalogs all that is Australian on the World Wide Web. Divided into commercial and non-commercial databases, visitors can

search or browse this enormous offering of the country's electronic resources.

Australia: City.Net

http://www.city.net/countries/australia/

If you're looking for information about cities, regions or states in Australia, or general information about Australia itself, this City.Net site links you up. Information on travel, sports, education and parks can be found here, along with guides and maps.

Australian Web Servers

http://www.csu.edu.au/links/ozmap.html

Charles Stuart University maintains this interactive map providing information about Web servers in Australia. Visitors also can access a geographically-categorized listing of Australian servers or indices offering links to tourist, weather and governmental resources.

Australian World Heritage Areas

http://kaos.erin.gov.au/land/conservation/wha/auswha.html

The World Heritage List contains 469 sites worldwide "with exceptional natural and/or cultural values." This page supplies information on the 11 Australian sites on the list. Click on a map to learn more about sites you are interested in.

The Bushwalking Page

http://www.anatomy.su.oz.au/danny/bushwalking/index.html

The Bushwalking Page provides hikers (bushwalkers in Aussie lingo) with everything they need to know to get out into the bush—weather reports, maps, environmental information, gear, books and advice. Links are made to U.S. backcountry web sites, but this is mostly an Australian page.

Information about Australia

http://www.anu.edu.au/foyer/aus.html

The Information about Australia page contains links to Australian guides, government sites and tourism resources. Obtain info regarding national parks, territorial governments, railroads, airlines and the 2000 Olympic games in Sydney.

NEW ZEALAND

New Zealand

http://archpropplan.auckland.ac.nz/misc/sources9.html

What exactly is a kiwi? You haven't been to New Zealand if you think it's only an egg-shaped fruit with green flesh. Use this page to jump to information—serious to frivolous—about the island country. Lob in some day mate! (drop in for a visit)

New Zealand on the Web

http://nz.com/

A group of homesick New Zealanders living abroad founded the New Zealand on the Web page to connect Web users all over the world to info from New Zealand. Take a virtual tour of New Zealand or contact New Zealanders at home or abroad. While you're at it, Aikiko International hopes you'll stop by and check out their Web page design and marketing services.

New Zealand Resources

http://www.lincoln.ac.nz/libr/nz/

This simply-designed page leads Net users looking for information on or from New Zealand to hundreds of resources arranged by topics such as social science, women, health and more. Links to other New Zealand collective pages are also provided.

OCEANIA/PACIFIC ISLANDS

Guam

http://ns.gov.gu/

The island of Guam, "where America's day begins," operates this official Web site to promote its culture and tourism and to provide mainlanders with some understanding of the island's status within the union. This site offers e-mail access to the government of Guam, information about Guam's Internet facilities, and entrance and customs requirements.

Vanuatu: A Small Place in the South Pacific

http://www.clark.net/pub/kiaman/vanuatu.html

Vanuatu is a very small island nation located in the South Pacific Ocean. Visitors to this page will discover maps, photos, historical notes and the CIA World Factbook for this tiny but exotic country.

TASMANIA

Tasmania—Tourism Information for the WWW

http://www.tas.gov.au/tourism/tasman.html

The Department of Tourism, Sport and Recreation in Hobart, Australia, provides tourism information on Tasmania here. Includes listings of special events, an image library, and links to an interactive tour and other Tasmanian servers.

EUROPE

Europe

http://www.tue.nl/europe/

Click on a European country and this service will connect you with a Web site for the country that contains a navigating map as the first page. Each map is additionally connected to an informational site about the country.

European Home Page

http://s700.uminho.pt/europa.html

The European Home Page provides an interactive map which links users to individual country's home pages by clicking on that nation's flag. There is also a text only version for visitors who cannot view graphics. Includes a link to the Beautiful Cultural European site which offers travel tips.

National Pages

http://info.fuw.edu.pl/national.html

This reference page contains links to the home pages of selected European nations and Japan. Visitors can just click a flag and go.

Virtual Tourist—Europe

http://www.vtourist.com/webmap/europe.htm

Netscape's Virtual Tourist page for Europe offers a clickable map of Europe that leads to listings of World Wide Web servers available in each country. Also contains links to sites on creating interactive graphics.

AUSTRIA

Austria: City.Net

http://www.city.net/countries/austria/

The City.Net information service maintains this site for its Austria resource index. Visitors will find links to national, regional and local organizations, culture and language guides and tourist information.

Information Servers in Austria

http://www.ifs.univie.ac.at/austria.html

This page links to detailed lists of Austrian information servers, organized by city. Visitors will also find listings of Austrian symposiums, seminars and conferences here.

BELGIUM

Belgian WWW/Gopher Resource Map

http://info1.vub.ac.be:8080/Belgium_map/index.html

This site provides an overview of all the Web and gopher servers in Belgium. Lists of academic, government, tourism, entertainment and other pages are listed. Connect directly to any site via an interactive map.

Belgium: Overview

http://pespmc1.vub.ac.be/BelgCul.html

Visitors will find an encyclopedia-style exploration of cultural, governmental and statistical information on Belgium at this site. Map imagery provides a detailed look at highways and railways.

BULGARIA

All about Bulgaria

http://www.cs.columbia.edu/~radev/bulginfo.html

Resources on Bulgaria are featured at this site, which includes Frequently Asked Questions (FAQs), an index to Bulgarian Web pages and the soc.culture.bulgaria newsgroup archive.

Bulgaria Information

http://www.bulgaria.com/

Learn about Bulgarian businesses, musical folklore, and educational and government institutions at this site, which spotlights the Southeastern European country. Those planning a Black Sea vacation will want to check out the travel facts as well.

Bulgaria on the Internet

http://pisa.rockefeller.edu:8080/Bulgaria/

At the Bulgaria on the Internet page, visitors can learn more about the royal family, connect to online newspapers and announcements, check out the Frequently Asked Questions (FAQ) file and link to a number of related sites and resources.

CROATIA

Republic of Croatia

http://tjev.tel.etf.hr/

The colorful home page for the Republic of Croatia is a comprehensive guide to the people, places and, yes, the computers of this newly-independent land. Visitors can tour the country's major cities and scenic wonders and find individual computer users in Croatia. In English.

CYPRUS

Cyprus

http://www.wam.umd.edu/~cyprus/tourist.html

If you can't afford a real break, at least catch a little virtual holiday fun at this site dedicated to tourist attractions of the Mediterranean island Cyprus. If all that name conjures up are images of olives and hairy men, then click here to see what you're missing!

Main Page for Cyprus

http://force.stwing.upenn.edu:8001/~durduran/cyprus.shtml

The Cyprus home page contains a tour of the island, maps and cultural information. Includes links to government servers, business information and pointers to organizations and political parties.

CZECH REPUBLIC

Czech Express Country Home Page

http://cech.cesnet.cz/

The Czech Express Country home page provides information about the culture, people and news events of the Czech Republic. Includes links to dozens of business, government, cultural and tourism information servers.

DENMARK

Clickable Map of Denmark

http://info.denet.dk/dkmap.html

The clickable map of Denmark found here provides an easy way for browsers to find Danish Web servers as well as information about Denmark. Click on a region to access cultural, commercial, educational and other information on the country.

FINLAND

Facts about Finland

http://www.funet.fi/Finland/index.html

At the Facts about Finland site, virtual world travelers can find information about Finland and Helsinki with corresponding maps. Maps of Europe and the world are also linked to this site. The bilingual pages have English translation.

Finland

http://www.csc.fi/tiko/finland.html

The Republic of Finland site features information about the country and its history, and includes links to a fact sheet, a clickable map and related Finnish Web sites.

Statistics Finland

http://www.stat.fi/sf/home.html

The Internet site for Finland's National Statistical Institute, this location provides the country's statistical news as well as publication and database information. Available in both Finnish and English.

Tampere Telephone Company: Finland page

http://www.tpo.fi/english/finland/index.html

The Tampere Telephone Company sponsers this Web page devoted to Finland, dubbed "large and clean" here. Read an overview of Finland here, or link to a clickable map, the Finland fact sheet and an index of Finnish Web servers.

FRANCE

FranceWeb Les Carnets de Route

http://www.francenet.fr/franceweb/
FWCarnetRoute.html

A directory of French cultural, commercial and computer-related sites on the Internet are compiled at this site, which tackles subjects as diverse as science, food, even French erotica. In French.

French Connection—AdmiNet

http://www.adminet.com/

AdmiNet is dedicated to providing online information about France's government authorities and public services. Its home page also contains links to resources of regional and cultural interest. In English and French.

Grenoble Research Libraries

http://www-pole.grenet.fr/POLE/REDOC/

The research libraries of Grenoble, France, offer their work to the world at large, particularly to anyone who needs to access research about the Alpine region. Information is in French.

Hapax: French Resources on the Web

http://hapax.be.sbc.edu/

Hapax is an experimental server providing pointers to a variety of French-related resources on the Web for university students and teachers. Visitors will find a substantial collection of French material, from art and history to humor and factbook information.

La France

http://www.urec.fr/france/france.html

Explore France via this map-based interface. A click on a French region produces a map of that area. From the smaller map, a click on the name of a town produces a list of its Web servers. The sites are also organized in an alphabetical listing by subject and by region. In French, with some English.

Liste des Serveurs World Wide Web en France

http://web.urec.fr/docs/www_list_fr.html

This site provides a comprehensive, alphabetical listing of Web servers in France, including commercial servers, regional information services, university pages and more. In French.

The Webfoot's Guide to France

http://www.webfoot.com/travel/guides/france/
france.html

Heading to France? This comprehensive online guide provides official French tourism information, the CIA factbook of the country, and current exchange rates. It also includes U.S. State Department travel warnings, of which there are very few.

GERMANY

Germany's Web Servers

http://www.leo.org/demap/

Visitors to this page will find a clickable map offering access to Web servers in Germany's cities. For those who prefer text only menus, a list of city servers is also available.

Germany: City.Net

http://www.city.net/countries/germany/

City.Net is an online guide to travel, entertainment, business and government information for communities worldwide. Visit this site for the service's Germany index, featuring links to city and state info and resources.

Germany.net

http://www.germany.net/index.html

Germany.net is a server designed for German speakers who want commercial information and advertising messages. The English page offers links about the country, its economy, German news and a pitch to companies that want to target the German market. Mostly in German with some English.

GREECE

Greece: City.Net

http://www.city.net/countries/greece/

City.Net's Greece page features information about Greek cities, islands and culture. It includes general factbook information about Greece, along with information for travelers, maps and a database of the Greek language.

Greek Tourist

http://www.Greece.org/hellas/index.html

Greece: The Traveler's Advisor offers a variety of useful info for browsers planning to take a trip to Greece. Check out general tourist tips for planning a trip, or take a virtual tour of Greece, complete with pictures.

HUNGARY

Hungarian Home Page

http://www.fsz.bme.hu/hungary/
homepage.html

A collection of links to Hungarian World Wide Web servers, searchable by geographic region or type of organization, can be found here. Also available are indices of Hungarian FTP servers, Telnet services and Hungary-related newsgroups.

Hungary Directory

http://www.hungary.com/hudir/

Access a comprehensive Internet directory for Hungary through HuDir, part of the larger Hungary Network. The searchable site offers thousands of links to information sorted by categories, ranging from the arts to travel. In English and Hungarian.

Hungary Network

http://www.hungary.com/

Hungary Network is a directory which ambitously claims to link to all Hungarian online resources. There's a section called Hungarian Who's Who Online for locating people, a government and diplomatic corner for political-minded visitors, and sections on business, travel and entertainment. In Hungarian and English.

Introduction to Hungary

http://www.fsz.bme.hu/hungary/intro.html

This Hungary introductory page is devoted to educating people about this country, its history and its people. Learn how Hungarians helped build Hollywood, why they were created by God to sit on horseback and why the Hungarian language is so different from other languages. See Editor's Choice.

ICELAND

Iceland

http://www.centrum.is/icerev/

The country of Iceland is the topic at hand here. Visitors can download daily news from the Icelandic media, browse through quarterly business and nature/travel magazines, order books from a publishing house and link to other Icelandic pages.

Iceland World Wide Web Servers Index

http://www.isnet.is/WWW/servers.html

ISnet, a joint service of Internet information providers NORDUnet and EUnet, maintains this site for its index of World Wide Web servers in Iceland. Visit here for an extensive collection of links to educational, governmental and commercial services.

ITALY

Italian WWW server map

http://www.pi.cnr.it/NIR-IT

This Web site indexes information on Italy taken from the U.S. Central Intelligence Agency's 1994 world fact book. Visitors can read about the country's geography, people, government, economy and defense forces here.

Italy: City.Net

http://www.city.net/countries/italy/

Browsers planning a trip to Italy can first take a virtual tour of Italian cities, islands and regions from this page. The page also includes an English to Italian dictionary and links to other City Net pages.

Windows On Italy

http://www.mi.cnr.it/WOI/

Windows on Italy, provided by the Italian National Research Council, offers a look at the historical, cultural and political aspects of the Southern European country. Visit here for daily news, links to Italian regions and pictures.

LATVIA

Clickable Map of Latvia

http://www.vernet.lv/Latvia/sites.html

Featured at this site is a clickable map of Latvia. Clicking on regions of the map of "the country of amber coasts," takes visitors to Internet sites at those locations. An index of Latvian resources also is available.

The Hornbill Web Page

http://www.latnet.lv/

This home page dedicated to the Eastern European state of Latvia provides a wealth of state-related information and resources. Visitors can read daily news and link to Latvia information servers and related sites of interest.

Latvia

http://www.ciesin.ee/LATVIA/

Are you considering a trip to Latvia? If so, stop by this page that features tourism information along with maps, jumps to various cities with pages and details about companies in the Eastern European country.

Latvia Online

http://www.vernet.lv/Latvia/

This Web site provides general information about Latvia, including a copy of the Northern European republic's constitution and data from the U.S. State Department's annual report on human rights. Includes travel information and links to directories of Latvian Web servers, news agencies and business pages.

LIECHTENSTEIN

Liechtenstein Links

http://www.cc.gatech.edu/gvu/people/Phd/Benjamin.Watson/links/liechtenstein.html

Liechtenstein Links gives browsers direct access to resources on Liechtenstein, including tourist information and maps as well as to media and business sources. This is also the place to find out how the country runs an online Internet lottery.

LITHUANIA

Mirror of Lithuania

http://www.mcs.com/~thomas/www/lt/

This is a collection of mirror sites for Internet servers in Lithuania. Visitors can locate various Lithuanian servers and select the nearest geographical mirror site for that location.

LUXEMBOURG

Home Page for Luxembourg

http://www.restena.lu/luxembourg/lux_welcome.html

A collection of links and resources to Web servers in the European nation of Luxembourg are available at this site. Visitors can hyperlink through a list of comprehensive topics and categories. In French and English.

Small is Beautiful—Welcome to Luxembourg

http://rzstud1.rz.uni-karlsruhe.de/~ujiw/lx.html

Luxemborg, "that small country in the middle of Europe," is the focus here, with essays on its culture and tourist attractions and links to other Luxembourg resources on the Net.

MACEDONIA

Soros-Home

http://www.soros.org.mk/

The Open Society Institute of Macedonia unveils the first Macedonian WWW server. Visitors can read and search news archives, then follow a link to the Republic of Macedonia home page or browse a list of other Web servers in Macedonia.

Virtual Macedonia

http://www.rit.edu/~bvs4997/Macedonia/

Visitors to this page will find an overview of Macedonia's past and its prospects for the future. Browsers can link to cultural particulars, facts and figures or take a photographic tour.

---

a2z EDITOR'S CHOICE

Introduction to Hungary

http://www.fsz.bme.hu/hungary/intro.html

Are Hungarians extraterrestrial beings? Nobel Prize-winning Italian physicist Enrico Fermi thought so—perhaps because the Hungarian language is so unique, or maybe because famous Hungarian composer Bela Bartok wrote such spacey music. Or so this Webmaster theorizes. Hundreds of factoids on religious practices, demographics, and a host of important dates in Hungarian history lines these pages on the people who, as legend has it, were created by God to sit on horseback. Hungry fans of Hungary will definitely want to sample tantalizing recipes for paprika chicken and, natch, the goulash.—*Reviewed by Joyce Slaton*

Do extra-terrestrial beings exist? - the Nobel Prize winning Italian physicist, Enrico Fermi, was once asked by his disciples in California. Of course, Fermi answered - they are already here among us, they are called Hungarians...

You are welcome here, in the homeland of the extra-terrestrial beings. Why did Fermi think this about us? Because Hollywood's dream factories were partly built by Hungarian producers, directors, writers and cameramen? Or because - as the saying goes - Hungarians were created by God to sit on horseback? Perhaps because Bela Bartok's music in his own time was considered extra-terrestrial by many? Or because of the Hungarian language, which does not resemble any world language and sounds so strange?

MOLDOVA

Virtual Moldova

http://www.info.polymtl.ca/zuse/tavi/www/Moldova.html

Virtual Moldova creates an info-environment for this Eastern European country, including a clickable map to select a specific regions. The page explores historical perspectives and shares present resources, taking visitors from one information destination to another.

NETHERLANDS

Holland City List

http://www.xxlink.nl/cities/

The Holland City Index allows users to click on the first letter of the city of their interest for a gateway into that location. The site also allows links to information on cities outside of the Netherlands.

Holland ExxPO

http://www.xxLINK.nl/exxpo/

If it's Dutch and it's on the Web, it probably can be found here. Holland ExxPO features a searchable database of resources, or visitors can browse an alphabetical listing of over 1,500 sites from the Netherlands. If checking out the sites inspires you to learn more, visit the Holland City Index or the geographical index to Dutch sites with a clickable map and an index of categories.

Netherlands Home

http://www.eeb.ele.tue.nl/dhp/

Browsers can use a clickable map to reach Web sites in the Netherlands here. The site includes links to sites about the country's government, politics, cities, education, media and commerce.

Statistics Netherlands

http://www.cbs.nl/

The government agency Statistics Netherlands collects, processes and analyzes data about the Dutch, then publishes it here. Visitors can read press releases, visit statistical links and access indexed data. In English and Dutch.

NORWAY

SN Horisont

http://www.oslonett.no/

Speakers of Norwegian will find a grab bag of info from Norway here: sports, news, Oslo-based Internet access providers and a general help file. If you don't speak the language, don't bother linking, Norwegian is the only option here.

Statistics Norway

http://www.ssb.no/

Statistics Norway holds a storehouse of statistical information about Norway's environment, popu-

lation, economic trends, public finances, and much more. Mostly in Norwegian, but plenty of English, too.

POLAND

Poland Network Resources

http://info.fuw.edu.pl/pzs/pzs.html

Web cruisers interested in Poland and Polish culture can access a multitude of resources via this robust repository. In addition to discussions groups, Internet providers and publications, here you'll find a comprehensive index of Polish Web sites.

Polish Home Page

http://info.fuw.edu.pl/poland.html

This Web site provides information about Poland and Polish culture. An extensive collection of pages and links here provide info on the country's government, geography, tourism, economy, media, sports, history and education. In English and Polish.

SunSITE Poland

http://sunsite.icm.edu.pl/

SunSITE Poland provides information about this European country's culture, tourism, and political, scientific and the academic scene. Text available in both English and Polish.

PORTUGAL

Portugal Guide

http://s700.uminho.pt/Portugal/portugal.html

A variety of useful information about Portugal is available at this Web site, with content ranging from historical information to soccer. Sections are divided into information useful to Portuguese and non-Portuguese people.

SAPO, Servidor de Apontadores Portugueses

http://sapo.ua.pt/

To discover electronic resources in Portugal, search this catalog of Portuguese servers. Link to commercial, cultural and governmental sites across the country. In Portuguese.

ROMANIA

Romanian Embassy—Washington, D.C.

http://www.embassy.org/romania/

Visitors to the Romanian Embassy on the Web will find a wealth of information about the country and its people. Frequently asked questions are answered, travel and tourism information is offered, and basic facts and images are presented.

RUSSIA

All Regions of Russia by Pictures

http://www.cs.toronto.edu/~mes/russia/photo.html

This Web site contains photos and an illustrated history of Russia, as well as an English/Russian dictionary and loads of other information about Russia, including maps, travel tips and current weather information.

Little Russia in San Antonio, TX

http://mars.uthscsa.edu/Russia/

Discover Russia on this page authored in San Antonio by a Russian immigrant who now teaches at the University of Texas Health and Science Center. Find Russian art, literature, musical treasures, tourist sights, computer games, Internet server network maps, even reprints of periodicals.

REESWeb : Russian and East European Studies

http://www.pitt.edu/~cjp/rsecon.html

The University Center for Russian and East European Studies at the University of Pittsburgh provides a page on business, economics and law resources. This is part of the World Wide Web Virtual Library and REESweb, which contains Russian and East European resources in a variety of areas.

Russia: City.Net

http://www.city.net/countries/russia/

The busy world catalogers at City.Net list Russia's major cities, with an extensive repository of information including travel guides and on-line excursions. Included are links to culture, language, education and maps.

Russian Web Servers

http://www.ras.ru/map.html

Access the growing list of Russian Web servers through a series of image maps on this page. Click on a region to view enlarged maps with more information about servers in that area. Visitors can also view a text list of servers.

Russian World Wide Web Servers

http://www.ac.msk.su/map_list.html

This index presents a listing of Russian servers arranged alphabetically by city. Includes a link to an interactive map of Russian sites.

SLOVAKIA

Slovakia Tour Guide

http://www.sanet.sk/Slovakia/TourGuide/

Slovakia Tour Guide site uses a clickable map of the Eastern European nation to direct visitors to information on over 30 destinations of political, historical or cultural significance. Take a virtual tour, or click on sites of geographic interest for quick info.

Slovakia Document Store

http://www.eunet.sk/slovakia/slovakia.html

This page offers an extensive collection of news and resources concerning the Central European Republic of Slovakia. Visitors and prospective travelers will find a topic index of information about business, travel, culture, events, demographics and much more.

Welcome to Slovakia

http://www.tuzvo.sk/

The Slovakia home page gives online visitors a virtual tour of this newly-independent European country, a translation and pronunciation guide to common words of greeting, information about the government, a round-up of daily news and a mailing list dedicated to helping visitors locate relatives in Slovakia.

SLOVENIA

Information Servers in Slovenia

http://www.ijs.si/slo/resources/

Information servers in the Eastern European nation Slovenia are the subject of this site. Search for information by subject, organization or protocol, or read general information about the country's economic, governmental and cultural resources.

SloWWWenia

http://www.ijs.si/slo.html

This guide to Slovenia, provided by the Jozef Stefan Institute of Ljubljana, Slovenia, offers an overview of the country's history, culture and natural landscape. Includes links to travel information, state research facilities, traditional food recipes and more.

SPAIN

Spain: City.Net

http://www.city.net/countries/spain/

Yet another country exploration by City.Net, this directory for Spain includes so many connections to tourist-friendly travel info and Spanish cities, it'll have you on the next plane. Want to travel further? Check out the rest of City.Net's catalog.

SWEDEN

Stockholm Resource Map

http://www.sunet.se/map/stockholm.html

Find links to Internet servers located in or concerning Sweden at the Stockholm Resource Map Site. Navigate the country's digital landscape with the Internet resource map provided here.

Swedish Page

http://www.it-kompetens.se/swedish.html

Visitors will learn about Sweden's culture, history, government and educational system here. The site also includes information on the Nobel prize, plus links to Swedish media. In English and Swedish.

SWITZERLAND

Information about Switzerland

http://www.ethz.ch/swiss/Switzerland_Info.html

An online Swiss almanac, the Information about Switzerland site provides vital statistics about the Alpine nation. The country's geography, history and government are all covered here in the brief factual style of an encyclopedia entry.

Switzerland—Home

http://heiwww.unige.ch/switzerland/

The Graduate Institute of International Studies, located in Switzerland, offers an interactive map of Switzerland providing a wide range of information on the country. Visitors can zoom into cities and learn more about them, access Swiss institutions, businesses, find out about upcoming events and tap into several directories.

UKRAINE

Ukraine

http://www.physics.mcgill.ca/WWW/oleh/ukr-info.html

The Ukraine page links users up to a plethora of sites on Ukrainian topics. Want to know what the Ukraine looks like? Then check out the map or maybe you'd rather see its coat of arms or flag? There's also historical outlines, people to meet and just about anything else you would want to know about this former Soviet country.

Ukraine: Frequently Asked Questions Plus Home Page

http://www.std.com/sabre/UKRAINE.html

Visitors to this site will find a Frequently Asked Questions (FAQ) file concerning the Ukraine—its laws, culture, publications, organizations and commerce. The site is maintained by the SABRE Foundation by virtue of a grant from the Eurasia Foundation.

UNITED KINGDOM

England: City.Net

http://city.net/countries/united_kingdom/england/

Excite's City.Net information service maintains this site for its England resource index. Visitors will find links to national, regional and local organizations, culture and language guides, tourist information, and much more.

The Gathering of the Clans

http://www.tartans.com/

The Gathering of the Clans home page is devoted to "all things Scottish," including history, culture and folklore, plus the basic facts on the country. Images of Scottish heraldry are featured.

Photos of Scotland

http://www.cs.ucl.ac.uk/misc/uk/scotland_photos.html

A collection of images from Scotland's countryside includes sweeping vistas and curling lochs (but no monsters that we could see). For those eager to traverse the moors and mountains of the region, links to mountain safety and equipment requirements are provided.

Scotland: Gateway to Scotland

http://www.geo.ed.ac.uk/home/scotland/scotland.html

The Department of Geography at the University of Edinburgh, Scotland maintains this site to provide an in-depth look at its country. Visit here to learn about Scotland's rich history, mountainous scenery and political structure. Links to information on the other countries of the United Kingdom are also available here.

UK Index

http://www.ukindex.co.uk/

UK Index is a searchable collection of United Kingdom-related sites on the Internet. It contains a quick reference guide and a beginner's guide, allowing visitors to register to receive a mailing list of sites related to their particular interests.

United Kingdom-Based World Wide Web Servers

http://src.doc.ic.ac.uk/all-uk.html

This site attempts to group together all World Wide Web servers in the U.K. Visitors can use a search engine or a sensitive map of the U.K. The authors make no claims of accuracy, but there's lots of links to be had here for the questing surfer.

United Kingdom: Comprehensive Resources

http://www.neosoft.com/~dlgates/uk/ukgeneral.html

The United Kingdom pages "are dedicated to all non-Brits who love the U.K. (and Brits who don't shy from an American source)." Webmasters here hope to become the most comprehensive Internet resource for U.K. info, and offer pointers to everything from universities and colleges to government and politics, travel and culture, right down to odder stuff like pictures of the royal family and whimsical pub signs.

Welsh World Wide Web Site

http://www.wales.com/

A Welsh site maintained by Web software innovators Technoleg Gwe at Bangor, North Wales, with links to many other Welsh Sites. Mae o werth ei ymweld!

LATIN AMERICA AND CARIBBEAN

CaribWeb Interactive Guide to the Caribbean
http://www.caribweb.com/caribweb/

Tired out from the daily grind of work and bills? Take yourself off on a virtual tour of the Caribbean through this UK-based site. Drop by the "electronic beach bar" for gossip with other "Caribophiles" or search the densely-packed database of restaurants, Yacht Charter companies and accommodations. Planning a romantic wedding? Carib Moon dishes the scoop on the legal formalities of tying the knot on these gorgeous islands. See Editor's Choice.

Directorio America Latina Global Net
http://www.dirglobal.net

This gateway provides pointers to extensive Latin American resources. Featured links lead to commercial, governmental, educational, cultural and tourism pages. In Spanish, with some English.

LANIC—Latin American Network Information Center
http://lanic.utexas.edu/

The University of Texas, Austin presents this Latin American information resource. Visitors will find links to educational, government and news organizations, plus country-specific Internet indices at this searchable site. Includes links to virtual libraries and research institutions' home pages.

Latin American Studies—World Wide Web Virtual Library
http://lanic.utexas.edu/las.html

This page contains the WWW Virtual Library entries for Latin American Studies. Visitors will find information indexed by country (from Argentina to Venezuela) and subject (from Art to Travel). The database is fully searchable.

MexPlaza
http://mexplaza.udg.mx/

MexPlaza is a collection of resources on Latin American culture, business and history. Visitors will find an art gallery, business articles, classified ads, shopping, a cultural museum and links to related sites. In Spanish and English.

BERMUDA

Forbes Guide to Bermuda
http://microstate.com/bermuda

This guide to Bermuda features articles on every aspect of life in Bermuda. Covered are the environment, tourist attractions, laws, government, military, economy, media, utilities, education, culture accommodations and restaurants.

NetWeb Bermuda—Home Page
http://www.bermuda.com/

NetWeb Bermuda provides an advertising and information dissemination resource for Bermuda businesses and personal users. Includes Bermuda-related pointers, travel info and personal home pages.

Welcome to the Bermuda Triangle
http://www.ibl.bm/

As you may know, the Eighth World Rugby Classic featured some of the best rugby ever seen in Bermuda. For the complete story on this and other Bermuda happenings, visit The Bermuda Triangle site, which has complete tourism and business info for the sunny island nation.

COSTA RICA

Costa Rica Photo Travel Journal
http://swissnet.ai.mit.edu/cr/

Take a look at "the canopy," the community of wildlife and plants living in the treetops of the Costa Rica rainforest. These images and a detailed guide to visiting the Central American country are provided here by a fellow traveler.

---

a2z **EDITOR'S CHOICE**

CaribWeb Interactive Guide to the Caribbean
http://www.caribweb.com/caribweb/

Daily grind got you down? No worries, a free Caribbean getaway—sans telemarketing trap—is right at your fingertips. (Just don't plan to get any sun while you're there.) This site of relevant links to the Caribbean arms virtual tourists with a database of hundreds of restaurants, hotels and beachy entertainment over seven balmy island locations. Better, it enables guests to do normal Caribbean things, like belly up to a virtual bar and chat with other lusty vacationers. Find out where to go, what to do, and, perhaps most importantly, what to drink. Specialized bars such as the Bare Bum Beach (do you even have to ask?) and the Hike, Bike and Brew offer fast friends a chance to share their getaway stories up close and personal—or to plot a bare-bum island adventure together. And those planning to take moonlight beach walks alone may be in luck with the True Romance Caribbean Personals page. Already got a honey and planning a romantic wedding? Carib Moon dishes the scoop on the legal formalities of tying the knot on the islands. Rum! Don't walk!—*Reviewed by Joyce Slaton*

The Source for Caribbean Travellers & Explorers

Welcome to this new resource for travellers and Caribophiles alike. Here you will find information from all the Caribbean Tourist board homepages and other relevant links to the caribbean.

Costa Rica Tourism and Living

http://merica.cool.co.cr/cgi-bin/turismo

Unless you hate the thought of virgin beaches, exotic jungles and free time on an island paradise, access this page of fun-in-the-sun info about Costa Rica. Provided by Inter@merica, a local Internet access provider.

CUBA

Cuba Internet Resources

http://ix.urz.uni-heidelberg.de/~pklee/Cuba/

A comprehensive listing of cultural, political, entertainment and current events resources by and for Cubans around the world, Cuba Internet Resources site can link the user to a world of information about the people, history and impact of the island nation.

Republic of Cuba Home Page

http://www.unipr.it/~davide/cuba/home.html

The Republic of Cuba Home Page is a lesson in Cuban culture, politics and economy. It includes links to newsgroups as well as to tourism information for this West Indies island which was the playground of socialites and mobsters in the 50s and 60s.

DOMINICAN REPUBLIC

Dominican Republic

http://www.codetel.net.do/

Find information on the Dominican Republic at this site hosted by the country's phone compay, Codetel. Follow Dominican politics or find out which beach to play on during your next vacation. In Spanish only.

GUATEMALA

About Guatemala

http://www.ualr.edu/~degonzalez/guatemala.html

This site offers a wealth of information about Guatemala. Read about the country's people, ancient and modern times, entertainment, adventures and native flora and fauna. News about surrounding countries is also provided here, including a collection of news articles and reports from around the American continent.

TRINIDAD & TOBAGO

Trinidad and Tobago

http://www.ugcs.caltech.edu/~benedett/trinidad/trinidad.html

Find a random assortment of information and links related to the Carribean island nations of Trinidad and Tobago here. News, entertainment and sports information appears in text, picture and map formats.

VIRGIN ISLANDS

The Webfoot's Guide to the British Virgin Islands

http://www.webfoot.com/travel/guides/bvi/bvi.html

The Webfoot's Guide to the British Virgin Islands contains everything you need to know before launching off to visit this tropical paradise. Check out travel advisories, temperature and precipitation at different times of the year, the currency exchange rates, sailing charters and diving sites.

MIDDLE EAST/ NORTH AFRICA

Middle East Resource Center

http://www.gpg.com/MERC/

Maintained by the Global Publishing Group, this site offers links to articles, poetry, books and publications related to Middle Eastern life. A chat area and links to other sites of interest are also featured, along with links to Middle East country pages.

Middle East Network Information Center—University of Texas

http://menic.utexas.edu/menic.html

The Center for Middle Eastern Studies at the University of Texas provides a comprehensive listing of information about and from the Middle East. Visitors can view information sorted by country, or they can take a look at Middle East centers and institutes.

Middle East—World Wide Web Virtual Library

http://menic.utexas.edu/mes.html

The World Wide Web Virtual library provides an index to sites in and about the Middle East here. The site is maintained by the Center for Middle Eastern Studies at the University of Texas at Austin.

EGYPT

Color Tour of Egypt

http://www.memphis.edu/egypt/egypt.html

Part of the University of Memphis Institute of Egyptian Art and Archaeology site, the Color Tour of Egypt features annotated images of Egyptian places and people. The page also links visitors to more information about the institute and an online exhibit.

Egypt

http://pages.prodigy.com/G/U/N/guardian/egypt.htm

"Egypt is a fascinating place." Yes, it is and the author of this in-depth site tells you all about it here, from ancient civilization to the present day. Spin through time and discover the history of this unique country's language, culture and technological advances. It's not all pyramids and camels out there, ya know.

Egyptian Info

http://santos.doc.ic.ac.uk/~mmg/EgyptianInfo.html

Ever been curious about Egypt? Visitors to this site can access an index of Egyptian online resources including travel info, businesses, recipes, music, newsgroups, mailing lists and Frequently Asked Questions (FAQ).

Egyptology Resources

http://www.newton.cam.ac.uk/egypt/

This page, maintained by the Newton Institute at the University of Cambridge in England, provides an abundance of Egypt-related resources. Visitors will find news, history and gossip, announcements of conferences and exhibitions, and an Egyptology bulletin board.

IRAN

Iranian Cultural & Information Center

http://tehran.stanford.edu/

The Iranian Cultural & Information Center, a service of Stanford University, provides resources for Iranians and members of Iranian/Persian studies programs. Visit here to learn about the country and link to a variety of online academic and cultural archives.

ISRAEL

The (Almost) Complete Guide to World Wide Web in Israel

http://gauss.technion.ac.il/~nyh/israel/

The (Almost) Complete Guide to the World Wide Web in Israel is dedicated to the memory of Israeli Prime Minister Yitzhak Rabin, with news reports on Israeli politics and links to related sites, including a Frequently Asked Questions (FAQ) file.

The SABRA Home Page of Israel— Welcome Page

http://www.sabra.net

The SABRA Home Page of Israel is a resource guide to Israeli information and culture. Visitors here will find a comprehensive listing of such topics as politics, education, food and finances. This page also offers access to SabraChat, a discussion group interested in Israeli life and people.

The Virtual Tour of Israel

http://dapsas.weizmann.ac.il/bcd/bcd_parent/
tour/tour.html

The Virtual Tour of Israel site features maps of Israel and links to each of the country's regions, including Tel Aviv and the Sharon Valley, Jerusalem, and the Coastal Plain and the Dead Sea.

The World Wide Web Server for Israel

http://www.il/

This index to Israeli Web sites provides pointers to a wealth of information about Israeli culture, education, organizations, events, news and entertainment. In English and Hebrew.

JORDAN

Hashemite Kingdom of Jordan

http://iconnect.com/jordan

The Hashemite Kingdom of Jordan page contains documents about Jordan in the areas of politics, human rights, economics and business. A copy of the constitution, the national charter and currency exchange information are included.

Jordan

http://www.iiconsulting.com/jordan/

Virtual globe trotters will find dozens of links to info about the Middle Eastern nation of Jordan—everything from history to culture to a tour guide with photos.

KUWAIT

Kuwait Sensitive Map

http://hsccwww.kuniv.edu.kw/

Visitors will find extensive information about Kuwait here. The site includes a factbook look at the country, a link to a daily newspaper, a clickable map and POW information from the Persian Gulf War. The site also includes links to numerous organizations, businesses and schools

LEBANON

Lebanon WWW Servers

http://www.sparc.com/lebanon.html

Find a variety of political, social and economic information about Middle Eastern nation of Lebanon at this site. Maps, photos and explanatory texts are offered here as well as links to other Lebanese Internet resources, including the American University of Beirut's World Wide Web server.

MOROCCO

Morocco Page

http://www.sas.upenn.edu/African_Studies/
Country_Specific/Morocco.html

For official U.S. intelligence on this North African nation, turn to the Morocco Page for U.S. State Department maps and travel advisories along with information on Moroccan languages, government and a Moroccan FAQ.

SAUDI ARABIA

Welcome to Saudi Arabia

http://darkwing.uoregon.edu/~kbatarfi/
saudi.html

An expatriate Saudi journalist studying in the United States maintains this guide to Saudi Arabia and the Arab World. Visitors will find a wealth of cultural, business and news resources as well as an in-depth guide to understanding Islam.

TURKEY

All about Turkey

http://web.syr.edu/~obalsoy/Turkiye/

Turkey's home page boasts a robust cultural bill of fare, featuring informational offerings ranging from the country's cuisine to its archaeology and museum exhibitions.

Turkey In Pictures

http://www.ege.edu.tr/~balsoy/Turkiye/
InPictures.html

Get to know Turkey through the images on this page. Visitors can browse the burgeoning photo archive by selecting from among regions of the country, or they can click to specific destinations.

NORTH AMERICA

Virtual Tourist—North America

http://wings.buffalo.edu/world/na.html

The Virtual Tourist leads online tours of World Wide Web servers across the globe. Find the gateway to North American server maps at this site and click your way to world travel.

CANADA

Canada: City.Net

http://www.city.net/countries/canada/

City.Net posts an index to its pages about Canada here. The extensive site includes city listings for provinces, territories, islands, county community organizations, government pages and general travel sites.

Canada Industry

http://info.ic.gc.ca/

At the Industry Canada page, the Canadian government presents info on subjects of national economic importance, such as industry sectors, marketplace rules and services, small businesses, and telecommunications, to name but a few.

Canada Info

http://www.clo.com/~canadainfo/

The Canadian Info page, maintained by the Canadian Almanac & Directory, is a collection of govermnenal and organizational resources from across the Great White North. There are links to over 20,000 associations, government departments, environmental agencies and more.

Canadian Geography from SchoolNet

http://www-nais.ccm.emr.ca/schoolnet/

Fun ways to learn more on the geography of America's northern neighbor crowd this page from SchoolNet with learning and teaching resources. Students can create their own interactive map of Canada, take a geography quiz, even ask questions of the never-before-stumped geographical genius the Harkster. In French and English.

Canadiana—The Canadian Resource Page

http://www.cs.cmu.edu/Web/Unofficial/
Canadiana/

Thinking about checking out Canada, eh? Before you jump on the plane, stop by Canadiana—The Canadian Resource Page for tons of links to information on Canada's government, business sector, arts scene, Web servers, culture, sports, newsgroups and much, much more.

Champlain: Canadian Information Explorer

http://champlain.gns.ca/champlain.html

Champlain's Canadian Information Explorer site provides information about Canada on the Internet. Search governmental sites—federal, provincial and municipal—as well as legal sites. In French and English.

Gateway to Canadian Geography

http://www-nais.ccm.emr.ca/

Canada's geographical, social and political landscapes are mapped here by the National Atlas Information Service. Examine digital and conventional cartographic products and services here. In English and French.

Statistics Canada—Statistique Canada

http://www.statcan.ca/

This site presents a statistical abstract of Canada. Includes listings by subject, products and services, new items and links to other Canadian government servers.

MEXICO

Consulado General de México en Nueva York
http://www.quicklink.com/mexico/

The Mexican Consulate General site contains information on Mexico's politics, culture and economy, including a newsletter and instructions on obtaining various Mexican documents. In Spanish and English.

Info Centro
http://www.infotec.conacyt.mx/

Find pointers to electronic Web resources from and about Mexico at the Info Centro page. Current events and upcoming conferences in Mexico, as well as links to tourist, business and government sites round out the selection. In Spanish and English.

Mexico: City.Net
http://www.city.net/countries/mexico/

This page from the City.Net Web site includes pointers to all of Mexico's cities that are online. The page also features links to cultural information about Mexico as well as maps and tourism resources.

Mexico Web Guide
http://mexico.web.com.mx/

Visit a new Mexican Web site each week at Mexico Web Guide. In addition to the featured site, visitors will find a directory of sites organized by subject. Find museums and government sites by browsing the lists or enter a search term to find a specific place. Spanish only.

Mexico's National Institute of Statistics, Geography and Informatics
http://www.inegi.gob.mx/

Mexico's National Institute of Statistics, Geography and Informatics offers details about the country through this home page. Stop by to check the latest figures estimating the population of the nation or the state of the economy. In English and Spanish.

UNITED STATES

United States: City.Net
http://www.city.net/countries/united_states/

City.Net is an online guide to travel, entertainment, business and government information for communities around the world. This site provides access to links for the U.S. and its territories. An extensive index of national information resources is also available.

Organization of American States Web
http://www.oas.org/

The Web page for the Organization of American States Web aims to further the mission of the group through strengthening the peace and security of the Western hemisphere. The organization includes the U.S. and the 35 sovereign states of Latin America. The site features history and news.

SOUTH AMERICA

ARGENTINA

Argentinian Secretariat of Science and Technology
http://www.secyt.gov.ar/

The Argentinian President depends on the Secretariat of Science and Technology to keep him updated on scientific matters that affect the country. This page links the guest to more on the secretariat and the state of sciences in Argentina, general Argentinian government information, biographical info on the men who hold the offices of President and Secretary, and the latest news, from the pampas to the palace. In English and Spanish.

BRAZIL

Brazil—Fundacao IBGE
http://www.ibge.gov.br/

Brazil's government agency for statistical, geographic and environmental info, Fundacao IBGE, features general facts about the nation through this page. Check in on the national economy or its environmental health.

CHILE

Welcome to Chile
http://sunsite.dcc.uchile.cl/chile/chile.html

The map-based interface found on this page links visitors to the universities of the Republic of Chile. There are also links to government, news, science, law, tourism and other information servers. In English.

COLUMBIA

Basic Colombia
http://www.univalle.edu.co/~servinfo/colombia.sp.html

Web tourists can access basic data about the country of Colombia, an outline of its character, maps, tourist information, its World Cup soccer team, or links to other pages dealing with the nation, this hyperlinked page is a compact reference. Spanish and English.

Columbia Sensitive Map
http://www.univalle.edu.co/MapaSens.html

This site contains general information about South America's country of Colombia, and a hyperlink map to information about universities in six Columbian cities. Includes links to related pages; in English and Spanish.

PERU

Peru
http://www.rcp.net.pe/peru/peru_ingles.html

Access the mysteries of Peru and her people on this page. A sensitive map takes you where you want to visit, but it will help to have that Spanish dictionary handy when you get there. In Spanish and English.

SURINAME

Gateway to Suriname
http://www.xs4all.nl/~ldirksz/index.html

Maintained in Amsterdam, these pages provide a wide range of information about the South American country, Suriname. Find news and commentary, especially on political topics, along with basic info on the country. Some information is in Dutch, some English, some both.

Tropical Rainforest in Suriname
http://www.euronet.nl/users/mbleeker/suri_eng.html

The Tropical Rainforest in Suriname site, part of a personal home page, contains information on the ecology, wildlife and native peoples of the rainforests of Northeastern South America. Includes profiles of indigenous tribes and links to other botanical sites for that region.

VENEZUELA

Venezuela's Web Server
http://venezuela.mit.edu/

This site contains the home page of Venezuela offering visitors information on travel and tourism, the country's history, economy and resources, as well as its business climate. Features include interactive maps, photos and links to related sites.

Venezuelan Institutions on the Net
http://venezuela.mit.edu/list.html

An extensive collection of Venezuelan Institutions join together to form this site with general info on Venezeualan schools, government, social organizations. There's even a link for Venezuelan music and folklore. In English and Spanish.

CULTURES

Aboriginal Page

http://www.vicnet.net.au/vicnet/COUNTRY/
ABORIG.HTM

Australia's indigenous Aboriginal people can trace their heritage back to the last Ice Age, a long and unique history spotlighted in the Aboriginal Page, a compendium of scores of links on the clannish and ecologically-minded Aborigines. News and historical information about the Aboriginal people of Australia compete with links to Australian Aboriginal rock art and musical theater programs, or guests can get just the basic facts on this fascinating culture.

Aboriginal Studies—World Wide Web Virtual Library

http://coombs.anu.edu.au/
WWWVL-Aboriginal.html

The Research Schools of Social Sciences & Pacific and Asian Studies at the Australian National University, Canberra, maintains this exhaustive page of Australian Aboriginal and native peoples links. Connections to history documents, native land title documents, works of art and culture predominate, with myriad links to Aboriginal publications.

Abyssinia CyberSpace Gateway

http://www.cs.indiana.edu/hyplan/dmulholl/
acg.html

A celebration of the collective cultures of East Africans, the Abyssinia CyberSpace Gateway explores the region and its people in links to info on the languages, the culture and the history of East Africans. Users can click on the country of their interest or access encyclopedic information on the area as a whole, gobbling up software, images and text as they choose.

Abzu Regional Index: Egypt

http://www-oi.uchicago.edu/OI/DEPT/RA/
ABZU/ABZU_REGINDX_EGYPT.HTML

Almost as good as poking around an archaeological site yourself, this site explores the fascinating history of Egypt. Check out links to Egypt archaeology projects, view Egyptian museum exhibits, or trace Egyptian history and culture from the days of papyrus to the Electronic Age.

African Studies Program, University of Wisconsin

http://www.wisc.edu/afr/main.html

Jump to servers from around the world which focus on Africa and African studies or just find out more on the UW program. Online libraries and archives of images and text from the Dark Continent draw both the tourist and the academic type to loads of information on African history, culture and attractions.

African Studies—World Wide Web Virtual Library

http://www.w3.org/pub/DataSources/
bySubject/AfricanStudies/africanWWW.html

The World Wide Web Virtual Library's African studies home page informs visitors about Southern African Web servers and allows them to link up with "historically Black" colleges. Also offered here are links to African art collections and cultural organizations as well as informational sources on various African regions and countries.

The Anti-Japanophile Home Page

http://www.sas.upenn.edu/~stevenso/
japan.html

Access to "almost anything and everything Japanese" is what this server promises to provide. Start with the latest news from Japan, then jump to official government pages from consulates and embassies to the Prime Minister's offering. Cheer on your favorite wrestler on linked sumo pages, bang your head to Japanese heavy metal or read up on Japan's chief menace, the Yakuza gangsters in this unusual non-tourist exploration.

Ariadnet

http://www.ariadne-t.gr/

Ariadnet, the Greek academic and research computer network, features information on the network's ten-year history along with links to information about Hellenic civilization, a guide to Athens and a gallery of local art.

Art of China

http://pasture.ecn.purdue.edu/~agenhtml/
agenmc/china/china.html

A beautifully-rendered image of warring dragons welcomes guests to this well-rounded cultural page serving up a variety of Chinese visual art images, musical selections and language resources. Take a virtual tour of China, ponder your Chinese zodiac sign or link to other Chinese-related sites.

Asian Studies—Australian National University Faculty of Asian Studies

http://online.anu.edu.au/asianstudies/

Online centers on Japan, Korea, Thailand and other Asian countries deliver the goods on Asia, with links to basic country information and more thorough sources, such as the World Wide Web Virtual Library. In addition, a comprehensive overview of the Asian Studies program at Australian National University is provided.

Assyria Online

http://www.cs.toronto.edu/~jatou/

Scratch the surface of thousands of years of history, culture and literature at Assyria Online. Ancient and modern civilizations are both represented here, from the history of Mesopotamian times to info on modern Assyrians of Sweden and Germany.

Bill's Aboriginal Links

http://www.bloorstreet.com/300block/
aborl.htm

Aboriginal culture in Australia, Canada, New Zealand and the U.S. is the focus of the hundreds of links provided by culture maven Bill. Find information on Aboriginal legislation and arts and links to Aboriginal-themed newsgroups along with maps of Aboriginal regions and environmental groups.

California Indian Library Collections

http://www.mip.berkeley.edu/cilc/brochure/
brochure.html

Thousands of texts concerning California's Native American population, both historical and modern, are archived in California's Indian Library collections and deposited in California libraries. Here, the collection is introduced, including information about sound recordings, photos and texts of historical value from the collections and contact info for collections administrators.

Canadian Heritage Information Network

http://www.chin.gc.ca/

Find out more about the Great White North at the Canadian Heritage Information Network with features that include a guide to Canadian museums and galleries, online Canadian cultural and historical exhibits, and information about Canadian publications and courses. In French and English.

Center for the Study of Southern Culture

http://imp.cssc.olemiss.edu/

Hey y'all, the University of Mississippi's Center for the Study of Southern Culture offers bachelor's and master's degrees on the history and culture of the American South. An overview of the program is presented, but the real draw is basic info on Southernisms like river baptism and invitations to Southern-styled conferences like the First International Conference on Elvis Presley.

Center For World Indigenous Studies Home Page

http://www.halcyon.com/FWDP/cwisinfo.html

The Center for World Indigenous Studies (CWIS) is an independent U.S. nonprofit organization dedicated to the understanding and appreciation of the world's indigenous peoples. Visitors to this site will find CWIS publications, activities, research and information on workshops and seminars.

Chinese Historical and Cultural Project, San Jose

http://www.dnai.com/~rutledge/CHCP_
home.html

On the Chinese Historical and Cultural Project page, find a multimedia curriculum and teacher's guide focusing on the Chinese people and culture. The curriculum includes lesson plans, hands-on activities and slides. A Chinese festival photo album is also here for perusal, and if you find yourself with free time on your hands, volunteer to be a dragon dancer in the next Chinese community event.

Chinese Philosophy Page

http://www-personal.monash.edu.au/~sab/index.html

Confucius say Chinese Philosophy page has enough links to turn the visitor into an expert on philosophy Chinese style, with philosophical texts and critical essays relating to Chinese thought, culture and language presented in full along with basic info on philosophical schools of thought such as Confucian and Daoist.

Cowboy Poetry

http://agricomm.com/agricomm/cp

The spirit of the Old West lives on in Cowboy Poetry, poems and prose which celebrate the uniquely American cowboy mystique. Poems by and about men and women who ride the range bring home the life of the cowboy, and other text spells out current gatherings and projects of interest to modern cowboys.

Culture and Society of Mexico

http://www.public.iastate.edu/~rjsalvad/scmfaq/scmfaq.html

The rich and varied heritage of Mexico is spotlighted in links to Mexican information centers on the Web offering insight on Mexican politics, languages and culture. Check out Mexico-related newsgroups for grassroots news, or read up on Mexico's indigenous tribes. In Spanish and English.

CultureNet

http://www.culturenet.ucalgary.ca/

CultureNet, an electronic information clearinghouse and publications service for cultural information, acts as a central resource for the Canadian cultural community. This site provides links to arts centers, schools and magazines.

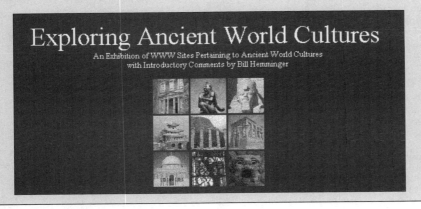

a2z   EDITOR'S CHOICE

Exploring Ancient World Cultures

http://cedar.evansville.edu/~wcweb/wc101/

This erudite Webmaster-professor first gives a brief lecture on why the study of ancient culture is important to the modern student, then goes on to uncover the mysteries of eight far-flung cultures from the ancient world. The Near East, India, Egypt, China, Greece, the Roman Empire, the Islamic World, and Medieval Europe are explored in this online classroom, which traces the cultural history that shaped the development of the modern world. Begin your journey to the past with an exploration of women in ancient times (when Egyptian women held the same legal rights as men), or with a search for the truth about Adam's legendary pre-Eve wife, Lilith. Your next stop might be one of the many museum sites indexed here, housing hundreds of art and archaeological treasures. The truly dedicated can complete online courses in world cultures or flip through an enormous collection of sacred texts from major world religions. While the Webmaster may not know where humankind is headed, he has a pretty good idea about where we've been.—*Reviewed by Joyce Slaton*

Exploring Ancient World Cultures
An Exhibition of WWW Sites Pertaining to Ancient World Cultures
with Introductory Comments by Bill Hemminger

Czech Page

http://www.columbia.edu/~js322/czech.html

Links to news and notes from Czech media spotlights what's hot and not in Czechoslovakia. For the hungry guest, yummy authentic Czechoslovakian recipes for dishes like Pork With Horseradish and Soup with Liver Dumplings are presented by former Czech Eleanor. In English and Czech.

Directorio America Latina Global Net

http://www.diglobal.net/

This gateway provides pointers to extensive Latin American resources. Featured links lead to commercial, governmental, educational, cultural and tourism pages. In Spanish, with some English.

Dunya: CyberMuslim Information Collective

http://www.uoknor.edu:80/cybermuslim/

Assalamu-alaikum and welcome to Dunya, where CyberMuslim Selim guides visitors to Muslim activist information, online Islamic newspapers and a primer on Islamic beliefs. Feel like chatting? Hook up with Muslim newsgroups to discuss Muslim religious practices or culture.

Exploring Ancient World Cultures

http://cedar.evansville.edu/~wcweb/wc101/

Explore the mysteries of eight far-flung cultures of the ancient world in an online classroom which traces the history of cultures which shaped the development of mankind. Follow cultural avenues into essay collections, museums and other Internet resources in this award-winning site. See Editor's Choice.

Fourth World Documentation Project Home Page

http://www.halcyon.com/FWDP/fourthw.html

The nations of the Fourth World, countries like Wales or Tibet which were forcefully incorporated into state unions, present the online community with international political and social commentary on Fourth World countries and their indigenous people. An overview of the far-reaching Fourth World Documentation Project is also available.

French Culture

http://www.culture.fr/

French culture, from newly discovered paleolithic cave paintings to the age of enlightenment to current Christmas traditions in France and Canada, is the topic at hand, and the French Ministry of Culture spreads the word. In French, with some English.

Friends and Partners Home Page

http://solar.rtd.utk.edu/friends/home.htmlopt-tables-unix-english-

Friends and Partners is a joint project between Russian and American citizens to create a meeting place for people of these two countries to learn about each other. This site includes links to a wide range of sites about art, health care, education, news, travel and much more. An electronic mailing list and an interactive coffee house are also provided for guests who want to take the chill off the Cold War themselves. See Editor's Choice.

Gaelic and Gaelic Culture Web

http://sunsite.unc.edu/gaelic/gaelic.html

The Gaelic and Gaelic Culture Web page is devoted to the study of the Gaels and the three Gaelic languages. Includes a look at the Celts and their six unique languages and the Celtic culture FAQ.

A Guide to the Great Sioux Nation

http://www.state.sd.us/state/executive/tourism/sioux/sioux.htm

This South Dakota online guide to the Great Sioux Nation provides information about landmarks and legends, artifacts, art and more from the fascinating Sioux culture. An index of links to an overview of each tribe is also featured, along with photos and maps.

The Gumbo Pages

http://www.gumbopages.com/index.html

Come to Southern Louisiana, where "alcohol, butter, cream and big piles of fried seafood are still good for you" and where the Gumbo Pages dish up a colorful collection of culinary and cultural information on New Orleans and Acadiana. Travelers' tips, music, culture, dining info, a Southern California survival guide and a number of mouth-watering Creole and Cajun recipes are among this site's features.

HELLAS Home Page

http://www.Greece.org/hellas/index.html

The HELLAS home page is designed as a resource for people of Greek ancestry. Links to subject areas such as travel and news are available, as well as news, pictures and news of interest to the Greek community.

Hispanic Heritage

http://www.clark.net/pub/jgbustam/heritage/heritage.html

Visitors to the Hispanic Pages in the USA site will find links to all Hispanic countries, Hispanic cybernauts on the Web and the Spanish language magazine, "Coloquio, Revista Cultural Hispana." Site features also include a review of famous Hispanics in the world and history.

Hmong Home Page

http://www.stolaf.edu/people/cdr/hmong/

Hmong culture originated in Southwestern China, but political pressure from imperialistic Chinese forced the Hmongs into Southeast Asia and the United States. Today, Hmongs are separated but still maintain a unique culture, explored in scores of links to Hmong languages, history and news. Find also a section on travel and study in Southeast Asia as well as photographic archives.

Icelandic Network for Education and Culture

http://www.ismennt.is/

The Icelandic Network for Education and Culture, Ismennt, offers pointers to some of the most interesting Icelandic people and places with Web presences. Stop by to read Viking sayings or read about Icelandic farming. In English and Icelandic.

India Network World Wide Web

http://india.bgsu.edu/index.html

The India Network and Research project distributes journals and publications to people interested in Asian Indian culture via e-mail. Visit this site to subscribe to this service or follow links to India-related Web resources.

Iranian Cultural & Information Center

http://tehran.stanford.edu/

Become an expert on Persian carpet patterns or learn how to make authentic Persian dishes at the Iranian Cultural & Information Center, a service of Stanford University. Those interested in Iranian/Persian culture can also check out art, sports and general cultural archives.

KampungNet: the Singapore Muslim Community Page

http://irdu.nus.sg/kampungnet/

KampungNet is an online community for Muslims living in Singapore. Visitors will find community news, arts and entertainment, publications and a list of Muslim buildings in the area. Available in English and Malay.

Kulturbox

http://www.kulturbox.de/

Berlin-based KULTURBOX is a regional Web server offering arts and entertainment resources from the German cultural community. Links to other German and international servers are provided. In German and English.

EDITOR'S CHOICE

Friends and Partners Home Page

http://solar.rtd.utk.edu/friends/home.htmlopt-tables-unix-english-

With an eye on communication opportunities afforded by the Internet, Friends and Partners is a joint project between Russian and American citizens who have created a virtual meeting place in order to learn more about each other. Links connect visitors to a wide range of sites exploring Russian and American art, health care, education, news, travel and more. Take some simple Russian pronunciation lessons and learn how to greet your new friends. Peruse the life-in-Russia column, "Moscow Life," or get a new take on the differences between everyday culture in Russia and America with anecdotes like this one from a Russian emigre praising American grocery stores: "I don't even have to carry heavy grocery packages, somebody always loads them in the trunk of my car. I just love it!!! And if you are a Russian woman, you fully understand that."—Reviewed by Joyce Slaton

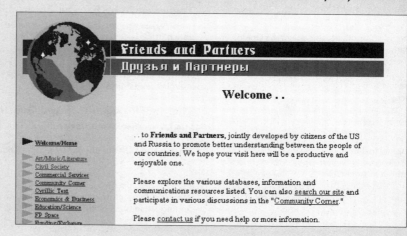

Latin American Studies—World Wide Web Virtual Library

http://lanic.utexas.edu/las.html

You could spend months navigating the hundreds of links on Latin America from the World Wide Web Virtual Library. Information is indexed by country (from Argentina to Venezuela) and subject (from Art to Travel), with a depth which incorporates all the diversity of Latin American culture.

List of Desi Home Pages

http://www.dallas.net/~noel/desis.html

This site provides an alphabetical listing of Indian and Desi personal home pages throughout the Internet. Includes links to information on Indian film, music, research institutions, and India.

MasterCard International Pointers

http://www.mastercard.com/home-g.htm

MasterCard presents a gateway to international culture for virtual travelers. Stories and legends from people of various cultures bring oral traditions to the Web and quotes from world thinkers link users to Web sites on similar topics.

Mito Arts Foundation

http://www.soum.co.jp/mito/

Japan's Mito Arts Foundation maintains this site as part of its effort to promote art, music and culture. Visitors will find information on the Art Tower Mito concept, as well as links to information on local art, music and theater presentations. Pages are offered in both Japanese and English.

Netherlands Institute for the Near East

http://www.leidenuniv.nl/nino/nino.html

The Netherlands Institute for the Near East in Leiden has long been a center of Oriental studies. Founded in 1939, it produces research and journals on Near East issues. Its home page has information about the institute, its publications and links to related sites.

Oneida Indian Nation

http://one-web.org/oneida/

This site contains the home page of the Oneida Indian Nation, one of the original members of the Iroquois Confederacy. Features include historical accounts, current news, information about ongoing projects and links to other native American resources.

Oriental Institute

http://www-oi.uchicago.edu/OI/default.html

The Oriental Institute at the University of Chicago is a museum and research body "devoted to the study of the ancient Near East." This site offers visitors a look at the institute's museum, its archives, archaeology and philology projects, plus related publications and databases.

Pacific Studies—World Wide Web Virtual Library

http://sunsite.anu.edu.au/spin/wwwvl-pacific/index.html

The Australian National University sponsors the Pacific Studies site, which offers links to Asia-Pacific cultural resources by nation, state or region. Visitors can also search the Asia-Pacific Studies Internet Resources database by keyword to access the library's voluminous collection of information on the countries and their people.

Pueblo Cultural Center

http://hanksville.phast.umass.edu/defs/independent/PCC/PCC.html

A visitor to the Indian Pueblo Cultural Center page will encounter the 19 Pueblo communities living in what is now called New Mexico. These Native Americans offer an educational look into their traditional social and political institutions as well as their everyday lives.

Russian and East European Studies—World Wide Web Virtual Library

http://www.pitt.edu:81/~cjp/rees.html

The states of the former Soviet Union, the Balkans and other Eastern European areas are the focus in this segment of the World Wide Web Virtual Library, with connections to generalized home pages for each country in the region as well as information arranged by topics like language, educational institutions or regional culture.

Southeast Asian Archive, University of California, Irvine

http://www.lib.uci.edu/sea/seahome.html

The often-unspoken history of Southeast Asian refugees fills the Southeast Asian Archive from the University of California, Irvine with multi-language library holdings which explore the culture and history of people from Cambodia, Laos and Vietnam in their countries of origin and in America. Link here to learn more about the collection and how you can get access.

Tennessee Bob's Famous French Links

http://www.utm.edu/departments/french/french.html

Take a whirlwind tour of France with Tennessee Bob, who guides guests from French art galleries and literature to newsgroups and language sites. In French and English.

Thailand: Frequently Asked Questions

http://www.nectec.or.th/soc.culture.thai/index.html

Did you know that the major religion of Thailand is Buddhism and that they have a particular fondness for poetry? You would if you had perused soc.culture.thai's FAQs, organized into types of info provided such as general or cultural, and presenting a complete picture of Thailand and Thai people.

Tribal Voice

http://www.tribal.com/

A group of Native Americans hosts this site, which explores traditional culture and history from a contemporary point of view. Includes opportunities for online "powwows" using the group's downloadable chat application and a gallery of digital tribal art.

Tropical Rainforest in Suriname

http://www.euronet.nl/users/mbleeker/suri_eng.html

The Tropical Rainforest in Suriname site, part of a personal home page, contains information on the ecology, wildlife and native peoples of the rainforests of Northeastern South America. Includes profiles of indigenous tribes and links to other botanical sites for that region.

UNESCO World Heritage List

http://www.cco.caltech.edu/~salmon/world.heritage.html

The 469 World Heritage Sites, as designated by the United Nations, range from the ancient city of Butrinti in Albania to the sacred city of Kandy in Sri Lanka. Many of these sites are hyperlinked, so visitors can learn more about them.

United Keetoowah Band

http://www.uark.edu/depts/comminfo/UKB/welcome.html

The United Keetoowah Band of the Cherokee Nation is online here with its latest council and tribe news. Browsers can also review an extensive 1993 federal report, "Burning Phoenix," which examines the reorganization of the band.

University of London School of Oriental and African Studies

http://www.soas.ac.uk/

The Federal University of London's School of Oriental and African Studies (SOAS) home page provides information about the school and its academic programs. Includes information on language and literature and facts about living in London. Visitors can request brochures electronically.

University of Pennsylvania Office of International Programs

http://pobox.upenn.edu/~oip/

The Office of International Programs is the coordinating office of the University of Pennsylvania's International Studies program. Visitors will find information on opportunities to study abroad, student fellowships and guidelines.

Vietnam VietGATE

http://www.saigon.com/

VietGATE provides info on Vietnamese culture via an online magazine and mailing lists. Visitors will find features on social issues and politics, as well as a variety of personal home pages here.

Vodoun (or Voodoo) Information Pages

http://www.vmedia.com/shannon/voodoo/voodoo.html

Angered at the depiction of Voudon in popular media as zombie-producing black magic, this site's author endeavors to present Voudon as a valid religion, explaining how French Catholic and African Yoruban beliefs melded to form the highly ritualistic religion. The facts on Voudon are presented evenhandedly, with non-sensational exploration of black magic, possession and Voudon's relationship with death. See Editor's Choice.

LANGUAGES AND LINGUISTICS

ARCHIVES AND INDICES

Dartmouth College Language Resource Center

http://www.dartmouth.edu/~hr/lrc/

The Language Resource Center at Dartmouth College maintains this site for a variety of language instruction resources. Visitors will find an overview of the center and an extensive index of educational materials for world languages from Arabic to Swahili.

Foreign Language Resources on the Web

http://www.itp.berkeley.edu/~thorne/HumanResources.html

Multi-language links guide the visitor from Arabic to Yiddish and to the most commonly-spoken languages in between. Dictionaries, cultural sites, and country information sites lend a cross-cultural perspective to this site from the language wizards at University of California, Berkeley.

Guides by Geographic Location

http://babel.uoregon.edu/yamada/geoguides.html

The Yamada Language Center at the University of Oregon provides language guides and annotated lists of news groups in a vast variety of languages spoken throughout the world. Visit here for language study resources, downloadable font archives, and even links to fictional languages from the "Star Trek" television series and "The Hobbit" trilogy.

Languages and Linguistics

http://english-www.hss.cmu.edu/langs/

The Languages and Linguistics gateway site serves up a host of links to electronic texts related to structural linguistics and linguistic theory. Web users who speak in tongues can look up hypertext dictionaries, instructional language guides and other linguistics resources here.

Languages and Translation FTP Server

ftp://ftp.willamette.edu/outgoing/tjones/

A variety of files concerned with languages are provided from this FTP server by Willamette University. Visit and find downloadable language dictionaries, lessons, and sound files for English, Italian, French and Spanish.

List of Language Lists

http://info.ox.ac.uk/departments/langcentre/langlists.html

Oxford's Language Center presents a comprehensive list of links to linguistics bulletin boards devoted to the study of individual languages and language groups. Contact info for each bulletin board's mailing list is given.

Oxford University Language Centre

http://info.ox.ac.uk/departments/langcentre/

Links to numerous online foreign language resources are provided on this page maintained by the Oxford University Language Centre. The page also describes the centre's mission and includes links to other Oxford sites.

Universal Survey of Languages

http://www.teleport.com/~napoleon/

Intended as a collaborative effort resulting in a major reference work, the Universal Survey of Languages serves linguistic beginners and experts alike. Find family tree of natural languages with basic info on many, information on invented languages like Esperanto and the Star Trek Ferengi dialogue and information on how to submit further information yourself to add to the site.

a2z EDITOR'S CHOICE

Vodoun (or Voodoo) Information Pages

http://www.vmedia.com/shannon/voodoo/voodoo.html

Angered at the popular media depiction of Voudon as zombie-producing black magic, this site's author presents the religion as valid, explaining how the French Catholic and African Yoruban beliefs of African slaves in Haiti melded to form it. The facts on Voudon are presented evenhandedly, with a glossary for the novitiate and descriptions of each of the major loa (living deities) and their sacrifices and tributes. Illustrations bring home the flavor of Voudon rituals, which utilize drumming, dancing, chanting and ecstatic trance to call upon the loa. Those who associate Voudon with black magic will also be interested in the non-sensational explanation of the limited role of black magic and evil spirits, called baka, in the religion. If Voudon is for you, check out the on-site calendar of ceremonies and plan your own rituals.—*Reviewed by Joyce Slaton*

Vodoun (or Voodoo) Information Pages

Introduction to Vodoun
Vodoun Creation Mythology
The Loa
The Houngan, Mambo and Hounfort
Basic Rituals of Vodoun
Possession
The Role of Black Magic
Vodoun and Death

Calendar of Vodoun Ceremonies
List of Loa
Glossary
Sources
Bibliography

Web-Accessible Linguistic Data Sources and Programs

http://linguist.tamu.edu/linguist/

Language and linguistics-oriented bulletin board and mailing list LINGUIST offers a collection of Internet-based linguistics resources, with links to related institutions and associations, language dictionaries and MUD sites, even online language classes. Allows visitors to add their links to the list.

The Yamada Language Guides

http://babel.uoregon.edu/yamada/guides.html

The Yamada Language Guides page presents an alphabetical archive of language resources on the Web, including a font archive and links to language-related newsgroups and mailing lists.

ASSOCIATIONS AND ORGANIZATIONS

The Yuen Ren Society

http://weber.u.washington.edu/~yuenren/

Located at Seattle's University of Washington, The Yuen Ren Society for the Promotion of Chinese Dialect Fieldwork offers info on its journal, "Treasury of Chinese Dialect Data," and details about upcoming conferences. Dialectology and general linguistic links are also featured.

COMPANIES

AmeriSpan Unlimited

http://www.amerispan.com/

Educational opportunities available through AmeriSpan Unlimited come to the Web through this page. It contains information about the company's Spanish immersion programs in Mexico, Central America and South America.

DICTIONARIES

Dictionaries List

http://math-www.uni-paderborn.de/HTML/Dictionaries.html

Learn how to whisper words of love or perhaps ask where the nearest bathroom is located in the language of your choice here, amongst the dozens of foreign language, technical and acronym dictionaries online. Foreign language offerings include Algerian/English, Slovene/English, German/English and many more.

English-Russian, Russian-English Dictionary

http://www.elvis.ru/cgi-bin/mtrans

Type in a word in English and instantly receive its Russian translation or translate from Russian to English using this form connected to a Russian-English dictionary. If you have a Cyrillic-capable browser, you may view this page and search results in Russian.

English-German Dictionary

http://www.tu-chemnitz.de/urz/netz/forms/dict.html

This interactive site allows visitors to find German equivalents for English words, and vice versa. Simply enter a word, German or English, and search (or suche). Instructions are in German only.

English-Estonian Dictionary

http://www.ibs.ee/dict/

Type an English or Estonian word into the form provided at this site and get a translation instantly. Includes over 17,000 entries.

Jeffrey's Japanese-English Dictionary Gateway

http://www.wg.omron.co.jp/cgi-bin/j-e

This English-to-Japanese conversion utility, maintained by an employee of Kyoto, Japan-based Omron Corporation, offers an easy-to-use keyword search database. Simply type in the target word in English and the utility provides the Japanese equivalent to users with browsers who can read Japanese. Includes Japanese-to-English conversions.

Jim Breen's Japanese Page

http://www.rdt.monash.edu.au/~jwb/japanese.html

A computer scientist posts a Japanese/English dictionary file he created here. Browsers of this extensive site also can download software and dozens of documents about handling Japanese text.

Russian-English Dictionary of Computer Terms

http://solar.rtd.utk.edu/cgi-bin/slovar

Translate computer terms from English to Russian or vice versa with this handy little device which proves geekiness transcends all cultures. You must have a Cyrillic decoder to receive Russian translations properly.

ENGLISH AS A SECOND LANGUAGE (ESL/EFL)

EFLWEB Home Page

http://www.u-net.com/eflweb/

EFLWEB produces English as a Foreign Language Magazine and this comprehensive Web site helpful for browsers interested in learning or teaching English as a second language. A set of FAQ answers common queries on learning and teaching English, but this site goes into far greater depth on the topic, presenting information on schools with EFL programs, reviews of EFL products and software and a calendar of related conferences.

English as a Second Language

http://www.lang.uiuc.edu/r-li5/esl/

The English language, with its non-standardized pronunciations and irregular verb conjugations, is very difficult to learn as a second language, but the resources here help to ease the load with links for people learning English for the first time. Listen to English dialogues to catch the rhythm of speech or hook up with ESL publications or writing labs and advisory pages, it's all here for the asking.

The Virtual English Language Center

http://www.comenius.com/index.html

Even native English speakers can improve their fluency with the lighthearted English examples and exercises provided here as a resource for students and teachers of English. Regard a sample from the Weekly Idiom section, which introduces English slang: "To screw"—"to treat very badly." Interactive fables make learning English fun and the center also provides an opportunity for English speakers to become e-mail penpals. See Editor's Choice.

GRAMMAR THEORY

Lexical Functional Grammar

http://clwww.essex.ac.uk/LFG/

This document page provides access to information about various aspects of the grammatical theory of Lexical Functional Grammar. Includes a description of the theory, links to publications, instructions to download documents and access to a mailing list.

INSTITUTES AND SCHOOLS

Department of Cognitive and Linguistic Sciences at Brown University

http://www.cog.brown.edu/

Brown's Cognitive and Linguistics Department describes undergraduate and graduate programs, courses of study, facilities and faculty profiles. Includes information on admissions, financial aid and links to other campus servers.

Foreign Languages Department, University of Toledo

http://131.183.82.151/home.html

The Department of Foreign Languages at the University of Toledo, Ohio, provides information here on its facilities, programs, faculty and students. Visit here to learn about the department, link to special foreign language home pages and request further information via a direct e-mail application. Includes links other university departments.

Gothenburg University, Linguistics Home Page

http://www.ling.gu.se/

Gothenburg University's Department of Linguistics offers department news and academic program overviews at this site. Find online linguistics resources in Swedish and English.

Hindi Program at Penn

http://philae.sas.upenn.edu/Hindi/hindi.html

Maintained by the Virtual Media Lab at the University of Pennsylvania, this site contains information on the school's Hindi language program. Visitors can access a general overview of the program, specific audio or video lessons, and photos from North India.

Language Learning Resource Center— CMU

http://ml.hss.cmu.edu/llrc

The Language Learning Resource Center at Carnegie Mellon University (CMU) in Pittsburgh maintains this informational site featuring an index to the languages taught at CMU and the resources available for each. Languages taught include: Chinese, French, German, Italian, Japanese, Russian, and Spanish.

Sabhal Mor Ostaig

http://www.smo.uhi.ac.uk/

Sabhal Mor Ostaig is a Gaelic educational facility located on the Scottish island of Skye. Visitors can access a Gaelic-English dictionary and take an online language course, or just learn more about the school. Provided in English and Gaelic.

UC-Berkeley East Asian Languages

http://central.itp.berkeley.edu/~eal/homepage.html

From this electronic brochure for the East Asian Languages department at the University of California-Berkeley, visitors can explore graduate and undergraduate course offerings here, as well as the charms of the university at large. In English.

UCL Department of Phonetics and Linguistics

http://www.phon.ucl.ac.uk/

The University College of London (UCL) Phonetics and Linguistics Department's home page provides information about the department, its educational programs and research activities. Stick around for bonus links to other language servers and university language departments as well.

University of Bristol Center for Theories of Language and Learning

http://www.bris.ac.uk/Depts/Philosophy/CTLL/

The U.K.'s University of Bristol's Centre for Theories of Language and Learning page investigates the links between language, learning and memory and provides this overview on the center as well as information on endangered languages and upcoming seminars as well as addresses of other researchers in the field.

University of Stuttgart Institute of Natural Language Processing

http://www.ims.uni-stuttgart.de/IMS.html

The Institute of Natural Language Processing at the University of Stuttgart, Germany, provides information here on its educational opportunities and course offerings at this site. Visitors can link to its staff listings, research area overviews, project activities and other administrative and academic resources. In German and English.

a2z EDITOR'S CHOICE

The Virtual English Language Center

http://www.comenius.com/index.html

Even native speakers can improve language skills with the lighthearted examples and exercises provided here for students and teachers of English, be it conventional, academic, or the high-tech jargon of science and technology. But this is no ordinary resource. Forget phrases like "good night" and "where's the bathroom?" How about looking up the meanings for "jerk around" and "out of it." Interactive fables make learning fun, too, with exercises based on traditional tales. And if you've a hankering to practice your new skills, register to find an e-mail pen-pal. Links to dictionaries, vocabulary pages and entertainment round out the site.—*Reviewed by Joyce Slaton*

University of Sussex Language Centre

http://www.sussex.ac.uk/langc/welcome.html

The Language Centre at the United Kingdom's University of Sussex maintains this site featuring an overview of the center's resources. English as a second language and foreign language courses are offered as is access to the CALL Library and its collection of downloadable language software.

LANGUAGES AND LANGUAGE TUTORIALS a2z

Akkadian

http://www.sron.ruu.nl/~jheise/akkadian/index.html

This tutorial on Akkadian, a dialect spoken in Mesopotamia in 3000 B.C., is provided here by the Netherland's Space Research Organization. Visitors will find instructional materials, sample texts and a downloadable user's dictionary.

The Arabic Tutor

http://www.teleport.com/~alquds

Visit here to learn about The Arabic Tutor, a language instruction software application for users of Microsoft's Windows operating system. Product news, ordering and price information, and a demonstration version of the program are available here. Includes free downloadable upgrades for licensed users.

A Beginning Course in Welsh

http://www.cs.brown.edu/fun/welsh/TOC.html

Hawddamor (welcome)! Brown University offers a complete online course in beginning conversational Welsh. Learn Welsh from the basics of pronouncing the consonant-heavy words to complicated conjugations, with help from a Welsh spell-checker and a Welsh-English dictionary which translates words and phrases instantly. Fi cadw pysgodyn i mewn fy llyfrdy (I have a fish in my library)!

Chinese-Language-Related Information Page

http://www.webcom.com/~bamboo/chinese/chinese.html

This is an extensive resource on Chinese language studies and the use of Chinese characters on computers. Learn how to read Chinese characters on the Web using available browser software, then use this capability to visit Chinese language sites on the Web such as radio broadcasts and library sites.

Croatian Language—Basic Phrases

http://tjev.tel.etf.hr/hrvatska/language/CroLang.html

Just the thing to have handy if you happen to be lost in Croatia, or need to ask where's the nearest police station, this guide to basic Croatian phrases can steer the non-native through any number of sticky situations with the simple phrases and pronunciation tips here.

The Cymdeithas Madog Home Page

http://tpowel.comdis.lsumc.edu/cymraeg/madog.htm

The Welsh Studies Institute of North America hopes more Americans will learn and enjoy the Welsh language. This page celebrates that aim, and offers info on its language courses, photos of Wales and Welsh cultural materials.

Esperanto—The International Language

http://wwwtios.cs.utwente.nl/esperanto/

Maintained by a Dutch computer researcher and linguist, this site outlines a wide variety of resources on Esperanto, the "international language" invented in 1887 to provide a common language between people who speak different languages. Visit here to find texts, audio files and plenty of other instructional materials.

The Esperanto Yellow Pages

http://www.cs.chalmers.se/pub/users/martinw/fla-pa/flavaj-pagxoj.html

The Esperanto Yellow Pages is an index of services and resources on the Internet related to the artificial language, such as Esperanto instructional pages, newsgroups, FTP sites and more. In Esperanto.

Gaelic and Gaelic Culture Web

http://sunsite.unc.edu/gaelic/gaelic.html

The Gaelic and Gaelic Culture Web page is devoted to the study of the Gaels and the three Gaelic languages. Includes a look at the Celts and their six unique languages.

Hebrew: A Living Language

http://www.macom.co.il/hebrew/

With a friendly "Shalom," Macom Networking of Jerusalem provides enough info on the ancient language of Hebrew to have you as fluent as an Israeli (well, close maybe). Begin with an overview of the alphabet and useful words and phrases, complete with sound files to aid in pronunciation. If you've ever needed to know how to request a small portion of falafel or assure a friend that "you and I will change the world," you'll find Macom's list of contemporary phrases a real life-saver. Hypertext Hebrew poetry exhibits the lyrical side of the language, and the "Words of Love" teaches neophytes how to communicate the difference between friendly fondness and red-hot passion. Hone your literary skills by reading a short story in the language, or find Hebrew-speaking friends at the online bulletin board.—*Reviewed by Joyce Slaton*

Hebrew: A Living Language

Welcome to the Hebrew pages of Macom Networking! This is a dynamic exhibit, and we are constantly adding to it. Please use our feedback buttons, they are scattered all over. Please come back for more visits, to see new stuff, phrase-of-the-day changes, and more! Add us to your Bookmark list. And please tell Hebrew schools in your area about us!

 HEBREW Pages

- The Hebrew Alphabet
- Verbs and Their Conjugation
- 1,2,3: Counting and Numbers
- A Short (hypertextual) Hebrew Story
- Search the Hebrew Pages

- Useful Words
- Useful Question Words
- Finding Your Way Around
- Fonts
- Hebrew Talk

- Contemporary phrases
- Traditional phrases
- New Phrase Of The Day
- POETRY
- Comments?

Gateway to Japan

http://condor.stcloud.msus.edu:20020/tojpn.html

Use the Kanji-capable Web browsers available for download to view a variety of Japanese language resources on the Web. Many links lead guests to sites offering Japanese instruction, but others concentrate on providing news, literature and cultural info in Japanese. In English and Japanese.

German Studies Trails on the Internet

http://www.uncg.edu/~lixlpurc/german.html

The Department of German and Russian Language Studies at the University of North Carolina at Greensboro maintains this site. Visitors will find a variety of World Wide Web-based interdisciplinary German resources for German arts, language and culture. In German and English.

Hebrew: A Living Language

http://www.macom.co.il/hebrew/

With a friendly shalom, Macom Networking of Jerusalem, Israel provides enough info on the ancient language of Hebrew to have you as fluent as a rabbi. Begin with an overview of the Hebrew alphabet, then move on to useful Hebrew words and phrases with sound bites to aid in pronunciation. Finish up with Hebrew stories and poetry. See Editor's Choice.

Integral Dutch Course

http://unicks.calvin.edu/dutchcourse.html

Learn Dutch using this online text-only course in the mechanics of the language. Each chapter is filled with illustrative examples and followed by practice exercises.

Japanese Language Information

http://www.mickey.ai.kyutech.ac.jp/cgi-bin/japanese

Browsers can study Japanese here. The page explains how to pronounce and write Japanese characters and includes links to books, magazines and software that will help hone Japanese language skills.

The Kamusi Project

http://www.yale.edu/swahili/

Intended to be a master resource for the African language Swahili, Yale's Kamusi Project hooks guests up to Swahili-English dictionaries, Swahili grammar notes and pronunciation guides and other Swahili resources. Guests can practice their newfound skills by singing along with Swahili songs or follow links to other African sites.

Kualono—Hawaiian Language Server

http://www.olelo.hawaii.edu/

Kualono, the server of the University of Hawaii's Hawaiian Language Center, serves the Hawaiian-speaking community. Find indigenous language resources, as well as opportunities for English speakers seeking to learn 'Olelo Hawai'i. In Hawaiian and English.

Noun Classification in Swahili

http://jefferson.village.virginia.edu/swahili/swahili.html

An extensive classification of nouns in the Swahili language is provided here by Ellen Contini-Morava, of the University of Virginia's Department of Anthropology linguistics program.

Slovene Alphabet

http://www.ijs.si/slo-chset.html

The Slovene alphabet looks a lot like the one English speakers are used to seeing, but the few differences are explained here, with attention to the pronunciation and written characteristics of characters. If the alphabet piques your interest, jump to English-Slovene dictionaries.

The Virtual English Language Center

http://www.comenius.com/index.html

Even native English speakers can improve their fluency with the lighthearted English examples and exercises provided here as a resource for students and teachers of English. Regard a sample from the Weekly Idiom section, which introduces English slang: "To screw"—"to treat very badly." Interactive fables make learning English fun and the center also provides an opportunity for English speakers to become e-mail penpals.

A Welsh Course

http://www.cs.brown.edu/fun/welsh/home.html

This conversational Welsh course is designed for beginners interested in learning the modern version of the language. Includes a detailed syllabus, lessons and links to other Welsh language education resources

PROFESSIONAL RESOURCES

Colibri Home Page

http://colibri.let.ruu.nl/

A resource for students, researchers and professionals in the fields of language, speech, logic and/or information, Colibri publishes a weekly newsletter and provides this Web site with online language and speech dictionaries and the latest news and notes from the linguistics front. Interested guests can also check out linguistics conferences and organizations.

Dartmouth College Language Resource Center

http://www.dartmouth.edu/~hr/lrc/

The Language Resource Center at Dartmouth College maintains this site for a variety of language instruction resources. Visitors will find an overview of the center and an extensive index of educational materials for world languages from Arabic to Swahili.

PUBLICATIONS AND INDUSTRY NEWS

Tecla

http://www.bbk.ac.uk/Departments/Spanish/TeclaHome.html

Visitors can read current and past issues of the magazine aimed at Spanish "learners and teachers" and improve their grasp of the language with Tecla's Spanish vocabulary extenders and educational essays.

SIGNAL FLAGGING

International Marine Signal Flags

http://155.187.10.12/flags/signal-flags.html

Find out how crews on ships at sea communicate with each other at the International Marine Signal Flags site. Visitors will find graphic representations of signal flags, as well as explanations of their specific meanings.

SOFTWARE

The Arabic Tutor

http://www.teleport.com/~alquds

Visit here to learn about The Arabic Tutor, a language instruction software application for users of Microsoft's Windows operating system. Product news, ordering and price information, and a demonstration version of the program are available here. Includes free downloadable upgrades for licensed users.

Freenet and Cyrillic

http://www.free.net/Docs/cyrillic/notes.en.html

In addition to negotiating the vagaries of the Internet, writers who use the Cyrillic alphabet must also convert their characters to the Arabic equivalent, and vice versa. This site provides instructions and some software to aid the conversion.

Gerdsooz, a Wireless Light Source

http://www.payvand.com/perdsooz/

Gerdsooz is a Persian script generator, using ASCII characters. "Now you can express yourself in Persian, to your friends, your spouse, or maybe that sweetheart of yours," the author writes. "You no longer have to send e-mails like: 'KhAnom man shomA rA khaily dost darm!'"

Lingsoft Home Page

http://www.lingsoft.fi/

Details on linguistic tools for text retrieval and information management systems may be found on the Lingsoft home page. Visitors can check out demos of the Finnish company's programs in action.

Reading Chinese on the Macintosh

http://www.dartmouth.edu/~hr/lrc/macchinese.html

Mac users can learn to read and edit Chinese documents with the instructions offered here. Apple Computer's Chinese language kit is explained from installation and configuration to operation.

Translate Instant Spanish

http://www.garlic.com/infobord/kadoch/main1.htm

Bilingual Software pitches its Spanish translation products at this promotional site. Here, visitors can download demonstrations of a program that automatically translates English text into Spanish.

Yamada Language Center Font Archive

http://babel.uoregon.edu/Yamada/fonts.html

This typeface archive, maintained by the Yamada Language Center at the University of Oregon, provides non-Latin character fonts. Download the fonts for creating documents using Czech, Hebrew, American Sign Language and other languages. A guide to built-in Macintosh capabilities is also included.

TRANSLATION SERVICES

Aquarius Directory of Translators and Interpreters

http://www.xs4all.nl/~jumanl/

Updated weekly, the Aquarius Directory is a World Wide Web search system for locating foreign language translators and interpreters. Search the database or sign up for Aquarius membership at this site. With over 368 languages offered and scores of translators online, you're sure to find the translating services you need. In need of a laugh? Check out Aquarius' offering of hilarious mistranslations.

Globalink

http://www.globalink.com/

Globalink offers translation services via modem, plus the "Language Assistant" series of software applications (the CD-ROM version of which features voice output). The Globalink home page is, appropriately, available in five languages.

Honyaku

http://www.crossroads.net/index.html

Japanese translators, or speakers of the language who are interested in translation will find a home at the Honyaku page. Visitors will find Honyaku mailing list and discussion group information, as well as an essay on translating for the Web and links to various Japanese language resources.

Translation Experts Ltd.

http://www.net-shopper.co.uk/software/ibm/trans/index.htm

This United Kingdom-based company, dedicated to language translation products and services, provides extensive company info here. Visitors can read detailed product and services descriptions, download software demos, or order online here.

The Translator's Home Companion

http://www.rahul.net/lai/companion.html

The Translator's Home Companion, a service of the Northern California Translator's Association, provides a variety of resources. Visit here for online library collections, text and dictionary reviews, software, links translation agencies, and more.

University of Twente Esperanto Translator

http://wwwtios.cs.utwente.nl/traduk/EO-EN/Translate/

The Tele-Informatics and Open Systems group at the University of Twente in the Netherlands maintains this Esperanto translator utility. Visitors can enter an Esperanto word or root to search for an English explanation, or vice versa.

Wordnet

http://www.ultranet.com/~wordnet/

Wordnet is a group of language experts who translate foreign languages for company' brochures, catalogs, presentations and legal agreements. Languages covered are: Spanish, French, German, Japanese and Chinese.

TRAVELERS' RESOURCES

Foreign Languages for Travelers

http://www.travlang.com/languages/

Forego forever the panic of being a helpless tourist unable to speak the most basic words of international languages at Foreign Languages for Travelers. This page offers basic instruction in 21 languages, offering sound bites of the most commonly-needed phrases to help you get it right. Access to foreign dictionaries and language pointers accompany travel-related info.

WORLD ALMANAC

CURRENCIES AND EXCHANGE RATES

Currency Converter

http://www.olsen.ch/cgi-bin/exmenu

Find out how much that Bahraini hotel room will cost in Australian dollars using this online conversion tool. Current exchange rates are offered, along with an auto-form that allows users to calculate exchange values for currencies in countries from Albania to Zimbabwe, and everything in between.

GRAB BAG

Canada Postal Code Lookup

http://www.mailposte.ca/english/pclookup/pclookup.html

Need to send a parcel to Canada? You can look up postal codes and rates from America's northern neighbor in this index from Canada's government-sponsored mail service, Canada Post Corporation. For the postal fancier, a complete history of postal services in Canada is here for perusal. Text available in French and English.

Date and Time Gateway

http://www.bsdi.com/date

Find the current time and date for cities around the world from in Greenwich Mean Time. City listings are arranged alphabetically within continental categories at this utilitarian site proudly displaying a "Most Boring Site" award.

How Far Is It?

http://www.indo.com/distance/

Plan your next escape by typing in where you are and where you want to go on this handy page, which uses the Geographic Name Server to find the latitude and longitude of two worldwide requested locations, and then calculates the distance between them. A map displaying the two locations is also provided along with "as the crow flies" distance between locations.

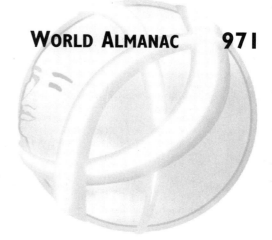

Geographic Nameserver

http://www.mit.edu:8001/geo/

The Massachusetts Institute of Technology maintains this site for keyword searches of its North American geography database. Visit here to find vital statistics on American cities, including latitude and longitude, elevation, zip codes, and more.

Local Times Around the World

http://www.hilink.com.au/times/

Is it too late to call your friend in Antigua, or are government offices still open in El Salvador? Find out what time it is right now in this exhaustive index which attempts to provide times for all world regions. Just click on a region and get the present time there as compared to Greenwich Mean Time.

National Flags

http://155.187.10.12/flags/nation-flags.html

Dozens of links are provided to images of national flags; from Argentina to Yemen. Just click on the country you want and get a full-color GIF image, courtesy of the Australian National Botanical Gardens.

U.S. Gazetteer

http://tiger.census.gov/cgi-bin/gazetteer

The U.S. Census Bureau's exhaustive cataloging of U.S. statistics has produced this almanac of city information, where questing users can type in a city or zip code and get back basic city information such as its location, population and a regional map, plus access to Census tables from the region covering such finer points as the ethnic makeup of its residents and what kind of housing exists.

U.S. Gazetteer at University of Buffalo

http://www.census.gov/cgi-bin/gazetteer

Type in the name of a city and get back factbook info on cities of that name in all the U.S. states with links to a U.S. map spotlighting the city's location and a more up-close mapped look at the region.

World Flags: An Incomplete Collection

http://www.adfa.oz.au/CS/flg/index.html

This site provides an admittedly less-than-comprehensive collection of flags for a world where boundaries change like the weather. Visitors can browse the archive, read about the patriotic customs of various nations or link to information about flag-waving associations around the globe.

MAPS

Color Landform Atlas of the United States

http://fermi.jhuapl.edu/states/states.html

Choose your path to information on U.S. states: do you want to check out maps of the each state and its counties or more textual resources from City.Net, Yahoo!, or Virtual Tourist? They're all here for each of the United States, plus a few resources for the U.S. as a whole.

Map Maker

http://www.pcug.co.uk/~MapMaker/

Freeware program Map Maker is designed for people in developing countries who need to create and manipulate maps on basic personal computers. This page allows browsers to download the software, a simple Geographical Information System.

National Atlas Information Service

http://www-nais.ccm.emr.ca/Home.html

Explore the geography of Canada with products from the National Atlas Information Service. Whether searching for a small town in Saskatchewan or a location of mineral deposits, the NAIS has maps to point the way.

The National Land Survey of Finland

http://www.nls.fi/

The National Land Survey of Finland outlines its mapping services here. Visitors will learn about its various departments, its use of geographic information systems and its satellite image center. In Finnish and English.

Thomas Bros. Maps

http://www.thomas.com/

Thomas Bros. Maps has been helping people find their way around California, Oregon, Washington, and Arizona since 1915 with its line of detailed electronic and print street maps. Visit here to find company information as well as the facts on its electronic and print maps and where to buy them.

Xerox PARC Map Viewer

http://mapweb.parc.xerox.com/map/

Pick a spot on this interactive world map to request a closer look and with every click get closer as maps zoom in on the exact place you're indicating. The map shows such features as borders and rivers, but if you need more detail on areas jump to the Geographic Name Server here.

APPENDIX A
GET THE FAQs:
FREQUENTLY ASKED QUESTIONS ABOUT a2z

http://a2z.lycos.com

Besides serving as a token attempt to emulate our online FAQs (that's shorthand for "Frequently Asked Questions," that most sacred of Web trends), these Q&A pages are for you, the inquisitive one, who always wants to know a little bit more.

Nice book, but what's a2z?

Launched on the World Wide Web in February 1996, a2z is the premier directory of the world's favorite places and spaces on the Internet. a2z complements the massive Lycos catalog and search engine by providing descriptions of, and links to, the most popular Web pages, gopher servers, and FTP sites on the planet.

With Lycos' powerful spider technology as its backbone, and a professional editorial team as its nerve center, a2z delivers the facts about sites on the Net—the who, what, why, when, where, and how—and lets you decide whether or not what's lurking beyond the hypertext is worth taking the time to visit.

Another Internet directory, eh?

Hey, not so fast! By combining the Lycos spider technology and the services of a full-time editorial team, a2z delivers what no other Internet directory does: the world's most popular sites, researched and described by professional journalists.

The spider helps to build a2z by seeking out the most linked-to sites in the Lycos catalog (which held an unmatched 50 million URLs at the time of this book's printing); the editorial team takes it from there, working up concise, straightforward site descriptions and carefully nesting each in a specific hierarchical branch of a thoughtfully developed category tree.

From archives in ancient architecture to a zany zoologist's personal home page, a2z makes it a snap to catch only the most rewarding URLs on the Web.

Uh…what's an URL?

That's Web talk for "uniform resource locator," a fancy way of giving an address on the Web. An URL (pronounced "Earl") tells your browser where to go to find the site you want.

But there's more…

a2z is also the proud host of an exclusive handful of original columns, written by certified Net stars (like Cybergrrl and Cool-Site-of-the-Day guru Glenn Davis), as well as our own crop of home-grown Web celebs. Our columnists (or Op-hEds, as we like to call them) lend their unique perspectives to provoke, inform, and entertain users on subjects ranging from the culture of pop to the politics of cool; from women and technology to life after 55. Come to a2z for the directory; stick around for the rants, conceits, and brainwork of the Op-hEds.

a2z sounds great, but how do I get there?

Easy. Punch **http://www.a2z.lycos.com** into your trusty Web browser's locater and away you go the home page. Once you're there, "bookmark" a2z for easy access next time around. Or if you just can't get enough, configure your browser to make a2z your own home page (instructions are given on-site), and we'll appear as if by magic every time you launch your browser.

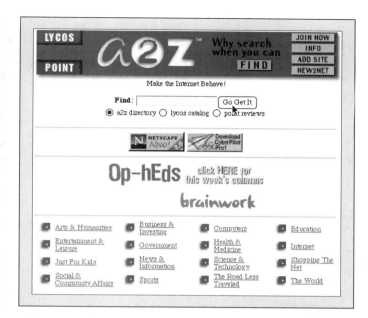

And once I'm there?

a2z facilitates two main approaches for finding information: browsing by subject or searching using a keyword query.

To use the search engine, simply enter the word or group of words that best describes what you're looking for—your *keywords*—directly into a "Find" text box, located on every page. The engine will immediately generate hyperlinked listings and descriptions for the 10 sites most relevant to your query. If you want to see more, click on the hyperlinked text for the "next 10 hits" at the bottom of the page. Consider the titles on display and read the a2z descriptions to help you decide which sites best suit your needs.

How do I know which keywords to use?

Formulating the best possible query will go a long way toward getting the results you want from a search. Most search engines—a2z and Lycos included—will ignore prepositions, articles, and conjunctions (like "of," "to," "from," "the," "a," "an," and "and"), so it's best not to use them. And try to be as precise as possible.

For example, let's say you're looking for some information about the film *On the Waterfront*. Simple, right? Well, maybe not; you might be surprised at the number of beachfront realtors turned up by your search if you simply use the film's title as your keyword search. Instead, try this combination: "waterfront," "marlon" and "brando." The sites you're looking for should appear at the very top of your results list.

What if I'm not sure what I want?

If you know exactly what you're looking for, using the search engine is a fast and easy way to go get it. But one of the most exhilarating aspects of the Web is the promise of all that wild and wonderful stuff you're likely to kick up each time you go browsing, or surfing, at random. To that end, a2z's hierarchical category trees make browsing an irresistable temptation.

To surf a2z, click through the category trees (like "News & Information") and subcategories ("Magazines & Periodicals") until you reach the specific subject you desire, or one that just strikes your fancy. Once there, you'll be treated to a2z's complete holdings of site descriptions. Offering links for titles from *Advertising Age* to the *Village Voice*, you'll find scrolling through the magazines listed in the directory can be a lot like an afternoon spent browsing the newsstand at your favorite bookstore.

But I still haven't found what I'm looking for...

As a directory of only the Web's most popular sites, a2z is by nature somewhat selective. While you may have no problem finding a description of "Mr. Showbiz" in a2z, a search for "Mr. Nefff's Mambo Karaoke Steakhouse" may prove less than fruitful. When it's time for the down-and-dirty search for obscurity, though, we've still got you covered. Twice over. a2z is part of the top-flight services and peripheral features gathered under the Lycos family umbrella. Each page of a2z links directly to Lycos Centispeed, the mother of all Internet search engines; and to a2z's savvy sister, Point Communications (you know, the "Top 5% of the Web" gang).

To get there directly, point to Lycos at **http://www.lycos.com**. You'll find Point at **http://point.lycos.com**.

And still more exclusive features complement the search and directory services of Lycos, a2z, and Point. Point Now keeps Webheads abreast of the latest developments in world news, its around-the-clock headline service linking to the Net's hottest news sources even as stories break. Lycos Road Maps enable users to instantly generate a street map for any U.S. address (great for directions to parties). And NetCarta WebMaps—the blueprints of the Web—allow users to see their favorite sites from a different perspective; the closest you'll get to a bird's eye view in cyberspace.

So, what are you looking for?

The definitive guides to numchucks and breakdancing? The definitive guide to breakdancing with numchucks? Whatever your pleasure, whatever your passion, a2z can't wait to help you find it, to help you make sense of it all, to separate the Borgs from the Borks from the Björks, so to speak. You've got the book. You've got the URL. So, what are you waiting for?

APPENDIX B
WHAT YOU NEED TO RUN THIS CD-ROM

To use this CD you will need a Web browser. If you do not currently have a browser installed on your computer, we have included several versions of Microsoft's Internet Explorer on this CD. Instructions for installation are included below.

RECOMMENDED PC SYSTEM

Pentium PC

Windows operating system

16MB RAM

15MB free space on your hard drive

4x CD-ROM drive

MINIMUM PC REQUIREMENTS

486 PC

Windows operating system

8MB RAM

8MB free space on your hard drive

2x CD-ROM drive

MACINTOSH SYSTEM REQUIREMENTS

Apple Macintosh or Power Macintosh (or clone) running System 7.0.1 or later

Apple OpenTransport or MacTCP and Thread Manager

Minimum of 8MB of RAM (16 preferred)

8MB free space on your hard drive (15 preferred)

2x CD-ROM drive (4x preferred)

And for all systems

A modem (14.4 bps or faster is recommended for optimum performance)

Note: Although a modem and Internet connection are not required to view the contents of the CD-ROM, you will need them to use the many Internet links we have included on the CD-ROM.

CD-ROM START INSTRUCTIONS

1. Place the CD-ROM in your CD-ROM drive.
2. Launch your Web browser.
3. From your Web browser, select Open File from the File menu. Select your CD-ROM drive (for PC users, usually drive D). Mac users, double-click on the CD-ROM icon— then select the folder called a2z. From within that folder, choose the file called index.htm.

INTERNET EXPLORER INSTALLATION INSTUCTIONS

MICROSOFT INTERNET EXPLORER 2.0.1 FOR MACINTOSH

Double-click the Internet Explorer Installer icon to install.

Note: Eudora Light is an Internet Mail client application that is included in Microsoft Internet Explorer 2.0.1 for Macintosh. Documentation for Eudora Light is not included. To download the Eudora Light Manual separately, visit the Microsoft Internet Explorer Web site at

http://http://www.microsoft.com/ie/iedl.htm#mac

MICROSOFT INTERNET EXPLORER 2.0 FOR WINDOWS 95

You must be using Microsoft Windows 95 to run Microsoft Internet Explorer 2.0.

If you're using a previous version of Microsoft Internet Explorer, click Open File to automatically upgrade your existing version.

If you're using a different browser, create a temporary folder on your hard disk, and then save the file in it. In that folder, double-click the Internet Explorer file to extract the program files.

INTERNET EXPLORER VERSION 2.01 FOR WINDOWS 3.1

Create a temporary directory on your computer. Save Microsoft Internet Explorer to the temporary directory. In File Manager, run Dlmini.exe to extract the program files.

Read the instructions below for LAN installations and for installing with existing TCP/IP connections.

In File Manager, run Setup.exe. Setup installs files in the directory you specify. If you want, you can delete the temporary directory you created.

Run Internet Explorer.

UPGRADING OVER VERSION 1.5 AND VERSION 1.6 BETA

The format of Iexplore.ini has changed, so Setup will make a backup copy of your current Iexplore.ini file to a file called Ie16ini.sav.

You will need to reapply any user-selectable settings, such as proxy servers, in the new version. Your Favorites and History list will be preserved.

Win32s is not required for this version, so if you installed Win32s specifically to run the version 1.6 beta, then you can remove it from your system. Please refer to the following URL for instructions on removing Win32s from your system:

http://www.microsoft.com/kb/faq/devtools/winsdk/ win32s/all.htm

LAN INSTALLATIONS

If you already have access to the Internet through your LAN, you will be able to use the Microsoft Internet Explorer to browse the Internet. (If you are not sure whether you currently have access, consult your network administrator.)

If you have access, your LAN administrator should provide you with proxy servers that also can be used, provided they are CERN compliant.

To install Internet Explorer, you need to do the following:

- Make sure you have the TCP/IP protocol installed.

- Proxy servers can also be used, provided they are CERN compliant. To enable use of a proxy server, choose Options from the View menu, and then on the Proxy tab, type the data needed for your proxy server.

INSTALLATION WITH EXISTING TCP/IP CONNECTIONS AND ISP ACCOUNTS

Microsoft Internet Explorer has been installed and tested with several of the most popular Internet access products available today.

In general, all that is required is that you configure the PATH command in your Autoexec.bat file so that Microsoft Internet Explorer can find the Winsock.dll file you are using to connect to the Internet. For example, if your Winsock.dll file is in the directory C:\Connect, add a line directly under your current PATH command that reads:

PATH=%PATH%;C:\CONNECT

WHAT'S ON THE CD-ROM?

The CD-ROM included with this book contains approximately 15,000 hyperlinked directory listings. Every section on the book—from health to software—allows you to select the Web address and instantly connect to the actual site. The CD-ROM also contains a hot button to connect directly to the Lycos search engine and Microsoft Internet Explorer for Mac and PC. The PC version of Internet Explorer is included for both Windows 3.x and Windows 95.

INDEX OF SITE NAMES

F

O